RESNICK & HALLIDAY'S

PHYSICS

for IIT-JEE

Vol. 1

RESNICK & HALLIDAY'S

PHYSICS

for IIT-JEE

Vol. 1

Adapted by:

Amit Gupta

BANSAL CLASSES

Kota, India

Resnick and Halliday's Physics For IIT-JEE

Other Wiley Editorial Offices:
John Wiley & Sons, Inc. 111 River Street, Hoboken, NJ 07030, USA
Wiley-VCH Verlag GmbH, Pappellaee 3, D-69469 Weinheim, Germany
John Wiley & Sons Australia Ltd, 42 McDougall Street, Milton, Queensland 4064, Australia
John Wiley & Sons (Asia) Pte Ltd, 2 Clementi Loop #02-01, Jin Xing Distripark, Singapore 129809
John Wiley & Sons Canada Ltd, 22 Worcester Road, Etobicoke, Ontario, Canada, M9W 1L1

First Edition: 2009
ISBN: 978-81-265-1942-2
www.wileyindia.com

Printed at: Rajiv Book Binding House, Delhi

Dedication

Everything that I know about teaching, I have learnt it from my esteemed teacher
Mr. V.K. Bansal.
I am deeply indebted to him.

Preface

Many students have asked me if a book exists , which contains all the topics and their in-depth analysis, in the same manner as that done at Bansal Classes (or is required for JEE)". I was unable to answer this question as there are many really good, authentic books written by well-known authors. However, if they come close in one aspect, they are lacking in some other. As the interest in IIT-JEE has increased tremendously in recent times, the requirement of a book that contains all the topics and their discussion from fundamental concepts was felt more. I feel great honor and satisfaction while presenting this book to all JEE aspirants and to our students at Bansal Classes. Honor, because I myself have studied and learnt Physics from the Resnick, Halliday and Walker's "Fundamentals of Physics". Satisfaction, because by adapting this book I, finally, have a definitive answer to my students' query.
The major changes in this adapted version of the classic text are:

- Inclusion of many small topics in all the chapters, which are an essential part of JEE, but were not given status of theory in the original book and have been treated only as problems. Hence, in this version, you will find in-depth discussion on topics such as Net Motion, Constrained Motion, Projection on an Inclined Plane, Calculation of Work for Non-Uniform Force, and so on.
- One new chapter has been created, namely, Circular Motion. The original book treats "Kinematics of Circular Motion" as part of the topic "Two and Three-dimensional Motion" and "Dynamics of Circular Motion" as the part of "Some Applications of Newton's laws". In this version I have collated the material from both the chapters, added some of my own and compiled them to form a new chapter called "Circular Motion".
- Another big change I have done is adding a number of quality solved examples. Although the original book does have many good examples, which illustrate basic use of the concepts, they are not sufficient to make students comfortable with the JEE-level problems.

The solved examples that are added in this adapted version may seem a bit high on complication level, but this is so only from conceptual view point, without using difficult mathematics. Also, great emphasis has been laid on explaining the solution of problems in such a way that the student will feel that it is his own thought process being reflected in the solution. Many solutions to the sample problems discuss not only the correct solution but also the most common wrong solutions as well. Almost all solutions are divided in four parts namely "**Conceptualize, Classify, Compute, Conclude**". The first section, "Conceptualize" explains the problem further with a little clue towards its solution. Sometimes, it also explains the mistake in popular wrong approach to the problem. The next part, "Classify", contains what equations and physics concepts should be used to solve the problem. In many simple problems, the two parts are merged. The next part, "Compute", contains the relevant equations and their solutions. Finally, there is "Conclude" which very often contains logical verification of the answer or justifies the prediction of answer done in "Conceptualize" part. These four C's are like four logical steps that the student is expected to develop for problem solving. These parts are being presented in a way that the students may want to try to solve the problem themselves just after reading the first part of solution, namely, "Conceptualize". In fact, I would suggest that they do so. If one is not successful after just reading "Conceptualize", he may read the next part of the solution, that is, "Classify", and again attempt the problem before reading the final solution presented in the third C, "Compute". Also a few topics and chapters are rearranged as per the syllabus and the order of classes followed at Bansals (and that holds true for most of the coaching classes).

Another major feature of this book is that it is packed with a lot of real-world physics. Having gone through the book, the student will realize that one can reason from basic physics concepts all the way to valid conclusions about the real world, and that understanding of the real world is where the fun is.

The book also provides the instructors with a tool by which they can teach students how to effectively read scientific material, identify fundamental concepts, reason through scientific questions and solve quantitative problems. This process is not easy for either students or instructors. Indeed, the course associated with this book may be one of the most challenging of all the courses taken by a student. However, it can also be one of the most rewarding because it reveals the world's fundamental clockwork from which all scientific and engineering applications spring.

Chapter Features

All the chapters open with a very interesting Puzzler. Further, as mentioned earlier, the text is divided into Solved Sample Problems, Checkpoints, Special Notes, Problem-solving Tactics, Review & Summary and End-of-Chapter Problems.

- **Opening puzzlers.** A curious puzzling situation opens each chapter and is explained somewhere within the chapter, to entice a student to read the chapter.
- **Checkpoints** are stopping points that effectively ask the student, "Can you answer this question with some reasoning based on the narrative or sample problem that you just read?" If not, then the student should go back over that previous material before traveling deeper into the chapter. *Answers to all checkpoints are in the back of the book.*
- **Sample problems** are chosen to demonstrate how problems can be solved with reasoned solutions rather than quick and simplistic plugging of numbers into an equation with no regard for what the equation means. The sample problems with the label "Build your skill" are problems which build on a concept. As explained earlier, each division (the four Cs) of the sample problems help the student to focus on the basic concepts at the root of the solution to a problem. In effect, these divisions say, "We start our solution by using this basic concept, a procedure that prepares us for solving many other problems.We don't start by grabbing an equation for a quick plug-and chug, a procedure that prepares us for nothing. We then go on and try to attempt the solution using this information."
- **Problem-solving tactics** contain helpful instructions to guide the student as to how to solve problems and avoid common errors.
- **Review & Summary** is a brief outline of the chapter contents that contains the essential concepts but which is not a substitute for reading the chapter.
- **Questions** are like the checkpoints and require reasoning and understanding rather than calculations. *Answers to all the questions are in the back of the book.*
- **Problems** are grouped under section titles and are labeled according to difficulty. *Answers to the problems are in the back of the book.*
- **Additional problems** are problems that are not ordered or sorted in any way so that a student must determine which part of the chapter is applicable for a given problem.

Amit Gupta
Bansal Classes, Kota
April 2009

Acknowledgement

First of all I would like to thank all my past and present students who made it possible for me to share this beautiful subject with them and helped me appreciate physics from different point of views. I also want to extend my thanks to Mr. Ankur Padia (Tirupati Publishers & Distributors), whose enterprise is the reason I started this work. Thanks are also due to my colleague Mr. Sunil Gupta, who has contributed to this work by helping in the selection of end-of-chapter problems.

My heartfelt thanks to the publishing team at John Wiley India, Mr Paras Bansal (Associate Publisher), Ms Sarah Rizvi, and Ms Nupoor Singh who made my first experience of writing a book a great one. Last but not the least, special thanks to my family, whose constant support and encouragement made this work possible.

Contents

Units and Dimensions

When an earthquake strikes a populated region, it can shake apart buildings and other structures or cause them to topple over. However, in some regions it can cause structures to sink into the ground until they are significantly submerged, as if the structures were on a dense fluid instead of solid ground.

How can a building sink into the ground?

The answer is in this chapter.

©AP/Wide World Photos

1-1 Introduction

Science and engineering are based on measurements and comparisons. Thus, we need rules about how things are measured and compared, and we need experiments to establish the units for those measurements and comparisons. One purpose of physics (and engineering) is to design and conduct those experiments.

For example, physicists strive to develop clocks of extreme accuracy so that any time or time interval can be precisely determined and compared. You may wonder whether such accuracy is actually needed or worth the effort. Here is one example of the worth: Without clocks of extreme accuracy, the Global Positioning System (GPS) that is now vital to worldwide navigation would be useless.

1-2 | Measuring Things

We discover physics by learning how to measure the quantities involved in physics. Among these quantities are length, time, mass, temperature, pressure, and electric current.

We measure each physical quantity in its own units, by comparison with a **standard.** The **unit** is a unique name we assign to measures of that quantity—for example, meter (m) for the quantity length. The standard corresponds to exactly 1.0 unit of the quantity. As you will see, the standard for length, which corresponds to exactly 1.0 m, is the distance traveled by light in a vacuum during a certain fraction of a second. We can define a unit and its standard in any way we care to. However, the important thing is to do so in such a way that scientists around the world will agree that our definitions are both sensible and practical.

Once we have set up a standard—say, for length—we must work out procedures by which any length whatever, be it the radius of a hydrogen atom, the wheelbase of a skateboard, or the distance to a star, can be expressed in terms of the standard. Rulers, which approximate our length standard, give us one such procedure for measuring length. However, many of our comparisons must be indirect. You cannot use a ruler, for example, to measure the radius of an atom or the distance to a star.

There are so many physical quantities that it is a problem to organize them. Fortunately, they are not all independent; for example, speed is the ratio of a length to a time. Thus, what we do is pick out—by international agreement—a small number of physical quantities, such as length and time, and assign standards to them alone. We then define all other physical quantities in terms of these *base quantities* and their standards (called *base standards*). Speed, for example, is defined in terms of the base quantities length and time and their base standards.

Base standards must be both accessible and invariable. If we define the length standard as the distance between one's nose and the index finger on an outstretched arm, we certainly have an accessible standard—but it will, of course, vary from person to person. The demand for precision in science and engineering pushes us to aim first for invariability. We then exert great effort to make duplicates of the base standards that are accessible to those who need them.

1-3 | The International System of Units

In 1971, the 14th General Conference on Weights and Measures picked seven quantities as base quantities, thereby forming the basis of the International System of Units, abbreviated SI from its French name and popularly known as the *metric system.* Table 1-1 shows the units for all the base quantities including length, mass, and time—that we use in the early chapters of this book.

TABLE 1-1

Set of Fundamental Quantities*

Physical Quantity	Units (SI)	Units (CGS)	Notations
Mass	kg (kilogram)	g	M
Length	m (meter)	m	L
Time	s (second)	s	T
Temperature	K (kelvin)	°C	θ
Current	A (ampere)	A	I or A
Luminous intensity	cd (candela)	—	cd
Amount of substance	moles	—	mol

Note: There are two supplementary quantities too: (a) Plane angle (radian) (b) Solid angle (steradian).
*A set of physical quantities which are completely independent of each other and all other physical quantities can be expressed in terms of these physical quantities is called Set of Fundamental Quantities.

All SI *derived units* are defined in terms of these base units. For example, the SI unit for power, called the **watt** (W), is defined in terms of the base units for mass, length, and time. Thus, as you will see in Chapter 8,

$$1 \text{ watt} = 1 \text{ W} = 1 \text{ kg} \cdot \text{m}^2/\text{s}^3 \tag{1-1}$$

where the last collection of unit symbols is read as kilogram-meter squared per second cubed.

To express the very large and very small quantities we often run into in physics, we use *scientific notation,* which employs powers of 10. In this notation,

$$3\,560\,000\,000 \text{ m} = 3.56 \times 10^9 \text{ m} \tag{1-2}$$

and

$$0.000\,000\,492 \text{ s} = 4.92 \times 10^{-7} \text{ s} \tag{1-3}$$

Scientific notation on computers sometimes takes on an even briefer look, as in 3.56 E9 and 4.92 E–7, where E stands for "exponent of ten." It is briefer still on some calculators, where E is replaced with an empty space.

As a further convenience when dealing with very large or very small measurements, we use the prefixes listed in Table 1-2. As you can see, each prefix represents a certain power of 10, to be used as a multiplication factor. Attaching a prefix to an SI unit has the effect of multiplying by the associated factor. Thus, we can express a particular electric power as

$$1.27 \times 10^9 \text{ watts} = 1.27 \text{ gigawatts} = 1.27 \text{ GW} \tag{1-4}$$

or a particular time interval as

$$2.35 \times 10^{-9} \text{ s} = 2.35 \text{ nanoseconds} = 2.35 \text{ ns} \tag{1-5}$$

Some prefixes, as used in milliliter, centimeter, kilogram, and megabyte, are probably familiar to you.

TABLE 1-2

Prefixes for SI Units

Factor	Prefix[a]	Symbol
10^{24}	yotta-	Y
10^{21}	zetta-	Z
10^{18}	exa-	E
10^{15}	peta-	P
10^{12}	tera-	T
10^{9}	**giga-**	**G**
10^{6}	**mega-**	**M**
10^{3}	**kilo-**	**k**
10^{2}	hecto-	h
10^{1}	deka-	da
10^{-1}	deci-	d
10^{-2}	**centi-**	**c**
10^{-3}	**milli-**	**m**
10^{-6}	**micro-**	**μ**
10^{-9}	**nano-**	**n**
10^{-12}	**pico-**	**p**
10^{-15}	femto-	f
10^{-18}	atto-	a
10^{-21}	zepto-	z
10^{-24}	yocto-	y

[a]The most frequently used prefixes are shown in bold type.

1-4 | Standards of SI Quantities

The four basic properties of standard units are:

1. They must be well defined.
2. They should be easily available and reproducible.
3. They should be invariant with time and space.
4. They should be accepted by all.

When you go through the standards please note that all standards do possess these four properties.

TABLE 1-3

Some Approximate Lengths

Measurement	Length in Meters
Distance to the first galaxies formed	2×10^{26}
Distance to the Andromeda galaxy	2×10^{22}
Distance to the nearby star Proxima Centauri	4×10^{16}
Distance to Pluto	6×10^{12}
Radius of Earth	6×10^{6}
Height of Mt. Everest	9×10^{3}
Thickness of this page	1×10^{-4}
Length of a typical virus	1×10^{-8}
Radius of a hydrogen atom	5×10^{-11}
Radius of a proton	1×10^{-15}

Length

In 1792, the newborn Republic of France established a new system of weights and measures. Its cornerstone was the meter, defined to be one ten-millionth of the distance from the north pole to the equator. Later, for practical reasons, this Earth standard was abandoned and the meter came to be defined as the distance between two fine lines engraved near the ends of a platinum–iridium bar, the **standard meter bar,** which was kept at the International Bureau of Weights and Measures near Paris. Accurate copies of the bar were sent to standardizing laboratories throughout the world. These **secondary standards** were used to produce other, still more accessible standards, so that ultimately every measuring device derived its authority from the standard meter bar through a complicated chain of comparisons.

Eventually, a standard more precise than the distance between two fine scratches on a metal bar was required. In 1960, a new standard for the meter, based on the wavelength of light, was adopted. Specifically, the standard for the meter was redefined to be 1 650 763.73 wavelengths of a particular orange-red light emitted by atoms of krypton-86 (a particular isotope, or type, of krypton) in a gas discharge tube. This awkward number of wavelengths was chosen so that the new standard would be close to the old meter-bar standard.

By 1983, however, the demand for higher precision had reached such a point that even the krypton-86 standard could not meet it, and in that year a bold step was taken. The meter was redefined as the distance traveled by light in a specified time interval. In the words of the 17th General Conference on Weights and Measures:

> The meter is the length of the path traveled by light in a vacuum during a time interval of 1/299 792 458 of a second.

This time interval was chosen so that the speed of light c is exactly

$$c = 299\,792\,458 \text{ m/s}$$

Measurements of the speed of light had become extremely precise, so it made sense to adopt the speed of light as a defined quantity and to use it to redefine the meter.

Table 1-3 shows a wide range of lengths, from that of the universe (top line) to those of some very small objects.

PROBLEM-SOLVING TACTICS

Tactic 1: Order of Magnitude The *order of magnitude* of a number is the power of ten when the number is expressed in scientific notation. For example, if $A = 2.3 \times 10^4$ and $B = 7.8 \times 10^4$, then the orders of magnitude of both A and B are 4.

Often, engineering and science professionals will estimate the result of a calculation to the *nearest* order of magnitude. For our example, the nearest order of magnitude is 4 for A and 5 for B. Such estimation is common when detailed or precise data required in the calculation are not known or easily found. Sample Problem 1-1 gives an example.

Sample Problem 1-1

The world's largest ball of string is about 2 m in radius. To the nearest order of magnitude, what is the total length L of the string in the ball?

Conceptualize/Classify: We could, of course, take the ball apart and measure the total length L, but that would take great effort and make the ball's builder most unhappy. Instead, because we want only the nearest order of magnitude, we can estimate any quantities required in the calculation.

Compute: Let us assume the ball is spherical with radius $R = 2$ m. The string in the ball is not closely packed (there are uncountable gaps between adjacent sections of string). To allow for these gaps, let us somewhat overestimate the cross-sectional area of the string by assuming the cross section is square, with an edge length $d = 4$ mm. Then, with a cross-sectional area of d^2 and a length L, the string occupies a total volume of

$$V = (\text{cross-sectional area})(\text{length}) = d^2L$$

This is approximately equal to the volume of the ball, given by $\frac{4}{3}\pi R^3$, which is about $4R^3$ because π is about 3. Thus, we have

$$d^2L = 4R^3$$

or

$$L = \frac{4R^3}{d^2} = \frac{4(2\text{ m})^3}{(4 \times 10^{-3}\text{ m})^2} = 2 \times 10^6\text{ m} \approx 10^6\text{ m} = 10^3\text{ km} \quad \text{(Answer)}$$

Conclude: To the nearest order of magnitude, the ball contains about 1000 km of string!

Time

Time has two aspects. For civil and some scientific purposes, we want to know the time of day so that we can order events in sequence. In much scientific work, we want to know how long an event lasts. Thus, any time standard must be able to answer two questions: "*When* did it happen?" and "What is its *duration*?" Table 1-4 shows some time intervals.

Any phenomenon that repeats itself is a possible time standard. Earth's rotation, which determines the length of the day, has been used in this way for centuries; Fig. 1-1 shows one novel example of a watch based on that rotation. A quartz clock, in which a quartz ring is made to vibrate continuously, can be calibrated against Earth's rotation via astronomical observations and used to measure time intervals in the laboratory. However, the calibration cannot be carried out with the accuracy called for by modern scientific and engineering technology.

To meet the need for a better time standard, atomic clocks have been developed. An atomic clock at the National Institute of Standards and Technology (NIST) in Boulder, Colorado, is the standard for Coordinated Universal Time (UTC) in the United States. Its time signals are available by shortwave radio (stations WWV and WWVH) and by telephone (303-499-7111). Time signals (and related information) are also available from the United States Naval Observatory at website http://tycho.usno.navy.mil/time.html (To set a clock extremely accurately at your particular location, you would have to account for the travel time required for these signals to reach you.)

Figure 1-2 shows variations in the length of one day on Earth over a 4-year period, as determined by comparison with a cesium (atomic) clock. Because the variation displayed by Fig. 1-2 is seasonal and repetitious, we suspect the rotating Earth when there is a difference between Earth and atom as timekeepers. The variation is due to tidal effects caused by the Moon and to large-scale winds.

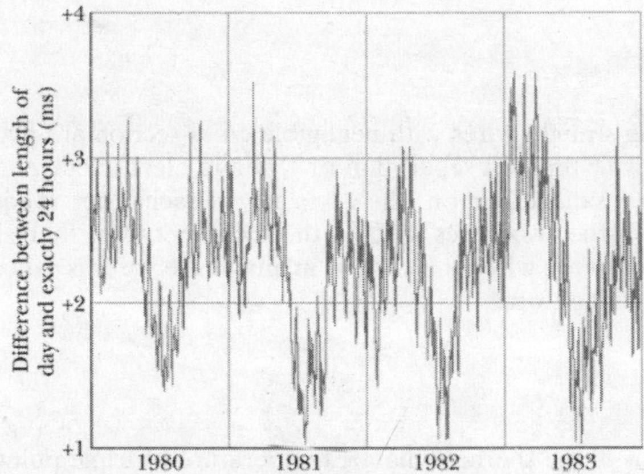

FIG. 1-2 Variations in the length of the day over a 4-year period. Note that the entire vertical scale amounts to only 3 ms (= 0.003 s).

TABLE 1-4

Some Approximate Time Intervals

Measurement	Time Interval in Seconds
Lifetime of the proton (predicted)	3×10^{40}
Age of the universe	5×10^{17}
Age of the pyramid of Cheops	1×10^{11}
Human life expectancy	2×10^{9}
Length of a day	9×10^{4}
Time between human heartbeats	8×10^{-1}
Lifetime of the muon	2×10^{-6}
Shortest lab light pulse	1×10^{-16}
Lifetime of the most unstable particle	1×10^{-23}
The Planck time[a]	1×10^{-43}

[a]This is the earliest time after the big bang at which the laws of physics as we know them can be applied.

FIG. 1-1 When the metric system was proposed in 1792, the hour was redefined to provide a 10-hour day. The idea did not catch on. The maker of this 10-hour watch wisely provided a small dial that kept conventional 12-hour time. Do the two dials indicate the same time? *(Steven Pitkin)*

FIG. 1-3 The international 1 kg standard of mass, a platinum–iridium cylinder 3.9 cm in height and in diameter. *(Courtesy Bureau International des Poids et Mesures, France)*

The 13th General Conference on Weights and Measures in 1967 adopted a standard second based on the cesium clock:

> One second is the time taken by 9 192 631 770 oscillations of the light (of a specified wavelength) emitted by a cesium-133 atom.

Atomic clocks are so consistent that, in principle, two cesium clocks would have to run for 6000 years before their readings would differ by more than 1 s. Even such accuracy pales in comparison with that of clocks currently being developed; their precision may be 1 part in 10^{18}—that is, 1 s in 1×10^{18} s (which is about 3×10^{10} y).

Mass

The Standard Kilogram

The SI standard of mass is a platinum–iridium cylinder (Fig. 1-3) kept at the International Bureau of Weights and Measures near Paris and assigned, by international agreement, a mass of 1 kilogram. Accurate copies have been sent to standardizing laboratories in other countries, and the masses of other bodies can be determined by balancing them against a copy. Table 1-5 shows some masses expressed in kilograms, ranging over about 83 orders of magnitude.

The U.S. copy of the standard kilogram is housed in a vault at NIST. It is removed, no more than once a year, for the purpose of checking duplicate copies that are used elsewhere. Since 1889, it has been taken to France twice for recomparison with the primary standard.

A Second Mass Standard

The masses of atoms can be compared with one another more precisely than they can be compared with the standard kilogram. For this reason, we have a second mass standard. It is the carbon-12 atom, which, by international agreement, has been assigned a mass of 12 **atomic mass units** (u). The relation between the two units is

$$1 \text{ u} = 1.660\,538\,86 \times 10^{-27} \text{ kg} \tag{1-6}$$

with an uncertainty of ±10 in the last two decimal places. Scientists can, with reasonable precision, experimentally determine the masses of other atoms relative to the mass of carbon-12. What we presently lack is a reliable means of extending that precision to more common units of mass, such as a kilogram.

TABLE 1-5

Some Approximate Masses

Object	Mass in Kilograms
Known universe	1×10^{53}
Our galaxy	2×10^{41}
Sun	2×10^{30}
Moon	7×10^{22}
Asteroid Eros	5×10^{15}
Small mountain	1×10^{12}
Ocean liner	7×10^{7}
Elephant	5×10^{3}
Grape	3×10^{-3}
Speck of dust	7×10^{-10}
Penicillin molecule	5×10^{-17}
Uranium atom	4×10^{-25}
Proton	2×10^{-27}
Electron	9×10^{-31}

Ampere

Suppose two long straight wires with negligible cross-section are placed parallel to each other in vacuum at a separation of 1 m and electric currents are established in the two in same direction. The wires attract each other. If equal currents are maintained in the two wires so that the force between them is 2×10^{-7} Newton per meter of the wires, the current in any of the wires is called 1 A. Here, Newton is the SI unit of force.

Kelvin

The fraction $^1/_{273.16}$ of the thermodynamic temperature of triple point of water is called 1 K.

Mole

The amount of a substance that contains as many units as there are number of atoms in 0.012 kg of carbon-12 is called a mole. This number (number of atoms in 0.012 kg of carbon-12) is called Avagadro constant and its best value available is $6.022\,045 \times 10^{23}$ with an uncertainty of about $0.000\,031 \times 10^{23}$.

Candela

The SI unit of luminous intensity is 1 cd which is the luminous intensity of a black body of surface area $1/600\,000$ m^2 placed at the temperature of freezing platinum and at a pressure of 101 325 N/m^2, in the direction perpendicular to its surface.

Derived physical quantities

The physical quantities that can be expressed in terms of fundamental physical quantities are called derived physical quantities; for example,

speed = distance/time

Dimensions

Dimensions are the powers to which fundamental physical quantities must be raised to express the physical quantity; for example,

$$\text{speed} = \text{distance/time} = \text{LT}^{-1}$$

Here, dimensions of L = 1 and that of T = −1.

1-5 | Applications of Dimensional Analysis

To find dimensions of a derived physical quantity

Dimensions of derived quantities

To find dimensions of derived quantities we should write a formula/equation which relates the unknown derived quantity with other known quantities. Thus, by expressing every quantity in terms of fundamental quantities we can find dimensions of unknown quantity by multiplication and division.

Example 1

Find the dimensional formulae of the following quantities:

1. Charge Q
2. Potential V
3. Resistance R
4. Universal constant of gravitation G
5. Coefficient of viscocity η

Some equations involving these quantities are

$$F = \frac{Gm_1 m_2}{r^2} \text{ and } F = -\eta A \frac{v_2 - v_1}{x_2 - x_1};\ Q = It,\ U = VIt \text{ and } V = RI;$$

where I denotes the electric current, t is time, U is energy, and the other symbols have their usual meanings.

Solution

1. $Q = It$

   Hence, [Q] = IT

2. $U = VIt$

   or, $ML^2T^{-2} = [V]IT$

   or, $[V] = ML^2I^{-1}T^{-3}$

3. $V = RI$

   or, $R = \frac{V}{I}$

   or, $[R] = \frac{ML^2I^{-1}T^{-3}}{I} = ML^2I^{-2}T^{-3}$

4. $F = G\frac{m_1m_2}{r^2}$

   or, $G = \frac{Fr^2}{m_1m_2}$

   or, $[G] = \frac{[F]L^2}{M^2} = \frac{MLT^{-2}L^2}{M^2} = M^{-1}L^3T^{-2}$

5. $F = -\eta A\frac{v_2 - v_1}{x_2 - x_1}$

   or, $MLT^{-2} = [\eta]L^2\frac{L/T}{L}$ or $[\eta] = ML^{-1}T^{-1}$

To derive a physical relation between different physical quantities

Example 2

The time of oscillaton T of a small drop of a liquid under surface tension (whose dimensions are those of force per unit length) depends upon the density d, the radius r, and the surface tension σ. Derive dimensionally the relationship $T \propto \sqrt{dr^3/\sigma}$.

Solution

First of all, let us find the dimensions of surface tension which is F/L

thus $$[MLT^{-2}]/L$$

$$S = [MT^{-2}]$$

Let $T \propto d^a r^b \sigma^c$, then substituting the dimension of various quantities, we get

$$[M^0L^0T^1] = [ML^{-3}]^a[L]^b[MT^{-2}]^c$$

$$= [M^aL^{-3a}][L^b][M^cT^{-2c}]$$

or $$[M^0L^0T^1] = [M^{a+c}L^{-3a+b}T^{-2c}]$$

Comparing the powers of similar quantities on both sides, we get

$$a + c = 0 \quad \text{(i)}$$

$$-3a + b = 0 \quad \text{(ii)}$$

and $$-2c = 1 \quad \text{(iii)}$$

From Eq. (iii) we get $c = -\frac{1}{2}$

From Eq. (i) we get $a = \frac{1}{2}$

From Eq. (ii) we get $b = \frac{3}{2}$

$$\therefore T \propto d^{1/2} r^{3/2} \sigma^{-1/2} \quad \text{or} \quad T \propto \sqrt{\frac{dr^3}{\sigma}}$$

Example 3

Stoke's formula says that force due to viscosity acting on a sphere of radius r moving in viscous liquid depends upon (i) coefficient of viscosity (η), (ii) radius of the sphere (r), and (iii) velocity (v). Find the relation dimensionally.

Solution

Let $F \propto \eta^a v^b r^c$, then substituting the dimensions of various quantities on both sides, we get

$$[MLT^{-2}] = [ML^{-1}T^{-1}]^a [LT^{-1}]^b [L]^c$$
$$= [M^a L^{-a+b+c} T^{-a-b}]$$

Comparing the powers of M, L, and T, we get

$a = 1, -a + b + c = 1$, and $-a-b = -2$

or, $b = 1$ and $c = 1-1+1 = 1$

$F \propto \eta^1 v^1 r^1$

or, $F = k(\eta r v)$ where k is a dimensionless constant.

Conversion of Units

We often need to change the units in which a physical quantity is expressed. We do so by a method called *chain-link conversion*. In this method, we multiply the original measurement by a **conversion factor** (a ratio of units that is equal to unity). For example, because 1 min and 60 s are identical time intervals, we have

$$\frac{1 \text{ min}}{60 \text{ s}} = 1 \quad \text{and} \quad \frac{60 \text{ s}}{1 \text{ min}} = 1$$

Thus, the ratios (1 min)/(60 s) and (60 s)/(1 min) can be used as conversion factors. This is *not* the same as writing $\frac{1}{60} = 1$ or $60 = 1$; each *number* and its *unit* must be treated together.

Because multiplying any quantity by unity leaves the quantity unchanged, we can introduce conversion factors wherever we find them useful. In chain-link conversion, we use the factors to cancel unwanted units. For example, to convert 2 min to seconds, we have

$$2 \text{ min} = (2 \text{ min})(1) = (2 \cancel{\text{min}})\left(\frac{60 \text{ s}}{1 \cancel{\text{min}}}\right) = 120 \text{ s} \qquad (1\text{-}7)$$

If you introduce a conversion factor in such a way that unwanted units do not cancel, invert the factor and try again. In conversions, the units obey the same algebraic rules as variables and numbers.

Appendix D gives conversion factors between SI and other systems of units, including non-SI units still used in the United States. However, the conversion factors are written in the style of "1 min = 60 s" rather than as a ratio. The following sample problem gives an example of how to set up such ratios.

Sample Problem 1-2

When, according to legend, Pheidippides ran from Marathon to Athens in 490 B.C. to bring word of the Greek victory over the Persians, he probably ran at a speed of about 23 rides per hour (rides/h). The ride is an ancient Greek unit for length, as are the stadium and the plethron: 1 ride was defined to be 4 stadia, 1 stadium was defined to be 6 plethra, and, in terms of a modern unit, 1 plethron is 30.8 m. How fast did Pheidippides run in kilometers per second (km/s)?

Conceptualize/Classify: In chain-link conversions, we write the conversion factors as ratios that will eliminate unwanted units.

Compute: Here we write

$$23 \text{ rides/h} = \left(23 \frac{\text{rides}}{\text{h}}\right)\left(\frac{4 \text{ stadia}}{1 \text{ ride}}\right)\left(\frac{6 \text{ plethra}}{1 \text{ stadium}}\right) \times \left(\frac{30.8 \text{ m}}{1 \text{ plethron}}\right)\left(\frac{1 \text{ km}}{1000 \text{ m}}\right)\left(\frac{1 \text{ h}}{3600 \text{ s}}\right)$$

$$= 4.7227 \times 10^{-3} \text{ km/s} \approx 4.7 \times 10^{-3} \text{ km/s} \qquad \text{(Answer)}$$

Sample Problem 1-3

The cran is a British volume unit for freshly caught herrings: 1 cran = 170.474 liters (L) of fish, about 750 herrings. Suppose that, to be cleared through customs in Saudi Arabia, a shipment of 1255 crans must be declared in terms of cubic covidos, where the covido is an Arabic unit of length: 1 covido = 48.26 cm. What is the required declaration?

Conceptualize/Classify: From Appendix D we see that 1 L is equivalent to 1000 cm^3. To convert from *cubic* centimeters to *cubic* covidos, we must *cube* the conversion ratio between centimeters and covidos.

Compute: We write the following chain-link conversion:

1255 crans

$$= (1255 \text{ crans})\left(\frac{170.474 \text{ L}}{1 \text{ cran}}\right)\left(\frac{1000 \text{ cm}^3}{1 \text{ L}}\right)\left(\frac{1 \text{ covido}}{48.26 \text{ cm}}\right)^3$$

$$= 1.903 \times 10^3 \text{ covidos}^3 \qquad \text{(Answer)}$$

PROBLEM-SOLVING TACTICS

Tactic 1: Significant Figures and Decimal Places If you calculated the answer to Sample Problem 1-2 without your calculator automatically rounding it off, the number 4.722 666 666 67 × 10^{-3} might have appeared in the display. The precision implied by this number is meaningless. We rounded the answer to 4.7×10^{-3} km/s so as not to imply that it is more precise than the given data. The given speed of 23 rides/h consists of two digits, called **significant figures.** Thus, we rounded the answer to two significant figures. In this book, final results of calculations are often rounded to match the least number of significant figures in the given data. (However, sometimes an extra significant figure is kept.) When the leftmost of the digits to be discarded is 5 or more, the last remaining digit is rounded up; otherwise it is retained as is. For example, 11.3516 is rounded to three significant figures as 11.4 and 11.3279 is rounded to three significant figures as 11.3. (The answers to sample problems in this book are usually presented with the symbol = instead of ≈ even if rounding is involved.)

When a number such as 3.15 or 3.15×10^3 is provided in a problem, the number of significant figures is apparent, but how about the number 3000? Is it known to only one significant figure (3×10^3)? Or is it known to as many as four significant figures (3.000×10^3)? In this book, we assume that all the zeros in such given numbers as 3000 are significant, but you had better not make that assumption elsewhere.

Don't confuse *significant figures* with *decimal places.* Consider the lengths 35.6 mm, 3.56 m, and 0.00356 m. They all have three significant figures but they have one, two, and five decimal places, respectively.

Sample Problem 1-4 Build your skill

Young's modulus of steel is 19×10^{10} N/m^2. Express it in dyne/cm^2. Here dyne is the CGS unit of force.

Solution: The unit of Young's modulus is N/m^2.

This suggests that it has dimensions Force/(distance)^2

Thus,
$$[Y] = \frac{[F]}{L^2} = \frac{MLT^{-2}}{L^2} = ML^{-1}T^{-2}$$

N/m^2 is in SI units.

So,
$$1 \text{ N/m}^2 = (1 \text{ kg})(1 \text{ m})^{-1}(1 \text{ s})^{-2}$$

and $1\ \text{dyne/cm}^2 = (1\ \text{g})\,(1\ \text{cm})^{-1}\,(1\ \text{s})^{-2}$

So $$\frac{1\ \text{N/m}^2}{1\ \text{dyne/cm}^2} = \left(\frac{1\ \text{kg}}{1\ \text{g}}\right)\left(\frac{1\ \text{m}}{1\ \text{cm}}\right)^{-1}\left(\frac{1\ \text{s}}{1\ \text{s}}\right)^{-2}$$

$$= 1000 \times \frac{1}{100} \times 1 = 10$$

or $1\ \text{N/m}^2 = 10\ \text{dyne/cm}^2$

or $19 \times 10^{10}\ \text{N/m}^2 = 19 \times 10^{11}\ \text{dyne/cm}^2$

To check dimensional corrections of a given physical relation between different physical quantities

If the dimensional equation or formula on the left hand side of a physical equation is equal to the dimensional formula on the right hand side then the relation is correct. This principle is called the principle of homogeneity.

Example 4

Check the accuracy of the equation

$$n = \frac{1}{2l}\sqrt{\frac{F}{\mu}}$$

where l is the length of the string, μ its mass per unit length, F the stretching force and n the frequency of vibration.

Solution

Dimensions of left hand side $n = \frac{1}{\text{T}} = \text{T}^{-1}$

Dimensions of right hand side $= \frac{1}{\left[\text{L}^1\right]}\left[\frac{\text{M}^1\text{L}^1\text{T}^{-2}}{\text{M}^1\text{L}^{-1}}\right] = \left[\text{L}^{-1}\right]\left[\text{LT}^{-1}\right] = \left[\text{T}^{-1}\right]$

As the dimensions of left and right hand sides are equal, the relation is correct.

Example 5

If velocity of light, acceleration due to gravity, and standard atmospheric pressure are taken as the fundamental units, what will be the value of

1. 9 m and
2. 30 s in new system of units. Given, velocity of light is 3×10^8 m/s, acceleration due to gravity 10 m/s^2, and standard atmospheric pressure is 10^5 N/m^2.

Solution

Velocity $[\text{V}] = [\text{L}^1\text{T}^{-1}]$

Acceleration $[a] = [\text{L}^1\text{T}^{-2}]$

Pressure $[\text{P}] = [\text{M}^1\text{L}^{-1}\text{T}^{-2}]$

It can be easily seen that $[\text{L}] = [\text{V}]^2[a]^{-1}[\text{P}]^0$

1. Let us call one unit of length as 1 keter in new system. Putting the values of V and a we get,

$$1 \text{ keter} = \frac{\left(3\times10^{8}\right)^{2}}{10} = 9\times10^{15} \text{ meter}$$

or $\quad 1 \text{ meter} = (1/9) \times 10^{-15}$

thus $\quad 9 \text{ meter} = 9 \times (1/9) \times 10^{-15} = 10^{-15} \text{ keter}$

It can be easily seen that

$$[T] = [V]^{1}[a]^{-1}[P]^{0}$$

2. Let us call one unit of time as 1 recond in new system putting the values of V and a we get

$$1 \text{ recond} = \frac{3\times10^{8}}{10} = 3\times10^{7} \text{ second}$$

or $\quad 1 \text{ second} = (1/3) \times 10^{-7}$

thus $\quad 30 \text{ second} = 30 \times (1/3) \times 10^{-7} = 10^{-6} \text{ recond}$

REVIEW & SUMMARY

Measurement in Physics Physics is based on measurement of physical quantities. Certain physical quantities have been chosen as **base quantities** (such as length, time, and mass); each has been defined in terms of a **standard** and given a **unit** of measure (such as meter, second, and kilogram). Other physical quantities are defined in terms of the base quantities and their standards and units.

SI Units The unit system emphasized in this book is the International System of Units (SI). The three physical quantities displayed in Table 1-1 are used in the early chapters. Standards, which must be both accessible and invariable, have been established for these base quantities by international agreement. These standards are used in all physical measurement, for both the base quantities and the quantities derived from them. Scientific notation and the prefixes of Table 1-2 are used to simplify measurement notation.

Changing Units Conversion of units may be performed by using *chain-link conversions* in which the original data are multiplied successively by conversion factors written as unity and the units are manipulated like algebraic quantities until only the desired units remain.

Length The meter is defined as the distance traveled by light during a precisely specified time interval.

Time The second is defined in terms of the oscillations of light emitted by an atomic (cesium-133) source. Accurate time signals are sent worldwide by radio signals keyed to atomic clocks in standardizing laboratories.

Mass The kilogram is defined in terms of a platinum–iridium standard mass kept near Paris. For measurements on an atomic scale, the atomic mass unit, defined in terms of the atom carbon-12, is usually used.

PROBLEMS

Standards of SI Quantities: Length

1 The micrometer (1 μm) is often called the *micron.* (a) How many microns make up 1.0 km? (b) What fraction of a centimeter equals 1.0 μm? (c) How many microns are in 1.0 yd?

2 Spacing in this book was generally done in units of points and picas: 12 points = 1 pica, and 6 picas = 1 inch. If a figure was misplaced in the page proofs by 0.80 cm, what was the misplacement in (a) picas and (b) points?

3 Earth is approximately a sphere of radius 6.37×10^{6} m. What are (a) its circumference in kilometers, (b) its surface area in square kilometers, and (c) its volume in cubic kilometers?

4 Antarctica is roughly semicircular, with a radius of 2000 km (Fig. 1-4). The average thickness of its ice cover is 3000 m. How many cubic centimeters of ice does Antarctica contain? (Ignore the curvature of Earth.)

Standards of SI Quantities: Time

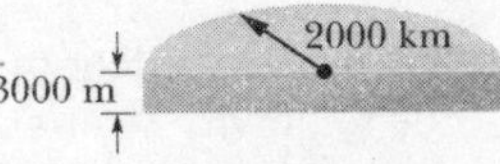

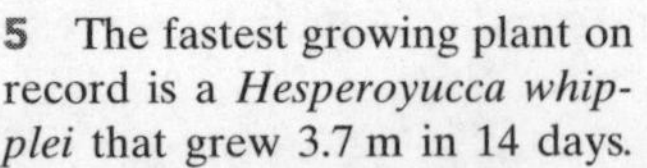

FIG. 1-4 Problem 4.

5 The fastest growing plant on record is a *Hesperoyucca whipplei* that grew 3.7 m in 14 days. What was its growth rate in micrometers per second?

6 A fortnight is a charming English measure of time equal to 2.0 weeks (the word is a contraction of "fourteen nights"). That is a nice amount of time in pleasant company but perhaps a painful string of microseconds in unpleasant company. How many microseconds are in a fortnight?

7 A lecture period (50 min) is close to 1 microcentury. (a) How long is a microcentury in minutes? (b) Using

$$\text{percentage difference} = \left(\frac{\text{actual} - \text{approximation}}{\text{actual}}\right)100$$

find the percentage difference from the approximation.

8 For about 10 years after the French Revolution, the French government attempted to base measures of time on multiples of ten: One week consisted of 10 days, one day consisted of 10 hours, one hour consisted of 100 minutes, and one minute consisted of 100 seconds. What are the ratios of (a) the French decimal week to the standard week and (b) the French decimal second to the standard second?

9 Three digital clocks A, B, and C run at different rates and do not have simultaneous readings of zero. Figure 1-5 shows simultaneous readings on pairs of the clocks for four occasions. (At the earliest occasion, for example, B reads 25.0 s and C reads 92.0 s.) If two events are 600 s apart on clock A, how far apart are they on (a) clock B and (b) clock C? (c) When clock A reads 400 s, what does clock B read? (d) When clock C reads 15.0 s, what does clock B read? (Assume negative readings for prezero times.)

312 512 A (s)
125 290
25.0 200 B (s)
92.0 142 C (s)

FIG. 1-5 Problem 9.

10 Suppose that, while lying on a beach near the equator watching the Sun set over a calm ocean, you start a stopwatch just as the top of the Sun disappears. You then stand, elevating your eyes by a height $H = 1.70$ m, and stop the watch when the top of the Sun again disappears. If the elapsed time is $t = 11.1$ s, what is the radius r of Earth?

Standards of SI Quantities: Mass

11 Gold, which has a density of 19.32 g/cm^3, is the most ductile metal and can be pressed into a thin leaf or drawn out into a long fiber. (a) If a sample of gold, with a mass of 27.63 g, is pressed into a leaf of 1.000 μm thickness, what is the area of the leaf? (b) If, instead, the gold is drawn out into a cylindrical fiber of radius 2.500 μm, what is the length of the fiber?

12 Iron has a density of 7.87 g/cm^3, and the mass of an iron atom is 9.27×10^{-26} kg. If the atoms are spherical and tightly packed, (a) what is the volume of an iron atom and (b) what is the distance between the centers of adjacent atoms?

13 Grains of fine California beach sand are approximately spheres with an average radius of 50 μm and are made of silicon dioxide, which has a density of 2600 kg/m^3. What mass of sand grains would have a total surface area (the total area of all the individual spheres) equal to the surface area of a cube 1.00 m on an edge?

14 During heavy rain, a section of a mountainside measuring 2.5 km horizontally, 0.80 km up along the slope, and 2.0 m deep slips into a valley in a mud slide. Assume that the mud ends up uniformly distributed over a surface area of the valley measuring 0.40 km $\times$ 0.40 km and that mud has a density of 1900 kg/m^3. What is the mass of the mud sitting above a 4.0 m^2 area of the valley floor?

15 Water is poured into a container that has a leak. The mass m of the water is given as a function of time t by $m = 5.00t^{0.8} - 3.00t + 20.00$, with $t \geq 0$, m in grams, and t in seconds. (a) At what time is the water mass greatest, and (b) what is that greatest mass? In kilograms per minute, what is the rate of mass change at (c) $t = 2.00$ s and (d) $t = 5.00$ s?

16 A vertical container with base area measuring 14.0 cm by 17.0 cm is being filled with identical pieces of candy, each with a volume of 50.0 mm^3 and a mass of 0.0200 g. Assume that the volume of the empty spaces between the candies is negligible. If the height of the candies in the container increases at the rate of 0.250 cm/s, at what rate (kilograms per minute) does the mass of the candies in the container increase?

Additional Problems

17 A *cord* is a volume of cut wood equal to a stack 8 ft long, 4 ft wide, and 4 ft high. How many cords are in 1.0 m^3?

18 One molecule of water (H_2O) contains two atoms of hydrogen and one atom of oxygen. A hydrogen atom has a mass of 1.0 u and an atom of oxygen has a mass of 16 u, approximately. (a) What is the mass in kilograms of one molecule of water? (b) How many molecules of water are in the world's oceans, which have an estimated total mass of 1.4×10^{21} kg?

19 A typical sugar cube has an edge length of 1 cm. If you had a cubical box that contained a mole of sugar cubes, what would its edge length be? (One mole = 6.02×10^{23} units.)

20 Using conversions and data in the chapter, determine the number of hydrogen atoms required to obtain 1.0 kg of hydrogen. A hydrogen atom has a mass of 1.0 u.

21 An astronomical unit (AU) is the average distance between Earth and the Sun, approximately 1.50×10^8 km. The speed of light is about 3.0×10^8 m/s. Express the speed of light in astronomical units per minute.

22 A person on a diet might lose 2.3 kg per week. Express the mass loss rate in milligrams per second, as if the dieter could sense the second-by-second loss.

23 A standard interior staircase has steps each with a rise (height) of 19 cm and a run (horizontal depth) of 23 cm. Research suggests that the stairs would be safer for descent if the run were, instead, 28 cm. For a particular staircase of total height 4.57 m, how much farther into the room would the staircase extend if this change in run were made?

24 The common Eastern mole, a mammal, typically has a mass of 75 g, which corresponds to about 7.5 moles of atoms. (A mole of atoms is 6.02×10^{23} atoms.) In atomic mass units (u), what is the average mass of the atoms in the common Eastern mole?

25 An *astronomical unit* (AU) is equal to the average distance from Earth to the Sun, about 92.9×10^6 mi. A *parsec* (pc) is the distance at which a length of 1 AU would subtend an angle of exactly 1 second of arc (Fig. 1-6). A *light-year* (ly) is the distance that light, traveling through a vacuum with a speed of 186 000 mi/s, would cover in 1.0 year. Express the Earth–Sun distance in (a) parsecs and (b) light-years.

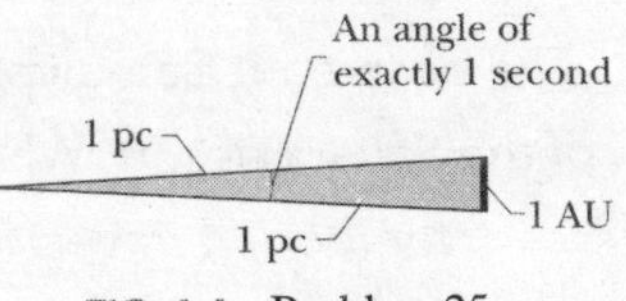

FIG. 1-6 Problem 25.

2 Vectors and Elementary Calculus

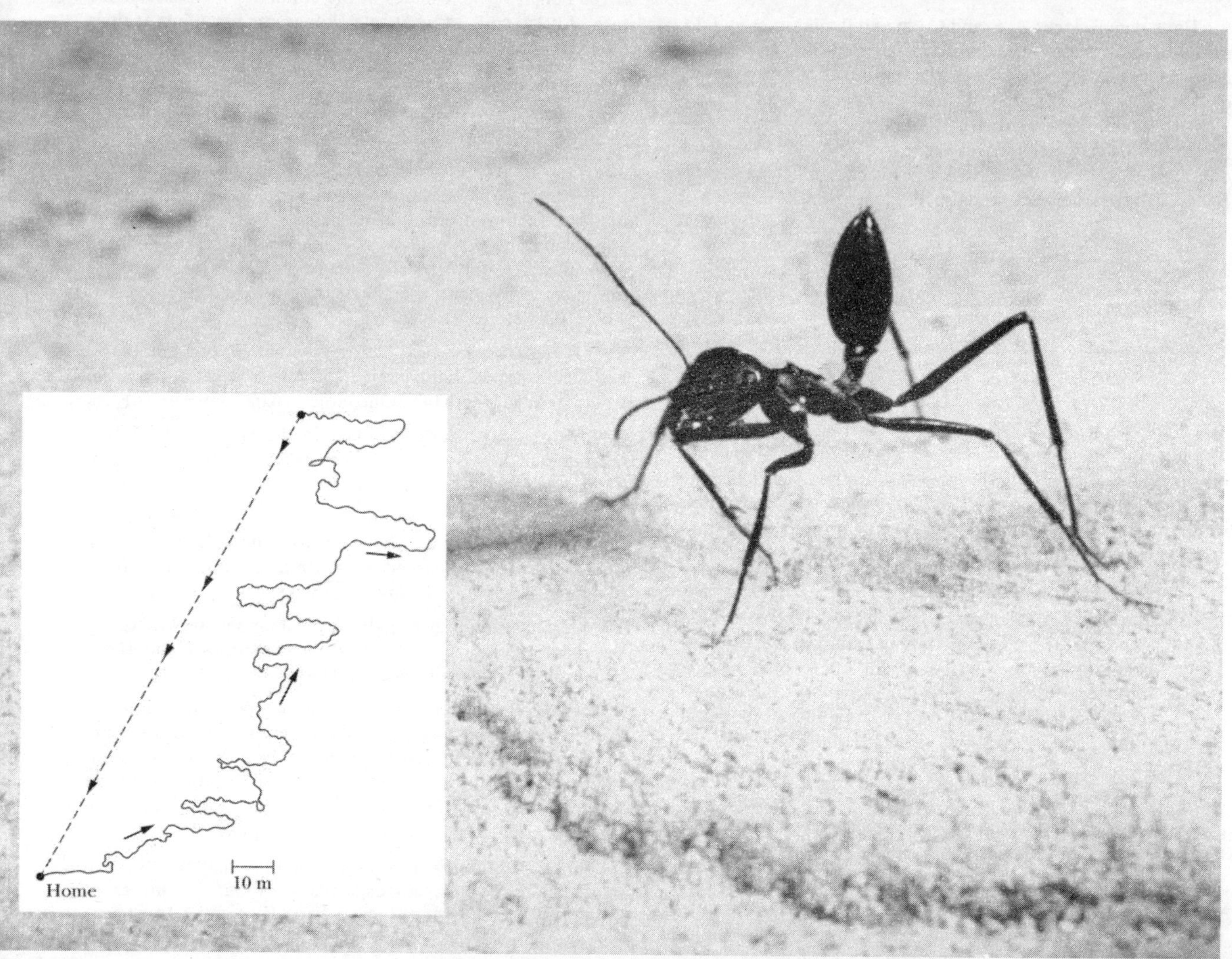

Courtesy Rudiger Wehner, Zoologisches Institut der Universitat Zurich

The desert ant Cataglyphis fortis *lives in the plains of the Sahara desert. When one of the ants forages for food, it travels from its home nest along a haphazard search path like the one shown here. The ant may travel more than 500 m along such a complicated path over flat, featureless sand that contains no landmarks. Yet, when the ant decides to return home, it turns and then runs directly home.*

How does the ant know the way home with no guiding clues on the desert plain?

The answer is in this chapter.

2-1 Introduction

In our study of physics, we often need mathematical tools to work with physical quantities. Two very important tools that we will be using are vectors and calculus. Physics deals with a great many quantities that have both size and direction, and it needs a special mathematical language—the language of vectors—to describe those quantities. This language is also used in engineering, the other sciences, and even in common speech. If you have ever given directions such as "Go five blocks down this street and then take a left," you have used the language of vectors. In fact, navigation of any sort is based on vectors, but physics and engineering also need vectors in special ways to explain phenomena involving rotation and magnetic forces, which we get to in later chapters.

The first part of this chapter deals with general properties of vector quantities. We discuss the addition and subtraction of vector quantities, together with some connon applications to physical situations. Vector quantities are used throughout this text. Therefore, it is imperative that you master the techniques discussed in this chapter.

Second part deals with calculus. Calculus is a branch of mathematics, which is a very important tool of physics. Calculus helps us to deal with quantities that are varying. Differential calculus helps in writing rate at any instant in an elegant manner. Integral calculus helps in adding variable quantities.

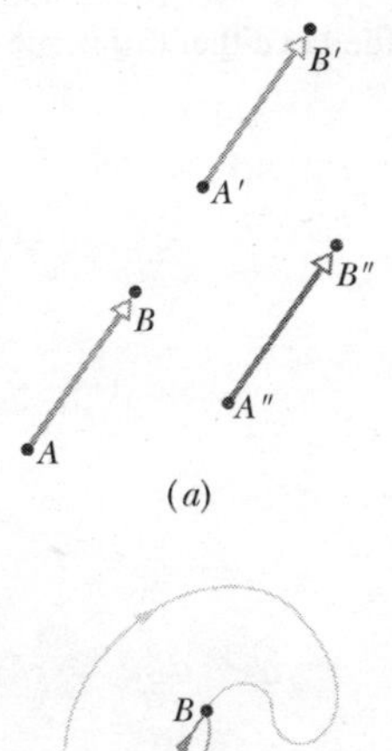

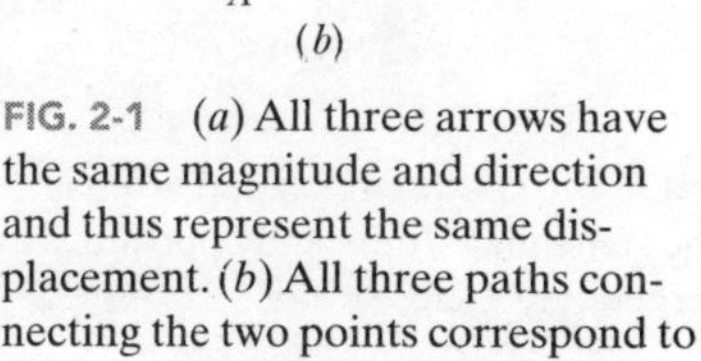

FIG. 2-1 (*a*) All three arrows have the same magnitude and direction and thus represent the same displacement. (*b*) All three paths connecting the two points correspond to the same displacement vector.

2-2 | Vector and Scalar Quantities

A particle moving along a straight line can move in only two directions. We can take its motion to be positive in one of these directions and negative in the other. For a particle moving in two or three dimensions, however, a plus sign or minus sign is no longer enough to indicate a direction. Instead, we must use a *vector.*

A **vector** has magnitude as well as direction, and vectors follow certain (vector) rules of combination, which we examine in this chapter.

A **vector quantity** is a quantity that has both a magnitude and a direction and thus can be represented with a vector. Some physical quantities that are vector quantities are displacement, velocity, and acceleration. You will see many more throughout this book, so learning the rules of vector combination now will help you greatly in later chapters.

Not all physical quantities involve a direction. Temperature, pressure, energy, mass, and time, for example, do not "point" in the spatial sense. We call such quantities **scalars,** and we deal with them by the rules of ordinary algebra. A single value, with a sign (as in a temperature of $-40°F$), specifies a scalar.

The simplest vector quantity is displacement, or change of position. A vector that represents a displacement is called, reasonably, a **displacement vector.** (Similarly, we have velocity vectors and acceleration vectors.) If a particle changes its position by moving from A to B in Fig. 2-1*a*, we say that it undergoes a displacement from A to B, which we represent with an arrow pointing from A to B. The arrow specifies the vector graphically. To distinguish vector symbols from other kinds of arrows in this book, we use the outline of a triangle as the arrowhead.

In Fig. 2-1*a*, the arrows from A to B, from A' to B', and from A'' to B'' have the same magnitude and direction. Thus, they specify identical displacement vectors and represent the same *change of position* for the particle. A vector can be shifted without changing its value *if* its length and direction are not changed.

The displacement vector tells us nothing about the actual path that the particle takes. In Fig. 2-1*b*, for example, all three paths connecting points A and B correspond to the same displacement vector, that of Fig. 2-1*a*. Displacement vectors represent only the overall effect of the motion, not the motion itself.

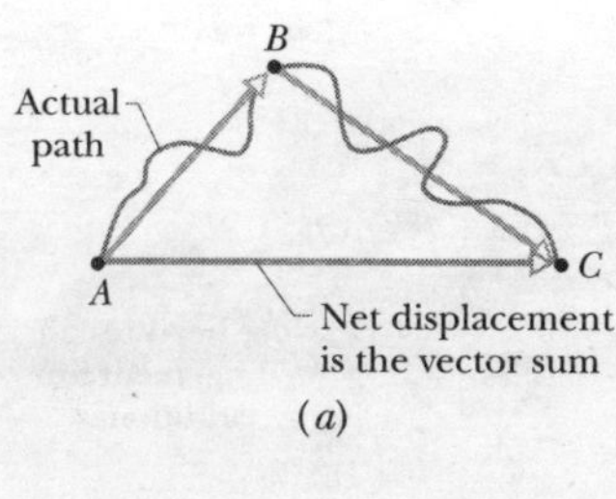

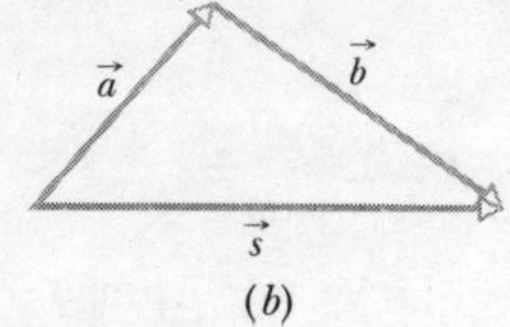

FIG. 2-2 (*a*) *AC* is the vector sum of the vectors *AB* and *BC*. (*b*) The same vectors relabeled.

2-3 | Vector Addition

Suppose that, as in the vector diagram of Fig. 2-2*a*, a particle moves from A to B and then later from B to C. We can represent its overall displacement (no matter

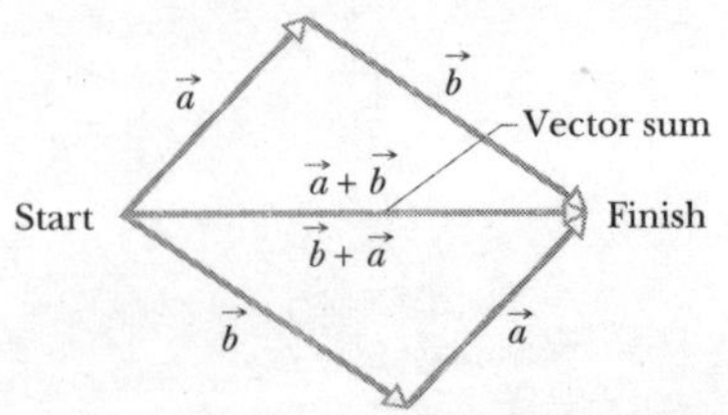

FIG. 2-3 The two vectors $\vec{a}$ and $\vec{b}$ can be added in either order; see Eq. 2-2.

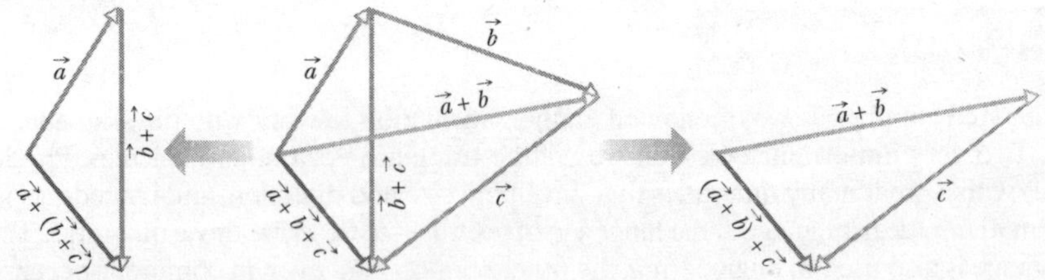

FIG. 2-4 The three vectors $\vec{a}$, $\vec{b}$, and $\vec{c}$ can be grouped in any way as they are added; see Eq. 2-3.

what its actual path) with two successive displacement vectors, AB and BC. The *net* displacement of these two displacements is a single displacement from A to C. We call AC the **vector sum** (or **resultant**) of the vectors AB and BC. This sum is not the usual algebraic sum.

In Fig. 2-2*b*, we redraw the vectors of Fig. 2-2*a* and relabel them in the way that we shall use from now on, namely, with an arrow over an italic symbol, as in $\vec{a}$. If we want to indicate only the magnitude of the vector (a quantity that lacks a sign or direction), we shall use the italic symbol, as in a, b, and s. (You can use just a handwritten symbol.) A symbol with an overhead arrow always implies both properties of a vector, magnitude and direction.

We can represent the relation among the three vectors in Fig. 2-2*b* with the *vector equation*

$$\vec{s} = \vec{a} + \vec{b} \tag{2-1}$$

which says that the vector $\vec{s}$ is the vector sum of vectors $\vec{a}$ and $\vec{b}$. The symbol + in Eq. 2-1 and the words "sum" and "add" have different meanings for vectors than they do in the usual algebra because they involve both magnitude *and* direction.

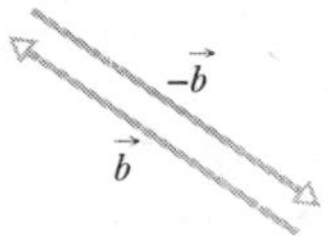

FIG. 2-5 The vectors $\vec{b}$ and $-\vec{b}$ have the same magnitude and opposite directions.

Figure 2-2 suggests a procedure for adding two-dimensional vectors $\vec{a}$ and $\vec{b}$ geometrically. (1) On paper, sketch vector $\vec{a}$ to some convenient scale and at the proper angle. (2) Sketch vector $\vec{b}$ to the same scale, with its tail at the head of vector $\vec{a}$, again at the proper angle. (3) The vector sum $\vec{s}$ is the vector that extends from the tail of $\vec{a}$ to the head of $\vec{b}$.

Vector addition, defined in this way, has two important properties. First, the order of addition does not matter. Adding $\vec{a}$ to $\vec{b}$ gives the same result as adding $\vec{b}$ to $\vec{a}$ (Fig. 2-3); that is,

$$\vec{a} + \vec{b} = \vec{b} + \vec{a} \quad \text{(commutative law)} \tag{2-2}$$

Second, when there are more than two vectors, we can group them in any order as we add them. Thus, if we want to add vectors $\vec{a}$, $\vec{b}$, and $\vec{c}$, we can add $\vec{a}$ and $\vec{b}$ first and then add their vector sum to $\vec{c}$. We can also add $\vec{b}$ and $\vec{c}$ first and then add *that* sum to $\vec{a}$. We get the same result either way, as shown in Fig. 2-4. That is,

$$(\vec{a} + \vec{b}) + \vec{c} = \vec{a} + (\vec{b} + \vec{c}) \quad \text{(associative law)} \tag{2-3}$$

The vector $-\vec{b}$ is a vector with the same magnitude as $\vec{b}$ but the opposite direction (see Fig. 2-5). Adding the two vectors in Fig. 2-5 would yield

$$\vec{b} + (-\vec{b}) = 0$$

Thus, adding $-\vec{b}$ has the effect of subtracting $\vec{b}$. We use this property to define the difference between two vectors: let $\vec{d} = \vec{a} - \vec{b}$. Then

$$\vec{d} = \vec{a} - \vec{b} = \vec{a} + (-\vec{b}) \quad \text{(vector subtraction)} \tag{2-4}$$

that is, we find the difference vector $\vec{d}$ by adding the vector $-\vec{b}$ to the vector $\vec{a}$. Figure 2-6 shows how this is done geometrically.

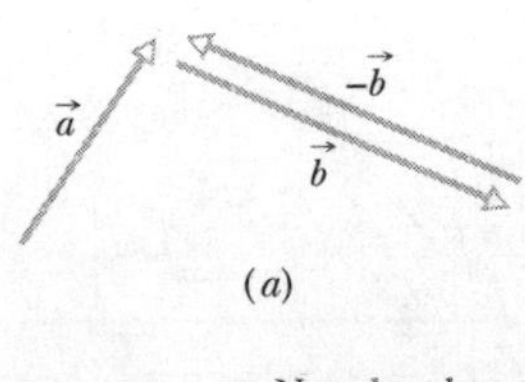

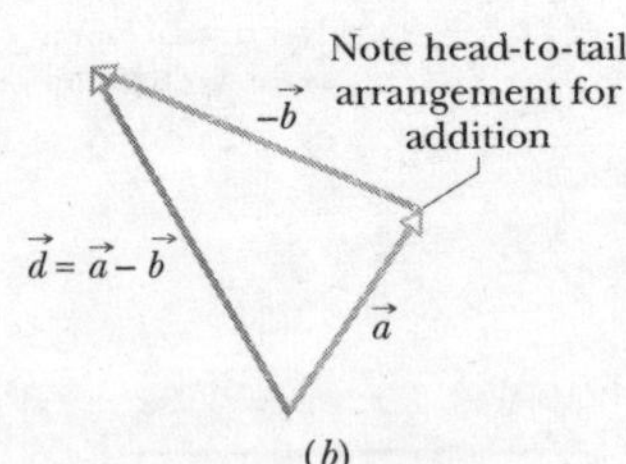

FIG. 2-6 (*a*) Vectors $\vec{a}$, $\vec{b}$, and $-\vec{b}$. (*b*) To subtract vector $\vec{b}$ from vector $\vec{a}$, add vector $-\vec{b}$ to vector $\vec{a}$.

As in the usual algebra, we can move a term that includes a vector symbol from one side of a vector equation to the other, but we must change its sign. For example, if we are given Eq. 2-4 and need to solve for $\vec{a}$, we can rearrange the equation as

$$\vec{d} + \vec{b} = \vec{a} \quad \text{or} \quad \vec{a} = \vec{d} + \vec{b}$$

Remember that, although we have used displacement vectors here, the rules for addition and subtraction hold for vectors of all kinds, whether they represent velocities, accelerations, or any other vector quantity. However, we can add only vectors of the same kind. For example, we can add two displacements, or two velocities, but adding a displacement and a velocity makes no sense. In the arithmetic of scalars, that would be like trying to add 21 s and 12 m.

CHECKPOINT 1 The magnitudes of displacements $\vec{a}$ and $\vec{b}$ are 3 m and 4 m, respectively, and $\vec{c} = \vec{a} + \vec{b}$. Considering various orientations of $\vec{a}$ and $\vec{b}$, what is (a) the maximum possible magnitude for $\vec{c}$ and (b) the minimum possible magnitude?

Sample Problem 2-1

In an orienteering class, you have the goal of moving as far (straight-line distance) from base camp as possible by making three straight-line moves. You may use the following displacements in any order: (a) $\vec{a}$, 2.0 km due east (directly toward the east); (b) $\vec{b}$, 2.0 km 30° north of east (at an angle of 30° toward the north from due east); (c) $\vec{c}$, 1.0 km due west. Alternatively, you may substitute either $-\vec{b}$ for $\vec{b}$ or $-\vec{c}$ for $\vec{c}$. What is the greatest distance you can be from base camp at the end of the third displacement?

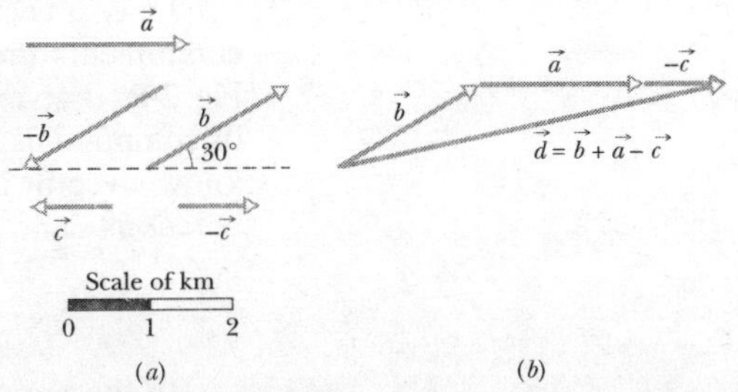

FIG. 2-7 (*a*) Displacement vectors; three are to be used. (*b*) Your distance from base camp is greatest if you undergo displacements $\vec{a}$, $\vec{b}$, and $-\vec{c}$, in any order.

Conceptualize/Classify: Using a convenient scale, we draw vectors $\vec{a}$, $\vec{b}$, $\vec{c}$, $-\vec{b}$, and $-\vec{c}$ as in Fig. 2-7*a*. We then mentally slide the vectors over the page, connecting three of them at a time in head-to-tail arrangements to find their vector sum $\vec{d}$. The tail of the first vector represents base camp. The head of the third vector represents the point at which you stop. The vector sum $\vec{d}$ extends from the tail of the first vector to the head of the third vector. Its magnitude d is your distance from base camp.

Compute: We find that distance d is greatest for a head-to-tail arrangement of vectors $\vec{a}$, $\vec{b}$, and $-\vec{c}$. They can be in any order, because their vector sum is the same for any order. The order shown in Fig. 2-7*b* is for the vector sum

$$\vec{d} = \vec{b} + \vec{a} + (-\vec{c})$$

Conclude: Using the scale given in Fig. 2-7*a*, we measure the length d of this vector sum, finding

$$d = 4.8 \text{ m} \qquad \text{(Answer)}$$

2-4 | Components of Vectors

Adding vectors geometrically can be tedious. A neater and easier technique involves algebra but requires that the vectors be placed on a rectangular coordinate system. The x and y axes are usually drawn in the plane of the page, as shown in Fig. 2-8*a*. The z axis comes directly out of the page at the origin; we ignore it for now and deal only with two-dimensional vectors.

A **component** of a vector is the projection of the vector on an axis. In Fig. 2-8*a*, for example, a_x is the component of vector $\vec{a}$ on (or along) the x axis and a_y is the component along the y axis. To find the projection of a vector along an axis, we draw perpendicular lines from the two ends of the vector to the axis, as shown. The projection of a vector on an x axis is its *x component*, and similarly the projection on the y axis is the *y component*. The process of finding the components of a vector is called **resolving the vector.**

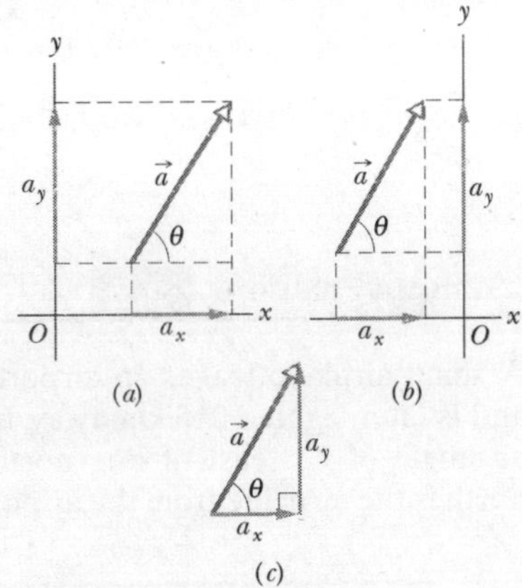

FIG. 2-8 (*a*) The components a_x and a_y of vector $\vec{a}$. (*b*) The components are unchanged if the vector is shifted, as long as the magnitude and orientation are maintained. (*c*) The components form the legs of a right triangle whose hypotenuse is the magnitude of the vector.

A component of a vector has the same direction (along an axis) as the vector. In Fig. 2-8, a_x and a_y are both positive because $\vec{a}$ extends in the positive direction of both axes. (Note the small arrowheads on the components, to indicate their direction.) If we were to reverse vector $\vec{a}$, then both components would be negative and their arrowheads would point toward negative x and y. Resolving vector $\vec{b}$ in Fig. 2-9 yields a positive component b_x and a negative component b_y.

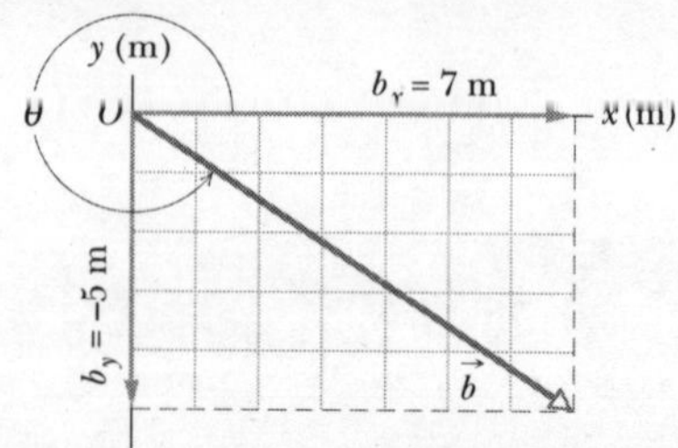

FIG. 2-9 The component of $\vec{b}$ on the x axis is positive, and that on the y axis is negative.

In general, a vector has three components, although for the case of Fig. 2-8*a* the component along the z axis is zero. As Figs. 2-8*a* and *b* show, if you shift a vector without changing its direction, its components do not change.

We can find the components of $\vec{a}$ in Fig. 2-8*a* geometrically from the right triangle there:

$$a_x = a \cos \theta \quad \text{and} \quad a_y = a \sin \theta \tag{2-5}$$

where θ is the angle that the vector $\vec{a}$ makes with the positive direction of the x axis, and a is the magnitude of $\vec{a}$. Figure 2-8*c* shows that $\vec{a}$ and its x and y components form a right triangle. It also shows how we can reconstruct a vector from its components: we arrange those components *head to tail*. Then we complete a right triangle with the vector forming the hypotenuse, from the tail of one component to the head of the other component.

Once a vector has been resolved into its components along a set of axes, the components themselves can be used in place of the vector. For example, $\vec{a}$ in Fig. 2-8*a* is given (completely determined) by a and θ. It can also be given by its components a_x and a_y. Both pairs of values contain the same information. If we know a vector in *component notation* (a_x and a_y) and want it in *magnitude-angle notation* (a and θ), we can use the equations to transform it.

$$a = \sqrt{a_x^2 + a_y^2} \quad \text{and} \quad \tan \theta = \frac{a_y}{a_x} \tag{2-6}$$

In the more general three-dimensional case, we need a magnitude and two angles (say, a, θ, and ϕ) or three components (a_x, a_y, and a_z) to specify a vector.

CHECKPOINT 2

In the figure, which of the indicated methods for combining the x and y components of vector $\vec{a}$ are proper to determine that vector?

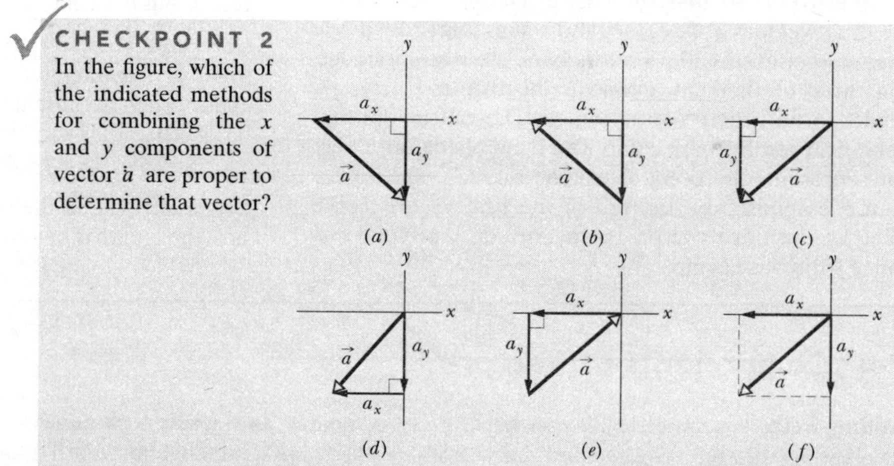

Sample Problem 2-2

A small airplane leaves an airport on an overcast day and is later sighted 215 km away, in a direction making an angle of 22° east of due north. How far east and north is the airplane from the airport when sighted?

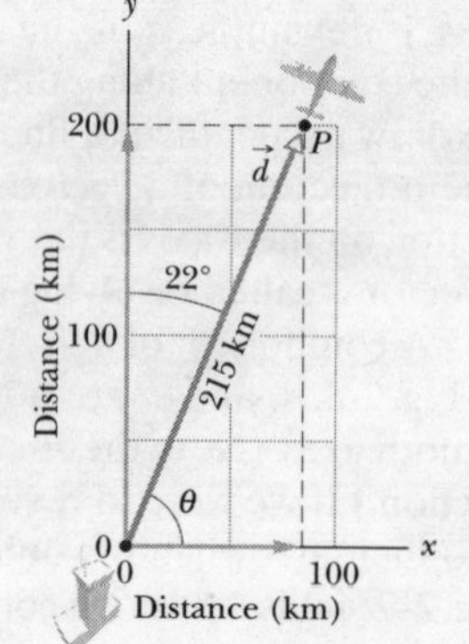

FIG. 2-10 A plane takes off from an airport at the origin and is later sighted at P.

Conceptualize/Classify: We are given the magnitude (215 km) and the angle (22° east of due north) of a vector and need to find the components of the vector.

Compute: We draw an xy coordinate system with the positive direction of x due east and that of y due north (Fig. 2-10). For convenience, the origin is placed at the airport. The airplane's displacement $\vec{d}$ points from the origin to where the airplane is sighted.

To find the components of $\vec{d}$, we use Eq. 2-5 with $\theta = 68°$ ($= 90° - 22°$):

$$d_x = d\cos\theta = (215\text{ km})(\cos 68°)$$
$$= 81\text{ km} \qquad \text{(Answer)}$$
$$d_y = d\sin\theta = (215\text{ km})(\sin 68°)$$
$$= 199\text{ km} \approx 2.0 \times 10^2\text{ km}. \qquad \text{(Answer)}$$

Conclude: Thus, the airplane is 81 km east and 2.0×10^2 km north of the airport.

Sample Problem 2-3

For two decades, spelunking teams sought a connection between the Flint Ridge cave system and Mammoth Cave, which are in Kentucky. When the connection was finally discovered, the combined system was declared the world's longest cave (more than 200 km long). The team that found the connection had to crawl, climb, and squirm through countless passages, traveling a net 2.6 km westward, 3.9 km southward, and 25 m upward. What was their displacement from start to finish?

Conceptualize/Classify: We have the components of a three-dimensional vector, and we need to find the vector's magnitude and two angles to specify the vector's direction.

Compute: Horizontal Components: We first draw the components as in Fig. 2-11*a*. The horizontal components (2.6 km west and 3.9 km south) form the legs of a horizontal right triangle. The team's horizontal displacement forms the hypotenuse of the triangle, and its magnitude d_h is given by the Pythagorean theorem:

$$d_h = \sqrt{(2.6\text{ km})^2 + (3.9\text{ km})^2} = 4.69\text{ km}$$

Also from the horizontal triangle in Fig. 2-11*a*, we see that this horizontal displacement is directed south of due west by an angle θ_h given by

$$\tan\theta_h = \frac{3.9\text{ km}}{2.6\text{ km}}$$

so $$\theta_h = \tan^{-1}\frac{3.9\text{ km}}{2.6\text{ km}} = 56° \qquad \text{(Answer)}$$

which is one of the two angles we need to specify the direction of the overall displacement.

Compute: Overall Displacement: To include the vertical component (25 m = 0.025 km), we now take a side view of Fig. 2-11*a*, looking northwest. We get Fig. 2-11*b*, where the vertical component and the horizontal displacement d_h form the legs of another right triangle. Now the team's overall displacement forms the hypotenuse of that triangle, with a magnitude d given by

$$d = \sqrt{(4.69\text{ km})^2 + (0.025\text{ km})^2} = 4.69\text{ km}$$
$$\approx 4.7\text{ km} \qquad \text{(Answer)}$$

This displacement is directed upward from the horizontal displacement by the angle

$$\theta_v = \tan^{-1}\frac{0.025\text{ km}}{4.69\text{ km}} = 0.3° \qquad \text{(Answer)}$$

Thus, the team's displacement vector had a magnitude of 4.7 km and was at an angle of 56° south of west and at an angle of 0.3° upward.

Conclude: The net vertical motion was, of course, insignificant compared with the horizontal motion. However, that fact would have been of no comfort to the team, which had to climb up and down countless times to get through the cave. The route they actually covered was quite different from the displacement vector.

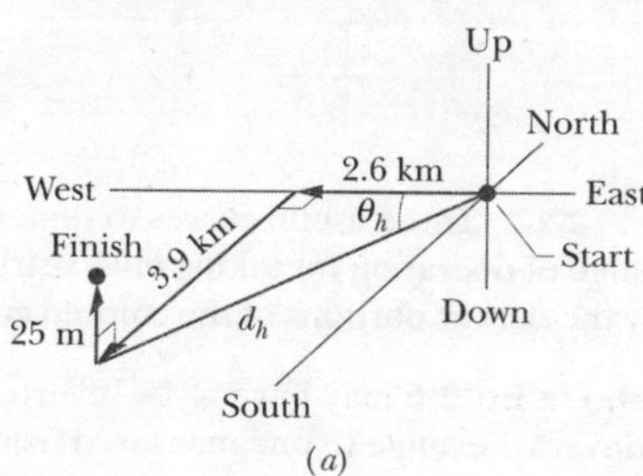

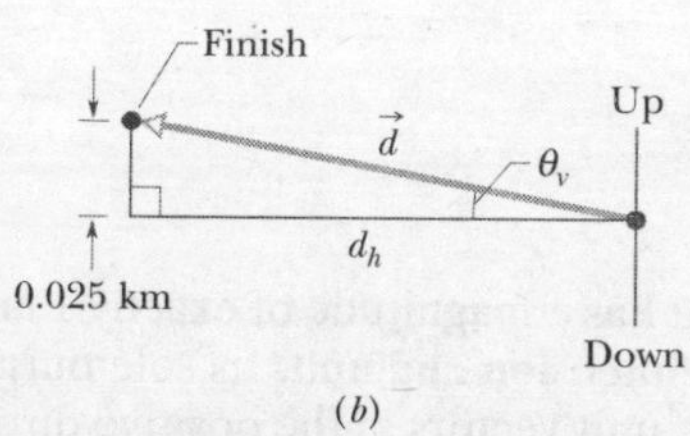

FIG. 2-11 (*a*) The components of the spelunking team's overall displacement and their horizontal displacement d_h. (*b*) A side view showing d_h and the team's overall displacement vector $\vec{d}$.

PROBLEM-SOLVING TACTICS

Tactic 1: Angles—Degrees and Radians Angles that are measured relative to the positive direction of the x axis are positive if they are measured in the counterclockwise direction and negative if measured clockwise. For example, 210° and −150° are the same angle.

Angles may be measured in degrees or radians (rad). To relate the two measures, recall that a full circle is 360° and 2π rad. To convert, say, 40° to radians, write

$$40° \frac{2\pi\text{ rad}}{360°} = 0.70\text{ rad}$$

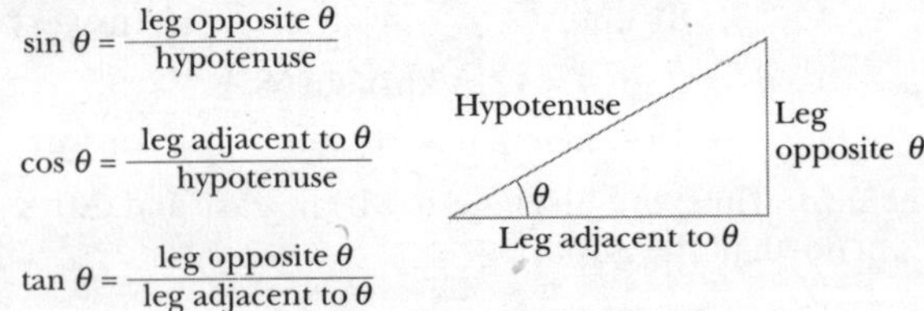

FIG. 2-12 A triangle used to define the trigonometric functions. See also Appendix E.

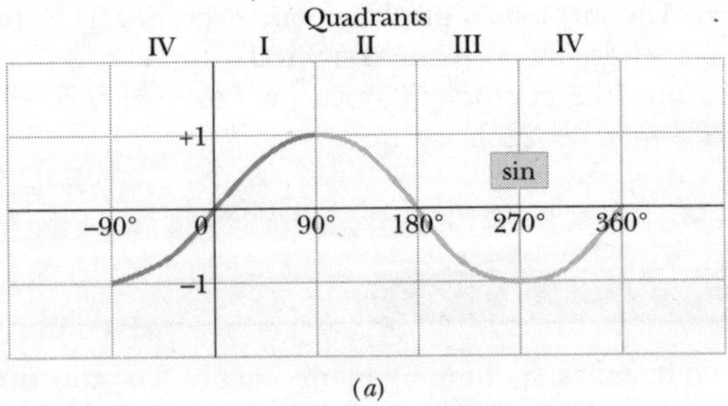

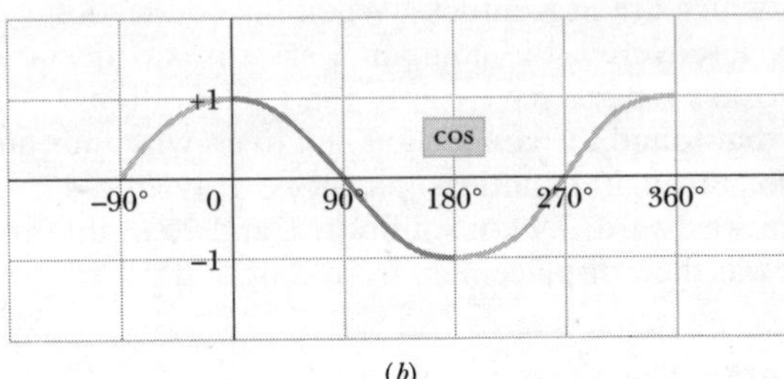

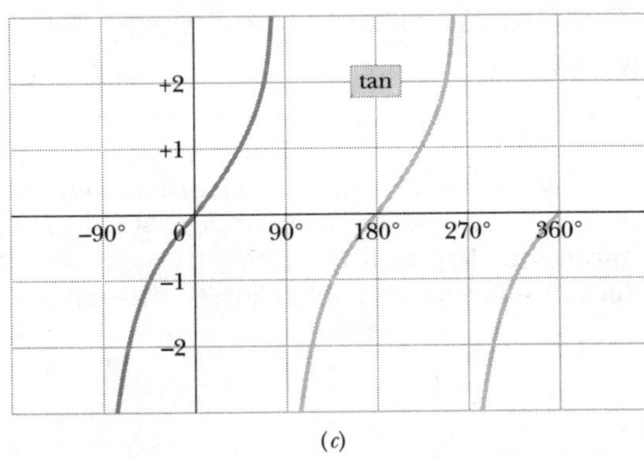

FIG. 2-13 Three useful curves to remember. A calculator's range of operation for taking *inverse* trig functions is indicated by the darker portions of the colored curves.

Tactic 2: *Trig Functions* You need to know the definitions of the common trigonometric functions—sine, cosine, and tangent—because they are part of the language of science and engineering. They are given in Fig. 2-12 in a form that does not depend on how the triangle is labeled.

You should also be able to sketch how the trig functions vary with angle, as in Fig. 2-13, in order to be able to judge whether a calculator result is reasonable. Even knowing the signs of the functions in the various quadrants can be of help.

Tactic 3: *Inverse Trig Functions* When the inverse trig functions $\sin^{-1}$, $\cos^{-1}$, and $\tan^{-1}$ are taken on a calculator, you must consider the reasonableness of the answer you get, because there is usually another possible answer that the calculator does not give. The range of operation for a calculator in taking each inverse trig function is indicated in Fig. 2-13. As an example, $\sin^{-1} 0.5$ has associated angles of 30° (which is displayed by the calculator, since 30° falls within its range of operation) and 150°. To see both values, draw a horizontal line through 0.5 in Fig. 2-13*a* and note where it cuts the sine curve.

How do you distinguish a correct answer? It is the one that seems more reasonable for the given situation. As an example, reconsider the calculation of θ_h in Sample Problem 2-3, where $\tan\theta_h = 3.9/2.6 = 1.5$. Taking $\tan^{-1} 1.5$ on your calculator tells you that $\theta_h = 56°$, but $\theta_h = 236°$ (= 180° + 56°) also has a tangent of 1.5. Which is correct? From the physical situation (Fig. 2-11*a*), 56° is reasonable and 236° is clearly not.

Tactic 4: *Measuring Vector Angles* The equations for $\cos\theta$ and $\sin\theta$ in Eq. 2-5 and for $\tan\theta$ in Eq. 2-6 are valid only if the angle is measured from the positive direction of the x axis. If it is measured relative to some other direction, then the trig functions in Eq. 2-5 may have to be interchanged and the ratio in Eq. 2-6 may have to be inverted. A safer method is to convert the angle to one measured from the positive direction of the x axis.

2-5 | Unit Vectors

A **unit vector** is a vector that has a magnitude of exactly 1 and points in a particular direction. **It lacks both dimension and unit.** Its sole purpose is to point—that is, to specify a direction. The unit vectors in the positive directions of the x, y, and z axes are labeled $\hat{\text{i}}$, $\hat{\text{j}}$, and $\hat{\text{k}}$, where the hat ˆ is used instead of an overhead arrow as for other vectors (Fig. 2-14). The arrangement of axes in Fig. 2-14 is said to be a **right-handed coordinate system.** The system remains right-handed if it is rotated rigidly. We use such coordinate systems exclusively in this book.

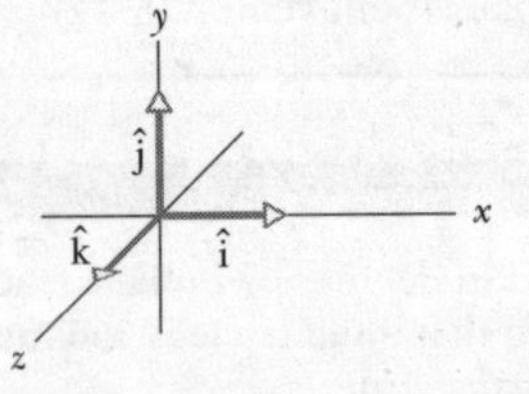

FIG. 2-14 Unit vectors $\hat{\text{i}}$, $\hat{\text{j}}$, and $\hat{\text{k}}$ define the directions of a right-handed coordinate system.

Unit vectors are very useful for expressing other vectors; for example, we can express $\vec{a}$ and $\vec{b}$ of Figs. 2-8 and 2-9 as

$$\vec{a} = a_x\hat{\text{i}} + a_y\hat{\text{j}} \tag{2-7}$$

and

$$\vec{b} = b_x\hat{\text{i}} + b_y\hat{\text{j}} \tag{2-8}$$

These two equations are illustrated in Fig. 2-15. The quantities $a_x\hat{i}$ and $a_y\hat{j}$ are vectors, called the **vector components** of $\vec{a}$. The quantities a_x and a_y are scalars, called the **scalar components** of $\vec{a}$ (or, as before, simply its **components**).

As an example, let us write the displacement $\vec{d}$ of the spelunking team of Sample Problem 2-3 in terms of unit vectors. First, superimpose the coordinate system of Fig. 2-14 on the one shown in Fig. 2-11*a*. Then the directions of $\hat{i}$, $\hat{j}$, and $\hat{k}$ are toward the east, up, and toward the south, respectively. Thus, displacement $\vec{d}$ from start to finish is neatly expressed in unit-vector notation as

$$\vec{d} = -(2.6\text{ km})\hat{i} + (0.025\text{ km})\hat{j} + (3.9\text{ km})\hat{k} \tag{2-9}$$

Here $-(2.6\text{ km})\hat{i}$ is the vector component $d_x\hat{i}$ along the x axis, and $-(2.6\text{ km})$ is the x component d_x.

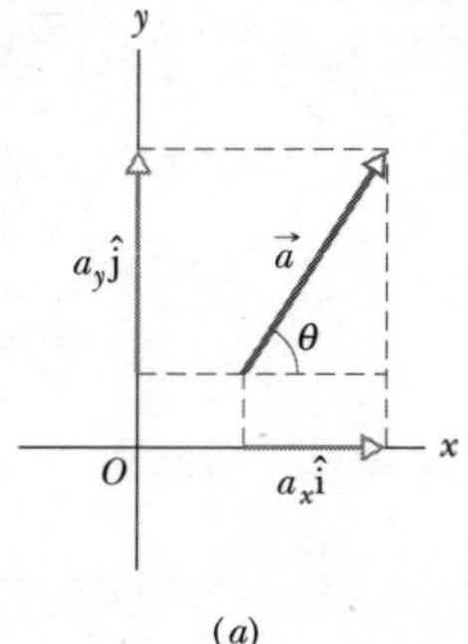

(*a*)

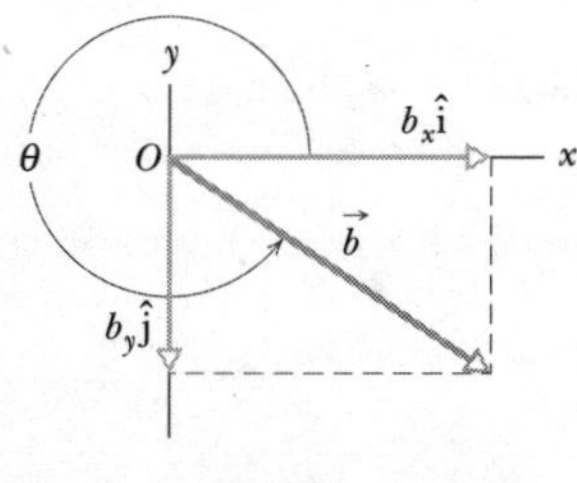

(*b*)

FIG. 2-15 (*a*) The vector components of vector $\vec{a}$. (*b*) The vector components of vector $\vec{b}$.

Representing Position Vector Using Unit Vectors

Position vector for a point is the vector for which tail is origin and head is the given point itself. Position vector of a point defines the position of the point with respect to the origin.

$$\overrightarrow{OP} = \vec{r}$$

$$\vec{r} = x\hat{i} + y\hat{j}$$

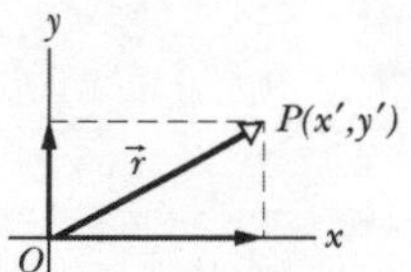

FIG. 2-16 Position vector of point *P*.

Representing Displacement Vector Using Unit Vectors

Change in position vector of a particle is known as displacement vector.

$$\overrightarrow{OP} = \vec{r}_1 = x_1\hat{i} + y_1\hat{j}$$

$$\overrightarrow{OQ} = \vec{r}_2 = x_2\hat{i} + y_2\hat{j}$$

$$\overrightarrow{PQ} = \vec{r}_2 - \vec{r}_1 = (x_2 - x_1)\hat{i} + (y_2 - y_1)\hat{j}$$

Thus we can represent a vector in space starting from (x_1, y_1) and ending at (x_2, y_2) as $(x_2 - x_1)\hat{i} + (y_2 - y_1)\hat{j}$

Components of Three Dimensional Vectors

$$\overrightarrow{OP} = \vec{r}$$

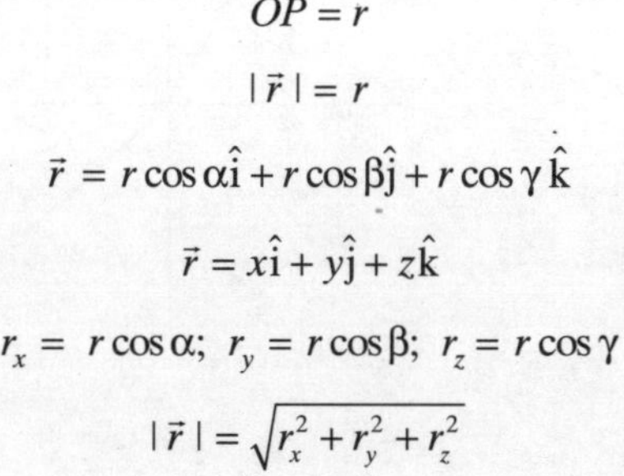

$$|\vec{r}| = r$$

$$\vec{r} = r\cos\alpha\hat{i} + r\cos\beta\hat{j} + r\cos\gamma\hat{k}$$

$$\vec{r} = x\hat{i} + y\hat{j} + z\hat{k}$$

$$r_x = r\cos\alpha;\ r_y = r\cos\beta;\ r_z = r\cos\gamma$$

$$|\vec{r}| = \sqrt{r_x^2 + r_y^2 + r_z^2}$$

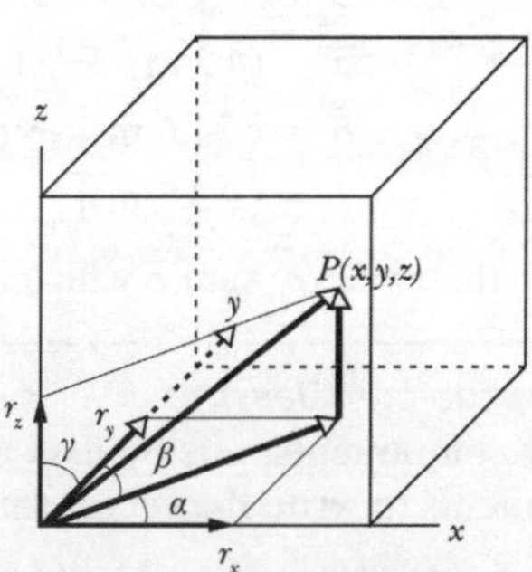

FIG. 2-17 These dimensional resolution of position vector $\overrightarrow{OP}$.

2-6 | Application of Unit Vector Form

Using a sketch, we can add vectors geometrically. On a vector-capable calculator, we can add them directly on the screen. A third way to add vectors is to combine their components axis by axis, which is the way we examine here.

To start, consider the statement

$$\vec{r} = \vec{a} + \vec{b} \tag{2-10}$$

which says that the vector $\vec{r}$ is the same as the vector $(\vec{a} + \vec{b})$. Thus, each component of $\vec{r}$ must be the same as the corresponding component of $(\vec{a} + \vec{b})$:

$$r_x = a_x + b_x \tag{2-11}$$

$$r_y = a_y + b_y \tag{2-12}$$

$$r_z = a_z + b_z \tag{2-13}$$

In other words, two vectors must be equal if their corresponding components are equal. Equations 2-10 to 2-13 tell us that to add vectors $\vec{a}$ and $\vec{b}$, we must (1) resolve the vectors into their scalar components; (2) combine these scalar components, axis by axis, to get the components of the sum $\vec{r}$; and (3) combine the components of $\vec{r}$ to get $\vec{r}$ itself. We have a choice in step 3. We can express $\vec{r}$ in unit-vector notation (as in Eq. 2-9) or in magnitude-angle notation (as in the answer to Sample Problem 2-3).

This procedure for adding vectors by components also applies to vector subtractions. Recall that a subtraction such as $\vec{d} = \vec{a} - \vec{b}$ can be rewritten as an addition $\vec{d} = \vec{a} + (-\vec{b})$. To subtract, we add $\vec{a}$ and $-\vec{b}$ by components, to get

$$d_x = a_x - b_x, \quad d_y = a_y - b_y, \quad \text{and} \quad d_z = a_z - b_z$$

where

$$\vec{d} = d_x\hat{\mathrm{i}} + d_y\hat{\mathrm{j}} + d_z\hat{\mathrm{k}}$$

CHECKPOINT 3 (a) In the figure here, what are the signs of the x components of $\vec{d}_1$ and $\vec{d}_2$? (b) What are the signs of the y components of $\vec{d}_1$ and $\vec{d}_2$? (c) What are the signs of the x and y components of $\vec{d}_1 + \vec{d}_2$?

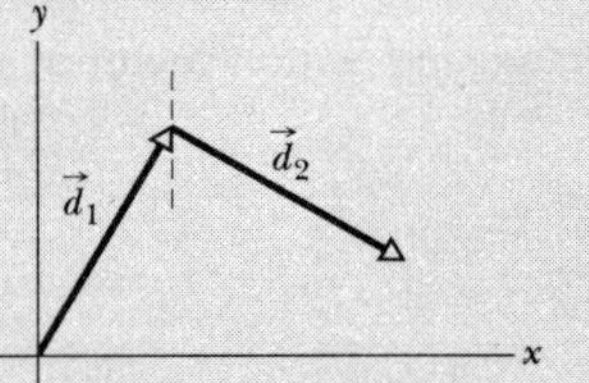

Sample Problem 2-4

Figure 2-18*a* shows the following three vectors:

$$\vec{a} = (4.2\text{ m})\hat{\mathrm{i}} - (1.5\text{ m})\hat{\mathrm{j}}$$

$$\vec{b} = (-1.6\text{ m})\hat{\mathrm{i}} + (2.9\text{ m})\hat{\mathrm{j}}$$

and

$$\vec{c} = (-3.7\text{ m})\hat{\mathrm{j}}$$

What is their vector sum $\vec{r}$ which is also shown?

Conceptualize/Classify: We can add the three vectors by components, axis by axis, and then combine the components to write the vector sum $\vec{r}$.

Compute: For the x axis, we add the x components of $\vec{a}$, $\vec{b}$, and $\vec{c}$, to get the x component of the vector sum $\vec{r}$:

$$r_x = a_x + b_x + c_x$$

$$= 4.2\text{ m} - 1.6\text{ m} + 0 = 2.6\text{ m}$$

Similarly, for the y axis,

$$r_y = a_y + b_y + c_y$$

$$= -1.5\text{ m} + 2.9\text{ m} - 3.7\text{ m} = -2.3\text{ m}$$

We then combine these components of $\vec{r}$ to write the vector in unit-vector notation:

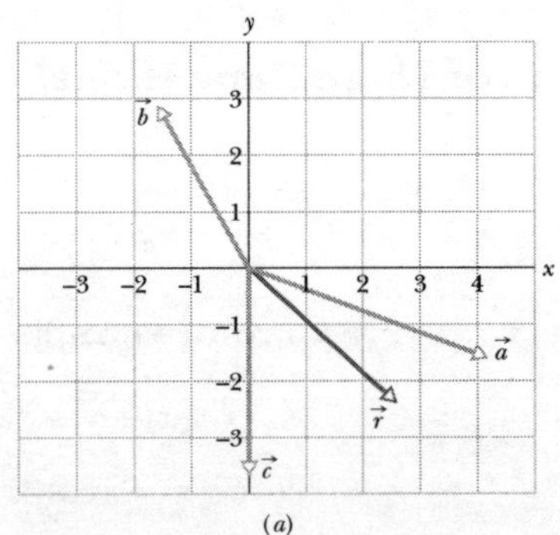

(*a*)

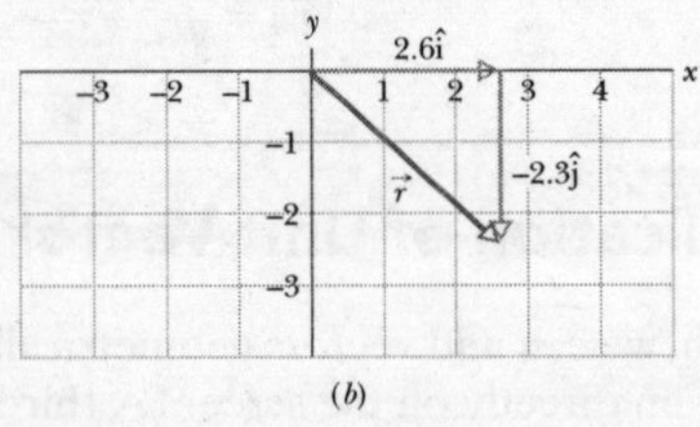

(*b*)

FIG. 2-18 Vector $\vec{r}$ is the vector sum of the other three vectors.

$$\vec{r} = (2.6\text{ m})\hat{i} - (2.3\text{ m})\hat{j} \qquad \text{(Answer)}$$

where $(2.6\text{ m})\hat{i}$ is the vector component of $\vec{r}$ along the x axis and $-(2.3\text{ m})\hat{j}$ is that along the y axis.

Figure 2-18*b* shows one way to arrange these vector components to form $\vec{r}$. (Can you sketch the other way?)

Conclude: We can also answer the question by giving the magnitude and an angle for $\vec{r}$. From Eq. 2-6, the magnitude is

$$r = \sqrt{(2.6\text{ m})^2 + (-2.3\text{ m})^2} \approx 3.5\text{ m} \qquad \text{(Answer)}$$

and the angle (measured from the $+x$ direction) is

$$\theta = \tan^{-1}\left(\frac{-2.3\text{ m}}{2.6\text{ m}}\right) = -41° \qquad \text{(Answer)}$$

Here the minus sign means clockwise direction.

Sample Problem 2-5

According to experiments, the desert ant shown in the chapter opening photograph keeps track of its movements along a mental coordinate system. When it wants to return to its home nest, it effectively sums its displacements along the axes of the system to calculate a vector that points directly home. As an example of the calculation, let's consider an ant making five runs of 6.0 cm each on an xy coordinate system, in the directions shown in Fig. 2-19*a*, starting from home. At the end of the fifth run, what are the magnitude and angle of the ant's net displacement vector $\vec{d}_{\text{net}}$, and what are those of the homeward vector $\vec{d}_{\text{home}}$ that extends from the ant's final position back to home?

Conceptualize/Classify: (1) To find the net displacement $\vec{d}_{\text{net}}$, we need to sum the five individual displacement vectors:

$$\vec{d}_{\text{net}} = \vec{d}_1 + \vec{d}_2 + \vec{d}_3 + \vec{d}_4 + \vec{d}_5$$

(2) We evaluate this sum for the x components alone,

$$d_{\text{net},x} = d_{1x} + d_{2x} + d_{3x} + d_{4x} + d_{5x} \qquad (2\text{-}14)$$

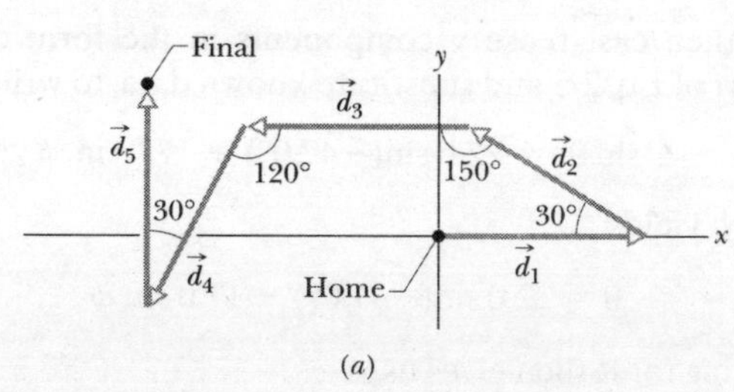

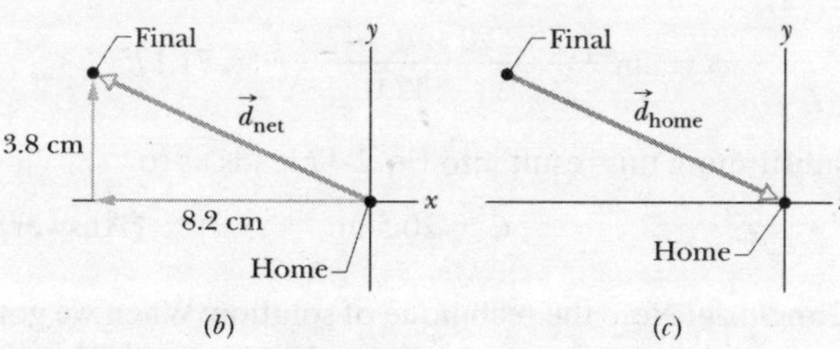

FIG. 2-19 (*a*) A search path of five runs. (*b*) The x and y components of $\vec{d}_{\text{net}}$. (*c*) Vector $\vec{d}_{\text{home}}$ points the way to the home nest.

and for the y components alone,

$$d_{\text{net},y} = d_{1y} + d_{2y} + d_{3y} + d_{4y} + d_{5y} \qquad (2\text{-}15)$$

(3) We construct $\vec{d}_{\text{net}}$ from its x and y components.

Compute: To evaluate Eq. 2-14, we apply the x part of Eq. 2-5 to each run:

$$\begin{aligned}
d_{1x} &= (6.0\text{ cm})\cos 0° = +6.0\text{ cm}\\
d_{2x} &= (6.0\text{ cm})\cos 150° = -5.2\text{ cm}\\
d_{3x} &= (6.0\text{ cm})\cos 180° = -6.0\text{ cm}\\
d_{4x} &= (6.0\text{ cm})\cos(-120°) = -3.0\text{ cm}\\
d_{5x} &= (6.0\text{ cm})\cos 90° = 0
\end{aligned}$$

Equation 2-14 then gives us

$$\begin{aligned}
d_{\text{net},x} &= +6.0\text{ cm} + (-5.2\text{ cm}) + (-6.0\text{ cm})\\
&\quad + (-3.0\text{ cm}) + 0\\
&= -8.2\text{ cm}
\end{aligned}$$

Similarly, we evaluate the individual y components of the five runs using the y part of Eq. 2-5. The results are shown in Table 2-1. Substituting the results into Eq. 2-15 then gives us

$$d_{\text{net},y} = +3.8\text{ cm}$$

Vector $\vec{d}_{\text{net}}$ and its x and y components are shown in Fig. 2-19*b*. To find the magnitude and angle of $\vec{d}_{\text{net}}$ from its components, we use Eq. 2-6. The magnitude is

$$\begin{aligned}
d_{\text{net}} &= \sqrt{d_{\text{net},x}^2 + d_{\text{net},y}^2}\\
&= \sqrt{(-8.2\text{ cm})^2 + (3.8\text{ cm})^2} = 9.0\text{ cm}
\end{aligned}$$

To find the angle (measured from the positive direction of x), we take an inverse tangent:

$$\begin{aligned}
\theta &= \tan^{-1}\left(\frac{d_{\text{net},y}}{d_{\text{net},x}}\right)\\
&= \tan^{-1}\left(\frac{3.8\text{ cm}}{-8.2\text{ cm}}\right) = -24.86°
\end{aligned}$$

Caution: Recall that taking an inverse tangent on a calculator may not give the correct answer. The answer $-24.86°$ indicates that the direction of $\vec{d}_{net}$ is in the fourth quadrant of our xy coordinate system. However, when we construct the vector from its components (Fig. 2-19*b*), we see that the direction of $\vec{d}_{net}$ is in the second quadrant. Thus, we must "fix" the calculator's answer by adding 180°:

$$\theta = -24.86° + 180° = 155.14° \approx 155°$$

Thus, the ant's displacement $\vec{d}_{net}$ has magnitude and angle

$$d_{net} = 9.0 \text{ cm at } 155° \qquad \text{(Answer)}$$

Vector $\vec{d}_{home}$ directed from the ant to its home has the same magnitude as $\vec{d}_{net}$ but the opposite direction (Fig. 2-19*c*). We already have the angle ($-24.86° \approx -25°$) for the direction opposite . Thus, has magnitude and angle

$$d_{home} = 9.0 \text{ cm at } -25° \qquad \text{(Answer)}$$

Conclude: A desert ant traveling more than 500 m from its home will actually make thousands of individual runs. Yet, it somehow knows how to calculate $\vec{d}_{home}$ (without studying this chapter).

TABLE 2-1

Run	d_x (cm)	d_y (cm)
1	+6.0	0
2	−5.2	+3.0
3	−6.0	0
4	−3.0	−5.2
5	0	+6.0
net	−8.2	+3.8

Sample Problem 2-6

A fellow camper is to walk away from you in a straight line (vector $\vec{A}$), turn, walk in a second straight line (vector $\vec{B}$) and then stop. How far must you walk in a straight line (vector $\vec{C}$) to reach her?

The three vectors (shown in Fig. 2-20) are related by

$$\vec{C} = \vec{A} + \vec{B} \qquad (2\text{-}16)$$

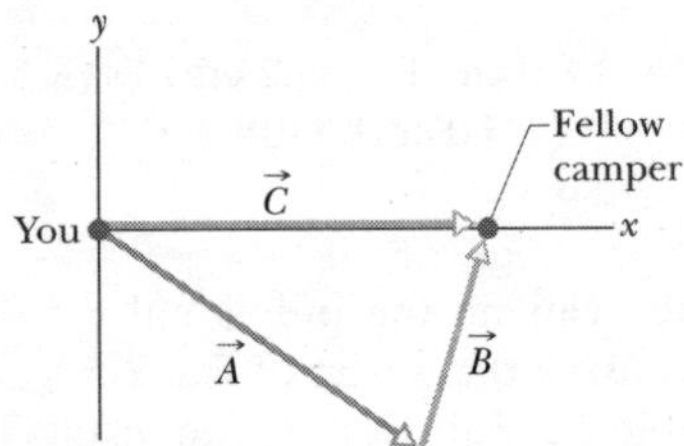

FIG. 2-20 $\vec{C}$ equals the sum $\vec{A} + \vec{B}$.

$\vec{A}$ has a magnitude of 22.0 m and is directed at an angle of $-47.0°$ (clockwise) from the positive direction of an x axis. $\vec{B}$ has a magnitude of 17.0 m and is directed counterclockwise from the positive direction of the x axis by angle ϕ. $\vec{C}$ is in the positive direction of the x axis. What is the magnitude of $\vec{C}$?

Conceptualize/Classify: We cannot answer the question by adding $\vec{A}$ and $\vec{B}$ directly on a vector-capable calculator, say, in the generic form of

$$[\text{magnitude } A \angle \text{ angle } A] + [\text{magnitude } B \angle \text{ angle } B]$$

because we do not know the value for the angle ϕ of $\vec{B}$. However, we *can* express Eq. 2-16 in terms of components for either the x axis or the y axis.

Compute: Since $\vec{C}$ is directed along the x axis, we choose that axis and write

$$C_x = A_x + B_x$$

We next express each x component in the form of the x part of Eq. 2-5 and substitute known data. We then have

$$C \cos 0° = 22.0 \cos(-47.0°) + 17.0 \cos \phi \qquad (2\text{-}17)$$

However, this hardly seems to help, because we still cannot solve for C without knowing ϕ.

Let us now express Eq. 2-16 in terms of components along the y axis:

$$C_y = A_y + B_y$$

We then cast these y components in the form of the y part of Eq. 2-5 and substitute known data, to write

$$C \sin 0° = 22.0 \sin(-47.0°) + 17.0 \sin \phi$$

which yields

$$0 = 22.0 \sin(-47.0°) + 17.0 \sin \phi$$

Solving for ϕ then gives us

$$\phi = \sin^{-1} - \frac{22.0 \sin(-47.0°)}{17.0} = 71.17°$$

Substituting this result into Eq. 2-17 leads us to

$$C = 20.5 \text{ m} \qquad \text{(Answer)}$$

Conclude: Note the technique of solution: When we got stuck with components on the x axis, we worked with components on the y axis, to evaluate ϕ. We next moved back to the x axis, to evaluate C.

Sample Problem 2-7 Build your skill

Find a vector of magnitude five time that of $\vec{A} = 12\hat{\imath} - 5\mathrm{j}$ and anti-parallel to $\vec{B} = 3\hat{\imath} - 4\hat{\jmath}$.

Solution: Lets represent our unknown vector as vector $\vec{C}$.

It is given
$$|\vec{C}| = 5|\vec{A}|$$
$$|\vec{A}| = \sqrt{12^2 + 5^2} = 13$$

hence $|\vec{C}| = 65$

Also, since vector $\vec{C}$ is opposite to vector $\vec{B}$
$$\hat{C} = -\hat{B}$$

$$\hat{B} = \frac{3\hat{\imath} - 4\hat{\jmath}}{\sqrt{3^2 + 4^2}} = \frac{3}{5}\hat{\imath} - \frac{4}{5}\hat{\jmath}$$

hence $C = -\frac{3}{5}\hat{\imath} + \frac{4}{5}\hat{\jmath}$

Thus $\vec{C} = |\vec{C}|\hat{C}$

gives us $\vec{C} = 65 \times \left(-\frac{3}{5}\hat{\imath} + \frac{4}{5}\hat{\jmath}\right) = -39\hat{\imath} + 52\hat{\jmath}$ (Answer)

Sample Problem 2-8 Build your skill

On a certain day rain was falling vertically with a speed of 30 m/s. A wind started blowing after some time with a speed of 10√3 m/s towards south. In which direction a girl waiting her for bus should hold her umbrella?

Solution: When wind blows it is easy to understand that velocity of wind will be added to the velocity of rain. The vector sum of the two velocities will given us final velocity of rain.

$$\vec{V}_F = \vec{V}_R + \vec{V}_W$$

where V_F is resultant velocity of rain, V_R is velocity of rain when there was no wind, and V_W is the velocity of wind.

Now consider vertical plane containing north south direction as our coordinate plane. Assigning positive y to vertically upward direction and positive x to north direction,

$$\vec{V}_W = -10\sqrt{3}\,\hat{\imath}$$
$$\vec{V}_R = -30\,\hat{\jmath}$$

Thus $\vec{V}_F = -10\sqrt{3}\hat{\imath} - 30\hat{\jmath}$

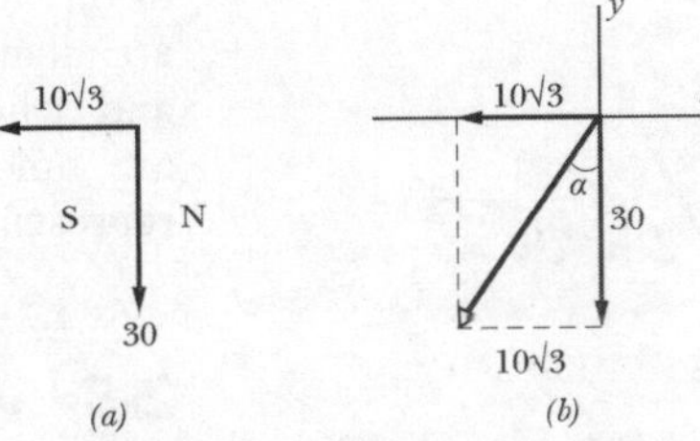

FIG. 2-21 Direction coordinates

$$\tan\alpha = \frac{10\sqrt{3}}{30} = \frac{1}{\sqrt{3}}$$

hence, $\alpha = 30°$ (Answer)

Thus, the girl should hold her umbrella at an angle of 30° to vertical.

CHECKPOINT 4 Find vector sum of forces $\vec{A}$ and $\vec{B}$. Magnitude of A is 130 N and is along $\overrightarrow{OA}$ where A is (3,–4,12) and $|B|$ = 200 N and is along vector $\overrightarrow{PQ}$ where Q is (–2,4,7) and P is (–2,8,10)

Solution:

$$\hat{A} = \frac{\overrightarrow{OA}}{|\overrightarrow{OA}|} = \frac{3\hat{\imath} - 4\hat{\jmath} + 12\hat{k}}{(13)}$$

$$\vec{A} = 30\hat{\imath} - 40\hat{\jmath} + 120\hat{k}$$

$$\hat{B} = \frac{\overrightarrow{PQ}}{|\overrightarrow{PQ}|} = \frac{-0\hat{\imath} + 4\hat{\jmath} + 3\hat{k}}{5}$$

$$\vec{B} = 160\hat{\jmath} + 120\hat{k}$$

2-7 | Vectors and the Laws of Physics

So far, in every figure that includes a coordinate system, the x and y axes are parallel to the edges of the book page. Thus, when a vector $\vec{a}$ is included, its components a_x and a_y are also parallel to the edges (as in Fig. 2-22a). *The only reason for that orientation of the axes is that it looks "proper"; there is no deeper reason.* We could, instead, rotate the axes (but not the vector $\vec{a}$) through an angle ϕ as in Fig. 2-22b, in which case the components would have new values, call them a'_x and a'_y. Since there are an infinite number of choices of ϕ, there are an infinite number of different pairs of components for $\vec{a}$.

Which then is the "right" pair of components? The answer is that they are all equally valid because each pair (with its axes) just gives us a different way of describing the same vector $\vec{a}$; all produce the same magnitude and direction for the vector. In Fig. 2-22 we have

$$a = \sqrt{a_x^2 + a_y^2} = \sqrt{a_x'^2 + a_y'^2} \tag{2-18}$$

and

$$\theta = \theta' + \phi \tag{2-19}$$

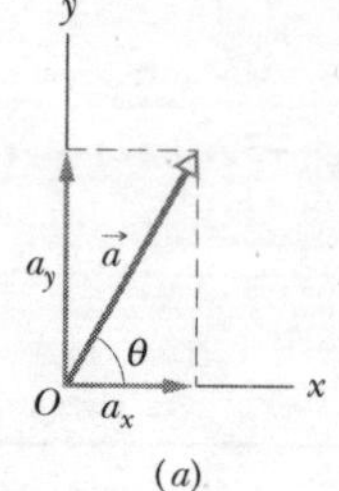

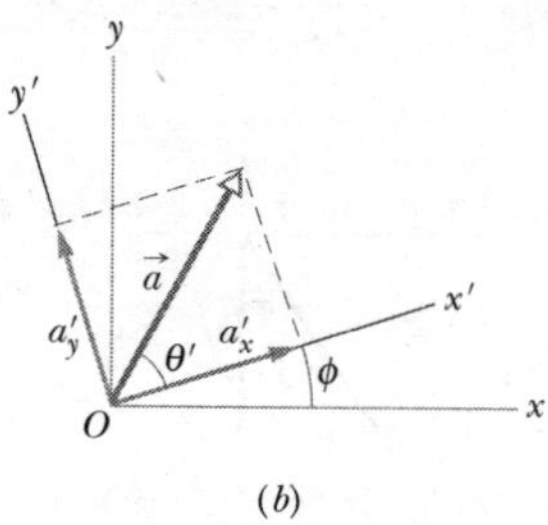

FIG. 2-22 (a) The vector $\vec{a}$ and its components. (b) The same vector, with the axes of the coordinate system rotated through an angle ϕ.

The point is that we have great freedom in choosing a coordinate system, because the relations among vectors do not depend on the location of the origin or on the orientation of the axes. This is also true of the relations of physics; they are all independent of the choice of coordinate system. Add to that the simplicity and richness of the language of vectors and you can see why the laws of physics are almost always presented in that language: one equation, like Eq. 2-10, can represent three (or even more) relations, like Eqs. 2-11, 2-12, and 2-13.

2-8 | Vector Multiplication

There are three ways in which vectors can be multiplied, but none is exactly like the usual algebraic multiplication. As you read this section, keep in mind that a vector-capable calculator will help you multiply vectors only if you understand the basic rules of that multiplication.

Multiplying a Vector by a Scalar

If we multiply a vector $\vec{a}$ by a scalar s, we get a new vector. Its magnitude is the product of the magnitude of $\vec{a}$ and the absolute value of s. Its direction is the direction of $\vec{a}$ if s is positive but the opposite direction if s is negative. To divide $\vec{a}$ by s, we multiply $\vec{a}$ by $1/s$.

Multiplying a Vector by a Vector

There are two ways to multiply a vector by a vector: one way produces a scalar (called the *scalar product*), and the other produces a new vector (called the *vector product*). (Students commonly confuse the two ways.)

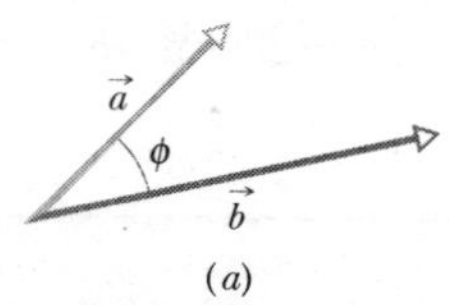

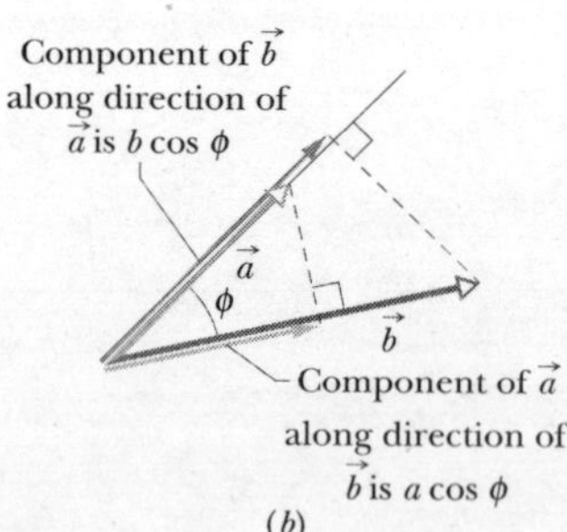

FIG. 2-23 (a) Two vectors $\vec{a}$ and $\vec{b}$, with an angle ϕ between them. (b) Each vector has a component along the direction of the other vector.

The Scalar Product

The **scalar product** of the vectors $\vec{a}$ and $\vec{b}$ in Fig. 2-23a is written as $\vec{a} \cdot \vec{b}$ and defined to be

$$\vec{a} \cdot \vec{b} = ab \cos \phi \tag{2-20}$$

where a is the magnitude of $\vec{a}$, b is the magnitude of $\vec{b}$, and ϕ is the angle between $\vec{a}$ and $\vec{b}$ (or, more properly, between the directions of $\vec{a}$ and $\vec{b}$). There are actually two such angles: ϕ and $360° - \phi$. Either can be used in Eq. 2-20, because their cosines are the same.

Note that there are only scalars on the right side of Eq. 2-20 (including the value of $\cos\phi$). Thus $\vec{a}\cdot\vec{b}$ on the left side represents a *scalar* quantity. Because of the notation, $\vec{a}\cdot\vec{b}$ is also known as the **dot product** and is spoken as "a dot b."

A dot product can be regarded as the product of two quantities: (1) the magnitude of one of the vectors and (2) the scalar component of the second vector along the direction of the first vector. For example, in Fig. 2-24*b*, $\vec{a}$ has a scalar component $a\cos\phi$ along the direction of $\vec{b}$; note that a perpendicular dropped from the head of $\vec{a}$ onto $\vec{b}$ determines that component. Similarly, $\vec{b}$ has a scalar component $b\cos\phi$ along the direction of $\vec{a}$.

If the angle ϕ between two vectors is 0°, the component of one vector along the other is maximum, and so also is the dot product of the vectors. If, instead, ϕ is 90°, the component of one vector along the other is zero, and so is the dot product.

Equation 2-20 can be rewritten as follows to emphasize the components:

$$\vec{a}\cdot\vec{b} = (a\cos\phi)(b) = (a)(b\cos\phi) \tag{2-21}$$

The commutative law applies to a scalar product, so we can write

$$\vec{a}\cdot\vec{b} = \vec{b}\cdot\vec{a}$$

When two vectors are in unit-vector notation, we write their dot product as

$$\vec{a}\cdot\vec{b} = (a_x\hat{i} + a_y\hat{j} + a_z\hat{k})\cdot(b_x\hat{i} + b_y\hat{j} + b_z\hat{k}) \tag{2-22}$$

which we can expand according to the distributive law: Each vector component of the first vector is to be dotted with each vector component of the second vector. By doing so, we can show that

$$\vec{a}\cdot\vec{b} = a_xb_x + a_yb_y + a_zb_z \tag{2-23}$$

When two vectors are perpendicular

1. $\theta = \pi/2 \Rightarrow \vec{a}\cdot\vec{b} = 0$

2. $\cos\theta = \dfrac{\vec{a}.\vec{b}}{|\vec{a}||\vec{b}|}$ (this is used to find the angle between two vectors.)

CHECKPOINT 5 Vectors $\vec{C}$ and $\vec{D}$ have magnitudes of 3 units and 4 units, respectively. What is the angle between the directions of $\vec{C}$ and $\vec{D}$ if $\vec{C}\cdot\vec{D}$ equals (a) zero, (b) 12 units, and (c) −12 units?

Sample Problem 2-9 Build your skill

If $\vec{a} = 3\hat{i} + 4\hat{j}$ and $\vec{b} = 2\hat{i} - \hat{j}$ then find angle between them.

Solution:

$$\cos\theta = \frac{\vec{a}.\vec{b}}{|\vec{a}||\vec{b}|};\ |\vec{a}| = 5;\ |\vec{b}| = \sqrt{5}$$

so

$$\cos\theta = \frac{6-4}{5\sqrt{5}} = \frac{2}{5\sqrt{5}}$$

$$\Rightarrow \theta = \cos^{-1}\left(\frac{2}{5\sqrt{5}}\right)$$

2-9 | Calculus

Introduction

Suppose on your eighth birthday at midnight you measured your height and found it to be 120 cm. One year later at midnight on your ninth birthday you again measure your height and find it to be 132 cm. Now if we say rate of increase of your height is 12 cm/year it does not mean that at the exact 11:59:59 pm you were 120 cm and as soon as clock moved to 12:00 midnight you streched and became 132 cm.

If we express your rate of growth as 1 cm/month we are not implying that every month at midnight of first you suddenly strech by 1 cm/month, since growth is a continuous process. If we assume you grow uniformly at all times the rate simply implies that if you grow Δh in time Δt at some point of time, the ratio $(\Delta h/\Delta t)$ will be 12 cm/year or/ cm/month or whatever unit you may choose.

Instantaneous Rate

We need to know the velocity of a particle at a particular instant in time rather than the average velocity over a finite time interval. When we say instantaneous velocity at a particular instant we are talking about the motion at a specific clock reading. But when we try to find how quickly something is moving that is, if we 'freeze time' we get undefined quantity as our answer, as $v = (\Delta h/\Delta t)$ and if time does not flow we get (0/0) as our answer, as nothing can move in 0 time. the calculus, explains how to describe an object's instantaneous velocity at any moment in time.

Differential calculus is a method of finding instantaneous rate. In many situations in physics, it is sometimes necessary to use the concept of instantaneous rate. The basic tool for this is calculus, invented by **Newton and Liebnitz** independently. The use of calculus is fundametal in the treatment of various problems in physics.

Sample Problem 2-10 Build your skill

A disk sliding along an inclined plane is found to have its position at any instant given by $x = 3t^2 + 1$, where x is in meters and t is in seconds. Compute its average velocity in the time interval between

1. 2 and 3 s

Solution: For $t = 3$ s, we have $\Delta t = 1$s

For 3 s, $x = 3(3)^2 + 1 = 28$ m and

$\Delta x = 28 \text{ m} - 13 \text{ m} = 15 \text{ m}$

For 2 s, $x = 3(2)^2 + 1 = 13$ m

Thus $$V_{\text{average}} = \frac{\Delta x}{\Delta t} = 15\,\text{m} / 1\,\text{s} = 15\,\text{m/s}$$

2. 2 and 2.1 s

Solution: For $t = 2.1$ s, we have $\Delta t = 0.1$ s

For 2.1 s, $x = 3(2.1)^2 + 1 = 14.23$ m

and $\Delta x = 1.23$ m

For 2 s, $x = 3(2)^2 + 1 = 13$ m

Thus $$V_{\text{average}} = \frac{\Delta x}{\Delta t} = 1.23\,\text{m} / 0.1\,\text{s} = 12.3\,\text{m/s}$$

3. 2 and 2.001 s

Solution: For $t = 2.001$ s, we have $\Delta t = 0.001$ s

For 2.001 s, $x = 3(2.001)^2 + 1 = 13.012003$ m and $\Delta x = 0.012003$ m

For 2 s, $x = 3(2)^2 + 1 = 13$ m

Thus $V_{\text{average}} = \Delta x/\Delta t = 0.012003 \text{ m}/0.001 \text{ s} = 12.003$ m/s

4. 2 and 2.00001 s

Solution: The student may verify that for $t = 2.00001$ s, $V_{\text{average}} = 12.00003$ m/s

5. Also find the instantaneuous velocity at 2 s.

Solution: In other words, the instantaneous velocity v equals the limiting value of the ratio $\Delta x/\Delta t$ as Δt approaches zero but it can not be zero as Δt being zero will mean Δx also becoming zero and velocity becoming undefined.

$$v = \lim_{\Delta t \to 0} \frac{\Delta x}{\Delta t}$$

In calculus notation, this limit is called the derivative of x with respect to t, written dx/dt.

$$v = \lim_{\Delta t \to 0} \frac{\Delta x}{\Delta t} = \frac{dx}{dt}$$

We note then that as Δt becomes smaller the velocity approaches the value of 12 m/s. We may thus expect that this is the instantaneous velocity at $t = 2$ s.

In fact, later we will see that when we take derivative of x with respect to t, we will get

$$v = \frac{dx}{dt} = \frac{d}{dt}(3t^2 + 1) = 6t$$

when we set $t = 2$ s, then we obtain $v = 12$ m/s

(Answer)

Sample Problem 2-11 Build your skill

Suppose $y(t)$ (that is, y as a function of t) is given by

$$y(t) = t^3$$

Find velocity (dy/dt) at $t = 3$ s.

Solution: Displacement at $t + \Delta t$ is

$$y(t + \Delta t) = (t + \Delta t)^3 = (t^3 + 3t^2\,\Delta t + 3t\,\Delta t^2 + \Delta t^3)$$

hence displacement from t to $(t + \Delta t)$ is Δy

$$\Delta y = y(t + \Delta t) - y(t) = (3t^2\,\Delta t + 3t\,\Delta t^2 + \Delta t^3)$$

Substituting this into Eq. 2-24 gives

$$\frac{dy}{dt} = \lim_{\Delta t \to 0} \frac{\Delta y}{\Delta t} = \lim_{\Delta t \to 0}[3t^2 + 3t\,\Delta t + \Delta t^2]$$

Here we can see that if we take very small value of Δt value of dy/dt will approach $3t^2$ as all other terms will become negligible and impossible to measure by any instrument available in this world.

hence, $\frac{dy}{dt} = 3t^2 \Rightarrow v = 3(3)^2 = 27 m/s$ (Answer)

Graphical Interpretation

To understand how graphical interpretation is made, consider Fig. 2-24*a*. We can easily find the average velocity for the interval during which the car moved from position A to position B (given by the slope of the secant 1) and for the interval during which it moved from A to F (given by the slope of the secant 2). As the car moved in positive direction in begning the slope of secant 1 is positive, but finally it lands on negative side, thats why slope of secant 2 is negative. Thus, the slope of the secant 1 which gives the value of the average velocity during the interval from A to B is a better representative of the initial velocity than is the value of the average velocity during the interval from A to F, which is the slope of secant 2. Now lets move point B to the left along the curve, toward point A, as in Fig. 2-24*b*. The secant 1 becomes steeper and steeper, and as the two points become extremely close together, the line becomes a tangent line to the curve at point A, indicated tangent 1 in Fig. 2-24*b*. The slope of this tangent line represents the velocity of the car at point A. We have determined the instantaneous velocity at the moment when it was at A. The instantaneous velocity can be positive, negative, or zero.

To avoid calculating instantaneous rates by complicated method we used previously we will remember some formulae which will give us the instantaneous rates directly. A useful formula to remember when $y = (ax + b)^n$, where a and b is a constant and n is any number as magnitude,

$$\frac{dy}{dx} = na(ax+b)^{n-1}$$

also it is easy to understand that $d\,[\text{constant}]/dx = 0$, as value of constant is not varying, so its rate of change is zero,

$$\frac{d}{dx}(a) = 0$$

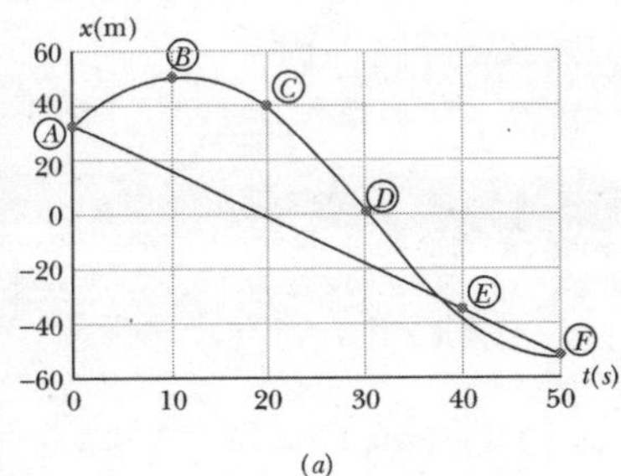

(*a*)

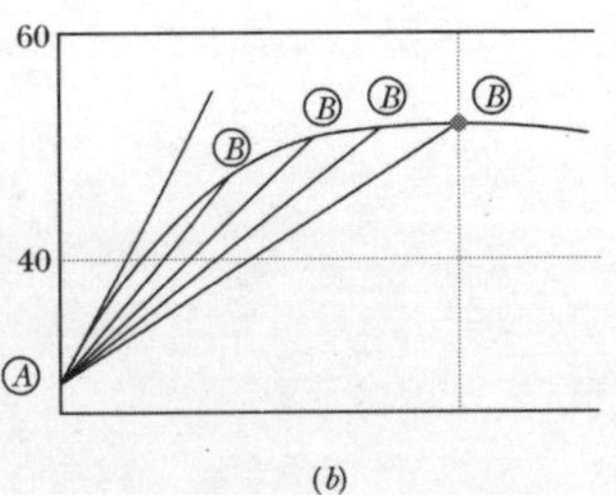

(*b*)

FIG. 2-24 Position-time graphs.

CHECKPOINT 6 If $s = (4t + 3)^4$, find velocity at $t = 1$ s

TABLE 2-2

Derivatives of Several Functions

$\frac{d}{dx}\left(e^{(ax+b)}\right) = ae^{(ax+b)}$	$\frac{d}{dx}\left(\cot(ax+b)\right) = -a\csc^2(ax+b)$
$\frac{d}{dx}\left(\sin(ax+b)\right) = a\cos(ax+b)$	$\frac{d}{dx}\left(\sec(ax+b)\right) = a\tan(ax+b)\sec(ax+b)$
$\frac{d}{dx}\left(\cos(ax+b)\right) = -a\sin(ax+b)$	$\frac{d}{dx}\left(\csc(ax+b)\right) = -a\cot(ax+b)\csc(ax+b)$
$\frac{d}{dx}\left(\tan(ax+b)\right) = a\sec^2(ax+b)$	$\frac{d}{dx}\left(\ln(ax+b)\right) = a/(ax+b)$

Note: The symbols *a*, *b* and *n* represent constants.

Special Properties of the Derivative

Derivative of the sum of two functions: If a function $f(x)$ is equal to the sum of two functions, the derivative of the sum is equal to the sum of the derivatives.

$$\frac{d}{dx}f(x) = \frac{d}{dx}[g(x) = h(x)] = \frac{dg}{dx} + \frac{dh}{dx} \quad (2\text{-}25)$$

Example 1

Find the derivative of

$$y(x) = 8x^5 + 4x^3 + 2x + 7$$

Solution

Applying Eq. 2-25 to each term independently and remembering that d/dx (constant) = 0,

we have,

$$\frac{dy}{dx} = 8(5)x^4 + 4(3)x^2 + 2(1)x^0 + 0$$

$$\frac{dy}{dx} = 40x^4 + 12x^2 + 2$$

CHECKPOINT 7 Find the derivative of $y = (3x + 4)^3 + \sin x$

Derivative of the product of two functions: If a function $f(x)$ is given by the product of two functions say, $g(x)$ and $h(x)$ the derivative of $f(x)$ is defined as

$$\frac{d}{dx}f(x) = \frac{d}{dx}[g(x)h(x)] = g\frac{dh}{dx} + h\frac{dg}{dx} \quad (2\text{-}26)$$

Example 2

Find the derivative of $y = x\sin x$.

Solution

Applying Eq. 2-25 to each term in the given expression,

we have,

$$\frac{dy}{dx} = x\frac{d}{dx}\sin x + \sin x\frac{dx}{dx}$$

$$\frac{dy}{dx} = x\cos x + \sin x$$

Example 3
Find the derivative of $y(x) = x^3/(x+1)^2$ with respect to x.

Solution
We can rewrite this function as $y(x) = x^3(x+1)^{-2}$ and apply Eq. 2-26

$$\frac{dy}{dx} = (x+1)^{-2}\frac{d}{dx}(x^3) + x^3\frac{d}{dx}(x+1)^{-2}$$

$$= (x+1)^{-2}3x^2 + x^3(-2)(x+1)^{-3}$$

$$\frac{dy}{dx} = \frac{3x^2}{(x+1)^2} - \frac{2x^3}{(x+1)^3}$$

Chain rule of differential calculus : If $y = f(x)$ and $x = g(z)$, then dy/dz can be writen as the product of two derivatives :

$$\frac{dy}{dz} = \frac{dy}{dx}\frac{dx}{dz}$$

Example 4
Given $y = \sqrt{x^2+2}$, find $\frac{dy}{dx}$.

Solution
Since $y = \sqrt{x^2+2}$ let us assume $x^2 + 2 = t \Rightarrow y = \sqrt{t}$

$$\frac{dy}{dx} = \frac{dy}{dt} \times \frac{dt}{dx}$$

$$\frac{dy}{dt} = \frac{d}{dt}t^{1/2} = \frac{1}{2\sqrt{t}}$$

$$\frac{dt}{dx} = \frac{d}{dx}(x^2+2) = 2x$$

$$\frac{dy}{dx} = \frac{x}{\sqrt{t}}$$

Now substitute the assumed value of t in this expression $\Rightarrow \frac{dy}{dx} = \frac{x}{\sqrt{x^2+2}}$

Example 5
Given $y = \ln(\sin x)$, find dy/dx.

Solution

Let $\sin x = t$

$$y = \ln t$$

$$\frac{dy}{dt} = \frac{1}{t} = \frac{1}{\sin x}$$

$$\frac{dt}{dx} = \cos x$$

$$\frac{dt}{dx} = \frac{dy}{dt} \times \frac{dt}{dx}$$

hence

$$\frac{dy}{dx} = \frac{1}{\sin x}\cos x$$

$$\frac{dy}{dx} = \cot x$$

Example 6

Given that velocity u is varying with distance as $u = cs^3$, find acceleration.

Solution

Acceleration, $$a = \frac{du}{dt} = \frac{du}{ds} \times \left(\frac{ds}{dt}\right)$$

$$\frac{du}{ds} = 3cs^2$$

$$\frac{ds}{dt} = u = cs^3$$

hence $$a = (3cs^2)(cs^3)$$

$$a = 3c^2s^5$$

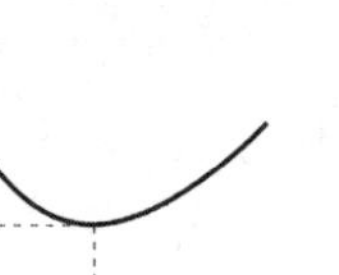

FIG. 2-25 Graphs depicting maxima and minima.

Maxima/Minima

Consider point A in graph-1 with slope zero, and also note that value of y_A is larger than its neighboring points. Consider point B in graph-2 its slope is zero, and also note that value of y_B is smaller than its neighboring points. This can be understood simply by thinking that when dy/dx is positive, y increases and when dy/dx is negative y decreases, hence at $dy/dx = 0$, it has stopped increasing and is about to start decreasing thus at $dy/dx = 0$, y has maximum value. Similar explanation should be given for Fig. 2-25*b*. Thus when $dy/dx = 0$, the y will either have maximum or minimum value compared to its neighbor.

Example 7

Find ratio of h and r so that material used for making cylindrical can is minimum.

Solution

Total surface area $2\pi r^2 + 2\pi rh = 2\pi r^2 + \frac{2v_0}{r}$

$$\therefore \quad \frac{dA}{dr} = 4\pi r - \frac{2v_0}{r^2} = 0$$

$$\therefore \quad \frac{r}{h} = \frac{1}{2} \Rightarrow 1:2$$

CHECKPOINT 8 Show that for $y = ax^2 + bx + c$, maximum or minimum value of y will occur when $x = -b/2a$.

2-10 | Integral Calculus

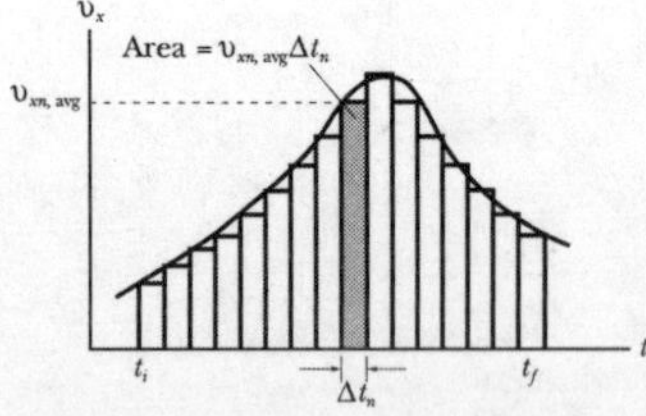

FIG. 2-26 Velocity dependence of a particle with respect to time.

The position of a particle can be obtained if its velocity dependence with time is given. In calculus, the method used to perform this task is referred to as either integration or finding the antiderivative. Graphically, it is equivalent to finding the area under a curve. Suppose the $v - t$ graph for a particle is as shown in Fig. 2-26. We want to find the displacement for time interval $t_f - t_i$. Let us divide the time interval $t_f - t_i$ into any small intervals, each of duration Δt_n. We can find the displacement Δx_n of the particle during any small interval, such as the one shaded in Fig. 2-26, by $\Delta xn = v_{xn,\,avg}\,\Delta xn$, where $v_{xn,\,avg}$ is the average velocity in that interval. Therefore, the displacement during this small interval is simply the area of the shaded rectangle. The total displacement for the interval $t_f - t_i$ is the sum of the areas of all the rectangles from t_i to t_f:

$$\Delta x = \sum_n v_{xn,avg} \Delta t_n$$

where the symbol Σ (uppercase Greek sigma) signifies a sum over all terms, that is, over all values of n.

Now, as the intervals are made smaller and smaller, the number of terms in the sum increases and the sum approaches a value equal to the area under the velocity-time graph. Therefore, in the limit $n \to \infty$, or $\Delta t_n \to 0$, the displacement is

$$\Delta x = \lim_{\Delta t_n \to 0} \sum_n v_{xn} \Delta t_n \tag{2-27}$$

Notice that we have replaced the average velocity $v_{xn,\,avg}$ with the instantaneous velocity $v_{xn,\,avg}$ in the sum. As you can see from Fig. 2-26, this approximation is valid in the limit of very small intervals. Therefore, if we know the $v_x - t$ graph for motion we can obtain the displacement during any time interval by measuring the area under the curve corresponding to that time interval. The limit of the sum shown in Eq. 2-27 is called a definite integral and is written

$$\lim_{\Delta t_n \to 0} \sum_n v_{xn} \Delta t_n = \int_{2_i}^{1_f} v_x(t)\, dt$$

where $v_x(t)$ denotes the velocity at any time t. If the explicit functional form of $v_x(t)$ is known and the limits are given, the integral can be evaluated.

To evaluate the value, we think of integration as the inverse of differentiation. As an example, consider the expression

$$f(x) = \frac{dy}{dx} = 3ax^2 + b \tag{2-28}$$

which was the result of differentiating the function

$$y(x) = ax^3 + bx + c$$

We can write Eq. 2-28 as $dy = f(x)\,dx = (3ax^2 + b)\,dx$ and obtain $y(x)$ by 'summing' over all values of x. Mathematically, we write this inverse operation as

$$y(x) = \int f(x)\, dx$$

For the function $f(x)$ given by Eq. 2-28, we have

$$y(x) = \int (3ax^2 + b)\,dx = ax^3 + bx + c$$

where c is a constant of the integration. This type of integral is called an indefinite integral because its value depends on the choice of c. A general indefinite integral $I(x)$ is defined as

$$I(x) = \int f(x)\,dx \tag{2-29}$$

where $f(x)$ is called the integrand and $f(x) = dI(x)/dx$. One common integral that arises in pratical situations has the form

$$\int x^n\,dx = \frac{x^{n+1}}{n+1} + c(n \neq -1)$$

This result is obvious, being that differentiation of the right-hand side with respect to x gives $f(x) = x^n$ directly. If the limits of the integration are known, this integral becomes a definite integral and is written.

$$\int_{x_1}^{x_2} x^n\,dx = \left.\frac{x^{n+1}}{n+1}\right|_{x_1}^{x_2} = \frac{x_2^{n+1} - x_1^{n+1}}{n+1}(n \neq -1)$$

For example,

1. $\int_0^a x^2\,dx = \left.\frac{x^3}{3}\right|_0^a = \frac{a^3}{3}$
2. $\int_3^5 x\,dx = \left.\frac{x^2}{2}\right|_3^5 = \frac{5^2 - 3^2}{2} = 8$
3. $\int_0^b x^{3/2}\,dx = \left.\frac{x^{5/2}}{5/2}\right|_0^b = \frac{2}{5}b^{5/2}$

TABLE 2-3

Some Indefinite Integrals

$\int (ax+b)^n\,dx = \frac{(ax+b)^{n+1}}{a(n+1)}$ (provided $n \neq 1$)	$\int e^{ax}\,dx = \frac{1}{a}e^{ax}$
$\int \frac{dx}{x} = \int x^{-1}\,dx = \ln x$	$\int \sin(ax+b)\,dx = \frac{1}{a}\cos(ax+b)$
$\int \frac{dx}{a+bx} = \frac{1}{b}\ln(a+bx)$	$\int \cos(ax+b)\,dx = \frac{1}{a}\sin(ax+b)$

Note: An arbitrary constant should be added to each of these integrals.

Approximations

For $x<<1$, the following approximations can be used:

$$(1+x)^n \approx 1+nx$$

For example $\quad (1.3)^{1/3} = (1+0.3)^{1/3} = 1+\frac{0.3}{3} = 1.1$

For example $\quad (104)^{1/2} = (100+4)^{1/2} = 10\,[1+0.04]^{1/2} = 10\,[-1+0.02] = 10.2$

For $x<<1$, the following approximations can be used:

$\tan x \approx \sin x \approx x, \qquad \cos x \approx 1 \qquad$ (x must be in radians)

For example $\quad \sin 2° = \sin\left(\frac{2\pi}{180}\right) = \frac{\pi}{90}$

REVIEW & SUMMARY

Scalars and Vectors *Scalars,* such as temperature, have magnitude only. They are specified by a number with a unit (10°C) and obey the rules of arithmetic and ordinary algebra. *Vectors,* such as displacement, have both magnitude and direction (5 m, north) and obey the rules of vector algebra.

Adding Vectors Geometrically Two vectors $\vec{a}$ and $\vec{b}$ may be added geometrically by drawing them to a common scale and placing them head to tail. The vector connecting the tail of the first to the head of the second is the vector sum $\vec{s}$. To subtract $\vec{b}$ from $\vec{a}$, reverse the direction of $\vec{b}$ to get $-\vec{b}$; then add $-\vec{b}$ to $\vec{a}$. Vector addition is commutative and obeys the associative law.

Components of a Vector The (scalar) *components* a_x and a_y of any two-dimensional vector $\vec{a}$ along the coordinate axes are found by dropping perpendicular lines from the ends of $\vec{a}$ onto the coordinate axes. The components are given by

$$a_x = a\cos\theta \quad \text{and} \quad a_y = a\sin\theta$$

where θ is the angle between the positive direction of the x axis and the direction of $\vec{a}$. The algebraic sign of a component indicates its direction along the associated axis. Given its components, we can find the magnitude and orientation of the vector $\vec{a}$ with

$$a = \sqrt{a_x^2 + a_y^2} \quad \text{and} \quad \tan\theta = \frac{a_y}{a_x}$$

Unit-Vector Notation *Unit vectors* $\hat{i}, \hat{j}$, and $\hat{k}$ have magnitudes of unity and are directed in the positive directions of the x, y, and z axes, respectively, in a right-handed coordinate system. We can write a vector $\vec{a}$ in terms of unit vectors as

$$\vec{a} = a_x\hat{i} + a_y\hat{j} + a_z\hat{k}$$

in which $a_x\hat{i}$, $a_y\hat{j}$, and $a_z\hat{k}$ are the **vector components** of $\vec{a}$ and a_x, a_y, and a_z are its **scalar components.**

Adding Vectors in Component Form To add vectors in component form, we use the rules

$$r_x = a_x + b_x \quad r_y = a_y + b_y \quad r_z = a_z + b_z$$

Here $\vec{a}$ and $\vec{b}$ are the vectors to be added, and $\vec{r}$ is the vector sum.

Product of a Scalar and a Vector The product of a scalar s and a vector $\vec{v}$ is a new vector whose magnitude is sv and whose direction is the same as that of $\vec{v}$ if s is positive, and opposite that of $\vec{v}$ if s is negative. To divide $\vec{v}$ by s, multiply $\vec{v}$ by $1/s$.

The Scalar Product The **scalar** (or **dot**) **product** of two vectors $\vec{a}$ and $\vec{b}$ is written $\vec{a}\vec{b}$ by

$$\vec{a}\cdot\vec{b} = ab\cos\phi$$

in which ϕ is the angle between the directions of $\vec{a}$ and $\vec{b}$. A scalar product is the product of the magnitude of one vector and the scalar component of the second vector along the direction of the first vector. In unit-vector notation,

$$\vec{a}\cdot\vec{b} = (a_x\hat{i} + a_y\hat{j} + a_z\hat{k})\cdot(b_x\hat{i} + b_y\hat{j} + b_z\hat{k})$$

which may be expanded according to the distributive law. Note that $\vec{a}\cdot\vec{b} = \vec{b}\cdot\vec{a}$.

The Vector Product The **vector** (or **cross**) **product** of two vectors $\vec{a}$ and $\vec{b}$ is written $\vec{a}\times\vec{b}$ and is a *vector* $\vec{c}$ whose magnitude c is given by

$$c = ab\sin\phi$$

in which ϕ is the smaller of the angles between the directions of $\vec{a}$ and $\vec{b}$. The direction of $\vec{c}$ is perpendicular to the plane defined by $\vec{a}$ and $\vec{b}$ and is given by a right-hand rule, as shown in Fig. 2-21. Note that $\vec{a}\times\vec{b} = -(\vec{b}\times\vec{a}$ In unit-vector notation,

$$\vec{a}\times\vec{b} = (a_x\hat{i} + a_y\hat{j} + a_z\hat{k})\times(b_x\hat{i} + b_y\hat{j} + b_z\hat{k})$$

which we may expand with the distributive law.

QUESTIONS

1 Being part of the "Gators," the University of Florida golfing team must play on a putting green with an alligator pit. Figure 2-27 shows an overhead view of one putting challenge of the team; an xy coordinate system is superimposed. Team members must putt from the origin to the hole, which is at xy coordinates (8 m, 12 m), but they can putt the golf ball using only one or more of the following displacements, one or more times:

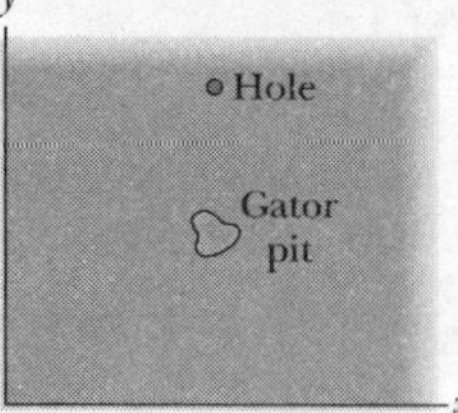

FIG. 2-27 Question 1.

$$\vec{d}_1 = (8\text{ m})\hat{i} + (6\text{ m})\hat{j},\ \vec{d}_2 = (6\text{ m})\hat{j},\ \vec{d}_3 = (8\text{ m})\hat{i}$$

The pit is at coordinates (8 m, 6 m). If a team member putts the ball into or through the pit, the member is automatically transferred to Florida State University, the arch rival. What sequence of displacements should a team member use to avoid the pit?

2 Equation 2-2 shows that the addition of two vectors $\vec{a}$ and $\vec{b}$ is commutative. Does that mean subtraction is commutative, so that $\vec{a} - \vec{b} = \vec{b} - \vec{a}$?

3 Can the sum of the magnitudes of two vectors ever be equal to the magnitude of the sum of the same two vectors? If no, why not? If yes, when?

4 The two vectors shown in Fig. 2-28 lie in an xy plane. What are the signs of the x and y components, respectively, of (a) $\vec{d}_1 + \vec{d}_2$, (b) $\vec{d}_1 - \vec{d}_2$, and (c) $\vec{d}_2 - \vec{d}_1$?

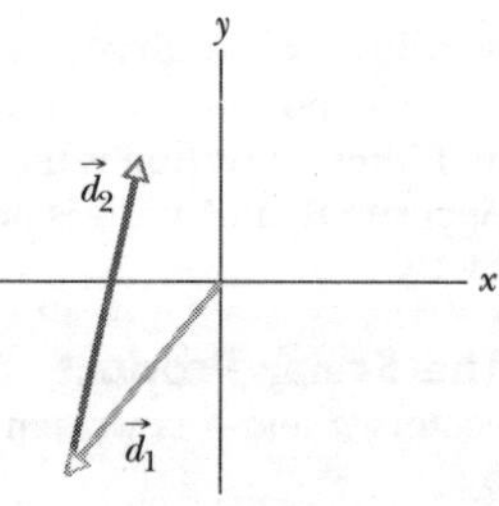

FIG. 2-28 Question 4.

5 If $\vec{d} = \vec{a} + \vec{b} + (-\vec{c})$, does (a) $\vec{a} + (-\vec{d}) = \vec{c} + (-\vec{b})$, (b) $\vec{a} = (-\vec{b}) + \vec{d} + \vec{c}$, and (c) $\vec{c} + (-\vec{d}) = \vec{a} + \vec{b}$?

6 Describe two vectors $\vec{a}$ and $\vec{b}$ such that

(a) $\vec{a} + \vec{b} = \vec{c}$ and $a + b = c$;

(b) $\vec{a} + \vec{b} = \vec{a} - \vec{b}$;

(c) $\vec{a} + \vec{b} = \vec{c}$ and $a^2 + b^2 = c^2$.

7 Which of the arrangements of axes in Fig. 2-29 can be labeled "right-handed coordinate system"? As usual, each axis label indicates the positive side of the axis.

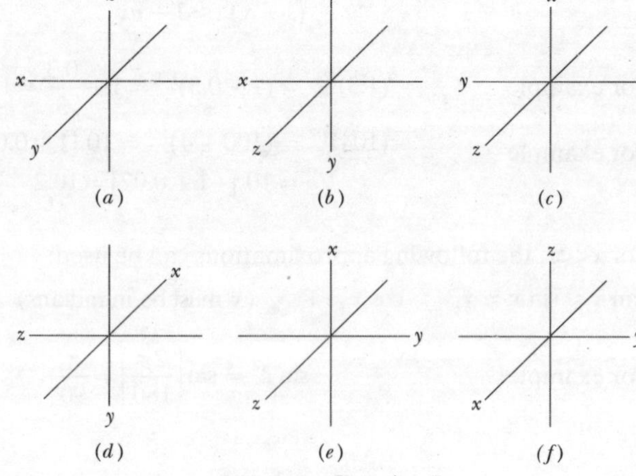

FIG. 2-29 Question 7.

8 Figure 2-30 shows vector $\vec{A}$ and four other vectors that have the same magnitude but differ in orientation. (a) Which of those other four vectors have the same dot product with $\vec{A}$? (b) Which have a negative dot product with $\vec{A}$?

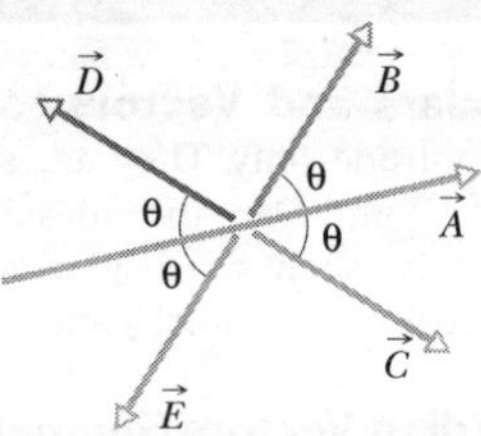

FIG. 2-30 Question 8.

9 If $\vec{F} = q(\vec{v} \times \vec{B})$ and $\vec{v}$ is perpendicular to $\vec{B}$, then what is the direction of $\vec{B}$ in the three situations shown in Fig. 3-31 when constant q is (a) positive and (b) negative?

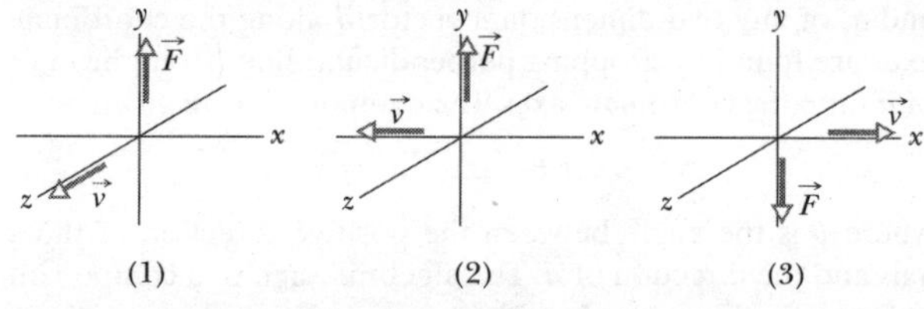

FIG. 2-31 Question 9.

10 If $\vec{a} \cdot \vec{b} = \vec{a} \cdot \vec{c}$, must $\vec{b}$ equal $\vec{c}$?

PROBLEMS

Components of Vectors

1 A displacement vector $\vec{r}$ in the xy plane is 15 m long and directed at angle $\theta = 30°$ in Fig. 2-32. Determine (a) the x component and (b) the y component of the vector.

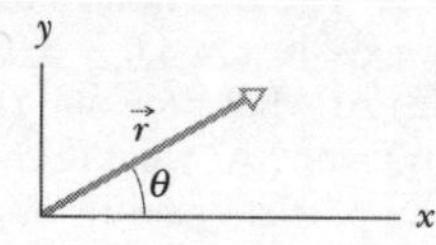

FIG. 2-32 Problem 1.

2 A room has dimensions 3.00 m (height) × 3.70 m × 4.30 m. A fly starting at one corner flies around, ending up at the diagonally opposite corner. (a) What is the magnitude of its displacement? (b) Could the length of its path be less than this magnitude? (c) Greater? (d) Equal? (e) Choose a suitable coordinate system and express the components of the displacement vector in that system in unit-vector notation. (f) If the fly walks, what is the length of the shortest path? (*Hint:* This can be answered without calculus. The room is like a box. Unfold its walls to flatten them into a plane.)

Application of Unit Vector Form

3 Two vectors are given by

$$\vec{a} = (4.0\text{ m})\hat{i} - (3.0\text{ m})\hat{j} + (1.0\text{ m})\hat{k}$$

and $$\vec{b} = (-1.0\text{ m})\hat{i} + (1.0\text{ m})\hat{j} + (4.0\text{ m})\hat{k}$$

In unit-vector notation, find (a) $\vec{a} + \vec{b}$, (b) $\vec{a} - \vec{b}$, and (c) a third vector $\vec{c}$ such that $\vec{a} - \vec{b} + \vec{c} = 0$.

4 An ant, crazed by the Sun on a hot Texas afternoon, darts over an xy plane scratched in the dirt. The x and y components of four consecutive darts are the following, all in centimeters: (30.0, 40.0), (b_x, −70.0), (−20.0, c_y), (−80.0, −70.0). The overall displacement of the four darts has the xy components (−140, −20.0). What are (a) b_x and (b) c_y? What are the (c) magnitude and (d) angle (relative to the positive direction of the x axis) of the overall displacement?

5 In a game of lawn chess, where pieces are moved between the centers of squares that are each 1.00 m on edge, a knight is moved in the following way: (1) two squares forward, one square rightward; (2) two squares leftward, one square forward; (3) two squares forward, one square leftward. What are (a) the magnitude and (b) the angle (relative to "forward") of the knight's overall displacement for the series of three moves?

6 If $\vec{B}$ is added to $\vec{C} = 3.0\hat{i} + 4.0\hat{j}$, the result is a vector in the positive direction of the y axis, with a magnitude equal to that of $\vec{C}$. What is the magnitude of $\vec{B}$?

7 Vector $\vec{A}$, which is directed along an x axis, is to be added to vector $\vec{B}$, which has a magnitude of 7.0 m. The sum is a third vector that is directed along the y axis, with a magnitude that is 3.0 times that of $\vec{A}$. What is that magnitude of $\vec{A}$?

8 Typical backyard ants often create a network of chemical trails for guidance. Extending outward from the nest, a trail branches (*bifurcates*) repeatedly, with 60° between the branches. If a roaming ant chances upon a trail, it can tell the way to the nest at any branch point: If it is moving away from the nest, it has two choices of path requiring a small turn in its travel direction, either 30° leftward or 30° rightward. If it is moving toward the nest, it has only one such choice. Figure 2-37 shows a typical ant trail, with lettered straight sections of 2.0 cm length and symmetric bifurcation of 60°. What are the (a) magnitude and (b) angle (relative to the positive direction of the superimposed x axis) of an ant's displacement from the nest (find it in the figure) if the ant enters the trail at point A? What are the (c) magnitude and (d) angle if it enters at point B?

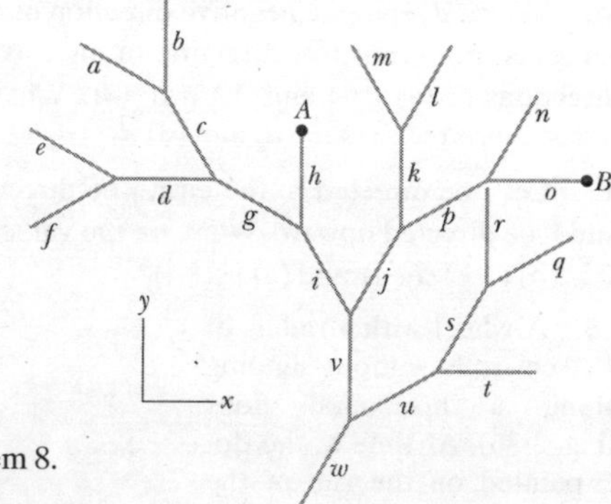

FIG. 2-33 Problem 8.

9 If $\vec{d}_1 + \vec{d}_2 = 5\vec{d}_3$, $\vec{d}_1 - \vec{d}_2 = 3\vec{d}_3$, and $\vec{d}_3 = 2\hat{i} + 4\hat{j}$, then what are, in unit-vector notation, (a) $\vec{d}_1$ and (b) $\vec{d}_2$?

10 In Fig. 2-34, a cube of edge length a sits with one corner at the origin of an xyz coordinate system. A *body diagonal* is a line that extends from one corner to another through the center. In unit-vector notation, what is the body diagonal that extends from the corner at (a) coordinates (0, 0, 0), (b) coordinates $(a, 0, 0)$, (c) coordinates $(0, a, 0)$, and (d) coordinates $(a, a, 0)$? (e) Determine the angles that the body diagonals make with the adjacent edges. (f) Determine the length of the body diagonals in terms of a.

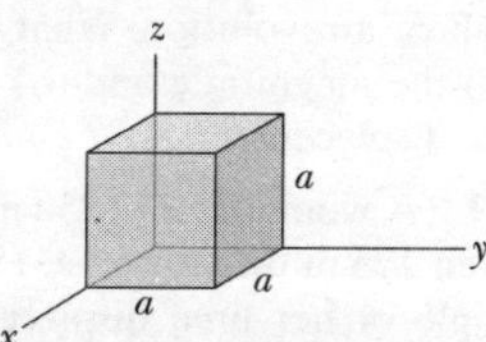

FIG. 2-34 Problem 10.

Multiplying Vectors

11 If $\vec{d}_1 = 3\hat{i} - 2\hat{j} + 4\hat{k}$ and $\vec{d}_2 = -5\hat{i} + 2\hat{j} - \hat{k}$, then what is $(\vec{d}_1 + \vec{d}_2) \cdot (\vec{d}_1 \times 4\vec{d}_2)$?

12 Three vectors are given by $\vec{a} = 3.0\hat{i} + 3.0\hat{j} - 2.0\hat{k}$, $\vec{b} = -1.0\hat{i} - 4.0\hat{j} + 2.0\hat{k}$, and $\vec{c} = 2.0\hat{i} + 2.0\hat{j} + 1.0\hat{k}$. Find (a) $\vec{a} \cdot (\vec{b} \times \vec{c})$ (b) $\vec{a} \cdot (\vec{b} + \vec{c})$ and (c) $\vec{a} \times (\vec{b} + \vec{c})$.

13 The three vectors in Fig. 2-35 have magnitudes $a = 3.00$ m, $b = 4.00$ m, and $c = 10.0$ m and angle $\theta = 30.0°$. What are (a) the x component and (b) the y component of $\vec{a}$; (c) the x component and (d) the y component of $\vec{b}$; and (e) the x component and (f) the y component of $\vec{c}$? If $\vec{c} = p\vec{a} + q\vec{b}$, what are the values of (g) p and (h) q?

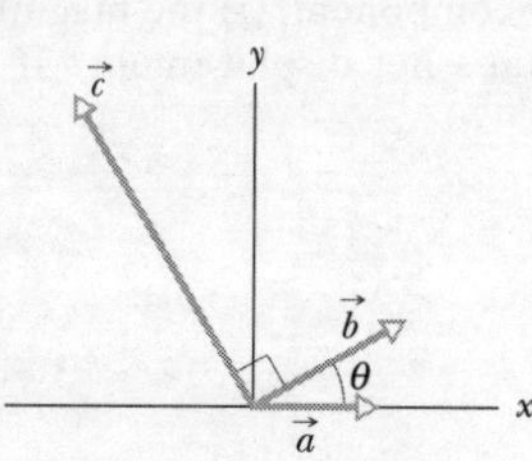

FIG. 2-35 Problem 13.

14 In a meeting of mimes, mime 1 goes through a displacement $\vec{d}_1 = (4.0 \text{ m})\hat{i} + (5.0 \text{ m})\hat{j}$ and mime 2 goes through a displacement $\vec{d}_2 = (-3.0 \text{ m})\hat{i} + (4.0 \text{ m})\hat{j}$. What are (a) $\vec{d}_1 \cdot \vec{d}_2$, (b) $(\vec{d}_1 + \vec{d}_2) \cdot \vec{d}_2$, and (c) the component of $\vec{d}_1$ along the direction of $\vec{d}_2$?

Additional Problems

15 A sailboat sets out from the U.S. side of Lake Erie for a point on the Canadian side, 90.0 km due north. The sailor, however, ends up 50.0 km due east of the starting point. (a) How far and (b) in what direction must the sailor now sail to reach the original destination?

16 Vector $\vec{d}_1$ is in the negative direction of a y axis, and vector $\vec{d}_2$ is in the positive direction of an x axis. What are the directions of (a) $\vec{d}_2/4$ and (b) $\vec{d}_1/(-4)$? What are the magnitudes of products (c) $\vec{d}_1 \cdot \vec{d}_2$ and (d) $\vec{d}_1 \cdot (\vec{d}_2/4)$?

17 Let $\hat{i}$ be directed to the east, $\hat{j}$ be directed to the north, and $\hat{k}$ be directed upward. What are the values of products (a) $\hat{i} \cdot \hat{k}$, (b) $(-\hat{k}) \cdot (-\hat{j})$, and (c) $\hat{j} \cdot (-\hat{j})$?

18 A wheel with a radius of 45.0 cm rolls without slipping along a horizontal floor (Fig. 2-36). At time t_1, the dot P painted on the rim of the wheel is at the point of contact between the wheel and the floor. At a later time t_2, the wheel has rolled through one-half of a revolution. What are (a) the magnitude and (b) the angle (relative to the floor) of the displacement of P?

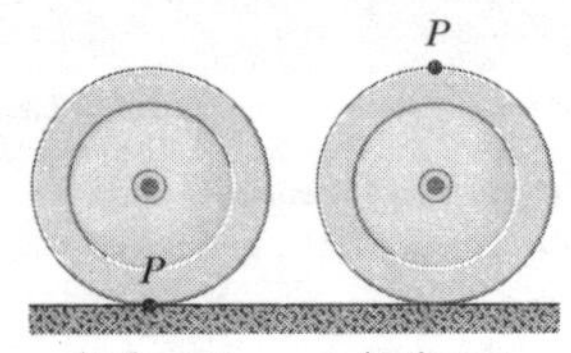

FIG. 2-36 Problem 18.

19 A woman walks 250 m in the direction 30° east of north, then 175 m directly east. Find (a) the magnitude and (b) the angle of her final displacement from the starting point. (c) Find the distance she walks. (d) Which is greater, that distance or the magnitude of her displacement?

20 If $\vec{B}$ is added to $\vec{A}$, the result is $6.0\hat{i} + 1.0\hat{j}$. If $\vec{B}$ is subtracted from $\vec{A}$, the result is $-4.0\hat{i} + 7.0\hat{j}$. What is the magnitude of $\vec{A}$?

21 A fire ant, searching for hot sauce in a picnic area, goes through three displacements along level ground: $\vec{d}_1$ for 0.40 m southwest (that is, at 45° from directly south and from directly west), $\vec{d}_2$ for 0.50 m due east, $\vec{d}_3$ for 0.60 m at 60° north of east. Let the positive x direction be east and the positive y direction be north. What are (a) the x component and (b) the y component of $\vec{d}_1$? What are (c) the x component and (d) the y component of $\vec{d}_2$? What are (e) the x component and (f) the y component of $\vec{d}_3$? What are (g) the x component, (h) the y component, (i) the magnitude, and (j) the direction of the ant's net displacement? If the ant is to return directly to the starting point, (k) how far and (l) in what direction should it move?

Instantaneous Velocity and Speed

22 The position function $x(t)$ of a particle moving along an x axis is $x = 4.0 - 6.0t^2$, with x in meters and t in seconds. (a) At what time and (b) where does the particle (momentarily) stop? At what (c) negative time and (d) positive time does the particle pass through the origin? (e) Graph x versus t for the range -5 s to $+5$ s. (f) To shift the curve rightward on the graph, should we include the term $+20t$ or the term $-20t$ in $x(t)$? (g) Does that inclusion increase or decrease the value of x at which the particle momentarily stops?

Acceleration

23 (a) If the position of a particle is given by $x = 20t - 5t^3$, where x is in meters and t is in seconds, when, if ever, is the particle's velocity zero? (b) When is its acceleration a zero? (c) For what time range (positive or negative) is a negative? (d) Positive?

24 The position of a particle moving along the x axis depends on the time according to the equation $x = ct^2 - bt^3$, where x is in meters and t in seconds. What are the units of (a) constant c and (b) constant b? Let their numerical values be 3.0 and 2.0, respectively. (c) At what time does the particle reach its maximum positive x position? From $t = 0.0$ s to $t = 4.0$ s, (d) what distance does the particle move and (e) what is its displacement? Find its velocity at times (f) 1.0 s, (g) 2.0 s, (h) 3.0 s, and (i) 4.0 s. Find its acceleration at times (j) 1.0 s, (k) 2.0 s, (l) 3.0 s, and (m) 4.0 s.

25 A salamander of the genus *Hydromantes* captures prey by launching its tongue as a projectile: The skeletal part of the tongue is shot forward, unfolding the rest of the tongue, until the outer portion lands on the prey, sticking to it. Fig. 2-37 shows the acceleration magnitude a versus time t for the acceleration phase of the launch in a typical situation. The indicated accelerations are $a_2 = 400 \text{ m/s}^2$ and $a_1 = 100 \text{ m/s}^2$. What is the outward speed of the tongue at the end of the acceleration phase?

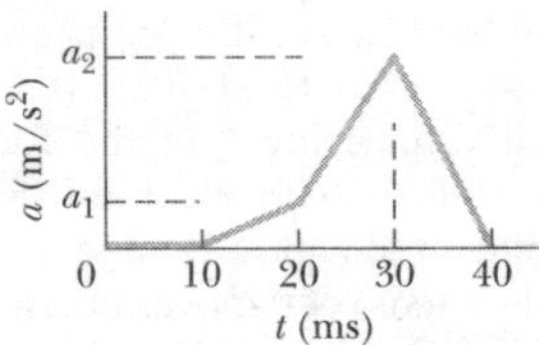

FIG. 2-37 Problem 25.

26 A particle's acceleration along an x axis is $a = 5.0t$, with t in seconds and a in meters per second squared. At $t = 2.0$ s, its velocity is $+17$ m/s. What is its velocity at $t = 4.0$ s?

27 A motorcyclist who is moving along an x axis directed toward the east has an acceleration given by $a = (6.1 - 1.2t)$ m/s^2 for $0 \leq t \leq 6.0$ s. At $t = 0$, the velocity and position of the cyclist are 2.7 m/s and 7.3 m. (a) What is the maximum speed achieved by the cyclist? (b) What total distance does the cyclist travel between $t = 0$ and 6.0 s?

Straight Line Motion

3

Jeremy Woodhouse/Masterfile

A woodpecker hammers its beak into the limb of a tree to search for insects to eat, to create storage space, or to audibly advertise for a mate. The motion toward the limb may be very rapid, but the stopping once the limb is reached is extremely rapid and would be fatal to a human. Thus, a woodpecker should seemingly fall from the tree either dead or unconscious every time it slams its beak into the tree. Not only does it survive, but it rapidly repeats the motion, sending out a rat-tat-tat signal through the air.

Why can a woodpecker survive the severe impacts with a tree limb?

The answer is in this chapter.

3-1 Introduction

One purpose of physics is to study the motion of objects—how fast they move, for example, and how far they move in a given amount of time. NASCAR engineers are fanatical about this aspect of physics as they determine the performance of their cars before and during a race. Geologists use this physics to measure tectonic-plate motion as they attempt to predict earthquakes. Medical researchers need this physics to map the blood flow through a patient when diagnosing a partially closed artery, and motorists use it to determine how they might slow sufficiently when their radar detector sounds a warning. There are countless other examples. In this chapter, we study the basic physics of motion where the object (race car, tectonic plate, blood cell, or any other object) moves along a single axis. Such motion is called *one-dimensional motion.*

3-2 | Motion

The world, and everything in it, moves. Even seemingly stationary things, such as a roadway, move with Earth's rotation, Earth's orbit around the Sun, the Sun's orbit around the center of the Milky Way galaxy, and that galaxy's migration relative to other galaxies. The classification and comparison of motions (called **kinematics**) is often challenging. What exactly do you measure, and how do you compare?

Before we attempt an answer, we shall examine some general properties of motion that is restricted in three ways.

1. The motion is along a straight line only. The line may be vertical, horizontal, or slanted, but it must be straight.
2. Forces (pushes and pulls) cause motion but will not be discussed until Chapter 5. In this chapter we discuss only the motion itself and changes in the motion. Does the moving object speed up, slow down, stop, or reverse direction? If the motion does change, how is time involved in the change?
3. The moving object is either a **particle** (by which we mean a point-like object such as an electron) or an object that moves like a particle (such that every portion moves in the same direction and at the same rate). A stiff pig slipping down a straight playground slide might be considered to be moving like a particle; however, a tumbling tumbleweed would not.

3-3 | Position and Displacement

To locate an object means to find its position relative to some reference point, often the **origin** (or zero point) of an axis such as the x axis in Fig. 3-1. The **positive direction** of the axis is in the direction of increasing numbers (coordinates), which is to the right in Fig. 3-1. The opposite is the **negative direction.**

For example, a particle might be located at $x = 5$ m, which means it is 5 m in the positive direction from the origin. If it were at $x = -5$ m, it would be just as far from the origin but in the opposite direction. On the axis, a coordinate of -5 m is less than a coordinate of -1 m, and both coordinates are less than a coordinate of $+5$ m. A plus sign for a coordinate need not be shown, but a minus sign must always be shown.

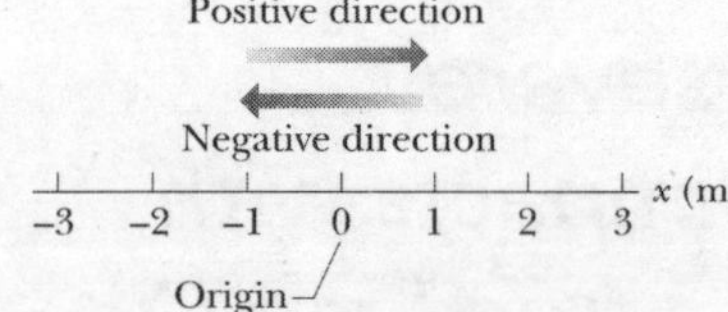

FIG. 3-1 Position is determined on an axis that is marked in units of length (here meters) and that extends indefinitely in opposite directions. The axis name, here x, is always on the positive side of the origin.

A change from position x_1 to position x_2 is called a **displacement** Δx, where

$$\Delta x = x_2 - x_1 \tag{3-1}$$

(The symbol Δ, the Greek uppercase delta, represents a change in a quantity, and it means the final value of that quantity minus the initial value.) When numbers are inserted for the position values x_1 and x_2 in Eq. 3-1, a displacement in the positive direction (to the right in Fig. 3-1) always comes out positive, and a displacement in the opposite direction (left in the figure) always comes out negative. For example, if the particle moves from $x_1 = 5$ m to $x_2 = 12$ m, then $\Delta x = (12 \text{ m}) - (5 \text{ m}) = +7$ m. The positive result indicates that the motion is in the positive direction. If, instead, the particle moves from $x_1 = 5$ m to $x_2 = 1$ m, then $\Delta x = (1 \text{ m}) - (5 \text{ m}) = -4$ m. The negative result indicates that the motion is in the negative direction.

The actual number of meters covered for a trip is irrelevant; displacement involves only the original and final positions. For example, if the particle moves from $x = 5$ m out to $x = 200$ m and then back to $x = 5$ m, the displacement from start to finish is $\Delta x = (5 \text{ m}) - (5 \text{ m}) = 0$.

A plus sign for a displacement need not be shown, but a minus sign must always be shown. If we ignore the sign (and thus the direction) of a displacement, we are left with the **magnitude** (or absolute value) of the displacement. For example, a displacement of $\Delta x = -4$ m has a magnitude of 4 m.

Displacement is an example of a **vector quantity,** which is a quantity that has both a direction and a magnitude. We explore vectors more fully in Chapter 3 (in fact, some of you may have already read that chapter), but here all we need is the idea that displacement has two features: (1) Its *magnitude* is the distance (such as the number of meters) between the original and final positions. (2) Its *direction,* from an original position to a final position, can be represented by a plus sign or a minus sign if the motion is along a single axis.

What follows is the first of many checkpoints you will see in this book. Each consists of one or more questions whose answers require some reasoning or a mental calculation, and each gives you a quick check of your understanding of a point just discussed. The answers are listed in the back of the book.

CHECKPOINT 1 Here are three pairs of initial and final positions, respectively, along an x axis. Which pairs give a negative displacement: (a) -3 m, $+5$ m; (b) -3 m, -7 m; (c) 7 m, -3 m?

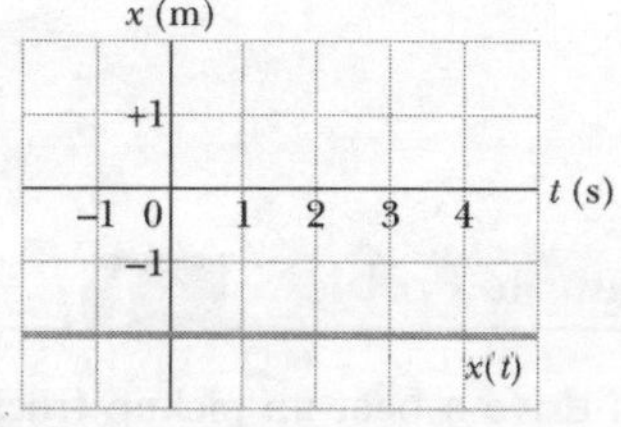

FIG. 3-2 The graph of $x(t)$ for an armadillo that is stationary at $x = -2$ m. The value of x is -2 m for all times t.

3-4 | Average Velocity and Average Speed

A compact way to describe position is with a graph of position x plotted as a function of time t—a graph of $x(t)$. (The notation $x(t)$ represents a function x of t, not the product x times t.) As a simple example, Fig. 3-2 shows the position function $x(t)$ for a stationary armadillo (which we treat as a particle) over a 7 s time interval. The animal's position stays at $x = -2$ m.

Figure 3-3*a* is more interesting, because it involves motion. The armadillo is apparently first noticed at $t = 0$ when it is at the position $x = -5$ m. It moves toward $x = 0$, passes through that point at $t = 3$ s, and then moves on to increasingly larger positive values of x. Figure 3-3*b* depicts the straight-line motion of the armadillo and is something like what you would see. The graph in Fig. 3-3*a* is more abstract and quite unlike what you would see, but it is richer in information. It also reveals how fast the armadillo moves.

Actually, several quantities are associated with the phrase "how fast." One of them is the **average velocity** v_{avg}, which is the ratio of the displacement Δx that occurs during a particular time interval Δt to that interval:

$$v_{\text{avg}} = \frac{\Delta x}{\Delta t} = \frac{x_2 - x_1}{t_2 - t_1} \tag{3-2}$$

The notation means that the position is x_1 at time t_1 and then x_2 at time t_2. A common unit for v_{avg} is the meter per second (m/s). You may see other units in the problems, but they are always in the form of length/time.

On a graph of x versus t, v_{avg} is the **slope** of the straight line that connects two particular points on the $x(t)$ curve: one is the point that corresponds to x_2 and t_2,

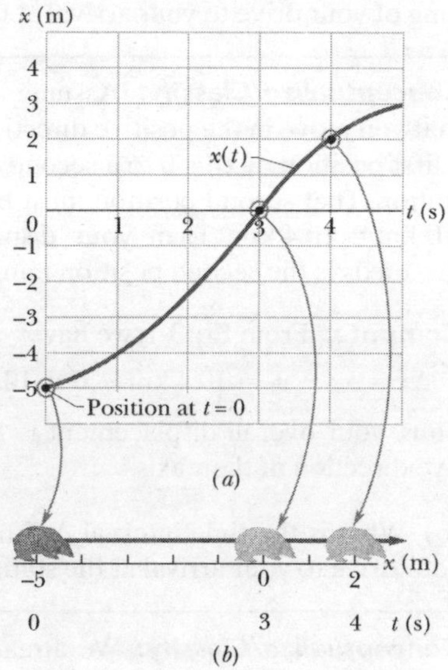

FIG. 3-3 (*a*) The graph of $x(t)$ for a moving armadillo. (*b*) The path associated with the graph. The scale below the x axis shows the times at which the armadillo reaches various x values.

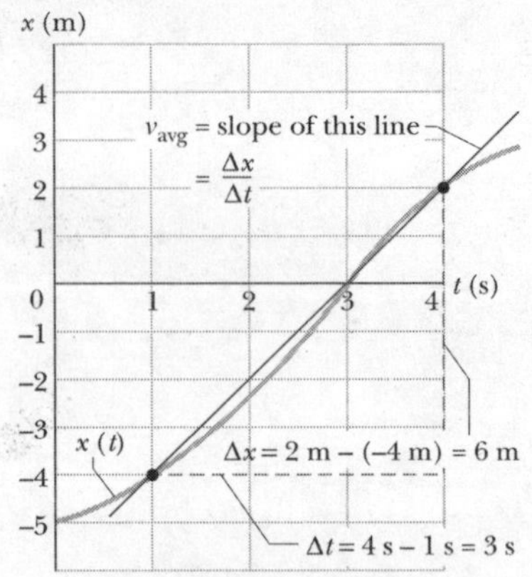

FIG. 3-4 Calculation of the average velocity between $t = 1$ s and $t = 4$ s as the slope of the line that connects the points on the $x(t)$ curve representing those times.

and the other is the point that corresponds to x_1 and t_1. Like displacement, v_{avg} has both magnitude and direction (it is another vector quantity). Its magnitude is the magnitude of the line's slope. A positive v_{avg} (and slope) tells us that the line slants upward to the right; a negative v_{avg} (and slope) tells us that the line slants downward to the right. The average velocity v_{avg} always has the same sign as the displacement Δx because Δt in Eq. 3-2 is always positive.

Figure 3-4 shows how to find v_{avg} in Fig. 3-3 for the time interval $t = 1$ s to $t = 4$ s. We draw the straight line that connects the point on the position curve at the beginning of the interval and the point on the curve at the end of the interval. Then we find the slope $\Delta x/\Delta t$ of the straight line. For the given time interval, the average velocity is

$$v_{avg} = \frac{6\text{ m}}{3\text{ s}} = 2\text{ m/s}$$

Average speed s_{avg} is a different way of describing "how fast" a particle moves. Whereas the average velocity involves the particle's displacement Δx, the average speed involves the total distance covered (for example, the number of meters moved), independent of direction; that is,

$$s_{avg} = \frac{\text{total distance}}{\Delta t} \tag{3-3}$$

Because average speed does *not* include direction, it lacks any algebraic sign. Sometimes s_{avg} is the same (except for the absence of a sign) as v_{avg}. However, as is demonstrated in Sample Problem 3-1, the two can be quite different.

Sample Problem 3-1

You drive a beat-up pickup truck along a straight road for 8.4 km at 70 km/h, at which point the truck runs out of gasoline and stops. Over the next 30 min, you walk another 2.0 km farther along the road to a gasoline station.

(a) What is your overall displacement from the beginning of your drive to your arrival at the station?

Conceptualize/Classify: Assume, for convenience, that you move in the positive direction of an x axis, from a first position of $x_1 = 0$ to a second position of x_2 at the station. That second position must be at $x_2 = 8.4$ km + 2.0 km = 10.4 km. Then your displacement Δx along the x axis is the second position minus the first position.

Compute: From Eq. 3-1, we have

$$\Delta x = x_2 - x_1 = 10.4\text{ km} - 0 = 10.4\text{ km}. \qquad \text{(Answer)}$$

Thus, your overall displacement is 10.4 km in the positive direction of the x axis.

(b) What is the time interval Δt from the beginning of your drive to your arrival at the station?

Conceptualize/Classify: We already know the walking time interval Δt_{wlk} (= 0.50 h), but we lack the driving time interval Δt_{dr}. However, we know that for the drive the displacement Δx_{dr} is 8.4 km and the average velocity $v_{avg,dr}$ is 70 km/h. Thus, this average velocity is the ratio of the displacement for the drive to the time interval for the drive.

Compute: We first write

$$v_{avg,dr} = \frac{\Delta x_{dr}}{\Delta t_{dr}}$$

Rearranging and substituting data then give us

$$\Delta t_{dr} = \frac{\Delta x_{dr}}{v_{avg,dr}} = \frac{8.4\text{ km}}{70\text{ km/h}} = 0.12\text{ h}$$

So,

$$\Delta t = \Delta t_{dr} + \Delta t_{wlk} = 0.12\text{ h} + 0.50\text{ h} = 0.62\text{ h} \qquad \text{(Answer)}$$

(c) What is your average velocity v_{avg} from the beginning of your drive to your arrival at the station? Find it both numerically and graphically.

Conceptualize/Classify: From Eq. 3-2 we know that v_{avg} *for the entire trip* is the ratio of the displacement of 10.4 km *for the entire trip* to the time interval of 0.62 h *for the entire trip.*

Compute: Here we find

$$v_{avg} = \frac{\Delta x}{\Delta t} = \frac{10.4\text{ km}}{0.62\text{ h}} = 16.8\text{ km/h} \approx 17\text{ km/h} \qquad \text{(Answer)}$$

To find v_{avg} graphically, first we graph the function $x(t)$ as shown in Fig. 3-5, where the beginning and arrival points on the graph are the origin and the point labeled as "Station." Your average velocity is the slope of the

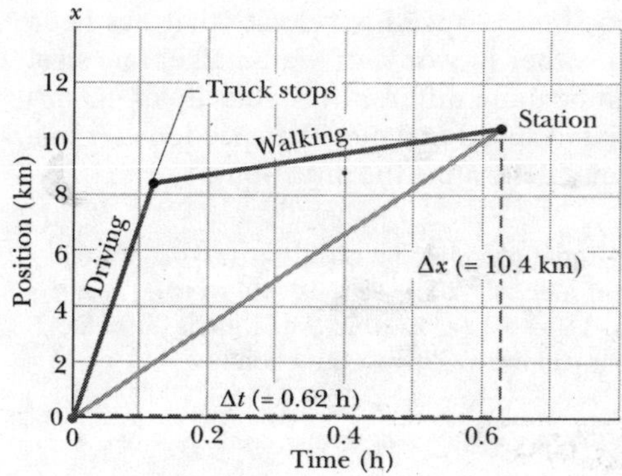

FIG. 3-5 The lines marked "Driving" and "Walking" are the position–time plots for the driving and walking stages. (The plot for the walking stage assumes a constant rate of walking.) The slope of the straight line joining the origin and the point labeled "Station" is the average velocity for the trip, from the beginning to the station.

straight line connecting those points; that is, v_{avg} is the ratio of the *rise* ($\Delta x = 10.4$ km) to the *run* ($\Delta t = 0.62$ h), which gives us $v_{avg} = 16.8$ km/h.

(d) Suppose that to pump the gasoline, pay for it, and walk back to the truck takes you another 45 min. What is your average speed from the beginning of your drive to your return to the truck with the gasoline?

Conceptualize/Classify: Your average speed is the ratio of the total distance you move to the total time interval you take to make that move.

Compute: The total distance is 8.4 km + 2.0 km + 2.0 km = 12.4 km. The total time interval is 0.12 h + 0.50 h + 0.75 h = 1.37 h. Thus, Eq. 3-3 gives us

$$s_{avg} = \frac{12.4 \text{ km}}{1.37 \text{ h}} = 9.1 \text{ km/h} \qquad \text{(Answer)}$$

PROBLEM-SOLVING TACTICS

Tactic 1: Do You Understand the Problem? The common difficulty is simply not understanding the problem. The best test of understanding is this: Can *you* explain the problem?

Write down the given data, with units, using the symbols of the chapter. (In Sample Problem 3-1, the given data allow you to find your net displacement Δx in part (a) and the corresponding time interval Δt in part (b).) Identify the unknown and its symbol. (In the sample problem, the unknown in part (c) is your average velocity v_{avg}.) Then find the connection between the unknown and the data. (The connection is provided by Eq. 3-2, the definition of average velocity.)

Tactic 2: Are the Units OK? Be sure to use a consistent set of units when putting numbers into the equations. In Sample Problem 3-1, the logical units in terms of the given data are kilometers for distances, hours for time intervals, and kilometers per hour for velocities. You may sometimes need to convert units.

Tactic 3: Is Your Answer Reasonable? Does your answer make sense, or is it far too large or far too small? Is the sign correct? Are the units appropriate? In part (c) of Sample Problem 3-1, for example, the correct answer is 17 km/h. If you find 0.00017 km/h, −17 km/h, 17 km/s, or 17 000 km/h, you should realize at once that you have done something wrong. The error may lie in your method, in your algebra, or in your keystroking of numbers on a calculator.

Tactic 4: Reading a Graph Figures 3-2, 3-3*a*, 3-4, and 3-5 are graphs you should be able to read easily. In each graph, the variable on the horizontal axis is the time t, with the direction of increasing time to the right. In each, the variable on the vertical axis is the position x of the moving particle with respect to the origin, with the positive direction of x upward. Always note the units (seconds or minutes; meters or kilometers) in which the variables are expressed.

3-5 | Instantaneous Velocity and Speed

You have now seen two ways to describe how fast something moves: average velocity and average speed, both of which are measured over a time interval Δt. However, the phrase "how fast" more commonly refers to how fast a particle is moving at a given instant—its **instantaneous velocity** (or simply **velocity**) v.

The velocity at any instant is obtained from the average velocity by shrinking the time interval Δt closer and closer to 0. As Δt dwindles, the average velocity approaches a limiting value, which is the velocity at that instant:

$$v = \lim_{\Delta t \to 0} \frac{\Delta x}{\Delta t} = \frac{dx}{dt} \qquad \text{(3-4)}$$

Note that v is the rate at which position x is changing with time at a given instant; that is, v is the derivative of x with respect to t. Also note that v at any instant is the slope of the position–time curve at the point representing that instant. Velocity is another vector quantity and thus has an associated direction.

Speed is the magnitude of velocity; that is, speed is velocity that has been stripped of any indication of direction, either in words or via an algebraic sign. (*Caution:* Speed and average speed can be quite different.) A velocity of +5 m/s and one of −5 m/s both have an associated speed of 5 m/s. The speedometer in a car measures speed, not velocity (it cannot determine the direction).

CHECKPOINT 2 The following equations give the position $x(t)$ of a particle in four situations (in each equation, x is in meters, t is in seconds, and $t > 0$): (1) $x = 3t - 2$; (2) $x = -4t^2 - 2$; (3) $x = 2/t^2$; and (4) $x = -2$. (a) In which situation is the velocity v of the particle constant? (b) In which is v in the negative x direction?

Sample Problem 3-2

Figure 3-6*a* is an $x(t)$ plot for an elevator cab that is initially stationary, then moves upward (which we take to be the positive direction of x), and then stops. Plot $v(t)$.

Conceptualize/Classify: We can find the velocity at any time from the slope of the $x(t)$ curve at that time.

Compute: The slope of $x(t)$, and so also the velocity, is zero in the intervals from 0 to 1 s and from 9 s on, so then the cab is stationary. During the interval *bc*, the slope is constant and nonzero, so then the cab moves with constant velocity. We calculate the slope of $x(t)$ then as

$$\frac{\Delta x}{\Delta t} = v = \frac{24\text{ m} - 4.0\text{ m}}{8.0\text{ s} - 3.0\text{ s}} = +4.0\text{ m/s}$$

The plus sign indicates that the cab is moving in the positive x direction. These intervals (where $v = 0$ and $v = 4$ m/s) are plotted in Fig. 3-6*b*. In addition, as the cab initially begins to move and then later slows to a stop, v varies as indicated in the intervals 1 s to 3 s and 8 s to 9 s. Thus, Fig. 3-6*b* is the required plot. (Figure 3-6*c* is considered in Section 3-6.)

Given a $v(t)$ graph such as Fig. 3-6*b*, we could "work backward" to produce the shape of the associated $x(t)$ graph (Fig. 3-6*a*). However, we would not know the actual values for x at various times, because the $v(t)$ graph indicates only *changes* in x. To find such a change in x during any interval, we must, in the language of calculus, calculate the area "under the curve" on the $v(t)$ graph for that interval. For example, during the interval 3 s to 8 s in which the cab has a velocity of 4.0 m/s, the change in x is

$$\Delta x = (4.0\text{ m/s})(8.0\text{ s} - 3.0\text{ s}) = +20\text{ m}$$

Conclude: (This area is positive because the $v(t)$ curve is above the t axis.) Figure 3-6*a* shows that x does indeed increase by 20 m in that interval. However, Fig. 3-6*b* does not tell us the *values* of x at the beginning and end of the interval. For that, we need additional information, such as the value of x at some instant.

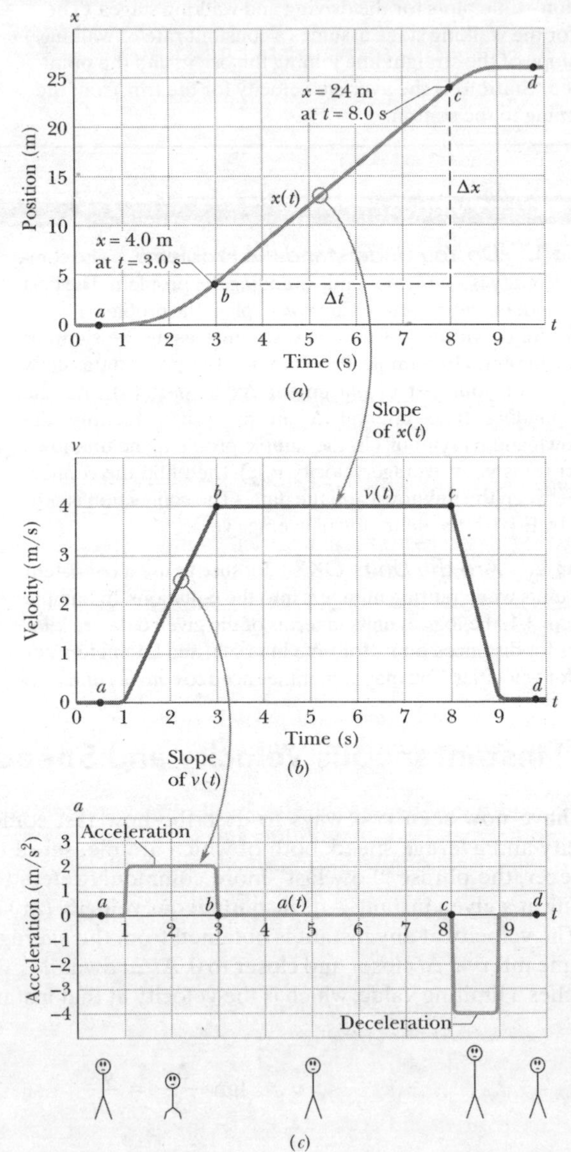

FIG. 3-6 (*a*) The $x(t)$ curve for an elevator cab that moves upward along an x axis. (*b*) The $v(t)$ curve for the cab. Note that it is the derivative of the $x(t)$ curve ($v = dx/dt$). (*c*) The $a(t)$ curve for the cab. It is the derivative of the $v(t)$ curve ($a = dv/dt$). The stick figures along the bottom suggest how a passenger's body might feel during the accelerations.

Sample Problem 3-3

The position of a particle moving on an x axis is given by

$$x = 7.8 + 9.2t - 2.1t^3 \quad (3\text{-}5)$$

with x in meters and t in seconds. What is its velocity at $t = 3.5$ s? Is the velocity constant, or is it continuously changing?

Conceptualize/Classify: Velocity is the first derivative (with respect to time) of the position function $x(t)$.

Compute: For simplicity, the units have been omitted from Eq. 3-5, but you can insert them if you like by changing the coefficients to 7.8 m, 9.2 m/s, and -2.1 m/s^3. Taking the derivative of Eq. 3-5, we write

$$v = \frac{dx}{dt} = \frac{d}{dt}(7.8 + 9.2t - 2.1t^3)$$

which becomes

$$v = 0 + 9.2 - (3)(2.1)t^2 = 9.2 - 6.3t^2 \quad (3\text{-}6)$$

At $t = 3.5$ s,

$$v = 9.2 - (6.3)(3.5)^2 = -68 \text{ m/s} \quad \text{(Answer)}$$

Conclude: At $t = 3.5$ s, the particle is moving in the negative direction of x (note the minus sign) with a speed of 68 m/s. Since the quantity t appears in Eq. 3-6, the velocity v depends on t and so is continuously changing.

3-6 | Acceleration

When a particle's velocity changes, the particle is said to undergo **acceleration** (or to accelerate). For motion along an axis, the **average acceleration** a_{avg} over a time interval Δt is

$$a_{avg} = \frac{v_2 - v_1}{t_2 - t_1} = \frac{\Delta v}{\Delta t} \quad (3\text{-}7)$$

where the particle has velocity v_1 at time t_1 and then velocity v_2 at time t_2. The **instantaneous acceleration** (or simply **acceleration**) is

$$a = \frac{dv}{dt} \quad (3\text{-}8)$$

In words, the acceleration of a particle at any instant is the rate at which its velocity is changing at that instant. Graphically, the acceleration at any point is the slope of the curve of $v(t)$ at that point. We can combine Eq. 3-8 with Eq. 3-4 to write

$$a = \frac{dv}{dt} = \frac{d}{dt}\left(\frac{dx}{dt}\right) = \frac{d^2x}{dt^2} \quad (3\text{-}9)$$

In words, the acceleration of a particle at any instant is the second derivative of its position $x(t)$ with respect to time.

A common unit of acceleration is the meter per second per second: m/(s · s) or m/s^2. Other units are in the form of length/(time · time) or length/time^2. Acceleration has both magnitude and direction (it is yet another vector quantity). Its algebraic sign represents its direction on an axis just as for displacement and velocity; that is, acceleration with a positive value is in the positive direction of an axis, and acceleration with a negative value is in the negative direction.

Figure 3-6*c* is a plot of the acceleration of the elevator cab discussed in Sample Problem 3-2. Compare this $a(t)$ curve with the $v(t)$ curve—each point on the $a(t)$ curve shows the derivative (slope) of the $v(t)$ curve at the corresponding time. When v is constant (at either 0 or 4 m/s), the derivative is zero and so also is the acceleration. When the cab first begins to move, the $v(t)$ curve has a positive derivative (the slope is positive), which means that $a(t)$ is positive. When the cab slows to a stop, the derivative and slope of the $v(t)$ curve are negative; that is, $a(t)$ is negative.

Next compare the slopes of the $v(t)$ curve during the two acceleration periods. The slope associated with the cab's slowing down (commonly called "deceleration") is steeper because the cab stops in half the time it took to get up to speed. The steeper slope means that the magnitude of the deceleration is larger than that of the acceleration, as indicated in Fig. 3-6*c*.

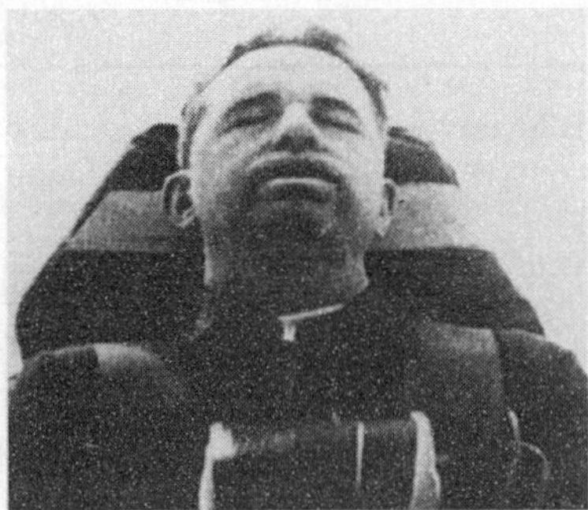

FIG. 3-7 Colonel J. P. Stapp in a rocket sled as it is brought up to high speed (acceleration out of the page) and then very rapidly braked (acceleration into the page). *(Courtesy U.S. Air Force)*

The sensations you would feel while riding in the cab of Fig. 3-6 are indicated by the sketched figures at the bottom. When the cab first accelerates, you feel as though you are pressed downward; when later the cab is braked to a stop, you seem to be stretched upward. In between, you feel nothing special. In other words, your body reacts to accelerations (it is an accelerometer) but not to velocities (it is not a speedometer). When you are in a car traveling at 90 km/h or an airplane traveling at 900 km/h, you have no bodily awareness of the motion. However, if the car or plane quickly changes velocity, you may become keenly aware of the change, perhaps even frightened by it. Part of the thrill of an amusement park ride is due to the quick changes of velocity that you undergo (you pay for the accelerations, not for the speed). A more extreme example is shown in the photographs of Fig. 3-7, which were taken while a rocket sled was rapidly accelerated along a track and then rapidly braked to a stop.

Large accelerations are sometimes expressed in terms of g units, with

$$1g = 9.8\ \text{m/s}^2 \qquad (g\ \text{unit}) \tag{3-10}$$

(As we shall discuss in Section 3-9, g is the magnitude of the acceleration of a falling object near Earth's surface.) On a roller coaster, you may experience brief accelerations up to $3g$, which is $(3)(9.8\ \text{m/s}^2)$, or about $29\ \text{m/s}^2$, more than enough to justify the cost of the ride.

PROBLEM-SOLVING TACTICS

Tactic 1: An Acceleration's Sign In common language, the sign of an acceleration has a nonscientific meaning: positive acceleration means that the speed of an object is increasing, and negative acceleration means that the speed is decreasing (the object is decelerating). In this book, however, the sign of an acceleration indicates a direction, not whether an object's speed is increasing or decreasing.

For example, if a car with an initial velocity $v = -25$ m/s is braked to a stop in 5.0 s, then $a_{avg} = +5.0\ \text{m/s}^2$. The acceleration is *positive*, but the car's speed has decreased. The reason is the difference in signs: the direction of the acceleration is opposite that of the velocity.

Here then is the proper way to interpret the signs:

If the signs of the velocity and acceleration of a particle are the same, the speed of the particle increases. If the signs are opposite, the speed decreases.

CHECKPOINT 3 A wombat moves along an x axis. What is the sign of its acceleration if it is moving (a) in the positive direction with increasing speed, (b) in the positive direction with decreasing speed, (c) in the negative direction with increasing speed, and (d) in the negative direction with decreasing speed?

Sample Problem 3-4 Build your skill

A particle's position on the x axis of Fig. 3-1 is given by

$$x = 4 - 27t + t^3$$

with x in meters and t in seconds.

(a) Because position x depends on time t, the particle must be moving. Find the particle's velocity function $v(t)$ and acceleration function $a(t)$.

Conceptualize/Classify: (1) To get the velocity function $v(t)$, we differentiate the position function $x(t)$ with respect to time. (2) To get the acceleration function $a(t)$, we differentiate the velocity function $v(t)$ with respect to time.

Compute: Differentiating the position function, we find

$$v = -27 + 3t^2 \qquad \text{(Answer)}$$

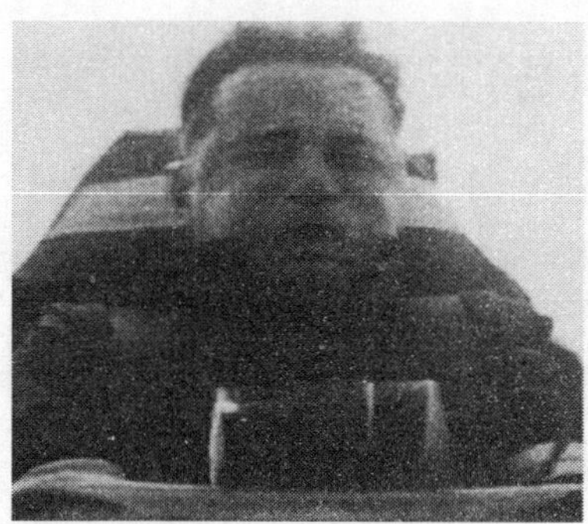

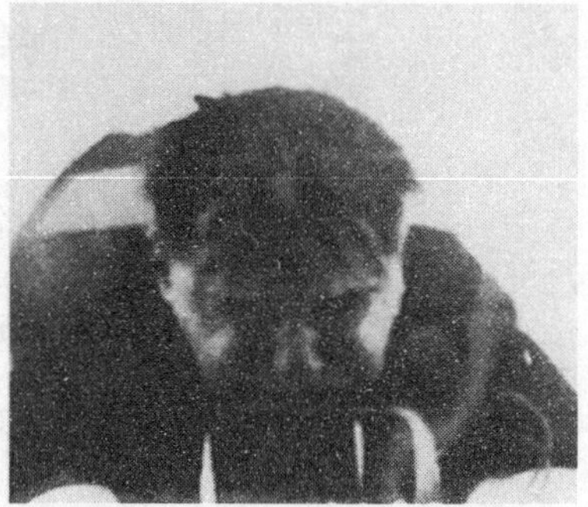

FIG. 3-7 *Continued*

with v in meters per second. Differentiating the velocity function then gives us

$$a = +6t \qquad \text{(Answer)}$$

with a in meters per second squared.

(b) Is there ever a time when $v = 0$?

Compute: Setting $v(t) = 0$ yields

$$0 = -27 + 3t^2$$

which has the solution

$$t = \pm 3 \text{ s} \qquad \text{(Answer)}$$

Thus, the velocity is zero both 3 s before and 3 s after the clock reads 0.

(c) Describe the particle's motion for $t \geq 0$.

Conclude: We need to examine the expressions for $x(t)$, $v(t)$, and $a(t)$.

At $t = 0$, the particle is at $x(0) = +4$ m and is moving with a velocity of $v(0) = -27$ m/s—that is, in the negative direction of the x axis. Its acceleration is $a(0) = 0$ because just then the particle's velocity is not changing.

For $0 < t < 3$ s, the particle still has a negative velocity, so it continues to move in the negative direction. However, its acceleration is no longer 0 but is increasing and positive. Because the signs of the velocity and the acceleration are opposite, the particle must be slowing.

Indeed, we already know that it stops momentarily at $t = 3$ s. Just then the particle is as far to the left of the origin in Fig. 3-1 as it will ever get. Substituting $t = 3$ s into the expression for $x(t)$, we find that the particle's position just then is $x = -50$ m. Its acceleration is still positive.

For $t > 3$ s, the particle moves to the right on the axis. Its acceleration remains positive and grows progressively larger in magnitude. The velocity is now positive, and it too grows progressively larger in magnitude.

3-7 | Constant Acceleration: A Special Case

In many types of motion, the acceleration is either constant or approximately so. For example, you might accelerate a car at an approximately constant rate when a traffic light turns from red to green. Then graphs of your position, velocity, and acceleration would resemble those in Fig. 3-8. (Note that $a(t)$ in Fig. 3-8*c* is constant, which requires that $v(t)$ in Fig. 3-8*b* have a constant slope.) Later when you brake the car to a stop, the acceleration (or deceleration in common language) might also be approximately constant.

Such cases are so common that a special set of equations has been derived for dealing with them. One approach to the derivation of these equations is given in this section. A second approach is given in the next section. Throughout both sections and later when you work on the homework problems, keep in mind that *these equations are valid only for constant acceleration (or situations in which you can approximate the acceleration as being constant).*

When the acceleration is constant, the average acceleration and instantaneous acceleration are equal and we can write Eq. 3-7, with some changes in notation, as

$$a = a_{\text{avg}} = \frac{v - v_0}{t - 0}$$

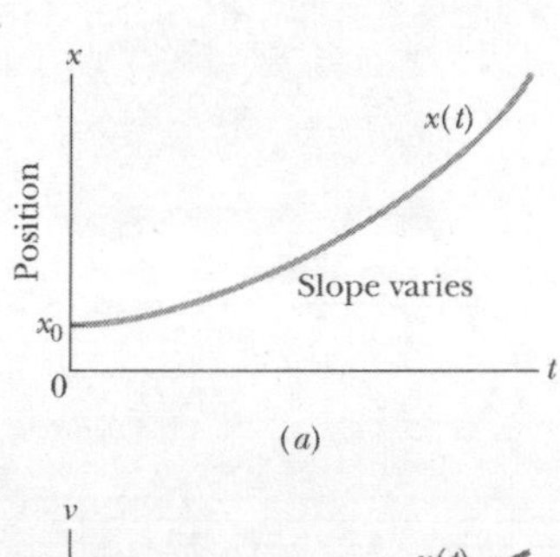

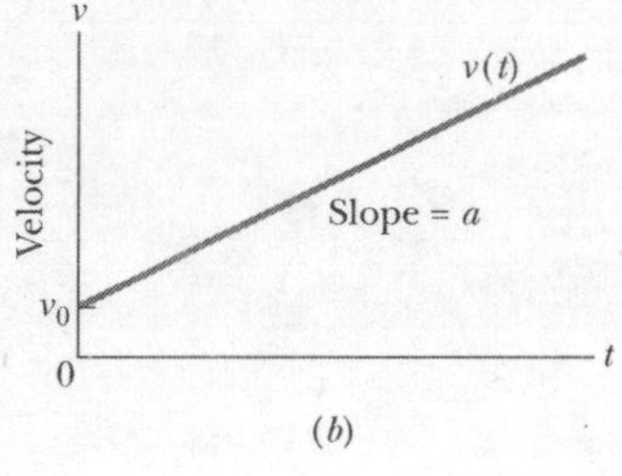

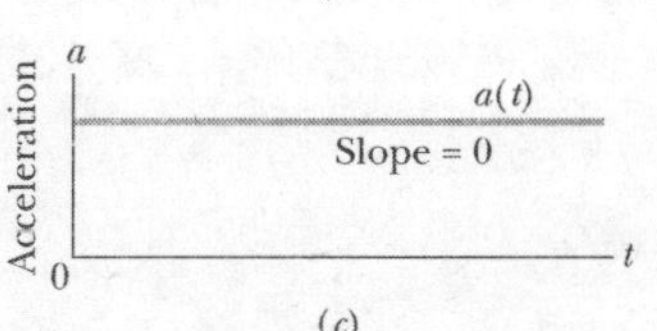

FIG. 3-8 (*a*) The position $x(t)$ of a particle moving with constant acceleration. (*b*) Its velocity $v(t)$, given at each point by the slope of the curve of $x(t)$. (*c*) Its (constant) acceleration, equal to the (constant) slope of the curve of $v(t)$.

Here v_0 is the velocity at time $t = 0$ and v is the velocity at any later time t. We can recast this equation as

$$v = v_0 + at \tag{3-11}$$

As a check, note that this equation reduces to $v = v_0$ for $t = 0$, as it must. As a further check, take the derivative of Eq. 3-11. Doing so yields $dv/dt = a$, which is the definition of a. Figure 3-8*b* shows a plot of Eq. 3-11, the $v(t)$ function; the function is linear and thus the plot is a straight line.

In a similar manner, we can rewrite Eq. 3-2 (with a few changes in notation) as

$$v_{avg} = \frac{x - x_0}{t - 0}$$

and then as

$$x = x_0 + v_{avg}t \tag{3-12}$$

in which x_0 is the position of the particle at $t = 0$ and v_{avg} is the average velocity between $t = 0$ and a later time t.

For the linear velocity function in Eq. 3-11, the *average* velocity over any time interval (say, from $t = 0$ to a later time t) is the average of the velocity at the beginning of the interval ($= v_0$) and the velocity at the end of the interval ($= v$). For the interval from $t = 0$ to the later time t then, the average velocity is

$$v_{avg} = \tfrac{1}{2}(v_0 + v) \tag{3-13}$$

Substituting the right side of Eq. 3-11 for v yields, after a little rearrangement,

$$v_{avg} = v_0 + \tfrac{1}{2}at \tag{3-14}$$

Finally, substituting Eq. 3-14 into Eq. 3-12 yields

$$x - x_0 = v_0t + \tfrac{1}{2}at^2 \tag{3-15}$$

As a check, note that putting $t = 0$ yields $x = x_0$, as it must. As a further check, taking the derivative of Eq. 3-15 yields Eq. 3-11, again as it must. Figure 3-8*a* shows a plot of Eq. 3-15; the function is quadratic and thus the plot is curved.

Equations 3-11 and 3-15 are the *basic equations for constant acceleration;* they can be used to solve any constant acceleration problem in this book. However, we can derive other equations that might prove useful in certain specific situations. First, note that as many as five quantities can possibly be involved in any problem about constant acceleration—namely, $x - x_0$, v, t, a, and v_0. Usually, one of these quantities is *not* involved in the problem, *either as a given or as an unknown.* We are then presented with three of the remaining quantities and asked to find the fourth.

Equations 3-11 and 3-15 each contain four of these quantities, but not the same four. In Eq. 3-11, the "missing ingredient" is the displacement $x - x_0$. In Eq. 3-15, it is the velocity v. These two equations can also be combined in three ways to yield three additional equations, each of which involves a different "missing variable." First, we can eliminate t to obtain

$$v^2 = v_0^2 + 2a(x - x_0) \tag{3-16}$$

This equation is useful if we do not know t and are not required to find it. Second, we can eliminate the acceleration a between Eqs. 3-11 and 3-15 to produce an equation in which a does not appear:

$$x - x_0 = \tfrac{1}{2}(v_0 + v)t \tag{3-17}$$

Finally, we can eliminate v_0, obtaining

$$x - x_0 = vt - \tfrac{1}{2}at^2 \tag{3-18}$$

Note the subtle difference between this equation and Eq. 3-15. One involves the initial velocity v_0; the other involves the velocity v at time t.

Table 3-1 lists the basic constant acceleration equations (Eqs. 3-11 and 3-15) as well as the specialized equations that we have derived. To solve a simple constant acceleration problem, you can usually use an equation from this list (*if* you have the list with you). Choose an equation for which the only unknown variable is the variable requested in the problem. A simpler plan is to remember only Eqs. 3-11 and 3-15, and then solve them as simultaneous equations whenever needed.

CHECKPOINT 4 The following equations give the position $x(t)$ of a particle in four situations: (1) $x = 3t - 4$; (2) $x = -5t^3 + 4t^2 + 6$; (3) $x = 2/t^2 - 4/t$; (4) $x = 5t^2 - 3$. To which of these situations do the equations of Table 3-1 apply?

TABLE 3-1

Equations for Motion with Constant Acceleration[a]

Equation Number	Equation	Missing Quantity
3-11	$v = v_0 + at$	$x - x_0$
3-15	$x - x_0 = v_0 t + \frac{1}{2}at^2$	v
3-16	$v^2 = v_0^2 + 2a(x - x_0)$	t
3-17	$x - x_0 = \frac{1}{2}(v_0 + v)t$	a
3-18	$x - x_0 = vt - \frac{1}{2}at^2$	v_0

[a]Make sure that the acceleration is indeed constant before using the equations in this table.

Sample Problem 3-5

The head of a woodpecker is moving forward at a speed of 7.49 m/s when the beak makes first contact with a tree limb. The beak stops after penetrating the limb by 1.87 mm. Assuming the acceleration to be constant, find the acceleration magnitude in terms of g.

Conceptualize/Classify: We can use the constant-acceleration equations; in particular, we can use Eq. 3-16 ($v^2 = v_0^2 + 2a(x - x_0)$), which relates velocity and displacement.

Compute: Because the woodpecker's head stops, the final velocity is $v = 0$. The initial velocity is $v_0 = 7.49$ m/s, and the displacement during the constant acceleration is $x - x_0 = 1.87 \times 10^{-3}$ m. Substituting these values into Eq. 3-16, we have

$$0^2 = (7.49 \text{ m/s})^2 + 2a\,(1.87 \times 10^{-3} \text{ m})$$

or

$$a = -1.500 \times 10^4 \text{ m/s}^2$$

Dividing by $g = 9.8$ m/s² and taking the absolute value, we find that the magnitude of the head's acceleration is

$$a = (1.53 \times 10^3)g \quad \text{(Answer)}$$

Conclude: This typical acceleration magnitude for a woodpecker is about 70 times the acceleration magnitude of Colonel Stapp in Fig. 3-7 and certainly would have been lethal to him. The ability of a woodpecker to withstand such huge acceleration magnitudes is not well understood, but there are two main arguments. (1) The woodpecker's motion is almost along a straight line. Some researchers believe that concussion can occur in humans and animals when the head is rapidly rotated around the neck (and brain stem), but that it is less likely in straight-line motion. (2) The woodpecker's brain is attached so well to the skull that there is little residual movement or oscillation of the brain just after the impact and no chance for the tissue connecting the skull and brain to tear.

Sample Problem 3-6 Build your skill

Figure 3-9 gives a particle's velocity v versus its position as it moves along an x axis with constant acceleration. What is its velocity at position $x = 0$?

Conceptualize/Classify: We can use the constant-acceleration equations; in particular, we can use Eq. 3-16 ($v^2 = v_0^2 + 2a(x - x_0)$), which relates velocity and position.

Compute (First try): Normally we want to use an equation that includes the requested variable. In Eq. 3-16, we can identify x_0 as 0 and v_0 as being the requested variable. Then we can identify a second pair of values as being v and x. From the graph, we have two such pairs: (1) $v = 8$ m/s and $x = 20$ m, and (2) $v = 0$ and $x = 70$ m. For example, we can write Eq. 3-16 as

$$(8 \text{ m/s})^2 = v_0^2 + 2a\,(20 \text{ m} - 0) \quad (3\text{-}19)$$

However, we know neither v_0 nor a.

Compute (Second try): Instead of directly involving the requested variable, let's use Eq. 3-16 with the two

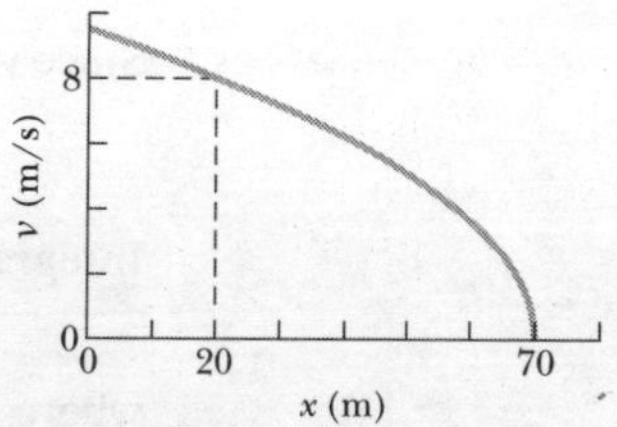

FIG. 3-9 Velocity versus position.

pairs of known data, identifying $v_0 = 8$ m/s and $x_0 = 20$ m as the first pair and $v = 0$ m/s and $x = 70$ m as the second pair. Then we can write

$$(0 \text{ m/s})^2 = (8 \text{ m/s})^2 + 2a(70 \text{ m} - 20 \text{ m})$$

which gives us $a = -0.64$ m/s². Substituting this value into Eq. 3-19 and solving for v_0 (the velocity associated with the position of $x = 0$), we find

$$v_0 = 9.5 \text{ m/s} \quad \text{(Answer)}$$

Conclude: Some problems involve an equation that includes the requested variable. A more challenging problem requires you to first use an equation that does *not* include the requested variable but that gives you a value needed to find it. Sometimes that procedure takes *physics courage* because it is so indirect. However, if you build your solving skills by solving lots of problems, the procedure gradually requires less courage and may even become obvious. Solving problems of any kind, whether physics or social, requires practice.

3-8 | Another Look at Constant Acceleration*

The first two equations in Table 3-1 are the basic equations from which the others are derived. Those two can be obtained by integration of the acceleration with the condition that a is constant. To find Eq. 3-11, we rewrite the definition of acceleration (Eq. 3-8) as

$$dv = a\, dt$$

We next write the *indefinite integral* (or *antiderivative*) of both sides:

$$\int dv = \int a\, dt$$

Since acceleration a is a constant, it can be taken outside the integration. We obtain

$$\int dv = a \int dt$$

or

$$v = at + C \tag{3-20}$$

To evaluate the constant of integration C, we let $t = 0$, at which time $v = v_0$. Substituting these values into Eq. 3-20 (which must hold for all values of t, including $t = 0$) yields

$$v_0 = (a)(0) + C = C$$

Substituting this into Eq. 3-20 gives us Eq. 3-11.

To derive Eq. 3-15, we rewrite the definition of velocity (Eq. 3-4) as

$$dx = v\, dt$$

and then take the indefinite integral of both sides to obtain

$$\int dx = \int v\, dt$$

Next, we substitute for v with Eq. 3-11:

$$\int dx = \int (v_0 + at)\, dt$$

Since v_0 is a constant, as is the acceleration a, this can be rewritten as

$$\int dx = v_0 \int dt + a \int t\, dt$$

Integration now yields

$$x = v_0 t + \tfrac{1}{2}at^2 + C' \tag{3-21}$$

where C' is another constant of integration. At time $t = 0$, we have $x = x_0$. Substituting these values in Eq. 3-21 yields $x_0 = C'$. Replacing C' with x_0 in Eq. 3-21 gives us Eq. 3-15.

3-9 | Free-Fall Acceleration

If you tossed an object either up or down and could somehow eliminate the effects of air on its flight, you would find that the object accelerates downward at a certain constant rate. That rate is called the **free-fall acceleration,** and its magnitude is represented by g. The acceleration is independent of the object's characteristics, such as mass, density, or shape; it is the same for all objects.

*This section is intended for students who have had integral calculus.

Two examples of free-fall acceleration are shown in Fig. 3-10, which is a series of stroboscopic photos of a feather and an apple. As these objects fall, they accelerate downward—both at the same rate g. Thus, their speeds increase at the same rate, and they fall together.

The value of g varies slightly with latitude and with elevation. At sea level in Earth's midlatitudes the value is 9.8 m/s^2 (or 32 ft/s^2), which is what you should use as an exact number for the problems in this book unless otherwise noted.

The equations of motion in Table 3-1 for constant acceleration also apply to free fall near Earth's surface; that is, they apply to an object in vertical flight, either up or down, when the effects of the air can be neglected. However, note that for free fall: (1) The directions of motion are now along a vertical y axis instead of the x axis, with the positive direction of y upward. (This is important for later chapters when combined horizontal and vertical motions are examined.) (2) The free-fall acceleration is negative—that is, downward on the y axis, toward Earth's center—and so it has the value $-g$ in the equations.

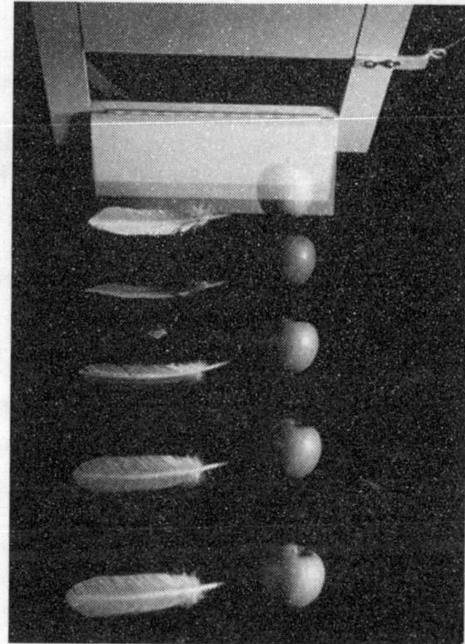

FIG. 3-10 A feather and an apple free fall in vacuum at the same magnitude of acceleration g. The acceleration increases the distance between successive images. In the absence of air, the feather and apple fall together. *(Jim Sugar/Corbis Images)*

The free-fall acceleration near Earth's surface is $a = -g = -9.8$ m/s^2, and the *magnitude* of the acceleration is $g = 9.8$ m/s^2. Do not substitute -9.8 m/s^2 for g.

Suppose you toss a tomato directly upward with an initial (positive) velocity v_0 and then catch it when it returns to the release level. During its *free-fall flight* (from just after its release to just before it is caught), the equations of Table 3-1 apply to its motion. The acceleration is always $a = -g = -9.8$ m/s^2, negative and thus downward. The velocity, however, changes, as indicated by Eqs. 3-11 and 3-16: during the ascent, the magnitude of the positive velocity decreases, until it momentarily becomes zero. Because the tomato has then stopped, it is at its maximum height. During the descent, the magnitude of the (now negative) velocity increases.

CHECKPOINT 5 (a) If you toss a ball straight up, what is the sign of the ball's displacement for the ascent, from the release point to the highest point? (b) What is it for the descent, from the highest point back to the release point? (c) What is the ball's acceleration at its highest point?

Sample Problem 3-7

On September 26, 1993, Dave Munday went over the Canadian edge of Niagara Falls in a steel ball equipped with an air hole and then fell 48 m to the water (and rocks). Assume his initial velocity was zero, and neglect the effect of the air on the ball during the fall.

(a) How long did Munday fall to reach the water surface?

Conceptualize/Classify: Because Munday's fall was a free fall, the constant-acceleration equations of Table 3-1 apply.

Compute: Let us place a y axis along the path of his fall, with $y = 0$ at his starting point and the positive direction up the axis (Fig. 3-11). Then the acceleration is $a = -g$ along that axis, and the water level is at $y = -48$ m (negative because it is below $y = 0$). Let the fall begin at time $t = 0$, with initial velocity $v_0 = 0$.

From Table 3-1 we choose Eq. 3-15 (but in y notation) because it contains the requested time t. We find

$$y - y_0 = v_0 t - \tfrac{1}{2}gt^2$$

$$-48\,\text{m} - 0 = 0t - \frac{1}{2}(9.8\,\text{m/s}^2)t^2$$

$$t^2 = 48/4.9$$

and $$t = 3.1\text{ s} \qquad \text{(Answer)}$$

Note that Munday's displacement $y - y_0$ is a negative quantity—Munday fell down, in the *negative direction* of the y axis (he did not fall up!). Also note that 48/4.9 has two square roots: 3.1 and -3.1. Here we choose the positive root because Munday obviously reaches the water surface *after* he begins to fall at $t = 0$.

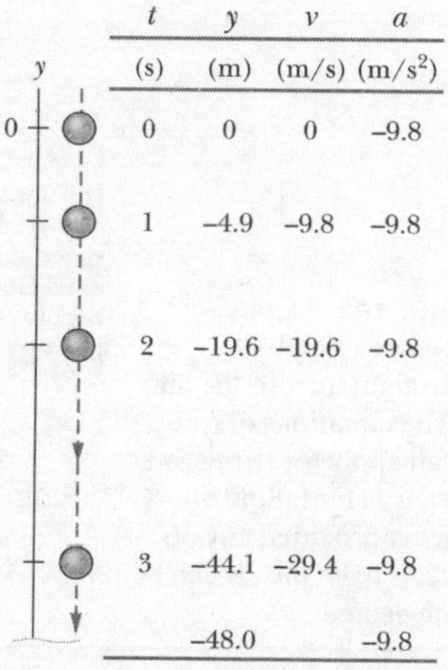

FIG. 3-11 The position, velocity, and acceleration of a freely falling object, here the steel ball ridden by Dave Munday over Niagara Falls.

(b) Munday could count off the three seconds of free fall but could not see how far he had fallen with each count. Determine his position at each full second.

Compute: We again use Eq. 3-15 but now we substitute, in turn, the values $t = 1.0$ s, 2.0 s, and 3.0 s, and solve for Munday's position y. The results are shown in Fig. 3-11.

(c) What was Munday's velocity as he reached the water surface?

Compute: To find the velocity from the original data without using the time of fall from (a), we rewrite Eq. 3-16 in y notation and then substitute known data:

$$v^2 = v_0^2 - 2g(y - y_0) = 0 - (2)(9.8 \text{ m/s}^2)(-48 \text{ m})$$

so $$v = -30.67 \text{ m/s} \approx -31 \text{ m/s} = -110 \text{ km/h} \quad \text{(Answer)}$$

We chose the negative root here because the velocity was in the negative direction.

(d) What was Munday's velocity at each count of one full second? Was he aware of his increasing speed?

Compute: To find the velocities from the original data without using the positions from (b), we let $a = -g$ in Eq. 3-11 and then substitute, in turn, the values $t = 1.0$ s, 2.0 s, and 3.0 s. Here is an example:

$$v = v_0 - gt$$
$$= 0 - (9.8 \text{ m/s}^2)(1.0 \text{ s}) = -9.8 \text{ m/s} \quad \text{(Answer)}$$

The other results are shown in Fig. 3-11.

Conclude: Once he was in free fall, Munday was unaware of the increasing speed because the acceleration during the fall was always -9.8 m/s^2, as noted in the last column of Fig. 3-11. He was, of course, sharply aware of hitting the water because then the acceleration abruptly changed. (Munday survived the fall but then faced stiff legal fines for his daredevil action.)

Sample Problem 3-8

In Fig. 3-12, a pitcher tosses a baseball up along a y axis, with an initial speed of 12 m/s.

(a) How long does the ball take to reach its maximum height?

Conceptualize/Classify: (1) Once the ball leaves the pitcher and before it returns to his hand, its acceleration is the free-fall acceleration $a = -g$. Because this is constant, Table 3-1 applies to the motion. (2) The velocity v at the maximum height must be 0.

Compute: Knowing v, a, and the initial velocity $v_0 = 12$ m/s, and seeking t, we solve Eq. 3-11, which contains those four variables. This yields

$$t = \frac{v - v_0}{a} = \frac{0 - 12 \text{ m/s}}{-9.8 \text{ m/s}^2} = 1.2 \text{ s.} \quad \text{(Answer)}$$

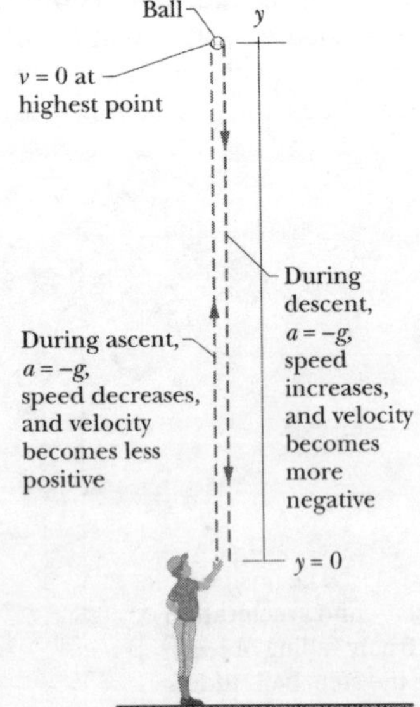

FIG. 3-12 A pitcher tosses a baseball straight up into the air. The equations of free fall apply for rising as well as for falling objects, provided any effects from the air can be neglected.

(b) What is the ball's maximum height above its release point?

Compute: We can take the ball's release point to be $y_0 = 0$. We can then write Eq. 3-16 in y notation, set $y - y_0 = y$ and $v = 0$ (at the maximum height), and solve for y. We get

$$y = \frac{v^2 - v_0^2}{2a} = \frac{0 - (12 \text{ m/s})^2}{2(-9.8 \text{ m/s}^2)} = 7.3 \text{ m} \quad \text{(Answer)}$$

(c) How long does the ball take to reach a point 5.0 m above its release point?

Compute: We know v_0, $a = -g$, and displacement $y - y_0 = 5.0$ m, and we want t, so we choose Eq. 3-15. Rewriting it for y and setting $y_0 = 0$ give us

$$y = v_0 t - \tfrac{1}{2}gt^2,$$

or $$5.0 \text{ m} = (12 \text{ m/s})t - (\tfrac{1}{2})(9.8 \text{ m/s}^2)t^2.$$

If we temporarily omit the units (having noted that they are consistent), we can rewrite this as

$$4.9t^2 - 12t + 5.0 = 0$$

Solving this quadratic equation for t yields

$$t = 0.53 \text{ s} \quad \text{and} \quad t = 1.9 \text{ s} \quad \text{(Answer)}$$

Conclude: There are two such times! This is not really surprising because the ball passes twice through $y = 5.0$ m, once on the way up and once on the way down.

PROBLEM-SOLVING TACTICS

Tactic 1: Meanings of Minus Signs In Sample Problems 3-7 and 3-8, we established a vertical axis (the y axis) and we chose—quite arbitrarily—its upward direction to be positive. We then chose the origin of the y axis (that is, the $y = 0$ position) to suit the problem. In Sample Problem 3-7, the origin was at the top of the falls, and in Sample Problem 3-8 it was at the pitcher's hand. A negative value of y then means that the body is below the chosen origin. A negative velocity means that the body is moving in the negative direction of the y axis—that is, downward. This is true no matter where the body is located.

We take the acceleration to be negative (-9.8 m/s^2) in all problems dealing with falling bodies. A negative acceleration means that, as time goes on, the velocity of the body becomes either less positive or more negative. This is true no matter where the body is located and no matter how fast or in what direction it is moving. In Sample Problem 3-8, the acceleration of the ball is negative (downward) throughout its flight, whether the ball is rising or falling.

Tactic 2: Unexpected Answers Mathematics often generates answers that you might not have thought of as possibilities, as in Sample Problem 3-8c. If you get more answers than you expect, do not automatically discard the ones that do not seem to fit. Examine them carefully for physical meaning. If time is your variable, even a negative value can mean something; negative time simply refers to time before $t = 0$, the (arbitrary) time at which you decided to start your stopwatch.

3-10 | Graphical Integration in Motion Analysis

When we have a graph of an object's acceleration versus time, we can integrate on the graph to find the object's velocity at any given time. Because acceleration a is defined in terms of velocity as $a = dv/dt$, the Fundamental Theorem of Calculus tells us that

$$v_1 - v_0 = \int_{t_0}^{t_1} a\,dt. \tag{3-22}$$

The right side of the equation is a definite integral (it gives a numerical result rather than a function), v_0 is the velocity at time t_0, and v_1 is the velocity at later time t_1. The definite integral can be evaluated from an $a(t)$ graph, such as in Fig. 3-13a. In particular,

$$\int_{t_0}^{t_1} a\,dt = \begin{pmatrix}\text{area between acceleration curve}\\ \text{and time axis, from } t_0 \text{ to } t_1\end{pmatrix} \tag{3-23}$$

If a unit of acceleration is 1 m/s^2 and a unit of time is 1 s, then the corresponding unit of area on the graph is

$$(1\ \text{m/s}^2)(1\ \text{s}) = 1\ \text{m/s}$$

which is (properly) a unit of velocity. When the acceleration curve is above the time axis, the area is positive; when the curve is below the time axis, the area is negative.

Similarly, because velocity v is defined in terms of the position x as $v = dx/dt$, then

$$x_1 - x_0 = \int_{t_0}^{t_1} v\,dt \tag{3-24}$$

where x_0 is the position at time t_0 and x_1 is the position at time t_1. The definite integral on the right side of Eq. 3-24 can be evaluated from a $v(t)$ graph, like that shown in Fig. 3-13b. In particular,

$$\int_{t_0}^{t_1} v\,dt = \begin{pmatrix}\text{area between velocity curve}\\ \text{and time axis, from } t_0 \text{ to } t_1\end{pmatrix} \tag{3-25}$$

If the unit of velocity is 1 m/s and the unit of time is 1 s, then the corresponding unit of area on the graph is

$$(1\ \text{m/s})(1\ \text{s}) = 1\ \text{m}$$

which is (properly) a unit of position and displacement. Whether this area is positive or negative is determined as described for the $a(t)$ curve of Fig. 3-13a.

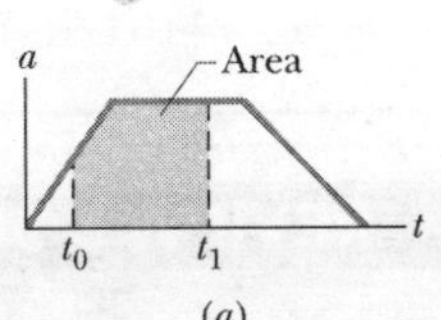

(a)

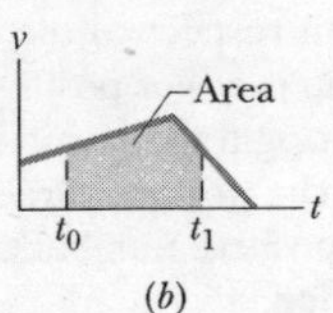

(b)

FIG. 3-13 The area between a plotted curve and the horizontal time axis, from time t_0 to time t_1, is indicated for (a) a graph of acceleration a versus t and (b) a graph of velocity v versus t.

Sample Problem 3-9

"Whiplash injury" commonly occurs in a rear-end collision where a front car is hit from behind by a second car. In the 1970s, researchers concluded that the injury was due to the occupant's head being whipped back over the top of the seat as the car was slammed forward. As a result of this finding, head restraints were built into cars, yet neck injuries in rear-end collisions continued to occur.

In a recent test to study neck injury in rear-end collisions, a volunteer was strapped to a seat that was then moved abruptly to simulate a collision by a rear car moving at 10.5 km/h. Figure 3-14*a* gives the accelerations of the volunteer's torso and head during the collision, which began at time $t = 0$. The torso acceleration was delayed by 40 ms because during that time interval the seat back had to compress against the volunteer. The head acceleration was delayed by an additional 70 ms. What was the torso speed when the head began to accelerate?

Conceptualize/Classify: We can calculate the torso speed at any time by finding an area on the torso $a(t)$ graph.

Compute: We know that the initial torso speed is $v_0 = 0$ at time $t_0 = 0$, at the start of the "collision." We want the torso speed v_1 at time $t_1 = 110$ ms, which is when the head begins to accelerate.

Combining Eqs. 3-22 and 3-23, we can write

$$v_1 - v_0 = \left(\begin{array}{c}\text{area between acceleration curve}\\ \text{and time axis, from } t_0 \text{ to } t_1\end{array}\right) \quad (3\text{-}26)$$

For convenience, let us separate the area into three regions (Fig. 3-14*b*). From 0 to 40 ms, region *A* has no area:

$$\text{area}_A = 0$$

From 40 ms to 100 ms, region *B* has the shape of a triangle, with area

$$\text{area}_B = \frac{1}{2}(0.060\,\text{s})\,(50\ \text{m/s}^2) = 1.5\,\text{m/s}$$

From 100 ms to 110 ms, region *C* has the shape of a rectangle, with area

$$\text{area}_C = (0.010\ \text{s})(50\ \text{m/s}^2) = 0.50\ \text{m/s}$$

Substituting these values and $v_0 = 0$ into Eq. 3-26 gives us

$$v_1 - 0 = 0 + 1.5\ \text{m/s} + 0.50\ \text{m/s}$$

or

$$v_1 = 2.0\ \text{m/s} = 7.2\ \text{km/h} \qquad \text{(Answer)}$$

Conclude: When the head is just starting to move forward, the torso already has a speed of 7.2 km/h. Researchers argue that it is this difference in speeds during the early stage of a rear-end collision that injures the neck. The backward whipping of the head happens later and could, especially if there is no head restraint, increase the injury.

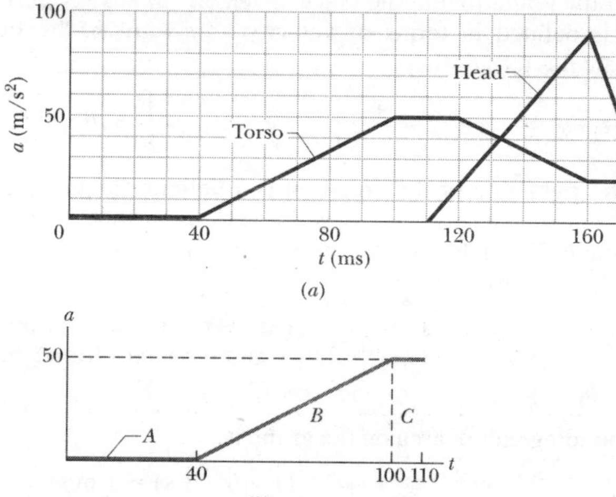

FIG. 3-14 (*a*) The $a(t)$ curve of the torso and head of a volunteer in a simulation of a rear-end collision. (*b*) Breaking up the region between the plotted curve and the time axis to calculate the area.

REVIEW & SUMMARY

Position The *position* x of a particle on an x axis locates the particle with respect to the **origin,** or zero point, of the axis. The position is either positive or negative, according to which side of the origin the particle is on, or zero if the particle is at the origin. The **positive direction** on an axis is the direction of increasing positive numbers; the opposite direction is the **negative direction.**

Displacement The *displacement* Δx of a particle is the change in its position:

$$\Delta x = x_2 - x_1$$

Displacement is a vector quantity. It is positive if the particle has moved in the positive direction of the x axis and negative if the particle has moved in the negative direction.

Average Velocity When a particle has moved from position x_1 to position x_2 during a time interval $\Delta t = t_2 - t_1$, its *average velocity* during that interval is

$$v_{\text{avg}} = \frac{\Delta x}{\Delta t} = \frac{x_2 - x_1}{t_2 - t_1}$$

The algebraic sign of v_{avg} indicates the direction of motion (v_{avg} is a vector quantity). Average velocity does not depend on the actual distance a particle moves, but instead depends on its original and final positions.

On a graph of x versus t, the average velocity for a time interval Δt is the slope of the straight line connecting the points on the curve that represent the two ends of the interval.

Average Speed The *average speed* s_{avg} of a particle during a time interval Δt depends on the total distance the particle moves in that time interval:

$$s_{avg} = \frac{\text{total distance}}{\Delta t}$$

Instantaneous Velocity The *instantaneous velocity* (or simply **velocity**) v of a moving particle is

$$v = \lim_{\Delta t \to 0} \frac{\Delta x}{\Delta t} = \frac{dx}{dt}$$

where Δx and Δt are defined by Eq. 3-2. The instantaneous velocity (at a particular time) may be found as the slope (at that particular time) of the graph of x versus t. **Speed** is the magnitude of instantaneous velocity.

Average Acceleration *Average acceleration* is the ratio of a change in velocity Δv to the time interval Δt in which the change occurs:

$$a_{avg} = \frac{\Delta v}{\Delta t}$$

The algebraic sign indicates the direction of a_{avg}.

Instantaneous Acceleration *Instantaneous acceleration* (or simply **acceleration**) a is the first time derivative of velocity $v(t)$ and the second time derivative of position $x(t)$:

$$a = \frac{dv}{dt} = \frac{d^2x}{dt^2}$$

On a graph of v versus t, the acceleration a at any time t is the slope of the curve at the point that represents t.

Constant Acceleration The five equations in Table 3-1 describe the motion of a particle with constant acceleration:

$$v = v_0 + at$$

$$x - x_0 = v_0 t + \tfrac{1}{2}at^2$$

$$v^2 = v_0^2 + 2a(x - x_0)$$

$$x - x_0 = \tfrac{1}{2}(v_0 + v)t$$

$$x - x_0 = vt - \tfrac{1}{2}at^2$$

These are *not* valid when the acceleration is not constant.

Free-Fall Acceleration An important example of straight-line motion with constant acceleration is that of an object rising or falling freely near Earth's surface. The constant acceleration equations describe this motion, but we make two changes in notation: (1) we refer the motion to the vertical y axis with $+y$ vertically *up*; (2) we replace a with $-g$, where g is the magnitude of the free-fall acceleration. Near Earth's surface, $g = 9.8 \text{ m/s}^2$ $(= 32 \text{ ft/s}^2)$.

QUESTIONS

1 Figure 3-15 shows four paths along which objects move from a starting point to a final point, all in the same time interval. The paths pass over a grid of equally spaced straight lines. Rank the paths according to (a) the average velocity of the objects and (b) the average speed of the objects, greatest first.

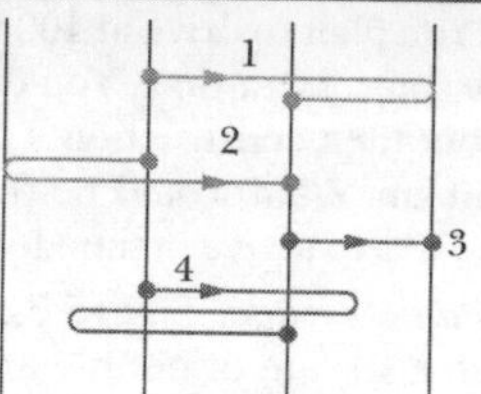

FIG. 3-15 Question 1.

2 Figure 3-16 is a graph of a particle's position along an x axis versus time. (a) At time $t = 0$, what is the sign of the particle's position? Is the particle's velocity positive, negative, or 0 at (b) $t = 1$ s, (c) $t = 2$ s, and (d) $t = 3$ s? (e) How many times does the particle go through the point $x = 0$?

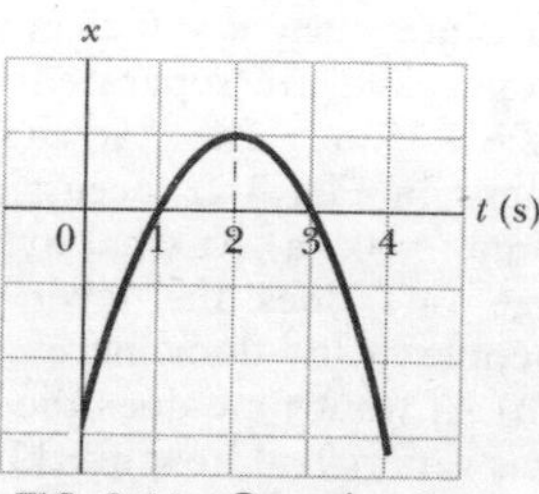

FIG. 3-16 Question 2.

3 Figure 3-17 gives the velocity of a particle moving on an x axis. What are (a) the initial and (b) the final directions of travel? (c) Does the particle stop momentarily? (d) Is the acceleration positive or negative? (e) Is it constant or varying?

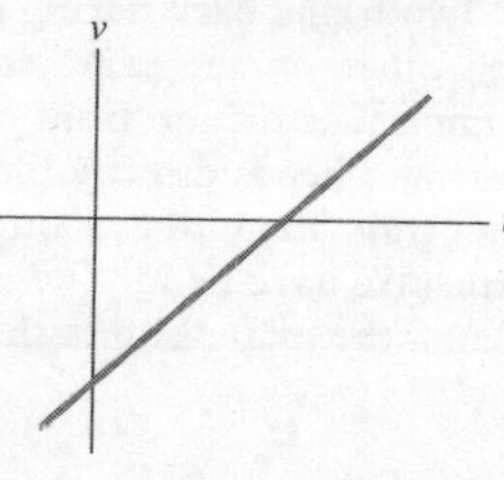

FIG. 3-17 Question 3.

4 Figure 3-18 gives the acceleration $a(t)$ of a Chihuahua as it chases a German shepherd along an axis. In which of the time periods indicated does the Chihuahua move at constant speed?

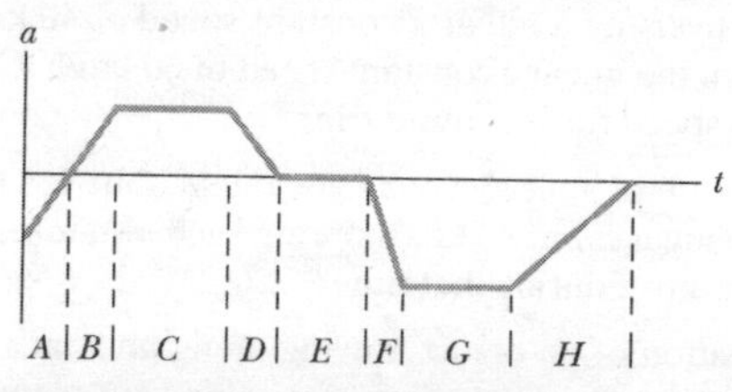

FIG. 3-18 Question 4.

5 Figure 3-19 gives the velocity of a particle moving along an axis. Point 1 is at the highest point on the curve; point 4 is at the lowest point; and points 2 and 6 are at the same height. What is the direction of travel at (a) time $t = 0$ and (b) point 4? (c) At which of the six numbered points does the particle reverse its direction of travel? (d) Rank the six points according to the magnitude of the acceleration, greatest first.

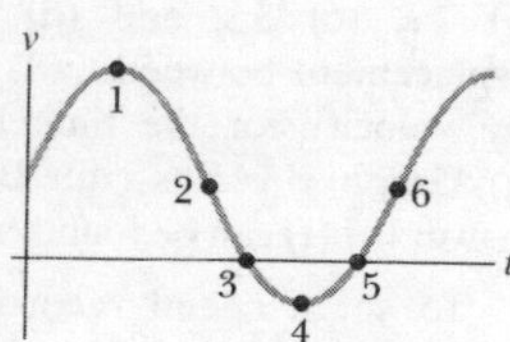

FIG. 3-19 Question 5.

6 The following equations give the velocity $v(t)$ of a particle in four situations: (a) $v = 3$; (b) $v = 4t^2 + 2t - 6$; (c) $v = 3t - 4$; (d) $v = 5t^2 - 3$. To which of these situations do the equations of Table 3-1 apply?

7 In Fig. 3-20, a cream tangerine is thrown directly upward past three evenly spaced windows of equal heights. Rank the windows according to (a) the average speed of the cream tangerine while passing them, (b) the time the cream tangerine takes to pass them, (c) the magnitude of the acceleration of the cream tangerine while passing them, and (d) the change Δv in the speed of the cream tangerine during the passage, greatest first.

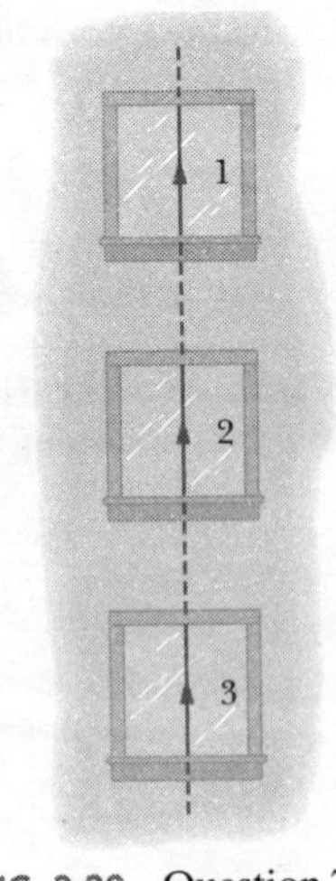

FIG. 3-20 Question 7.

8 At $t = 0$, a particle moving along an x axis is at position $x_0 = -20$ m. The signs of the particle's initial velocity v_0 (at time t_0) and constant acceleration a are, respectively, for four situations: (1) +, +; (2) +, −; (3) −, +; (4) −, −. In which situations will the particle (a) stop momentarily, (b) pass through the origin, and (c) never pass through the origin?

9 Hanging over the railing of a bridge, you drop an egg (no initial velocity) as you throw a second egg downward. Which curves in Fig. 3-21 give the velocity $v(t)$ for (a) the dropped egg and (b) the thrown egg? (Curves A and B are parallel; so are C, D, and E; so are F and G.)

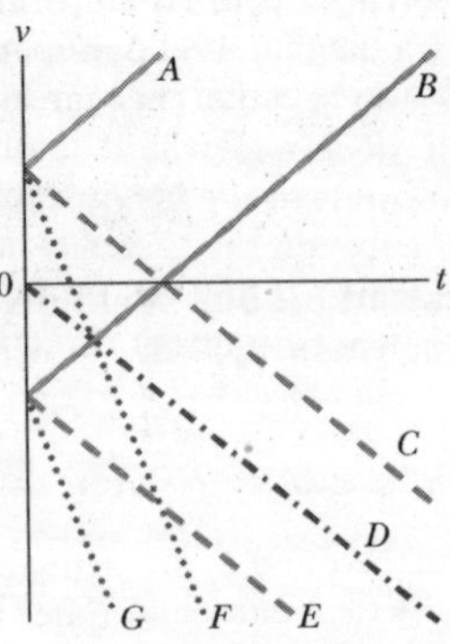

FIG. 3-21 Question 9.

PROBLEMS

Average Velocity and Average Speed

1 An automobile travels on a straight road for 40 km at 30 km/h. It then continues in the same direction for another 40 km at 60 km/h. (a) What is the average velocity of the car during this 80 km trip? (Assume that it moves in the positive x direction.) (b) What is the average speed? (c) Graph x versus t and indicate how the average velocity is found on the graph.

2 A car travels up a hill at a constant speed of 40 km/h and returns down the hill at a constant speed of 60 km/h. Calculate the average speed for the round trip.

3 During a hard sneeze, your eyes might shut for 0.50 s. If you are driving a car at 90 km/h during such a sneeze, how far does the car move during that time?

4 The position of an object moving along an x axis is given by $x = 3t - 4t^2 + t^3$, where x is in meters and t in seconds. Find the position of the object at the following values of t: (a) 1 s, (b) 2 s, (c) 3 s, and (d) 4 s. (e) What is the object's displacement between $t = 0$ and $t = 4$ s? (f) What is its average velocity for the time interval from $t = 2$ s to $t = 4$ s? (g) Graph x versus t for $0 \le t \le 4$ s and indicate how the answer for (f) can be found on the graph.

5 To set a speed record in a measured (straight-line) distance d, a race car must be driven first in one direction (in time t_1) and then in the opposite direction (in time t_2). (a) To eliminate the effects of the wind and obtain the car's speed v_c in a windless situation, should we find the average of d/t_1 and d/t_2 (method 1) or should we divide d by the average of t_1 and t_2? (b) What is the fractional difference in the two methods when a steady wind blows along the car's route and the ratio of the wind speed v_w to the car's speed v_c is 0.0240?

6 You are to drive to an interview in another town, at a distance of 300 km on an expressway. The interview is at 11:15 A.M. You plan to drive at 100 km/h, so you leave at 8:00 A.M. to allow some extra time. You drive at that speed for the first 100 km, but then construction work forces you to slow to 40 km/h for 40 km. What would be the least speed needed for the rest of the trip to arrive in time for the interview?

7 *Panic escape*. Figure 3-22 shows a general situation in which a stream of people attempt to escape through an exit door that turns out to be locked. The people move toward the door at speed $v_s = 3.50$ m/s, are each $d = 0.25$ m in depth, and are separated by $L = 1.75$ m. The arrangement in Fig. 3-22 occurs at time $t = 0$. (a) At what average rate does the layer of people at the door increase? (b) At what time does the layer's depth reach 5.0 m? (The answers reveal how quickly such a situation becomes dangerous.)

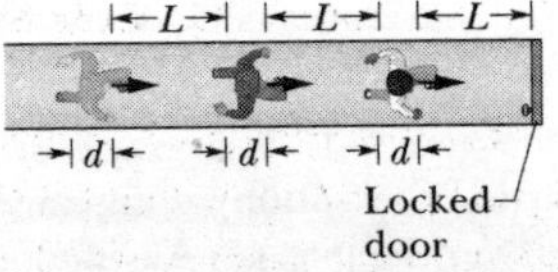

FIG. 3-22 Problem 7.

8 Two trains, each having a speed of 30 km/h, are headed at each other on the same straight track. A bird that can fly 60 km/h flies off the front of one train when they are 60 km apart and heads directly for the other train. On reaching the other train, the bird flies directly back to the first train, and so forth. (We have no idea *why* a bird would behave in this way.) What is the total distance the bird travels before the trains collide?

9 *Traffic shock wave.* An abrupt slowdown in concentrated traffic can travel as a pulse, termed a *shock wave,* along the line of cars, either downstream (in the traffic direction) or upstream, or it can be stationary. Figure 3-23 shows a uniformly spaced line of cars moving at speed v = 25.0 m/s toward a uniformly spaced line of slow cars moving at speed v_s = 5.00 m/s. Assume that each faster car adds length L = 12.0 m (car length plus buffer zone) to the line of slow cars when it joins the line, and assume it slows abruptly at the last instant. (a) For what separation distance d between the faster cars does the shock wave remain stationary? If the separation is twice that amount, what are the (b) speed and (c) direction (upstream or downstream) of the shock wave?

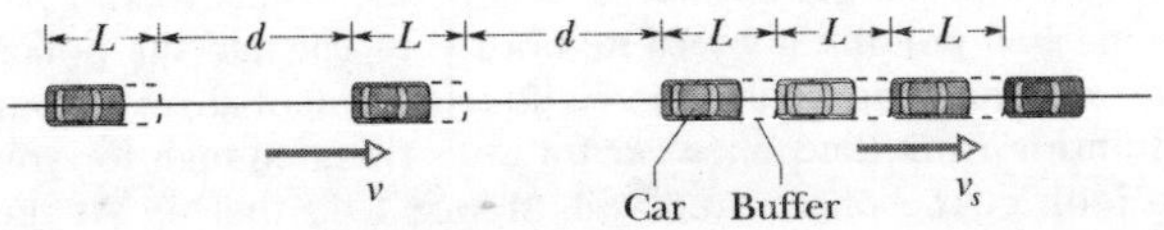

FIG. 3-23 Problem 9.

10 You drive on Interstate 10 from San Antonio to Houston, half the *time* at 55 km/h and the other half at 90 km/h. On the way back you travel half the *distance* at 55 km/h and the other half at 90 km/h. What is your average speed (a) from San Antonio to Houston, (b) from Houston back to San Antonio, and (c) for the entire trip? (d) What is your average velocity for the entire trip? (e) Sketch x versus t for (a), assuming the motion is all in the positive x direction. Indicate how the average velocity can be found on the sketch.

Instantaneous Velocity and Speed

11 (a) If a particle's position is given by $x = 4 - 12t + 3t^2$ (where t is in seconds and x is in meters), what is its velocity at t = 1 s? (b) Is it moving in the positive or negative direction of x just then? (c) What is its speed just then? (d) Is the speed increasing or decreasing just then? (Try answering the next two questions without further calculation.) (e) Is there ever an instant when the velocity is zero? If so, give the time t; if not, answer no. (f) Is there a time after t = 3 s when the particle is moving in the negative direction of x? If so, give the time t; if not, answer no.

12 An electron moving along the x axis has a position given by $x = 16te^{-t}$ m, where t is in seconds. How far is the electron from the origin when it momentarily stops?

13 The position of a particle moving along the x axis is given in centimeters by $x = 9.75 + 1.50t^3$, where t is in seconds. Calculate (a) the average velocity during the time interval t = 2.00 s to t = 3.00 s; (b) the instantaneous velocity at t = 2.00 s; (c) the instantaneous velocity at t = 3.00 s; (d) the instantaneous velocity at t = 2.50 s; and (e) the instantaneous velocity when the particle is midway between its positions at t = 2.00 s and t = 3.00 s. (f) Graph x versus t and indicate your answers graphically.

Acceleration

14 The position of a particle moving along an x axis is given by $x = 12t^2 - 2t^3$, where x is in meters and t is in seconds. Determine (a) the position, (b) the velocity, and (c) the acceleration of the particle at t = 3.0 s. (d) What is the maximum positive coordinate reached by the particle and (e) at what time is it reached? (f) What is the maximum positive velocity reached by the particle and (g) at what time is it reached? (h) What is the acceleration of the particle at the instant the particle is not moving (other than at t = 0)? (i) Determine the average velocity of the particle between t = 0 and t = 3 s.

15 From t = 0 to t = 5.00 min, a man stands still, and from t = 5.00 min to t = 10.0 min, he walks briskly in a straight line at a constant speed of 2.20 m/s. What are (a) his average velocity v_{avg} and (b) his average acceleration a_{avg} in the time interval 2.00 min to 8.00 min? What are (c) v_{avg} and (d) a_{avg} in the time interval 3.00 min to 9.00 min? (e) Sketch x versus t and v versus t, and indicate how the answers to (a) through (d) can be obtained from the graphs.

Constant Acceleration: A Special Case

16 A world's land speed record was set by Colonel John P. Stapp when in March 1954 he rode a rocket-propelled sled that moved along a track at 1020 km/h. He and the sled were brought to a stop in 1.4 s. (See Fig. 3-7.) In terms of g, what acceleration did he experience while stopping?

17 A certain elevator cab has a total run of 190 m and a maximum speed of 305 m/min, and it accelerates from rest and then back to rest at 1.22 m/s². (a) How far does the cab move while accelerating to full speed from rest? (b) How long does it take to make the nonstop 190 m run, starting and ending at rest?

18 Figure 3-24 depicts the motion of a particle moving along an x axis with a constant acceleration. The figure's vertical scaling is set by x_s = 6.0 m. What are the (a) magnitude and (b) direction of the particle's acceleration?

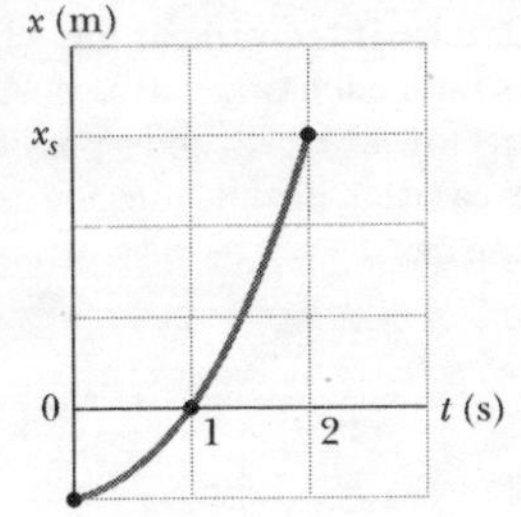

FIG. 3-24 Problem 18.

19 (a) If the maximum acceleration that is tolerable for passengers in a subway train is 1.34 m/s² and subway stations are located 806 m apart, what is the maximum speed a subway train can attain between stations? (b) What is the travel time between stations? (c) If a subway train stops for 20 s at each station, what is the maximum average speed of the train, from one start-up to the next? (d) Graph x, v, and a versus t for the interval from one start-up to the next.

20 Cars A and B move in the same direction in adjacent lanes. The position x of car A is given in Fig. 3-25, from time t = 0 to t = 7.0 s. The figure's vertical scaling is set by x_s = 32.0 m. At t = 0, car B is at x = 0, with a velocity of 12 m/s and a negative constant acceleration a_B. (a) What must a_B be such that the cars are (momentarily) side by side (momentarily at the

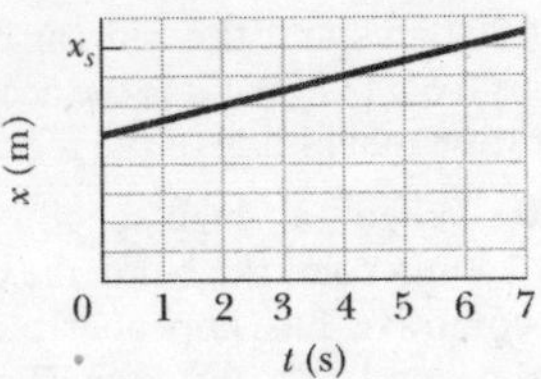

FIG. 3-25 Problem 20.

same value of x) at $t = 4.0$ s? (b) For that value of a_B, how many times are the cars side by side? (c) Sketch the position x of car B versus time t on Fig. 3-25. How many times will the cars be side by side if the magnitude of acceleration a_B is (d) more than and (e) less than the answer to part (a)?

21 You are driving toward a traffic signal when it turns yellow. Your speed is the legal speed limit of $v_0 = 55$ km/h; your best deceleration rate has the magnitude $a = 5.18$ m/s^2. Your best reaction time to begin braking is $T = 0.75$ s. To avoid having the front of your car enter the intersection after the light turns red, should you brake to a stop or continue to move at 55 km/h if the distance to the intersection and the duration of the yellow light are (a) 40 m and 2.8 s, and (b) 32 m and 1.8 s? Give an answer of brake, continue, either (if either strategy works), or neither (if neither strategy works and the yellow duration is inappropriate).

22 As two trains move along a track, their conductors suddenly notice that they are headed toward each other. Figure 3-26 gives their velocities v as functions of time t as the conductors slow the trains. The figure's vertical scaling is set by $v_s = 40.0$ m/s. The slowing processes begin when the trains are 200 m apart. What is their separation when both trains have stopped?

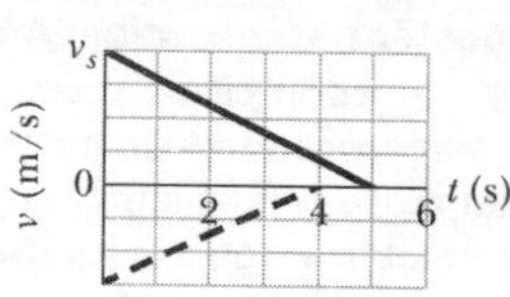

FIG. 3-26 Problem 22.

23 In Fig. 3-27, two cars, identical except for the color, move toward each other in adjacent lanes and parallel to an x axis. At time $t = 0$, the red car is at $x_r = 0$ and the green car is at $x_g = 220$ m. If the red car has a constant velocity of 20 km/h, the cars pass each other at $x = 44.5$ m, and if it has a constant velocity of 40 km/h, they pass each other at $x = 76.6$ m. What are (a) the initial velocity and (b) the acceleration of the green car?

FIG. 3-27 Problems 23 and 24.

24 Figure 3-27 shows a red car and a green car that move toward each other. Figure 3-28 is a graph of their motion, showing the positions $x_{g0} = 270$ m and $x_{r0} = -35.0$ m at time $t = 0$. The green car has a constant speed of 20.0 m/s and the red car begins from rest. What is the acceleration magnitude of the red car?

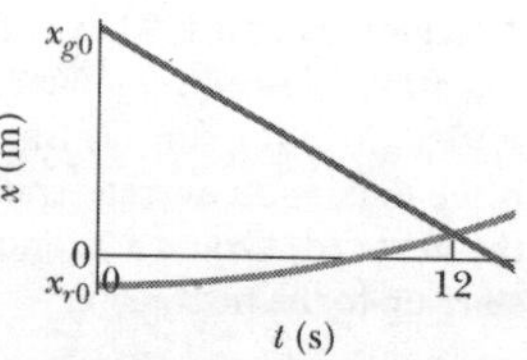

FIG. 3-28 Problem 24.

25 When a high-speed passenger train traveling at 161 km/h rounds a bend, the engineer is shocked to see that a locomotive has improperly entered onto the track from a siding and is a distance $D = 676$ m ahead (Fig. 3-29). The locomotive is moving at 29.0 km/h. The engineer of the high-speed train immediately applies the brakes. (a) What must be the magnitude of the resulting constant deceleration if a collision is to be just avoided? (b) Assume that the engineer is at $x = 0$ when, at $t = 0$, he first spots the locomotive. Sketch $x(t)$ curves for the locomotive and high-speed train for the cases in which a collision is just avoided and is not quite avoided.

FIG. 3-29 Problem 42.

26 You are arguing over a cell phone while trailing an unmarked police car by 25 m; both your car and the police car are traveling at 110 km/h. Your argument diverts your attention from the police car for 2.0 s (long enough for you to look at the phone and yell, "I won't do that!"). At the beginning of that 2.0 s, the police officer begins braking suddenly at 5.0 m/s^2. (a) What is the separation between the two cars when your attention finally returns? Suppose that you take another 0.40 s to realize your danger and begin braking. (b) If you too brake at 5.0 m/s^2, what is your speed when you hit the police car?

Free-Fall Acceleration

27 A hoodlum throws a stone vertically downward with an initial speed of 12.0 m/s from the roof of a building, 30.0 m above the ground. (a) How long does it take the stone to reach the ground? (b) What is the speed of the stone at impact?

28 (a) With what speed must a ball be thrown vertically from ground level to rise to a maximum height of 50 m? (b) How long will it be in the air? (c) Sketch graphs of y, v, and a versus t for the ball. On the first two graphs, indicate the time at which 50 m is reached.

29 A hot-air balloon is ascending at the rate of 12 m/s and is 80 m above the ground when a package is dropped over the side. (a) How long does the package take to reach the ground? (b) With what speed does it hit the ground?

30 A bolt is dropped from a bridge under construction, falling 90 m to the valley below the bridge. (a) In how much time does it pass through the last 20% of its fall? What is its speed (b) when it begins that last 20% of its fall and (c) when it reaches the valley beneath the bridge?

31 A key falls from a bridge that is 45 m above the water. It falls directly into a model boat, moving with constant velocity, that is 12 m from the point of impact when the key is released. What is the speed of the boat?

32 At time $t = 0$, apple 1 is dropped from a bridge onto a roadway beneath the bridge; somewhat later, apple 2 is thrown down from the same height. Figure 3-30 gives the vertical positions y of the apples versus t during the falling, until both apples have hit the roadway. With approximately what speed is apple 2 thrown down?

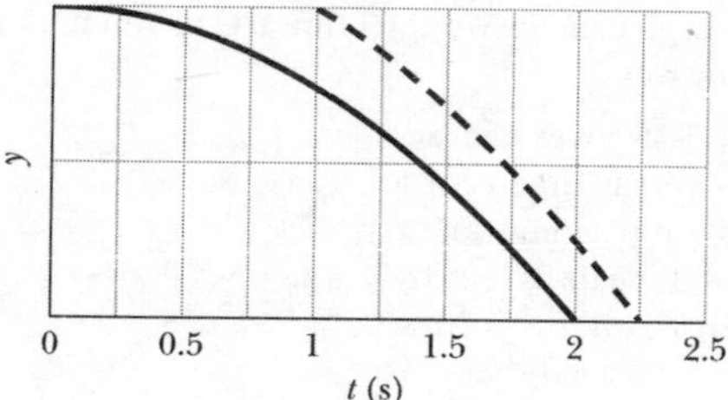

FIG. 3-30 Problem 32.

33 As a runaway scientific balloon ascends at 19.6 m/s, one of its instrument packages breaks free of a harness and free-falls. Figure 3-31 gives the vertical velocity of the package versus time, from before it breaks free to when it reaches the ground. (a) What maximum height above the break-free point does it rise? (b) How high is the break-free point above the ground?

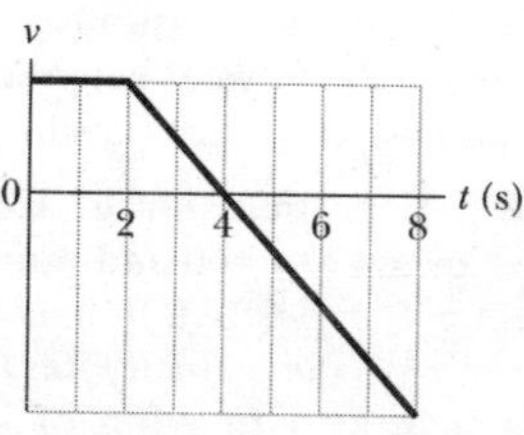

FIG. 3-31 Problem 33.

34 Figure 3-32 shows the speed v versus height y of a ball tossed directly upward, along a y axis. Distance d is 0.40 m. The speed at height y_A is v_A. The speed at height y_B is $\frac{1}{3}v_A$. What is speed v_A?

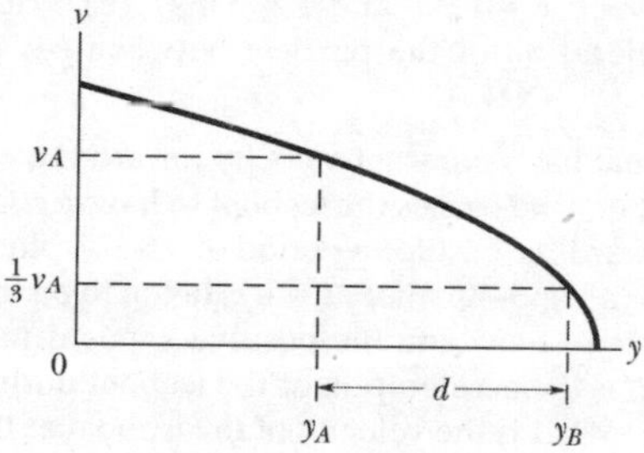

FIG. 3-32 Problem 34.

35 A ball of moist clay falls 15.0 m to the ground. It is in contact with the ground for 20.0 ms before stopping. (a) What is the magnitude of the average acceleration of the ball during the time it is in contact with the ground? (Treat the ball as a particle.) (b) Is the average acceleration up or down?

36 Water drips from the nozzle of a shower onto the floor 200 cm below. The drops fall at regular (equal) intervals of time, the first drop striking the floor at the instant the fourth drop begins to fall. When the first drop strikes the floor, how far below the nozzle are the (a) second and (b) third drops?

37 An object falls a distance h from rest. If it travels $0.50h$ in the last 1.00 s, find (a) the time and (b) the height of its fall. (c) Explain the physically unacceptable solution of the quadratic equation in t that you obtain.

38 A drowsy cat spots a flowerpot that sails first up and then down past an open window. The pot is in view for a total of 0.50 s, and the top-to-bottom height of the window is 2.00 m. How high above the window top does the flowerpot go?

39 A ball is shot vertically upward from the surface of another planet. A plot of y versus t for the ball is shown in Fig. 3-33, where y is the height of the ball above its starting point and $t = 0$ at the instant the ball is shot. The figure's vertical scaling is set by $y_s = 30.0$ m. What are the magnitudes of (a) the free-fall acceleration on the planet and (b) the initial velocity of the ball?

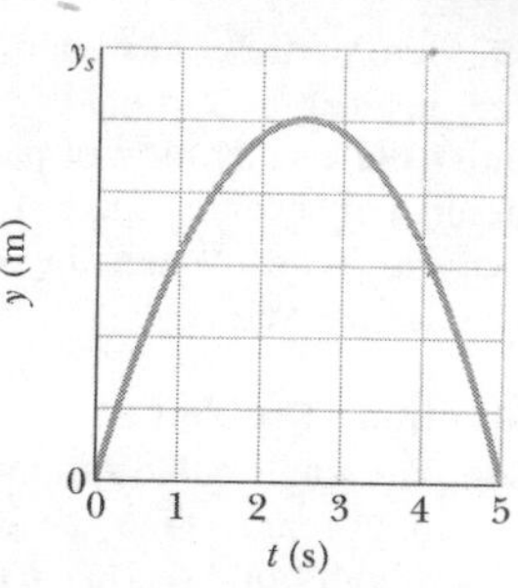

FIG. 3-33 Problem 39.

40 A steel ball is dropped from a building's roof and passes a window, taking 0.125 s to fall from the top to the bottom of the window, a distance of 1.20 m. It then falls to a sidewalk and bounces back past the window, moving from bottom to top in 0.125 s. Assume that the upward flight is an exact reverse of the fall. The time the ball spends below the bottom of the window is 2.00 s. How tall is the building?

41 A basketball player grabbing a rebound jumps 76.0 cm vertically. How much total time (ascent and descent) does the player spend (a) in the top 15.0 cm of this jump and (b) in the bottom 15.0 cm? Do your results explain why such players seem to hang in the air at the top of a jump?

Graphical Integration in Motion Analysis

42 In Sample Problem 3-9, at maximum head acceleration, what is the speed of (a) the head and (b) the torso?

43 In a forward punch in karate, the fist begins at rest at the waist and is brought rapidly forward until the arm is fully extended. The speed $v(t)$ of the fist is given in Fig. 3-34 for someone skilled in karate. How far has the fist moved at (a) time $t = 50$ ms and (b) when the speed of the fist is maximum?

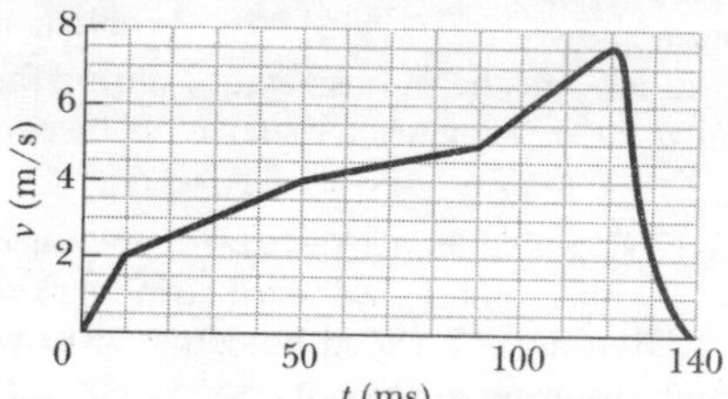

FIG. 3-34 Problem 43.

44 When a soccer ball is kicked toward a player and the player deflects the ball by "heading" it, the acceleration of the head during the collision can be significant. Figure 3-35 gives the measured acceleration $a(t)$ of a soccer player's head for a bare head and a helmeted head, starting from rest. At time $t = 7.0$ ms, what is the difference in the speed acquired by the bare head and the speed acquired by the helmeted head?

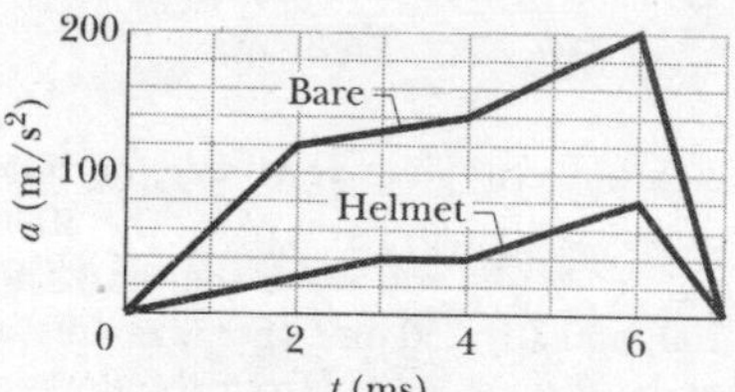

FIG. 3-35 Problem 44.

45 Two particles move along an x axis. The position of particle 1 is given by $x = 6.00t^2 + 3.00t + 2.00$ (in meters and seconds); the acceleration of particle 2 is given by $a = -8.00t$ (in meters per seconds squared and seconds) and, at $t = 0$, its velocity is 20 m/s. When the velocities of the particles match, what is their velocity?

Additional Problems

46 The single cable supporting an unoccupied construction elevator breaks when the elevator is at rest at the top of a 120-m-high building. (a) With what speed does the elevator strike the ground? (b) How long is it falling? (c) What is its speed when it passes the halfway point on the way down? (d) How long has it been falling when it passes the halfway point?

47 Two diamonds begin a free fall from rest from the same height, 1.0 s apart. How long after the first diamond begins to fall will the two diamonds be 10 m apart?

48 A motorcycle is moving at 30 m/s when the rider applies the brakes, giving the motorcycle a constant deceleration. During the 3.0 s interval immediately after braking begins, the speed decreases to 15 m/s. What distance does the motorcycle travel from the instant braking begins until the motorcycle stops?

49 At time $t = 0$, a rock climber accidentally allows a piton to fall freely from a high point on the rock wall to the valley below him. Then, after a short delay, his climbing partner, who is 10 m higher on the wall, throws a piton downward. The positions y of the pitons versus t during the falling are given in Fig. 3-36. With what speed is the second piton thrown?

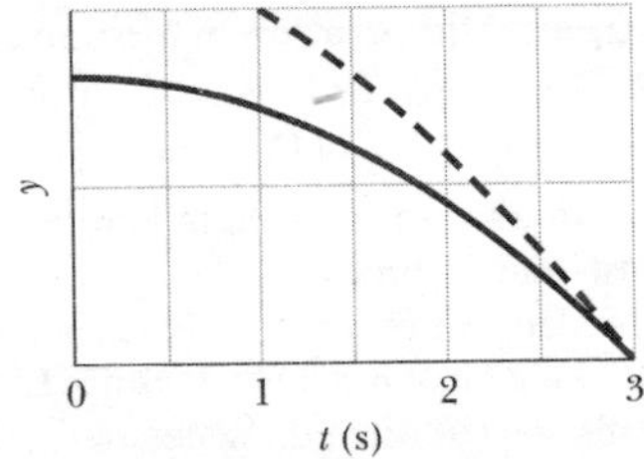

FIG. 3-36 Problem 49.

50 Figure 3-37 shows a simple device for measuring your reaction time. It consists of a cardboard strip marked with a scale and two large dots. A friend holds the strip *vertically*, with thumb and forefinger at the dot on the right in Fig. 3-37. You then position your thumb and forefinger at the other dot (on the left in Fig. 3-37), being careful not to touch the strip. Your friend releases the strip, and you try to pinch it as soon as possible after you see it begin to fall. The mark at the place where you pinch the strip gives your reaction time. (a) How far from the lower dot should you place the 50.0 ms mark? How much higher should you place the marks for (b) 100, (c) 150, (d) 200, and (e) 250 ms? (For example, should the 100 ms marker be 2 times as far from the dot as the 50 ms marker? If so, give an answer of 2 times. Can you find any pattern in the answers?)

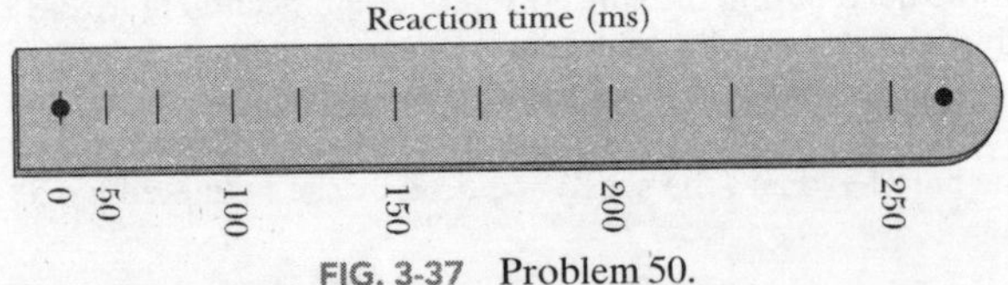

FIG. 3-37 Problem 50.

51 Figure 3-38 gives the acceleration a versus time t for a particle moving along an x axis. The a-axis scale is set by $a_s = 12.0\ \text{m/s}^2$. At $t = -2.0$ s, the particle's velocity is 7.0 m/s. What is its velocity at $t = 6.0$ s?

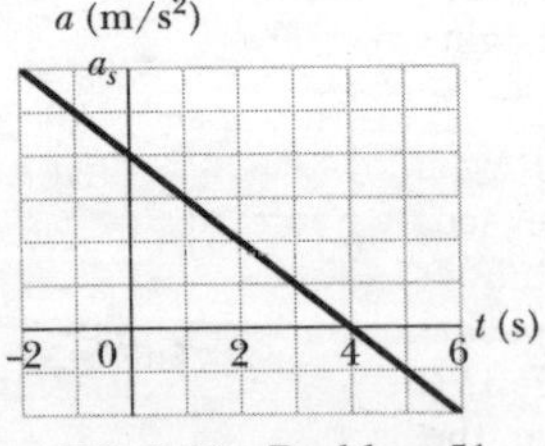

FIG. 3-38 Problem 51.

52 A certain juggler usually tosses balls vertically to a height H. To what height must they be tossed if they are to spend twice as much time in the air?

53 A particle starts from the origin at $t = 0$ and moves along the positive x axis. A graph of the velocity of the particle as a function of the time is shown in Fig. 3-39; the v-axis scale is set by $v_s = 4.0$ m/s. (a) What is the coordinate of the particle at $t = 5.0$ s? (b) What is the velocity of the particle at $t = 5.0$ s? (c) What is the acceleration of the particle at $t = 5.0$ s? (d) What is the average velocity of the particle between $t = 1.0$ s and $t = 5.0$ s? (e) What is the average acceleration of the particle between $t = 1.0$ s and $t = 5.0$ s?

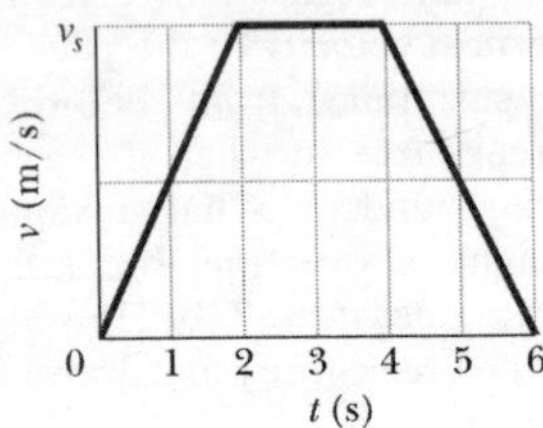

FIG. 3-39 Problem 53.

54 An iceboat has a constant velocity toward the east when a sudden gust of wind causes the iceboat to have a constant acceleration toward the east for a period of 3.0 s. A plot of x versus t is shown in Fig. 3-40, where $t = 0$ is taken to be the instant the wind starts to blow and the positive x axis is toward the east. (a) What is the acceleration of the iceboat during the 3.0 s interval? (b) What is the velocity of the iceboat at the end of the 3.0 s interval? (c) If the acceleration remains constant for an additional 3.0 s, how far does the iceboat travel during this second 3.0 s interval?

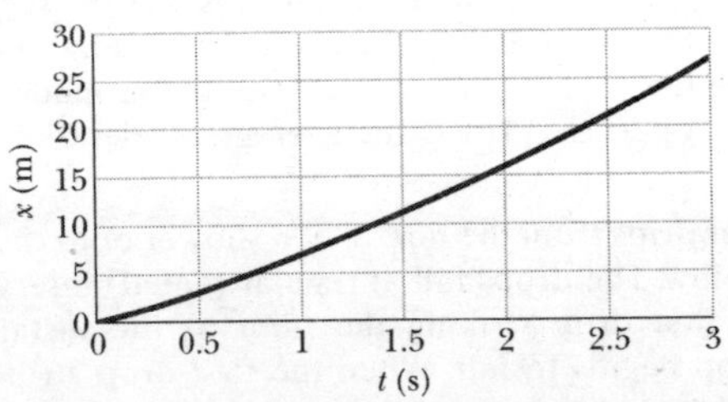

FIG. 3-40 Problem 54.

55 A ball is thrown vertically downward from the top of a 36.6-m-tall building. The ball passes the top of a window that is 12.2 m above the ground 2.00 s after being thrown. What is the speed of the ball as it passes the top of the window?

56 A parachutist bails out and freely falls 50 m. Then the parachute opens, and thereafter she decelerates at $2.0\ \text{m/s}^2$.

She reaches the ground with a speed of 3.0 m/s. (a) How long is the parachutist in the air? (b) At what height does the fall begin?

57 The Zero Gravity Research Facility at the NASA Glenn Research Center includes a 145 m drop tower. This is an evacuated vertical tower through which, among other possibilities, a 1 m diameter sphere containing an experimental package can be dropped. (a) How long is the sphere in free fall? (b) What is its speed just as it reaches a catching device at the bottom of the tower? (c) When caught, the sphere experiences an average deceleration of 25*g* as its speed is reduced to zero. Through what distance does it travel during the deceleration?

58 A ball is thrown *down* vertically with an initial *speed* of v_0 from a height of h. (a) What is its speed just before it strikes the ground? (b) How long does the ball take to reach the ground? What would be the answers to (c) part a and (d) part b if the ball were thrown *upward* from the same height and with the same initial speed? Before solving any equations, decide whether the answers to (c) and (d) should be greater than, less than, or the same as in (a) and (b).

4 Two- and Three-Dimensional Motion

Source: Rob Tringali/Sports Chrome Inc.

When a high fly ball is hit to the outfield, how does the outfielder in the area know where to be in order to catch it? Often the outfielder will jog or run at a measured pace to the catch site, arriving just as the ball does. Playing experience surely helps, but some other factor seems to be involved.

What clue is hidden in the ball's motion?

The answer is in this chapter.

4-1 Introduction

In this chapter we continue looking at the aspect of physics that analyzes motion, but now the motion can be in two or three dimensions. For example, medical researchers and aeronautical engineers might concentrate on the physics of the two- and three-dimensional turns taken by fighter pilots in dogfights because a modern high-performance jet can take a tight turn so quickly that the pilot immediately loses consciousness. A sports engineer might focus on the physics of basketball. For example, in a *free throw* (where a player gets an uncontested shot at the basket from about 4.3 m), a player might employ the *overhand push shot,* in which the ball is pushed away from about shoulder height and then released. Or the player might use an *underhand loop shot,* in which the ball is brought upward from about the belt-line level and released. The first technique is the overwhelming choice among professional players, but the legendary Rick Barry set the record for free-throw shooting with the underhand technique.

Motion in three dimensions is not easy to understand. For example, you are probably good at driving a car along a freeway (one-dimensional motion) but would probably have a difficult time in landing an airplane on a runway (three-dimensional motion) without a lot of training.

In our study of two- and three-dimensional motion, we start with position and displacement.

4-2 | Position and Displacement

One general way of locating a particle (or particle-like object) is with a **position vector** $\vec{r}$, which is a vector that extends from a reference point (usually the origin) to the particle. In the unit-vector notation of Section 3-5, $\vec{r}$ can be written

$$\vec{r} = x\hat{i} + y\hat{j} + z\hat{k} \tag{4-1}$$

where $x\hat{i}$, $y\hat{j}$, and $z\hat{k}$ are the vector components of $\vec{r}$ and the coefficients x, y, and z are its scalar components.

The coefficients x, y, and z give the particle's location along the coordinate axes and relative to the origin; that is, the particle has the rectangular coordinates (x, y, z). For instance, Fig. 4-1 shows a particle with position vector

$$\vec{r} = (-3\text{ m})\hat{i} + (2\text{ m})\hat{j} + (5\text{ m})\hat{k}$$

and rectangular coordinates $(-3\text{ m}, 2\text{ m}, 5\text{ m})$. Along the x axis the particle is 3 m from the origin, in the $-\hat{i}$ direction. Along the y axis it is 2 m from the origin, in the $+\hat{j}$ direction. Along the z axis it is 5 m from the origin, in the $+\hat{k}$ direction.

As a particle moves, its position vector changes in such a way that the vector always extends to the particle from the reference point (the origin). If the position vector changes—say, from $\vec{r}_1$ to $\vec{r}_2$ during a certain time interval—then the particle's **displacement** $\Delta\vec{r}$ during that time interval is

$$\Delta\vec{r} = \vec{r}_2 - \vec{r}_1 \tag{4-2}$$

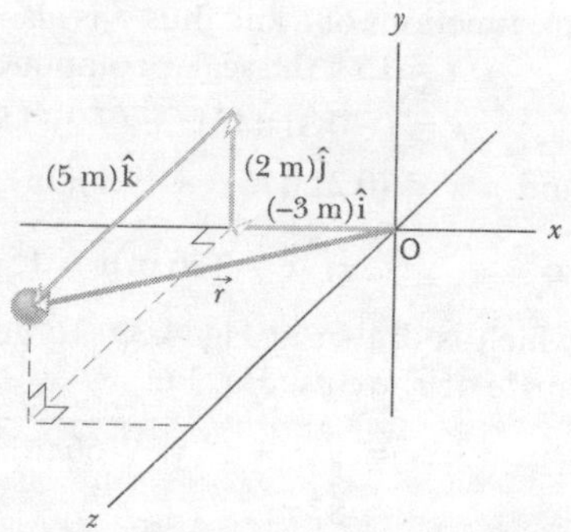

FIG. 4-1 The position vector $\vec{r}$ for a particle is the vector sum of its vector components.

Using the unit-vector notation of Eq. 4-1, we can rewrite this displacement as

$$\Delta\vec{r} = (x_2\hat{i} + y_2\hat{j} + z_2\hat{k}) - (x_1\hat{i} + y_1\hat{j} + z_1\hat{k})$$

or as

$$\Delta\vec{r} = (x_2 - x_1)\hat{i} + (y_2 - y_1)\hat{j} + (z_2 - z_1)\hat{k} \tag{4-3}$$

where coordinates (x_1, y_1, z_1) correspond to position vector $\vec{r}_1$ and coordinates (x_2, y_2, z_2) correspond to position vector $\vec{r}_2$. We can also rewrite the displacement by substituting Δx for $(x_2 - x_1)$, Δy for $(y_2 - y_1)$, and Δz for $(z_2 - z_1)$:

$$\Delta\vec{r} = \Delta x\hat{i} + \Delta y\hat{j} + \Delta z\hat{k} \tag{4-4}$$

Sample Problem 4-1

In Fig. 4-2, the position vector for a particle initially is

$$\vec{r}_1 = (-3.0\text{ m})\hat{\text{i}} + (2.0\text{ m})\hat{\text{j}} + (5.0\text{ m})\hat{\text{k}}$$

and then later is

$$\vec{r}_2 = (9.0\text{ m})\hat{\text{i}} + (2.0\text{ m})\hat{\text{j}} + (8.0\text{ m})\hat{\text{k}}$$

What is the particle's displacement $\Delta\vec{r}$ from $\vec{r}_1$ to $\vec{r}_2$?

Conceptualize/Classify: The displacement $\Delta\vec{r}$ is obtained by subtracting the initial $\vec{r}_1$ from the later $\vec{r}_2$.

Compute: The subtraction gives us

$$\begin{aligned}\Delta\vec{r} &= \vec{r}_2 - \vec{r}_1\\ &= [9.0 - (-3.0)]\hat{\text{i}} + [2.0 - 2.0]\hat{\text{j}} + [8.0 - 5.0]\hat{\text{k}}\\ &= (12\text{ m})\hat{\text{i}} + (3.0\text{ m})\hat{\text{k}} \qquad \text{(Answer)}\end{aligned}$$

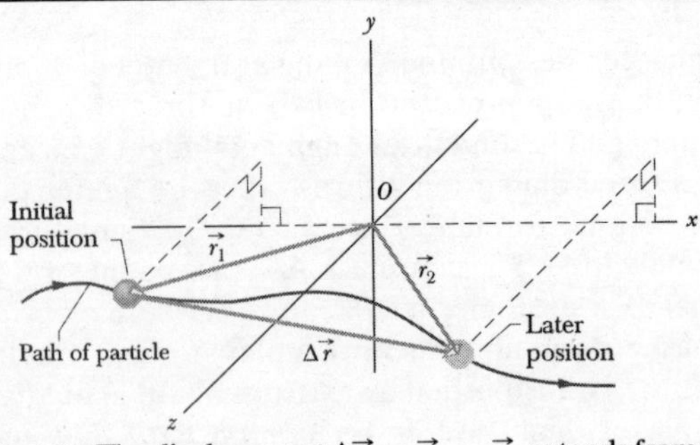

FIG. 4-2 The displacement $\Delta\vec{r} = \vec{r}_2 - \vec{r}_1$ extends from the head of the initial position vector $\vec{r}_1$ to the head of the later position vector $\vec{r}_2$.

Conclude: This displacement vector is parallel to the xz plane because it lacks a y component.

Sample Problem 4-2

A rabbit runs across a parking lot on which a set of coordinate axes has, strangely enough, been drawn. The coordinates (meters) of the rabbit's position as functions of time t (seconds) are given by

$$x = -0.31t^2 + 7.2t + 28 \qquad (4\text{-}5)$$

and

$$y = 0.22t^2 - 9.1t + 30 \qquad (4\text{-}6)$$

(a) At $t = 15$ s, what is the rabbit's position vector $\vec{r}$ in unit-vector notation and in magnitude-angle notation?

Conceptualize/Classify: The x and y coordinates of the rabbit's position, as given by Eqs. 4-5 and 4-6, are the scalar components of the rabbit's position vector $\vec{r}$.

Compute: We can write

$$\vec{r}(t) = x(t)\hat{\text{i}} + y(t)\hat{\text{j}} \qquad (4\text{-}7)$$

(We write $\vec{r}(t)$ rather than $\vec{r}$ because the components are functions of t, and thus $\vec{r}$ is also.)

At $t = 15$ s, the scalar components are

$$x = (-0.31)(15)^2 + (7.2)(15) + 28 = 66\text{ m}$$

and $y = (0.22)(15)^2 - (9.1)(15) + 30 = -57\text{ m}$

so

$$\vec{r} = (66\text{ m})\hat{\text{i}} - (57\text{ m})\hat{\text{j}} \qquad \text{(Answer)}$$

which is drawn in Fig. 4-3a. To get the magnitude and angle of $\vec{r}$, we use Eq. 3-6:

$$r = \sqrt{x^2 + y^2} = \sqrt{(66\text{ m})^2 + (-57\text{ m})^2}$$
$$= 87\text{ m} \qquad \text{(Answer)}$$

and $$\theta = \tan^{-1}\frac{y}{x} = \tan^{-1}\left(\frac{-57\text{ m}}{66\text{ m}}\right) = -41°$$

(Answer)

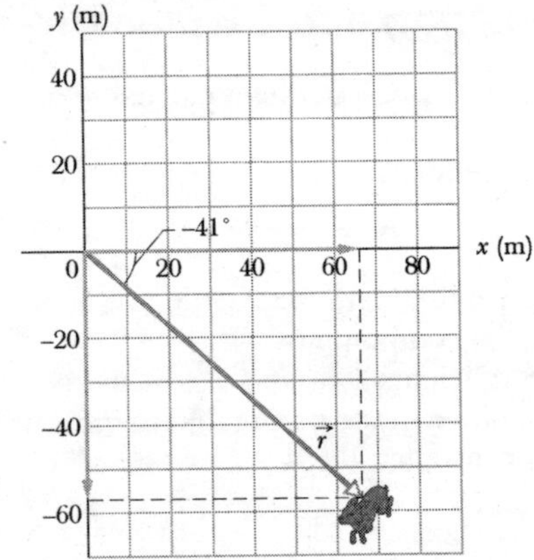

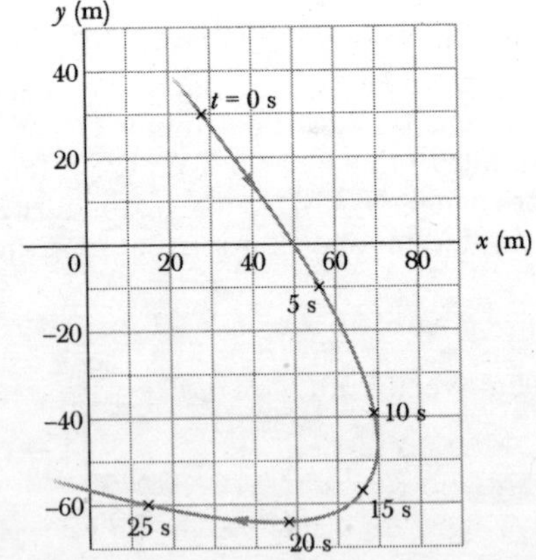

FIG. 4-3 (a) A rabbit's position vector $\vec{r}$ at time $t = 15$ s. The scalar components of $\vec{r}$ are shown along the axes. (b) The rabbit's path and its position at five values of t.

Conclude: Although $\theta = 139°$ has the same tangent as $-41°$, the components of $\vec{r}$ indicate that the desired angle is $139° - 180° = -41°$.

(b) Graph the rabbit's path for $t = 0$ to $t = 25$ s.

Drawing: We can repeat part (a) for several values of t and then plot the results. Figure 4-3*b* shows the plots for five values of t and the path connecting them. We can also plot Eqs. 4-5 and 4-6 on a calculator.

4-3 | Average Velocity and Instantaneous Velocity

If a particle moves from one point to another, we might need to know how fast it moves. Just as in Chapter 2, we can define two quantities that deal with "how fast": *average velocity* and *instantaneous velocity.* However, here we must consider these quantities as vectors and use vector notation.

If a particle moves through a displacement $\Delta\vec{r}$ in a time interval Δt, then its **average velocity** $\vec{v}_{avg}$ is

$$\text{average velocity} = \frac{\text{displacement}}{\text{time interval}}$$

or

$$\vec{v}_{avg} = \frac{\Delta\vec{r}}{\Delta t} \tag{4-8}$$

This tells us that the direction of $\vec{v}_{avg}$ (the vector on the left side of Eq. 4-8) must be the same as that of the displacement $\Delta\vec{r}$ (the vector on the right side). Using Eq. 4-4, we can write Eq. 4-8 in vector components as

$$\vec{v}_{avg} = \frac{\Delta x\hat{i} + \Delta y\hat{j} + \Delta z\hat{k}}{\Delta t} = \frac{\Delta x}{\Delta t}\hat{i} + \frac{\Delta y}{\Delta t}\hat{j} + \frac{\Delta z}{\Delta t}\hat{k} \tag{4-9}$$

For example, if the particle in Sample Problem 4-1 moves from its initial position to its later position in 2.0 s, then its average velocity during that move is

$$\vec{v}_{avg} = \frac{\Delta\vec{r}}{\Delta t} = \frac{(12\text{ m})\hat{i} + (3.0\text{ m})\hat{k}}{2.0\text{ s}} = (6.0\text{ m/s})\hat{i} + (1.5\text{ m/s})\hat{k}$$

That is, the average velocity (a vector quantity) has a component of 6.0 m/s along the x axis and a component of 1.5 m/s along the z axis.

When we speak of the **velocity** of a particle, we usually mean the particle's **instantaneous velocity** $\vec{v}$ at some instant. This $\vec{v}$ is the value that $\vec{v}_{avg}$ approaches in the limit as we shrink the time interval Δt to 0 about that instant. Using the language of calculus, we may write $\vec{v}$ as the derivative

$$\vec{v} = \frac{d\vec{r}}{dt} \tag{4-10}$$

Figure 4-4 shows the path of a particle that is restricted to the xy plane. As the particle travels to the right along the curve, its position vector sweeps to the right. During time interval Δt, the position vector changes from $\vec{r}_1$ to $\vec{r}_2$ and the particle's displacement is $\Delta\vec{r}$.

To find the instantaneous velocity of the particle at, say, instant t_1 (when the particle is at position 1), we shrink interval Δt to 0 about t_1. Three things happen as we do so. (1) Position vector $\vec{r}_2$ in Fig. 4-4 moves toward $\vec{r}_1$ so that $\Delta\vec{r}$ shrinks toward zero. (2) The direction of $\Delta\vec{r}/\Delta t$ (and thus of $\vec{v}_{avg}$) approaches the direction of the line tangent to the particle's path at position 1. (3) The average velocity $\vec{v}_{avg}$ approaches the instantaneous velocity $\vec{v}$ at t_1.

In the limit as $\Delta t \to 0$, we have $\vec{v}_{avg} \to \vec{v}$ and, most important here, $\vec{v}_{avg}$ takes on the direction of the tangent line. Thus, $\vec{v}$ has that direction as well:

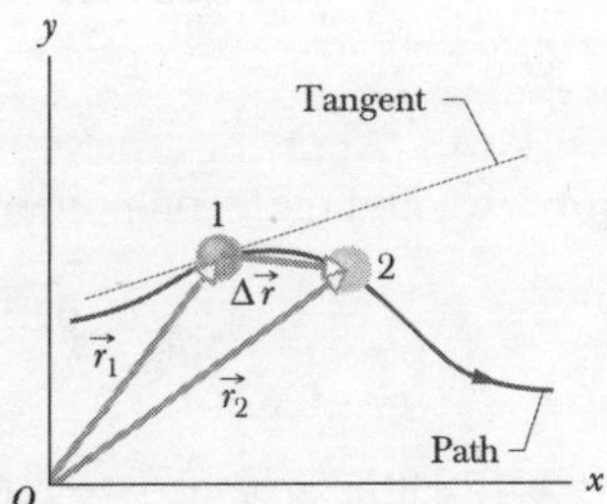

FIG. 4-4 The displacement $\Delta\vec{r}$ of a particle during a time interval Δt, from position 1 with position vector $\vec{r}_1$ at time t_1 to position 2 with position vector $\vec{r}_2$ at time t_2. The tangent to the particle's path at position 1 is shown.

The direction of the instantaneous velocity $\vec{v}$ of a particle is always tangent to the particle's path at the particle's position.

The result is the same in three dimensions: $\vec{v}$ is always tangent to the particle's path.

To write Eq. 4-10 in unit-vector form, we substitute for $\vec{r}$ from Eq. 4-1:

$$\vec{v} = \frac{d}{dt}(x\hat{\mathrm{i}} + y\hat{\mathrm{j}} + z\hat{\mathrm{k}}) = \frac{dx}{dt}\hat{\mathrm{i}} + \frac{dy}{dt}\hat{\mathrm{j}} + \frac{dz}{dt}\hat{\mathrm{k}}$$

This equation can be simplified somewhat by writing it as

$$\vec{v} = v_x\hat{\mathrm{i}} + v_y\hat{\mathrm{j}} + v_z\hat{\mathrm{k}} \tag{4-11}$$

where the scalar components of $\vec{v}$ are

$$v_x = \frac{dx}{dt}, \quad v_y = \frac{dy}{dt}, \quad \text{and} \quad v_z = \frac{dz}{dt} \tag{4-12}$$

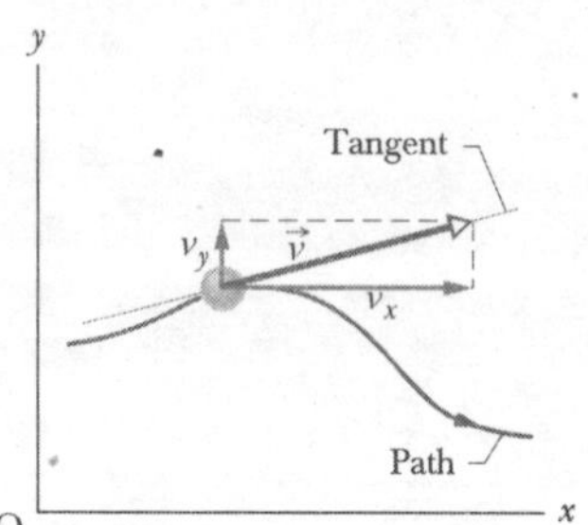

FIG. 4-5 The velocity $\vec{v}$ of a particle, along with the scalar components of $\vec{v}$.

For example, dx/dt is the scalar component of $\vec{v}$ along the x axis. Thus, we can find the scalar components of $\vec{v}$ by differentiating the scalar components of $\vec{r}$.

Figure 4-5 shows a velocity vector $\vec{v}$ and its scalar x and y components. Note that $\vec{v}$ is tangent to the particle's path at the particle's position. *Caution:* When a position vector is drawn, as in Figs. 4-1 through 4-4, it is an arrow that extends from one point (a "here") to another point (a "there"). However, when a velocity vector is drawn, as in Fig. 4-5, it does *not* extend from one point to another. Rather, it shows the instantaneous direction of travel of a particle at the tail, and its length (representing the velocity magnitude) can be drawn to any scale.

CHECKPOINT 1 The figure shows a circular path taken by a particle. If the instantaneous velocity of the particle is $\vec{v} = (2\text{ m/s})\hat{\mathrm{i}} - (2\text{ m/s})\hat{\mathrm{j}}$, through which quadrant is the particle moving at that instant if it is traveling (a) clockwise and (b) counterclockwise around the circle? For both cases, draw $\vec{v}$ on the figure.

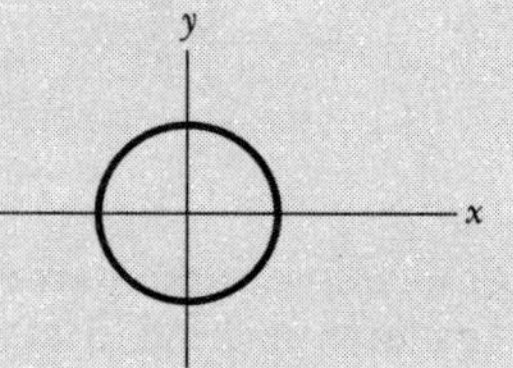

Sample Problem 4-3

For the rabbit in Sample Problem 4-2 find the velocity $\vec{v}$ at time $t = 15$ s.

Conceptualize/Classify: We can find $\vec{v}$ by taking derivatives of the components of the rabbit's position vector.

Compute: Applying the v_x part of Eq. 4-12 to Eq. 4-5, we find the x component of $\vec{v}$ to be

$$v_x = \frac{dx}{dt} = \frac{d}{dt}(-0.31t^2 + 7.2t + 28)$$
$$= -0.62t + 7.2 \tag{4-13}$$

At $t = 15$ s, this gives $v_x = -2.1$ m/s. Similarly, applying the v_y part of Eq. 4-12 to Eq. 4-6, we find

$$v_y = \frac{dy}{dt} = \frac{d}{dt}(0.22t^2 - 9.1t + 30)$$
$$= 0.44t - 9.1 \tag{4-14}$$

At $t = 15$ s, this gives $v_y = -2.5$ m/s. Equation 4-11 then yields

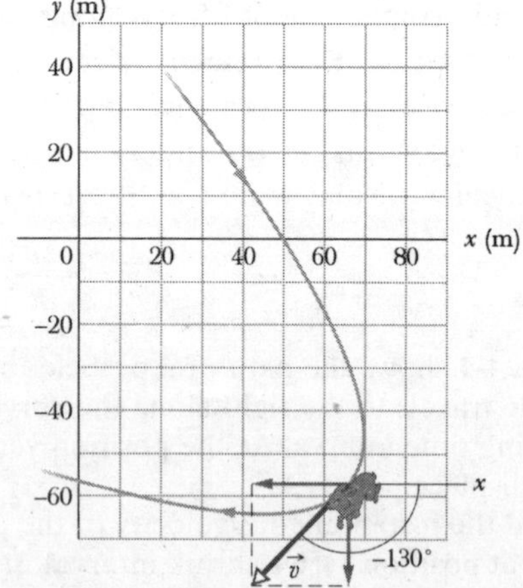

FIG. 4-6 The rabbit's velocity $\vec{v}$ at $t = 15$ s.

$$\vec{v} = (-2.1\text{ m/s})\hat{\mathrm{i}} + (-2.5\text{ m/s})\hat{\mathrm{j}} \quad \text{(Answer)}$$

which is shown in Fig. 4-6, tangent to the rabbit's path and in the direction the rabbit is running at $t = 15$ s.

To get the magnitude and angle of $\vec{v}$, either we use a vector-capable calculator or we follow Eq. 3-6 to write

$$v = \sqrt{v_x^2 + v_y^2} = \sqrt{(-2.1\text{ m/s})^2 + (-2.5\text{ m/s})^2}$$
$$= 3.3\text{ m/s} \qquad \text{(Answer)}$$

and

$$\theta = \tan^{-1}\frac{v_y}{v_x} = \tan^{-1}\left(\frac{-2.5\text{ m/s}}{-2.1\text{ m/s}}\right)$$
$$= \tan^{-1} 1.19 = -130^\circ. \qquad \text{(Answer)}$$

Conclude: This angle is -130° or $-130^\circ + 180^\circ = 50^\circ$

4-4 | Average Acceleration and Instantaneous Acceleration

When a particle's velocity changes from $\vec{v}_1$ to $\vec{v}_2$ in a time interval Δt, its **average acceleration** $\vec{a}_{avg}$ during Δt is

$$\text{average acceleration} = \frac{\text{change in velocity}}{\text{time interval}}$$

or

$$\vec{a}_{avg} = \frac{\vec{v}_2 - \vec{v}_1}{\Delta t} = \frac{\Delta\vec{v}}{\Delta t} \qquad (4\text{-}15)$$

If we shrink Δt to zero about some instant, then in the limit $\vec{a}_{avg}$ approaches the **instantaneous acceleration** (or **acceleration**) $\vec{a}$ at that instant; that is,

$$\vec{a} = \frac{d\vec{v}}{dt} \qquad (4\text{-}16)$$

If the velocity changes in *either* magnitude *or* direction (or both), the particle must have an acceleration.

We can write Eq. 4-16 in unit-vector form by substituting Eq. 4-11 for $\vec{v}$ to obtain

$$\vec{a} = \frac{d}{dt}(v_x\hat{\text{i}} + v_y\hat{\text{j}} + v_z\hat{\text{k}})$$
$$= \frac{dv_x}{dt}\hat{\text{i}} + \frac{dv_y}{dt}\hat{\text{j}} + \frac{dv_z}{dt}\hat{\text{k}}$$

We can rewrite this as

$$\vec{a} = a_x\hat{\text{i}} + a_y\hat{\text{j}} + a_z\hat{\text{k}} \qquad (4\text{-}17)$$

where the scalar components of $\vec{a}$ are

$$a_x = \frac{dv_x}{dt}, \quad a_y = \frac{dv_y}{dt}, \quad \text{and} \quad a_z = \frac{dv_z}{dt} \qquad (4\text{-}18)$$

To find the scalar components of $\vec{a}$, we differentiate the scalar components of $\vec{v}$.

Figure 4-7 shows an acceleration vector $\vec{a}$ and its scalar components for a particle moving in two dimensions. *Caution:* When an acceleration vector is drawn, as in Fig. 4-7, it does *not* extend from one position to another. Rather, it shows the direction of acceleration for a particle located at its tail, and its length (representing the acceleration magnitude) can be drawn to any scale.

CHECKPOINT 2 Here are four descriptions of the position (in meters) of a puck as it moves in an xy plane:

(1) $x = -3t^2 + 4t - 2$ and $y = 6t^2 - 4t$

(2) $x = -3t^3 - 4t$ and $y = -5t^2 + 6$

(3) $\vec{r} = 2t^2\hat{\text{i}} - (4t + 3)\hat{\text{j}}$

(4) $\vec{r} = (4t^3 - 2t)\hat{\text{i}} + 3\hat{\text{j}}$

Are the x and y acceleration components constant? Is acceleration $\vec{a}$ constant?

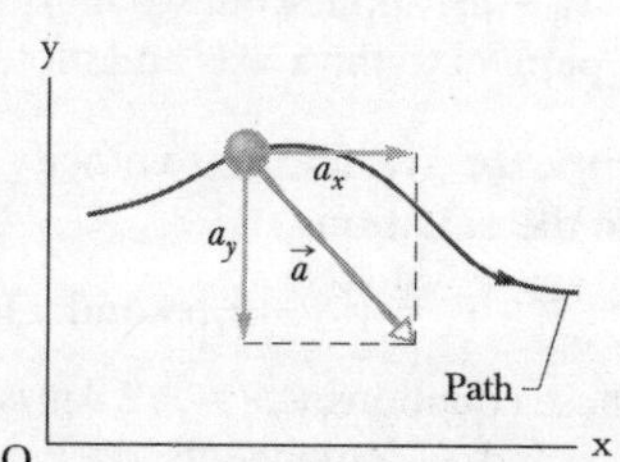

FIG. 4-7 The acceleration $\vec{a}$ of a particle and the scalar components of $\vec{a}$.

Sample Problem 4-4

For the rabbit in Sample Problems 4-2 and 4-3, find the acceleration $\vec{a}$ at time $t = 15$ s.

Conceptualize/Classify: We can find $\vec{a}$ by taking derivatives of the rabbit's velocity components.

Compute: Applying the a_x part of Eq. 4-18 to Eq. 4-13, we find the x component of $\vec{a}$ to be

$$a_x = \frac{dv_x}{dt} = \frac{d}{dt}(-0.62t + 7.2) = -0.62 \text{ m/s}^2$$

Similarly, applying the a_y part of Eq. 4-18 to Eq. 4-14 yields the y component as

$$a_y = \frac{dv_y}{dt} = \frac{d}{dt}(0.44t - 9.1) = 0.44 \text{ m/s}^2$$

We see that the acceleration does not vary with time (it is a constant) because the time variable t does not appear in the expression for either acceleration component. Equation 4-17 then yields

$$\vec{a} = (-0.62 \text{ m/s}^2)\hat{\text{i}} + (0.44 \text{ m/s}^2)\hat{\text{j}} \quad \text{(Answer)}$$

which is superimposed on the rabbit's path in Fig. 4-8.

To get the magnitude and angle of $\vec{a}$, either we use a vector-capable calculator or we follow Eq. 3-6. For the magnitude we have

$$a = \sqrt{a_x^2 + a_y^2} = \sqrt{(-0.62 \text{ m/s}^2)^2 + (0.44 \text{ m/s}^2)^2}$$
$$= 0.76 \text{ m/s}^2 \quad \text{(Answer)}$$

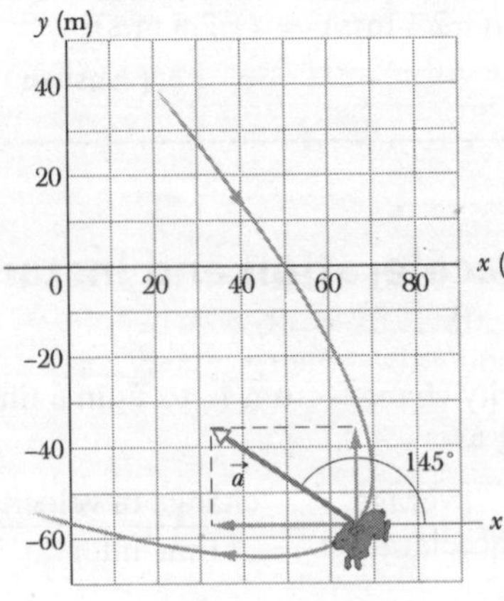

FIG. 4-8 The acceleration $\vec{a}$ of the rabbit at $t = 15$ s. The rabbit happens to have this same acceleration at all points on its path.

For the angle we have

$$\theta = \tan^{-1}\frac{a_y}{a_x} = \tan^{-1}\left(\frac{0.44 \text{ m/s}^2}{-0.62 \text{ m/s}^2}\right) = -35°$$

Conclude: However, this angle, indicates that $\vec{a}$ is directed to the right and downward in Fig. 4-8. Yet, we know from the components that $\vec{a}$ must be directed to the left and upward. To find the other angle that has the same tangent as $-35°$ but is not displayed on a calculator, we add 180°:

$$-35° + 180° = 145° \quad \text{(Answer)}$$

This *is* consistent with the components of $\vec{a}$. Note that $\vec{a}$ has the same magnitude and direction throughout the rabbit's run because the acceleration is constant.

Sample Problem 4-5

A particle with velocity $\vec{v}_0 = -2.0\hat{\text{i}} + 4.0\hat{\text{j}}$ (in meters per second) at $t = 0$ undergoes a constant acceleration $\vec{a}$ of magnitude $a = 3.0$ m/s² at an angle $\theta = 130°$ from the positive direction of the x axis. What is the particle's velocity $\vec{v}$ at $t = 5.0$ s?

Conceptualize: Here the values are not given in unit vector format.

Classify: Because the acceleration is constant, Eq. 2-11 ($v = v_0 + at$) applies, but we must use it separately for motion parallel to the x axis and motion parallel to the y axis.

Compute: We find the velocity components v_x and v_y from the equations

$$v_x = v_{0x} + a_x t \quad \text{and} \quad v_y = v_{0y} + a_y t$$

In these equations, v_{0x} ($= -2.0$ m/s) and v_{0y} ($= 4.0$ m/s) are the x and y components of $\vec{v}_0$, and a_x and a_y are the x and y components of $\vec{a}$. To find a_x and a_y, we resolve $\vec{a}$ either with a vector-capable calculator or with Eq. 3-5:

$$a_x = a\cos\theta = (3.0 \text{ m/s}^2)(\cos 130°) = -1.93 \text{ m/s}^2$$
$$a_y = a\sin\theta = (3.0 \text{ m/s}^2)(\sin 130°) = +2.30 \text{ m/s}^2$$

When these values are inserted into the equations for v_x and v_y, we find that, at time $t = 5.0$ s,

$$v_x = -2.0 \text{ m/s} + (-1.93 \text{ m/s}^2)(5.0 \text{ s}) = -11.65 \text{ m/s}$$
$$v_y = 4.0 \text{ m/s} + (2.30 \text{ m/s}^2)(5.0 \text{ s}) = 15.50 \text{ m/s}$$

Thus, at $t = 5.0$ s, we have, after rounding,

$$\vec{v} = (-12 \text{ m/s})\hat{\text{i}} + (16 \text{ m/s})\hat{\text{j}} \quad \text{(Answer)}$$

Following Eq. 3-6, we find that the magnitude and angle of $\vec{v}$ are

$$v = \sqrt{v_x^2 + v_y^2} = 19.4 \approx 19 \text{ m/s} \quad \text{(Answer)}$$

and

$$\theta = \tan^{-1}\frac{v_y}{v_x} = 127° \approx 130° \quad \text{(Answer)}$$

Conclude: Now sketch the vector $\vec{v}$ with its components to see whether angle is reasonable.with the components.

4-5 | Projectile Motion

We next consider a special case of two-dimensional motion: A particle moves in a vertical plane with some initial velocity $\vec{v}_0$ but its acceleration is always the free-fall acceleration $\vec{g}$, which is downward. Such a particle is called a **projectile** (meaning that it is projected or launched), and its motion is called **projectile motion.** A projectile might be a tennis ball (Fig. 4-9) or baseball in flight, but it is not an airplane or a duck in flight. Many sports (from golf and football to lacrosse and racquetball) involve the projectile motion of a ball, and much effort is spent in trying to control that motion for an advantage. For example, the racquetball player who discovered the Z-shot in the 1970s easily won his games because the ball's peculiar flight to the rear of the court always perplexed his opponents.

FIG. 4-9 A stroboscopic photograph of a yellow tennis ball bouncing off a hard surface. Between impacts, the ball has projectile motion. *Source:* Richard Megna/Fundamental Photographs.

Our goal here is to analyze projectile motion using the tools for two-dimensional motion described in Sections 4-2 through 4-4 and making the assumption that air has no effect on the projectile. Figure 4-10, which is analyzed in the next section, shows the path followed by a projectile when the air has no effect. The projectile is launched with an initial velocity $\vec{v}_0$ that can be written as

$$\vec{v}_0 = v_{0x}\hat{\mathrm{i}} + v_{0y}\hat{\mathrm{j}} \tag{4-19}$$

The components v_{0x} and v_{0y} can then be found if we know the angle θ_0 between $\vec{v}_0$ and the positive x direction:

$$v_{0x} = v_0 \cos\theta_0 \quad \text{and} \quad v_{0y} = v_0 \sin\theta_0 \tag{4-20}$$

During its two-dimensional motion, the projectile's position vector $\vec{r}$ and velocity vector $\vec{v}$ change continuously, but its acceleration vector $\vec{a}$ is constant and *always* directed vertically downward. The projectile has *no* horizontal acceleration.

Projectile motion, like that in Figs. 4-9 and 4-10, looks complicated, but we have the following simplifying feature (known from experiment):

> In projectile motion, the horizontal motion and the vertical motion are independent of each other; that is, neither motion affects the other.

This feature allows us to break up a problem involving two-dimensional motion into two separate and easier one-dimensional problems, one for the horizontal motion (with *zero acceleration*) and one for the vertical motion (with *constant downward acceleration*). Here are two experiments that show that the horizontal motion and the vertical motion are independent.

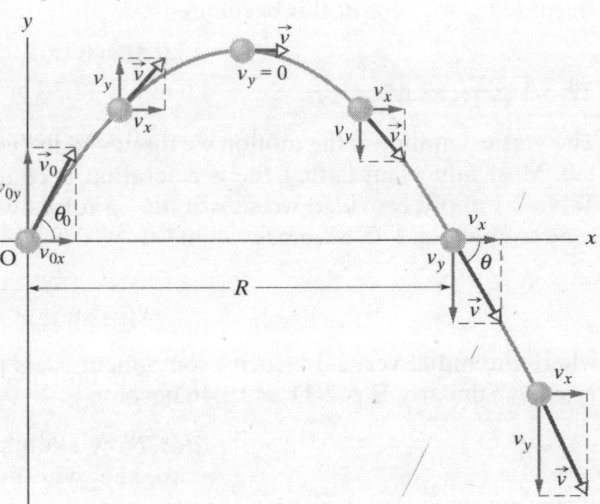

FIG. 4-10 The path of a projectile that is launched at $x_0 = 0$ and $y_0 = 0$, with an initial velocity $\vec{v}_0$. The initial velocity and the velocities at various points along its path are shown, along with their components. Note that the horizontal velocity component remains constant but the vertical velocity component changes continuously. The *range R* is the horizontal distance the projectile has traveled *when it returns to its launch height.*

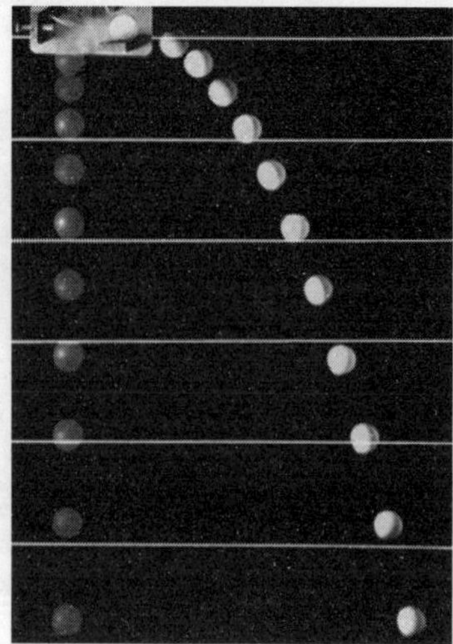

FIG. 4-11 One ball is released from rest at the same instant that another ball is shot horizontally to the right. Their vertical motions are identical. *Source:* Richard Megna/ Fundamental Photographs.

Two Golf Balls

Figure 4-11 is a stroboscopic photograph of two golf balls, one simply released and the other shot horizontally by a spring. The golf balls have the same vertical motion, both falling through the same vertical distance in the same interval of time. *The fact that one ball is moving horizontally while it is falling has no effect on its vertical motion;* that is, the horizontal and vertical motions are independent of each other.

A Great Student Rouser

Figure 4-12 shows a demonstration that has enlivened many a physics lecture. It involves a blowgun G, using a ball as a projectile. The target is a can suspended from a magnet M, and the tube of the blowgun is aimed directly at the can. The experiment is arranged so that the magnet releases the can just as the ball leaves the blowgun.

If g (the magnitude of the free-fall acceleration) were zero, the ball would follow the straight-line path shown in Fig. 4-12 and the can would float in place after the magnet released it. The ball would certainly hit the can.

However, g is *not* zero, but the ball *still* hits the can! As Fig. 4-12 shows, during the time of flight of the ball, both ball and can fall the same distance h from their zero-g locations. The harder the demonstrator blows, the greater is the ball's initial speed, the shorter the flight time, and the smaller the value of h.

CHECKPOINT 3 At a certain instant, a fly ball has velocity $\vec{v} = 25\hat{\imath} - 4.9\hat{\jmath}$ (the x axis is horizontal, the y axis is upward, and $\vec{v}$ is in meters per second). Has the ball passed its highest point?

4-6 | Projectile Motion Analyzed

Now we are ready to analyze projectile motion, horizontally and vertically.

The Horizontal Motion

Because there is *no acceleration* in the horizontal direction, the horizontal component v_x of the projectile's velocity remains unchanged from its initial value v_{0x} throughout the motion, as demonstrated in Fig. 4-13. At any time t, the projectile's horizontal displacement $x - x_0$ from an initial position x_0 is given by Eq. 2-15 with $a = 0$, which we write as

$$x - x_0 = v_{0x}t$$

Because $v_{0x} = v_0 \cos \theta_0$, this becomes

$$x - x_0 = (v_0 \cos \theta_0)t \tag{4-21}$$

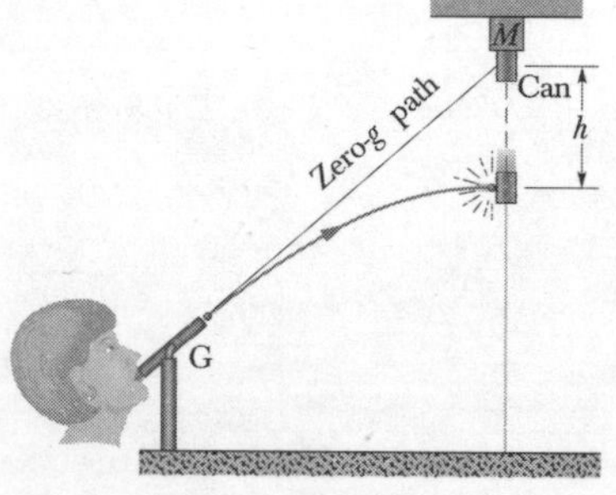

FIG. 4-12 The projectile ball always hits the falling can. Each falls a distance h from where it would be were there no free-fall acceleration.

The Vertical Motion

The vertical motion is the motion we discussed in Section 2-9 for a particle in free fall. Most important is that the acceleration is constant. Thus, the equations of Table 2-1 apply, provided we substitute $-g$ for a and switch to y notation. Then, for example, Eq. 2-15 becomes

$$\begin{aligned} y - y_0 &= v_{0y}t - \tfrac{1}{2}gt^2 \\ &= (v_0 \sin \theta_0)t - \tfrac{1}{2}gt^2 \end{aligned} \tag{4-22}$$

where the initial vertical velocity component v_{0y} is replaced with the equivalent $v_0 \sin \theta_0$. Similarly, Eqs. 2-11 and 2-16 become

$$v_y = v_0 \sin \theta_0 - gt \tag{4-23}$$

and $$v_y^2 = (v_0 \sin \theta_0)^2 - 2g(y - y_0) \tag{4-24}$$

As is illustrated in Fig. 4-10 and Eq. 4-23, the vertical velocity component behaves just as for a ball thrown vertically upward. It is directed upward initially, and its magnitude steadily decreases to zero, *which marks the maximum height of the path.* The vertical velocity component then reverses direction, and its magnitude becomes larger with time.

FIG. 4-13 The vertical component of this skateboarder's velocity is changing but not the horizontal component, which matches the skateboard's velocity. As a result, the skateboard stays underneath him, allowing him to land on it. *Source:* Jamie Budge/Liaison/ Getty Images, Inc.

Equation of the Path

We can find the equation of the projectile's path (its **trajectory**) by eliminating time t between Eqs. 4-21 and 4-22. Solving Eq. 4-21 for t and substituting into Eq. 4-22, we obtain, after a little rearrangement,

$$y = (\tan \theta_0)x - \frac{gx^2}{2(v_0 \cos \theta_0)^2} \quad \text{(trajectory)} \tag{4-25}$$

This is the equation of the path shown in Fig. 4-10. In deriving it, for simplicity we let $x_0 = 0$ and $y_0 = 0$ in Eqs. 4-21 and 4-22, respectively. Because g, θ_0, and v_0 are constants, Eq. 4-25 is of the form $y = ax + bx^2$, in which a and b are constants. This is the equation of a parabola, so the path is *parabolic*.

The following equation can be considered to be quadratic in x as

$$\left(\frac{g}{2u^2 \cos^2 \theta}\right)x^2 - (\tan \theta)x + y = 0$$

Thus, for every value of y we can have maximum two values of x. This simply means that a projectile can pass through same height for two different x coordinates.

This equation can be considered to be quadratic in $\tan \theta$ as

$$\left(\frac{gx^2}{2u^2}\right)\tan^2 \theta - x \tan \theta + \left(y + \frac{gx^2}{2u^2}\right) = 0$$

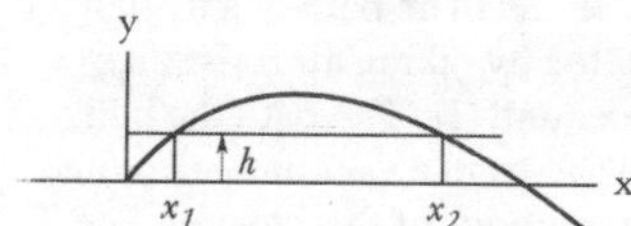

FIG. 4-14 (*a*) Particle passing the same height twice during projectile motion.

Thus, for every value of (x, y) we can have two angles of projection. This means we can hit a given target by using two different angles of projection.

The equation of trajectory can also be modified to give following result.

$$y = x \tan \theta \left[1 - \frac{x}{R}\right] \tag{i}$$

Writing the equation of a trajectory in standard form

$$y = x \tan \theta - \frac{gx^2}{2u^2 \cos^2 \theta}$$

Taking $\tan \theta$ common and doing some manipulation we can write Eq. (i) as.

$$y = x \tan \theta \left[1 - \frac{x}{R}\right]$$

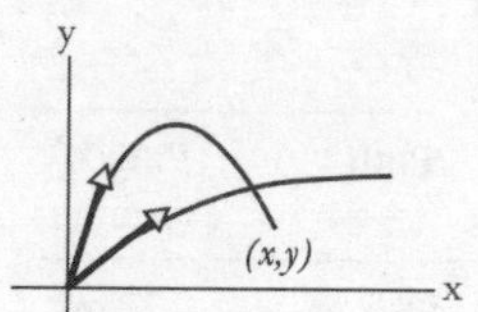

FIG. 4-14 (*b*) Particle passing the same point twice for two different angles of projection.

CHECKPOINT 4 A particle is thrown over a triangle from one end of a horizontal base and after grazing the vertex falls on the other end of the base. If α and β be the base angles and θ the angle of projection, prove that $\tan \theta = \tan \alpha + \tan \beta$.

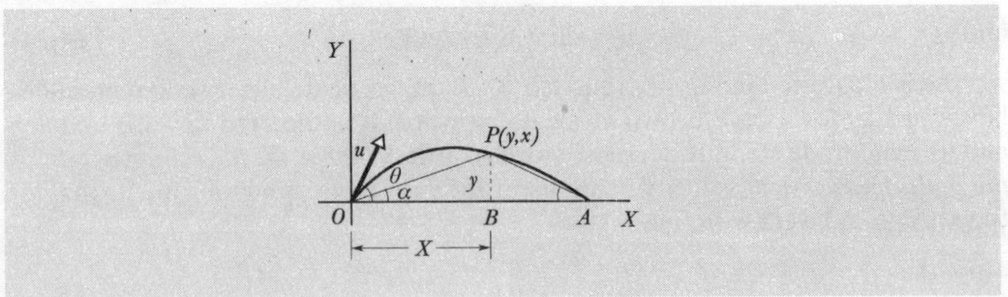

The Horizontal Range

The *horizontal range* R of the projectile, as Fig. 4-10 shows, is the *horizontal* distance the projectile has traveled when it returns to its initial (launch) height. To find range R, let us put $x - x_0 = R$ in Eq. 4-21 and $y - y_0 = 0$ in Eq. 4-22, obtaining

$$R = (v_0 \cos \theta_0)t$$

and

$$0 = (v_0 \sin \theta_0)t - \tfrac{1}{2}gt^2$$

Eliminating t between these two equations yields

$$R = \frac{2v_0^2}{g} \sin \theta_0 \cos \theta_0$$

Using the identity $\sin 2\theta_0 = 2 \sin \theta_0 \cos \theta_0$ (see Appendix E), we obtain

$$R = \frac{v_0^2}{g} \sin 2\theta_0 \qquad \text{(4-26)}$$

Caution: This equation does *not* give the horizontal distance traveled by a projectile when the final height is not the launch height.

Note that R in Eq. 4-26 has its maximum value when $\sin 2\theta_0 = 1$, which corresponds to $2\theta_0 = 90°$ or $\theta_0 = 45°$.

The horizontal range R is maximum for a launch angle of 45°.

However, when the launch and landing heights differ, as in shot put, hammer throw, and basketball, a launch angle of 45° does not yield the maximum horizontal distance.

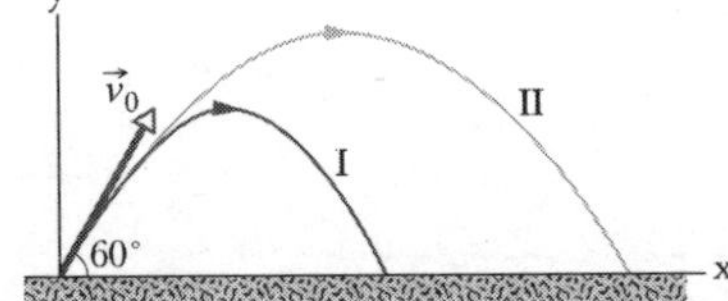

FIG. 4-15 (I) The path of a fly ball calculated by taking air resistance into account. (II) The path the ball would follow in a vacuum, calculated by the methods of this chapter. See Table 4-1 for corresponding data. (Adapted from "The Trajectory of a Fly Ball," by Peter J. Brancazio, *The Physics Teacher,* January 1985.)

TABLE 4-1

Two Fly Balls[a]

	Path I (Air)	Path II (Vacuum)
Range	98.5 m	177 m
Maximum height	53.0 m	76.8 m
Time of flight	6.6 s	7.9 s

[a]See Fig. 4-15. The launch angle is 60° and the launch speed is 44.7 m/s.

The Effects of the Air

We have assumed that the air through which the projectile moves has no effect on its motion. However, in many situations, the disagreement between our calculations and the actual motion of the projectile can be large because the air resists (opposes) the motion. Figure 4-15, for example, shows two paths for a fly ball that leaves the bat at an angle of 60° with the horizontal and an initial speed of 44.7 m/s. Path I (the baseball player's fly ball) is a calculated path that approximates normal conditions of play, in air. Path II (the physics professor's fly ball) is the path the ball would follow in a vacuum.

CHECKPOINT 5 A fly ball is hit to the outfield. During its flight (ignore the effects of the air), what happens to its (a) horizontal and (b) vertical components of velocity? What are the (c) horizontal and (d) vertical components of its acceleration during ascent, during descent, and at the topmost point of its flight?

Sample Problem 4-6

In Fig. 4-16, a rescue plane flies at 198 km/h (= 55.0 m/s) and constant height h = 500 m toward a point directly over a victim, where a rescue capsule is to land.

(a) What should be the angle ϕ of the pilot's line of sight to the victim when the capsule release is made?

Conceptualize: You can hold an eraser between your fingers and while moving your hand just release it. You will see that the eraser is moving on a curved path. Once the capsule is released it will experience only gravity. Also it will have same initial velocity as that of the plane due to inertia.

Classify: Once released, the capsule is a projectile, so its horizontal and vertical motions can be considered separately (we need not consider the actual curved path of the capsule).

Compute: In Fig. 4-15, we see that ϕ is given by

$$\phi = \tan^{-1}\frac{x}{h} \qquad (4\text{-}27)$$

where x is the horizontal coordinate of the victim (and of the capsule when it hits the water) and h = 500 m. We should be able to find x with Eq. 4-21:

$$x - x_0 = (v_0 \cos \theta_0)t \qquad (4\text{-}28)$$

Here we know that $x_0 = 0$ because the origin is placed at the point of release. Because the capsule is *released* and not shot from the plane, its initial velocity $\vec{v}_0$ is equal to the plane's velocity. Thus, we know also that the initial velocity has magnitude v_0 = 55.0 m/s and angle $\theta_0 = 0°$ (measured relative to the positive direction of the x axis). However, we do not know the time t the capsule takes to move from the plane to the victim.

To find t, we next consider the *vertical* motion and specifically Eq. 4-22:

$$y - y_0 = (v_0 \sin \theta_0)t - \tfrac{1}{2}gt^2 \qquad (4\text{-}29)$$

Here the vertical displacement $y - y_0$ of the capsule is −500 m (the negative value indicates that the capsule moves *downward*). So,

$$-500\text{ m} = (55.0\text{ m/s})(\sin 0°)t - \tfrac{1}{2}(9.8\text{ m/s}^2)t^2$$

Solving for t, we find t = 10.1 s. Using that value in Eq. 4-28 yields

$$x - 0 = (55.0\text{ m/s})(\cos 0°)(10.1\text{ s})$$

or

$$x = 555.5\text{ m}$$

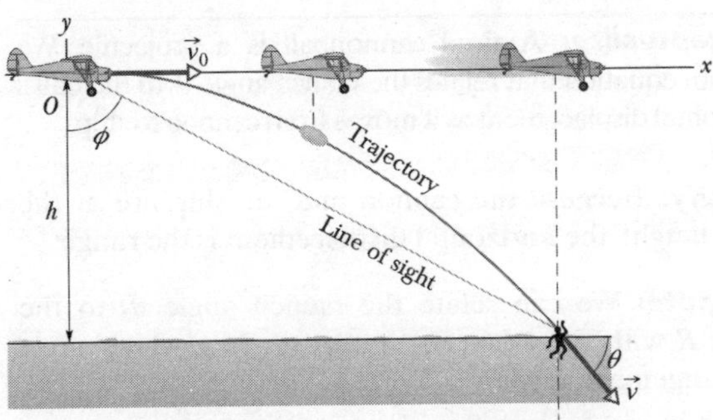

FIG. 4-16 A plane drops a rescue capsule while moving at constant velocity in level flight. While falling, the capsule remains under the plane.

Then Eq. 4-27 gives us

$$\phi = \tan^{-1}\frac{555.5\text{ m}}{500\text{ m}} = 48.0° \qquad \text{(Answer)}$$

(b) As the capsule reaches the water, what is its velocity $\vec{v}$ in unit-vector notation and in magnitude-angle notation?

Classify: (1) The horizontal and vertical components of the capsule's velocity are independent. (2) Component v_x does not change from its initial value $v_{0x} = v_0 \cos \theta_0$ because there is no horizontal acceleration. (3) Component v_y changes from its initial value $v_{0y} = v_0 \sin \theta_0$ because there is a vertical acceleration.

Compute: When the capsule reaches the water,

$$v_x = v_0 \cos \theta_0 = (55.0\text{ m/s})(\cos 0°) = 55.0\text{ m/s}$$

Using Eq. 4-23 and the capsule's time of fall t = 10.1 s, we also find that when the capsule reaches the water,

$$\begin{aligned} v_y &= v_0 \sin \theta_0 - gt \\ &= (55.0\text{ m/s})(\sin 0°) - (9.8\text{ m/s}^2)(10.1\text{ s}) \\ &= -99.0\text{ m/s} \qquad (4\text{-}30) \end{aligned}$$

Thus, at the water

$$\vec{v} = (55.0\text{ m/s})\hat{i} - (99.0\text{ m/s})\hat{j} \qquad \text{(Answer)}$$

Using Eq. 3-6 as a guide, we find that the magnitude and the angle of $\vec{v}$ are

$$v = 113\text{ m/s} \quad \text{and} \quad \theta = -60.9° \qquad \text{(Answer)}$$

Conclude: Since it is moving on a curved path, it must form an angle.

Sample Problem 4-7

Figure 4-17 shows a pirate ship 560 m from a fort defending a harbor entrance. A defense cannon, located at sea level, fires balls at initial speed $v_0 = 82$ m/s.

(a) At what angle θ_0 from the horizontal must a ball be fired to hit the ship?

Conceptualize: A fired cannonball is a projectile. We want an equation that relates the launch angle θ_0 to the ball's horizontal displacement as it moves from cannon to ship.

Classify: Because the cannon and the ship are at the same height, the horizontal displacement is the range.

Compute: We can relate the launch angle θ_0 to the range R with Eq. 4-26 ($R = (v_0^2/g)\sin 2\theta_0$), which, after rearrangement, gives

$$\theta_0 = \frac{1}{2}\sin^{-1}\frac{gR}{v_0^2} = \frac{1}{2}\sin^{-1}\frac{(9.8\text{ m/s}^2)(560\text{ m})}{(82\text{ m/s})^2}$$

$$= \frac{1}{2}\sin^{-1} 0.816 \qquad (4\text{-}31)$$

One solution of $\sin^{-1}$ (54.7°) is displayed by a calculator; we subtract it from 180° to get the other solution (125.3°). Thus, Eq. 4-31 gives us

$$\theta_0 = 27° \quad \text{and} \quad \theta_0 = 63° \qquad \text{(Answer)}$$

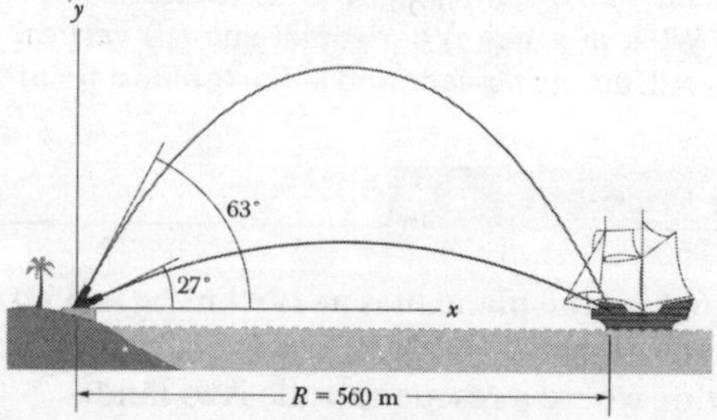

FIG. 4-17 A pirate ship under fire.

Conclude: We have already learnt that there are two possible angles for same range and they are complementary as we can check

(b) What is the maximum range of the cannonballs?

Compute: We have seen that maximum range corresponds to an elevation angle θ_0 of 45°. Thus,

$$R = \frac{v_0^2}{g}\sin 2\theta_0 = \frac{(82\text{ m/s})^2}{9.8\text{ m/s}^2}\sin(2 \times 45°)$$

$$= 686\text{ m} \approx 690\text{ m} \qquad \text{(Answer)}$$

Conclude: As the pirate ship sails away, the two elevation angles at which the ship can be hit draw together, eventually merging at $\theta_0 = 45°$ when the ship is 690 m away. Beyond that distance the ship is safe.

Sample Problem 4-8

Suppose a batsman B hits a high fly ball to the outfield, directly toward an outfielder F and with a launch speed of $v_0 = 40$ m/s and a launch angle of $\theta_0 = 35°$. During the flight, a line from the outfielder to the ball makes an angle ϕ with the ground. Plot elevation angle ϕ versus time t, assuming that the outfielder is

(a) already positioned to catch the ball,
(b) is 6.0 m too close to the batter, and
(c) is 6.0 m too far away.

Conceptualize: While trying to catch a ball which has gone to great height you can imagine that angle of line of sight increases as ball moves. If we neglect air drag, the ball is a projectile for which the vertical motion and the horizontal motion can be analyzed separately.

Classify: Assuming the ball is caught at approximately the height it is hit, the horizontal distance traveled by the ball is the range R, given by Eq. 4-26 ($R = (v_0^2/g)\sin 2\theta_0$).

Compute: The ball can be caught if the outfielder's distance from the batter is equal to the range R of the ball. Using Eq. 4-26, we find

$$R = \frac{v_0^2}{g}\sin 2\theta_0 = \frac{(40\text{ m/s})^2}{9.8\text{ m/s}^2}\sin(70°) = 153.42\text{ m}$$

$$(4\text{-}32)$$

FIG. 4-18 The elevation angle ϕ for a ball hit toward an outfielder is (*a*) defined and (*b*) plotted versus time t.

Figure 4-18*a* shows a snapshot of the ball in flight when the ball is at height y and horizontal distance x from the batter (who is at the origin). The horizontal distance of the ball from the outfielder is $R - x$, and the elevation angle ϕ of the ball in the outfielder's view is given by $\tan\phi = y/(R - x)$. For the height y, we use Eq. 4-22 ($y - y_0 = (v_0 \sin\theta_0)t - \frac{1}{2}gt^2$), setting $y_0 = 0$. For the horizontal distance x, we substitute with Eq. 4-21

$(x - x_0 = (v_0 \cos \theta_0)t)$, setting $x_0 = 0$. Thus, using $v_0 = 40$ m/s and $\theta_0 = 35°$, we have

$$\phi = \tan^{-1} \frac{(40 \sin 35°)t - 4.9t^2}{153.42 - (40 \cos 35°)t} \qquad (4\text{-}33)$$

Graphing this function versus t gives the middle plot in Fig. 4-18b. We see that the ball's angle in the outfielder's view increases at an almost steady rate throughout the flight.

If the outfielder is 6.0 m too close to the batter, we replace the distance of 153.42 m in Eq. 4-33 with 153.42 m − 6.0 m = 147.42 m. Regraphing the function gives the "Too close" plot in Fig. 4-18b. Now the elevation angle of the ball rapidly increases toward the end of the flight as the ball soars over the outfielder's head. If the outfielder is 6.0 m too far away from the batter, we replace the distance of 153.42 m in Eq. 4-33 with 159.42 m. The resulting plot is labeled "Too far" in the figure: The angle first increases and then rapidly decreases.

Conclude: Thus, if a ball is hit directly toward an outfielder, the player can tell from the change in the ball's elevation angle ϕ whether to stay put, run toward the batter, or back away from the batter.

Sample Problem 4-9

At time $t = 0$, a golf ball is shot from ground level into the air, as indicated in Fig. 4-19a. The angle θ between the ball's direction of travel and the positive direction of the x axis is given in Fig. 4-19b as a function of time t. The ball lands at $t = 6.00$ s. What is the magnitude v_0 of the ball's launch velocity, at what height $(y - y_0)$ above the launch level does the ball land, and what is the ball's direction of travel just as it lands?

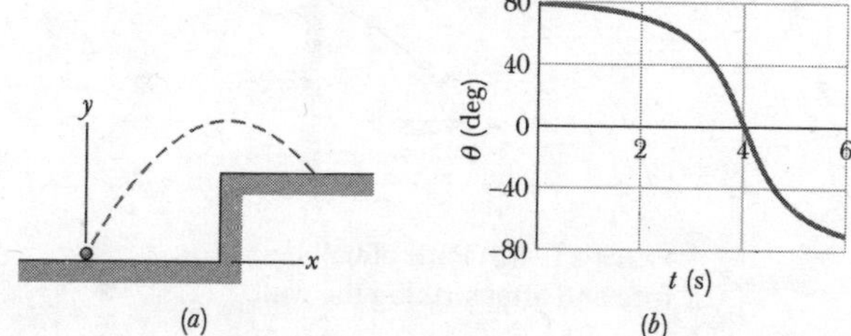

FIG. 4-19 (a) Path of a golf ball shot onto a plateau. (b) The angle θ that gives the ball's direction of motion during the flight is plotted versus time t.

Conceptualize: The ball is a projectile, and so its horizontal and vertical motions can be considered separately. The horizontal component v_x $(= v_0 \cos \theta_0)$ of the ball's velocity does not change during the flight. The vertical component v_y of its velocity *does* change and is zero when the ball reaches maximum height.

Classify: The ball's direction of travel at any time during the flight is at the angle of its velocity vector $\vec{v}$ just then. That angle is given by $\tan \theta = v_y/v_x$, with the velocity components evaluated at that time.

Compute: When the ball reaches its maximum height, $v_y = 0$. So, the direction of the velocity $\vec{v}$ is horizontal, at angle $\theta = 0°$. From the graph, we see that this condition occurs at $t = 4.0$ s. We also see that the launch angle θ_0 (at $t = 0$) is 80°. Using Eq. 4-23 $(v_y = v_0 \sin \theta_0 - gt)$, with $t = 4.0$ s, $g = 9.8$ m/s^2, $\theta_0 = 80°$, and $v_y = 0$, we find

$$v_0 = 39.80 \approx 40 \text{ m/s} \qquad \text{(Answer)}$$

The ball lands at $t = 6.00$ s. Using Eq. 4-22 $(y - y_0 = (v_0 \sin \theta_0)t - \frac{1}{2}gt^2)$ with $t = 6.00$ s, we obtain

$$y - y_0 = 58.77 \text{ m} \approx 59 \text{ m} \qquad \text{(Answer)}$$

Conclude: Just as the ball lands, its horizontal velocity v_x is still $v_0 \cos \theta_0$; substituting for v_0 and θ_0 gives us $v_x = 6.911$ m/s. We find its vertical velocity just then by using Eq. 4-23 $(v_y = v_0 \sin \theta_0 - gt)$ with $t = 6.00$ s, which yields $v_y = -19.60$ m/s. Thus, the angle of the ball's direction of travel at landing is

$$\theta = \tan^{-1} \frac{v_y}{v_x} = \tan^{-1} \frac{-19.60 \text{ m/s}}{6.911 \text{ m/s}} \approx -71° \qquad \text{(Answer)}$$

Sample Problem 4-10

A boy stands 4 m away from a vertical wall and throws a ball that leaves the boy's hand at $h = 1.05$ m above the ground with initial velocity $v_0 = 10\sqrt{2}$ m/s at an angle of 45° with the horizontal. After striking the wall elastically the ball rebounds. At what distance from the foot of the wall does the ball hit the ground? ($g = 10$ m/s)

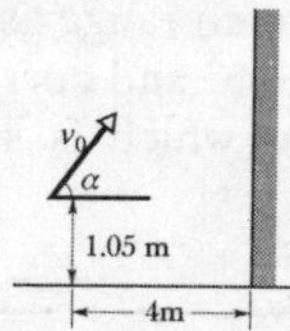

FIG. 4-20 Boy throwing a ball towards a wall.

Conceptualize: Looking at Fig. (4-20) we can imagine it is going to be a projectile motion broken in two paths. Both paths will be parabola. Time of collision with the wall will be negligible. Elatic collision with the wall will reverse direction of its horizontal component without affecting the vertical component.

Classify: Since vertical component is unaffected the motion in vertical direction is simple. Also, during motion the horizontal component of velocity changes only in direction.

Compute: Vertical motion is simply like a person has thrown a ball with speed of 10 m/s in upward direction from height of 1.05 m. Hence time of flight can be calculated. Here we are assuming upward direction to be positive.

Initial velocity, $u_y = 10\sqrt{2}\sin 45^\circ = 10$

Acceleration, $a_y = -10$

Displacement, $s = -1.05$

$$-1.25 = 10t - 5t^2$$

$$5t^2 - 10t - 1.25 = 0$$

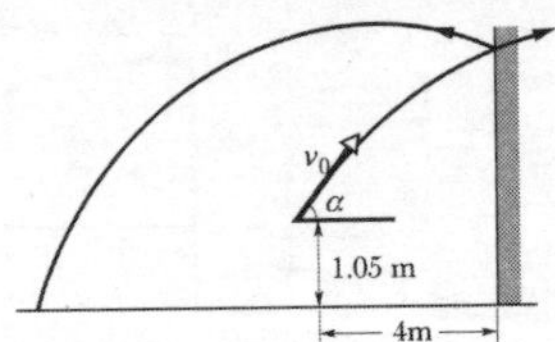

FIG. 4-21 (*a*) Path of ball before and after striking the wall.

Solving we get time of flight = 2.1 s.
Consdering horizontal motion of ball before colliding with wall.

Time before collision

$$t = 4/u_x = 0.4$$

Thus time remaining to return is 1.7 s.
Hence horizontal distance travelled in this time is = $1.7 \times 10 = 17$ m

Conclude: Answer seems to be satisfactory in magnitude.

In Case Of: If there had been no wall the ball would have gone 21 m away from the feet of the boy. The only effect of the wall is to reverse the direction of horizontal motion.

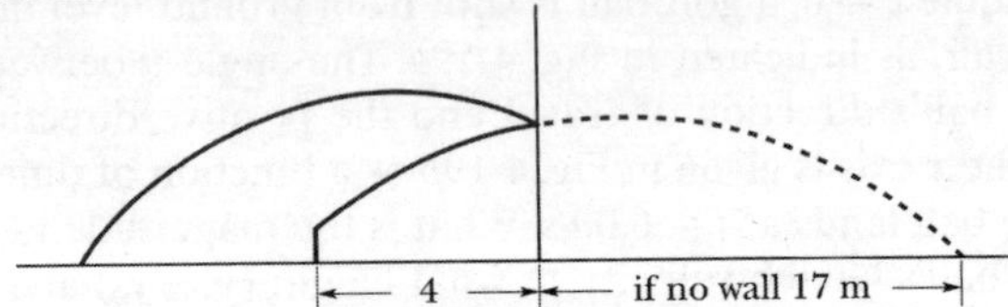

FIG. 4-22 (*b*) Path of the ball if there was no wall.

Sample Problem 4-11

We have a fire extinguishing hose pipe which disposes water at the speed of 10 m/s. A very high building is on fire. The safe distance from the building on ground is 5 m, (as some explosion might occur). How high can this water strike the building. (take $g = 10$ m/s²)

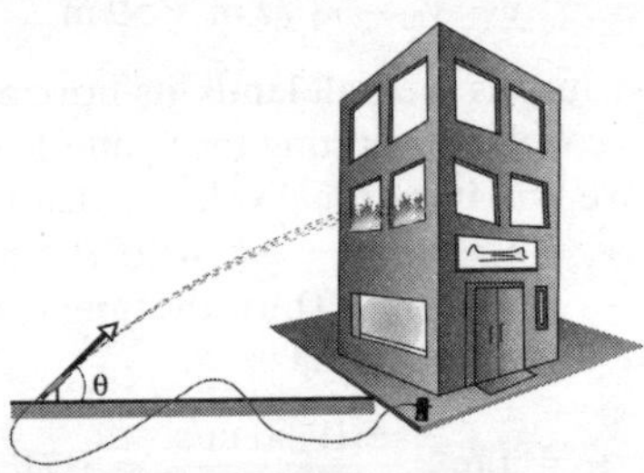

Conceptualize: Here we must understand that taking range of projectile as 10 m and making projectile hit the building when it is at maximum height is wrong. By doing this we are not acheiving maximum y for given $x = 5$ m. This just makes highest point of path to like on $x = 5$, But there may be other path for which y will be maximum for given x.

Classify: This problem will be solved by using equation of trajectory by putting $x = 5$ m and maximising y by varying θ.

Compute: $$y = x\tan\theta - \frac{gx^2}{2u^2\cos^2\theta}$$

Putting we get $x = 5$ m

$$y = 5\tan\theta - \frac{10 \times 5^2 \sec^2\theta}{2 \times 10^2}$$

$$1.25\tan^2\theta - 5\tan\theta + (y + 1.25) = 0$$

for real roots discriminant must be positive.

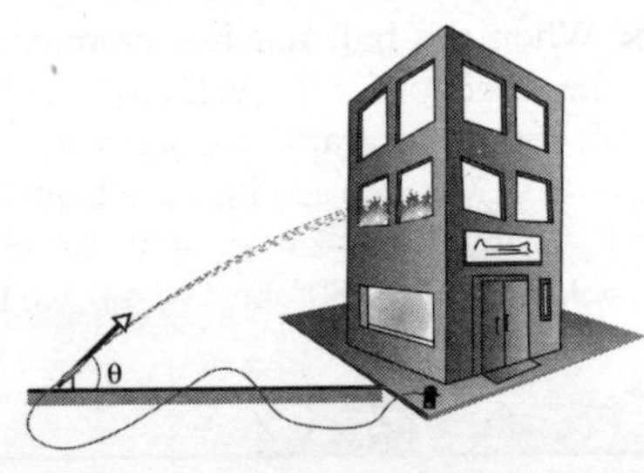

$$5^2 - 4x1.25\ (y + 1.25) > 0$$

Solving $3.75 \geq y$
hence maximum $y = 3.75$ m

Conclude: If we have taken range as 10 m then angle of projection will be $\theta = 45^\circ$ and corresponding maximum height $H = 2.5$ m which is smaller than our answer.

Sample Problem 4-12

A stone is being thrown at a speed of 10 m/s from the top of a 15 m high building. Find how far from the foot of building can the stone be thrown.

Conceptualize: We must understand that by taking angle of projection 45° we will not get maximum distance from foot of building, as this value maximizes x on some level. If we make angle of projection 0° even then time for which it will travel will reduce. If we take angles close to 90° time of travelling increases but horizontal component of velocity reduces.

Classify: This problem will be solved by using equation of trajectory by putting $y = -15$ m and maximizing x by varying θ.

Compute:

$$y = x\tan\theta - \frac{gx^2\sec^2\theta}{2u^2}$$

$$-15 = x\tan\theta - \frac{10x^2(\tan^2\theta+1)}{2\times10\times10}$$

$$-300 = 20x\tan\theta - x^2\tan^2\theta - x^2$$

$$\tan^2\theta(x^2) - \tan\theta(20x) + (x^2-300) = 0$$

for $\tan\theta$ to be real, discriminant must be positive

$$(20x^2) - 4x^2(x^2-300) \geq 0$$

$$20 \geq x$$

hence $x_{max} = 20$

Conclude: What if $\theta = 0°$

then x is $\sqrt{\frac{2\times15}{10}}\times10 = 17.3$

and when $\theta = 45°$, x is $5(1+\sqrt{7})$

Both the quatities are less than the maximum value found by us.

4-7 | Projection on Inclined Plane

Suppose there is an inclined plane making an angle θ with horizontal and a particle is projected at an angle α from horizontal. Now we have to take our x axis along inclind plane as distances along the incline have to be measured. This choice of x makes our y as line perpendicular to x. Now taking components along x and y we break motion in two orthoganal axes.

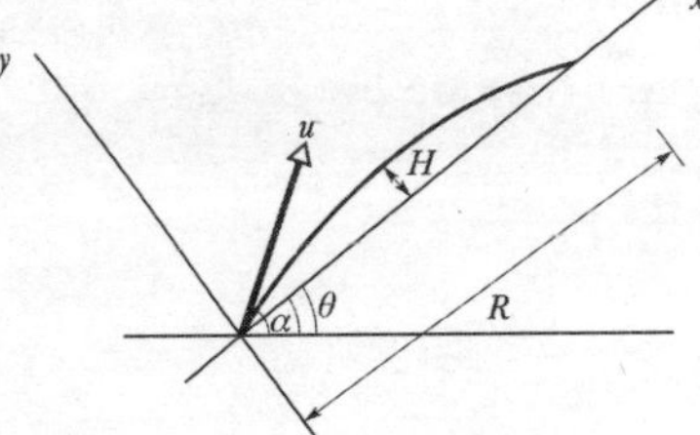

FIG. 4-23 A projectile being launched from the foot of an incline.

x axis	y axis
$u_x = u\cos(\alpha-\theta)$	$u_y = u\sin(\alpha-\theta)$
$a_x = -g\sin\theta$	$a_y = -g\cos\theta$
velocity at any time t	velocity at any time t
$v_x = u\cos(\alpha-\theta) - g\sin\theta t$	$v_y = u\sin(\alpha-\theta) - g\cos\theta t$

We can see that both motions are accelerated motion. Also it is very important ot note that our choice of x and y has net altered the projectile motion by any means. It is still same as original projectile motion with constant acceleration let's find different parameters.

Time of Flight

Displacement in y direction $s_y = 0$

$$0 = u\sin(\alpha-\theta)T - \frac{1}{2}g\cos\theta T^2$$

$$T = \frac{2u\sin(\alpha-\theta)}{g\cos\theta}$$

Maximum Height (relative to inclined plane)

Point where $v_y = 0$ has maximum height

$$(0)^2 = u^2 \sin^2(\alpha - \theta) - 2g\cos\theta H$$

$$H = \frac{u^2 \sin^2(\alpha - \theta)}{2g\cos\theta}$$

Range Along Inclined Plane

Remember that still horizontal motion is unaccelerated motion with constant velocity so distance l covered along horizontal by the time it strikes the incline.

So,

$$l = u\cos\alpha T$$

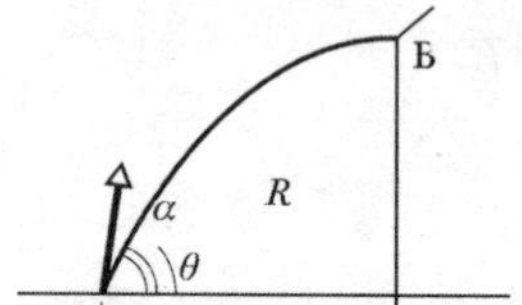

FIG. 4-24 Path of the projectile, projected from the foot of an incline O landing at point B.

Looking at Fig. 4-24 consider triangle OAB with OB being range R such that

$$R = \frac{l}{\cos\theta}$$

$$R = \frac{u\cos\alpha}{\cos\theta} \times \frac{2u\sin(\alpha - \theta)}{g\cos\theta}$$

$$R = \frac{2u^2 \sin(\alpha - \theta)\cos\alpha}{g\cos^2\theta}$$

CHECKPOINT 6 Find maximum value of range on an incline of angle θ with horizontal.

$$R = \frac{u^2[\sin(2\alpha - \theta) - \sin\theta]}{g\cos^2\theta}$$

CHECKPOINT 7 **Projection from top of inclined plane:** Inclined plane is at an angle θ with horizontal and a particle is projected from top at an angle α with horizontal as shown in figure. Find all corresponding results for time of flight, maximum height, and range along inclined plane.

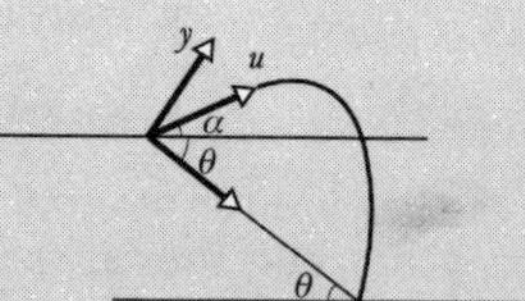

Sample Problem 4-13 Build your skill

A particle is projected up an inclined plane. Plane is inclined at an angle θ with horizontal and particle is projected at an angle α with horizontal. If particle strikes the plane horizontally then prove that

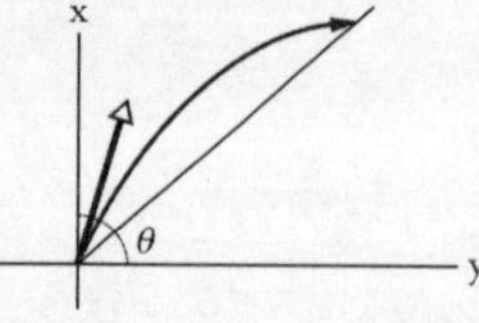

$$T = \frac{2u\sin(\alpha + \theta)}{g\cos\theta}$$

$$\tan\alpha = 2\tan\theta$$

Solution: We know time of flight considering vertical motion

$u = v \sin \alpha$

$a = -g$

$v = 0$

$\sin \alpha \cos \theta = 2 \sin \alpha \cos \theta - 2 \cos \alpha \sin \theta$

$2 \cos \alpha \sin \theta = \sin \alpha \cos \theta$

$2 \tan \theta = \tan \alpha$

Line of greatest slope: When projection is not along line of greatest slope then 3-D motion and three comp. One will not be affected by gravity (v_Z). A 3-D view of an incline plane is given below. Here y direction is perpendicular to the plane of incline.

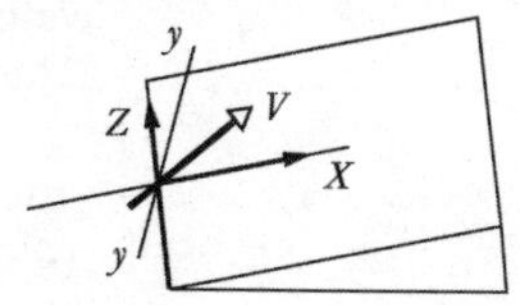

4-8 | Relative Motion

A person travelling by train may ask his co-passenger 'Dilli aa gaya kya' (Has Delhi come?). This statement seems to claim that Delhi is moving towards our passenger. We may say that his understanding of world is wrong as all of us know that 'actually' it is the train which is moving not the huge Delhi city.

If we observe from passenger's point of view we will realise that relative to him all parts of train are at rest, which means relative to him train is at rest. Still when passenger gets down from the train, he is in different city, thus it must be the cities which are moving.

The point is that when a person standing on ground says that 'actually' it is the train (hence passengers sitting in train) which is moving and reaching Delhi (which of course is stationary), he is also right. The difference here is of refrence frame.

Relative Motion in One Dimension

Suppose you see a duck flying north at 30 km/h. To another duck flying alongside, the first duck seems to be stationary. In other words, the velocity of a particle depends on the **reference frame** of whoever is observing or measuring the velocity. For our purposes, a reference frame is the physical object to which we attach our coordinate system. In everyday life, that object is the ground. For example, the speed listed on a speeding ticket is always measured relative to the ground. The speed relative to the police officer would be different if the officer were moving while making the speed measurement.

Suppose that Arun (at the origin of frame A in Fig. 4-25) is parked by the side of a highway, watching car P (the "particle") speed past. Babita (at the origin of frame B) is driving along the highway at constant speed and is also watching car P. Suppose that they both measure the position of the car at a given moment. From Fig. 4-25 we see that

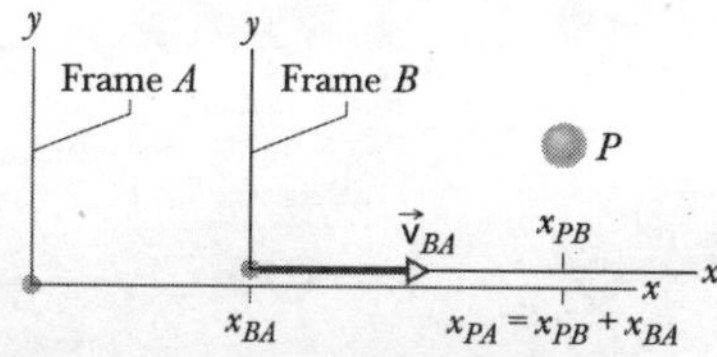

FIG. 4-25 Arun (frame A) and Babita (frame B) watch car P, as both B and P move at different velocities along the common x axis of the two frames. At the instant shown, x_{BA} is the coordinate of B in the A frame. Also, P is at coordinate x_{PB} in the B frame and coordinate $x_{PA} = x_{PB} + x_{BA}$ in the A frame.

$$x_{PA} = x_{PB} + x_{BA} \tag{4-40}$$

The equation is read: "The coordinate x_{PA} of P as measured by A *is equal to* the coordinate x_{PB} of P as measured by B *plus* the coordinate x_{BA} of B as measured by A." Note how this reading is supported by the sequence of the subscripts.

Taking the time derivative of Eq. 4-40, we obtain

$$\frac{d}{dt}(x_{PA}) = \frac{d}{dt}(x_{PB}) + \frac{d}{dt}(x_{BA})$$

Thus, the velocity components are related by

$$v_{PA} = v_{PB} + v_{BA} \tag{4-41}$$

This equation is read: "The velocity v_{PA} of P as measured by A *is equal to* the velocity v_{PB} of P as measured by B *plus* the velocity v_{BA} of B as measured by A." The term v_{BA} is the velocity of frame B relative to frame A.

Here we consider only frames that move at constant velocity relative to each other. In our example, this means that Babita (frame B) drives always at constant velocity v_{BA} relative to Arun (frame A). Car P (the moving particle), however, can change speed and direction (that is, it can accelerate).

To relate an acceleration of P as measured by Babita and by Arun, we take the time derivative of Eq. 4-41:

$$\frac{d}{dt}(v_{PA}) = \frac{d}{dt}(v_{PB}) + \frac{d}{dt}(v_{BA})$$

Because v_{BA} is constant, the last term is zero and we have

$$a_{PA} = a_{PB} \tag{4-42}$$

In other words:

Observers on different frames of reference that move at constant velocity relative to each other will measure the same acceleration for a moving particle.

World as seen by observer on ground | World as seen by B

V_B → 60 km/h | 60 km/h ← → 60 km/h

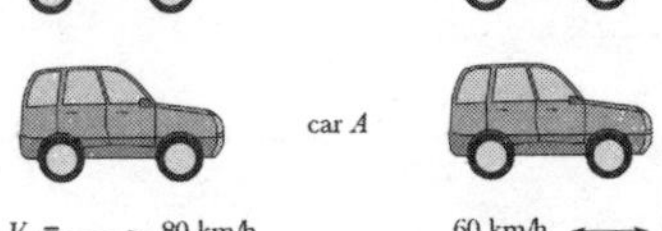

V_A = → 80 km/h | 60 km/h ← → 80 km/h

Babita | 20 km/h to right

(a) (b)

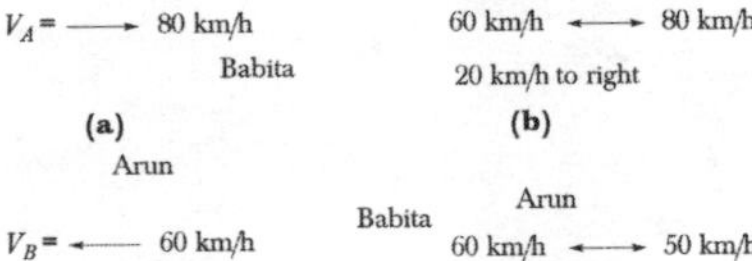

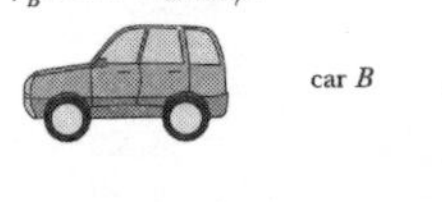

V_A = → 80 km/h | 80 km/h → 60 km/h

120 km/h to right

FIG. 4-26

Let's see how we use this concept in daily life. Suppose that car A travelling on a straight road at 80 km/h passes car B going in the same direction at 60 km/h (Fig. 4-26*a*). Then, velocity of A relative to B is given by

$$\begin{aligned} v_A - v_B &= 80 \text{ km/h} - 60 \text{ km/h} \\ &= 20 \text{ km/h (to the right in Fig. 4-26}b) \end{aligned}$$

We know that if somebody passes us in same direction we don't find them moving very fast. If A and B are travelling in opposite directions, Fig. 4-26*c*, we show this by giving one velocity a positive sign, say v_A, and the other a negative sign. Hence we can write

$$\begin{aligned} v_A - v_B &= +80 \text{ km/h} - (-60 \text{ km/h}) \\ &= (80 + 60) \text{ km/h} \\ &= 140 \text{ km/h} \qquad \text{(to the right in Fig. 4-26}d) \end{aligned}$$

We know that if somebody passes by in opposite direction, we find them moving really fast. In effect, in both cases, to find the velocity of A relative to B, we have applied B's velocity reversed to both cars. It is then just as if B is at rest and A has two velocities v_A and v_B, which are subtracted when v_A and v_B are in the same direction and added when they are in opposite directions. When the velocities are not in the same straight line, they must be added by the parallelogram law.

Sample Problem 4-14

In Fig. 4-25, suppose that Babita's velocity relative to Arun is a constant $v_{BA} = 52$ km/h and car P is moving in the negative direction of the x axis.

(a) If Arun measures a constant $v_{PA} = -78$ km/h for car P, what velocity v_{PB} will Babita measure?

Conceptualize/Classify: We can attach a frame of reference A to Arun and a frame of reference B to Babita. Because the frames move at constant velocity relative to each other along one axis, we can use Eq. 4-41 ($v_{PA} = v_{PB} + v_{BA}$) to relate v_{PB} to v_{PA} and v_{BA}.

Compute: We find

$$-78 \text{ km/h} = v_{PB} + 52 \text{ km/h}$$

Thus, $$v_{PB} = -130 \text{ km/h} \qquad \text{(Answer)}$$

Conclude: If car P were connected to Babita's car by a cord wound on a spool, the cord would be unwinding at a speed of 130 km/h as the two cars separated.

(b) If car P brakes to a stop relative to Arun (and thus relative to the ground) in time $t = 10$ s at constant acceleration, what is its acceleration a_{PA} relative to Arun?

Conceptualize/Classify: To calculate the acceleration of car P *relative to Arun,* we must use the car's velocities *relative to Arun.* Because the acceleration is constant, we can use Eq. 2-11 ($v = v_0 + at$) to relate the acceleration to the initial and final velocities of P.

Compute: The initial velocity of P relative to Arun is $v_{PA} = -78$ km/h and the final velocity is 0. Thus,

$$a_{PA} = \frac{v - v_0}{t} = \frac{0 - (-78 \text{ km/h})}{10 \text{ s}} \frac{1 \text{ m/s}}{3.6 \text{ km/h}}$$

$$= 2.2 \text{ m/s}^2 \qquad \text{(Answer)}$$

(c) What is the acceleration a_{PB} of car P relative to Babita during the braking?

Classify: To calculate the acceleration of car P *relative to Babita,* we must use the car's velocities *relative to Babita.*

Compute: We know the initial velocity of P relative to Babita from part (a) ($v_{PB} = -130$ km/h). The final velocity of P relative to Babita is -52 km/h (this is the velocity of the stopped car relative to the moving Babita). Thus,

$$a_{PB} = \frac{v - v_0}{t} = \frac{-52 \text{ km/h} - (-130 \text{ km/h})}{10 \text{ s}} \frac{1 \text{ m/s}}{3.6 \text{ km/h}}$$

$$= 2.2 \text{ m/s}^2 \qquad \text{(Answer)}$$

Conclude: We should have foreseen this result: Because Arun and Babita have a constant relative velocity, they must measure the same acceleration for the car.

Relative Motion in Two Dimensions

In two dimensional situation, consider three observers at rest O, A and B. Position of B from reference frame of A is $\vec{r}_{BA}$. We must understand that if A wants to go and meet B he needs to look only at $\vec{r}_{BA}$ and decide direction of his velocity which will take him to B. For A, origin of reference frame is not O it is A itself. From our knowledge of vectors we can deduce that

$$\vec{r}_B = \vec{r}_A + \vec{r}_{BA} \text{ thus } \vec{r}_{BA} = \vec{r}_B - \vec{r}_A \qquad \text{(i)}$$

Position vector of B with respect to A is defined as $\vec{r}_{BA}$ Differentiating this equation with respect to time we get

$$\vec{v}_{BA} = \vec{v}_B - \vec{v}_A \qquad \text{(ii)}$$

On further differentiating we get

$$\vec{a}_{BA} = \vec{a}_B - \vec{a}_A \qquad \text{(iii)}$$

Our two observers are again watching a moving particle P from the origins of reference frames A and B, while B moves at a constant velocity $\vec{v}_{BA}$ relative to A. (The corresponding axes of these two frames remain parallel.) Figure 4-27 shows a certain instant during the motion. At that instant, the position vector of the origin of B relative to the origin of A is $\vec{r}_{BA}$. Also, the position vectors of particle P are $\vec{r}_{PA}$ relative to the origin of A and $\vec{r}_{PB}$ relative to the origin of B. From the arrangement of heads and tails of those three position vectors, we can relate the vectors with

$$\vec{r}_{PA} = \vec{r}_{PB} + \vec{r}_{BA} \qquad \text{(4-43)}$$

By taking the time derivative of this equation, we can relate the velocities $\vec{v}_{PA}$ and $\vec{v}_{PB}$ of particle P relative to our observers:

$$\vec{v}_{PA} = \vec{v}_{PB} + \vec{v}_{BA} \qquad \text{(4-44)}$$

By taking the time derivative of this relation, we can relate the accelerations $\vec{a}_{PA}$ and $\vec{a}_{PB}$ of the particle P relative to our observers. However, note that because $\vec{v}_{BA}$ is constant, its time derivative is zero. Thus, we get

$$\vec{a}_{PA} = \vec{a}_{PB} \qquad \text{(4-45)}$$

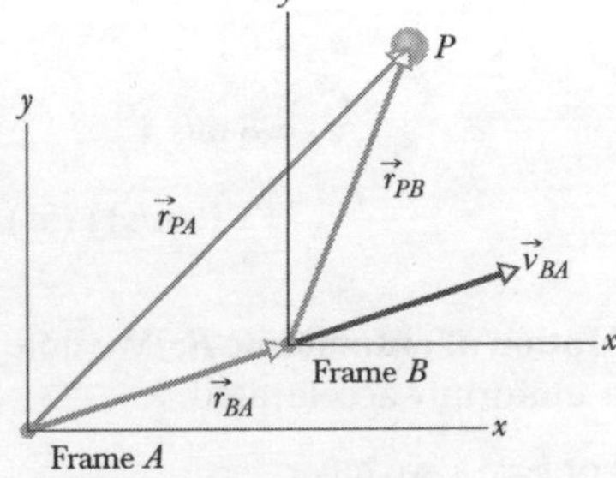

FIG. 4-27 Frame B has the constant two-dimensional velocity $\vec{v}_{BA}$ relative to frame A. The position vector of B relative to A is $\vec{r}_{BA}$. The position vectors of particle P are $\vec{r}_{PA}$ relative to A and $\vec{r}_{PB}$ relative to B.

As for one-dimensional motion, we have the following rule: Observers on different frames of reference that move at constant velocity relative to each other will measure the *same* acceleration for a moving particle.

Sample Problem 4-15

Automobile A is traveling east at the constant speed of 8 m/s. As automobile A crosses the intersection shown, automobile B starts from rest 55 m north of the intersection and moves south with a constant acceleration of 2 m/s². Determine the position, velocity, and acceleration of B relative to A 5 s after A crosses the intersection.

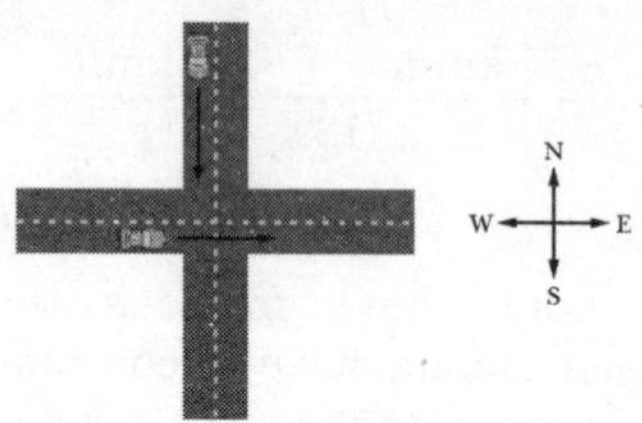

Top view of an intersection.

Conceptualize/Classify: We choose x and y axes with origin at the intersection of the two streets and with positive senses directed respectively east and north.

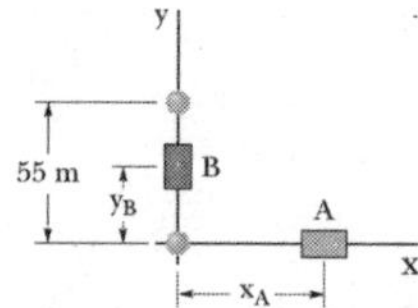

Compute: Motion of automobile A:

For $t = 5$ s, we have

$$a_A = 0$$

$$v_A = 8 \text{ m/s } \mathbf{i}$$

$$r_A = +(8\text{m/s})\,\mathbf{i}\,(5\text{s}) = 40 \text{ m } \mathbf{i}$$

Motion of automobile B: We note that the motion of B is uniformly accelerated.

For $t = 5$ s, we have

$$a_B = 2 \text{ m/s}^2\,(-\mathbf{j})$$

$$v_B = (2 \text{ m/s}^2)\,(-\mathbf{j})\,(5 \text{ s}) = 10 \text{ m/s}\,(-\mathbf{j})$$

$$r_B = 55 - 1/2\,(2 \text{ m/s}^2)\,(5 \text{ s})^2 = 30 \text{ m}\,(\mathbf{j})$$

Motion of B relative to A: We draw the triangle corresponding to the vector equation $\vec{r}_{BA} = \vec{r}_B - \vec{r}_A$ and obtain the magnitude and direction of the position vector of B relative to A.

$$\vec{r}_{BA} = 30 \text{ m}\,(\mathbf{j}) - 40 \text{ m}$$

$$|\vec{r}_{BA}| = 50 \text{ m}$$

$$\alpha = 37^\circ$$

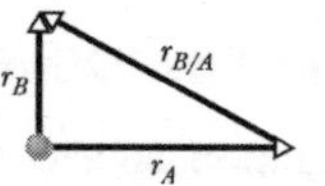

Position vector of B with respect to A.

Proceeding in a similar fashion, we find the velocity and acceleration of B relative to A.

$$\vec{v}_{BA} = 10 \text{ m/s}\,(-\mathbf{j}) - 8 \text{ m/s}$$

$$|\vec{v}_{BA}| = \sqrt{164}$$

$$\beta = \tan^{-1}(5/4)$$

Velocity of B with respect to A.

$$\vec{a}_{B/A} = 1.2 \text{ m/s}^2\,(-\mathbf{j})$$

Conclude: Since there is no x and y axes given we can not leave answer in unit vector notation.

CHECKPOINT 8 Two particles located at position vector $\boldsymbol{r}_a$ and $\boldsymbol{r}_b$ are moving with constant velocity $\boldsymbol{v}_a$ and $\boldsymbol{v}_b$. How these four vectors should be related so the particles can meet.

Sample Problem 4-16

Two particles are launched from two high rise buildings simultaneously as shown in Fig. 4-28. Find minimum distance between these two particles.

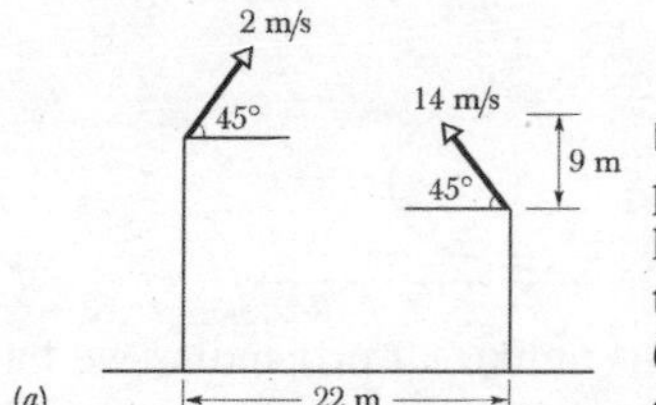

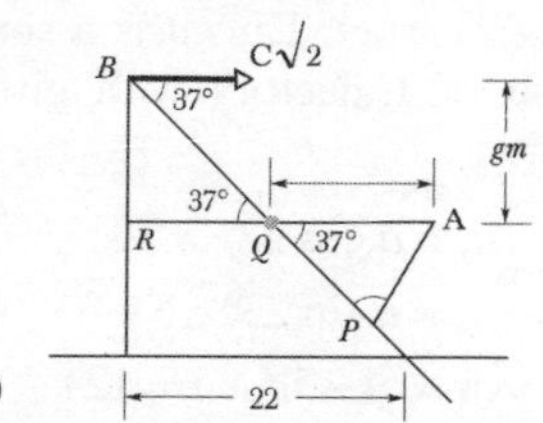

FIG. 4-28 (*a*) Two projectiles being launched from the top of two buildings (*b*) motion of *B* as observed by *A*.

Conceptualize: Here we have problem dealing with minimum distance between two particles. When we try to visualize the motion and variation of distance between them we will realize that it is very complicated. Both particles will be undergoing projectile motion in a parabolic trajectory.

Classify: This a problem that can be solved by considering reference frame attached to one of the particles. This will ensure that we have to look at motion of only one particle as other will be at rest. This is a problem which involves not only relative velocity but also relative acceleration.

Compute: We start by finding acceleration. $\vec{a}_B = -\hat{j}, \vec{a}_A = -g\hat{j}$ hence $\vec{a}_{BA} = \vec{a}_B - \vec{a}_A = 0$

If acceleration of *B* with respect to *A* is zero then *B* is moving on a straight path with constant velocity in reference frame attached to *A*. You can recall from our discusion on kinematics in two dimensions that even for change in direction we need acceleration. If acceleration is zero it means path has to be straight line.

First we will find velocity vector *B* with respect to *A*

$$\vec{v}_B = \sqrt{2}\hat{i} + \sqrt{2}\hat{j}$$

$$\vec{v}_A = -7\sqrt{2}\hat{i} + 7\sqrt{2}\hat{j}$$

hence $\quad \vec{v}_{B/A} = 8\sqrt{2}\hat{i} - 6\sqrt{2}\hat{j}$

Let's make a pictoral representation of *B*'s motion as seen by *A*.

Particle *B* will be going along *BB*' as seen from *A*'s reference frame. We can see from Fig. 4-28(b) that minimum distance will be equal to the length of perpendicular dropped from *A* on path of *B*, that is length of *AP*.

Consider $\quad \dfrac{RB}{RQ} = \tan 37^\circ$

Therefore, $\quad \therefore RQ = \dfrac{9 \times 4}{3} = 12 \text{ m}$

As $\quad RQ + QA = RA$

hence $\quad QA = 10 \text{ m}$

and consider $\quad PA = QA \sin 37^\circ$

$PA = 6 \text{ m}$ (Answer)

Conclude: Motion of a projectile as seen by other projectile is straight line as proven. To find minimum distance between two particles it is always better to take a reference frame attached to one of the particles as it will simplify the visualizetion since only one of the two will be moving now.

In Case of: We take refrence frame attached to *B* rather than to *A*.

Solution: $\quad \vec{v}_{AB} = -8\sqrt{2}\hat{i} + 6\sqrt{2}\hat{j}$

We get same answer. Also you can see from Fig. 4-28*c*, it is the same geometry too.

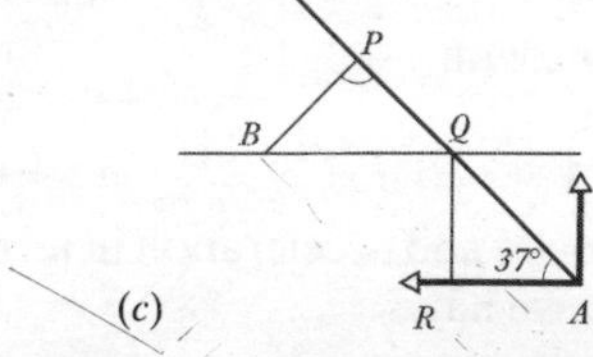

Sample Problem 4-17

Aladin starts flying on his magic carpet which has an acceleration of 26 m/s at an angle of 23° with horizontal.

$$\sin 23^\circ = \frac{5}{13}$$

Aladin on his magic carpet.

Princess Jasmine is standing on ground watching her sweetheart. Aladin throws a normal stone (one that obeys laws of physics unlike the magic carpet) at an angle of 23° to the horizontal, at velocity of 13 m/s.

(a) Find equation of trajectory of stone in reference frame of ground attached to Princess Jasmine taking *x* and *y* coordinates as shown.

Conceptualize/Classify: Princess Jasmine is attached to ground frame, thus motion of stone in her frame is going to be a simple projectile since magic carpet was at rest when stone was projected it means initial velocity of stone in ground frame will be equal to initial velocity in frame attached to magic carpet. Thus it is a simple problem of finding equation of trajectory with given velocity and angle of prejection.

Compute: $u_x = u \cos 23^\circ = 12$

$u_y = u \sin 23^\circ = 5$

$y = 5t - 5t^2 \mid x = 12\,t$

Note: Acceleration of stone is going to be g = 10 m/s^2. Acceleration of magic carpet will not be transferred to stone. As it is said that it is a normal stone, and thus subjected only to force of gravity. Thus it is freely falling object as all projectiles are.

Hence $$y = \frac{5x}{12} - \frac{5x^2}{144}$$

b) Find equation of trajectory in frame attached to Aladin.

Conceptualize: This problem involves a reference frame attached to an acceleration of observer. The observer is looking at an object which is also accelerating in ground frame (as all projectiles are accelerated motion). Initial relative velocity is same as given in the problem. Furthermore it involves acceleration component in both directions. Thus we need to seperate x and y motion as done in projectile motion.

Classify:

In x-coordinate frame	In y-coordinate frame
acceleration of stone, $a_s = 0$	$a_s = -10$
acceleration of magic carpet, $a_{mc} = 26 \cos 23 = 24$	$a_{mc} = -10$
acceleration of stone with respect to carpet, $a_{sm} = a_s - a_m = -24$	$a_{sm} = 0$

Separating the velocity and acceleration in terms of x and y coordinated, we have

Velocity of stone, $u_s = 12$	$u_s = 5$
Velocity of magic carpet, $u_m = 0$	$u_m = 0$
Velocity of stone with respect to magic carpet, $u_{sm} = 12$	$u_{sm} = 5$
hence $x = 12\,t - 12\,t^2$	hence $y = 5\,t$

thus eliminating time,

$$x = \frac{12y}{5} - \frac{12y^2}{25}$$

Compute: If we draw trajectory using the above equation We get figure

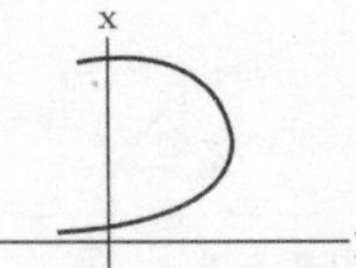

It is a parabola but unlike all projectiles we have seen here x and y are swapped.

Conclude: From solutions of a and b part we can see that path of a particle depends not only on parameters of particle motion but also on the motion of observer. Princess Jasmine is observing a normal parabola since she was observing no acceleration along x and y. While Aladin is observing a parabola rotated by 90° with respect to orignal he observes no acceleration along y but uniform acceleration along x.

(c) Find time when Aladin sees stone directly overhead. Find time when Princess Jasmine sees stone at the initial horizontal level.

Solution: For Princes Jasmine when y becomes zero, stone is at initial horizontal level putting $y = 0$ in $t = 1$ s.

For Aladin to be directly overhead putting $x = 0$ in $t = 1$ s.

In Case Of: How do we explain Aladin observing stone directly overhead at the same time Princess Jasmine sees stone at initial horizontal level.

Solution: Princes Jasmine will observe Aladin going in a straight line. After one second x co-ordinate of Aladin will be

$$x_A = 1/2 \times 24 \times 1^2 = 12$$

And x coordinate of stone

$$x_x = 12 \times 1 = 12$$

Thus they are equal !

Here is a figure representing motion of stone and magic carpet in frame of Princes Jasmine.

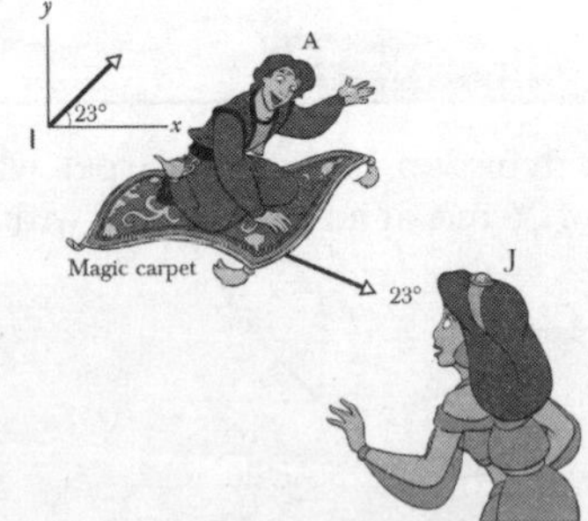

CHECKPOINT 9 Refering to the above problem make figure of stone and Princes Jasmine's motion as observed by Aladin and reconcile the fact that how when he observes stone directly overhead, Princes Jasmine is seeing stone at initial horizontal level.

4-9 | Net Motion

Suppose Priya is walking in a train moving along the track at a constant velocity. If we ask, "How fast is Priya walking?" This question is not well defined. Do we mean her velocity as measured by Tarun, a passenger on the train, or her velocity as measured by Girish, who is standing on the ground and looking into the train as it passes by ? The answer to the question "How fast?" depends on the observer.

Priya is walking from one end of the car to the other during a time interval Δt. The displacement of Priya as measured by Tarun–her displacement relative to the train is $\Delta\vec{r}_{PT} = \vec{v}_{PT}\,\Delta t$. During the same time interval, the train's displacement relative to the ground is $\Delta\vec{r}_{TR} = \vec{v}_{TG}\,\Delta t$. As measured by Girish, Priya's displacement is partly due to her motion relative to the train and partly due to the motion of the train relative to the ground. Figure shows that $\Delta\vec{r}_{PT} + \Delta\vec{r}_{TG} = \Delta\vec{r}_{PG}$. Dividing by the time interval Δt gives the relationship between the three velocities.

$$\vec{v}_{PT} + \vec{v}_{TG} = \vec{v}_{TG}$$

V_{PT} is velocity of Priya with respect to train. It is also called velocity of Priya in train at rest. This way of writing is correct since when we make train as our reference frame it is assumed to be at rest.

Concept of net motion is of enormous practical interest to pilots of aircraft, sailors, and captains of ocean liners. The pilot of an airplane is ultimately concerned with the motion of the plane with respect to the ground – the take off and landing points are fixed points on the ground. However, the controls of the plane (engines, rudder, and spoilers) affect the motion of the plane with respect to air. A sailor has to consider three different velocities of the boat: with respect to the shore (for launching and landing), with respect to air (for the behavior of the sails), and with respect to water (for the behavior of the rudder).

Sample Problem 4-18

Flight from Delhi to Chennai

An airplane flies from Delhi to Chennai (1770 km) in 4.4 h when no wind blows. On a day with a Northerly wind blowing, the plane makes the trip in 4.0 h. (a) What is the wind speed ? (b) If a southern wind blows at the same speed, how long does the trip take ?

Conceptualize/Classify: We assume the plane has the same airspeed – the same speed relative to the air – in both cases. Once the plane is up in the air, the behavior of the wings, rudder etc., depends on relative velocity of wind ; the ground speed is irrelevant. But it is not irrelevant for the passengers, who are interested in a displacement relative to the ground. Northern wind means wind coming from north and going towards south.

Compute: Let $\vec{v}_{PG}$ and $\vec{v}_{PA}$ represent the velocity of the plane relative to the ground and the velocity of the plane relative to the air, respectively. The wind velocity – the velocity of the air relative to the ground – can be written as $\vec{v}_{AG}$ Then $\vec{v}_{PA} + \vec{v}_{AG} = \vec{v}_{PG}$.

$$\vec{v}_{PA} = \vec{v}_{PG} = \frac{1770\text{ km}}{4.4\text{ h}} = 400\text{ km/h}$$

(a) On the day with the northern wind

$$\vec{v}_{PG} = \frac{1770\text{ km}}{4.0\text{ h}} = 440\text{ km/h}$$

We expect v_{PA} to be the same regardless of whether there is a wind or not. $\vec{v}_{PG}$ and $\vec{v}_{AG}$ are in the same direction, which we label as the +x-direction then,

$$\vec{v}_{PA} + \vec{v}_{AG} = \vec{v}_{PG}$$

$$v_{AGx} = v_{PGx} - v_{PAx} = 440\text{ km/h} - 400\text{ km/h} = 40\text{ km/h}$$
$$v_{AGy} = 0,$$

so the wind speed is $v_{AG} = 40$ km/h.

(b) With a 40 km/h southern the velocity of the plane with respect to the ground is,

$$v_{PGx} = v_{PAx} + v_{AGx} = 400\text{ km/h} + (-40\text{ km/h}) = 360\text{ km/h}$$

The ground speed of the plane is 360 km/h and the trip takes

$$\frac{1770\text{ km}}{360\text{ km/h}} = 4.9\text{ h} \qquad \text{(Answer)}$$

Sample Problem 4-19

A boat crossing a 250 m wide river moves with a speed of 5 km/h in still water. The river flows at uniform speed of 4 km/h due east.

(a) If the boat is steered towards north, determine the velocity of the boat relative to an observer standing on ground.

Conceptualize: If you swim across a river while the current takes you downstream, you will not be able to move directly across the river, but will end up downstream .

Classify: We can categorize this problem as one involving net motion, where the velocity of the boat will be net effect of its own propulsion and due to flow of river.

Compute: The velocity of the boat relative to the water $\mathbf{v}_{bw}$, is same as velocity of boat if water was still, $\mathbf{v}_{we}$ is the velocity of the river relative to the Earth. We need to find $\mathbf{v}_{be}$, the velocity of the boat relative to the Earth.

Writing equation of net motion $\mathbf{v}_{be} = \mathbf{v}_{bw} + \mathbf{v}_{we}$ three vectors are shown in Fig. 4-29*a*. The quantity $\mathbf{v}_{bw}$ is due north; $\mathbf{v}_{we}$ is due east; and the vector sum of the two, $\mathbf{v}_{be}$, is at an angle θ as defined in Fig. 4-29*a*.

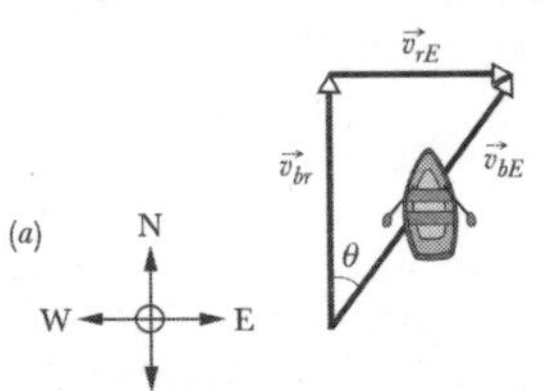

FIG. 4-29 (*a*) A boat steered across the stream (*b*) A boat being steered such that it travels across the river

The speed v_{bE} of the both relative to the Earth is

$$\vec{v}_{bE} = \sqrt{\vec{v}_{br}^2 + \vec{v}_{rE}^2} = \sqrt{4^2 + 5^2} = \sqrt{41} \text{ km/h}$$

Direction of $\vec{v}_{bE}$: $\quad \theta = \tan^{-1}(0.8)$

Conclude: Notice that the speed of $1\sqrt{41}$ km/h is faster than boat speed of 5 km/h in still water. The current velocity adds to the boat's to give a higher speed.

Notice in Fig. 4-29*a* that your resultant velocity is at an angle to the direction straight across the river, so boat will end up downstream.

(b) If the boat travels with the same speed of 5 km/h in still water, and is to travel due north that is directly across the river as shown in Fig. 4-29*b*, at what angle it should be steered?

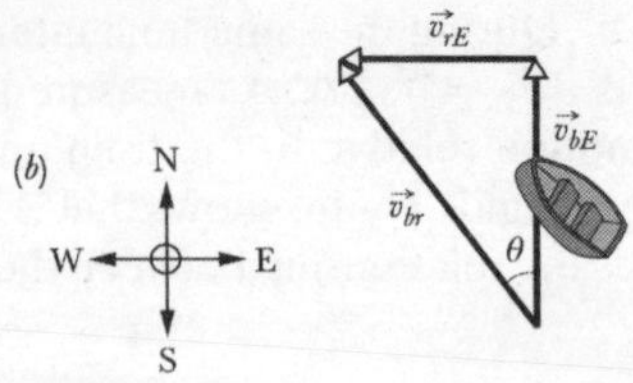

Conceptualize/Classify: We should now aim the boat upstream so as to go straight across the river.

Compute: Writing equation of net motion $\mathbf{v}_{be} = \mathbf{v}_{bw} + \mathbf{v}_{we}$ three vectors are shown in Fig. 4-29*b*. As in part (*a*), we know $\mathbf{v}_{we}$ and the magnitude of the vector $\mathbf{v}_{bw}$, and we want $\mathbf{v}_{be}$ to be directed across the river. Note the difference

$$\vec{v}_{bE} = \sqrt{\vec{v}_{br}^2 - \vec{v}_{rE}^2} = \sqrt{5^2 - 4^2} = 3 \text{ km/h}$$

Direction in which the boat is heading: $\theta = 53°$

Conclude: The boat must head upstream so as to move directly across the river. The boat must move 53° west of north. The boat will be aimed upstream at larger angles for faster currents.

(c) Imagine that the two boats in parts (*a*) and (*b*) are racing across the river. Which boat arrives at the opposite bank first?

Solution: In part (*a*), the velocity of 5 km/h is aimed directly across the river while in part (*b*), the velocity aimed directly across the river has a magnitude of only 3 km/h. Therefore, the boat in part (*a*) has a larger velocity component directly across the river and arrives first.

Sample Problem 4-20

In Fig. 4-30*a*, a plane moves due east while the pilot points the plane somewhat south of east, toward a steady wind that blows to the northeast. The plane has velocity $\vec{v}_{PW}$ relative to the wind, with an airspeed (speed relative to the wind) of 215 km/h, directed at angle θ south of east. The wind has velocity $\vec{v}_{WG}$ relative to the ground with speed 65.0 km/h, directed 20° east of north. What is the magnitude of the velocity given, cos 20° and sin 16.5° $\vec{v}_{PG}$ of the plane relative to the ground, and what is θ?

Conceptualize: The situation is like the one in Fig. 4-27. Here the moving particle *P* is the plane, frame *A* is attached to the ground (call it *G*), and frame *B* is "attached" to the wind (call it *W*).

Classify: We need a vector diagram like Fig. 4-22 but with three velocity vectors.

Compute: First we construct a sentence that relates the three vectors shown in Fig. 4-30*b*:

velocity of plane relative to ground (*PG*)	=	velocity of plane relative to wind (*PW*)	+	velocity of wind relative to ground (*WG*)

This relation is written in vector notation as

$$\vec{v}_{PG} = \vec{v}_{PW} + \vec{v}_{WG} \tag{4-46}$$

We need to resolve the vectors into components on the coordinate system of Fig. 4-30*b* and then solve Eq. 4-46 axis by axis. For the *y* components, we find

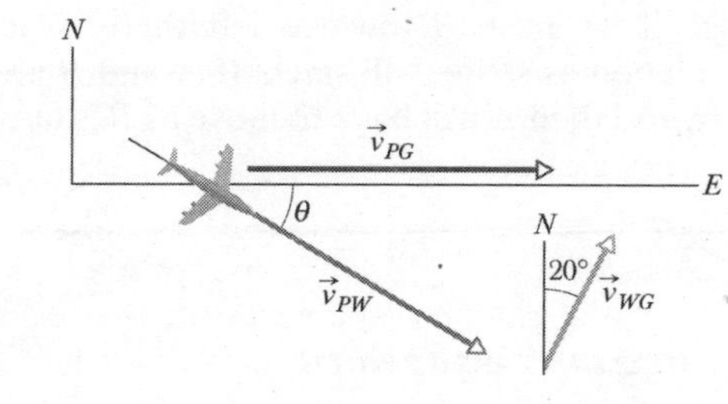

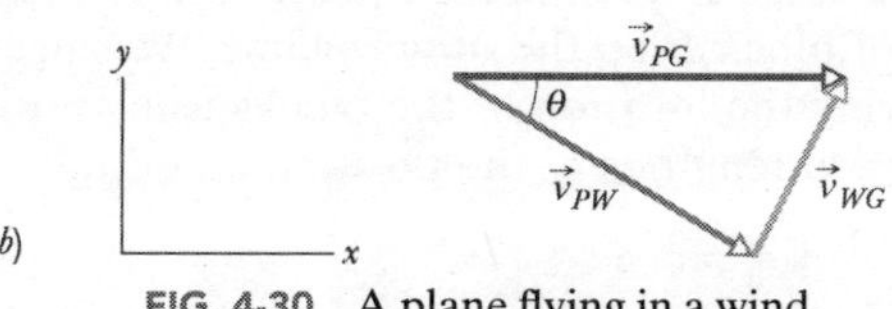

FIG. 4-30 A plane flying in a wind.

$$v_{PG,y} = v_{PW,y} + v_{WG,y}$$

or $\quad 0 = -(215 \text{ km/h}) \sin \theta + (65.0 \text{ km/h})(\cos 20.0°)$

Solving for θ gives us

$$\theta = \sin^{-1} \frac{(65.0 \text{ km/h})(\cos 20.0°)}{215 \text{ km/h}} = 16.5° \quad \text{(Answer)}$$

Similarly, for the x components we find

$$v_{PG,x} = v_{PW,x} + v_{WG,x}$$

Here, because $\vec{v}_{PG}$ is parallel to the x axis, the component $v_{PG,x}$ is equal to the magnitude v_{PG}. Substituting this notation and the value $\theta = 16.5°$, we find

$$v_{PG} = (215 \text{ km/h})(\cos 16.5°) + (65.0 \text{ km/h})(\sin 20.0°)$$
$$= 228 \text{ km/h} \quad \text{(Answer)}$$

4-10 | Constraint Motion

When two or more bodies are connected then their motion is interdependent to maintain connection. For example, if we have a block kept on incline plane and we want the block to maintain contact with it the block can not have velocity and acceleration in direction perpendicular to the incline.

If we have two block kept touching each other on horizontal surface as shown then they must have same velocity and acceleration to maintain the contact.

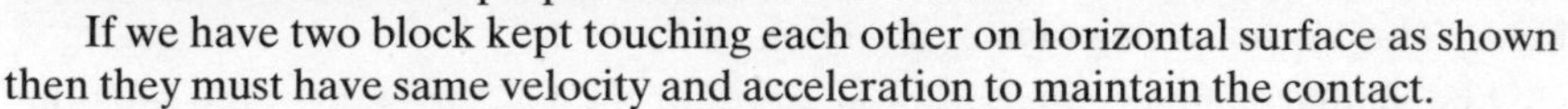

If we keep a block on wedge which can move then again constraint is defined in refrence frame attached to wedge. The block can not have any acceleration in y direction in reference frame attached to wedge.

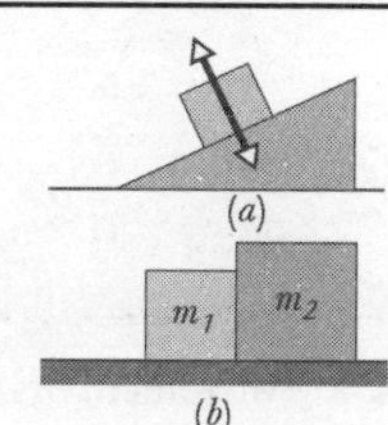

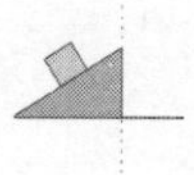

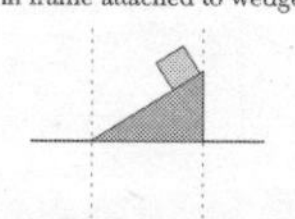

FIG. 4-31 Constraint motion. (a) A block on inclined plane. (b) Two blocks touching each other on horizontal surface. (c) Constraint defined in reference frame attached to wedge.

Sample Problem 4-21

Find relation between velocity and acceleration of rod and wedge.

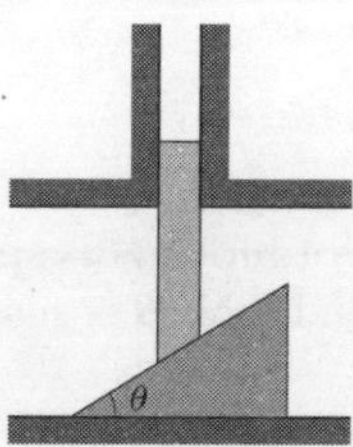

Conceptualize: Let's imagine what happens when wedge is pushed towards left. We make a superimposing diagram on the initial diagram.

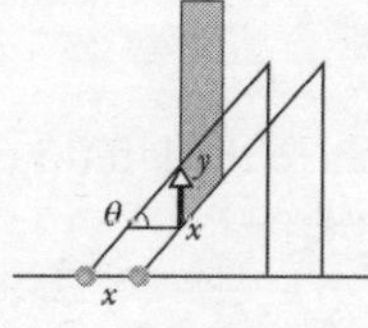

Classify: Here there are three constraints involved (a) the wedge can move only horizontally, (b) the rod can move only vertically, and (c) the rod and wedge to remain in contact. Thus their motion has to be related using geometry.

Compute: We can see that when wedge moves x along horizontal direction rod rises by y.

$$\tan \theta = \frac{y}{x} \Rightarrow y = x \tan \theta$$

hence $v_R = v_w \tan \theta$ differentiating and $a_R = a_w \tan \theta$

Conclude: The rod should not have any acceleration with respect to wedge perpendicular to incline.

When two bodies are connected by inextensible rope then their motion is interdependent if we want rope to remain taut. If we connect two block as shown in diagram and pull block B towards right block A must cover same distance as B to keep string tight.

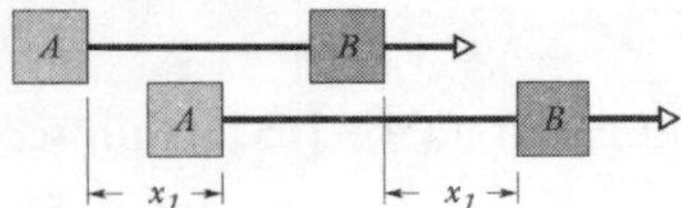

Although if we push B towards left there is no constraint relation as string will slack. If A and B are connected by rod then A will have to move as B is moving is both the above cases.

Mathematical Analysis (constraint equation)

The movement of block A downward along the inclined plane in Fig. 4-32 will cause a corresponding movement of block B up the other incline. We can show this mathematically by first specifying the location of the blocks using position coordinates x_A and x_B. If the total card length is l_o, the position coordinates are related by the equation.

$$\mathrm{x_A} + l_{\mathrm{CD}} + \mathrm{x_B} = l_{\mathrm{T}}$$

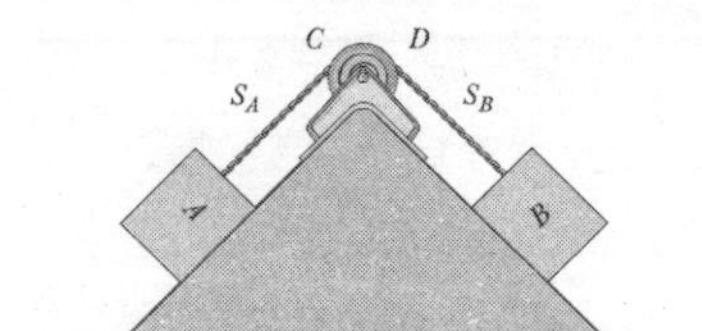

FIG. 4-32 Movement of block along inclined plane.

Here l_{CD} is the length of the cord passing over arc CD. Differentiating this expression, realizing that l_{CD} and l_O remain constant, while x_A and x_B measure the lengths of the changing segments of the cord, we have

$$\frac{dx_B}{dt} + \frac{dx_A}{dt} = 0 \quad \text{or} \quad v_{\mathrm{B}} = -v_{\mathrm{A}}$$

The negative sign indicates that when block A has a velocity downward, that is in the direction of positive x_A, it causes a corresponding upward velocity of block B; that is, B moves in the negative x_B direction.

In a similar manner, time differentiation of the velocities gives the relation between the accelerations, that is

$$a_B = -a_A$$

CHECKPOINT 10 If velocity of A is 2 m/s downwards what is the velocity of B.

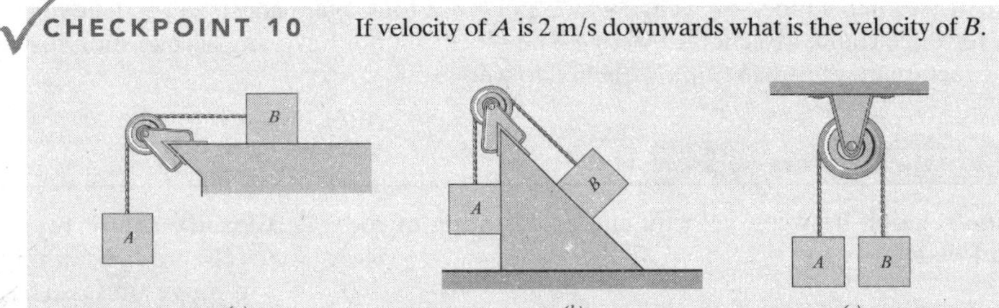

A more complicated example involving constrained motion of two blocks is shown in (Fig. a). In this case, the position of block A is specified by x_A, and the position of the end of the cord from which block B is suspended is defined by x_B.

During the motion, the segments PQR of the cord in (Fig. a) remain constant. If l_O represents the total length of cord minus these segments, then the position coordinates can be related by the equation

$$2s_B + h + s_A = l$$

Since l and h are constant during the motion, the two time derivatives yield

$$2v_B = -v_A \qquad 2a_B = -a_A$$

Hence, when B moves downward ($+s_B$), A moves to the left ($-s_A$) at two times the motion.

Sample Problem 4-22

Determine the speed of block A in Fig. 4-33 if block B has an upward speed of 6 ft/s.

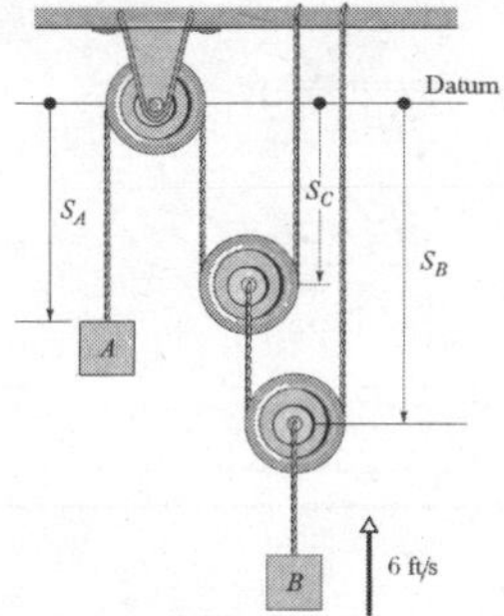

FIG. 4-33 A complicated arrangement involving three pulleys, two blocks, and a rope.

Conceptualize:/Classify : As shown, the positions of blocks A and B are defined using the coordinates x_A. Since the system has two cords which change length, it will be necessary to use a third coordinate, x_C, in order to relate x_A to x_B. In other words, the length of one of the cords can be expressed in terms of x_A and x_C, and the length of the other cord can be expressed in terms of s_B and s_C.

Compute: For the two cords, lengths are l_1 and l_2, we have

$$x_A + 2x_C = l_1,\; x_B + (x_B - x_C) = l_2$$

Eliminating x_C yields an equation defining the positions of both blocks, that is,

$$x_A + 4x_B = 2l_2 + l_1$$

Time Derivative: The time derivative gives

$$v_A + 4v_B = 0$$

so that when $u_B = -6$ ft/s (upward),

$$v_A = +24 \text{ ft/s} = +24 \text{ ft/s} \downarrow \qquad \text{(Answer)}$$

Sample Problem 4-23

A man at A is pulling a block B as shown in Fig. 4-34 by walking to the right with a constant velcoity $\upsilon_A = 0.5$ m/s. Determine the velocity and acceleration of the block B when it reaches the window elevation at E. The rope is 30 m long and passes over a small pulley at P.

Conceptualize/Classify: This problem is unlike the previous examples, since rope segment PA changes both direction and magnitude. However, the ends of the rope, which define the positions of S and A, are specified by means of the x and y coordinates measured from fixed points and directed along the paths of motion of the ends of the rope.

Compute: The x and y coordinates may be related since the rope has a fixed length $l = 30$ m, which at all times is equal to the length of segment PA plus CP. Using the Pythagorean theorem to determine l_{DA}, we have l_{DA}, we have $l_{DA} = \sqrt{(15)^2 + x^2}$; also, $l_{CD} = 15 - y$. Hence,

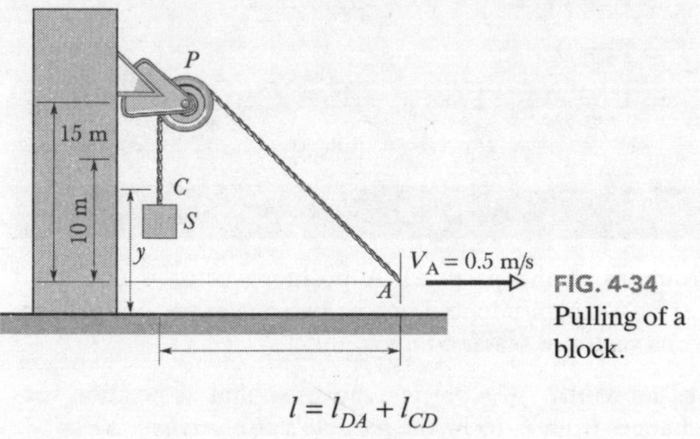

FIG. 4-34 Pulling of a block.

$$30 = \sqrt{(15)^2 + x^2} + (15 - y)$$

$$y = \sqrt{225 + x^2} - 15 \qquad \text{(i)}$$

Time Derivative: Taking the time derivative, where $\upsilon_S = dy/dt$ and $\upsilon_A = dx/dt$, yields

$$v_s = \frac{dy}{dt} = \frac{1}{2}\frac{2x}{\sqrt{225 + x^2}}\frac{dx}{dt} = \frac{x}{\sqrt{225 + x^2}}v_A \qquad \text{(ii)}$$

At $y = 10$ m, x is determined from Eq. i, that is $x = 20$ m. Hence, from Eq. ii with $U_A = 0.5$ m/s.

$$v_s = \frac{20}{\sqrt{225 + (20)^2}}0.5 = 0.4 \text{ m/s} = 400 \text{ mm/s} \uparrow \quad \text{(Answer)}$$

The acceleration is determined by taking the time derivative of Eq. ii. Since υ_A is constant, then $a_A = d\upsilon_A/dt = 0$, and we have

$$a_s = \frac{d^2y}{dt^2} = \left[\frac{-x^2}{(225 + x^2)^{3/2}}\frac{dx}{dt} + \frac{1}{(225 + x^2)^{1/2}}\frac{dx}{dt}\right]v_A = \frac{225u_A^2}{(225 + x^2)^{3/2}}$$

At $x = 20$ m, with $\upsilon_A = 0.5$ m/s, the acceleration beomes

$$a_s = \frac{225(0.5 \text{ m/s})^2}{[225 + (20)^2]^{3/2}} = 0.00360 \text{ m/s}^2 = 3.60 \text{ mm/s}^2 \uparrow \quad \text{(Answer)}$$

Conclude: Note that the constant velocity at A causes the other end C of the rope to have this acceleration since v_A causes segment DA to change its direction.

Sample Problem 4-24 Build your skill

The boy at C stands near the edge of the pier and pulls in the rope horizontally at constant speed v_B. Determine how fast the raft approaches the pier at the instant the rope length BR is d.

Given: $v_B = 6$ m/s; $h = 8$ m; $d = 50$ m

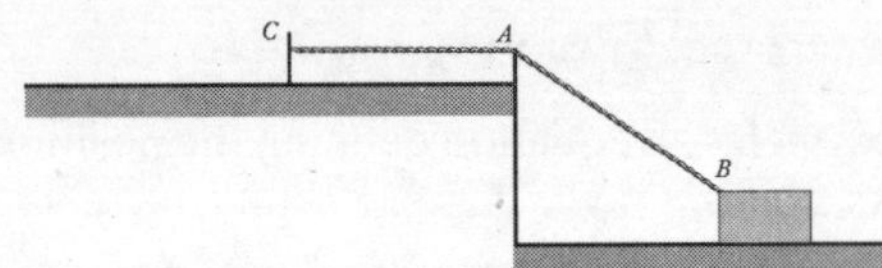

Solution:

$$x_B = \sqrt{a^2 - h^2}$$

$$L = x_C + \sqrt{h^2 + x_B^2}$$

$$0 = v_C + \frac{x_B v_B}{\sqrt{h^2 + x_B^2}}$$

$$v_B = -v_c \left(\frac{\sqrt{h^2 + x_B^2}}{x_B} \right)$$

$$v_B = -6.078 \text{ m/s}$$

Positive means to the right, negative to the left.

Sample Problem 4-25

Find velocity vector of m_1 if m_2 is pulled with constant velocity $v_2 = 2$ m/s.

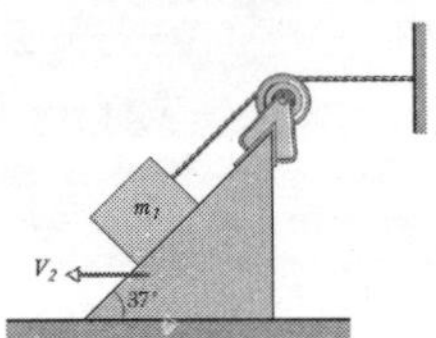

Conceptualize: This problem involves two constraints. One involves the rope and other is involves m_1 and m_2 remaining in constact with each other.

Classify: These two constraints can be understood easily if we shift our refrence frame to the to the wedge. By doing this we will be able to simplify motion of block m_1 and thus solve constraint of rope easily.

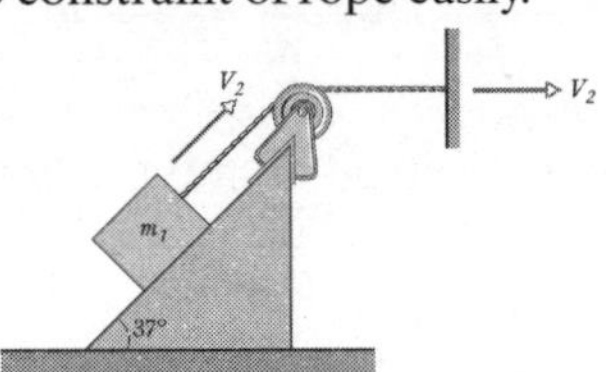

Compute: In refrence frame of attached to wedge wall will move horizontally towards left with speed v_2 as shown.

Thus, it can be easily deduced that m_1 will move with velocity v_2 upwards. But this is velocity of m_1 on frame attached to m_2 using relation ship of net motion.

$$\vec{v}_1 = \vec{v}_{12} + \vec{v}_2$$

we can get $\vec{v}_1$ as shown

Solving we get $|\vec{v}_1| = v_2$

Conclude: We can check that this velocity vector satisfies condition of m_1 having no component of velocity perpendicular to incline with respect to the wedge.

CHECKPOINT 11 If $V_2 = 2$ m/s upwards; $v_P = 1$ m/s upwards. Find the velocity of block 1 and block 3 ?

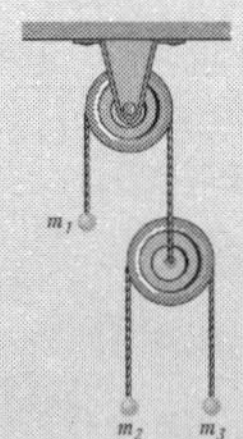

Solution:

$$\Rightarrow V_2 - V_P = V_P - V_3$$

$$\Rightarrow V_3 = 0$$

$$\Rightarrow V_1 = -V_P = 1 \text{ m/s} \downarrow$$

REVIEW & SUMMARY

Position Vector The location of a particle relative to the origin of a coordinate system is given by a *position vector* $\vec{r}$, which in unit-vector notation is

$$\vec{r} = x\hat{i} + y\hat{j} + z\hat{k}$$

Here $x\hat{i}$, $y\hat{j}$, and $z\hat{k}$ are the vector components of position vector $\vec{r}$, and x, y, and z are its scalar components (as well as the coordinates of the particle). A position vector is described either by a magnitude and one or two angles for orientation, or by its vector or scalar components.

Displacement If a particle moves so that its position vector changes from $\vec{r}_1$ to $\vec{r}_2$, the particle's *displacement* $\Delta\vec{r}$ is

$$\Delta\vec{r} = \vec{r}_2 - \vec{r}_1$$

The displacement can also be written as

$$\Delta\vec{r} = (x_2 - x_1)\hat{\text{i}} + (y_2 - y_1)\hat{\text{j}} + (z_2 - z_1)\hat{\text{k}}$$
$$= \Delta x\hat{\text{i}} + \Delta y\hat{\text{j}} + \Delta z\hat{\text{k}}$$

Average Velocity and Instantaneous Velocity If a particle undergoes a displacement $\Delta\vec{r}$ in time interval Δt, its *average velocity* $\vec{v}_{avg}$ for that time interval is

$$\vec{v}_{avg} = \frac{\Delta\vec{r}}{\Delta t}$$

As Δt in Eq. 4-8 is shrunk to 0, $\vec{v}_{avg}$ reaches a limit called either the *velocity* or the *instantaneous velocity* $\vec{v}$:

$$\vec{v} = \frac{d\vec{r}}{dt}$$

which can be rewritten in unit-vector notation as

$$\vec{v} = v_x\hat{\text{i}} + v_y\hat{\text{j}} + v_z\hat{\text{k}}$$

where $v_x = dx/dt$, $v_y = dy/dt$, and $v_z = dz/dt$. The instantaneous velocity $\vec{v}$ of a particle is always directed along the tangent to the particle's path at the particle's position.

Average Acceleration and Instantaneous Acceleration If a particle's velocity changes from $\vec{v}_1$ to $\vec{v}_2$ in time interval Δt, its *average acceleration* during Δt is

$$\vec{a}_{avg} = \frac{\vec{v}_2 - \vec{v}_1}{\Delta t} = \frac{\Delta\vec{v}}{\Delta t}$$

As Δt in Eq. 4-15 is shrunk to 0, $\vec{a}_{avg}$ reaches a limiting value called either the *acceleration* or the *instantaneous acceleration* $\vec{a}$:

$$\vec{a} = \frac{d\vec{v}}{dt}$$

In unit-vector notation,

$$\vec{a} = a_x\hat{\text{i}} + a_y\hat{\text{j}} + a_z\hat{\text{k}}$$

where $a_x = dv_x/dt$, $a_y = dv_y/dt$, and $a_z = dv_z/dt$.

Projectile Motion *Projectile motion* is the motion of a particle that is launched with an initial velocity $\vec{v}_0$. During its flight, the particle's horizontal acceleration is zero and its vertical acceleration is the free-fall acceleration $-g$. (Upward is taken to be a positive direction.) If $\vec{v}_0$ is expressed as a magnitude (the speed v_0) and an angle θ_0 (measured from the horizontal), the particle's equations of motion along the horizontal x axis and vertical y axis are

$$x - x_0 = (v_0 \cos\theta_0)t$$

$$y - y_0 = (v_0 \sin\theta_0)t - \tfrac{1}{2}gt^2$$

$$v_y = v_0 \sin\theta_0 - gt$$

$$v_y^2 = (v_0 \sin\theta_0)^2 - 2g(y - y_0)$$

The **trajectory** (path) of a particle in projectile motion is parabolic and is given by

$$y = (\tan\theta_0)x - \frac{gx^2}{2(v_0\cos\theta_0)^2}$$

if x_0 and y_0 of Eqs. 4-21 to 4-24 are zero. The particle's **horizontal range** R, which is the horizontal distance from the launch point to the point at which the particle returns to the launch height, is

$$R = \frac{v_0^2}{g}\sin 2\theta_0$$

Uniform Circular Motion If a particle travels along a circle or circular arc of radius r at constant speed v, it is said to be in *uniform circular motion* and has an acceleration $\vec{a}$ of constant magnitude

$$a = \frac{v^2}{r}$$

The direction of $\vec{a}$ is toward the center of the circle or circular arc, and $\vec{a}$ is said to be *centripetal.* The time for the particle to complete a circle is

$$T = \frac{2\pi r}{v}$$

T is called the *period of revolution,* or simply the *period,* of the motion.

Relative Motion When two frames of reference A and B are moving relative to each other at constant velocity, the velocity of a particle P as measured by an observer in frame A usually differs from that measured from frame B. The two measured velocities are related by

$$\vec{v}_{PA} = \vec{v}_{PB} + \vec{v}_{BA}$$

where $\vec{v}_{BA}$ is the velocity of B with respect to A. Both observers measure the same acceleration for the particle:

$$\vec{a}_{PA} = \vec{a}_{PB}$$

QUESTIONS

1 Figure 4-35 shows the initial position i and the final position f of a particle. What are the (a) initial position vector $\vec{r}_i$ and (b) final position vector $\vec{r}_f$, both in unit-vector notation? (c) What is the x component of displacement $\Delta\vec{r}$?

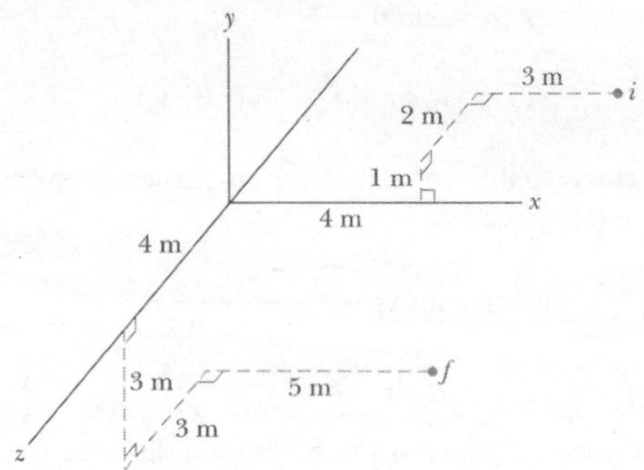

FIG. 4-35 Question 1.

2 Figure 4-36 shows the path taken by a skunk foraging for trash food, from initial point i. The skunk took the same time T to go from each labeled point to the next along its path. Rank points a, b, and c according to the magnitude of the average velocity of the skunk to reach them from initial point i, greatest first.

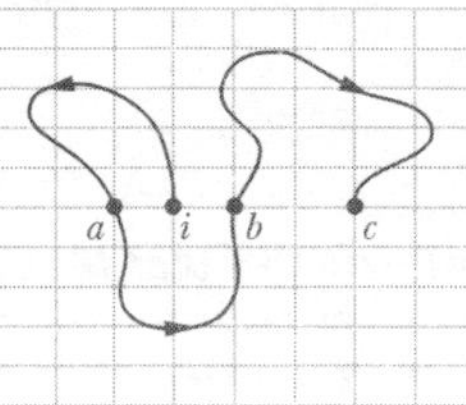

FIG. 4-36 Question 2.

3 You are to launch a rocket, from just above the ground, with one of the following initial velocity vectors: (1) $\vec{v}_0 = 20\hat{i} + 70\hat{j}$, (2) $\vec{v}_0 = -20\hat{i} + 70\hat{j}$, (3) $\vec{v}_0 = 20\hat{i} - 70\hat{j}$, (4) $\vec{v}_0 = -20\hat{i} - 70\hat{j}$. In your coordinate system, x runs along level ground and y increases upward. (a) Rank the vectors according to the launch speed of the projectile, greatest first. (b) Rank the vectors according to the time of flight of the projectile, greatest first.

4 Figure 4-37 shows three situations in which identical projectiles are launched (at the same level) at identical initial speeds and angles. The projectiles do not land on the same terrain, however. Rank the situations according to the final speeds of the projectiles just before they land, greatest first.

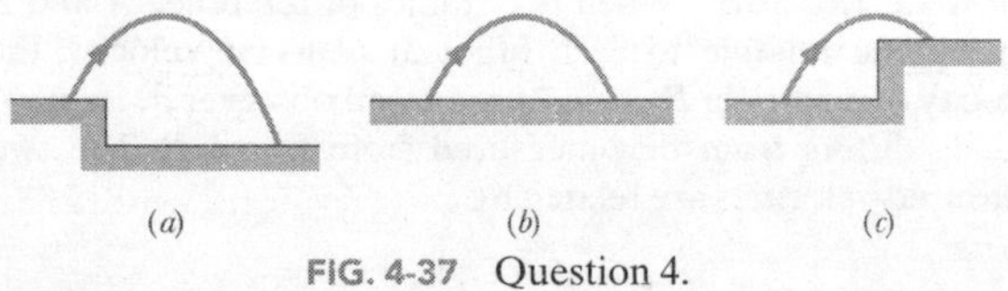

FIG. 4-37 Question 4.

5 When Paris was shelled from 100 km away with the WWI long-range artillery piece "Big Bertha," the shells were fired at an angle greater than 45° to give them a greater range, possibly even twice as long as at 45°. Does that result mean that the air density at high altitudes increases with altitude or decreases?

6 In Fig. 4-38, a cream tangerine is thrown up past windows 1, 2, and 3, which are identical in size and regularly spaced vertically. Rank those three windows according to (a) the time the cream tangerine takes to pass them and (b) the average speed of the cream tangerine during the passage, greatest first.

The cream tangerine then moves down past windows 4, 5, and 6, which are identical in size and irregularly spaced horizontally. Rank those three windows according to (c) the time the cream tangerine takes to pass them and (d) the average speed of the cream tangerine during the passage, greatest first.

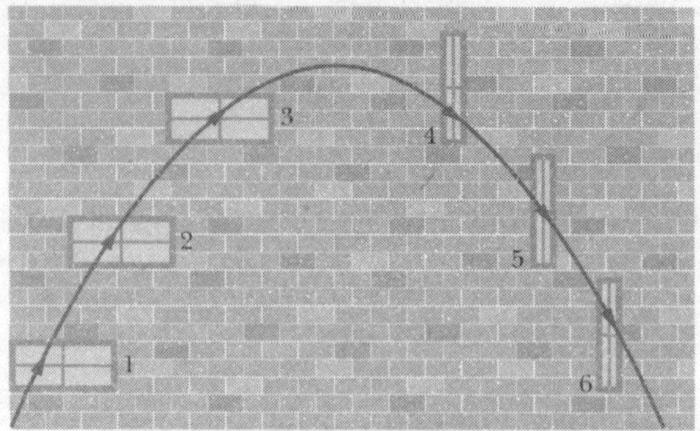

FIG. 4-38 Question 6.

7 Figure 4-39 shows three paths for a football kicked from ground level. Ignoring the effects of air, rank the paths according to (a) time of flight, (b) initial vertical velocity component, (c) initial horizontal velocity component, and (d) initial speed, greatest first.

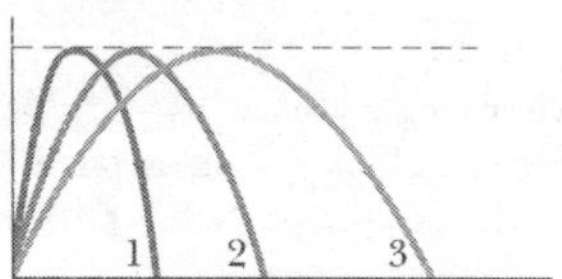

FIG. 4-39 Question 7.

8 The only good use of a fruitcake is in catapult practice. Curve 1 in Fig. 4-40 gives the height y of a catapulted fruitcake versus the angle θ between its velocity vector and its acceleration vector during flight. (a) Which of the lettered points on that curve corresponds to the landing of the fruitcake on the ground? (b) Curve 2 is a similar plot for the same launch speed but for a different launch angle. Does the fruitcake now land farther away or closer to the launch point?

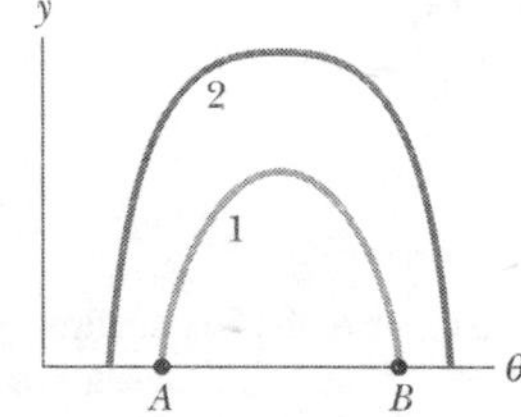

FIG. 4-40 Question 8.

9 An airplane flying horizontally at a constant speed of 350 km/h over level ground releases a bundle of food supplies. Ignore the effect of the air on the bundle. What are the bundle's initial (a) vertical and (b) horizontal components of velocity? (c) What is its horizontal component of velocity just before hitting the ground? (d) If the airplane's speed were, instead, 450 km/h, would the time of fall be longer, shorter, or the same?

10 A ball is shot from ground level over level ground at a certain initial speed. Figure 4-41 gives the range R of the ball versus its launch angle θ_0. Rank the three lettered points on the plot according to (a) the total flight time of the ball and (b) the ball's speed at maximum height, greatest first.

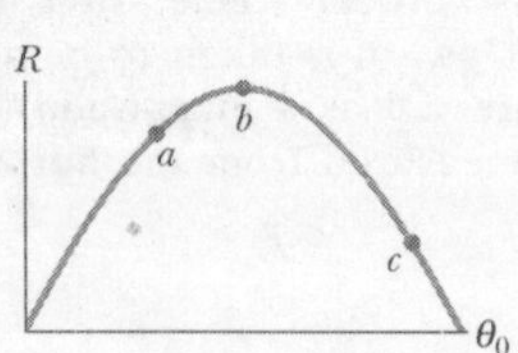

FIG. 4-41 Question 10.

PROBLEMS

Position and Displacement

1 The minute hand of a wall clock measures 10 cm from its tip to the axis about which it rotates. The magnitude and angle of the displacement vector of the tip are to be determined for three time intervals. What are the (a) magnitude and (b) angle from a quarter after the hour to half past, the (c) magnitude and (d) angle for the next half hour, and the (e) magnitude and (f) angle for the hour after that?

Average Velocity and Instantaneous Velocity

2 A train at a constant 60.0 km/h moves east for 40.0 min, then in a direction 50.0° east of due north for 20.0 min, and then west for 50.0 min. What are the (a) magnitude and (b) angle of its average velocity during this trip?

3 A plane flies 483 km east from city A to city B in 45.0 min and then 966 km south from city B to city C in 1.50 h. For the total trip, what are the (a) magnitude and (b) direction of the plane's displacement, the (c) magnitude and (d) direction of its average velocity, and (e) its average speed?

4 Figure 4-42 gives the path of a squirrel moving about on level ground, from point A (at time $t = 0$), to points B (at $t = 5.00$ min), C (at $t = 10.0$ min), and finally D (at $t = 15.0$ min). Consider the average velocities of the squirrel from point A to each of the other three points. Of them, what are the (a) magnitude and (b) angle of the one with the least magnitude and the (c) magnitude and (d) angle of the one with the greatest magnitude?

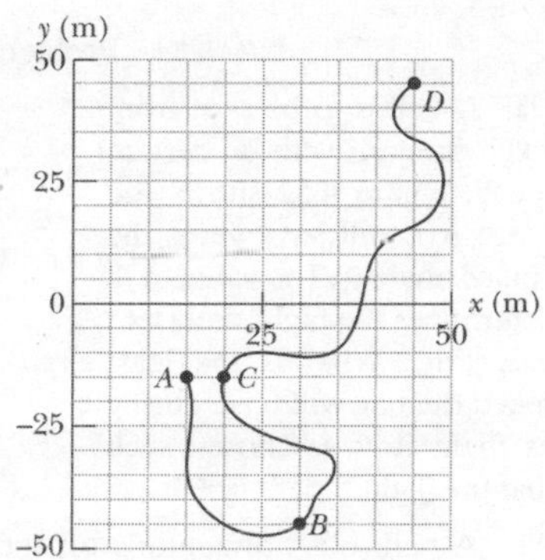

FIG. 4-42 Problem 4.

5 The position vector $\vec{r} = 5.00t\hat{i} + (et + ft^2)\hat{j}$ locates a particle as a function of time t. Vector $\vec{r}$ is in meters, t is in seconds, and factors e and f are constants. Figure 4-43 gives the angle θ of the particle's direction of travel as a function of t (θ is measured from the positive x direction). What are (a) e and (b) f, including units?

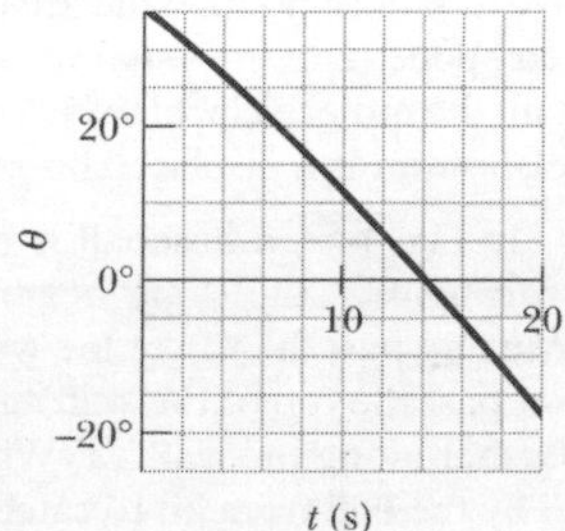

FIG. 4-43 Problem 5.

Average Acceleration and Instantaneous Acceleration

6 The position $\vec{r}$ of a particle moving in an xy plane is given by $\vec{r} = (2.00t^3 - 5.00t)\hat{i} + (6.00 - 7.00t^4)\hat{j}$, with $\vec{r}$ in meters and t in seconds. In unit-vector notation, calculate (a) $\vec{r}$, (b) $\vec{v}$, and (c) $\vec{a}$ for $t = 2.00$ s. (d) What is the angle between the positive direction of the x axis and a line tangent to the particle's path at $t = 2.00$ s?

7 At one instant a bicyclist is 40.0 m due east of a park's flagpole, going due south with a speed of 10.0 m/s. Then 30.0 s later, the cyclist is 40.0 m due north of the flagpole, going due east with a speed of 10.0 m/s. For the cyclist in this 30.0 s interval, what are the (a) magnitude and (b) direction of the displacement, the (c) magnitude and (d) direction of the average velocity, and the (e) magnitude and (f) direction of the average acceleration?

8 The acceleration of a particle moving only on a horizontal xy plane is given by $\vec{a} = 3t\hat{i} + 4t\hat{j}$, where $\vec{a}$ is in meters per second-squared and t is in seconds. At $t = 0$, the position vector $\vec{r} = (20.0 \text{ m})\hat{i} + (40.0 \text{ m})\hat{j}$ locates the particle, which then has the velocity vector $\vec{v} = (5.00 \text{ m/s})\hat{i} + (2.00 \text{ m/s})\hat{j}$. At $t = 4.00$ s, what are (a) its position vector in unit-vector notation and (b) the angle between its direction of travel and the positive direction of the x axis?

9 In Fig. 4-44, particle A moves along the line $y = 30$ m with a constant velocity $\vec{v}$ of magnitude 3.0 m/s and parallel to the x axis. At the instant particle A passes the y axis, particle B leaves the origin with zero initial speed and constant acceleration $\vec{a}$ of magnitude 0.40 m/s². What angle θ between $\vec{a}$ and the positive direction of the y axis would result in a collision?

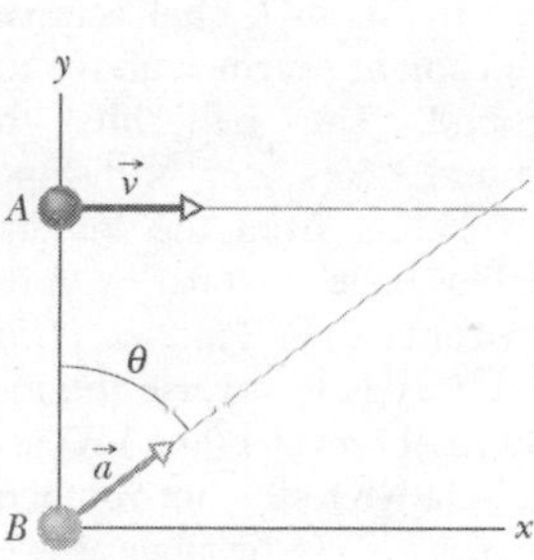

FIG. 4-44 Problem 9.

Projectile Motion Analyzed

10 A dart is thrown horizontally with an initial speed of 10 m/s toward point P, the bull's-eye on a dart board. It hits at point Q on the rim, vertically below P, 0.19 s later. (a) What is the distance PQ? (b) How far away from the dart board is the dart released?

11 In Fig. 4-45, a stone is projected at a cliff of height h with an initial speed of 42.0 m/s directed at angle $\theta_0 = 60.0°$ above the horizontal. The stone strikes at A, 5.50 s after launching. Find (a) the height h of the cliff, (b) the speed of the stone just before impact at A, and (c) the maximum height H reached above the ground.

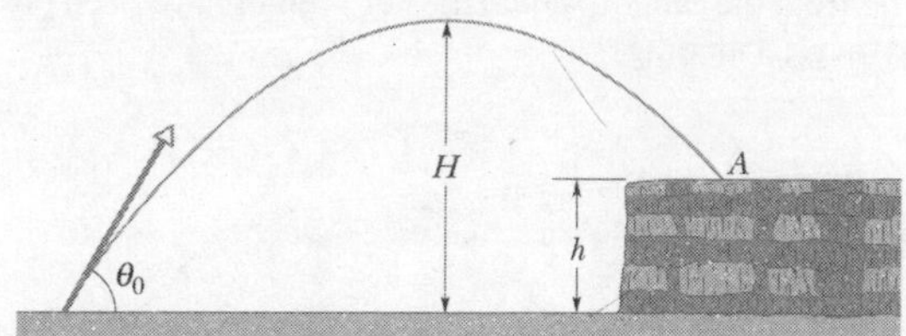

FIG. 4-45 Problem 11.

12 A certain airplane has a speed of 290.0 km/h and is diving at an angle of $\theta = 30.0°$ below the horizontal when the pilot releases a radar decoy (Fig. 4-46). The horizontal distance between the release point and the point where the decoy strikes the ground is $d = 700$ m. (a) How long is the decoy in the air? (b) How high was the release point?

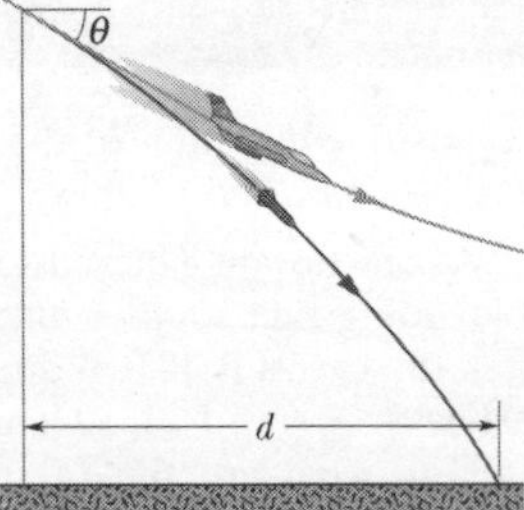

FIG. 4-46 Problem 12.

13 A plane, diving with constant speed at an angle of 53.0° with the vertical, releases a projectile at an altitude of 730 m. The projectile hits the ground 5.00 s after release. (a) What is the speed of the plane? (b) How far does the projectile travel horizontally during its flight? What are the (c) horizontal and (d) vertical components of its velocity just before striking the ground?

14 A soccer ball is kicked from the ground with an initial speed of 19.5 m/s at an upward angle of 45°. A player 55 m away in the direction of the kick starts running to meet the ball at that instant. What must be his average speed if he is to meet the ball just before it hits the ground?

15 In Fig. 4-47, a ball is thrown leftward from the left edge of the roof, at height h above the ground. The ball hits the ground 1.50 s later, at distance $d = 25.0$ m from the building and at angle $\theta = 60.0°$ with the horizontal. (a) Find h. (*Hint:* One way is to reverse the motion, as if on videotape.) What are the (b) magnitude and (c) angle relative to the horizontal of the velocity at which the ball is thrown? (d) Is the angle above or below the horizontal?

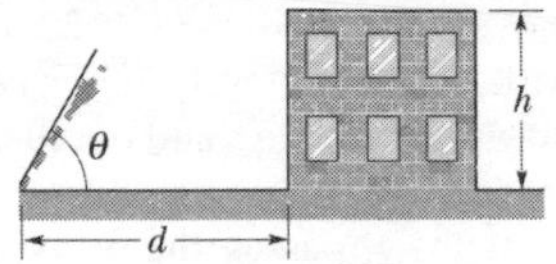

FIG. 4-47 Problem 15.

16 A golf ball is struck at ground level. The speed of the golf ball as a function of the time is shown in Fig. 4-48, where $t = 0$ at the instant the ball is struck. (a) How far does the golf ball travel horizontally before returning to ground level? (b) What is the maximum height above ground level attained by the ball?

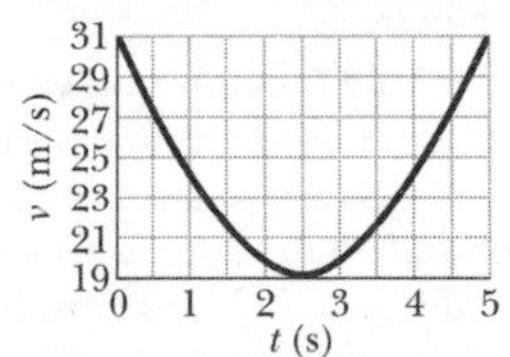

FIG. 4-48 Problem 16.

17 In 1939 or 1940, Emanuel Zacchini took his human-cannonball act to an extreme: After being shot from a cannon, he soared over three Ferris wheels and into a net (Fig. 4-49). (a) Treating him as a particle, calculate his clearance over the first wheel. (b) If he reached maximum height over the middle wheel, by how much did he clear it? (c) How far from the cannon should the net's center have been positioned (neglect air drag)?

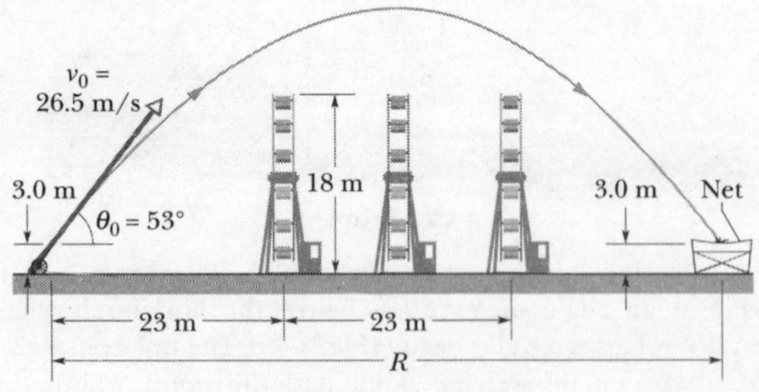

FIG. 4-49 Problem 17.

18 In Fig. 4-50, a ball is thrown up onto a roof, landing 4.00 s later at height $h = 20.0$ m above the release level. The ball's path just before landing is angled at $\theta = 60.0°$ with the roof. (a) Find the horizontal distance d it travels. What are the (b) magnitude and (c) angle (relative to the horizontal) of the ball's initial velocity?

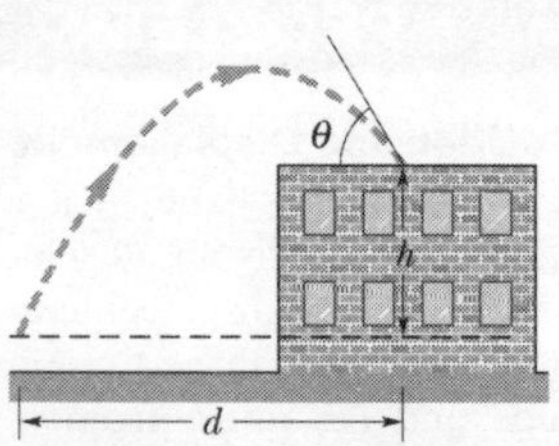

FIG. 4-50 Problem 18.

19 A ball is to be shot from level ground toward a wall at distance x (Fig. 4-51a). Figure 4-51b shows the y component v_y of the ball's velocity just as it would reach the wall, as a function of that distance x. What is the launch angle?

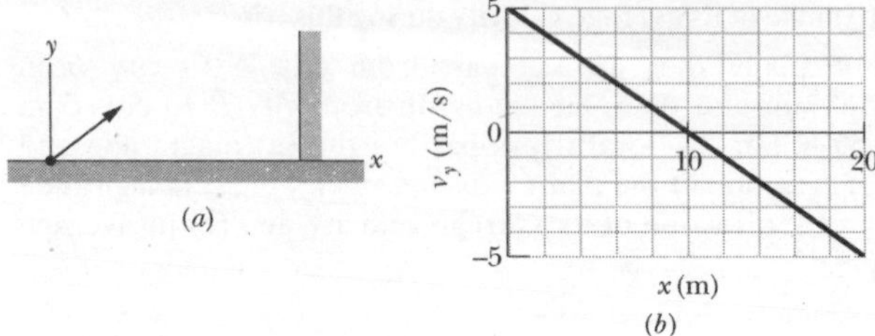

FIG. 4-51 Problem 19.

20 A ball is to be shot from level ground with a certain speed. Figure 4.52 shows the range R it will have verus the launch angle θ_0. The value of θ_0 determines the flight time; let t max time. What is the least speed the ball will have during its flight if θ_0 is chosen such that the flight time is $0.500t_{max}$?

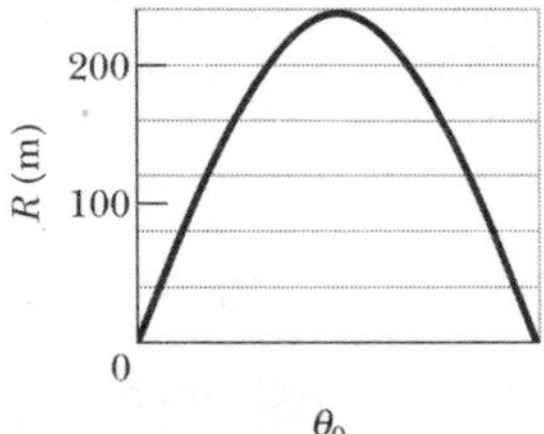

FIG. 4-52 Problem 20.

21 A ball rolls horizontally off the top of a stairway with a speed of 1.52 m/s. The steps are 20.3 cm high and 20.3 cm wide. Which step does the ball hit first?

22 Two seconds after being projected from ground level, a projectile is displaced 40 m horizontally and 53 m vertically above its launch point. What are the (a) horizontal and (b) vertical components of the initial velocity of the projectile? (c) At the instant the projectile achieves its maximum height above ground level, how far is it displaced horizontally from the launch point?

23 In Fig. 4-53, a baseball is hit at a height $h = 1.00$ m and then caught at the same height. It travels alongside a wall, moving up past the top of the wall 1.00 s after it is hit and then down past the top of the wall 4.00 s later, at distance $D = 50.0$ m farther along the wall. (a) What horizontal distance is traveled by the ball from hit to catch? What are the (b) magnitude and (c) angle (relative to the horizontal) of the ball's velocity just after being hit? (d) How high is the wall?

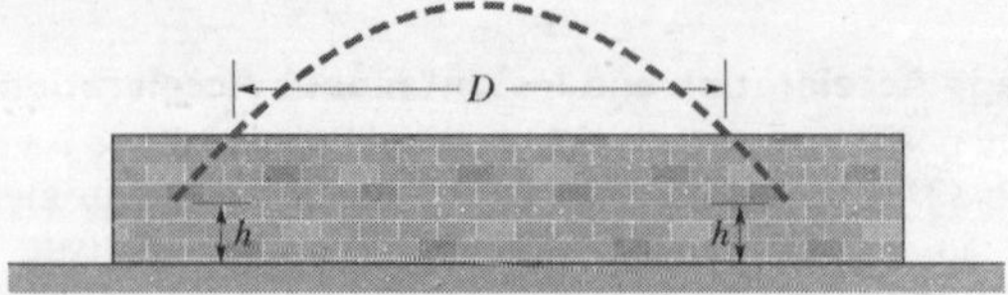

FIG. 4-53 Problem 23.

Relative Motion in One Dimension

24 A suspicious-looking man runs as fast as he can along a moving sidewalk from one end to the other, taking 2.50 s. Then security agents appear, and the man runs as fast as he can back along the sidewalk to his starting point, taking 10.0 s. What is the ratio of the man's running speed to the sidewalk's speed?

Relative Motion in Two Dimensions

25 Snow is falling vertically at a constant speed of 8.0 m/s. At what angle from the vertical do the snowflakes appear to be falling as viewed by the driver of a car traveling on a straight, level road with a speed of 50 km/h?

26 A 200-m-wide river flows due east at a uniform speed of 2.0 m/s. A boat with a speed of 8.0 m/s relative to the water leaves the south bank pointed in a direction 30° west of north. What are the (a) magnitude and (b) direction of the boat's velocity relative to the ground? (c) How long does the boat take to cross the river?

27 Two highways intersect as shown in Fig. 4-54. At the instant shown, a police car P is distance $d_P = 800$ m from the intersection and moving at speed $v_P = 80$ km/h. Motorist M is distance $d_M = 600$ m from the intersection and moving at speed $v_M = 60$ km/h. (a) In unit-vector notation, what is the velocity of the motorist with respect to the police car? (b) For the instant shown in Fig. 4-43, what is the angle between the velocity found in (a) and the line of sight between the two cars? (c) If the cars maintain their velocities, do the answers to (a) and (b) change as the cars move nearer the intersection?

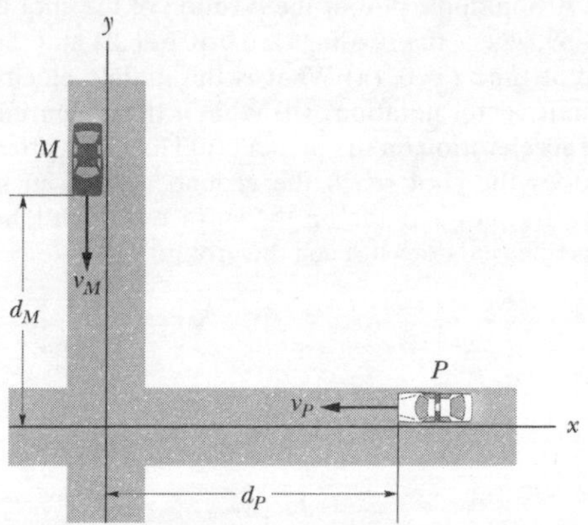

FIG. 4-54 Problem 27.

28 In the overhead view of Fig. 4-55, Jeeps P and B race along straight lines, across flat terrain, and past stationary border guard A. Relative to the guard, B travels at a constant speed of 20.0 m/s, at the angle $\theta_2 = 30.0°$. Relative to the guard, P has accelerated from rest at a constant rate of 0.400 m/s² at the angle $\theta_1 = 60.0°$. At a certain time during the acceleration, P has a speed of 40.0 m/s. At that time, what are the (a) magnitude and (b) direction of the velocity of P relative to B and the (c) magnitude and (d) direction of the acceleration of P relative to B?

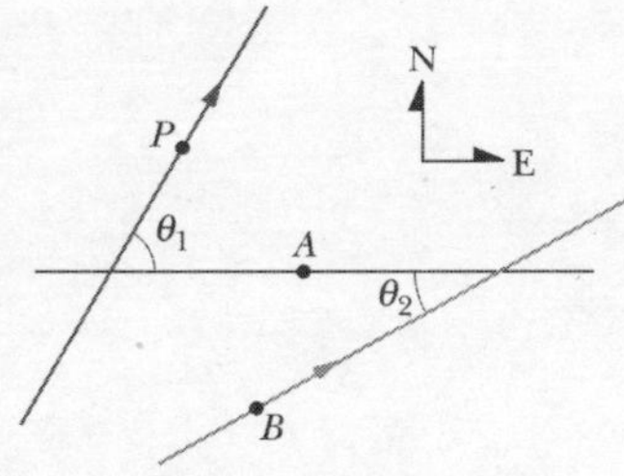

FIG. 4-55 Problem 28.

29 Ship A is located 4.0 km north and 2.5 km east of ship B. Ship A has a velocity of 22 km/h toward the south, and ship B has a velocity of 40 km/h in a direction 37° north of east. (a) What is the velocity of A relative to B in unit-vector notation with $\hat{i}$ toward the east? (b) Write an expression (in terms of $\hat{i}$ and $\hat{j}$) for the position of A relative to B as a function of t, where $t = 0$ when the ships are in the positions described above. (c) At what time is the separation between the ships least? (d) What is that least separation?

Additional Problems

30 You are kidnapped by chemistry majors (who are upset because you told them chemistry is not a real science). Although blindfolded, you can tell the speed of their car (by the whine of the engine), the time of travel (by mentally counting off seconds), and the direction of travel (by turns along the rectangular street system). From these clues, you know that you are taken along the following course: 50 km/h for 2.0 min, turn 90° to the right, 20 km/h for 4.0 min, turn 90° to the right, 20 km/h for 60 s, turn 90° to the left, 50 km/h for 60 s, turn 90° to the right, 20 km/h for 2.0 min, turn 90° to the left, 50 km/h for 30 s. At that point, (a) how far are you from your starting point, and (b) in what direction relative to your initial direction of travel are you?

31 In Fig. 4-56, a ball is shot directly upward from the ground with an initial speed of $v_0 = 7.00$ m/s. Simultaneously, a construction elevator cab begins to move upward from the ground with a constant speed of $v_c = 3.00$ m/s. What maximum height does the ball reach relative to (a) the ground and (b) the cab floor? At what rate does the speed of the ball change relative to (c) the ground and (d) the cab floor?

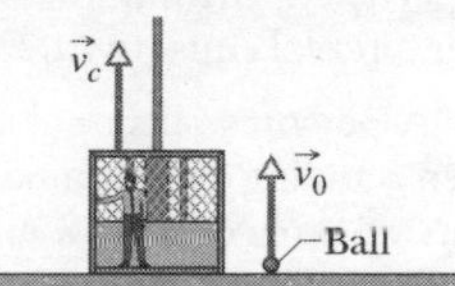

FIG. 4-56 Problem 31.

32 In Fig. 4-57a, a sled moves in the negative x direction at constant speed v_s while a ball of ice is shot from the sled with a velocity $\vec{v}_0 = v_{0x}\hat{i} + v_{0y}\hat{j}$ relative to the sled. When the ball lands, its horizontal displacement Δx_{bg} relative to the ground (from its launch position to its landing position) is measured. Figure 4-57b gives Δx_{bg} as a function of v_s. Assume the ball lands at approximately its launch height. What are the values of (a) v_{0x} and (b) v_{0y}? The ball's displacement Δx_{bs} relative to the sled can also be measured. Assume that the sled's velocity is not changed when the ball is shot. What is Δx_{bs} when v_s is (c) 5.0 m/s and (d) 15 m/s?

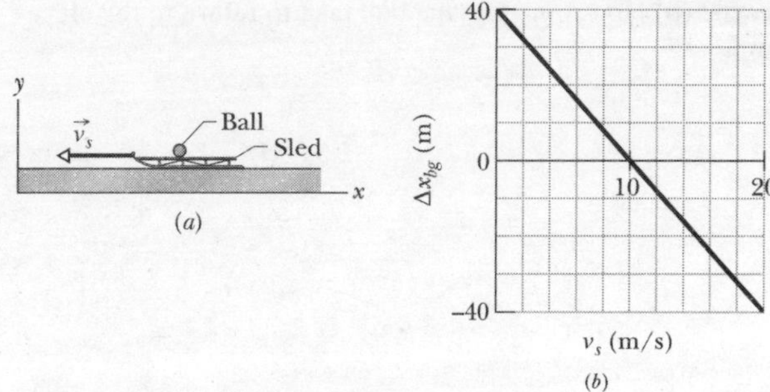

FIG. 4-57 Problem 32.

33 A woman who can row a boat at 6.4 km/h in still water faces a long, straight river with a width of 6.4 km and a current of 3.2 km/h. Let $\hat{i}$ point directly across the river and $\hat{j}$ point directly downstream. If she rows in a straight line to a point directly opposite her starting position, (a) at what angle to $\hat{i}$ must she point the boat and (b) how long will she take? (c) How long will she take if, instead, she rows 3.2 km *down* the river and then back to her starting point? (d) How long if she rows 3.2 km *up* the river and then back to her starting point? (e) At what angle to $\hat{i}$ should she point the boat if she wants to cross the river in the shortest possible time? (f) How long is that shortest time?

34 An iceboat sails across the surface of a frozen lake with constant acceleration produced by the wind. At a certain instant the boat's velocity is $(6.30\hat{i} - 8.42\hat{j})$ m/s. Three seconds later, because of a wind shift, the boat is instantaneously at rest. What is its average acceleration for this 3 s interval?

35 Figure 4-58 shows the straight path of a particle across an xy coordinate system as the particle is accelerated from rest during time interval Δt_1. The acceleration is constant. The xy coordinates for point A are (4.00 m, 6.00 m); those for point B are (12.0 m, 18.0 m). (a) What is the ratio a_y/a_x of the acceleration components? (b) What are the coordinates of the particle if the motion is continued for another interval equal to Δt_1?

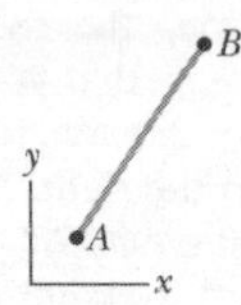

FIG. 4-58 Problem 35.

36 A person walks up a stalled 15-m-long escalator in 90 s. When standing on the same escalator, now moving, the person is carried up in 60 s. How much time would it take that person to walk up the moving escalator? Does the answer depend on the length of the escalator?

37 The range of a projectile depends not only on v_0 and θ_0 but also on the value g of the free-fall acceleration, which varies from place to place. In 1936, Jesse Owens established a world's running broad jump record of 8.09 m at the Olympic Games at Berlin (where $g = 9.8128 \text{ m/s}^2$). Assuming the same values of v_0 and θ_0, by how much would his record have differed if he had competed instead in 1956 at Melbourne (where $g = 9.7999 \text{ m/s}^2$)?

38 An elevator without a ceiling is ascending with a constant speed of 10 m/s. A boy on the elevator shoots a ball directly upward, from a height of 2.0 m above the elevator floor, just as the elevator floor is 28 m above the ground. The initial speed of the ball with respect to the elevator is 20 m/s. (a) What maximum height above the ground does the ball reach? (b) How long does the ball take to return to the elevator floor?

39 Suppose that a space probe can withstand the stresses of a $20g$ acceleration. (a) What is the minimum turning radius of such a craft moving at a speed of one-tenth the speed of light? (b) How long would it take to complete a 90° turn at this speed?

40 A wooden boxcar is moving along a straight railroad track at speed v_1. A sniper fires a bullet (initial speed v_2) at it from a high-powered rifle. The bullet passes through both lengthwise walls of the car, its entrance and exit holes being exactly opposite each other as viewed from within the car. From what direction, relative to the track, is the bullet fired? Assume that the bullet is not deflected upon entering the car, but that its speed decreases by 20%. Take $v_1 = 85$ km/h and $v_2 = 650$ m/s. (Why don't you need to know the width of the boxcar?)

41 The position $\vec{r}$ of a particle moving in the xy plane is given by $\vec{r} = 2t\hat{i} + 2\sin[(\pi/4 \text{ rad/s})t]\hat{j}$, where $\vec{r}$ is in meters and t is in seconds. (a) Calculate the x and y components of the particle's position at $t = 0, 1.0, 2.0, 3.0$, and 4.0 s and sketch the particle's path in the xy plane for the interval $0 \le t \le 4.0$ s. (b) Calculate the components of the particle's velocity at $t = 1.0$, 2.0, and 3.0 s. Show that the velocity is tangent to the path of the particle and in the direction the particle is moving at each time by drawing the velocity vectors on the plot of the particle's path in part (a). (c) Calculate the components of the particle's acceleration at $t = 1.0, 2.0$, and 3.0 s.

42 A track meet is held on a planet in a distant solar system. A shot-putter releases a shot at a point 2.0 m above ground level. A stroboscopic plot of the position of the shot is shown in Fig. 4-59, where the readings are 0.50 s apart and the shot is released at time $t = 0$. (a) What is the initial velocity of the shot in unit-vector notation? (b) What is the magnitude of the free-fall acceleration on the planet? (c) How long after it is released does the shot reach the ground? (d) If an identical throw of the shot is made on the surface of Earth, how long after it is released does it reach the ground?

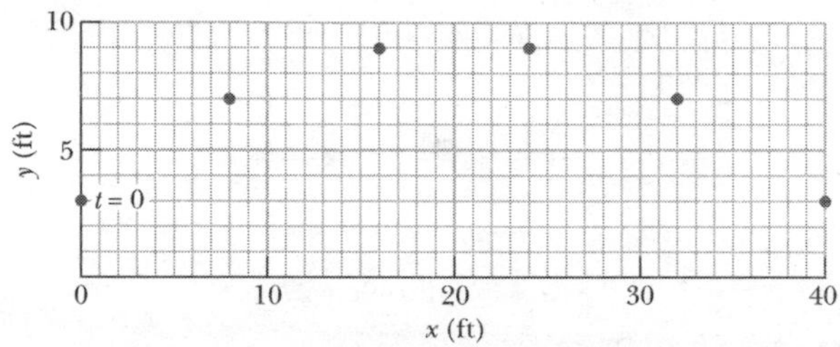

FIG. 4-59 Problem 42.

Newton's Laws of Motion

5

Blue Water Photo/Index Stock

Many roller-coaster enthusiasts prefer riding in the first car because they enjoy being the first to go over an "edge" and onto a downward slope. However, many other enthusiasts prefer the rear car—they claim that going over the edge is far more frightening there. The roller coaster is certainly moving faster when the last car is dragged over the edge by the rest of the roller coaster. But there seems to be some other, more subtle element that brings out the fear as that last car comes to the edge.

What is the subtle fear factor in riding the last car in a roller coaster?

The answer is in this chapter.

5-1 | Introduction

We have seen that part of physics is a study of motion, including accelerations, which are changes in velocities. Physics is also a study of what can *cause* an object to accelerate. That cause is a **force,** which is, loosely speaking, a push or pull on the object. The force is said to *act* on the object to change its velocity. For example, when a car accelerates, a force from the road acts on the tires to cause the car's acceleration. When a car slams into a telephone pole, a force on the car from the pole causes the car to stop. Science, engineering, legal, and medical journals are filled with articles about forces on objects, including people.

5-2 | Newtonian Mechanics

The relation between a force and the acceleration it causes was first understood by Isaac Newton (1642–1727) and is the subject of this chapter. The study of that relation, as Newton presented it, is called *Newtonian mechanics.* We shall focus on its three primary laws of motion.

Newtonian mechanics does not apply to all situations. If the speeds of the interacting bodies are very large—an appreciable fraction of the speed of light—we must replace Newtonian mechanics with Einstein's special theory of relativity, which holds at any speed, including those near the speed of light. If the interacting bodies are on the scale of atomic structure (for example, they might be electrons in an atom), we must replace Newtonian mechanics with quantum mechanics. Physicists now view Newtonian mechanics as a special case of these two more comprehensive theories. Still, it is a very important special case because it applies to the motion of objects ranging in size from the very small (almost on the scale of atomic structure) to astronomical (galaxies and clusters of galaxies).

5-3 | Newton's First Law

Before Newton formulated his mechanics, it was thought that some influence, a "force," was needed to keep a body moving at constant velocity. Similarly, a body was thought to be in its "natural state" when it was at rest. For a body to move with constant velocity, it seemingly had to be propelled in some way, by a push or a pull. Otherwise, it would "naturally" stop moving.

These ideas were reasonable. If you send a puck sliding across a wooden floor, it does indeed slow and then stop. If you want to make it move across the floor with constant velocity, you have to continuously pull or push it.

Send a puck sliding over the ice of a skating rink, however, and it goes a lot farther. You can imagine longer and more slippery surfaces, over which the puck would slide farther and farther. In the limit you can think of a long, extremely slippery surface (said to be a **frictionless surface**), over which the puck would hardly slow. (We can in fact come close to this situation by sending a puck sliding over a horizontal air table, across which it moves on a film of air.)

From these observations, we can conclude that a body will keep moving with constant velocity if no force acts on it. That leads us to the first of Newton's three laws of motion:

> **Newton's First Law:** If no force acts on a body, the body's velocity cannot change; that is, the body cannot accelerate.

In other words, if the body is at rest, it stays at rest. If it is moving, it continues to move with the same velocity (same magnitude *and* same direction).

5-4 | Force

We now wish to define the unit of force. We know that a force can cause the acceleration of a body. Thus, we shall define the unit of force in terms of the acceleration that a force gives to a standard reference body, which we take to be the standard kilogram of Fig. 1-3. This body has been assigned, exactly and by definition, a mass of 1 kg.

We put the standard body on a horizontal frictionless table and pull the body to the right (Fig. 5-1) so that, by trial and error, it eventually experiences a measured acceleration of 1 m/s^2. We then declare, as a matter of definition, that the force we are exerting on the standard body has a magnitude of 1 newton (abbreviated N).

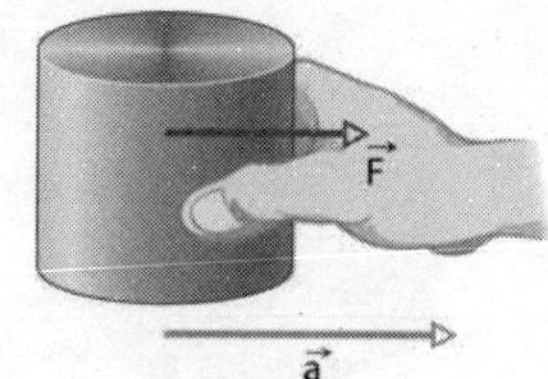

FIG. 5-1 A force $\vec{F}$ on the standard kilogram gives that body an acceleration $\vec{a}$.

We can exert a 2 N force on our standard body by pulling it so that its measured acceleration is 2 m/s^2, and so on. Thus in general, if our standard body of 1 kg mass has an acceleration of magnitude a, we know that a force F must be acting on it and that the magnitude of the force (in newtons) is equal to the magnitude of the acceleration (in meters per second per second).

Thus, a force is measured by the acceleration it produces. However, acceleration is a vector quantity, with both magnitude and direction. Is force also a vector quantity? We can easily assign a direction to a force (just assign the direction of the acceleration), but that is not sufficient. We must prove by experiment that forces are vector quantities. Actually, that has been done: forces are indeed vector quantities; they have magnitudes and directions, and they combine according to the vector rules of Chapter 2.

This means that when two or more forces act on a body, we can find their **net force,** or **resultant force,** by adding the individual forces vectorially. A single force that has the magnitude and direction of the net force has the same effect on the body as all the individual forces together. This fact is called the **principle of superposition for forces.** The world would be quite strange if, for example, you and a friend were to pull on the standard body in the same direction, each with a force of 1 N, and yet somehow the net pull was 14 N.

In this book, forces are most often represented with a vector symbol such as $\vec{F}$, and a net force is represented with the vector symbol $\vec{F}_{net}$. As with other vectors, a force or a net force can have components along coordinate axes. When forces act only along a single axis, they are single-component forces. Then we can drop the overhead arrows on the force symbols and just use signs to indicate the directions of the forces along that axis.

Instead of the wording used in Section 5-3, the more proper statement of Newton's first law is in terms of a *net* force:

> **Newton's First Law:** If no *net* force acts on a body ($\vec{F}_{net} = 0$), the body's velocity cannot change; that is, the body cannot accelerate.

There may be multiple forces acting on a body, but if their net force is zero, the body cannot accelerate.

Inertial Reference Frames

Newton's first law is not true in all reference frames, but we can always find reference frames in which it (as well as the rest of Newtonian mechanics) is true. Such frames are called **inertial reference frames,** or simply **inertial frames.**

> An inertial reference frame is one in which Newton's laws hold.

For example, we can assume that the ground is an inertial frame provided we can neglect Earth's astronomical motions (such as its rotation).

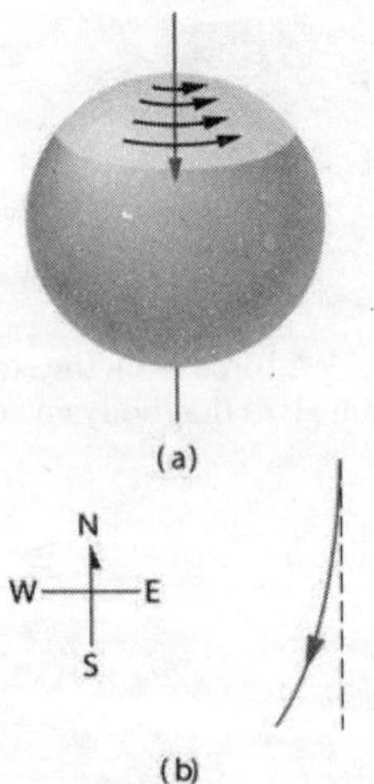

FIG. 5-2 (*a*) The path of a puck sliding from the north pole as seen from a stationary point in space. Earth rotates to the east. (*b*) The path of the puck as seen from the ground.

That assumption works well if, say, a puck is sent sliding along a *short* strip of frictionless ice—we would find that the puck's motion obeys Newton's laws. However, suppose the puck is sent sliding along a *long* ice strip extending from the north pole (Fig. 5-2*a*). If we view the puck from a stationary frame in space, the puck moves south along a simple straight line because Earth's rotation around the north pole merely slides the ice beneath the puck. However, if we view the puck from a point on the ground so that we rotate with Earth, the puck's path is not a simple straight line. Because the eastward speed of the ground beneath the puck is greater the farther south the puck slides, from our ground-based view the puck appears to be deflected westward (Fig. 5-2*b*). However, this apparent deflection is caused not by a force as required by Newton's laws but by the fact that we see the puck from a rotating frame. In this situation, the ground is a **noninertial frame.**

In this book we usually assume that the ground is an inertial frame and that measured forces and accelerations are from this frame. If measurements are made in, say, an elevator that is accelerating relative to the ground, then the measurements are being made in a noninertial frame and the results can be surprising.

5-5 | Mass

Everyday experience tells us that a given force produces different magnitudes of acceleration for different bodies. Put a baseball and a bowling ball on the floor and give both the same sharp kick. Even if you don't actually do this, you know the result: The baseball receives a noticeably larger acceleration than the bowling ball. The two accelerations differ because the mass of the baseball differs from the mass of the bowling ball—but what, exactly, is mass?

We can explain how to measure mass by imagining a series of experiments in an inertial frame. In the first experiment we exert a force on a standard body, whose mass m_0 is defined to be 1.0 kg. Suppose that the standard body accelerates at 1.0 m/s². We can then say the force on that body is 1.0 N.

We next apply that same force (we would need some way of being certain it is the same force) to a second body, body X, whose mass is not known. Suppose we find that this body X accelerates at 0.25 m/s². We know that a *less massive* baseball receives a *greater acceleration* than a more massive bowling ball when the same force (kick) is applied to both. Let us then make the following conjecture: The ratio of the masses of two bodies is equal to the inverse of the ratio of their accelerations when the same force is applied to both. For body X and the standard body, this tells us that

$$\frac{m_X}{m_0} = \frac{a_0}{a_X}.$$

Solving for m_X yields

$$m_X = m_0 \frac{a_0}{a_X} = (1.0 \text{ kg}) \frac{1.0 \text{ m/s}^2}{0.25 \text{ m/s}^2} = 4.0 \text{ kg}.$$

Our conjecture will be useful, of course, only if it continues to hold when we change the applied force to other values. For example, if we apply an 8.0 N force to the standard body, we obtain an acceleration of 8.0 m/s². When the 8.0 N force is applied to body X, we obtain an acceleration of 2.0 m/s². Our conjecture then gives us

$$m_X = m_0 \frac{a_0}{a_X} = (1.0 \text{ kg}) \frac{8.0 \text{ m/s}^2}{2.0 \text{ m/s}^2} = 4.0 \text{ kg},$$

consistent with our first experiment. Many experiments yielding similar results indicate that our conjecture provides a consistent and reliable means of assigning a mass to any given body.

Our measurement experiments indicate that mass is an *intrinsic* characteristic of a body—that is, a characteristic that automatically comes with the existence of the body. They also indicate that mass is a scalar quantity. However, the nagging question remains: What, exactly, is mass?

Since the word *mass* is used in everyday English, we should have some intuitive understanding of it, maybe something that we can physically sense. Is it a body's size, weight, or density? The answer is no, although those characteristics are sometimes confused with mass. We can say only that *the mass of a body is the characteristic that relates a force on the body to the resulting acceleration.* Mass has no more familiar definition; you can have a physical sensation of mass only when you try to accelerate a body, as in the kicking of a baseball or a bowling ball.

5-6 | Newton's Second Law

All the definitions, experiments, and observations we have discussed so far can be summarized in one neat statement:

Newton's Second Law: The *net force* on a body is equal to the product of the body's mass and its acceleration, where acceleration is being observed from inertial reference frame.

In equation form,

$$\vec{F}_{net} = m\vec{a} \quad \text{(Newton's second law)} \tag{5-1}$$

This equation is simple, but we must use it cautiously. First, we must be certain about which body we are applying it to. Then $\vec{F}_{net}$ must be the vector sum of *all* the forces that act on *that* body. Only forces that act on *that* body are to be included in the vector sum, not forces acting on other bodies that might be involved in the given situation. For example, if you are in a Mumbai local train, the net force on *you* is the vector sum of all the pushes and pulls on *your* body. It does not include any push or pull on another passenger from you.

Like other vector equations, Eq. 5-1 is equivalent to three component equations, one for each axis of an *xyz* coordinate system:

$$F_{net,x} = ma_x, \quad F_{net,y} = ma_y, \quad \text{and} \quad F_{net,z} = ma_z \tag{5-2}$$

Each of these equations relates the net force component along an axis to the acceleration along that same axis. For example, the first equation tells us that the sum of all the force components along the x axis causes the x component a_x of the body's acceleration, but causes no acceleration in the y and z directions. Turned around, the acceleration component a_x is caused only by the sum of the force components along the x axis. In general,

The acceleration component along a given axis is caused *only by* the sum of the force components along that *same* axis, and not by force components along any other axis.

TABLE 5-1

Units in Newton's Second Law (Eqs. 5-1 and 5-2)

System	Force	Mass	Acceleration
SI	newton (N)	kilogram (kg)	m/s^2
CGS[a]	dyne	gram (g)	cm/s^2

[a]1 dyne = $1\ g \cdot cm/s^2$.

Equation 5-1 tells us that if the net force on a body is zero, the body's acceleration $\vec{a} = 0$. If the body is at rest, it stays at rest; if it is moving, it continues to move at constant velocity. In such cases, any forces on the body *balance* one another, and both the forces and the body are said to be in *equilibrium.* Commonly, the forces are also said to *cancel* one another, but the term "cancel" is tricky. It does *not* mean that the forces cease to exist (canceling forces is not like canceling dinner reservations). The forces still act on the body.

For SI units, Eq. 5-1 tells us that

$$1\ \text{N} = (1\ \text{kg})(1\ \text{m/s}^2) = 1\ \text{kg}\cdot\text{m/s}^2 \tag{5-3}$$

Some force units in other systems of units are given in Table 5-1 and Appendix D.

Free-Body Diagram

To solve problems with Newton's second law, we often draw a **free-body diagram** in which the only body shown is the one for which we are summing forces. A sketch of the body itself is preferred by some teachers but, to save space in these chapters, we shall usually represent the body with a dot. Also, each force on the body is drawn as a vector arrow with its tail on the body. A coordinate system is usually included, and the acceleration of the body is sometimes shown with a vector arrow (labeled as an acceleration). Remember not to show "*ma*"as one of the net forces in a free-body diagram, as it is not force acting on an object; *m* is the effect of net forces acting on an object.

A **system** consists of one or more bodies, and any force on the bodies inside the system from bodies outside the system is called an **external force.** If the bodies making up a system are rigidly connected to one another, we can treat the system as one composite body, and the net force $\vec{F}_{\text{net}}$ on it is the vector sum of all external forces. (We do not include **internal forces**—that is, forces between two bodies inside the system.) For example, a connected railroad engine and car form a system. If, say, a tow line pulls on the front of the engine, the force due to the tow line acts on the whole engine–car system. Just as for a single body, we can relate the net external force on a system to its acceleration with Newton's second law, $\vec{F}_{\text{net}} = m\vec{a}$, where m is the total mass of the system.

CHECKPOINT 1 The figure here shows two horizontal forces acting on a block on a frictionless floor. If a third horizontal force $\vec{F}_3$ also acts on the block, what are the magnitude and direction of $\vec{F}_3$ when the block is (a) stationary and (b) moving to the left with a constant speed of 5 m/s?

3 N 5 N

Sample Problem 5-1

In the overhead view of Fig. 5-3*a*, a 2.0 kg cookie tin is accelerated at 3.0 m/s² in the direction shown by $\vec{a}$, over a frictionless horizontal surface. The acceleration is caused by three horizontal forces, only two of which are shown: $\vec{F}_1$ of magnitude 10 N and $\vec{F}_2$ of magnitude 20 N. What is the third force $\vec{F}_3$ in unit-vector notation and in magnitude-angle notation?

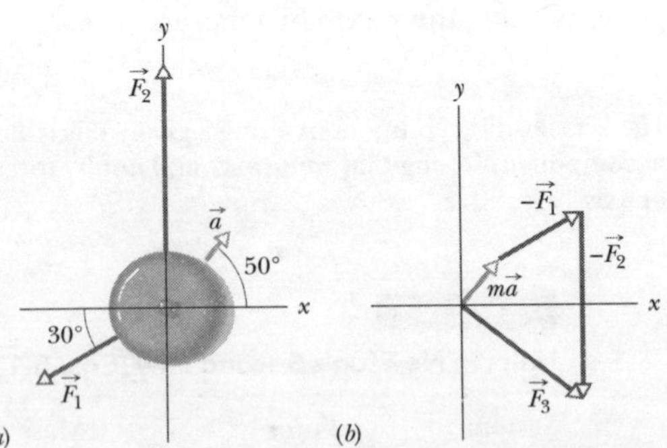

FIG. 5-3 (*a*) An overhead view of two of three horizontal forces that act on a cookie tin, resulting in acceleration $\vec{a}$. $\vec{F}_3$ is not shown. (*b*) An arrangement of vectors $m\vec{a}$, $-\vec{F}_1$, and $-\vec{F}_2$ to find force $\vec{F}_3$.

Conceptualize/Classify: The net force $\vec{F}_{\text{net}}$ on the tin is the sum of the three forces and is related to the acceleration $\vec{a}$ via Newton's second law ($\vec{F}_{\text{net}} = m\vec{a}$). Thus,

$$\vec{F}_1 + \vec{F}_2 + \vec{F}_3 = m\vec{a} \tag{5-4}$$

which gives us

$$\vec{F}_3 = m\vec{a} - \vec{F}_1 - \vec{F}_2 \qquad (5\text{-}5)$$

Compute: Because this is a two-dimensional problem, we *cannot* find $\vec{F}_3$ merely by substituting the magnitudes for the vector quantities on the right side of Eq. 5-5. Instead, we must vectorially add $m\vec{a}$, $-\vec{F}_1$ (the reverse of $\vec{F}_1$), and $-\vec{F}_2$ (the reverse of $\vec{F}_2$), as shown in Fig. 5-3*b*. We know both magnitude and angle for all three vectors. However, here we shall evaluate the right side of Eq. 5-5 in terms of components, first along the x axis and then along the y axis.

***x* components:** Along the x axis we have

$$\begin{aligned} F_{3,x} &= ma_x - F_{1,x} - F_{2,x} \\ &= m(a\cos 50°) - F_1\cos(-150°) - F_2\cos 90° \end{aligned}$$

Then, substituting known data, we find

$$\begin{aligned} F_{3,x} &= (2.0\text{ kg})(3.0\text{ m/s}^2)\cos 50° - (10\text{ N})\cos(-150°) \\ &\quad - (20\text{ N})\cos 90° \\ &= 12.5\text{ N} \end{aligned}$$

***y* components:** Similarly, along the y axis we find

$$\begin{aligned} F_{3,y} &= ma_y - F_{1,y} - F_{2,y} \\ &= m(a\sin 50°) - F_1\sin(-150°) - F_2\sin 90° \\ &= (2.0\text{ kg})(3.0\text{ m/s}^2)\sin 50° - (10\text{ N})\sin(-150°) \\ &\quad - (20\text{ N})\sin 90° \\ &= -10.4\text{ N} \end{aligned}$$

Vector: In unit-vector notation, we can write

$$\begin{aligned} \vec{F}_3 &= F_{3,x}\hat{i} + F_{3,y}\hat{j} = (12.5\text{ N})\hat{i} - (10.4\text{ N})\hat{j} \\ &\approx (13\text{ N})\hat{i} - (10\text{ N})\hat{j} \qquad \text{(Answer)} \end{aligned}$$

We can also use Eq. 3-6 to obtain the magnitude and the angle (from the positive direction of the x axis) as

$$F_3 = \sqrt{F_{3,x}^2 + F_{3,y}^2} = 16\text{ N}$$

and

$$\theta = \tan^{-1}\frac{F_{3,y}}{F_{3,x}} = -40° \qquad \text{(Answer)}$$

5-7 | Newton's Third Law

Two bodies are said to *interact* when they push or pull on each other—that is, when a force acts on each body due to the other body. For example, suppose you position a book B so it leans against a crate C (Fig. 5-4*a*). Then the book and crate interact: There is a horizontal force $\vec{F}_{BC}$ on the book from the crate (or due to the crate) and a horizontal force $\vec{F}_{CB}$ on the crate from the book (or due to the book). This pair of forces is shown in Fig. 5-4*b*. Newton's third law states that

Newton's Third Law: When two bodies interact, the forces on the bodies from each other are always equal in magnitude and opposite in direction.

For the book and crate, we can write this law as the scalar relation

$$F_{BC} = F_{CB} \qquad \text{(equal magnitudes)}$$

or as the vector relation

$$\vec{F}_{BC} = -\vec{F}_{CB} \qquad \text{(equal magnitudes and opposite directions)}$$

where the minus sign means that these two forces are in opposite directions. We can call the forces between two interacting bodies a **third-law force pair.** These third law pair forces are always of same nature. When any two bodies interact in any situation, a third-law force pair is present. The book and crate in Fig. 5-11*a* are stationary, but the third law would still hold if they were moving and even if they were accelerating.

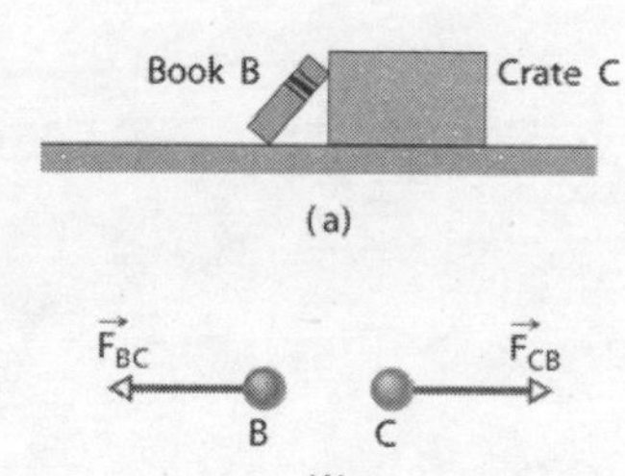

FIG. 5-4 (*a*) Book B leans against crate C. (*b*) Forces $\vec{F}_{BC}$ (the force on the book from the crate) and $\vec{F}_{CB}$ (the force on the crate from the book) have the same magnitude and are opposite in direction.

5-8 | Some Particular Forces

Now we will learn about the nature and behaviour of major forces that we will encounter in mechanics.

The Gravitational Force

A **gravitational force** $\vec{F}_g$ on a body is a certain type of pull that is directed toward a second body. In these early chapters, we do not discuss the nature of this force and usually consider situations in which the second body is Earth. Thus, when we speak of *the* gravitational force $\vec{F}_g$ on a body, we usually mean a force that pulls on it directly toward the center of Earth—that is, directly down toward the ground. We shall assume that the ground is an inertial frame.

Suppose a body of mass m is in free fall with the free-fall acceleration of magnitude g. Then, if we neglect the effects of the air, the only force acting on the body is the gravitational force $\vec{F}_g$. We can relate this downward force and downward acceleration with Newton's second law ($\vec{F} = m\vec{a}$). We place a vertical y axis along the body's path, with the positive direction upward. For this axis, Newton's second law can be written in the form $F_{\text{net},y} = ma_y$, which, in our situation, becomes

$$-F_g = m(-g)$$

or

$$F_g = mg \tag{5-6}$$

In words, the magnitude of the gravitational force is equal to the product mg.

This same gravitational force, with the same magnitude, still acts on the body even when the body is not in free fall but is, say, at rest on a pool table or moving across the table. (For the gravitational force to disappear, Earth would have to disappear.)

We can write Newton's second law for the gravitational force in these vector forms:

$$\vec{F}_g = -F_g\hat{j} = -mg\hat{j} = m\vec{g} \tag{5-7}$$

where $\hat{j}$ is the unit vector that points upward along a y axis, directly away from the ground, and $\vec{g}$ is the free-fall acceleration (written as a vector), directed downward.

The weight of an object arises because of gravitational pull of earth. Using W for the magnitude of the weight, m for the mass of the object, and M_E for the mass of the earth, it follows from Newton's law of gravitation.

$$W = G\,\frac{M_E m}{r^2} \tag{5-8}$$

Equation (5-8) emphasize that an object has weight whether or not it is resting on the earth's surface, because the gravitational force is acting even when the distance r is not equal to the radius R_E of the earth. However, the gravitational force becomes weaker as r increases

Mass and weight are not the same quantity. Mass measures inertia as already discussed in Section 5.3. As such, mass is an intrinsic property of matter and does not change as an object moves from one location to another. On the other hand weight is the gravitational force acting on the object and can vary, depending on how far the object is above the earth's surface.

The relation between weight W and mass m can be written in one of two ways as shown in Fig. 5-5.

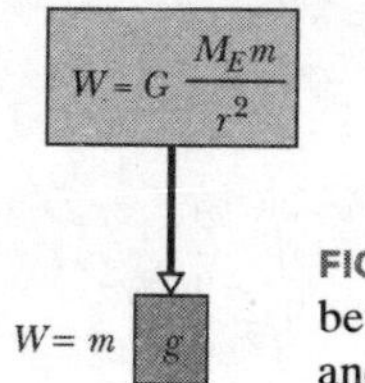

FIG. 5-5 Relation between weight W and mass M.

Equation 5-10 is Newton's law of universal gravitation, while Eq. 5-8 is Newton's second law. These expressions make the difference between mass and weight clear. The weight of an object whose mass is m depends on the values for the universal graviation constant G, the mass M_E of the earth, and the distance r. These three parameters together determine the acceleration g due to gravity. The specific value of $g = 9.80\ \text{m/s}^2$ applies only when r equals the radius R_E of the earth.

When we write force due to earth's attraction on a body as mg, the g here does not mean acceleration due to gravity. Symbol 'g' is used to represent GM/R_E^2.

The **weight** W of a body is the magnitude of the net force required to prevent the body from falling freely, as measured by someone on the ground. For example, to keep a ball at rest in your hand while you stand on the ground, you must provide an upward force to balance the gravitational force on the ball from Earth. Suppose the magnitude of the gravitational force is 2.0 N. Then the magnitude of your upward force must be 2.0 N, and thus the weight W of the ball is 2.0 N. We also say that the ball *weighs* 2.0 N and speak about the ball *weighing* 2.0 N.

A ball with a weight of 3.0 N would require a greater force from you—namely, a 3.0 N force—to keep it at rest. The reason is that the gravitational force you must balance has a greater magnitude—namely, 3.0 N. We say that this second ball is *heavier* than the first ball.

Now let us generalize the situation. Consider a body that has an acceleration zero relative to the ground, which we again assume to be an inertial frame. Two forces act on the body: a downward gravitational force $\vec{F}_g$ and a balancing upward force of magnitude W. We can write Newton's second law for a vertical y axis, with the positive direction upward, as

$$F_{\text{net},y} = ma_y$$

In our situation, this becomes

$$W - F_g = m(0) \tag{5-9}$$

or

$$W = F_g \quad \text{(weight, with ground as inertial frame)} \tag{5-10}$$

The weight W of a body is equal to the magnitude F_g of the gravitational force on the body.

This equation tells us (assuming the ground is an inertial frame) that substituting mg for F_g from Eq. 5-6, we find

$$W = mg \quad \text{(weight)} \tag{5-11}$$

which relates a body's weight to its mass.

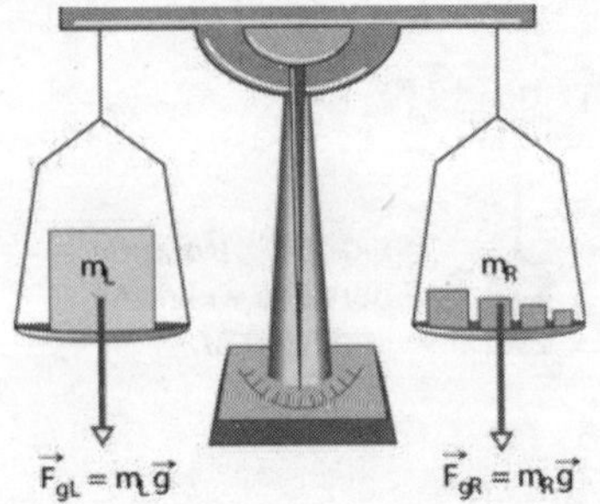

FIG. 5-6 An equal-arm balance. When the device is in balance, the gravitational force $\vec{F}_{gL}$ on the body being weighed (on the left pan) and the total gravitational force $\vec{F}_{gR}$ on the reference bodies (on the right pan) are equal. Thus, the mass m_L of the body being weighed is equal to the total mass m_R of the reference bodies.

To *weigh* a body means to measure its weight. One way to do this is to place the body on one of the pans of an equal-arm balance (Fig. 5-6) and then place reference bodies (whose masses are known) on the other pan until we strike a balance (so that the gravitational forces on the two sides match). The masses on the pans then match, and we know the mass of the body. If we know the value of g for the location of the balance, we can also find the weight of the body with Eq. 5-11.

We can also weigh a body with a spring scale (Fig. 5-7). The body stretches a spring, moving a pointer along a scale that has been calibrated and marked in either mass or weight units. (Most bathroom scales in the United States work this way and are marked in the force unit pounds.) If the scale is marked in mass units, it is accurate only where the value of g is the same as where the scale was calibrated.

The weight of a body must be measured when the body is not accelerating vertically relative to the ground. For example, you can measure your weight on a scale in your bathroom or on a fast train. However, if you repeat the measurement with the scale in an accelerating elevator, the reading differs from your weight because of the acceleration. Such a measurement is called an *apparent weight.*

Caution: Weight is the magnitude of a force and is related to mass by Eq. 5-11. If you move a body to a point where the value of g is different, the body's mass (an intrinsic property) is not different but the weight is. For example, the weight of a bowling ball having a mass of 7.2 kg is 71 N on Earth but only 12 N on the Moon. The mass is the same on Earth and Moon, but the free-fall acceleration on the Moon is only 1.6 m/s^2.

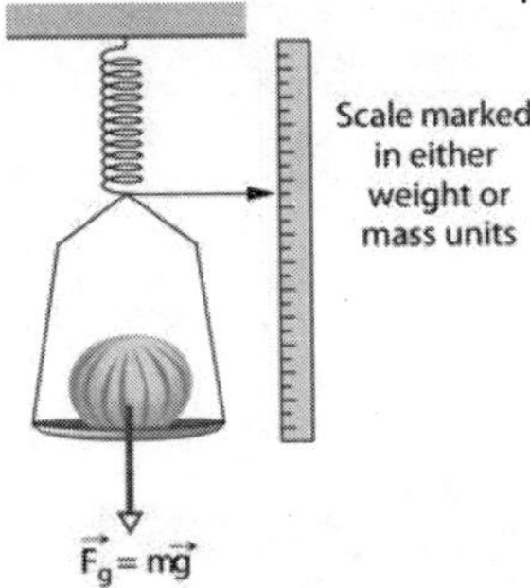

FIG. 5-7 A spring scale. The reading is proportional to the *weight* of the object on the pan, and the scale gives that weight if marked in weight units. If, instead, it is marked in mass units, the reading is the object's weight only if the value of g at the location where the scale is being used is the same as the value of g at the location where the scale was calibrated.

Normal Contact Force

If you stand on a mattress, Earth pulls you downward, but you remain stationary. The reason is that the mattress, because it deforms downward due to you, pushes up on you. Similarly, if you stand on a floor, it deforms (it is compressed, bent, or buckled ever so slightly) and pushes up on you. Even a seemingly rigid concrete floor does this (if it is not sitting directly on the ground, enough people on the floor could break it).

The push on you from the mattress or floor is a **normal force** $\vec{F}_N$. The name comes from the mathematical term *normal,* meaning perpendicular: The force on you from, say, the floor is perpendicular to the floor.

When a body presses against a surface, the surface (even a seemingly rigid one) deforms and pushes on the body with a normal force $\vec{F}_N$ that is perpendicular to the surface.

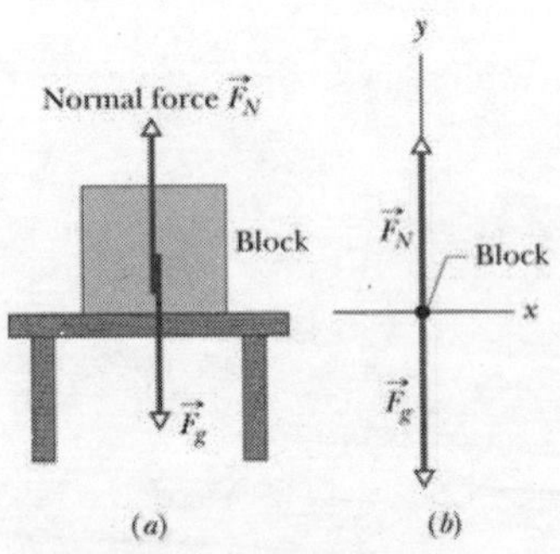

FIG. 5-8 (*a*) A block resting on a table experiences a normal force $\vec{F}_N$ perpendicular to the tabletop. (*b*) The free-body diagram for the block.

Figure 5-8*a* shows an example. A block of mass m presses down on a table, deforming it somewhat because of the gravitational force $\vec{F}_g$ on the block. The table pushes up on the block with normal force $\vec{F}_N$. The free-body diagram for the block is given in Fig. 5-8*b*. Forces $\vec{F}_g$ and $\vec{F}_N$ are the only two forces on the block and they are both vertical. Thus, for the block we can write Newton's second law for a positive-upward y axis ($F_{net,y} = ma_y$) as

$$F_N - F_g = ma_y$$

From Eq. 5-8, we substitute mg for F_g, finding

$$F_N - mg = ma_y$$

Then the magnitude of the normal force is

$$F_N = mg + ma_y = m(g + a_y) \tag{5-12}$$

for any vertical acceleration a_y of the table and block (they might be in an accelerating elevator). If the table and block are not accelerating relative to the ground, then $a_y = 0$ and Eq. 5-12 yields

$$F_N = mg \qquad (5\text{-}13)$$

According to Newton's third law, there is also a normal contact force exerted on the table by the block; this normal contact force acts downward and is of equal magnitude. In everyday language, we might say that the table "feels the block's weight". That is not a correct statement in the language of physics. The table cannot experience the gravitational pull on the block by earth; the table can only experience forces exerted on the table. What the table does experience is the normal contact force – a contact force – exerted on the table by the block.

If the table's surface is horizontal, the normal force on the block will be vertical and equal in magnitude to the block's weight. If the surface of the table is not horizontal, the normal force is not vertical and is not equal in magnitude to the weight of the block. Always remember that the normal force is perpendicular to the contact surfce (Fig. 5-9*b*). If there are other vertical forces acting on the block, then the normal force is not equal in magnitude to the block's weight (Fig. 5-9*c*). We can never assume anything about the magnitude of the normal contact force as it is self adjusting in nature.

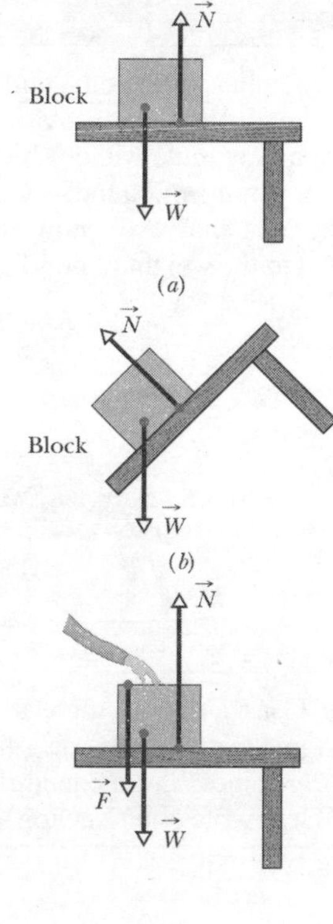

FIG. 5-9 Forces acting on a block kept on a table.

CHECKPOINT 2 In Fig. 5-8, is the magnitude of the normal force $\vec{F}_N$ greater than, less than, or equal to mg if the block and table are in an elevator moving upward (a) at constant speed and (b) at increasing speed?

PROBLEM-SOLVING TACTICS

Tactic 1: Normal Force Equation 5-13 for the normal force on a body holds only when $\vec{F}_N$ is directed upward and the body's vertical acceleration is zero; so we do *not* apply it for other orientations of $\vec{F}_N$ or when the vertical acceleration is not zero. Instead, we must derive a new expression for $\vec{F}_N$ from Newton's second law.

We are free to move $\vec{F}_N$ around in a figure as long as we maintain its orientation. For example, in Fig. 5-8*a* we can slide it downward so that its head is at the boundary between block and tabletop. However, $\vec{F}_N$ is least likely to be misinterpreted when its tail is either at that boundary or somewhere within the block (as shown). An even better technique is to draw a free-body diagram as in Fig. 5-8*b*, with the tail of directly on the dot or sketch representing the block.

Tactic 2: Dimensions and Vectors When you are dealing with forces, you cannot just add or subtract their magnitudes to find their net force unless they happen to be directed *along the same axis.* If they are not, you must use vector addition, either by means of a vector-capable calculator or by finding components along axes, one axis at a time, as is done in Sample Problem 5-1.

Tactic 3: Reading Force Problems Read the problem statement several times until you have a good mental picture of what the situation is, what data are given, and what is requested. If you know what the problem is about but don't know what to do next, put the problem aside and reread the text. If you are hazy about Newton's second law, reread that section. Study the sample problems. And remember that solving physics problems (like repairing cars and designing computer chips) takes training.

Tactic 4: Draw Two Types of Figures You may need two figures. One is a rough sketch of the actual situation. When you draw the forces, place the tail of each force vector either on the boundary of or within the body on which that force acts. The other figure is a free-body diagram: the forces on a *single* body are drawn, with the body represented by a dot or a sketch. Place the tail of each force vector on the dot or sketch.

Tactic 5: What Is Your System? If you are using Newton's second law, you must know what body or system you are applying it to. In Sample Problem 5-1, it is the cookie tin.

Tactic 6: Choose Your Axes Wisely Often, we can save a lot of work by choosing one of our coordinate axes to coincide with one of the forces.

Sample Problem 5-2 Build your skill

Mr. Shekh Chilli is riding on a mule, holding a heavy bundle on his head. When you advise him to keep bundle on mule he may say mule will not be able to hold combined weight of my body and bundle. Convince him using free-body diagrams that even now mule is experiencing a force equal to the weight of bundle and Shekh Chilli.

Solution: Considering all three as particles kept on each other and making free-body diagrams N_{BS} is not third law pair of mBg. Since B is in equilibrium we can write $m_B g - N_{BS} = 0$ We can write using Newton's second Law.

we get $N_{BS} = m_B g$

Since N_{BS} and N_{SB} are third law pair

$$N_{SB} = N_{BS} = m_B g$$

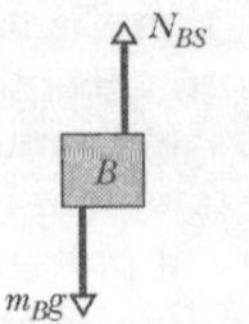

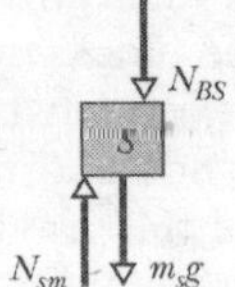

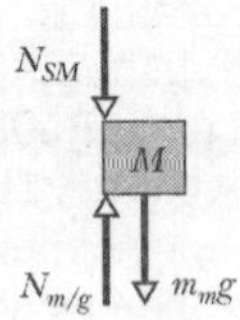

Similarly S is in equilibrium

so $N_{SB} + m_S g - N_{sm} = 0$

Solving we get $N_{sm} = (m_s + m_B)g$

Since N_{sm} and N_{ms} are third law pairs

$$N_{ms} = N_{sm} = (m_s + m_B)\,g$$

Thus mule is experiencing normal contact force (N_{mS}) by Shekh Chilli which is equal to the magnitude of the combined weight of Shekh Chilli and bundle.

CHECKPOINT 3 If the system in Fig. (*a*) is given an acceleration $a = 5\text{m/s}^2$, find the forces on the sphere of mass m, assuming no friction.

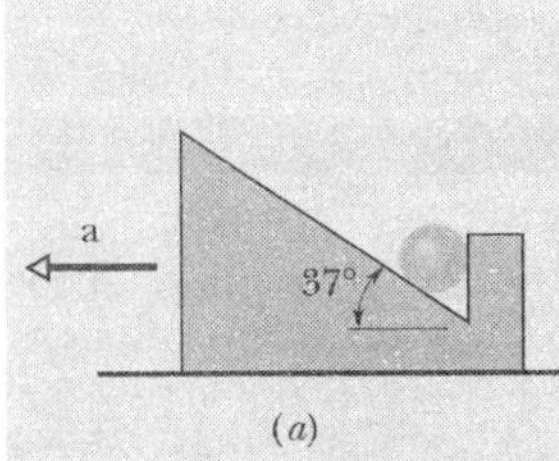

(*a*)

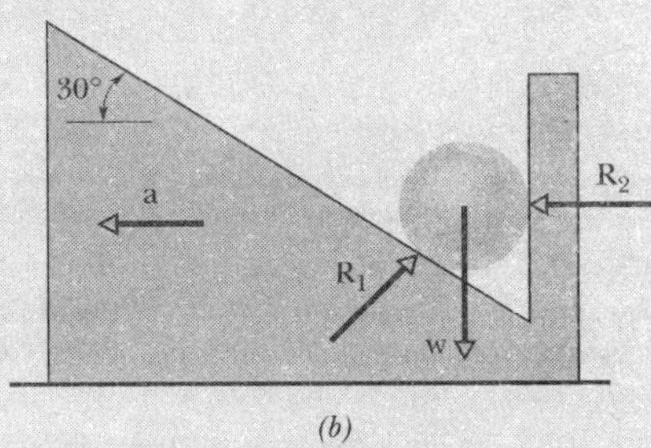

(*b*)

Solution: From the above figures $EF_{ver} = R_1 \cos 37° - w = ma_{ver}$

$EF_{hor} = R_2 - R_1 \sin 30° = ma$. Thus, the acting forces are

$$R_1 = \frac{mg}{\cos 37°} = 1.2mg$$

$$R_2 = R_1 \sin 37° + ma$$
$$= (1.2mg)(0.6) + ma$$
$$= 12.2\,mg\,?$$

and the weight, w.

Sample Problem 5-3 Build your skill

In Fig. 5-10*a*, a passenger of mass $m = 72.2$ kg stands on a platform scale in an elevator cab. We are concerned with the scale readings when the cab is stationary and when it is moving up or down.

(a) Find a general solution for the scale reading, whatever the vertical motion of the cab.

Conceptualize: The reading is equal to the magnitude of the normal force $\vec{F}_N$ on the passenger from the scale. The only other force acting on the passenger is the gravitational force $\vec{F}_g$, as shown in the free-body diagram of Fig. 5-10.

Classify: We can relate the forces on the passenger to his acceleration $\vec{a}$ by using Newton's second law

($\vec{F}_{\text{net}} = m\vec{a}$). However, recall that we can use this law only in an inertial frame. If the cab accelerates, then it is not an inertial frame. So we choose the ground to be our inertial frame and make any measure of the passenger's acceleration relative to it.

Compute: Please note that ma is not being shown in free-body diagrams **as *ma* is not the force, it is the effect of the net force acting on the person**. Only two actual forces act on the person in elevator — normal contact force by the scale's surface, and weight. Because the two forces on the passenger and his acceleration are all directed vertically, along the y axis in Fig. 5-10*b*, we can use Newton's second law written for y components

$$(F_{\text{net},y} = ma_y)$$

$$F_N - F_g = ma$$

or

$$F_N = F_g + ma \qquad (5\text{-}14)$$

This tells us that the scale reading, which is equal to F_N, depends on the vertical acceleration. Substituting mg for F_g gives us

$$F_N = m(g + a) \qquad \text{(Answer)} \qquad (5\text{-}15)$$

for any choice of acceleration a.

In Case Of: (1) What does the scale read if the cab is stationary or moving upward at a constant 0.50 m/s?

Solution: For any constant velocity (zero or otherwise), the acceleration a of the passenger is zero.

Substituting this and other known values into Eq. 5-28, we find

$$F_N = (72.2 \text{ kg})(9.8 \text{ m/s}^2 + 0) = 708 \text{ N} \qquad \text{(Answer)}$$

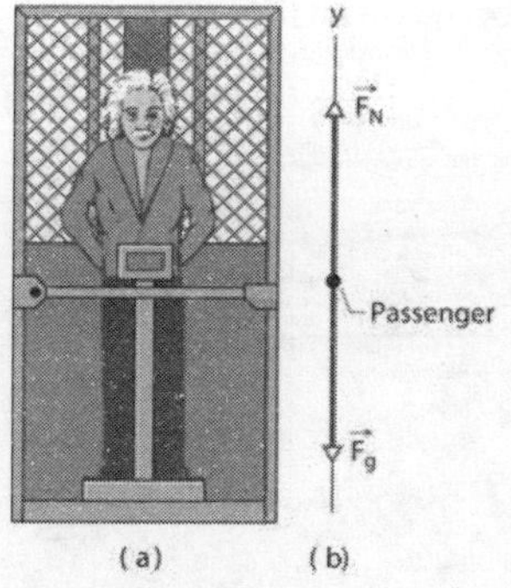

FIG. 5-10 (*a*) A passenger stands on a platform scale that indicates either his weight or his apparent weight. (*b*) The free-body diagram for the passenger, showing the normal force $\vec{F}_N$ on him from the scale and the gravitational force $\vec{F}_g$.

This is the weight of the passenger and is equal to the magnitude F_g of the gravitational force on him.

In Case Of: (2) What does the scale read if the cab accelerates upward at 3.20 m/s² and downward at 3.20 m/s²?

Solution: For $a = 3.20$ m/s², Eq. 5-28 gives

$$F_N = (72.2 \text{ kg})(9.8 \text{ m/s}^2 + 3.20 \text{ m/s}^2)$$
$$= 939 \text{ N} \qquad \text{(Answer)}$$

and for $a = -3.20$ m/s², it gives

$$F_N = (72.2 \text{ kg})(9.8 \text{ m/s}^2 - 3.20 \text{ m/s}^2)$$
$$= 477 \text{ N} \qquad \text{(Answer)}$$

Conclude: For an upward acceleration (either the cab's upward speed is increasing or its downward speed is decreasing), the scale reading is greater than the passenger's weight. That reading is a measurement of an apparent weight, because it is made in a noninertial frame. For a downward acceleration (either decreasing upward speed or increasing downward speed), the scale reading is less than the passenger's weight.

(b) During the upward acceleration discussed above, what is the magnitude F_{net} of the net force on the passenger, and what is the magnitude $a_{p,\text{cab}}$ of his acceleration as measured in the frame of the cab? Does $\vec{F}_{\text{net}} = m\vec{a}_{p,\text{cab}}$?

Conceptualize/Classify: The magnitude F_g of the gravitational force on the passenger does not depend on the motion of the passenger or the cab; so, from part (1), F_g is 708 N. From part (2), the magnitude F_N of the normal force on the passenger during the upward acceleration is the 939 N reading on the scale.

Compute: Thus, the net force on the passenger is

$$F_{\text{net}} = F_N - F_g = 939 \text{ N} - 708 \text{ N} = 231 \text{ N} \qquad \text{(Answer)}$$

Conclude: However, his acceleration $a_{\text{p,cab}}$ relative to the frame of the cab is zero. Thus, in the noninertial frame of the accelerating cab, F_{net} is not equal to $ma_{\text{p,cab}}$, and Newton's second law does not hold.

CHECKPOINT 4 If cable of lift break what will be the reading shown by scale. Explain your result qualitatively.

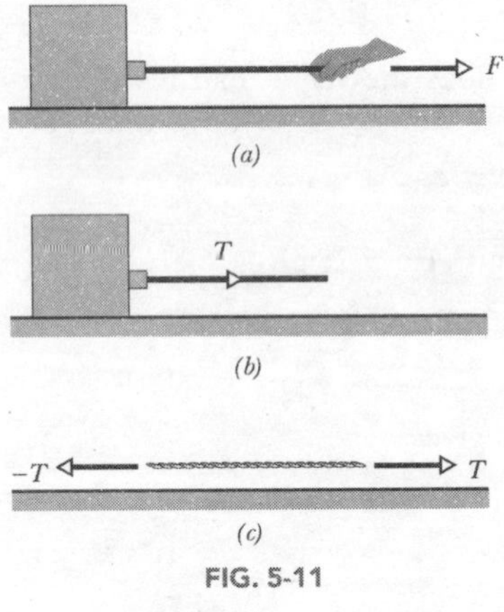

FIG. 5-11

FIG. 5-12 A frictional force $\vec{f}$ opposes the attempted slide of a body over a surface.

Tension Force

Force is often applied by means of strings or ropes that are used to pull an object. For instance, Fig. 5-11*a* shows a force *F* being applied to the right end of a rope attached to a crate.

When the cord (or a rope, cable, or other such object) is pulled taut, the cord pulls on the body with a force *P* directed away from the body and along the cord (Fig. 5-11*a*). The force is often called a *tension force* because the cord is said to be in a state of *tension* (or to be *under tension*), which means that it is being pulled taut. Each particle in the rope is applying a force on its neighbor. We can think of a string as composed of short section interacting by contact forces. Each section pulls the sections to either side of it, and by Newton's third law, it is pulled by the adjacent section. The magnitude of the force acting between adjacent sections is called tension. There is no direction associated with tension. The *tension in the cord* is the magnitude *T* of the force on the body. For example, if the force on the body from the cord has magnitude $T = 50$ N, the tension in the cord is 50 N.

According to Newton's third law, the crate applies a reaction force on the rope. The reaction force has the same magnitude as *F* but is oppositely directed. In other words, a force – *F* acts on the left end of the rope. Thus, forces of equal magnitude act on opposite ends of the rope, as in Fig. 5-11*c*, and tend to pull it apart. Here we have used the concept of a "massless" rope without mentioning. In reality, a massless rope does not exist, but it is a useful approximation. According to the second law, a net force is required to accelerate an object that has mass. In contrast, no net force is needed to acclerate a massless rope, since $\Sigma F = ma$ and $m = 0$ kg. So in above situation force acting on the ends of rope will be equal and appositely directed. In this book we will assume that a rope connecting one object to another is massless, unless stated otherwise. Tension force in a rope remains same from one end to the other even when the rope passes around smooth objects such as a smooth pulley in Fig. 5-13. Also, if a free pulley is massless then tension remains same even if there is friction between pulley and rope.We assume ropes and strings in our physics problems to be of infinite strength unless otherwise mentioned. Also, it is important to remember that ropes can change tension instantaneously.

A cord is often said to be *massless* (meaning its mass is negligible compared to the body's mass) and *unstretchable.* The cord then exists only as a connection between two bodies. It pulls on both bodies with the same force magnitude *T*, even if the bodies and the cord are accelerating and even if the cord runs around a *massless, frictionless pulley* (Figs. 5-14*b* and *c*). Although the string may have a non-zero acceleration, the net force on an ideal string is zero because it has zero mass; if m=0, then $\vec{F}_t = m\vec{a} = 0$ for a cord with acceleration $\vec{a}$.

(a)

(b)

FIG. 5-13 (*a*) Rope passing over a smooth pulley. (*b*) Tension in rope.

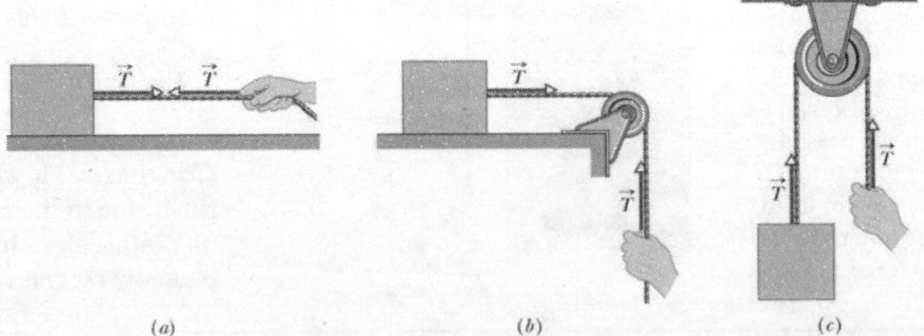

FIG. 5-14 (*a*) The cord, pulled taut, is under tension. If its mass is negligible, the cord pulls on the body and the hand with force $\vec{T}$, even if the cord runs around a massless, frictionless pulley as in (*b*) and (*c*).

Ideal Pulleys

A pulley can change the direction of the force exerted by a cord. We know that to lift something heavy, it is easier to stand on the ground and pull down on the rope than to pull up on the rope as shown in figure. An ideal pulley has no mass and no friction. An ideal pulley exerts no tangential force on the cord. As a result, the tension of an ideal cord that runs through an ideal pulley is the same on both sides of the pulley. An ideal pulley can change the direction of the force exerted by a cord without changing the magnitude. As long as real pulley has a small mass and negligible amount of friction, we can consider it as an ideal pulley.

Let's make a free-body diagrams for a short segment of the cord at the top of the pulley. Choosing the x axis to be horizontal, the normal force has no x-component. Applying Newton's second law along the x-axis : $\Sigma F_x = T_1 \cos\theta - T_2 \cos\theta = ma_x$. For $m = 0$, $T_1 = T_2$. The same reasoning can be applied to any segment of cord in contact with the pulley to show that the tensions are the same on either side of the pulley. Thus an ideal cord that passes over an ideal pulley has the same tension at its ends. Such a pulley has negligible mass compared to the bodies and negligible friction on its axle opposing its rotation. If the cord wraps halfway around a pulley, as in Fig. 5-9c, the net force on the pulley from the cord has the magnitude $2T$.

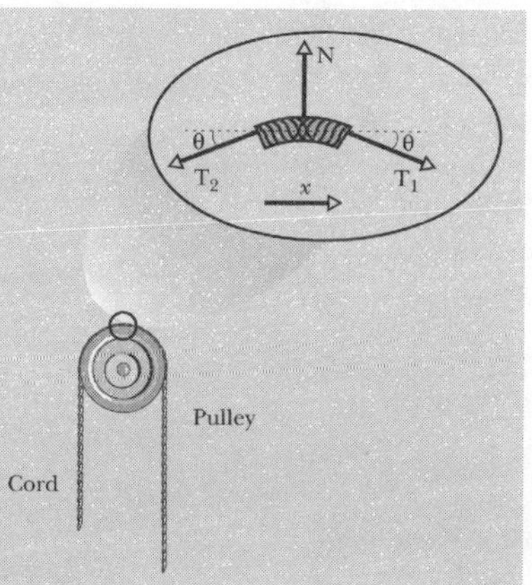

CHECKPOINT 5 The suspended body in Fig. 5-14c weighs 75 N. Is T equal to, greater than, or less than 75 N when the body is moving upward (a) at constant speed, (b) at increasing speed, and (c) at decreasing speed?

Spring Force

Many springs follow Hooke's law for small extension and compression. That is , the extension or compression – the increase or decrease in length from the relaxed length – is proportional to the force applied to the ends of the spring.

Hooke's law for an ideal spring :

$$F = k\,\Delta L$$

In above equation, F is the magnitude of the force exerted on each end of the spring and ΔL is the modulus of change in length of the spring from its relaxed length. The constant k is called the spring constant for a particular spring. The SI units of a spring constant are N/m. The spring constant is a measure of how tough it is to stretch or compress a spring. A stiffer spring has a larger spring constant because larger forces must be exerted on the spring to stretch or compress it.

When we say an ideal spring, we mean a spring that obeys Hooke's law and is also massless. Since we have assumed spring to be massles we know forces acting on both ends have to be equal and opposite, to have net force on spring to be zero.

Suppose we keep an ideal spring aligned with the x axis. One end is fixed in place and the other end can move along the x axis (Fig. 5-15). We choose the origin so that moveable end is at $x = 0$ when the spring is relaxed. Then the force exerted by the moveable end of the spring on whatever is attached as given in Fig. 5-15. F_x is the force exerted by the moveable end when its position is x ; the spring is relaxed at $x = 0$.

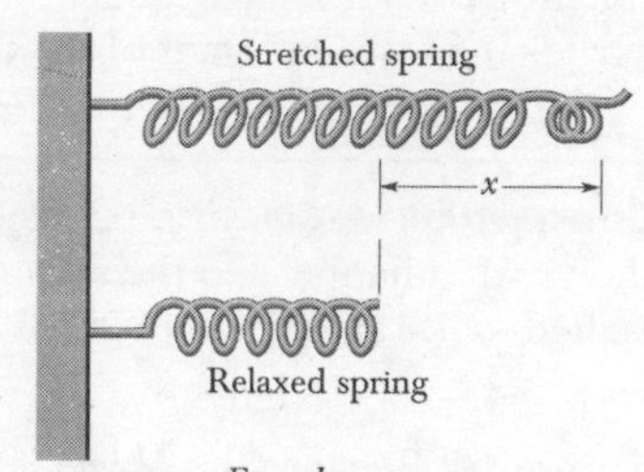

FIG. 5-15 Ideal spring aligned with x axis.

The negative sign indicates the direction of the force. The moveable end of the spring always pushes or pulls toward its relaxed position. If it is displaced in the positive x-direction, the force it exerts is the negative x-direction (back toward $x = 0$). If it is displaced in the negative x-direction, the force it exerts is in the positive x-direction (again, back toward $x = 0$).

PROBLEM-SOLVING TACTICS

Tactic 1: If we look at free-body diagram of the spring we will note that force on spring must act from both ends.

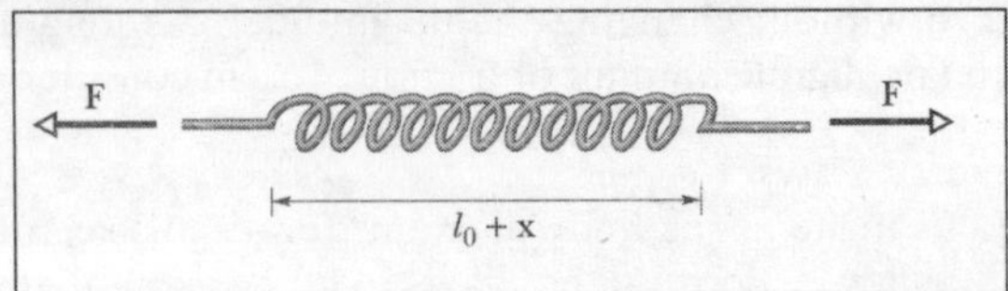

l_0 is natural length of spring

Example

Let's say Rahul and Sachin are pulling a spring from two ends as shown. Rahul moves x_2 and Sachin moves x_1.

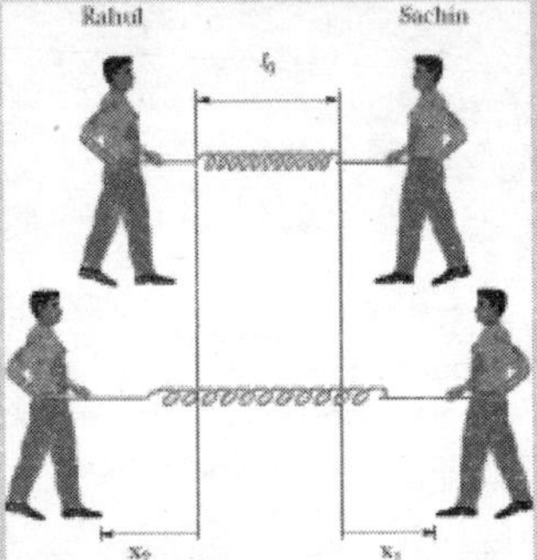

FIG. 5-16 Rahul and Sachin pulling a spring from two ends.

The force acting on Rahul and Sachin is $k(x_1 + x_2)$, not kx_2 on Rahul and kx_1 on Sachin. Force due to spring is kx where x is defined as $|l - l_0|$, where l is present length and l_0 is natural length.

Sample Problem 5-4

The spring is hanging vertically (Fig. 5-17a), and a sphere of mass m is attached to its lower end. Under the pull of the weight, the spring stretches a distance d from its equilibrium position (Fig. 5-17b) If a spring is stretched 2.0 cm by a suspended obect having a mass of 0.5 kg, what is the force constant of the spring.

Conceptualize/Classify: Consider Fig. 5-17b, which shows what happens to the spring when the object is attached to it. The object in Fig. 5-17b is in equilibrium.

Compute: Because the object is in equilibrium, the net force on it is zero. Thus, the upward spring force must be equal to the weight. (Fig. 5-17c).

$$|\vec{F}_s| = kx = mg$$

$$k = \frac{mg}{x} = \frac{(0.5\text{ kg})(10\ m/s^2)}{2.0 \times 10^{-2}\text{ m}} = 2.5 \times 10\text{ N/m}$$

(a) (b) (c)

FIG. 5-17 Spring hanging vertically with a sphere of mass M attached to lower end.

Conclude: When springs are connected in parallel then we can replace them by single spring of spring constant k_e where $k_e = k_1 + k_2$. Here we present the proof.

(a) This situation is shown in Fig. 5-17*d* If the force F pulls the mass m by y, the stretch in each spring will be same as y.

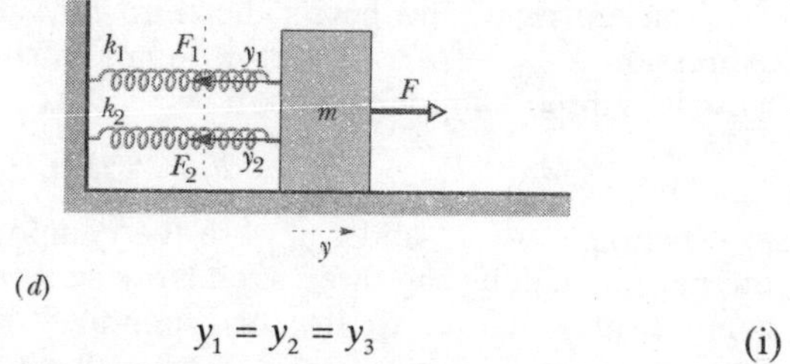

(*d*)

$$y_1 = y_2 = y_3 \qquad \text{(i)}$$

Now for an equivalent spring $F = k_e y$ and as spring constants are not equal so $F_1 = F_2$.

For equilibrium,

$$F = F_1 + F_2 \Rightarrow k_e y = k_1 y_1 + k_2 y_2$$

which in the light of Eq. (i) reduces to

$$k_e = k_1 + k_2$$

For more than two springs $k = k_1 + k_2 + k_3 +$ ......

(b) When springs are connected in series then we can replace them by single spring of spring consant k_e where $1/k_e = 1/k_1 + 1/k_2$.

Here we present the proof. This situation is shown in Fig. 5-17*e*, as springs are massless, so force in the springs will be same

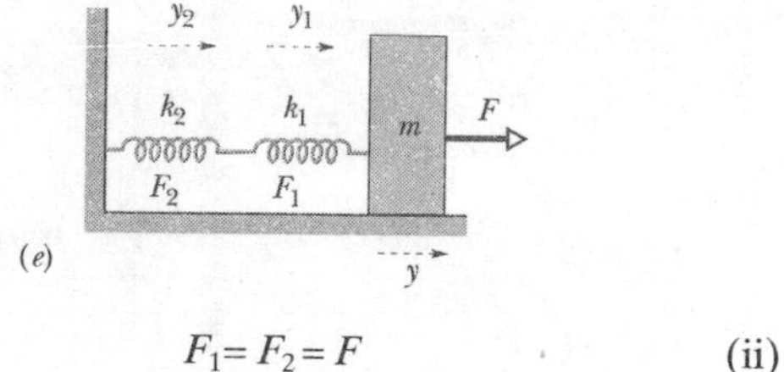

(*e*)

$$F_1 = F_2 = F \qquad \text{(ii)}$$

Now for equivalent spring $F = k_e y$. As spring constants are not equal so extensions will not be equal, but total extension y can be written as sum of two extensions $y = y_1 + y_2$

or $$\frac{F}{k} = \frac{F_1}{k_1} + \frac{F_2}{k_2} \qquad \left[as\ for\ F = ky, y = \frac{F}{k}\right]$$

For more than two springs

$$\frac{1}{k} = \frac{1}{k_1} + \frac{1}{k_2} + \ldots\ldots\ldots$$

5-9 | Applying Newton's Laws

The rest of this chapter consists of sample problems. You should pore over them, learning their procedures for attacking a problem. Especially important is knowing how to translate a sketch of a situation into a free-body diagram with appropriate axes, so that Newton's laws can be applied.

Sample Problem 5-5 Build your skill

Figure 5-18 shows a block S (the *sliding block*) with mass $M = 3.3$ kg. The block is free to move along a horizontal frictionless surface and connected, by a cord that wraps over a frictionless pulley, to a second block H (the *hanging block*), with mass $m = 2.1$ kg. The cord and pulley have negligible masses compared to the blocks (they are "massless"). The hanging block H falls as the sliding block S accelerates to the right. Find (a) the acceleration of block S, (b) the acceleration of block H, and (c) the tension in the cord.

Q *What is this problem all about?*

You are given two bodies—sliding block and hanging block—but must also consider *Earth,* which pulls on both bodies. (Without Earth, nothing would happen here.) A total of five forces act on the blocks, as shown in Fig. 5-19:

1. The cord pulls to the right on sliding block S with a force of magnitude T.
2. The cord pulls upward on hanging block H with a force of the same magnitude T. This upward force keeps block H from falling freely.
3. Earth pulls down on block S with the gravitational force $\vec{F}_{gS}$, which has a magnitude equal to Mg.
4. Earth pulls down on block H with the gravitational force $\vec{F}_{gH}$, which has a magnitude equal to mg.
5. The table pushes up on block S with a normal force $\vec{F}_N$.

There is another thing you should note. We assume that the cord does not stretch, so that if block H falls 1 mm in a certain time, block S moves 1 mm to the right in that same time. This means that the blocks move together and their accelerations have the same magnitude a.

Q *How do I classify this problem? Should it suggest a particular law of physics to me?*

Yes. Forces, masses, and accelerations are involved, and they should suggest Newton's second law of motion, $\vec{F}_{net} = m\vec{a}$. That is our starting key idea.

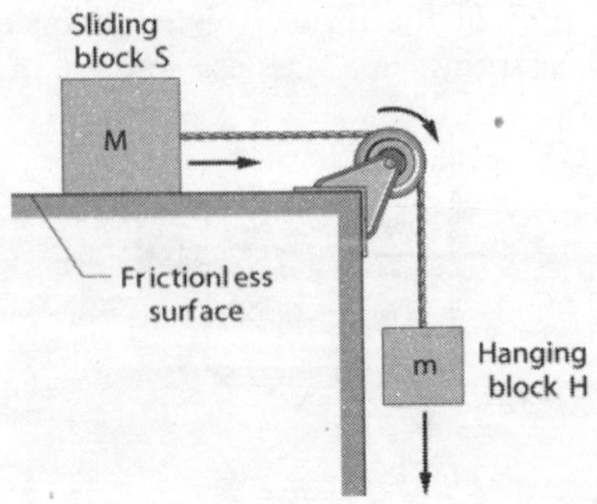

FIG. 5-18 A block S of mass M is connected to a block H of mass m by a cord that wraps over a pulley.

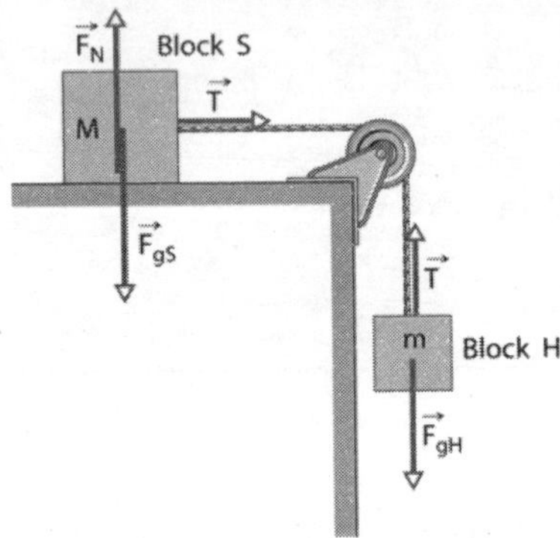

FIG. 5-19 The forces acting on the two blocks of Fig. 5-18.

Q *If I apply Newton's second law to this problem, to which body should I apply it?*

We focus on two bodies, the sliding block and the hanging block. Although they are *extended objects* (they are not points), we can still treat each block as a particle because every part of it moves in exactly the same way. A second key idea is to apply Newton's second law separately to each block.

Q *What about the pulley?*

We cannot represent the pulley as a particle because different parts of it move in different ways. When we discuss rotation, we shall deal with pulleys in detail. Meanwhile, we eliminate the pulley from consideration by assuming its mass to be negligible compared with the masses of the two blocks. Its only function is to change the cord's orientation.

Q *OK. Now how do I apply $\vec{F}_{\text{net}} = m\vec{a}$ to the sliding block?*

Represent block S as a particle of mass M and draw *all* the forces that act *on* it, as in Fig. 5-20*a*. This is the block's free-body diagram. Next, draw a set of axes. It makes sense to draw the x axis parallel to the table, in the direction in which the block moves.

Q *Thanks, but you still haven't told me how to apply $\vec{F}_{\text{net}} = m\vec{a}$ to the sliding block. All you've done is explain how to draw a free-body diagram.*

You are right, and here's the third key idea: The expression $\vec{F}_{\text{net}} = M\vec{a}$ is a vector equation, so we can write it as three component equations:

$$F_{\text{net},x} = Ma_x \quad F_{\text{net},y} = Ma_y \quad F_{\text{net},z} = Ma_z \tag{5-16}$$

in which $F_{\text{net},x}$, $F_{\text{net},y}$, and $F_{\text{net},z}$ are the components of the net force along the three axes. Now we apply each component equation to its corresponding direction. Because block S does not accelerate vertically, $F_{\text{net},y} = Ma_y$ becomes

$$F_N - F_{gS} = 0 \quad \text{or} \quad F_N = F_{gS}$$

Thus in the y direction, the magnitude of the normal force is equal to the magnitude of the gravitational force.

No force acts in the z direction, which is perpendicular to the page.

In the x direction, there is only one force component, which is T. Thus, $F_{\text{net},x} = Ma_x$ becomes

$$T = Ma \tag{5-17}$$

This equation contains two unknowns, T and a; so we cannot yet solve it. Recall, however, that we have not said anything about the hanging block.

Q *I agree. How do I apply $\vec{F}_{\text{net}} = m\vec{a}$ to the hanging block?*

We apply it just as we did for block S: Draw a free-body diagram for block H, as in Fig. 5-20*b*. Then apply $\vec{F}_{\text{net}} = m\vec{a}$ in component form. This time, because the acceleration is along the y axis, we use the y part of Eq. 5-16 ($F_{\text{net},y} = ma_y$) to write

$$T - F_{gH} = ma_y$$

We can now substitute mg for F_{gH} and $-a$ for a_y (negative because block H accelerates in the negative direction of the y axis). We find

$$T - mg = -ma \tag{5-18}$$

Now note that Eqs. 5-17 and 5-18 are simultaneous equations with the same two unknowns, T and a. Subtracting these equations eliminates T. Then solving for a yields

$$a = \frac{m}{M + m}g \tag{5-19}$$

Substituting this result into Eq. 5-17 yields

$$T = \frac{Mm}{M + m}g \tag{5-20}$$

Putting in the numbers gives, for these two quantities,

$$a = \frac{m}{M + m}g = \frac{2.1 \text{ kg}}{3.3 \text{ kg} + 2.1 \text{ kg}}(9.8 \text{ m/s}^2)$$
$$= 3.8 \text{ m/s}^2. \qquad \text{(Answer)}$$

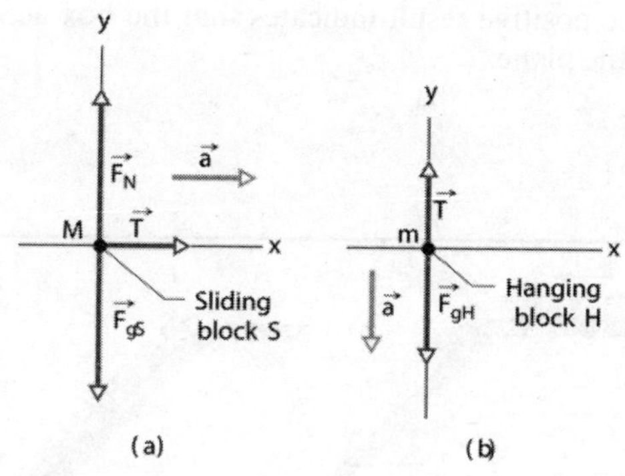

FIG. 5-20 (*a*) A free-body diagram for block *S* of Fig. 5-13. (*b*) A free-body diagram for block *H* of Fig. 5-13.

and
$$T = \frac{Mm}{M+m}g = \frac{(3.3\text{ kg})(2.1\text{ kg})}{3.3\text{ kg} + 2.1\text{ kg}}(9.8\text{ m/s}^2)$$

$$= 13\text{ N} \qquad \text{(Answer)}$$

Q *The problem is now solved, right?*

That's a fair question, but the problem is not really finished until we have examined the results to see whether they make sense. (If you made these calculations on the job, wouldn't you want to see whether they made sense before you turned them in?)

Look first at Eq. 5-19. Note that it is dimensionally correct and that the acceleration a will always be less than g. This is as it must be, because the hanging block is not in free fall. The cord pulls upward on it.

Look now at Eq. 5-20, which we can rewrite in the form

$$T = \frac{M}{M+m}mg \qquad (5\text{-}21)$$

In this form, it is easier to see that this equation is also dimensionally correct, because both T and mg have dimensions of forces. Equation 5-21 also lets us see that the tension in the cord is always less than mg, and thus is always less than the gravitational force on the hanging block. That is a comforting thought because, if T were *greater* than mg, the hanging block would accelerate upward.

We can also check the results by studying special cases, in which we can guess what the answers must be. A simple example is to put $g = 0$, as if the experiment were carried out in interstellar space. We know that in that case, the blocks would not move from rest, there would be no forces on the ends of the cord, and so there would be no tension in the cord. Do the formulas predict this? Yes, they do. If you put $g = 0$ in Eqs. 5-19 and 5-20, you find $a = 0$ and $T = 0$. Two more special cases you might try are $M = 0$ and $m \rightarrow \infty$.

Sample Problem 5-6

In Fig. 5-21*a*, a cord pulls on a box of biscuits up along a frictionless plane inclined at $\theta = 30°$. The box has mass $m = 5.00$ kg, and the force from the cord has magnitude $T = 25.0$ N. What is the box's acceleration component a along the inclined plane?

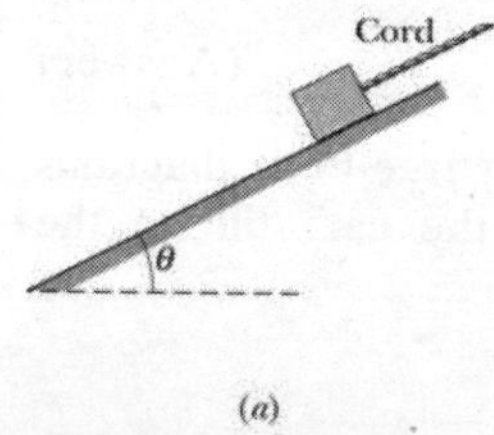

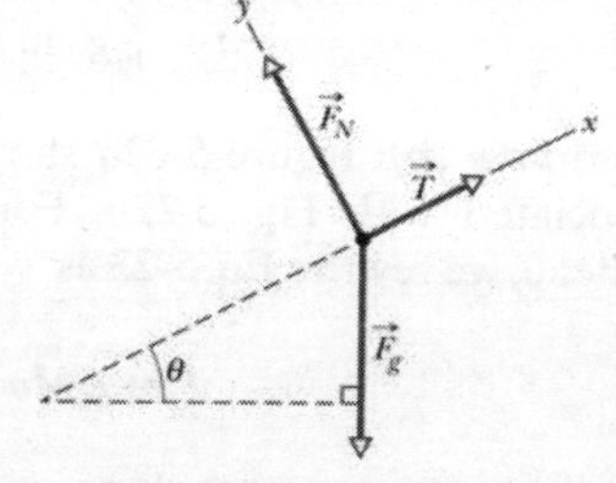

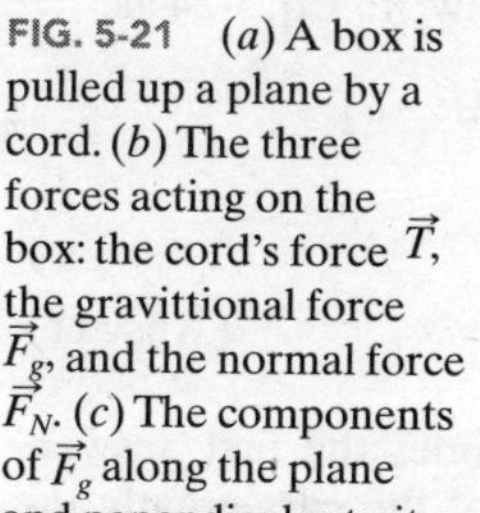

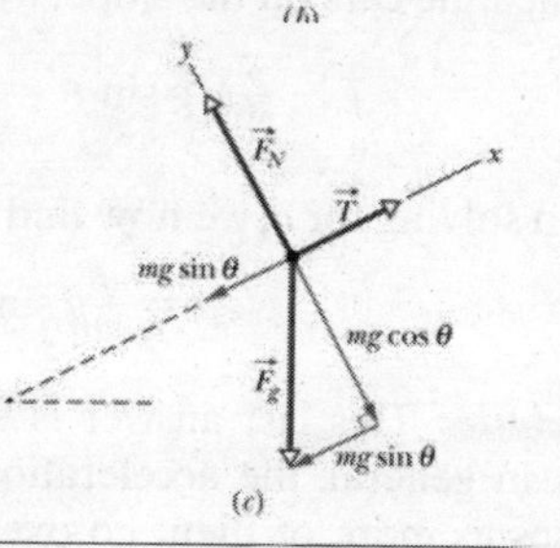

FIG. 5-21 (*a*) A box is pulled up a plane by a cord. (*b*) The three forces acting on the box: the cord's force $\vec{T}$, the gravittional force $\vec{F}_g$, and the normal force $\vec{F}_N$. (*c*) The components of $\vec{F}_g$ along the plane and pependicular to it.

Conceptualize: The acceleration along the plane is set by the force components along the plane (not by force components perpendicular to the plane), as expressed by Newton's second law (Eq. 5-1).

Classify: For convenience, we draw a coordinate system and a free-body diagram as shown in Fig. 5-21*b*. The positive direction of the x axis is up the plane. Force $\vec{T}$ from the cord is up the plane and has magnitude $T = 25.0$ N. The gravitational force $\vec{F}_g$ is downward and has magnitude $mg = (5.00\text{ kg})(9.8\text{ m/s}^2) = 49.0$ N. More important, its component along the plane is down the plane and has magnitude $mg \sin\theta$ as indicated in Fig. 5-21*c*. (To see why that trig function is involved, compare the right triangles in Figs. 5-21*b* and *c*.) To indicate the direction, we can write the component as $-mg \sin\theta$. The normal force $\vec{F}_N$ is perpendicular to the plane and thus does not determine acceleration along the plane.

Compute: We write Newton's second law ($\vec{F}_{net} = m\vec{a}$) for motion along the x axis as

$$T - mg\sin\theta = ma \qquad (5\text{-}22)$$

Substituting data and solving for a, we find

$$a = 0.100 \text{ m/s}^2 \quad \text{(Answer)}$$

Here, the positive result indicates that the box accelerates up the plane.

Sample Problem 5-7

Let's return to the chapter opening question: What produces the tear factor in the last car of a traditional gravity-driven roller coaster? Let's consider a coaster having 10 identical cars with total mass M and massless interconnections. Figure 5-22*a* shows the coaster just after the first car has begun its descent along a frictionless slope with an angle θ. Figure 5-22*b* shows the coaster just before the last car begins its descent. What is the acceleration of the coaster in these two situations?

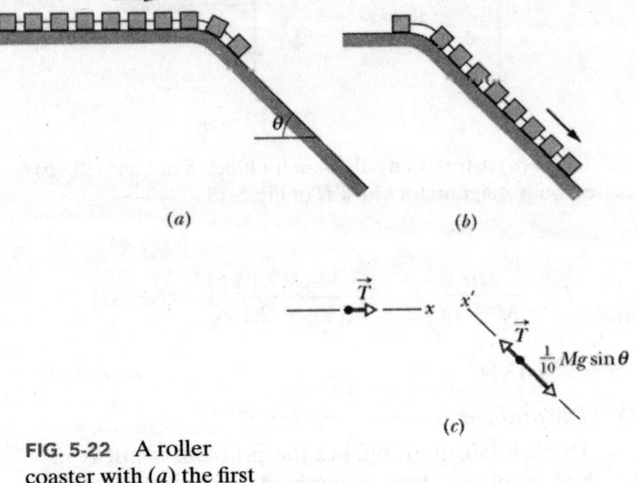

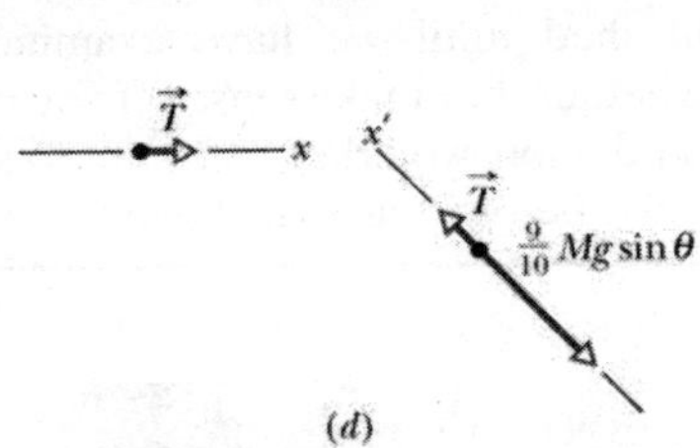

FIG. 5-22 A roller coaster with (*a*) the first car on a slope and (*b*) all but the last car on the slope. (*c*) Free-body diagrams for the cars on the plateau and the car on the slope in (*a*). (*d*) Free-body diagrams for (*b*).

Conceptualize/Classify: When the motion is along a single axis, we write that law in component form (such as $F_{\text{net},x} = ma_x$) and we use only force components along that axis. (3) When several objects move together at the same velocity and with the same acceleration, they can be regarded as a single composite object. *Internal forces* act between the individual objects, but only *external forces* can cause the composite object to accelerate.

Compute (a): Figure 5-22*c* shows free-body diagrams associated with Fig. 5-22*a*, with convenient axes superimposed. The tilted x' axis has its positive direction up the slope. T is the magnitude of the interconnection force between the car on the slope and the cars still on the plateau. Because the coaster consists of 10 identical cars with total mass M, the mass of the car on the slope is $\frac{1}{10}M$ and the mass of the cars on the plateau is $\frac{9}{10}M$. Only a single *external* force acts along the x axis on the nine-car composite—namely, the interconnection force with magnitude T. (The forces between the nine cars are internal forces.) Thus, Newton's second law for motion along the x axis ($F_{\text{net},x} = ma_x$) becomes

$$T = \tfrac{9}{10}Ma \quad (5\text{-}23)$$

where a is the magnitude of the acceleration a_x along the x axis.

Along the tilted x' axis, two forces act on the car on the slope: the interconnection force with magnitude T (in the positive direction of the axis) and the x' component of the gravitational force (in the negative direction of the axis). From Sample Problem 5-5, we know to write that gravitational component as $-mg \sin\theta$, where m is the mass. Because we know that the car accelerates *down* the slope in the negative x' direction with magnitude a, we can write the acceleration as $-a$. Thus, for this car, with mass $\frac{1}{10}M$ we write Newton's second law for motion along the x' axis as

$$T - \tfrac{1}{10}Mg\sin\theta = \tfrac{1}{10}M(-a) \quad (5\text{-}24)$$

Substituting for T from Eq. 5-23 and solving for a, we have

$$a = \tfrac{1}{10}g\sin\theta \quad \text{(Answer)}$$

Compute (b): Figure 5-22*d* shows free-body diagrams associated with Fig. 5-22*b*. For the car still on the plateau, we rewrite Eq. 5-23 as

$$T = \tfrac{1}{10}Ma$$

For the nine cars on the slope, we rewrite Eq. 5-24 as

$$T - \tfrac{9}{10}Mg\sin\theta = \tfrac{9}{10}M(-a)$$

Again solving for a, we now find

$$a = \tfrac{9}{10}g\sin\theta \quad \text{(Answer)}$$

Conclude: This last answer is 9 times the first answer. Thus, in general, the acceleration of the cars greatly increases as more of them go over the edge and onto the slope. That increase in acceleration occurs regardless of your car choice, but your interpretation of the acceleration depends on the choice. In the first car, most of the acceleration occurs on the slope and is due to the component of the gravitational force along the slope, which is reasonable. In the last car, most of the acceleration occurs on the plateau and is due to the push on you from the back of your seat. That push rapidly increases as you approach the edge, giving you the frightening sensation that you are about to be hurled off the plateau and into the air.

CHECKPOINT 6 A car accelerates down a hill (Fig. 5-23), going from rest to 30.0 m/s in 6.00 s. During the acceleration, a toy ($m = 0.1$ kg) hangs by a string from the car's ceiling. The acceleration is such that the string remains perpendicular to the ceiling. Determine the angle θ.

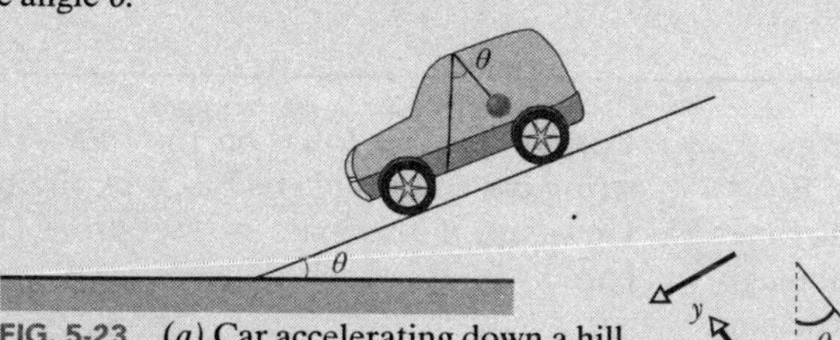

FIG. 5-23 (*a*) Car accelerating down a hill.

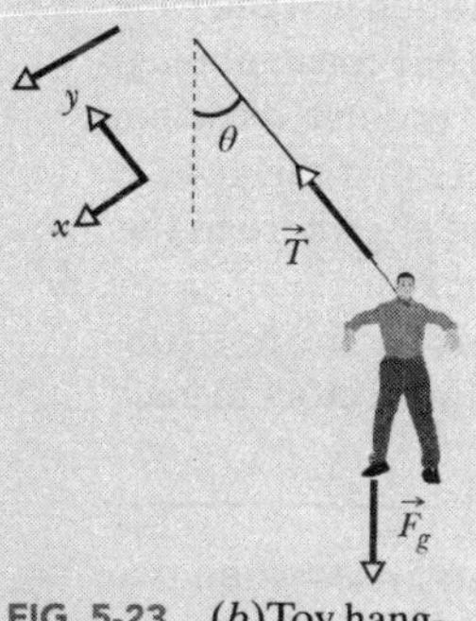

FIG. 5-23 (*b*) Toy hanging from car's ceiling.

Solution:

$\vec{a} = 5.00\, m/s^2$

Choose the x axis pointing down the slope and using

$v = u + at$; 30.0 m/s = 0 + a (6.00 s)

a = 5.00 m/s

Consider forces on the toy

$\Sigma F_x = ma_x$; $mg \sin\theta = m\left(5.00\ \text{m/s}^2\right)$ hence θ=30°

Sample Problem 5-8 Build your skill

In Fig. 5-24*a*, a constant horizontal force $\vec{F}_{app}$ of magnitude 20 N is applied to block A of mass $m_A = 4.0$ kg, which pushes against block B of mass $m_B = 6.0$ kg. The blocks slide over a frictionless surface, along an x axis.

(a) What is the acceleration of the blocks?

Conceptualize: Because force $\vec{F}_{app}$ is applied directly to block A, we use Newton's second law to relate that force to the acceleration $\vec{a}$ of block A. Because the motion is along the x axis, we use that law for x components ($F_{net,x} = ma_x$), writing it as

$$F_{app} = m_A a$$

However, this is seriously wrong because $\vec{F}_{app}$ is not the only horizontal force acting on block A. There is also the force $\vec{F}_{AB}$ from block B (Fig. 5-24*b*).

Classify: Let us now include force $\vec{F}_{AB}$ by writing, again for the x axis,

$$F_{app} - F_{AB} = m_A a$$

(We use the minus sign to include the direction of $\vec{F}_{AB}$.) Because F_{AB} is a second unknown, we cannot solve this equation for a.

Compute: Because of the direction in which force $\vec{F}_{app}$ is applied, the two blocks form a rigidly connected system. We can relate the net force *on the system* to the acceleration *of the system* with Newton's second law. Here, once again for the x axis, we can write that law as

$$F_{app} = (m_A + m_B)a$$

where now we properly apply $\vec{F}_{app}$ to the system with total mass $m_A + m_B$. Solving for a and substituting known values, we find

$$a = \frac{F_{app}}{m_A + m_B} = \frac{20\text{ N}}{4.0\text{ kg} + 6.0\text{ kg}} = 2.0\text{ m/s}^2$$

(Answer)

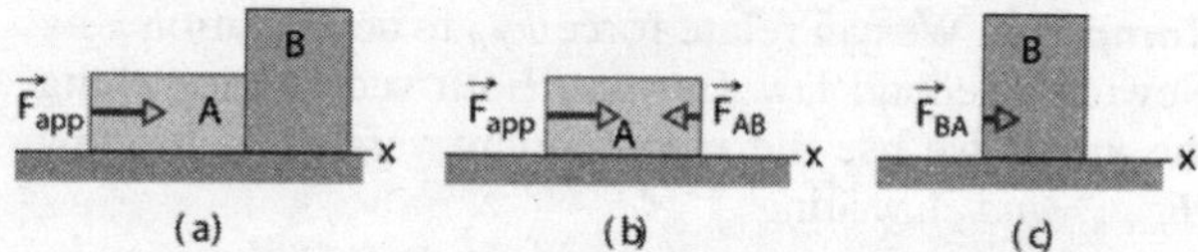

FIG. 5-24 (*a*) A constant horizontal force $\vec{F}_{app}$ is applied to block A, which pushes against block B. (*b*) Two horizontal forces act on block A. (*c*) Only one horizontal force acts on block B.

Conclude: Thus, the acceleration of the system and of each block is in the positive direction of the x axis and has the magnitude 2.0 m/s^2.

(b) What is the (horizontal) force $\vec{F}_{BA}$ on block B from block A (Fig. 5-20c)?

Classify: We can relate the net force on block B to the block's acceleration with Newton's second law.

Compute: Here we can write that law, still for components along the x axis, as

$$F_{BA} = m_B a,$$

which, with known values, gives

$$F_{BA} = (6.0 \text{ kg})(2.0 \text{ m/s}^2) = 12 \text{ N}. \quad \text{(Answer)}$$

Conclude: Thus, force $\vec{F}_{BA}$ is in the positive direction of the x axis and has a magnitude of 12 N.

Sample Problem 5-9

In Fig. 5-25a, a hand H pulls on a taut horizontal rope R (of mass m = 0.200 kg) that is attached to a block B (of mass M = 5.00 kg). The resulting acceleration a of the rope and block across the frictionless surface has constant magnitude 0.300 m/s^2 and is directed in the positive direction of the x axis indicated in the figure. Note that this rope is not "massless" like those in Fig. 5-10 and elsewhere in this chapter. We return to this feature in part (d).

(a) Identify all the third-law force pairs for the horizontal forces in Fig. 5-5 1a and show how the vectors in each pair are related.

Conceptualize: A third-law force pair arises when two bodies *interact*; the forces of the pair are equal in magnitude and opposite in direction, and the force on each body is due to the other body.

Classify: The "exploded view" of Fig. 5-25b shows that here there are two such force pairs for the horizontal forces. At the hand-rope boundary, we have the force $\vec{F}_{RH}$ on the rope from the hand and the force $\vec{F}_{HR}$ on the hand from the rope. These forces are equal and opposite in direction, so they are related by

$$\vec{F}_{RH} = -\vec{F}_{HR} \quad \text{(Answer)}$$

Similarly, at the rope-block boundary we have

$$\vec{F}_{BR} = -\vec{F}_{RB} \quad \text{(Answer)}$$

(b) What is the magnitude of the force $\vec{F}_{BR}$ on the block from the rope?

Classify: We know that the block has an acceleration a in the positive direction of the x axis. The only force acting on the block along that axis is F_{BR}.

Compute: We can relate force F_{BR} to acceleration a by Newton's second law. Because both vectors are along the x axis, we use the x component version of the law ($F_{net,\,x} = ma._x$), writing

$$F_{BR} = Ma$$

Substituting nown values, we find that the magnitude of F_{BR} is

$$F_{BR} = (5.00 \text{ kg})(0.300 \text{ m/s}^2) = 1.50 \text{ N} \quad \text{(Answer)}$$

Conclude: The force on the block is less than $\vec{F}$; the string does not pull the block by the full applied force. However, if the mass of the string is negligible compared with the block, $\vec{F}_{MR} = \vec{F}$.

We make free-body diagram of a section of an actual rope (that is, its mass cannot be neglected considering tension at B to be F′ and tension at A to be $A.F.$

(c) What is the magnitude of the force $\vec{F}_{RB}$ on the rope from the block?

Classify: From (a), we know that $\vec{F}_{RB} = \vec{F}_{BR}$, so $\vec{F}_{RB}$ has the magnitude

$$F_{RB} = \vec{F}_{BR} = 1.50 \text{ N} \quad \text{(Answer)}$$

(d) What is the magnitude of the force $\vec{F}_{RH}$ on the rope from the hand?

Classify: With the rope taut, the rope and block form a system on which $\vec{F}_{RH}$ acts.

Compute: The mass of the system is $m + M$. For this system, Newton's second law for x components gives us

$$F_{RH} = (m+M)a \quad (5\text{-}25)$$
$$= (0.200 \text{ kg} + 5.00 \text{ kg})(0.300 \text{ m/s}^2) = 1.56 \text{ N} \quad \text{(Answer)}$$

Conclude: Now note that the magnitude of the force F_{RH} on the rope from the hand (1.56 N) is greater than the magnitude of the force $\vec{F}_{BR}$ on the block from the

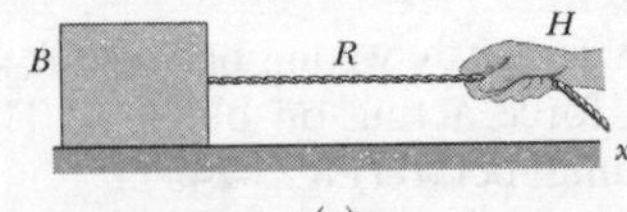

(a)

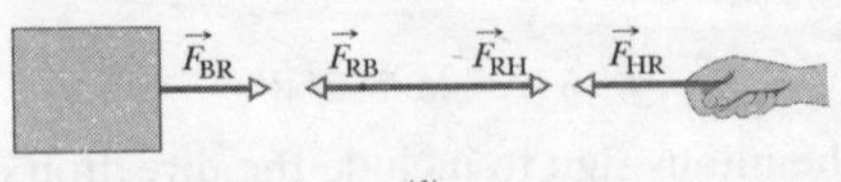

(b)

FIG. 5-25 (a) Hand H pulls on rope R, which is attached to block B. (b) An exploded view of block, rope, and hand, with the forces between block and rope and between rope and hand.

rope (1.50 N, from part (b) above). The reason is that $\vec{F}_{BR}$ must accelerate only the block but $\vec{F}_{RH}$ must accelerate both the block and the rope, and the rope's mass m is *not* negligible. If we let $m \rightarrow 0$ in Eq. 5-25, then we find 1.50 N, the same magnitude as at the other end. We often assume that an interconnecting rope is massless so that we can approximate the forces at its two ends as having the same magnitude.

If there are external forces on the rope, or if the rope is accelerating, the tension generally varies along the rope.

CHECKPOINT 7 A uniform rope of mass M and length L hangs from the limb of a tree. Find the tension at distance x from the bottom.

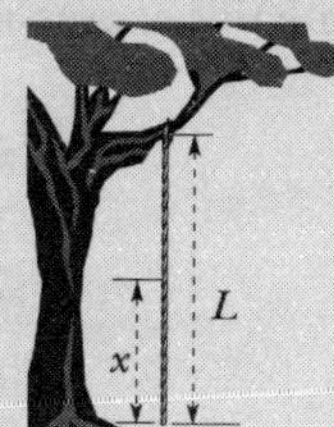

Sample Problem 5-10

The Atwood Machine

When two objects of are attached by an ideal string passing over an ideal pulley as shown, the arrangement is called an Atwood machine. Determine the magnitude of the acceleration of the block of mass m and the tension in the string.

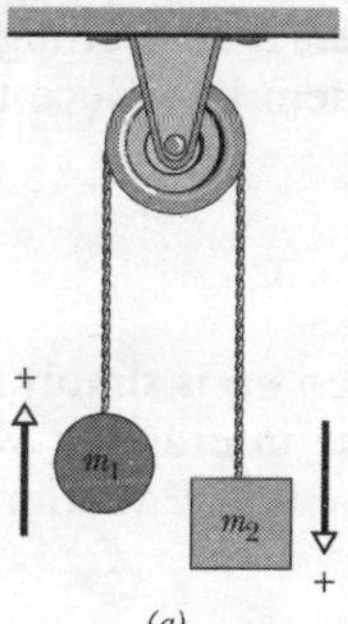

FIG. 5-26 Atwood machine.

Conceptualize: When one block will move upward, the other block will move downward, their accelerations are of equal magnitude as we have learnt in constraint motion.

Classify: The blocks in the Atwood machine are experiencing the gravitational force and the forces exerted by the strings connected to them.

Compute: The free-body diagrams for the two objects are as shown in Fig. 5-26*b* the tension exerted by the string is in upward direction and the weight is acting downward.

We define upward as the positive direction for object 1. We define downward as the positive direction for object 2. According to this sign convention, the net force exerted on object 1 is $T - m_1g$, and the net force exerted on object 2 is $m_2g - T$.

Applying Newton's second law to object 1:

$$T m_1g = m_1a \tag{i}$$

Applying Newton's second law to object 2:

$$m_2g - T = m_2a \tag{ii}$$

Add Eq. (ii) to Eq. (i),

$$-m_1g + m_2g = m_1a + m_2a$$

Solve for the acceleration:

$$a = \left[\frac{m_2 - m_1}{m_1 + m_2}\right]g \tag{iii}$$

Substitute Eq. (iii) into Eq. (i) to find T:

$$T = m_1(g + a_y) = \left[\frac{2m_1m_2}{m_1 + m_2}\right]g \tag{iv}$$

Conclude: Note that if m_2 is lighter than m_1 then sign of acceleration will be negative thus making m_2 go up and m_1 go down.

In Case Of: What if the objects have equal masses, that is, $m_1 = m_2$?

Solution: If we have the same mass on both sides, the system is balanced and should not accelerate. Mathematically, we see that if $m_1 = m_2$, Eq. (iii) gives us $a_y = 0$.

In Case Of: What if one of the masses is much larger than the other : $m_1 >> m_2$?

Solution: In the case in which one mass is infinitely larger than the other, we can ignore the effect of the smaller mass. Therefore, the larger mass should simply fall as if the smaller mass were not there. We see that if $m_1 >> m_2$, Eq. (iii) gives us $a_y = -g$.

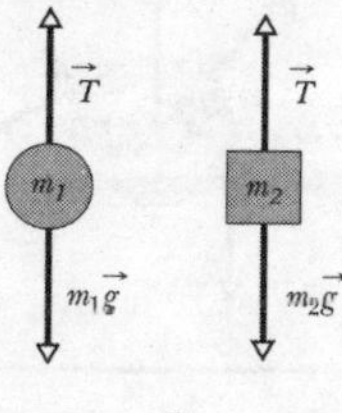

Sample Problem 5-11

A sphere of mass m_1 and a block of mass m_2 are attached by a lightweight cord that passes over a ideal pulley. The block lies on a frictionless incline of angle θ. Find the acceleration of the two objects and the tension in the cord.

Conceptualize/Classify: If m_2 moves down the incline, m_1 moves upward with same magnitude of acceleration.

Compute: Making the free-body diagrams

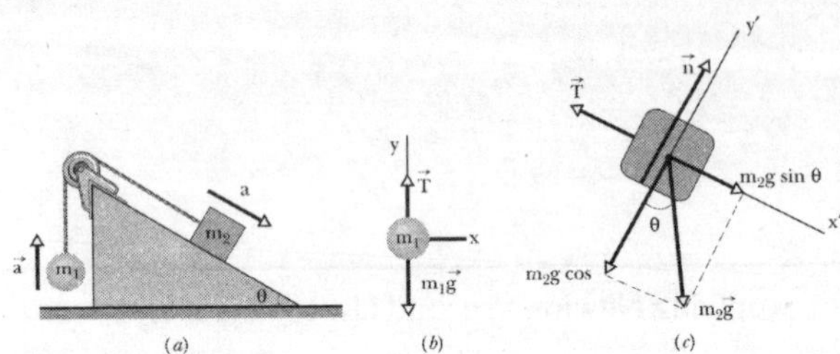

FIG. 5-27 (*a*) Sphere and block attached by light weight cord over a pulley. (*b*, *c*) Free-body diagrams.

Substitute this expression for a into Eq. (v) to find T: Apply Newton's second law on the sphere along the vertical, and choosing the upward direction as positive.

$$T - m_{x}g = m_1 a = m_1 a \quad \text{(i)}$$

For the block applying Newton's second law along the incline as in Fig. 5-27*c*

$$m_2 g \sin\theta - T = m_2 a_x = m_2 a \quad \text{(ii)}$$

$$N - m_2 g \cos\theta = 0 \quad \text{(iii)}$$

If the two objects have same accelerations of equal magnitude a, solve Eq. (ii) for T.

$$T = m_1(g + a) \quad \text{(iv)}$$

Subsituting this expression for T into Eq. (iii), solve for a.

$$m_2 g \sin\theta - m_1(g + a) = m_2 a \quad \text{(v)}$$

Substitute this expression for a into Eq. (v) to find T.

$$T = \frac{m_1 m_2 g(\sin\theta + 1)}{m_1 + m_2} \quad \text{(vi)}$$

$$a = \frac{m_2 g \sin\theta - m_1 g}{m_1 + m_2} \quad \text{(vii)}$$

Conclude: The block will accelerate down the incline if $m_2 \sin\theta > m_1$. If $m_1 > m_2 \sin\theta$, the block will accelerate up the incline

In Case Of: What happens in this situation if $\theta = 90°$?

Solution: If $\theta = 90°$, the inclined plane becomes vertical and there is no interaction between its surface and m_2. Therefore, this problem becomes the Atwood machine of Sample Problem 5-10. Letting $\theta \to 90°$ in Eqs. (vi) and (vii) causes them to reduce to Eqs. (iii) and (iv) of *Example ( )*.

In Case Of: What if $m_1 = 0$?

Solution: If $m_1 = 0$, then m_2 is simply sliding down an inclined plane without interacting with m_1 through the string, keeping $m_1 \to 0$ in Equation (6) gives $a = g \sin\theta$.

Sample Problem 5-12

Find force acting as the pulley due to rod that attaches it to incline given $\theta = 37°$ and $m_1 = m_2$.

Conceptualize: The pulley is in equilibrium and ropes passing over pulley must be applying forces on pulley.

Classify: This is an equilibrium model. Forces applied by ropes and the rod on pulley should cancel act. We have to rember that they are vectors.

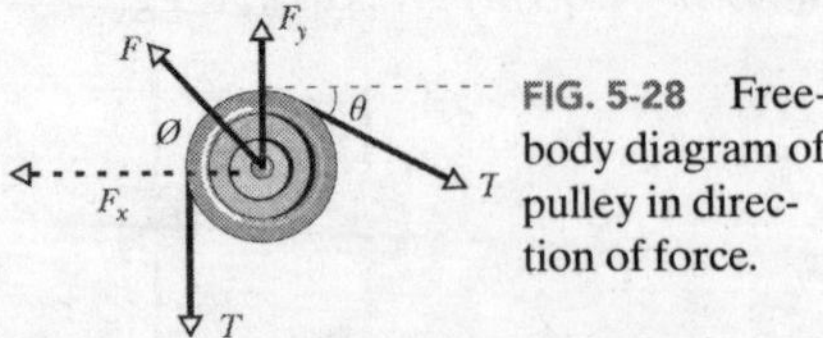

FIG. 5-28 Free-body diagram of pulley in direction of force.

Compute: We construct free-body diagram of pulley in direction of force due to rod on the pulley is unknown we cannot say that it is along the rod only.

Thus, we take components of force F along horizontal and vertical direction and call them F_x and F writing Newton's second law

$$F_y - T\sin\theta - T = 0 \qquad F_y = T(1 + \sin\theta)$$

Conclude: Answer is coming of the some order as tension.

$$|\vec{F}| = \sqrt{F_y^2 + F_y^2}$$

$$|\vec{F}| = T\sqrt{2 + 2\sin\theta}$$

Sample Problem 5-13

In following setup pulley strings and spring are light. Initially all masses are in equilibrium and at rest.

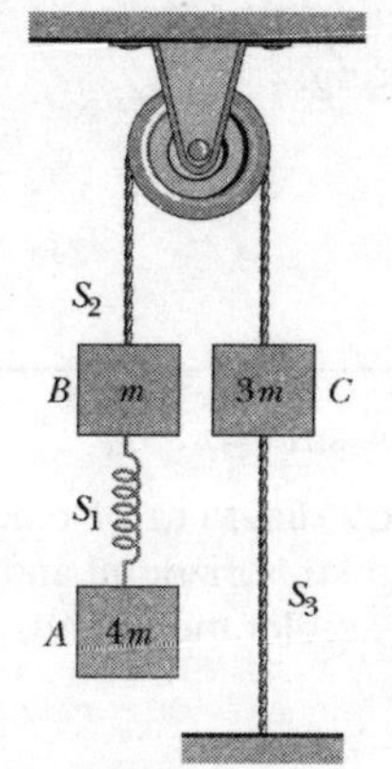

FIG. 5-29 Setup of masses hanging from a pulley.

(a) Find tension in spring and tension in ropes

Conceptualize: We know by inspecting the Fig. 5-29 that total gravitational pull on left will be larger than the gravitational pull on right.

Classify: As given in question this problem involves three bodies in equilibrium, hence can be modeled as particle in equilibrium.

Compute: Let's make free-body diagrams of all three bodies. Tension on string on both sides of pulley is going to be same as we have learnt in earlier examples.

Applying Newton's second law to block A,

$$4mg - T_1 = 0$$

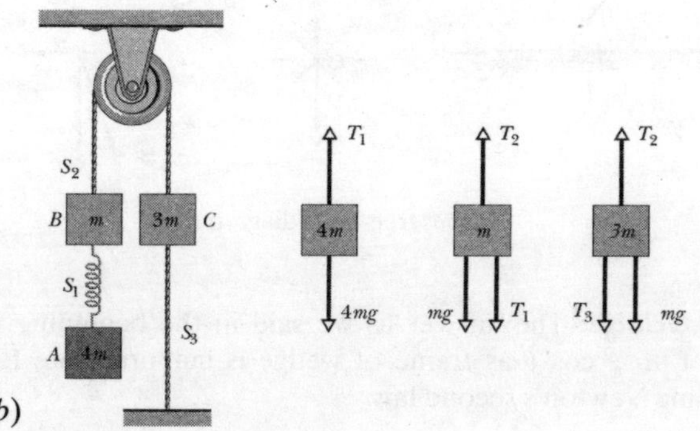

Applying Newton's second law to block B,

$$mg + T_1 - T_2 = 0$$

Applying Newton's second law to block C,

$$T_3 + 3mg - T_2 = 0$$

Solving

$$T_1 = 4\,mg$$
$$T_2 = 5\,mg$$
$$T_3 = 2\,mg$$

Here spring is behaving same as string except that it is stretched while string cannot stretch.

(b) Find acceleration of masses immediately after the string S_3 is cut.

Conceptualize/Classify: The most important point in this problem is that any object of finite mass cannot change its position instantaneously, as this require infinite velocity. No finite mass can achieve infinite velocity instantaneously as it requires infinite acceleration, hence infinite force.

Thus, immediately after cutting the string S_3 all masses will remain at same position and force due to spring will not change. As force of spring is $k\,x$ and x is $u - l_0$. At the same time it is emphasized that tension in string S_2 will change instantaneously (tension is a self adjusting force), to maintain constraint relation between blocks B and C since they have same magnitude of accleration. We can identify all the forces acting on all objects. Only tension T in string S_2 is unknown force all other forces are known.

Compute: Considering free-body diagrams

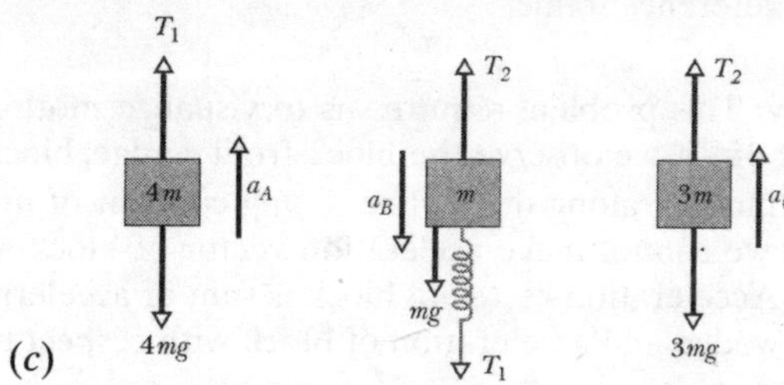

We know from part (a) that tension in spring is T_1 and $T_1 = 4\,mg$

Writing Newton's second law for A

$$4\,mg - T_1 = 4ma_A'$$

Writing Newton's second law for B

$$T_1 + mg - T_2' = ma_B'$$

Writing Newton's second law for C

$$T_2' - 3mg = 3ma_C'$$

Quantities which may have different value from part (a) are represented using symbol $'$, for example a tenstion in string S_2 is T_2', others which have same value as part (a) have been retained with same symbol.

$$\text{as } a_B' = a_C'$$

Solving we get $a_A' = 0$ $a_B' = a_C' = g/2$

Conclude: If we would have taken T_2' unchanged, string S_2 would have slacked as acceleration of C will be larger than acceleration of B. We can also see that tension in string has changed instantaneously. Tension in a string is a self adjusting force and it adusts instantaneously to avoid slacking.

Sample Problem 5-14

There is no friction at any contact and hence wedge is free to move. Find force acting on wedge due to block. Also, find acceleration of wedge.

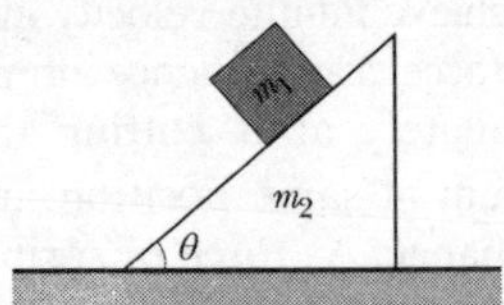

Conceptualize: From earlier problems you may want to directly reach to conclusion that answer is $m_1 g \cos\theta$. But it you go back and check the solution you will find it was solved in reference frame of ground as wedge was not moving. Horizontal component of normal contact force applied by block on wedge will accelerate the wedge. Thus, reference frame attached to wedge is non-inertial reference frame.

Classify: This problem requires us to visualize motion of mass m_1. If we observe the block from wedge, block will be moving along the incline. Using concept of net motion we cannot make accleration vector of block as shown. Acceleration vector of block is sum of acceleration of wedge and acceleration of block with respect to wedge ($a \rightarrow_{b/w}$)

$\vec{a_f} \equiv$ a_w, $a_{b/w}$

Wedge is constrained to move along horizontal plane.

$$\vec{a}_f = \vec{a}_{b/w} + \vec{a}_w$$

Compute: Consider free-body diagram of wedge. Take horizontal component of normal contact force and apply Newton's second law

$$N \sin\theta = m_2 a_w$$

Consider free-body diagra m of block and acceleration vector of block, take horizontal and vertical component of forces and acceleration, and apply Newton's second law.

$$a_x = a_{b/w} \cos\theta + a_w$$
$$a_y = a_{b/w} \sin\theta$$

$$N \sin\theta = m_1 (a_{b/w} \cos\theta - a_w)$$
$$m_1 g - N\cos\theta = m_1 (a_{b/w} \sin\theta)$$

Solving we get

$$N = \frac{m_1 m_2 g \cos\theta}{(m_2 + m_1 \sin^2\theta)}$$
$$a_w = \frac{m_1 g \cos\theta \sin\theta}{(m_2 + m_1 \sin^2\theta)}, \quad a_{b/w} = \frac{(m_1 + m_2) g \sin\theta}{(m_1 \sin^2\theta + m_2)}$$

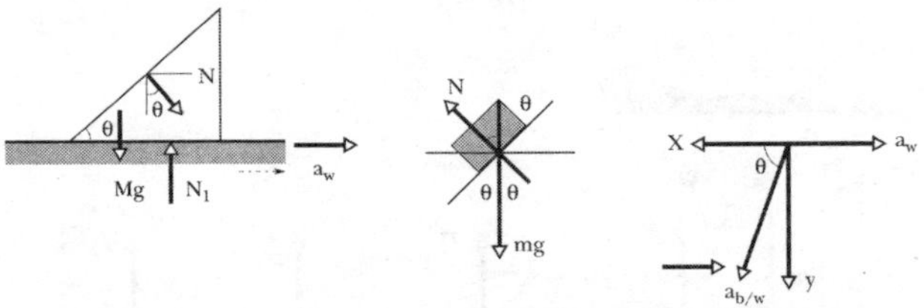

Various free-body diagrams.

Conclude: The answer as we said in the beginning is not $m_1 g \cos\theta$ as frame of wedge is inappropriate for using Newton's second law.

In Case Of: Wedge is of infinite mass. Answer our answer should become $m_1 g \cos\theta$ as wedge will remain stationary and hence an inertial reference frame.

Sample Problem 5-15

What horizontal force must be applied to the cart shown in Fig. 5-30 so that the blocks remain stationary relative to the cart ? Assume all surfaces, wheels, and pulley are frictionless.

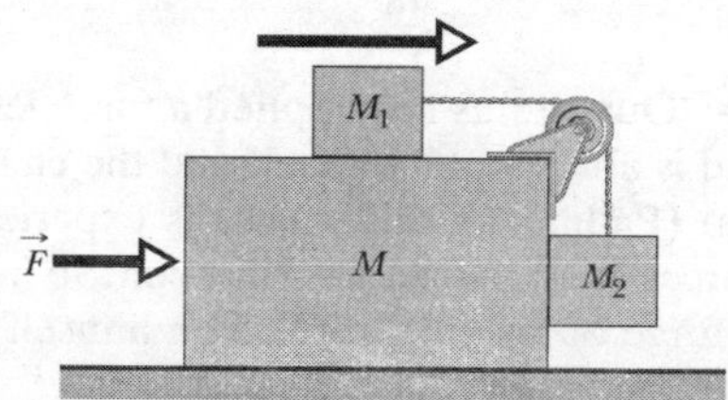

FIG. 5-30 System of blocks, pulley, and cart.

Conceptualize/Classify: It is easy to see that all the bodies will be having same acceleration, as the blocks are supposed to be at rest with respect to the cart. Since no horizontal force is acting on the block m_1 it must be accelerated due to the force exerted by the string.

Compute: Writing Newton's second law for different blocks

For m_1 along horizontal: $T = m_1 a$

For m_2 along vertical: $T - m_2 g = 0$

Eliminating T,

$$a = \frac{m_2 g}{m_1}$$

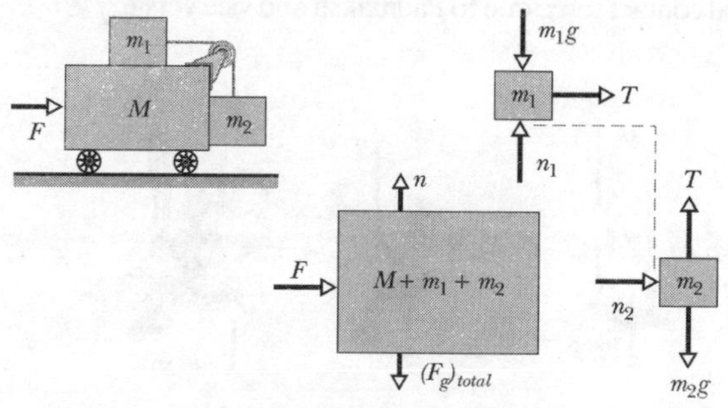

Various free-body diagrams

For all three blocks:

$$F = (M + m_1 + m_2)a$$

$$= (M + m_1 + m_2)\left[\frac{m_2 g}{m_1}\right] \qquad \text{(Answer)}$$

Conclude: You may be wondering what happened to the normal contact force between block m_2 and cart. The point is this normal contact force is internal to the system for which we have written above equation. Although we can see in free-body diagram the cause of horizontal acceleration for block m_2 is this normal only.

Sample Problem 5-16

An ingenious child named Padmaksh wants to pluck a mango from a tree without climbing the tree. He sits on a chair connected to a light rope that passes over a smooth branch (Fig.5-23). The rope also has a light spring balance attached in the middle. Now Padmaksh pulls on the loose end of the rope so that the spring scale reads 252 N. Padmaksh's mass is 32 kg, and the chair's mass is 16 kg. Assume Padmaksh's feet are not touching the ground. (a) Draw free-body diagrams for Padmaksh and the chair considered as separate systems, and another diagram for Padmaksh and the chair considered as one system. (b) Find the magnitude and direction of acceleration of the system.

(*a*)

FIG. 5-31 (*a*) A child sitting on a chair hanging from a tree through a rope and pulley arrangement. (*b*) A child sitting on a chair hanging from a tree through a rope and pulley arrangement.

(a) Conceptualize: When Padmaksh pulls the rope downward by applying force in vertically downward direction, the rope also applies the same force on his hands according to Newton's third law. Also the chair will be experiencing normal contact force due to Padmaksh and vice versa.

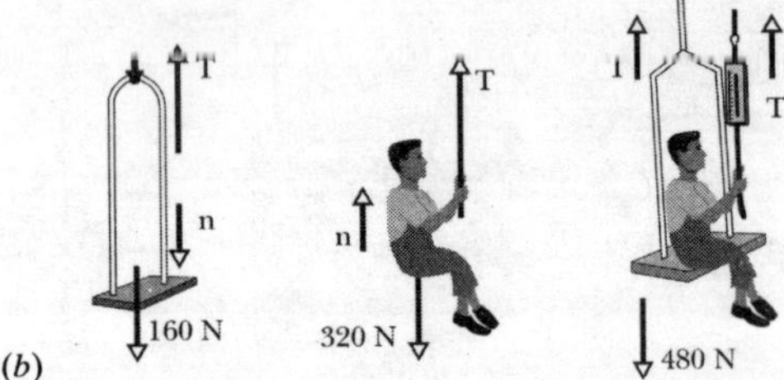

(b) Conceptualize/Classify: It is easy to see that both Padmaksh and chair will be having same acceleration. As the Padmaksh is supposed to be at rest with respect to the chair. It is evident from the fig() that it will be easier to solve the problem by taking Padmaksh and the chair as the system, as number of unkowns will be minimum.

Compute: First consider Padmaksh and the chair as the system. Note that two ropes support the system, and $T = 252$ N in each rope.

Applying $\Sigma F = ma$; $2T - 480 = ma$, where

$$m = 32 \text{ kg} + 16 \text{ kg} = 48 \text{ kg}$$

Solving for a gives

$$a = \frac{504 - 480}{48} = 0.5 \text{m/s}^2$$

Conclude: Our genius has applied a force less than his weight and is able to pull himself and the chair because the system (Padmaksh and chair) is experiencing two tension forces, both in upward direction. So he is getting twice the force of his pull, applied on himself by this ingenious arrangement.

In Case Of: Find the force Padmaksh exerts on the chair. Applying, $\Sigma F = ma$ on Padmaksh:

where $\Sigma F = n + T - mg$

$$\Sigma F = n + T - 320 = ma$$

where $m = 32$ kg

$$n = ma + 320 - T = 32\,(0.5) + 320 - 252 = 84 \text{ N}$$

CHECKPOINT 8 In the situation described in the example above (a) Assume Padmaksh is momentarily at rest and he stops pulling down on the rope. Padmaksh passes the free end of the rope to another child, of mass 42 kg, standing on the ground, who holds it tightly. Describe the subsequent motion.
(b) Instead, assume Padmaksh is momentarily at rest and he ties the end of the rope to a strong hook projecting from the tree trunk. In which case does the rope have more chances of breaking.

Sample Problem 5-17

A light smooth pulley fixed to the ceiling of an elevator car carries a thread whose ends are attached to the loads m_1 and m_2 ($m_1 > m_2$). The car starts going up with an acceleration a. Assuming the masses of the pulley and the thread, as well as the friction, to be negligible find:

(a) the acceleration of m_1 relative to the ground.

(b) the force exerted by the pulley on the ceiling of the car.

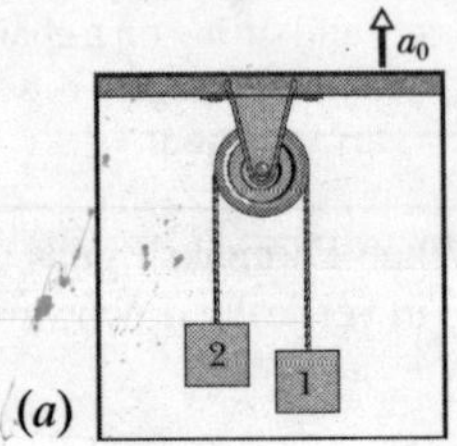

FIG. 5-32 (*a*) Pulley fixed to ceiling of an elevator car. (*b*) free-body diagrams.

Conceptualize: In frame of pulley of objects 1 and 2 will have same magnitude of acceleration. This acceleration cannot be used for Newton's second law because lift and pulley are accelerated and hence noninertial reference frame.

Classify: We have to find acceleration of objects 1 and 2 in ground frame. Using constraint equation, we can find relation between accelerations of the object.

Compute: Let x_1 and x_2 be the co-ordinate of the blocks. x_3 is co-ordinate of pulley.

All co-ordinates are written from a fixed reference line as shown.

$x_1 - x_3$ is length of rope on right

$x_2 - x_3$ is length of rope on left

$x_1 - x_3 + x_2 - x_3 = L$

and differentiating we get

$$v_1 - v_2 - 2(-v) = 0 \qquad a_2 - a_1 = 2a$$

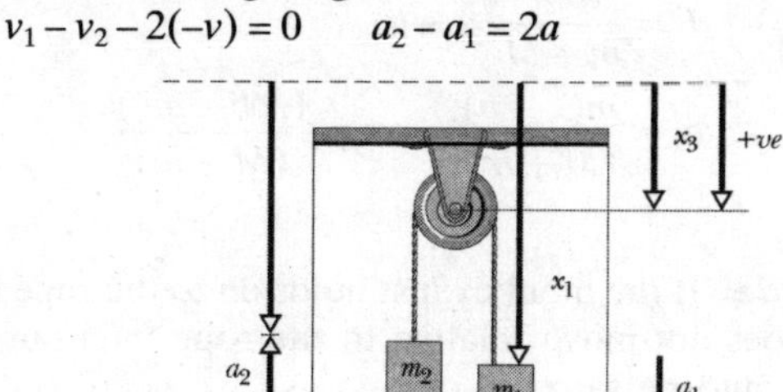

From the free-body diagrams of m_1 and m_2

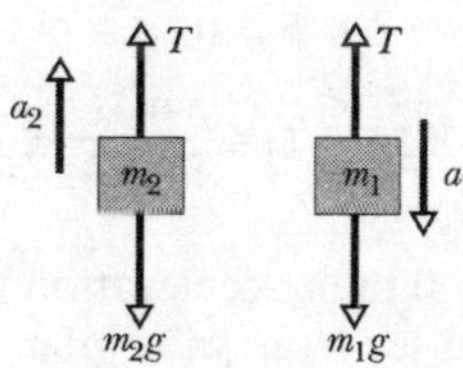

$$m_1 g - T = m_1 a_1$$

and $$T - m_2 g = m_2 a_2$$

Adding, $$(m_1 - m_2)\,g = m_1 a_1 + m_2 a_2$$

$$= m_1 a_1 + m_2(2a + a_1)$$

or $$a_1 = \frac{(m_1 - m_2)g - 2m_2 a}{m_1 \quad m_2}$$

(b) $$F = 2T = 2m_1(g - a_1) = 2m_1$$

$$\left[g \frac{(m_1 - m_2)g - 2m_2 a}{m_1 + m_2}\right]$$

or $$F = \frac{4m_1 m_2}{m_1 + m_2}(g + a)$$

Conclude: We can check that acceleration of objects 1 and 2 in reference frame of lift are coming out to be equal in magnitude and opposite in direction.

Soultion: Acceleration of object 1 relative to the car is written as $a_{1/\text{car}}$

$$a_{1/\text{car}} = a_1 - (-a) = a_1 + a$$

or $$a_{1/\text{car}} = \frac{(m_1 - m_2)g - 2m_2 a}{m_1 + m_2} + a = \frac{m_1 - m_2}{m_1 + m_2}(g + a)$$

Acceleration of object 2 relative to the car is written as $a_{2/\text{car}}$

$$a_{2/\text{car}} = a_2 - a = \frac{m_1 - m_2}{m_1 + m_2}(g + a)$$

In Case Of: What if acceleration of lift is zero?

Solution: We get same result as

$$a_1 = \frac{(m_1 - m_2)g}{m_1 + m_2} \text{ downward}$$

and $$a_2 = \frac{(m_1 - m_2)g}{(m_1 + m_2)} \text{ upward}$$

In Case Of: What if lift falls freely, that is $a = -g$?

Solution: We should find that tension will be zero and both objects will fall freely.

Sample Problem 5-18

A monkey of mass m is climbing on a rope passing over a light frictionless pulley. The opposite end of the rope is tied to a weight of mass M lying on a smooth horizontal plane (Fig. 5-33). Find the accelerations of both bodies (relative to the plane) and the tension in the rope for the two cases (neglect mass of pulley and rope). Given that the monkey moves upward with an acceleration b relative to the rope.

Conceptualize: The main issue in this problem is difference between pulling on a rope rather than holding on to the rope.

Classify: As monkey pulls the rope downward, the rope moves relative to him. Thus we can't say that monkey and the block kept on horizontal surface will have same acceleration. Thus constraint relation between them is not valid. If monkey would have simply held on the rope then constraint relation would have been valid.

Compute: Let a be the absolute upward acceleration of the monkey and a be the absolute downward acceleration of the rope. Obviously a is also the rightward acceleration of M. Then $b = a - (-a')$ (since relative acceleration is the vector difference between the absolute accelerations) or $$b = a + a'$$

Considering upward motion of the monkey

$$T\text{-}mg = ma \qquad \text{(i)}$$

Considering rightward motion of M

$$T - Ma' = Ma' = M(b - a)$$

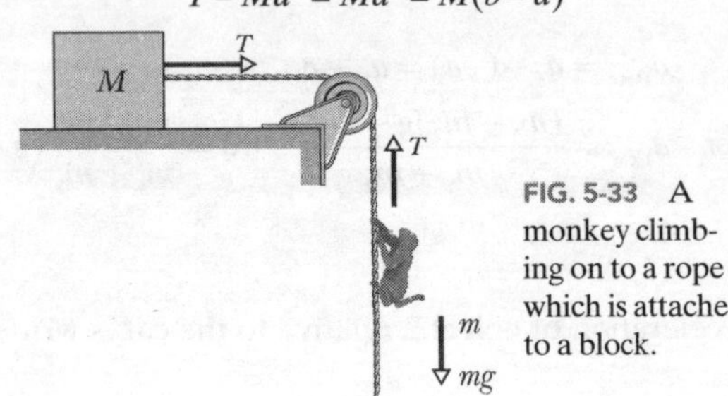

FIG. 5-33 A monkey climbing on to a rope which is attached to a block.

Eliminating a between (i) and (ii) we get T in terms of b.

$$T = \frac{mM}{m+M}(g+b)$$

$$a' = \frac{m(g+b)}{(M+m)} \qquad a = \frac{(Mb - mg)}{(M+m)}$$

Conclude: If the monkey just holds on to the rope that is, he does not move relative to the rope then our answer should be same as of eg(). All we need to do is keep $b = 0$ in the result.

Hence,

$$b = 0$$

$$T = \frac{mM}{m+M}g$$

Also, if $b = 0$ then acceleration of monkey is downward as you can see from value of a'.

5-10 | Fictitious force

Motion in Accelerated Frames

Till now we have restricted ourselves to apply Newton's laws of motion, only to describe observations that are made in an inertial frame of reference. In this part, we learn how Newton's laws can be applied by an observer in a noninertial reference frame. For example,consider a block kept on smooth surface of a compartment of train. When the train is moving at constant velocity it is an inertial frame. An observer on the train observes the block initially at rest to remain at rest.

On the accelerating train, the block accelerates toward the back of the train. We might conclude based on Newton's second law *F= ma* that a force is acting the block to cause it to accelerate, but the Newton's second law is not applicable from this frame. So we cannot relate observed acceleration with the Force acting on the block.

If we still want to use Newton's second law we apply a fictitious force, acting in backward direction, that is, opposite to the acceleration of noninertial reference frame. This force explains the motion of block toward the back of car. The fictious force is equal to $-ma$, where a is the acceleration of the noninertial reference frame. Fictitious force appears to act on an object in the same way as a real force, but real forces are always interactions between two objects. On the other hand there is no second object for a fictitious force.

Sample Problem 5-19

A small ball of mass m hangs by a cord from the ceiling of a compartment of a train that is accelerating to the right as shown in Fig. 5-34. Analyze the situations for two observers A and B.

Conceptualize: The observer A on the ground, is inertial frame. He sees the compartment is accelerating and knows that the deviation of the cord provides the ball, required horizontal force. The noninertial observer on the compartment, cannot see the car's motion so that he is not aware of its acceleration. Because he does not know of this acceleration, he will say that Newton's second law is not valid as the object has net horizontal force (the horizontal component of tension) but no horizontal acceleration.

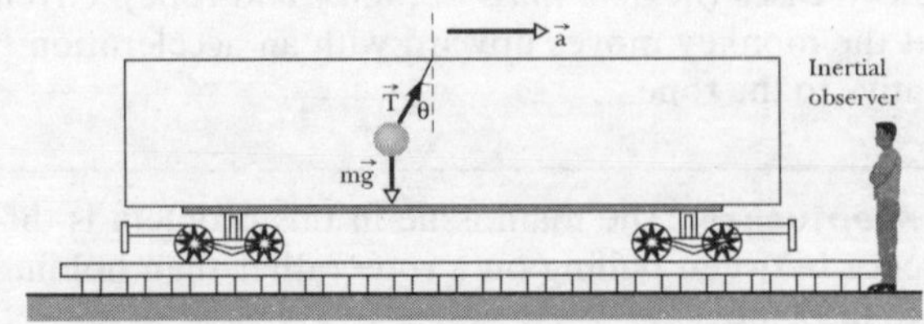

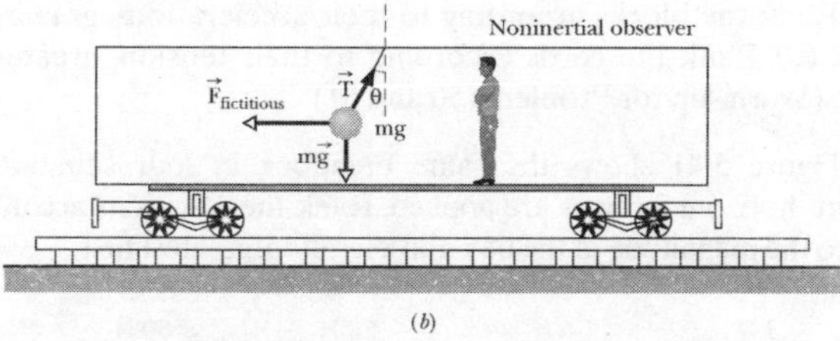

FIG. 5-34 A ball hanging inside a accelerating compartment is being observed by two observes.

Classify: For the inertial observer, ball has a net force in the horizontal direction and is in equilibrium in the vertical direction. For the noninertial observer, we apply fictitious force toward left and consider it to be in equilibrium.

Compute: According to the inertial observer A, the ball experiences two forces T, exerted by the cord and the weight.

Applying Newton's second law in horizontal and vertical direction we get

inertial observer
$$T\sin\theta - mg = 0$$
$$T\cos\theta = ma$$

According to the noninertial observer B riding in the car (Fig. 5-34b), the ball is always at rest and so its acceleration is zero. The noninertial observer applies a fictitious force in the horizontal direction of magnitude ma toward left. This fictious force balances the horizontal component of T and thus the net force on the ball is zero.

Applying Newton's second law in in horizontal and vertical direction we get

Noninertial observer
$$T\sin\,\theta - mg = 0$$
$$T\cos\,\theta - ma = 0$$

These expressions are equivalent to Eqs. (1) and (2).

Conclude: The noninertial observer B obtains the same equations as the inertial observer. The physical explanation of the cord's deflection, however, differs in the two frames of reference.

QUESTIONS

1 In Fig. 5-35, forces $\vec{F}_1$ and $\vec{F}_2$ are applied to a lunchbox as it slides at constant velocity over a frictionless floor. We are to decrease angle θ without changing the magnitude of $\vec{F}_1$. For constant velocity, should we increase, decrease, or maintain the magnitude of $\vec{F}_2$?

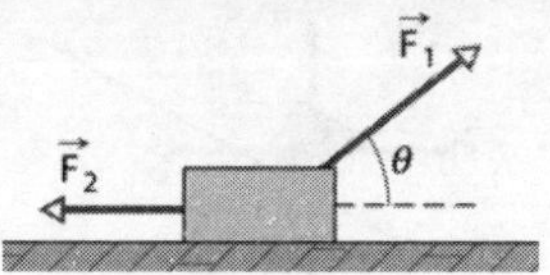

FIG. 5-35 Question 1.

2 At time $t = 0$, constant $\vec{F}$ begins to act on a rock moving through deep space in the $+x$ direction. (a) For time $t > 0$, which are possible functions $x(t)$ for the rock's position: (1) $x = 4t - 3$, (2) $x = -4t^2 + 6t - 3$, (3) $x = 4t^2 + 6t - 3$? (b) For which function is $\vec{F}$ directed opposite the rock's initial direction of motion?

3 Figure 5-36 shows overhead views of four situations in which forces act on a block that lies on a frictionless floor. If the force magnitudes are chosen properly, in which situations is it possible that the block is (a) stationary and (b) moving with a constant velocity?

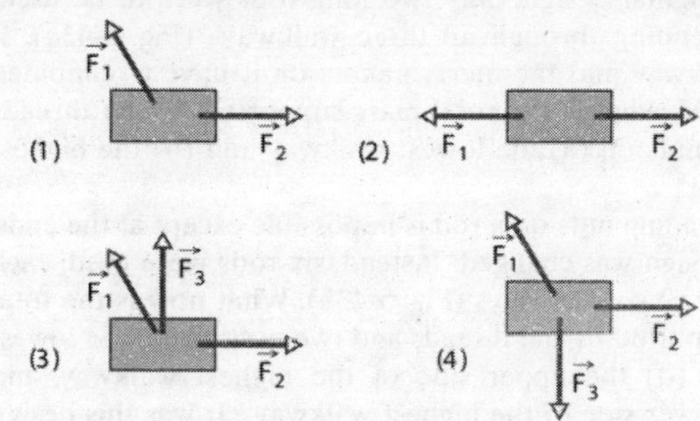

FIG. 5-36 Question 3.

4 Two horizontal forces,

$$\vec{F}_1 = (3\text{ N})\hat{\imath} - (4\text{ N})\hat{\jmath} \quad \text{and} \quad \vec{F}_2 = -(1\text{ N})\hat{\imath} - (2\text{ N})\hat{\jmath}$$

pull a banana split across a frictionless lunch counter. Without using a calculator, determine which of the vectors in the free-body diagram of Fig. 5-37 best represent (a) $\vec{F}_1$ and (b) $\vec{F}_2$. What is the net-force component along (c) the x axis and (d) the y axis? Into which quadrants do (e) the net-force vector and (f) the split's acceleration vector point?

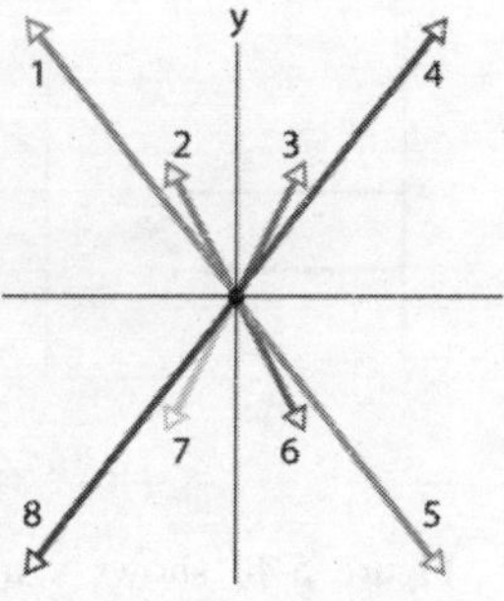

FIG. 5-37 Question 4.

5 Figure 5-38 gives the free-body diagram for four situations in which an object is pulled by several forces across a frictionless floor, as seen from overhead. In which situations does the object's acceleration $\vec{a}$ have (a) an x component and (b) a y component? (c) In each situation, give the direction of $\vec{a}$ by naming either a quadrant or a direction along an axis. (This can be done with a few mental calculations.)

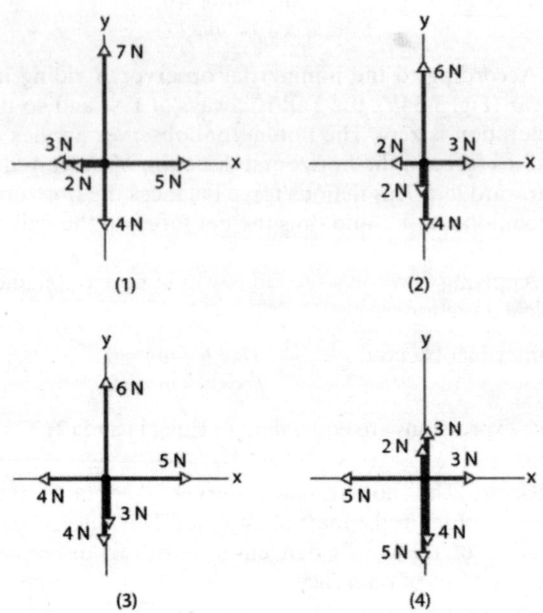

FIG. 5-38 Question 5.

6 Figure 5-39 gives three graphs of velocity component $v_x(t)$ and three graphs of velocity component $v_y(t)$. The graphs are not to scale. Which $v_x(t)$ graph and which $v_y(t)$ graph best correspond to each of the four situations in Question 5 and Fig. 5-24?

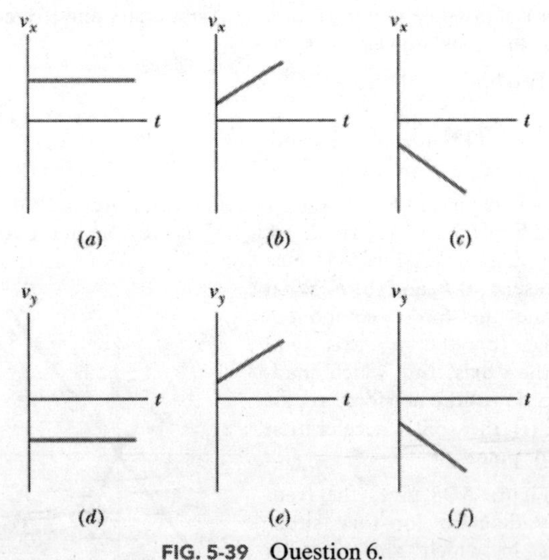

FIG. 5-39 Question 6.

7 Figure 5-40 shows a train of four blocks being pulled across a frictionless floor by force $\vec{F}$. What total mass is accelerated to the right by (a) force $\vec{F}$, (b) cord 3, and (c) cord 1? (d) Rank the blocks according to their accelerations, greatest first. (e) Rank the cords according to their tension, greatest first. (Warm-up for Problems 50 and 51)

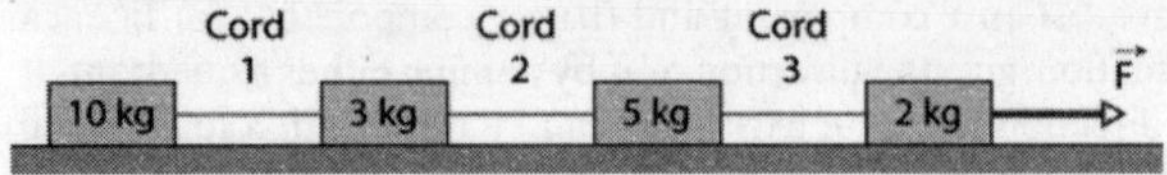

FIG. 5-40 Question 7.

8 Figure 5-41 shows the same breadbox in four situations where horizontal forces are applied. Rank the situations according to the magnitude of the box's acceleration, greatest first.

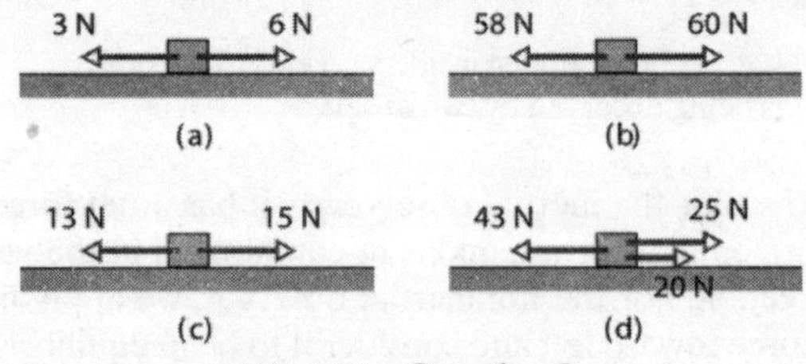

FIG. 5-41 Question 8.

9 A vertical force $\vec{F}$ is applied to a block of mass m that lies on a floor. What happens to the magnitude of the normal force $\vec{F}_N$ on the block from the floor as magnitude F is increased from zero if force $\vec{F}$ is (a) downward and (b) upward?

10 Figure 5-42 shows four choices for the direction of a force of magnitude F to be applied to a block on an inclined plane. The directions are either horizontal or vertical. (For choices a and b, the force is not enough to lift the block off the plane.) Rank the choices according to the magnitude of the normal force on the block from the plane, greatest first.

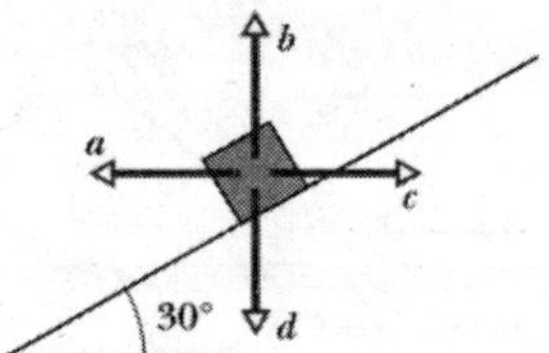

FIG. 5-42 Question 10.

11 July 17, 1981, Kansas City: The newly opened Hyatt Regency is packed with people listening and dancing to a band playing favorites from the 1940s. Many of the people are crowded onto the walkways that hang like bridges across the wide atrium. Suddenly two of the walkways collapse, falling onto the merrymakers on the main floor.

The walkways were suspended one above another on vertical rods and held in place by nuts threaded onto the rods. In the original design, only two long rods were to be used, each extending through all three walkways (Fig. 5-43*a*). If each walkway and the merrymakers on it have a combined mass of M, what is the total mass supported by the threads and two nuts on (a) the lowest walkway and (b) the highest walkway?

Threading nuts on a rod is impossible except at the ends, so the design was changed: Instead, six rods were used, each connecting two walkways (Fig. 5-43*b*). What now is the total mass supported by the threads and two nuts on (c) the lowest walkway, (d) the upper side of the highest walkway, and (e) the lower side of the highest walkway? It was this design that failed.

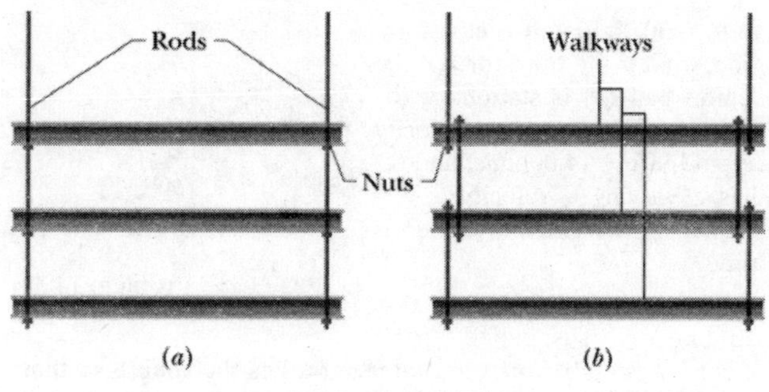

FIG. 5-43 Question 11.

12 Figure 5-44 shows three blocks being pushed across a frictionless floor by horizontal force $\vec{F}$. What total mass is accelerated to the right by (a) force $\vec{F}$, (b) force $\vec{F}_{21}$ on block 2 from block 1, and (c) force $\vec{F}_{32}$ on block 3 from block 2? (d) Rank the blocks according to their acceleration magnitudes, greatest first. (e) Rank forces $\vec{F}$, $\vec{F}_{21}$, and $\vec{F}_{32}$ according to magnitude, greatest first. (Warm-up for Problem 53)

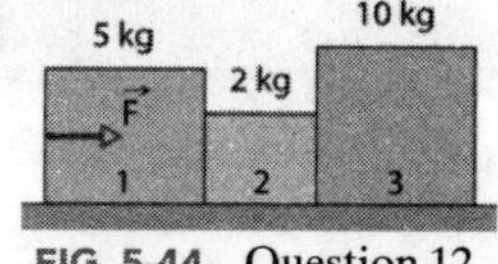

FIG. 5-44 Question 12.

PROBLEMS

Newton's Second Law

1 While two forces act on it, a particle is to move at the constant velocity $\vec{v} = (3\text{ m/s})\hat{\text{i}} - (4\text{ m/s})\hat{\text{j}}$. One of the forces is $\vec{F}_1 = (2\text{ N})\hat{\text{i}} + (-6\text{ N})\hat{\text{j}}$. What is the other force?

2 A 2.0 kg particle moves along an x axis, being propelled by a variable force directed along that axis. Its position is given by $x = 3.0\text{ m} + (4.0\text{ m/s})t + ct^2 - (2.0\text{ m/s}^3)t^3$, with x in meters and t in seconds. The factor c is a constant. At $t = 3.0$ s, the force on the particle has a magnitude of 36 N and is in the negative direction of the axis. What is c?

3 Two horizontal forces $\vec{F}_1$ and $\vec{F}_2$ act on a 4.0 kg disk that slides over frictionless ice, on which an xy coordinate system is laid out. Force $\vec{F}_1$ is in the positive direction of the x axis and has a magnitude of 7.0 N. Force $\vec{F}_2$ has a magnitude of 9.0 N. Figure 5-45 gives the x component v_x of the velocity of the disk as a function of time t during the sliding. What is the angle between the constant directions of forces $\vec{F}_1$ and $\vec{F}_2$?

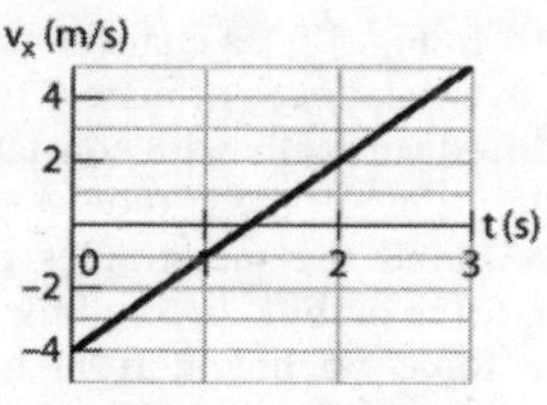

FIG. 5-45 Problem 3.

Some Particular Forces

4 (a) An 11.0 kg salami is supported by a cord that runs to a spring scale, which is supported by a cord hung from the ceiling (Fig. 5-46a). What is the reading on the scale, which is marked in weight units? (b) In Fig. 5-46b the salami is supported by a cord that runs around a pulley and to a scale. The opposite end of the scale is attached by a cord to a wall. What is the reading on the scale? (c) In Fig. 5-46c the wall has been replaced with a second 11.0 kg salami, and the assembly is stationary. What is the reading on the scale?

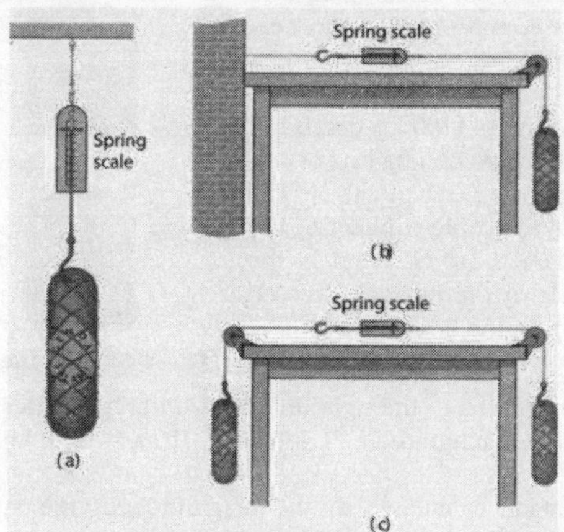

FIG. 5-46 Problem 4.

5 A block with a weight of 3.0 N is at rest on a horizontal surface. A 1.0 N upward force is applied to the block by means of an attached vertical string. What are the (a) magnitude and (b) direction of the force of the block on the horizontal surface?

6 Figure 5-47 shows an arrangement in which four disks are suspended by cords. The longer, top cord loops over a frictionless pulley and pulls with a force of magnitude 98 N on the wall to which it is attached. The tensions in the shorter cords are $T_1 = 58.8$ N, $T_2 = 49.0$ N, and $T_3 = 9.8$ N. What are the masses of (a) disk A, (b) disk B, (c) disk C, and (d) disk D?

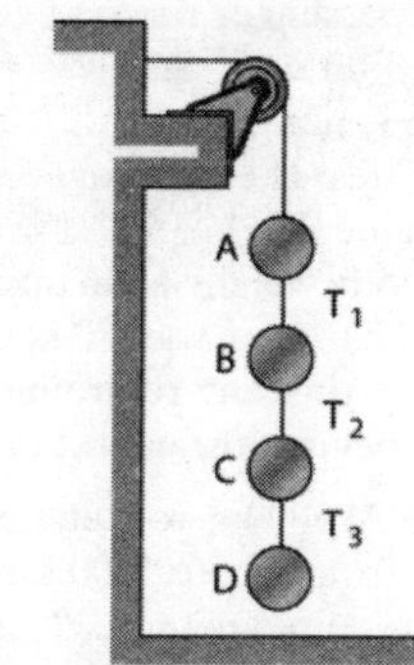

FIG. 5-47 Problem 6.

Applying Newton's Laws

7 A customer sits in an amusement park ride in which the compartment is to be pulled downward in the negative direction of a y axis with an acceleration magnitude of $1.24g$, with $g = 9.80\text{ m/s}^2$. A 0.567 g coin rests on the customer's knee. Once the motion begins and in unit-vector notation, what is the coin's acceleration relative to (a) the ground and (b) the customer? (c) How long does the coin take to reach the compartment ceiling, 2.20 m above the knee? In unit-vector notation, what are (d) the actual force on the coin and (e) the apparent force according to the customer's measure of the coin's acceleration?

8 In Fig. 5-48, let the mass of the block be 8.5 kg and the angle θ be 30°. Find (a) the tension in the cord and (b) the normal force acting on the block. (c) If the cord is cut, find the magnitude of the resulting acceleration of the block.

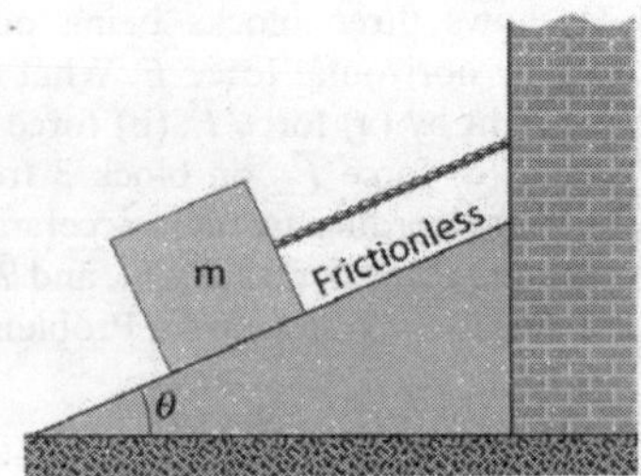

FIG. 5-48 Problem 8.

9 A constant horizontal force $\vec{F}_a$ pushes a 2.00 kg FedEx package across a frictionless floor on which an xy coordinate system has been drawn. Figure 5-49 gives the package's x and y velocity components versus time t. What are the (a) magnitude and (b) direction of $\vec{F}_a$?

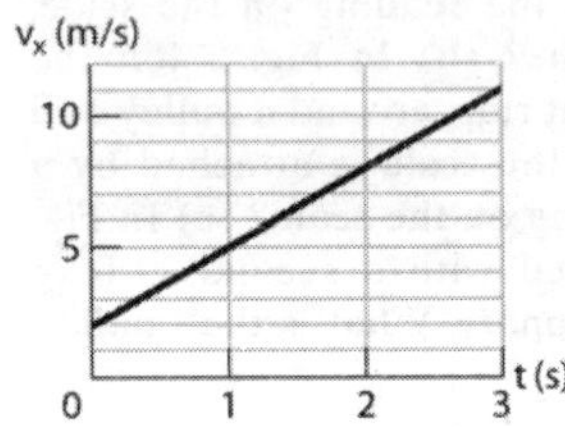

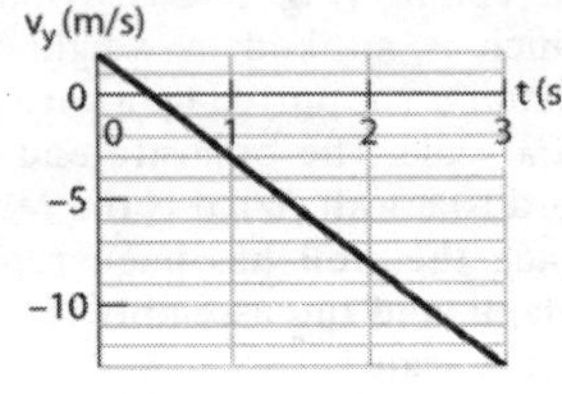

FIG. 5-49 Problem 9.

10 In April 1974, John Massis of Belgium managed to move two passenger railroad cars. He did so by clamping his teeth down on a bit that was attached to the cars with a rope and then leaning backward while pressing his feet against the railway ties. The cars together weighed 700 kN (about 80 tons). Assume that he pulled with a constant force that was 2.5 times his body weight, at an upward angle θ of 30° from the horizontal. His mass was 80 kg, and he moved the cars by 1.0 m. Neglecting any retarding force from the wheel rotation, find the speed of the cars at the end of the pull.

11 A 500 kg rocket sled can be accelerated at a constant rate from rest to 1600 km/h in 1.8 s. What is the magnitude of the required net force?

12 In Fig. 5-50, a crate of mass m = 100 kg is pushed at constant speed up a frictionless ramp (θ = 30.0°) by a horizontal force $\vec{F}$. What are the magnitudes of (a) $\vec{F}$ and (b) the force on the crate from the ramp?

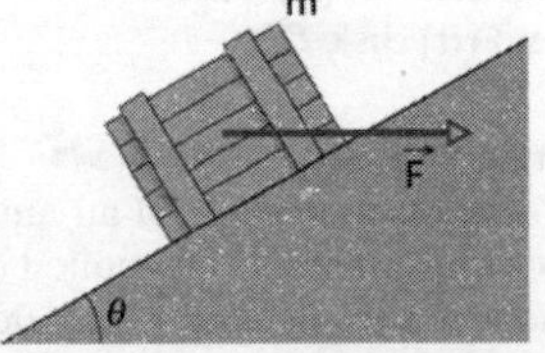

FIG. 5-50 Problem 12.

13 A 40 kg girl and an 8.4 kg sled are on the frictionless ice of a frozen lake, 15 m apart but connected by a rope of negligible mass. The girl exerts a horizontal 5.2 N force on the rope. What are the acceleration magnitudes of (a) the sled and (b) the girl? (c) How far from the girl's initial position do they meet?

14 Figure 5-51 shows an overhead view of a 0.0250 kg lemon half and two of the three horizontal forces that act on it as it is on a frictionless table. Force $\vec{F}_1$ has a magnitude of 6.00 N and is at θ_1 = 30.0°. Force $\vec{F}_2$ has a magnitude of 7.00 N and is at θ_2 = 30.0°. In unit-vector notation, what is the third force if the lemon half (a) is stationary, (b) has constant velocity $\vec{v} = (13.0\hat{i} - 14.0\hat{j})$ m/s, and (c) has varying velocity $\vec{v} = (13.0t\hat{i} - 14.0t\hat{j})$ m/s², where t is time?

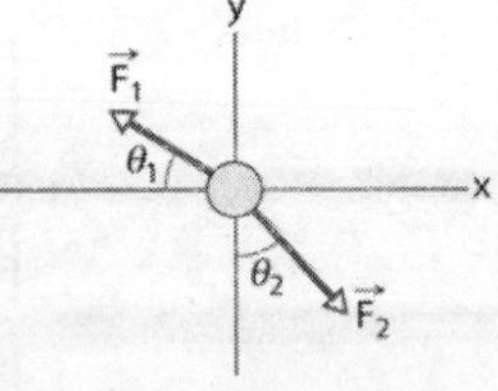

FIG. 5-51 Problem 14.

15 A sphere of mass 3.0 × 10^{-4} kg is suspended from a cord. A steady horizontal breeze pushes the sphere so that the cord makes a constant angle of 37° with the vertical. Find (a) the push magnitude and (b) the tension in the cord.

16 An elevator cab and its load have a combined mass of 1600 kg. Find the tension in the supporting cable when the cab, originally moving downward at 12 m/s, is brought to rest with constant acceleration in a distance of 42 m.

17 Using a rope that will snap if the tension in it exceeds 387 N, you need to lower a bundle of old roofing material weighing 449 N from a point 6.1 m above the ground. (a) What magnitude of the bundle's acceleration will put the rope on the verge of snapping? (b) At that acceleration, with what speed would the bundle hit the ground?

18 An elevator cab is pulled upward by a cable. The cab and its single occupant have a combined mass of 2000 kg. When that occupant drops a coin, its acceleration relative to the cab is 8.00 m/s² downward. What is the tension in the cable?

19 In Fig. 5-52, a chain consisting of five links, each of mass 0.100 kg, is lifted vertically with constant acceleration of magnitude a = 2.50 m/s². Find the magnitudes of (a) the force on link 1 from link 2, (b) the force on link 2 from link 3, (c) the force on link 3 from link 4, and (d) the force on link 4 from link 5. Then find the magnitudes of (e) the force $\vec{F}$ on the top link from the person lifting the chain and (f) the *net* force accelerating each link.

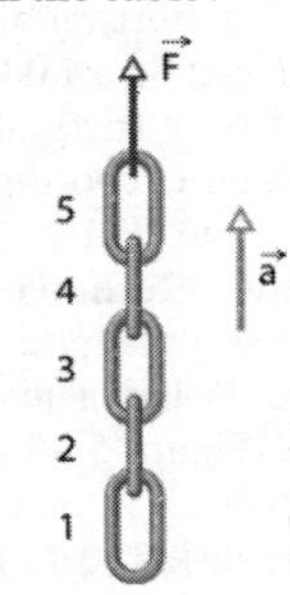

FIG. 5-52 Problem 19.

20 In Fig. 5-53, elevator cabs A and B are connected by a short cable and can be pulled upward or lowered by the cable above cab A. Cab A has mass 1700 kg; cab B has mass 1300 kg. A 12.0 kg box of catnip lies on the floor of cab A. The tension in the cable connecting the cabs is 1.91 × 10^4 N. What is the magnitude of the normal force on the box from the floor?

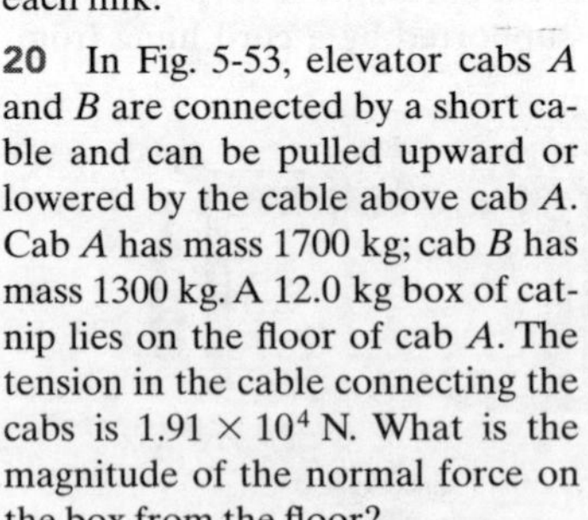

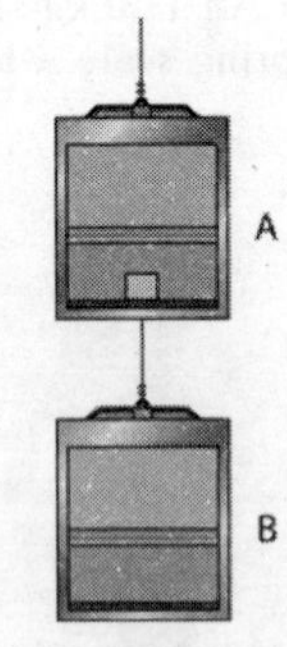

FIG. 5-53 Problem 20.

21 In Fig. 5-54, three connected blocks are pulled to the right on a horizontal frictionless table by a force of magnitude T_3 = 65.0 N. If m_1 = 12.0 kg, m_2 = 24.0 kg, and m_3 = 31.0 kg, calculate (a) the magnitude of the system's acceleration, (b) the tension T_1, and (c) the tension T_2.

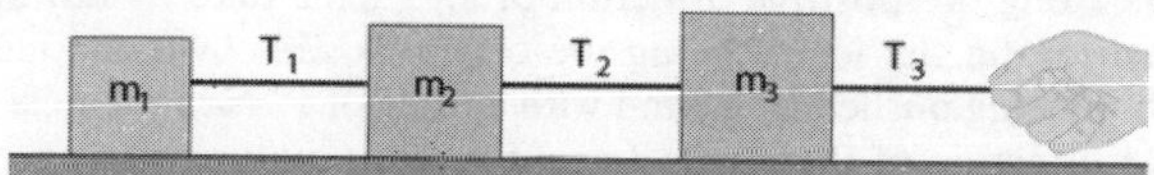

FIG. 5-54 Problem 21.

22 In Fig. 5-55*a*, a constant horizontal force $\vec{F}_a$ is applied to block *A*, which pushes against block *B* with a 20.0 N force directed horizontally to the right. In Fig. 5-55*b*, the same force $\vec{F}_a$ is applied to block *B*; now block *A* pushes on block *B* with a 10.0 N force directed horizontally to the left. The blocks have a combined mass of 12.0 kg. What are the magnitudes of (a) their acceleration in Fig. 5-54*a* and (b) force $\vec{F}_a$?

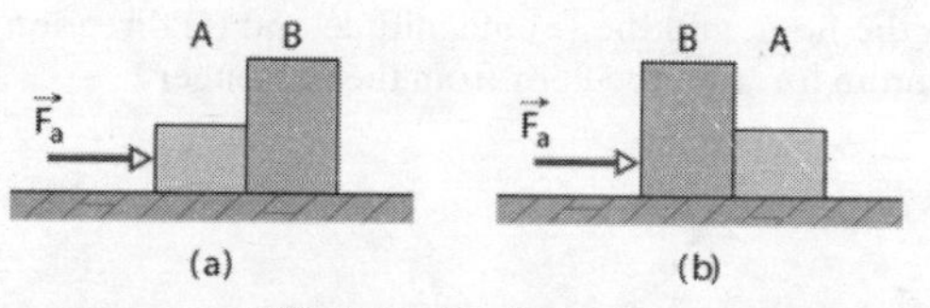

FIG. 5-55 Problem 22.

23 Two blocks are in contact on a frictionless table. A horizontal force is applied to the larger block, as shown in Fig. 5-56. (a) If $m_1 =$ 2.3 kg, $m_2 = 1.2$ kg, and $F = 3.2$ N, find the magnitude of the force between the two blocks. (b) Show that if a force of the same magnitude *F* is applied to the smaller block but in the opposite direction, the magnitude of the force between the blocks is 2.1 N, which is not the same value calculated in (a). (c) Explain the difference.

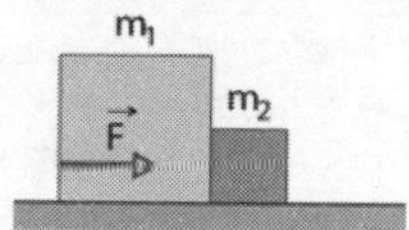

FIG. 5-56 Problem 23.

24 In Fig. 5-57, three ballot boxes are connected by cords, one of which wraps over a pulley having negligible friction on its axle and negligible mass. The three masses are $m_A =$ 30.0 kg, $m_B = 40.0$ kg, and m_C = 10.0 kg. When the assembly is released from rest, (a) what is the tension in the cord connecting *B* and *C*, and (b) how far does *A* move in the first 0.250 s (assuming it does not reach the pulley)?

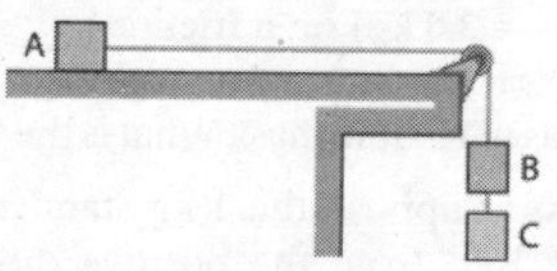

FIG. 5-57 Problem 24.

25 Figure 5-58 shows two blocks connected by a cord (of negligible mass) that passes over a frictionless pulley (also of negligible mass). The arrangement is known as *Atwood's machine.* One block has mass $m_1 =$ 1.30 kg; the other has mass $m_2 = 2.80$ kg. What are (a) the magnitude of the blocks' acceleration and (b) the tension in the cord?

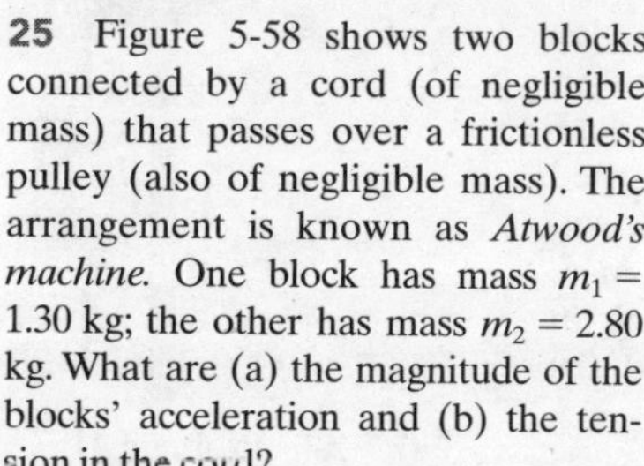

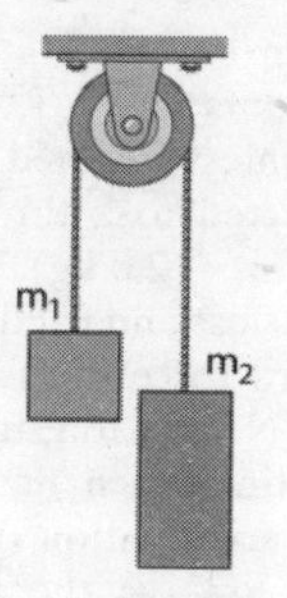

FIG. 5-58 Problem 25.

26 A 10 kg monkey climbs up a massless rope that runs over a frictionless tree limb and back down to a 15 kg package on the ground (Fig. 5-59). (a) What is the magnitude of the least acceleration the monkey must have if it is to lift the package off the ground? If, after the package has been lifted, the monkey stops its climb and holds onto the rope, what are the (b) magnitude and (c) direction of the monkey's acceleration and (d) the tension in the rope?

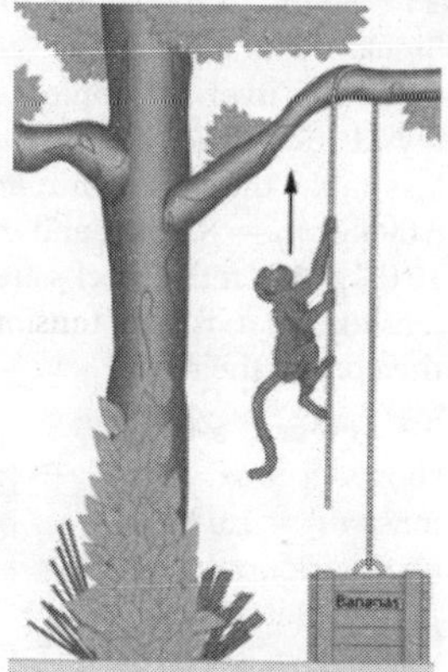

FIG. 5-59 Problem 26.

27 A block of mass $m_1 = 3.70$ kg on a frictionless plane inclined at angle $\theta = 30.0°$ is connected by a cord over a massless, frictionless pulley to a second block of mass $m_2 = 2.30$ kg (Fig. 5-60). What are (a) the magnitude of the acceleration of each block, (b) the direction of the acceleration of the hanging block, and (c) the tension in the cord?

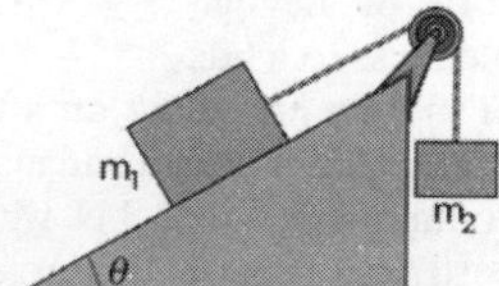

FIG. 5-60 Problem 27.

28 Figure 5-61 shows a man sitting in a bosun's chair that dangles from a massless rope, which runs over a massless, frictionless pulley and back down to the man's hand. The combined mass of man and chair is 95.0 kg. With what force magnitude must the man pull on the rope if he is to rise (a) with a constant velocity and (b) with an upward acceleration of 1.30 m/s²? (*Hint:* A free-body diagram can really help.) If the rope on the right extends to the ground and is pulled by a co-worker, with what force magnitude must the co-worker pull for the man to rise (c) with a constant velocity and (d) with an upward acceleration of 1.30 m/s²? What is the magnitude of the force on the ceiling from the pulley system in (e) part a, (f) part b, (g) part c, and (h) part d?

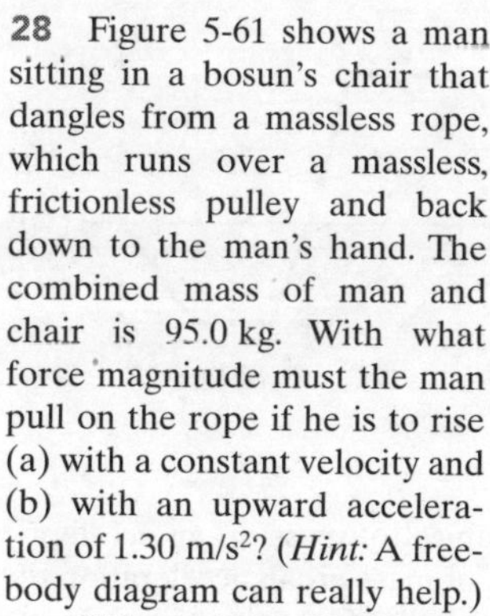

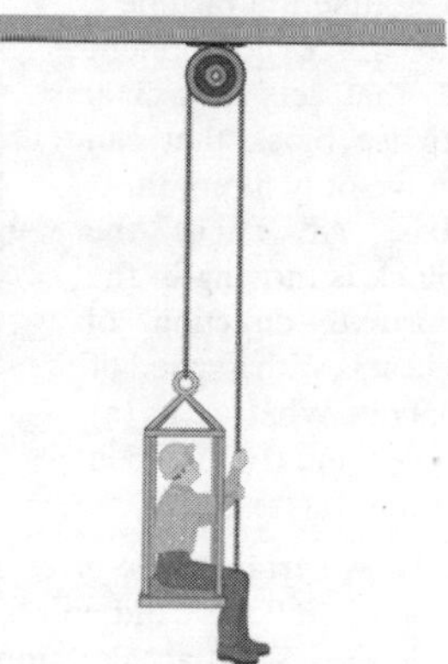
FIG. 5-61 Problem 28.

29 A hot-air balloon of mass *M* is descending vertically with downward acceleration of magnitude *a*. How much mass (ballast) must be thrown out to give the balloon an upward acceleration of magnitude *a*? Assume that the upward force from the air (the lift) does not change because of the decrease in mass.

30 Figure 5-64 shows *Atwood's machine,* in which two containers are connected by a cord (of negligible mass) passing over a frictionless pulley (also of negligible mass). At time $t = 0$, container 1 has mass 1.30 kg and container 2 has mass 2.80 kg, but container 1 is losing mass (through a leak) at the constant rate of 0.200 kg/s. At what rate is the acceleration magnitude of the containers changing at (a) $t = 0$ and (b) $t = 3.00$ s? (c) When does the acceleration reach its maximum value?

31 Figure 5-62 shows three blocks attached by cords that loop over frictionless pulleys. Block B lies on a frictionless table; the masses are m_A = 6.00 kg, m_B = 8.00 kg, and m_C = 10.0 kg. When the blocks are released, what is the tension in the cord at the right?

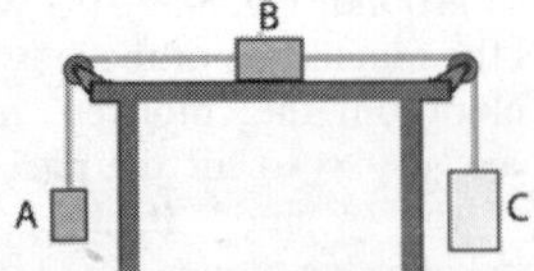

FIG. 5-62 Problem 31.

32 Figure 5-63 shows a box of mass m_2 = 1.0 kg on a frictionless plane inclined at angle θ = 30°. It is connected by a cord of negligible mass to a box of mass m_1 = 3.0 kg on a horizontal frictionless surface. The pulley is frictionless and massless. (a) If the magnitude of horizontal force $\vec{F}$ is 2.3 N, what is the tension in the connecting cord? (b) What is the largest value the magnitude of $\vec{F}$ may have without the cord becoming slack?

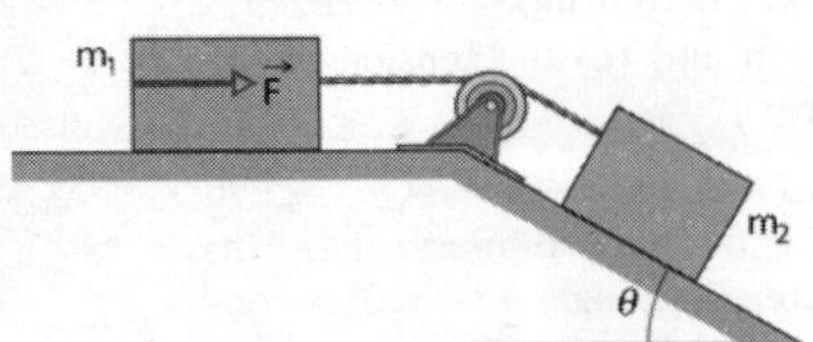

FIG. 5-63 Problem 32.

33 Figure 5-64 gives, as a function of time t, the force component F_x that acts on a 3.00 kg ice block that can move only along the x axis. At t = 0, the block is moving in the positive direction of the axis, with a speed of 3.0 m/s. What are its (a) speed and (b) direction of travel at t = 11 s?

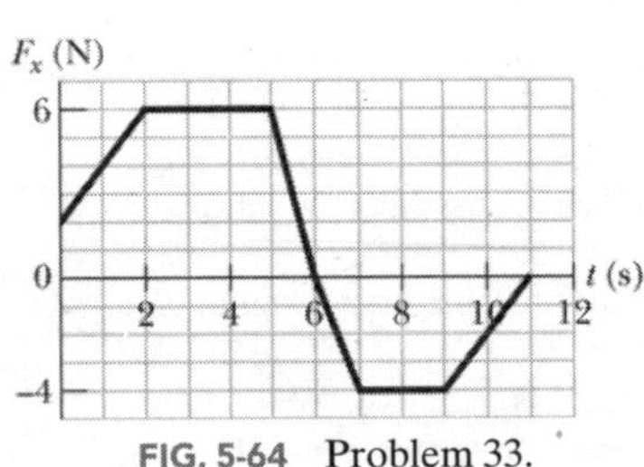

FIG. 5-64 Problem 33.

34 A certain force gives an object of mass m_1 an acceleration of 12.0 m/s² and an object of mass m_2 an acceleration of 3.30 m/s². What acceleration would the force give to an object of mass (a) $m_2 - m_1$ and (b) $m_2 + m_1$?

35 In Fig. 5-65, a force $\vec{F}$ of magnitude 12 N is applied to a FedEx box of mass m_2 = 1.0 kg. The force is directed up a plane tilted by θ = 37°. The box is connected by a cord to a UPS box of mass m_1 = 3.0 kg on the floor. The floor, plane, and pulley are frictionless, and the masses of the pulley and cord are negligible. What is the tension in the cord?

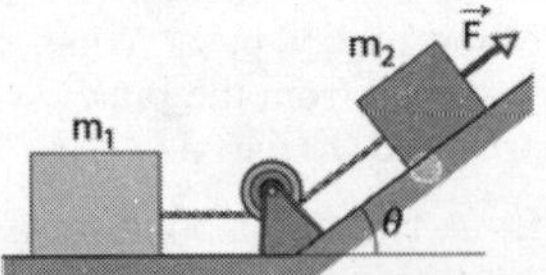

FIG. 5-65 Problem 35.

36 A certain particle has a weight of 22 N at a point where g = 9.8 m/s². What are its (a) weight and (b) mass at a point where g = 4.9 m/s²? What are its (c) weight and (d) mass if it is moved to a point in space where g = 0?

37 For sport, a 12 kg armadillo runs onto a large pond of level, frictionless ice. The armadillo's initial velocity is 5.0 m/s along the positive direction of an x axis. Take its initial position on the ice as being the origin. It slips over the ice while being pushed by a wind with a force of 17 N in the positive direction of the y axis. In unit-vector notation, what are the animal's (a) velocity and (b) position vector when it has slid for 3.0 s?

38 A 50 kg passenger rides in an elevator cab that starts from rest on the ground floor of a building at t = 0 and rises to the top floor during a 10 s interval. The cab's acceleration as a function of the time is shown in Fig. 5-66, where positive values of the acceleration mean that it is directed upward. What are the (a) magnitude and (b) direction (up or down) of the maximum force on the passenger from the floor, the (c) magnitude and (d) direction of the minimum force on the passenger from the floor, and the (e) magnitude and (f) direction of the maximum force on the floor from the passenger?

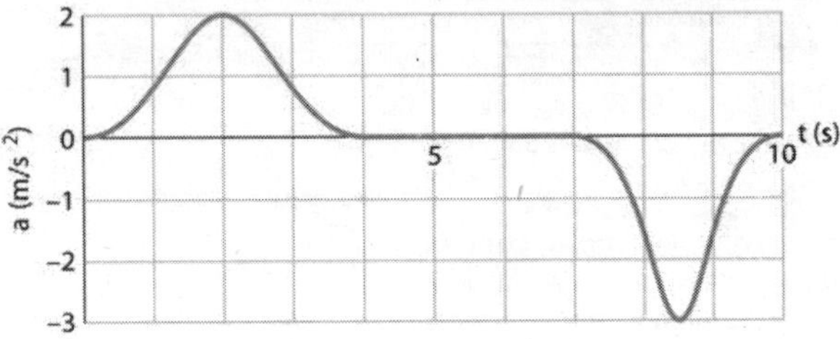

FIG. 5-66 Problem 38.

39 Figure 5-67 shows a box of dirty money (mass m_1 = 3.0 kg) on a frictionless plane inclined at angle θ_1 = 30°. The box is connected via a cord of negligible mass to a box of laundered money (mass m_2 = 2.0 kg) on a frictionless plane inclined at angle θ_2 = 60°. The pulley is frictionless and has negligible mass. What is the tension in the cord?

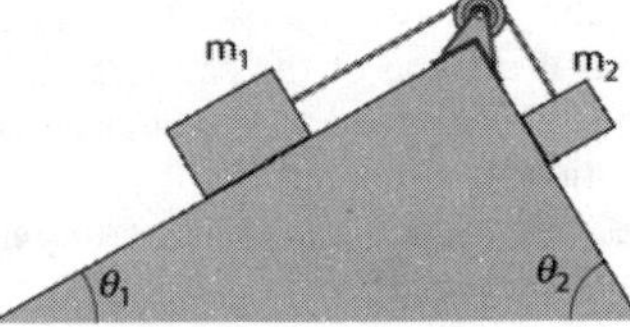

FIG. 5-67 Problem 39.

40 Suppose the 1 kg standard body accelerates at 4.00 m/s² at 160° from the positive direction of an x axis due to two forces; one is $\vec{F}_1$ = (2.50 N)$\hat{i}$ + (4.60 N)$\hat{j}$. What is the other force (a) in unit-vector notation and as (b) a magnitude and (c) an angle?

41 In Fig. 5-68, a tin of antioxidants (m_1 = 1.0 kg) on a frictionless inclined surface is connected to a tin of corned beef (m_2 = 2.0 kg). The pulley is massless and frictionless. An upward force of magnitude F = 6.0 N acts on the corned beef tin, which has a downward acceleration of 5.5 m/s². What are (a) the tension in the connecting cord and (b) angle β?

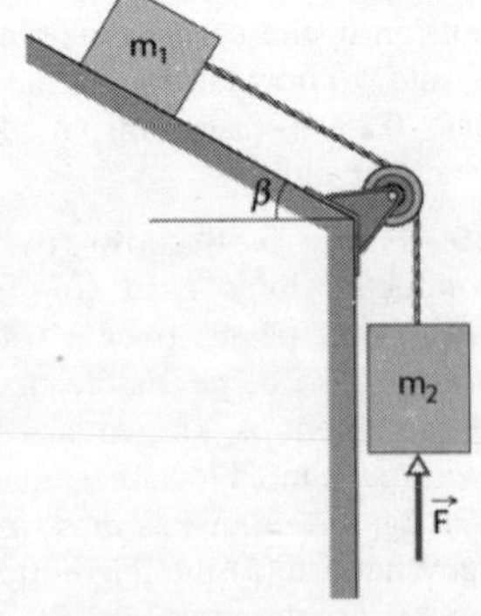

FIG. 5-68 Problem 41.

Friction

6

Will & Deni McIntyre/Stone/Getty Images

The Great Pyramid, built about 4500 years ago, consists of about 2 300 000 stone blocks, most with a mass of 2000 to 3000 kg. How did the engineers and workers manage to lift the stones into place to construct this pyramid, which is over 140 m high? Some researchers argue that during the construction a large team of men would pull a block up a giant earthen ramp that ran at a modest angle up one side of the pyramid. However, no evidence (such as rubble or painted pictures) exists to support this theory. Other researchers argue that a spiral ramp ran around the pyramid. However, such a ramp would have been highly unstable and, besides, maneuvering a 2000 kg stone around the 90° corners along the ramp would have been daunting, if not impossible.

How did the ancient people move the blocks up and into position?

The answer is in this chapter.

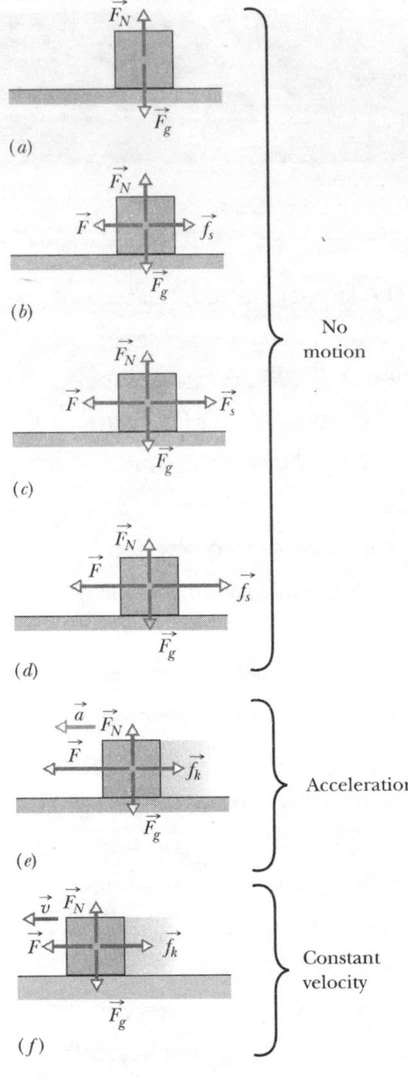

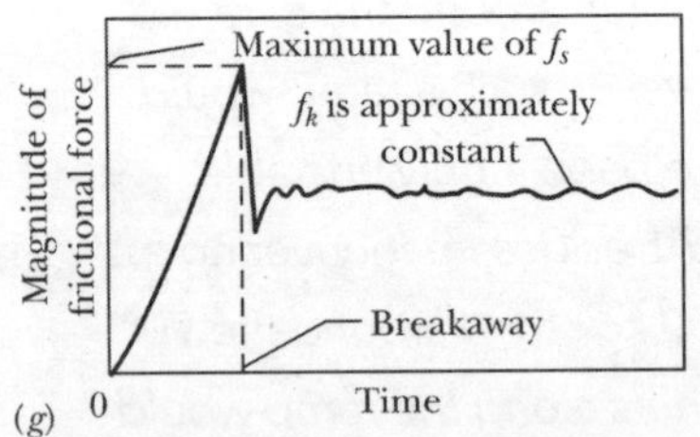

FIG. 6-1 (*a*) The forces on a stationary block. (*b–d*) An external force $\vec{F}$, applied to the block, is balanced by a static frictional force $\vec{f}_s$. As F is increased, f_s also increases, until f_s reaches a certain maximum value. (*e*) The block then "breaks away," accelerating suddenly in the direction of $\vec{F}$. (*f*) If the block is now to move with constant velocity, F must be reduced from the maximum value it had just before the block broke away. (*g*) Some experimental results for the sequence (*a*) through (*f*).

6-1 | Introduction

Frictional forces are unavoidable in our daily lives. If we were not able to counteract them, they would stop every moving object and bring to a halt every rotating shaft. About 20% of the gasoline used in an automobile is needed to counteract friction in the engine and in the drive train. On the other hand, if friction were totally absent, we could not get an automobile to go anywhere, and we could not walk or ride a bicycle. We could not hold a pencil, and, if we could, it would not write. Nails and screws would be useless, woven cloth would fall apart, and knots would untie.

Here we deal with the frictional forces that exist between dry solid surfaces, either stationary relative to each other or moving across each other at slow speeds. Consider three simple thought experiments:

1. Send a book sliding across a long horizontal counter. As expected, the book slows and then stops. This means the book must have an acceleration parallel to the counter surface, in the direction opposite the book's velocity. From Newton's second law, then, a force must act on the book parallel to the counter surface, in the direction opposite its velocity. That force is a frictional force.
2. Push horizontally on the book to make it travel at constant velocity along the counter. Can the force from you be the only horizontal force on the book? No, because then the book would accelerate. From Newton's second law, there must be a second force, directed opposite your force but with the same magnitude, so that the two forces balance. That second force is a frictional force, directed parallel to the counter.
3. Push horizontally on a heavy crate. The crate does not move. From Newton's second law, a second force must also be acting on the crate to counteract your force. Moreover, this second force must be directed opposite your force and have the same magnitude as your force, so that the two forces balance. That second force is a frictional force. Push even harder. The crate still does not move. Apparently the frictional force can change in magnitude so that the two forces still balance. Now push with all your strength. The crate begins to slide. Evidently, there is a maximum magnitude of the frictional force. When you exceed that maximum magnitude, the crate slides.

Figure 6-1 shows a similar situation. In Fig. 6-1*a*, a block rests on a tabletop, with the gravitational force $\vec{F}_g$ balanced by a normal force $\vec{F}_N$. In Fig. 6-1*b*, you exert a force $\vec{F}$ on the block, attempting to pull it to the left. In response, a frictional force $\vec{f}_s$ is directed to the right, exactly balancing your force. The force $\vec{f}_s$ is called the **static frictional force.** The block does not move.

Figures 6-1*c* and 6-1*d* show that as you increase the magnitude of your applied force, the magnitude of the static frictional force $\vec{f}_s$ also increases and the block remains at rest. When the applied force reaches a certain magnitude, however, the block "breaks away" from its intimate contact with the tabletop and accelerates leftward (Fig. 6-1*e*). The frictional force that then opposes the motion is called the **kinetic frictional force** $\vec{f}_k$.

Usually, the magnitude of the kinetic frictional force, which acts when there is motion, is less than the maximum magnitude of the static frictional force, which acts when there is no motion. Thus, if you wish the block to move across the surface with a constant speed, you must usually decrease the magnitude of the applied force once the block begins to move, as in Fig. 6-1*f*. As an example, Fig. 6-1*g* shows the results of an experiment in which the force on a block was slowly increased until breakaway occurred. Note the reduced force needed to keep the block moving at constant speed after breakaway.

A frictional force is, in essence, the vector sum of many forces acting between the surface atoms of one body and those of another. When two ordinary surfaces are placed together, only the high points touch each other. (It is like having the Alps of Switzerland turned over and placed down on the Alps of Austria.) The actual *micro*scopic area of contact is much less than the apparent *macro*scopic contact area, perhaps by a factor of 10^4. Nonetheless, many contact points do cold-weld together. These welds produce static friction when an applied force attempts to slide the surfaces relative to each other.

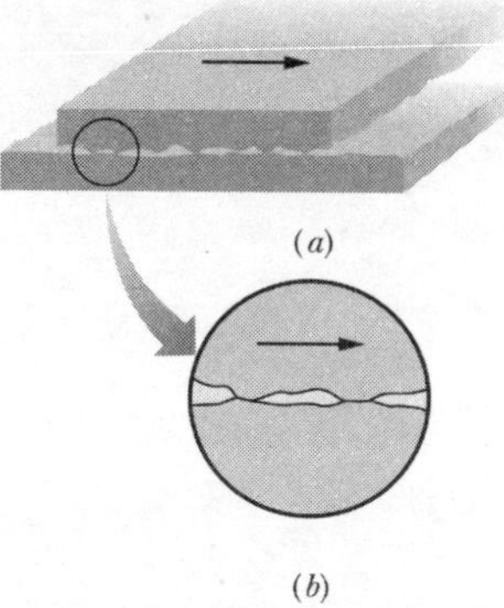

FIG. 6-2 The mechanism of sliding friction. (*a*) The upper surface is sliding to the right over the lower surface in this enlarged view. (*b*) A detail, showing two spots where cold-welding has occurred. Force is required to break the welds and maintain the motion.

If two highly polished and carefully cleaned metal surfaces are brought together in a very good vacuum (to keep them clean), they cannot be made to slide over each other. Because the surfaces are so smooth, many atoms of one surface contact many atoms of the other surface, and the surfaces *cold-weld* together instantly, forming a single piece of metal. If a machinist's specially polished gage blocks are brought together in air, there is less atom-to-atom contact, but the blocks stick firmly to each other and can be separated only by means of a wrenching motion. Usually, however, this much atom-to-atom contact is not possible. Even a highly polished metal surface is far from being flat on the atomic scale. Moreover, the surfaces of everyday objects have layers of oxides and other contaminants that reduce cold-welding.

If the applied force is great enough to pull one surface across the other, there is first a tearing of welds (at breakaway) and then a continuous re-forming and tearing of welds as movement occurs and chance contacts are made (Fig. 6-2). The kinetic frictional force $\vec{f}_k$ that opposes the motion is the vector sum of the forces at those many chance contacts.

If the two surfaces are pressed together harder, many more points cold-weld. Now getting the surfaces to slide relative to each other requires a greater applied force: The static frictional force $\vec{f}_s$ has a greater maximum value. Once the surfaces are sliding, there are many more points of momentary cold-welding, so the kinetic frictional force $\vec{f}_k$ also has a greater magnitude.

Often, the sliding motion of one surface over another is "jerky" because the two surfaces alternately stick together and then slip. Such repetitive *stick-and-slip* can produce squeaking or squealing, as when tires skid on dry pavement, fingernails scratch along a chalkboard, or a rusty hinge is opened. It can also produce beautiful sounds, as when a bow is drawn properly across a violin string. Frictional force always acts tangentially to the contact surface.

6-1a | Properties of Friction

Experiments show that when a dry and unlubricated body presses against a surface in the same condition and a force $\vec{F}$ attempts to slide the body along the surface, the resulting frictional force has three properties:

Property 1. If the body does not move, then the static frictional force $\vec{f}_s$ and the component of $\vec{F}$ that is parallel to the surface balance each other. They are equal in magnitude, and $\vec{f}_s$ is directed opposite to that component of $\vec{F}$.

Property 2. The magnitude of $\vec{f}_s$ has a maximum value $f_{s,\max}$ that is given by where μ_s is the **coefficient of static friction** and F_N is the magnitude of the normal force on the body from the surface. If the magnitude of the component of $\vec{F}$ that is parallel to the surface exceeds $f_{s,\max}$, then the body begins to slide along the surface.

$$f_{s,\max} = \mu_s F_N \tag{6-1}$$

Property 3. If the body begins to slide along the surface, then magnitude of frictional force rapidly decreases to a value f_k given by

$$f_k = \mu_k F_N \tag{6-2}$$

where μ_k is the **coefficient of kinetic friction.** Thereafter, during the sliding, a kinetic frictional force $\vec{f}_k$ with magnitude given by Eq. 6-2 opposes the motion.

The magnitude F_N of the normal force appears in properties 2 and 3 as a measure of how firmly the body presses against the surface. If the body presses harder, then, by Newton's third law, F_N is greater. Properties 1 and 2 are worded in terms of a single applied force $\vec{F}$, but they also hold for the net force of several applied forces acting on the body. Equations 6-1 and 6-2 are *not* vector equations; the direction of $\vec{f}_s$ or $\vec{f}_k$ is always parallel to the surface and opposed to the attempted sliding, and the normal force $\vec{F}_N$ is perpendicular to the surface.

The coefficients μ_s and μ_k are dimensionless and must be determined experimentally. Their values depend on certain properties of both the body and the surface; hence, they are usually referred to with the preposition "between," as in "the value of μ_s *between* an egg and a Teflon-coated skillet is 0.04, but that *between* rock-climbing shoes and rock is as much as 1.2." We assume that the value of μ_k does not depend on the speed at which the body slides along the surface.

The coefficients of friction are considered independent of the area of contact between the surfaces. We may think that having larger area of contact might increase the friction force. Although this will increase points in contact as in Fig. 6-2, but the weight of the object is now distributed over a larger area and the individual points cold welded as strongly. Thus these effects cancel each other, the friction force is independent of the area.

CHECKPOINT 1 A block lies on a floor. (a) What is the magnitude of the frictional force on it from the floor? (b) If a horizontal force of 5 N is now applied to the block, but the block does not move, what is the magnitude of the frictional force on it? (c) If the maximum value $f_{s,\max}$ of the static frictional force on the block is 10 N, will the block move if the magnitude of the horizontally applied force is 8 N? (d) If it is 12 N? (e) What is the magnitude of the frictional force in part (c)?

6-2 | Static Friction

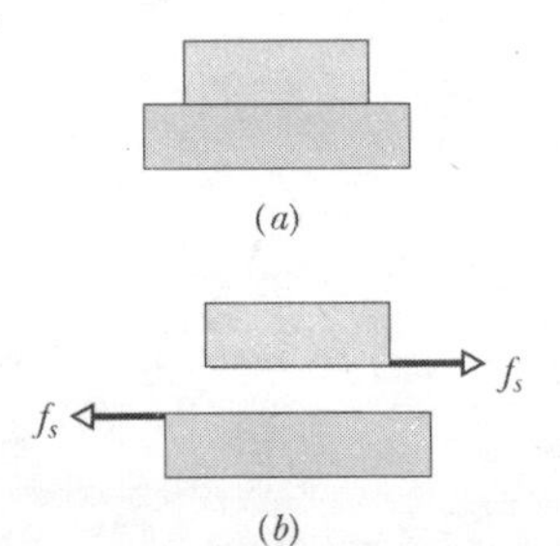

FIG. 6-3 Two books kept on top of each other.

Static friction acts when two contact sufaces are not moving relative to each other. For example, if we keep two books one on top of the other (Fig. 6-3) and we slowly push the lower book, both the books move together, the force moving the upper book is friction. Since the books are moving with respect to ground but they are not moving with respect to each other, this force of friction between two books is of static nature Similarly when we walk on ground the friction force acting on the foot is of static nature. You may be surprise but the foot in contact with ground is not moving while the other foot is moving. During this time friction acting between foot and ground is static friction (Fig. 6-4).

If we are increasing our speed then static friction is acting in forward direction. This happens because we try to pull our leg backward while walking in forward direction. This means foot is trying to move in backward direction with respect to ground and ground applies friction in forward direction on foot to oppose the direction of relative motion.

Both the direction and magnitude of static friction are self-adjusting such that relative motion is opposed.

In fact, in the previous case of books also, we can see that static friction by acting in forward direction on upper book has given it some motion so it can move with the lower book. Another point to be noted here is that even the third law pair of the static friction is opposing relative motion by trying to slow down the lower book (which is being accelerated externally).

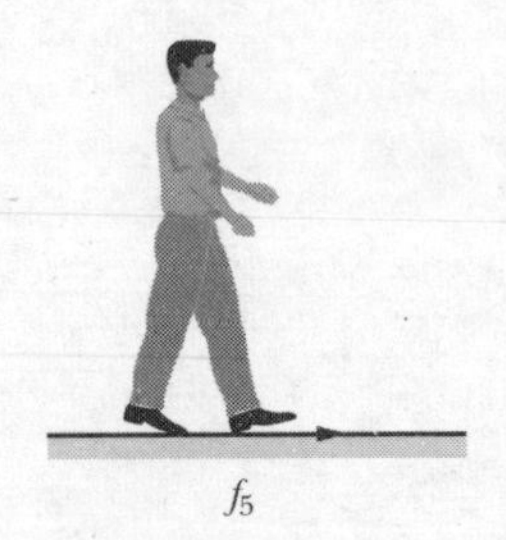

FIG. 6-4 Person walking due to static friction.

In Fig. 6-5*a* and *b* we are assuming block is stationary and we can see in that static friction is acting in such direction as to oppose the relative motion. *F* represents external force and f_S represents friction.

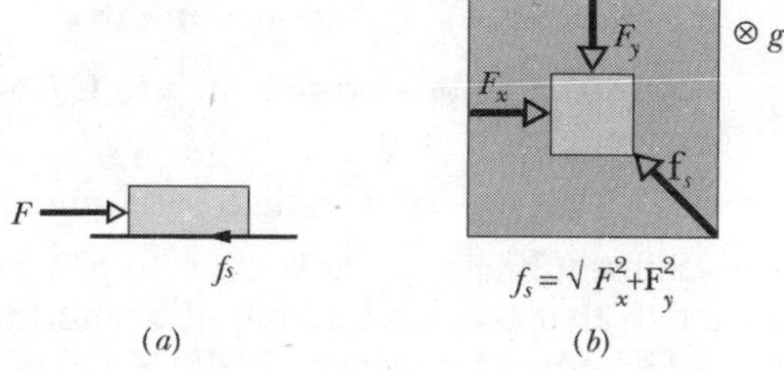

FIG. 6-5 Stationary block and static friction.

The magnitude of the static friction between any two surfaces in contact can have the values

$$f_s < \mu_s N \tag{6-3}$$

where the dimensionless constant μ_s is known as the coefficient of static friction. N is the magnitude of the normal contact force exerted by one surface on the other. The equality in Eq. 6-3 holds when the surfaces are on the verge of slipping, that is, when $f_s = f_{s,max} = \mu_s N$. This situation is called impending motion. The inequality holds when the surfaces are not on the verge of slipping. Maximum strength of the joints formed is directly proportional to the normal contact force because higher the normal contact force, higher is the joint strength that is, $f_{s,\max} \propto N$.

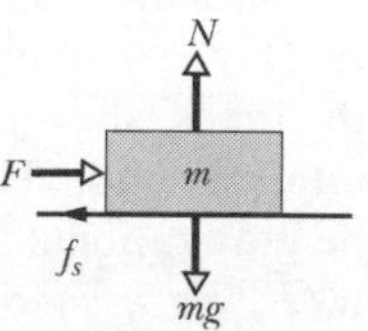

FIG. 6-6 Forces acting on block of mass m.

It also depends on the roughness of contact surface $f_{s,\max}$ (also called f_{limiting}) = $\mu_s N$. Magnitude of static friction is self-adjusting such that relative motion does not start (but still it has maximum value). Let us say we are applying force F on a block kept on horizontal rough surface (Fig. 6-6) with coefficient of static friction μ_s = 0.1 and mass of block is 5 kg. When applied force F is less than 5 N the value of static friction is not 5 N. It is the maximum value of friction. But when applied force F is more than 5 N, the value of static friction is 5 N as given in Table 6-1.

TABLE 6-1

Values of Limiting and Static Friction on Application of Force

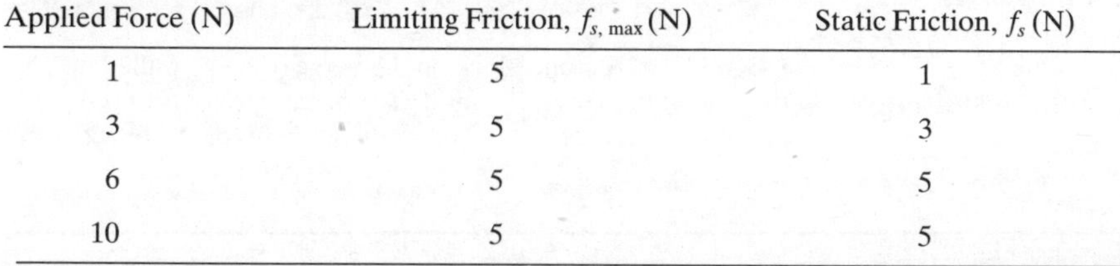

Applied Force (N)	Limiting Friction, $f_{s,\max}$ (N)	Static Friction, f_s (N)
1	5	1
3	5	3
6	5	5
10	5	5

CHECKPOINT 2 We pull the block kept on rough horizontal surface by applying 100 N force at 37° with horizontal. Find force of friction acting on the block. Given m = 20 kg, μ_s = 0.5.

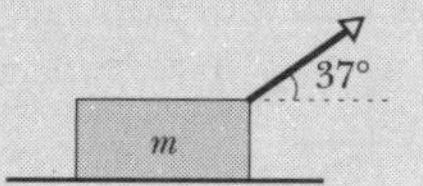

Sample Problem 6-1

Experimental determination of μ_s

Although many ingenious schemes have been attributed to the building of the Great Pyramid, the stone blocks were probably hauled up the side of the pyramid by men pulling on ropes. Figure 6-7a represents a 2000 kg stone block in the process of being pulled up the finished (smooth) side of the Great Pyramid, which forms a plane inclined at angle θ = 53°. The block is secured to a wood sled and is pulled by multiple ropes (only one is shown). The sled's track is lubricated with water to decrease the coefficient of static friction to 0.40. Assume negligible friction at the (lubricated) point where the ropes pass over the edge at the top of the side. If each man on top of the pyramid pulls with a (reasonable) force of 832 N, how many men are needed to put the block on the verge of moving?

Conceptualize: Because the block is on the *verge* of moving, the static frictional force must be at its maximum possible value; that is, $f_s = f_{s,\max}$.

Classify: Because the block is on the verge of moving *up* the plane, the frictional force must be *down* the plane (to oppose the pending motion).

Compute: We know that the component of the gravitational force down the plane is $mg \sin\theta$ and the component perpendicular to (and inward from) the plane is $mg \cos\theta$ (Fig. 6-7*b*). Figure 6-7*c* is a free-body diagram for the block, showing the force $\vec{F}$ applied by the ropes, the static frictional force $\vec{f_s}$, and the two components of the gravitational force. We can write Newton's second law ($\vec{F}_{\text{net}} = m\vec{a}$) for forces along the x axis as

$$F - mg \sin\theta - f_s = m(0) \tag{6-4}$$

Because the block is on the verge of sliding and the frictional force is at the maximum possible value $f_{s,\max}$, we use Eq. 6-1 to replace f_s with $\mu_s F_N$:

$$f_s = f_{s,\max} = \mu_s F_N \tag{6-5}$$

from which $\mu_s = \dfrac{f_s}{N}$

From Figure 6-7*c*, we see that along the y axis Newton's second law becomes

$$F_N - mg \cos\theta = m(0) \tag{6-6}$$

Solving Eq. 6-6 for F_N and substituting the result into Eq. 6-5, we have

$$f_s = \mu_s mg \cos\theta \tag{6-7}$$

Substituting this expression into Eq. 6-4 and solving for F lead to

$$F = \mu_s mg \cos\theta + mg \sin\theta \tag{6-8}$$

Substituting $m = 2000$ kg, $\theta - 53°$, and $\mu_s = 0.40$, we find that the force required to put the stone block on the verge of moving is 20800 N. Dividing this by the assumed pulling force of 832 N from each man, we find that the required number of men is

$$N = \frac{20800 \text{ N}}{832 \text{ N}} = 25 \text{ men} \qquad \text{(Answer)}$$

Conclude: Once the stone block began to move, the friction was kinetic friction and the coefficient was about 0.20. You can show that the required number of men was then 22. Thus, the huge stone blocks of the Great Pyramid could be pulled up into position by reasonably small teams of men.

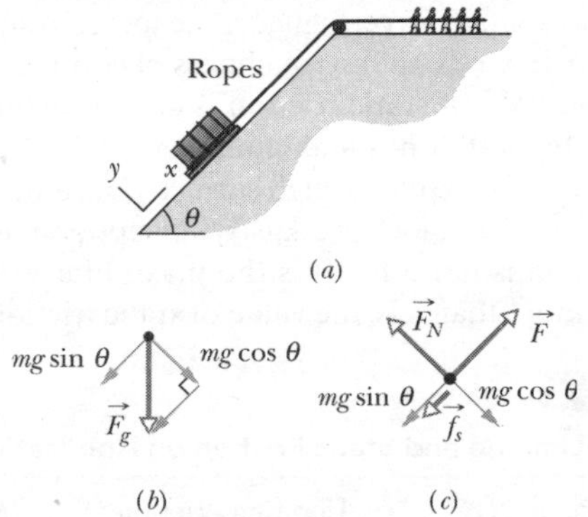

FIG. 6-7 (*a*) A stone block on the verge of being pulled up the side of the Great Pyramid. (*b*) The components of the gravitational force. (*c*) A free-body diagram for the block.

Sample Problem 6-2

A block of mass m_1 is kept on a fixed inclined plane and attached to a block of mass m_2 by a rope as shown in Figure 6.8. The incline makes angle θ with horizontal and coefficient of friction is m. Find range of m_2 for which m_1 remains at rest (given $\theta > \tan^{-1}\mu_s$).

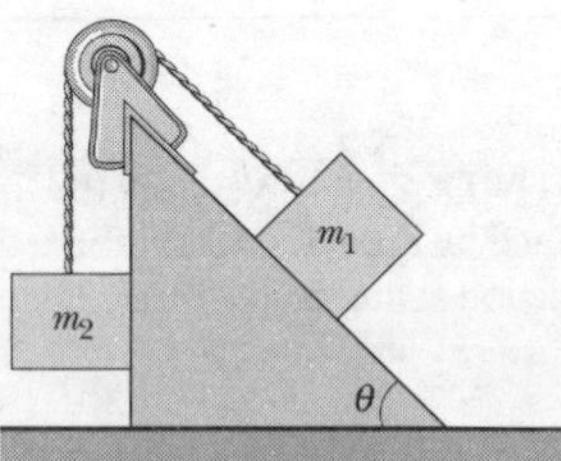

FIG. 6-8 (*a*) A block of mass m_1 is kept on a fixed rough inclined plane and attached to a block of mass m_2 by a rope. (*b*) and (*c*) Free-body diagrams.

Conceptualize: This problem is about finding range. If we make m_2 very light such that m_2 becomes zero m_1 will tend to go down the inclined plane hence friction will act in upward direction. On the other hand, if we make m_2 very heavy then m_1 will definitely move up with the friction acting downward.

Classify: It involves static friction as it is given in the problem that m_1 remains at rest and also m_1 at rest implies that m_2 must be at rest. Also from above discussion it is clear that static friction is going to change direction. So we need to solve this problem in two parts.

(*a*) To find minimum value we should assume block m_1 is in impending state to go down.

(*b*) To find maximum value we should assume block m_1 is in impending state to go up.

Compute : (*a*) If m_2 is small then m_1 will tend to go down the incline for the smallest possible value of m_2, for equilibrium m_1 will experience maximum friction upward. Making free-body diagram.

For equilibrium of m_2

$$T = m_2 g$$

(*b*)

For equilibrium of m_1 along incline

$$T + \mu_s N - m_1 g \sin\theta = 0$$

and perpendicular to incline

$$m_1 g \cos\theta - N = 0$$

Solving above $m_2 = m_1 (\sin\theta - \mu_s \cos\theta)$

Compute : (*b*) Now if m_2 is increased friction on m_1 will decrease as tension is increasing, but if we keep on increasing m_2 then friction will become directed down the incline and for maximum value of m_1 it will be directed downward and equal to $f_{s,\max}$ because m_1 is about to move up.

Making free-body diagram.

For equilibrium of m_2

$$T = m_2 g \qquad \text{(i)}$$

For equilibrium of m_1 along incline

$$T - \mu_s N - m_1 g \sin\theta = 0 \qquad \text{(ii)}$$

and perpendicular to incline

$$m_1 g \cos\theta - N = 0 \qquad \text{(iii)}$$

Solving Eqs. (i), (ii), and (iii).

$$m_2 = m_1 (\sin\theta + \mu_s \cos\theta)$$

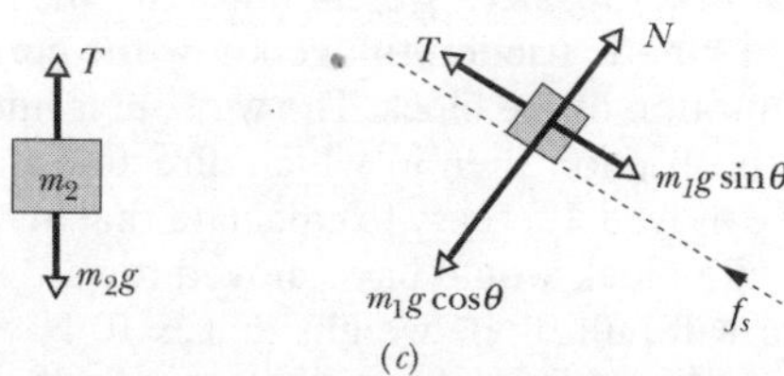

(*c*)

Conclude: As expected we are getting two different values of m_2 for two different independing states of motion of m_1.

In Case Of: $m_2 = m_1 \sin\theta$, find value of friction force acting on m_1.

Friction force is not required as $T = m_2 g$ balances m_2 and $T = m_1 g \sin\theta$ balances m_1. At this value of m_2 friction shifts the direction, hence it is zero of this value. If we have mass m_2 lower than this m_1 tends to go down with friction acting up the incline and vice versa.

6-3 | Kinetic Friction

Kinectic friction acts when there is relative motion between two surfaces in contact. It acts always opposite to the relative velocity as we can see in Fig. 6-9. The magnitude is not self adjusting as in static friction it is always is equal to $\mu_k N$.

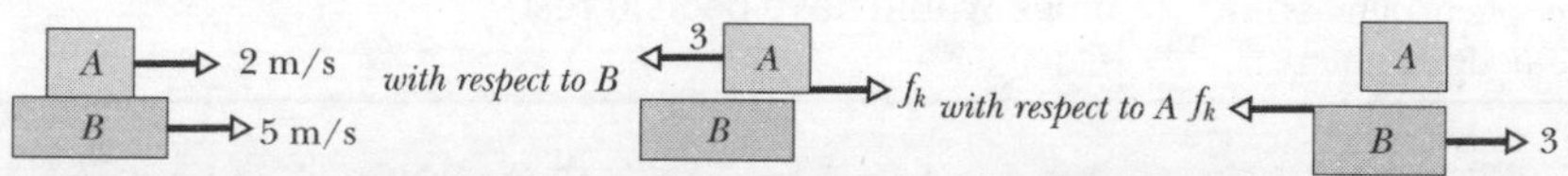

FIG. 6-9 Two blocks kept one on another with the given instantaneous velocities.

Sample Problem 6-3 Build your skill

Find unit vector in direction of friction force acting on block.

Given, $\vec{v}_P = 7\hat{i} - 2\hat{j}, \quad \vec{v}_B = 3\hat{i} + \hat{j}$

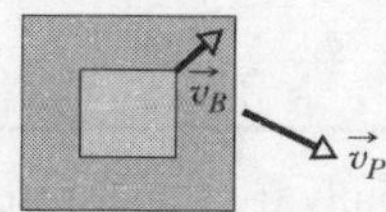

Top view of a block kept on a moving platform.

Solution: $\vec{v}_{B/P} = 3\hat{i} + \hat{j} - (7\hat{i} - 2\hat{j})$

Friction on B due to P must be (opposite of the velocity of B with respact to P

Friction on B due to p $\hat{f}_k = -\gamma_{B/P} = -\frac{4}{5}\hat{i} + \frac{3}{5}\hat{j}$

Sample Problem 6-4

A block m_1 of mass 10 kg kept on a rough, horizontal surface is connected to a sphere m_2 of mass 1 kg by a string over an ideal pulley as shown in Fig. 6-10*a*. A force F of magnitude 50 N at an angle 37° with the horizontal is applied to the block as shown and the block slides to the right. The coefficient of kinetic friction between the block and surface is 0.1. Determine the magnitude of the acceleration of the two objects.

Conceptualize/Classify: We cannot write the correct direction of kinetic friction till we know the correct direction of motion of the block. The way out is imagine if there was no friction then in which direction the bock would have moved. It is easy to calculate that in absence of friction the block would have moved toward right as the sphere will pull by its weight that is 10 N which is smaller than the horizontal component of F 40N.

Compute: Now we can draw free-body diagrams for the two objects. as shown in Fig. 6-10*b* and Fig. 6-10*c*. The applied force has x and y components 40 N and 30 N, respectively. The magnitudes of the acceleration of the block and the acceleration of the sphere is $\vec{a}$.

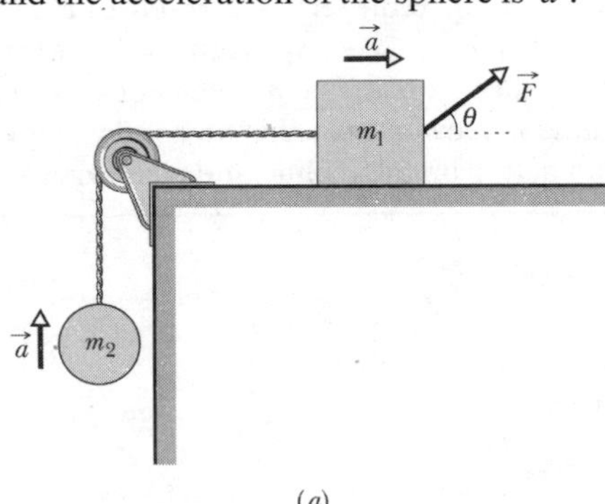

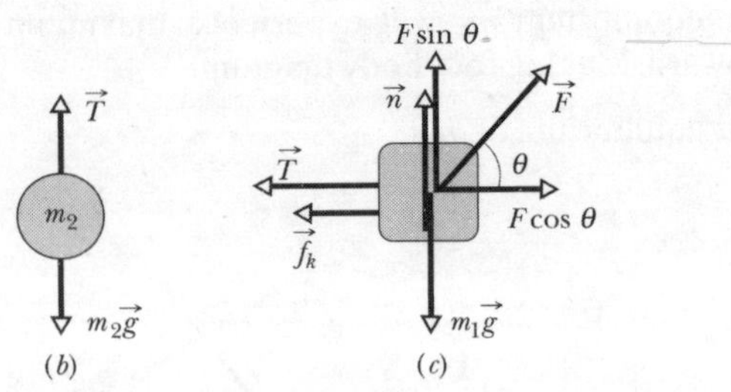

FIG. 6-10 (*a*) A block of mass m_1 connected to sphere of mass m_2 by a string over an ideal pulley. (*b*) and (*c*) Free-body diagrams.

Applying Newton's second law to the block in the horizontal direction:

$$F\cos\theta - f_k - T = m_1 a \qquad \text{(i)}$$

Applying Newton's second law to the block in the vertical direction:

$$N + F\sin\theta - m_1 g = 0 \qquad \text{(ii)}$$

Applying Newton's second law to the ball in the vertical direction :

$$T - m_2 g = m_2 a \qquad \text{(iii)}$$

Solve Eq. (ii) for N: $N = m_1 g - F\sin\theta$

Substitute N into $f_k = \mu_k N$

$$f_k = \mu_k(m_1 g - F\sin\theta) = 0.1(100 - 30) = 7 \qquad \text{(iv)}$$

$$40 - 7 - 1(a + g) = 10a$$

Substitute Eq. (iv) and the value of T from Eq. (iii) into Eq. (i)

and solving for $\vec{a}$:

$$\vec{a} = 23/11 \text{ m/s}^2$$

Conclude: If friction force would have been larger the block would have been at rest.

CHECKPOINT 3 Solve the previous problem for $\mu_k = 0.8$.

6-4 | Some More Applications

In this section, we are going to see new problems which involve the following variations, where:

1. nature of friction may change during the course of motion,
2. variation in magnitude of static friction when blocks are in contact,
3. magnitude of applied force is varied.

Sample Problem 6-5

Blocks are given velocities as shown in Fig. 6-11*a* at $t = 0$ s, find velocity and position of 10 kg block at

(*a*) $t = 1$s and (*b*) $t = 4$s

Conceptualize: Initially frictional force acting on 10 kg (Fig. 6-11*a*) block is kinetic friction acting opposite to the velocity. We can also imagine that as time passes velocities

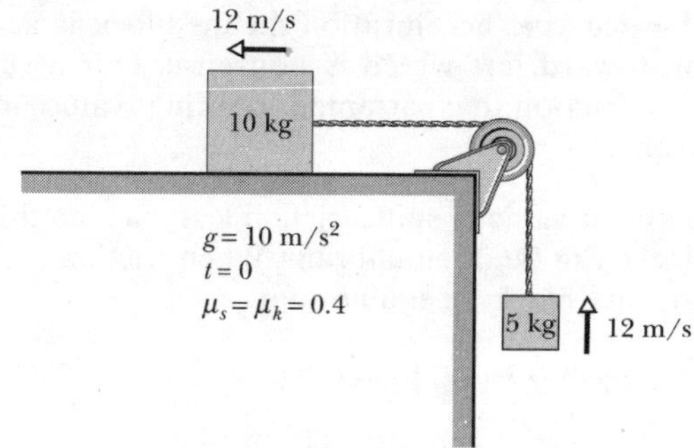

FIG. 6-11 (*a*) A block kept on rough horizontal rough table and attached to another block of mass 5 kg are shown moving with initial speeds (*b*) and (*c*) Free-body diagrams.

of the blocks will keep on decreasing as both the forces (friction and tension) on 10 kg block are opposing the motion.

Classify: This problem looks similar to the previous example except that a horizontal force on 10 kg block is missing. So to find acceleration initially we will proceed similiar to the previous example.

Compute: Kinetic friction acts opposite to relative velocity so on the 10 kg block it will act toward right.

Making free-body diagram as shown in Fig. 6-11*b*.

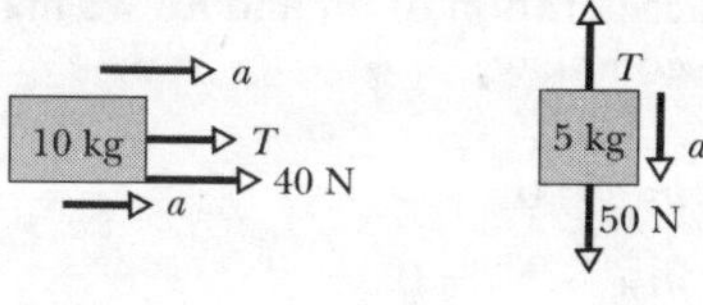

(*b*)

Both the blocks will have same acceleration. Writing Newton's second law for both blocks:

(*a*) $40 + T = 10a$, $\quad 50 - T = 5a$.

Solving we get $a = 6\ m/s^2$

Writing parameters of motion

$$u = 12\ m/s; \qquad a = -6\ m/s^2$$

Applying equations for uniform acceleration at $t = 1s$, we get

$$v = 12 - 6 \times 1 = 6\ m/s; \quad s = 12 \times 1 - 3 \times 1 = 9\ m$$

(*b*) $t = 4s$

Classify: This part seems to be very simple as we have to put value of time $t = 4s$ in previous equation and should get the answer.

$$v = -12\ m/s$$

Which means the direction of *motion changed during* these 3 seconds ($t = 1$ to $t = 4s$). Since kinetic friction acts opposite to the relative velocity, it must have changed the direction. If kinetic friction changes direction then value of acceleration will be different, so we have to first of all find when and where the blocks stop.

When we do that we have to make new free-body diagram and proceed further.

Compute:

$u = 12\ m/s$; $\quad a = -6\ m/s^2$ (till velocity becomes zero)

$v = 0 \Rightarrow t = 2\ s \quad ; \quad s = 12 \times 2 - 3 \times 4 = 12\ m$ toward left

New free-body diagram after $t = 2$ s.

The 10 kg block has tendency to move toward right hence friction will act toward left and applying Newton's second law we get,

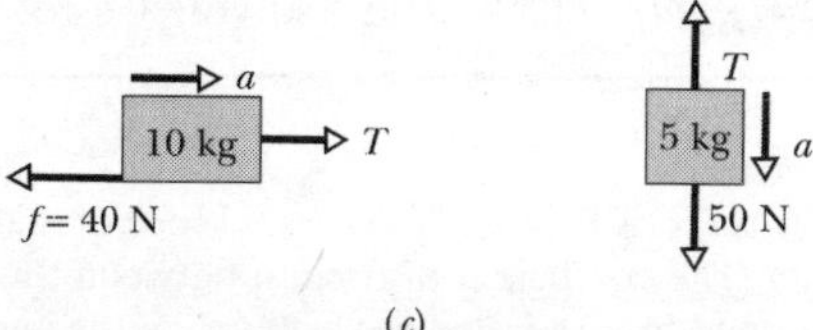

(*c*)

$$50 - T = 5a$$

$$T - 40 = 10a$$

$a = 2/3\ m/s^2$ (after $t = 2$ s)

$u =$ m/s, $a = 2/3\ m/s^2$, $\Delta t = 2$ s

applying equation for uniform acceleration, we get

$$s = \frac{1}{2} \times \frac{2}{3} \times 4 = 1.33\ m$$

Total displacement will be, $12 - 1.33 = 10.67$ m

Conclude: We have learnt that kinetic friction opposes relative velocity not relative acceleration. We have also seen that kinetic friction changes direction when motion is reverses, so in problems involving kinetic friction we should not take acceleration as constant.

(*c*) In the same question, if $\mu_s = 0.6$ and all other parameters are same. Find velocity of blocks at $t = 4$ s.

Conceptualize: The effect of different coefficient of static friction will come only when block is at rest. Kinetic friction acts on the block while it is moving, which has same value as in previous question, thus at $t = 2$ s blocks will stop.

Classify: At the instant when the blocks are at rest the force of friction on 10 kg block is static. Now we must check whether it will allow the motion or not.

Compute: At $t = 2$ s

Making free-body diagram

Direction of static friction on the 10 kg block will be toward left as it tends to go toward right due to tension. Now writing Newton's second law.

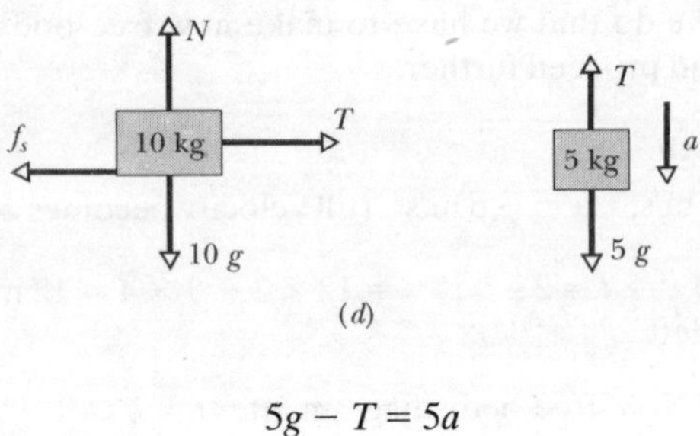

$$5g - T = 5a$$

$$T - f_s = 10a$$

Let's assume friction has limiting value that is,

$f_s = \mu_s N = 60$ N and solving we get $a = -\dfrac{2}{3}$ m/s^2

The negative acceleration means block is accelerating toward lcft which is nonsense. Our assumption that friction has attained limiting value must be wrong.

Here, for value of static friction less than limiting value, blocks can be in equilibrium When friction is 50 N we can have blocks in equilibrium.

Thus answer is $v = 0$ as after $t = 2$ s. the blocks will not move.

Conclude: When $\mu_s \neq \mu_k$ then to find wether relative motion can start or not we must check using ms. Once relative motion starts, we use mk to find friction.

CHECKPOINT 4 A block of mass m slips on a rough horizontal table under the action of a horizontal force applied to it. The coefficient of friction between the block and the table is μ. The table does not move on the floor. Find the total frictional force applied by the floor on the legs of the table. Do you need the friction coefficient between the table and the floor or the mass of the table ?

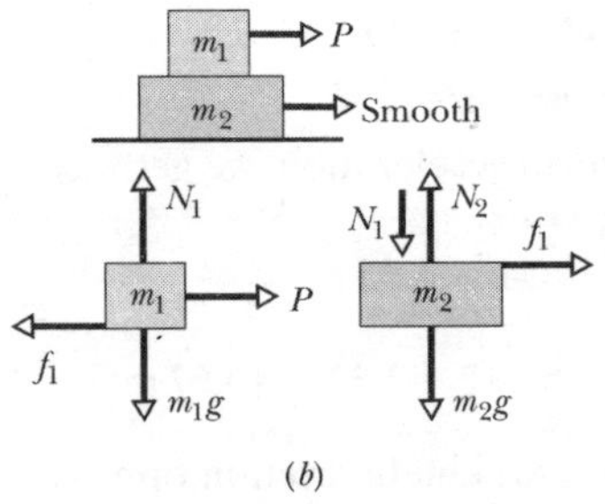

FIG. 6-12 Two blocks kept one over the other undergoing friction.

Block over block

Consider two blocks kept one over the other as in Fig. 6-12 where m_1 is kept on top of m_2. Let's say coefficient of friction between m_1 and m_2 is m_1 and between m_2 and ground is m_2. To find acceleration of m_1 and m_2 we make their free-body diagram and write Newton's second law.

along y axis $\quad N_1 - m_1 g = 0$

$$N_1 + m_2 g - N_2 = 0$$

gives $\quad N_1 = m_1 g$

$$N_2 = (m_1 + m_2)\, g$$

along x axis $\quad P_1 - f_1 = m_1 a_1$

$$f_1 = m_2 a_2$$

and we know $\quad f_1 \leq \mu_1 N_1$

We have got two equations and three unknowns in equations along x direction. This problem cannot be solved unless we make some assumptions.

Case I: If we assume both blocks are moving together then friction between them need not be equal to maximum value. Thus, taking $a_1 = a_2$, we are down to two unknowns and we can solve the equations, but we must verify our answer by checking $f_1 \leq \mu_1 N_1$. If this check fails we go to next possibility.

Case II: If we assume blocks are moving relative to each other, then friction between them must have reached maximum value

$$a_1 \neq a_2 \text{ but } f_1 = \mu_1 N_1$$

Again we get two unknowns and two equations. We can solve it, but we must verify our answer.

We will check the answer by verifying that friction is opposite the direction of relative motion.

Sample Problem 6-6 Build your skill

(a) Friction coefficient between blocks is 0.5 and between ground and 10 kg block is 0.2. Find acceleration of blocks if force $F = 40$ N is applied on 5 kg block as shown.

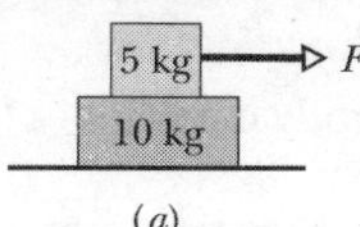

(*a*)

FIG. 6-13 Free-body diagrams.

Solution: First we find the values of limiting friction at all contact surfaces. ($f_{s,\max}$)

5 kg $f_{s\max} = 25$ N

10 kg $f_{s\max} = 30$ N

(*b*)

The only driving force that the 10 kg block can experience is the one applied by the lower surface of 5 kg block on 10 kg block.

The maximum value of this force is 25 N. This is lower than the minimum force required to move with respect to ground.

Hence only the 5 kg block will move

25 ← 5 kg → 40 N

$a_A = 3\text{ m/s}^2,\ a_B = 0\text{ m/s}^2$

25 ← 10 kg → 25 N

(*c*)

(b) Friction coefficient between the blocks is 0.5 and ground is smooth, if force of 30 N is applied on the upper block as shown. Find accelerations of the blocks.

$\mu_1 = 0.5$ A 5 kg → 30 N

Smooth 10 kg B

(*d*)

Solution:

Conceptualize: Maximum friction force between blocks is 25 N and ground is smooth. 10 kg block must move because some force on upper surface will act on it.

5 kg $f_{1,\max} = 25$ N

10 kg $f_{2,\max} = 0$ N

B can either move with same velocity and acceleration as *A* or it can move relative to *A*.

Classify: Let's assume *B* moves with *A* and solve

Compute: Making free-body diagram

Writing Newton's second law $30 - f = 5a$

$$f = 10\,a$$

Solving $a = 2\text{ m/s}^2$ and $f = 20$ N

f ← 5 kg → 30 N

10 kg → *f*

(*e*)

Now check if this acceleration is possible by verifying $f \le f_1$

Writing Newton's second law

→2

f ← 5 kg → 30   10 kg → *f* →2

(*f*)

$30 - f = 5 \times 2 \quad f = 10 \times 2 = 20$ N

$f = 20 < 25$

(c) Friction coefficient between the blocks is 0.5 and ground is smooth, if force of 60 N is applied on the upper block as shown find accelerations of the blocks.

Conclude: Hence our assumption is true. We can try by assuming they are not moving together and solve the equations to get an absurd result.

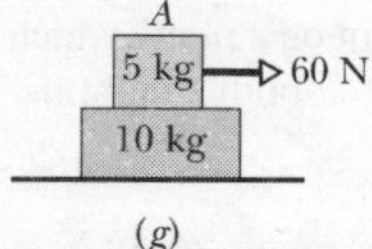

(*g*)

Classify: Let's assume they have same acceleration. The value of acceleration is $60/(10+5) = 4\text{ m/s}^2$.

Compute: Making free-body diagram

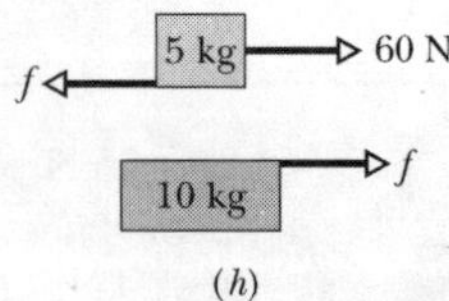

(h)

Writing Newton's second law

$$60 - f = 5 \times 4 \qquad f = 10 \times 4 = 40\text{ N}$$

Solving $a = 4$ m/s² and $f = 40$ N while limiting value of friction is 25 N, hence our assumption is wrong.

Let's say they are not moving together.

$$a_1 = 7\text{ m/s}^2,\ a_2 = 2.5\text{ m/s}^2$$

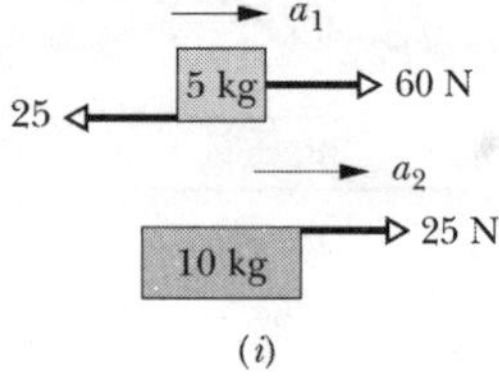

(i)

Conclude: If we look at 5 kg block from frame attached to 10 kg block we will find it is moving toward right and friction is acting towards left. This is satisfying friction's tendency to oppose relative motion.

In Case Of: In part (a) if we assume they are moving seperately solve, how do we verify that answer is incorrect. If we assume they are moving seperately friction attains maximum value.

Again making free-body diagram

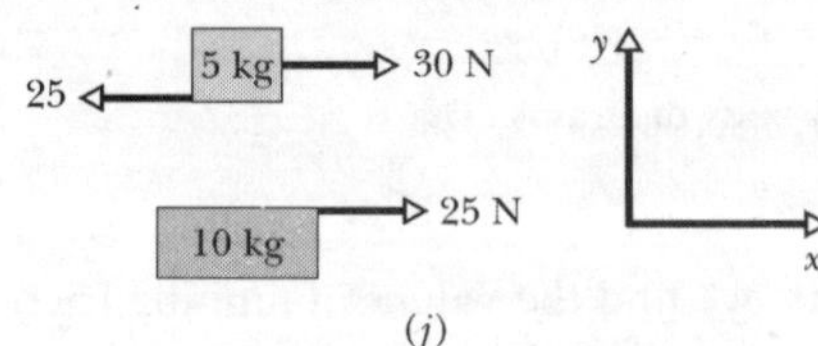

(j)

$$a_1 = \frac{30 - 25}{5} = 1\text{ m/s}^2$$

$$a_2 = \frac{25}{10} = 25\text{ m/s}^2$$

If we look at 5 kg block from reference frame attached to 10 kg block we get

$$a_{1/2} = a_1 - a_2 = -1.5\text{ m/s}^2$$

that is 5 kg block will be moving towards left and friction on it also acting in same direction. This is not possible as friction must oppose relative motion.

CHECKPOINT 5 Find maximum force for which the blocks of the above problem can move together.

Sample Problem 6-7

A bar of mass m_1 is placed on a plank of mass m_2, which rests on a smooth horizontal plane (Fig. 6-14*a*). The coefficient of friction between the surfaces of the bar and the plank is equal to k. The plank is subjected to the horizontal force F depending on time t as $F = at$ (a is a constant).

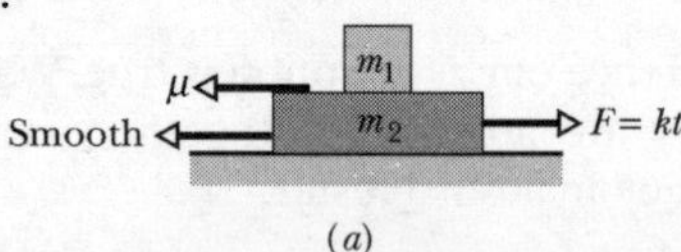

(a)

FIG. 6-14 (*a*) A bar kept on a plank which is subjected to a horizontal force. (*b*) Free-body diagram.

Find :

(1) the moment of time t_0 at which the plank starts sliding from under the bar ;

(2) the acceleration of the bar a_1 and that of plank a_2 in during motion.

Conceptualize/Classify: This problem is similar to problems that we have already solved. Here as the force F grows, so does the static friction force f. However, the friction force f has the limiting value $f_{limit} = km_1g$ unless this value is reached, both bodies move together with equal accelerations. But as soon as the force f reaches this limit, mass m_2 starts sliding under mass m_1.

Compute: Let us make free-body diagram

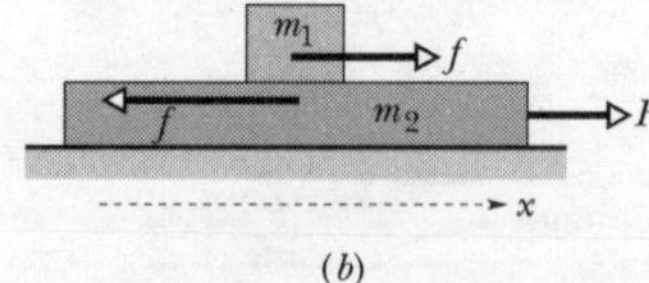

(b)

Writing Newton's second law for the plank and the bar, having taken the positive direction of the x axis as shown in Fig. 6-14*b*

$$f = m_1a_1, \quad F - f = m_2a_2 \qquad \text{(i)}$$

acceleration of m_2 must be always greater than equal to the acceleration of m_1 that is $a_2\ a_1$ where the sign "="

corresponds to the moment $t = t_0$. Hence, when $f = k\,m_1\,g$ then sliding begins putting $f = km_1 g$ in Eq. (i) we get,

$$t_0 = (m_1 + m_2)\frac{kg}{a}$$

When $t \le t_0$, then

$$a_1 = a_2 = \frac{at}{(m_1 + m_2)}$$

and when $t\ \ t_0$, then they seperate. Only force acting on m_1 is friction, whose value is constant.

thus $a_1 = kg =$ constant,

Now m_2 is experiencing force F and constant friction

thus $at - k\,m_1\,g = m_2\,a_2$

Solving we get

$$a_2 = \frac{(at - km_1 g)}{m_2}$$

Conclude: You may have been tempted to think that when external force F ($F = at$) is equal to $k\,m_1\,g$ slipping will begin. You can check that at this instant t_2 they are moving with same acceleration .

$$a\,t_2 = k\,m_1\,g$$

$$t_2 = \frac{km_1 g}{a}$$

Let's find force of friction between the blocks at this instant.

$$k\,m_1\,g - f = m_2\,a$$

$$f = m_1\,a$$

Solving for friction

$$f = \frac{km_1 g}{\left(1 + \frac{m_2}{m_1}\right)}$$

Since friction is less than the maximum value slipping has not yet begin.

CHECKPOINT 6 Plot a_1 and a_2 as function of time.

REVIEW & SUMMARY

Friction When a force $\vec{F}$ tends to slide a body along a surface, a **frictional force** from the surface acts on the body. The frictional force is parallel to the surface and directed so as to oppose the sliding. It is due to bonding between the body and the surface.

If the body does not slide, the frictional force is a **static frictional force** $\vec{f}_s$. If there is sliding, the frictional force is a **kinetic frictional force** $\vec{f}_k$.

1. If a body does not move, the static frictional force $\vec{f}_s$ and the component of $\vec{F}$ parallel to the surface are equal in magnitude, and $\vec{f}_s$ is directed opposite that component. If the component increases, f_s also increases.

2. The magnitude of $\vec{f}_s$ has a maximum value $f_{s,\max}$ given by

$$f_{s,\max} = \mu_s F_N$$

where μ_s is the **coefficient of static friction** and F_N is the magnitude of the normal force. If the component of $\vec{F}$ parallel to the surface exceeds $f_{s,\max}$, the body slides on the surface.

3. If the body begins to slide on the surface, the magnitude of the frictional force rapidly decreases to a constant value f_k given by

$$f_k = \mu_k F_N$$

where μ_k is the **coefficient of kinetic friction.**

QUESTIONS

1 In Fig. 6-15, horizontal force $\vec{F}_1$ of magnitude 10 N is applied to a box on a floor, but the box does not slide. Then, as the magnitude of vertical force $\vec{F}_2$ is increased from zero, do the following quantities increase, decrease, or stay the same: (a) the magnitude of the frictional force $\vec{f}_s$ on the box; (b) the magnitude of the normal force $\vec{F}_N$ on the box from the floor; (c) the maximum value $f_{s,\max}$ of the magnitude of the static frictional force on the box? (d) Does the box eventually slide?

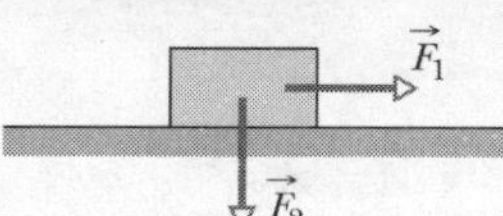

FIG. 6-15 Question 1.

2 In three experiments, three different horizontal forces are applied to the same block lying on the same countertop. The force magnitudes are $F_1 = 12$ N, $F_2 = 8$ N, and $F_3 = 4$ N. In each experiment, the block remains stationary in spite of the applied force. Rank the forces according to (a) the magnitude f_s of the static frictional force on the block from the countertop and (b) the maximum value $f_{s,\max}$ of that force, greatest first.

3 In Fig. 6-16, if the box is stationary and the angle θ between the horizontal and force $\vec{F}$ is increased somewhat, do the following quantities increase, decrease, or remain the same: (a) F_x; (b) f_s; (c) F_N; (d) $f_{s,max}$? (e) If, instead, the box is sliding and θ is increased, does the magnitude of the frictional force on the box increase, decrease, or remain the same?

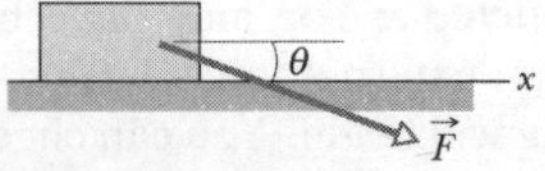

FIG. 6-16 Question 3.

4 Repeat Question 3 for force $\vec{F}$ angled upward instead of downward as drawn.

5 If you press an apple crate against a wall so hard that the crate cannot slide down the wall, what is the direction of (a) the static frictional force $\vec{f}_s$ on the crate from the wall and (b) the normal force $\vec{F}_N$ on the crate from the wall? If you increase your push, what happens to (c) f_s, (d) F_N, and (e) $f_{s,max}$?

6 In Fig. 6-17, a block of mass m is held stationary on a ramp by the frictional force on it from the ramp. A force $\vec{F}$, directed up the ramp, is then applied to the block and gradually increased in magnitude from zero. During the increase, what happens to the direction and magnitude of the frictional force on the block?

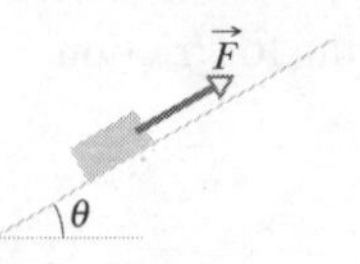

FIG. 6-17 Question 6.

7 Reconsider Question 6 but with the force $\vec{F}$ now directed down the ramp. As the magnitude of $\vec{F}$ is increased from zero, what happens to the direction and magnitude of the frictional force on the block?

8 In Fig. 6-18, a horizontal force of 100 N is to be applied to a 10 kg slab that is initially stationary on a frictionless floor, to accelerate the slab. A 10 kg block lies on top of the slab; the coefficient of friction μ between the block and the slab is not known, and the block might slip. (a) Considering that possibility, what is the possible range of values for the magnitude of the slab's acceleration a_{slab}? (*Hint:* You don't need written calculations; just consider extreme values for μ.) (b) What is the possible range for the magnitude a_{block} of the block's acceleration?

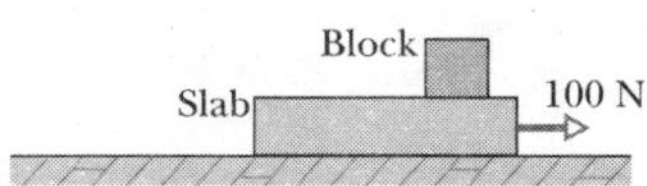

FIG. 6-18 Question 8.

9 A person riding a Ferris wheel moves through positions at (1) the top, (2) the bottom, and (3) midheight. If the wheel rotates at a constant rate, rank these three positions according to (a) the magnitude of the person's centripetal acceleration, (b) the magnitude of the net centripetal force on the person, and (c) the magnitude of the normal force on the person, greatest first.

10 In 1987, as a Halloween stunt, two sky divers passed a pumpkin back and forth between them while they were in free fall just west of Chicago. The stunt was great fun until the last sky diver with the pumpkin opened his parachute. The pumpkin broke free from his grip, plummeted about 0.5 km, ripped through the roof of a house, slammed into the kitchen floor, and splattered all over the newly remodeled kitchen. From the sky diver's viewpoint and from the pumpkin's viewpoint, why did the sky diver lose control of the pumpkin?

11 Figure 6-19 shows the path of a park ride that travels at constant speed through five circular arcs of radii R_0, $2R_0$, and $3R_0$. Rank the arcs according to the magnitude of the centripetal force on a rider traveling in the arcs, greatest first.

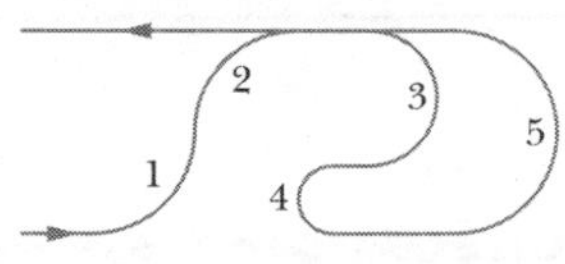

FIG. 6-19 Question 11.

PROBLEMS

Properties of Friction

1 A slide-loving pig slides down a certain 7° slide in twice the time it would take to slide down a frictionless 7° slide. What is the coefficient of kinetic friction between the pig and the slide?

2 A 3.5 kg block is pushed along a horizontal floor by a force $\vec{F}$ of magnitude 15 N at an angle $\theta = 37°$ with the horizontal (Fig. 6-20). The coefficient of kinetic friction between the block and the floor is 0.25. Calculate the magnitudes of (a) the frictional force on the block from the floor and (b) the block's acceleration.

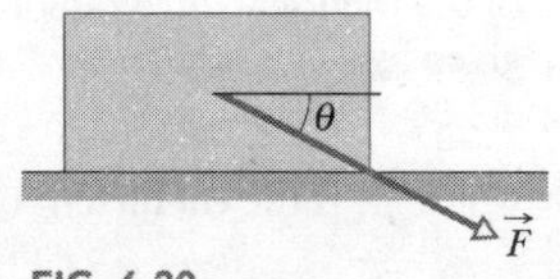

FIG. 6-20 Problems 2 and 11.

3 A 2.5 kg block is initially at rest on a horizontal surface. A horizontal force $\vec{F}$ of magnitude 6.0 N and a vertical force $\vec{P}$ are then applied to the block (Fig. 6-21). The coefficients of friction for the block and surface are $\mu_s = 0.40$ and $\mu_k = 0.25$. Determine the magnitude of the frictional force acting on the block if the magnitude of $\vec{P}$ is (a) 8.0 N, (b) 10 N, and (c) 12 N.

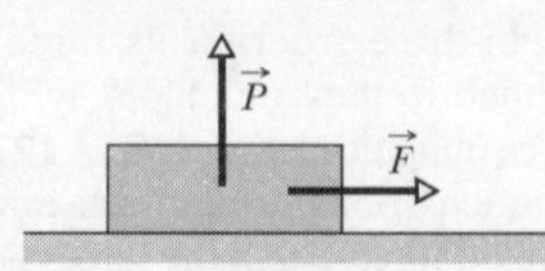

FIG. 6-21 Problem 3.

4 You testify as an *expert witness* in a case involving an accident in which car A slid into the rear of car B, which was stopped at a red light along a road headed down a hill (Fig. 6-22). You find that the slope of the hill is $\theta = 12.0°$, that the cars were separated by distance $d = 24.0$ m when the driver of car A put the car into a slide (it lacked any automatic anti-brake-lock system), and that the speed of car A at the onset of braking was $v_0 = 18.0$ m/s. With what speed did car A hit car B if the coefficient of kinetic friction was (a) 0.60 (dry road surface) and (b) 0.10 (road surface covered with wet leaves)?

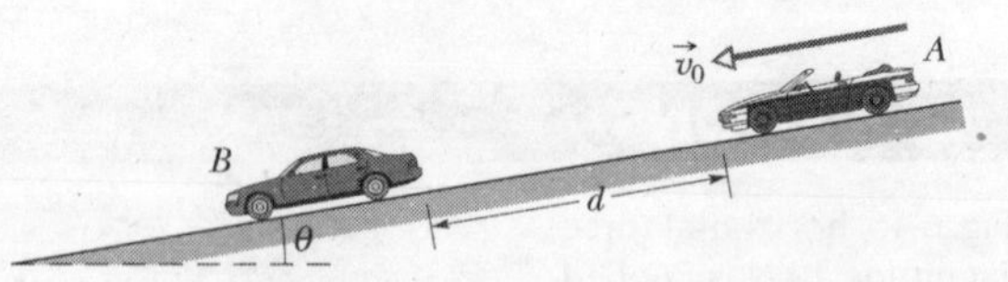

FIG. 6-22 Problem 4.

5 A 12 N horizontal force $\vec{F}$ pushes a block weighing 5.0 N against a vertical wall (Fig. 6-23). The coefficient of static friction between the wall and the block is 0.60, and the coefficient of kinetic

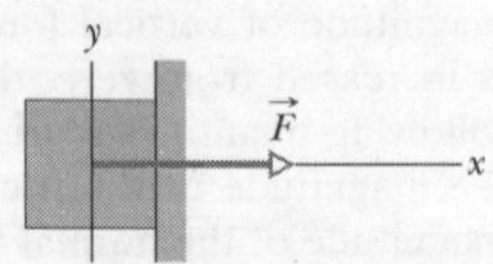

FIG. 6-23 Problem 5.

friction is 0.40. Assume that the block is not moving initially. (a) Will the block move? (b) In unit-vector notation, what is the force on the block from the wall?

6 A 4.10 kg block is pushed along a floor by a constant applied force that is horizontal and has a magnitude of 40.0 N. Figure 6-24 gives the block's speed v versus time t as the block moves along an x axis on the floor. The scale of the figure's vertical axis is set by $v_s = 5.0$ m/s. What is the coefficient of kinetic friction between the block and the floor?

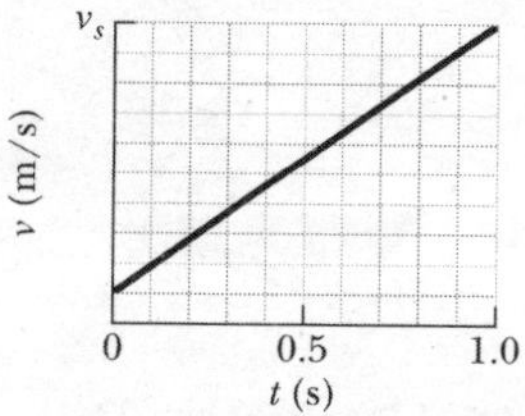

FIG. 6-24 Problem 6.

7 An initially stationary box of sand is to be pulled across a floor by means of a cable in which the tension should not exceed 1100 N. The coefficient of static friction between the box and the floor is 0.35. (a) What should be the angle between the cable and the horizontal in order to pull the greatest possible amount of sand, and (b) what is the weight of the sand and box in that situation?

8 In Fig. 6-25, a force $\vec{P}$ acts on a block weighing 45 N. The block is initially at rest on a plane inclined at angle $\theta = 15°$ to the horizontal. The positive direction of the x axis is up the plane. The coefficients of friction between block and plane are $\mu_s = 0.50$ and $\mu_k = 0.34$. In unit-vector notation, what is the frictional force on the block from the plane when $\vec{P}$ is (a) $(-5.0\text{ N})\hat{i}$, (b) $(-8.0\text{ N})\hat{i}$, and (c) $(-15\text{ N})\hat{i}$?

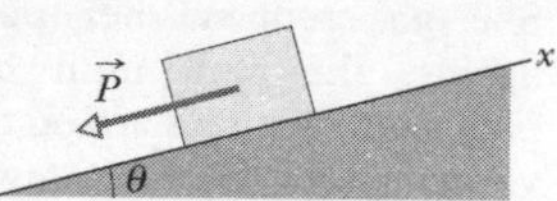

FIG. 6-25 Problem 8.

9 In Fig. 6-26, a box of Cheerios (mass $m_C = 1.0$ kg) and a box of Wheaties (mass $m_W = 3.0$ kg) are accelerated across a horizontal surface by a horizontal force $\vec{F}$ applied to the Cheerios box. The magnitude of the frictional force on the Cheerios box is 2.0 N, and the magnitude of the frictional force on the Wheaties box is 4.0 N. If the magnitude of $\vec{F}$ is 12 N, what is the magnitude of the force on the Wheaties box from the Cheerios box?

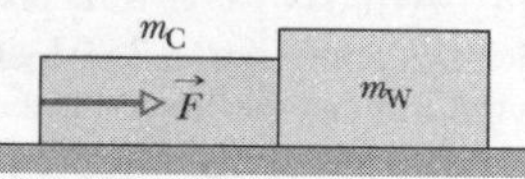

FIG. 6-26 Problem 9.

10 Block B in Fig. 6-27 weighs 711 N. The coefficient of static friction between block and table is 0.25; angle θ is 30°; assume that the cord between B and the knot is horizontal. Find the maximum weight of block A for which the system will be stationary.

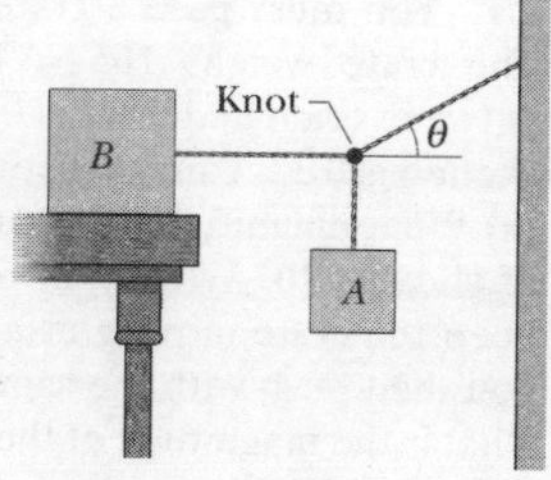

FIG. 6-27 Problem 10.

11 A block is pushed across a floor by a constant force that is applied at downward angle θ (Fig. 6-20). Figure 6-28 gives the acceleration magnitude a versus a range of values for the coefficient of kinetic friction μ_k between block and floor: $a_1 = 3.0$ m/s², $\mu_{k2} = 0.20$, and $\mu_{k3} = 0.40$. What is the value of θ?

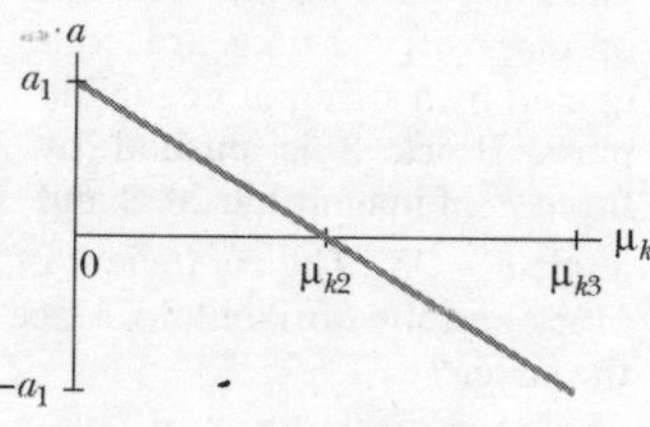

FIG. 6-28 Problem 11.

12 When the three blocks in Fig. 6-29 are released from rest, they accelerate with a magnitude of 0.500 m/s². Block 1 has mass M, block 2 has $2M$, and block 3 has $2M$. What is the coefficient of kinetic friction between block 2 and the table?

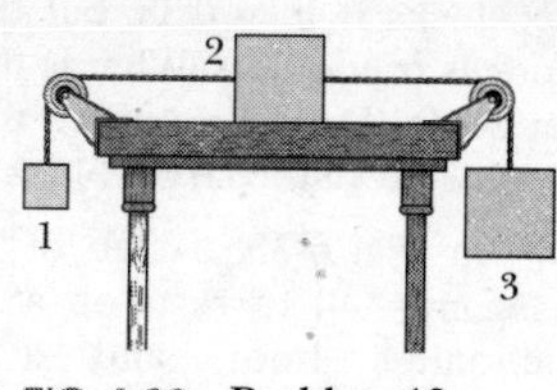

FIG. 6-29 Problem 12.

13 In Fig. 6-30, a sled is held on an inclined plane by a cord pulling directly up the plane. The sled is to be on the verge of moving up the plane. In Fig. 6-31, the magnitude F required of the cord's force on the sled is plotted versus a range of values for the coefficient of static friction μ_s between sled and plane: $F_1 = 2.0$ N, $F_2 = 5.0$ N, and $\mu_2 = 0.50$. At what angle θ is the plane inclined?

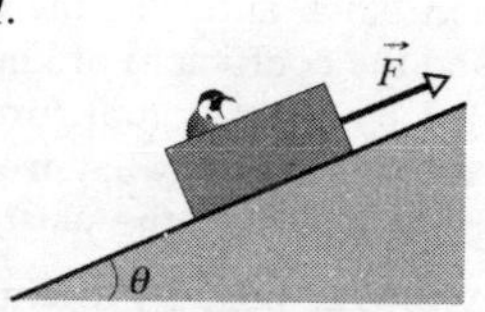

FIG. 6-30 Problems 13.

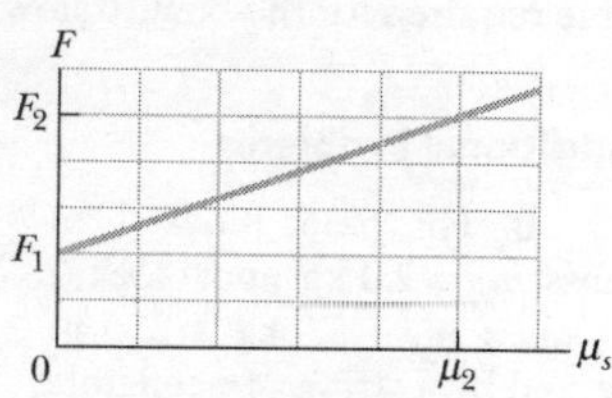

FIG. 6-31 Problem 13.

14 Body A in Fig. 6-32 weighs 102 N, and body B weighs 32 N. The coefficients of friction between A and the incline are $\mu_s = 0.56$ and $\mu_k = 0.25$. Angle θ is 40°. Let the positive direction of an x axis be up the incline. In unit-vector notation, what is the acceleration of A if A is initially (a) at rest, (b) moving up the incline, and (c) moving down the incline?

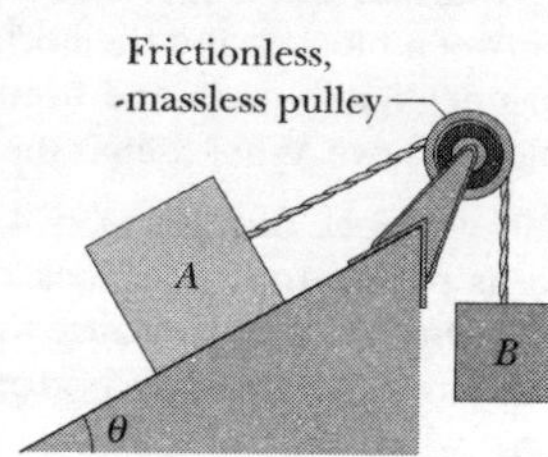

FIG. 6-32 Problem 14.

15 In Fig. 6-33, blocks A and B have weights of 44 N and 22 N, respectively. (a) Determine the minimum weight of block C to keep A from sliding if μ_s between A and the table is 0.20. (b) Block C suddenly is lifted off A. What is the acceleration of block A if μ_k between A and the table is 0.15?

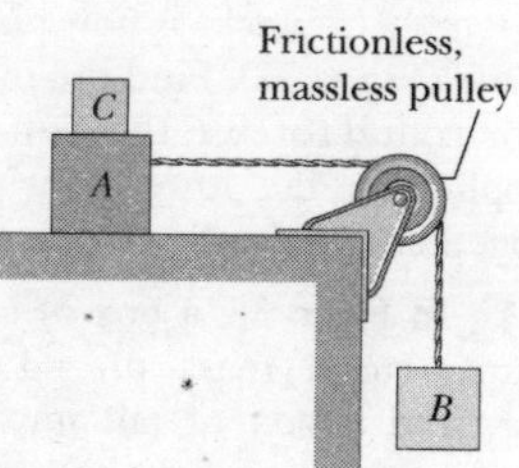

FIG. 6-33 Problem 15.

16 The two blocks ($m = 16$ kg and $M = 88$ kg) in Fig. 6-34 are not attached to each other. The coefficient of static friction between

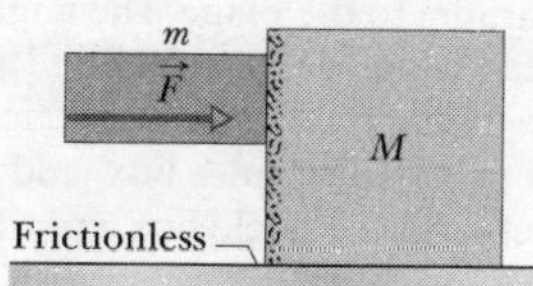

FIG. 6-34 Problem 16.

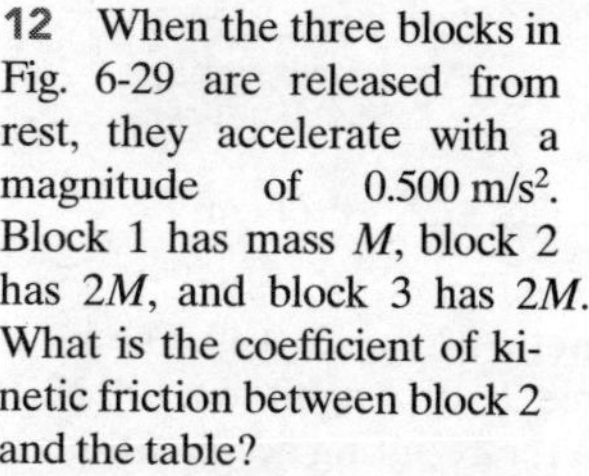

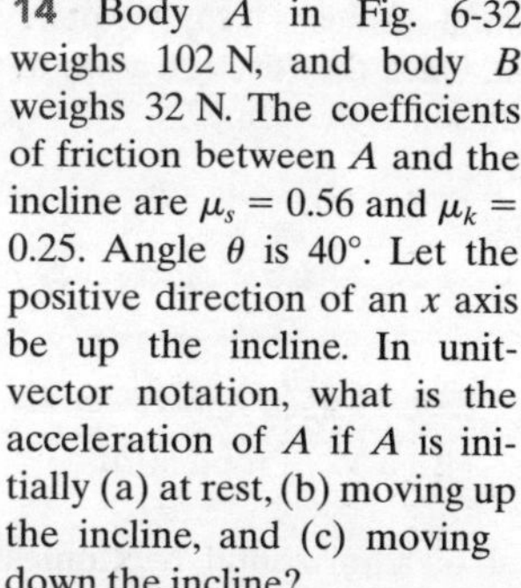

the blocks is $\mu_s = 0.38$, but the surface beneath the larger block is frictionless. What is the minimum magnitude of the horizontal force $\vec{F}$ required to keep the smaller block from slipping down the larger block?

17 In Fig. 6-35, a slab of mass $m_1 = 40$ kg rests on a frictionless floor, and a block of mass $m_2 = 10$ kg rests on top of the slab. Between block and slab, the coefficient of static friction is 0.60, and the coefficient of kinetic friction is 0.40. The block is pulled by a horizontal force $\vec{F}$ of magnitude 100 N. In unit-vector notation, what are the resulting accelerations of (a) the block and (b) the slab?

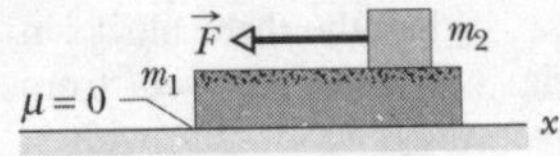

FIG. 6-35 Problem 17.

18 A 1000 kg boat is traveling at 90 km/h when its engine is shut off. The magnitude of the frictional force $\vec{f}_k$ between boat and water is proportional to the speed v of the boat: $f_k = 70v$, where v is in meters per second and f_k is in newtons. Find the time required for the boat to slow to 45 km/h.

Additional Problems

19 In Fig. 6-36, block 1 of mass $m_1 = 2.0$ kg and block 2 of mass $m_2 = 3.0$ kg are connected by a string of negligible mass and are initially held in place. Block 2 is on a frictionless surface tilted at $\theta = 30°$. The coefficient of kinetic friction between block 1 and the horizontal surface is 0.25. The pulley has negligible mass and friction. Once they are released, the blocks move. What then is the tension in the string?

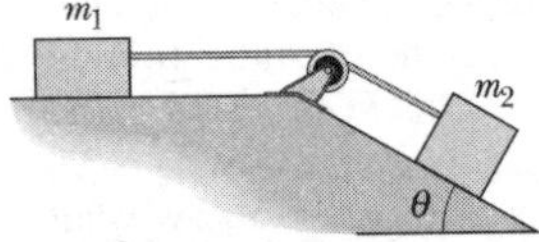

FIG. 6-36 Problem 19.

20 A block of mass $m_t = 4.0$ kg is put on top of a block of mass $m_b = 5.0$ kg. To cause the top block to slip on the bottom one while the bottom one is held fixed, a horizontal force of at least 12 N must be applied to the top block. The assembly of blocks is now placed on a horizontal, frictionless table (Fig. 6-37). Find the magn-itudes of (a) the maximum horizontal force $\vec{F}$ that can be applied to the lower block so that the blocks will move together and (b) the resulting acceleration of the blocks.

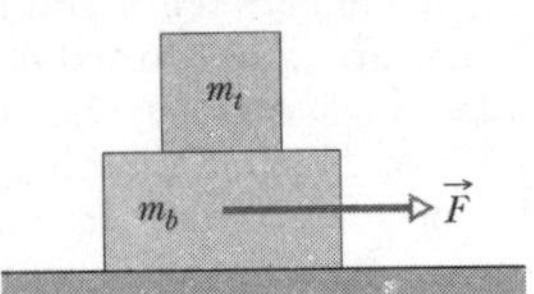

FIG. 6-37 Problem 20.

21 In Fig. 6-38, a box of ant aunts (total mass $m_1 = 1.65$ kg) and a box of ant uncles (total mass $m_2 = 3.30$ kg) slide down an inclined plane while attached by a massless rod parallel to the plane. The angle of incline is $\theta = 30.0°$. The coefficient of kinetic friction between the aunt box and the incline is $\mu_1 = 0.226$; that between the uncle box and the incline is $\mu_2 = 0.113$. Compute (a) the tension in the rod and (b) the magnitude of the common acceleration of the two boxes. (c) How would the answers to (a) and (b) change if the uncles trailed the aunts?

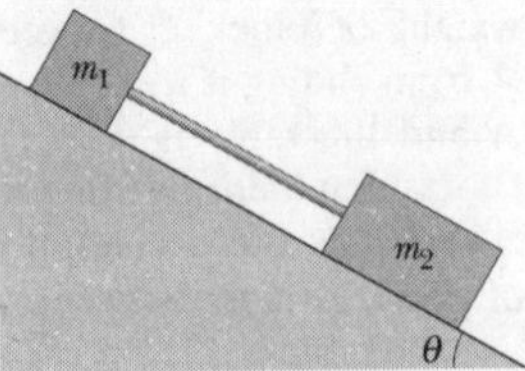

FIG. 6-38 Problem 21.

22 In Fig. 6-39, a crate slides down an inclined right-angled trough. The coefficient of kinetic friction between the crate and the trough is μ_k. What is the acceleration of the crate in terms of μ_k, θ, and g?

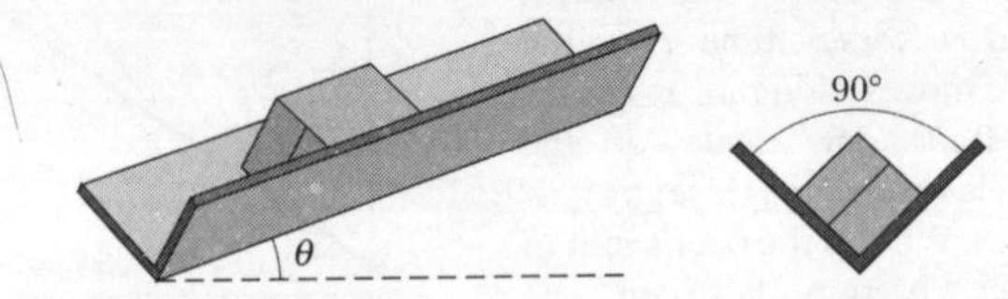

FIG. 6-39 Problem 22.

23 In Fig. 6-40, a 49 kg rock climber is climbing a "chimney." The coefficient of static friction between her shoes and the rock is 1.2; between her back and the rock is 0.80. She has reduced her push against the rock until her back and her shoes are on the verge of slipping. (a) Draw a free-body diagram of her. (b) What is the magnitude of her push against the rock? (c) What fraction of her weight is supported by the frictional force on her shoes?

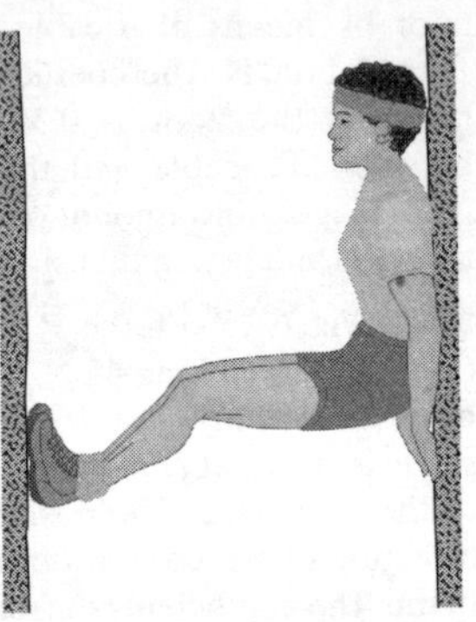
FIG. 6-40 Problem 23.

24 A 100 N force, directed at an angle θ above a horizontal floor, is applied to a 25.0 kg chair sitting on the floor. If $\theta = 0°$, what are (a) the horizontal component F_h of the applied force and (b) the magnitude F_N of the normal force of the floor on the chair? If $\theta = 30.0°$, what are (c) F_h and (d) F_N? If $\theta = 60.0°$, what are (e) F_h and (f) F_N? Now assume that the coefficient of static friction between chair and floor is 0.420. Does the chair slide or remain at rest if θ is (g) 0°, (h) 30.0°, and (i) 60.0°?

25 You must push a crate across a floor to a docking bay. The crate weighs 165 N. The coefficient of static friction between crate and floor is 0.510, and the coefficient of kinetic friction is 0.32. Your force on the crate is directed horizontally. (a) What magnitude of your push puts the crate on the verge of sliding? (b) With what magnitude must you then push to keep the crate moving at a constant velocity? (c) If, instead, you then push with the same magnitude as the answer to (a), what is the magnitude of the crate's acceleration?

26 In Fig. 6-41, block 1 of mass $m_1 = 2.0$ kg and block 2 of mass $m_2 = 1.0$ kg are connected by a string of negligible mass. Block 2 is pushed by force $\vec{F}$ of magnitude 20 N and angle $\theta = 35°$. The coefficient of kinetic friction between each block and the horizontal surface is 0.20. What is the tension in the string?

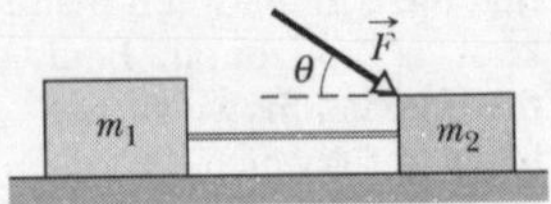

FIG. 6-41 Problem 26.

27 In Fig. 6-42 a fastidious worker pushes directly along the handle of a mop with a force $\vec{F}$. The handle is at an angle θ

with the vertical, and μ_s and μ_k are the coefficients of static and kinetic friction between the head of the mop and the floor. Ignore the mass of the handle and assume that all the mop's mass m is in its head. (a) If the mop head moves along the floor with a constant velocity, then what is F? (b) Show that if θ is less than a certain value θ_0, then $\vec{F}$ (still directed along the handle) is unable to move the mop head. Find θ_0.

FIG. 6-42 Problem 27.

28 In Fig. 6-43, a block weighing 22 N is held at rest against a vertical wall by a horizontal force $\vec{F}$ of magnitude 60 N. The coefficient of static friction between the wall and the block is 0.55, and the coefficient of kinetic friction between them is 0.38. In six experiments, a second force $\vec{P}$ is applied to the block and directed parallel to the wall with these magnitudes and directions: (a) 34 N, up, (b) 12 N, up, (c) 48 N, up, (d) 62 N, up, (e) 10 N, down, and (f) 18 N, down. In each experiment, what is the magnitude of the frictional force on the block? In which does the block move (g) up the wall and (h) down the wall? (i) In which is the frictional force directed down the wall?

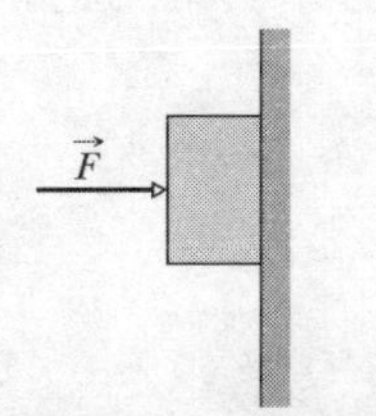

FIG. 6-43 Problem 28.

29 A 1.5 kg box is initially at rest on a horizontal surface when at $t = 0$ a horizontal force $\vec{F} = (1.8t)\hat{\mathrm{i}}$ N (with t in seconds) is applied to the box. The acceleration of the box as a function of time t is given by $\vec{a} = 0$ for $0 \le t \le 2.8$ s and $\vec{a} = (1.2t - 2.4)\hat{\mathrm{i}}$ m/s² for $t > 2.8$ s. (a) What is the coefficient of static friction between the box and the surface? (b) What is the coefficient of kinetic friction between the box and the surface?

30 A trunk with a weight of 220 N rests on the floor. The coefficient of static friction between the trunk and the floor is 0.41, and the coefficient of kinetic friction is 0.32. (a) What is the magnitude of the minimum horizontal force with which a person must push on the trunk to start it moving? (b) Once the trunk is moving, what magnitude of horizontal force must the person apply to keep it moving with constant velocity? (c) If the person continued to push with the force used to start the motion, what would be the magnitude of the trunk's acceleration?

31 The friction coefficient between the board and the floor shown in Fig. 6-44 is μ. Find the maximum force that the man can exert on the rope so that the board does not slip on the floor.

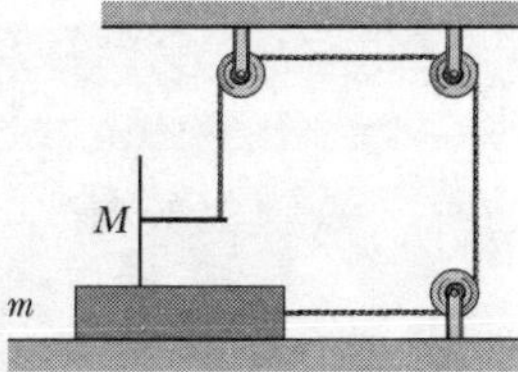

FIG. 6-44 Problem 31.

32 Find the acceleration of the block of mass M in the situation of Fig. 6-45 The coefficient of friction between the two blocks is μ_1 and that between the bigger block and the ground is μ_2.

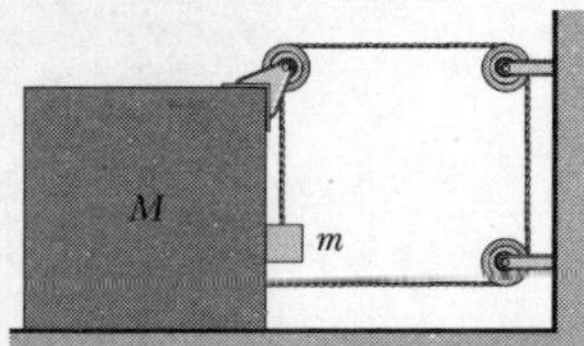

FIG. 6-45 Problem 32.

33 Fig. 6-46 shows a small block of mass m kept at the left end of a larger block of mass M and length l. The system can slide on a horizontal road. The system is started toward right with an initial velocity v_0. The friction coefficient between the road and the bigger block is μ and that between the blocks is $\mu/2$. Find the time elapsed before the smaller block separates from the bigger block. Neglect dimenstions of smaller block.

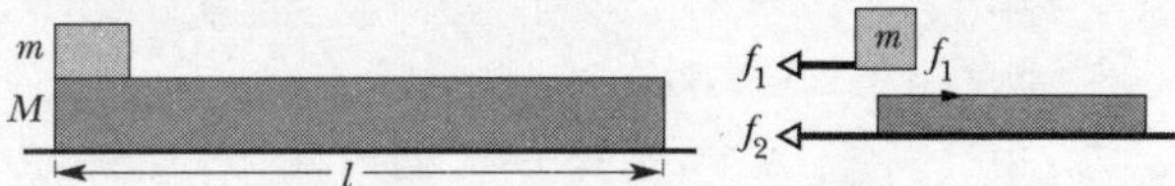

FIG. 6-46 Problem 33.

7 Circular Motion

UPI Photo/Dilip Vishwanat/Landov LLC

The driver of a funny car prepares for a timed run along a quarter-mile track by spinning the wheels, to make the tires and track sticky so that traction is high. Then the driver waits at the starting line until the countdown on the Christmas tree lights reaches green. The car's forward surge is so powerful that the car is effectively launched like a horizontal rocket. The science and engineering of funny cars is now so advanced that winning and losing is often determined by elapsed times differing by only 1 ms.

What property of a car determines the winning time?

7-1 | Introduction

A cameraman is shooting the formula-1 race event. One of the participants, say Louis Hamilton is going on a curved path of the track. If the cameraman is given two choices O_1 and O_2 for standing, (Fig. 7-1) which one should he choose and why?

Obviously the answer is O_2 because θ_2 is less than θ_1 which means he has to cover less angle in same time. At this point, we may not have much idea about circular motion or angular kinematics but it is clear that the decision was based on analysis of angular variables.

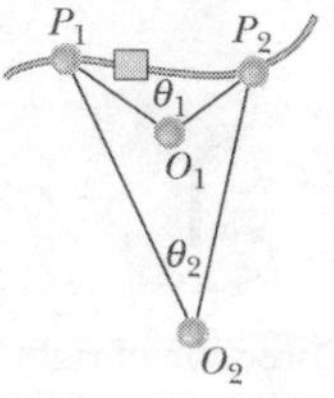

FIG. 7-1 (θ_2 and θ_1 are angles substended by Louis Hamilton while going from P_1 to P_2 on O_2 and O_1).

Radian Measure:

We are familiar with measuring angles in degrees, but in many situations measuing angles in radian becomes more convenient. One such situation is when we measure the angular displacement or angular velocity of a particle with the distance traveled by, or the speed of particle.

In Fig. 7-2, an angle θ between two radii of a circle define an arc of length s. We say that θ is the angle subtended by the arc. The arc length is proportional to both the radius of the circle and to the angle subtended. The angle θ in radians is defined as

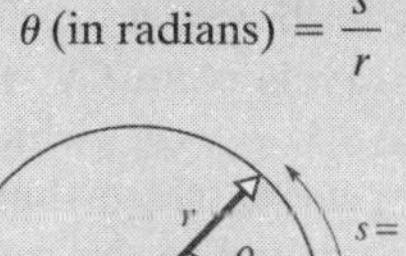

$$\theta \text{ (in radians)} = \frac{s}{r}$$

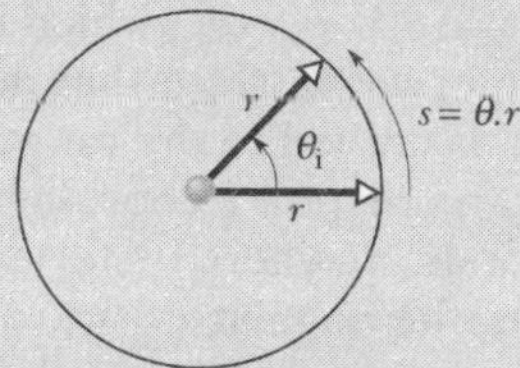

FIG. 7-2 Measuring angle in radians.

where r is the radius of the circle. Since an angle in radians is defined by the ratio of two lengths, it is a dimensionless quantity (a pure number).

7-2 | Angular Variables

Angular Displacement

Angle subtended by a moving particle at a fixed point is defined as angular displacement about that fixed point. Thus in the introductory section angular displacement of car about O_1 is θ_1 and about O_2 is θ_2. Angular displacement is measured in radians and is a dimensionless quantity.

Angular displacement depends on the choice of reference frame. If another driver observes the Louis Hamilton's car he will definitely see different angle subtended by his car. It is important to note that angular displacement depends not only on both reference frame but it also depends on the location of observers in the frame. The linear displacement is same for both observers at different positions in same frame, for example, O_1 and O_2 will observe same linear displacement but will observe different angular displacement, although both points are in the same ground frame.

It may be a bit surprising, but small angular displacement is considered to be a vector quantity. Direction of angular displacement vector is decided by right-hand rule which says that we twirl our right-hand fingers in sense of motion then direction in which our thumb is pointing (Fig. 7-3), gives the direction of angular displacement vector. It may look confusing that direction of vector is nowhere near the actual

FIG. 7-3 Direction of right hand thumb is the direction of the vector.

motion, but if we pay attention to a few facts we will see that perhaps this is the best way to represent angular displacement vector. Let's say the vector in Fig. 7-3 represents angular displacement . It holds three informations which can completely describe the angular motion of the particle.

The vector nature of angular quantities is further discussed in Chapter 10

1. The unique plane perpendicular to the vector direction represents the plane of motion of particle.
2. If the thumb represents direction of the vector then direction of our fingers will give us the sense of rotation.
3. Length of the vector will represent the magnitude of angular displacement.

It is important to note that the, plane of circular motion of particles will remain fixed in general. This means that the direction of angular variables will remain fixed (although sense may become positive or negative). Thus even though angular variables are vectors but we need not worry too much as there directions will remain unchanged. This situation is much like one-dimensional motion where variables are vectors but we do not use vector notation, we simply use signs +ve and −ve to represent sense. To conclude, the study of angular kinematics is like one dimensional motion, that is, the use of vector notation is not needed, rather the sign +ve or −ve is sufficient to represent the sense or direction.

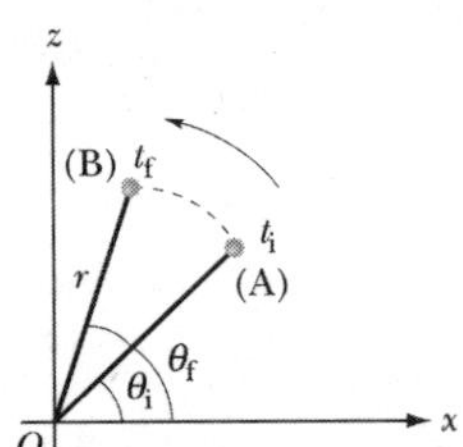

FIG. 7-4 Measuring angular displacement.

In Fig. 7-4, as the particle travels from (A) to (B) in a time Δt, the radius vector sweeps out an angle of $\Delta\theta = \theta_f - \theta_i$, which is equal to the angular displacement during the time interval Δt. Note that neither the angular position nor the angular displacement is limited to the range $0 < \theta < 2\pi$. For example, if the particle in Fig. 7-4 starts at polar coordinates (r, θ) makes two trips around a circular path, and ends up where it started, its angular displacement is described as $\theta = 4\pi$. Thus, the angular position does not get reset to zero each time the particle crosses the x-axis. The number of revolutions completed by the particles in a time interval is the angular displacement during the interval divided by 2π.

Angular Velocity

The rate of change of angular displacement is called angular velocity. We define the average angular speed $\overline{\omega}$, as the ratio of the angular displacement to the time interval Δt:

$$\overline{\omega} = \frac{\theta_f - \theta_i}{t_f - t_i} = \frac{\Delta t}{\Delta t} \qquad (7\text{-}1)$$

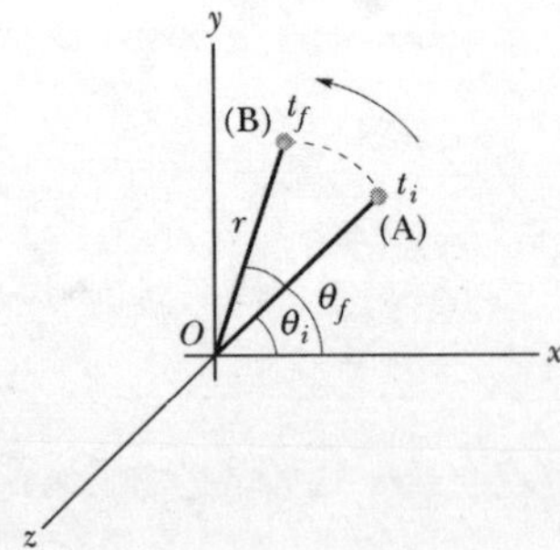

FIG. 7-5 Measuring angular displacement.

In analogy to the translational speed, the instantaneous angular speed $\overline{\omega}$ is defined as the limit of the ratio in Eq. 7-1 as Δt approaches zero:

$$\overline{\omega} = \lim_{\Delta t \to 0} \frac{\Delta\theta}{\Delta t} = \frac{d\theta}{dt} \qquad (7\text{-}2)$$

Angular speed has units of rad/s (or s_{-1} because radian have no dimensions). Let us adopt the convention that the fixed axis of rotation for an object is the z-axis, as in Fig.7-5.

Angular Acceleration

The rate of change of angular velocity is called angular acceleration. If the instantaneous angular speed of a particle changes from ω_i to ω_f in the time interval Δt, then the particle is said to undergo an angular acceleration. The average angular acceleration, $\overrightarrow{\alpha}$, of a particle moving in a circular path is defined as the ratio of the change in the angular speed to the time interval Δt :

$$\overline{\alpha} = \frac{\omega_f - \omega_i}{t_f - t_i} = \frac{\Delta\omega}{dt} \quad (7\text{-}3)$$

In analogy to the translational accelertion, the instantaneous angular acceleration is defined as the limit of the ratio $\Delta\omega/\Delta t$ as Δt approaches zero:

$$\overline{\alpha} = \lim_{\Delta t \to 0} \frac{\Delta\omega}{\Delta t} = \frac{d\omega}{dt} \quad (7\text{-}4)$$

Angular acceleration has units of rad/s^2, or s^{-2} and dimensions T^{-2}. The direction of angular acceleration is same as of angular velocity if angular velocity is increasing and if angular velocity is decreasing, the direction of angular acceleration is opposite. For uniform angular acceleration, the following equations can be proven very easily.

$$\omega = \omega_0 + \alpha t$$

$$\theta = \omega_0 t + \frac{1}{2}\alpha t^2 \quad (7\text{-}5)$$

$$\omega^2 = \omega_0^2 + 2\alpha\theta$$

where, ω_0 and ω are the angular velocities at time $t = 0$ and $t = t$ respectively. Similarly, α and θ represent the angular acceleration and angular displacement at time t.

7-3 | Relation Between Angular Velocity and Linear Velocity

When the motion of a particle is represented using angular variables, it does not mean that its motion cannot be described using linear parameters. Both the representations are valid and anyone can be adopted to analyze the situation. For example, during a cricket match, motion of the ball, for a fielder chasing it, is better understood using linear variables such as velocity, acceleration and so on. While for a cameraperson the motion of the same ball is better understood using its angular velocity, angular acceleration and so on, with respect to his position.

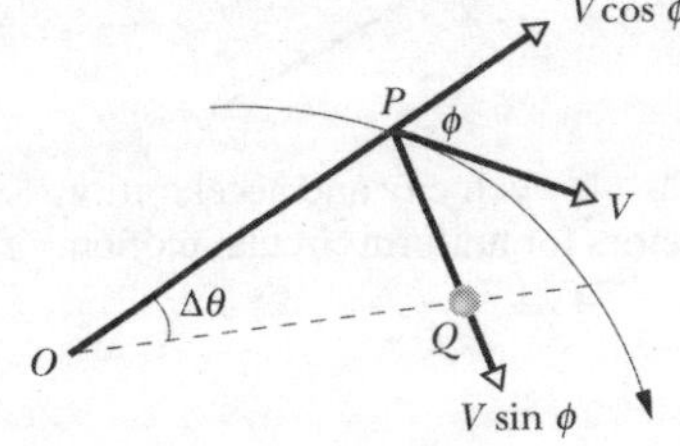

FIG. 7-6 Particle P moving with a speed V along a curved path.

Consider a particle P moving with a speed V along a curve (Fig. 7-6) and an observer is located at O. Let OP represent an imaginary line joining particle P to the observer O. The velocity vector makes an angle θ with OP at this instant. Note that the component, $V\sin\phi$ (component of velocity perpendicular to OP) is the cause of angular displacement. In other words, if only $V\cos\phi$ existed, we need not turn our heads to keep the particle in our line of sight.

If only $V\sin\phi$ exists then PQ is the distance travelled by particle in time Δt.

$$PQ = (V\sin\phi)\,\Delta t$$

Looking at the triangle OPQ it can be seen that for very small angle $\Delta\theta$.

$$PQ = OP\,(\Delta\theta)$$

Solving we get $$\frac{\Delta\theta}{\Delta t} = \frac{V\sin\phi}{\text{OP}}$$

Under the limit $\Delta t \to 0$, $\dfrac{\Delta\theta}{\Delta t}$ becomes $\dfrac{d\theta}{dt}$ which is the instantaneous angular velocity.

Thus we can write,

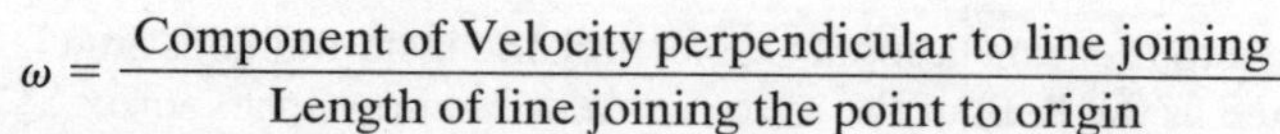

$$\omega = \frac{\text{Component of Velocity perpendicular to line joining}}{\text{Length of line joining the point to origin}}$$

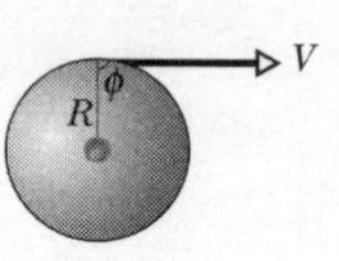

FIG. 7-7 Example of a particle undergoing circular motion

For example, in circular (Fig. 7-7) motion we can derive relation between angular velocity and speed. Velocity is always perpendicular to the line joining the center and particle. Thus, angular velocity of particle with respect to the center is,

$$\omega = \frac{V \sin \phi}{R} \tag{7-6}$$

$$\text{Since } \phi = 90°, \omega = \frac{V}{R}$$

CHECKPOINT 1 A projectile is launched at speed u making an angle θ with the horizontal. Find angular velocity of projectile at the time when it reaches same level, with respect to the point of projection at the time of landing.

7-4 | A Particle in Uniform Circular Motion

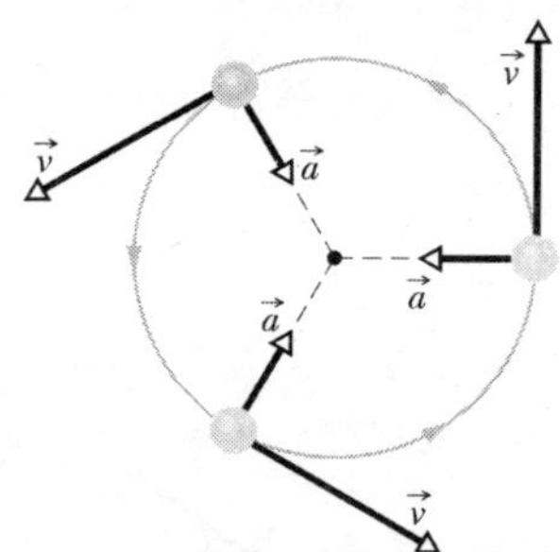

FIG. 7-8 Velocity and acceleration vectors for uniform circular motion.

A particle is in **uniform circular motion** if it travels around a circle or a circular arc at constant (*uniform*) speed. Although the speed does not vary, *the particle is accelerating* because the velocity changes in direction.

Figure 7-8 shows the relationship between the velocity and acceleration vectors at various stages during uniform circular motion. Both vectors have constant magnitude, but their directions change continuously. The velocity is always directed tangent to the circle in the direction of motion. The acceleration is always directed *radially inward.* Because of this, the acceleration associated with uniform circular motion is called a **centripetal** (meaning "center seeking") **acceleration.** As we prove next, the magnitude of this acceleration $\vec{a}$ is

$$a = \frac{v^2}{r} \quad \text{(centripetal acceleration)} \tag{7-7}$$

where r is the radius of the circle and v is the speed of the particle.

In addition, during this acceleration at constant speed, the particle travels the circumference of the circle (a distance of $2\pi r$) in time

$$T = \frac{2\pi r}{v} \quad \text{(period)} \tag{7-8}$$

T is called the *period of revolution,* or simply the *period,* of the motion. It is, in general, the time for a particle to go around a closed path exactly once.

Proof of Eq. 7-7

To find the magnitude and direction of the acceleration for uniform circular motion, we consider Fig. 7-9. In Fig. 7-9*a*, particle p moves at constant speed v around a circle of radius r. At the instant shown, p has coordinates x_p and y_p.

Recall that the velocity $\vec{v}$ of a moving particle is always tangent to the particle's path at the particle's position. In Fig. 7-9*a*, that means $\vec{v}$ is perpendicular to a radius r drawn to the particle's position. Then the angle θ that $\vec{v}$ makes with a vertical at p equals the angle θ that radius r makes with the x axis.

The scalar components of $\vec{v}$ are shown in Fig. 7-9*b*. With them, we can write the velocity $\vec{v}$ as

$$\vec{v} = v_x\hat{i} + v_y\hat{j} = (-v \sin \theta)\hat{i} + (v \cos \theta)\hat{j} \tag{7-9}$$

Now, using the right triangle in Fig. 7-9*a*, we can replace $\sin\theta$ with y_p/r and $\cos\theta$ with x_p/r to write

$$\vec{v} = \left(-\frac{vy_p}{r}\right)\hat{i} + \left(\frac{vx_p}{r}\right)\hat{j} \tag{7-10}$$

To find the acceleration $\vec{a}$ of particle p, we must take the time derivative of this equation. Noting that speed v and radius r do not change with time, we obtain

$$\vec{a} = \frac{d\vec{v}}{dt} = \left(-\frac{v}{r}\frac{dy_p}{dt}\right)\hat{i} + \left(\frac{v}{r}\frac{dx_p}{dt}\right)\hat{j} \tag{7-11}$$

Now note that the rate dy_p/dt at which y_p changes is equal to the velocity component v_y. Similarly, $dx_p/dt = v_x$, and, again from Fig. 7-9*b*, we see that $v_x = -v\sin\theta$ and $v_y = v\cos\theta$. Making these substitutions in Eq. 7-11, we find

$$\vec{a} = \left(-\frac{v^2}{r}\cos\theta\right)\hat{i} + \left(-\frac{v^2}{r}\sin\theta\right)\hat{j} \tag{7-12}$$

This vector and its components are shown in Fig. 7-9*c*. We find

$$a = \sqrt{a_x^2 + a_y^2} = \frac{v^2}{r}\sqrt{(\cos\theta)^2 + (\sin\theta)^2} = \frac{v^2}{r}\sqrt{1} = \frac{v^2}{r}$$

as we wanted to prove. To orient $\vec{a}$, we find the angle ϕ shown in Fig. 7-9*c*:

$$\tan\phi = \frac{a_y}{a_x} = \frac{-(v^2/r)\sin\theta}{-(v^2/r)\cos\theta} = \tan\theta$$

Thus, $\phi = \theta$, which means that $\vec{a}$ is directed along the radius r of Fig. 7-9*a*, toward the circle's center, as we wanted to prove.

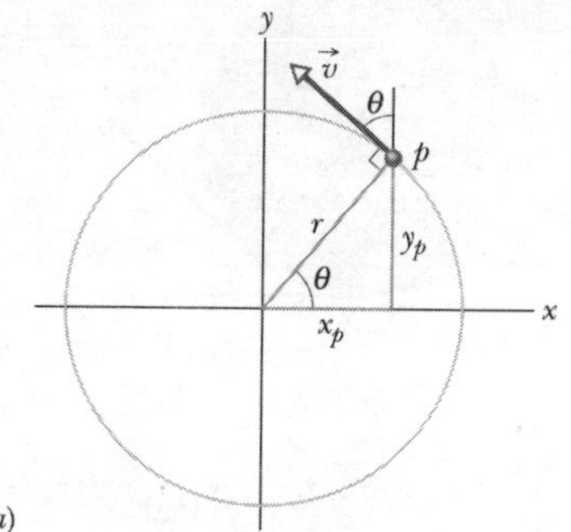

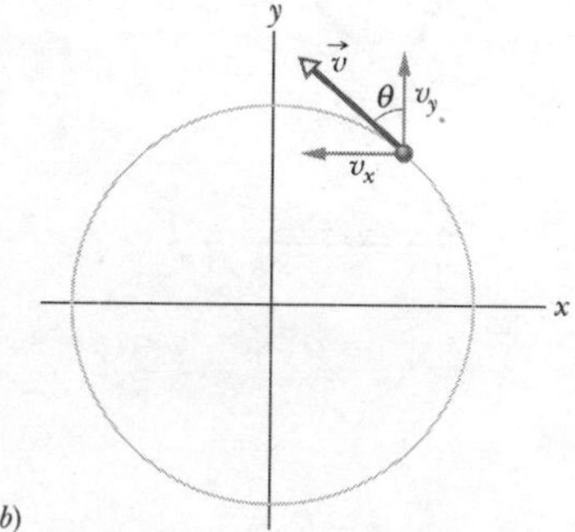

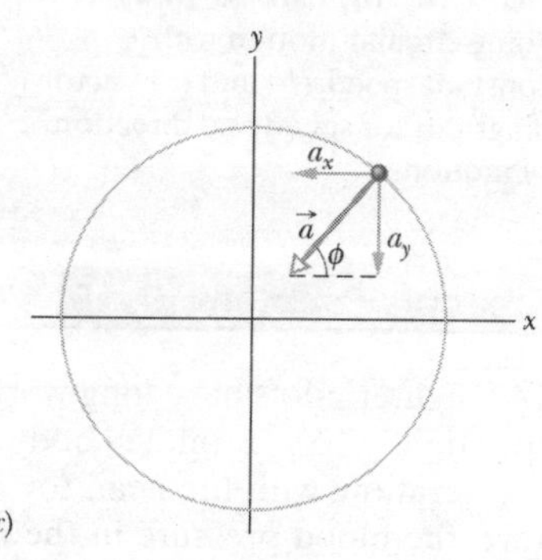

FIG. 7-9 Particle p moves in counterclockwise uniform circular motion. (*a*) Its position and velocity $\vec{v}$ at a certain instant. (*b*) Velocity $\vec{v}$. (*c*) Acceleration $\vec{a}$.

Deriving $a = v^2/r$ Geometrically

Consider a particle moving with constant speed v in a circle of radius r, Fig. (7-10*a*). If it travels from A to B in a short interval of time δt then, (since distance = speed × time).

$$\text{arc } AB = v\delta t$$

Also, by the definition of an angle in radians

$$\text{arc } AB = r\delta\theta \ (\delta\theta = \angle AOB)$$

$$r\delta\theta = v\delta t$$

$$\delta\theta = v\delta t/r \tag{7-13}$$

The vectors $\vec{v}_A$ and $\vec{v}_B$ drawn tangentially at A and B represent the velocities at these points. The change of velocity between A and B is $\vec{v}_B - \vec{v}_A$

But $$\vec{v}_B - \vec{v}_A = \vec{v}_B + (-\vec{v}_A)$$

So to subtract vector $\vec{v}_A$ from vector $\vec{v}_B$ we add vectors v_B and '$-\vec{v}_A$' by the parallelogram law. In Fig. 7-10*b*, PQ represents $\vec{v}_B$ in magnitude (v) and direction (BD); QR represents '$-\vec{v}_A$' in magnitude (v) and direction (CA). The change of velocity, as can be seen in Fig. 7-10*b* is a vector represented by PR.

Since one vector $(-\vec{v}_A)$ is perpendicular to OA and the other $(\vec{v}_B)$ is perpendicular to OB, $\angle PQR = \angle AOB = \delta\theta$. If δt is very small, $\delta\theta$ will also be small and PQ in Fig. 7-10*b* will have almost the same length as arc PR in Fig. 7-10*c* which subtends angle $\delta\theta$ at the center of a circle of radius v.

Arc $PR = v\delta\theta$ (from definition of radian) and so

$$PR = v\delta\theta$$

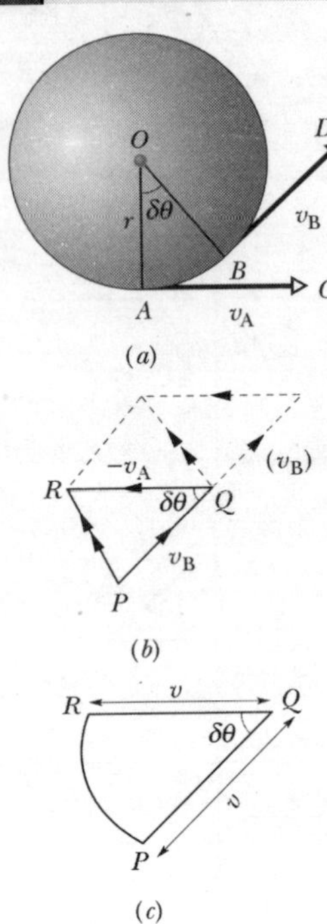

FIG. 7-10 (*a*) Particle undergoing circular motion with constant speed. (*b*) and (*c*) Vector diagrams for speed and direction of motion.

But from Eq. 7-13 $\quad \delta\theta = \dfrac{v\,\delta t}{r}$

Hence $\quad PR = \dfrac{v^2}{r}\,\delta t$

The magnitude of acceleration a between A and B is

$$a = \frac{\text{Change of velocity}}{\text{Time interval}} = \frac{PR}{\delta t}$$

Therefore $\quad a = \dfrac{v^2}{r}$

If ω is the angular velocity of the body, $v = r\omega$ and we can also write

$$a = \omega^2 r$$

The direction of acceleration is toward the center O of the circle, as can be seen if δt is made so small that A and B almost coincide; r is then perpendicular to $\vec{v}_A$(or $\vec{v}_B$), that is, along AO (or BO). We say the body has a centripetal acceleration (that is, center-seeking).

CHECKPOINT 2 An object moves at constant speed along a circular path in a horizontal xy plane, with the center at the origin. When the object is at $x = -2$ m, its velocity is $-(4\text{ m/s})\hat{j}$. Give the object's (a) velocity and (b) acceleration at $y = 2$ m.

Sample Problem 7-1

IAF fighter pilots have long worried about taking a turn too tightly. As a pilot's body undergoes centripetal acceleration, with the head toward the center of curvature, the blood pressure in the brain decreases, leading to loss of brain function.

There are several warning signs. When the centripetal acceleration is $2g$ or $3g$, the pilot feels heavy. At about $4g$, the pilot's vision switches to black and white and narrows to "tunnel vision." If that acceleration is sustained or increased, vision ceases and, soon after, the pilot is unconscious—a condition known as *g*-LOC for "*g*-induced loss of consciousness."

What is the magnitude of the acceleration, in g units, of a pilot whose aircraft enters a horizontal circular turn with a velocity of $\vec{v}_i = (400\hat{i} + 300\hat{j})$ m/s and 25 s later leaves the turn with a velocity of $\vec{v}_f = (-400\hat{i} - 300\hat{j})$ m/s? Assume speed is constant.

Conceptualize/Classify: We assume the turn is made with uniform circular motion. Then the pilot's acceleration is centripetal and has magnitude a given by Eq. $a = v^2/R$, where R is the circle's radius. Also, the time required to complete a full circle is the period given by Eq. $T = 2\pi R/v$.

Compute: Because we do not know radius R, let's solve Eq. 7-8 for R and substitute into Eq. 7-7. We find

$$a = \frac{2\pi v}{T}$$

Speed v here is the (constant) magnitude of the velocity during the turning. Let's substitute the components of the initial velocity into:

$$v = \sqrt{v_x^2 + v_y^2}$$

$$v = \sqrt{(400\text{ m/s})^2 + (300\text{ m/s})^2} = 500\text{ m/s}$$

To find the period T of the motion, first note that the final velocity is the reverse of the initial velocity. This means the aircraft leaves on the opposite side of the circle from the initial point and must have completed half a circle in the given 25 s. Thus a full circle would have taken $T = 50$ s.

Substituting these values into our equation for a, we find

$$a = \frac{2\pi(500\text{ m/s})}{50\text{ s}} = 62.83\text{ m/s}^2 \approx 6.4\text{ g} \qquad \text{(Answer)}$$

Conclude: Thus the pilot may have fainted.

7-5 | The Particle in Non-Uniform Circular Motion

Now we consider the motion of a particle along a curve where the direction and magnitude of velocity changes as shown in Fig. 7-11. Remember that the velocity vector is always tangent to the path but the acceleration vector $\vec{a}$ can be at any angle with respect to the path. At any instant, this vector can be resolved into two components: a radial component $\vec{a}_r$ and a tangential component $\vec{a}_t$. The direction perpendicular to the velocity is called radial direction and acceleration along this direction is actually responsible for the change in direction of velocity.

Direction changing comp.
θ
V
$a \sin \theta$
a
Magnitude changing comp.
$a \cos \theta$

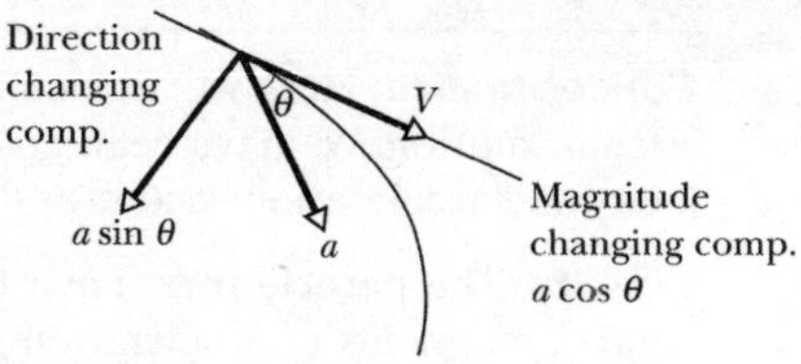

FIG. 7-11 A particle moving on a general curve with varying speed.

Centripetal Condition

When the component of acceleration perpendicular to velocity is v^2/r and always directed toward a fixed point, with r remaining constant, under such conditions, the particle will undergo circular motion about that fixed point with radius r.

$$\vec{a}_c = \vec{a}_r = v^2/r$$

We call the radial component of the acceleration as the centripetal acceleration as was discussed earlier. Please note that for undergoing circular motion of radius r we do not need to have constant speed. The forces providing centripetal acceleration will vary to give the required value, for maintaining circular motion. If the radial component of acceleration does not satisfy the above condition for fixed r and is not directed toward a fixed point, then the particle will undergo motion on an arbitrary path.

The tangential component of acceleration causes a change in the speed v of the particle. This component, which is parallel to the instantaneous velocity and its magnitude, is given by

$$a_t = \frac{d|\vec{v}|}{dt} = \frac{d(\omega R)}{dt} = \frac{R d\omega}{dt} = R\alpha \quad \text{(Tangential acceleration)}$$

Where α is the angular acceleration along the direction of velocity vector $\vec{v}$.

We can recall from previous section that under uniform circular motion the acceleration has only the radial component and no tangential component. The total acceleration vector $\vec{a}$ can be written as the vector sum of the component vectors:

$$\vec{a} = \vec{a}_r + \vec{a}_t \quad \text{(Total acceleration)}$$

PROBLEM-SOLVING TACTICS

Tactic 1: Magnitude of acceleration is same as magnitude of rate of change of velocity.

$$|\vec{a}| = \frac{|d\vec{V}|}{dt} = \sqrt{a_t^2 + a_r^2} \quad \text{or} \quad \left|\frac{d\vec{V}}{dt}\right| = \sqrt{(\alpha R)^2 + (\omega^2 R)^2}$$

Tactic 2: Rate of change of magnitude of velocity is called tangential acceleration.

$\vec{a}_t = \dfrac{d|\vec{V}|}{dt}$ Note: $\vec{a}_t$ is not the magnitude of acceleration.

So, $|\vec{a}|$ is the magnitude of rate of change of velocity and $\vec{a}_t$ is the rate of change of magnitude of velocity (a).

Sample Problem 7-2

A particle is undergoing circular motion with speed V and radius R. The angle between acceleration and velocity vectors is θ at certian instant. Find magnitude of tangential component of acceleration in terms of V, R and θ at this instant.

Conceptualize: Here we are dealing with non-uniform circular motion. We have been given angle between velocity and acceleration vectors as θ.

Classify: The particle must have tangential and centripetal components of acceleration as shown in Fig. 7-12.

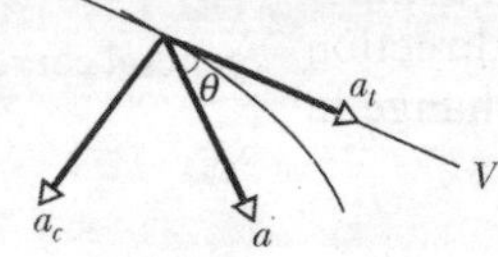

FIG. 7-12 Tangential and centripetal components of acceleration.

Compute: Let's assume that the magnitude of particle's acceleration is a.

$$a_c = \frac{V^2}{R} = a \sin \theta \qquad \text{(i)}$$

Hence $$a = \frac{V^2}{R \sin \theta}$$

The tangential component of acceleration is given by $a_t = a \cos \theta$

Substituting the value of a from (i), we get

$$a_1 = \frac{V^2 \cos \theta}{R \sin \theta} = \frac{V^2}{R} \cos \theta$$

Conclude: It is important to remember that for motion along all paths, the component of acceleration along the velocity vector is responsible for change in magnitude of velocity.

CHECKPOINT 3 Which of the situations described by the figure is possible?

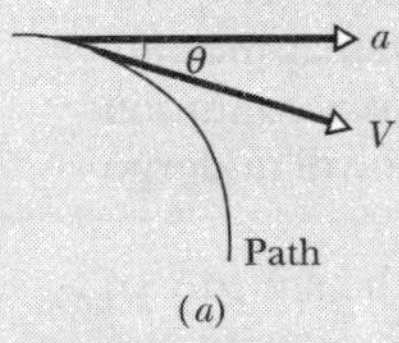

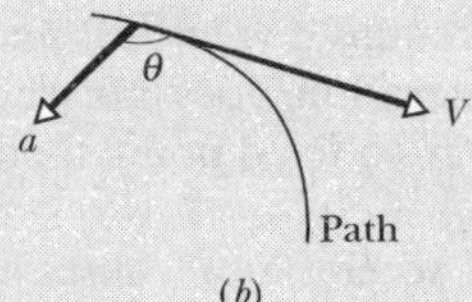

Sample Problem 7-3

A car is increasing its speed at constant rate of 0.1 m/s². The car passes over a convex circular overbridge (Fig. 7-13) of radius 40 m. At the moment the car is at the top of the overbridge, its speed is 2 m/s. What are the magnitude and direction of the total acceleration vector at this instant?

Conceptualize: Think about your experience of driving over such an overbridge.

Classify: The car is moving along a curved path, with variable speed. Thus car have both tangential and radial acceleration. The radial acceleration is given by Eq. 7-7, with v = 2m/s and r = 40 m. The radial acceleration vector is directed straight downward, and the tangential acceleration vector has magnitude 0.1 m/s² and is horizontal.

Compute: Evaluate the radial acceleration:

$$a_r = \frac{v^2}{r} = \frac{(2\ \text{m/s})^2}{40\ \text{m}} = 0.1\ \text{m/s}^2$$

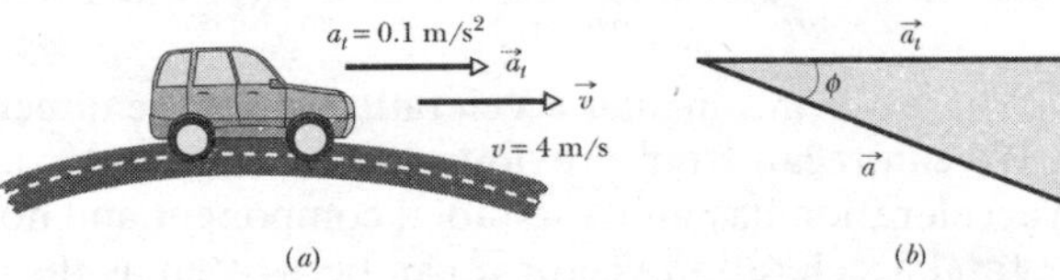

FIG. 7-13 (*a*) Car accelerating over a convex overbridge. (*b*) Free-body diagram.

The magnitude of $\vec{a}$ is given by

$$|\vec{a}| = \sqrt{a_t^2 + a_r^2} = \sqrt{2}\ \text{m/s}^2$$

The angle ϕ (see Fig. 7-13*b*) between $\vec{a}$ and the horizontal is given by

$$\phi = \tan^{-1} \frac{a_r}{a_t} = 45°$$

Radius of Curvature

When a particle undergoes any general motion along any arbitrary path, we can define a geometrical quantity called radius of curvature. Let's say a particle going along any arbitrary path passes through point A. When the particle crosses this point, it satisfies centripetal condition of moving on an imaginary circle of radius R_C, then we say radius of curvature of the path at A is R_C (Fig. 7-14).

If a_r represents the component of acceleration perpendicular to velocity,

then
$$a_r = \frac{V^2}{R_C}$$

Where R_C is radius of curvature of the imaginary circle touching the curve at A.

and
$$R_C = \frac{V^2}{a_r} = \frac{V^2}{a_1}$$

Hence
$$a_r = a_1$$

FIG. 7-14 Path of a particle moving along an imaginary circle satisfying centripetal condition.

In general, R_C *at any point on the path can be defined as*

$$R_C = \frac{(\text{Speed})^2}{\text{Component of acceleration perpendicular to velocity}}$$

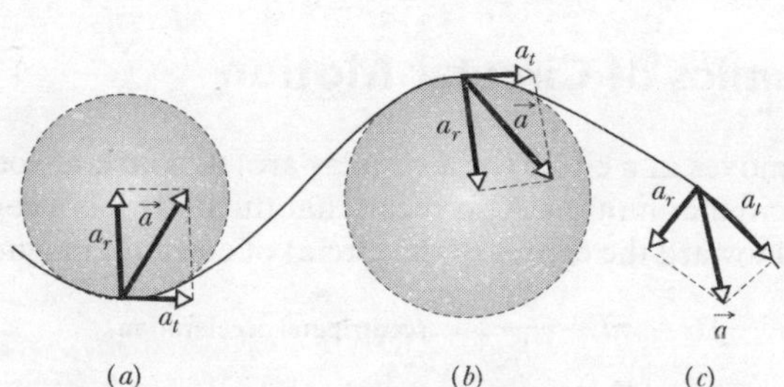

FIG. 7-15 At each of three points (A), (B), and (C) in active figure (7-14c), we draw dashed circles that represent the curvature of the actual path at each point. The radius of the circles is equal to the path's radius of curvature at each point direction and in magnitude.

CHECKPOINT 4 A projectile is launched horizontally with 20 ms^{-1} from some height. Find R_C at $t = 2$ s.

Sample Problem 7-4

A particle is moving along a parabola $y = 4x^2$ with a constant speed of 2 m/s.

(a) Find acceleration at $x = 0$

(b) Find unit vector of acceleration at $x = 1/8$.

Conceptualize: Looking at the Fig. 7-16*a*, we can see that particle is going on a curved path with no tangential component of acceleration, as speed is constant. This means that the acceleration will have only radial component, or putting it simply, acceleration will always be perpendicular to velocity.

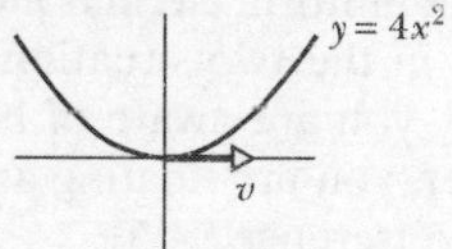

FIG. 7-16*a* A particle moving on a parabolic path.

(a) Compute: We can write y component of velocity v as

$$v_y = \frac{dy}{dt} = \frac{dy}{dx} \times \frac{dx}{dt}$$

Substituting the value of $y = 4x^2$ in the above relation, we get

$$v_y = \frac{d(4x^2)}{dx} \times \frac{dx}{dt}$$

Differentiating first term on RHS with respect to x, we get

$$v_y = 8 \times v_x \qquad \text{(i)}$$

where, $v_x = \dfrac{dx}{dt}$ (component of velocity along x direction)

Differentiating v_y with respect to time we get

$$a_y = \frac{dv_y}{dt} = \frac{dv_y}{dx} \times \frac{dx}{dt}$$

where, a_x is the y component of acceleration.

Substitutive Eq. (i) in above relation we get

$$a_y = \frac{d(8 \times v_x)}{dx} \times v_x$$

$$a_y = v_x^2 8 + 8x \times v_x \times \frac{dv_x}{dx}$$

At $x = 0$, the particle is at origin and therefore it has velocity only along x-axis that is, $v_x = 2x$

$$a_y = (2)^2 \times 8 = 32 \text{ m/s}^2$$

(b) Compute: Slope of curve $= \frac{dy}{dx} = 8x$

At $x = \frac{1}{8}$, slope = 1

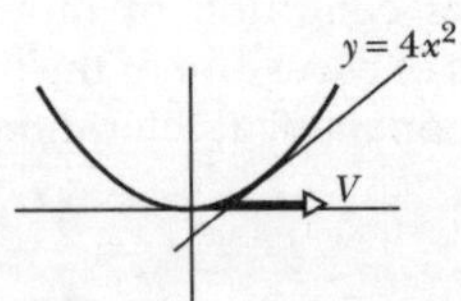

FIG. 7-16b A particle moving on a parabolic path.

Now since acceleration is perpendicular to velocity at every point it is also perpendicular to the slope of curve

$$\therefore \hat{a} = -\hat{i} + \hat{j}$$

Conclude: It is not necessary that at constant speed a particle should undergo only circular motion or straight line motion. As the acceleration is perpendicular to velocity but is not satisfying condition for centripetal acceleration then the particle moves on some other curve with constant speed.

7-6 | Dynamics of Circular Motion

When a body moves in a circle (or a circular arc) at constant speed v, it is said to be in uniform circular motion. Also recall that the body has a centripetal acceleration (directed toward the center of the circle) of constant magnitude given by

$$a = \frac{v^2}{R} \quad \text{(centripetal acceleration)} \tag{7-14}$$

where R is the radius of the circle.

Let us examine two examples of uniform circular motion:

1. *Rounding a curve in a car.* You are sitting in the center of the rear seat of a car moving at a constant high speed along a flat road. When the driver suddenly turns left, rounding a corner in a circular arc, you slide across the seat toward the right and then jam against the car wall for the rest of the turn. What is going on?

   While the car moves in the circular arc, it is in uniform circular motion; that is, it has an acceleration that is directed toward the center of the circle. By Newton's second law, a force must cause this acceleration. Moreover, the force must also be directed toward the center of the circle. Thus, it is a **centripetal force,** where the adjective indicates the direction. In this example, the centripetal force is a frictional force on the tires from the road; it makes the turn possible.

   If you are to move in uniform circular motion along with the car, there must also be a centripetal force on you. However, apparently the frictional force on you from the seat was not great enough to make you go in a circle with the car. Thus, the seat slid beneath you, until the right wall of the car jammed into you. Then its push on you provided the needed centripetal force on you, and you joined the car's uniform circular motion.

2. *Orbiting Earth.* This time you are a passenger in the space shuttle *Atlantis.* As it and you orbit Earth, you float through your cabin. What is going on?

   Both you and the shuttle are in uniform circular motion and have accelerations directed toward the center of the circle. Again by Newton's second law, centripetal forces must cause these accelerations. This time the centripetal forces are gravitational pulls (the pull on you and the pull on the shuttle) exerted by Earth and directed radially inward, toward the center of Earth.

In both car and shuttle you are in uniform circular motion, acted on by a centripetal force—yet your sensations in the two situations are quite different. In the car, jammed up against the wall, you are aware of being compressed by the wall. In the orbiting shuttle, however, you are floating around with no sensation of any force acting on you. Why this difference?

The difference is due to the nature of the two centripetal forces. In the car, the centripetal force is the push on the part of your body touching the car wall. You can sense the compression on that part of your body. In the shuttle, the centripetal force is Earth's gravitational pull on every atom of your body. Thus, there is no compression (or pull) on any one part of your body and no sensation of a force acting on you. (The sensation is said to be one of "weightlessness," but that description is tricky. The pull on you by Earth has certainly not disappeared and, in fact, is only a little less than it would be with you on the ground.)

Another example of a centripetal force is shown in Fig. 7-17. There a carrom stricker moves around in a circle at constant speed v while tied to a string looped around a central peg. This time the centripetal force is the radially inward pull on the stricker from the string. Without that force, the stricker would slide off in a straight line instead of moving in a circle.

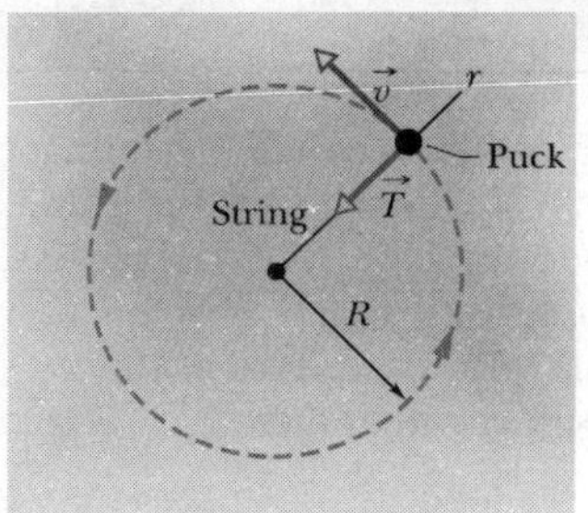

FIG. 7-17 An over head view of a carrom stricker moving with constant speed v in a circular path of radius R on a horizontal frictionless surface. The centripetal force on the stricker is $\vec{T}$, the pull from the string, directed inward along the radial axis r extending through the stricker.

Note again that a centripetal force is not a new kind of force. The name merely indicates the direction of the force. It can, in fact, be a frictional force, a gravitational force, the force from a car wall or a string, or any other force. For any situation:

> A centripetal force accelerates a body by changing the direction of the body's velocity without changing the body's speed.

From Newton's second law and the equation, $a = v^2/R$, we can write the magnitude F of a centripetal force (or a net centripetal force) as

$$F = m\frac{v^2}{R} \quad \text{(magnitude of centripetal force)} \qquad (7\text{-}15)$$

Because the speed v^2 here is constant, the magnitude of acceleration adn force are also constants.

However, the directions of the centripetal acceleration and force are not constant; they vary continuously so as to always point toward the center of the circle. For this reason,the force and acceleration vectors are sometimes drawn along a radial axis r that moves with the body and always extends from the center of the circle to the body, as in Fig. 7-17. The positive direction of the axis is radially outward, but the acceleration and force vectors point radially inward.

Steps for Solving Problems

1. Identify the plane of circular motion.
2. Locate the center and calculate the radius.
3. Make free-body diagram.
4. Resolve forces only and always along these three directions :
   (a) In the plane along radial direction.
   (b) In the plane along tangential direction.
   (c) Perpendicular to the plane of circular motion.

(a) Add the force assuming radially inward direction as positive

Therefore $$\sum F_r = \frac{mV^2}{R}$$

$$F = ma$$
$$= \frac{mv^2}{R}$$

(b) 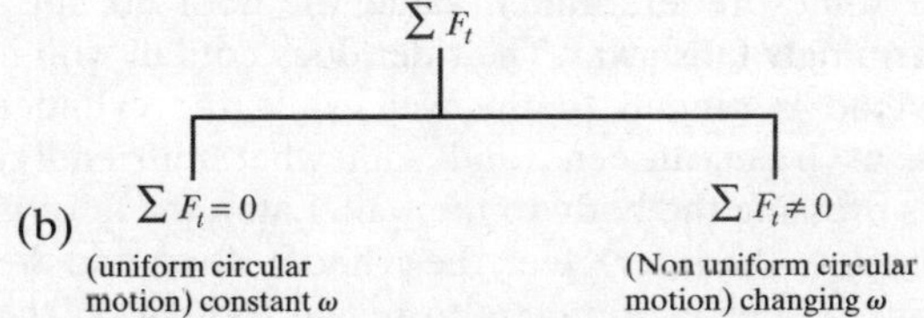

(c) Since plane cannot be accelerating then $\sum F_1 = 0$. If plane accelerates then actually it will not be circular motion from ground frame.

Sample Problem 7-5

In a 1901 circus performance, Allo "Dare Devil" Diavolo introduced the stunt of riding a bicycle in a loop-the-loop (Fig. 7-18*a*). Assuming that the loop is a circle with radius $R = 2.7$ m, what is the least speed v Diavolo could have at the top of the loop to remain in contact with it there?

(*a*)

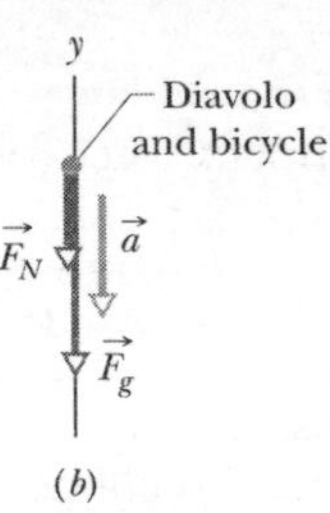

(*b*)

FIG. 7-18 (*a*) Contemporary advertisement for Diavolo and (*b*) free-body diagram for the performer at the top of the loop. *(Photograph in part a reproduced with permission of Circus World Museum)*

Conceptualize: We can assume that Diavolo and his bicycle travel through the top of the loop as a single particle in uniform circular motion.

Classify: Thus, at the top, the acceleration $\vec{a}$ of this particle must have the magnitude $a = v^2/R$ given by Eq. 7-14 and be directed downward, toward the center of the circular loop.

Compute: The forces on the particle when it is at the top of the loop are shown in the free-body diagram of Fig 7-18*b*. The gravitational force $\vec{F}_g$ is directed downward along a y axis; so is the normal force $\vec{F}_N$ on the particle from the loop; so also is the centripetal acceleration of the particle. Thus, Newton's second law for y components ($F_{\text{net},y} = ma_y$) gives us

$$-F_N - F_g = m(-a)$$

and

$$-F_N - mg = m\left(-\frac{v^2}{R}\right) \tag{7-16}$$

If the particle has the *least speed* v needed to remain in contact, then it is on the *verge of losing contact* with the loop (falling away from the loop), which means that $F_N = 0$ at the top of the loop (the particle and loop touch but without any normal force). Substituting 0 for F_N in Eq. 7-16, solving for v, and then substituting known values give us

$$v = \sqrt{gR} = \sqrt{(9.8\ \text{m/s}^2)(2.7\ \text{m})}$$
$$= 5.1\ \text{m/s} \qquad \text{(Answer)}$$

Conclude: Diavolo made certain that his speed at the top of the loop was greater than 5.1 m/s so that he did not lose contact with the loop and fall away from it. Note that this speed requirement is independent of the mass of Diavolo and his bicycle. Had he feasted on, say, momos before his performance, he still would have had to exceed only 5.1 m/s to maintain contact as he passed through the top of the loop.

Sample Problem 7-6 Build your skill

Even some seasoned roller-coaster riders blanch at the thought of riding the Rotor, which is essentially a large, hollow cylinder that is rotated rapidly around its central axis (Fig. 7-19). Before the ride begins, a rider enters the cylinder through a door on the side and stands on a floor, up against a canvas-covered wall. The door is closed, and as the cylinder begins to turn, the rider, wall, and floor move in unison. When the rider's speed reaches some predetermined value, the floor abruptly and alarmingly falls away. The rider does not fall with it but instead is pinned to the wall while the cylinder rotates, as if an unseen (and somewhat unfriendly) agent is pressing the body to the wall. Later, the floor is eased back to the rider's feet, the cylinder slows, and the rider sinks a few centimeters to regain footing on the floor. (Some riders consider all this to be fun.)

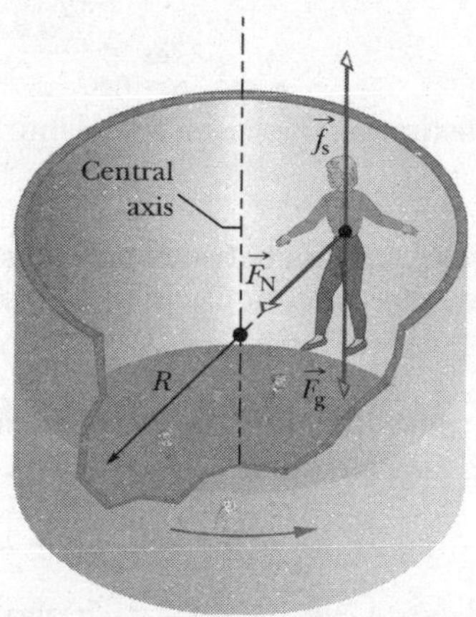

FIG. 7-19 A Rotor in an amusement park, showing the forces on a rider. The centripetal force is the normal force $\vec{F}_N$ with which the wall pushes inward on the rider.

Suppose that the coefficient of static friction μ_s between the rider's clothing and the canvas is 0.40 and that the cylinder's radius R is 2.1 m.

(a) What minimum speed v must the cylinder and rider have if the rider is not to fall when the floor drops?

Conceptualize: The gravitational force $\vec{F}_g$ on the rider tends to slide her down the wall, but she does not move because a frictional force from the wall acts upward on her (Fig. 7-19).

Classify: If she is to be on the verge of sliding down, that upward force must be a *static* frictional force $\vec{f}_s$ at its maximum value $\mu_s F_N$, where F_N is the magnitude of the normal force $\vec{F}_N$ on her from the cylinder (Fig. 7-19). This normal force is directed horizontally toward the central axis of the cylinder and is the centripetal force that causes the rider to move in a circular path, with centripetal acceleration of magnitude $a = v^2/R$ and directed toward the center of the circle. We want speed v in that last expression, for the condition that the rider is on the verge of sliding.

Compute: Vertical forces: We first place a vertical y axis through the rider, with the positive direction upward. We can then apply Newton's second law to the rider, writing it for y components ($F_{\text{net},y} = ma_y$) as

$$f_s - mg = m(0)$$

where m is the rider's mass and mg is the magnitude of $\vec{F}_g$. Because the rider is on the verge of sliding, we substitute the maximum value $\mu_s F_N$ for f_s in this equation, getting

$$\mu_s F_N - mg = 0$$

or

$$F_N = \frac{mg}{\mu_s} \tag{7-17}$$

Radial forces: Next we place a radial r axis through the rider, with the positive direction outward. We can then write Newton's second law for components along that axis as

$$-F_N = m\left(-\frac{v^2}{R}\right) \tag{7-18}$$

Substituting Eq. 7-17 for F_N and then solving for v, we find

$$v = \sqrt{\frac{gR}{\mu_s}} = \sqrt{\frac{(9.8\ \text{m/s}^2)(2.1\ \text{m})}{0.40}}$$

$$= 7.17\ \text{m/s} \approx 7.2\ \text{m/s} \qquad \text{(Answer)}$$

Note that the result is independent of the rider's mass; it holds for anyone riding the Rotor, from a child to a sumo wrestler, which is why no one has to "weigh in" to ride the Rotor.

(b) If the rider's mass is 49 kg, what is the magnitude of the centripetal force on her?

Compute: According to Eq. 7-18,

$$F_N = m\frac{v^2}{R} = (49\ \text{kg})\frac{(7.17\ \text{m/s})^2}{2.1\ \text{m}}$$

$$\approx 1200\ \text{N} \qquad \text{(Answer)}$$

Conclude: Although this force is directed toward the central axis, the rider has an overwhelming sensation that the force pinning her against the wall is directed radially outward. Her sensation stems from the fact that she is in a noninertial frame (she and it are accelerating). As measured from such frames, forces can be illusionary. The illusion is part of the Rotor's attraction.

Sample Problem 7-7

In spite of the extreme care taken in engineering a roller coaster, an unlucky few of the millions of people who ride roller coasters each year end up with a medical condition called *roller-coaster headache*. Symptoms, which might not appear for several days, include vertigo and headache, both severe enough to require medical treatment.

Let's investigate the probable cause by designing the track for our own *induction roller coaster* (which can be accelerated by magnetic forces even on a horizontal track). To create an initial thrill, we want each passenger to leave the loading point with acceleration g along the horizontal track. To increase the thrill, we also want that first section of track to form a circular arc (Fig. 7-20), so that the passenger also experiences a centripetal acceleration. As the passenger accelerates along the arc, the magnitude of this centripetal acceleration increases alarmingly. When the magnitude a of the net acceleration reaches $4g$ at some point P and angle θ_P along the arc, we want the passenger then to move in a straight line, along a tangent to the arc.

(a) What angle θ_P should the arc subtend so that a is $4g$ at point P?

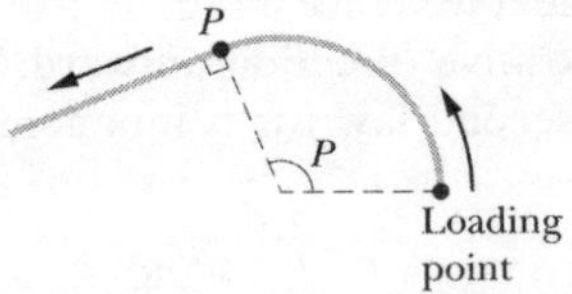

FIG. 7-20 An overhead view of a horizontal track for a roller coaster. The track begins as a circular arc at the loading point and then, at point P, continues along a tangent to the arc.

Conceptualize/Classify: (1) At any given time, the passenger's net acceleration $\vec{a}$ is the vector sum of the tangential acceleration $\vec{a}_t$ along the track and the radial acceleration $\vec{a}_r$ toward the arc's center of curvature. (2) The value of a_r at any given time depends on the angular speed ω according to Eq. $a_r = \omega^2 r$, where r is the radius of the circular arc. (3) An angular acceleration α around the arc is associated with the tangential acceleration a_t along the track according to Eq. $a_t = \alpha r$. (4) Because a_t and r are constant, so is α and thus we can use the constant angular-acceleration equations.

Compute: Because we are trying to determine a value for angular position θ, let's choose the following equation from among the constant angular–acceleration equations:

$$\omega^2 = \omega_0^2 + 2\alpha(\theta - \theta_0) \tag{7-19}$$

For the angular acceleration α,

$$\alpha = \frac{a_t}{r} \tag{7-20}$$

We also substitute $\omega_0 = 0$ and $\theta_0 = 0$, and we find

$$\omega^2 = \frac{2a_t\theta}{r} \tag{7-21}$$

Substituting this result for ω^2 into

$$a_r = \omega^2 r \tag{7-22}$$

gives a relation between the radial acceleration, the tangential acceleration, and the angular position θ:

$$a_r = 2a_t\theta \tag{7-23}$$

Because $\vec{a}_t$ and $\vec{a}_r$ are perpendicular vectors, their sum has the magnitude

$$a = \sqrt{a_t^2 + a_r^2} \tag{7-24}$$

Substituting for a_r from Eq. 7-23 and solving for θ lead to

$$\theta = \tfrac{1}{2}\sqrt{\frac{a^2}{a_t^2} - 1} \tag{7-25}$$

When a reaches the design value of $4g$, angle is the angle θ_P we want. Substituting $a = 4g$, $\theta = \theta_P$, and $a_t = g$ into Eq. 7-25, we find

$$\theta_P = \tfrac{1}{2}\sqrt{\frac{(4g)^2}{g^2} - 1} = 1.94 \text{ rad} = 111° \qquad \text{(Answer)}$$

(b) What is the magnitude a of the passenger's net acceleration at point P and after point P?

At P, a has the design value of $4g$. Just after P is reached, the passenger moves in a straight line and no longer has centripetal acceleration. Thus, the passenger has only the acceleration magnitude g along the track. Hence,

$$a = 4g \text{ at } P \quad \text{and} \quad a = g \text{ after } P \qquad \text{(Answer)}$$

Conclude: Roller-coaster headache can occur when a passenger's head undergoes an abrupt change in acceleration, with the acceleration magnitude large before or after the change. The reason is that the change can cause the brain to move relative to the skull, tearing the veins that bridge the brain and skull. Our design to increase the acceleration from g to $4g$ along the path to P might harm the passenger, but the abrupt change in acceleration as the passenger passes through point P is more likely to cause roller-coaster headache.

Sample Problem 7-8

A ball of mass 0.5 kg is attached to a light string of length 2 m. The ball is whirled on a horizontal smooth surface in a circle of radius 2 m as shown in Fig. 7-21. If the string can withstand tension upto 100 N, what is the maximum speed at which the ball can be whirled.

Conceptualize/Classify: A stronger cord can whirl the ball faster before the string breaks. Also more massive the ball probability of the string breaking at same speed is also very high.

Compute: Only radial force is acting on the ball, so we need to write only one equation, $\sum F_r = \frac{mV^2}{R}$. Furthermore, the maximum speed the ball can attain corresponds to the maximum tension that the string can withstand:

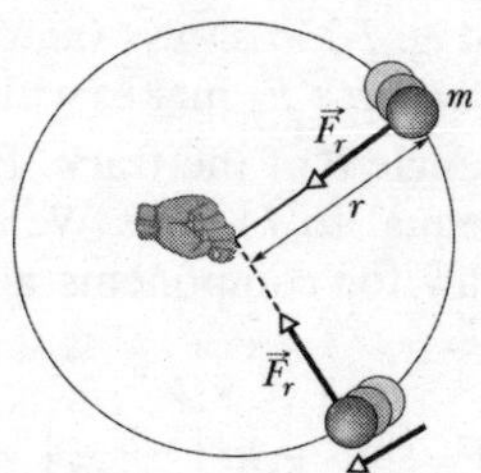

FIG. 7-21 Ball attached to light string and whirled along a circular path

$$T_{max} = \frac{mv_{max}^2}{r} \quad (7\text{-}26)$$

Solve for v

$$v_{max} = \sqrt{\frac{T_{max}r}{m}} = \sqrt{\frac{(100\text{ N})(2\text{ m})}{0.5\text{ kg}}} = 20\text{ m/s}$$

Conclude: Eq. 7-26 shows that increase in mass or speed increases the chances of breaking the cord as we had conceptualized in the begining.

Sample Problem 7-9 The Concial Pendulum

A particle of mass m is suspended from a string of length L. The particle revolves with constant speed v in a horizontal circle .The string sweeps out the surface of a cone of semi vertex angle θ. The system shown is commonly known as a conical pendulum. Find an expression for v in terms of L, g and θ.

Conceptualize: Looking at the motion of the ball in Fig. 7-22*a* we can see that particle is undergoing circular motion in horizontal plane. We can also locate the center and the radius of circle is given as *r*.

Classify: From the geometry in Fig. 7-22*a*, we have $r = L \sin \theta$.

Making free-body diagram and resolving forces along these three directions :

(a) In the horizontal plane along radial direction
(b) In the vertical plane

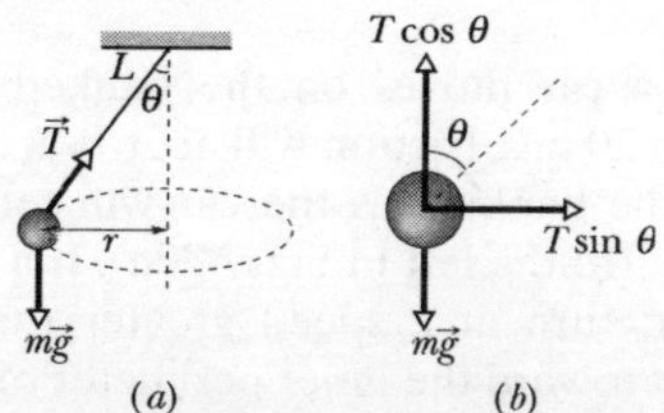

FIG. 7-22 Conical pendulum

Compute: Since plane cannot be accelerating, then $\sum F_{\parallel} = 0$ in the vertical direction, that is $T\cos\theta - mg = 0$ gives

$$T\cos\theta = mg \quad \text{(i)}$$

Add the force assuming radially in ward direction as positive

$$T\sin 0 = mv^2/r \quad \text{(ii)}$$

$T\sin\theta$ represents the radial or centripetal acceleration. Divide Eq. (ii) by equation (i) and use $\sin\theta/\cos\theta = \tan\theta$;

$$\tan\theta = \frac{v^2}{rg}$$

Solve for v

$$v = \sqrt{rg\tan\theta}$$
$$= \sqrt{Lg\sin\theta\tan\theta}$$

Conclude: When θ is 90º the string is horizontal and the speed is infinite. Thus the string cannot be horizontal. The gravitational force on the ball is being balanced by the vertical component of the tension. When string becomes horizontal there would be no force to balance the weight. Also note that the speed is not dependent on the mass of the ball.

Sample Problem 7-10

Curved portions of highways are always banked (tilted) to prevent cars from sliding off the highway. When a highway is dry, the frictional force between the tires and the road surface may be enough to prevent sliding. When the highway is wet, however, the frictional force may be negligible, and banking is then essential. Figure 6-13*a* represents a car of mass m as it moves at a constant speed v of 20 m/s around a banked circular track of radius $R = 200$ m. (It is a normal car, rather than a race car, which means any vertical force from the passing air

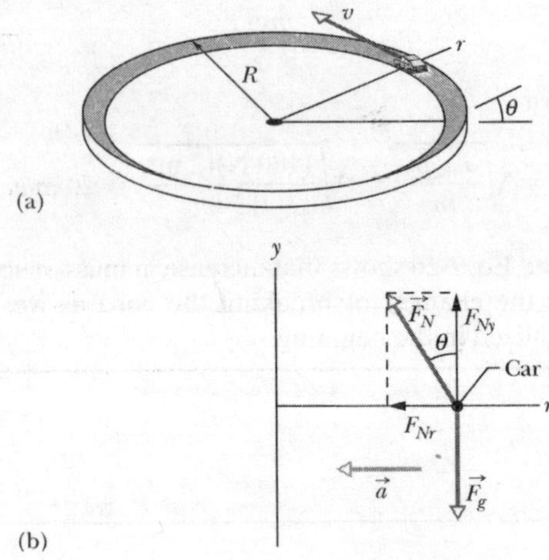

FIG. 7-23 (*a*) A car moves around a curved banked road at constant speed *v*. The bank angle is exaggerated for clarity. (*b*) A free-body diagram for the car, assuming that friction between tires and road is zero and that the car lacks negative lift. The radially inward component F_{Nr} of the normal force (along radial axis *r*) provides the necessary centripetal force and radial acceleration.

is negligible.) If the frictional force from the track is negligible, what bank angle θ prevents sliding?

Conceptualize: Figure (7-23) shows the banked roadway, with center of the circular path. The car is not moving on a horizontal surface, that is, it will experience a normal contact force which is not vertical. The track is banked so as to tilt the normal force $\vec{F}_N$ on the car toward the center of the circle (Fig. 7-23).

Classify: A closer observation will reveal that this problem is exact copy of conical pendulum problem with N replacing *T*. Thus, $\vec{F}_N$ now has a centripetal component of magnitude F_{Nr}, directed inward along a radial axis *r*. We want to find the value of the bank angle θ such that this centripetal component keeps the car on the circular track without need of friction.

Compute: On a horizontal (unbanked) road, friction between car and road provides the centripetal acceleration. Here the horizontal component of normal force *N* is toward the center of the curve and as in the previous conical pendulum problem, is providing centripetal acceleration. Similar to the conical pendulum problem the vertical component is balancing the weight.

Radial forces: As Fig. 7-23*b* shows (and as you should verify), the angle that force $\vec{F}_N$ makes with the vertical is equal to the bank angle θ of the track. Thus, the radial component F_{Nr} is equal to $F_N \sin\theta$. We can now write Newton's second law for components along the *r* axis ($F_{\text{net},r} = ma_r$) as

$$-F_N \sin\theta = m\left(-\frac{v^2}{R}\right) \qquad (7\text{-}27)$$

We cannot solve this equation for the value of θ because it also contains the unknowns F_N and *m*.

Vertical forces: We next consider the forces and acceleration along the *y* axis in Fig. 7-23*b*. The vertical component of the normal force is $F_{Ny} = F_N \cos\theta$, the gravitational force $\vec{F}_g$ on the car has the magnitude *mg*, and the acceleration of the car along the *y* axis is zero. Thus we can write Newton's second law for components along the *y* axis ($F_{\text{net},y} = ma_y$) as

$$F_N \cos\theta - mg = m(0)$$

from which

$$F_N \cos\theta = mg \qquad (7\text{-}28)$$

Combining results, Eq. 7-28 also contains the unknowns F_N and *m*, but note that dividing Eq. 7-27 by Eq. 7-28 neatly eliminates both those unknowns. Doing so, replacing $(\sin\theta)/(\cos\theta)$ with $\tan\theta$, and solving for θ then yield

$$\theta = \tan^{-1}\frac{v^2}{gR}$$

$$= \tan^{-1}\frac{(20\text{ m/s})^2}{(10\text{ m/s}^2)(200\text{ m})} = 0.2\text{ rad} \quad \text{(Answer)}$$

Conclude: If a car moves on the banked turn at a speed less than 20 m/s, friction will act toward the outer perimeter of the banking as the car will tend to slide down the bank (to the left in Fig. 7-23*a*). If a car moves on the banked turn at a speed greater than 20 m/s, friction will act toward the inner perimeter of the banking as the car will tend to go outward of the curve (to the left in Fig. 7-23*a*). Also the result shows that for designing the banking we need not consider the different vehicles having different mass as final answer is independent of mass.

Sample Problem 7-11

Particle *A* is suspended by a string tied at point *O* from the roof of a room. The same particle is also tied to one of the walls of that room, at point *B* (Fig. 7-24*a*). Find the tension in *OA* before and after *AB* is cut.

Conceptualize/ Classify: Before cutting the rope it is a simple equilibrium problem. After cutting the rope the particle will move on a circular path. Our analysis for both situations has to be different.

Compute: Case 1: Consider the free-body diagram of the particle before cutting in all directions (Fig. 7-24*b*). Resolving forces vertically and horizontally and applying equilibrium model

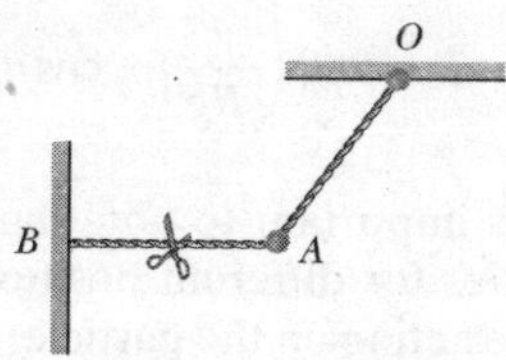

FIG. 7-24a Particle suspended from the roof and tied to wall of room by means of a string.

$$T_1 = \cos\theta - mg = 0 \qquad (7\text{-}29)$$

$$T_1 \sin\theta - T_2 = 0 \qquad (7\text{-}30)$$

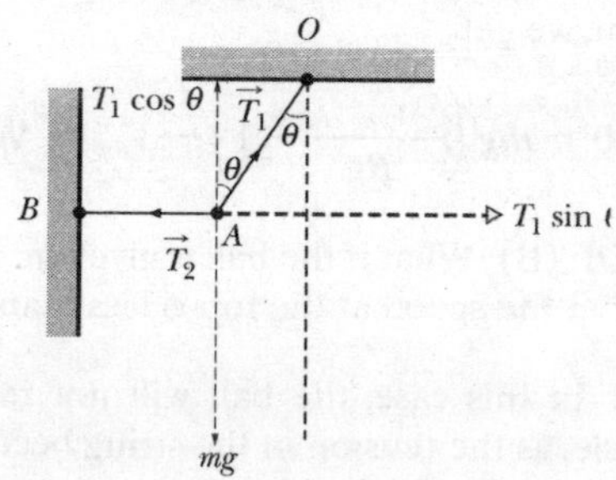

FIG. 7-24b Free-body diagram.

From Eq. 7-29, we have

$$T_1 = \frac{mg}{\cos\theta}$$

Case 2: Making new free-body diagram (Fig. 7-24*c*). Tension in the rope can change instantaneously. We cannot resolve forces in vertical and horizontal direction because acceleration of the particle is unknown. We can resolve forces along the length of rope and perpendicular to the rope. We know that radical acceleration of the particle will be zero as after cutting the rope, particle will come to rest.

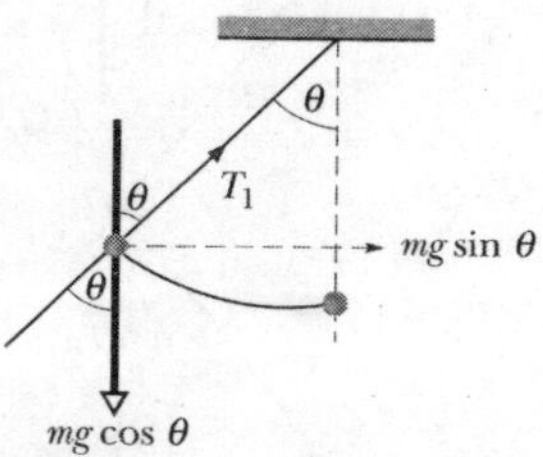

FIG. 7-24c Free-body diagrams.

Conclude: Writing Newton's second law along the string

$$T_1 - mg\cos\theta = m\,v^2/l$$

As $v = 0$ after cutting

$$T_1 - mg\cos\theta = 0$$

In Case Of: In case we want to write Newton's second law in vertical direction, how do we go about it?

Solution: It is easy to find that tangential acceleration $a_t = g\sin\theta$ and we know $a_c = 0$ as centripetal acceleration is zero after cutting. Taking component of forces and acceleration in vertical direction

$$mg - T_1\cos\theta = m\,a_t\sin\theta$$

$$T_1\cos\theta = mg\,(1 - \sin^2\theta)$$

thus $\quad T_1 = mg\cos\theta$

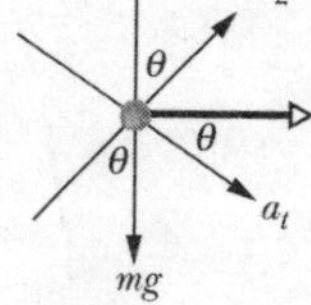

FIG. 7-24d

7-7 | Nonuniform Circular Motion

Previously, we learnt that particle moving with varying speed on a circular path has a tangential component of acceleration , in addition to the radial component. Therefore, the net force acting on the particle should have both radial and a tangential component. The total force exerted on the particle is $\sum\vec{F} = \sum\vec{F}_r + \sum\vec{F}_t$ as shown in active Fig. 7-25. The vector $\sum\vec{F}_r$ is directed toward the center and provides the radial acceleration which changes the direction of velocity. The vector $\sum\vec{F}_t$, tangent to the circle, provides the tangential acceleration, which causes change in the particle's speed with time.

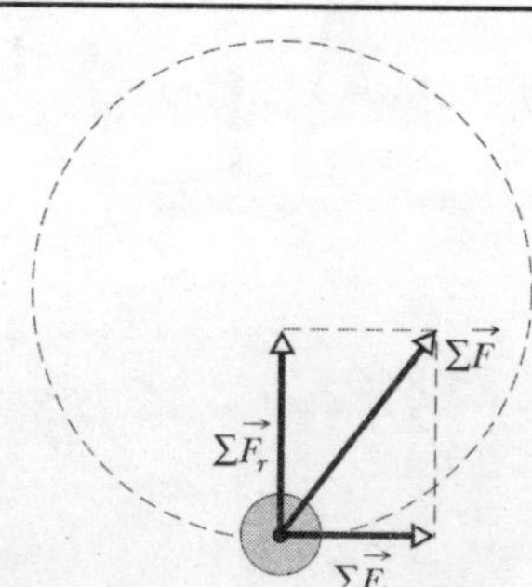

FIG. 7-25 Forces acting on a particle moving with varying speed on a circular path.

Sample Problem 7-12

A small ball of mass m is attached to a string of length R and moves in a vertical circle with a speed v m/s about a fixed point O as illustrated in Fig. 7-26. Find the tension in the string, when it makes an angle θ with the vertical, in terms of v, θ and g.

Conceptualize: The speed of the ball is not uniform in this example as the gravitational force has a tangential component, at almost all points on the path.

Classify: It is not a uniform circular motion.

Compute: Making the free-body diagram, we see that the only forces acting on the spere are the weight and the tension exerted by the cord. Tension is always acting radially inward. We need to resolve mg into a tangential component $mg\sin\theta$ and a radial component $mg\cos\theta$.

Apply Newton's second law to the ball in the tangential direction:

$$mg\sin\theta = ma_t$$

$$a_t = g\sin\theta$$

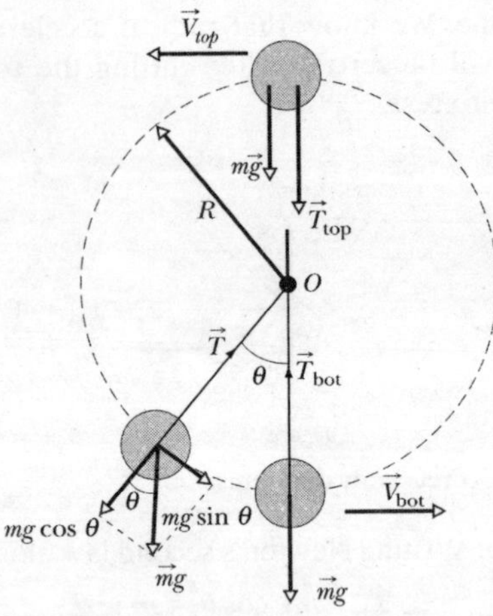

FIG. 7-26 Ball of mass m suspended at center by a string undergoing circular motion.

Apply Newton's second law to the forces acting on the ball in the radial direction

$$T - mg\cos\theta = \frac{mv^2}{R}$$

$$T = mg\left(\frac{v^2}{Rg} + \cos\theta\right)$$

Conclude: It is important to note that v in the expression above varies for different positions as there is net tangential force acting on the particle.

In Case Of: (A) What speed would the ball have at the top of the circle if the tension in the cord becomes zero at this point ?

Solution: Keeping tension equal to zero in the above expression, we get

$$0 = mg\left(\frac{v_{top}^2}{Rg} - 1\right) \rightarrow v_{top} = \sqrt{gR}$$

In Case Of: (B) What if the ball is given an initial velocity such that the speed at the top is less than this value ?

Solution: In this case, the ball will not reach the top of the circle, as the tension in the string becomes zero at some lower point. The ball becomes a projectile as only force acting is gravity and ball has some oblique velocity.

7-8 | Centrifugal Force

Consider a car traveling on a highway at a high speed and approaching a curved road. As the car takes the right turn, a passenger slides to the left and hits the door. What causes him to move toward the door ?

This phenomenon can be explained without using fictitious force. Before the car takes the turn, the passenger is moving in a straight line path. As the car enters the turn and travels a curved path, the passenger is still moving along the original straight line path due to inertia. If a sufficiently large force which satisfies the centripetal condition acts on the passenger, toward the center of curvature in he can move in a curved path along with the car. But the frictional force between the seat and car is not larger enough,to satisfy centripetal condition, so the seat follows a curved path and the passenger continues in the original straight line path. Therefore, from reference frame of an observer in the car, the passenger slides to the right relative to the seat. Finally, he encounters the door, which provides a sufficient force which satisfies the centripetal condition, allowing him to follow the same curved path as the car.

This can also be explained using by using concept of fictitious force and using reference frame attached to the car. Since car is accelerating toward right an observer sitting in car must apply a fictitious force toward left (Newton's second law). The force acting toward the left pushes the passenger away from the center of the circular path. This fictitious force is called the "centrifugal force,". This fictitious force is due to the centripetal acceleration associated with the changing direction of the car's velocity vector.

CHECKPOINT 5 Consider a car is moving on circular path of radius R with speed v. A block kept inside the frictionless surface of car is touching the right wall as shown. Write Newton's second law from the reference frame attached to observer A and B.

CHECKPOINT 6 Abead slides freely along a curved wire lying on a horizontal plane at constant speed as shown in the figure. (i) Draw the vectors representing the force exerted by the wire on the bead at points A, B, and C. (ii) Suppose the bead in the figure speeds up with constant tangential acceleration as it moves toward the right. Draw the vectors representing the force on the bead at points A, B and C.

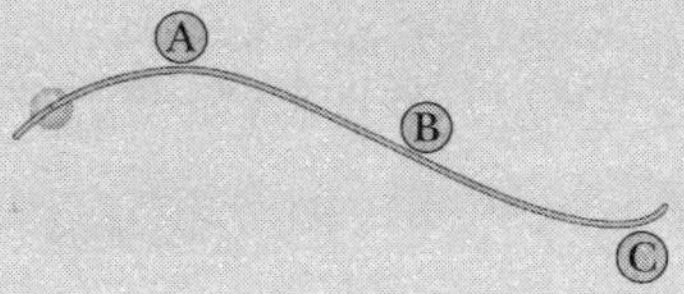

REVIEW & SUMMARY

Angular Displacement A body that rotates about a rotation axis, changing its angular position from θ_1 to θ_2, undergoes an **angular displacement**

$$\Delta\theta = \theta_2 - \theta_1$$

where $\Delta\theta$ is positive for counterclockwise rotation and negative for clockwise rotation.

Angular Velocity and Speed If a body rotates through an angular displacement $\Delta\theta$ in a time interval Δt, its **average angular velocity** ω_{avg} is

$$\omega_{avg} = \frac{\Delta\theta}{\Delta t}$$

The **(instantaneous) angular velocity** ω of the body is

$$\omega = \frac{d\theta}{dt}$$

Both ω_{avg} and ω are vectors, with directions given by the **right-hand rule** of Fig. 10-6. They are positive for counterclockwise rotation and negative for clockwise rotation. The magnitude of the body's angular velocity is the **angular speed.**

Angular Acceleration If the angular velocity of a body changes from ω_1 to ω_2 in a time interval $\Delta t = t_2 - t_1$, the **average angular acceleration** α_{avg} of the body is

$$\alpha_{avg} = \frac{\omega_2 - \omega_1}{t_2 - t_1} = \frac{\Delta\omega}{\Delta t}$$

The **(instantaneous) angular acceleration** α of the body is

$$\alpha = \frac{d\omega}{dt}$$

Both α_{avg} and α are vectors.

The Kinematic Equations for Constant Angular Acceleration *Constant angular acceleration* (α = constant) is an important special case of rotational motion. The appropriate kinematic equations, given in Table 10-1, are

$$\omega = \omega_0 + \alpha t$$

$$\theta - \theta_0 = \omega_0 t + \tfrac{1}{2}\alpha t^2$$

$$\omega^2 = \omega_0^2 + 2\alpha(\theta - \theta_0)$$

$$\theta - \theta_0 = \tfrac{1}{2}(\omega_0 + \omega)t$$

$$\theta - \theta_0 = \omega t - \tfrac{1}{2}\alpha t^2$$

Linear and Angular Variables Related A point in a rigid rotating body, at a *perpendicular distance r* from the rotation axis, moves in a circle with radius r. If the body rotates through an angle θ, the point moves along an arc with length s given by

$$s = \theta r \quad \text{(radian measure)}$$

where θ is in radians.

The linear velocity $\vec{v}$ of the point is tangent to the circle; the point's linear speed v is given by

$$v = \omega r \quad \text{(radian measure)}$$

where ω is the angular speed (in radians per second) of the body.

The linear acceleration $\vec{a}$ of the point has both *tangential* and *radial* components. The tangential component is

$$a_t = \alpha r \quad \text{(radian measure)}$$

where α is the magnitude of the angular acceleration (in radians per second-squared) of the body. The radial component of $\vec{a}$ is

$$a_r = \frac{v^2}{r} = \omega^2 r \quad \text{(radian measure)}$$

If the point moves in uniform circular motion, the period T of the motion for the point and the body is

$$T = \frac{2\pi r}{v} = \frac{2\pi}{\omega} \quad \text{(radian measure)}$$

Uniform Circular Motion If a particle moves in a circle or a circular arc of radius R at constant speed v, the particle is said to be in **uniform circular motion.** It then has a **centripetal acceleration** $\vec{a}$ with magnitude given by

$$a = \frac{v^2}{R}$$

This acceleration is due to a net **centripetal force** on the particle, with magnitude given by

$$F = \frac{mv^2}{R}$$

where m is the particle's mass. The vector quantities $\vec{a}$ and $\vec{F}$ are directed toward the center of curvature of the particle's path.

QUESTIONS

1 A person riding a Ferris wheel moves through positions at (1) the top, (2) the bottom, and (3) midheight. If the wheel rotates at a constant rate, rank these three positions according to (a) the magnitude of the person's centripetal acceleration, (b) the magnitude of the net centripetal force on the person, and (c) the magnitude of the normal force on the person, greatest first.

2 Figure 6-18 shows the path of a park ride that travels at constant speed through five circular arcs of radii R_0, $2R_0$, and $3R_0$. Rank the arcs according to the magnitude of the centripetal force on a rider traveling in the arcs, greatest first.

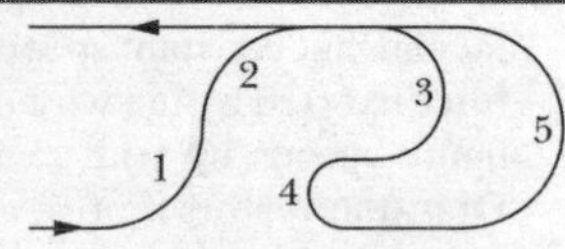

FIG. 7-27 Question 2.

PROBLEMS

1 What is the smallest radius of an unbanked (flat) track around which a bicyclist can travel if her speed is 29 km/h and the μ_s between tires and track is 0.32?

2 A cat dozes on a stationary merry-go-round, at a radius of 5.4 m from the center of the ride. Then the operator turns on the ride and brings it up to its proper turning rate of one complete rotation every 6.0 s. What is the least coefficient of static friction between the cat and the merry-go-round that will allow the cat to stay in place, without sliding?

3 Suppose the coefficient of static friction between the road and the tires on a car is 0.60 and the car has no negative lift. What speed will put the car on the verge of sliding as it rounds a level curve of 30.5 m radius?

4 A circular-motion addict of mass 80 kg rides a Ferris wheel around in a vertical circle of radius 10 m at a constant speed of 6.1 m/s. (a) What is the period of the motion? What is the magnitude of the normal force on the addict from the seat when both go through (b) the highest point of the circular path and (c) the lowest point?

5 A roller-coaster car has a mass of 1200 kg when fully loaded with passengers. As the car passes over the top of a circular hill of radius 18 m, its speed is not changing. At the top of the hill, what are the (a) magnitude F_N and (b) direction (up or down) of the normal force on the car from the track if the car's speed is $v = 11$ m/s? What are (c) F_N and (d) the direction if $v = 14$ m/s?

6 In Fig. 7-28, a car is driven at constant speed over a circular hill and then into a circular valley with the same radius. At the top of the hill, the normal force on the driver from the car seat is 0. The driver's mass is 70.0 kg. What is the magnitude of the normal force on the driver from the seat when the car passes through the bottom of the valley?

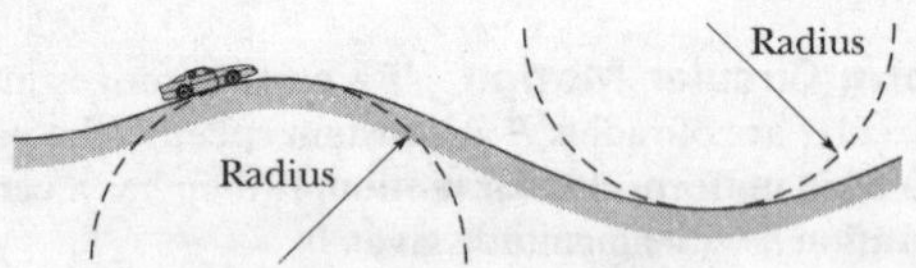

FIG. 7-28 Problem 6.

7 A student of weight 667 N rides a steadily rotating Ferris wheel (the student sits upright). At the highest point, the magnitude of the normal force $\vec{F}_N$ on the student from the seat is 556 N. (a) Does the student feel "light" or "heavy" there? (b) What is the magnitude of $\vec{F}_N$ at the lowest point? If the wheel's speed is doubled, what is the magnitude F_N at the (c) highest and (d) lowest point?

8 In designing circular rides for amusement parks, mechanical engineers must consider how small variations in certain parameters can alter the net force on a passenger. Consider a passenger of mass m riding around a horizontal circle of radius r at speed v. What is the variation dF in the net force magnitude for (a) a variation dr in the radius with v held constant, (b) a variation dv in the speed with r held constant, and (c) a variation dT in the period with r held constant?

9 An airplane is flying in a horizontal circle at a speed of 133 km/h (Fig. 7-29). If its wings are tilted at angle $\theta = 40°$ to the horizontal, what is the radius of the circle in which the plane is flying? Assume that the required force is provided entirely by an "aerodynamic lift" that is perpendicular to the wing surface (take $\tan 40° = 0.84$).

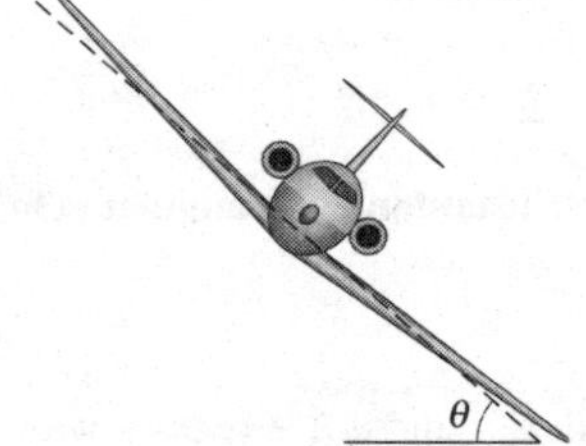

FIG. 7-29 Problem 9.

10 An 85.0 kg passenger is made to move along a circular path of radius $r = 3.50$ m in uniform circular motion. (a) Figure 7-30a is a plot of the required magnitude F of the net centripetal force for a range of possible values of the passenger's speed v. What is the plot's slope at $v = 8.30$ m/s? (b) Figure 7-30b is a plot of F for a range of possible values of T, the period of the motion. What is the plot's slope at $T = 2.50$ s?

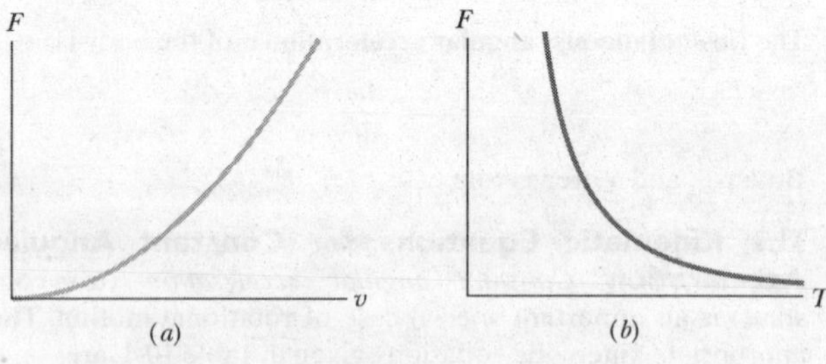

FIG. 7-30 Problem 10.

11 A puck of mass $m = 1.50$ kg slides in a circle of radius $r = 20.0$ cm on a frictionless table while attached to a hanging cylinder of mass $M = 2.50$ kg by a cord through a hole in the table (Fig. 7-31). What speed keeps the cylinder at rest?

12 *Brake or turn?* Figure 7-32 depicts an overhead view of a car's path as the car travels toward a wall. Assume that the driver begins to brake the car when the distance to the wall is $d = 107$ m, and take the car's mass as $m = 1400$ kg, its initial speed as $v_0 = 35$ m/s, and the coefficient of static friction as $\mu_s = 0.50$. Assume that the car's weight is distributed evenly on the four wheels, even during braking. (a) What magnitude of static friction is needed (between tires and road) to stop the car just as it reaches the wall? (b) What is the maximum possible static friction $f_{s,\max}$? (c) If the coefficient of kinetic friction between the (sliding) tires and the road is $\mu_k = 0.40$, at what speed will the car hit the wall? To avoid the crash, a driver could elect to turn the car so that it just barely misses the wall, as shown in the figure. (d) What magnitude of frictional force would be required to keep the car in a circular path of radius d and at the given speed v_0? (e) Is the required force less than $f_{s,\max}$ so that a circular path is possible?

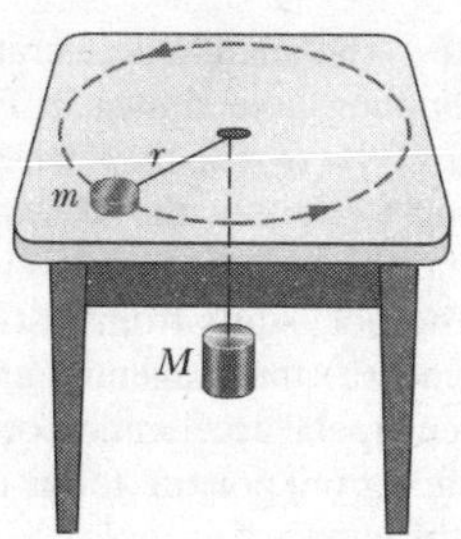

FIG. 7-31 Problem 11.

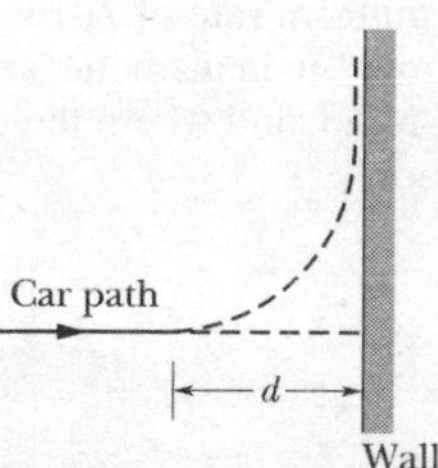

FIG. 7-32 Problem 12.

13 A bolt is threaded onto one end of a thin horizontal rod, and the rod is then rotated horizontally about its other end. An engineer monitors the motion by flashing a strobe lamp onto the rod and bolt, adjusting the strobe rate until the bolt appears to be in the same eight places during each full rotation of the rod (Fig. 7-33). The strobe rate is 2000 flashes per second; the bolt has mass 30 g and is at radius 3.5 cm. What is the magnitude of the force on the bolt from the rod?

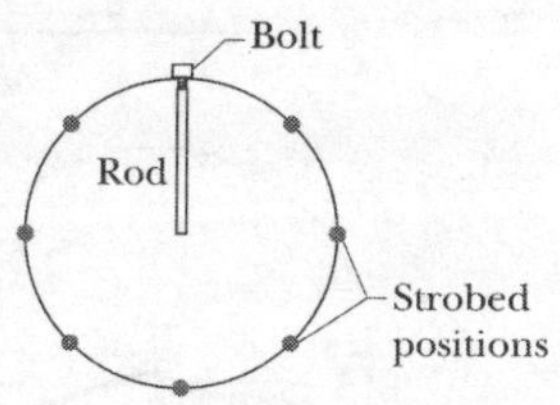

FIG. 7-33 Problem 13.

14 A banked circular highway curve is designed for traffic moving at 60 km/h. The radius of the curve is 200 m. Traffic is moving along the highway at 40 km/h on a rainy day. What is the minimum coefficient of friction between tires and road that will allow cars to take the turn without sliding off the road? (Assume the cars do not have negative lift.)

15 In Fig. 7-34, a 1.34 kg ball is connected by means of two massless strings, each of length $L = 1.70$ m, to a vertical, rotating rod. The strings are tied to the rod with separation $d = 1.70$ m and are taut. The tension in the upper string is 35 N. What are the (a) tension in the lower string, (b) magnitude of the net force $\vec{F}_{net}$ on the ball, and (c) speed of the ball? (d) What is the direction of $\vec{F}_{net}$?

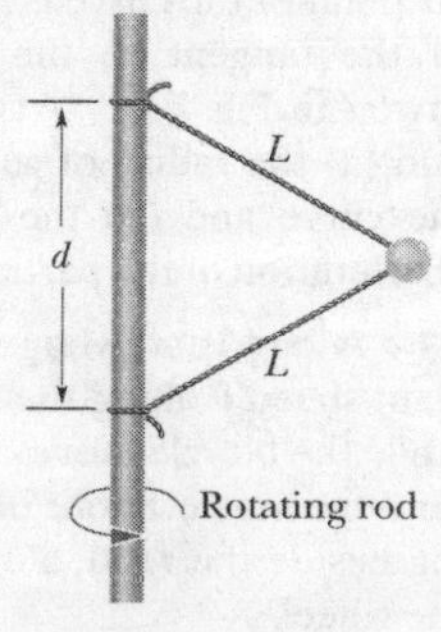

FIG. 7-34 Problem 15.

16 Figure 7-35 shows a *conical pendulum,* in which the bob (the small object at the lower end of the cord) moves in a horizontal circle at constant speed. (The cord sweeps out a cone as the bob rotates.) The bob has a mass of 0.040 kg, the string has length $L = 0.90$ m and negligible mass, and the bob follows a circular path of circumference 0.94 m. What are (a) the tension in the string and (b) the period of the motion?

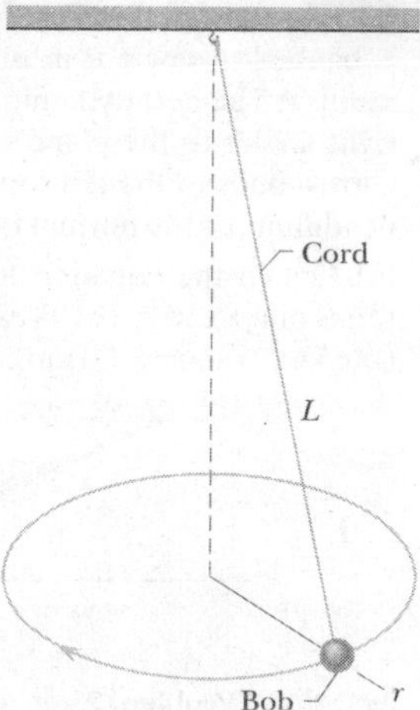

FIG. 7-35 Problem 16.

17 In Fig. 7-36, a stuntman drives a car (without negative lift) over the top of a hill, the cross section of which can be approximated by a circle of radius $R = 250$ m. What is the greatest speed at which he can drive without the car leaving the road at the top of the hill?

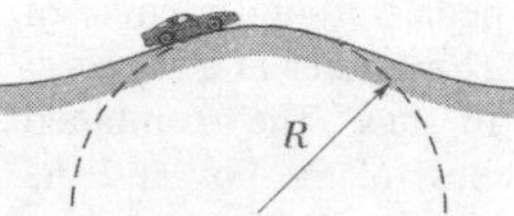

FIG. 7-36 Problem 17.

18 A car weighing 10.7 kN and traveling at 13.4 m/s without negative lift attempts to round an unbanked curve with a radius of 61.0 m. (a) What magnitude of the frictional force on the tires is required to keep the car on its circular path? (b) If the coefficient of static friction between the tires and the road is 0.350, is the attempt at taking the curve successful?

19 A certain string can withstand a maximum tension of 40 N without breaking. A child ties a 0.37 kg stone to one end and, holding the other end, whirls the stone in a vertical circle of radius 0.91 m, slowly increasing the speed until the string breaks. (a) Where is the stone on its path when the string breaks? (b) What is the speed of the stone as the string breaks?

20 When a small 2.0 g coin is placed at a radius of 5.0 cm on a horizontal turntable that makes three full revolutions in 3.14 s, the coin does not slip. What are (a) the coin's speed, the (b) magnitude and (c) direction (radially inward or outward) of the coin's acceleration, and the (d) magnitude and (e) direction (inward or outward) of the frictional force on the coin? The coin is on the verge of slipping if it is placed at a radius of 10 cm. (f) What is the coefficient of static friction between coin and turntable?

21 A child places a picnic basket on the outer rim of a merry-go-round that has a radius of 4.6 m and revolves once every 30 s. (a) What is the speed of a point on that rim? (b) What is the lowest value of the coefficient of static friction between basket and merry-go-round that allows the basket to stay on the ride?

22 In the Bohr model of the hydrogen atom an electron is pictured rotating in a circle (with a radius of 0.5×10^{-10} m) about the positive nucleus of the atom. The centripetal force is furnished by the electric attraction of the positive nucleus for the negative electron. How large is this force if the electron is moving with a speed of 2.3×10^6 m/s ? (The mass of an electron is 9×10^{-31}kg.)

23 As indicated in Fig. 7-37 a plane flying at constant speed is banked at angle θ in order to fly in a horizontal circle of radius r. The aerodynamic lift force acts gernerally upward at right angles to the plane's wings and fuselage. This lift force corresponds to the tension provided by the string in a conical pendulum, or the normal force of a banked road.

(a) Obtain the equation for the required banking angle θ in terms of v, r and g. (b) What is the required angle for $v = 60$ m/s (216 km/h) and $r = 1.0$ km ?

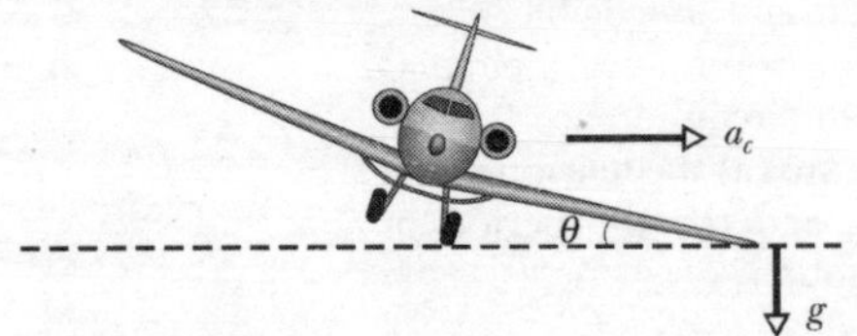

FIG. 7-37 Problem 23.

24 A boy on a bicycle pedals around a circle of 22 m radius at a speed of 10 m/s. The combined mass of the boy and the bicycle combined mass of the boy and the bicycle is 80 kg. (a) What is the centripetal force exerted by the pavement on the bicycle ? (b)What is the upward force exerted by the pavement on the bicycle ? See Fig. 7-38.

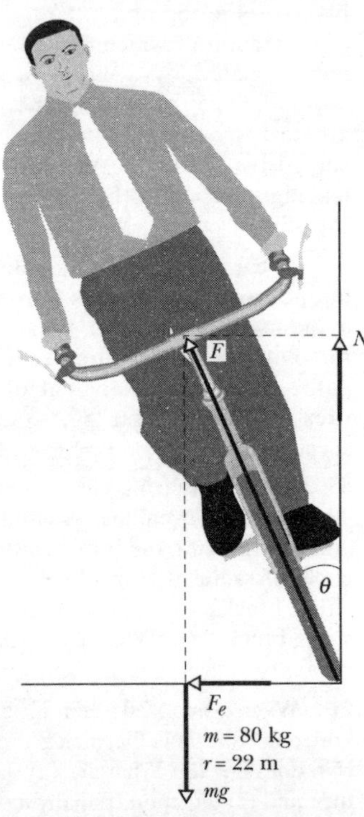

FIG. 7-38 Problem 24.

25 At the equator, the effective value of g is smaller than at the poles. One reason for this is the centripetal acceleration due to the earth's rotation. The magnitude of the centripetal acceleration must be subtracted from the magnitude of the acceleration due purely to gravity in order to obtain the effective value of g. (a) Calculate the fractional diminution of g at the equator. Express your result as a percentage. (b) How short would the earth's period of rotation have to be in order for objects at the equator to the "weightless" (that is, in order for the effective value of g to be zero) ? (c) How would be the period found in part *b* compare with that of a satellite skimming the surface of an airless earth ?

26 A particle is to slide alopg horizontal circular path on the inside of the funnel. The surface of the funnel is frictionless. How fast must the particle be moving (in terms of r and θ) if it is to execute this motion ?

27 The designer of a roller coaster wishes the riders to experience "Weightlessness" as they round the top of one hill. How fast must the car be going if the radius of curvature at the hilltop is 20 m ?

28 The angular acceleration of the toppling pole shown in Fig. 7-39 is given by $\alpha = \text{k} \sin \theta$, where θ is the angle between the axis of the pole and the vertical, and k is a constant. The pole starts from rest at $\theta = 0$. Find (a) the tangential and (b) the centripetal acceleration of the upper end of the pole in terms of k, θ and (the length of the pole).

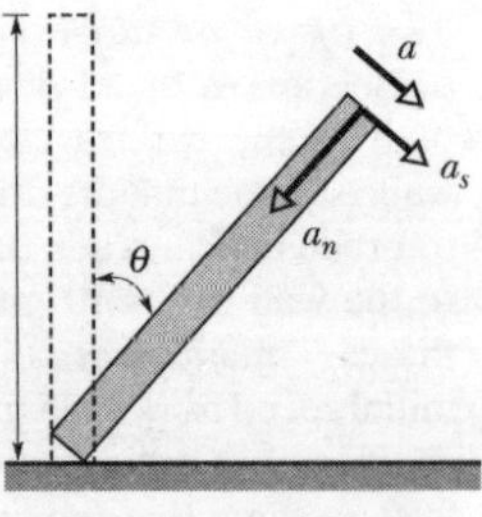

FIG. 7-39 Problem 28.

29 A wet open umbrella is held upright as shown in Fig. 7-40*a* and is twirled about the handle at a uniform rate of 21 rev in 44s. If the rim of the umbrella is a circle 1 m in diameter, and the height of the rim above the floor is 1.5 m, find where the drops of water spun off the rim hit the floor.

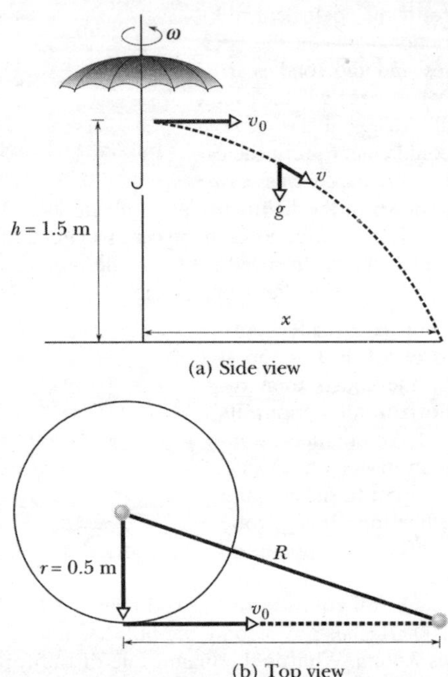

FIG. 7-40 Problem 29.

30 A particle whose mass is 2 kg moves with a speed of 44 m/s on a curved path. The resultant force acting on the particle at a particular point of the curve is 30 N at 60° to the tangent to the curve, as shwon in Fig. 7-41. At the point, find (a) the radius of curvature of the curve and (b) the tangential acceleration of the particle.

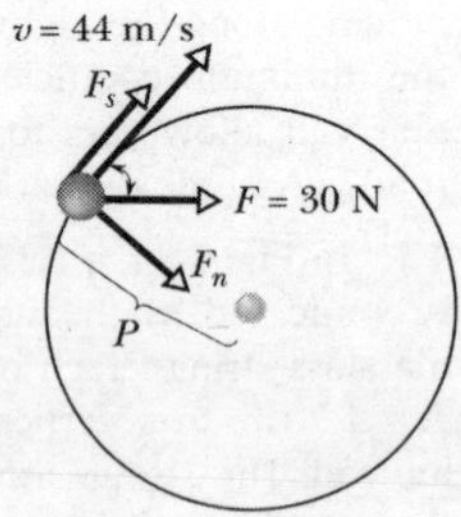

FIG. 7-41 Problem 30.

31 A bug is crawling with constant speed v along the spoke of a bicycle wheel, of radius a, while the bicycle moves down the road with constant speed V. Find the accelerations of the bug, as observed by a man standing beside the road, along the perpendicular to the spoke of the wheel.

32 At the instant $\theta = \theta_l$ in the Fig. 7-42, the boy's center of mass G has a downward speed v_G. Determine the rate of increase in his speed and the tension in each of the two supporting cords of the swing at this instant. The boy has a weight W. Neglect his size and the mass of the seat and cords.

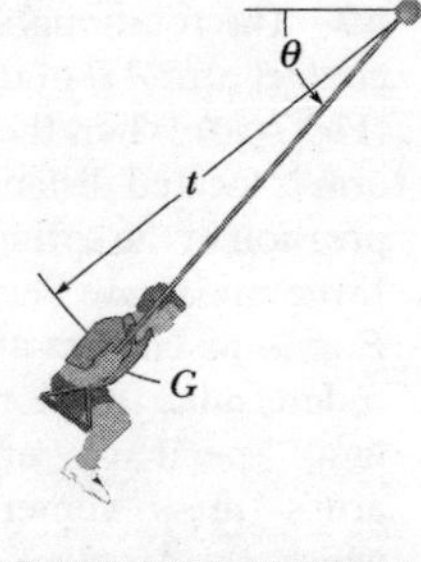

FIG. 7-42 Problem 32.

Given:

$W = 60 \text{ lb}$

$\theta_l = 60 \text{ deg}$

$l = 10 \text{ ft}$

$v_G = 15 \text{ ft/s}$

$g = 32.2 \text{ ft s}^2$

33 If the crest of the hill has a radius of curvature p (Fig. 7-43), determine the maximum constant speed at which the car can travel over it without leaving the surface of the road. Neglect the size of the car in the calculation. The car has mass m.

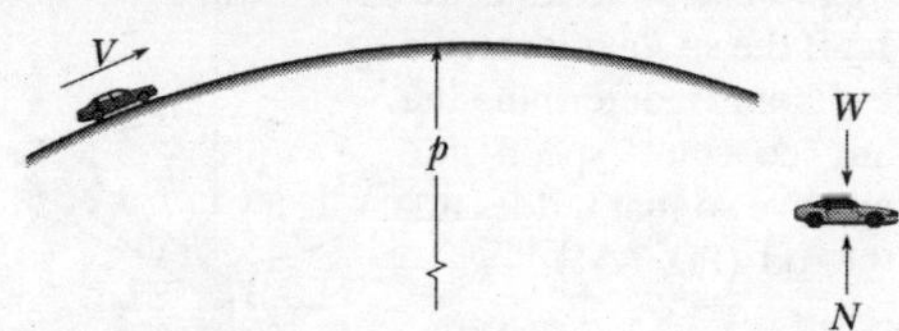

FIG. 7-43 Problem 33.

Given:

$p = 40\, m$

$m = 1700 \text{ kg}$

$g = 10 \text{ m/s}^2$

34 The airplane, traveling at constant speed v is executing a horizontal turn (Fig. 4-44). If the plane is banked at angle θ when the pilot experiences only a normal force on the seat of the plane, determine the radius of curvature p of the turn. Also, what is the normal force of the seat on the pilot if he has mass M? (Units used: $\text{kN} = 10^3\text{N}$)

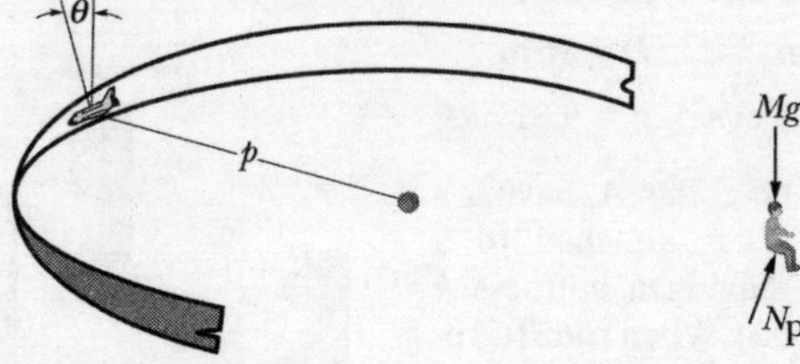

FIG. 7-44 Problem 34.

Given:

$v = 50 \text{ m/s}$

$\theta = 15 \text{ deg}$

$M = 70 \text{ kg}$

$g = 9.815 \text{ m/s}^2$

35 The man has weight W and lies against the cushion for which the coefficient of static friction is μ_s, (Fig. 7-45). Determine the resultant normal and frictional forces the cushion exerts on him if, due to rotation about the z axis, he has constant speed v. Neglect the size of the man.

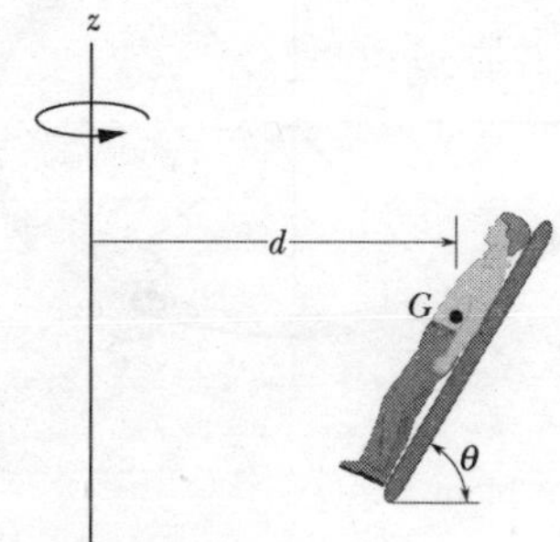

FIG. 7-45 Problem 35.

$W = 150 \text{ lb}$

$\mu_s = 0.5$

$v = 20 \text{ ft/s}$

$\theta = 60 \text{ deg}$

$d = 8 \text{ ft}$

36 Determine the constant speed of the passengers on the amusement-park ride if it is observed that the supporting cables are directed at angle q from the vertical (Fig. 7-46). Each chair including its passenger has a mass m_c. Also, what are the components of force in the n, t, and b directions which the chair exerts on a passenger of mass m_p during the motion?

FIG. 7-46 Problem 36.

Given:

$\theta = 30 \text{ deg}$	$d = 4 \text{ m}$
$m_c = 80 \text{ kg}$	$b = 6 \text{ m}$
$m_p = 50 \text{ kg}$	$g = 9.81 \text{ m/s}^2$

37 A collar having a mass M and negligible size slides over the surface of a horizontal circular rod for which the coefficient of kinetic friction is μ_k, (Fig. 7-47). If the collar is given a

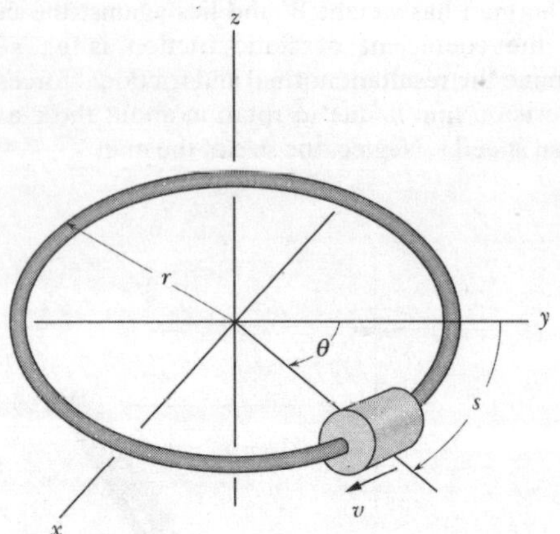

FIG. 7-47 Problem 37.

speed v_1 and then released at $\theta = 0$ deg, determine how far, d, it slides on the rod before coming to rest.

Given:

$M = 0.75$ kg $\quad r = 100$ mm

$\mu_k = 0.3 \quad g = 9.81\ \text{m/s}^2$

$v_1 = 4$ m/s

38 The smooth block B, having mass M, is attached to the vertex A of the right circular cone using a light cord. The cone is rotating at a constant angular rate about the z axis such that the block attains speed v (Fig. 7-48). At this speed, determine the tension in the cord and the reaction which the cone exerts on the block. Neglect the size of the block.

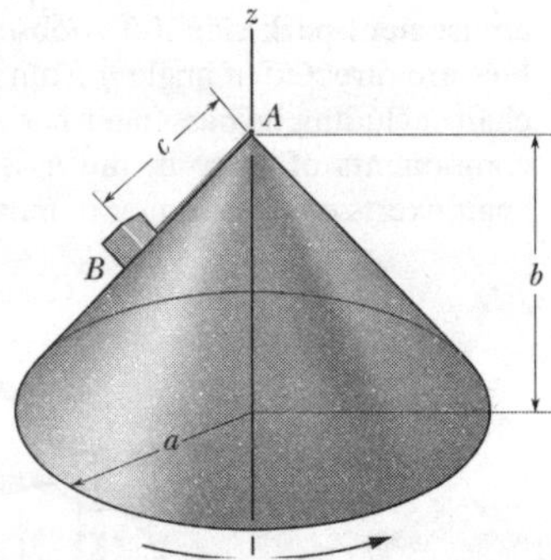

FIG. 7-48 Problem 38.

Given:

$M = 0.2$ kg $\quad v = 0.5$ m/s

$a = 300$ mm $\quad$ b = 400 mm

$c = 200$ mm $\quad g = 9.81\ \text{m/s}^2$

39 The pendulum bob B of mass M is released from rest when $\theta = 0°$ (Fig. 7-49). Determine the initial tension in the cord and also at the instant the bob reaches point D, $\theta = \theta_1$. Neglect the size of the bob.

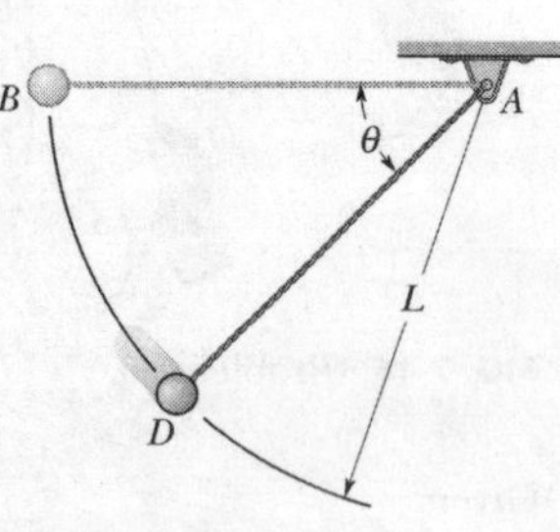

FIG. 7-49 Problem 39.

Given:

$M = 3$ kg $\quad \theta_1 = 45$ deg

$L = 2$ m $\quad g = 9.81\ \text{m/s}^2$

40 The rotational speed of the disk is controlled by a smooth contact arm AB of mass M which is spring-mounted on the disk (Fig. 7-50). When the disk is at rest, the center of mass G of the arm is located distance d from the center O, and the preset compression in the spring is a. If the initial gap between B and the contact at C is b, determine the (controlling) speed v_G of the arm's mass center, G, which will close the gap. The disk rotates in the horizontal plane. The spring has a stiffness k and its ends are attached to the contact arm at D and to the disk at E.

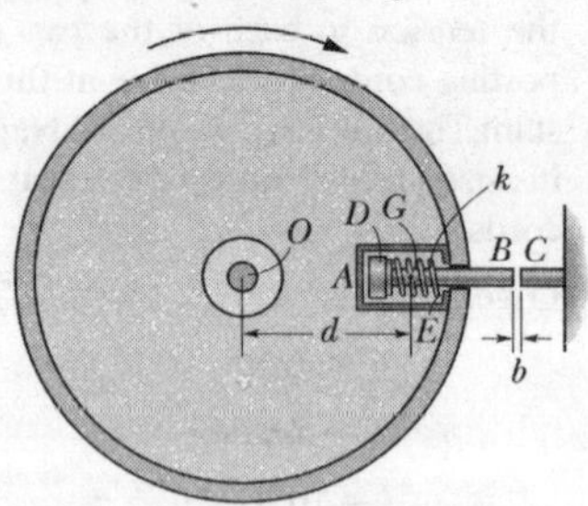

FIG. 7-50 Problem 40.

Given:

$M = 30$ gm $\quad a = 20$ mm $\quad b = 10$ mm $\quad d = 150$ mm $\quad k = 50$ N/m

41 The spool S of mass M fits loosely on the inclined rod for which the coefficient of static friction is μ_s. If the spool is located a distance d from A, determine the maximum constant speed the spool can have so that it does not slip up the rod (Fig. 7-51).

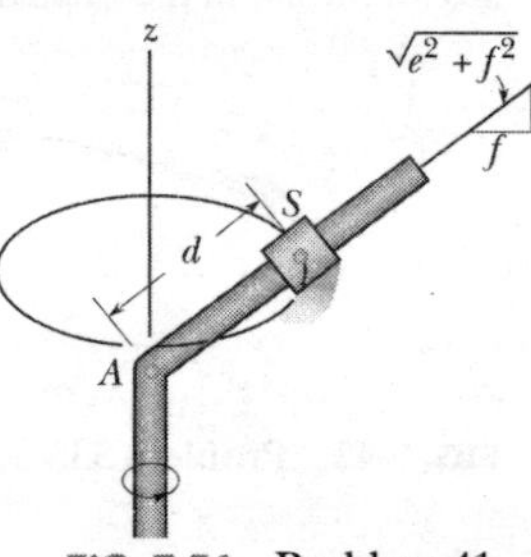

FIG. 7-51 Problem 41.

Given:

$M = 2$ kg $\quad e = 3$

$\mu_k = 0.2 \quad f = 4$

$d = 0.25$ m $\quad g = 9.81\ \text{m/s}^2$

42 The man has mass M and sits a distance d from the center of the rotating platform (Fig. 7-52). Due to the rotation his speed is increased from rest by the rate v'. If the coefficient of static friction between his clothes and the platform is μ_s, determine the time required to cause him to slip.

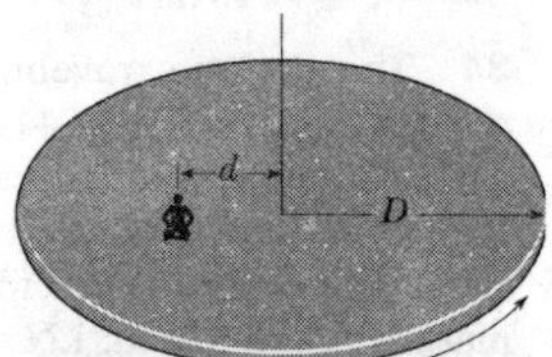

FIG. 7-52 Problem 42.

Given:

$M = 80$ kg $\quad \mu e = 0.3$

$d = 3$ m $\quad D = 10$ m

$v' = 0.4\ \text{m/s}^2 \quad g = 9.81\ \text{m/s}^2$

43 The collar A, having a mass M, is attached to a spring having a stiffness k (Fig. 7-53). When rod BC rotates about the vertical axis, the collar slides outward along the smooth rod DE. If the spring is unstretched when $x = 0$, determine the constant speed of the collar in order that $x = x_1$. Neglect the size of the collar.

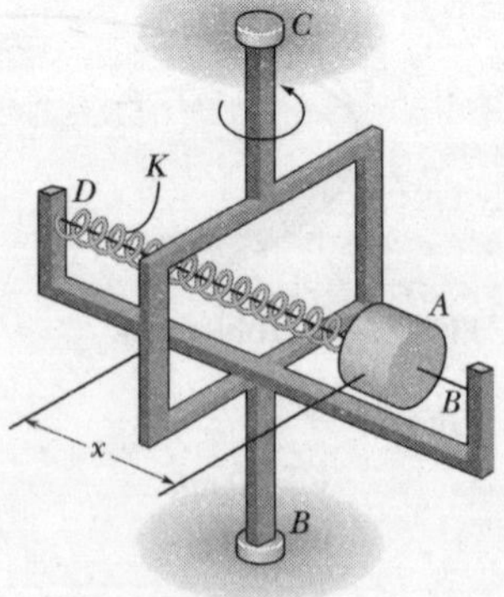

FIG. 7-53 Problem 43.

Given:

$M = 0.75$ kg

$k = 200$ N/m

$x_f = 100$ mm

$g = 9.81$ m/s^2

44 The block has weight W and it is free to move along the smooth slot in the rotating disk. The spring has stiffness k and an unstretched length δ (Fig. 7-54). Determine the force of the spring on the block and the tangential component of force which the slot exerts on the side of the block is at rest with respect to the disk and is traveling with constant speed v.

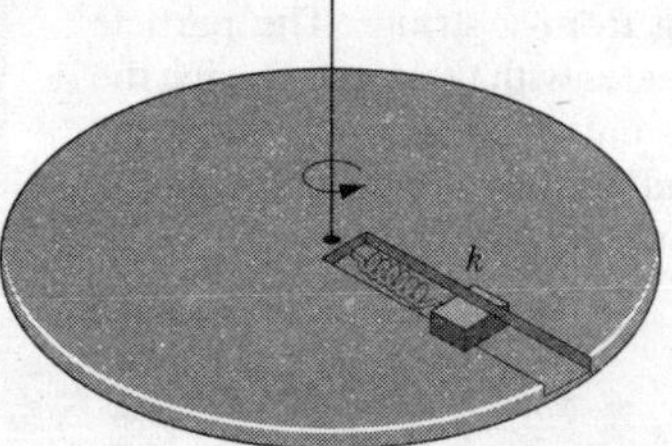

FIG. 7-54 Problem 44.

$W = 2$ lb

$k = 2.5$ lb/ft

$\delta = 1.25$ ft

$v = 12$ ft/s

45 The particle has mass M and is confined to move along the smooth horizontal slot due to the rotation of the arm OA (Fig. 7-55). Determine the force of the rod on the particle and the normal force of the slot on the particle when $\theta = \theta_1$. The rod is rotating with a constant angular velocity θ'. Assume the particle contacts only one side of the slot at any instant.

Given:

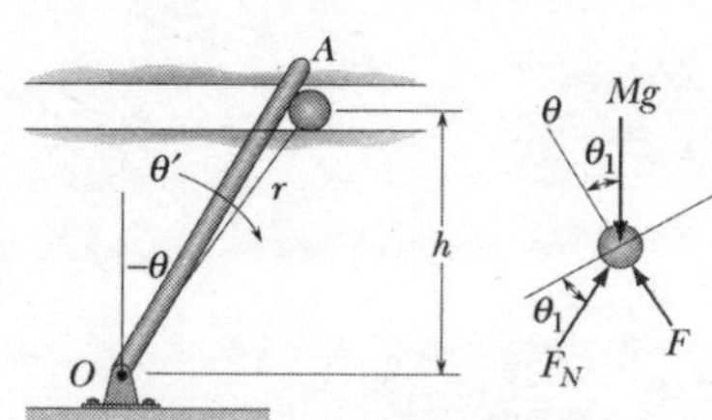

FIG. 7-55 Problem 45.

$M = 0.5$ kg $\quad \theta_1 = 30$ deg

$\theta' = 2$ rad/s $\quad \theta' = 0$ rad/s

$h = 0.5$ m $\quad g = 9.81$ m/s^2

46 A chain of mass m, radius r (mass uniformly distributed) is kept on a cone (Fig. 7-56). If the chain moves by an angular velocity ω, then find the tension in the chain due to rotation.

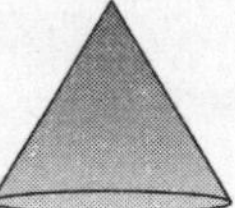
FIG. 7-56 Problem 46.

47 A hemispherical bowl of radius R is rotated about its axis of symmetry which is kept vertical. A small block is kept at a position where the radius makes an angle θ with the vertical. The block rotates with the bowl without slipping. The friction coefficient between the block and the bowl surface is μ. Find the range of angular speed for which the block will not slip.

48 A particle is projected with a velocity u making an angle θ with the horizontal. What is the radius of curvature of the parabola where the particle makes an angle θ /2 with the horiozontal.?

49 A small block of mass m is placed on the rotating conical surface at the radius $r = 0.2$ m shown in Fig. 7-57. Determine the maximum angular velocity ω of the cone about the vertical axis for which the block will not slip. Friction between block and surface is 0.8.

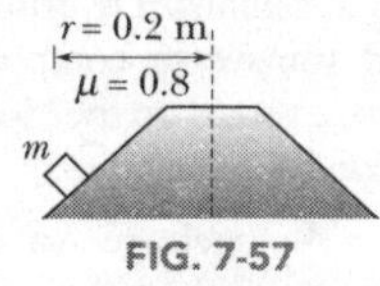

FIG. 7-57 Problem 49.

50 The two balls of mass m_A = 10 kg and m_B = 15 kg are connected by an elastic string and supported on a turntable as shown in Fig. 7-58. When the turn is at rest, the tension in the string is $T = 100$ N and the balls exert this same force on each of the stops. What forces wil they exert on the stops when the turntable is rotating uniformly about vertical axis oo′ at 60 rpm ?

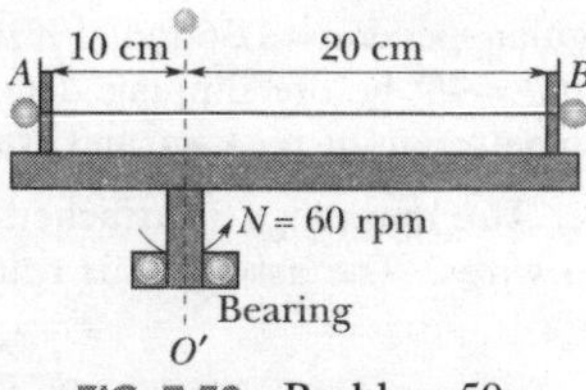

FIG. 7-58 Problem 50.

51 An elastic cord having an unstretched length L, stiffness k, and mass per unit length λ is stretched around the drum of radius r ($2\pi > L$). Determine the angular velocity of the cord due to the rotation of the drum, which will allow the cord to loosen its contact with the drum. See Fig. 7-59.

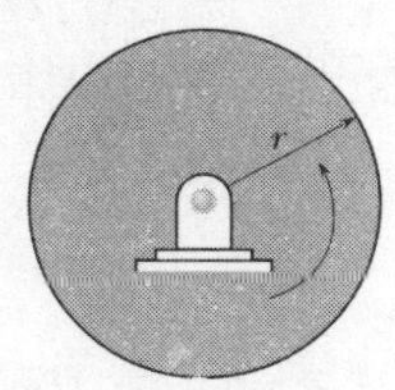

FIG. 7-59 Problem 51.

52 A small 0.25 kg collar C may slide on a semicircular rod which is made to rotate about the vertical axis y-y' at a constant rate of 7.5 rad/s (Fig. 7-60). Determine the values of θ for which the collar will not slide on the rod, assuming no friction between the collar and the rod.

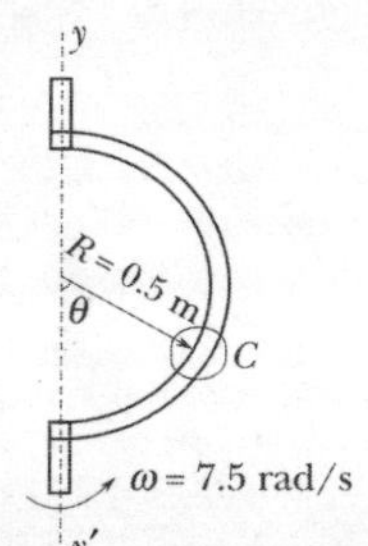

FIG. 7-60 Problem 52.

53 Block A has a mass of $M_A = 15$ kg and B has mass of $M_B = 45$ kg. They are on a rotating surface and connected by a string as shown in Fig. 7-61. Determine the value of ω at which radial sliding will occur. The coefficient of friction between blocks surface is 0.25.

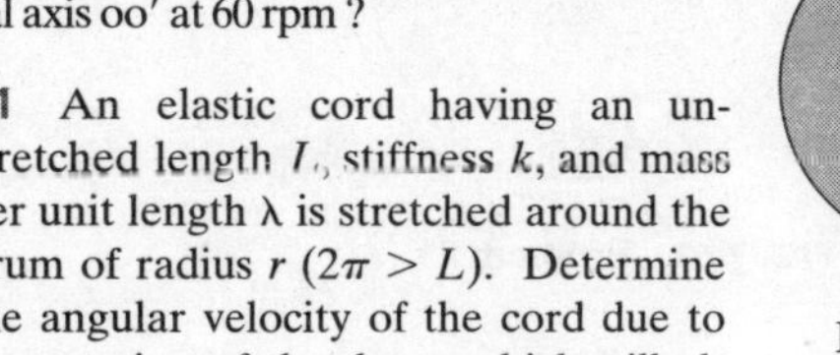

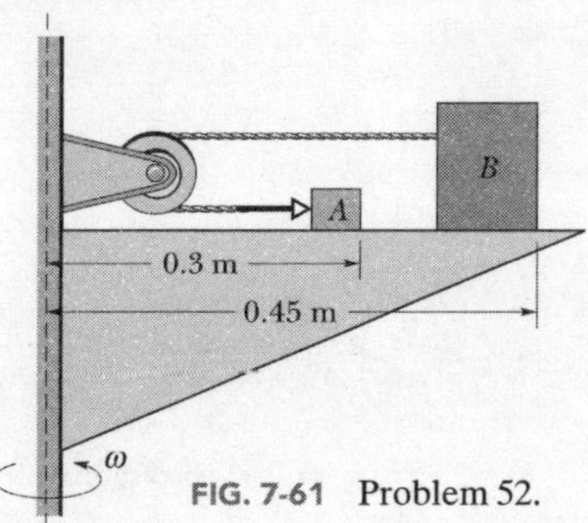

FIG. 7-61 Problem 52.

54 The motion of a 2 kg block B in horizontal plane is defined by the relations together $r = 3t^2 - t^3$ and $\theta = 2t^2$ where r is in meters, t in seconds and θ is in radians. Determine the radial and transverse components of the force exerted on the block when $t = 1$ second. See Fig. 7-62.

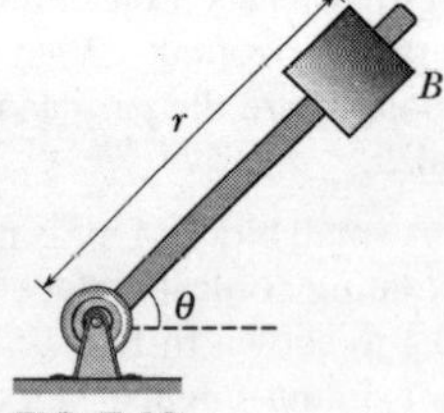

FIG. 7-62 Problem 54.

55 A package of mass m is placed inside a drum that rotates in the vertical plane at the constant angular speed $\omega = 1.36$ rad/s. If the package reaches the position $\theta = 45°$ before slipping, determine the coefficient of friction between the package and drum. See Fig. 7-63.

56 The mass at C is attached to the vertical pole AB by two wires. The assembly is rotating about AB at the constant angular speed ω. If the force in wire BC is twice the force in AC, determine the value of ω. See Fig. 7-64.

57 A cone with an apex angle of $2\alpha = 60°$ rotates at uniform speed about its vertical axis. On it lays a particle of mass m hanging from a string. The particle rotates with the cone. Derive the formula for tension in the string and for the pressure force on the cone. See Fig. 7-65.

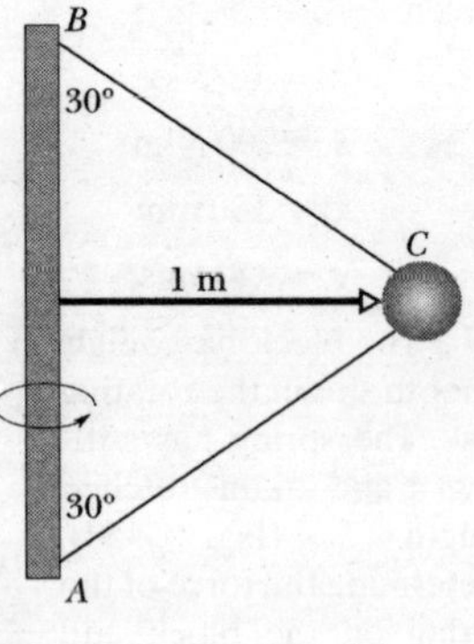

FIG. 7-64 Problem 56.

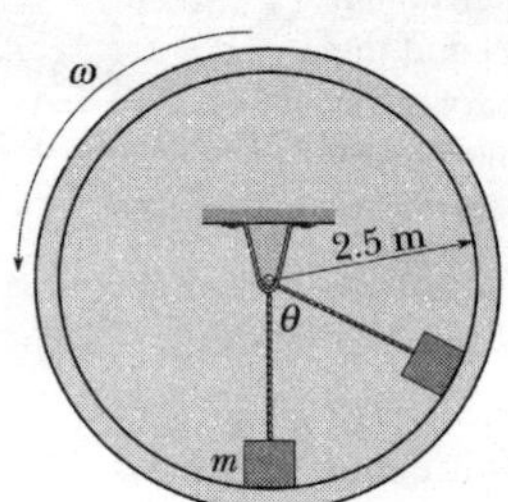

FIG. 7-63 Problem 55.

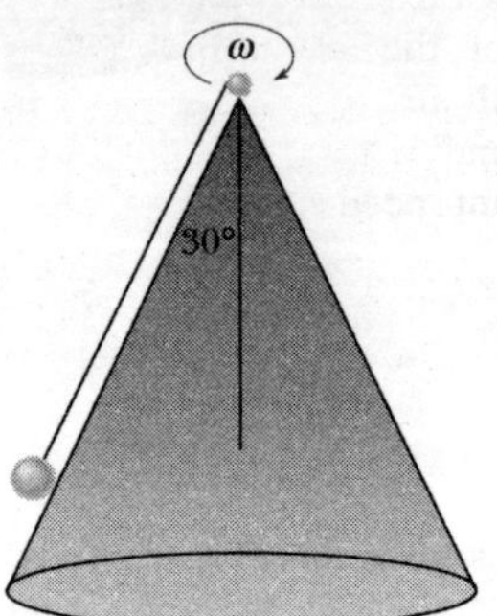

FIG. 7-65 Problem 57.

Some Physical Properties

Air (dry, at 20°C and 1 atm)	
Density	1.21 kg/m^3
Specific heat at constant pressure	1010 J/kg · K
Ratio of specific heats	1.40
Speed of sound	343 m/s
Electrical breakdown strength	3×10^6 V/m
Effective molar mass	0.0289 kg/mol
Water	
Density	1000 kg/m^3
Speed of sound	1460 m/s
Specific heat at constant pressure	4190 J/kg · K
Heat of fusion (0°C)	333 kJ/kg
Heat of vaporization (100°C)	2260 kJ/kg
Index of refraction (λ = 589 nm)	1.33
Molar mass	0.0180 kg/mol
Earth	
Mass	5.98×10^{24} kg
Mean radius	6.37×10^6 m
Free-fall acceleration at Earth s surface	9.8 m/s^2
Standard atmosphere	1.01×10^5 Pa
Period of satellite at 100 km altitude	86.3 min
Radius of the geosynchronous orbit	42 200 km
Escape speed	11.2 km/s
Magnetic dipole moment	8.0×10^{22} A · m^2
Mean electric field at surface	150 V/m, down
Distance to	
Moon	3.82×10^8 m
Sun	1.50×10^{11} m
Star nearest the Sun	4.04×10^{16} m
Galactic center	2.2×10^{20} m
Andromeda galaxy	2.1×10^{22} m
Edge of the observable universe	$\sim 10^{26}$ m

The Greek Alphabet

Alpha	A	α	Iota	I	ι	Rho	P	ρ
Beta	B	β	Kappa	K	κ	Sigma	Σ	σ
Gamma	Γ	γ	Lambda	Λ	λ	Tau	T	τ
Delta	Δ	δ	Mu	M	μ	Upsilon	Y	υ
Epsilon	E	ϵ	Nu	N	ν	Phi	Φ	ϕ, φ
Zeta	Z	ζ	Xi	Ξ	ξ	Chi	X	χ
Eta	H	η	Omicron	O	o	Psi	Ψ	ψ
Theta	Θ	θ	Pi	Π	π	Omega	Ω	ω

8 Work, Power, and Energy

Courtesy Mark Reid, USGS

When an avalanche of rocks moves down a mountainside and into a valley, friction between the moving rocks and the land slow and eventually stop the flow. The runout (the distance the rocks can move across a valley) is typically 2/3 of the height from which the rocks descended. However, in large avalanches, where a large amount of material comes down a mountainside, the runout can be 30 times as much, which can take a seemingly safe community by fatal surprise.

Why can large avalanches have such long runouts?

The answer is in this chapter.

8-1 Introduction

One of the fundamental goals of physics is to investigate something that everyone talks about: energy. The topic is obviously important. Indeed, our civilization is based on acquiring and effectively using energy.

For example, everyone knows that any type of motion requires energy: Flying across the Pacific Ocean requires it. Lifting material to the top floor of an office building or to an orbiting space station requires it. Throwing a fastball requires it. We spend a tremendous amount of money to acquire and use energy. Wars have been started because of energy resources. Wars have been ended because of a sudden, overpowering use of energy by one side. Everyone knows many examples of energy and its use, but what does the term *energy* really mean?

The term *energy* is so broad that a clear definition is difficult to write. Technically, energy is a scalar quantity associated with the state (or condition) of one or more objects. However, this definition is too vague to be of help to us now.

A looser definition might at least get us started. Energy is a number that we associate with a system of one or more objects. If a force changes one of the objects by, say, making it move, then the energy number changes. After countless experiments, scientists and engineers realized that if the scheme by which we assign energy numbers is planned carefully, the numbers can be used to predict the outcomes of experiments and, even more important, to build machines, such as flying machines. This success is based on a wonderful property of our universe: Energy can be transformed from one type to another and transferred from one object to another, but the total amount is always the same (energy is *conserved*). No exception to this *principle of energy conservation* has ever been found.

Think of the many types of energy as being numbers representing money in many types of bank accounts. Rules have been made about what such money numbers mean and how they can be changed. You can transfer money numbers from one account to another or from one system to another, perhaps electronically with nothing material actually moving. However, the total amount (the total of all the money numbers) can always be accounted for: It is always conserved.

In this chapter we focus on only one type of energy (*kinetic energy*) and on only one way in which energy can be transferred (*work*). We also examine a few other types of energy and how the principle of energy conservation can be written as equations to be solved.

Kinetic energy K is energy associated with the *state of motion* of an object. The faster the object moves, the greater is its kinetic energy. When the object is stationary, its kinetic energy is zero.

For an object of mass m whose speed v is well below the speed of light,

$$K = \tfrac{1}{2}mv^2 \qquad \text{(kinetic energy)} \tag{8-1}$$

For example, a 3.0 kg duck flying past us at 2.0 m/s has a kinetic energy of $6.0\ \text{kg}\cdot\text{m}^2/\text{s}^2$; that is, we associate that number with the duck's motion.

The SI unit of kinetic energy (and every other type of energy) is the **joule** (J), named for James Prescott Joule, an English scientist of the 1800s. It is defined directly from Eq. 8-1 in terms of the units for mass and velocity:

$$1\ \text{joule} = 1\ \text{J} = 1\ \text{kg}\cdot\text{m}^2/\text{s}^2 \tag{8-2}$$

Thus, the flying duck has a kinetic energy of 6.0 J.

8-2 | Work

If you accelerate an object to a greater speed by applying a force to the object, you increase the kinetic energy K (= $\frac{1}{2}mv^2$) of the object. Similarly, if you decelerate the object to a lesser speed by applying a force, you decrease the kinetic energy of the object. We account for these changes in kinetic energy by saying that your force has transferred energy *to* the object from yourself or *from* the object to yourself. In such a transfer of energy via a force, **work** W is said to be *done on the object by the force.* More formally, we define work as follows:

> Work W is energy transferred to or from an object by means of a force acting on the object. Energy transferred to the object is positive work, and energy transferred from the object is negative work.

"Work," then, is transferred energy; "doing work" is the act of transferring the energy. Work has the same units as energy and is a scalar quantity.

The term *transfer* can be misleading. It does not mean that anything material flows into or out of the object; that is, the transfer is not like a flow of water. Rather, it is like the electronic transfer of money between two bank accounts: The number in one account goes up while the number in the other account goes down, with nothing material passing between the two accounts.

Note that we are not concerned here with the common meaning of the word "work," which implies that *any* physical or mental labor is work. According to our everyday understanding of the word "work", a teacher's sitting on a chair and contemplating how to present this idea to you is work, your reading these lines is work. If you push hard against a wall, you tire because of the continuously repeated muscle contractions that are required, and you are, in the common sense, working. However, such effort does not cause an energy transfer to or from the wall and thus is not work done on the wall as defined here.

To avoid confusion in this chapter, we shall use the symbol W only for work and shall represent a weight with its equivalent mg.

We define work on a system by an agent exerting a force $\vec{F}$ as scalar product of $\vec{F}$ and very small displacement d of point of application of force.

$$dW = \vec{F} \cdot \vec{ds}$$

Here it is important to note that a particle may be subjected to many forces. It may have some instantaneous velocity which causes very small displacement $d\,\vec{s}$ in very small time. Work done by $\vec{F}_1$ is $dw = \vec{F}_1 d\,\vec{s}$. Here Force $\vec{F}_1$ may not be the cause of small displacement $d\,\vec{s}$ Work is relative quantity because displacement is relative. (Remember force is not dependent on choice of reference frame).

CHECKPOINT 1 A lift is going up with constant velocity u. Calculate work from reference frame of ground and lift in time t.

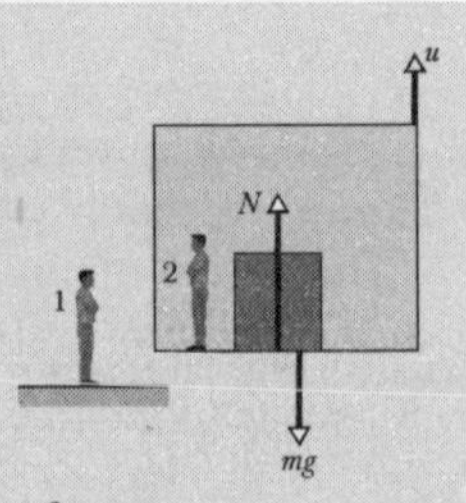

Solution: Particle is in equilibrium $N\text{-}mg = 0 \Rightarrow N = \text{mg}$

Work Done in reference frame of lift is zero as displacement of block is zero.

Work Done in ground reference frame = $N.ut$

We can observe that work is dependent on reference frame.

8-3 | Calculation of Work for Uniform Force

$$dW = \vec{F}.d\vec{S}$$

For uniform force, can be taken out of integral. Hence, $W = \int \vec{F}.d\vec{S} = \vec{F}.\int d\vec{S}$

Thus $W = \vec{F}\cdot\vec{s}$ (*This is true only for uniform forces*)

$$W = F(S\cos\theta)$$

here $S\cos\theta$ is component of displacement along force. Alternately we can write

$$W = (F\cos\theta)S$$

Here $F\cos\theta$ is component of force along displacement.

Relation Between Work and Kinetic Energy for Uniform Forces

Let us consider a bead that can slide along a frictionless wire that is stretched along a horizontal x axis (Fig. 8-1). A constant force $\vec{F}$, directed at an angle ϕ to the wire, accelerates the bead along the wire. We can relate the force and the acceleration with Newton's second law, written for components along the x axis:

$$F_x = ma_x \tag{8-3}$$

where m is the bead's mass. As the bead moves through a displacement $\vec{d}$, the force changes the bead's velocity from an initial value $\vec{v}_0$ to some other value $\vec{v}$. Because the force is constant, we know that the acceleration is also constant. Thus, for components along the x axis,

$$v^2 = v_0^2 + 2a_x d \tag{8-4}$$

Solving this equation for a_x, substituting into Eq. 8-3, and rearranging then give us

$$\tfrac{1}{2}mv^2 - \tfrac{1}{2}mv_0^2 = F_x d \tag{8-5}$$

The first term on the left side of the equation is the kinetic energy K_f of the bead at the end of the displacement d, and the second term is the kinetic energy K_i of the bead at the start of the displacement. Thus, the left side of Eq. 8-5 tells us the kinetic energy has been changed by the force, and the right side tells us the change is equal to $F_x d$. Therefore, the work W done on the bead by the force (the energy transfer due to the force) is

$$W = F_x d \tag{8-6}$$

If we know values for F_x and d, we can use this equation to calculate the work W done on the bead by the force.

> To calculate the work a force does on an object as the object moves through some displacement, we use only the force component along the object's displacement. The force component perpendicular to the displacement does zero work.

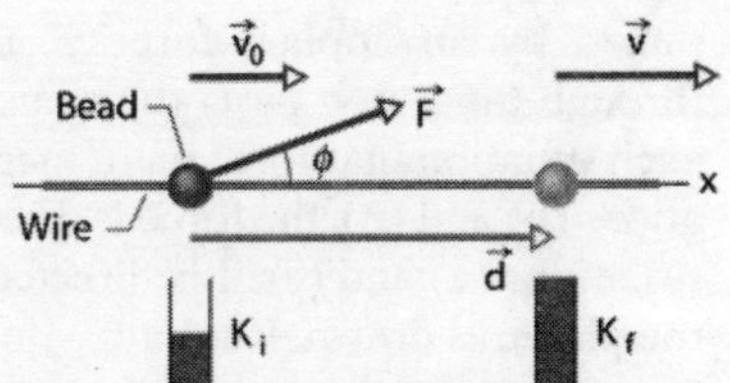

FIG. 8-1 A constant force $\vec{F}$ directed at angle ϕ to the displacement $\vec{d}$ of a bead on a wire accelerates the bead along the wire, changing the velocity of the bead from $\vec{v}_0$ to $\vec{v}$. A "kinetic energy gauge" indicates the resulting change in the kinetic energy of the bead, from the value K_i to the value K_f.

From Fig. 8-1, we see that we can write F_x as $F\cos\phi$, where ϕ is the angle between the directions of the displacement $\vec{d}$ and the force $\vec{F}$. Thus,

$$W = Fd\cos\phi \quad \text{(work done by a constant force)} \tag{8-7}$$

Because the right side of this equation is equivalent to the scalar (dot) product $\vec{F}\cdot\vec{d}$, we can also write

$$W = \vec{F}\cdot\vec{d} \quad \text{(work done by a constant force)} \tag{8-8}$$

where F is the magnitude of $\vec{F}$. (You may wish to review the discussion of scalar products.) Equation 8-8 is especially useful for calculating the work when $\vec{F}$ and $\vec{d}$ are given in unit-vector notation.

Cautions: There are two restrictions to using Eqs. 8-6 through 8-8 to calculate work done on an object by a force. First, the force must be a *constant force;* that is, it must not change in magnitude or direction as the object moves. (Later, we shall discuss what to do with a *variable force* that changes in magnitude.) Second, the object must be *particle-like.* This means that the object must be *rigid;* all parts of it must move together, in the same direction. In this chapter we consider only particle-like objects, such as the bed and its occupant being pushed in Fig. 8-2.

A force does positive work when it has a vector component in the same direction as the displacement, and it does negative work when it has a vector component in the opposite direction. It does zero work when it has no such vector component.

Signs for work. The work done on an object by a force can be either positive work or negative work. For example, if the angle ϕ in Eq. 8-7 is less than 90°, then cos ϕ is positive and thus so is the work. If ϕ is greater than 90° (up to 180°), then cos ϕ is negative and thus so is the work. (Can you see that the work is zero when $\phi = 90°$?) These results lead to a simple rule. To find the sign of the work done by a force, consider the force vector component that is parallel to the displacement:

Units for work. Work has the SI unit of the joule, the same as kinetic energy. However, from Eqs. 8-6 and 8-7 we can see that an equivalent unit is the newton-meter (N · m). The corresponding unit in the British system is the foot-pound (ft · lb). Extending Eq. 8-2, we have

$$1\ \text{J} = 1\ \text{kg} \cdot \text{m}^2/\text{s}^2 = 1\ \text{N} \cdot \text{m} = 0.738\ \text{ft} \cdot \text{lb} \qquad (8\text{-}9)$$

Net work done by several forces. When two or more forces act on an object, the **net work** done on the object is the sum of the work done by the individual forces. We can calculate the net work in two ways. (1) We can find the work done by each force and then sum those works. (2) Alternatively, we can first find the net force $\vec{F}_{net}$ of those forces. Then we can use Eq. 8-7, substituting the magnitude F_{net} for F and also the angle between the directions of $\vec{F}_{net}$ and $\vec{d}$ for ϕ. Similarly, we can use Eq. 8-8 with $\vec{F}_{net}$ substituted for $\vec{F}$.

Sample Problem 8-1 Build your skill

Fig. 8-2 shows four situations in which the same box is pulled by an applied force $\vec{F}$ up a frictionless ramp through (and then past) the same vertical distance h. In each situation that force has a magnitude of 10 N. In situations (b) and (d), the force is directed along the plane; in situations (a) and (c), it is directed at an angle $\theta = 37°$ to the plane, as drawn. Rank the situations according to the work done on the box in the vertical distance h by the applied force. Also, discuss whether answer depends on the initial speed of box or the presence of other forces.

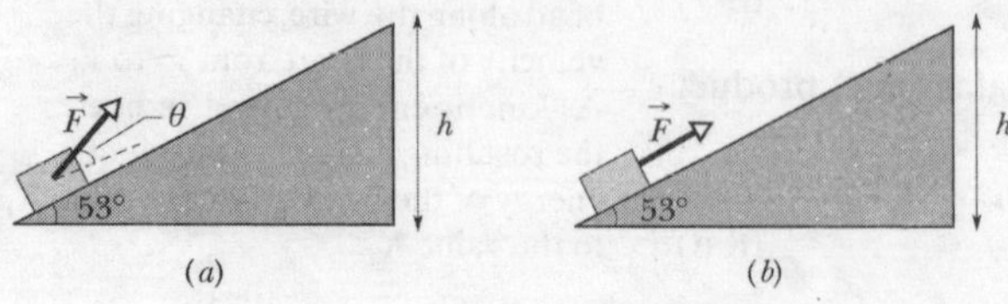

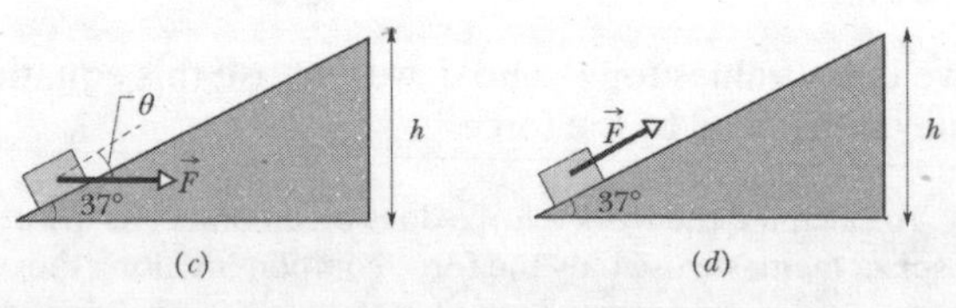

FIG. 8-2 Boxes being pulled on inclines by applying forces in different directions.

Solution: (b) and (d) will have larger work than (a) and (c), respectively, because displacement in (b) and (a) is same and similarly displacement in (d) and (a) is also same, but in (b) and (d) force is acting along displacement. Thus, scalar product of force and displacement will be larger. Now we compare (b) and (d) by comparing magnitude of displacement; we can see easily that displacement is larger for (d). Thus, by similar argument, we can prove that displacement of (c) is larger than (a).

Hence $\qquad W_d > W_b,\ W_c > W_a$

Numerical calculations will also reveal that our arguments were correct. And we will find relation between w_b and w_c

$$w_d = F\, h \operatorname{cosec} 37° = \frac{5Fh}{3}$$

$$w_d = F\ h\ \operatorname{cosec}\ 37° = \frac{5Fh}{4}$$

$$w_c = (F\ \cos 37°)\ (h\ \operatorname{cosec}\ 37°) = \frac{4Fh}{3}$$

$$w_d = (F\ \cos\ 37°)\ (h\ \operatorname{cosec}\ 53°) = F\ h$$

In order to derive the relations for work done, we first need to calculate the displacement, that is, the length of the ramp in terms of vertical distance 'h'. Also, in situations and the force 'F' also needs to be resolved along the direction of displacement to determine the work done.

Hence, $w_d > w_c > w_b > w_a$ (Answer)

Sample Problem 8-2 Build your skill

A force $\vec{F} = (3.00\text{ N})\,\hat{\text{i}} + (7.00\text{ N})\,\hat{\text{j}} + (7.00\text{ N})$ acts on a 2.00 kg mobile object that moves from an initial position of $\vec{r}_i = (3.00\text{ m})\,\hat{\text{i}} - (2.00\text{ m})\,\hat{\text{j}} + (5.00\text{ m})\,\hat{\text{k}}$ to a final position of $\vec{r}_f = +\,(5.00\text{ m})\,\hat{\text{i}} + (4.00\text{ m})\,\hat{\text{j}} + (7.00\text{ m})\,\hat{\text{k}}$ in 4.00 s. Find the work done on the object by the force in the 4.00 s interval.

Solution: We know that displacement vector is equal to change in position vector.

Thus, $\vec{S} = \vec{r}_f - \vec{r}_i$

$$= (2\hat{\text{i}} + 6\hat{\text{j}} + 2\hat{\text{k}})\,\text{m}$$

Thus, the work done by force $\vec{F}$ is given by

$$W = \vec{F} \cdot \vec{S}$$

so, $W = \left(3\hat{\text{i}} + 7\hat{\text{j}} + 7\hat{\text{k}}\right) \cdot \left(2\hat{\text{i}} + 6\hat{\text{j}} + 2\hat{\text{k}}\right)$

$$= (6 + 42 + 14)\,\text{J}$$

$$= 62\text{ J}$$

(Answer)

Work–Kinetic Energy Theorem

Equation 8-10 relates the change in kinetic energy of the bead (from an initial $K_i = \frac{1}{2}mv_0^2$ to a later $K_f = \frac{1}{2}mv^2$) to the work $W\,(= F_x d)$ done on the bead. For such particle-like objects, we can generalize that equation. Let ΔK be the change in the kinetic energy of the object, and let W be the net work done on it. Then

$$\Delta K = K_f - K_i = W \tag{8-10}$$

which says that

$$\begin{pmatrix}\text{change in the kinetic}\\ \text{energy of a particle}\end{pmatrix} = \begin{pmatrix}\text{net work done on}\\ \text{the particle}\end{pmatrix}$$

We can also write

$$K_f = K_i + W \tag{8-11}$$

which says that

$$\begin{pmatrix}\text{kinetic energy after}\\ \text{the net work is done}\end{pmatrix} = \begin{pmatrix}\text{kinetic energy}\\ \text{before the net work}\end{pmatrix} + \begin{pmatrix}\text{the net}\\ \text{work done}\end{pmatrix}$$

These statements are known traditionally as the **work–kinetic energy theorem** for particles. They hold for both positive and negative work: If the net work done on a particle is positive, then the particle's kinetic energy increases by the amount of the work. If the net work done is negative, then the particle's kinetic energy decreases by the amount of the work.

For example, if the kinetic energy of a particle is initially 5 J and there is a net transfer of 2 J to the particle (positive net work), the final kinetic energy is 7 J. If, instead, there is a net transfer of 2 J from the particle (negative net work),

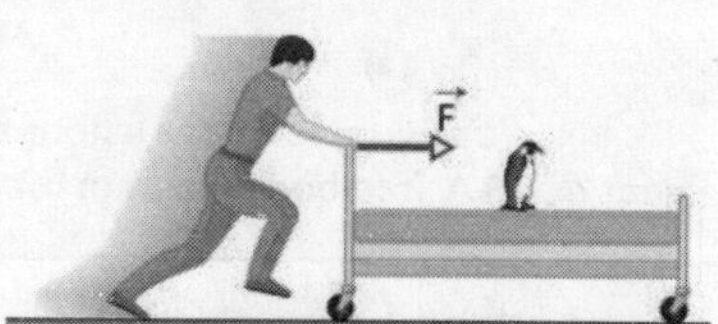

FIG. 8-3 A contestant in a bed race. We can approximate the bed and its occupant as being a particle for the purpose of calculating the work done on them by the force applied by the

Sample Problem 8-3

Figure 8-4*a* shows two industrial spies sliding an initially stationary 64.6 kg floor safe a displacement $\vec{d}$ of magnitude 0.50 m, straight toward their truck. The push $\vec{F}_1$ of spy 001 is 12.0 N, directed at an angle of 53°downward from the horizontal; the pull $\vec{F}_2$ of spy 002 is 10.0 N, directed at 37° above the horizontal. The magnitudes and directions of these forces do not change as the safe moves, and the floor and safe make frictionless contact.

(a) What is the net work done on the safe by forces $\vec{F}_1$ and $\vec{F}_2$ during the displacement $\vec{d}$?

Conceptualize: The net work W done on the safe by the two forces is the sum of the work they do individually.

Classify: The forces are constant in both magnitude and direction, we can use either Eq. 8-7 ($W = Fd \cos \phi$) or Eq. 8-8 ($W = \vec{F} \cdot \vec{d}$) to calculate those work. Since we know the magnitudes and directions of the forces, we choose Eq. 8-71.

Compute: From Eq. 8-7 and the free-body diagram for the safe in Fig. 8-4*b*, the work done by $\vec{F}_1$ is

$$W_1 = F_1 d \cos \phi_1 = (12.0 \text{ N})(8.50 \text{ m})(\cos 53°)$$
$$= 61.2 \text{ J}$$

and the work done by $\vec{F}_2$ is

$$W_2 = F_2 d \cos \phi_2 = (10.0 \text{ N})(8.50 \text{ m})(\cos .37°)$$
$$= 68 \text{ J}$$

Thus, the net work W is

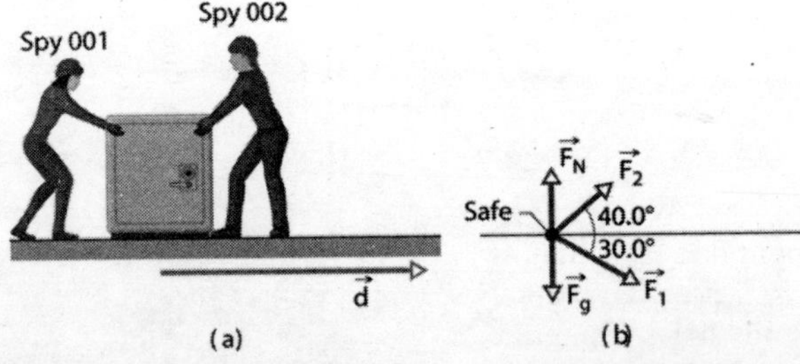

FIG. 8-4 (*a*) Two spies move a floor safe through a displacement $\vec{d}$. (*b*) A free-body diagram for the safe.

$$W = W_1 + W_2 = 61.8 \text{ J} + 68 \text{ J}$$
$$= 129.2 \text{ J} \quad \text{(Answer)}$$

Conclude: Since net force has component along the displacement, work should have been positive as the answer is now going to be.

During the 8.50 m displacement, therefore, the spies transfer 129 J of energy to the kinetic energy of the safe.

In Case Of: (a)The work W_g done on the safe by the gravitational force $\vec{F}_g$ and what is the work W_N done on the safe by the normal force $\vec{F}_N$ from the floor?

Solution: Because these forces are constant in both magnitude and direction, we can find the work they do with Eq. 8-7.

Thus, with mg as the magnitude of the gravitational force, we write

$$W_g = mgd \cos 90° = mgd(0) = 0 \quad \text{(Answer)}$$

and

$$W_N = F_N d \cos 90° = F_N d(0) = 0 \quad \text{(Answer)}$$

We should have known this result. Because these forces are perpendicular to the displacement of the safe, they do zero work on the safe and do not transfer any energy to or from it.

In Case Of: (b)The safe is initially stationary. What is its speed v_f at the end of the 8.50 m displacement?

Conceptualize: The speed of the safe changes because its kinetic energy is changed when energy is transferred to it by $\vec{F}_1$ and $\vec{F}_2$.

Compute: We relate the speed to the work done by combining Eqs. 8-10 and 8-1:

$$W = K_f - K_i = \tfrac{1}{2}mv_f^2 - \tfrac{1}{2}mv_i^2$$

The initial speed v_i is zero, and we now know that the work done is 129.2 J. Solving for v_f and then substituting known data, we find that

$$v_f = \sqrt{\frac{2W}{m}} = \sqrt{\frac{2(153.4 \text{ J})}{225 \text{ kg}}}$$
$$= 2 \text{ m/s} \quad \text{(Answer)}$$

Work Done by the Gravitational Force

We next examine the work done on an object by the gravitational force acting on it. Figure 8-5 shows a particle-like tomato of mass m that is thrown upward with initial speed v_0 and thus with initial kinetic energy $K_i = \frac{1}{2}mv_0^2$. As the tomato rises, it is slowed by a gravitational force $\vec{F}_g$; that is, the tomato's kinetic energy decreases because $\vec{F}_g$ does work on the tomato as it rises. Because we can treat the tomato as a particle, we can use Eq. $W = Fd \cos \phi$ to express the work done during a displacement $\vec{d}$. For the force magnitude F, we use mg as the magnitude of $\vec{F}_g$. Thus, the work W_g done by the gravitational force $\vec{F}_g$ is

$$W_g = mgd \cos \phi \quad \text{(work done by gravitational force)} \tag{8-12}$$

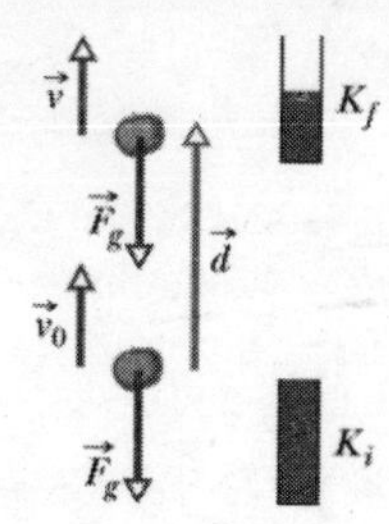

FIG. 8-5 Because the gravitational force $\vec{F}_g$ acts on it, a particle-like tomato of mass m thrown upward slows from velocity $\vec{v}_0$ to velocity $\vec{v}$ during displacement $\vec{d}$. A kinetic energy gauge indicates the resulting change in the kinetic energy of the tomato, from $K_i (= \frac{1}{2}mv_0^2)$ to $K_f (= \frac{1}{2}mv^2)$.

For a rising object, force $\vec{F}_g$ is directed opposite the displacement $\vec{d}$, as indicated in Fig. 8-5. Thus, $\phi = 180°$ and

$$W_g = mgd \cos 180° = mgd(-1) = -mgd \tag{8-13}$$

The minus sign tells us that during the object's rise, the gravitational force acting on the object transfers energy in the amount mgd from the kinetic energy of the object. This is consistent with the slowing of the object as it rises.

After the object has reached its maximum height and is falling back down, the angle ϕ between force $\vec{F}_g$ and displacement $\vec{d}$ is zero. Thus,

$$W_g = mgd \cos 0° = mgd(+1) = +mgd \tag{8-14}$$

The plus sign tells us that the gravitational force now transfers energy in the amount mgd to the kinetic energy of the object. This is consistent with the speeding up of the object as it falls. (Actually, energy transfers associated with lifting and lowering an object involve the full object–Earth system.)

Work Done in Lifting and Lowering an Object

Now suppose we lift a particle-like object by applying a vertical force $\vec{F}$ to it. During the upward displacement, our applied force does positive work W_a on the object while the gravitational force does negative work W_g on it. Our applied force tends to transfer energy to the object while the gravitational force tends to transfer energy from it. By Eq. 8-10, the change ΔK in the kinetic energy of the object due to these two energy transfers is

$$\Delta K = K_f - K_i = W_a + W_g \tag{8-15}$$

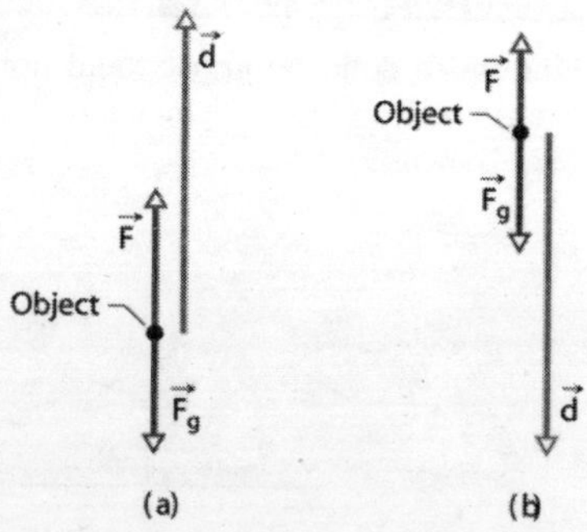

FIG. 8-6 (*a*) An applied force $\vec{F}$ lifts an object. The object's displacement $\vec{d}$ makes an angle $\phi = 180°$ with the gravitational force $\vec{F}_g$ on the object. The applied force does positive work on the object. (*b*) An applied force $\vec{F}$ lowers an object. The displacement $\vec{d}$ of the object makes an angle $\phi = 0°$ with the gravitational force $\vec{F}_g$. The applied force does negative work on the object.

in which K_f is the kinetic energy at the end of the displacement and K_i is that at the start of the displacement. This equation also applies if we lower the object, but then the gravitational force tends to transfer energy *to* the object while our force tends to transfer energy *from* it.

In one common situation, the object is stationary before and after the lift—for example, when you lift a book from the floor to a shelf. Then K_f and K_i are both zero, and Eq. 8-15 reduces to

$$W_a + W_g = 0$$

or

$$W_a = -W_g \tag{8-16}$$

Note that we get the same result if K_f and K_i are not zero but are still equal. Either way, the result means that the work done by the applied force is the negative of the work done by the gravitational force; that is, the applied force transfers the same amount of energy to the object as the gravitational force transfers from the object. Using Eq. 8-12, we can rewrite Eq. 8-16 as

$$W_a = -mgd \cos \phi \qquad \text{(work done in lifting and lowering; } K_f = K_i\text{)} \qquad (8\text{-}17)$$

with ϕ being the angle between $\vec{F}_g$ and $\vec{d}$. If the displacement is vertically upward (Fig. 8-6*a*), then $\phi = 180°$ and the work done by the applied force equals *mgd*. If the displacement is vertically downward (Fig. 8-6*b*), then $\phi = 0°$ and the work done by the applied force equals $-mgd$.

Equations 8-16 and 8-17 apply to any situation in which an object is lifted or lowered, with the object stationary before and after the lift. They are independent of the magnitude of the force used. For example, if you lift a mug from the floor to over your head, your force on the mug varies considerably during the lift. Still, because the mug is stationary before and after the lift, the work your force does on the mug is given by Eqs. 8-16 and 8-17, where, in Eq. 8-17, *mg* is the weight of the mug and *d* is the distance you lift it.

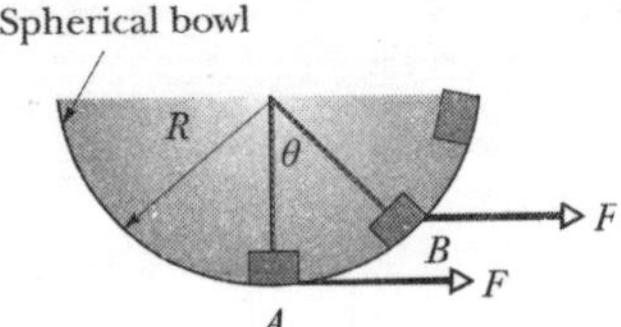

FIG. 8-7 Application of force on a block of mass *m* along a spherical bowl.

Here are few simple examples where we calculate work done by uniform forces acting on an object. We take a small block of mass *m* from *A* to *B* along a fixed smooth spherical bowl by applying horizontal force *F* on it. Let's say arc *AB* substends angle θ on *O* (Fig. 8-7). The horizontal component of displacement is $R(\sin\theta)$ and vertical component of displacement is $R(1 - \cos \theta)$. Then work done by gravity W_g can be very easily written as product of force and component and vertical component of displacement. Since they are opposite to each other, our answer will have negative sign

$$W_g = -mgR\,(1 - \cos \theta)$$

Similarly, work done by force *F* will be, $W_f = FR(\sin\theta)$.

Sample Problem 8-4 Build your skill

Find work done by gravity, and normal when block comes from *A* to *B* on a smooth inclined plan as shown in Fig. 8-8*a*.

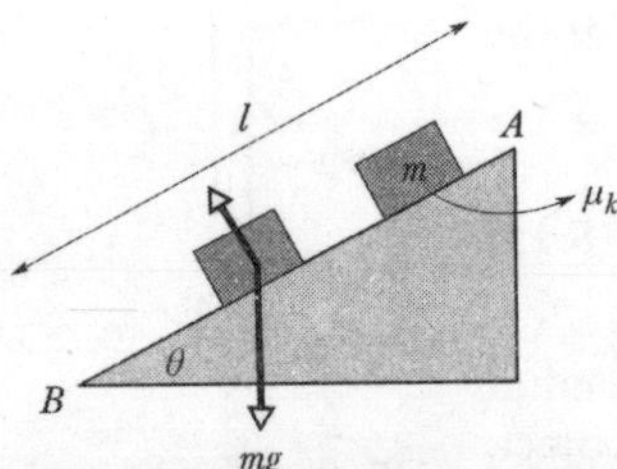

FIG. 8-8 (*a*) A block moving from point *A* to point *B* on a smooth inclined plane.

Solution: $W_g = mg\,(l \sin\theta) = (mg \sin\theta)l$

$W_N = 0$ (because displacement is perpendicular to force)

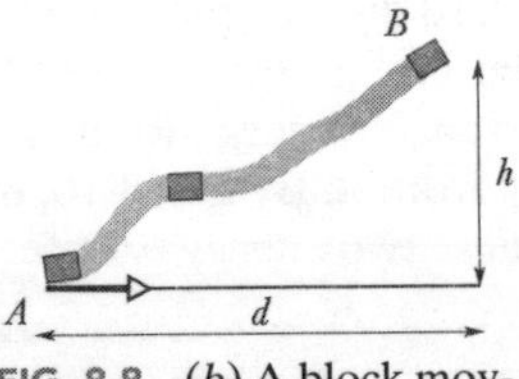

FIG. 8-8 (*b*) A block moving on a random path.

We can see that work done is dependent only on the final displacement vector. It is completely independent of the type of path (Fig. 8-8*b*). Infact we can see that work depends only on component of displacement along force and force in case of uniform force. For example in when we take the block from *A* to *B* by applying constant horizontal force, F_1, work done by gravity and force F_1 will not be dependent on the path *AB*. Work done by gravity will be $-mgh$ *as* long as *B* is height *h* above *A*. Similarly, work done by F_1 will remain $F_1 \times d$ as long as horizontal distance between *A* and *B* is *d*.

Sample Problem 8-5

An initially stationary 15.0 kg crate of cheese wheels is pulled, via a cable, a distance $d = 5.70$ m up a frictionless ramp to a height h of 2.50 m, where it stops (Fig. 8-9*a*).

(a) How much work W_g is done on the crate by the gravitational force $\vec{F}_g$ during the lift?

Conceptualize/Classify: We treat the crate as a particle and use $W_g = mgd \cos \phi$ to find the work W_g done by $\vec{F}_g$.

Compute: We do not know the angle ϕ between the directions of $\vec{F}_g$ and displacement $\vec{d}$. However, from the crate's free-body diagram in Fig. 8-9*b*, we find that ϕ is $\theta + 90°$, where θ is the (unknown) angle of the ramp. Eq. 8-12 then gives us

$$W_g = mgd \cos(\theta + 90°) = -mgd \sin \theta \quad (8\text{-}18)$$

where we have used a trigonometric identity to simplify the expression. The result seems to be useless because θ is unknown. But (continuing with physics courage) we see from Fig. 8-9*a* that $d \sin \theta = h$, where h is a known quantity. With this substitution, Eq. 8-18 gives us

$$\begin{aligned} W_g &= -mgh \quad (8\text{-}19) \\ &= -(15.0\text{ kg})(9.8\text{ m/s}^2)(2.50\text{ m}) \\ &= -368\text{ J} \quad \text{(Answer)} \end{aligned}$$

Conclude: Note that Eq. 8-19 tells us that the work W_g done by the gravitational force depends on the vertical displacement but (surprisingly) not on the horizontal displacement.

(b) How much work W_T is done on the crate by the force $\vec{T}$ from the cable during the lift?

Conceptualize/Classify: We cannot just substitute the force magnitude $\vec{T}$ for F in Eq. 8-7 ($W = Fd \cos \phi$) because we do not know the value of T.

Classify: However, to get us going we can treat the crate as a particle and then apply the work–kinetic energy theorem ($\Delta K = W$) to it. Because the crate is stationary before and after the lift, the change ΔK in its kinetic energy is zero.

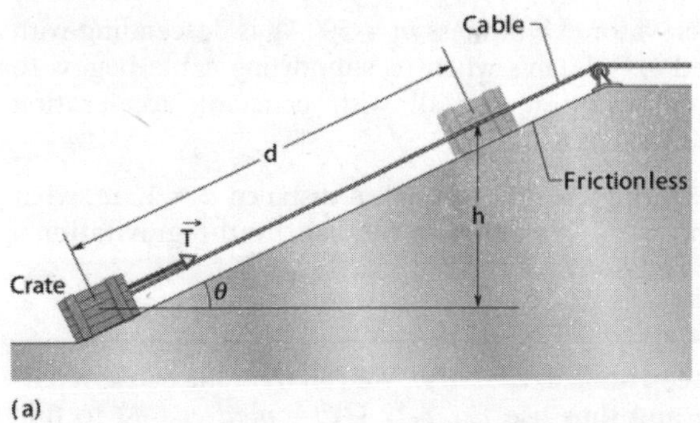

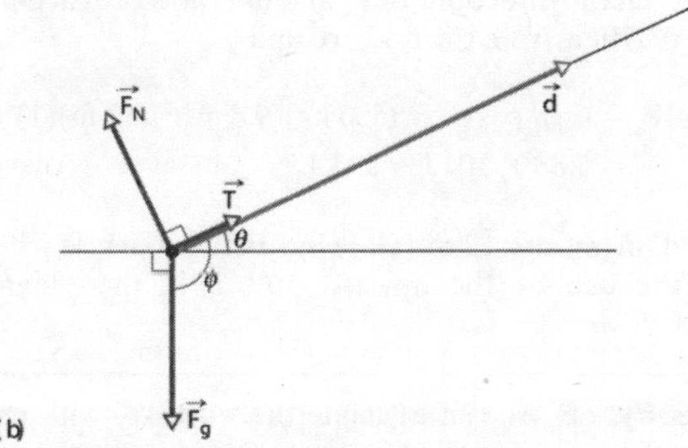

FIG. 8-9 (*a*) A crate is pulled up a frictionless ramp by a force $\vec{T}$ parallel to the ramp. (*b*) A free-body diagram for the crate, showing also the displacement $\vec{d}$.

Compute: For the net work W done on the crate, we must sum the works done by all three forces acting on the crate. From (a), the work W_g done by the gravitational force $\vec{F}_g$ is -368 J. The work W_N done by the normal force $\vec{F}_N$ on the crate from the ramp is zero because $\vec{F}_N$ is perpendicular to the displacement. We want the work W_T done by $\vec{T}$. Thus, the work–kinetic energy theorem gives us

$$\Delta K = W_T + W_g + W_N$$

or

$$0 = W_T - 368\text{ J} + 0$$

and so

$$W_T = 368\text{ J} \quad \text{(Answer)}$$

Conclude: Here, without the knowledge of force, we have been able to find the work done by that force, by using knowledge of other parameters.

Sample Problem 8-6 Build your skill

An elevator cab of mass $m = 500$ kg is descending with speed $v_i = 4.0$ m/s when its supporting cable begins to slip, allowing it to fall with constant acceleration $\vec{a} = \vec{g}/5$ (Fig. 8-10*a*).

(a) During the fall through a distance $d = 12$ m, what is the work W_g done on the cab by the gravitational force $\vec{F}_g$?

Conceptualize/Classify: We can treat the cab as a particle and thus use Eq. 8-12 ($W_g = mgd \cos \phi$) to find the work W_g.

Compute: From Fig. 8-10*b*, we see that the angle between the directions of $\vec{F}_g$ and the cab's displacement $\vec{d}$ is 0°. Then, from Eq. 8-12, we find

$$W_g = mgd \cos 0° = (500 \text{ kg})(9.8 \text{ m/s}^2)(12 \text{ m})(1)$$
$$= 5.88 \times 10^4 \text{ J} \approx 59 \text{ kJ} \qquad \text{(Answer)}$$

(b) During the 12 m fall, what is the work W_T done on the cab by the upward pull $\vec{T}$ of the elevator cable?

Classify: (1) We can calculate the work W_T with using $W = Fd \cos \phi$ if we first find an expression for the magnitude T of the cable's pull. (2) We can find that expression by writing Newton's second law for components along the y axis in Fig. 8-10*b* ($F_{\text{net},y} = ma_y$).

Compute: We get

$$T - F_g = ma$$

Solving for T, substituting mg for F_g, and then substituting the result in Eq. 8-7, we obtain

$$W_T = Td \cos \phi = m(a + g)d \cos \phi$$

Next, substituting $-g/5$ for the (downward) acceleration a and then 180° for the angle ϕ between the directions of forces $\vec{T}$ and $m\vec{g}$, we find

$$W_T = m\left(-\frac{g}{5} + g\right) d \cos \phi = \frac{4}{5} mgd \cos \phi$$

$$= \frac{4}{5}(500 \text{ kg})(9.8 \text{ m/s}^2)(12 \text{ m}) \cos 180°$$

$$= -4.70 \times 10^4 \text{ J} \approx -47 \text{ kJ} \qquad \text{(Answer)}$$

Conclude: Note that W_T is not simply the negative of W_g. The reason is that, because the cab accelerates during the fall, its speed changes during the fall, and thus its kinetic energy also changes. Therefore, Eq. 8-16 (which assumes that the initial and final kinetic energies are equal) does *not* apply here.

(c) What is the net work W done on the cab during the fall?

Classify: The net work is the sum of the works done by the forces acting on the cab:

Compute: $W = W_g + W_T = 5.88 \times 10^4 \text{ J} - 4.70 \times 10^4 \text{ J}$

$$= 1.18 \times 10^4 \text{ J} \approx 12 \text{ kJ} \qquad \text{(Answer)}$$

(d) What is the cab's kinetic energy at the end of the 12 m fall?

Classify: The kinetic energy changes *because* of the net work done on the cab, according to $K_f = K_i + W$.

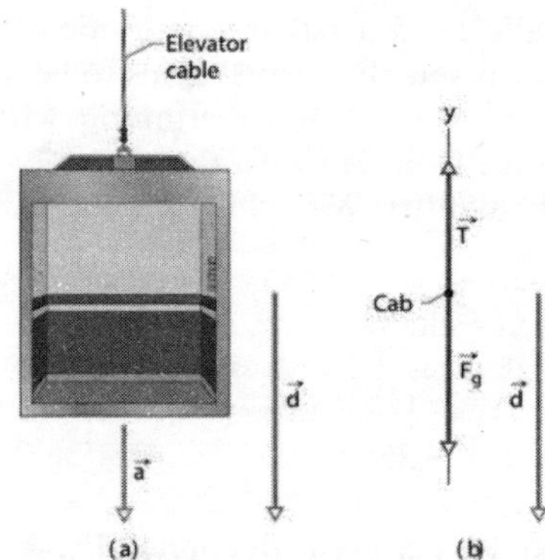

FIG. 8-10 An elevator cab, descending with speed v_i, suddenly begins to accelerate downward. (*a*) It moves through a displacement $\vec{d}$ with constant acceleration $\vec{a} = \vec{g}/5$. (*b*) A free-body diagram for the cab, displacement included.

Compute: From Eq. 8-1, we can write the kinetic energy at the start of the fall as $K_i = \frac{1}{2}mv_i^2$. We can then write Eq. 8-11 as

$$K_f = K_i + W = \tfrac{1}{2}mv_i^2 + W$$
$$= \tfrac{1}{2}(500 \text{ kg})(4.0 \text{ m/s})^2 + 1.18 \times 10^4 \text{ J}$$
$$= 1.58 \times 10^4 \text{ J} \approx 16 \text{ kJ} \qquad \text{(Answer)}$$

Conclude: Since total work in part (c) is positive, the kinetic energy has increased.

8-4 | Work Done by a Spring Force

We next want to examine the work done on a particle-like object by a particular type of *variable force*—namely, a **spring force**, the force from a spring. Many forces in nature have the same mathematical form as the spring force. Thus, by examining this one force, you can gain an understanding of many others.

The Spring Force

Figure 8-11*a* shows a spring in its **relaxed state**—that is, neither compressed nor extended. One end is fixed, and a particle-like object—a block, say—is attached to the other, free end. If we stretch the spring by pulling the block to the right as in Fig. 8-11*b*, the spring pulls on the block toward the left. (Because a spring force acts to restore the relaxed state, it is sometimes said to be a *restoring force.*) If we compress the spring by pushing the block to the left as in Fig. 8-11*c*, the spring now pushes on the block toward the right.

To a good approximation for many springs, the force $\vec{F}_s$ from a spring is proportional to the displacement $\vec{d}$ of the free end from its position when the spring is in the relaxed state. The *spring force* is given by

$$\vec{F}_s = -k\vec{d} \qquad \text{(Hooke's law)} \tag{8-20}$$

which is known as **Hooke's law** after Robert Hooke, an English scientist of the late 1600s. The minus sign in Eq. 8-20 indicates that the direction of the spring force is always opposite the direction of the displacement of the spring's free end. The constant k is called the **spring constant** (or **force constant**) and is a measure of the stiffness of the spring. The larger k is, the stiffer the spring; that is, the larger k is, the stronger the spring's pull or push for a given displacement. The SI unit for k is the newton per meter.

In Fig. 8-11 an x axis has been placed parallel to the length of the spring, with the origin ($x = 0$) at the position of the free end when the spring is in its relaxed state. For this common arrangement, we can write Eq. 8-20 as

$$F_x = -kx \qquad \text{(Hooke's law)} \tag{8-21}$$

where we have changed the subscript. If x is positive (the spring is stretched toward the right on the x axis), then F_x is negative (it is a pull toward the left). If x is negative (the spring is compressed toward the left), then F_x is positive (it is a push toward the right). Note that a spring force is a *variable force* because it is a function of x, the position of the free end. Thus F_x can be symbolized as $F(x)$. Also note that Hooke's law is a *linear* relationship between F_x and x.

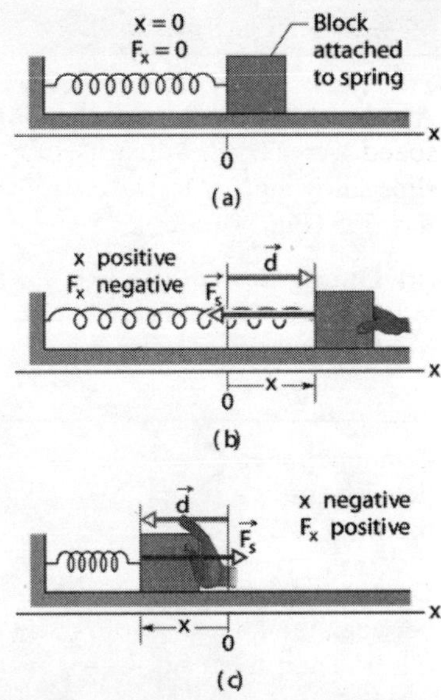

FIG. 8-11 (*a*) A spring in its relaxed state. The origin of an x axis has been placed at the end of the spring that is attached to a block. (*b*) The block is displaced by $\vec{d}$, and the spring is stretched by a positive amount x. Note the restoring force $\vec{F}_s$ exerted by the spring. (*c*) The spring is compressed by a negative amount x. Again, note the restoring force.

The Work Done by a Spring Force

To find the work done by the spring force as the block in Fig. 8-11*a* moves, let us make two simplifying assumptions about the spring. (1) It is *massless;* that is, its mass is negligible relative to the block's mass. (2) It is an *ideal spring;* that is, it obeys Hooke's law exactly. Let us also assume that the contact between the block and the floor is frictionless and that the block is particle-like.

We give the block a rightward jerk to get it moving and then leave it alone. As the block moves rightward, the spring force F_x does work on the block, decreasing the kinetic energy and slowing the block. However, we *cannot* find this work by using $W = Fd\cos\phi$ because that equation assumes a constant force. The spring force is a variable force.

To find the work done by the spring, we use calculus. Let the block's initial position be x_i and its later position x_f. Then divide the distance between those two positions into many segments, each of tiny length Δx. Label these segments, starting from x_i, as segments 1, 2, and so on. As the block moves through a segment, the spring force hardly varies because the segment is so short that x hardly varies. Thus, we can approximate the force magnitude as being constant within the segment. Label these magnitudes as F_{x1} in segment 1, F_{x2} in segment 2, and so on.

With the force now constant in each segment, we *can* find the work done within each segment by using Eq. 8-7. Here $\phi = 180°$, and so $\cos\phi = -1$. Then the work done is $-F_{x1}\,\Delta x$ in segment 1, $-F_{x2}\,\Delta x$ in segment 2, and so on. The net work W_s done by the spring, from x_i to x_f, is the sum of all these works:

$$W_s = \sum -F_{xj}\,\Delta x \tag{8-22}$$

where j labels the segments. In the limit as Δx goes to zero, Eq. 8-22 becomes

$$W_s = \int_{x_i}^{x_f} -F_x\,dx \tag{8-23}$$

From Eq. 8-21, the force magnitude F_x is kx. Thus, substitution leads to

$$\begin{aligned} W_s &= \int_{x_i}^{x_f} -kx\,dx = -k\int_{x_i}^{x_f} x\,dx \\ &= (-\tfrac{1}{2}k)[x^2]_{x_i}^{x_f} = (-\tfrac{1}{2}k)(x_f^2 - x_i^2) \end{aligned} \tag{8-24}$$

Multiplied out, this yields

$$W_s = \tfrac{1}{2}kx_i^2 - \tfrac{1}{2}kx_f^2 \quad \text{(work by a spring force)} \tag{8-25}$$

This work W_s done by the spring force can have a positive or negative value, depending on whether the *net* transfer of energy is to or from the block as the block moves from x_i to x_f. *Caution:* The final position x_f appears in the *second* term on the right side of Eq. 8-25. Therefore, Eq. 8-25 tells us:

> Work W_s is positive if the block ends up closer to the relaxed position ($x = 0$) than it was initially. It is negative if the block ends up farther away from $x = 0$. It is zero if the block ends up at the same distance from $x = 0$.

If $x_i = 0$ and if we call the final position x, then Eq. 8-25 becomes

$$W_s = -\tfrac{1}{2}kx^2 \quad \text{(work by a spring force)} \tag{8-26}$$

The Work Done by an Applied Force

Now suppose that we displace the block along the x axis while continuing to apply a force $\vec{F}_a$ to it. During the displacement, our applied force does work W_a on the block while the spring force does work W_s. By Eq. 8-10, the change ΔK in the kinetic energy of the block due to these two energy transfers is

$$\Delta K = K_f - K_i = W_a + W_s \tag{8-27}$$

in which K_f is the kinetic energy at the end of the displacement and K_i is that at the start of the displacement. If the block is stationary before and after the displacement, then K_f and K_i are both zero and Eq. 8-27 reduces to

$$W_a = -W_s \tag{8-28}$$

> If a block that is attached to a spring is stationary before and after a displacement, then the work done on it by the applied force displacing it is the negative of the work done on it by the spring force.

Caution: If the block is not stationary before and after the displacement, then this statement is *not* true.

Sample Problem 8-7

A spring is kept compressed by a small length x_1 from its natural length l_0. Now it is further pushed towards wall by an amount x_2, so that total compression becomes $x_1 + x_2$. Find the total work done by spring on block during this compression.

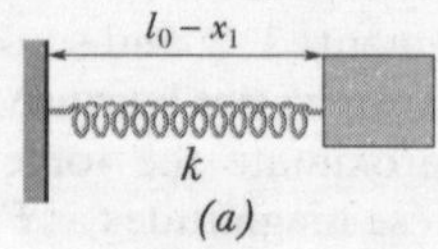

(a)

Conceptualize/classify: Spring will try to push the block towards right because of the restoring force k and block is moving towards left so the final work done by spring on block is going to be negative.

Compute: $\vec{F} = kx\hat{i} \quad d\vec{s} = dx(-\hat{i})$

Now, work done by the spring through the displacement $d\vec{s} = dx(-\hat{i})$

We know $\quad dW = \vec{F}.d\vec{S} = -kx\,dx$

Integrating the above relation from the initial compression x_1 to the final compression x_1+x_2, gives the total work done

$$W = -k\int_{x_1}^{(x_1+x_2)} x\,dx = -\frac{1}{2}k\left[(x_1+x_2)^2 - x_1^2\right]$$

$$-\frac{1}{2}k\,(x_2^2 + 2x_1x_2)$$

(b)

Conclude: The work is negative as the direction of force and displacement is opposite.

Sample Problem 8-8

A block is connected to a spring which is in its relaxed state (natural length l_0). Find maximum extension of spring.

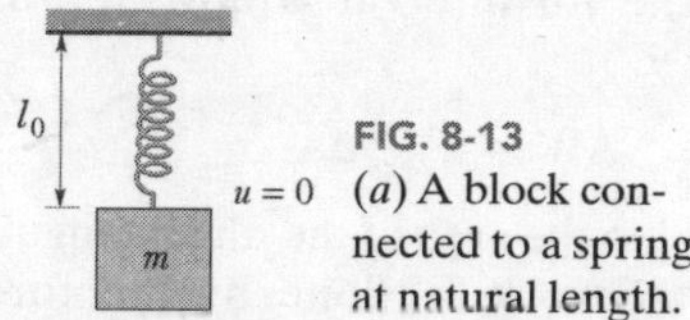

FIG. 8-13 (a) A block connected to a spring at natural length.

Conceptualize: Forces that will act on the block are spring force (acting upwards) and gravity (downwards). Initially spring force will be small compared to gravity. So, particle will go down increasing its speed. After some time, net force on particle will become upwards as spring force will become larger than weight of the block. Hence, it will start deaccelerating and finally comes to rest.

Classify: Maximum extension occurs when the block steps. While it is moving downward, the extension in the spring keeps on increasing. We will use work energy theorem as we know that the initial and final kinetic energy of the block is zero.

Compute: Work done for displacement x due to gravitational pull is mgx. Work done for displacement x of the spring is $-1/2\ kx^2$. The negative sign indicates that the force due to spring is acting in a direction opposite to the gravitational force on the block.

Now, writing work-energy theorem for the system

$$W = mgx - \frac{1}{2}kx^2 = 0$$

FIG. 8-13 (b) The block connected to the spring which has extended.

Because the change in kinetic energy is zero

$$mgx - \frac{1}{2}kx^2 = 0$$

Thus, the maximum extension in the spring is

$$x = \frac{2mg}{k}$$

Conclude: It is very important to remember that at maximum displacement, acceleration is not zero rather that velocity is zero.

Sample Problem 8-9

In the previous problem, find the maximum velocity.

Conceptualize/Classify: Velocity of the block will keep on increasing till the weight is greater than the spring force. When spring force becomes equal to weight of the block, it will have maximum velcoity at the instant, as after this the velocity starts to decrease.

Compute: Let us say that the extension of spring is x_2 when spring force is equal to weight of the block. Therefore,

$$Kx_2 = mg$$

thus,

$$x_2 = \frac{mg}{K}$$

Work done by gravity mgx_2

So, the work done by spring form $-\frac{1}{2}kx_2^2$

Applying work–kinetic energy theorem

$$mgx_2 - \frac{1}{2}kx_2^2 = \frac{1}{2}m\,v_{\text{mass}}^2 - 0$$

Substituting the value of $x_2 = mg/k$ in the above equation and solving we get

$$v_{\max} = \sqrt{\frac{mg^2}{k}}$$

Conclude: We can check that velocity of block is lower at any other point.

8-5 I Calculation of Work for Non-Uniform Force

One-Dimensional Analysis

Let us return to the situation of Fig. 8-2 but now consider the force to be in the positive direction of the x axis and the force magnitude to vary with position x. Thus, as the bead (particle) moves, the magnitude $F(x)$ of the force doing work on it changes. Only the magnitude of this variable force changes, not its direction, and the magnitude at any position does not change with time.

Figure 8-14*a* shows a plot of such a *one-dimensional variable force.* We want an expression for the work done on the particle by this force as the particle moves from an initial point x_i to a final point x_f. However, we *cannot* use the equation $W = Fd\cos\phi$ because it applies only for a constant force $\vec{F}$. Here, again, we shall use calculus. We divide the area under the curve of Fig. 8-14*a* into a number of narrow strips of width Δx (Fig. 8-14*b*). We choose Δx small enough to permit us to take the force $F(x)$ as being reasonably constant over that interval. We let $F_{j,\text{avg}}$ be the average value of $F(x)$ within the jth interval. Then in Fig. 8-14*b*, $F_{j,\text{avg}}$ is the height of the jth strip.

With $F_{j,\text{avg}}$ considered constant, the increment (small amount) of work ΔW_j done by the force in the jth interval is now approximately given by Eq. 8-7 and is

$$\Delta W_j = F_{j,\text{avg}}\,\Delta x \tag{8-29}$$

In Fig. 8-14*b*, ΔW_j is then equal to the area of the jth rectangular, shaded strip.

To approximate the total work W done by the force as the particle moves from x_i to x_f, we add the areas of all the strips between x_i and x_f in Fig. 8-14*b*:

$$W = \sum \Delta W_j = \sum F_{j,\text{avg}}\,\Delta x \tag{8-30}$$

Equation 8-30 is an approximation because the broken "skyline" formed by the tops of the rectangular strips in Fig. 8-14*b* only approximates the actual curve of $F(x)$.

We can make the approximation better by reducing the strip width Δx and using more strips (Fig. 8-14*c*). In the limit, we let the strip width approach zero; the number of strips then becomes infinitely large and we have, as an exact result,

$$W = \lim_{\Delta x \to 0} \sum F_{j,\text{avg}}\,\Delta x \tag{8-31}$$

This limit is exactly what we mean by the integral of the function $F(x)$ between the limits x_i and x_f. Thus, Eq. 8-31 becomes

$$W = \int_{x_i}^{x_f} F(x)\,dx \qquad \text{(work: variable force)} \tag{8-32}$$

If we know the function $F(x)$, we can substitute it into Eq. 8-32, introduce the proper limits of integration, carry out the integration, and thus find the work. (Appendix E contains a list of common integrals.) Geometrically, the work is equal to the area between the $F(x)$ curve and the x axis, between the limits x_i and x_f (shaded in Fig. 8-14*d*).

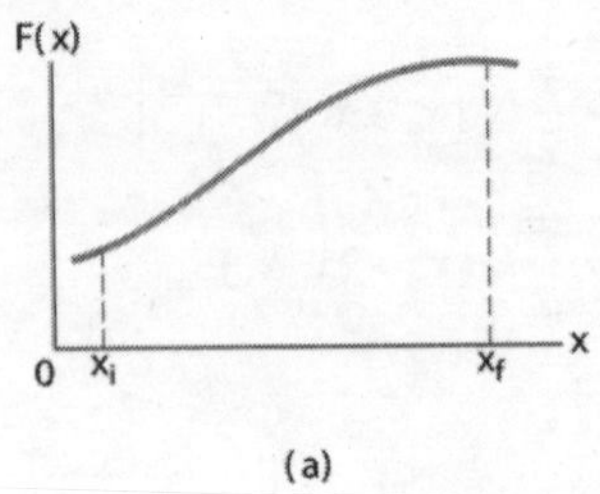

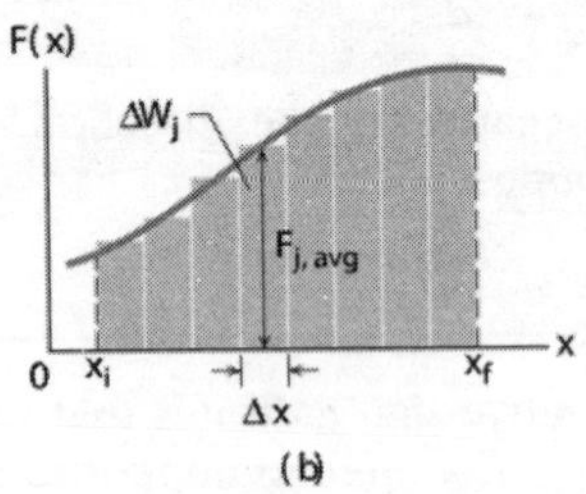

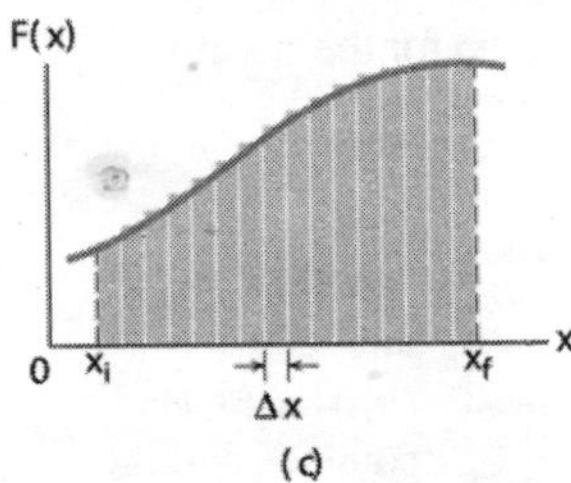

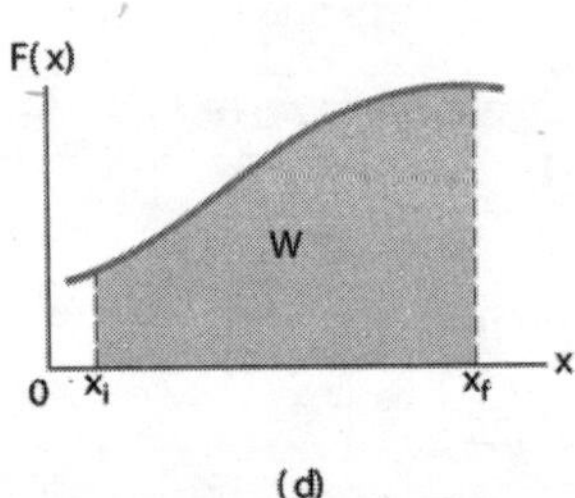

FIG. 8-14 (*a*) A one-dimensional force $\vec{F}(x)$ plotted against the displacement x of a particle on which it acts. The particle moves from x_i to x_f. (*b*) Same as (*a*) but with the area under the curve divided into narrow strips. (*c*) Same as (*b*) but with the area divided into narrower strips. (*d*) The limiting case. The work done by the force is given by Eq. 8-32 and is represented by the shaded area between the curve and the x axis and between x_i and x_f.

Three-Dimensional Analysis

Consider now a particle that is acted on by a three-dimensional force

$$\vec{F} = F_x\hat{\imath} + F_y\hat{\jmath} + F_z\hat{k} \tag{8-33}$$

in which the components F_x, F_y, and F_z can depend on the position of the particle; that is, they can be functions of that position. However, we make three simplifications: F_x may depend on x but not on y or z, F_y may depend on y but not on x or z, and F_z may depend on z but not on x or y. Now let the particle move through an incremental displacement

$$d\vec{r} = dx\hat{\mathrm{i}} + dy\hat{\mathrm{j}} + dz\hat{\mathrm{k}} \tag{8-34}$$

The increment of work dW done on the particle by $\vec{F}$ during the displacement $d\vec{r}$ is,

$$dW = \vec{F}\cdot d\vec{r} = F_x\,dx + F_y\,dy + F_z\,dz \tag{8-35}$$

The work W done by $\vec{F}$ while the particle moves from an initial position r_i having coordinates (x_i, y_i, z_i) to a final position r_f having coordinates (x_f, y_f, z_f) is then

$$W = \int_{r_i}^{r_f} dW = \int_{x_i}^{x_f} F_x\,dx + \int_{y_i}^{y_f} F_y\,dy + \int_{z_i}^{z_f} F_z\,dz \tag{8-36}$$

If $\vec{F}$ has only an x component, then the y and z terms in Eq. 8-36 are zero and the equation reduces to Eq. 8-32.

Work–Kinetic Energy Theorem with a Variable Force

Equation 8-32 gives the work done by a variable force on a particle in a one-dimensional situation. Let us now make certain that the calculated work is indeed equal to the change in kinetic energy of the particle, as the work–kinetic energy theorem states.

Consider a particle of mass m, moving along an x axis and acted on by a net force $F(x)$ that is directed along that axis. The work done on the particle by this force as the particle moves from position x_i to position x_f is given by Eq. 8-32 as

$$W = \int_{x_i}^{x_f} F(x)\,dx = \int_{x_i}^{x_f} ma\,dx \tag{8-37}$$

in which we use Newton's second law to replace $F(x)$ with ma. We can write the quantity $ma\,dx$ in Eq. 8-37 as

$$ma\,dx = m\frac{dv}{dt}\,dx \tag{8-38}$$

From the chain rule of calculus, we have

$$\frac{dv}{dt} = \frac{dv}{dx}\frac{dx}{dt} = \frac{dv}{dx}v \tag{8-39}$$

and Eq. 8-38 becomes

$$ma\,dx = m\frac{dv}{dx}v\,dx = mv\,dv \tag{8-40}$$

Substituting Eq. 8-40 into Eq. 8-37 yields

$$W = \int_{v_i}^{v_f} mv\,dv = m\int_{v_i}^{v_f} v\,dv$$

$$= \tfrac{1}{2}mv_f^2 - \tfrac{1}{2}mv_i^2 \tag{8-41}$$

Note that when we change the variable from x to v we are required to express the limits on the integral in terms of the new variable. Note also that because the mass m is a constant, we are able to move it outside the integral.

Recognizing the terms on the right side of Eq. 8-41 as kinetic energies allows us to write this equation as

$$W = K_f - K_i = \Delta K$$

which is the work–kinetic energy theorem.

Sample Problem 8-10

A 2.0 kg block moves along the x axis on a horizontal frictionless surface, accelerated by a force $F(x)$ that varies with the block's position as shown in Fig. 8-15.

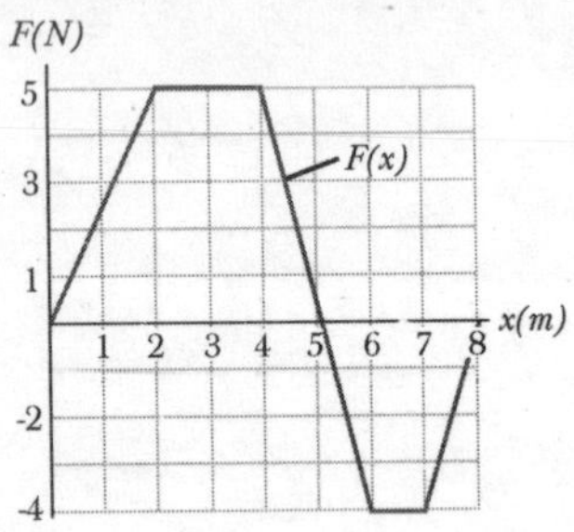

FIG. 8-15 Force experienced by the block plotted against position.

How much work is done on the block by the force as the block moves from its initial point at $x = 0$ to $x = 5$ m ?

Conceptualize: The work done by one-dimensional force is given by

$$W = \int_{x_i}^{x_f} F(x)\,dx$$

We have to calculate work done from $x = 0$ to $x = 5$ although graph goes till $x = 8$, and $F(x)$ is given by Fig. 8-15

Classify: We can easily evaluate the integral graphically from figure to do so, we make use of the fact that the area between the plot of $F(x)$ and the x axis between the limits $x_i = 0$ and $x_f = 5$, m is the value of integral.

Compute: Note that we can split that area into three parts: a right triangle at the left (from $x = 0$ to $x = 2$ m), a central rectangle (from $x = 2$ m to $x = 4$ m), and a triangle at the right (from $x = 4$ m to $x = 5$ m).

Recall that the area of a triangle is given by 1/2 (base) (height). The work $w_{0.5}$ that is done on the block from $x = 0$ and $x = 5$ m is then

$$w_{0.5} = \frac{1}{2}(2\,\text{m})(5\,\text{N}) + (2\,\text{m})(5\,\text{N}) + \frac{1}{2}(1\,\text{m})(5\,\text{m})$$

$$= 17.5\,\text{J} \qquad \text{(Answer)}$$

Conclude: Since force is always (from $x = 0$ to $x = 5$) acting along the displacement, in this particular case the work done should be positive and we see that it is positive.

Sample Problem 8-11

A particle moves from point $A(2, 1)$ to point $B(4, 4)$ along a straight line AB.

One of the force acting on the particle is a variable and is given by $\vec{F}\hat{i} = x_i + y^2\hat{j}$. Find the work done by this force.

Conceptualize: Since force is dependent on x and y coordinate, so we cannot use the relation $W = \vec{F}.\vec{S}$.

Classify: In order to solve this problem, we need to write the displacement $d\vec{s}$ in terms of small change in x and y coordinates.

Compute: If x-coordinate changes by dx and y coordinate by dy then the total displacement vector is vector sum of $dx\hat{i}$ and $dy\hat{j}$.

$$d\vec{s} = dx\hat{i} + dy\hat{j}$$

Thus, the small work dw done during this displacement by the force is given by

$$dw = \vec{F}\cdot\vec{ds}$$

Substituting the value of $\vec{F}$ and $\vec{ds}$, we get

$$dw = \left(x\hat{i} + y^2\hat{j}\right)\left(dx\hat{i} + dy^2\hat{j}\right)$$

On integrating $\int dw = w = \int\left(xdx + y^2dy\right)$

$$W = \int_2^4 x\,dx + \int_1^4 y^2\,dy$$

$$= \left.\frac{x^2}{2}\right|_2^4 + \left.\frac{y^3}{3}\right|_1^4$$

$$= \frac{16-4}{2} + \frac{64-1}{3}$$

$$= 6 + 21$$

$$= 27\,\text{J} \qquad \text{(Answer)}$$

Conclude: The work is coming out positive as you can verify that force and displacement vector are at an angle less than 90°.

8-6 | Validity of Work–Kinetic Energy Theorem in Inertial Reference Frames

Newton's second law of motion holds only in inertial reference frames. Another reference frame moving with a constant velocity relative to any inertial reference frame, is also considered an inertial reference frame. Many physical quantities when observed from different inertial frames, always give the same magnitude. For example, mass, time, length, acceleration, and force. Other quantities such as displacement, velocity, and hence kinetic energy have different values when measured in different inertial frames.

Two observers in different inertial frames will observe the same change in velocity vector in a given period of a moving particle. Thus, they will measure the same acceleration for a moving particle. But the change in kinetic energy for both observers will be different. The same observers in different inertial frames however are measuring different velocities, that is, they have measured different values for the displacement of a particle in a given period. But interestingly they measured the same values for the forces acting on the particle as force is independent of reference frame. *To conclude, two observers in two different inertial frames will observe same force but different displacement for a given particle.* Thus, they will measure different values for the work done on the particle.

Following example will clarify the above discussion and we will see how work–kinetic energy theorem is valid in different inertial frames.

Sample Problem 8-12

A worker on a railway cart is pushing a box. The cart is moving at a constant speed of 20 m/s by some external agent. The box has a mass of 25 kg, and is being pushed forward over a distance of 2 m on the cart by the worker at constant acceleration, increasing its speed from 0 to 2 m/s relative to car. (a) What will be the value of change in kinetic energy and work done by worker as calculated by Tenzing, who is standing on the cart.

Conceptualize/Classify: Fig. 8-16(*a*) shows the starting and finishing positions according to Tenzing who is riding on the cart.

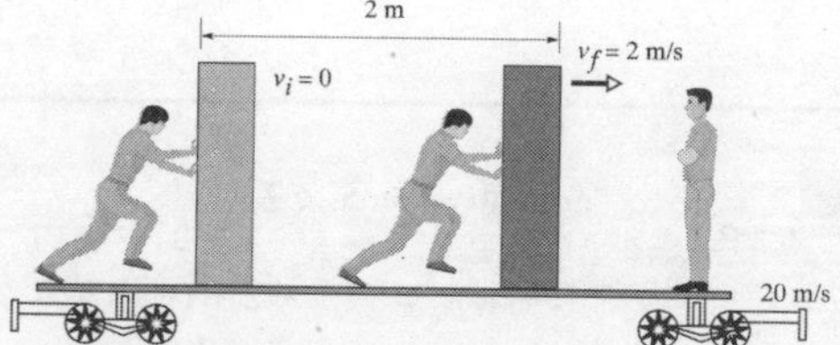

FIG. 8-16 (*a*) A worker pushing a box on a moving railway cart being observed from the cart itself.

Compute: The change in kinetic energy (Δk) as calculated by Tenzing is given by

$$\Delta K = K\hat{f} - K\hat{i} = 1/2\ (25\text{ kg})\ (2\text{ m/s}^2) - 0 = 50\text{ J}$$

because the initial velocity of the box is zero ($v_i = 0$) and its final velocity is 2 m/s ($v_f = 2$ m/s).*

The assumed constant acceleration of the box can be found from equation $v_f^2 - v_i^2 = 2\,as$ which gives

$$v_i = 0$$
$$v_f = 2\text{ m/s}$$
$$a = \frac{v_f^2 - v_i^2}{2s} = \frac{\left(2\text{ m/s}^2\right) - 0}{2(2\text{m})} = 1\text{ m/s}^2$$

This acceleration is due to the force applied by the worker. We can find net force applied by the worker

$$F = ma = (25\text{ kg})\ (1\text{ m/s}^2) = 25\text{ N}$$

As the box moves through a displacement of 2 m, the work done on the box by this force is

$$W = Fs = (25)\ (2\text{ m}) = 50\text{ J} \qquad \text{(Answer)}$$

Conclude: The observer on the train finds that $W = \Delta K$ and thus the work-energy theorem is valid.

(b) How does Girish standing on the ground interpret a similar measurement?

Conceptualize/Classify: Fig. 8-16(*b*) shows the starting and finishing positions according to Girish who is standing on the ground.

Compute: (We are using primed symbols to represent the measurements of the ground-based observer.) When the box is at rest on the railroad car, it is moving forward with a velocity of $v_1' = 20$ m/s according to Girish. After the box is pushed, the ground-based

*Note: Remember here that the observe is also riding on the cart, so in determining the kinetic energy, we have to consider velocity from tenzing's reference frame.

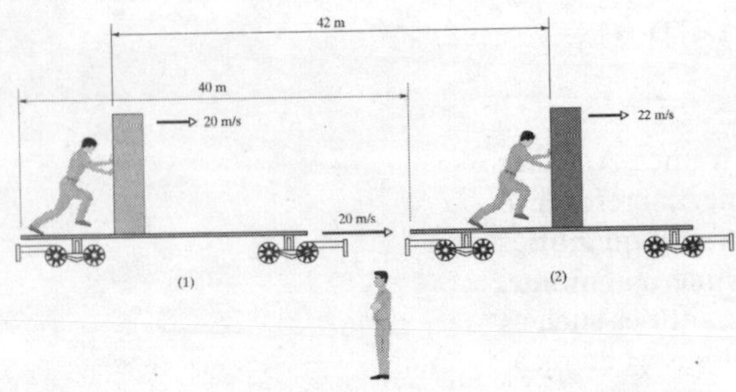

FIG. 8-16 (*b*) A worker pushing a box on a moving railway cart being observed from ground by Girish.

observer concludes its speed to be $v\hat{f}' = 22$ m/s. Girish determines the change in kinetic energy to be

$$\Delta K' = K_f' - K_i' = 1/2\, m v_f'^2 - 1/2\, m v_i'^2 = 1/2\,(25 \text{ kg})\,(22 \text{ m/s})^2 - 1/2\,(25 \text{ kg})\,(20 \text{ m/s})^2$$

$$= 1050 \text{ J}$$

As expected, this is different from what the observer on the train, Tenzing, measured for the change in kinetic energy ($\Delta K = 50$ J).

Let us calculate the work done on the box according to the ground-based observer Girish. The total displacement of the box also depends on the observer's reference frame, as Fig. 8-16(*b*) shows. To Girish, the force is exerted over a larger distance of 42 m because at a speed of 20 m/s, the train travels 40.0 m in 2 *s*, and the total displacement $\Delta s'$ of the box in this time is 40 m + 2 m = 42 m.

Force, on the other hand, is independent of reference frame, so for Girish, $F' = F = 25$ N. So, Girish, concludes that the work done by worker is

$$W' = F'\Delta s' = (25 \text{ N})\,(42 \text{ m}) = 1050 \text{ J} \quad \text{(Answer)}$$

Conclude: The work-energy theorem also holds for the ground-based observer. Even though the two observers find different values for displacements and velocities and thus calculate different values of work and kinetic energy but each finally concludes that work done is equal to change in kinetic energy.

8-7 | Work–Kinetic Theorem for a System (Collection of Particles)

While verifying work–kinetic energy theorem for a system of many particles, we must remember that work done by all the forces (external and internal) must be considered.

Otherwise this equation should be used separately on individual particles. (Although total work done by static friction, tension, and normal contact force that is by action and reaction on a system will always add up to zero.)

Sample Problem 8-13 Build your skill

Two block are kept over one another as shown in Fig. 8-17 Ground is smooth and friction coefficient between blocks is 0.5. Lower block is pulled by a uniform horizontal force of 15 N magnitude. Find final speed of blocks. Apply work–kinetic energy theorem on the blocks separately and verify that work done by friction between blocks adds to zero.

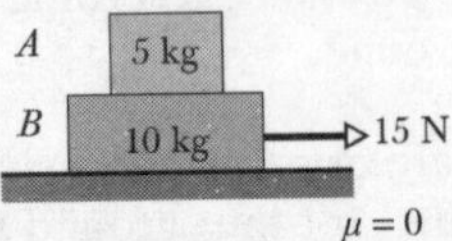

FIG. 8-17 Two block are kept over one another and Lower block is pulled by a uniform horizontal force.

Solution (i) For individual bodies

5 kg → 5

$$w_A = 5 \times 2$$

$$w_B = 15 \times 2 + (-5) \times 2$$

$$\Sigma W = 30 = kE_{\text{sys}} = 1/2 \times 10v^2 + 1/2 \times 5v^2$$

$$v = 2$$

(ii) We know work done by static friction will be zero because action–reaction will be in opposite direction but displacement of contact point will be same. Thus, $\vec{f}_A . d\vec{s}_A + \vec{f}_B . d\vec{s}_B = 0$ because $d\vec{s}_A = d\vec{s}_B$ but $\vec{f}_A = -\vec{f}_B$

Thus, $15 \times 2 = (1/2) \times 10v^2 + (1/2) \times 5v^2$

$v = 2$ (Answer)

8-8 | Potential Energy

One job of physics is to identify the different types of energy in the world, especially those that are of common importance. One general type of energy is **potential energy** U. Technically, potential energy is energy that can be associated with the configuration (arrangement) of a system of objects that exert forces on one another.

This is a pretty formal definition of something that is actually familiar to you. An example might help better than the definition: A bungee-cord jumper plunges from a staging platform (Fig. 8-18). The system of objects consists of Earth and the jumper. The force between the objects is the gravitational force. The configuration of the system changes (the separation between the jumper and Earth decreases—that is, of course, the thrill of the jump). We can account for the jumper's motion and increase in kinetic energy by defining a **gravitational potential energy** U. This is the energy associated with the state of separation between two objects that attract each other by the gravitational force, here the jumper and Earth.

When the jumper begins to stretch the bungee cord near the end of the plunge, the system of objects consists of the cord and the jumper. The force between the objects is an elastic (spring-like) force. The configuration of the system changes (the cord stretches). We can account for the jumper's decrease in kinetic energy and the cord's increase in length by defining an **elastic potential energy** U. This is the energy associated with the state of compression or extension of an elastic object, here the bungee cord.

Physics determines how the potential energy of a system can be calculated so that energy might be stored or put to use. For example, before any particular bungee-cord jumper takes the plunge, someone (probably a mechanical engineer) must determine the correct cord to be used by calculating the gravitational and elastic potential energies that can be expected. Then the jump is only thrilling and not fatal.

FIG. 8-18 The kinetic energy of a bungee-cord jumper increases during the free fall, and then the cord begins to stretch, slowing the jumper. *(KOFUJIWARA/amana images/ Getty Images News and Sport Services)*

8-8a | Work and Potential Energy

We have discussed the relation between work and a change in kinetic energy. Now we shall discuss the relation between work and a change in potential energy.

Let us throw a tomato upward (Fig. 8-19). We already know that as the tomato rises, the work W_g done on the tomato by the gravitational force is negative because the force transfers energy *from* the kinetic energy of the tomato. We can now finish the story by saying that this energy is transferred by the gravitational force *to* the gravitational potential energy of the tomato–Earth system.

The tomato slows, stops, and then begins to fall back down because of the gravitational force. During the fall, the transfer is reversed: The work W_g done on the tomato by the gravitational force is now positive—that force transfers energy *from* the gravitational potential energy of the tomato–Earth system *to* the kinetic energy of the tomato.

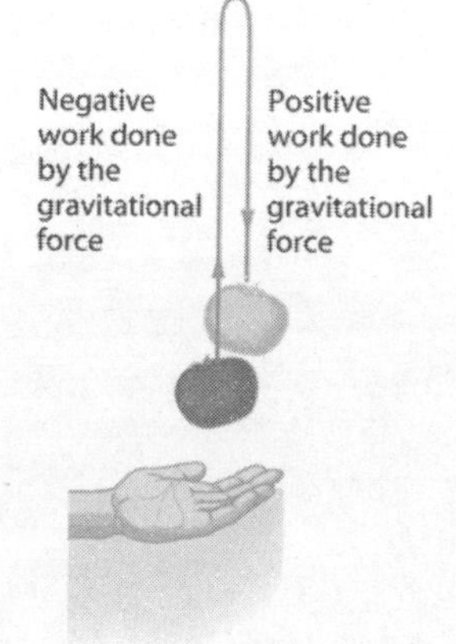

FIG. 8-19 A tomato is thrown upward. As it rises, the gravitational force does negative work on it, decreasing its kinetic energy. As the tomato descends, the gravitational force does positive work on it, increasing its kinetic energy.

For either rise or fall, the change ΔU in gravitational potential energy is defined as being equal to the negative of the work done on the tomato by the gravitational force. Using the general symbol W for work, we write this as

$$\Delta U = -W \tag{8-42}$$

This equation also applies to a block–spring system, as in Fig. 8-20. If we abruptly shove the block to send it moving rightward, the spring force acts leftward and thus does negative work on the block, transferring energy from the kinetic energy of the block to the elastic potential energy of the spring–block

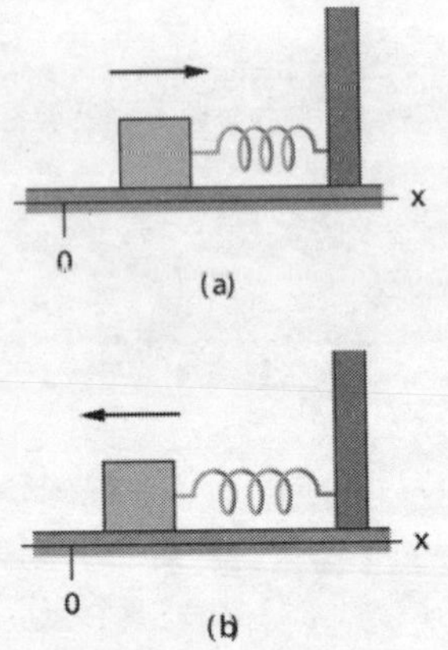

FIG. 8-20 A block, attached to a spring and initially at rest at $x = 0$, is set in motion toward the right. (*a*) As the block moves rightward (as indicated by the arrow), the spring force does negative work on it. (*b*) Then, as the block moves back toward $x = 0$, the spring force does positive work on it.

system. The block slows and eventually stops, and then begins to move leftward because the spring force is still leftward. The transfer of energy is then reversed—it is from potential energy of the spring–block system to kinetic energy of the block.

Conservative and Nonconservative Forces

Let us list the key elements of the two situations we just discussed:

1. The *system* consists of two or more objects.
2. A *force* acts between a particle-like object (tomato or block) in the system and the rest of the system.
3. When the system configuration changes, the force does *work* (call it W_1) on the particle-like object, transferring energy between the kinetic energy K of the object and some other type of energy of the system.
4. When the configuration change is reversed, the force reverses the energy transfer, doing work W_2 in the process.

In a situation in which $W_1 = -W_2$ is always true, the other type of energy is a potential energy and the force is said to be a **conservative force.** As you might suspect, the gravitational force and the spring force are both conservative (since otherwise we could not have spoken of gravitational potential energy and elastic potential energy, as we did previously).

A force that is not conservative is called a **nonconservative force.** The kinetic frictional force and drag force are nonconservative. For an example, let us send a block sliding across a floor that is not frictionless. During the sliding, a kinetic frictional force from the floor slows the block by transferring energy from its kinetic energy to a type of energy called *thermal energy* (which has to do with the random motions of atoms and molecules). We know from experiment that this energy transfer cannot be reversed (thermal energy cannot be transferred back to kinetic energy of the block by the kinetic frictional force). Thus, although we have a system (made up of the block and the floor), a force that acts between parts of the system, and a transfer of energy by the force, the force is not conservative. Therefore, thermal energy is not a potential energy.

When only conservative forces act on a particle-like object, we can greatly simplify otherwise difficult problems involving motion of the object. The next section, in which we develop a test for identifying conservative forces, provides one means for simplifying such problems.

8-8b | Path Independence of Conservative Forces

The primary test for determining whether a force is conservative or nonconservative is this: Let the force act on a particle that moves along any *closed path,* beginning at some initial position and eventually returning to that position (so that the particle makes a *round trip* beginning and ending at the initial position). The force is conservative only if the total energy it transfers to and from the particle during the round trip along this and any other closed path is zero. In other words:

> The net work done by a conservative force on a particle moving around any closed path is zero.

We know from experiment that the gravitational force passes this *closed-path test.* An example is the tossed tomato of Fig. 8-21. The tomato leaves the launch point with speed v_0 and kinetic energy $\frac{1}{2}mv_0^2$. The gravitational force acting on the tomato slows it, stops it, and then causes it to fall back down. When the tomato returns to the launch point, it again has speed v_0 and kinetic energy $\frac{1}{2}mv_0^2$. Thus, the gravitational force transfers as much energy *from* the tomato during the ascent as it transfers *to* the tomato during the descent back to the launch point. The net work done on the tomato by the gravitational force during the round trip is zero.

An important result of the closed-path test is that:

> The work done by a conservative force on a particle moving between two points does not depend on the path taken by the particle.

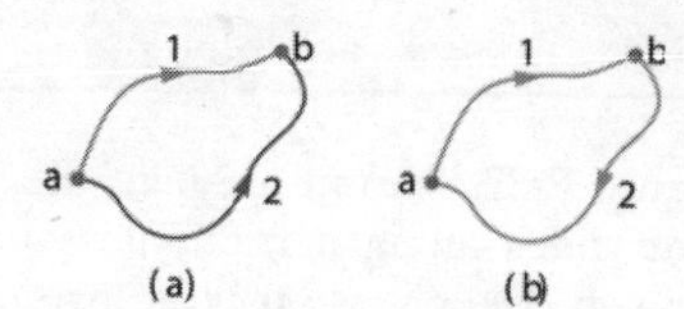

FIG. 8-21 (*a*) As a conservative force acts on it, a particle can move from point a to point b along either path 1 or path 2. (*b*) The particle moves in a round trip, from point a to point b along path 1 and then back to point a along path 2.

For example, suppose that a particle moves from point a to point b in Fig. 8-21a along either path 1 or path 2. If only a conservative force acts on the particle, then the work done on the particle is the same along the two paths. In symbols, we can write this result as

$$W_{ab,1} = W_{ab,2} \tag{8-43}$$

where the subscript ab indicates the initial and final points, respectively, and the subscripts 1 and 2 indicate the path.

This result is powerful because it allows us to simplify difficult problems when only a conservative force is involved. Suppose you need to calculate the work done by a conservative force along a given path between two points, and the calculation is difficult or even impossible without additional information. You can find the work by substituting some other path between those two points for which the calculation is easier and possible. Sample Problem 8-14 gives an example, but first we need to prove Eq. 8-43.

Proof of Equation 8-43

Figure 8-21b shows an arbitrary round trip for a particle that is acted upon by a single force. The particle moves from an initial point a to point b along path 1 and then back to point a along path 2. The force does work on the particle as the particle moves along each path. Without worrying about where positive work is done and where negative work is done, let us just represent the work done from a to b along path 1 as $W_{ab,1}$ and the work done from b back to a along path 2 as $W_{ba,2}$. If the force is conservative, then the net work done during the round trip must be zero:

$$W_{ab,1} + W_{ba,2} = 0$$

and thus

$$W_{ab,1} = -W_{ba,2} \tag{8-44}$$

In words, the work done along the outward path must be the negative of the work done along the path back.

Let us now consider the work $W_{ab,2}$ done on the particle by the force when the particle moves from a to b along path 2, as indicated in Fig. 8-21a. If the force is conservative, that work is the negative of $W_{ba,2}$:

$$W_{ab,2} = -W_{ba,2} \tag{8-45}$$

Substituting $W_{ab,2}$ for $-W_{ba,2}$ in Eq. 8-44, we obtain

$$W_{ab,1} = W_{ab,2}$$

which is what we set out to prove.

CHECKPOINT 2 The figure shows three paths connecting points a and b. A single force $\vec{F}$ does the indicated work on a particle moving along each path in the indicated direction. On the basis of this information, is force $\vec{F}$ conservative?

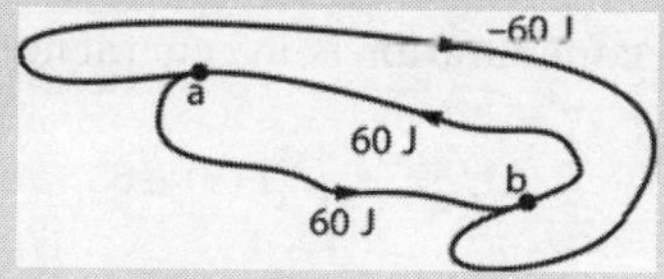

Sample Problem 8-14

Figure 8-22a shows a 2.0 kg block of slippery cheese that slides along a frictionless track from point a to point b. The cheese travels through a total distance of 2.0 m along the track, and a net vertical distance of 0.80 m. How much work is done on the cheese by the gravitational force during the slide?

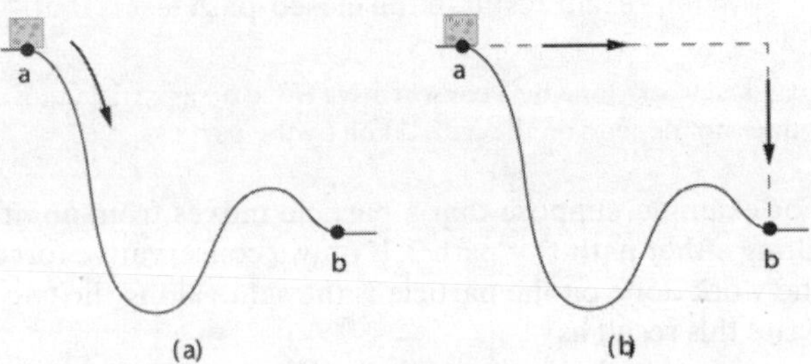

FIG. 8-22 (a) A block of cheese slides along a frictionless track from point a to point b. (b) Finding the work done on the cheese by the gravitational force is easier along the dashed path than along the actual path taken by the cheese; the result is the same for both paths.

Conceptualize: We *cannot* calculate the work by using the equation $W_g = mgd \cos \phi$. The reason is that the angle ϕ between the directions of the gravitational force $\vec{F}_g$ and the displacement $\vec{d}$ varies along the track in an unknown way. (Even if we did know the shape of the track and could calculate ϕ along it, the calculation could be very difficult.)

Classify: Because $\vec{F}_g$ is a conservative force, we can find the work by choosing some other path between a and b—one that makes the calculation easy.

Compute: Let us choose the dashed path in Fig. 8-22b; it consists of two straight segments. Along the horizontal segment, the angle ϕ is a constant 90°. Even though we do not know the displacement along that horizontal segment, the work W_h done there is

$$W_h = mgd \cos 90° = 0$$

Along the vertical segment, the displacement d is 0.80 m and, with $\vec{F}_g$ and $\vec{d}$ both downward, the angle ϕ is a constant 0°. Thus, for the work W_v done along the vertical part of the dashed path,

$$W_v = mgd \cos 0°$$
$$= (2.0 \text{ kg})(9.8 \text{ m/s}^2)(0.80 \text{ m})(1) = 15.7 \text{ J}$$

The total work done on the cheese by $\vec{F}_g$ as the cheese moves from point a to point b along the dashed path is then

$$W = W_h + W_v = 0 + 15.7 \text{ J} \approx 16 \text{ J} \quad \text{(Answer)}$$

Conclude: This should also be the kinetic energy as the cheese slides along the track from a and reaches b.

8-8c | Determining Potential Energy Values

Here we find equations that give the value of the two types of potential energy discussed in this chapter: gravitational potential energy and elastic potential energy. However, first we must find a general relation between a conservative force and the associated potential energy.

Consider a particle-like object that is part of a system in which a conservative force acts. When that force does work W on the object, the change ΔU in $\vec{F}$ the potential energy associated with the system is the negative of the work done. We wrote this fact as $\Delta U = -W$. For the most general case, in which the force may vary with position, we may write the work W as in Eq. 8-32:

$$W = \int_{x_i}^{x_f} F(x)\, dx \tag{8-46}$$

This equation gives the work done by the force when the object moves from point x_i to point x_f, changing the configuration of the system. (Because the force is conservative, the work is the same for all paths between those two points.)

Substituting Eq. 8-46 into Eq. 8-42, we find that the change in potential energy due to the change in configuration is, in general notation,

$$\Delta U = -\int_{x_i}^{x_f} F(x)\, dx \tag{8-47}$$

Gravitational Potential Energy

We first consider a particle with mass m moving vertically along a y axis (the positive direction is upward). As the particle moves from point y_i to point y_f, the gravitational force $\vec{F}_g$ does work on it. To find the corresponding change in the gravitational potential energy of the particle–Earth system, we use Eq. 8-47 with two changes: (1) We integrate along the y axis instead of the x axis, because the gravitational force acts vertically. (2) We substitute $-mg$ for the force symbol F, because $\vec{F}_g$ has the magnitude mg and is directed down the y axis. We then have

$$\Delta U = -\int_{y_i}^{y_f} (-mg)\, dy = mg \int_{y_i}^{y_f} dy = mg\Big[y\Big]_{y_i}^{y_f}$$

which yields

$$\Delta U = mg(y_f - y_i) = mg\,\Delta y \qquad (8\text{-}48)$$

Only *changes* ΔU in gravitational potential energy (or any other type of potential energy) are physically meaningful. However, to simplify a calculation or a discussion, we sometimes would like to say that a certain gravitational potential value U is associated with a certain particle–Earth system when the particle is at a certain height y. To do so, we rewrite Eq. 8-48 as

$$U - U_i = mg(y - y_i) \qquad (8\text{-}49)$$

Then we take U_i to be the gravitational potential energy of the system when it is in a **reference configuration** in which the particle is at a **reference point** y_i. Usually we take $U_i = 0$ and $y_i = 0$. Doing this changes Eq. 8-49 to

$$U(y) = mgy \qquad \text{(gravitational potential energy)} \qquad (8\text{-}50)$$

This equation tells us:

The gravitational potential energy associated with a particle–Earth system depends only on the vertical position y (or height) of the particle relative to the reference position $y = 0$, not on the horizontal position.

Elastic Potential Energy

We next consider the block–spring system shown in Fig. 8-22, with the block moving on the end of a spring of spring constant k. As the block moves from point x_i to point x_f, the spring force $F_x = -kx$ does work on the block. To find the corresponding change in the elastic potential energy of the block–spring system, we substitute $-kx$ for $F(x)$ in Eq. 8-47. We then have

$$\Delta U = -\int_{x_i}^{x_f} (-kx)\, dx = k \int_{x_i}^{x_f} x\, dx = \tfrac{1}{2}k\Big[x^2\Big]_{x_i}^{x_f}$$

or

$$\Delta U = \tfrac{1}{2}kx_f^2 - \tfrac{1}{2}kx_i^2 \qquad (8\text{-}51)$$

To associate a potential energy value U with the block at position x, we choose the reference configuration to be when the spring is at its relaxed length and the block is at $x_i = 0$. Then the elastic potential energy U_i is 0, and Eq. 8-51 becomes

$$U - 0 = \tfrac{1}{2}kx^2 - 0$$

which gives us

$$U(x) = \tfrac{1}{2}kx^2 \qquad \text{(elastic potential energy)} \qquad (8\text{-}52)$$

CHECKPOINT 3 A particle is to move along an x axis from $x = 0$ to x_1 while a conservative force, directed along the x axis, acts on the particle. The figure shows three situations in which the x component of that force varies with x. The force has the same maximum magnitude F_1 in all three situations. Rank the situations according to the change in the associated potential energy during the particle's motion, most positive first.

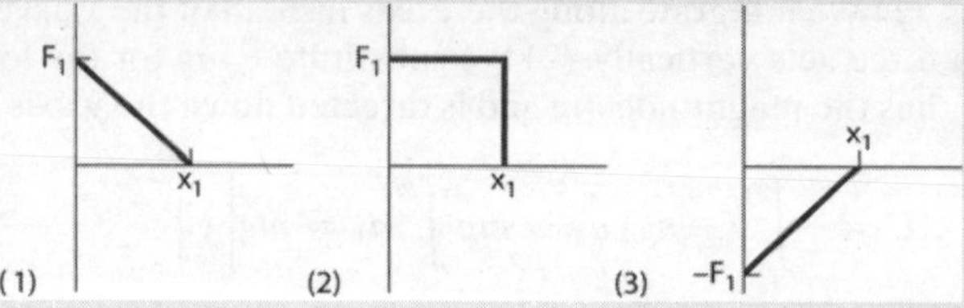

PROBLEM-SOLVING TACTICS

Tactic 1:* *Using the Term "Potential Energy" A potential energy is associated with a system as a whole. However, you might see statements that associate it with only part of the system. For example, you might read, "An apple hanging in a tree has a gravitational potential energy of 30 J." Such statements are often acceptable, but you should always keep in mind that the potential energy is actually associated with a system—here the apple–Earth system. Also keep in mind that assigning a particular potential energy value, such as 30 J here, to an object or even a system makes sense *only* if the reference potential energy value is known, as explored in Sample Problem 8-2.

Sample Problem 8-15

A 2.0 kg sloth hangs 5.0 m above the ground (Fig. 8-23). (a) What is the gravitational potential energy U of the sloth–Earth system if we take the reference point $y = 0$ to be (1) at the ground, (2) at a balcony floor that is 3.0 m above the ground, (3) at the limb, and (4) 1.0 m above the limb? Take the gravitational potential energy to be zero at $y = 0$.

Conceptualize/Classify: Once we have chosen the reference point for $y = 0$, we can calculate the gravitational potential energy U of the system *relative to that reference point* with Eq. 8-50.

Compute: For choice (1) the sloth is at $y = 5.0$ m, and

$$U = mgy = (2.0\text{ kg})(9.8\text{ m/s}^2)(5.0\text{ m})$$
$$= 98\text{ J} \qquad \text{(Answer)}$$

For the other choices, the values of U are

(2) $U = mgy = mg(2.0\text{ m}) = 39\text{ J}$

(3) $U = mgy = mg(0) = 0\text{ J}$,

(4) $U = mgy = mg(-1.0\text{ m})$

$$= -19.6\text{ J} \approx -20\text{ J} \qquad \text{(Answer)}$$

(b) The sloth drops to the ground. For each choice of reference point, what is the change ΔU in the potential energy of the sloth–Earth system due to the fall?

Conceptualize/Classify: The *change* in potential energy does not depend on the choice of the reference point for $y = 0$; instead, it depends on the change in height Δy.

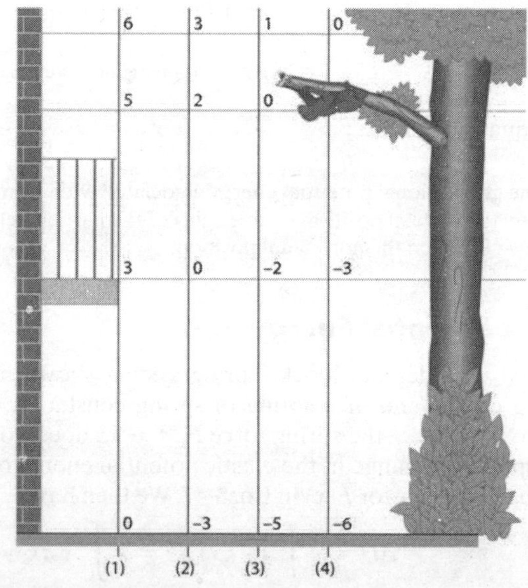

FIG. 8-23 Four choices of reference point $y = 0$. Each y axis is marked in units of meters. The choice affects the value of the potential energy U of the sloth–Earth system. However, it does not affect the change ΔU in potential energy of the system if the sloth moves by, say, falling.

Compute: For all four situations, we have the same $\Delta y = -5.0$ m. Thus, for (1) to (4), Eq. 8-48 tells us that

$$\Delta U = mg\,\Delta y = (2.0\text{ kg})(9.8\text{ m/s}^2)(-5.0\text{ m})$$
$$= -98\text{ J} \qquad \text{(Answer)}$$

Conclude: As sloth is going down, its potential decreases.

8-9 | Work Energy Theorem

As we have learnt from work–kinetic energy theorem, if some forces are acting on a body then some of the work done by individual forces acting on it is equal to change in kinetic energy.

$$W_1 + W_2 + \cdots\cdots + W_n = KE_f - KF_i$$

If some of them is conservative and others are non-conservative then for conservative forces we can write potential energy

$$\Sigma W_c + \Sigma W_{nc} = KE_f - KE_i$$

$$\Sigma \{-(U_f - U_i)\} + \Sigma W_{nc} = KE_f - KE_i$$

$$\Sigma W_{nc} = KE_f - KE_i + \Sigma(U_f - U_i)$$

The term on RHS is often called mechanical energy. To conclude, effect of a force can either be written as work on LHS or it can come as potential energy on RHS.

CHECKPOINT 4 The figure shows four situations—one in which an initially stationary block is dropped and three in which the block is allowed to slide down frictionless ramps. (a) Rank the situations according to the kinetic energy of the block at point B, greatest first. (b) Rank them according to the speed of the block at point B, greatest first.

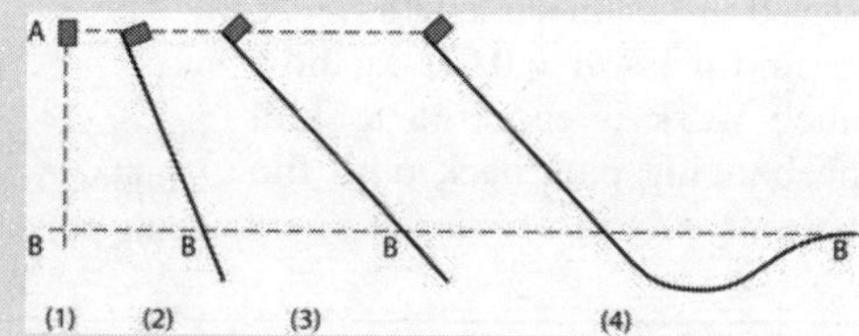

Sample Problem 8-16 Build your skill

In Fig. 8-24, a child of mass m is released from rest at the top of a water slide, at height h = 8.5 m above the bottom of the slide. Assuming that the slide is frictionless because of the water on it, find the child's speed at the bottom of the slide.

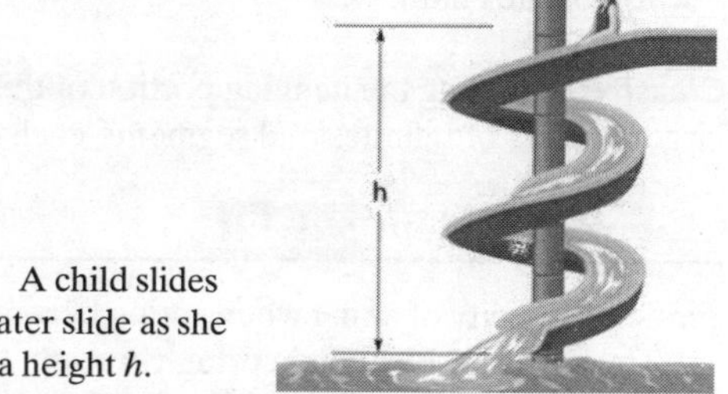

FIG. 8-24 A child slides down a water slide as she descends a height h.

Conceptualize: We cannot find her speed at the bottom by using her acceleration along the slide as we might have in earlier chapters because we do not know the slope (angle) of the slide. However, because that speed is related to her kinetic energy, perhaps we can use the principle of conservation of mechanical energy to get the speed. Then we would not need to know the slope.

Classify: Mechanical energy is conserved in a system *if* the system is isolated and *if* only conservative forces cause energy transfers within it. Let's check.

Forces: Two forces act on the child. The *gravitational force,* a conservative force, does work on her. The *normal force* on her from the slide does no work because its direction at any point during the descent is always perpendicular to the direction in which the child moves.

System: Because the only force doing work on the child is the gravitational force, we choose the child–Earth system as our system, which we can take to be isolated.

Thus, we have only a conservative force doing work in an isolated system, so we *can* use the principle of conservation of mechanical energy.

Compute: Let the mechanical energy be $E_{mec,t}$ when the child is at the top of the slide and $E_{mec,b}$ when she is at the bottom. Then the conservation principle tells us

$$E_{mec,b} = E_{mec,t} \tag{8-53}$$

To show both kinds of mechanical energy, we have

$$K_b + U_b = K_t + U_t \tag{8-54}$$

or

$$\tfrac{1}{2}mv_b^2 + mgy_b = \tfrac{1}{2}mv_t^2 + mgy_t$$

Dividing by m and rearranging yield

$$v_b^2 = v_t^2 + 2g(y_t - y_b)$$

Putting $v_t = 0$ and $y_t - y_b = h$ leads to

$$v_b = \sqrt{2gh} = \sqrt{(2)(9.8\text{ m/s}^2)(8.5\text{ m})}$$

$$= 13\text{ m/s} \qquad \text{(Answer)}$$

This is the same speed that the child would reach if she fell 8.5 m vertically. On an actual slide, some frictional forces would act and the child would not be moving quite so fast.

Conclude: Although this problem is hard to solve directly with Newton's laws, using conservation of mechanical energy makes the solution much easier. However, if we were asked to find the time taken for the child to reach the bottom of the slide, energy methods would be of no use; we would need to know the shape of the slide, and we would have a difficult problem.

PROBLEM-SOLVING TACTICS

Tactic 2: Conservation of Mechanical Energy Asking the following questions will help you to solve problems involving the principle of conservation of mechanical energy.

For what system is mechanical energy conserved? You should be able to separate your system from its environment. Imagine drawing a closed surface such that whatever is inside is your system and whatever is outside is the environment of that system.

Is friction or drag present? If friction or drag is present, mechanical energy is not conserved.

Is your system isolated? The principle of conservation of mechanical energy applies only to isolated systems. That means that no *external forces* (forces exerted by objects outside the system) should do work on the objects in the system.

What are the initial and final states of your system? The system changes from some initial configuration to some final configuration. You apply the principle of conservation of mechanical energy by saying that E_{mec} has the same value in both these configurations. Be very clear about what these two configurations are.

Sample Problem 8-17

In Fig. 8-25, a chain is held on a frictionless table with one fourth of its length hanging over the edge. If the chain has length $L = 28$ cm and mass $m = 0.012$ kg, how much work is required to pull the hanging part back onto the table?

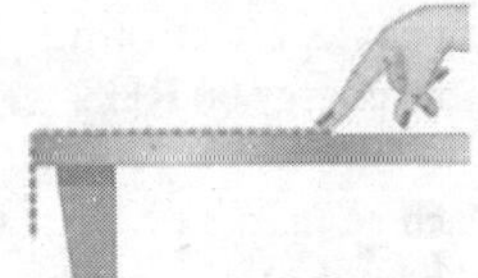

FIG. 8-25 A chain hanging from a table is being pulled up.

Conceptualize: The work done required to pull the chain back onto the table is the change in the gravitational potential energy, that is, stored in the hanging portion of the chain.

Classify: Dividing the hanging portion of the chain into a large number of infinitesimal segments, each of length dy.

Compute: We note that the mass of a segment is (m/L) dy and the potential energy of a segment when it is a distance below the table top is

$$dU = (m/L)\, g|y|\, dy = -(m/L)\, gy\, dy$$

The $-$ve sign is because y is negative-valued (we have $+y$ upward and the origin is at the tabletop). The total potential energy is obtained by integrating the above relation with respect to y.

$$U = -\frac{m\,g}{L}\int_{-L/4}^{0} y\, dy = \frac{1}{2}\frac{m\,g}{L}(L/4)^2 = m\,g\,L/32$$

The work required to pull the chain onto the table is therefore

$$W = \Delta U = mgL/32 = (0.012\,\text{kg})(9.8\,\text{m/s}^2)(0.28\,\text{m})/32 = 0.0010\,\text{J}$$

Conclude: As the potential energy as increased, the work has to be done and so the work is coming out as positive.

Sample Problem 8-18

Find the velocity of a ring when spring becomes horizontal. The spring is ideal and spring constant $K = 400$ N m. Mass of ring is 10 kg. Natural length of spring is 4 m. The ring initially holded in the position shown in Fig. 8-26.

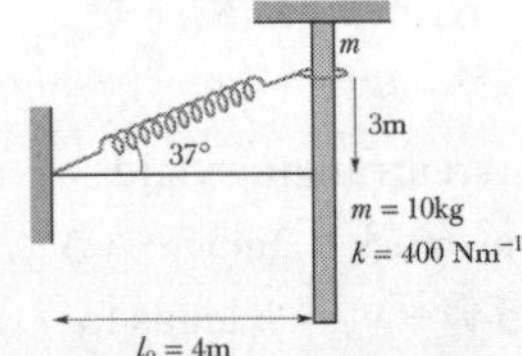

FIG. 8-26 A ring moving on a vertical rod attached to a spring.

Conceptualize: The ring will move downward under the action of two forces (1) the gravitational pull on the ring and (2) the vertical component of the spring force

Classify: As the ring is going down, its kinetic energy will keep on increasing due to positive work being done by spring and gravity. We spring as part of the system, so we can write potential energy of spring rather than work done by spring force on the ring.

Compute: According to work-energy theorem,

$$W = K_f - K_i + U_{sf} - U_{si}$$

Here U_s represents PE of spring at its initial and final position. Work done by gravity, $W_g = mgh = (10\text{ kg})\ (10\text{ m/s}^{-2})\ (3\text{ m}) = 300\text{ J} = \text{W}$. $K_i = 0$ since the particle is at rest initially and $k_f = 1/2\ mv^2{}_f$ (v_f is the final velocity). Initial length of spring is hypotenuse of the right triangle whose extention is $x_i = 5 - 4 = 1$ m.

Finally, when spring becomes horizontal, the extension $x_f = 0$ the spring reaches its natural length. Putting all the values in equation

$$300 = \left(\frac{1}{2} \times 10v_f^2 - 0\right) + \left(0 - \frac{1}{2} \times 400 \times (1)^2\right)$$

Solving we get $v_f = 10$ m/s.

Conclude: This speed should be greater than if the ring would have gained if fall freely over 3 m distance. This is because the ring (using the relation $v_f^2 - v_i^2 = 2gh$ and $v_i = 0$) has gained kinetic energy due to gravity and also due to spring's loss of potential energy.

The answer for falling freely for 3 m speed is

$$v_f = \sqrt{2\times10\times3} = \sqrt{60}$$

Thus, as expected, our answer is larger than $\sqrt{60}$.

No Friction Involved

To compete in a bowling-ball-hurling contest, you first squat and cup your hands under the ball on the floor. Then you rapidly straighten up while also pulling your hands up sharply, launching the ball upward at about face level. During your upward motion, your applied force on the ball obviously does work; that is, it is an external force that transfers energy, but to what system?

To answer, wc check to see which energies change. There is a change ΔK in the ball's kinetic energy and, because the ball and Earth become more separated, there is a change ΔU in the gravitational potential energy of the ball–Earth system. To include both changes, we need to consider the ball–Earth system. Then your force is an external force doing work on that system, and the work is

$$W = \Delta K + \Delta U \tag{8-55}$$

or

$$W = \Delta E_{mec} \quad \text{(work done on system, no friction involved)} \tag{8-56}$$

where ΔE_{mec} is the change in the mechanical energy of the system. These two equations, which are represented in Fig. 8-27, are equivalent energy statements for work done on a system by an external force when friction is not involved.

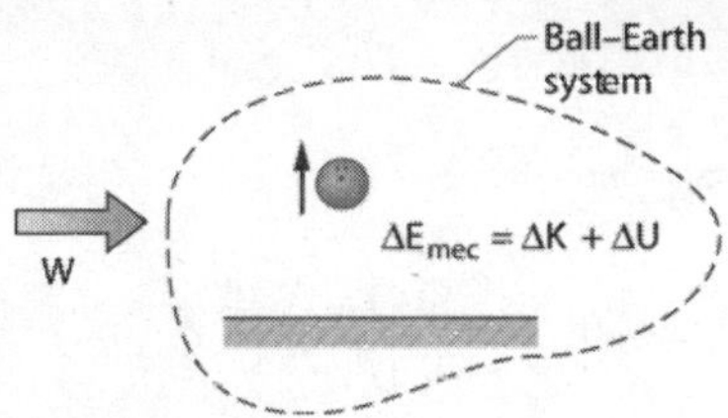

FIG. 8-27 Positive work W is done on a system of a bowling ball and Earth, causing a change ΔE_{mec} in the mechanical energy of the system, a change ΔK in the ball's kinetic energy, and a change ΔU in the system's gravitational potential energy.

Friction Involved

We next consider the example in Fig. 8-28*a*. A constant horizontal force $\vec{F}$ pulls a block along an x axis and through a displacement of magnitude d, increasing the block's velocity from $\vec{v}_0$ to $\vec{v}$. During the motion, a constant kinetic frictional force $\vec{f}_k$ from the floor acts on the block. Let us first choose the block as our system and apply Newton's second law to it. We can write that law for components along the x axis ($F_{net,x} = ma_x$) as

$$F - f_k = ma \tag{8-57}$$

Because the forces are constant, the acceleration $\vec{a}$ is also constant. Thus, we can use Eq.

$$v^2 = v_0^2 + 2ad$$

Solving this equation for a, substituting the result into Eq. 8-57, and rearranging then give us

$$Fd = \tfrac{1}{2}mv^2 - \tfrac{1}{2}mv_0^2 + f_k d \tag{8-58}$$

or, because $\frac{1}{2}mv^2 - \frac{1}{2}mv_0^2 = \Delta K$ for the block,

$$Fd = \Delta K + f_k d \tag{8-59}$$

In a more general situation (say, one in which the block is moving up a ramp), there can be a change in potential energy. To include such a possible change, we generalize Eq. 8-59 by writing

$$Fd = \Delta E_{mec} + f_k d \tag{8-60}$$

By experiment we find that the block and the portion of the floor along which it slides become warmer as the block slides. The temperature of an object is related to the object's thermal energy E_{th} (the energy associated with the random motion of the atoms and molecules in the object). Here, the thermal energy of the block and floor increases because (1) there is friction between them and (2) there is sliding. Recall that friction is due to the cold-welding between two surfaces. As the block slides over the floor, the sliding causes repeated tearing and re-forming of the welds between the block and the floor, which makes the block and floor warmer. Thus, the sliding increases their thermal energy E_{th}.

Through experiment, we find that the increase ΔE_{th} in thermal energy is equal to the product of the magnitudes f_k and d:

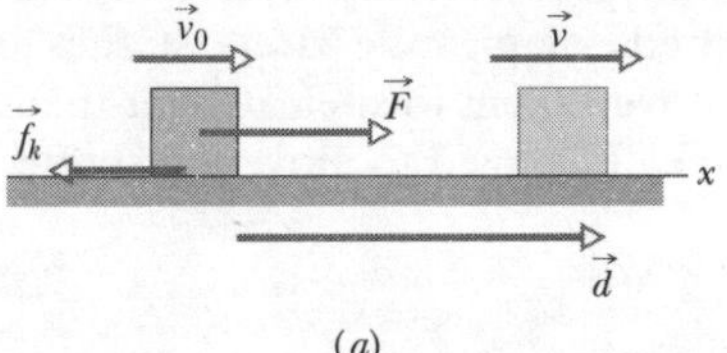

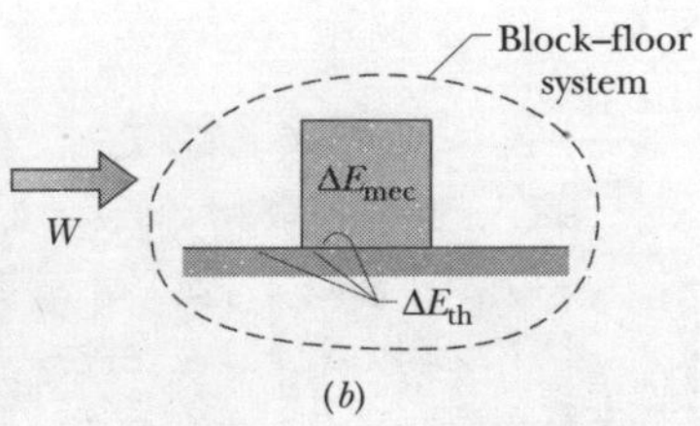

FIG. 8-28 (*a*) A block is pulled across a floor by force $\vec{F}$ while a kinetic frictional force $\vec{f}_k$ opposes the motion. The block has velocity $\vec{v}_0$ at the start of a displacement $\vec{d}$ and velocity $\vec{v}$ at the end of the displacement. (*b*) Positive work W is done on the block–floor system by force $\vec{F}$, resulting in a change ΔE_{mec} in the block's mechanical energy and a change ΔE_{th} in the thermal energy of the block and floor.

$$\Delta E_{th} = f_k d \qquad \text{(increase in thermal energy by sliding)} \qquad (8\text{-}61)$$

Thus, we can rewrite Eq. 8-60 as

$$Fd = \Delta E_{mec} + \Delta E_{th} \qquad (8\text{-}62)$$

Fd is the work W done by the external force $\vec{F}$ (the energy transferred by the force), but on which system is the work done (where are the energy transfers made)? To answer, we check to see which energies change. The block's mechanical energy changes, and the thermal energies of the block and floor also change. Therefore, the work done by force $\vec{F}$ is done on the block–floor system. That work is

$$W = \Delta E_{mec} + \Delta E_{th} \qquad \text{(work done on system, friction involved)} \qquad (8\text{-}63)$$

This equation, which is represented in Fig. 8-28*b*, is the energy statement for the work done on a system by an external force when friction is involved.

CHECKPOINT 5 In three trials, a block is pushed by a horizontal applied force across a floor that is not frictionless, as in Fig. 8-28*a*. The magnitudes F of the applied force and the results of the pushing on the block's speed are given in the table. In all three trials, the block is pushed through the same distance d. Rank the three trials according to the change in the thermal energy of the block and floor that occurs in that distance d, greatest first.

Trial	F	Result on Block's Speed
a	5.0 N	decreases
b	7.0 N	remains constant
c	8.0 N	increases

Sample Problem 8-19

The prehistoric people of Easter Island carved hundreds of gigantic stone statues in a quarry and then moved them to sites all over the island (Fig. 8-29). How they managed to move the statues by as much as 10 km without the use of sophisticated machines has been hotly debated. They most likely cradled each statue in a wooden sled and then pulled the sled over a "runway" consisting of almost identical logs acting as rollers. In a modern reenactment of this technique, 25 men were able to move a 9000 kg Easter Island–type statue 45 m over level ground in 2 min.

FIG. 8-29 Easter Island stone statues. *(©LMR Group/Alamy Images)*

(a) Estimate the work the net force $\vec{F}$ from the men did during the 45 m displacement of the statue, and determine the system on which that force did the work.

Conceptualize/Classify: (1) We can calculate the work done with Eq. $W = Fd \cos \phi$. (2) To determine the system on which the work is done we see which energies change.

Compute: In Eq. $W = Fd$ cos, d is the distance 45 m, F is the magnitude of the net force on the statue from the 25 men, and $\phi = 0°$. Let us estimate that each man pulled with a force magnitude equal to twice his weight, which we take to be the same value mg for all the men. Thus, the magnitude of the net force from the men was $F = (25)(2mg) = 50mg$. Estimating a man's mass as 80 kg, we can then write equation as

$$W = Fd\cos\phi = 50mgd\cos\phi$$
$$= (50)(80\text{ kg})(9.8\text{ m/s}^2)(45\text{ m})\cos 0°$$
$$= 1.8\times 10^6\text{ J} \approx 2\text{ MJ} \qquad \text{(Answer)}$$

Conclude: Because the statue moved, there was certainly a change ΔK in its kinetic energy during the motion. We can easily guess that there must have been considerable kinetic friction between the sled, logs, and ground, resulting in a change ΔE_{th} in their thermal energies. Thus, the system on which the work was done consisted of the statue, sled, logs, and ground.

(b) What was the increase ΔE_{th} in the thermal energy of the system during the 45 m displacement?

Conceptualize/Classify: We can relate ΔE_{th} to the work W done by $\vec{F}$ with the energy statement of Eq. 8-63 for a system that involves friction:

$$W = \Delta E_{mec} + \Delta E_{th}$$

Compute: We know the value of W from (a). The change ΔE_{mec} in the statue's mechanical energy was zero because the statue was stationary at the beginning and the end of the move and its elevation did not change. Thus, we find

$$\Delta E_{th} = W = 1.8\times 10^6\text{ J} \approx 2\text{ MJ} \quad \text{(Answer)}$$

(c) Estimate the work that would have been done by the 25 men if they had moved the statue 10 km across level ground on Easter Island. Also estimate the total change ΔE_{th} that would have occurred in the statue–sled–logs–ground system.

Compute: We calculate W as in (a), but with 1×10^4 m substituted for d. Also, we again equate ΔE_{th} to W. We get

$$W = \Delta E_{th} = 3.9\times 10^8\text{ J} \approx 400\text{ MJ} \quad \text{(Answer)}$$

Conclude: This would have been a staggering amount of energy for the men to have transferred during the movement of a statue. Still, the 25 men *could* have moved the statue 10 km without some mysterious energy source.

Sample Problem 8-20

A food shipper pushes a wood crate of cabbage heads (total mass $m = 14$ kg) across a concrete floor with a constant horizontal force $\vec{F}$ of magnitude 40 N. In a straight-line displacement of magnitude $d = 0.50$ m, the speed of the crate decreases from $v_0 = 0.60$ m/s to $v = 0.20$ m/s.

(a) How much work is done by force $\vec{F}$, and on what system does it do the work?

Conceptualize/Classify: Because the applied force $\vec{F}$ is constant, we can calculate the work it does by using Eq. $W = Fd\cos\phi$.

Compute: Substituting given data, including the fact that force $\vec{F}$ and displacement $\vec{d}$ are in the same direction, we find

$$W = Fd\cos\phi = (40\text{ N})(0.50\text{ m})\cos 0°$$
$$= 20\text{ J} \qquad \text{(Answer)}$$

Conclude: We can determine the system on which the work is done to see which energies change. Because the crate's speed changes, there is certainly a change ΔK in the crate's kinetic energy. Is there friction between the floor and the crate, and thus a change in thermal energy? Note that $\vec{F}$ and the crate's velocity have the same direction. Thus, if there is no friction, then $\vec{F}$ should be accelerating the crate to a *greater* speed. However, the crate is *slowing,* so there must be friction and a change ΔE_{th} in thermal energy of the crate and the floor. Therefore, the system on which the work is done is the crate–floor system, because both energy changes occur in that system.

(b) What is the increase ΔE_{th} in the thermal energy of the crate and floor?

Conceptualize/Classify: We can relate ΔE_{th} to the work W done by $\vec{F}$ with the energy statement of Eq. 8-63 for a system that involves friction:

$$W = \Delta E_{mec} + \Delta E_{th} \qquad (8\text{-}64)$$

Compute: We know the value of W from (a). The change ΔE_{mec} in the crate's mechanical energy is just the change in its kinetic energy because no potential energy changes occur, so we have

$$\Delta E_{mec} = \Delta K = \tfrac{1}{2}mv^2 - \tfrac{1}{2}mv_0^2$$

Substituting this into Eq. 8-64 and solving for ΔE_{th}, we find

$$\Delta E_{th} = W - (\tfrac{1}{2}mv^2 - \tfrac{1}{2}mv_0^2) = W - \tfrac{1}{2}m(v^2 - v_0^2)$$
$$= 20\text{ J} - \tfrac{1}{2}(14\text{ kg})[(0.20\text{ m/s})^2 - (0.60\text{ m/s})^2]$$
$$= 22.2\text{ J} \approx 22\text{ J} \qquad \text{(Answer)}$$

Sample Problem 8-21 Build your skill

If block of mass m goes round in horizontal circle find work done by friction (given coefficient of friction is m_k) for one turn.

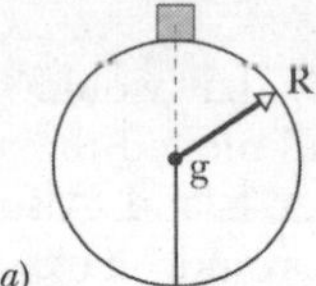

FIG. 8-30 (*a*) A block moving in a horizontal circular path. (*b*) The figure shows the work done by the block.

Solution: At all points of time direction of friction is varying but it is always opposite to displacement. Thus

$$dW = \vec{F}.d\vec{S}$$
$$\hat{F} = -\hat{S}$$

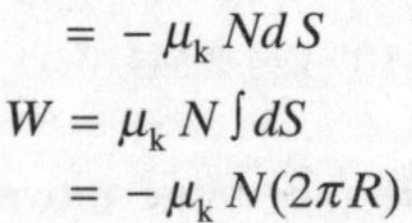

$$= -\mu_k N dS$$
$$W = \mu_k N \int dS$$
$$= -\mu_k N(2\pi R)$$

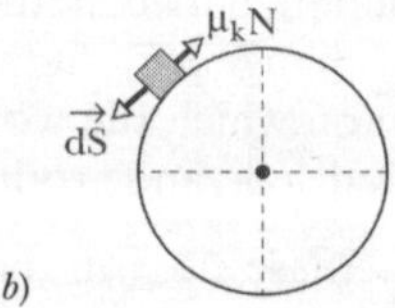

8-10 | Conservation of Energy

FIG. 8-31 To descend, the rock climber must transfer energy from the gravitational potential energy of a system consisting of him, his gear, and Earth. He has wrapped the rope around metal rings so that the rope rubs against the rings. This allows most of the transferred energy to go to the thermal energy of the rope and rings rather than to his kinetic energy. *(Tyler Stableford/The Image Bank/ Getty Images)*

We now have discussed several situations in which energy is transferred to or from objects and systems, much like money is transferred between accounts. In each situation we assume that the energy that was involved could always be accounted for; that is, energy could not magically appear or disappear. In more formal language, we assumed (correctly) that energy obeys a law called the **law of conservation of energy,** which is concerned with the **total energy** E of a system. That total is the sum of the system's mechanical energy, thermal energy, and any type of *internal energy* in addition to thermal energy. (We have not yet discussed other types of internal energy.) The law states that

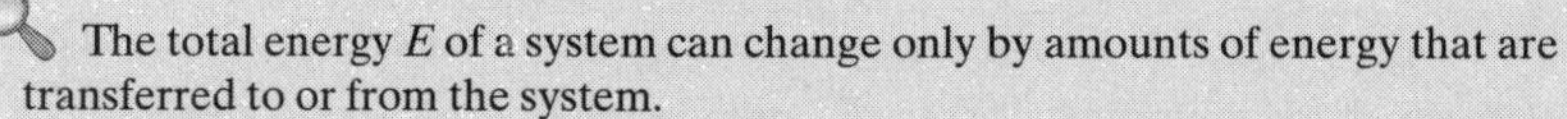

The total energy E of a system can change only by amounts of energy that are transferred to or from the system.

The only type of energy transfer that we have considered is work W done on a system. Thus, for us at this point, this law states that

$$W = \Delta E = \Delta E_{mec} + \Delta E_{th} + \Delta E_{int} \quad (8\text{-}65)$$

where ΔE_{mec} is any change in the mechanical energy of the system, ΔE_{th} is any change in the thermal energy of the system, and ΔE_{int} is any change in any other type of internal energy of the system. Included in ΔE_{mec} are changes ΔK in kinetic energy and changes ΔU in potential energy (elastic, gravitational, or any other type we might find).

This law of conservation of energy is *not* something we have derived from basic physics principles. Rather, it is a law based on countless experiments. Scientists and engineers have never found an exception to it.

Isolated System

If a system is isolated from its environment, there can be no energy transfers to or from it. For that case, the law of conservation of energy states:

The total energy E of an isolated system cannot change.

Many energy transfers may be going on *within* an isolated system—between, say, kinetic energy and a potential energy or between kinetic energy and thermal energy. However, the total of all the types of energy in the system cannot change.

We can use the rock climber in Fig. 8-31 as an example, approximating him, his gear, and Earth as an isolated system. As he rappels down the rock face, changing the configuration of the system, he needs to control the transfer of energy from the gravitational potential energy of the system. (That energy cannot just disappear.) Some of it is transferred to his kinetic energy. However, he obviously does not want very much transferred to that type or he will be moving too quickly, so he has wrapped the rope around metal rings to produce friction between the rope and the rings as he moves down. The sliding of the rings on the rope then transfers the gravitational potential energy of the system to thermal energy of the rings and rope in a way that he can control. The total energy of the climber–gear–Earth system (the total of its gravitational potential energy, kinetic energy, and thermal energy) does not change during his descent.

For an isolated system, the law of conservation of energy can be written in two ways. First, by setting $W = 0$ in Eq. 8-66, we get

$$\Delta E_{\text{mec}} + \Delta E_{\text{th}} + \Delta E_{\text{int}} = 0 \quad \text{(isolated system)} \tag{8-66}$$

We can also let $\Delta E_{\text{mec}} = E_{\text{mec},2} - E_{\text{mec},1}$, where the subscripts 1 and 2 refer to two different instants—say, before and after a certain process has occurred. Then Eq. 8-66 becomes

$$E_{\text{mec},2} = E_{\text{mec},1} - \Delta E_{\text{th}} - \Delta E_{\text{int}} \tag{8-67}$$

Equation 8-67 tells us:

> In an isolated system, we can relate the total energy at one instant to the total energy at another instant *without considering the energies at intermediate times.*

This fact can be a very powerful tool in solving problems about isolated systems when you need to relate energies of a system before and after a certain process occurs in the system.

In earlier section we discussed a special situation for isolated systems—namely, the situation in which nonconservative forces (such as a kinetic frictional force) do not act within them. In that special situation, ΔE_{th} and ΔE_{int} are both zero, and so Eq. 8-67 reduces to Eq. 8-67. In other words, the mechanical energy of an isolated system is conserved when nonconservative forces do not act in it.

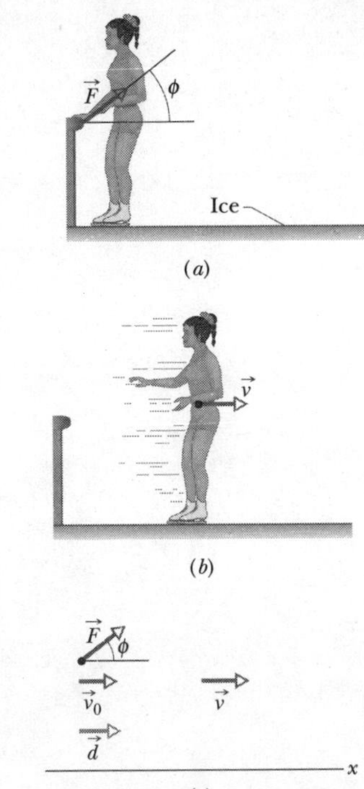

FIG. 8-32 (*a*) As a skater pushes herself away from a railing, the force on her from the railing is $\vec{F}$. (*b*) After the skater leaves the railing, she has velocity $\vec{v}$. (*c*) External force $\vec{F}$ acts on the skater, at angle ϕ with a horizontal x axis. When the skater goes through displacement $\vec{d}$, her velocity is changed from $\vec{v}_0 (= 0)$ to $\vec{v}$ by the horizontal component of $\vec{F}$.

External Forces and Internal Energy Transfers

An external force can change the kinetic energy or potential energy of an object without doing work on the object—that is, without transferring energy to the object. Instead, the force is responsible for transfers of energy from one type to another inside the object.

Figure 8-32 shows an example. An initially stationary ice-skater pushes away from a railing and then slides over the ice (Figs. 8-32*a* and *b*). Her kinetic energy increases because of an external force $\vec{F}$ on her from the rail. However, that force does not transfer energy from the rail to her. Thus, the force does no work on her. Rather, her kinetic energy increases as a result of internal transfers from the biochemical energy in her muscles.

Figure 8-33 shows another example. An engine increases the speed of a car with four-wheel drive (all four wheels are made to turn by the engine). During the acceleration, the engine causes the tires to push backward on the road surface. This push produces frictional forces $\vec{f}$ that act on each tire in the forward direction. The net external force $\vec{F}$ from the road, which is the sum of these frictional forces, accelerates the car, increasing its kinetic energy. However, $\vec{F}$ does not transfer energy from the road to the car and so does no work on the car.

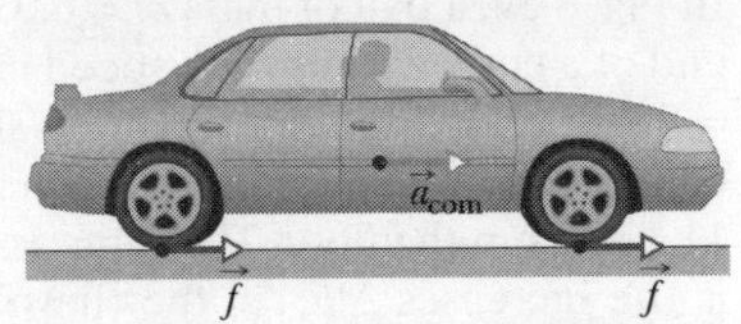

FIG. 8-33 A vehicle accelerates to the right using four-wheel drive. The road exerts four frictional forces (two of them shown) on the bottom surfaces of the tires. Taken together, these four forces make up the net external force $\vec{F}$ acting on the car.

Rather, the car's kinetic energy increases as a result of internal transfers from the energy stored in the fuel.

In situations like these two, we can sometimes relate the external force $\vec{F}$ on an object to the change in the object's mechanical energy if we can simplify the situation. Consider the ice-skater example. During her push through distance d in Fig. 8-32*c*, we can simplify by assuming that the acceleration is constant, her speed changing from $v_0 = 0$ to v. (That is, we assume $\vec{F}$ has constant magnitude F and angle ϕ.) After the push, we can simplify the skater as being a particle and neglect the fact that the exertions of her muscles have increased the thermal energy in her muscles and changed other physiological features. Then we can apply the equation $\frac{1}{2}mv^2 - \frac{1}{2}mv_0^2 = F_x d$ to write

$$K - K_0 = (F\cos\phi)d$$

or

$$\Delta K = Fd\cos\phi \tag{8-68}$$

If the situation also involves a change in the elevation of an object, we can include the change ΔU in gravitational potential energy by writing

$$\Delta U + \Delta K = Fd\cos\phi \tag{8-69}$$

The force on the right side of this equation does no work on the object but is still responsible for the changes in energy shown on the left side.

Power

Power is defined as the rate at which work is done by a force. In a more general sense, power P is the rate at which energy is transferred by a force from one type to another. If an amount of energy ΔE is transferred in an amount of time Δt, the **average power** due to the force is

$$P_{avg} = \frac{\Delta E}{\Delta t} \tag{8-70}$$

Similarly, the **instantaneous power** due to the force is

$$P = \frac{dE}{dt} \tag{8-71}$$

Sample Problem 8-22

In Fig. 8-34, a ball of mass $m = 6.0$ kg slides onto the left end of a curved ramp with speed $v_o = 7.8$ m/s at height $y_o = 8.5$ m above the floor. It then slides to the right and comes to a momentary stop when it reaches a height $y = 11.1$ m from the floor. The ramp is not frictionless. What is the increases ΔE_{th} in the thermal energy of the ball and ramp because of the sliding?

Conceptualize/Classify: A Key Idea to get us started is to examine all the forces on the ball, and then see if we have an isolated system or a system on which an external force is doing work.

Compute: The normal force on the ball from the ramp does no work on the ball, because its direction is always perpendicular to that of the ball's displacement. The gravitational force on the ball does do work as the ball's elevation changes. Because there is friction between the ball and the ramp, the sliding increases their thermal energy.

Conclude: The ball—ramp—Earth system includes all these forces and e nergy transfers in one isolated system. Then a second Key Idea is that, because the system is isolated, its total energy cannot change. We can apply the

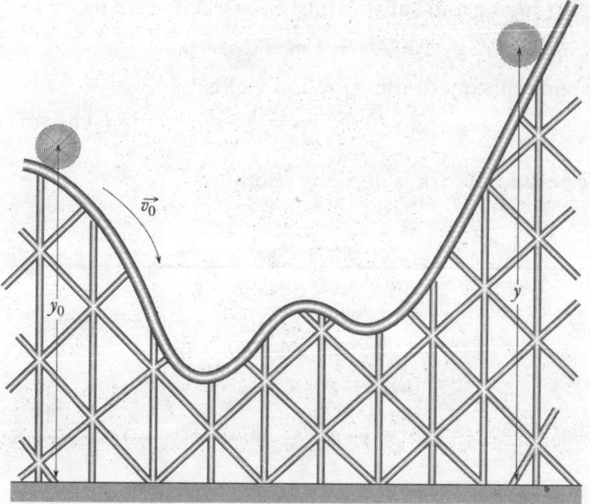

FIG. 8-34 A ball slides along a curved ramp, starting with speed v_0 at the height y_0 and reaching a height y at which it momentarily stops.

law of conservation of energy in the form of Eq. 8-72 to this system:

$$\Delta E_{mec} + \Delta E_{th} = 0 \quad (8\text{-}72)$$

where the energy changes occur between the initial state and the state when the ball stops momentarily. Also, the change ΔK in the kinetic energy of the ball and the change ΔU in the gravitational potential energy of the system, where

$$\Delta K = 0 - \frac{1}{2}mv_0^2$$

and

$$\Delta U = mgy - mgy_0$$

Substituting these expressions into Eq. 8-72 and solving for ΔE_{th} yields

$$\Delta E_{th} = \frac{1}{2}mv_0^2 - mg\,(y - y_0)$$

$$= \frac{1}{2}(6.0\text{ Kg})(7.8\text{ m/s})^2$$

$$- (6.0\text{ Kg})(9.8\text{ m/s}^2)(11.1\text{ m} - 8.5\text{ m})$$

$$\approx 30\text{ J} \quad \text{(Answer)}$$

Sample Problem 8-23

In Fig. 8-35, a 2.0 kg package of tamales slides along a floor with speed $v_1 = 4.0$ m/s. It then runs into and compresses a spring, until the package momentarily stops. Its path to the initially relaxed spring is frictionless, but as it compresses the spring, a kinetic frictional force from the floor, of magnitude 15 N, acts on the package. If $k = 10\,000$ N/m, by what distance d is the spring compressed when the package stops?

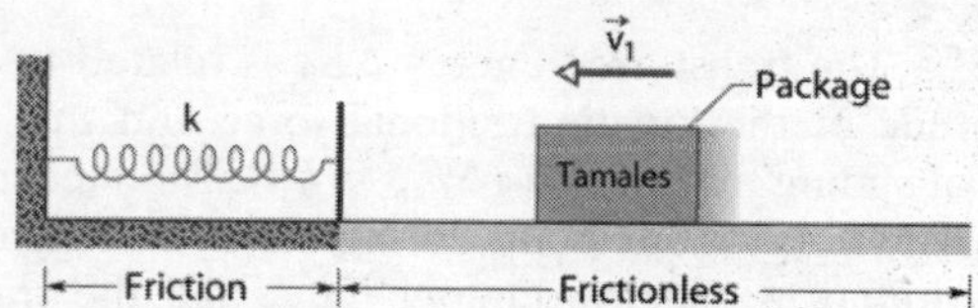

FIG. 8-35 A package slides across a frictionless floor with velocity $\vec{v}_1$ toward a spring of spring constant k. When the package reaches the spring, a frictional force from the floor acts on the package.

Conceptualize: We need to examine all the forces and then to determine whether we have an isolated system or a system on which an external force is doing work.

Classify: *Forces:* The normal force on the package from the floor does no work on the package because the direction of this force is always perpendicular to the direction of the package's displacement. For the same reason, the gravitational force on the package does no work. As the spring is compressed, however, a spring force does work on the package, transferring energy to elastic potential energy of the spring. The spring force also pushes against a rigid wall. Because there is friction between the package and the floor, the sliding of the package across the floor increases their thermal energies.

System: The package–spring–floor–wall system includes all these forces and energy transfers in one isolated system. Therefore, because the system is isolated, its total energy cannot change. We can then apply the law of conservation of energy in the form of Eq. 8-73 to the system:

$$E_{mec,2} = E_{mec,1} - \Delta E_{th} \quad (8\text{-}73)$$

Compute: In Eq. 8-73, let subscript 1 correspond to the initial state of the sliding package and subscript 2 correspond to the state in which the package is momentarily stopped and the spring is compressed by distance d. For both states the mechanical energy of the system is the sum of the package's kinetic energy ($K = ½\,mv^2$) and the spring's potential energy ($U = ½\,kx^2$). For state 1, $U = 0$ (because the spring is not compressed), and the package's speed is v_1. Thus, we have

$$E_{mec,1} = K_1 + U_1 = \tfrac{1}{2}mv_1^2 + 0$$

For state 2, $K = 0$ (because the package is stopped), and the compression distance is d. Therefore, we have

$$E_{mec,2} = K_2 + U_2 = 0 + \tfrac{1}{2}kd^2$$

Finally, by Eq. 8-61, we can substitute $f_k d$ for the change ΔE_{th} in the thermal energy of the package and the floor. We can now rewrite Eq. 8-42 as

$$\tfrac{1}{2}kd^2 = \tfrac{1}{2}mv_1^2 - f_k d$$

Rearranging and substituting known data give us

$$5000d^2 + 15d - 16 = 0$$

Solving this quadratic equation yields

$$d = 0.055 \text{ m} = 5.5 \text{ cm} \qquad \text{(Answer)}$$

Conclude: Work is done by friction.

Sample Problem 8-24

Figure 8-36*a* shows the mountain slope and the valley along which a rock avalanche moves. The rocks have a total mass m, fall from a height $y = H$, move a distance d_1 along a slope of angle $\theta = 45°$, and then move a distance d_2 along a flat valley. What is the ratio d_2/H of the runout to the fall height if the coefficient of kinetic friction has the reasonable value of 0.60?

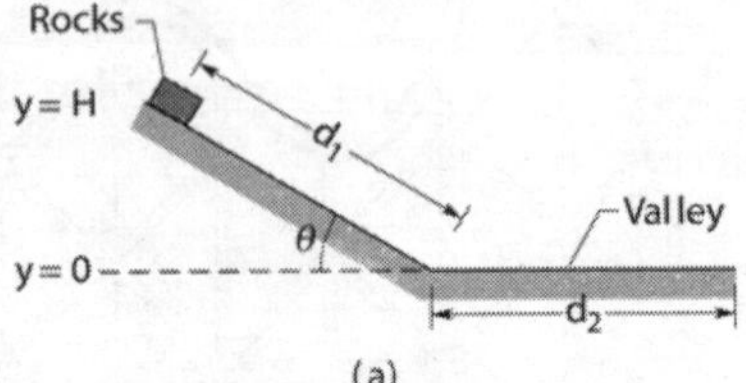

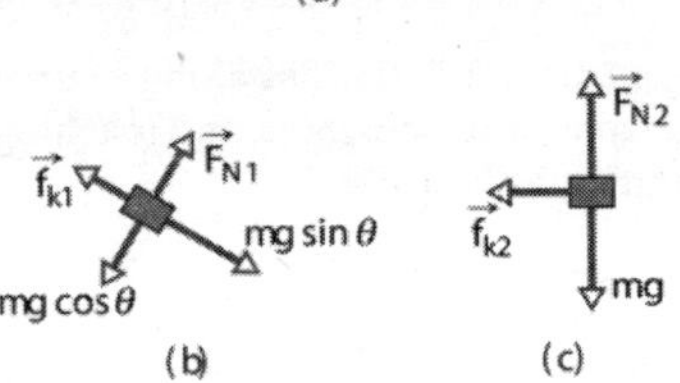

FIG. 8-36 (*a*) The path a rock avalanche takes down a mountainside and across a valley floor. The forces on the rock material along (*b*) the mountainside and (*c*) the valley floor.

Conceptualize: The mechanical energy E_{mec} of the rocks–Earth system is the sum of the kinetic energy ($K = 1/2\ mv^2$)and the gravitational potential energy ($U = mgy$). The mechanical energy is not conserved during the slide because a (nonconservative) frictional force acts on the rocks, transferring an amount of energy ΔE_{th} to the thermal energy of the rocks and ground.

Classify: The transferred energy ΔE_{th} is related to the magnitude of the kinetic frictional force and the distance of sliding by Eq. 8-74 ($\Delta E_{th} = f_k d$). The mechanical energy $E_{mec,2}$ at any point during the slide is related to the initial mechanical energy $E_{mec,1}$ and the transferred energy ΔE_{th} by Eq. 8-74, which can be rewritten as $E_{mec,2} = E_{mec,1} - \Delta E_{th}$.

Compute: The final mechanical energy $E_{mec,2}$ is equal to the initial mechanical energy $E_{mec,1}$ minus the amount ΔE_{th} lost to thermal energy:

$$E_{mec,2} = E_{mec,1} - \Delta E_{th} \qquad (8\text{-}74)$$

Initially the rocks have potential energy $U = mgH$ and kinetic energy $K = 0$, and so the initial mechanical energy is $E_{mec,1} = mgH$. Finally (when the rocks stop) the rocks have potential energy $U = 0$ and kinetic energy $K = 0$, and so $E_{mec,2} = 0$. The amount of energy transferred to thermal energy is $\Delta E_{th,1} = f_{k1}d_1$ during the slide down the slope and $\Delta E_{th,2} = f_{k2}d_2$ during the runout across the valley. Substituting these expressions into Eq. 8-74, we have

$$0 = mgH - f_{k1}d_1 - F_{k2}d_2 \qquad (8\text{-}75)$$

From Fig. 8-36*a*, we see that $d_1 = H/(\sin\theta)$. To obtain expressions for the kinetic frictional forces, we use the equation ($f_k = \mu_k F_N$). On an inclined plane the normal force offsets the component $mg\cos\theta$ of the gravitational force (Fig. 8-36*b*). Similarly, on a horizontal surface the normal force offsets the full magnitude mg of the gravitational force (Fig. 8-32*c*). Substituting these expressions into Eq. 8-75 and solving for the ratio d_2/H, we find

$$0 = mgH - \mu_k(mg\cos\theta)\frac{H}{\sin\theta} - \mu_k mgd_2$$

and

$$\frac{d_2}{H} = \left(\frac{1}{\mu_k} - \frac{1}{\tan\theta}\right) \qquad (8\text{-}76)$$

Substituting $\mu_k = 0.60$ and $\theta = 45°$, we find

$$\frac{d_2}{H} = 0.67 \qquad \text{(Answer)}$$

Conclude: Our result is typical for a small avalanche. However, for a large avalanche, the ratio d_2/H may be as large as 20. If you substitute this ratio into Eq. 8-76 and solve for the coefficient of kinetic friction, you find $\mu_k = 0.05$. Researchers do not understand how a large avalanche of jagged, tumbling rocks can have a value of μ_k small enough to rival that of very slippery ice. One of the most promising ideas is that the material is continuously levitated by a thin layer of small oscillating debris and thus almost never touches the mountain slope or valley floor until the avalanche stops.

Sample Problem 8-25

In Fig. 8-37*a*, a 20 kg block is about to collide with a spring at its relaxed length. As the block compresses the spring, a kinetic frictional force between the block and floor acts on the block. Figure 8-37*b* gives the block's kinetic energy $K(x)$ and the spring's potential energy $U(x)$ as functions of the block's position x as the spring is compressed. What is the coefficient of kinetic friction μ_k between the block and floor?

Conceptualize: The mechanical energy E_{mec} $(= K + U)$ is not conserved during the compression because the nonconservative frictional force acts on the block, transferring an amount of energy ΔE_{th} to the thermal energy of the block and floor.

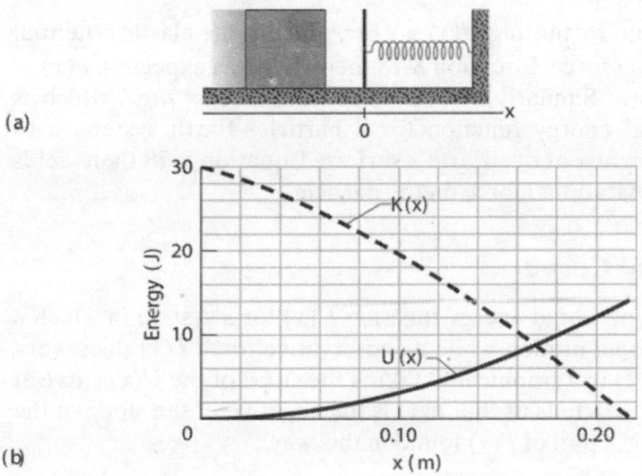

FIG. 8-37 (*a*) Block on the verge of colliding with a spring. (*b*) The change of kinetic energy K and potential energy U as the spring is compressed and the block slows to a stop.

Classify: The transferred energy ΔE_{th} is related to the magnitude of the kinetic frictional force and the distance of sliding by Eq. 8-61 ($\Delta E_{th} = f_k d$). The mechanical energy $E_{mec,2}$ at any point during the compression is related to the initial mechanical energy $E_{mec,1}$ and ΔE_{th} by Eq. 8-67, which can be rewritten as $E_{mec,2} = E_{mec,1} - \Delta E_{th}$.

Compute: Finding ΔE_{th}: From Fig. 8-33*b*, we see that when the block is at $x = 0$ and is on the verge of compressing the spring, its kinetic energy is $K = 30$ J and the spring's potential energy is $U = 0$. Thus, the sum of K and U is

$$E_{mec,1} = 30 \text{ J}$$

The spring is at its maximum compression when the block stops—that is, when the kinetic energy drops to 0. From the figure we see that this occurs at $x \approx 0.215$ m, at which $K = 0$ and $U = 14$ J. Thus, at the stopping point, the sum of K and U is

$$E_{mec,2} = 14 \text{ J}$$

To find the amount of energy transferred to thermal energy, we write $E_{mec,2} = E_{mec,1} - \Delta E_{th}$ as

$$14 \text{ J} - 30 \text{ J} - \Delta E_{th}$$

or

$$\Delta E_{th} = 16 \text{ J}$$

Finding μ_k: We know that a kinetic frictional force is given by $f_k = \mu_k F_N$, where the normal force is given by $F_N = mg$. Here, the frictional force f_k transfers 16 J to thermal energy over distance $d = 0.215$ m, according to $\Delta E_{th} = f_k d$. Pulling these several expressions together, we write

$$\Delta E_{th} = f_k d = \mu_k F_N d = \mu_k mgd$$

and then substitute the data $\Delta E_{th} = 16$ J, $m = 20$ kg, $g = 9.8 \text{ m/s}^2$, and $d = 0.215$ m, finding

$$\mu_k = 0.38 \qquad \text{(Answer)}$$

Conclude: This is similar to numerical interpretelations made earlier except that information is given graphically.

8-11 | Relation Between Conservative Force and Potential Energy

Once again we consider a particle that is part of a system in which a conservative force acts. This time suppose that the particle is constrained to move along an x axis while the conservative force does work on it. We can learn a lot about the motion of the particle from a plot of the system's potential energy $U(x)$. However, before we discuss such plots, we need one more relationship.

Finding the Force Analytically

Equation 8-77 tells us how to find the change ΔU in potential energy between two points in a one-dimensional situation if we know the force $F(x)$. Now we want to go the other way; that is, we know the potential energy function $U(x)$ and want to find the force.

For one-dimensional motion, the work W done by a force that acts on a particle as the particle moves through a distance Δx is $F(x)\,\Delta x$. We can then write

$$\Delta U(x) = -W = -F(x)\,\Delta x \tag{8-77}$$

Solving for $F(x)$ and passing to the differential limit yield

$$F(x) = -\frac{dU(x)}{dx} \quad \text{(one-dimensional motion)} \tag{8-78}$$

which is the relation we sought.

We can check this result by putting $U(x) = \frac{1}{2}kx^2$, which is the elastic potential energy function for a spring force. Equation 8-78 then yields, as expected, $F(x) = -kx$, which is Hooke's law. Similarly, we can substitute $U(x) = mgx$, which is the gravitational potential energy function for a particle–Earth system, with a particle of mass m at height x above Earth's surface. Equation 8-78 then yields $F = -mg$, which is the gravitational force on the particle.

The Potential Energy Curve

Figure 8-38*a* is a plot of a potential energy function $U(x)$ for a system in which a particle is in one-dimensional motion while a conservative force $F(x)$ does work on it. We can easily find $F(x)$ by (graphically) taking the slope of the $U(x)$ curve at various points. (Equation 8-78 tells us that $F(x)$ is the negative of the slope of the $U(x)$ curve.) Figure 8-38*b* is a plot of $F(x)$ found in this way.

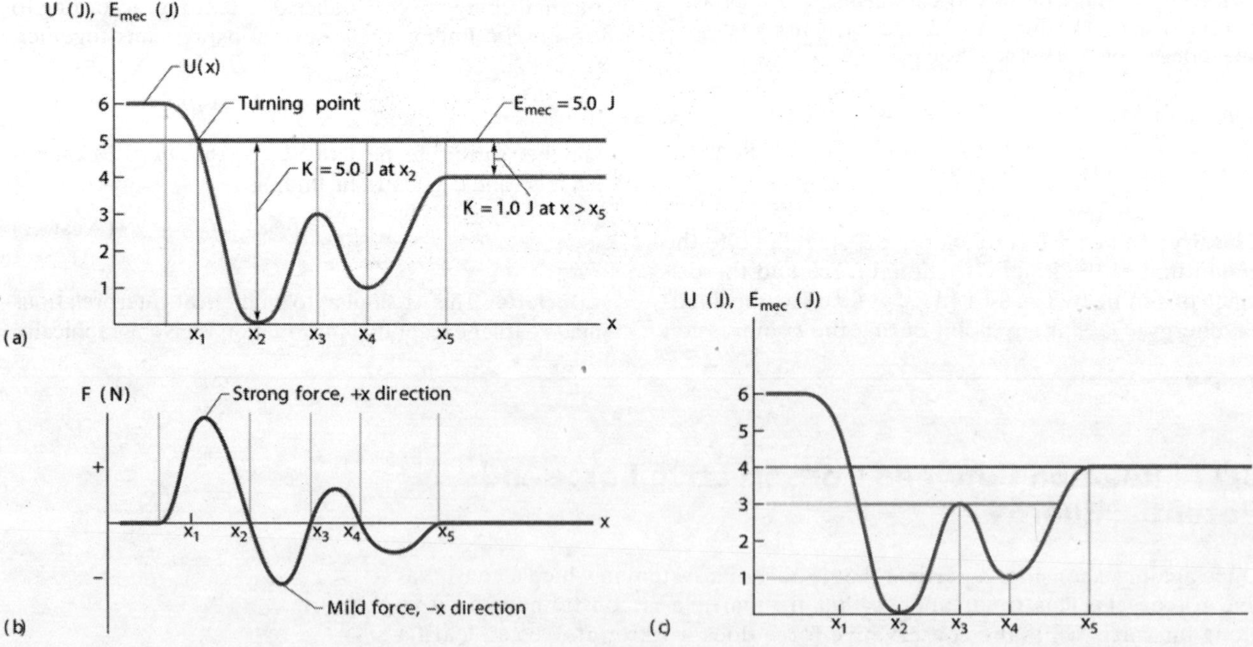

FIG. 8-38 (*a*) A plot of $U(x)$, the potential energy function of a system containing a particle confined to move along an x axis. There is no friction, so mechanical energy is conserved. (*b*) A plot of the force $F(x)$ acting on the particle, derived from the potential energy plot by taking its slope at various points. (*c*) The $U(x)$ plot of (*a*) with three possible values of E_{mec} shown.

Turning Points

In the absence of a nonconservative force, the mechanical energy E of a system has a constant value given by

$$U(x) + K(x) = E_{\text{mec}} \tag{8-79}$$

Here $K(x)$ is the *kinetic energy function* of a particle in the system (this $K(x)$ gives the kinetic energy as a function of the particle's location x). We may rewrite Eq. 8-79 as

$$K(x) = E_{\text{mec}} - U(x) \tag{8-80}$$

Suppose that E_{mec} (which has a constant value, remember) happens to be 5.0 J. It would be represented in Fig. 8-38*a* by a horizontal line that runs through the value 5.0 J on the energy axis. (It is, in fact, shown there.)

Equation 8-80 tells us how to determine the kinetic energy K for any location x of the particle: On the $U(x)$ curve, find U for that location x and then subtract U from E_{mec}. For example, if the particle is at any point to the right of x_5, then $K =$ 1.0 J. The value of K is greatest (5.0 J) when the particle is at x_2 and least (0 J) when the particle is at x_1.

Since K can never be negative (because v^2 is always positive), the particle can never move to the left of x_1, where $E_{\text{mec}} - U$ is negative. Instead, as the particle moves toward x_1 from x_2, K decreases (the particle slows) until $K = 0$ at x_1 (the particle stops there).

Note that when the particle reaches x_1, the force on the particle, given by Eq. 8-78, is positive (because the slope dU/dx is negative). This means that the particle does not remain at x_1 but instead begins to move to the right, opposite its earlier motion. Hence x_1 is a **turning point,** a place where $K = 0$ (because $U = E$) and the particle changes direction. There is no turning point (where $K = 0$) on the right side of the graph. When the particle heads to the right, it will continue indefinitely.

Equilibrium Points

Figure 8-38*c* shows three different values for E_{mec} superposed on the plot of the potential energy function $U(x)$ of Fig. 8-38*a*. Let us see how they change the situation. If $E_{\text{mec}} = 4.0$ J (purple line), the turning point shifts from x_1 to a point between x_1 and x_2. Also, at any point to the right of x_5, the system's mechanical energy is equal to its potential energy; thus, the particle has no kinetic energy and by Eq. 8-78, no force acts on it, and so it must be stationary. A particle at such a position is said to be in **neutral equilibrium.** (A marble placed on a horizontal tabletop is in that state.)

If $E_{\text{mec}} = 3.0$ J (pink line), there are two turning points: One is between x_1 and x_2, and the other is between x_4 and x_5. In addition, x_3 is a point at which $K = 0$. If the particle is located exactly there, the force on it is also zero, and the particle remains stationary. However, if it is displaced even slightly in either direction, a nonzero force pushes it farther in the same direction, and the particle continues to move. A particle at such a position is said to be in **unstable equilibrium.** (A marble balanced on top of a bowling ball is an example.)

Next consider the particle's behavior if $E_{\text{mec}} = 1.0$ J (green line). If we place it at x_4, it is stuck there. It cannot move left or right on its own because to do so would require a negative kinetic energy. If we push it slightly left or right, a restoring force appears that moves it back to x_4. A particle at such a position is said to be in **stable equilibrium.** (A marble placed at the bottom of a hemispherical bowl is an example.) If we place the particle in the cup-like *potential well* centered at x_2, it is between two turning points. It can still move somewhat, but only partway to x_1 or x_3.

CHECKPOINT 6 The figure gives the potential energy function $U(x)$ for a system in which a particle is in one-dimensional motion. (a) Rank regions AB, BC, and CD according to the magnitude of the force on the particle, greatest first. (b) What is the direction of the force when the particle is in region AB?

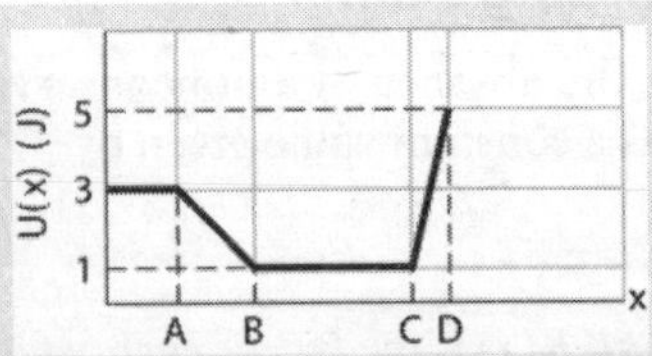

Sample Problem 8-26

A 2.00 kg particle moves along an x axis in one-dimensional motion while a conservative force along that axis acts on it. The potential energy $U(x)$ associated with the force is plotted in Fig. 8-39*a*. That is, if the particle were placed at any position between $x = 0$ and $x = 7.00$ m, it would have the plotted value of U. At $x = 6.5$ m, the particle has velocity $\vec{v}_0 = (-4.00 \text{ m/s})\hat{\text{i}}$.

(a) From Fig. 8-39*a*, determine the particle's speed at $x_1 = 4.5$ m.

Conceptualize/Classify: (1) The particle's kinetic energy is given by $K = \frac{1}{2}mv^2$. (2) Because only a conservative force acts on the particle, the mechanical energy $E_{mec} (= K + U)$ is conserved as the particle moves. (3) Therefore, on a plot of $U(x)$ such as Fig. 8-39*a*, the kinetic energy is equal to the difference between E_{mec} and U.

Compute: At $x = 6.5$ m, the particle has kinetic energy

$$K_0 = \tfrac{1}{2}mv_0^2 = \tfrac{1}{2}(2.00 \text{ kg})(4.00 \text{ m/s})^2$$
$$= 16.0 \text{ J}$$

Because the potential energy there is $U = 0$, the mechanical energy is

$$E_{mec} = K_0 + U_0 = 16.0 \text{ J} + 0 = 16.0 \text{ J}$$

This value for E_{mec} is plotted as a horizontal line in Fig. 8-39*a*. From that figure we see that at $x = 4.5$ m, the potential energy is $U_1 = 7.0$ J. The kinetic energy K_1 is the difference between E_{mec} and U_1:

$$K_1 = E_{mec} - U_1 = 16.0 \text{ J} - 7.0 \text{ J} = 9.0 \text{ J}$$

Because $K_1 = \frac{1}{2}mv_1^2$, we find

$$v_1 = 3.0 \text{ m/s} \qquad \text{(Answer)}$$

(b) Where is the particle's turning point located?

Conceptualize/Classify: The turning point is where the force momentarily stops and then reverses the particle's motion. That is, it is where the particle momentarily has $v = 0$ and thus $K = 0$.

Classify: Because K is the difference between E_{mec} and U, we want the point in Fig. 8-39*a* where the plot of U rises to meet the horizontal line of E_{mec}, as shown in Fig. 8-39*b*. Because the plot of U is a straight line in Fig. 8-39*b*, we can draw nested right triangles as shown and then write the proportionality of distances

$$\frac{16 - 7.0}{d} = \frac{20 - 7.0}{4.0 - 1.0}$$

which gives us $d = 2.08$ m. Thus, the turning point is at

$$x = 4.0 \text{ m} - d = 1.9 \text{ m} \qquad \text{(Answer)}$$

(c) Evaluate the force acting on the particle when it is in the region $1.9 \text{ m} < x < 4.0$ m.

Conceptualize/Classify: The force is given by Eq. $F(x) = -dU(x)/dx$. The equation states that the force is equal to the negative of the slope on a graph of $U(x)$.

Compute: For the graph of Fig. 8-39*b*, we see that for the range $1.0 \text{ m} < x < 4.0$ m the force is

$$F = -\frac{20 \text{ J} - 7.0 \text{ J}}{1.0 \text{ m} - 4.0 \text{ m}} = 4.3 \text{ N} \qquad \text{(Answer)}$$

Thus, the force has magnitude 4.3 N and is in the positive direction of the x axis. This result is consistent with the fact that the initially leftward-moving particle is stopped by the force and then sent rightward.

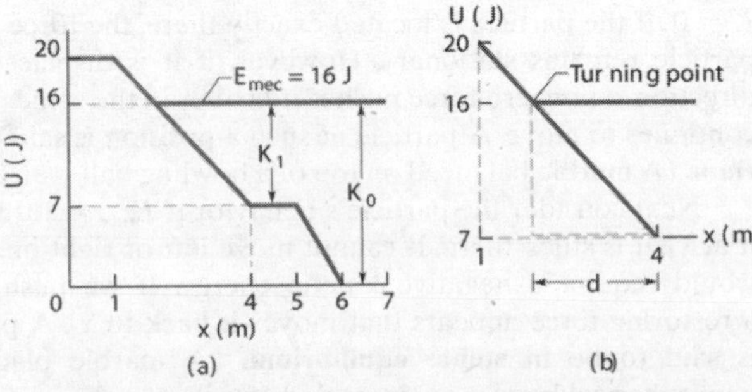

FIG. 8-39 (*a*) A plot of potential energy U versus position x. (*b*) A section of the plot used to find where the particle turns around.

If potential energy is given as function of all three co-ordinates x, y, and z, we use the following method.

$$\vec{F} = -\vec{\nabla}(U)$$

$$\vec{\nabla} \text{ represents } \frac{\partial}{\partial x}\hat{i} + \frac{\partial}{\partial y}\hat{j} + \frac{\partial}{\partial z}\hat{k}$$

CHECKPOINT 7 If $U = 4x^2y + 2yz^2$, find force.

8-12 | Vertical Circular motion

A particle of mass m is kept in fixed smooth sphere of radius R and projected horizontally from the bottom point A with speed u. Let us find the minimum speed so that it can reach the point B.

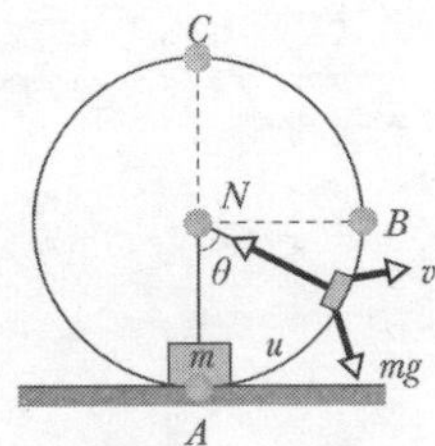

FIG. 8-40 A particle of is kept in a fixed smooth sphere of radius and is undergoing circular motion in a vertical plane.

Since we have to determine the minimum speed which will provide it just the sufficient kinetic energy so that it comes to rest at B, thus $K = 0$. Taking gravitational potential energy at A to be zero, we can write using work-energy theorem.

$$(k_f - k_i) + (U_f - U_i) = 0$$

$$\left(0 - \frac{1}{2}mu^2\right) + (mgR - 0) = 0$$

Hence, $$u = \sqrt{2gR}$$

Now let us find the speed required to reach C. If we again use work-energy theorem as used above, we get

$$\left[0 - mu^2\right] + \left[mg\ (2R) - 0\right] = 0$$

Solving we get, $\mu = \sqrt{4gR}$

We will show that this answer is wrong, because the particle may leave contact with the sphere (Fig. 8-48) before reaching C. We must find the equation describing variation of normal contact force. It will be a good time to go and review Sample problem 7-12.

As the particle is undergoing circular motion, we can write centripetal condition at any θ with vertical.

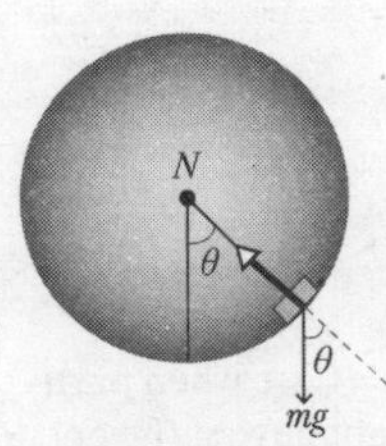

FIG. 8-41 Free-body diagram of a particle undergoing circular motion inside a fixed sphere.

$$N - mg\ \cos\ \theta = \frac{mV^2}{R}$$

Where N is the normal contact force and mg cos θ represents the normal component of weight mg at that point.

Solving for N, we get, $$N = mg \cos\theta + \frac{mV^2}{R} \tag{8-81}$$

This cquation is valid for the complete circle, that is, for values of θ from 0 to 2π. It is important to note that for $O < \theta < \pi/2$, N will never be zero as both mg cos θ and mV^2/R are positive. Hence, it will be in contact and will have circular motion till it crosses B. To find speed we have to write the work–kinetic energy theorem when particle is at angle θ with vertical. Work done by gravity should be equal to change in kinetic energy.

$$-mg\left(R\left(1 - \cos\theta\right)\right) = \frac{mV^2}{2} - \frac{mu^2}{2}$$

Where V is the final velocity and μ is the initial velocity

Solving we get $\qquad V^2 = u^2 - 2gR\left(1 - \cos\theta\right)$

$$V^2 = u^2 - 2gR + 2gR\cos\theta$$

We can put this value of V in Eq. 8-81

Thus, $\qquad N = mg\cos\theta + \dfrac{m\left(u^2 2gR + 2gR\cos\theta\right)}{R}$

Solving we get, $\qquad N = \dfrac{m}{R}\left[u^2 - 2gR + 3gR\cos\theta\right]$

Now we have a direct relation between normal N and angle, θ.

We can see that if we want to find minimum value of speed to reach point B, there is no need to check the equation; what then matters is the kinetic energy. As normal will not become zero:

for $\qquad 0 < \theta < \dfrac{\pi}{2}$

On comparing, we get

$$v^2 = u^2 - 2gR + 2gR\cos\theta$$

$$N = \frac{m}{R}\left[u^2 - 2gR + 3\cos\theta gR\right]$$

we can see that for positive cos θ, N will be greater than V. The region AB ends to values of θ from 0 to $\pi/2$ and will have positive cos θ. Thus, in the region AB when speed becomes zero, normal will have positive value. So, for the region AB, we should check speed. On the other hand, when cos θ has negative values, N will have smaller values than V. The region BC corresponds to values of θ from $\pi/2$ to π and will give negative values of cos θ. Thus, in the region BC, when N becomes zero, speed is non-zero so for the region BC we should check value of N rather than V. Now we will discuss the motion of particle after being projected with different speeds.

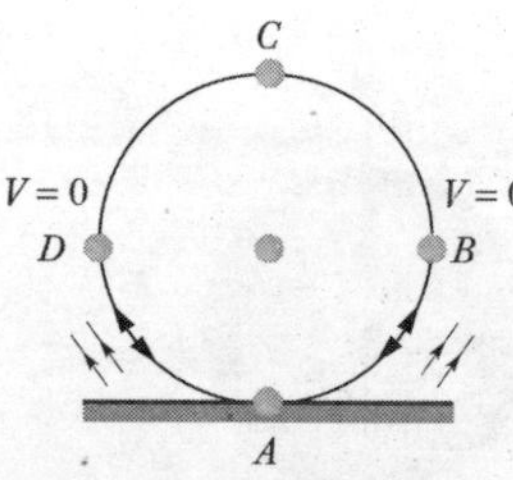

FIG. 8-42 Case when particle does not have sufficient energy to reach point B.

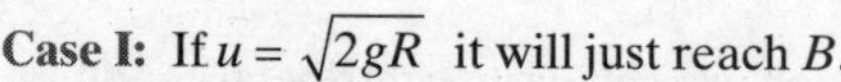

Case I: If $u = \sqrt{2gR}$ it will just reach B.

It will execute an oscillatory motion from A to B then return to A continue to D and so on.

Case II: If we project the particle with velocity u where $u < \sqrt{2gR}$.

The body will not reach B but its velocity will become zero before it reaches B and it will execute oscillatory motion from right extreme to left extreme.

When we provide velocity larger than $\sqrt{2gR}$, the particle will cross B and now major concern is of normal contact force as it will become zero before speed becomes zero. This is why minimum velocity to reach C is not $\sqrt{4gR}$ as we are considering speed and not normal contact force; whereas to reach C it is necessary that 'N' does not become zero. Corresponding to point C, θ is equal to π.

We are checking for 'π' as $\cos \pi$ has a maximum negative value (–1). If N is not zero at this point, then for all θ the normal will never be zero.

Thus, for the minimum speed to reach point C, we keep $\theta = \pi$ and $N = 0$

$$0 = u^2 - 2gR + 3gR\,(-1)$$

Solving we get $u = \sqrt{5gR}$

So, we find that the minimum speed to required to reach point C is $\sqrt{5gR}$ and not $u = \sqrt{4gR}$.

Case III: If $u > \sqrt{5gR}$

The body will freely move in a circle as 'N' will never be zero.

Case IV: If $u = \sqrt{5gR}$, then we say that the body just completes the circle.

We can also find speed at C $\quad v^2 = 5gR - 2gR - 2gR$

solving we get $\quad v = \sqrt{gR}$

We have already solved that at $C, N = 0$ for $\sqrt{5gR}$.

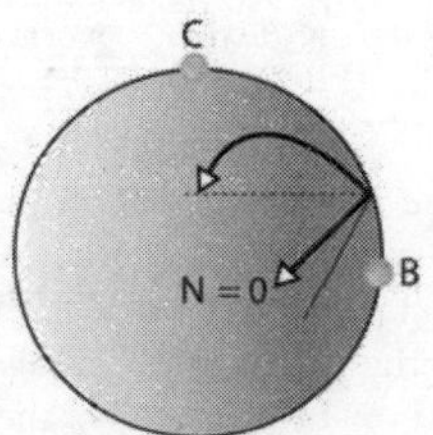

FIG. 8-43 Case when particle leaves circular motion between B and C and starts circular motion.

Case V: If $\sqrt{5gR} > u > \sqrt{2gR}$ then it will leave circular motion between B and C and start a projectile motion.

For the above mentioned value, the normal will become zero somewhere between B and C. At this point, velocity is non zero. So, the particle will leave circular motion and will become a projectile.

For a mass tied by a light rod about O. Here problem is simply of energy because rod can both pull and push so we can have any value of tension with any sign. Different results are given below considering only energy.

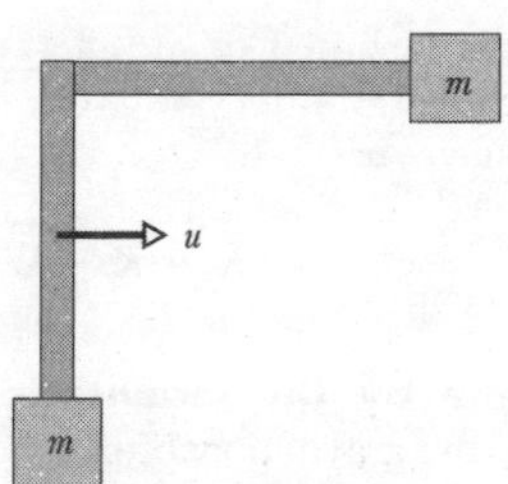

FIG. 8-44 A particle attached to a rigid rod in a vertical plane.

Case I: $u < \sqrt{2gR}$ – Pendulum.

Case II: $u = \sqrt{2gR}$ will reach B and come back.

Case III: $\sqrt{4gR} > u > \sqrt{2gR}$. The body will continue to move in a circular motion as tension of a rod can go negative which is allowed as the rod instead of pulling the body will push it.

$$A \rightarrow P \rightarrow Q \rightarrow P \rightarrow A \rightarrow P' \rightarrow Q'$$

Case IV: $u = \sqrt{4gR}$ $\qquad V = 0, T \rightarrow -\text{ve}$

The body will stop at the top.

Case V: $u > \sqrt{4gR}$.

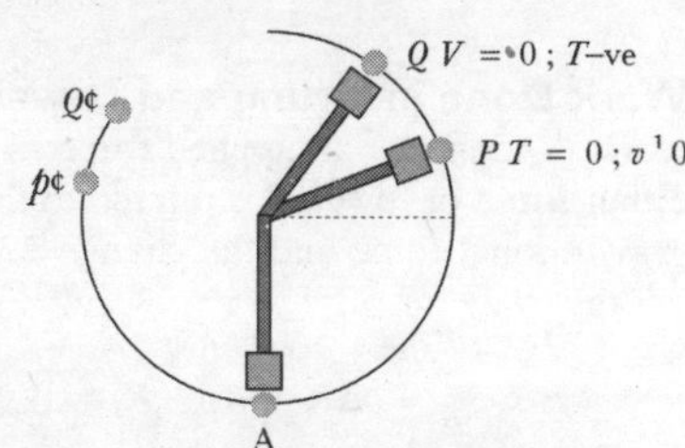

FIG. 8-45 Various cases for a particle to attached to a rigid rod in vertical plane.

REVIEW & SUMMARY

Kinetic Energy The **kinetic energy** K associated with the motion of a particle of mass m and speed v, where v is well below the speed of light, is

$$K = \tfrac{1}{2}mv^2 \quad \text{(kinetic energy)}$$

Work **Work** W is energy transferred to or from an object via a force acting on the object. Energy transferred to the object is positive work, and from the object, negative work.

Work Done by a Constant Force The work done on a particle by a constant force $\vec{F}$ during displacement $\vec{d}$ is

$$W = Fd\cos\phi = \vec{F}\cdot\vec{d} \quad \text{(work, constant force)}$$

in which ϕ is the constant angle between the directions of $\vec{F}$ and $\vec{d}$. Only the component of $\vec{F}$ that is along the displacement $\vec{d}$ can do work on the object. When two or more forces act on an object, their **net work** is the sum of the individual works done by the forces, which is also equal to the work that would be done on the object by the net force $\vec{F}_{net}$ of those forces.

Work and Kinetic Energy For a particle, a change ΔK in the kinetic energy equals the net work W done on the particle:

$$\Delta K = K_f - K_i = W \quad \text{(work–kinetic energy theorem)}$$

in which K_i is the initial kinetic energy of the particle and K_f is the kinetic energy after the work is done. Equation 8-10 rearranged gives us

$$K_f = K_i + W$$

Work Done by the Gravitational Force The work W_g done by the gravitational force $\vec{F}_g$ on a particle-like object of mass m as the object moves through a displacement $\vec{d}$ is given by

$$W_g = mgd\cos\phi$$

in which ϕ is the angle between $\vec{F}_g$ and $\vec{d}$.

Work Done in Lifting and Lowering an Object The work W_a done by an applied force as a particle-like object is either lifted or lowered is related to the work W_g done by the gravitational force and the change ΔK in the object's kinetic energy by

$$\Delta K = K_f - K_i = W_a + W_g$$

If $K_f = K_i$, then the above equation reduces to

$$W_a = -W_g$$

which tells us that the applied force transfers as much energy to the object as the gravitational force transfers from it.

Spring Force The force $\vec{F}_s$ from a spring is

$$\vec{F}_s = -k\vec{d} \quad \text{(Hooke's law)}$$

where $\vec{d}$ is the displacement of the spring's free end from its position when the spring is in its **relaxed state** (neither compressed nor extended), and k is the **spring constant** (a measure of the spring's stiffness). If an x axis lies along the spring, with the origin at the location of the spring's free end when the spring is in its relaxed state, Hooke's law can be written as

$$F_x = -kx \quad \text{(Hooke's law)}$$

A spring force is thus a variable force: It varies with the displacement of the spring's free end.

Work Done by a Spring Force If an object is attached to the spring's free end, the work W_s done on the object by the spring force when the object is moved from an initial position x_i to a final position x_f is

$$W_s = \tfrac{1}{2}kx_i^2 - \tfrac{1}{2}kx_f^2$$

If $x_i = 0$ and $x_f = x$, then

$$W_s = -\tfrac{1}{2}kx^2$$

Work Done by a Variable Force When the force $\vec{F}$ on a particle-like object depends on the position of the object, the work done by $\vec{F}$ on the object while the object moves from an initial position r_i with coordinates (x_i, y_i, z_i) to a final position r_f with coordinates (x_f, y_f, z_f) must be found by integrating the force. If we assume that component F_x may depend on x but not on y or z, component F_y may depend on y but not on x or z, and component F_z may depend on z but not on x or y, then the work is

$$W = \int_{x_i}^{x_f} F_x\,dx + \int_{y_i}^{y_f} F_y\,dy + \int_{z_i}^{z_f} F_z\,dz$$

If $\vec{F}$ has only an x component, then

$$W = \int_{x_i}^{x_f} F(x)\,dx$$

Conservative Forces A force is a **conservative force** if the net work it does on a particle moving around any closed path, from an initial point and then back to that point, is zero. Equivalently, a force is conservative if the net work it does on a particle moving between two points does not depend on the path taken by the particle. The gravitational force and the spring force are conservative forces; the kinetic frictional force is a **nonconservative force.**

Potential Energy A **potential energy** is energy that is associated with the configuration of a system in which a conservative force acts. When the conservative force does work W on a particle within the system, the change ΔU in the potential energy of the system is

$$\Delta U = -W$$

If the particle moves from point x_i to point x_f, the change in the potential energy of the system is

$$\Delta U = -\int_{x_i}^{x_f} F(x)\,dx$$

Gravitational Potential Energy The potential energy associated with a system consisting of Earth and a nearby particle is **gravitational potential energy.** If the particle moves from height y_i to height y_f, the change in the gravitational potential energy of the particle–Earth system is

$$\Delta U = mg(y_f - y_i) = mg\,\Delta y$$

If the **reference point** of the particle is set as $y_i = 0$ and the corresponding gravitational potential energy of the system is set as $U_i = 0$, then the gravitational potential energy U when the particle is at any height y is

$$U(y) = mgy$$

Elastic Potential Energy **Elastic potential energy** is the energy associated with the state of compression or extension of an elastic object. For a spring that exerts a spring force $F = -kx$ when its free end has displacement x, the elastic potential energy is

$$U(x) = \tfrac{1}{2}kx^2$$

The **reference configuration** has the spring at its relaxed length, at which $x = 0$ and $U = 0$.

Mechanical Energy The **mechanical energy** E_{mec} of a system is the sum of its kinetic energy K and potential energy U:

$$E_{mec} = K + U$$

An *isolated system* is one in which no *external force* causes energy changes. If only conservative forces do work within an isolated system, then the mechanical energy E_{mec} of the system cannot change. This **principle of conservation of mechanical energy** is written as

$$K_2 + U_2 = K_1 + U_1$$

in which the subscripts refer to different instants during an energy transfer process. This conservation principle can also be written as

$$\Delta E_{mec} = \Delta K + \Delta U = 0$$

Potential Energy Curves If we know the potential energy function $U(x)$ for a system in which a one-dimensional force $F(x)$ acts on a particle, we can find the force as

$$F(x) = -\frac{dU(x)}{dx}$$

If $U(x)$ is given on a graph, then at any value of x, the force $F(x)$ is the negative of the slope of the curve there and the kinetic energy of the particle is given by

$$K(x) = E_{mec} - U(x)$$

where E_{mec} is the mechanical energy of the system. A **turning point** is a point x at which the particle reverses its motion (there, $K = 0$). The particle is in **equilibrium** at points where the slope of the $U(x)$ curve is zero (there, $F(x) = 0$).

Work Done on a System by an External Force Work W is energy transferred to or from a system by means of an external force acting on the system. When more than one force acts on a system, their *net work* is the transferred energy. When friction is not involved, the work done on the system and the change ΔE_{mec} in the mechanical energy of the system are equal:

$$W = \Delta E_{mec} = \Delta K + \Delta U$$

When a kinetic frictional force acts within the system, then the thermal energy E_{th} of the system changes. (This energy is associated with the random motion of atoms and molecules in the system.) The work done on the system is then

$$W = \Delta E_{mec} + \Delta E_{th}$$

The change ΔE_{th} is related to the magnitude f_k of the frictional force and the magnitude d of the displacement caused by the external force by

$$\Delta E_{th} = f_k d$$

Power The **power** due to a force is the *rate* at which that force transfers energy. If an amount of energy ΔE is transferred by a force in an amount of time Δt, the **average power** of the force is

$$P_{avg} = \frac{\Delta E}{\Delta t}$$

The **instantaneous power** due to a force is

$$P = \frac{dE}{dt}$$

QUESTIONS

1 Is positive or negative work done by a constant force $\vec{F}$ on a particle during a straight-line displacement $\vec{d}$ if (a) the angle between $\vec{F}$ and $\vec{d}$ is 30°; (b) the angle is 100°; (c) $\vec{F} = 2\hat{i} - 3\hat{j}$ and $\vec{d} = -4\hat{i}$?

2 In three situations, a briefly applied horizontal force changes the velocity of a hockey puck that slides over frictionless ice. The overhead views of Fig. 8-46 indicate, for each situation, the puck's initial speed v_i, its final speed v_f, and the directions of the corresponding velocity vectors. Rank the situations according to the work done on the puck by the applied force, most positive first and most negative last.

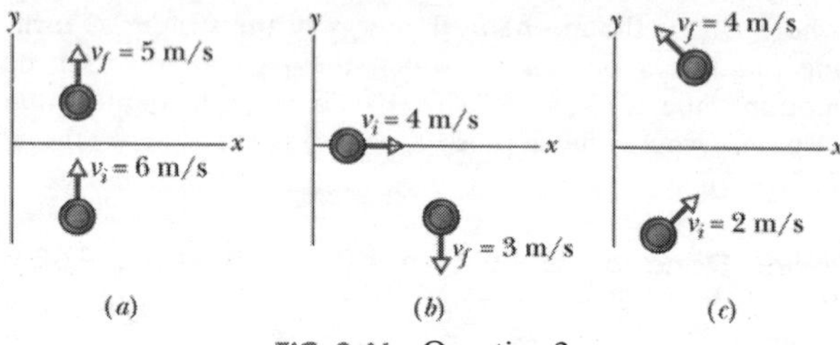

FIG. 8-46 Question 2.

3 Rank the following velocities according to the kinetic energy a particle will have with each velocity, greatest first: (a) $\vec{v} = 4\hat{i} + 3\hat{j}$, (b) $\vec{v} = -4\hat{i} + 3\hat{j}$, (c) $\vec{v} = -3\hat{i} + 4\hat{j}$, (d) $\vec{v} = 3\hat{i} - 4\hat{j}$, (e) $\vec{v} = 5\hat{i}$, and (f) $v = 5$ m/s at 30° to the horizontal.

4 Figure 8-47*a* shows two horizontal forces that act on a block that is sliding to the right across a frictionless floor. Figure 8-47*b* shows three plots of the block's kinetic energy K versus time t. Which of the plots best corresponds to the following three situations: (a) $F_1 = F_2$, (b) $F_1 > F_2$, (c) $F_1 < F_2$?

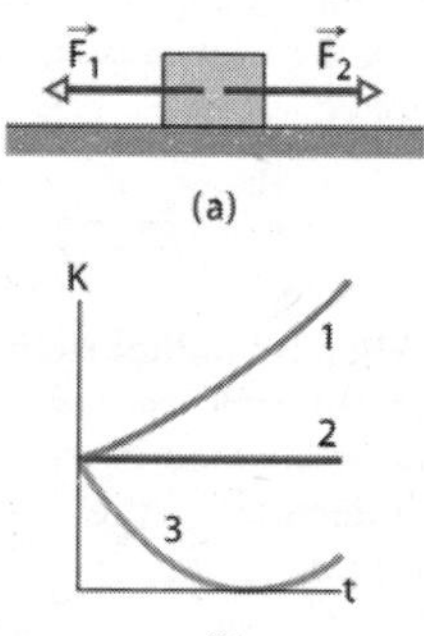

FIG. 8-47 Question 4.

5 In Fig. 8-48, a greased pig has a choice of three frictionless slides along which to slide to the ground. Rank the slides according to how much work the gravitational force does on the pig during the descent, greatest first.

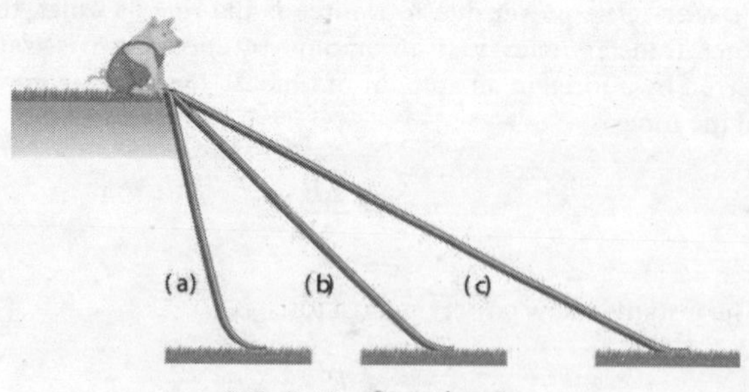

FIG. 8-48 Question 5.

6 Figure 8-54*a* shows four situations in which a horizontal force acts on the same block, which is initially at rest. The force magnitudes are $F_2 = F_4 = 2F_1 = 2F_3$. The horizontal component v_x of the block's velocity is shown in Fig. 8-49*b* for the four situations. (a) Which plot in Fig. 8-49*b* best corresponds to which force in Fig. 8-49*a*? (b) Which plot in Fig. 8-49*c* (for kinetic energy K versus time t) best corresponds to which plot in Fig. 8-49*b*?

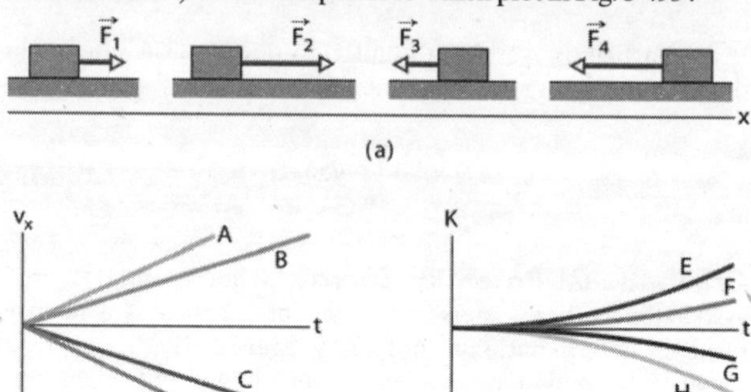

FIG. 8-49 Question 6.

7 Figure 8-50 shows four graphs (drawn to the same scale) of the x component F_x of a variable force (directed along an x axis) versus the position x of a particle on which the force acts. Rank the graphs according to the work done by the force on the particle from $x = 0$ to $x = x_1$, from most positive work first to most negative work last.

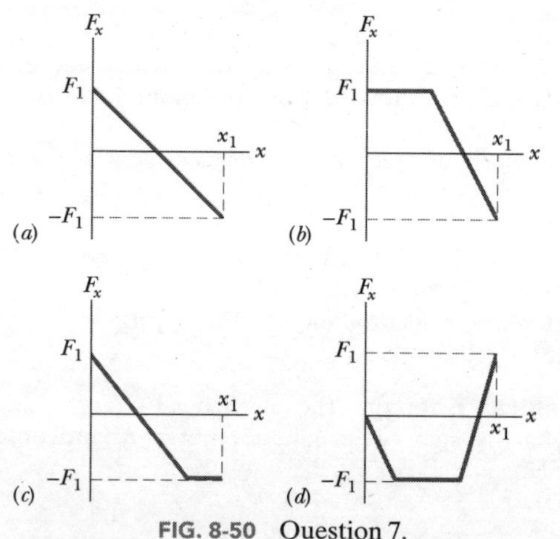

FIG. 8-50 Question 7.

8 Figure 8-51 gives the x component F_x of a force that can act on a particle. If the particle begins at rest at $x = 0$, what is its coordinate when it has (a) its greatest kinetic energy, (b) its greatest speed, and (c) zero speed? (d) What is the particle's direction of travel after it reaches $x = 6$ m?

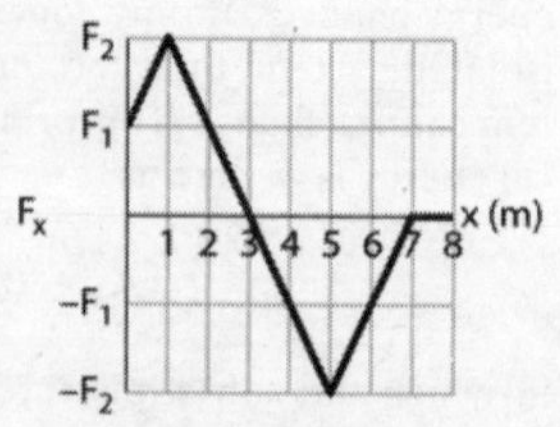

FIG. 8-51 Question 8.

9 Spring A is stiffer than spring B ($k_A > k_B$). The spring force of which spring does more work if the springs are compressed (a) the same distance and (b) by the same applied force?

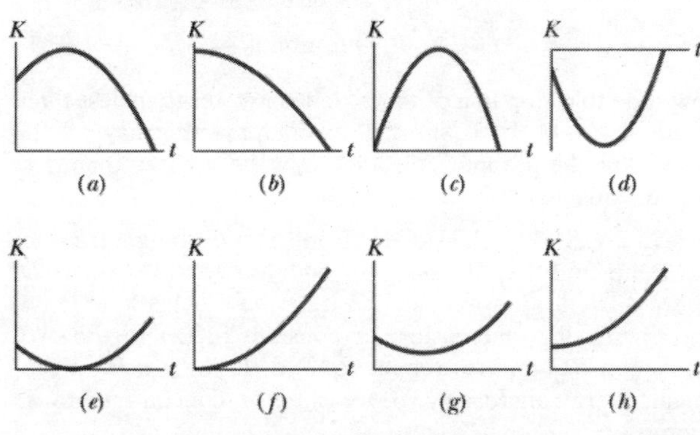

FIG. 8-52 Question 9.

10 Figure 8-53 shows one direct path and four indirect paths from point i to point f. Along the direct path and three of the indirect paths, only a conservative force F_c acts on a certain object. Along the fourth indirect path, both F_c and a nonconservative force F_{nc} act on the object. The change ΔE_{mec} in the object's mechanical energy (in joules) in going from i to f is indicated along each straight-line segment of the indirect paths. What is ΔE_{mec} (a) from i to f along the direct path and (b) due to F_{nc} along the one path where it acts?

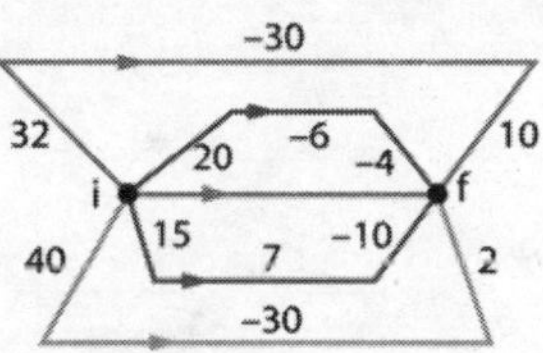

FIG. 8-53 Question 10.

11 In Fig. 8-54, a small, initially stationary block is released on a frictionless ramp at a height of 3.0 m. Hill heights along the ramp are as shown. The hills have identical circular tops, and the block does not fly off any hill. (a) Which hill is the first the block cannot cross? (b) What does the block do after failing to cross that hill? On which hilltop is (c) the centripetal acceleration of the block greatest and (d) the normal force on the block least?

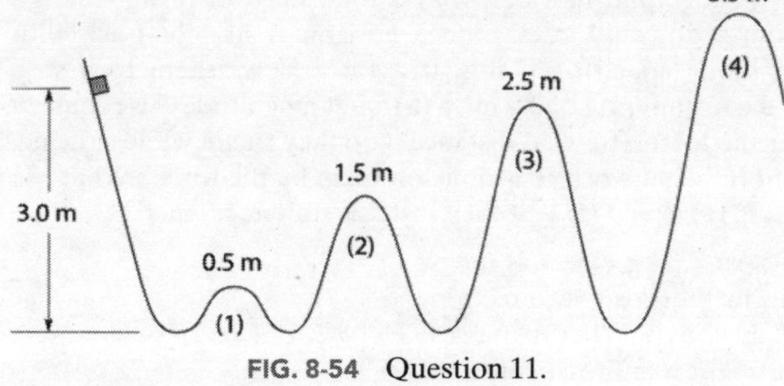

FIG. 8-54 Question 11.

12 In Fig. 8-55, a horizontally moving block can take three frictionless routes, differing only in elevation, to reach the dashed finish line. Rank the routes according to (a) the speed of the block at the finish line and (b) the travel time of the block to the finish line, greatest first.

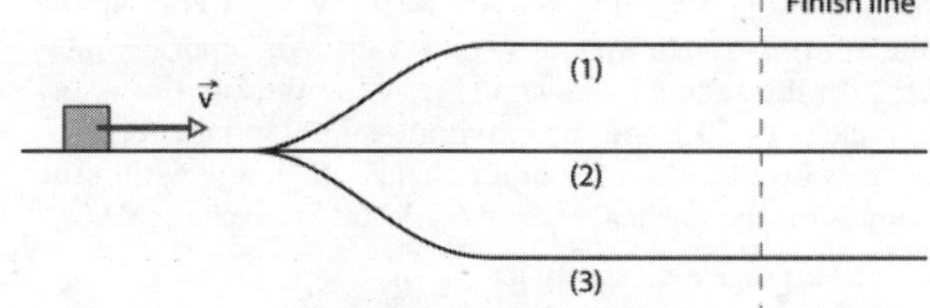

FIG. 8-55 Question 12.

13 Figure 8-56 gives the potential energy function of a particle. (a) Rank regions AB, BC, CD, and DE according to the magnitude of the force on the particle, greatest first. What value must the mechanical energy E_{mec} of the particle not exceed if the particle is to be (b) trapped in the potential well at the left, (c) trapped in the potential well at the right, and (d) able to move between the two potential wells but not to the right of point H? For the situation of (d), in which of regions BC, DE, and FG will the particle have (e) the greatest kinetic energy and (f) the least speed?

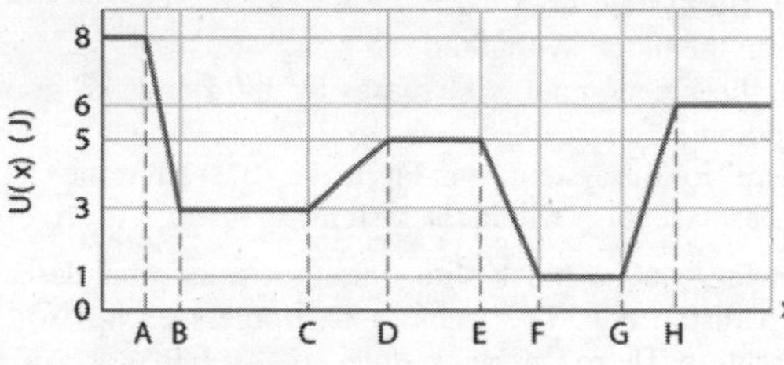

FIG. 8-56 Question 13.

14 Figure 8-57 shows three situations involving a plane that is not frictionless and a block sliding along the plane. The block begins with the same speed in all three situations and slides until the kinetic frictional force has stopped it. Rank the situations according to the increase in thermal energy due to the sliding, greatest first.

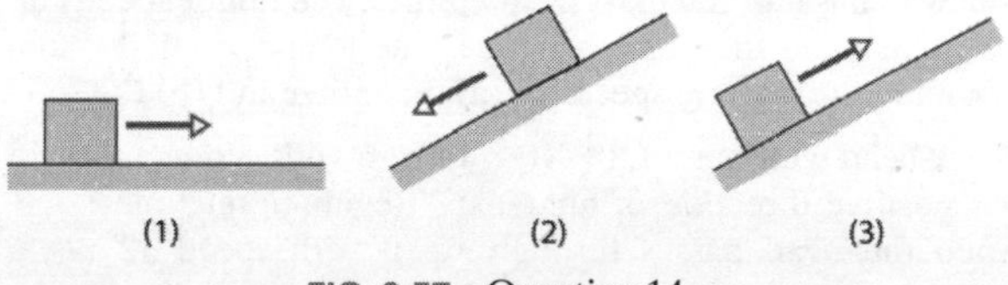

FIG. 8-57 Question 14.

15 In Fig. 8-58a, you pull upward on a rope that is attached to a cylinder on a vertical rod. Because the cylinder fits tightly on the rod, the cylinder slides along the rod with consid-

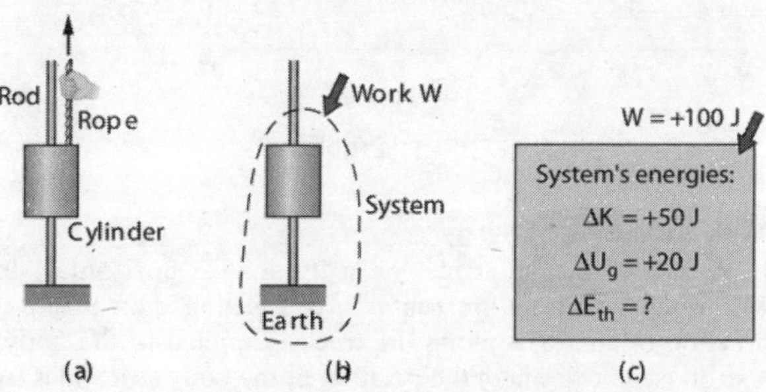

FIG. 8-58 Question 15.

erable friction. Your force does work $W = +100$ J on the cylinder–rod–Earth system (Fig. 8-58*b*). An "energy statement" for the system is shown in Fig. 8-58*c*: the kinetic energy K increases by 50 J, and the gravitational potential energy U_g increases by 20 J. The only other change in energy within the system is for the thermal energy E_{th}. What is the change ΔE_{th}?

16 The arrangement shown in Fig. 8-59 is similar to that in Question 6. Here you pull downward on the rope that is attached to the cylinder, which fits tightly on the rod. Also, as the cylinder descends, it pulls on a block via a second rope, and the block slides over a lab table. Again consider the cylinder–rod–Earth system, similar to that shown in Fig. 8-59*b*. Your work on the system is 200 J. The system does work of 60 J on the block. Within the system, the kinetic energy increases by 130 J and the gravitational potential energy decreases by 20 J. (a) Draw an "energy statement" for the system, as in Fig. 8-59*c*. (b) What is the change in the thermal energy within the system?

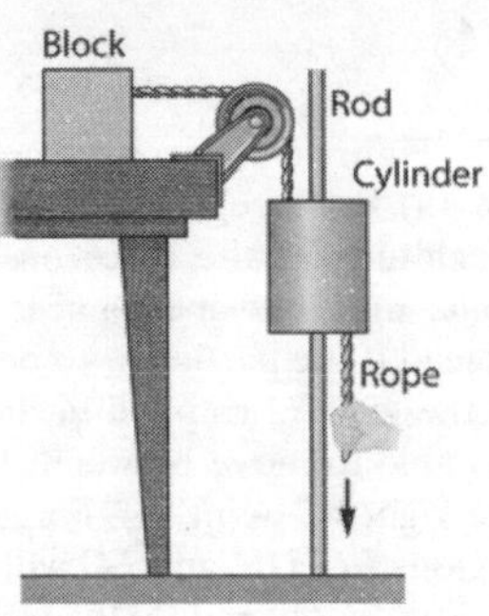

FIG. 8-59 Question 16.

17 In Fig. 8-60, a block slides along a track that descends through distance h. The track is frictionless except for the lower section. There the block slides to a stop in a certain distance D because of friction. (a) If we decrease h, will the block now slide to a stop in a distance that is greater than, less than, or equal to D? (b) If, instead, we increase the mass of the block, will the stopping distance now be greater than, less than, or equal to D?

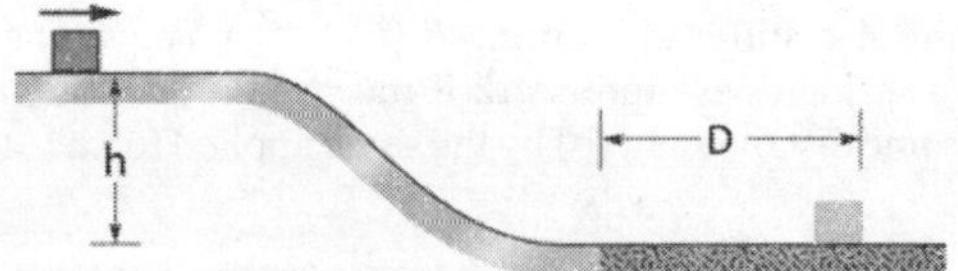

FIG. 8-60 Question 17.

18 In Fig. 8-61, a block slides from A to C along a frictionless ramp, and then it passes through horizontal region CD, where a frictional force acts on it. Is the block's kinetic energy increasing, decreasing, or constant in (a) region AB, (b) region BC, and (c) region CD? (d) Is the block's mechanical energy increasing, decreasing, or constant in those regions?

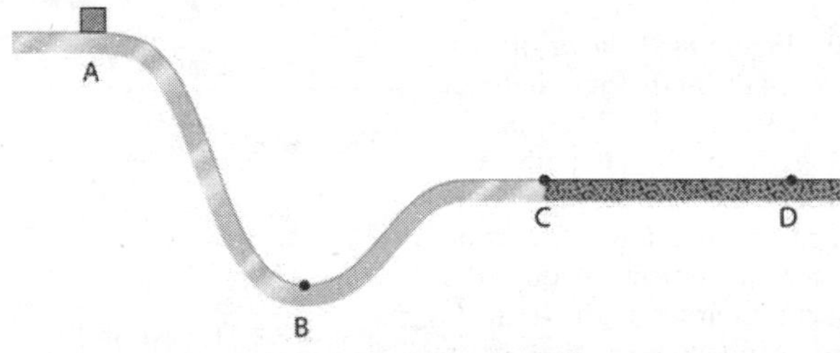

FIG. 8-61 Question 18.

PROBLEMS

Kinetic Energy

1 A father racing his son has half the kinetic energy of the son, who has half the mass of the father. The father speeds up by 1.0 m/s and then has the same kinetic energy as the son. What are the original speeds of (a) the father and (b) the son?

2 A bead with mass 1.8×10^{-2} kg is moving along a wire in the positive direction of an x axis. Beginning at time $t = 0$, when the bead passes through $x = 0$ with speed 12 m/s, a constant force acts on the bead. Figure 8-62 indicates the bead's position at times $t_0 = 0$, $t_1 = 1.0$ s, $t_2 = 2.0$ s, and $t_3 = 3.0$ s. The bead momentarily stops at $t = 3.0$ s. What is the kinetic energy of the bead at $t = 10$ s?

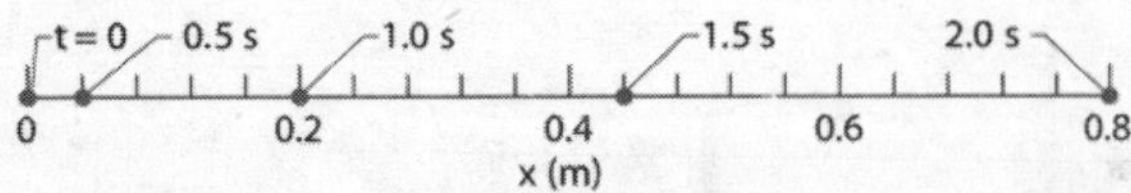

FIG. 8-62 Problem 2.

Work and Kinetic Energy

3 A 3.0 kg body is at rest on a frictionless horizontal air track when a constant horizontal force $\vec{F}$ acting in the positive direction of an x axis along the track is applied to the body. A stroboscopic graph of the position of the body as it slides to the right is shown in Fig. 8-63. The force $\vec{F}$ is applied to the body at $t = 0$, and the graph records the position of the body at 0.50 s intervals. How much work is done on the body by the applied force $\vec{F}$ between $t = 0$ and $t = 2.0$ s?

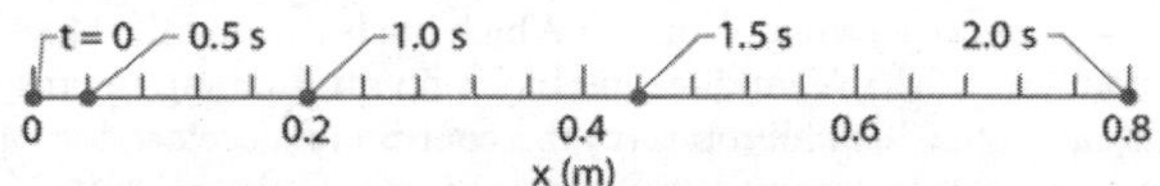

FIG. 8-63 Problem 3.

4 A luge and its rider, with a total mass of 85 kg, emerge from a downhill track onto a horizontal straight track with an initial speed of 37 m/s. If a force slows them to a stop at a constant rate of 2.0 m/s², (a) what magnitude F is required for the force, (b) what distance d do they travel while slowing, and (c) what work W is done on them by the force? What are (d) F, (e) d, and (f) W if they, instead, slow at 4.0 m/s²?

5 An 8.0 kg object is moving in the positive direction of an x axis. When it passes through $x = 0$, a constant force directed along the axis begins to act on it. Fig. 8-64 gives its kinetic energy K versus position x as it moves from $x = 0$ to $x = 5.0$ m; $K_0 = 30.0$ J. The force continues

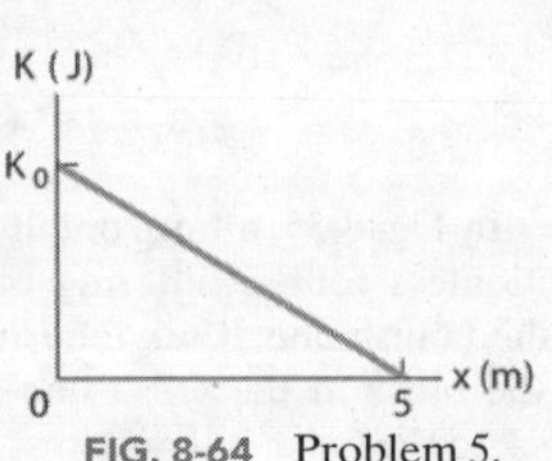

FIG. 8-64 Problem 5.

to act. What is v when the object moves back through $x = -3.0$ m?

6 Figure 8-65 shows three forces applied to a trunk that moves leftward by 3.00 m over a frictionless floor. The force magnitudes are $F_1 = 5.00$ N, $F_2 = 9.00$ N, and $F_3 = 3.00$ N, and the indicated angle is $\theta = 60.0°$. During the displacement, (a) what is the net work done on the trunk by the three forces and (b) does the kinetic energy of the trunk increase or decrease?

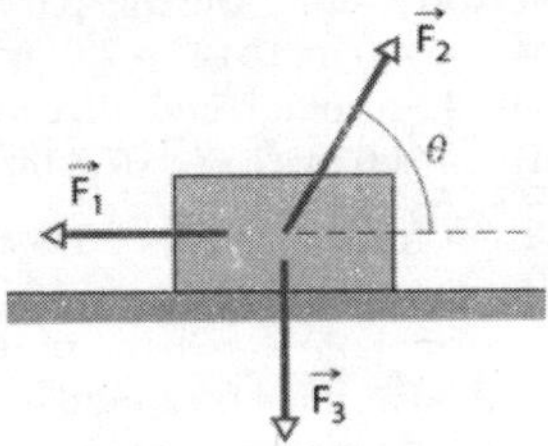

FIG. 8-65 Problem 6.

7 A can of bolts and nuts is pushed 2.00 m along an x axis by a broom along the greasy (frictionless) floor of a car repair shop in a version of shuffleboard. Figure 8-66 gives the work W done on the can by the constant horizontal force from the broom, versus the can's position x. The scale of the figure's vertical axis is set by $W_s = 6.0$ J. (a) What is the magnitude of that force? (b) If the can had an initial kinetic energy of 3.00 J, moving in the positive direction of the x axis, what is its kinetic energy at the end of the 2.00 m?

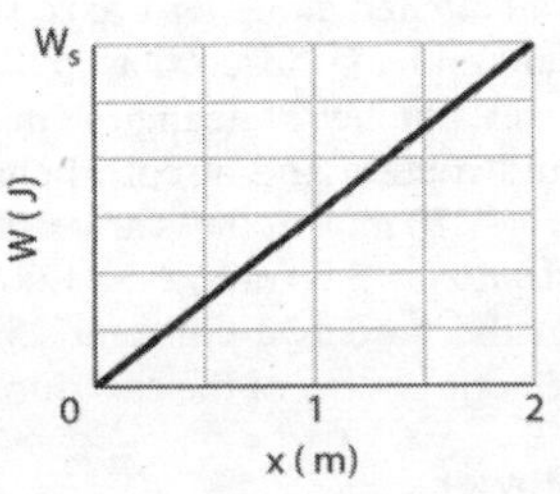

FIG. 8-66 Problem 7.

8 A 12.0 N force with a fixed orientation does work on a particle as the particle moves through displacement $\vec{d} = (2.00\hat{i} - 4.00\hat{j} + 3.00\hat{k})$m. What is the angle between the force and the displacement if the change in the particle's kinetic energy is (a) +30.0 J and (b) −30.0 J?

Work Done by the Gravitation

9 In Fig. 8-67, a horizontal force $\vec{F}_a$ of magnitude 20.0 N is applied to a 3.00 kg psychology book as the book slides a distance $d = 0.500$ m up a frictionless ramp at angle $\theta = 30.0°$. (a) During the displacement, what is the net work done on the book by $\vec{F}_a$, the gravitational force on the book, and the normal force on the book? (b) If the book has zero kinetic energy at the start of the displacement, what is its speed at the end of the displacement?

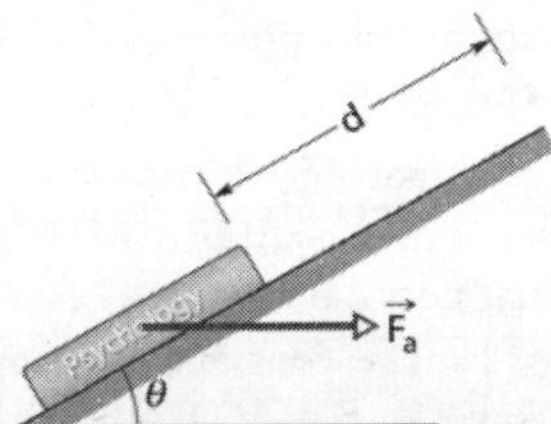

FIG. 8-67 Problem 9.

10 In Fig. 8-68, a constant force $\vec{F}_a$ of magnitude 82.0 N is applied to a 3.00 kg shoe box at angle $\phi = 53.0°$, causing the box to move up a frictionless ramp at constant speed. How much work is done on the box by $\vec{F}_a$ when the box has moved through vertical distance $h = 0.150$ m?

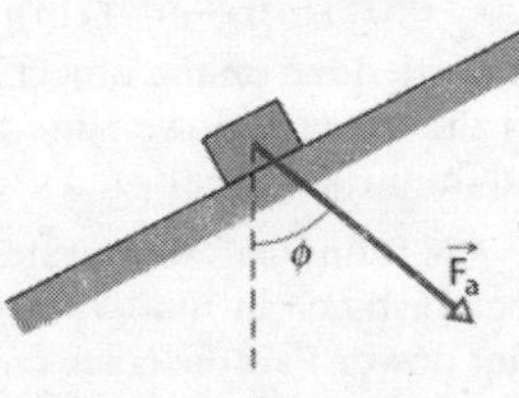

FIG. 8-68 Problem 10.

11 A block is sent up a frictionless ramp along which an x axis extends upward. Fig. 8-69 gives the kinetic energy of the block as a function of position x; the scale of the figure's vertical axis is set by $K_s = 40.0$ J. If the block's initial speed is 4.00 m/s, what is the normal force on the block?

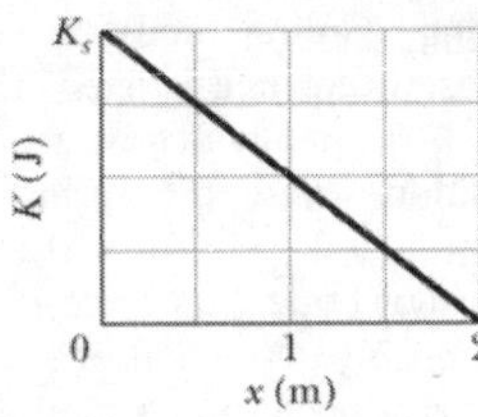

FIG. 8-69 Problem 11.

12 In Fig. 8-70, a 0.250 kg block of cheese lies on the floor of a 900 kg elevator cab that is being pulled upward by a cable through distance $d_1 = 2.40$ m and then through distance $d_2 = 10.5$ m. (a) Through d_1, if the normal force on the block from the floor has constant magnitude $F_N = 3.00$ N, how much work is done on the cab by the force from the cable? (b) Through d_2, if the work done on the cab by the (constant) force from the cable is 92.61 kJ, what is the magnitude of F_N?

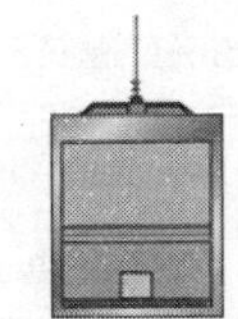

FIG. 8-70 Problem 12.

Work Done by a Spring Force

13 The only force acting on a 2.0 kg body as it moves along a positive x axis has an x component $F_x = -6x$ N, with x in meters. The velocity at $x = 3.0$ m is 8.0 m/s. (a) What is the velocity of the body at $x = 4.0$ m? (b) At what positive value of x will the body have a velocity of 5.0 m/s?

14 Figure 8-71 gives spring force F_x versus position x for the spring–block arrangement of Fig. 8-11. The scale is set by $F_s = 160.0$ N. We release the block at $x = 12$ cm. How much work does the spring do on the block when the block moves from $x_i = +8.0$ cm to (a) $x = +5.0$ cm, (b) $x = -5.0$ cm, (c) $x = -8.0$ cm, and (d) $x = -10.0$ cm?

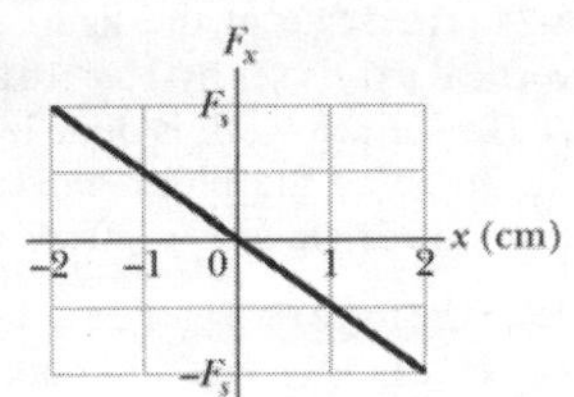

FIG. 8-71 Problem 14.

15 In the arrangement of Fig. 8-11, we gradually pull the block from $x = 0$ to $x = +3.0$ cm, where it is stationary. Figure 8-72 gives the work that our force does on the block. The scale of the figure's vertical axis is set by $W_s = 1.0$ J. We then pull the block out to $x = +5.0$ cm and release it from rest. How much work does the spring do on the block when the block moves from $x_i = +5.0$ cm to (a) $x = +4.0$ cm, (b) $x = -2.0$ cm, and (c) $x = -5.0$ cm?

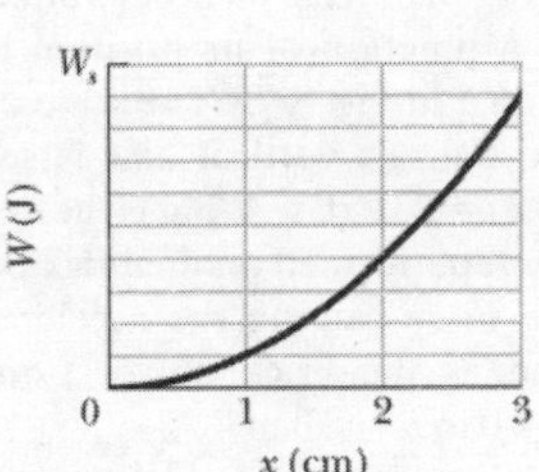

FIG. 8-72 Problem 15.

16 In Fig. 8-11a, a block of mass m lies on a horizontal frictionless surface and is attached to one end of a horizontal

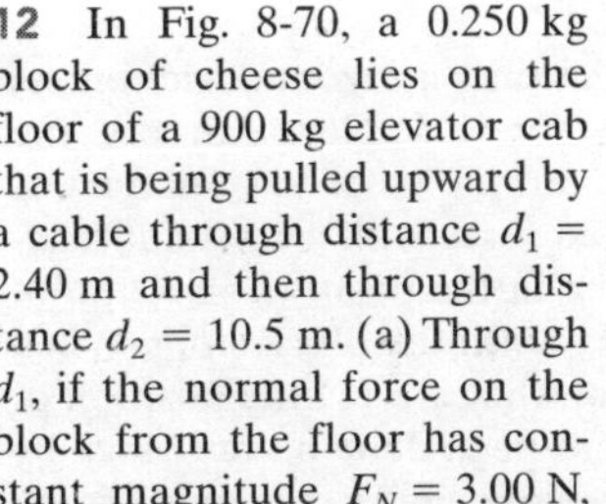

spring (spring constant k) whose other end is fixed. The block is initially at rest at the position where the spring is unstretched ($x = 0$) when a constant horizontal force $\vec{F}$ in the positive direction of the x axis is applied to it. A plot of the resulting kinetic energy of the block versus its position x is shown in Fig. 8-73. The scale of the figure's vertical axis is set by $K_s = 4.0$ J. (a) What is the magnitude of $\vec{F}$? (b) What is the value of k?

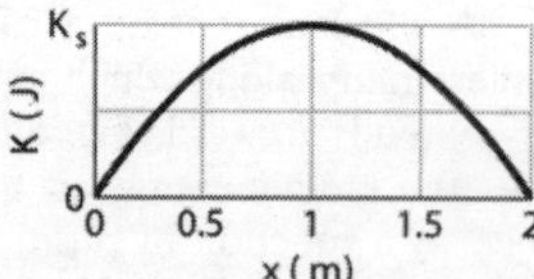

FIG. 8-73 Problem 16.

17 The block in Fig. 8-11a lies on a horizontal frictionless surface, and the spring constant is 50 N/m. Initially, the spring is at its relaxed length and the block is stationary at position $x = 0$. Then an applied force with a constant magnitude of 3.0 N pulls the block in the positive direction of the x axis, stretching the spring until the block stops. When that stopping point is reached, what are (a) the position of the block, (b) the work that has been done on the block by the applied force, and (c) the work that has been done on the block by the spring force? During the block's displacement, what are (d) the block's position when its kinetic energy is maximum and (e) the value of that maximum kinetic energy?

Work Done by a General Variable Force

18 A 5.0 kg block moves in a straight line on a horizontal frictionless surface under the influence of a force that varies with position as shown in Fig. 8-74. The scale of the figure's vertical axis is set by $F_s = 10.0$ N. How much work is done by the force as the block moves from the origin to $x = 8.0$ m?

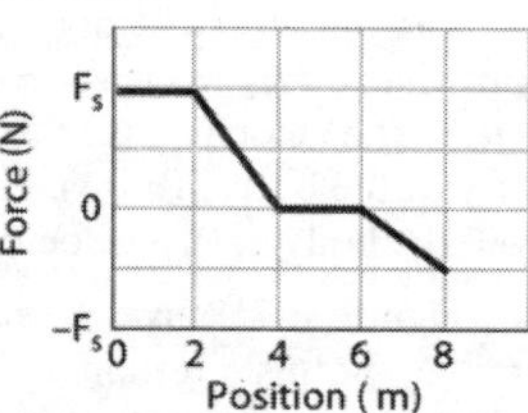

FIG. 8-74 Problem 18.

19 The force on a particle is directed along an x axis and given by $F = F_0(x/x_0 - 1)$. Find the work done by the force in moving the particle from $x = 0$ to $x = 2x_0$ by (a) plotting $F(x)$ and measuring the work from the graph and (b) integrating $F(x)$.

20 A 10 kg brick moves along an x axis. Its acceleration as a function of its position is shown in Fig. 8-75. The scale of the figure's vertical axis is set by $a_s = 20.0$ m/s². What is the net work performed on the brick by the force causing the acceleration as the brick moves from $x = 0$ to $x = 8.0$ m?

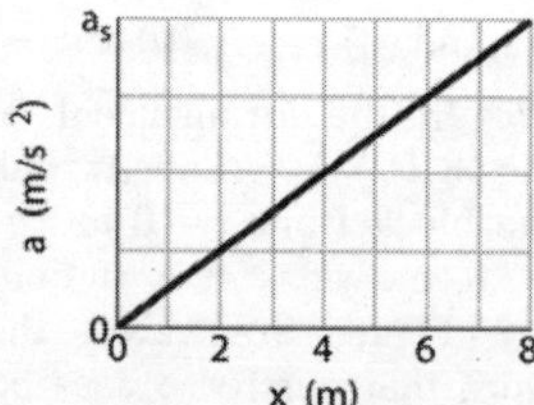

FIG. 8-75 Problem 20.

21 A single force acts on a 3.0 kg particle-like object whose position is given by $x = 3.0t - 4.0t^2 + 1.0t^3$, with x in meters and t in seconds. Find the work done on the object by the force from $t = 0$ to $t = 4.0$ s.

22 Figure 8-76 gives the acceleration of a 2.00 kg particle as an applied force $\vec{F}_a$ moves it from rest along an x axis from $x = 0$ to $x = 9.0$ m. The scale of the figure's vertical axis is set by $a_s = 6.0$ m/s². How much work has the force done on the particle when the particle reaches (a) $x = 4.0$ m, (b) $x = 7.0$ m, and (c) $x = 9.0$ m? What is the particle's speed and direction of travel when it reaches (d) $x = 4.0$ m, (e) $x = 7.0$ m, and (f) $x = 9.0$ m?

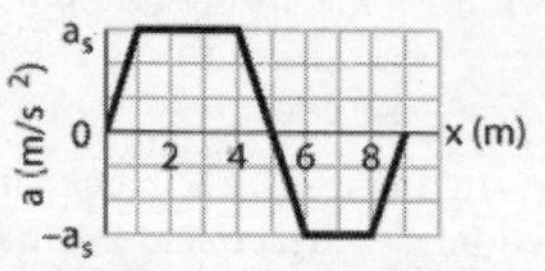

FIG. 8-76 Problem 22.

23 A force $\vec{F} = (cx - 3.00x^2)\hat{i}$ acts on a particle as the particle moves along an x axis, with $\vec{F}$ in newtons, x in meters, and c a constant. At $x = 0$, the particle's kinetic energy is 20.0 J; at $x = 3.00$ m, it is 11.0 J. Find c.

24 Figure 8-77 shows a cord attached to a cart that can slide along a frictionless horizontal rail aligned along an x axis. The left end of the cord is pulled over a pulley, of negligible mass and friction and at cord height $h = 1.20$ m, so the cart slides from $x_1 = 3.00$ m to $x_2 = 1.00$ m. During the move, the tension in the cord is a constant 25.0 N. What is the change in the kinetic energy of the cart during the move?

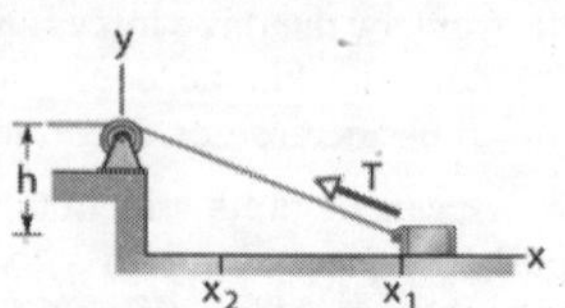

FIG. 8-77 Problem 24.

Power

25 A fully loaded, slow-moving freight elevator has a cab with a total mass of 1200 kg, which is required to travel upward 54 m in 3.0 min, starting and ending at rest. The elevator's counterweight has a mass of only 950 kg, and so the elevator motor must help. What average power is required of the force the motor exerts on the cab via the cable?

26 (a) At a certain instant, a particle-like object is acted on by a force $\vec{F} = (4.0\text{ N})\hat{i} - (2.0\text{ N})\hat{j} + (9.0\text{ N})\hat{k}$ while the object's velocity is $\vec{v} = -(2.0\text{ m/s})\hat{i} + (4.0\text{ m/s})\hat{k}$. What is the instantaneous rate at which the force does work on the object? (b) At some other time, the velocity consists of only a y component. If the force is unchanged and the instantaneous power is -12 W, what is the velocity of the object?

27 A machine carries a 4.0 kg package from an initial position of $\vec{d}_i = (0.50\text{ m})\hat{i} + (0.75\text{ m})\hat{j} + (0.20\text{ m})\hat{k}$ at $t = 0$ to a final position of $\vec{d}_f = (7.50\text{ m})\hat{i} + (12.0\text{ m})\hat{j} + (7.20\text{ m})\hat{k}$ at $t = 12$ s. The constant force applied by the machine on the package is $\vec{F} = (2.00\text{ N})\hat{i} + (4.00\text{ N})\hat{j} + (6.00\text{ N})\hat{k}$. For that displacement, find (a) the work done on the package by the machine's force and (b) the average power of the machine's force on the package.

28 A force $\vec{F} = (3.00\text{ N})\hat{i} + (7.00\text{ N})\hat{j} + (7.00\text{ N})\hat{k}$ acts on a 2.00 kg mobile object that moves from an initial position of $\vec{d}_i = (3.00\text{ m})\hat{i} - (2.00\text{ m})\hat{j} + (5.00\text{ m})\hat{k}$ to a final position of $\vec{d}_f = -(5.00\text{ m})\hat{i} + (4.00\text{ m})\hat{j} + (7.00\text{ m})\hat{k}$ in 4.00 s. Find (a) the work done on the object by the force in the 4.00 s interval, (b) the average power due to the force during that interval, and (c) the angle between vectors $\vec{d}_i$ and $\vec{d}_f$.

29 A funny car accelerates from rest through a measured track distance in time T with the engine operating at a constant power P. If the track crew can increase the engine power by a differential amount dP, what is the change in the time required for the run?

Determining Potential Energy Values

30 In Fig. 8-78, a frictionless roller-coaster car of mass $m = 825$ kg tops the first hill with speed $v_0 = 17.0$ m/s at height $h = 42.0$ m. How much work does the gravitational force do on the car from that point to (a) point A, (b) point B, and (c) point C? If the gravitational potential energy of the car–Earth system is taken to be zero at C, what is its value when the car is at (d) B and (e) A? (f) If mass m were doubled, would the change in the gravitational potential energy of the system between points A and B increase, decrease, or remain the same?

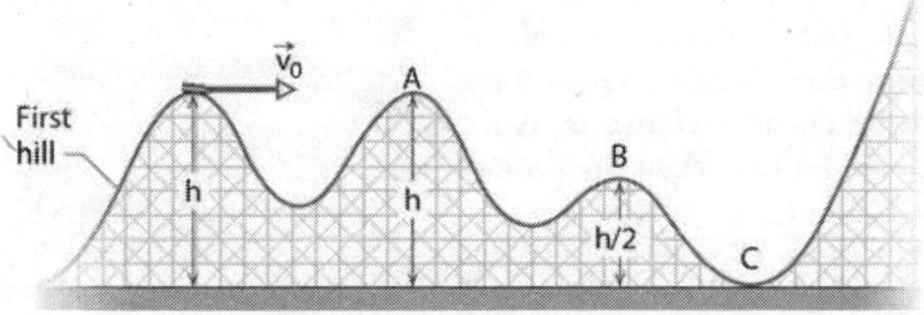

FIG. 8-78 Problems 30.

31 Figure 8-79 shows a thin rod, of length $L = 2.00$ m and negligible mass, that can pivot about one end to rotate in a vertical circle. A ball of mass $m = 5.00$ kg is attached to the other end. The rod is pulled aside to angle $\theta_0 = 30.0°$ and released with initial velocity $\vec{v}_0 = 0$. As the ball descends to its lowest point, (a) how much work does the gravitational force do on it and (b) what is the change in the gravitational potential energy of the ball–Earth system? (c) If the gravitational potential energy is taken to be zero at the lowest point, what is its value just as the ball is released? (d) Do the magnitudes of the answers to (a) through (c) increase, decrease, or remain the same if angle θ is increased?

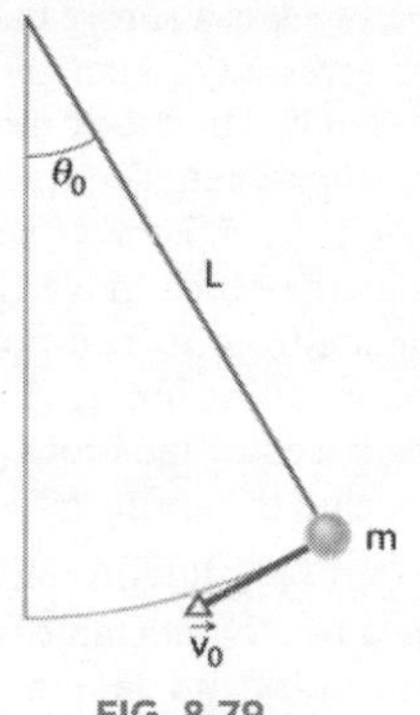

FIG. 8-79 Problems 31.

32 In Fig. 8-80, a small block of mass $m = 0.032$ kg can slide along the frictionless loop-the-loop, with loop radius $R = 12$ cm. The block is released from rest at point P, at height $h = 5.0R$ above the bottom of the loop. How much work does the gravitational force do on the block as the block travels from point P to (a) point Q and (b) the top of the loop? If the gravitational potential energy of the block–Earth system is taken to be zero at the bottom of the loop, what is that potential energy when the block is (c) at point P, (d) at point Q, and (e) at the top of the loop? (f) If, instead of merely being released, the block is given some initial speed downward along the track, do the answers to (a) through (e) increase, decrease, or remain the same?

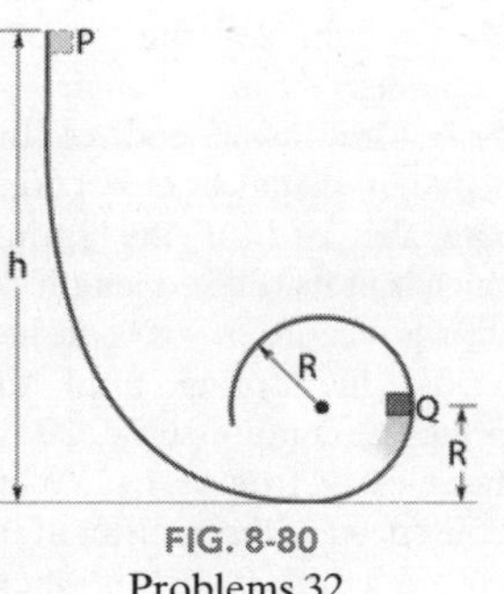

FIG. 8-80 Problems 32.

Conservation of Mechanical Energy

33 A 5.0 g marble is fired vertically upward using a spring gun. The spring must be compressed 8.0 cm if the marble is to just reach a target 20 m above the marble's position on the compressed spring. (a) What is the change ΔU_g in the gravitational potential energy of the marble–Earth system during the 20 m ascent? (b) What is the change ΔU_s in the elastic potential energy of the spring during its launch of the marble? (c) What is the spring constant of the spring?

34 A 700 g block is released from rest at height h_0 above a vertical spring with spring constant $k = 400$ N/m and negligible mass. The block sticks to the spring and momentarily stops after compressing the spring 19.0 cm. How much work is done (a) by the block on the spring and (b) by the spring on the block? (c) What is the value of h_0? (d) If the block were released from height $2.00h_0$ above the spring, what would be the maximum compression of the spring?

35 In Problem 8, what are the magnitudes of (a) the horizontal component and (b) the vertical component of the *net* force acting on the block at point Q? (c) At what height h should the block be released from rest so that it is on the verge of losing contact with the track at the top of the loop? (*On the verge of losing contact* means that the normal force on the block from the track has just then become zero.) (d) Graph the magnitude of the normal force on the block at the top of the loop versus initial height h, for the range $h = 0$ to $h = 6R$.

36 A single conservative force $\vec{F} = (6.0x - 12)\hat{\imath}$ N, where x is in meters, acts on a particle moving along an x axis. The potential energy U associated with this force is assigned a value of 27 J at $x = 0$. (a) Write an expression for U as a function of x, with U in joules and x in meters. (b) What is the maximum positive potential energy? At what (c) negative value and (d) positive value of x is the potential energy equal to zero?

37 The string in Fig. 8-81 is $L = 120$ cm long, has a ball attached to one end, and is fixed at its other end. The distance d from the fixed end to a fixed peg at point P is 75.0 cm. When the initially stationary ball is released with the string horizontal as shown, it will swing along the dashed arc. What is its speed when it reaches (a) its lowest point and (b) its highest point after the string catches on the peg?

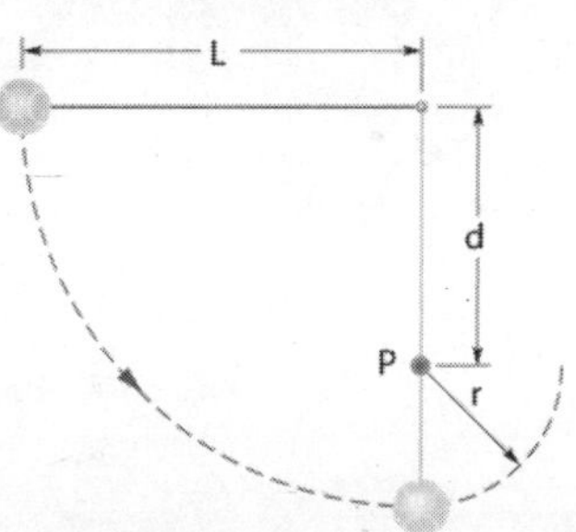

FIG. 8-81 Problems 37.

38 A block of mass $m = 2.0$ kg is dropped from height $h = 40$ cm onto a spring of spring constant $k = 1960$ N/m (Fig. 8-82). Find the maximum distance the spring is compressed.

39 At $t = 0$ a 1.0 kg ball is thrown from a tall tower with $\vec{v} = (18 \text{ m/s})\hat{\imath} + (24 \text{ m/s})\hat{\jmath}$. What is ΔU of the ball–Earth system between $t = 0$ and $t = 6.0$ s (still free fall)?

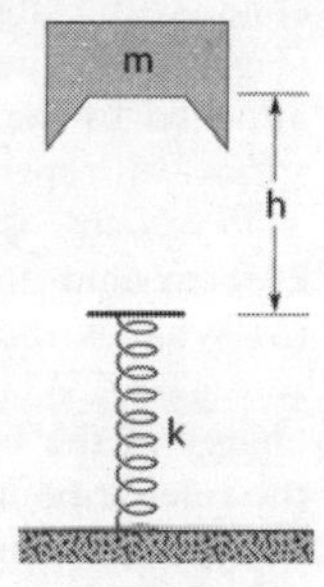

FIG. 8-82 Problem 38.

40 A 60 kg skier starts from rest at height $H = 20$ m above the end of a ski-jump ramp (Fig. 8-83) and leaves the ramp at angle $\theta = 28°$. Neglect the effects of air resistance and assume the ramp is frictionless. (a) What is the maximum height h of his jump above the end of the ramp? (b) If he increased his weight by putting on a backpack, would h then be greater, less, or the same?

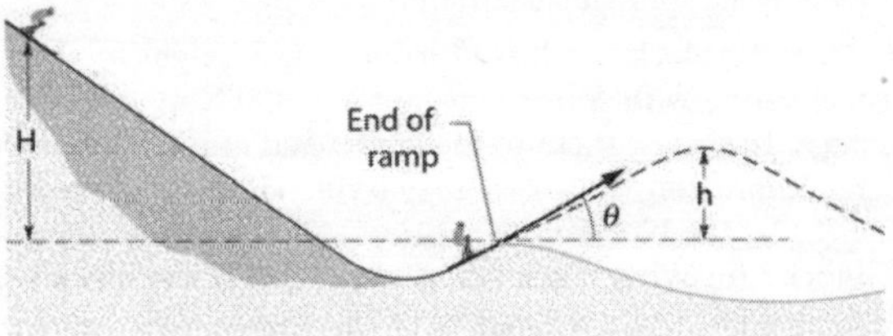

FIG. 8-83 Problem 40.

41 A 2.0 kg breadbox on a frictionless incline of angle $\theta = 40°$ is connected, by a cord that runs over a pulley, to a light spring of spring constant $k = 120$ N/m, as shown in Fig. 8-84. The box is released from rest when the spring is unstretched. Assume that the pulley is massless and frictionless. (a) What is the speed of the box when it has moved 10 cm down the incline? (b) How far down the incline from its point of release does the box slide before momentarily stopping, and what are the (c) magnitude and (d) direction (up or down the incline) of the box's acceleration at the instant the box momentarily stops?

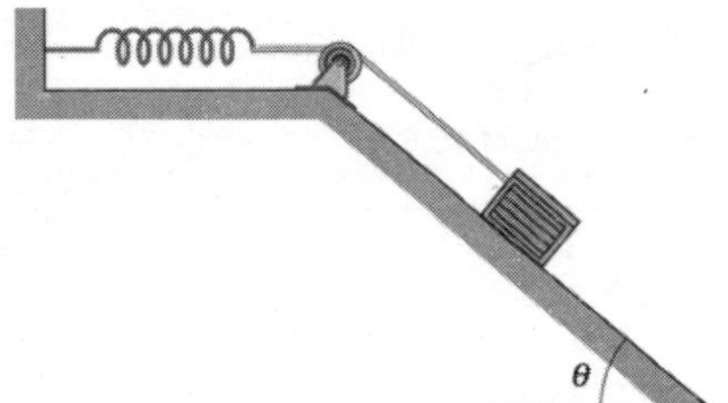

FIG. 8-84 Problem 41.

42 A block with mass $m = 2.00$ kg is placed against a spring on a frictionless incline with angle $\theta = 30.0°$ (Fig. 8-85). (The block is not attached to the spring.) The spring, with spring constant $k = 19.6$ N/cm, is compressed 20.0 cm and then released. (a) What is the elastic potential energy of the compressed spring? (b) What is the change in the gravitational potential energy of the block–Earth system as the block moves from the release point to its highest point on the incline? (c) How far along the incline is the highest point from the release point?

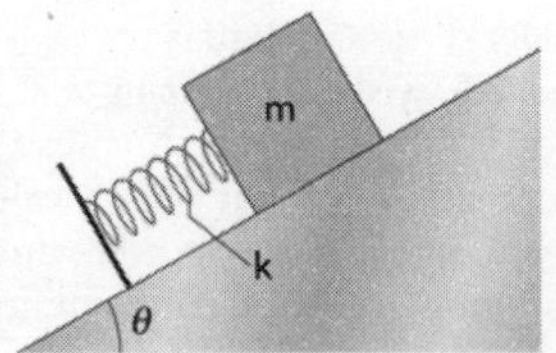

FIG. 8-85 Problem 42.

43 Figure 8-86*a* applies to the spring in a cork gun (Fig. 8-86*b*); it shows the spring force as a function of the stretch or compression of the spring. The spring is compressed by 5.5 cm and used to propel a 3.8 g cork from the gun. (a) What is the speed of the cork if it is released as the spring passes through its relaxed position? (b) Suppose, instead, that the cork sticks to the spring and stretches it 1.5 cm before separation occurs. What now is the speed of the cork at the time of release?

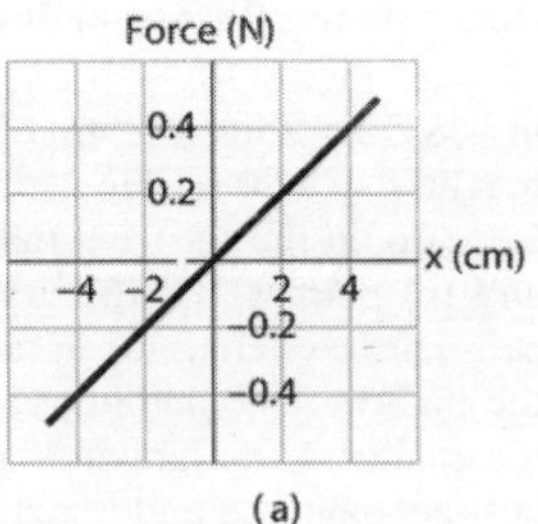

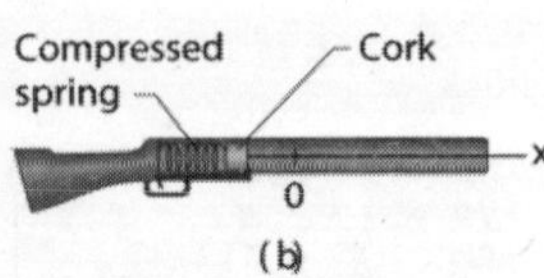

FIG. 8-86 Problem 43.

44 In Fig. 8-87, a block of mass $m = 12$ kg is released from rest on a frictionless incline of angle $\theta = 30°$. Below the block is a spring that can be compressed 2.0 cm by a force of 270 N. The block momentarily stops when it compresses the spring by 5.5 cm. (a) How far does the block move down the incline from its rest position to this stopping point? (b) What is the speed of the block just as it touches the spring?

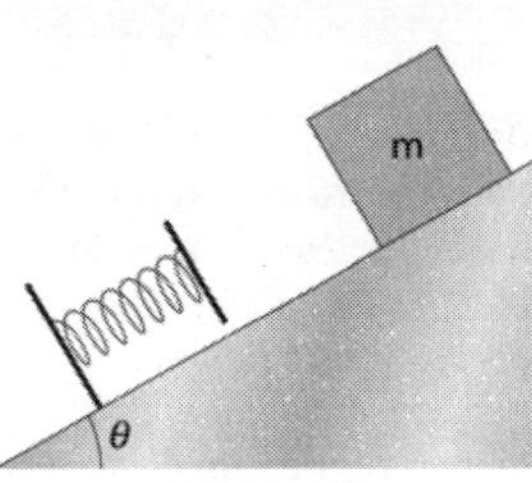

FIG. 8-87 Problems 44.

45 In Fig. 8-88, a chain is held on a frictionless table with one-fourth of its length hanging over the edge. If the chain has length $L = 28$ cm and mass $m = 0.012$ kg, how much work is required to pull the hanging part back onto the table?

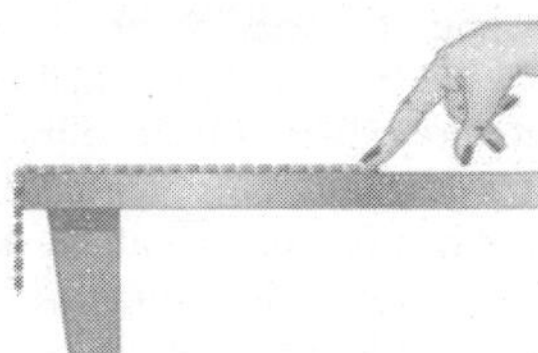

FIG. 8-88 Problem 45.

46 In Fig. 8-89, a spring with $k = 170$ N/m is at the top of a frictionless incline of angle $\theta = 37.0°$. The lower end of the incline is distance $D = 1.00$ m from the end of the spring, which is at its relaxed length. A 2.00 kg canister is pushed against the spring until the spring is compressed 0.200 m and released from rest. (a) What is the speed of the canister at the instant the spring returns to its relaxed length (which is when the canister loses contact with the spring)? (b) What is the speed of the canister when it reaches the lower end of the incline?

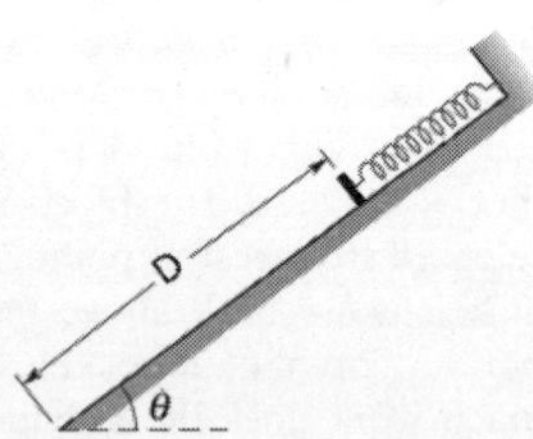

FIG. 8-89 Problem 46.

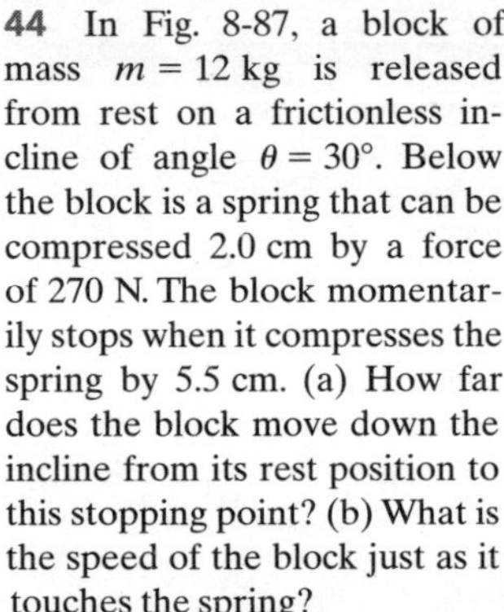

47 Two children are playing a game in which they try to hit a small box on the floor with a marble fired from a spring-loaded gun that is mounted on a table. The target box is horizontal distance

$D = 2.20$ m from the edge of the table; see Fig. 8-90. Bobby compresses the spring 1.10 cm, but the center of the marble falls 27.0 cm short of the center of the box. How far should Rhoda compress the spring to score a direct hit? Assume that neither the spring nor the ball encounters friction in the gun.

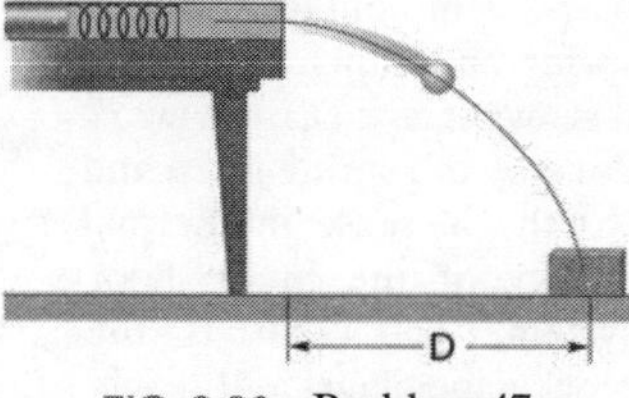

FIG. 8-90 Problem 47.

48 A uniform cord of length 25 cm and mass 15 g is initially stuck to a ceiling. Later, it hangs vertically from the ceiling with only one end still stuck. What is the change in the gravitational potential energy of the cord with this change in orientation? (*Hint:* Consider a differential slice of the cord and then use integral calculus.)

49 A boy is initially seated on the top of a hemispherical ice mound of radius $R = 13.8$ m. He begins to slide down the ice, with a negligible initial speed (Fig. 8-91). Approximate the ice as being frictionless. At what height does the boy lose contact with the ice?

FIG. 8-91 Problem 49.

50 In Fig. 8 92, a block of mass $m = 3.20$ kg slides from rest a distance d down a frictionless incline at angle $\theta = 30.0°$ where it runs into a spring of spring constant 431 N/m. When the block momentarily stops, it has compressed the spring by 21.0 cm. What are (a) distance d and (b) the distance between the point of the first block–spring contact and the point where the block's speed is greatest?

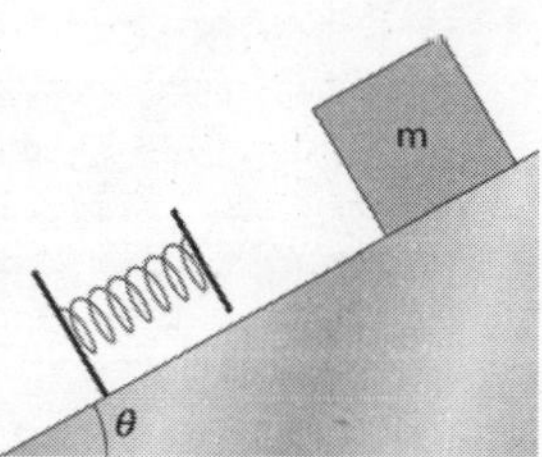

FIG. 8-92 Problems 50.

Reading a Potential Energy Curve

51 The potential energy of a diatomic molecule (a two-atom system like H_2 or O_2) is given by

$$U = \frac{A}{r^{12}} - \frac{B}{r^6}$$

where r is the separation of the two atoms of the molecule and A and B are positive constants. This potential energy is associated with the force that binds the two atoms together. (a) Find the *equilibrium separation*—that is, the distance between the atoms at which the force on each atom is zero. Is the force repulsive (the atoms are pushed apart) or attractive (they are pulled together) if their separation is (b) smaller and (c) larger than the equilibrium separation?

52 Figure 8-93 shows a plot of potential energy U versus position x of a 0.90 kg particle that can travel only along an x axis. (Nonconservative forces are not involved.) Three values are $U_A = 15.0$ J, $U_B = 35.0$ J, and $U_C = 45.0$ J. The particle is released at $x = 4.5$ m with an initial speed of 7.0 m/s, headed in the negative x direction. (a) If the particle can reach $x = 1.0$ m, what is its speed there, and if it cannot, what is its turning point? What are the (b) magnitude and (c) direction of the force on the particle as it begins to move to the left of $x = 4.0$ m? Suppose, instead, the particle is headed in the positive x direction when it is released at $x = 4.5$ m at speed 7.0 m/s. (d) If the particle can reach $x = 7.0$ m, what is its speed there, and if it cannot, what is its turning point? What are the (e) magnitude and (f) direction of the force on the particle as it begins to move to the right of $x = 5.0$ m?

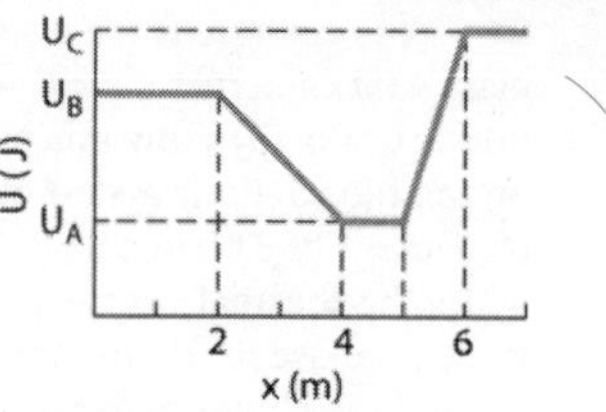

FIG. 8-93 Problem 52.

53 Figure 8-94 shows a plot of potential energy U versus position x of a 0.200 kg particle that can travel only along an x axis under the influence of a conservative force. The graph has these values: $U_A = 9.00$ J, $U_C = 20.00$ J, and $U_D = 24.00$ J. The particle is released at the point where U forms a "potential hill" of "height" $U_B = 12.00$ J, with kinetic energy 4.00 J. What is the speed of the particle at (a) $x = 3.5$ m and (b) $x = 6.5$ m? What is the position of the turning point on (c) the right side and (d) the left side?

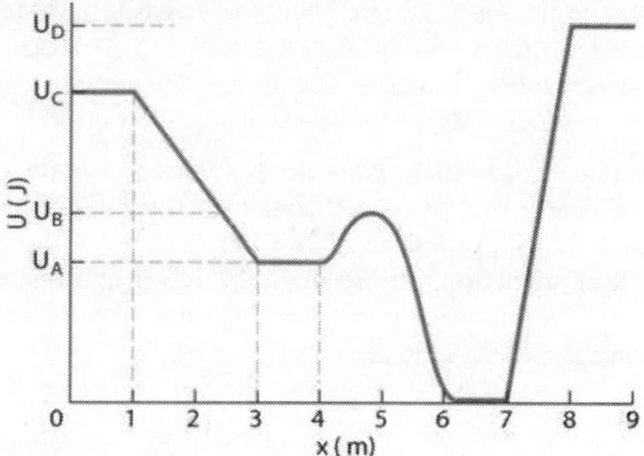

FIG. 8-94 Problem 53.

54 A single conservative force $F(x)$ acts on a 1.0 kg particle that moves along an x axis. The potential energy $U(x)$ associated with $F(x)$ is given by

$$U(x) = -4x\,e^{-x/4}\text{ J}$$

where x is in meters. At $x = 5.0$ m the particle has a kinetic energy of 2.0 J. (a) What is the mechanical energy of the system? (b) Make a plot of $U(x)$ as a function of x for $0 \le x \le 10$ m, and on the same graph draw the line that represents the mechanical energy of the system. Use part (b) to determine (c) the least value of x the particle can reach and (d) the greatest value of x the particle can reach. Use part (b) to determine (e) the maximum kinetic energy of the particle and (f) the value of x at which it occurs. (g) Determine an expression in newtons and meters for $F(x)$ as a function of x. (h) For what (finite) value of x does $F(x) = 0$?

Work Done on a System by an External Force

55 A worker pushed a 27 kg block 9.2 m along a level floor at constant speed with a force directed 32° below the horizontal. If the coefficient of kinetic friction between block and floor was 0.20, what were (a) the work done by the worker's force and (b) the increase in thermal energy of the block– floor system?

56 A horizontal force of magnitude 35.0 N pushes a block of mass 4.00 kg across a floor where the coefficient of kinetic friction is 0.600. (a) How much work is done by that applied force on the block–floor system when the block slides through a displacement of 3.00 m across the floor? (b) During that displacement, the thermal energy of the block increases by 40.0 J. What is the increase in thermal energy of the floor? (c) What is the increase in the kinetic energy of the block?

Conservation of Energy

57 In Fig. 8-95, a block slides down an incline. As it moves from point A to point B, which are 5.0 m apart, force $\vec{F}$ acts on the block, with magnitude 2.0 N and directed down the incline. The magnitude of the frictional force acting on the block is 10 N. If the kinetic energy of the block increases by 35 J between A and B, how much work is done on the block by the gravitational force as the block moves from A to B?

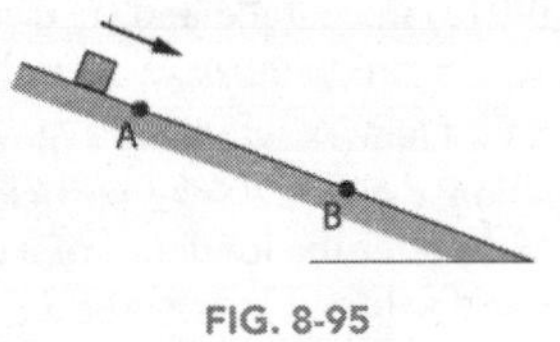

FIG. 8-95 Problems 57.

58 You push a 2.0 kg block against a horizontal spring, compressing the spring by 15 cm. Then you release the block, and the spring sends it sliding across a tabletop. It stops 75 cm from where you released it. The spring constant is 200 N/m. What is the block–table coefficient of kinetic friction?

59 In Fig. 8-96, a block slides along a track from one level to a higher level after passing through an intermediate valley. The track is frictionless until the block reaches the higher level. There a frictional force stops the block in a distance d. The block's initial speed v_0 is 6.0 m/s, the height difference h is 1.1 m, and μ_k is 0.60. Find d.

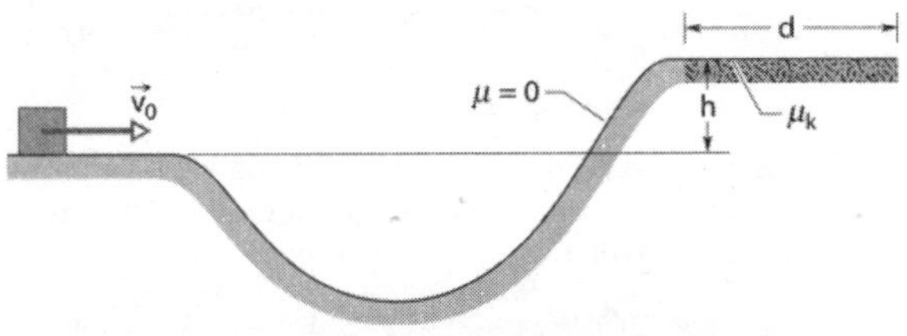

FIG. 8-96 Problem 59.

60 In Fig. 8-97, a 3.5 kg block is accelerated from rest by a compressed spring of spring constant 640 N/m. The block leaves the spring at the spring's relaxed length and then travels over a horizontal floor with a coefficient of kinetic friction $\mu_k = 0.25$. The frictional force stops the block in distance $D = 7.8$ m. What are (a) the increase in the thermal energy of the block–floor system, (b) the maximum kinetic energy of the block, and (c) the original compression distance of the spring?

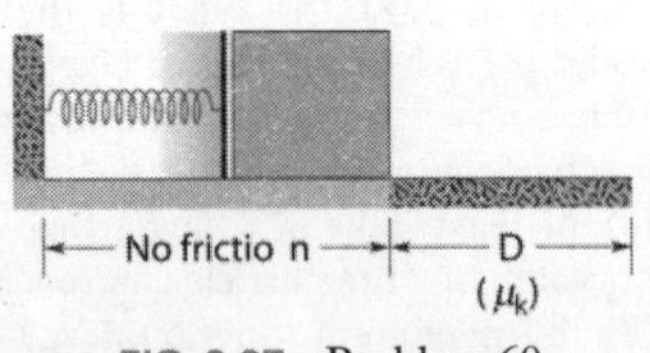

FIG. 8-97 Problem 60.

61 In Fig. 8-98, a block of mass $m = 2.5$ kg slides head on into a spring of spring constant $k = 320$ N/m. When the block stops, it has compressed the spring by 7.5 cm. The coefficient of kinetic friction between block and floor is 0.25. While the block is in contact with the spring and being brought to rest, what are (a) the work done by the spring force and (b) the increase in thermal energy of the block–floor system? (c) What is the block's speed just as it reaches the spring?

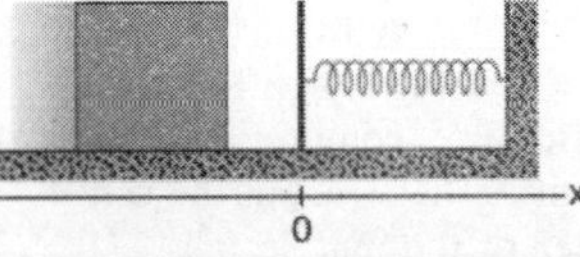

FIG. 8-98 Problem 61.

62 In Fig. 8-99, a block is released from rest at height $d = 40$ cm and slides down a frictionless ramp and onto a first plateau, which has length d and where the coefficient of kinetic friction is 0.50. If the block is still moving, it then slides down a second frictionless ramp through height $d/2$ and onto a lower plateau, which has length $d/2$ and where the coefficient of kinetic friction is again 0.50. If the block is still moving, it then slides up a frictionless ramp until it (momentarily) stops. Where does the block stop? If its final stop is on a plateau, state which one and give the distance L from the left edge of that plateau. If the block reaches the ramp, give the height H above the lower plateau where it momentarily stops.

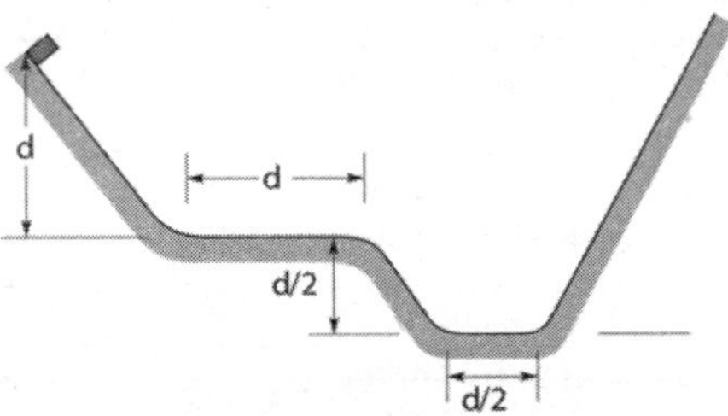

FIG. 8-99 Problem 62.

63 A particle can slide along a track with elevated ends and a flat central part, as shown in Fig. 8-100. The flat part has length $L = 40$ cm. The curved portions of the track are frictionless, but for the flat part the coefficient of kinetic friction is $\mu_k = 0.20$. The particle is released from rest at point A, which is at height $h = L/2$. How far from the left edge of the flat part does the particle finally stop?

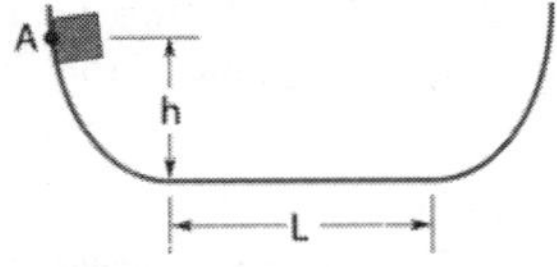

FIG. 8-100 Problem 63.

64 In Fig. 8-101, a block slides along a path that is without friction until the block reaches the section of length $L = 0.75$ m, which begins at height $h = 2.0$ m on a ramp of angle $\theta = 30°$. In that section, the coefficient of kinetic friction is 0.40. The block passes through point A with a speed of 8.0 m/s. If the block can reach point B (where the friction ends), what is its speed there, and if it cannot, what is its greatest height above A?

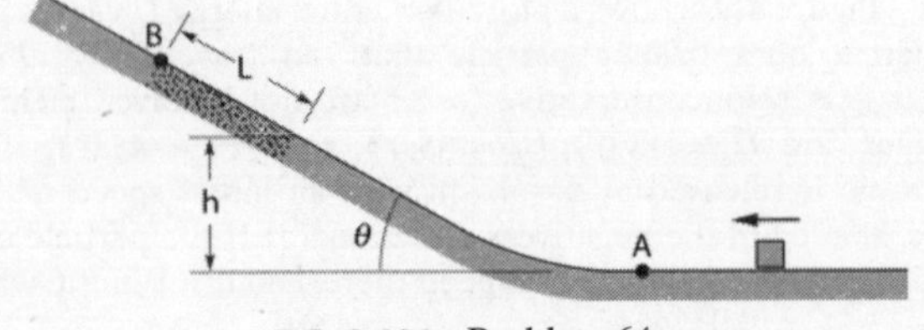

FIG. 8-101 Problem 64.

65 The cable of the 1800 kg elevator cab in Fig. 8-102 snaps when the cab is at rest at the first floor, where the cab bottom is a distance $d = 3.7$ m above a spring of spring constant $k = 0.15$ MN/m. A safety device clamps the cab against guide rails so that a constant frictional force of 4.4 kN opposes the cab's motion. (a) Find the speed of the cab just before it hits the spring. (b) Find the maximum distance x that the spring is compressed (the frictional force still acts during this compression). (c) Find the distance that the cab will bounce back up the shaft. (d) Using conservation of energy, find the approximate total distance that the cab will move before coming to rest. (Assume that the frictional force on the cab is negligible when the cab is stationary.)

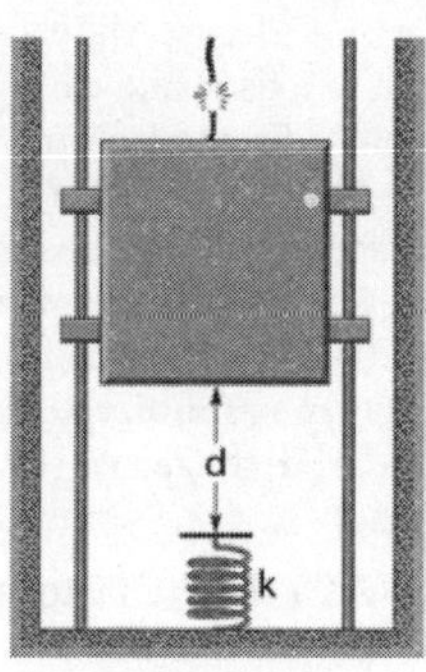

FIG. 8-102 Problem 65.

Additional Problems

66 A 250 g block is dropped onto a relaxed vertical spring that has a spring constant of $k = 2.5$ N/cm (Fig. 8-103). The block becomes attached to the spring and compresses the spring 12 cm before momentarily stopping. While the spring is being compressed, what work is done on the block by (a) the gravitational force on it and (b) the spring force? (c) What is the speed of the block just before it hits the spring? (Assume that friction is negligible.) (d) If the speed at impact is doubled, what is the maximum compression of the spring?

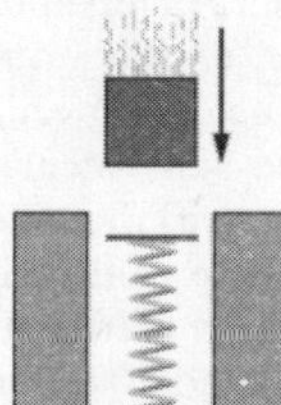
FIG. 8-103 Problem 66.

67 How much work is done by a force $\vec{F} = (2x \text{ N})\hat{i} + (3 \text{ N})\hat{j}$, with x in meters, that moves a particle from a position $\vec{r}_i = (2 \text{ m})\hat{i} + (3 \text{ m})\hat{j}$ to a position $\vec{r}_f = -(4 \text{ m})\hat{i} - (3 \text{ m})\hat{j}$?

68 In Fig. 8-104, a cord runs around two massless, frictionless pulleys. A canister with mass $m = 20$ kg hangs from one pulley, and you exert a force $\vec{F}$ on the free end of the cord. (a) What must be the magnitude of $\vec{F}$ if you are to lift the canister at a constant speed? (b) To lift the canister by 2.0 cm, how far must you pull the free end of the cord? During that lift, what is the work done on the canister by (c) your force (via the cord) and (d) the gravitational force? (*Hint:* When a cord loops around a pulley as shown, it pulls on the pulley with a net force that is twice the tension in the cord.)

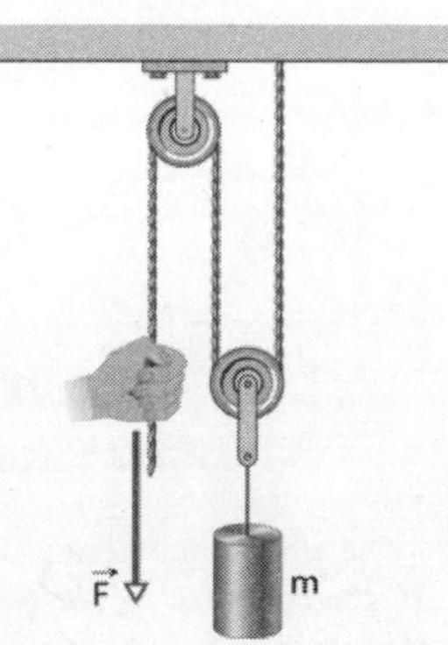

FIG. 8-104 Problem 68.

69 A constant force of magnitude 10 N makes an angle of 150° (measured counterclockwise) with the positive x direction as it acts on a 2.0 kg object moving in an xy plane. How much work is done on the object by the force as the object moves from the origin to the point having position vector $(2.0 \text{ m})\hat{i} - (4.0 \text{ m})\hat{j}$?

70 A 230 kg crate hangs from the end of a rope of length $L = 12.0$ m. A horizontal push on the crate with a varying force $\vec{F}$ to move it distance $d = 4.00$ m to the side (Fig. 8-105). (a) What is the magnitude of $\vec{F}$ when the crate is in this final position? During the crate's displacement, what are (b) the total work done on it, (c) the work done by the gravitational force on the crate, and (d) the work done by the pull on the crate from the rope? (e) Knowing that the crate is motionless before and after its displacement, use the answers to (b), (c), and (d) to find the work your force $\vec{F}$ does on the crate. (f) Why is the work of your force not equal to the product of the horizontal displacement and the answer to (a)?

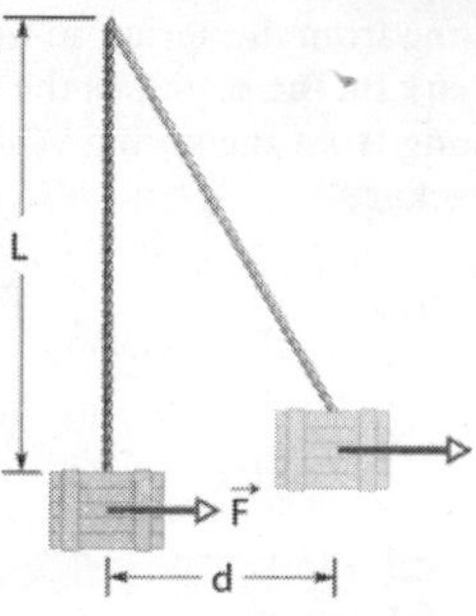

FIG. 8-105 Problem 70.

71 The only force acting on a 2.0 kg body as the body moves along an x axis varies as shown in Fig. 8-106. The scale of the figure's vertical axis is set by $F_s = 4.0$ N. The velocity of the body at $x = 0$ is 4.0 m/s. (a) What is the kinetic energy of the body at $x = 3.0$ m? (b) At what value of x will the body have a kinetic energy of 8.0 J? (c) What is the maximum kinetic energy of the body between $x = 0$ and $x = 5.0$ m?

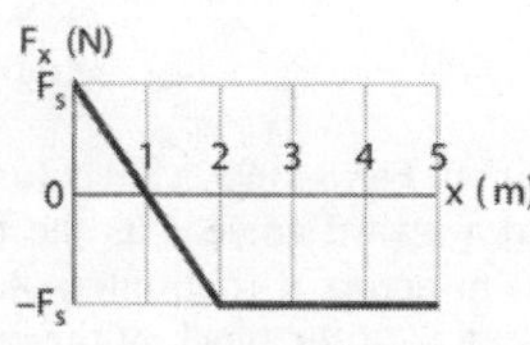

FIG. 8-106 Problem 71.

72 Figure 8-107 shows a cold package of hot dogs sliding rightward across a frictionless floor through a distance $d = 20.0$ cm while three forces act on the package. Two of them are horizontal and have the magnitudes $F_1 = 5.00$ N and $F_2 = 1.00$ N; the third is angled down by $\theta = 60.0°$ and has the magnitude $F_3 = 4.00$ N. (a) For the 20.0 cm displacement, what is the N; the third is angled down by $\theta = 60.0°$ and has the magnitude $F_3 = 4.00$ N. (a) For the 20.0 cm displacement, what is the *net* work done on the package by the three applied forces, the gravitational force on the package, and the normal force on the package? (b) If the package has a mass of 2.0 kg and an initial kinetic energy of 0, what is its speed at the end of the displacement?

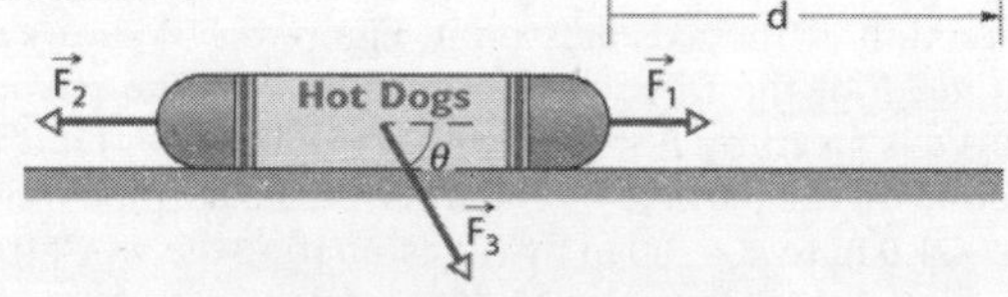

FIG. 8-107 Problem 72.

73 A frightened child is restrained by her mother as the child slides down a frictionless playground slide. If the force on the child from the mother is 100 N up the slide, the child's kinetic energy increases by 30 J as she moves down the slide a distance of 1.8 m. (a) How much work is done on the child by the gravitational force during the 1.8 m descent? (b) If the child is not restrained by her mother, how much will the child's kinetic energy increase as she comes down the slide that same distance of 1.8 m?

74 A spring with a pointer attached is hanging next to a scale marked in millimeters. Three different packages are hung from the spring, in turn, as shown in Fig. 8-108. (a) Which mark on the scale will the pointer indicate when no package is hung from the spring? (b) What is the weight W of the third package?

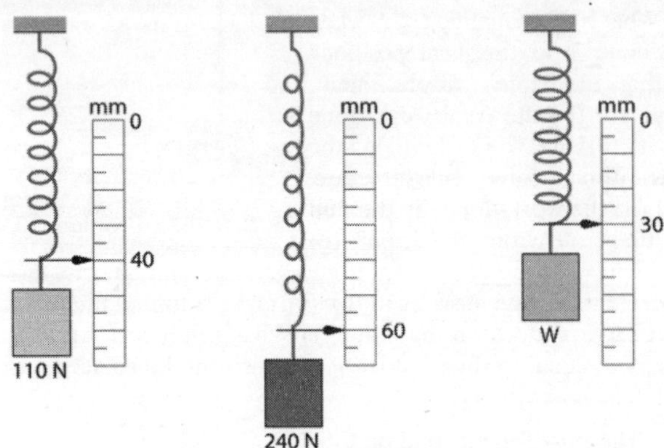

FIG. 8-108 Problem 74.

75 In Fig. 8-109*a*, a 2.0 N force is applied to a 4.0 kg block at a downward angle θ as the block moves rightward through 1.0 m across a frictionless floor. Find an expression for the speed v_f of the block at the end of that distance if the block's initial velocity is (a) 0 and (b) 1.0 m/s to the right. (c) The situation in Fig. 8-115*b* is similar in that the block is initially moving at 1.0 m/s to the right, but now the 2.0 N force is directed downward to the left. Find an expression for the speed v_f of the block at the end of the 1.0 m distance. (d) Graph all three expressions for v_f versus downward angle θ for $\theta = 0°$ to $\theta = 90°$. Interpret the graphs.

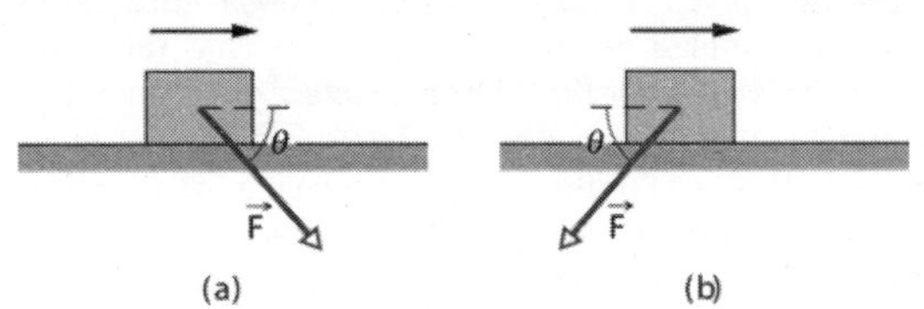

FIG. 8-109 Problem 75.

76 As a particle moves along an x axis, a force in the positive direction of the axis acts on it. Figure 8-110 shows the magnitude F of the force versus position x of the particle. The curve is given by $F = a/x^2$, with $a = 9.0\ \text{N}\cdot\text{m}^2$. Find the work done on the particle by the force as the particle moves from $x = 1.0$ m to $x = 3.0$ m by (a) estimating the work from the graph and (b) integrating the force function.

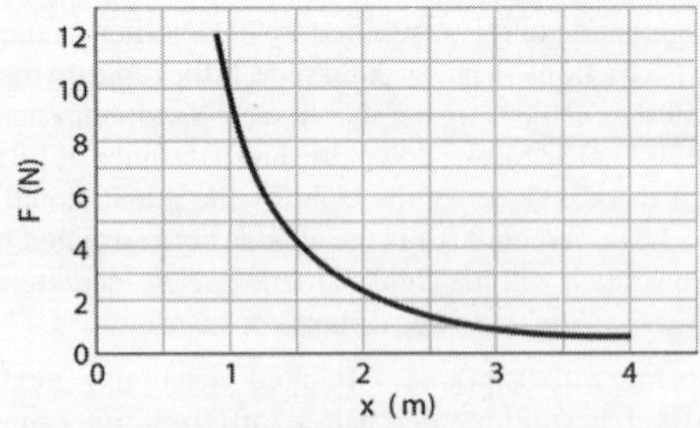

FIG. 8-110 Problem 76.

77 A CD case slides along a floor in the positive direction of an x axis while an applied force $\vec{F}_a$ acts on the case. The force is directed along the x axis and has the x component $F_{ax} = 9x - 3x^2$, with x in meters and F_{ax} in newtons. The case starts at rest at the position $x = 0$, and it moves until it is again at rest. (a) Plot the work $\vec{F}_a$ does on the case as a function of x. (b) At what position is the work maximum, and (c) what is that maximum value? (d) At what position has the work decreased to zero? (e) At what position is the case again at rest?

78 At a certain factory, 300 kg crates are dropped vertically from a packing machine onto a conveyor belt moving at 1.20 m/s (Fig. 8-111). (A motor maintains the belt's constant speed.) The coefficient of kinetic friction between the belt and each crate is 0.400. After a short time, slipping between the belt and the crate ceases, and the crate then moves along with the belt. For the period of time during which the crate is being brought to rest relative to the belt, calculate, for a coordinate system at rest in the factory, (a) the kinetic energy supplied to the crate, (b) the magnitude of the kinetic frictional force acting on the crate, and (c) the energy supplied by the motor. (d) Explain why answers (a) and (c) differ.

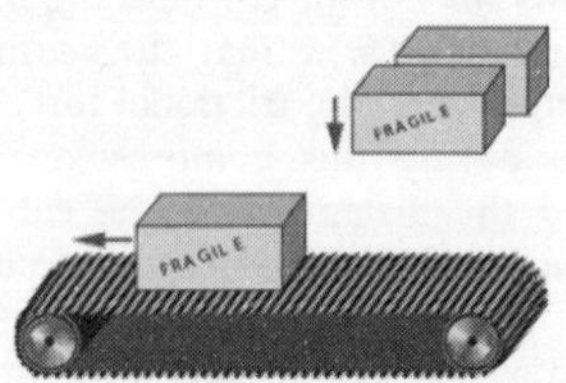

FIG. 8-111 Problem 78.

79 In Fig. 8-112, a small block is sent through point A with a speed of 7.0 m/s. Its path is without friction until it reaches the section of length $L = 12$ m, where the coefficient of kinetic friction is 0.70. The indicated heights are $h_1 = 6.0$ m and $h_2 = 2.0$ m. What are the speeds of the block at (a) point B and (b) point C? (c) Does the block reach point D? If so, what is its speed there; if not, how far through the section of friction does it travel?

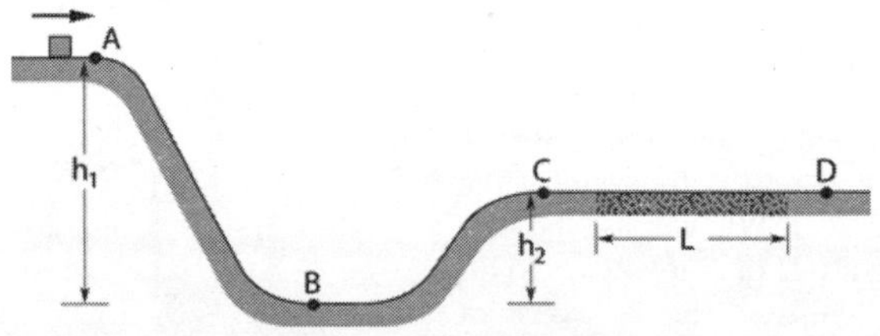

FIG. 8-112 Problem 79.

80 The only force acting on a particle is conservative force $\vec{F}$. If the particle is at point A, the potential energy of the system associated with $\vec{F}$ and the particle is 40 J. If the particle moves from point A to point B, the work done on the particle by $\vec{F}$ is +25 J. What is the potential energy of the system with the particle at B?

81 A constant horizontal force moves a 50 kg trunk 6.0 m up a 30° incline at constant speed. The coefficient of kinetic friction between the trunk and

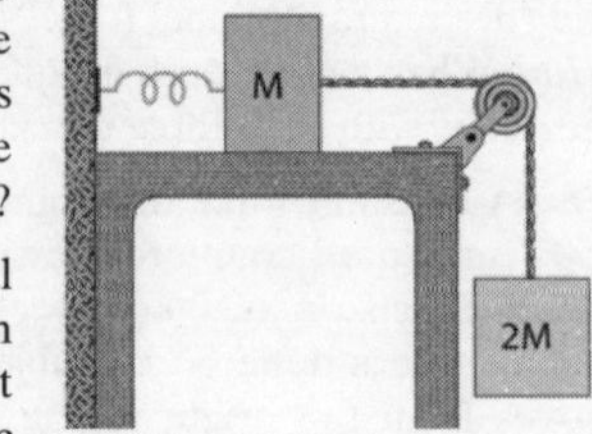

FIG. 8-113 Problem 81.

the incline is 0.20. What are (a) the work done by the applied force and (b) the increase in the thermal energy of the trunk and incline?

82 Two blocks, of masses $M = 2.0$ kg and $2M$, are connected to a spring of spring constant $k = 200$ N/m that has one end fixed, as shown in Fig. 8-64. The horizontal surface and the pulley are frictionless, and the pulley has negligible mass. The blocks are released from rest with the spring relaxed. (a) What is the combined kinetic energy of the two blocks when the hanging block has fallen 0.090 m? (b) What is the kinetic energy of the hanging block when it has fallen that 0.090 m? (c) What maximum distance does the hanging block fall before momentarily stopping?

83 The temperature of a plastic cube is monitored while the cube is pushed 3.0 m across a floor at constant speed by a horizontal force of 15 N. The thermal energy of the cube increases by 20 J. What is the increase in the thermal energy of the floor along which the cube slides?

84 In Fig. 8-114, a 1400 kg block of granite is pulled up an incline at a constant speed of 1.34 m/s by a cable and winch. The indicated distances are $d_1 = 40$ m and $d_2 = 30$ m. The coefficient of kinetic friction between the block and the incline is 0.40. What is the power due to the force applied to the block by the cable?

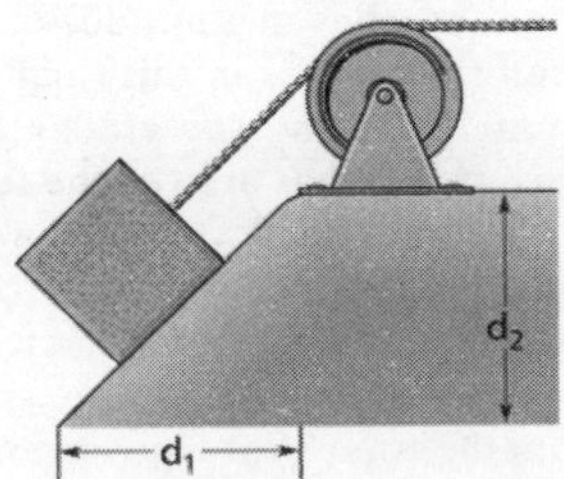

FIG. 8-114 Problem 84.

85 A 30 g bullet moving a horizontal velocity of 500 m/s comes to a stop 12 cm within a solid wall. (a) What is the change in the bullet's mechanical energy? (b) What is the magnitude of the average force from the wall stopping it?

86 A locomotive with a power capability of 1.5 MW can accelerate a train from a speed of 10 m/s to 25 m/s in 6.0 min. (a) Calculate the mass of the train. Find (b) the speed of the train and (c) the force accelerating the train as functions of time (in seconds) during the 6.0 min interval. (d) Find the distance moved by the train during the interval.

87 A river descends 15 m through rapids. The speed of the water is 3.2 m/s upon entering the rapids and 13 m/s upon leaving. What percentage of the gravitational potential energy of the water–Earth system is transferred to kinetic energy during the descent? (*Hint:* Consider the descent of, say, 10 kg of water.)

88 The magnitude of the gravitational force between a particle of mass m_1 and one of mass m_2 is given by

$$F(x) = G\frac{m_1 m_2}{x^2}$$

where G is a constant and x is the distance between the particles. (a) What is the corresponding potential energy function $U(x)$? Assume that $U(x) \to 0$ as $x \to \infty$ and that x is positive. (b) How much work is required to increase the separation of the particles from $x = x_1$ to $x = x_1 + d$?

89 A particle can move along only an x axis, where conservative forces act on it (Fig. 8-115 and the following table). The particle is released at $x = 5.00$ m with a kinetic energy of $K = 14.0$ J and a potential energy of $U = 0$. If its motion is in the negative direction of the x axis, what are its (a) K and (b) U at $x = 2.00$ m and its (c) K and (d) U at $x = 0$? If its motion is in the positive direction of the x axis, what are its (e) K and (f) U at $x = 11.0$ m, its (g) K and (h) U at $x = 12.0$ m, and its (i) K and (j) U at $x = 13.0$ m? (k) Plot $U(x)$ versus x for the range $x = 0$ to $x = 13.0$ m.

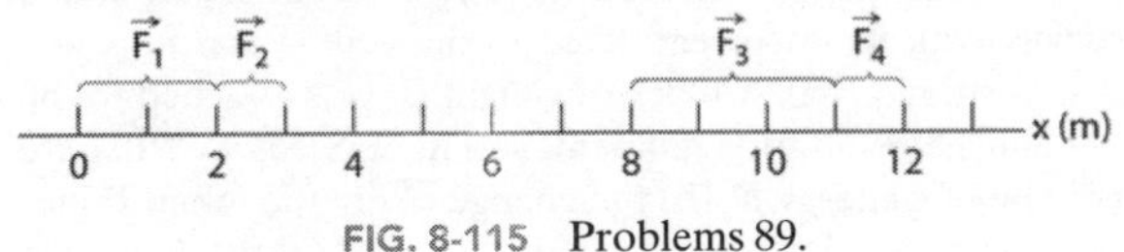

FIG. 8-115 Problems 89.

Next, the particle is released from rest at $x = 0$. What are (l) its kinetic energy at $x = 5.0$ m and (m) the maximum positive position x_{max} it reaches? (n) What does the particle do after it reaches x_{max}?

Range	Force
0 to 2.00 m	$\vec{F}_1 = +(3.00\text{ N})\hat{i}$
2.00 m to 3.00 m	$\vec{F}_2 = +(5.00\text{ N})\hat{i}$
3.00 m to 8.00 m	$F = 0$
8.00 m to 11.0 m	$\vec{F}_3 = -(4.00\text{ N})\hat{i}$
11.0 m to 12.0 m	$\vec{F}_4 = -(1.00\text{ N})\hat{i}$
12.0 m to 15.0 m	$F = 0$

90 We move a particle along an x axis, first outward from $x = 1.0$ m to $x = 4.0$ m and then back to $x = 1.0$ m, while an external force acts on it. That force is directed along the x axis, and its x component can have different values for the outward trip and for the return trip. Here are the values (in newtons) for four situations, where x is in meters:

Outward	Inward
(a) +3.0	−3.0
(b) +5.0	+5.0
(c) $+2.0x$	$-2.0x$
(d) $+3.0x^2$	$+3.0x^2$

Find the net work done on the particle by the external force *for the round trip* for each of the four situations. (e) For which, if any, is the external force conservative?

91 A conservative force $F(x)$ acts on a 2.0 kg particle that moves along an x axis. The potential energy $U(x)$ associated with $F(x)$ is graphed in Fig. 8-116. When the particle is at

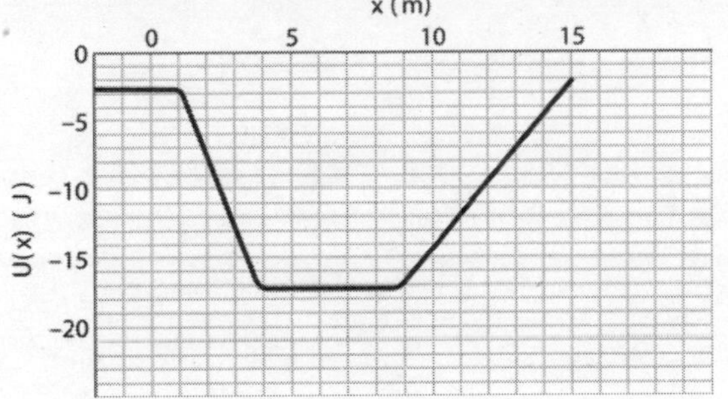

FIG. 8-116 Problem 91.

$x = 2.0$ m, its velocity is -1.5 m/s. What are the (a) magnitude and (b) direction of $F(x)$ at this position? Between what positions on the (c) left and (d) right does the particle move? (e) What is the particle's speed at $x = 7.0$ m?

92 A spring with spring constant $k = 200$ N/m is suspended vertically with its upper end fixed to the ceiling and its lower end at position $y = 0$. A block of weight 20 N is attached to the lower end, held still for a moment, and then released. What are (a) the kinetic energy K, (b) the change (from the initial value) in the gravitational potential energy ΔU_g, and (c) the change in the elastic potential energy ΔU_e of the spring–block system when the block is at $y = -5.0$ cm? What are (d) K, (e) ΔU_g, and (f) ΔU_e when $y = -10$ cm, (g) K, (h) ΔU_g, and (i) ΔU_e when $y = -15$ cm, and (j) K, (k) ΔU_g, and (l) ΔU_e when $y = -20$ cm?

93 Each second, 1200 m^3 of water passes over a waterfall 100 m high. Three-fourths of the kinetic energy gained by the water in falling is transferred to electrical energy by a hydroelectric generator. At what rate does the generator produce electrical energy? (The mass of 1 m^3 of water is 1000 kg.)

94 A massless rigid rod of length L has a ball of mass m attached to one end (Fig. 8-117). The other end is pivoted in such a way that the ball will move in a vertical circle. First, assume that there is no friction at the pivot. The system is launched downward from the horizontal position A with initial speed v_0. The ball just barely reaches point D and then stops. (a) Derive an expression for v_0 in terms of L, m, and g. (b) What is the tension in the rod when the ball passes through B? (c) A little grit is placed on the pivot to increase the friction there. Then the ball just barely reaches C when launched from A with the same speed as before. What is the decrease in the mechanical energy during this motion? (d) What is the decrease in the mechanical energy by the time the ball finally comes to rest at B after several oscillations?

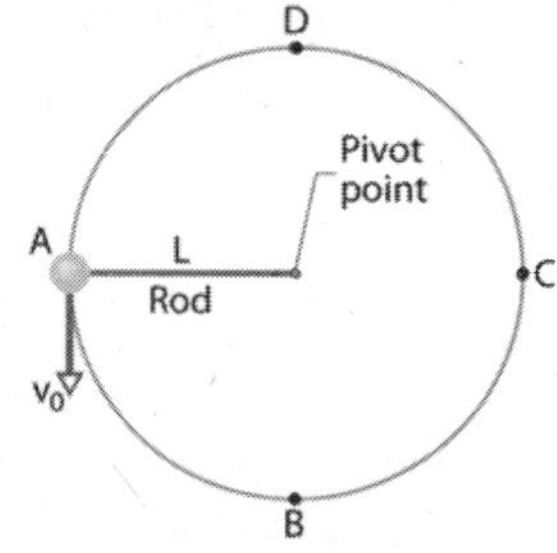

FIG. 8-117 Problem 94.

95 Conservative force $F(x)$ acts on a particle that moves along an x axis. Figure 8-118 shows how the potential energy $U(x)$ associated with force $F(x)$ varies with the position of the particle. (a) Plot $F(x)$ for the range $0 < x < 6$ m. (b) The mechanical energy E of the system is 4.0 J. Plot the kinetic energy $K(x)$ of the particle directly on Fig. 8-122.

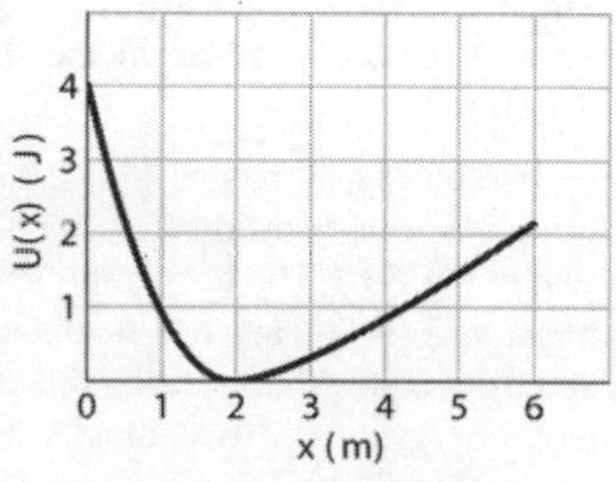

FIG. 8-118 Problem 95.

96 A 230 kg crate hangs from the end of a 13.0 m rope. You push horizontally on the crate with a varying force $\vec{F}$ to move it 5.00 m to the side (Fig. 8-119). (a) What is the magnitude of $\vec{F}$ when the crate is in this final position ? During the crate's displacement, what are (b) the total work done on it, (c) the work done by the gravitational force on the crate, and (d) the work done by the pull on the crate from the rope ? (e) Knowing that the crate is motionless before and after its displacement, use the answers to (b), (c) and (d) to find the work your force $\vec{F}$ does on the crate. (f) Why is the work of your force not equal to the product of the horizontal displacement and the answer to (a) ?

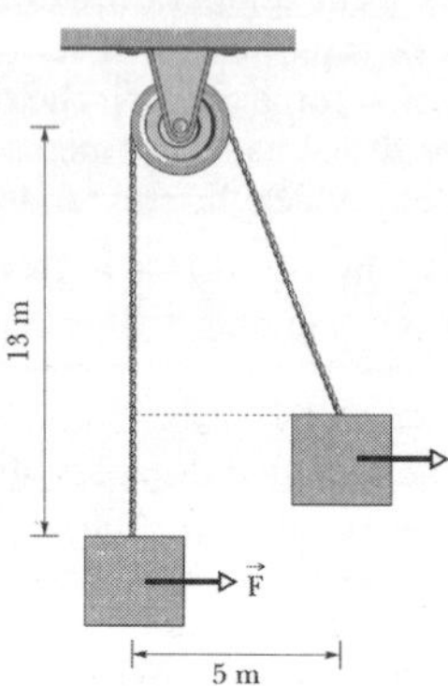

FIG. 8-119 Problem 96.

97 A body of mass m was slowly pulled up the hill (Fig. 8-120) by a force $\vec{F}$ which at each point was directed along a tangent to the trajectory. Find the work performed by this force, if the height of the hill is h, the length of its basel, and the coefficient of friction k.

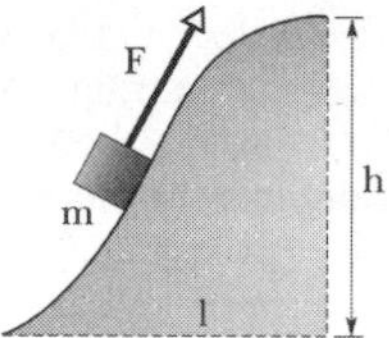

FIG. 8-120 Problem 97.

Center of Mass

9

©franzfoto.com/Alamy Images

The males of the bighorn sheep (Ovis canadensis) fight one another to gain the attention of the females. Two males repeatedly run at each other at full speed with their heads lowered so that the horns collide, until one of them finally gives up. Such clashes can be costly because if a horn breaks, the male will likely be seriously hurt or killed in the next collision. But even without a broken horn, both sheep should seemingly fall to the ground with concussions.

How can the head-banging sheep withstand such violent clashes?

The answer is in this chapter.

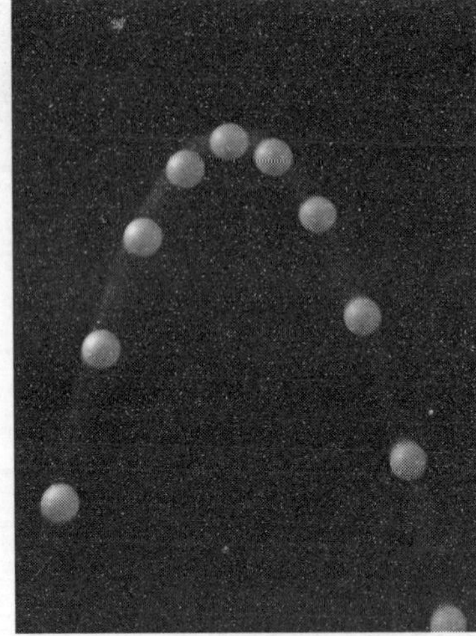

(a)

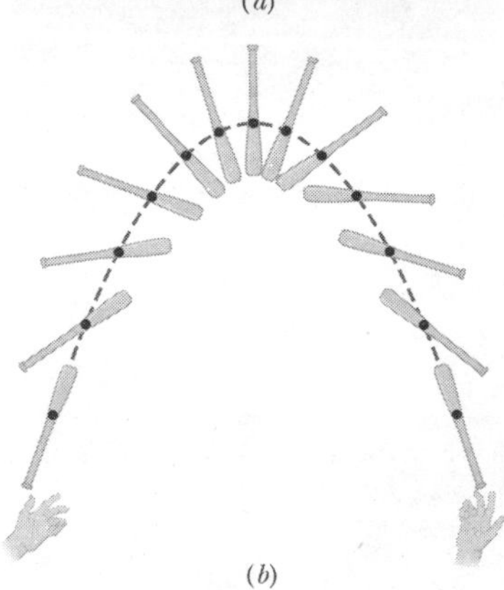

(b)

FIG. 9-1 (a) A ball tossed into the air follows a parabolic path. (b) The center of mass (black dot) of a baseball bat flipped into the air follows a parabolic path, but all other points of the bat follow more complicated curved paths. *(a: Richard Megna/Fundamental Photographs)*

9-1 Introduction

Every mechanical engineer hired as an expert witness to reconstruct a traffic accident uses physics. Every trainer who coaches a ballerina on how to leap uses physics. Indeed, analyzing complicated motion of any sort requires simplification via an understanding of physics. In this chapter we discuss how the complicated motion of a system of objects, such as a car or a ballerina, can be simplified if we determine a special point of the system—the *center of mass* of that system.

Here is a quick example. If you toss a ball into the air without much spin on the ball (Fig. 9-1*a*), its motion is simple—it follows a parabolic path, as we discussed in Chapter 4, and the ball can be treated as a particle. If, instead, you flip a baseball bat into the air (Fig. 9-1*b*), its motion is more complicated. Because every part of the bat moves differently, along paths of many different shapes, you cannot represent the bat as a particle. Instead, it is a system of particles each of which follows its own path through the air. However, the bat has one special point—the center of mass—that *does* move in a simple parabolic path. The other parts of the bat move around the center of mass. (To locate the center of mass, balance the bat on an outstretched finger; the point is above your finger, on the bat's central axis.)

You cannot make a career of flipping baseball bats into the air, but you can make a career of advising long-jumpers or dancers on how to leap properly into the air while either moving their arms and legs or rotating their torso. Your starting point would be the person's center of mass because of its simple motion.

9-2 | The Center of Mass

We define the **center of mass** (com) of a system of particles (such as a person) in order to predict the possible motion of the system.

> The center of mass of a system of particles is the point that moves as though (1) all of the system's mass were concentrated there and (2) all external forces were applied there.

In this section we discuss how to determine where the center of mass of a system of particles is located. We start with a system of only a few particles, and then we consider a system of a great many particles (a solid body, such as a baseball bat). Later in the chapter, we discuss how the center of mass of a system moves when external forces act on the system.

Systems of Particles

Figure 9-2*a* shows two particles of masses m_1 and m_2 separated by distance d. We have arbitrarily chosen the origin of an x axis to coincide with the particle of mass m_1. We *define* the position of the center of mass (com) of this two-particle system to be

$$x_{com} = \frac{m_2}{m_1 + m_2} d \tag{9-1}$$

Suppose, as an example, that $m_2 = 0$. Then there is only one particle, of mass m_1, and the center of mass must lie at the position of that particle; Eq. 9-1 dutifully reduces to $x_{com} = 0$. If $m_1 = 0$, there is again only one particle (of mass m_2), and we have, as we expect, $x_{com} = d$. If $m_1 = m_2$, the center of mass should be halfway between the two particles; Eq. 9-1 reduces to $x_{com} = \frac{1}{2}d$, again as we expect. Finally, Eq. 9-1 tells us that if neither m_1 nor m_2 is zero, x_{com} can have only values that lie between zero and d; that is, the center of mass must lie somewhere between the two particles.

Figure 9-2*b* shows a more generalized situation, in which the coordinate system has been shifted leftward. The position of the center of mass is now defined as

$$x_{com} = \frac{m_1 x_1 + m_2 x_2}{m_1 + m_2} \tag{9-2}$$

Note that if we put $x_1 = 0$, then x_2 becomes d and Eq. 9-2 reduces to Eq. 9-1, as it must. Note also that in spite of the shift of the coordinate system, the center of mass is still the same distance from each particle.

We can rewrite Eq. 9-2 as

$$x_{com} = \frac{m_1 x_1 + m_2 x_2}{M} \tag{9-3}$$

in which M is the total mass of the system. (Here, $M = m_1 + m_2$.) We can extend this equation to a more general situation in which n particles are strung out along the x axis. Then the total mass is $M = m_1 + m_2 + \cdots + m_n$, and the location of the center of mass is

$$x_{com} = \frac{m_1 x_1 + m_2 x_2 + m_3 x_3 + \cdots + m_n x_n}{M} = \frac{1}{M}\sum_{i=1}^{n} m_i x_i \tag{9-4}$$

The subscript i is an index that takes on all integer values from 1 to n.

If the particles are distributed in three dimensions, the center of mass must be identified by three coordinates. By extension of Eq. 9-4, they are

$$x_{com} = \frac{1}{M}\sum_{i=1}^{n} m_i x_i, \qquad y_{com} = \frac{1}{M}\sum_{i=1}^{n} m_i y_i, \qquad z_{com} = \frac{1}{M}\sum_{i=1}^{n} m_i z_i \tag{9-5}$$

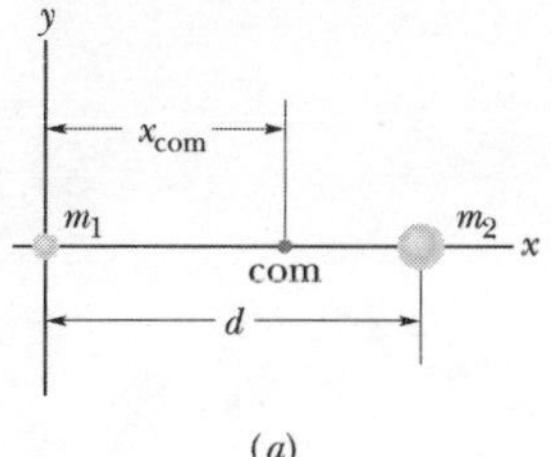

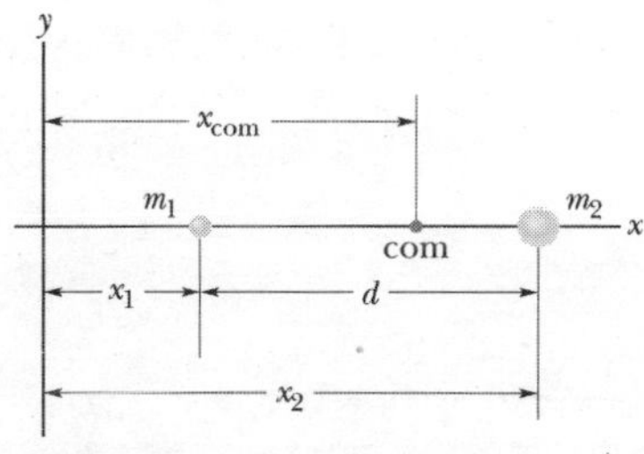

FIG. 9-2 (*a*) Two particles of masses m_1 and m_2 are separated by distance d. The dot labeled com shows the position of the center of mass, calculated from Eq. 9-1. (*b*) The same as (*a*) except that the origin is located farther from the particles. The position of the center of mass is calculated from Eq. 9-2. The location of the center of mass with respect to the particles is the same in both cases.

We can also define the center of mass with the language of vectors. First recall that the position of a particle at coordinates x_i, y_i, and z_i is given by a position vector:

$$\vec{r}_i = x_i\hat{\mathrm{i}} + y_i\hat{\mathrm{j}} + z_i\hat{\mathrm{k}} \tag{9-6}$$

Here the index identifies the particle, and $\hat{\mathrm{i}}$, $\hat{\mathrm{j}}$, and $\hat{\mathrm{k}}$ are unit vectors pointing, respectively, in the positive direction of the x, y, and z axes. Similarly, the position of the center of mass of a system of particles is given by a position vector:

$$\vec{r}_{com} = x_{com}\hat{\mathrm{i}} + y_{com}\hat{\mathrm{j}} + z_{com}\hat{\mathrm{k}} \tag{9-7}$$

The three scalar equations of Eq. 9-5 can now be replaced by a single vector equation,

$$\vec{r}_{com} = \frac{1}{M}\sum_{i=1}^{n} m_i \vec{r}_i \tag{9-8}$$

where again M is the total mass of the system. You can check that this equation is correct by substituting Eqs. 9-6 and 9-7 into it, and then separating out the x, y, and z components. The scalar relations of Eq. 9-5 result.

Solid Bodies

An ordinary object, such as a baseball bat, contains so many particles (atoms) that we can best treat it as a continuous distribution of matter. The "particles" then become differential mass elements dm, the sums of Eq. 9-5 become integrals, and the coordinates of the center of mass are defined as

$$x_{com} = \frac{1}{M}\int x\,dm, \qquad y_{com} = \frac{1}{M}\int y\,dm, \qquad z_{com} = \frac{1}{M}\int z\,dm \tag{9-9}$$

where M is now the mass of the object.

Evaluating these integrals for most common objects (such as a television set or a moose) would be difficult, so here we consider only *uniform* objects. Such objects have uniform *density,* or mass per unit volume; that is, the density ρ

(Greek letter rho) is the same for any given element of an object as for the whole object. From Eq. 1-8, we can write

$$\rho = \frac{dm}{dV} = \frac{M}{V} \tag{9-10}$$

where dV is the volume occupied by a mass element dm, and V is the total volume of the object. Substituting $dm = (M/V)\,dV$ from Eq. 9-10 into Eq. 9-9 gives

$$x_{\text{com}} = \frac{1}{V}\int x\,dV, \qquad y_{\text{com}} = \frac{1}{V}\int y\,dV, \qquad z_{\text{com}} = \frac{1}{V}\int z\,dV \tag{9-11}$$

You can bypass one or more of these integrals if an object has a point, a line, or a plane of symmetry. The center of mass of such an object then lies at that point, on that line, or in that plane. For example, the center of mass of a uniform sphere (which has a point of symmetry) is at the center of the sphere (which is the point of symmetry). The center of mass of a uniform cone (whose axis is a line of symmetry) lies on the axis of the cone. The center of mass of a banana (which has a plane of symmetry that splits it into two equal parts) lies somewhere in that plane.

The center of mass of an object need not lie within the object. There is no dough at the com of a doughnut, and no iron at the com of a horseshoe.

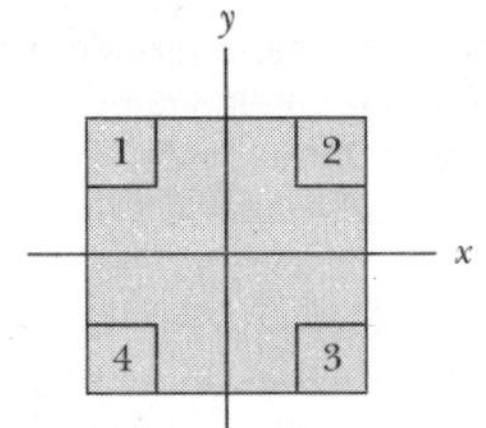

CHECKPOINT 1 The figure shows a uniform square plate from which four identical squares at the corners will be removed. (a) Where is the center of mass of the plate originally? Where is it after removal of (b) square 1; (c) squares 1 and 2; (d) squares 1 and 3; (e) squares 1, 2 and 3; (f) all four squares? Answer in terms of quardrants, axes, or points (without caluculation, of course).

Sample Problem 9-1

Three particles of masses $m_1 = 1.2$ kg, $m_2 = 2.5$ kg, and $m_3 = 3.4$ kg form an equilateral triangle of edge length $a = 140$ cm. Where is the center of mass of this system?

Conceptualize/classify: We are dealing with particles instead of an extended solid body, so we can use Eq. 9-5 to locate their center of mass. The particles are in the plane of the equilateral triangle, so we need only the first two equations.

Compute: We can simplify the calculations by choosing the x and y axes so that one of the particles is located at the origin and the x axis coincides with one of the triangle's sides (Fig. 9-3). The three particles then have the following coordinates:

Particle	Mass (kg)	x (cm)	y (cm)
1	1.2	0	0
2	2.5	140	0
3	3.4	70	120

The total mass M of the system is 7.1 kg.

From Eq. 9-5, the coordinates of the center of mass are

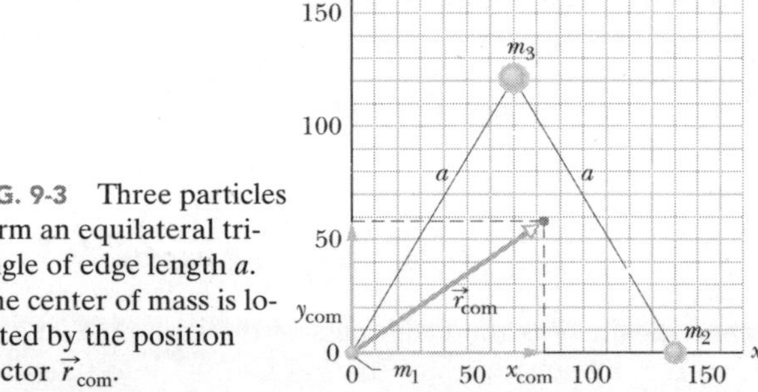

FIG. 9-3 Three particles form an equilateral triangle of edge length a. The center of mass is located by the position vector $\vec{r}_{\text{com}}$.

$$x_{\text{com}} = \frac{1}{M}\sum_{i=1}^{3} m_i x_i = \frac{m_1x_1 + m_2x_2 + m_3x_3}{M}$$

$$= \frac{(1.2\text{ kg})(0) + (2.5\text{ kg})(140\text{ cm}) + (3.4\text{ kg})(70\text{ cm})}{7.1\text{ kg}}$$

$$= 83\text{ cm} \qquad \text{(Answer)}$$

and $$y_{\text{com}} = \frac{1}{M}\sum_{i=1}^{3} m_i y_i = \frac{m_1y_1 + m_2y_2 + m_3y_3}{M}$$

$$= \frac{(1.2\text{ kg})(0) + (2.5\text{ kg})(0) + (3.4\text{ kg})(120\text{ cm})}{7.1\text{ kg}}$$

$$= 58\text{ cm} \qquad \text{(Answer)}$$

Conclude: In Fig. 9-3, the center of mass is located by the position vector $\vec{r}_{\text{com}}$, which has components x_{com} and y_{com}.

Sample Problem 9-2 Build your skill

Figure 9-4a shows a uniform metal plate P of radius $2R$ from which a disk of radius R has been stamped out (removed) in an assembly line. Using the xy coordinate system shown, locate the center of mass com_P of the plate.

Conceptualize: Let us roughly locate the center of plate P by using symmetry. We note that the plate is symmetric about the x axis (we get the portion below that axis by rotating the upper portion about the axis). Thus, com_P must be on the x axis. The plate (with the disk removed) is not symmetric about the y axis. However, because there is somewhat more mass on the right of the y axis, com_P must be somewhat to the right of that axis. Thus, the location of com_P should be roughly as indicated in Fig. 9-4a.

Classify Plate P is an extended solid body, so we can use Eqs. 9-11 to find the actual coordinates of com_P. However, that procedure is difficult. Here is a much easier way: In working with centers of mass, we can assume that the mass of a *uniform* object is concentrated in a particle at the object's center of mass.

Compute: First, put the stamped-out disk (call it disk S) back into place (Fig. 9-4b) to form the original composite plate (call it plate C). Because of its circular symmetry, the center of mass com_S for disk S is at the center of S, at $x = -R$ (as shown). Similarly, the center of mass com_C for composite plate C is at the center of C, at the origin (as shown). We then have the following:

Plate	Center of Mass	Location of com	Mass
P	com_P	$x_P = ?$	m_P
S	com_S	$x_S = -R$	m_S
C	com_C	$x_C = 0$	$m_C = m_S + m_P$

Assume that mass m_S of disk S is concentrated in a particle at $x_S = -R$, and mass m_P is concentrated in a particle at x_P (Fig. 9-4c). Next treat these two particles as a two-particle system, using Eq. 9-2 to find their center of mass x_{S+P}. We get

$$x_{S+P} = \frac{m_S x_S + m_P x_P}{m_S + m_P} \qquad (9\text{-}12)$$

Next note that the combination of disk S and plate P is composite plate C. Thus, the position x_{S+P} of com_{S+P} must coincide with the position x_C of com_C, which is at the origin; so $x_{S+P} = x_C = 0$. Substituting this into Eq. 9-12 and solving for x_P, we get

$$x_P = -x_S \frac{m_S}{m_P} \qquad (9\text{-}13)$$

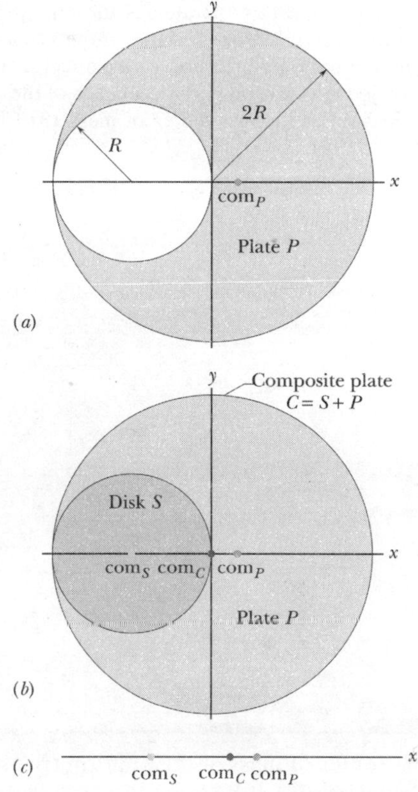

FIG. 9-4 (a) Plate P is a metal plate of radius $2R$, with a circular hole of radius R. The center of mass of P is at point com_P. (b) Disk S has been put back into place to form a composite plate C. The center of mass com_S of disk S and the center of mass com_C of plate C are shown. (c) The center of mass com_{S+P} of the combination of S and P coincides with com_C, which is at $x = 0$.

We can relate these masses to the face areas of S and P by noting that

$$\text{mass} = \text{density} \times \text{volume}$$
$$= \text{density} \times \text{thickness} \times \text{area}$$

Then $$\frac{m_S}{m_P} = \frac{\text{density}_S}{\text{density}_P} \times \frac{\text{thickness}_S}{\text{thickness}_P} \times \frac{\text{area}_S}{\text{area}_P}$$

Because the plate is uniform, the densities and thicknesses are equal; we are left with

$$\frac{m_S}{m_P} = \frac{\text{area}_S}{\text{area}_P} = \frac{\text{area}_S}{\text{area}_C - \text{area}_S}$$

$$= \frac{\pi R^2}{\pi(2R)^2 - \pi R^2} = \frac{1}{3}$$

Substituting this and $x_S = -R$ into Eq. 9-13, we have

$$x_P = \tfrac{1}{3}R \qquad \text{(Answer)}$$

Conlude: As expected the location of COM is towords right. Here we have replaced the bodies by their own COMs to calculate the COM of the combined body.

PROBLEM-SOLVING TACTICS

Tactic 1: Center-of-Mass Problems Sample Problems 9-1 and 9-2 provide three strategies for simplifying center-of-mass problems. (1) Make full use of the symmetry of the object, be it about a point, a line, or a plane. (2) If the object can be divided into several parts, treat each of these parts as a particle, located at its own center of mass. (3) Choose your axes wisely: If your system is a group of particles, choose one of the particles as your origin. If your system is a body with a line of symmetry, let that be your x or y axis. The choice of origin can be completely arbitrary because the location of the center of mass is the same regardless of the origin from which it is measured.

CHECKPOINT 2 Find location of COM of the arrangement of regular hexagon having point masses at five vertices.

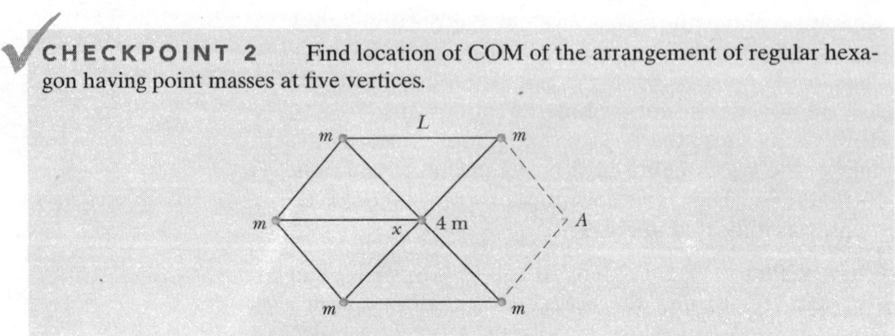

Sample Problem 9-3 Build your skill

Find the center of mass of the uniform triangular plate that is, shown in Fig. 9-5.

Solution: Figure 9-5*a* shows the plate divided into thin slats, parallel to one side of the triangle. The Key Idea here is that, from symmetry, the center of mass of a thin, uniform slat is at its mid-point. Thus, the center of mass of the triangular plate must lie somewhere along the line that connects the midpoints of all slats.

That bisecting line also connects the upper vertex with the midpoint of the opposite side. The plate would balance if it were placed on a knife-edge coinciding with this line of symmetry.

In Figs. 9-5*b* and 9-5*c*, we subdivide the plate into slats parallel to the other two sides of the triangle. Again, the center of mass must lie somewhere along each of the bisecting lines shown. Hence the center of mass of the plate must lie at the intersection of these three symmetry lines, as Fig. 9-5*d* shows. That intersection is the only point that the three lines have in common.

You can check this conclusion experimentally by taking advantage of the (correct) intuitive notion that an object suspended from one of its points will orient itself so that its center of mass lies vertically below that point. Suspend the triangle from each vertex in turn, and draw a line vertically downward from the suspension point, as in Fig. 9-5*e*. The center of mass of the triangle will be at the intersection of the three lines.

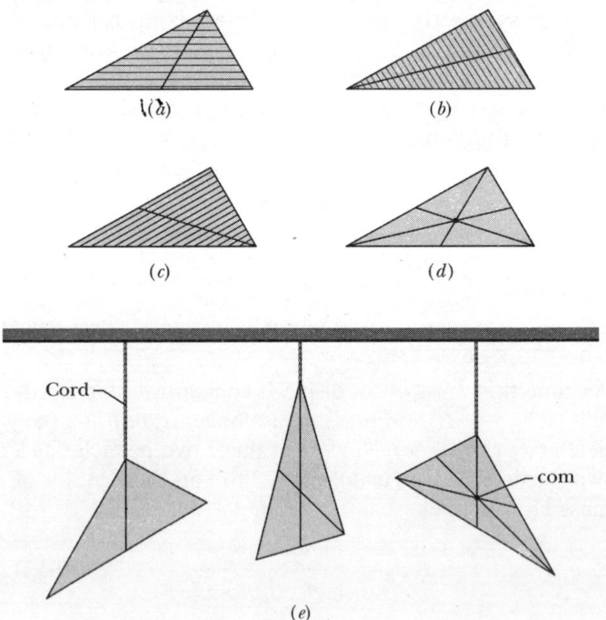

FIG. 9-5 Sample Problem 9-3. In (*a*), (*b*), and (*c*), the triangular plate is divided into thin slats, parallel to one side. The center of mass must lie along the bisecting line shown, (*d*) The dot, the only point common to all three lines, is the position of the center of mass, (*e*) Finding the center of mass by suspending the triangle from each vertex in turn.

Sample Problem 9-4

Locate the center of mass of the uniform circular wire segment shown in Fig 9-6.

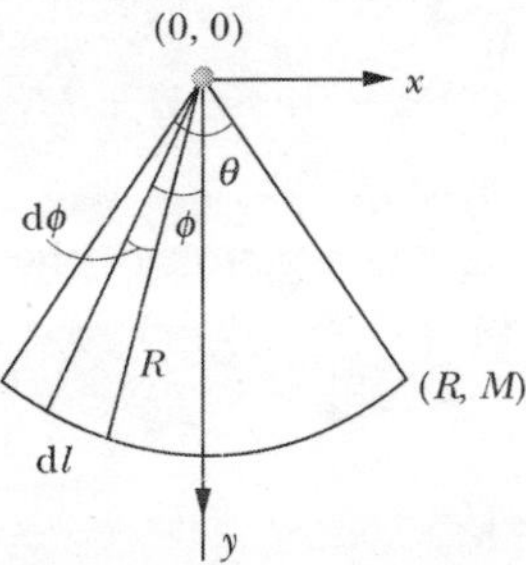

FIG. 9-6 Uniform circular wire segment subtending angle θ at the center.

Conceptualize: By symmetry, we can see that the center of mass must lie on the angle θ bisector.

Classify: This problem can be solved by taking differential elements subtending angle $d\theta$ at the center.

Solution: A differential element circular arc is selected as shown in the figure. This element is located at angle ϕ from the bisector and is substending angle $d\phi$ on the center. The differential length of the element is $dL = R\, d\phi$, and its co-ordinates are $\tilde{x} = R\cos\phi$ and $\tilde{y} = R\sin\phi$

Applying above equations and integrating with respect to ϕ where ϕ can attain any value from $-\frac{\theta}{2}$ to $\frac{\theta}{2}$, we obtain:

$$\bar{x} = \frac{\int_L \tilde{x}dL}{\int_L dL} = \frac{\int_{\theta/2}^{\theta/2}(R\cos\phi)R\,d\phi}{\int_{\theta/2}^{\theta/2}R\,d\phi} = 0 \qquad \text{(Answer)}$$

$$\bar{y} = \frac{\int_L ydL}{\int_L dL} = \frac{\int_{\theta/2}^{\theta/2}(R\sin\phi)R\,d\phi}{\int_{\theta/2}^{\theta/2}R\,d\phi} = \frac{2R\sin(\theta/2)}{\theta} \qquad \text{(Answer)}$$

Conclude: If the ring is complete, then the center of mass should lie on the center and it can be verified by putting $\theta = 2\pi$ in the answer. Aslo, for half ring we can put $\theta = \pi$ and we get,

For half ring $y = \frac{2R}{\pi}$

Sample Problem 9-5

Locate the center of mass for a semicircular plate as shown in Fig 9-7.

Conceptualize: By symmetry, we can see that the center of mass must lie on the angle θ bisector.

Classify: This problem can be solved by taking differential elements subtending angle $d\theta$ at the center.

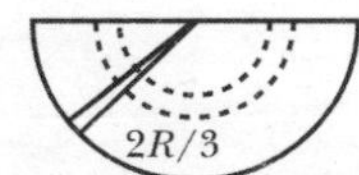

FIG. 9-7 Semicircular plate with center of mass on angle bisector.

Compute: We choose the element in the shape of a triangle ambiguous (Actually the shape is a circular sector; however, neglecting small curved part can be neglected, the element becomes triangular.)

The area of the element is

$$dA = \frac{1}{2}(R)(R\,d\theta) = \frac{R^2}{2}d\theta$$

and using the results of conceptual example, the center of mass of the (triangular) element is located at distance

$$r = \frac{2}{3}R$$

Applying the results of center of mass of half ring, we obtain:

$$y = \frac{2(2R/3)}{\pi} = \frac{4R}{3\pi}$$

Conclude: We have used the result for ring and the triangular plate. Similarly, in other situations also, we can use known results to find center of mass of unknown bodies.

TABLE 9-1

Geometry	Location of center of mass
Thin hemispherical shell	$\frac{R}{2}$ from the center
Hollow cone of height H	$\frac{2H}{3}$ from the trip of the cone
Solid cone of height h	$\frac{3h}{4}$ from the tip of the cone
Solid hemisphere	$3R/8$ from the center

Sample Problem 9-6

The U-shaped object pictured in Fig. 9-8. has outer dimensions of 100 mm on each side, and each of its three sides is 20 mm wide. It was cut from a uniform sheet of plastic 6.0 mm thick. Locate the center of mass of this object.

Conceptualize/Classify: A key idea here is to break the U-shaped object up into pieces, each having an easily located center of mass of that piece, and then use Eq. to locate the center of mass of the whole object.

Compute: As shown in Fig. 9-8 we can think of the U-shaped object as made up of two vertical bars, each 100 mm long 20 mm wide, joined together by one horizontal bar 60 mm long and 20 mm wide. Let's place the origin of our coordinate system at the lower-left rear corner of the U, with the x-axis across its base and the y-axis along its left edge. To locate the center of mass of each of the bars, we will use the key idea that the center of mass of a symmetric object of uniform density is located at its geometric center. This means that the center of mass of each bar is exactly halfway from either end, halfway from either side, and halfway between the top and bottom surfaces of the plastic sheet. Putting a dot at the center of each of the bars, A, B and C, we can now write down their locations in the coordinate system pictured there:

TABLE 9-2

Object	Mass	X (mm)	Y (mm)	Z (mm)
Left bar	M_A	90	50	3
Right bar	M_B	90	50	3
Bottom bar	M_C	50	10	3

To learn more about the relative masses of the three bars, we can use the key idea that the mass of each bar is proportional to its volume since the bars have a uniform common density. In this case, the relationship is even simpler: since the three bars are of the same width and thickness, each one's mass is directly proportional to its length, so

$$M_A = M_B = M \text{ and } M = M(60\text{ mm}) / (100\text{ mm}) = 0.6\,M$$

and $M_{sys} = M_A + M_B + M_C = M + M + 0.6\,M = 2.6\,M$

Replacing each bar by a point mass at its center of mass, Eq. gives us the location of the center of mass of the entire U-shaped object.

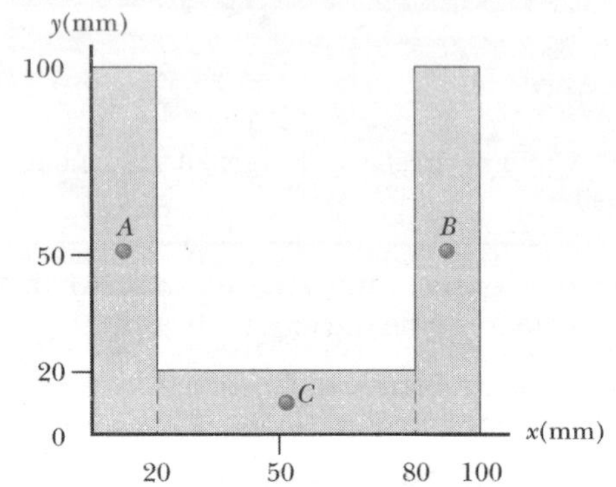

FIG. 9-8 U-shaped object.

$$X_{com} = \frac{M_A X_A + M_B X_B + M_C X_C}{M_{sys}}$$

$$= \frac{M(10\text{ mm}) + M(90\text{ mm}) + 0.6M(50\text{ mm})}{2.6M}$$

$$= 50\text{ mm} \qquad \text{(Answer)}$$

$$Y_{com} = \frac{M_A Y_A + M_B Y_B + M_C Y_C}{M_{sys}}$$

$$= \frac{M(50\text{ mm}) + M(50\text{ mm}) + 0.6M(10\text{ mm})}{2.6M}$$

$$Y_{com} = 41\text{ mm}$$

so $$Z_{com} = \frac{M\,(3.0\text{ mm}) + M\,(3.0\text{ mm}) + 0.6\,M\,(3.0\text{ mm})}{2.6\,M}$$

$$= \frac{(7.8\text{ mm})\,M}{2.6\,M} = 3\text{ mm}$$

$$R_{com} = (50\text{ mm})\hat{i} + (41\text{ mm})\hat{j} + (3\text{ mm})\hat{k}$$

9-3 | Newton's Second Law for a System of Particles

Now that we know how to locate the center of mass of a system of particles, we discuss how external forces can move a center of mass. Let us start with a simple system of two billiard balls.

If you roll a cue ball at a second billiard ball that is, at rest, you expect that the two-ball system will continue to have some forward motion after impact. You would be surprised, for example, if both balls came back toward you or if both moved to the right or to the left.

What continues to move forward, its steady motion completely unaffected by the collision, is the center of mass of the two-ball system. If you focus on this point—which is always halfway between these bodies because they have identical masses—you can easily convince yourself by trial at a billiard table that this is so. No matter whether the collision is glancing, head-on, or somewhere in between, the center of mass continues to move forward, as if the collision had never occurred. Let us look into this center-of-mass motion in more detail.

To do so, we replace the pair of billiard balls with an assemblage of n particles of (possibly) different masses. We are interested not in the individual motions of these particles but *only* in the motion of the center of mass of the assemblage. Although the center of mass is just a point, it moves like a particle whose mass is equal to the total mass of the system; we can assign a position, a velocity, and an acceleration to it. We state (and shall prove next) that the vector equation that governs the motion of the center of mass of such a system of particles is

$$\vec{F}_{net} = M\vec{a}_{com} \quad \text{(system of particles)} \tag{9-14}$$

This equation is Newton's second law for the motion of the center of mass of a system of particles. Note that its form is the same as the form of the equation ($\vec{F}_{net} = m\vec{a}$) for the motion of a single particle. However, the three quantities that appear in Eq. 9-14 must be evaluated with some care:

1. $\vec{F}_{net}$ is the net force of *all external forces* that act on the system. Forces on one part of the system from another part of the system (*internal forces*) are not included in Eq. 9-14.
2. M is the *total mass* of the system. We assume that no mass enters or leaves the system as it moves, so that M remains constant. The system is said to be **closed.**
3. $\vec{a}_{com}$ is the acceleration of the *center of mass* of the system. Equation 9-14 gives no information about the acceleration of any other point of the system.

Equation 9-14 is equivalent to three equations involving the components of $\vec{F}_{net}$ and $\vec{a}_{com}$ along the three coordinate axes. These equations are

$$F_{net,x} = Ma_{com,x} \qquad F_{net,y} = Ma_{com,y} \qquad F_{net,z} = Ma_{com,z} \tag{9-15}$$

Now we can go back and examine the behavior of the billiard balls. Once the cue ball has begun to roll, no net external force acts on the (two-ball) system. Thus, because $\vec{F}_{net} = 0$, Eq. 9-14 tells us that $\vec{a}_{com} = 0$ also. Because acceleration is the rate of change of velocity, we conclude that the velocity of the center of mass of the system of two balls does not change. When the two balls collide, the forces that come into play are *internal* forces, on one ball from the other. Such forces do not contribute to the net force $\vec{F}_{net}$, which remains zero. Thus, the center of mass of the system, which was moving forward before the collision, must continue to move forward after the collision, with the same speed and in the same direction.

Equation 9-14 applies not only to a system of particles but also to a solid body, such as the bat of Fig. 9-1*b*. In that case, M in Eq. 9-14 is the mass of the bat and $\vec{F}_{net}$ is the gravitational force on the bat. Equation 9-14 then tells us that $\vec{a}_{com} = \vec{g}$. In other words, the center of mass of the bat moves as if the bat were a single particle of mass M, with force $\vec{F}_g$ acting on it.

FIG. 9-9 A fireworks rocket explodes in flight. In the absence of air drag, the center of mass of the fragments would continue to follow the original parabolic path, until fragments began to hit the ground.

Figure 9-9 shows another interesting case. Suppose that at a fireworks display, a rocket is launched on a parabolic path. At a certain point, it explodes into fragments. If the explosion had not occurred, the rocket would have continued along the trajectory shown in the figure. The forces of the explosion are *internal* to the system (at first the system is just the rocket, and later it is its fragments); that is, they are forces on parts of the system from other parts. If we ignore air drag, the net *external* force $\vec{F}_{net}$ acting on the system is the gravitational force on the system, regardless of whether the rocket explodes. Thus, from Eq. 9-14, the acceleration $\vec{a}_{com}$ of the center of mass of the fragments (while they are in flight) remains equal to $\vec{g}$. This means that the center of mass of the fragments follows the same parabolic trajectory that the rocket would have followed had it not exploded.

When a ballet dancer leaps across the stage in a grand jeté, she raises her arms and stretches her legs out horizontally as soon as her feet leave the stage (Fig. 9-10). These actions shift her center of mass upward through her body. Although the shifting center of mass faithfully follows a parabolic path across the stage, its movement relative to the body decreases the height that is, attained by her head and torso, relative to that of a normal jump. The result is that the head and torso follow a nearly horizontal path, giving an illusion that the dancer is floating.

Proof of Equation 9-14

Now let us prove this important equation. From Eq. 9-8 we have, for a system of n particles,

$$M\vec{r}_{com} = m_1\vec{r}_1 + m_2\vec{r}_2 + m_3\vec{r}_3 + \cdots + m_n\vec{r}_n \tag{9-16}$$

in which M is the system's total mass and $\vec{r}_{com}$ is the vector locating the position of the system's center of mass.

Differentiating Eq. 9-16 with respect to time gives

$$M\vec{v}_{com} = m_1\vec{v}_1 + m_2\vec{v}_2 + m_3\vec{v}_3 + \cdots + m_n\vec{v}_n \tag{9-17}$$

Here $\vec{v}_i$ $(= d\vec{r}_i/dt)$ is the velocity of the ith particle, and $\vec{v}_{com}$ $(= d\vec{r}_{com}/dt)$ is the velocity of the center of mass.

Differentiating Eq. 9-17 with respect to time leads to

$$M\vec{a}_{com} = m_1\vec{a}_1 + m_2\vec{a}_2 + m_3\vec{a}_3 + \cdots + m_n\vec{a}_n \tag{9-18}$$

Here $\vec{a}_i$ $(= d\vec{v}_i/dt)$ is the acceleration of the ith particle, and $\vec{a}_{com}$ $(= d\vec{v}_{com}/dt)$ is the acceleration of the center of mass. Although the center of mass is just a

FIG. 9-10 A grand jeté. (Adapted from *The Physics of Dance,* by Kenneth Laws, Schirmer Books, 1984.)

geometrical point, it has a position, a velocity, and an acceleration, as if it were a particle.

From Newton's second law, $m_i\vec{a}_i$ is equal to the resultant force $\vec{F}_i$ that acts on the *i*th particle. Thus, we can rewrite Eq. 9-18 as

$$M\vec{a}_{com} = \vec{F}_1 + \vec{F}_2 + \vec{F}_3 + \cdots + \vec{F}_n \qquad (9\text{-}19)$$

Among the forces that contribute to the right side of Eq. 9-19 will be forces that the particles of the system exert on each other (internal forces) and forces exerted on the particles from outside the system (external forces). By Newton's third law, the internal forces form third-law force pairs and cancel out in the sum that appears on the right side of Eq. 9-19. What remains is the vector sum of all the *external* forces that act on the system. Equation 9-19 then reduces to Eq. 9-14, the relation that we set out to prove.

CHECKPOINT 3 Two skaters on frictionless ice hold opposite ends of a pole of negligible mass. An axis runs along the pole, and the origin of the axis is at the center of mass of the two-skater system. One skater, Fred, weighs twice as much as the other skater, Ethel. Where do the skaters meet if (a) Fred pulls hand over hand along the pole so as to draw himself to Ethel, (b) Ethel pulls hand over hand to draw herself to Fred, and (c) both skaters pull hand over hand?

Sample Problem 9-7

The three particles in Fig. 9-11*a* are initially at rest. Each experiences an *external* force due to bodies outside the three-particle system. The directions are indicated, and the magnitudes are $F_1 = 6.0$ N, $F_2 = 0$ N, and $F_3 = 8$ N. What is the acceleration of the center of mass of the system, and in what direction does it move?

Conceptualize: The position of the center of mass, calculated by the method of Sample Problem 9-1, is marked by a dot in the figure.

Classify: We can treat the center of mass as if it were a real particle, with a mass equal to the system's total mass $M = 16$ kg. We can also treat the three external forces as if they act at the center of mass (Fig. 9-11*b*).

Compute: We can now apply Newton's second law ($\vec{F}_{net} = m\vec{a}$) to the center of mass, writing

$$\vec{F}_{net} = M\vec{a}_{com} \qquad (9\text{-}20)$$

or

$$\vec{F}_1 + \vec{F}_2 + \vec{F}_3 = M\vec{a}_{com} \qquad (9\text{-}21)$$

so

$$\vec{a}_{com} = \frac{\vec{F}_1 + \vec{F}_2 + \vec{F}_3}{M} \qquad (9\text{-}21)$$

Equation 9-20 tells us that the acceleration $\vec{a}_{com}$ of the center of mass is in the same direction as the net external force $\vec{F}_{net}$ on the system (Fig. 9-8*b*). Because the particles are initially at rest, the center of mass must

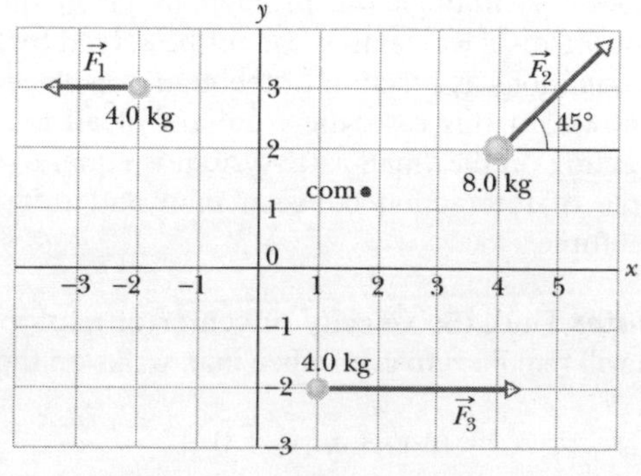

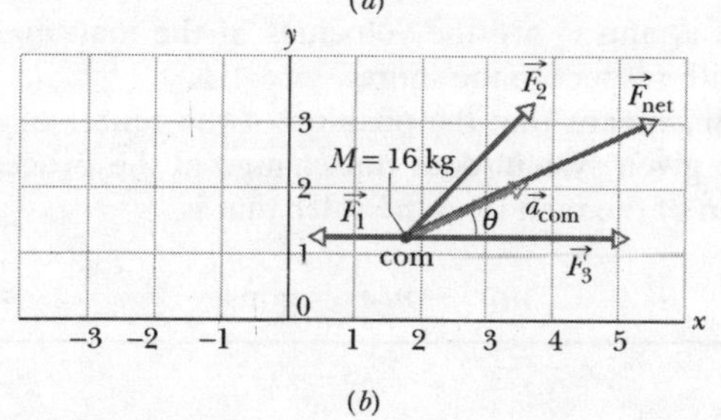

FIG. 9-11 (*a*) Three particles, initially at rest in the positions shown, are acted on by the external forces shown. The center of mass (com) of the system is marked. (*b*) The forces are now transferred to the center of mass of the system, which behaves like a particle with a mass *M* equal to the total mass of the system. The net external force $\vec{F}_{net}$ and the acceleration $\vec{a}_{com}$ of the center of mass are shown.

also be at rest. As the center of mass then begins to accelerate, it must move off in the common direction of $\vec{a}_{com}$ and $\vec{F}_{net}$.

We can evaluate the right side of Eq. 9-21 directly on a vector-capable calculator, or we can rewrite Eq. 9-21 in component form, find the components of $\vec{a}_{com}$, and then find $\vec{a}_{com}$. Along the x axis, we have

$$a_{com,x} = \frac{F_{1x} + F_{2x} + F_{3x}}{M}$$

$$= \frac{-6.0\text{ N} + (12\text{ N})\cos 45° + \text{N}}{16\text{ kg}} = 0.500\text{ m/s}^2$$

Along the y axis, we have

$$a_{com,y} = \frac{F_{1y} + F_{2y} + F_{3y}}{M}$$

$$= \frac{0 + (12\text{ N})\sin 45° + 0}{16\text{ kg}} = 0.00\text{ m/s}^2$$

From these components, we find that $\vec{a}_{com}$ has the magnitude

$$a_{com} = \sqrt{(a_{com,x})^2 + (a_{com,y})^2}$$
$$= 0.707\text{ m/s}^2 \approx 0.707\text{ m/s}^2 \quad \text{(Answer)}$$

and the angle (from the positive direction of the x axis)

$$\theta = \tan^{-1}\frac{a_{com,y}}{a_{com,x}} = 45° \quad \text{(Answer)}$$

Conclude: If we would have calculated the individual accelereations and then calculated the individual accel-ereations and then calculated acceleration of COM we would have got the same result.

Sample Problem 9-8

A man of mass m_1 is located on a raft of mass m_2 which is floating on the surface of a lake. The man travels a distance l on the raft and then stops. The resistance of the water is negligible. Find the corresponding displacement of the raft and displacement of the man relative to the ground.

Conceptualize: If you have ever walked on a stationary raft or boat, you can imagine that as you go forward the raft goes backward.

Categorize: Although the problem is given only in terms of the displacements, it cannot be solved by kinematics equations as function of the man's displacement is unknown. In this case, the resultant of all external forces acting on the "man-raft" system is equal to zero; the force of interaction between man and raft is an internal force.

Compute: Thus, the velocity of center of mass of the system will remain zero even when man walks on the raft.

$$m_1v_1 + m_2v_2 = 0$$

where v_1 and v_2 are the velocities of the man and the raft with respect to the shore.

This means that the position of the center of mass of the given system does not change in the process of motion of the man (and the raft), that is,

$$m_1r_1 + m_2r_2 = \text{const}$$

where r_1 and r_2 are the position vectors describing the positions of the center of mass of the man and the raft relative to a certain point on the shore. From this equality, we find the relationship between the change of the vectors r_1 and r_2:

$$m_1\Delta r_1 + m_2\Delta r_2 = 0$$

The vectors Δr_1 and Δr_2 represent the displacements of the man and the raft with respect to the shore. Also, the displacement of the man relative to the shore may be represented in the form $\Delta r_1 = \Delta r_2 + \Delta r'_1$, where $\Delta r'_1$ is the displacement of the man relative to the raft, l.

We can find the displacement of the raft using all above relations and rearranging them a

$$\Delta r_2 = -\frac{m_1}{m_1 + m_2}\Delta r'$$

$$\Delta r_2 = -\frac{m_1}{m_1 + m_2}l$$

Conclude: It can be seen from this that the displacement $\Delta r'_2$ of the raft does not depend on the nature of the man's motion, that is, on the function $\Delta r'(t)$. Thus, he may have walked in any pattern at any speed, the displacement of the raft will be same if he stops at the other end. If we make $m_1 \gg m_2$, then as we expect, answer should be zero because the man will not be able to move the infinetly heavy raft.

Sample Problem 9-9

Find distance moved by wedge of mass M when block having mass m reaches ground. Assume all surfaces are frictionless.

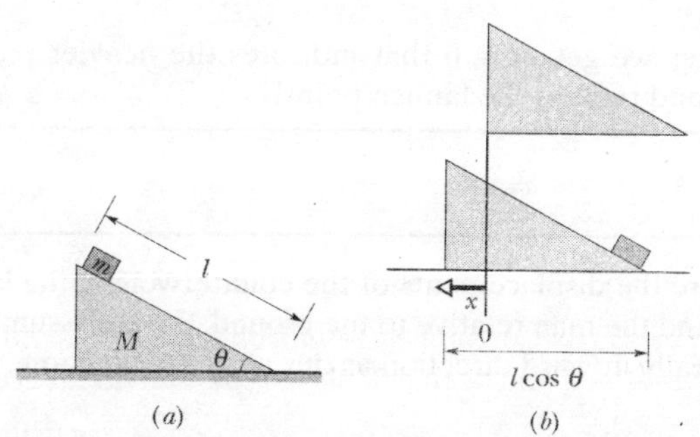

FIG. 9-12 (*a*) A block kept on a smooth wedge. (*b*) Movement of block on the wedge and simultaneously the wedge also shifts.

Conceptualize: It can be imagined with the help of Fig. 9-12 that when block slides down on the wedge, the wedge will start moving toward left. The horizontal component of the normal contact force due to the block will push the wedge toward left.

Classify: You may want to proceed directly by calculating accleration and then displacements. In fact if you have time go ahead do it; may be when you have gone through that painful and tediuous solution you will be able to appreciate concept of momentum better!! So here comes our hero!!!

Compute: Since no external force will act in horizontal direction, so momentum of the system consisting of the block and wedge remains conserved. Since initially both the bodies are at rest, the velocity of center of mass initially is zero and its x component will remain zero. Hence, center of mass displacement of the center of mass along x will remain zero. Thus, similar to the previous example, we can say that the $M\Delta\vec{x}_1 + m\Delta\vec{x}_2 = 0$. $\Delta\vec{x}_1$ is the x component of the displacement of the wedge with respect to ground

Considering direction along right to be positive $\Delta\vec{x}_1 = -x$, $\Delta\vec{x}_2$ is the x component of the displacement of the block with respect to ground $\Delta\vec{x}_2 = (l\cos\theta - x)$

Putting the value of Δx_1 and Δx_2, we get

$$-Mx + m(l\cos\theta - x) = 0$$

$$ml\cos\theta = x(M+m)$$

$$x = \frac{ml\cos\theta}{(M+m)}$$

Conclude: If we make $\theta = 0$, we get same result as in the previous example because the wedge becomes raft. If we make $M \gg m$, then as we expect, answer should be zero because the small block will not be able to move the infinetly heavy wedge.

Sample Problem 9-10 Build your skill

A missile fired into the air suddenly explodes into several fragments as shown in Fig. 9.13.

(a) What can be said about the motion of the center of mass of the system after the explosion?

Solution: Neglecting air resistance, the only external force on the missile is the gravitational force.

Therefore, if the missile did not explode, it would continue to move along the parabolic path indicated by the dashed line in figure. Because the forces caused by the explosion are internal, they will not affect the motion of the center of mass of the system (the pieces). Therefore, even after the explosion, the center of mass of the fragments follows the same parabolic path that the projectile would have followed if no explosion had occurred.

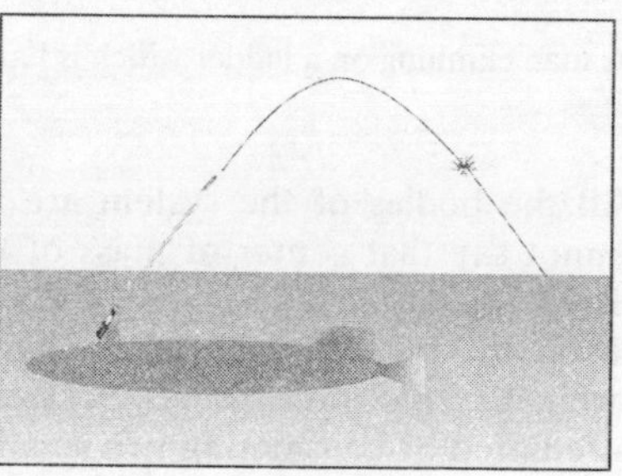

FIG. 9-13 A missile being fired from a submarine.

(b) If the missile did not explode, it would have landed at a distance R from its launch point.

Suppose the explosion splits it into two pieces of mass ratio 1:2. Lighter piece lands at a distance $3R$ from the launch point. Where does the heavier piece land?

Solution: As discussed in part (A), the center of mass of the two-piece system lands at a distance R from the launch point. One of the pieces lands at a further distance $2R$ from the landing point (or a distance $3R$ from the launch point) to the right in the figure. Applying the equation for locating the center of mass of the two piece system, $Mx_{com} = (M/3)x_1 + (2M/3)x_2$ launch point as origin

Give that

$$x_{com} = R \text{ and } x_1 = 3R$$

solving, we get $x_2 = 0$ that indicates the heavier piece will land right at the launch point!

Sample Problem 9-11

A rope passing over a pulley has a ladder of mass M and a man of mass m on the ladder at one end. On the other end, a counterweight of mass $M + m$ is attached. Initially everything is at rest. The man climbs upward by distance l on the ladder and then stops. Ignoring the masses of the pulley and the rope, as well as the friction in the pulley axis, find the work done by the man?

Conceptualize: It is easy to understand that since man is going upward against gravity, he has to do some work. The ladder will also move down as the man pulls it down for pushing himself up the ladder. The displacement of the man on the ladder that is, with respect to ladder, so his absolute displacement is going to be different. This also leads to the point that counterbalance has to come down as it is constrained to move according to the motion of the ladder.

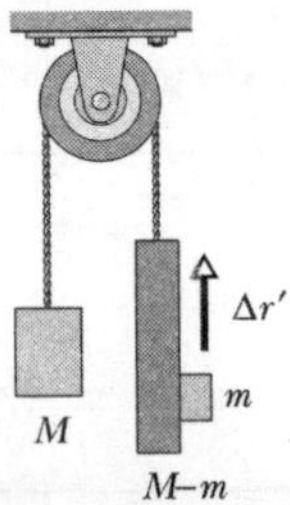

FIG. 9-14 A man climbing on a ladder which is hanging from a rope.

Classify: All the bodies of the system are intially at rest. We cannot say that center of mass of the whole system will remain stationary because the ceiling will apply force on the pulley, which is not equal to the combined weight of the three bodies. So, this problem has to be attempted by considering two smaller sytems that is, ladder-man and the counterweight.

Compute: The rope tension and total gravitational pull is same on the left and on the right hand side, thus they will have same free-body diagram. Thus, center of mass of the right and the left will have same velocity and same displacements at all points of time. Δr_1, Δr_2, and Δr_3 are the displacements of the counterweight, the ladder, and the man relative to the ground. We are assuming vertically upward direction as our positive direction.

Thus, the displacement of the center of mass of ladder–man system, Δr_{lm} is related to Δr_2 and Δr_3 as

$$(M + m)\,\Delta r_{lm} = M\Delta r_2 + m\Delta r_3$$

Also, the displacement of center of mass of the counterweight must be equal to the displacement of the center of mass of ladder–man system, Δr_{lm}

$$\Delta r_1 = \Delta r_{lm}$$

Due to constraint, the displacement of the ladder is equal to the displacement of the counterweight and opposite in the direction, as the counterweight and the ladder are connected by the same rope, so

$$\Delta r_1 = \Delta r_2$$

The displacement of the man in ground frame, Δr_3 will be equal to the vector sum of the displacement of man with respect to ladder, $\Delta r'$ and displacement of the ladder, Δr_2

$$\Delta r_3 = \Delta r_2 + \Delta r'$$

Solving for Δr_2 and keeping $\Delta r' = 1$ we get, $\Delta r_2 = -ml/(2(m + M))$

thus $\Delta r_1 = ml/(2(m + M))$ and
$\Delta r_3 = (2M + m)l/\,(2(m + M))$

So, the $\Delta PE_1 = (M + m)g \times ml/(2(m + M)) = mlg/2$

$\Delta PE_2 = Mg \times \{-ml/(2(m + M))\} = -mMgl/(2(m + M))$

and $\Delta PE_3 = mg(2M + m)l/(2(m + M))$

The value of increase in potential energy of the system is equal to the work done by man as there is no change in kinetic energy.

We would like to emphasize and remind you although the internal forces are incapable of changing momentum of the system but they can change the mechanical energy.

$$WD = \Delta PE_1 + \Delta PE_2 + \Delta PE_3 = mgl \quad \text{(Answer)}$$

Conclude: Although final answer may look very surprising that the work done by man is independent of the mass of the ladder, nevertheless this is what we should have expected in the first place. Why?

If the ladder would have been infinitely heavy, then answer would have been same as above; right? Similarly, if ladder would have had zero mass it can be shown by putting $M = 0$ in displacement equations that both man and counterweight would have risen by $l/2$ and hence same answer. Finally, you can think that as we increase the mass of ladder, the amount of distances that the ladder and the counterweight rise decreases and vice versa.

9-4 | Linear Momentum

In this section, we discuss only a single particle instead of a system of particles, in order to define two important quantities. Then in Section 9-5, we extend those definitions to systems of many particles.

The first definition concerns a familiar word—*momentum*—that has several meanings in everyday language but only a single precise meaning in physics and engineering. The **linear momentum** of a particle is a vector quantity $\vec{p}$ that is, defined as

$$\vec{p} = m\vec{v} \quad \text{(linear momentum of a particle)} \qquad (9\text{-}22)$$

in which m is the mass of the particle and $\vec{v}$ is its velocity. (The adjective *linear* is often dropped, but it serves to distinguish $\vec{p}$ from *angular* momentum, which is introduced in Chapter 11 and which is associated with rotation.) Since m is always a positive scalar quantity, Eq. 9-22 tells us that $\vec{p}$ and $\vec{v}$ have the same direction. From Eq. 9-22, the SI unit for momentum is the kilogram-meter per second (kg · m/s).

Newton expressed his second law of motion in terms of momentum:

> The time rate of change of the momentum of a particle is equal to the net force acting on the particle and is in the direction of that force.

In equation form this becomes

$$\vec{F}_{net} = \frac{d\vec{p}}{dt} \qquad (9\text{-}23)$$

In words, Eq. 9-23 says that the net external force $\vec{F}_{net}$ on a particle changes the particle's linear momentum $\vec{p}$. Conversely, the linear momentum can be changed only by a net external force. If there is no net external force, $\vec{p}$ *cannot* change. As we shall see in Section 9-7, this last fact can be an extremely powerful tool in solving problems.

Manipulating Eq. 9-23 by substituting for $\vec{p}$ from Eq. 9-22 gives, for constant mass m,

$$\vec{F}_{net} = \frac{d\vec{p}}{dt} = \frac{d}{dt}(m\vec{v}) = m\frac{d\vec{v}}{dt} = m\vec{a}$$

Thus, the relations $\vec{F}_{net} = d\vec{p}/dt$ and $\vec{F}_{net} = m\vec{a}$ are equivalent expressions of Newton's second law of motion for a particle.

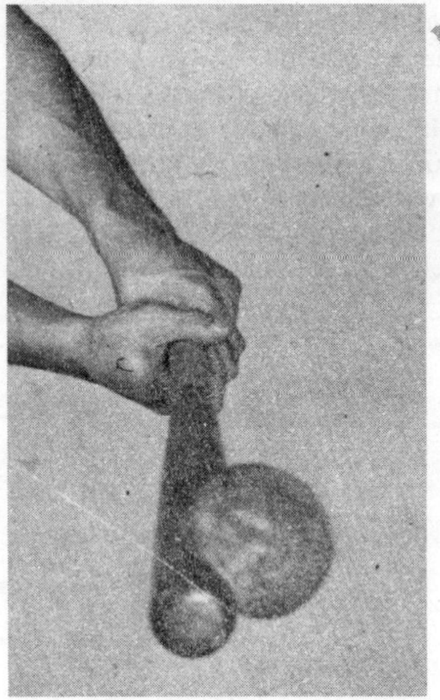

FIG. 9-15 The collision of a ball with a bat collapses part of the ball. *(Photo by Harold E. Edgerton. ©The Harold and Esther Edgerton Family Trust, courtesy of Palm Press, Inc.)*

CHECKPOINT 4 The figure gives the magnitude p of the linear momentum versus time t for a particle moving along an axis. A force directed along the axis acts on the particle. (a) Rank the four regions indicated according to the magnitude of the force, greatest first. (b) In which region is the particle slowing?

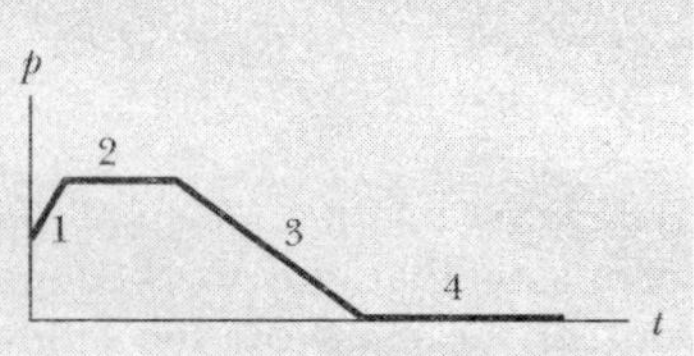

9-5 | The Linear Momentum of a System of Particles

Let's extend the definition of linear momentum to a system of particles. Consider a system of n particles, each with its own mass, velocity, and linear momentum. The particles may interact with each other, and external forces may act on them. The system as a whole has a total linear momentum $\vec{P}$, which is defined to be the vector sum of the individual particles' linear momenta. Thus,

$$\vec{P} = \vec{p}_1 + \vec{p}_2 + \vec{p}_3 + \cdots + \vec{p}_n$$
$$= m_1\vec{v}_1 + m_2\vec{v}_2 + m_3\vec{v}_3 + \cdots + m_n\vec{v}_n \quad (9\text{-}24)$$

If we compare this equation with Eq. 9-17, we see that

$$\vec{P} = M\vec{v}_{com} \quad \text{(linear momentum, system of particles)}, \quad (9\text{-}25)$$

which is another way to define the linear momentum of a system of particles:

> The linear momentum of a system of particles is equal to the product of the total mass M of the system and the velocity of the center of mass.

If we take the time derivative of Eq. 9-25, we find

$$\frac{d\vec{P}}{dt} = M\frac{d\vec{v}_{com}}{dt} = M\vec{a}_{com} \quad (9\text{-}26)$$

Comparing Eqs. 9-14 and 9-26 allows us to write Newton's second law for a system of particles in the equivalent form

$$\vec{F}_{net} = \frac{d\vec{P}}{dt} \quad \text{(system of particles)} \quad (9\text{-}27)$$

where $\vec{F}_{net}$ is the net external force acting on the system. This equation is the generalization of the single-particle equation $\vec{F}_{net} = d\vec{p}/dt$ to a system of many particles. In words, the equation says that the net external force $\vec{F}_{net}$ on a system of particles changes the linear momentum $\vec{P}$ of the system. Conversely, the linear momentum can be changed only by a net external force. If there is no net external force, $\vec{P}$ *cannot* change.

Sample Problem 9-12 Build your skill

A boat is moving at constant speed through the water. The passengers on the boat want to arrive at the shore early. They decide to try to speed up the boat by gathering at the front and running together toward the back of the boat. They stop running when they reach the back of the boat. After they have all stopped running, is the speed of the boat (*a*) higher than it was before they started running, (*b*) unchanged from what it was before they started running, (*c*) lower than it was before they started running, or (*d*) impossible to determine?

Conceptualize/Classify: (i) While they are running toward the back, is the speed of the boat (*a*) higher than it was before, (*b*) unchanged, (*c*) lower than it was before, or (*d*) impossible to determine? (ii) The passengers stop running when they reach the back of the boat. After they have all stopped running, is the speed of the boat (*a*) higher than it was before they started running, (*b*) unchanged from what it was before they started running, (*c*) lower than it was before they started running, or (*d*) impossible to determine?

Compute: (i) (*a*) This effect is the same one as the man walking on the raft that we just discussed. The boat – passengers system is isolated. If all the passengers start running one way, the speed of the boat increases the other way. (ii) (*b*) Once they stop running, the momentum of the system is the same as it was before they started running; you cannot change the momentum of an isolated system by means of internal forces.

Conclude: In case you are thinking that the passengers could run to the back repeatedly to take advantage of the speed increase but while they are running, it must be remembered that they will slow the ship down every time they return to the front.

CHECKPOINT 5 In the previous question what happens to the work done by the passengers?

Sample Problem 9-13 Build your skill

If we pull this rod from one end then at any point on rod there will be a tension (internal force) driving the remaining body.

$$T = \left(\frac{F}{m}\right) \times \left(\left(\frac{m}{l}\right)x\right)$$

Note: From the above discussion, we can understand that momentum of a system depends only on external forces and internal forces cannot affect net momentum of system. But internal forces can still contribute in changing energy of system and momentum of parts of system. For example, in chin–up exercise on horizontal bar, force is required to generate momentum in vertical direction but it is not doing work. Increase in PE during rising up is due to work done by internal force of body. But internal forces alone cannot change momentum of the body.

Sample Problem 9-14

A long plank of mass M is kept on a smooth horizontal surface and a block of mass m is kept on it with initial velocity u as shown in the figure. Find total work done by friction between the plank and the block assuming plank is sufficiently long.

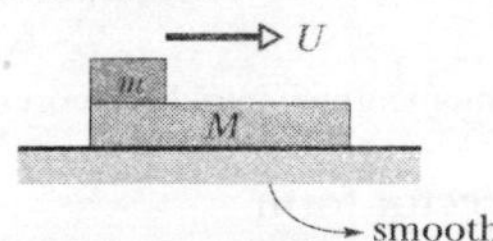

FIG. 9-16 Block of mass m kept on a long plank of mass M.

Conceptualize: When the block moves relative to the plank, the friction acting on it tries to slow it down, acting toward left. The Newton's third law pair of this friction will act on the plank towrds right and will try to make the plank go fast. Thus, we can say that at some point of time they will attain a common velocity, after that friction will not act and the common velocity that will be attained is the final velocity they will have.

Classify: If we can find the common velocity, then we can calculate work done by friction as it is the only force acting on the system. Work done by kinetic friction cannot be calculated directly. Now the question arises what is this problem doing in the chapter of momentum. Here is the answer and the solution to our example.

Compute: If we take the plank and the block as one system then the only force acting on the system is the frictional force which is an internal force, hence it cannot affect the momentum of the system although it can change the energy of the system. Thus, it is a very simple problem involving momentum conservation.

$$mu = mV + MV$$

$$V = \frac{mu}{M + m}$$

Since work done by friction is responsible for change in kinetic energy, so

final kinetic energy of system − initial kinetic energy = work done

$$W = \left(\frac{1}{2}\right)(M + m)V^2 - \left(\frac{1}{2}\right)mu^2$$

$$W = \frac{-Mmu^2}{2[M + m]}$$

Conclude: As expected, the work done by friction is negative and it has decreased the total KE of the system.

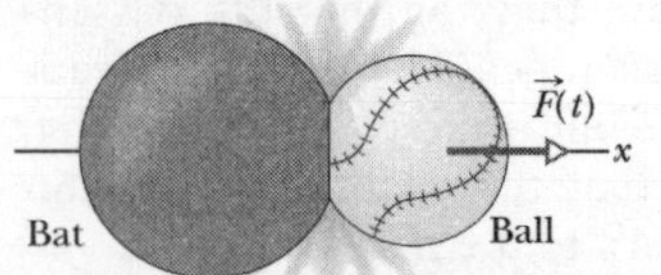

FIG. 9-17 Force $\vec{F}(t)$ acts on a ball as the ball and a bat collide.

9-6 | Impulse and Momentum

The momentum $\vec{p}$ of any particle-like body cannot change unless a net external force changes it. For example, we could push on the body to change its momentum. More dramatically, we could arrange for the body to collide with a baseball bat. In such a *collision* (or *crash*), the external force on the body is brief, has large magnitude, and suddenly changes the body's momentum. Collisions occur commonly in our world, but before we get to them, we need to consider a simple collision in which a moving particle-like body (a *projectile*) collides with some other body (a *target*).

Single Collision

Let the projectile be a ball and the target be a bat. The collision is brief, and the ball experiences a force that is, great enough to slow, stop, or even reverse its motion. Figure 9-17 depicts the collision at one instant. The ball experiences a force $\vec{F}(t)$ that varies during the collision and changes the linear momentum $\vec{p}$ of the ball. That change is related to the force by Newton's second law written in the form $\vec{F} = d\vec{p}/dt$. Thus, in time interval dt, the change in the ball's momentum is

$$d\vec{p} = \vec{F}(t)\, dt \tag{9-28}$$

We can find the net change in the ball's momentum due to the collision if we integrate both sides of Eq. 9-28 from a time t_i just before the collision to a time t_f just after the collision:

$$\int_{t_i}^{t_f} d\vec{p} = \int_{t_i}^{t_f} \vec{F}(t)\, dt \tag{9-29}$$

The left side of this equation gives us the change in momentum: $\vec{p}_f - \vec{p}_i = \Delta\vec{p}$. The right side, which is a measure of both the magnitude and the duration of the collision force, is called the **impulse** $\vec{J}$ of the collision:

$$\vec{J} = \int_{t_i}^{t_f} \vec{F}(t)\, dt \quad \text{(impulse defined)} \tag{9-30}$$

Thus, the change in an object's momentum is equal to the impulse on the object:

$$\Delta\vec{p} = \vec{J} \quad \text{(linear momentum–impulse theorem)} \tag{9-31}$$

This expression can also be written in the vector form

$$\vec{p}_f - \vec{p}_i = \vec{J} \tag{9-32}$$

and in such component forms as

$$\Delta p_x = J_x \tag{9-33}$$

and

$$p_{fx} - p_{ix} = \int_{t_i}^{t_f} F_x\, dt \tag{9-34}$$

If we have a function for $\vec{F}(t)$, we can evaluate $\vec{J}$ (and thus the change in momentum) by integrating the function. If we have a plot of $\vec{F}$ versus time t, we can evaluate $\vec{J}$ by finding the area between the curve and the t axis, such as in Fig. 9-18*a*. In many situations we do not know how the force varies with time but we do know the average magnitude F_{avg} of the force and the duration $\Delta t\ (= t_f - t_i)$ of the collision. Then we can write the magnitude of the impulse as

$$J = F_{avg}\, \Delta t \tag{9-35}$$

The average force is plotted versus time as in Fig. 9-18*b*. The area under that curve is equal to the area under the curve for the actual force $F(t)$ in Fig. 9-18*a* because both areas are equal to impulse magnitude J.

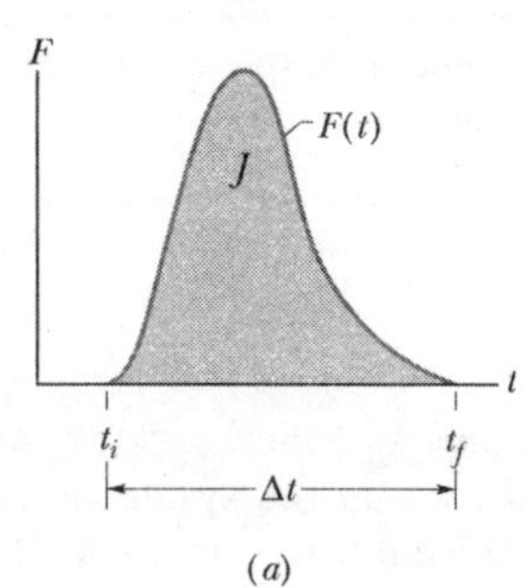

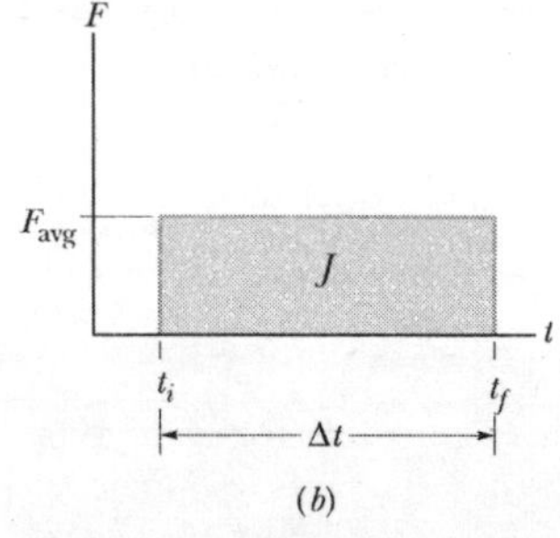

FIG. 9-18 (*a*) The curve shows the magnitude of the time-varying force $F(t)$ that acts on the ball in the collision of Fig. 9-8. The area under the curve is equal to the magnitude of the impulse $\vec{J}$ on the ball in the collision. (*b*) The height of the rectangle represents the average force F_{avg} acting on the ball over the time interval Δt. The area within the rectangle is equal to the area under the curve in (*a*) and thus is also equal to the magnitude of the impulse $\vec{J}$ in the collision.

Instead of the ball, we could have focused on the bat in Fig. 9-17. At any instant, Newton's third law tells us that the force on the bat has the same magnitude but the opposite direction as the force on the ball. From Eq. 9-30, this means that the impulse on the bat has the same magnitude but the opposite direction as the impulse on the ball.

CHECKPOINT 6 A paratrooper whose chute fails to open lands in snow; he is hurt slightly. Had he landed on bare ground, the stopping time would have been 10 times shorter and the collision lethal. Does the presence of the snow increase, decrease, or leave unchanged the values of (a) the paratrooper's change in momentum, (b) the impulse stopping the paratrooper, and (c) the force stopping the paratrooper?

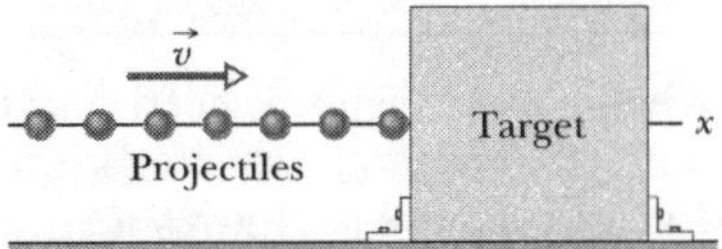

FIG. 9-19 A steady stream of projectiles, with identical linear momenta, collides with a target, which is fixed in place. The average force F_{avg} on the target is to the right and has a magnitude that depends on the rate at which the projectiles collide with the target or, equivalently, the rate at which mass collides with the target.

Series of Collisions

Now let's consider the force on a body when it undergoes a series of identical, repeated collisions. For example, as a prank, we might adjust one of those machines that fire tennis balls to fire them at a rapid rate directly at a wall. Each collision would produce a force on the wall, but that is, not the force we are seeking. We want the average force F_{avg} on the wall during the bombardment—that is, the average force during a large number of collisions.

In Fig. 9-19, a steady stream of projectile bodies, with identical mass m and linear momenta $m\vec{v}$, moves along an x axis and collides with a target body that is, fixed in place. Let n be the number of projectiles that collide in a time interval Δt. Because the motion is along only the x axis, we can use the components of the momenta along that axis. Thus, each projectile has initial momentum mv and undergoes a change Δp in linear momentum because of the collision. The total change in linear momentum for n projectiles during interval Δt is $n\,\Delta p$. The resulting impulse $\vec{J}$ on the target during Δt is along the x axis and has the same magnitude of $n\,\Delta p$ but is in the opposite direction. We can write this relation in component form as

$$J = -n\,\Delta p \tag{9-36}$$

where the minus sign indicates that J and Δp have opposite directions.

By rearranging Eq. 9-35 and substituting Eq. 9-36, we find the average force F_{avg} acting on the target during the collisions:

$$F_{avg} = \frac{J}{\Delta t} = -\frac{n}{\Delta t}\Delta p = -\frac{n}{\Delta t}m\,\Delta v \tag{9-37}$$

This equation gives us F_{avg} in terms of $n/\Delta t$, the rate at which the projectiles collide with the target, and Δv, the change in the velocity of those projectiles.

If the projectiles stop upon impact, then in Eq. 9-37 we can substitute, for Δv,

$$\Delta v = v_f - v_i = 0 - v = -v \tag{9-38}$$

where v_i $(= v)$ and v_f $(= 0)$ are the velocities before and after the collision, respectively. If, instead, the projectiles bounce (rebound) directly backward from the target with no change in speed, then $v_f = -v$ and we can substitute

$$\Delta v = v_f - v_i = -v - v = -2v \tag{9-39}$$

In time interval Δt, an amount of mass $\Delta m = nm$ collides with the target. With this result, we can rewrite Eq. 9-37 as

$$F_{avg} = -\frac{\Delta m}{\Delta t}\Delta v \tag{9-40}$$

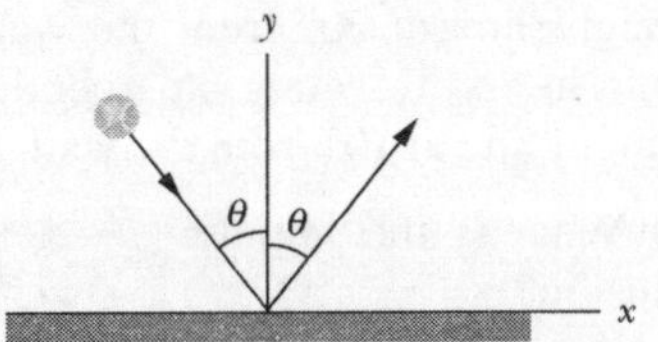

FIG. 9-20 Path followed during collision of a mass with target.

CHECKPOINT 7 The figure shows an overhead view of a ball bouncing from a vertical wall without any change in its speed. Consider the change $\Delta\vec{p}$ in the ball's linear momentum. (a) Is Δp_x positive, negative, or zero? (b) Is Δp_y positive, negative, or zero? (c) What is the direction of $\Delta\vec{p}$?

Sample Problem 9-15

When a male bighorn sheep runs head-first into another male, the rate at which its speed drops to zero is dramatic. Figure 9-21 gives a typical graph of the acceleration a versus time t for such a collision, with the acceleration taken as negative to correspond to an initially positive velocity. The peak acceleration has magnitude 34 m/s² and the duration of the collision is 0.27 s. Assume that the sheep's mass is 90.0 kg. What are the magnitudes of the impulse and average force due to the collision?

Conceptualize: Consider the sheep as the point masses undergoing collision and the change in momentum due to impulse. Impulse is defined as being the integration of force with respect to time, according to Eq. 9-30 ($\vec{J} = \int \vec{F}(t)\,dt$). (2) Average force is related to the impulse and the elapsed time by Eq. 9-35 ($J = F_{avg}\,\Delta t$).

Compute: We do not have a function for the force that we can integrate. However, we do have a graph of a versus t that we can transform to be F versus t by multiplying the scale on the acceleration axis by the mass of 90.0 kg. Then we can graphically integrate by finding the area between the plot and the time axis. Since the plot is in the shape of a triangle, we have for the impulse magnitude

$$J = \text{area} = \tfrac{1}{2}(0.27\text{ s})(90.0\text{ kg})(34.0\text{ m/s}^2)$$
$$= 4.13 \times 10^2\text{ N}\cdot\text{s} \approx 4.1 \times 10^2\text{ N}\cdot\text{s} \quad \text{(Answer)}$$

For the magnitude of the average force, we can write

$$F_{avg} = \frac{J}{\Delta t} = \frac{4.13 \times 10^2\text{ N}\cdot\text{s}}{0.27\text{ s}}$$
$$= 1.5 \times 10^3\text{ N} \quad \text{(Answer)}$$

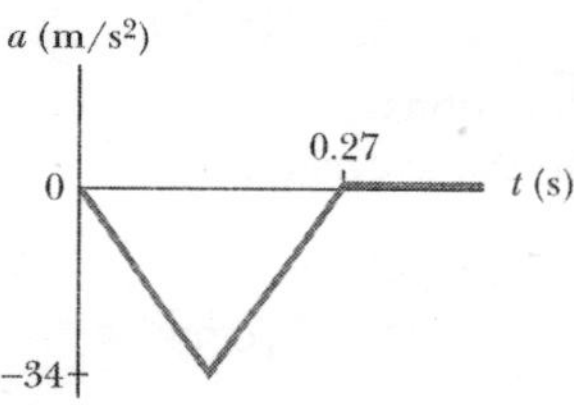

FIG. 9-21 The acceleration versus time of a bighorn sheep during a collision with another male.

Conclude: The impulse is equal to the change in the sheep's momentum during the collision. So, the size of the impulse depends on the sheep's mass and its speed right before the collision. To win the fight, a male wants a large momentum magnitude. However, if the sheep were to hit skull-to-skull or skull-to-horn, the collision duration would be 1/10 of what we just used and thus the average force would be 10 times what we just calculated. Such a large force would result in concussion or even death; neither result would win the favors of onlooking female sheep. A male avoids such results by having flexible horns that yield somewhat during the collision. Such yielding prolongs the collision and decreases the force to about 1500 N, which the skull, brain, and muscles can withstand. Thus, if a horn breaks during a collision, the next collision could be fatal.

Sample Problem 9-16

Race-car wall collision. Figure 9-22*a* is an overhead view of the path taken by a race car driver as his car collides with the racetrack wall. Just before the collision, he is traveling at speed $v_i = 70$ m/s along a straight line at 30° from the wall. Just after the collision, he is traveling at speed $v_f = 50$ m/s along a straight line at 10° from the wall. His mass m is 80 kg.

(a) What is the impulse $\vec{J}$ on the driver due to the collision?

Conceptualize: We can treat the driver as a particle-like body and thus apply the physics of this section. However, we cannot calculate $\vec{J}$ directly from Eq. 9-30 because we do not know anything about the force $\vec{F}(t)$ on the driver during the collision. That is, we do not have a function of $\vec{F}(t)$ or a plot for it and thus cannot integrate to find $\vec{J}$.

Classify: However, we *can* find $\vec{J}$ from the change in the driver's linear momentum $\vec{p}$ via Eq. 9-32 ($\vec{J} = \vec{p}_f - \vec{p}_i$).

Compute: Figure 9-15*b* shows the driver's momentum $\vec{p}_i$ before the collision (at angle 30° from the positive x

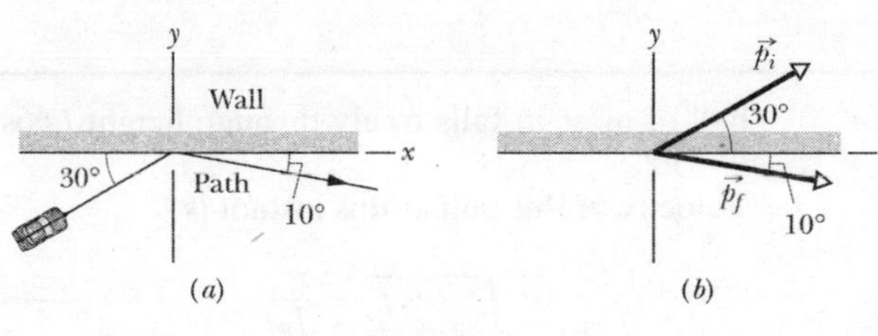

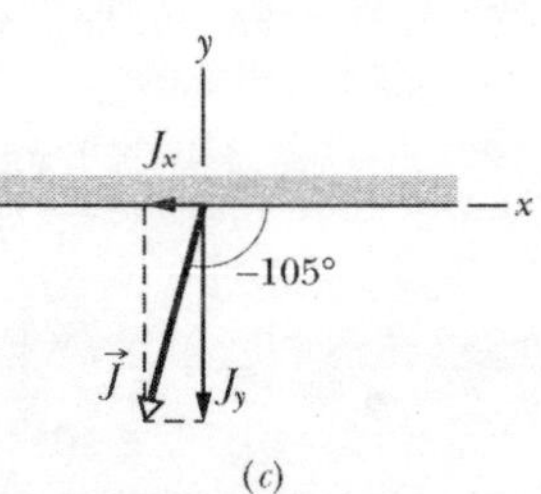

FIG. 9-22 (*a*) Overhead view of the path taken by a race car and its driver as the car slams into the racetrack wall. (*b*) The initial momentum $\vec{p}_i$ and final momentum $\vec{p}_f$ of the driver. (*c*) The impulse $\vec{J}$ on the driver during the collision.

direction) and his momentum $\vec{p}_f$ after the collision (at angle −10°). From Eqs. 9-32 and 9-22 ($\vec{p} = m\vec{v}$), we can write

$$\vec{J} = \vec{p}_f - \vec{p}_i = m\vec{v}_f - m\vec{v}_i = m(\vec{v}_f - \vec{v}_i) \quad (9\text{-}41)$$

We could evaluate the right side of this equation directly on a vector-capable calculator because we know m is 80 kg, $\vec{v}_f$ is 50 m/s at −10°, and $\vec{v}_i$ is 70 m/s at 30°. Instead, here we evaluate Eq. 9-41 in component form.

***x* component:** Along the x axis we have

$$\begin{aligned} J_x &= m(v_{fx} - v_{ix}) \\ &= (80\text{ kg})[(50\text{ m/s})\cos(-10°) - (70\text{ m/s})\cos 30°] \\ &= -910\text{ kg}\cdot\text{m/s} \end{aligned}$$

***y* component:** Along the y axis,

$$\begin{aligned} J_y &= m(v_{fy} - v_{iy}) \\ &= (80\text{ kg})[(50\text{ m/s})\sin(-10°) - (70\text{ m/s})\sin 30°] \\ &= -3495\text{ kg}\cdot\text{m/s} \approx -3500\text{ kg}\cdot\text{m/s} \end{aligned}$$

Impulse: The impulse is then

$$\vec{J} = (-910\hat{\mathrm{i}} - 3500\hat{\mathrm{j}})\text{ kg}\cdot\text{m/s} \quad \text{(Answer)}$$

which means the impulse magnitude is

$$J = \sqrt{J_x^2 + J_y^2} = 3616\text{ kg}\cdot\text{m/s} \approx 3600\text{ kg}\cdot\text{m/s}.$$

The angle of $\vec{J}$ is given by

$$\theta = \tan^{-1}\frac{J_y}{J_x} \quad \text{(Answer)}$$

which a calculator evaluates as 75.4°. Recall that the physically correct result of an inverse tangent might be the displayed answer plus 180°. We can tell which is correct here by drawing the components of $\vec{J}$ (Fig. 9-22*c*). We find that θ is actually 75.4° + 180° = 255.4°, which we can write as

$$\theta = -105° \quad \text{(Answer)}$$

(b) The collision lasts for 14 ms. What is the magnitude of the average force on the driver during the collision?

Classify: From Eq. 9-35 ($J = F_{avg}\,\Delta t$), the magnitude F_{avg} of the average force is the ratio of the impulse magnitude J to the duration Δt of the collision.

Compute: We have

$$\begin{aligned} F_{avg} &= \frac{J}{\Delta t} = \frac{3616\text{ kg}\cdot\text{m/s}}{0.014\text{ s}} \\ &= 2.583 \times 10^5\text{ N} \approx 2.6 \times 10^5\text{ N} \quad \text{(Answer)} \end{aligned}$$

Using $F = ma$ with m = 80 kg, you can show that the magnitude of the driver's average acceleration during the collision is about $3.22 \times 10^3\text{ m/s}^2 = 329g$. We can guess that the collision will probably be fatal.

Conclude: Mechanical engineers attempt to reduce the chances of a fatality by designing and building racetrack walls with more "give," so that a collision lasts longer. For example, if the collision here lasted 10 times longer and the other data remained the same, the magnitudes of the average force and average acceleration would be 10 times less and probably survivable.

CHECKPOINT 8 A block of mass m is hanging from an inextensible string and another block of mass m is hanging from a spring as shown. When a particle of mass m is fired toward the block, it immediately sticks to the larger block. Find the velocity of combined mass immediately after this collision.

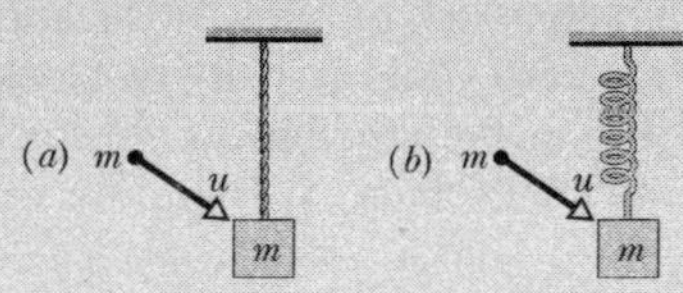

Sample Problem 9-17

A ball of mass $m_1 = 100$ g is suspended from point A by an inextensible thread, each of length $l = 32/35$ m. Now the same ball is drawn aside and held at the same level as A but at a distance $\frac{\sqrt{3}}{2}t$ from A, as shown in Fig. 9-23. Now the ball is released, calculate velocity u_1 which the ball have at the lowest point of its path at point C.

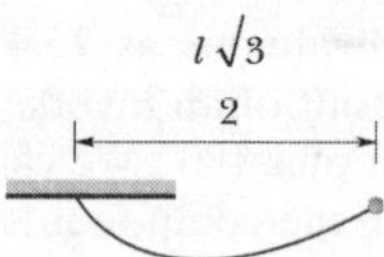

FIG. 9-23 (*a*) A ball attached to a slack string is released. (*b*) Free-body diagram.

Conceptualize: We know that a slack string cannot apply any force, thus the ball falls freely, vertically downward, like a particle dropped from some height, till thread becomes taut. After the thread becomes taut, the ball undergoes circular motion around the point of suspension as the tight thread will ensure constant distance from the point of suspension.

Classify: When the thread becomes taut it will apply an impulsive force on the particle along the length of the rope. Thus, we cannot use momentum conservation or energy conservation as the impulsive force due to jerk in the rope is a dissipative force.

Compute: Now we can think that component of velocity of the ball perpendicular to the rope will remain unchanged during the jerk as there is no impulse on the ball perpendicular to the thread. At that instant inclination θ of the thread with the vertical is given by

$$\sin\theta \frac{[(\sqrt{3}/2)l]}{l} = \frac{\sqrt{3}}{2} \text{ or } \theta = 60°$$

or ball of mass m falls freely through height $l\cos\theta = l/2$.

∴ Velocity of this ball at this instant is

$$v_0 = \sqrt{2g \times \frac{l}{2}} = \sqrt{gl}$$

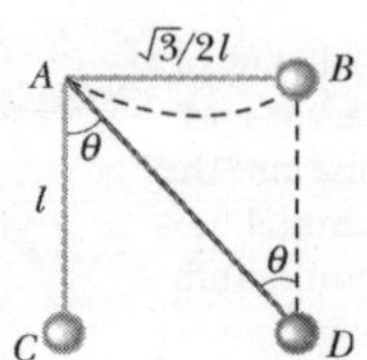

Here D is the position just after jeck and before reaching lowest point C.

It can be resolved into two components:

(i) $\sqrt{gl}\cos\theta$, along the thread. But thread is inextensible, hence this component decreases to zero (due to tension developed in the thread).

(ii) $\sqrt{gl}\sin\theta$ (perpendicular to the thread). Due to this component, ball starts to move along circle whose center is at A.

We can use conservation of energy from just after jerk till it reaches the lowest point. So, the kinetic energy of the ball just after jerk at point D is $\frac{1}{2}m_1(\sqrt{gl}\sin\theta)^2$ and potential energy stored is given as $m_1gl(1-\cos\theta)$.

Using law of conservation of energy, we get

$$\frac{1}{2}m_1u_1^2 = \frac{1}{2}m_1(\sqrt{gl}\sin\theta)^2 + m_1g(l - l\cos\theta)$$

where u_1 is velocity at lowest point that is, at C.

Putting the values and solving equation, we get

$$\Rightarrow u_1 = 4 \text{ m/s}$$

Sample Problem 9-18 Build your skill

(a) Consider a block of mass M kept on a rough surface being hit by a particle of mass m, find the velocity of combined mass immediately after the particle stucks with the block.

(b) Consider a block of mass M connected to a spring kept on smooth surface being hit by a particle of mass m, find the velocity of combined mass immediately after the particle stucks with the block.

Solution:

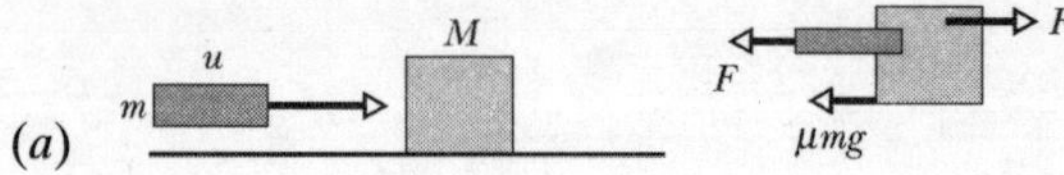

Impulse of μmg is negligible thus momentum is conserved just after collision.

According to conservation of momentum initial momentum = final momentum

Initially block of mass M is stationary so its initial velocity is zero while velocity of block of mass m is 'u'. After collision, both the blocks are stuck and move with a common final velocity v. Therefore, $mu + 0 = (m + M)v$

$$mu = (m + M)v \Rightarrow v = \frac{mu}{M + m}$$

$$\Rightarrow v = \frac{mu}{m + M}$$

(b) 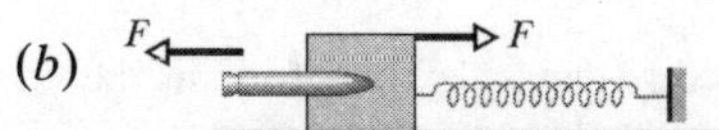

Spring force will be very small and impulse by it is negligible thus momentum is conserved just after collision.

$$v = \frac{mu}{M + m}$$

Sample Problem 9-19

An engineer has been hired to design wall to protect a hillside home from a possible snow avalanche. The engineer makes these assumptions: Snow in an avalanche has a density **ρ** of 500 kg/m^3, would hit the wall perpendicularly at a speed of 20 m/s and then stop, and would hit it at the rate of 1000 m^3/s. For these assumptions, what would be the magnitude of the average force on the wall from the snow?

Conceptualize: A key idea here is that the snow hits the wall as a steady stream of bodies, as in Fig. 10-5.

Classify: Thus, we can use Eq. (10-13) to find the magnitude of the average force on the wall. However, because the snow hits in a continuous flow, we take a differential limit of $\Delta m/\Delta t$ and write

$$F_{avg} = -\frac{dm}{dt}\Delta v \qquad (10\text{-}48)$$

Compute: Because the snow stops on hitting the wall, we use Eq. (10-11) ($\Delta v = -v$) for the change Δv in the velocity of the snow. We are given the volume rate $dV/dt = 1000$ m^3/s at which snow collides with the wall. We can find the mass rate dm/dt from

$$\frac{\text{mass}}{\text{second}} = \frac{\text{mass}}{\text{volume}} \times \frac{\text{volume}}{\text{second}}$$

or

$$\frac{dm}{dt} = \rho\frac{dV}{dt}$$

Substituting $-v$ for Δv and $\rho dV/dt$ for dm/dt in Eq. (10-48), we find

$$F_{avg} = \rho v\frac{dV}{dt} = (500\text{ kg/m}^3)(20\text{ m/s})(1000\text{ m}^3\text{/s})$$
$$= 10 \times 10^7\text{ N}$$

Conclude: The answer suggests why avalanches typically flatten homes and other structures in their paths.

This equation gives the average force F_{avg} in terms of $\Delta m/\Delta t$, the rate at which mass collides with the target. Here again we can substitute for Δv from Eq. 9-38 or 9-39 depending on what the projectiles do.

9-7 | Conservation of Momentum

Suppose that the net external force $\vec{F}_{net}$ (and thus the net impulse $\vec{J}$) acting on a system of particles is zero (the system is isolated) and that no particles leave or enter the system (the system is closed). Putting $\vec{F}_{net} = 0$ in Eq. 9-27 then yields $d\vec{P}/dt = 0$, or

> If no net external force acts on a system of particles, the total linear momentum $\vec{P}$ of the system cannot change.

$$\vec{P} = \text{constant} \quad \text{(closed, isolated system)} \qquad (9\text{-}42)$$

In words,
This result is called the **law of conservation of linear momentum.** It can also be written as

$$\vec{P}_i = \vec{P}_f \quad \text{(closed, isolated system)} \qquad (9\text{-}43)$$

In words, this equation says that, for a closed, isolated system,

$$\begin{pmatrix}\text{total linear momentum}\\ \text{at some initial time } t_i\end{pmatrix} = \begin{pmatrix}\text{total linear momentum}\\ \text{at some later time } t_f\end{pmatrix}$$

If the component of the net *external* force on a closed system is zero along an axis, then the component of the linear momentum of the system along that axis cannot change.

Caution: Momentum should not be confused with energy. In the sample problems of this section, momentum is conserved but energy is definitely not.

Equations 9-42 and 9-43 are vector equations and, as such, each is equivalent to three equations corresponding to the conservation of linear momentum in three mutually perpendicular directions as in, say, an xyz coordinate system. Depending on the forces acting on a system, linear momentum might be conserved in one or two directions but not in all directions. However,

As an example, suppose that you toss a grapefruit across a room. During its flight, the only external force acting on the grapefruit (which we take as the system) is the gravitational force $\vec{F}_g$, which is directed vertically downward. Thus, the vertical component of the linear momentum of the grapefruit changes, but since no horizontal external force acts on the grapefruit, the horizontal component of the linear momentum cannot change.

CHECKPOINT 9 An initially stationary device lying on a frictionless floor explodes into two pieces, which then slide across the floor. One piece slides in the positive direction of an x axis. (a) What is the sum of the momenta of the two pieces after the explosion? (b) Can the second piece move at an angle to the x axis? (c) What is the direction of the momentum of the second piece?

Sample Problem 9-20

One-dimensional explosion: Figure 9-24a shows a space hauler and cargo module, of total mass M, traveling along an x axis in deep space. They have an initial velocity $\vec{v}_i$ of magnitude 2100 km/h relative to the Sun. With a small explosion, the hauler ejects the cargo module, of mass $0.20M$ (Fig. 9-24b). The hauler then travels 500 km/h faster than the module along the x axis; that is, the relative speed v_{rel} between the hauler and the module is 500 km/h. What then is the velocity $\vec{v}_{HS}$ of the hauler relative to the Sun?

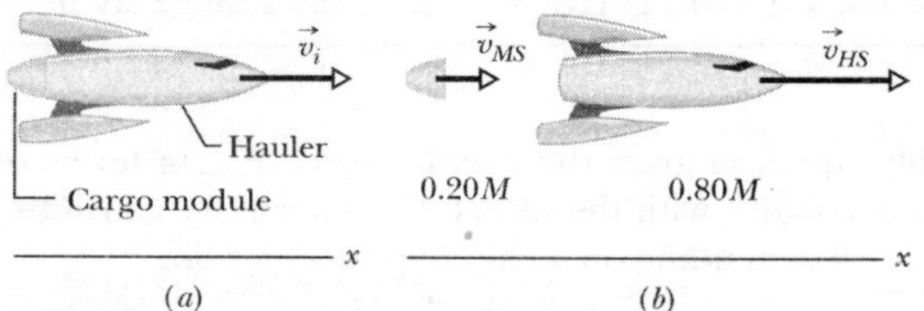

FIG. 9-24 (*a*) A space hauler, with a cargo module, moving at initial velocity $\vec{v}_i$. (*b*) The hauler has ejected the cargo module. Now the velocities relative to the Sun are $\vec{v}_{MS}$ for the module and $\vec{v}_{HS}$ for the hauler.

Conceptualize/Classify: Because the hauler–module system is closed and isolated, its total linear momentum is conserved; that is,

$$\vec{P}_i = \vec{P}_f \tag{9-44}$$

where the subscripts i and f refer to values before and after the ejection, respectively.

Compute: Because the motion is along a single axis, we can write momenta and velocities in terms of their x components, using a sign to indicate direction. Before the ejection, we have

$$P_i = Mv_i \tag{9-45}$$

Let v_{MS} be the velocity of the ejected module relative to the Sun. The total linear momentum of the system after the ejection is then

$$P_f = (0.20M)v_{MS} + (0.80M)v_{HS} \tag{9-46}$$

where the first term on the right is the linear momentum of the module and the second term is that of the hauler.

We do not know the velocity v_{MS} of the module relative to the Sun, but we can relate it to the known velocities with

$$\begin{pmatrix}\text{velocity of}\\ \text{hauler relative}\\ \text{to Sun}\end{pmatrix} = \begin{pmatrix}\text{velocity of}\\ \text{hauler relative}\\ \text{to module}\end{pmatrix} + \begin{pmatrix}\text{velocity of}\\ \text{module relative}\\ \text{to Sun}\end{pmatrix}$$

In symbols, this gives us

$$v_{HS} = v_{rel} + v_{MS} \tag{9-47}$$

or

$$v_{MS} = v_{HS} - v_{rel}$$

Substituting this expression for v_{MS} into Eq. 9-46, and then substituting Eqs. 9-45 and 9-46 into Eq. 9-44, we find

$$Mv_i = 0.20M(v_{HS} - v_{\text{rel}}) + 0.80Mv_{HS}$$

which gives us

$$v_{HS} = v_i + 0.20v_{\text{rel}}$$

or

$$v_{HS} = 2100 \text{ km/h} + (0.20)(500 \text{ km/h})$$
$$= 2200 \text{ km/h} \qquad \text{(Answer)}$$

The increase in velocity is expected as during the pushng the module the hauler must have applied force on the module and which according to Newton's third law would have applied equal and opposite force on the module.

Sample Problem 9-21

Two-dimensional explosion: A firecracker placed inside a coconut of mass M, initially at rest on a frictionless floor, blows the coconut into three pieces that slide across the floor. An overhead view is shown in Fig. 9-25*a*. Piece C, with mass $0.30M$, has final speed $v_{fC} = 5.0$ m/s.

(a) What is the speed of piece B, with mass $0.20M$?

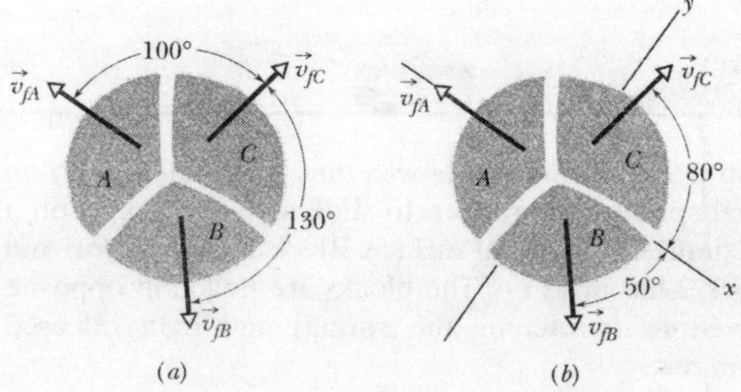

FIG. 9-25 Three pieces of an exploded coconut move off in three directions along a frictionless floor. (*a*) An overhead view of the event. (*b*) The same with a two-dimensional axis system imposed.

Conceptualize/Classify: First we need to see whether linear momentum is conserved. We note that (1) the coconut and its pieces form a closed system, (2) the explosion forces are internal to that system, and (3) no net external force acts on the system. Therefore, the linear momentum of the system is conserved.

Compute: To get started, we superimpose an xy coordinate system as shown in Fig. 9-25*b*, with the negative direction of the x axis coinciding with the direction of $\vec{v}_{fA}$. The x axis is at 80° with the direction of $\vec{v}_{fC}$ and 50° with the direction of $\vec{v}_{fB}$.

Linear momentum is conserved separately along each axis. Let's use the y axis and write

$$P_{iy} = P_{fy} \qquad (9\text{-}48)$$

where subscript i refers to the initial value (before the explosion), and subscript y refers to the y component of $\vec{P}_i$ or $\vec{P}_f$.

The component P_{iy} of the initial linear momentum is zero, because the coconut is initially at rest. To get an expression for P_{fy}, we find the y component of the final linear momentum of each piece, using the y-component version of Eq. 9-22 ($p_y = mv_y$):

$$p_{fA,y} = 0$$

$$p_{fB,y} = -0.20Mv_{fB,y} = -0.20Mv_{fB} \sin 50°$$

$$p_{fC,y} = 0.30Mv_{fC,y} = 0.30Mv_{fC} \sin 80°$$

(Note that $p_{fA,y} = 0$ because of our choice of axes.) Equation 9-48 can now be written as

$$P_{iy} = P_{fy} = p_{fA,y} + p_{fB,y} + p_{fC,y}$$

Then, with $v_{fC} = 5.0$ m/s, we have

$$0 = 0 - 0.20Mv_{fB} \sin 50° + (0.30M)(5.0 \text{ m/s}) \sin 80°$$

from which we find

$$v_{fB} = 9.64 \text{ m/s} \approx 9.6 \text{ m/s} \qquad \text{(Answer)}$$

(b) What is the speed of piece A?

Compute: Because linear momentum is also conserved along the x axis, we have

$$P_{ix} = P_{fx} \qquad (9\text{-}49)$$

where $P_{ix} = 0$ because the coconut is initially at rest. To get P_{fx}, we find the x components of the final momenta, using the fact that piece A must have a mass of $0.50M$ ($= M - 0.20M - 0.30M$):

$$p_{fA,x} = -0.50Mv_{fA}$$

$$p_{fB,x} = 0.20Mv_{fB,x} = 0.20Mv_{fB} \cos 50°$$

$$p_{fC,x} = 0.30Mv_{fC,x} = 0.30Mv_{fC} \cos 80°$$

Equation 9-49 can now be written as

$$P_{ix} = P_{fx} = p_{fA,x} + p_{fB,x} + p_{fC,x}$$

Then, with $v_{fC} = 5.0$ m/s and $v_{fB} = 9.64$ m/s, we have

$$0 = -0.50Mv_{fA} + 0.20M(9.64 \text{ m/s}) \cos 50° + 0.30M(5.0 \text{ m/s}) \cos 80°$$

from which we find

$$v_{fA} = 3.0 \text{ m/s} \qquad \text{(Answer)}$$

PROBLEM-SOLVING TACTICS

Tactic 1: Conservation of Linear Momentum For problems involving the conservation of linear momentum, first make sure that you have chosen a closed, isolated system. *Closed* means that no matter (no particles) passes through the system boundary in any direction. *Isolated* means that the net external force acting on the system is zero. If it is not isolated, then remember that each component of linear momentum is conserved separately if the corresponding component of the net external force is zero. So, you might conserve one component and not another.

Next, select two appropriate states of the system (which you may choose to call the initial state and the final state) and write expressions for the linear momentum of the system in each of these two states. In writing these expressions, make sure that you know what inertial reference frame you are using, and make sure also that you include the entire system, not missing any part of it and not including objects that do not belong to your system.

Finally, set your expressions for $\vec{P}_i$ and $\vec{P}_f$ equal to each other and solve for what is requested.

Sample Problem 9-22

Figure 9-26 shows two blocks that are connected by an ideal spring and are free to slide along an x axis on a frictionless horizontal surface. Block 1 has mass m_1 and block 2 has mass m_2. The blocks are pulled in opposite directions (stretching the spring) and then released from rest.

(a) What is the ratio v_1/v_2 of the velocity of block 1 to the velocity of block 2 as the separation between the blocks decreases?

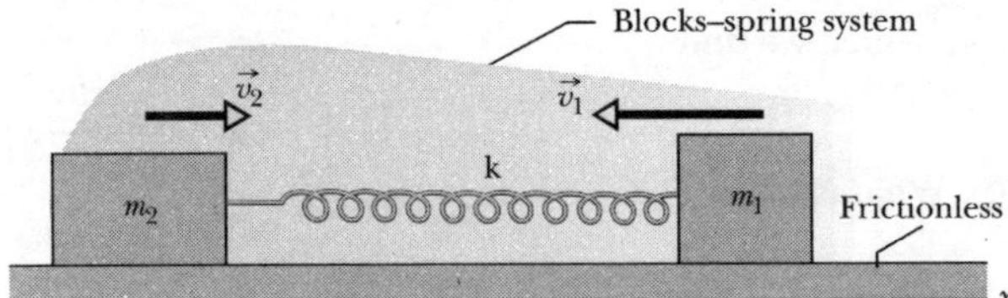

FIG. 9-26 Two blocks, which are on a frictionless surface and connected by a spring, are pulled away from each other and then released from rest. The blocks-spring system is indicated.

Conceptualize: The blocks are to be treated as particles as there is no requirement to find motion as function of time we need not attempt the problem from force analyses. Later we will solve same problem and derive position as function of time in Chapter 15.

Classify: We can use the law of conservation of linear momentum. If so, maybe we can relate the velocities of the blocks by relating their momenta. To make this check, we consider the system consisting of the two blocks and the spring. Then the spring force that accelerates the blocks is internal to the system and so cannot change the total linear momentum P of the system; thus, we need not consider that force. What *can* change P is an external force. The only *external* forces acting on the system are vertical, so the horizontal component of P cannot change as the blocks move.

Compute: We will apply the law of conservation of momentum in the form $P_i = P_f$, for x components of the momenta. We let i correspond to the release of the blocks from rest. Each block has a momentum of zero just then, so $P_i = 0$. We also let f correspond to any instant as the blocks approach each other. Then the total momentum is the sum of momenta m_1v_1 for block 1 and m_2v_2 for block 2. For our system, we can now write the conservation law as

$$0 = m_1v_1 + m_2v_2 \tag{9-50}$$

which gives us

$$\frac{v_1}{v_2} = -\frac{m_2}{m_1} \tag{9-51}$$

The minus sign tells us that the two velocities always have opposite signs. Equation 9-51 holds at every instant after release, no matter what the actual speeds of the blocks are.

(b) What is the ratio K_1/K_2 of the kinetic energies of the blocks as their separation decreases?

Solution: The key idea here is that we can find the ratio of the kinetic energies by using the definition of kinetic energy, that is,

$$\frac{K_1}{K_2} = -\frac{\frac{1}{2}m_1v_1^2}{\frac{1}{2}m_2v_2^2} = \frac{m_1}{m_2}\left(\frac{v_1}{v_2}\right)^2$$

Substituting for v_1/v_1 from Eq. 9-51 and simplifying, we find

$$\frac{K_1}{K_2} = \frac{m_2}{m_1} \tag{9-52}$$

Conclude: As the blocks move toward each other and the stretch of the spring decreases, energy is transferred from the elastic potential energy of the spring to the kinetic energies K_1 and K_2 of the blocks. Although K_1 and K_2 then increase, Eq. 9-52 tells us that their ratio does not change but is preset by the ratio of the masses. After the spring reaches its rest length and begins to be compressed by the blocks, the energy transfer is reversed, but Eq. 9-52 still holds.

Equations 9-50 through 9-52 apply to other situations in which two bodies attract (or repel) each other. For example, they apply to a stone falling toward Earth. The stone corresponds to, say, block 1 in Fig. 9-26, and Earth to block 2. The gravitational force between the stone and Earth corresponds to the mutual force between the blocks that is, provided by the spring in Fig. 9-18. Our reference frame is the frame in which the center of mass of the stone-Earth system is stationary. *In this frame,* Eq. 9-50 tells us that the magnitudes of the linear momenta of the stone and Earth remain equal to each other throughout the fall. Equations 9-51 and 9-52 tell us that, because m_2 ª m_1, the stone has much greater speed and kinetic energy than Earth during the fall, again *in the given frame.*

Sample Problem 9-23

Find speed of the wedge when block of mass m is about to reach the ground. Assuming all surfaces are frictionless. Mass of the block, m and of wedge, M is 1 kg each. Length of incline is l = 0.51 m and it is at an angle 37° to the horizontal.

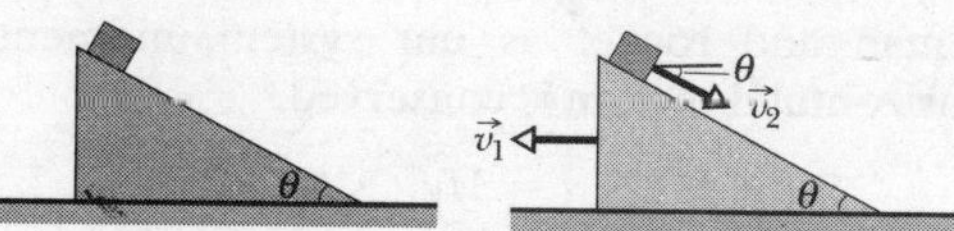

FIG. 9-27 (*a*) A block kept on a smooth wedge. (*b*) Block comes down and the wedge moves to the right with velocity V_1

Conceptualize: Please go back and review 9-22. There we had to just find displacement here we have to find velocity.

Classify: As discussed already, solving the problem by calculating accleration and then displacements and velocities is a painful and tediuous solution. We will attempt this by conserving momentum and energy; here energy can be conserved as no dissipative force is present in the system.

Compute: Let us say that the block has velocity v_2' with respect to the wedge v_1 and the wedge has velocity with respect to ground. Considering direction of motion along right horizontal to be +ve value of X-component of velocity for block and wedge can be given as

$$\vec{v}_{2x} = v'_2 \cos\theta - v_1 \quad \text{(of block)}$$

and

$$\vec{v}_{1x} = -v_1 \quad \text{(of wedge)}$$

Similarly, considering direction of motion along vertically downward +ve y axis, we can find Y-component of velocity for block and wedge that is,

$$v_{2y} = v'_2 \sin\theta \quad \text{(of block)}$$

and

$$\vec{v}_{1y} = 0 \quad \text{(of wedge)}$$

Thus, net velocity of block is

$$V_2^2 = (v_2'\cos\theta - v_1)^2 + (v_2'\sin\theta)^2$$

Since no external force will act in horizontal direction, so momentum of the system consisting of the block and wedge remains conserved in horizontal direction. Initially both the bodies are at rest the velocity of center of mass initially is zero and its x component will remain zero.

$$-Mv_1 + m(v_2'\cos\theta - v) = 0$$

Also from conservation of energy,

$$mgl\sin\theta = \frac{1}{2}mv_1^2 + \frac{1}{2}mv_2^2$$

[Work done by normal force on system is zero]

Now putting the value of v_2 we get

$$mgl\sin\theta = \frac{1}{2}mv_1^2 + \frac{1}{2}m[(v_2'\cos\theta - v_1)^2 + (v_2'\sin\theta)^2]$$

from Eq. we get $\quad v_2'\cos\theta - v_1 = \dfrac{Mv_1}{m}$

and $\quad v_2' = \left(\dfrac{M+m}{m\cos\theta}\right)v_1$

Using above results, we get

$$mgl\sin\theta = \frac{1}{2}Mv_1^2 + \frac{1}{2}m\left(\frac{M^2v_1^2}{m^2} + \frac{(M+m)^2\sin^2\theta\, v_1^2}{m^2\cos^2\theta}\right)$$

Solving we get v_1 = 1.2 m/s

Conclude: If we make θ = 0, we get same result as in the previous example because the wedge becomes raft. If we make $M \gg m$, then as we expect, answer should be zero because the small block will not be able to move the infinitely heavy wedge.

In Case Of: Comment on the magnitude of normal due to ground N.

It must be less than $(M + m)g$ as the center of mass of the system must be accelerating downwards as the block has a component of acceleration vertically downward.

Sample Problem 9-24

Problems involving impulsive forces: "Relative means after the event"

Illustration: John Rambo is strapped on a trolley which is travelling at the speed u on a smooth horizontal surface; he is carrying a shoulder fired rocket launcher. The combined mass of John Rambo, rocket launcher and trolley is M. The launcher has a rocket of mass m (which makes the total mass as $M + m$). The muzzle velocity of rocket is V. What will be the velocities of Rambo and rocket just after firing?

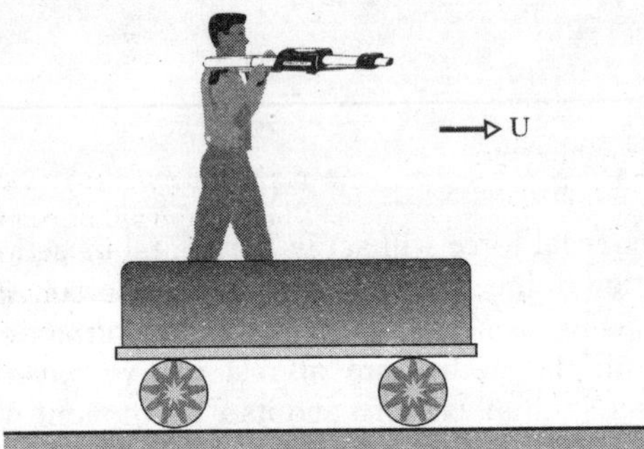

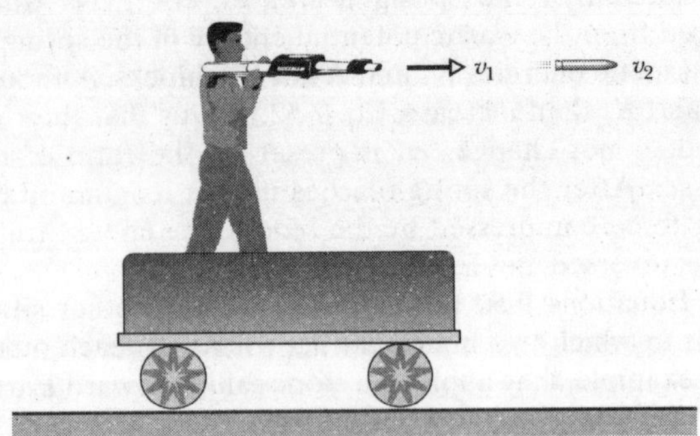

FIG. 9-28 (*a*) Rambo strapped on a trolley travelling at speed u with rocket launcher on his shoulder. (*b*) Velocity after rocket is fired.

Conceptualize: We know that the recoil of firing will apply a impulse on Rambo toward left. Thus, we should expect Rambo to be moving slowly or moving toward left.

Classify: Firing will involve large impulsive forces of explosion which cannot be analyzed directly. Taking man and rocket as one system, then momentum along horizontal direction is conserved.

Compute: Let us say v_2 and v_1 are the velocities of the rocket and Rambo, respectively, just after firing. Muzzle velocity means the velocity of the projectile with respect to the launcher. But as soon as the velocity of rocket increases from u to v_2, the velocity of Rambo would also be changed to v_1 as the force of explosion acts simultaneously on both the launcher and the rocket according to Newton's third law. So, the equation of relative velocity is written in terms of velocities just after firing.

Using Eq. and rearranging, we get

$$v_2 - v_1 = V_0$$

Taking man and rocket as our system, momentum along horizontal direction is conserved.

$$(m + M)\,u = Mv_1 + Mv_2$$

Solving we get,

$$v_2 = u\left(\frac{MV_0}{M+m}\right) \quad \text{and} \quad v_1 = u - \left(\frac{MV_0}{M+m}\right)$$

Conclude: As expected, the velocity of the Rambo has decreased or if $\dfrac{mV_0}{(M+m)} > u$ he would be going toward left. Also, if we assume M to be very large in comparison to m, then there will be no change in the velocity of Rambo. Also, the rocket will have a higher velocity as all the energy of explosion will be going only to the rocket. This situation is like that of firing a 9 mm shot from a gun mounted on 80 ton Battle Tank.

Sample Problem 9-25

A pan of mass m = 1.5 kg and a block of mass M = 3 kg are connected with each other by a flexible, light and inextensible string, passing over a small, light, and frictionless pulley. Initially the block is resting over a horizontal floor as shown in figure. At t = 0, an inelastic ball of mass m_0 = 0.5 kg collides with the pan with velocity v_0 = 16 m/s

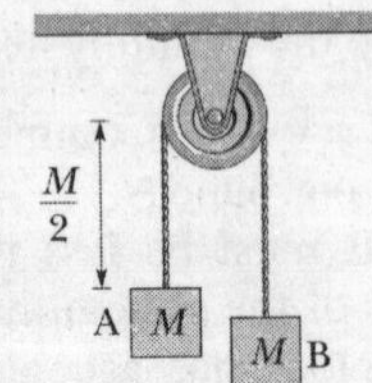

(vertically downward). Calculate the maximum height, upto which the block rises.

Conceptualize: When ball strikes the pan, it does not rebound because collision of these two is inelastic or the ball gets stuck with the pan. Simultaneously block is jerked into motion due to impulsive reaction exerted by the string. As the pan and ball start to move downward, the block starts to move up with the same speed, due to constraint of the rope.

Classify: Here we cannot conserve momentum of system consisting of the pulley as the ceiling may apply an impulsive force on the system. Ceiling is not considered as part of system as it has an infinite mass and zero velocity which gives indeterminate momentum. Thus, this problem will be attempted by writing impulse due to string on two blocks.

Compute: Let impulsive reaction of the string be J. After collision, let the pan and ball start to move downward, at the same time the block starts to move up with the same speed v_1 (as that of pan and ball going down).

Considering downward direction as positive, the impulse momentum equation of ball and pan is $-J = (m + m_0)\, v_1 - m_0 v_0$, the impulse momentum equation for block $-J = M(-v_1) - 0$.

Putting the values and solving above two equations, we get

From above two equations, $v_1 = 1.6$ m/s.

Since mass M of block is greater than combined mass $(m + m)$ of pan and ball, therefore, block retards and comes to instantaneous rest at highest point. Let that retardation be α,

$$\alpha = \frac{M - (m + m_0)}{M + (m + m_0)} g = 2 \text{ m/s}^2$$

Considering upward motion of block from floor to highest point and using,

$$u = v_1 = 1.6 \text{ m/s}, a = -\alpha = -2 \text{ m/s}^2, v = 0$$

We can find the distance it travels before coming to rest, using equation $v_2 = u_2 + 2\,as$

Putting the value in equation and solving, we get

$$s = h = 0.64 \text{ m}$$

Conclude: Since the dissipative forces of jerk and inelastic collision are occuring, energy of the system decreased from its initial value. Which can be verified by checking initial gravitational potential energy of the system and the final gravitational potential energy of the system.

9-8 | Collisions

In Section 9-6, we considered the collision of two particle-like bodies but focused on only one of the bodies at a time. For the next several sections we switch our focus to the system itself, with the assumption that the system is closed and isolated. In Section 9-7, we discussed a rule about such a system: The total linear momentum $\vec{P}$ of the system cannot change because there is no net external force to change it. This is a very powerful rule because it can allow us to determine the results of a collision *without* knowing the details of the collision (such as how much damage is done).

Collision

Collision is an event in which strong force acts between two or more bodies for a short time.

1. In a collision, we consider a situation before and after the collision. The duration of collision is negligible as compared to the time for which event is observed.
2. *In a collision effect of external non-impulsive forces (example, gravity, spring) can be neglected because they are very small compared to interaction forces and time of collision is very small.*
3. When two bodies collide, they exert force on each other through point of contact, which is perpendicular to the plane of contact. The direction of force of interaction is line of collision.
4. In case of collision, if the external impulsive forces are not acting in a direction of collision, the total momentum of system in that direction remains conserved

$$m_1\vec{u} + m_2\vec{u} = m_1\vec{v} + m_2\vec{v}$$

5. After collision only the components of velocity along the line of collision changes, the perpendicular components of velocity remain unaffected.

6. According to initial velocities and line of collision, collision can be of two types:
   (*A*) Head on collision (*B*) Oblique collision

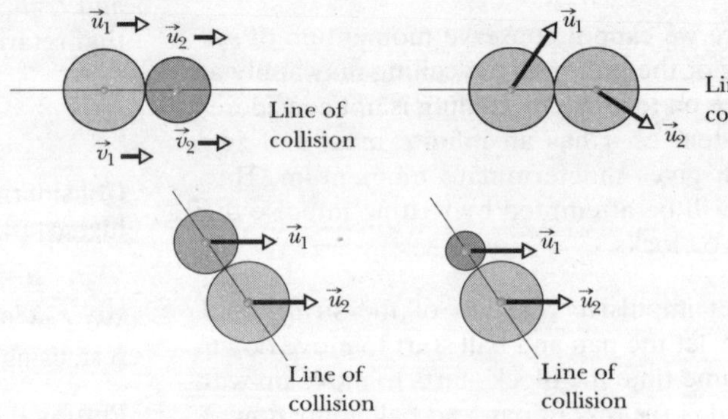

$\vec{u}_1$ $\vec{u}_2$ Line of collision $\vec{v}_1$ $\vec{v}_2$ $\vec{u}_1$ Line of collision $\vec{u}_2$ $\vec{u}_1$ $\vec{u}_2$ Line of collision $\vec{u}_1$ $\vec{u}_2$ Line of collision

FIG. 9-29 Head-on and oblique collision.

Head-on collision occurs when the direction of motion of the two colliding particles is along a line passing through the center of mass of the particles. This line is called the line of collision (Fig. 9-29*a*). When the motion of one or both of the particles is at an angle with the line of collision (Fig. 9-29*b*), the collision is said to be oblique collision.

We shall also be interested in the total kinetic energy of a system of two colliding bodies. If that total happens to be unchanged by the collision, then the kinetic energy of the system is *conserved* (it is the same before and after the collision). Such a collision is called an **elastic collision.** In everyday collisions of common bodies, such as two cars or a ball and a bat, some energy is always transferred from kinetic energy to other forms of energy, such as thermal energy or energy of sound. Thus, the kinetic energy of the system is *not* conserved. Such a collision is called an **inelastic collision.**

Consider the two smooth particles *A* and *B* undergoing the head-on collision

1. Let's say the particles have the initial momentum as shown in Fig. 9-29*a*. Collision will occur if $v_{Ai} > v_{Bi}$
2. During the collision, the bodies must be thought of as deformable or non- rigid. The bodies will undergo a period of deformation during which they exert an equal but opposite deformation impulse $\int P\,dt$ on each other (Fig. 9-29*b*). Thus, their velocity will vary continuously such that velocity of *A* will decrease and velocity of *B* will increase.
3. When both particles will have a common velocity *v*, the deformation of both particles will be maximum.
4. After achieving common velocity, a period of restitution occurs in which the bodies try to return to their original shapes. The equal and opposite restitution impulse $\int R\,dt$ pushes the particles apart from one another (Fig. (*d*)). The deformation impulse is always greater than that of restitution, that is, $\int P\,dt. > \int R\,dt.$
5. Once the restitution impulse stops acting, the particles will have a final velocity and hence momentum and kinetic energy.

Let us determine their final velcoities $(v_A)_2$ and $(v_B)_2$. Only the internal impulses of deformation and restitution occur and no external impulse is acting.

Apply the principle of impulse and momentum to each particle. During the deformation phase for particle *A*, we have

$$-\int P\,\mathrm{dt} = m_A v - m_A (v_A)_1 \qquad \int P\,\mathrm{dt} = m_B v - m_B (v_B)_1$$

For the restitution phase.

$$-\int R\,dt = m_A(v_A)_2 - m_A v \qquad \int R\,dt = m_B(v_B)_2 - m_B v$$

The ratio of the restitution impulse to the deformation impulse is called the coefficient of restitution, *e*. From the above equations, this value for particle *A* is

$$e = \frac{\int R\,dt}{\int P\,dt} = \frac{v - (v_A)_2}{(v_A)_1 - v} \quad \text{and} \quad e = \frac{\int R\,dt}{\int P\,dt} = \frac{(v_B)_2 - v}{v - (v_B)_1}$$

If the unknown v is eliminated from the above two equations, the coefficient of restitution can be expressed in terms of the particles' initial and final velocities as

$$e = \frac{(v_B)_2 - (v_A)_2}{(v_A)_1 - (v_B)_1}$$

It is important to choose a positive direction and then use it consistently while writing all quantities with sign. We have defined the positive direction to the right, if a negative value comes as a result from the solution, it indicates motion is to the left.

When applying the equation, the sense of an unknown velocity can be assumed. If the solution yields a negative magnitude, the velocity acts in the opposite sense.

Newton's Law for Collision

1. $\dfrac{v_2 - v_1}{u_2 - u_1} = -e$

v_1 and $v_2 \rightarrow$ components of velocities of colliding points of the bodies, along the line of contact, after collision (with sign)

u_1 and $u_2 \rightarrow$ components of velocities of colliding points of the bodies, along the line of contact, before collision (with sign)

$e \rightarrow$ coefficient of restitution

Coefficient of Restitution: In general, e has a value between zero and one, and one should be aware of the physical meaning of these two limits.

Example of sign convention:

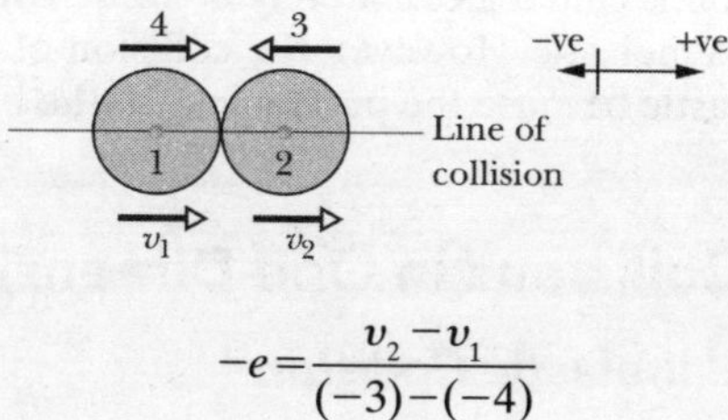

$$-e = \frac{v_2 - v_1}{(-3)-(-4)}$$

2. This law is valid even when momentum of the system is not conserved.
3. For $e = 1$ perfectly elastic collision.

Perfectly Elastic Collision ($e = 1$): If the collision between the two bodies is perfectly elastic, the deformation impulse ($\int P\,dt$.) is equal and opposite to the restitution impulse ($\int R\,dt$). Although in reality, the condition $e = 1$ for an elastic collision can never be achieved.

for	$0 < e < 1$	inelastic collision
for	$e = 0$	perfectly inelastic collision (bodies will move together)

Perfectly inelastic collision ($e = 0$): The collision is said to be perfectly in elastic when $e = 0$. In this case of colliding bodies, there is no tendency to regain shape. The event of collision is over when they have maximum deformation. Thus, restitution impulse $\int R\, dt = 0$, so that after collision both bodies stick together and move with a common velocity. In this case, the loss of kinetic energy is maximum as energy is lost during deformation.

4. $v_2 - v_1 = e\,(u_2 - u_1)$

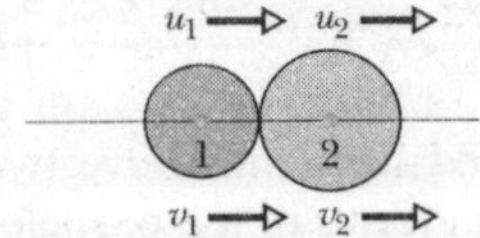

It can also be expressed as

Relative velocity of receding after impact = e [Relative velocity of approach before impact]

From the above discussion it should be clear that the principle of work and energy is not useful for the analysis of this problem. Using the particle's velocities before and after collision, the energy lost during collision can be calculated. This energy loss $\Sigma U_{1\text{-}2} = \Sigma T_2 - \Sigma T_1$, occurs because some part of the initial kinetic energy of the bodies is converted into thermal energy as well as creating sound and deformation of the material when the collision occurs. If the collision is perfectly elastic, no energy is lost in the collision; whereas if the collision is perfectly inelastic, the energy lost during collision is a maximum.

However, in some situations, we can *approximate* a collision of common bodies as elastic. Suppose that you drop a Superball onto a hard floor. If the collision between the ball and floor (or Earth) were elastic, the ball would lose no kinetic energy because of the collision and would rebound to its original height. However, the actual rebound height is somewhat short, showing that at least some kinetic energy is lost in the collision and thus that the collision is somewhat inelastic. Still, we might choose to neglect that small loss of kinetic energy to approximate the collision as elastic.

The inelastic collision of two bodies always involves a loss in the kinetic energy of the system. The greatest loss occurs if the bodies stick together, in which case the collision is called a **completely inelastic collision.** The collision of a baseball and a bat is inelastic. However, the collision of a wet putty ball and a bat is completely inelastic because the putty sticks to the bat.

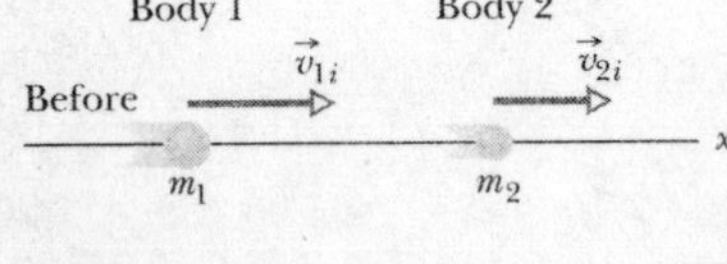

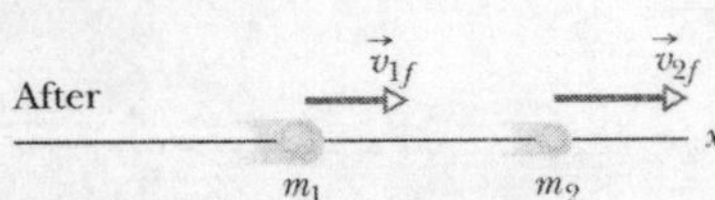

FIG. 9-30 Bodies 1 and 2 move along an x axis, before and after they have an inelastic collision.

9-9 | Inelastic Collisions in One Dimension

One-Dimensional Inelastic Collision

Figure 9-30 shows two bodies just before and just after they have a one-dimensional collision. The velocities before the collision (subscript i) and after the collision (subscript f) are indicated. The two bodies form our system, which is closed and isolated. We can write the law of conservation of linear momentum for this two-body system as

$$\begin{pmatrix}\text{total momentum } \vec{P}_i \\ \text{before the collision}\end{pmatrix} = \begin{pmatrix}\text{total momentum } \vec{P}_f \\ \text{after the collision}\end{pmatrix}$$

which we can symbolize as

$$\vec{p}_{1i} + \vec{p}_{2i} = \vec{p}_{1f} + \vec{p}_{2f} \qquad \text{(conservation of linear momentum)} \qquad (9\text{-}53)$$

Because the motion is one-dimensional, we can drop the overhead arrows for vectors and use only components along the axis, indicating direction with a sign. Thus, from $p = mv$, we can rewrite Eq. 9-53 as

$$m_1 v_{1i} + m_2 v_{2i} = m_1 v_{1f} + m_2 v_{2f} \tag{9-54}$$

If we know values for, say, the masses, the initial velocities, and one of the final velocities, we can find the other final velocity with Eq. 9-54.

One-Dimensional Completely Inelastic Collision

Figure 9-31 shows two bodies before and after they have a completely inelastic collision (meaning they stick together). The body with mass m_2 happens to be initially at rest ($v_{2i} = 0$). We can refer to that body as the *target* and to the incoming body as the *projectile*. After the collision, the stuck-together bodies move with velocity V. For this situation, we can rewrite Eq. 9-54 as

$$m_1 v_{1i} = (m_1 + m_2)V \tag{9-55}$$

or

$$V = \frac{m_1}{m_1 + m_2} v_{1i} \tag{9-56}$$

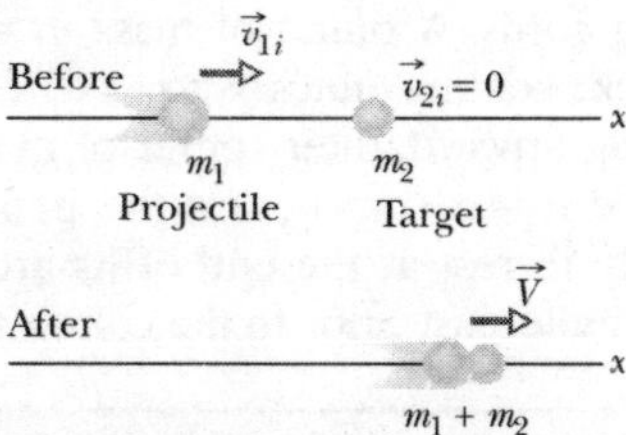

FIG. 9-31 A completely inelastic collision between two bodies. Before the collision, the body with mass m_2 is at rest and the body with mass m_1 moves directly toward it. After the collision, the stuck-together bodies move with the same velocity $\vec{V}$.

If we know values for, say, the masses and the initial velocity v_{1i} of the projectile, we can find the final velocity V with Eq. 9-56. Note that V must be less than v_{1i} because the mass ratio $m_1/(m_1 + m_2)$ must be less than unity.

Velocity of Center of Mass

In a closed, isolated system, the velocity $\vec{v}_{com}$ of the center of mass of the system cannot be changed by a collision because, with the system isolated, there is no net external force to change it. To get an expression for $\vec{v}_{com}$, let us return to the two-body system and one-dimensional collision of Fig. 9-19. From Eq. 9-25 ($\vec{P} = M\vec{v}_{com}$), we can relate $\vec{v}_{com}$ to the total linear momentum $\vec{P}$ of that two-body system by writing

$$\vec{P} = M\vec{v}_{com} = (m_1 + m_2)\vec{v}_{com} \tag{9-57}$$

The total linear momentum $\vec{P}$ is conserved during the collision; so it is given by either side of Eq. 9-53. Let us use the left side to write

$$\vec{P} = \vec{p}_{1i} + \vec{p}_{2i} \tag{9-58}$$

Substituting this expression for $\vec{P}$ in Eq. 9-57 and solving for $\vec{v}_{com}$ give us

$$\vec{v}_{com} = \frac{\vec{P}}{m_1 + m_2} = \frac{\vec{p}_{1i} + \vec{p}_{2i}}{m_1 + m_2} \tag{9-59}$$

The right side of this equation is a constant, and $\vec{v}_{com}$ has that same constant value before and after the collision.

For example, in a series of freeze frames, the motion of the center of mass for the completely inelastic collision of Fig. 9-31. Body 2 is the target, and its initial linear momentum in Eq. 9-59 is $\vec{p}_{2i} = m_2\vec{v}_{2i} = 0$. Body 1 is the projectile, and its initial linear momentum in Eq. 9-56 is $\vec{p}_{1i} = m_1\vec{v}_{1i}$. Note that as the series of freeze frames progresses to and then beyond the collision, the center of mass moves at a constant velocity to the right. After the collision, the common final speed V of the bodies is equal to $\vec{v}_{com}$ because then the center of mass travels with the stuck-together bodies.

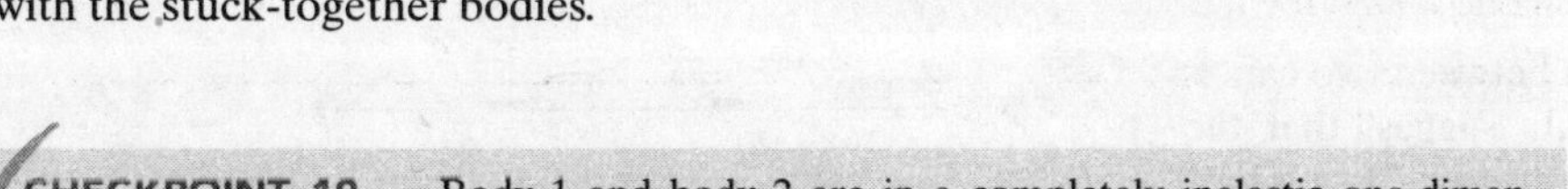

CHECKPOINT 10 Body 1 and body 2 are in a completely inelastic one-dimensional collision. What is their final momentum if their initial momenta are, respectively, (a) 10 kg · m/s and 0; (b) 10 kg · m/s and 4 kg · m/s; (c) 10 kg · m/s and −4 kg · m/s?

Sample Problem 9-26 Build your skill

The *ballistic pendulum* was used to measure the speeds of bullets before electronic timing devices were developed. The version shown in Fig. 9-32 consists of a large block of wood of mass $M = 5.4$ kg, hanging from two long cords. A bullet of mass $m = 9.5$ g is fired into the block, coming quickly to rest. The *block + bullet* then swing upward, their center of mass rising a vertical distance $h = 6.3$ cm before the pendulum comes momentarily to rest at the end of its arc. What is the speed of the bullet just prior to the collision?

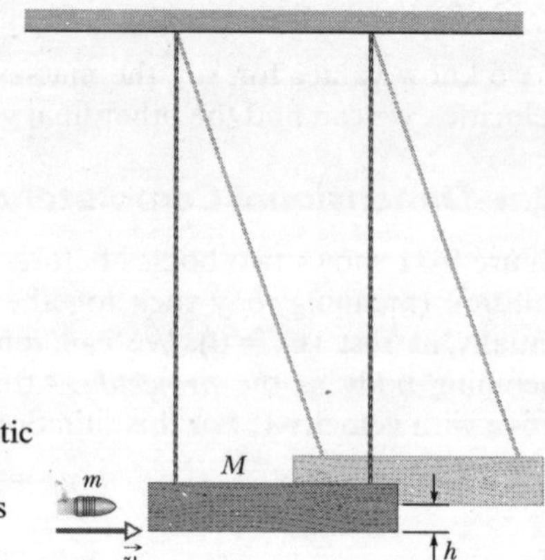

FIG. 9-32 A ballistic pendulum, used to measure the speeds of bullets.

Conceptualize/Classify: We can see that the bullet's speed v must determine the rise height h. However, we cannot use the conservation of mechanical energy to relate these two quantities because surely energy is transferred from mechanical energy to other forms (such as thermal energy and energy to break apart the wood) as the bullet penetrates the block. Nevertheless, we can split this complicated motion into two steps that we can separately analyze: (1) the bullet–block collision and (2) the bullet–block rise, during which mechanical energy *is* conserved.

Compute step 1: Because the collision within the bullet–block system is so brief, we can make two important assumptions: (1) During the collision, the gravitational force on the block and the force on the block from the cords are still balanced. Thus, during the collision, the net external impulse on the bullet–block system is zero. Therefore, the system is isolated and its total linear momentum is conserved. (2) The collision is one-dimensional in the sense that the direction of the bullet and block *just after the collision* is in the bullet's original direction of motion.

Because the collision is one-dimensional, the block is initially at rest, and the bullet sticks in the block, we use Eq. 9-56 to express the conservation of linear momentum. Replacing the symbols there with the corresponding symbols here, we have

$$V = \frac{m}{m+M}v \qquad (9\text{-}60)$$

Compute step 2: As the bullet and block now swing up together, the mechanical energy of the bullet–block–Earth system is conserved. (This mechanical energy is not changed by the force of the cords on the block, because that force is always directed perpendicular to the block's direction of travel.) Let's take the block's initial level as our reference level of zero gravitational potential energy. Then conservation of mechanical energy means that the system's kinetic energy at the start of the swing must equal its gravitational potential energy at the highest point of the swing. Because the speed of the bullet and block at the start of the swing is the speed V immediately after the collision, we may write this conservation as

$$\tfrac{1}{2}(m+M)V^2 = (m+M)gh$$

Compute steps: Substituting for V from Eq. 9-60 leads to

$$v = \frac{m+M}{m}\sqrt{2gh}$$

$$= \left(\frac{0.0095\text{ kg} + 5.4\text{ kg}}{0.0095\text{ kg}}\right)\sqrt{(2)(9.8\text{ m/s}^2)(0.063\text{ m})}$$

$$= 630\text{ m/s} \qquad \text{(Answer)}$$

Conclude: The ballistic pendulum is a kind of "transformer," exchanging the high speed of a light object (the bullet) for the low—and thus more easily measurable—speed of a massive object (the block).

Sample Problem 9-27 Build your skill

The most dangerous type of collision between two cars is a head-on collision. Surprisingly, data suggest that the risk of fatality to a driver is less if that driver has a passenger in the car. Let's see why.

Before — Car 1 $\vec{v}_{1i}$, m_1 — Car 2 $\vec{v}_{2i}$, m_2 — x

FIG. 9-33 Two cars about to collide head-on.

Figure 9-33 represents two identical cars about to collide head-on in a completely inelastic, one-dimensional collision along an x axis. During the collision, the two cars form a closed system. Let's make the reasonable assumption that during the collision the impulse between the cars is so great that we can neglect the relatively minor impulses due to the frictional forces on the tires from the road. Then we can assume that there is no net external force on the two-car system.

The x component of the initial velocity of car 1 along the x axis is $v_{1i} = +25$ m/s, and that of car 2 is $v_{2i} = -25$ m/s. During the collision, the force (and thus the impulse) on each car causes a change Δv in the car's velocity. The probability of a driver being killed depends on the magnitude of Δv for that driver's car. We want to calculate the changes Δv_1 and Δv_2 in the velocities of the two cars.

(a) First, let each car carry only a driver. The total mass of car 1 (including driver 1) is $m_1 = 1400$ kg, and the total mass of car 2 (including driver 2) is $m_2 = 1400$ kg. What are the changes Δv_1 and Δv_2 in the velocities of the cars?

Conceptualize: Because the system is closed and isolated, its total linear momentum is conserved.

Classify: From Eq. 9-54, we can write this as

$$m_1 v_{1i} + m_2 v_{2i} = m_1 v_{1f} + m_2 v_{2f} \quad (9\text{-}61)$$

Since the collision is completely inelastic, the two cars stick together and thus have the same velocity V after the collision. Substituting V for v_{1f} and v_{2f} into Eq. 9-61 and solving for V, we have

$$V = \frac{m_1 v_{1i} + m_2 v_{2i}}{m_1 + m_2} \quad (9\text{-}62)$$

Substitution of the given data then results in

$$V = \frac{(1400\text{ kg})(+25\text{ m/s}) + (1400\text{ kg})(-25\text{ m/s})}{1400\text{ kg} + 1400\text{ kg}} = 0$$

Thus, the change in the velocity of car 1 is

$$\Delta v_1 = v_{1f} - v_{1i} = V - v_{1i}$$
$$= 0 - (+25\text{ m/s}) = -25\text{ m/s} \quad \text{(Answer)}$$

and the change in the velocity of car 2 is

$$\Delta v_2 = v_{2f} - v_{2i} = V - v_{2i}$$
$$= 0 - (-25\text{ m/s}) = +25\text{ m/s} \quad \text{(Answer)}$$

(b) Next, we reconsider the collision, but this time with an 80 kg passenger in car 1. What are Δv_1 and Δv_2 now?

Compute: Repeating our steps but now substituting $m_1 = 1480$ kg, we find that

$$V = 0.694\text{ m/s}$$

which gives

$$\Delta v_1 = -24.3\text{ m/s}$$

and

$$\Delta v_2 = +25.7\text{ m/s} \quad \text{(Answer)}$$

(c) The magnitude of Δv_1 is less with the passenger in the car. Because the probability of a driver being killed depends on Δv_1, we can reason that the probability is less for driver 1.

The data on head-on car collisions do not include values of Δv, but they do include the car masses and whether or not a collision was fatal. Fitting a function to the collected data, researchers have found that the fatality risk r_1 of driver 1 is given by

$$r_1 = c\left(\frac{m_2}{m_1}\right)^{1.79} \quad (9\text{-}63)$$

where c is a constant. Justify why the ratio m_2/m_1 appears in this equation, and then use the equation to compare the fatality risks for driver 1 with and without the passenger.

Compute: We first rewrite Eq. 9-61 as

$$m_1(v_{1f} - v_{1i}) = -m_2(v_{2f} - v_{2i})$$

Substituting $\Delta v_1 = v_{1f} - v_{1i}$ and $\Delta v_2 = v_{2f} - v_{2i}$ and rearranging give us

$$\frac{m_2}{m_1} = -\frac{\Delta v_1}{\Delta v_2} \quad (9\text{-}64)$$

A driver's fatality risk depends on the change Δv for that driver. In Eq. 9-64, we see that the ratio of Δv values in a collision is the inverse of the ratio of the masses, and this is the reason researchers can link fatality risk to the ratio of masses in Eq. 9-63.

From part (a) and Eq. 9-63, *without* the passenger, driver 1 has a fatality risk of

$$r_1 = c\left(\frac{1400\text{ kg}}{1400\text{ kg}}\right)^{1.79} = c \quad (9\text{-}65)$$

From part (b) and Eq. 9-63, *with* the passenger, driver 1 has a fatality risk of

$$r_1' = c\left(\frac{1400\text{ kg}}{1400\text{ kg} + 80\text{ kg}}\right)^{1.79} = 0.9053c$$

Substituting for c from Eq. 9-65, we find

$$r_1' = 0.9053 r_1 \approx 0.91 r_1 \quad \text{(Answer)}$$

Conclude: In words, the fatality risk for driver 1 is about 9% less when a passenger is in the car.

9-10 | Elastic Collisions in One Dimension

As we discussed in Section 9-8, everyday collisions are inelastic but we can approximate some of them as being elastic; that is, we can approximate that the total kinetic energy of the colliding bodies is conserved and is not transferred to other forms of energy:

$$\begin{pmatrix}\text{total kinetic energy}\\ \text{before the collision}\end{pmatrix} = \begin{pmatrix}\text{total kinetic energy}\\ \text{after the collision}\end{pmatrix}$$

This does not mean that the kinetic energy of each colliding body cannot change. Rather, it means this:

In an elastic collision, the kinetic energy of each colliding body may change, but the total kinetic energy of the system does not change.

For example, the collision of a cue ball with an object ball in a game of pool can be approximated as being an elastic collision. If the collision is head-on (the cue ball heads directly toward the object ball), the kinetic energy of the cue ball can be transferred almost entirely to the object ball. (Still, the fact that the collision makes a sound means that at least a little of the kinetic energy is transferred to the energy of the sound.)

Stationary Target

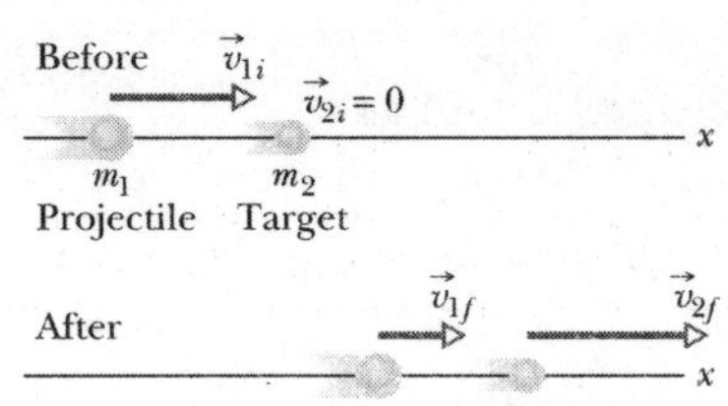

FIG. 9-34 Body 1 moves along an x-axis before having an elastic collision with body 2, which is initially at rest. Both bodies move along that axis after the collision.

Figure 9-34 shows two bodies before and after they have a one-dimensional collision, like a head-on collision between pool balls. A projectile body of mass m_1 and initial velocity v_{1i} moves toward a target body of mass m_2 that is, initially at rest ($v_{2i} = 0$). Let's assume that this two-body system is closed and isolated. Then the net linear momentum of the system is conserved, and from Eq. 9-54 we can write that conservation as

$$m_1 v_{1i} = m_1 v_{1f} + m_2 v_{2f} \qquad \text{(linear momentum)} \tag{9-66}$$

If the collision is also elastic, then the total kinetic energy is conserved and we can write that conservation as

$$\tfrac{1}{2}m_1 v_{1i}^2 = \tfrac{1}{2}m_1 v_{1f}^2 + \tfrac{1}{2}m_2 v_{2f}^2 \qquad \text{(kinetic energy)} \tag{9-67}$$

In each of these equations, the subscript i identifies the initial velocities and the subscript f the final velocities of the bodies. If we know the masses of the bodies and if we also know v_{1i}, the initial velocity of body 1, the only unknown quantities are v_{1f} and v_{2f}, the final velocities of the two bodies. With two equations at our disposal, we should be able to find these two unknowns.

To do so, we rewrite Eq. 9-66 as

$$m_1(v_{1i} - v_{1f}) = m_2 v_{2f} \tag{9-68}$$

and Eq. 9-67 as*

$$m_1(v_{1i} - v_{1f})(v_{1i} + v_{1f}) = m_2 v_{2f}^2 \tag{9-69}$$

After dividing Eq. 9-69 by Eq. 9-68 and doing some more algebra, we obtain

$$v_{1f} = \frac{m_1 - m_2}{m_1 + m_2} v_{1i} \tag{9-70}$$

and

$$v_{2f} = \frac{2m_1}{m_1 + m_2} v_{1i} \tag{9-71}$$

We note from Eq. 9-71 that v_{2f} is always positive (the initially stationary target body with mass m_2 always moves forward). From Eq. 9-70 we see that v_{1f} may be of either sign (the projectile body with mass m_1 moves forward if $m_1 > m_2$ but rebounds if $m_1 < m_2$).

Let us look at a few special situations.

* In this step, we use the identity $a^2 - b^2 = (a - b)(a + b)$. It reduces the amount of algebra needed to solve the simaltaneous equations (Eqs. 9-68 and 9-69).

1. ***Equal masses*** If $m_1 = m_2$, Eqs. 9-70 and 9-71 reduce to

$$v_{1f} = 0 \quad \text{and} \quad v_{2f} = v_{1i}$$

which we might call a pool player's result. It predicts that after a head-on collision of bodies with equal masses, body 1 (initially moving) stops dead in its tracks and body 2 (initially at rest) takes off with the initial speed of body 1. In head-on collisions, bodies of equal mass simply exchange velocities. This is true even if body 2 is not initially at rest.

2. ***A massive target*** In Fig. 9-23, a massive target means that $m_2 \gg m_1$. For example, we might fire a golf ball at a stationary cannonball. Equations 9-70 and 9-71 then reduce to

$$v_{1f} \approx -v_{1i} \quad \text{and} \quad v_{2f} \approx \left(\frac{2m_1}{m_2}\right) v_{1i} \tag{9-72}$$

This tells us that body 1 (the golf ball) simply bounces back along its incoming path, its speed essentially unchanged. Initially stationary body 2 (the cannonball) moves forward at a low speed, because the quantity in parentheses in Eq. 9-72 is much less than unity. All this is what we should expect.

3. ***A massive projectile*** This is the opposite case; that is, $m_1 \gg m_2$. This time, we fire a cannonball at a stationary golf ball. Equations 9-70 and 9-71 reduce to

$$v_{1f} \approx v_{1i} \quad \text{and} \quad v_{2f} \approx 2v_{1i} \tag{9-73}$$

Equation 9-73 tells us that body 1 (the cannonball) simply keeps on going, scarcely slowed by the collision. Body 2 (the golf ball) charges ahead at twice the speed of the cannonball.

You may wonder: Why twice the speed? As a starting point in thinking about the matter, recall the collision described by Eq. 9-72, in which the velocity of the incident light body (the golf ball) changed from $+v$ to $-v$, a velocity *change* of $2v$. The same *change* in velocity (but now from zero to $2v$) occurs in this example also.

Moving Target

Now that we have examined the elastic collision of a projectile and a stationary target, let us examine the situation in which both bodies are moving before they undergo an elastic collision.

For the situation of Fig. 9-35, the conservation of linear momentum is written as

$$m_1v_{1i} + m_2v_{2i} = m_1v_{1f} + m_2v_{2f} \tag{9-74}$$

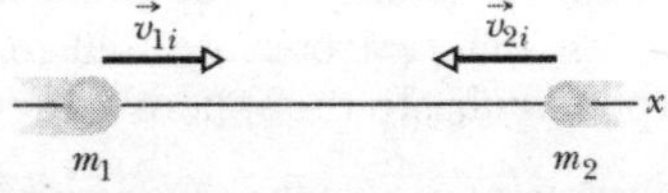

FIG. 9-35 Two bodies headed for a one-dimensional elastic collision.

and the conservation of kinetic energy is written as

$$\tfrac{1}{2}m_1v_{1i}^2 + \tfrac{1}{2}m_2v_{2i}^2 = \tfrac{1}{2}m_1v_{1f}^2 + \tfrac{1}{2}m_2v_{2f}^2 \tag{9-75}$$

To solve these simultaneous equations for v_{1f} and v_{2f}, we first rewrite Eq. 9-74 as

$$m_1(v_{1i} - v_{1f}) = -m_2(v_{2i} - v_{2f}) \tag{9-76}$$

and Eq. 9-75 as

$$m_1(v_{1i} - v_{1f})(v_{1i} + v_{1f}) = -m_2(v_{2i} - v_{2f})(v_{2i} + v_{2f}) \tag{9-77}$$

After dividing Eq. 9-77 by Eq. 9-76 and doing some more algebra, we obtain

$$v_{1f} = \frac{m_1 - m_2}{m_1 + m_2}v_{1i} + \frac{2m_2}{m_1 + m_2}v_{2i} \tag{9-78}$$

and

$$v_{2f} = \frac{2m_1}{m_1 + m_2}v_{1i} + \frac{m_2 - m_1}{m_1 + m_2}v_{2i} \tag{9-79}$$

Note that the assignment of subscripts 1 and 2 to the bodies is arbitrary. If we exchange those subscripts in Fig. 9-35 and in Eqs. 9-78 and 9-79, we end up with the same set of equations. Note also that if we set $v_{2i} = 0$, body 2 becomes a stationary target as in Fig. 9-34, and Eqs. 9-78 and 9-79 reduce to Eqs. 9-70 and 9-71, respectively.

CHECKPOINT 11 What is the final linear momentum of the target in Fig. 9-23 if the initial linear momentum of the projectile is 6 kg·m/s and the final linear momentum of the projectile is (a) 2 kg·m/s and (b) −2 kg·m/s? (c) What is the final kinetic energy of the target if the initial and final kinetic energies of the projectile are, respectively, 5 J and 2 J?

Sample Problem 9-28

Two metal spheres, suspended by vertical cords, initially just touch, as shown in Fig. 9-36. Sphere 1, with mass $m_1 = 30$ g, is pulled to the left to height $h_1 = 8.0$ cm, and then released from rest. After swinging down, it undergoes an elastic collision with sphere 2, whose mass $m_2 = 75$ g. What is the velocity v_{1f} of sphere 1 just after the collision?

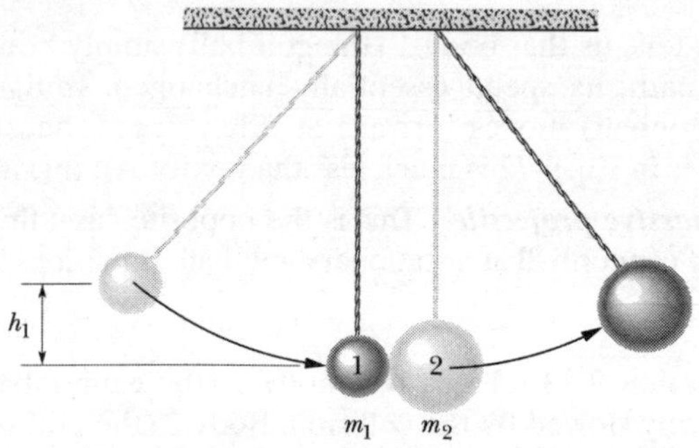

FIG. 9-36 Two metal spheres suspended by cords just touch when they are at rest. Sphere 1, with mass m_1, is pulled to the left to height h_1 and then released.

Conceptualize: We can imagine that as sphere 1 descends, it will gain kinetic energy and then collide with sphere 2.

Classify: We can split this complicated motion into two steps that we can analyze separately: (1) the descent of sphere 1 (in which mechanical energy is conserved) and (2) the two-sphere collision (in which momentum is conserved).

Compute 1: As sphere 1 swings down, the mechanical energy of the sphere–Earth system is conserved. (The mechanical energy is not changed by the force of the cord on sphere 1 because that force is always directed perpendicular to the sphere's direction of travel.)

Calculate: Let us take the lowest level as our reference level of zero gravitational potential energy. Then the kinetic energy of sphere 1 at the lowest level must equal the gravitational potential energy of the system when sphere 1 is at height h_1. Thus,

$$\tfrac{1}{2}m_1v_{1i}^2 = m_1gh_1$$

which we solve for the speed v_{1i} of sphere 1 just before the collision:

$$v_{1i} = \sqrt{2gh_1} = \sqrt{(2)(9.8\ \text{m/s}^2)(0.080\ \text{m})} = 1.252\ \text{m/s}$$

Compute 2: Here we can make two assumptions in addition to the assumption that the collision is elastic. First, we can assume that the collision is one-dimensional because the motions of the spheres are approximately horizontal from just before the collision to just after it. Second, because the collision is so brief, we can assume that the two-sphere system is closed and isolated. This means that the total linear momentum of the system is conserved.

Thus, we can use Eq. 9-70 to find the velocity of sphere 1 just after the collision:

$$v_{1f} = \frac{m_1 - m_2}{m_1 + m_2}v_{1i} = \frac{0.030\ \text{kg} - 0.075\ \text{kg}}{0.030\ \text{kg} + 0.075\ \text{kg}}(1.252\ \text{m/s}) = -0.537\ \text{m/s} \approx -0.54\ \text{m/s} \qquad \text{(Answer)}$$

Conclude: The minus sign tells us that sphere 1 moves to the left just after the collision.

9-11 | Collisions in Two Dimensions

When two bodies collide, the impulse between them determines the directions in which they then travel. In particular, when the collision is not head-on, the bodies do not end up traveling along their initial axis. For such two-dimensional collisions in a closed, isolated system, the total linear momentum must still be conserved:

$$\vec{P}_{1i} + \vec{P}_{2i} = \vec{P}_{1f} + \vec{P}_{2f} \tag{9-80}$$

If the collision is also elastic (a special case), then the total kinetic energy is also conserved:

$$K_{1i} + K_{2i} = K_{1f} + K_{2f} \tag{9-81}$$

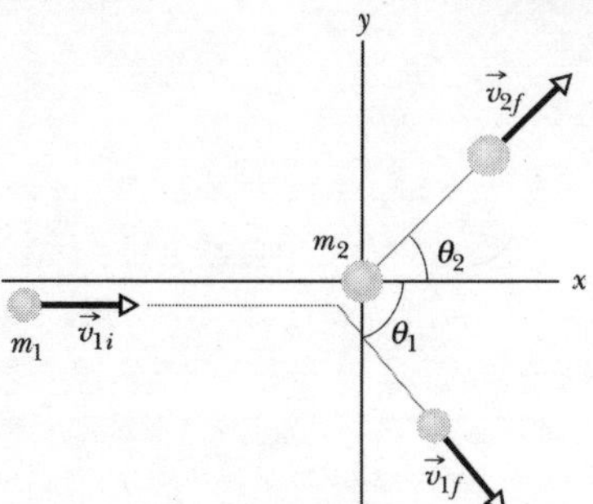

FIG. 9-37 An elastic collision between two bodies in which the collision is not head-on. The body with mass m_2 (the target) is initially at rest.

Equation 9-80 is often more useful for analyzing a two-dimensional collision if we write it in terms of components on an xy coordinate system. For example, Fig. 9-37 shows a *glancing collision* (it is not head-on) between a projectile body and a target body initially at rest. The impulses between the bodies have sent the bodies off at angles θ_1 and θ_2 to the x axis, along which the projectile initially traveled. In this situation we would rewrite Eq. 9-80 for components along the x axis as

$$m_1 v_{1i} = m_1 v_{1f} \cos\theta_1 + m_2 v_{2f} \cos\theta_2 \tag{9-82}$$

and along the y axis as

$$0 = -m_1 v_{1f} \sin\theta_1 + m_2 v_{2f} \sin\theta_2 \tag{9-83}$$

We can also write Eq. 9-81 (for the special case of an elastic collision) in terms of speeds:

$$\tfrac{1}{2} m_1 v_{1i}^2 = \tfrac{1}{2} m_1 v_{1f}^2 + \tfrac{1}{2} m_2 v_{2f}^2 \quad \text{(kinetic energy)} \tag{9-84}$$

Equations 9-82 to 9-83 contain seven variables: two masses, m_1 and m_2; three speeds, v_{1i}, v_{1f}, and v_{2f}, and two angles, θ_1 and θ_2. If we know any four of these quantities, we can solve the three equations for the remaining three quantities

Oblique Collision

When oblique collision occurs between two smooth bodies, the bodies have velocities of unknown directions and unknown magnitudes after collision. Provided the initial velocities are known, four unknowns present in the problem can be calculated. As shown in Fig. 9-38(a), these unknowns way be represented either as $(v_A)_2$, $(v_B)_2$, θ_2, and ϕ_2, or as the x and y components of the final velocities.

If the y-axis is taken as the plane of contact and the x-axis along the line of collision, the impulsive forces of deformation and restitution act only in the x direction, Fig. 9-38(b). Resolving the velocity or momentum vectors into components along the x- and y-axes (Fig. 9-38(b)), it is possible to write four independent scalar equations in order to determine $(v_{Ax})_2$, $(v_{Ay})_2$, $(v_{Bx})_2$, and $(v_{By})_2$.

FIG. 9-38 Oblique collision (a) Bodies just before collision. (b) Bodies during and just after collision.

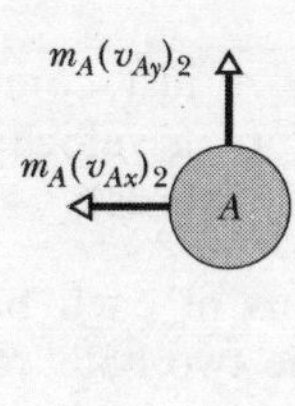

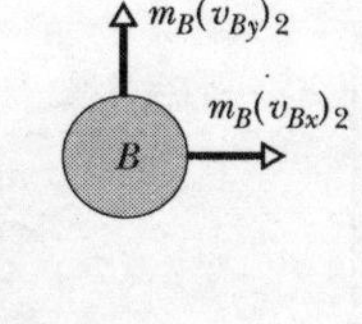

1. Momentum of the system is conserved along x direction as no external impulse is acting on the system.
2. The coefficient of restitution, $e = ((v_{Bx})_2 - (v_{Ax})_2/(v_{Ax})_1 - (v_{Bx})_1$, relates the relative-velocity components of the particles along the line of collision (x-axis).
3. Momentum of particle A is conserved along the y-axis, perpendicular to the line of collision, since no impulse acts on particle A in this direction.
4. Momentum of particle B is conserved along the y-axis, perpendicular to the line of collision, since no impulse acts on particle B in this direction.

CHECKPOINT 12 Suppose that the projectile has an initial momentum of 6 kg·m/s, a final x component of momentum of 4 kg·m/s, and a final y component of momentum of −3 kg·m/s. For the target, what then are (a) the final x component of momentum and (b) the final y component of momentum?

Sample Problem 9-29

A small steel ball A is suspended by an inextensible thread of length l = 1.5 m from O. Another identical ball is thrown vertically downward such that its surface remains just in contact with thread during downward motion and collides elastically with the suspended ball. If the suspended ball just completes vertical circle after collision, calculate the velocity of the falling ball just before collision.

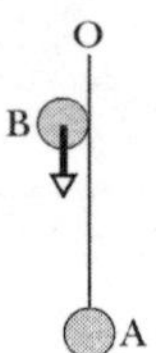

Conceptualize: The ball A is constrained by the thread to move on a path such that it has constant distance from O, such path is a circle around O. After collision with ball B, the ball A will start moving in a vertical circle about point O as the collision will impart horizontal velocity to the ball A.

Classify: Since ball A just completes vertical circle after collision, therefore its velocity just after collision is $\sqrt{5gl}$ (horizontally rightwards).

Compute: Let radius of each ball be r and let line joining centers of the two balls make angle sin θ with the vertical at the instant of collision

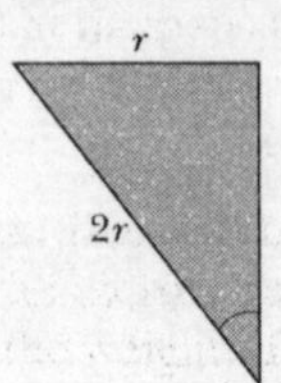

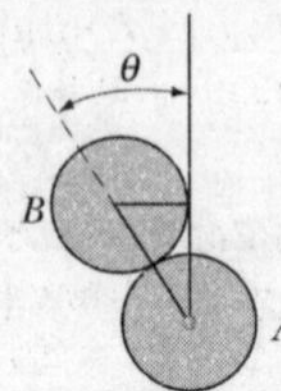

$$\sin\theta = \frac{r}{2r} \quad \text{or} \quad \theta = 30^\circ$$

Let velocity of ball B (just before collision) be v_0. This velocity can be resolved into two components, (i) v_0 cos 30°, along the line joining the centers of the two balls and (ii) v_0 sin 30° normal to this line. Impulse J due to collision acts along v_0 cos 30° and changes this component of velocity of ball B. Along v_0 sin 30°, there is no impulse thus this component of velocity of ball B remains unchanged.

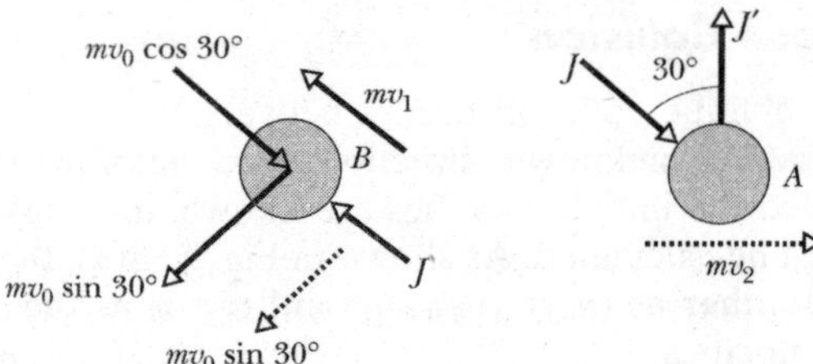

Ball A experiences two simultaneous impulses one vertically upward impulse exerted by thread on ball A is called J' and other is the impulsive interaction J between the balls.

The component of velocity of ball B along line of collision v_1 is given by

$$J - mv_0 \cos 30^\circ = mv_1$$

or

$$v_1 = \frac{J}{m} - v_0 \cos 30^\circ$$

Velocity v_2 of ball A is horizontal and is given by J sin 30° = mv_2

or

$$v_2 = \frac{J}{2m}$$

Since the balls collide elastically, therefore, coefficient of restitution is $e = 1$.

As $e = \dfrac{v_2 - v_1}{u_1 - u_2}$, where u_1, u_2, and v_1, v_2 are the components of initial and final velocities along the line of collision.

Component of velocity v of ball A along the line of collision between two balls is $v_2 \sin 30°$ (away from ball B).

Hence, $$e = \frac{v_2 \sin 30° - (-v_1)}{v_0 \cos 30° - 0} = 1$$

Putting the value of v_2 and v_1 in above equation, we get

$$J = 1.6\, m v_0 \cos 30°$$

$\therefore \quad v_1 = 0.6\, v_0 \cos 30°$ and $v_2 = 0.8\, v_0 \cos 30°$

Since ball A just completes vertical circle, therefore

$$v_2 = \sqrt{5gl}$$

$$0.8 v_0 \cos 30° = \sqrt{5gl} \text{ or } v_0 = 12.5 \text{ ms}^{-1}$$

Conclude: We are able to use the Newton's law of collision even when system is experiencing external impulse.

9-12 | C-Frame

We can attach a frame of reference, to the center of mass of a system, this is called the center of mass or C-frame of reference. Relative to this frame, the center of mass is at rest ($v_{com} = 0$) and according to equation $P = Mv_{com}$, the total momentum of a system of particles in the C-frame of reference is always zero.

$$\vec{P} = \sum_i \vec{P}_i = 0 \text{ in the } C\text{-frame of reference.}$$

The C-frame is important because many situations can be more simply analyzed in the C-frame. It is clear that the C-frame moves with a velocity v_{com} relative to the ground frame. When no external forces act on a system, the C-frame becomes a inertial frame.

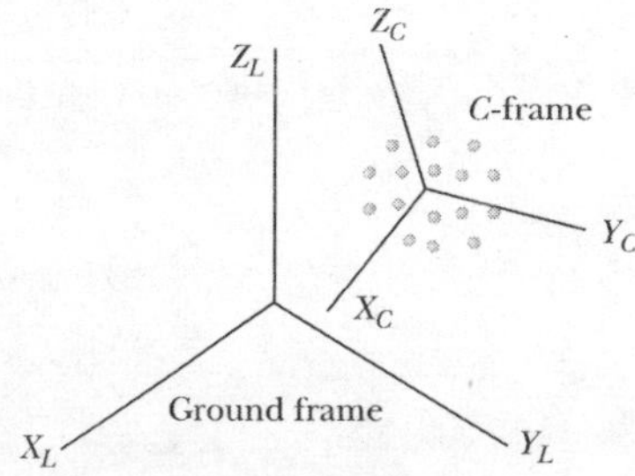

FIG. 9-39 Velocity of two particles relative to center of mass.

Sample Problem 9-30 Build your skill

The velocities of two particles of masses m_1 and m_2 relative to an observer in an initial frame are v_1 and v_2. Determine the velocity of the center of mass relative to the observer and the velocity of each particle relative to the center of mass.

Solution: From definition

$$v_{com} = \frac{dr_{com}}{dt} = \frac{1}{M}\sum_i m_i \frac{dr_i}{dt} = \frac{\sum_i m_i v_i}{M}$$

the velocity of the center of mass relative to the observer is

$$v_{com} = \frac{m_1 v_1 + m_2 v_2}{m_1 + m_2}$$

The velocities of each particle relative to the center of mass, using the relative motion equations for velocities is

$$v'_1 = v_1 - v_{cm} = v_1 - \frac{m_1 v_1 + m_2 v_2}{m_1 + m_2}$$

$$= \frac{m_2(v_1 - v_2)}{m_1 + m_2} = \frac{m_2 v_{12}}{m_1 + m_2}$$

$$v'_2 = v_2 - v_{cm} = \frac{m_1(v_2 + v_1)}{m_1 + m_2} = -\frac{m_1 v_{12}}{m_1 + m_2}$$

where $v_{12} = v_1 - v_2$ is the relative velocity of the two particles.

Thus, in the C-frame, the two particles appear to be moving in opposite directions with velocities inversely proportional to their masses.

Also relative to the center of mass, the two particles move with equal but opposite momentum since

$$p'_1 - m_1 v'_1 = \frac{m_1 m_2 v_{12}}{(m_1 + m_2)} = -p'_1$$

The expressions for two particle problems are much simpler when they are related to the C-frame of reference.

Let us find relation between kinetic energy of a system from ground frame and C-frame; we have a system consisting of many particles, let's say speed of the

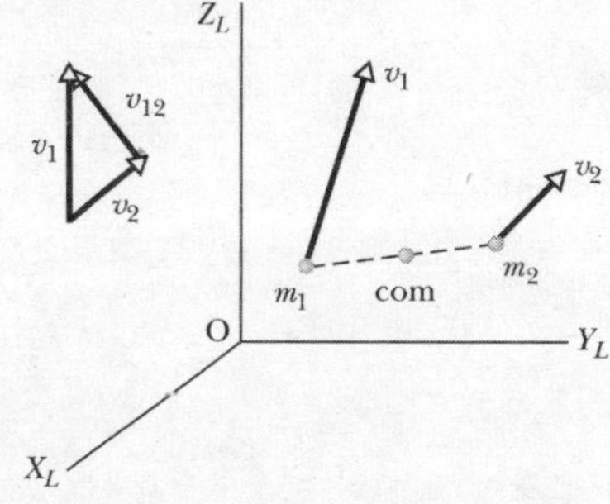

FIG. 9-40 Velocity of two particles relative to center of mass.

ith particle is v_i. Then kinetic energy of system, K, in ground frame will be summation of individual kinetic energy.

$$K_s = \sum\left(\frac{1}{2}m_i v_i^2\right)$$

$$\text{now } v_1 = v_{i/c} + v_c$$

where v_i is velocity of the ith particle in ground frame, $v_{i/c}$ is velocity of the ith particle in reference to frame attached to the center of mass and v_c is velocity of center of mass in ground frame.

$$k_s = \frac{1}{2}\sum m_i(\vec{v}_{ic} + \vec{v}_c)^2$$

$$k_s = \frac{1}{2}\sum m_i \vec{v}_{i/c}^{\,2} + \frac{1}{2}\sum m_i \vec{v}_c^{\,2} + \frac{1}{2}\times 2\left(\sum m_i \cdot \vec{v}_{i/c} \cdot \vec{v}_c\right)$$

$$k_s = \sum \frac{1}{2} m_i \vec{v}_{i/c}^{\,2} + \frac{1}{2}\left(\sum m_i\right)\vec{v}_c^{\,2} + \left(\sum m_i \cdot \vec{v}_{i/c}\right)\vec{v}_c$$

we can take v_c out of summation in second and third term as it is constant. Now third term becomes zero, as $\sum m_i \vec{v}_{i/c} = M\vec{v}_{c/c}$

$v_{c/c}$ is velocity of center of mass in frame of COM, which is zero. Also, it represents momentum of system in C-frame which is zero

$$\left(\frac{1}{2}\sum m_i \vec{v}_{i/c}^{\,2}\right) = k_{a/c}$$

Thus, we get $k_s = k_{s/c} + \frac{1}{2}mv_c^2$

where $k_{s/c}$ means kinetic energy of system in C-frame. This important conclusion will be again useful in rotational dynamics; we can do little manipulation to write the equation as

$$k_s = k_{s/c} + \frac{P_c^2}{2M}$$

A System of Two Particles

Suppose the masses of the particles are equal to m_1 and m_2 and their velocities in the K reference frame be $\vec{v}_1$ and $\vec{v}_2$, respectively. Let us find the expressions defining their momenta and the total kinetic energy in the C-frame.

The momentum of the first particle in the C-system is

$$p_{1/c} = m_1 \vec{v}_{1/c} = m_1(\vec{v}_1 - \vec{v}_c)$$

where v_c is the velocity of the center of mass of the system in the ground frame. Substituting in this formula expression $\vec{v}_1 = \dfrac{m_1\vec{v}_1 + m_2\vec{v}_2}{m_1 + m_2}$

$$\vec{p}_{1/c} = \mu(\vec{v}_1 - \vec{v}_2)$$

where μ is the so-called reduced mass of the system.

$$\mu = \frac{m_1 m_2}{m_1 + m_2}$$

Similarly, the momentum of the second particle in the C-frame is

$$\vec{p}_{2/c} = \mu(\vec{v}_2 - \vec{v}_1)$$

Thus, the momenta of the two particles in the *C*-frame are equal in magnitude and opposite in direction; the modulus of the momentum of each particle is

$$\vec{p}_{1/c} = \mu v_{rel}$$

where $v_{rel} = |\vec{v}_1 - \vec{v}_2|$ is the velocity of one particle relative to another.

Finally, let us consider kinetic energy. The total kinetic energy of the two particles in the *C*-frame is

$$k_{s/c} = k_1 + k_2 = \frac{\vec{p}^2}{2m_1} + \frac{\vec{p}^2}{2m_2}$$

According to the equation $\mu = \dfrac{m_1 m_2}{m_1 + m_2}$ or $\dfrac{1}{m_2} + \dfrac{1}{m_2} = \dfrac{1}{\mu}$

then $k_{s/c} = \dfrac{\vec{p}^2}{2\mu_1} = \dfrac{\mu v_{rel}^2}{2}$

as $k_S = k_{s/c} + k_c$, we get k_s

$$k_s = \frac{\mu v_{rel}^2}{2} + \frac{m v_c^2}{2}$$

Sample Problem 9-31 Build your skill

Two particles of mass m_1, m_2 moving with initial velocity u_1 and u_2 collide head-on. Find minimum kinetic energy that system has during collision. Thus prove that maximum kinetic energy is lost in perfectly inelastic collision

Solution:

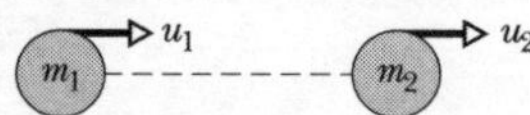

In *C*-frame, initial kinetic energy of system if

$\dfrac{1}{2}\mu(u_2 - u_1)^2$ where $\mu = \dfrac{m_1 m_2}{m_1 + m_2}$

During collision, at the instant of maximum deformation, we get minimum kinetic energy in *C*-frame as they attain same velocity thus relative velocity becomes zero.

When an isolated system has minimum kinetic energy in *C*-frame, it will also have minimum kinetic energy in ground frame as velocity of center of mass is constant.

Thus, minimum kinetic energy during collision is

$$\frac{1}{2}(m_1 + m_2)v_c^2$$

where $v_c = \dfrac{(m_1 u_1 + m_2 u_2)}{m_1 + m_2}$

In perfectly inelastic collision, since both the particles move together, the relative velocity becomes zero. Thus, final kinetic energy is $\frac{1}{2} m_s v_c^2$ as velocity of center of mass is constant. This is the minimum possible kinetic energy that a system will have because in all other cases there will be one more term adding in the kinetic energy of system because of particles having relative velocity.

Sample Problem 9-32

Two blocks of mass m_1 and m_2 connected by an ideal spring of spring constant k are kept on a smooth horizontal surface. Find maximum extension of the spring when the block m_2 is given an initial velocity of u toward right as shown in figure.

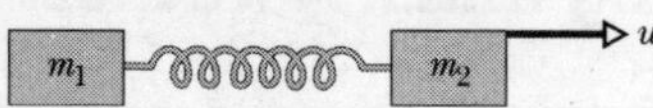

Conceptualize: When a block of mass m_2 is given an initial velocity of u toward right, the spring extends and pulls the block toward left and the same extended spring will pull the block m_1 toward right. Initially the force acting on m_2 will reduce its speed and the force acting on m_1 will increase its speed. Thus, we can see that initally the extension will be increasing.

Classify: If we consider the two blocks and spring as one system, then total mechanical energy must be conserved as there is no dissipative force present. Also, momentum will be conserved as there is no external force present.

Compute: Now there will be an instant when the blocks will have same velocity, that is, the velocity of m_1 has increased sufficiently to become equal to the velocity of m which have been decreasing continuously. At this moment, the spring will have maximum extension as till this point distance between the blocks was continuously increasing as the m had larger velocity. Now it will start decresing as m will be moving faster than m and it will reduce the distance between the two blocks. Thus, when $v_1 = v_2$, extension is maximum. This can also be understood alternatively by looking at m from reference frame attached to m. To an observer sitting on m_1 the block m, will be closest or farthest when it is relatively at rest.

Since no external force is present, velocity of center of mass is given as going to be constant and

$$v_c = \frac{(m_2 u)}{m_1 + m_2}$$

From the reference frame of center of mass the initial

$$\text{KE} = \frac{1}{2}\mu(v_{2i} - v_{1i})^2 = \frac{1}{2}\frac{m_1 m_2}{m_1 + m_2}(u)^2$$

From the reference frame of center of mass the final

$$\text{KE} = \frac{1}{2}\mu(v_{2f} - v_{1f})^2 = 0$$

Thus, equating initial and final energy in C-frame, we get

$$\frac{1}{2}\frac{m_1 m_2}{m_1 + m_2}(u)^2 = 0 + \frac{1}{2}Kx^2$$

Thus, maximum extension is

$$x = u\sqrt{\frac{m_1 m_2}{k(m_1 + m_2)}}$$

Conclude: This problem can be thought exactly as the opposite of the previous example as here the maximum extension is occuring when the relative velocity is zero.

9-13 | Impulse Momentum Equation for Continuous Processes

Momentum and the flow of mass

Analyzing a system having mass flowing in or out may become really confusing if we try to apply Newton's laws directly. A rocket is the best example of such a system.

These problems can be handled easily using $F = dP/dt$, provided that we keep clearly in mind exactly what is included in the system. When this equation is applied in the integral form,

$$\int_{t_a}^{t_b} \mathrm{F}dt = \mathrm{P}(t_b) - \mathrm{P}(t_a)$$

it is essential to deal with the same set of particles throughout the time interval t_a to t_b; that is, of all the particles which are originally in the system are taken in account. Thus, the mass of the system does not change during the time of interest.

9-14 | Systems with Varying Mass: A Rocket

In the systems we have dealt with so far, we have assumed that the total mass of the system remains constant. Sometimes, as in a rocket, it does not. Most of the mass of a rocket on its launching pad is fuel, all of which will eventually be burned and ejected from the nozzle of the rocket engine.

We handle the variation of the mass of the rocket as the rocket accelerates by applying Newton's second law, not to the rocket alone but to the rocket and its ejected combustion products taken together. The mass of *this* system does *not* change as the rocket accelerates.

Finding the Acceleration

Assume that we are at rest relative to an inertial reference frame, watching a rocket accelerate through deep space with no gravitational or atmospheric drag forces acting on it. For this one-dimensional motion, let M be the mass of the rocket and v its velocity at an arbitrary time t (see Fig. 9-41a).

Figure 9-41b shows how things stand a time interval dt later. The rocket now has velocity $v + dv$ and mass $M + dM$, where the change in mass dM is a *negative quantity.* The exhaust products released by the rocket during interval dt have mass $-dM$ and velocity U relative to our inertial reference frame.

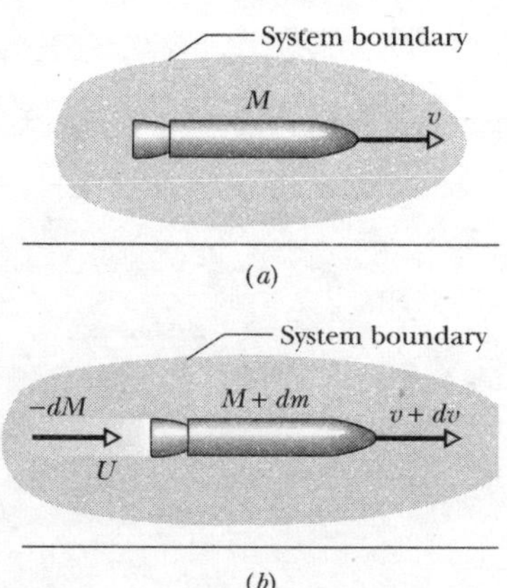

FIG. 9-41 (a) An accelerating rocket of mass M at time t, as seen from an inertial reference frame. (b) The same but at time $t + dt$. The exhaust products released during interval dt are shown.

To analyze the motion of the rocket in detail, we must equate the external force acting on the system, F, with the rate of change of momentum, dP/dt. Consider the rocket at time t. Between t and $t + \Delta t$, a mass of fuel Δm is burned and expelled as gas with velocity u relative to the rocket. The exhaust velocity u is determined by the nature of the propellants, the throttling of the engine, etc., but it is independent of the velocity of the rocket.

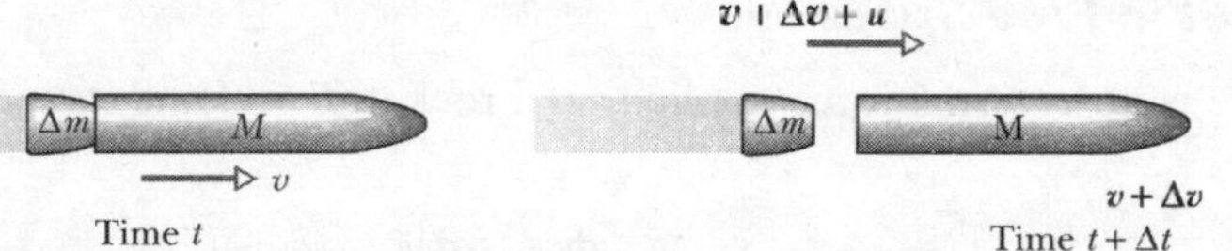

The sketches below show the system at time t and $t + \Delta t$. The system consists of Δm plus the remaining mass of the rocket M. Hence the total mass is $M + \Delta m$. The velocity of the rocket at time t is $v(t)$, and at $t + \Delta t$, it is $v + \Delta v$. The initial momentum is

$$P(t) = (M + \Delta m)\, v$$

and the final momentum is

$$P(t + \Delta t) = M(v + \Delta v) + \Delta m\,(v + \Delta v + u)$$

The change in momentum is

$$\begin{aligned}\Delta P &= P(t + \Delta t) - P(t) \\ &= M\,\Delta v + (\Delta m)u\end{aligned}$$

Therefore, for a short time interval

$$\frac{dP}{dt} = \lim_{\Delta t \to 0} \frac{\Delta P}{\Delta t}$$

$$= M\frac{\Delta v}{dt} + u\frac{dm}{dt}$$

Note that we have defined u to be positive in the direction of v. In most rocket applications u is negative, opposite to v. It is inconvenient to have both m and M in the equations. dm/dt is the rate of increase exhaust mass. Since this mass comes out of the rocket,

$$\frac{dm}{dt} = -\frac{dM}{dt}$$

Using above equation, and equating the external force to dP/dt, we obtain the fundamental rocket equation.

$$F = M\frac{dv}{dt} - u\frac{dM}{dt}$$

It may be useful to point out two minor subtleties in our development. The first is that the velocities have been expressed with respect to an inertial frame and not with frame of reference attached to the rocket. The second is that we took the final velocity of the element of exhaust gas to be $v + \Delta v + u$ rather than $v + u$. This is correct (consult example on spring gun recoil if you need help in analyzing explaination), but actually it makes no difference here, since either of the expression will yield the same final result when the limit is taken. Here are the two examples on rocket problem.

Rocket in Free Space

If there is no external force applied on a rocket, $F = 0$ and its motion is given by

$$M\frac{dv}{dt} = u\frac{dM}{dt}$$

or
$$\frac{dv}{dt} = \frac{u}{M}\frac{dM}{dt}$$

Generally, the exhaust velocity u is constant, and hence it is easy to integrate the equation of motion.

$$\int_{t_0}^{t_f} \frac{dv}{dt}\,dt = u\int_{t_0}^{t_f} \frac{1}{M}\frac{dM}{dt}\,dt$$

$$= u\int_{M_0}^{M_f} \frac{dM}{M}$$

$$v_f - v_0 = u \ln\frac{M_f}{M_0}$$

or

$$= -u \ln\frac{M_o}{M_f}$$

If $v_0 = 0$, then

$$v_f = -u \ln\frac{M_o}{M_f}$$

The final velocity is independent of how the mass is released - the fuel can be expelled rapidly or slowly without affecting v_f. The only important quantities are the exhaust velocity and the ratio of initial to final mass.

Sample Problem 9-33

A rocket whose initial mass M_i is 850 kg consumes fuel at the rate $R = 2.3$ kg/s. The speed v_{rel} of the exhaust gases relative to the rocket engine is 2800 m/s. What thrust does the rocket engine provide?

Conceptualize/Classify: Thrust T is equal to the product of the fuel consumption rate R and the relative speed v_{rel} at which exhaust gases are expelled, as given by Eq. 9-87.

Compute: Here we find

$$T = Rv_{rel} = (2.3 \text{ kg/s})(2800 \text{ m/s})$$
$$= 6440 \text{ N} \approx 6400 \text{ N}. \qquad \text{(Answer)}$$

(b) What is the initial acceleration of the rocket?

Conceptualize/Classify:: We can relate the thrust T of a rocket to the magnitude a of the resulting acceleration with $T = Ma$, where M is the rocket's mass. However, M decreases and a increases as fuel is consumed. Because we want the initial value of a here, we must use the intial value M_i of the mass.

Compute: We find

$$a = \frac{T}{M_i} = \frac{6440 \text{ N}}{850 \text{ kg}} = 7.6 \text{ m/s}^2 \qquad \text{(Answer)}$$

Conclude: To be launched from Earth's surface, a rocket must have an initial acceleration greater than $g = 9.8$ m/s^2. Put another way, the thrust T of the rocket engine must exceed the initial gravitational force on the rocket, which here has the magnitude $M_i g$, which gives us (850 kg)(9.8 m/s^2), or 8330 N. Because the acceleration or thrust requirement is not met (here $T = 6400$ N), our rocket could not be launched from Earth's surface by itself; it would require another, more powerful, rocket.

Sample Problem 9-34

Frieght car and hopper:

Sand falls from a stationary hopper onto a freight car which is moving with uniform velocity V_r. The sand falls at the rate μ. How much force is needed to keep the freight car moving at the speed V_0?

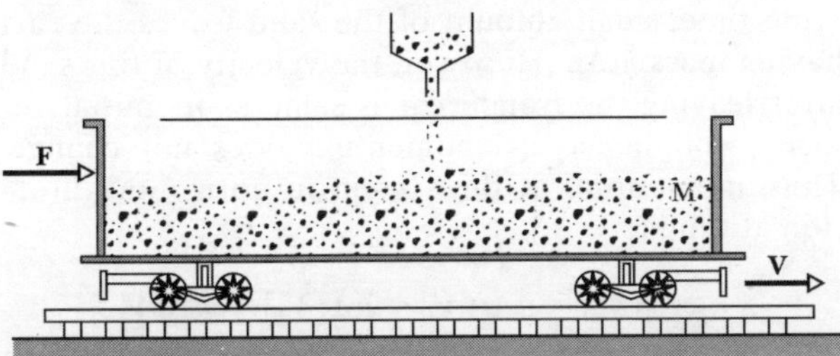

Conceptualize: Although the velocity of the cart is constant but it may not remain so when the sand falls in a. The falling sand will apply force of friction on the cart; to counter this force we have to apply equal and opposite force on the cart.

Classify: The required force on the cart cannot be calculated using F=ma as the force on the cart due to sand is unknown. This problem will be solved by taking falling sand and cart as one system.

Compute: At time t, the total mass of the frieght car including the mass of sand present inside it is M.

$$M = M_0 + \mu t$$

Let us consider the freight car, the sand inside it and small amount of sand which is going to fall in time Δt onto the car as one system. This small amount of the sand is in mid air, falling freely and does not have any horizontal component of velocity. Thus, momentum of the system in horizontal direction at time t is:

$$P_i \, (M_0 + \mu t) \, V_0 + \mu\Delta t(0)$$

Once the small amount of the sand joins the remainings and in the car, it will have same velocity as the car due to impulsive friction.

Thus, momentum of the system in horizontal direction at time $(t + \Delta t)$ is: $P_f = (M + \mu\Delta t) \, V_0$

$$\text{Using } F = dp/dt = \frac{p_f - p_i}{\Delta t}$$

$$\text{or} \quad F\Delta t = P_f - P_i$$
$$F\Delta t = \mu\Delta t \, V_0$$

The required force is $F = \mu V_0$

In case of: What would happen if the upper surface of the freight car was slippery ?

Answer: The required force is $F = 0$ because sand particles will not move and fall down as there is no friction, hence no force. In this case, the initial speed of the sand is 0.

Sample Problem 9-35

Leaky Frieght car:
Now consider a related case. The same freight car is leaking sand at the rate μ; what force is needed to keep the freight car moving uniformly with speed v?

Conceptualize/Classify: The required force on the cart cannot be calculated using $F = ma$ as the force on the cart due to sand is unkown. This problem will be solved by taking falling sand and cart as system.

Compute: At time t, the total mass of the frieght car including the mass of sand present inside it is M.

$$M = M_0 - \mu t$$

Let us consider the freight car and the sand inside it as our system. Thus, momentum of the system in horizontal direction at time t is: $P_i = (M_0 - \mu t)\, V_0$. Now consider small amount of the sand leaving the cart in time Δt, having mass $\mu\Delta t$. However, the velocity of the sand after leaving the freight car is same as that of its initial velocity, and its momentum does not change.

Thus, momentum of the system in horizontal direction at time $(t + \Delta t)$ is:

$$P_f = \{M_0 - \mu\,(t + \Delta t)\}\, V_0 + \mu\Delta t\, V_0 = (M_0 - \mu t)\, V_0$$

$$\text{Using } F = dP/dt = \frac{\Delta P}{\Delta t}$$

or

$$= \frac{P_f - P_i}{\Delta t}$$

$$F\Delta t = P_f - P_i$$

$$F\Delta t = 0$$

Since $dP/dt = 0$, no force is required. (The sand does change its momentum when it hits the ground, and there is a resulting force on the ground, but that does not affect the motion of the freight car.}

The required force is zero.

Conclude: The falling sand need not apply any force on the cart while leaving it, so the required force on the cart is zero. Although the mass is varying but no force is required.

Sample Problem 9-36

Leaky Frieght car and Hopper

Sand falls from a stationary hopper onto a freight car which is moving with uniform velocity V_0. The sand falls at the rate μ into the car and the same freight car is leaking sand at the rate rate μ, thus keeping its mass constant. How much force is needed to keep the freight car moving at the speed V_0?

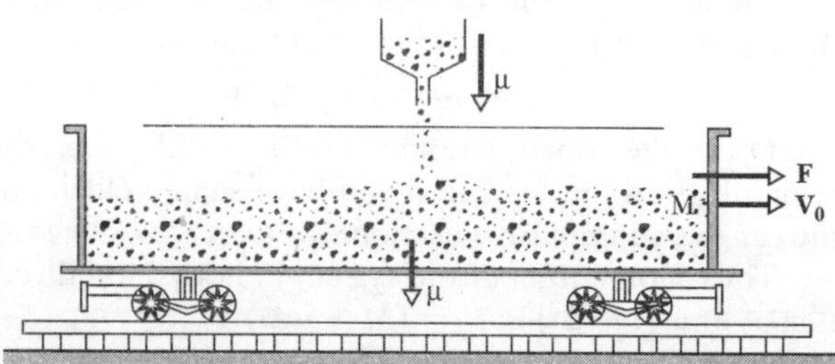

Solution: At time t, the total mass of the frieght car including the mass of sand present inside it is M_0. Let us consider the freight car, the sand inside it and small amount of sand which is going to fall from hopper onto the car in time Δt as one system. This small amount of the sand is in mid air, falling freely right now and does not have any horizontal component of velocity.

Thus, momentum of the system in horizontal direction at time t is : $P_i = M_0V_0 + \mu\Delta t\,(0)$. Once the small amount, $\mu\Delta t$ of the sand joins the remaining sand in the car, it will have same velocity as that of the car due to impulsive friction. Also, during the same time, small amount of the sand leaves the cart having mass, $\mu\Delta t$. However, the velocity of this sand after leaving the freight car is same as its initial velocity, and hence its momentum does not change. Thus, momentum of the system in horizontal direction at time $(t + \Delta t)$ is:

$$P_f = \{(M_0 - \mu\Delta t)\, V_0 + \mu\Delta t\, V_0\} + \mu\Delta t\, V_0$$

$$\text{Using } F = \frac{\Delta P}{\Delta t} = \frac{P_f - P_i}{\Delta t}$$

or

$$F\Delta t = P_f - P_i$$

$$F\Delta t = \mu\Delta t V_0$$

CHECKPOINT 13 A spaceship of mass m_0 moves in absence of external forces with a constant velocity v_0. To change the direction of motion of spaceship a jet engine is switched on. It starts ejecting a gas jet with velocity u which is constant relative to the spaceship and directed at right angles to the spaceship motion. The engine is shut down when mass of spaceship decreases to m. Through what angle α did the motion direction of motion of the spaceship deviate due to the jet engine operation?

Sample Problem 9-37

A uniform chain $A'B'$ of length $2l$ having mass λ per unit length is hanging from ceiling by two light, inextensible threads AA' and BB' of equal length as shown in Fig. 9-42. Distance AB is very small. Thread BB' is burnt at $t = 0$, calculate tension in thread AA' at time t.

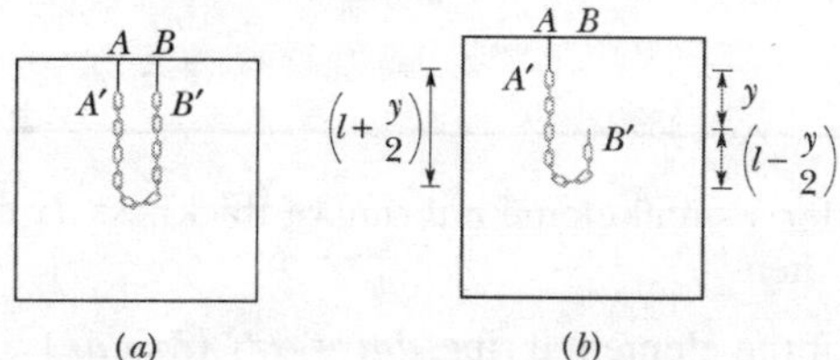

FIG. 9-42 (*a*) Uniform chain AB hanging from ceiling. (*b*) Direction of movement of chain after getting burnt at one end.

Conceptualize: When thread is burnt, end B' of chain starts moving under gravity while $A'$is at rest.

Hence, length of left side vertical part of chain increases.

Classify: Tension in thread AA' is due to two factors:

(i) due to weight of left side vertical part of chain and
(ii) due to rate of change of momentum of the chain when its links transfers from right to left part. So, we will try to find the mass on the left side as function of time and apply impulse momentum equation for continuous processes to the chain on left side.

Compute: Consider downward motion of end B' as shown in Fig. 9-42*b*.

Initial relative velocity, $u = 0$

Acceleration, $a' = g$

Using equation of motion, $y = ut + \frac{1}{2}at^2$

we calculate relative displacement of end B' in time t is

$$y = \frac{1}{2}gt^2 \; [u = 0 \text{ and } a' = g]$$

or

$$y = \frac{1}{2}gt^2$$

Mass of left vertical part of chain at time t,

Since λ = mass $\Rightarrow$ mass = λ x length

length

$$m = \left(l + \frac{y}{2}\right)\lambda$$

Putting values of y, we get

$$m = \lambda l + \frac{1}{4}\lambda gt^2$$

Let a rate of increase of mass in left part be $\mu = \frac{d}{dt}m$,

Using the value of m from above, we get

$$\mu = \frac{1}{2}\lambda gt$$

Change in velocity of a link when it transfers from right to left vertical part, $\Delta v = gt$

$\therefore$ Rate of change of momentum,

$$\frac{dp}{dt} = \mu\,\Delta v = \frac{1}{2}\lambda g^2 t^2$$

Weight of left vertical part $= mg = \left[\lambda l + \frac{1}{4}\lambda gt^2\right]g$

$\therefore$ Required tension $T = mg + \frac{dp}{dt}$

Putting values from above equation, we get

$$T = \lambda lg + \frac{3}{4}\lambda g^2 t^2$$

Conclude: The tension is more than the weight of the left side as every part joining the chain from right part applies impulse on it in vertically downward direction as chain applies force on the element to stop its vertically downward motion.

9-15 | Some Extra Derivations

Sample Problem 9-38

Determine the position of center of mass of thin hemispherical shell of mass M and radius R, assuming uniform mass distribution.

Solution: In this case, consider a small circular strip of thickness ds. The thickness of ring substends angle $d\theta$ at the center of the hemisphere as shown in Fig. 9-43. Radius of ring element is $R\cos\theta$. Mass of the element is

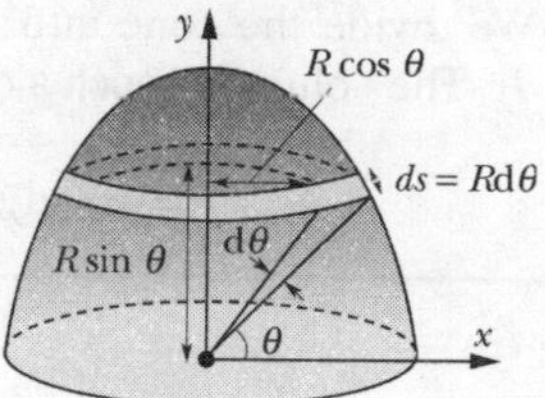

FIG. 9-43 Thin hemispherical shell.

dm = mass per unit area × area of circular strip

$$= \frac{M}{2\pi R^2} \times (2\pi R \cos\theta)\, R\, d\theta$$

Then $x_{com} = 0$ from symmetry of diagram

and $y_{com} = \frac{1}{M}\int_0^{\pi/2} dm R \sin\theta$

Putting value of dm, we get

$$= \frac{1}{M}\int_0^{\pi/2} \frac{M}{2\pi R^2}(2\pi R\cos\theta\, R\, d\theta)\, R\sin\theta$$

$$= R\int_0^{\pi/2} \sin\theta\cos\theta\, d\theta$$

$$= \frac{R}{2}$$

Sample Problem 9-39

Determine the center of mass of a uniform hollow cone of height H and semi vertex angle α as shown in Fig. 9-44.

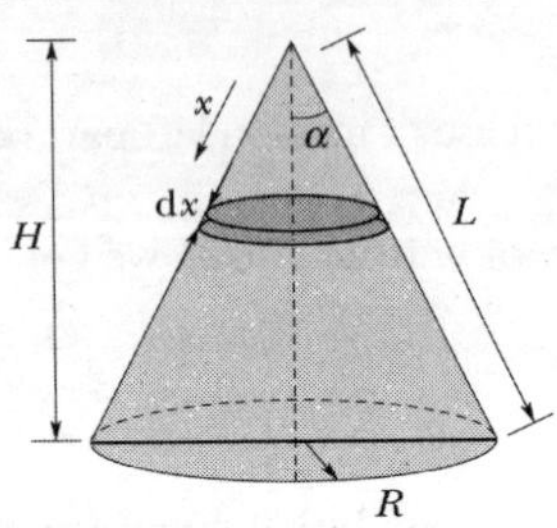

FIG. 9-44 Uniform hollow cone.

Assuming mass per unit area $= \sigma = \left(\frac{M}{\pi RL}\right)$

Consider a small elemental ring of thickness dx and radius r, then

Mass of the elemental ring, $dm = \alpha \times (2\pi r\, dx)$

$$y = x\cos\theta$$

$$dy = dx\cos\theta$$

$$r = y\tan\theta$$

$$y_{com} = \frac{\int_0^H y\left(\frac{M}{\pi RL}\right) \times 2\pi r dx}{M}$$

$$y_{com} = \frac{2H}{3} \text{ from the tip of the cone}$$

Sample Problem 9-40

Determine the center of mass of a uniform solid cone of height h and semiangle α as shown in Fig. 9-45.

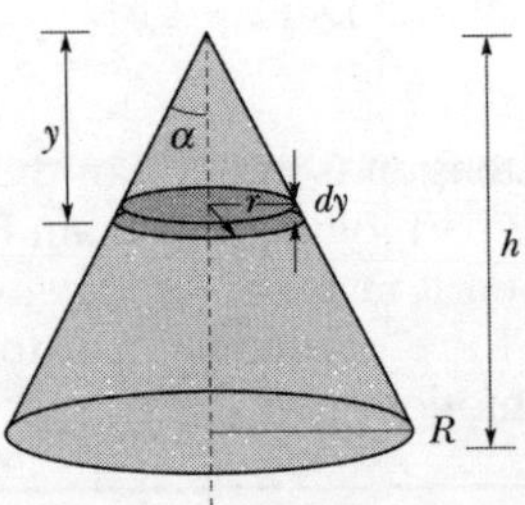

FIG. 9-45

Solution: We place the apex of the cone at the origin. It is clear that the center of mass will lie along the y-axis. We divide the cone into disc of radius x and thickness dy. The volume of such a disc is

$$dV = \pi x_2\, dy = \pi(y\tan\alpha)^2\, dy$$

The mass of the elemental disc is $dm = \rho\, dV$. First we will determine the total mass of the cone M here y goes from 0 to H, that is, total height of cone.

$$M = \int dm = \pi\rho\tan^2\alpha\int_0^h y^2 dy$$

$$= \pi\rho\tan^2\alpha\frac{h^3}{3} \tag{9-85}$$

The position of the center of mass is given by

$$y_{CM} = \frac{1}{M}\int_0^h y\, dm = \frac{1}{M}\pi\rho\tan^2\alpha\int_0^h y^3 dy$$

$$= \frac{1}{M}\pi\rho\tan^2\alpha\frac{h^4}{4} \tag{9-86}$$

From equations (9-85) and (9-86), we have

$$y_{CM} = \frac{3h}{4}$$

This explains element of solid cone as disc and compares it with next problems element as ring.

Sample Problem 9-41

A hemispherical object of uniform density has radius R. Prove by integration that its center of mass lies along its axis of symmetry at a distance $3R/8$ from the center of the plane surface.

Solution: As shown in Fig.(9-46), we choose a coordinate system with the origin at the center of the flat face and we let the yz plane be the plane of the face. We now imagine slicing the hemisphere into discs parallel to the yz plane. A disc of thickness dx, located at a distance x from the plane face, has a radius $\sqrt{R^2 - x^2}$. Therefore, the mass of the disk $dm = \pi\rho(R^2 - x^2)dx$, where ρ is the mass density of the hemisphere. The center of mass of the hemisphere has an x coordinate x_{cm} given by

$$x_{CM} = \frac{\int_0^R \frac{dm}{dx} dx}{\int_0^R \frac{dm}{dx} dx}$$

$$= \frac{\int_0^R \pi\rho x(R^2 - x^2)dx}{\int_0^R \pi\rho(R^2 - x^2)dx}$$

$$= \frac{\left(\frac{x^2R^2}{2} - \frac{x^4}{4}\right)\Big|_0^R}{\left(xR^2 - \frac{x^3}{3}\right)\Big|_0^R} = \frac{\frac{R^4}{4}}{\frac{2R^3}{3}} = \frac{3R}{8}$$

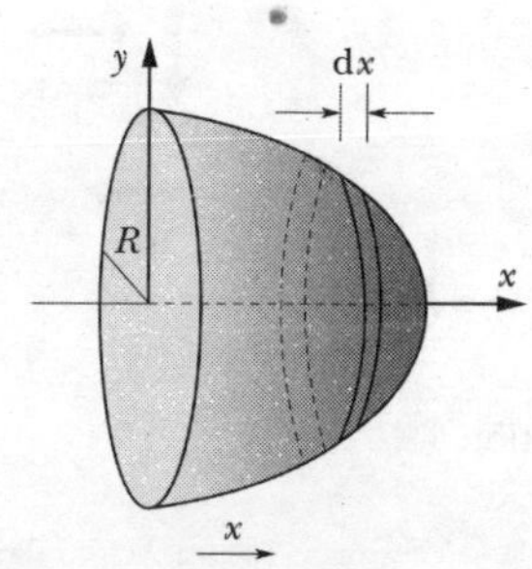

FIG. 9-46 Hemispherical object of uniform density.

$$y_{com} = z_{com} = 0$$

QUESTIONS

1 Figure 9-47 shows an overhead view of three particles on which external forces act. The magnitudes and directions of the forces on two of the particles are indicated. What are the magnitude and direction of the force acting on the third particle if the center of mass of the three-particle system is (a) stationary, (b) moving at a constant velocity rightward, and (c) accelerating rightward?

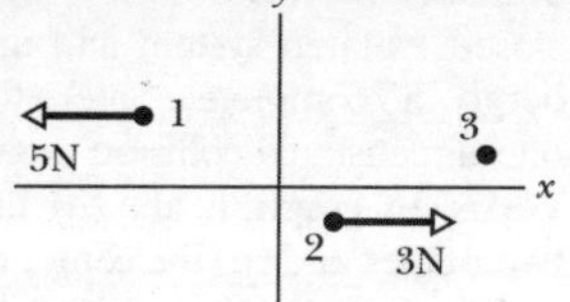

FIG. 9-47 Question 1.

2 Figure 9-48 shows an overhead view of four particles of equal mass sliding over a frictionless surface at constant velocity. The directions of the velocities are indicated; their magnitudes are equal. Consider pairing the particles. Which pairs form a system with a center of mass that (a) is stationary, (b) is stationary and at the origin, and (c) passes through the origin?

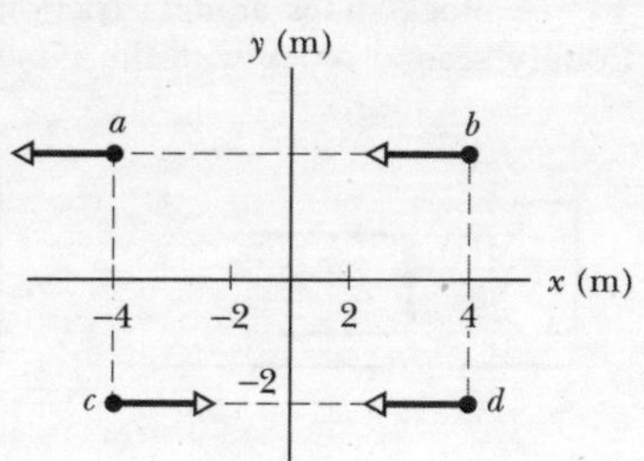

FIG. 9-48 Question 2.

3 The free-body diagrams in Fig. 9-49 give, from overhead views, the horizontal forces acting on three boxes of chocolates as the boxes move over a frictionless confectioner's counter. For each box, is its linear momentum conserved along the x axis and the y axis?

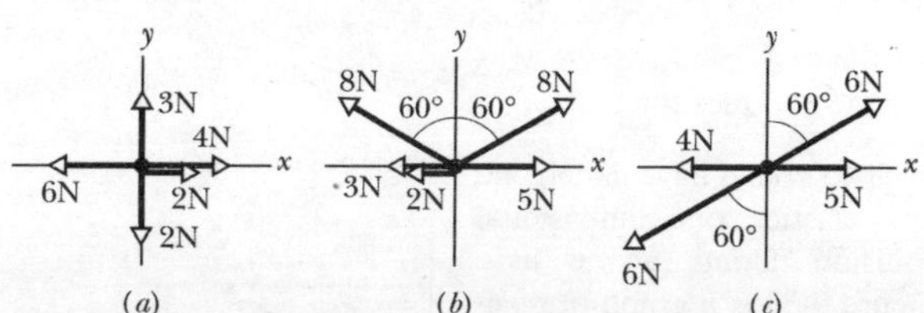

FIG. 9-49 Question 3.

4 Figure 9-50 shows four groups of three or four identical particles that move parallel to either the x axis or the y axis, at identical speeds. Rank the groups according to center-of-mass speed, greatest first.

5 Consider a box, like that in Sample Problem 9-6, which explodes into two pieces while moving with a constant positive velocity along an x axis. If one piece, with mass m_1, ends up with positive velocity $\vec{v}_1$, then the second piece, with mass m_2, could end up with (a) a positive velocity $\vec{v}_2$ (Fig. 9-51a), (b) a negative velocity $\vec{v}_2$ (Fig. 9-51b), or (c) zero velocity (Fig. 9-51c). Rank those three possible results for the second piece according to the corresponding magnitude of $\vec{v}_1$, greatest first.

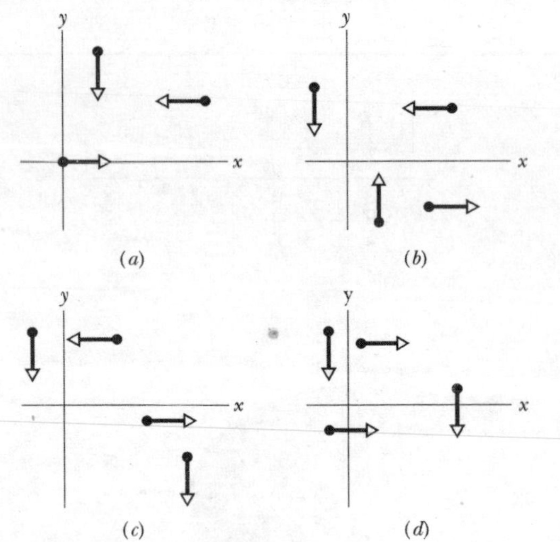

FIG. 9-50 Question 4.

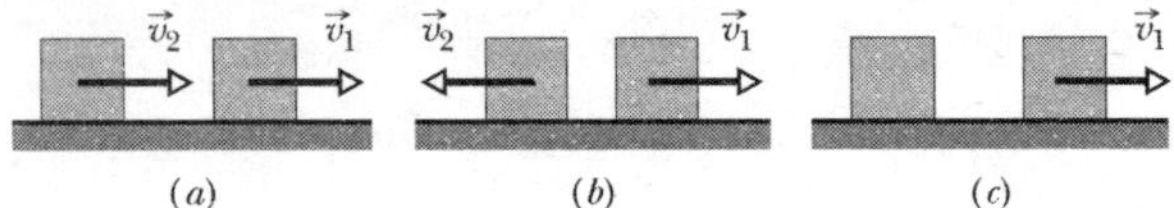

FIG. 9-51 Question 5.

6 Figure 9-52 shows graphs of force magnitude versus time for a body involved in a collision. Rank the graphs according to the magnitude of the impulse on the body, greatest first.

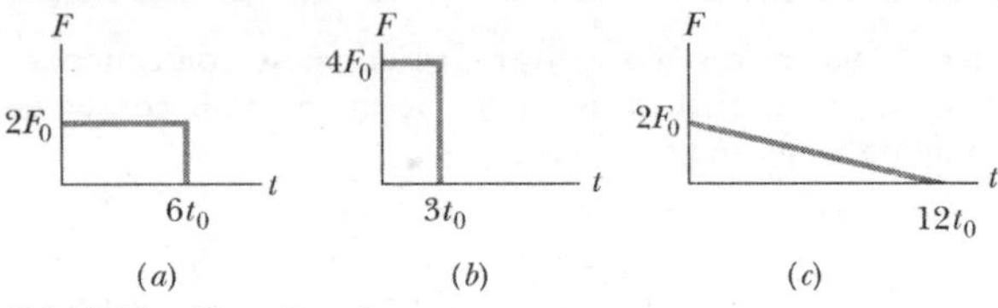

FIG. 9-52 Question 6.

7 Two bodies have undergone an elastic one-dimensional collision along an x axis. Figure 9-53 is a graph of position versus time for those bodies and for their center of mass. (a) Were both bodies initially moving, or was one initially stationary? Which line segment corresponds to the motion of the center of mass (b) before the collision and (c) after the collision? (d) Is the mass of the body that was moving faster before the collision greater than, less than, or equal to that of the other body?

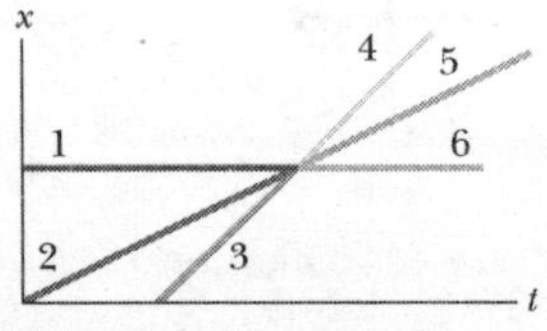

FIG. 9-53 Question 7.

8 Figure 9-44: A block on a horizontal floor is initially either stationary, sliding in the positive direction of an x axis, or sliding in the negative direction of that axis. Then the block explodes into two pieces that slide along the x axis. Assume the block and the two pieces form a closed, isolated system. Six choices for a graph of the momenta of the block and the pieces are given, all versus time t. Determine which choices represent physically impossible situations and explain why.

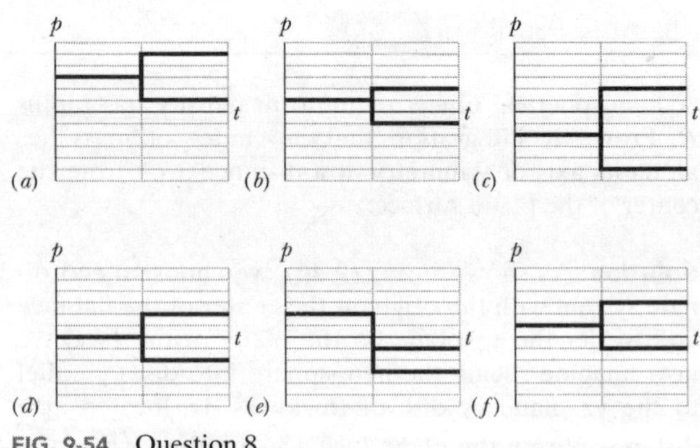

FIG. 9-54 Question 8.

9 Block 1 with mass m_1 slides along an x axis across a frictionless floor and then undergoes an elastic collision with a stationary block 2 with mass m_2. Figure 9-55 shows a plot of position x versus time t of block 1 until the collision occurs at position x_c and time t_c. In which of the lettered regions on the graph will the plot be continued (after the collision) if (a) $m_1 < m_2$ and (b) $m_1 > m_2$? (c) Along which of the numbered dashed lines will the plot be continued if $m_1 = m_2$?

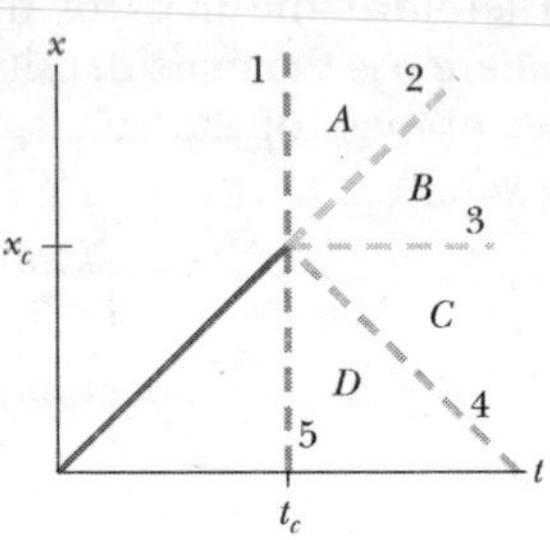

FIG. 9-55 Question 9.

10 Figure 9-56 shows four graphs of position versus time for two bodies and their center of mass. The two bodies form a closed, isolated system and undergo a completely inelastic, one-dimensional collision on an x axis. In graph 1, are (a) the two bodies and (b) the center of mass moving in the positive or negative direction of the x axis? (c) Which graphs correspond to a physically impossible situation? Explain.

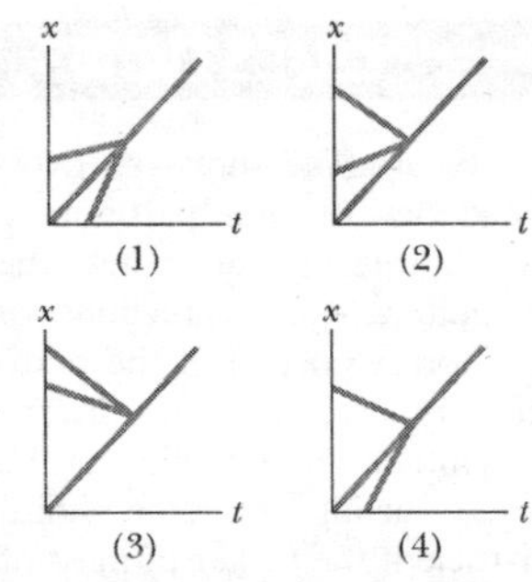

FIG. 9-56 Question 10.

11 A block slides along a frictionless floor and into a stationary second block with the same mass. Figure 9-57 shows

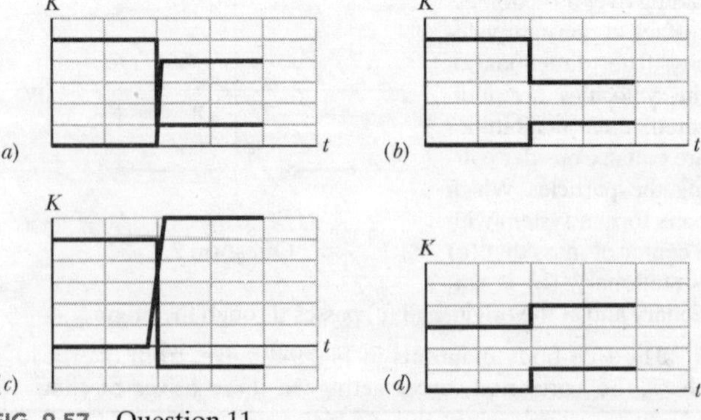

FIG. 9-57 Question 11.

four choices for a graph of the kinetic energies K of the blocks. (a) Determine which represent physically impossible situations. Of the others, which best represents (b) an elastic collision and (c) an inelastic collision?

12 Figure 9-58 shows a snapshot of block 1 as it slides along an x axis on a frictionless floor, before it undergoes an elastic collision with stationary block 2. The figure also shows three possible positions of the center of mass (com) of the two-block system at the time of the snapshot. (Point B is halfway between the centers of the two blocks.) Is block 1 stationary, moving forward, or moving backward after the collision if the com is located in the snapshot at (a) A, (b) B, and (c) C?

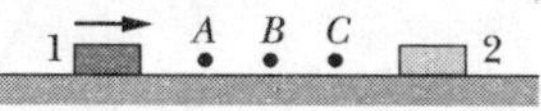

FIG. 9-58 Question 12.

PROBLEMS

The Center of Mass

1 What are (a) the x coordinate and (b) the y coordinate of the center of mass for the uniform plate shown in Fig. 9-59 if $L = 5.0$ cm?

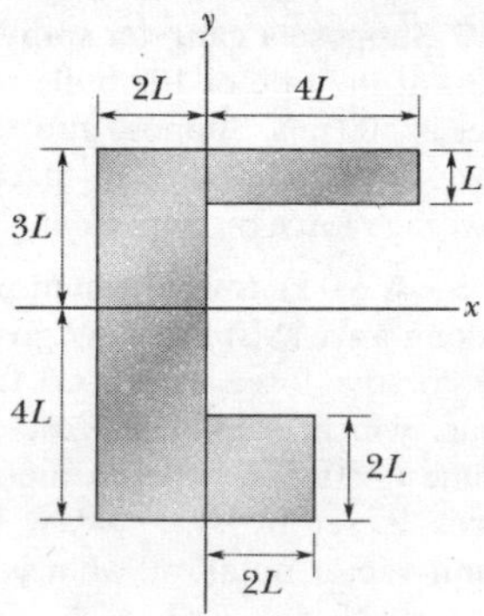

FIG. 9-59 Problem 1.

2 In Fig. 9-60, three uniform thin rods, each of length $L =$ 22 cm, form an inverted U. The vertical rods each have a mass of 14 g; the horizontal rod has a mass of 42 g. What are (a) the x coordinate and (b) the y coordinate of the system's center of mass?

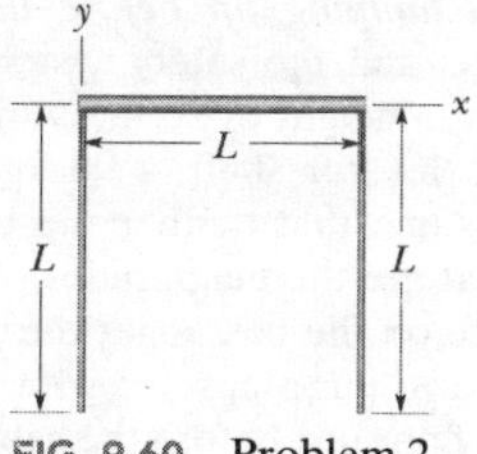

FIG. 9-60 Problem 2.

3 Figure 9-61 shows a cubical box that has been constructed from uniform metal plate of negligible thickness. The box is open at the top and has edge length $L = 40$ cm. Find (a) the x coordinate, (b) the y coordinate, and (c) the z coordinate of the center of mass of the box.

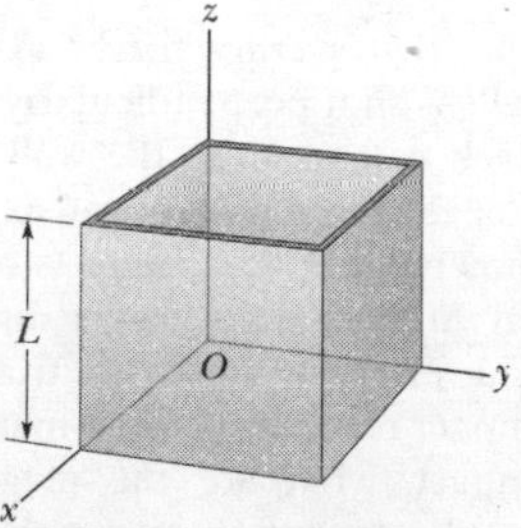

FIG. 9-61 Problem 3.

4 A uniform soda can of mass 0.140 kg is 12.0 cm tall and filled with 1.31 kg of soda (Fig. 9-62). Then small holes are drilled in the top and bottom (with negligible loss of metal) to drain the soda. What is the height h of the com of the can and contents (a) initially and (b) after the can loses all the soda? (c) What happens to h as the soda drains out? (d) If x is the height of the remaining soda at any given instant, find x when the com reaches its lowest point.

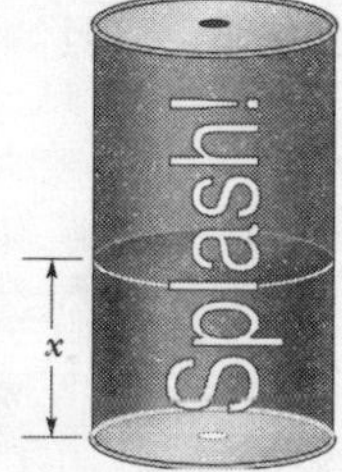

FIG. 9-62 Problem 4.

Newton's Second Law for a System of Particles

5 Two skaters, one with mass 65 kg and the other with mass 40 kg, stand on an ice rink holding a pole of length 10 m and negligible mass. Starting from the ends of the pole, the skaters pull themselves along the pole until they meet. How far does the 40 kg skater move?

6 A stone is dropped at $t = 0$. A second stone, with twice the mass of the first, is dropped from the same point at $t =$ 100 ms. (a) How far below the release point is the center of mass of the two stones at $t = 300$ ms? (Neither stone has yet reached the ground.) (b) How fast is the center of mass of the two-stone system moving at that time?

7 A 1000 kg automobile is at rest at a traffic signal. At the instant the light turns green, the automobile starts to move with a constant acceleration of 4.0 m/s^2. At the same instant a 2000 kg truck, traveling at a constant speed of 8.0 m/s, overtakes and passes the automobile. (a) How far is the com of the automobile–truck system from the traffic light at $t =$ 3.0 s? (b) What is the speed of the com then?

8 Figure 9-63 shows an arrangement with an air track, in which a cart is connected by a cord to a hanging block. The cart has mass $m_1 = 0.600$ kg, and its center is initially at xy coordinates $(-0.500\text{ m},\ 0\text{ m})$; the block has mass $m_2 =$ 0.400 kg, and its center is initially at xy coordinates $(0,\ -0.100\text{ m})$. The mass of the cord and pulley are negligible.

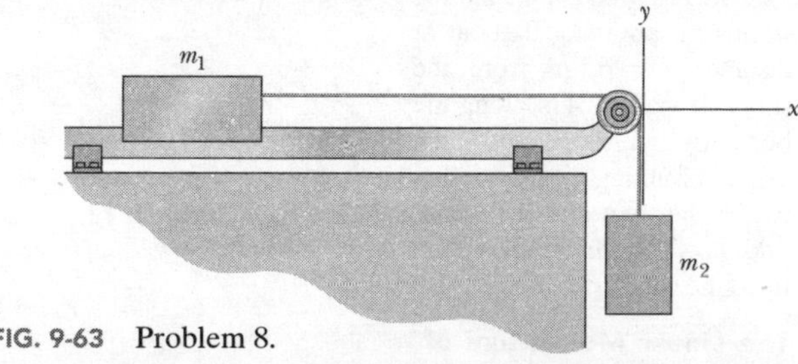

FIG. 9-63 Problem 8.

The cart is released from rest, and both cart and block move until the cart hits the pulley. The friction between the cart and the air track and between the pulley and its axle is negligible. (a) In unit-vector notation, what is the acceleration of the center of mass of the cart–block system? (b) What is the velocity of the com as a function of time t? (c) Sketch the path taken by the com. (d) If the path is curved, determine whether it bulges upward to the right or downward to the left, and if it is straight, find the angle between it and the x axis.

9 In Figure 9-64, two particles are launched from the origin of the coordinate system at time $t = 0$. Particle 1 of mass $m_1 = 5.00$ g is shot directly along the x axis on a frictionless floor,

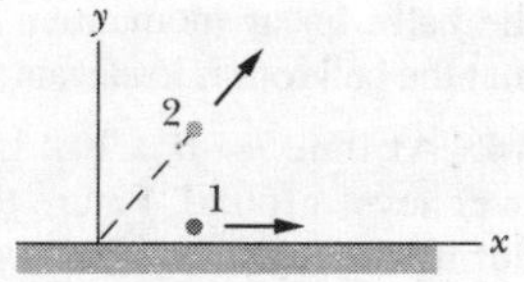

FIG. 9-64 Problem 9.

with constant speed 10.0 m/s. Particle 2 of mass $m_2 = 3.00$ g is shot with a velocity of magnitude 20.0 m/s, at an upward angle such that it always stays directly above particle 1. (a) What is the maximum height H_{max} reached by the com of the two-particle system? In unit-vector notation, what are the (b) velocity and (c) acceleration of the com when the com reaches H_{max}?

10 A shell is shot with an initial velocity $\vec{v}_0$ of 20 m/s, at an angle of $\theta_0 = 60°$ with the horizontal. At the top of the trajectory, the shell explodes into two fragments of equal mass (Fig. 9-65). One fragment, whose speed immediately after the explosion is zero, falls vertically. How far from the gun does the other fragment land, assuming that the terrain is level and that air drag is negligible?

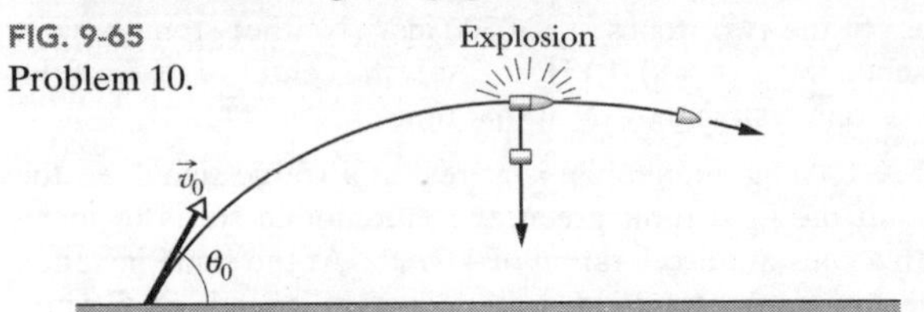

FIG. 9-65 Problem 10.

11 Ricardo, of mass 80 kg, and Carmelita, who is lighter, are enjoying Lake Merced at dusk in a 30 kg canoe. When the canoe is at rest in the placid water, they exchange seats, which are 3.0 m apart and symmetrically located with respect to the canoe's center. If the canoe moves 40 cm horizontally relative to a pier post, what is Carmelita's mass?

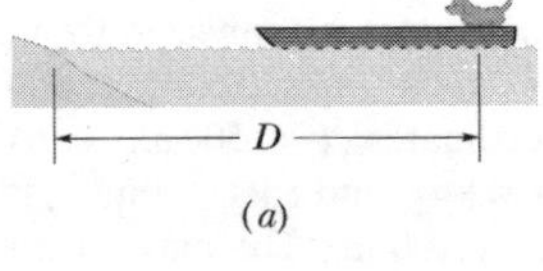

12 In Fig. 9-66*a*, a 4.5 kg dog stands on an 18 kg flatboat at distance $D = 6.1$ m from the shore. It walks 2.4 m along the boat toward shore and then stops. Assuming no friction between the boat and the water, find how far the dog is then from the shore. (*Hint:* See Fig. 9-66*b*.)

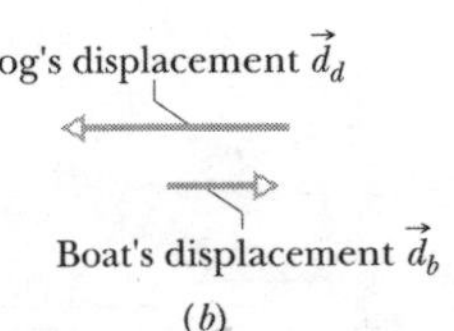

FIG. 9-66 Problem 12.

The Linear Momentum of a System of Particles

13 Figure 9-67 gives an overhead view of the path taken by a 0.165 kg cue ball as it bounces from a rail of a pool table. The ball's initial speed is 2.00 m/s, and the angle θ_1 is 30.0°. The bounce reverses the y component of the ball's velocity but does not alter the x component. What are (a) angle θ_2 and (b) the change in the ball's linear momentum in unit-vector notation? (The fact that the ball rolls is irrelevant to the problem.)

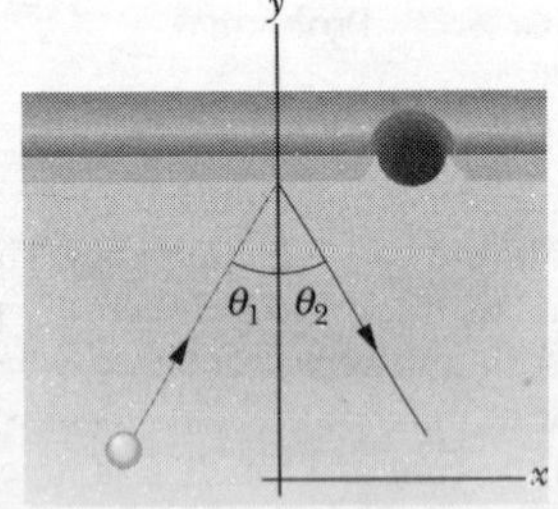

FIG. 9-67 Problem 13.

14 At time $t = 0$, a ball is struck at ground level and sent over level ground. Figure 9-68 gives momentum p versus t during the flight ($p_0 = 6.0$ kg · m/s and $p_1 = 4.0$ kg · m/s). At what initial angle is the ball launched?

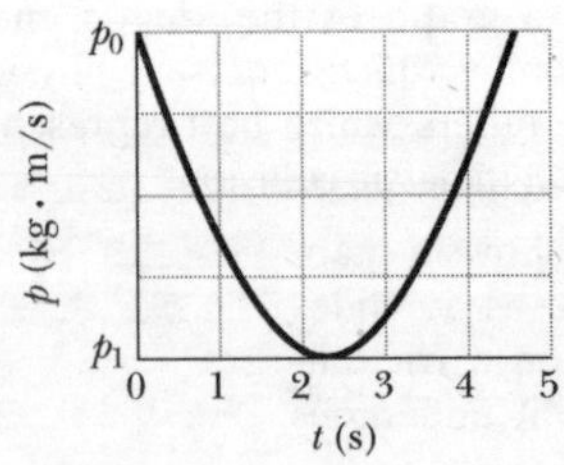

FIG. 9-68 Problem 14.

Collision and Impulse

15 Suppose a gangster sprays Superman's chest with 3 g bullets at the rate of 100 bullets/min, and the speed of each bullet is 500 m/s. Suppose too that the bullets rebound straight back with no change in speed. What is the magnitude of the average force on Superman's chest?

16 A 5.0 kg toy car can move along an x axis; Fig. 9-69 gives F_x of the force acting on the car, which begins at rest at time $t = 0$. The scale on the F_x axis is set by $F_{xs} = 5.0$ N. In unit-vector notation, what is $\vec{p}$ at (a) $t = 4.0$ s and (b) $t = 7.0$ s, and (c) what is v at $t = 9.0$ s?

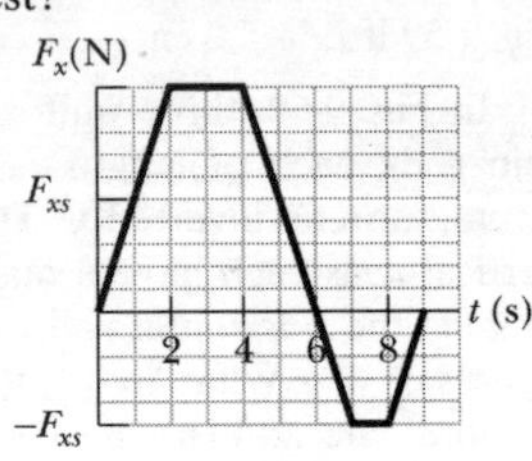

FIG. 9-69 Problem 16.

17 *Jumping up before the elevator hits.* After the cable snaps and the safety system fails, an elevator cab free-falls from a height of 36 m. During the collision at the bottom of the elevator shaft, a 90 kg passenger is stopped in 5.0 ms. (Assume that neither the passenger nor the cab rebounds.) What are the magnitudes of the (a) impulse and (b) average force on the passenger during the collision? If the passenger were to jump upward with a speed of 7.0 m/s relative to the cab floor just before the cab hits the bottom of the shaft, what are the magnitudes of the (c) impulse and (d) average force (assuming the same stopping time)?

18 *Two average forces.* A steady stream of 0.250 kg snowballs is shot perpendicularly into a wall at a speed of 4.00 m/s. Each ball sticks to the wall. Figure 9-70 gives the magnitude F of the force on the wall as a function of time t for two of the snowball impacts. Impacts occur with a repetition time interval $\Delta t_r = 50.0$ ms, last a duration time interval $\Delta t_d = 10$ ms, and produce isosceles triangles on the graph, with each impact reaching a force maximum $F_{max} = 200$ N. During each impact, what are the magnitudes of (a) the impulse and (b) the average force on the wall? (c) During a time interval

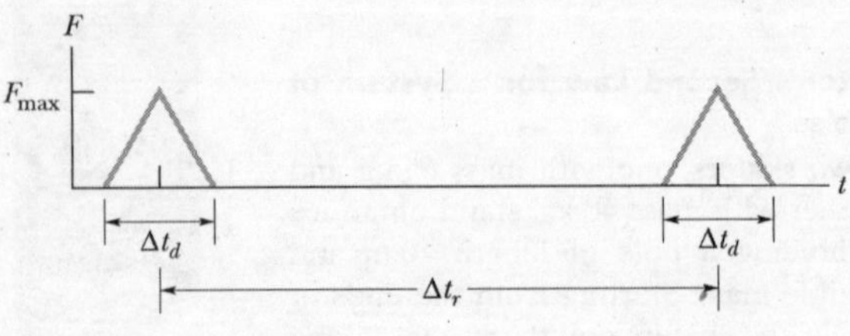

FIG. 9-70 Problem 18.

of many impacts, what is the magnitude of the average force on the wall?

19 A 0.25 kg puck is initially stationary on an ice surface with negligible friction. At time $t = 0$, a horizontal force begins to move the puck. The force is given by $\vec{F} = (12.0 - 3.00t^2)\hat{i}$, with $\vec{F}$ in newtons and t in seconds, and it acts until its magnitude is zero. (a) What is the magnitude of the impulse on the puck from the force between $t = 0.500$ s and $t = 1.25$ s? (b) What is the change in momentum of the puck between $t = 0$ and the instant at which $F = 0$?

Conservation of Linear Momentum

20 A 4.0 kg mess kit sliding on a frictionless surface explodes into two 2.0 kg parts: 3.0 m/s, due north, and 5.0 m/s, 30° north of east. What is the original speed of the mess kit?

21 Figure 9-71 shows a two-ended "rocket" that is, initially stationary on a frictionless floor, with its center at the origin of an x axis. The rocket consists of a central block C (of mass $M = 6.00$ kg) and blocks L and R (each of mass $m = 2.00$ kg) on the left and right sides. Small explosions can shoot either of the side blocks away from block C and along the x axis. Here is the sequence: (1) At time $t = 0$, block L is shot to the left with a speed of 3.00 m/s *relative* to the velocity that the explosion gives the rest of the rocket. (2) Next, at time $t = 0.80$ s, block R is shot to the right with a speed of 3.00 m/s *relative* to the velocity that block C then has. At $t = 2.80$ s, what are (a) the velocity of block C and (b) the position of its center?

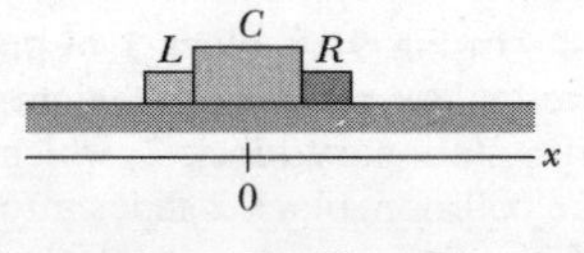

FIG. 9-71 Problem 21.

22 An object, with mass m and speed v relative to an observer, explodes into two pieces, one three times as massive as the other; the explosion takes place in deep space. The less massive piece stops relative to the observer. How much kinetic energy is added to the system during the explosion, as measured in the observer's reference frame?

23 A vessel at rest at the origin of an xy coordinate system explodes into three pieces. Just after the explosion, one piece, of mass m, moves with velocity $(-30\text{ m/s})\hat{i}$ and a second piece, also of mass m, moves with velocity $(-30\text{ m/s})\hat{j}$. The third piece has mass 3 m. Just after the explosion, what are the (a) magnitude and (b) direction of the velocity of the third piece?

24 In Fig. 9-72, a stationary block explodes into two pieces L and R that slide across a frictionless floor and then into regions with friction, where they stop. Piece L, with a mass of 2.0 kg, encounters a coefficient of kinetic friction $\mu_L = 0.40$ and slides to a stop in distance $d_L = 0.15$ m. Piece R encounters a coefficient of kinetic friction $\mu_R = 0.50$ and slides to a stop in distance $d_R = 0.25$ m. What was the mass of the block?

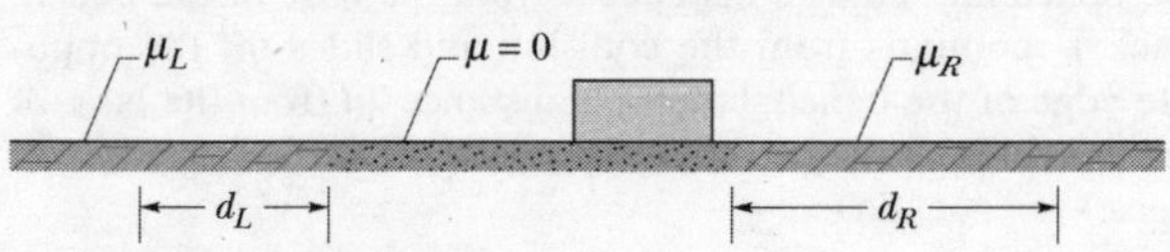

FIG. 9-72 Problem 24.

25 A 20.0 kg body is moving through space in the positive direction of an x axis with a speed of 200 m/s when, due to an internal explosion, it breaks into three parts. One part, with a mass of 10.0 kg, moves away from the point of explosion with a speed of 100 m/s in the positive y direction. A second part, with a mass of 4.00 kg, moves in the negative x direction with a speed of 500 m/s. (a) In unit-vector notation, what is the velocity of the third part? (b) How much energy is released in the explosion? Ignore effects due to the gravitational force.

26 Particle A and particle B are held together with a compressed spring between them. When they are released, the spring pushes them apart, and they then fly off in opposite directions, free of the spring. The mass of A is 2.00 times the mass of B, and the energy stored in the spring was 60 J. Assume that the spring has negligible mass and that all its stored energy is transferred to the particles. Once that transfer is complete, what are the kinetic energies of (a) particle A and (b) particle B?

Inelastic Collisions in One Dimension

27 In Fig. 9-73*a*, a 3.50 g bullet is fired horizontally at two blocks at rest on a frictionless table. The bullet passes through block 1 (mass 1.20 kg) and embeds itself in block 2 (mass 1.80 kg). The blocks end up with speeds $v_1 = 0.630$ m/s and $v_2 = 1.40$ m/s (Fig. 9-73*b*). Neglecting the material removed from block 1 by the bullet, find the speed of the bullet as it (a) leaves and (b) enters block 1.

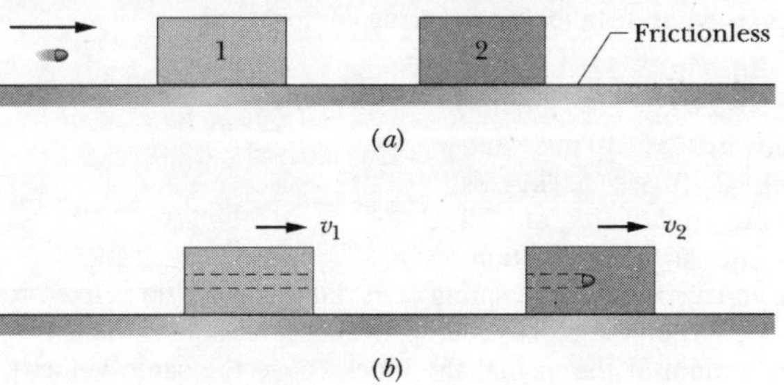

FIG. 9-73 Problem 27.

28 In Fig. 9-74, a 10 g bullet moving directly upward at 1000 m/s strikes and passes through the center of mass of a 5.0 kg block initially at rest. The bullet emerges from the block moving directly upward at 400 m/s. To what maximum height does the block then rise above its initial position?

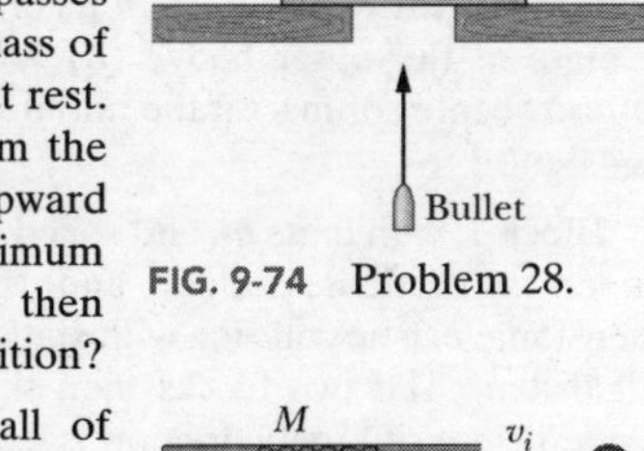

FIG. 9-74 Problem 28.

29 In Fig. 9-75, a ball of mass $m = 60$ g is shot with speed $v_i = 22$ m/s into the barrel of a spring gun of mass $M = 240$ g initially at rest on a frictionless surface. The ball sticks in the barrel at the point of maximum compression of the spring. Assume that the increase in thermal energy due to friction between the ball and the barrel is negligible. (a) What is the speed of the spring gun after the ball stops in the barrel? (b) What

FIG. 9-75 Problem 29.

fraction of the initial kinetic energy of the ball is stored in the spring?

30 A completely inelastic collision occurs between two balls of wet putty that move directly toward each other along a vertical axis. Just before the collision, one ball, of mass 3.0 kg, is moving upward at 20 m/s and the other ball, of mass 2.0 kg, is moving downward at 12 m/s. How high do the combined two balls of putty rise above the collision point? (Neglect air drag.)

31 A 5.0 kg block with a speed of 3.0 m/s collides with a 10 kg block that has a speed of 2.0 m/s in the same direction. After the collision, the 10 kg block travels in the original direction with a speed of 2.5 m/s. (a) What is the velocity of the 5.0 kg block immediately after the collision? (b) By how much does the total kinetic energy of the system of two blocks change because of the collision? (c) Suppose, instead, that the 10 kg block ends up with a speed of 4.0 m/s. What then is the change in the total kinetic energy? (d) Account for the result you obtained in (c).

32 In Fig. 9-76, block 2 (mass 1.0 kg) is at rest on a frictionless surface and touching the end of an unstretched spring of spring constant 200 N/m. The other end of the spring is fixed to a wall. Block 1 (mass 2.0 kg), traveling at speed $v_1 = 4.0$ m/s, collides with block 2, and the two blocks stick together. When the blocks momentarily stop, by what distance is the spring compressed?

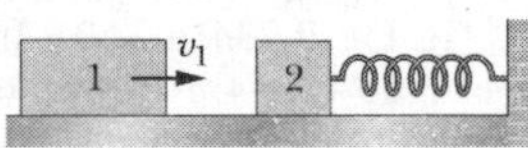

FIG. 9-76 Problem 32.

33 In Fig. 9-77, block 1 (mass 2.0 kg) is moving rightward at 10 m/s and block 2 (mass 5.0 kg) is moving rightward at 3.0 m/s. The surface is frictionless, and a spring with a spring constant of 1120 N/m is fixed to block 2. When the blocks collide, the compression of the spring is maximum at the instant the blocks have the same velocity. Find the maximum compression.

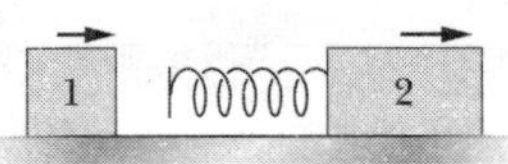

FIG. 9-77 Problems 33 and 63.

Elastic Collisions in One Dimension

34 A body of mass 2.0 kg makes an elastic collision with another body at rest and continues to move in the original direction but with one-fourth of its original speed. (a) What is the mass of the other body? (b) What is the speed of the two-body center of mass if the initial speed of the 2.0 kg body was 4.0 m/s?

35 Block 1, with mass m_1 and speed 4.0 m/s, slides along an x axis on a frictionless floor and then undergoes a one-dimensional elastic collision with stationary block 2, with mass $m_2 = 0.40m_1$. The two blocks then slide into a region where the coefficient of kinetic friction is 0.50; there they stop. How far into that region do (a) block 1 and (b) block 2 slide?

36 In Fig. 9-78, particle 1 of mass $m_1 = 0.30$ kg slides rightward along an x axis on a frictionless floor with a speed of 2.0 m/s. When it reaches $x = 0$, it undergoes a one-dimensional elastic collision with stationary particle 2 of mass $m_2 = 0.40$ kg. When particle 2 then reaches a wall at $x_w = 70$ cm, it bounces from the wall with no loss of speed. At what position on the x axis does particle 2 then collide with particle 1?

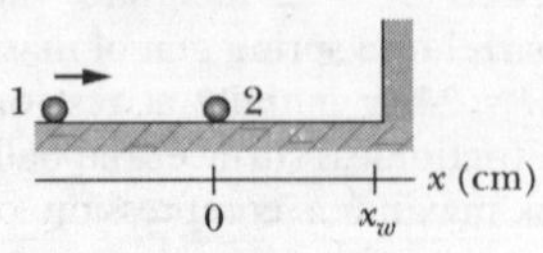

FIG. 9-78 Problem 36.

37 A steel ball of mass 0.500 kg is fastened to a cord that is, 70.0 cm long and fixed at the far end. The ball is then released when the cord is horizontal (Fig. 9-79). At the bottom of its path, the ball strikes a 2.50 kg steel block initially at rest on a frictionless surface. The collision is elastic. Find (a) the speed of the ball and (b) the speed of the block, both just after the collision.

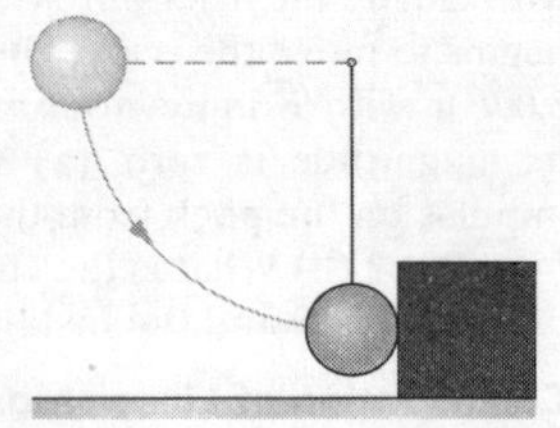

FIG. 9-79 Problem 37.

38 In Fig. 9-80, block 1 of mass m_1 slides from rest along a frictionless ramp from height $h = 2.50$ m and then collides with stationary block 2, which has mass $m_2 = 2.00m_1$. After the collision, block 2 slides into a region where the coefficient of kinetic friction μ_k is 0.500 and comes to a stop in distance d within that region. What is the value of distance d if the col-

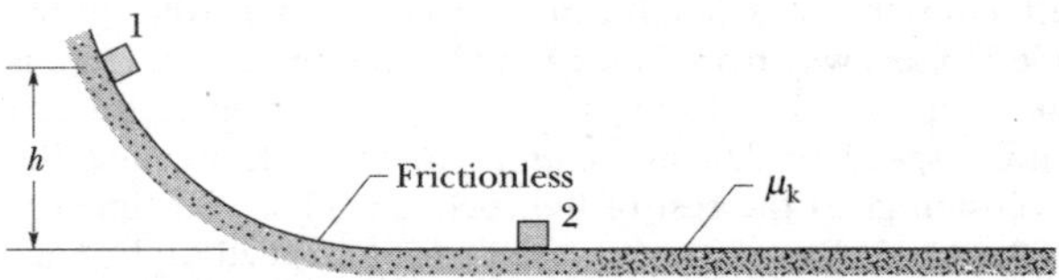

FIG. 9-80 Problem 38.

39 A small ball of mass m is aligned above a larger ball of mass $M = 0.63$ kg (with a slight separation, as with the baseball and basketball of Fig. 9-81a), and the two are dropped simultaneously from a height of $h = 1.8$ m. Assume the radius of each ball is negligible relative to h.) (a) If the larger ball rebounds elastically from the floor and then the small ball rebounds elastically from the larger ball, what value of m results in the larger ball stopping when it collides with the small ball? (b) What height does the small ball then reach (Fig. 9-81b)?

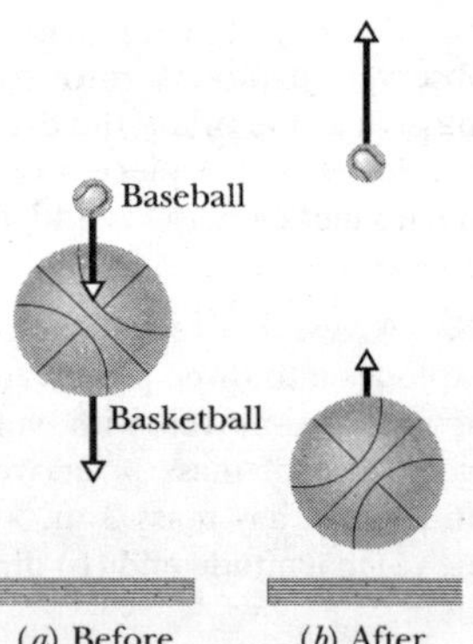

FIG. 9-81 Problem 39.

40 In Fig. 9-82, puck 1 of mass $m_1 = 0.20$ kg is sent sliding across a frictionless lab bench, to undergo a one-dimensional elastic collision with stationary puck 2. Puck 2 then slides off the bench and lands a distance d from the base of the bench. Puck 1 rebounds from the collision and slides off the opposite edge of the bench, landing a distance $2d$ from the base of the bench. What is the mass of puck 2? (*Hint:* Be careful with signs.)

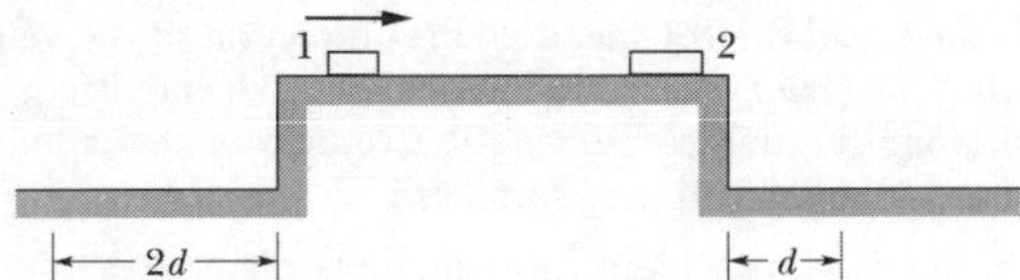

FIG. 9-82 Problem 40.

Collisions in Two Dimensions

41 A projectile proton with a speed of 500 m/s collides elastically with a target proton initially at rest. The two protons then move along perpendicular paths, with the projectile path at 60° from the original direction. After the collision, what are the speeds of (a) the target proton and (b) the projectile proton?

42 Two 2.0 kg bodies, A and B, collide. The velocities before the collision are $\vec{v}_A = (15\hat{i} + 30\hat{j})$ m/s and $\vec{v}_B = (-10\hat{i} + 5.0\hat{j})$ m/s. After the collision, $\vec{v}'_A = (-5.0\hat{i} + 20\hat{j})$ m/s. What are (a) the final velocity of B and (b) the change in the total kinetic energy (including sign)?

43 Ball B, moving in the positive direction of an x axis at speed v, collides with stationary ball A at the origin. A and B have different masses. After the collision, B moves in the negative direction of the y axis at speed $v/2$. (a) In what direction does A move? (b) Show that the speed of A cannot be determined from the given information.

44 After a completely inelastic collision, two objects of the same mass and same initial speed move away together at half their initial speed. Find the angle between the initial velocities of the objects.

Systems with Varying Mass: A Rocket

45 Consider a rocket that is, in deep space and at rest relative to an inertial reference frame. The rocket's engine is to be fired for a certain interval. What must be the rocket's *mass ratio* (ratio of initial to final mass) over that interval if the rocket's original speed relative to the inertial frame is to be equal to (a) the exhaust speed (speed of the exhaust products relative to the rocket) and (b) 2.0 times the exhaust speed?

46 A rocket that is, in deep space and initially at rest relative to an inertial reference frame has a mass of 2.55×10^5 kg, of which 1.81×10^5 kg is fuel. The rocket engine is then fired for 250 s while fuel is consumed at the rate of 480 kg/s. The speed of the exhaust products relative to the rocket is 3.27 km/s. (a) What is the rocket's thrust? After the 250 s firing, what are (b) the mass and (c) the speed of the rocket?

47 In Fig. 9-83, two long barges are moving in the same direction in still water, one with a speed of 10 km/h and the other with a speed of 20 km/h. While they are passing each other, coal is shoveled from the slower to the faster one at a rate of 1000 kg/min. How much additional force must be provided by the driving engines of (a) the faster barge and (b) the slower barge if neither is to change speed? Assume that the shoveling is always perfectly sideways and that the frictional forces between the barges and the water do not depend on the mass of the barges.

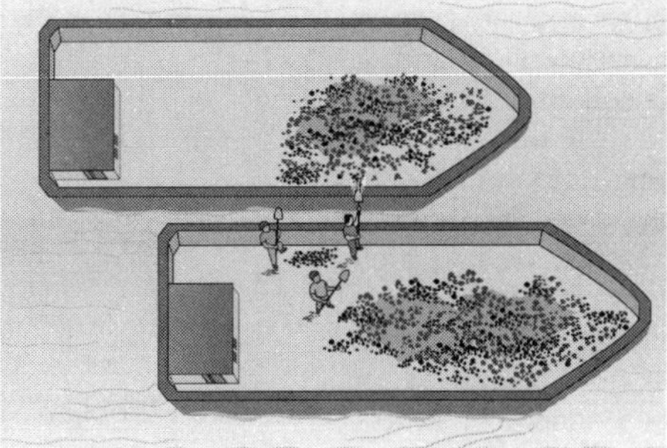

FIG. 9-83 Problem 47.

Additional Problems

48 *Speed amplifier.* In Fig. 9-84, block 1 of mass m_1 slides along an x axis on a frictionless floor with a speed of $v_{1i} = 4.00$ m/s. Then it undergoes a one-dimensional elastic collision with stationary block 2 of mass $m_2 = 0.500m_1$. Next, block 2 undergoes a one-dimensional elastic collision with stationary block 3 of mass $m_3 = 0.500m_2$. (a) What then is the speed of block 3? Are (b) the speed, (c) the kinetic energy, and (d) the momentum of block 3 greater than, less than, or the same as the initial values for block 1?

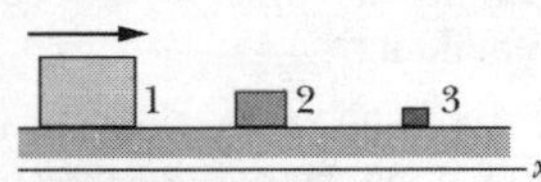

FIG. 9-84 Problem 48.

49 *Speed deamplifier.* In Fig. 9-85, block 1 of mass m_1 slides along an x axis on a frictionless floor at speed 4.00 m/s. Then it undergoes a one-dimensional elastic collision with stationary block 2 of mass $m_2 = 2.00m_1$. Next, block 2 undergoes a one-dimensional elastic collision with stationary block 3 of mass $m_3 = 2.00m_2$. (a) What then is the speed of block 3? Are (b) the speed, (c) the kinetic energy, and (d) the momentum of block 3 greater than, less than, or the same as the initial values for block 1?

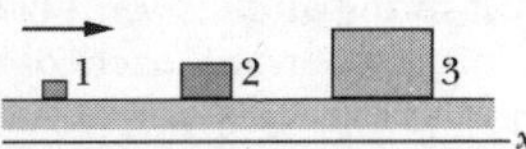

FIG. 9-85 Problem 49.

50 *"Relative" is an important word.* In Fig. 9-86, block L of mass $m_L = 1.00$ kg and block R of mass $m_R = 0.500$ kg are held in place with a compressed spring between them. When the blocks are released, the spring sends them sliding across a frictionless floor. (The spring has negligible mass and falls to the floor after the blocks leave it.) (a) If the spring gives block L a release speed of 1.20 m/s *relative* to the floor, how far does block R travel in the next 0.800 s? (b) If, instead, the spring gives block L a release speed of 1.20 m/s *relative* to the velocity that the spring gives block R, how far does block R travel in the next 0.800 s?

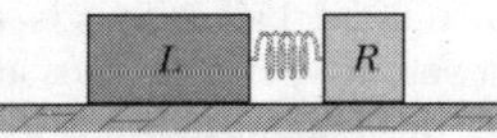

FIG. 9-86 Problem 50.

51 *Pancake collapse of a tall building.* In the section of a tall building shown in Fig. 9-87a, the infrastructure of any given floor K must support the weight W of all higher floors. Normally the infrastructure is constructed with a safety factor s so that it can withstand an even greater downward force of

sW. If, however, the support columns between K and L suddenly collapse and allow the higher floors to free-fall together onto floor K (Fig. 9-87b), the force in the collision can exceed sW and, after a brief pause, cause K to collapse onto floor J, which collapses on floor I, and so on until the ground is reached. Assume that the floors are separated by $d = 4.0$ m and have the same mass. Also assume that when the floors above K free-fall onto K, the collision lasts 1.5 ms. Under these simplified conditions, what value must the safety factor s exceed to prevent pancake collapse of the building?

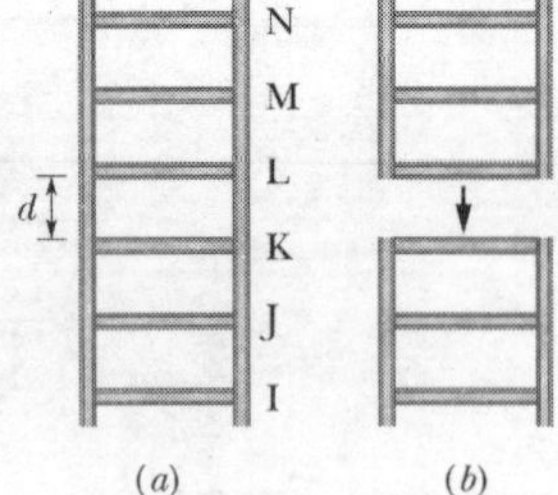

FIG. 9-87 Problem 51.

52 A 1400 kg car moving at 5.3 m/s is initially traveling north along the positive direction of a y axis. After completing a 90° right-hand turn in 4.6 s, the inattentive operator drives into a tree, which stops the car in 350 ms. In unit-vector notation, what is the impulse on the car (a) due to the turn and (b) due to the collision? What is the magnitude of the average force that acts on the car (c) during the turn and (d) during the collision? (e) What is the direction of the average force during the turn?

53 Two blocks of masses 1.0 kg and 3.0 kg are connected by a spring and rest on a frictionless surface. They are given velocities toward each other such that the 1.0 kg block travels initially at 1.7 m/s toward the center of mass, which remains at rest. What is the initial speed of the other block?

54 A 75 kg man is riding on a 39 kg cart traveling at a velocity of 2.3 m/s. He jumps off with zero horizontal velocity relative to the ground. What is the resulting change in the cart's velocity, including sign?

55 In the arrangement of Fig. 9-87, billiard ball 1 moving at a speed of 2.2 m/s undergoes a glancing collision with identical billiard ball 2 that is, at rest. After the collision, ball 2 moves at speed 1.1 m/s, at an angle of $\theta_2 = 60°$. What are (a) the magnitude and (b) the direction of the velocity of ball 1 after the collision? (c) Do the given data suggest the collision is elastic or inelastic?

56 A rocket is moving away from the solar system at a speed of 6.0×10^3 m/s. It fires its engine, which ejects exhaust with a speed of 3.0×10^3 m/s relative to the rocket. The mass of the rocket at this time is 4.0×10^4 kg, and its acceleration is 2.0 m/s². (a) What is the thrust of the engine? (b) At what rate, in kilograms per second, is exhaust ejected during the firing?

57 The three balls in the overhead view of Fig. 9-75 are identical. Balls 2 and 3 touch each other and are aligned perpendicular to the path of ball 1. The velocity of ball 1 has magnitude $v_0 = 10$ m/s and is directed at the contact point of balls 1 and 2. After the collision, what are the (a) speed and (b) direction of the velocity of ball 2, the (c) speed and (d) direction of the velocity of ball 3, and the (e) speed and (f) direction of the velocity of ball 1? (*Hint:* With friction absent, each impulse is directed along the line connecting the centers of the colliding balls, normal to the colliding surfaces.)

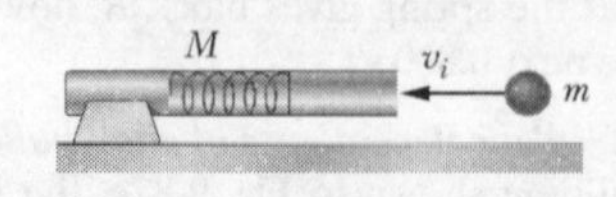

FIG. 9-75 Problem 57.

58 In Fig. 9-88, two identical containers of sugar are connected by a cord that passes over a frictionless pulley. The cord and pulley have negligible mass, each container and its sugar together have a mass of 500 g, the centers of the containers are separated by 50 mm, and the containers are held fixed at the same height. What is the horizontal distance between the center of container 1 and the center of mass of the two-container system (a) initially and (b) after 20 g of sugar is transferred from container 1 to container 2? After the transfer and after the containers are released, (c) in what direction and (d) at what acceleration magnitude does the center of mass move?

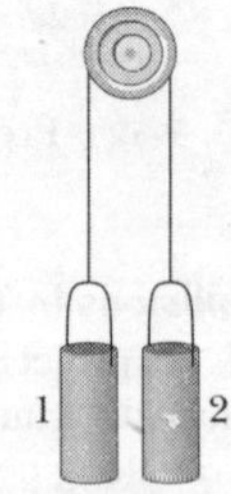

FIG. 9-88 Problem 58.

59 The script for an action movie calls for a small race car (of mass 1500 kg and length 3.0 m) to accelerate along a flattop boat (of mass 4000 kg and length 14 m), from one end of the boat to the other, where the car will then jump the gap between the boat and a somewhat lower dock. You are the technical advisor for the movie. The boat will initially touch the dock, as in Fig. 9-89; the boat can slide through the water without significant resistance; both the car and the boat can be approximated as uniform in their mass distribution. Determine what the width of the gap will be just as the car is about to make the jump.

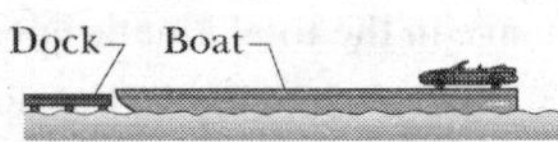

FIG. 9-89 Problem 59.

60 In Fig. 9-90, block 1 slides along an x axis on a frictionless floor with a speed of 0.75 m/s. When it reaches stationary block 2, the two blocks undergo an elastic collision. The following table gives the mass and length of the (uniform) blocks and also the locations of their centers at time $t = 0$. Where is the center of mass of the two-block system located (a) at $t = 0$, (b) when the two blocks first touch, and (c) at $t = 4.0$ s?

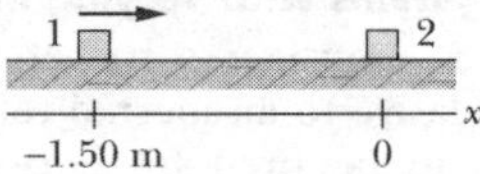

FIG. 9-90 Problem 60.

Block	Mass (kg)	Length (cm)	Center at $t = 0$
1	0.25	5.0	$x = -1.50$ m
2	0.50	6.0	$x = 0$

61 In Fig. 9-91, an 80 kg man is on a ladder hanging from a balloon that has a total mass of 320 kg (including the basket passenger). The balloon is initially stationary relative to the ground. If the man on the ladder begins to climb at 2.5 m/s relative to the ladder, (a) in what direction and (b) at what speed does the balloon move? (c) If the man then stops climbing, what is the speed of the balloon?

62 During a lunar mission, it is necessary to increase the speed of a spacecraft by 2.2 m/s when it is moving at 400 m/s relative to the Moon. The speed of the exhaust products from the rocket engine is 1000 m/s relative to the spacecraft. What fraction of the initial mass of the spacecraft must be burned and ejected to accomplish the speed increase?

63 In Fig. 9-77, block 1 (mass 6.0 kg) is moving rightward at 8.0 m/s and block 2 (mass 4.0 kg) is moving rightward at 2.0 m/s. The surface is frictionless, and a spring with a spring constant of 8000 N/m is fixed to block 2. Eventually block 1 overtakes block 2. At the instant block 1 is moving rightward at 6.4 m/s, what are (a) the speed of block 2 and (b) the elastic potential energy of the spring?

64 Particle 1 with mass 3.0 kg and velocity $(5.0\text{ m/s})\hat{i}$ undergoes a one-dimensional elastic collision with particle 2 with mass 2.0 kg and velocity $(-6.0\text{ m/s})\hat{i}$. After the collision, what are the velocities of (a) particle 1 and (b) particle 2?

FIG. 9-91 Problem 61.

65 At a certain instant, four particles have the xy coordinates and velocities given in the following table. At that instant, what are the (a) x and (b) y coordinates of their center of mass and (c) the velocity of their center of mass?

Particle	Mass (kg)	Position (m)	Velocity (m/s)
1	2.0	0, 3.0	$-9.0\hat{j}$
2	4.0	3.0, 0	$6.0\hat{i}$
3	3.0	0, −2.0	$6.0\hat{j}$
4	12	−1.0, 0	$-2.0\hat{i}$

66 Figure 9-92 shows two 22.7 kg ice sleds that are placed a short distance apart, one directly behind the other. A 3.63 kg cat initially standing on one sled jumps to the other one and then back to the first. Both jumps are made at a speed of 3.05 m/s relative to the ice. What are the final speeds of (a) the first sled and (b) the other sled?

FIG. 9-92 Problem 66.

Rigid Body Dynamics-I

David Wrobel/Visuals Unlimited

The snapping shrimp stuns its prey (tiny crabs) by clamping its oversized claw shut but not on the prey itself. Instead, the prey is stunned by a powerful sound wave generated by the moving part of the claw as it nears the stationary part of the claw. The sound (a snap resembling the pop of popcorn) can be heard by a diver and, with enough shrimp, can be loud enough to hide a submarine from sonar detection. The sound wave can also produce very faint flashes of light, what is generally called sound-produced light or sonoluminescence. However, some researchers have dubbed the shrimp-produced light shrimpoluminescence.

How can a shrimp claw generate such a powerful sound wave?

The answer is in this chapter.

10-1 Introduction

A rigid body may be defined as a system of particles such that the distances between the particles do not vary with time. This condition is satisfied approximately only by bodies which exist in nature; however, the majority of solid objects, deform so little in shape and size under ordinary conditions that these deformations may be entirely neglected for applying laws of motion on the body. This chapter and the next will help us understand simple motions of rigid bodies.

10-2 | Kinematics of Rigid Body

Translation Motion

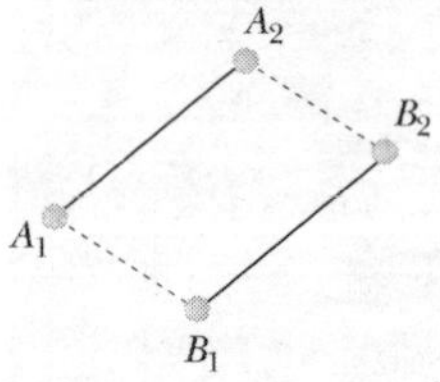

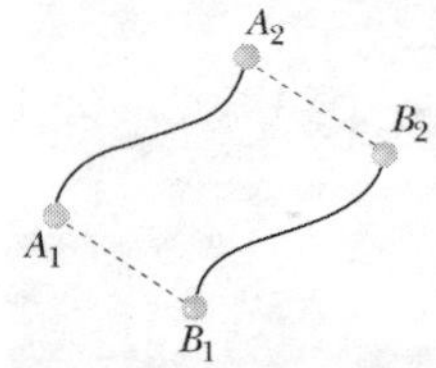

FIG. 10-1 Rectilinear translation.

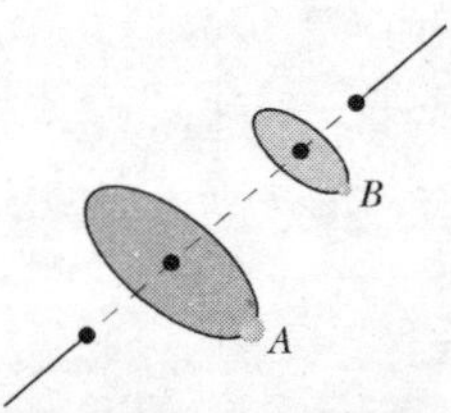

FIG. 10-2 Curvilinear translation.

A motion is said to be translation if any straight line inside the body shifts parallel to itself during the motion. It can also be observed that in a translation all the particles forming the body move along parallel paths. If these paths are straight lines, the motion is said to be a rectilinear translation Fig. 10-1; if the paths are curved lines, the motion is a curvilinear translation Fig. 10-2. Examples: a car traveling along a straight section of a road, a Ferries wheel cage and so on.

When moving translationary, all the points on the solid traverse equal distances in the same time interval. Therefore, velocities, as well as accelerations, of all points on the body at the given moment of time are same vectors. This fact allows the study of translation of a solid to be simplified to the study of motion of an individual point on that body, that is, it becomes the problem of kinematics of a point.

Rotation about a Fixed Axis

As we have discussed, one focus of physics is motion. However, so far we have examined only the motion of **Translation**, in which an object moves along a straight or curved line, as in Fig.10-4*a*. We now turn to the motion of **rotation**, in which an object turns about an axis, as in Fig. 10-4*b*.

You see rotation in nearly every machine, you use it every time you open a beverage can with a pull tab, and you pay to experience it every time you go to an amusement park. Rotation is the key to many fun activities, such as hitting a long drive in golf (the ball needs to rotate in order for the air to keep it aloft longer) and throwing a curveball in baseball (the ball needs to rotate in order for the air to push it left or right). Rotation is also the key to more serious matters, such as metal failure in aging airplanes.

In this motion, the particles forming the rigid body move in parallel planes along circles centered on the same fixed axis called the axis of rotation, Fig. 10-3. If this axis, intersects the rigid body, the particles located on the axis have zero velocity and zero acceleration.

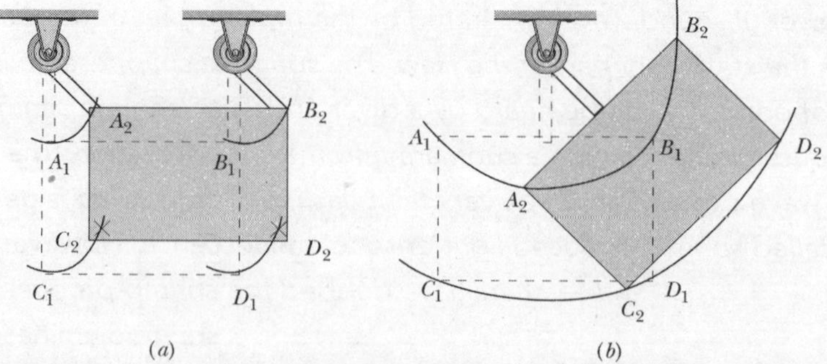

FIG. 10-3 (*a*) Curvilinear translation. (*b*) Rotation.

Rotation should not be confused with certain types of curvilinear translation. For example, the plate shown in Fig. 10-3*a* is in curvilinear translation, with all its particles moving along parallel circles, while the plate shown in Fig. 10-3*b* is in rotation, with all its particles moving along concentric circles.

In the first case, any given straight line drawn on the plate will shift parallel to itself, whereas in the second case, point *O* remains fixed.

Because each particle moves in a given plane, the rotation of a body about a fixed axis is said to be a plane motion.

General Plane

There are many other types of plane motion, that is, motion in which all the particles of the body move in parallel planes. Any plane motion which is neither a rotation nor a translation is referred to as a general plane motion. Two examples of general plane motion.

For this chapter we will focus only on rotation about a fixed axis.

We wish to examine the rotation of a rigid body about a fixed axis. A **rigid body** is a body that can rotate with all its parts locked together and without any change in its shape. A **fixed axis** means that the rotation occurs about an axis that does not move. Thus, we shall not examine an object like the Sun, because the parts of the Sun (a ball of gas) are not locked together. We also shall not examine an object like a bowling ball rolling along a lane, because the ball rotates about a moving axis (the ball's motion is a mixture of rotation and translation).

Figure 10-5 shows a rigid body of arbitrary shape in rotation about a fixed axis, called the **axis of rotation** or the **rotation axis.** In pure rotation (*angular motion*), every point of the body moves in a circle whose center lies on the axis of rotation, and every point moves through the same angle during a particular time interval. In pure translation (*linear motion*), every point of the body moves in a straight line, and every point moves through the same *linear distance* during a particular time interval.

We deal now—one at a time—with the angular equivalents of the linear quantities position, displacement, velocity, and acceleration.

(*a*)

(*b*)

FIG. 10-4 Figure skater Sasha Cohen in motion of (*a*) pure translation in a fixed direction and (*b*) pure rotation about a vertical axis. (*a: Mike Segar/Reuters/Landov LLC; b: Elsa/Getty Images, Inc.*)

10-3 | The Rotational Variables

We begin our discussion of rotation by defining the variables for the motion.

Angular Position

Figure 10-6 shows a *reference line*, fixed in the body, perpendicular to the rotation axis and rotating with the body. The **angular position** of this line is the angle of the line relative to a fixed direction, which we take as the **zero angular position.** In Fig. 10-7, the angular position θ is measured relative to the positive direction of the x axis. From geometry, we know that θ is given by

$$\theta = \frac{s}{r} \quad \text{(radian measure)} \tag{10-1}$$

Here s is the length of a circular arc that extends from the x axis (the zero angular position) to the reference line, and r is the radius of the circle.

An angle defined in this way is measured in **radians** (rad) rather than in revolutions (rev) or degrees. The radian, being the ratio of two lengths, is a pure number and thus has no dimension. Because the circumference of a circle of radius r is $2\pi r$, there are 2π radians in a complete circle:

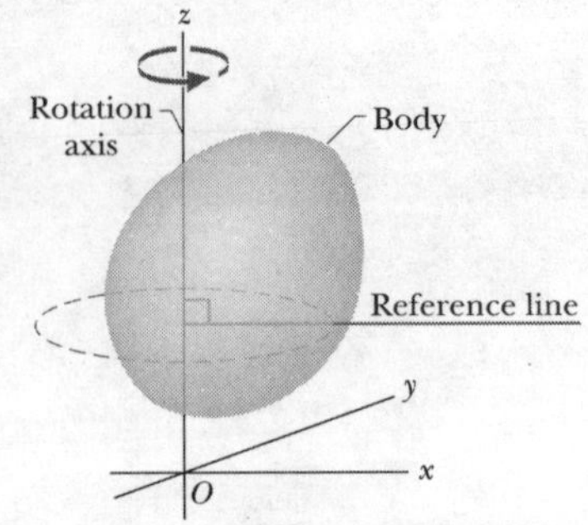

FIG. 10-5 A rigid body of arbitrary shape in pure rotation about the z axis of a coordinate system. The position of the *reference line* with respect to the rigid body is arbitrary, but it is perpendicular to the rotation axis. It is fixed in the body and rotates with the body.

$$1 \text{ rev} = 360° = \frac{2\pi r}{r} = 2\pi \text{ rad} \tag{10-2}$$

and thus

$$1 \text{ rad} = 57.3° = 0.159 \text{ rev} \tag{10-3}$$

We do *not* reset θ to zero with each complete rotation of the reference line about the rotation axis. If the reference line completes two revolutions from the zero angular position, then the angular position θ of the line is $\theta = 4\pi$ rad.

For pure translation along an x axis, we can know all there is to know about a moving body if we know $x(t)$, its position as a function of time. Similarly, for pure rotation, we can know all there is to know about a rotating body if we know $\theta(t)$, the angular position of the body's reference line as a function of time.

Angular Displacement

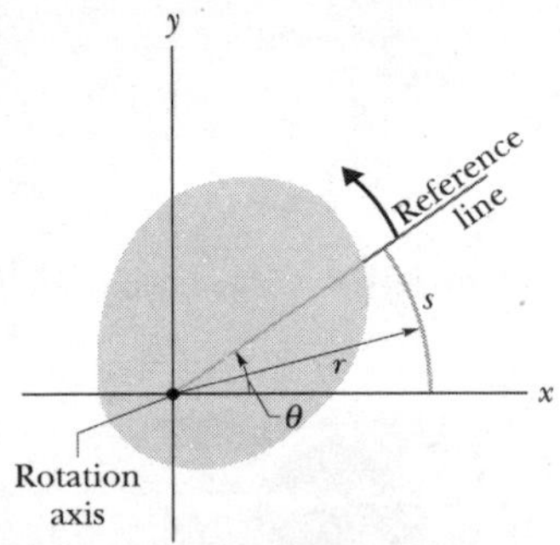

FIG. 10-6 The rotating rigid body of Fig. 10-5 in cross section, viewed from above. The plane of the cross section is perpendicular to the rotation axis, which now extends out of the page, toward you. In this position of the body, the reference line makes an angle θ with the x axis.

If the body of Fig. 10-6 rotates about the rotation axis as in Fig. 10-7, changing the angular position of the reference line from θ_1 to θ_2, the body undergoes an **angular displacement** $\Delta\theta$ given by

$$\Delta\theta = \theta_2 - \theta_1 \tag{10-4}$$

This definition of angular displacement holds not only for the rigid body as a whole but also for *every particle within that body.*

If a body is in translational motion along an x axis, its displacement Δx is either positive or negative, depending on whether the body is moving in the positive or negative direction of the axis. Similarly, the angular displacement $\Delta\theta$ of a rotating body is either positive or negative, according to the following rule: The phrase "*clocks are negative*" can help you remember this rule (they certainly are negative when their alarms sound off early in the morning).

An angular displacement in the counterclockwise direction is positive, and one in the clockwise direction is negative.

CHECKPOINT 1 A disk can rotate about its central axis like a merry-go-round. Which of the following pairs of values for its initial and final angular positions, respectively, give a negative angular displacement: (a) -3 rad, $+5$ rad, (b) -3 rad, -7 rad, (c) 7 rad, -3 rad?

Angular Velocity

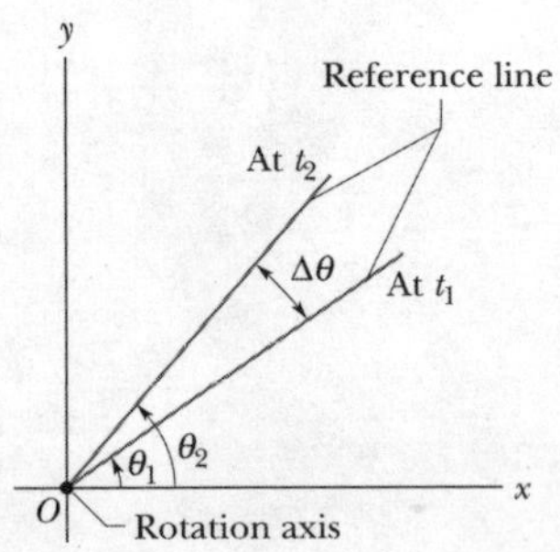

FIG. 10-7 The reference line of the rigid body of Figs. 10-5 and 10-6 is at angular position θ_1 at time t_1 and at angular position θ_2 at a later time t_2. The quantity $\Delta\theta$ $(= \theta_2 - \theta_1)$ is the angular displacement that occurs during the interval Δt $(= t_2 - t_1)$. The body itself is not shown.

Suppose that our rotating body is at angular position θ_1 at time t_1 and at angular position θ_2 at time t_2 as in Fig. 10-7. We define the **average angular velocity** of the body in the time interval Δt from t_1 to t_2 to be

$$\omega_{avg} = \frac{\theta_2 - \theta_1}{t_2 - t_1} = \frac{\Delta\theta}{\Delta t} \tag{10-5}$$

in which $\Delta\theta$ is the angular displacement that occurs during Δt (ω is the lowercase Greek letter omega).

The **(instantaneous) angular velocity** ω, with which we shall be most concerned, is the limit of the ratio in Eq. 10-5 as Δt approaches zero. Thus,

$$\omega = \lim_{\Delta t \to 0} \frac{\Delta\theta}{\Delta t} = \frac{d\theta}{dt} \tag{10-6}$$

If we know $\theta(t)$, we can find the angular velocity ω by differentiation.

Equations 10-5 and 10-6 hold not only for the rotating rigid body as a whole but also for *every particle of that body* because the particles are all locked together. The unit of angular velocity is commonly the radian per second (rad/s) or the revolution per second (rev/s).

If a particle moves in translation along an x axis, its linear velocity v is either positive or negative, depending on whether the particle is moving in the positive or negative direction of the axis. Similarly, the angular velocity ω of a rotating rigid body is either positive or negative, depending on whether the body is rotating counterclockwise (positive) or clockwise (negative). The magnitude of instantaneous angular velocity is equal to the **angular speed**.

Angular Acceleration

If the angular velocity of a rotating body is not constant, then the body has an angular acceleration. Let ω_2 and ω_1 be its angular velocities at times t_2 and t_1, respectively. The **average angular acceleration** of the rotating body in the interval from t_1 to t_2 is defined as

$$\alpha_{\text{avg}} = \frac{\omega_2 - \omega_1}{t_2 - t_1} = \frac{\Delta\omega}{\Delta t} \tag{10-7}$$

in which $\Delta\omega$ is the change in the angular velocity that occurs during the time interval Δt. The **(instantaneous) angular acceleration** α, with which we shall be most concerned, is the limit of this quantity as Δt approaches zero. Thus,

$$\alpha = \lim_{\Delta t \to 0} \frac{\Delta\omega}{\Delta t} = \frac{d\omega}{dt} \tag{10-8}$$

Equations 10-7 and 10-8 also hold for *every particle of that body.* The unit of angular acceleration is commonly the radian per second-squared (rad/s^2) or the revolution per second-squared (rev/s^2).

10-4 | Are Angular Quantities Vectors?

We can describe the position, velocity, and acceleration of a single particle by means of vectors. If the particle is confined to a straight line, however, we do not really need vector notation. Such a particle has only two directions available to it, and we can indicate these directions with plus and minus signs.

In the same way, a rigid body rotating about a fixed axis can rotate only clockwise or counterclockwise as seen along the axis, and again we can select between the two directions by means of plus and minus signs. The question arises: "Can we treat the angular displacement, velocity, and acceleration of a rotating body as vectors?" The answer is a qualified "yes" (see the caution below, in connection with angular displacements).

Consider the angular velocity. Fig. 10-8*a* shows a vinyl record rotating on a turntable. The record has a constant angular speed ω (= $33\frac{1}{3}$ rev/min) in the clockwise direction. We can represent its angular velocity as a vector $\vec{\omega}$ pointing along the axis of rotation, as in Fig. 10-8*b*. Here's how: We choose the length of this vector according to some convenient scale, for example, with 1 cm corresponding to 10 rev/min. Then we establish a direction for the vector $\vec{\omega}$ by using a **right-hand rule**, as Fig. 10-8*c* shows: Curl your right hand about the rotating record, your fingers pointing *in the direction of rotation.* Your extended thumb will then point in the direction of the angular velocity vector. If the record were to rotate in the opposite sense, the right-hand rule would tell you that the angular velocity vector then points in the opposite direction.

It is not easy to get used to representing angular quantities as vectors. We instinctively expect that something should be moving *along* the direction of a

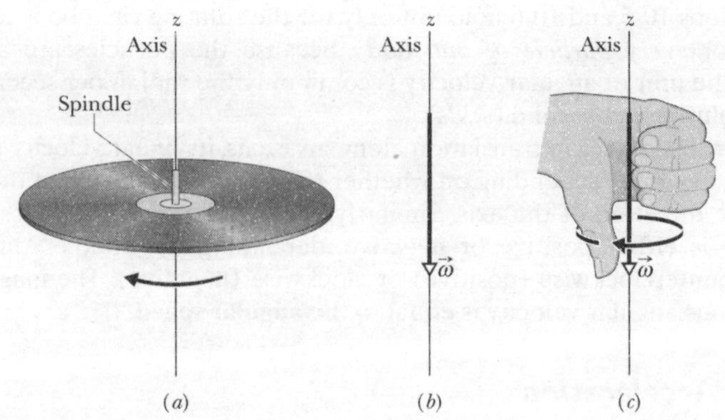

FIG. 10-8 (*a*) A record rotating about a vertical axis that coincides with the axis of the spindle. (*b*) The angular velocity of the rotating record can be represented by the vector $\vec{\omega}$, lying along the axis and pointing down, as shown. (*c*) We establish the direction of the angular velocity vector as downward by using a right-hand rule. When the fingers of the right hand curl around the record and point the way it is moving, the extended thumb points in the direction of $\vec{\omega}$.

vector. That is not the case here. Instead, something (the rigid body) is rotating *around* the direction of the vector. In the world of pure rotation, a vector defines an axis of rotation, not a direction in which something moves. Nonetheless, the vector also defines the motion. Furthermore, it obeys all the rules for vector manipulation. The angular acceleration $\vec{\alpha}$ is another vector, and it too obeys those rules.

In this chapter we consider only rotations that are about a fixed axis. For such situations, we need not consider vectors—we can represent angular velocity with ω and angular acceleration with α, and we can indicate direction with an implied plus sign for counterclockwise or an explicit minus sign for clockwise.

Now for the caution: Angular *displacements* (unless they are very small) *cannot* be treated as vectors. Why not? We can certainly give them both magnitude and direction, as we did for the angular velocity vector in Fig. 10-8. However, to be represented as a vector, a quantity must *also* obey the rules of vector addition, one of which says that if you add two vectors, the order in which you add them does not matter. Angular displacements fail this test.

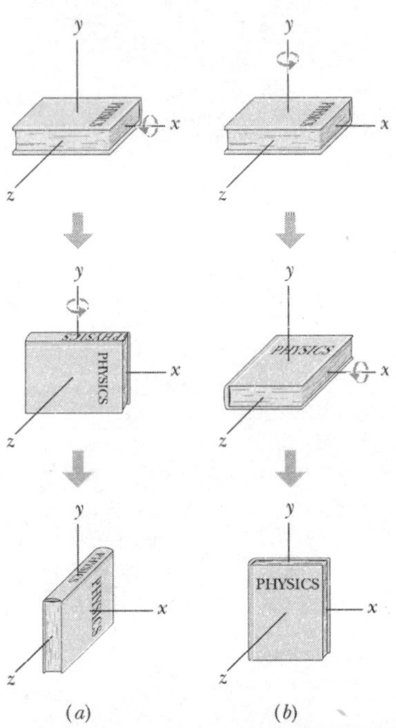

FIG. 10-9 (*a*) From its initial position, at the top, the book is given two successive 90° rotations, first about the (horizontal) x axis and then about the (vertical) y axis. (*b*) The book is given the same rotations, but in the reverse order.

Figure 10-9 gives an example. An initially horizontal book is given two 90° angular displacements, first in the order of Fig. 10-9*a* and then in the order of Fig. 10-9*b*. Although the two angular displacements are identical, their order is not, and the book ends up with different orientations. Here's another example. Hold your right arm downward, palm toward your thigh. Keeping your wrist rigid, (1) lift the arm forward until it is horizontal, (2) move it horizontally until it points toward the right, and (3) then bring it down to your side. Your palm faces forward. If you start over, but reverse the steps, which way does your palm end up facing? From either example, we must conclude that the addition of two angular displacements depends on their order and they cannot be vectors.

10-5 | Rotation with Constant Angular Acceleration

In pure translation, motion with a *constant linear acceleration* (for example, that of a falling body) is an important special case. In Table 3-1, we displayed a series of equations that hold for such motion.

In pure rotation, the case of *constant angular acceleration* is also important, and a parallel set of equations holds for this case also. We shall not derive them here, but simply write them from the corresponding linear equations, substituting equivalent angular quantities for the linear ones. This is done in Table 10-1, which lists both sets of equations (Eqs. 3-11 and 3-15 to 3-18; 10-9 to 10-13).

Recall that Eqs. 3-11 and 3-15 are basic equations for constant linear acceleration—the other equations in the Linear list can be derived from them. Similarly, Eqs. 10-9 and 10-10 are the basic equations for constant angular acceleration, and the other equations in the Angular list can be derived from them. To solve a simple

TABLE 10-1

Equations of Motion for Constant Linear Acceleration and for Constant Angular Acceleration

Equation Number	Linear Equation	Missing Variable		Angular Equation	Equation Number
(3-11)	$v = v_0 + at$	$x - x_0$	$\theta - \theta_0$	$\omega = \omega_0 + \alpha t$	(10-9)
(3-15)	$x - x_0 = v_0 t + \frac{1}{2}at^2$	v	ω	$\theta - \theta_0 = \omega_0 t + \frac{1}{2}\alpha t^2$	(10-10)
(3-16)	$v^2 = v_0^2 + 2a(x - x_0)$	t	t	$\omega^2 = \omega_0^2 + 2\alpha(\theta - \theta_0)$	(10-11)
(3-17)	$x - x_0 = \frac{1}{2}(v_0 + v)t$	a	α	$\theta - \theta_0 = \frac{1}{2}(\omega_0 + \omega)t$	(10-12)
(3-18)	$x - x_0 = vt - \frac{1}{2}at^2$	v_0	ω_0	$\theta - \theta_0 = \omega t - \frac{1}{2}\alpha t^2$	(10-13)

problem involving constant angular acceleration, you can usually use an equation from the Angular list (*if* you have the list). Choose an equation for which the only unknown variable will be the variable requested in the problem. A better plan is to remember only Eqs. 10-9 and 10-10, and then solve them as simultaneous equations whenever needed. An example is given in Sample Problem 10-4.

CHECKPOINT 2 In four situations, a rotating body has angular position $\theta(t)$ given by (a) $\theta = 3t - 4$, (b) $\theta = -5t^3 + 4t^2 + 6$, (c) $\theta = 2/t^2 - 4/t$, and (d) $\theta = 5t^2 - 3$. To which situations do the angular equations of Table 10-1 apply?

Sample Problem 10-1

A grindstone (Fig. 10-10) rotates at constant angular acceleration $\alpha = 0.35$ rad/s^2. At time $t = 0$, it has an angular velocity of $\omega_0 = -4.6$ rad/s and a reference line on it is horizontal, at the angular position $\theta_0 = 0$.

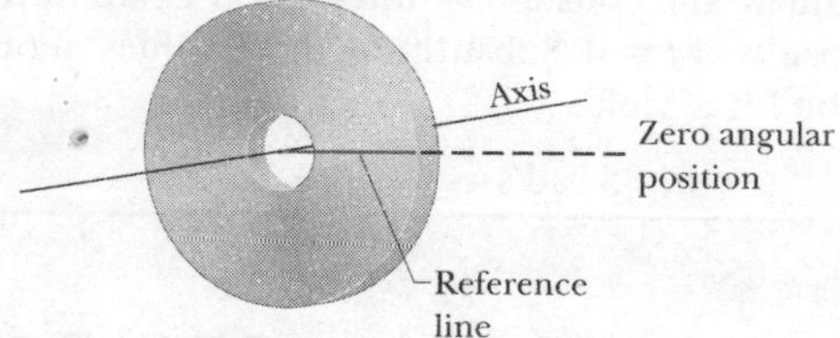

FIG. 10-10 A grindstone. At $t = 0$ the reference line (which we imagine to be marked on the stone) is horizontal.

(a) At what time after $t = 0$ is the reference line at the angular position $\theta = 5.0$ rev?

Conceptualize/Classify: The angular acceleration is constant, so we can use the rotation equations of Table 10-1. We choose Eq. 10-10,

$$\theta - \theta_0 = \omega_0 t + \tfrac{1}{2}\alpha t^2$$

because the only unknown variable it contains is the desired time t.

Compute: Substituting known values and setting $\theta_0 = 0$ and $\theta = 5.0 \text{ rev} = 10\pi$ rad give us

$$10\pi \text{ rad} = (-4.6 \text{ rad/s})t + \tfrac{1}{2}(0.35 \text{ rad/s}^2)t^2$$

(We converted 5.0 rev to 10π rad to keep the units consistent.) Solving this quadratic equation for t, we find

$$t = 32 \text{ s} \qquad \text{(Answer)}$$

(b) Describe the grindstone's rotation between $t = 0$ and $t = 32$ s.

Conceptualize/Classify: The wheel is initially rotating in the negative (clockwise) direction with angular velocity $\omega_0 = -4.6$ rad/s, but its angular acceleration α is positive. This initial opposition of the signs of angular velocity and angular acceleration means that the wheel slows in its rotation in the negative direction, stops, and then reverses to rotate in the positive direction. After the reference line comes back through its initial orientation of $\theta = 0$, the wheel turns an additional 5.0 rev by time $t = 32$ s.

(c) At what time t does the grindstone momentarily stop?

Classify: We again go to the table of equations for constant angular acceleration, and again we need an equation that contains only the desired unknown variable t.

Compute: However, now the equation must also contain the variable ω, so that we can set it to 0 and then solve for the corresponding time t. We choose Eq. 10-9, which yields

$$t = \frac{\omega - \omega_0}{\alpha} = \frac{0 - (-4.6 \text{ rad/s})}{0.35 \text{ rad/s}^2} = 13 \text{ s} \qquad \text{(Answer)}$$

Sample Problem 10-2

A child's top is spun with angular acceleration

$$\alpha = 5t^3 - 4t$$

with t in seconds and α in radians per second-squared. At $t = 0$, the top has angular velocity 5 rad/s, and a reference line on it is at angular position $\theta = 2$ rad.

(a) Obtain an expression for the angular velocity $\omega(t)$ of the top.

Conceptualize/Classify: By definition, $\alpha(t)$ is the derivative of $\omega(t)$ with respect to time. Thus, we can find $\omega(t)$ by integrating $\alpha(t)$ with respect to time.

Compute: Equation 10-8 tells us

$$d\omega = \alpha\, dt$$

so

$$\int d\omega = \int \alpha\, dt$$

From this we find

$$\omega = \int (5t^3 - 4t)\, dt = \tfrac{5}{4}t^4 - \tfrac{4}{2}t^2 + C$$

To evaluate the constant of integration C, we note that $\omega = 5$ rad/s at $t = 0$. Substituting these values in our expression for ω yields

$$5 \text{ rad/s} = 0 - 0 + C$$

so $C = 5$ rad/s. Then

$$\omega = \tfrac{5}{4}t^4 - 2t^2 + 5 \qquad \text{(Answer)}$$

(b) Obtain an expression for the angular position $\theta(t)$ of the top.

Conceptualize/Classify: By definition, $\omega(t)$ is the derivative of $\theta(t)$ with respect to time. Therefore, we can find $\theta(t)$ by integrating $\omega(t)$ with respect to time.

Compute: Since Eq. 10-6 tells us that

$$d\theta = \omega\, dt$$

we can write

$$\theta = \int \omega\, dt = \int (\tfrac{5}{4}t^4 - 2t^2 + 5)\, dt$$

$$= \tfrac{1}{4}t^5 - \tfrac{2}{3}t^3 + 5t + C'$$

$$= \tfrac{1}{4}t^5 - \tfrac{2}{3}t^3 + 5t + 2 \qquad \text{(Answer)}$$

where C' has been evaluated by noting that $\theta = 2$ rad at $t = 0$.

Conclude: The results are being obtained using integration, as angular acceleration is variable.

10-6 | Relating the Linear and Angular Variables

In uniform circular motion, a particle travels at constant linear speed v along a circle and around an axis of rotation. When a rigid body, such as a merry-go-round, rotates around an axis, each particle in the body moves in its own circle around that axis. Since the body is rigid, all the particles make one revolution in the same amount of time; that is, they all have the same angular speed ω.

However, the farther a particle is from the axis, the greater the circumference of its circle is, and so the faster its linear speed v must be. You can notice this on a merry-go-round. You turn with the same angular speed ω regardless of your distance from the center, but your linear speed v increases noticeably if you move to the outside edge of the merry-go-round.

We often need to relate the linear variables s, v, and a for a particular point in a rotating body to the angular variables θ, ω, and α for that body. The two sets of variables are related by r, the *perpendicular distance* of the point from the rotation axis. This perpendicular distance is the distance between the point and the rotation axis, measured along a perpendicular to the axis. It is also the radius r of the circle traveled by the point around the axis of rotation.

The Position

If a reference line on a rigid body rotates through an angle θ, a point within the body at a position r from the rotation axis moves a distance s along a circular arc, where s is given by Eq. 10-1:

$$s = \theta r \quad \text{(radian measure)} \tag{10-14}$$

This is the first of our linear–angular relations. *Caution:* The angle θ here must be measured in radians because Eq. 10-14 is itself the definition of angular measure in radians.

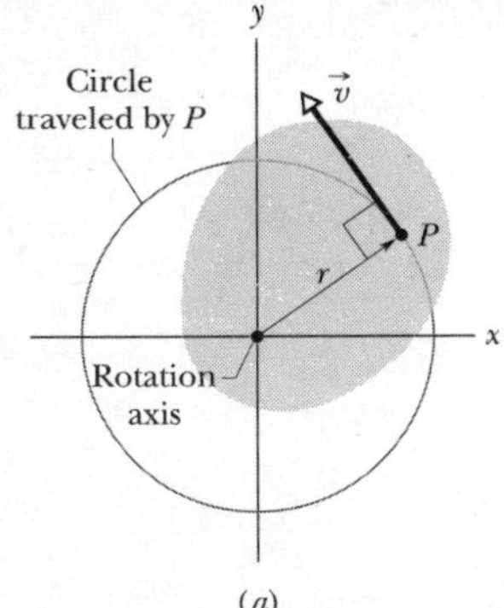

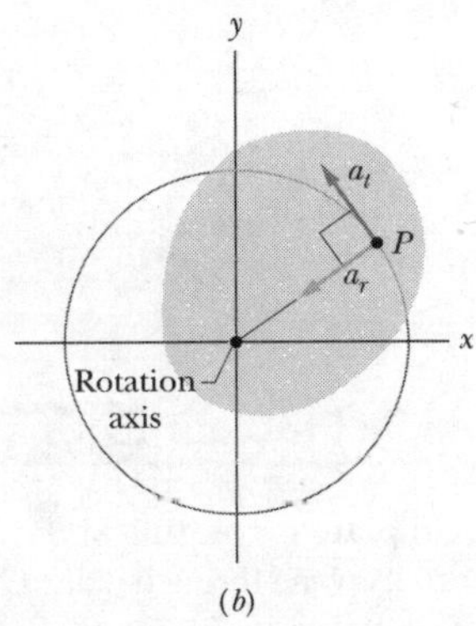

FIG. 10-11 The rotating rigid body of Fig. 10-5, shown in cross section viewed from above. Every point of the body (such as P) moves in a circle around the rotation axis. (*a*) The linear velocity $\vec{v}$ of every point is tangent to the circle in which the point moves. (*b*) The linear acceleration $\vec{a}$ of the point has (in general) two components: tangential a_t and radial a_r.

The Speed

Differentiating Eq. 10-14 with respect to time—with r held constant—leads to

$$\frac{ds}{dt} = \frac{d\theta}{dt} r.$$

However, ds/dt is the linear speed (the magnitude of the linear velocity) of the point in question, and $d\theta/dt$ is the angular speed ω of the rotating body. So

$$v = \omega r \quad \text{(radian measure)} \tag{10-15}$$

Caution: The angular speed ω must be expressed in radian measure.

Equation 10-15 tells us that since all points within the rigid body have the same angular speed ω, points with greater radius r have greater linear speed v. Figure 10-11*a* reminds us that the linear velocity is always tangent to the circular path of the point in question.

If the angular speed ω of the rigid body is constant, then Eq. 10-15 tells us that the linear speed v of any point within it is also constant. Thus, each point within the body undergoes uniform circular motion. The period of revolution T for the motion of each point and for the rigid body itself is given by

$$T = \frac{2\pi r}{v} \tag{10-16}$$

This equation tells us that the time for one revolution is the distance $2\pi r$ traveled in one revolution divided by the speed at which that distance is traveled. Substituting for v from Eq. 10-15 and canceling r, we find also that

$$T = \frac{2\pi}{\omega} \quad \text{(radian measure)} \tag{10-17}$$

This equivalent equation says that the time for one revolution is the angular distance $2\pi r$ traveled in one revolution divided by the angular speed (or rate) at which that angle is traveled.

The Acceleration

Differentiating Eq. 10-15 with respect to time—again with r held constant—leads to

$$\frac{dv}{dt} = \frac{d\omega}{dt} r. \tag{10-18}$$

Here we run up against a complication. In Eq. 10-18, dv/dt represents only the part of the linear acceleration that is responsible for changes in the *magnitude* v of the linear velocity $\vec{v}$. Like $\vec{v}$, that part of the linear acceleration is tangent to the path of the point in question. We call it the *tangential component* a_t of the linear acceleration of the point, and we write

$$a_t = \alpha r \quad \text{(radian measure)} \tag{10-19}$$

where $\alpha = d\omega/dt$. *Caution:* The angular acceleration α in Eq. 10-19 must be expressed in radian measure.

In addition, a particle (or point) moving in a circular path has a *radial component* of linear acceleration, $a_r = v^2/r$ (directed radially inward), that is responsible for changes in the *direction* of the linear velocity $\vec{v}$. By substituting for v from Eq. 10-15, we can write this component as

$$a_r = \frac{v^2}{r} = \omega^2 r \qquad \text{(radian measure)} \tag{10-20}$$

Thus, as Fig. 10-11*b* shows, the linear acceleration of a point on a rotating rigid body has, in general, two components. The radially inward component a_r (given by Eq. 10-20) is present whenever the angular velocity of the body is not zero. The tangential component a_t (given by Eq. 10-19) is present whenever the angular acceleration is not zero.

CHECKPOINT 3 A cockroach rides
angular speed of this system (*merry-g*
cockroach have (a) radial acceleration an
ing, does the cockroach have (c) radial ac

Velocity, acceleration and displacement has no meaning for a rigid body undergoing pure rotational motion. But angular parameters are defined.

Sample Problem 10-3

A rigid plate is rotating about an axis passing perpendicular to its plane through point O as shown in Fig. 10-12 Find angular velocity of point B with respect to point A. Angular velocity of rigid body is ω.

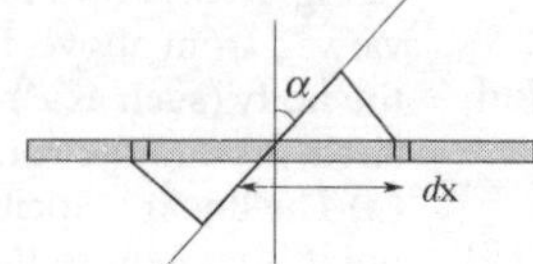

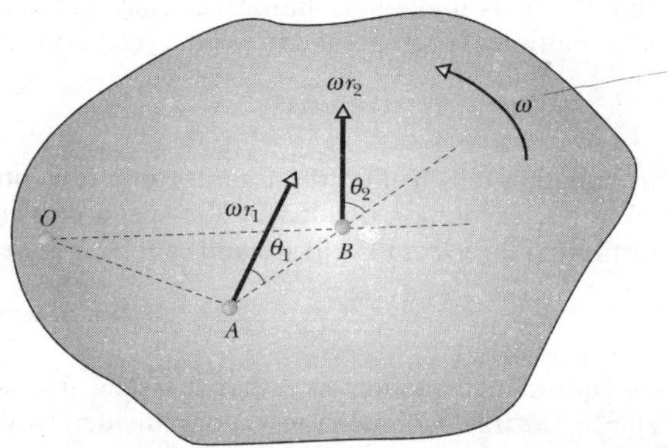

FIG. 10-12 Rigid plate rotating about an axis perpendicular to its plane.

Conceptualize: All particles of rigid body are undergoing circular motion with same angular velocity ω about point O. We cannot say that since A and B have same angular velocity their relative angular velocity will be zero. Looking at the velocities of A and B it can be seen that their relative velocity is not zero, (as their velocity vectors are nonparellel). This means A must move with respect to B, but since they lie on rigid body their distance cannot change. Let's try to recall a motion where distance does not change; there is only one such motion, it is called circular motion. Thus A must be undergoing circular motion with respect to B. If we use same argument for B, we can say B is undergoing circular motion. Since our choice of A and B is random we can genralize and say that all the particle lying on rigid body are undergoing circular motion with respect to any particle lying on rigid body.

Conceptualize/Classify: To find relative angular velocity we will use the following steps:

Compute: As shown velocities of A and B will be perpendicular to OA and OB, respectively. Let's say $\vec{v}_A$ makes angle θ_1, with AB and $\vec{v}_B$ makes angle θ_2 with AB. For triangle OAB, we can say

$$\angle B = \frac{\pi}{2} - \theta_2$$

$$\angle A = \frac{\pi}{2} + \theta_1$$

To use Eq. ( ) we need compound of velocity of B with respect to A perpendicular to AB.

$$V_{\perp A} = \omega r_1 \sin\theta_1 \quad (r_1 = OA)$$

$$V_{\perp B} = \omega r_2 \sin\theta_2 \quad (r_2 = OB)$$

Hence angular velocity of B with respect to A is $\omega_{B/A}$

$$\omega_{B/A} = \frac{\omega r_2 \sin\theta_2 - \omega r_1 \sin\theta_1}{AB}$$

We can write projection formula

$$AB = OA \cos A + OB \cos B$$

$$= -r_1 \cos\left(\frac{\pi}{2} + \theta_1\right) + r_2 \cos\left(\frac{\pi}{2} - \theta_2\right)$$

Hence, $$AB = r_1 \sin \theta_1 + r_2 \sin \theta_2$$

thus $$\omega_{B/A} = \omega$$

Conclude: We can see that the answer is independent of choice of points A and B. Thus, angular velocity of a particle lying on rigid body with respect to another particle is same as angular velocity of rigid body. It is important to note that even sense is same.

In Case Of: Let's find relative velocity component of B with respect to A along AB.

Solution: $V_{\parallel} = \omega r_2 \cos \theta_2 - \omega r_1 \cos \theta_1$

Using sine rule it can be shown

$$\frac{r_2}{\sin\left(\frac{\pi}{2} + \theta_1\right)} = \frac{r_1}{\sin\left(\frac{\pi}{2} - \theta_2\right)}$$

Hence $$r_2 \cos \theta_2 = r_1 \cos \theta_1$$

Thus $$V_{\parallel} = 0$$

This is expected as distance between particles lying on rigid body cannot change, so component of relative velocity along line joining is zero.

In Case Of: Angular velocity of O with respect to A.

Solution: Its trivial to show that velocity of O with respect to A is ωr, and it is perpendicular to OA.

$$\omega_{O/A} = \frac{\omega r_1}{r_1} = \omega$$

Thus A is rotating with angular velocity ω about O and O is rotating with angular veocity ω about A.

10-7 | Kinetic Energy of Rotation

The rapidly rotating blade of a table saw certainly has kinetic energy due to that rotation. How can we express the energy? We cannot apply the familiar formula $K = \frac{1}{2}mv^2$ to the saw as a whole because that would give us the kinetic energy only of the saw's center of mass, which is zero.

Instead, we shall treat the table saw (and any other rotating rigid body) as a collection of particles with different speeds. We can then add up the kinetic energies of all the particles to find the kinetic energy of the body as a whole. In this way we obtain, for the kinetic energy of a rotating body,

$$K = \tfrac{1}{2}m_1v_1^2 + \tfrac{1}{2}m_2v_2^2 + \tfrac{1}{2}m_3v_3^2 + \cdots$$

$$= \sum \tfrac{1}{2}m_iv_i^2 \qquad (10\text{-}21)$$

in which m_i is the mass of the ith particle and v_i is its speed. The sum is taken over all the particles in the body.

The problem with Eq. 10-21 is that v_i is not the same for all particles. We solve this problem by substituting for v from Eq. $v = \omega r$, so that we have

$$K = \sum \tfrac{1}{2}m_i(\omega r_i)^2 = \tfrac{1}{2}\left(\sum m_ir_i^2\right)\omega^2 \qquad (10\text{-}22)$$

in which ω *is* the same for all particles.

The quantity in parentheses on the right side of Eq. 10-22 tells us how the mass of the rotating body is distributed about its axis of rotation. We call that quantity the **rotational inertia** (or **moment of inertia**) I of the body with respect to the axis of rotation. It is a constant for a particular rigid body and a particular rotation axis. (That axis must always be specified if the value of I is to be meaningful.)

We may now write

$$I = \sum m_ir_i^2 \quad \text{(rotational inertia)} \qquad (10\text{-}23)$$

and substitute into Eq. 10-22, obtaining

$$K = \tfrac{1}{2}I\omega^2 \qquad \text{(radian measure)} \qquad (10\text{-}24)$$

as the expression we seek. Because we have used the relation $v = \omega r$ in deriving Eq. 10-24, ω must be expressed in radian measure. The SI unit for I is the kilogram–square meter ($kg \cdot m^2$).

Equation 10-24, which gives the kinetic energy of a rigid body in pure rotation, is the angular equivalent of the formula $K = \tfrac{1}{2}Mv_{com}^2$, which gives the kinetic energy of a rigid body in pure translation. In both formulas there is a factor of 1/2. Where mass M appears in one equation, I (which involves both mass and its distribution) appears in the other. Finally, each equation contains as a factor the square of a speed—translational or rotational as appropriate. The kinetic energies of translation and of rotation are not different kinds of energy. They are both kinetic energy, expressed in ways that are appropriate to the motion at hand.

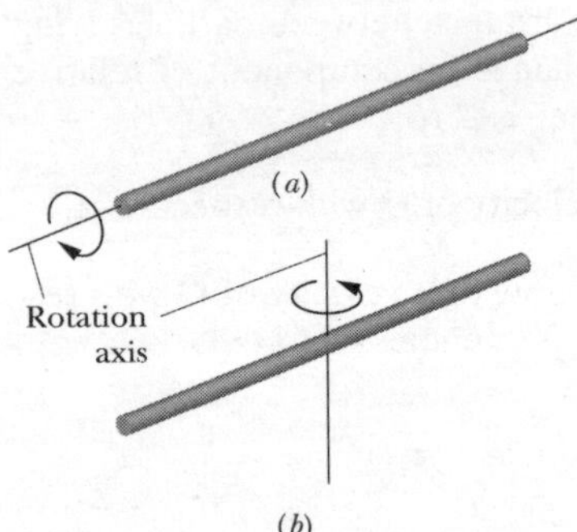

FIG. 10-13 A long rod is much easier to rotate about (*a*) its central (longitudinal) axis than about (*b*) an axis through its center and perpendicular to its length. The reason for the difference is that the mass is distributed closer to the rotation axis in (*a*) than in (*b*).

We noted previously that the rotational inertia of a rotating body involves not only its mass but also how that mass is distributed. Here is an example that you can literally feel. Rotate a long, fairly heavy rod (a pole, a length of lumber, or something similar), first around its central (longitudinal) axis (Fig. 10-13*a*) and then around an axis perpendicular to the rod and through the center (Fig. 10-13*b*). Both rotations involve the very same mass, but the first rotation is much easier than the second. The reason is that the mass is distributed much closer to the rotation axis in the first rotation. As a result, the rotational inertia of the rod is much smaller in Fig. 10-13*a* than in Fig. 10-13*b*. In general, smaller rotational inertia means easier rotation.

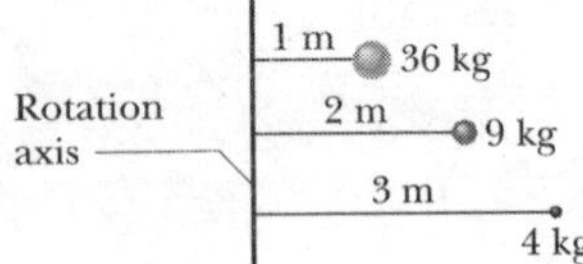

CHECKPOINT 4 The figure shows three small spheres that rotate about a vertical axis. The perpendicular distance between the axis and the center of each sphere is given. Rank the three spheres according to their rotational inertia about that axis, greatest first.

10-8 | Calculating the Moment of Inertia

If a rigid body consists of a few particles, we can calculate its rotational inertia about a given rotation axis with Eq. $I = \sum m_i r_i^2$; that is, we can find the product mr^2 for each particle and then sum the products. (Recall that r is the perpendicular distance a particle is from the given rotation axis.)

If a rigid body consists of a great many adjacent particles (it is *continuous,* like a Frisbee), using Eq. 10-23 would require a computer. Thus, instead, we replace the sum in Eq. 10-23 with an integral and define the rotational inertia of the body as

$$I = \int r^2\, dm \qquad \text{(rotational inertia, continuous body)} \qquad (10\text{-}25)$$

Table 10-2 gives the results of such integration for nine common body shapes and the indicated axes of rotation.

Parallel-Axis Theorem

Suppose we want to find the rotational inertia I of a body of mass M about a given axis. In principle, we can always find I with the integration of Eq. 10-25. However, there is a shortcut if we happen to already know

TABLE 10-2

Some Rotational Inertias

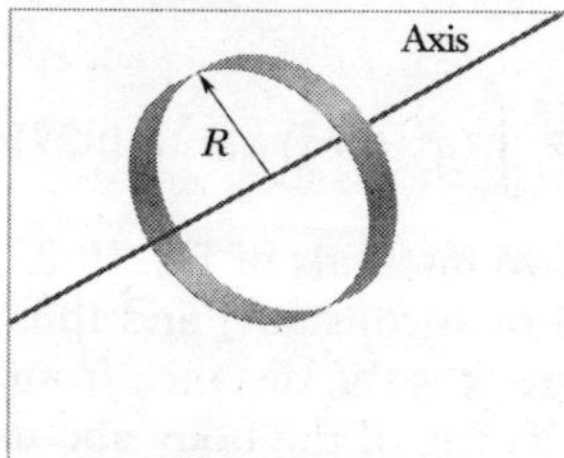 Hoop about central axis $I = MR^2$ (a)	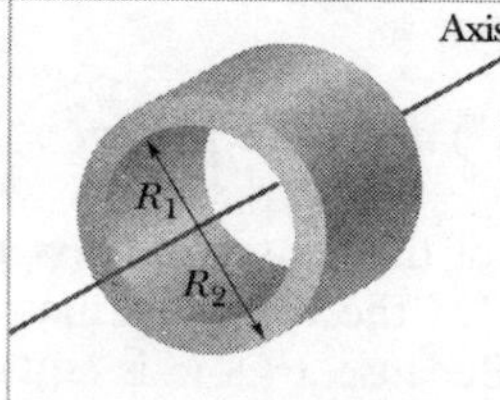 Annular cylinder (or ring) about central axis $I = \frac{1}{2}M(R_1^2 + R_2^2)$ (b)	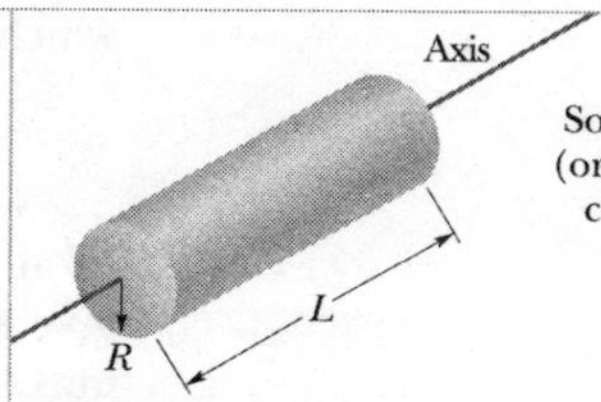 Solid cylinder (or disk) about central axis $I = \frac{1}{2}MR^2$ (c)
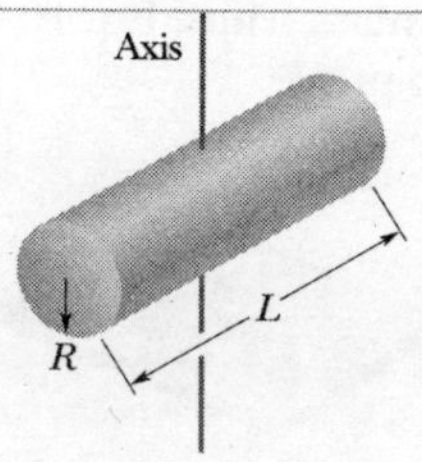 Solid cylinder (or disk) about central diameter $I = \frac{1}{4}MR^2 + \frac{1}{12}ML^2$ (d)	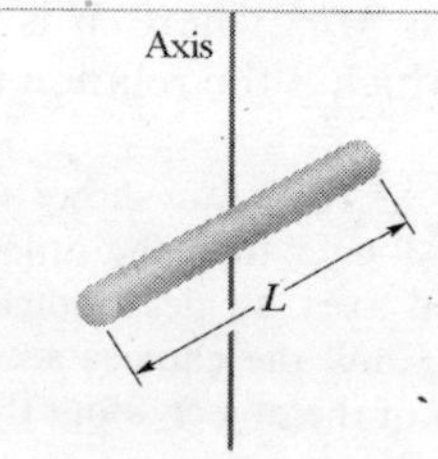 Thin rod about axis through center perpendicular tolength $I = \frac{1}{12}ML^2$ (e)	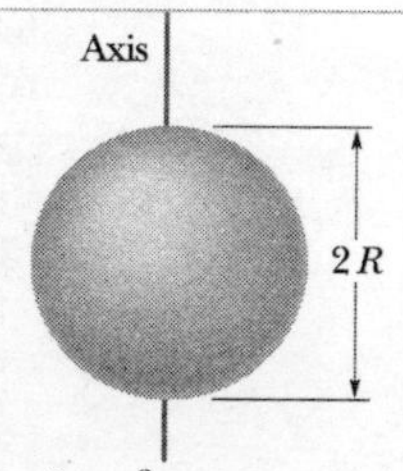 Solid sphere about any diameter $I = \frac{2}{5}MR^2$ (f)
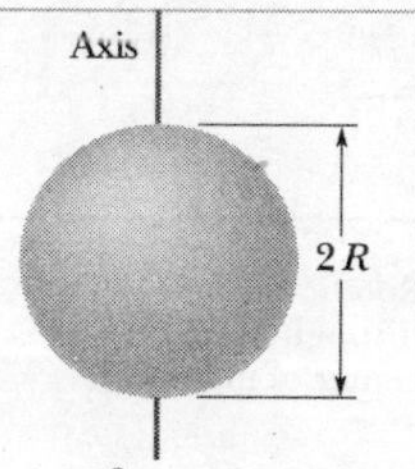 Thin spherical shell about any diameter $I = \frac{2}{3}MR^2$ (g)	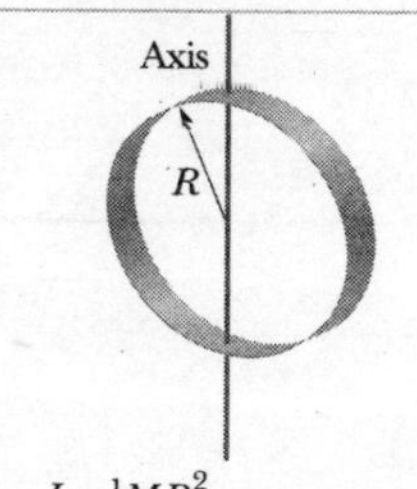 Hoop about any diameter $I = \frac{1}{2}MR^2$ (h)	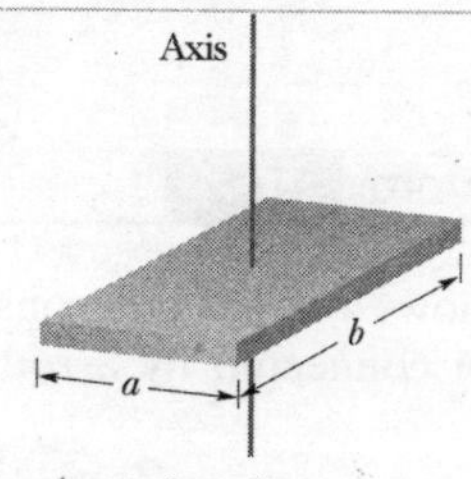 Slab about perpendicular axis through center $I = \frac{1}{12}M(a^2 + b^2)$ (i)

the rotational inertia I_{com} of the body about a *parallel* axis that extends through the body's center of mass. Let h be the perpendicular distance between the given axis and the axis through the center of mass (remember these two axes must be parallel). Then the rotational inertia I about the given axis is

$$I = I_{com} + Mh^2 \quad \text{(parallel-axis theorem)} \tag{10-26}$$

This equation is known as the **parallel-axis theorem.** We shall now prove it and then put it to use in Checkpoint 5 and Sample Problem 10-4.

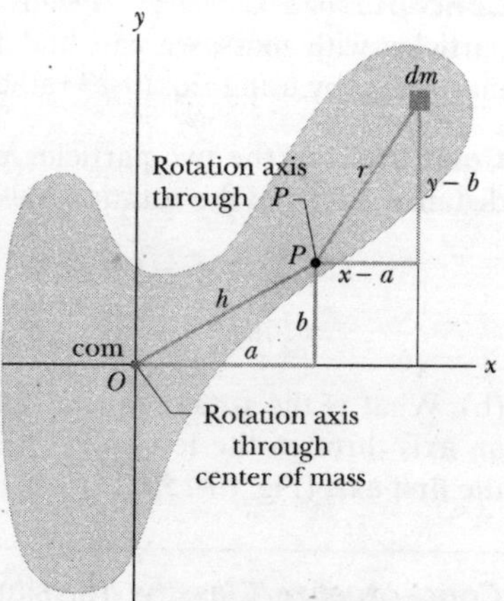

FIG. 10-14 A rigid body in cross section, with its center of mass at O. The parallel-axis theorem (Eq. 10-26) relates the rotational inertia of the body about an axis through O to that about a parallel axis through a point such as P, a distance h from the body's center of mass. Both axes are perpendicular to the plane of the figure.

Proof of the Parallel-Axis Theorem

Let O be the center of mass of the arbitrarily shaped body shown in cross section in Fig. 10-14. Place the origin of the coordinates at O. Consider an axis through O perpendicular to the plane of the figure, and another axis through point P parallel to the first axis. Let the x and y coordinates of P be a and b.

Let dm be a mass element with the general coordinates x and y. The rotational inertia of the body about the axis through P is then, from Eq. 10-25,

$$I = \int r^2\,dm = \int [(x-a)^2 + (y-b)^2]\,dm$$

which we can rearrange as

$$I = \int (x^2+y^2)\,dm - 2a\int x\,dm - 2b\int y\,dm + \int (a^2+b^2)\,dm \quad (10\text{-}27)$$

From the definition of the center of mass, the middle two integrals of Eq. 10-27 give the coordinates of the center of mass (multiplied by a constant) and thus must each be zero. Because $x^2 + y^2$ is equal to R^2, where R is the distance from O to dm, the first integral is simply I_{com}, the rotational inertia of the body about an axis through its center of mass. Inspection of Fig. 10-14 shows that the last term in Eq. 10-27 is Mh^2, where M is the body's total mass. Thus, Eq. 10-27 reduces to Eq. 10-26, which is the relation that we set out to prove.

CHECKPOINT 5 The figure shows a book-like object (one side is longer than the other) and four choices of rotation axes, all perpendicular to the face of the object. Rank the choices according to the rotational inertia of the object about the axis, greatest first.

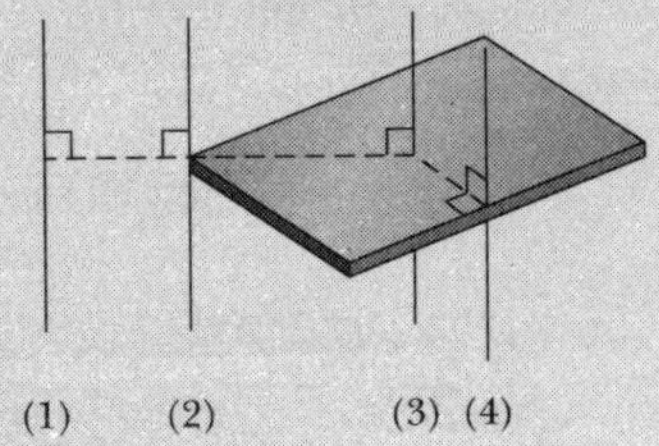

Sample Problem 10-4

Figure 10-15a shows a rigid body consisting of two particles of mass m connected by a rod of length L and negligible mass.

(a) What is the rotational inertia I_{com} about an axis through the center of mass, perpendicular to the rod as shown?

Conceptualize/Classify: Because we have only two particles with mass, we can find the body's rotational inertia I_{com} by using Eq. 10-23 rather than by integration.

Compute: For the two particles, each at perpendicular distance ½L from the rotation axis, we have

$$I = \sum m_i r_i^2 = (m)(\tfrac{1}{2}L)^2 + (m)(\tfrac{1}{2}L)^2$$

$$= \tfrac{1}{2}mL^2 \qquad \text{(Answer)}$$

(b) What is the rotational inertia I of the body about an axis through the left end of the rod and parallel to the first axis (Fig. 10-15b)?

Conceptualize/Classify: This situation is simple enough for us to find I using either of two techniques. The first is similar to the one used in part (a). The other, more powerful one, is to apply the parallel-axis theorem.

First technique: We calculate I as in part (a), except here the perpendicular distance r_i is zero for the particle on the left and L for the particle on the right. Now Eq. 10-23 gives us

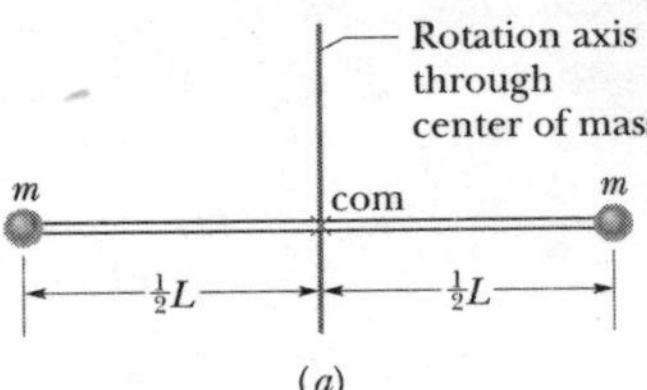

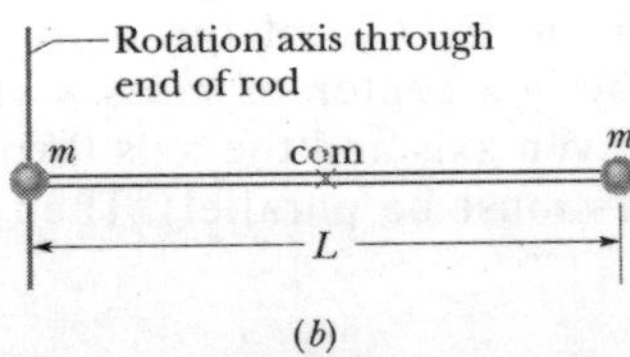

FIG. 10-15 A rigid body consisting of two particles of mass m joined by a rod of negligible mass.

$$I = m(0)^2 + mL^2 = mL^2 \qquad \text{(Answer)}$$

Second technique: Because we already know I_{com} about an axis through the center of mass and because the axis here is parallel to that "com axis," we can apply the parallel-axis theorem (Eq. 10-26). We find

$$I = I_{com} + Mh^2 = \tfrac{1}{2}mL^2 + (2m)(\tfrac{1}{2}L)^2$$

$$= mL^2 \qquad \text{(Answer)}$$

Conclude: The answer is same from both the techniques as expected.

Sample Problem 10-5

Figure 10-16*a* shows a thin, uniform rod of mass M and length L, on an x axis with the origin at the rod's center.

(a) What is the rotational inertia of the rod about the perpendicular rotation axis through the center?

Conceptualize/Classify: Because the rod is uniform, its center of mass is at its center. Therefore, we are looking for I_{com}.

Compute: Because the rod is a continuous object, we must use the integral of Eq. 10-25,

$$I = \int r^2\,dm \tag{10-28}$$

to find the rotational inertia.

Compute: We want to integrate with respect to coordinate x (not mass m as indicated in the integral), so we must relate the mass dm of an element of the rod to its length dx along the rod. (Such an element is shown in Fig. 10-16*a*.) Because the rod is uniform, the ratio of mass to length is the same for all the elements and for the rod as a whole. Thus, we can write

$$\frac{\text{Element's mass } dm}{\text{Element's length } dx} = \frac{\text{Rod's mass } M}{\text{Rod's length } L}$$

or

$$dm = \frac{M}{L}\,dx$$

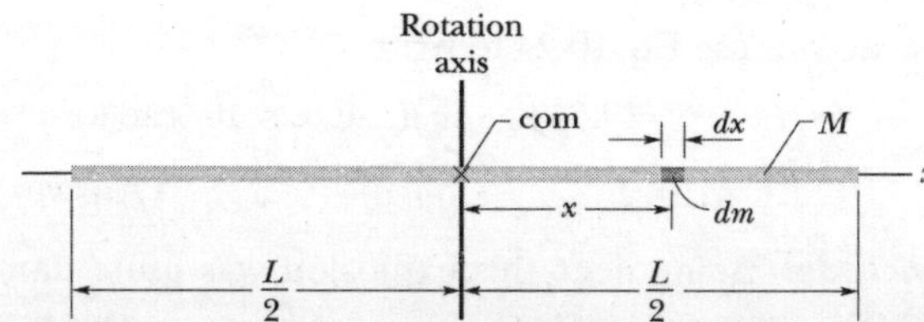

FIG. 10-16 (*a*) A uniform rod of length L and mass M. An element of mass dm and length dx is represented.

We can now substitute this result for dm and x for r in Eq. 10-28. Then we integrate from end to end of the rod (from $x = -L/2$ to $x = L/2$) to include all the elements. We find

$$I = \int_{x=-L/2}^{x=+L/2} x^2\left(\frac{M}{L}\right)dx$$

$$= \frac{M}{3L}\Big[x^3\Big]_{-L/2}^{+L/2} = \frac{M}{3L}\left[\left(\frac{L}{2}\right)^3 - \left(-\frac{L}{2}\right)^3\right]$$

$$= \tfrac{1}{12}ML^2 \qquad \text{(Answer)}$$

This agrees with the result given in Table 10-2*e*.

(b) What is the rod's rotational inertia I about a new rotation axis that is perpendicular to the rod and through the left end?

Conceptualize/Classify: We can find I by shifting the origin of the x axis to the left end of the rod and then integrating from $x = 0$ to $x = L$. However, here we shall use a more powerful (and easier) technique by applying the parallel-axis theorem (Eq. 10-26).

Compute: If we place the axis at the rod's end so that it is parallel to the axis through the center of mass, then we can use the parallel-axis theorem (Eq. 10-26). We know from part (a) that I_{com} is $\frac{1}{12}ML^2$. From Fig. 10-16*a*, the perpendicular distance h between the new rotation axis and the center of mass is $\frac{1}{2}L$. Equation 10-26 then gives us

$$I = I_{com} + Mh^2 = \tfrac{1}{12}ML^2 + (M)(\tfrac{1}{2}L)^2$$

$$= \tfrac{1}{3}ML^2 \qquad \text{(Answer)}$$

Actually, this result holds for any axis through the left or right end that is perpendicular to the rod, whether it is parallel to the axis as shown in Fig. 10-16*a* or not.

(c) Find moment of inertia of the uniform red about axis VV' passing through center at on angle α with the red.

Conceptualize: $dI = \dfrac{M}{L}dx\,(x\sin\alpha)^2$

Classify: Let's take an element of length dx at distance x from center. The perpendicular distance from axis is $x\sin\theta$.

Moment of inertia of the element is

$$dI = \frac{M}{L}(x\sin\alpha)^2\,dx$$

Integrating we get

$$I = \frac{M}{L}\sin^2\alpha\int_{-L/2}^{L/2} x^2\,dx$$

$$= \frac{M}{L}\sin^2\alpha \times \frac{1}{3} \times \frac{L^3}{4}$$

$$= \frac{1}{12}ML^2\sin^2\alpha$$

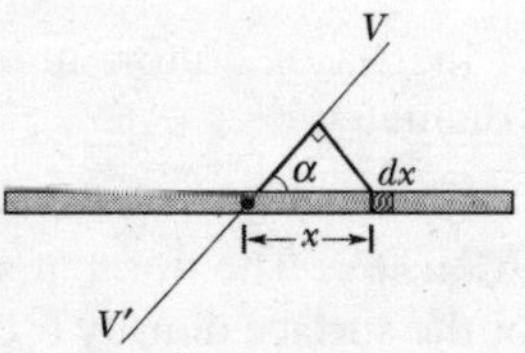

FIG. 10-16 (*b*) Moment of inertia of element dx.

Sample Problem 10-6

Large machine components that undergo prolonged, high-speed rotation are first examined for the possibility of failure in a *spin test system.* In this system, a component is *spun up* (brought up to high speed) while inside a cylindrical arrangement of lead bricks and containment liner, all within a steel shell that is closed by a lid clamped into place. If the rotation causes the component to shatter, the soft lead bricks are supposed to catch the pieces for later analysis.

FIG. 10-17 Some of the destruction caused by the explosion of a rapidly rotating steel disk. *(Courtesy Test Devices, Inc.)*

In 1985, Test Devices, Inc. (www.testdevices.com) was spin testing a sample of a solid steel rotor (a disk) of mass M = 272 kg and radius R = 38.0 cm. When the sample reached an angular speed ω of 14 000 rev/min, the test engineers heard a dull thump from the test system, which was located one floor down and one room over from them. Investigating, they found that lead bricks had been thrown out in the hallway leading to the test room, a door to the room had been hurled into the adjacent parking lot, one lead brick had shot from the test site through the wall of a neighbor's kitchen, the structural beams of the test building had been damaged, the concrete floor beneath the spin chamber had been shoved downward by about 0.5 cm, and the 900 kg lid had been blown upward through the ceiling and had then crashed back onto the test equipment (Fig. 10-17). The exploding pieces had not penetrated the room of the test engineers only by luck.

How much energy was released in the explosion of the rotor?

Conceptualize: The released energy was equal to the rotational kinetic energy K of the rotor just as it reached the angular speed of 14 000 rev/min.

Classify: We can find K with Eq. $K = \frac{1}{2} I\omega^2$, but first we need an expression for the rotational inertia I. Because the rotor was a disk that rotated like a merry-go-round, I is given by the expression in Table 10-2c ($I = \frac{1}{2} MR^2$).

Compute: Thus, we have

$$I = \tfrac{1}{2}MR^2 = \tfrac{1}{2}(272\text{ kg})(0.38\text{ m})^2 = 19.64\text{ kg}\cdot\text{m}^2$$

The angular speed of the rotor was

$$\omega = (14\,000\text{ rev/min})(2\pi\text{ rad/rev})\left(\frac{1\text{ min}}{60\text{ s}}\right)$$
$$= 1.466 \times 10^3\text{ rad/s}$$

Now we can use Eq. 10-24 to write

$$K = \tfrac{1}{2}I\omega^2 = \tfrac{1}{2}(19.64\text{ kg}\cdot\text{m}^2)(1.466 \times 10^3\text{ rad/s})^2$$
$$= 2.1 \times 10^7\text{ J} \qquad \text{(Answer)}$$

Conclude: Being near this explosion was quite dangerous.

CHECKPOINT 6 Find the moment of inertia of a half uniform ring (mass m, radius r) about center.

Sample Problem 10-7

Find moment of inertia of hollow uniform sphere of mass M about a diameter.

Conceptualize/Classify: The total mass M is given by the integral of the surface density σ over the area of the shell $M = \int \sigma dA$. Since the shell is homogeneous, the surface density σ is constant. Therefore, $M = \sigma\int dA = \sigma A = 4\pi R^2\sigma$ This implies that $\sigma = M/4\pi R^2$.

Compute: Refer to Fig. 10-18. The hoop shown has a radius r = R sin θ and therefore a circumference of $2\pi R$ sin θ. The width of the hoop is $R\,d\theta$, so the area

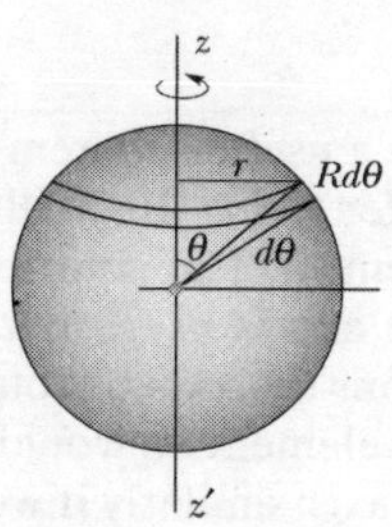

FIG. 10-18 Hollow uniform sphere of mass M.

$dA = (2\pi R \sin\theta)(R\, d\theta)$, and the mass $dM = \sigma dA = (M/4\pi R^2)(2R^2 \sin\theta\, d\theta) = (M/2)\sin\theta\, d\theta$.

We use dI to denote the moment of inertia of the hoop about the axis ZZ'. The perpendicular distance from the axis to each part of the hoop is $R\sin\theta$. Therefore $dI = (R\sin\theta)^2$ and $dM = (MR^2/2)\sin^3\theta\, d\theta$.

The moment of inertia of the entire shell is the moment of inertia of the various hoops.

$$dI = \frac{M}{2}\sin\theta\, d\theta\, R^2 \sin^2\theta$$

Integrating over whole sphere:

$$I = \frac{MR^2}{2}\int_0^{\pi} \sin^3\theta\, d\theta$$

We can write

$$\sin^3\theta = \frac{-\sin 3\theta + 3\sin\theta}{4}$$

$$I = \frac{MR^2}{8}\left[-\int_0^{\pi}\sin 3\theta\, d\theta + 3\int_0^{\pi}\sin\theta\, d\theta\right]$$

$$= \frac{MR^2}{8}\left[-\frac{2}{3} + 6\right]$$

$$= \frac{2}{3}MR^2 \qquad \text{(Answer)}$$

Conclude: We have derived the result by adding moment of inertia of rings.

Sample Problem 10-8

Find the moment of inertia of solid sphere about a diameter as shown in Fig. 10-19.

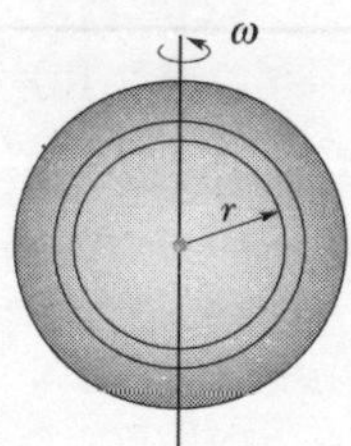

FIG. 10-19 Solid sphere.

Conceptualize/Classify: The sphere can be considered as made up of many concentric thin shells. From previous example, a spherical subshell of radius r has moment of inertia:

$$dI = \frac{2}{3}dmr^2$$

We can now solve by integrating over the whole volume.

Compute:

$$dm = \frac{M}{\frac{4}{3}\pi R^3} \times 4\pi r^2 dr$$

$$= \frac{3M}{R^3} r^2 dr$$

$$dI = \frac{2}{3} \times \frac{3M}{R^3} r^2 (dr) r^2$$

$$= \frac{2M}{R^3}\int_0^R r^4 dr$$

$$= \frac{2MR^2}{5} \qquad \text{(Answer)}$$

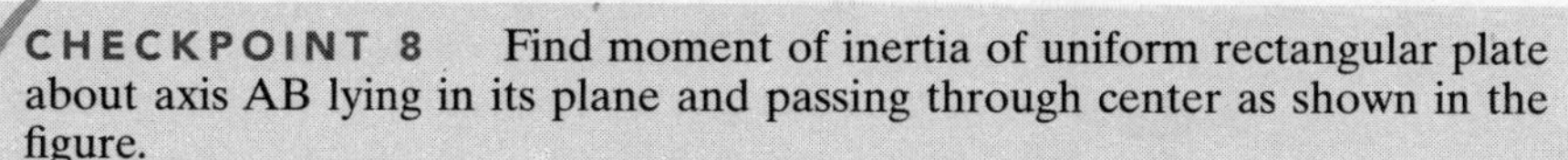

CHECKPOINT 7 Find moment of inertia of a uniform solid sphere about a tangent.

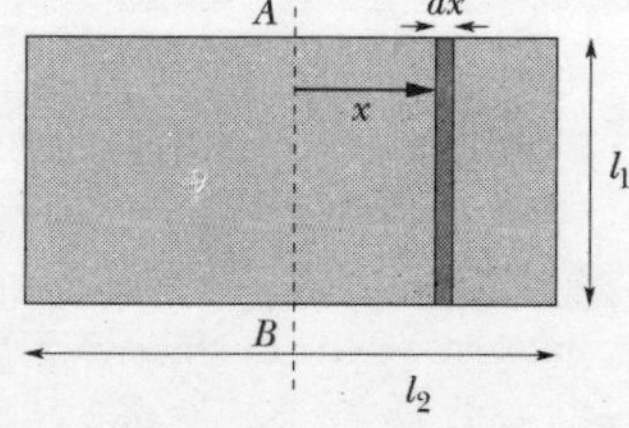

CHECKPOINT 8 Find moment of inertia of uniform rectangular plate about axis AB lying in its plane and passing through center as shown in the figure.

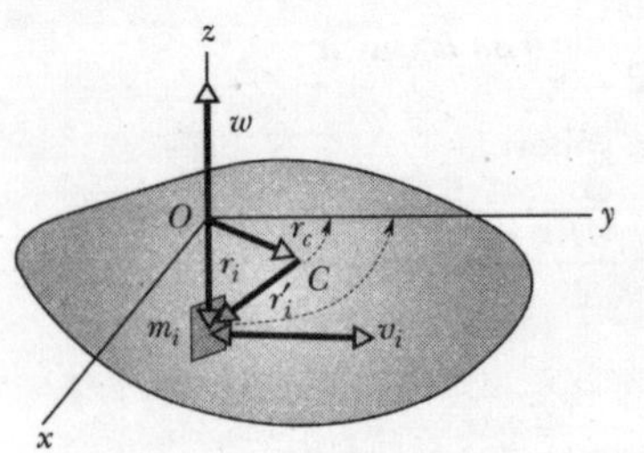

FIG. 10-20 Rotating slab and its representative mass element.

Perpendicular Axis Theorem

Before proceeding further, we demonstrate a useful theorem about moments of inertia for thin, slablike objects. We may refer to Fig. 10-20 illustrating the rotating slab and its representative mass element m. The contribution of m_i to the moment of inertia I_z with respect to the z axis is $m_i r_i^2$, that is the mass of the particle times the square of its distance from the axis of rotation. If we should consider rotation about the x axis, the mass element m_i would contribute $m_i y_i^2$ to the moment of inertia with respect to the x axis; similarly it would give $m_i x_i^2$ with respect to the y axis. Thus,

$$I_x = \sum m_i y_i^2$$

$$I_y = \sum m_i x_i^2$$

By addition we obtain

$$I_x + I_y = \sum m_i (x_i^2 + y_i^2) = \sum m_i r_i^2 = I_z$$

This proves the perpendicular axis theorem, true for plane, thin rigid bodies.

Sample Problem 10-9 Build your skill

Use the perpendicular-axis theorem to relate the moment of inertia of a thin uniform circular disk (about any diameter) to its moment of inertia about find its central axis.

Solution: A thin uniform-density disk of radius R is confined to the xy plane, as shown in Fig. 10-21. The perpendicular-axis theorem implies that $I_{xO} = I_{yO} = I_{zO}$. But by symmetry $I_{xO} = I_{yO} = I_{zd} I_d$ denotes the moment of inertia about any diameter. Therefore, we have $2I_d = I_{zO}$. The moment of inertia of a solid cylinder or disk of radius R about the symmetry axis is $\frac{1}{2}MR^2$. Thus,

$$I_{zo} = \frac{1}{2}MR^2$$

and

$$I_d = \frac{1}{4}MR^2$$

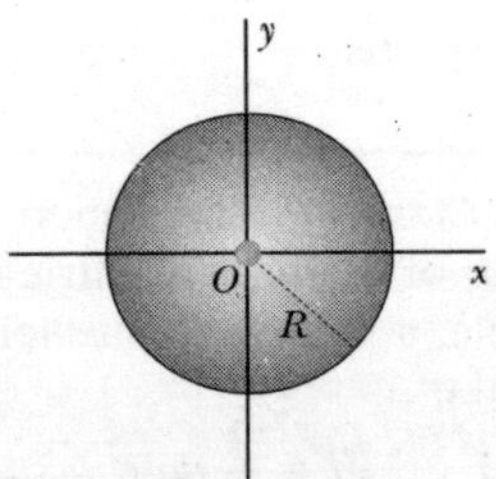

FIG. 10-21 Thin uniform circular disc.

CHECKPOINT 9 Find moment of inertia of a uniform ring about chord AA' at distance $R/2$ from center.

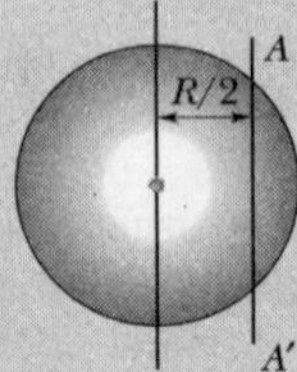

Sample Problem 10-10

Find moment of inertia of a uniform rectangular plate about axis zz' passing through center and perpendicular to the plane plate shown in Fig. 10-22*a*.

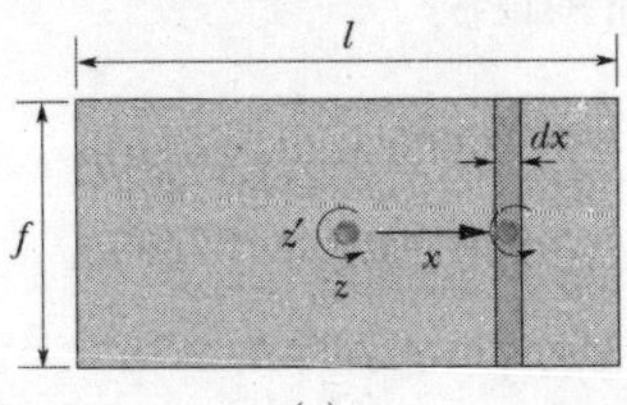

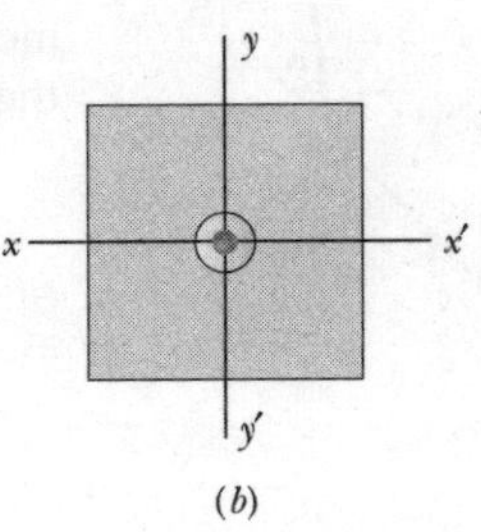

FIG. 10-22a Uniform rectangular plate in *x-y* plane.

$$I_{xx'} = \frac{Mf^2}{12}; \quad I_{yy} = \frac{Ml^2}{12}$$

Conceptualize: Imagine twirling your note book about its center by keeping index finger of two hands on two faces of the note book.

Classify: This is a simple problem using theorem of perpendicular axes (Fig. 10-22*b*).

Hence

$$I_{zz} = I_{xx} + I_{yy}$$

$$I_{zz'} = M\left(\frac{f^2 l^2}{12}\right)$$

CHECKPOINT 10 Find moment of inertia in above case about axes 7 and 8 lying in plane of the plate.

Radius of Gyration

$K = \sqrt{\dfrac{I}{M}}$ When I is MI about an axis, K is radius of gyration about that axis.

10-9 | Torque

A doorknob is located as far as possible from the door's hinge line for a good reason. If you want to open a heavy door, you must certainly apply a force; that alone, however, is not enough. Where you apply that force and in what direction you push are also important. If you apply your force nearer to the hinge line than the knob, or at any angle other than 90° to the plane of the door, you must use a greater force to move the door than if you apply the force at the knob and perpendicular to the door's plane.

Figure 10-23*a* shows a cross section of a body that is free to rotate about an axis passing through O and perpendicular to the cross section. A force $\vec{F}$ is applied at point P, whose position relative to O is defined by a position vector $\vec{r}$. The directions of vectors $\vec{F}$ and $\vec{r}$ make an angle ϕ with each other. (For simplicity, we consider only forces that have no component parallel to the rotation axis; thus, $\vec{F}$ is in the plane of the page.)

To determine how $\vec{F}$ results in a rotation of the body around the rotation axis, we resolve $\vec{F}$ into two components (Fig. 10-23*b*). One component, called the *radial component* F_r, points along $\vec{r}$. This component does not cause rotation, because it acts along a line that extends through O. (If you pull on a door parallel to the plane of the door, you do not rotate the door.) The other component of $\vec{F}$, called the *tangential component* F_t, is perpendicular to $\vec{r}$ and has magnitude $F_t = F \sin \phi$. This component *does* cause rotation. (If you pull on a door perpendicular to its plane, you can rotate the door.)

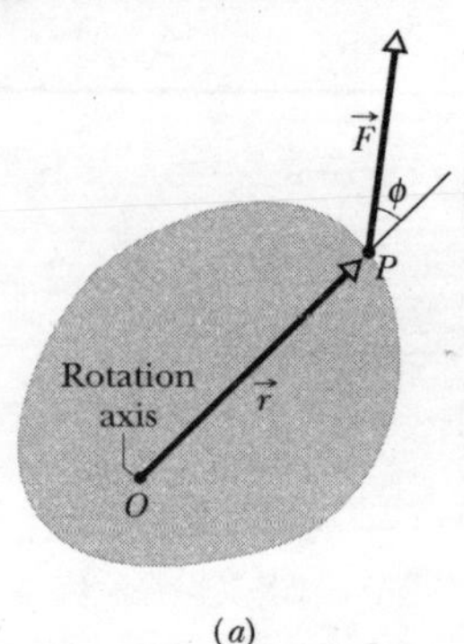

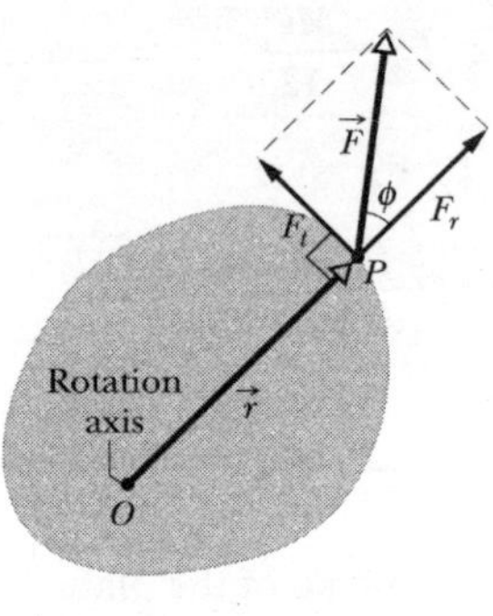

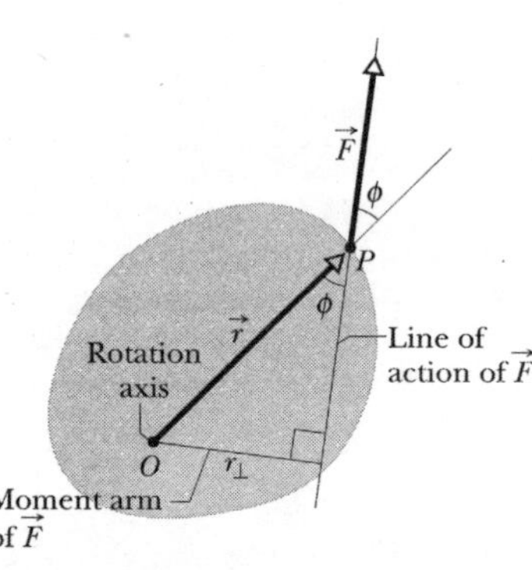

FIG. 10-23 (*a*) A force $\vec{F}$ acts at point P on a rigid body that is free to rotate about an axis through O; the axis is perpendicular to the plane of the cross section shown here. (*b*) The torque due to this force is $(r)(F \sin \phi)$. We can also write it as rF_t, where F_t is the tangential component of $\vec{F}$. (*c*) The torque can also be written as $r_\perp F$, where $r_\perp$ is the moment arm of $\vec{F}$.

The ability of $\vec{F}$ to rotate the body depends not only on the magnitude of its tangential component F_t, but also on just how far from O the force is applied. To include both these factors, we define a quantity called **torque** τ as the product of the two factors and write it as

$$\tau = (r)(F \sin \phi) \tag{10-29}$$

Two equivalent ways of computing the torque are

$$\tau = (r)(F \sin \phi) = rF_t \tag{10-30}$$

and

$$\tau = (r \sin \phi)(F) = r_\perp F \tag{10-31}$$

where $r_\perp$ is the perpendicular distance between the rotation axis at O and an extended line running through the vector $\vec{F}$ (Fig. 10-23*c*). This extended line is called the **line of action** of $\vec{F}$, and $r_\perp$ is called the **moment arm** of $\vec{F}$. Figure 10-23*b* shows that we can describe r, the magnitude of $\vec{r}$, as being the moment arm of the force component F_t.

Torque, which comes from the Latin word meaning "to twist," may be loosely identified as the turning or twisting action of the force $\vec{F}$. When you apply a force to an object—such as a screwdriver or torque wrench—with the purpose of turning that object, you are applying a torque. The SI unit of torque is the newton-meter (N · m). *Caution:* The newton-meter is also the unit of work. Torque and work, however, are quite different quantities and must not be confused. Work is often expressed in joules (1 J = 1 N · m), but torque never is.

In the next section, we shall discuss torque in a general way as being a vector quantity. Here, however, because we consider only rotation around a single axis, we do not need vector notation. Instead, a torque has either a positive or negative value depending on the direction of rotation it would give a body initially at rest: If the body would rotate counterclockwise, the torque is positive. If the object would rotate clockwise, the torque is negative.

Torques obey the superposition principle for forces: When several torques act on a body, the **net torque** (or **resultant torque**) is the sum of the individual torques. The symbol for net torqueis τ_{net}.

CHECKPOINT 11 The figure shows an overhead view of a meter stick that can pivot about the dot at the position marked 20 (for 20 cm). All five forces on the stick are horizontal and have the same magnitude. Rank the forces according to the magnitude of the torque they produce, greatest first.

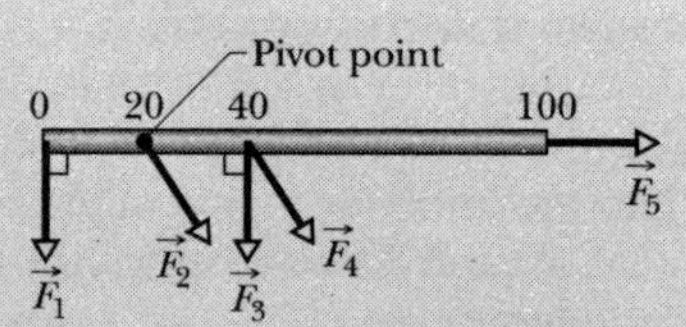

10-10 | Vector Product and Torque

In the previous section, we defined torque τ for a rigid body that can rotate around a fixed axis, with each particle in the body forced to move in a path that is a circle centered on that axis. We now expand the definition of torque to apply it to an individual particle that moves along any path relative to a fixed *point* (rather than a fixed axis). The path need no longer be a circle, and we must write the torque as a vector $\vec{\tau}$ that may have any direction.

Figure 11-24*a* shows such a particle at point A in an xy plane. A single force $\vec{F}$ in that plane acts on the particle, and the particle's position relative to the origin O is given by position vector $\vec{r}$. The torque $\vec{\tau}$ acting on the particle relative to the fixed point O is a vector quantity defined as

$$\vec{\tau} = \vec{r} \times \vec{F} \quad \text{(torque defined)} \tag{10-32}$$

We can evaluate the vector (or cross) product in this definition of $\vec{\tau}$ by using the rules for such products. To find the direction of $\vec{\tau}$, we slide the vector $\vec{F}$ (without changing its direction) until its tail is at the origin O, so that the two vectors in the vector product are tail to tail as in Fig. 10-24*b*. We then use the right-hand rule for vector products, sweeping the fingers of the right hand from $\vec{r}$ (the first vector in the product) into $\vec{F}$ (the second vector). The outstretched right thumb then gives the direction of $\vec{\tau}$. In Fig. 10-24*b*, the direction of $\vec{\tau}$ is in the positive direction of the z axis.

To determine the magnitude of $\vec{\tau}$, we apply the general result of Eq. $c = ab \sin \phi$, finding

$$\tau = rF \sin \phi \tag{10-33}$$

where ϕ is the smaller angle between the directions of $\vec{r}$ and $\vec{F}$ when the vectors are tail to tail. From Fig. 10-24*b*, we see that Eq. 10-33 can be rewritten as

$$\tau = rF_{\perp} \tag{10-34}$$

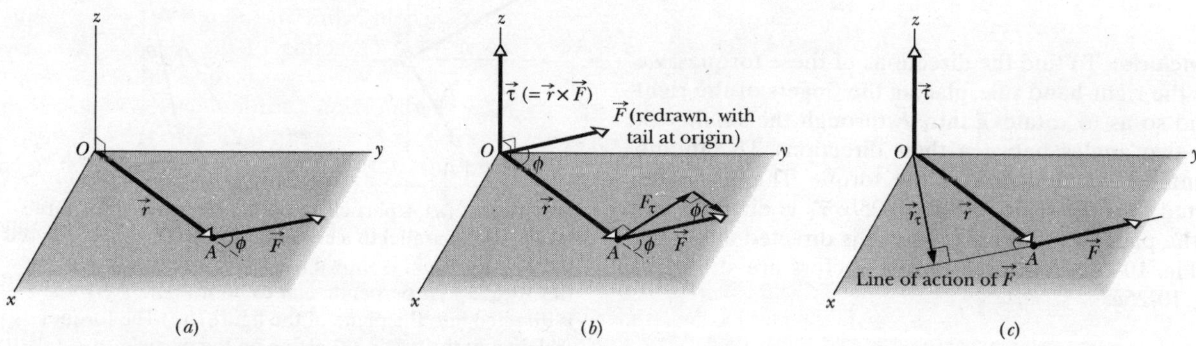

FIG. 10-24 Defining torque. (*a*) A force $\vec{F}$, lying in an xy plane, acts on a particle at point A. (*b*) This force produces a torque $\vec{\tau}\ (= \vec{r} \times \vec{F})$ on the particle with respect to the origin O. By the right-hand rule for vector (cross) products, the torque vector points in the positive direction of z. Its magnitude is given by $rF_{\perp}$ in (*b*) and by $r_{\perp}F$ in (*c*).

where $F_{\perp}\ (= F \sin \phi)$ is the component of $\vec{F}$ perpendicular to $\vec{r}$. From Fig. 10-24*c*, we see that Eq. 10-33 can also be rewritten as

$$\tau = r_{\perp}(F = r \sin \phi) \tag{10-35}$$

where $r_{\perp}\ (= r \sin \phi)$ is the moment arm of $\vec{F}$ (the perpendicular distance between O and the line of action of $\vec{F}$).

CHECKPOINT 12 The position vector $\vec{r}$ of a particle points along the positive direction of a z axis. If the torque on the particle is (a) zero, (b) in the negative direction of x, and (c) in the negative direction of y, in what direction is the force causing the torque?

Sample Problem 10-11

In Fig. 10-25*a*, three forces, each of magnitude 2.0 N, act on a particle. The particle is in the xz plane at point A given by position vector $\vec{r}$, where $r = 3.0$ m and $\theta = 30°$. Force $\vec{F}_1$ is parallel to the x axis, force $\vec{F}_2$ is parallel to the z axis, and force $\vec{F}_3$ is parallel to the y axis. What is the torque, about the origin O, due to each force?

Conceptualize/Classify: Because the three force vectors do not lie in a plane, we cannot evaluate their torques. Instead, we must use vector (or cross) products, with magnitudes given by Eq. $\tau = rF \sin \phi$ and directions given by the right-hand rule for vector products.

Compute: Because we want the torques with respect to the origin O, the vector $\vec{r}$ required for each cross product is the given position vector. To determine the angle ϕ between the direction of $\vec{r}$ and the direction of each force, we shift the force vectors of

Fig. 10-25a, each in turn, so that their tails are at the origin. Figures 10-25b, c, and d, which are direct views of the xz plane, show the shifted force vectors $\vec{F}_1$, $\vec{F}_2$, and $\vec{F}_3$, respectively. (Note how much easier the angles are to see.) In Fig. 10-25d, the angle between the directions of $\vec{r}$ and $\vec{F}_3$ is 90° and the symbol ⊗ means $\vec{F}_3$ is directed into the page. If it were directed out of the page, it would be represented with the symbol ⊙.

Now, applying Eq. 10-33 for each force, we find the magnitudes of the torques to be

$$\tau_1 = rF_1 \sin\phi_1 = (3.0\ \text{m})(2.0\ \text{N})(\sin 150°) = 3.0\ \text{N}\cdot\text{m}$$

$$\tau_2 = rF_2 \sin\phi_2 = (3.0\ \text{m})(2.0\ \text{N})(\sin 120°) = 5.2\ \text{N}\cdot\text{m}$$

and $$\tau_3 = rF_3 \sin\phi_3 = (3.0\ \text{m})(2.0\ \text{N})(\sin 90°) = 6.0\ \text{N}\cdot\text{m} \quad \text{(Answer)}$$

Conclude: To find the directions of these torques, we use the right-hand rule, placing the fingers of the right hand so as to rotate $\vec{r}$ into $\vec{F}$ through the *smaller* of the two angles between their directions. The thumb points in the direction of the torque. Thus $\vec{\tau}_1$ is directed into the page in Fig. 10-25b; $\vec{\tau}_2$ is directed out of the page in Fig. 10-25c; and $\vec{\tau}_3$ is directed as shown in Fig. 10-25d. All three torque vectors are shown in Fig. 10-25e.

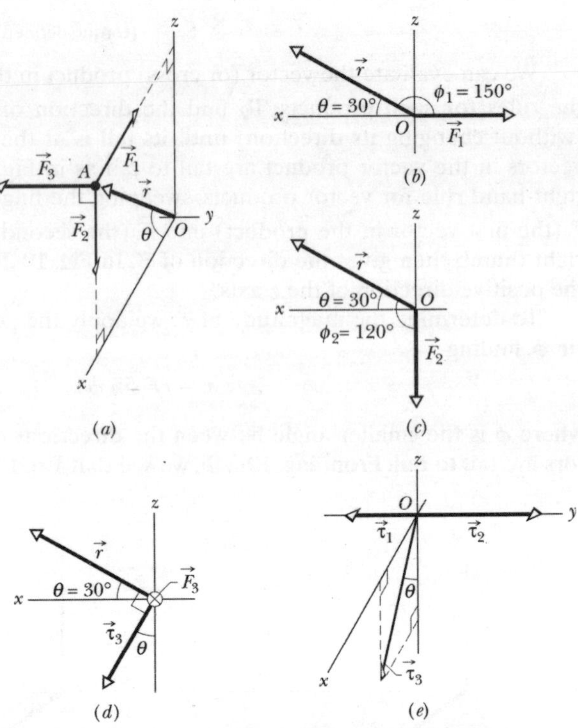

FIG. 10-25 (a) A particle at point A is acted on by three forces, each parallel to a coordinate axis. The angle ϕ (used in finding torque) is shown (b) for $\vec{F}_1$ and (c) for $\vec{F}_2$. (d) Torque $\vec{\tau}_3$ is perpendicular to both $\vec{r}$ and $\vec{F}_3$ (force $\vec{F}_3$ is directed into the plane of the figure). (e) The torques (relative to the origin O) acting on the particle.

PROBLEM-SOLVING TACTICS

Tactic 1:* *Vector Products and Torques Equation 10-33 for torques is our first application of the vector (or cross) product.

Keep in mind that a torque is calculated *with respect to* (or *about*) a point, which must be known if the value of the torque is to be meaningful. Changing the point can change the torque in both magnitude and direction. For example, in Sample Problem 10-1, the torques due to the three forces are calculated about the origin O. You can show that the torques due to the same three forces are all zero if they are calculated about point A (at the position of the particle), because then $r = 0$ for each force.

CHECKPOINT 13 Find torque due to gravity at any time t about point of projection, if a body of mass m is projected at an angle θ with u at $t = 0$.

$$\tau_0 = mg\, u \cos\theta\, t$$

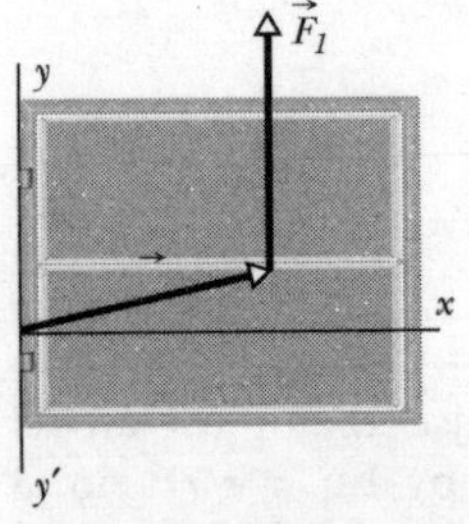

FIG. 10-26 Application of upward force on a door.

Let's again take example of door. We are applying a force F_1 on the door in vertically upward direction (Fig. 10-26).

When we apply this force we know that door has no tendency to rotate about its axis yy', but considering our defination of torque as $\vec{r} \times \vec{F}_1$ we can see that $\vec{\tau}_1$ is coming out to be nonzero. This contradication is arising because the door (and almost all the rigid bodies in this chapter) is constrained to rotate only about one axis, that is, y axis. The torque we are getting due to force $\vec{F}$ has component along this axis. Only those torques which are parallel to a particular axis have ability to produce rotation about that axis. To further understand concept of multiple axes consider rotation of your palm about wrist (Fig. 10-27a).

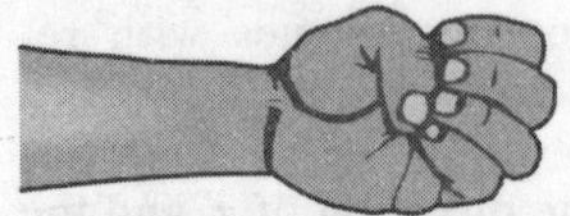

FIG. 10-27a Rotation of palm about wrist.

This complicated motion is in Fig. 10-27*a* result of rotation about mainly two orthogonal axes as shown in Fig. But these complicated rotations are not our focus at this level. We are going to restrict ourselves only on rotations about single axis like rotation of ones forearm about elbow (Fig. 10-27*b*). To conclude, only those components of torque vector that are useful in producing rotation which are parallel to the axis of rotation.

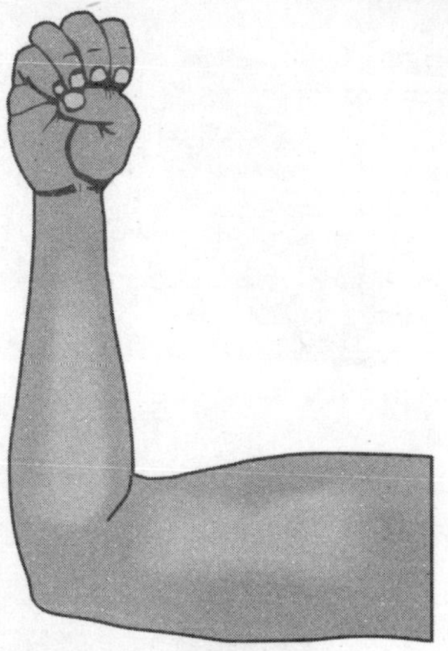

FIG. 10-27*b* Rotation of forearm about elbow

10-11 | The Center of Gravity

The gravitational force on an extended body is the vector sum of the gravitational forces acting on the individual elements (the atoms) of the body. Instead of considering all those individual elements, we can say that

> The gravitational force $\vec{F}_g$ on a body effectively acts at a single point, called the **center of gravity** (cog) of the body.

Here the word "effectively" means that if the forces on the individual elements were somehow turned off and force $\vec{F}_g$ at the center of gravity were turned on, the net force and the net torque (about any point) acting on the body would not change.

Until now, we have assumed that the gravitational force $\vec{F}_g$ acts at the center of mass (com) of the body. This is equivalent to assuming that the center of gravity is at the center of mass. Recall that, for a body of mass M, the force $\vec{F}_g$ is equal to $M\vec{g}$, where $\vec{g}$ is the acceleration that the force would produce if the body were to fall freely. In the proof that follows, we show that

> If $\vec{g}$ is the same for all elements of a body, then the body's center of gravity (cog) is coincident with the body's center of mass (com).

This is approximately true for everyday objects because $\vec{g}$ varies only a little along Earth's surface and decreases in magnitude only slightly with altitude. Thus, for objects like a mouse or a moose, we have been justified in assuming that the gravitational force acts at the center of mass. After the following proof, we shall resume that assumption.

Proof

First, we consider the individual elements of the body. Figure 10-28*a* shows an extended body, of mass M, and one of its elements, of mass m_i. A gravitational force $\vec{F}_{gi}$ acts on each such element and is equal to $m_i\vec{g}_i$. The subscript on $\vec{g}_i$ means $\vec{g}_i$ is the gravitational acceleration *at the location of the element i* (it can be different for other elements).

In Fig. 10-28*a*, each force $\vec{F}_{gi}$ produces a torque τ_i on the element about the origin O, with moment arm x_i. Using Eq. $\tau = r_\perp F$, we can write torque τ_i as

$$\tau_i = x_i F_{gi} \tag{10-36}$$

The net torque on all the elements of the body is then

$$\tau_{\text{net}} = \sum \tau_i = \sum x_i F_{gi} \tag{10-37}$$

Next, we consider the body as a whole. Figure 10-28*b* shows the gravitational force $\vec{F}_g$ acting at the body's center of gravity. This force produces a torque τ on the body about O, with moment arm x_{cog}. Again using Eq. $\tau = r_\perp F$, we can write this torque as

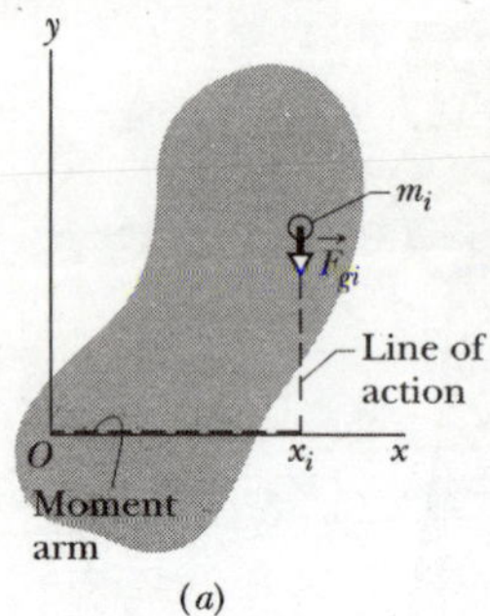

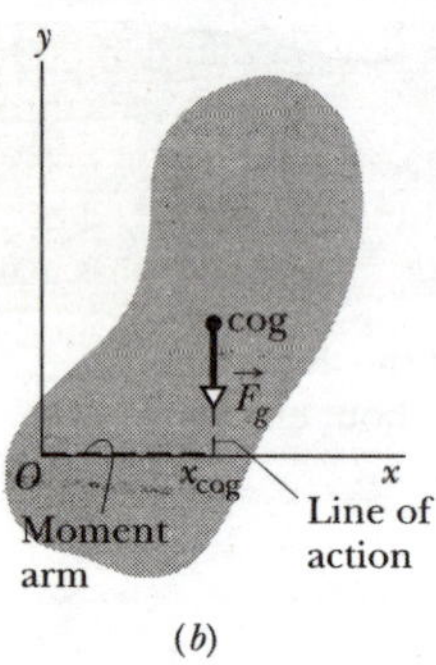

FIG. 10-28 (*a*) An element of mass m_i in an extended body. The gravitational force $\vec{F}_{gi}$ on the element has moment arm x_i about the origin O of the coordinate system. (*b*) The gravitational force $\vec{F}_g$ on a body is said to act at the center of gravity (cog) of the body. Here $\vec{F}_g$ has moment arm x_{cog} about origin O.

$$\tau = x_{cog}F_g \tag{10-38}$$

The gravitational force $\vec{F}_g$ on the body is equal to the sum of the gravitational forces $\vec{F}_{gi}$ on all its elements, so we can substitute ΣF_{gi} for F_g in Eq. 10-38 to write

$$\tau = x_{cog}\sum F_{gi} \tag{10-39}$$

Now recall that the torque due to force $\vec{F}_g$ acting at the center of gravity is equal to the net torque due to all the forces $\vec{F}_{gi}$ acting on all the elements of the body. (That is how we defined the center of gravity.) Thus, τ in Eq. 10-39 is equal to τ_{net} in Eq. 10-37. Putting those two equations together, we can write

$$x_{cog}\sum F_{gi} = \sum x_i F_{gi}$$

Substituting $m_i g_i$ for F_{gi} gives us

$$x_{cog}\sum m_i g_i = \sum x_i m_i g_i \tag{10-40}$$

Now here is a key idea: If the accelerations g_i at all the locations of the elements are the same, we can cancel g_i from this equation to write

$$x_{cog}\sum m_i = \sum x_i m_i \tag{10-41}$$

The sum Σm_i of the masses of all the elements is the mass M of the body. Therefore, we can rewrite Eq. 10-41 as

$$x_{cog} = \frac{1}{M}\sum x_i m_i \tag{10-42}$$

The right side of this equation gives the coordinate x_{com} of the body's center of mass (Eq. 9-4). We now have what we sought to prove:

$$x_{cog} = x_{com} \tag{10-43}$$

A practical use of this result is that in order to balance an object, the pivot point must be at the center of gravity.

Effective Point of Application of Forces

Equivalent force: In the cases when the total torque of all external forces turns out to be perpendicular to the resultant force, that is, $\tau \perp F$, all external forces may be replaced by a F acting along a certain straight line. In fact, if the total torque relative to some point O is perpendicular to F, that is, $OM \perp F$, then we can always find a vector $\vec{r}_0 \perp \tau$ (Fig. 10-29), such that with the given τ and F

$$\tau = \vec{r}_0 \times F$$

Here the choice of $\vec{r}_0$ is not unambiguous: adding any vector $\vec{r}$ parallel to F, we do not violate the last equality. This means that this equality defines not a point of "application" of the force F, but a line along which it acts. Knowing the moduli τ and F of the corresponding vectors, we can find the arm l of the force F (Fig. 10-29):

$$l = \frac{\tau}{F}$$

Thus, if $\tau \perp F$, then the system of forces acting on various points of a solid may be replaced by one equivalent force which is equal to the resultant force F and produces a torque equal to the total torque τ of all external forces.

This implies that the equivalent force mg of the gravitational forces passes through the centre of inertia of the body. It is customary to say that the equivalent force of gravity is "applied" to the center of inertia of a body, or to its center of gravity. Clearly, the torque of this force relative to the center of inertia of a body is equal to zero.

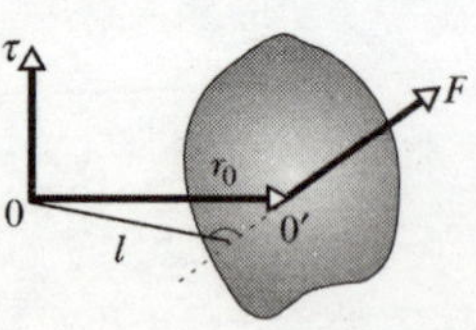

FIG. 10-29 All forces are replaced by one force and one torque.

10-12 | The Rigid Object Under a Net Torque

A torque can cause rotation of a rigid body, as when you use a torque to rotate a door. Here we want to relate the net torque τ_{net} on a rigid body to the angular acceleration α that torque causes about a rotation axis. We do so by analogy with Newton's second law ($F_{net} = ma$) for the acceleration a of a body of mass m due to a net force F_{net} along a coordinate axis. We replace F_{net} with τ_{net}, m with I, and a with α in radian measure, writing

$$\tau_{net} = I\alpha \quad \text{(Newton's second law for rotation} \qquad (10\text{-}44)$$

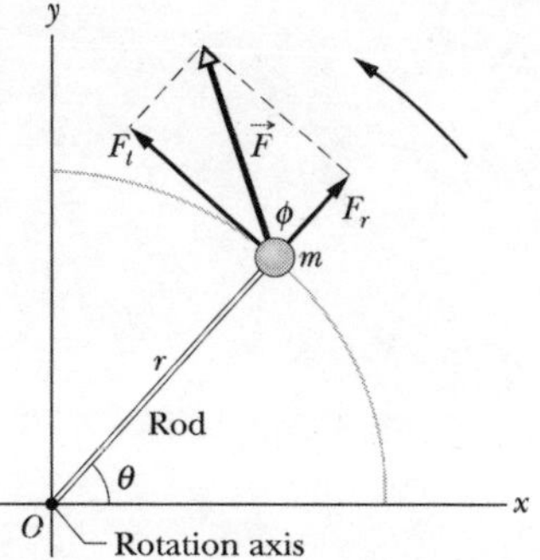

FIG. 10-30 A simple rigid body, free to rotate about an axis through O, consists of a particle of mass m fastened to the end of a rod of length r and negligible mass. An applied force $\vec{F}$ causes the body to rotate.

Proof of Equation 10-44

We prove Eq. 10-44 by first considering the simple situation shown in Fig. 10-30. The rigid body there consists of a particle of mass m on one end of a massless rod of length r. The rod can move only by rotating about its other end, around a rotation axis (an axle) that is perpendicular to the plane of the page. Thus, the particle can move only in a circular path that has the rotation axis at its center.

A force $\vec{F}$ acts on the particle. However, because the particle can move only along the circular path, only the tangential component F_t of the force (the component that is tangent to the circular path) can accelerate the particle along the path. We can relate F_t to the particle's tangential acceleration a_t along the path with Newton's second law, writing

$$F_t = ma_t$$

The torque acting on the particle is,

$$\tau = F_t r = ma_t r$$

From Eq. $a_t = \alpha r$ we can write this as

$$\tau = m(\alpha r)r = (mr^2)\alpha \qquad (10\text{-}45)$$

The quantity in parentheses on the right is the rotational inertia of the particle about the rotation axis.. Thus, Eq. 10-45 reduces to

$$\tau = I\alpha \quad \text{(radian measure)} \qquad (10\text{-}46)$$

For the situation in which more than one force is applied to the particle, we can generalize Eq. 10-46 as

$$\tau_{net} = I\alpha \quad \text{(radian measure)} \qquad (10\text{-}47)$$

which we set out to prove. We can extend this equation to any rigid body rotating about a fixed axis, because any such body can always be analyzed as an assembly of single particles.

CHECKPOINT 14 The Figure shows an overhead view of a meter stick that can pivot about the point indicated, which is to the left of the stick's midpoint. Two horizontal forces, $\vec{F}_1$ and $\vec{F}_2$, are applied to the stick. Only $\vec{F}_1$ is shown. Force $\vec{F}_2$ is perpendicular to the stick and is applied at the right end. If the stick is not to turn, (a) what should be the direction of $\vec{F}_2$, and (b) should F_2 be greater than, less than, or equal to F_1?

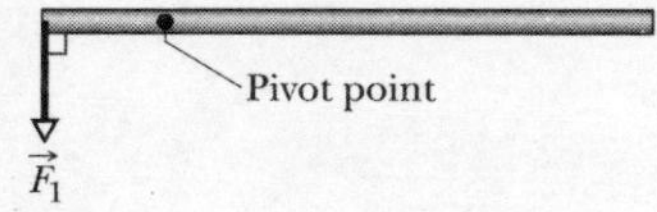

Let's demonstrate that the total torque of all internal forces relative to any point is equal to zero. The internal forces refer to the forces of interaction between the particles of the given system. In accordance with Newton's third law these forces are pairwise equal in magnitude and are opposite. Internal forces must be acting in accordance with third law and should be along line joining the two particles in direction and lie on the same straight line as shown in Fig. (10-31) We can see that length of moment arm is same.

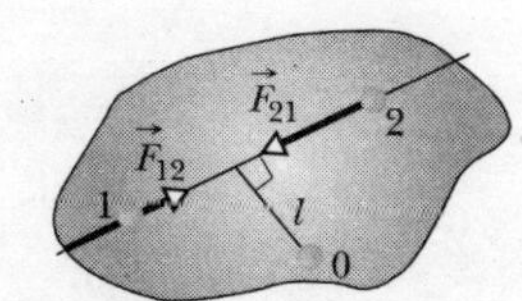

FIG. 10-31 Length of moment arm for action reaction is equal

$$|\vec{\tau}_{12}| = F_{12}\, l = |\vec{\tau}_{21}| = F_{21}\, l$$

but $$\hat{\tau}_{12} = -\hat{\tau}_{21}$$

Consequently, the torque of each pair of interaction are equal in magnitude and opposite in direction, that is, they cancel each other, and hence the total torque of all internal forces always equals zero.

Also note that $\Sigma\tau = I\alpha$ has been derived assuming body is rigid. You should recall that taking out of summation in Eq. 10-45 implies that all particles have same angular acceleration which in turn implies that our collection of particles is a rigid body.

10-13 | Work and Rotational Kinetic Energy

When a force F causes a rigid body of mass m to accelerate along a coordinate axis, the force does work W on the body. Thus, the body's kinetic energy ($K = \frac{1}{2}mv^2$) can change. Suppose it is the only energy of the body that changes, then we relate the change ΔK in kinetic energy to the work W with the work–kinetic energy theorem, writing

$$\Delta K = K_f - K_i = \tfrac{1}{2}mv_f^2 - \tfrac{1}{2}mv_i^2 = W \qquad \text{(work–kinetic energy theorem)} \qquad (10\text{-}48)$$

For motion confined to an x axis, we can calculate the work,

$$W = \int_{x_i}^{x_f} F\,dx \qquad \text{(work, one-dimensional motion)} \qquad (10\text{-}49)$$

This reduces to $W = Fd$ when F is constant and the body's displacement is d. The rate at which the work is done is the power, which we can write as,

$$P = \frac{dW}{dt} = Fv \qquad \text{(power, one-dimensional motion)} \qquad (10\text{-}50)$$

Now let us consider a rotational situation that is similar. When a torque accelerates a rigid body in rotation about a fixed axis, the torque does work W on the body. Therefore, the body's rotational kinetic energy ($K = \frac{1}{2}I\omega^2$) can change. Suppose that it is the only energy of the body that changes. Then we can still relate the change ΔK in kinetic energy to the work W with the work–kinetic energy theorem, except now the kinetic energy is a rotational kinetic energy:

$$\Delta K = K_f - K_i = \tfrac{1}{2}I\omega_f^2 - \tfrac{1}{2}I\omega_i^2 = W \qquad \text{(work–kinetic energy theorem)} \qquad (10\text{-}51)$$

Here, I is the rotational inertia of the body about the fixed axis and ω_i and ω_f are the angular speeds of the body before and after the work is done, respectively.

Also, we can calculate the work with a rotational equivalent of Eq. 10-49,

$$W = \int_{\theta_i}^{\theta_f} \tau\,d\theta \qquad \text{(work, rotation about fixed axis)} \qquad (10\text{-}52)$$

where τ is the torque doing the work W, and θ_i and θ_f are the body's angular positions before and after the work is done, respectively. When τ is constant, Eq. 10-52 reduces to

$$W = \tau(\theta_f - \theta_i) \qquad \text{(work, constant torque)} \qquad (10\text{-}53)$$

The rate at which the work is done is the power, which we can find with the rotational equivalent of Eq. 10-50,

$$P = \frac{dW}{dt} = \tau\omega \quad \text{(power, rotation about fixed axis)} \tag{10-54}$$

Table 10-3 summarizes the equations that apply to the rotation of a rigid body about a fixed axis and the corresponding equations for translational motion.

TABLE 10-3

Some Corresponding Relations for Translational and Rotational Motion

Pure Translation (Fixed Direction)		Pure Rotation (Fixed Axis)	
Position	x	Angular position	θ
Velocity	$v = dx/dy$	Angular velocity	$\omega = d\theta/dt$
Acceleration	$a = dv/dt$	Angular acceleration	$\alpha = d\omega/dt$
Mass	m	Rotational inertia	I
Newton's second law	$F_{net} = ma$	Newton's second law	$\tau_{net} = I\alpha$
Work	$W = \int F\,dx$	Work	$W = \int \tau\,d\theta$
Kinetic energy	$K = \frac{1}{2}mv^2$	Kinetic energy	$K = \frac{1}{2}I\omega^2$
Power (constant force)	$P = Fv$	Power (constant torque)	$P = \tau\omega$
Work–kinetic energy theorem	$W = \Delta K$	Work–kinetic energy theorem	$W = \Delta K$

Proof of Eqs. 10-51 through 10-54

Let us again consider the situation of Fig. 10-30, in which force $\vec{F}$ rotates a rigid body consisting of a single particle of mass m fastened to the end of a massless rod. During the rotation, force $\vec{F}$ does work on the body. Let us assume that the only energy of the body that is changed by $\vec{F}$ is the kinetic energy. Then we can apply the work–kinetic energy theorem of Eq. 10-48:

$$\Delta K = K_f - K_i = W \tag{10-55}$$

Using $K = \frac{1}{2}mv^2$ and Eq. $v = \omega r$, we can rewrite Eq. 10-55 as

$$\Delta K = \tfrac{1}{2}mr^2\omega_f^2 - \tfrac{1}{2}mr^2\omega_i^2 = W \tag{10-56}$$

The rotational inertia for this one-particle body is $I = mr^2$. Substituting this into Eq. 10-57 yields

$$\Delta K = \tfrac{1}{2}I\omega_f^2 - \tfrac{1}{2}I\omega_i^2 = W$$

which is Eq. 10-51. We derived it for a rigid body with one particle, but it holds for any rigid body rotated about a fixed axis.

We next relate the work W done on the body in Fig. 10-30 to the torque τ on the body due to force $\vec{F}$. When the particle moves a distance ds along its circular path, only the tangential component F_t of the force accelerates the particle along the path. Therefore, only F_t does work on the particle. We write that work dW as $F_t\,ds$. However, we can replace ds with $r\,d\theta$, where $d\theta$ is the angle through which the particle moves. Thus we have

$$dW = F_t r\,d\theta \tag{10-57}$$

From Eq. 10-30, we see that the product $F_t r$ is equal to the torque τ, so we can rewrite Eq. 10-57 as

$$dW = \tau \, d\theta \tag{10-58}$$

The work done during a finite angular displacement from θ_i to θ_f is then

$$W = \int_{\theta_i}^{\theta_f} \tau \, d\theta$$

which is Eq. 10-52. It holds for any rigid body rotating about a fixed axis. Equation 10-53 comes directly from Eq. 10-52.

We can find the power P for rotational motion from Eq. 10-58:

$$P = \frac{dW}{dt} = \tau \frac{d\theta}{dt} = \tau\omega$$

which is Eq. 10-54,

Application of $\tau_{axis} = I_{axis}\,\alpha$

Equations to be used: Following equations are going to be very useful for solving problems of rotational dynamics for fixed axis.

1. $\tau_{\text{axis}} = I_{\text{axis}}\,\alpha$

2. $\vec{F}_{\text{ext}} = M\vec{a}_{\text{cm}}$

3. $\vec{P}_{\text{sys}} = M\vec{V}_{\text{cm}}$ and $F_{\text{ext}} = \dfrac{d\vec{P}_{\text{sys}}}{dt}$

4. Rotational kinetic energy $= \dfrac{1}{2} I_{\text{axis}}\,\omega^2$
   (r is distance of any point from axis)

5. $a_r = \omega^2 r$

6. $a_r = \alpha r$

7. $\tau = \dfrac{d\vec{L}_{\text{sys}}}{dt}$

Steps for Solving Problems

1. Select a body or bodies to be analyzed.
2. For each body, draw free body diagram.
3. Identify axis of rotation.
4. Assume angular acceleration of the body about the axis of rotation.
5. Write torque about the axis of rotation.
6. Use $\tau_{\text{axis}} = \tau_{\text{axis}}\alpha$ with sign.
7. If required use other equations.
8. Continue to repeat steps 1–7 till you have equal number of unknowns and equations.

Sample Problem 10-12 Build your skill

Figure 10-32*a* shows a uniform disk, with mass $M = 2.5$ kg and radius $R = 20$ cm, mounted on a fixed horizontal axle. A block with mass $m = 1.2$ kg hangs from a massless cord that is wrapped around the rim of the disk. Find the acceleration of the falling block, the angular acceleration of the disk, and the tension in the cord. The cord does not slip, and there is no friction at the axle.

Conceptualize/Classify: Taking the block as a system, we can relate its acceleration a to the forces acting on it with Newton's second law ($\vec{F}_{net} = m\vec{a}$). (Taking the disk as a system, we can relate its angular acceleration α to the torque acting on it with Newton's second law for rotation ($\tau_{net} = I\alpha$).

Classify: To combine the motions of block and disk, we use the fact that the linear acceleration a of the block and the (tangential) linear acceleration a_t of the disk rim are equal.

Forces on block: The forces are shown in the block's free-body diagram in Fig. 10-32*b*: The force from the cord is $\vec{T}$, and the gravitational force is $\vec{F}_g$, of magnitude mg.

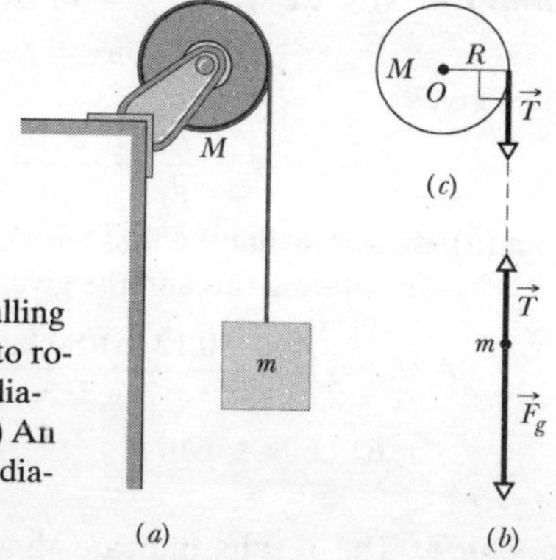

FIG. 10-32 (*a*) The falling block causes the disk to rotate. (*b*) A free-body diagram for the block. (*c*) An incomplete free-body diagram for the disk.

Compute: We can now write Newton's second law for components along a vertical y axis ($F_{net,y} = ma_y$) as

$$T - mg = ma \tag{10-59}$$

However, we cannot solve this equation for a because it also contains the unknown T.

Torque on disk: Previously, when we got stuck on the y axis, we switched to the x axis. Here, we switch to the rotation of the disk. To calculate the torques and the rotational inertia I, we take the rotation axis to be perpendicular to the disk and through its center, at point O in Fig. 10-32*c*.

The torques are then given by Eq. $\tau = rF_t$. The gravitational force on the disk and the force on the disk from the axle both act at the center of the disk and thus at distance $r = 0$, so their torques are zero. The force $\vec{T}$ on the disk due to the cord acts at distance $r = R$ and is tangent to the rim of the disk. Therefore, its torque is $-RT$, negative because the torque rotates the disk clockwise from rest. From Table 10-2*c*, the rotational inertia I of the disk is $1/2\ MR^2$. Thus we can write $\tau_{net} = I\alpha$ as

$$-RT = \tfrac{1}{2}MR^2\alpha \tag{10-60}$$

This equation seems useless because it has two unknowns, α and T, neither of which is the desired a. However, mustering physics courage, we can make it useful with this fact: Because the cord does not slip, the linear acceleration a of the block and the (tangential) linear acceleration a_t of the rim of the disk are equal. Then, by Eq. $a_t = \alpha r$ we see that here $\alpha = a/R$. Substituting this in Eq. 10-60 yields

$$T = -\tfrac{1}{2}Ma \tag{10-61}$$

Combining results: Combining Eqs. 10-59 and 10-61 leads to

$$a = -g\frac{2m}{M + 2m} = -(9.8\ \text{m/s}^2)\frac{(2)(1.2\ \text{kg})}{2.5\ \text{kg} + (2)(1.2\ \text{kg})}$$

$$= -4.8\ \text{m/s}^2 \qquad \text{(Answer)}$$

We then use Eq. 10-61 to find T:

$$T = -\tfrac{1}{2}Ma = -\tfrac{1}{2}(2.5\ \text{kg})(-4.8\ \text{m/s}^2)$$

$$= 6.0\ \text{N} \qquad \text{(Answer)}$$

Conclude: As we should expect, acceleration a of the falling block is less than g, and tension T in the cord ($= 6.0$ N) is less than the gravitational force on the hanging block ($= mg = 11.8$ N). We can see also that a and T depend on the mass of the disk but not on its radius. As a check, we note that the formulas derived above predict $a = -g$ and $T = 0$ for the case of a massless disk ($M = 0$). This is what we would expect; the block simply falls as a free-body. From Eq. 10-19, the angular acceleration of the disk is

$$\alpha = \frac{a}{R} = \frac{-4.8\ \text{m/s}^2}{0.20\ \text{m}} = -24\ \text{rad/s}^2 \qquad \text{(Answer)}$$

Sample Problem 10-13

To throw an 80 kg opponent with a basic judo hip throw, you intend to pull his uniform with a force $\vec{F}$ and a moment arm $d_1 = 0.30$ m from a pivot point (rotation axis) on your right hip (Fig. 10-33). You wish to rotate him about the pivot point with an angular acceleration α of -6.0 rad/s^2—that is, with an angular acceleration that is *clockwise* in the figure. Assume that his rotational inertia I relative to the pivot point is 15 kg · m^2.

(a) What must the magnitude of $\vec{F}$ be if, before you throw him, you bend your opponent forward to bring his center of mass to your hip (Fig. 10-33*a*)?

Conceptualize: We can relate your pull $\vec{F}$ on your opponent to the given angular acceleration α via Newton's second law for rotation ($\tau_{net} = I\alpha$).

Classify: As his feet leave the floor, we can assume that only three forces act on him: your pull $\vec{F}$, a force $\vec{N}$ on him from you at the pivot point (this force is not indicated in Fig. 10-33), and the gravitational force $\vec{F}_g$. To use $\tau_{net} = I\alpha$, we need the corresponding three torques, each about the pivot point.

Compute: From Eq. $\tau = r_\perp F$, the torque due to your pull $\vec{F}$ is equal to $-d_1F$, where d_1 is the moment arm $r_\perp$ and the sign indicates the clockwise rotation this torque tends to cause. The torque due to $\vec{N}$ is zero, because $\vec{N}$ acts at the pivot point and thus has moment arm $r_\perp = 0$.

To evaluate the torque due to $\vec{F}_g$, we can assume that $\vec{F}_g$ acts at your opponent's center of mass. With the center of mass at the pivot point, $\vec{F}_g$ has moment arm $r_\perp = 0$ and thus the torque due to $\vec{F}_g$ is zero. Thus, the only torque on your opponent is due to your pull $\vec{F}$, and we can write $\tau_{net} = I\alpha$ as

$$-d_1F = I\alpha$$

We then find

$$F = \frac{-I\alpha}{d_1} = \frac{-(15\text{ kg}\cdot\text{m}^2)(-6.0\text{ rad/s}^2)}{0.30\text{ m}}$$

$$= 300\text{ N} \qquad \text{(Answer)}$$

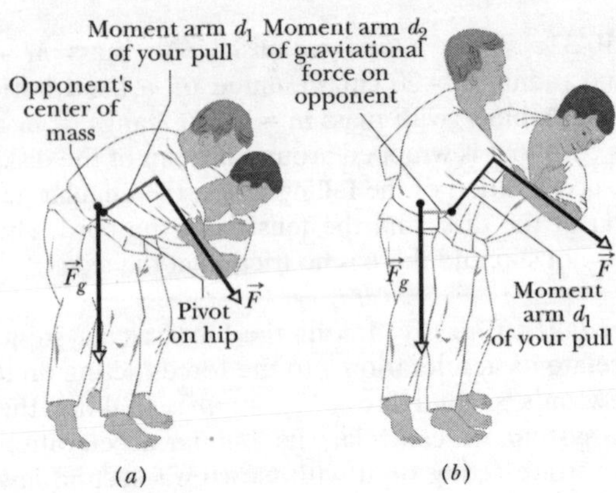

FIG. 10-33 A judo hip throw (*a*) correctly executed and (*b*) incorrectly executed.

(b) What must be the magnitude of $\vec{F}$ be if your opponent remains upright before you throw him, so that $\vec{F}_g$ has a moment arm $d_2 = 0.12$ m (Fig. 10-33*b*)?

Conceptualize/Classify: Because the moment arm for $\vec{F}_g$ is no longer zero, the torque due to $\vec{F}_g$ is now equal to d_2mg and is positive because the torque attempts counterclockwise rotation.

Compute: Now we write $\tau_{net} = I\alpha$ as

$$-d_1F + d_2mg = I\alpha$$

which gives

$$F = -\frac{I\alpha}{d_1} + \frac{d_2mg}{d_1}$$

From (a), we know that the first term on the right is equal to 300 N. Substituting this and the given data, we have

$$F = 300\text{ N} + \frac{(0.12\text{ m})(80\text{ kg})(9.8\text{ m/s}^2)}{0.30\text{ m}}$$

$$= 613.6\text{ N} \approx 610\text{ N} \qquad \text{(Answer)}$$

Conclude: The results indicate that you will have to pull much harder if you do not initially bend your opponent to bring his center of mass to your hip. A good judo fighter knows this lesson from physics.

Sample Problem 10-14

A tall, cylindrical chimney starts facking over as shown in Fig. 10-34. Treat the chimney as a thin ridgid rod of length $L = 55.0$ m. At the instant it makes an angle of $\theta = 35.0°$ with the vertical, what is its angular speed ω_f?

Conceptualize: You can imagine keeping a pencil vertical and then releasing it. The path coverd by the pencil shall be the same as that of the chimney in this problem.

As the rod tips over, it's weight of the causes rod to fall faster.

Classify: During the rotation, the mechanical energy (the sum of the rotational kinetic energy K and the gravitational potential energy U) does not change.

$$K = \frac{1}{2}I\omega^2$$

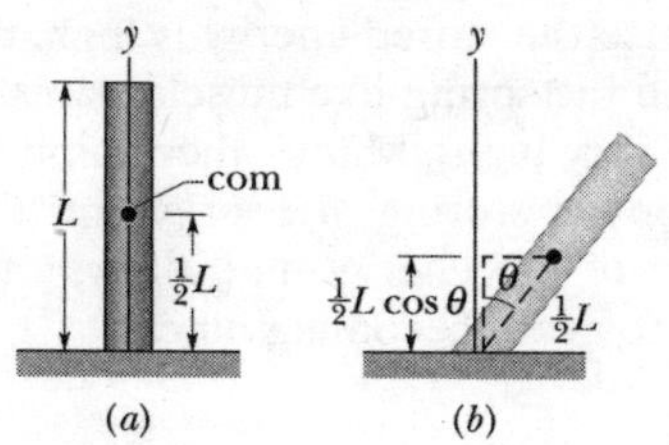

FIG. 10-34 (a) A cylindrical chimney. (b) The height of its center of mass is determined with the right triangle.

Conservation of mechanical energy: As the center of mass of the chimney falls, energy is transferred from gravitational potential energy U to rotational kinetic energy K but the total amount does not change. We can write this fact as

$$K_f + U_f = K_i + U_i \qquad (10\text{-}62)$$

Compute: Rotational kinetic energy: The kinetic energy K is initially zero but its value thereafter $(= \frac{1}{2}I\omega^2)$ depends on the rotational inertia I. If we had a thin rod rotating around its center of mass (at its center), we know from Table 10-2 that $(I_{com} = \frac{1}{12}mL^2)$ where m is the rod's mass and L is the rod's length. However, our rod-like chimney rotates around one end, at a distance of $L/2$ from the center, and so we use the parallel-axis theorem to find

$$I = \tfrac{1}{12}mL + m\left(\frac{L}{2}\right)^2 = \tfrac{1}{3}mL^2 \qquad (10\text{-}63)$$

Substituting this into $(K = \frac{1}{2}I\omega^2)$ tells us

$$K_f = \tfrac{1}{2}(\tfrac{1}{3}mL^2)\omega^2 \qquad (10\text{-}64)$$

Potential energy: The potential energy $U (= mgy)$ depends on the height of each segment of the chimney. However, we can calculate U by assuming that all of the mass is concentrated at the chimney's com, which is initially at height ½L. So the initial potential energy is

$$U_i = \tfrac{1}{2}mgL \qquad (10\text{-}65)$$

When the chimney has rotated through angle θ, Fig. 10-34b tells us that the center is at height $\frac{1}{2}L\cos\theta$. So, the potential energy is now

$$U_f = \tfrac{1}{2}mgL\cos\theta \qquad (10\text{-}66)$$

Angular speed: After substituting Eqs. 10-66, 10-65, and 10-64 into Eq. 10-62 and setting $K_i = 0$, we solve for ω_f and find

$$\omega = \sqrt{\frac{3g}{L}(1-\cos\theta)} = \sqrt{\frac{3(9.8\ \text{m/s}^2)}{55.0\ \text{m}}(1-\cos 35.0°)}$$
$$= 0.311\ \text{rad/s} \qquad \text{(Answer)}$$

Conclude: We can see from the equation that angular velocity increases as angle increases.

The bottom portion of a chimney tends to rotate around the base faster than the top portion, and the chimney is likely to break apart during the rotation, with the top half lagging behind the bottom half.

Sample Problem 10-15

In the oversized claw of a snapping shrimp, the dactylus (the large, mobile section of the claw) is drawn away from the propodius (the opposing, stationary part of the claw) by a muscle that is gradually put under tension (Fig. 10-35). Energy stored in the muscle increases as the tension increases. The sudden release of the dactylus allows it to rotate about a pivot point, to slam shut on the propodius in a time interval Δt of only 290 μs. In particular, the *plunger* on the dactylus runs into a cavity on the propodius, causing water to squirt out of the cavity so quickly that the water undergoes *cavitation*. That is, the water vaporizes to form bubbles of water vapor. These bubbles rapidly grow as they enter the surrounding water and then they suddenly collapse, emitting an intense sound wave. The combination of these sound waves from many bubbles can stun the shrimp's prey.

The peak angular speed ω of the dactylus is about 2×10^3 rad/s and its rotational inertia I is about $3 \times 10^{-11}\ \text{kg}\cdot\text{m}^2$. At what average rate is energy transferred from the muscle to the rotation?

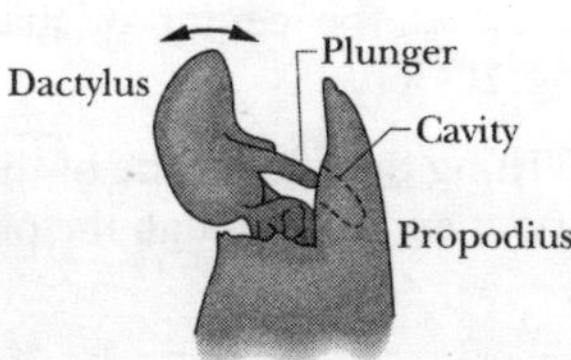

FIG. 10-35 The oversized claw of a snapping shrimp. The dactylus is first pulled away from the opposing section of the propodius and then allowed to snap back to it, thrusting the plunger into the cavity.

Conceptualize/Classify: Rotational kinetic energy is given by Eq. $K = \frac{1}{2}I\omega^2$. Average power is given by Eq. $P_{avg} = \Delta E/\Delta t$.

Compute: When the angular speed reaches its peak value, the rotational kinetic energy is

$$K = \tfrac{1}{2}I\omega^2 = \tfrac{1}{2}(3\times10^{-11}\ \text{kg}\cdot\text{m}^2)(2\times10^3\ \text{rad/s})^2$$
$$= 6\times10^{-5}\ \text{J}$$

The average power is then

$$P_{avg} = \frac{\Delta E}{\Delta t} = \frac{6 \times 10^{-5}\,\text{J}}{290 \times 10^{-6}\,\text{s}}$$

$$= 0.2\ \text{W} \qquad \text{(Answer)}$$

Conclude: This power greatly exceeds what any fast-acting muscle in the shrimp can produce. However, in the claw the shrimp effectively locks the dactylus against a spring so that it can gradually increase the tension and stored energy (the power of this stage is low). Then, once the stored energy is high, the dactylus is released and the spring-like muscle slams it shut (the power is now very high). Many other animals make use of such low-power storing of energy and then a high-power release of the energy that allows them to capture lunch or to avoid becoming lunch.

Sample Problem 10-16

A uniform rod of length L and mass M pivoted about its end as shown in Fig. 10-36, and is free to rotate in the vertical plane about the pivot. The rod is released from rest in the horizontal position. (a)What is the initial angular acceleration of the rod ?

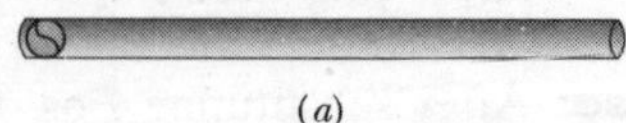

(a)

FIG. 10-36a A uniform rod in vertical plane with horizontal axis is released.

Conceptualize: It is easy to imagine that rod rotates clockwise, around the pivot at the left end, when it is released.

Classify: The rod will be experiencing two forces one is the weight, effectively acting on center of mass and the other is the force due to hinge or pivot, acting through the hinge. When we write torque about the pivot the torque due to second force will become zero because its moment arm is zero. Now the torque is due to only the gravitational force on the rod, for the rotation axis considered crossing the pivot. The rod is a rigid body under a net torque.

Compute: We know the gravitational force acts effectively at the center of mass of the rod as shown in Fig. 10-36*b*.

Writing the magnitude of the torque due to the weight about an axis through the pivot.

$$\tau = Mg\left(\frac{L}{2}\right)$$

Use Eq. 10-44 to obtain the angular acceleration of the rod:

$$\alpha = \frac{\tau}{I} = \frac{Mg(L/2)}{\frac{1}{3}ML^2} = \frac{3g}{2L}$$

(b) Find the initial acceleration of the right end of the rod?

Compute: Using Eq. 10-44 with $r = L$ for the initial acceleration of the right end of the rod.

$$a_t = L\alpha = \frac{3}{2}g$$

Conclude: These values are the initial values of the angular and translational accelerations. Once the rod begins to rotate, the gravitational force is no longer perpendicular to the rod and the values of the two acceleration changes as shown in part (c)

(c) Find normal contact force due to hinge when rod has rotated through angle θ as shown shown in Fig. 10-36*b*.

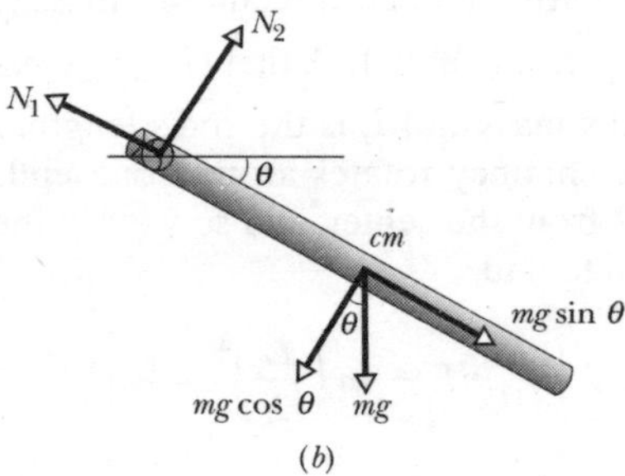

(b)

Compute: We know the gravitational force effectively acts at the centerof mass of the rod as shown in Fig. 10-36*b*. Writing the magnitude of the torque due to the weight about an axis through the pivot.

$$mg \cos\theta \times \frac{l}{2} = \frac{ml^2}{3} \times \alpha$$

$$\alpha = \frac{3g\cos\theta}{2l}$$

By energy conservation

$$mg\frac{l}{2}\sin\theta = \frac{1}{2}\frac{ml^2}{3}\omega^2$$

$$\omega = \sqrt{\frac{3g\sin\theta}{l}}$$

$$a_r = \omega^2\frac{l}{2} = \frac{3g\sin\theta}{l} \times \frac{l}{2} = \frac{3g\sin\theta}{2}$$

$$a_t = \alpha\frac{l}{2} = \frac{3g\cos\theta}{4}$$

$$N_1 - mg\sin\theta = m\frac{3g\sin\theta}{2}$$

hence $$N_1 = \frac{5mg\sin\theta}{2}$$

$$mg\cos\theta - N_2 = m\frac{3g\cos\theta}{2}$$

hence $$N_2 = \frac{mg\cos\theta}{4}$$

$$N = \sqrt{N_1^{\,2} + N_2^{\,2}} \quad |\vec{p}| = m\omega\frac{l}{2} = \frac{m\sqrt{3gl}\sin\theta}{2}$$

Sample Problem 10-17

Atwood machine with a massive pulley

Consider the system shown in Fig. 10-37 with $M_1 = 20.0$ kg, $M_2 = 12.5$ kg, $R = 0.200$ m, and the mass of the uniform pulley $M = 5.00$ kg. The string is light and inextensible and does not slip on the pulley. Find the acceleration a for the arrangement as shown in Fig. 10-37. The pulley axis is frictionless.

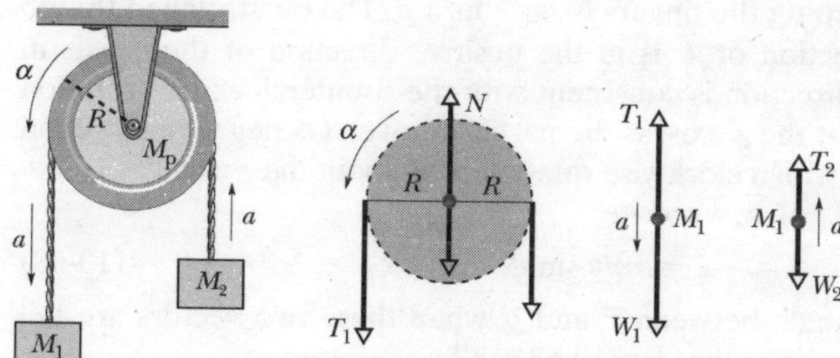

FIG. 10-37 Atwood machine with massive pulley.

Conceptualize: It is a good time to go and look at previous examples, and realise that this problem is different from them as the pulley in this problem is going to rotate so that string does not slip over the pulley, in other words the effect of the pulley is to be included.

Classify: It can be concluded that tension in the two ends of the rope is going to be different. For further clarification you can again read the section, where we specified that tension being same is under specific assumptions.

Compute: Force diagrams for three masses and the points of application of the forces on the pulley are shown in Fig. 10-37. The pulley evidently undergoes pure rotation about its axle, so we take the axis of rotation to be the axle.

Applying Newton's second law on masses

$$W_1 - T_1 = M_1 a$$
$$T_2 - W_2 = M_2 a$$

Writing equation for pulley about axle $T_1R - T_2R = I\alpha$

Note that in the torque equation, α must be positive counterclockwise to correspond to our convention that torque out of the paper is positive. Applying Newton's second law on pulley $N - T_1 - T_2 - W_p = 0$

N is the force on the axle, and the last equation simply assures that the pulley does not fall. Since we don't need to know N, it does not contribute to the solution. Since the rope does not slip, the constraint equation can relate a and α. The velocity of the rope v must be equal to the velocity of a point on the surface of the wheel, that is, ωR,

$v = \omega R$, from which it follows that

$$a = \alpha R$$

We can now eliminate T_1, T_2, and α;

$$W_1 - W_2 - (T_1 - T_2) = (M_1 + M_2)a$$

$$T_1 - T_2 = \frac{I\alpha}{R} = \frac{Ia}{R^2}$$

$$W_1 - W_2 - \frac{Ia}{R^2} = (M_1 + M_2)a$$

The pulley is a simple disk, we have

$$I = \frac{M_P R^2}{2}$$

and it follows that

$$a = \frac{(M_1 - M_2)g}{M_1 + M_2 + M_p/2}$$
$$= \frac{(20 - 12.5)10}{20 + 12.5 + 2.5}$$
$$= \frac{75}{35} = 2.14$$

Conclude: The pulley increases the total inertial mass of the system, but in comparison with the hanging weights. The answer becomes same if we keep mass of pulley to be zero, thus tension on both sides also becomes zero.

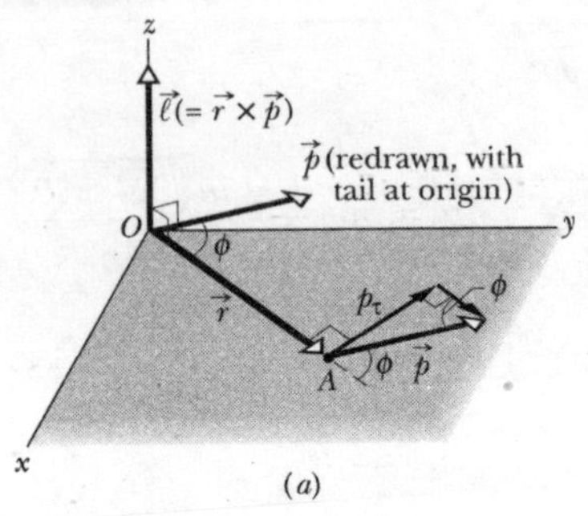

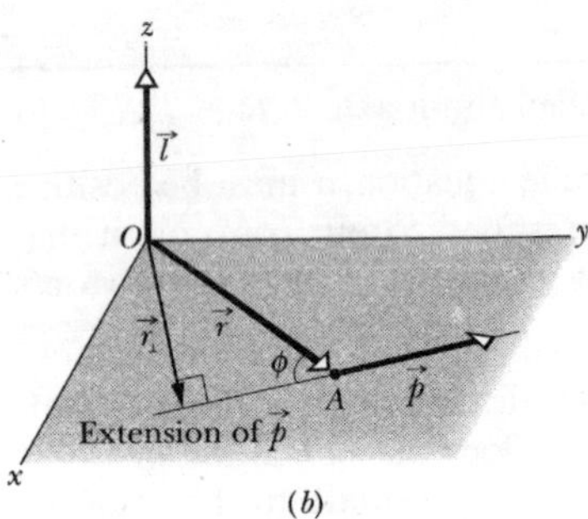

FIG. 10-38 Defining angular momentum. A particle passing through point A has linear momentum $\vec{p}(=m\vec{v})$, with the vector $\vec{p}$ lying in an xy plane. The particle has angular momentum $\vec{\ell}\,(=\vec{r}\times\vec{p})$ with respect to the origin O. By the right-hand rule, the angular momentum vector points in the positive direction of z. (a) The magnitude of $\vec{\ell}$ is given by $\ell = rp_\perp = rmv_\perp$. (b) The magnitude of $\vec{\ell}$ is also given by $\ell = r_\perp p = r_\perp mv$.

10-14 | Angular Momentum

Recall that the concept of linear momentum $\vec{p}$ and the principle of conservation of linear momentum are extremely powerful tools. They allow us to predict the outcome of, say, a collision of two cars without knowing the details of the collision. Here we begin a discussion of the angular counterpart of $\vec{p}$, winding up later with the angular counterpart of the conservation principle.

Figure 10-38 shows a particle of mass m with linear momentum $\vec{p}\,(=m\vec{v})$ as it passes through point A in an xy plane. The **angular momentum** $\vec{\ell}$ of this particle with respect to the origin O is a vector quantity defined as

$$\vec{\ell} = \vec{r}\times\vec{p} = m(\vec{r}\times\vec{v}) \qquad \text{(angular momentum defined)} \qquad (10\text{-}67)$$

where $\vec{r}$ is the position vector of the particle with respect to O. As the particle moves relative to O in the direction of its momentum $\vec{p}\,(=m\vec{v})$, position vector $\vec{r}$ rotates around O. Note carefully that to have angular momentum about O, the particle does *not* itself have to rotate around O. Angular momentum bears the same relation to linear momentum that torque does to force. The SI unit of angular momentum is the kilogram-meter-squared per second ($kg \cdot m^2/s$), equivalent to the joule-second ($J \cdot s$).

To find the direction of the angular momentum vector $\vec{\ell}$ in Fig. 10-38, we slide the vector $\vec{p}$ until its tail is at the origin O. Then we use the right-hand rule for vector products, sweeping the fingers from $\vec{r}$ into $\vec{p}$. The outstretched thumb then shows that the direction of $\vec{\ell}$ is in the positive direction of the z axis in Fig. 10-38. This positive direction is consistent with the counterclockwise rotation of position vector $\vec{r}$ about the z axis, as the particle moves. (A negative direction of $\vec{\ell}$ would be consistent with a clockwise rotation of $\vec{r}$ about the z axis.)

To find the magnitude of $\vec{\ell}$, we write

$$\ell = rmv\sin\phi \qquad (10\text{-}68)$$

where ϕ is the smaller angle between $\vec{r}$ and $\vec{p}$ when these two vectors are tail to tail. From Fig. 10-38*a*, we see that Eq. 10-68 can be rewritten as

$$\ell = rp_\perp = rmv_\perp \qquad (10\text{-}69)$$

where $p_\perp$ is the component of $\vec{p}$ perpendicular to $\vec{r}$ and $v_\perp$ is the component of $\vec{v}$ perpendicular to $\vec{r}$. From Fig. 10-38*b*, we see that Eq. 10-68 can also be rewritten as

$$\ell = r_\perp p = r_\perp mv \qquad (10\text{-}70)$$

where $r_\perp$ is the perpendicular distance between O and the extension of $\vec{p}$.

Just as is true for torque, angular momentum has meaning only with respect to a specified origin. Moreover, if the particle in Fig. 10-38 did not lie in the xy plane, or if the linear momentum $\vec{p}$ of the particle did not also lie in that plane, the angular momentum $\vec{\ell}$ would not be parallel to the z axis. The direction of the angular momentum vector is always perpendicular to the plane formed by the position and linear momentum vectors $\vec{r}$ and $\vec{p}$.

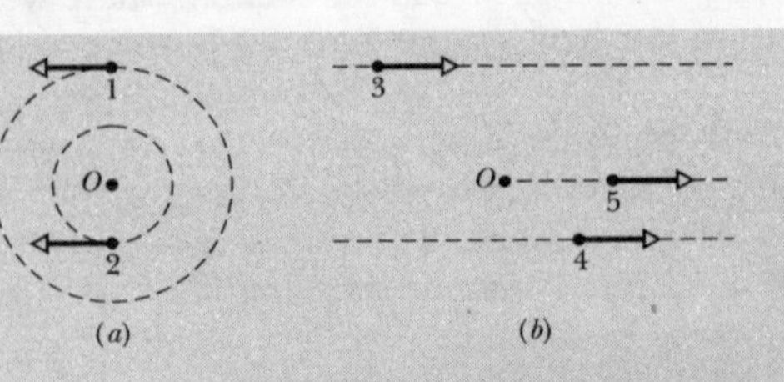

CHECKPOINT 15 In part *a* of the figure, particles 1 and 2 move around point O in opposite directions, in circles with radii 2 m and 4 m. In part *b*, particles 3 and 4 travel in the same direction, along straight lines at perpendicular distances of 4 m and 2 m from point O. Particle 5 moves directly away from O. All five particles have the same mass and the same constant speed. (a) Rank the particles according to the magnitudes of their angular momentum about point O, greatest first. (b) Which particles have negative angular momentum about point O?

Sample Problem 10-18

Figure 10-39 shows an overhead view of two particles moving at constant momentum along horizontal paths. Particle 1, with momentum magnitude $p_1 = 5.0$ kg·m/s, has position vector $\vec{r}_1$ and will pass 2.0 m from point O. Particle 2, with momentum magnitude $p_2 = 2.0$ kg·m/s, has position vector $\vec{r}_2$ and will pass 4.0 m from point O. What are the magnitude and direction of the net angular momentum $\vec{L}$ about point O of the two-particle system?

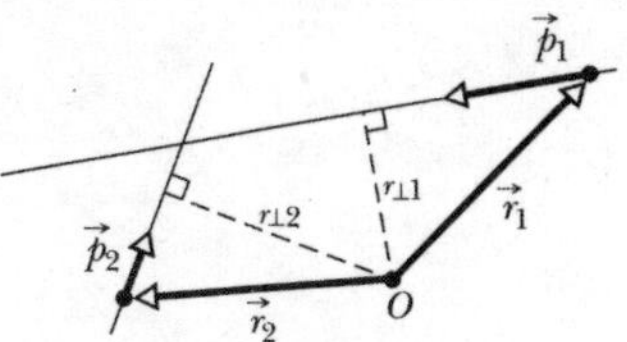

FIG. 10-39 Two particles pass near point O.

Conceptualize/Classify: To find $\vec{L}$, we can first find the individual angular momenta $\vec{\ell}_1$ and $\vec{\ell}_2$ and then add them. To evaluate their magnitudes, we can use any one of Eqs. 10-18 through 10-21. However, Eq. 10-21 is easiest, because we are given the perpendicular distances $r_{1\perp}$ (= 2.0 m) and $r_{2\perp}$ (= 4.0 m) and the momentum magnitudes p_1 and p_2.

Compute: For particle 1, Eq. 10-21 yields

$$\ell_1 = r_{\perp 1}p_1 = (2.0 \text{ m})(5.0 \text{ kg}\cdot\text{m/s}) = 10 \text{ kg}\cdot\text{m}^2\text{/s}$$

To find the direction of vector $\vec{\ell}_1$, we use Eq. 10-18 and the right-hand rule for vector products. For $\vec{r}_1 \times \vec{p}_1$, the vector product is out of the page, perpendicular to the plane of Fig. 10-39. This is the positive direction, consistent with the counterclockwise rotation of the particle's position vector $\vec{r}_1$ around O as particle 1 moves. Thus, the angular momentum vector for particle 1 is

$$\ell_1 = +10 \text{ kg}\cdot\text{m}^2\text{/s}$$

Similarly, the magnitude of $\vec{\ell}_2$ is

$$\ell_2 = r_{\perp 2}p_2 = (4.0 \text{ m})(2.0 \text{ kg}\cdot\text{m/s}) = 8.0 \text{ kg}\cdot\text{m}^2\text{/s}$$

and the vector product $\vec{r}_2 \times \vec{p}_2$ is into the page, which is the negative direction, consistent with the clockwise rotation of $\vec{r}_2$ around O as particle 2 moves. Thus, the angular momentum vector for particle 2 is

$$\ell_2 = -8.0 \text{ kg}\cdot\text{m}^2\text{/s}.$$

The net angular momentum for the two-particle system is

$$L = \ell_1 + \ell_2 = +10 \text{ kg}\cdot\text{m}^2\text{/s} + (-8.0 \text{ kg}\cdot\text{m}^2\text{/s}) = +2.0 \text{ kg}\cdot\text{m}^2\text{/s} \quad \text{(Answer)}$$

Conclude: The plus sign means that the system's net angular momentum about point O is out of the page.

10-15 | Newton's Second Law in Angular Form

Newton's second law written in the form

$$\vec{F}_{\text{net}} = \frac{d\vec{p}}{dt} \quad \text{(single particle)} \tag{10-71}$$

expresses the close relation between force and linear momentum for a single particle. We have seen enough of the parallelism between linear and angular quantities to be pretty sure that there is also a close relation between torque and angular momentum. Guided by Eq. 10-71, we can even guess that it must be

$$\vec{\tau}_{\text{net}} = \frac{d\vec{\ell}}{dt} \quad \text{(single particle)} \tag{10-72}$$

Equation 10-72 is indeed an angular form of Newton's second law for a single particle:

Equation 10-72 has no meaning unless the torques $\vec{\tau}$ and the angular momentum $\vec{\ell}$ are defined with respect to the same origin.

The (vector) sum of all the torques acting on a particle is equal to the time rate of change of the angular momentum of that particle.

Proof of Equation 10-72

We start with Eq. 10-67, the definition of the angular momentum of a particle:

$$\vec{\ell} = m(\vec{r} \times \vec{v})$$

where $\vec{r}$ is the position vector of the particle and $\vec{v}$ is the velocity of the particle. Differentiating[1] each side with respect to time t yields

$$\frac{d\vec{\ell}}{dt} = m\left(\vec{r} \times \frac{d\vec{v}}{dt} + \frac{d\vec{r}}{dt} \times \vec{v}\right) \tag{10-73}$$

However, $d\vec{v}/dt$ is the acceleration $\vec{a}$ of the particle, and $d\vec{r}/dt$ is its velocity $\vec{v}$. Thus, we can rewrite Eq. 10-24 as

$$\frac{d\vec{\ell}}{dt} = m(\vec{r} \times \vec{a} + \vec{v} \times \vec{v})$$

Now $\vec{v} \times \vec{v} = 0$ (the vector product of any vector with itself is zero because the angle between the two vectors is necessarily zero). This leads to

$$\frac{d\vec{\ell}}{dt} = m(\vec{r} \times \vec{a}) = \vec{r} \times m\vec{a}$$

We now use Newton's second law ($\vec{F}_{net} = m\vec{a}$) to replace $m\vec{a}$ with its equal, the vector sum of the forces that act on the particle, obtaining

$$\frac{d\vec{\ell}}{dt} = \vec{r} \times \vec{F}_{net} = \sum(\vec{r} \times \vec{F}) \tag{10-74}$$

Here the symbol Σ indicates that we must sum the vector products $\vec{r} \times \vec{F}$ for all the forces. However, from Eq. 10-40, we know that each one of those vector products is the torque associated with one of the forces. Therefore, Eq. 10-74 tells us that

$$\vec{\tau}_{net} = \frac{d\vec{\ell}}{dt}$$

This is Eq. 10-72, the relation that we set out to prove.

CHECKPOINT 16 The figure shows the position vector $\vec{r}$ of a particle at a certain instant, and four choices for the direction of a force that is to accelerate the particle. All four choices lie in the xy plane. (a) Rank the choices according to the magnitude of the time rate of change ($d\vec{\ell}/dt$) they produce in the angular momentum of the particle about point O, greatest first. (b) Which choice results in a negative rate of change about O?

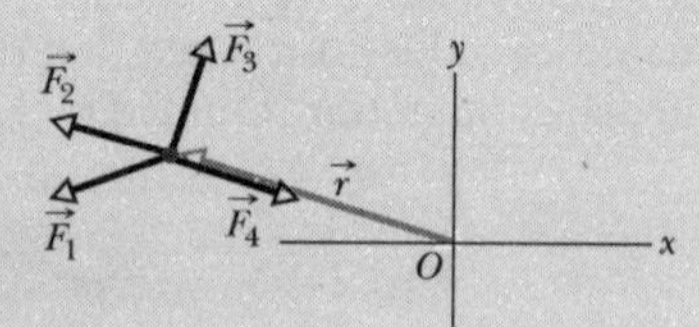

[1]In differentiating a vector product, be sure not to change the order of the two quantities (here $\vec{r}$ and $\vec{v}$) that form that product.

Sample Problem 10-19 Build your skill

In Fig. 10-40, a penguin of mass m falls from rest at point A, a horizontal distance D from the origin O of an xyz coordinate system. (The positive direction of the z axis is directly outward from the plane of the figure.)

(a) What is the angular momentum $\vec{\ell}$ of the falling penguin about O?

Conceptualize/Classify: We can treat the penguin as a particle, and thus its angular momentum $\vec{\ell}$ is given by Eq. 11-18 ($\vec{\ell} = \vec{r} \times \vec{p}$), where $\vec{r}$ is the penguin's position vector (extending from O to the penguin) and $\vec{p}$ is the penguin's linear momentum. (The penguin has *angular* momentum about O even though it moves in a straight line, because vector $\vec{r}$ rotates about O as the penguin falls.)

Compute: To find the magnitude of $\vec{\ell}$, we can use any one of the scalar equations derived from Eq. 11-18—namely, Eqs. 11-19 through 11-21. However, Eq. 11-21 ($\ell = r_\perp mv$) is easiest because the perpendicular distance $r_\perp$ between O and an extension of vector $\vec{p}$ is the given distance D. The speed of an object that has fallen from rest for a time t is $v = gt$. We can now write Eq. 11-21 in terms of given quantities as

$$\ell = r_\perp mv = Dmgt \qquad \text{(Answer)}$$

To find the direction of $\vec{\ell}$, we use the right-hand rule for the vector product $\vec{r} \times \vec{p}$ in Eq. 11-18.

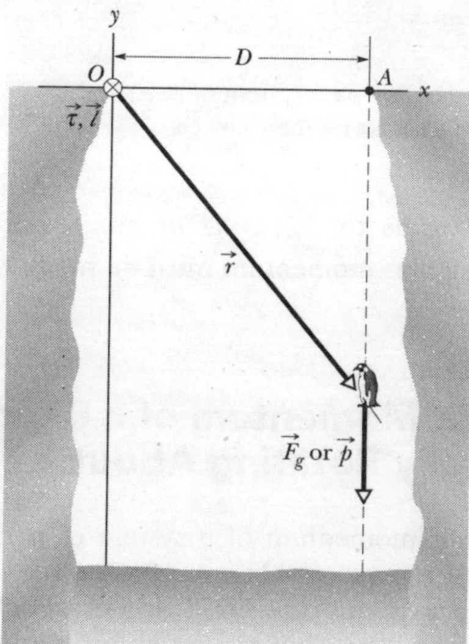

FIG. 10-40 A penguin falls vertically from point A. The torque $\vec{\tau}$ and the angular momentum $\vec{\ell}$ of the falling penguin with respect to the origin O are directed into the plane of the figure at O.

Mentally shift $\vec{p}$ until its tail is at the origin, and then use the fingers of your right hand to rotate $\vec{r}$ into $\vec{p}$ through the smaller angle between the two vectors. Your outstretched thumb then points into the plane of the figure, indicating that the product $\vec{r} \times \vec{p}$ and thus also $\vec{\ell}$ are directed into that plane, in the negative direction of the z axis. We represent $\vec{\ell}$ with an encircled cross ⊗ at O. The vector $\vec{\ell}$ changes with time in magnitude only; its direction remains unchanged.

(b) About the origin O, what is the torque $\vec{\tau}$ on the penguin due to the gravitational force $\vec{F}_g$?

Conceptualize/Classify: (1) The torque is given by Eq. 11-14 ($\vec{\tau} = \vec{r} \times \vec{F}$), where now the force is $\vec{F}_g$. (2) Force $\vec{F}_g$ causes a torque on the penguin, even though the penguin moves in a straight line, because $\vec{r}$ rotates about O as the penguin moves.

Compute: To find the magnitude of $\vec{\tau}$, we can use any one of the scalar equations derived from Eq. 11-14—namely, Eqs. 11-15 through 11-17. However, Eq. 11-17 ($\tau = r_\perp F$) is easiest because the perpendicular distance $r_\perp$ between O and the line of action of $\vec{F}_g$ is the given distance D. So, substituting D and using mg for the magnitude of $\vec{F}_g$, we can write Eq. 11-17 as

$$\tau = DF_g = Dmg \qquad \text{(Answer)}$$

Using the right-hand rule for the vector product $\vec{r} \times \vec{F}$ in Eq. 11-14, we find that the direction of $\vec{\tau}$ is the negative direction of the z axis, the same as $\vec{\ell}$.

Conclude: The results we obtained in parts (a) and (b) must be consistent with Newton's second law in the angular form of Eq. 11-23 ($\vec{\tau}_{net} = d\vec{\ell}/dt$). To check the magnitudes we got, we write Eq. 11-23 in component form for the z axis and then substitute our result $\ell = Dmgt$. We find

$$\tau = \frac{d\ell}{dt} = \frac{d(Dmgt)}{dt} = Dmg$$

which is the magnitude we found for $\vec{\tau}$. To check the directions, we note that Eq. 11-23 tells us that $\vec{\tau}$ and $d\vec{\ell}/dt$ must have the same direction. So $\vec{\tau}$ and $\vec{\ell}$ must also have the same direction, which is what we found.

10-16 | The Angular Momentum of a System of Particles

Now we turn our attention to the angular momentum of a system of particles with respect to an origin. The total angular momentum $\vec{L}$ of the system is the (vector) sum of the angular momenta of the individual particles (here with label i):

$$\vec{L} = \vec{\ell}_1 + \vec{\ell}_2 + \vec{\ell}_3 + \cdots + \vec{\ell}_n = \sum_{i=1}^{n} \vec{\ell}_i \tag{10-75}$$

With time, the angular momenta of individual particles may change because of interactions between the particles or with the outside. We can find the resulting change in $\vec{L}$ by taking the time derivative of Eq. 10-75. Thus,

$$\frac{d\vec{L}}{dt} = \sum_{i=1}^{n} \frac{d\vec{\ell}_i}{dt} \tag{10-76}$$

From Eq. 10-72, we see that $d\vec{\ell}_i/dt$ is equal to the net torque $\vec{\tau}_{\text{net},i}$ on the ith particle. We can rewrite Eq. 10-76 as

$$\frac{d\vec{L}}{dt} = \sum_{i=1}^{n} \vec{\tau}_{\text{net},i} \tag{10-77}$$

That is, the rate of change of the system's angular momentum $\vec{L}$ is equal to the vector sum of the torques on its individual particles. Those torques include *internal torques* (due to forces between the particles) and *external torques* (due to forces on the particles from bodies external to the system). However, the forces between the particles always come in third-law force pairs so their torques sum to zero. Thus, the only torques that can change the total angular momentum $\vec{L}$ of the system are the external torques acting on the system.

Let $\vec{\tau}_{\text{net}}$ represent the net external torque, the vector sum of all external torques on all particles in the system. Then we can write Eq. 10-77 as

$$\vec{\tau}_{\text{net}} = \frac{d\vec{L}}{dt} \quad \text{(system of particles)} \tag{10-78}$$

which is Newton's second law in angular form. It says:

> The net external torque $\vec{\tau}_{\text{net}}$ acting on a system of particles is equal to the time rate of change of the system's total angular momentum $\vec{L}$.

Equation 10-78 is analogous to $\vec{F}_{\text{net}} = d\vec{P}/dt$ but requires extra caution: Torques and the system's angular momentum must be measured relative to the same origin.

10-17 | The Angular Momentum of a Rigid Body Symmetrically Rotating About a Fixed Axis

We next evaluate the angular momentum of a system of particles that form a rigid body that rotates about a fixed axis. Figure 10-41a shows such a body. The fixed axis of rotation is a z axis, and the body rotates about it with constant angular speed ω. We wish to find the angular momentum of the body about that axis.

We can find the angular momentum by summing the z components of the angular momenta of the mass elements in the body. In Fig. 10-41a, a typical mass element, of mass Δm_i, moves around the z axis in a circular path. The position of the mass element is located relative to the origin O by position vector $\vec{r}_i$. The radius of the mass element's circular path is $r_{\perp i}$, the perpendicular distance between the element and the z axis.

The magnitude of the angular momentum $\vec{\ell}_i$ of this mass element, with respect to O, is given by Eq. 10-68:

$$\ell_i = (r_i)(p_i)(\sin 90°) = (r_i)(\Delta m_i\, v_i)$$

where p_i and v_i are the linear momentum and linear speed of the mass element, and 90° is the angle between $\vec{r}_i$ and $\vec{p}_i$. The angular momentum vector $\vec{\ell}_i$ for the mass element in Fig. 10-41*a* is shown in Fig. 10-41*b*; its direction must be perpendicular to those of $\vec{r}_i$ and $\vec{p}_i$.

We are interested in the component of $\vec{\ell}_i$ that is parallel to the rotation axis, here the z axis. That z component is

$$\ell_{iz} = \ell_i \sin\theta = (r_i \sin\theta)(\Delta m_i\, v_i) = r_{\perp i}\, \Delta m_i\, v_i$$

The z component of the angular momentum for the rotating rigid body as a whole is found by adding up the contributions of all the mass elements that make up the body. Thus, because $v = \omega r_\perp$, we may write

$$L_z = \sum_{i=1}^{n} \ell_{iz} = \sum_{i=1}^{n} \Delta m_i\, v_i r_{\perp i} = \sum_{i=1}^{n} \Delta m_i (\omega r_{\perp i}) r_{\perp i}$$

$$= \omega \left(\sum_{i=1}^{n} \Delta m_i\, r_{\perp i}^2 \right) \qquad (10\text{-}79)$$

We can remove ω from the summation here because it has the same value for all points of the rotating rigid body.

The quantity $\Sigma\, \Delta m_i\, r_{\perp i}^2$ in Eq. 10-79 is the rotational inertia I of the body about the fixed axis (see Eq. 10-82). Thus Eq. 10-79 reduces to

$$L = I\omega \qquad \text{(rigid body, fixed axis)} \qquad (10\text{-}80)$$

We have dropped the subscript z, but you must remember that the angular momentum defined by Eq. 10-80 is the angular momentum about the rotation axis. Also, I in that equation is the rotational inertia about that same axis.

Table 10-4, which supplements Table 10-3, extends our list of corresponding linear and angular relations.

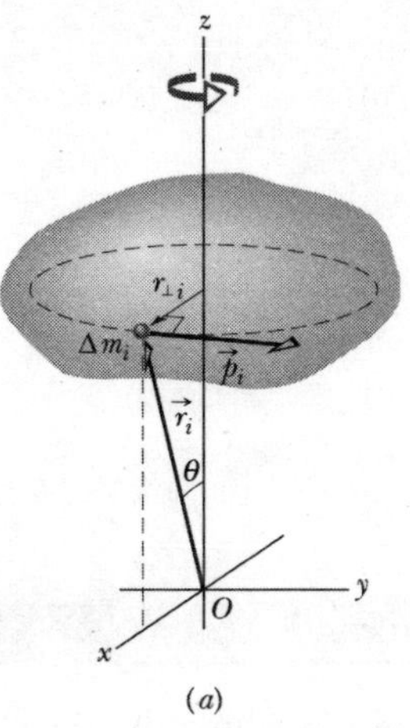

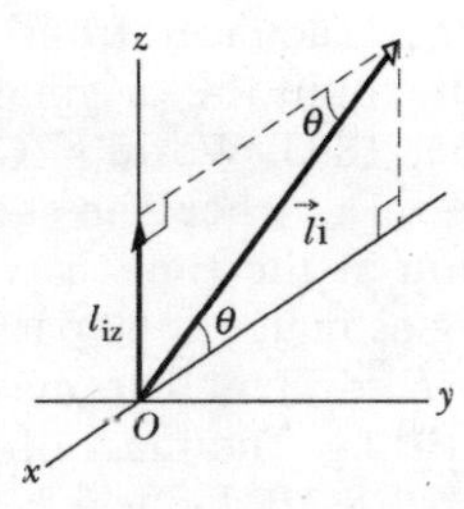

FIG. 10-41 (*a*) A rigid body rotates about a z axis with angular speed ω. A mass element of mass Δm_i within the body moves about the z axis in a circle with radius $r_{\perp i}$. The mass element has linear momentum $\vec{p}_i$, and it is located relative to the origin O by position vector $\vec{r}_i$. Here the mass element is shown when $r_{\perp i}$ is parallel to the x axis. (*b*) The angular momentum $\vec{\ell}_i$, with respect to O, of the mass element in (*a*). The z component ℓ_{iz} is also shown.

TABLE 10-4

More Corresponding Variables and Relations for Translational and Rotational Motion[a]

Translational		Rotational	
Force	$\vec{F}$	Torque	$\vec{\tau}\ (= \vec{r} \times \vec{F})$
Linear momentum	$\vec{p}$	Angular momentum	$\vec{\ell}\ (= \vec{r} \times \vec{p})$
Linear momentum[b]	$\vec{P}\ (= \Sigma \vec{p}_i)$	Angular momentum[b]	$\vec{L}\ (= \Sigma \vec{\ell}_i)$
Linear momentum[b]	$\vec{P} = M\vec{v}_{com}$	Angular momentum[c]	$L = I\omega$
Newton's second law[b]	$\vec{F}_{net} = \dfrac{d\vec{P}}{dt}$	Newton's second law[b]	$\vec{\tau}_{net} = \dfrac{d\vec{L}}{dt}$
Conservation law[d]	$\vec{P}$ = a constant	Conservation law[d]	$\vec{L}$ = a constant

[a]See also Table 10-3.

[b]For systems of particles, including rigid bodies.

[c]For a rigid body about a fixed axis, with L being the component along that axis.

[d]For a closed, isolated system.

CHECKPOINT 17

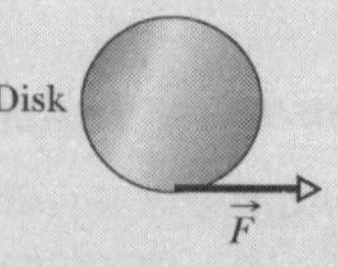

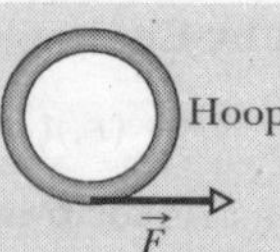

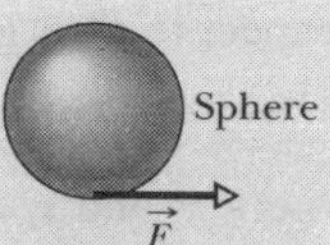

In the figure, a disk, a hoop, and a solid sphere are made to spin about fixed central axes (like a top) by means of strings wrapped around them, with the strings producing the same constant tangential force $\vec{F}$ on all three objects. The three objects have the same mass and radius, and they are initially stationary. Rank the objects according to (a) their angular momentum about their central axes and (b) their angular speed, greatest first, when the strings have been pulled for a certain time t.

Sample Problem 10-20

George Washington Gale Ferris, Jr., a civil engineering graduate from Rensselaer Polytechnic Institute, built the original Ferris wheel (Fig. 10-42) for the 1893 World's Columbian Exposition in Chicago. The wheel, an astounding engineering construction at the time, carried 36 wooden cars, each holding as many as 60 passengers, around a circle of radius $R = 38$ m. The mass of each car was about 1.1×10^4 kg. The mass of the wheel's structure was about 6.0×10^5 kg, which was mostly in the circular grid from which the cars were suspended. The wheel made a complete rotation at an angular speed ω_F in about 2 min.

(a) Estimate the magnitude L of the angular momentum of the wheel and its passengers while the wheel rotated at ω_F.

FIG. 10-42 The original Ferris wheel. *(From "Shepp's World's Fair Photographed" by James W. Shepp and Daniel P. Shepp, Globe Publishing Co., Chicago and Philadelphia, 1893).*

Conceptualize/Classify: We can treat the wheel, cars, and passengers as a rigid object rotating about a fixed axis, at the wheel's axle. Then Eq. 10-80 ($L = I\omega$) gives the magnitude of the angular momentum of that object. We need to find ω_F and the rotational inertia I of this object.

Compute (Rotational inertia): To find I, let us start with the loaded cars. Because we can treat them as particles, at distance R from the axis of rotation, we know from Eq. 10-82 that their rotational inertia is $I_{pc} = M_{pc}R^2$, where M_{pc} is their total mass. Let us assume that the 36 cars are each filled with 60 passengers, each of mass 70 kg. Then their total mass is

$$M_{pc} = 36[1.1 \times 10^4 \text{ kg} + 60(70 \text{ kg})] = 5.47 \times 10^5 \text{ kg}$$

and their rotational inertia is

$$I_{pc} = M_{pc}R^2 = (5.47 \times 10^5 \text{ kg})(38 \text{ m})^2 = 7.90 \times 10^8 \text{ kg}\cdot\text{m}^2.$$

Next we consider the structure of the wheel. Let us assume that the rotational inertia of the structure is due mainly to the circular grid suspending the cars. Further, let us assume that the grid forms a hoop of radius R, with a mass M_{hoop} of 3.0×10^5 kg (half the wheel's mass). From Table 10-2a, the rotational inertia of the hoop is

$$I_{\text{hoop}} = M_{\text{hoop}}R^2 = (3.0 \times 10^5 \text{ kg})(38 \text{ m})^2 = 4.33 \times 10^8 \text{ kg}\cdot\text{m}^2.$$

The combined rotational inertia I of the cars, passengers, and hoop is then

$$I = I_{pc} + I_{\text{hoop}} = 7.90 \times 10^8 \text{ kg}\cdot\text{m}^2 + 4.33 \times 10^8 \text{ kg}\cdot\text{m}^2 = 1.22 \times 10^9 \text{ kg}\cdot\text{m}^2.$$

Angular speed: To find the rotational speed ω_F, we use $\omega_{\text{avg}} = \Delta\theta/\Delta t$. Here the wheel goes through an angular displacement of $\Delta\theta = 2\pi$ rad in a time period $\Delta t = 2$ min. Thus, we have

$$\omega_F = \frac{2\pi \text{ rad}}{(2 \text{ min})(60 \text{ s/min})} = 0.0524 \text{ rad/s}.$$

Angular momentum: Now we can find the magnitude L of the angular momentum with Eq. 10-80:

$$L = I\omega_F = (1.22 \times 10^9\ \text{kg}\cdot\text{m}^2)(0.0524\ \text{rad/s})$$
$$= 6.39 \times 10^7\ \text{kg}\cdot\text{m}^2/\text{s} \approx 6.4 \times 10^7\ \text{kg}\cdot\text{m}^2/\text{s} \quad \text{(Answer)}$$

(b) If the fully loaded wheel is rotated from rest to ω_F in a time period $\Delta t_1 = 5.0$ s, what is the magnitude τ_{avg} of the average net external torque acting on it?

Conceptualize/Classify: The average net external torque is related to the change DL in the angular momentum of the loaded wheel by Eq. (i) ($\vec{\tau}_{net} = d\vec{L}/dt$).

Compute: Because the wheel rotates about a fixed axis to reach angular speed ω_F in time period Δt_1, we can rewrite Eq. (i) as $\tau_{avg} = \Delta L/\Delta t_1$. The change ΔL is from zero to the answer for part (a). Thus, we have

$$\tau_{avg} = \frac{\Delta L}{\Delta t_1} = \frac{6.39 \times 10^7\ \text{kg}\cdot\text{m}^2/\text{s} - 0}{5.0\ \text{s}}$$
$$\approx 1.3 \times 10^7\ \text{N}\cdot\text{m} \quad \text{(Answer)}$$

Sample Problem 10-21 Build your skill

Consider a particle of mass m sliding freely in the x direction with velocity $v = v\hat{\imath}$, as shown in Fig. 10-43.

(a) What is its angular momentum $\vec{L}_A$ about origin A and its angular momentum $\vec{L}_B$ about point B?

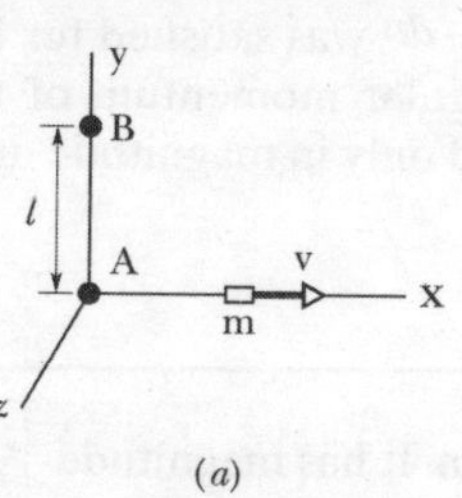

FIG. 10-43 (*a*) A particle of mass *m* sliding freely in the *x* direction, from point *A*. (*b*) The position vector r_A from origin *A* to the current position of block. (*c*) The position vector r_B resolved into components r_x and r_y.

Solution: As shown in Fig. 10-43 the position vector from origin A to the block, r_A is

$$\vec{r}_A = x\hat{\imath}$$
$$\vec{L}_A = m\vec{r}_A \times \vec{v}$$
$$= 0$$

Since $\vec{r}_A$ is parallel to $\vec{v}$, their cross product is zero

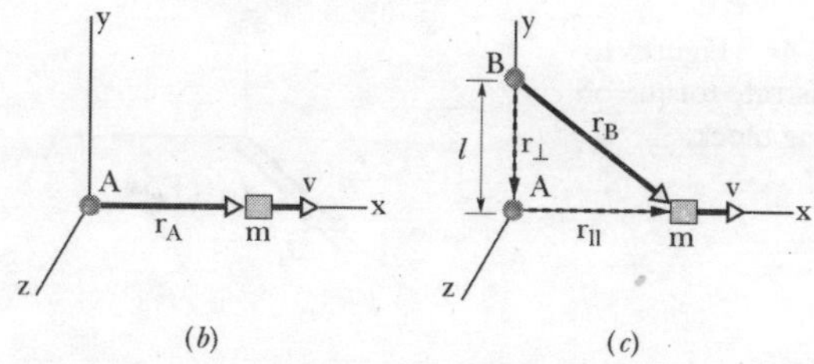

Now writing position vector of particle from B, we can solve the position vector $\vec{r}_B$ into a component $\vec{r}_x$ parallel to and a component $\vec{r}_y$ perpendicular to $\vec{v}$.

Since $\vec{r}_x \times \vec{v} = 0$, only $\vec{r}_y$ gives a contribution to $\vec{L}_B$.

$$\vec{L}_B = m\vec{r}_B \times \vec{v} \quad \text{(Answer)}$$

$$\vec{L}_B = mlv\hat{k} \quad \text{(Answer)}$$

Sample Problem 10-22

In the above example, find torque on the sliding block about A and about B.

Solution: If the block is sliding freely, v does not change, and $\vec{L}_A$, $\vec{L}_B$ is therefore constant, as we expect, since there is no torque acting on the block about A or B. Suppose now that the block in the previous example slows down because of a uniform force $\vec{F}_g = -f\hat{\imath}$. Find the torque on the block about A and B directly and using dL/dt.

Conceptualize/Classify: Angular momentum about A is zero and will remain so, even if speed changes. Thus angular momentum is constant and torque is zero. For B we will go to direct calculation.

Compute: From direct calculation, we can see that torgue about A is

$$\vec{\tau}_A = \vec{r}_A \times \vec{f} = 0$$

As the force and the position vector are parellel, momentum is constant and torgue should be zero.

Compute: For torque about B we go directly to the required equation

$$\vec{\tau}_B = \vec{r}_B \times \vec{f}$$

Thus $\vec{\tau}_B = -lf\hat{k}$

Now we will varify Eq. by directly calculating $\frac{d\vec{L}_B}{dt}$ and equate it to $\vec{\tau}_B$.As the speed of the block decreases, $\vec{L}_B$ remains along the positive z direction but its magnitude decreases. Therefore, the vector $\Delta\vec{L}_B$ which representing change in $\vec{L}_B$ is points in the negative z direction, as shown in the lower figure. Since $\vec{\tau} = d\vec{L}/dt$, the vectors $\vec{\tau}$ and $\Delta\vec{L}$ are always parallel, thus direction of $\Delta\vec{L}_B$ is the same the direction of $\vec{\tau}_B$.

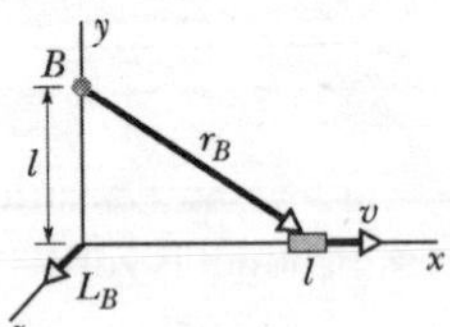

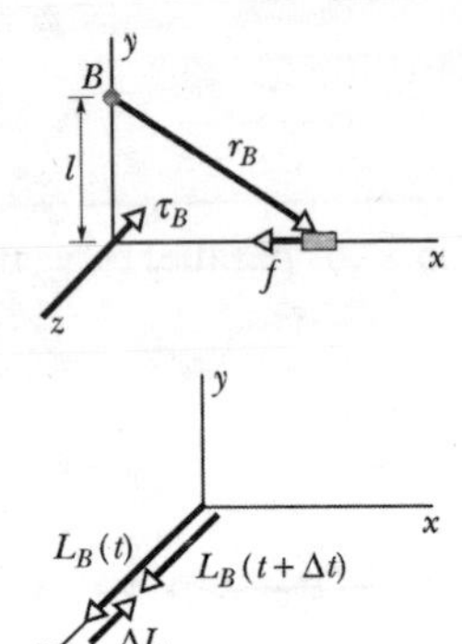

FIG. 10-44 Figures to demonstrate torque on a slliding block.

Hence,

$$\Delta\vec{L}_B = ml\Delta v\hat{k} \qquad \text{(i)}$$

here$\Delta v < 0$ as v is decreasing. Dividing Eq. (i) by Δt and taking the limit $\Delta t \to 0$, we have

$$\frac{d\vec{L}_B}{dt} = ml\frac{dv}{dt}\hat{k} \qquad \text{(ii)}$$

By Newton's second law, $m\ dv/dt = -f$ and Eq. (ii) becomes

$$\frac{dL_B}{dt} = -lf\hat{k} = \tau_B$$

as we expected the result is matching.

Conclude : It is important to remember that since $\vec{\tau}$ and $\vec{L}$ depend on the choice of origin, the same origin must be used for both when applying the relation $\vec{\tau} = d\vec{L}/dt$. When we used A and B as the origin $\vec{\tau} = d\vec{L}/dt$ was satisfied for both the points seperately. The angular momentum of the block in this example changed only in magnitude and not in direction.

Sample Problem 10-23 Build your skill

Angular momentum of the conical pendulum. The conical pendulum is in steady circular motion with constant angular velocity ω as shown in figure. Mass of the particle is m and string makes angle α with vertical. Find angular momentum of the particle about the center C of the circle and the hinge O about which the string is attached.

Conceptualize/Classify: We start by finding L_c, angular mometnum of mass m about point c. We can see that velocity of the particle is always going to be perpendicular to the line joining particle with the center C. Also both vectors r and v are, lying on horizontal (x,y) plane so the angular momentum, L_c will be in the positive z direction. It has magnitude $|r_\perp||p| = |r||p| = rp$, where r is the radius of the circular motion as we can see from Fig. 10-1

$$|p| = Mv = Mr\omega,$$

We know $L_c = rx\,p$ we have $L_c = Mr^2\omega\hat{k}$

Now let us evaluate the angular momentum L_O about the point O located at the hinge.

$$L_O = r' \times p$$

Velocity of the particle is perpendicular to the line op as shown in figure

$$|L_o| = |r' \times p||r'||p| = l|p|$$

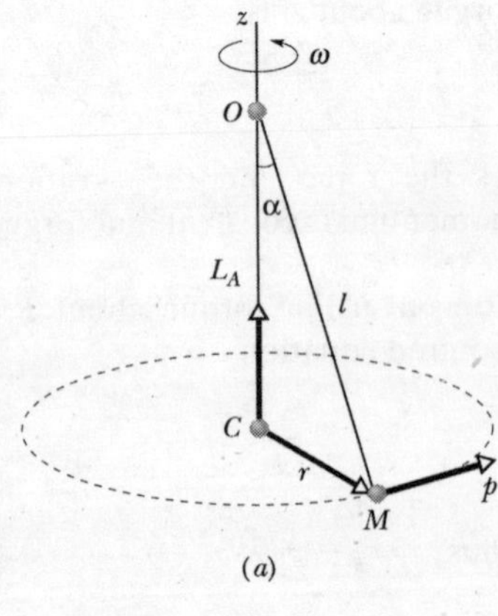

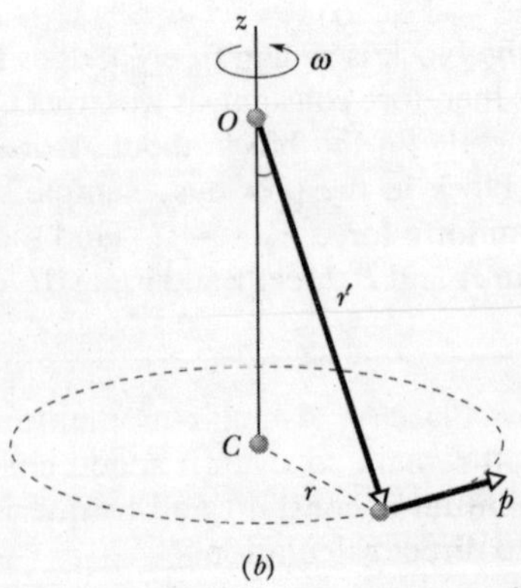

FIG. 10-45 A conical pendulum in steady circular motion with a constant angular velocity.

$$|L_O| = Mlr\omega,$$

where $|r'| = l$, is the length of the string.
It can be again seen that the magnitude of L depends on the choice of the origin.

(b) Also check whether the L is changing or is constant.

Solution: We must note that L_C is constant, both in magnitude and direction. The magnitude of L_O is constant, but its direction is not constant as can be seen from Fig. 10-45 L_O is always perpendicular to the plane containing r' and p. As the particle moves the plane containing r' and p vector hanges, thus changing the direction of L_O. Fig. 10-45 shows L_O at different times. As the bob swings around, L_O rotates as shown in Fig. 10-45. The vertical component of L_O is not moving, but the horizontal component rotates in the circle with the bob.

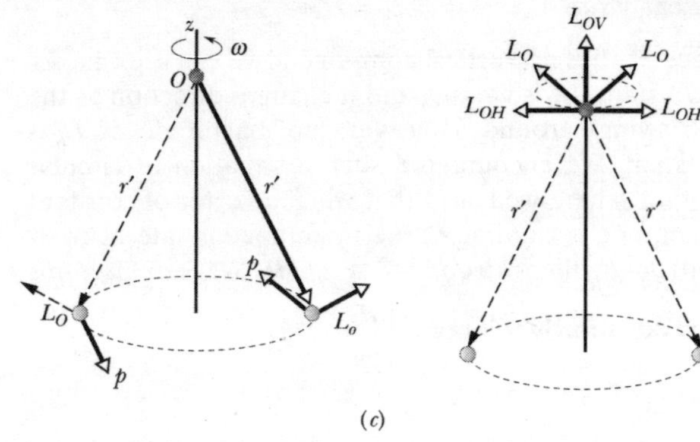

We can draw the angular momentum at any position we choose, only the magnitude and direction of L have to be same.

Sample Problem 10-24

Calculate torque on the conical pendulum about C and about O in the previous example.

Conceptualize: In last problem we calculated the angular momentum of a conical pendulum about two different points. As the angular momrntum about C is not changing in magnitude or direction we should expect to get $\vec{\tau}_A$ to be zero. The magnitude of L_O is constant, but its direction is varying so we should expect to get a non zero $\vec{\tau}_o$.

Classify: Now we shall show that the relation $\vec{\tau} =$ ***dL/dt*** is satisfied by calculating torque and change in angular momentum separately as we did in sample problem 10-23.

Compute: Figure 10-46 shows the free-body diagram of the particle.

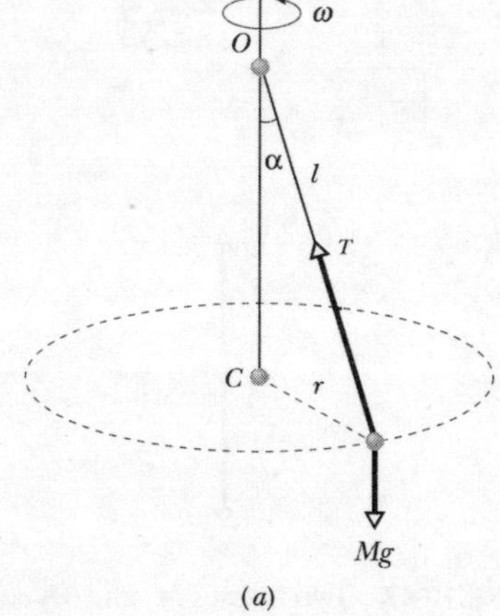

FIG. 10-46 (*a*) Torque on the conical pendulum in steady circular motion with a constant angular velocity. (*b*) and (*c*) show the radial component L_r.

Resolving forces for uniform circular motion since there is no vertical acceleration

$$T\cos\alpha - Mg = 0$$

The total force F on the bob is radially inward:

$$F = -T\sin\alpha\,\hat{r}.$$

The torque on M about C is $\vec{\tau}_C = r_C \times F = 0$ since r_C and F are both in the radial direction.

Hence and we know from Sample Problem 10-23 that L_C is constant and therefore

$$\frac{dL_C}{dt} = 0$$

As we already know from sample problem 10-23 the problem is very different if we take the origin at O as angular momentum about O is changing.
The torque about O is $\vec{\tau}_O$ $\quad \vec{\tau}_O = r_O \times F.$

Hence

$$|\tau_0| = l\cos\alpha\, F = l\cos\alpha\, T\sin\alpha$$

$$(\text{as we know } T\cos\alpha = Mg)$$

$$|\tau_O| = Mgl\sin\alpha$$

The direction of $\vec{\tau}_o$ is always along the velocity of M,

$$\vec{\tau}_O = Mgl\sin\alpha\hat{\theta}$$

$\hat{\theta}$ is the unit vector in tangential direction We want to show that the relation $\vec{\tau}_O = dL_O/dt$ is satisfied.

From sample problem 10-23, we know that L_O has constant magnitude $Mlrw$. As the Fig. 10-46 shows, L_O has a vertical component $L_{BV} = Mlrw\sin\alpha$ and a horizontal radial component $L_{BH} = Mlrw\cos\alpha$.

We can write $L_0 = L_v + L_h$

Since $\vec{\tau}_O$ has no vertical component we can see that L_V is constant. L_H is varying and it changes direction as the bob swings around. However, the magnitude of L_h is constant. We encountered such a situation in circular motion, where we learnt that when a vector of constant magnitude is rotating at the intantaneous rate of rotation $d\theta/dt$, then $|dA/dt| = A\ d\theta/dt$. We can use this relation directly to obtain $\left|\frac{dL_r}{dt}\right| = L_r\omega$ ·

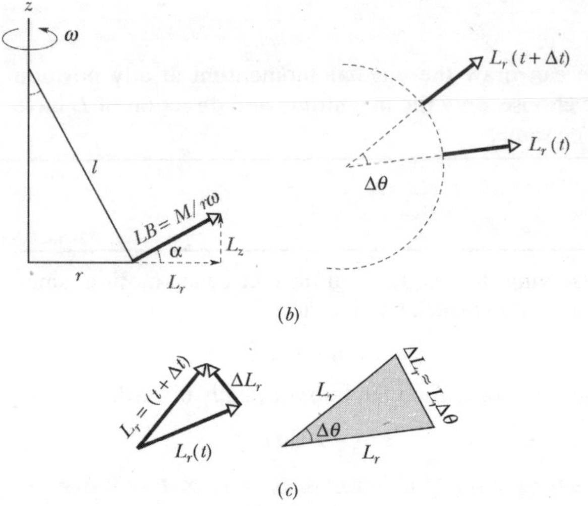

Since we shall use this result frequently, we will derive it again using geometry.

The vector diagrams in Fig. 10-46(*b*) and (*c*) show radial component L_r at some time t and at $t + \Delta t$ During the interval Δt, the bob moves through angle $\Delta\theta = \omega\Delta t$ and the vector L_r rotates through the same angle. The magnitude of the vector difference $\Delta L_r = L_r(t+\Delta t) - L_r(t)$ (*t*) is given approximately by

$$|\Delta L_r| \approx L_r\Delta\theta.$$

In the limit $\Delta t \to 0$, we have

$$|\Delta L_r| / \Delta t = \frac{dL_r}{dt}$$

thus, $$\frac{dL_r}{dt} = L_r\frac{d\theta}{dt} = L_r\omega$$

Since $L_r = Ml r\omega \cos\alpha$ we have

$$\left|\frac{dL_r}{dt}\right| = L_r\omega$$

$Mr\omega^2 = T\sin\alpha$, and $T\cos\alpha = Mg$, we get

$$\frac{dL_r}{dt} = Mlr\omega^2 \cos\alpha$$

Conclude: This agrees with the magnitude of L_O derived earlier. Furthermore, as the vector drawings indicate, dL_r/dt lies in the tangential direction, parallel to τ_O, as we expect.

Sample Problem 10-25

A ball of mass M_1 and a block of mass M_2 are connected by a string that passes over a pulley as shown in Fig. 10-47. The pulley is uniform disc of radius R, and the mass M. Find the acceleration of the two objects, using the concepts of angular momentum and torque.

Conceptualize: If the block M_1 moves upward, the block M_2 moves downward, and the pulley will rotate counterclockwise. This problem is same as sample problem 10-xx we have already solved, except that now we have to use angular momentum and torque to find accleration.

Classify: We define the blocks and pulley as our system. We consider the axle of the pulley as our axis. We can write the angular momentum of the system considering the ball and the block that are moving translationally and the pulley which is undergoing pure rotation. The external torque on the system about the axis is due to the weights of the blocks.

Compute: Due to the constraint the blocks have same speed v. We can find angular momentum using the definition of angular momentum about the axle. Using $L = rxP$

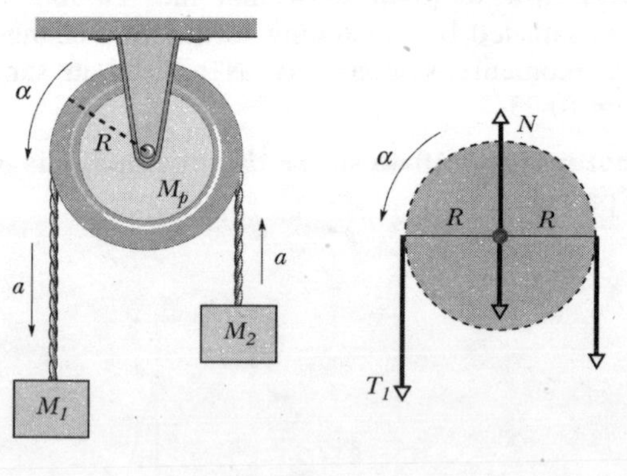

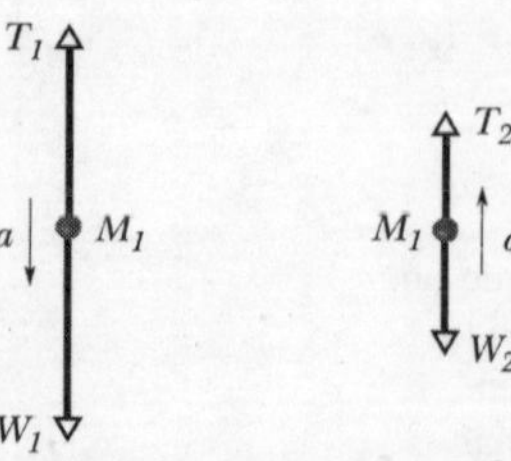

FIG. 10-47 Two masses M_1 and M_2 connected by a string that passes over a pulley.

$$P_1 = -M_1 v\hat{j} \text{ and } r_1 = -R\hat{i} - y_1\hat{j}$$

Using $\boldsymbol{L} = \boldsymbol{rxP}$ the angular momentum of block 1 is $m_1 v R\hat{k}$

$$P_2 = -M_2 v\hat{j} \text{ and } r_2 = R\hat{i} \times y_2\hat{j}$$

Using $\boldsymbol{L} = \boldsymbol{rxP}$ the angular momentum of block 2 is $M_2 v R\hat{k}$ about our chosen axis.

The angular momentum of the pulley can be found using $L = Iw$

Thus, the angular momentum of the pulley about our chosen axis is $MR^2\omega\hat{k}/2$.

We calculate the external torque acting on the system about the pulley axle. The force is being exerted by the axle on the pulley but it does not produce torque about the axle as it the length of moment arm is zero. The gravitational force $M_1\vec{g}$ acting on block 1 produces a torque about the axle equal to $M_1 gR\hat{k}$, and the gravitational force $M_2\vec{g}$ acting on block 2 produces a torque about the axle equal in magnitude to $-M_2 gR\hat{k}$ where R is the moment arm of the force about the axle. Thus the total external torque about the pulley axle is

$$\sum \tau_{ext} = M_1 gR\hat{k} - M_2 gR\hat{k}$$

Write an expression for the total angular momentum of the system:

Substitute this expression and the total external torque

$$L = (M_1 vR + M_2 vR + MvR)\hat{k} \quad \text{(i)}$$

using

$$\sum \tau_{ext} = \frac{dL}{dt}$$

$$M_1 gR\hat{k} - M_2 gR\hat{k} = \frac{d}{dt}[(M_1 + M_2 + M)vR]\hat{k}$$

$$M_1 gR - M_2 gR = (M_1 + M_2 + M)R\frac{dv}{dt} \quad \text{(ii)}$$

Recognizing that $dv/dt = a$, solve Eq. (ii) for a:

$$a = \frac{M_1 g}{M_1 + M_2 + M}$$

Conclude: Answer is same as for Sample Problem 10-17. Evaluating the net torque about the axle, we did not include the forces that the string exerts on the objects because these forces are internal to the system. Instead we analyzed the system as a whole. Only external torques contribute to the change in the system's angular momentum. While solving the same problem previously as sample problem 10-17 we could not have taken pulley and masses as the system is valid only for rigid systems. Here we can consider the pulley, ropes and blocks as one system although they are not a single rigid body because this equation is valid even for non-rigid system.

10-18 | Conservation of Angular Momentum

So far we have discussed two powerful conservation laws, the conservation of energy and the conservation of linear momentum. Now we meet a third law of this type, involving the conservation of angular momentum. We start from Eq. 10-78 ($\vec{\tau}_{net} = d\vec{L}/dt$), which is Newton's second law in angular form. If no net external torque acts on the system, this equation becomes $d\vec{L}/dt = 0$, or

$$\vec{L} = \text{a constant} \quad \text{(isolated system)} \quad (10\text{-}81)$$

This result, called the **law of conservation of angular momentum,** can also be written as

$$\begin{pmatrix}\text{net angular momentum}\\ \text{at some initial time } t_i\end{pmatrix} = \begin{pmatrix}\text{net angular momentum}\\ \text{at some later time } t_f\end{pmatrix}$$

or

$$\vec{L}_i = \vec{L}_f \quad \text{(isolated system)} \quad (10\text{-}82)$$

Equations 10-81 and 10-82 tell us:

If the net external torque acting on a system is zero, the angular momentum $\vec{L}$ of the system remains constant, no matter what changes take place within the system.

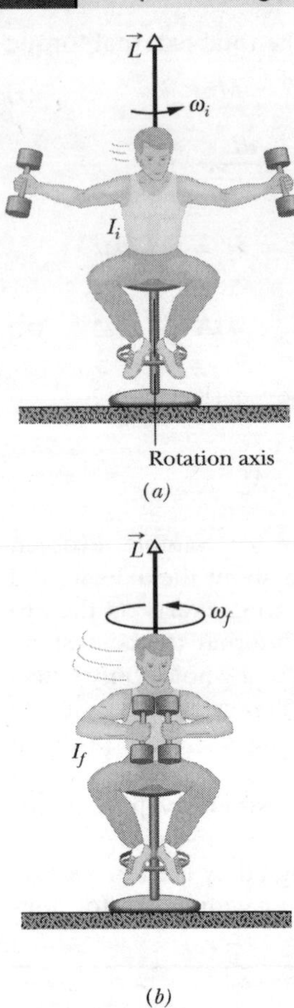

FIG. 10-48 (*a*) The student has a relatively large rotational inertia about the rotation axis and a relatively small angular speed. (*b*) By decreasing his rotational inertia, the student automatically increases his angular speed. The angular momentum $\vec{L}$ of the rotating system remains unchanged.

Equations 10-81 and 10-82 are vector equations; as such, they are equivalent to three component equations corresponding to the conservation of angular momentum in three mutually perpendicular directions. Depending on the torques acting on a system, the angular momentum of the system might be conserved in only one or two directions but not in all directions:

> If the component of the net *external* torque on a system along a certain axis is zero, then the component of the angular momentum of the system along that axis cannot change, no matter what changes take place within the system.

We can apply this law to the isolated body in Fig. 10-48, which rotates around the z axis. Suppose that the initially rigid body somehow redistributes its mass relative to that rotation axis, changing its rotational inertia about that axis. Equations 10-81 and 10-82 state that the angular momentum of the body cannot change. Substituting Eq. 10-80 (for the angular momentum along the rotational axis) into Eq. 10-82, we write this conservation law as

$$I_i\omega_i = I_f\omega_f \tag{10-83}$$

Here the subscripts refer to the values of the rotational inertia I and angular speed ω before and after the redistribution of mass.

Like the other two conservation laws that we have discussed, Eqs. 10-81 and 10-82 hold beyond the limitations of Newtonian mechanics. They hold for particles whose speeds approach that of light (where the theory of special relativity reigns), and they remain true in the world of subatomic particles (where quantum physics reigns). No exceptions to the law of conservation of angular momentum have ever been found.

We now discuss four examples involving this law.

1. ***The spinning volunteer*** Figure 10-48 shows a student seated on a stool that can rotate freely about a vertical axis. The student, who has been set into rotation at a modest initial angular speed ω_i, holds two dumbbells in his outstretched hands. His angular momentum vector $\vec{L}$ lies along the vertical rotation axis, pointing upward.

   The instructor now asks the student to pull in his arms; this action reduces his rotational inertia from its initial value I_i to a smaller value I_f because he moves mass closer to the rotation axis. His rate of rotation increases markedly, from ω_i to ω_f. The student can then slow down by extending his arms once more, moving the dumbbells outward.

   No net external torque acts on the system consisting of the student, stool, and dumbbells. Thus, the angular momentum of that system about the rotation axis must remain constant, no matter how the student maneuvers the dumbbells. In Fig. 10-48*a*, the student's angular speed ω_i is relatively low and his rotational inertia I_i is relatively high. According to Eq. 10-83, his angular speed in Fig. 10-48*b* must be greater to compensate for the decreased I_f.

2. ***The springboard diver*** Figure 10-49 shows a diver doing a forward one-and-a-half-somersault dive. As you should expect, her center of mass follows a parabolic path. She leaves the springboard with a definite angular momentum $\vec{L}$ about an axis through her center of mass, represented by a vector pointing into the plane of Fig. 10-49, perpendicular to the page. When she is in the air, no net external torque acts on her about her center of mass, so her angular momentum about her center of mass cannot change. By pulling her arms and legs into the closed *tuck position,* she can considerably reduce her rotational

inertia about the same axis and thus, according to Eq. 10-83, considerably increase her angular speed. Pulling out of the tuck position (into the *open layout position*) at the end of the dive increases her rotational inertia and thus slows her rotation rate so she can enter the water with little splash. Even in a more complicated dive involving both twisting and somersaulting, the angular momentum of the diver must be conserved, in both magnitude *and* direction, throughout the dive.

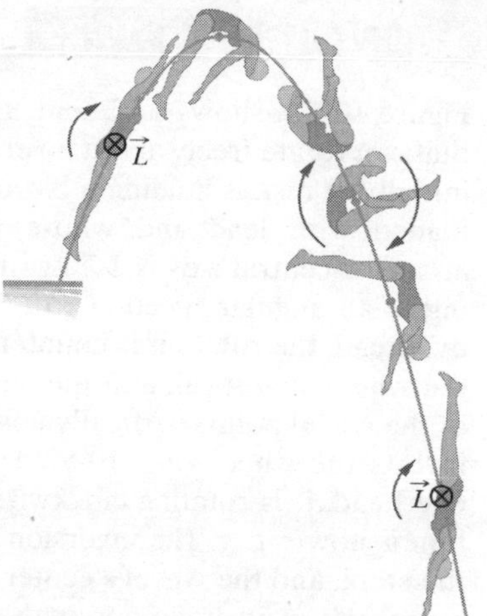

FIG. 10-49 The diver's angular momentum $\vec{L}$ is constant throughout the dive, being represented by the tail ⊗ of an arrow that is perpendicular to the plane of the figure. Note also that her center of mass (see the dots) follows a parabolic path.

3. ***Long jump*** When an athlete takes off from the ground in a running long jump, the forces on the launching foot give the athlete an angular momentum with a forward rotation around a horizontal axis. Such rotation would not allow the jumper to land properly: In the landing, the legs should be together and extended forward at an angle so that the heels mark the sand at the greatest distance. Once airborne, the angular momentum cannot change (it is conserved) because no external torque acts to change it. However, the jumper can shift most of the angular momentum to the arms by rotating them in windmill fashion (Fig. 10-50). Then the body remains upright and in the proper orientation for landing.

FIG. 10-50 Windmill motion of the arms during a long jump helps maintain body orientation for a proper landing.

4. ***Tour jeté*** In a tour jeté, a ballet performer leaps with a small twisting motion on the floor with one foot while holding the other leg perpendicular to the body (Fig. 10-51*a*). The angular speed is so small that it may not be perceptible to the audience. As the performer ascends, the outstretched leg is brought down and the other leg is brought up, with both ending up at angle θ to the body (Fig. 10-51*b*). The motion is graceful, but it also serves to increase the rotation because bringing in the initially outstretched leg decreases the performer's rotational inertia. Since no external torque acts on the airborne performer, the angular momentum cannot change. Thus, with a decrease in rotational inertia, the angular speed must increase. When the jump is well executed, the performer seems to suddenly begin to spin and rotates 180° before the initial leg orientations are reversed in preparation for the landing. Once a leg is again outstretched, the rotation seems to vanish.

FIG. 10-51 (*a*) Initial phase of a tour jeté: large rotational inertia and small angular speed. (*b*) Later phase: smaller rotational inertia and larger angular speed.

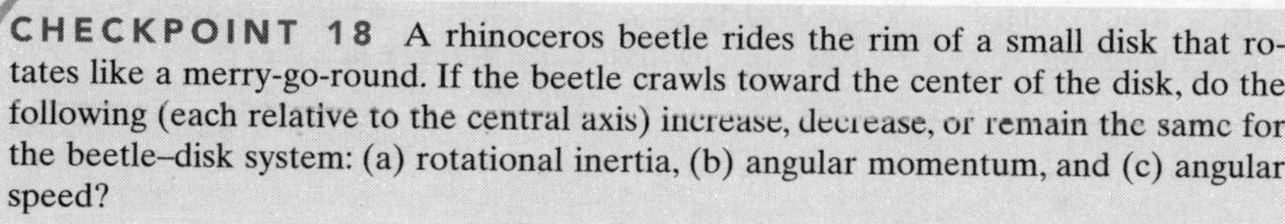

CHECKPOINT 18 A rhinoceros beetle rides the rim of a small disk that rotates like a merry-go-round. If the beetle crawls toward the center of the disk, do the following (each relative to the central axis) increase, decrease, or remain the same for the beetle–disk system: (a) rotational inertia, (b) angular momentum, and (c) angular speed?

Sample Problem 10-26

Figure 10-52*a* shows a student, again sitting on a stool that can rotate freely about a vertical axis. The student, initially at rest, is holding a bicycle wheel whose rim is loaded with lead and whose rotational inertia I_{wh} about its central axis is 1.2 kg·m². The wheel is rotating at an angular speed ω_{wh} of 3.9 rev/s; as seen from overhead, the rotation is counterclockwise. The axis of the wheel is vertical, and the angular momentum $\vec{L}_{wh}$ of the wheel points vertically upward. The student now inverts the wheel (Fig. 10-52*b*) so that, as seen from overhead, it is rotating clockwise. Its angular momentum is now $-\vec{L}_{wh}$. The inversion results in the student, the stool, and the wheel's center rotating together as a composite rigid body about the stool's rotation axis, with rotational inertia $I_b = 6.8$ kg·m². (The fact that the wheel is also rotating about its center does not affect the mass distribution of this composite body; thus, I_b has the same value whether or not the wheel rotates.) With what angular speed ω_b and in what direction does the composite body rotate after the inversion of the wheel?

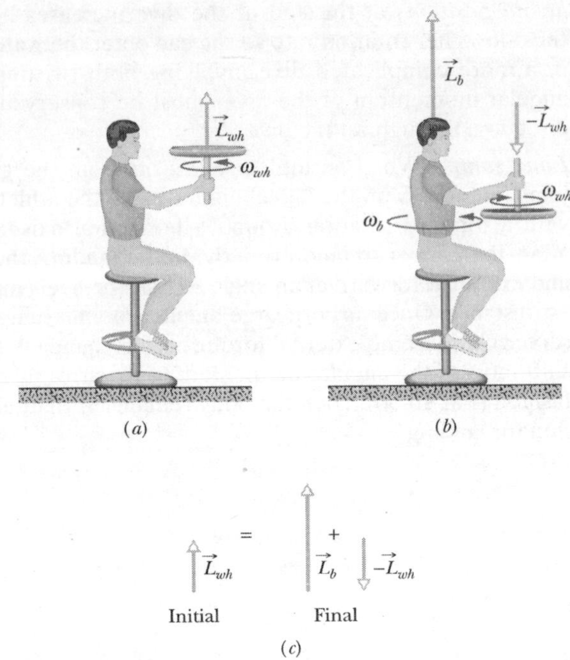

FIG. 10-52 (*a*) A student holds a bicycle wheel rotating around a vertical axis. (*b*) The student inverts the wheel, setting himself into rotation. (*c*) The net angular momentum of the system must remain the same in spite of the inversion.

Conceptualize: The angular speed ω_b we seek is related to the final angular momentum $\vec{L}_b$ of the composite body about the stool's rotation axis by Eq. 10-80 ($L = I\omega$).

The initial angular speed ω_{wh} of the wheel is related to the angular momentum $\vec{L}_{wh}$ of the wheel's rotation about its center by the same equation.

Classify: The vector addition of $\vec{L}_b$ and $\vec{L}_{wh}$ gives the total angular momentum $\vec{L}_{tot}$ of the system of student, stool, and wheel.

As the wheel is inverted, no net *external* torque acts on that system to change $\vec{L}_{tot}$ about any vertical axis. (torque due to forces between the student and the wheel as the student inverts the wheel are *internal* to the system). So, the system's total angular momentum is conserved about any vertical axis.

Compute: The conservation of $\vec{L}_{tot}$ is represented with vectors in Fig. 10-52*c*. We can also write this conservation in terms of components along a vertical axis as

$$L_{b,f} + L_{wh,f} = L_{b,i} + L_{wh,i}, \qquad (10\text{-}84)$$

where *i* and *f* refer to the initial state (before inversion of the wheel) and the final state (after inversion). Because inversion of the wheel inverted the angular momentum vector of the wheel's rotation, we substitute $-L_{wh,i}$ for $L_{wh,f}$. Then, if we set $L_{b,i} = 0$ (because the student, the stool, and the wheel's center were initially at rest), Eq. 10-35 yields

$$L_{b,f} = 2L_{wh,i}.$$

Using Eq. 10-31, we next substitute $I_b\omega_b$ for $L_{b,f}$ and $I_{wh}\omega_{wh}$ for $L_{wh,i}$ and solve for ω_b, finding

$$\omega_b = \frac{2I_{wh}}{I_b}\omega_{wh}$$

$$= \frac{(2)(1.2 \text{ kg}\cdot\text{m}^2)(3.9 \text{ rev/s})}{6.8 \text{ kg}\cdot\text{m}^2} = 1.4 \text{ rev/s}. \qquad \text{(Answer)}$$

Conclude: This positive result tells us that the student rotates counterclockwise about the stool axis as seen from overhead. If the student wishes to stop rotating, he has only to invert the wheel once more.

Sample Problem 10-27

In Fig. 10-53, a cockroach with mass m rides on a disk of mass $6.00m$ and radius R. The disk rotates like a merry-go-round around its central axis at angular speed $\omega_i = 1.50$ rad/s. The cockroach is initially at radius $r = 0.800R$, but then it crawls out to the rim of the disk. Treat the cockroach as a particle. What then is the angular speed?

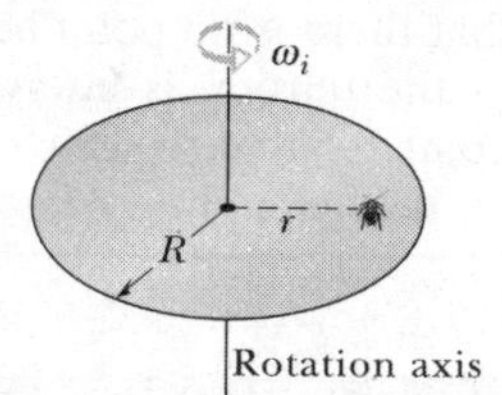

FIG. 10-53 A cockroach rides at radius r on a disk rotating like a merry-go-round.

Conceptualize: The cockroach's crawl changes the mass distribution (and thus the rotational inertia) of the cockroach–disk system.

Classify: The angular momentum of the system does not change because there is no external torque to change it. (The forces and torques due to the cockroach's crawl are internal to the system.)

We want to find the final angular speed. Our key is to equate the final angular momentum L_f to the initial angular momentum L_i, because both involve angular speed. They also involve rotational inertia I.

Compute: So, let's start by finding the rotational inertia of the system of cockroach and disk before and after the crawl.

The rotational inertia of a disk rotating about its central axis is given by Table 10-2c as ½MR^2. Substituting 6.00m for the mass M, our disk here has rotational inertia

$$I_d = 3.00mR^2 \tag{10-85}$$

(We don't have values for m and R, but we shall continue with physics courage.)

From Eq. 10-82, we know that the rotational inertia of the cockroach (a particle) is equal to mr^2. Substituting the cockroach's initial radius ($r = 0.800R$) and final radius ($r = R$), we find that its initial rotational inertia about the rotation axis is

$$I_{ci} = 0.64mR^2 \tag{10-86}$$

and its final rotational inertia about the rotation axis is

$$I_{cf} = mR^2 \tag{10-87}$$

So, the cockroach–disk system initially has the rotational inertia

$$I_i = I_d + I_{ci} = 3.64mR^2 \tag{10-88}$$

and finally has the rotational inertia

$$I_f = I_d + I_{cf} = 4.00mR^2 \tag{10-89}$$

Next, we use Eq. 10-80 ($L = I\omega$) to write the fact that the system's final angular momentum L_f is equal to the system's initial angular momentum L_i:

$$I_f\omega_f = I_i\omega_i$$

or

$$4.00mR^2\omega_f = 3.64mR^2(1.50 \text{ rad/s})$$

After canceling the unknowns m and R, we come to

$$\omega_f = 1.37 \text{ rad/s} \quad \text{(Answer)}$$

Conclude: Note that the angular speed decreased because part of the mass moved outward from the rotation axis. Thus, increasing moment of inertia and decreasing angular velocity to keep angular momentum conserved. It can also be understood from force that while moving out the tangential component of force that cockroach applies on the disc is producing torque in opposite sense of the angular velocity.

Sample Problem 10-28 Build your skill

On a horizontal smooth plane there is a fixed vertical cylinder and a particle A connected to the cylinder by a thread AB (Fig. 10-54) top view. The particle is set in motion with the initial velocity v as shown in the figure. Is there any fixed point here relative to which the angular momentum of the particle is constant in the process of motion?

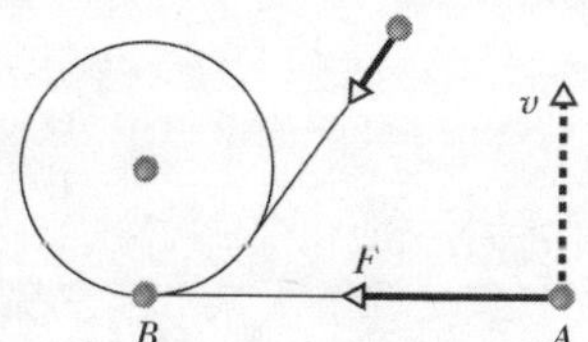

FIG. 10-54 Fixed vertical cylinder on a smooth plane.

Solution: The only force acting on the particle A in this case is the tension F of the thread. It is easy to see that there is no point here relative to which the torque of the tension is always zero. Therefore, there is no point relative to which the angular momentum of the particle would be constant. The tension acting on the particle is along the string. Thus any point lying on the line of string, will have zero torque due to tension, about itself. Since particle is moving this line keeps on changing. This example illustrates that sometimes a point relative to which the angular mometnum of a particle is constant cannot be found at all.

Sample Problem 10-29

Two identical small balls of radius r_1 are mounted on a rough horizontal light bar along which they can slide (Fig. 10-55). Initially the spheres are brought together and connected by a thread. Then the whole assembly is set into rotation about a vertical axis with angular velocity ω_0. After a period of free rotation, the thread is burned up, the spheres fly apart toward the ends of the bar. If length of bar on either side of axis is l, find the angular velocity of the assembley when the balls reach the ends.

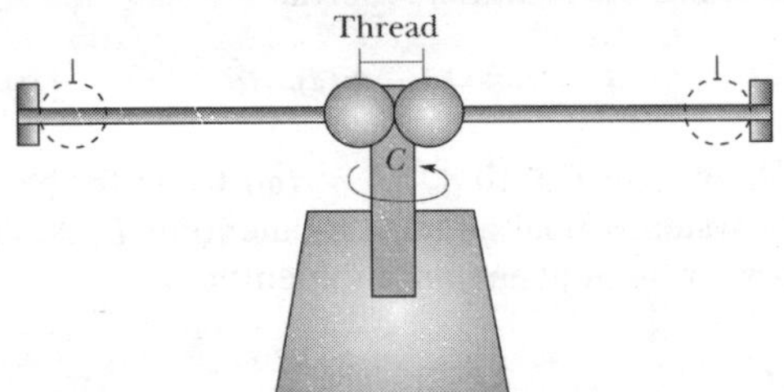

FIG. 10-55 Identical balls mounted in light bar.

Conceptualize: It is easy to imagine that balls will move symmetrically towards the ends.

Classify: The observed phenomenon is a direct result of the conservation of angular momentum. As this assembly behaves as a system experiencing zero torque.

Compute: As given the sizes of spheres are negligible. Then, using the law of conservation of angular momentum relative to the point C in the initial and final states of the system,

$$2\,m\,[r_1 v_1] = 2m\,[r_2 v_2]$$

it follows that,

$$r_1^2\,\omega_1 = r_2^2\omega_2$$

Conclude: It is seen that as the distance r from the spheres to the rotation axis grows, the angular velocity of the assembly decreases (as $1/r^2$). And vice versa, if the distance between the spheres decreases (due to some internal forces), the angular velocity of the assembly increases.

Note that the final result is quite independent of the nature of internal forces (here the friction forces between the spheres and the bar).

Sample Problem 10-30 Build your skill

Disc 1 (Fig. 10-56) rotates about a smooth vertical axis with the angular velcotiy ω_1. Disc 2 rotating with the angular velocity ω_2 is kept on disc 1 while rotating in the same direction. Find the change in the rotational kinetic energy of the system given that the moments of inertia of the discs relative to the rotation axis are equal to I_1 and I_2 respectively. The contact surfaces of the discs are rough.

Conceptualize: It is easy to imagine that finally disks will start rotating with same angular velocity. Friction between the two disks will slow down the faster disks and speed up the slower disks.

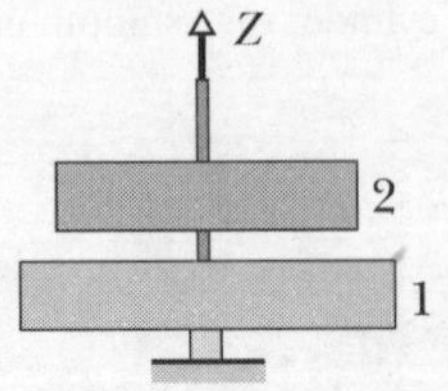

FIG. 10-56 Two discs rotating about vertical axis.

Classify: It is easy to understand that we can conserve angular momentum of the assembly about the axis as friction between the two disks will be providing internal torque.

Compute: Let us say the final angular velocity of rotation of the assembly is. From the law of conservation of the angular momentum relative to the axis is

$$I_1\omega_1 + I_2\omega_2 = (I_1 + I_2)\,\omega, \text{ thus}$$

$$\omega = (I_1\omega_1 + I_2\omega_2)\,/\,(I_1 + I_2) \tag{10-90}$$

Note that ω_1, ω_2 and ω are algebraic quantities. If $\omega > 0$, the corresponding vector coincides with the positive direction of the z axis, and vice versa.

Initial kinetic energy $I_1\omega^2{}_1/2 + I_1\omega^2{}_1/2$

Final kinetic energy $(I_1 + I_2)\,\omega^2/2$

The change in the kinetic energy of rotation for this system is

$$\Delta T = (I_1 + I_2)\omega^2/2 - (I_1\omega_1^2/2 + I_2\omega_2^2/2)$$

Replacing ω_2 by its expression, we get

$$\Delta T = -\frac{I_1 + I_2}{2(I_1 + I_2)}(\omega_{1z} - \omega_{2z})^2 \quad (10\text{-}91)$$

Conclude: The minus sign shows that the kinetic energy of the system decreases.

Note that the result in Eqs. 10-90 and 10-91 are quite similar in form and meaning to the case of absolutely inelastic collision.

Sample Problem 10-31

A smooth rod of length l rotates freely in a horizontal plane with the angular velocity about a stationary vertical axis O as shown in (Fig. 10-57) The moment of inertia of the rod is equal to I relative to the axis . A small ring of mass m is located on the rod close to the rotation axis and is tied to it by a thread. When the thread is burned, the ring starts sliding radially outwards along the rod. Find the velocity v of the ring relative to the rod as a function of its distance r from the rotation axis.

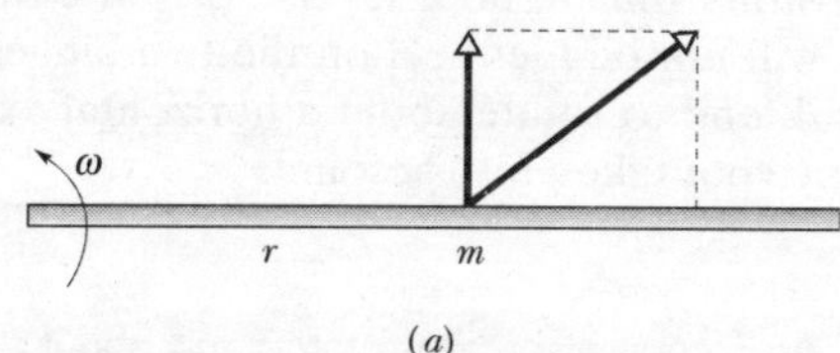

FIG. 10-57 (a) Smooth rod rotating freely.

Conceptualize: Considering the rod and the ring as our system. The system is experiencing no external torque about the axis hence the angular momentum relative to the rotation axis does not vary. There is no nonconservative force or impulse occuring so in the process of motion the kinetic energy of the system does not vary.

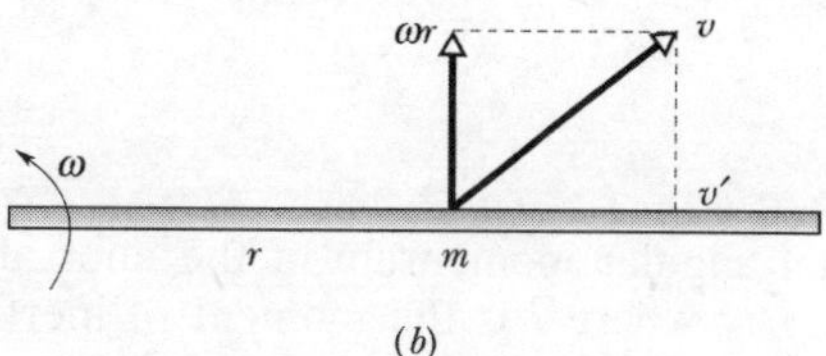

Compute: Hence, we can conserve angular momentum about the axis and kinetic energy of the system.

$$I\omega_0 = (I + mr^2)\omega \quad 1/2(I\omega_0^2) = (1/2)\,I\omega^2 + (1/2)\,m/v^2$$

where $v^2 = v_2 + \omega^2 r^2$ (Fig.). From these equation we obtain

$$v' = w_0 r / \sqrt{1 + mr^2 / I}$$

Conclude: If we keep $r = 0$ we get $v = 0$ which is the situation at the begining.

Sample Problem 10-32

Who isn't familiar with the sound of doors banging in sudden dust and rain storms. The regular banging of a door against its stopper can loosen and damage the hinges of the door. The proper choice of the distance of the doorstop from the hinges can remove all the impulses acting ont the hinges. In the Fig. 10-58 consider the door as a uniform rectangular plate hinged about a frictionless vertical axis. If the length of the door is l, find the distance of the doorstop from the hinges.

Conceptualize: Imagine that door is rotating anti clockwise and is going to strike the doorstop with angular velocity ω_0.

Classify: The forces on the door during impact are F_d, due to the stop, and F' and F'' due to the hinge. F' is the small radial force which provides the centripetal acceleration of the swinging door.

Compute: F' and F_d are the large impulsive forces which bring the door to rest immedietely when it bangs against the stop. The force on the hinges is equal and opposite to F' and F''. To minimise the damage to the hinges we should make F' as small as possible.

Now to derive an expression for F', we shall use impulse momentum equation and angular impulse momentum equation for the door.

since $dL = \tau\, dt$, we have $L_{\text{final}} - L_{\text{initial}} = \int_{ij}^{ij} \tau\, dt$

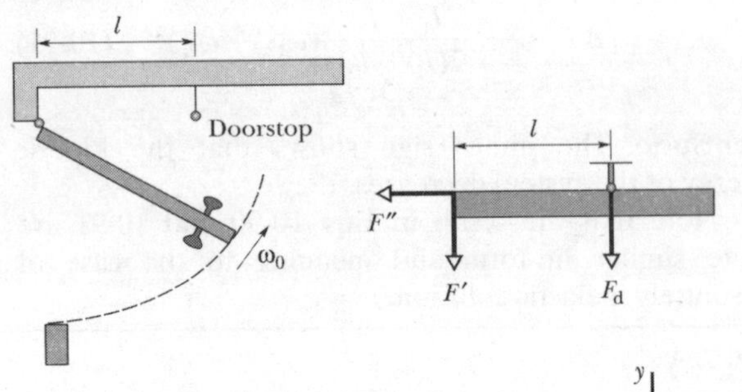

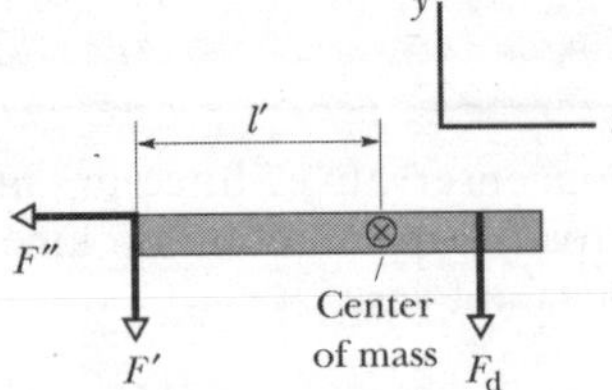

FIG. 10-58 Banging of door and center of mass.

The initial angular momentum of the door about the hinges is $I\omega_0$, where I is the moment of inertia about the hinges. Since the door comes to rest just after the impact, $L_{\text{final}} = 0$. The torque on the door during the collision is in counterclockwise sense and thus $\tau = -lF_d$, and we obtain $I\omega_0 = l \int F_d\, dt$,

where the integral is over the duration of the collision Also, from linear impulse momentum equation

$$P_{\text{final}} - P_{\text{initial}} = \int F\, dt$$

where F is the total force. The momentum in the y direction immediately before the collision is $MV_y = Ml$ ω'_0, where l' is the distance from the hinges to the center of mass of the door. $P_{\text{final}} = 0$, and the y component of F is $F_y = -(F' + F_d)$. Hence.

$$Ml'\omega = \int (F' + F_d)\, dt$$

According to the equation $\int F_d\, dt = I\omega_0/l$ and substituting this in Eq. ( ) gives

$$\int F'\, dt = \left(Ml' - \frac{1}{l} \right) \omega_0 1/l\ \omega_0$$

by choosing the impact force can be made zero.

If the door is uniform, and of width d, then $I = Md^2/3$ and $l' = d/2$. In this case $l = 2/3\ d$.

Conclude: The stop must be at the height of the center of mass rather than at floor level. Otherwise the impact forces will not be identical on the two hinges and the door will tend to rotate about a horizontal axis, an effect we have not taken into account.

CHECKPOINT 19 A rod of mass 12 m and length l lying on a smooth horizontal plane can rotate freely about a stationary, vertical axis passing through the rod's end. A disc of mass m moving along the plane with speed u hits the rod's end perpendicularly and gets stuck there. Find the angular velocity of the system.

Sample Problem 10-33

Angular momentum of a rotating skew rod

Consider a uniform rigid rod of mass m and length a. The midpoint of the rod point O, is attached to a vertical axis which rotates at angular speed ω. The rod is skewed at angle α, as shown in the sketch. Find the angular momentum of the rod about the mid point of the rod .

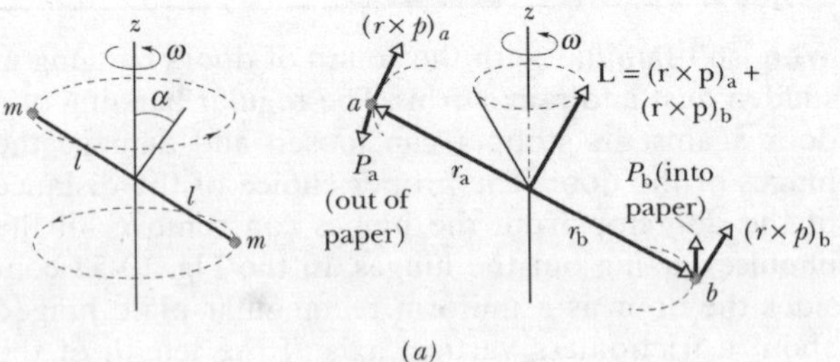

FIG. 10-59 Angular momentum of a rotating skew rod.

Conceptualize: This rod is same as the rod of eg(), where we found moment of interia about the same axis. Do not use $L=I\omega$ as this is valid only for bodies symmetric about the axis and it is very clear that this is not symmetric about the axis.

Classify: The most direct method is to calculate the angular mometnum from the definition $L = \Sigma(r_j \times p_j)$. Consider an element of length dx at distance x from the center. Each element moves in a circle of radius

$$r = x \cos \alpha$$

with angular speed ω.

Compute: The momentum of element is $|p| = dm(\omega x \cos \alpha)$, tangential to the circular path. Taking the midpoint of the skew rod as origin, $|r|=l$. r lies along the rod and is perpendicular to p.

$$dL = r \times p = |r| \times |p| \qquad \text{hence } |dL| = dm\, \omega\, l^2 \cos \omega$$

dL is perpendicular to the skew rod and for all elements it will be in the same direction thus integrating over the whole rod we get

$$|L| = m\omega\, l^2 \cos \alpha / 12$$

Conclude: L is perpendicular to the skew rod and lies in the plane of the rod and the z axis,and it turns with the rod, and its tip traces out a circle about the z axis. as shown in the left hand drawing below.

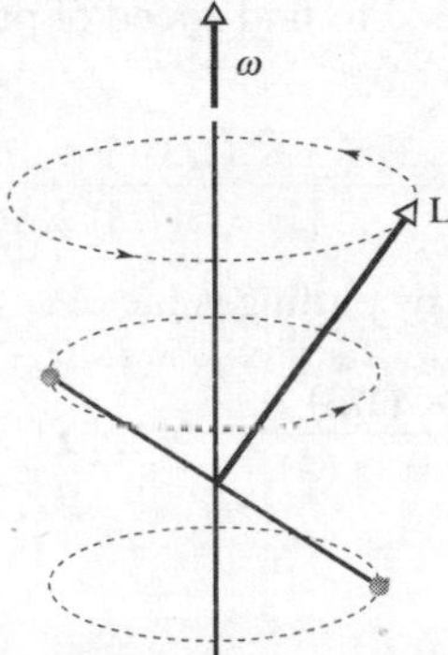

We encountered a similar situation in sample problem 10-xx with the conical pendulum. Note that $|L|$ is not equal to $I\omega$. You can recall from sample problem 10-xx that $I = (ml^2/12)\cos^2 \omega$. $|L| = I\omega$ is generally not true for nonsymmetric bodies.

(b) Find torque on the rotating skew rod

Conceptualize: As we have seen in the first part of this problem that horizontal component of angular momentum vector is changing the direction, so there is requirement of torque to achieve that change. Although if we use Eq. 10-xx it may appear tht since v is constant and angular acceleration is zero and so the torque is zero. At the end of solution we will explain the apperent failure of $\tau = I\alpha$

Classify: We will be using geometric arguments which will emphasizes the connection between torque and the rate of change of angular momentum.

Compute: As in sample problem 10-xx, we resolve L into a verical component $L_v = L \cos \alpha$ and a horizontal component $L_h = L \sin \alpha$ as shown in the figureh. Since L_v is constant, there is no torque about the z axis. L_h vis constant in magnitude but is rotating with the rod. The rate of change of L is due to this component only. Once again we are dealing with a rotating vector. From sample problem 10-xx, we should know that $dL_h/dt = \omega L_h$. We will derive this result once more since it is important to be able to visualize the rotation of L_h. From the vector diagram we have

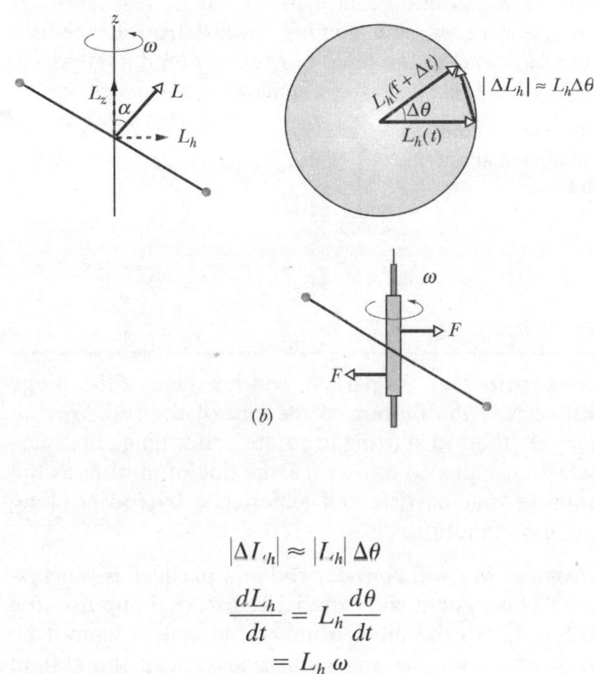

$$|\Delta L_h| \approx |L_h|\, \Delta\theta$$

$$\frac{dL_h}{dt} = L_h \frac{d\theta}{dt}$$
$$= L_h\, \omega$$

The torque is given by

$$\tau = \frac{dL_h}{dt}$$
$$= L_h\, \omega$$
$$= \omega\, L \sin \alpha$$

The torque τ is in the tangential direction in the horizontal plane and rotates with the rod.

Conclude: From the equation $\tau = I\alpha$ we may have thought that torque on a rotating system always causes the speed of rotation to change. The equation $\tau = I\alpha$ is useful only when angular acceleration and torque vectors are parallel. In this problem the speed of rotation is constant, and the torque causes the direction of L to change. Furthermore, it illustrates that torque and angular momentum are real vectors which can be resolved into components along any axes we choose. Also it is important to note that the torque is being produced by the forces on the rotating bearing of the skew rod.

Find the torque in case of $\alpha = 0$ or $\alpha = \pi/2$.

Solution: $\tau = 0$, this is because body becomes symmetric and angular momentum have only vertical component which is constant.

Sample Problem 10-34

A uniform rod of mass m and length l is hinged about one of its end. The hinge is smooth and rod lies on a smooth horizontal surface as shown in Fig. 10-61. A particle of mass m is coming towards rod at speed u perpendicular to the length of rod (a) Find angular velocity of the rod just after impact

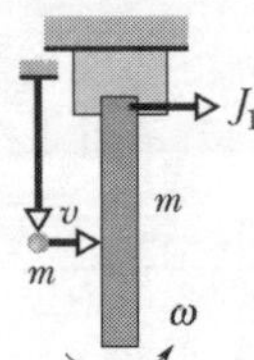

FIG. 10-61 Uniform rod hinged about one end.

Conceptualize: As particle will hit the rod the hinge will restrict the motion of the end of the rod. We can imagine the rod starting to rotate about hinge and particle continuing to move on same line of motion as the Impulse that particle will experience by rod is along the line of motion.

Classify: We will consider rod and particle as our system. This system will experience external impulse due to hinge. So the momentum of the system cannot be conserved. But the angular momentum of the system about hinge will remain conserved as torque due to impulse at hinge is zero.

Compute: By conserving angular momentum about hinge

$$mux = mvx + \frac{ml^2\omega}{3}$$

here v is the speed of particle after the collision and ω is the angular velocity of rod after? as shown in Fig. We can also write Newton's law of collision remembering that it is the velocity of contact points that is required.

$$\frac{\omega x - v}{0 - u} = -e$$

Solving the two Eqs. we get $\omega = \dfrac{3ux(l + e)}{(l^2 + 3x^2)}$

(b) Also find impulse due to hinge on rod during collision.

Conceptualize: Coefficient of restitution is e and perpendicular distance of line of motion from hinge is x. Consider $e = 1/3$, $u = 3$ m/s, and $l = 1$ m, $m = 2$ kg and $x = 1/3$ m.

Classify: Now to find impulse due to hinge J_1, we will consider rod and particle as our system and write Impulse momentum equation.

Compute: We should remember that impulse between rod and particle during collision need not be considered since it will be in internal impulse thus we can write.

$$\vec{J}_1 = (\vec{P}_{\text{rod}\,f} + \vec{P}_{\text{Particle}\,f}) - (\vec{P}_{\text{rod}\,i} + \vec{P}_{\text{Particle}\,i})$$

$$\vec{P}_{\text{Particle}\,i} = 6\,\text{Nm} \quad \vec{P}_{\text{rod}\,i} = 0$$

For $P_{\text{Particle}\,f}$ we need to find speed of particle from part (a)

$$\omega = \frac{3 \times 3 \times (1/3)(1 + 1/3)}{[1^2 + 3(1/3)^2]}$$

Now solving for v by putting value of ω

$$\frac{3 \times (1/3) - v}{0 - (3)} = -(1/3)$$

Solving $v = 0$

Hence $P_{\text{Particle}\,f} = 0$

For $\vec{P}_{\text{rod}\,f}$ we need velocity of center of mass of rod as $\vec{P}_{\text{rod}\,f} = MV_{\text{cm}}$ thus

$$V_{cm} = \omega \times r_c = \omega \times \frac{l}{2} = \frac{3}{2}\,\text{rod}\,s^{-1}$$

thus, $\quad P_{rf} = 2 \times \dfrac{3}{2} = 3$ kg m/s

Hence, $\quad J_1 = (3 + 0) - (0 + 6) = -3$

Conclude: The negative sign on impulse means that impulse on the rod by the hinge is toward left. This means the end attached to the axis must have tried to move toward right and hinge opposed the motion by applying impulse toward left.

In Case Of: What will be the sign of J_1 if particle hits the rod close to the other end.

Solution: The sign will be positive as the end attached to the hinge will have tendency to go left and hence the hinge will apply impulse toward right.

Sample Problem 10-35

A horizontal, homogeneous cylinder of mass M and radius R is pivoted about its axis M, and radius R is pivoted about its axis of symmetry. As shown in Fig. 10-60*a*, a string is wrapped several times around the cylinder and tied to a body of mas m resting on a support positioned so that the string has no slack. The body m is carefuly lifted vertically at distance h, and then released.

(a) Just before the string becomes taut, evaluate the angular velocity ω_0 of the cylinder, the speed v_0 of the falling body m, and the kinetic energy K_0 of the system.

(b) Evaluate the corresponding quantities, ω_1, v_1, and K_1, for the instant just after the string becomes taut.

Conceptualize: Since string is slack it is easy to imagine that block will feel freel for distance λ. Till this time tension in string will be zero.

Classify: (a) Just before the string becomes taut, the cylinder is still at rest. Since the tension remained zero nothing has caused the cylinder to begin turning. That is, $\omega_0 = 0$. Since the string has exerted no force on the body of mass m, it has fallen freely with accln g thus $v_0 = \sqrt{2gh}$. Same result can be derived by writing work kinetic energy theorem for the system. The kinetic energy of the system is given by

$$K_0 = \frac{1}{2}mv_0^2 + \frac{1}{2}I_c\omega_0^2 = mgh.$$

solving we get $v_0 = \sqrt{2gh}$

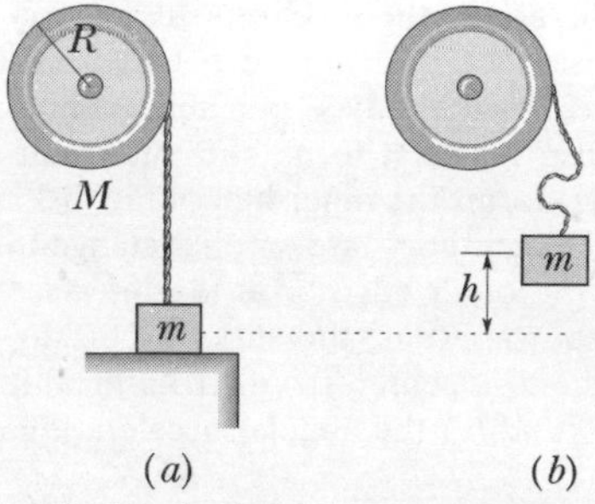

FIG. 10-60 Cylinder pivoted about its axis.

Conceptualize/Classify: (b) The end attached to the block will be moving and it will pull the part of string touching the cylinder as the string becomes taut.

Thus when string becomes tight an impulse/jerk will develop in the string. This jerk will start the motion of cylinder. There will be also an impulse due to axis of the cylinder. Here we can take cylinder, string and block as our system. We will take axle of cylinder as the axis for writing angular momentum.

Compute: The impulse due to jerk in string will produce internal angular impulse, and the impulse due to l the will produce zero angular impulse about the axle. Furthermore, the angular momentum of the system must be conserved, since the impulse due to the snap of the string is of very short duration and the weight mg contributes negligibly in that time. The string is assumed to be inextensible, so $v_1 = \omega_1 R$.

Thus we have $L_1 = mv_1R + 1/2\ MR^2\omega\ 1 = L_0$, where $L_0 = mv_0\ R = m\ \sqrt{2gh}\ R$. Solving for the angular speed, we find

$$\omega_1 = \frac{v_0}{R[1+(M/2m)]} = \frac{\sqrt{2gh}}{R[1+(M/2m)]}$$

The corresponding speed is given by

$$v_1 = \omega_1 R = \frac{v_0}{1+(M/2m)]} = \frac{\sqrt{2gh}}{[1+(M/2m)]}$$

The final kinetic energy K_1 is given by

$$K_1 = \frac{1}{2}mv_1^2 + \frac{1}{2}I_c\omega_1^2$$

$$= \frac{1}{2}mv_1^2 + \frac{1}{2}\left(\frac{1}{2}MR^2\right)$$

$$\left(\frac{v_1^2}{R^2}\right) = \frac{1}{2}\left(m + \frac{M}{2}\right)v_1^2 = \frac{1}{2}$$

$$\left(\frac{mv_0^2}{1+(M/2m)}\right) = \frac{K_0}{1+(M/2m)}$$

Conclude: The final kinetic energy is less than initial because whenever impulses occur in a system energy does not remain conserved.

QUESTIONS

1 Figure 10-62 is a graph of the angular velocity versus time for a disk rotating like a merry-go-round. For a point on the disk rim, rank the instants *a*, *b*, *c*, and *d* according to the magnitude of the (a) tangential and (b) radial acceleration, greatest first.

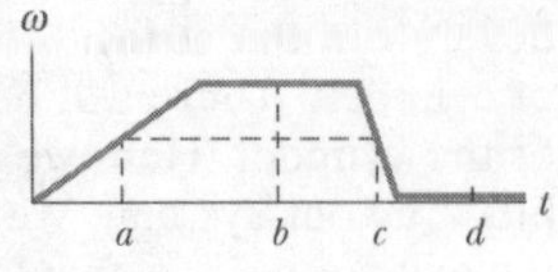

FIG. 10-62 Question 1.

2 Figure 10-63*b* is a graph of the angular position of the rotating disk of Fig. 10-63*a*. Is the angular velocity of the disk positive, negative, or zero at (a) $t = 1$ s, (b) $t = 2$ s, and (c) $t = 3$ s? (d) Is the angular acceleration positive or negative?

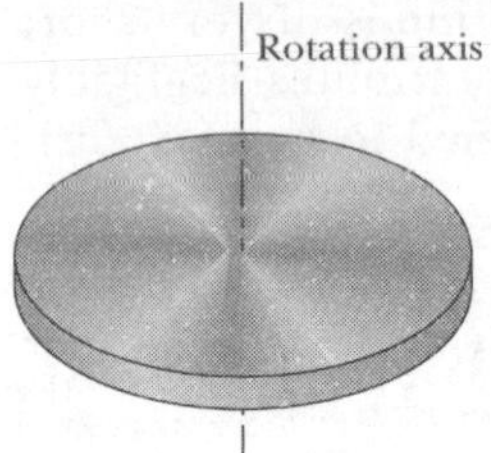

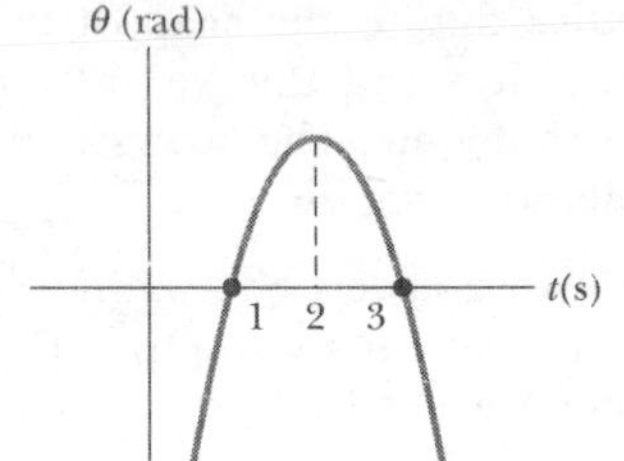

FIG. 10-63 Question 2.

3 Figure 10-64 shows a uniform metal plate that had been square before 25% of it was snipped off. Three lettered points are indicated. Rank them according to the rotational inertia of the plate around a perpendicular axis through them, greatest first.

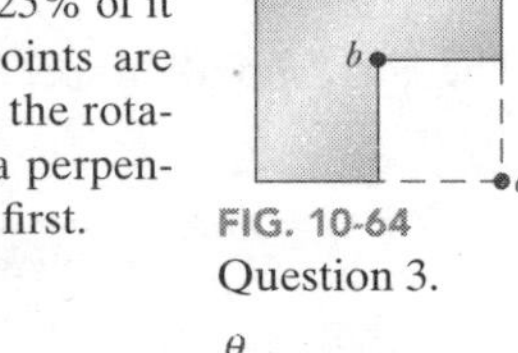

FIG. 10-64 Question 3.

4 Figure 10-65 shows plots of angular position θ versus time t for three cases in which a disk is rotated like a merry-go-round. In each case, the rotation direction changes at a certain angular position θ_{change}. (a) For each case, determine whether θ_{change} is clockwise or counterclockwise from $\theta = 0$, or whether it is at $\theta = 0$. For each case, determine (b) whether ω is zero before, after, or at $t = 0$ and (c) whether α is positive, negative, or zero.

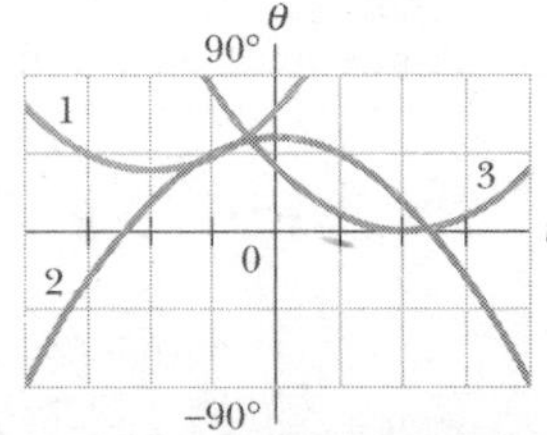

FIG. 10-65 Question 4.

5 Figure 10-66*a* is an overhead view of a horizontal bar that can pivot; two horizontal forces act on the bar, but it is stationary. If the angle between the bar and $\vec{F}_2$ is now decreased from 90° and the bar is still not to turn, should F_2 be made larger, made smaller, or left the same?

6 Figure 10-66*b* shows an overhead view of a horizontal bar that is rotated about the pivot point by two horizontal forces, $\vec{F}_1$ and $\vec{F}_2$, with $\vec{F}_2$ at angle ϕ to the bar. Rank the following values of ϕ according to the magnitude of the angular acceleration of the bar, greatest first: 90°, 70°, and 110°.

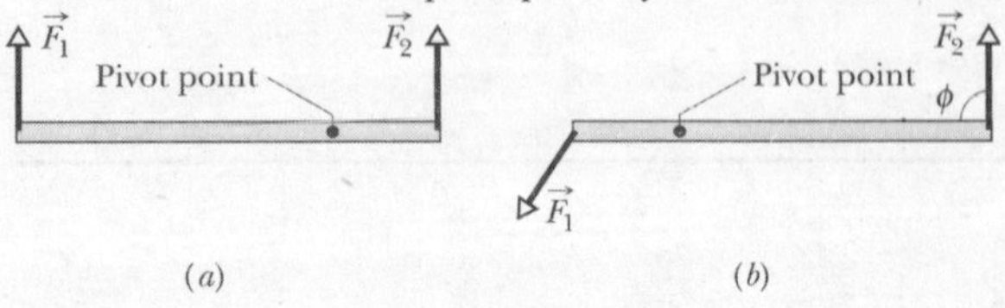

FIG. 10-66 Questions 5 and 6.

7 In Fig. 10-67, two forces $\vec{F}_1$ and $\vec{F}_2$ act on a disk that turns about its center like a merry-go-round. The forces maintain the indicated angles during the rotation, which is counterclockwise and at a constant rate. However, we are to decrease the angle θ of $\vec{F}_1$ without changing the magnitude of $\vec{F}_1$. (a) To keep the angular speed constant, should we increase, decrease, or maintain the magnitude of $\vec{F}_2$? Do forces (b) $\vec{F}_1$ and (c) $\vec{F}_2$ tend to rotate the disk clockwise or counterclockwise?

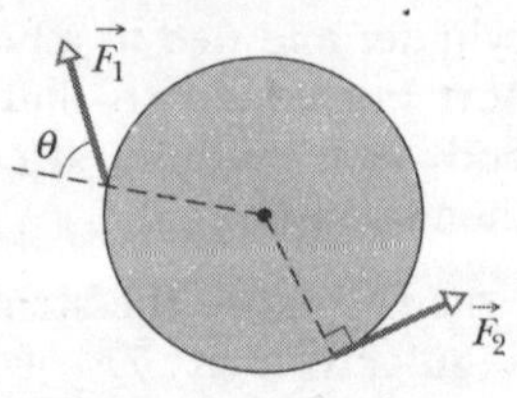

FIG. 10-67 Question 7.

8 In the overhead view of Fig. 10-68, five forces of the same magnitude act on a strange merry-go-round; it is a square that can rotate about point *P*, at midlength along one of the edges. Rank the forces according to the magnitude of the torque they create about point *P*, greatest first.

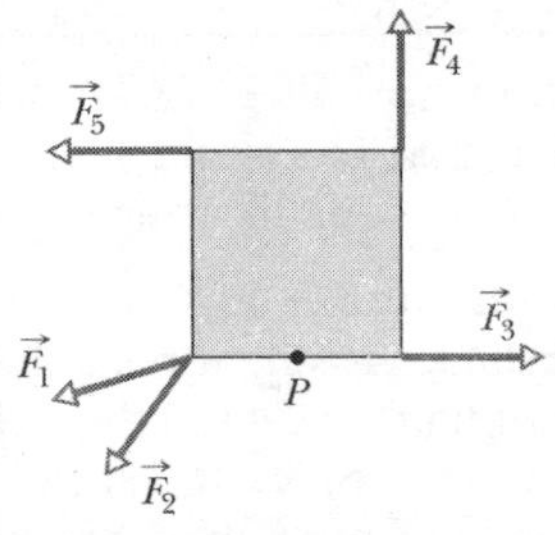

FIG. 10-68 Question 8.

9 A force is applied to the rim of a disk that can rotate like a merry-go-round, so as to change its angular velocity. Its initial and final angular velocities, respectively, for four situations are: (a) −2 rad/s, 5 rad/s; (b) 2 rad/s, 5 rad/s; (c) −2 rad/s, −5 rad/s; and (d) 2 rad/s, −5 rad/s. Rank the situations according to the work done by the torque due to the force, greatest first.

10 Figure 10-69 shows three flat disks (of the same radius) that can rotate about their centers like merry-go-rounds. Each disk consists of the same two materials, one denser than the other (density is mass per unit volume). In disks 1 and 3, the denser material forms the outer half of the disk area. In disk 2, it forms the inner half of the disk area. Forces with identical magnitudes are applied tangentially to the disk, either at the outer edge or at the interface of the two materials, as shown. Rank the disks according to (a) the torque about the disk center, (b) the rotational inertia about the disk center, and (c) the angular acceleration of the disk, greatest first.

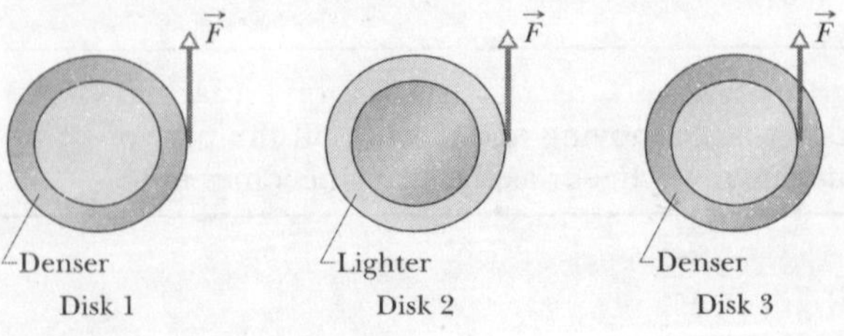

FIG. 10-69 Question 10.

PROBLEMS

1 A diver makes 2.5 revolutions on the way from a 10-m-high platform to the water. Assuming zero initial vertical velocity, find the average angular velocity during the dive.

2 The angular position of a point on the rim of a rotating wheel is given by $\theta = 4.0t - 3.0t^2 + t^3$, where θ is in radians and t is in seconds. What are the angular velocities at (a) $t = 2.0$ s and (b) $t = 4.0$ s? (c) What is the average angular acceleration for the time interval that begins at $t = 2.0$ s and ends at $t = 4.0$ s? What are the instantaneous angular accelerations at (d) the beginning and (e) the end of this time interval?

3 When a slice of buttered toast is accidentally pushed over the edge of a counter, it rotates as it falls. If the distance to the floor is 76 cm and for rotation less than 1 rev, what are the (a) smallest and (b) largest angular speeds that cause the toast to hit and then topple to be butter-side down?

4 The wheel in Fig. 10-70 has eight equally spaced spokes and a radius of 30 cm. It is mounted on a fixed axle and is spinning at 2.5 rev/s. You want to shoot a 20-cm-long arrow parallel to this axle and through the wheel without hitting any of the spokes. Assume that the arrow and the spokes are very thin. (a) What minimum speed must the arrow have? (b) Does it matter where between the axle and rim of the wheel you aim? If so, what is the best location?

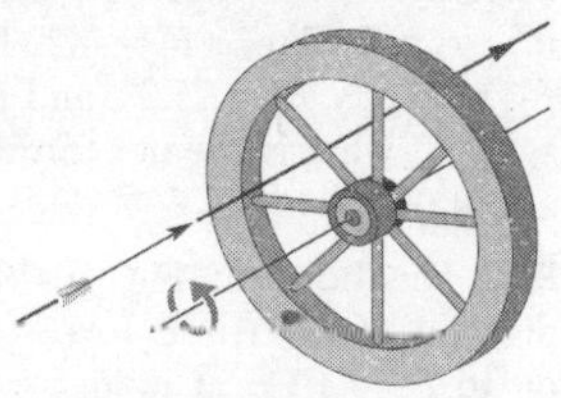

FIG. 10-70 Problem 4.

5 The angular acceleration of a wheel is $\alpha = 6.0t^4 - 4.0t^2$, with α in radians per second-squared and t in seconds. At time $t = 0$, the wheel has an angular velocity of +2.0 rad/s and an angular position of +1.0 rad. Write expressions for (a) the angular velocity (rad/s) and (b) the angular position (rad) as functions of time (s).

Rotation with Constant Angular Acceleration

6 A merry-go-round rotates from rest with an angular acceleration of 1.50 rad/s^2. How long does it take to rotate through (a) the first 2.00 rev and (b) the next 2.00 rev?

7 At $t = 0$, a flywheel has an angular velocity of 4.7 rad/s, a constant angular acceleration of -0.25 rad/s^2, and a reference line at $\theta_0 = 0$. (a) Through what maximum angle θ_{max} will the reference line turn in the positive direction? What are the (b) first and (c) second times the reference line will be at $\theta = \frac{1}{2}\theta_{max}$? At what (d) negative time and (e) positive time will the reference line be at $\theta = -10.5$ rad? (f) Graph θ versus t, and indicate the answers to (a) through (e) on the graph.

8 A disk rotates about its central axis starting from rest and accelerates with constant angular acceleration. At one time it is rotating at 10 rev/s; 60 revolutions later, its angular speed is 15 rev/s. Calculate (a) the angular acceleration, (b) the time required to complete the 60 revolutions, (c) the time required to reach the 10 rev/s angular speed, and (d) the number of revolutions from rest until the time the disk reaches the 10 rev/s angular speed.

9 A flywheel turns through 40 rev as it slows from an angular speed of 1.5 rad/s to a stop. (a) Assuming a constant angular acceleration, find the time for it to come to rest. (b) What is its angular acceleration? (c) How much time is required for it to complete the first 20 of the 40 revolutions?

Relating the Linear and Angular Variables

10 Between 1911 and 1990, the top of the leaning bell tower at Pisa, Italy, moved toward the south at an average rate of 1.2 mm/y. The tower is 55 m tall. In radians per second, what is the average angular speed of the tower's top about its base?

11 An astronaut is being tested in a centrifuge. The centrifuge has a radius of 10 m and, in starting, rotates according to $\theta = 0.30t^2$, where t is in seconds and θ is in radians. When $t = 5.0$ s, what are the magnitudes of the astronaut's (a) angular velocity, (b) linear velocity, (c) tangential acceleration, and (d) radial acceleration?

12 An early method of measuring the speed of light makes use of a rotating slotted wheel. A beam of light passes through one of the slots at the outside edge of the wheel, as in Fig. 10-71, travels to a distant mirror, and returns to the wheel just in time to pass through the next slot in the wheel. One such slotted wheel has a radius of 5.0 cm and 500 slots around its edge. Measurements taken when the mirror is $L = 500$ m from the wheel indicate a speed of light of 3.0×10^5 km/s. (a) What is the (constant) angular speed of the wheel? (b) What is the linear speed of a point on the edge of the wheel?

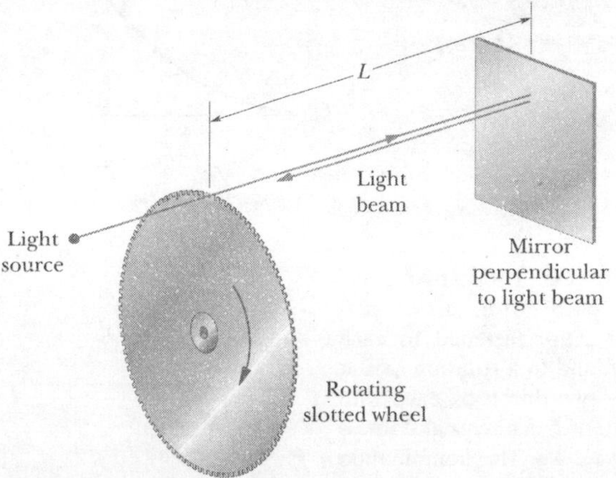

FIG. 10-71 Problem 12.

13 In Fig. 10-72, wheel A of radius $r_A = 10$ cm is coupled by belt B to wheel C of radius $r_C = 25$ cm. The angular speed of wheel A is increased from rest at a constant rate of 1.6 rad/s^2. Find the time needed for wheel C to reach an angular speed of 100 rev/min, assuming the belt does not slip. (*Hint:* If the belt does not slip, the linear speeds at the two rims must be equal.)

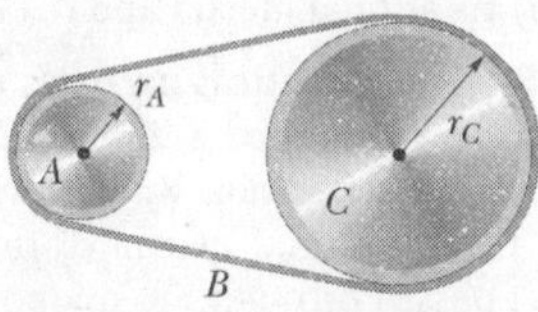

FIG. 10-72 Problem 13.

14 A record turntable is rotating at $33\frac{1}{3}$ rev/min. A watermelon seed is on the turntable 6.0 cm from the axis of rotation. (a) Calculate the acceleration of the seed, assuming that it does not slip. (b) What is the minimum value of the coefficient of static friction between the seed and the turntable if the seed is not to slip? (c) Suppose that the turntable achieves its angular speed by starting from rest and undergoing a constant angular acceleration for 0.25 s. Calculate the minimum coefficient of static friction required for the seed not to slip during the acceleration period.

15 Figure 10-73 gives angular speed versus time for a thin rod that rotates around one end. The scale on the ω axis is set by $\omega_s = 6.0$ rad/s. (a) What is the magnitude of the rod's angular acceleration? (b) At $t = 4.0$ s, the rod has a rotational kinetic energy of 1.60 J. What is its kinetic energy at $t = 0$?

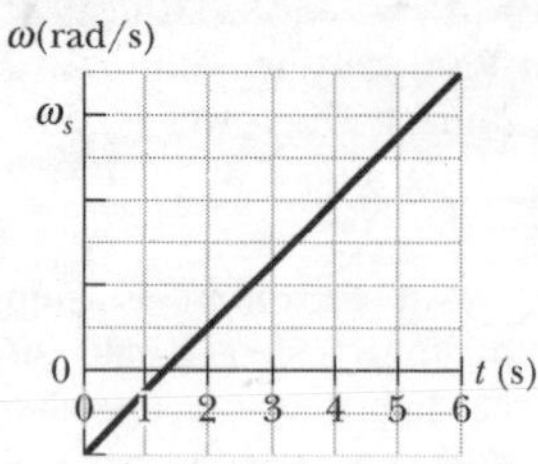

FIG. 10-73 Problem 15.

Calculating the Rotational Inertia

16 Figure 10-74*a* shows a disk that can rotate about an axis at a radial distance *h* from the center of the disk. Figure 10-74*b* gives the rotational inertia *I* of the disk about the axis as a function of that distance *h*, from the center out to the edge of the disk. The scale on the *I* axis is set by $I_A = 0.050$ kg·m² and $I_B = 0.150$ kg·m². What is the mass of the disk?

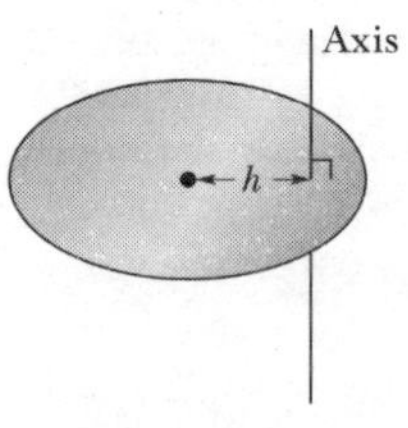

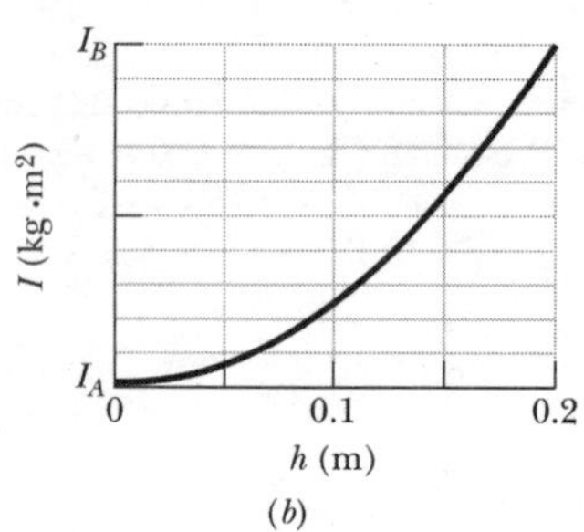

FIG. 10-74 Problem 16.

17 In Fig. 10-75, two particles, each with mass $m =$ 0.85 kg, are fastened to each other, and to a rotation axis at *O*, by two thin rods, each with length $d = 5.6$ cm and mass $M = 1.2$ kg. The combination rotates around the rotation axis with angular speed $\omega =$ 0.30 rad/s. Measured about *O*, what are the combination's (a) rotational inertia and (b) kinetic energy?

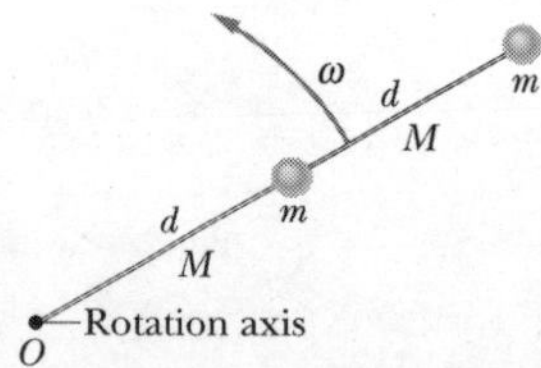

FIG. 10-75 Problem 17.

18 Four identical particles of mass 0.50 kg each are placed at the vertices of a 2.0 m × 2.0 m square and held there by four massless rods, which form the sides of the square. What is the rotational inertia of this rigid body about an axis that (a) passes through the midpoints of opposite sides and lies in the plane of the square, (b) passes through the midpoint of one of the sides and is perpendicular to the plane of the square, and (c) lies in the plane of the square and passes through two diagonally opposite particles?

19 The uniform solid block in Fig. 10-76 has mass 0.172 kg and edge lengths $a = 3.5$ cm, $b = 8.4$ cm, and $c = 1.4$ cm. Calculate its rotational inertia about an axis through one corner and perpendicular to the large faces.

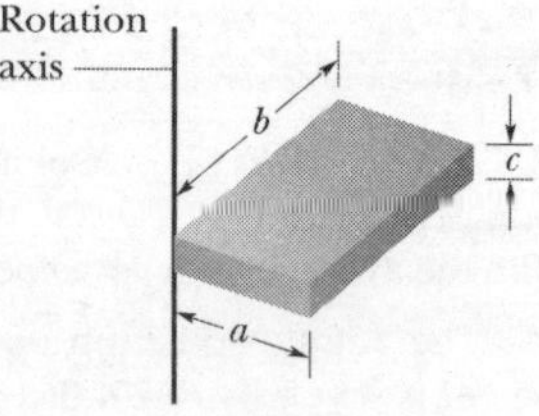

FIG. 10-76 Problem 19.

20 The masses and coordinates of four particles are as follows: 50 g, $x = 2.0$ cm, $y =$ 2.0 cm; 25 g, $x = 0$, $y = 4.0$ cm; 25 g, $x = -3.0$ cm, $y = -3.0$ cm; 30 g, $x = -2.0$ cm, $y = 4.0$ cm. What are the rotational inertias of this collection about the (a) *x*, (b) *y*, and (c) *z* axes? (d) Suppose the answers to (a) and (b) are *A* and *B*, respectively. Then what is the answer to (c) in terms of *A* and *B*?

Torque

21 The body in Fig. 10-77 is pivoted at *O*, and two forces act on it as shown. If $r_1 = 1.30$ m, $r_2 = 2.15$ m, $F_1 = 4.20$ N, $F_2 = 4.90$ N, $\theta_1 = 75.0°$, and $\theta_2 = 60.0°$, what is the net torque about the pivot?

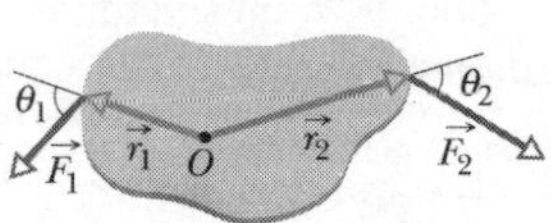

FIG. 10-77 Problem 21.

22 The body in Fig. 10-78 is pivoted at *O*. Three forces act on it: $F_A = 10$ N at point *A*, 8.0 m from *O*; $F_B = 16$ N at *B*, 4.0 m from *O*; and $F_C = 19$ N at *C*, 3.0 m from *O*. What is the net torque about *O*?

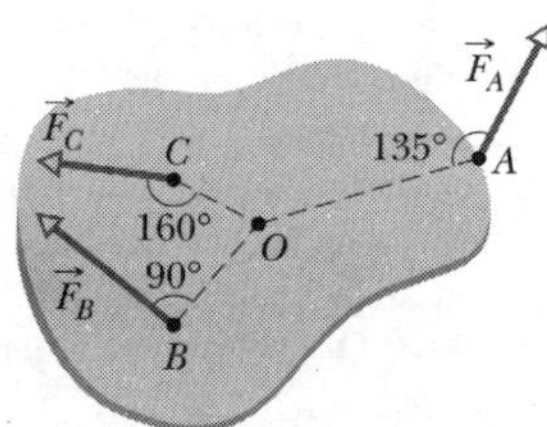

FIG. 10-78 Problem 22.

Newton's Second Law for Rotation

23 Figure 10-79 shows particles 1 and 2, each of mass *m*, attached to the ends of a rigid massless rod of length $L_1 + L_2$, with $L_1 = 20$ cm and $L_2 = 80$ cm. The rod is held horizontally on the fulcrum and then released. What are the magnitudes of the initial accelerations of (a) particle 1 and (b) particle 2?

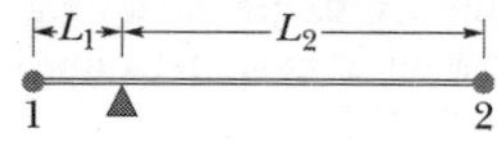

FIG. 10-79 Problem 23.

24 In Fig. 10-80*a*, an irregularly shaped plastic plate with uniform thickness and density (mass per unit volume) is to be rotated around an axle that is perpendicular to the plate face and through point *O*. The rotational inertia of the plate about that axle is measured with the following method. A circular disk of mass 0.500 kg and radius 2.00 cm is glued to the plate, with its center aligned with point *O* (Fig. 10-80*b*). A string is wrapped around the edge of the disk the way a string is wrapped around a top. Then the string is pulled for 5.00 s. As a result, the disk and plate are rotated by a constant force of 0.400 N that is applied by the string tangentially to the edge of the disk. The resulting angular speed is 114 rad/s. What is the rotational inertia of the plate about the axle?

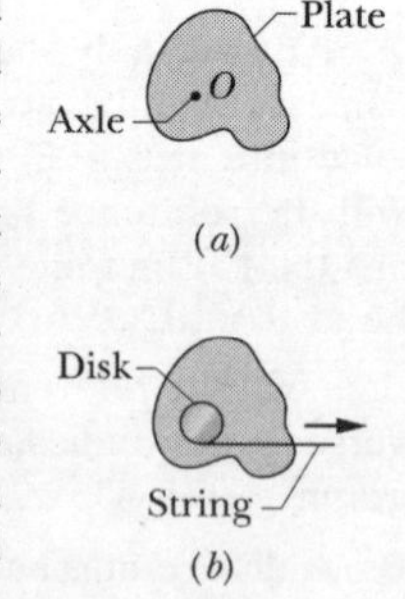

FIG. 10-80 Problem 24.

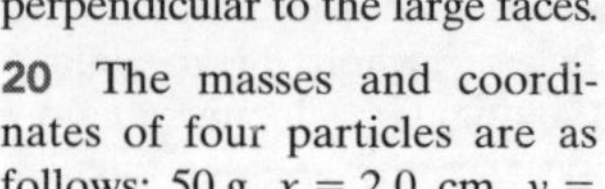

25 In Fig. 10-81, a cylinder having a mass of 2.0 kg can rotate about its central axis through point O. Forces are applied as shown: $F_1 = 6.0$ N, $F_2 = 4.0$ N, $F_3 = 2.0$ N, and $F_4 = 5.0$ N. Also, $r = 5.0$ cm and $R = 12$ cm. Find the (a) magnitude and (b) direction of the angular acceleration of the cylinder. (During the rotation, the forces maintain their same angles relative to the cylinder.)

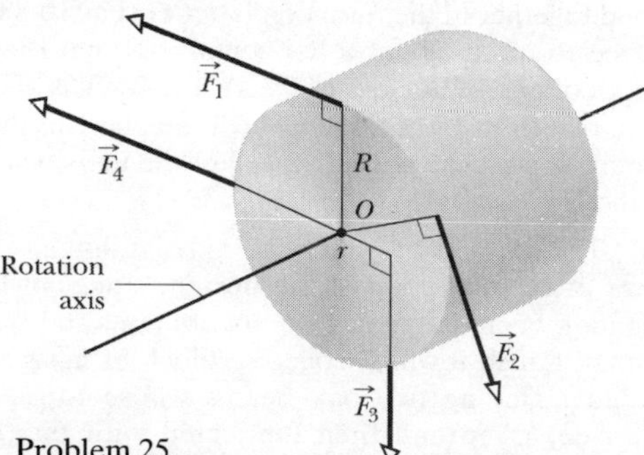

FIG. 10-81 Problem 25.

26 In Fig. 10-82, block 1 has mass $m_1 = 460$ g, block 2 has mass $m_2 = 500$ g, and the pulley, which is mounted on a horizontal axle with negligible friction, has radius $R = 5.00$ cm. When released from rest, block 2 falls 75.0 cm in 5.00 s without the cord slipping on the pulley. (a) What is the magnitude of the acceleration of the blocks? What are (b) tension T_2 and (c) tension T_1? (d) What is the magnitude of the pulley's angular acceleration? (e) What is its rotational inertia?

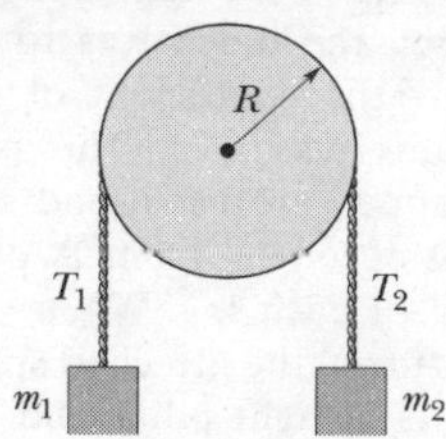

FIG. 10-82 Problems 26.

27 In a judo foot-sweep move, you sweep your opponent's left foot out from under him while pulling on his gi (uniform) toward that side. As a result, your opponent rotates around his right foot and onto the mat. Figure 10-83 shows a simplified diagram of your opponent as you face him, with his left foot swept out. The rotational axis is through point O. The gravitational force $\vec{F}_g$ on him effectively acts at his center of mass, which is a horizontal distance $d = 28$ cm from point O. His mass is 70 kg, and his rotational inertia about point O is 65 kg · m². What is the magnitude of his initial angular acceleration about point O if your pull $\vec{F}_a$ on his gi is (a) negligible and (b) horizontal with a magnitude of 300 N and applied at height $h = 1.4$ m?

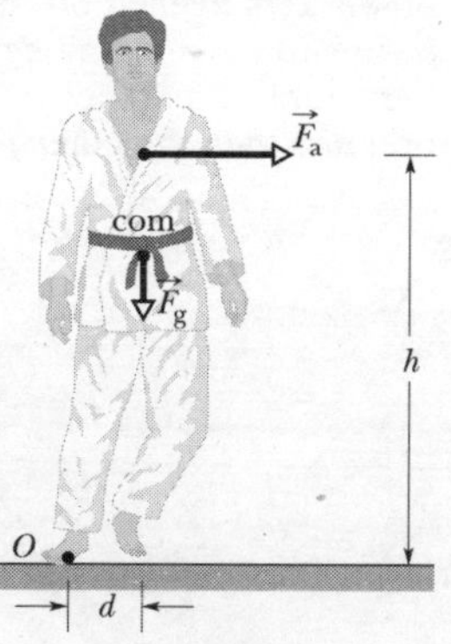

FIG. 10-83 Problem 27.

28 A pulley, with a rotational inertia of 1.0×10^{-3} kg · m² about its axle and a radius of 10 cm, is acted on by a force applied tangentially at its rim. The force magnitude varies in time as $F = 0.50t + 0.30t^2$, with F in newtons and t in seconds. The pulley is initially at rest. At $t = 3.0$ s what are (a) its angular acceleration and (b) its angular speed?

Work and Rotational Kinetic Energy

29 A uniform cylinder of radius 10 cm and mass 20 kg is mounted so as to rotate freely about a horizontal axis that is parallel to and 5.0 cm from the central longitudinal axis of the cylinder. (a) What is the rotational inertia of the cylinder about the axis of rotation? (b) If the cylinder is released from rest with its central longitudinal axis at the same height as the axis about which the cylinder rotates, what is the angular speed of the cylinder as it passes through its lowest position?

30 A meter stick is held vertically with one end on the floor and is then allowed to fall. Find the speed of the other end just before it hits the floor, assuming that the end on the floor does not slip. (*Hint:* Consider the stick to be a thin rod and use the conservation of energy principle.)

31 In Fig. 10-84, three 0.0100 kg particles have been glued to a rod of length $L = 6.00$ cm and negligible mass and can rotate around a perpendicular axis through point O at one end. How much work is required to change the rotational rate (a) from 0 to 20.0 rad/s, (b) from 20.0 rad/s to 40.0 rad/s, and (c) from 40.0 rad/s to 60.0 rad/s? (d) What is the slope of a plot of the assembly's kinetic energy (in joules) versus the square of its rotation rate (in radians-squared per second squared)?

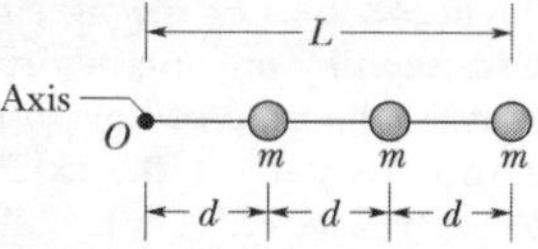

FIG. 10-84 Problems 31

32 Figure 10-85 shows a rigid assembly of a thin hoop (of mass m and radius $R = 0.150$ m) and a thin radial rod (of mass m and length $L = 2.00R$). The assembly is upright, but if we give it a slight nudge, it will rotate around a horizontal axis in the plane of the rod and hoop, through the lower end of the rod. Assuming that the energy given to the assembly in such a nudge is negligible, what would be the assembly's angular speed about the rotation axis when it passes through the upside-down (inverted) orientation?

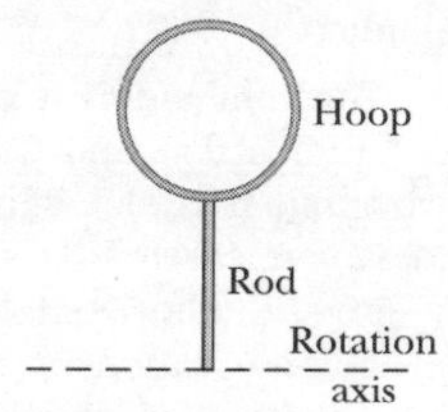

FIG. 10-85 Problem 32.

33 A uniform spherical shell of mass $M = 4.5$ kg and radius $R = 8.5$ cm can rotate about a vertical axis on frictionless bearings (Fig. 10-86). A massless cord passes around the equator of the shell, over a pulley of rotational inertia $I = 3.0 \times 10^{-3}$ kg · m² and radius $r = 5.0$ cm, and is attached to a small object of mass $m = 0.60$ kg. There is no friction on the pulley's axle; the cord does not slip on the pulley. What is the speed of the object when it has fallen 82 cm after being released from rest? Use energy considerations.

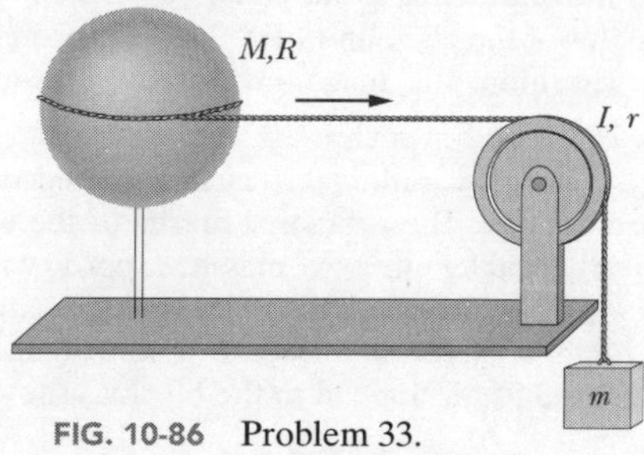

FIG. 10-86 Problem 33.

Additional Problems

34 George Washington Gale Ferris, Jr., a civil engineering graduate from Rensselaer Polytechnic Institute, built the original Ferris wheel for the 1893 World's Columbian Exposition in Chicago. The wheel, an astounding engineering construction at the time, carried 36 wooden cars, each holding up to 60 passengers, around a circle 76 m in diameter. The cars were loaded 6 at a time, and once all 36 cars were full, the wheel made a complete rotation at constant angular speed in about 2 min. Estimate the amount of work that was required of the machinery to rotate the passengers alone.

35 At 7:14 A.M. on June 30, 1908, a huge explosion occurred above remote central Siberia, at latitude 61° N and longitude 102° E; the fireball thus created was the brightest flash seen by anyone before nuclear weapons. The *Tunguska Event,* which according to one chance witness "covered an enormous part of the sky," was probably the explosion of a *stony asteroid* about 140 m wide. (a) Considering only Earth's rotation, determine how much later the asteroid would have had to arrive to put the explosion above Helsinki at longitude 25° E. This would have obliterated the city. (b) If the asteroid had, instead, been a *metallic asteroid,* it could have reached Earth's surface. How much later would such an asteroid have had to arrive to put the impact in the Atlantic Ocean at longitude 20° W? (The resulting tsunamis would have wiped out coastal civilization on both sides of the Atlantic.)

36 The thin uniform rod in Fig. 10-87 has length 2.0 m and can pivot about a horizontal, frictionless pin through one end. It is released from rest at angle $\theta =$ 40° above the horizontal. Use the principle of conservation of energy to determine the angular speed of the rod as it passes through the horizontal position.

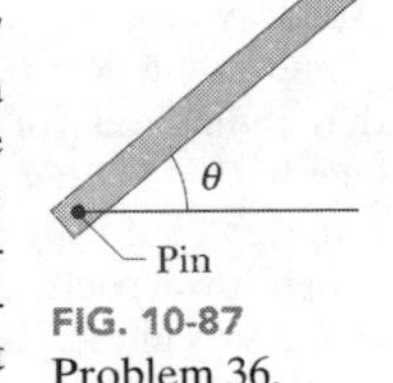

FIG. 10-87 Problem 36.

37 A high-wire walker always attempts to keep his center of mass over the wire (or rope). He normally carries a long, heavy pole to help: If he leans, say, to his right (his com moves to the right) and is in danger of rotating around the wire, he moves the pole to his left (its com moves to the left) to slow the rotation and allow himself time to adjust his balance. Assume that the walker has a mass of 70.0 kg and a rotational inertia of $15.0\ \text{kg}\cdot\text{m}^2$ about the wire. What is the magnitude of his angular acceleration about the wire if his com is 5.0 cm to the right of the wire and (a) he carries no pole and (b) the 14.0 kg pole he carries has its com 10 cm to the left of the wire?

38 A bicyclist of mass 70 kg puts all his mass on each downward-moving pedal as he pedals up a steep road. Take the diameter of the circle in which the pedals rotate to be 0.40 m, and determine the magnitude of the maximum torque he exerts about the rotation axis of the pedals.

39 A wheel of radius 0.20 m is mounted on a frictionless horizontal axis. The rotational inertia of the wheel about the axis is $0.050\ \text{kg}\cdot\text{m}^2$. A massless cord wrapped around the wheel is attached to a 2.0 kg block that slides on a horizontal frictionless surface. If a horizontal force of magnitude $P = 3.0$ N is applied to the block as shown in Fig. 10-54, what is the magnitude of the angular acceleration of the wheel? Assume the cord does not slip on the wheel.

40 A rigid body is made of three identical thin rods, each with length $L = 0.600$ m, fastened together in the form of a letter **H** (Fig. 10-88). The body is free to rotate about a horizontal axis that runs along the length of one of the legs of the **H**. The body is allowed to fall from rest from a position in which the plane of the **H** is horizontal. What is the angular speed of the body when the plane of the **H** is vertical?

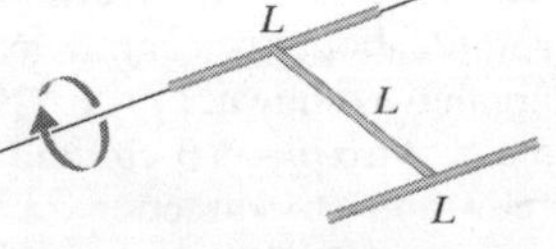

FIG. 10-88 Problem 40.

41 The method by which the massive lintels (top stones) were lifted to the top of the upright stones at Stonehenge has long been debated. One possible method was tested in a small Czech town. A concrete block of mass 5124 kg was pulled up along two oak beams whose top surfaces had been debarked and then lubricated with fat (Fig. 10-89). The beams were 10 m long, and each extended from the ground to the top of one of the two upright pillars onto which the block was to be raised. The pillars were 3.9 m high; the coefficient of static friction between block and beams was 0.22. The pull on the block was via ropes wrapped around it and around the top ends of two spruce logs of length 4.5 m. A platform was strung at the opposite end of each log. When enough workers sat or stood on a platform, the attached spruce log would pivot about the top of its upright pillar and pull one end of the block a short distance up a beam. For each log, the rope holding the block was approximately perpendicular to the log; the distance between the pivot point and the point where the rope wrapped around the log was 0.70 m. Assuming that each worker had a mass of 85 kg, find the smallest number of workers needed on the two platforms so that the block begins to move up along the beams. (About half this number could actually move the block by moving first one end of it and then the other.)

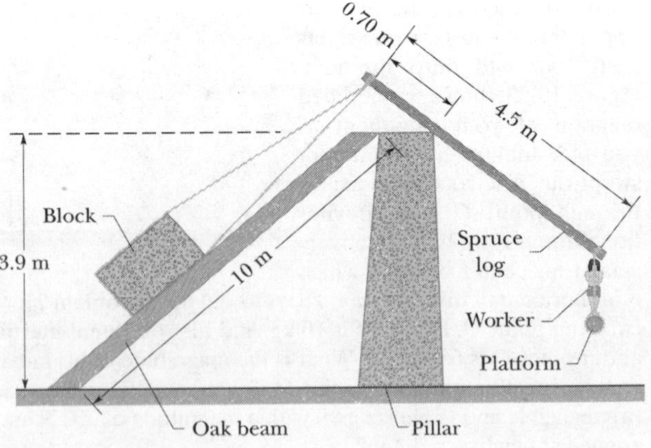

FIG. 10-89 Problem 41.

42 A yo-yo-shaped device mounted on a horizontal frictionless axis is used to lift a 30 kg box as shown in Fig. 10-90. The outer radius R of the device is 0.50 m, and the radius r of the hub is 0.20 m. When a constant horizontal force $\vec{F}_{app}$ of magnitude 140 N is applied to a rope wrapped around the outside of the device, the box, which is suspended from a rope wrapped around the hub, has an upward acceleration of magnitude 0.80 m/s². What is the rotational inertia of the device about its axis of rotation?

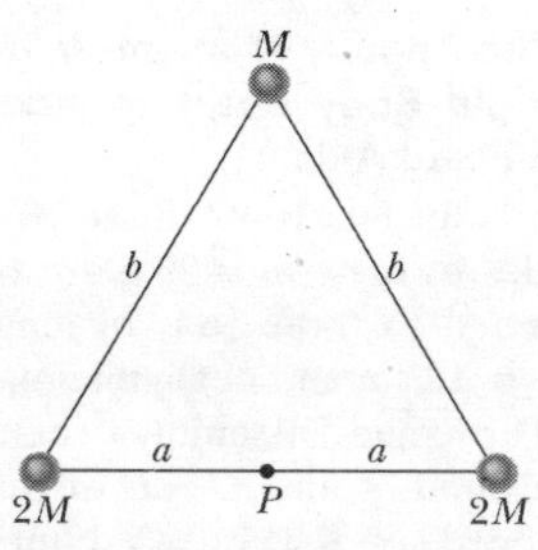

FIG. 10-90 Problem 42.

43 The rigid body shown in Fig. 10-91 consists of three particles connected by massless rods. It is to be rotated about an axis perpendicular to its plane through point P. If $M = 0.40$ kg, $a = 30$ cm, and $b = 50$ cm, how much work is required to take the body from rest to an angular speed of 5.0 rad/s?

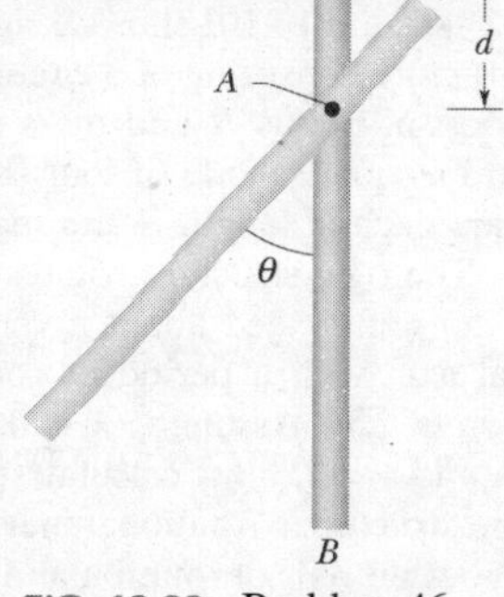

FIG. 10-91 Problem 43.

44 *Beverage engineering.* The pull tab was a major advance in the engineering design of beverage containers. The tab pivots on a central bolt in the can's top. When you pull upward on one end of the tab, the other end presses downward on a portion of the can's top that has been scored. If you pull upward with a 10 N force, approximately what is the magnitude of the force applied to the scored section? (You will need to examine a can with a pull tab.)

45 Cheetahs running at top speed have been reported at an astounding 114 km/h (about 71 mi/h) by observers driving alongside the animals. Imagine trying to measure a cheetah's speed by keeping your vehicle abreast of the animal while also glancing at your speedometer, which is registering 114 km/h. You keep the vehicle a constant 8.0 m from the cheetah, but the noise of the vehicle causes the cheetah to continuously veer away from you along a circular path of radius 92 m. Thus, you travel along a circular path of radius 100 m. (a) What is the angular speed of you and the cheetah around the circular paths? (b) What is the linear speed of the cheetah along its path? (If you did not account for the circular motion, you would conclude erroneously that the cheetah's speed is 114 km/h, and that type of error was apparently made in the published reports.)

46 In Fig. 10-92, a thin uniform rod (mass 3.0 kg, length 4.0 m) rotates freely about a horizontal axis A that is perpendicular to the rod and passes through a point at distance $d = 1.0$ m from the end of the rod. The kinetic energy of the rod as it passes through the vertical position is 20 J. (a) What is the rotational inertia of the rod about axis A? (b) What is the (linear) speed of the end B of the rod as the rod passes through the vertical position? (c) At what angle θ will the rod momentarily stop in its upward swing?

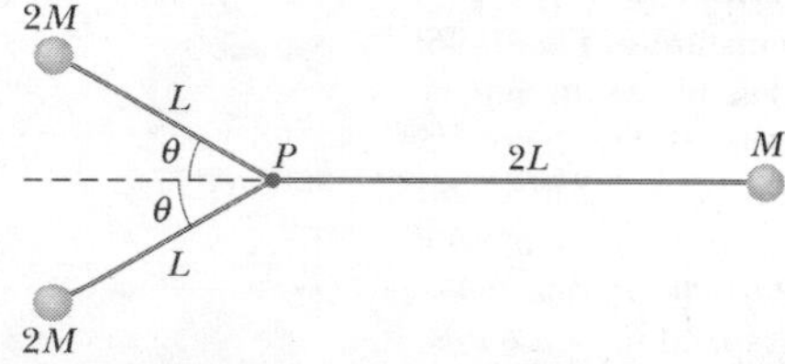

FIG. 10-92 Problem 46.

47 The rigid object shown in Fig. 10-93 consists of three balls and three connecting rods, with $M = 1.6$ kg, $L = 0.60$ m, and $\theta = 30°$. The balls may be treated as particles, and the connecting rods have negligible mass. Determine the rotational kinetic energy of the object if it has an angular speed of 1.2 rad/s about (a) an axis that passes through point P and is perpendicular to the plane of the figure and (b) an axis that passes through point P, is perpendicular to the rod of length $2L$, and lies in the plane of the figure.

FIG. 10-93 Problem 47.

48 In Fig. 10-94, four pulleys are connected by two belts. Pulley A (radius 15 cm) is the drive pulley, and it rotates at 10 rad/s. Pulley B (radius 10 cm) is connected by belt 1 to pulley A. Pulley B' (radius 5 cm) is concentric with pulley B and is rigidly attached to it. Pulley C (radius 25 cm) is connected by belt 2 to pulley B'. Calculate (a) the linear speed of a point on belt 1, (b) the angular speed of pulley B, (c) the angular speed of pulley B', (d) the linear speed of a point on belt 2, and (e) the angular speed of pulley C. (*Hint:* If the belt between two pulleys does not slip, the linear speeds at the rims of the two pulleys must be equal.)

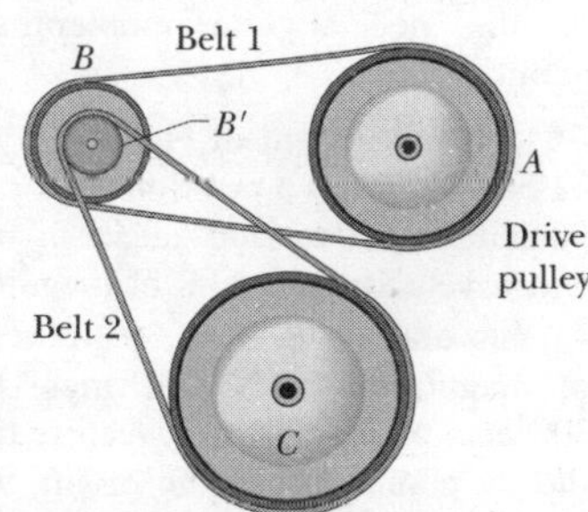

FIG. 10-94 Problem 48.

49 Two thin rods (each of mass 0.20 kg) are joined together to form a rigid body as shown in Fig. 10-95. One of the rods has length $L_1 = 0.40$ m, and the other has length $L_2 = 0.50$ m. What is the rotational inertia of this rigid body about (a) an axis that is perpendicular to the plane of the paper and passes through the center of the shorter rod and (b) an axis that is perpendicular to the plane of the paper and passes through the center of the longer rod?

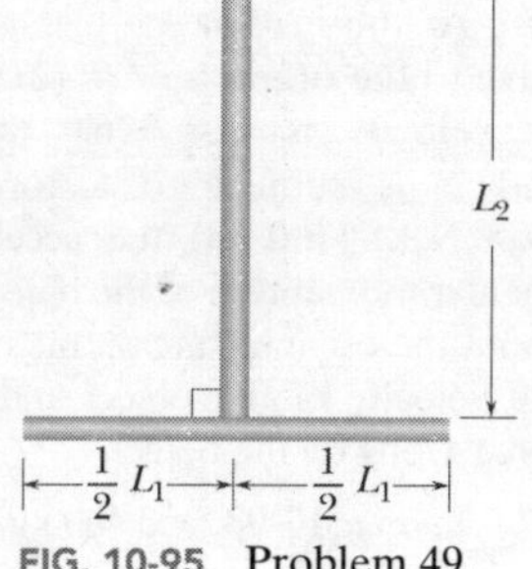

FIG. 10-95 Problem 49.

Torque Revisited

50 In unit-vector notation, what is the net torque about the origin on a flea located at coordinates (0, −4.0 m, 5.0 m) when forces $\vec{F}_1 = (3.0\text{ N})\hat{k}$ and $\vec{F}_2 = (-2.0\text{ N})\hat{j}$ act on the flea?

51 In unit-vector notation, what is the torque about the origin on a jar of jalapeño peppers located at coordinates (3.0 m, −2.0 m, 4.0 m) due to (a) force $\vec{F}_1 = (3.0\text{ N})\hat{i} - (4.0\text{ N})\hat{j} + (5.0\text{ N})\hat{k}$, (b) force $\vec{F}_2 = (-3.0\text{ N})\hat{i} - (4.0\text{ N})\hat{j} - (5.0\text{ N})\hat{k}$, and (c) the vector sum of $\vec{F}_1$ and $\vec{F}_2$? (d) Repeat part (c) for the torque about the point with coordinates (3.0 m, 2.0 m, 4.0 m).

52 Force $\vec{F} = (2.0\text{ N})\hat{i} - (3.0\text{ N})\hat{k}$ acts on a pebble with position vector $\vec{r} = (0.50\text{ m})\hat{j} - (2.0\text{ m})\hat{k}$ relative to the origin. In unit-vector notation, what is the resulting torque on the pebble about (a) the origin and (b) the point (2.0 m, 0, −3.0 m)?

Angular Momentum

53 In the instant of Fig. 10-96, two particles move in an xy plane. Particle P_1 has mass 6.5 kg and speed $v_1 = 2.2$ m/s, and it is at distance $d_1 = 1.5$ m from point O. Particle P_2 has mass 3.1 kg and speed $v_2 = 3.6$ m/s, and it is at distance $d_2 = 2.8$ m from point O. What are the (a) magnitude and (b) direction of the net angular momentum of the two particles about O?

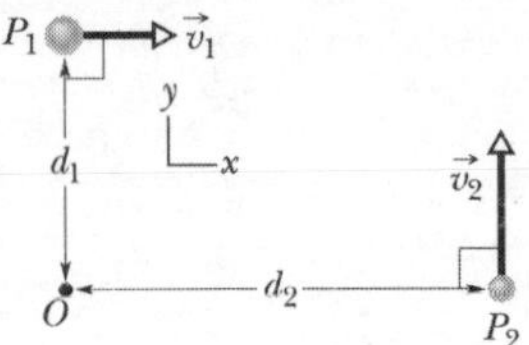

FIG. 10-96 Problem 53.

54 At the instant of Fig. 10-97, a 2.0 kg particle P has a position vector $\vec{r}$ of magnitude 3.0 m and angle $\theta_1 = 45°$ and a velocity vector $\vec{v}$ of magnitude 4.0 m/s and angle $\theta_2 = 30°$. Force $\vec{F}$, of magnitude 2.0 N and angle $\theta_3 = 30°$, acts on P. All three vectors lie in the xy plane. About the origin, what are the (a) magnitude and (b) direction of the angular momentum of P and the (c) magnitude and (d) direction of the torque acting on P?

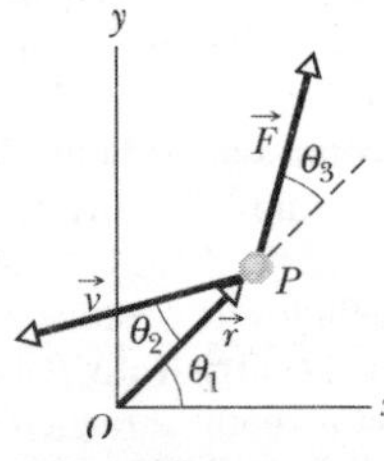

FIG. 10-97 Problem 54.

55 At one instant, force $\vec{F} = 4.0\hat{j}$ N acts on a 0.25 kg object that has position vector $\vec{r} = (2.0\hat{i} - 2.0\hat{k})$ m and velocity vector $\vec{v} = (-5.0\hat{i} + 5.0\hat{k})$ m/s. About the origin and in unit-vector notation, what are (a) the object's angular momentum and (b) the torque acting on the object?

56 At the instant the displacement of a 2.00 kg object relative to the origin is $\vec{d} = (2.00\text{ m})\hat{i} + (4.00\text{ m})\hat{j} - (3.00\text{ m})\hat{k}$, its velocity is $\vec{v} = -(6.00\text{ m/s})\hat{i} + (3.00\text{ m/s})\hat{j} + (3.00\text{ m/s})\hat{k}$ and it is subject to a force $\vec{F} = (6.00\text{ N})\hat{i} - (8.00\text{ N})\hat{j} + (4.00\text{ N})\hat{k}$. Find (a) the acceleration of the object, (b) the angular momentum of the object about the origin, (c) the torque about the origin acting on the object, and (d) the angle between the velocity of the object and the force acting on the object.

57 In Fig. 10-98, a 0.400 kg ball is shot directly upward at initial speed 40.0 m/s. What is its angular momentum about P, 2.00 m horizontally from the launch point, when the ball is (a) at maximum height and (b) halfway back to the ground? What is the torque on the ball about P due to the gravitational force when the ball is (c) at maximum height and (d) halfway back to the ground?

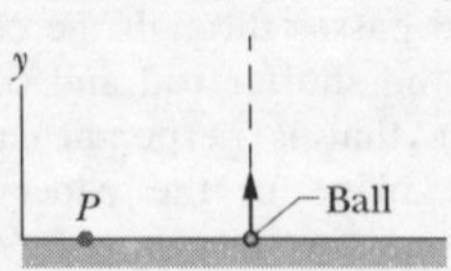

FIG. 10-98 Problem 57.

Newton's Second Law in Angular Form

58 A particle is acted on by two torques about the origin: $\vec{\tau}_1$ has a magnitude of 2.0 N·m and is directed in the positive direction of the x axis, and $\vec{\tau}_2$ has a magnitude of 4.0 N·m and is directed in the negative direction of the y axis. In unit-vector notation, find $d\vec{\ell}/dt$, where $\vec{\ell}$ is the angular momentum of the particle about the origin.

59 At time t, $\vec{r} = 4.0t^2\hat{i} - (2.0t + 6.0t^2)\hat{j}$ gives the position of a 3.0 kg particle relative to the origin of an xy coordinate system ($\vec{r}$ is in meters and t is in seconds). (a) Find an expression for the torque acting on the particle relative to the origin. (b) Is the magnitude of the particle's angular momentum relative to the origin increasing, decreasing, or unchanging?

The Angular Momentum of a Rigid Body Rotating About a Fixed Axis

60 In Fig. 10-99, three particles of mass $m = 23$ g are fastened to three rods of length $d = 12$ cm and negligible mass. The rigid assembly rotates around point O at angular speed $\omega = 0.85$ rad/s. About O, what are (a) the rotational inertia of the assembly, (b) the magnitude of the angular momentum of the middle particle, and (c) the magnitude of the angular momentum of the asssembly?

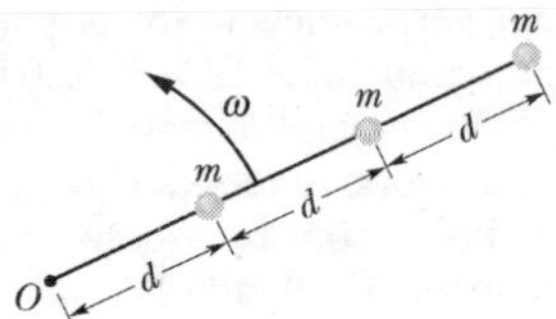

FIG. 10-99 Problem 60.

61 Figure 10-100 gives the torque τ that acts on an initially stationary disk that can rotate about its center like a merry-go-round. The scale on the τ axis is set by $\tau_s = 4.0$ N·m. What is the angular momentum of the disk about the rotation axis at times (a) $t = 7.0$ s and (b) $t = 20$ s?

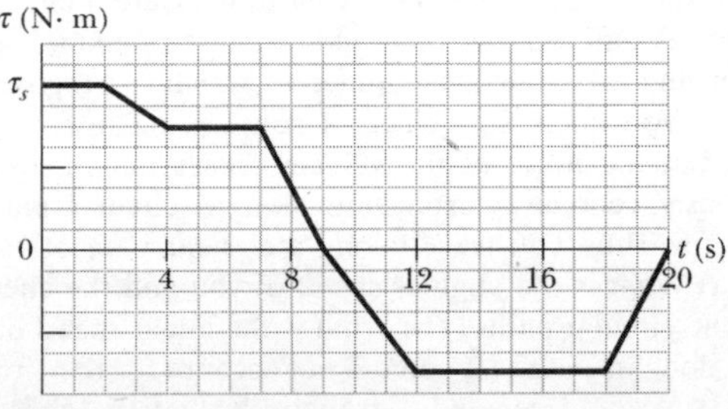

FIG. 10-100 Problem 61.

62 Figure 10-101 shows a rigid structure consisting of a circular hoop of radius R and mass m, and a square made of four thin bars, each of length R and mass m. The rigid structure rotates at a constant speed about a vertical axis, with a period of rotation of 2.5 s. Assuming $R = 0.50$ m and $m = 2.0$ kg, calculate (a) the structure's rotational inertia about the axis of rotation and (b) its angular momentum about that axis.

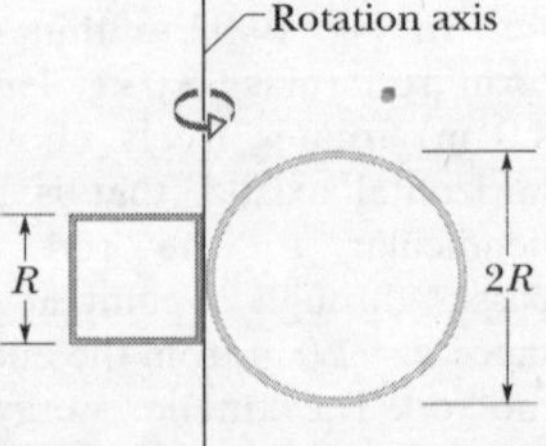

FIG. 10-101 Problem 62.

63 A disk with a rotational inertia of $7.00\ \text{kg}\cdot\text{m}^2$ rotates like a merry-go-round while undergoing a torque given by $\tau = (5.00 + 2.00t)\ \text{N}\cdot\text{m}$. At time $t = 1.00$ s, its angular momentum is $5.00\ \text{kg}\cdot\text{m}^2/\text{s}$. What is its angular momentum at $t = 3.00$ s?

Conservation of Angular Momentum

64 A man stands on a platform that is rotating (without friction) with an angular speed of 1.2 rev/s; his arms are outstretched and he holds a brick in each hand. The rotational inertia of the system consisting of the man, bricks, and platform about the central vertical axis of the platform is $6.0\ \text{kg}\cdot\text{m}^2$. If by moving the bricks the man decreases the rotational inertia of the system to $2.0\ \text{kg}\cdot\text{m}^2$, what are (a) the resulting angular speed of the platform and (b) the ratio of the new kinetic energy of the system to the original kinetic energy? (c) What source provided the added kinetic energy?

65 A Texas cockroach first rides at the center of a circular disk that rotates freely like a merry-go-round without external torques. The cockroach then walks out to the edge of the disk, at radius R. Figure 10-102 gives the angular speed ω of the cockroach–disk system during the walk. The scale on the ω axis is set by $\omega_a = 5.0$ rad/s and $\omega_b = 6.0$ rad/s. When the cockroach is on the edge at radius R, what is the ratio of the bug's rotational inertia to that of the disk, both calculated about the rotation axis?

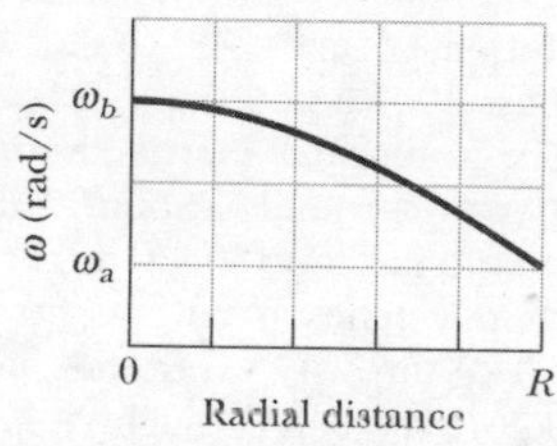

FIG. 10-102 Problem 65.

66 Two disks are mounted (like a merry-go-round) on low-friction bearings on the same axle and can be brought together so that they couple and rotate as one unit. The first disk, with rotational inertia $3.30\ \text{kg}\cdot\text{m}^2$ about its central axis, is set spinning counterclockwise at 450 rev/min. The second disk, with rotational inertia $6.60\ \text{kg}\cdot\text{m}^2$ about its central axis, is set spinning counterclockwise at 900 rev/min. They then couple together. (a) What is their angular speed after coupling? If instead the second disk is set spinning clockwise at 900 rev/min, what are their (b) angular speed and (c) direction of rotation after they couple together?

67 The rotational inertia of a collapsing spinning star drops to $\frac{1}{3}$ its initial value. What is the ratio of the new rotational kinetic energy to the initial rotational kinetic energy?

68 A track is mounted on a large wheel that is free to turn with negligible friction about a vertical axis (Fig. 10-103). A toy train of mass m is placed on the track and, with the system initially at rest, the train's electrical power is turned on. The train reaches speed 0.15 m/s with respect to the track. What is the angular speed of the wheel if its mass is $1.1m$ and its radius is 0.43 m? (Treat the wheel as a hoop, and neglect the mass of the spokes and hub.)

FIG. 10-103 Problem 68.

69 A Texas cockroach of mass 0.17 kg runs counterclockwise around the rim of a lazy Susan (a circular disk mounted on a vertical axle) that has radius 15 cm, rotational inertia $5.0 \times 10^{-3}\ \text{kg}\cdot\text{m}^2$, and frictionless bearings. The cockroach's speed (relative to the ground) is 2.0 m/s, and the lazy Susan turns clockwise with angular velocity $\omega_0 = 2.8$ rad/s. The cockroach finds a bread crumb on the rim and, of course, stops. (a) What is the angular speed of the lazy Susan after the cockroach stops? (b) Is mechanical energy conserved as it stops?

70 In a long jump, an athlete leaves the ground with an initial angular momentum that tends to rotate her body forward, threatening to ruin her landing. To counter this tendency, she rotates her outstretched arms to "take up" the angular momentum (Fig. 11-19). In 0.700 s, one arm sweeps through 0.500 rev and the other arm sweeps through 1.000 rev. Treat each arm as a thin rod of mass 4.0 kg and length 0.60 m, rotating around one end. In the athlete's reference frame, what is the magnitude of the total angular momentum of the arms around the common rotation axis through the shoulders?

71 A uniform thin rod of length 0.500 m and mass 4.00 kg can rotate in a horizontal plane about a vertical axis through its center. The rod is at rest when a 3.00 g bullet traveling in the rotation plane is fired into one end of the rod. As viewed from above, the bullet's path makes angle $\theta = 60.0°$ with the rod (Fig. 10-104). If the bullet lodges in the rod and the angular velocity of the rod is 10 rad/s immediately after the collision, what is the bullet's speed just before impact?

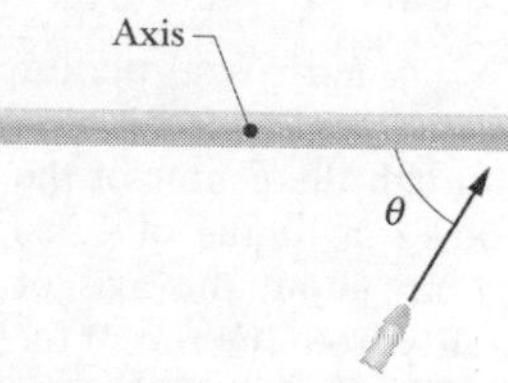

FIG. 10-104 Problem 71.

72 A cockroach of mass m lies on the rim of a uniform disk of mass $4.00m$ that can rotate freely about its center like a merry-go-round. Initially the cockroach and disk rotate together with an angular velocity of 0.260 rad/s. Then the cockroach walks halfway to the center of the disk. (a) What then is the angular velocity of the cockroach–disk system? (b) What is the ratio K/K_0 of the new kinetic energy of the system to its initial kinetic energy? (c) What accounts for the change in the kinetic energy?

73 Figure 10-105 is an overhead view of a thin uniform rod of length 0.800 m and mass M rotating horizontally at angular speed 20.0 rad/s about an axis through its center. A particle of mass $M/3.00$ initially attached to one end is ejected from the rod and travels along a path that is perpendicular to the rod at the instant of ejection. If the particle's speed v_p is 6.00 m/s greater than the speed of the rod end just after ejection, what is the value of v_p?

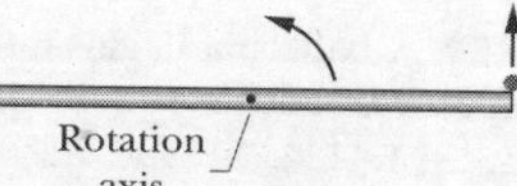

FIG. 10-105 Problem 73.

74 In Fig. 10-106, a 1.0 g bullet is fired into a 0.50 kg block attached to the end of a 0.60 m nonuniform rod of mass 0.50 kg.

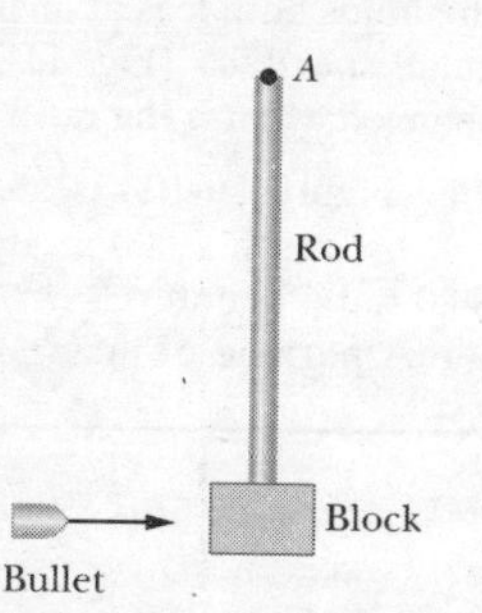

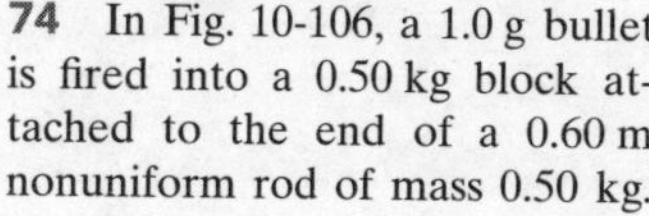

FIG. 10-106 Problem 74.

The block–rod–bullet system then rotates in the plane of the figure, about a fixed axis at A. The rotational inertia of the rod alone about that axis at A is $0.060\ \text{kg}\cdot\text{m}^2$. Treat the block as a particle. (a) What then is the rotational inertia of the block–rod–bullet system about point A? (b) If the angular speed of the system about A just after impact is 4.5 rad/s, what is the bullet's speed just before impact?

75 A uniform disk of mass $10m$ and radius $3.0r$ can rotate freely about its fixed center like a merry-go-round. A smaller uniform disk of mass m and radius r lies on top of the larger disk, concentric with it. Initially the two disks rotate together with an angular velocity of 20 rad/s. Then a slight disturbance causes the smaller disk to slide outward across the larger disk, until the outer edge of the smaller disk catches on the outer edge of the larger disk. Afterward, the two disks again rotate together (without further sliding). (a) What then is their angular velocity about the center of the larger disk? (b) What is the ratio K/K_0 of the new kinetic energy of the two-disk system to the system's initial kinetic energy?

76 A horizontal platform in the shape of a circular disk rotates on a frictionless bearing about a vertical axle through the center of the disk. The platform has a mass of 150 kg, a radius of 2.0 m, and a rotational inertia of 300 $\text{kg}\cdot\text{m}^2$ about the axis of rotation. A 60 kg student walks slowly from the rim of the platform toward the center. If the angular speed of the system is 1.5 rad/s when the student starts at the rim, what is the angular speed when she is 0.50 m from the center?

77 The uniform rod (length 0.60 m, mass 1.0 kg) in Fig. 10-107 rotates in the plane of the figure about an axis through one end, with a rotational inertia of $0.12\ \text{kg}\cdot\text{m}^2$. As the rod swings through its lowest position, it collides with a 0.20 kg putty wad that sticks to the end of the rod. If the rod's angular speed just before collision is 2.4 rad/s, what is the angular speed of the rod–putty system immediately after collision?

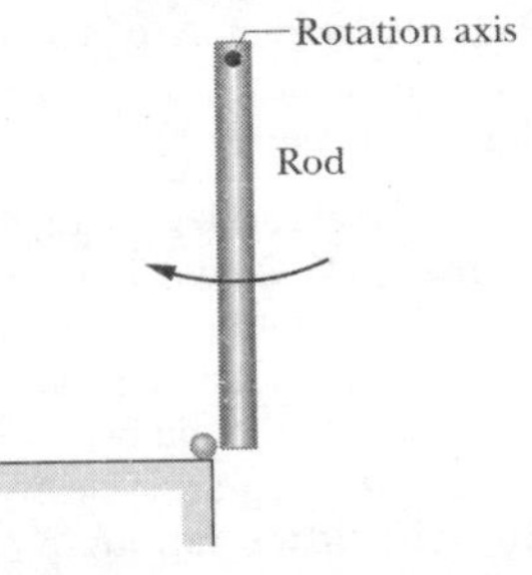

FIG. 10-107 Problem 77.

78 A ballerina begins a tour jeté (Fig. 11-20a) with angular speed ω_i and a rotational inertia consisting of two parts: $I_{leg} = 1.44\ \text{kg}\cdot\text{m}^2$ for her leg extended outward at angle $\theta = 90.0°$ to her body and $I_{trunk} = 0.660\ \text{kg}\cdot\text{m}^2$ for the rest of her body (primarily her trunk). Near her maximum height she holds both legs at angle $\theta = 30.0°$ to her body and has angular speed ω_f (Fig. 11-20b). Assuming that I_{trunk} has not changed, what is the ratio ω_f/ω_i?

79 Figure 10-108 is an overhead view of a thin uniform rod of length 0.600 m and mass M rotating horizontally at 80.0 rad/s counterclockwise about an axis through its center. A particle of mass $M/3.00$ and traveling horizontally at speed 40.0 m/s hits the rod and sticks. The particle's path is perpendicular to the rod at the instant of the hit, at a distance d from the rod's center. (a) At what value of d are rod and particle stationary after the hit? (b) In which direction do rod and particle rotate if d is greater than this value?

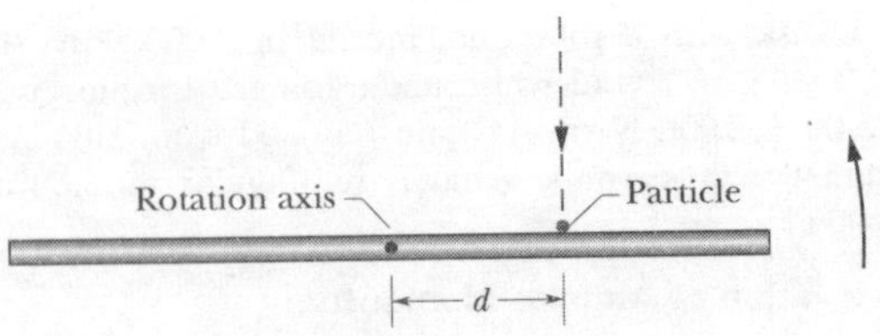

FIG. 10-108 Problem 79.

80 In Fig. 10-109, a 30 kg child stands on the edge of a stationary merry-go-round of mass 100 kg and radius 2.0 m. The rotational inertia of the merry-go-round about its rotation axis is $150\ \text{kg}\cdot\text{m}^2$. The child catches a ball of mass 1.0 kg thrown by a friend. Just before the ball is caught, it has a horizontal velocity $\vec{v}$ of magnitude 12 m/s, at angle $\phi = 37°$ with a line tangent to the outer edge of the merry-go-round, as shown. What is the angular speed of the merry-go-round just after the ball is caught?

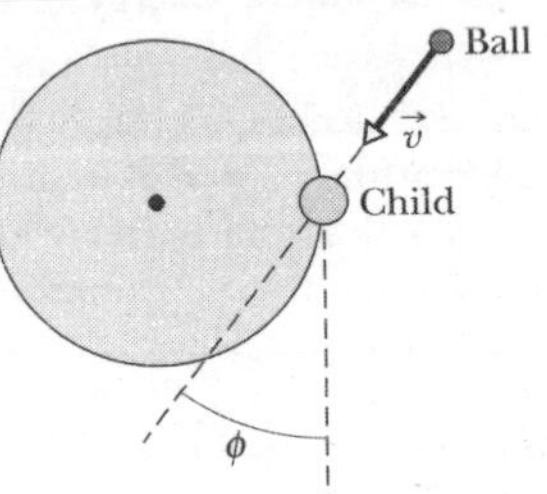

FIG. 10-109 Problem 80.

81 In Fig. 10-110, a small 50 g block slides down a frictionless surface through height $h = 20$ cm and then sticks to a uniform rod of mass 100 g and length 40 cm. The rod pivots about point O through angle θ before momentarily stopping. Find θ.

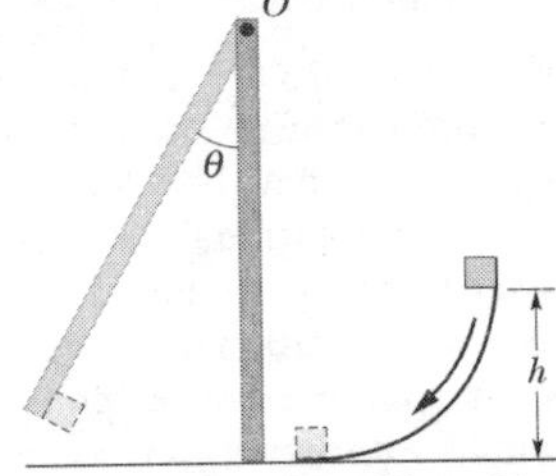

FIG. 10-110 Problem 81.

82 Two 2.00 kg balls are attached to the ends of a thin rod of length 50.0 cm and negligible mass. The rod is free to rotate in a vertical plane without friction about a horizontal axis through its center. With the rod initially horizontal (Fig. 10-111), a 50.0 g wad of wet putty drops onto one of the balls, hitting it with a speed of 3.00 m/s and then sticking to it. (a) What is the angular speed of the system just after the putty wad hits? (b) What is the ratio of the kinetic energy of the system after the collision to that of the putty wad just before? (c) Through what angle will the system rotate before it momentarily stops?

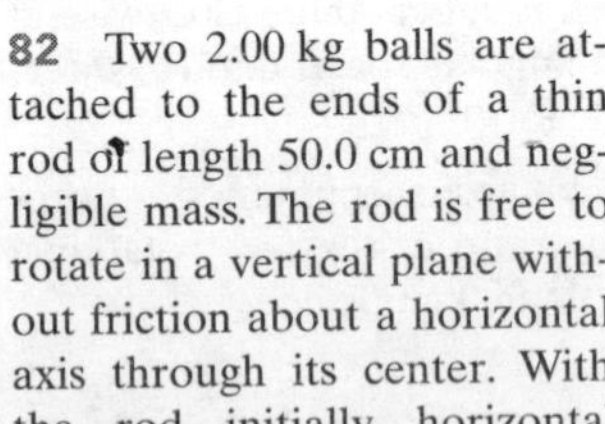

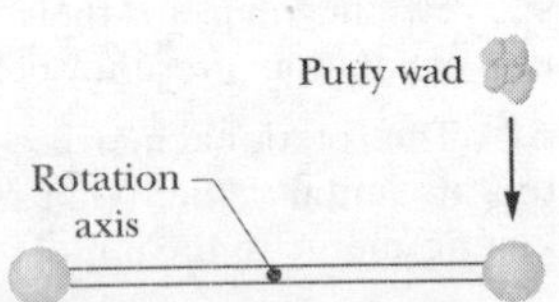

FIG. 10-111 Problem 82.

Rigid Body Dynamics—II  

The famous tower in Pisa, Italy, began to lean toward the south even during its construction, which spanned two centuries. The leaning increased with time but only at the snail's pace of 0.001° per year. In recent years, when the tilt reached 5.5°, the tower was closed to tourists because authorities feared that it would soon collapse. But doesn't collapse require that the tower's center of mass move out beyond the base of the tower? That would not have happened for many more years.

> *So, what was the danger to the tower?*

The answer is in this chapter.

PhotoDisc, Inc/Getty Images, Inc.

11-1 | Introduction

In Chapter 10 we discussed pure rotational motion of rigid body. We learnt many new concepts and new physical quantities namely moment of inertia, torque, and angular momentum. In this chapter, we will discuss general plane motion of rigid body popularly known as combined rotation and translation. Our methods and tools of analyzing this type of motion are going to be similar as discussed in the previous chapter. We will also develop new understanding of equilibrium and stability.

11-2 | Kinematics of Combined Rotation and Translation

FIG. 11-1 The self-righting Segway Human Transporter. *(Justin Sullivan/ Getty Images News and Sport Services)*

As we discussed in Chapter 10, physics includes the study of rotation. Arguably, the most important application of that physics is in the rolling motion of wheels and wheel-like objects. This applied physics has long been used. For example, when the prehistoric people of Easter Island moved their gigantic stone statues from the quarry and across the island, they dragged them over logs acting as rollers. Much later, when settlers moved westward across America in the 1800s, they rolled their possessions first by wagon and then later by train. Today, like it or not, the world is filled with cars, trucks, motorcycles, bicycles, and other rolling vehicles.

The physics and engineering of rolling have been around for so long that you might think no fresh ideas remain to be developed. However, skateboards and in-line skates were invented and engineered fairly recently, to become huge financial successes. Street luge is now catching on, and the self-righting Segway (Fig. 11-1) may change the way people move around in large cities. Applying the physics of rolling can still lead to surprises and rewards. Our starting point in exploring that physics is to simplify rolling motion.

11-3 | Rolling as Translation and Rotation Combined

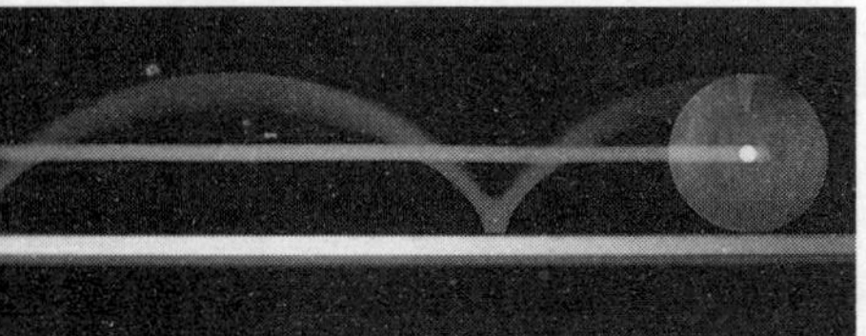

FIG. 11-2 A time-exposure photograph of a rolling disk. Small lights have been attached to the disk, one at its center and one at its edge. The latter traces out a curve called a *cycloid. (Richard Megna/ Fundamental Photographs)*

Here we consider only objects that *roll smoothly* along a surface; that is, the objects roll without slipping or bouncing on the surface. Figure 11-2 shows how complicated smooth rolling motion can be: Although the center of the object moves in a straight line parallel to the surface, a point on the rim certainly does not. However, we can study this motion by treating it as a combination of translation of the center of mass and rotation of the rest of the object around that center.

To see how we do this, pretend you are standing on a sidewalk watching the bicycle wheel of Fig. 11-3 as it rolls along a street. As shown, you see the center of mass O of the wheel move forward at constant speed v_{com}. The point P on the street where the wheel makes contact with the street surface also moves forward at speed v_{com}, so that P always remains directly below O.

During a time interval t, you see both O and P move forward by a distance s. The bicycle rider sees the wheel rotate through an angle θ about the center of the wheel, with the point of the wheel that was touching the street at the beginning of t moving through arc length s. Equation 11-1 relates the arc length s to the rotation angle θ:

$$s = \theta R \tag{11-1}$$

where R is the radius of the wheel. The linear speed v_{com} of the center of the wheel (the center of mass of this uniform wheel) is ds/dt. The angular speed ω of the wheel about its center is $d\theta/dt$. Thus, differentiating Eq. 11-1 with respect to time (with R held constant) gives us

$$v_{com} = \omega R \quad \text{(smooth rolling motion)} \tag{11-2}$$

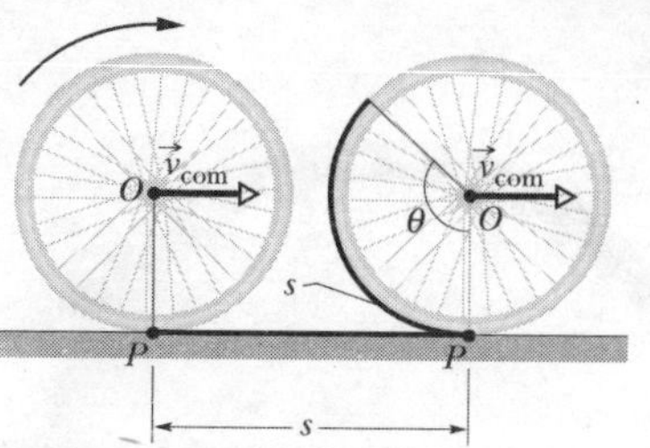

FIG. 11-3 The center of mass O of a rolling wheel moves a distance s at velocity $\vec{v}_{com}$ while the wheel rotates through angle θ. The point P at which the wheel makes contact with the surface over which the wheel rolls also moves a distance s.

Figure 11-4 shows that the rolling motion of a wheel is a combination of purely translational and purely rotational motions. Figure 11-4*a* shows the purely rotational motion (as if the rotation axis through the center were stationary): Every point on the wheel rotates about the center with angular speed ω. (This is the type of motion we considered in Chapter 10.) Every point on the outside edge of the wheel has linear speed v_{com} given by Eq. 11-2. Figure 11-4*b* shows the purely translational motion (as if the wheel did not rotate at all): Every point on the wheel moves to the right with speed v_{com}.

The combination of Figs. 11-4*a* and 11-4*b* yields the actual rolling motion of the wheel, Fig. 11-4*c*. Note that in this combination of motions, the portion of the wheel at the bottom (at point P) is stationary and the portion at the top (at point T) is moving at speed $2v_{com}$, faster than any other portion of the wheel. These results are demonstrated in Fig. 11-5, which is a time exposure of a rolling bicycle wheel. You can tell that the wheel is moving faster near its top than near its bottom because the spokes are more blurred at the top than at the bottom.

The motion of any round body rolling smoothly over a surface can be separated into purely rotational and purely translational motions, as in Figs. 11-4*a* and 11-4*b*.

Let's consider a bicycle going on a straight road in a straight line. The motion of any arbitarary point on wheel is quite complicated. To make the visualization of motion simple we apply concept of net motion. We understand that motion of center of the wheel can be easily observed by us and in this case it is a straight line motion. If we put an observer on the bicycle and ask him to describe the motion of any point. On the wheel he will describe it as pure rotational motion about the axle. In other words, he will observe all the particles on the wheel undergoing circular motion with same angular velocity, angular acceleration, and undergoing same angular displacement about point lying on acceleration. Thus, we can say,

$$\vec{r}_P = \vec{r}_A + \vec{r}_{P/A}$$
$$\vec{S}_P = \vec{S}_{P/A} + \vec{S}_A$$
$$\vec{V}_P = \vec{V}_{P/A} + \vec{V}_A$$
$$\vec{a}_P = \vec{a}_{P/A} + \vec{a}_A$$

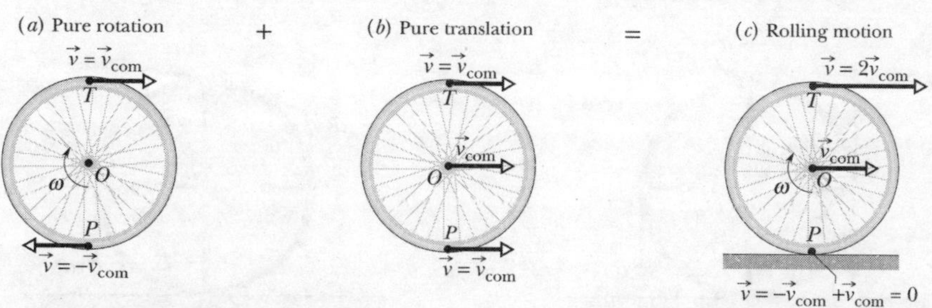

FIG. 11-4 Rolling motion of a wheel as a combination of purely rotational motion and purely translational motion. (*a*) The purely rotational motion: All points on the wheel move with the same angular speed ω. Points on the outside edge of the wheel all move with the same linear speed $v = v_{com}$. The linear velocities $\vec{v}$ of two such points, at top (T) and bottom (P) of the wheel, are shown. (*b*) The purely translational motion: All points on the wheel move to the right with the same linear velocity $\vec{v}_{com}$. (*c*) The rolling motion of the wheel is the combination of (*a*) and (*b*).

Here $\vec{S}_{P/A} = \theta_P \vec{r}_{P/A}$, $\vec{V}_{P/A} = \omega \vec{r}_{P/A}$, and $\vec{a}_{P/A} = \alpha \vec{r}_{P/A}$

Thus, our strategy for solving problems in this chapter will involve finding angular parameters of motion of P about A and finding linear parameter of motion of A.

If A is center of mass we can find its acceleration using

$$\vec{F}_{ext} = M\vec{a}_{com}$$

Later we will prove that we will be able to use $T_{ext} = I\,\alpha$ about center of mass even if it is accelerating.

FIG. 11-5 A photograph of a rolling bicycle wheel. The spokes near the wheel's top are more blurred than those near the bottom because the top ones are moving faster, as Fig. 11-4c shows. *(Courtesy Alice Halliday)*

PROBLEM-SOLVING TACTICS

Tactic 1: Do not relate v and ω of wheel by writing $v = \omega R$. It is possible to have one without having the other. If we lock the cycle and pull it we will have translational motion of the wheel and no rotation. If we keep it on stand and rotate the wheel we will have angular velocity but no linear velocity. These two parameters are completely independent of each other.

Let's say the bicycle is going at velocity V and wheel is rotating with angular velocity ω. The figures below help us finding velocity of any arbitnary point. All points on wheel must have a velocity perpendicular to the line joining the center in frame attached to the center.

Kinematics

1. Velocity

with respect to center

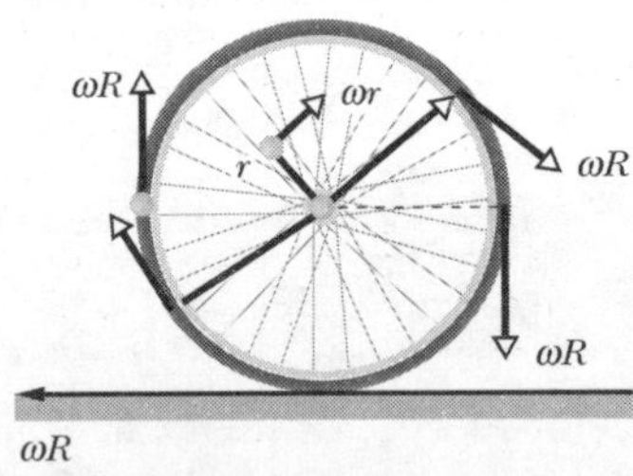

with respect to ground

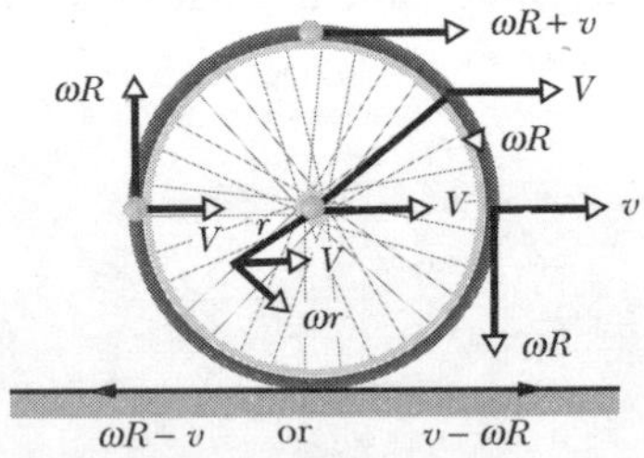

2. Acceleration

with respect to center

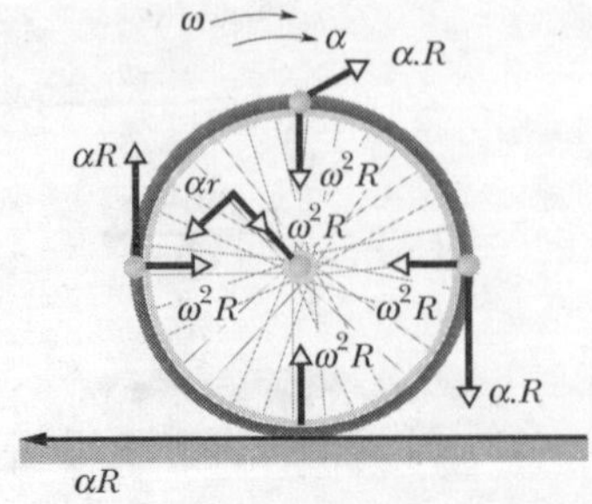

with respect to ground

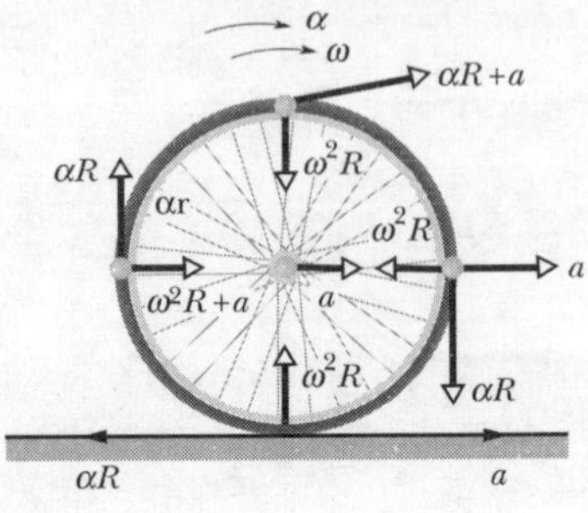

Rolling and Sliding

Case 1 $V_{com} > \omega R$

The friction will be kinetic in nature and its magnitude can be determined by using $f_k = \mu_k N$. Direction will be opposite to V_{com} (point of contact A is moving forward with respect to ground this is how brakes stop a car).

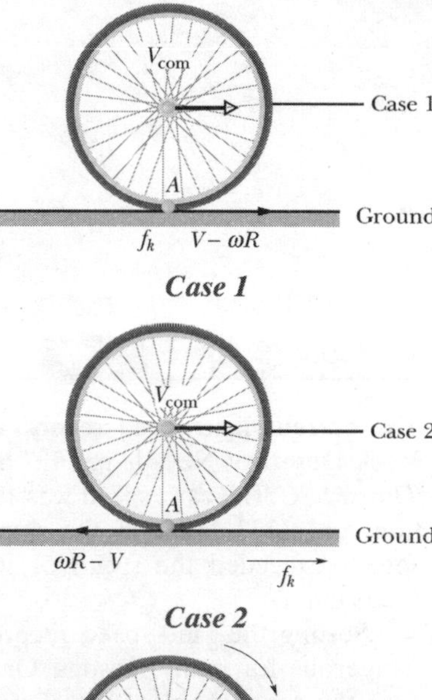

Case 2 $V_{com} < \omega R$

The friction will be kinetic in nature and its magnitude can be determined using $f_k = \mu_k N$. Direction will be same as V_{com} (point of contact A is moving backward with respect to ground. This is how a car accelerates because of friction).

Case 3 $V_{com} < \omega r$

Known as perfect rolling maximum problems when we come across this situation.

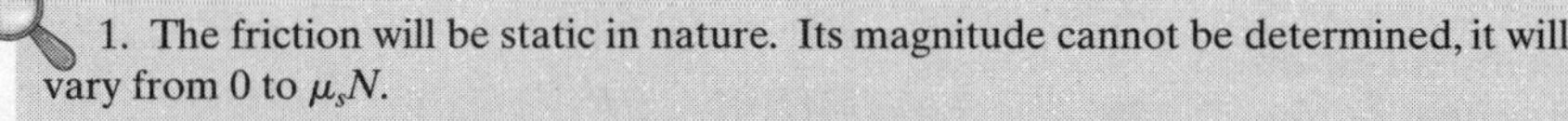

1. The friction will be static in nature. Its magnitude cannot be determined, it will vary from 0 to $\mu_s N$.

2. Even its direction cannot be predicted. We can assume any direction and answer will come with sign. For example, if assumed that friction is acting toward left and the value comes to be −3 it means it is acting toward right.

3. The total work done by static friction is zero. Thus, mechanical energy of the system will remain conserved.

When the rolling body is in contact with moving object.

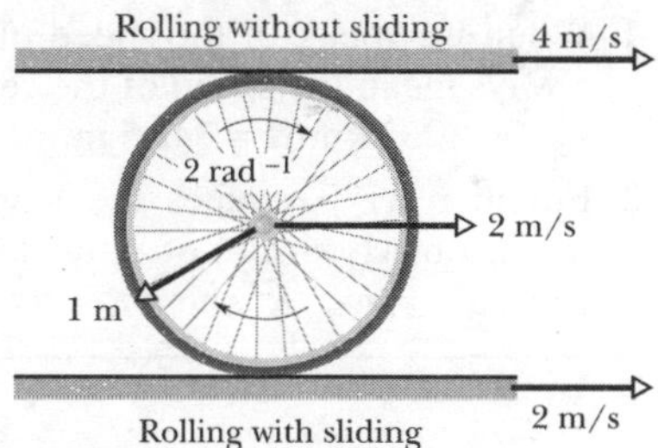

11-4 | Kinetic Energy of Combined Translation and Rotation

Let us now calculate the kinetic energy of the rolling wheel as measured by the stationary observer. If we view the rolling as pure rotation about an axis through P in Fig. 11-6, then from Eq. 10-34 we have

$$K = \tfrac{1}{2} I_P \omega^2 \tag{11-3}$$

in which ω is the angular speed of the wheel and I_P is the rotational inertia of the wheel about the axis through P. From the parallel-axis theorem of Eq. 10-36 ($I = I_{com} + Mh^2$), we have

$$I_P = I_{com} + MR^2 \tag{11-4}$$

in which M is the mass of the wheel, I_{com} is its rotational inertia about an axis through its center of mass, and R (the wheel's radius) is the perpendicular distance h. Substituting Eq. 11-4 into Eq. 11-3, we obtain

$$K = \tfrac{1}{2} I_{com} \omega^2 + \tfrac{1}{2} MR^2 \omega^2$$

and using the relation $v_{com} = \omega R$ (Eq. 11-2) yields

$$K = \tfrac{1}{2} I_{com} \omega^2 + \tfrac{1}{2} M v_{com}^2 \tag{11-5}$$

We can interpret the term $1/2\ I_{com}\omega^2$ as the kinetic energy associated with the rotation of the wheel about an axis through its center of mass (Fig. 11-4a),

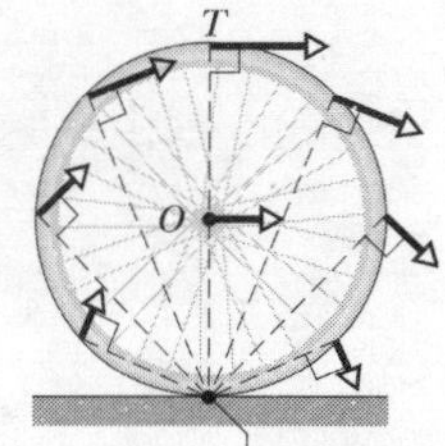

FIG. 11-6 Rolling can be viewed as pure rotation, with angular speed ω, about an axis that always extends through P. The vectors show the instantaneous linear velocities of selected points on the rolling wheel. You can obtain the vectors by combining the translational and rotational motions as in Fig. 11-4.

and the term $1/2Mv_{com}^2$ as the kinetic energy associated with the translational motion of the wheel's center of mass (Fig. 11-4*b*). Thus, we have the following rule:

> A rolling object has two types of kinetic energy: a rotational kinetic energy ($1/2\ I_{com}\omega^2$) due to its rotation about its center of mass and a translational kinetic energy ($1/2\ Mv_{com}^2$) due to translation of its center of mass.

Sample Problem 11-1

The current land-speed record was set in the Black Rock Desert of Nevada in 1997 by the jet-powered car *Thrust SSC*. The car's speed was 1222 km/h in one direction and 1233 km/h in the opposite direction. Both speeds exceeded the speed of sound at that location (1207 km/h).

Setting the land-speed record was obviously very dangerous for many reasons. One of them had to do with the car's wheels. Approximate each wheel on the car *Thrust SSC* as a disk of uniform thickness and mass $M = 170$ kg, and assume smooth rolling. When the car's speed was 1233 km/h, what was the kinetic energy of each wheel?

Conceptualize/Classify: Equation 11-5 gives the kinetic energy of a rolling object, but we need three ideas to use it:

1. When we speak of the speed of a rolling object, we always mean the speed of the center of mass, so here $v_{com} = 1233$ km/h $= 342.5$ m/s.
2. Equation 11-5 requires the angular speed ω of the rolling object, which we can relate to v_{com} with Eq. 11-2, writing $\omega = v_{com}/R$, where R is the wheel's radius.
3. Equation 11-5 also requires the rotational inertia I_{com} of the object about its center of mass. From Table 10-2*c*, we find that, for a uniform disk, $I_{com} = 1/2MR^2$.

Compute: Now Eq. 11-5 gives us

$$K = \tfrac{1}{2}I_{com}\omega^2 + \tfrac{1}{2}Mv_{com}^2$$
$$= (\tfrac{1}{2})(\tfrac{1}{2}MR^2)(v_{com}/R)^2 + \tfrac{1}{2}Mv_{com}^2 = \tfrac{3}{4}Mv_{com}^2$$
$$= \tfrac{3}{4}(170\ \text{kg})(342.5\ \text{m/s})^2$$
$$= 1.50 \times 10^7\ \text{J} \qquad \text{(Answer)}$$

Conclude: (Note that the wheel's radius R cancels out of the calculation.)

This answer gives one measure of the danger when the land-speed record was set by *Thrust SSC:* The kinetic energy of each (cast aluminum) wheel on the car was huge, almost as much as the kinetic energy (2.1×10^7 J) of the spinning steel disk that exploded in Sample Problem 10-8. Had a wheel hit any hard obstacle along the car's path, the wheel would have exploded the way the steel disk did, with the car and driver moving faster than sound!

11-5 | Forces of Rolling

Friction and Rolling

If a wheel rolls at constant speed, as in Fig. 11-3, it has no tendency to slide at the point of contact *P*, and thus no frictional force acts there. However, if a net force acts on the rolling wheel to speed it up or to slow it, then that net force causes acceleration $\vec{a}_{com}$ of the center of mass along the direction of travel. It also causes the wheel to rotate faster or slower, which means it causes an angular acceleration α. These accelerations tend to make the wheel slide at *P*. Thus, a frictional force must act on the wheel at *P* to oppose that tendency.

If the wheel *does not* slide, the force is a *static* frictional force $\vec{f}_s$ and the motion is smooth rolling. We can then relate the magnitudes of the linear acceleration $\vec{a}_{com}$ and the angular acceleration α by differentiating Eq. 11-2 with respect to time (with R held constant). On the left side, dv_{com}/dt is a_{com}, and on the right side $d\omega/dt$ is α. So, for smooth rolling we have

$$a_{com} = \alpha R \quad \text{(smooth rolling motion)} \qquad (11\text{-}6)$$

If the wheel *does* slide when the net force acts on it, the frictional force that acts at P in Fig. 11-3 is a *kinetic* frictional force $\vec{f}_k$. The motion then is not smooth rolling, and Eq. 11-6 does not apply to the motion. In this chapter we discuss only smooth rolling motion.

Figure 11-7 shows an example in which a wheel is being made to rotate faster while rolling to the right along a flat surface, as on a bicycle at the start of a race. The faster rotation tends to make the bottom of the wheel slide to the left at point P. A frictional force at P, directed to the right, opposes this tendency to slide. If the wheel does not slide, that frictional force is a static frictional force $\vec{f}_s$ (as shown), the motion is smooth rolling, and Eq. 11-6 applies to the motion. (Without friction, bicycle races would be stationary and very boring.)

If the wheel in Fig. 11-7 were made to rotate slower, as on a slowing bicycle, we would change the figure in two ways: The directions of the center-of-mass acceleration $\vec{a}_{com}$ and the frictional force $\vec{f}_s$ at point P would now be to the left.

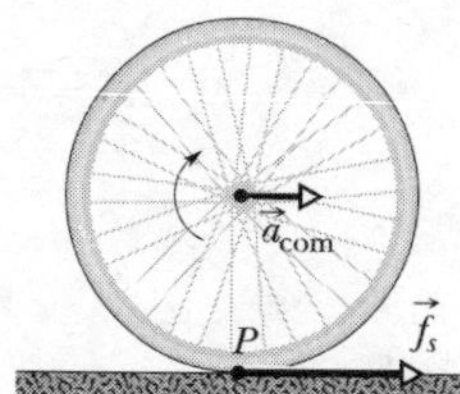

FIG. 11-7 A wheel rolls horizontally without sliding while accelerating with linear acceleration $\vec{a}_{com}$. A static frictional force $\vec{f}_s$ acts on the wheel at P, opposing its tendency to slide.

Rolling Down a Ramp

Figure 11-8 shows a round uniform body of mass M and radius R rolling smoothly down a ramp at angle θ, along an x axis. We want to find an expression for the body's acceleration $a_{com,x}$ down the ramp. We do this by using Newton's second law in both its linear version ($F_{net} = Ma$) and its angular version ($\tau_{net} = I\alpha$).

We start by drawing the forces on the body as shown in Fig. 11-8:

1. The gravitational force $\vec{F}_g$ on the body is directed downward. The tail of the vector is placed at the center of mass of the body. The component along the ramp is $F_g \sin\theta$, which is equal to $Mg \sin\theta$.
2. A normal force $\vec{F}_N$ is perpendicular to the ramp. It acts at the point of contact P, but in Fig. 11-8 the vector has been shifted along its direction until its tail is at the body's center of mass.
3. A static frictional force $\vec{f}_s$ acts at the point of contact P and is directed up the ramp. (Do you see why? If the body were to slide at P, it would slide *down* the ramp. Thus, the frictional force opposing the sliding must be *up* the ramp.)

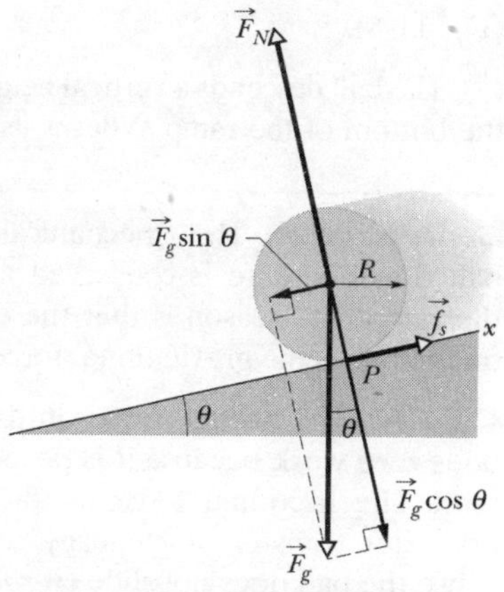

FIG. 11-8 A round uniform body of radius R rolls down a ramp. The forces that act on it are the gravitational force $\vec{F}_g$, a normal force $\vec{F}_N$, and a frictional force $\vec{f}_s$ pointing up the ramp. (For clarity, vector $\vec{F}_N$ has been shifted in the direction it points until its tail is at the center of the body.)

We can write Newton's second law for components along the x axis in Fig. 11-8 ($F_{net,x} = ma_x$) as

$$f_s - Mg\sin\theta = Ma_{com,x} \qquad (11\text{-}7)$$

This equation contains two unknowns, f_s and $a_{com,x}$. (We should *not* assume that f_s is at its maximum value $f_{s,max}$. All we know is that the value of f_s is just right for the body to roll smoothly down the ramp, without sliding.)

We now wish to apply Newton's second law in angular form to the body's rotation about its center of mass. First, we shall use Eq. 10-41 ($\tau = r_\perp F$) to write the torques on the body about that point. The frictional force $\vec{f}_s$ has moment arm R and thus produces a torque Rf_s, which is positive because it tends to rotate the body counterclockwise in Fig. 11-8. Forces $\vec{F}_g$ and $\vec{F}_N$ have zero moment arms about the center of mass and thus produce zero torques. So we can write the angular form of Newton's second law ($\tau_{net} = I\alpha$) about an axis through the body's center of mass as

$$Rf_s = I_{com}\alpha \qquad (11\text{-}8)$$

This equation contains two unknowns, f_s and α.

Because the body is rolling smoothly, we can use Eq. 11-6 ($a_{com} = \alpha R$) to relate the unknowns $a_{com,x}$ and α. But we must be cautious because here $a_{com,x}$ is negative (in the negative direction of the x axis) and α is positive (counter-clockwise). Thus, we substitute $-a_{com,x}/R$ for α in Eq. 11-8. Then, solving for f_s, we obtain

$$f_s = -I_{com}\frac{a_{com,x}}{R^2} \tag{11-9}$$

Substituting the right side of Eq. 11-9 for f_s in Eq. 11-7, we then find

$$a_{com,x} = -\frac{g\sin\theta}{1 + I_{com}/MR^2} \tag{11-10}$$

We can use this equation to find the linear acceleration $a_{com,x}$ of any body rolling along an incline of angle θ with the horizontal.

CHECKPOINT 1 Disks A and B are identical and roll across a floor with equal speeds. Then disk A rolls up an incline, reaching a maximum height h, and disk B moves up an incline that is identical except that it is frictionless. Is the maximum height reached by disk B greater than, less than, or equal to h?

Sample Problem 11-2

A uniform ball, of mass $M = 6.00$ kg and radius R, rolls smoothly from rest down a ramp at angle $\theta = 30.0°$ (Fig. 11-8).

(a) The ball descends a vertical height $h = 1.20$ m to reach the bottom of the ramp. What is its speed at the bottom?

Conceptualize: The mechanical energy E of the ball–Earth system is conserved as the ball rolls down the ramp. The reason is that the only force doing work on the ball is the gravitational force, a conservative force.

Classify: The normal force on the ball from the ramp does zero work because it is perpendicular to the ball's path. The frictional force on the ball from the ramp does not transfer any energy to thermal energy because the ball does not slide (it *rolls smoothly*).

Therefore, we can write the conservation of mechanical energy ($E_f = E_i$) as

$$K_f + U_f = K_i + U_i \tag{11-11}$$

where subscripts f and i refer to the final values (at the bottom) and initial values (at rest), respectively. The gravitational potential energy is initially $U_i = Mgh$ (where M is the ball's mass) and finally $U_f = 0$. The kinetic energy is initially $K_i = 0$. For the final kinetic energy K_f, we need an additional idea: Because the ball rolls, the kinetic energy involves both translation *and* rotation, so we include them both by using the right side of Eq. 11-5.

Compute: Substituting into Eq. 11-11 gives us

$$(\tfrac{1}{2}I_{com}\omega^2 + \tfrac{1}{2}Mv_{com}^2) + 0 = 0 + Mgh \tag{11-12}$$

where I_{com} is the ball's rotational inertia about an axis through its center of mass, v_{com} is the requested speed at the bottom, and ω is the angular speed there.

Because the ball rolls smoothly, we can use Eq. 11-2 to substitute v_{com}/R for ω to reduce the unknowns in Eq. 11-12. Doing so, substituting $\frac{2}{5}MR^2$ for I_{com} (from Table 10-2f), and then solving for v_{com} give us

$$v_{com} = \sqrt{(\tfrac{10}{7})gh} = \sqrt{(\tfrac{10}{7})(9.8\text{ m/s}^2)(1.20\text{ m})}$$
$$= 4.10\text{ m/s} \qquad \text{(Answer)}$$

Conclude: Note that the answer does not depend on M or R.

(b) What are the magnitude and direction of the frictional force on the ball as it rolls down the ramp?

Conceptualize/Classify: Because the ball rolls smoothly, Eq. 11-9 gives the frictional force on the ball.

Compute: Before we can use Eq. 11-9, we need the ball's acceleration $a_{com,x}$ from Eq. 11-10:

$$a_{com,x} = -\frac{g\sin\theta}{1 + I_{com}/MR^2} = -\frac{g\sin\theta}{1 + \frac{2}{5}MR^2/MR^2}$$
$$= -\frac{(9.8\text{ m/s}^2)\sin 30.0°}{1 + \frac{2}{5}} = -3.50\text{ m/s}^2$$

Note that we needed neither mass M nor radius R to find $a_{com,x}$. Thus, any size ball with any uniform mass would have this acceleration down a 30.0° ramp, provided the ball rolls smoothly.

We can now solve Eq. 11-9 as

$$f_s = -I_{com}\frac{a_{com,x}}{R^2} = -\tfrac{2}{5}MR^2\frac{a_{com,x}}{R^2} = -\tfrac{2}{5}Ma_{com,x}$$
$$= -\tfrac{2}{5}(6.00\text{ kg})(-3.50\text{ m/s}^2) = 8.40\text{ N} \qquad \text{(Answer)}$$

Conclude: Note that we needed mass M but not radius R. Thus, the frictional force on any 6.00 kg ball rolling smoothly down a 30.0° ramp would be 8.40 N regardless of the ball's radius.

11-6 | Torques About a Center of Mass

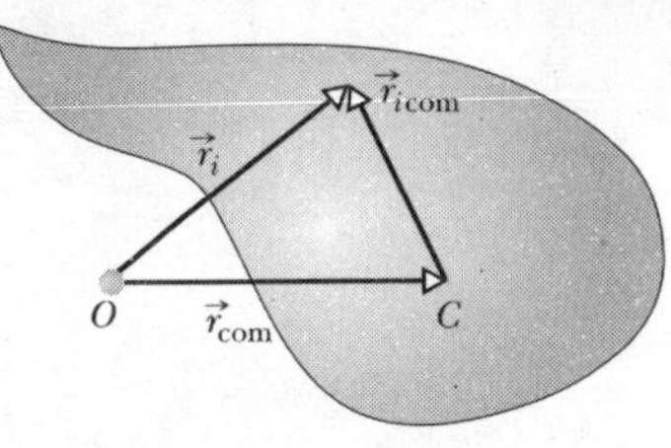

FIG. 11-9 Position vectors of center of mass and a random point with respect to origin. Position vector of the random point with respect to center of mass.

Some caution is needed in choosing the point to be used for writing the equation $\tau_{net} = I\alpha$. Although we can use a point fixed in inertial space there is another convinient point about which $\tau_{net} = I\alpha$ can be used even if it is accelerated. As in Chapter. 6 we derived

$$\sum \mathbf{F}_{ext} = M\mathbf{a}_{com} \qquad \text{we will also derive} \qquad \tau_{net} = I_{com}\,\alpha$$

$$\tau_{net} = \sum \mathbf{r}_{i/com} \times \mathbf{F}_{ext} = I_{com} \qquad \tau_{net} = I_{com}\,\alpha$$

where the torques are taken about the center of mass. These two points, the fixed point and the center of mass, can always be used. Other points, particularly accelerated points, can be used only with great care, and sometimes a "fictitious force" must be introduced.

Proof: Let's say that the center of mass is moving with accleration $\vec{a}$. If we take center of mass as our reference frame, then we have to apply pseudo force $-M_i\,\vec{a}$ on all the particles. Now torque will not only involve torque due to external forces about center of mass but it will also involve torque due to psuedo forces about center of mass.

$$\tau_{pseudo,i} = -\vec{r}_i \times m_i\vec{a}$$

Torque about center of mass

$$
\begin{aligned}
&= \sum \tau_{pseudo,i} = \sum(\vec{r}_i \times m_i\vec{a}) = -\sum(m_i\vec{r}_i) \times \vec{a} \\
&= -M\left(\frac{\sum(m_i\vec{r}_i)}{M}\right) \times \vec{a} \\
&= -M(\vec{r}_{com} \times \vec{a}) \\
&= -(\vec{r}_{com} \times (M\vec{a})) = 0 \\
&= 0
\end{aligned}
$$

Theorem: Angular momentum of a body about any point A or an axis A = angular momentum of the body about center of mass for an axis parallel to axis A + angular momentum of center of mass about axis A.

Angular momentum of a body about any point A or an axis A will be sum of angular momenta of indivdual particles $\vec{L} = \sum m_i(\vec{r}_i \times \vec{v}_i)$

We can write $\quad \vec{r}_i = [\vec{r}_{icom} + \vec{r}_{com}] \quad$ and $\quad \vec{v}_i = [\vec{v}_{icom} + \vec{v}_{com}]$

$$
\begin{aligned}
\vec{L} &= \sum m_i[\vec{r}_{icom} + \vec{r}_{com}] \times [\vec{v}_{icom} + \vec{v}_{com}] \\
&= \sum m_i(\vec{r}_{icom} \times \vec{v}_{icom}) + \sum m_i(\vec{r}_{com} \times \vec{v}_{icom}) + \\
&\quad \sum m_i(\vec{r}_{icom} \times \vec{v}_{com}) + \sum m_i(\vec{r}_{com} \times \vec{v}_{com}) \\
&= \sum \vec{r}_{icom} \times (m_i\vec{v}_{icom}) + \vec{r}_{com} \times \\
&\quad \sum m_i\vec{v}_{icom} + \left(\sum m_i\vec{r}_{icom}\right) \times \vec{v}_{com} + (\vec{r}_{com} \times \vec{v}_{com})\sum m_i
\end{aligned}
$$

$\sum m_i\,\vec{v}_{com}$ means momentum of the body with respect to center of mass which is zero

$(\sum m_i\, r_{com})$ means Position vector of the center of mass of the body with respect to which is zero

$$= \vec{L}_{body\text{-}com} + \vec{r}_{com} \times \vec{O} + \vec{O} \times \vec{v}_{com} + \vec{L}_{com}$$

$$\vec{L}_{body} = \vec{L}_{body\text{-}com} + \vec{L}_{com}$$

Pure Rolling of Uniform Circular Bodies

First we will take problems involving pure rolling only, that is, rolling without sliding. In this case force of friction will be static. The magnitude will be unknown but it has to be less than $\mu_s N$. As far as direction is concerned we can assume any direction, the answer will come with correct sign. We will have kinematic relation equating velocity of contact points and thus tangential accelerations of contact points. Many times rather than explicitly saying that pure rolling is taking place, we will find problems stating that "friction is sufficient to prevent any slipping" or simply no slipping is taking place at any contact or just "friction is sufficient".

Plane Motion of Rigid Body

During plane motion of a rigid body, the center of mass C of a rigid body moves in a certain plane while the angular velocity vector ω of the body always remains perpendicular to that plane. This means that motion of the body can be interpreted as purely rotational motion about the axis passing through the center of mass of the body in the C frame. Thus, we have the following two equations describing plane motion of a rigid body:

$$\mathbf{F} = ma_c; \quad \tau_c = I_c\alpha$$

where m is the mass of the body, $\mathbf{F}$ is the resultant of all external forces. I_C and τ_C are the moment of inertia and the total torque of all external forces, both quantities are being expressed relative to the axis passing through the center of mass of the body. It should be remembered that the torque τ_{com} includes only external forces.

Summary of dynamical formulas for fixed axis motion:

1. Pure rotation about an axis – no translation.

$$L = I\omega$$
$$\tau = T\alpha$$
$$K = (1/2)I\omega^2$$

2. Rotation and translation (subscripts 0 refers to center mass)

$$L_Z = I_0\omega + (\mathbf{R} \times MV)$$
$$\tau_Z = \tau_0 + (\mathbf{R} \times \mathbf{F})$$
$$\alpha_Z = I_0\alpha$$
$$K = \frac{1}{2}I_0\omega + \frac{1}{2}MV^2$$

11-7 | The Yo-Yo

A yo-yo is a physics lab that you can fit in your pocket. If a yo-yo rolls down its string for a distance h, it loses potential energy in amount mgh but gains kinetic energy in both translational ($1/2\ Mv^2_{com}$) and rotational ($1/2\ I_{com}\omega^2$) forms. As it climbs back up, it loses kinetic energy and regains potential energy.

In a modern yo-yo, the string is not tied to the axle but is looped around it. When the yo-yo "hits" the bottom of its string, an upward force on the axle from the string stops the descent. The yo-yo then spins, axle inside loop, with only rotational kinetic energy. The yo-yo keeps spinning ("sleeping") until you "wake it" by jerking on the string, causing the string to catch on the axle and the yo-yo to climb back up. The rotational kinetic energy of the yo-yo at the bottom of its string (and thus the sleeping time) can be considerably increased by throwing the yo-yo downward so that it starts down the string with initial speeds v_{com} and ω instead of rolling down from rest.

To find an expression for the linear acceleration a_{com} of a yo-yo rolling down a string, we could use Newton's second law just as we did for the body rolling down a ramp in Fig. 11-8. The analysis is the same except for the following:

1. Instead of rolling down a ramp at angle θ with the horizontal, the yo-yo rolls down a string at angle $\theta = 90°$ with the horizontal.
2. Instead of rolling on its outer surface at radius R, the yo-yo rolls on an axle of radius R_0 (Fig. 11-10*a*).
3. Instead of being slowed by frictional force $\vec{f}_s$, the yo-yo is slowed by the force $\vec{T}$ on it from the string (Fig. 11-10*b*).

The analysis would again lead us to Eq. 11-10. Therefore, let us just change the notation in Eq. 11-10 and set $\theta = 90°$ to write the linear acceleration as

$$a_{com} = -\frac{g}{1 + I_{com}/MR_0^2} \qquad (11\text{-}13)$$

where I_{com} is the yo-yo's rotational inertia about its center and M is its mass. A yo-yo has the same downward acceleration when it is climbing back up.

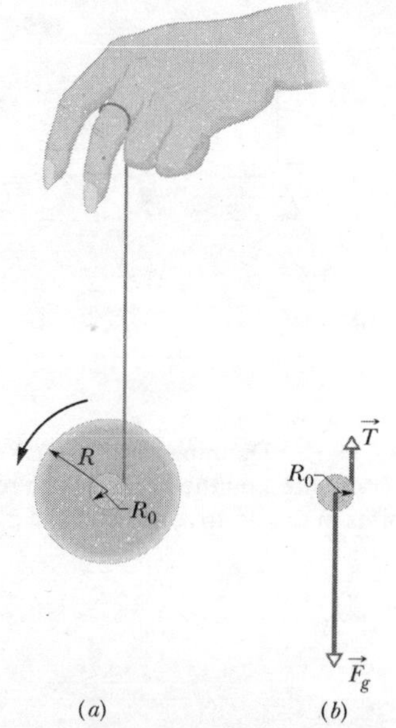

FIG. 11-10 (*a*) A yo-yo, shown in cross section. The string, of assumed negligible thickness, is wound around an axle of radius R_0. (*b*) A free-body diagram for the falling yo-yo. Only the axle is shown.

11-8 | Torque Revisited

In Chapter 10 we defined torque τ for a rigid body that can rotate around a fixed axis, with each particle in the body forced to move in a path that is a circle centered on that axis. We now expand the definition of torque to apply it to an individual particle that moves along any path relative to a fixed *point* (rather than a fixed axis). The path need no longer be a circle, and we must write the torque as a vector $\vec{\tau}$ that may have any direction.

Figure 11-11*a* shows such a particle at point A in an xy plane. A single force $\vec{F}$ in that plane acts on the particle, and the particle's position relative to the origin O is given by position vector $\vec{r}$. The torque $\vec{\tau}$ acting on the particle relative to the fixed point O is a vector quantity defined as

$$\vec{\tau} = \vec{r} \times \vec{F} \quad \text{(torque defined)} \qquad (11\text{-}14)$$

We can evaluate the vector (or cross) product in this definition of $\vec{\tau}$ by using the rules for such products given in Section 3-8. To find the direction of $\vec{\tau}$, we slide the vector $\vec{F}$ (without changing its direction) until its tail is at the origin O, so that the two vectors in the vector product are tail to tail as in Fig. 11-11*b*. We then use the right-hand rule for vector products in Fig. 3-21*a*, sweeping the fingers of the right hand from $\vec{r}$ (the first vector in the product) into $\vec{F}$ (the second vector). The outstretched right thumb then gives the direction of $\vec{\tau}$. In Fig. 11-11*b*, the direction of $\vec{\tau}$ is in the positive direction of the z axis.

To determine the magnitude of $\vec{\tau}$, we apply the general result of Eq. 3-27 ($c = ab \sin \phi$), finding

$$\tau = rF \sin \phi \qquad (11\text{-}15)$$

where ϕ is the smaller angle between the directions of $\vec{r}$ and $\vec{F}$ when the vectors are tail to tail. From Fig. 11-11*b*, we see that Eq. 11-15 can be rewritten as

$$\tau = rF_{\perp} \qquad (11\text{-}16)$$

where $F_{\perp}$ ($= F \sin \phi$) is the component of $\vec{F}$ perpendicular to $\vec{r}$. From Fig. 11-11*c*, we see that Eq. 11-15 can also be rewritten as

$$\tau = r_{\perp}F \qquad (11\text{-}17)$$

where $r_{\perp}$ ($= r \sin \phi$) is the moment arm of $\vec{F}$ (the perpendicular distance between O and the line of action of $\vec{F}$).

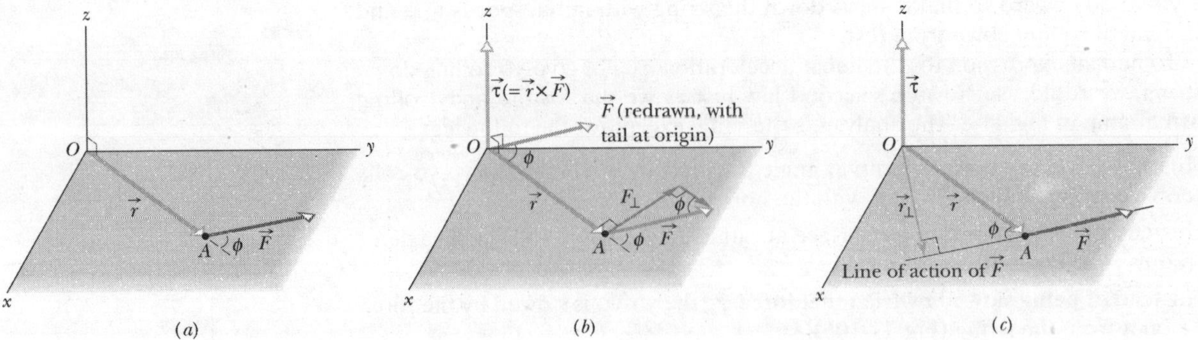

FIG. 11-11 Defining torque. (*a*) A force $\vec{F}$, lying in an *xy* plane, acts on a particle at point *A*. (*b*) This force produces a torque $\vec{\tau}\ (=\vec{r}\times\vec{F})$ on the particle with respect to the origin *O*. By the right-hand rule for vector (cross) products, the torque vector points in the positive direction of *z*. Its magnitude is given by $rF_\perp$ in (*b*) and by $r_\perp F$ in (*c*).

CHECKPOINT 2 The position vector $\vec{r}$ of a particle points along the positive direction of a *z* axis. If the torque on the particle is (a) zero, (b) in the negative direction of *x*, and (c) in the negative direction of *y*, in what direction is the force causing the torque?

Sample Problem 11-3

A double pulley of mass *m*, outer radius *R* and inner radius $r = R/4$ and radius of gyration, *R*/2, is kept on rough surface. A light inextensible string is wound on the inner pulley and the other end passes over a fixed light pulley and is attached to a mass *m* as shown in Fig. 11-12 slipping is taking place between double pulley and string and double pulley and ground. Find acceleration of the block.

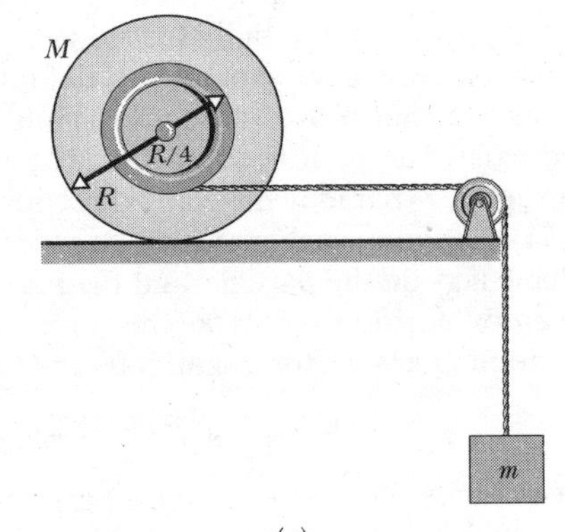

Conceptualize: It is easy to imagine that gravity pulls toward right.

Classify: Since friction is sufficient between double pulley and ground this is a problem involving pure rolling. Also no slipping between string and the pulley means that the lowest point of the smaller pulley and string will always have same velocity.

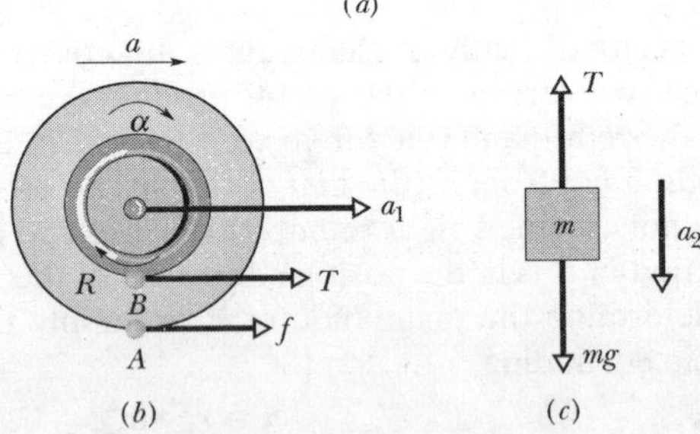

FIG. 11-12 (*a*) A double pulley attached to a hanging block. (*b*) and (*c*) Free-body diagram of the block and double pulley.

Compute: Make free-body diagram of the double pulley and the block.

Write Newton's second law for block and double pulley

$$Mg - T = Ma_2 \tag{i}$$

$$T + f = Ma_1 \tag{ii}$$

Applying $\tau_{\text{com}}^{\text{ext}} = I_{\text{com}}\,\alpha$

α for the double pulley. Remember that direction of α is opposite to the sense of torque

$$\frac{TR}{4} + fR = M\left(\frac{R}{2}\right)^2(-\alpha) \tag{iii}$$

$$a_1 - \alpha_1 R = 0 \tag{iv}$$

For pure rolling contact point must remain at rest with respect to ground. The block and center of mass of double pulley are not directly connected by a rope, hence they will not have same acceleration. Point *B* on smaller pulley and block will have same acceleration and speed all the time.

We can write $\quad a_2 = a_1 - \alpha_1\left(\dfrac{R}{4}\right) \quad$ (v) using Eqs. (iv) and (v)

$$a_2 = \frac{3a_1}{4} \qquad \text{(vi)}$$

Eq. (iii) can be written as $T + 4f = -M\alpha_1 R$

$$T + 4f = -Ma_1$$

adding to (ii) gives $f = -\frac{2T}{5}$

from (ii) it gives $T = \frac{5Ma_1}{3}$

from (i) and (vi) $Mg - \frac{5Ma_1}{3} = \frac{3Ma_1}{4}$

solving for a_1 we get $a_1 = \frac{12g}{29}$

Thus, $a_2 = 9g/29$ (Answer)

Conclude: Our arbitrary assumption about the direction of friction has not affected the answer, you may try the whole problem again assuming direction of friction in opposite direction.

Sample Problem 11-4

Fig. 11-13 shows a uniform cylinder at rest on a rough horizontal rug that is pulled out from under it with an acceleration perpendicular to the axis of the cylinder. Find force of friction on cylinder, assuming it does not slip ?

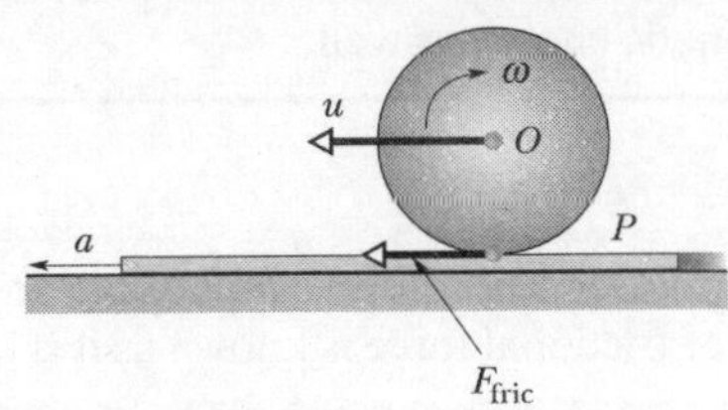

FIG. 11-13 A rug under the cylinder is being pulled.

Conceptualize: Imagine pulling a paper from under a ball, the friction should act toward left to prevent slipping.

Classify: When rug is pulled from under the cylinder, there will be tendency of slipping between rug and cylinder and friction will appear to prevent the slipping. Since it is given there is no slipping between cylinder and rug we can assume that force of friction will be static in nature.

Compute: Making free-body diagram of the cylinder, we realize the only horizontal force on the cylinder is that of friction at *P*. Writing Newton's second law for center of mass of the cylinder

$$F_{\text{fric}} = M\frac{dv_c}{dt}$$

Let us take the center of mass, point *O*, for evaluating the torque

$$F_{\text{fric}}R = I_c\frac{d\omega}{dt} = \frac{1}{2}MR^2\frac{d\omega}{dt}$$

$$a_P = \frac{dv_c}{dt} + R\frac{d\omega}{dt}$$

Since we have rolling without slipping, the tangential acceleration of the contact points are equal

$$a_p = a_{\text{rug}} \qquad \text{hence} \qquad a = \frac{dv_c}{dt} + R\frac{d\omega}{dt}$$

where $a_{\text{rug}} = a$

So that using $M\frac{dv_c}{dt} = \frac{1}{2}MR\frac{d\omega}{dt}$

we obtain $\frac{3}{2}R\frac{d\omega}{dt} = a$

giving $\frac{dv_c}{dt} = \frac{a}{3}$ and $F_{\text{fric}} = M\frac{a}{3}$

Conclude:. The direction of friction is coming as expected.

In Case Of: We take torque about *P*. The force of gravity and reaction at the surface pass through the point *P*, as does also the friction force, so the net torque about $P = 0$. Therefore, we say.

$$\alpha = 0, \quad \omega = \text{const} = \left(MR^2 + I_c\right)\omega$$

We recognize this as obviously wrong; the motion certainly is not with constant ω .This is wrong because *p* is an accelerated point and we cannot use $\tau = I\alpha$ about an accelerated point except the center of mass.

Sample Problem 11-5

A uniform sphere of radius *r* starts rolling down without slipping from the top of another fixed sphere of radius *R* (Fig. 11-14). Find the angular velocity of the sphere, and angle with vertical after it leaves the surface of the fixed sphere.

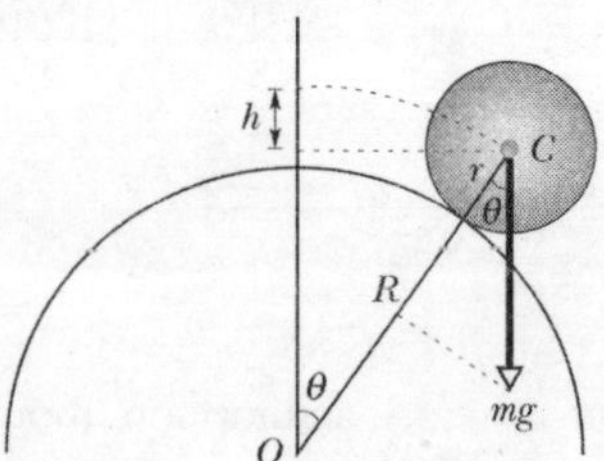

FIG. 11-14 A ball kept on a fixed sphere rolls down.

Conceptualize: Imagine keeping a small ball on top of a basketball, after moving some distance it leaves the basketball, also its speed keeps on increasing.

Classify: At the moment of breaking off the normal contact force between the two spheres will become zero. We can conserve energy as the friction acting is static hence no loss of mechanical energy. This problem can be categorized as vertical circular motion, where dimensions of body are not negligible.

Compute: Let us write the equation of motion for the center of the sphere at the moment of breaking off.

$mg\cos\theta = mV^2/(R + r)$, (remember $N = 0$ at this instant)

where v is the velocity of the center of the sphere at that moment, and θ is the corresponding angle The velocity v can be found from the energy conservation law:

$$mgh = mV^2 + I\omega^2/2$$

where I is the moment of inertia of the sphere relative to the axis passing through the sphere's center. In addition,

$v = \omega r$, for pure rolling contact point should have zero velocity;

$$h = (R + r)(1 - \cos\theta), \text{ from geometry}$$

From these four equations we obtain

$$\omega = \sqrt{10g(R + r)/17r^2}\ \theta = \cos^{-1}(10/17)$$

Conclude: The center of small ball is undergoing vertical circular motion but is not because the ball will have rotational kinetic energy as well.

Rolling with Slipping

Rolling with slipping of uniform circular bodies in this case α and a_{com} are independent of each other, but the magnitude of frictional force is known as it is kinetic.

$$f = \mu_k N$$

Complications arise due to the sense of direction. If relative velocities of contact points are known, then direction of friction can be ascertained easily otherwise we have to take cases and solve as we used to in Chapter 6. If any quantity comes negative we have to reject the solution and start again with opposite direction.

Sample Problem 11-6

A uniform cylinder is set in motion with back spin, on a rough horizontal surface, as shown in Fig. 11-15. If given velocity is u and angular velocity is ω_0, find relation between ω_0 and u so the uniform cylinder can come back.

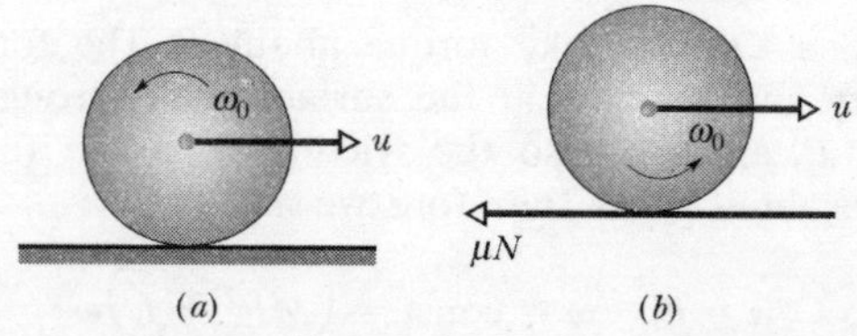

FIG. 11-15 (*a*) Cylinder on rough surface moves forward with back spin. (*b*) Fricton on the cylinder with back spin.

Conceptualize: Imagine pushing a ball while giving it a reverse spin on ground, if you have ever tried it you know that, we have to give it larger spin for it to come back.

Classify: It is a problem involving rolling with sliding, as in the begining the speed of contact point will be toward right. Friction will be kinetic and act toward left.

Compute: Making free-body diagram only horizontal force acting on the cylinder is kinetic friction.

thus, $f = \mu N = \mu mg$ applying Newton's second law we get, $a = -\mu g$

We can write $\tau = I\alpha$ about center of the uniform cylinder

$$\mu mgR = mk^2\alpha \text{ solving, } \alpha = -\frac{mgR}{k^2}$$

Writing speed and angular velocity at any arbitrary time t

$$V = u - \mu gt$$

$$\text{and } \omega = \omega_0 - \frac{\mu gRt}{k^2} \quad \text{(i)}$$

Now if the angular speed remains in same direction at the instant the velocity becomes zero, friction will still be acting toward left and at the next instant the ball will start coming back due to the acceleration provided by the force of friction. Thus $w > 0$ when $v = 0$.

If reverse happens that is w becomes zero before the velocity becomes zero, the ball will start pure rolling and continue to move toward right.

So, at $t = t_1$ $V = 0$, putting value of

$$t_1 = \frac{\mu}{\mu g} \text{ in Eq. (i)}$$

$$\omega = \omega_0 - \frac{\mu R}{k^2} \quad \text{thus} \quad \omega_0 > \frac{\mu R}{k^2} \qquad \text{(Answer)}$$

Conclude: As expected answer is implying that angular velocity should be larger than a particular value.

Sample Problem 11-7

A uniform rod is hanging from the ceiling, by two threads as shown in Fig. 11-16. Find tension in string *AP* immediately after string *BQ* is broken.

Conceptualize: It is easy to imagine that rod will start rotating clockwise due to gravity. The motion of rod will be such that point *P* will undergo circular motion about *A*.

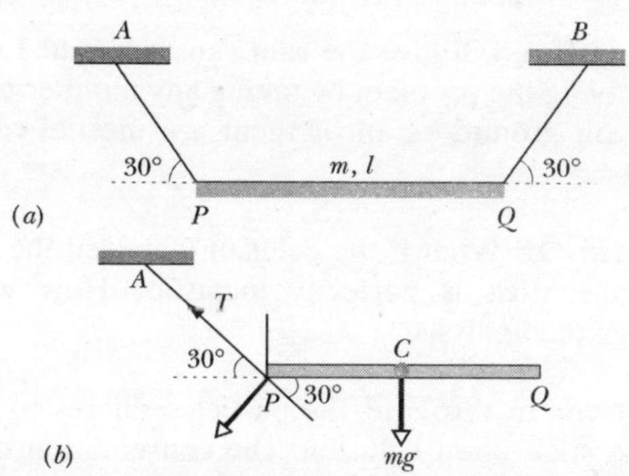

FIG. 11-16 (*a*) A rod is hanging by two symmetric threads. (*b*) Free-body diagram of a rod.

Classify: This is a problem in which center of mass is moving and we do not have any fixed point, but we do have constraint on point *P*'s motion, that is, it will undergo circular motion about *A*. We will write torque about center of mass of the rod due to tension in string *AP*.

Compute: τ about center of mass $\tau = (T \sin 30°)\,(l/2)$

$$\tau = \frac{ml^2}{12}\alpha \quad \text{we get} \quad \alpha = \frac{3T}{ml}$$

X and *Y* components of center of mass's are

$$a_{\text{com}} = \frac{T\cos 30°}{m} \qquad a_{\text{com}} = \frac{mg - T\sin 30°}{m}$$

Immediately after cutting the speed of point *P* is zero, hence its centripetal acceleration, that is, acceleration toward *P* must be zero. Thus, acceleration of *P* immediately after cutting must be perpendicular to *AP*. Thus, writting net acceleration of *P* perpendicular to *AP* using $\vec{a}_P = \vec{a}_{P/C} + \vec{a}_C = 0$

$$a_{P/C} = \alpha\left(\frac{1}{2}\right)\cos 60°$$

$$\text{thus} \quad a_{\text{center of mass}}\cos 30° - a_{\text{center of mass}}\cos 60° + \alpha\left(\frac{1}{2}\right)\cos 60° = 0$$

$$\frac{3T}{4m} - \left(\frac{g}{2} = \frac{T}{4m}\right) + \frac{3T}{ml} \times \frac{l}{2} \times \frac{1}{2} = 0$$

Solving we get $T = \dfrac{2mg}{7}$ (Answer)

Conclude: The tension is less than *mg* as the center of mass will be accelerating down.

Sample Problem 11-8

A 1 kg particle traveling at 3.0 m/s strikes a 2 kg uniform rod of length 4 m that is lying on a smooth surface as shown in Fig. 11-17. Assume the collision is elastic and the particle and rod are smooth. Find the speed of the particle, the speed of the rod, and the angular speed of the rod just after the collision.

Conceptualize: The two figures show the situation just befor hitting and just after collision. The rod will undergo combined translational and rotational motion. The only force exerted by the rod on the particle is the normal contact force, which is parallel to the original path of the particle. Thus the particle will continue on original line of motion. Also the speed of particle must be smaller as some of its kinetic energy will be transferred to the rod.

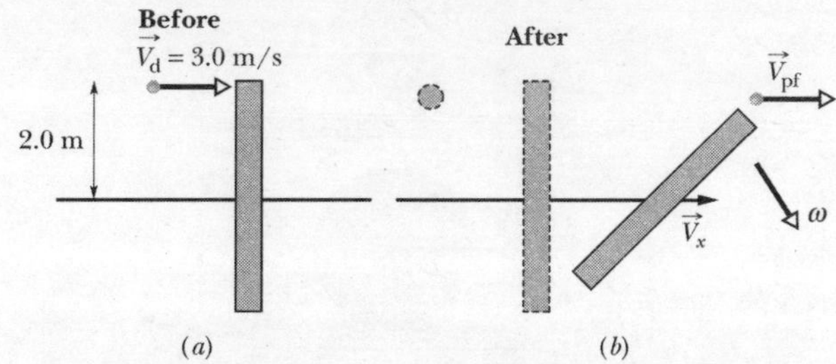

FIG. 11-17 Particle collides with a rod kept on a horizontal plane.

Classify: Because the surface is frictionless, the particle and rod will not experience any external horizontal force.

Compute: We have three unknowns, namely v_{pf}, v_r, and v_{pi} so we need three equations to solve. Applying the law of the conservation of linear momentum to the system:

$$m_p\, v_{pi} = m_p\, v_{pf} + m_r\, v_r \quad \text{(i)}$$

Substituting the values and solving, we get

$$3 \text{ kg . m/s} - (1 \text{ kg})\, v_{pf} = (2 \text{ kg})\, v_r$$

Since no external force is present there is no external torque acting about any point, we can apply the law of conservation of angular momentum on the system of rod and particle, about any point lying on ground. We take point O lying on ground on the line of motion of the particle as our reference point for writing angular momentum. Assuming clockwise sense as positive, apply conservation of angular momentum to the system:

$$m_p\, v_{pi}\,(0) = m_p\, v_{pf}\,(0) + m_r\, v_r\, l + I\omega \quad \text{(ii)}$$

Substituting the known values

$$0 = 0 - (2v_r\,.\,2m) + (32/3 \text{ kg}\,.\,m^2)\omega$$

Applying Newton's law of collision and remembering that velocities written are those of the colliding point not of the center of mass. So we have to write the velocity of the end point of the rod which is

$$wl + V_{\text{com}}$$

We can also say that kinetic energy of the system is conserved; in this case, the kinetic energy consists of translational and rotational forms.

Solving Eqs. simultaneously, we find that $v_d = 2.3$ m/s, $v_s = 1.3$ m/s, and $\omega = -2.0$ rad/s.

Conclude: These values seem reasonable. The particle is moving more slowly after the collision than that was before the collision.

In Case Of: What if we would have solved the problem by conserving angular momentum about some other point like P which is lying directly behind the center of mass of the rod.

Solution: Only Eq. (2) will alter. As the rod's center of mass is moving on the line passing through point P the angular momentum of center of mass of the rod will be zero with respect to point P.

$$m_p v_{pi}(2) = m_p v_{pf}(2) - m_r v_r(0) + I\omega$$

Solving Eqs. will give the same answer. Infact you can try solving the problem by taking any number of points lying on ground as all of them are inertial reference points.

In Case Of: What if the collision between the particle and the stick is perfectly inelastic? How will that change the analysis ?

Solution: In this case, the particle adheres to the end of the stick upon collision. The conservation of linear momentum will change as

$$m_d v_{di} = (m_d + m_s)v_{\text{com}}$$

When you solve this you will find that energy of the system has decreased.

Sample Problem 11-9

We take a uniform cylinder, rotating with angular velocity ω and keep it carefully on a rough thin plank. The plank is kept at rest on a smooth horizontal surface. Find final velocity of the plank. Both bodies have same mass.

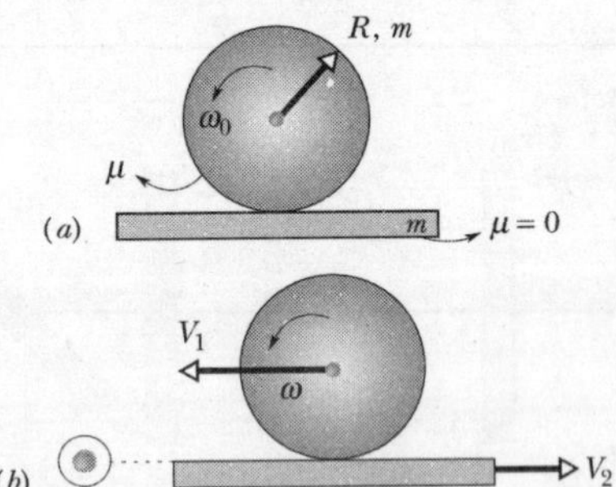

FIG. 11-18 (*a*) A rotating uniform cylinder kept on a plank. (*b*) Conserving angular momentum about point O.

Conceptualize: We can imagine that friction on the cylinder will act toward left reducing its angular velocity and moving it toward left. The reaction of the above-mentioned friction will be acting on the plank toward right. Final velocity of the contact point of cylinder and plank will be same, as pure rolling will start between cylinder and plank due to friction between them.

Classify: Considering the cylinder and the plank as our system we can see that no external horizontal force is acting on the system so the momentum of the system can be conserved. Angular momentum of the cylinder can also be conserveđ by about a point O as net external torque due to friction will be zero.

Compute:

Conserving momentum $\quad 0 + 0 = -mv_1 + mv_2$

For pure rolling the velocity of contact point of cylinder is $-v_1 + \omega R$ and that of plank is v_2, will be same $-v_1 + \omega R = v_2$.

Conserving angular momentum of cylinder about point O,

$$mR^2\omega_o/2 = mR^2\omega/2 + mv_1 R$$

angular momentum of plank will be zero as it is thin.

Solving we get, $v_1 = \frac{R\omega_0}{4}$; $v_2 = \frac{R\omega_0}{4}$

Conclude: The mechanical energy of the system must have reduced as the friction force acting is kinetic in nature. Verify this by writing final kinetic energy.

11-9 | Rigid Body in Equilibrium

Equilibrium

A balancing rock. Although its perch seems precarious, the rock is in static equilibrium. *(Symon Lobsang/Photis/Jupiter Images Corp.)*

Consider these objects: (1) a book resting on a table, (2) a hockey puck sliding with constant velocity across a frictionless surface, (3) the rotating blades of a ceiling fan, and (4) the wheel of a bicycle that is traveling along a straight path at constant speed. For each of these four objects,

1. The linear momentum $\vec{P}$ of its center of mass is constant.
2. Its angular momentum $\vec{L}$ about its center of mass, or about any other point, is also constant.

We say that such objects are in **equilibrium.** The two requirements for equilibrium are then

$$\vec{P} = \text{a constant} \quad \text{and} \quad \vec{L} = \text{a constant} \tag{11-18}$$

Our concern in this chapter is with situations in which the constants in Eq. 11-1 are zero; that is, we are concerned largely with objects that are not moving in any way—either in translation or in rotation—in the reference frame from which we observe them. Such objects are in **static equilibrium.** Of the four objects mentioned at the beginning of this section, only one—the book resting on the table—is in static equilibrium.

The balancing rock is another example of an object that, for the present at least, is in static equilibrium. It shares this property with countless other structures, such as cathedrals, houses, filing cabinets, and taco stands, that remain stationary over time.

If a body returns to a state of static equilibrium after having been displaced from that state by a force, the body is said to be in *stable* static equilibrium. A marble placed at the bottom of a hemispherical bowl is an example. However, if a small force can displace the body and end the equilibrium, the body is in *unstable* static equilibrium.

For example, suppose we balance a domino with the domino's center of mass vertically above the supporting edge, as in Fig. 11-19*a*. The torque about the supporting edge due to the gravitational force $\vec{F}_g$ on the domino is zero because the line of action of $\vec{F}_g$ is through that edge. Thus, the domino is in equilibrium. Of course, even a slight force on it due to some chance disturbance ends the equilibrium. As the line of action of $\vec{F}_g$ moves to one side of the supporting edge (as in Fig. 11-19*b*), the torque due to $\vec{F}_g$ increases the rotation of the domino. Therefore, the domino in Fig. 11-19*a* is in unstable static equilibrium.

The domino in Fig. 11-19*c* is not quite as unstable. To topple this domino, a force would have to rotate it through and then beyond the balance position of Fig. 11-19*a*, in which the center of mass is above a supporting edge. A slight force will not topple this domino, but a vigorous flick of the finger against the domino certainly will. (If we arrange a chain of such upright dominos, a finger flick against the first can cause the whole chain to fall.)

The child's square block in Fig. 11-19*d* is even more stable because its center of mass would have to be moved even farther to get it to pass above a supporting edge. A flick of the finger may not topple the block. (This is why you never see a chain of toppling square blocks.) The worker in Fig. 11-20 is like both the

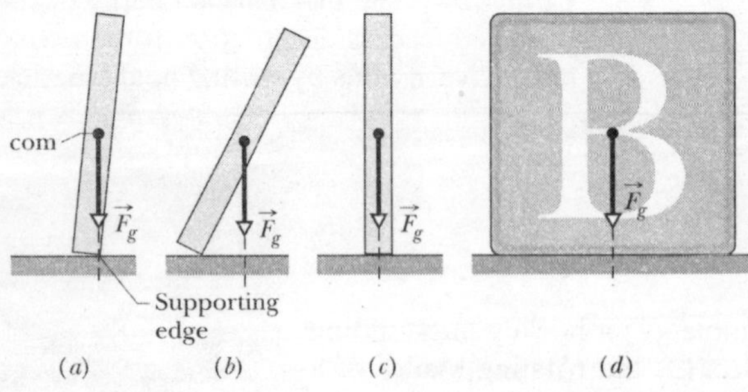

FIG. 11-19 (*a*) A domino balanced on one edge, with its center of mass vertically above that edge. The gravitational force $\vec{F}_g$ on the domino is directed through the supporting edge. (*b*) If the domino is rotated even slightly from the balanced orientation, then $\vec{F}_g$ causes a torque that increases the rotation. (*c*) A domino upright on a narrow side is somewhat more stable than the domino in (*a*). (*d*) A square block is even more stable.

FIG. 11-20 A construction worker balanced on a steel beam is in static equilibrium but is more stable parallel to the beam than perpendicular to it. *(Robert Brenner/PhotoEdit)*

domino and the square block: Parallel to the beam, his stance is wide and he is stable; perpendicular to the beam, his stance is narrow and he is unstable (and at the mercy of a chance gust of wind).

The analysis of static equilibrium is very important in engineering practice. The design engineer must isolate and identify all the external forces and torques that may act on a structure and, by good design and wise choice of materials, ensure that the structure will remain stable under these loads. Such analysis is necessary to ensure, for example, that bridges do not collapse under their traffic and wind loads and that the landing gear of aircraft will function after the shock of rough landings.

11-10 | The Requirements of Equilibrium

The translational motion of a body is governed by Newton's second law in its linear momentum form, given by Eq. 9-27 as

$$\vec{F}_{\text{net}} = \frac{d\vec{P}}{dt} \tag{11-19}$$

If the body is in translational equilibrium—that is, if $\vec{P}$ is a constant—then $d\vec{P}/dt = 0$ and we must have

$$\vec{F}_{\text{net}} = 0 \quad \text{(balance of forces)} \tag{11-20}$$

The rotational motion of a body is governed by Newton's second law in its angular momentum form, given by Eq. 11-29 as

$$\vec{\tau}_{\text{net}} = \frac{d\vec{L}}{dt} \tag{11-21}$$

If the body is in rotational equilibrium—that is, if $\vec{L}$ is a constant—then $d\vec{L}/dt = 0$ and we must have

$$\vec{\tau}_{\text{net}} = 0 \quad \text{(balance of torques)} \tag{11-22}$$

Thus, the two requirements for a body to be in equilibrium are as follows:

1. The vector sum of all the external forces that act on the body must be zero.
2. The vector sum of all external torques that act on the body, measured about *any* possible point, must also be zero.

These requirements obviously hold for *static* equilibrium. They also hold for the more general equilibrium in which $\vec{P}$ and $\vec{L}$ are constant but not zero.

Equations 11-3 and 11-5, as vector equations, are each equivalent to three independent component equations, one for each direction of the coordinate axes:

Balance of forces	Balance of torques
$F_{\text{net},x} = 0$	$\tau_{\text{net},x} = 0$
$F_{\text{net},y} = 0$	$\tau_{\text{net},y} = 0$
$F_{\text{net},z} = 0$	$\tau_{\text{net},z} = 0$

(11-23)

We shall simplify matters by considering only situations in which the forces that act on the body lie in the *xy* plane. This means that the only torques that can act on the body must tend to cause rotation around an axis parallel to the *z* axis. With this assumption, we eliminate one force equation and two torque equations from Eq. 11-6, leaving

$$F_{\text{net},x} = 0 \quad \text{(balance of forces)} \tag{11-24}$$

$$F_{\text{net},y} = 0 \quad \text{(balance of forces)} \tag{11-25}$$

$$\tau_{\text{net},z} = 0 \quad \text{(balance of torques)} \tag{11-26}$$

Here, $\tau_{\text{net},z}$ is the net torque that the external forces produce either about the *z* axis or about *any* axis parallel to it.

A hockey puck sliding at constant velocity over ice satisfies Eqs. 11-24, 111-25, and 11-9 and is thus in equilibrium *but not in static equilibrium.* For static equilibrium, the linear momentum $\vec{P}$ of the puck must be not only constant but also zero; the puck must be at rest on the ice. Thus, there is another requirement for static equilibrium:

3. The linear momentum $\vec{P}$ of the body must be zero.

CHECKPOINT 3 The figure gives six overhead views of a uniform rod on which two or more forces act perpendicularly to the rod. If the magnitudes of the forces are adjusted properly (but kept nonzero), in which situations can the rod be in static equilibrium?

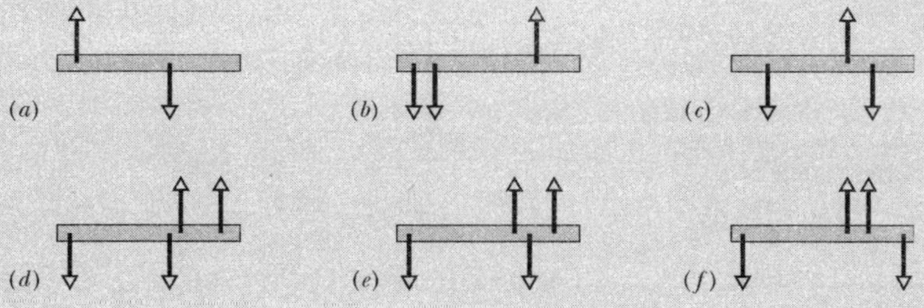

Some Examples of Static Equilibrium

In this section we examine four sample problems involving static equilibrium. In each, we select a system of one or more objects to which we apply the equations of equilibrium (Eqs. 11-7, 11-8, and 11-9). The forces involved in the equilibrium are all in the xy plane, which means that the torques involved are parallel to the z axis. Thus, in applying Eq. 11-9, the balance of torques, we select an axis parallel to the z axis about which to calculate the torques. Although Eq. 11-9 is satisfied for *any* such choice of axis, you will see that certain choices simplify the application of Eq. 11-9 by eliminating one or more unknown force terms.

CHECKPOINT 4 The figure gives an overhead view of a uniform rod in static equilibrium. (a) Can you find the magnitudes of unknown forces $\vec{F}_1$ and $\vec{F}_2$ by balancing the forces? (b) If you wish to find the magnitude of force $\vec{F}_2$ by using a balance of torques equation, where should you place a rotational axis to eliminate $\vec{F}_1$ from the equation? (c) The magnitude of $\vec{F}_2$ turns out to be 65 N. What then is the magnitude of $\vec{F}_1$?

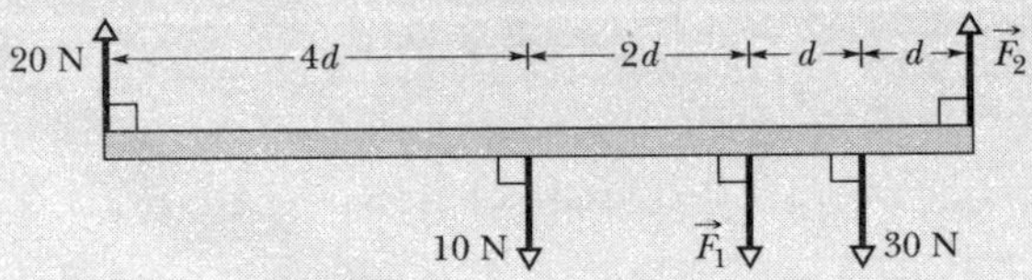

Sample Problem 11-10 Build your skill

In Fig. 11-21a, a uniform beam, of length L and mass $m = 1.8$ kg, is at rest on two scales. A uniform block, with mass $M = 2.7$ kg, is at rest on the beam, with its center a distance $L/4$ from the beam's left end. What do the scales read?

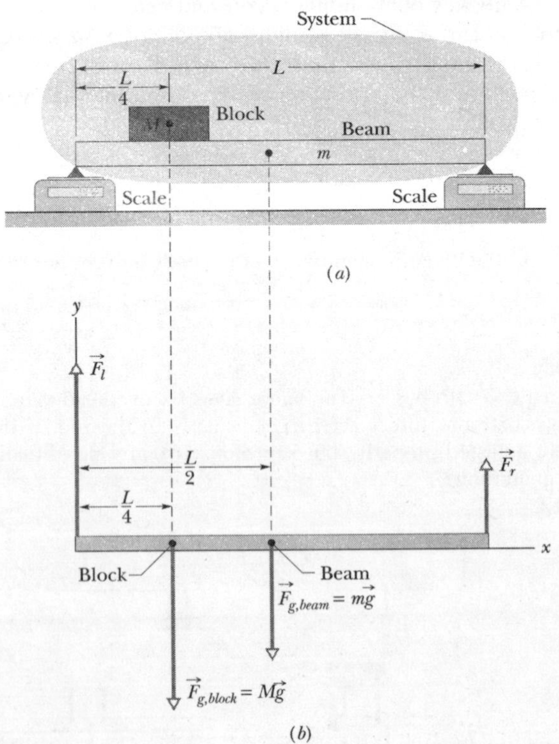

FIG. 11-21 (a) A beam of mass m supports a block of mass M. (b) A free-body diagram, showing the forces that act on the system *beam + block*.

Conceptualize: The first steps in the solution of *any* problem about static equilibrium are these: Clearly define the system to be analyzed and then draw a free-body diagram of it, indicating all the forces on the system. Here, let us choose the system as the beam and block taken together. Then the forces on the system are shown in the free-body diagram of Fig. 11-21b. (Choosing the system takes experience, and often there can be more than one good choice; see item 2 of Problem-Solving Tactic 1 below.)

Classify: Because the system is in static equilibrium, we can apply the balance of forces equations (Eqs. 11-24 and 11-25) and the balance of torques equation (Eq. 11-26) to it.

Compute: The normal forces on the beam from the scales are $\vec{F}_l$ on the left and $\vec{F}_r$ on the right. The scale readings that we want are equal to the magnitudes of those forces. The gravitational force $\vec{F}_{g,beam}$ on the beam acts at the beam's center of mass and is equal to $m\vec{g}$. Similarly, the gravitational force $\vec{F}_{g,block}$ on the block acts at the block's center of mass and is equal to $M\vec{g}$. However, to simplify Fig. 11-21b, the block is represented by a dot within the boundary of the beam and $\vec{F}_{g,block}$ is drawn with its tail on that dot. (This shift of vector $\vec{F}_{g,block}$ along its line of action does not alter the torque due to $\vec{F}_{g,block}$ about any axis perpendicular to the figure.)

The forces have no x components, so Eq. 11-24 ($F_{net,x} = 0$) provides no information. For the y components, Eq. 11-25 ($F_{net,y} = 0$) gives us

$$F_l + F_r - Mg - mg = 0 \qquad (11\text{-}27)$$

This equation contains two unknowns, the forces F_l and F_r, so we also need to use Eq. 11-6, the balance of torques equation. We can apply it to *any* rotation axis perpendicular to the plane of Fig. 11-21. Let us choose a rotation axis through the left end of the beam. We shall also use our general rule for assigning signs to torques: If a torque would cause an initially stationary body to rotate clockwise about the rotation axis, the torque is negative. If the rotation would be counterclockwise, the torque is positive. Finally, we shall write the torques in the form $r_\perp F$, where the moment arm $r_\perp$ is 0 for $\vec{F}_l$, $L/4$ for $M\vec{g}$, $L/2$ for $m\vec{g}$, and L for $\vec{F}_r$.

We now can write the balancing equation ($\tau_{net,z} = 0$) as

$$(0)(F_l) - (L/4)(Mg) - (L/2)(mg) + (L)(F_r) = 0$$

which gives us

$$\begin{aligned} F_r &= \tfrac{1}{4}Mg + \tfrac{1}{2}mg \\ &= \tfrac{1}{4}(2.7\ \text{kg})(9.8\ \text{m/s}^2) + \tfrac{1}{2}(1.8\ \text{kg})(9.8\ \text{m/s}^2) \\ &= 15.44\ \text{N} \approx 15\ \text{N} \qquad \text{(Answer)} \end{aligned}$$

Now, solving for F_l and substituting this result, we find

$$\begin{aligned} F_l &= (M + m)g - F_r \\ &= (2.7\ \text{kg} + 1.8\ \text{kg})(9.8\ \text{m/s}^2) - 15.44\ \text{N} \\ &= 28.66\ \text{N} \approx 29\ \text{N} \qquad \text{(Answer)} \end{aligned}$$

Conclude: *Note the strategy in the solution:* When we wrote an equation for the balance of force components, we got stuck with two unknowns. If we had written an equation for the balance of torques around some *arbitrary* axis, we would have again gotten stuck with those two unknowns. However, because we chose the axis to pass through the point of application of one of the unknown forces, here $\vec{F}_l$, we did not get stuck. Our choice neatly eliminated that force from the torque equation, allowing us to solve for the other unknown force magnitude F_r. Then we returned to the equation for the balance of force components to find the remaining unknown force magnitude.

Sample Problem 11-11

In Fig. 11-22*a*, a ladder of length $L = 12$ m and mass $m = 45$ kg leans against a slick (frictionless) wall. The ladder's upper end is at height $h = 9.3$ m above the pavement on which the lower end rests (the pavement is not frictionless). The ladder's center of mass is $L/3$ from the lower end. A firefighter of mass $M = 72$ kg climbs the ladder until her center of mass is $L/2$ from the lower end. What then are the magnitudes of the forces on the ladder from the wall and the pavement?

Conceptualize/Classify: First, we choose our system as being the firefighter and ladder, together, and then we draw the free-body diagram of Fig. 11-22*b*. Because the system is in static equilibrium, the balancing equations (Eqs. 11-24 through 11-26) apply to it.

Compute: In Fig. 11-22*b*, the firefighter is represented with a dot within the boundary of the ladder. The gravitational force on her is represented with its equivalent $M\vec{g}$, and that vector has been shifted along its line of action, so that its tail is on the dot. (The shift does not alter a torque due to $M\vec{g}$ about any axis perpendicular to the figure.)

The only force on the ladder from the wall is the horizontal force $\vec{F}_w$ (there cannot be a frictional force along a frictionless wall). The force $\vec{F}_p$ on the ladder from the pavement has a horizontal component $\vec{F}_{px}$ that is a static frictional force and a vertical component $\vec{F}_{py}$ that is a normal force.

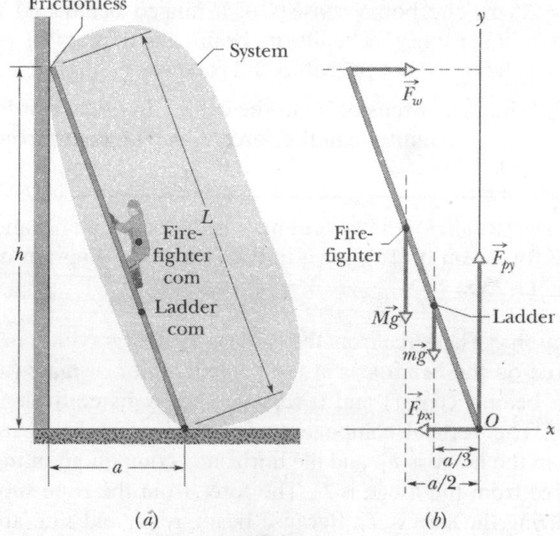

FIG. 11-22 (*a*) A firefighter climbs halfway up a ladder that is leaning against a frictionless wall. The pavement beneath the ladder is not frictionless. (*b*) A free-body diagram, showing the forces that act on the *firefighter* + *ladder* system. The origin O of a coordinate system is placed at the point of application of the unknown force $\vec{F}_p$ (whose vector components $\vec{F}_{px}$ and $\vec{F}_{py}$ are shown).

To apply the balancing equations, let's start with Eq. 11-26 ($\tau_{net,z} = 0$). To choose an axis about which to calculate the torques, note that we have unknown forces ($\vec{F}_w$ and $\vec{F}_p$) at the two ends of the ladder. To eliminate, say, $\vec{F}_p$ from the calculation, we place the axis at point O, perpendicular to the figure. We also place the origin of an xy coordinate system at O. We can find torques about O with any of Eqs. 10-39 through 10-41, but Eq. 10-41 ($\tau = r_\perp F$) is easiest to use here.

To find the moment arm $r_\perp$ of $\vec{F}_w$, we draw a line of action through that vector (horizontal dashed line in Fig. 11-22*b*). Then $r_\perp$ is the perpendicular distance between O and the line of action. In Fig. 11-22*b*, $r_\perp$ extends along the y axis and is equal to the height h. We similarly draw lines of action for $M\vec{g}$ and $m\vec{g}$ and see that their moment arms extend along the x axis. For the distance a shown in Fig. 11-22*a*, the moment arms are $a/2$ (the firefighter is halfway up the ladder) and $a/3$ (the ladder's center of mass is one-third of the way up the ladder), respectively. The moment arms for $\vec{F}_{px}$ and $\vec{F}_{py}$ are zero.

Now, with torques written in the form $r_\perp F$, the balancing equation $\tau_{\text{net},z} = 0$ becomes

$$-(h)(F_w) + (a/2)(Mg) + (a/3)(mg) + (0)(F_{px}) + (0)(F_{py}) = 0 \qquad (11\text{-}27)$$

(Recall our rule: A positive torque corresponds to counterclockwise rotation and a negative torque corresponds to clockwise rotation.)

Using the Pythagorean theorem, we find that

$$a = \sqrt{L^2 - h^2} = 7.58 \text{ m}$$

Then Eq. 11-27 gives us

$$F_w = \frac{ga(M/2 + m/3)}{h} = \frac{(9.8 \text{ m/s}^2)(7.58 \text{ m})(72/2 \text{ kg} + 45/3 \text{ kg})}{9.3 \text{ m}} = 407 \text{ N} \approx 410 \text{ N} \qquad \text{(Answer)}$$

Now we need to use the force balancing equations. The equation $F_{\text{net},x} = 0$ gives us

$$F_w - F_{px} = 0$$

so

$$F_{px} = F_w = 410 \text{ N} \qquad \text{(Answer)}$$

The equation $F_{\text{net},y} = 0$ gives us

$$F_{py} - Mg - mg = 0$$

so

$$F_{py} = (M + m)g = (72 \text{ kg} + 45 \text{ kg})(9.8 \text{ m/s}^2) = 1146.6 \text{ N} \approx 1100 \text{ N} \qquad \text{(Answer)}$$

Sample Problem 11-12

Figure 11-23*a* shows a safe, of mass $M = 430$ kg, hanging by a rope from a boom with dimensions $a = 1.9$ m and $b = 2.5$ m. The boom consists of a hinged beam and a horizontal cable. The uniform beam has a mass m of 85 kg; the masses of the cable and rope are negligible.

(a) What is the tension T_c in the cable? In other words, what is the magnitude of the force $\vec{T}_c$ on the beam from the cable?

Conceptualize: The system here is the beam alone, and the forces on it are shown in the free-body diagram of Fig. 11-23*b*.

Classify: The force from the cable is $\vec{T}_c$. The gravitational force on the beam acts at the beam's center of mass (at the beam's center) and is represented by its equivalent $m\vec{g}$. The vertical component of the force on the beam from the hinge is $\vec{F}_v$, and the horizontal component of the force from the hinge is $\vec{F}_h$. The force from the rope supporting the safe is $\vec{T}_r$. Because beam, rope, and safe are stationary, the magnitude of $\vec{T}_r$ is equal to the weight of the safe: $T_r = Mg$. We place the origin O of an xy coordinate system at the hinge. Because the system is in static equilibrium, the balancing equations apply to it.

Compute: Let us start with Eq. 11-27 ($\tau_{\text{net},z} = 0$). Note that we are asked for the magnitude of force $\vec{T}_c$ and not of forces $\vec{F}_h$ and $\vec{F}_v$ acting at the hinge, at point O. To eliminate $\vec{F}_h$ and $\vec{F}_v$ from the torque calculation,

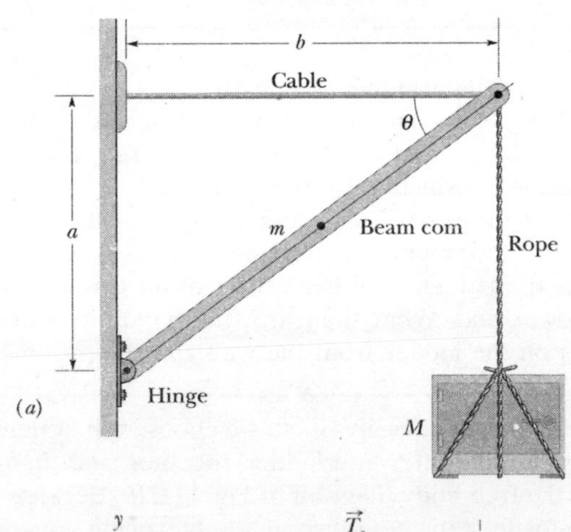

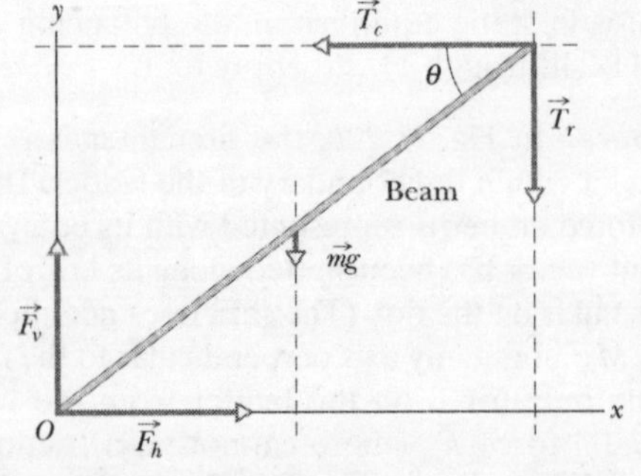

FIG. 11-23 (*a*) A heavy safe is hung from a boom consisting of a horizontal steel cable and a uniform beam. (*b*) A free-body diagram for the beam.

we should calculate torques about an axis that is perpendicular to the figure at point O. Then $\vec{F}_h$ and $\vec{F}_v$ will have moment arms of zero. The lines of action for $\vec{T}_c$, $\vec{T}_r$, and $m\vec{g}$ are dashed in Fig. 11-23*b*. The corresponding moment arms are a, b, and $b/2$.

Writing torques in the form of $r_\perp F$ and using our rule about signs for torques, the balancing equation $\tau_{\text{net},z} = 0$ becomes

$$(a)(T_c) - (b)(T_r) - (\tfrac{1}{2}b)(mg) = 0$$

Substituting Mg for T_r and solving for T_c, we find that

$$T_c = \frac{gb(M + \frac{1}{2}m)}{a}$$

$$= \frac{(9.8\text{ m/s}^2)(2.5\text{ m})(430\text{ kg} + 85/2\text{ kg})}{1.9\text{ m}}$$

$$= 6093\text{ N} \approx 6100\text{ N} \qquad \text{(Answer)}$$

(b) Find the magnitude F of the net force on the beam from the hinge.

Conceptualize/Classify: Now we want F_h and F_v so we can combine them to get F. Because we know T_c, we apply the force balancing equations to the beam.

Compute: For the horizontal balance, we write $F_{\text{net},x} = 0$ as

$$F_h - T_c = 0$$

and so

$$F_h = T_c = 6093\text{ N}$$

For the vertical balance, we write $F_{\text{net},y} = 0$ as

$$F_v - mg - T_r = 0$$

Substituting Mg for T_r and solving for F_v, we find that

$$F_v = (m + M)g = (85\text{ kg} + 430\text{ kg})(9.8\text{ m/s}^2)$$
$$= 5047\text{ N}$$

From the Pythagorean theorem, we now have

$$F = \sqrt{F_h^2 + F_v^2}$$
$$= \sqrt{(6093\text{ N})^2 + (5047\text{ N})^2} \approx 7900\text{ N} \qquad \text{(Answer)}$$

Conclude: Note that F is substantially greater than either the combined weights of the safe and the beam, 5000 N, or the tension in the horizontal wire, 6100 N.

Sample Problem 11-13

Let's assume that the Tower of Pisa is a uniform hollow cylinder of radius $R = 9.8$ m and height $h = 60$ m. The center of mass is located at height $h/2$, along the cylinder's central axis. In Fig. 11-24*a*, the cylinder is upright. In Fig. 11-24*b*, it leans rightward (toward the tower's southern wall) by $\theta = 5.5°$, which shifts the com by a distance d. Let's assume that the ground exerts only two forces on the tower. A normal force $\vec{F}_{NL}$ acts on the left (northern) wall, and a normal force $\vec{F}_{NR}$ acts on the right (southern) wall. By what percent does the magnitude F_{NR} increase because of the leaning?

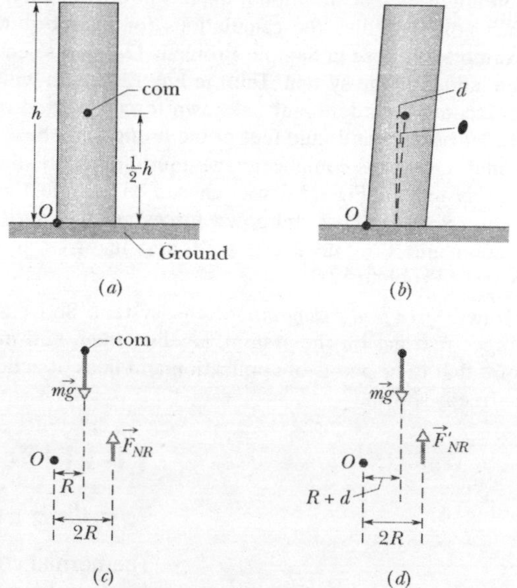

FIG. 11-24 A cylinder modeling the Tower of Pisa: (*a*) upright and (*b*) leaning, with the center of mass shifted rightward. The forces and moment arms to find torques about a pivot at point O for the cylinder (*c*) upright and (*d*) leaning.

Conceptualize: Because the tower is still standing, it is in equilibrium and thus the sum of torques calculated around any point must be zero.

Calssify: Because we want to calculate F_{NR} on the right side and do not know or want F_{NL} on the left side, we use a pivot point on the left side to calculate torques. The forces on the upright tower are represented in Fig. 11-24*c*. The gravitational force $m\vec{g}$, taken to act at the com, has a vertical line of action and a moment arm of R (the perpendicular distance from the pivot to the line of action).

Compute: About the pivot, the torque associated with this force would tend to create clockwise rotation and thus is negative. The normal force $\vec{F}_{NR}$ on the southern wall also has a vertical line of action, and its moment arm is $2R$. About the pivot, the torque associated with this force would tend to create counterclockwise rotation and thus is positive. We now can write the torque-balancing equation ($\tau_{\text{net},z} = 0$) as

$$-(R)(mg) + (2R)(F_{NR}) = 0$$

which yields

$$F_{NR} = \tfrac{1}{2}mg \qquad (11\text{-}28)$$

We should have been able to guess this result: With the center of mass located on the central axis (the cylinder's line of symmetry), the right side supports half the cylinder's weight.

In Fig. 11-24*b*, the com is shifted rightward by distance

$$d = \tfrac{1}{2}h \tan\theta$$

The only change in the balance of torques equation is that the moment arm for the gravitational force is now $R + d$ and the normal force at the right has a new magnitude F'_{NR} (Fig. 11-24*d*). Thus, we write

$$-(R + d)(mg) + (2R)(F'_{NR}) = 0$$

which gives us

$$F'_{NR} = \frac{(R + d)}{2R}mg \qquad (11\text{-}29)$$

Dividing Eq. 11-21 by Eq. 11-20 and then substituting for d, we obtain

$$\frac{F'_{NR}}{F_{NR}} = \frac{R + d}{R} = 1 + \frac{d}{R} = 1 + \frac{0.5h\tan\theta}{R}$$

Substituting the values of $h = 60$ m, $R = 9.8$ m, and $\theta = 5.5°$ leads to

$$\frac{F'_{NR}}{F_{NR}} = 1.29$$

Conclude: Thus, our simple model predicts that, although the tilt is modest, the normal force on the tower's southern wall has increased by about 30%. One danger to the tower is that the force may cause the southern wall to buckle and explode outward.

PROBLEM-SOLVING TACTICS

Tactic 1: Static Equilibrium Problems Here is a list of steps for solving static equilibrium problems:

1. Draw a *sketch* of the problem.
2. Select the *system* to which you will apply the laws of equilibrium, drawing a closed curve around the system on your sketch to fix it clearly in your mind. In some situations you can select a single object as the system; it is the object you wish to be in equilibrium. In other situations, you might include additional objects in the system *if* their inclusion simplifies the calculations for equilibrium. For example, suppose in Sample Problem 12-2 you select only the ladder as the system. Then in Fig. 12-6*b* you will have to account for additional unknown forces exerted on the ladder by the hands and feet of the firefighter. These additional unknowns complicate the equilibrium calculations. The system of Fig. 12-6 was chosen to include the firefighter so that those unknown forces are *internal* to the system and thus need not be found in order to solve Sample Problem 12-2.
3. Draw a *free-body diagram* of the system. Show all the forces that act on the system, labeling them and making sure that their points of application and lines of action are correctly shown.
4. Draw in the *x and y axes* of a coordinate system with at least one axis parallel to one or more unknown force. Resolve into components the forces that do not lie along one of the axes. In all our sample problems it made sense to choose the *x* axis horizontal and the *y* axis vertical.
5. Write the two *balance of forces equations,* using symbols throughout.
6. Choose one or more rotation axes perpendicular to the plane of the figure and write the *balance of torques equation* for each axis. If you choose an axis that passes through the line of action of an unknown force, the equation will be simplified because that force will not appear in it.
7. *Solve* your equations *algebraically* for the unknowns. Some students feel more confident in substituting numbers with units in the independent equations at this stage, especially if the algebra is particularly involved. However, experienced problem solvers prefer the algebra, which reveals the dependence of solutions on the various variables.
8. Finally, *substitute numbers* with units in your algebraic solutions, obtaining numerical values for the unknowns.
9. Look at your answer—does it make sense? Is it obviously too large or too small? Is the sign correct? Are the units appropriate?

11-11 | Toppling

Toppling of a Box on an Inclined Plane

The normal contact force's line of action is not always predictable. For example, the forces acting on the box in Fig. 11-25 are its weight $\vec{W}$, friction $\vec{f}$, and the normal force

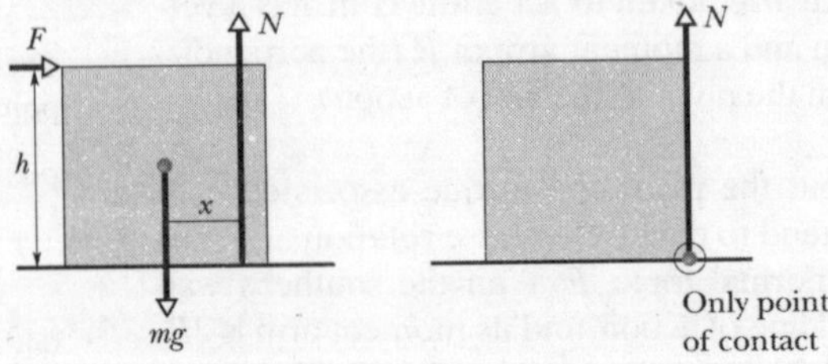

FIG. 11-25 A box being pushed by horizontal force and shifting of normal.

exerted by the ground, $\vec{N}$. Weight acts at the body's center of mass. Friction acts along the surface where the crate and the plane are in contact. Normal reaction is a contact force. It does not act at a single point, but it is distributed on the surface. Actually, it is the resultant of a large number of small normal forces acting all over the base of the crate. The normal forces are not uniformly distributed across the base, but we can find an effective point of application by taking $\vec{\tau}_{net} = 0$, if the body is not toppling.

Sample Problem 11-14

The crate in Fig 11-26. has dimensions l by h and the ramp is inclined at θ to the horizontal. Find the maximum θ for which it does not topple. Coefficient of friction between ramp and crate is μ.

Conceptualize: When we keep a box on a very steep incline the box topples downward. We can also conclude that the leftmost part of the box lifts before it topples. This means that normal contact force must have shifted toward right.

Classify: The crate is in equilibrium. By applying force and torque balance, we may find where the normal force acts.

Compute: We choose the x axis to be along the slope and the y axis to be perpendicular to it. The sum of force components in each direction must be zero.

$$0 = \sum F_x = f - W \sin\theta$$

and

$$0 = \sum F_y = n - W \cos\theta$$

We consider the net torque about the center of mass of the crate. Three forces exert torque :

1. The weight acts at the center of mass and so exerts no torque about it.
2. The friction force acts along the surface between crate and ramp and exerts a torque $fh/2$, out of the paper (Fig. 11-26).
3. The normal force acts at an unknown distance x from the downhill edge of the crate and exerts a torque $n[(l/2) - x]$ into the page.

These torques sum to zero.

$$0 = \sum \tau = \left[f(h/2) - n\{(l/2) - x\} \right]$$

From force balance, we have $f = W \sin\theta$ and $N = W \cos\theta$:

so $$W \sin\theta (h/2) = W \cos\theta \left[(l/2) - x \right]$$

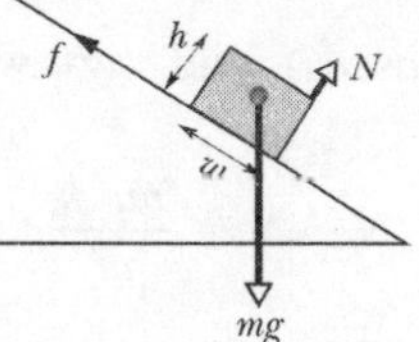

FIG. 11-26 A crate resting on an incline.

When the crate is about to topple the x will become zero, as the effective point of application of the normal will be the right edge.

$$\theta = \tan^{-1}\left(\frac{1}{h}\right)$$

Conclude: We can see that a taller box will overturn more easily than a shorter box.

In Case Of: Given $\tan\phi = \mu$, if $\phi > \theta$; first slip $\theta > \phi$; first topple.

Sample Problem 11-15

A car of mass m traveling at speed v moves on a horizontal track. The center of mass of the car describes a circle of radius r. If $2a$ is the separation of the inner and outer wheels and h is the height of the center of mass above the ground, show that the limiting speed beyond which the car will overturn is given by

$$v^2 = \frac{gra}{h}$$

FIG. 11-27 Car turning at a crossing.

Conceptualize: Fig. 11.27 shows the rear view of the car that is turning toward left. If you have watched any action movie where cars overturns you may know that it will overturn outward of the curve when traveling at a high speed.

Classify: Frictional force on the tyres provides a centripetal force while turning. When car is going at a high speed the inner tyres will loose contact with the ground. We can consider car in equilibrium in its own frame.

Compute: As it will be a noninertial reference frame, we have to apply pseudo centrifugal force

$$\sum F_x = f_1 + f_2 - \frac{mv^2}{r} = 0 \qquad \text{(i)}$$

$$\sum F_y = N_1 + N_2 - mg = 0 \qquad \text{(ii)}$$

From condition of rotational equilibrium, sum of moments about center of mass G must be zero.

$$\sum \tau = (f_1 + f_2)h + \frac{N_1\omega}{2} - \frac{N_2\omega}{2} = 0 \qquad \text{(iii)}$$

$$f_1 + f_2 = (N_1 - N_2)\frac{a}{h} \qquad \text{(iv)}$$

On combining Eqs. (i) and (iv) we can eliminate $(f_1 + f_2)$, to obtain

$$N_2 - N_1 = \frac{mv^2h}{ar} \qquad \text{(v)}$$

Now we can solve Eqs. (ii) and (v) simultaneously to obtain

$$2N_1 = mg - \frac{mv^2h}{r} \quad \text{and} \quad 2N_2 = mg + \frac{mv^2h}{r}$$

The inner wheels will leave the ground when N_1 becomes zero, that is,

$$mg = \frac{mv^2h}{ar}$$

$$\text{or} \quad v^2 = \frac{gra}{h}$$

Conclude: As expected in Eq. (v) we can see that as v increases the N_1 will decrease and car will overturn outwardly.

In Case Of: If frictional force is not sufficient to provide centripetal acceleration, sideways skidding will occur instead of overturning.

$$f_1 + f_2 \le \mu(N_1 + N_2)$$

Equality sign holds when skidding starts.

$$N_1 + N_2 = mg$$

$$\text{and} \quad f_1 + f_2 = \frac{mv^2}{r}$$

Therefore, the limiting speed at which skidding occurs is given by $v^2 + \mu gr$. If the car is to skid rather than overturn,

$$\mu gr < \frac{gra}{h} \quad \text{or} \quad \mu < \frac{a}{h}$$

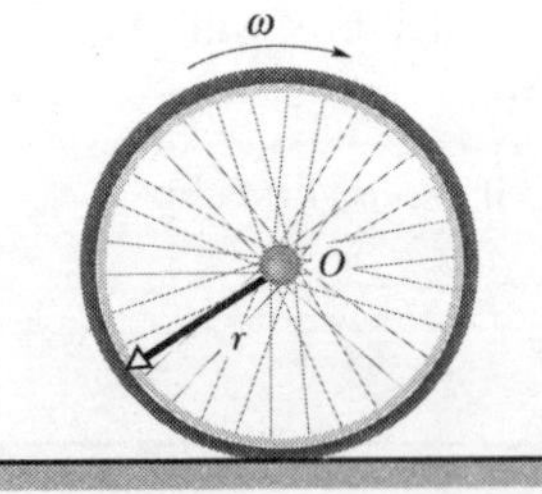

(a)

(b)

FIG. 11-28 A wheel undergoing rolling.

11-12 | Instantaneous Center of Zero Velocity

Instantaneous Center of Zero Velocity

The velocity of an arbitrary point, B on a rigid body, at a given instant can be obtained easily if we can find the reference point, A that has zero velocity at that instant In this case, $\mathbf{v}_A = \mathbf{0}$, and using the net motion equation, $\mathbf{v}_B = \mathbf{v}_A + \mathbf{v}_{B/A}$, and $\mathbf{v}_{B/A}, = \omega \times \mathbf{r}_{BA}$. Point A is called the instantaneous center of zero velocity (IC) and it lies on the instantaneous axis of zero velocity. This axis is perpendicular to the plane of the motion. The body appears to rotate about this axis instantaneously. Position vector of point B with respect to the IC is $\mathbf{r}_{BC}$. Then the magnitude of $\mathbf{v}_B$ is simply $v_B = \omega \mathbf{r}_{B/IC}$, where ω is the angular velocity of the body. Since all the particles are undergoing circular motion, the direction of $\mathbf{v}_B$ is always perpendicular to $\mathbf{r}_{B/IC}$.

For example, consider a wheel which rolls without slipping, Fig. 11-28*a*. In this case, the point of contact with the ground has zero velocity. Hence, this point represents the IC for the wheel, Fig. 11-28*b*. If it is imagined that the wheel is momentarily pinned at this point, the velocities of points A, B, O, and so on, can be found using $= \omega r$. Here the radial distances $\mathbf{r}_{A/IC}$, $\mathbf{r}_{O/IC}$ and $\mathbf{r}_{B/IC}$, as shown in Fig. 11-28*b*, must be determined from the geometry of the wheel.

The instantaneous center of zero veocity for the body can only be used for an instant of time. Since the body changes its position from one instant to another, then for each position of the body a unique instantaneous center must be determined.

Although the *IC* may be conveniently used to determine the velocity of any point in a body, it generally does not have zero acceleration and therefore it should not be used for finding the accelerations of points in a body.

Location of the IC

If the location of the *IC* is unknown, it may be determined by using the fact that the relative position vector extending from the *IC* to a point is always perpendicular to the velocity of the point. Several possibilities exist.

CHECKPOINT 5 Suggest a method to locate *IC* for the following situations.

1. Given the velocity of a point on the body and the angular velocity of the body
2. Given the lines of action of two nonparallel velocities.
3. Given the magnitude and direction of two parallel velocities.

Solution: **1.** In this case, if $\mathbf{v}_B$ and ω are known, the *IC* is located along the line drawn perpendicular to at $\mathbf{v}_B$ at B, such that the distance from B to the *IC* is $r_{B/C} = v_B/\omega$, fig. (a). Note that the *IC* lies on that side of B which causes rotation about the *IC*, which is consistent with the direction of motion caused by ω and $\mathbf{v}_B$.

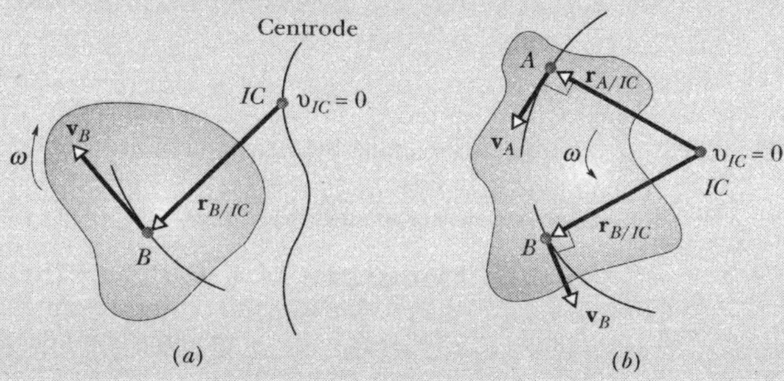

2. Given the lines of action of two nonparallel velocities. Consider the body in Fig. (b), where the lines of action of the velocities $\mathbf{v}_A$ and $\mathbf{v}_B$ are known. Draw two lines from points A and B that are perpendicular to v_A and v_B. Extending these perpendiculars to their point of intersection as shown locates the *IC* at the instant considered. The magnitudes $\mathbf{r}_{A/IC}$ and $\mathbf{r}_{B/IC}$ are generally determined from the geometry of the body and trigonometry. Furthermore, if the magnitude and sense of $\mathbf{v}_A$ are known, then the angular velocity of the body is determined from $v_A = \omega r_{A/IC}$. Once computed, ω can then be used to determine $v_B = \omega r_{B/IC}$.
3. When the velocities of points A and B are parallel and have known magnitudes v_A and v_B, then the location of the *IC* is determined by proportional triangles. Examples are shown in Fig. (c) and (d). In both cases $r_{A/IC} = v_A/\omega$ and $r_{B/IC} = v_B/\omega$. If d is a known distance between points A and B, then in Fig. (c), $r_{A/IC} + r_{B/IC} = d$ and in Fig. (d), $r_{B/IC} - r_{A/IC} = d$. As a special case, note that if the body is translating, $\mathbf{v}_A = \mathbf{v}_B$ and the *IC* would be located at infinity, in which case $r_{A/IC} = r_{B/IC} \to \infty$ This being the case, $\omega = v_A/\infty = v_B/\infty = 0$ as expected.

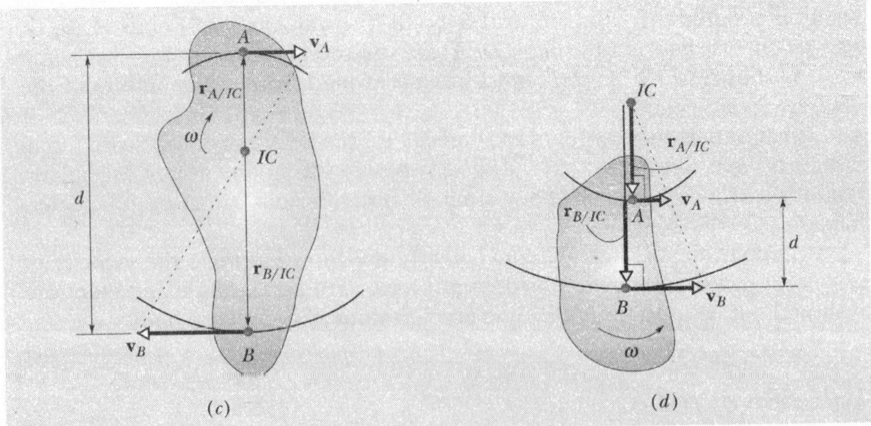

Sample Problem 11-16 Build your skill

A cylinder of radius r is rolling purely on ground, find whether particles having velocity greater than v_c are more than particles having velocity less than v_c.

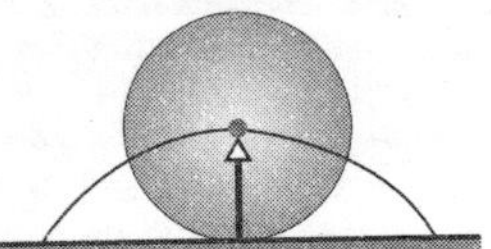

FIG. 11-29 A cylinder rolling without sliding on ground.

Solution: The points lying below this arc are the ones having velocity less than v_c as their distance from the *IC* which is in contact with the ground is less than r. Thus, it is clear that these points are less in number than those having distance larger than r and thus having velocity greater than v_c.

REVIEW & SUMMARY

Rolling Bodies For a wheel of radius R rolling smoothly,

$$v_{\text{com}} = \omega R$$

where v_{com} is the linear speed of the wheel's center of mass and ω is the angular speed of the wheel about its center. The wheel may also be viewed as rotating instantaneously about the point P of the "road" that is in contact with the wheel. The angular speed of the wheel about this point is the same as the angular speed of the wheel about its center. The rolling wheel has kinetic energy

$$K = \tfrac{1}{2}I_{\text{com}}\omega^2 + \tfrac{1}{2}Mv_{\text{com}}^2$$

where I_{com} is the rotational moment of the wheel about its center of mass and M is the mass of the wheel. If the wheel is being accelerated but is still rolling smoothly, the acceleration of the center of mass $\vec{a}_{\text{com}}$ is related to the angular acceleration α about the center with

$$a_{\text{com}} = \alpha R$$

If the wheel rolls smoothly down a ramp of angle θ, its acceleration along an x axis extending up the ramp is

$$a_{\text{com},x} = -\frac{g \sin \theta}{1 + I_{\text{com}}/MR^2}$$

Torque as a Vector In three dimensions, *torque* $\vec{\tau}$ is a vector quantity defined relative to a fixed point (usually an origin); it is

$$\vec{\tau} = \vec{r} \times \vec{F}$$

where $\vec{F}$ is a force applied to a particle and $\vec{r}$ is a position vector locating the particle relative to the fixed point. The magnitude of $\vec{\tau}$ is given by

$$\tau = rF \sin \phi = rF_\perp = r_\perp F$$

where ϕ is the angle between $\vec{F}$ and $\vec{r}$, $F_\perp$ is the component of $\vec{F}$ perpendicular to $\vec{r}$, and $r_\perp$ is the moment arm of $\vec{F}$. The direction of $\vec{\tau}$ is given by the right-hand rule.

Angular Momentum of a Particle The *angular momentum* $\vec{\ell}$ of a particle with linear momentum p, mass m, and linear velocity $\vec{v}$ is a vector quantity defined relative to a fixed point (usually an origin) as

$$\vec{\ell} = \vec{r} \times \vec{p} = m(\vec{r} \times \vec{v})$$

The magnitude of $\vec{\ell}$ is given by

$$\begin{aligned}\ell &= rmv \sin \phi \\ &= rp_\perp = rmv_\perp \\ &= r_\perp p = r_\perp mv\end{aligned}$$

where ϕ is the angle between $\vec{r}$ and $\vec{p}$, $p_\perp$ and $v_\perp$ are the components of $\vec{p}$ and $\vec{v}$ perpendicular to $\vec{r}$, and $r_\perp$ is the perpendicular distance between the fixed point and the extension of $\vec{p}$. The direction of $\vec{\ell}$ is given by the right-hand rule for cross products.

Newton's Second Law in Angular Form Newton's second law for a particle can be written in angular form as

$$\vec{\tau}_{net} = \frac{d\vec{\ell}}{dt}$$

where $\vec{\tau}_{net}$ is the net torque acting on the particle and $\vec{\ell}$ is the angular momentum of the particle.

Angular Momentum of a System of Particles The angular momentum $\vec{L}$ of a system of particles is the vector sum of the angular momenta of the individual particles:

$$\vec{L} = \vec{\ell}_1 + \vec{\ell}_2 + \cdots + \vec{\ell}_n = \sum_{i=1}^{n} \vec{\ell}_i$$

The time rate of change of this angular momentum is equal to the net external torque on the system (the vector sum of the torques due to interactions of the particles of the system with particles external to the system):

$$\vec{\tau}_{net} = \frac{d\vec{L}}{dt} \qquad \text{(system of particles)}$$

Angular Momentum of a Rigid Body For a rigid body rotating about a fixed axis, the component of its angular momentum parallel to the rotation axis is

$$L = I\omega \qquad \text{(rigid body, fixed axis)}$$

Conservation of Angular Momentum The angular momentum $\vec{L}$ of a system remains constant if the net external torque acting on the system is zero:

$$\vec{L} = \text{a constant} \qquad \text{(isolated system)}$$

or

$$\vec{L}_i = \vec{L}_f \qquad \text{(isolated system)}$$

This is the **law of conservation of angular momentum.**

Precession of a Gyroscope A spinning gyroscope can precess about a vertical axis through its support at the rate

$$\Omega = \frac{Mgr}{I\omega}$$

where M is the gyroscope's mass, r is the moment arm, I is the rotational inertia, and ω is the spin rate.

QUESTIONS

1 In Fig. 11-30, three forces of the same magnitude are applied to a particle at the origin ($\vec{F}_1$ acts directly into the plane of the figure). Rank the forces according to the magnitudes of the torques they create about (a) point P_1, (b) point P_2, and (c) point P_3, greatest first.

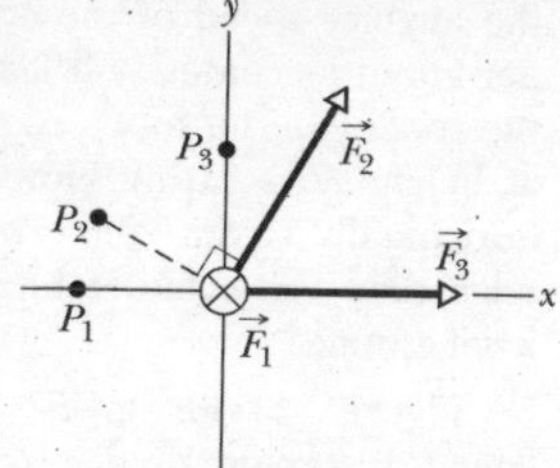

FIG. 11-30 Question 1.

2 The position vector $\vec{r}$ of a particle relative to a certain point has a magnitude of 3 m, and the force $\vec{F}$ on the particle has a magnitude of 4 N. What is the angle between the directions of $\vec{r}$ and $\vec{F}$ if the magnitude of the associated torque equals (a) zero and (b) 12 N·m?

3 What happens to the initially stationary yo-yo in Fig. 11-31 if you pull it via its string with (a) force $\vec{F}_2$ (the line of action passes through the point of contact on the table, as indicated), (b) force $\vec{F}_1$ (the line of action passes above the point of contact), and (c) force $\vec{F}_3$ (the line of action passes to the right of the point of contact)?

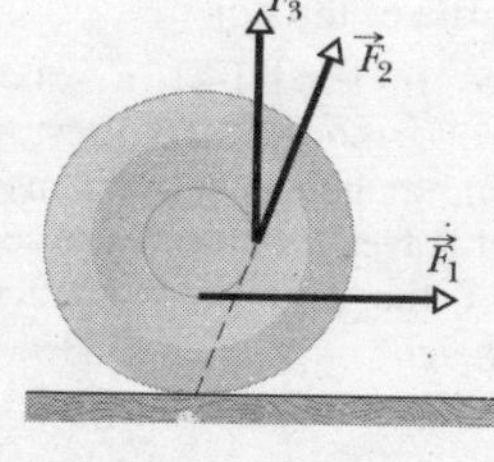

FIG. 11-31 Question 3.

4 Figure 11-32 shows two particles A and B at xyz coordinates (1 m, 1 m, 0) and (1 m, 0, 1 m). Acting on each particle are three numbered forces, all of the same magnitude and each directed parallel to an axis. (a) Which of the forces produce a torque about the origin that is directed parallel to y? (b) Rank the forces according to the magnitudes of the torques they produce on the particles about the origin, greatest first.

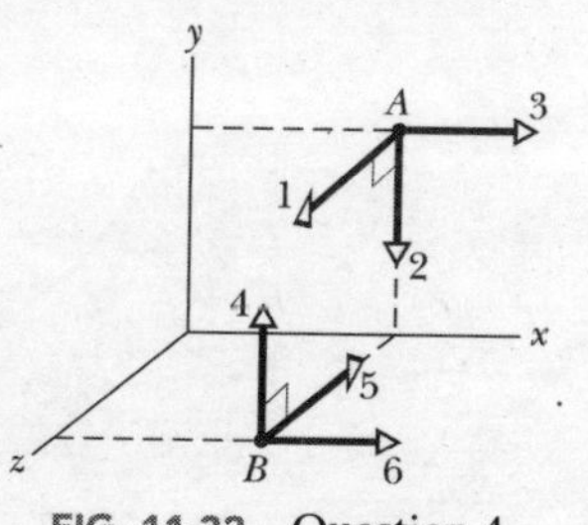

FIG. 11-32 Question 4.

5 Figure 11-33 shows three particles of the same mass and the same constant speed moving as indicated by the velocity vectors. Points a, b, c, and d form a square, with point e at the center. Rank the points according to the magnitude of the net angular momentum of the three-particle system when measured about the points, greatest first.

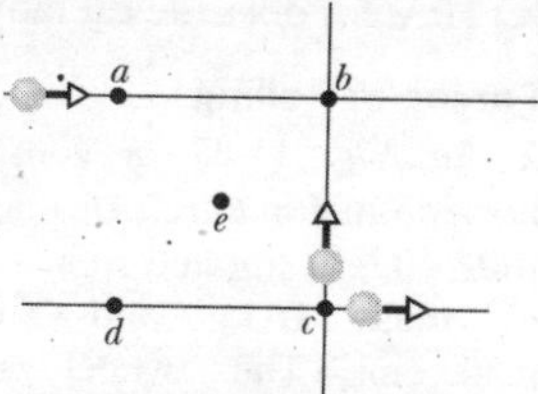

FIG. 11-33 Question 5.

6 Figure 11-34 shows a particle moving at constant velocity $\vec{v}$ and five points with their xy coordinates. Rank the points according to the magnitude of the angular momentum of the particle measured about them, greatest first.

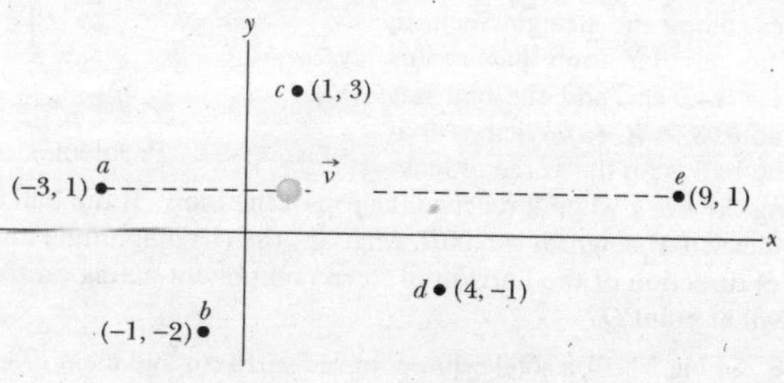

FIG. 11-34 Question 6.

7 Figure 11-35 gives the angular momentum magnitude L of a wheel versus time t. Rank the four lettered time intervals according to the magnitude of the torque acting on the wheel, greatest first.

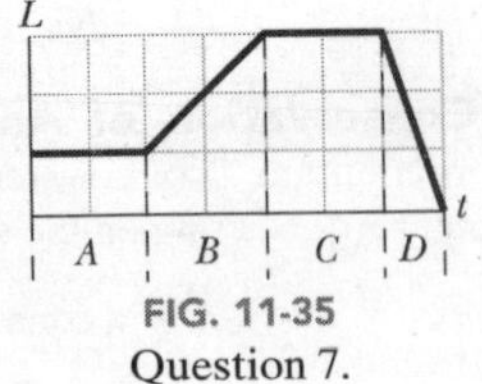

FIG. 11-35 Question 7.

8 The angular momenta $\ell(t)$ of a particle in four situations are (1) $\ell = 3t + 4$; (2) $\ell = -6t^2$; (3) $\ell = 2$; (4) $\ell = 4/t$. In which situation is the net torque on the particle (a) zero, (b) positive and constant, (c) negative and increasing in magnitude ($t > 0$), and (d) negative and decreasing in magnitude ($t > 0$)?

9 A rhinoceros beetle rides the rim of a horizontal disk rotating counterclockwise like a merry-go-round. If the beetle then walks along the rim in the direction of the rotation, will the magnitudes of the following quantities (each measured about the rotation axis) increase, decrease, or remain the same (the disk is still rotating in the counterclockwise direction): (a) the angular momentum of the beetle–disk system, (b) the angular momentum and angular velocity of the beetle, and (c) the angular momentum and angular velocity of the disk? (d) What are your answers if the beetle walks in the direction opposite the rotation?

10 Figure 11-36 shows an overhead view of a rectangular slab that can spin like a merry-go-round about its center at O. Also shown are seven paths along which wads of bubble gum can be thrown (all with the same speed and mass) to stick onto the stationary slab. (a) Rank the paths according to the angular speed that the slab (and gum) will have after the gum sticks, greatest first. (b) For which paths will the angular momentum of the slab (and gum) about O be negative from the view of Fig. 11-35?

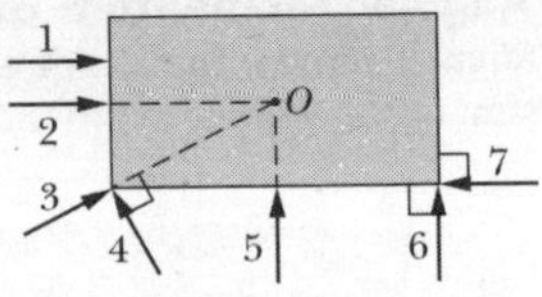

FIG. 11-36 Question 10.

PROBLEMS

Rolling as Translation and Rotation Combined

1 An automobile traveling at 80.0 km/h has tires of 75.0 cm diameter. (a) What is the angular speed of the tires about their axles? (b) If the car is brought to a stop uniformly in 30.0 complete turns of the tires (without skidding), what is the magnitude of the angular acceleration of the wheels? (c) How far does the car move during the braking?

Forces of Rolling

2 In Fig. 11-37, a constant horizontal force $\vec{F}_{app}$ of magnitude 10 N is applied to a wheel of mass 10 kg and radius 0.30 m. The wheel rolls smoothly on the horizontal surface, and the acceleration of its center of mass has magnitude 0.60 m/s^2. (a) In unit-vector notation, what is the frictional force on the wheel? (b) What is the rotational inertia of the wheel about the rotation axis through its center of mass?

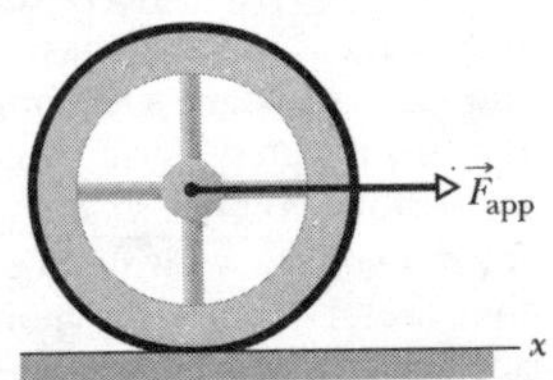

FIG. 11-37 Problem 2.

3 In Fig. 11-38, a solid brass ball of mass 0.280 g will roll smoothly along a loop-the-loop track when released from rest along the straight section. The circular loop has radius $R = 14.0$ cm, and the ball has radius $r \ll R$. (a) What is h if the ball is on the verge of leaving the track when it reaches the top of the loop? If the ball is released at height $h = 6.00R$, what are the (b) magnitude and (c) direction of the horizontal force component acting on the ball at point Q?

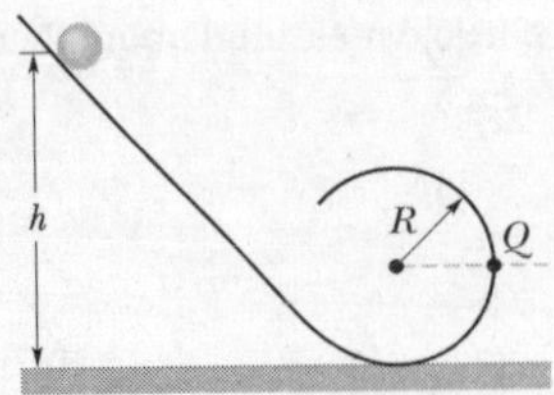

FIG. 11-38 Problem 3.

4 In Fig. 11-39, a solid cylinder of radius 10 cm and mass 12 kg starts from rest and rolls without slipping a distance $L = 6.0$ m down a roof that is inclined at the angle $\theta = 30°$. (a) What is the angular speed of the cylinder about its center as it leaves the roof? (b) The roof's edge is at height $H = 5.0$ m. How far horizontally from the roof's edge does the cylinder hit the level ground?

FIG. 11-39 Problem 4.

5 Figure 11-40 gives the speed v versus time t for a 0.500 kg object of radius 6.00 cm that rolls smoothly down a 30° ramp. The scale on the velocity axis is set by $v_s = 4.0$ m/s. What is the rotational inertia of the object?

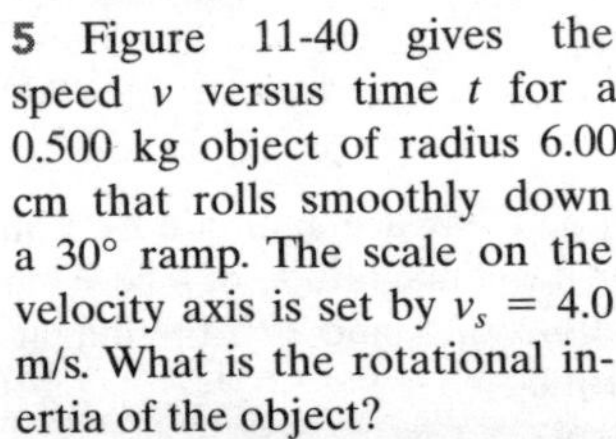

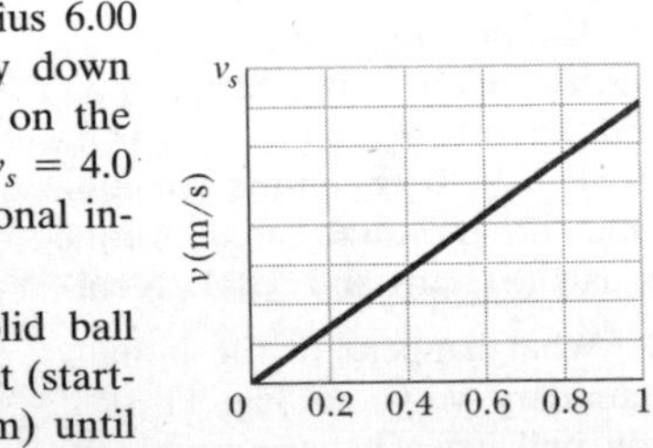

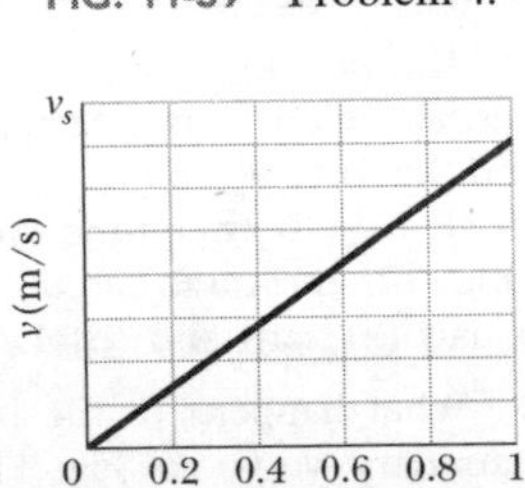

FIG. 11-40 Problem 5.

6 In Fig. 11-41, a solid ball rolls smoothly from rest (starting at height $H = 6.0$ m) until it leaves the horizontal section at the end of the track, at height $h = 2.0$ m. How far horizontally from point A does the ball hit the floor?

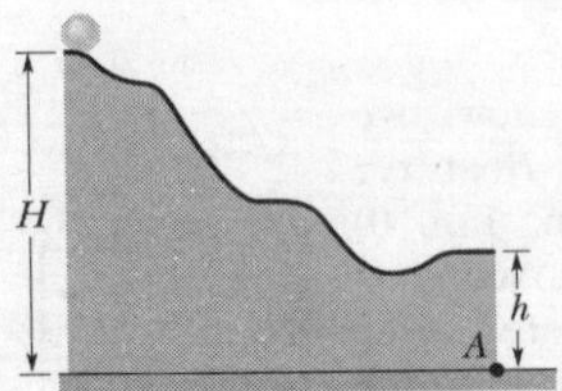

FIG. 11-41 Problem 6.

7 Figure 11-42 shows the potential energy $U(x)$ of a solid ball that can roll along an x axis. The scale on the U axis is set by $U_s = 100$ J. The ball is uniform, rolls smoothly, and has a mass of 0.400 kg. It is released at $x = 7.0$ m headed in the negative direction of the x axis with a mechanical energy of 75 J. (a) If the ball can reach $x = 0$ m, what is its speed there, and if it cannot, what is its turning point? Suppose, instead, it is headed in the positive direction of the x axis when it is released at $x = 7.0$ m with 75 J. (b) If the ball can reach $x = 13$ m, what is its speed there, and if it cannot, what is its turning point?

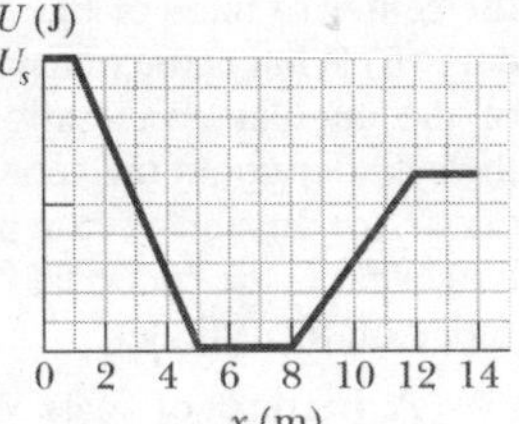

FIG. 11-42 Problem 7.

8 A bowler throws a bowling ball of radius $R = 11$ cm along a lane. The ball (Fig. 11-43) slides on the lane with initial speed $v_{com,0} = 8.5$ m/s and initial angular speed $\omega_0 = 0$. The coefficient of kinetic friction between the ball and the lane is 0.21. The kinetic frictional force $\vec{f}_k$ acting on the ball causes a linear acceleration of the ball while producing a torque that causes an angular acceleration of the ball. When speed v_{com} has decreased enough and angular speed ω has increased enough, the ball stops sliding and then rolls smoothly. (a) What then is v_{com} in terms of ω? During the sliding, what are the ball's (b) linear acceleration and (c) angular acceleration? (d) How long does the ball slide? (e) How far does the ball slide? (f) What is the linear speed of the ball when smooth rolling begins?

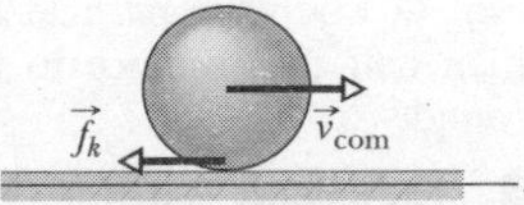

FIG. 11-43 Problem 8.

9 In Fig. 11-44, a small, solid, uniform ball is to be shot from point P so that it rolls smoothly along a horizontal path, up along a ramp, and onto a plateau. Then it leaves the plateau horizontally to land on a game board, at a horizontal distance d from the right edge of the plateau. The vertical heights are $h_1 = 5.00$ cm and $h_2 = 1.60$ cm. With what speed must the ball be shot at point P for it to land at $d = 6.00$ cm?

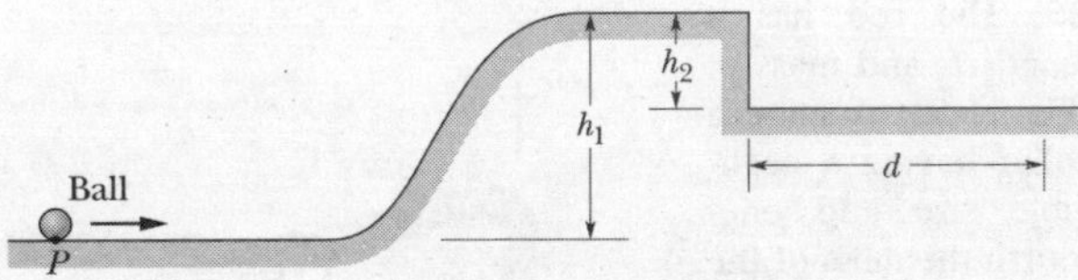

FIG. 11-44 Problem 9.

10 *Nonuniform ball.* In Fig. 11-45, a ball of mass M and radius R rolls smoothly from rest down a ramp and onto a circular loop of radius 0.48 m. The initial height of the ball is $h = 0.36$ m. At the loop bottom, the magnitude of the normal force on the ball is $2.00Mg$. The ball consists of an outer spherical shell (of a certain uniform density) that is glued to a central sphere (of a different uniform density). The rotational inertia of the ball can be expressed in the general form $I = \beta MR^2$, but β is not 0.4 as it is for a ball of uniform density. Determine β.

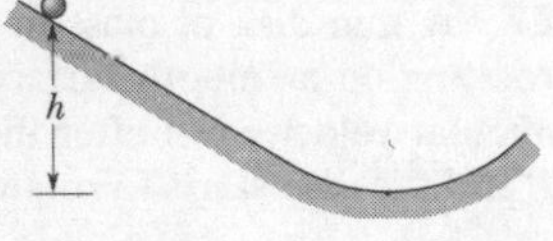

FIG. 11-45 Problem 10.

11 In 1980, over San Francisco Bay, a large yo-yo was released from a crane. The 116 kg yo-yo consisted of two uniform disks of radius 32 cm connected by an axle of radius 3.2 cm. What was the magnitude of the acceleration of the yo-yo during (a) its fall and (b) its rise? (c) What was the tension in the cord on which it rolled? (d) Was that tension near the cord's limit of 52 kN? Suppose you build a scaled-up version of the yo-yo (same shape and materials but larger). (e) Will the magnitude of your yo-yo's acceleration as it falls be greater than, less than, or the same as that of the San Francisco yo-yo? (f) How about the tension in the cord?

12 A bola consists of three massive, identical spheres connected to a common point by identical lengths of sturdy string (Fig. 11-46a). To launch this native South American weapon, you hold one of the spheres overhead and then rotate that hand about its wrist so as to rotate the other two spheres in a horizontal path about the hand. Once you manage sufficient rotation, you cast the weapon at a target. Initially the bola rotates around the previously held sphere at angular speed ω_i but then quickly changes so that the spheres rotate around the common connection point at angular speed ω_f (Fig. 11-46b). (a) What is the ratio ω_f/ω_i? (b) In the center-of-mass frame, what is the ratio K_f/K_i of the corresponding rotational kinetic energies?

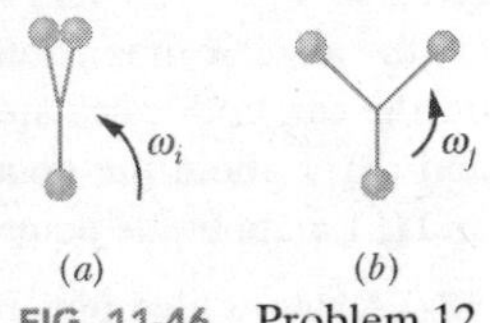

FIG. 11-46 Problem 12.

13 During a jump to his partner, an aerialist is to make a quadruple somersault lasting a time $t = 1.87$ s. For the first and last quarter-revolution, he is in the extended orientation shown in Fig. 11-47, with rotational inertia $I_1 = 19.9$ kg·m² around his center of mass (the dot). During the rest of the flight he is in a tight tuck, with rotational inertia $I_2 = 3.93$ kg·m². What must be his angular speed ω_2 around his center of mass during the tuck?

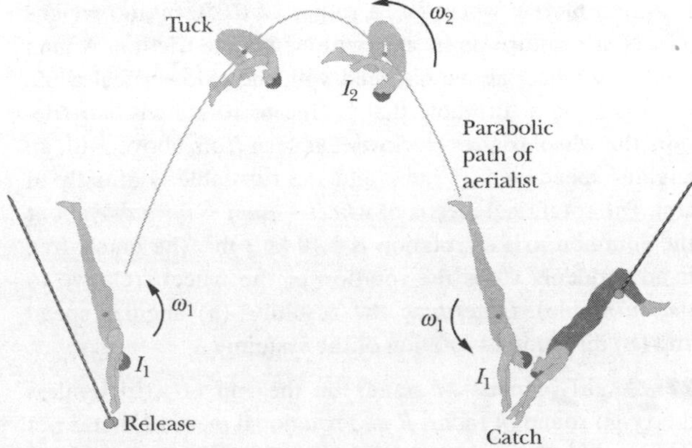

FIG. 11-47 Problem 13.

14 Wheels A and B in Fig. 11-48 are connected by a belt that does not slip. The radius of B is 3.00 times the radius of A. What would be the ratio of the rotational inertias I_A/I_B if the two wheels had (a) the same angular momentum about their central axes and (b) the same rotational kinetic energy?

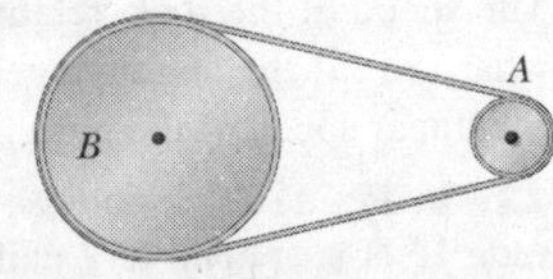

FIG. 11-48 Problem 14.

15 A body of radius R and mass m is rolling smoothly with speed v on a horizontal surface. It then rolls up a hill to a maximum height h. (a) If $hv = 3v^2/4g$, what is the body's rotational inertia about the rotational axis through its center of mass? (b) What might the body be?

16 If Earth's polar ice caps fully melted and the water returned to the oceans, the oceans would be deeper by about 30 m.What effect would this have on Earth's rotation? Make an estimate of the resulting change in the length of the day.

17 A 3.0 kg toy car moves along an x axis with a velocity given by $\vec{v} = -2.0t$ m/s, with t in seconds. For $t > 0$, what are (a) the angular momentum $\vec{L}$ of the car and (b) the torque $\vec{\tau}$ on the car, both calculated about the origin? What are (c) $\vec{L}$ and (d) $\vec{\tau}$ about the point (2.0 m, 5.0 m, 0)? What are (e) $\vec{L}$ and (f) $\vec{\tau}$ about the point (2.0 m, – 5.0 m, 0)?

18 A thin-walled pipe rolls along the floor.What is the ratio of its translational kinetic energy to its rotational kinetic energy about the central axis parallel to its length?

19 A solid sphere of weight 36.0 N rolls up an incline at an angle of 30.0°. At the bottom of the incline the center of mass of the sphere has a translational speed of 4.90 m/s. (a) What is the kinetic energy of the sphere at the bottom of the incline? (b) How far does the sphere travel up along the incline? (c) Does the answer to (b) depend on the sphere's mass?

20 An automobile has a total mass of 1700 kg. It accelerates from rest to 40 km/h in 10 s. Assume each wheel is a uniform 32 kg disk. Find, for the end of the 10 s interval, (a) the rotational kinetic energy of each wheel about its axle, (b) the total kinetic energy of each wheel, and (c) the total kinetic energy of the automobile.

21 With axle and spokes of negligible mass and a thin rim, a certain bicycle wheel has a radius of 0.350 m and weighs 37.0 N; it can turn on its axle with negligible friction. A man holds the wheel above his head with the axle vertical while he stands on a turntable that is free to rotate without friction; the wheel rotates clockwise, as seen from above, with an angular speed of 57.7 rad/s, and the turntable is initially at rest. The rotational inertia of *wheel + man + turntable* about the common axis of rotation is 2.10 kg · m^2. The man's free hand suddenly stops the rotation of the wheel (relative to the turntable). Determine the resulting (a) angular speed and (b) direction of rotation of the system.

22 A girl of mass M stands on the rim of a frictionless merry-go-round of radius R and rotational inertia I that is not moving. She throws a rock of mass m horizontally in a direction that is tangent to the outer edge of the merrygo-round. The speed of the rock, relative to the ground, is v. Afterward, what are (a) the angular speed of the merrygo-round and (b) the linear speed of the girl?

23 In Fig. 11-49, a constant horizontal force F_{app} of magnitude 12 N is applied to a uniform solid cylinder by fishing line wrapped around the cylinder. The mass of the cylinder is 10 kg, its radius is 0.10 m, and the cylinder rolls smoothly on the horizontal surface. (a) What is the magnitude of the acceleration of the center of mass of the cylinder? (b) What is the magnitude of the angular acceleration of the cylinder about the center of mass? (c) In unit-vector notation, what is the frictional force acting on the cylinder?

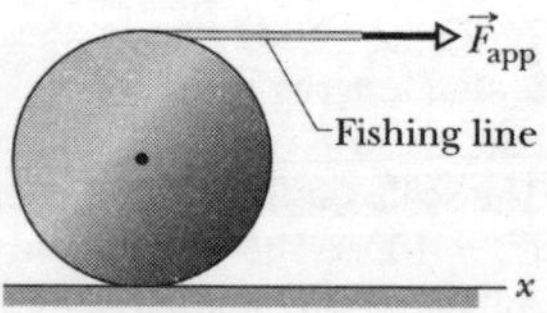

FIG. 11-49 Problem 23.

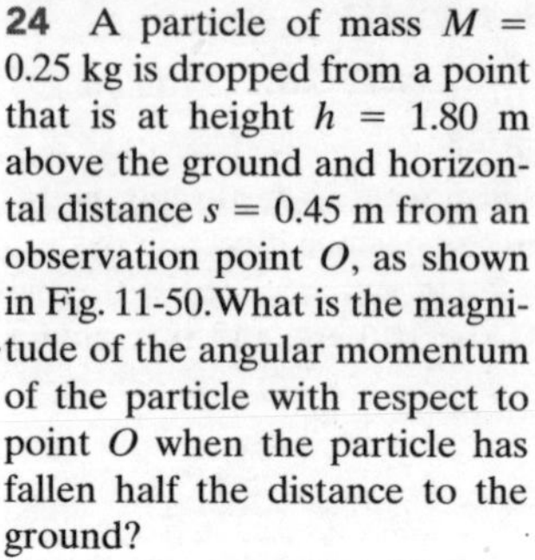

24 A particle of mass M = 0.25 kg is dropped from a point that is at height h = 1.80 m above the ground and horizontal distance s = 0.45 m from an observation point O, as shown in Fig. 11-50.What is the magnitude of the angular momentum of the particle with respect to point O when the particle has fallen half the distance to the ground?

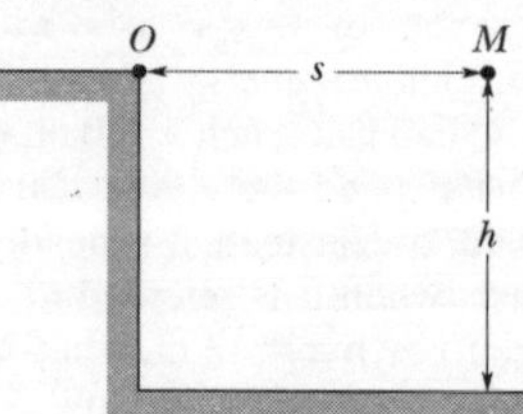

FIG. 11-50 Problem 24.

25 The slender rod of mass $M = 4$ kg rests on a smooth floor. If it is kicked so as to receive a horizontal impulse $I = 8$ Ns at point A as shown in Fig. 11-51, determine its angular velocity and the speed of its mass center.

Given:

$l_1 = 2$ m

$l_2 = 1.75$ m

$\theta = 60$ deg

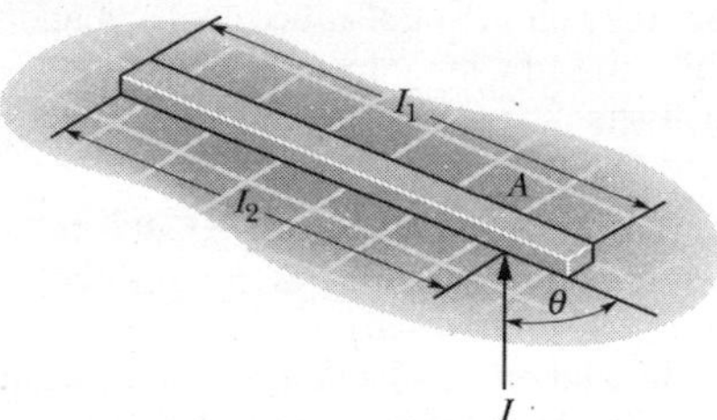

FIG. 11-51 Problem 25.

26 The rod has a length L and mass m (Fig. 11-52). A smooth collar having a negligible size and one-fourth the mass of the rod is placed on the rod at its midpoint. If the rod is freely rotating with angular velocity ω about its end and the collar is released, determine the rod's angular velocity just before the collar flies off the rod. Also, what is the speed of the collar as it leaves the rod?

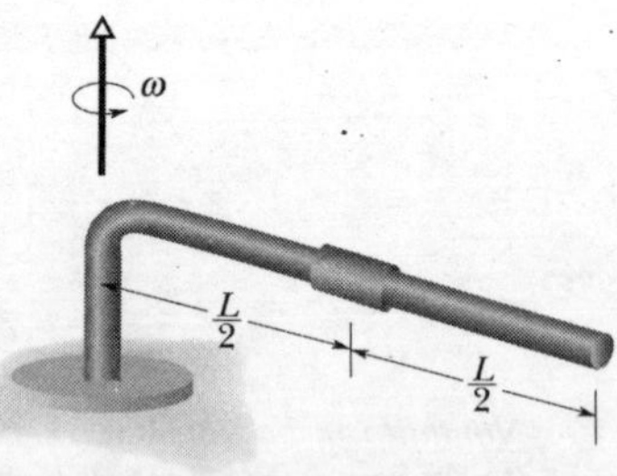

FIG. 11-52 Problem 26.

27 A thin disk of mass m has an angular velocity $\omega 1$ while rotating on a smooth surface (Fig. 11-53). Determine its new angular velocity just after the hook at its edge strikes the peg P and the disk starts to rotate about P without rebounding.

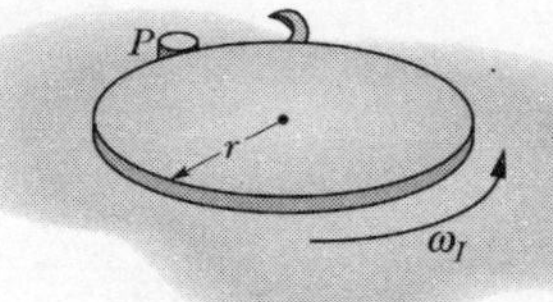

FIG. 11-53 Problem 27.

28 The truck carries the spool which has mass m and radius of gyration k_G (Fig. 11-54). Determine the angular acceleration of the spool if it is not tied down on the truck and the truck begins to accelerate at the rate a_{At}. Assume the spool does not slip on the bed of the truck.

Given:

$m = 50$ kg $\quad r = 2$ m

$k_G = 1$ m $\quad g = 10$ m/s^2

$a_{At} = 2$ m/s^2

FIG. 11-54 Problem 28.

29 The truck carries the spool which has weight W and radius of gyration k_G (Fig. 11-55). Determine the angular acceleration of the spool if it is not tied down on the truck and the truck begins to accelerate at the rate a_{At}. The coefficients of static and kinetic friction between the spool and the truck bed are μ_s and μ_k, respectively.

Given:

$W = 20$ kg $\quad g = 10$ m/s^2

$k_G = 1$ m $\quad \mu_s = 0.15$

$a_{At} = 2$ m/s^2 $\quad \mu_k = 0.1$

$r = 2$ m

Since $F = 16$ N $< F_{max} = 30$ N then our no-slip is occuring

FIG. 11-55 Problem 29.

30 The spool has mass M and radius of gyration k_G (Fig. 11-56). It rests on the inclined surface for which the coefficient of kinetic friction is μ_k. If the spool is released from rest and slips at A, determine the initial tension in the cord and the angular acceleration of the spool.

Given:

$M = 75$ kg $\quad k_G = 0.380$ m $\quad a = 0.3$ m

$\mu_k = 0.15$ $\quad \theta = 30°$ $\quad b = 0.6$ m

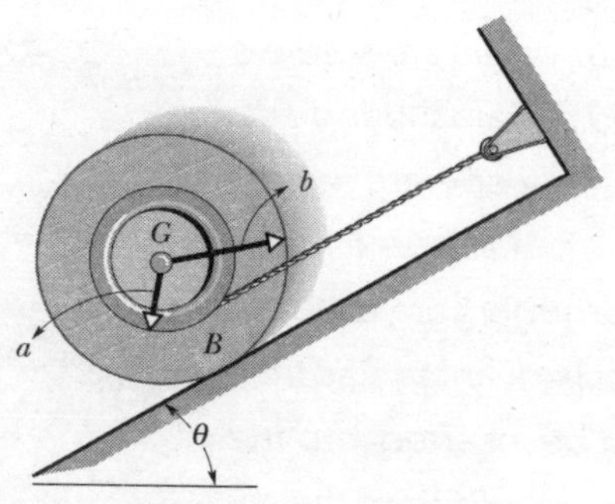

FIG. 11-56 Problem 30.

31 A uniform rod having weight W is pin-supported at A from a roller which rides on horizontal track (Fig. 11-57). If the rod is originally at rest, and horizontal force **F** is applied to the roller, determine the acceleration of the roller. Neglect the mass of the roller and its size d in the computations.

Given:

$W = 10$ lb

$F = 15$ lb

$l = 2$ ft

$g = 32.2$ ft/s^2

$a_G = 4.83$ ft/s^2 $\quad \alpha = 145$ rad/s^2 $\quad a_A = 193$ ft/s^2

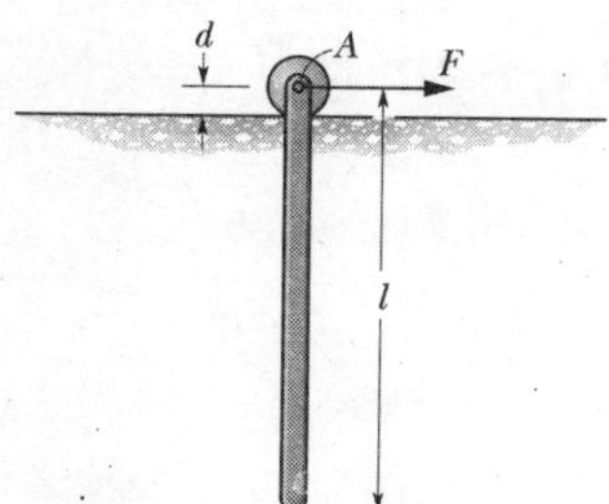

FIG. 11-57 Problem 31.

12 Elasticity

Paratroopers are soldiers trained in parachuting and generally operate as part of an airborne force. Paratroopers are used for tactical advantage as they can be inserted into the battlefield from the air, thereby allowing them to be positioned in areas not accessible by land. If the paratrooper lands at a higher speed his leg may break.

PhotoDisc, Inc/Getty Images, Inc.

How much impact can he withstand while landing?

The answer is in this chapter.

12-1 | Introduction

Indeterminate Structures

For the problems of previous chapters section, we have only three independent equations at our disposal, usually two balance of forces equations and one balance of torques equation about a given rotation axis. Thus, if a problem has more than three unknowns, we cannot solve it.

It is easy to find such problems. In Sample Problem 11-11, for example, we could have assumed that there is friction between the wall and the top of the ladder. Then there would have been a vertical frictional force acting where the ladder touches the wall, making a total of four unknown forces. With only three equations, we could not have solved this problem.

Consider also an unsymmetrically loaded car. What are the forces—all different—on the four tires? Again, we cannot find them because we have only three independent equations. Similarly, we can solve an equilibrium problem for a table with three legs but not for one with four legs. Problems like these, in which there are more unknowns than equations, are called **indeterminate.**

Yet solutions to indeterminate problems exist in the real world. If you rest the tires of the car on four platform scales, each scale will register a definite reading, the sum of the readings being the weight of the car. What is eluding us in our efforts to find the individual forces by solving equations?

The problem is that we have assumed—without making a great point of it—that the bodies to which we apply the equations of static equilibrium are perfectly rigid. By this we mean that they do not deform when forces are applied to them. Strictly, there are no such bodies. The tires of the car, for example, deform easily under load until the car settles into a position of static equilibrium.

We have all had experience with a wobbly restaurant table, which we usually level by putting folded paper under one of the legs. If a big enough elephant sat on such a table, however, you may be sure that if the table did not collapse, it would deform just like the tires of a car. Its legs would all touch the floor, the forces acting upward on the table legs would all assume definite (and different) values as in Fig. 12-1, and the table would no longer wobble. How do we find the values of those forces acting on the legs?

To solve such indeterminate equilibrium problems, we must supplement equilibrium equations with some knowledge of *elasticity,* the branch of physics and engineering that describes how real bodies deform when forces are applied to them. The next section provides an introduction to this subject.

FIG. 12-1 The table is an indeterminate structure. The four forces on the table legs differ from one another in magnitude and cannot be found from the laws of static equilibrium alone.

CHECKPOINT 1 A horizontal uniform bar of weight 10 N is to hang from a ceiling by two wires that exert upward forces $\vec{F}_1$ and $\vec{F}_2$ on the bar. The figure shows four arrangements for the wires. Which arrangements, if any, are indeterminate (so that we cannot solve for numerical values of $\vec{F}_1$ and $\vec{F}_2$)?

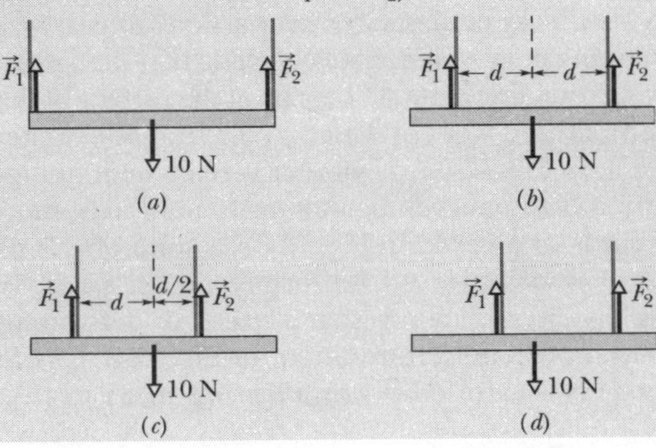

Elasticity

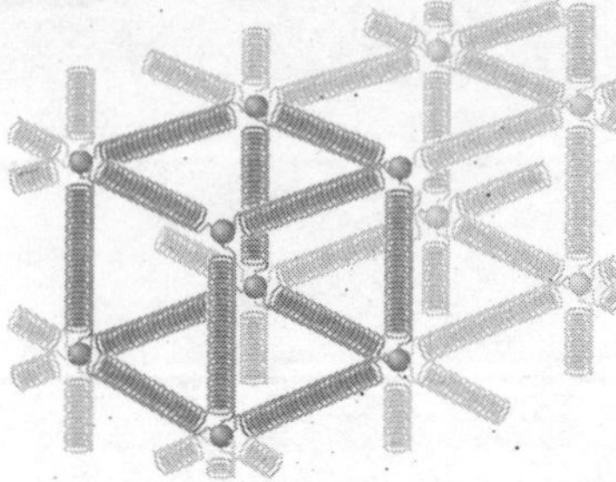

FIG. 12-2 The atoms of a metallic solid are distributed on a repetitive three-dimensional lattice. The springs represent interatomic forces.

When a large number of atoms come together to form a metallic solid, such as an iron nail, they settle into equilibrium positions in a three-dimensional *lattice,* a repetitive arrangement in which each atom is a well-defined equilibrium distance from its nearest neighbors. The atoms are held together by interatomic forces that are modeled as tiny springs in Fig. 12-2. The lattice is remarkably rigid, which is another way of saying that the "interatomic springs" are extremely stiff. It is for this reason that we perceive many ordinary objects, such as metal ladders, tables, and spoons, as perfectly rigid. Of course, some ordinary objects, such as garden hoses or rubber gloves, do not strike us as rigid at all. The atoms that make up these objects *do not* form a rigid lattice like that of Fig. 12-2 but are aligned in long, flexible molecular chains, each chain being only loosely bound to its neighbors.

All real "rigid" bodies are to some extent **elastic,** which means that we can change their dimensions slightly by pulling, pushing, twisting, or compressing them. To get a feeling for the orders of magnitude involved, consider a vertical steel rod 1 m long and 1 cm in diameter attached to a factory ceiling. If you hang a subcompact car from the free end of such a rod, the rod will stretch but only by about 0.5 mm, or 0.05%. Furthermore, the rod will return to its original length when the car is removed.

If you hang two cars from the rod, the rod will be permanently stretched and will not recover its original length when you remove the load. If you hang three cars from the rod, the rod will break. Just before rupture, the elongation of the rod will be less than 0.2%. Although deformations of this size seem small, they are important in engineering practice. (Whether a wing under load will stay on an airplane is obviously important.)

12-2 | Stress and Strain

Undeformed material, have the molecules in a state of equilibrium and all parts of the body are in mechanical equilibrium. When a deformation occurs, the arrangement of the molecules is changed, and the body ceases to be in its original state of equilibrium. Therefore those forces arise which tend to bring the body back to equilibrium. These internal forces which occur when a body is deformed are called internal stresses. If no deformation occurs, there are no internal stresses.

The internal stresses are due to molecular forces, that is, the forces of interaction between the molecules. These molecular forces have a very short range of action. Their effect extends only to the neighboring molecules, or in other words the range of these forces is same as the distance between the molecules. On the other hand the theory of elasticity is a macroscopic theory, and the only distances considered are those which are large compared with the distances between the molecules. The range of action of the molecular forces should therefore be taken as zero in the theory of elasticity. We can say that the forces that cause the internal stresses are, with regard to the theory of elasticity, "near-action" forces, which act from any point only to neighboring points. Hence, we conclude that the forces exerted on one part of the body by surrounding parts act only on at the surface of that part.

Figure 12-3 shows three ways in which a solid might change its dimensions when forces act on it. In Fig. 12-3*a*, a cylinder is stretched. In Fig. 12-3*b*, a cylinder is deformed by a force perpendicular to its long axis, much as we might deform a pack of cards or a book. In Fig. 12-3*c*, a solid object placed in a fluid under high pressure is compressed uniformly on all sides. What the three deformation types have in common is that a **stress,** or deforming force per unit area, produces a **strain,** or unit deformation. In Fig. 12-3, *tensile stress* (associated with stretching) is illustrated in (*a*), *shearing stress* in (*b*), and *hydraulic stress* in (*c*).

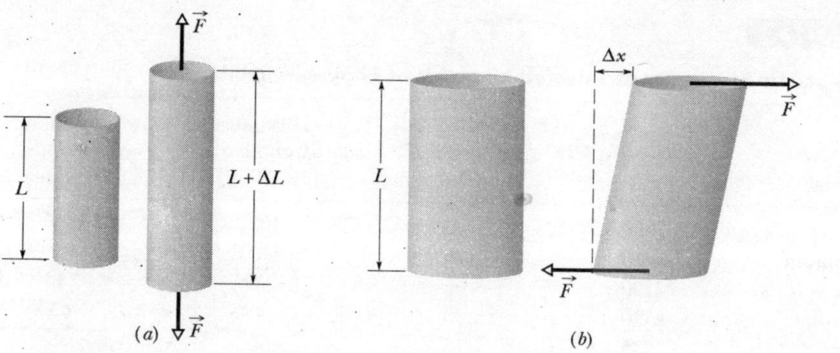

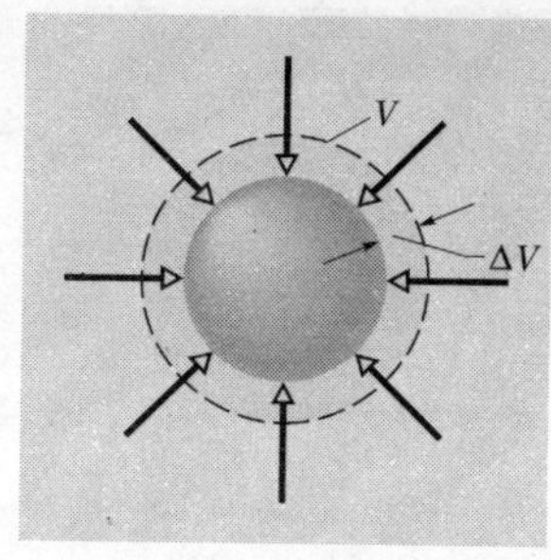

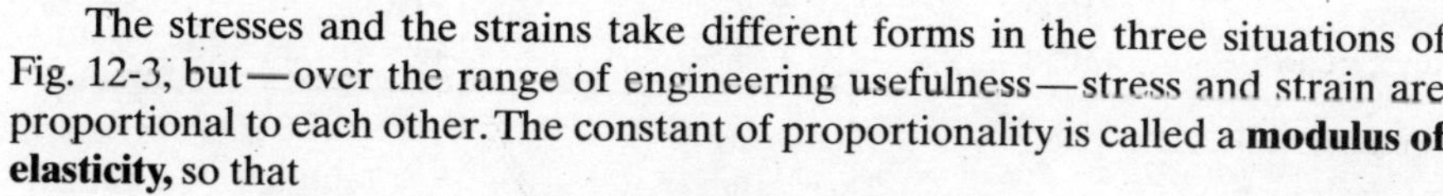

The stresses and the strains take different forms in the three situations of Fig. 12-3, but—over the range of engineering usefulness—stress and strain are proportional to each other. The constant of proportionality is called a **modulus of elasticity,** so that

$$\text{stress} = \text{modulus} \times \text{strain} \tag{12-1}$$

In a standard test of tensile properties, the tensile stress on a test cylinder (like that in Fig. 12-4) is slowly increased from zero to the point at which the cylinder fractures, and the strain is carefully measured and plotted. The result is a graph of stress versus strain like that in Fig. 12-5. For a substantial range of applied stresses, the stress–strain relation is linear, and the specimen recovers its original dimensions when the stress is removed; it is here that Eq. 12-1 applies. If the stress is increased beyond the **yield strength** S_y of the specimen, the specimen becomes permanently deformed. If the stress continues to increase, the specimen eventually ruptures, at a stress called the **ultimate strength** S_u.

FIG. 12-3 (*a*) A cylinder subject to *tensile stress* stretches by an amount ΔL. (*b*) A cylinder subject to *shearing stress* deforms by an amount Δx, somewhat like a pack of playing cards would. (*c*) A solid sphere subject to uniform *hydraulic stress* from a fluid shrinks in volume by an amount ΔV. All the deformations shown are greatly exaggerated.

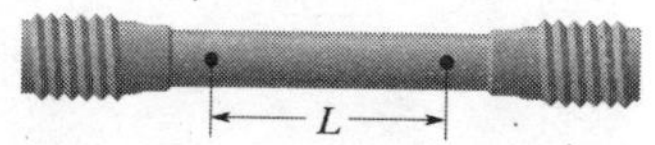

FIG. 12-4 A test specimen used to determine a stress–strain curve such as that of Fig. 12-5. The change ΔL that occurs in a certain length L is measured in a tensile stress–strain test.

Tension and Compression

For simple tension or compression, the stress on the object is defined as F/A, where F is the magnitude of the force applied perpendicularly to an area A on the object. The strain, or unit deformation, is then the dimensionless quantity $\Delta L/L$, the fractional (or sometimes percentage) change in a length of the specimen. If the specimen is a long rod and the stress does not exceed the yield strength, then not only the entire rod but also every section of it experiences the same strain when a given stress is applied. Because the strain is dimensionless, the modulus in Eq. 12-1 has the same dimensions as the stress—namely, force per unit area.

The modulus for tensile and compressive stresses is called the **Young's modulus** and is represented in engineering practice by the symbol E. Equation 12-1 becomes

$$\frac{F}{A} = E\frac{\Delta L}{L} \tag{12-2}$$

The strain $\Delta L/L$ in a specimen can often be measured conveniently with a *strain gage* (Fig. 12-6). This simple and useful device, which can be attached directly to operating machinery with an adhesive, is based on the principle that its electrical properties are dependent on the strain it undergoes.

Although the Young's modulus for an object may be almost the same for tension and compression, the object's ultimate strength may well be different for the two types of stress. Concrete, for example, is very strong in compression but is so weak in tension that it is almost never used in that manner. Table 12-1 shows the Young's modulus and other elastic properties for some materials of engineering interest.

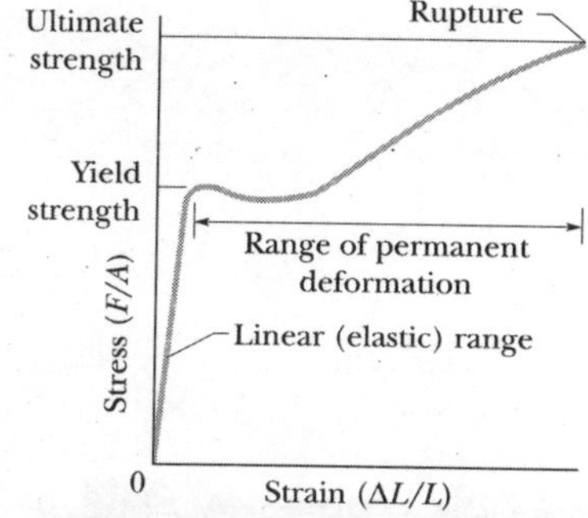

FIG. 12-5 A stress–strain curve for a steel test specimen such as that of Fig. 12-4. The specimen deforms permanently when the stress is equal to the *yield strength* of the specimen's material. It ruptures when the stress is equal to the *ultimate strength* of the material.

FIG. 12-6 A strain gage of overall dimensions 9.8 mm by 4.6 mm. The gage is fastened with adhesive to the object whose strain is to be measured; it experiences the same strain as the object. The electrical resistance of the gage varies with the strain, permitting strains up to 3% to be measured. *(Courtesy Vishay Micro-Measurements Group, Raleigh, NC)*

TABLE 12-1

Some Elastic Properties of Selected Materials of Engineering Interest

Material	Density ρ (kg/m^3)	Young's Modulus E (10^9 N/m^2)	Ultimate Strength S_u (10^6 N/m^2)	Yield Strength S_y (10^6 N/m^2)
Steel[a]	7860	200	400	250
Aluminum	2710	70	110	95
Glass	2190	65	50[b]	—
Concrete[c]	2320	30	40[b]	—
Wood[d]	525	13	50[b]	—
Bone	1900	9[b]	170[b]	—
Polystyrene	1050	3	48	—

[a]Structural steel (ASTM-A36).
[b]In compression.
[c]High strength.
[d]Douglas fir.

Shearing

In the case of shearing, the stress is also a force per unit area, but the force vector lies in the plane of the area rather than perpendicular to it. The strain is the dimensionless ratio $\Delta x/L$, with the quantities defined as shown in Fig. 12-3*b*. The corresponding modulus, which is given the symbol G in engineering practice, is called the **shear modulus**. For shearing, Eq. 12-1 is written as

$$\frac{F}{A} = G\frac{\Delta x}{L} \tag{12-3}$$

Shearing stresses play a critical role in the buckling of shafts that rotate under load and in bone fractures caused by bending.

Hydraulic Stress

In Fig. 12-3*c*, the stress is the fluid pressure p on the object, and, as you will see in later chapters, pressure is a force per unit area. The strain is $\Delta V/V$, where V is the original volume of the specimen and ΔV is the absolute value of the change in volume. The corresponding modulus, with symbol B, is called the **bulk modulus** of the material. The object is said to be under *hydraulic compression,* and the pressure can be called the *hydraulic stress.* For this situation, we write Eq. 12-1 as

$$p = B\frac{\Delta V}{V} \tag{12-4}$$

The bulk modulus is 2.2×10^9 N/m^2 for water and 1.6×10^{11} N/m^2 for steel. The pressure at the bottom of the Pacific Ocean, at its average depth of about 4000 m, is 4.0×10^7 N/m^2. The fractional compression $\Delta V/V$ of a volume of water due to this pressure is 1.8%; that for a steel object is only about 0.025%. In general, solids—with their rigid atomic lattices—are less compressible than liquids, in which the atoms or molecules are less tightly coupled to their neighbors.

Sample Problem 12-1

One end of a steel rod of radius $R = 9.5$ mm and length $L = 81$ cm is held in a vise. A force of magnitude $F = 62$ kN is then applied perpendicularly to the end face (uniformly across the area) at the other end. What are the stress on the rod and the elongation ΔL and strain of the rod?

Conceptualize/Classify: The stress is the ratio of the magnitude F of the perpendicular force to the area A. The ratio is the left side of Eq. 12-2. The elongation ΔL is related to the stress and Young's modulus E by Eq. 12-2 ($F/A = E\,\Delta L/L$). Strain is the ratio of the elongation to the initial length L.

Compute: To find the stress, we write

$$\text{Stress} = \frac{F}{A} = \frac{F}{\pi R^2} = \frac{6.2 \times 10^4\ \text{N}}{(\pi)(9.5 \times 10^{-3}\ \text{m})^2}$$

$$= 2.2 \times 10^8 \text{ N/m}^2 \qquad \text{(Answer)}$$

The yield strength for structural steel is 2.5×10^8 N/m², so this rod is dangerously close to its yield strength.

We find the value of Young's modulus for steel in Table 12-1. Then from Eq. 12-2 we find the elongation:

$$\Delta L = \frac{(F/A)L}{E} = \frac{(2.2 \times 10^8 \text{ N/m}^2)(0.81 \text{ m})}{2.0 \times 10^{11} \text{ N/m}^2}$$

$$= 8.9 \times 10^{-4} \text{ m} = 0.89 \text{ mm} \qquad \text{(Answer)}$$

For the strain, we have

$$\frac{\Delta L}{L} = \frac{8.9 \times 10^{-4} \text{ m}}{0.81 \text{ m}}$$

$$= 1.1 \times 10^{-3} = 0.11\% \qquad \text{(Answer)}$$

Conclude: You can see that at just 0.1% strain the rod is at yield point. This is the reason we cannot see any change in the dimensions of the metal objects under normal situations.

Sample Problem 12-2

A table has three legs that are 1.00 m in length and a fourth leg that is longer by $d = 0.50$ mm, so that the table wobbles slightly. A steel cylinder with mass $M = 290$ kg is placed on the table (which has a mass much less than M) so that all four legs are compressed but unbuckled and the table is level but no longer wobbles. The legs are wooden cylinders with cross-sectional area $A = 1.0$ cm²; Young's modulus is $E = 1.3 \times 10^{10}$ N/m². What are the magnitudes of the forces on the legs from the floor?

Conceptualize/Classify: We take the table plus steel cylinder as our system. The situation is like that in Fig. 12-1, except now we have a steel cylinder on the table. If the tabletop remains level, the legs must be compressed in the following ways: Each of the short legs must be compressed by the same amount (call it ΔL_3) and thus by the same force of magnitude F_3. The single long leg must be compressed by a larger amount ΔL_4 and thus by a force with a larger magnitude F_4. In other words, for a level tabletop, we must have

$$\Delta L_4 = \Delta L_3 + d \qquad (12\text{-}5)$$

From Eq. 12-2, we can relate a change in length to the force causing the change with $\Delta L = FL/AE$, where L is the original length of a leg. We can use this relation to replace ΔL_4 and ΔL_3 in Eq. 12-5. However, note that we can approximate the original length L as being the same for all four legs.

Compute: Making those replacements and that approximation gives us

$$\frac{F_4 L}{AE} = \frac{F_3 L}{AE} + d \qquad (12\text{-}6)$$

We cannot solve this equation because it has two unknowns, F_4 and F_3.

To get a second equation containing F_4 and F_3, we can use a vertical y axis and then write the balance of vertical forces ($F_{\text{net},y} = 0$) as

$$3F_3 + F_4 - Mg = 0 \qquad (12\text{-}7)$$

where Mg is equal to the magnitude of the gravitational force on the system. (*Three* legs have force $\vec{F}_3$ on them.) To solve the simultaneous Eq. 12-6 and 12-7 for, say, F_3, we first use Eq. 12-7 to find that $F_4 = Mg - 3F_3$. Substituting that into Eq. 12-6 then yields, after some algebra,

$$F_3 = \frac{Mg}{4} - \frac{dAE}{4L}$$

$$= \frac{(290 \text{ kg})(9.8 \text{ m/s}^2)}{4}$$

$$- \frac{(5.0 \times 10^{-4} \text{ m})(10^{-4} \text{ m}^2)(1.3 \times 10^{10} \text{ N/m}^2)}{(4)(1.00 \text{ m})}$$

$$= 548 \text{ N} \approx 5.5 \times 10^2 \text{ N} \qquad \text{(Answer)}$$

From Eq. 12-7 we then find

$$F_4 = Mg - 3F_3 = (290 \text{ kg})(9.8 \text{ m/s}^2) - 3(548 \text{ N})$$

$$\approx 1.2 \text{ kN} \qquad \text{(Answer)}$$

Conclude: You can show that to reach their equilibrium configuration, the three short legs are each compressed by 0.42 mm and the single long leg by 0.92 mm.

12-3 | Energy

Let's consider a rod of relaxed length l_0 fixed at one end with the wall as shown in Fig. 12-7. Now on the free end we apply a force varying slowly such that the rod is always in equilibrium.

When the stress in the rod is σ, the force we will be applying is F, where $F = A\sigma$.

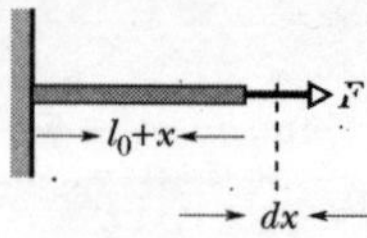

FIG. 12-7 A rod attached to a wall is being pulled by force F.

At this instant, the rod has extended by x so the strain in the rod is $S = \frac{x}{l}$.

Young's Modulus is given by

$$Y = \frac{\sigma}{\left(\frac{x}{l}\right)} \Rightarrow \sigma = \frac{Yx}{l} \text{ therefore } F = \frac{YAx}{l}$$

Thus, work done by the external force to extend the rod further by dx is Fdx.

$$\text{Therefore, } \int Fdx = \int_0^x \frac{YAx}{l} dx$$

$$W = \frac{1}{2}\frac{YA}{l}x^2 = \frac{1}{2}\left(\frac{Yx}{l}\right)\left(\frac{x}{l}\right)(lA) = \frac{1}{2} \times \sigma \times S \times \text{Volume}$$

This is also the energy stored in the rod in form of potential energy as the internal forces are conservative in nature till the elastic region. Thus elastic potential energy stored in the rod is

$$U = \frac{1}{2} \times \sigma \times S \times \text{Volume}$$

Sample Problem 12-3

Find strain in the rod of mass m, cross-sectional area A and Young's modulus being Y, under its own weight.

Conceptualize/Classify: As gravity will be pulling the rod as a whole downward there will be tension in the rod. But the lower points will have lesser tension than the upper points as they have to support lesser weights.

Compute: Tension in the rod at distance x from the lower end is T,

where $$T = \left(\frac{mx}{l}\right)g$$

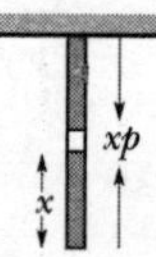

FIG. 12-8 Tension in rod of mass m.

m/l, mass per unit length

Thus stress at distance x from the lower end is $\sigma = T/A$

Thus, strain at this point is

$$S = \frac{\sigma}{Y} = \frac{\left(\frac{mxg}{lA}\right)}{Y}$$

We can write strain at distance x as $\frac{ds}{dx}$, here ds is change in length in an element of length dx.

$$\frac{ds}{dx} = \frac{\left(\frac{mxg}{lA}\right)}{Y} \qquad (12\text{-}8)$$

$$\int_0^{\Delta L} ds = \int_0^L \left(\frac{mgx}{lAY}\right) dx$$

Here ΔL is the total change in the length of the rod.

$$\Delta L = \frac{mg}{lAY}\left(\frac{l^2}{2}\right)$$

Hence, total strain in the rod is $\frac{mg}{2AY}$

Also find the elastic potential energy stored in the rod.

Compute: Now the energy stored in the element at distance x from the lower end is

$$dU = \frac{1}{2} \times \frac{mgx}{lA} \times \frac{ds}{dx} \times Adx$$

$$\text{As we know } \frac{ds}{dx} = \frac{\left(\frac{mxg}{lA}\right)}{Y} \text{ from Eq. 12-8}$$

$$\int_0^{U_0} dU = \frac{m^2g^2}{2l^2AY}\int_0^l x^2\, dx$$

$$U_0 = \frac{m^2g^2}{2l^2AY} \times \frac{l^3}{3}$$

$$= \frac{m^2g^2l}{6AY}$$

Conclude: The answers are dimensionally correct.

Sample Problem 12-4

A solid sphere is initially kept in open air, and the pressure exerted on it by air is 1.0×10^5 N/m^2 (atmospheric pressure). The sphere is lowered into the ocean to a depth where the pressure is 200 times the atmospheric pressure. The volume of the sphere in air is 0.5 m^3. What is the change in the volume once the sphere is submerged? Given that bulk modulus is 6.1×10^{10} N/m^2.

Conceptualize/Classify: What happens when you squeeze a tennis ball in your hand its volume reduces as it shrinks. We can expect same thing to happen to the sphere when it is subjected to high pressure from the ocean water. We need to perform a simple calculation using Eq. 12-8.

Compute: Substitute the numerical values:

The negative sign indicates that the volume of the sphere decreases.

$$\Delta V = -\frac{V_i \Delta P}{B}$$

$$\Delta V = -\frac{(0.50\ \text{m}^3)(2.0 \times 10^7\ \text{N/m}^2 - 1.0 \times 10^5\ \text{N/m}^2)}{6.1 \times 10^{10}\ \text{N/m}^2}$$

$$= -1.6 \times 10^{-4}\ \text{m}^3 \qquad \text{(Answer)}$$

12-4 | Poisson's Ratio

When a length of wire is stretched, its cross-sectional area becomes smaller. Now there will be axial strain $\Delta l/l$ along the length of the wire and a lateral strain in the directions perpendicular to the length. For a wire of circular cross-section, if the radius was r before stretching and $(r - \Delta r)$ after stretching, the strain perpendicular to the length is $\Delta r/r$. The ratio of these two strains is called Poisson's ratio, κ.

$$\kappa = \left(\frac{\Delta r}{r}\right) \times \left(\frac{l}{\Delta l}\right) = \frac{\textit{lateral strain}}{\textit{axial strain}} \qquad (12\text{-}9)$$

Poisson's ratio, like Young's modulus and shear modulus, is a property of the solid and does not depend on its shape.

Relation between Poisson's Ratio and Young's Modulus

Imagine we have submerged a small solid object deep into a liquid so that it experiences uniform pressure P from all directions. This pressure will apply compressive force on the object reducing its size but keeping its shape unaltered. For example, if the cube of side a in Fig. 12-9 experiences an equal inward force Pl^2 on each of its six faces, there is an equal compression in the x, y and z directions, resulting in a cube with slightly shorter sides.

If the force was acting only in one dimension then the length of a side becomes $l - \Delta l$ from l. The volume of the cube becomes $(l - \Delta l)^3$ changed from l^3. Since Δl is very much smaller than l for practical values of pressures, thus terms in $(\Delta l)^2$ and $(\Delta l)^3$ may be neglected.

$$(l - \Delta l)^3 \approx l^3 - 3l^2\,\Delta l$$

The fractional change in volume $\Delta V/V = 3\Delta l/l$

As usual, stress/strain is constant for small deformations, and we can define the bulk modulus B of the material of the cube as

$$B = \frac{PV}{\Delta V}$$

Since the change in volume has occurred as a result of the application of three separate linear forces in the x, y and z directions, the bulk modulus can be related to Young's modulus. If the forces Pl^2 in the x, y and z direction are each applied in turn, each causes an extension in the two perpendicular directions by an amount given by Poisson's ratio. When the forces Pl^2 in the $\pm\, x$ directions are applied to the cube, the length of the sides parallel to the x axis becomes $l - \Delta l$, and the length of the other sides becomes $l + \kappa\Delta l$. The volume of the cube is now

$$(l - \Delta l) \times (l + \kappa\Delta l)^2 \approx l^3 - l^2\Delta l\,(1 - 2\kappa)$$

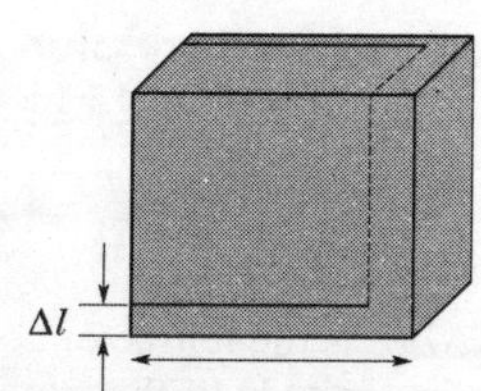

FIG. 12-9 A cube immersed in a liquid, being compressed from all sides.

and the fractional change in volume is $\Delta V/V = \Delta l(1 - 2\kappa)/l$

as $\Delta l/l = P/Y$, we can write $\Delta l(1 - 2\kappa)/l = P(1 - 2\kappa)/Y$.

The fractional change in volume, when forces Pl^2 are applied to all six faces of the cube, is simply three times this amount. The fractional change in volume is also given by the bulk modulus, and it follows that

$$B = \frac{PV}{\Delta V} = \frac{Y}{3(1 - 2\kappa)}$$

Thus,
$$B = \frac{Y}{3(1 - 2\kappa)}$$

The mechanical properties:

The mechanical properties of a material govern its behavior under the action of external forces. When engineers select a material for a particular application they give special attention to these properties. Four important mechanical properties are strength, rigdity, ductility and toughness. Strength tells us the maximum magnitude of applied force a material can withstand before breaking.

Rigidity tells us about the resistance material offers against distortion in its shape or size, or both. A stiff material is not very flexible. There is no such thing as a perfectly stiff or rigid (unyielding) material. All materials deform when subjected to force, although the deformation may be very small.

Ductility means the ease with which the material can be hammered, pressed, bent, rolled, cut or stretched into useful shapes.

A tough material is one that is not brittle, that is, it does not crack readily.

Steel has all four properties, putty has none of them. Glass is strong and stiff but not tough or ductile. Which properties would you ascribe to rubber, nylon and diamond?

REVIEW & SUMMARY

Elastic Moduli Three **elastic moduli** are used to describe the elastic behavior (deformations) of objects as they respond to forces that act on them. The **strain** (fractional change in length) is linearly related to the applied **stress** (force per unit area) by the proper modulus, according to the general relation

$$\text{stress} = \text{modulus} \times \text{strain}$$

Tension and Compression When an object is under tension or compression, Eq. 12-1 is written as

$$\frac{F}{A} = E\frac{\Delta L}{L}$$

where $\Delta L/L$ is the tensile or compressive strain of the object, F is the magnitude of the applied force $\vec{F}$ causing the strain, A is the cross-sectional area over which $\vec{F}$ is applied (perpendicular to A, as in Fig. 12-3a), and E is the **Young's modulus** for the object. The stress is F/A.

Shearing When an object is under a shearing stress, Eq. 12-1 is written as

$$\frac{F}{A} = G\frac{\Delta x}{L}$$

where $\Delta x/L$ is the shearing strain of the object, Δx is the displacement of one end of the object in the direction of the applied force $\vec{F}$ (as in Fig. 12-3b), and G is the **shear modulus** of the object. The stress is F/A.

Hydraulic Stress When an object undergoes *hydraulic compression* due to a stress exerted by a surrounding fluid, Eq. 12-1 is written as

$$p = B\frac{\Delta V}{V}$$

where p is the pressure (*hydraulic stress*) on the object due to the fluid, $\Delta V/V$ (the strain) is the absolute value of the fractional change in the object's volume due to that pressure, and B is the **bulk modulus** of the object.

PROBLEMS

1 A horizontal aluminum rod 4.8 cm in diameter projects 5.3 cm from a wall. A 1200 kg object is suspended from the end of the rod. The shear modulus of aluminum is 3.0×10^{10} N/m². Neglecting the rod's mass, find (a) the shear stress on the rod and (b) the vertical deflection of the end of the rod.

2 Figure 12-10 shows the stress–strain curve for a material. The scale of the stress axis is set by $s = 300$, in units of 10^6 N/m². What are (a) the Young's modulus and (b) the approximate yield strength for this material?

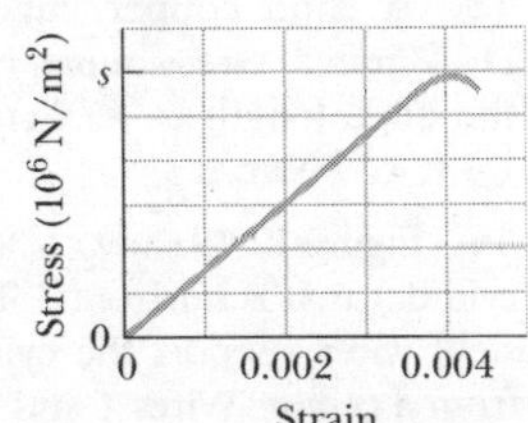

FIG. 12-10 Problem 2.

3 In Fig. 12-11, a 103 kg uniform log hangs by two steel wires, A and B, both of radius 1.20 mm. Initially, wire A was 2.50 m long and 2.00 mm shorter than wire B. The log is now horizontal. What are the magnitudes of the forces on it from (a) wire A and (b) wire B? (c) What is the ratio d_A/d_B?

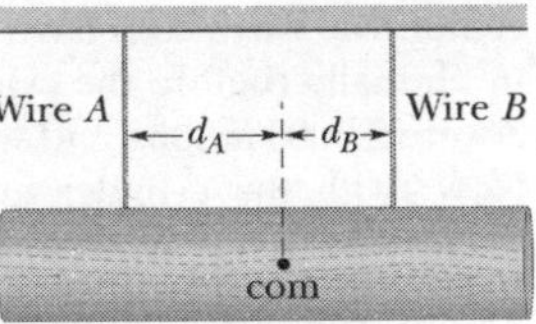

FIG. 12-11 Problem 3.

4 Figure 12-12 shows the stress versus strain plot for an aluminum wire that is stretched by a machine pulling in opposite directions at the two ends of the wire. The scale of the stress axis is set by $s = 7.0$, in units of 10^7 N/m². The wire has an initial length of 0.800 m and an initial cross-sectional area of 2.00×10^{-6} m². How much work does the force from the machine do on the wire to produce a strain of 1.00×10^{-3}?

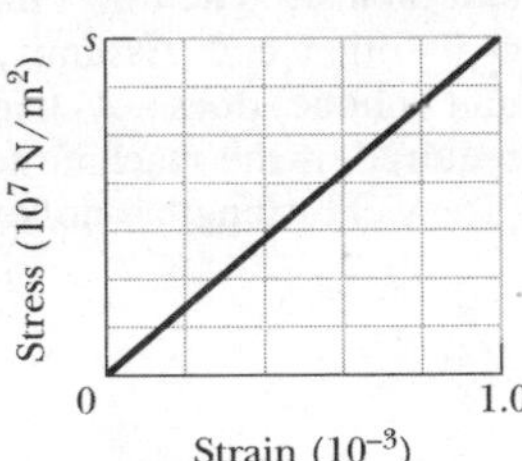

FIG. 12-12 Problem 4.

5 In Fig. 12-13, a lead brick rests horizontally on cylinders A and B. The areas of the top faces of the cylinders are related by $A_A = 2A_B$; the Young's moduli of the cylinders are related by $E_A = 2E_B$. The cylinders had identical lengths before the brick was placed on them. What fraction of the brick's mass is supported (a) by cylinder A and (b) by cylinder B? The horizontal distances between the center of mass of the brick and the centerlines of the cylinders are d_A for cylinder A and d_B for cylinder B. (c) What is the ratio d_A/d_B?

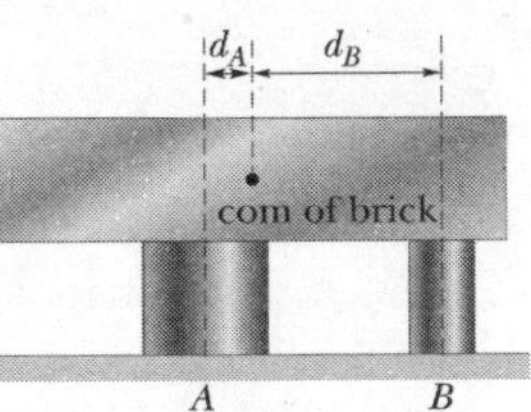

FIG. 12-13 Problem 5.

6 Figure 12-14 shows an approximate plot of stress versus strain for a spider-web thread, out to the point of breaking at a strain of 2.00. The vertical axis scale is set by $a = 0.12$ GN/m², $b = 0.30$ GN/m², and $c = 0.80$ GN/m². Assume that the thread has an initial length of 0.80 cm, an initial cross-sectional area of 8.0×10^{-12} m², and (during stretching) a constant volume. Assume also that when the single thread snares a flying insect, the insect's kinetic energy is transferred to the stretching of the thread. (a) How much kinetic energy would put the thread on the verge of breaking? What is the kinetic energy of (b) a fruit fly of mass 6.00 mg and speed 1.70 m/s and (c) a bumble bee of mass 0.388 g and speed 0.420 m/s? Would (d) the fruit fly and (e) the bumble bee break the thread?

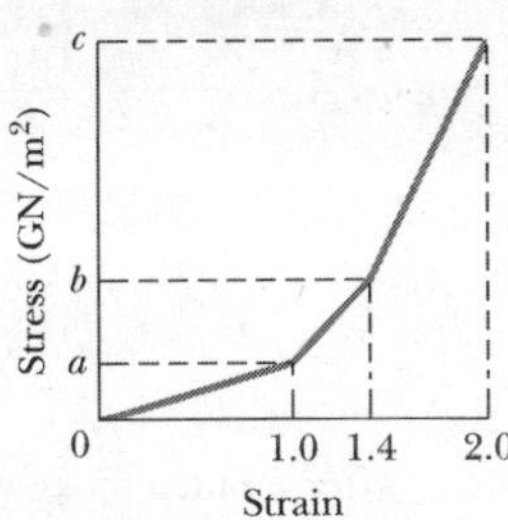

FIG. 12-14 Problem 6.

7 A tunnel of length $L = 150$ m, height $H = 7.2$ m, and width 5.8 m (with a flat roof) is to be constructed at distance $d = 60$ m beneath the ground. (See Fig. 12-15.) The tunnel roof is to be supported entirely by square steel columns, each with a cross-sectional area of 960 cm². The mass of 1.0 cm³ of the ground material is 2.8 g. (a) What is the total weight of the ground material the columns must support? (b) How many columns are needed to keep the compressive stress on each column at one-half its ultimate strength?

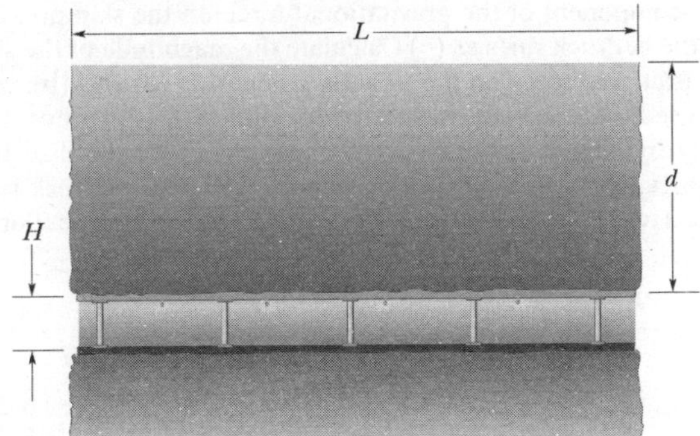

FIG. 12-15 Problem 7.

8 Figure 12-16 represents an insect caught at the midpoint of a spider-web thread. The thread breaks under a stress of 8.20×10^8 N/m² and a strain of 2.00. Initially, it was horizontal and had a length of 2.00 cm and a cross-sectional area of 8.00×10^{-12} m². As the thread was stretched under the weight of the insect, its volume remained constant. If the weight of the insect puts the thread on the verge of breaking, what is the insect's mass? (A spider's web is built to break if a potentially harmful insect, such as a bumble bee, becomes snared in the web.)

FIG. 12-16 Problem 8.

9 Figure 12-17 is an overhead view of a rigid rod that turns about a vertical axle until the identical rubber stoppers A and B are forced against rigid walls at distances $r_A = 7.0$ cm and $r_B = 4.0$ cm from the axle. Initially the stoppers touch the walls without being compressed. Then force $\vec{F}$ of magnitude 220 N is applied perpendicular to the rod at a distance $R = 5.0$ cm from the axle. Find the magnitude of the force compressing (a) stopper A and (b) stopper B.

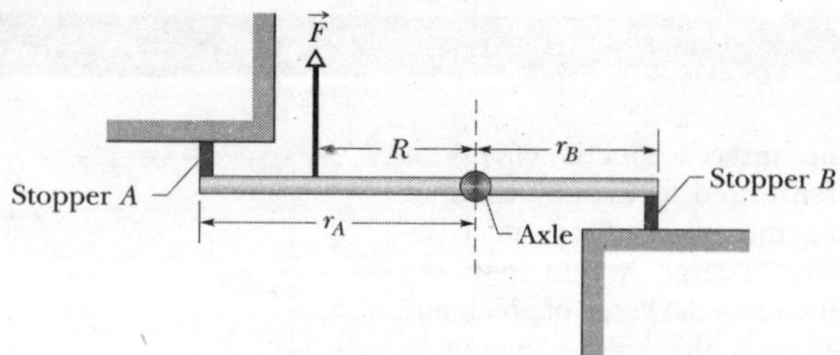

FIG. 12-17 Problem 9.

10 After a fall, a 95 kg rock climber finds himself dangling from the end of a rope that had been 15 m long and 9.6 mm in diameter but has stretched by 2.8 cm. For the rope, calculate (a) the strain, (b) the stress, and (c) the Young's modulus.

11 In Fig. 12-18, a rectangular slab of slate rests on a bedrock surface inclined at angle $\theta = 26°$. The slab has length $L = 43$ m, thickness $T = 2.5$ m, and width $W = 12$ m, and 1.0 cm³ of it has a mass of 3.2 g. The coefficient of static friction between slab and bedrock is 0.39. (a) Calculate the component of the gravitational force on the slab parallel to the bedrock surface. (b) Calculate the magnitude of the static frictional force on the slab. By comparing (a) and (b), you can see that the slab is in danger of sliding. This is prevented only by chance protrusions of bedrock. (c) To stabilize the slab, bolts are to be driven perpendicular to the bedrock surface (two bolts are shown). If each bolt has a cross-sectional area of 6.4 cm² and will snap under a shearing stress of 3.6×10^8 N/m², what is the minimum number of bolts needed? Assume that the bolts do not affect the normal force.

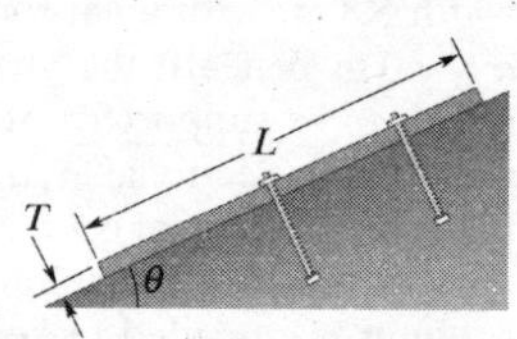

FIG. 12-18 Problem 11.

12 A mine elevator is supported by a single steel cable 2.5 cm in diameter. The total mass of the elevator cage and occupants is 670 kg. By how much does the cable stretch when the elevator hangs by (a) 12 m of cable and (b) 362 m of cable? (Neglect the mass of the cable.)

13 A solid copper cube has an edge length of 85.5 cm. How much stress must be applied to the cube to reduce the edge length to 85.0 cm? The bulk modulus of copper is 1.4×10^{11} N/m².

14 Figure 12-19 shows a 300 kg cylinder that is horizontal. Three steel wires support the cylinder from a ceiling. Wires 1 and 3 are attached at the ends of the cylinder, and wire 2 is attached at the center. The wires each have a cross-sectional area of 2.00×10^{-6} m². Initially (before the cylinder was put in place) wires 1 and 3 were 2.0000 m long and wire 2 was 6.00 mm longer than that. Now (with the cylinder in place) all three wires have been stretched. What is the tension in (a) wire 1 and (b) wire 2?

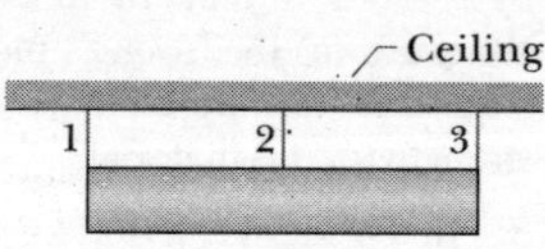

FIG. 12-19 Problem 14.

15 A cylindrical aluminum rod, with an initial length of 0.8000 m and radius 1000.0 μm, is clamped in place at one end and then stretched by a machine pulling parallel to its length at its other end. Assuming that the rod's density (mass per unit volume) does not change, find the force magnitude that is required of the machine to decrease the radius to 999.9 μm. (The yield strength is not exceeded.)

Newtonian Gravitation

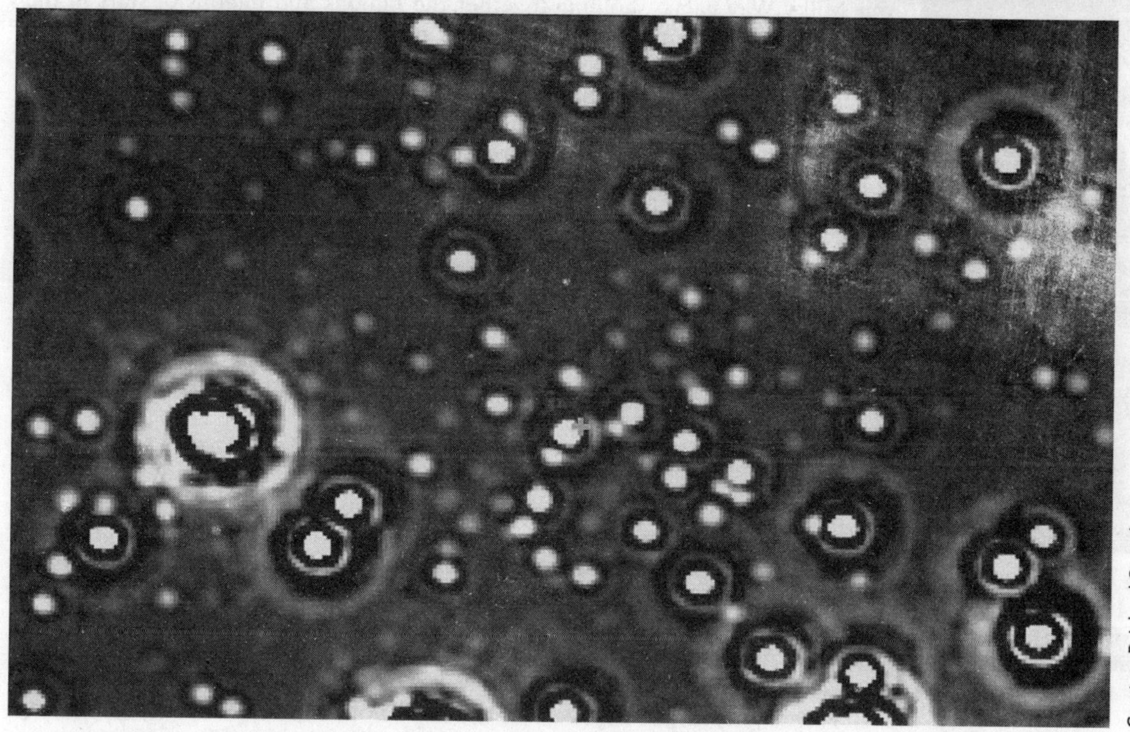

Courtesy Reinhard Genzel

This is an image of the stars near our Milky Way galaxy's center, which is marked with a small cross. Note that nothing shows up exactly at the center, but slightly off center (at the 8:00 position) there is a small circle. That circle is the image of a star known as S2. The other circles are also images of stars (the halos around them are artificially produced by the method of processing the images). Most stars in our galaxy move so slowly that we cannot actually see them move relative to one another, not even over a lifetime of observations. However, S2 is very different—we can see it move. In fact, it is moving so rapidly that it makes a complete trip around the Galaxy's center in only 15.2 years. There must be something huge at the center, yet we see nothing there.

What monster lies at our galaxy's center?

The answer is in this chapter.

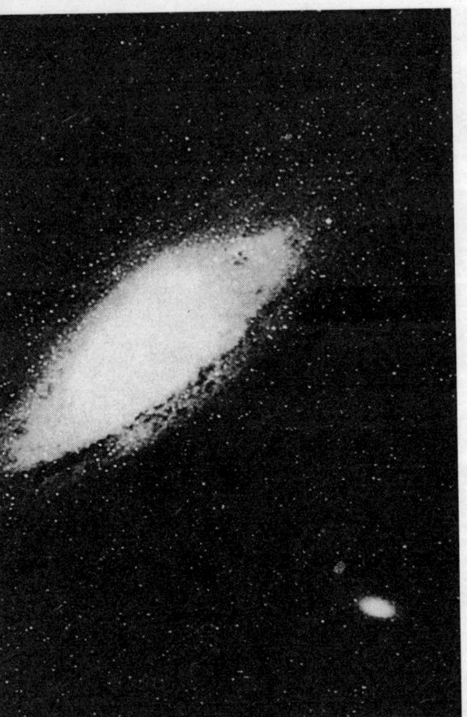

FIG. 13-1 The Andromeda Galaxy. Located 2.3×10^6 light-years from us, and faintly visible to the naked eye, it is very similar to our home galaxy, the Milky Way. *(Courtesy NASA)*

13-1 WHAT IS PHYSICS?

One of the long-standing goals of physics is to understand the gravitational force—the force that holds you to Earth, holds the Moon in orbit around Earth, and holds Earth in orbit around the Sun. It also reaches out through the whole of our Milky Way galaxy, holding together the billions and billions of stars in the Galaxy and the countless molecules and dust particles between stars. We are located somewhat near the edge of this disk-shaped collection of stars and other matter, 2.6×10^4 light-years (2.5×10^{20} m) from the galactic center, around which we slowly revolve.

The gravitational force also reaches across intergalactic space, holding together the Local Group of galaxies, which includes, in addition to the Milky Way, the Andromeda Galaxy (Fig. 13-1) at a distance of 2.3×10^6 light-years away from Earth, plus several closer dwarf galaxies, such as the Large Magellanic Cloud. The Local Group is part of the Local Supercluster of galaxies that is being drawn by the gravitational force toward an exceptionally massive region of space called the Great Attractor. This region appears to be about 3.0×10^8 light-years from Earth, on the opposite side of the Milky Way. And the gravitational force is even more far-reaching because it attempts to hold together the entire universe, which is expanding.

This force is also responsible for some of the most mysterious structures in the universe: *black holes.* When a star considerably larger than our Sun burns out, the gravitational force between all its particles can cause the star to collapse in on itself and thereby to form a black hole. The gravitational force at the surface of such a collapsed star is so strong that neither particles nor light can escape from the surface (thus the term "black hole"). Any star coming too near a black hole can be ripped apart by the strong gravitational force and pulled into the hole. Enough captures like this yields a *supermassive black hole.* Such mysterious monsters appear to be common in the universe.

Although the gravitational force is still not fully understood, the starting point in our understanding of it lies in the *law of gravitation* of Isaac Newton.

13-2 | Newton's Law of Gravitation

Physicists like to study seemingly unrelated phenomena to show that a relationship can be found if the phenomena are examined closely enough. This search for unification has been going on for centuries. In 1665, the 23-year-old Isaac Newton made a basic contribution to physics when he showed that the force that holds the Moon in its orbit is the same force that makes an apple fall. We take this knowledge so much for granted now that it is not easy for us to comprehend the ancient belief that the motions of earthbound bodies and heavenly bodies were different in kind and were governed by different laws.

Newton concluded not only that Earth attracts both apples and the Moon but also that every body in the universe attracts every other body; this tendency of bodies to move toward each other is called **gravitation.** Newton's conclusion takes a little getting used to, because the familiar attraction of Earth for earthbound bodies is so great that it overwhelms the attraction that earthbound bodies have for each other. For example, Earth attracts an apple with a force magnitude of about 0.8 N. You also attract a nearby apple (and it attracts you), but the force of attraction has less magnitude than the weight of a speck of dust.

Newton proposed a *force law* that we call **Newton's law of gravitation:** Every particle attracts any other particle with a **gravitational force** of magnitude

$$F = G\frac{m_1 m_2}{r^2} \quad \text{(Newton's law of gravitation)} \qquad (13\text{-}1)$$

Here m_1 and m_2 are the masses of the particles, r is the distance between them, and G is the **gravitational constant,** with a value that is now known to be

$$G = 6.67 \times 10^{-11}\ \mathrm{N \cdot m^2/kg^2} = 6.67 \times 10^{-11}\ \mathrm{m^3/kg \cdot s^2} \tag{13-2}$$

In Fig. 13-2*a*, $\vec{F}$ is the gravitational force acting on particle 1 (mass m_1) due to particle 2 (mass m_2). The force is directed toward particle 2 and is said to be an *attractive force* because particle 1 is attracted toward particle 2. The magnitude of the force is given by Eq. 13-1.

We can describe $\vec{F}$ as being in the positive direction of an r axis extending radially from particle 1 through particle 2 (Fig. 13-2*b*). We can also describe $\vec{F}$ by using a radial unit vector $\hat{r}$ (a dimensionless vector of magnitude 1) that is directed away from particle 1 along the r axis (Fig. 13-2*c*). From Eq. 13-1, the force on particle 1 is then

$$\vec{F} = G\frac{m_1 m_2}{r^2}\hat{r} \tag{13-3}$$

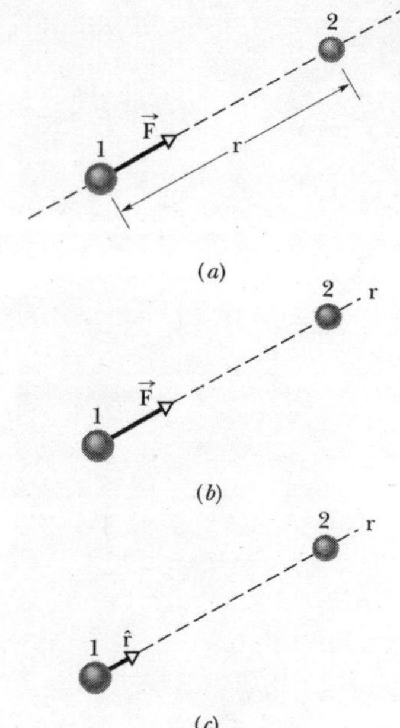

FIG. 13-2 (*a*) The gravitational force $\vec{F}$ on particle 1 due to particle 2 is an attractive force because particle 1 is attracted to particle 2. (*b*) Force $\vec{F}$ is directed along a radial coordinate axis r extending from particle 1 through particle 2. (*c*) $\vec{F}$ is in the direction of a unit vector $\hat{r}$ along the r axis.

The gravitational force on particle 2 due to particle 1 has the same magnitude as the force on particle 1 but the opposite direction. These two forces form a third-law force pair, and we can speak of the gravitational force *between* the two particles as having a magnitude given by Eq. 13-1. This force between two particles is not altered by other objects, even if they are located between the particles. Put another way, no object can shield either particle from the gravitational force due to the other particle.

The strength of the gravitational force—that is, how strongly two particles with given masses at a given separation attract each other—depends on the value of the gravitational constant G. If G—by some miracle—were suddenly multiplied by a factor of 10, you would be crushed to the floor by Earth's attraction. If G were divided by this factor, Earth's attraction would be so weak that you could jump over a building.

Although Newton's law of gravitation applies strictly to particles, we can also apply it to real objects as long as the sizes of the objects are small relative to the distance between them. The Moon and Earth are far enough apart so that, to a good approximation, we can treat them both as particles—but what about an apple and Earth? From the point of view of the apple, the broad and level Earth, stretching out to the horizon beneath the apple, certainly does not look like a particle.

Newton solved the apple–Earth problem by proving an important theorem called the *shell theorem:*

> A uniform spherical shell of matter attracts a particle that is outside the shell as if all the shell's mass were concentrated at its center.

Earth can be thought of as a nest of such shells, one within another and each shell attracting a particle outside Earth's surface as if the mass of that shell were at the center of the shell. Thus, from the apple's point of view, Earth *does* behave like a particle, one that is located at the center of Earth and has a mass equal to that of Earth.

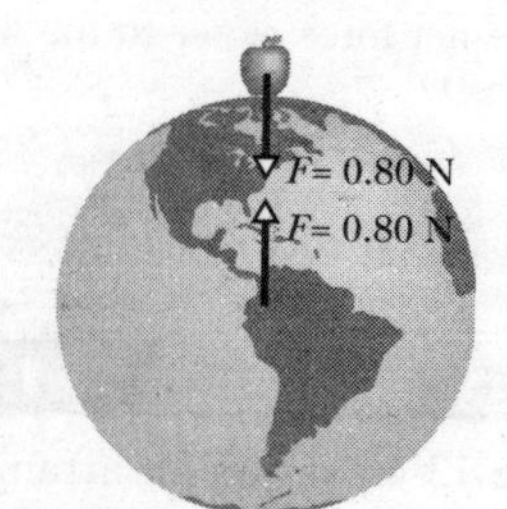

FIG. 13-3 The apple pulls up on Earth just as hard as Earth pulls down on the apple.

Suppose that, as in Fig. 13-3, Earth pulls down on an apple with a force of magnitude 0.80 N. The apple must then pull up on Earth with a force of magnitude 0.80 N, which we take to act at the center of Earth. Although the forces are matched in magnitude, they produce different accelerations when the apple is released. The accelerations of the apple is about 9.8 m/s^2, the familiar acceleration of a falling body near Earth's surface. The acceleration of Earth, however, measured in a reference frame attached to the center of mass of the apple–Earth system, is only about 1×10^{-25} m/s^2.

CHECKPOINT 1 A particle is to be placed, in turn, outside four objects, each of mass m: (1) a large uniform solid sphere, (2) a large uniform spherical shell, (3) a small uniform solid sphere, and (4) a small uniform shell. In each situation, the distance between the particle and the center of the object is d. Rank the objects according to the magnitude of the gravitational force they exert on the particle, greatest first.

13-3 | Gravitation and the Principle of Superposition

Given a group of particles, we find the net (or resultant) gravitational force on any one of them from the others by using the **principle of superposition.** This is a general principle that says a net effect is the sum of the individual effects. Here, the principle means that we first compute the individual gravitational forces that act on our selected particle due to each of the other particles. We then find the net force by adding these forces vectorially, as usual.

For n interacting particles, we can write the principle of superposition for the gravitational forces on particle 1 as

$$\vec{F}_{1,\text{net}} = \vec{F}_{12} + \vec{F}_{13} + \vec{F}_{14} + \vec{F}_{15} + \cdots + \vec{F}_{1n} \tag{13-4}$$

Here $\vec{F}_{1,\text{net}}$ is the net force on particle 1 and, for example, $\vec{F}_{13}$ is the force on particle 1 from particle 3. We can express this equation more compactly as a vector sum:

$$\vec{F}_{1,\text{net}} = \sum_{i=2}^{n} \vec{F}_{1i} \tag{13-5}$$

What about the gravitational force on a particle from a real (extended) object? This force is found by dividing the object into parts small enough to treat as particles and then using Eq. 13-5 to find the vector sum of the forces on the particle from all the parts. In the limiting case, we can divide the extended object into differential parts each of mass dm and each producing a differential force $d\vec{F}$ on the particle. In this limit, the sum of Eq. 13-5 becomes an integral and we have

$$\vec{F}_1 = \int d\vec{F} \tag{13-6}$$

in which the integral is taken over the entire extended object and we drop the subscript "net." If the extended object is a uniform sphere or a spherical shell, we can avoid the integration of Eq. 13-6 by assuming that the object's mass is concentrated at the object's center and using Eq. 13-1.

CHECKPOINT 2 The figure shows four arrangements of three particles of equal masses. (a) Rank the arrangements according to the magnitude of the net gravitational force on the particle labeled m, greatest first. (b) In arrangement 2, is the direction of the net force closer to the line of length d or to the line of length D?

Sample Problem 13-1

Figure 13-4a shows an arrangement of three particles, particle 1 of mass $m_1 = 6.0$ kg and particles 2 and 3 of mass $m_2 = m_3 = 4.0$ kg, and distance $a = 2.0$ cm. What is the net gravitational force $\vec{F}_{1,\text{net}}$ on particle 1 due to the other particles?

Conceptualize/Classify: Because we have particles, the magnitude of the gravitational force on particle 1 due to either of the other particles is given by Eq. 13-1 ($F = Gm_1m_2/r^2$). The direction of either gravitational force on particle 1 is toward the particle responsible for it. Because the forces are not along a single axis, we *cannot* simply add or subtract their magnitudes or their components to get the net force. Instead, we must add them as vectors.

Compute: From Eq. 13-1, the magnitude of the force $\vec{F}_{12}$ on particle 1 from particle 2 is

$$F_{12} = \frac{Gm_1m_2}{a^2}$$
$$= \frac{(6.67 \times 10^{-11}\ \text{m}^3/\text{kg}\cdot\text{s}^2)(6.0\ \text{kg})(4.0\ \text{kg})}{(0.020\ \text{m})^2}$$
$$= 4.00 \times 10^{-6}\ \text{N}$$

Similarly, the magnitude of force $\vec{F}_{13}$ on particle 1 from particle 3 is

$$F_{13} = \frac{Gm_1m_3}{(2a)^2}$$
$$= \frac{(6.67 \times 10^{-11}\ \text{m}^3/\text{kg}\cdot\text{s}^2)(6.0\ \text{kg})(4.0\ \text{kg})}{(0.040\ \text{m})^2}$$
$$= 1.00 \times 10^{-6}\ \text{N}$$

Force $\vec{F}_{12}$ is directed in the positive direction of the y axis (Fig. 13-4*b*) and has only the y component F_{12}. Similarly, $\vec{F}_{13}$ is directed in the negative direction of the x axis and has only the x component $-F_{13}$.

To find the net force $\vec{F}_{1,\text{net}}$ on particle 1, we must add the two forces as vectors. We can do so on a vector-capable calculator. However, here we note that $-F_{13}$ and F_{12} are actually the x and y components of $\vec{F}_{1,\text{net}}$.

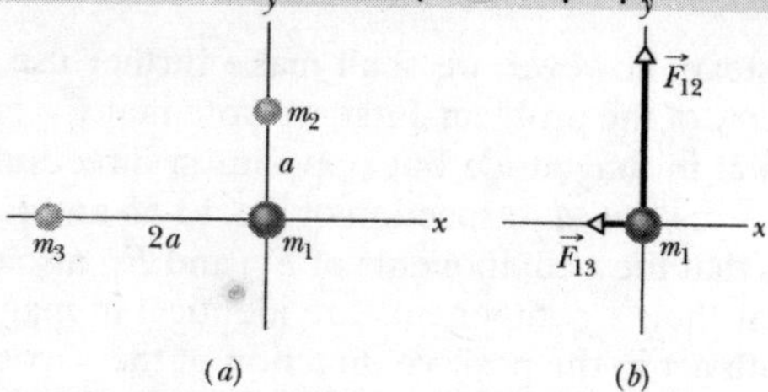

FIG. 13-4 (*a*) An arrangement of three particles. (*b*) The forces acting on the particle of mass m_1 due to the other particles.

Therefore, we can use Eq. 3-6 to find first the magnitude and then the direction of $\vec{F}_{1,\text{net}}$. The magnitude is

$$F_{1,\text{net}} = \sqrt{(F_{12})^2 + (-F_{13})^2}$$
$$= \sqrt{(4.00 \times 10^{-6}\ \text{N})^2 + (-1.00 \times 10^{-6}\ \text{N})^2}$$
$$= 4.1 \times 10^{-6}\ \text{N} \qquad \text{(Answer)}$$

Relative to the positive direction of the x axis, Eq. 3-6 gives the direction of $\vec{F}_{1,\text{net}}$ as

$$\theta = \tan^{-1}\frac{F_{12}}{-F_{13}} = \tan^{-1}\frac{4.00 \times 10^{-6}\ \text{N}}{-1.00 \times 10^{-6}\ \text{N}} = -76°$$

Conclude: Is this a reasonable direction? No, because the direction of $\vec{F}_{1,\text{net}}$ must be between the directions of $\vec{F}_{12}$ and $\vec{F}_{13}$. Recall from Chapter 3 (Problem-Solving Tactic 3) that a calculator displays only one of the two possible answers to a $\tan^{-1}$ function. We find the other answer by adding 180°:

$$-76° + 180° = 104° \qquad \text{(Answer)}$$

which *is* a reasonable direction for $\vec{F}_{1,\text{net}}$.

Sample Problem 13-2 Build your skill

Figure 13-5*a* shows an arrangement of five particles, with masses $m_1 = 8.0$ kg, $m_2 = m_3 = m_4 = m_5 = 2.0$ kg, and with $a = 2.0$ cm and $\theta = 30°$. What is the net gravitational force $\vec{F}_{1,\text{net}}$ on particle 1 due to the other particles?

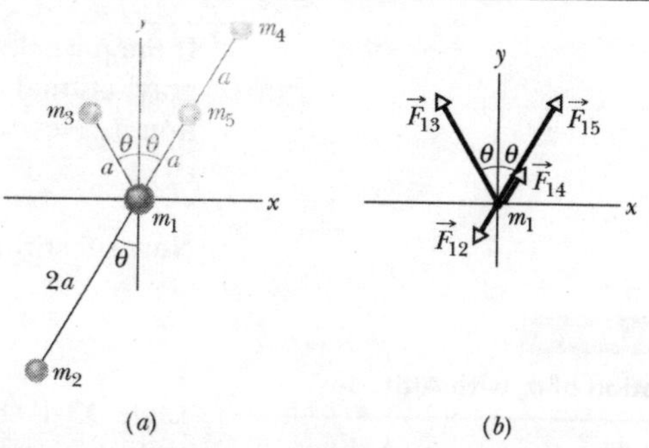

FIG. 13-5 (*a*) An arrangement of five particles. (*b*) The forces acting on the particle of mass m_1 due to the other four particles.

Conceptualize/Classify: Because we have particles, the magnitude of the gravitational force on particle 1 due to either of the other particles is given by Eq. 13-1 ($F = Gm_1m_2/r^2$). The direction of a gravitational force on particle 1 is toward the particle responsible for the force. We can use symmetry to eliminate unneeded calculations.

Compute: For the magnitudes of the forces on particle 1, first note that particles 2 and 4 have equal masses and equal distances of $r = 2a$ from particle 1. Thus, from Eq. 13-1, we find

$$F_{12} = F_{14} = \frac{Gm_1m_2}{(2a)^2} \qquad (13\text{-}7)$$

Similarly, since particles 3 and 5 have equal masses and are both distance $r = a$ from particle 1, we find

$$F_{13} = F_{15} = \frac{Gm_1m_3}{a^2} \qquad (13\text{-}8)$$

We could now substitute known data into these two equations to evaluate the magnitudes of the forces, indicate the directions of the forces on the free-body diagram of Fig. 13-5*b*, and then find the net force either (1) by resolving the vectors into x and y components, finding the net x and net y components, and then vectorially combining them or (2) by adding the vectors directly on a vector-capable calculator.

Instead, however, we shall make further use of the symmetry of the problem. First, we note that $\vec{F}_{12}$ and $\vec{F}_{14}$ are equal in magnitude but opposite in direction; thus, those forces *cancel.* Inspection of Fig. 13-5*b* and Eq. 13-8 reveals that the *x* components of $\vec{F}_{13}$ and $\vec{F}_{15}$ also *cancel,* and that their *y* components are identical in magnitude and both act in the positive direction of the *y* axis. Thus, $\vec{F}_{1,net}$ acts in that same direction, and its magnitude is twice the *y* component of $\vec{F}_{13}$:

$$F_{1,net} = 2F_{13}\cos\theta = 2\frac{Gm_1m_3}{a^2}\cos\theta$$

$$= \frac{2(6.67\times10^{-11}\ \text{m}^3/\text{kg}\cdot\text{s}^2)(8.0\ \text{kg})(2.0\ \text{kg})}{(0.020\ \text{m})^2}\cos 30°$$

$$= 4.6\times10^{-6}\ \text{N} \qquad \text{(Answer)}$$

Conclude: Note that the presence of particle 5 along the line between particles 1 and 4 does not alter the gravitational force on particle 1 from particle 4.

PROBLEM-SOLVING TACTICS

Tactic 1:* *Drawing Gravitational Force Vectors When you are given a diagram of particles, such as Fig. 13-4*a*, and asked to find the net gravitational force on one of them, you should usually draw a free-body diagram showing only the particle of concern and the forces on *it alone,* as in Fig. 13-4*b*. If, instead, you choose to superimpose the force vectors on the given diagram, be sure to draw the vectors with either all tails (preferably) or all heads on the particle experiencing those forces. If you draw the vectors elsewhere, you invite confusion—and confusion is guaranteed if you draw the vectors on the particles *causing* the forces.

Tactic 2:* *Simplifying a Sum of Forces with Symmetry In Sample Problem 13-2 we used the symmetry of the situation: By realizing that particles 2 and 4 are positioned symmetrically about particle 1, and thus that $\vec{F}_{12}$ and $\vec{F}_{14}$ cancel, we avoided calculating either force. By realizing that the *x* components of $\vec{F}_{13}$ and $\vec{F}_{15}$ cancel and that their *y* components are identical and add, we saved even more effort.

In problems with symmetry, you can save much effort and reduce the chance of error by identifying which calculations are not needed because of the symmetry. Such identification is a skill acquired only by doing many homework problems.

13-4 | Gravitation Near Earth's Surface

Let us assume that Earth is a uniform sphere of mass *M*. The magnitude of the gravitational force from Earth on a particle of mass *m*, located outside Earth a distance *r* from Earth's center, is then given by Eq. 13-1 as

$$F = G\frac{Mm}{r^2} \qquad (13\text{-}9)$$

If the particle is released, it will fall toward the center of Earth, as a result of the gravitational force $\vec{F}$, with an acceleration we shall call the **gravitational acceleration** $\vec{a}_g$. Newton's second law tells us that magnitudes *F* and a_g are related by

$$F = ma_g \qquad (13\text{-}10)$$

Now, substituting *F* from Eq. 13-9 into Eq. 13-10 and solving for a_g, we find

$$a_g = \frac{GM}{r^2} \qquad (13\text{-}11)$$

TABLE 13-1

Variation of a_g with Altitude

Altitude (km)	a_g (m/s²)	Altitude Example
0	9.83	Mean Earth surface
8.8	9.80	Mt. Everest
36.6	9.71	Highest crewed balloon
400	8.70	Space shuttle orbit
35 700	0.225	Communications satellite

Table 13-1 shows values of a_g computed for various altitudes above Earth's surface. Notice a_g is significant even at 400 km.

Since Section 5-4, we have assumed that Earth is an inertial frame by neglecting its rotation. This simplification has allowed us to assume that the free-fall acceleration *g* of a particle is the same as the particle's gravitational acceleration (which we now call a_g). Furthermore, we assumed that *g* has the constant value 9.8 m/s² any place on Earth's surface. However, any *g* value measured at a given location will differ from the a_g value calculated with Eq. 13-11 for that location for three reasons: (1) Earth's mass is not distributed uniformly, (2) Earth is not a perfect sphere, and (3) Earth rotates. Moreover, because *g* differs from a_g, the same three reasons mean that the measured weight *mg* of a particle differs from the magnitude of the gravitational force on the particle as given by Eq. 13-9. Let us now examine those reasons.

1. ***Earth's mass is not uniformly distributed.*** The density (mass per unit volume) of Earth varies radially as shown in Fig. 13-6, and the density of the crust (outer section) varies from region to region over Earth's surface. Thus, g varies from region to region over the surface.
2. ***Earth is not a sphere.*** Earth is approximately an ellipsoid, flattened at the poles and bulging at the equator. Its equatorial radius is greater than its polar radius by 21 km. Thus, a point at the poles is closer to the dense core of Earth than is a point on the equator. This is one reason the free-fall acceleration g increases as one proceeds, at sea level, from the equator toward either pole.
3. ***Earth is rotating.*** The rotation axis runs through the north and south poles of Earth. An object located on Earth's surface anywhere except at those poles must rotate in a circle about the rotation axis and thus must have a centripetal acceleration directed toward the center of the circle. This centripetal acceleration requires a centripetal net force that is also directed toward that center.

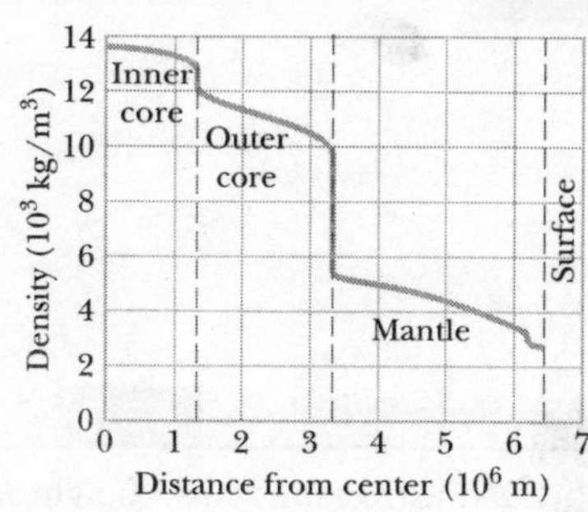

FIG. 13-6 The density of Earth as a function of distance from the center. The limits of the solid inner core, the largely liquid outer core, and the solid mantle are shown, but the crust of Earth is too thin to show clearly on this plot.

To see how Earth's rotation causes g to differ from a_g, let us analyze a simple situation in which a crate of mass m is on a scale at the equator. Figure 13-7*a* shows this situation as viewed from a point in space above the north pole.

Figure 13-7*b*, a free-body diagram for the crate, shows the two forces on the crate, both acting along a radial r axis that extends from Earth's center. The normal force $\vec{F}_N$ on the crate from the scale is directed outward, in the positive direction of the r axis. The gravitational force, represented with its equivalent $m\vec{a}_g$, is directed inward. Because it travels in a circle about the center of Earth as Earth turns, the crate has a centripetal acceleration $\vec{a}$ directed toward Earth's center. From Eq. 10-23 ($a_r = \omega^2 r$), we know this acceleration is equal to $\omega^2 R$, where ω is Earth's angular speed and R is the circle's radius (approximately Earth's radius). Thus, we can write Newton's second law for forces along the r axis ($F_{\text{net},r} = ma_r$) as

$$F_N - ma_g = m(-\omega^2 R) \qquad (13\text{-}12)$$

The magnitude F_N of the normal force is equal to the weight mg read on the scale. With mg substituted for F_N, Eq. 13-12 gives us

$$mg = ma_g - m(\omega^2 R) \qquad (13\text{-}13)$$

which says

$$\begin{pmatrix}\text{measured}\\ \text{weight}\end{pmatrix} = \begin{pmatrix}\text{magnitude of}\\ \text{gravitational force}\end{pmatrix} - \begin{pmatrix}\text{mass times}\\ \text{centripetal acceleration}\end{pmatrix}$$

Thus, the measured weight is less than the magnitude of the gravitational force on the crate, because of Earth's rotation.

To find a corresponding expression for g and a_g, we cancel m from Eq. 13-13 to write

$$g = a_g - \omega^2 R \qquad (13\text{-}14)$$

which says

$$\begin{pmatrix}\text{free-fall}\\ \text{acceleration}\end{pmatrix} = \begin{pmatrix}\text{gravitational}\\ \text{acceleration}\end{pmatrix} - \begin{pmatrix}\text{centripetal}\\ \text{acceleration}\end{pmatrix}$$

Thus, the measured free-fall acceleration is less than the gravitational acceleration because of Earth's rotation.

The difference between accelerations g and a_g is equal to $\omega^2 R$ and is greatest on the equator (for one reason, the rad0ius of the circle traveled by the crate is

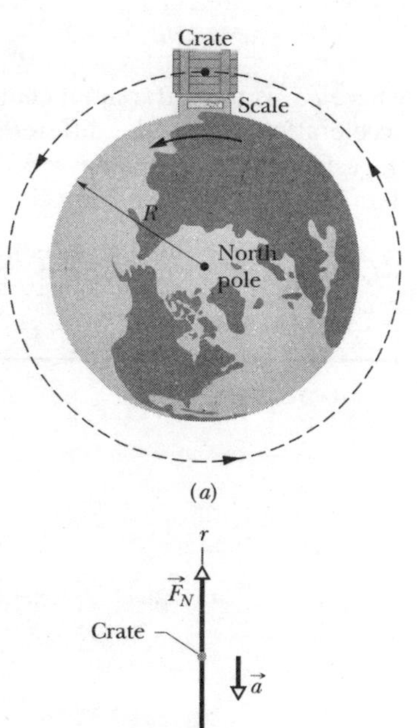

FIG. 13-7 (*a*) A crate sitting on a scale at Earth's equator, as seen by an observer positioned on Earth's rotation axis at some point above the north pole. (*b*) A free-body diagram for the crate, with a radial r axis extending from Earth's center. The gravitational force on the crate is represented with its equivalent $m\vec{a}_g$. The normal force on the crate from the scale is $\vec{F}_N$. Because of Earth's rotation, the crate has a centripetal acceleration $\vec{a}$ that is directed toward Earth's center.

greatest there). To find the difference, we can use Eq. 10-5 ($\omega = \Delta\theta/\Delta t$) and Earth's radius $R = 6.37 \times 10^6$ m. For one rotation of Earth, θ is 2π rad and the time period Δt is about 24 h. Using these values (and converting hours to seconds), we find that g is less than a_g by only about 0.034 m/s^2 (small compared to 9.8 m/s^2). Therefore, neglecting the difference in accelerations g and a_g is often justified. Similarly, neglecting the difference between weight and the magnitude of the gravitational force is also often justified.

Sample Problem 13-3

(a) An astronaut whose height h is 1.70 m floats "feet down" in an orbiting space shuttle at distance $r = 6.77 \times 10^6$ m away from the center of Earth. What is the difference between the gravitational acceleration at her feet and at her head?

Conceptualize: We can approximate Earth as a uniform sphere of mass M_E. Then, from Eq. 13-11, the gravitational acceleration at any distance r from the center of Earth is

$$a_g = \frac{GM_E}{r^2} \tag{13-15}$$

Classify: We might simply apply this equation twice, first with $r = 6.77 \times 10^6$ m for the feet and then with $r = 6.77 \times 10^6$ m + 1.70 m for the head. However, a calculator may give us the same value for a_g twice, and thus a difference of zero, because h is so much smaller than r. Here's a more promising approach: Because we have a differential change dr in r between the astronaut's feet and head, we should differentiate Eq. 13-15 with respect to r.

Compute: The differentiation gives us

$$da_g = -2\frac{GM_E}{r^3}\,dr \tag{13-16}$$

where da_g is the differential change in the gravitational acceleration due to the differential change dr in r. For the astronaut, $dr = h$ and $r = 6.77 \times 10^6$ m. Substituting data into Eq. 13-16, we find

$$da_g = -2\frac{(6.77 \times 10^{-11}\ \text{m}^3/\text{kg}\cdot\text{s}^2)(5.98 \times 10^{24}\ \text{kg})}{(6.77 \times 10^6\ \text{m})^3}(1.70\ \text{m})$$

$$= -4.37 \times 10^{-6}\ \text{m/s}^2 \qquad \text{(Answer)}$$

where the M_E value is taken from Appendix C. This result means that the gravitational acceleration of the astronaut's feet toward Earth is slightly greater than the gravitational acceleration of her head toward Earth. This difference in acceleration tends to stretch her body, but the difference is so small that the stretching is unnoticeable.

(b) If the astronaut is now "feet down" at the same orbital radius $r = 6.77 \times 10^6$ m about a black hole of mass $M_h = 1.99 \times 10^{31}$ kg (10 times our Sun's mass), what is the difference between the gravitational acceleration at her feet and at her head? The black hole has a mathematical surface (*event horizon*) of radius $R_h = 2.95 \times 10^4$ m. Nothing, not even light, can escape from that surface or anywhere inside it. Note that the astronaut is well outside the surface (at $r = 229R_h$).

Compute: We again have a differential change dr in r between the astronaut's feet and head, so we can again use Eq. 13-16. However, now we substitute $M_h = 1.99 \times 10^{31}$ kg for M_E. We find

$$da_g = -2\frac{(6.67 \times 10^{-11}\ \text{m}^3/\text{kg}\cdot\text{s}^2)(1.99 \times 10^{31}\ \text{kg})}{(6.77 \times 10^6\ \text{m})^3}(1.70\ \text{m})$$

$$= -14.5\ \text{m/s}^2 \qquad \text{(Answer)}$$

Conclude: This means that the gravitational acceleration of the astronaut's feet toward the black hole is noticeably larger than that of her head. The resulting tendency to stretch her body would be bearable but quite painful. If she drifted closer to the black hole, the stretching tendency would increase drastically.

13-5 | Gravitation Inside Earth

Newton's shell theorem can also be applied to a situation in which a particle is located *inside* a uniform shell, to show the following:

> A uniform shell of matter exerts no *net* gravitational force on a particle located inside it.

Caution: This statement does *not* mean that the gravitational forces on the particle from the various elements of the shell magically disappear. Rather, it means that the *sum* of the force vectors on the particle from all the elements is zero.

If Earth's mass were uniformly distributed, the gravitational force acting on a particle would be a maximum at Earth's surface and would decrease as the particle moved outward, away from the planet. If the particle were to move inward, perhaps down a deep mine shaft, the gravitational force would change for two reasons. (1) It would tend to increase because the particle would be moving closer to the center of Earth. (2) It would tend to decrease because the thickening shell of material lying outside the particle's radial position would not exert any net force on the particle.

For a uniform Earth, the second influence would prevail and the force on the particle would steadily decrease to zero as the particle approached the center of Earth. However, for the real (nonuniform) Earth, the force on the particle actually increases as the particle begins to descend. The force reaches a maximum at a certain depth and then decreases as the particle descends farther.

Sample Problem 13-4

In *Pole to Pole,* an early science fiction story by George Griffith, three explorers attempt to travel by capsule through a naturally formed (and, of course, fictional) tunnel directly from the south pole to the north pole (Fig. 13-8). According to the story, as the capsule approaches Earth's center, the gravitational force on the explorers becomes alarmingly large and then, exactly at the center, it suddenly but only momentarily disappears. Then the capsule travels through the second half of the tunnel, to the north pole.

Check Griffith's description by finding the gravitational force on the capsule of mass m when it reaches a distance r from Earth's center. Assume that Earth is a sphere of uniform density ρ (mass per unit volume).

Conceptualize/Classify: Newton's shell theorem gives us three ideas:

1. When the capsule is at radius r from Earth's center, the portion of Earth that lies outside a sphere of radius r does *not* produce a net gravitational force on the capsule.
2. The portion of Earth that lies inside that sphere *does* produce a net gravitational force on the capsule.
3. We can treat the mass M_{ins} of that inside portion of Earth as being the mass of a particle located at Earth's center.

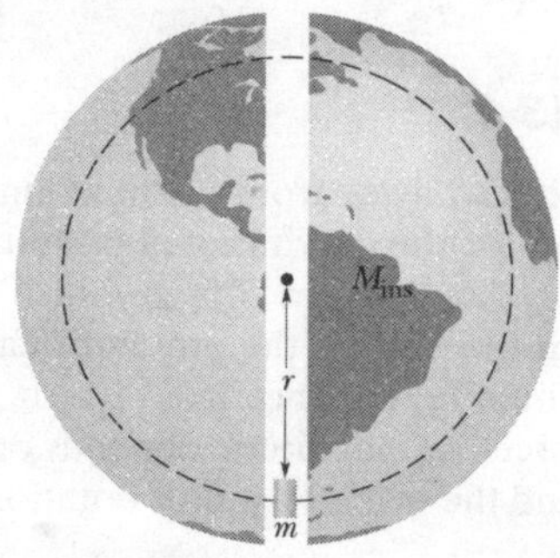

FIG. 13-8 A capsule of mass m falls from rest through a tunnel that connects Earth's south and north poles. When the capsule is at distance r from Earth's center, the portion of Earth's mass that is contained in a sphere of that radius is M_{ins}.

Compute: All three ideas tell us that we can write Eq. 13-1, for the magnitude of the gravitational force on the capsule, as

$$F = \frac{GmM_{ins}}{r^2} \qquad (13\text{-}17)$$

To write the mass M_{ins} in terms of the radius r, we note that the volume V_{ins} containing this mass is $\frac{4}{3}\pi r^3$. Also, because we're assuming an Earth of uniform density, the density $\rho_{ins} = M_{ins}/V_{ins}$ is Earth's density ρ. Thus, we have

$$M_{ins} = \rho V_{ins} = \rho \frac{4\pi r^3}{3} \qquad (13\text{-}18)$$

Then, after substituting this expression into Eq. 13-17 and canceling, we have

$$F = \frac{4\pi Gm\rho}{3} r \quad \text{(Answer)} \qquad (13\text{-}19)$$

This equation tells us that the force magnitude F depends linearly on the capsule's distance r from Earth's center. Thus, as r decreases, F also decreases (opposite of Griffith's description), until it is zero at Earth's center. At least Griffith got the zero-at-the-center detail correct.

Equation 13-19 can also be written in terms of the force vector $\vec{F}$ and the capsule's position vector $\vec{r}$ along a radial axis extending from Earth's center. Let K represent the collection of constants $4\pi Gm\rho/3$. Then, Eq. 13-19 becomes

$$\vec{F} = -K\vec{r} \qquad (13\text{-}20)$$

in which we have inserted a minus sign to indicate that $\vec{F}$ and $\vec{r}$ have opposite directions. Equation 13-20 has the form of Hooke's law (Eq. 7-20, $\vec{F} = -k\vec{d}$).

Conclude: Thus, under the idealized conditions of the story, the capsule would oscillate like a block on a spring, with the center of the oscillation at Earth's center. After the capsule had fallen from the south pole to Earth's center, it would travel from the center to the north pole (as Griffith said) and then back again, repeating the cycle forever.

13-6 | Gravitational Potential Energy

In Section 8-4, we discussed the gravitational potential energy of a particle–Earth system. We were careful to keep the particle near Earth's surface, so that we could regard the gravitational force as constant. We then chose some reference

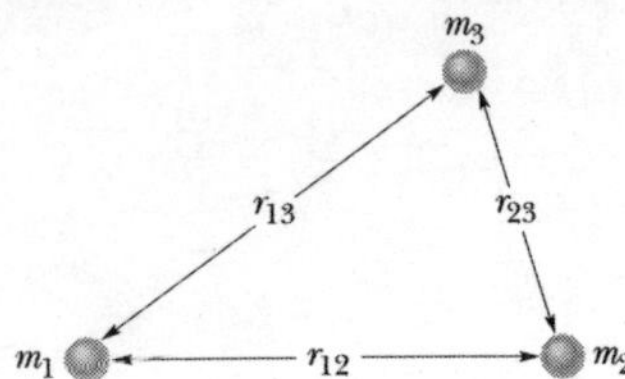

FIG. 13-9 A system consisting of three particles. The gravitational potential energy *of the system* is the sum of the gravitational potential energies of all three pairs of particles.

configuration of the system as having a gravitational potential energy of zero. Often, in this configuration the particle was on Earth's surface. For particles not on Earth's surface, the gravitational potential energy decreased when the separation between the particle and Earth decreased.

Here, we broaden our view and consider the gravitational potential energy U of two particles, of masses m and M, separated by a distance r. We again choose a reference configuration with U equal to zero. However, to simplify the equations, the separation distance r in the reference configuration is now large enough to be approximated as *infinite.* As before, the gravitational potential energy decreases when the separation decreases. Since $U = 0$ for $r = \infty$, the potential energy is negative for any finite separation and becomes progressively more negative as the particles move closer together.

With these facts in mind and as we shall justify next, we take the gravitational potential energy of the two-particle system to be

$$U = -\frac{GMm}{r} \quad \text{(gravitational potential energy)} \tag{13-21}$$

Note that $U(r)$ approaches zero as r approaches infinity and that for any finite value of r, the value of $U(r)$ is negative.

The potential energy given by Eq. 13-21 is a property of the system of two particles rather than of either particle alone. There is no way to divide this energy and say that so much belongs to one particle and so much to the other. However, if $M \gg m$, as is true for Earth (mass M) and a baseball (mass m), we often speak of "the potential energy of the baseball." We can get away with this because, when a baseball moves in the vicinity of Earth, changes in the potential energy of the baseball–Earth system appear almost entirely as changes in the kinetic energy of the baseball, since changes in the kinetic energy of Earth are too small to be measured. Similarly, in Section 13-8 we shall speak of "the potential energy of an artificial satellite" orbiting Earth, because the satellite's mass is so much smaller than Earth's mass. When we speak of the potential energy of bodies of comparable mass, however, we have to be careful to treat them as a system.

If our system contains more than two particles, we consider each pair of particles in turn, calculate the gravitational potential energy of that pair with Eq. 13-21 as if the other particles were not there, and then algebraically sum the results. Applying Eq. 13-21 to each of the three pairs of Fig. 13-9, for example, gives the potential energy of the system as

$$U = -\left(\frac{Gm_1m_2}{r_{12}} + \frac{Gm_1m_3}{r_{13}} + \frac{Gm_2m_3}{r_{23}}\right) \tag{13-22}$$

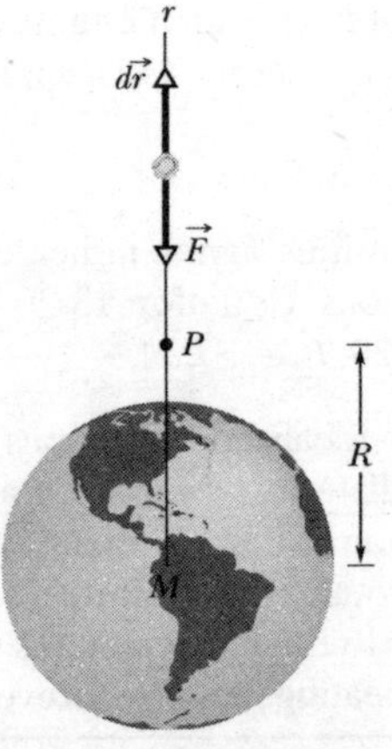

FIG. 13-10 A baseball is shot directly away from Earth, through point P at radial distance R from Earth's center. The gravitational force $\vec{F}$ on the ball and a differential displacement vector $d\vec{r}$ are shown, both directed along a radial r axis.

Proof of Equation 13-21

Let us shoot a baseball directly away from Earth along the path in Fig. 13-10. We want to find an expression for the gravitational potential energy U of the ball at point P along its path, at radial distance R from Earth's center. To do so, we first find the work W done on the ball by the gravitational force as the ball travels from point P to a great (infinite) distance from Earth. Because the gravitational force $\vec{F}(r)$ is a variable force (its magnitude depends on r), we must use the techniques of Section 7-8 to find the work. In vector notation, we can write

$$W = \int_R^\infty \vec{F}(r) \cdot d\vec{r} \tag{13-23}$$

The integral contains the scalar (or dot) product of the force $\vec{F}(r)$ and the differential displacement vector $d\vec{r}$ along the ball's path. We can expand that product as

$$\vec{F}(r) \cdot d\vec{r} = F(r)\, dr \cos\phi \tag{13-24}$$

where ϕ is the angle between the directions of $\vec{F}(r)$ and $d\vec{r}$. When we substitute

180° for ϕ and Eq. 13-1 for $F(r)$, Eq. 13-24 becomes

$$\vec{F}(r)\cdot d\vec{r} = -\frac{GMm}{r^2}\,dr$$

where M is Earth's mass and m is the mass of the ball.

Substituting this into Eq. 13-23 and integrating give us

$$W = -GMm\int_R^\infty \frac{1}{r^2}\,dr = \left[\frac{GMm}{r}\right]_R^\infty$$

$$= 0 - \frac{GMm}{R} = -\frac{GMm}{R} \qquad (13\text{-}25)$$

where W is the work required to move the ball from point P (at distance R) to infinity. Equation 8-1 ($\Delta U = -W$) tells us that we can also write that work in terms of potential energies as

$$U_\infty - U = -W$$

Because the potential energy U_∞ at infinity is zero, U is the potential energy at P, and W is given by Eq. 13-25, this equation becomes

$$U = W = -\frac{GMm}{R}$$

Switching R to r gives us Eq. 13-21, which we set out to prove.

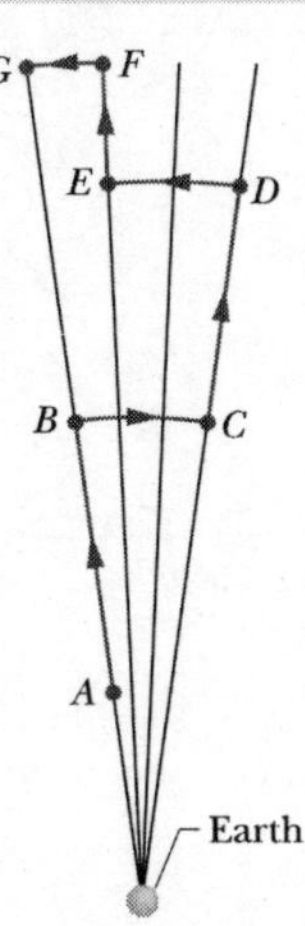

FIG. 13-11 Near Earth, a baseball is moved from point A to point G along a path consisting of radial lengths and circular arcs.

Path Independence

In Fig. 13-11, we move a baseball from point A to point G along a path consisting of three radial lengths and three circular arcs (centered on Earth). We are interested in the total work W done by Earth's gravitational force $\vec{F}$ on the ball as it moves from A to G. The work done along each circular arc is zero, because the direction of $\vec{F}$ is perpendicular to the arc at every point. Thus, W is the sum of only the works done by $\vec{F}$ along the three radial lengths.

Now, suppose we mentally shrink the arcs to zero. We would then be moving the ball directly from A to G along a single radial length. Does that change W? No. Because no work was done along the arcs, eliminating them does not change the work. The path taken from A to G now is clearly different, but the work done by $\vec{F}$ is the same.

We discussed such a result in a general way in Section 8-3. Here is the point: The gravitational force is a conservative force. Thus, the work done by the gravitational force on a particle moving from an initial point i to a final point f is independent of the path taken between the points. From Eq. 8-1, the change ΔU in the gravitational potential energy from point i to point f is given by

$$\Delta U = U_f - U_i = -W \qquad (13\text{-}26)$$

Since the work W done by a conservative force is independent of the actual path taken, the change ΔU in gravitational potential energy is *also independent* of the path taken.

Potential Energy and Force

In the proof of Eq. 13-21, we derived the potential energy function $U(r)$ from the force function $\vec{F}(r)$. We should be able to go the other way—that is, to start from the potential energy function and derive the force function. Guided by Eq. 8-22 ($F(x) = -dU(x)/dx$), we can write

$$F = -\frac{dU}{dr} = -\frac{d}{dr}\left(-\frac{GMm}{r}\right)$$

$$= -\frac{GMm}{r^2} \qquad (13\text{-}27)$$

This is Newton's law of gravitation (Eq. 13-1). The minus sign indicates that the force on mass m points radially inward, toward mass M.

Escape Speed

If you fire a projectile upward, usually it will slow, stop momentarily, and return to Earth. There is, however, a certain minimum initial speed that will cause it to move upward forever, theoretically coming to rest only at infinity. This minimum initial speed is called the (Earth) **escape speed.**

Consider a projectile of mass m, leaving the surface of a planet (or some other astronomical body or system) with escape speed v. The projectile has a kinetic energy K given by $\frac{1}{2}mv^2$ and a potential energy U given by Eq. 13-21:

$$U = -\frac{GMm}{R}$$

in which M is the mass of the planet and R is its radius.

When the projectile reaches infinity, it stops and thus has no kinetic energy. It also has no potential energy because an infinite separation between two bodies is our zero-potential-energy configuration. Its total energy at infinity is therefore zero. From the principle of conservation of energy, its total energy at the planet's surface must also have been zero, and so

$$K + U = \tfrac{1}{2}mv^2 + \left(-\frac{GMm}{R}\right) = 0$$

This yields

$$v = \sqrt{\frac{2GM}{R}} \tag{13-28}$$

Note that v does not depend on the direction in which a projectile is fired from a planet. However, attaining that speed is easier if the projectile is fired in the direction the launch site is moving as the planet rotates about its axis. For example, rockets are launched eastward at Cape Canaveral to take advantage of the Cape's eastward speed of 1500 km/h due to Earth's rotation.

Equation 13-28 can be applied to find the escape speed of a projectile from any astronomical body, provided we substitute the mass of the body for M and the radius of the body for R. Table 13-2 shows some escape speeds.

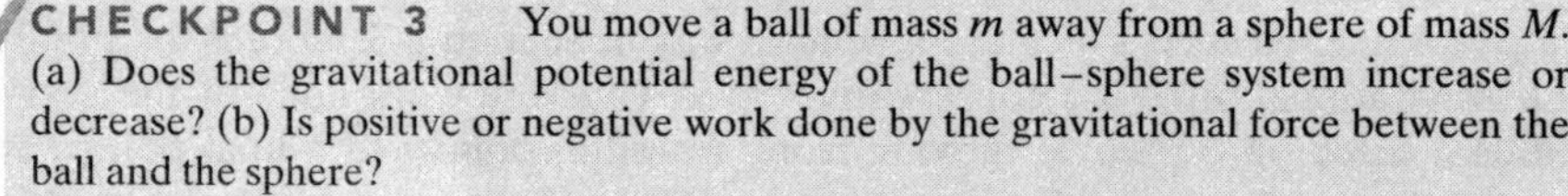

CHECKPOINT 3 You move a ball of mass m away from a sphere of mass M. (a) Does the gravitational potential energy of the ball–sphere system increase or decrease? (b) Is positive or negative work done by the gravitational force between the ball and the sphere?

TABLE 13-2

Some Escape Speeds

Body	Mass (kg)	Radius (m)	Escape Speed (km/s)
Ceres[a]	1.17×10^{21}	3.8×10^5	0.64
Earth's moon[a]	7.36×10^{22}	1.74×10^6	2.38
Earth	5.98×10^{24}	6.37×10^6	11.2
Jupiter	1.90×10^{27}	7.15×10^7	59.5
Sun	1.99×10^{30}	6.96×10^8	618
Sirius B[b]	2×10^{30}	1×10^7	5200
Neutron star[c]	2×10^{30}	1×10^4	2×10^5

[a]The most massive of the asteroids.

[b]A *white dwarf* (a star in a final stage of evolution) that is a companion of the bright star Sirius.

[c]The collapsed core of a star that remains after that star has exploded in a *supernova* event.

Sample Problem 13-5

An asteroid, headed directly toward Earth, has a speed of 12 km/s relative to the planet when the asteroid is 10 Earth radii from Earth's center. Neglecting the effects of Earth's atmosphere on the asteroid, find the asteroid's speed v_f when it reaches Earth's surface.

Conceptualize/Classify: Because we are to neglect the effects of the atmosphere on the asteroid, the mechanical energy of the asteroid–Earth system is conserved during the fall. Thus, the final mechanical energy (when the asteroid reaches Earth's surface) is equal to the initial mechanical energy. With kinetic energy K and gravitational potential energy U, we can write this as

$$K_f + U_f = K_i + U_i \qquad (13\text{-}29)$$

Also, if we assume the system is isolated, the system's linear momentum must be conserved during the fall. Therefore, the momentum change of the asteroid and that of Earth must be equal in magnitude and opposite in sign. However, because Earth's mass is so much greater than the asteroid's mass, the change in Earth's speed is negligible relative to the change in the asteroid's speed. So, the change in Earth's kinetic energy is also negligible. Thus, we can assume that the kinetic energies in Eq. 13-29 are those of the asteroid alone.

Compute: Let m represent the asteroid's mass and M represent Earth's mass (5.98×10^{24} kg). The asteroid is initially at distance $10R_E$ and finally at distance R_E, where R_E is Earth's radius (6.37×10^6 m). Substituting Eq. 13-21 for U and $\frac{1}{2}mv^2$ for K, we rewrite Eq. 13-29 as

$$\tfrac{1}{2}mv_f^2 - \frac{GMm}{R_E} = \tfrac{1}{2}mv_i^2 - \frac{GMm}{10R_E}.$$

Rearranging and substituting known values, we find

$$\begin{aligned} v_f^2 &= v_i^2 + \frac{2GM}{R_E}\left(1 - \frac{1}{10}\right) \\ &= (12 \times 10^3 \text{ m/s})^2 \\ &\quad + \frac{2(6.67 \times 10^{-11} \text{ m}^3/\text{kg}\cdot\text{s}^2)(5.98 \times 10^{24} \text{ kg})}{6.37 \times 10^6 \text{ m}} 0.9 \\ &= 2.567 \times 10^8 \text{ m}^2/\text{s}^2 \end{aligned}$$

and

$$v_f = 1.60 \times 10^4 \text{ m/s} = 16 \text{ km/s} \qquad \text{(Answer)}$$

Conclude: At this speed, the asteroid would not have to be particularly large to do considerable damage at impact. If it were only 5 m across, the impact could release about as much energy as the nuclear explosion at Hiroshima. Alarmingly, about 500 million asteroids of this size are near Earth's orbit, and in 1994 one of them apparently penetrated Earth's atmosphere and exploded 20 km above the South Pacific (setting off nuclear-explosion warnings on six military satellites). The impact of an asteroid 500 m across (there may be a million of them near Earth's orbit) could end modern civilization and almost eliminate humans worldwide.

13-7 | Planets and Satellites: Kepler's Laws

The motions of the planets, as they seemingly wander against the background of the stars, have been a puzzle since the dawn of history. The "loop-the-loop" motion of Mars, shown in Fig. 13-12, was particularly baffling. Johannes Kepler (1571–1630), after a lifetime of study, worked out the empirical laws that govern these motions. Tycho Brahe (1546–1601), the last of the great astronomers to make observations without the help of a telescope, compiled the extensive data from which Kepler was able to derive the three laws of planetary motion that now bear Kepler's name. Later, Newton (1642–1727) showed that his law of gravitation leads to Kepler's laws.

FIG. 13-12 The path seen from Earth for the planet Mars as it moved against a background of the constellation Capricorn during 1971. The planet's position on four days is marked. Both Mars and Earth are moving in orbits around the Sun so that we see the position of Mars relative to us; this relative motion sometimes results in an apparent loop in the path of Mars.

In this section we discuss each of Kepler's three laws. Although here we apply the laws to planets orbiting the Sun, they hold equally well for satellites, either natural or artificial, orbiting Earth or any other massive central body.

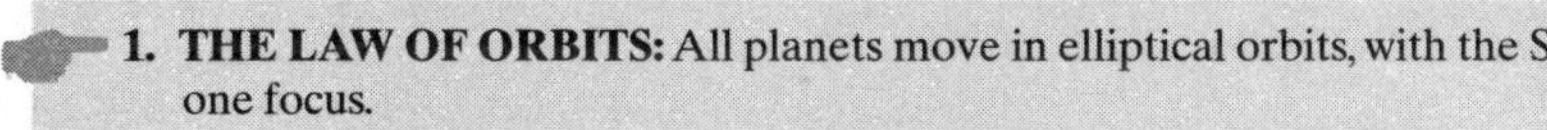

1. THE LAW OF ORBITS: All planets move in elliptical orbits, with the Sun at one focus.

Figure 13-13 shows a planet of mass m moving in such an orbit around the Sun, whose mass is M. We assume that $M \gg m$, so that the center of mass of the planet–Sun system is approximately at the center of the Sun.

The orbit in Fig. 13-13 is described by giving its **semimajor axis** a and its **eccentricity** e, the latter defined so that ea is the distance from the center of the ellipse to either focus F or F'. *An eccentricity of zero corresponds to a circle,* in

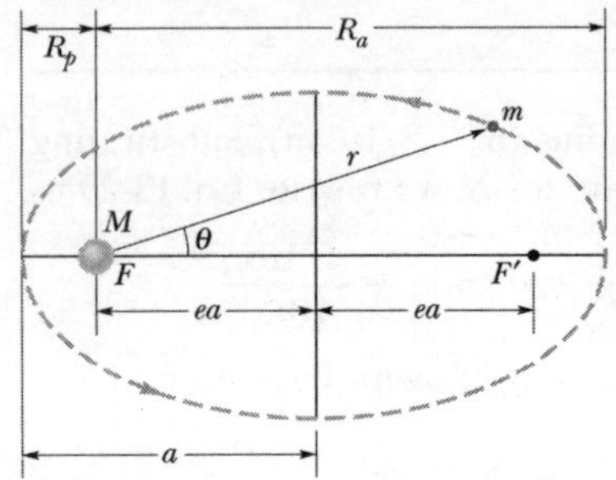

FIG. 13-13 A planet of mass m moving in an elliptical orbit around the Sun. The Sun, of mass M, is at one focus F of the ellipse. The other focus is F', which is located in empty space. Each focus is a distance ea from the ellipse's center, with e being the eccentricity of the ellipse. The semimajor axis a of the ellipse, the perihelion (nearest the Sun) distance R_p, and the aphelion (farthest from the Sun) distance R_a are also shown.

which the two foci merge to a single central point. The eccentricities of the planetary orbits are not large; so if the orbits are drawn to scale, they look circular. The eccentricity of the ellipse of Fig. 13-13, which has been exaggerated for clarity, is 0.74. The eccentricity of Earth's orbit is only 0.0167.

2. THE LAW OF AREAS: A line that connects a planet to the Sun sweeps out equal areas in the plane of the planet's orbit in equal time intervals; that is, the rate dA/dt at which it sweeps out area A is constant.

Qualitatively, this second law tells us that the planet will move most slowly when it is farthest from the Sun and most rapidly when it is nearest to the Sun. As it turns out, Kepler's second law is totally equivalent to the law of conservation of angular momentum. Let us prove it.

The area of the shaded wedge in Fig. 13-14*a* closely approximates the area swept out in time Δt by a line connecting the Sun and the planet, which are separated by distance r. The area ΔA of the wedge is approximately the area of a triangle with base $r\Delta\theta$ and height r. Since the area of a triangle is one-half of the base times the height, $\Delta A \approx \frac{1}{2}r^2\,\Delta\theta$. This expression for ΔA becomes more exact as Δt (hence $\Delta\theta$) approaches zero. The instantaneous rate at which area is being swept out is then

$$\frac{dA}{dt} = \tfrac{1}{2}r^2\frac{d\theta}{dt} = \tfrac{1}{2}r^2\omega \qquad (13\text{-}30)$$

in which ω is the angular speed of the rotating line connecting Sun and planet.

Figure 13-14*b* shows the linear momentum $\vec{p}$ of the planet, along with the radial and perpendicular components of $\vec{p}$. From Eq. 11-20 ($L = rp_\perp$), the magnitude of the angular momentum $\vec{L}$ of the planet about the Sun is given by the product of r and $p_\perp$, the component of $\vec{p}$ perpendicular to r. Here, for a planet of mass m,

$$L = rp_\perp = (r)(mv_\perp) = (r)(m\omega r)$$
$$= mr^2\omega \qquad (13\text{-}31)$$

where we have replaced $v_\perp$ with its equivalent ωr (Eq. 10-18). Eliminating $r^2\omega$ between Eqs. 13-30 and 13-31 leads to

$$\frac{dA}{dt} = \frac{L}{2m}. \qquad (13\text{-}32)$$

3. THE LAW OF PERIODS: The square of the period of any planet is proportional to the cube of the semimajor axis of its orbit.

If dA/dt is constant, as Kepler said it is, then Eq. 13-32 means that L must also be constant—angular momentum is conserved. Kepler's second law is indeed

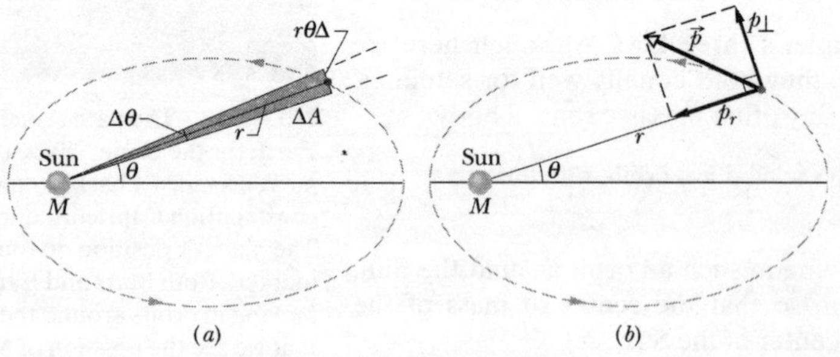

FIG. 13-14 (*a*) In time Δt, the line r connecting the planet to the Sun moves through an angle $\Delta\theta$, sweeping out an area ΔA (shaded). (*b*) The linear momentum $\vec{p}$ of the planet and the components of $\vec{p}$.

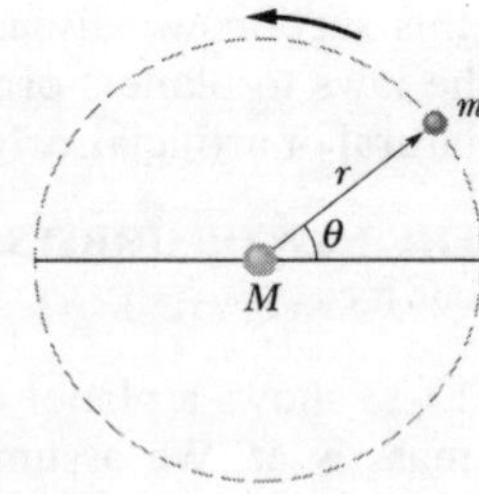

FIG. 13-15 A planet of mass m moving around the Sun in a circular orbit of radius r.

equivalent to the law of conservation of angular momentum.

To see this, consider the circular orbit of Fig. 13-15, with radius r (the radius of a circle is equivalent to the semimajor axis of an ellipse). Applying Newton's second law ($F = ma$) to the orbiting planet in Fig. 13-15 yields

$$\frac{GMm}{r^2} = (m)(\omega^2 r) \quad (13\text{-}33)$$

Here we have substituted from Eq. 13-1 for the force magnitude F and used Eq. 10-23 to substitute $\omega^2 r$ for the centripetal acceleration. If we now use Eq. 10-20 to replace ω with $2\pi/T$, where T is the period of the motion, we obtain Kepler's third law:

$$T^2 = \left(\frac{4\pi^2}{GM}\right) r^3 \quad \text{(law of periods)} \quad (13\text{-}34)$$

The quantity in parentheses is a constant that depends only on the mass M of the central body about which the planet orbits.

TABLE 13-3

Kepler's Law of Periods for the Solar System

Planet	Semimajor Axis a (10^{10} m)	Period T (y)	T^2/a^3 (10^{-34} y^2/m^3)
Mercury	5.79	0.241	2.99
Venus	10.8	0.615	3.00
Earth	15.0	1.00	2.96
Mars	22.8	1.88	2.98
Jupiter	77.8	11.9	3.01
Saturn	143	29.5	2.98
Uranus	287	84.0	2.98
Neptune	450	165	2.99
Pluto	590	248	2.99

CHECKPOINT 4 Satellite 1 is in a certain circular orbit around a planet, while satellite 2 is in a larger circular orbit. Which satellite has (a) the longer period and (b) the greater speed?

Sample Problem 13-6

Comet Halley orbits the Sun with a period of 76 years and, in 1986, had a distance of closest approach to the Sun, its *perihelion distance* R_p, of 8.9×10^{10} m. Table 13-3 shows that this is between the orbits of Mercury and Venus.

(a) What is the comet's farthest distance from the Sun, which is called its *aphelion distance* R_a?

Conceptualize/Classify: From Fig. 13-13, we see that $R_a + R_p = 2a$, where a is the semimajor axis of the orbit. Thus, we can find R_a if we first find a. We can relate a to the given period via the law of periods (Eq. 13-34) if we simply substitute the semimajor axis a for r.

Compute: Making that substitution and then solving for a, we have

$$a = \left(\frac{GMT^2}{4\pi^2}\right)^{1/3} \quad (13\text{-}35)$$

If we substitute the mass M of the Sun, 1.99×10^{30} kg, and the period T of the comet, 76 years or 2.4×10^9 s, into Eq. 13-35, we find that $a = 2.7 \times 10^{12}$ m. Now we have

$$\begin{aligned} R_a &= 2a - R_p \\ &= (2)(2.7 \times 10^{12}\text{ m}) - 8.9 \times 10^{10}\text{ m} \\ &= 5.3 \times 10^{12}\text{ m} \qquad \text{(Answer)} \end{aligned}$$

Table 13-3 shows that this is a little less than the semimajor axis of the orbit of Pluto. Thus, the comet does not get farther from the Sun than Pluto.

(b) What is the eccentricity e of the orbit of comet Halley?

Conceptualize/Classify: We can relate e, a, and R_p via Fig. 13-13, in which we see that $ea = a - R_p$.

Compute: We have

$$\begin{aligned} e &= \frac{a - R_p}{a} = 1 - \frac{R_p}{a} \\ &= 1 - \frac{8.9 \times 10^{10}\text{ m}}{2.7 \times 10^{12}\text{ m}} = 0.97 \qquad \text{(Answer)} \end{aligned}$$

Conclude: This tells us that, with an eccentricity approaching unity, this orbit must be a long thin ellipse.

Sample Problem 13-7

Let's return to the story that opens this chapter. Figure 13-16 shows the observed orbit of the star S2 as the star moves around a mysterious and unobserved object called Sagittarius A* (pronounced "A star"), which is at the center of the Milky Way galaxy. S2 orbits Sagittarius A* with a period of $T = 15.2$ y and with a semimajor axis of $a = 5.50$ light-days ($= 1.42 \times 10^{14}$ m). What is the mass M of Sagittarius A*? What is Sagittarius A*?

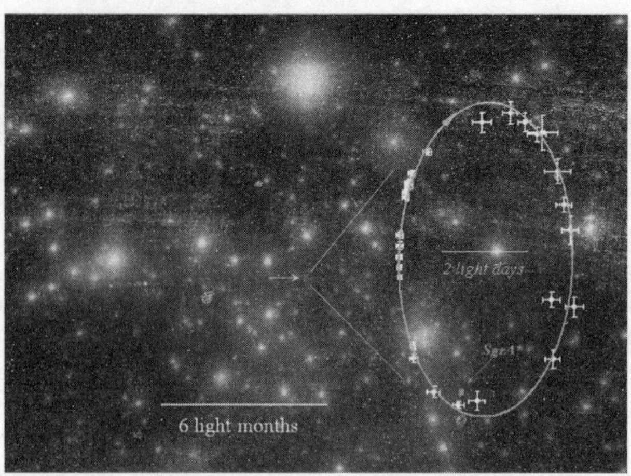

FIG. 13-16 The orbit of star S2 about Sagittarius A* (Sgr A*). The elliptical orbit appears skewed because we do not see it from directly above the orbital plane. Uncertainties in the location of S2 are indicated by the crossbars. *(Courtesy Reinhard Genzel)*

Conceptualize/Classify: The period T and the semimajor axis a of the orbit are related to the mass M of Sagittarius A* according to Kepler's law of periods. From Eq. 13-34, with a replacing the radius r of a circular orbit, we have

$$T^2 = \left(\frac{4\pi^2}{GM}\right)a^3 \quad (13\text{-}36)$$

Compute: Solving Eq. 13-36 for M and substituting the given data lead us to

$$M = \frac{4\pi^2 a^3}{GT^2}$$

$$= \frac{4\pi^2(1.42 \times 10^{14}\text{ m})^3}{(6.67 \times 10^{-11}\text{ N}\cdot\text{m}^2/\text{kg}^2)[(15.2\text{ y})(3.16 \times 10^7\text{ s/y})]^2}$$

$$= 7.35 \times 10^{36}\text{ kg} \quad \text{(Answer)}$$

To figure out what Sagittarius A* might be, let's divide this mass by the mass of our Sun ($M_{\text{Sun}} = 1.99 \times 10^{30}$ kg) to find that

$$M = (3.7 \times 10^6)M_{\text{Sun}}$$

Conclude: Sagittarius A* has a mass of 3.7 million Suns! However, it cannot be seen. Thus, it is an extremely compact object. Such a huge mass in such a small object leads to the reasonable conclusion that this object is a *supermassive* black hole. In fact, evidence is mounting that a supermassive black hole lurks at the center of most galaxies. (Movies of the stars orbiting Sagittarius A* are available on the Web; search under "black hole galactic center.")

Equation 13-34 holds also for elliptical orbits, provided we replace r with a, the semimajor axis of the ellipse. This law predicts that the ratio T^2/a^3 has essentially the same value for every planetary orbit around a given massive body. Table 13-3 shows how well it holds for the orbits of the planets of the solar system.

13-8 | Satellites: Orbits and Energy

As a satellite orbits Earth in an elliptical path, both its speed, which fixes its kinetic energy K, and its distance from the center of Earth, which fixes its gravitational potential energy U, fluctuate with fixed periods. However, the mechanical energy E of the satellite remains constant. (Since the satellite's mass is so much smaller than Earth's mass, we assign U and E for the Earth–satellite system to the satellite alone.)

The potential energy of the system is given by Eq. 13-21:

$$U = -\frac{GMm}{r}$$

(with $U = 0$ for infinite separation). Here r is the radius of the satellite's orbit, assumed for the time being to be circular, and M and m are the masses of Earth and the satellite, respectively.

To find the kinetic energy of a satellite in a circular orbit, we write Newton's second law ($F = ma$) as

$$\frac{GMm}{r^2} = m\frac{v^2}{r} \quad (13\text{-}37)$$

where v^2/r is the centripetal acceleration of the satellite. Then, from Eq. 13-37, the kinetic energy is

$$K = \tfrac{1}{2}mv^2 = \frac{GMm}{2r} \tag{13-38}$$

which shows us that for a satellite in a circular orbit,

$$K = -\frac{U}{2} \quad \text{(circular orbit)} \tag{13-39}$$

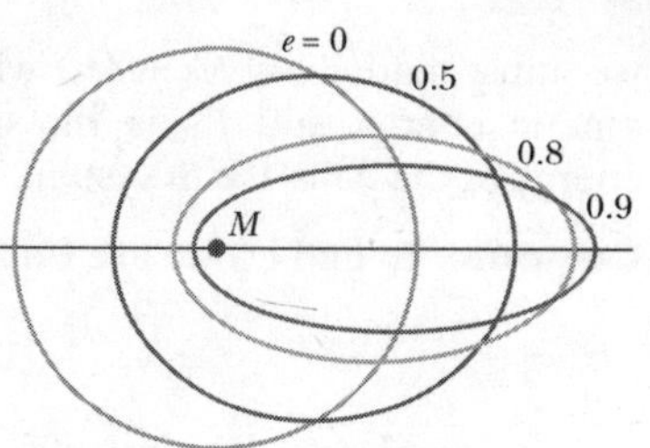

FIG. 13-17 Four orbits with different eccentricities e about an object of mass M. All four orbits have the same semimajor axis a and thus correspond to the same total mechanical energy E.

The total mechanical energy of the orbiting satellite is

$$E = K + U = \frac{GMm}{2r} - \frac{GMm}{r}$$

or

$$E = -\frac{GMm}{2r} \quad \text{(circular orbit)} \tag{13-40}$$

This tells us that for a satellite in a circular orbit, the total energy E is the negative of the kinetic energy K:

$$E = -K \quad \text{(circular orbit)} \tag{13-41}$$

For a satellite in an elliptical orbit of semimajor axis a, we can substitute a for r in Eq. 13-40 to find the mechanical energy:

$$E = -\frac{GMm}{2a} \quad \text{(elliptical orbit)} \tag{13-42}$$

Equation 13-42 tells us that the total energy of an orbiting satellite depends only on the semimajor axis of its orbit and not on its eccentricity e. For example,

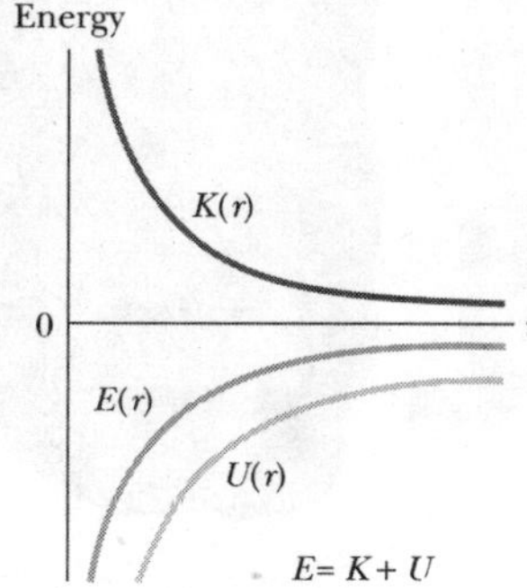

FIG. 13-18 The variation of kinetic energy K, potential energy U, and total energy E with radius r for a satellite in a circular orbit. For any value of r, the values of U and E are negative, the value of K is positive, and $E = -K$. As $r \to \infty$, all three energy curves approach a value of zero.

CHECKPOINT 5 In the figure here, a space shuttle is initially in a circular orbit of radius r about Earth. At point P, the pilot briefly fires a forward-pointing thruster to decrease the shuttle's kinetic energy K and mechanical energy E. (a) Which of the dashed elliptical orbits shown in the figure will the shuttle then take? (b) Is the orbital period T of the shuttle (the time to return to P) then greater than, less than, or the same as in the circular orbit?

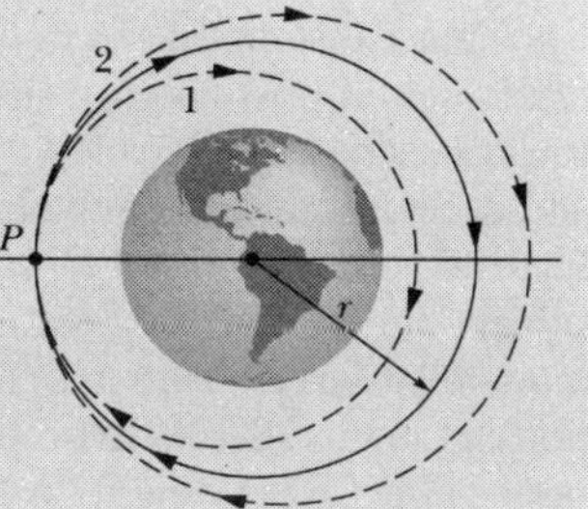

Sample Problem 13-8

A playful astronaut releases a bowling ball, of mass $m = 7.20$ kg, into circular orbit about Earth at an altitude h of 350 km.

(a) What is the mechanical energy E of the ball in its orbit?

Conceptualize/Classify: We can get E from the orbital energy, given by Eq. 13-40 ($E = -GMm/2r$), if we first find the orbital radius r.

Compute: The orbital radius must be

$$r = R + h = 6370 \text{ km} + 350 \text{ km} = 6.72 \times 10^6 \text{ m}$$

in which R is the radius of Earth. Then, from Eq. 13-40, the mechanical energy is

$$E = -\frac{GMm}{2r}$$

$$= -\frac{(6.67 \times 10^{-11} \text{ N}\cdot\text{m}^2/\text{kg}^2)(5.98 \times 10^{24} \text{ kg})(7.20 \text{ kg})}{(2)(6.72 \times 10^6 \text{ m})}$$

$$= -2.14 \times 10^8 \text{ J} = -214 \text{ MJ} \qquad \text{(Answer)}$$

(b) What is the mechanical energy E_0 of the ball on the launchpad at Cape Canaveral? From there to the orbit, what is the change ΔE in the ball's mechanical energy?

Conceptualize/Classify: On the launchpad, the ball is *not* in orbit and thus Eq. 13-40 does *not* apply. Instead, we must find $E_0 = K_0 + U_0$, where K_0 is the ball's kinetic energy and U_0 is the gravitational potential energy of the ball–Earth system.

Compute: To find U_0, we use Eq. 13-21 to write

$$U_0 = -\frac{GMm}{R}$$
$$= -\frac{(6.67 \times 10^{-11}\ \text{N}\cdot\text{m}^2/\text{kg}^2)(5.98 \times 10^{24}\ \text{kg})(7.20\ \text{kg})}{6.37 \times 10^6\ \text{m}}$$
$$= -4.51 \times 10^8\ \text{J} = -451\ \text{MJ}$$

The kinetic energy K_0 of the ball is due to the ball's motion with Earth's rotation. You can show that K_0 is less than 1 MJ, which is negligible relative to U_0. Thus, the mechanical energy of the ball on the launchpad is

$$E_0 = K_0 + U_0 \approx 0 - 451\ \text{MJ} = -451\ \text{MJ} \quad \text{(Answer)}$$

The *increase* in the mechanical energy of the ball from launchpad to orbit is

$$\Delta E = E - E_0 = (-214\ \text{MJ}) - (-451\ \text{MJ})$$
$$= 237\ \text{MJ} \quad \text{(Answer)}$$

Conclude: This is worth a few dollars at your utility company. Obviously the high cost of placing objects into orbit is not due to their required mechanical energy.

four orbits with the same semimajor axis are shown in Fig. 13-17; the same satellite would have the same total mechanical energy E in all four orbits. Figure 13-18 shows the variation of K, U, and E with r for a satellite moving in a circular orbit about a massive central body.

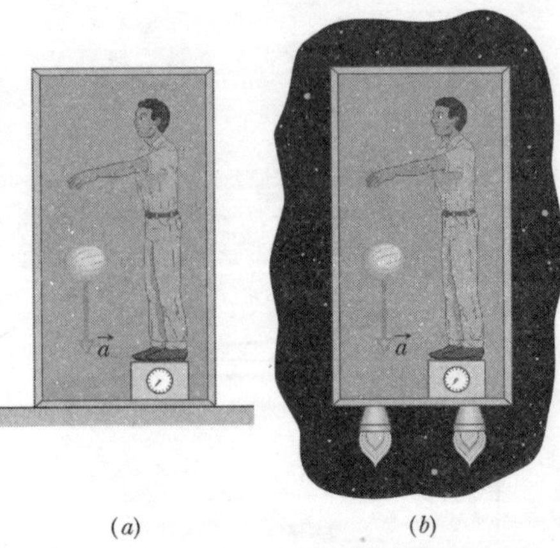

FIG. 13-19 (*a*) A physicist in a box resting on Earth sees a cantaloupe falling with acceleration $a = 9.8\ \text{m/s}^2$. (*b*) If he and the box accelerate in deep space at $9.8\ \text{m/s}^2$, the cantaloupe has the same acceleration relative to him. It is not possible, by doing experiments within the box, for the physicist to tell which situation he is in. For example, the platform scale on which he stands reads the same weight in both situations.

13-9 | Einstein and Gravitation

Principle of Equivalence

Albert Einstein once said: "I was . . . in the patent office at Bern when all of a sudden a thought occurred to me: 'If a person falls freely, he will not feel his own weight.' I was startled. This simple thought made a deep impression on me. It impelled me toward a theory of gravitation."

Thus Einstein tells us how he began to form his **general theory of relativity.** The fundamental postulate of this theory about gravitation (the gravitating of objects toward each other) is called the **principle of equivalence,** which says that gravitation and acceleration are equivalent. If a physicist were locked up in a small box as in Fig. 13-19, he would not be able to tell whether the box was at rest on Earth (and subject only to Earth's gravitational force), as in Fig. 13-19*a*, or accelerating through interstellar space at $9.8\ \text{m/s}^2$ (and subject only to the force producing that acceleration), as in Fig. 13-19*b*. In both situations he would feel the same and would read the same value for his weight on a scale. Moreover, if he watched an object fall past him, the object would have the same acceleration relative to him in both situations.

Curvature of Space

We have thus far explained gravitation as due to a force between masses. Einstein showed that, instead, gravitation is due to a curvature of space that is caused by the masses. (As is discussed later in this book, space and time are entangled, so the curvature of which Einstein spoke is really a curvature of *spacetime,* the combined four dimensions of our universe.)

Picturing how space (such as vacuum) can have curvature is difficult. An analogy might help: Suppose that from orbit we watch a race in which two boats begin on Earth's equator with a separation of 20 km and head due south (Fig. 13-20*a*). To the sailors, the boats travel along flat, parallel paths. However, with time the boats draw together until, nearer the south pole, they touch. The sailors in the boats can interpret this drawing together in terms of a force acting on the boats. Looking on from space, however, we can see that the boats draw together simply because of the curvature of Earth's surface. We can see this because we are viewing the race from "outside" that surface.

Figure 13-20*b* shows a similar race: Two horizontally separated apples are dropped from the same height above Earth. Although the apples may appear to travel along parallel paths, they actually move toward each other because they both

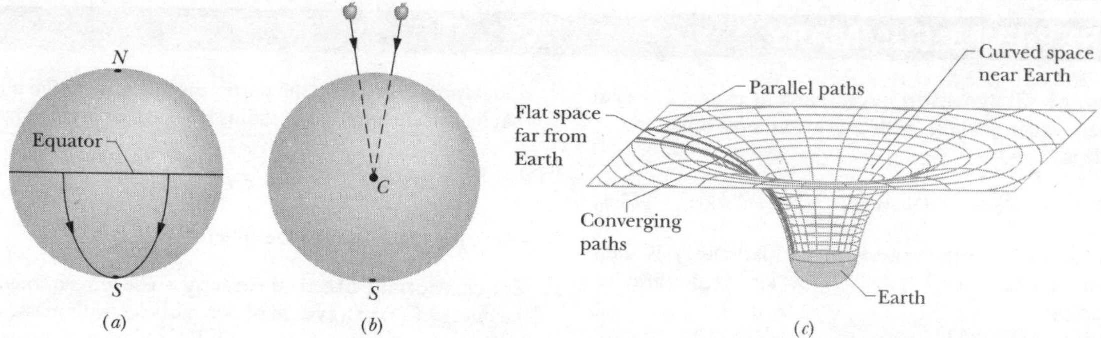

fall toward Earth's center. We can interpret the motion of the apples in terms of the gravitational force on the apples from Earth. We can also interpret the motion in terms of a curvature of the space near Earth, a curvature due to the presence of Earth's mass. This time we cannot see the curvature because we cannot get "outside" the curved space, as we got "outside" the curved Earth in the boat example. However, we can depict the curvature with a drawing like Fig. 13-20*c*; there the apples would move along a surface that curves toward Earth because of Earth's mass.

FIG. 13-20 (*a*) Two objects moving along lines of longitude toward the south pole converge because of the curvature of Earth's surface. (*b*) Two objects falling freely near Earth move along lines that converge toward the center of Earth because of the curvature of space near Earth. (*c*) Far from Earth (and other masses), space is flat and parallel paths remain parallel. Close to Earth, the parallel paths begin to converge because space is curved by Earth's mass.

When light passes near Earth, the path of the light bends slightly because of the curvature of space there, an effect called *gravitational lensing.* When light passes a more massive structure, like a galaxy or a black hole having large mass, its path can be bent more. If such a massive structure is between us and a quasar (an extremely bright, extremely distant source of light), the light from the quasar can bend around the massive structure and toward us (Fig. 13-21*a*). Then, because the light seems to be coming to us from a number of slightly different directions in the sky, we see the same quasar in all those different directions. In some situations, the quasars we see blend together to form a giant luminous arc, which is called an *Einstein ring* (Fig. 13-21*b*).

Should we attribute gravitation to the curvature of spacetime due to the presence of masses or to a force between masses? Or should we attribute it to the actions of a type of fundamental particle called a *graviton,* as conjectured in some modern physics theories? We just don't know.

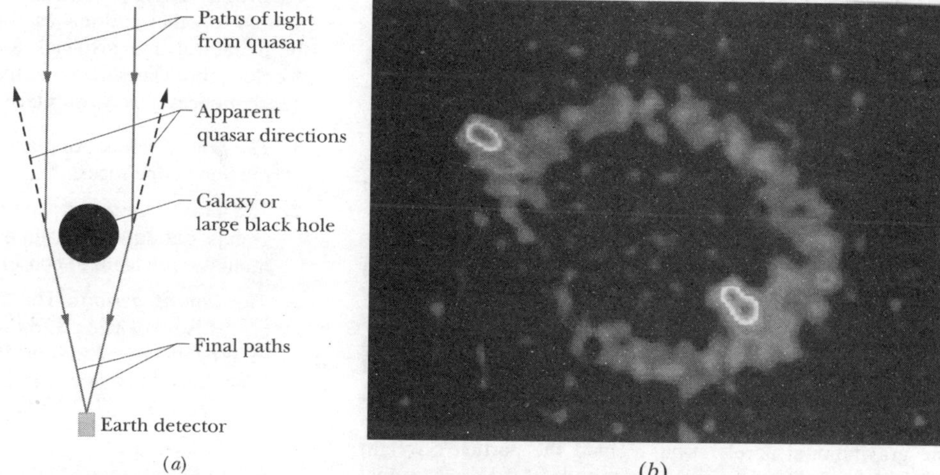

FIG. 13-21 (*a*) Light from a distant quasar follows curved paths around a galaxy or a large black hole because the mass of the galaxy or black hole has curved the adjacent space. If the light is detected, it appears to have originated along the backward extensions of the final paths (dashed lines). (*b*) The Einstein ring known as MG1131+0456 on the computer screen of a telescope. The source of the light (actually, radio waves, which are a form of invisible light) is far behind the large, unseen galaxy that produces the ring; a portion of the source appears as the two bright spots seen along the ring. (*Courtesy National Radio Astronomy Observatory*)

REVIEW & SUMMARY

The Law of Gravitation Any particle in the universe attracts any other particle with a **gravitational force** whose magnitude is

$$F = G\frac{m_1 m_2}{r^2} \quad \text{(Newton's law of gravitation)} \qquad (13\text{-}1)$$

where m_1 and m_2 are the masses of the particles, r is their separation, and G ($= 6.67 \times 10^{-11}\ \text{N}\cdot\text{m}^2/\text{kg}^2$) is the *gravitational constant.*

Gravitational Behavior of Uniform Spherical Shells Equation 13-1 holds only for particles. The gravitational force between extended bodies must generally be found by adding (integrating) the individual forces on individual particles within the bodies. However, if either of the bodies is a uniform spherical shell or a spherically symmetric solid, the net gravitational force it exerts on an *external* object may be computed as if all the mass of the shell or body were located at its center.

Superposition Gravitational forces obey the **principle of superposition;** that is, if n particles interact, the net force $\vec{F}_{1,\text{net}}$ on a particle labeled particle 1 is the sum of the forces on it from all the other particles taken one at a time:

$$\vec{F}_{1,\text{net}} = \sum_{i=2}^{n} \vec{F}_{1i} \qquad (13\text{-}5)$$

in which the sum is a vector sum of the forces $\vec{F}_{1i}$ on particle 1 from particles 2, 3, . . . , n. The gravitational force $\vec{F}_1$ on a particle from an extended body is found by dividing the body into units of differential mass dm, each of which produces a differential force $d\vec{F}$ on the particle, and then integrating to find the sum of those forces:

$$\vec{F}_1 = \int d\vec{F} \qquad (13\text{-}6)$$

Gravitational Acceleration The *gravitational acceleration* a_g of a particle (of mass m) is due solely to the gravitational force acting on it. When the particle is at distance r from the center of a uniform, spherical body of mass M, the magnitude F of the gravitational force on the particle is given by Eq. 13-1. Thus, by Newton's second law,

$$F = ma_g \qquad (13\text{-}10)$$

which gives

$$a_g = \frac{GM}{r^2} \qquad (13\text{-}11)$$

Free-Fall Acceleration and Weight Because Earth's mass is not distributed uniformly, because the planet is not perfectly spherical, and because it rotates, the actual free-fall acceleration $\vec{g}$ of a particle near Earth differs slightly from the gravitational acceleration $\vec{a}_g$, and the particle's weight (equal to mg) differs from the magnitude of the gravitational force acting on the particle as computed with Eq. 13-1.

Gravitation Within a Spherical Shell A uniform shell of matter exerts no net gravitational force on a particle located inside it. This means that if a particle is located inside a uniform solid sphere at distance r from its center, the gravitational force exerted on the particle is due only to the mass M_{ins} that lies inside a sphere of radius r. This mass is given by

$$M_{\text{ins}} = \rho\frac{4\pi r^3}{3} \qquad (13\text{-}18)$$

where ρ is the density of the sphere.

Gravitational Potential Energy The gravitational potential energy $U(r)$ of a system of two particles, with masses M and m and separated by a distance r, is the negative of the work that would be done by the gravitational force of either particle acting on the other if the separation between the particles were changed from infinite (very large) to r. This energy is

$$U = -\frac{GMm}{r} \quad \text{(gravitational potential energy)} \qquad (13\text{-}21)$$

Potential Energy of a System If a system contains more than two particles, its total gravitational potential energy U is the sum of terms representing the potential energies of all the pairs. As an example, for three particles, of masses m_1, m_2, and m_3,

$$U = -\left(\frac{Gm_1m_2}{r_{12}} + \frac{Gm_1m_3}{r_{13}} + \frac{Gm_2m_3}{r_{23}}\right) \qquad (13\text{-}22)$$

Escape Speed An object will escape the gravitational pull of an astronomical body of mass M and radius R (that is, it will reach an infinite distance) if the object's speed near the body's surface is at least equal to the **escape speed,** given by

$$v = \sqrt{\frac{2GM}{R}} \qquad (13\text{-}28)$$

Kepler's Laws Gravitational attraction holds the solar system together and makes possible orbiting Earth satellites, both natural and artificial. Such motions are governed by Kepler's three laws of planetary motion, all of which are direct consequences of Newton's laws of motion and gravitation:

1. ***The law of orbits.*** All planets move in elliptical orbits with the Sun at one focus.
2. ***The law of areas.*** A line joining any planet to the Sun sweeps out equal areas in equal time intervals. (This statement is equivalent to conservation of angular momentum.)
3. ***The law of periods.*** The square of the period T of any planet is proportional to the cube of the semimajor axis a of its orbit. For circular orbits with radius r,

$$T^2 = \left(\frac{4\pi^2}{GM}\right)r^3 \quad \text{(law of periods)} \qquad (13\text{-}34)$$

where M is the mass of the attracting body—the Sun in the case of the solar system. For elliptical planetary orbits, the semimajor axis a is substituted for r.

Energy in Planetary Motion When a planet or satellite with mass m moves in a circular orbit with radius r, its potential energy U and kinetic energy K are given by

$$U = -\frac{GMm}{r} \quad \text{and} \quad K = \frac{GMm}{2r} \qquad (13\text{-}21, 13\text{-}38)$$

The mechanical energy $E = K + U$ is then

$$E = -\frac{GMm}{2r} \qquad (13\text{-}40)$$

For an elliptical orbit of semimajor axis a,

$$E = -\frac{GMm}{2a} \qquad (13\text{-}42)$$

Einstein's View of Gravitation Einstein pointed out that gravitation and acceleration are equivalent. This **principle of equivalence** led him to a theory of gravitation (the **general theory of relativity**) that explains gravitational effects in terms of a curvature of space.

QUESTIONS

1 In Fig. 13-22, a central particle is surrounded by two circular rings of particles, at radii r and R, with $R > r$. All the particles have mass m. What are the magnitude and direction of the net gravitational force on the central particle due to the particles in the rings?

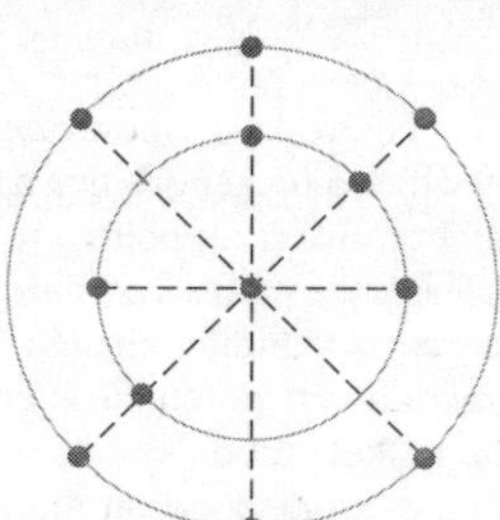

FIG. 13-22 Question 1.

2 In Fig. 13-23, two particles, of masses m and $2m$, are fixed in place on an axis. (a) Where on the axis can a third particle of mass $3m$ be placed (other than at infinity) so that the net gravitational force on it from the first two particles is zero: to the left of the first two particles, to their right, between them but closer to the more massive particle, or between them but closer to the less massive particle? (b) Does the answer change if the third particle has, instead, a mass of $16m$? (c) Is there a point off the axis (other than infinity) at which the net force on the third particle would be zero?

FIG. 13-23 Question 2.

3 Figure 13-24 shows three situations involving a point particle P with mass m and a spherical shell with a uniformly distributed mass M. The radii of the shells are given. Rank the situations according to the magnitude of the gravitational force on particle P due to the shell, greatest first.

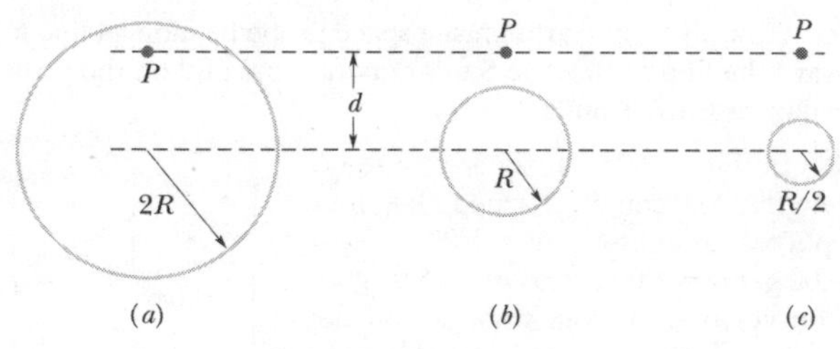

FIG. 13-24 Question 3.

4 Figure 13-25 shows three arrangements of the same identical particles, with three of them placed on a circle of radius 0.20 m and the fourth one placed at the center of the circle. (a) Rank the arrangements according to the magnitude of the net gravitational force on the central particle due to the other three particles, greatest first. (b) Rank them according to the gravitational potential energy of the four-particle system, least negative first.

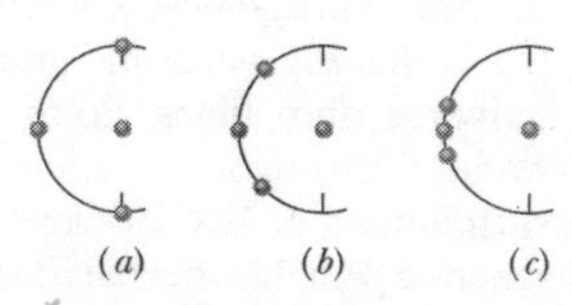

FIG. 13-25 Question 4.

5 In Fig. 13-26, a central particle of mass M is surrounded by a square array of other particles, separated by either distance d or distance $d/2$ along the perimeter of the square. What are the magnitude and direction of the net gravitational force on the central particle due to the other particles?

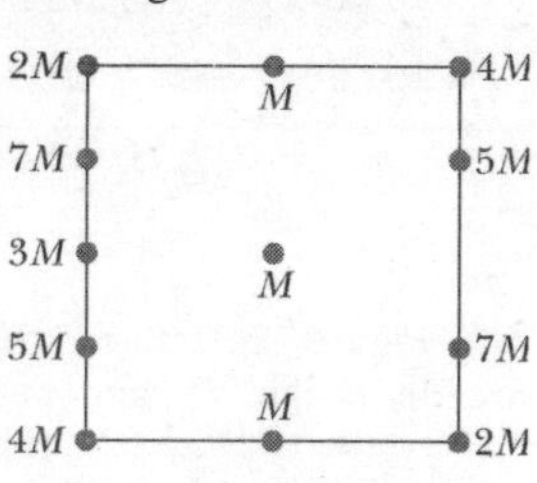

FIG. 13-26 Question 5.

6 Figure 13-27 gives the gravitational acceleration a_g for four planets as a function of the radial distance r from the center of the planet, starting at the surface of the planet (at radius R_1, R_2, R_3, or R_4). Plots 1 and 2 coincide for $r \geq R_2$; plots 3 and 4 coincide for $r \geq R_4$. Rank the four planets according to (a) mass and (b) mass per unit volume, greatest first.

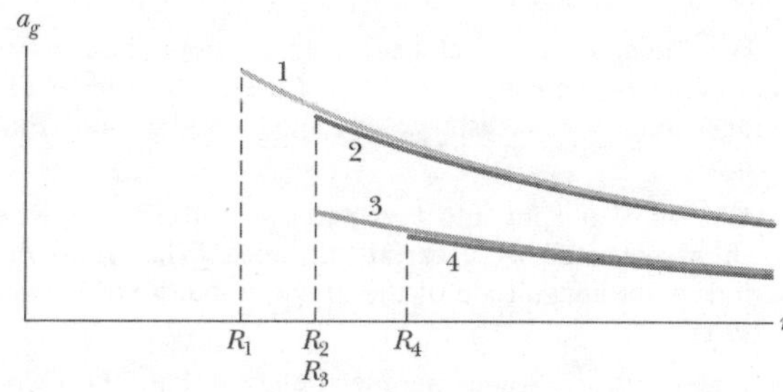

FIG. 13-27 Question 6.

7 Figure 13-28 shows three particles initially fixed in place, with B and C identical and positioned symmetrically about the y axis, at distance d from A. (a) In what direction is the net gravitational force $\vec{F}_{net}$ on A? (b) If we move C directly away from the origin, does $\vec{F}_{net}$ change in direction? If so, how and what is the limit of the change?

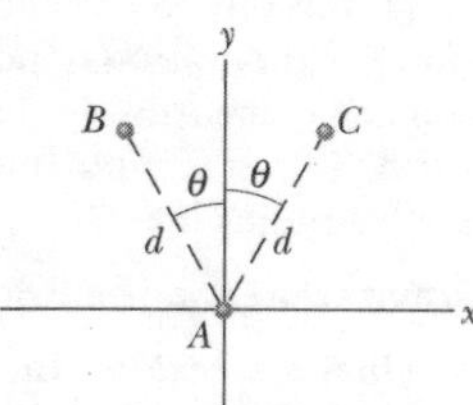

FIG. 13-28 Question 7.

8 In Fig. 13-29, three particles are fixed in place. The mass of B is greater than the mass of C. Can a fourth particle (particle D) be placed somewhere so that the net gravitational force on particle A from particles B, C, and D is zero? If so, in which quadrant should it be placed and which axis should it be near?

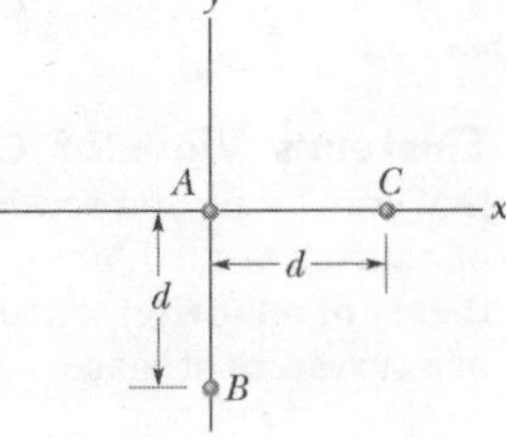

FIG. 13-29 Question 8.

9 Rank the four systems of equal-mass particles shown in Checkpoint 2 according to the absolute value of the gravitational potential energy of the system, greatest first.

10 In Fig. 13-30, a particle of mass m (not shown) is to be moved from an infinite distance to one of the three possible locations a, b, and c. Two other particles, of masses m and $2m$, are fixed in place. Rank the three possible locations according to the work done by the net gravitational force on the moving particle due to the fixed particles, greatest first.

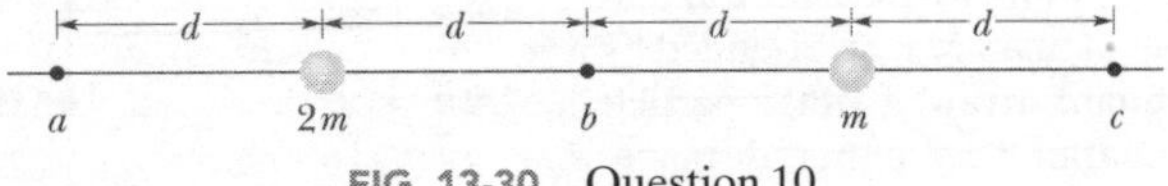

FIG. 13-30 Question 10.

11 Figure 13-31 shows three uniform spherical planets that are identical in size and mass. The periods of rotation T for the planets are given, and six lettered points are indicated—three points are on the equators of the planets and three points are on the north poles. Rank the points according to the value of the free-fall acceleration g at them, greatest first.

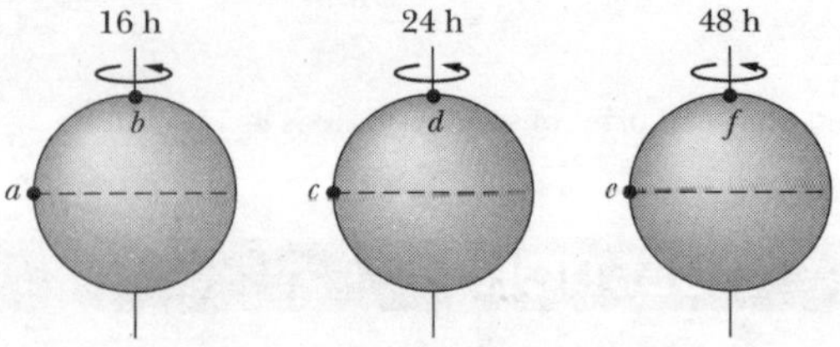

FIG. 13-31 Question 11.

12 Figure 13-32 shows six paths by which a rocket orbiting a moon might move from point a to point b. Rank the paths according to (a) the corresponding change in the gravitational potential energy of the rocket–moon system and (b) the net work done on the rocket by the gravitational force from the moon, greatest first.

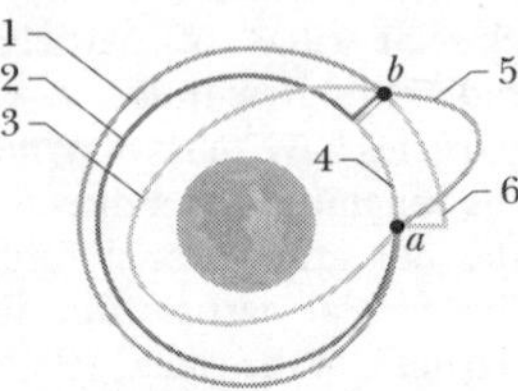

FIG. 13-32 Question 12.

PROBLEMS

Newton's Law of Gravitation

1 What must the separation be between a 5.2 kg particle and a 2.4 kg particle for their gravitational attraction to have a magnitude of 2.3×10^{-12} N?

2 The Sun and Earth each exert a gravitational force on the Moon. What is the ratio F_{Sun}/F_{Earth} of these two forces? (The average Sun–Moon distance is equal to the Sun–Earth distance.)

3 A mass M is split into two parts, m and $M - m$, which are then separated by a certain distance. What ratio m/M maximizes the magnitude of the gravitational force between the parts?

4 *Moon effect.* Some people believe that the Moon controls their activities. If the Moon moves from being directly on the opposite side of Earth from you to being directly overhead, by what percent does (a) the Moon's gravitational pull on you increase and (b) your weight (as measured on a scale) decrease? Assume that the Earth–Moon (center-to-center) distance is 3.82×10^8 m and Earth's radius is 6.37×10^6 m.

Gravitation and the Principle of Superposition

5 *One dimension.* In Fig. 13-33, two point particles are fixed on an x axis separated by distance d. Particle A has mass m_A and particle B has mass $3.00m_A$. A third particle C, of mass $75.0m_A$, is to be placed on the x axis and near particles A and B. In terms of distance d, at what x coordinate should C be placed so that the net gravitational force on particle A from particles B and C is zero?

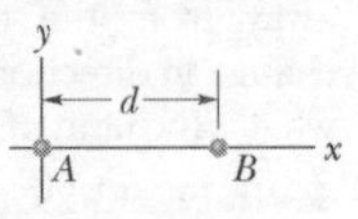

FIG. 13-33 Problem 5.

6 In Fig. 13-34, three 5.00 kg spheres are located at distances $d_1 = 0.300$ m and $d_2 = 0.400$ m. What are the (a) magnitude and (b) direction (relative to the positive direction of the x axis) of the net gravitational force on sphere B due to spheres A and C?

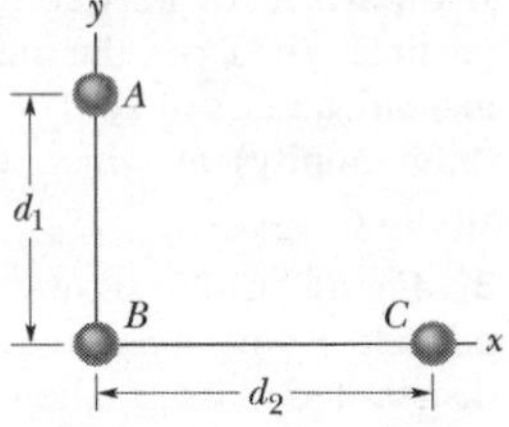

FIG. 13-34 Problem 6.

7 How far from Earth must a space probe be along a line toward the Sun so that the Sun's gravitational pull on the probe balances Earth's pull?

8 In Fig. 13-35, a square of edge length 20.0 cm is formed by four spheres of masses $m_1 = 5.00$ g, $m_2 = 3.00$ g, $m_3 = 1.00$ g, and $m_4 = 5.00$ g. In unit-vector notation, what is the net gravitational force from them on a central sphere with mass $m_5 = 2.50$ g?

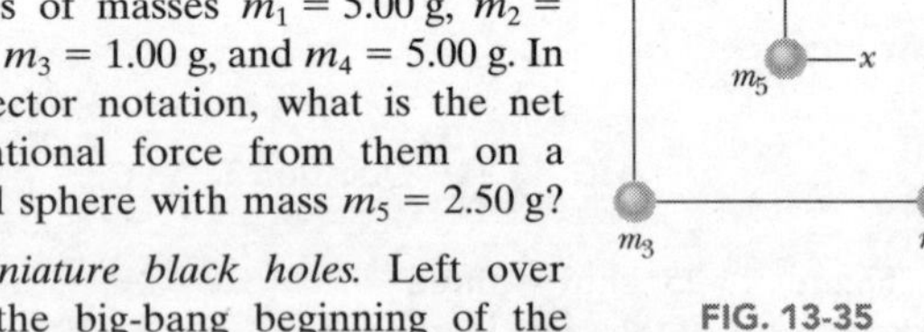

FIG. 13-35 Problem 8.

9 *Miniature black holes.* Left over from the big-bang beginning of the universe, tiny black holes might still wander through the universe. If one with a mass of 1×10^{11} kg (and a radius of only 1×10^{-16} m) reached Earth, at what distance from your head would its gravitational pull on you match that of Earth's?

10 In Fig. 13-36*a*, particle *A* is fixed in place at $x = -0.20$ m on the *x* axis and particle *B*, with a mass of 1.0 kg, is fixed in place at the origin. Particle *C* (not shown) can be moved along the *x* axis, between particle *B* and $x = \infty$. Figure 13-36*b* shows the *x* component $F_{net,x}$ of the net gravitational force on particle *B* due to particles *A* and *C*, as a function of position *x* of particle *C*. The plot actually extends to the right, approaching an asymptote of -4.17×10^{-10} N as $x \to \infty$. What are the masses of (a) particle *A* and (b) particle *C*?

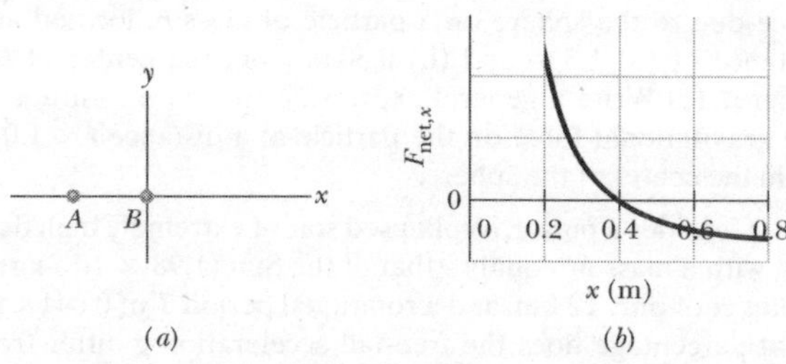

FIG. 13-36 Problem 10.

11 As seen in Fig. 13-37, two spheres of mass *m* and a third sphere of mass *M* form an equilateral triangle, and a fourth sphere of mass m_4 is at the center of the triangle. The net gravitational force on that central sphere from the three other spheres is zero. (a) What is *M* in terms of *m*? (b) If we double the value of m_4, what then is the magnitude of the net gravitational force on the central sphere?

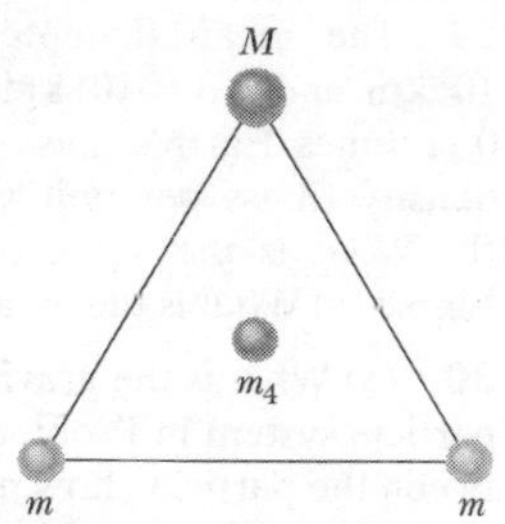

FIG. 13-37 Problem 11.

12 Three point particles are fixed in position in an *xy* plane. Two of them, particle *A* of mass 6.00 g and particle *B* of mass 12.0 g, are shown in Fig. 13-38, with a separation of $d_{AB} = 0.500$ m at angle $\theta = 30°$. Particle *C*, with mass 8.00 g, is not shown. The net gravitational force acting on particle *A* due to particles *B* and *C* is 2.77×10^{-14} N at an angle of $-163.8°$ from the positive direction of the *x* axis. What are (a) the *x* coordinate and (b) the *y* coordinate of particle *C*?

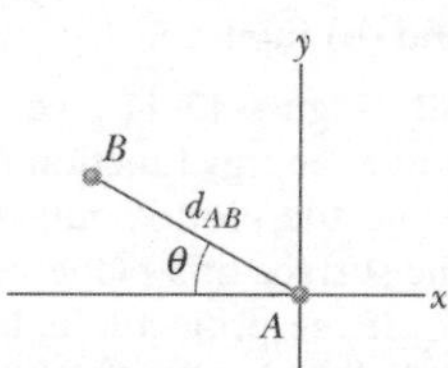

FIG. 13-38 Problem 12.

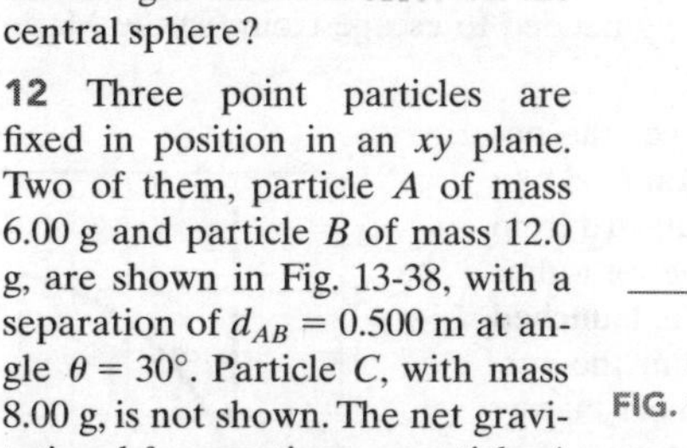

13 Figure 13-39 shows a spherical hollow inside a lead sphere of radius $R = 4.00$ cm; the surface of the hollow passes through the center of the sphere and "touches" the right side of the sphere. The mass of the sphere before hollowing was $M = 2.95$ kg. With what gravitational force does the hollowed-out lead sphere attract a small sphere of mass $m = 0.431$ kg that lies at a distance $d = 9.00$ cm from the center of the lead sphere, on the straight line connecting the centers of the spheres and of the hollow?

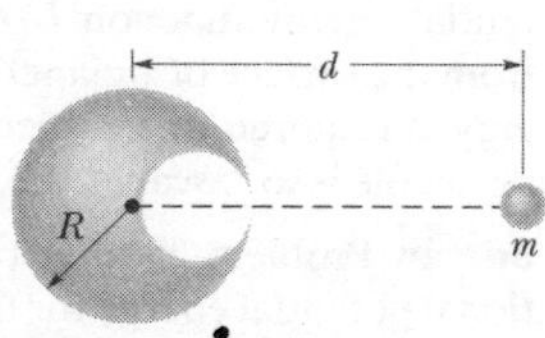

FIG. 13-39 Problem 13.

14 *Two dimensions.* In Fig. 13-40, three point particles are fixed in place in an *xy* plane. Particle *A* has mass m_A, particle *B* has mass $2.00m_A$, and particle *C* has mass $3.00m_A$. A fourth particle *D*, with mass $4.00m_A$, is to be placed near the other three particles. In terms of distance *d*, at what (a) *x* coordinate and (b) *y* coordinate should particle *D* be placed so that the net gravitational force on particle *A* from particles *B*, *C*, and *D* is zero?

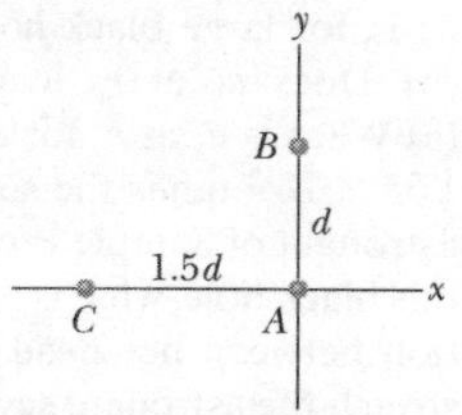

FIG. 13-40 Problem 14.

15 *Three dimensions.* Three point particles are fixed in place in an *xyz* coordinate system. Particle *A*, at the origin, has mass m_A. Particle *B*, at *xyz* coordinates (2.00*d*, 1.00*d*, 2.00*d*), has mass $2.00m_A$, and particle *C*, at coordinates (−1.00*d*, 2.00*d*, −3.00*d*), has mass $3.00m_A$. A fourth particle *D*, with mass $4.00m_A$, is to be placed near the other particles. In terms of distance *d*, at what (a) *x*, (b) *y*, and (c) *z* coordinate should *D* be placed so that the net gravitational force on *A* from *B*, *C*, and *D* is zero?

16 In Fig. 13-41, a particle of mass $m_1 = 0.67$ kg is a distance $d = 23$ cm from one end of a uniform rod with length $L = 3.0$ m and mass $M = 5.0$ kg. What is the magnitude of the gravitational force $\vec{F}$ on the particle from the rod?

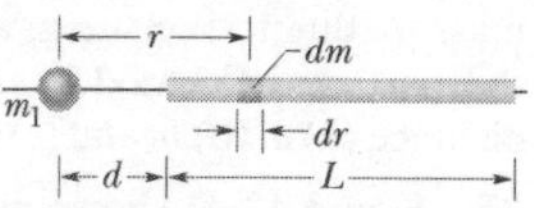

FIG. 13-41 Problem 16.

Gravitation Near Earth's Surface

17 At what altitude above Earth's surface would the gravitational acceleration be 4.9 m/s²?

18 *Mile-high building.* In 1956, Frank Lloyd Wright proposed the construction of a mile-high building in Chicago. Suppose the building had been constructed. Ignoring Earth's rotation, find the change in your weight if you were to ride an elevator from the street level, where you weigh 600 N, to the top of the building.

19 (a) What will an object weigh on the Moon's surface if it weighs 100 N on Earth's surface? (b) How many Earth radii must this same object be from the center of Earth if it is to weigh the same as it does on the Moon?

20 *Mountain pull.* A large mountain can slightly affect the direction of "down" as determined by a plumb line. Assume that we can model a mountain as a sphere of radius $R = 2.00$ km and density (mass per unit volume) 2.6×10^3 kg/m³. Assume also that we hang a 0.50 m plumb line at a distance of 3*R* from the sphere's center and such that the sphere pulls horizontally on the lower end. How far would the lower end move toward the sphere?

21 One model for a certain planet has a core of radius *R* and mass *M* surrounded by an outer shell of inner radius *R*, outer radius 2*R*, and mass 4*M*. If $M = 4.1 \times 10^{24}$ kg and $R = 6.0 \times 10^6$ m, what is the gravitational acceleration of a particle at points (a) *R* and (b) 3*R* from the center of the planet?

22 The radius R_h and mass M_h of a black hole are related by $R_h = 2GM_h/c^2$, where c is the speed of light. Assume that the gravitational acceleration a_g of an object at a distance $r_o = 1.001R_h$ from the center of a black hole is given by Eq. 13-11 (it is, for large black holes). (a) In terms of M_h, find a_g at r_o. (b) Does a_g at r_o increase or decrease as M_h increases? (c) What is a_g at r_o for a very large black hole whose mass is 1.55×10^{12} times the solar mass of 1.99×10^{30} kg? (d) If the astronaut of Sample Problem 13-3 is at r_o with her feet toward this black hole, what is the difference in gravitational acceleration between her head and her feet? (e) Is the tendency to stretch the astronaut severe?

23 Certain neutron stars (extremely dense stars) are believed to be rotating at about 1 rev/s. If such a star has a radius of 20 km, what must be its minimum mass so that material on its surface remains in place during the rapid rotation?

Gravitation Inside Earth

24 Two concentric spherical shells with uniformly distributed masses M_1 and M_2 are situated as shown in Fig. 13-42. Find the magnitude of the net gravitational force on a particle of mass m, due to the shells, when the particle is located at radial distance (a) a, (b) b, and (c) c.

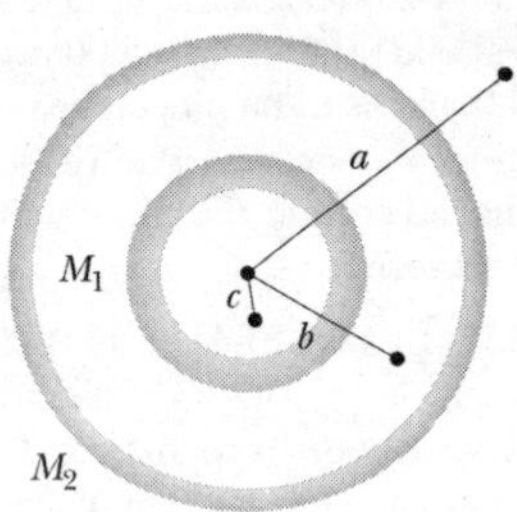

FIG. 13-42 Problem 24.

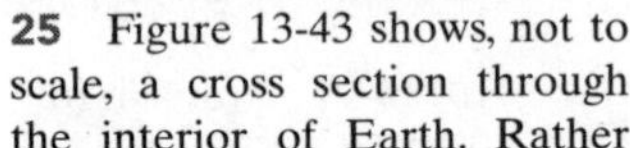

25 Figure 13-43 shows, not to scale, a cross section through the interior of Earth. Rather than being uniform throughout, Earth is divided into three zones: an outer *crust*, a *mantle*, and an inner *core*. The dimensions of these zones and the masses contained within them are shown on the figure. Earth has a total mass of 5.98×10^{24} kg and a radius of 6370 km. Ignore rotation and assume that Earth is spherical. (a) Calculate a_g at the surface. (b) Suppose that a bore hole (the *Mohole*) is driven to the crust–mantle interface at a depth of 25.0 km; what would be the value of a_g at the bottom of the hole? (c) Suppose that Earth were a uniform sphere with the same total mass and size. What would be the value of a_g at a depth of 25.0 km? (Precise measurements of a_g are sensitive probes of the interior structure of Earth, although results can be clouded by local variations in mass distribution.)

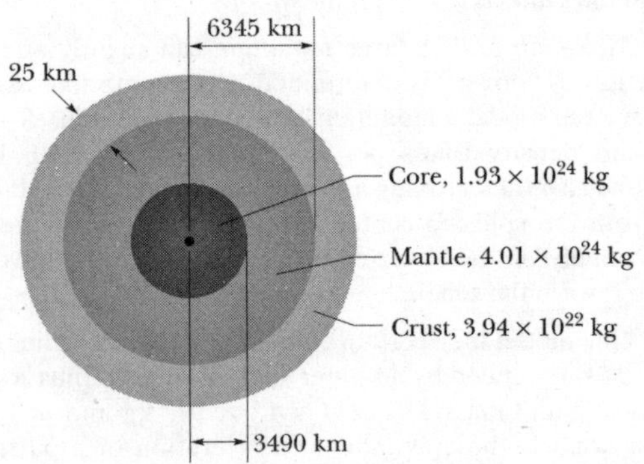

FIG. 13-43 Problem 25.

26 Assume a planet is a uniform sphere of radius R that (somehow) has a narrow radial tunnel through its center (Fig. 13-8). Also assume we can position an apple anywhere along the tunnel or outside the sphere. Let F_R be the magnitude of the gravitational force on the apple when it is located at the planet's surface. How far from the surface is there a point where the magnitude of the gravitational force on the apple is $\frac{1}{2}F_R$ if we move the apple (a) away from the planet and (b) into the tunnel?

27 A solid uniform sphere has a mass of 1.0×10^4 kg and a radius of 1.0 m. What is the magnitude of the gravitational force due to the sphere on a particle of mass m located at a distance of (a) 1.5 m and (b) 0.50 m from the center of the sphere? (c) Write a general expression for the magnitude of the gravitational force on the particle at a distance $r \leq 1.0$ m from the center of the sphere.

28 Consider a pulsar, a collapsed star of extremely high density, with a mass M equal to that of the Sun (1.98×10^{30} kg), a radius R of only 12 km, and a rotational period T of 0.041 s. By what percentage does the free-fall acceleration g differ from the gravitational acceleration a_g at the equator of this spherical star?

Gravitational Potential Energy

29 The mean diameters of Mars and Earth are 6.9×10^3 km and 1.3×10^4 km, respectively. The mass of Mars is 0.11 times Earth's mass. (a) What is the ratio of the mean density (mass per unit volume) of Mars to that of Earth? (b) What is the value of the gravitational acceleration on Mars? (c) What is the escape speed on Mars?

30 (a) What is the gravitational potential energy of the two-particle system in Problem 1? If you triple the separation between the particles, how much work is done (b) by the gravitational force between the particles and (c) by you?

31 What multiple of the energy needed to escape from Earth gives the energy needed to escape from (a) the Moon and (b) Jupiter?

32 Figure 13-44 gives the potential energy function $U(r)$ of a projectile, plotted outward from the surface of a planet of radius R_s. If the projectile is launched radially outward from the surface with a mechanical energy of -2.0×10^9 J, what are (a) its kinetic energy at radius $r = 1.25R_s$ and (b) its *turning point* (see Section 8-6) in terms of R_s?

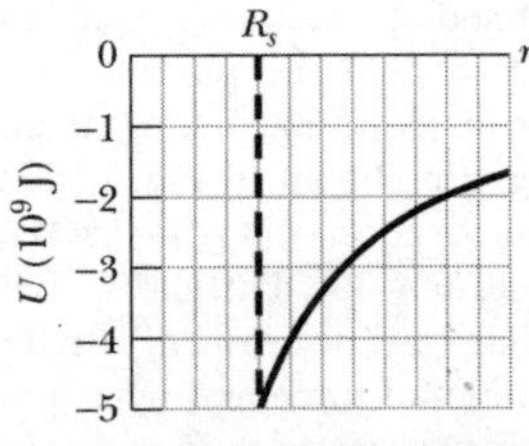

FIG. 13-44 Problems 32 and 33.

33 Figure 13-44 gives the potential energy function $U(r)$ of a projectile, plotted outward from the surface of a planet of radius R_s. What least kinetic energy is required of a projectile launched at the surface if the projectile is to "escape" the planet?

34 In Problem 3, what ratio m/M gives the least gravitational potential energy for the system?

35 The three spheres in Fig. 13-45, with masses $m_A = 80$ g, $m_B = 10$ g, and $m_C = 20$ g, have their centers on a common line, with $L = 12$ cm and $d = 4.0$ cm. You move sphere B along the line until its center-to-center separation from C is $d = 4.0$ cm. How much work is done on sphere B (a) by you and (b) by the net gravitational force on B due to spheres A and C?

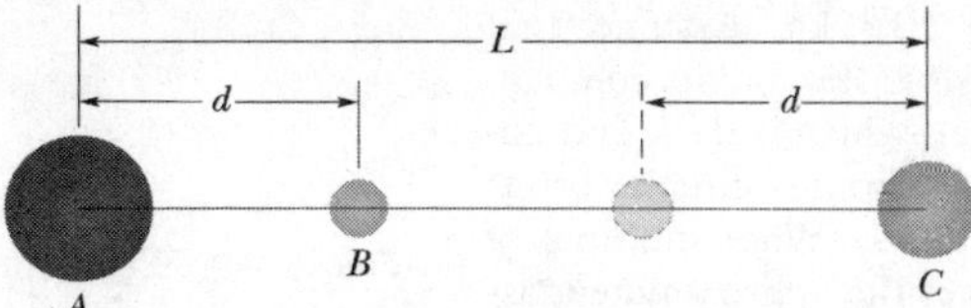

FIG. 13-45 Problem 35.

36 A projectile is shot directly away from Earth's surface. Neglect the rotation of Earth. What multiple of Earth's radius R_E gives the radial distance a projectile reaches if (a) its initial speed is 0.500 of the escape speed from Earth and (b) its initial kinetic energy is 0.500 of the kinetic energy required to escape Earth? (c) What is the least initial mechanical energy required at launch if the projectile is to escape Earth?

37 (a) What is the escape speed on a spherical asteroid whose radius is 500 km and whose gravitational acceleration at the surface is 3.0 m/s^2? (b) How far from the surface will a particle go if it leaves the asteroid's surface with a radial speed of 1000 m/s? (c) With what speed will an object hit the asteroid if it is dropped from 1000 km above the surface?

38 Zero, a hypothetical planet, has a mass of 5.0×10^{23} kg, a radius of 3.0×10^6 m, and no atmosphere. A 10 kg space probe is to be launched vertically from its surface. (a) If the probe is launched with an initial energy of 5.0×10^7 J, what will be its kinetic energy when it is 4.0×10^6 m from the center of Zero? (b) If the probe is to achieve a maximum distance of 8.0×10^6 m from the center of Zero, with what initial kinetic energy must it be launched from the surface of Zero?

39 Two neutron stars are separated by a distance of 1.0×10^{10} m. They each have a mass of 1.0×10^{30} kg and a radius of 1.0×10^5 m. They are initially at rest with respect to each other. As measured from that rest frame, how fast are they moving when (a) their separation has decreased to one-half its initial value and (b) they are about to collide?

40 In deep space, sphere A of mass 20 kg is located at the origin of an x axis and sphere B of mass 10 kg is located on the axis at $x = 0.80$ m. Sphere B is released from rest while sphere A is held at the origin. (a) What is the gravitational potential energy of the two-sphere system just as B is released? (b) What is the kinetic energy of B when it has moved 0.20 m toward A?

41 Figure 13-46 shows four particles, each of mass 20.0 g, that form a square with an edge length of $d = 0.600$ m. If d is reduced to 0.200 m, what is the change in the gravitational potential energy of the four-particle system?

FIG. 13-46 Problem 41.

42 Figure 13-47a shows a particle A that can be moved along a y axis from an infinite distance to the origin. That origin lies at the midpoint between particles B and C, which have identical masses, and the y axis is a perpendicular bisector between them. Distance D is 0.3057 m. Figure 13-47b shows the potential energy U of the three-particle system as a function of the position of particle A along the y axis. The curve actually extends rightward and approaches an asymptote of -2.7×10^{-11} J as $y \to \infty$. What are the masses of (a) particles B and C and (b) particle A?

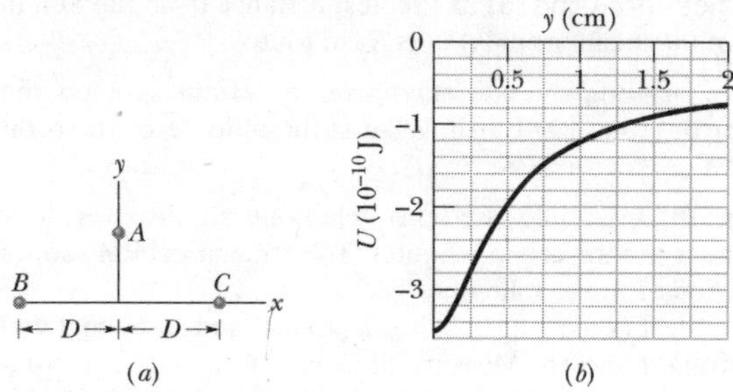

FIG. 13-47 Problem 42.

Planets and Satellites: Kepler's Laws

43 The Martian satellite Phobos travels in an approximately circular orbit of radius 9.4×10^6 m with a period of 7 h 39 min. Calculate the mass of Mars from this information.

44 The first known collision between space debris and a functioning satellite occurred in 1996: At an altitude of 700 km, a year-old French spy satellite was hit by a piece of an Ariane rocket that had been in orbit for 10 years. A stabilizing boom on the satellite was demolished, and the satellite was sent spinning out of control. Just before the collision and in kilometers per hour, what was the speed of the rocket piece relative to the satellite if both were in circular orbits and the collision was (a) head-on and (b) along perpendicular paths?

45 The Sun, which is 2.2×10^{20} m from the center of the Milky Way galaxy, revolves around that center once every 2.5×10^8 years. Assuming each star in the Galaxy has a mass equal to the Sun's mass of 2.0×10^{30} kg, the stars are distributed uniformly in a sphere about the galactic center, and the Sun is at the edge of that sphere, estimate the number of stars in the Galaxy.

46 The mean distance of Mars from the Sun is 1.52 times that of Earth from the Sun. From Kepler's law of periods, calculate the number of years required for Mars to make one revolution around the Sun; compare your answer with the value given in Appendix C.

47 A satellite, moving in an elliptical orbit, is 360 km above Earth's surface at its farthest point and 180 km above at its closest point. Calculate (a) the semimajor axis and (b) the eccentricity of the orbit.

48 A satellite is put in a circular orbit about Earth with a radius equal to one-half the radius of the Moon's orbit. What is its period of revolution in lunar months? (A lunar month is the period of revolution of the Moon.)

49 (a) What linear speed must an Earth satellite have to be in a circular orbit at an altitude of 160 km above Earth's surface? (b) What is the period of revolution?

50 The Sun's center is at one focus of Earth's orbit. How far from this focus is the other focus, (a) in meters and (b) in terms of the solar radius, 6.96×10^8 m? The eccentricity is 0.0167, and the semimajor axis is 1.50×10^{11} m.

51 A comet that was seen in April 574 by Chinese astronomers on a day known by them as the Woo Woo day was spotted again in May 1994. Assume the time between observations is the period of the Woo Woo day comet and take its eccentricity as 0.11. What are (a) the semimajor axis of the comet's orbit and (b) its greatest distance from the Sun in terms of the mean orbital radius R_P of Pluto?

52 An orbiting satellite stays over a certain spot on the equator of (rotating) Earth. What is the altitude of the orbit (called a *geosynchronous orbit*)?

53 In 1610, Galileo used his telescope to discover four prominent moons around Jupiter. Their mean orbital radii a and periods T are as follows:
(a) Plot log a (y axis) against log T (x axis) and show that you get a straight line. (b) Measure the slope of the line and compare it with the value that you expect from Kepler's third law. (c) Find the mass of Jupiter from the intercept of this line with the y axis.

Name	a (10^8 m)	T (days)
Io	4.22	1.77
Europa	6.71	3.55
Ganymede	10.7	7.16
Callisto	18.8	16.7

54 In 1993 the spacecraft *Galileo* sent home an image (Fig. 13-48) of asteroid 243 Ida and a tiny orbiting moon (now known as Dactyl), the first confirmed example of an asteroid–moon system. In the image, the moon, which is 1.5 km wide, is 100 km from the center of the asteroid, which is 55 km long. The shape of the moon's orbit is not well known; assume it is circular with a period of 27 h. (a) What is the mass of the asteroid? (b) The volume of the asteroid, measured from the *Galileo* images, is 14 100 km^3. What is the density (mass per unit volume) of the asteroid?

FIG. 13-48 Problem 54. A tiny moon (at right) orbits asteroid 243 Ida. *(Courtesy NASA)*

55 In a certain binary-star system, each star has the same mass as our Sun, and they revolve about their center of mass. The distance between them is the same as the distance between Earth and the Sun. What is their period of revolution in years?

56 *Hunting a black hole.* Observations of the light from a certain star indicate that it is part of a binary (two-star) system. This visible star has orbital speed v = 270 km/s, orbital period T = 1.70 days, and approximate mass $m_1 = 6M_s$, where M_s is the Sun's mass, 1.99×10^{30} kg. Assume that the visible star and its companion star, which is dark and unseen, are both in circular orbits (Fig. 13-49). What multiple of M_s gives the approximate mass m_2 of the dark star?

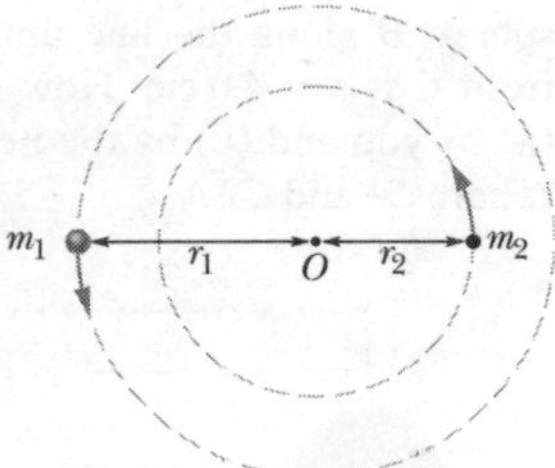

FIG. 13-49 Problem 56.

57 A 20 kg satellite has a circular orbit with a period of 2.4 h and a radius of 8.0×10^6 m around a planet of unknown mass. If the magnitude of the gravitational acceleration on the surface of the planet is 8.0 m/s^2, what is the radius of the planet?

58 The presence of an unseen planet orbiting a distant star can sometimes be inferred from the motion of the star as we see it. As the star and planet orbit the center of mass of the star–planet system, the star moves toward and away from us with what is called the *line of sight velocity,* a motion that can be detected. Figure 13-50 shows a graph of the line of sight velocity versus time for the star 14 Herculis. The star's mass is believed to be 0.90 of the mass of our Sun. Assume that only one planet orbits the star and that our view is along the plane of the orbit. Then approximate (a) the planet's mass in terms of Jupiter's mass m_J and (b) the planet's orbital radius in terms of Earth's orbital radius r_E.

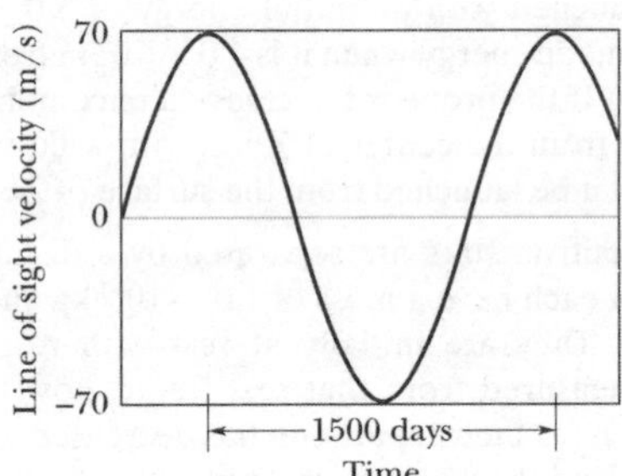

FIG. 13-50 Problem 58.

59 Three identical stars of mass M form an equilateral triangle that rotates around the triangle's center as the stars move in a common circle about that center. The triangle has edge length L. What is the speed of the stars?

Satellites: Orbits and Energy

60 Two Earth satellites, A and B, each of mass m, are to be launched into circular orbits about Earth's center. Satellite A is to orbit at an altitude of 6370 km. Satellite B is to orbit at an altitude of 19 110 km. The radius of Earth R_E is 6370 km. (a) What is the ratio of the potential energy of satellite B to that of satellite A, in orbit? (b) What is the ratio of the kinetic energy of satellite B to that of satellite A, in orbit? (c) Which satellite has the greater total energy if each has a mass of 14.6 kg? (d) By how much?

61 An asteroid, whose mass is 2.0×10^{-4} times the mass of Earth, revolves in a circular orbit around the Sun at a distance that is twice Earth's distance from the Sun. (a) Calculate the period of revolution of the asteroid in years. (b) What is the ratio of the kinetic energy of the asteroid to the kinetic energy of Earth?

62 A satellite orbits a planet of unknown mass in a circle of radius 2.0×10^7 m. The magnitude of the gravitational force on the satellite from the planet is $F = 80$ N. (a) What is the kinetic energy of the satellite in this orbit? (b) What would F be if the orbit radius were increased to 3.0×10^7 m?

63 (a) At what height above Earth's surface is the energy required to lift a satellite to that height equal to the kinetic energy required for the satellite to be in orbit at that height? (b) For greater heights, which is greater, the energy for lifting or the kinetic energy for orbiting?

64 In Fig. 13-51, two satellites, A and B, both of mass $m = 125$ kg, move in the same circular orbit of radius $r = 7.87 \times 10^6$ m around Earth but in opposite senses of rotation and therefore on a collision course. (a) Find the total mechanical energy $E_A + E_B$ of the *two satellites + Earth* system before the collision. (b) If the collision is completely inelastic so that the wreckage remains as one piece of tangled material (mass $= 2m$), find the total mechanical energy immediately after the collision. (c) Just after the collision, is the wreckage falling directly toward Earth's center or orbiting around Earth?

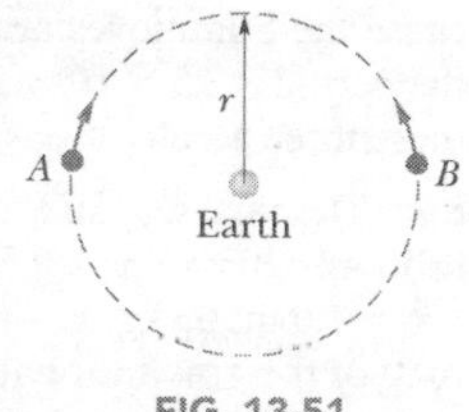

FIG. 13-51 Problem 64.

65 A satellite is in a circular Earth orbit of radius r. The area A enclosed by the orbit depends on r^2 because $A = \pi r^2$. Determine how the following properties of the satellite depend on r: (a) period, (b) kinetic energy, (c) angular momentum, and (d) speed.

66 One way to attack a satellite in Earth orbit is to launch a swarm of pellets in the same orbit as the satellite but in the opposite direction. Suppose a satellite in a circular orbit 500 km above Earth's surface collides with a pellet having mass 4.0 g. (a) What is the kinetic energy of the pellet in the reference frame of the satellite just before the collision? (b) What is the ratio of this kinetic energy to the kinetic energy of a 4.0 g bullet from a modern army rifle with a muzzle speed of 950 m/s?

67 What are (a) the speed and (b) the period of a 220 kg satellite in an approximately circular orbit 640 km above the surface of Earth? Suppose the satellite loses mechanical energy at the average rate of 1.4×10^5 J per orbital revolution. Adopting the reasonable approximation that the satellite's orbit becomes a "circle of slowly diminishing radius," determine the satellite's (c) altitude, (d) speed, and (e) period at the end of its 1500th revolution. (f) What is the magnitude of the average retarding force on the satellite? Is angular momentum around Earth's center conserved for (g) the satellite and (h) the satellite–Earth system (assuming that system is isolated)?

68 Two small spaceships, each with mass $m = 2000$ kg, are in the circular Earth orbit of Fig. 13-52, at an altitude h of 400 km. Igor, the commander of one of the ships, arrives at any fixed point in the orbit 90 s ahead of Picard, the commander of the other ship. What are the (a) period T_0 and (b) speed v_0 of the ships? At point P in Fig. 13-52, Picard fires an instantaneous burst in the forward direction, *reducing* his ship's speed by 1.00%. After this burst, he follows the elliptical orbit shown dashed in the figure. What are the (c) kinetic energy and (d) potential energy of his ship immediately after the burst? In Picard's new elliptical orbit, what are (e) the total energy E, (f) the semimajor axis a, and (g) the orbital period T? (h) How much earlier than Igor will Picard return to P?

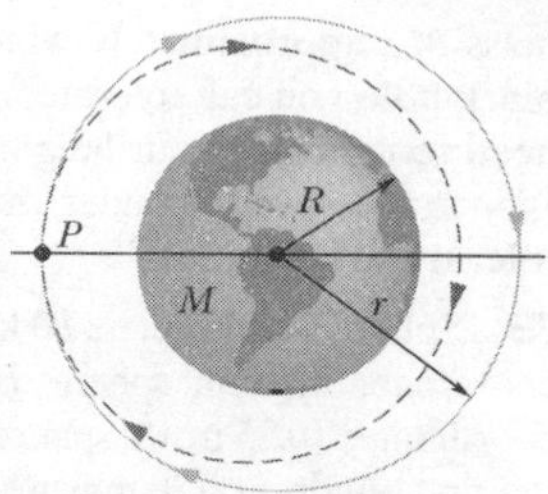

FIG. 13-52 Problem 68.

Einstein and Gravitation

69 In Fig. 13-19b, the scale on which the 60 kg physicist stands reads 220 N. How long will the cantaloupe take to reach the floor if the physicist drops it (from rest relative to himself) at a height of 2.1 m above the floor?

Additional Problems

70 The mysterious visitor that appears in the enchanting story *The Little Prince* was said to come from a planet that "was scarcely any larger than a house!" Assume that the mass per unit volume of the planet is about that of Earth and that the planet does not appreciably spin. Approximate (a) the free-fall acceleration on the planet's surface and (b) the escape speed from the planet.

71 Figure 13-53 is a graph of the kinetic energy K of an asteroid versus its distance r from Earth's center, as the asteroid falls directly in toward that center. (a) What is the (approximate) mass of the asteroid? (b) What is its speed at $r = 1.945 \times 10^7$ m?

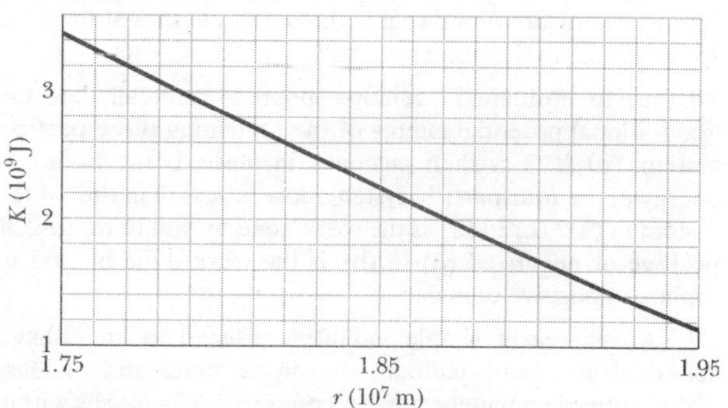

FIG. 13-53 Problem 71.

72 The radius R_h of a black hole is the radius of a mathematical sphere, called the event horizon, that is centered on the black hole. Information from events inside the event horizon cannot reach the outside world. According to Einstein's general theory of relativity, $R_h = 2GM/c^2$, where M is the mass of the black hole and c is the speed of light.

Suppose that you wish to study a black hole near it, at a radial distance of $50R_h$. However, you do not want the difference in gravitational acceleration between your feet and your head to exceed 10 m/s² when you are feet down (or head down) toward the black hole. (a) As a multiple of our Sun's mass M_S, approximately what is the limit to the mass of the black hole you can tolerate at the given radial distance? (You need to estimate your height.) (b) Is the limit an upper limit (you can tolerate smaller masses) or a lower limit (you can tolerate larger masses)?

73 Sphere A with mass 80 kg is located at the origin of an xy coordinate system; sphere B with mass 60 kg is located at coordinates (0.25 m, 0); sphere C with mass 0.20 kg is located in the first quadrant 0.20 m from A and 0.15 m from B. In unit-vector notation, what is the gravitational force on C due to A and B?

74 A satellite is in elliptical orbit with a period of 8.00×10^4 s about a planet of mass 7.00×10^{24} kg. At aphelion, at radius 4.5×10^7 m, the satellite's angular speed is 7.158×10^{-5} rad/s. What is its angular speed at perihelion?

75 In a shuttle craft of mass $m = 3000$ kg, Captain Janeway orbits a planet of mass $M = 9.50 \times 10^{25}$ kg, in a circular orbit of radius $r = 4.20 \times 10^7$ m. What are (a) the period of the orbit and (b) the speed of the shuttle craft? Janeway briefly fires a forward-pointing thruster, reducing her speed by 2.00%. Just then, what are (c) the speed, (d) the kinetic energy, (e) the gravitational potential energy, and (f) the mechanical energy of the shuttle craft? (g) What is the semi-major axis of the elliptical orbit now taken by the craft? (h) What is the difference between the period of the original circular orbit and that of the new elliptical orbit? (i) Which orbit has the smaller period?

76 A typical neutron star may have a mass equal to that of the Sun but a radius of only 10 km. (a) What is the gravitational acceleration at the surface of such a star? (b) How fast would an object be moving if it fell from rest through a distance of 1.0 m on such a star? (Assume the star does not rotate.)

77 Four uniform spheres, with masses $m_A = 40$ kg, $m_B = 35$ kg, $m_C = 200$ kg, and $m_D = 50$ kg, have (x, y) coordinates of (0, 50 cm), (0, 0), (−80 cm, 0), and (40 cm, 0), respectively. In unit-vector notation, what is the net gravitational force on sphere B due to the other spheres?

78 (a) In Problem 77, remove sphere A and calculate the gravitational potential energy of the remaining three-particle system. (b) If A is then put back in place, is the potential energy of the four-particle system more or less than that of the system in (a)? (c) In (a), is the work done by you to remove A positive or negative? (d) In (b), is the work done by you to replace A positive or negative?

79 A very early, simple satellite consisted of an inflated spherical aluminum balloon 30 m in diameter and of mass 20 kg. Suppose a meteor having a mass of 7.0 kg passes within 3.0 m of the surface of the satellite. What is the magnitude of the gravitational force on the meteor from the satellite at the closest approach?

80 A uniform solid sphere of radius R produces a gravitational acceleration of a_g on its surface. At what distance from the sphere's center are there points (a) inside and (b) outside the sphere where the gravitational acceleration is $a_g/3$?

81 A projectile is fired vertically from Earth's surface with an initial speed of 10 km/s. Neglecting air drag, how far above the surface of Earth will it go?

82 A 50 kg satellite circles planet Cruton every 6.0 h. The magnitude of the gravitational force exerted on the satellite by Cruton is 80 N. (a) What is the radius of the orbit? (b) What is the kinetic energy of the satellite? (c) What is the mass of planet Cruton?

83 In a double-star system, two stars of mass 3.0×10^{30} kg each rotate about the system's center of mass at radius 1.0×10^{11} m. (a) What is their common angular speed? (b) If a meteoroid passes through the system's center of mass perpendicular to their orbital plane, what minimum speed must it have at the center of mass if it is to escape to "infinity" from the two-star system?

84 An object lying on Earth's equator is accelerated (a) toward the center of Earth because Earth rotates, (b) toward the Sun because Earth revolves around the Sun in an almost circular orbit, and (c) toward the center of our galaxy because the Sun moves around the galactic center. For the latter, the period is 2.5×10^8 y and the radius is 2.2×10^{20} m. Calculate these three accelerations as multiples of $g = 9.8$ m/s^2.

85 The masses and coordinates of three spheres are as follows: 20 kg, $x = 0.50$ m, $y = 1.0$ m; 40 kg, $x = -1.0$ m, $y = -1.0$ m; 60 kg, $x = 0$ m, $y = -0.50$ m. What is the magnitude of the gravitational force on a 20 kg sphere located at the origin due to these three spheres?

86 With what speed would mail pass through the center of Earth if falling in the tunnel of Sample Problem 13-4?

87 The orbit of Earth around the Sun is *almost* circular: The closest and farthest distances are 1.47×10^8 km and 1.52×10^8 km respectively. Determine the corresponding variations in (a) total energy, (b) gravitational potential energy, (c) kinetic energy, and (d) orbital speed. (*Hint:* Use conservation of energy and conservation of angular momentum.)

88 A spaceship is on a straight-line path between Earth and the Moon. At what distance from Earth is the net gravitational force on the spaceship zero?

89 An object of mass m is initially held in place at radial distance $r = 3R_E$ from the center of Earth, where R_E is the radius of Earth. Let M_E be the mass of Earth. A force is applied to the object to move it to a radial distance $r = 4R_E$, where it again is held in place. Calculate the work done by the applied force during the move by integrating the force magnitude.

90 The fastest possible rate of rotation of a planet is that for which the gravitational force on material at the equator just barely provides the centripetal force needed for the rotation. (Why?) (a) Show that the corresponding shortest period of rotation is

$$T = \sqrt{\frac{3\pi}{G\rho}}$$

where ρ is the uniform density (mass per unit volume) of the spherical planet. (b) Calculate the rotation period assuming a density of 3.0 g/cm^3, typical of many planets, satellites, and asteroids. No astronomical object has ever been found to be spinning with a period shorter than that determined by this analysis.

91 (a) If the legendary apple of Newton could be released from rest at a height of 2 m from the surface of a neutron star with a mass 1.5 times that of our Sun and a radius of 20 km, what would be the apple's speed when it reached the surface of the star? (b) If the apple could rest on the surface of the star, what would be the approximate difference between the gravitational acceleration at the top and at the bottom of the apple? (Choose a reasonable size for an apple; the answer indicates that an apple would never survive near a neutron star.)

92 Some people believe that the positions of the planets at the time of birth influence the newborn. Others deride this belief and claim that the gravitational force exerted on a baby by the obstetrician is greater than the force exerted by the planets. To check this claim, calculate the magnitude of the gravitational force exerted on a 3 kg baby (a) by a 70 kg obstetrician who is 1 m away and roughly approximated as a point mass, (b) by the massive planet Jupiter ($m = 2 \times 10^{27}$ kg) at its closest approach to Earth ($= 6 \times 10^{11}$ m), and (c) by Jupiter at its greatest distance from Earth ($= 9 \times 10^{11}$ m). (d) Is the claim correct?

93 A certain triple-star system consists of two stars, each of mass m, revolving in the same circular orbit of radius r around a central star of mass M (Fig. 13-54). The two orbiting stars are always at opposite ends of a diameter of the orbit. Derive an expression for the period of revolution of the stars.

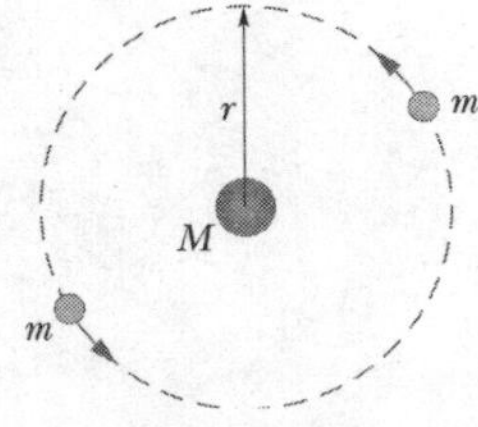

FIG. 13-54 Problem 93.

94 A 150.0 kg rocket moving radially outward from Earth has a speed of 3.70 km/s when its engine shuts off 200 km above Earth's surface. (a) Assuming negligible air drag, find the rocket's kinetic energy when the rocket is 1000 km above Earth's surface. (b) What maximum height above the surface is reached by the rocket?

95 Planet Roton, with a mass of 7.0×10^{24} kg and a radius of 1600 km, gravitationally attracts a meteorite that is initially at rest relative to the planet, at a distance great enough to take as infinite. The meteorite falls toward the planet. Assuming the planet is airless, find the speed of the meteorite when it reaches the planet's surface.

96 Two 20 kg spheres are fixed in place on a y axis, one at $y = 0.40$ m and the other at $y = -0.40$ m. A 10 kg ball is then released from rest at a point on the x axis that is at a great distance (effectively infinite) from the spheres. If the only forces acting on the ball are the gravitational forces from the spheres, then when the ball reaches the (x, y) point (0.30 m, 0), what are (a) its kinetic energy and (b) the net force on it from the spheres, in unit-vector notation?

97 A satellite of mass 125 kg is in a circular orbit of radius 7.00×10^6 m around a planet. If the period is 8050 s, what is the mechanical energy of the satellite?

98 In his 1865 science fiction novel *From the Earth to the Moon*, Jules Verne described how three astronauts are shot to the Moon by means of a huge gun. According to Verne, the aluminum capsule containing the astronauts is accelerated by ignition of nitrocellulose to a speed of 11 km/s along the gun barrel's length of 220 m. (a) In g units, what is the average acceleration of the capsule and astronauts in the gun barrel? (b) Is that acceleration tolerable or deadly to the astronauts?

A modern version of such gun-launched spacecraft (although without passengers) has been proposed. In this modern version, called the SHARP (Super High Altitude Research Project) gun, ignition of methane and air shoves a piston along the gun's tube, compressing hydrogen gas that then launches a rocket. During this launch, the rocket moves 3.5 km and reaches a speed of 7.0 km/s. Once launched, the rocket can be fired to gain additional speed. (c) In g units, what would be the average acceleration of the rocket within the launcher? (d) How much additional speed is needed (via the rocket engine) if the rocket is to orbit Earth at an altitude of 700 km?

99 Several planets (Jupiter, Saturn, Uranus) are encircled by rings, perhaps composed of material that failed to form a satellite. In addition, many galaxies contain ring-like structures. Consider a homogeneous thin ring of mass M and outer radius R (Fig. 13-55). (a) What gravitational attraction does it exert on a particle of mass m located on the ring's central axis a distance x from the ring center? (b) Suppose the particle falls from rest as a result of the attraction of the ring of matter. What is the speed with which it passes through the center of the ring?

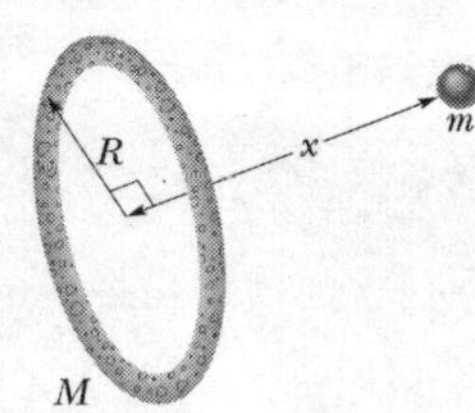

FIG. 13-55 Problem 99.

100 Four identical 1.5 kg particles are placed at the corners of a square with sides equal to 20 cm. What is the magnitude of the net gravitational force on any one of the particles due to the others?

101 We watch two identical astronomical bodies A and B, each of mass m, fall toward each other from rest because of the gravitational force on each from the other. Their initial center-to-center separation is R_i. Assume that we are in an inertial reference frame that is stationary with respect to the center of mass of this two-body system. Use the principle of conservation of mechanical energy ($K_f + U_f = K_i + U_i$) to find the following when the center-to-center separation is $0.5R_i$: (a) the total kinetic energy of the system, (b) the kinetic energy of each body, (c) the speed of each body relative to us, and (d) the speed of body B relative to body A.

Next assume that we are in a reference frame attached to body A (we ride on the body). Now we see body B fall from rest toward us. From this reference frame, again use $K_f + U_f = K_i + U_i$ to find the following when the center-to-center separation is $0.5R_i$: (e) the kinetic energy of body B and (f) the speed of body B relative to body A. (g) Why are the answers to (d) and (f) different? Which answer is correct?

102 What is the percentage change in the acceleration of Earth toward the Sun when the alignment of Earth, Sun, and Moon changes from an eclipse of the Sun (with the Moon between Earth and Sun) to an eclipse of the Moon (Earth between Moon and Sun)?

103 A planet requires 300 (Earth) days to complete its circular orbit around its sun, which has a mass of 6.0×10^{30} kg. What are the planet's (a) orbital radius and (b) orbital speed?

104 A particle of comet dust with mass m is a distance R from Earth's center and a distance r from the Moon's center. If Earth's mass is M_E and the Moon's mass is M_m, what is the sum of the gravitational potential energy of the particle–Earth system and the gravitational potential energy of the particle–Moon system?

14 Fluids

Warren Bolster/Stone/Getty Images

In short, how does a surfer surf?

The answer is in this chapter.

A surfer patiently kneels on his surfboard to catch the next big wave. When he spots a wave building in height as it heads his way, he rapidly paddles toward shore so that he is moving almost as fast as the wave as the wave begins to sweep under him. Then he stands up on the board, continuously adjusting his balance. How does he manage to continue riding the wave? How, instead, can he move up or down the front of the wave?

14-1 | Introduction

What is a Fluid?

A **fluid,** in contrast to a solid, is a substance that can flow. Fluids conform to the boundaries of any container in which we put them. They do so because a fluid cannot sustain a force that is tangential to its surface. (A fluid is a substance that flows because it cannot withstand a shearing stress. It can, however, exert a force in the direction perpendicular to its surface.) Some materials, such as pitch, take a long time to conform to the boundaries of a container, but they do so eventually; thus, we classify even those materials as fluids.

You may wonder why we lump liquids and gases together and call them fluids. After all (you may say), liquid water is as different from steam as it is from ice. Actually, it is not. Ice, like other crystalline solids, has its constituent atoms organized in a fairly rigid three-dimensional array called a crystalline lattice. In neither steam nor liquid water, however, is there any such orderly long-range arrangement.

14-2 | Density and Pressure

When we discuss rigid bodies, we are concerned with particular lumps of matter, such as wooden blocks, baseballs, or metal rods. Physical quantities that we find useful, and in whose terms we express Newton's laws, are *mass* and *force.* We might speak, for example, of a 3.6 kg block acted on by a 25 N force.

With fluids, we are more interested in the extended substance and in properties that can vary from point to point in that substance. It is more useful to speak of **density** and **pressure** than of mass and force.

Density

To find the density ρ of a fluid at any point, we isolate a small volume element ΔV around that point and measure the mass Δm of the fluid contained within that element. The **density** is then

$$\rho = \frac{\Delta m}{\Delta V} \qquad (14\text{-}1)$$

In theory, the density at any point in a fluid is the limit of this ratio as the volume element ΔV at that point is made smaller and smaller. In practice, we assume that a fluid sample is large relative to atomic dimensions and thus is "smooth" (with uniform density), rather than "lumpy" with atoms. This assumption allows us to write Eq. 14-1 as

$$\rho = \frac{m}{V} \quad \text{(uniform density)} \qquad (14\text{-}2)$$

where m and V are the mass and volume of the sample.

Density is a scalar property; its SI unit is the kilogram per cubic meter. Table 14-1 shows the densities of some substances and the average densities of some objects. Note that the density of a gas (see Air in the table) varies considerably with pressure, but the density of a liquid (see Water) does not; that is, gases are readily *compressible* but liquids are not.

TABLE 14-1

Some Densities

Material or Object	Density (kg/m³)	Material or Object	Density (kg/m³)
Interstellar space	10^{-20}	Iron	7.9×10^3
Best laboratory vacuum	10^{-17}	Mercury (the metal, not the planet)	13.6×10^3
Air: 20°C and 1 atm pressure	1.21	Earth: average	5.5×10^3
20°C and 50 atm	60.5	core	9.5×10^3
Styrofoam	1×10^2	crust	2.8×10^3
Ice	0.917×10^3	Sun: average	1.4×10^3
Water: 20°C and 1 atm	0.998×10^3	core	1.6×10^5
20°C and 50 atm	1.000×10^3	White dwarf star (core)	10^{10}
Seawater: 20°C and 1 atm	1.024×10^3	Uranium nucleus	3×10^{17}
Whole blood	1.060×10^3	Neutron star (core)	10^{18}

Pressure

Let a small pressure-sensing device be suspended inside a fluid-filled vessel, as in Fig. 14-1*a*. The sensor (Fig. 14-1*b*) consists of a piston of surface area ΔA riding in a close-fitting cylinder and resting against a spring. A readout arrangement allows us to record the amount by which the (calibrated) spring is compressed by the surrounding fluid, thus indicating the magnitude ΔF of the force that acts normal to the piston. We define the **pressure** on the piston from the fluid as

$$p = \frac{\Delta F}{\Delta A} \tag{14-3}$$

In theory, the pressure at any point in the fluid is the limit of this ratio as the surface area ΔA of the piston, centered on that point, is made smaller and smaller. However, if the force is uniform over a flat area A, we can write Eq. 14-3 as

$$p = \frac{F}{A} \quad \text{(pressure of uniform force on flat area)} \tag{14-4}$$

where F is the magnitude of the normal force on area A. (When we say a force is uniform over an area, we mean that the force is evenly distributed over every point of the area.)

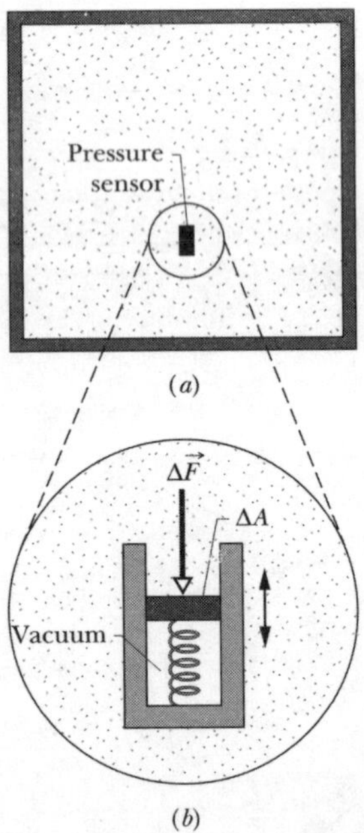

FIG. 14-1 (*a*) A fluid-filled vessel containing a small pressure sensor, shown in (*b*). The pressure is measured by the relative position of the movable piston in the sensor.

We find by experiment that at a given point in a fluid at rest, the pressure p defined by Eq. 14-4 has the same value no matter how the pressure sensor is oriented. Pressure is a scalar, having no directional properties. It is true that the force acting on the piston of our pressure sensor is a vector quantity, but Eq. 14-4 involves only the *magnitude* of that force, a scalar quantity.

The SI unit of pressure is the newton per square meter, which is given a special name, the **pascal** (Pa). In metric countries, tire pressure gauges are calibrated in kilopascals. The pascal is related to some other common (non-SI) pressure units as follows:

$$1 \text{ atm} = 1.01 \times 10^5 \text{ Pa} = 760 \text{ torr} = 14.7 \text{ lb/in.}^2$$

The *atmosphere* (atm) is, as the name suggests, the approximate average pressure of the atmosphere at sea level. The *torr* (named for Evangelista Torricelli, who invented the mercury barometer in 1674) was formerly called the *millimeter of mercury* (mm Hg). The pound per square inch is often abbreviated psi. Table 14-2 shows some pressures.

TABLE 14-2

Some Pressures

	Pressure (Pa)		Pressure (Pa)
Center of the Sun	2×10^{16}	Automobile tire[a]	2×10^5
Center of Earth	4×10^{11}	Atmosphere at sea level	1.0×10^5
Highest sustained laboratory pressure	1.5×10^{10}	Normal blood systolic pressure[a,b]	1.6×10^4
Deepest ocean trench (bottom)	1.1×10^8	Best laboratory vacuum	10^{-12}
Spike heels on a dance floor	10^6		

[a]Pressure in excess of atmospheric pressure.
[b]Equivalent to 120 torr on the physician's pressure gauge.

Sample Problem 14-1

A living room has floor dimensions of 3.5 m and 4.2 m and a height of 2.4 m.

(a) What does the air in the room weigh when the air pressure is 1.0 atm?

Conceptualize: The air's weight is equal to mg, where m is its mass.

Classify: Mass m is related to the air density ρ and the air volume V by Eq. 14-2 ($\rho = m/V$).

Compute: Putting the two ideas together and taking the density of air at 1.0 atm from Table 14-1, we find

$$mg = (\rho V)g$$
$$= (1.21 \text{ kg/m}^3)(3.5 \text{ m} \times 4.2 \text{ m} \times 2.4 \text{ m})(9.8 \text{ m/s}^2)$$
$$= 418 \text{ N} \approx 420 \text{ N.} \qquad \text{(Answer)}$$

Conclude: This is the weight of about 110 cans of Pepsi.

(b) What is the magnitude of the atmosphere's downward force on the top of your head, which we take to have an area of 0.040 m^2?

Conceptualize/Classify: When the fluid pressure p on a surface of area A is uniform, the fluid force on the surface can be obtained from Eq. 14-4 ($p = F/A$).

Compute: Although air pressure varies daily, we can approximate that $p = 1.0$ atm. Then Eq. 14-4 gives

$$F = pA = (1.0 \text{ atm})\left(\frac{1.01 \times 10^5 \text{ N/m}^2}{1.0 \text{ atm}}\right)(0.040 \text{ m}^2)$$
$$= 4.0 \times 10^3 \text{ N} \qquad \text{(Answer)}$$

Conclude: This large force is equal to the weight of the column of air that covers the top of your head and extends all the way to the top of the atmosphere.

14-3 | Fluids at Rest

Figure 14-2a shows a tank of water—or other liquid—open to the atmosphere. As every diver knows, the pressure *increases* with depth below the air–water interface. The diver's depth gauge, in fact, is a pressure sensor much like that of Fig. 14-1b. As every mountaineer knows, the pressure *decreases* with altitude as one ascends into the atmosphere. The pressures encountered by the diver and the mountaineer are usually called *hydrostatic pressures,* because they are due to fluids that are static (at rest). Here we want to find an expression for hydrostatic pressure as a function of depth or altitude.

Let us look first at the increase in pressure with depth below the water's surface. We set up a vertical y axis in the tank, with its origin at the air–water interface and the positive direction upward. We next consider a water sample contained in an imaginary right circular cylinder of horizontal base (or face) area A, such that y_1 and y_2 (both of which are *negative* numbers) are the depths below the surface of the upper and lower cylinder faces, respectively.

Figure 14-2b shows a free-body diagram for the water in the cylinder. The water is in *static equilibrium;* that is, it is stationary and the forces on it balance. Three forces act on it vertically: Force $\vec{F}_1$ acts at the top surface of the

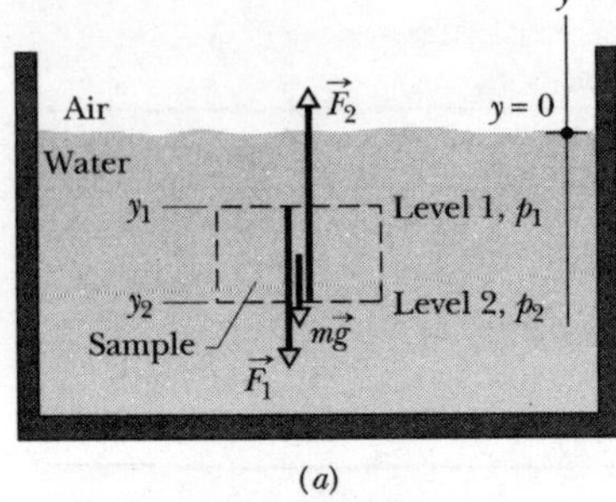

(a)

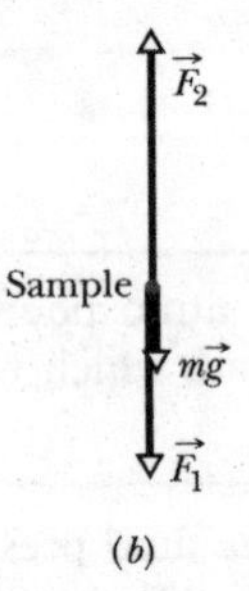

(b)

FIG. 14-2 (a) A tank of water in which a sample of water is contained in an imaginary cylinder of horizontal base area A. Force $\vec{F}_1$ acts at the top surface of the cylinder; force $\vec{F}_2$ acts at the bottom surface of the cylinder; the gravitational force on the water in the cylinder is represented by $m\vec{g}$. (b) A free-body diagram of the water sample.

cylinder and is due to the water above the cylinder. Similarly, force $\vec{F}_2$ acts at the bottom surface of the cylinder and is due to the water below the cylinder. The gravitational force on the water in the cylinder is represented by $m\vec{g}$, where m is the mass of the water in the cylinder. The balance of these forces is written as

$$F_2 = F_1 + mg \tag{14-5}$$

We want to transform Eq. 14-5 into an equation involving pressures. From Eq. 14-4, we know that

$$F_1 = p_1 A \quad \text{and} \quad F_2 = p_2 A \tag{14-6}$$

The mass m of the water in the cylinder is, from Eq. 14-2, $m = \rho V$, where the cylinder's volume V is the product of its face area A and its height $y_1 - y_2$. Thus, m is equal to $\rho A(y_1 - y_2)$. Substituting this and Eq. 14-6 into Eq. 14-5, we find

$$p_2 A = p_1 A + \rho A g(y_1 - y_2)$$

or

$$p_2 = p_1 + \rho g(y_1 - y_2) \tag{14-7}$$

This equation can be used to find pressure both in a liquid (as a function of depth) and in the atmosphere (as a function of altitude or height). For the former, suppose we seek the pressure p at a depth h below the liquid surface. Then we choose level 1 to be the surface, level 2 to be a distance h below it (as in Fig. 14-3), and p_0 to represent the atmospheric pressure on the surface. We then substitute

$$y_1 = 0, \quad p_1 = p_0 \quad \text{and} \quad y_2 = -h, \quad p_2 = p$$

into Eq. 14-7, which becomes

$$p = p_0 + \rho g h \quad \text{(pressure at depth } h\text{)} \tag{14-8}$$

Note that the pressure at a given depth in the liquid depends on that depth but not on any horizontal dimension.

> The pressure at a point in a fluid in static equilibrium depends on the depth of that point but not on any horizontal dimension of the fluid or its container.

Thus, Eq. 14-8 holds no matter what the shape of the container. If the bottom surface of the container is at depth h, then Eq. 14-8 gives the pressure p there.

In Eq. 14-8, p is said to be the total pressure, or **absolute pressure,** at level 2. To see why, note in Fig. 14-3 that the pressure p at level 2 consists of two contributions: (1) p_0, the pressure due to the atmosphere, which bears down on the liquid, and (2) ρgh, the pressure due to the liquid above level 2, which bears down on level 2. In general, the difference between an absolute pressure and an atmospheric pressure is called the **gauge pressure.** (The name comes from the use of a gauge to measure this difference in pressures.) For the situation of Fig. 14-3, the gauge pressure is ρgh.

Equation 14-7 also holds above the liquid surface: It gives the atmospheric pressure at a given distance above level 1 in terms of the atmospheric pressure p_1 at level 1 (*assuming* that the atmospheric density is uniform over that distance). For example, to find the atmospheric pressure at a distance d above level 1 in Fig. 14-3, we substitute

$$y_1 = 0, \quad p_1 = p_0 \quad \text{and} \quad y_2 = d, \quad p_2 = p$$

Then with $\rho = \rho_{air}$, we obtain

$$p = p_0 - \rho_{air} g d$$

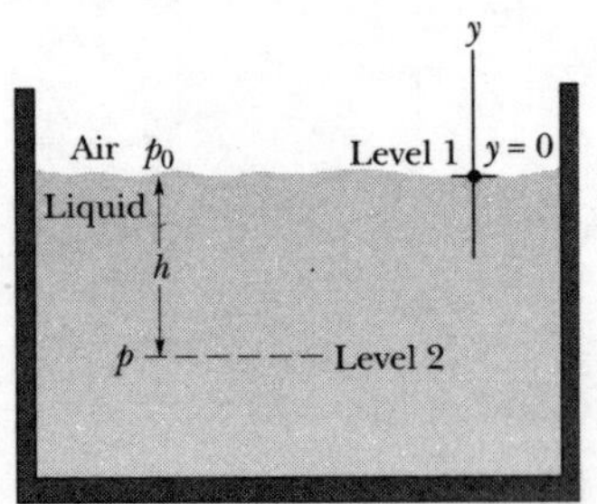

FIG. 14-3 The pressure p increases with depth h below the liquid surface according to Eq. 14-8.

CHECKPOINT 1 The figure shows four containers of olive oil. Rank them according to the pressure at depth h, greatest first.

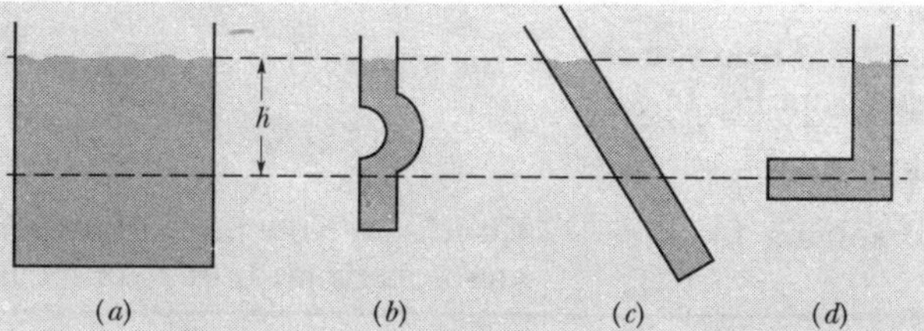

Sample Problem 14-2

A novice scuba diver practicing in a swimming pool takes enough air from his tank to fully expand his lungs before abandoning the tank at depth L and swimming to the surface. He ignores instructions and fails to exhale during his ascent. When he reaches the surface, the difference between the external pressure on him and the air pressure in his lungs is 9.3 kPa. From what depth does he start? What potentially lethal danger does he face?

Conceptualize: Exhaling reduces pressure inside the lungs. This means that while he was down inside the pool he must have had high pressure inside the lungs.

Classify: The pressure at depth h in a liquid of density ρ is given by Eq. 14-8 ($p = p_0 + \rho gh$), where the gauge pressure ρgh is added to the atmospheric pressure p_0.

Compute: Here, when the diver fills his lungs at depth L, the external pressure on him (and thus the air pressure within his lungs) is greater than normal and given by Eq. 14-8 as

$$p = p_0 + \rho gL$$

where p_0 is atmospheric pressure and ρ is the water's density (998 kg/m^3, from Table 14-1). As he ascends, the external pressure on him decreases, until it is atmospheric pressure p_0 at the surface. His blood pressure also decreases, until it is normal. However, because he does not exhale, the air pressure in his lungs remains at the value it had at depth L. At the surface, the pressure difference between the higher pressure in his lungs and the lower pressure on his chest is

$$\Delta p = p - p_0 = \rho gL$$

from which we find

$$L = \frac{\Delta p}{\rho g} = \frac{9300 \text{ Pa}}{(998 \text{ kg/m}^3)(9.8 \text{ m/s}^2)}$$

$$= 0.95 \text{ m} \qquad \text{(Answer)}$$

Conclude: This is not deep! Yet, the pressure difference of 9.3 kPa (about 9% of atmospheric pressure) is sufficient to rupture the diver's lungs and force air from them into the depressurized blood, which then carries the air to the heart, killing the diver. If the diver follows instructions and gradually exhales as he ascends, he allows the pressure in his lungs to equalize with the external pressure, and then there is no danger.

Sample Problem 14-3

The U-tube in Fig. 14-4 contains two liquids in static equilibrium: Water of density ρ_w (= 998 kg/m^3) is in the right arm, and oil of unknown density ρ_x is in the left. Measurement gives l = 135 mm and d = 12.3 mm. What is the density of the oil?

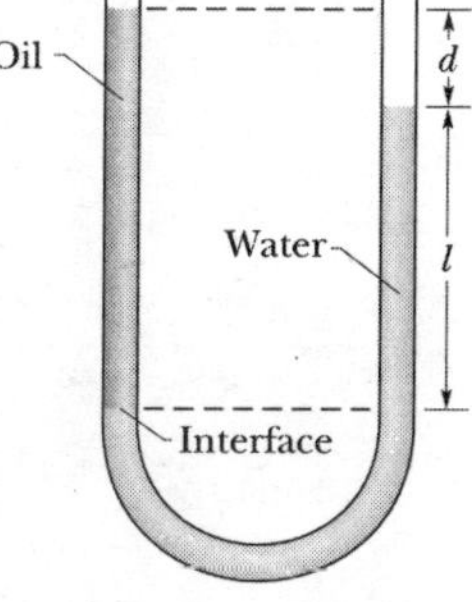

FIG. 14-4 The oil in the left arm stands higher than the water in the right arm because the oil is less dense than the water. Both fluid columns produce the same pressure p_{int} at the level of the interface.

Conceptualize: You may be tempted to think that their should not be any difference in the level in two arms. But it is also important to note that it happens when the density is same.

Classify: The pressure p_{int} at the level of the oil–water interface in the left arm depends on the density ρ_x and height of the oil above the interface. The water in the right arm *at the same level* must be at the same pressure p_{int}. The reason is that, because the water is in static equilibrium, pressures at points in the water at the same level must be the same even if the points are separated horizontally.

Compute: In the right arm, the interface is a distance l below the free surface of the *water,* and we have, from Eq. 14-8,

$$p_{int} = p_0 + \rho_w gl \qquad \text{(right arm)}$$

In the left arm, the interface is a distance $l + d$ below the free surface of the *oil,* and we have, again from Eq. 14-8,

$$p_{int} = p_0 + \rho_x g(l + d) \quad \text{(left arm)}$$

Equating these two expressions and solving for the unknown density yield

$$\rho_x = \rho_w \frac{l}{l + d} = (998 \text{ kg/m}^3) \frac{135 \text{ mm}}{135 \text{ mm} + 12.3 \text{ mm}}$$

$$= 915 \text{ kg/m}^3 \qquad \text{(Answer)}$$

Conclude: Note that the answer does not depend on the atmospheric pressure p_0 or the free-fall acceleration g.

14-4 | Measuring Pressure

The Mercury Barometer

Figure 14-5*a* shows a very basic *mercury barometer,* a device used to measure the pressure of the atmosphere. The long glass tube is filled with mercury and inverted with its open end in a dish of mercury, as the figure shows. The space above the mercury column contains only mercury vapor, whose pressure is so small at ordinary temperatures that it can be neglected.

We can use Eq. 14-7 to find the atmospheric pressure p_0 in terms of the height h of the mercury column. We choose level 1 of Fig. 14-2 to be that of the air–mercury interface and level 2 to be that of the top of the mercury column, as labeled in Fig. 14-5*a*. We then substitute

$$y_1 = 0, \quad p_1 = p_0 \quad \text{and} \quad y_2 = h, \quad p_2 = 0$$

into Eq. 14-7, finding that

$$p_0 = \rho g h \qquad (14\text{-}9)$$

where ρ is the density of the mercury.

For a given pressure, the height h of the mercury column does not depend on the cross-sectional area of the vertical tube. The fanciful mercury barometer of Fig. 14-5*b* gives the same reading as that of Fig. 14-5*a*; all that counts is the vertical distance h between the mercury levels.

Equation 14-9 shows that, for a given pressure, the height of the column of mercury depends on the value of g at the location of the barometer and on the density of mercury, which varies with temperature. The height of the column (in millimeters) is numerically equal to the pressure (in torr) *only* if the barometer is at a place where g has its accepted standard value of 9.80665 m/s^2 *and* the temperature of the mercury is 0°C. If these conditions do not prevail (and they rarely do), small corrections must be made before the height of the mercury column can be transformed into a pressure.

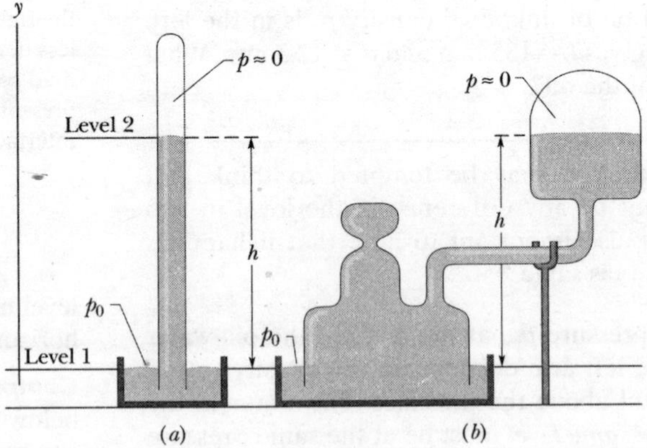

FIG. 14-5 (*a*) A mercury barometer. (*b*) Another mercury barometer. The distance h is the same in both cases.

The Open-Tube Manometer

An *open-tube manometer* (Fig. 14-6) measures the gauge pressure p_g of a gas. It consists of a **U**-tube containing a liquid, with one end of the tube connected to the vessel whose gauge pressure we wish to measure and the other end open to the atmosphere. We can use Eq. 14-7 to find the gauge pressure in terms of the height h shown in Fig. 14-6. Let us choose levels 1 and 2 as shown in Fig. 14-6. We then substitute

$$y_1 = 0, \quad p_1 = p_0 \quad \text{and} \quad y_2 = -h, \quad p_2 = p$$

into Eq. 14-7, finding that

$$p_g = p - p_0 = \rho g h \tag{14-10}$$

where ρ is the density of the liquid in the tube. The gauge pressure p_g is directly proportional to h.

The gauge pressure can be positive or negative, depending on whether $p > p_0$ or $p < p_0$. In inflated tires or the human circulatory system, the (absolute) pressure is greater than atmospheric pressure, so the gauge pressure is a positive quantity, sometimes called the *overpressure.* If you suck on a straw to pull fluid up the straw, the (absolute) pressure in your lungs is actually less than atmospheric pressure. The gauge pressure in your lungs is then a negative quantity.

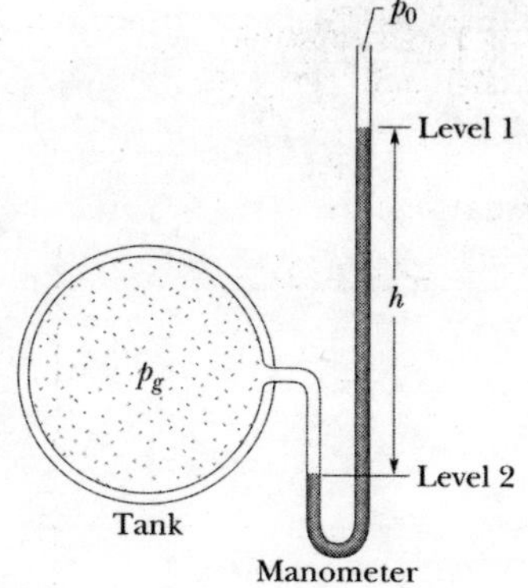

FIG. 14-6 An open-tube manometer, connected to measure the gauge pressure of the gas in the tank on the left. The right arm of the **U**-tube is open to the atmosphere.

14-5 | Pascal's Principle

When you squeeze one end of a tube to get toothpaste out the other end, you are watching **Pascal's principle** in action. This principle is also the basis for the Heimlich maneuver, in which a sharp pressure increase properly applied to the abdomen is transmitted to the throat, forcefully ejecting food lodged there. The principle was first stated clearly in 1652 by Blaise Pascal (for whom the unit of pressure is named):

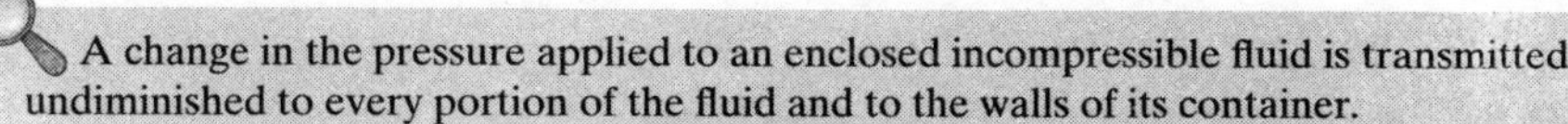
A change in the pressure applied to an enclosed incompressible fluid is transmitted undiminished to every portion of the fluid and to the walls of its container.

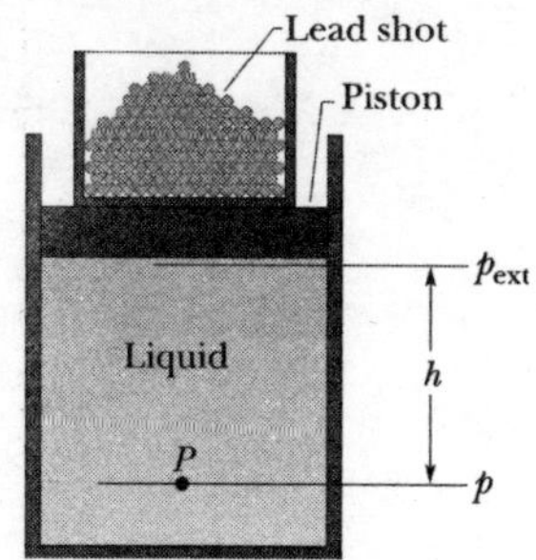

FIG. 14-7 Lead shot (small balls of lead) loaded onto the piston create a pressure p_{ext} at the top of the enclosed (incompressible) liquid. If p_{ext} is increased, by adding more lead shot, the pressure increases by the same amount at all points within the liquid.

Demonstrating Pascal's Principle

Consider the case in which the incompressible fluid is a liquid contained in a tall cylinder, as in Fig. 14-7. The cylinder is fitted with a piston on which a container of lead shot rests. The atmosphere, container, and shot exert pressure p_{ext} on the piston and thus on the liquid. The pressure p at any point P in the liquid is then

$$p = p_{ext} + \rho g h \tag{14-11}$$

Let us add a little more lead shot to the container to increase p_{ext} by an amount Δp_{ext}. The quantities ρ, g, and h in Eq. 14-11 are unchanged, so the pressure change at P is

$$\Delta p = \Delta p_{ext} \tag{14-12}$$

This pressure change is independent of h, so it must hold for all points within the liquid, as Pascal's principle states.

Pascal's Principle and the Hydraulic Lever

Figure 14-8 shows how Pascal's principle can be made the basis of a hydraulic lever. In operation, let an external force of magnitude $\vec{F}_i$ be directed downward on the left-hand (or input) piston, whose surface area is A_i. An incompressible liquid in the device then produces an upward force of magnitude $\vec{F}_o$ on the right-hand (or output) piston, whose surface area is A_o. To keep the system

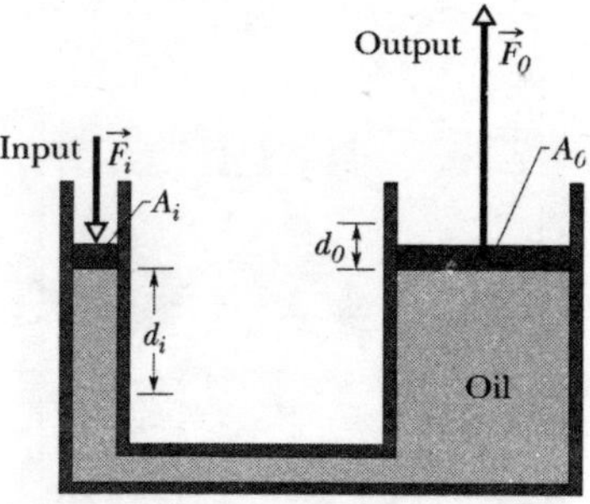

FIG. 14-8 A hydraulic arrangement that can be used to magnify a force $\vec{F}_i$. The work done is, however, not magnified and is the same for both the input and output forces.

in equilibrium, there must be a downward force of magnitude $\vec{F}_o$ on the output piston from an external load (not shown). The force $\vec{F}_i$ applied on the left and the downward force $\vec{F}_o$ from the load on the right produce a change Δp in the pressure of the liquid that is given by

$$\Delta p = \frac{F_i}{A_i} = \frac{F_o}{A_o},$$

so

$$F_o = F_i \frac{A_o}{A_i}. \tag{14-13}$$

Equation 14-13 shows that the output force F_o on the load must be greater than the input force F_i if $A_o > A_i$, as is the case in Fig. 14-8.

If we move the input piston downward a distance d_i, the output piston moves upward a distance d_o, such that the same volume V of the incompressible liquid is displaced at both pistons. Then

$$V = A_i d_i = A_o d_o,$$

which we can write as

$$d_o = d_i \frac{A_i}{A_o}. \tag{14-14}$$

This shows that, if $A_o > A_i$ (as in Fig. 14-8), the output piston moves a smaller distance than the input piston moves.

From Eqs. 14-13 and 14-14 we can write the output work as

$$W = F_o d_o = \left(F_i \frac{A_o}{A_i}\right)\left(d_i \frac{A_i}{A_o}\right) = F_i d_i, \tag{14-15}$$

which shows that the work W done *on* the input piston by the applied force is equal to the work W done *by* the output piston in lifting the load placed on it.

The advantage of a hydraulic lever is this:

With a hydraulic lever, a given force applied over a given distance can be transformed to a greater force applied over a smaller distance.

The product of force and distance remains unchanged so that the same work is done. However, there is often tremendous advantage in being able to exert the larger force. Most of us, for example, cannot lift an automobile directly but can with a hydraulic jack, even though we have to pump the handle farther than the automobile rises and in a series of small strokes.

14-6 | Archimedes' Principle

FIG. 14-9 A thin-walled plastic sack of water is in static equilibrium in the pool. The gravitational force on the sack must be balanced by a net upward force on it from the surrounding water.

Figure 14-9 shows a student in a swimming pool, manipulating a very thin plastic sack (of negligible mass) that is filled with water. She finds that the sack and its contained water are in static equilibrium, tending neither to rise nor to sink. The downward gravitational force $\vec{F}_g$ on the contained water must be balanced by a net upward force from the water surrounding the sack.

This net upward force is a **buoyant force** $\vec{F}_b$. It exists because the pressure in the surrounding water increases with depth below the surface. Thus, the pressure near the bottom of the sack is greater than the pressure near the top, which means the forces on the sack due to this pressure are greater in magnitude near the bottom of the sack than near the top. Some of the forces are represented in Fig. 14-10*a*, where the space occupied by the sack has been left empty. Note that the force vectors drawn near the bottom of that space (with upward components) have longer lengths than those drawn near the top of the sack (with downward components). If we vectorially add all the forces on the sack from the water, the horizontal components cancel and the vertical components add to yield the upward buoyant force $\vec{F}_b$ on the sack. (Force $\vec{F}_b$ is shown to the right of the pool in Fig. 14-10*a*.)

Because the sack of water is in static equilibrium, the magnitude of $\vec{F}_b$ is equal to the magnitude $m_f g$ of the gravitational force $\vec{F}_g$ on the sack of water: $F_b = m_f g$. (Subscript f refers to *fluid,* here the water.) In words, the magnitude of the buoyant force is equal to the weight of the water in the sack.

In Fig. 14-10*b*, we have replaced the sack of water with a stone that exactly fills the hole in Fig. 14-10*a*. The stone is said to *displace* the water, meaning that the stone occupies space that would otherwise be occupied by water. We have changed nothing about the shape of the hole, so the forces at the hole's surface must be the same as when the water-filled sack was in place. Thus, the same upward buoyant force that acted on the water-filled sack now acts on the stone; that is, the magnitude F_b of the buoyant force is equal to $m_f g$, the weight of the water displaced by the stone.

Unlike the water-filled sack, the stone is not in static equilibrium. The downward gravitational force $\vec{F}_g$ on the stone is greater in magnitude than the upward buoyant force, as is shown in the free-body diagram in Fig. 14-10*b*. The stone thus accelerates downward, sinking to the bottom of the pool.

Let us next exactly fill the hole in Fig. 14-10*a* with a block of lightweight wood, as in Fig. 14-10*c*. Again, nothing has changed about the forces at the hole's surface, so the magnitude F_b of the buoyant force is still equal to $m_f g$, the weight of the displaced water. Like the stone, the block is not in static equilibrium. However, this time the gravitational force $\vec{F}_g$ is lesser in magnitude than the buoyant force (as shown to the right of the pool), and so the block accelerates upward, rising to the top surface of the water.

Our results with the sack, stone, and block apply to all fluids and are summarized in **Archimedes' principle:**

> When a body is fully or partially submerged in a fluid, a buoyant force $\vec{F}_b$ from the surrounding fluid acts on the body. The force is directed upward and has a magnitude equal to the weight $m_f g$ of the fluid that has been displaced by the body.

The buoyant force on a body in a fluid has the magnitude

$$F_b = m_f g \quad \text{(buoyant force)} \tag{14-16}$$

where m_f is the mass of the fluid that is displaced by the body.

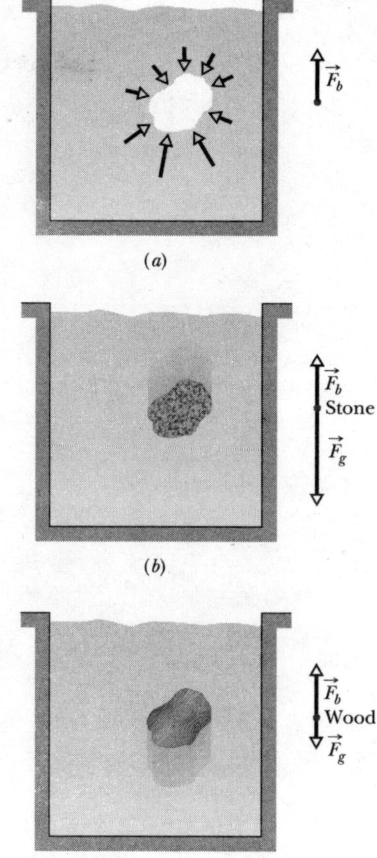

FIG. 14-10 (*a*) The water surrounding the hole in the water produces a net upward buoyant force on whatever fills the hole. (*b*) For a stone of the same volume as the hole, the gravitational force exceeds the buoyant force in magnitude. (*c*) For a lump of wood of the same volume, the gravitational force is less than the buoyant force in magnitude.

Floating

When we release a block of lightweight wood just above the water in a pool, the block moves into the water because the gravitational force on it pulls it downward. As the block displaces more and more water, the magnitude F_b of the upward buoyant force acting on it increases. Eventually, F_b is large enough to equal the magnitude F_g of the downward gravitational force on the block, and the block comes to rest. The block is then in static equilibrium and is said to be *floating* in the water. In general,

> When a body floats in a fluid, the magnitude F_b of the buoyant force on the body is equal to the magnitude F_g of the gravitational force on the body.

We can write this statement as

$$F_b = F_g \quad \text{(floating)} \tag{14-17}$$

From Eq. 14-16, we know that $F_b = m_f g$. Thus,

When a body floats in a fluid, the magnitude F_g of the gravitational force on the body is equal to the weight $m_f g$ of the fluid that has been displaced by the body.

We can write this statement as

$$F_g = m_f g \quad \text{(floating)} \tag{14-18}$$

In other words, a floating body displaces its own weight of fluid.

Apparent Weight in a Fluid

If we place a stone on a scale that is calibrated to measure weight, then the reading on the scale is the stone's weight. However, if we do this underwater, the upward buoyant force on the stone from the water decreases the reading. That reading is then an apparent weight. In general, an **apparent weight** is related to the actual weight of a body and the buoyant force on the body by

$$\begin{pmatrix}\text{apparent}\\ \text{weight}\end{pmatrix} = \begin{pmatrix}\text{actual}\\ \text{weight}\end{pmatrix} - \begin{pmatrix}\text{magnitude of}\\ \text{buoyant force}\end{pmatrix},$$

which we can write as

$$\text{weight}_{\text{app}} = \text{weight} - F_b \quad \text{(apparent weight)} \tag{14-19}$$

If, in some test of strength, you had to lift a heavy stone, you could do it more easily with the stone underwater. Then your applied force would need to exceed only the stone's apparent weight, not its larger actual weight, because the upward buoyant force would help you lift the stone.

The magnitude of the buoyant force on a floating body is equal to the body's weight. Equation 14-19 thus tells us that a floating body has an apparent weight of zero—the body would produce a reading of zero on a scale. (When astronauts prepare to perform a complex task in space, they practice the task floating underwater, where their apparent weight is zero as it is in space.)

CHECKPOINT 2 A penguin floats first in a fluid of density ρ_0, then in a fluid of density $0.95\rho_0$, and then in a fluid of density $1.1\rho_0$. (a) Rank the densities according to the magnitude of the buoyant force on the penguin, greatest first. (b) Rank the densities according to the amount of fluid displaced by the penguin, greatest first.

Sample Problem 14-4

In Fig. 14-11*a*, a surfer rides on the front side of a wave, at a point where a tangent to the wave has a slope of $\theta = 30.0°$. The combined mass of surfer and surfboard is $m = 83.0$ kg, and the board has a submerged volume of $V = 2.50 \times 10^{-2}$ m³. The surfer maintains his position on the wave as the wave moves at constant speed toward shore. What are the magnitude and direction (relative to the positive direction of the x axis in Fig. 14-11*b*) of the drag force on the surfboard from the water?

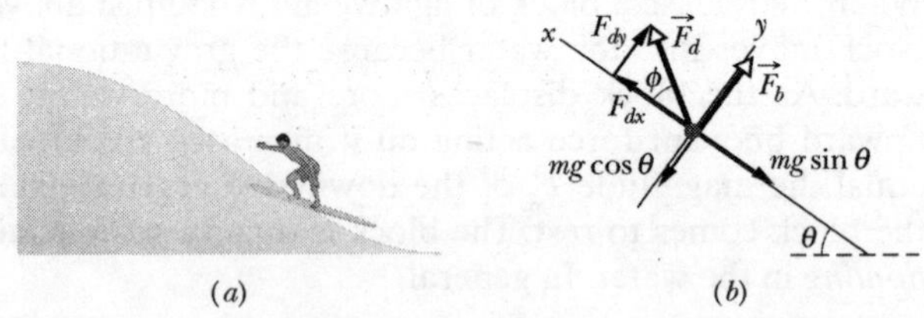

FIG. 14-11 (*a*) Surfer. (*b*) Free-body diagram showing the forces on the surfer–surfboard system.

Conceptualize: It may look bit perplexing at first that how the surfer is experiencing a drag force, that is, a force opposite to the velocity and still moving with constant velocity. But paying close attention to the question you will realize that the wave has a slope.

The buoyancy force on the surfer has a magnitude F_b equal to the weight of the seawater displaced by the submerged volume of the surfboard. The direction of the force is perpendicular to the surface at the surfer's location.

Classify: By Newton's second law, because the surfer moves at constant speed toward the shore, the (vector) sum of the buoyancy force $\vec{F}_b$ the gravitational force $\vec{F}_g$, and the drag force $\vec{F}_d$ must be 0.

Compute: The forces and their components are shown in the free-body diagram of Fig. 14-11*b*. The gravitational force $\vec{F}_g$ is downward and has a component of $mg \sin\theta$ down the slope and a component of $mg \cos\theta$ perpendicular to the slope. A drag force $\vec{F}_d$ from the water acts on the surfboard because water is continuously forced up into the wave as the wave continues to move toward the shore. This push on the surfboard is upward and to the rear, at angle ϕ to the x axis. The buoyancy force $\vec{F}_b$ is perpendicular to the water surface; its magnitude depends on the mass m_f of the water displaced by the surfboard, as given by Eq. 14-16 ($F_b = m_f g$). From Eq. 14-2 ($\rho = m/V$), we can write the mass in terms of the seawater density ρ_w and the submerged volume V of the surfboard: $m_f = \rho_w V$. From Table 14-1, seawater density ρ_w is 1.024×10^3 kg/m³. Thus, the magnitude of the buoyant force is

$$\begin{aligned} F_b &= m_f g = \rho_w V g \\ &= (1.024 \times 10^3 \text{ kg/m}^3)(2.50 \times 10^{-2} \text{ m}^3)(9.8 \text{ m/s}^2) \\ &= 2.509 \times 10^2 \text{ N} \end{aligned}$$

So, Newton's second law for the y axis,

$$F_{dy} + F_b - mg\cos\theta = m(0)$$

becomes

$$F_{dy} + 2.509 \times 10^2 \text{ N} - (83 \text{ kg})(9.8 \text{ m/s}^2)\cos 30.0° = 0$$

yielding

$$F_{dy} = 453.5 \text{ N}$$

Similarly, Newton's second law $\vec{F}_{\text{net}} = m\vec{a}$ for the x axis,

$$F_{dx} - mg\sin\theta = m(0)$$

yields $$F_{dx} = 406.7 \text{ N}$$

Combining the two components of the drag force tells us that the force has magnitude

$$\begin{aligned} F_d &= \sqrt{(406.7 \text{ N})^2 + (453.5 \text{ N})^2} \\ &= 609 \text{ N} \qquad \text{(Answer)} \end{aligned}$$

and angle

$$\phi = \tan^{-1}\left(\frac{453.5 \text{ N}}{406.7 \text{ N}}\right) = 48.1° \qquad \text{(Answer)}$$

Conclude: Wipeout avoided: If the surfer tilts the board slightly forward, the magnitude of the drag force decreases and angle ϕ changes. The result is that the net force is no longer zero and the surfer moves down the face of the wave. The descent is somewhat self-adjusting because, as the surfer descends, the tilt angle θ of the wave surface decreases and thus so does the component of the gravitational force $mg \sin\theta$ pulling the surfer down the slope. So, the surfer can adjust the board to re-establish equilibrium, now lower on the wave. Similarly, by tilting the board slightly backward, the surfer increases the drag and moves up the face of the wave. If the surfer is still on the lower part of the wave, then both θ and $mg \sin\theta$ increase and again the surfer can control the forces and re-establish equilibrium.

Sample Problem 14-5

In Fig. 14-12, a block of density $\rho = 800$ kg/m³ floats face down in a fluid of density $\rho_f = 1200$ kg/m³. The block has height $H = 6.0$ cm.

(a) By what depth h is the block submerged?

Conceptualize: Floating requires that the upward buoyant force on the block match the downward gravitational force on the block.

Classify: The buoyant force is equal to the weight $m_f g$ of the fluid displaced by the submerged portion of the block.

H h

FIG. 14-12 Block of height H floats in a fluid, to a depth of h.

Compute: From Eq. 14-16, we know that the buoyant force has the magnitude $F_b = m_f g$, where m_f is the mass of the fluid displaced by the block's submerged volume V_f. From Eq. 14-2 ($\rho = m/V$), we know that the mass of the displaced fluid is $m_f = \rho_f V_f$. We don't know V_f but if we symbolize the block's face length as L and its width as W, then from Fig. 14-12 we see that the submerged volume must be $V_f = LWh$. If we now combine our three expressions, we find that the upward buoyant force has magnitude

$$F_b = m_f g = \rho_f V_f g = \rho_f LWhg \qquad (14\text{-}20)$$

Similarly, we can write the magnitude F_g of the gravitational force on the block, first in terms of the block's mass m, then in terms of the block's density ρ and (full) volume V, and then in terms of the block's dimensions L, W, and H (the full height):

$$F_g = mg = \rho Vg = \rho_f LWHg \qquad (14\text{-}21)$$

The floating block is stationary. Thus, writing Newton's second law for components along a vertical y axis ($F_{\text{net},y} = ma_y$), we have

$$F_b - F_g = m(0)$$

or from Eqs. 14-20 and 14-21,

$$\rho_f LWhg - \rho LWHg = 0$$

which gives us

$$h = \frac{\rho}{\rho_f} H = \frac{800 \text{ kg/m}^3}{1200 \text{ kg/m}^3}(6.0 \text{ cm})$$

$$= 4.0 \text{ cm} \qquad \text{(Answer)}$$

(b) If the block is held fully submerged and then released, what is the magnitude of its acceleration?

Conceptualize/Classify: The gravitational force on the block is the same but now, with the block fully submerged, the volume of the displaced water as $V = LWH$. (The full height of the block is used.) This means that the value of F_b is now larger, and the block will no longer be stationary but will accelerate upward.

Compute: Now Newton's second law yields

$$F_b - F_g = ma$$

or

$$\rho_f LWHg - \rho LWHg = \rho LWHa$$

where we inserted ρLWH for the mass m of the block. Solving for a leads to

$$a = \left(\frac{\rho_f}{\rho} - 1\right)g = \left(\frac{1200 \text{ kg/m}^3}{800 \text{ kg/m}^3} - 1\right)(9.8 \text{ m/s}^2)$$

$$= 4.9 \text{ m/s}^2 \qquad \text{(Answer)}$$

Conclude: As expected answer is coming such that the block is accelerating upward.

Sample Problem 14-6

Buoyant force on a submerged object

A spherical buoy has a diameter of 2 m, and mass 100 kg, and is anchored to the seafloor with a cable as shown in Fig. 14-13*a*. The buoy is completely immersed in water as illustrated. For this condition what is the tension of the cable?

Conceptualize: This is a simple problem involving a body in equilibrium. This body will be experiencing weight, tension, and buoyant force.

Classify: We first draw a free-body diagram of the buoy as shown in Fig. 14-13*b*, where F_B is the buoyant force acting on the buoy, W is the weight of the buoy, and T is the tension in the cable.

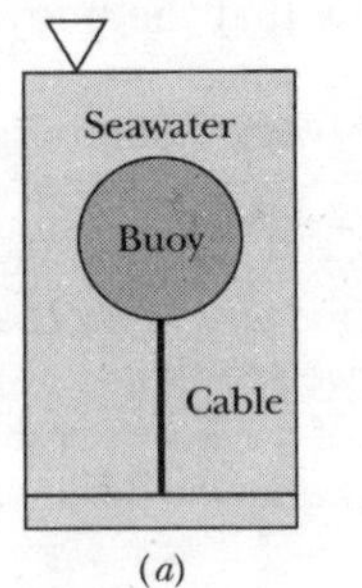

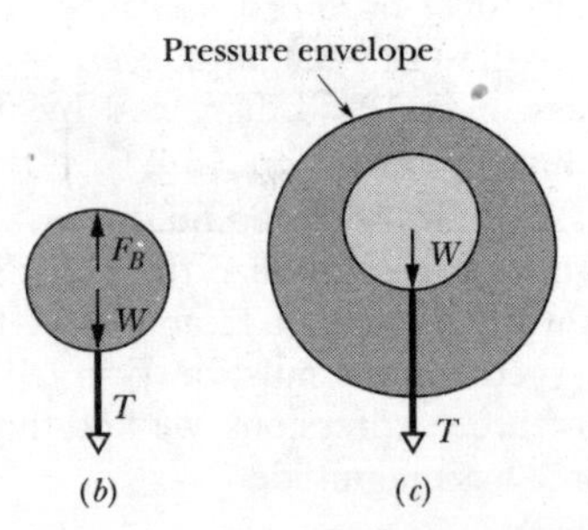

FIG. 14-13

Compute: For equilibrium it follows that

$$T = F_B - W$$

$$F_B = \gamma V g \qquad \text{(i)}$$

From Eq. (i) and taking for water, $\gamma = (1000 \text{ kg/m}^3$ and $V = \pi d^3/6)$ gives

$$F_B = (1000 \text{ kg/m}^3)[(\pi/6)(2 \text{ m})^3(10 \text{ m/s}^2)] = 41888 \text{ N}$$

The tension in the cable can now be calculated as

$$T = 41888 \text{ N} - 1000 \text{ N} = 40888 \text{ N} \qquad \text{(Answer)}$$

Conclude: Note that we replaced the effect of the hydrostatic pressure force on the body by the buoyant force, F_B. Another correct free-body diagram of the buoy is shown in Fig. 14-13*c*. The net effect of the pressure forces on the surface of the buoy is equal to the upward force of magnitude, F_B (the buoyant force). *Do not include both the buoyant force and the hydrostatic pressure effects in your calculations — use one or the other.*

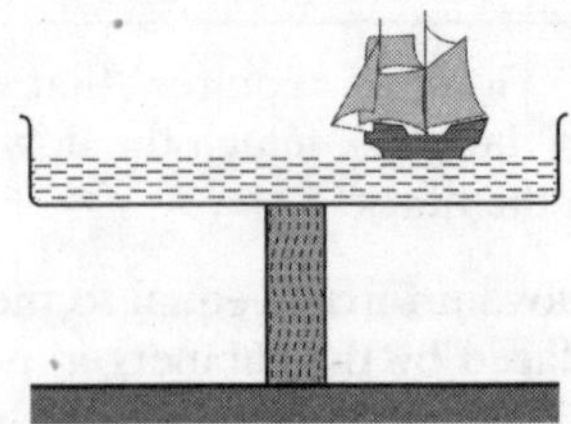

CHECKPOINT 3 A wooden block floats vertically in a glass filled with water. How will the level of the water in the glass change if the block is kept in a horizontal position?

CHECKPOINT 4 A vessel filled with water is placed exactly in middle of a thin wall as shown in figure. Will the system topple if a small wooden boat carrying some weight is floated in the vessel?

Sample Problem 14-7 Build your skill

A homogeneous piece of ice floats in a glass filled with water. How will the level of the water in the glass change when the ice melts?

Solution: Since the piece of ice floats, the weight of the water displaced by it is equal to the weight of the ice itself or the weight of the water it produces upon melting. For this reason the water formed by the piece of ice will occupy a volume equal to that of the submerged portion, and the level of the water will not change.

CHECKPOINT 5 A piece of ice is floating in a tub filled with water. How will the level of the water in the tub change when the ice melts ? Consider the following cases:

(1) A stone is frozen in the ice.

(2) The ice contains an air bubble.

Sample Problem 14-8 Build your skill

A vessel with a body floating in it is kept in an elevator accelerating downward with acceleration a such that $a < g$. Will the body rise or sink further in the vessel?

The force of buoyancy on the body can be written as $F = \rho V_2 (g - a)$, where V_2 is the volume of the submerged portion of the body in the lift. As pressure at a point h below the surface will become $\rho(g - a)h$ instead of ρgh. Applying the Newton's second Law, remembering that the body was accelerating upward at a.

$$Mg - \rho V_2 (g - a) = Ma$$

Hence, $V_2 = \dfrac{M}{\rho}$ thus $V_2 = V$, as in a stationary vessel, $V = \dfrac{M}{\rho}$. Thus, the body does not rise to the surface.

Sample Problem 14-9 Build your skill

Mercury is poured into two communicating identical cylindrical vessels, then equal amount of water is poured in both the vessels above the mercury. The level of the water in both vessels becomes same. Will the level of the water and the mercury be the same if a piece of wood is dropped into one vessel and some water equal in weight to this piece is added to the other?

Solution: Before the piece of wood is droped the level of the mercury was same, as the level of the water in both the vessel is same.

The piece of wood applies the same force as the water added, on the mercury. So the level of the mercury in both vessels will be same.

The submerged portion of the piece of wood occupies the same volume as the equal weight of the water. As water that will be displaced by this piece is equal to its weight which is equal to the amount of water added. Therefore, if the cross sections of the vessels are the same, the level of the water in both vessels will coincide.

Sample Problem 14-10

Water is filled to a height H behind a dam of width w as shown in Fig. 14-14a. Determine the resultant force exerted by the water on the dam.

Conceptualize: Pressure is varying with depth. We cannot calculate the force on the dam by water by simply multiplying the area by the pressure at some depth.

Classify: So we will use integration to solve this example. We will consider elements at some depth, write pressure there and integrate over the full depth of water.

Compute: Let's consider a vertical y axis, starting from the bottom of the dam. Let's consider a thin horizontal strip at a height y above the bottom, such as shown in Fig. 14-14. We need to consider force due to the

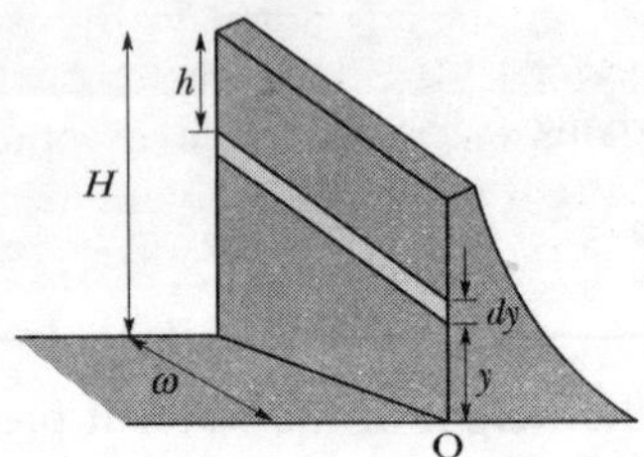

FIG. 14-14 Water exerts a force on a dam

pressure of the water only as atmospheric pressure acts on both sides of the dam.

The pressure due to the water at the depth h:

$$P = \rho gh = \rho g(H - y)$$

The force exerted on the shaded strip of area $dA = wdy$:

$$dF = P\,dA = \rho g(H - y)\,\omega dy$$

Integrate to find the total force on the dam:

$$F = \int P\,dA = \int_0^H \rho g\,(H - y)\omega dy = 1/2\ \rho g\omega H^2$$

Conclude: Note that the thickness of the dam shown in Fig. 14-14 increases with depth. This design accounts for the increasing pressure that water exerts on the dam walls as the depth increases.

Find the total torque exerted by the water on dam about a horizontal axis through O. Also find the effective line of action of the total force exerted by the water is at a distance 1/3 H above O.

Classify: We will use integration to solve this example. We will consider elements at some depth, write pressure there and thus write torque about the axis passing through O, then integrate over the full depth of water.

Conclude: The torque is $\tau = \int d = \int rdF$

From the figure $\tau = \int_0^H y[\rho g(H - y)wdy] = \frac{1}{6}\rho gwH^3$

The total force is given as $\frac{1}{2}\rho gwH^3$

If this were applied at a height y_{eff} such that the torque remains unchanged, we have

$$\frac{1}{6}\rho gwH^3 = y_{\text{eff}}\left[\frac{1}{2}\rho gwH^2\right] \text{ and } y_{\text{eff}} = \frac{1}{3}H$$

Sample Problem 14-11 Build your skill

Three vessels having different shapes are shown in Fig. 14-15*a*, having the base area and the same weight when empty. The vessels are filled with mercury to the same level. Neglecting the effect of the atmosphere, find (a) which vessel has the maximum and which vessel has the minimum pressure at the bottom, or if the pressure is the same?

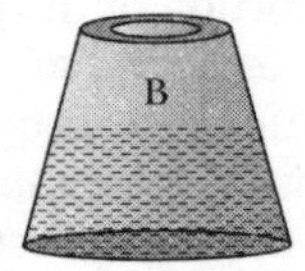

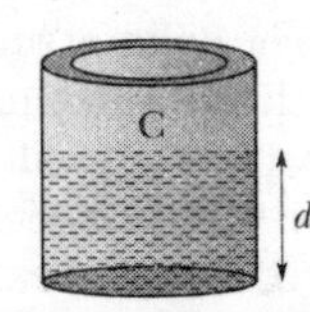

FIG. 14-15*a* Three differently shaped vessels filled with water to same level.

Solution: (a) The mercury at the bottom of each vessel is at the same depth d below the surface. Neglecting the pressure at the surface, the pressures at the bottom must be equal hence:

$$P = \rho gd$$

Solution: (b) Which vessel shows the maximum weight when weighed on a weighing scale or do they all weigh the same? The weight of each filled vessel is equal to the weight of the vessel itself plus the weight of the mercury inside. The vessels themselves are of equal weights, but vessel A holds more mercury than C, while vessel B holds less mercury than C. Vessel A weighs the most and vessel B weighs the least.

(c) As the mercury exerts the same downward force on the bottom of each vessel, then why does the vessels weigh differently ?

Solution: In vessel C, forces due to fluid pressure on the sides of the container are horizontal. Forces on any two diametrically opposite points on the walls of the container are equal and opposite; thus, the net force on the container walls is zero. The force on the bottom is

$$F = PA = (\rho gd)\,(\pi r^2)$$

The volume of water in the cylinder is $V = \pi r^2 d$, so

$$F = \rho gV = (\rho V)\,g = mg$$

The force on the bottom of vessel C is equal to the weight of the water, as expected. The forces due to fluid pressure on the sides of the containers A and B have vertical components also. Hence, the force between the fluid and the base of container will not be equal to the weight of the fluid. These containers support the fluid by exerting an upward force equal in magnitude to the weight of the fluid but some force is being applied by the sidewalls and the remaining by the bottom. Fig. 14-15*b* shows the forces acting on each container due to the water.

The force on the bottom of vessel A is less than the weight of the mercury in the container, while the force on the bottom of vessel B is greater than the weight of the mercury. In vessel A, the forces on the container walls have downward components as well as horizontal components. The sum of the downward components of the forces on the walls and the downward force on the bottom of the container is equal to the weight of the water. Similarly, the forces on the walls of vessel B have upward components. In each case, the total force on the bottom and sides of the container due to the water is equal to the weight of the water.

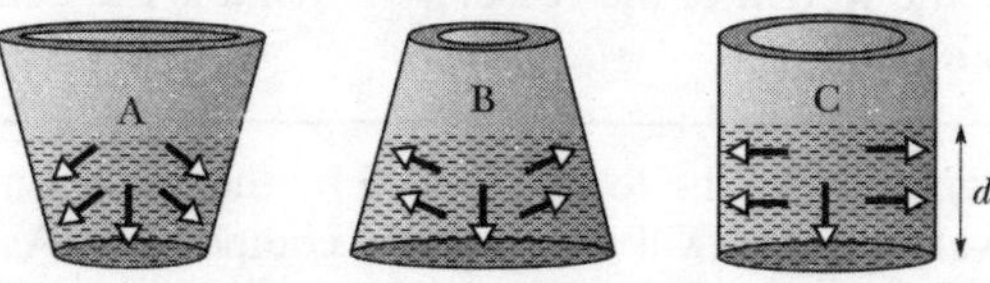

FIG. 14-15*b* Forces exerted on the containers by the water.

Hydrostatic Force on a Curved Surface

Vessels may have walls and even bottoms which are nonplanar. Although theoretically speaking, the resultant fluid force on a surface can be determined by integration, as was done for the plane surfaces. This is generally a really tough process and we cannot offer simple, general formulas. Here we discuss an alternative approach where we will find the horizontal and vertical components of the forces by considering the fluid volume enclosed by the curved surface in equilibrium.

For example, consider the curved portion *BC* of the open tank, having a unit length perpendicular to the plane of the paper, as shown in Fig. (14-16*a*). To find the resultant fluid force acting on this section, we consider entire fluid that is enclosed by the surface *BC*, the horizontal plane surface *AB*, and the vertical plane surface *AC* as a separate body. Imagine that this body is seperated by the remaining fluid mass by an imaginary surface. The free-body diagram for the body is shown in Fig. 14-16*b*. From the discussion of forces on planar surfaces, we know the magnitude and the effective point of application of forces F_1 and F_2. The weight, W of the mass of fluid enclosed by the imaginary surface is a product of density of the fluid and the enclosed volume and acts through the center of gravity (CG) of the mass of fluid contained within the imaginary surface. The forces F_H and F_V represent the components of the force that the tank exerts on the fluid.

In order for this force system to be in translational and rotational equilibrium, the horizontal component F_H must be equal in magnitude and collinear with F_2, and the vertical component F_V equal in magnitude and collinear with the resultant of the vertical forces F_1 and W. Thus,

$$F_H = F_2$$

$$F_V = F_1 = W$$

and the magnitude of the resultant is obtained from the equation:

$$F_R = \sqrt{(F_H)^2 + (F_V)^2}$$

From the principles of equilibrium discussed earlier, it is known that when a body is held in equilibrium by three nonparallel forces their lines of action intersect at a common point, and should be coplanar. Although our analysis is being done for the fluid, by Newton's third law the force experienced by the curved surface is equal and opposite to F_R . The desired fluid force is shown in Fig. 14-16*c*.

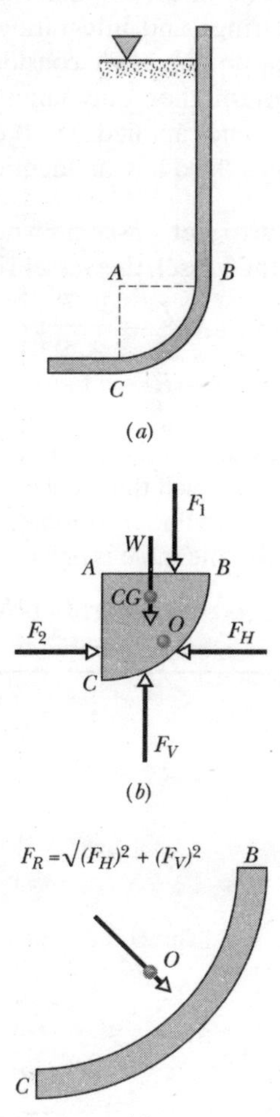

FIG. 14-16 (*a*) Curved portion of an open tank. (*b*) Free-body diagram of the body of fluid enclosed in the space *ABC* as shown in part (*a*). (*c*) Force on the curved wall of the tank due to fluid.

Sample Problem 14-12

A conical vessel without a bottom tightly stands on a table. A liquid is poured into the vessel and as soon as its level reaches the height h, the pressure of the liquid raises the vessel. The radius of the bottom greater base of the vessel is R, the semi-vertex angle of the cone is α, and the weight of the vessel is W. What is the density of the liquid?

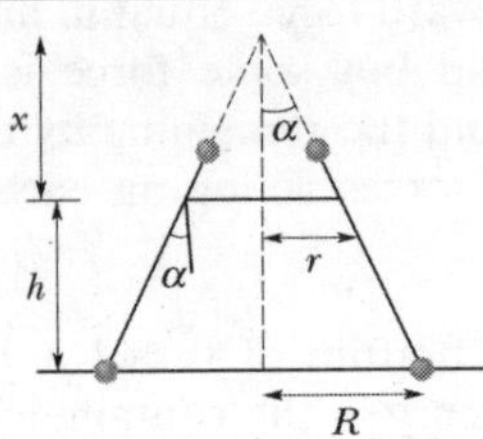

FIG. 14-17a A frustum without any bottom filled with fluid.

Conceptualize: The forces applied by the liquid on the side walls of cone will have vertical components. As the amount of liquid increases, this force will increase till it lifts the vessel.

Classify: We need to calculate the force mentioned above. The direct solution may appear to be taking elemental rings and integrating the force. But there is a faster approach. If we consider the liquid as a system in equilibrium, then only unknown force acting on it will be the one applied by the sidewalls. According to Newton's third law, an identical force acts on the vessel.

Compute: Let's assume when the height of the liquid is h in the vessel, the vessel rises.

$$\tan\alpha = \frac{r}{x} = \frac{R}{x+h}$$

on solving $r = R - h\tan\alpha$ (i)

The pressure on the "bottom" of the vessel is ρgh and the force with which the hatched portion (the truncated cone minus the cylinder volume) of the liquid (Fig. 14.17b) presses on the table is $\rho gh\pi$

$$(R^2 - r^2) = \rho gh\pi\,(2Rh\tan\alpha - h^2\tan^2\alpha)$$

According to Newton's third law, an identical force acts on the liquid. For equilibrium of the liquid at the moment when the vessel starts rising

$$W + W_1 = \rho gh\pi\,(2Rh\tan\alpha - h^2\tan^2\alpha)$$

where W_1 is the weight of the hatched portion of the liquid

$$W_1 = \frac{\rho gh}{3}\{\pi R^2 + \pi(R - h\tan\alpha)^2 + \pi R(R - h\tan\alpha)\} - \rho gh\pi(R - h\tan\alpha)^2$$

Therefore, $$\rho = \frac{W}{\pi gh^2\tan\alpha\left(R - \dfrac{h\tan\alpha}{3}\right)}$$

Conclude: If the vessel would have been a cylinder it will be impossible to make it lifted up by putting liquid in the vessel. We can verify this by keeping value of α as zero. We get required density as infinite, which is meaningless.

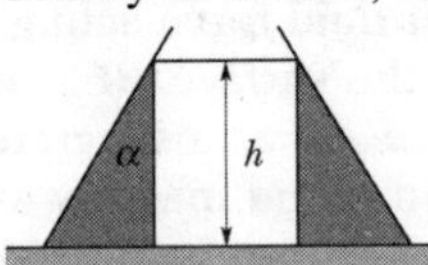

FIG. 14-17b Dividing fluid in two parts for calculating the volume of the fluid.

Linear Accelerated Motion

We consider an open container of a liquid that is moving along a straight line with a constant acceleration a as shown in Fig. 14-18.

Let's consider a small horizontal cylinder of length dx and cross-sectional area A located at y distance below the free surface of the fluid. This cylinder is accelerating in ground frame with an accleration a hence the net horizontal force acting on it should be equal to the product of mass (dm) and acceleration.

$$dm = Adx\rho$$

$$P_2A - P_1A = (Adx\rho)\,a$$

If we say that the right face of the cylinder is y below the free surface of the fluid then the left surface is $y + dy$ below the surface of liquid. Thus,

$$P_2 - P_1 = \rho g dy$$

therefore, $$\frac{dy}{dx} = \frac{a}{g}$$

As the slope of the free surface is coming out to be constant, we can say that it must be a straight line.

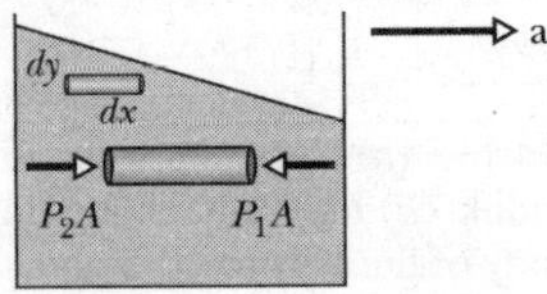

FIG. 14-18 Linear accelerated motion of the vessel containing fluid.

$$\tan\theta = \frac{a}{g} \tag{14-22}$$

If the container has acceleration along y also, then the slope of this line is given by the relationship.

$$\frac{dy}{dx} = -\frac{a_x}{g + a_y}$$

Along a free surface, the pressure is constant, so that for the accelerating mass shown in Fig. 14-19, the free surface will be inclined if $a_x \neq 0$. In addition, all lines parallel to the free surface will have same pressure.

For the special circumstance in which $a_x = 0$, $a_y \neq 0$. which corresponds to the mass of fluid accelerating in the vertical direction, the fluid surface will be horizontal. However, we see that the pressure variatio is not $\rho g dy$, but is given by the equation.

$$dP = \rho(g + a_y)\, dy$$

Thus, the pressure on the bottom of a liquid-filled tank which is resting on the floor of an elevator that is accelerating upward will be more than, if the, tank would have been at rest (or moving with a constant velocity). It is to be noted that for a freely falling fluid mass ($a_y = -g$), the pressure variation in all three coordinate directions are zero, which means that the pressure throughout will be same. The pressure throughout a "blob" of a liquid floating in an orbiting space shuttle (a form of free fall) is zero. The only force holding the liquid together is surface tension.

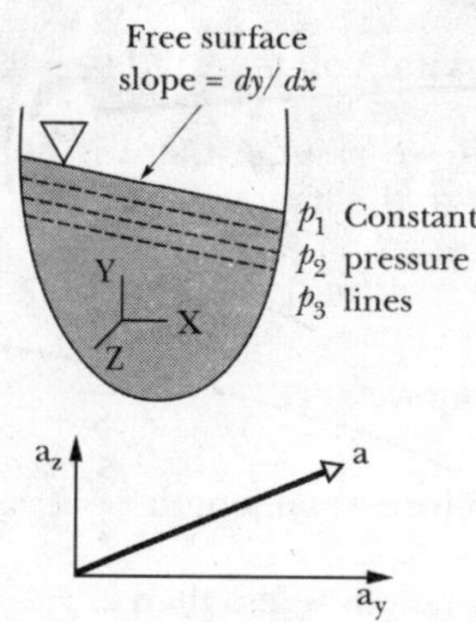

FIG. 14-19 A vessel accelerating in at some angle with horizontal.

Sample Problem 14-13

The cross section of a tank kept on a vehicle is shown in Fig 14-20*a*. The rectangular tank is open to the atmosphere. During motion of the vehicle, the tank is subjected to a constant linear acceleration, a = 2.5 m/s². How much fluid will be left inside the tank if initially the tank is half filled. The vessel is 5 m wide and 2 m high.

Conceptualize: As discussed earlier, the fluid will have an inclined free surface as shown in the figures, having angle θ with horizontal. You can imagine that if we accelerate it at a higher rate more fluid will get spilled in the process as it will rise higher.

Classify: If the height of the liquid on the left wall is greater than 2 m the fluid will be spilled out.

Compute: Using Eq. (14-22), we can find the angle that the fluid will make with the horizontal.

$$\tan\theta = \frac{2.5}{10} = \frac{1}{4}$$

Let's assume that the dimension of tank in the plane perpendicular to the page is *d*.

From the geometry its easy to see that free surface on right-hand side will go down and the same will rise on left-hand side. Thus, if we assume that fluid on right-hand side has not touched the floor, we will have fluid taking a shape as shown in Fig 14-20*b*. The cuboid part will have volume $x \times 5 \times d$, where x is the height above the bottom.

The wedge part will have the volume $\frac{1}{2} \times h \times 5 \times d$, where h can be found in the following:

$$(h/5) = \tan\theta = (1/4)$$

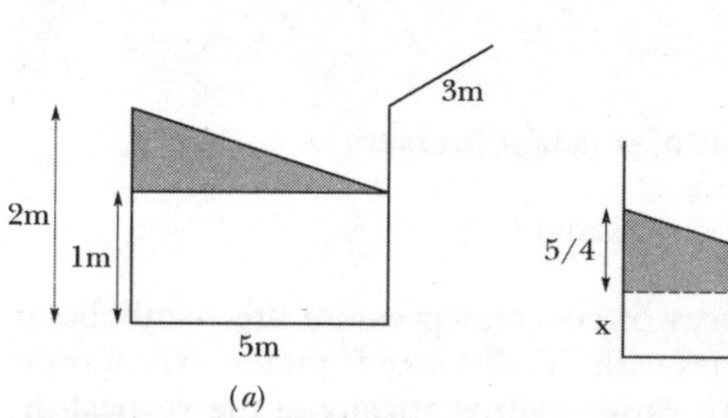

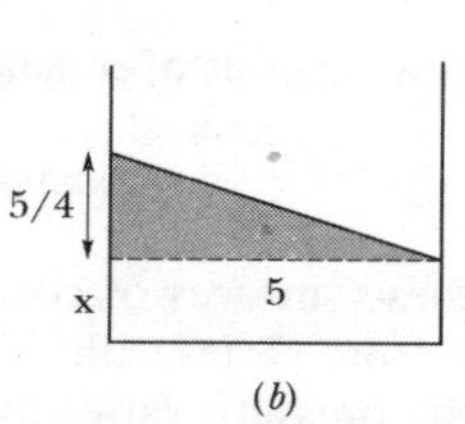

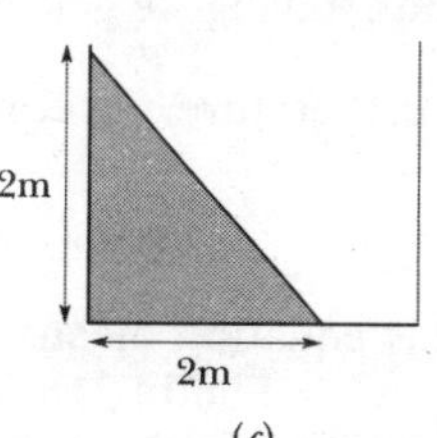

FIG. 14-20

Thus total volume will be $\frac{1}{2} \times (5/4) \times 5 \times d + x \times 5 \times d$

and if we assume there is no spilling than it must be equal to the final volume.

$$\frac{1}{2} \times (5/4) \times 5 \times d + x \times 5 \times d = 1 \times 5 \times d$$

Solving we get $\quad x = \frac{3}{8}$

Therefore, total length $\frac{5}{4} + \frac{3}{8} = \frac{10+3}{8} = \frac{13}{8} < 2$

Thus, height is less than 2.

Hence, water will not spill.

Conclude: The answer may sound little anti-climax as there is no spill, but at least we know that as acceleration inceases, the chances of spilling will also increase.

In Case Of: How much fluid will be left inside the tank if the vehicle accelerates at accleration, $a = 10$ m/s^2?

Classify: If the height of the liquid on the left wall is greater than 2 m the fluid will be spilled out.

Compute: Using Eq. (14-22) we can find the angle that the fluid will make with the horizontal.

$$\tan\theta = \frac{10}{10} = 1, \text{ thus } \quad \theta = \frac{\pi}{4}$$

In this case, fluid cannot remain inside. Fluid having an inclined free surface at 45° angle, and covering the bottom of length 5 m, will also be 5 m high. This will require the wall to be of 5 m height, which is just 2 m for the given vessel. Instead, if we think it other way round to keep in contact with the left-hand side wall, bottom will have to be covered only 2 m with the fluid as shown in Fig. 14-20*c*.

Fluid inside = $(1/2) \times 2 \times 2 \times d$ m^3

Remain inside = $2d$ m^3

Thus, volume of fluid gone outside = $3d$ m^3

CHECKPOINT 6 If the vessel is closed from the top and now accelerated at 10 m/s^2, then what length of the floor will be uncovered?

Rotating Vessel

Consider a cylinderical vessel, rotating at constant angular velocity about its axis. If it contains fluid then after an initial irregular shape, it will rotate with the tank as a rigid body. The acceleration of fluid particles located at a distance r from the axis of rotation will be equal to $\omega^2 r$, and the direction of the acceleration is toward the axis of rotation as shown in Fig. 14-21.

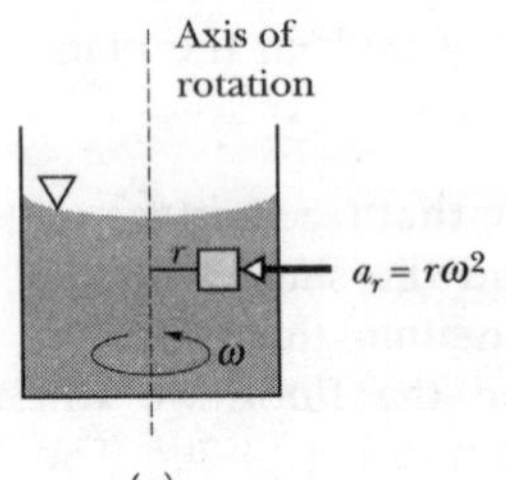

The fluid particles will be undergoing circular motion.

Let's consider a small horizontal cylinder of length dr and cross-sectional area A located y below the free surface of the fluid and r from the axis (Fig. 14-19*a*). This cylinder is accelerating in ground frame with accleration $\omega^2 r$ toward the axis; hence, the net horizontal force acting on it should be equal to the product of mass (dm) and acceleration.

$$dm = Adr\rho$$

$$P_2A - P_1A = (Adr\rho)\,\omega^2 r$$

If we say that the left face of the cylinder is y below the free surface of the fluid then the right surface is $y + dy$ below the surface of liquid. Thus,

$$P_2 - P_1 = \rho g\, dy$$

Thus, solving we get $\quad \frac{dy}{dr} = \frac{r\omega^2}{g}$

and, therefore, the equation for surfaces of constant pressure is

$$y = \frac{\omega^2 r^2}{2g} + \text{constant}$$

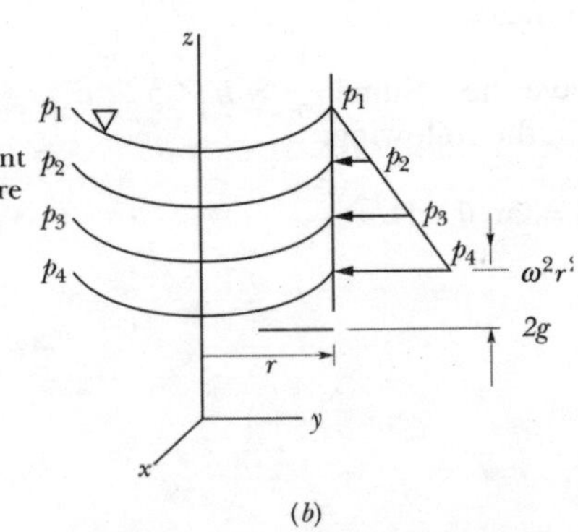

FIG. 14-21 (*a*)A cylinder containing fluid is rotating about its axis. (*b*)Constant pressure lines in the rotating cylinder.

This equation means that these surfaces of constant pressure are parabolic as shown in Fig. 14-21*b*. The pressure varies with the distance from the axis of rotation, but at a fixed radius, the pressure varies hydrostatically in the vertical direction as shown in Fig. 14-21*b*.

Sample Problem 14-14

Free Surface Shape of Liquid in a Rotating Tank
The angular velocity, ω, of a rotating body or shaft can be measured by attaching an open cylinder of liquid, as shown in Fig. 14-22a, and measuring the change in the fluid level, $H - h_0$, caused by the rotation of the fluid. Determine the relationship between this change in fluid level and the angular velocity. Assume no fluid is spilling out of the vessel.

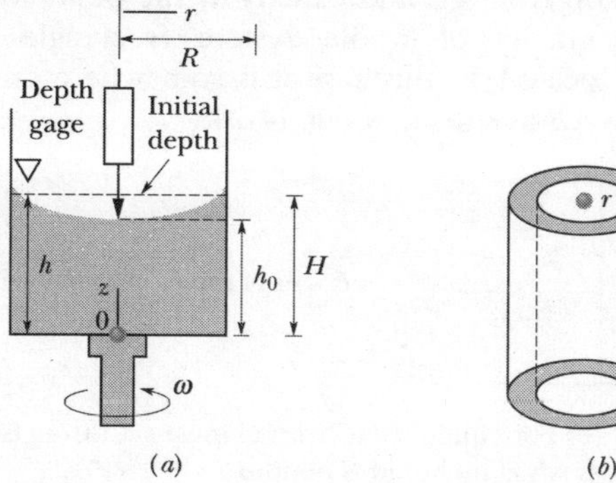

FIG. 14-22

Conceptualize/Classify: We know from the previous discussion that the free surface of fluid will have parabolic shape. Thus, fluid at the axis will be lower than the fluid around it.

Compute: The height, h, of the free surface above the tank bottom can be determined as follows:

$$h = \frac{\omega^2 r^2}{2g} + h_0$$

The initial volume of fluid in the tank, V_i, is equal to

$$V_i = \pi R^2 H$$

The volume of the fluid with the rotating tank can be found by considering a differential element of cyliderical shape as shown in Fig. 14-22b. This cylindrical shell is taken at some arbitrary radius, r, and thickness dr. Thus, its volume is

$$dV = 2\pi rh\, dr$$

The total volume is, therefore,

$$V = 2\pi \int_0^R r\left(\frac{\omega^2 r^2}{2g} + h_0\right) dr = \frac{\pi\omega^2 R^4}{4g} + \pi R^2 h_0$$

Since the volume of the fluid in the tank must remain constant (given that none spills over the top), it follows that

$$\pi R^2 H = \frac{\pi\omega^2 R^4}{4g} + \pi R^2 h_0$$

or

$$H - h_0 = \frac{\omega^2 R^2}{4g} \qquad \text{(Answer)}$$

Conclude: This is the relationship we were looking for. It shows that the change in depth could indeed be used to determine the rotational speed.

14-7 | Buoyant Force

The location of the line of action of the buoyant force can be determined by adding torques of the forces due to pressure forces, with respect to some convenient axis. The buoyant force must pass through the center of mass of the displaced volume, as shown in Fig. 14-23a, as it was in translational and rotational equilibrium. The point through which the buoyant force acts is called the center of buoyancy.

These same results apply to floating bodies which are only partially submerged, as shown in Fig. 14-23b, if the density of the fluid above the liquid surface is very small compared with the liquid in which the body floats. As the fluid above the surface is usually air, for practial purposes this condition is satisfied.

In the above discussion, the fluid is assumed to have a constant density. If a body is immersed in a fluid in which density varies with depth, such as having multiple layers of fluid, the magnitude of the buoyant force remains equal to the weight of the displaced fluid and the buoyant force passes through the center of mass of the displaced volume.

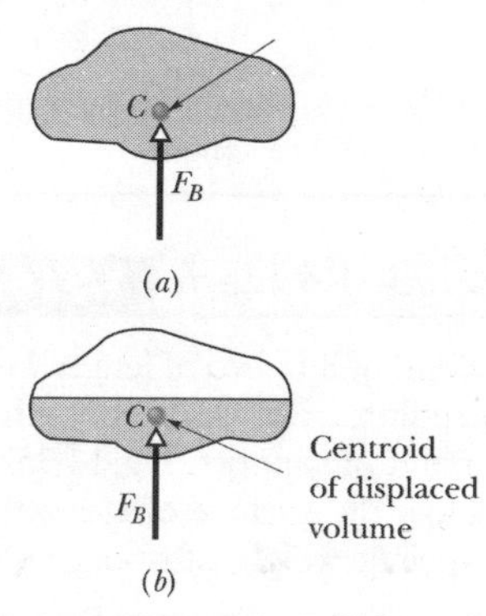

FIG. 14-23 Buoyant force passing through center of mass of the displaced volume when a body is (a) totally submerged and (b) partially submerged. The fluid is assumed to have constant density.

Sample Problem 14-15 Build your skill

A square with side b and rectangle with sides b and $2b$ are cut out from two plates of equal thickness with densities of 3.5 g/cm^3 and 2 g/cm^3, the square being cut out of the heavier material. The square and the rectangle are fastened together in the form of the letter L and placed upside down on the bottom of an empty vessel (Fig. 14-24a). Will the object be stable if the vessel is filled with water?

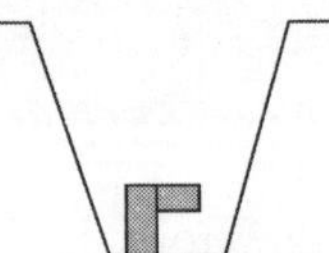

FIG. 14-24 (a) A geometric body kept in vessel and fluid is poured

Solution: The inverted L will be stable on the bottom of the empty vessel, since a perpendicular dropped from the center of gravity b(see Fig. 14-24b) is within the limits of the supporting area. As water is poured into the vessel, the bouyant force acting on the rectangle will grow in magnitude (it is assumed that the water can flow between the base of the block and the bottom of the vessel). When the depth of the water in the vessel is 0.5r, the sum of the torques of the forces which tend to turn the body clockwise will be equal to the sum of those acting in the opposite direction. As the vessel is filled further, the block will fall.

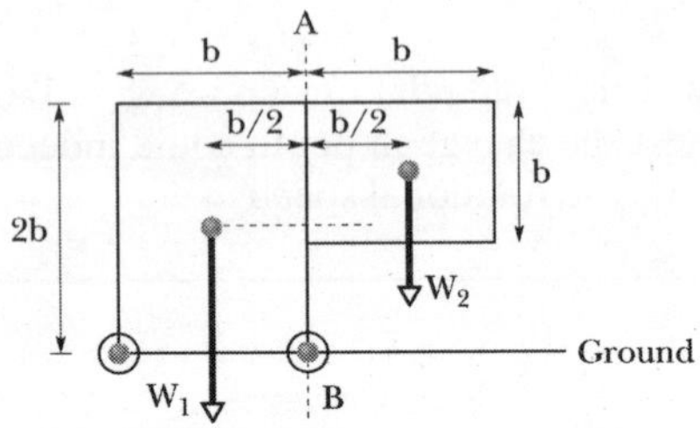

FIG. 14-24 (b) Weight acting through the Center of mass of the square and rectangle.

Initially, $W_1 = 2b^2(2) = 4b^2$

$W_2 = 3.5\, b^2$

First we need to find exact location of normal. Normal must develop from ground exactly at the point where center of gravity of whole system (rectangle and square) is located. In this case it is somewhere on left side of line AB as shown in Fig. 14-24c.

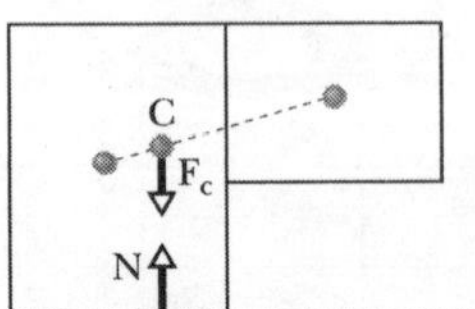

FIG. 14-24 (c) For equilibrium Normal must act through the center of mass when no liquid is poured

Now we can say that whole system is in rotational equilibrium.

When we start pouring liquid gradually, normal force decreases according to the following equation:

$$B+N = F_C = (W_1+W_2)$$

here B is bouyant force on rectangular body.

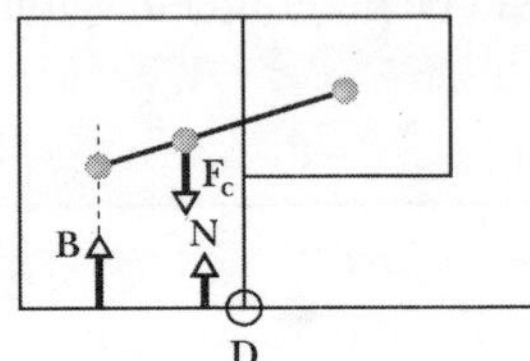

FIG. 14-24 (d) For equilibrium Normal must shift when liquid is poured

Sample Problem 14-16

One end of a board of length l is hinged on top of a stone protruding from water. Length a of the board is above the point of support (Fig. 14-25a). What part of the board is below the surface of the water in equilibrium state, if the specific weight of wood is γ?

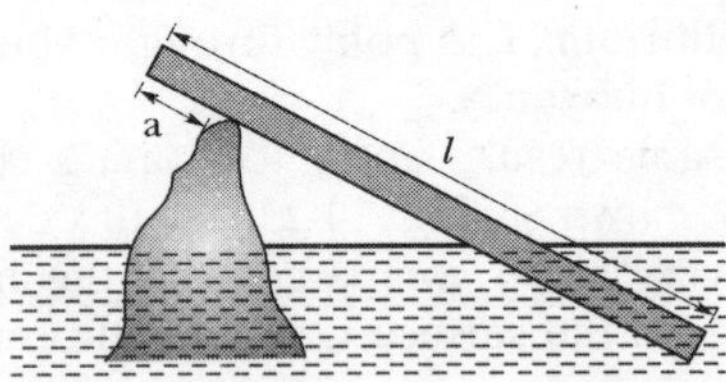

FIG. 14-25 (a) A board partially submerged inside the fluid.

Conceptualize: The rod is experiencing no net force and torque.

Classify: We cannot solve this problem by equating net force to zero, as the force applied by the stone is unknown. Thus, we will balance the torques of the forces acting on the board with respect to point C (Fig. 14-25b). This will exclude the force applied by the stone, as the moment arm for this force will be zero.

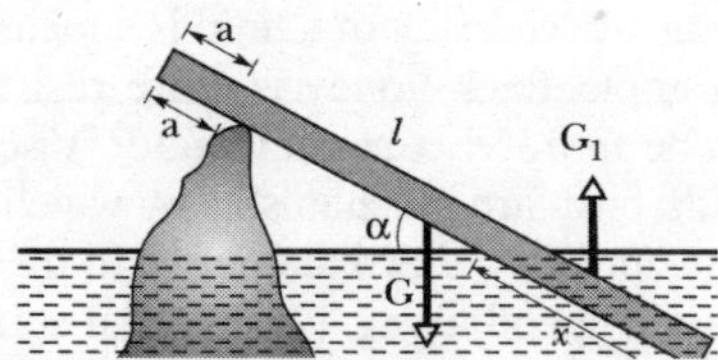

FIG. 14-25 (*b*) Free-body diagram of the board

Here B_1 is the buoyant force applied by the water on the submerged portion and is equal to the volume of submerged portion multiplied by the density of water.

$$B_1 = Ax\gamma_0$$

The length of moment arm is $\left(l - a - \dfrac{x}{2}\right)\cos\alpha$

Weight of the board is $W = A/\gamma$. Here A is the cross-sectional area of the board and γ the specific weight of the water. Equating torque, we get

$$B_1\left(l - a - \frac{x}{2}\right)\cos\alpha = M\left(\frac{1}{2} - a\right)\cos\alpha$$

Hence, $$x = (l - a) \pm \sqrt{(l - a)^2 - \frac{\gamma}{\gamma_0}l(l - 2a)}$$

Since $x < l - a$, only one solution is valid :

$$x = (l - a) - \sqrt{(l - a)^2 - \frac{\gamma}{\gamma_0}l(l - 2a)}$$

Conclude: The value of weight and bouyant force are not equal as their must be some force acting on the board due to the stone.

Stability

The center of buoyancy and center of gravity do not necessarily coincide so the floating or submerged body may not be in stable equilibrium. A small rotation can cause the buoyant force to produce either a restoring or overturning torque. For example, for the completely submerged body as shown in Fig. 14-26*a*, which has a center of gravity below the center of buoyancy, a rotation from its equilibrium position will create a restoring torque by the buoyant force, F_B, which causes the body to rotate back to its original position. Thus, if the center of gravity falls below the center of buoyancy, the body is stable.

However, as shown in Fig. 14-26*b*, if the center of gravity of the completely submerged body is above the center of buoyancy, the resulting torque formed by the weight and the buoyant force will cause the body to overturn and move to a new equilibrium position. Thus, a completely submerged body with its center of gravity above its center of buoyancy is in an unstable equilibrium position.

For floating bodies, the stability problem is more complicated, as the body rotates the location of the center of buoyancy may change.

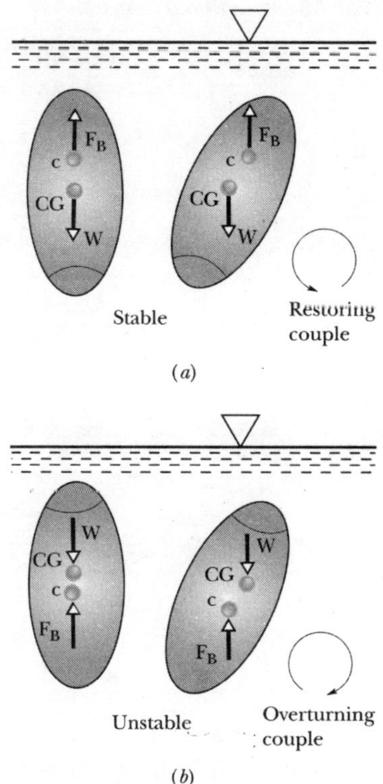

FIG. 14-26 Different situations where rotational equilibrium of body is discussed

14-8 | Fluid Dynamics

Ideal Fluids in Motion

The motion of *real fluids* is very complicated and not yet fully understood. Instead, we shall discuss the motion of an **ideal fluid,** which is simpler to handle mathematically and yet provides useful results. Here are four assumptions that we make about our ideal fluid; they all are concerned with *flow:*

1. ***Steady flow*** In *steady* (or *laminar*) *flow,* the velocity of the moving fluid at any fixed point does not change with time, either in magnitude or in direction. The gentle flow of water near the center of a quiet stream is steady; the flow in a chain of rapids is not. Figure 14-27 shows a transition from steady flow to *nonsteady* (or *nonlaminar* or *turbulent*) *flow* for a rising stream of smoke. The speed of the smoke particles increases as they rise and, at a certain critical speed, the flow changes from steady to nonsteady.
2. ***Incompressible flow*** We assume, as for fluids at rest, that our ideal fluid is incompressible; that is, its density has a constant, uniform value.

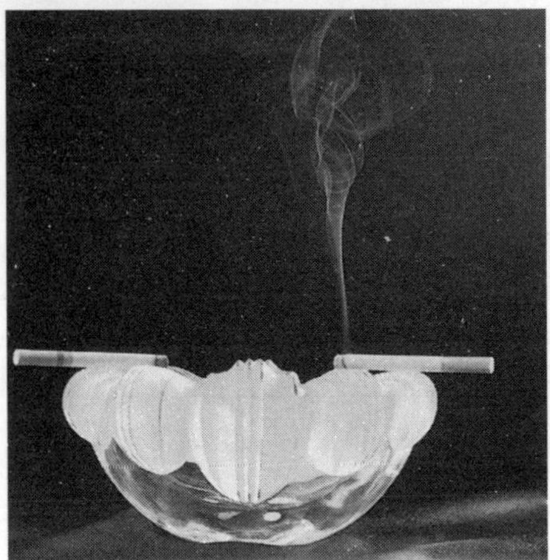

FIG. 14-27 At a certain point, the rising flow of smoke and heated gas changes from steady to turbulent. *(Will McIntyre/Photo Researchers)*

3. ***Nonviscous flow*** Roughly speaking, the viscosity of a fluid is a measure of how resistive the fluid is to flow. For example, thick honey is more resistive to flow than water, and so honey is said to be more viscous than water. Viscosity is the fluid analog of friction between solids; both are mechanisms by which the kinetic energy of moving objects can be transferred to thermal energy. In the absence of friction, a block could glide at constant speed along a horizontal surface. In the same way, an object moving through a nonviscous fluid would experience no *viscous drag force*—that is, no resistive force due to viscosity; it could move at constant speed through the fluid. The British scientist Lord Rayleigh noted that in an ideal fluid a ship's propeller would not work, but, on the other hand, in an ideal fluid a ship (once set into motion) would not need a propeller!
4. ***Irrotational flow*** Although it need not concern us further, we also assume that the flow is *irrotational.* To test for this property, let a tiny grain of dust move with the fluid. Although this test body may (or may not) move in a circular path, in irrotational flow the test body will not rotate about an axis through its own center of mass. For a loose analogy, the motion of a Ferris wheel is rotational; that of its passengers is irrotational.

We can make the flow of a fluid visible by adding a *tracer.* This might be a dye injected into many points across a liquid stream (Fig. 14-28) or smoke particles added to a gas flow (Fig. 14-27). Each bit of a tracer follows a *streamline,* which is the path that a tiny element of the fluid would take as the fluid flows. We already know that the velocity of a particle is always tangent to the path taken by the particle. Here the particle is the fluid element, and its velocity $\vec{v}$ is always tangent to a streamline (Fig. 14-29). For this reason, two streamlines can never intersect; if they did, then an element arriving at their intersection would have two different velocities simultaneously—an impossibility.

The Equation of Continuity

You may have noticed that you can increase the speed of the water emerging from a garden hose by partially closing the hose opening with your thumb. Apparently the speed v of the water depends on the cross-sectional area A through which the water flows.

Here we wish to derive an expression that relates v and A for the steady flow of an ideal fluid through a tube with varying cross section, like that in Fig. 14-30. The flow there is toward the right, and the tube segment shown (part of a longer tube) has length L. The fluid has speeds v_1 at the left end of the segment and A_2 at the right end. The tube has cross-sectional areas A_1 at the left end and A_2 at the right end. Suppose that in a time interval Δt a volume ΔV of fluid enters the

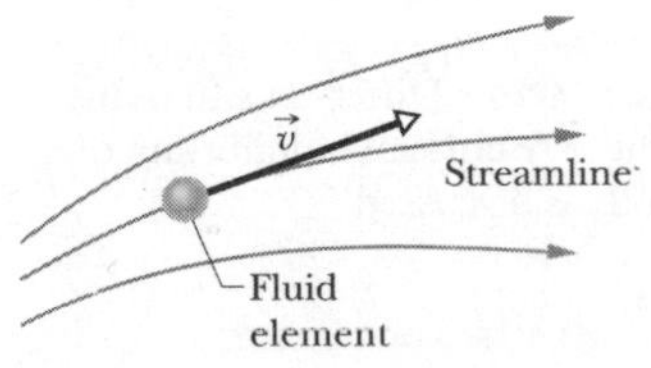

FIG. 14-29 A fluid element traces out a streamline as it moves. The velocity vector of the element is tangent to the streamline at every point.

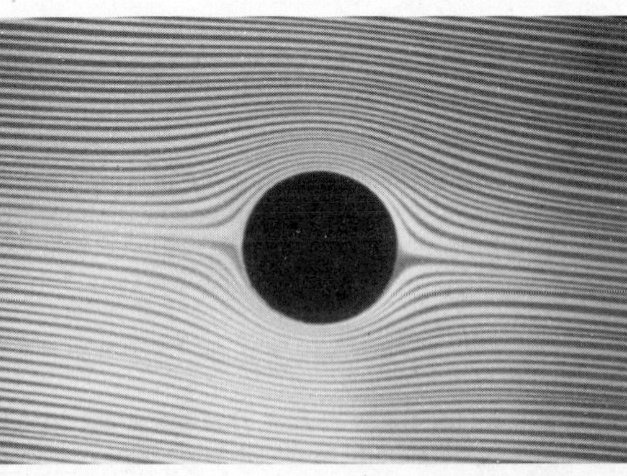

FIG. 14-28 The steady flow of a fluid around a cylinder, as revealed by a dye tracer that was injected into the fluid upstream of the cylinder. *(Courtesy D.H. Peregrine, University of Bristol)*

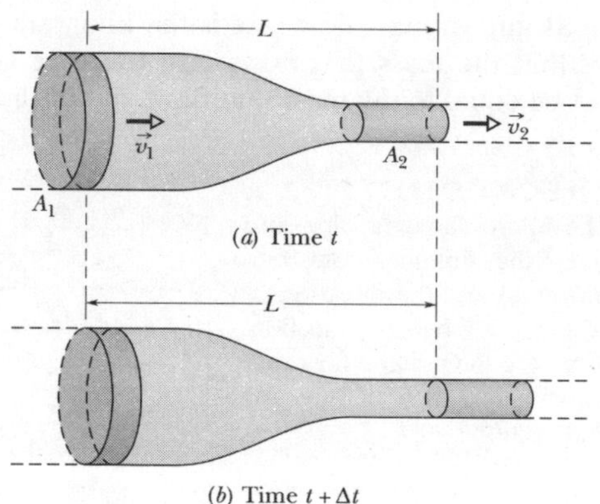

FIG. 14-30 Fluid flows from left to right at a steady rate through a tube segment of length L. The fluid's speed is v_1 at the left side and v_2 at the right side. The tube's cross-sectional area is A_1 at the left side and A_2 at the right side. From time t in (a) to time $t + \Delta t$ in (b), the amount of fluid shown in purple enters at the left side and the equal amount of fluid shown in green emerges at the right side.

tube segment at its left end (that volume is colored purple in Fig. 14-30). Then, because the fluid is incompressible, an identical volume ΔV must emerge from the right end of the segment (it is colored green in Fig. 14-30).

We can use this common volume ΔV to relate the speeds and areas. To do so, we first consider Fig. 14-31, which shows a side view of a tube of *uniform* cross-sectional area A. In Fig. 14-31*a*, a fluid element e is about to pass through the dashed line drawn across the tube width. The element's speed is v, so during a time interval Δt, the element moves along the tube a distance $\Delta x = v\,\Delta t$. The volume ΔV of fluid that has passed through the dashed line in that time interval Δt is

$$\Delta V = A\,\Delta x = Av\,\Delta t \tag{14-23}$$

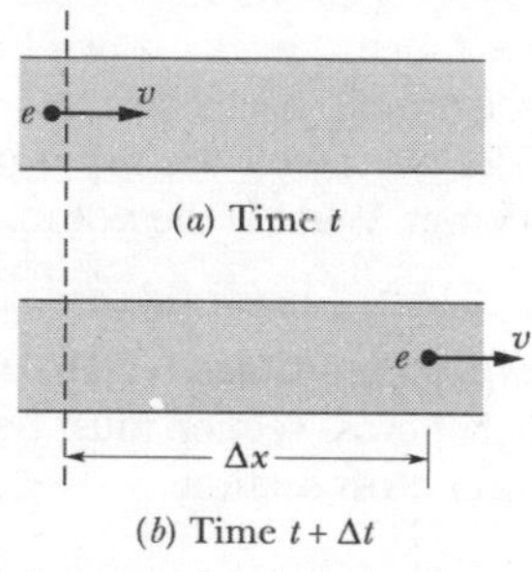

FIG. 14-31 Fluid flows at a constant speed v through a tube. (a) At time t, fluid element e is about to pass the dashed line. (b) At time $t + \Delta t$, element e is a distance $\Delta x = v\,\Delta t$ from the dashed line.

Applying Eq. 14-23 to both the left and right ends of the tube segment in Fig. 14-30, we have

$$\Delta V = A_1 v_1\,\Delta t = A_2 v_2\,\Delta t$$

or

$$A_1 v_1 = A_2 v_2 \quad \text{(equation of continuity)} \tag{14-24}$$

This relation between speed and cross-sectional area is called the **equation of continuity** for the flow of an ideal fluid. It tells us that the flow speed increases when we decrease the cross-sectional area through which the fluid flows (as when we partially close off a garden hose with a thumb).

Equation 14-24 applies not only to an actual tube but also to any so-called *tube of flow,* or imaginary tube whose boundary consists of streamlines. Such a tube acts like a real tube because no fluid element can cross a streamline; thus, all the fluid within a tube of flow must remain within its boundary. Figure 14-32 shows a tube of flow in which the cross-sectional area increases from area A_1 to area A_2 along the flow direction. From Eq. 14-24 we know that, with the increase in area, the speed must decrease, as is indicated by the greater spacing between streamlines at the right in Fig. 14-32. Similarly, you can see that in Fig. 14-28 the speed of the flow is greatest just above and just below the cylinder.

We can rewrite Eq. 14-24 as

$$R_V = Av = \text{a constant} \quad \text{(volume flow rate, equation of continuity)} \tag{14-25}$$

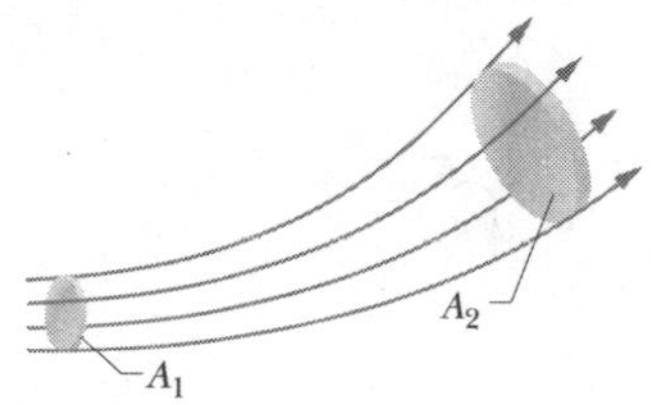

FIG. 14-32 A tube of flow is defined by the streamlines that form the boundary of the tube. The volume flow rate must be the same for all cross sections of the tube of flow.

in which R_V is the **volume flow rate** of the fluid (volume past a given point per unit time). Its SI unit is the cubic meter per second (m^3/s). If the density ρ of the fluid is uniform, we can multiply Eq. 14-25 by that density to get the **mass flow rate** R_m (mass per unit time):

$$R_m = \rho R_V = \rho Av = \text{a constant} \quad \text{(mass flow rate)} \tag{14-26}$$

The SI unit of mass flow rate is the kilogram per second (kg/s). Equation 14-26 says that the mass that flows into the tube segment of Fig. 14-30 each second must be equal to the mass that flows out of that segment each second.

CHECKPOINT 7
The figure shows a pipe and gives the volume flow rate (in cm^3/s) and the direction of flow for all but one section. What are the volume flow rate and the direction of flow for that section?

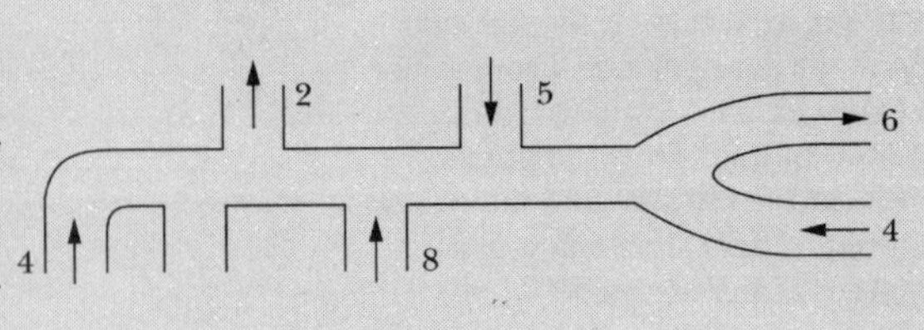

Sample Problem 14-17

Figure 14-33 shows how the stream of water emerging from a faucet "necks down" as it falls. The indicated cross-sectional areas are $A_0 = 1.2\ \text{cm}^2$ and $A = 0.35\ \text{cm}^2$. The two levels are separated by a vertical distance $h = 45$ mm. What is the volume flow rate from the tap?

Conceptualize/Classify: The volume flow rate through the higher cross section must be the same as that through the lower cross section.

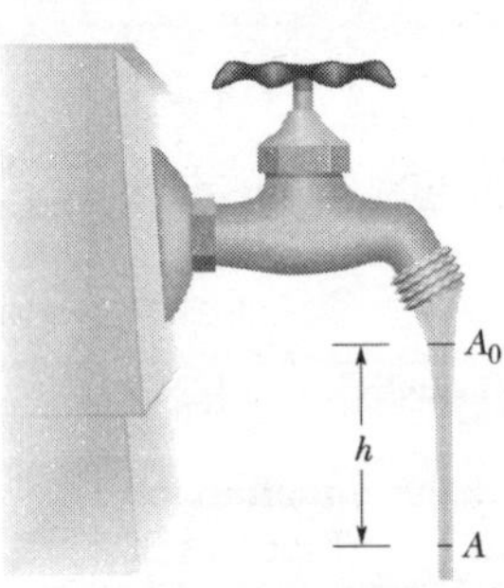

FIG. 14-33 As water falls from a tap, its speed increases. Because the volume flow rate must be the same at all horizontal cross sections of the stream, the stream must "neck down" (narrow).

Compute: From Eq. 14-25, we have

$$A_0 v_0 = Av \tag{14-27}$$

where v_0 and v are the water speeds at the levels corresponding to A_0 and A. We can also write, because the water is falling freely with acceleration g,

$$v^2 = v_0^2 + 2gh \tag{14-28}$$

Eliminating v between Eqs. 14-27 and 14-28 and solving for v_0, we obtain

$$v_0 = \sqrt{\frac{2ghA^2}{A_0^2 - A^2}}$$

$$= \sqrt{\frac{(2)(9.8\ \text{m/s}^2)(0.045\ \text{m})(0.35\ \text{cm}^2)^2}{(1.2\ \text{cm}^2)^2 - (0.35\ \text{cm}^2)^2}}$$

$$= 0.286\ \text{m/s} = 28.6\ \text{cm/s}.$$

From Eq. 14-25, the volume flow rate R_V is then

$$R_V = A_0 v_0 = (1.2\ \text{cm}^2)(28.6\ \text{cm/s})$$

$$= 34\ \text{cm}^3/\text{s} \qquad \text{(Answer)}$$

14-9 | Bernoulli's Equation

Figure 14-34 represents a tube through which an ideal fluid is flowing at a steady rate. In a time interval Δt, suppose that a volume of fluid ΔV, colored purple in Fig. 14-34, enters the tube at the left (or input) end and an identical volume, colored green in Fig. 14-34, emerges at the right (or output) end. The emerging volume must be the same as the entering volume because the fluid is incompressible, with an assumed constant density ρ.

Let y_1, v_1, and p_1 be the elevation, speed, and pressure of the fluid entering at the left, and y_2, v_2, and p_2 be the corresponding quantities for the fluid emerging at the right. By applying the principle of conservation of energy to the fluid, we shall show that these quantities are related by

$$p_1 + \tfrac{1}{2}\rho v_1^2 + \rho g y_1 = p_2 + \tfrac{1}{2}\rho v_2^2 + \rho g y_2 \tag{14-29}$$

In general, the term $\tfrac{1}{2}\rho v^2$ is called the fluid's **kinetic energy density** (kinetic energy per unit volume). We can also write Eq. 14-29 as

$$p + \tfrac{1}{2}\rho v^2 + \rho g y = \text{a constant} \quad \text{(Bernoulli's equation)} \tag{14-30}$$

Equations 14-29 and 14-30 are equivalent forms of **Bernoulli's equation,** after Daniel Bernoulli, who studied fluid flow in the 1700s.[1] Like the equation of continuity (Eq. 14-25), Bernoulli's equation is not a new principle but simply the reformulation of a familiar principle in a form more suitable to fluid mechanics. As a check, let us apply Bernoulli's equation to fluids at rest, by putting $v_1 = v_2 = 0$ in Eq. 14-29. The result is

$$p_2 = p_1 + \rho g(y_1 - y_2)$$

which is Eq. 14-7.

A major prediction of Bernoulli's equation emerges if we take y to be a constant ($y = 0$, say) so that the fluid does not change elevation as it flows. Equation 14-29 then becomes

$$p_1 + \tfrac{1}{2}\rho v_1^2 = p_2 + \tfrac{1}{2}\rho v_2^2 \qquad (14\text{-}31)$$

which tells us that:

> If the speed of a fluid element increases as the element travels along a horizontal streamline, the pressure of the fluid must decrease, and conversely.

Put another way, where the streamlines are relatively close together (where the velocity is relatively great), the pressure is relatively low, and conversely.

The link between a change in speed and a change in pressure makes sense if you consider a fluid element. When the element nears a narrow region, the higher pressure behind it accelerates it so that it then has a greater speed in the narrow region. When it nears a wide region, the higher pressure ahead of it decelerates it so that it then has a lesser speed in the wide region.

Bernoulli's equation is strictly valid only to the extent that the fluid is ideal. If viscous forces are present, thermal energy will be involved. We take no account of this in the derivation that follows.

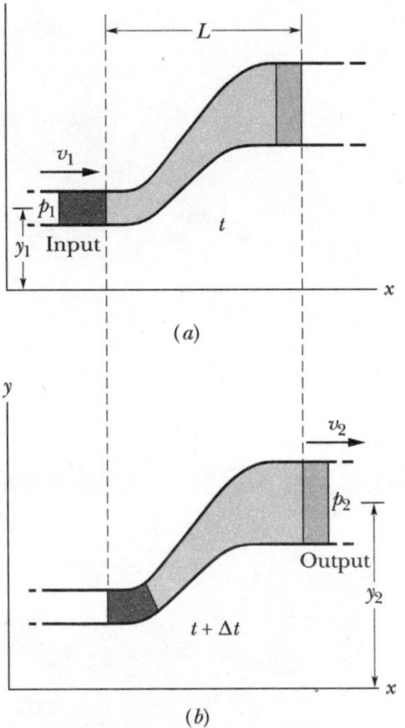

FIG. 14-34 Fluid flows at a steady rate through a length L of a tube, from the input end at the left to the output end at the right. From time t in (*a*) to time $t + \Delta t$ in (*b*), the amount of fluid shown in purple enters the input end and the equal amount shown in green emerges from the output end.

Proof of Bernoulli's Equation

Let us take as our system the entire volume of the (ideal) fluid shown in Fig. 14-34. We shall apply the principle of conservation of energy to this system as it moves from its initial state (Fig. 14-34*a*) to its final state (Fig. 14-34*b*). The fluid lying between the two vertical planes separated by a distance L in Fig. 14-34 does not change its properties during this process; we need be concerned only with changes that take place at the input and output ends.

First, we apply energy conservation in the form of the work–kinetic energy theorem,

$$W = \Delta K \qquad (14\text{-}32)$$

which tells us that the change in the kinetic energy of our system must equal the net work done on the system. The change in kinetic energy results from the change in speed between the ends of the tube and is

$$\begin{aligned} \Delta K &= \tfrac{1}{2}\Delta m\, v_2^2 - \tfrac{1}{2}\Delta m\, v_1^2 \\ &= \tfrac{1}{2}\rho\, \Delta V(v_2^2 - v_1^2) \end{aligned} \qquad (14\text{-}33)$$

in which $\Delta m\ (= \rho\, \Delta V)$ is the mass of the fluid that enters at the input end and leaves at the output end during a small time interval Δt.

The work done on the system arises from two sources. The work W_g done by the gravitational force ($\Delta m\, \vec{g}$) on the fluid of mass Δm during the vertical lift of the mass from the input level to the output level is

[1]For irrotational flow (which we assume), the constant in Eq. 14-32 has the same value for all points within the tube of flow; the points do not have to lie along the same streamline. Similarly, the points 1 and 2 in Eq. 14-31 can lie anywhere within the tube of flow.

$$W_g = -\Delta m\, g(y_2 - y_1)$$
$$= -\rho g\, \Delta V(y_2 - y_1) \qquad (14\text{-}34)$$

This work is negative because the upward displacement and the downward gravitational force have opposite directions.

Work must also be done *on* the system (at the input end) to push the entering fluid into the tube and *by* the system (at the output end) to push forward the fluid that is located ahead of the emerging fluid. In general, the work done by a force of magnitude F, acting on a fluid sample contained in a tube of area A to move the fluid through a distance Δx, is

$$F\,\Delta x = (pA)(\Delta x) = p(A\,\Delta x) = p\,\Delta V$$

The work done on the system is then $p_1\,\Delta V$, and the work done by the system is $-p_2\,\Delta V$. Their sum W_p is

$$W_p = -p_2\,\Delta V + p_1\,\Delta V$$
$$= -(p_2 - p_1)\,\Delta V \qquad (14\text{-}35)$$

The work–kinetic energy theorem of Eq. 14-32 now becomes

$$W = W_g + W_p = \Delta K$$

Substituting from Eqs. 14-33, 14-34, and 14-35 yields

$$-\rho g\,\Delta V(y_2 - y_1) - \Delta V(p_2 - p_1) = \tfrac{1}{2}\rho\,\Delta V(v_2^2 - v_1^2)$$

This, after a slight rearrangement, matches Eq. 14-29, which we set out to prove.

CHECKPOINT 8 Water flows smoothly through the pipe shown in the figure, descending in the process. Rank the four numbered sections of pipe according to (a) the volume flow rate R_V through them, (b) the flow speed v through them, and (c) the water pressure p within them, greatest first.

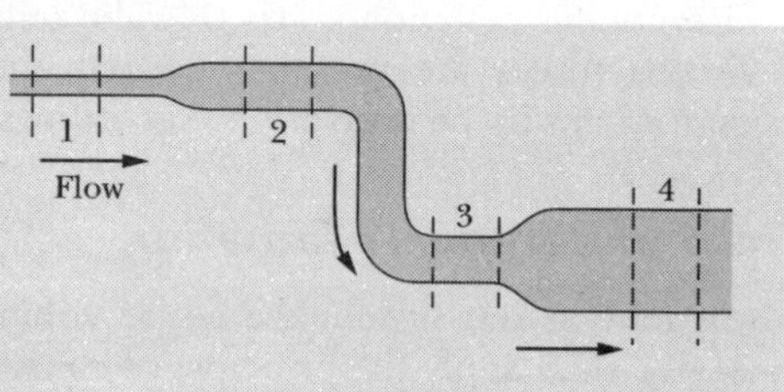

Sample Problem 14-18

Ethanol of density $\rho = 791\ \text{kg/m}^3$ flows smoothly through a horizontal pipe that tapers (as in Fig. 14-30) in cross-sectional area from $A_1 = 1.20 \times 10^{-3}\ \text{m}^2$ to $A_2 = A_1/2$. The pressure difference between the wide and narrow sections of pipe is 4120 Pa. What is the volume flow rate R_V of the ethanol?

Conceptualize: (1) Because the fluid flowing through the wide section of pipe must entirely pass through the narrow section, the volume flow rate R_V must be the same in the two sections. Thus, from Eq. 14-27,

$$R_V = v_1 A_1 = v_2 A_2 \qquad (14\text{-}36)$$

However, with two unknown speeds, we cannot evaluate this equation for R_V.

Classify: Because the flow is smooth, we can apply Bernoulli's equation. From Eq. 14-29, we can write

$$p_1 + \tfrac{1}{2}\rho v_1^2 + \rho g y = p_2 + \tfrac{1}{2}\rho v_2^2 + \rho g y \qquad (14\text{-}37)$$

where subscripts 1 and 2 refer to the wide and narrow sections of pipe, respectively, and y is their common elevation. This equation hardly seems to help because it does not contain the desired R_V and it contains the unknown speeds v_1 and v_2.

Compute: There is a neat way to make Eq. 14-37 work for us: First, we can use Eq. 14-36 and the fact that $A_2 = A_1/2$ to write

$$v_1 = \frac{R_V}{A_1} \quad \text{and} \quad v_2 = \frac{R_V}{A_2} = \frac{2R_V}{A_1} \qquad (14\text{-}38)$$

Then we can substitute these expressions into Eq. 14-37 to eliminate the unknown speeds and introduce the desired volume flow rate. Doing this and solving for R_V yield

$$R_V = A_1\sqrt{\frac{2(p_1 - p_2)}{3\rho}} \qquad (14\text{-}39)$$

We still have a decision to make: We know that the pressure difference between the two sections is 4120 Pa, but does that mean that $p_1 - p_2$ is 4120 Pa or -4120 Pa? We could guess the former is true, or otherwise the square root in Eq. 14-39 would give us an imaginary number. Instead of guessing, however, let's try some reasoning. From Eq. 14-36 we see that speed v_2 in the narrow section (small A_2) must be greater than speed v_1 in the wider section (larger A_1). Recall that if the speed of a fluid increases as the fluid travels along a horizontal path (as here), the pressure of the fluid must decrease. Thus, p_1 is greater than p_2, and $p_1 - p_2 = 4120$ Pa. Inserting this and known data into Eq. 14-39 gives

$$R_V = 1.20 \times 10^{-3}\,\text{m}^2\sqrt{\frac{(2)(4120\text{ Pa})}{(3)(791\text{ kg/m}^3)}}$$

$$= 2.24 \times 10^{-3}\,\text{m}^3\text{/s} \qquad \text{(Answer)}$$

Conclude: This is a simple application of equation of continuity.

Sample Problem 14-19

In the old West, a desperado fires a bullet into an open water tank (Fig. 14-35), creating a hole a distance h below the water surface. What is the speed v of the water exiting the tank?

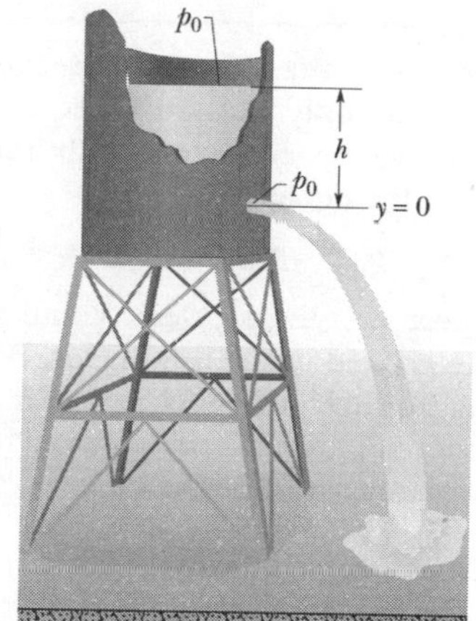

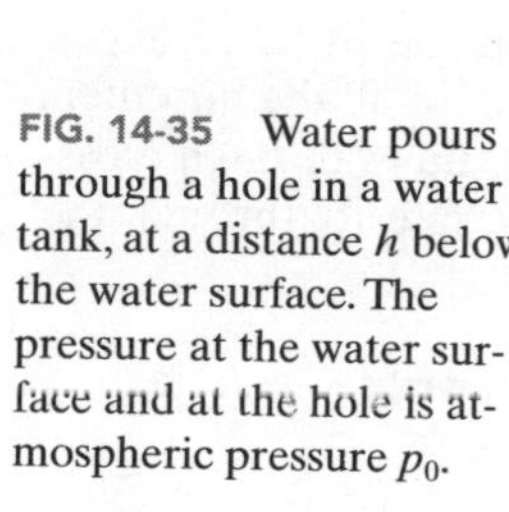

FIG. 14-35 Water pours through a hole in a water tank, at a distance h below the water surface. The pressure at the water surface and at the hole is atmospheric pressure p_0.

Conceptualize: This situation is essentially that of water moving (downward) with speed v_0 through a wide pipe (the tank) of cross-sectional area A and then moving (horizontally) with speed v through a narrow pipe (the hole) of cross-sectional area a.

Classify: Because the water flowing through the wide pipe must entirely pass through the narrow pipe, the volume flow rate R_V must be the same in the two "pipes." We can also relate v to v_0 (and to h) through Bernoulli's equation (Eq. 14-29).

Compute: From Eq. 14-27,

$$R_V = av = Av_0$$

and thus

$$v_0 = \frac{a}{A}v$$

Because $a \ll A$, we see that $v_0 \ll v$. To apply Bernoulli's equation, we take the level of the hole as our reference level for measuring elevations (and thus gravitational potential energy). Noting that the pressure at the top of the tank and at the bullet hole is the atmospheric pressure p_0 (because both places are exposed to the atmosphere), we write Eq. 14-29 as

$$p_0 + \tfrac{1}{2}\rho v_0^2 + \rho gh = p_0 + \tfrac{1}{2}\rho v^2 + \rho g(0) \qquad (14\text{-}40)$$

(Here the top of the tank is represented by the left side of the equation and the hole by the right side. The zero on the right indicates that the hole is at our reference level.) Before we solve Eq. 14-40 for v, we can use our result that $v_0 \ll v$ to simplify it: We assume that v_0^2, and thus the term $\frac{1}{2}\rho v_0^2$ in Eq. 14-40, is negligible relative to the other terms, and we drop it. Solving the remaining equation for v then yields

$$v = \sqrt{2gh} \qquad \text{(Answer)}$$

Conclude: This is the same speed that an object would have when falling a height h from rest. This is because the work done by atmospheric pressure cancells with pressure at top of the tank and at the hole.

Sample Problem 14-20 Build your skill

Many types of race cars depend on *negative lift* (or *downforce*) to push them down against the track surface so they can take turns quickly without sliding out into the track wall. Part of the negative lift is the *ground force*, which is a force due to the airflow beneath the car. As the race car in Fig. 14-36 moves forward at 27.25 m/s, air is forced to flow over and under the car (Fig. 14-36). The air forced to flow under the car enters through a vertical cross-sectional area $A_0 = 0.0330\text{ m}^2$ at the front of the car (Fig. 14-36) and then flows beneath the car where the vertical cross-sectional area is $A_1 = 0.0310\text{ m}^2$. Treat this flow as steady flow through a stationary horizontal pipe that decreases in cross-sectional area from A_0 to A_1 (Fig. 14-36).

(a) At the moment it passes through A_0, the air is at atmospheric pressure p_0. At what pressure p_1 is the air as it moves through A_1?

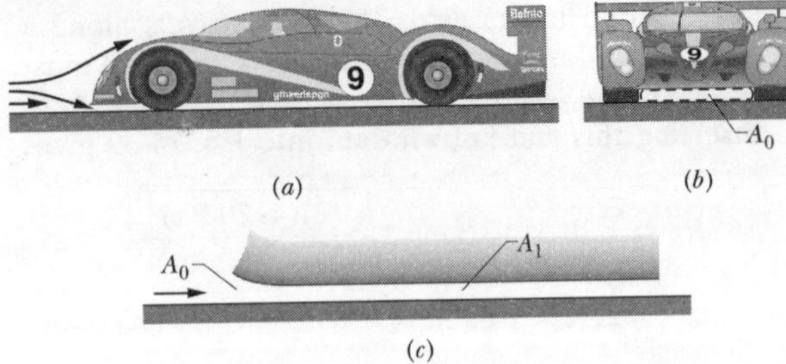

FIG. 14-36 (*a*) Air flows above and below a race car. (*b*) The flow beneath the car enters through vertical cross-sectional area A_0. (*c*) The flow is then constrained as in a pipe that narrows to vertical cross-sectional area A_1.

Conceptualize/Classify: Because the flow is steady, we can apply Bernoulli's equation (Eq. 14-29) to the flow. To be consistent with the given subscripts, we write the equation as

$$p_0 + \tfrac{1}{2}\rho v_0^2 + \rho g y = p_1 + \tfrac{1}{2}\rho v_1^2 + \rho g y \qquad (14\text{-}41)$$

where ρ is the air density and y is the distance above the ground of the flowing air. Because all the air entering through cross-sectional area A_0 flows through cross-sectional area A_1, the volume flow rate R_V through the two areas must be the same.

Compute: From Eq. 14-25, we can write

$$A_0 v_0 = A_1 v_1,$$

or

$$v_1 = v_0 \frac{A_0}{A_1} \qquad (14\text{-}42)$$

Substituting Eq. 14-42 into Eq. 14-41 and rearranging give us

$$p_1 = p_0 - \tfrac{1}{2}\rho v_0^2\left(\frac{A_0^2}{A_1^2} - 1\right) \qquad (14\text{-}43)$$

The speed of the air as it enters A_0 at the front of the car is equal to 27.25 m/s, the speed of the car as it moves forward through the air. Substituting this speed, the air density $\rho = 1.21$ kg/m³, and the values for A_0 and A_1 into Eq. 14-43, we find

$$p_1 = p_0 - \tfrac{1}{2}(1.21\ \text{kg/m}^3)(27.25\ \text{m/s})^2\left(\frac{(0.0330\ \text{m}^2)^2}{(0.0310\ \text{m}^2)^2} - 1\right)$$

$$= p_0 - 59.838\ \text{Pa} \approx p_0 - 59.8\ \text{Pa} \qquad \text{(Answer)}$$

Conclude: Thus, the air pressure beneath the car is 59.8 Pa less than atmospheric pressure.

(b) If the horizontal cross-sectional area of the car is $A_h = 4.86\ \text{m}^2$, what is the magnitude of the net vertical force $F_{\text{net},y}$ on the car due to the air pressures above and below the car?

Conceptualize/Classify: The pressure on a surface is the force per unit area, as given by the equation $p = F/A$.

Compute: Here we are concerned with the top and bottom surfaces of the car, where we take both surfaces to have area A_h. Above the car the air is at atmospheric pressure p_0 and presses down on the car with a vertical component

$$F_{y,\text{above}} = -p_0 A_h$$

Below the car, the air is at pressure $p_1 = p_0 - 59.838$ Pa and presses up on the car with a vertical component

$$F_{y,\text{below}} = (p_0 - 59.838\ \text{Pa})A_h$$

The net vertical force is then

$$\begin{aligned} F_{\text{net},y} &= F_{y,\text{below}} + F_{y,\text{above}} \\ &= (p_0 - 59.838\ \text{Pa})A_h - p_0 A_h \\ &= -(59.838\ \text{Pa})(4.86\ \text{m}^2) = -291\ \text{N} \qquad \text{(Answer)} \end{aligned}$$

Conclude: Danger of drafting – This net downward force, which is due to the reduced air pressure beneath the car, is the ground effect acting on the car. It is about 30% of the total negative lift that helps hold the car on the track. Without negative lift, a car must greatly slow for turns or else it will slide outward into the track wall. In a race, a driver can reduce the air drag on his car by closely following another car, a procedure known as *drafting.* However, the leading car disrupts the steady flow of air under the trailing car, eliminating the ground effect on the trailing car. If the trailing driver does not anticipate that elimination and slow accordingly, sliding into the track wall may be unavoidable.

Sample Problem 14-21

A pump is designed as a horizontal cylinder of area A with a tight fitting piston also having same area and an outlet orifice of area a. Determine the velocity of outflow of a liquid from the pump if the piston moves with a constant velocity under the action of a force F. The density of the liquid is ρ.

Conceptualize: This whole arrangement is exactly like an injection. As we push the piston by applying force F the liquid inside it will be forced out of the orifice. Harder we push, faster the liquid should spurt out.

Classify: We can use work kinetic energy theorem as work done by the pushing force will be equal to change in kinetic energy. As we assume the liquid to be ideal, we can say that no loss of energy will take place.

Compute: Let's assume the piston is moving with speed u. As the piston will cover the distance ut during the time t (Fig. 14-37a), the force F will perform the work $W = Fut$. The mass of the liquid flowing out during the time t is ρAut.

The outflow velocity of the liquid v can be found from the continuity equation $Au = av$.

The change in the kinetic energy of the liquid during the time t is

$$\frac{1}{2}M(v^2 - u^2)$$

Where v is velocity of liquid coming out, work done by force is Fut which increases velocity of liquid coming out.

$$\text{Therefore, } F\,u\,t = \frac{1}{2}M\,(v^2 - u^2) = \rho\,Aut\left(\frac{v^2}{2} - \frac{u^2}{2}\right)$$

This change should be equal to the work performed by the force F:

$$F\,u\,t = \rho\,Aut\left(\frac{v^2}{2} - \frac{u^2}{2}\right)$$

$$F - \rho A[v^2 - u^2] \qquad (14\text{-}44)$$

we also have

$$u = \frac{av}{A} \qquad (14\text{-}45)$$

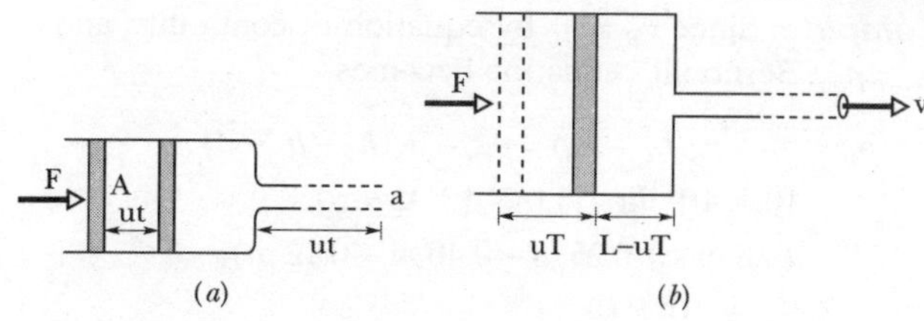

FIG. 14-37 (a) and (b) As the piston moves a distance ut in time t the fluid is ejected from the other side.

Eq. (11-44) and (11-45) implies

$$v^2 = \frac{2F}{\rho A}\left(\frac{1}{1 - \frac{a}{A}}\right)$$

If a $\ll A$, then $v = \sqrt{\frac{2F}{A\rho}}$

Upon eliminating u, we find that

$$v^2 = \frac{2F}{A\rho} \times \frac{1}{1 - \frac{a^2}{A^2}}$$

Conclude: The same result can be obtained by using Bernoulli's equation, as it is based on conservation of energy.

Sample Problem 14-22

Figure 14-38 shows a *siphon,* which is a device for removing liquid from a container. Tube ABC must initially be filled, but once this has been done, liquid will flow through the tube until the liquid surface in the container is level with the tube opening at A. The liquid has density 1000 kg/m^3 and negligible viscosity. The distances shown are h_1 = 25 cm, d = 12 cm, and h_2 = 40 cm. (a) With what speed does the liquid emerge from the tube at C? (b) If the atmospheric pressure is 1.0×10^5 Pa, what is the pressure in the liquid at the topmost point B? (c) Theoretically, what is the greatest possible height h_1 that a siphon can lift water?

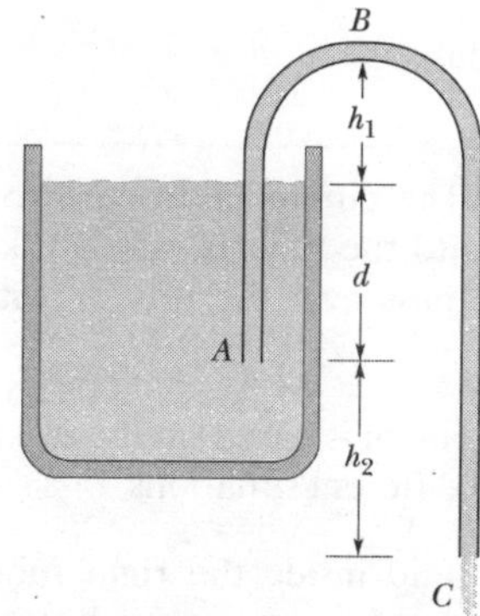

FIG. 14-38 A standard siphon arrangement

Conceptualize: You may have used siphon and you may recollect that lower the exit point of the fluid is, faster the fluid flows out.

Classify: We consider a point D on the surface of the liquid in the container, in the same tube of flow with points A, B, and C. Applying Bernoulli's equation to points D and C, we obtain

$$p_D + \frac{1}{2}\rho v_D^2 = \rho g h_D = p_C + \frac{1}{2}\rho v_C^2 + \rho g h_C$$

Compute: Which leads to

$$v_C = \sqrt{\frac{2(p_D - p_C)}{\rho} + \Delta 2g(h_D - h_C) + \Delta v_D^2} \approx \sqrt{2g\,(d + \Delta h_2)}.$$

where in the last step we set $p_d = p_c = p_{\text{air}}$ and $vd/vc \approx 0$. Plugging in the values, we obtain

$$v_c = \sqrt{2(9.8\text{ m/s}^2)(0.40\text{ m} + 0.12\text{ m})} = 3.2\text{ m/s}.$$

Conclude: The result confirms our experience.

(b) ***Classify:*** We now consider points B and C:

$$p_B + \frac{1}{2}\rho v_B^2 = \rho g h_B = p_C + \frac{1}{2}\rho v_C^2 + \rho g h_C.$$

Compute: Since $v_B = v_C$ by equation of continuity, and $p_C = p_{air}$, Bernoulli's equation becomes

$$p_B = p_C + \rho g(h_C - h_B) = p_{air} - \rho g(h_1 + h_2 + d)$$
$$= 10 \times 10^5 \text{ Pa} - (1.0 \times 10^3 \text{ kg/m}^3)$$
$$(9.8 \text{ m/s}^2)(0.25 \text{ m} + 0.40 \text{ m} + 0.12 \text{ m})$$
$$= 9.2 \times 10^4 \text{ Pa}$$

(c) **Compute:** Since $p_B \geq 0$, we must let $p_{air} - \rho g(h_1 + d + h_2) \geq 0$, which yields

$$h_1 \leq h_{1,max} = \frac{p_{air}}{\rho g} - d - h_2 = 10.3 \text{ m}$$

CHECKPOINT 9 A siphon of uniform diameter is used to drain water from a tank as illustrated in the figure. Assuming steady flow without friction, consider a small hole in the hose at location D as indicated. When the siphon is used, will water leak out of the hose, or will air leak into the hose and thus causing the siphon to stop?

Sample Problem 14-23

Figure 14-39 shows a device called Pitot's tube. It measures the velocity of moving fluids. Determine the velocity of the fluid in terms of the density ρ, the density of the fluid in manometer (U-tube) σ and the height 'h'.

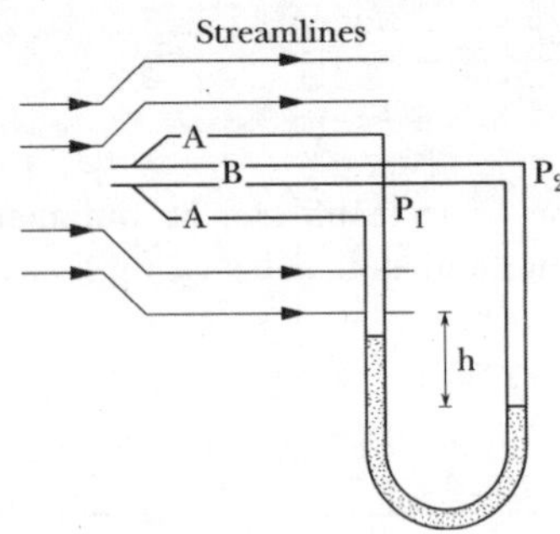

FIG. 14-39 Pitot tube.

Conceptualize: The difference in the two tubes is that liquid will flow into the tube B with full kinetic energy while it will just pass over the tube A without directly entering into it.

Classify: This problem is based on the use of Bernoulli's principle, on two different situations.

Compute: The fluid inside the right tube must be at rest as the fluid exactly at the end is in contact with the fluid in Pitot tube, which is at rest.

The velocity v_1 is the fluid velocity v_f. The velocity v_2 of the fluid at point B is zero and the pressure in the right arm is P_2 (called stagnation pressure).

Thus using Bernoulli's principle

$$p_1 + \frac{1}{2}\rho v_1^2 = P_2 + \frac{1}{2}\rho v_2^2$$

We get

$$P_2 = P_1 + \frac{1}{2}\rho v_f^2$$

On the other hand, the openings at point A is not along the flow lines, so we don't need to use Bernoulli's equation. We can simply say that the pressure just outside the opening is same as that within the Pitot tube.

Therefore, the pressure at the left arm of the manometer is same as the fluid pressre P_f, that is, $P_1 = P_f$.

Also $$P_2 = P_1 + (\rho - \sigma)\, gh \tag{14-46}$$

Generally $\sigma \ll \rho$, so it is ignored.

Thus $$P_2 = P_f + \rho gh \tag{14-47}$$

From Eqs. (14-46) and (14-47), $\frac{1}{2}\sigma v_f^2 = \rho gh$

or $$v_f = \sqrt{\frac{2\rho gh}{\sigma}}$$

Conclude: Thus we can see that we have measured the fluid velocity as this was the only difference between the two tubes leading to the pressure difference between the tubes.

Sample Problem 14-24

A tank has two outlets (i) a rounded orifice A of diameter D and (ii) a pipe B with well rounded entry and of length L, as shown in Fig. 14-40. For a height of water H in the tank determine the (a) discharge from the outlets A and B, (b) velocities in the two outlets at levels 1 and 2 indicated in Fig. 14-40.

Conceptualize: The difference in the two situations is that in part (i) pressure at the point 1 and all points below it will be atmospheric. On the other hand in part (ii) only at point 2 pressure will be atmospheric.

Classify: This problem is based on the use of Bernoulli's principle, on two different situations.

Compute:
(a) Rounded orifice A: Applying Bernoulli's equation to a point on the water surface 3 and point 1, we get

$$0 + 0 + H = \frac{p_1}{\gamma} + \frac{V_{1a}^2}{2g} + 0$$

As the orifice discharges to atmosphere, $\frac{p_1}{\gamma} = 0$

and $V_{1a} = \sqrt{2gH}$. The discharge $Q_a = \frac{\pi}{4} D^2 \sqrt{2gH}$

At point 2, the pressure is atmospheric and hence by applying Bernoulli's equation between points 3 and 2, we get

$$0 + 0 + (H + L) = 0 + \frac{V_{2a}^2}{2g} + 0$$

or $\quad V_{2a} = \sqrt{2g(H + L)}$

FIG. 14-40

As the discharge is Q_a, the diameter at 2 will be smaller than D.

(b) Pipe:

By applying Bernoulli's equation between points 3 and 2.

$$0 + 0 + (H + L) = 0 + \frac{V_{2b}^2}{2g} + 0$$

or $\quad V_{2b} = \sqrt{2g(H + L)}$

As the pipe size is uniform from points 1 to 2, by continuity equation

$$V_{1b} + V_{2b} = \sqrt{2g(H + L)}$$

thus the results are:

	Orifice	Pipe
Velocity at 1 =	$\sqrt{2gH}$	$\sqrt{2g(H + L)}$
Velocity at 2 =	$\sqrt{2g(H + L)}$	$\sqrt{2g(H + L)}$
Discharge Q =	$\frac{\pi}{4} D^2 \sqrt{2gH}$	$\frac{\pi}{4} D^2 \sqrt{2g(H + L)}$

Conclude: We can see that velocity at point 2 is same in both the cases, this could have been directly concluded by applying Bernoulli's equation between points 3 and 2 in both parts.

Sample Problem 14-25 Build your skill

A *venturi meter* is used to measure the flow speed of a fluid in a pipe. The meter is connected between two sections of the pipe (Fig. 14-41); the cross-sectional area A of the entrance and exit of the meter matches the pipe's cross-sectional area. Between the entrance and exit, the fluid flows from the pipe with speed V and then through a narrow "throat" of cross-sectional area a with speed v. A manometer connects the wider portion of the meter to the narrower portion. The change in the fluid's speed is accompanied by a change Δp in the fluid's pressure, which causes a height difference h of the liquid in the two arms of the manometer. (Here Δp means pressure in the throat minus pressure in the pipe.) (a) By applying Bernoulli's equation and the equation of continuity to points 1 and 2 in Fig. 14-41, show that

$$V = \sqrt{\frac{2a^2 \Delta p}{\rho(a^2 - A^2)}},$$

where ρ is the density of the fluid. (b) Suppose that the fluid is fresh water, that the cross-sectional areas are 64 cm^2 in the pipe and 32 cm^2 in the throat, and that the pressure is 55 kPa in the pipe and 41 kPa in the throat. What is the rate of water flow in cubic meters per second?

Solution: (a) The continuity equation yields $Av = aV$, and Bernoulli's equation yields $\Delta p + \frac{1}{2}\rho v^2 = \frac{1}{2}\rho V^2$, where $\Delta p = p_1 - p_2$. The first equation gives $V = (A/a)v$.

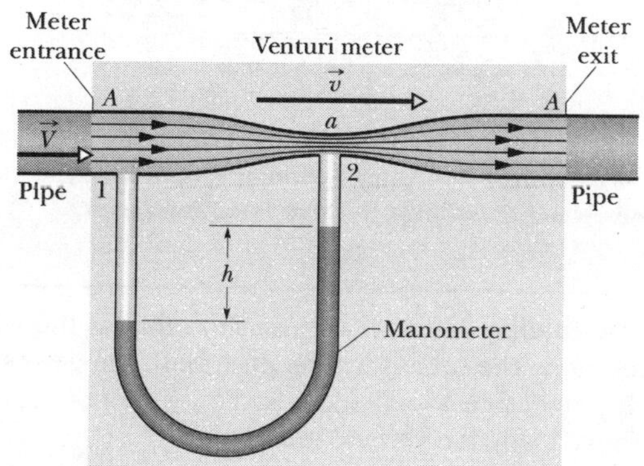

FIG. 14-41 Venturi Meter

We use this to substitute for V in the second equation, and obtain $\Delta p + \frac{1}{2}\rho v^2 = \frac{1}{2}\rho(A/a)^2 v^2$. We solve for v. The result is

$$v = \sqrt{\frac{2\Delta p}{\rho\,((A/a)^2 - 1)}} = \sqrt{\frac{2a^2\Delta p}{\rho\,(A^2 - a^2)}}.$$

(b) We substitute values to obtain

$$v = \sqrt{\frac{2(32 \times 10^{-4}\ \text{m}^2)^2(55 \times 10^3\ \text{Pa} - 41 \times 10^3\ \text{Pa})}{(1000\ \text{kg/m}^3)((64 \times 10^{-4}\ \text{m}^2)^2 - (32 \times 10^{-4}\ \text{m}^2)^2)}} = 3.06\ \text{m/s}$$

Consequently, the flow rate is

$$Av = (64 \times 10^{-4}\ \text{m}^2)\,(3.06\ \text{m/s}) = 2.0 \times 10^{-2}\ \text{m}^3/\text{s}$$

Sample Problem 14-26

Figure 14-42*a* shows a self-acting water lifting device called a hydraulic ram. Its working is based on the phenomenon of hydraulic impact — when a liquid flowing along a tube is suddenly stopped, then their is a sharp increase in the pressure of the liquid. Its flow can be suddenly stopped, for example, by the shutting of a valve that discharges the water from the tube. A tube with a length of $l = 2$ metres and a diameter of $d = 20$ cm is lowered into a brook with a current velocity of $v = 4$ m/s.

First, let valve V_2 be open and valve V_1 be shut. A sharp increase in pressure will cause valve V_1 to open (valve V_2 will close at the same time) and the water will flow up into vessel A. The pressure drops, valve V_1 shuts and V_2 opens. The water in the tube assumes its course and the phenomenon is repeated in the previous sequence.

Find the amount of water raised by the ram in one hour to a height of $h = 30$ m if each valve opens thirty times a minute.

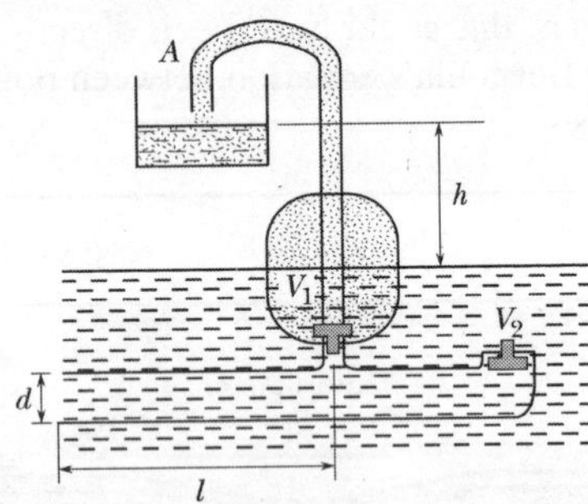

FIG. 14-42 (*a*) A self-acting hydraulic ram in which, as valve 2 closes, water flows through valve 1 and reaches *A*.

Conceptualize: Here we can imagine that as the water rushes along the tube it will be push both the valves but due to the design V_2 will close and V_1 will open. Thus, it will move along the vertical tube.

Classify: Now this problem involves conservation of mechanical energy as in the ideal fluid there is no loss of mechanical energy.

Compute: Thus on the basis of the law of conservation of energy, we can write

$$\frac{Mv^2}{2} = \text{mgh}$$

where M is the mass of the water in the tube stopped by valve V_2 and m is the mass of the water raised to the height h.

Therefore, $$\frac{\rho l \pi d^2}{4} \times \frac{v^2}{2} = \rho V_0 gh$$

where V_0 is the volume of mass m.

The average volume raised in two seconds is

$$V_0 = \frac{l\pi d^2 v^2}{8gh} = 1.7 \times 10^{-3}\ \text{m}^3$$

One hour of ram operation will raise

$$V = 1.7 \times 10^{-3} \times 30 \times 60 \cong 3\text{m}^3$$

Conclude: Above device converts kinetic energy of water into potential energy. When water comes inside tube, it has some kinetic energy and exerts impulsive force on wall "V_1" and this way valve open and gain potential. This process repeats once in two seconds.

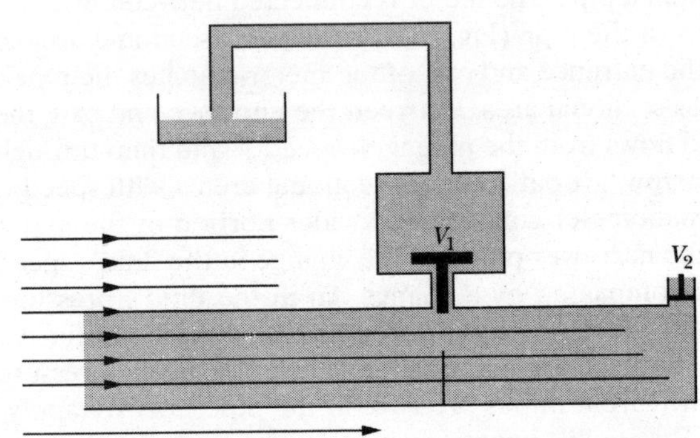

FIG. 14-42 (*b*) Flow lines in the ram.

Sample Problem 14-27

A hole is cut in the ice in the middle of a large lake. The ice is 2 m thick. What length of rope is required to scoop up a bucketful of water?

Solution: The ice can be supported by the edge of the shore only in small ponds. It will be floating in the middle of a large lake. The ratio between the densities of the ice and the water is 0.9. Therefore, nine-tenths of the entire thickness of the ice will be under the water. Thus distance from the surface of the ice to the water is 0.2 m.

Sample Problem 14-28 Build your skill

A ship passing through a loch rises to a higher level in a chamber of the loch into which water is pumped from the side of the lower level (Fig. 14-43). When will the pumps perform more work: when a large ship is in the chamber, or a small boat?

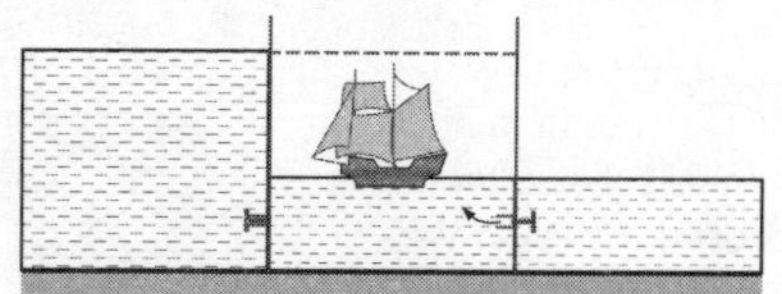

FIG. 14-43 Ship passing through a loch.

Solution: In both cases the pumps perform identical work, since the same amount of pumped in water rises to the same level.

Sample Problem 14-29 Build your skill

Mercury is poured into two communicating cylindrical vessels with different cross sections, then some amount of water is poured in both the vessels above the mercury so the level of the water in both vessels becomes same. Will the level of the water and the mercury be the same if a piece of wood is dropped into one vessel and some water equal in weight to this piece is added to the other?

Solution: If the cross sections are different, the water will be higher and the mercury lower in the vessel with a smaller cross section. This will occur because the pressure on the surface of the mercury will increase differently when amounts of water equal in weight and volume are added to the vessels with various cross sections.

REVIEW AND SUMMARY

Density The **density** ρ of any material is defined as the material's mass per unit volume:

$$\rho = \frac{\Delta m}{\Delta V}$$

Usually, where a material sample is much larger than atomic dimensions, we can write Eq. 14-1 as

$$\rho = \frac{m}{V}$$

Fluid Pressure A **fluid** is a substance that can flow; it conforms to the boundaries of its container because it cannot withstand shearing stress. It can, however, exert a force perpendicular to its surface. That force is described in terms of **pressure** p:

$$p = \frac{\Delta F}{\Delta A}$$

in which ΔF is the force acting on a surface element of area ΔA. If the force is uniform over a flat area, Eq. 14-3 can be written as

$$p = \frac{F}{A}$$

The force resulting from fluid pressure at a particular point in a fluid has the same magnitude in all directions. **Gauge pressure** is the difference between the actual pressure (or *absolute pressure*) at a point and the atmospheric pressure.

Pressure Variation with Height and Depth Pressure in a fluid at rest varies with vertical position y. For y measured positive upward,

$$p_2 = p_1 + \rho g(y_1 - y_2)$$

The pressure in a fluid is the same for all points at the same level. If h is the *depth* of a fluid sample below some reference level at which the pressure is p_0, Eq. 14-7 becomes

$$p = p_0 + \rho g h$$

where p is the pressure in the sample.

Pascal's Principle A change in the pressure applied to an enclosed fluid is transmitted undiminished to every portion of the fluid and to the walls of the containing vessel.

Archimedes' Principle When a body is fully or partially submerged in a fluid, a buoyant force $\vec{F}_b$ from the surrounding fluid acts on the body. The force is directed upward and has a magnitude given by

$$F_b = m_f g,$$

where m_f is the mass of the fluid that has been displaced by the body (that is, the fluid that has been pushed out of the way by the body).

When a body floats in a fluid, the magnitude F_b of the (upward) buoyant force on the body is equal to the magnitude F_g of the (downward) gravitational force on the body. The **apparent weight** of a body on which a buoyant force acts is related to its actual weight by

$$\text{weight}_{\text{app}} = \text{weight} - F_b.$$

Flow of Ideal Fluids An **ideal fluid** is incompressible and lacks viscosity, and its flow is steady and irrotational. A *streamline* is the path followed by an individual fluid particle. A *tube of flow* is a bundle of streamlines. The flow within any tube of flow obeys the **equation of continuity:**

$$R_V = Av = \text{a constant},$$

in which R_V is the **volume flow rate,** A is the cross-sectional area of the tube of flow at any point, and v is the speed of the fluid at that point. The **mass flow rate** R_m is

$$R_m = \rho R_V = \rho A v = \text{a constant}.$$

Bernoulli's Equation Applying the principle of conservation of mechanical energy to the flow of an ideal fluid leads to **Bernoulli's equation:**

$$p + \tfrac{1}{2}\rho v^2 + \rho g y = \text{a constant}$$

along any tube of flow.

QUESTIONS

1 *The teapot effect.* Water poured slowly from a teapot spout can double back under the spout for a considerable distance before detaching and falling. (The water layer is held against the underside of the spout by atmospheric pressure.) In Fig. 14-44, in the water layer inside the spout, point a is at the top of the layer and point b is at the bottom of the layer; in the water layer outside the spout, point c is at the top of the layer and point d is at the bottom of the layer. Rank those four points according to the gauge pressure in the water there, most positive first.

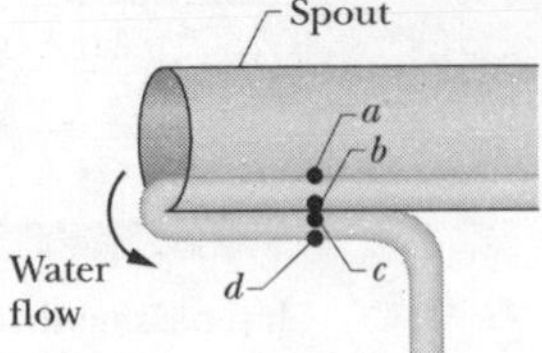

FIG. 14-44 Question 1.

2 Figure 14-45 shows a tank filled with water. Five horizontal floors and ceilings are indicated; all have the same area and are located at distances L, $2L$, or $3L$ below the top of the tank. Rank them according to the force on them due to the water, greatest first.

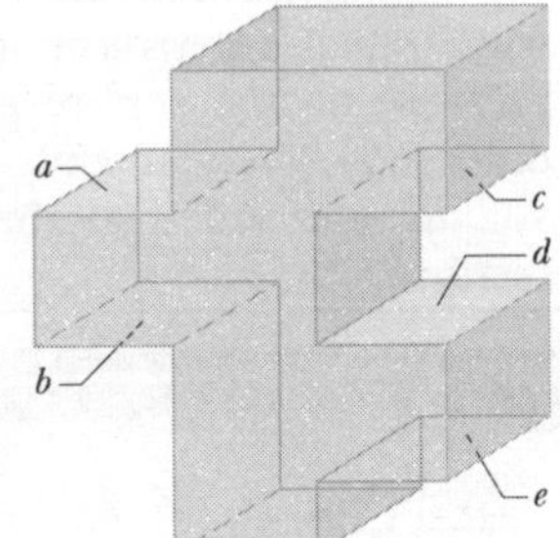

FIG. 14-45 Question 2.

3 We fully submerge an irregular 3 kg lump of material in a certain fluid. The fluid that would have been in the space now occupied by the lump has a mass of 2 kg. (a) When we release the lump, does it move upward, move downward, or remain in place? (b) If we next fully submerge the lump in a less dense fluid and again release it, what does it do?

4 Figure 14-46 shows four situations in which a red liquid and a gray liquid are in a U-tube. In one situation the liquids cannot be in static equilibrium. (a) Which situation is that? (b) For the other three situations, assume static equilibrium. For each, is the density of the red liquid greater than, less than, or equal to the density of the gray liquid?

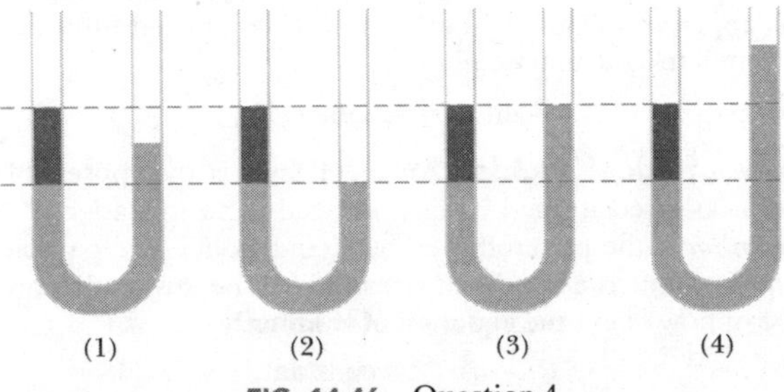

FIG. 14-46 Question 4.

5 A boat with an anchor on board floats in a swimming pool that is somewhat wider than the boat. Does the pool water level move up, move down, or remain the same if the anchor is (a) dropped into the water or (b) thrown onto the surrounding ground? (c) Does the water level in the pool move upward, move downward, or remain the same if, instead, a cork is dropped from the boat into the water, where it floats?

6 Figure 14-47 shows three identical open-top containers filled to the brim with water; toy ducks float in two of them. Rank the containers and contents according to their weight, greatest first.

FIG. 14-47 Question 6.

7 Water flows smoothly in a horizontal pipe. Figure 14-48 shows the kinetic energy K of a water element as it moves along an x axis that runs along the pipe. Rank the three lettered sections of the pipe according to the pipe radius, greatest first.

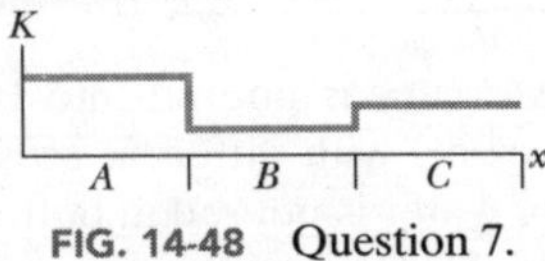

FIG. 14-48 Question 7.

8 The gauge pressure p_g versus depth h is plotted in Fig. 14-49 for three liquids. For a rigid plastic bead fully submerged in each liquid, rank the plots according to the magnitude of the buoyant force on the bead, greatest first.

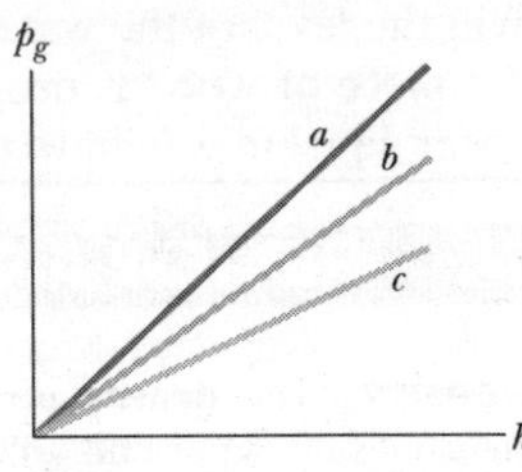

FIG. 14-49 Question 8.

9 Figure 14-50 shows four arrangements of pipes through which water flows smoothly toward the right. The radii of the pipe sections are indicated. In which arrangements is the net work done on a unit volume of water moving from the leftmost section to the rightmost section (a) zero, (b) positive, and (c) negative?

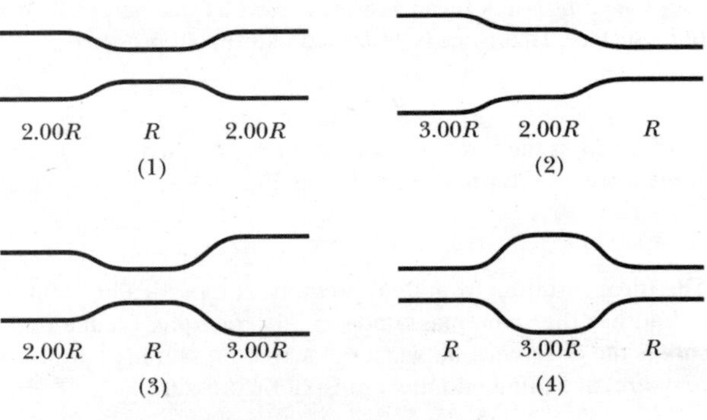

FIG. 14-50 Question 9.

10 A rectangular block is pushed face-down into three liquids, in turn. The apparent weight W_{app} of the block versus depth h in the three liquids is plotted in Fig. 14-51. Rank the liquids according to their weight per unit volume, greatest first.

FIG. 14-51 Question 10.

PROBLEMS

Density and Pressure

1 Find the pressure increase in the fluid in a syringe when a nurse applies a force of 42 N to the syringe's circular piston, which has a radius of 1.1 cm.

2 Three liquids that will not mix are poured into a cylindrical container. The volumes and densities of the liquids are 0.50 L, 2.6 g/cm^3; 0.25 L, 1.0 g/cm^3; and 0.40 L, 0.80 g/cm^3. What is the force on the bottom of the container due to these liquids? One liter = 1 L = 1000 cm^3. (Ignore the contribution due to the atmosphere.)

3 An office window has dimensions 3.4 m by 2.1 m. As a result of the passage of a storm, the outside air pressure drops to 0.96 atm, but inside the pressure is held at 1.0 atm. What net force pushes out on the window?

4 You inflate the front tires on your car to 28 psi. Later, you measure your blood pressure, obtaining a reading of 120/80, the readings being in mm Hg. In metric countries (which is to say, most of the world), these pressures are customarily reported in kilopascals (kPa). In kilopascals, what are (a) your tire pressure and (b) your blood pressure?

5 A fish maintains its depth in fresh water by adjusting the air content of porous bone or air sacs to make its average density the same as that of the water. Suppose that with its air sacs collapsed, a fish has a density of 1.08 g/cm^3. To what fraction of its expanded body volume must the fish inflate the air sacs to reduce its density to that of water?

6 A partially evacuated airtight container has a tight-fitting lid of surface area 77 m^2 and negligible mass. If the force required to remove the lid is 480 N and the atmospheric pressure is 1.0×10^5 Pa, what is the internal air pressure?

7 In 1654 Otto von Guericke, inventor of the air pump, gave a demonstration before the noblemen of the Holy Roman Empire in which two teams of eight horses could not pull apart two evacuated brass hemispheres. (a) Assuming the hemispheres have (strong) thin walls, so that R in Fig. 14-52 may be considered both the inside and outside radius, show that the force $\vec{F}$ required to pull apart the hemispheres has magnitude $F = \pi R^2 \, \Delta p$, where Δp is the difference between the pressures outside and inside the sphere. (b) Taking R as 30 cm, the inside pressure as 0.10 atm, and the outside pressure as 1.00 atm, find the force magnitude the teams of horses would have had to exert to pull apart the hemispheres. (c) Explain why one team of horses could have proved the point just as well if the hemispheres were attached to a sturdy wall.

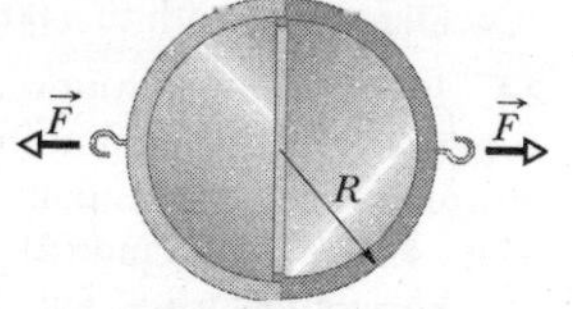

FIG. 14-52 Problem 7.

Fluids at Rest

8 Calculate the hydrostatic difference in blood pressure between the brain and the foot in a person of height 1.83 m. The density of blood is 1.06×10^3 kg/m^3.

9 At a depth of 10.9 km, the Challenger Deep in the Marianas Trench of the Pacific Ocean is the deepest site in any ocean. Yet, in 1960, Donald Walsh and Jacques Piccard reached the Challenger Deep in the bathyscaph *Trieste.* Assuming that seawater has a uniform density of 1024 kg/m^3, approximate the hydrostatic pressure (in atmospheres) that the *Trieste* had to withstand.

10 The maximum depth d_{max} that a diver can snorkel is set by the density of the water and the fact that human lungs can function against a maximum pressure difference (between inside and outside the chest cavity) of 0.050 atm. What is the difference in d_{max} for fresh water and the water of the Dead Sea (the saltiest natural water in the world, with a density of 1.5×10^3 kg/m^3)?

11 Crew members attempt to escape from a damaged submarine 100 m below the surface. What force must be applied to a pop-out hatch, which is 1.2 m by 0.60 m, to push it out at that depth? Assume that the density of the ocean water is 1024 kg/m^3 and the internal air pressure is at 1.00 atm.

12 The plastic tube in Fig. 14-53 has a cross-sectional area of 5.00 cm^2. The tube is filled with water until the short arm (of length d = 0.800 m) is full. Then the short arm is sealed and more water is gradually poured into the long arm. If the seal will pop off when the force on it exceeds 9.80 N, what total height of water in the long arm will put the seal on the verge of popping?

FIG. 14-53 Problems 12 and 75.

13 What gauge pressure must a machine produce in order to suck mud of density 1800 kg/m^3 up a tube by a height of 1.5 m?

14 *The bends during flight.* Anyone who scuba dives is advised not to fly within the next 24 h because the air mixture for diving can introduce nitrogen to the bloodstream. Without allowing the nitrogen to come out of solution slowly, any sudden air-pressure reduction (such as during airplane ascent) can result in the nitrogen forming bubbles in the blood, creating the *bends*, which can be painful and even fatal. Military special operation forces are especially at risk. What is the change in pressure on such a special-op soldier who must scuba dive at a depth of 20 m in seawater one day and parachute at an altitude of 7.6 km the next day? Assume that the average air density within the altitude range is 0.87 kg/m^3.

15 *Giraffe bending to drink.* In a giraffe with its head 2.0 m above its heart, and its heart 2.0 m above its feet, the (hydrostatic) gauge pressure in the blood at its heart is 250 torr. Assume that the giraffe stands upright and the blood density is 1.06×10^3 kg/m^3. In torr (or mm Hg), find the (gauge) blood pressure (a) at the brain (the pressure is enough to perfuse the brain with blood, to keep the giraffe from fainting) and (b) at the feet (the pressure must be countered by tight-fitting skin acting like a pressure stocking). (c) If the giraffe were to lower its head to drink from a pond without splaying its legs and moving slowly, what would be the increase in the blood pressure in the brain? (Such action would probably be lethal.)

16 In Fig. 14-54, an open tube of length L = 1.8 m and cross-sectional area A = 4.6 cm^2 is fixed to the top of a cylindrical barrel of diameter D = 1.2 m and height H = 1.8 m. The barrel and tube are filled with water (to the top of the

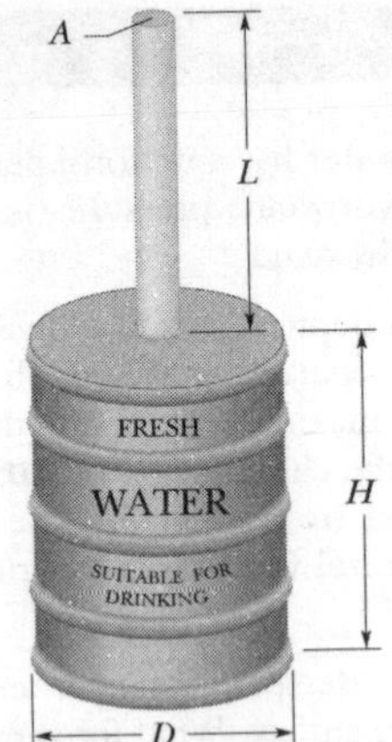

FIG. 14-54 Problem 16.

tube). Calculate the ratio of the hydrostatic force on the bottom of the barrel to the gravitational force on the water contained in the barrel. Why is that ratio not equal to 1.0? (You need not consider the atmospheric pressure.)

17 *Blood pressure in Argentinosaurus.* (a) If this long-necked, gigantic sauropod had a head height of 21 m and a heart height of 9.0 m, what (hydrostatic) gauge pressure in its blood was required at the heart such that the blood pressure at the brain was 80 torr (just enough to perfuse the brain with blood)? Assume the blood had a density of 1.06×10^3 kg/m^3. (b) What was the blood pressure (in torr or mm Hg) at the feet?

18 *Snorkeling by humans and elephants.* When a person snorkels, the lungs are connected directly to the atmosphere through the snorkel tube and thus are at atmospheric pressure. In atmospheres, what is the difference Δp between this internal air pressure and the water pressure against the body if the length of the snorkel tube is (a) 20 cm (standard situation) and (b) 4.0 m (probably lethal situation)? In the latter, the pressure difference causes blood vessels on the walls of the lungs to rupture, releasing blood into the lungs. As depicted in Fig. 14-55, an elephant can safely snorkel through its trunk while swimming with its lungs 4.0 m below the water surface because the membrane around its lungs contains connective tissue that holds and protects the blood vessels, preventing rupturing.

FIG. 14-55 Problem 18.

19 Two identical cylindrical vessels with their bases at the same level each contain a liquid of density 1.30×10^3 kg/m^3. The area of each base is 4.00 cm^2, but in one vessel the liquid height is 0.854 m and in the other it is 1.560 m. Find the work done by the gravitational force in equalizing the levels when the two vessels are connected.

20 *g-LOC in dogfights.* When a pilot takes a tight turn at high speed in a modern fighter airplane, the blood pressure at the brain level decreases, blood no longer perfuses the brain, and the blood in the brain drains. If the heart maintains the (hydrostatic) gauge pressure in the aorta at 120 torr (or mm Hg) when the pilot undergoes a horizontal centripetal acceleration of $4g$, what is the blood pressure (in torr) at the brain, 30 cm radially inward from the heart? The perfusion in the brain is small enough that the vision switches to black and white and narrows to "tunnel vision" and the pilot can undergo *g*-LOC ("*g*-induced loss of consciousness"). Blood density is 1.06×10^3 kg/m^3.

21 In analyzing certain geological features, it is often appropriate to assume that the pressure at some horizontal *level of compensation,* deep inside Earth, is the same over a large region and is equal to the pressure due to the gravitational force on the overlying material. Thus, the pressure on the level of compensation is given by the fluid pressure formula. This model requires, for one thing, that mountains have *roots* of continental rock extending into the denser mantle (Fig. 14-56). Consider a mountain of height H = 6.0 km on a continent of thickness T = 32 km. The continental rock has a density of 2.9 g/cm^3, and beneath this rock the mantle has a density of 3.3 g/cm^3. Calculate the depth D of the root. (*Hint:* Set the pressure at points a and b equal; the depth y of the level of compensation will cancel out.)

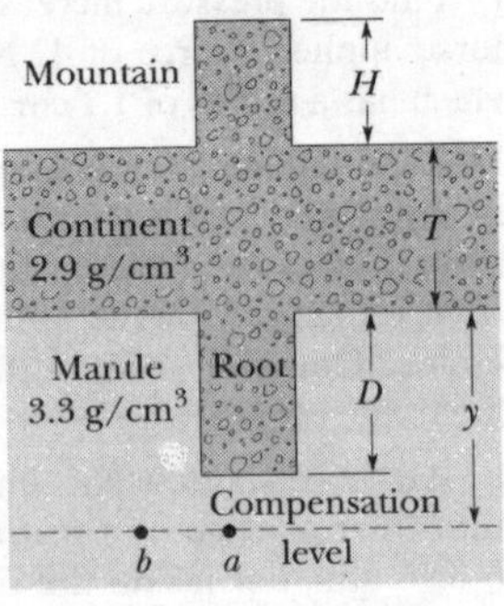

FIG. 14-56 Problem 21.

22 The L-shaped tank shown in Fig. 14-57 is filled with water and is open at the top. If d = 5.0 m, what is the force due to the water (a) on face A and (b) on face B?

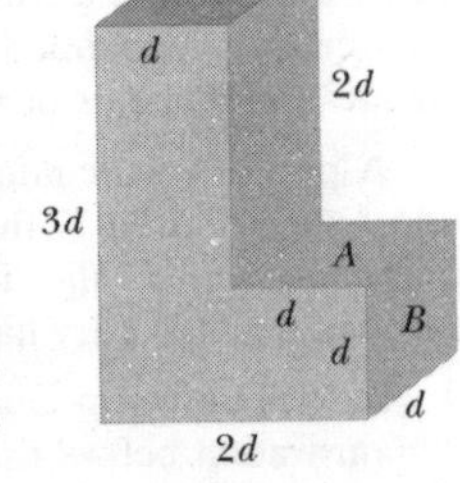

FIG. 14-57 Problem 22.

23 A large aquarium of height 5.00 m is filled with fresh water to a depth of 2.00 m. One wall of the aquarium consists of thick plastic 8.00 m wide. By how much does the total force on that wall increase if the aquarium is next filled to a depth of 4.00 m?

24 In Fig. 14-58, water stands at depth D = 35.0 m behind the vertical upstream face of a dam of width W = 314 m. Find (a) the net horizontal force on the dam from the gauge pressure of the water and (b) the net torque due to that force about a line through O parallel to the width of the dam. (c) Find the moment arm of this torque.

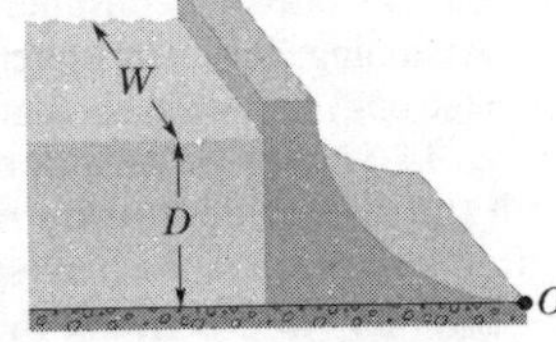

FIG. 14-58 Problem 24.

Measuring Pressure

25 In one observation, the column in a mercury barometer (as is shown in Fig. 14-5*a*) has a measured height h of 740.35 mm. The temperature is −5.0°C, at which temperature the density of mercury ρ is 1.3608×10^4 kg/m^3. The free-fall acceleration g at the site of the barometer is 9.7835 m/s^2. What is the atmospheric pressure at that site in pascals and in torr (which is the common unit for barometer readings)?

26 To suck lemonade of density 1000 kg/m^3 up a straw to a maximum height of 4.0 cm, what minimum gauge pressure (in atmospheres) must you produce in your lungs?

27 What would be the height of the atmosphere if the air density (a) were uniform and (b) decreased linearly to zero with height? Assume that at sea level the air pressure is 1.0 atm and the air density is 1.3 kg/m^3.

Pascal's Principle

28 A piston of cross-sectional area a is used in a hydraulic press to exert a small force of magnitude f on the enclosed liquid. A connecting pipe leads to a larger piston of cross-sectional area A (Fig. 14-59). (a) What force magnitude F will the larger piston sustain without moving? (b) If the piston diameters are 3.80 cm and 53.0 cm, what force magnitude on the small piston will balance a 20.0 kN force on the large piston?

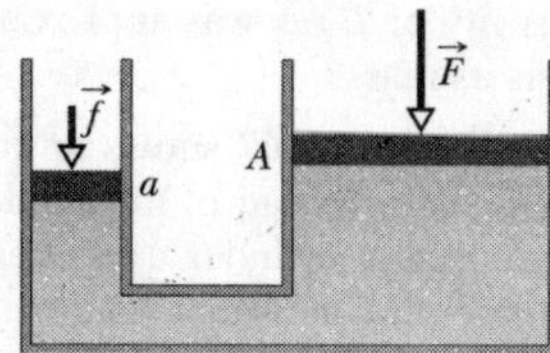

FIG. 14-59 Problem 28.

29 In Fig. 14-60, a spring of spring constant 3.00×10^4 N/m is between a rigid beam and the output piston of a hydraulic lever. An empty container with negligible mass sits on the input piston. The input piston has area A_i, and the output piston has area $18.0A_i$. Initially the spring is at its rest length. How many kilograms of sand must be (slowly) poured into the container to compress the spring by 5.00 cm?

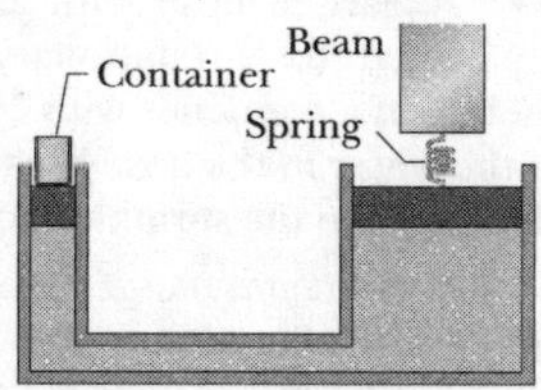

FIG. 14-60 Problem 29.

Archimedes' Principle

30 In Fig. 14-61, a cube of edge length L = 0.600 m and mass 450 kg is suspended by a rope in an open tank of liquid of density 1030 kg/m^3. Find (a) the magnitude of the total downward force on the top of the cube from the liquid and the atmosphere, assuming atmospheric pressure is 1.00 atm, (b) the magnitude of the total upward force on the bottom of the cube, and (c) the tension in the rope. (d) Calculate the magnitude of the buoyant force on the cube using Archimedes' principle. What relation exists among all these quantities?

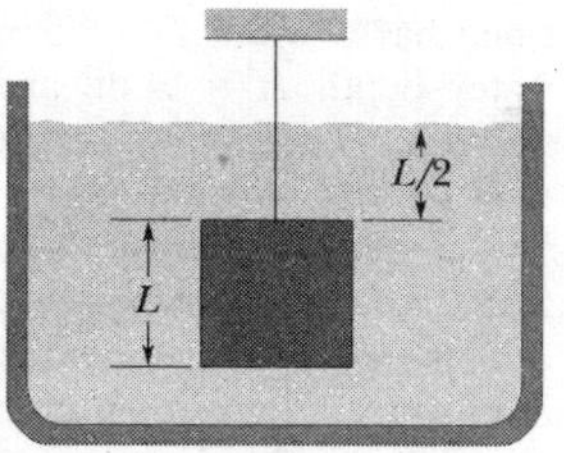

FIG. 14-61 Problem 30.

31 An iron anchor of density 7870 kg/m^3 appears 200 N lighter in water than in air. (a) What is the volume of the anchor? (b) How much does it weigh in air?

32 A boat floating in fresh water displaces water weighing 35.6 kN. (a) What is the weight of the water this boat displaces when floating in salt water of density 1.10×10^3 kg/m^3? (b) What is the difference between the volume of fresh water displaced and the volume of salt water displaced?

33 Three children, each of weight 356 N, make a log raft by lashing together logs of diameter 0.30 m and length 1.80 m. How many logs will be needed to keep them afloat in fresh water? Take the density of the logs to be 800 kg/m^3.

34 A 5.00 kg object is released from rest while fully submerged in a liquid. The liquid displaced by the submerged object has a mass of 3.00 kg. How far and in what direction does the object move in 0.200 s, assuming that it moves freely and that the drag force on it from the liquid is negligible?

35 A block of wood floats in fresh water with two-thirds of its volume V submerged and in oil with $0.90V$ submerged. Find the density of (a) the wood and (b) the oil.

36 A flotation device is in the shape of a right cylinder, with a height of 0.500 m and a face area of 4.00 m^2 on top and bottom, and its density is 0.400 times that of fresh water. It is initially held fully submerged in fresh water, with its top face at the water surface. Then it is allowed to ascend gradually until it begins to float. How much work does the buoyant force do on the device during the ascent?

37 A hollow sphere of inner radius 8.0 cm and outer radius 9.0 cm floats half-submerged in a liquid of density 800 kg/m^3. (a) What is the mass of the sphere? (b) Calculate the density of the material of which the sphere is made.

38 *Lurking alligators.* An alligator waits for prey by floating with only the top of its head exposed, so that the prey cannot easily see it. One way it can adjust the extent of sinking is by controlling the size of its lungs. Another way may be by swallowing stones (*gastrolithes*) that then reside in the stomach. Figure 14-62 shows a highly simplified model (a "rhombohedron gater") of mass 130 kg that roams with its head partially exposed. The top head surface has area 0.20 m^2. If the alligator were to swallow stones with a total mass of 1.0% of its body mass (a typical amount), how far would it sink?

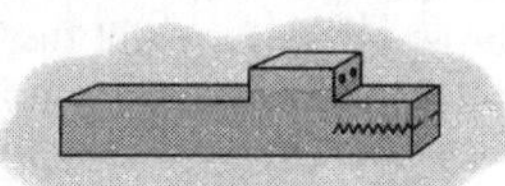

FIG. 14-62 Problem 38.

39 What fraction of the volume of an iceberg (density 917 kg/m^3) would be visible if the iceberg floats (a) in the ocean (salt water, density 1024 kg/m^3) and (b) in a river (fresh water, density 1000 kg/m^3)? (When salt water freezes to form ice, the salt is excluded. So, an iceberg could provide fresh water to a community.)

40 A small solid ball is released from rest while fully submerged in a liquid and then its kinetic energy is measured when it has moved 4.0 cm in the liquid. Fig. 14-63 gives the results after many liquids are used: The kinetic energy K is plotted versus the liquid density ρ_{liq}, and K_s = 1.60 J sets the scale on the vertical axis. What are (a) the density and (b) the volume of the ball?

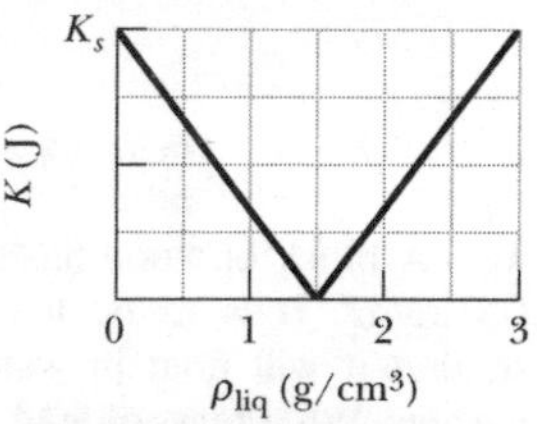

FIG. 14-63 Problem 40.

41 A hollow spherical iron shell floats almost completely submerged in water. The outer diameter is 60.0 cm, and the density of iron is 7.87 g/cm^3. Find the inner diameter.

42 In Fig. 14-64a, a rectangular block is gradually pushed face-down into a liquid. The block has height d; on the bottom and top the face area is A = 5.67 cm^2. Figure 14-43b gives the apparent weight W_{app} of the block as a function of the depth h of its lower face. The scale on the vertical axis is set by W_s = 0.20 N. What is the density of the liquid?

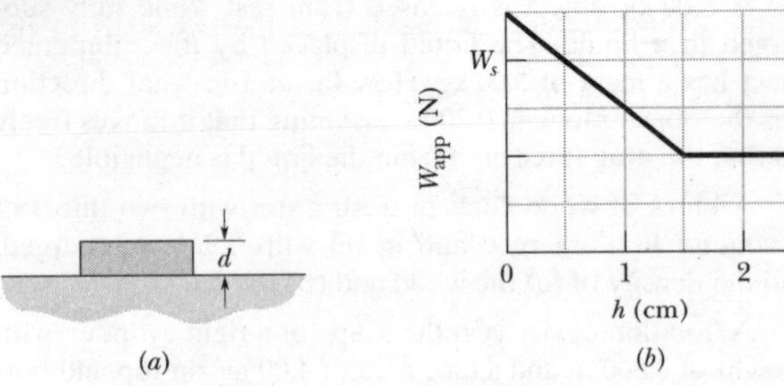

FIG. 14-64 Problem 42.

43 An iron casting containing a number of cavities weighs 6000 N in air and 4000 N in water. What is the total volume of all the cavities in the casting? The density of iron (that is, a sample with no cavities) is 7.87 g/cm^3.

44 Suppose that you release a small ball from rest at a depth of 0.600 m below the surface in a pool of water. If the density of the ball is 0.300 that of water and if the drag force on the ball from the water is negligible, how high above the water surface will the ball shoot as it emerges from the water? (Neglect any transfer of energy to the splashing and waves produced by the emerging ball.)

45 The volume of air space in the passenger compartment of an 1800 kg car is 5.00 m^3. The volume of the motor and front wheels is 0.750 m^3, and the volume of the rear wheels, gas tank, and trunk is 0.800 m^3; water cannot enter these two regions. The car rolls into a lake. (a) At first, no water enters the passenger compartment. How much of the car, in cubic meters, is below the water surface with the car floating (Fig. 14-65)? (b) As water slowly enters, the car sinks. How many cubic meters of water are in the car as it disappears below the water surface? (The car, with a heavy load in the trunk, remains horizontal.)

FIG. 14-65 Problem 45.

46 A block of wood has a mass of 3.67 kg and a density of 600 kg/m^3. It is to be loaded with lead (1.14×10^4 kg/m^3) so that it will float in water with 0.900 of its volume submerged. What mass of lead is needed if the lead is attached to (a) the top of the wood and (b) the bottom of the wood?

47 When researchers find a reasonably complete fossil of a dinosaur, they can determine the mass and weight of the living dinosaur with a scale model sculpted from plastic and based on the dimensions of the fossil bones. The scale of the model is 1/20; that is, lengths are 1/20 actual length, areas are $(1/20)^2$ actual areas, and volumes are $(1/20)^3$ actual volumes. First, the model is suspended from one arm of a balance and weights are added to the other arm until equilibrium is reached. Then the model is fully submerged in water and enough weights are removed from the second arm to reestablish equilibrium (Fig. 14-66). For a model of a particular *T. rex* fossil, 637.76 g had to be removed to reestablish equilibrium. What was the volume of (a) the model and (b) the actual *T. rex*? (c) If the density of *T. rex* was approximately the density of water, what was its mass?

FIG. 14-66 Problem 47.

48 Figure 14-67 shows an iron ball suspended by thread of negligible mass from an upright cylinder that floats partially submerged in water. The cylinder has a height of 6.00 cm, a face area of 12.0 cm^2 on the top and bottom, and a density of 0.30 g/cm^3, and 2.00 cm of its height is above the water surface. What is the radius of the iron ball?

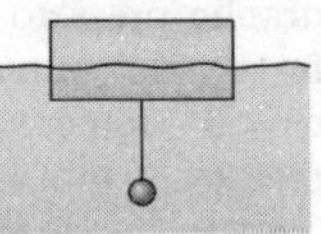

FIG. 14-67 Problem 48.

The Equation of Continuity

49 A garden hose with an internal diameter of 1.9 cm is connected to a (stationary) lawn sprinkler that consists merely of a container with 24 holes, each 0.13 cm in diameter. If the water in the hose has a speed of 0.91 m/s, at what speed does it leave the sprinkler holes?

50 Two streams merge to form a river. One stream has a width of 8.2 m, depth of 3.4 m, and current speed of 2.3 m/s. The other stream is 6.8 m wide and 3.2 m deep, and flows at 2.6 m/s. If the river has width 10.5 m and speed 2.9 m/s, what is its depth?

51 *Canal effect.* Figure 14-68 shows an anchored barge that extends across a canal by distance d = 30 m and into the water by distance b = 12 m. The canal has a width D = 55 m, a water depth H = 14 m, and a uniform water-flow speed v_i = 1.5 m/s. Assume that the flow around the barge is uniform. As the water passes the bow, the water level undergoes a dramatic dip known as the canal effect. If the dip has depth h = 0.80 m, what is the water speed alongside the boat through the vertical cross sections at (a) point a and (b) point b? The erosion due to the speed increase is a common concern to hydraulic engineers.

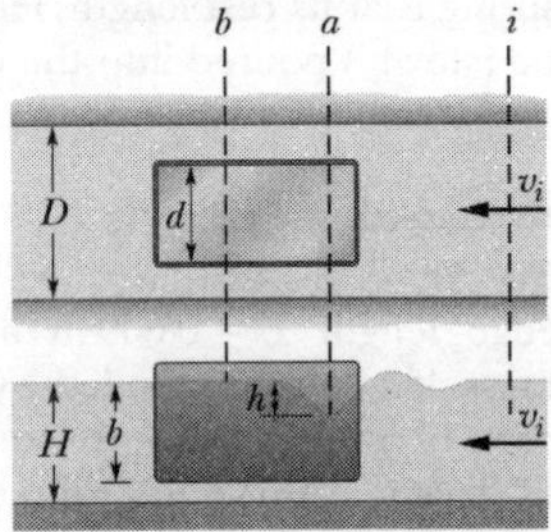

FIG. 14-68 Problem 51.

52 Figure 14-69 shows two sections of an old pipe system that runs through a hill, with distances $d_A = d_B = 30$ m and D = 110 m. On each side of the hill, the pipe radius is 2.00 cm. However, the radius of the pipe inside the hill is no longer known. To determine it, hydraulic engineers first establish that water flows through the left and right sections at 2.50 m/s. Then they release a dye in the water at point A and find that it takes 88.8 s to reach point B. What is the average radius of the pipe within the hill?

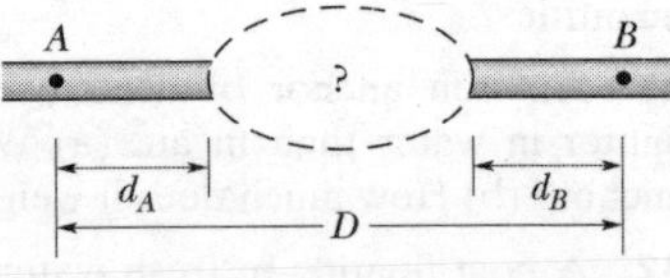

FIG. 14-69 Problem 52.

53 Water is pumped steadily out of a flooded basement at a speed of 5.0 m/s through a uniform hose of radius 1.0 cm.

The hose passes out through a window 3.0 m above the waterline. What is the power of the pump?

54 The water flowing through a 1.9 cm (inside diameter) pipe flows out through three 1.3 cm pipes. (a) If the flow rates in the three smaller pipes are 26, 19, and 11 L/min, what is the flow rate in the 1.9 cm pipe? (b) What is the ratio of the speed in the 1.9 cm pipe to that in the pipe carrying 26 L/min?

Bernoulli's Equation

55 Water is moving with a speed of 5.0 m/s through a pipe with a cross-sectional area of 4.0 cm^2. The water gradually descends 10 m as the pipe cross-sectional area increases to 8.0 cm^2. (a) What is the speed at the lower level? (b) If the pressure at the upper level is 1.5×10^5 Pa, what is the pressure at the lower level?

56 The intake in Fig. 14-70 has cross-sectional area of 0.74 m^2 and water flow at 0.40 m/s. At the outlet, distance $D = 180$ m below the intake, the cross-sectional area is smaller than at the intake and the water flows out at 9.5 m/s. What is the pressure difference between inlet and outlet?

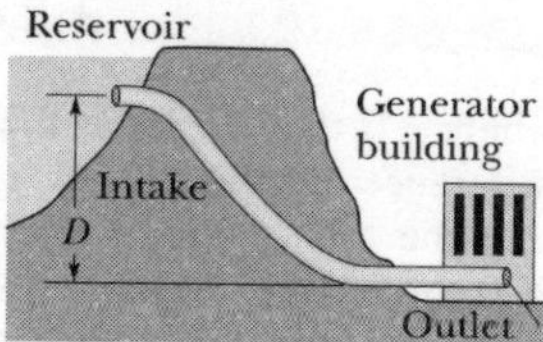

FIG. 14-70 Problem 56.

57 A water pipe having a 2.5 cm inside diameter carries water into the basement of a house at a speed of 0.90 m/s and a pressure of 170 kPa. If the pipe tapers to 1.2 cm and rises to the second floor 7.6 m above the input point, what are the (a) speed and (b) water pressure at the second floor?

58 Models of torpedoes are sometimes tested in a horizontal pipe of flowing water, much as a wind tunnel is used to test model airplanes. Consider a circular pipe of internal diameter 25.0 cm and a torpedo model aligned along the long axis of the pipe. The model has a 5.00 cm diameter and is to be tested with water flowing past it at 2.50 m/s. (a) With what speed must the water flow in the part of the pipe that is unconstricted by the model? (b) What will the pressure difference be between the constricted and unconstricted parts of the pipe?

59 A cylindrical tank with a large diameter is filled with water to a depth $D = 0.30$ m. A hole of cross-sectional area $A = 6.5$ cm^2 in the bottom of the tank allows water to drain out. (a) What is the rate at which water flows out, in cubic meters per second? (b) At what distance below the bottom of the tank is the cross-sectional area of the stream equal to one-half the area of the hole?

60 Suppose that two tanks, 1 and 2, each with a large opening at the top, contain different liquids. A small hole is made in the side of each tank at the same depth h below the liquid surface, but the hole in tank 1 has half the cross-sectional area of the hole in tank 2. (a) What is the ratio ρ_1/ρ_2 of the densities of the liquids if the mass flow rate is the same for the two holes? (b) What is the ratio R_{V1}/R_{V2} of the volume flow rates from the two tanks? (c) At one instant, the liquid in tank 1 is 12.0 cm above the hole. If the tanks are to have *equal* volume flow rates, what height above the hole must the liquid in tank 2 be just then?

61 How much work is done by pressure in forcing 1.4 m^3 of water through a pipe having an internal diameter of 13 mm if the difference in pressure at the two ends of the pipe is 1.0 atm?

62 In Fig. 14-71, water flows through a horizontal pipe and then out into the atmosphere at a speed $v_1 = 15$ m/s. The diameters of the left and right sections of the pipe are 5.0 cm and 3.0 cm. (a) What volume of water flows into the atmosphere during a 10 min period? In the left section of the pipe, what are (b) the speed v_2 and (c) the gauge pressure?

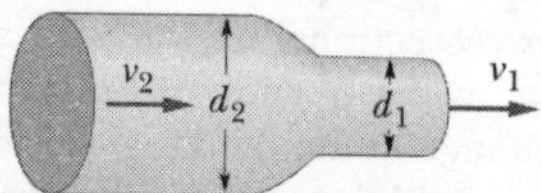

FIG. 14-71 Problem 62.

63 In Fig. 14-72, the fresh water behind a reservoir dam has depth $D = 15$ m. A horizontal pipe 4.0 cm in diameter passes through the dam at depth $d = 6.0$ m. A plug secures the pipe opening. (a) Find the magnitude of the frictional force between plug and pipe wall. (b) The plug is removed. What water volume exits the pipe in 3.0 h?

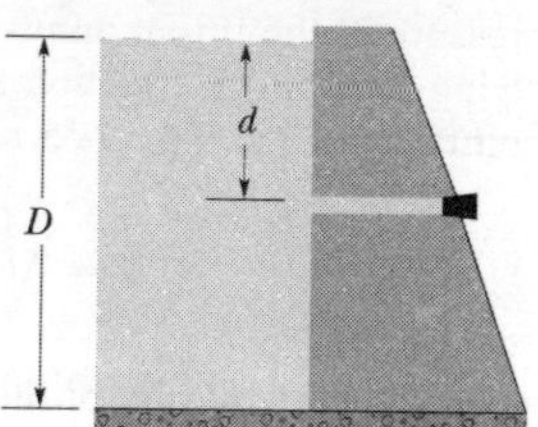

FIG. 14-72 Problem 63.

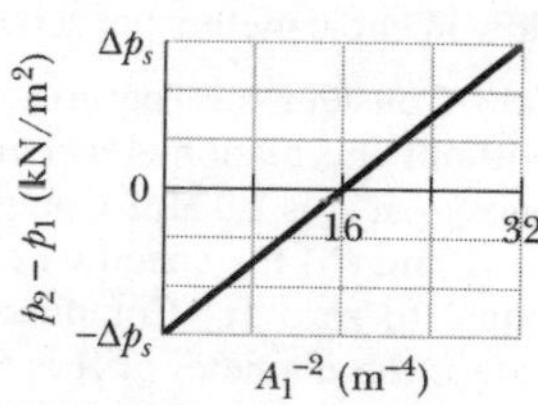

FIG. 14-73 Problem 64.

64 Fresh water flows horizontally from pipe section 1 of cross-sectional area A_1 into pipe section 2 of cross-sectional area A_2. Figure 14-73 gives a plot of the pressure difference $p_2 - p_1$ versus the inverse area squared A_1^{-2} that would be expected for a volume flow rate of a certain value if the water flow were laminar under all circumstances. The scale on the vertical axis is set by $\Delta p_s = 300$ kN/m^2. For the conditions of the figure, what are the values of (a) A_2 and (b) the volume flow rate?

65 Figure 14-74 shows a stream of water flowing through a hole at depth $h = 10$ cm in a tank holding water to height $H = 40$ cm. (a) At what distance x does the stream strike the floor? (b) At what depth should a second hole be made to give the same value of x? (c) At what depth should a hole be made to maximize x?

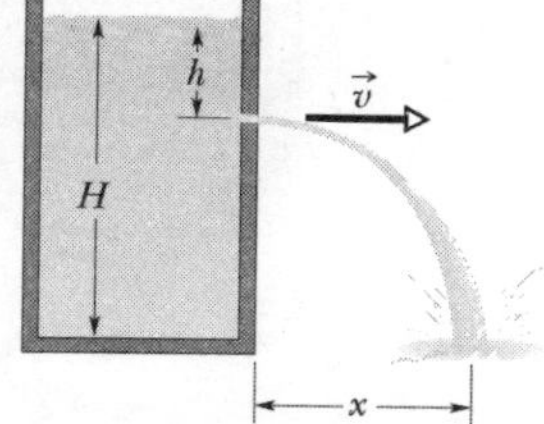

FIG. 14-74 Problem 65.

66 In Fig. 14-75, water flows steadily from the left pipe section (radius $r_1 = 2.00R$), through the middle section (radius R), and into the right section (radius $r_3 = 3.00R$). The speed of the water in the middle section is 0.500 m/s. What is the net work done on 0.400 m^3 of the water as it moves from the left section to the right section?

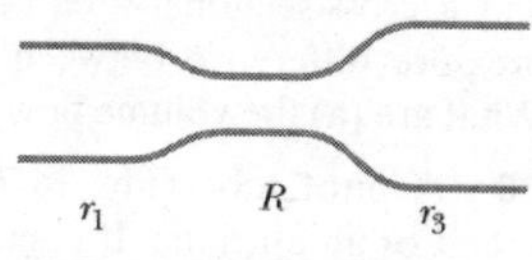

FIG. 14-75 Problem 66.

67 A *venturi meter* is used to measure the flow speed of a fluid in a pipe. The meter is connected between two sections of the pipe (Fig. 14-76); the cross-sectional area A of the entrance and exit of the meter matches the pipe's cross-sectional

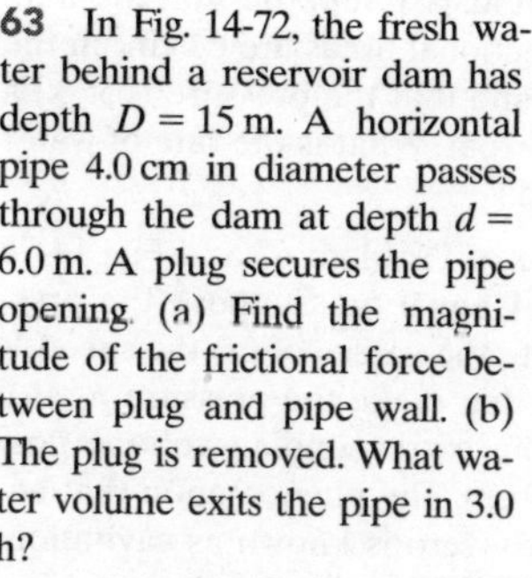

area. Between the entrance and exit, the fluid flows from the pipe with speed V and then through a narrow "throat" of cross-sectional area a with speed v. A manometer connects the wider portion of the meter to the narrower portion. The change in the fluid's speed is accompanied by a change Δp in the fluid's pressure, which causes a height difference h of the liquid in the two arms of the manometer. (Here Δp means pressure in the throat minus pressure in the pipe.) (a) By applying Bernoulli's equation and the equation of continuity to points 1 and 2 in Fig. 14-55, show that

$$V = \sqrt{\frac{2a^2\,\Delta p}{\rho(a^2 - A^2)}},$$

where ρ is the density of the fluid. (b) Suppose that the fluid is fresh water, that the cross-sectional areas are 64 cm^2 in the pipe and 32 cm^2 in the throat, and that the pressure is 55 kPa in the pipe and 41 kPa in the throat. What is the rate of water flow in cubic meters per second?

68 Consider the venturi tube of Problem 67 and Fig. 14-76 without the manometer. Let A equal $5a$. Suppose the pressure p_1 at A is 2.0 atm. Compute the values of (a) the speed V at A and (b) the speed v at a that make the pressure p_2 at a equal to zero. (c) Compute the corresponding volume flow rate if the diameter at A is 5.0 cm. The phenomenon that occurs at a when p_2 falls to nearly zero is known as cavitation. The water vaporizes into small bubbles.

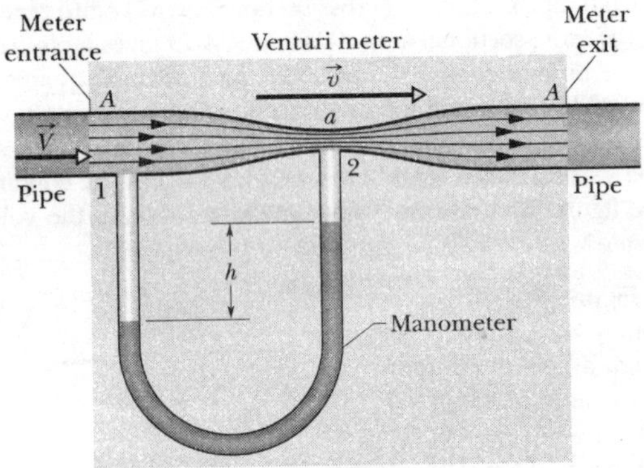

FIG. 14-76 Problems 67 and 68.

69 A liquid of density 900 kg/m^3 flows through a horizontal pipe that has a cross-sectional area of 1.90×10^{-2} m^2 in region A and a cross-sectional area of 9.50×10^{-2} m^2 in region B. The pressure difference between the two regions is 7.20×10^3 Pa. What are (a) the volume flow rate and (b) the mass flow rate?

70 A pitot tube (Fig. 14-77) is used to determine the airspeed of an airplane. It consists of an outer tube with a number of small holes B (four are shown) that allow air into the tube; that tube is connected to one arm of a U-tube. The other arm of the U-tube is connected to hole A at the front end of the device, which points in the direction the plane is headed. At A the air becomes stagnant so that $v_A = 0$. At B, however, the speed of the air presumably equals the airspeed v of the plane. (a) Use Bernoulli's equation to show that

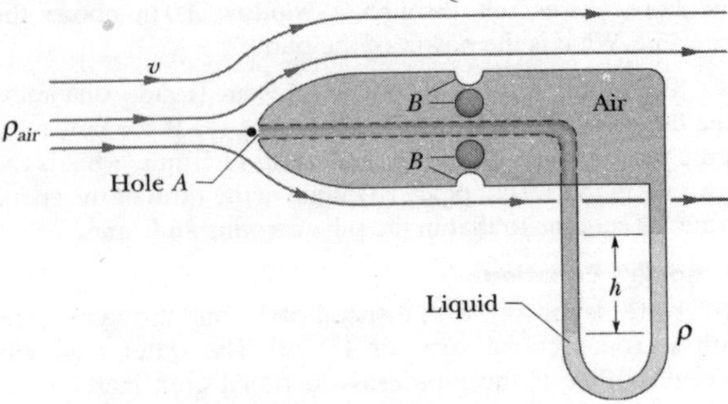

FIG. 14-77 Problems 70 and 71.

$$v = \sqrt{\frac{2\rho g h}{\rho_{air}}},$$

where ρ is the density of the liquid in the U-tube and h is the difference in the liquid levels in that tube. (b) Suppose that the tube contains alcohol and the level difference h is 26.0 cm. What is the plane's speed relative to the air? The density of the air is 1.03 kg/m^3 and that of alcohol is 810 kg/m^3.

71 A pitot tube (see Problem 70) on a high-altitude aircraft measures a differential pressure of 180 Pa. What is the aircraft's airspeed if the density of the air is 0.031 kg/m^3?

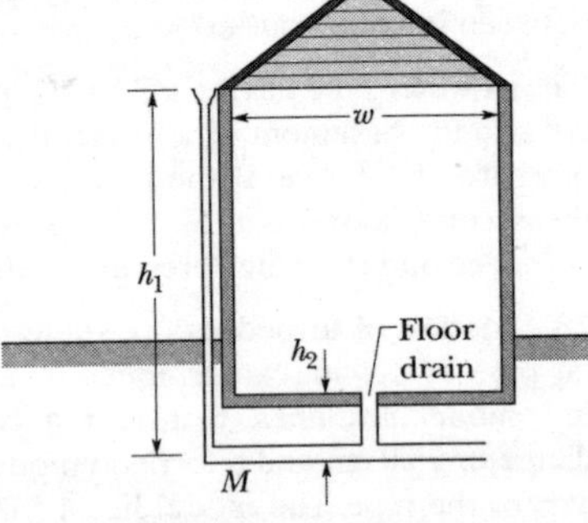

FIG. 14-78 Problem 72.

72 A very simplified schematic of the rain drainage system for a home is shown in Fig. 14-78. Rain falling on the slanted roof runs off into gutters around the roof edge; it then drains through downspouts (only one is shown) into a main drainage pipe M below the basement, which carries the water to an even larger pipe below the street. In Fig. 14-57, a floor drain in the basement is also connected to drainage pipe M. Suppose the following apply:

1. the downspouts have height $h_1 = 11$ m,
2. the floor drain has height $h_2 = 1.2$ m,
3. pipe M has radius 3.0 cm,
4. the house has side width $w = 30$ m and front length $L = 60$ m,
5. all the water striking the roof goes through pipe M,
6. the initial speed of the water in a downspout is negligible,
7. the wind speed is negligible (the rain falls vertically).

At what rainfall rate, in centimeters per hour, will water from pipe M reach the height of the floor drain and threaten to flood the basement?

Additional Problems

73 A glass ball of radius 2.00 cm sits at the bottom of a container of milk that has a density of 1.03 g/cm^3. The normal force on the ball from the container's lower surface has magnitude 9.48×10^{-2} N. What is the mass of the ball?

74 When you cough, you expel air at high speed through the trachea and upper bronchi so that the air will remove excess mucus lining the pathway. You produce the high speed by this procedure: You breathe in a large amount of air, trap it by closing the glottis (the narrow opening in the larynx), increase the air pressure by contracting the lungs, partially collapse the trachea and upper bronchi to narrow the pathway, and then expel the air through the pathway by suddenly reopening the glottis. Assume that during the expulsion the volume flow rate is 7.0×10^{-3} m³/s. What multiple of the speed of sound v_s (= 343 m/s) is the airspeed through the trachea if the trachea diameter (a) remains its normal value of 14 mm and (b) contracts to 5.2 mm?

75 Figure 14-53 shows a modified U-tube: the right arm is shorter than the left arm. The open end of the right arm is height d = 10.0 cm above the laboratory bench. The radius throughout the tube is 1.50 cm. Water is gradually poured into the open end of the left arm until the water begins to flow out the open end of the right arm. Then a liquid of density 0.80 g/cm³ is gradually added to the left arm until its height in that arm is 8.0 cm (it does not mix with the water). How much water flows out of the right arm?

76 Caught in an avalanche, a skier is fully submerged in flowing snow of density 96 kg/m³. Assume that the average density of the skier, clothing, and skiing equipment is 1020 kg/m³. What percentage of the gravitational force on the skier is offset by the buoyant force from the snow?

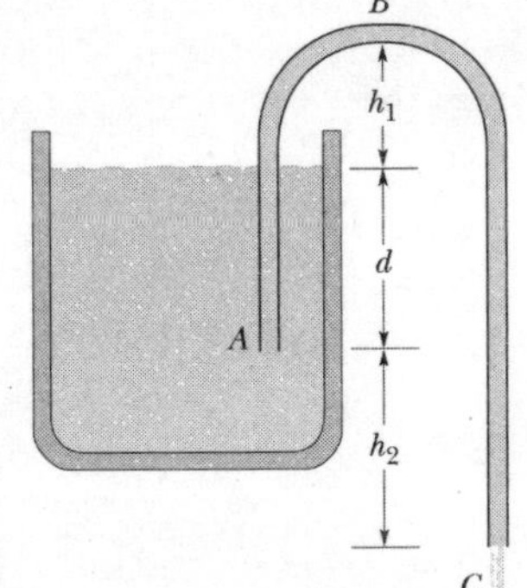

FIG. 14-79 Problem 77.

77 Figure 14-79 shows a *siphon,* which is a device for removing liquid from a container. Tube ABC must initially be filled, but once this has been done, liquid will flow through the tube until the liquid surface in the container is level with the tube opening at A. The liquid has density 1000 kg/m³ and negligible viscosity. The distances shown are h_1 = 25 cm, d = 12 cm, and h_2 = 40 cm. (a) With what speed does the liquid emerge from the tube at C? (b) If the atmospheric pressure is 1.0×10^5 Pa, what is the pressure in the liquid at the topmost point B? (c) Theoretically, what is the greatest possible height h_1 that a siphon can lift water?

78 Suppose that your body has a uniform density of 0.95 times that of water. (a) If you float in a swimming pool, what fraction of your body's volume is above the water surface?

Quicksand is a fluid produced when water is forced up into sand, moving the sand grains away from one another so they are no longer locked together by friction. Pools of quicksand can form when water drains underground from hills into valleys where there are sand pockets. (b) If you float in a deep pool of quicksand that has a density 1.6 times that of water, what fraction of your body's volume is above the quicksand surface? (c) In particular, are you submerged enough to be unable to breathe?

79 If a bubble in sparkling water accelerates upward at the rate of 0.225 m/s² and has a radius of 0.500 mm, what is its mass? Assume that the drag force on the bubble is negligible.

80 What is the acceleration of a rising hot-air balloon if the ratio of the air density outside the balloon to that inside is 1.39? Neglect the mass of the balloon fabric and the basket.

81 A tin can has a total volume of 1200 cm³ and a mass of 130 g. How many grams of lead shot of density 11.4 g/cm³ could it carry without sinking in water?

82 A simple open U-tube contains mercury. When 11.2 cm of water is poured into the right arm of the tube, how high above its initial level does the mercury rise in the left arm?

83 An object hangs from a spring balance. The balance registers 30 N in air, 20 N when this object is immersed in water, and 24 N when the object is immersed in another liquid of unknown density. What is the density of that other liquid?

84 In an experiment, a rectangular block with height h is allowed to float in four separate liquids. In the first liquid, which is water, it floats fully submerged. In liquids A, B, and C, it floats with heights $h/2$, $2h/3$, and $h/4$ above the liquid surface, respectively. What are the *relative densities* (the densities relative to that of water) of (a) A, (b) B, and (c) C?

85 About one-third of the body of a person floating in the Dead Sea will be above the waterline. Assuming that the human body density is 0.98 g/cm³, find the density of the water in the Dead Sea. (Why is it so much greater than 1.0 g/cm³?)

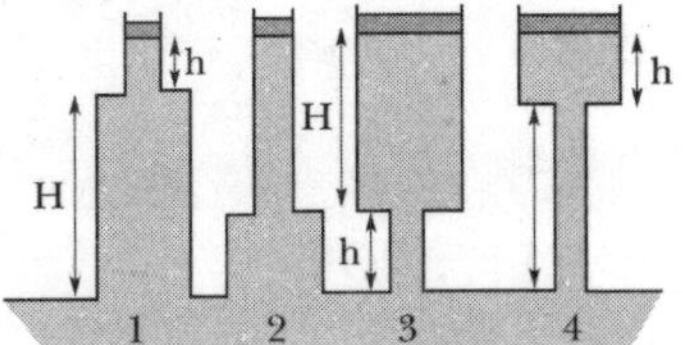

FIG. 14-80 Problem 86.

86 Four piston pumps are made of pipe sections with a large and a small diameters. The pumps lifted water to the same height H + h (Fig. 14-80). Which of the pistons should be pulled with a greater force to keep it in equilibrium? Disregard the weight of the pistons.

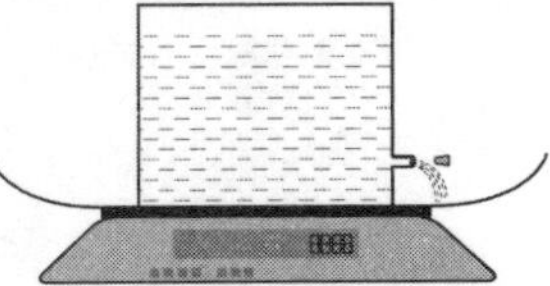
FIG. 14-81 Problem 87.

87 A vessel with water is placed on a pan of a weighing machine Fig. 14-81. Will the reading change if the cock is opened? The outflowing water gets onto the same pan on which the vessel is placed and comes to rest immedietely after falling on to it.

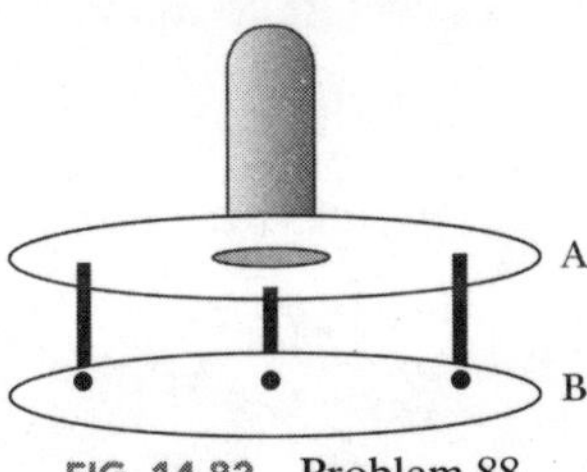

FIG. 14-82 Problem 88.

88 The demonstration device shown in (Fig. 14-82)

consists of two disks A and B. The hole in the centre of disk A is connected by a pipe to a cylinder containing compressed air. Disk B hangs on three pins along which it can move freely up and down. If a stream of compressed air is passed through the pipe, the lower disk will begin to knock against the upper one. Explain the cause of this phenomenon.

89 A water clock (Clepsydra) used in ancient Greece is designed as a vessel with a small orifice O (Fig. 14-83). The time is determined according to the level of the water in the vessel. What should the shape of the vessel be for the time scale to be uniform ?

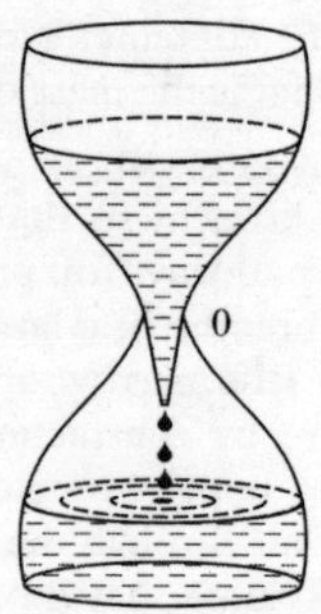

FIG. 14-83 Problem 89.

Simple Harmonic Motion 15

REUTERS/Richard Chung/Landov LLC

If a tall building sways slowly in a wind, the occupants may not even notice the motion, but if the swaying repeats more than 10 times per second, it becomes annoying and may even cause motion sickness. One reason is that when a person is standing, the head tends to sway even more than the feet, setting off motion sensors in the balancing region of the inner ear. Various mechanisms are employed to decrease a building's sway. For example, the large ball (5.4×10^5 kg) seen in this photograph hangs on the 92nd floor of one of the world's tallest buildings.

How can the ball counter the building's sway?

The answer is in this chapter.

15-1 | Introduction

Our hearts beat, our lungs oscillate, we shiver when we are cold, we sometimes snore, we can hear and speak because our eardrums and larynges vibrate. We cannot even say "vibration" properly without the tip of the tongue oscillating.

Our world is filled with oscillations in which objects move back and forth repeatedly. Many oscillations are merely amusing or annoying, but many others are financially important or dangerous. Here are a few examples: When a bat hits a baseball, the bat may oscillate enough to sting the batter's hands or even to break apart. When wind blows past a power line, the line may oscillate ("gallop" in electrical engineering terms) so severely that it rips apart, shutting off the power supply to a community. When an airplane is in flight, the turbulence of the air flowing past the wings makes them oscillate, eventually leading to metal fatigue and even failure. When a train travels around a curve, its wheels oscillate horizontally ("hunt" in mechanical engineering terms) as they are forced to turn in new directions (you can hear the oscillations).

When an earthquake occurs near a city, buildings may be set oscillating so severely that they are shaken apart. When an arrow is shot from a bow, the feathers at the end of the arrow manage to snake around the bow staff without hitting it because the arrow oscillates. When a coin drops into a metal collection plate, the coin oscillates with such a familiar ring that the coin's denomination can be determined from the sound. When a rodeo cowboy rides a bull, the cowboy oscillates wildly as the bull jumps and turns (at least the cowboy hopes to be oscillating).

The study and control of oscillations are two of the primary goals of both physics and engineering. In this chapter we discuss a basic type of oscillation called *simple harmonic motion.*

Periodic Motion

Any motion in which all the parameters of motion are repeated after a definite time interval is called periodic motion. The time which elapses between successive passages in the same direction through any point is termed the periodic time, or the period, of the motion.

The number of periods comprised in 1s is called the frequency; thus, if T is the period and n is the frequency of a periodic motion, we have $n = 1/T$.

The motion of the hands of a clock is periodic; the period of the motion of the minute hand being 1 h or 3600 s. The bob of a pendulum moves periodically, the period being equal to the time of one complete (to and fro) oscillation. Periodic motion can be along any path.

Oscillatory Motion

If in a case of periodic motion particle moves to and fro on the same path, the motion is said to be oscillatory motion. A body that undergoes oscillatory motion always does so about a stable equilibrium position. When it is moved away from this position and released, it experiences a net force or torque to pull it back toward equilibrium position. But by the time it gets there, the restoring force/torque would have done some positive work on it. Thus, it must have gained some kinetic energy, so it overshoots the equilibrium position. Now it stops somewhere on the other side, and is again pulled back toward equilibrium. Imagine a ball rolling back and forth in a round bowl or a pendulum that swings back and forth past its lowest position.

CHECKPOINT 1 A particle hanging from a thread is launched horizontally such that it completes the circle. Is the motion periodic or oscillatory?

CHECKPOINT 2 A particle hanging from a thread is launched horizontally with small speed such that it does not even reach to the horizontal level. Is the motion periodic or oscillatory?

Important Characteristics of Oscillatory Motion

1. When a particle in stable equilibrium is disturbed, then it has tendency to return to equilibrium position and this tendency is exhibited as oscillatory motion.
2. The force on the body acts toward the mean position, that is, force is always opposite to the displacement vector of the particle with respect to mean position. (This force is known as restoring force.)

$$\hat{F} = -\hat{r},\ \hat{\tau} = -\hat{\theta}$$

   where $\hat{r}$ and $\hat{\theta}$ are displacements and angular displacement from mean position.
3. Energy is also conserved. If energy is not conserved then the particle will not be able to repeat the parameters of the motion.

15-2 | Simple Harmonic Motion

Sinusoidal Vibrations

Our study will be mostly related to sinusoidal vibrations which we will show later that they arise when net force experienced by an oscillating body has magnitude proportional to the distance from the mean position or torque is directly proportional to the angular displacement from mean position. There are two reasons for this – one physical, one mathematical, and both basic to the whole subject. The physical reason is that purely sinusoidal vibrations are common in many types of mechanical systems. Such motion is almost always possible if the displacements are small enough. If, for example, we have a body attached to a spring, the force exerted on it at a displacement x from equilibrium is actually

$$F(x) = -\ k_1x+k_2x^2+k_3x^3+.........$$

where k_1, k_2, k_3, etc., are a set of constants, and we can always find a range of values of x within which the sum of the terms in x^2, x^3, etc., is negligible, compared to the term $-k_1x$. If the body is of mass m and the mass of the spring is negligible, the equation of motion of the body then becomes

$$m\frac{d^2x}{dt^2} = -\ k_1x$$

It is easy to verify that above equation is satisfied by an equation of the form

$$x = A\sin(\omega t+\phi_0)$$

where $\omega = (k_1/m)^{1/2}$. Thus, sinusoidal vibration or simple harmonic motion (SHM) is likely possible in small vibrations. But we should remember that in general it is only an approximation (although perhaps a very close one) to the true motion.

The second reason is the mathematical one. The actual importance of purely sinusoidal vibrations is proved in a famous theorem given by the French mathematician J.B. Fourier in 1807. According to Fourier's theorem, any periodic function with a period T can be considered as a sum of pure sinusoidal vibrations of periods T, $T/2$, $T/3$, etc., with appropriately chosen amplitudes. A thorough familiarity with sinusoidal vibrations will be a stepping stone for our understanding of every conceivable problem involving periodic phenomena.

Derivation of Equation of Simple Harmonic Motion

As we know, in SHM, magnitude is directly proportional to distance from the mean position and is directed toward it. Considering origin at the mean position and displacing the particle along x axis, the net force on the particle F is given by

$$F = -kx, \quad \text{where } k \text{ is a constant.}$$

$$ma = -kx$$

$$a = -\frac{k}{m}x = -\omega^2 x \quad \text{Considering } \frac{k}{m} = \omega^2$$

$$\frac{d^2x}{dt^2} + \omega^2 x = 0.$$

This is a differential form of equation of SHM.

$$\frac{dv}{dt} = -\omega^2 x$$

$$v\frac{dv}{dt} = -\omega^2 xv$$

$$v\frac{dv}{dt} = -\omega^2 x\frac{dx}{dt}$$

Multiplying both sides by x, we get

$$vdv = -\omega^2 x\mathrm{d}x$$

Integrating we get

$$\frac{v^2}{2} = -\frac{\omega^2 x^2}{2} + C_1$$

Here C_1 is constant of integration

$$v^2 = C_1 - \omega^2 x^2$$

$$v = \sqrt{C_1 - \omega^2 x^2}$$

$$\frac{dx}{dt} = \sqrt{C_1 - \omega^2 x^2}$$

$$\frac{dx}{\sqrt{C_1 - \omega^2 x^2}} = dt$$

$$\frac{dx}{\omega\sqrt{\left(\frac{C_1}{\omega}\right)^2 - x^2}} = dt$$

Integration of the above relation gives

$$\frac{1}{\omega} = \sin^{-1}\left(\frac{x\omega}{\sqrt{C_1}}\right) = t + C_2$$

where C_2 is another constant of integration

$$\sin^{-1}\left(\frac{x\omega}{\sqrt{C_1}}\right) = \omega t + \omega C_2$$

$$x = \frac{\sqrt{C_1}}{\omega}\sin(\omega t + \omega C_2)$$

$$x = A\sin(\omega t + \phi)$$

where $A = \dfrac{\sqrt{C_1}}{\omega}$ and $\phi = \omega C_2$

So, the sinusoidal function of the form of the above equation of an SHM and thus V_a represents SHM.

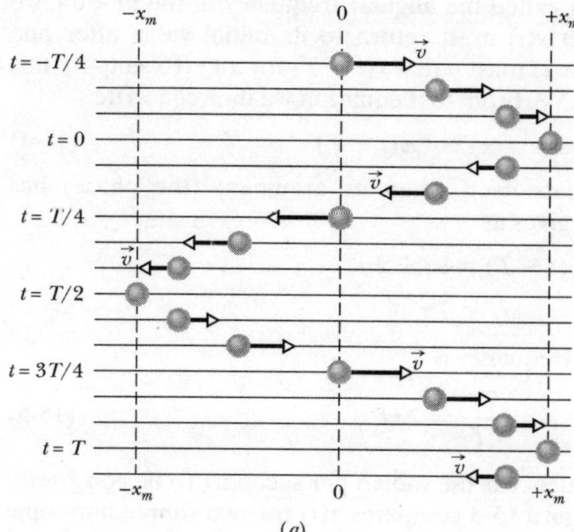

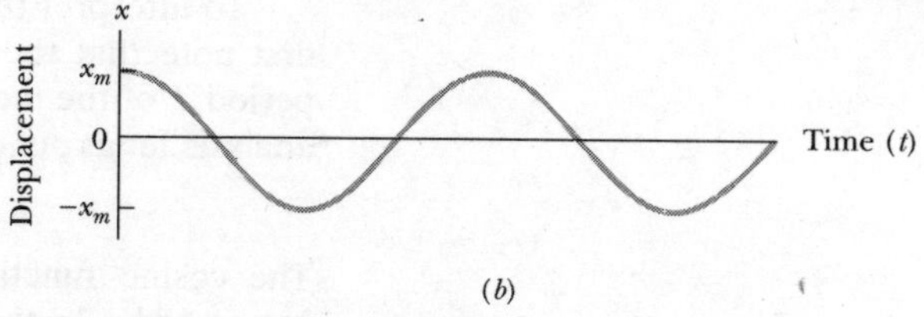

FIG. 15-1 (*a*) A sequence of "snapshots" (taken at equal time intervals) showing the position of a particle as it oscillates back and forth about the origin of an x axis, between the limits $+x_m$ and $-x_m$. The vector arrows are scaled to indicate the speed of the particle. The speed is maximum when the particle is at the origin and zero when it is at $\pm x_m$. If the time t is chosen to be zero when the particle is at $+x_m$, then the particle returns to $+x_m$ at $t = T$, where T is the period of the motion. The motion is then repeated. (*b*) A graph of x as a function of time for the motion of (*a*).

Figure 15-1*a* shows a sequence of "snapshots" of a simple oscillating system, a particle moving repeatedly back and forth about the origin of an x axis. In this section we simply describe the motion. Later, we shall discuss how to attain such motion.

One important property of oscillatory motion is its **frequency,** or number of oscillations that are completed each second. The symbol for frequency is f, and its SI unit is the **hertz** (abbreviated Hz), where

$$1 \text{ hertz} = 1 \text{ Hz} = 1 \text{ oscillation per second} = 1 \text{ s}^{-1} \tag{15-1}$$

Related to the frequency is the **period** T of the motion, which is the time for one complete oscillation (or **cycle**); that is,

$$T = \frac{1}{f} \tag{15-2}$$

Any motion that repeats itself at regular intervals is called **periodic motion** or **harmonic motion.** We are interested here in motion, that repeats itself in a particular way—namely, like that in Fig. 15-1*a*. For such motion, the displacement x of the particle from the origin is given as a function of time by

$$x(t) = x_m \cos(\omega t + \phi) \quad \text{(displacement)} \tag{15-3}$$

in which x_m, ω, and ϕ are constants. This motion is called **simple harmonic motion** (SHM), a term that means the periodic motion is a sinusoidal function of time. Equation 15-3, in which the sinusoidal function is a cosine function, is graphed in Fig. 15-1*b*. (You can get that graph by rotating Fig. 15-1*a* counterclockwise by 90° and then connecting the successive locations of the particle with a curve.) The quantities that determine the shape of the graph are displayed in Fig. 15-2 with their names. We now shall define those quantities.

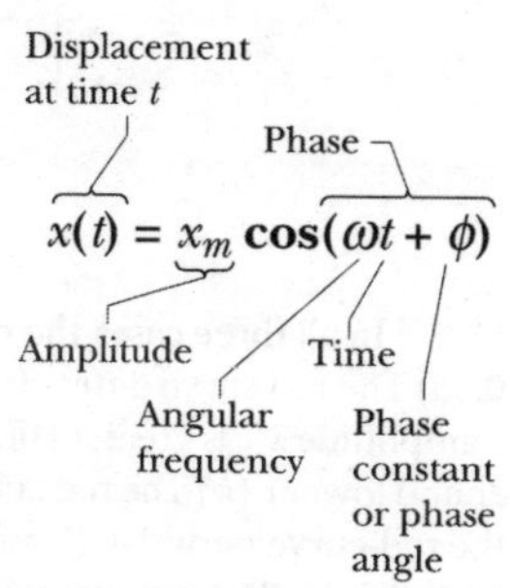

FIG. 15-2 A handy reference to the quantities in Eq. 15-3 for simple harmonic motion.

The quantity x_m, called the **amplitude** of the motion, is a positive constant whose value depends on how the motion was started. The subscript m stands for *maximum* because the amplitude is the magnitude of the maximum displacement of the particle in either direction. The cosine function in Eq. 15-3 varies between the limits ± 1; so the displacement $x(t)$ varies between the limits $\pm x_m$.

The time-varying quantity $(\omega t + \phi)$ in Eq. 15-3 is called the **phase** of the motion, and the constant ϕ is called the **phase constant** (or **phase angle**). The value of ϕ depends on the displacement and velocity of the particle at time $t = 0$. For the $x(t)$ plots of Fig. 15-3*a*, the phase constant ϕ is zero.

To interpret the constant ω, called the **angular frequency** of the motion, we first note that the displacement $x(t)$ must return to its initial value after one period T of the motion; that is, $x(t)$ must equal $x(t+T)$ for all t. To simplify this analysis, let us put $\phi = 0$ in Eq. 15-3. From that equation we then can write

$$x_m \cos \omega t = x_m \cos \omega(t + T) \tag{15-4}$$

The cosine function first repeats itself when its argument (the phase) has increased by 2π rad; so Eq. 15-4 gives us

$$\omega(t + T) = \omega t + 2\pi$$

or

$$\omega T = 2\pi$$

Thus, from Eq. 15-2 the angular frequency is

$$\omega = \frac{2\pi}{T} = 2\pi f \tag{15-5}$$

The SI unit of angular frequency is the radian per second. (To be consistent, then, ϕ must be in radians.) Figure 15-3 compares $x(t)$ for two simple harmonic motions that differ either in amplitude, in period (and thus in frequency and angular frequency), or in phase constant.

CHECKPOINT 3 A particle undergoing simple harmonic oscillation of period T (like that in Fig. 15-1) is at $-x_m$ at time $t = 0$. Is it at $-x_m$, at $+x_m$, at 0, between $-x_m$ and 0, or between 0 and $+x_m$ when (a) $t = 2.00T$, (b) $t = 3.50T$, and (c) $t = 5.25T$?

Velocity of SHM

By differentiating Eq. 15-3, we can find an expression for the velocity of a particle moving with SHM that is,

$$v(t) = \frac{dx(t)}{dt} = \frac{d}{dt}[x_m \cos(\omega t + \phi)]$$

or

$$v(t) = -\omega x_m \sin(\omega t + \phi) \quad \text{(velocity)} \tag{15-6}$$

Figure 15-4*a* is a plot of Eq. 15-3 with $\phi = 0$. Figure 15-4*b* shows Eq. 15-6, also with $\phi = 0$. Analogous to the amplitude x_m in Eq. 15-3, the positive quantity

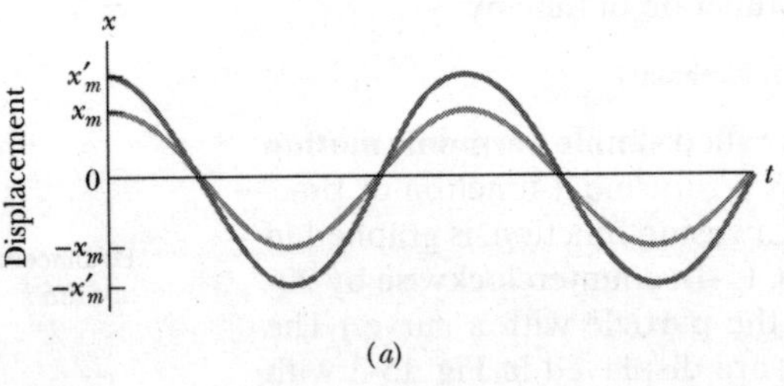

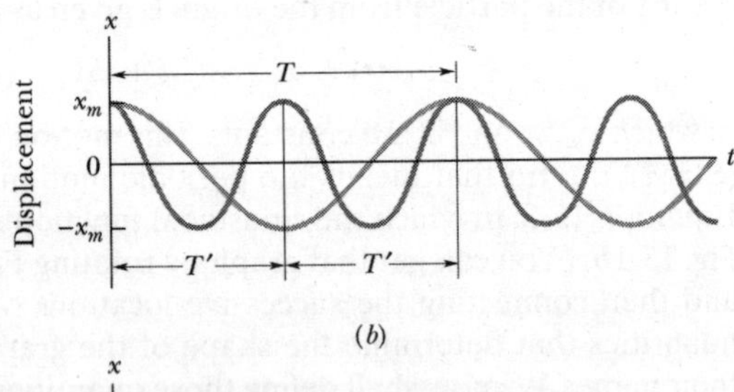

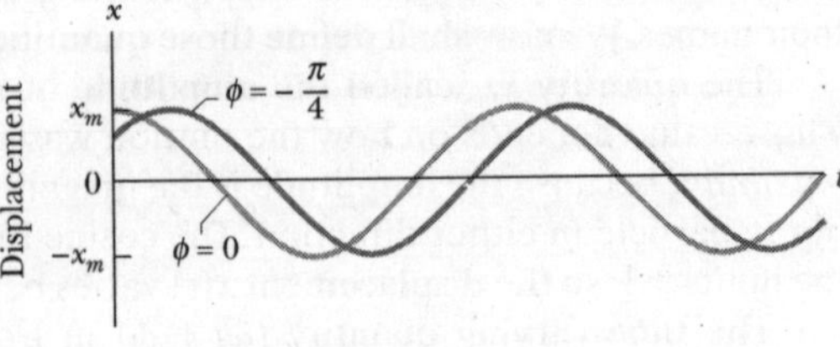

FIG. 15-3 In all three cases, the blue curve is obtained from Eq. 15-3 with $\phi = 0$. (*a*) The red curve differs from the blue curve *only* in that the red-curve amplitude x'_m is greater (the red-curve extremes of displacement are higher and lower). (*b*) The red curve differs from the blue curve *only* in that the red-curve period is $T' = T/2$ (the red curve is compressed horizontally). (*c*) The red curve differs from the blue curve *only* in that for the red curve $\phi = -\pi/4$ rad rather than zero (the negative value of ϕ shifts the red curve to the right).

ωx_m in Eq. 15-6 is called the **velocity amplitude** v_m. As you can see in Fig. 15-4*b*, the velocity of the oscillating particle varies between the limits $\pm v_m = \pm\omega x_m$. Note also in that figure that the curve of $v(t)$ is *shifted* (to the left) from the curve of $x(t)$ by one-quarter period; when the magnitude of the displacement is greatest (that is, $x(t) = x_m$), the magnitude of the velocity is least (that is, $v(t) = 0$). When the magnitude of the displacement is least (that is, zero), the magnitude of the velocity is greatest (that is, $v_m = \omega x_m$).

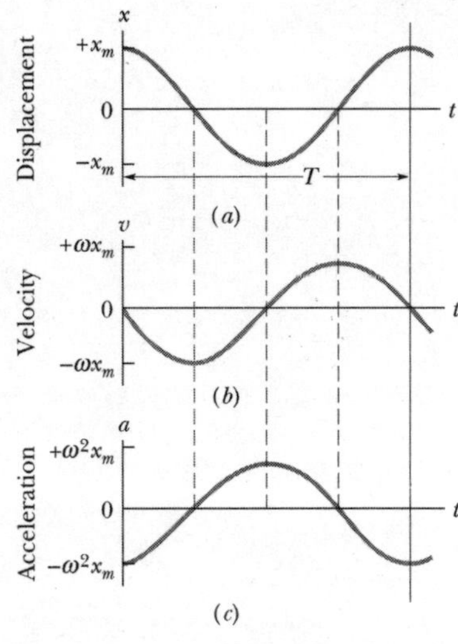

FIG. 15-4 (*a*) The displacement $x(t)$ of a particle oscillating in SHM with phase angle ϕ equal to zero. The period T marks one complete oscillation. (*b*) The velocity $v(t)$ of the particle. (*c*) The acceleration $a(t)$ of the particle.

Acceleration of SHM

Knowing the velocity $v(t)$ for simple harmonic motion, we can find an expression for the acceleration of the oscillating particle by differentiating once more. Thus, we have, from Eq. 15-6,

$$a(t) = \frac{dv(t)}{dt} = \frac{d}{dt}[-\omega x_m \sin(\omega t + \phi)]$$

or

$$a(t) = -\omega^2 x_m \cos(\omega t + \phi) \quad \text{(acceleration)} \qquad (15\text{-}7)$$

Figure 15-4*c* is a plot of Eq. 15-7 for the case $\phi = 0$. The positive quantity $\omega^2 x_m$ in Eq. 15-7 is called the **acceleration amplitude** a_m; that is, the acceleration of the particle varies between the limits $\pm a_m = \pm\omega^2 x_m$, as Fig. 15-4*c* shows. Note also that the acceleration curve $a(t)$ is shifted (to the left) by $\frac{1}{4}T$ relative to the velocity curve $v(t)$.

We can combine Eqs. 15-3 and 15-7 to yield

$$a(t) = -\omega^2 x(t) \qquad (15\text{-}8)$$

which is the hallmark of SHM:

> In SHM, the acceleration is proportional to the displacement but opposite in sign, and the two quantities are related by the square of the angular frequency.

Thus, as Fig. 15-4 shows, when the displacement has its greatest positive value, the acceleration has its greatest negative value, and conversely. When the displacement is zero, the acceleration is also zero.

PROBLEM-SOLVING TACTICS

Tactic 1:* *Phase Angles Note the effect of the phase angle ϕ on a plot of $x(t)$. When $\phi = 0$, $x(t)$ has a graph like that in Fig. 15-4*a*, a typical cosine curve. Increasing ϕ shifts the curve leftward along the t axis. (You might remember this with the symbol ↑φ←, where the up arrow indicates an increase in ϕ and the left arrow indicates the resulting shift in the curve.) Decreasing ϕ shifts the curve rightward, as shown in Fig. 15-3*c* for $\phi = -\pi/4$.

Two plots of SHM with different phase angles are said to have a *phase difference;* each is said to be *phase-shifted* from the other, or *out of phase* with the other. The curves in Fig. 15-3*c*, for example, have a phase difference of $\pi/4$ rad; that is, one curve is phase-shifted from the other by $\pi/4$ rad.

Because SHM repeats after each period T and the cosine function repeats after each 2π rad, one period T represents a phase difference of 2π rad. In Fig. 15-4, $x(t)$ is phase-shifted to the right from $v(t)$ by one-quarter period, or $-\pi/2$ rad; it is shifted to the right from $a(t)$ by one-half period, or $-\pi$ rad. A phase shift of 2π rad causes a curve of SHM to coincide with itself; that is, it looks unchanged.

15-3 | Force Law for Simple Harmonic Motion

Once we know how the acceleration of a particle varies with time, we can use Newton's second law to learn what force must act on the particle to give it that acceleration. If we combine Newton's second law and Eq. 15-8, we find, for SHM,

$$F = ma = -(m\omega^2)x \qquad (15\text{-}9)$$

This result—a restoring force that is proportional to the displacement but opposite in sign—is familiar. It is Hooke's law,

$$F = -kx \tag{15-10}$$

for a spring, the spring constant here being

$$k = m\omega^2 \tag{15-11}$$

We can infact take Eq. 15-10 as an alternative definition of SHM. It says:

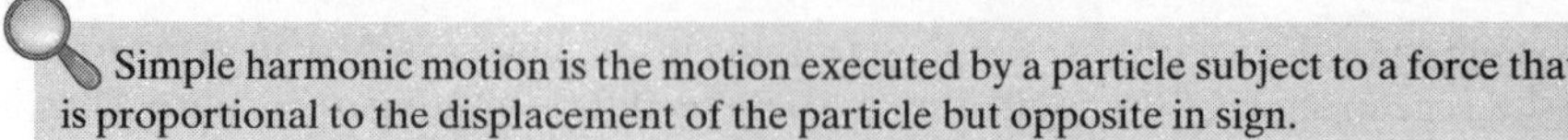

Simple harmonic motion is the motion executed by a particle subject to a force that is proportional to the displacement of the particle but opposite in sign.

The block–spring system of Fig. 15-5 forms a **linear simple harmonic oscillator** (linear oscillator, for short), where "linear" indicates that F is proportional to x rather than to some other power of x. The angular frequency ω of the SHM of the block is related to the spring constant k and the mass m of the block by Eq. 15-11, which yields

$$\omega = \sqrt{\frac{k}{m}} \quad \text{(angular frequency)} \tag{15-12}$$

By combining Eqs. 15-5 and 15-12, we can write, for the **period** of the linear oscillator of Fig. 15-5,

$$T = 2\pi\sqrt{\frac{m}{k}} \quad \text{(period)} \tag{15-13}$$

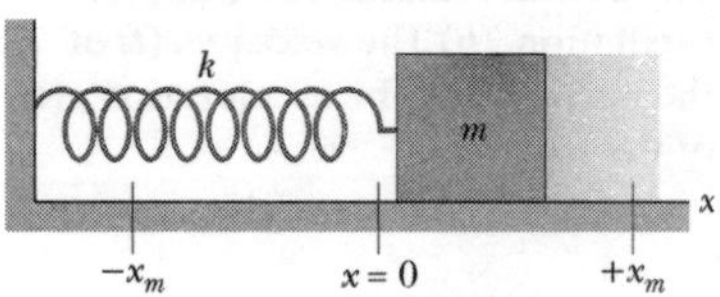

FIG. 15-5 A linear simple harmonic oscillator. The surface is frictionless. Like the particle of Fig. 15-1, the block moves in simple harmonic motion once it has been either pulled or pushed away from the $x = 0$ position and released. Its displacement is then given by Eq. 15-3.

Equations 15-12 and 15-13 tell us that a large angular frequency (and thus a small period) goes with a stiff spring (large k) and a light block (small m).

Every oscillating system, be it a diving board or a violin string, has some element of "springiness" and some element of "inertia" or mass, and thus resembles a linear oscillator. In the linear oscillator of Fig. 15-5, these elements are located in separate parts of the system: The springiness is entirely in the spring, which we assume to be massless, and the inertia is entirely in the block, which we assume to be rigid. In a violin string, however, the two elements are both within the string.

CHECKPOINT 4 Which of the following relationships between the force F on a particle and the particle's position x implies simple harmonic oscillation: (a) $F = -5x$, (b) $F = -400x^2$, (c) $F = 10x$, (d) $F = 3x^2$?

Sample Problem 15-1

A block whose mass m is 680 g is fastened to a spring whose spring constant k is 65 N/m. The block is pulled a distance $x = 11$ cm from its equilibrium position at $x = 0$ on a frictionless surface and released from rest at $t = 0$.

(a) What are the angular frequency, the frequency, and the period of the resulting motion?

Conceptualize/Classify: The block–spring system forms a linear simple harmonic oscillator, with the block undergoing SHM.

Compute: The angular frequency is given by Eq. 15-12:

$$\omega = \sqrt{\frac{k}{m}} = \sqrt{\frac{65\text{ N/m}}{0.68\text{ kg}}} = 9.78\text{ rad/s}$$

$$\approx 9.8\text{ rad/s.} \quad \text{(Answer)}$$

The frequency follows from Eq. 15-5, which yields

$$f = \frac{\omega}{2\pi} = \frac{9.78\text{ rad/s}}{2\pi\text{ rad}} = 1.56\text{ Hz} \approx 1.6\text{ Hz} \quad \text{(Answer)}$$

The period follows from Eq. 15-2, which yields

$$T = \frac{1}{f} = \frac{1}{1.56\text{ Hz}} = 0.64\text{ s} = 640\text{ ms} \quad \text{(Answer)}$$

(b) What is the amplitude of the oscillation?

Conceptualize: With no friction involved, the mechanical energy of the spring–block system is conserved.

Classify: The block is released from rest 11 cm from its equilibrium position, with zero kinetic energy and the elastic potential energy of the system at a maximum. Thus, the block will have zero kinetic energy whenever it is again 11 cm from its equilibrium position, which means it will never be farther than 11 cm from that position. Its maximum displacement is 11 cm:

$$x_m = 11 \text{ cm} \qquad \text{(Answer)}$$

(c) What is the maximum speed v_m of the oscillating block, and where is the block when it has this speed?

Conceptualize/Classify: The maximum speed v_m is the velocity amplitude ωx_m in Eq. 15-6.

Compute: Thus, we have

$$v_m = \omega x_m = (9.78 \text{ rad/s})(0.11 \text{ m}) = 1.1 \text{ m/s} \qquad \text{(Answer)}$$

Conclude: This maximum speed occurs when the oscillating block is rushing through the origin; compare Figs. 15-4*a* and 15-4*b*, where you can see that the speed is a maximum whenever $x = 0$.

(d) What is the magnitude a_m of the maximum acceleration of the block?

Conceptualize/Classify: The magnitude a_m of the maximum acceleration is the acceleration amplitude $\omega^2 x_m$ in Eq. 15-7.

Compute: So, we have

$$a_m = \omega^2 x_m = (9.78 \text{ rad/s})^2(0.11 \text{ m}) = 11 \text{ m/s}^2 \qquad \text{(Answer)}$$

Conclude: This maximum acceleration occurs when the block is at the ends of its path. At those points, the force acting on the block has its maximum magnitude; compare Figs. 15-4*a* and 15-4*c*, where you can see that the magnitudes of the displacement and acceleration are maximum at the same times.

(e) What is the phase constant ϕ for the motion?

Compute: Equation 15-3 gives the displacement of the block as a function of time. We know that at time $t = 0$, the block is located at $x = x_m$. Substituting these *initial conditions,* as they are called, into Eq. 15-3 and canceling x_m give us

$$1 = \cos\phi \qquad (15\text{-}14)$$

Taking the inverse cosine then yields

$$\phi = 0 \text{ rad} \qquad \text{(Answer)}$$

(Any angle that is an integer multiple of 2π rad also satisfies Eq. 15-14; we chose the smallest angle.)

(f) What is the displacement function $x(t)$ for the spring–block system?

Compute: The function $x(t)$ is given in general form by Eq. 15-3. Substituting known quantities into that equation gives us

$$\begin{aligned} x(t) &= x_m \cos(\omega t + \phi) \\ &= (0.11 \text{ m}) \cos[(9.8 \text{ rad/s})t + 0] \\ &= 0.11 \cos(9.8t) \qquad \text{(Answer)} \end{aligned}$$

where x is in meters and t is in seconds.

15-4 | Simple Harmonic Motion and Uniform Circular Motion

In 1610, Galileo, using his newly constructed telescope, discovered the four principal moons of Jupiter. Over weeks of observation, each moon seemed to him to be moving back and forth relative to the planet in what today we would call simple harmonic motion; the disk of the planet was the midpoint of the motion. The record of Galileo's observations, written in his own hand, is still available. A. P. French of MIT used Galileo's data to work out the position of the moon Callisto relative to Jupiter. In the results shown in Fig. 15-6, the circles are based on Galileo's observations and the curve is a best fit to the data. The curve strongly suggests Eq. 15-3, the displacement function for SHM. A period of about 16.8 days can be measured from the plot.

Actually, Callisto moves with essentially constant speed in an essentially circular orbit around Jupiter. Its true motion—far from being simple harmonic—is uniform circular motion. What Galileo saw—and what you can see with a

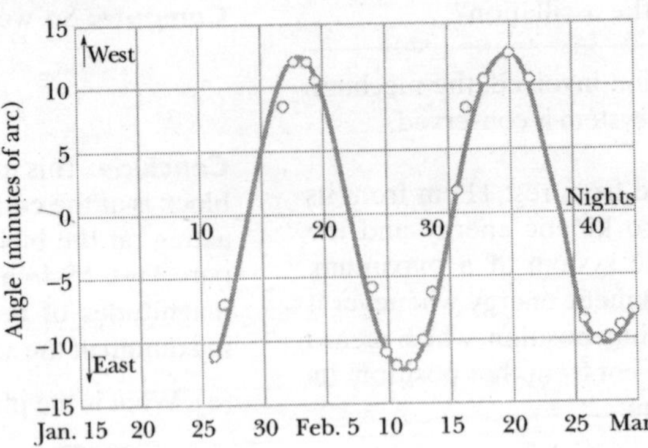

FIG. 15-6 The angle between Jupiter and its moon Callisto as seen from Earth. The circles are based on Galileo's 1610 measurements. The curve is a best fit, strongly suggesting simple harmonic motion. At Jupiter's mean distance from Earth, 10 minutes of arc corresponds to about 2×10^6 km. (Adapted from A. P. French, *Newtonian Mechanics*, W. W. Norton & Company, New York, 1971, p. 288.)

good pair of binoculars and a little patience—is the projection of this uniform circular motion on a line in the plane of the motion. We are led by Galileo's remarkable observations to the conclusion that simple harmonic motion is uniform circular motion viewed edge-on. In more formal language:

Simple harmonic motion is the projection of uniform circular motion on a diameter of the circle in which the circular motion occurs.

Figure 15-7*a* gives an example. It shows a *reference particle P′* moving in uniform circular motion with (constant) angular speed ω in a *reference circle.* The radius x_m of the circle is the magnitude of the particle's position vector. At any time t, the angular position of the particle is $\omega t + \phi$, where ϕ is its angular position at $t = 0$.

The projection of particle P' onto the x axis is a point P, which we take to be a second particle. The projection of the position vector of particle P' onto the x axis gives the location $x(t)$ of P. Thus, we find

$$x(t) = x_m \cos(\omega t + \phi)$$

which is precisely Eq. 15-3. Our conclusion is correct. If reference particle P' moves in uniform circular motion, its projection particle P moves in SHM along a diameter of the circle.

Figure 15-7*b* shows the velocity $\vec{v}$ of the reference particle. From Eq. $v = \omega r$, the magnitude of the velocity vector is ωx_m; its projection on the x axis is

$$v(t) = -\omega x_m \sin(\omega t + \phi)$$

which is exactly Eq. 15-6. The minus sign appears because the velocity component of P in Fig. 15-7*b* is directed to the left, in the negative direction of x.

Figure 15-7*c* shows the radial acceleration $\vec{a}$ of the reference particle. From Eq. $a_r = \omega^2 r$, the magnitude of the radial acceleration vector is $\omega^2 x_m$; its projection on the x axis is

$$a(t) = -\omega^2 x_m \cos(\omega t + \phi)$$

which is exactly Eq. 15-7. Thus, whether we look at the displacement, the velocity, or the acceleration, the projection of uniform circular motion is indeed simple harmonic motion.

One of the best ways of describing an SHM is to consider it as the projection of uniform circular motion. Imagine, for example, that a disk of radius A rotates about a horizontal axis at the rate of ω rad/s. Suppose that a peg P is attached to the edge of the disk and that a horizontalbeam of parallel light casts a shadow of the peg on a vertical screen, as shown in Fig. 15-8*a*. Then this shadow performs SHM with period $2\pi/\omega$ and amplitude A along a vertical line on the screen.

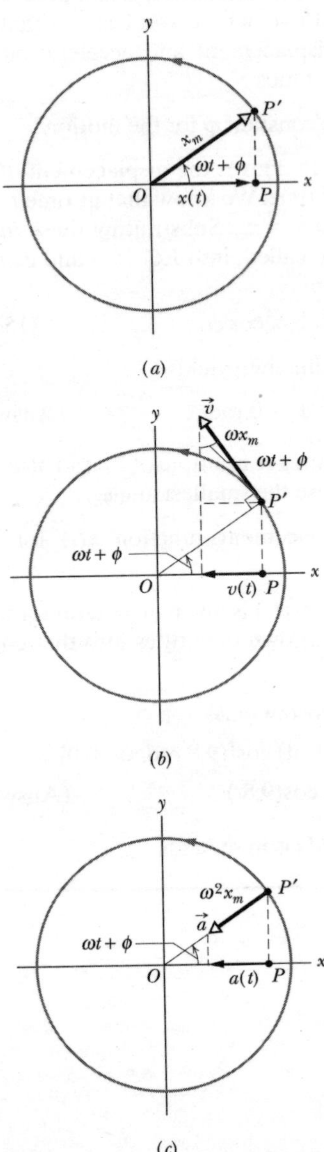

FIG. 15-7 (*a*) A reference particle P' moving with uniform circular motion in a reference circle of radius x_m. Its projection P on the x axis executes simple harmonic motion. (*b*) The projection of the velocity $\vec{v}$ of the reference particle is the velocity of SHM. (*c*) The projection of the radial acceleration $\vec{a}$ of the reference particle is the acceleration of SHM.

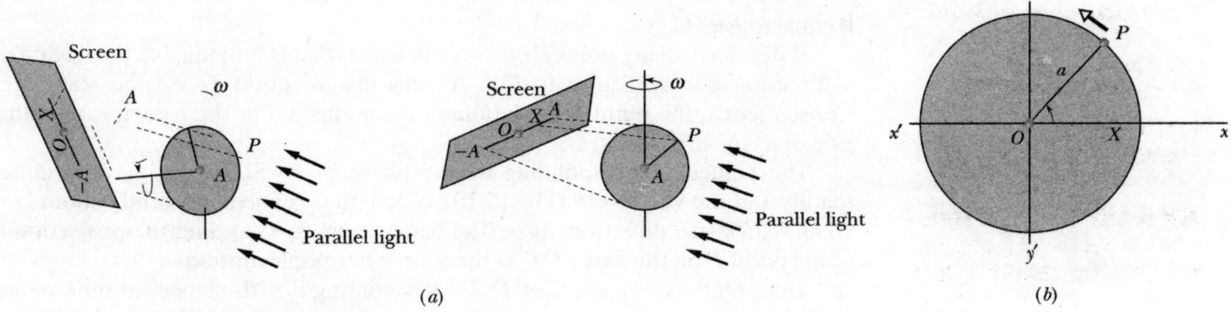

FIG. 15-8 Shadow of point P on a vertical wall undergoing SHM.

More abstractly, we can imagine SHM as being the geometrical projection of a uniform circular motion. (By geometrical projection we mean simply the process of drawing a perpendicular to a given line from the instantaneous position of the point P.) Let the tracing point, P, revolve uniformly at a constant distance OP from O, the direction of motion being anticlockwise. Through O we draw the rectangular axes $X'OX$ and $Y'OY$. From P draw PQ perpendicular to OY. Thus, OQ is the component of OP resolved parallel to OY. As P revolves about O, the point Q moves up and down along $Y'OY$, its motion being of the simple harmonic type. When P passes across the axis $X'OX$, Q will pass through O. When P passes across the axis $Y'OY$, Q will be at its position of maximum displacement from its mean position, O.

The maximum displacement of Q will thus be equal to the radius a of the circular path of point P; it is termed the amplitude of the SHM.

The phase of the SHM at any instant is equal to the angle which has been swept out by the line OP. If we measure the phase from the particular position of OP when Q is moving in a certain direction (say upward) through O, the angle $XOP = \theta$ is equal to the phase of the SHM.

The displacements of Q for various values of the phase angle θ, are shown by the curve to the right of Fig. 15-9. The x coordinate is equal to the circular measure of the angle XOP, and the distance OQ is plotted along the y axis.

Let the amplitude $OP = a$, while $OQ = y$. Then $y/a = RP/OP = \sin\theta$. Therefore, $y = a\sin\theta$. The graph is plotted to the right of the figure as described by this equation.

Further, if OP completes a rotation (that is rotate through an angle 2π) in the period T, then we have $\theta = 2\pi t/T$, and therefore $y = a\sin(2\pi t/T)$.

When the tracing point P crosses the axis OX, it is moving, for the instant, parallel to the axis OY. Consequently, at this instant the point Q is moving along OY with a velocity equal to that of the tracing point P in its circular path. The velocity

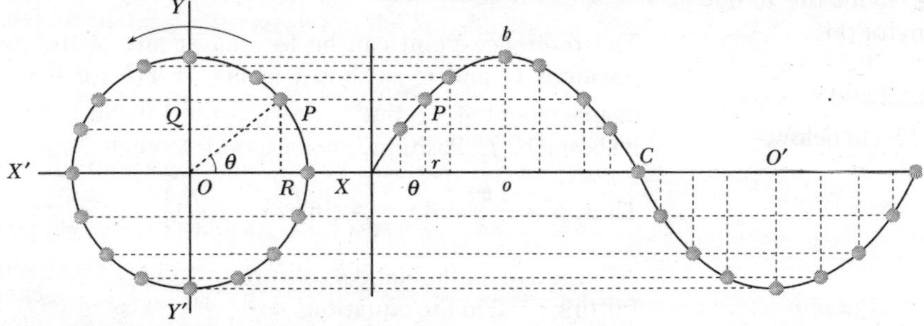

FIG. 15-9 Location of Q plotted as function of time with corresponding positions of tracing point P.

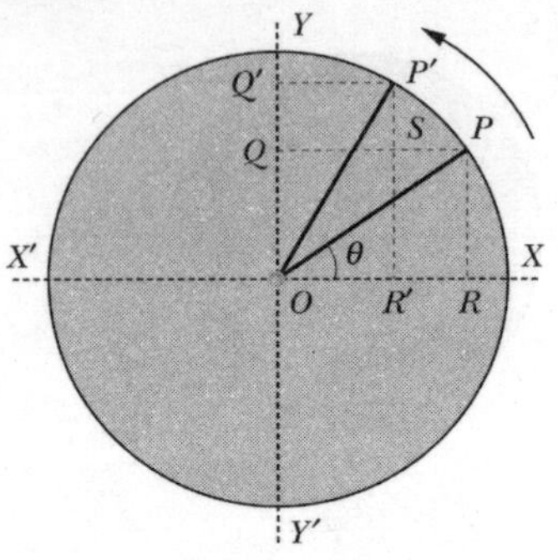

FIG. 15-10 Taking shadow of tracing point P on X axis rather than Y axis.

of P is equal $2\pi a/T$. Hence, the velocity of Q as it passes through its mean position O is equal to $2\pi a/T$.

When the tracing point P crosses the axis OY, it is moving, for the instant, in a direction perpendicular to OY. At this instant point Q will be stationary. Consequently, the point Q is stationary for an instant at the extreme, on either side of its mean position O.

The velocity corresponding to any phase of an SHM can be determined readily. Let the vector OP (Fig. 15-10), of length a, revolve uniformly about O in an anticlockwise direction, its period being equal to T; and let the projection Q of the point P on the axis YOY' is the simple harmonic motion.

Thus, $OQ = y = a \sin (2\pi t/T)$. Differentiating it with respect to time we get

$$\frac{dy}{dt} = v\frac{2\pi a}{T}\cos\left(\frac{2\pi t}{T}\right)$$

This gives the instantaneous velocity of the simple harmonic motion at the time t. In terms of the phase angle θ, the velocity is equal to $2\pi a/T \cos\theta$. When $\theta = 0$, $\cos\theta = 1$, and the velocity is equal to $2\pi a/T$, as already discussed; when $\theta = \pi/2$, $\cos\theta = 0$, and the velocity is equal to zero and so on.

Thus, a point executing a SHM moves with a maximum velocity equal to $2\pi a/T$ on passing through its mean position. Its velocity diminishes as it moves away from its mean position, being equal to $(2\pi a/T)\cos\theta$ when the phase angle is θ, and attaining the value zero at the extreme position. Subsequently, as the point returns toward its mean position, its velocity increases, and once more attains the value $2\pi a/T$ on moving through the mean position.

The use of a uniform circular motion as a purely geometrical basis for describing SHM embodies more than we have so far chosen to recognize. This circular motion, once we have set it up, defines SHM of amplitude A and angular frequency ω along any straight line in the plane of the circle.

Sample Problem 15-2

Write equation of SHM of angular frequency ω and amplitude A if the particle is situated at $A/\sqrt{2}$ at $t = 0$ and is going toward mean position.

Conceptualize: Since angular frequency and amplitude are given, we have two of the three quantities required for the equation of SHM.

Classify: Thus, we need to find out the value of initial phase, ϕ from the given information about the initial conditions. We will use phasor diagram for this.

Compute: At $t = 0$, particle was at $A/\sqrt{2}$ and was going toward mean position as shown in Fig. 15-11a below.

$-A$ —— M ← $A/\sqrt{2}$ —— A

(a)

FIG. 15-11a Particle at $t = 0$.

The same situation is described by making reference point on a circle of radius A as shown in Fig. 15-11b below.

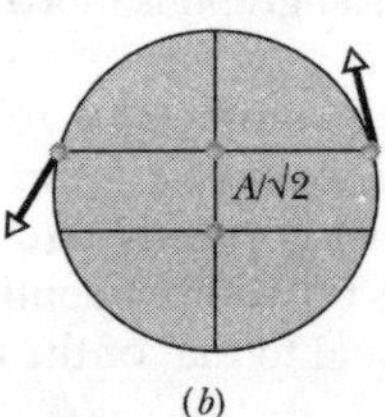

(b)

FIG. 15-11b Phasor diagram of particle at $t = 0$.

The reference point can be located at any of the two positions G and H as shown in Fig. 15-11b for having displacement $A/\sqrt{2}$, but to move toward mean position it should be H. Position H corresponds to angle $3\pi/4$.

Thus, $\phi = \frac{3\pi}{4}$ and $x = A\sin\left(\omega t + \frac{3\pi}{4}\right)$

Alternative mathematical solution:
Putting $t = 0$ in the equation

$$x = A\sin(\omega t + \phi)$$

We get

$$\frac{A}{\sqrt{2}} = A \sin \phi$$

Thus,

$$\phi = \frac{\pi}{4}, \frac{3\pi}{4}$$

but at $t = 0$; $v < 0$ so $\frac{\pi}{4}$ is rejected, hence

$$x = A \sin\left(\omega t + \frac{3\pi}{4}\right)$$

Conclude: The ease of using phasor diagram is quite evident in this solution.

Sample Problem 15-3

At $t = 0$, the displacement $x(0)$ of the block in a linear oscillator like that of Fig. 15-5 is -8.50 cm. (Read $x(0)$ as "x at time zero.") The block's velocity $v(0)$ then is -0.920 m/s, and its acceleration $a(0)$ is $+47.0$ m/s^2.

(a) What is the angular frequency ω of this system?

Conceptualize/Classify: With the block in SHM, Eqs. 15-3, 15-6, and 15-7 give its displacement, velocity, and acceleration, respectively, and each contains v.

Compute: Let's substitute $t = 0$ into each to see whether we can solve any one of them for ω. We find

$$x(0) = x_m \cos \phi \qquad (15\text{-}15)$$

$$v(0) = -\omega x_m \sin \phi \qquad (15\text{-}16)$$

and

$$a(0) = -\omega^2 x_m \cos \phi \qquad (15\text{-}17)$$

In Eq. 15-15, ω has disappeared. In Eqs. 15-16 and 15-17, we know values for the left sides, but we do not know x_m and ϕ. However, if we divide Eq. 15-17 by Eq. 15-15, we neatly eliminate both x_m and ϕ and can then solve for ω as

$$\omega = \sqrt{-\frac{a(0)}{x(0)}} = \sqrt{-\frac{47.0 \text{ m/s}^2}{-0.0850 \text{ m}}}$$

$$= 23.5 \text{ rad/s} \qquad \text{(Answer)}$$

(b) What are the phase constant ϕ and amplitude x_m?

Compute: We know ω and want ϕ and x_m. If we divide Eq. 15-16 by Eq. 15-15, we find

$$\frac{v(0)}{x(0)} = \frac{-\omega x_m \sin \phi}{x_m \cos \phi} = -\omega \tan \phi$$

Solving for $\tan \phi$, we find

$$\tan \phi = -\frac{v(0)}{\omega x(0)} = -\frac{-0.920 \text{ m/s}}{(23.5 \text{ rad/s})(-0.0850 \text{ m})}$$

$$= -0.461$$

This equation has two solutions:

$$\phi = -25° \quad \text{and} \quad \phi = 180° + (-25°) = 155°$$

(Normally only the first solution here is displayed by a calculator.) To choose the proper solution, we test them both by using them to compute values for the amplitude x_m. From Eq. 15-15, we find that if $\phi = -25°$, then

$$x_m = \frac{x(0)}{\cos \phi} = \frac{-0.0850 \text{ m}}{\cos(-25°)} = -0.094 \text{ m}$$

We find similarly that if $\phi = 155°$, then $x_m = 0.094$ m. Because the amplitude of SHM must be a positive constant, the correct phase constant and amplitude here are

$$\phi = 155° \quad \text{and} \quad x_m = 0.094 \text{ m} = 9.4 \text{ cm} \quad \text{(Answer)}$$

PROBLEM-SOLVING TACTICS

Tactic 2: *Identifying SHM* In linear SHM the acceleration a and displacement x of the system are related by an equation of the form

$$a = -(\text{a positive constant})x$$

which says that the acceleration is proportional to the displacement from the equilibrium position but is in the opposite direction. Once you find such an expression for an oscillating system, you can immediately compare it with Eq. 15-8, identify the positive constant as being equal to ω^2, and so quickly get an expression for the angular frequency of the motion. With Eq. 15-5 you then can find the period T and the frequency f.

In some problems you might derive an expression for the force F as a function of displacement x. If the motion is linear SHM, the force and displacement are related by

$$F = -(\text{a positive constant})x$$

which says that the force is proportional to the displacement but is in the opposite direction. Once you have found such an expression, you can immediately compare it with Eq. 15-10 and identify the positive constant as being k. If you know the mass that is involved, you can then use Eqs. 15-12, 15-13, and 15-5 to find the angular frequency ω, period T, and frequency f.

CHECKPOINT 5 Find the distance traveled by a particle executing SHM with time period T and amplitude A in time $T/12$ after starting from rest.

Sample Problem 15-4

A particle is moving on y axis under a variable force $F = -ky + C$.

(a) Can the motion of the particle be called SHM? Hence or otherwise write y position of particle as function of time.

Conceptualize: This force is not the standard form of the SHM, that is, $F = -kx$. But still the relation between force and displacement is linear.

Classify: The equation can be written in a standard format by just shifting the origin.

Compute: We can write the force as

$$F = -k\left(y - \frac{C}{k}\right)$$

let us define $s = y - \dfrac{C}{k}$ (i)

where s is the displacement from mean position because at $y = \dfrac{C}{k}$, F is zero.

Thus, the mean position is at $y = \left(\dfrac{C}{k}\right)$

Thus, force can be written as $F = -ks$ (ii)

which is the equation of SHM about $y = \dfrac{C}{k}$

Differentiating Eq. (i) with respect to time twice

we get $\dfrac{d^2y}{dt^2} = \dfrac{d^2s}{dt^2}$

Thus, force $F = m\dfrac{d^2y}{dt^2}$ can also be written as $F = m\dfrac{d^2s}{dt^2}$

Substituting in Eq. (ii)

$$m\frac{d^2s}{dt^2} = -ks$$

Comparing with standard equation we know that the solution of the above SHM equation is

$$s = A\sin(\omega t + \phi)$$

Where $\omega = \sqrt{\dfrac{k}{m}}$

Replacing with value of $s = y - \dfrac{C}{k}$

We get, $y = A\sin(\omega t + \phi) + \dfrac{C}{k}$

Conclude: This particle is undergoing SHM about $y = \frac{C}{k}$. Since no information is given about initial position and velocity of the particle, we have to keep initial phase ϕ and amplitude A as unknown.

(b) If in the previous question $F = -10y + 20$, and mass m of the particle is 2.5 kg and is released from rest from $y = +3$, at $t = 0$. Write the equation of SHM.

Conceptualize/Classify: Since information is given about initial position and velocity of the particle, we just need to find initial phase ϕ and amplitude.

Compute: From previous discussion, we can write

$$y = A\sin(\omega t + \phi) + \frac{C}{k}$$

where $k = 10$, $m = 2.5$ kg, and $C = 20$, thus $\omega = \sqrt{\dfrac{k}{m}}$ gives us $\omega = 2$

Mean position is at $y = 2$ as force at this point is zero

$$F = -10 \times 2 + 20 = 0$$

$$y = A\sin(2t + \phi) + 2$$

at $t = 0$, the particle is at $y = 3$ and is at rest thus its extreme position is $y = 3$. The distance between the mean position and extreme position is 1 m. Thus, amplitude $A = 1$.

Thus, at $t = 0$

$$y = 1\sin\phi + 2 = 3$$

$$\sin\phi = 1 \Rightarrow \phi = \frac{\pi}{2}$$

$$y = A\sin(2t + \phi) + 2 \ (\text{as } A = 1, \phi = \frac{\pi}{2})$$

$$y = \cos 2t + 2 \qquad \text{(Answer)}$$

Conclude: This particle is undergoing SHM about $y = 2$. Since information is given about initial position and velocity of the particle, we are able to find initial phase ϕ and amplitude A.

15-5 | Energy in Simple Harmonic Motion

We already know that the energy of a linear oscillator transfers back and forth between kinetic energy and potential energy, while the sum of the two—the mechanical energy E of the oscillator—remains constant. We now consider this situation quantitatively.

The potential energy of a linear oscillator like that of Fig. 15-5 is associated entirely with the spring. Its value depends on how much the spring is stretched or compressed—that is, on $x(t)$. We can use Eqs. 8-11 and 15-3 to find

$$U(t) = \tfrac{1}{2}kx^2 = \tfrac{1}{2}kx_m^2 \cos^2(\omega t + \phi) \qquad (15\text{-}18)$$

Caution: A function written in the form $\cos^2 A$ (as here) means $(\cos A)^2$ and is *not* the same as one written $\cos A^2$, which means $\cos(A^2)$.

The kinetic energy of the system of Fig. 15-5 is associated entirely with the block. Its value depends on how fast the block is moving—that is, on $v(t)$. We can use Eq. 15-6 to find

$$K(t) = \tfrac{1}{2}mv^2 = \tfrac{1}{2}m\omega^2 x_m^2 \sin^2(\omega t + \phi) \qquad (15\text{-}19)$$

If we use Eq. 15-12 to substitute k/m for ω^2, we can write Eq. 15-19 as

$$K(t) = \tfrac{1}{2}mv^2 = \tfrac{1}{2}kx_m^2 \sin^2(\omega t + \phi) \qquad (15\text{-}20)$$

The mechanical energy follows from Eqs. 15-18 and 15-20 and is

$$\begin{aligned} E &= U + K \\ &= \tfrac{1}{2}kx_m^2 \cos^2(\omega t + \phi) + \tfrac{1}{2}kx_m^2 \sin^2(\omega t + \phi) \\ &= \tfrac{1}{2}kx_m^2 [\cos^2(\omega t + \phi) + \sin^2(\omega t + \phi)] \end{aligned}$$

For any angle α,

$$\cos^2 \alpha + \sin^2 \alpha = 1$$

Thus, the quantity in the square brackets above is unity and we have

$$E = U + K = \tfrac{1}{2}kx_m^2 \qquad (15\text{-}21)$$

The mechanical energy of a linear oscillator is indeed constant and independent of time. The potential energy and kinetic energy of a linear oscillator are shown as functions of time t in Fig. 15-12*a*, and they are shown as functions of displacement x in Fig. 15-12*b*.

You might now understand why an oscillating system normally contains an element of springness and an element of inertia; The former stores its potential energy and the latter stores its kinetic energy.

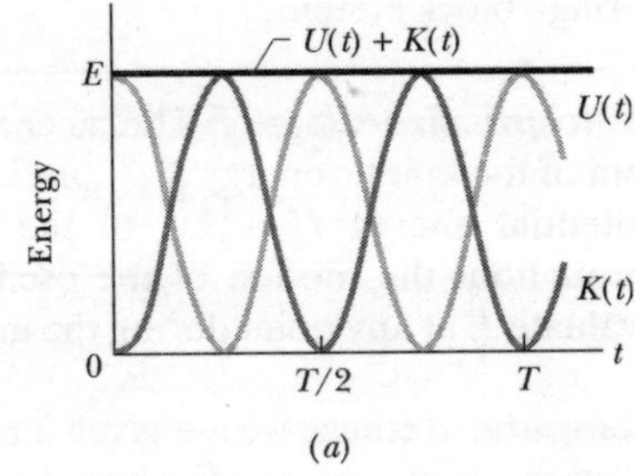

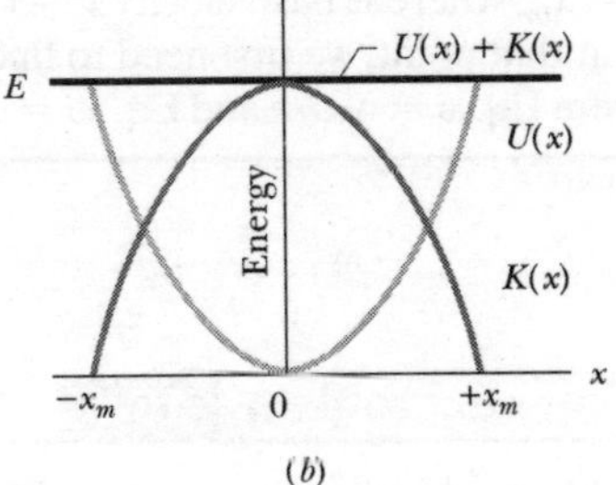

FIG. 15-12 (*a*) Potential energy $U(t)$, kinetic energy $K(t)$, and mechanical energy E as functions of time t for a linear harmonic oscillator. Note that all energies are positive and that the potential energy and the kinetic energy peak twice during every period. (*b*) Potential energy $U(x)$, kinetic energy $K(x)$, and mechanical energy E as functions of position x for a linear harmonic oscillator with amplitude x_m. For $x = 0$ the energy is all kinetic, and for $x = \pm x_m$ it is all potential.

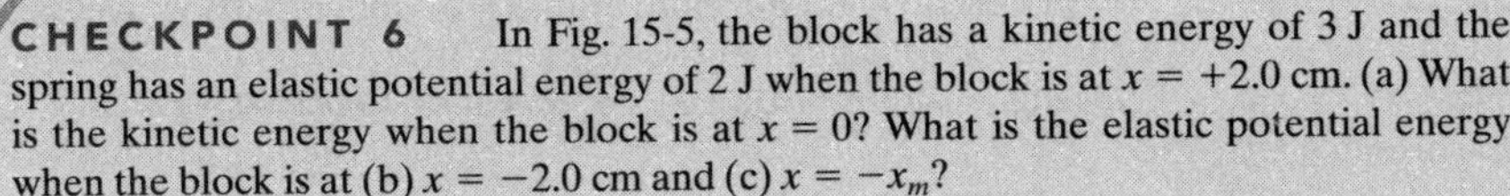

CHECKPOINT 6 In Fig. 15-5, the block has a kinetic energy of 3 J and the spring has an elastic potential energy of 2 J when the block is at $x = +2.0$ cm. (a) What is the kinetic energy when the block is at $x = 0$? What is the elastic potential energy when the block is at (b) $x = -2.0$ cm and (c) $x = -x_m$?

Sample Problem 15-5

The huge ball that appears in this chapter's opening photograph hangs from four cables and swings like a pendulum when the building sways in the wind. When the building sways—say, eastward—the massive pendulum does also but delayed enough so that as it finally swings eastward, the building is swaying westward. Thus, the pendulum's motion is out of step with the building's motion, tending to counter it.

Many other buildings have other types of *mass dampers*, as these anti-sway devices are called. Some, like the John Hancock building in Boston, have a large block oscillating at the end of a spring and on a lubricated track. The principle is the same as with the pendulum: The motion of the oscillator is out of step with the motion of the building.

Suppose the block has mass $m = 2.72 \times 10^5$ kg and is designed to oscillate at frequency $f = 10.0$ Hz and with amplitude $x_m = 20.0$ cm.

(a) What is the total mechanical energy E of the spring–block system?

Conceptualize/Classify: The mechanical energy E (the sum of the kinetic energy $K = \frac{1}{2}mv^2$ of the block and the potential energy $U = \frac{1}{2}kx^2$ of the spring) is constant throughout the motion of the oscillator. Thus, we can evaluate E at any point during the motion.

Compute: Because we are given amplitude x_m of the oscillations, let's evaluate E when the block is at position $x = x_m$, where it has velocity $v = 0$. However, to evaluate U at that point, we first need to find the spring constant k. From Eq. $\omega = \sqrt{k/m}$ and Eq. $\omega = 2\pi f$, we find

$$k = m\omega^2 = m(2\pi f)^2$$
$$= (2.72 \times 10^5 \text{ kg})(2\pi)^2(10.0 \text{ Hz})^2$$
$$= 1.073 \times 10^9 \text{ N/m}$$

We can now evaluate E as

$$E = K + U = \tfrac{1}{2}mv^2 + \tfrac{1}{2}kx^2$$
$$= 0 + \tfrac{1}{2}(1.073 \times 10^9 \text{ N/m})(0.20 \text{ m})^2$$
$$= 2.147 \times 10^7 \text{ J} \approx 2.1 \times 10^7 \text{ J} \qquad \text{(Answer)}$$

(b) What is the block's speed as it passes through the equilibrium point?

Compute: We want the speed at $x = 0$, where the potential energy is $U = \frac{1}{2}kx^2 = 0$ and the mechanical energy is entirely kinetic energy. So, we can write

$$E = K + U = \tfrac{1}{2}mv^2 + \tfrac{1}{2}kx^2$$
$$2.147 \times 10^7 \text{ J} = \tfrac{1}{2}(2.72 \times 10^5 \text{ kg})v^2 + 0$$

or $$v = 12.6 \text{ m/s} \qquad \text{(Answer)}$$

Conclude: Because E is entirely kinetic energy, this is the maximum speed v_m.

Sample Problem 15-6

A block of mass 4 m is attached to a vertical spring of spring constant K. The block is made by glueing two blocks of mass 3 m and 4 m, respectively. Initially, the block is in equilibirium and at rest. At $t = 0$, the part of the block having mass 3 m falls down. Considering hanging point on ceiling as $y = 0$ and downward direction as positive y, find y-coordinate of mass 'm' as a function of time.

Conceptualize: As the original block (mass 4 m) is in equilibrium, the combined mass will be streching the spring by $4mg/k$. Thus, the spring will be $4mg/k$ below the natural length. As the bigger block falls, the smaller block will experience a force larger than its weight in upward direction.

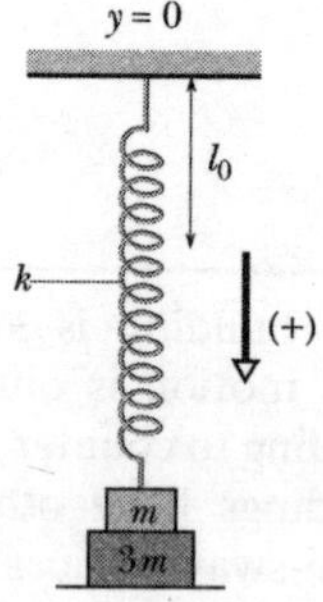

Classify: The block remaining attached to the spring will be undergoing SHM. To find equation of SHM, we need to find angular frequency, amplitude, and initial phase.

Compute: When the extension in the spring is x, the net force on the block is $mg - kx = \dfrac{md^2x}{dt^2}$, again as $x = 0$ is not position of equilibrium, we have to shift origin to the position of equilibrium.

Defining $x = \left(\dfrac{mg}{k} + s\right)$ as at $s = 0$ or $x = mg/k$ is position of equilibrium putting in the equation we get $mg - k\left(\dfrac{mg}{k} + s\right) = \dfrac{md^2s}{dt^2}$ which on solving gives

$$\frac{d^2s}{dt^2} = -\left(\frac{k}{m}\right)s$$

$$S = A\sin(\omega t + \phi) \text{ with } \omega = \sqrt{\frac{k}{m}}$$

Now we have to find A. As we have defined A as distance between $v = 0$ and $a = 0$. At $t = 0$, the block was at rest with extension of spring being $4mg/k$ and at the

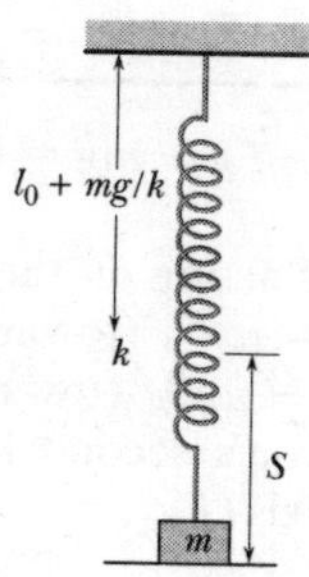

new equilibrium position extension of spring being mg/k. Thus,

$$A = \frac{3\,mg}{k}$$

Now we have to find the initial phase. As the particle is at rest at $t = 0$ on positive side, the initial phase will be $\frac{\pi}{2}$.

$$\phi = \frac{\pi}{2}$$

Thus, the y coordinate of the block

$$y = l_0 + \frac{mg}{k} + s$$

Substituting, all the values from above, we get

$$y = l_0 + \frac{mg}{k} + \frac{3\,mg}{k}\sin\left[\sqrt{\frac{k}{m}}\,t + \frac{\pi}{2}\right]$$

Conclude: At time $t = 0$, the distance of the block from the ceiling is $l_0 + 4\,mg/k$, which can be verified by putting $t = 0$ in the equation.

Sample Problem 15-7

Find time period of motion when elastic spring is replaced by an elastic string of long natural length in previous example and everything else remains same.

Conceptualize: The difference in this problem from the previous one is that when the block goes above equilibrium position, the string will stop applying force as the elastic string will slack.

Classify: Thus, the block will not be undergoing SHM for its whole period as the block goes above the natural length position the only force acting on it will be gravity. But as no dissipative force is acting on the system, the motion is still periodic oscillations.

Compute: First we need to find the duration for which the string is applying force and the motion of the block is described by equations of SHM.

The block will not be doing SHM after it crosses natural length which is mg/k above the natural length. Depicting this on phasor diagram, we can see that it will leave SHM at $A/3$. Thus, it will be undergoing SHM for the angle $\alpha = \pi + 2\theta$ angle on phasor diagram which represents motion through I to J to G.

where $\theta = \sin^{-1}(1/3)$, thus time taken by the body under SHM is α/ω.

Now the remaining motion is free fall under gravity. The particle returns to the same point from where the string got slacked and resumes SHM as the string becomes tight and starts applying force. To find velocity at the instant the string slacks, we can use the equation

$$v = \omega\sqrt{A^2 - x^2}, \text{ where}$$

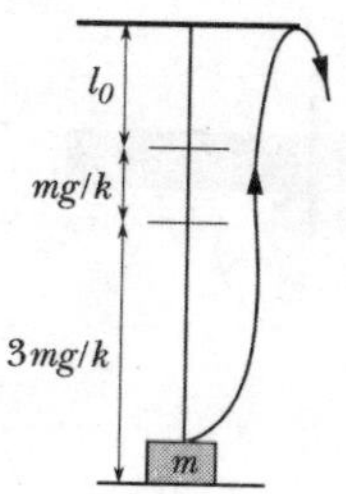

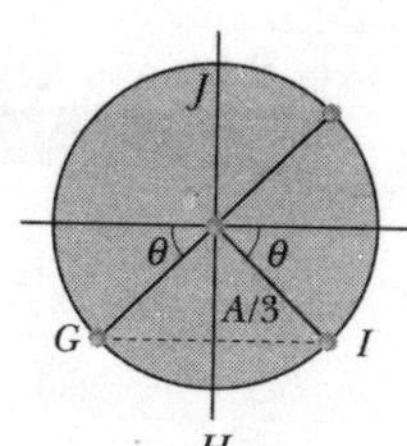

$$x = mg/k,\ \omega = \sqrt{\frac{k}{m}},\ \text{and } A = 3\,mg/k$$

$$v = \sqrt{\frac{9m^2g^2}{k^2} - \frac{m^2g^2}{k^2}}\sqrt{\frac{k}{m}}$$

$$v = 2\sqrt{2}\,\frac{mg}{k}\sqrt{\frac{k}{m}} \quad \sqrt{A^2 - x^2}$$

$$= 2\sqrt{2}\,g\sqrt{\frac{m}{k}}$$

The time it will take to come back is t_1.

$$t_1 = \frac{2v_1}{g} = 4\sqrt{2}\sqrt{\frac{m}{k}} \text{ (using } V = u + at)$$

Thus, total time for one complete oscillation is

$$T = 4\sqrt{2}\sqrt{\frac{m}{k}} + \left(\pi + 2\sin^{-1}(1/3)\right)\sqrt{m/k}$$

Conclude: The motion cannot be described as SHM as for some part of the motion, the block is not experiencing force proportional to distance.

Sample Problem 15-8

In Fig. 15-13*a*, a uniform bar with mass m lies symmetrically across two rapidly rotating, fixed rollers, A and B, with distance $L = 2.0$ cm between the bar's center of mass and each roller. The rollers, whose directions of rotation are shown in the figure, slip against the bar with coefficient of kinetic friction $\mu_k = 0.40$. Suppose the bar is displaced horizontally by a distance x, as shown in Fig. 15-13*b*, and then released. What is the angular frequency ω of the resulting horizontal simple harmonic (back and forth) motion of the bar?

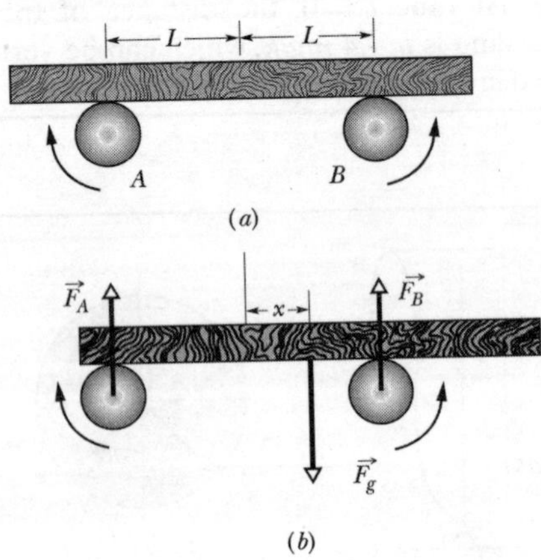

FIG.15–13 (*a*) A bar is in equilibrium on two rotating rollers, *A* and *B*, that slip beneath it. (*b*) The bar is displaced from equilibrium by a distance *x* and then released.

Conceptualize: This situation seems very different from other SHM situations we have analyzed. However, the key idea here is that we can find ω if we find an expression for the horizontal acceleration a of the bar as a function of x and then compare it with $a = -\omega^2 x$.

Classify: Since vertical forces (as shown in Fig. 15-13*b*), horizontal frictional forces, and torques all act on the bar, we shall apply Newton's second law both vertically and horizontally, and then in angular form about one of the contact points between bar and roller.

Compute: The vertical forces acting on the bar are the gravitational force $\vec{F}_g$ (with magnitude mg) and supporting forces $\vec{F}_A$ due to roller A and $\vec{F}_B$ due to roller B. Since there is no vertical acceleration of the bar, Newton's second law for components along a vertical y axis ($F_{\text{net},y} = ma_y$) gives us

$$F_A + F_B - mg = 0 \tag{15-22}$$

The horizontal forces acting on the bar are the kinetic frictional forces $f_{kA} = \mu_k F_A$ (toward the right) due to roller A and $f_{kB} = -\mu_k F_B$ (toward the left) due to roller B. Thus, Newton's second law for components along a horizontal x axis ($F_{\text{net},y} = ma_x$) gives us

$$\mu_k F_A - \mu_k F_B = ma$$

$$a = \frac{\mu_k F_A - \mu_k F_B}{m} \tag{15-23}$$

We now consider torques about an axis perpendicular to the plane of Fig. 15-13 and through the contact point between the bar and roller A. The bar experiences no angular acceleration about that axis, so Newton's second law for torque about such an axis ($\tau_{\text{net}} = I\alpha$) gives us

$$F_A(0) + F_B 2L - mg(L+x) + f_{kA}(0) + f_{kB}(0) = 0 \tag{15-24}$$

where the forces $\vec{F}_A$, $\vec{F}_B$, $m\vec{g}$, $\vec{f}_{kA}$, and $\vec{f}_{kB}$ have moment arms about that axis of 0, $2L$, $L + x$, 0 and 0, respectively.

Solving Eq. 15-24 for F_B and then solving Eq. 15-22 for F_A, we find

$$F_B = \frac{mg(L+x)}{2L} \quad \text{and} \quad F_A = \frac{mg(L-x)}{2L}$$

Substituting these results into Eq. 15-23 yields

$$a = -\frac{\mu_k g}{L} x \tag{15-25}$$

Comparison of Eq. 15-25 with $a = -\omega^2 x$ reveals that the bar must be undergoing SHM with angular frequency ω given by

$$\omega^2 = \frac{\mu_k g}{L}$$

Thus,

$$\omega = \sqrt{\frac{\mu_k g}{L}} = \sqrt{\frac{(0.40)(9.8\ \text{m/s}^2)}{0.020\ \text{m}}}$$

$$= 14\ \text{rad/s}$$

Conclude: There is another amazing point that the rollers will be experiencing kinetic friction which can slow them down. There must be some external torque on the rollers to maintain the motion of the rollers.

REVIEW & SUMMARY

Frequency The *frequency* f of periodic, or oscillatory, motion is the number of oscillations per second. In the SI system, it is measured in hertz:

$$1 \text{ hertz} = 1 \text{ Hz} = 1 \text{ oscillation per second} = 1 \text{ s}^{-1}$$

Period The *period* T is the time required for one complete oscillation, or **cycle.** It is related to the frequency by

$$T = \frac{1}{f}$$

Simple Harmonic Motion In *simple harmonic motion* (SHM), the displacement $x(t)$ of a particle from its equilibrium position is described by the equation

$$x = x_m \cos(\omega t + \phi) \text{ (displacement)}$$

in which x_m is the **amplitude** of the displacement, the quantity $(\omega t + \phi)$ is the **phase** of the motion, and ϕ is the **phase constant.** The **angular frequency** ω is related to the period and frequency of the motion by

$$\omega = \frac{2\pi}{T} = 2\pi f \text{ (angular frequency)}$$

Differentiating Eq. 15-3 leads to equations for the particle's SHM velocity and acceleration as functions of time:

$$v = -\omega x_m \sin(\omega t + \phi) \text{ (velocity)}$$

and $$a = -\omega^2 x_m \cos(\omega t + \phi) \text{ (acceleration)}$$

In Eq. 15-6, the positive quantity ωx_m is the **velocity amplitude** v_m of the motion. In Eq. 15-7, the positive quantity $\omega^2 x_m$ is the **acceleration amplitude** a_m of the motion.

The Linear Oscillator A particle with mass m that moves under the influence of a Hooke's law restoring force given by $F = -kx$ exhibits simple harmonic motion with

$$\omega = \sqrt{\frac{k}{m}} \text{ (angular frequency)}$$

and $$T = 2\pi\sqrt{\frac{m}{k}} \text{ (period)}$$

Such a system is called a **linear simple harmonic oscillator.**

Energy A particle in simple harmonic motion has, at any time, kinetic energy $K = 1/2\ mv^2$ and potential energy $U = 1/2\ kx^2$. If no friction is present, the mechanical energy $E = K + U$ remains constant even though K and U change.

QUESTIONS

1 The acceleration $a(t)$ of a particle undergoing SHM is graphed in Fig. 15-14. (a) Which of the labeled points corresponds to the particle at $-x_m$? (b) At point 4, is the velocity of the particle positive, negative, or zero? (c) At point 5, is the particle at $-x_m$, at $+x_m$, at 0, between $-x_m$ and 0, or between 0 and $+x_m$?

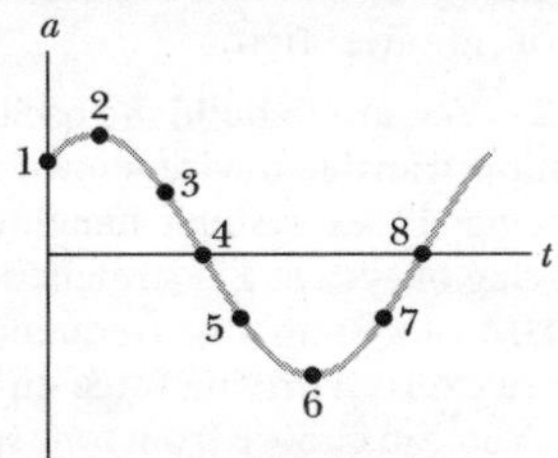

FIG. 15-14 Question 1.

2 Which of the following relationships between the acceleration a and the displacement x of a particle involve SHM: (a) $a = 0.5x$, (b) $a = 400x^2$, (c) $a = -20x$, (d) $a = -3x^2$?

3 Which of the following describe ϕ for the SHM of Fig. 15-15*a*:

(a) $-\pi < \phi < -\pi/2$,

(b) $\pi < \phi < 3\pi/2$,

(c) $-3\pi/2 < \phi < -\pi$?

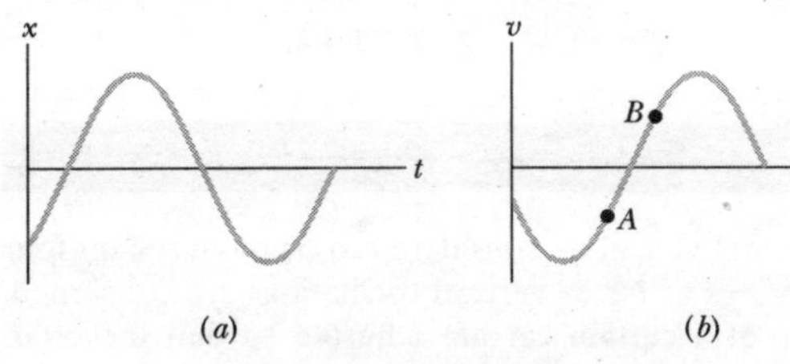

FIG. 15-15 Questions 3 and 4.

4 The velocity $v(t)$ of a particle undergoing SHM is graphed in Fig. 15-15*b*. Is the particle momentarily stationary, headed toward $-x_m$, or headed toward $+x_m$ at (a) point A on the graph and (b) point B? Is the particle at $-x_m$, at $+x_m$, at 0, between $-x_m$ and 0, or between 0 and $+x_m$ when its velocity is represented by (c) point A and (d) point B? Is the speed of the particle increasing or decreasing at (e) point A and (f) point B?

5 Figure 15-16 shows the $x(t)$ curves for three experiments involving a particular spring–box system oscillating in SHM. Rank the curves according to (a) the system's angular frequency, (b) the spring's potential energy at time $t = 0$, (c) the box's kinetic energy at $t = 0$, (d) the box's speed at $t = 0$, and (e) the box's maximum kinetic energy, greatest first.

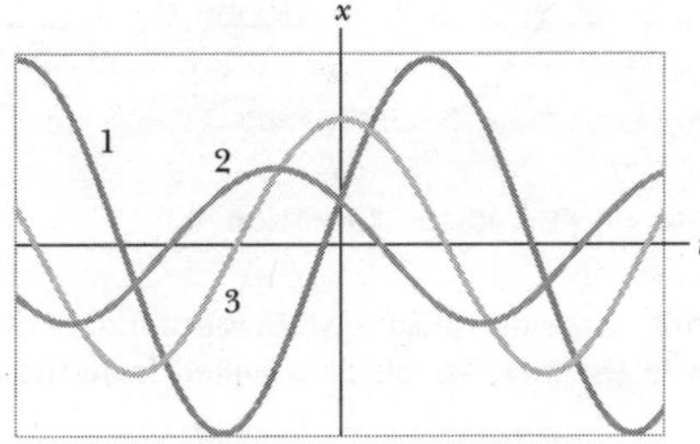

FIG. 15-16 Question 5.

6 Figure 15-17 gives, for three situations, the displacements $x(t)$ of a pair of simple harmonic oscillators (A and B) that are identical except for phase. For each pair, what phase shift (in radians and in degrees) is needed to shift the curve for A to coincide with the curve for B? Of the many possible answers, choose the shift with the smallest absolute magnitude.

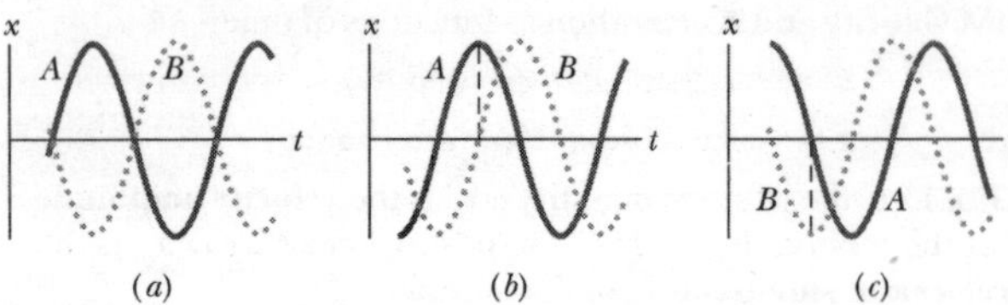

FIG. 15-17 Question 6.

7 You are to complete Fig. 15-18a so that it is a plot of velocity v versus time t for the spring–block oscillator that is shown in Fig. 15-18b for $t = 0$. (a) In Fig. 15-18a, at which lettered point or in what region between the points should the (vertical) v axis intersect the t axis? (For example, should it intersect at point A, or maybe in the region between points A and B?) (b) If the block's velocity is given by $v = -v_m \sin(\omega t + \phi)$, what is the value of ϕ? Make it positive, and if you cannot specify the value (such as $+\pi/2$ rad), then give a range of values (such as between 0 and $\pi/2$).

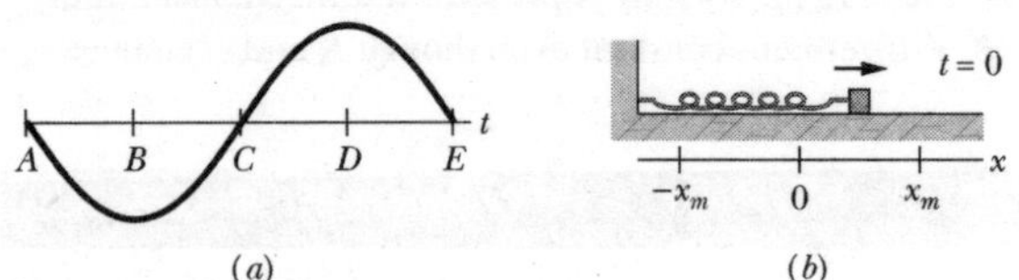

FIG. 15-18 Question 7.

8 You are to complete Fig. 15-19a so that it is a plot of acceleration a versus time t for the spring–block oscillator that is shown in Fig. 15-19b for $t = 0$. (a) In Fig. 15-19a, at which lettered point or in what region between the points should the (vertical) a axis intersect the t axis? (For example, should it intersect at point A, or maybe in the region between points A and B?) (b) If the block's acceleration is given by $a = -a_m \cos(\omega t + \phi)$, what is the value of ϕ? Make it positive, and if you cannot specify the value (such as $+\pi/2$ rad), then give a range of values (such as between 0 and $\pi/2$).

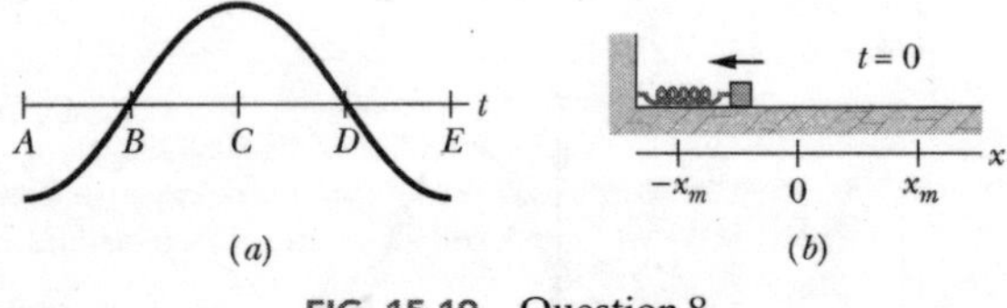

FIG. 15-19 Question 8.

9 In Fig. 15-20, a spring–block system is put into SHM in two experiments. In the first, the block is pulled from the equilibrium position through a displacement d_1 and then released. In the second, it is pulled from the equilibrium position through a greater displacement d_2 and then released. Are the (a) amplitude, (b) period, (c) frequency, (d) maximum kinetic energy, and (e) maximum potential energy in the second experiment greater than, less than, or the same as those in the first experiment?

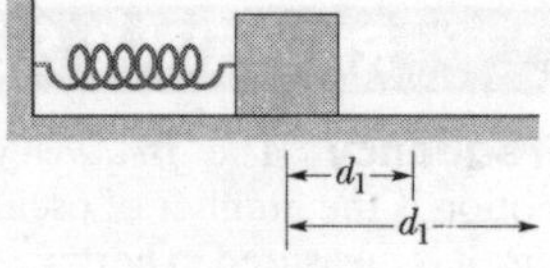

FIG. 15-20 Question 9.

10 Figure 15-21 shows plots of the kinetic energy K versus position x for three harmonic oscillators that have the same mass. Rank the plots according to (a) the corresponding spring constant and (b) the corresponding period of the oscillator, greatest first.

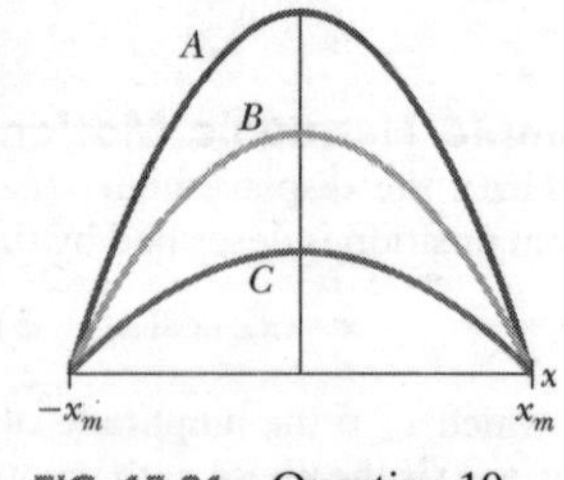

FIG. 15-21 Question 10.

11 Figure 15-22 shows three physical pendulums consisting of identical uniform spheres of the same mass that are rigidly connected by identical rods of negligible mass. Each pendulum is vertical and can pivot about suspension point O. Rank the pendulums according to period of oscillation, greatest first.

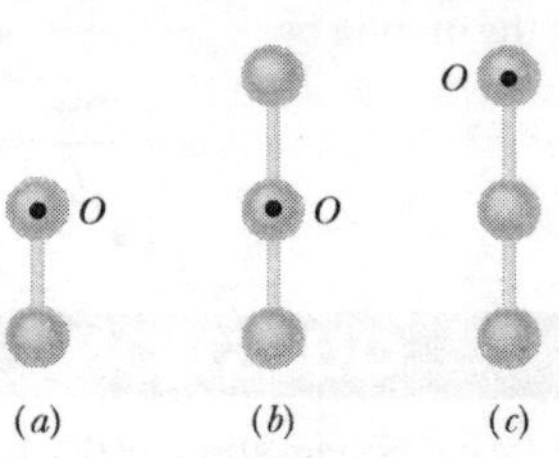

FIG. 15-22 Question 11.

12 You are to build the oscillation transfer device shown in Fig. 15-23. It consists of two spring–block systems hanging from a flexible rod. When the spring of system 1 is stretched and then released, the resulting SHM of system 1 at frequency f_1 oscillates the rod. The rod then exerts a driving force on system 2, at the same frequency f_1. You can choose from four springs with spring constants k of 1600, 1500, 1400, and 1200 N/m, and four blocks with masses m of 800, 500, 400, and 200 kg. Mentally determine which spring should go with which block in each of the two systems to maximize the amplitude of oscillations in system 2.

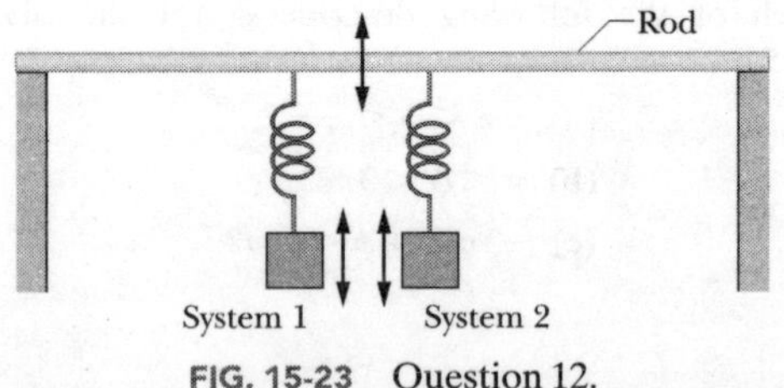

FIG. 15-23 Question 12.

PROBLEMS

The Force Law for Simple Harmonic Motion

1 An object undergoing simple harmonic motion takes 0.25 s to travel from one point of zero velocity to the next such point. The distance between those points is 36 cm. Calculate the (a) period, (b) frequency, and (c) amplitude of the motion.

2 An automobile can be considered to be mounted on four identical springs as far as vertical oscillations are concerned. The springs of a certain car are adjusted so that the oscillations have a frequency of 3.00 Hz. (a) What is the spring constant of each spring if the mass of the car is 1450 kg and the mass is evenly distributed over the springs? (b) What will be the oscillation frequency if five passengers, averaging 73.0 kg each, ride in the car with an even distribution of mass?

3 An oscillator consists of a block of mass 0.500 kg connected to a spring. When set into oscillation with amplitude 35.0 cm, the oscillator repeats its motion every 0.500 s. Find the (a) period, (b) frequency, (c) angular frequency, (d) spring constant, (e) maximum speed, and (f) magnitude of the maximum force on the block from the spring.

4 What is the phase constant for the harmonic oscillator with the position function $x(t)$ given in Fig. 15-24 if the position function has the form $x = x_m \cos(\omega t + \phi)$? The vertical axis scale is set by $x_s = 6.0$ cm.

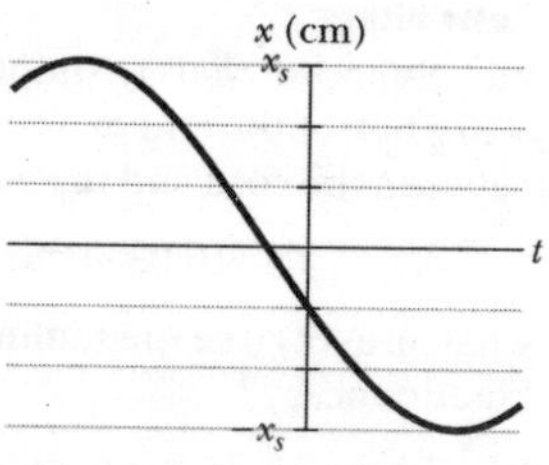

FIG. 15-24 Problem 4.

5 The function $x = (6.0 \text{ m}) \cos[(3\pi \text{ rad/s})t + \pi/3 \text{ rad}]$ gives the simple harmonic motion of a body. At $t = 2.0$ s, what are the (a) displacement, (b) velocity, (c) acceleration, and (d) phase of the motion? Also, what are the (e) frequency and (f) period of the motion?

6 What is the phase constant for the harmonic oscillator with the velocity function $v(t)$ given in Fig. 15-25 if the position function $x(t)$ has the form $x = x_m \cos(\omega t + \phi)$? The vertical axis scale is set by $v_s = 4.0$ cm/s.

FIG. 15-25 Problem 6.

7 In Fig. 15-26, two identical springs of spring constant 7580 N/m are attached to a block of mass 0.245 kg. What is the frequency of oscillation on the frictionless floor?

FIG. 15-26 Problems 7 and 16.

8 Figure 15-27 shows block 1 of mass 0.200 kg sliding to the right over a frictionless elevated surface at a speed of 8.00 m/s. The block undergoes an elastic collision with stationary block 2, which is attached to a spring of spring constant 1208.5 N/m. (Assume that the spring does not affect the collision.) After the collision, block 2 oscillates in SHM with a period of 0.140 s, and block 1 slides off the opposite end of the elevated surface, landing a distance d from the base of that surface after falling height $h = 4.90$ m. What is the value of d?

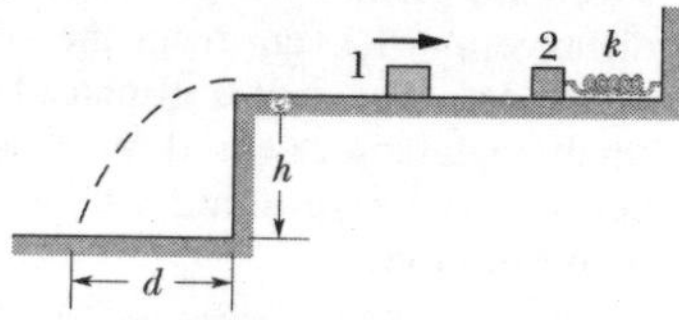

FIG. 15-27 Problem 8.

9 An oscillator consists of a block attached to a spring ($k = 400$ N/m). Initially, the position (measured from the system's equilibrium location), velocity, and acceleration of the block are $x = 0.100$ m, $v = -13.6$ m/s, and $a = -123$ m/s^2. Calculate (a) the frequency of oscillation, (b) the mass of the block, and (c) the amplitude of the motion (d) the initial phase

ans (d) 165.5°.

10 At a certain harbor, the tides cause the ocean surface to rise and fall a distance d (from highest level to lowest level) in simple harmonic motion, with a period of 12.5 h. How long does it take for the water to fall a distance $0.250d$ from its highest level?

11 A block is on a horizontal surface (a shake table) that is moving back and forth horizontally with simple harmonic motion of frequency 2.0 Hz. The coefficient of static friction between block and surface is 0.50. How great can the amplitude of the SHM be if the block is not to slip along the surface?

12 Two particles execute simple harmonic motion of the same amplitude and frequency along close parallel lines. They pass each other moving in opposite directions each time their displacement is half their amplitude. What is their phase difference?

13 Two particles oscillate in simple harmonic motion along a common straight-line segment of length A. Each particle has a period of 1.5 s, but they differ in phase by $\pi/6$ rad. (a) How far apart are they (in terms of A) 0.50 s after the lagging particle leaves one end of the path? (b) Are they then moving in the same direction, toward each other, or away from each other?

14 Figure 15-28a is a partial graph of the position function $x(t)$ for a simple harmonic oscillator with an angular frequency of 1.20 rad/s; Fig. 15-28b is a partial graph of the corresponding velocity function $v(t)$. The vertical axis scales are set by $x_s = 5.0$ cm and $v_s = 5.0$ cm/s. What is the phase constant of the SHM if the position function $x(t)$ is given the form $x = x_m \cos(\omega t + \phi)$?

FIG. 15-28 Problem 14.

15 A block rides on a piston that is moving vertically with simple harmonic motion. (a) If the SHM has period 1.0 s, at what amplitude of motion will the block and piston separate? (b) If the piston has an amplitude of 5.0 cm, what is the maximum frequency for which the block and piston will be in contact continuously?

16 In Fig. 15-26, two springs are attached to a block that can oscillate over a frictionless floor. If the left spring is removed, the block oscillates at a frequency of 30 Hz. If, instead, the spring on the right is removed, the block oscillates at a frequency of 45 Hz. At what frequency does the block oscillate with both springs attached?

17 In Fig. 15-29, two blocks ($m = 1.8$ kg and $M = 10$ kg) and a spring ($k = 200$ N/m) are arranged on a horizontal, frictionless surface. The coefficient of static friction between the two blocks is 0.40. What amplitude of simple harmonic motion of the spring–blocks system puts the smaller block on the verge of slipping over the larger block?

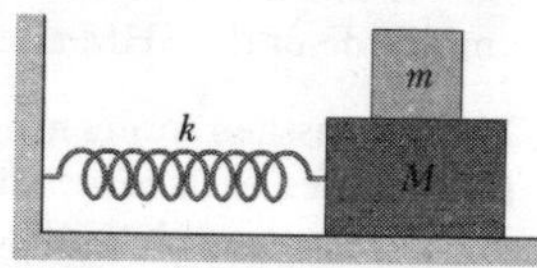

FIG. 15-29 Problem 17.

18 In Fig. 15-30, a block weighing 14.0 N, which can slide without friction on an incline at angle $\theta = 40.0°$, is connected to the top of the incline by a massless spring of unstretched length 0.450 m and spring constant 120 N/m. (a) How far from the top of the incline is the block's equilibrium point? (b) If the block is pulled slightly down the incline and released, what is the period of the resulting oscillations?

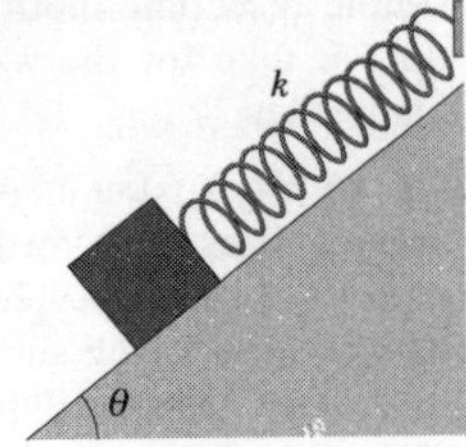

FIG. 15-30 Problem 18.

Energy in Simple Harmonic Motion

19 Figure 15-31 shows the kinetic energy K of a simple harmonic oscillator versus its position x. The vertical axis scale is set by $K_s = 4.0$ J. What is the spring constant?

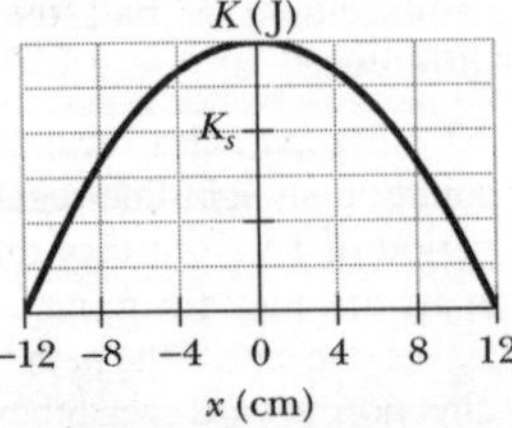

FIG. 15-31 Problem 19.

20 A 10 g particle undergoes SHM with an amplitude of 2.0 mm, a maximum acceleration of magnitude 8.0×10^3 m/s^2, and an unknown phase constant ϕ. What are (a) the period of the motion, (b) the maximum speed of the particle, and (c) the total mechanical energy of the oscillator? What is the magnitude of the force on the particle when the particle is at (d) its maximum displacement and (e) half its maximum displacement?

21 A block of mass $M = 5.4$ kg, at rest on a horizontal frictionless table, is attached to a rigid support by a spring of constant $k = 6000$ N/m. A bullet of mass $m = 9.5$ g and velocity $\vec{v}$ of magnitude 630 m/s strikes and is embedded in the block (Fig. 15-32). Assuming the compression of the spring is negligible until the bullet is embedded, determine (a) the speed of the block immediately after the collision and (b) the amplitude of the resulting simple harmonic motion.

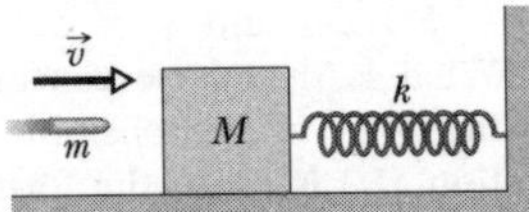

FIG. 15-32 Problem 21.

22 In Fig. 15-33, block 2 of mass 2.0 kg oscillates on the end of a spring in SHM with a period of 20 ms. The position of the block is given by $x = (1.0 \text{ cm}) \cos(\omega t + \pi/2)$. Block 1 of mass 4.0 kg slides toward block 2 with a velocity of magnitude 6.0 m/s, directed along the spring's length. The two blocks undergo a completely inelastic collision at time $t = 5.0$ ms. (The duration of the collision is much less than the period of motion.) What is the amplitude of the SHM after the collision?

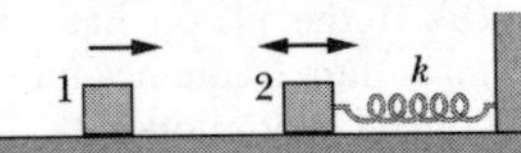

FIG. 15-33 Problem 22.

23 A massless spring hangs from the ceiling with a small object attached to its lower end. The object is initially held at rest in a position y_i such that the spring is at its rest length. The object is then released from y_i and oscillates up and down, with its lowest position being 10 cm below y_i. (a) What is the frequency of the oscillation? (b) What is the speed of the object when it is 8.0 cm below the initial position? (c) An object of mass 300 g is attached to the first object, after which the system oscillates with half the original frequency. What is the mass of the first object? (d) How far below y_i is the new equilibrium (rest) position with both objects attached to the spring?

An Angular Simple Harmonic Oscillator

24 A 95 kg solid sphere with a 15 cm radius is suspended by a vertical wire. A torque of 0.20 N · m is required to rotate the sphere through an angle of 0.85 rad and then maintain that orientation. What is the period of the oscillations that result when the sphere is then released?

Pendulums

25 Suppose that a simple pendulum consists of a small 60.0 g bob at the end of a cord of negligible mass. If the angle θ between the cord and the vertical is given by

$$\theta = (0.0800 \text{ rad}) \cos[(4.43 \text{ rad/s})t + \phi]$$

what are (a) the pendulum's length and (b) its maximum kinetic energy?

26 In Fig. 15-34, the pendulum consists of a uniform disk with radius $r = 10.0$ cm and mass 500 g attached to a uniform rod with length $L = 500$ mm and mass 270 g. (a) Calculate the rotational inertia of the pendulum about the pivot point. (b) What is the distance between the pivot point and the center of mass of the pendulum? (c) Calculate the period of oscillation.

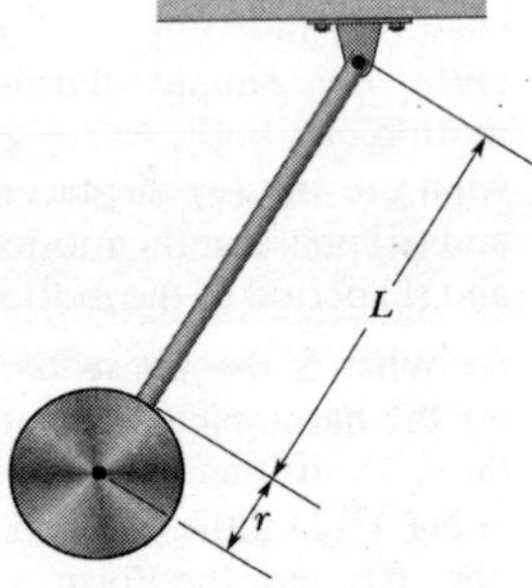

FIG. 15-34 Problem 26.

27 A physical pendulum consists of a meter stick that is pivoted at a small hole drilled through the stick a distance d from the 50 cm mark. The period of oscillation is 2.5 s. Find d.

28 In Fig. 15-35, a physical pendulum consists of a uniform solid disk (of radius $R = 2.35$ cm) supported in a vertical plane by a pivot located a distance $d = 1.75$ cm from the center of the disk. The disk is displaced by a small angle and released. What is the period of the resulting simple harmonic motion?

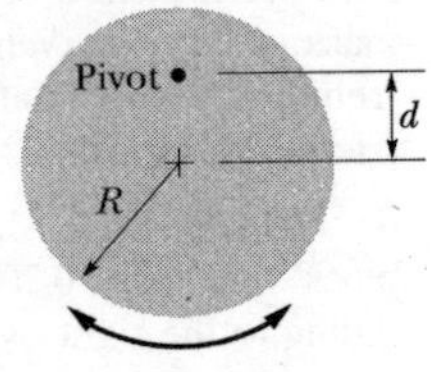

FIG. 15-35 Problem 28.

29 A physical pendulum consists of two meter-long sticks joined together as shown in Fig. 15-36. What is the pendulum's period of oscillation about a pin inserted through point A at the center of the horizontal stick?

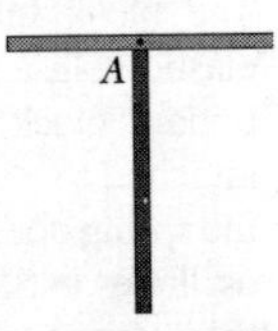

FIG. 15-36 Problem 29.

30 A thin uniform rod (mass = 0.50 kg) swings about an axis that passes through one end of the rod and is perpendicular to the plane of the swing. The rod swings with a period of 1.5 s and an angular amplitude of 10°. (a) What is the length of the rod? (b) What is the maximum kinetic energy of the rod as it swings?

31 In Fig. 15-37, a stick of length $L = 1.85$ m oscillates as a physical pendulum. (a) What value of distance x between the stick's center of mass and its pivot point O gives the least period? (b) What is that least period?

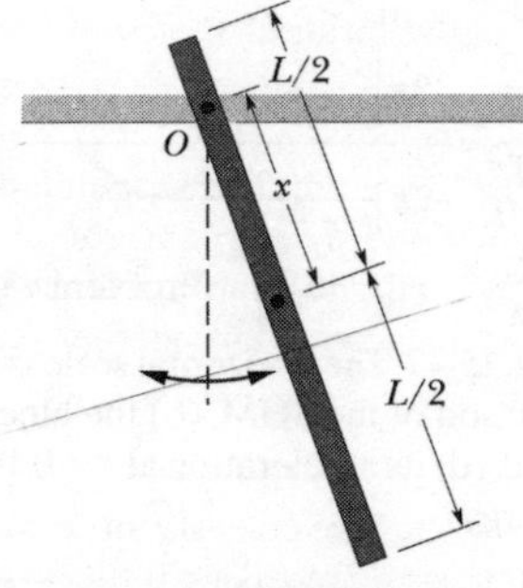

FIG. 15-37 Problem 31.

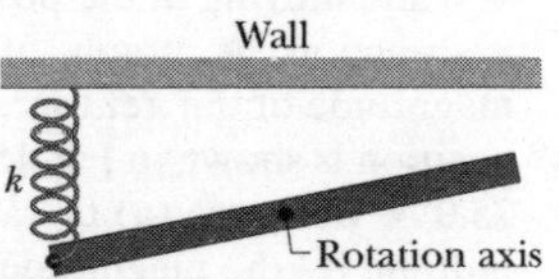

FIG. 15-38 Problem 32.

32 The 3.00 kg cube in Fig. 15-38 has edge lengths $d = 6.00$ cm and is mounted on an axle through its center. A spring ($k = 1200$ N/m) connects the cube's upper corner to a rigid wall. Initially the spring is at its rest length. If the cube is rotated 3° and released, what is the period of the resulting SHM?

33 In the overhead view of Fig. 15-39, a long uniform rod of mass 0.600 kg is free to rotate in a horizontal plane about a vertical axis through its center. A spring with force constant $k = 1850$ N/m is connected horizontally between one end of the rod and a fixed wall. When the rod is in equilibrium, it is parallel to the wall. What is the period of the small oscillations that result when the rod is rotated slightly and released?

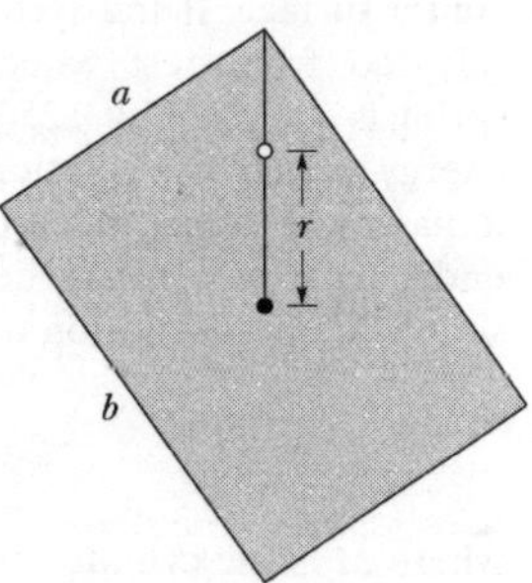

FIG. 15-39 Problem 33.

34 A rectangular block, with face lengths $a = 35$ cm and $b = 45$ cm, is to be suspended on a thin horizontal rod running through a narrow hole in the block. The block is then to be set swinging about the rod like a pendulum, through small angles so that it is in SHM. Figure 15-40 shows one possible position of the hole, at distance r from the block's center, along a line connecting the center with a corner. (a) Plot the period of the pendulum versus distance r along that line such that the minimum in the curve is apparent. (b) For what value of r does that minimum occur? There is actually a line of points around the block's center for which the period of swinging has the same minimum value. (c) What shape does that line make?

FIG. 15-40 Problem 34.

35 A pendulum is formed by pivoting a long thin rod about a point on the rod. In a series of experiments, the period is measured as a function of the distance x between the pivot point and the rod's center. (a) If the rod's length is $L = 2.20$ m and its mass is $m = 22.1$ g, what is the minimum period? (b) If x is chosen to minimize the period and then L is increased, does the period increase, decrease, or remain the same? (c) If, instead, m is increased without L increasing, does the period increase, decrease, or remain the same?

36 In Fig. 15-41, a 2.50 kg disk of diameter $D = 42.0$ cm is supported by a rod of length $L = 76.0$ cm and negligible mass that is pivoted at its end. (a) With the massless torsion spring unconnected, what is the period of oscillation? (b) With the torsion spring connected, the rod is vertical at equilibrium. What is the torsion constant of the spring if the period of oscillation has been decreased by 0.500 s?

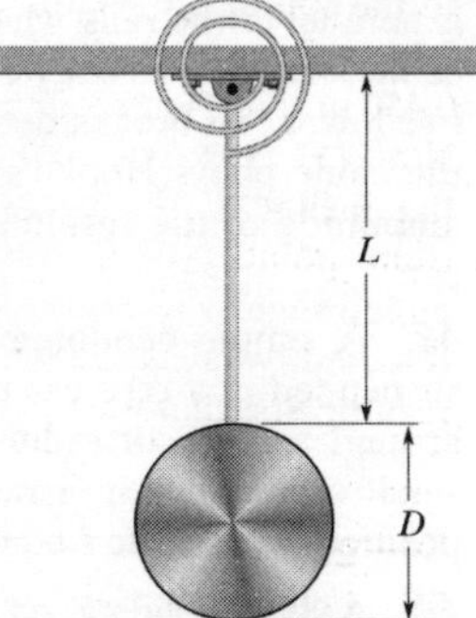

FIG. 15-41 Problem 36.

Additional Problems

37 Figure 15-42 shows the kinetic energy K of a simple pendulum versus its angle θ from the vertical. The vertical axis scale is set by $K_s = 10.0$ mJ. The pendulum bob has mass 0.200 kg. What is the length of the pendulum?

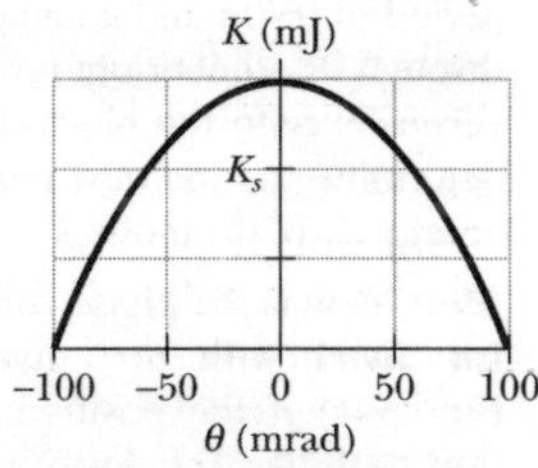

FIG. 15-42 Problem 37.

38 Although California is known for earthquakes, it has large regions dotted with precariously balanced rocks that would be easily toppled by even a mild earthquake. The rocks have stood this way for thousands of years, suggesting that major earthquakes have not occurred in those regions during that time. If an earthquake were to put such a rock into sinusoidal oscillation (parallel to the ground) with a frequency of 2.2 Hz, an oscillation amplitude of 1.0 cm would cause the rock to topple. What would be the magnitude of the maximum acceleration of the oscillation, in terms of g?

39 A 4.00 kg block is suspended from a spring with $k = 500$ N/m. A 50.0 g bullet is fired into the block from directly below with a speed of 150 m/s and becomes embedded in the block. (a) Find the amplitude of the resulting SHM. (b) What percentage of the original kinetic energy of the bullet is transferred to mechanical energy of the oscillator?

40 A 55.0 g block oscillates in SHM on the end of a spring with $k = 1500$ N/m according to $x = x_m \cos(\omega t + \phi)$. How long does the block take to move from position $+0.800x_m$ to (a) position $+0.600x_m$ and (b) position $-0.800x_m$?

FIG. 15-43 Problem 41.

41 A wheel is free to rotate about its fixed axle. A spring is attached to one of its spokes a distance r from the axle, as shown in Fig. 15-43. (a) Assuming that the wheel is a hoop of mass m and radius R, what is the angular frequency ω of small oscillations of this system in terms of m, R, r, and the spring constant k? What is ω if (b) $r = R$ and (c) $r = 0$?

42 In Fig. 15-44, three 10 000 kg ore cars are held at rest on a mine railway using a cable that

FIG. 15-44 Problem 42.

is parallel to the rails, which are inclined at angle $\theta = 30°$. The cable stretches 15 cm just before the coupling between the two lower cars breaks, detaching the lowest car. Assuming that the cable obeys Hooke's law, find the (a) frequency and (b) amplitude of the resulting oscillations of the remaining two cars.

43 A simple pendulum of length 20 cm and mass 5.0 g is suspended in a race car traveling with constant speed 70 m/s around a circle of radius 50 m. If the pendulum undergoes small oscillations in a radial direction about its equilibrium position, what is the frequency of oscillation?

44 A block sliding on a horizontal frictionless surface is attached to a horizontal spring with a spring constant of 600 N/m. The block executes SHM about its equilibrium position with a period of 0.40 s and an amplitude of 0.20 m. As the block slides through its equilibrium position, a 0.50 kg putty wad is dropped vertically onto the block. If the putty wad sticks to the block, determine (a) the new period of the motion and (b) the new amplitude of the motion.

45 What is the phase constant for SMH with $a(t)$ given in Fig. 15-45 if the position function $x(t)$ has the form $x = x_m \cos(\omega t + \phi)$ and $a_s = 4.0$ m/s^2?

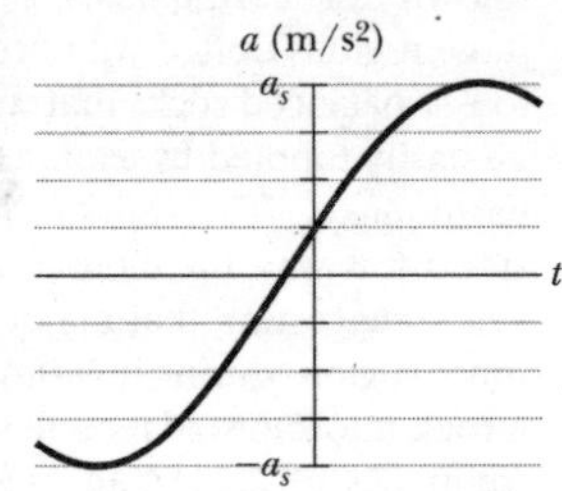

FIG. 15-45 Problem 45.

46 A torsion pendulum consists of a metal disk with a wire running through its center and soldered in place. The wire is mounted vertically on clamps and pulled taut. Figure 15-46*a* gives the magnitude τ of the torque needed to rotate the disk about its center (and thus twist the wire) versus the rotation angle θ. The vertical axis scale is set by $\tau_s = 4.0 \times 10^{-3}$ N·m. The disk is rotated to $\theta = 0.200$ rad and then released. Figure 15-46*b* shows the resulting oscillation in terms of angular position θ versus time t. The horizontal axis scale is set by $t_s = 0.40$ s. (a) What is the rotational inertia of the disk about its center? (b) What is the maximum angular speed $d\theta/dt$ of the disk? (*Caution:* Do not confuse the (constant) angular frequency of the SHM with the (varying) angular speed of the rotating disk, even though they usually have the same symbol ω. *Hint:* The potential energy U of a torsion pendulum is equal to $1/2\kappa\theta^2$, analogous to $U = 1/2kx^2$ for a spring.)

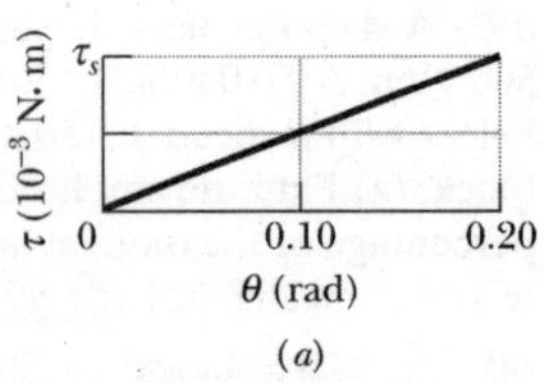

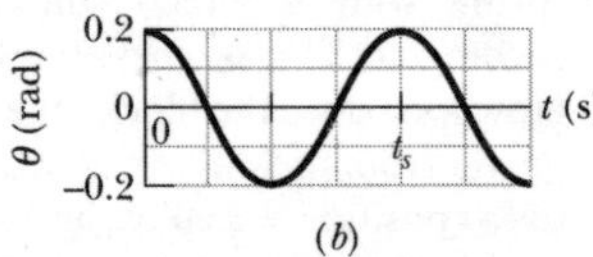

FIG. 15-46 Problem 46.

47 A spider can tell when its web has captured, say, a fly because the fly's thrashing causes the web threads to oscillate. A spider can even determine the size of the fly by the frequency of the oscillations. Assume that a fly oscillates on the *capture thread* on which it is caught like a block on a spring. What is the ratio of oscillation frequency for a fly with mass m to a fly with mass $2.5m$?

48 A simple harmonic oscillator consists of a block attached to a spring with $k = 200$ N/m. The block slides on a frictionless surface, with equilibrium point $x = 0$ and amplitude 0.20 m. A graph of the block's velocity v as a function of time t is shown in Fig. 15-47. The horizontal scale is set by $t_s = 0.20$ s. What are (a) the period of the SHM, (b) the block's mass, (c) its displacement at $t = 0$, (d) its acceleration at $t = 0.10$ s, and (e) its maximum kinetic energy?

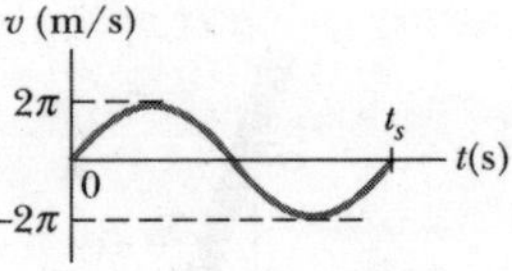

FIG. 15-47 Problem 48.

49 A simple harmonic oscillator consists of a 0.50 kg block attached to a spring. The block slides back and forth along a straight line on a frictionless surface with equilibrium point $x = 0$. At $t = 0$ the block is at $x = 0$ and moving in the positive x direction. A graph of the magnitude of the net force $\vec{F}$ on the block as a function of its position is shown in Fig. 15-48. The vertical scale is set by $F_s = 75.0$ N. What are (a) the amplitude and (b) the period of the motion, (c) the magnitude of the maximum acceleration, and (d) the maximum kinetic energy?

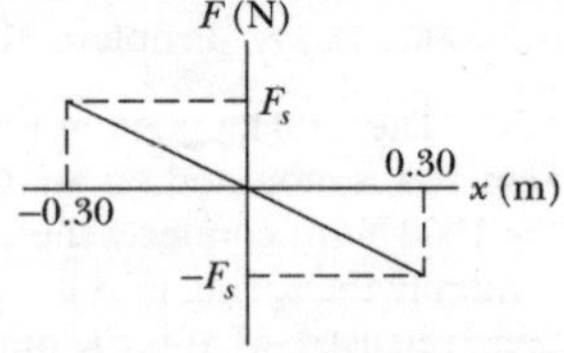

FIG. 15-48 Problem 49.

50 In Fig. 15-49, a solid cylinder attached to a horizontal spring ($k = 3.00$ N/m) rolls without slipping along a horizontal surface. If the system is released from rest when the spring is stretched by 0.250 m, find (a) the translational kinetic energy and (b) the rotational kinetic energy of the cylinder as it passes through the equilibrium position. (c) Show that under these conditions the cylinder's center of mass executes simple harmonic motion with period

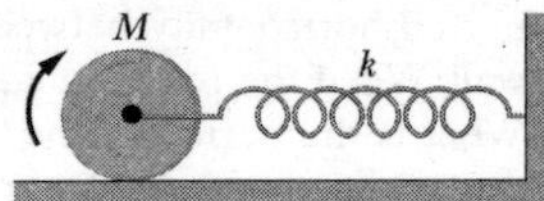

FIG. 15-49 Problem 50.

$$T = 2\pi\sqrt{\frac{3M}{2k}}$$

where M is the cylinder mass. (*Hint:* Find the time derivative of the total mechanical energy.)

51 A block weighing 10.0 N is attached to the lower end of a vertical spring ($k = 200.0$ N/m), the other end of which is attached to a ceiling. The block oscillates vertically and has a kinetic energy of 2.00 J as it passes through the point at which the spring is unstretched. (a) What is the period of the oscillation? (b) Use the law of conservation of energy to determine the maximum distance the block moves both above and below the point at which the spring is unstretched. (These are not necessarily the same.) (c) What is the amplitude of the oscillation? (d) What is the maximum kinetic energy of the block as it oscillates?

52 A 2.0 kg block executes SHM while attached to a horizontal spring of spring constant 200 N/m. The maximum speed of the block as it slides on a horizontal frictionless surface is 3.0 m/s. What are (a) the amplitude of the block's motion, (b) the magnitude of its maximum acceleration, and (c) the magnitude of its minimum acceleration? (d) How long does the block take to complete 7.0 cycles of its motion?

53 The vibration frequencies of atoms in solids at normal temperatures are of the order of 10^{13} Hz. Imagine the atoms to be connected to one another by springs. Suppose that a single silver atom in a solid vibrates with this frequency and that all the other atoms are at rest. Compute the effective spring constant. One mole of silver (6.02×10^{23} atoms) has a mass of 108 g.

54 The center of oscillation of a physical pendulum has this interesting property: If an impulse (assumed horizontal and in the plane of oscillation) acts at the center of oscillation, no oscillations are felt at the point of support. Baseball players (and players of many other sports) know that unless the ball hits the bat at this point (called the "sweet spot" by athletes), the oscillations due to the impact will sting their hands. To prove this property, let the stick in Fig. 15-11*a* simulate a baseball bat. Suppose that a horizontal force $\vec{F}$ (due to impact with the ball) acts toward the right at *P*, the center of oscillation. The batter is assumed to hold the bat at *O*, the pivot point of the stick. (a) What acceleration does the point *O* undergo as a result of $\vec{F}$? (b) What angular acceleration is produced by $\vec{F}$ about the center of mass of the stick? (c) As a result of the angular acceleration in (b), what linear acceleration does point *O* undergo? (d) Considering the magnitudes and directions of the accelerations in (a) and (c), convince yourself that *P* is indeed the "sweet spot."

16 Mechanical Waves

In 2001, a sleek footbridge across the Thames River was opened in London to connect the Tate Modern art gallery with the vicinity of St. Paul's Cathedral and to mark the new millennium. However, soon after the first surge of pedestrians began to walk over it, the Millennium Bridge, as it is called, began to oscillate so much that many of the pedestrians had difficulty keeping their balance. Similar oscillations can occur in a mosh pit on a standard wood floor, especially if the participants are pogoing or body slamming.

Sion Touhig/Getty Images News and Sport Services

What causes such oscillations, which can be the nightmare of structural engineers?

The answer is in this chapter.

Bruno Vincent/Reportage/Getty Images, Inc.

16-1 | Introduction

One of the primary subjects of physics is waves. To see how important waves are in the modern world, just consider the music industry. Every piece of music you hear, from some retro-punk band playing in a campus dive to the most eloquent concerto playing on the Web, depends on performers producing waves and your detecting those waves. In between production and detection, the information carried by the waves might need to be transmitted (as in a live performance on the Web) or recorded and then reproduced (as with CDs, DVDs, or the other devices currently being developed in engineering labs worldwide). The financial importance of controlling music waves is staggering, and the rewards to engineers who develop new control techniques can be rich.

This chapter focuses on waves traveling along a stretched string, such as on a guitar. The next chapter focuses on sound waves, such as those produced by a guitar string being played. Before we do all this, though, our first job is to classify the countless waves of the everyday world into basic types.

16-2 | Propogation of Distance and Wave Equation

Types of Waves

Waves are of three main types:

1. ***Mechanical waves.*** These waves are most familiar because we encounter them almost constantly; common examples include water waves, sound waves, and seismic waves. All these waves have two central features: They are governed by Newton's laws, and they can exist only within a material medium, such as water, air, and rock.
2. ***Electromagnetic waves.*** These waves are less familiar, but you use them constantly; common examples include visible and ultraviolet light, radio and television waves, microwaves, x rays, and radar waves. These waves require no material medium to exist. Light waves from stars, for example, travel through the vacuum of space to reach us. All electromagnetic waves travel through a vacuum at the same speed $c = 299\,792\,458$ m/s.
3. ***Matter waves.*** Although these waves are commonly used in modern technology, they are probably very unfamiliar to you. These waves are associated with electrons, protons, and other fundamental particles, and even atoms and molecules. Because we commonly think of these particles as constituting matter, such waves are called matter waves.

Much of what we discuss in this chapter applies to waves of all kinds. However, for specific examples we shall refer to mechanical waves.

Transverse and Longitudinal Waves

A wave sent along a stretched, taut string is the simplest mechanical wave. If you give one end of a stretched string a single up-and-down jerk, a wave in the form of a single *pulse* travels along the string, as in Fig. 16-1*a*. This pulse and its motion can occur because the string is under tension. When you pull your end of the string upward, it begins to pull upward on the adjacent section of the string via tension between the two sections. As the adjacent section moves upward, it begins to pull the next section upward, and so on. Meanwhile, you have pulled down on your end of the string. As each section moves upward in turn, it begins to be pulled back downward by neighboring sections that are already on the way down. The net result is that a distortion in the string's shape (the pulse) moves along the string at some velocity $\vec{v}$.

If you move your hand up and down in continuous simple harmonic motion, a continuous wave travels along the string at velocity $\vec{v}$. Because the motion of your hand is a sinusoidal function of time, the wave has a sinusoidal shape at any

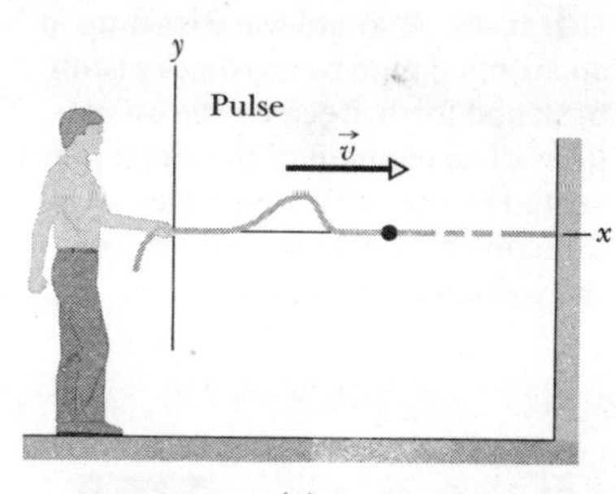

(*a*)

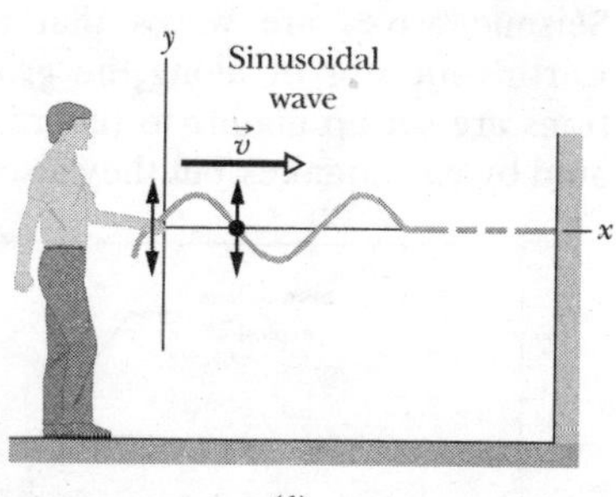

(*b*)

FIG. 16-1 (*a*) A single pulse is sent along a stretched string. A typical string element (marked with a dot) moves up once and then down as the pulse passes. The element's motion is perpendicular to the wave's direction of travel, so the pulse is a *transverse wave*. (*b*) A sinusoidal wave is sent along the string. A typical string element moves up and down continuously as the wave passes. This too is a transverse wave.

given instant, as in Fig. 16-1*b*; that is, the wave has the shape of a sine curve or a cosine curve.

We consider here only an "ideal" string, in which no friction-like forces within the string cause the wave to die out as it travels along the string. In addition, we assume that the string is so long that we need not consider a wave rebounding from the far end.

One way to study the waves of Fig. 16-1 is to monitor the **wave forms** (shapes of the waves) as they move to the right. Alternatively, we could monitor the motion of an element of the string as the element oscillates up and down while a wave passes through it. We would find that the displacement of every such oscillating string element is *perpendicular* to the direction of travel of the wave, as indicated in Fig. 16-1*b*. This motion is said to be **transverse,** and the wave is said to be a **transverse wave.**

Figure 16-2 shows how a sound wave can be produced by a piston in a long, air-filled pipe. If you suddenly move the piston rightward and then leftward, you can send a pulse of sound along the pipe. The rightward motion of the piston moves the elements of air next to it rightward, changing the air pressure there. The increased air pressure then pushes rightward on the elements of air somewhat farther along the pipe. Moving the piston leftward reduces the air pressure next to it. As a result, first the elements nearest the piston and then farther elements move leftward. Thus, the motion of the air and the change in air pressure travel rightward along the pipe as a pulse.

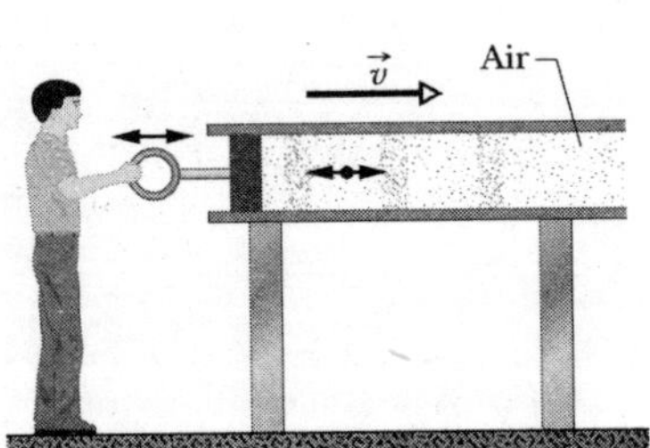

FIG. 16-2 A sound wave is set up in an air-filled pipe by moving a piston back and forth. Because the oscillations of an element of the air (represented by the dot) are parallel to the direction in which the wave travels, the wave is a *longitudinal wave.*

If you push and pull on the piston in simple harmonic motion, as is being done in Fig. 16-2, a sinusoidal wave travels along the pipe. Because the motion of the elements of air is parallel to the direction of the wave's travel, the motion is said to be **longitudinal,** and the wave is said to be a **longitudinal wave.** In this chapter we focus on transverse waves, and string waves in particular; in Chapter 17 we focus on longitudinal waves, and sound waves in particular.

Both a transverse wave and a longitudinal wave are said to be **traveling waves** because they both travel from one point to another, as from one end of the string to the other end in Fig. 16-1 and from one end of the pipe to the other end in Fig. 16-2. Note that it is the wave that moves from end to end, not the material (string or air) through which the wave moves.

Sample Problem 16-1

Seismic waves are waves that travel either through Earth's interior or along the ground. Seismology stations are set up mainly to record seismic waves generated by earthquakes, but they also record seismic waves generated by any large release of energy near Earth's surface, such as an explosion. As the seismic waves travel past a station, they oscillate a recording pen and the pen traces out a graph. Figure 16-3*a* is one of the graphs created by seismic waves from the mysterious sinking of the Russian submarine *Kursk* in August 2000. The first oscillations of the pen are marked with an arrow and were of small amplitude. Much stronger oscillations began about 134 s later.

From this, analysts concluded that the first seismic waves were generated by an onboard explosion, possibly

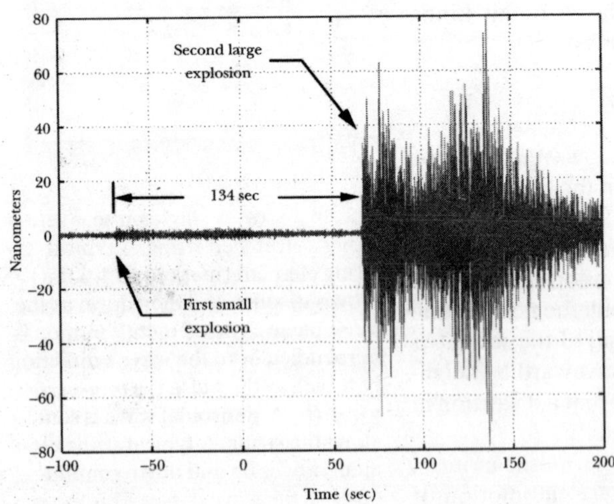

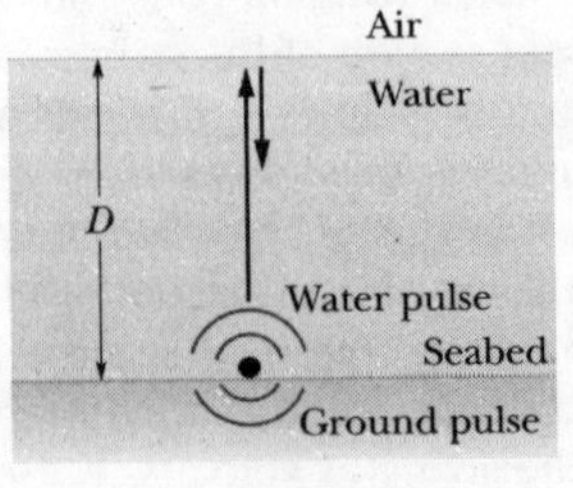

FIG. 16-3 (*a*) Graph made by a recording device as seismic waves from the *Kursk* passed the device. Amplitude is plotted vertically; time increases rightward. *(Courtesy of Jay Pulli/BBN Technologies)* (*b*) With the submarine sitting at depth D, the large explosion sent pulses both into the ground and up through the water.

a torpedo that failed to launch when fired. The explosion presumably breached the hull, started a fire, and sank the submarine. The later, much stronger seismic waves were generated after the submarine was sunk and were possibly generated when the fire caused several of the powerful missiles on board to explode simultaneously. These stronger waves arrived at seismology stations as pulses separated by a time interval Δt of about 0.11 s. To what depth D did the submarine sink?

Conceptualize/Classify: The speed of a sound is equal to the distance traveled divided by the travel time.

Compute: Let us assume that the stronger explosion occurred after the *Kursk* was sitting on the ocean floor (the seabed). That explosion sent a pulse into the seabed and a pulse upward through the water (Fig. 16-3*b*). The pulse traveling through the water "bounced" several times between the water surface and the seabed. Each time it hit the seabed, it sent another pulse into the ground, and seismology stations detected those ground pulses as they arrived one after another. Thus, the time Δt between any two detected ground pulses was equal to the round-trip time for the water pulse to travel up to the water surface and back to the seabed. From the equation $v_{avg} = \Delta x/\Delta t$, we can relate the speed v of the water pulse to the round-trip distance $2D$ and the round-trip time Δt as

$$v = \frac{2D}{\Delta t}$$

or

$$D = \frac{v\,\Delta t}{2} \tag{16-1}$$

Waves travel through seawater at about 1500 m/s. Substituting this value and $\Delta t = 0.11$ s in Eq. 16-1, we find that the seismic data predicted the sunken *Kursk* was at a depth of approximately

$$D = \frac{(1500 \text{ m/s})(0.11 \text{ s})}{2}$$

$$= 82.5 \text{ m} \approx 83 \text{ m} \qquad \text{(Answer)}$$

Conclude: In fact, the wreck was discovered at a depth of about 115 m.

16-3 | Wave Equation

Suppose we have a continuous, homogeneous string stretching from $x = 0$ to infinity. The string is attached at $x = 0$ to an oscillator, vibrating at constant frequency, that is shaking the string and thus producing the traveling wave along the string. Suppose that the displacement $y(t)$ of the output terminal is given by the harmonic oscillation

$$y(t) = A \sin \omega t \tag{16-2}$$

We wish to find the displacemetn $\Psi(x, t)$ of a moving part located at position x, where x is anywhere between $x = 0$ and infinity. We can easily find $\Psi(x, t)$ at $x = 0$. Since the string is tied directly to the oscillator, the displacement of the string at $x = 0$ is equal to $y(t)$:

$$\Psi(0, t) = y\,(t) = A \sin \omega t \tag{16-3}$$

We assume that wave travels with constant velocity as long as the properties of the medium remain constant. We also understand that the motion of a part of string at position x, at time t is the same as that of the string at $x = 0$ at some earlier time t'. Here t' is earlier than t by the time that the wave takes to travel the distance x at speed of wave v:

$$t' = t - \frac{x}{v}$$

Thus we have the form of a traveling sinusoidal wave,

$$\begin{aligned}\Psi(x, t) &= \Psi(0, t') \\ &= A \sin \omega t' \\ &= A \sin \omega \left(t - \frac{x}{v}\right) \\ &= A \sin \left(\omega t - \frac{\omega x}{v}\right)\end{aligned}$$

Note that at fixed x, $\Psi(x, t)$ is a harmonic oscillation in time.

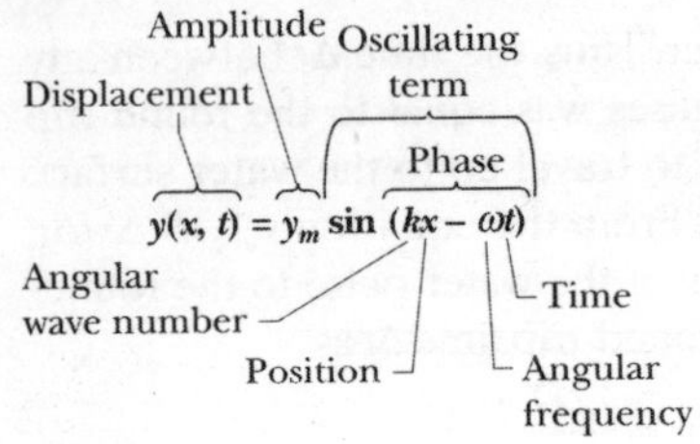

FIG. 16-4 The names of the quantities in Eq. 16-4, for a transverse sinusoidal wave.

Parameters

Wavelength and Frequency

To completely describe a wave on a string (and the motion of any element along its length), we need a function that gives the shape of the wave. This means that we need a relation in the form $y = h(x, t)$, in which y is the transverse displacement of any string element as a function h of the time t and the position x of the element along the string. In general, a sinusoidal shape like the wave in Fig. 16-1b can be described with h being either a sine or cosine function; both give the same general shape for the wave. In this chapter we use the sine function.

Imagine a sinusoidal wave like that of Fig. 16-1b traveling in the positive direction of an x axis. As the wave sweeps through succeeding elements (that is, very short sections) of the string, the elements oscillate parallel to the y axis. At time t, the displacement y of the element located at position x is given by

$$y(x, t) = y_m \sin(kx - \omega t) \tag{16-4}$$

Because this equation is written in terms of position x, it can be used to find the displacements of all the elements of the string as a function of time. Thus, it can tell us the shape of the wave at any given time and how that shape changes as the wave moves along the string.

The names of the quantities in Eq. 16-4 are displayed in Fig. 16-4 and defined next. Before we discuss them, however, let us examine Fig. 16-5, which shows five "snapshots" of a sinusoidal wave traveling in the positive direction of an x axis. The movement of the wave is indicated by the rightward progress of the short arrow pointing to a high point of the wave. From snapshot to snapshot, the short arrow moves to the right with the wave shape, but the string moves *only* parallel to the y axis. To see that, let us follow the motion of the red-dyed string element at $x = 0$. In the first snapshot (Fig. 16-5a), this element is at displacement $y = 0$. In the next snapshot, it is at its extreme downward displacement because a *valley* (or extreme low point) of the wave is passing through it. It then moves back up through $y = 0$. In the fourth snapshot, it is at its extreme upward displacement because a *peak* (or extreme high point) of the wave is passing through it. In the fifth snapshot, it is again at $y = 0$, having completed one full oscillation.

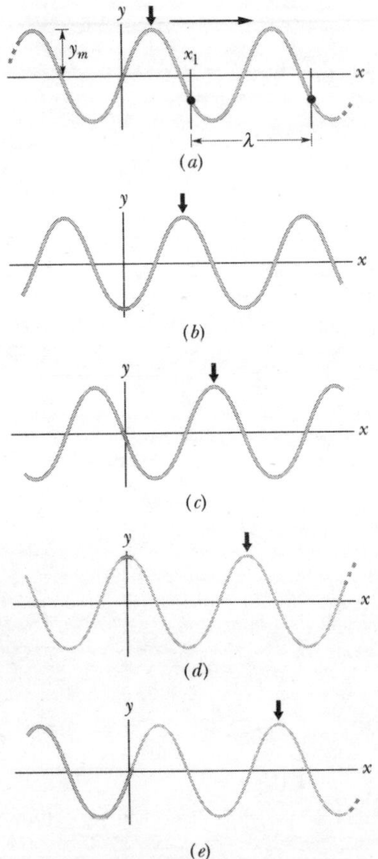

FIG. 16-5 Five "snapshots" of a string wave traveling in the positive direction of an x axis. The amplitude y_m is indicated. A typical wavelength λ, measured from an arbitrary position x_1, is also indicated.

Amplitude and Phase The **amplitude** y_m of a wave, such as that in Fig. 16-5, is the magnitude of the maximum displacement of the elements from their equilibrium positions as the wave passes through them. (The subscript m stands for maximum.) Because y_m is a magnitude, it is always a positive quantity, even if it is measured downward instead of upward as drawn in Fig. 16-5a.

The **phase** of the wave is the *argument* $kx - \omega t$ of the sine in Eq. 16-4. As the wave sweeps through a string element at a particular position x, the phase changes linearly with time t. This means that the sine also changes, oscillating between $+1$ and -1. Its extreme positive value ($+1$) corresponds to a peak of the wave moving through the element; at that instant the value of y at position x is y_m. Its extreme negative value (-1) corresponds to a valley of the wave moving through the element; at that instant the value of y at position x is $-y_m$. Thus, the sine function and the time-dependent phase of a wave correspond to the oscillation of a string element, and the amplitude of the wave determines the extremes of the element's displacement.

Wavelength and Angular Wave Number The **wavelength** λ of a wave is the distance (parallel to the direction of the wave's travel) between repetitions of the shape of the wave (or *wave shape*). A typical wavelength is marked in Fig. 16-5a, which is a snapshot of the wave at time $t = 0$. At that time, Eq. 16-4 gives, for the description of the wave shape,

$$y(x,0) = y_m \sin kx \tag{16-5}$$

By definition, the displacement y is the same at both ends of this wavelength—that is, at $x = x_1$ and $x = x_1 + \lambda$. Thus, by Eq. 16-5,

$$\begin{aligned} y_m \sin kx_1 &= y_m \sin k(x_1 + \lambda) \\ &= y_m \sin(kx_1 + k\lambda) \end{aligned} \tag{16-6}$$

A sine function begins to repeat itself when its angle (or argument) is increased by 2π rad, so in Eq. 16-6 we must have $k\lambda = 2\pi$, or

$$k = \frac{2\pi}{\lambda} \quad \text{(angular wave number)} \tag{16-7}$$

We call k the **angular wave number** of the wave; its SI unit is the radian per meter, or the inverse meter. (Note that the symbol k here does *not* represent a spring constant as previously.)

Notice that the wave in Fig. 16-5 moves to the right by $1/4\lambda$ from one snapshot to the next. Thus, by the fifth snapshot, it has moved to the right by 1λ.

Phase Difference

Suppose the oscillation of the particle at $x = 0$ is simple harmonic of angular frequency ω. Its displacement with time t will be given by $y = a \sin \omega t$, where a is the amplitude of the oscillation. If the wave generated travels from left to right, a particle at P, distance x from O, will lag in phase by some phase angle β. As all the disturbances reaching the point p take time $t_1 = x/c$, after passing through O. For the displacement y of the particle at P, we can write

FIG. 16-6 Particles at x_1 and at x_2 are in phase.

AQ:1

$$y = a \sin (\omega t - \beta)$$

thus $\beta = \omega t_1 = \omega x/c$. Substituting for β in the above equation, we get

$$\begin{aligned} y &= a \sin (\omega t - \beta x/c) \\ &= a \sin (\omega t - kx) \end{aligned}$$

where $k = \omega/c$

If the wave traveled in the opposite direction, the vibration at P would lead on that at O by β and the displacement y at P would be written as

$$y = a \sin (\omega t + kx)$$

This is the equation for a wave traveling from right to left.

Phase difference between x_2 and x_1 is $\Delta\phi = \frac{\omega}{V}(x_2\ x_1)$. Note that for wave traveling in positive direction x_2 is behind x_1 by this amount and vice versa that is, for wave traveling in negative direction x_1 is behind x_2 by this amount.

Phase Constant

When a sinusoidal traveling wave is given by the wave function of Eq. 16-4, the wave near $x = 0$ looks like Fig. 16-7*a* when $t = 0$. Note that at $x = 0$, the displacement is $y = 0$ and the slope is at its maximum positive value. We can generalize Eq. 16-4 by inserting a **phase constant** ϕ in the wave function:

$$y = y_m \sin(kx - \omega t + \phi) \tag{16-8}$$

The value of ϕ can be chosen so that the function gives some other displacement and slope at $x = 0$ when $t = 0$. For example, a choice of $\phi = +\pi/5$ rad gives the displacement and slope shown in Fig. 16-7*b* when $t = 0$. The wave is still sinusoidal with the same values of y_m, k, and ω, but it is now shifted from what you see in Fig. 16-7*a* (where $\phi = 0$).

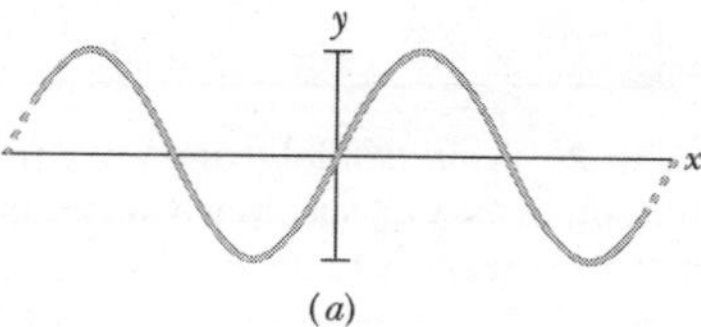

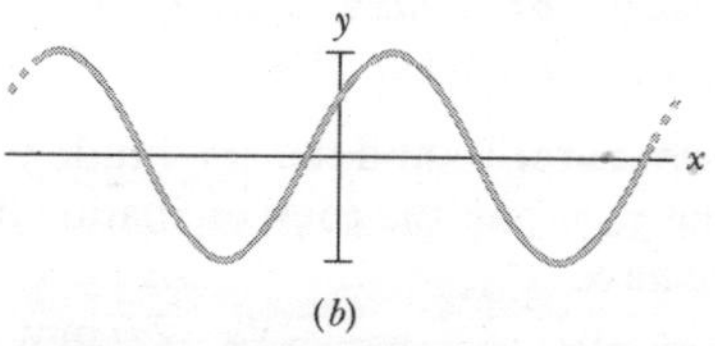

FIG. 16-7 A sinusoidal traveling wave at $t = 0$ with a phase constant ϕ of (*a*) 0 and (*b*) $\pi/5$ rad.

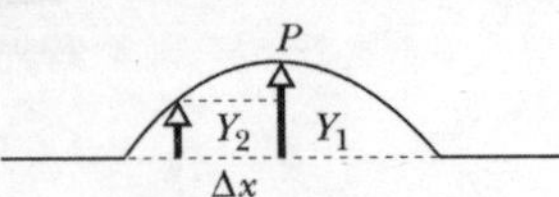

FIG. 16-8 Disturbance reaches P traveling distance dx and taking it from y_1 to y_2 height.

Velocity of Particle and Slope

Let us study Fig. 16-8 which shows a moving particle. In time Δt particle at p will move $y_1 - y_2$ downward or in other words wave would have traveled dx in the same time.

$\Delta t = \dfrac{y_1 - y_2}{V_p} = -\dfrac{\Delta y}{v_p}$ and $\Delta t = \dfrac{\Delta x}{c}$ equating the time durations and applying limit Δt approach zero, we get

$V_p = -\left[\dfrac{\partial y}{\partial x}\right]c$ partial derivative is being used as the y depends on both x and t.

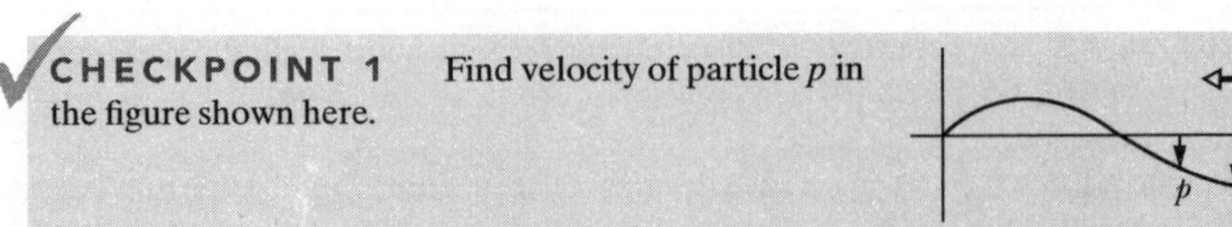

CHECKPOINT 1 Find velocity of particle p in the figure shown here.

Sample Problem 16-2

A sinusoidal wave moving along a siring in the positive direction of an x axis was recorded on video tape. The curves in Fig. 16-9 represent the wave in two freeze-frames of the tape, first as the solid curve and their, 1.0 ms later, as the dotted curve. The grid lines along the x axis are 1.0 cm apart. Each string element oscillated vertically (perpendicular to the x axis) a total distance of 4.0 mm as the wave passed through it. The wave moved a distance $d = 3.16$ cm to the right in the 1.0 ms time interval. Write an equation for this wave in the form

$$y(x, t) = y_m \sin(kx \pm wt) \qquad (16\text{–}9)$$

where ± indicates that the proper sign must be determined.

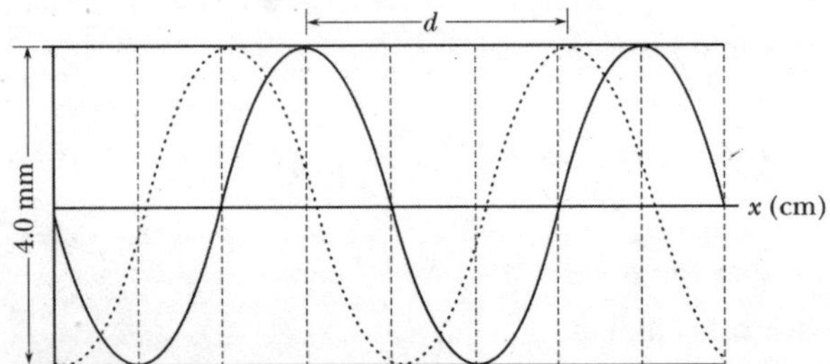

FIG. 16-9 A sinusoidal string wave traveling in the positive direction of an x axis is shown at two instants, between which the wave travels distance d.

(a) *Conceptualize/Classify:* We need to find values for y_m, k, and ω in Eq. 16-9.

Compute: To find the amplitude y_m, we use the key idea that y_m is half the total oscillation distance of 4.0 mm, so we have

$$y_m = 2.0 \text{ mm}$$

(b) *Conceptualize/Classify:* To find angular wave number k, we used two key ideas: First, k is related to the wavelength λ by $k = 2\pi/\Lambda$. Second, we can determine λ from Fig. 16-9 by measuring the distance (parallel to the x axis) between repetitions of the wave shape.

Compute: Let's use, say, the solid curve and pick the point at which it crosses the x axis at the third vertical grid line from the left. That curve makes an identical crossing 4 grid lines to the right of the first point. Thus, $\lambda = 4 \times 1.0$ cm $= 4.0$ cm, and so

$$k = \frac{2\pi}{\lambda} = \frac{2\pi}{0.040 \text{ m}} = 157 \text{ m}^{-1} \approx 160 \text{ m}^{-1}$$

(c) *Conceptualize/Classify:* To find angular frequency ω, we again need two **key ideas**: First, ω is related to k and the wave speed v by $v - \omega/k$. Second, v is the ratio of the distance d traveled by the wave to the time interval Δt required for the travel.

Compute: From equation $v - \omega/k$ and the given data, we get

$$\omega = kv = k\frac{d}{\Delta t} = (157 \text{ m}^{-1})\frac{0.0316 \text{ m}}{0.0010 \text{ s}} = 496.1 \text{ s}^{-1} \approx 500 \text{ s}^{-1}$$

(d) *Conceptualize/Classify:* An additional key idea is that, because the wave is moving in the positive direction of the x axis, we must use the minus sign in Eq. 16-9

Compute: We can now rewrite that equation as

$$y(x, t) = (2.0 \text{ mm}) \sin[(160 \text{ m}^{-1})x - (5000 \text{ s}^{-1})t] \quad \text{(Answer)}$$

with y in millimeters, x in meters, and t in seconds.

Conclude: In this question all the information was given graphically and we got the result in form of equation. We can verify the result by putting values of time as 0 and 1 ms and drawing the shape and matching it with the given figure.

16-4 | Speed of Waves on String

Speed of a Traveling Wave

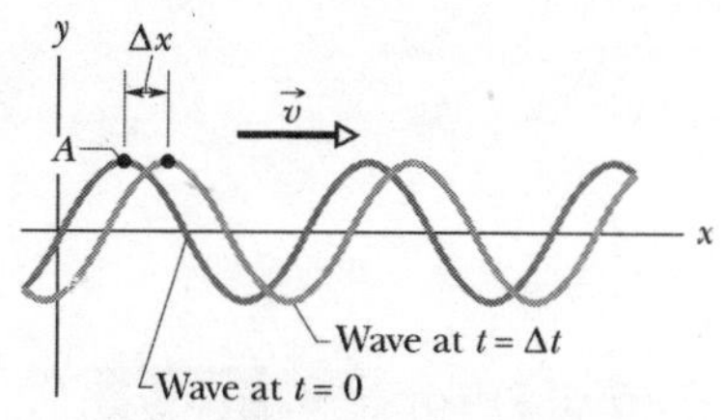

FIG. 16-10 Two snapshots of the wave of Fig. 16-5, at time $t = 0$ and then at time $t = \Delta t$. As the wave moves to the right at velocity $\vec{v}$, the entire curve shifts a distance Δx during Δt. Point A "rides" with the wave form, but the string elements move only up and down.

Figure 16-10 shows two snapshots of the wave of Eq. 16-4, taken a small time interval Δt apart. The wave is traveling in the positive direction of x (to the right in Fig. 16-10), the entire wave pattern moving a distance Δx in that direction during the interval Δt. The ratio $\Delta x/\Delta t$ (or, in the differential limit, dx/dt) is the **wave speed** v. How can we find its value?

As the wave in Fig. 16-10 moves, each point of the moving wave form, such as point A marked on a peak, retains its displacement y. (Points on the string do not retain their displacement, but points on the wave *form* do.) If point A retains its displacement as it moves, the phase in Eq. 16-4 giving it that displacement must remain a constant:

$$kx - \omega t = \text{a constant} \tag{16-10}$$

Note that although this argument is constant, both x and t are changing. In fact, as t increases, x must also, to keep the argument constant. This confirms that the wave pattern is moving in the positive direction of x.

To find the wave speed v, we take the derivative of Eq. 16-10, getting

$$k\frac{dx}{dt} - \omega = 0$$

or

$$\frac{dx}{dt} = v = \frac{\omega}{k} \tag{16-11}$$

Using equation $k = 2\pi/\lambda$ and equation $\omega = 2\pi/T$, we can rewrite the wave speed as

$$v = \frac{\omega}{k} = \frac{\lambda}{T} = \lambda f \quad \text{(wave speed)} \tag{16-12}$$

The equation $v = \lambda/T$ tells us that the wave speed is one wavelength per period; the wave moves a distance of one wavelength in one period of oscillation.

Equation 16-4 describes a wave moving in the positive direction of x. We can find the equation of a wave traveling in the opposite direction by replacing t in Eq. 16-4 with $-t$. This corresponds to the condition

$$kx + \omega t = \text{a constant} \tag{16-13}$$

which (compare Eq. 16-10) requires that x *decrease* with time. Thus, a wave traveling in the negative direction of x is described by the equation

$$y(x, t) = y_m \sin(kx + \omega t) \tag{16-14}$$

If you analyze the wave of Eq. 16-14 as we have just done for the wave of Eq. 16-4, you will find for its velocity

$$\frac{dx}{dt} = -\frac{\omega}{k} \tag{16-15}$$

The minus sign (compare Eq. 16-11) verifies that the wave is indeed moving in the negative direction of x and justifies our switching the sign of the time variable.

Consider now a wave of arbitrary shape, given by

$$y(x, t) = h(kx \pm \omega t) \tag{16-16}$$

where h represents *any* function, the sine function being one possibility. Our previous analysis shows that all waves in which the variables x and t enter into the combination $kx \pm \omega t$ are traveling waves. Furthermore, all traveling waves *must* be of the form of Eq. 16-16. Thus, $y(x, t) = \sqrt{ax + bt}$ represents a possible (though perhaps physically a little bizarre) traveling wave. The function $y(x, t) = \sin(ax^2 - bt)$, on the other hand, does *not* represent a traveling wave.

CHECKPOINT 2 Here are the equations of three waves: (1) $y(x, t) = 2\sin(4x - 2t)$, (2) $y(x, t) = \sin(3x - 4t)$, (3) $y(x, t) = 2\sin(3x - 3t)$. Rank the waves according to their (a) wave speed and (b) maximum speed perpendicular to the wave's direction of travel (the transverse speed), greatest first.

Sample Problem 16-3

A wave traveling along a string is described by

$$y(x, t) = 0.00327\sin(72.1x - 2.72t) \qquad (16\text{-}17)$$

in which the numerical constants are in SI units (0.00327 m, 72.1 rad/m, and 2.72 rad/s).

(a) What is the amplitude of this wave?

Conceptualize: Equation 16-15 is of the same form as Eq. 16-4,

$$y = y_m \sin(kx - \omega t) \qquad (16\text{-}18)$$

so we have a sinusoidal wave.

Classify: By comparing the two equations, we can find the amplitude.

Compute: We see that

$$y_m = 0.00327 \text{ m} = 3.27 \text{ mm} \qquad \text{(Answer)}$$

(b) What are the wavelength, period, and frequency of this wave?

Compute: By comparing Eqs. 16-17 and 16-18, we see that the angular wave number and angular frequency are

$$k = 72.1 \text{ rad/m} \quad \text{and} \quad \omega = 2.72 \text{ rad/s}$$

We then relate wavelength λ to k via Eq. 16-5:

$$\lambda = \frac{2\pi}{k} = \frac{2\pi \text{ rad}}{72.1 \text{ rad/m}}$$

$$= 0.0871 \text{ m} = 8.71 \text{ cm} \qquad \text{(Answer)}$$

Next, we relate T to ω with Eq. 16-10:

$$T = \frac{2\pi}{\omega} = \frac{2\pi \text{rad}}{2.72 \text{ rad/s}} = 2.31 \text{ s} \qquad \text{(Answer)}$$

and from Eq. 16-11 we have

$$f = \frac{1}{T} = \frac{1}{2.31 \text{ s}} = 0.433 \text{ Hz} \qquad \text{(Answer)}$$

(c) What is the velocity of this wave?

Compute: The speed of the wave is given by Eq. 16-12:

$$v = \frac{\omega}{k} = \frac{2.72 \text{ rad/s}}{72.1 \text{ rad/m}} = 0.0377 \text{ m/s}$$

$$= 3.77 \text{ cm/s} \qquad \text{(Answer)}$$

Conclude: Because the phase in Eq. 16-17 contains the position variable x, the wave is moving along the x axis. Also, because the wave equation is written in the form of Eq. 16-4, the *minus* sign in front of the ωt term indicates that the wave is moving in the *positive* direction of the x axis. (Note that the quantities calculated in (b) and (c) are independent of the amplitude of the wave.)

(d) What is the displacement y at $x = 22.5$ cm and $t = 18.9$ s?

Compute: Equation 16-17 gives the displacement as a function of position x and time t. Substituting the given values into the equation yields

$$y = 0.00327\sin(72.1 \times 0.225 - 2.72 \times 18.9)$$

$$= (0.00327 \text{ m})\sin(-35.1855 \text{ rad})$$

$$= (0.00327 \text{ m})(0.588)$$

$$= 0.00192 \text{ m} = 1.92 \text{ mm} \qquad \text{(Answer)}$$

Thus, the displacement is positive.

Sample Problem 16-4

In Sample Problem 16-3*d*, we showed that at $t = 18.9$ s the transverse displacement y of the element of the string at $x = 0.255$ m due to the wave of Eq. 16-17 is 1.92 mm.

(a) What is u, the transverse velocity of the same element of the string, at that time? (This velocity, which is associated with the transverse oscillation of an element of the string, is in the y direction. Do not confuse it with v, the constant velocity at which the *wave form* travels along the x axis.)

Conceptualize/Classify: The transverse velocity u is the rate at which the displacement y of the element is changing. In general, that displacement is given by

$$y(x, t) = y_m \sin(kx - \omega t) \qquad (16\text{-}19)$$

For an element at a certain location x, we find the rate of change of y by taking the derivative of Eq. 16-19 with respect to t while treating x as a constant. A derivative taken while one (or more) of the variables is treated as a constant is called a *partial derivative* and is represented by the symbol $\partial/\partial x$ rather than d/dx.

Compute: Here we have

$$u = \frac{\partial y}{\partial t} = -\omega y_m \cos(kx - \omega t) \qquad (16\text{-}20)$$

Next, substituting numerical values from Sample Problem 16-3, we obtain

$$u = (-2.72 \text{ rad/s})(3.27 \text{ mm}) \cos(-35.1855 \text{ rad})$$
$$= 7.20 \text{ mm/s} \qquad \text{(Answer)}$$

Conclude: Thus, at $t = 18.9$ s, the element of the string at $x = 22.5$ cm is moving in the positive direction of y with a speed of 7.20 mm/s.

(b) What is the transverse acceleration a_y of the same element at that time?

Conceptualize/Classify: The transverse acceleration a_y is the rate at which the transverse velocity of the element is changing.

Compute: From Eq. 16-20, again treating x as a constant but allowing t to vary, we find

$$a_y = \frac{\partial u}{\partial t} = -\omega^2 y_m \sin(kx - \omega t)$$

Comparison with Eq. 16-19 shows that we can write this as

$$a_y = -\omega^2 y$$

We see that the transverse acceleration of an oscillating string element is proportional to its transverse displacement but opposite in sign. This is completely consistent with the action of the element itself—namely, that it is moving transversely in simple harmonic motion. Substituting numerical values yields

$$a_y = -(2.72 \text{ rad/s})^2(1.92 \text{ mm})$$
$$= -14.2 \text{ mm/s}^2 \qquad \text{(Answer)}$$

Conclude: Thus, at $t = 18.9$ s, the element of string at $x = 22.5$ cm is displaced from its equilibrium position by 1.92 mm in the positive y direction and has an acceleration of magnitude 14.2 mm/s² in the negative y direction.

PROBLEM-SOLVING TACTICS

Tactic 1: Evaluating Large Phases Sometimes, as in Sample Problems 16-2*d* and 16-3, an angle much greater than 2π rad (or 360°) crops up and you are asked to find its sine or cosine. Adding or subtracting an integral multiple of 2π rad to such an angle does not change the value of any of its trigonometric functions. In Sample Problem 16-3*d*, for example, we used the angle -35.1855 rad in a sine function. Adding $(6)(2\pi \text{ rad})$ to this angle yields

$$-35.1855 \text{ rad} + (6)(2\pi \text{ rad}) = 2.51361 \text{ rad}$$

an angle of less than 2π rad that has the same trigonometric functions as -35.1855 rad (Fig. 16-11). As an example, the sine of both 2.51361 rad and -35.1855 rad is 0.588.

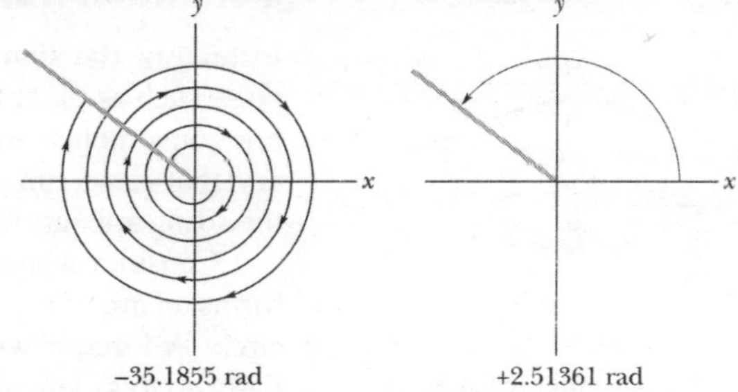

FIG. 16-11 These two angles are different, but all their trigonometric functions are identical.

Caution: Do not round off large angles if you intend to take their sines or cosines. In taking the sine of a very large angle, you are throwing away most of the angle and taking the sine of what is left over. If, for example, you were to round -35.1855 rad to -35 rad (a change of 0.5% and normally a reasonable step), you would be changing the sine of the angle by 27%. Also, if you change a large angle from degrees to radians, be sure to use an exact conversion factor (such as $180° = \pi$ rad) rather than an approximate one (such as $57.3° \approx 1$ rad).

Wave Speed on a Stretched String

The speed of a wave is related to the wave's wavelength and frequency by Eq. 16-12, but *it is set by the properties of the medium.* If a wave is to travel through a medium such as water, air, steel, or a stretched string, it must cause the particles of that medium to oscillate as it passes. For that to happen, the medium must possess both mass (so that there can be kinetic energy) and elasticity (so that there can be potential energy). Thus, the medium's mass and elasticity properties determine how fast the wave can travel in the medium. Conversely, it should be possible to calculate the speed of the wave through the medium in terms of these properties. We do so now for a stretched string, in two ways.

Dimensional Analysis

In dimensional analysis, we carefully examine the dimensions of all the physical quantities that enter into a given situation to determine the quantities they produce. In this case, we examine mass and elasticity to find a speed v, which has the dimension of length divided by time, or LT^{-1}.

For the mass, we use the mass of a string element, which is the mass m of the string divided by the length l of the string. We call this ratio the *linear density* μ of the string. Thus, $\mu = m/l$, its dimension being mass divided by length, ML^{-1}.

You cannot send a wave along a string unless the string is under tension, which means that it has been stretched and pulled taut by forces at its two ends. The tension τ in the string is equal to the common magnitude of those two forces. As a wave travels along the string, it displaces elements of the string by causing additional stretching, with adjacent sections of string pulling on each other because of the tension. Thus, we can associate the tension in the string with the stretching (elasticity) of the string. The tension and the stretching forces it produces have the dimension of a force—namely, MLT^{-2} (from $F = ma$).

We need to combine μ (dimension ML^{-1}) and τ (dimension MLT^{-2}) to get v (dimension LT^{-1}). A little juggling of various combinations suggests

$$v = C\sqrt{\frac{\tau}{\mu}} \tag{16-21}$$

in which C is a dimensionless constant that cannot be determined with dimensional analysis. In our second approach to determining wave speed, you will see that Eq. 16-21 is indeed correct and that $C = 1$.

Derivation from Newton's Second Law

Instead of the sinusoidal wave of Fig. 16-1*b*, let us consider a single symmetrical pulse such as that of Fig. 16-12, moving from left to right along a string with speed v. For convenience, we choose a reference frame in which the pulse remains stationary; that is, we run along with the pulse, keeping it constantly in view. In this frame, the string appears to move past us, from right to left in Fig. 16-12, with speed v.

Consider a small string element of length Δl within the pulse, an element that forms an arc of a circle of radius R and subtending an angle 2θ at the center of that circle. A force $\vec{\tau}$ with a magnitude equal to the tension in the string pulls tangentially on this element at each end. The horizontal components of these forces cancel, but the vertical components add to form a radial restoring force $\vec{F}$. In magnitude,

$$F = 2(\tau \sin \theta) \approx \tau(2\theta) = \tau\frac{\Delta l}{R} \quad \text{(force)} \tag{16-22}$$

where we have approximated $\sin \theta$ as θ for the small angles θ in Fig. 16-12. From that figure, we have also used $2\theta = \Delta l/R$. The mass of the element is given by

$$\Delta m = \mu\,\Delta l \quad \text{(mass)} \tag{16-23}$$

where μ is the string's linear density.

At the moment shown in Fig. 16-12, the string element Δl is moving in an arc of a circle. Thus, it has a centripetal acceleration toward the center of that circle, given by

$$a = \frac{v^2}{R} \quad \text{(acceleration)} \tag{16-24}$$

Equations 16-22, 16-23, and 16-24 contain the elements of Newton's second law. Combining them in the form

$$\text{force} = \text{mass} \times \text{acceleration}$$

FIG. 16-12 A symmetrical pulse, viewed from a reference frame in which the pulse is stationary and the string appears to move right to left with speed v. We find speed v by applying Newton's second law to a string element of length Δl, located at the top of the pulse.

gives
$$\frac{\tau \Delta l}{R} = (\mu \Delta l)\frac{v^2}{R}$$
Solving this equation for the speed v yields
$$v = \sqrt{\frac{\tau}{\mu}} \quad \text{(speed)} \qquad (16\text{-}25)$$
in exact agreement with Eq. 16-21 if the constant C in that equation is given the value unity. Equation 16-25 gives the speed of the pulse in Fig. 16-12 and the speed of *any* other wave on the same string under the same tension.

Equation 16-25 tells us:

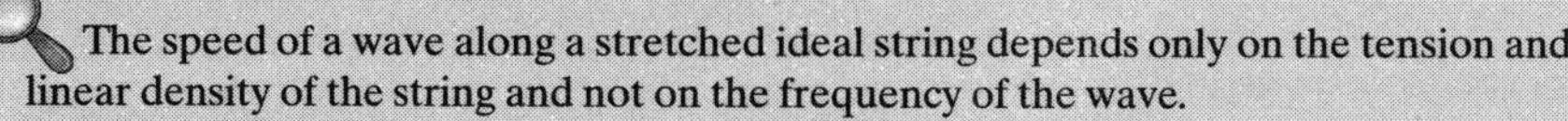
The speed of a wave along a stretched ideal string depends only on the tension and linear density of the string and not on the frequency of the wave.

The *frequency* of the wave is fixed entirely by whatever generates the wave (for example, the person in Fig. 16-1*b*). The *wavelength* of the wave is then fixed by Eq. 16-12 in the form $\lambda = v/f$.

CHECKPOINT 3 You send a traveling wave along a particular string by oscillating one end. If you increase the frequency of the oscillations, do (a) the speed of the wave and (b) the wavelength of the wave increase, decrease, or remain the same? If, instead, you increase the tension in the string, do (c) the speed of the wave and (d) the wavelength of the wave increase, decrease, or remain the same?

Sample Problem 16-5

In Fig. 16-13, two strings have been tied together with a knot and then stretched between two rigid supports. The strings have linear densities $\mu_1 = 1.4 \times 10^{-4}$ kg/m and $\mu_2 = 2.8 \times 10^{-4}$ kg/m. Their lengths are $L_1 = 3.0$ m and $L_2 = 2.0$ m, and string 1 is under a tension of 400 N. Simultaneously, on each string a pulse is sent from the rigid support end, toward the knot. Which pulse reaches the knot first?

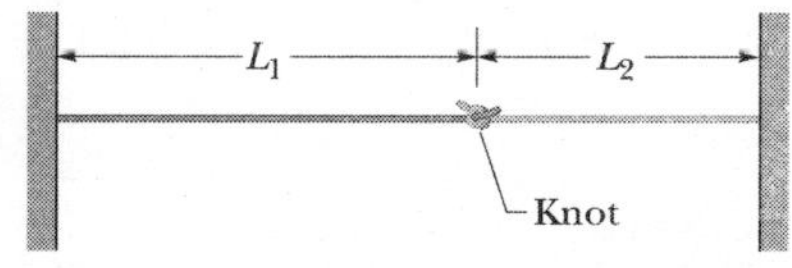

FIG. 16-13 Two strings, of lengths L_1 and L_2, tied together with a knot and stretched between two rigid supports.

Conceptualize/Classify:

1. The time t taken by a pulse to travel a length L is $t = L/v$, where v is the constant speed of the pulse.
2. The speed of a pulse on a stretched string depends on the string's tension τ and linear density μ, and is given by equation $v = \sqrt{\tau/\mu}$.
3. Because the two strings are stretched together, they must both be under the same tension τ (= 400 N).

Compute: Putting these three ideas together gives us, as the time for the pulse on string 1 to reach the knot,
$$t_1 = \frac{L_1}{v_1} = L_1\sqrt{\frac{\mu_1}{\tau}} = (3.0\text{ m})\sqrt{\frac{1.4 \times 10^{-4}\text{ kg/m}}{400\text{ N}}}$$
$$= 1.77 \times 10^{-3}\text{ s}.$$
Similarly, the data for the pulse on string 2 give us
$$t_2 = L_2\sqrt{\frac{\mu_2}{\tau}} = 1.67 \times 10^{-3}\text{ s}$$
Thus, the pulse on string 2 reaches the knot first.

Conclude: Now look back at the second point. The linear density of string 2 is greater than that of string 1, so the pulse on string 2 must be slower than that on string 1. Could we have guessed the answer from that fact alone? No, because from the first point we see that the distance traveled by a pulse also matters.

16-5 | General Equation of Wave

The Wave Equation

As a wave passes through any element on a stretched string, the element moves perpendicularly to the wave's direction of travel. By applying Newton's second law to the element's motion, we can derive a general differential equation, called the *wave equation*, that governs the travel of waves of any type.

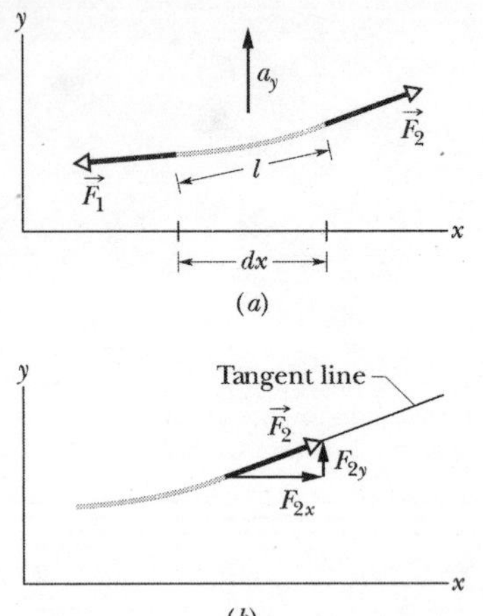

FIG. 16-14 (*a*) A string element as a sinusoidal transverse wave travels on a stretched string. Forces $\vec{F}_1$ and $\vec{F}_2$ act at the left and right ends, producing acceleration $\vec{a}$ having a vertical component a_y. (*b*) The force at the element's right end is directed along a tangent to the element's right side.

Figure 16-14*a* shows a snapshot of a string element of mass dm and length ℓ as a wave travels along a string of linear density μ that is stretched along a horizontal x axis. Let us assume that the wave amplitude is small so that the element can be tilted only slightly from the x axis as the wave passes. The force $\vec{F}_2$ on the right end of the element has a magnitude equal to tension τ in the string and is directed slightly upward. The force $\vec{F}_1$ on the left end of the element also has a magnitude equal to the tension τ but is directed slightly downward. Because of the slight curvature of the element, these two forces produce a net force that causes the element to have an upward acceleration a_y. Newton's second law written for y components ($F_{\text{net},y} = ma_y$) gives us

$$F_{2y} - F_{1y} = dm\, a_y \tag{16-26}$$

Let's analyze this equation in parts.

Mass. The element's mass dm can be written in terms of the string's linear density μ and the element's length ℓ as $dm = \mu\ell$. Because the element can have only a slight tilt, $\ell \approx dx$ (Fig. 16-14*a*) and we have the approximation

$$dm = \mu\, dx \tag{16-27}$$

Acceleration. The acceleration a_y in Eq. 16-26 is the second derivative of the displacement y with respect to time:

$$a_y = \frac{d^2y}{dt^2} \tag{16-28}$$

Forces. Figure 16-14*b* shows that $\vec{F}_2$ is tangent to the string at the right end of the string element. Thus we can relate the components of the force to the string slope S_2 at the right end as

$$\frac{F_{2y}}{F_{2x}} = S_2 \tag{16-29}$$

We can also relate the components to the magnitude F_2 ($= \tau$) with

$$F_2 = \sqrt{F_{2x}^2 + F_{2y}^2}$$

or

$$\tau = \sqrt{F_{2x}^2 + F_{2y}^2} \tag{16-30}$$

However, because we assume that the element is only slightly tilted, $F_{2y} \ll F_{2x}$ and therefore we can rewrite Eq. 16-30 as

$$\tau = F_{2x} \tag{16-31}$$

Substituting this into Eq. 16-29 and solving for F_{2y} yield

$$F_{2y} = \tau S_2 \tag{16-32}$$

Similar analysis at the left end of the string element gives us

$$F_{1y} = \tau S_1 \tag{16-33}$$

We can now substitute Eqs. 16-27, 16-28, 16-32, and 16-33 into Eq. 16-26 to write

$$\tau S_2 - \tau S_1 = (\mu dx)\frac{d^2y}{dt^2}$$

or

$$\frac{S_2 - S_1}{dx} = \frac{\mu}{\tau}\frac{d^2y}{dt^2} \tag{16-34}$$

Because the string element is short, slopes S_2 and S_1 differ by only a differential amount dS, where S is the slope at any point:

$$S = \frac{dy}{dx} \tag{16-35}$$

First replacing $S_2 - S_1$ in Eq. 16-34 with dS and then using Eq. 16-35 to substitute dy/dx for S, we find

$$\frac{dS}{dx} = \frac{\mu}{\tau}\frac{d^2y}{dt^2}$$

$$\frac{d(dy/dx)}{dx} = \frac{\mu}{\tau}\frac{d^2y}{dt^2}$$

and
$$\frac{\partial^2 y}{\partial x^2} = \frac{\mu}{\tau}\frac{\partial^2 y}{\partial t^2} \tag{16-36}$$

In the last step, we switched to the notation of partial derivatives because on the left we differentiate only with respect to x and on the right we differentiate only with respect to t. Finally, substituting from equation $v = \sqrt{\tau/\mu}$, we find

$$\frac{\partial^2 y}{\partial x^2} = \frac{1}{v^2}\frac{\partial^2 y}{\partial t^2} \quad \text{(wave equation)} \tag{16-37}$$

This is the general differential equation that governs the travel of waves of all types.

16-6 | Phasors

We can represent a string wave (or any other type of wave) vectorially with a **phasor.** In essence, a phasor is a vector that has a magnitude equal to the amplitude of the wave and that rotates around an origin; the angular speed of the phasor is equal to the angular frequency ω of the wave. For example, the wave

$$y_1(x, t) = y_{m1}\sin(kx - \omega t) \tag{16-38}$$

is represented by the phasor shown in Fig. 16-15a. The magnitude of the phasor is the amplitude y_{m1} of the wave. As the phasor rotates around the origin at angular speed ω, its projection y_1 on the vertical axis varies sinusoidally, from a maximum of y_{m1} through zero to a minimum of $-y_{m1}$ and then back to y_{m1}. This variation corresponds to the sinusoidal variation in the displacement y_1 of any point along the string as the wave passes through that point.

When two waves travel along the same string in the same direction, we can represent them and their resultant wave in a *phasor diagram*. The phasors in Fig. 16-15b represent the wave of Eq. 16-38 and a second wave given by

$$y_2(x, t) = y_{m2}\sin(kx - \omega t + \phi) \tag{16-39}$$

This second wave is phase-shifted from the first wave by phase constant ϕ. Because the phasors rotate at the same angular speed ω, the angle between the two phasors is always ϕ. If ϕ is a *positive* quantity, then the phasor for wave 2 *lags* the phasor for wave 1 as they rotate, as drawn in Fig. 16-15b. If ϕ is a negative quantity, then the phasor for wave 2 *leads* the phasor for wave 1.

Because waves y_1 and y_2 have the same angular wave number k and angular frequency ω,

$$y'(x, t) = y'_m\sin(kx - \omega t + \beta) \tag{16-40}$$

where y'_m is the amplitude of the resultant wave and β is its phase constant. To find the values of y'_m and β, we would have to sum the two combining waves. To do this on a phasor diagram, we vectorially add the two phasors at any instant during their rotation, as in Fig. 16-15c where phasor y_{m2} has been shifted to the head of phasor y_{m1}. The magnitude of the vector sum equals the amplitude y'_m in Eq. 16-40. The angle between the vector sum and the phasor for y_1 equals the phase constant β in Eq. 16-40.

We can use phasors to combine waves *even if their amplitudes are different.*

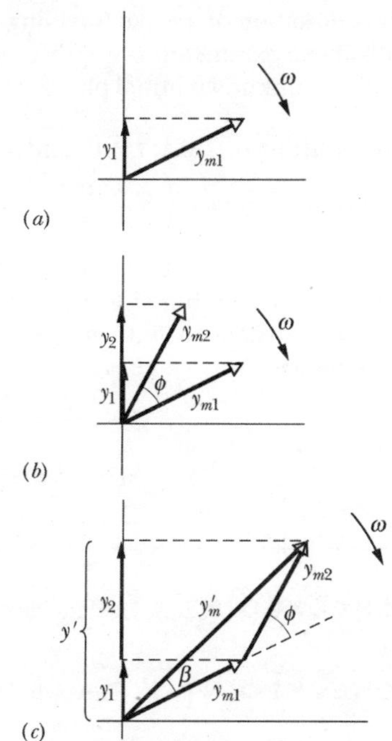

FIG. 16-15 (a) A phasor of magnitude y_{m1} rotating about an origin at angular speed ω represents a sinusoidal wave. The phasor's projection y_1 on the vertical axis represents the displacement of a point through which the wave passes. (b) A second phasor, also of angular speed ω but of magnitude y_{m2} and rotating at a constant angle ϕ from the first phasor, represents a second wave, with a phase constant ϕ. (c) The resultant wave is represented by the vector sum y'_m of the two phasors.

Sample Problem 16-6

A sinusoidal wave with amplitude $A = 0.5$ mm and wavelength $\lambda = 0.4$ m, is traveling on a string with speed $V = 12$m/s. At $t = 0$ particle at $x = 0.1$ m is located at $y = 0.25$ mm and going down. (a) Find equation of wave and (b) plot the sinusoidal wave at $t = 0$.

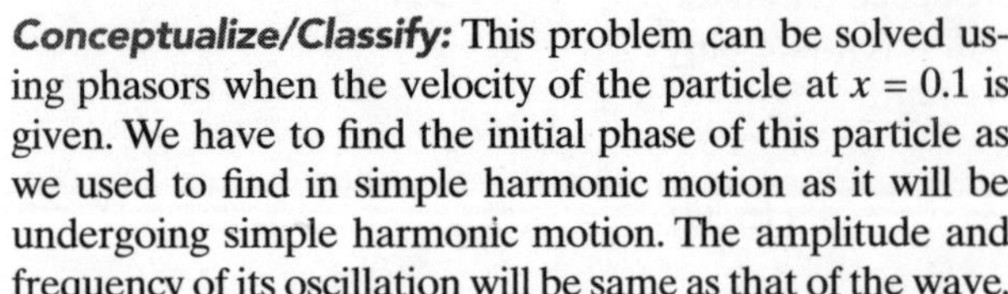

Conceptualize/Classify: This problem can be solved using phasors when the velocity of the particle at $x = 0.1$ is given. We have to find the initial phase of this particle as we used to find in simple harmonic motion as it will be undergoing simple harmonic motion. The amplitude and frequency of its oscillation will be same as that of the wave.

Compute: Angular frequency $\omega = 2\pi \frac{V}{\lambda} = 2\pi \frac{12}{0.4}$ rad/s $= 60\pi$ rad/s. Wave number $k = 2\pi/\lambda = 5\pi$ rad/s, amplitude $A = 0.5$ mm.

Thus, equation of a wave traveling in positive x direction with above parameters is $y = 0.5(\text{mm}) \sin(60\pi t - 5\pi x + \phi)$, here ϕ is unknown initial phase.

Now, putting $x = 0.1$, $t = 0$, and $y = 0.25$ mm in above equation we get $\sin\left(\phi - \frac{\pi}{2}\right) = 0.5$

We can have have two values $\pi/6$ and $5\pi/6$ satisfying argument of sine function, by making phasor we realize that for particle to have negative velocity $5\pi/6$ is the right choice.

$$\therefore \phi - \frac{\pi}{2} = \frac{5\pi}{6}$$

$$\phi = \frac{5\pi}{6} + \frac{\pi}{2} = \frac{5\pi + 3\pi}{6} = \frac{4\pi}{3}$$

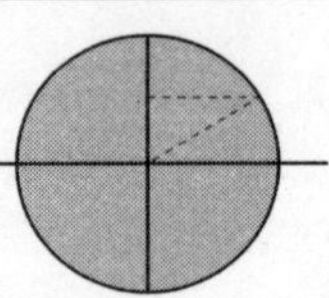

FIG. 16-16*a* Phasor is coming to be in first quadrant.

$$y = A \sin(60\pi t - 5\pi x + \frac{4\pi}{3})$$

(b) *Compute:* To plot the wave function at $t = 0$ we need to locate the point $x = 0$.

$$y = A \sin \frac{4\pi}{3} \quad \text{thus we get} \quad y = -\frac{\sqrt{3}A}{2}$$

If we proceed with this information we have two possible shapes. To decide which of them is the actual possible shape we should see the motion of the particle at $x = 0$

$$\text{therefore,} \quad V = A \cos(\frac{4\pi}{3} - 5\pi x)$$

at $x = 0$; velocity is downward, hence Fig. 16-16*b* is the correct representation.

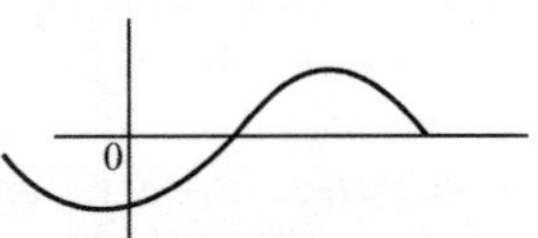

FIG. 16-16*b* Shape of string at $t = 0$.

CHECKPOINT 4 Find closest two particles to $x = 0.1$ having same velocity as $x = 0.1$ at $t = 0$.

CHECKPOINT 5 At what time after $t = 0$, will $x = 0.2$ m will be at $y = 0.25$ mm and going up for first time.

16-7 | Superposition

Principle of Superposition for Waves

It often happens that two or more waves pass simultaneously through the same region. When we listen to a concert, for example, sound waves from many instruments fall simultaneously on our eardrums. The electrons in the antennas of our radio and television receivers are set in motion by the net effect of many electromagnetic waves from many different broadcasting centers. The water of a lake or harbor may be churned up by waves in the wakes of many boats.

Suppose that two waves travel simultaneously along the same stretched string. Let $y_1(x, t)$ and $y_2(x, t)$ be the displacements that the string would experience if each wave traveled alone. The displacement of the string when the waves overlap is then the algebraic sum

$$y'(x, t) = y_1(x, t) + y_2(x, t) \tag{16-41}$$

This summation of displacements along the string means that

> Overlapping waves algebraically add to produce a **resultant wave** (or **net wave**).

This is another example of the **principle of superposition,** which says that when several effects occur simultaneously, their net effect is the sum of the individual effects.

Figure 16-17 shows a sequence of snapshots of two pulses traveling in opposite directions on the same stretched string. When the pulses overlap, the resultant pulse is their sum. Moreover,

> Overlapping waves do not in any way alter the travel of each other.

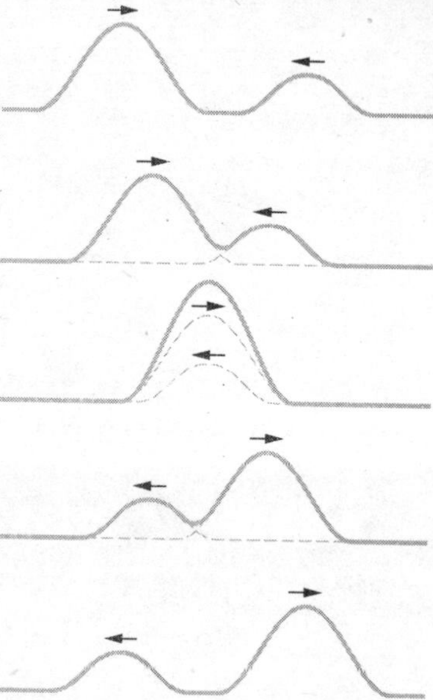

FIG. 16-17 A series of snapshots that show two pulses traveling in opposite directions along a stretched string. The superposition principle applies as the pulses move through each other.

The most important and amazing features of the wave is that two pulses traveling in opposite directions, can pass right through each other and emerge from the encounter with their separate original identities.

Figure 16-18 shows such superpositions. Their are two symmetrical pulses traveling in opposite directions. These pulses have exact same shape, except that one is in positive y and the other is in negative y. As they pass through each other, there is an instant at which the whole string is straight; it appears as if the pulses had destroyed each other. But we know that each pulse was carrying some energy, which did not get disappeared unless some dissipative force is present. According to principle of superposition the pulses do reappear with exact same shape as before. The question arises that how can the pulses remember the original shape when the string was straight, (and apparently they were dead) so they are recovered intact in their original form? The answer lies in the different velocities of the different parts of the string. The velocities also add as the displacements add. The velocity distribution of a symmetrical positive pulse traveling to the right is exactly Q:2 the same as that of a similar negative pulse traveling to the left. This can also be understood from the Eq. () as the signs of both $\partial y/\partial x$ and $\partial x/\partial t$ will be reversed hence v_y will not change. This can also be seen by making sketches of the two pulses as they appear at two successive instants as shown in Fig. 16-18*b*. Thus the transverse displacements cancel, but the transverse velocities add, and for this one instant the whole energy of the system resides in the kinetic energy associated with these velocities.

It is convenient to assume simple geometric shapes such as the rectangle, triangle, and trapezoid etc. as shown in Fig. 16-18*c* for pulses. With a triangular

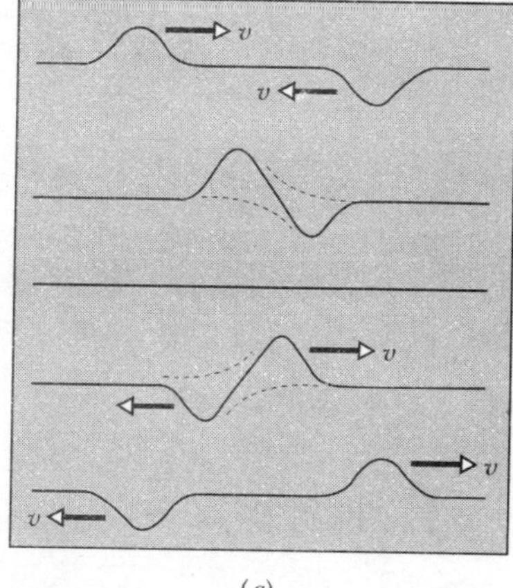

(*a*)

(*b*)

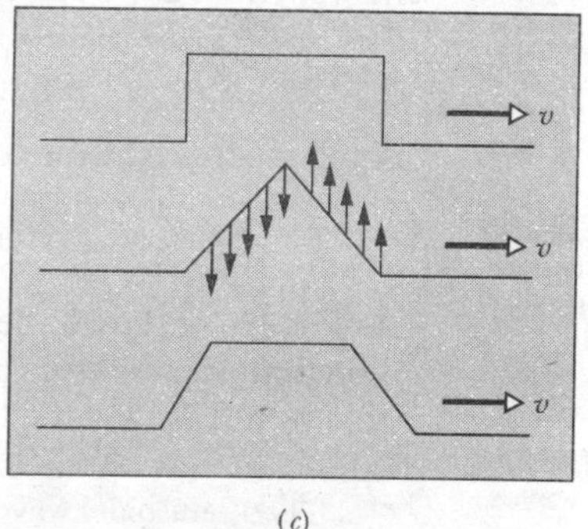

(*c*)

FIG. 16-18 (*a*) Two opposing waves traveling in opposite directions. (*b*) Superimposition of velocities. (*c*) Superimposition of velocities and shape of pulse.

pulse, for example, the transverse velocity is the same for all points along each side of the pulse, and the effects of superposing such pulses are easily analyzed. It should be realized, however, that such shapes and corners (such as the trapezoid) mean discontinuous changes in transverse velocity, which in turn means infinite accelerations which is not possible.

Any real pulse, therefore, has rounded corners and sloping sides, whatever shape it may have otherwise.

16-8 | Interference

Interference of Waves

Suppose we send two sinusoidal waves of the same wavelength and amplitude in the same direction along a stretched string. The superposition principle applies. What resultant wave does it predict for the string?

The resultant wave depends on the extent to which the waves are *in phase* (in step) with respect to each other—that is, how much one wave form is shifted from the other wave form. If the waves are exactly in phase (so that the peaks and valleys of one are exactly aligned with those of the other), they combine to double the displacement of either wave acting alone. If they are exactly out of phase (the peaks of one are exactly aligned with the valleys of the other), they combine to cancel everywhere, and the string remains straight. We call this phenomenon of combining waves **interference,** and the waves are said to **interfere.** (These terms refer only to the wave displacements; the travel of the waves is unaffected.)

Let one wave traveling along a stretched string be given by

$$y_1(x, t) = y_m \sin(kx - \omega t) \tag{16-42}$$

and another, shifted from the first, by

$$y_2(x, t) = y_m \sin(kx - \omega t + \phi) \tag{16-43}$$

These waves have the same angular frequency ω (and thus the same frequency f), the same angular wave number k (and thus the same wavelength λ), and the same amplitude y_m. They both travel in the positive direction of the x axis, with the same speed, given by Eq. 16-25. They differ only by a constant angle ϕ, the phase constant. These waves are said to be *out of phase* by ϕ or to have a *phase difference* of ϕ, or one wave is said to be *phase-shifted* from the other by ϕ.

From the principle of superposition (Eq. 16-41), the resultant wave is the algebraic sum of the two interfering waves and has displacement

$$\begin{aligned} y'(x, t) &= y_1(x, t) + y_2(x, t) \\ &= y_m \sin(kx - \omega t) + y_m \sin(kx - \omega t + \phi) \end{aligned} \tag{16-44}$$

In Appendix E we see that we can write the sum of the sines of two angles α and β as

$$\sin \alpha + \sin \beta = 2 \sin \tfrac{1}{2}(\alpha + \beta) \cos \tfrac{1}{2}(\alpha - \beta) \tag{16-45}$$

Applying this relation to Eq. 16-44 leads to

$$y'(x, t) = [2y_m \cos \tfrac{1}{2}\phi] \sin(kx - \omega t + \tfrac{1}{2}\phi) \tag{16-46}$$

As Fig. 16-19 shows, the resultant wave is also a sinusoidal wave traveling in the direction of increasing x. It is the only wave you would actually see on the string (you would *not* see the two interfering waves of Eqs. 16-42 and 16-43).

Displacement

$$\underbrace{y'(x,t)}_{} = \underbrace{[2y_m \cos \tfrac{1}{2}\phi]}_{\text{Magnitude gives amplitude}} \underbrace{\sin(kx - \omega t + \tfrac{1}{2}\phi)}_{\text{Oscillating term}}$$

FIG. 16-19 The resultant wave of Eq. 16-44, due to the interference of two sinusoidal transverse waves, is also a sinusoidal transverse wave, with an amplitude and an oscillating term.

> If two sinusoidal waves of the same amplitude and wavelength travel in the *same* direction along a stretched string, they interfere to produce a resultant sinusoidal wave traveling in that direction.

The resultant wave differs from the interfering waves in two respects: (1) its phase constant is $1/2\phi$, and (2) its amplitude y'_m is the magnitude of the quantity in the brackets in Eq. 16-46:

$$y'_m = |2y_m \cos \tfrac{1}{2}\phi| \qquad \text{(amplitude)} \qquad (16\text{-}47)$$

If $\phi = 0$ rad (or 0°), the two interfering waves are exactly in phase, as in Fig. 16-20*a*. Then Eq. 16-46 reduces to

$$y'(x, t) = 2y_m \sin(kx - \omega t) \qquad (\phi = 0) \qquad (16\text{-}48)$$

This resultant wave is plotted in Fig. 16-20*d*. Note from both that figure and Eq. 16-48 that the amplitude of the resultant wave is twice the amplitude of either interfering wave. That is the greatest amplitude the resultant wave can have, because the cosine term in Eqs. 16-46 and 16-47 has its greatest value (unity) when $\phi = 0$. Interference that produces the greatest possible amplitude is called *fully constructive interference.*

If $\phi = \pi$ rad (or 180°), the interfering waves are exactly out of phase as in Fig. 16-20*b*. Then $\cos 1/2\phi$ becomes $\cos \pi/2 = 0$, and the amplitude of the resultant wave as given by Eq. 16-47 is zero. We then have, for all values of x and t,

$$y'(x, t) = 0 \qquad (\phi = \pi \text{ rad}) \qquad (16\text{-}49)$$

The resultant wave is plotted in Fig. 16-20*e*. Although we sent two waves along the string, we see no motion of the string. This type of interference is called *fully destructive interference*.

Because a sinusoidal wave repeats its shape every 2π rad, a phase difference $\phi = 2\pi$ rad (or 360°) corresponds to a shift of one wave relative to the other wave by a distance equivalent to one wavelength. Thus, phase differences can be described in terms of wavelengths as well as angles. For example, in Fig. 16-20*b* the waves may be said to be 0.50 wavelength out of phase. Table 16-1 shows some other examples of phase differences and the interference they produce. Note that when interference is neither fully constructive nor fully destructive, it is called *intermediate interference*. The amplitude of the resultant wave is then intermediate

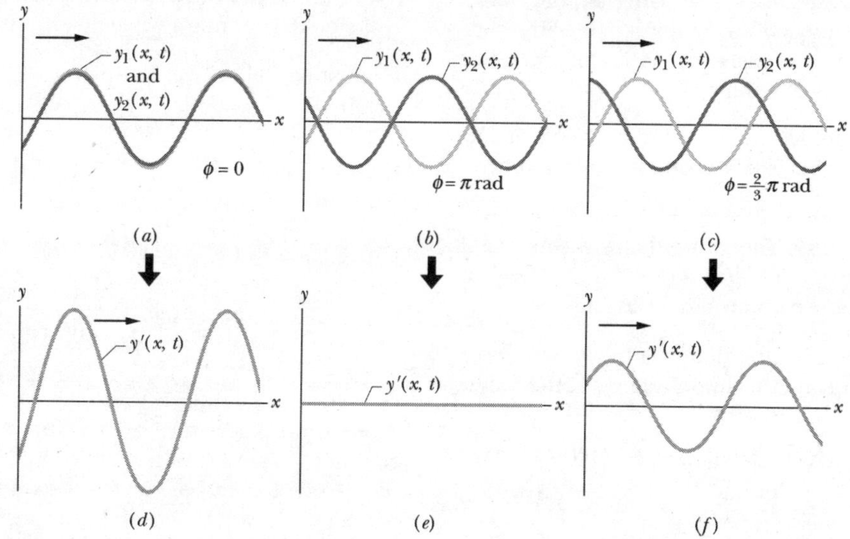

FIG. 16-20 Two identical sinusoidal waves, $y_1(x, t)$ and $y_2(x, t)$, travel along a string in the positive direction of an x axis. They interfere to give a resultant wave $y'(x, t)$. The resultant wave is what is actually seen on the string. The phase difference ϕ between the two interfering waves is (*a*) 0 rad or 0°, (*b*) π rad or 180°, and (*c*) $2/3\pi$ rad or 120°. The corresponding resultant waves are shown in (*d*), (*e*), and (*f*).

TABLE 16-1

Phase Difference and Resulting Interference Types[a]

Phase Difference, in			Amplitude of Resultant Wave	Type of Interference
Degrees	Radians	Wavelengths		
0	0	0	$2y_m$	Fully constructive
120	$\frac{2}{3}\pi$	0.33	y_m	Intermediate
180	π	0.50	0	Fully destructive
240	$\frac{4}{3}\pi$	0.67	y_m	Intermediate
360	2π	1.00	$2y_m$	Fully constructive
865	15.1	2.40	$0.60y_m$	Intermediate

[a]The phase difference is between two otherwise identical waves, with amplitude y_m, moving in the same direction.

between 0 and $2y_m$. For example, from Table 16-1, if the interfering waves have a phase difference of 120° ($\phi = 2/3\pi$ rad = 0.33 wavelength), then the resultant wave has an amplitude of y_m, the same as that of the interfering waves (see Figs. 16-20*c* and *f*).

Two waves with the same wavelength are in phase if their phase difference is zero or any integer number of wavelengths. Thus, the integer part of any phase difference *expressed in wavelengths* may be discarded. For example, a phase difference of 0.40 wavelength is equivalent in every way to one of 2.40 wavelengths, and so the simpler of the two numbers can be used in computations.

CHECKPOINT 6 Here are four possible phase differences between two identical waves, expressed in wavelengths: 0.20, 0.45, 0.60, and 0.80. Rank them according to the amplitude of the resultant wave, greatest first.

Sample Problem 16-7

Two identical sinusoidal waves, moving in the same direction along a stretched string, interfere with each other. The amplitude y_m of each wave is 9.8 mm, and the phase difference ϕ between them is 100°.

(a) What is the amplitude y'_m of the resultant wave due to the interference, and what is the type of this interference?

Conceptualize/Classify: These are identical sinusoidal waves traveling in the *same direction* along a string, so they interfere to produce a sinusoidal traveling wave.

Compute: Because they are identical, the waves have the *same amplitude.* Thus, the amplitude y'_m of the resultant wave is given by Eq. 16-47:

$$y'_m = |2y_m \cos \tfrac{1}{2}\phi| = |(2)(9.8 \text{ mm}) \cos(100°/2)|$$
$$= 13 \text{ mm} \qquad \text{(Answer)}$$

Conclude: We can tell that the interference is *intermediate* in two ways. The phase difference is between 0 and 180°, and, correspondingly, the amplitude y'_m is between 0 and $2y_m$ (= 19.6 mm).

(b) What phase difference, in radians and wavelengths, will give the resultant wave an amplitude of 4.9 mm?

Compute: Now we are given y'_m and seek ϕ. From Eq. 16-47,

$$y'_m = |2y_m \cos \tfrac{1}{2}\phi|$$

we now have

$$4.9 \text{ mm} = (2)(9.8 \text{ mm}) \cos \tfrac{1}{2}\phi$$

which gives us (with a calculator in the radian mode)

$$\phi = 2 \cos^{-1} \frac{4.9 \text{ mm}}{(2)(9.8 \text{ mm})}$$
$$= \pm 2.636 \text{ rad} \approx \pm 2.6 \text{ rad} \qquad \text{(Answer)}$$

Conclude: There are two solutions because we can obtain the same resultant wave by letting the first wave *lead* (travel ahead of) or *lag* (travel behind) the second wave by 2.6 rad. In wavelengths, the phase difference is

$$\frac{\phi}{2\pi \text{ rad/wavelength}} = \frac{\pm 2.636 \text{ rad}}{2\pi \text{ rad/wavelength}}$$
$$= \pm 0.42 \text{ wavelength} \qquad \text{(Answer)}$$

Sample Problem 16-8

Two sinusoidal waves $y_1(x, t)$ and $y_2(x, t)$ have the same wavelength and travel together in the same direction along a string. Their amplitudes are $y_{m1} = 4.0$ mm and $y_{m2} = 3.0$ mm, and their phase constants are 0 and $\pi/3$ rad, respectively. What are the amplitude y'_m and phase constant β of the resultant wave? Write the resultant wave in the form of Eq. 16-40.

Conceptualize: The two waves have a number of properties in common: Because they travel along the same string, they must have the same speed v, as set by the tension and linear density of the string according to Eq. 16-25. With the same wavelength λ, they must have the same angular wave number k $(= 2\pi/\lambda)$. Also, with the same wave number k and speed v, they must have the same angular frequency ω $(= kv)$.

Classify: The waves (call them waves 1 and 2) can be represented by phasors rotating at the same angular speed ω about an origin. Because the phase constant for wave 2 is *greater* than that for wave 1 by $\pi/3$, phasor 2 must *lag* phasor 1 by $\pi/3$ rad in their clockwise rotation, as shown in Fig. 16-21*a*. The resultant wave due to the interference of waves 1 and 2 can then be represented by a phasor that is the vector sum of phasors 1 and 2.

Compute: To simplify the vector summation, we drew phasors 1 and 2 in Fig. 16-21*a* at the instant when phasor 1 lies along the horizontal axis. We then drew lagging phasor 2 at positive angle $\pi/3$ rad. In Fig. 16-21*b* we shifted phasor 2 so its tail is at the head of phasor 1. Then we can draw the phasor y'_m of the resultant wave from the tail of phasor 1 to the head of phasor 2. The phase constant β is the angle phasor y'_m makes with phasor 1.

To find values for y'_m and β, we can sum phasors 1 and 2 directly on a vector-capable calculator (by adding a vector of magnitude 4.0 and angle 0 rad to a vector of magnitude 3.0 and angle $\pi/3$ rad) or we can add the vectors by components. For the horizontal components we have

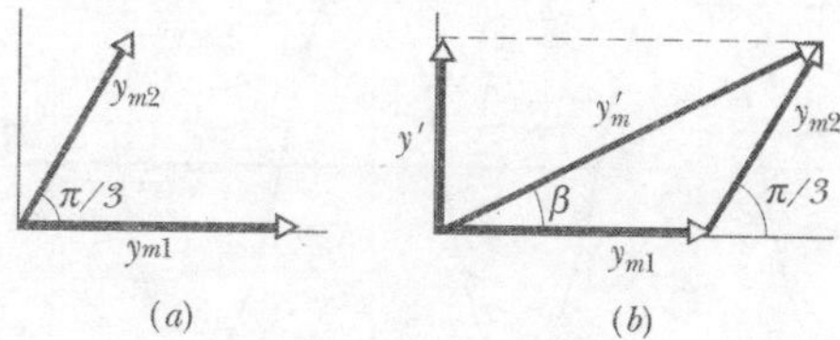

FIG. 16-21 (*a*) Two phasors of magnitudes y_{m1} and y_{m2} and with phase difference $\pi/3$. (*b*) Vector addition of these phasors at any instant during their rotation gives the magnitude y'_m of the phasor for the resultant wave.

$$y'_{mh} = y_{m1}\cos 0 + y_{m2}\cos \pi/3$$
$$= 4.0 \text{ mm} + (3.0 \text{ mm})\cos \pi/3 = 5.50 \text{ mm}$$

For the vertical components we have

$$y'_{mv} = y_{m1}\sin 0 + y_{m2}\sin \pi/3$$
$$= 0 + (3.0 \text{ mm})\sin \pi/3 = 2.60 \text{ mm}$$

Thus, the resultant wave has an amplitude of

$$y'_m = \sqrt{(5.50 \text{ mm})^2 + (2.60 \text{ mm})^2}$$
$$= 6.1 \text{ mm} \qquad \text{(Answer)}$$

and a phase constant of

$$\beta = \tan^{-1}\frac{2.60 \text{ mm}}{5.50 \text{ mm}} = 0.44 \text{ rad} \qquad \text{(Answer)}$$

From Fig. 16-21*b*, phase constant β is a *positive* angle relative to phasor 1. Thus, the resultant wave *lags* wave 1 in their travel by phase constant $\beta = +0.44$ rad. From Eq. 16-40, we can write the resultant wave as

$$y'(x, t) = (6.1 \text{ mm})\sin(kx - \omega t + 0.44 \text{ rad}) \qquad \text{(Answer)}$$

Conclude: Use of phasor has made the solution very simple compared to direct trigonometric equation.

Sample Problem 16-9

Two sinusoidal waves with the same amplitude of 4.0 mm and the same wavelength traveled together along a string that is stretched along an x axis; the *resultant wave* due to their interference was recorded on video tape. The curves in Fig. 16-22 represent the *resultant* wave in two freezeframes, first as the solid curve and then, 1.0 ms later, as the dotted curve. The grid lines along the x axis are 1.0 cm apart, and the string elements oscillated vertically (perpendicular to the x axis) by 6.0 mm as the resultant wave passed through them. That wave moved a distance $d = 4.20$ cm to the right in the 1.0 ms time interval. Write equations for the two interfering waves and for their resultant wave.

Conceptualize: From Fig. 16-22, we see that the resultant wave is a sinusoidal wave that moves in the positive direction of the x axis.

Classify: The interfering waves must both move in that direction and we can write them as

$$y_1(x, t) = y_m \sin(kx - \omega t) \qquad (16\text{-}50)$$

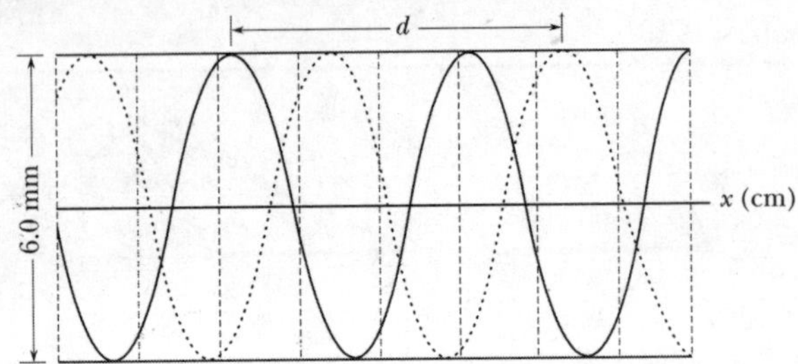

FIG. 16-22 The resultant wave of two sinusoidal string waves traveling along an x axis is shown at two instants, between which the resultant wave travels distance d.

and $$y_2(x,t) = y_m \sin(kx - \omega t + \phi) \qquad (16\text{-}51)$$

where y_{m}, = 4.0 mm. We can now write the resultant wave as

$$y'(x,t) = [2y_{m}, \cos \tfrac{1}{2}\phi] \sin(kx - \omega t + \tfrac{1}{2}\phi) \qquad (16\text{-}52)$$

The amplitude $2y_m \cos \frac{1}{2}\phi$ of the resultant wave is half the total oscillation distance of 6.0 mm, so we have

$$2y_m \cos \tfrac{1}{2}\phi = 3.0 \text{ mm}$$

Substituting $y_m = 4.0$ mm and solving for ϕ, we get

$$\phi = 2\cos^{-1}\frac{3.0 \text{ mm}}{2(4.0 \text{ mm})} = 136° \approx 2.4 \text{ rad}$$

Thus, the phase constant in Eq. 16-51 is $\phi = 2.4$ rad and the phase constant in Eq. 16-52 is $\frac{1}{2}\phi = \frac{1}{2}(2.4 \text{ rad}) \approx 1.2$ rad.

To find the angular wave number k, we use two key ideas. First, the common value of k in Eqs. 16-50, 16-51, and 16-52 is related to the common wavelength λ by equation $k = 2\pi/\lambda$. Second, the wavelength λ can be measured in Fig. 16-21 as the distance (parallel to the x axis) between repetitions of the wave shape. Let's use the solid curve and pick any point at which it crosses the x axis. That curve makes an identical crossing 3.0 cm to the right (or left) from the first point. Thus, $\lambda = 3.0$ cm, and

$$k = \frac{2\pi}{\lambda} = \frac{2\pi}{0.030 \text{ m}} = 209 \text{ m}^{-1} = 210 \text{ m}^{-1}$$

To find the common angular frequency ω, we use two more key ideas: The common value of ω in Eqs. 16-50, 16-51, and 16-52 is related to k and the common wave speed v by equation $v = \omega/k$. That wave speed v is the ratio of the distance d traveled by the resultant wave to the time interval Δt required for that travel. Thus, we have

$$\omega = kv = k\frac{d}{\Delta t} = (209 \text{ m}^{-1})\frac{0.0420 \text{ m}}{0.0010 \text{ s}} = 8778 \text{ s}^{-1} \approx 8800 \text{ s}^{-1}$$

We can now write Eqs. 16-50 and 16-51 for the interfering waves as

$$y_1(x,t) = (4.0 \text{ mm}) \sin(210x - 88007)$$

and

$$y_2(x,t) = (4.0 \text{ mm}) \sin(210x - 8800t + 2.4 \text{ rad}) \qquad \text{(Answer)}$$

with x in meters and t in seconds. We can also write Eq. 16-52 for the resultant wave as

$$y'(x,t) = (3.0 \text{ mm}) \sin(210x - 8800t + 1.2 \text{ rad}) \qquad \text{(Answer)}$$

again with x in meters and t in seconds.

Conclude: The phase difference between two waves must be 2.4 rad, although the two wave equations can have any value of initial phase.

16-9 | Standing Waves

We have already discussed two sinusoidal waves of the same wavelength and amplitude traveling *in the same direction* along a stretched string. What if they travel in opposite directions? We can again find the resultant wave by applying the superposition principle.

Figure 16-23 suggests the situation graphically. It shows the two combining waves, one traveling to the left in Fig. 16-23*a*, the other to the right in Fig. 16-23*b*. Figure 16-23*c* shows their sum, obtained by applying the superposition principle graphically. The outstanding feature of the resultant wave is that there are places along the string, called **nodes,** where the string never moves. Four such nodes are marked by dots in Fig. 16-23*c*. Halfway between adjacent nodes are **antinodes,** where the amplitude of the resultant wave is a maximum. Wave patterns such as that of Fig. 16-23*c* are called **standing waves** because the wave patterns do not move left or right; the locations of the maxima and minima do not change.

> If two sinusoidal waves of the same amplitude and wavelength travel in *opposite* directions along a stretched string, their interference with each other produces a standing wave.

To analyze a standing wave, we represent the two combining waves with the equations

$$y_1(x,t) = y_m \sin(kx - \omega t) \qquad (16\text{-}53)$$

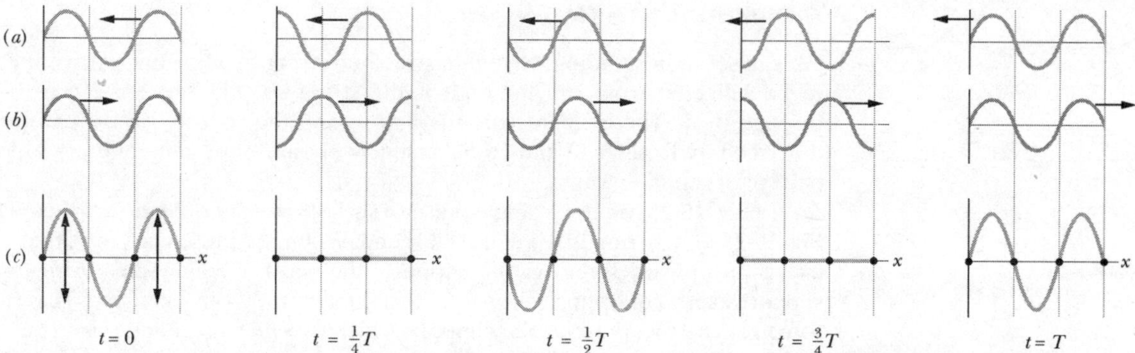

FIG. 16-23 (*a*) Five snapshots of a wave traveling to the left, at the times t indicated below part (*c*) (T is the period of oscillation). (*b*) Five snapshots of a wave identical to that in (*a*) but traveling to the right, at the same times t. (*c*) Corresponding snapshots for the superposition of the two waves on the same string. At $t = 0, \frac{1}{2}T$, and T, fully constructive interference occurs because of the alignment of peaks with peaks and valleys with valleys. At $t = \frac{1}{4}T$ and $\frac{3}{4}T$, fully destructive interference occurs because of the alignment of peaks with valleys. Some points (the nodes, marked with dots) never oscillate; some points (the antinodes) oscillate the most.

and

$$y_2(x, t) = y_m \sin(kx + \omega t) \tag{16-54}$$

The principle of superposition gives, for the combined wave,

$$y'(x, t) = y_1(x, t) + y_2(x, t) = y_m \sin(kx - \omega t) + y_m \sin(kx + \omega t)$$

Applying the trigonometric relation of Eq. 16-45 leads to

$$y'(x, t) = [2y_m \sin kx] \cos \omega t \tag{16-55}$$

which is displayed in Fig. 16-24. This equation does not describe a traveling wave because it is not of the form of Eq. 16-16. Instead, it describes a standing wave.

$$\overbrace{y'(x,t)}^{\text{Displacement}} = \underbrace{[2y_m \sin kx]}_{\substack{\text{Magnitude gives}\\ \text{amplitude}\\ \text{at position } x}} \underbrace{\cos \omega t}_{\text{Oscillating term}}$$

FIG. 16-24 The resultant wave of Eq. 16-53 is a standing wave and is due to the interference of two sinusoidal waves of the same amplitude and wavelength that travel in opposite directions.

The quantity $2y_m \sin kx$ in the brackets of Eq. 16-55 can be viewed as the amplitude of oscillation of the string element that is located at position x. However, since an amplitude is always positive and $\sin kx$ can be negative, we take the absolute value of the quantity $2y_m \sin kx$ to be the amplitude at x.

In a traveling sinusoidal wave, the amplitude of the wave is the same for all string elements. That is not true for a standing wave, in which the amplitude *varies with position*. In the standing wave of Eq. 16-55, for example, the amplitude is zero for values of kx that give $\sin kx = 0$. Those values are

$$kx = n\pi, \quad \text{for} \quad n = 0, 1, 2, \ldots. \tag{16-56}$$

Substituting $k = 2\pi/\lambda$ in this equation and rearranging, we get

$$x = n\frac{\lambda}{2}, \quad \text{for} \quad n = 0, 1, 2, \ldots \quad \text{(nodes)} \tag{16-57}$$

as the positions of zero amplitude—the nodes—for the standing wave of Eq. 16-55. Note that adjacent nodes are separated by $\lambda/2$, half a wavelength.

The amplitude of the standing wave of Eq. 16-55 has a maximum value of $2y_m$, which occurs for values of kx that give $|\sin kx| = 1$. Those values are

$$\begin{aligned} kx &= \tfrac{1}{2}\pi, \tfrac{3}{2}\pi, \tfrac{5}{2}\pi, \ldots \\ &= (n + \tfrac{1}{2})\pi, \quad \text{for} \quad n = 0, 1, 2, \ldots. \end{aligned} \tag{16-58}$$

Substituting $k = 2\pi/\lambda$ in Eq. 16-58 and rearranging, we get

$$x = \left(n + \frac{1}{2}\right)\frac{\lambda}{2}, \quad \text{for} \quad n = 0, 1, 2, \ldots \quad \text{(antinodes)} \tag{16-59}$$

as the positions of maximum amplitude—the antinodes—of the standing wave of Eq. 16-55. The antinodes are separated by $\lambda/2$ and are located halfway between pairs of nodes.

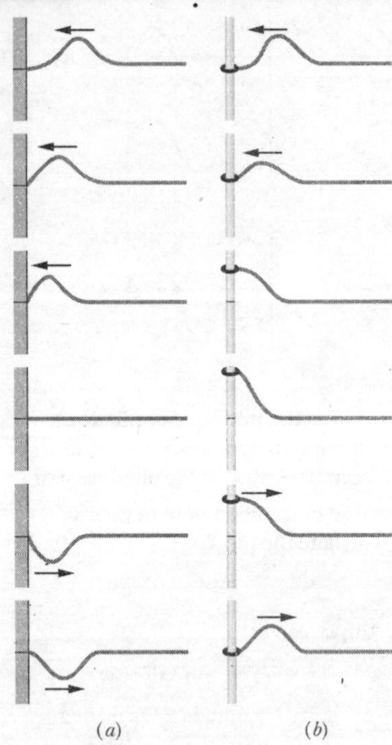

FIG. 16-25 (*a*) A pulse incident from the right is reflected at the left end of the string, which is tied to a wall. Note that the reflected pulse is inverted from the incident pulse. (*b*) Here the left end of the string is tied to a ring that can slide without friction up and down the rod. Now the pulse is not inverted by the reflection.

Reflections at a Boundary

We can set up a standing wave in a stretched string by allowing a traveling wave to be reflected from the far end of the string so that the wave travels back through itself. The incident (original) wave and the reflected wave can then be described by Eqs. 16-52 and 16-53, respectively, and they can combine to form a pattern of standing waves.

In Fig. 16-25, we use a single pulse to show how such reflections take place. In Fig. 16-25*a*, the string is fixed at its left end. When the pulse arrives at that end, it exerts an upward force on the support (the wall). By Newton's third law, the support exerts an opposite force of equal magnitude on the string. This second force generates a pulse at the support, which travels back along the string in the direction opposite that of the incident pulse. In a "hard" reflection of this kind, there must be a node at the support because the string is fixed there. The reflected and incident pulses must have opposite signs, so as to cancel each other at that point.

In Fig. 16-25*b*, the left end of the string is fastened to a light ring that is free to slide without friction along a rod. When the incident pulse arrives, the ring moves up the rod. As the ring moves, it pulls on the string, stretching the string and producing a reflected pulse with the same sign and amplitude as the incident pulse. Thus, in such a "soft" reflection, the incident and reflected pulses reinforce each other, creating an antinode at the end of the string; the maximum displacement of the ring is twice the amplitude of either of these pulses.

CHECKPOINT 7 Two waves with the same amplitude and wavelength interfere in three different situations to produce resultant waves with the following equations:

1. $y'(x, t) = 4\sin(5x - 4t)$
2. $y'(x, t) = 4\sin(5x)\cos(4t)$
3. $y'(x, t) = 4\sin(5x + 4t)$

In which situation are the two combining waves traveling (a) toward positive x, (b) toward negative x, and (c) in opposite directions?

AQ:1

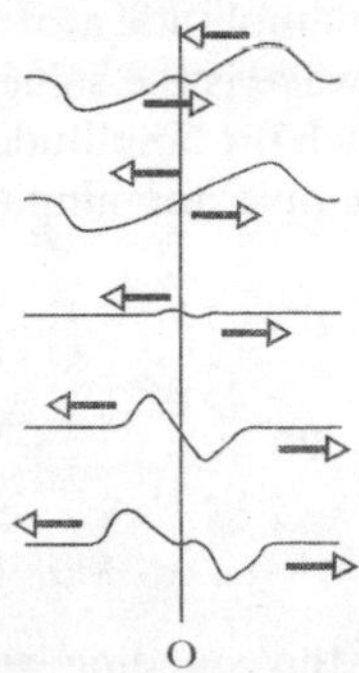

FIG. 16-26 Overlap of two wave pulses—one right side up, one inverted—traveling in opposite directions. Time increases from top to bottom.

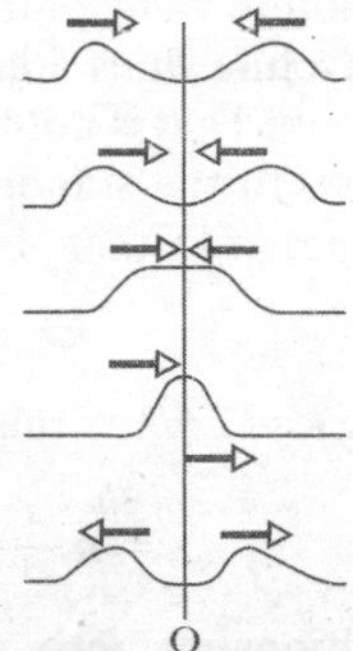

FIG. 16-27 Overlap of two wave pulses – both right side up – traveling in opposite directions. Time increases from top to bottom. Compare with Fig. 16-26.

FIG. 16-28 A string attached to a rigid wall.

Mathematical Description of Generation of Standing Wave Due to Reflection of a Traveling Wave

Rigid wall: Not capable of transferring energy

Suppose we have a continuous, homogeneous string stretching from $x = 0$ to $x = l$ as shown in Fig. 16-28. The string is attached at $x = 0$ to an oscillator, vibrating at constant frequency, that is shaking the string and thus producing the traveling wave along the string. Suppose that the displacement $y(t)$ of the output terminal is given by the harmonic oscillation

$$y(t) = A \sin \omega t$$

Since the string is tied directly to the oscillator, the displacement of the string at $x = 0$ is equal to $y(t)$:

$$y_i(0, t) = y(t) = A \sin(\omega t + \phi)$$

The displacemetn $y_i(x, t)$ of a moving part located at position x, where x is anywhere between $x = 0$ and l.

$$y_i(x, t) = A \sin\left(\omega t - \frac{\omega x}{V} + \phi\right)$$

$$y_i(x, t) = A \sin\left(\omega t - \frac{\omega l}{V} + \phi\right)$$

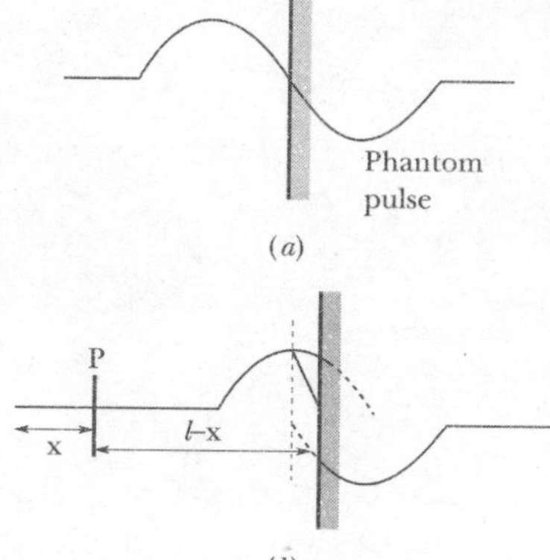

FIG. 16-29 Pulse on the right hand side of the wall represents phantom pulse which later on superimposes with the original pulse.

When this disturbance reaches $x = l$, it will get inverted upon reflection as shown in Fig. 16.29. This can also be understood from the concept of phantom pulse.

$$y_r(l, t) = -y_i(l, t)$$

and the point on the wall will become source of a new wave.

Pulse:

Now we have to find the equationof the reflected wave, $y_r(x, t)$.

$$y_r(l, t) = -A \sin\left(\omega t - \frac{\omega l}{V} + \phi\right)$$

$$= A \sin\left(\omega t - \frac{\omega l}{V} + \phi + \pi\right)$$

Particle at x is at distance of $(l - x)$ from the wall which is the source of inverted wave. Thus it is $\omega\left(\frac{l - x}{V}\right)$ behind in phase with the source.

Therefore, $y_r(x, t) = A \sin\left[\{\omega t - \left(\frac{\omega l}{V}\right) + \phi + \pi\} - \omega\frac{(l - x)}{V}\right]$

After some time both waves will exist in the medium and we will have superposition of the two waves.

$$y = y_i + y_r$$

$$y = 2A \cos\left(kx - \frac{\pi}{2} - kl\right) \sin\left(wt + + \frac{\pi}{2} - kl\right)$$

This is an equation of a standing wave. We can verify that at $x = l$, that is at the wall net displacement y is zero at all times by putting $x = l$ in this equation.

Free end: Not capable of transferring energy

If wall is replaced by free end with frictionless rod and massless ring as shown in figure 16.30. then $y_r(l, t) = y_i(l, t)$

$$y_i(l, t) = A \sin\left(\omega t - \frac{\omega l}{V} + \phi\right)$$

thus $$y_r(l, t) = A \sin\left(\omega t - \frac{\omega l}{V} + \phi\right)$$

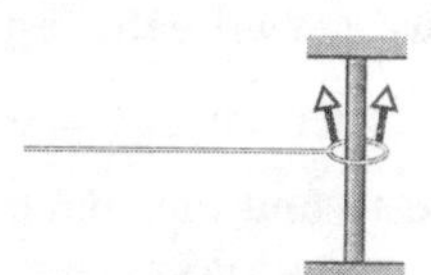
FIG. 16-30 A string tied to a free end:

Particle at x is at distance of $(l - x)$ from the wall which is the source of inverted wave. Thus it is $\omega\left(\frac{l - x}{V}\right)$ behind in phase with the source.

$$y_r(x,t) = A\sin(\omega t - kl + \phi - k(l-x))$$

$$y_r(x,t) = A\sin(\omega t - kx + \phi - 2kl)$$

After some time both waves will exist in the medium and we will have superposition of the two waves.

$$y = y_i + y_r$$

$$y = 2A\cos(kx - kl)\sin(\omega t + \phi - kl)$$

This is an equation of astanding wave. We can verify that at $x = l$, that is, at the free end net displacement y is maximum(it is antinode) by putting $x = l$ in this equation.

Sample Problem 16-10

Two sinusoidal waves with the same amplitude and wavelength travel along a string that is stretched along an x axis; the *resultant wave* due to their superposition was recorded on video tape. The curves in Fig. 16-31 represent the resultant wave in four freezeframes in the sequence of a, b, c, and d, with 1.0 ms elapsing between curves a and d. The grid lines along the x axis are 1.0 cm apart, and the string elements oscillated perpendicular to the x axis by 16.0 mm (between the extreme displacements shown by curves a and d) as the resultant wave passed through them. Write equations for the two superposition waves and for their resultant wave.

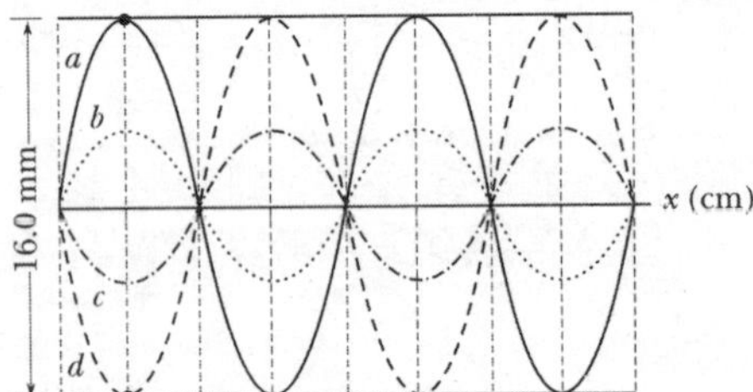

FIG. 16-31 The resultant wave of two sinusoidal string waves traveling along an x axis is shown at four instants (a, b, c, and d).

Conceptualize: Figure 16-31, shows a standing wave and so the two waves must be traveling in opposite directions.

Classify: The two waves have the forms given by:

$$y_1(x,t) = y_m \sin(kx - \omega t) \qquad (16\text{-}60)$$

and

$$y_2(x,t) = y_m \sin(kx + \omega t) \qquad (16\text{-}61)$$

Hence, we can write the resultant wave as

$$y'(x,t) = (2y_m, \sin kx)\cos\omega t \qquad (16\text{-}62)$$

We need to find the common values of y_m, k, and ω in the three equations.

Compute: To find y_m, we use the key idea that the amplitude of a standing wave is a maximum at an antinode, and there the amplitude is $2y_m$. Here the maximum amplitude of the standing wave is 8.0 mm, so

$$y_m = 4.0 \text{ mm}$$

To find the angular wave number k, we use two more key ideas. First, the common angular wave number k in Eqs. 16-60, 16-61 and 16-62 is related to the common wavelength λ by equation $k = 2\pi/\lambda$. Second, the nodes in a standing wave are separated by 0.50λ. Because the antinodes in Fig. 16-31 are separated by 2.0 cm, we have $\lambda = 2 \times 2.0$ cm $= 4.0$ cm. Then

$$k = \frac{2\pi}{\lambda} = \frac{2\pi}{0.040 \text{ m}} = 157 \text{ m}^{-1} \approx 160 \text{ m}^{-1}$$

To find the common angular frequency ω, we again use two more key ideas: We can relate the common value of ω in Eqs. 16-60, 16-61, and 16-62 to the period T of the standing wave with equation $\omega = 2\pi/T$. A string element at an antinode takes time T to move through a full oscillation from one extreme and back to the first extreme. According to the given data, the string element at the dot on curve a in Fig. 16-31 takes 1.0 ms to move to the position of the dot on curve d, which is one-half a full oscillation. Thus, $T = 2.0$ ms, and

$$\omega = \frac{2\pi}{T} = \frac{2\pi}{0.0020 \text{ s}} = 3142 \text{ s}^{-1} \approx 3100 \text{ s}^{-1}$$

Now we can write Eqs. 16-60 and 16-61 for the interfering waves as

$$y_1(x,t) = (4.0 \text{ mm})\sin(160x - 3100t)$$

and

$$y_2(x,t) = (4.0 \text{ mm})\sin(160x - 3100t) \qquad \text{(Answer)}$$

with x in meters and t in seconds. We can also write the standing wave of Eq. 16-62 as

$$y'(x,t) = (8.0 \text{ mm})(\sin 160x)(\cos 3100t) \qquad \text{(Answer)}$$

again with x in meters and t in seconds.

16-10 | Normal Modes of Vibrations

Standing Waves and Resonance

Consider a string, such as a guitar string, that is stretched between two clamps. Suppose we send a continuous sinusoidal wave of a certain frequency along the string, say, toward the right. When the wave reaches the right end, it reflects and begins to travel back to the left. That left-going wave then overlaps the wave that is still traveling to the right. When the left-going wave reaches the left end, it reflects again and the newly reflected wave begins to travel to the right, overlapping the left-going and right-going waves. In short, we very soon have many overlapping traveling waves, which interfere with one another.

For certain frequencies, the interference produces a standing wave pattern (or **oscillation mode**) with nodes and large antinodes like those in Fig. 16-31. Such a standing wave is said to be produced at **resonance,** and the string is said to *resonate* at these certain frequencies, called **resonant frequencies.** If the string is oscillated at some frequency other than a resonant frequency, a standing wave is not set up. Then the interference of the right-going and left-going traveling waves results in only small (perhaps imperceptible) oscillations of the string.

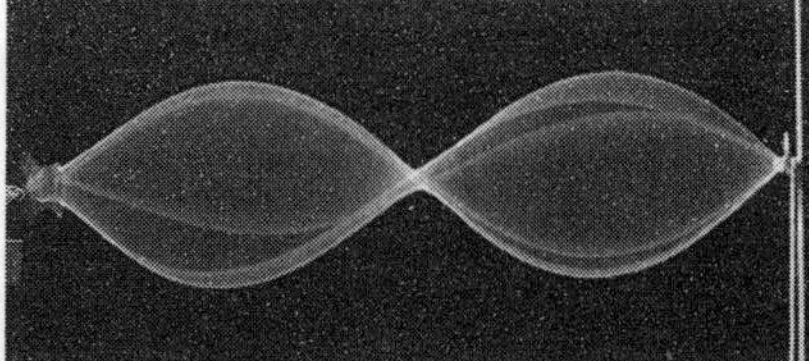
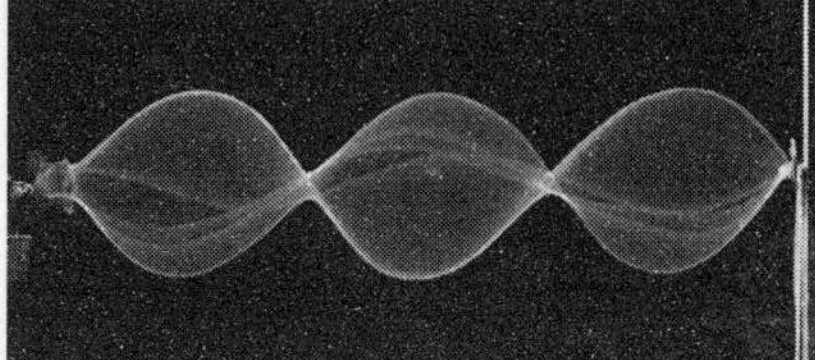
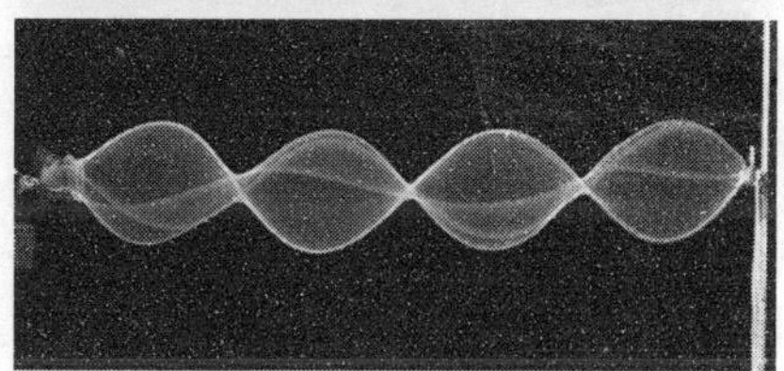

FIG. 16-31 Stroboscopic photographs reveal (imperfect) standing wave patterns on a string being made to oscillate by an oscillator at the left end. The patterns occur at certain frequencies of oscillation. *(Richard Megna/Fundamental Photographs)*

Let a string be stretched between two clamps separated by a fixed distance L. To find expressions for the resonant frequencies of the string, we note that a node must exist at each of its ends, because each end is fixed and cannot oscillate. The simplest pattern that meets this key requirement is that in Fig. 16-32*a*, which shows the string at both its extreme displacements (one solid and one dashed, together forming a single "loop"). There is only one antinode, which is at the center of the string. Note that half a wavelength spans the length L, which we take to be the string's length. Thus, for this pattern, $\lambda/2 = L$. This condition tells us that if the left-going and right-going traveling waves are to set up this pattern by their interference, they must have the wavelength $\lambda = 2L$.

A second simple pattern meeting the requirement of nodes at the fixed ends is shown in Fig. 16-32*b*. This pattern has three nodes and two antinodes and is said to be a two-loop pattern. For the left-going and right-going waves to set it up, they must have a wavelength $\lambda = L$. A third pattern is shown in Fig. 16-32*c*. It has four nodes, three antinodes, and three loops, and the wavelength is $\lambda = \frac{2}{3}L$. We could continue this progression by drawing increasingly more complicated patterns. In each step of the progression, the pattern would have one more node and one more antinode than the preceding step, and an additional $\lambda/2$ would be fitted into the distance L.

Thus, a standing wave can be set up on a string of length L by a wave with a wavelength equal to one of the values

$$\lambda = \frac{2L}{n}, \qquad \text{for } n = 1, 2, 3, \ldots. \tag{16-63}$$

The resonant frequencies that correspond to these wavelengths follow from Eq. 16-15:

$$f = \frac{v}{\lambda} = n\frac{v}{2L}, \qquad \text{for } n = 1, 2, 3, \ldots. \tag{16-64}$$

Here v is the speed of traveling waves on the string.

Equation 16-24 tells us that the resonant frequencies are integer multiples of the lowest resonant frequency, $f = v/2L$, which corresponds to $n = 1$. The oscillation mode with that lowest frequency is called the *fundamental mode* or the *first harmonic.* The *second harmonic* is the oscillation mode with $n = 2$, the *third harmonic* is that with $n = 3$, and so on. The frequencies associated with these modes are often labeled f_1, f_2, f_3, and so on. The collection of all possible oscillation modes is called the **harmonic series**, and n is called the **harmonic number** of the nth harmonic.

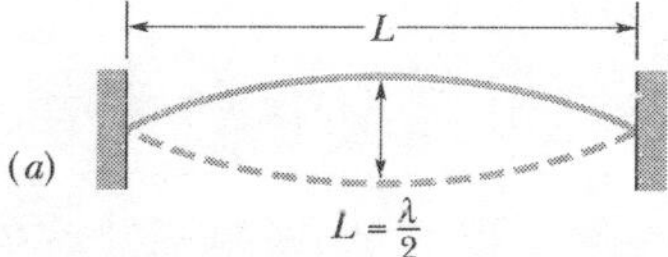

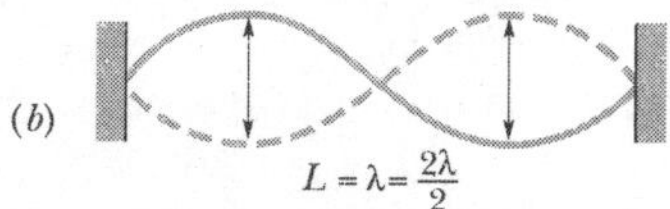

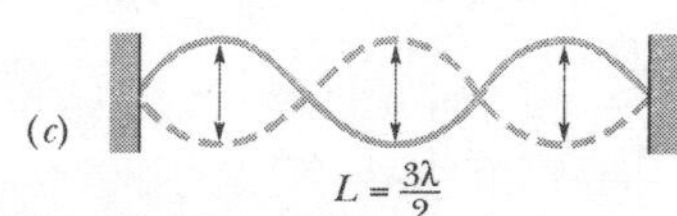

FIG. 16-32 A string, stretched between two clamps, is made to oscillate in standing wave patterns. (*a*) The simplest possible pattern consists of one *loop,* which refers to the composite shape formed by the string in its extréme displacements (the solid and dashed lines). (*b*) The next simplest pattern has two loops. (*c*) The next has three loops.

FIG. 16-33 One of many possible standing wave patterns for a kettledrum head, made visible by dark powder sprinkled on the drumhead. As the head is set into oscillation at a single frequency by a mechanical oscillator at the upper left of the photograph, the powder collects at the nodes, which are circles and straight lines in this two-dimensional example. *(Courtesy Thomas D. Rossing, Northern Illinois University)*

For a given string under a given tension, each resonant frequency corresponds to a particular oscillation pattern. Thus, if the frequency is in the audible range, you can hear the shape of the string. Resonance can also occur in two dimensions (such as on the surface of the kettledrum in Fig. 16-33) and in three dimensions (such as in the wind-induced swaying and twisting of a tall building).

Footbridges and Mosh Pits

When the Millennium Bridge over the Thames River was first opened to pedestrians, the bridge did not initially exhibit oscillations. The footsteps of the pedestrians produced vertical and horizontal forces on the bridge that tended to set up the second harmonic on the bridge (which is much like the second harmonic on a string), but the pedestrians were few and their walking was uncoordinated. However, once their number exceeded a critical value, the second harmonic suddenly became noticeable and walking became difficult. To keep their balance, many pedestrians began to time their steps to the bridge's swaying, which then became even worse and led to the bridge being closed until damping devices could be added.

Similar structural oscillations occur when an audience on a football stadium deck or in a concert hall begins to sway or stomp in a coordinated fashion. Perhaps the worse situation can occur in a mosh pit on a lightweight suspended floor. When the crowded dancers begin to pogo, in which their coordinated jumps are in time with the music's beat, they can set up resonance in the floor, which typically has a resonant frequency of 2 Hz. Resonance can then quickly build as more people are forced to coordinate their motion with the oscillations, which might become large enough to break the floor and cause it to collapse. To avoid that possibility, modern building codes commonly require that suspended dance floors be built with resonant frequencies no lower than 5 Hz.

CHECKPOINT 8 In the following series of resonant frequencies, one frequency (lower than 400 Hz) is missing: 150, 225, 300, 375 Hz. (a) What is the missing frequency? (b) What is the frequency of the seventh harmonic?

Sample Problem 16-11 Build your skill

Figure 16-34 shows a pattern of resonant oscillation of a string of mass $m = 2.500$ g and length $L = 0.800$ m and that is under tension $\tau = 325.0$ N. What is the wavelength λ of the transverse waves producing the standing-wave pattern, and what is the harmonic number n? What is the frequency f of the transverse waves and of the oscillations of the moving string elements? What is the maximum magnitude of the transverse velocity u_m of the element oscillating at coordinate $x = 0.180$ m (note the x axis in the figure)? At what point during the element's oscillation is the transverse velocity maximum?

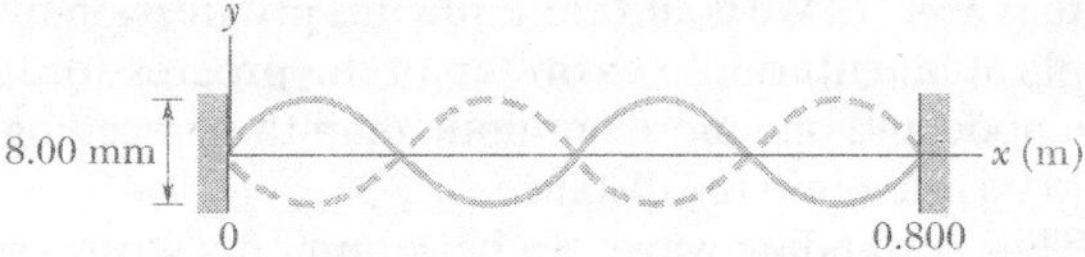

FIG. 16-34 Resonant oscillation of a string under tension.

Conceptualize: The traverse waves that produce a standing-wave pattern must have a wavelength such that an integer number n of half-wavelengths fit into the length L of the string. The frequency of those waves and of the oscillations of the string elements is given by equation $f = nv/2L$.

Classify: The displacement of a string element as a function of position x and time t is given by equation 16-55:

$$y'(x,t) = [2y_m \sin kx] \cos \omega t \qquad (16\text{-}65)$$

Compute: Wavelength and harmonic number: In Fig. 16-36, the solid line, which is effectively a snapshot (or freeze frame) of the oscillations, reveals that 2 full wavelengths fit into the length $L = 0.800$ m of the string. Thus, we have

$$2\lambda = L$$

or

$$\lambda = \frac{L}{2} \qquad (16\text{-}66)$$

$$= \frac{0.800 \text{ m}}{2} = 0.400 \text{ m} \qquad \text{(Answer)}$$

By counting the number of loops (or half-wavelengths) in Fig. 16-34, we see that the harmonic number is

$$n = 4 \qquad \text{(Answer)}$$

We reach the same conclusion by comparing Eqs. 16-66 and $\lambda = 2L/n$. Thus, the string is oscillating in its fourth harmonic.

Frequency: We can get the frequency f of the transverse waves from equation $v = \lambda f$ if we first find the speed v of the waves. That speed is given by Eq. 16-25, but we must substitute m/L for the unknown linear density μ. We obtain

$$v = \sqrt{\frac{\tau}{\mu}} = \sqrt{\frac{\tau}{m/L}} = \sqrt{\frac{\tau L}{m}}$$

$$= \sqrt{\frac{(325\text{ N})(0.800\text{ m})}{2.50 \times 10^{-3}\text{ kg}}} = 322.49\text{ m/s}$$

After rearranging Eq. 16-12, we write

$$f = \frac{v}{\lambda} = \frac{322.49\text{ m/s}}{0.400\text{ m}}$$

$$= 806.2\text{ Hz} \approx 806\text{ Hz} \qquad \text{(Answer)}$$

Note that we get the same answer by substituting into Eq. 16-64:

$$f = n\frac{v}{2L} = 4\frac{322.49\text{ m/s}}{2(0.800\text{ m})}$$

$$= 806\text{ Hz} \qquad \text{(Answer)}$$

Now note that this 806 Hz is not only the frequency of the waves producing the fourth harmonic but also the frequency of the string elements that oscillate vertically in Fig. 16-34. It is also the frequency of the sound you would hear from the string.

Transverse velocity: The displacement y' of the string element located at coordinate x is given by Eq. 16-65 as a function of time t. The term $\cos\omega t$ contains the dependence on time and thus provides the "motion" of the standing wave. The term $2y_m \sin kx$ sets the extent of the motion—that is, the amplitude. The greatest amplitude occurs at an antinode, where $\sin kx$ is $+1$ or -1 and thus the greatest amplitude is $2y_m$. From Fig. 16-34, we see that $2y_m = 4.00$ mm, which tells us that $y_m = 2.00$ mm.

We want the transverse velocity—the velocity of a string element parallel to the y axis. To find it, we take the time derivative of Eq. 16-65:

$$u(x, t) = \frac{\partial y'}{\partial t} = \frac{\partial}{\partial t}[(2y_m \sin kx)\cos\omega t]$$

$$= [-2y_m\omega \sin kx]\sin\omega t \qquad (16\text{-}67)$$

Here the term $\sin\omega t$ provides the variation with time and the term $-2y_m\omega \sin kx$ provides the extent of that variation. We want the absolute magnitude of that extent:

$$u_m = |-2y_m\omega \sin kx|$$

To evaluate this for the element at $x = 0.180$ m, we first note that $y_m = 2.00$ mm, $k = 2\pi/\lambda = 2\pi/(0.400\text{ m})$, and $\omega = 2\pi f = 2\pi(806.2\text{ Hz})$. Then the maximum speed of the element at $x = 0.180$ m is

$$u_m = \left| -2(2.00 \times 10^{-3}\text{ m})(2\pi)(806.2\text{ Hz}) \times \sin\left(\frac{2\pi}{0.400\text{ m}}(0.180\text{ m})\right)\right|$$

$$= 6.26\text{ m/s} \qquad \text{(Answer)}$$

Conclude: To determine when the string element has this maximum speed, we could investigate Eq. 16-67. However, a little thought can save a lot of work. The element is undergoing simple harmonic motion and must come to a momentary stop at its extreme upward position and extreme downward position. It has the greatest speed as it zips through the midpoint of its oscillation, just as a block does in a block–spring oscillator.

PROBLEM-SOLVING TACTICS

Tactic 2: Harmonics on a String When you need to obtain information about a certain harmonic on a stretched string of given length L, first draw that harmonic (as in Fig. 16-32). If you are asked about, say, the fifth harmonic, you need to draw five loops between the fixed support points. That would mean that five loops, each of length $\lambda/2$, occupy the length L of the string. Thus, $5(\lambda/2) = L$, and $\lambda = 2L/5$. You can then use equation $f = v/\lambda$ to find the frequency of the harmonic.

Keep in mind that the wavelength of a harmonic is set only by the length L of the string, but the frequency depends also on the wave speed v, which is set by the tension and the linear density of the string via Eq. 16-25.

Sample Problem 16-12

Find the second longest resonance wavelength for which $\frac{3l}{8}$ is antinode.

Conceptualize: If we try normal frequencies for string with both rigid ends we can solve this problem simply by trial and error.

Classify: We can consider rope of length $\frac{3l}{8}$ with one end rigid and one end free. Also we can consider a rope of length l with both ends rigid. The frequencies which satisfies both equations simultaneously are the required frequency.

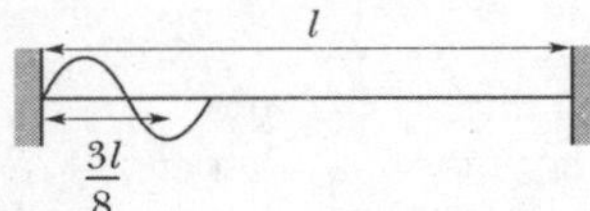

FIG. 16-35 A string connected at both ends with rigid wall.

Compute: All posible frequencies which will satisfy condition of both ends rigid

$$f_1 = \frac{m}{2f}\sqrt{\frac{T}{\mu}}$$

All posible frequencies which will satisfy condition of rope of length $\frac{3l}{8}$ with one end rigid and one end free

$$f_2 = \frac{2n+1}{4\left(\frac{3l}{8}\right)}\sqrt{\frac{T}{\mu}}$$

only those vibrations will have resonance which satisfy $f_1 = f_2$

$$\frac{2n+1}{4\left(\frac{3l}{8}\right)}\sqrt{\frac{T}{\mu}} = f = \frac{m}{2f}\sqrt{\frac{T}{\mu}}$$

Therefore $\quad 8n + 4 = 3m$

$$3m - 8n = 4$$

m	n
4	1
12	4
20	7

The second row has the second lowest frequency, hence second largest wavelength.

Therefore on putting value $\lambda = 6\,l$

Conclude: We can verify the answer by checking for the above value that result in satisfying both the conditions.

Sonometer

The Eq. 16-64 may be verified experimentally using a sonometer. Sonometer consists of a wire under tension, arranged on a hollow wooden box as in Fig. 16-36. The vibrations of the wire are passed by the movable bridges to the box and then to the air inside it. In order to verify the relationship between f and l, the bridges are moved so that different lengths between them excite at their different fundamental frequencies when plucked at the center. The frequencies may be found by measuring length of wire which vibrate in resonance with tuning forks of known frequencies. The product $f \times l$ should be constant within the limits of experimetal error.

To check that $f \propto \sqrt{T}$, the same length of wire is subjected to different tensions by changing the hanging mass.

The relation between f and $l/\sqrt{\mu}$ requires the use of wires of different diameters and materials but of the same vibrating length and under the same tension.

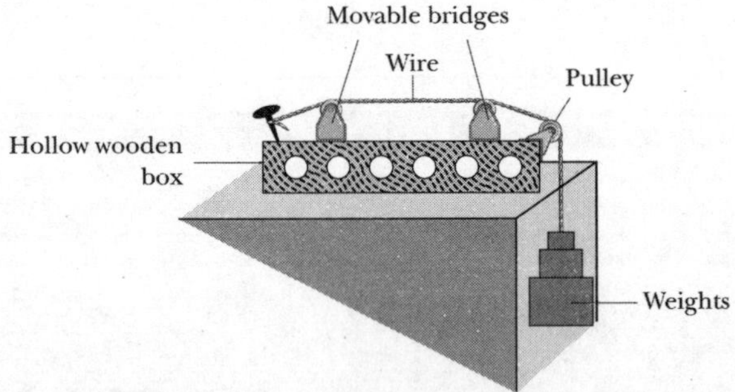

FIG. 16-36 Sonometer.

16-11 | Energy and Power of a Wave

Energy and Power of a Wave Traveling Along a String

When we set up a wave on a stretched string, we provide energy for the motion of the string. As the wave moves away from us, it transports that energy as both kinetic energy and elastic potential energy. Let us consider each form in turn.

Kinetic Energy

A string element of mass dm, oscillating transversely in simple harmonic motion as the wave passes through it, has kinetic energy associated with its transverse velocity $\vec{u}$. When the element is rushing through its $y = 0$ position (element b in Fig. 16-37), its transverse velocity—and thus its kinetic energy—is a maximum. When the element is at its extreme position $y = y_m$ (as is element a), its transverse velocity—and thus its kinetic energy—is zero.

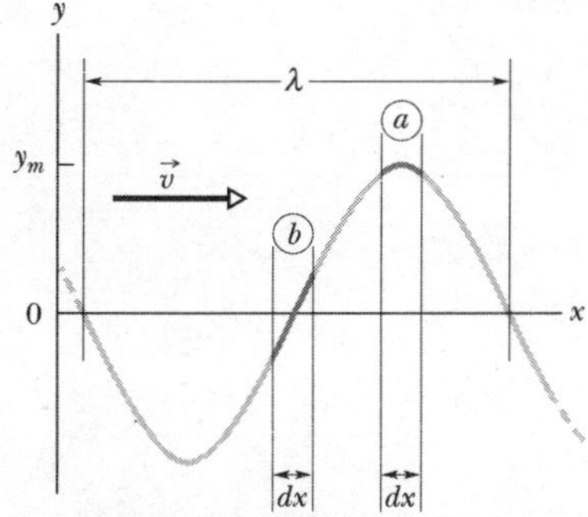

FIG. 16-37 A snapshot of a traveling wave on a string at time $t = 0$. String element a is at displacement $y = y_m$, and string element b is at displacement $y = 0$. The kinetic energy of the string element at each position depends on the transverse velocity of the element. The potential energy depends on the amount by which the string element is stretched as the wave passes through it.

Elastic Potential Energy

To send a sinusoidal wave along a previously straight string, the wave must necessarily stretch the string. As a string element of length dx oscillates transversely, its length must increase and decrease in a periodic way if the string element is to fit the sinusoidal wave form. Elastic potential energy is associated with these length changes, just as for a spring.

When the string element is at its $y = y_m$ position (element a in Fig. 16-37), its length has its normal undisturbed value dx, so its elastic potential energy is zero. However, when the element is rushing through its $y = 0$ position, it has maximum stretch and thus maximum elastic potential energy.

Energy Transport

The oscillating string element thus has both its maximum kinetic energy and its maximum elastic potential energy at $y = 0$. In the snapshot of Fig. 16-37, the regions of the string at maximum displacement have no energy, and the regions at zero displacement have maximum energy. As the wave travels along the string, forces due to the tension in the string continuously do work to transfer energy from regions with energy to regions with no energy.

Suppose we set up a wave on a string stretched along a horizontal x axis so that Eq. 16-4 describes the string's displacement. We might send a wave along the string by continuously oscillating one end of the string, as in Fig. 16-1b. In doing so, we continuously provide energy for the motion and stretching of the string—as the string sections oscillate perpendicularly to the x axis, they have kinetic energy and elastic potential energy. As the wave moves into sections that were previously at rest, energy is transferred into those new sections. Thus, we say that the wave *transports* the energy along the string.

Calculation of Kinetic Energy and Potential Energy

Rate of Energy Transmission

The kinetic energy dK associated with a string element of mass dm is given by

$$dK = \tfrac{1}{2}\, dm\, u^2 \qquad (16\text{-}68)$$

where u is the transverse speed of the oscillating string element. To find u, we differentiate Eq. 16 2 with respect to time while holding x constant:

$$u = \frac{\partial y}{\partial t} = -\omega y_m \cos(kx - \omega t) \qquad (16\text{-}69)$$

Using this relation and putting $dm = \mu\, dx$, we rewrite Eq. 16-66 as

$$dK = \tfrac{1}{2}(\mu\, dx)(-\omega y_m)^2 \cos^2(kx - \omega t) \qquad (16\text{-}70)$$

The potential energy can be calculated by finding the amount by which the deformed string is longer than when it is straight. This extension, multiplied by tension T, is the work done in the deformation (Fig. 16-38). Thus, for the segment, we have potential energy = $T\,(ds - dx)$

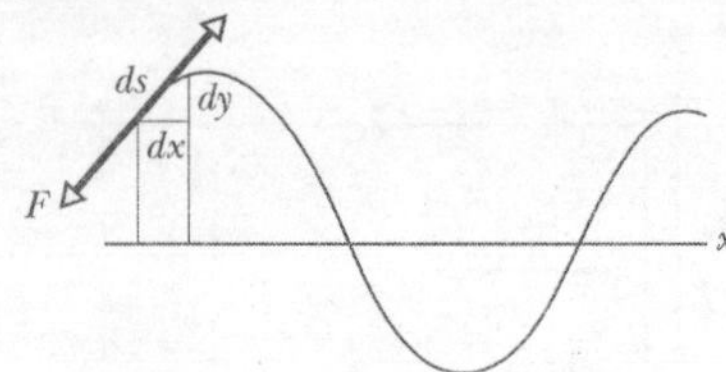

FIG. 16-38 A small element in a string.

where $ds = (dx^2 + dy^2)^{1/2}$

$$= dx\left[1 + \left(\frac{\partial y}{\partial x}\right)^2\right]^{1/2}$$

If we assume that the transverse displacements are small, so that $\frac{\partial y}{\partial x} \ll 1$, we can approximate the above expression using the binomial expansion to two terms, thus getting

$$ds - dx \approx \frac{1}{2}\left(\frac{\partial y}{\partial x}\right)^2 dx$$

Therefore,

$$\text{potential energy} \approx \frac{1}{2}\,T\left(\frac{\partial y}{\partial x}\right)^2 dx$$

Hence, we have

$$\text{potential-energy density} \equiv \frac{dU}{dx} \equiv \frac{1}{2}\,T\left(\frac{\partial y}{\partial x}\right)^2 \qquad (16\text{-}71)$$

It is worth noting that the kinetic-energy and potential-energy densities, as given by Eqs. 16-70 and 16-71, are equal since $T = \mu v^2$.

It is very interesting to note that both kinetic energy and potential energy are varying similarly, that is, when kinetic energy becomes zero potential energy also becomes zero and when kinetic energy becomes maximum potential energy also becomes maximum. We can see in Fig. 16-39 that part (a) has maximum kinetic energy as it is passing through mean position and it also has maximum potential energy as the stretch is maximum.

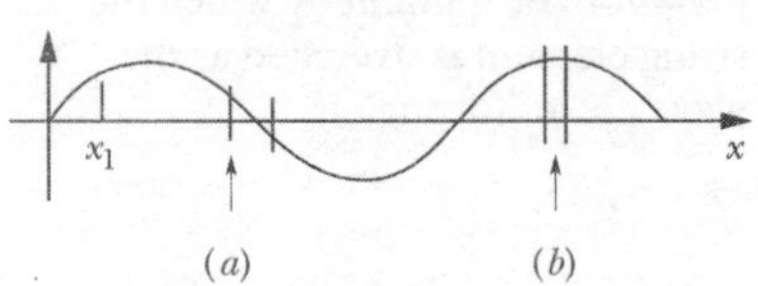

FIG. 16-39 A small element in a string is having maximum kinetic and potential energy at mean position and minimum kinetic and potential energy at extreme position.

Looking at part (b) we can see it has minimum kinetic energy as it is at extreme position and it also has minimum potential energy as the stretch at (b) is minimum.

The total kinetic energy in the segment of string between $x = 0$ and $x = \lambda$ is thus

$$K = \frac{1}{2}\,\mu u_0^2 \int_0^\lambda \cos^2\left(\frac{2\pi x}{\lambda}\right)dx$$

Where u_0 represents maximum particle velocity, $u_0 = wy_m$

that is, $$K = \frac{1}{4}\,(\lambda\mu)u_0^2$$

This, then, is the kinetic energy associated with one complete wavelength of the disturbance. (You can easily verify that the same answer is obtained by integrating the kinetic-energy density between any two values of x separated by λ at a given instant.)

The potential energy over the same portion of the string must, as we have already seen, be equal to the kinetic energy.

$$U = \pi^2 A^2\,\mu v^2 \lambda$$

which is equal in magnitude to K, as given by Eq. (16-70),

The total energy per wavelength, E, can be written

$$E = \frac{1}{2}\,(\lambda\mu)u_0^2 \qquad (16\text{-}72)$$

and is thus equal to the kinetic energy that a piece of the string of length λ would have if all of it were moving with the maximum transverse velocity u_0 associated with the wave.

Although we have chosen to make the calculation for a sinusoidal wave, equivalent results can be calculated for other kinds of waveform.

Power

Imagine that one end of a very long string is being oscillated transversely so as to generate a sinusoidal wave traveling out along the string. The calculations of the previous section clearly require that this process must involve a continuing input of energy. For each new length λ of the string that is set in motion by the wave, the amount of energy given by Eq. (16-72) must be supplied. The work equivalent to this energy must therefore be supplied by the the source at the end of the string. Let us see how this can be verified. Power flowing along x direction will be given by product of y component of tension and velocity of particle at x. Thus, instantaneous power transferred from left part to the right part is P_i.

$$P_i = (T \sin \theta)\left(\frac{\partial y}{\partial t}\right)$$

$$P_i = -T\left(\frac{\partial y}{\partial x}\right)\left(\frac{\partial y}{\partial t}\right) \qquad (16\text{-}73)$$

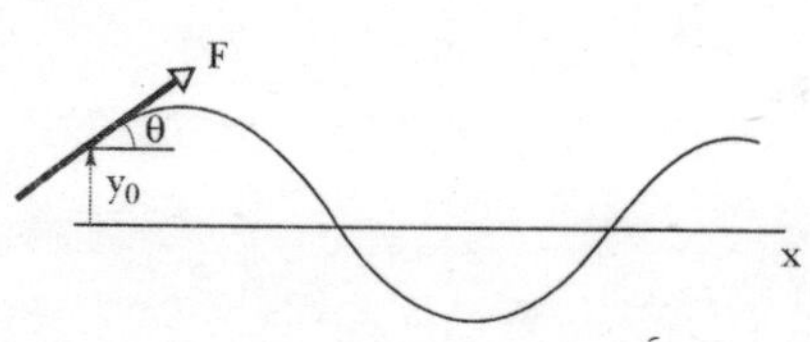

FIG. 16-40 Force doing work.

Minus sign is appearing because tension is acting downward.

Suppose now that we have, in particular, a sinusoidal wave described by the equation

$$y(x, t) = A \sin 2\pi\nu\left(t - \frac{x}{v}\right)$$

Then at any given value of x we have

On differentiating with respect to x we have

$$\frac{\partial y}{\partial x} = -\frac{2\pi\nu A}{v} \cos 2\pi\nu\left(t - \frac{x}{v}\right)$$

Therefore,

$$F_y = -\frac{2\pi\nu AT}{v} \cos 2\pi\nu t$$

Q:2 We can find instantaneous power for a sine wave $y = A \sin(\omega t - kx)$ by using eq. ( )

$$P_i = -T\,(AK \cos(\omega t - kx))\,[A\omega \cos(\omega t - kx)]$$

$$P_{\text{inst.}} = TA^2 k\omega \cos^2(\omega t - kx)$$

To find average power over one time period, we use $P_{\text{avg}} = \dfrac{\int_0^t P dt}{T_0}$

$$P_{\text{avg}} = \frac{A^2\omega^2 c}{2}$$

This is the average energy flowing through any point in one time period.

Energy and Power in Standing Wave

For standing wave we can still use Eqs. 16-70, 16-71, and 16-73, because during the derivation it was never assumed that wave is progressive. Only assumption was that string remains elastic. Let's assume a standing wave $y = A \cos kx \sin \omega t$

Thus, we get kinetic energy of small element of length dx as

$$dk = 1/2\,(\mu dx)A^2\omega^2 \cos^2 kx \cos^2 \omega t$$

Similarly, potential energy

$$dU = \frac{1}{2} T\, dx A^2 k^2 \sin^2 kx \sin^2 \omega t$$

Total energy of a small element of length dx is

$$dE = dk + dU$$

$$dE = \frac{\mu A^2 \omega^2}{2}(\cos^2 kx \ \cos^2 \omega t + \sin^2 kx \ \sin^2 \omega t)dx \qquad (16\text{-}74)$$

We can see that energy of a small element is dependent on time, that is, it is varying. We may have expected that energy of an element is constant but it is not, so we will show in next part that power is tsranmitting in stationary wave.

$$P_i = -T\left(\frac{\partial y}{\partial x}\right) \times \left(\frac{\partial y}{\partial t}\right)$$

$$P_i = -T[-AK \sin \omega t \sin kx]\,(A\omega \cos kx \cos \omega t)$$

$$P_i = TA^2 \omega k \sin \omega t \cos \omega t \sin kx \cos kx$$

Again you can see that energy is flowing through all parts except nodes and anti-nodes as at nodes $\cos kx = 0$ and at antinodes $\sin kx = 0$.

At only nodes and anti-nodes power transmitted is zero. This can be explained simply by observing that node is always at rest, so no energy can be transferred across it. At anti-node slope is zero so the force of tension is always along x and hence perpendicular to the velocity of particle which is always along y.

Thus, it is very important to understand that energy is flowing in stationary wave except at nodes and anti-nodes. Total energy from one node to the adjacent node remains constant and we can find energy of half loop from a anti-node to node by integrating Eq. (16-74) from 0 to $\lambda/4$

$$\int dE = E = \frac{\mu A^2 \omega^2}{2}\left[\cos^2 \omega t \int_0^{\lambda/4} \cos^2 kx\,dx + \sin^2 \omega t \int_0^{\lambda/4} \sin^2 kx\,dx\right]$$

$$E = \frac{\mu A^2 \omega^2}{2}\left[\cos^2 \omega t\left(\frac{1}{2}\right)\left(\frac{\lambda}{4}\right) + \sin^2 \omega t\left(\frac{1}{2}\right)\left(\frac{\lambda}{4}\right)\right]$$

$$E = \frac{\mu^2 A^2 \omega^2 \lambda}{16}$$

You can see that it is constant for half loop measured from a node to anti-node or from anti-node to a node.

Transmission

Consider a transverse wave propogating on a string which is further connected by another string, on which the wave has different speeds of propagation. Let the undisplaced strings lie along the x direction and the point where the strings are joined be at position x equal to zero. The string on the left-hand side have a wave of angular frequency ω propogating at speed v_1 having wavenumber k_1, and the string on the right-hand side of the joint propagates waves at a speed v_2 corresponding to wavenumber k_2. Some important points are as follows:-

1. The frequency of the waves on the two separate parts of the string must be the same; otherwise the join could not stay intact. At $x = 0$ the strings must go up and down together.
2. The tension in the strings must also be the same everywhere; otherwise the joint would move in the x direction.
3. The total disturbance on the left-hand string is the sum of the incident wave $A_i \cos(\omega t - k_1 x)$ and the reflected wave $A_r \cos(\omega t + k_1 x)$, where A_i and A_r are the respective amplitudes. The total wave on the left-hand string is thus given by
$$y_L = A_i \cos(\omega t - k_1 x) + A_r \cos(\omega t + k_1 x)$$
4. The disturbance on the right-hand string is a progressive wave given by
$$y_R = A_t \cos(\omega t - k_2 x) \tag{16-75}$$
where A_t is the amplitude of the transmitted wave.

We assume that there are no phase differences between the incident, reflected, and transmitted waves at $x = 0$. At $x = 0$, where the strings join , the string is continuous so at all times the displacement on the left at $x = 0$ must be equal to the displacement on the right at $x = 0$. Also, in order to make the forces on a very small section at the join equal and opposite, the slopes of the string either side of the join must be the same $(\partial y/\partial x)_L = (\partial y/\partial x)_R$ at $x = 0$. The conditions that the displacement and its derivative be continuous at the join are the boundary conditions that must be satisfied when the propagating wave meets the discontinuity.

The boundary condition on string continuity applied at time $t = 0$ gives

$$A_i + A_r = A_t$$

and the equal-slope condition applied at time $t = \pi/2\omega$ gives

$$k_1A_i - k_1A_r = k_2A_t$$

Manipulation of these two equations gives

$$\frac{A_r}{A_i} = \frac{k_1 - k_2}{k_1 + k_2} \tag{16-76}$$

and

$$\frac{A_t}{A_i} = \frac{2k_1}{k_1 + k_2}$$

We have now determined the amplitudes of the transmitted and reflected waves in terms of the amplitude of the incident wave. This was done by assuming that the phases of all three waves were equal at $x = 0$. A_t has the same sign as A_i since their ratio is always positive. However, A_r may have a different sign then A_i depending on the values of k_1 and k_2. If $k_2 > k_1$, there is a phase difference of π between incident and reflected waves; adding π to the phase of the reflected wave in Eq. (16-75) is equivalent to changing the sign of A_r.

Whether or not there is a phase change of π on reflection is determined by the sign of $(k_1 - k_2)$. The wavenumber on the right is greater than on the left if the speed of the waves on the right is less than on the left. Thus, from Eq. (16-76), the phase change is zero if the string on the right is lighter than on the left, or π if it is heavier.

Figure 16-41 shows at time $t = 0$ a wave of amplitude A_i incident on the join at $x = 0$ between two strings. The string on the right has a smaller value of mass per unit length μ than the string on the left. If the string on the right is very heavy, the join does not move and k_2 tends to infinity. For this situation A_t is zero, the phase change is π and we have standing waves set up.

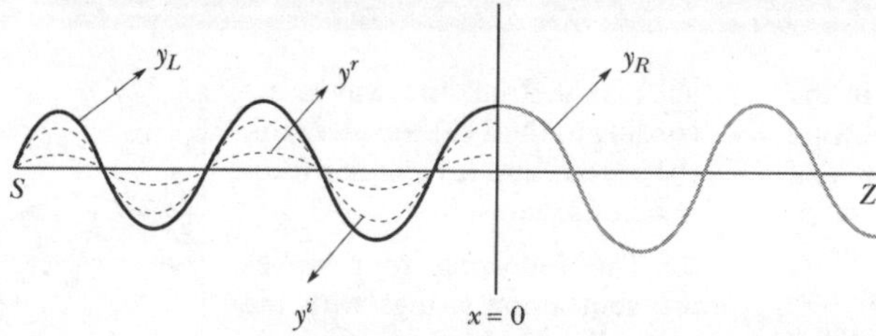

FIG. 16-41 Two different mass density strings connected.

REVIEW & SUMMARY

Transverse and Longitudinal Waves Mechanical waves can exist only in material media and are governed by Newton's laws. **Transverse** mechanical waves, like those on a stretched string, are waves in which the particles of the medium oscillate perpendicular to the wave's direction of travel. Waves in which the particles of the medium oscillate parallel to the wave's direction of travel are **longitudinal** waves.

Sinusoidal Waves A sinusoidal wave moving in the positive direction of an x axis has the mathematical form

$$y(x, t) = y_m \sin(kx - \omega t)$$

where y_m is the **amplitude** of the wave, k is the **angular wave number,** ω is the **angular frequency,** and $kx - \omega t$ is the **phase.** The **wavelength** λ is related to k by

$$k = \frac{2\pi}{\lambda}$$

Finally, the **wave speed** v is related to these other parameters by

$$v = \frac{\omega}{k} = \frac{\lambda}{T} = \lambda f$$

Equation of a Traveling Wave Any function of the form

$$y(x, t) = h(kx \pm \omega t)$$

can represent a **traveling wave** with a wave speed given by Eq. 16-13 and a wave shape given by the mathematical form of h. The plus sign denotes a wave traveling in the negative direction of the x axis, and the minus sign a wave traveling in the positive direction.

Wave Speed on Stretched String The speed of a wave on a stretched string is set by properties of the string. The speed on a string with tension τ and linear density μ is

$$v = \sqrt{\frac{\tau}{\mu}}$$

Power The **average power** of, or average rate at which energy is transmitted by, a sinusoidal wave on a stretched string is given by

$$P_{avg} = \tfrac{1}{2}\mu v \omega^2 y_m^2$$

Superposition of Waves When two or more waves traverse the same medium, the displacement of any particle of the medium is the sum of the displacements that the individual waves would give it.

Interference of Waves Two sinusoidal waves on the same string exhibit **interference,** adding or canceling according to the principle of superposition. If the two are traveling in the same direction and have the same amplitude y_m and frequency (hence the same wavelength) but differ in phase by a **phase constant** ϕ, the result is a single wave with this same frequency:

$$y'(x,t) = [2y_m \cos \tfrac{1}{2}\phi] \sin(kx - \omega t + \tfrac{1}{2}\phi)$$

If $\phi = 0$, the waves are exactly in phase and their interference is fully constructive; if $\phi = \pi$ rad, they are exactly out of phase and their interference is fully destructive.

Phasors A wave $y(x, t)$ can be represented with a **phasor.** This is a vector that has a magnitude equal to the amplitude y_m of the wave and that rotates about an origin with an angular speed equal to the angular frequency ω of the wave. The projection of the rotating phasor on a vertical axis gives the displacement y of a point along the wave's travel.

Standing Waves The interference of two identical sinusoidal waves moving in opposite directions produces **standing waves.** For a string with fixed ends, the standing wave is given by

$$y'(x,t) = [2y_m \sin kx] \cos \omega t$$

Standing waves are characterized by fixed locations of zero displacement called **nodes** and fixed locations of maximum displacement called **antinodes.**

Resonance Standing waves on a string can be set up by reflection of traveling waves from the ends of the string. If an end is fixed, it must be the position of a node. This limits the frequencies at which standing waves will occur on a given string. Each possible frequency is a **resonant frequency,** and the corresponding standing wave pattern is an **oscillation mode.** For a stretched string of length L with fixed ends, the resonant frequencies are

$$f = \frac{v}{\lambda} = n\frac{v}{2L}, \qquad \text{for } n = 1, 2, 3, \ldots.$$

The oscillation mode corresponding to $n = 1$ is called the *fundamental mode* or the *first harmonic*; the mode corresponding to $n = 2$ is the *second harmonic*; and so on.

QUESTIONS

1 Figure 16-42*a* gives a snapshot of a wave traveling in the direction of positive x along a string under tension. Four string elements are indicated by the lettered points. For each of those elements, determine whether, at the instant of the snapshot, the element is moving upward or downward or is momentarily at rest. (*Hint:* Imagine the wave as it moves through the four string elements, as if you were watching a video of the wave as it traveled rightward.)

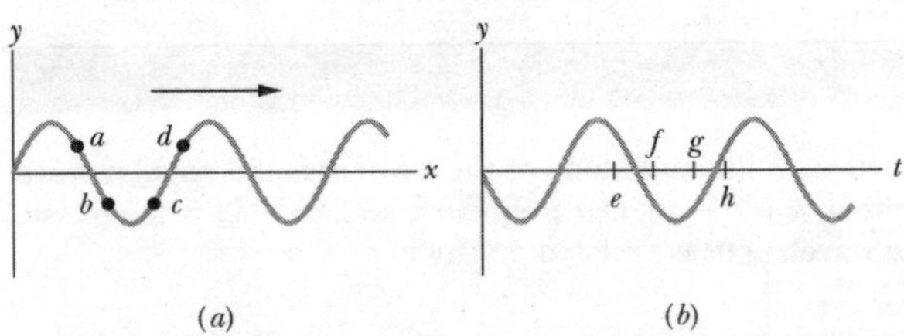

FIG. 16-42 Question 1.

Figure 16-42*b* gives the displacement of a string element located at, say, $x = 0$ as a function of time. At the lettered times, is the element moving upward or downward or is it momentarily at rest?

2 Figure 16-43 shows three waves that are *separately* sent along a string that is stretched under a certain tension along an x axis. Rank the waves according to their (a) wavelengths, (b) speeds, and (c) angular frequencies, greatest first.

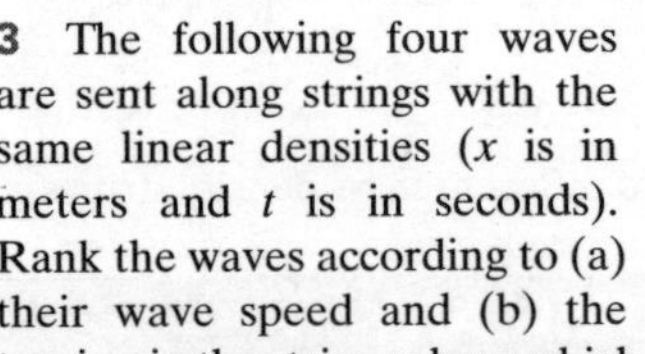

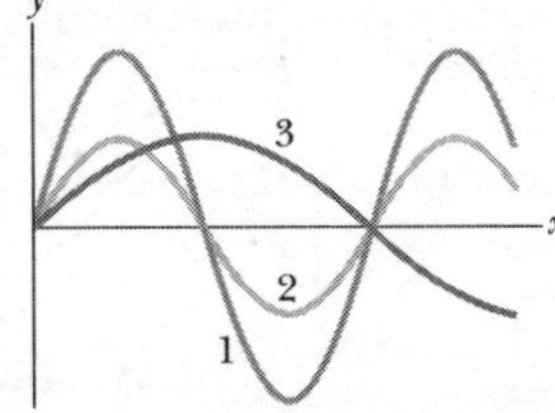

FIG. 16-43 Question 2.

3 The following four waves are sent along strings with the same linear densities (x is in meters and t is in seconds). Rank the waves according to (a) their wave speed and (b) the tension in the strings along which they travel, greatest first:

(1) $y_1 = (3 \text{ mm}) \sin(x - 3t)$, (3) $y_3 = (1 \text{ mm}) \sin(4x - t)$,
(2) $y_2 = (6 \text{ mm}) \sin(2x - t)$, (4) $y_4 = (2 \text{ mm}) \sin(x - 2t)$.

4 In Fig. 16-44, wave 1 consists of a rectangular peak of height 4 units and width d, and a rectangular valley of depth 2 units and width d. The wave travels rightward along an x axis. Choices 2, 3, and 4 are similar waves, with the same heights, depths, and widths, that will travel leftward along that axis and through wave 1. Right-going wave 1 and one of the left-going waves will interfere as they pass through each other. With which left-going wave will the interference give, for an instant, (a) the deepest valley, (b) a flat line, and (c) a flat peak $2d$ wide?

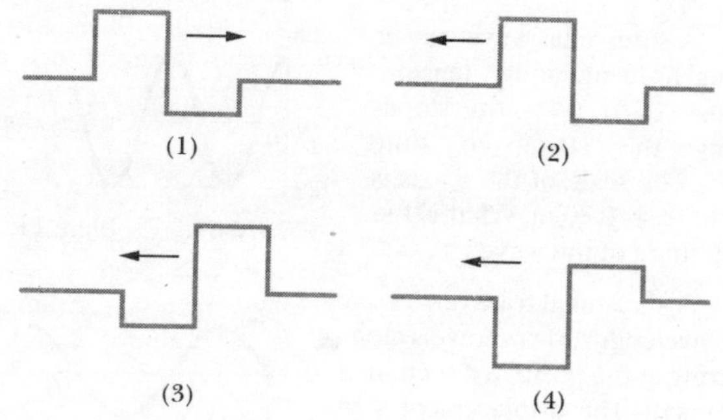

FIG. 16-44 Question 4.

5 A sinusoidal wave is sent along a cord under tension, transporting energy at the average rate of $P_{avg,1}$. Two waves, identical to that first one, are then to be sent along the cord with a phase difference ϕ of either 0, 0.2 wavelength, or 0.5 wavelength. (a) With only mental calculation, rank those choices of ϕ according to the average rate at which the waves will transport energy, greatest first. (b) For the first choice of ϕ, what is the average rate in terms of $P_{avg,1}$?

6 The amplitudes and phase differences for four pairs of waves of equal wavelengths are (a) 2 mm, 6 mm, and π rad; (b) 3 mm, 5 mm, and π rad; (c) 7 mm, 9 mm, and π rad; (d) 2 mm, 2 mm, and 0 rad. Each pair travels in the same direction along the same string. Without written calculation, rank the four pairs according to the amplitude of their resultant wave, greatest first. (*Hint:* Construct phasor diagrams.)

7 If you start with two sinusoidal waves of the same amplitude traveling in phase on a string and then somehow phase-shift one of them by 5.4 wavelengths, what type of interference will occur on the string?

8 If you set up the seventh harmonic on a string, (a) how many nodes are present, and (b) is there a node, antinode, or some intermediate state at the midpoint? If you next set up the sixth harmonic, (c) is its resonant wavelength longer or shorter than that for the seventh harmonic, and (d) is the resonant frequency higher or lower?

9 Figure 16-45 shows phasor diagrams for three situations in which two waves travel along the same string. All six waves have the same amplitude. Rank the situations according to the amplitude of the net wave on the string, greatest first.

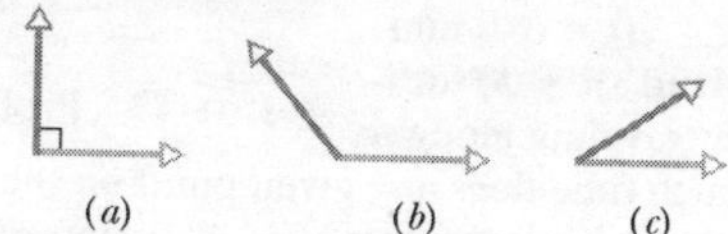

FIG. 16-45 Question 9.

10 (a) If a standing wave on a string is given by

$$y'(t) = (3 \text{ mm}) \sin(5x) \cos(4t)$$

is there a node or an antinode of the oscillations of the string at $x = 0$? (b) If the standing wave is given by

$$y'(t) = (3 \text{ mm}) \sin(5x + \pi/2) \cos(4t)$$

is there a node or an antinode at $x = 0$?

11 Strings A and B have identical lengths and linear densities, but string B is under greater tension than string A. Figure 16-46 shows four situations, (*a*) through (*d*), in which standing wave patterns exist on the two strings. In which situations is there the possibility that strings A and B are oscillating at the same resonant frequency?

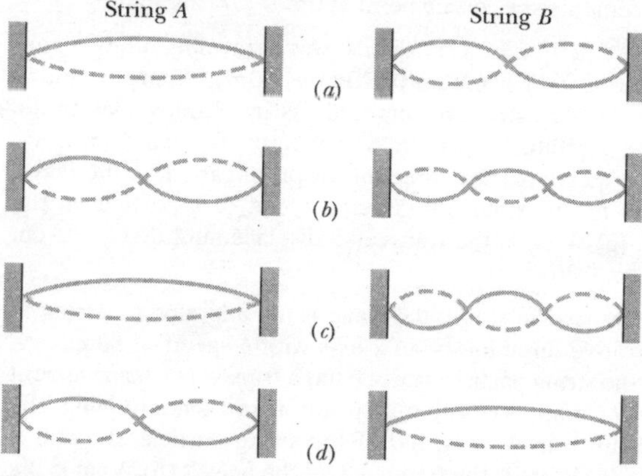

FIG. 16-46 Question 11.

PROBLEMS

sec. 16-1 The Speed of a Traveling Wave

1 A sand scorpion can detect the motion of a nearby beetle (its prey) by the waves the motion sends along the sand surface (Fig. 16-47). The waves are of two types: transverse waves traveling at $v_t = 50$ m/s and longitudinal waves traveling at $v_l = 150$ m/s. If a sudden motion sends out such waves, a scorpion can tell the distance of the beetle from the difference Δt in the arrival times of the waves at its leg nearest the beetle. If $\Delta t = 4.0$ ms, what is the beetle's distance?

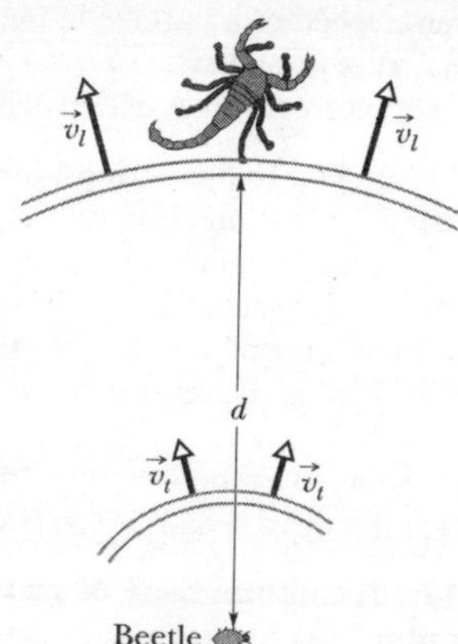

FIG. 16-47 Problem 1.

2 A sinusoidal wave travels along a string. The time for a particular point to move from maximum displacement to zero is 0.170 s. What are the (a) period and (b) frequency? (c) The wavelength is 1.40 m; what is the wave speed?

3 *A human wave.* During sporting events within large, densely packed stadiums, spectators will send a wave (or pulse) around the stadium (Fig. 16-48). As the wave reaches a group of spectators, they stand with a cheer and then sit. At any instant, the width w of the wave is the distance from the leading edge (people are just about to stand) to the trailing edge (people have just sat down). Suppose a human wave travels a distance of 853 seats around a stadium in 39 s, with spectators requiring about 1.8 s to respond to the wave's passage by standing and then sitting. What are (a) the wave speed v (in seats per second) and (b) width w (in number of seats)?

FIG. 16-48 Problem 3.

4 If $y(x, t) = (6.0 \text{ mm}) \sin(kx + (600 \text{ rad/s})t + \phi)$ describes a wave traveling along a string, how much time does any given point on the string take to move between displacements $y = +2.0$ mm and $y = -2.0$ mm?

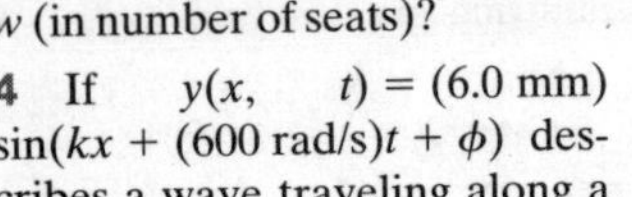

5 Figure 16-49 shows the transverse velocity u versus time t of the point on a string at $x = 0$, as a wave passes through it. The scale on the vertical axis is set by $u_s = 4.0$ m/s. The wave has form $y(x, t) = y_m \sin(kx - \omega t + \phi)$. What is ϕ? (*Caution:* A calculator does not always give the proper inverse trig function, so check your answer by substituting it and an assumed value of ω into $y(x, t)$ and then plotting the function.)

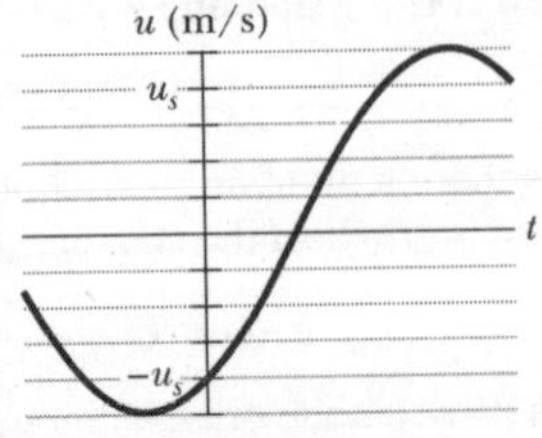

FIG. 16-49 Problem 5.

6 A sinusoidal wave of frequency 500 Hz has a speed of 350 m/s. (a) How far apart are two points that differ in phase by $\pi/3$ rad? (b) What is the phase difference between two displacements at a certain point at times 1.00 ms apart?

7 The equation of a transverse wave traveling along a very long string is $y = 6.0 \sin(0.020\pi x + 4.0\pi t)$, where x and y are expressed in centimeters and t is in seconds. Determine (a) the amplitude, (b) the wavelength, (c) the frequency, (d) the speed, (e) the direction of propagation of the wave, and (f) the maximum transverse speed of a particle in the string. (g) What is the transverse displacement at $x = 3.5$ cm when $t = 0.26$ s?

8 A transverse sinusoidal wave is moving along a string in the positive direction of an x axis with a speed of 80 m/s. At $t = 0$, the string particle at $x = 0$ has a transverse displacement of 4.0 cm from its equilibrium position and is not moving. The maximum transverse speed of the string particle at $x = 0$ is 16 m/s. (a) What is the frequency of the wave? (b) What is the wavelength of the wave? If the wave equation is of the form $y(x, t) = y_m \sin(kx \pm \omega t + \phi)$, what are (c) y_m, (d) k, (e) ω, (f) ϕ, and (g) the correct choice of sign in front of ω?

9 The function $y(x, t) = (15.0 \text{ cm}) \cos(\pi x - 15\pi t)$, with x in meters and t in seconds, describes a wave on a taut string. What is the transverse speed for a point on the string at an instant when that point has the displacement $y = +12.0$ cm?

10 A sinusoidal wave moving along a string is shown twice in Fig. 16-50, as crest A travels in the positive direction of an x axis by distance $d = 6.0$ cm in 4.0 ms. The tick marks along the axis are separated by 10 cm; height $H = 6.00$ mm. If the wave equation is of the form $y(x, t) = y_m \sin(kx \pm \omega t)$, what are (a) y_m, (b) k, (c) ω, and (d) the correct choice of sign in front of ω?

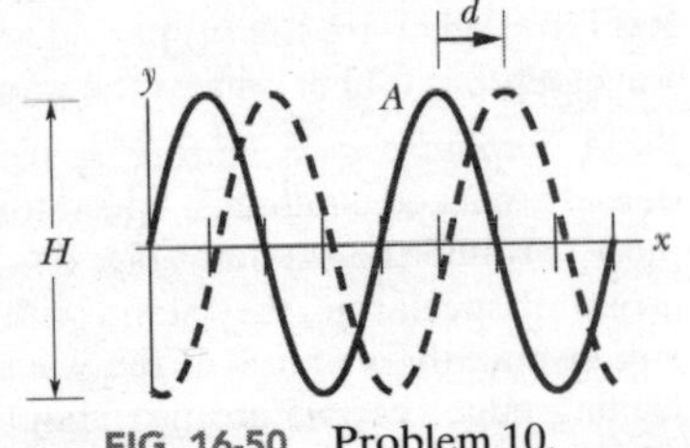

FIG. 16-50 Problem 10.

11 A sinusoidal wave travels along a string under tension. Figure 16-51 gives the slopes along the string at time $t = 0$. The scale of the x axis is set by $x_s = 0.80$ m. What is the amplitude of the wave?

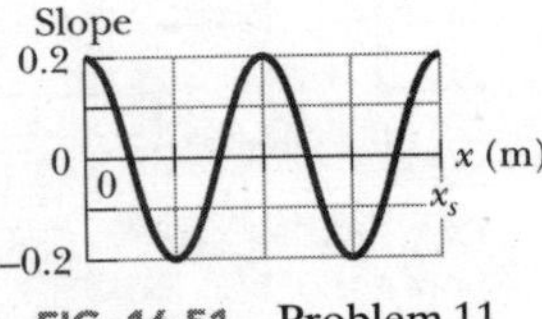

FIG. 16-51 Problem 11.

12 A sinusoidal transverse wave of wavelength 20 cm travels along a string in the positive direction of an x axis. The displacement y of the string particle at $x = 0$ is given in Fig. 16-52 as a function of time t. The scale of the vertical axis is set by $y_s = 4.0$ cm. The wave equation is to be in the form $y(x, t) = y_m \sin(kx \pm \omega t + \phi)$. (a) At $t = 0$, is a plot of y versus x in the shape of a positive sine function or a negative sine function? What are (b) y_m, (c) k, (d) ω, (e) ϕ, (f) the sign in front of ω, and (g) the speed of the wave? (h) What is the transverse velocity of the particle at $x = 0$ when $t = 5.0$ s?

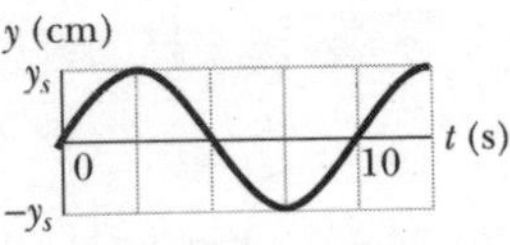

FIG. 16-52 Problem 12.

sec. 16-2 Wave Speed on a Stretched String

13 A stretched string has a mass per unit length of 5.00 g/cm and a tension of 10.0 N. A sinusoidal wave on this string has an amplitude of 0.12 mm and a frequency of 100 Hz and is traveling in the negative direction of an x axis. If the wave equation is of the form $y(x, t) = y_m \sin(kx \pm \omega t)$, what are (a) y_m, (b) k, (c) ω, and (d) the correct choice of sign in front of ω?

14 The equation of a transverse wave on a string is

$$y = (2.0 \text{ mm}) \sin[(20 \text{ m}^{-1})x - (600 \text{ s}^{-1})t]$$

The tension in the string is 15 N. (a) What is the wave speed? (b) Find the linear density of this string in grams per meter.

15 A sinusoidal transverse wave is traveling along a string in the negative direction of an x axis. Figure 16-53 shows a plot of the displacement as a function of position at time $t = 0$; the scale of the y axis is set by $y_s = 4.0$ cm. The string tension is 3.6 N, and its linear density is 25 g/m. Find the (a) amplitude, (b) wavelength, (c) wave speed, and (d) period of the wave. (e) Find the maximum transverse speed of a particle in the string. If the wave is of the form $y(x, t) = y_m \sin(kx \pm \omega t + \phi)$, what are (f) k, (g) ω, (h) ϕ, and (i) the correct choice of sign in front of ω?

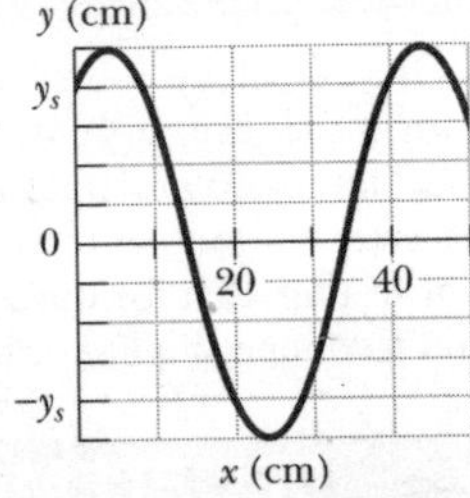

FIG. 16-53 Problem 15.

16 In Fig. 16-54*a*, string 1 has a linear density of 3.00 g/m, and string 2 has a linear density of 5.00 g/m. They are under tension due to the hanging block of mass $M = 500$ g. Calculate the wave speed on (a) string 1 and (b) string 2. (*Hint:* When a string loops halfway around a pulley, it pulls on the pulley with a net force that is twice the tension in the string.) Next the block is divided into two blocks (with $M_1 + M_2 = M$) and the apparatus is rearranged as shown in Fig. 16-54*b*. Find (c) M_1 and (d) M_2 such that the wave speeds in the two strings are equal.

17 A uniform rope of mass m and length L hangs from a ceiling. (a) Show that the speed of a transverse wave on the rope is a function of y, the distance from the lower end, and is given by $v = \sqrt{gy}$. (b) Show that the time a transverse wave takes to travel the length of the rope is given by $t = 2\sqrt{L/g}$.

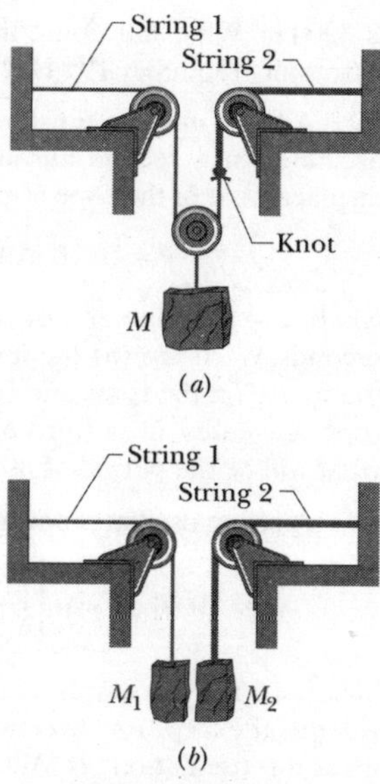

FIG. 16-54 Problem 16.

sec. 16-3 Energy and Power of a Wave Traveling Along a String

18 A string along which waves can travel is 2.70 m long and has a mass of 260 g. The tension in the string is 36.0 N. What must be the frequency of traveling waves of amplitude 7.70 mm for the average power to be 85.0 W?

19 A sinusoidal wave is sent along a string with a linear density of 2.0 g/m. As it travels, the kinetic energies of the mass elements along the string vary. Figure 16-55*a* gives the rate dK/dt at which kinetic energy passes through the string elements at a particular instant, plotted as a function of distance x along the string. Figure 16-55*b* is similar except that it gives the rate at which kinetic energy passes through a particular mass element (at a particular location), plotted as a function of time t. For both figures, the scale on the vertical (rate) axis is set by $R_s = 10$ W. What is the amplitude of the wave?

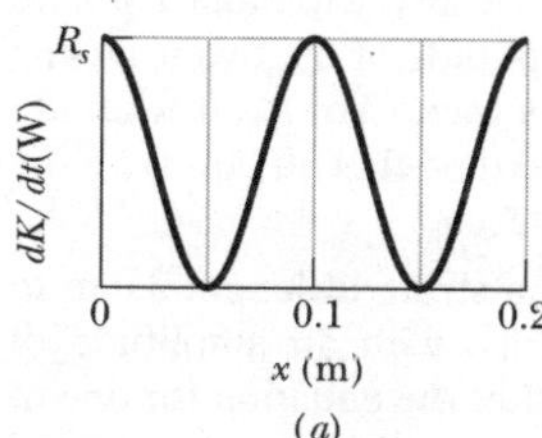

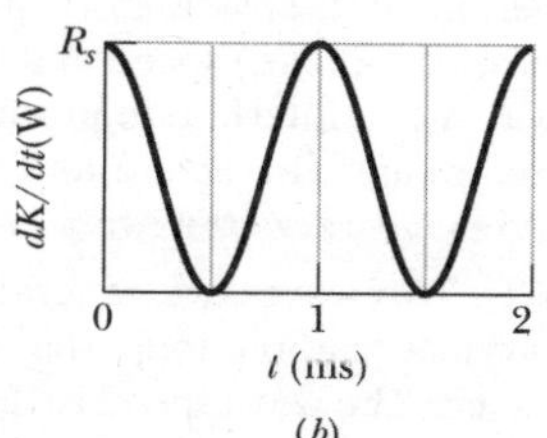

FIG. 16-55 Problem 19.

sec. 16-4 The Wave Equation

20 Use the wave equation to find the speed of a wave given by

$$y(x, t) = (3.00 \text{ mm}) \sin[(4.00 \text{ m}^{-1})x - (7.00 \text{ s}^{-1})t]$$

21 Use the wave equation to find the speed of a wave given by

$$y(x, t) = (2.00 \text{ mm})[(20 \text{ m}^{-1})x - (4.0 \text{ s}^{-1})t]^{0.5}$$

22 Use the wave equation to find the speed of a wave given in terms of the general function $h(x, t)$:

$$y(x, t) = (4.00 \text{ mm})\, h[(30 \text{ m}^{-1})x + (6.0 \text{ s}^{-1})t]$$

sec. 16-5 Interference of Waves

23 Two identical traveling waves, moving in the same direction, are out of phase by $\pi/2$ rad. What is the amplitude of the resultant wave in terms of the common amplitude y_m of the two combining waves?

24 What phase difference between two identical traveling waves, moving in the same direction along a stretched string, results in the combined wave having an amplitude 1.50 times that of the common amplitude of the two combining waves? Express your answer in (a) degrees, (b) radians, and (c) wavelengths.

25 Two sinusoidal waves with the same amplitude of 9.00 mm and the same wavelength travel together along a string that is stretched along an x axis. Their resultant wave is shown twice in Fig. 16-56, as valley A travels in the negative direction of the x axis by distance $d = 56.0$ cm in 8.0 ms. The tick marks along the axis are separated by 10 cm, and height H is 8.0 mm. Let the equation for one wave be of the form $y(x, t) = y_m \sin(kx \pm \omega t + \phi_1)$, where $\phi_1 = 0$ and you must choose the correct sign in front of ω. For the equation for the other wave, what are (a) y_m, (b) k, (c) ω, (d) ϕ_2, and (e) the sign in front of ω?

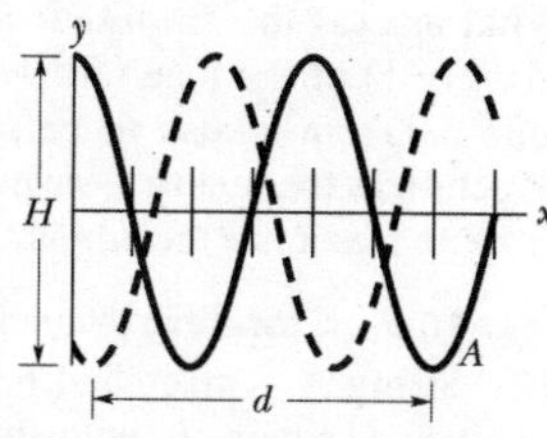

FIG. 16-56 Problem 25.

26 A sinusoidal wave of angular frequency 1200 rad/s and amplitude 3.00 mm is sent along a cord with linear density 2.00 g/m and tension 1200 N. (a) What is the average rate at which energy is transported by the wave to the opposite end of the cord? (b) If, simultaneously, an identical wave travels along an adjacent, identical cord, what is the total average rate at which energy is transported to the opposite ends of the two cords by the waves? If, instead, those two waves are sent along the *same* cord simultaneously, what is the total average rate at which they transport energy when their phase difference is (c) 0, (d) 0.4π rad, and (e) π rad?

sec. 16-6 Phasors

27 Two sinusoidal waves of the same frequency travel in the same direction along a string. If $y_{m1} = 3.0$ cm, $y_{m2} = 4.0$ cm, $\phi_1 = 0$, and $\phi_2 = \pi/2$ rad, what is the amplitude of the resultant wave?

28 Two sinusoidal waves of the same frequency are to be sent in the same direction along a taut string. One wave has an amplitude of 5.0 mm, the other 8.0 mm. (a) What phase difference ϕ_1 between the two waves results in the smallest amplitude of the resultant wave? (b) What is that smallest amplitude? (c) What phase difference ϕ_2 results in the largest amplitude of the resultant wave? (d) What is that largest amplitude? (e) What is the resultant amplitude if the phase angle is $(\phi_1 - \phi_2)/2$?

29 Two sinusoidal waves of the same period, with amplitudes of 5.0 and 7.0 mm, travel in the same direction along a stretched string; they produce a resultant wave with an amplitude of 9.0 mm. The phase constant of the 5.0 mm wave is 0. What is the phase constant of the 7.0 mm wave?

30 Four waves are to be sent along the same string, in the same direction:

$$y_1(x, t) = (4.00 \text{ mm}) \sin(2\pi x - 400\pi t)$$
$$y_2(x, t) = (4.00 \text{ mm}) \sin(2\pi x - 400\pi t + 0.7\pi)$$
$$y_3(x, t) = (4.00 \text{ mm}) \sin(2\pi x - 400\pi t + \pi)$$
$$y_4(x, t) = (4.00 \text{ mm}) \sin(2\pi x - 400\pi t + 1.7\pi)$$

What is the amplitude of the resultant wave?

31 These two waves travel along the same string:

$$y_1(x,t) = (4.60 \text{ mm}) \sin(2\pi x - 400\pi t)$$
$$y_2(x,t) = (5.60 \text{ mm}) \sin(2\pi x - 400\pi t + 0.80\pi \text{ rad}).$$

What are (a) the amplitude and (b) the phase angle (relative to wave 1) of the resultant wave? (c) If a third wave of amplitude 5.00 mm is also to be sent along the string in the same direction as the first two waves, what should be its phase angle in order to maximize the amplitude of the new resultant wave?

sec. 16-7 Standing Waves and Resonance

32 String A is stretched between two clamps separated by distance L. String B, with the same linear density and under the same tension as string A, is stretched between two clamps separated by distance $4L$. Consider the first eight harmonics of string B. For which of these eight harmonics of B (if any) does the frequency match the frequency of (a) A's first harmonic, (b) A's second harmonic, and (c) A's third harmonic?

33 A string fixed at both ends is 8.40 m long and has a mass of 0.120 kg. It is subjected to a tension of 96.0 N and set oscillating. (a) What is the speed of the waves on the string? (b) What is the longest possible wavelength for a standing wave? (c) Give the frequency of that wave.

34 Two sinusoidal waves with identical wavelengths and amplitudes travel in opposite directions along a string with a speed of 10 cm/s. If the time interval between instants when the string is flat is 0.50 s, what is the wavelength of the waves?

35 A nylon guitar string has a linear density of 7.20 g/m and is under a tension of 150 N. The fixed supports are distance D = 90.0 cm apart. The string is oscillating in the standing wave pattern shown in Fig. 16-57. Calculate the (a) speed, (b) wavelength, and (c) frequency of the traveling waves whose superposition gives this standing wave.

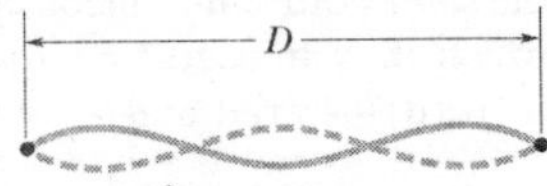

FIG. 16-57 Problem 35.

36 A string under tension τ_i oscillates in the third harmonic at frequency f_3, and the waves on the string have wavelength λ_3. If the tension is increased to $\tau_f = 4\tau_i$ and the string is again made to oscillate in the third harmonic, what then are (a) the frequency of oscillation in terms of f_3 and (b) the wavelength of the waves in terms of λ_3?

37 A string that is stretched between fixed supports separated by 75.0 cm has resonant frequencies of 420 and 315 Hz, with no intermediate resonant frequencies. What are (a) the lowest resonant frequency and (b) the wave speed?

38 If a transmission line in a cold climate collects ice, the increased diameter tends to cause vortex formation in a passing wind. The air pressure variations in the vortexes tend to cause the line to oscillate (*gallop*), especially if the frequency of the variations matches a resonant frequency of the line. In long lines, the resonant frequencies are so close that almost any wind speed can set up a resonant mode vigorous enough to pull down support towers or cause the line to *short out* with an adjacent line. If a transmission line has a length of 347 m, a linear density of 3.35 kg/m, and a tension of 65.2 MN, what are (a) the frequency of the fundamental mode and (b) the frequency difference between successive modes?

39 One of the harmonic frequencies for a particular string under tension is 325 Hz. The next higher harmonic frequency is 390 Hz. What harmonic frequency is next higher after the harmonic frequency 195 Hz?

40 A rope, under a tension of 200 N and fixed at both ends, oscillates in a second-harmonic standing wave pattern. The displacement of the rope is given by

$$y = (0.10 \text{ m})(\sin \pi x/2) \sin 12\pi t$$

where $x = 0$ at one end of the rope, x is in meters, and t is in seconds. What are (a) the length of the rope, (b) the speed of the waves on the rope, and (c) the mass of the rope? (d) If the rope oscillates in a third-harmonic standing wave pattern, what will be the period of oscillation?

41 A string oscillates according to the equation

$$y' = (0.50 \text{ cm}) \sin\left[\left(\frac{\pi}{3} \text{ cm}^{-1}\right)x\right] \cos[(40\pi \text{ s}^{-1})t]$$

What are the (a) amplitude and (b) speed of the two waves (identical except for direction of travel) whose superposition gives this oscillation? (c) What is the distance between nodes? (d) What is the transverse speed of a particle of the string at the position x = 1.5 cm when t = 9/8 s?

42 A standing wave pattern on a string is described by

$$y(x,t) = 0.040 (\sin 5\pi x)(\cos 40\pi t)$$

where x and y are in meters and t is in seconds. For $x \geq 0$, what is the location of the node with the (a) smallest, (b) second smallest, and (c) third smallest value of x? (d) What is the period of the oscillatory motion of any (nonnode) point? What are the (e) speed and (f) amplitude of the two traveling waves that interfere to produce this wave? For $t \geq 0$, what are the (g) first, (h) second, and (i) third time that all points on the string have zero transverse velocity?

43 Two waves are generated on a string of length 3.0 m to produce a three-loop standing wave with an amplitude of 1.0 cm. The wave speed is 100 m/s. Let the equation for one of the waves be of the form $y(x,t) = y_m \sin(kx + \omega t)$. In the equation for the other wave, what are (a) y_m, (b) k, (c) ω, and (d) the sign in front of ω?

44 For a certain transverse standing wave on a long string, an antinode is at $x = 0$ and an adjacent node is at x = 0.10 m. The displacement $y(t)$ of the string particle at x = 0 is shown in Fig. 16-58, where the scale of the y axis is set by y_s = 4.0 cm. When t = 0.50 s, what is the displacement of the string particle at (a) x = 0.20 m and (b) x = 0.30 m? What is the transverse velocity of the string particle at x = 0.20 m at (c) t = 0.50 s and (d) t = 1.0 s? (e) Sketch the standing wave at t = 0.50 s for the range x = 0 to x = 0.40 m.

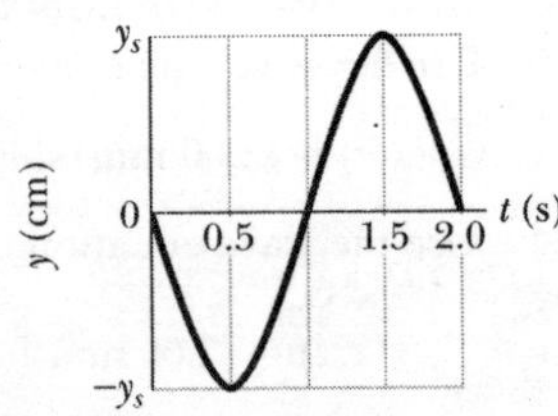

FIG. 16-58 Problem 44.

45 A generator at one end of a very long string creates a wave given by

$$y = (6.0 \text{ cm}) \cos \frac{\pi}{2} [(2.00 \text{ m}^{-1})x + (8.00 \text{ s}^{-1})t]$$

and a generator at the other end creates the wave

$$y = (6.0 \text{ cm}) \cos \frac{\pi}{2} [(2.00 \text{ m}^{-1})x - (8.00 \text{ s}^{-1})t]$$

Calculate the (a) frequency, (b) wavelength, and (c) speed of each wave. For $x \geq 0$, what is the location of the node having the (d) smallest, (e) second smallest, and (f) third smallest value of x? For $x \geq 0$, what is the location of the antinode having the (g) smallest, (h) second smallest, and (i) third smallest value of x?

46 Two sinusoidal waves with the same amplitude and wavelength travel through each other along a string that is stretched along an x axis. Their resultant wave is shown twice in Fig. 16-59, as the antinode A travels from an extreme upward displacement to an extreme downward displacement in 6.0 ms. The tick marks along the axis are separated by 10 cm; height H is 1.80 cm. Let the equation for one of the two waves be of the form $y(x, t) = y_m \sin(kx + \omega t)$. In the equation for the other wave, what are (a) y_m, (b) k, (c) ω, and (d) the sign in front of ω?

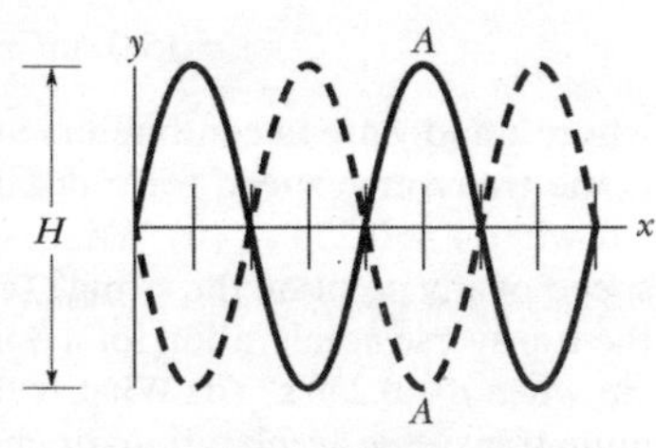

FIG. 16-59 Problem 46.

47 In Fig. 16-60, a string, tied to a sinusoidal oscillator at P and running over a support at Q, is stretched by a block of mass m. Separation $L = 1.20$ m, linear density $\mu = 1.6$ g/m, and the oscillator frequency $f = 120$ Hz. The amplitude of the motion at P is small enough for that point to be considered a node. A node also exists at Q. (a) What mass m allows the oscillator to set up the fourth harmonic on the string? (b) What standing wave mode, if any, can be set up if $m = 1.00$ kg?

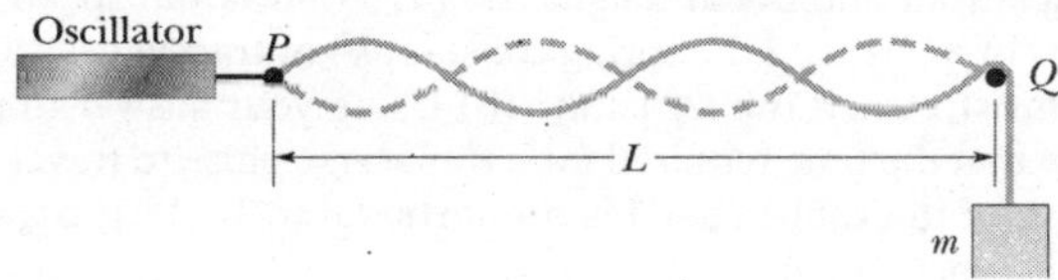

FIG. 16-60 Problems 47 and 49.

48 In Fig. 16-61, an aluminum wire, of length $L_1 = 60.0$ cm, cross-sectional area 1.00×10^{-2} cm^2, and density 2.60 g/cm^3, is joined to a steel wire, of density 7.80 g/cm^3 and the same cross-sectional area. The compound wire, loaded with a block of mass $m = 10.0$ kg, is arranged so that the distance L_2 from the joint to the supporting pulley is 86.6 cm. Transverse waves are set up on the wire by an external source of variable frequency; a node is located at the pulley. (a) Find the lowest frequency that generates a standing wave having the joint as one of the nodes. (b) How many nodes are observed at this frequency?

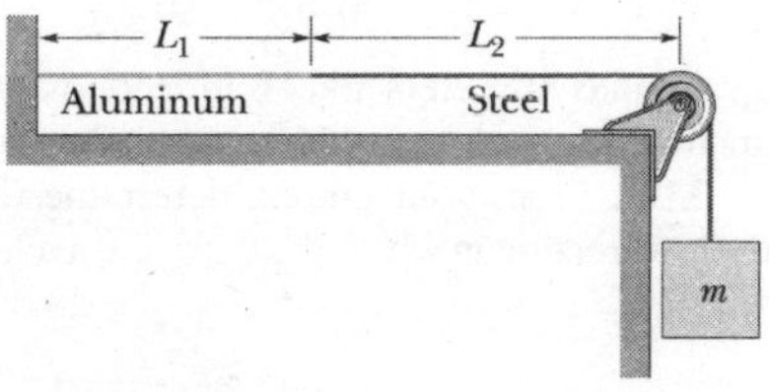

FIG. 16-61 Problem 48.

49 In Fig. 16-60, a string, tied to a sinusoidal oscillator at P and running over a support at Q, is stretched by a block of mass m. The separation L between P and Q is 1.20 m, and the frequency f of the oscillator is fixed at 120 Hz. The amplitude of the motion at P is small enough for that point to be considered a node. A node also exists at Q. A standing wave appears when the mass of the hanging block is 286.1 g or 447.0 g, but not for any intermediate mass. What is the linear density of the string?

Additional Problems

50 Three sinusoidal waves of the same frequency travel along a string in the positive direction of an x axis. Their amplitudes are y_1, $y_1/2$, and $y_1/3$, and their phase constants are 0, $\pi/2$, and π, respectively. What are the (a) amplitude and (b) phase constant of the resultant wave? (c) Plot the wave form of the resultant wave at $t = 0$, and discuss its behavior as t increases.

51 Figure 16-62 shows the displacement y versus time t of the point on a string at $x = 0$, as a wave passes through that point. The scale of the y axis is set by $y_s = 6.0$ mm. The wave has form $y(x, t) = y_m \sin(kx - \omega t + \phi)$. What is ϕ? (*Caution:* A calculator does not always give the proper inverse trig function, so check your answer by substituting it and an assumed value of ω into $y(x, t)$ and then plotting the function.)

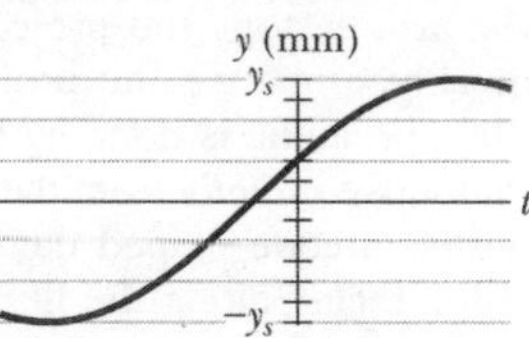

FIG. 16-62 Problem 51.

52 Figure 16-63 shows transverse acceleration a_y versus time t of the point on a string at $x = 0$, as a wave written in the form $y(x, t) = y_m \sin(kx - \omega t + \phi)$ passes through that point. The scale of the vertical axis is set by $a_s = 400$ m/s^2. What is ϕ? (*Caution:* A calculator does not always give the proper inverse trig function, so check your answer by substituting it and an assumed value of ω into $y(x, t)$ and then plotting the function.)

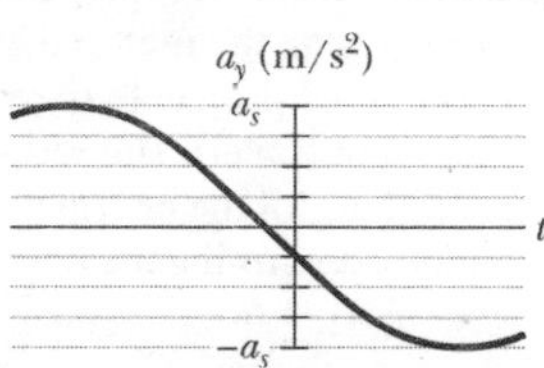

FIG. 16-63 Problem 52.

53 At time $t = 0$ and at position $x = 0$ m along a string, a traveling sinusoidal wave with an angular frequency of 440 rad/s has displacement $y = +4.5$ mm and transverse velocity $u = -0.75$ m/s. If the wave has general form $y(x, t) = y_m \sin(kx - \omega t + \phi)$, what is phase constant ϕ?

54 A single pulse, given by $h(x - 5.0t)$, is shown in Fig. 16-64 for $t = 0$. The scale of the vertical axis is set by $h_s = 2$. Here x is in centimeters and t is in seconds. What are the (a) speed and (b) direction of travel of the pulse? (c) Plot $h(x - 5t)$ as a function of x for $t = 2$ s. (d) Plot $h(x - 5t)$ as a function of t for $x = 10$ cm.

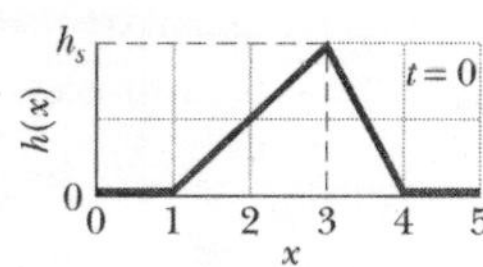

FIG. 16-64 Problem 54.

55 Two sinusoidal 120 Hz waves, of the same frequency and amplitude, are to be sent in the positive direction of an x axis that is directed along a cord under tension. The waves can be sent in phase, or they can be phase-shifted. Figure 16-65 shows the amplitude y' of the resulting wave versus the distance of the shift (how far one wave is shifted from the other wave). The scale of the vertical axis is set by $y'_s = 6.0$ mm. If the equations for the two waves are of the form $y(x, t) = y_m \sin(kx \pm \omega t)$, what are (a) y_m, (b) k, (c) ω, and (d) the correct choice of sign in front of ω?

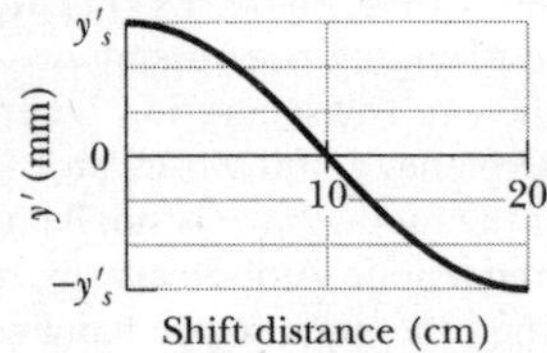

FIG. 16-65 Problem 55.

56 Energy is transmitted at rate P_1 by a wave of frequency f_1 on a string under tension τ_1. What is the new energy transmission rate P_2 in terms of P_1 (a) if the tension is increased to $\tau_2 = 4\tau_1$ and (b) if, instead, the frequency is decreased to $f_2 = f_1/2$?

57 *Body armor*. When a high-speed projectile such as a bullet or bomb fragment strikes modern body armor, the fabric of the armor stops the projectile and prevents penetration by quickly spreading the projectile's energy over a large area. This spreading is done by longitudinal and transverse pulses that move *radially* from the impact point, where the projectile pushes a cone-shaped dent into the fabric. The longitudinal pulse, racing along the fibers of the fabric at speed v_l ahead of the denting, causes the fibers to thin and stretch, with material flowing radially inward into the dent. One such radial fiber is shown in Fig. 16-66*a*. Part of the projectile's energy goes into this motion and stretching. The transverse pulse, moving at a slower speed v_t, is due to the denting. As the projectile increases the dent's depth, the dent increases in radius, causing the material in the fibers to move in the same direction as the projectile (perpendicular to the transverse pulse's direction of travel). The rest of the projectile's energy goes into this motion. All the energy that does not eventually go into permanently deforming the fibers ends up as thermal energy.

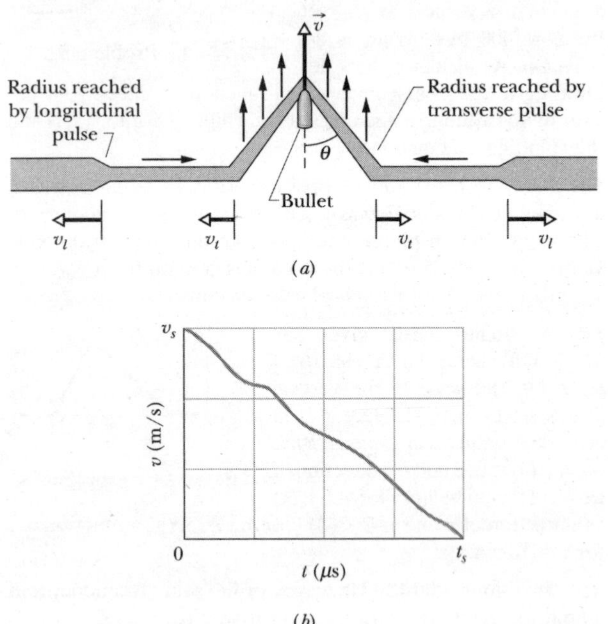

FIG. 16-66 Problem 57.

Figure 16-66*b* is a graph of speed v versus time t for a bullet of mass 10.2 g fired from a .38 Special revolver directly into body armor. The scales of the vertical and horizontal axes are set by $v_s = 300$ m/s and $t_s = 40.0$ μs. Take $v_l = 2000$ m/s, and assume that the half-angle θ of the conical dent is 60°. At the end of the collision, what are the radii of (a) the thinned region and (b) the dent (assuming that the person wearing the armor remains stationary)?

58 A wave on a string is described by

$$y(x, t) = 15.0 \sin(\pi x/8 - 4\pi t)$$

where x and y are in centimeters and t is in seconds. (a) What is the transverse speed for a point on the string at $x = 6.00$ cm when $t = 0.250$ s? (b) What is the maximum transverse speed of any point on the string? (c) What is the magnitude of the transverse acceleration for a point on the string at $x = 6.00$ cm when $t = 0.250$ s? (d) What is the magnitude of the maximum transverse acceleration for any point on the string?

59 A certain transverse sinusoidal wave of wavelength 20 cm is moving in the positive direction of an x axis. The transverse velocity of the particle at $x = 0$ as a function of time is shown in Fig. 16-67, where the scale of the vertical axis is set by $u_s = 5.0$ cm/s. What are the (a) wave speed, (b) amplitude, and (c) frequency? (d) Sketch the wave between $x = 0$ and $x = 20$ cm at $t = 2.0$ s.

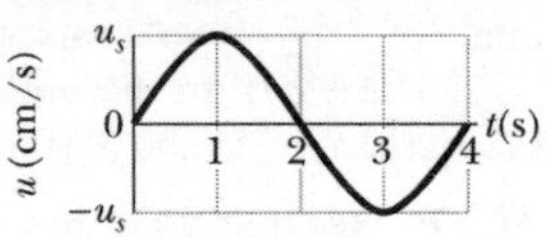

FIG. 16-67 Problem 59.

60 The type of rubber band used inside some baseballs and golf balls obeys Hooke's law over a wide range of elongation of the band. A segment of this material has an unstretched length ℓ and a mass m. When a force F is applied, the band stretches an additional length $\Delta\ell$. (a) What is the speed (in terms of m, $\Delta\ell$, and the spring constant k) of transverse waves on this stretched rubber band? (b) Using your answer to (a), show that the time required for a transverse pulse to travel the length of the rubber band is proportional to $1/\sqrt{\Delta\ell}$ if $\Delta\ell \ll \ell$ and is constant if $\Delta\ell \gg \ell$.

61 The speed of electromagnetic waves (which include visible light, radio, and x rays) in vacuum is 3.0×10^8 m/s. (a) Wavelengths of visible light waves range from about 400 nm in the violet to about 700 nm in the red. What is the range of frequencies of these waves? (b) The range of frequencies for shortwave radio (for example, FM radio and VHF television) is 1.5 to 300 MHz. What is the corresponding wavelength range? (c) X ray wavelengths range from about 5.0 nm to about 1.0×10^{-2} nm. What is the frequency range for X rays?

62 A traveling wave on a string is described by

$$y = 2.0 \sin\left[2\pi\left(\frac{t}{0.40} + \frac{x}{80}\right)\right]$$

where x and y are in centimeters and t is in seconds. (a) For $t = 0$, plot y as a function of x for $0 \le x \le 160$ cm. (b) Repeat (a) for $t = 0.05$ s and $t = 0.10$ s. From your graphs, determine (c) the wave speed and (d) the direction in which the wave is traveling.

Longitudinal Waves

Andoni Canela/Age Fotostock America, Inc.

Echoes can be enchanting in certain outdoor settings and annoying in rooms where they make speech unintelligible, but they always mimic the source of the sound. For example, the sound of a handclap returns as the sound of a handclap. However, an echo in front of these steps up the side of a pyramid in the Mayan ruins at Chichen Itza, Mexico, is remarkably different because the handclap returns as a musical note descending in frequency.

What causes this musical echo, said to be a chirped echo?

The answer is in this chapter.

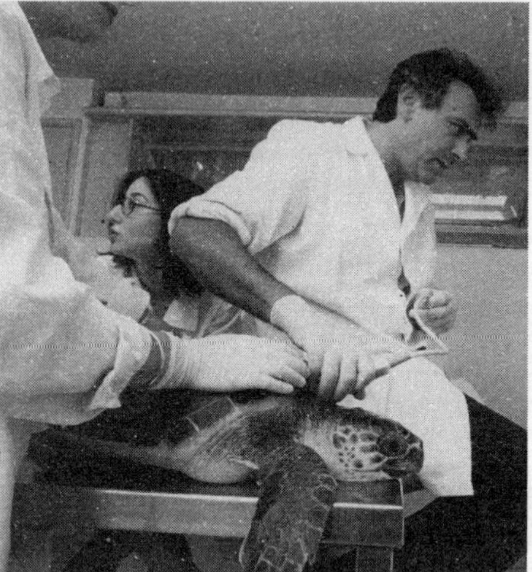

FIG. 17-1 A loggerhead turtle is being checked with ultrasound (which has a frequency above your hearing range); an image of its interior is being produced on a monitor off to the right. *(Mauro Fermariello/SPL/Photo Researchers)*

17-1 | Sound

As we already know, mechanical waves are waves that require a material medium to exist. There are two types of mechanical waves: *Transverse waves* involve oscillations perpendicular to the direction in which the wave travels; *longitudinal waves* involve oscillations parallel to the direction of wave travel.

In this book, a **sound wave** is defined roughly as any longitudinal wave. Seismic prospecting teams use such waves to probe Earth's crust for oil. Ships carry sound-ranging gear (sonar) to detect underwater obstacles. Submarines use sound waves to stalk other submarines, largely by listening for the characteristic noises produced by the propulsion system. Figure 17-1 suggests how sound waves can be used to explore the soft tissues of an animal or human body. In this chapter we shall focus on sound waves that travel through the air and that are audible to people.

Figure 17-2 illustrates several ideas that we shall use in our discussions. Point S represents a tiny sound source, called a *point source,* that emits sound waves in all directions. The *wavefronts* and *rays* indicate the direction of travel and the spread of the sound waves. **Wavefronts** are surfaces over which the oscillations due to the sound wave have the same value; such surfaces are represented by whole or partial circles in a two-dimensional drawing for a point source. **Rays** are directed lines perpendicular to the wavefronts that indicate the direction of travel of the wavefronts. The short double arrows superimposed on the rays of Fig. 17-2 indicate that the longitudinal oscillations of the air are parallel to the rays.

Near a point source like that of Fig. 17-2, the wavefronts are spherical and spread out in three dimensions, and there the waves are said to be *spherical.* As the wavefronts move outward and their radii become larger, their curvature decreases. Far from the source, we approximate the wavefronts as planes (or lines on two-dimensional drawings), and the waves are said to be *planar.*

17-2 | The Speed of Sound

The speed of any mechanical wave, transverse or longitudinal, depends on both an inertial property of the medium (to store kinetic energy) and an elastic property of the medium (to store potential energy). Thus, we can generalize the speed of a transverse wave along a stretched string, by writing

$$v = \sqrt{\frac{\tau}{\mu}} = \sqrt{\frac{\text{elastic property}}{\text{inertial property}}} \tag{17-1}$$

where (for transverse waves) τ is the tension in the string and μ is the string's linear density. If the medium is air and the wave is longitudinal, we can guess that the inertial property, corresponding to μ, is the volume density ρ of air. What shall we put for the elastic property?

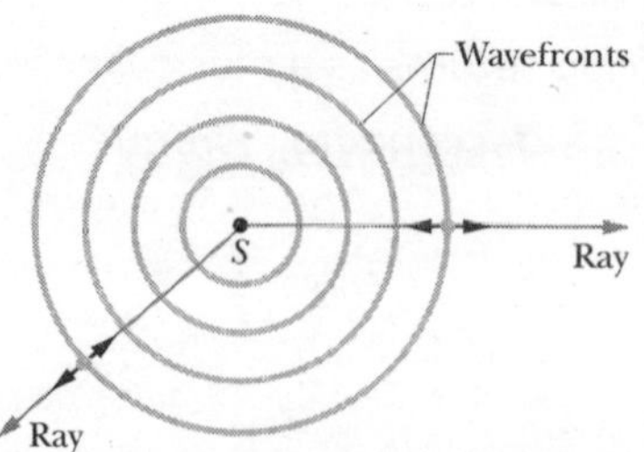

FIG. 17-2 A sound wave travels from a point source S through a three-dimensional medium. The wavefronts form spheres centered on S; the rays are radial to S. The short, double-headed arrows indicate that elements of the medium oscillate parallel to the rays.

In a stretched string, potential energy is associated with the periodic stretching of the string elements as the wave passes through them. As a sound wave passes through air, potential energy is associated with periodic compressions and expansions of small volume elements of the air. The property that determines the extent to which an element of a medium changes in volume when the pressure (force per unit area) on it changes is the **bulk modulus** B, defined as

$$B = -\frac{\Delta p}{\Delta V/V} \quad \text{(definition of bulk modulus)} \tag{17-2}$$

Here $\Delta V/V$ is the fractional change in volume produced by a change in pressure Δp. As explained earlier the SI unit for pressure is the newton per square meter, which is given a special name, the *pascal* (Pa). From Eq. 17-2 we see that the unit for B is also the pascal. The signs of Δp and ΔV are always opposite: When we increase the pressure on an element (Δp is positive), its volume decreases (ΔV is negative). We include a minus sign in Eq. 17-2 so that B is always a positive quantity. Now substituting B for τ and ρ for μ in Eq. 17-1 yields

$$v = \sqrt{\frac{B}{\rho}} \quad \text{(speed of sound)} \tag{17-3}$$

as the speed of sound in a medium with bulk modulus B and density ρ. Table 17-1 lists the speed of sound in various media.

The density of water is almost 1000 times greater than the density of air. If this were the only relevant factor, we would expect from Eq. 17-3 that the speed of sound in water would be considerably less than the speed of sound in air. However, Table 17-1 shows us that the reverse is true. We conclude (again from Eq. 17-3) that the bulk modulus of water must be more than 1000 times greater than that of air. This is indeed the case. Water is much more incompressible than air, which (see Eq. 17-2) is another way of saying that its bulk modulus is much greater.

TABLE 17-1

The Speed of Sound[a]

Medium	Speed (m/s)
Gases	
Air (0°C)	331
Air (20°C)	343
Helium	965
Hydrogen	1284
Liquids	
Water (0°C)	1402
Water (20°C)	1482
Seawater[b]	1522
Solids	
Aluminum	6420
Steel	5941
Granite	6000

[a]At 0°C and 1 atm pressure, except where noted.

[b]At 20°C and 3.5% salinity.

Formal Derivation of Eq. 17-3

We now derive Eq. 17-3 by direct application of Newton's laws. Let a single pulse in which air is compressed travel (from right to left) with speed v through the air in a long tube, like that in Fig. 16-2. Let us run along with the pulse at that speed, so that the pulse appears to stand still in our reference frame. Figure 17-3*a* shows the situation as it is viewed from that frame. The pulse is standing still, and air is moving at speed v through it from left to right.

Let the pressure of the undisturbed air be p and the pressure inside the pulse be $p + \Delta p$, where Δp is positive due to the compression. Consider an element of air of thickness Δx and face area A, moving toward the pulse at speed v. As this element enters the pulse, the leading face of the element encounters a region of higher pressure, which slows the element to speed $v + \Delta v$, in which Δv is negative. This slowing is complete when the rear face of the element reaches the pulse, which requires time interval

$$\Delta t = \frac{\Delta x}{v} \tag{17-4}$$

Let us apply Newton's second law to the element. During Δt, the average force on the element's trailing face is pA toward the right, and the average force on the leading face is $(p + \Delta p)A$ toward the left (Fig. 17-3*b*). Therefore, the average net force on the element during Δt is

$$\begin{aligned} F &= pA - (p + \Delta p)A \\ &= -\Delta p\, A \quad \text{(net force)} \end{aligned} \tag{17-5}$$

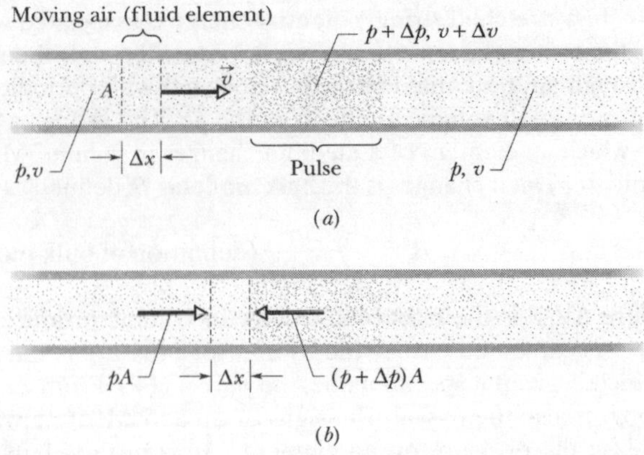

FIG. 17-3 A compression pulse is sent from right to left down a long air-filled tube. The reference frame of the figure is chosen so that the pulse is at rest and the air moves from left to right. (*a*) An element of air of width Δx moves toward the pulse with speed v. (*b*) The leading face of the element enters the pulse. The forces acting on the leading and trailing faces (due to air pressure) are shown.

The minus sign indicates that the net force on the air element is directed to the left in Fig. 17-3*b*. The volume of the element is $A\,\Delta x$, so with the aid of Eq. 17-4, we can write its mass as

$$\Delta m = \rho\,\Delta V = \rho A\,\Delta x = \rho A v\,\Delta t \quad \text{(mass)} \tag{17-6}$$

The average acceleration of the element during Δt is

$$a = \frac{\Delta v}{\Delta t} \quad \text{(acceleration)} \tag{17-7}$$

Thus, from Newton's second law ($F = ma$), we have, from Eqs. 17-5, 17-6, and 17-7,

$$-\Delta p\,A = (\rho A v\,\Delta t)\frac{\Delta v}{\Delta t}$$

which we can write as

$$\rho v^2 = -\frac{\Delta p}{\Delta v/v} \tag{17-8}$$

The air that occupies a volume $V\,(= Av\,\Delta t)$ outside the pulse is compressed by an amount $\Delta V\,(= A\,\Delta v\,\Delta t)$ as it enters the pulse. Thus,

$$\frac{\Delta V}{V} = \frac{A\,\Delta v\,\Delta t}{Av\,\Delta t} = \frac{\Delta v}{v} \tag{17-9}$$

Substituting Eq. 17-9 and then Eq. 17-2 into Eq. 17-8 leads to

$$\rho v^2 = -\frac{\Delta p}{\Delta v/v} = -\frac{\Delta p}{\Delta V/V} = B$$

Solving for v yields Eq. 17-3 for the speed of the air toward the right in Fig. 17-3, and thus for the actual speed of the pulse toward the left.

Sample Problem 17-1

When a sound pulse, as from a handclap, is produced at the foot of the stairs at the Mayan pyramid shown in the chapter's opening photograph, the sound waves reflect from the steps in succession, the closest (lowest) one first (Fig. 17-4*a*) and the farthest (highest) one last (Fig. 17-4*b*). The depth and height of the steps are $d = 0.263$ m, and the speed of sound is 343 m/s. The paths taken by the sound waves to and from the steps near the bottom of the stairs are approximately horizontal. The slanted paths taken by the sound waves to and from the steps near the top are approximately 45° to the horizontal. At what frequency f_{bot} do the echo pulses arrive at the listener from the bottom steps? At what frequency f_{top} do they arrive from the top steps a short time later?

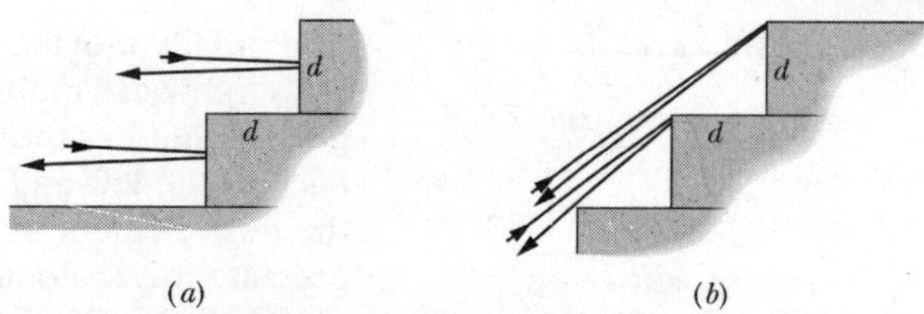

FIG. 17-4 Sound waves reflect from (*a*) the bottom steps and (*b*) the top steps of a tall flight of stairs.

Conceptualize: The frequency f at which the pulses return to the listener is the inverse of the time Δt between successive pulses.

Classify: The time interval Δt required by sound to travel a given distance L is related to the speed of sound v by $v = L/\Delta t$.

Compute: In Fig. 17-4*a* at the bottom of the stairs, the sound wave that reflects from the higher step travels a distance $L = 2d$ more than the sound wave that reflects from the lower step. (The higher wave must travel twice across the step's depth.) So, the arrivals of the echo pulses at the listener are separated by the time interval

$$\Delta t_{bot} = \frac{L}{v} = \frac{2d}{v} \tag{17-10}$$

$$= \frac{2(0.263 \text{ m})}{343 \text{ m/s}} = 1.533 \times 10^{-3} \text{ s}$$

The frequency f_{bot} at which the pulses arrive at the listener is

$$f_{bot} = \frac{1}{\Delta t_{bot}} \tag{17-11}$$

$$= \frac{1}{1.533 \times 10^{-3} \text{ s}} = 652 \text{ Hz} \qquad \text{(Answer)}$$

The time interval Δt_{bot} is too short for a listener to distinguish the individual pulses. Instead, the frequency f_{bot} is brought to consciousness—the listener hears a musical note of frequency 652 Hz.

In Fig. 17-4*b* at the top of the stairs, the slanted approach and return of the sound waves means that the wave reflected from the higher step travels a distance $L = 2\sqrt{2}d$ more than the wave that reflects from the lower step. (The travel is twice along the hypotenuse of a right triangle with equal legs of length d.) So, now the arrivals of the echo pulses at the listener are separated by the time interval

$$\Delta t_{top} = \frac{L}{v} = \frac{2\sqrt{2}d}{v} \tag{17-12}$$

$$= \frac{2\sqrt{2}(0.263 \text{ m})}{343 \text{ m/s}} = 2.168 \times 10^{-3} \text{ s}$$

and the frequency that is brought to consciousness is

$$f_{top} = \frac{1}{\Delta t_{top}}$$

$$= \frac{1}{2.168 \times 10^{-3} \text{ s}} = 461 \text{ Hz} \qquad \text{(Answer)}$$

Conclude: Thus, a handclap in front of the stairs produces an echo that begins with a frequency of 652 Hz and ends with a frequency of 461 Hz. You might be able to hear such a musical echo from other stairs or even from a picket fence if you stand alongside it.

17-3 | Traveling Sound Waves

Here we examine the displacements and pressure variations associated with a sinusoidal sound wave traveling through air. Figure 17-5*a* displays such a wave traveling rightward through a long air-filled tube. We can produce such a wave by

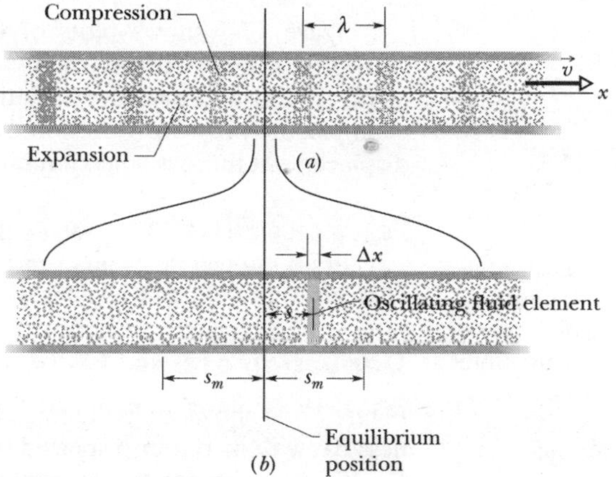

FIG. 17-5 (*a*) A sound wave, traveling through a long air-filled tube with speed v, consists of a moving, periodic pattern of expansions and compressions of the air. The wave is shown at an arbitrary instant. (*b*) A horizontally expanded view of a short piece of the tube. As the wave passes, an air element of thickness Δx oscillates left and right in simple harmonic motion about its equilibrium position. At the instant shown in (*b*), the element happens to be displaced a distance s to the right of its equilibrium position. Its maximum displacement, either right or left, is s_m.

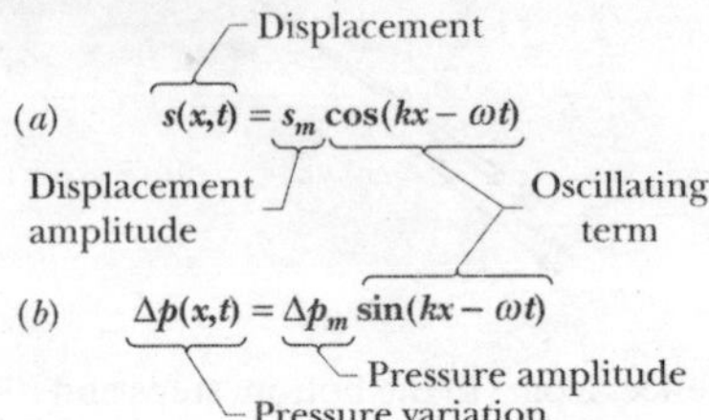

FIG. 17-6 (*a*) The displacement function and (*b*) the pressure-variation function of a traveling sound wave consist of an amplitude and an oscillating term.

sinusoidally moving a piston at the left end of the tube (as in Fig. 16-2). The piston's rightward motion moves the element of air next to the piston face and compresses that air; the piston's leftward motion allows the element of air to move back to the left and the pressure to decrease. As each element of air pushes on the next element in turn, the right–left motion of the air and the change in its pressure travel along the tube as a sound wave.

Consider the thin element of air of thickness Δx shown in Fig. 17-5*b*. As the wave travels through this portion of the tube, the element of air oscillates left and right in simple harmonic motion about its equilibrium position. Thus, the oscillations of each air element due to the traveling sound wave are like those of a string element due to a transverse wave, except that the air element oscillates *longitudinally* rather than *transversely.* Because string elements oscillate parallel to the y axis, we write their displacements in the form $y(x, t)$. Similarly, because air elements oscillate parallel to the x axis, we could write their displacements in the confusing form $x(x, t)$, but we shall use $s(x, t)$ instead.

To show that the displacements $s(x, t)$ are sinusoidal functions of x and t, we can use either a sine function or a cosine function. In this chapter we use a cosine function, writing

$$s(x, t) = s_m \cos(kx - \omega t) \tag{17-13}$$

Figure 17-6*a* labels the various parts of this equation. In it, s_m is the **displacement amplitude**—that is, the maximum displacement of the air element to either side of its equilibrium position (see Fig. 17-5*b*). The angular wave number k, angular frequency ω, frequency f, wavelength λ, speed v, and period T for a sound (longitudinal) wave are defined and interrelated exactly as for a transverse wave, except that λ is now the distance (again along the direction of travel) in which the pattern of compression and expansion due to the wave begins to repeat itself (see Fig. 17-5*a*). (We assume s_m is much less than λ.)

As the wave moves, the air pressure at any position x in Fig. 17-5*a* varies sinusoidally, as we prove next. To describe this variation we write

$$\Delta p(x, t) = \Delta p_m \sin(kx - \omega t) \tag{17-14}$$

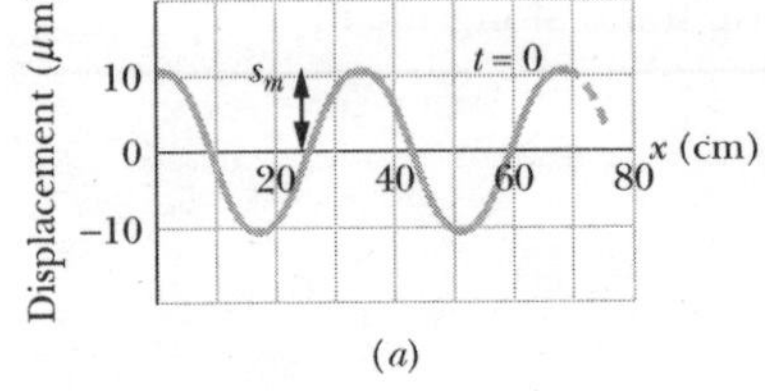

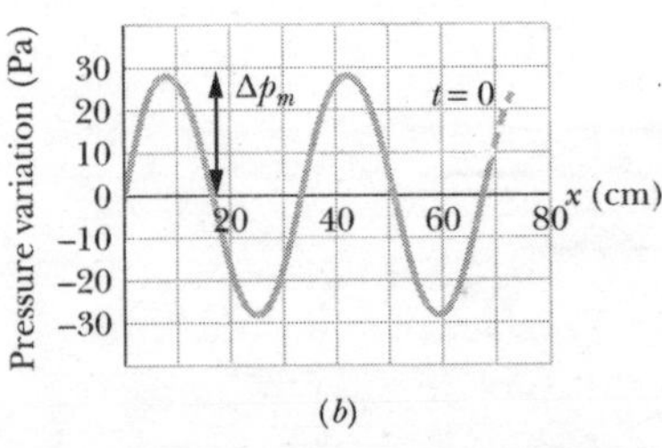

FIG. 17-7 (*a*) A plot of the displacement function (Eq. 17-13) for $t = 0$. (*b*) A similar plot of the pressure-variation function (Eq. 17-14). Both plots are for a 1000 Hz sound wave whose pressure amplitude is at the threshold of pain; see Sample Problem 17-2.

Figure 17-6*b* labels the various parts of this equation. A negative value of Δp in Eq. 17-14 corresponds to an expansion of the air, and a positive value to a compression. Here Δp_m is the **pressure amplitude,** which is the maximum increase or decrease in pressure due to the wave; Δp_m is normally very much less than the pressure p present when there is no wave. As we shall prove, the pressure amplitude Δp_m is related to the displacement amplitude s_m in Eq. 17-13 by

$$\Delta p_m = (v\rho\omega)s_m \tag{17-15}$$

Figure 17-7 shows plots of Eqs. 17-13 and 17-14 at $t = 0$; with time, the two curves would move rightward along the horizontal axes. Note that the displacement and pressure variation are $\pi/2$ rad (or 90°) out of phase. Thus, for example, the pressure variation Δp at any point along the wave is zero when the displacement there is a maximum.

CHECKPOINT 1 When the oscillating air element in Fig. 17-5*b* is moving rightward through the point of zero displacement, is the pressure in the element at its equilibrium value, just beginning to increase, or just beginning to decrease?

Derivation of Eqs. 17-14 and 17-15

Figure 17-5*b* shows an oscillating element of air of cross-sectional area A and thickness Δx, with its center displaced from its equilibrium position by distance s. From Eq. 17-2 we can write, for the pressure variation in the displaced element,

$$\Delta p = -B\frac{\Delta V}{V} \quad (17\text{-}16)$$

The quantity V in Eq. 17-16 is the volume of the element, given by

$$V = A\,\Delta x \quad (17\text{-}17)$$

The quantity ΔV in Eq. 17-16 is the change in volume that occurs when the element is displaced. This volume change comes about because the displacements of the two faces of the element are not quite the same, differing by some amount Δs. Thus, we can write the change in volume as

$$\Delta V = A\,\Delta s \quad (17\text{-}18)$$

Substituting Eqs. 17-17 and 17-18 into Eq. 17-16 and passing to the differential limit yield

$$\Delta p = -B\frac{\Delta s}{\Delta x} = -B\frac{\partial s}{\partial x} \quad (17\text{-}19)$$

The symbols ∂ indicate that the derivative in Eq. 17-19 is a *partial derivative*, which tells us how s changes with x when the time t is fixed. From Eq. 17-13 we then have, treating t as a constant,

$$\frac{\partial s}{\partial x} = \frac{\partial}{\partial x}[s_m \cos(kx - \omega t)] = -ks_m \sin(kx - \omega t)$$

Substituting this quantity for the partial derivative in Eq. 17-19 yields

$$\Delta p = Bks_m \sin(kx - \omega t)$$

Setting $\Delta p_m = Bks_m$, this yields Eq. 17-14, which we set out to prove.

Using Eq. 17-3, we can now write

$$\Delta p_m = (Bk)s_m = (v^2\rho k)s_m$$

Equation 17-15, which we also wanted to prove, follows at once if we substitute ω/v for k from Eq. 16-13.

Sample Problem 17-2

The maximum pressure amplitude Δp_m that the human ear can tolerate in loud sounds is about 28 Pa (which is very much less than the normal air pressure of about 10^5 Pa). What is the displacement amplitude s_m for such a sound in air of density $\rho = 1.21\ \text{kg/m}^3$, at a frequency of 1000 Hz and a speed of 343 m/s?

Conceptualize/Classify: The displacement amplitude s_m of a sound wave is related to the pressure amplitude Δp_m of the wave according to Eq. 17-15.

Compute: Solving that equation for s_m yields

$$s_m = \frac{\Delta p_m}{v\rho\omega} = \frac{\Delta p_m}{v\rho(2\pi f)}$$

Substituting known data then gives us

$$s_m = \frac{28\ \text{Pa}}{(343\ \text{m/s})(1.21\ \text{kg/m}^3)(2\pi)(1000\ \text{Hz})}$$
$$= 1.1 \times 10^{-5}\ \text{m} = 11\ \mu\text{m} \qquad \text{(Answer)}$$

Conclude: That is only about one-seventh the thickness of this page. Obviously, the displacement amplitude of even the loudest sound that the ear can tolerate is very small.

The pressure amplitude Δp_m for the *faintest* detectable sound at 1000 Hz is 2.8×10^{-5} Pa. Proceeding as above leads to $s_m = 1.1 \times 10^{-11}$ m or 11 pm, which is about one-tenth the radius of a typical atom. The ear is indeed a sensitive detector of sound waves.

17-4 | Intensity and Characteristics

If you have ever tried to sleep while someone played loud music nearby, you are well aware that there is more to sound than frequency, wavelength, and speed. There is also intensity. The **intensity** I of a sound wave at a surface is the average

Sound can cause the wall of a drinking glass to oscillate. If the sound produces a standing wave of oscillations and if the intensity of the sound is large enough, the glass will shatter. *(Ben Rose/The Image Bank/Getty Images)*

rate per unit area at which energy is transferred by the wave through or onto the surface. We can write this as

$$I = \frac{P}{A} \tag{17-20}$$

where P is the time rate of energy transfer (the power) of the sound wave and A is the area of the surface intercepting the sound. As we shall derive shortly, the intensity I is related to the displacement amplitude s_m of the sound wave by

$$I = \tfrac{1}{2}\rho v \omega^2 s_m^2 \tag{17-21}$$

Variation of Intensity with Distance

How intensity varies with distance from a real sound source is often complex. Some real sources (like loudspeakers) may transmit sound only in particular directions, and the environment usually produces echoes (reflected sound waves) that overlap the direct sound waves. In some situations, however, we can ignore echoes and assume that the sound source is a point source that emits the sound *isotropically*—that is, with equal intensity in all directions. The wavefronts spreading from such an isotropic point source S at a particular instant are shown in Fig. 17-8.

Let us assume that the mechanical energy of the sound waves is conserved as they spread from this source. Let us also center an imaginary sphere of radius r on the source, as shown in Fig. 17-8. All the energy emitted by the source must pass through the surface of the sphere. Thus, the time rate at which energy is transferred through the surface by the sound waves must equal the time rate at which energy is emitted by the source (that is, the power P_s of the source). From Eq. 17-20, the intensity I at the sphere must then be

$$I = \frac{P_s}{4\pi r^2} \tag{17-22}$$

where $4\pi r^2$ is the area of the sphere. Equation 17-22 tells us that the intensity of sound from an isotropic point source decreases with the square of the distance r from the source.

CHECKPOINT 2 The figure indicates three small patches 1, 2, and 3 that lie on the surfaces of two imaginary spheres; the spheres are centered on an isotropic point source S of sound. The rates at which energy is transmitted through the three patches by the sound waves are equal. Rank the patches according to (a) the intensity of the sound on them and (b) their area, greatest first.

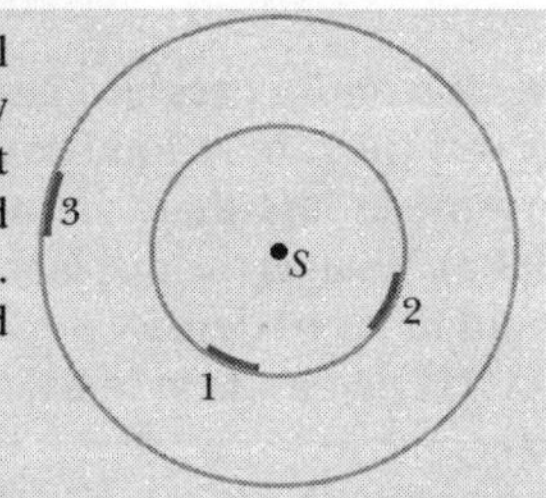

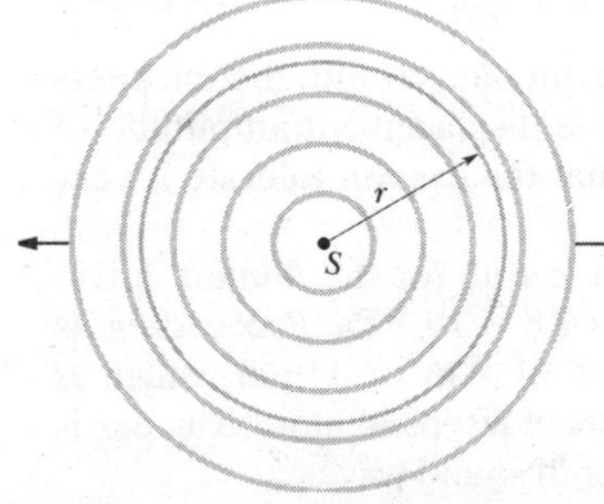

FIG. 17-8 A point source S emits sound waves uniformly in all directions. The waves pass through an imaginary sphere of radius r that is centered on S.

The Decibel Scale

You saw in Sample Problem 17-2 that the displacement amplitude at the human ear ranges from about 10^{-5} m for the loudest tolerable sound to about 10^{-11} m for the faintest detectable sound, a ratio of 10^6. From Eq. 17-21 we see that the intensity of a sound varies as the *square* of its amplitude, so the ratio of intensities at these two limits of the human auditory system is 10^{12}. Humans can hear over an enormous range of intensities.

We deal with such an enormous range of values by using logarithms. Consider the relation

$$y = \log x$$

in which x and y are variables. It is a property of this equation that if we *multiply* x by 10, then y increases by 1. To see this, we write

$$y' = \log(10x) = \log 10 + \log x = 1 + y$$

Similarly, if we multiply x by 10^{12}, y increases by only 12.

Thus, instead of speaking of the intensity I of a sound wave, it is much more convenient to speak of its **sound level** β, defined as

$$\beta = (10 \text{ dB}) \log \frac{I}{I_0} \qquad (17\text{-}23)$$

TABLE 17-2

Some Sound Levels (dB)

Hearing threshold	0
Rustle of leaves	10
Conversation	60
Rock concert	110
Pain threshold	120
Jet engine	130

Here dB is the abbreviation for **decibel,** the unit of sound level, a name that was chosen to recognize the work of Alexander Graham Bell. I_0 in Eq. 17-23 is a standard reference intensity ($= 10^{-12}$ W/m^2), chosen because it is near the lower limit of the human range of hearing. For $I = I_0$, Eq. 17-23 gives $\beta = 10 \log 1 = 0$, so our standard reference level corresponds to zero decibels. Then β increases by 10 dB every time the sound intensity increases by an order of magnitude (a factor of 10). Thus, $\beta = 40$ corresponds to an intensity that is 10^4 times the standard reference level. Table 17-2 lists the sound levels for a variety of environments.

Derivation of Eq. 17-21

Consider, in Fig. 17-5*a*, a thin slice of air of thickness dx, area A, and mass dm, oscillating back and forth as the sound wave of Eq. 17-13 passes through it. The kinetic energy dK of the slice of air is

$$dK = \tfrac{1}{2}\, dm\, v_s^2 \qquad (17\text{-}24)$$

Here v_s is not the speed of the wave but the speed of the oscillating element of air, obtained from Eq. 17-13 as

$$v_s = \frac{\partial s}{\partial t} = -\omega s_m \sin(kx - \omega t)$$

Using this relation and putting $dm = \rho A\, dx$ allow us to rewrite Eq. 17-24 as

$$dK = \tfrac{1}{2}(\rho A\, dx)(-\omega s_m)^2 \sin^2(kx - \omega t) \qquad (17\text{-}25)$$

Dividing Eq. 17-25 by dt gives the rate at which kinetic energy moves along with the wave. For transverse waves, dx/dt is the wave speed v, so we have

$$\frac{dK}{dt} = \tfrac{1}{2}\rho A v \omega^2 s_m^2 \sin^2(kx - \omega t) \qquad (17\text{-}26)$$

The *average* rate at which kinetic energy is transported is

$$\left(\frac{dK}{dt}\right)_{\text{avg}} = \tfrac{1}{2}\rho A v \omega^2 s_m^2 [\sin^2(kx - \omega t)]_{\text{avg}}$$

$$= \tfrac{1}{4}\rho A v \omega^2 s_m^2 \qquad (17\text{-}27)$$

To obtain this equation, we have used the fact that the average value of the square of a sine (or a cosine) function over one full oscillation is 1/2.

We assume that *potential* energy is carried along with the wave at this same average rate. The wave intensity I, which is the average rate per unit area at which energy of both kinds is transmitted by the wave, is then, from Eq. 17-27,

$$I = \frac{2(dK/dt)_{\text{avg}}}{A} = \tfrac{1}{2}\rho v \omega^2 s_m^2$$

which is Eq. 17-21, the equation we set out to derive.

Sample Problem 17-3

An electric spark jumps along a straight line of length $L = 10$ m, emitting a pulse of sound that travels radially outward from the spark. (The spark is said to be a *line source* of sound.) The power of the emission is $P_s = 1.6 \times 10^4$ W.

(a) What is the intensity I of the sound when it reaches a distance $r = 12$ m from the spark?

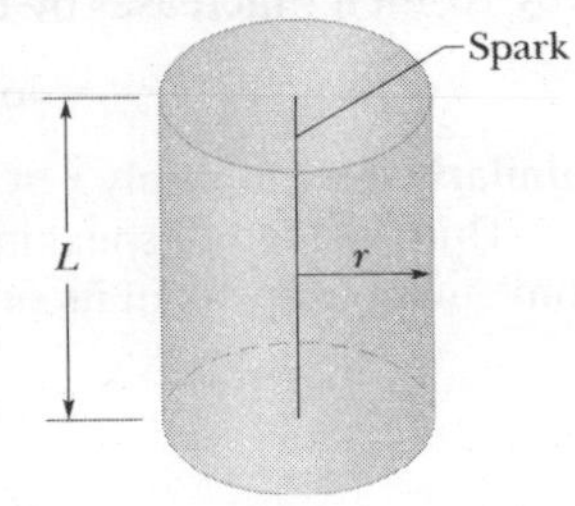

FIG. 17-9 A spark along a straight line of length L emits sound waves radially outward. The waves pass through an imaginary cylinder of radius r and length L that is centered on the spark.

Conceptualize: Let us center an imaginary cylinder of radius $r = 12$ m and length $L = 10$ m (open at both ends) on the spark, as shown in Fig. 17-9. Then the intensity I at the cylindrical surface is the ratio P/A, where P is the time rate at which sound energy passes through the surface and A is the surface area.

Classify: We assume that the principle of conservation of energy applies to the sound energy. This means that the rate P at which energy is transferred through the cylinder must equal the rate P_s at which energy is emitted by the source.

Compute: Putting these ideas together and noting that the area of the cylindrical surface is $A = 2\pi rL$, we have

$$I = \frac{P}{A} = \frac{P_s}{2\pi rL} \tag{17-28}$$

This tells us that the intensity of the sound from a line source decreases with distance r (and not with the square of distance r as for a point source). Substituting the given data, we find

$$I = \frac{1.6 \times 10^4 \text{ W}}{2\pi(12 \text{ m})(10 \text{ m})}$$

$$= 21.2 \text{ W/m}^2 \approx 21 \text{ W/m}^2 \qquad \text{(Answer)}$$

(b) At what time rate P_d is sound energy intercepted by an acoustic detector of area $A_d = 2.0$ cm², aimed at the spark and located a distance $r = 12$ m from the spark?

Compute: We know that the intensity of sound at the detector is the ratio of the energy transfer rate P_d there to the detector's area A_d:

$$I = \frac{P_d}{A_d} \tag{17-29}$$

We can imagine that the detector lies on the cylindrical surface of (a). Then the sound intensity at the detector is the intensity I (= 21.2 W/m²) at the cylindrical surface. Solving Eq. 17-35 for P_d gives us

$$P_d = (21.2 \text{ W/m}^2)(2.0 \times 10^{-4} \text{ m}^2) = 4.2 \text{ mW} \qquad \text{(Answer)}$$

Sample Problem 17-4

Many veteran rockers suffer from acute hearing damage because of the high sound levels they endured for years while playing music near loudspeakers or listening to music on headphones. Some, like Ted Nugent, can no longer hear in a damaged ear. Others, like Peter Townshend of the Who, have a continuous ringing sensation (tinnitus). Recently, many rockers, such as Lars Ulrich of Metallica (Fig. 17-10), began wearing special earplugs to protect their hearing during performances. If an earplug decreases the sound level of the sound waves by 20 dB, what is the ratio of the final intensity I_f of the waves to their initial intensity I_i?

FIG. 17-10 Lars Ulrich of Metallica is an advocate for the organization HEAR (Hearing Education and Awareness for Rockers), which warns about the damage high sound levels can have on hearing. *(Tim Mosenfelder/ Getty Images News and Sport Services)*

Conceptualize/Classify: For both the final and initial waves, the sound level β is related to the intensity by the definition of sound level in Eq. 17-23.

Compute: For the final waves we have

$$\beta_f = (10 \text{ dB}) \log \frac{I_f}{I_0}$$

and for the initial waves we have

$$\beta_i = (10\text{ dB})\log\frac{I_i}{I_0}$$

The difference in the sound levels is

$$\beta_f - \beta_i = (10\ dB)\left(\log\frac{I_f}{I_0} - \log\frac{I_i}{I_0}\right) \quad (17\text{-}30)$$

Using the identity

$$\log\frac{a}{b} - \log\frac{c}{d} = \log\frac{ad}{bc}$$

we can rewrite Eq. 17-30 as

$$\beta_f - \beta_i = (10\ dB)\log\frac{I_f}{I_i} \quad (17\text{-}31)$$

Rearranging and then substituting the given decrease in sound level as $\beta_f - \beta_i = -20$ dB, we find

$$\log\frac{I_f}{I_i} = \frac{\beta_f - \beta_i}{10\ dB} = \frac{-20\ dB}{10\ dB} = -2.0$$

We next take the antilog of the far left and far right sides of this equation. (Although the antilog $10^{-2.0}$ can be evaluated mentally, you could use a calculator by keying in 10^-2.0 or using the 10^x key.) We find

$$\frac{I_f}{I_i} = \log^{-1}(-2.0) = 0.010 \qquad \text{(Answer)}$$

Conclude: Thus, the earplug reduces the intensity of the sound waves to 0.010 of their initial intensity, which is a decrease of two orders of magnitude.

Pitch

This is also a sensation experienced by a listener. It depends mainly on the frequency of vibration of the air, which of course is the same as that of the source of sound. Frequency is a physical quantity and is measured in hertz (Hz), one vibration per second is known as one hertz. A high frequency produces a high-pitched note and a low frequency gives a low-pitched note.

Quality of Timber

The same note played on two different instruments does not sound the same and different waveforms are obtained on a CRO. The notes are said to have different quality or timber. This is due to the fact that with one exception (a tuning fork), sounds are never 'pure notes', that is, of one frequency; their waveforms are not sinusoidal. They consist of a main or fundamental note which usually predominates and others, generally with smaller intensities, called overtones. The fundametal is the component of lowest frequency and the overtones have frequencies that are multiples of the fundametal frequency. The number and intensities of the overtones determine the quality of a sound.

17-5 | 3-D Propagation

Waves in Two and Three Dimensions

Although $\xi = f(x - vt)$ represents a wave motion propagating along the x axis, we do not necessarily have to interpret it as meaning a wave concentrated on the x axis. If the physical disturbance described by ξ is present over all space, then at a given time t, the function $\xi = f(x - vt)$ gives the same value at all points having the same x. x = const. represents a plane perpendicular to the x axis (Fig. 17-11), which contains all the points in the plane perpendicular to the x axis. This plane is called a wavefront. Therefore, in three dimensions the expression $\xi = f(x - vt)$ describes a plane wave propagating parallel to the x axis.

We must note that for a plane wave the direction of propagation is important which is represented by unit vector of the wave velocity vector $\hat{a}$, perpendicular to the plane of the wave. This vector may not lie along any of the three coordinate axes. It is therefore convenient to express the plane wave equation. in a form that does not require the $\hat{a}$ to be along any of the axes. In the case of Fig. 17-11, the unit vector $\hat{a}$ is parallel to the x axis. If $\boldsymbol{r}$ is the position vector of any point in the wave front, we can see that

$$x = \hat{a} \cdot \boldsymbol{r}$$

and therefore we may write equation

$$\xi = f(\hat{a} \cdot \boldsymbol{r} - vt)$$

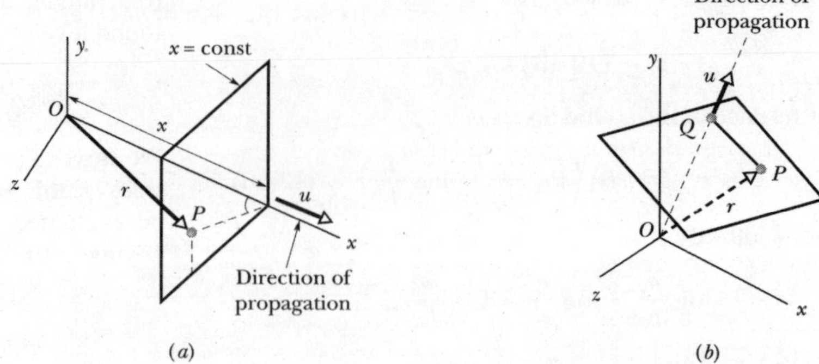

FIG. 17-11 (*a*) Plane wave propagating along the *x* axis (*b*) Plane wave propagating arbitrary direction.

The Propagation Vector

Suppose we have a harmonic traveling plane wave propagating in a homogeneous dispersive medium in the direction of the unit vector $\hat{c}$, (along the line *c*). Suppose that at the origin the wave function has the time dependence

$$\Psi(0, t) = \sin \omega t \tag{17-32}$$

Then at a plane at some distance c from the origin the disturbance is given by

$$\Psi(c, t) = A \sin(\omega t - kc) \tag{17-33}$$

We need to write this wave function in terms of general coordinates *x*, *y*, *z*, instead by the distance *c* along the propagation direction. Let $\vec{r} = x\hat{i} + y\hat{j} + z\hat{k}$ denote a point in space as measured from the origin of the *x*, *y*, *z* system. Thus the quantity *kc* in Eq. 17-33 can be written

$$kc = k(\hat{c} \cdot \boldsymbol{r}) = (k\hat{c}) \cdot \boldsymbol{r} \equiv \boldsymbol{k} \cdot \boldsymbol{r} \tag{17-34}$$

The quantity $k\hat{c}$ is called the propagation vector $\boldsymbol{k}$;

$$\vec{k} = k\hat{c} \tag{17-35}$$

The magnitude of $\boldsymbol{k}$ is $(2\pi/\lambda)$; the direction of $\boldsymbol{k}$ is $\hat{c}$, along the wave propagation direction. Eq.17-34 becomes for a wave having 3-D velocity vector.

$$k\hat{c} = \boldsymbol{k} \cdot \boldsymbol{r} = k_x x + k_y y + k_z z$$

The physical meaning of the wavenumber *k* is the increase in phase per unit displacement along the propagation direction $\hat{v}$. So that *kc* is the phase increased in distance *c*. The meaning of k_x is the increased phase per unit displacement along the $+x$ axis, that is, along $\hat{i}$ makes an angle θ with $\hat{c}$. Suppose that the wavelength is λ. Then if one moves along the direction $\hat{c}$ by a distance λ (at fixed time), the phase increases by 2π. If instead one advances along $\hat{i}$, one must travel a distance $\lambda/\cos\theta$ before a increases by one wavelength. Then the phase has increased by 2π in a distance along $\hat{i}$ that is larger than λ by a factor $(\cos\theta)^{-1}$.

In the case of a harmonic or sinusoidal plane wave propagating in the direction $\boldsymbol{u}$, we write.

$$\Psi = A \sin[k(\hat{u} \cdot \boldsymbol{r} - vt)] = \text{A} \sin(k_x x + k_y y + k_z z - \omega t)$$

where k_x, k_y, and k_z, are the components of $\boldsymbol{k}$ satisfying the relation

$$k_x^2 + k_y^2 + k_z^2 = k^2 = \omega^2/v^2$$

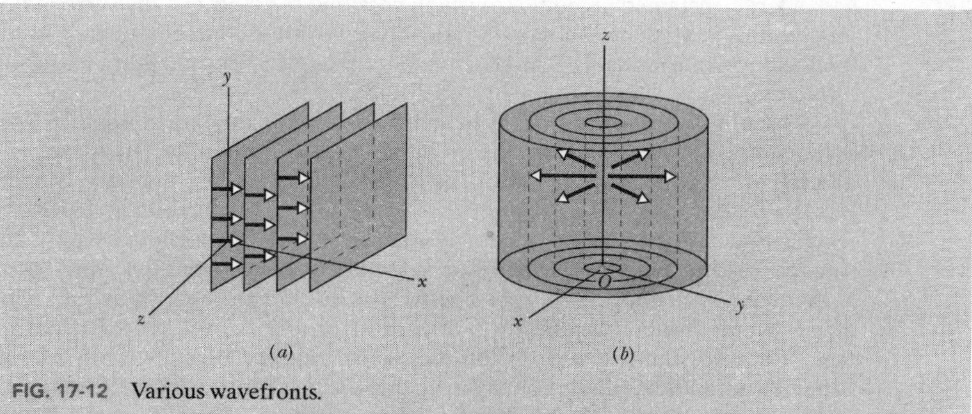

FIG. 17-12 Various wavefronts.

The plane waves in Fig. 17-11, although contain the three coordinates x, y, z, are really 1-D problems, since the propagation is along one particular direction and the physical situation is the same in all planes perpendicular to the direction of propagation (Fig. 17-12*a*). But in nature there are other kinds of waves that propagate in several directions as shown in Fig. 17-12.

Spherical Wave

Let's say point source (Fig. 17-13) is emanating power H isotropically. All particles at dist r from O are in same phase. Wave fronts are sphere with center at O.

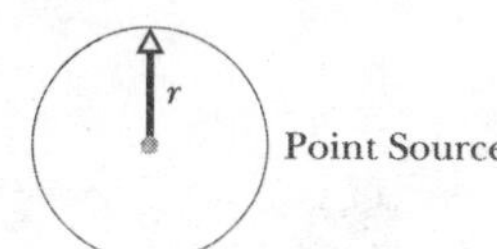

FIG. 17-13 Point source emanating power H.

Intensity at distance R is I, where $$I = \frac{H}{4\pi R^2}$$

Equating with the formula for intensity derived earlier

$$\text{Therefore,} \quad \frac{H}{4\pi r^2} = \frac{p_0^2 C}{2B}$$

$$\text{Thus, excess pressure amplitude becomes,} \; p_0 = \frac{D}{r}, \text{ where } D = \sqrt{\frac{HB}{2\pi c}}$$

$$\text{Therefore,} \quad p = \frac{D}{r} \sin(\omega t - \vec{k} \cdot \vec{r} + \phi)$$

17-6 | Standing Waves

Sources of Musical Sound

Musical sounds can be set up by oscillating strings (guitar, piano, violin), membranes (kettledrum, snare drum), air columns (flute, oboe, pipe organ, and the digeridoo of Fig. 17-14), wooden blocks or steel bars (marimba, xylophone), and many other oscillating bodies. Most common instruments involve more than a single oscillating part.

Standing waves can be set up on a stretched string that is fixed at both ends. They arise because waves traveling along the string are reflected back onto the string at each end. If the wavelength of the waves is suitably matched to the length of the string, the superposition of waves traveling in opposite directions produces a standing wave pattern (or oscillation mode). The wavelength required of the waves for such a match is one that corresponds to a *resonant frequency* of the string. The advantage of setting up standing waves is that the string then oscillates

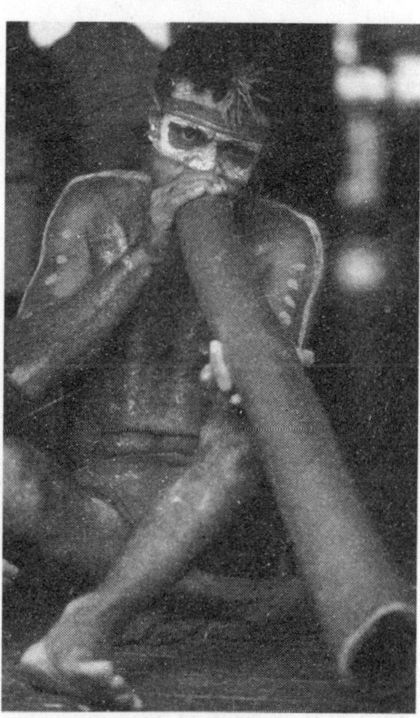

FIG. 17-14 The air column within a digeridoo ("a pipe") oscillates when the instrument is played. *(Alamy Images)*

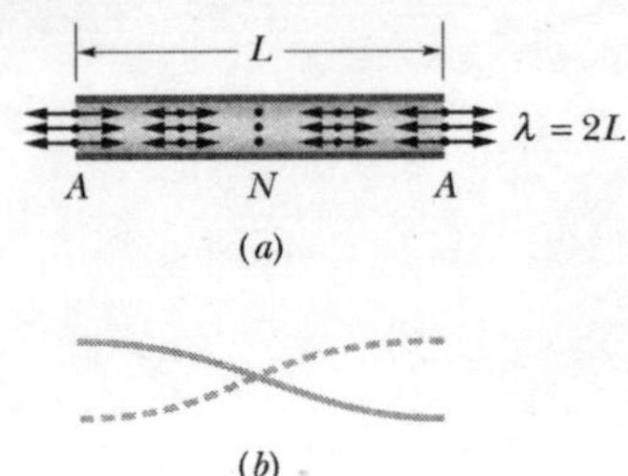

FIG. 17-15 (*a*) The simplest standing wave pattern of displacement for (longitudinal) sound waves in a pipe with both ends open has an antinode (A) across each end and a node (N) across the middle. (The longitudinal displacements represented by the double arrows are greatly exaggerated.) (*b*) The corresponding standing wave pattern for (transverse) string waves.

with a large, sustained amplitude, pushing back and forth against the surrounding air and thus generating a noticeable sound wave with the same frequency as the oscillations of the string. This production of sound is of obvious importance to, say, a guitarist.

We can set up standing waves of sound in an air-filled pipe in a similar way. As sound waves travel through the air in the pipe, they are reflected at each end and travel back through the pipe. (The reflection occurs even if an end is open, but the reflection is not as complete as when the end is closed.) If the wavelength of the sound waves is suitably matched to the length of the pipe, the superposition of waves traveling in opposite directions through the pipe sets up a standing wave pattern. The wavelength required of the sound waves for such a match is one that corresponds to a resonant frequency of the pipe. The advantage of such a standing wave is that the air in the pipe oscillates with a large, sustained amplitude, emitting at any open end a sound wave that has the same frequency as the oscillations in the pipe. This emission of sound is of obvious importance to, say, an organist.

Many other aspects of standing sound wave patterns are similar to those of string waves: The closed end of a pipe is like the fixed end of a string in that there must be a node (zero displacement) there, and the open end of a pipe is like the end of a string attached to a freely moving ring, in that there must be an antinode there. (Actually, the antinode for the open end of a pipe is located slightly beyond the end, but we shall not dwell on that detail.)

The simplest standing wave pattern that can be set up in a pipe with two open ends is shown in Fig. 17-15*a*. There is an antinode across each open end, as required. There is also a node across the middle of the pipe. An easier way of representing this standing longitudinal sound wave is shown in Fig. 17-15*b*—by drawing it as a standing transverse string wave.

The standing wave pattern of Fig. 17-15*a* is called the *fundamental mode* or *first harmonic*. For it to be set up, the sound waves in a pipe of length L must have a wavelength given by $L = \lambda/2$, so that $\lambda = 2L$. Several more standing sound wave patterns for a pipe with two open ends are shown in Fig. 17-16*a* using string wave representations. The *second harmonic* requires sound waves of wavelength $\lambda = L$, the *third harmonic* requires wavelength $\lambda = 2L/3$, and so on.

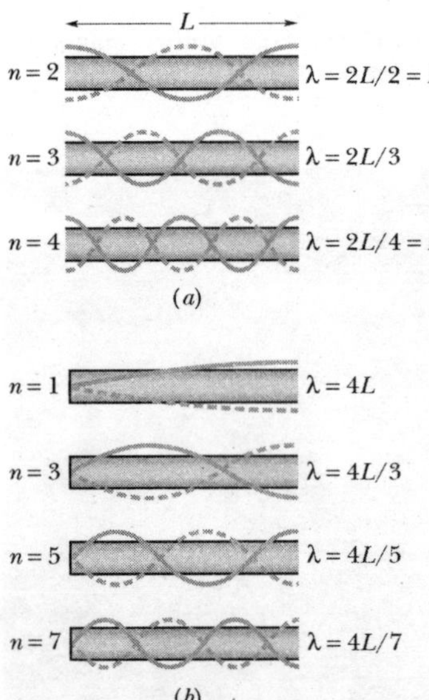

FIG. 17-16 Standing wave patterns for string waves superimposed on pipes to represent standing sound wave patterns in the pipes. (*a*) With *both* ends of the pipe open, any harmonic can be set up in the pipe. (*b*) With only *one* end open, only odd harmonics can be set up.

More generally, the resonant frequencies for a pipe of length L with two open ends correspond to the wavelengths

$$\lambda = \frac{2L}{n}, \qquad \text{for } n = 1, 2, 3, \ldots \tag{17-36}$$

where n is called the *harmonic number*. Letting v be the speed of sound, we write the resonant frequencies for a pipe with two open ends as

$$f = \frac{v}{\lambda} = \frac{nv}{2L}, \qquad \text{for } n = 1, 2, 3, \ldots \quad \text{(pipe, two open ends)} \tag{17-37}$$

Figure 17-16*b* shows (using string wave representations) some of the standing sound wave patterns that can be set up in a pipe with only one open end. As required, across the open end there is an antinode and across the closed end there is a node. The simplest pattern requires sound waves having a wavelength given by $L = \lambda/4$, so that $\lambda = 4L$. The next simplest pattern requires a wavelength given by $L = 3\lambda/4$, so that $\lambda = 4L/3$, and so on.

More generally, the resonant frequencies for a pipe of length L with only one open end correspond to the wavelengths

$$\lambda = \frac{4L}{n}, \qquad \text{for } n = 1, 3, 5, \ldots \tag{17-38}$$

in which the harmonic number n *must be an odd number*. The resonant frequencies are then given by

$$f = \frac{v}{\lambda} = \frac{nv}{4L}, \quad \text{for } n = 1, 3, 5, \ldots \quad \text{(pipe, one open end)} \qquad (17\text{-}39)$$

Note again that only odd harmonics can exist in a pipe with one open end. For example, the second harmonic, with $n = 2$, cannot be set up in such a pipe. Note also that for such a pipe the adjective in a phrase such as "the third harmonic" still refers to the harmonic number n (and not to, say, the third possible harmonic).

The length of a musical instrument reflects the range of frequencies over which the instrument is designed to function, and smaller length implies higher frequencies. Figure 17-17, for example, shows the saxophone and violin families, with their frequency ranges suggested by the piano keyboard. Note that, for every instrument, there is overlap with its higher- and lower-frequency neighbors.

In any oscillating system that gives rise to a musical sound, whether it is a violin string or the air in an organ pipe, the fundamental and one or more of the higher harmonics are usually generated simultaneously. Thus, you hear them together—that is, superimposed as a net wave. When different instruments are played at the same note, they produce the same fundamental frequency but different intensities for the higher harmonics. For example, the fourth harmonic of middle C might be relatively loud on one instrument and relatively quiet or even missing on another. Thus, because different instruments produce different net waves, they sound different to you even when they are played at the same note. That would be the case for the two net waves shown in Fig. 17-18, which were produced at the same note by different instruments.

CHECKPOINT 3 Pipe A, with length L, and pipe B, with length $2L$, both have two open ends. Which harmonic of pipe B has the same frequency as the fundamental of pipe A?

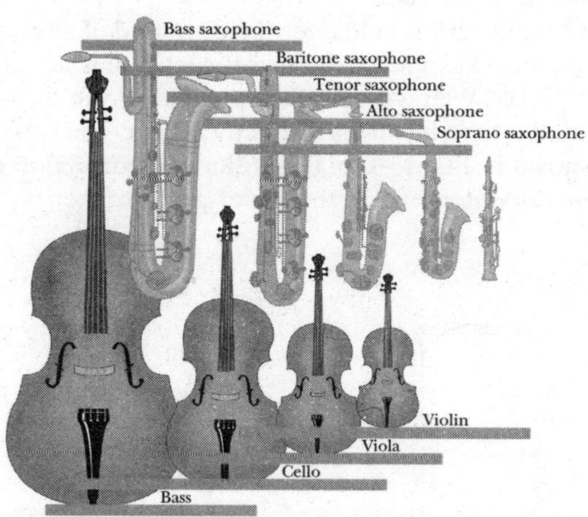

FIG. 17-17 The saxophone and violin families, showing the relations between instrument length and frequency range. The frequency range of each instrument is indicated by a horizontal bar along a frequency scale suggested by the keyboard at the bottom; the frequency increases toward the right.

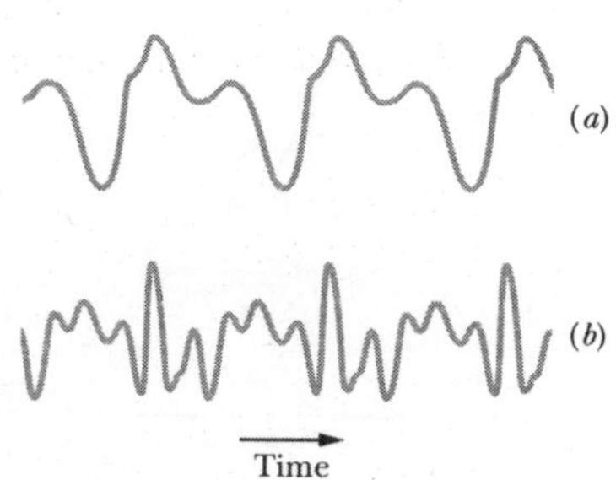

FIG. 17-18 The wave forms produced by (a) a flute and (b) an oboe when played at the same note, with the same first harmonic frequency.

Sample Problem 17-5

Weak background noises from a room set up the fundamental standing wave in a cardboard tube of length $L = 67.0$ cm with two open ends. Assume that the speed of sound in the air within the tube is 343 m/s.

(a) What frequency do you hear from the tube?

Conceptualize: With both pipe ends open, we have a symmetric situation in which the standing wave has an antinode at each end of the tube.

Classify: The standing wave pattern (in string wave style) is that of Fig. 17-15*b*.

Compute: The frequency is given by Eq. 17-37 with $n = 1$ for the fundamental mode:

$$f = \frac{nv}{2L} = \frac{(1)(343 \text{ m/s})}{2(0.670 \text{ m})} = 256 \text{ Hz} \qquad \text{(Answer)}$$

Conclude: If the background noises set up any higher harmonics, such as the second harmonic, you also hear frequencies that are *integer* multiples of 256 Hz.

(b) If you jam your ear against one end of the tube, what fundamental frequency do you hear from the tube?

Conceptualize: With your ear effectively closing one end of the tube, we have an asymmetric situation—an antinode still exists at the open end, but a node is now at the other (closed) end.

Classify: The standing wave pattern is the top one in Fig. 17-16*b*.

Compute: The frequency is given by Eq. 17-39 with $n = 1$ for the fundamental mode:

$$f = \frac{nv}{4L} = \frac{(1)(343 \text{ m/s})}{4(0.670 \text{ m})} = 128 \text{ Hz} \qquad \text{(Answer)}$$

Conclude: If the background noises set up any higher harmonics, they will be *odd* multiples of 128 Hz. That means that the frequency of 256 Hz (which is an even multiple) cannot now occur.

End-correction of Pipes

The air at the open end of a pipe is free to move. So the vibrations at this end of a sounding pipe extend a little into the air outside the pipe. The antinode of the stationary wave due to any note is then a small distance e away from the open end in practice, known as the end-correction. So the fundamental wavelength λ in the case of a closed pipe is given by $\lambda/4 = l + e$, where l is the length of the pipe, Fig. 17-19. In the case of an open pipe sounding its fundamental note, the wavelength λ is given by $\lambda/2 = l + e + e$, since two end-corrections are required, Fig. 17-19*b*. So $\lambda = 2(l + 2e)$.

Calculation shows that $e = 0.6r$, where r is the radius of the pipe. So the wider the pipe, the greater is the end-correction.

Resonance Tube Experiment, Measurement of Velocity of Sound and 'End-correction' of Tube

If a tuning-fork is held over the open end of a tube T filled with water, resonance is obtained at some position as the level of water is gradually lowered as shown in Fig. 17-19*c*. We recognise the resonance from the sound heard from the vibrating air in the tube becomes distinctly louder. The stationary wave which sets up then is shown in Fig. 17-19*c*. If e is the end-correction of the tube and l is the length from the water level to the top of the tube, then

$$l + e = \frac{\lambda}{4}$$

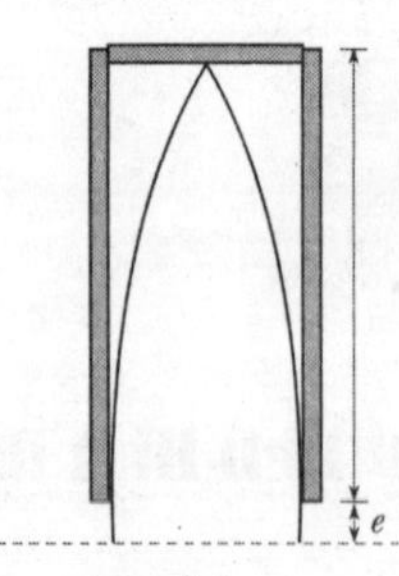

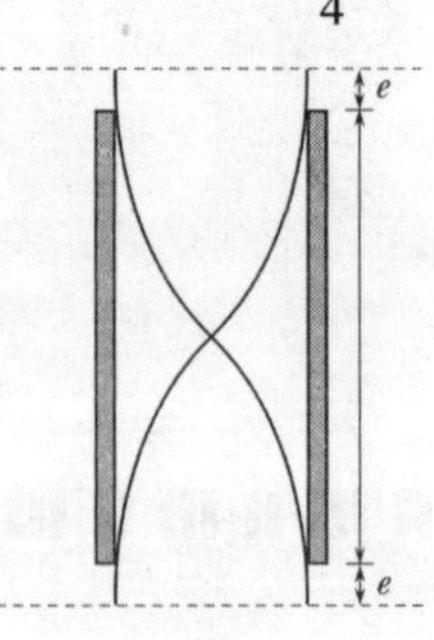

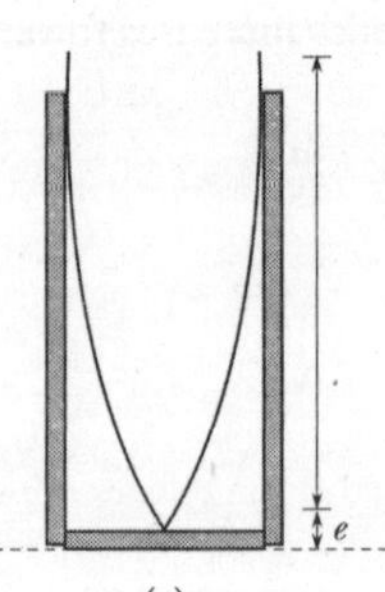

FIG. 17-19 (*a*) and (*b*) End-correction of pipes. (*c*) Resonance tube experiment.

But
$$\lambda = \frac{c}{f}$$
where f is the frequency of the fork and c is the velocity of sound in air.
$$l + e = \frac{c}{4f} \qquad (1)$$

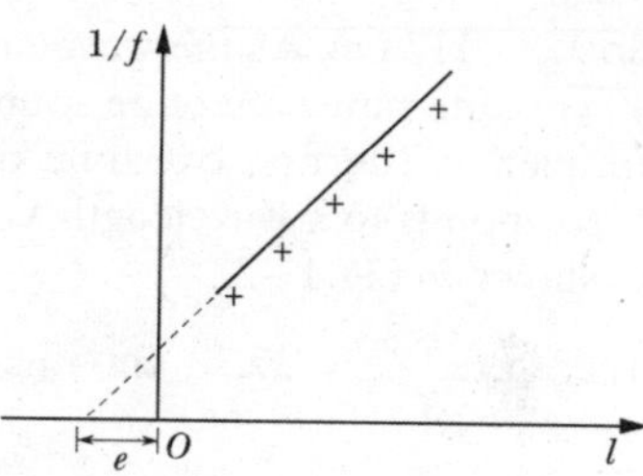

FIG. 17-20 Plot of $1/f$ vs l

If different tuning-forks of known frequency are used, and the corresponding values of l are measured when resonance occurs,we can plot a graph from Eq. (1) of $1/f$ against l Fig. 17-20. From Eq. (1), theslope of the line is $4/c$. So we can find speed of sound c. Also, the intercept of the line on the x axis of l is e, so the end-correction can also be found.

The experiment can also be performed by one fork only if the tube is sufficiently long. In this case the level of the water is lowered even after the first resonance, until resonance is again obtained at a lower water level w_1, as shown in Fig. 17-21. The stationary wave that sets up is shown in Fig. 17-21 and the new length to the top from w_1 is l_1.

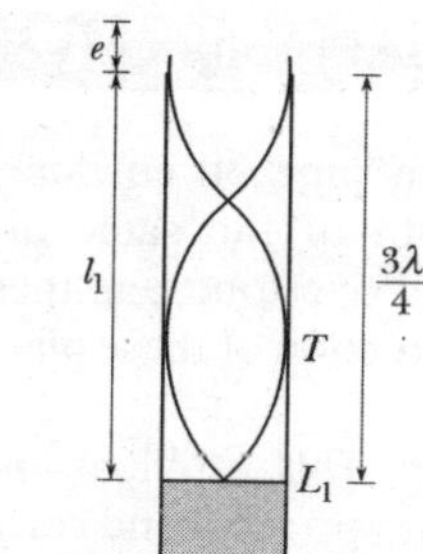

FIG. 17-21 Resonance tube

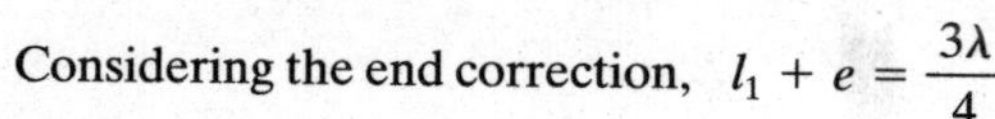

Considering the end correction, $l_1 + e = \frac{3\lambda}{4}$

But from Eq. (1)
$$l_1 - l = \frac{\lambda}{2}$$

Subtracting, $l_1 - l = \frac{\lambda}{2}$

$$\therefore \quad \lambda = 2(l_1 - l)$$
$$\therefore \quad c = f\lambda = 2f(l_1 - l)$$

In this method for c, therefore, the end-correction e is eliminated. The magnitude of e can be found from Eqs. (1) and (2). Thus, from (1),

$$3l + 3e = \frac{3\lambda}{4} = l_1 + e, \text{ from} \qquad (2)$$

$$\therefore \quad 2e = l_1 - 3l \quad \text{or} \quad e = \frac{l_1 - 3l}{2}$$

So e can be found from measurements of $l_1$and l.

Sample Problem 17-6

Resonance in Pipes: A cylindrical pipe of length 28 cm closed at one end is found to be at resonance when a tuning fork of frequency 850 Hz is sounded near the open end. Find the mode of vibration of the air in the pipe, and calculate the value of the end-correction (take the speed of sound in air as 340 m/s).

Conceptualize: We can draw the first three possibilities for resonance remembering that open end is adisplacement node.

Classify: This problem involves using Eq. 17-39 with possible end correction.

Compute: Let λ be the wavelength of the sound in the pipe.

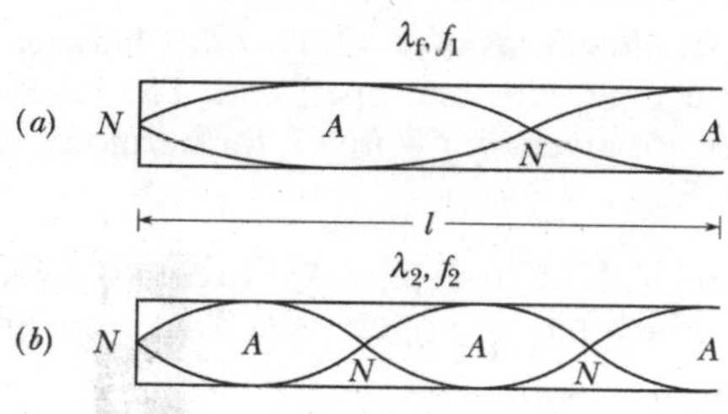

FIG. 17-22 Organ pipe with various modes of vibrations.

Then $\lambda = \frac{c}{f} = \frac{340}{850} = 0.4 \text{ m} = 40 \text{ cm}$

If the pipe is resonating at its fundametal frequency f_0, the stationary wave in the pipe is shown in Fig. 17-22a and the wavelength λ_0 is given by $\lambda_0/4 = 28$ cm.

So $\lambda_0 = 112$ cm. As the wavelength of the sound is just 40 cm , the pipe cannot be sounding at its fundamental frequency. The first overtone of the pipe is $3f_0$, which corresponds to a wavelength λ_1 given by $3\lambda_1/4 = 28$ cm as shown in Fig. 17-22.

Therefore, $\lambda_1 = 37.33$ cm this is close to the actual wavelength

Consequently, allowing for the effect of an end correction, the pipe can be considered sounding at its first overtone.

Let e = the end-correction in centimeters.

Then $$28 + e = \frac{3\lambda_1}{4}$$

Thus, $$28 + e = \frac{3}{4} \times 40 \qquad \text{so,} \qquad e = 2 \text{ cm}$$

Conclude: This answer seems to be of the reasonable order of magnitude.

Sample Problem 17-7 Build your skill

An open pipe 30 cm long and a closed pipe 23 cm long both of the same diameter, are each sounding their first overtone, and these are in unison. What is the end-correction of these pipes?

Solution: This problem involves using Eqs. 17-37 and 17-39 with possible end correction.

Suppose c is the speed of sound in air, and f is the frequency of the note. The wavelength, λ, is then c/f. When the open pipe is sounding its first overtone, the length of the pipe plus end-corrections = λ.

Therefore, $$\frac{c}{f} = 30 + 2e \qquad (17\text{-}40)$$

since there are *two end-corrections*.
When the closed pipe is sounding its first overtone,

$$\frac{3\lambda}{4} = 23 + e$$

$$\therefore \quad \frac{3c}{4} = 23 + e \qquad (17\text{-}41)$$

From Eqs. 17-40 and 17-41, it follows that

$$23 + e = \frac{3}{4}(30 + 2e)$$

Therefore, $92 + 4e = 90 + 6e$ so, $e = 1$ cm

Sample Problem 17-8

The two pipes in Fig. 17-23 are submerged in seawater at 20°C. Pipe A, with length $L_A = 1.50$ m and one open end, contains a small sound source that is to set up the standing wave with the second lowest resonant frequency of that pipe.

(a) What is resonant frequency?

Conceptualize/Classify: Only odd harmonics can exist in a pipe with one open end. The resonant frequencies are given by $f = nv/4L$ for harmonic numbers $n = 1, 3, 5, \ldots$.

(b) Sound leaking from pipe A is to set up resonance in pipe B, which has two open ends. That resonance is to be at the second lowest resonant frequency of pipe B. What is the required length L_B of pipe B?

Conceptualize/Classify: Any harmonic can exist in a pipe with two open ends. The resonant frequencies are given by $f = nv/2L$ for harmonic numbers $n = 1, 2, 3, \ldots$.

Compute: Because resonant frequency increases with increasing n, the second lowest resonant frequency corresponds to $n = 2$, the second lowest choice of n. Therefore, we can write

$$f = \frac{2v}{2L_B}$$

Solving for L_B and substituting known data yield

$$L_B = \frac{v}{f} = \frac{1522 \text{ m/s}}{761 \text{ Hz}} = 2.00 \text{ m} \quad \text{(Answer)}$$

Compute: Because resonant frequency increases with increasing n, the second lowest resonant frequency corresponds to $n = 3$, the second lowest choice of n.

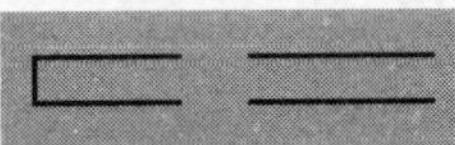

FIG. 17-23 Two pipes submerged in seawater. A sound source in pipe A sets up acoustic resonance in that pipe. Sound then leaks from pipe A into pipe B.

Caution: The frequency is the *second* lowest but, becauses = 3, it is for the *third* harmonic of pipe *A*. Using the speed of sound in seawater from Table 17-1, we then have

$$f = \frac{nv}{4L_A} = \frac{(3)(1522 \text{ m/s})}{(4)(1.50 \text{ m})} = 761 \text{ Hz} \qquad \text{(Answer)}$$

Standing Waves in Rods

A rod clamped in the middle and disturbed parallel to the length at one end will vibrate as shown in Fig. 17-24*a*. For clarity, the displacements have been drawn in the transverse direction although they are actually parallel to the rod. The midpoint of the rod will be a displacement node as it is restricted by the clamp and the ends of the rod are displacement antinodes as they are free to vibrate. The vibrations in the set-up are similiar to those in a pipe open at both ends. The fundamental mode is shown in Fig. 17-24 having wavelength $2L$. Other normal modes can be produced by clamping the rod at different points. For example, when the rod is clamped at a distance $L/4$ from one end, the second normal mode (Fig. 17-24*b*) is observed.

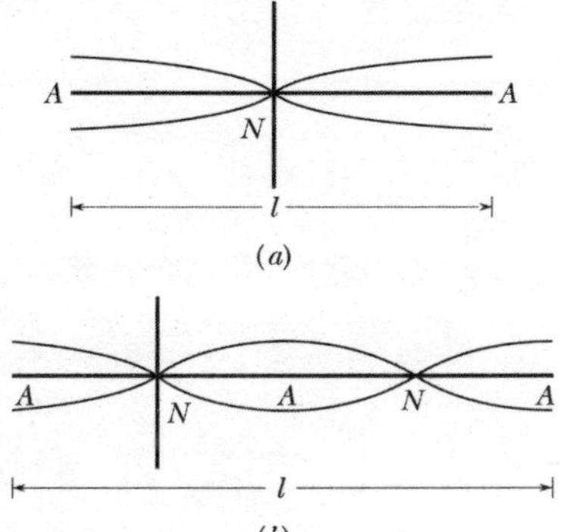

FIG. 17-24 Vibrations in a rod clamped in the middle & disturbed parallel to it's length.

17-7 | Interference

Like transverse waves, sound waves can undergo interference. Let us consider, in particular, the interference between two identical sound waves traveling in the same direction. Figure 17-25 shows how we can set up such a situation: Two point sources S_1 and S_2 emit sound waves that are in phase and of identical wavelength λ. Thus, the sources themselves are said to be in phase; that is, as the waves emerge from the sources, their displacements are always identical. We are interested in the waves that then travel through point P in Fig. 17-25. We assume that the distance to P is much greater than the distance between the sources so that we can approximate the waves as traveling in the same direction at P.

If the waves traveled along paths with identical lengths to reach point P, they would be in phase there. As with transverse waves, this means that they would undergo fully constructive interference there. However, in Fig. 17-25, path L_2 traveled by the wave from S_2 is longer than path L_1 traveled by the wave from S_1. The difference in path lengths means that the waves may not be in phase at point P. In other words, their phase difference ϕ at P depends on their **path length difference** $\Delta L = |L_2 - L_1|$.

To relate phase difference ϕ to path length difference ΔL, we recall that a phase difference of 2π rad corresponds to one wavelength. Thus, we can write the proportion

$$\frac{\phi}{2\pi} = \frac{\Delta L}{\lambda} \tag{17-42}$$

from which

$$\phi = \frac{\Delta L}{\lambda} 2\pi \tag{17-43}$$

Fully constructive interference occurs when ϕ is zero, 2π, or any integer multiple of 2π. We can write this condition as

$$\phi = m(2\pi), \qquad \text{for } m = 0, 1, 2, \ldots \text{ (fully constructive interference)} \tag{17-44}$$

From Eq. 17-43, this occurs when the ratio $\Delta L/\lambda$ is

$$\frac{\Delta L}{\lambda} = 0, 1, 2, \ldots \qquad \text{(fully constructive interference)} \tag{17-45}$$

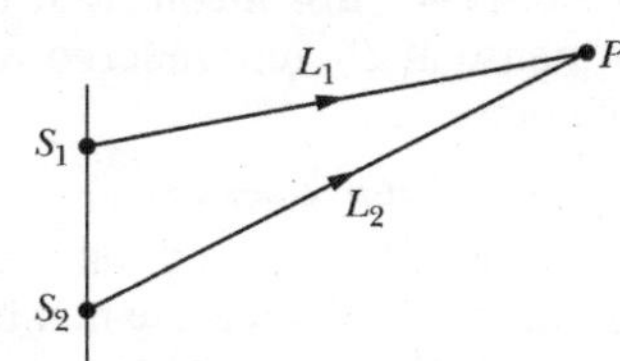

FIG. 17-25 Two point sources S_1 and S_2 emit spherical sound waves in phase. The rays indicate that the waves pass through a common point P.

For example, if the path length difference $\Delta L = |L_2 - L_1|$ in Fig. 17-25 is equal to 2λ, then $\Delta L/\lambda = 2$ and the waves undergo fully constructive interference at point

P. The interference is fully constructive because the wave from S_2 is phase-shifted relative to the wave from S_1 by 2λ, putting the two waves *exactly in phase* at P.

Fully destructive interference occurs when ϕ is an odd multiple of π, a condition we can write as

$$\phi = (2m + 1)\pi, \quad \text{for } m = 0, 1, 2, \ldots \text{ (fully destructive interference)} \tag{17-46}$$

From Eq. 17-35, this occurs when the ratio $\Delta L/\lambda$ is

$$\frac{\Delta L}{\lambda} = 0.5, 1.5, 2.5, \ldots \quad \text{(fully destructive interference)} \tag{17-47}$$

For example, if the path length difference $\Delta L = |L_2 - L_1|$ in Fig. 17-25 is equal to 2.5λ, then $\Delta L/\lambda = 2.5$ and the waves undergo fully destructive interference at point P. The interference is fully destructive because the wave from S_2 is phase-shifted relative to the wave from S_1 by 2.5 wavelengths, which puts the two waves *exactly out of phase* at P.

Of course, two waves could produce intermediate interference as, say, when $\Delta L/\lambda = 1.2$. This would be closer to fully constructive interference ($\Delta L/\lambda = 1.0$) than to fully destructive interference ($\Delta L/\lambda = 1.5$).

Sample Problem 17-9 Build your skill

In Fig. 17-26*a*, two point sources S_1 and S_2, which are in phase and separated by distance $D = 1.5\lambda$, emit identical sound waves of wavelength λ.

(a) What is the path length difference of the waves from S_1 and S_2 at point P_1, which lies on the perpendicular bisector of distance D, at a distance greater than D from the sources? What type of interference occurs at P_1?

Solution: Because the waves travel identical distances to reach P_1, their path length difference is

$$\Delta L = 0 \quad \text{(Answer)}$$

From Eq. 17-45, this means that the waves undergo fully constructive interference at P_1.

(b) What are the path length difference and type of interference at point P_2 in Fig. 17-26*a*?

Solution: The wave from S_1 travels the extra distance D $(= 1.5\lambda)$ to reach P_2. Thus, the path length difference is

$$\Delta L = 1.5\lambda \quad \text{(Answer)}$$

From Eq. 17-47, this means that the waves are exactly out of phase at P_2 and undergo fully destructive interference there.

(c) Figure 17-26*b* shows a circle with a radius much greater than D, centered on the midpoint between sources S_1 and S_2. What is the number of points N around this circle at which the interference is fully constructive?

Conceptualize: Imagine that, starting at point a, we move clockwise along the circle to point d. As we move

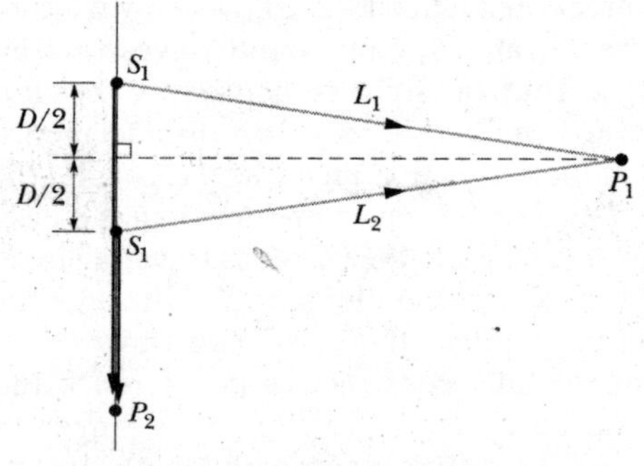

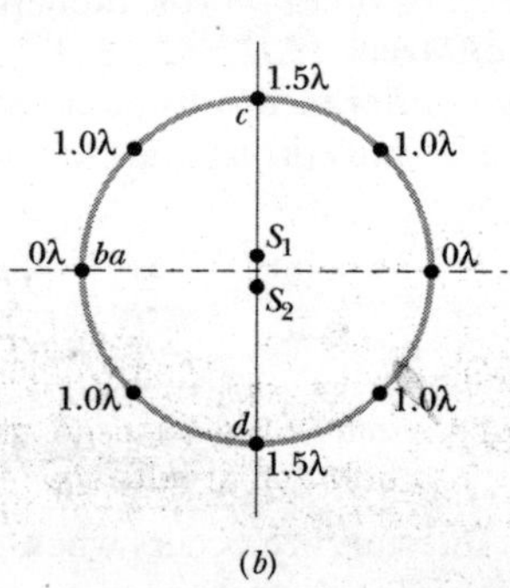

FIG. 17-26 (*a*) Two point sources S_1 and S_2, separated by distance D, emit spherical sound waves in phase. The waves travel equal distances to reach point P_1. Point P_2 is on the line extending through S_1 and S_2. (*b*) The path length difference (in terms of wavelength) between the waves from S_1 and S_2, at eight points on a large circle around the sources.

to point d, the path length difference ΔL increases and so the type of interference changes.

Classify: From (a), we know that the path length difference is $\Delta L = 0\lambda$ at point a. From (b), we know that $\Delta L = 1.5\lambda$ at point d. Thus, there must be one point along the circle between a and d at which $\Delta L = \lambda$, as indicated in Fig. 17-26b. From Eq. 17-45, fully constructive interference occurs at that point. Also, there can be no other point along the way from point a to point d at which fully constructive interference occurs, because there is no other integer than 1 between 0 and 1.5.

Compute: We can now use symmetry to locate the other points of fully constructive interference along the rest of the circle. Symmetry about line cd gives us point b, at which $\Delta L = 0\lambda$. Also, there are three more points at which $\Delta L = \lambda$. In all we have

$$N = 6 \qquad \text{(Answer)}$$

Conclude: Using the above discussion we can also find number of minimas. Two minimas are located on y axis and four minimas each in a quadrant between points of path differences 0 and $1l$.

Sample Problem 17-10

A sound source emits two sinusoidal sound waves, both of wavelength A, along paths A and B in Fig. 17-27. The sound traveling along path B is reflected from five surfaces as shown and then merges at point Q with the sound that traveled along path A, For what values of d (in wavelengths) are the waves exactly out of phase when they merge at point Q? For what values of d are the waves exactly in phase at point Q?

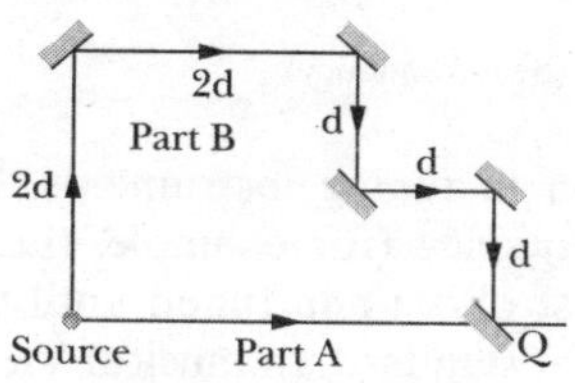

FIG. 17-27 A sound source sends sound waves along paths A and B. The wave moving along path B is reflected five times and then travels with the wave moving along path A.

Conceptualize: Because the two waves emerge from the same source, they must emerge in phase with each other.

Classify: When they merge at point Q their phase difference can depend only on the path length difference ΔL between the two paths they followed.

Compute: To reach Q, the wave following path A travels distance $3d$, and the wave following path B travels distance $7d$. Thus, their path length difference ΔL is $4d$.

If the waves are to be exactly out of phase at Q, we must have

$$\frac{\Delta L}{\lambda} = 0.5, 1.5, 2.5, \ldots$$

Substituting $\Delta L = 4d$ and solving for d then give us

$$d = \frac{1}{8}\lambda, \frac{3}{8}\lambda, \frac{5}{8}\lambda, \ldots \qquad \text{(Answer)}$$

Similarly, if the waves are to be exactly in phase at point Q, we must have

$$\frac{\Delta L}{\lambda} = 0, 1, 2, 3, \ldots$$

We can eliminate 0 from the list (which implies that there is no path difference in Fig. 17-27). Then solving for d, we find

$$d = \frac{1}{4}\lambda, \frac{1}{2}\lambda, \frac{3}{4}\lambda, \ldots \qquad \text{(Answer)}$$

17-8 | Beats

If we listen, a few minutes apart, to two sounds whose frequencies are, say, 552 and 564 Hz, most of us cannot tell one from the other. However, if the sounds reach our ears simultaneously, what we hear is a sound whose frequency is 558 Hz, the *average* of the two combining frequencies. We also hear a striking variation in the intensity of this sound—it increases and decreases in slow, wavering **beats** that repeat at a frequency of 12 Hz, the *difference* between the two combining frequencies. Figure 17-28 shows this beat phenomenon.

Let the time-dependent variations of the displacements due to two sound waves of equal amplitude s_m be

$$s_1 = s_m \cos \omega_1 t \qquad \text{and} \qquad s_2 = s_m \cos \omega_2 t \qquad (17\text{-}48)$$

where $\omega_1 > \omega_2$. From the superposition principle, the resultant displacement is

$$s = s_1 + s_2 = s_m(\cos \omega_1 t + \cos \omega_2 t)$$

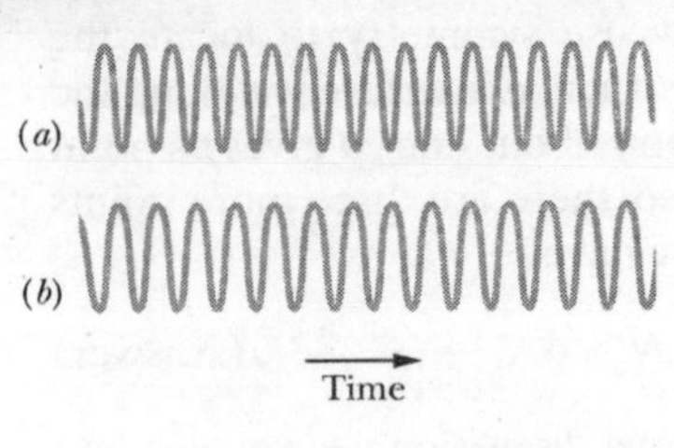

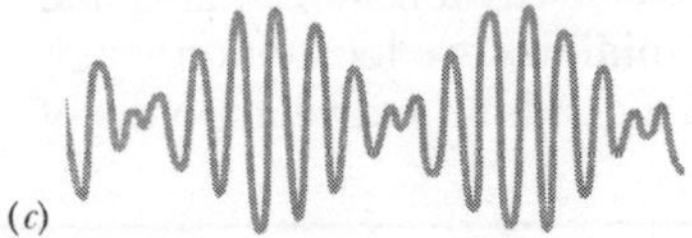

FIG. 17-28 (a, b) The pressure variations Δp of two sound waves as they would be detected separately. The frequencies of the waves are nearly equal. (c) The resultant pressure variation if the two waves are detected simultaneously.

Using the trigonometric identity (see Appendix E)

$$\cos\alpha + \cos\beta = 2\cos[\tfrac{1}{2}(\alpha - \beta)]\cos[\tfrac{1}{2}(\alpha + \beta)]$$

allows us to write the resultant displacement as

$$s = 2s_m \cos[\tfrac{1}{2}(\omega_1 - \omega_2)t]\cos[\tfrac{1}{2}(\omega_1 + \omega_2)t] \qquad (17\text{-}49)$$

If we write

$$\omega' = \tfrac{1}{2}(\omega_1 - \omega_2) \quad \text{and} \quad \omega = \tfrac{1}{2}(\omega_1 + \omega_2) \qquad (17\text{-}50)$$

we can then write Eq. 17-43 as

$$s(t) = [2s_m \cos\omega' t]\cos\omega t \qquad (17\text{-}51)$$

We now assume that the angular frequencies ω_1 and ω_2 of the combining waves are almost equal, which means that $\omega \gg \omega'$ in Eq. 17-50. We can then regard Eq. 17-51 as a cosine function whose angular frequency is ω and whose amplitude (which is not constant but varies with angular frequency ω') is the absolute value of the quantity in the brackets.

A maximum amplitude will occur whenever $\cos\omega' t$ in Eq. 17-51 has the value +1 or −1, which happens twice in each repetition of the cosine function. Because $\cos\omega' t$ has angular frequency ω', the angular frequency ω_{beat} at which beats occur is $\omega_{beat} = 2\omega'$. Then, with the aid of Eq. 17-50, we can write

$$\omega_{beat} = 2\omega' = (2)(\tfrac{1}{2})(\omega_1 - \omega_2) = \omega_1 - \omega_2$$

Because $\omega = 2\pi f$, we can recast this as

$$f_{beat} = f_1 - f_2 \qquad \text{(beat frequency)} \qquad (17\text{-}52)$$

Musicians use the beat phenomenon in tuning instruments. If an instrument is sounded against a standard frequency (for example, the note called "concert *A*" played on an orchestra's first oboe) and tuned until the beat disappears, the instrument is in tune with that standard. In musical Vienna, concert *A* (440 Hz) is available as a telephone service for the city's many musicians.

Sample Problem 17-11

When an emperor penguin returns from a search for food, how can it find its mate among the thousands of penguins huddled together for warmth in the harsh Antarctic weather? It is not by sight, because penguins all look alike, even to a penguin.

The answer lies in the way penguins vocalize. Most birds vocalize by using only one side of their two-sided vocal organ, called the *syrinx*. Emperor penguins, however, vocalize by using both sides simultaneously. Each side sets up acoustic standing waves in the bird's throat and mouth, much like in a pipe with two open ends. Suppose that the frequency of the first harmonic produced by side *A* is $f_{A1} = 432$ Hz and the frequency of the first harmonic produced by side *B* is $f_{B1} = 371$ Hz. What is the beat frequency between those two first-harmonic frequencies and between the two second-harmonic frequencies?

Conceptualize/Classify: The beat frequency between two frequencies is their difference, as given by Eq. 17-52 ($f_{beat} = f_1 - f_2$).

Compute: For the two first-harmonic frequencies f_{A1} and f_{B1}, the beat frequency is

$$f_{beat,1} = f_{A1} - f_{B1} = 432 \text{ Hz} - 371 \text{ Hz} = 61 \text{ Hz} \qquad \text{(Answer)}$$

Because the standing waves in the penguin are effectively in a pipe with two open ends, the resonant frequencies are given by Eq. 17-37 ($f = nv/2L$), in which L is the (unknown) length of the effective pipe. The first-harmonic frequency is $f_1 = v/2L$, and the second-harmonic frequency is $f_2 = 2v/2L$. Comparing these two frequencies, we see that, in general,

$$f_2 = 2f_1$$

For the penguin, the second harmonic of side *A* has frequency $f_{A2} = 2f_{A1}$ and the second harmonic of side *B* has frequency $f_{B2} = 2f_{B1}$. Using Eq. 17-52 with frequencies f_{A2} and f_{B2}, we find that the corresponding beat frequency is

$$f_{beat,2} = f_{A2} - f_{B2} = 2f_{A1} - 2f_{B1} = 2(432 \text{ Hz}) - 2(371 \text{ Hz}) = 122 \text{ Hz} \qquad \text{(Answer)}$$

Conclude: Experiments indicate that penguins can perceive such large beat frequencies (humans cannot). Thus, a penguin's cry can be rich with different harmonics and different beat frequencies, allowing the voice to be recognized even among the voices of thousands of other, closely huddled penguins.

17-9 | The Doppler Effect

A police car is parked by the side of the highway, sounding its 1000 Hz siren. If you are also parked by the highway, you will hear that same frequency. However, if there is relative motion between you and the police car, either toward or away from each other, you will hear a different frequency. For example, if you are driving *toward* the police car at 120 km/h (about 75 mi/h), you will hear a *higher* frequency (1096 Hz, an *increase* of 96 Hz). If you are driving *away from* the police car at that same speed, you will hear a *lower* frequency (904 Hz, a *decrease* of 96 Hz).

These motion-related frequency changes are examples of the **Doppler effect.** The effect was proposed (although not fully worked out) in 1842 by Austrian physicist Johann Christian Doppler. It was tested experimentally in 1845 by Buys Ballot in Holland, "using a locomotive drawing an open car with several trumpeters."

The Doppler effect holds not only for sound waves but also for electromagnetic waves, including microwaves, radio waves, and visible light. Here, however, we shall consider only sound waves, and we shall take as a reference frame the body of air through which these waves travel. This means that we shall measure the speeds of a source S of sound waves and a detector D of those waves *relative to that body of air.* (Unless otherwise stated, the body of air is stationary relative to the ground, so the speeds can also be measured relative to the ground.) We shall assume that S and D move either directly toward or directly away from each other, at speeds less than the speed of sound.

If either the detector or the source is moving, or both are moving, the emitted frequency f and the detected frequency f' are related by

$$f' = f\frac{v \pm v_D}{v \pm v_S} \quad \text{(general Doppler effect)} \qquad (17\text{-}53)$$

where v is the speed of sound through the air, v_D is the detector's speed relative to the air, and v_S is the source's speed relative to the air. The choice of plus or minus signs is set by this rule:

When the motion of detector or source is toward the other, the sign on its speed must give an upward shift in frequency. When the motion of detector or source is away from the other, the sign on its speed must give a downward shift in frequency.

In short, *toward* means *shift up,* and *away* means *shift down.*

Here are some examples of the rule. If the detector moves toward the source, use the plus sign in the numerator of Eq. 17-53 to get a shift up in the frequency. If it moves away, use the minus sign in the numerator to get a shift down. If it is stationary, substitute 0 for v_D. If the source moves toward the detector, use the minus sign in the denominator of Eq. 17-53 to get a shift up in the frequency. If it moves away, use the plus sign in the denominator to get a shift down. If the source is stationary, substitute 0 for v_S.

FIG. 17-29 A stationary source of sound S emits spherical wavefronts, shown one wavelength apart, that expand outward at speed v. A sound detector D, represented by an ear, moves with velocity $\vec{v}_D$ toward the source. The detector senses a higher frequency because of its motion.

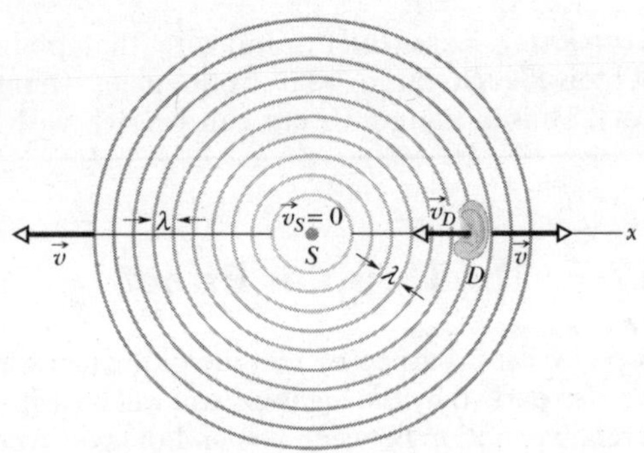

Next, we derive equations for the Doppler effect for the following two specific situations and then derive Eq. 17-53 for the general situation.

1. When the detector moves relative to the air and the source is stationary relative to the air, the motion changes the frequency at which the detector intercepts wavefronts and thus changes the detected frequency of the sound wave.
2. When the source moves relative to the air and the detector is stationary relative to the air, the motion changes the wavelength of the sound wave and thus changes the detected frequency (recall that frequency is related to wavelength).

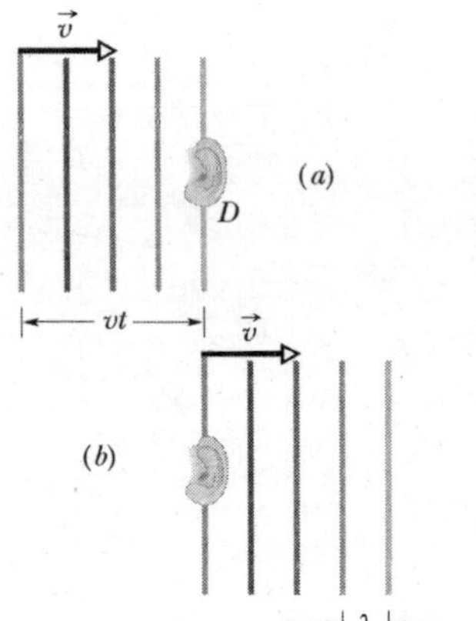

FIG. 17-30 The wavefronts of Fig. 17-28, assumed planar, (a) reach and (b) pass a stationary detector D; they move a distance vt to the right in time t.

Moving Detector and Stationary Source

In Fig. 17-29, a detector D (represented by an ear) is moving at speed v_D toward a stationary source S that emits spherical wavefronts, of wavelength λ and frequency f, moving at the speed v of sound in air. The wavefronts are drawn one wavelength apart. The frequency detected by detector D is the rate at which D intercepts wavefronts (or individual wavelengths). If D were stationary, that rate would be f, but since D is moving into the wavefronts, the rate of interception is greater, and thus the detected frequency f' is greater than f.

Let us for the moment consider the situation in which D is stationary (Fig. 17-30). In time t, the wavefronts move to the right a distance vt. The number of wavelengths in that distance vt is the number of wavelengths intercepted by D in time t, and that number is vt/λ. The rate at which D intercepts wavelengths, which is the frequency f detected by D, is

$$f = \frac{vt/\lambda}{t} = \frac{v}{\lambda} \qquad (17\text{-}54)$$

In this situation, with D stationary, there is no Doppler effect—the frequency detected by D is the frequency emitted by S.

Now let us again consider the situation in which D moves in the direction opposite the wavefront velocity (Fig. 17-31). In time t, the wavefronts move to the right a distance vt as previously, but now D moves to the left a distance $v_D t$. Thus, in this time t, the distance moved by the wavefronts relative to D is $vt + v_D t$. The number of wavelengths in this relative distance $vt + v_D t$ is the number of wavelengths intercepted by D in time t and is $(vt + v_D t)/\lambda$. The *rate* at which D intercepts wavelengths in this situation is the frequency f', given by

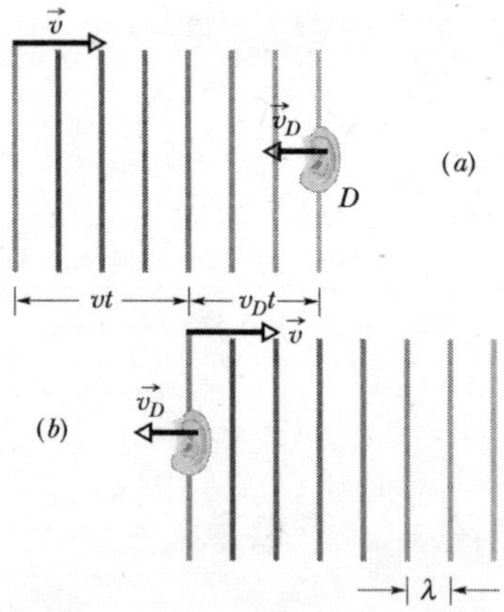

FIG. 17-31 Wavefronts traveling to the right (a) reach and (b) pass detector D, which moves in the opposite direction. In time t, the wavefronts move a distance vt to the right and D moves a distance $v_D t$ to the left.

$$f' = \frac{(vt + v_D t)/\lambda}{t} = \frac{v + v_D}{\lambda} \qquad (17\text{-}55)$$

From Eq. 17-54, we have $\lambda = v/f$. Then Eq. 17-47 becomes

$$f' = \frac{v + v_D}{v/f} = f\frac{v + v_D}{v} \qquad (17\text{-}56)$$

Note that in Eq. 17-56, $f' > f$ unless $v_D = 0$ (the detector is stationary).

Similarly, we can find the frequency detected by D if D moves away from the source. In this situation, the wavefronts move a distance $vt - v_D t$ relative to D in time t, and f' is given by

$$f' = f\frac{v - v_D}{v} \qquad (17\text{-}57)$$

In Eq. 17-57, $f' < f$ unless $v_D = 0$. We can summarize Eqs. 17-56 and 17-57 with

$$f' = f\frac{v \pm v_D}{v} \text{ (detector moving, source stationary)} \qquad (17\text{-}58)$$

Moving Source and Stationary Detector

Let detector D be stationary with respect to the body of air, and let source S move toward D at speed v_S (Fig. 17-32). The motion of S changes the wavelength of the sound waves it emits and thus the frequency detected by D.

To see this change, let $T\ (= 1/f)$ be the time between the emission of any pair of successive wavefronts W_1 and W_2. During T, wavefront W_1 moves a distance vT and the source moves a distance $v_S T$. At the end of T, wavefront W_2 is emitted. In the direction in which S moves, the distance between W_1 and W_2, which is the wavelength λ' of the waves moving in that direction, is $vT - v_S T$. If D detects those waves, it detects frequency f' given by

$$f' = \frac{v}{\lambda'} = \frac{v}{vT - v_S T} = \frac{v}{v/f - v_S/f}$$

$$= f\frac{v}{v - v_S} \qquad (17\text{-}59)$$

Note that f' must be greater than f unless $v_S = 0$.

In the direction opposite that taken by S, the wavelength λ' of the waves is $vT + v_S T$. If D detects those waves, it detects frequency f' given by

$$f' = f\frac{v}{v + v_S} \qquad (17\text{-}60)$$

Now f' must be less than f unless $v_S = 0$.

We can summarize Eqs. 17-59 and 17-60 with

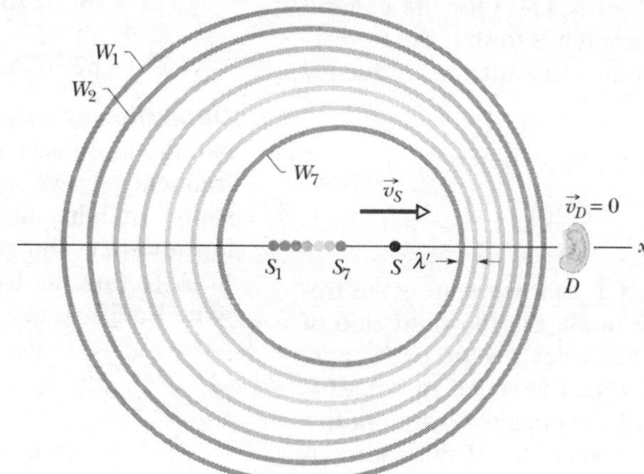

FIG. 17-32 A detector D is stationary, and a source S is moving toward it at speed v_S. Wavefront W_1 was emitted when the source was at S_1, wavefront W_7 when it was at S_7. At the moment depicted, the source is at S. The detector senses a higher frequency because the moving source, chasing its own wavefronts, emits a reduced wavelength λ' in the direction of its motion.

$$f' = f\frac{v}{v \pm v_S} \text{ (source moving, detector stationary)} \qquad (17\text{-}61)$$

General Doppler Effect Equation

We can now derive the general Doppler effect equation by replacing f in Eq. 17-61 (the source frequency) with f' of Eq. 17-58 (the frequency associated with motion of the detector). The result is Eq. 17-53 for the general Doppler effect.

That general equation holds not only when both detector and source are moving but also in the two specific situations we just discussed. For the situation in which the detector is moving and the source is stationary, substitution of $v_S = 0$ into Eq. 17-53 gives us Eq. 17-58, which we previously found. For the

CHECKPOINT 4 The figure indicates the directions of motion of a sound source and a detector for six situations in stationary air. For each situation, is the detected frequency greater than or less than the emitted frequency, or can't we tell without more information about the actual speeds?

	Source	Detector		Source	Detector
(a)	⟶	• 0 speed	(d)	⟵	⟵
(b)	⟵	• 0 speed	(e)	⟶	⟵
(c)	⟶	⟶	(f)	⟵	⟶

Sample Problem 17-12 Build your skill

Bats navigate and search out prey by emitting, and then detecting reflections of, ultrasonic waves, which are sound waves with frequencies greater than can be heard by a human. Suppose a bat emits ultrasound at frequency $f_{be} = 82.52$ kHz while flying with velocity $\vec{v}_b = (9.00 \text{ m/s})\hat{\imath}$ as it chases a moth that flies with velocity $\vec{v}_m = (8.00 \text{ m/s})\hat{\imath}$. What frequency f_{md} does the moth detect? What frequency f_{bd} does the bat detect in the returning echo from the moth?

Conceptualize The frequency is shifted by the relative motion of the bat and moth.

Classify: Because they move along a single axis, the shifted frequency is given by Eq. 17-53 for the general Doppler effect. Motion *toward* tends to shift the frequency *up*, and motion *away* tends to shift the frequency *down*.

Compute: The general Doppler equation is

$$f' = f\frac{v \pm v_D}{v \pm v_S} \tag{17-62}$$

Here, the detected frequency f' that we want is the frequency f_{md} detected by the moth. On the right side of the equation, the emitted frequency f is the bat's emission frequency $f_{be} = 82.52$ kHz, the speed of sound is $v = 343$ m/s, the speed v_D of the detector is the moth's speed $v_m = 8.00$ m/s, and the speed v_S of the source is the bat's speed $v_b = 9.00$ m/s.

These substitutions into Eq. 17-62 are easy to make. However, the decisions about the plus and minus signs can be tricky. Think in terms of *toward* and *away.* We have the speed of the moth (the detector) in the numerator of Eq. 17-62. The moth moves *away* from the bat, which tends to lower the detected frequency. Because the speed is in the numerator, we choose the minus sign to meet that tendency (the numerator becomes smaller). These reasoning steps are shown in Table 17-3.

We have the speed of the bat in the denominator of Eq. 17-62. The bat moves *toward* the moth, which tends to increase the detected frequency. Because the speed is in the denominator, we choose the minus sign to meet that tendency (the denominator becomes smaller).

With these substitutions and decisions, we have

$$f_{md} = f_{be}\frac{v - v_m}{v - v_b}$$

$$= (82.52 \text{ kHz})\frac{343 \text{ m/s} - 8.00 \text{ m/s}}{343 \text{ m/s} - 9.00 \text{ m/s}}$$

$$= 82.767 \text{ kHz} \approx 82.8 \text{ kHz} \qquad \text{(Answer)}$$

Detection of echo by bat: In the echo back to the bat, the moth acts as a source of sound, emitting at the frequency f_{md} we just calculated. So now the moth is the source (moving *away*) and the bat is the detector (moving *toward*). The reasoning steps are shown in Table 17-3. To find the frequency f_{bd} detected by the bat, we write Eq. 17-62 as

$$f_{bd} = f_{md}\frac{v + v_b}{v + v_m}$$

$$= (82.767 \text{ kHz})\frac{343 \text{ m/s} + 9.00 \text{ m/s}}{343 \text{ m/s} + 8.00 \text{ m/s}}$$

$$= 83.00 \text{ kHz} \approx 83.0 \text{ kHz} \qquad \text{(Answer)}$$

Conclude: The sound is also heard by the moth so it has also got chances of defending itself. Some moths evade bats by "jamming" the detection system with ultrasonic clicks.

TABLE 17-3

Bat to Moth		Echo Back to Bat	
Detector	Source	Detector	Source
moth	bat	bat	moth
speed $v_D = v_m$	speed $v_S = v_b$	speed $v_D = v_b$	speed $v_S = v_m$
away	toward	toward	away
shift down	shift up	shift up	shift down
numerator	denominator	numerator	denominator
minus	minus	plus	plus

Sample Problem 17-13

A engine is continuously emitting sound of frequency 1.2 kHz moving uniformly along a straight track. A stationary listener is situated off the track at a perpendicular distance of $l = 350$ m. The velocity of engine is equal to 50 m/s and the velocity of sound is 350 m/s. Find the frequency of sound received by the listener at the moment when the engine gets closest to him.

Conceptualize: This problem is based on the fact that sound takes finite time to reach from the engine to the listener. You can imagine it like this, suppose you are running along a straight path and you are throwing balls of diffferent colors toward your friend standing off the path at some distance. By the time the first ball reaches your friend you will be at some other position throwing some other ball.

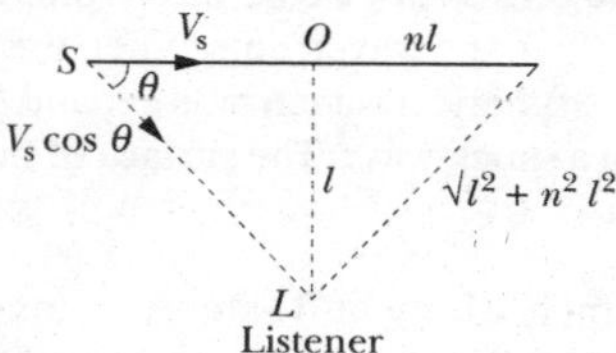

FIG. 17-33 An engine moving on a railway track and sound is listened by listener, L.

Classify: Similarly, the frequency emitted by the engine when it is closest to the listener does not reach instantaneously. Sound takes finite time to reach the listener from engine. The frequency heard when the engine is closest, was emitted from some previous position of the engine.

Compute: Let the velocity of engine make an angle θ with the line joining engine and listener, and the sound emitted by the engine at this moment, reaches the listener exactly at the same instant, when the engine is closest to the listener. Thus the time in which sound reaches the listener along SL is equal to the time when engine reaches point O from point s. From Fig. 17-33

$$\cos\theta = \frac{SO}{SL} = \frac{v_s t}{ct} = \frac{v_s}{c} \qquad \text{(i)}$$

(a) The component of velocity, along the direction of sound propogation will effect the wavelength. Thus V_s $\cos\theta$ should be used in the equation of doppler effect. Frequency heard by the listener is

$$f_L = f_S\left(\frac{c}{c - v_S\cos\theta}\right) \qquad \text{(ii)}$$

$$= f_S\left(\frac{c}{c - v_S^2/c}\right)$$

$$= f_S\left(\frac{c}{1 - v_S^2/c^2}\right)$$

On substituting numerical values, we get

$$f_L = 1.225 \text{ kHz}$$

Conclude: Since the sound heard by the listener was emitted while approaching the listener the frequency observed should have been higher than the source frequency.

In Case Of: Find the location of the engine and at the moment when the listener receives actual frequency of the engine.

Solution: When the source is at O, the velocity component of source toward listener is $v_S \cos 90° = 0$. Hence from Eq. (ii)

$$f_L = f_S\left(\frac{c}{c - v_S\cos 90°}\right) = f_S$$

Time taken by sound to reach the listener is l/c

Distance moved by engine in this time

$$= \left(\frac{l}{c}\right)v_S = \left(\frac{50}{35} \times 70 = 50 \text{ m}\right)$$

Thus, engine is located at distance of 50 m from the nearest point when the listener hears the actual frquency.

situation in which the source is moving and the detector is stationary, substitution of $v_D = 0$ into Eq. 17-53 gives us Eq. 17-61, which we previously found. Thus, Eq. 17-53 is the equation to remember.

17-10 | Supersonic Speeds, Shock Waves

If a source is moving toward a stationary detector at a speed equal to the speed of sound—that is, if $v_S = v$—Eqs. 17-53 and 17-61 predict that the detected frequency f' will be infinitely great. This means that the source is moving so fast that it keeps pace with its own spherical wavefronts, as Fig. 17-34*a* suggests. What happens when the speed of the source *exceeds* the speed of sound?

For such *supersonic* speeds, Eqs. 17-53 and 17-61 no longer apply. Figure 17-34*b* depicts the spherical wavefronts that originated at various positions of the source. The radius of any wavefront in this figure is vt, where v is the speed of sound and t is the time that has elapsed since the source emitted that wave-

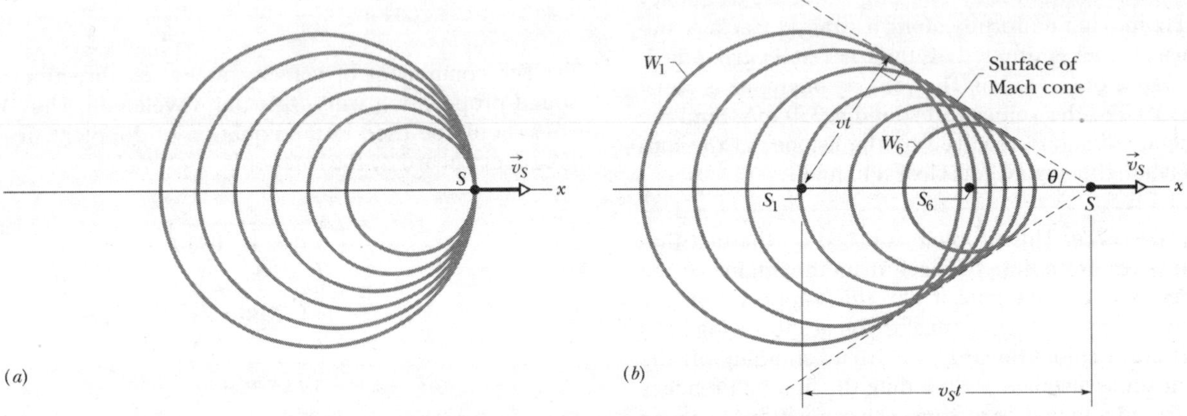

FIG. 17-34 (*a*) A source of sound *S* moves at speed v_S equal to the speed of sound and thus as fast as the wavefronts it generates. (*b*) A source *S* moves at speed v_S faster than the speed of sound and thus faster than the wavefronts. When the source was at position S_1 it generated wavefront W_1, and at position S_6 it generated W_6. All the spherical wavefronts expand at the speed of sound v and bunch along the surface of a cone called the Mach cone, forming a shock wave. The surface of the cone has half-angle θ and is tangent to all the wavefronts.

front. Note that all the wavefronts bunch along a *V*-shaped envelope in the two-dimensional drawing of Fig. 17-34*b*. The wavefronts actually extend in three dimensions, and the bunching actually forms a cone called the *Mach cone*. A *shock wave* is said to exist along the surface of this cone, because the bunching of wavefronts causes an abrupt rise and fall of air pressure as the surface passes through any point. From Fig. 17-34*b*, we see that the half-angle θ of the cone, called the *Mach cone angle*, is given by

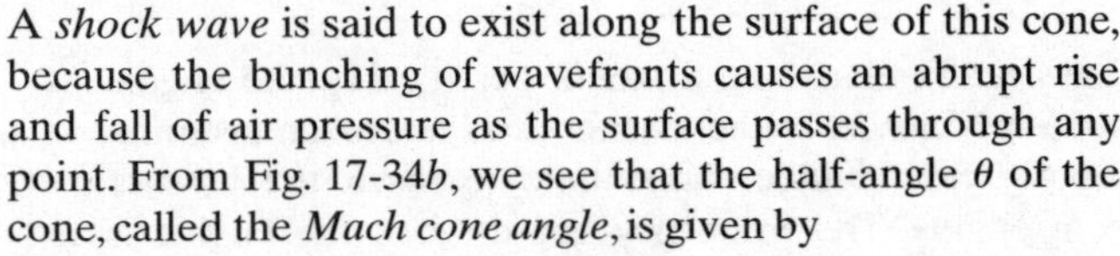

$$\sin\theta = \frac{vt}{v_S t} = \frac{v}{v_S} \quad \text{(Mach cone angle)} \qquad (17\text{-}63)$$

The ratio v_S/v is called the *Mach number*. When you hear that a particular plane has flown at Mach 2.3, it means that its speed was 2.3 times the speed of sound in the air through which the plane was flying. The shock wave generated by a supersonic aircraft (Fig. 17-35) or projectile produces a burst of sound, called a *sonic boom*, in which the air pressure first suddenly increases and then suddenly decreases below normal

FIG. 17-35 Shock waves produced by the wings of a Navy FA 18 jet. The shock waves are visible because the sudden decrease in air pressure in them caused water molecules in the air to condense, forming a fog. (*U.S. Navy photo by Ensign John Gay*)

REVIEW & SUMMARY

Sound Waves Sound waves are longitudinal mechanical waves that can travel through solids, liquids, or gases. The speed v of a sound wave in a medium having **bulk modulus** B and density ρ is

$$v = \sqrt{\frac{B}{\rho}} \quad \text{(speed of sound)}$$

In air at 20°C, the speed of sound is 343 m/s.

A sound wave causes a longitudinal displacement s of a mass element in a medium as given by

$$s = s_m \cos(kx - \omega t)$$

where s_m is the **displacement amplitude** (maximum displacement) from equilibrium, $k = 2\pi/\lambda$, and $\omega = 2\pi f$, λ and f being the wavelength and frequency, respectively, of the sound wave. The sound wave also causes a pressure change Δp of the medium from the equilibrium pressure:

$$\Delta p = \Delta p_m \sin(kx - \omega t)$$

where the **pressure amplitude** is

$$\Delta p_m = (v\rho\omega)s_m$$

Interference The interference of two sound waves with identical wavelengths passing through a common point depends on their phase difference ϕ there. If the sound waves were emitted in phase and are traveling in approximately the same direction, ϕ is given by

$$\phi = \frac{\Delta L}{\lambda} 2\pi$$

where ΔL is their **path length difference** (the difference in the distances traveled by the waves to reach the common point). Fully constructive interference occurs when ϕ is an integer multiple of 2π,

$$\phi = m(2\pi), \quad \text{for } m = 0, 1, 2, \ldots$$

and, equivalently, when ΔL is related to wavelength λ by

$$\frac{\Delta L}{\lambda} = 0, 1, 2, \ldots$$

Fully destructive interference occurs when ϕ is an odd multiple of π,

$$\phi = (2m + 1)\pi, \quad \text{for } m = 0, 1, 2, \ldots$$

and, equivalently, when ΔL is related to λ by

$$\frac{\Delta L}{\lambda} = 0.5, 1.5, 2.5, \ldots$$

Sound Intensity The **intensity** I of a sound wave at a surface is the average rate per unit area at which energy is transferred by the wave through or onto the surface:

$$I = \frac{P}{A}$$

where P is the time rate of energy transfer (power) of the sound wave and A is the area of the surface intercepting the sound. The intensity I is related to the displacement amplitude s_m of the sound wave by

$$I = \tfrac{1}{2}\rho v\omega^2 s_m^2$$

The intensity at a distance r from a point source that emits sound waves of power P_s is

$$I = \frac{P_s}{4\pi r^2}$$

Sound Level in Decibels The *sound level* β in *decibels* (dB) is defined as

$$\beta = (10\text{ dB}) \log \frac{I}{I_0}$$

where I_0 ($= 10^{-12}$ W/m^2) is a reference intensity level to which all intensities are compared. For every factor-of-10 increase in intensity, 10 dB is added to the sound level.

Standing Wave Patterns in Pipes Standing sound wave patterns can be set up in pipes. A pipe open at both ends will resonate at frequencies

$$f = \frac{v}{\lambda} = \frac{nv}{2L} \quad n = 1, 2, 3, \ldots$$

where v is the speed of sound in the air in the pipe. For a pipe closed at one end and open at the other, the resonant frequencies are

$$f = \frac{v}{\lambda} = \frac{nv}{4L} \quad n = 1, 3, 5, \ldots$$

Beats *Beats* arise when two waves having slightly different frequencies, f_1 and f_2, are detected together. The beat frequency is

$$f_{\text{beat}} = f_1 - f_2$$

The Doppler Effect The *Doppler effect* is a change in the observed frequency of a wave when the source or the detector moves relative to the transmitting medium (such as air). For sound the observed frequency f' is given in terms of the source frequency f by

$$f' = f\frac{v \pm v_D}{v \pm v_S} \quad \text{(general Doppler effect)}$$

where v_D is the speed of the detector relative to the medium, v_S is that of the source, and v is the speed of sound in the medium. The signs are chosen such that f' tends to be *greater* for motion toward and *less* for motion away.

Shock Wave If the speed of a source relative to the medium exceeds the speed of sound in the medium, the Doppler equation no longer applies. In such a case, shock waves result. The half-angle θ of the Mach cone is given by

$$\sin\theta = \frac{v}{v_S} \quad \text{(Mach cone angle)}$$

QUESTIONS

1 In Fig. 17-36, three long tubes (A, B, and C) are filled with different gases under different pressures. The ratio of the bulk modulus to the density is indicated for each gas in terms of a basic value B_0/ρ_0. Each tube has a piston at its left end that can send a sound pulse through the tube (as in Fig. 16-2). The three pulses are sent simultaneously. Rank the tubes according to the time of arrival of the pulses at the open right ends of the tubes, earliest first.

FIG. 17-36 Question 1.

2 In Fig. 17-37, two point sources S_1 and S_2, which are in phase, emit identical sound waves of wavelength 2.0 m. In terms of wavelengths, what is the phase difference between the waves arriving at point P if (a) $L_1 = 38$ m and $L_2 = 34$ m, and (b) $L_1 = 39$ m and $L_2 = 36$ m? (c) Assuming that the source separation is much smaller than L_1 and L_2, what type of interference occurs at P in situations (a) and (b)?

FIG. 17-37 Question 2.

3 In a first experiment, a sinusoidal sound wave is sent through a long tube of air, transporting energy at the average rate of $P_{avg,1}$. In a second experiment, two other sound waves, identical to the first one, are to be sent simultaneously through the tube with a phase difference ϕ of either 0, 0.2 wavelength, or 0.5 wavelength between the waves. (a) With only mental calculation, rank those choices of ϕ according to the average rate at which the waves will transport energy, greatest first. (b) For the first choice of ϕ, what is the average rate in terms of $P_{avg,1}$?

4 Pipe A has length L and one open end. Pipe B has length $2L$ and two open ends. Which harmonics of pipe B have a frequency that matches a resonant frequency of pipe A?

5 For a particular tube, here are four of the six harmonic frequencies below 1000 Hz: 300, 600, 750, and 900 Hz. What two frequencies are missing from the list?

6 The sixth harmonic is set up in a pipe. (a) How many open ends does the pipe have (it has at least one)? (b) Is there a node, antinode, or some intermediate state at the midpoint?

7 In Fig. 17-38, pipe A is made to oscillate in its third harmonic by a small internal sound source. Sound emitted at the right end happens to resonate four nearby pipes, each with only one open end (they are *not* drawn to scale). Pipe B oscillates in its lowest harmonic, pipe C in its second lowest harmonic, pipe D in its third lowest harmonic, and pipe E in its fourth lowest harmonic. Without computation, rank all five pipes according to their length, greatest first. (*Hint:* Draw the standing waves to scale and then draw the pipes to scale.)

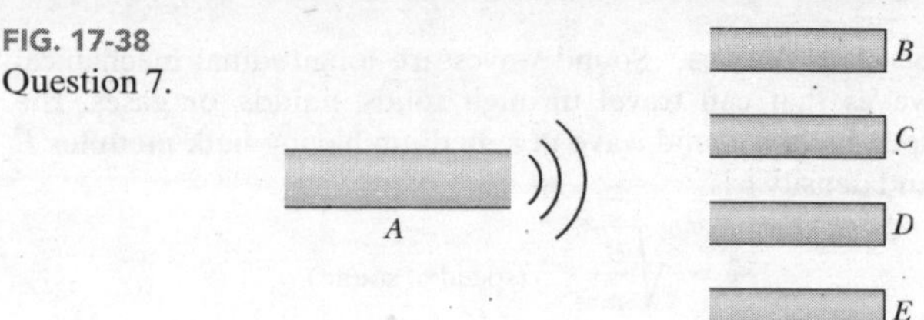

FIG. 17-38 Question 7.

8 Figure 17-39 shows a stretched string of length L and pipes a, b, c, and d of lengths L, $2L$, $L/2$, and $L/2$, respectively. The string's tension is adjusted until the speed of waves on the string equals the speed of sound waves in the air. The fundamental mode of oscillation is then set up on the string. In which pipe will the sound produced by the string cause resonance, and what oscillation mode will that sound set up?

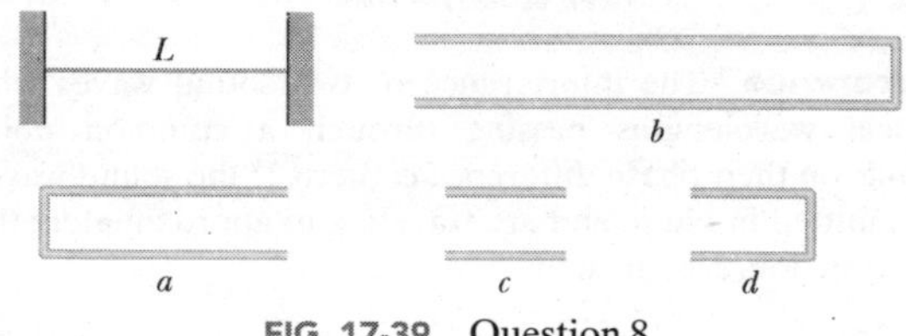

FIG. 17-39 Question 8.

9 Figure 17-40 shows a moving sound source S that emits at a certain frequency, and four stationary sound detectors. Rank the detectors according to the frequency of the sound they detect from the source, greatest first.

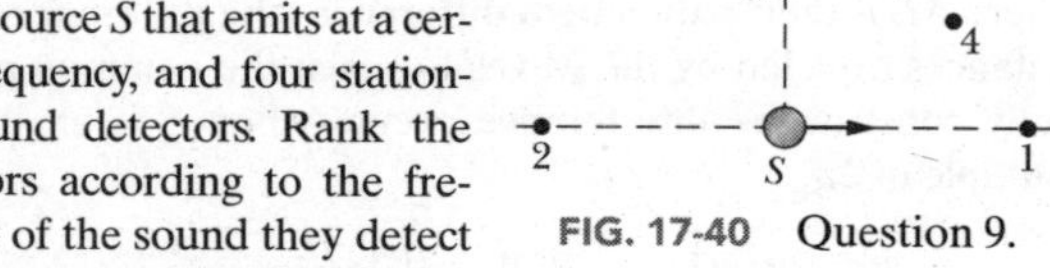

FIG. 17-40 Question 9.

10 A friend rides, in turn, the rims of three fast merry-go-rounds while holding a sound source that emits isotropically at a certain frequency. You stand far from each merry-go-round. The frequency you hear for each of your friend's three rides varies as the merry-go-round rotates. The variations in frequency for the three rides are given by the three curves in Fig. 17-41. Rank the curves according to (a) the linear speed v of the sound source, (b) the angular speeds ω of the merry-go-rounds, and (c) the radii r of the merry-go-rounds, greatest first.

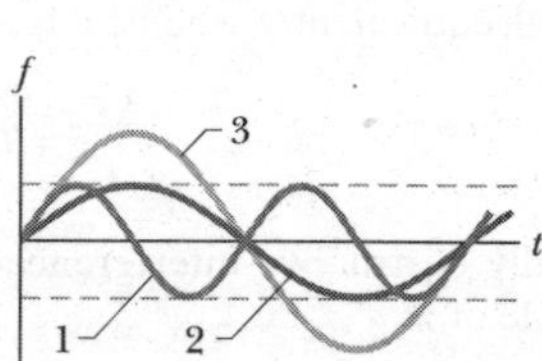

FIG. 17-41 Question 10.

PROBLEMS

Where needed in the problems, use

speed of sound in air = 343 m/s

and density of air = 1.21 kg/m^3

unless otherwise specified.

The Speed of Sound

1 When the door of the Chapel of the Mausoleum in Hamilton, Scotland, is slammed shut, the last echo heard by someone standing just inside the door reportedly comes 15 s later. (a) If that echo were due to a single reflection off a wall opposite the door, how far from the door would that wall be? (b) If, instead, the wall is 25.7 m away, how many reflections (back and forth) correspond to the last echo?

2 A column of soldiers, marching at 120 paces per minute, keep in step with the beat of a drummer at the head of the column. The soldiers in the rear end of the column are striding forward with the left foot when the drummer is advancing with the right foot. What is the approximate length of the column?

3 A stone is dropped into a well. The splash is heard 3.00 s later. What is the depth of the well?

4 *Hot chocolate effect.* Tap a metal spoon inside a mug of water and note the frequency f_i you hear. Then add a spoonful of powder (say, chocolate mix or instant coffee) and tap again as you stir the powder. The frequency you hear has a lower value f_s because the tiny air bubbles released by the powder change the water's bulk modulus. As the bubbles reach the water surface and disappear, the frequency gradually shifts back to its initial value. During the effect, the bubbles don't appreciably change the water's density or volume or the sound's wavelength. Rather, they change the value of dV/dp—that is, the differential change in volume due to the differential change in the pressure caused by the sound wave in the water. If $f_s/f_i = 0.333$, what is the ratio $(dV/dp)_s/(dV/dp)_i$?

5 Earthquakes generate sound waves inside Earth. Unlike a gas, Earth can experience both transverse (S) and longitudinal (P) sound waves. Typically, the speed of S waves is about 4.5 km/s, and that of P waves 8.0 km/s. A seismograph records P and S waves from an earthquake. The first P waves arrive 3.0 min before the first S waves. If the waves travel in a straight line, how far away does the earthquake occur?

6 A man strikes one end of a thin rod with a hammer. The speed of sound in the rod is 15 times the speed of sound in air. A woman, at the other end with her ear close to the rod, hears the sound of the blow twice with a 0.12 s interval between; one sound comes through the rod and the other comes through the air alongside the rod. If the speed of sound in air is 343 m/s, what is the length of the rod?

Traveling Sound Waves

$$\Delta p = (1.50 \text{ Pa}) \sin \pi[(0.900 \text{ m}^{-1})x - (315 \text{ s}^{-1})t]$$

Find the (a) pressure amplitude, (b) frequency, (c) wavelength, and (d) speed of the wave.

7 If the form of a sound wave traveling through air is

$$s(x, t) = (6.0 \text{ nm}) \cos(kx + (3000 \text{ rad/s})t + \phi)$$

how much time does any given air molecule along the path take to move between displacements $s = +2.0$ nm and $s = -2.0$ nm?

8 *Underwater illusion.* One clue used by your brain to determine the direction of a source of sound is the time delay Δt between the arrival of the sound at the ear closer to the source and the arrival at the farther ear. Assume that the source is distant so that a wavefront from it is approximately planar when it reaches you, and let D represent the separation between your ears. (a) If the source is located at angle θ in front of you (Fig. 17-42), what is Δt in terms of D and the speed of sound v in air? (b) If you are submerged in water and the sound source is directly to your right, what is Δt in terms of D and the speed of sound v_w in water? (c) Based on the time-delay clue, your brain interprets the submerged sound to arrive at an angle θ from the forward direction. Evaluate θ for fresh water at 20°C.

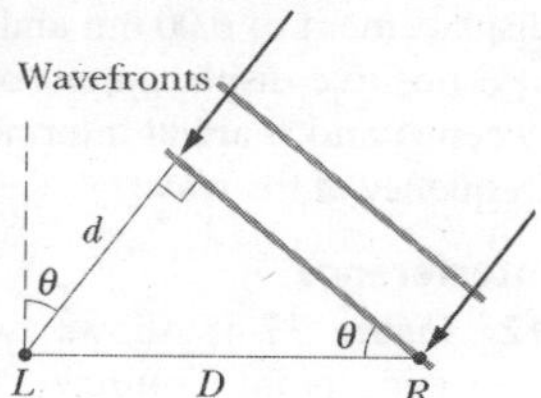

FIG. 17-42 Problem 8.

9 A handclap on stage in an amphitheater sends out sound waves that scatter from terraces of width $w = 0.75$ m (Fig. 17-43). The sound returns to the stage as a periodic series of pulses, one from each terrace; the parade of pulses sounds like a played note. (a) Assuming that all the rays in Fig. 17-42 are horizontal, find the frequency at which the pulses return (that is, the frequency of the perceived note). (b) If the width w of the terraces were smaller, would the frequency be higher or lower?

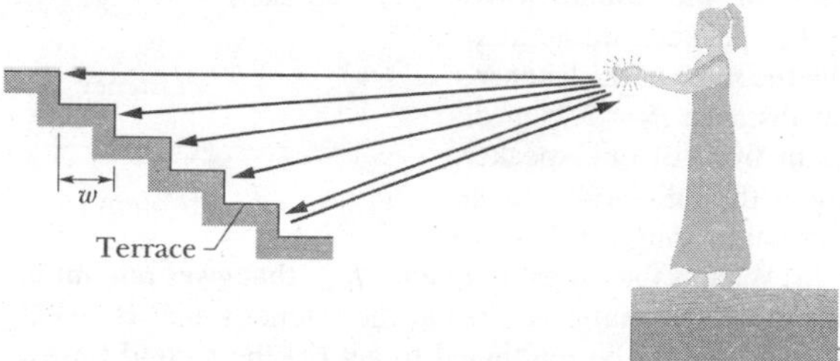

FIG. 17-43 Problem 9.

10 Figure 17-44 shows the output from a pressure monitor mounted at a point along the path taken by a sound wave of a single frequency traveling at 343 m/s through air with a uniform density of 1.21 kg/m^3. The vertical axis scale is set by $\Delta p_s = 4.0$ mPa. If the *displacement* function of the wave is written as $s(x, t) = s_m \cos(kx - \omega t)$, what are (a) s_m, (b) k, and (c) ω? The air is then cooled so that its density is 1.35

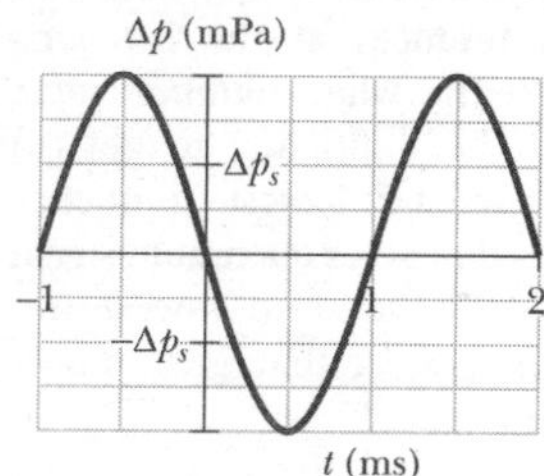

FIG. 17-44 Problem 10.

kg/m^3 and the speed of a sound wave through it is 320 m/s. The sound source again emits the sound wave at the same frequency and same pressure amplitude. What now are (d) s_m, (e) k, and (f) ω?

11 A sound wave of the form $s = s_m \cos(kx - \omega t + \phi)$ travels at 343 m/s through air in a long horizontal tube. At one instant, air molecule A at $x = 2.000$ m is at its maximum positive displacement of 6.00 nm and air molecule B at $x = 2.070$ m is at a positive displacement of 2.00 nm. All the molecules between A and B are at intermediate displacements. What is the frequency of the wave?

Interference

12 Figure 17-45 shows two isotropic point sources of sound, S_1 and S_2. The sources emit waves in phase at wavelength 0.50 m; they are separated by $D = 1.75$ m. If we move a sound detector along a large circle centered at the midpoint between the sources, at how many points do waves arrive at the detector (a) exactly in phase and (b) exactly out of phase?

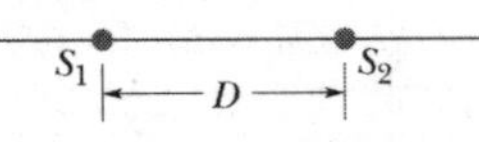

FIG. 17-45 Problems 12.

13 In Fig. 17-46, sound with a 40.0 cm wavelength travels rightward from a source and through a tube that consists of a straight portion and a half-circle. Part of the sound wave travels through the half-circle and then rejoins the rest of the wave, which goes directly through the straight portion. This rejoining results in interference. What is the smallest radius r that results in an intensity minimum at the detector?

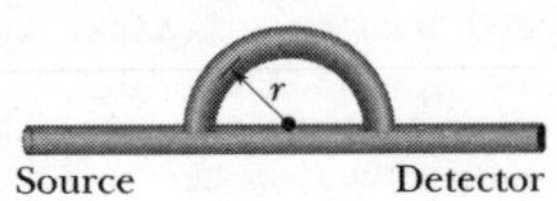

FIG. 17-46 Problem 13.

14 In Fig. 17-47, two speakers separated by distance $d_1 = 2.00$ m are in phase. Assume the amplitudes of the sound waves from the speakers are approximately the same at the listener's ear at distance $d_2 = 3.75$ m directly in front of one speaker. Consider the full audible range for normal hearing, 20 Hz to 20 kHz. (a) What is the lowest frequency $f_{\min,1}$ that gives minimum signal (destructive interference) at the listener's ear? By what number must $f_{\min,1}$ be multiplied to get (b) the second lowest frequency $f_{\min,2}$ that gives minimum signal and (c) the third lowest frequency $f_{\min,3}$ that gives minimum signal? (d) What is the lowest frequency $f_{\max,1}$ that gives maximum signal (constructive interference) at the listener's ear? By what number must $f_{\max,1}$ be multiplied to get (e) the second lowest frequency $f_{\max,2}$ that gives maximum signal and (f) the third lowest frequency $f_{\max,3}$ that gives maximum signal?

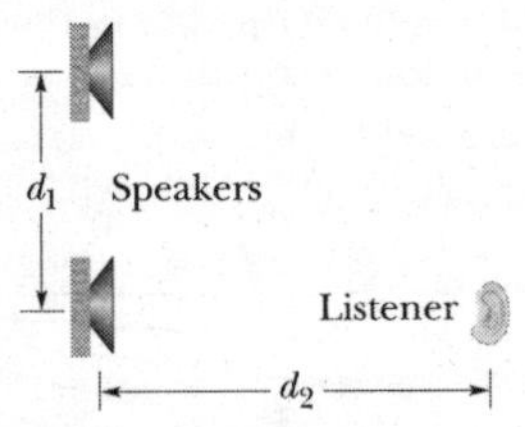

FIG. 17-47 Problem 14.

15 In Fig. 17-48, sound waves A and B, both of wavelength λ, are initially in phase and traveling rightward, as indicated by the two rays. Wave A is reflected from four surfaces but ends up traveling in its original direction. Wave B ends in that direction after reflecting from two surfaces. Let distance L in the figure be expressed as a multiple q of λ: $L = q\lambda$. What are the (a) smallest and (b) second smallest values of q that put A and B exactly out of phase with each other after the reflections?

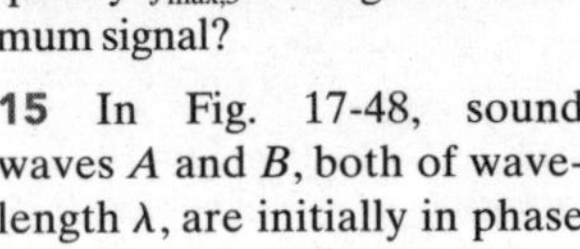

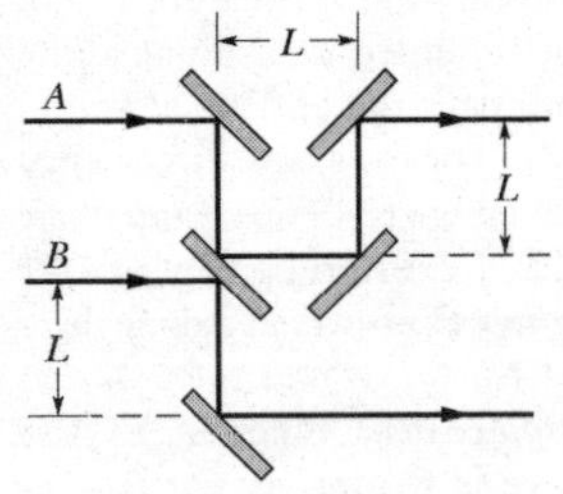

FIG. 17-48 Problem 15.

16 Two loudspeakers are located 3.35 m apart on an outdoor stage. A listener is 18.3 m from one and 19.5 m from the other. During the sound check, a signal generator drives the two speakers in phase with the same amplitude and frequency. The transmitted frequency is swept through the audible range (20 Hz to 20 kHz). (a) What is the lowest frequency $f_{\min,1}$ that gives minimum signal (destructive interference) at the listener's location? By what number must $f_{\min,1}$ be multiplied to get (b) the second lowest frequency $f_{\min,2}$ that gives minimum signal and (c) the third lowest frequency $f_{\min,3}$ that gives minimum signal? (d) What is the lowest frequency $f_{\max,1}$ that gives maximum signal (constructive interference) at the listener's location? By what number must $f_{\max,1}$ be multiplied to get (e) the second lowest frequency $f_{\max,2}$ that gives maximum signal and (f) the third lowest frequency $f_{\max,3}$ that gives maximum signal?

17 Figure 17-49 shows four isotropic point sources of sound that are uniformly spaced on an x axis. The sources emit sound at the same wavelength λ and same amplitude s_m, and they emit in phase. A point P is shown on the x axis. Assume that as the sound waves travel to P, the decrease in their amplitude is negligible. What multiple of s_m is the amplitude of the net wave at P if distance d in the figure is (a) $\lambda/4$, (b) $\lambda/2$, and (c) λ?

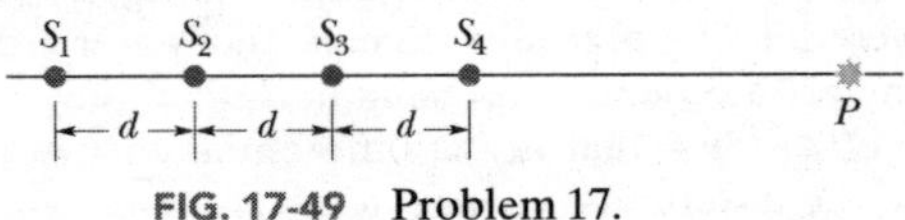

FIG. 17-49 Problem 17.

18 Figure 17-50 shows two point sources S_1 and S_2 that emit sound of wavelength $\lambda = 2.00$ m. The emissions are isotropic and in phase, and the separation between the sources is $d = 16.0$ m. At any point P on the x axis, the wave from S_1 and the wave from S_2 interfere. When P is very far away ($x \approx \infty$), what are (a) the phase difference between the arriving waves from S_1 and S_2 and (b) the type of interference they produce? Now move point P along the x axis toward S_1. (c) Does the phase difference between the waves increase or decrease? At what distance x do the waves have a phase difference of (d) 0.50λ, (e) 1.00λ, and (f) 1.50λ?

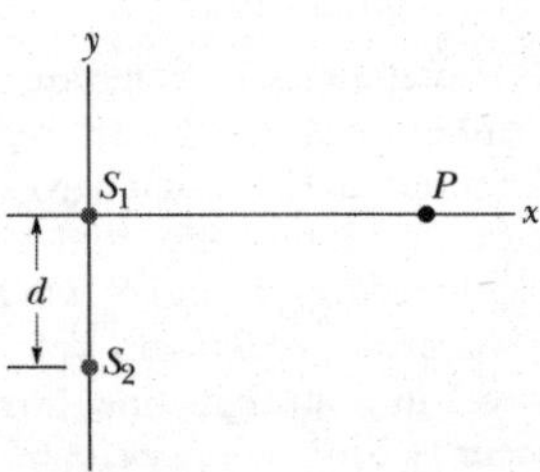

FIG. 17-50 Problem 18.

Intensity and Sound Level

19 A source emits sound waves isotropically. The intensity of the waves 2.50 m from the source is 1.91×10^{-4} W/m^2.

Assuming that the energy of the waves is conserved, find the power of the source.

20 Two sounds differ in sound level by 1.00 dB. What is the ratio of the greater intensity to the smaller intensity?

21 A sound wave of frequency 300 Hz has an intensity of 1.00 $\mu W/m^2$. What is the amplitude of the air oscillations caused by this wave?

22 The source of a sound wave has a power of 1.00 μW. If it is a point source, (a) what is the intensity 3.00 m away and (b) what is the sound level in decibels at that distance?

23 A certain sound source is increased in sound level by 30.0 dB. By what multiple is (a) its intensity increased and (b) its pressure amplitude increased?

24 Approximately a third of people with normal hearing have ears that continuously emit a low-intensity sound outward through the ear canal. A person with such *spontaneous otoacoustic emission* is rarely aware of the sound, except perhaps in a noise-free environment, but occasionally the emission is loud enough to be heard by someone else nearby. In one observation, the sound wave had a frequency of 1665 Hz and a pressure amplitude of 1.13×10^{-3} Pa. What were (a) the displacement amplitude and (b) the intensity of the wave emitted by the ear?

25 When you "crack" a knuckle, you suddenly widen the knuckle cavity, allowing more volume for the synovial fluid inside it and causing a gas bubble suddenly to appear in the fluid. The sudden production of the bubble, called "cavitation," produces a sound pulse—the cracking sound. Assume that the sound is transmitted uniformly in all directions and that it fully passes from the knuckle interior to the outside. If the pulse has a sound level of 62 dB at your ear, estimate the rate at which energy is produced by the cavitation.

26 *Party hearing.* As the number of people at a party increases, you must raise your voice for a listener to hear you against the *background noise* of the other partygoers. However, once you reach the level of yelling, the only way you can be heard is if you move closer to your listener, into the listener's "personal space." Model the situation by replacing you with an isotropic point source of fixed power P and replacing your listener with a point that absorbs part of your sound waves. These points are initially separated by $r_i = 1.20$ m. If the background noise increases by $\Delta\beta = 5$ dB, the sound level at your listener must also increase. What separation r_f is then required?

27 A point source emits 30.0 W of sound isotropically. A small microphone intercepts the sound in an area of 0.750 cm^2, 200 m from the source. Calculate (a) the sound intensity there and (b) the power intercepted by the microphone.

28 Two atmospheric sound sources A and B emit isotropically at constant power. The sound levels β of their emissions are plotted in Fig. 17-51 versus the radial distance r from the sources. The vertical axis scale is set by $\beta_1 = 85.0$ dB and $\beta_2 = 65.0$ dB. What are (a) the ratio of the larger power to the smaller power and (b) the sound level difference at $r = 10$ m?

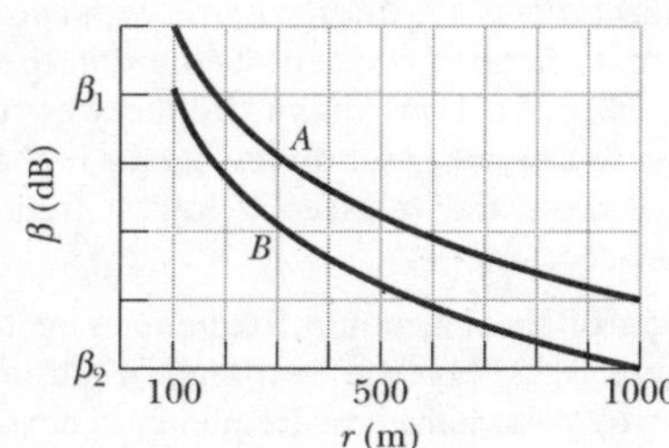

FIG. 17-51 Problem 28.

29 A sound source sends a sinusoidal sound wave of angular frequency 3000 rad/s and amplitude 12.0 nm through a tube of air. The internal radius of the tube is 2.00 cm. (a) What is the average rate at which energy (the sum of the kinetic and potential energies) is transported to the opposite end of the tube? (b) If, simultaneously, an identical wave travels along an adjacent, identical tube, what is the total average rate at which energy is transported to the opposite ends of the two tubes by the waves? If, instead, those two waves are sent along the *same* tube simultaneously, what is the total average rate at which they transport energy when their phase difference is (c) 0, (d) 0.40π rad, and (e) π rad?

Sources of Musical Sound

30 The crest of a *Parasaurolophus* dinosaur skull contains a nasal passage in the shape of a long, bent tube open at both ends. The dinosaur may have used the passage to produce sound by setting up the fundamental mode in it. (a) If the nasal passage in a certain *Parasaurolophus* fossil is 2.0 m long, what frequency would have been produced? (b) If that dinosaur could be recreated (as in *Jurassic Park*), would a person with a hearing range of 60 Hz to 20 kHz be able to hear that fundamental mode and, if so, would the sound be high or low frequency? Fossil skulls that contain shorter nasal passages are thought to be those of the female *Parasaurolophus.* (c) Would that make the female's fundamental frequency higher or lower than the male's?

31 (a) Find the speed of waves on a violin string of mass 800 mg and length 22.0 cm if the fundamental frequency is 920 Hz. (b) What is the tension in the string? For the fundamental, what is the wavelength of (c) the waves on the string and (d) the sound waves emitted by the string?

32 The water level in a vertical glass tube 1.00 m long can be adjusted to any position in the tube. A tuning fork vibrating at 686 Hz is held just over the open top end of the tube, to set up a standing wave of sound in the air-filled top portion of the tube. (That air-filled top portion acts as a tube with one end closed and the other end open.) (a) For how many different positions of the water level will sound from the fork set up resonance in the tube's air-filled portion, which acts as a pipe with one end closed (by the water) and the other end open? What are the (b) least and (c) second least water heights in the tube for resonance to occur?

33 In Fig. 17-52, S is a small loudspeaker driven by an audio oscillator with a frequency that is varied from 1000 Hz to

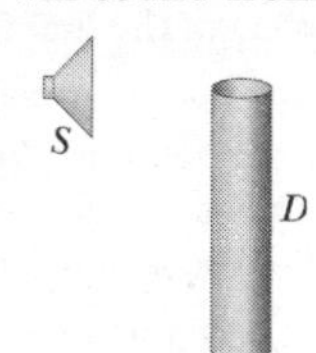

FIG. 17-52 Problem 33.

2000 Hz, and D is a cylindrical pipe with two open ends and a length of 45.7 cm. The speed of sound in the air-filled pipe is 344 m/s. (a) At how many frequencies does the sound from the loudspeaker set up resonance in the pipe? What are the (b) lowest and (c) second lowest frequencies at which resonance occurs?

34 One of the harmonic frequencies of tube A with two open ends is 325 Hz. The next-highest harmonic frequency is 390 Hz. (a) What harmonic frequency is next highest after the harmonic frequency 195 Hz? (b) What is the number of this next-highest harmonic?

One of the harmonic frequencies of tube B with only one open end is 1080 Hz. The next-highest harmonic frequency is 1320 Hz. (c) What harmonic frequency is next highest after the harmonic frequency 600 Hz? (d) What is the number of this next-highest harmonic?

35 A violin string 30.0 cm long with linear density 0.650 g/m is placed near a loudspeaker that is fed by an audio oscillator of variable frequency. It is found that the string is set into oscillation only at the frequencies 880 and 1320 Hz as the frequency of the oscillator is varied over the range 500–1500 Hz. What is the tension in the string?

36 A tube 1.20 m long is closed at one end. A stretched wire is placed near the open end. The wire is 0.330 m long and has a mass of 9.60 g. It is fixed at both ends and oscillates in its fundamental mode. By resonance, it sets the air column in the tube into oscillation at that column's fundamental frequency. Find (a) that frequency and (b) the tension in the wire.

37 A well with vertical sides and water at the bottom resonates at 7.00 Hz and at no lower frequency. (The air-filled portion of the well acts as a tube with one closed end and one open end.) The air in the well has a density of 1.10 kg/m^3 and a bulk modulus of 1.33×10^5 Pa. How far down in the well is the water surface?

38 Pipe A, which is 1.20 m long and open at both ends, oscillates at its third lowest harmonic frequency. It is filled with air for which the speed of sound is 343 m/s. Pipe B, which is closed at one end, oscillates at its second lowest harmonic frequency. This frequency of B happens to match the frequency of A. An x axis extends along the interior of B, with $x = 0$ at the closed end. (a) How many nodes are along that axis? What are the (b) smallest and (c) second smallest value of x locating those nodes? (d) What is the fundamental frequency of B?

Beats

39 A tuning fork of unknown frequency makes 3.00 beats per second with a standard fork of frequency 384 Hz. The beat frequency decreases when a small piece of wax is put on a prong of the first fork. What is the frequency of this fork?

40 Two identical piano wires have a fundamental frequency of 600 Hz when kept under the same tension. What fractional increase in the tension of one wire will lead to the occurrence of 6.0 beats/s when both wires oscillate simultaneously?

41 You have five tuning forks that oscillate at close but different frequencies. What are the (a) maximum and (b) minimum number of different beat frequencies you can produce by sounding the forks two at a time, depending on how the frequencies differ?

The Doppler Effect

42 A whistle of frequency 540 Hz moves in a circle of radius 60.0 cm at an angular speed of 15.0 rad/s. What are the (a) lowest and (b) highest frequencies heard by a listener a long distance away, at rest with respect to the center of the circle?

43 An acoustic burglar alarm consists of a source emitting waves of frequency 28.0 kHz. What is the beat frequency between the source waves and the waves reflected from an intruder walking at an average speed of 0.950 m/s directly away from the alarm?

44 A sound source A and a reflecting surface B move directly toward each other. Relative to the air, the speed of source A is 29.9 m/s, the speed of surface B is 65.8 m/s, and the speed of sound is 329 m/s. The source emits waves at frequency 1200 Hz as measured in the source frame. In the reflector frame, what are the (a) frequency and (b) wavelength of the arriving sound waves? In the source frame, what are the (c) frequency and (d) wavelength of the sound waves reflected back to the source?

45 In Fig. 17-53, a French submarine and a U.S. submarine move toward each other during maneuvers in motionless water in the North Atlantic. The French sub moves at speed $v_F = 50.00$ km/h, and the U.S. sub at $v_{US} = 70.00$ km/h. The French sub sends out a sonar signal (sound wave in water) at 1.000×10^3 Hz. Sonar waves travel at 5470 km/h. (a) What is the signal's frequency as detected by the U.S. sub? (b) What frequency is detected by the French sub in the signal reflected back to it by the U.S. sub?

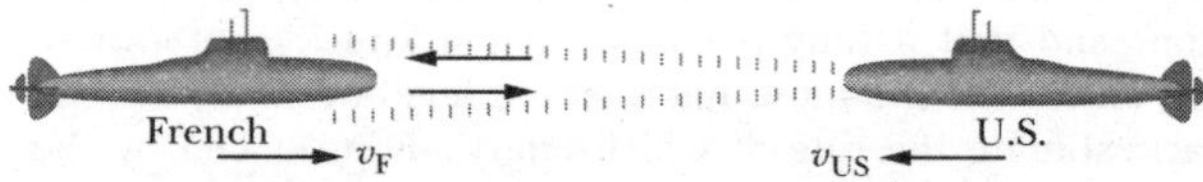

FIG. 17-53 Problem 45.

46 A stationary detector measures the frequency of a sound source that first moves at constant velocity directly toward the detector and then (after passing the detector) directly away from it. The emitted frequency is f. During the approach the detected frequency is f'_{app} and during the recession it is f'_{rec}. If $(f'_{app} - f'_{rec})/f = 0.500$, what is the ratio v_s/v of the speed of the source to the speed of sound?

47 A bat is flitting about in a cave, navigating via ultrasonic bleeps. Assume that the sound emission frequency of the bat is 39 000 Hz. During one fast swoop directly toward a flat wall surface, the bat is moving at 0.025 times the speed of sound in air. What frequency does the bat hear reflected off the wall?

48 Figure 17-54 shows four tubes with lengths 1.0 m or 2.0 m, with one or two open ends as drawn. The third harmonic is set up in each tube, and some of the sound that escapes from them is detected by detector D, which moves directly away from the tubes. In terms of the speed of sound v, what speed must the detector have such that the detected frequency of the sound from (a) tube 1,

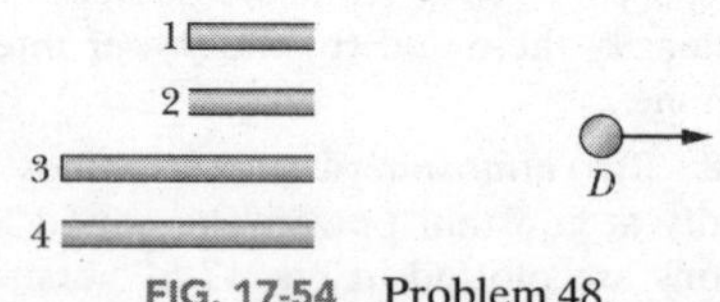

FIG. 17-54 Problem 48.

(b) tube 2, (c) tube 3, and (d) tube 4 is equal to the tube's fundamental frequency?

49 A girl is sitting near the open window of a train that is moving at a velocity of 10.00 m/s to the east. The girl's uncle stands near the tracks and watches the train move away. The locomotive whistle emits sound at frequency 500.0 Hz. The air is still. (a) What frequency does the uncle hear? (b) What frequency does the girl hear? A wind begins to blow from the east at 10.00 m/s. (c) What frequency does the uncle now hear? (d) What frequency does the girl now hear?

50 Two trains are traveling toward each other at 30.5 m/s relative to the ground. One train is blowing a whistle at 500 Hz. (a) What frequency is heard on the other train in still air? (b) What frequency is heard on the other train if the wind is blowing at 30.5 m/s toward the whistle and away from the listener? (c) What frequency is heard if the wind direction is reversed?

51 A 2000 Hz siren and a civil defense official are both at rest with respect to the ground. What frequency does the official hear if the wind is blowing at 12 m/s (a) from source to official and (b) from official to source?

Supersonic Speeds, Shock Waves

52 The shock wave off the cockpit of the FA 18 in Fig. 17-24 has an angle of about 60°. The airplane was traveling at about 1350 km/h when the photograph was taken. Approximately what was the speed of sound at the airplane's altitude?

53 A jet plane passes over you at a height of 5000 m and a speed of Mach 1.5. (a) Find the Mach cone angle (the sound speed is 331 m/s). (b) How long after the jet passes directly overhead does the shock wave reach you?

54 A plane flies at 1.25 times the speed of sound. Its sonic boom reaches a man on the ground 1.00 min after the plane passes directly overhead. What is the altitude of the plane? Assume the speed of sound to be 330 m/s.

Additional Problems

55 In Fig. 17-55, sound of wavelength 0.850 m is emitted isotropically by point source S. Sound ray 1 extends directly to detector D, at distance $L = 10.0$ m. Sound ray 2 extends to D via a reflection (effectively, a "bouncing") of the sound at a flat surface. That reflection occurs on a perpendicular bisector to the SD line, at distance d from the line. Assume that the reflection shifts the sound wave by 0.500λ. For what least value of d (other than zero) do the direct sound and the reflected sound arrive at D (a) exactly out of phase and (b) exactly in phase?

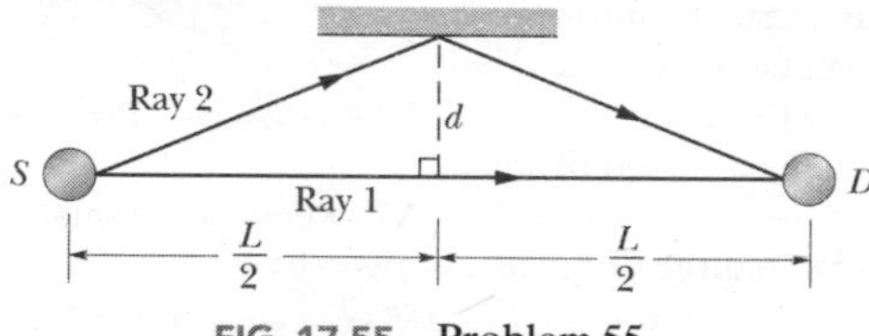

FIG. 17-55 Problem 55.

56 A sinusoidal sound wave moves at 343 m/s through air in the positive direction of an x axis. At one instant, air molecule A is at its maximum displacement in the negative direction of the axis while air molecule B is at its equilibrium position. The separation between those molecules is 15.0 cm, and the molecules between A and B have intermediate displacements in the negative direction of the axis. (a) What is the frequency of the sound wave?

In a similar arrangement, for a different sinusoidal sound wave, air molecule C is at its maximum displacement in the positive direction while molecule D is at its maximum displacement in the negative direction. The separation between the molecules is again 15.0 cm, and the molecules between C and D have intermediate displacements. (b) What is the frequency of the sound wave?

57 In Fig. 17-56, sound waves A and B, both of wavelength λ, are initially in phase and traveling rightward, as indicated by the two rays. Wave A is reflected from four surfaces but ends up traveling in its original direction. What multiple of wavelength λ is the smallest value of distance L in the figure that puts A and B exactly out of phase with each other after the reflections?

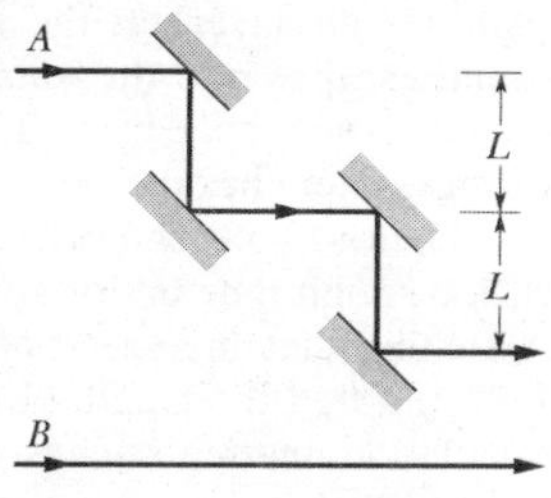

FIG. 17-56 Problem 57.

58 A trumpet player on a moving railroad flatcar moves toward a second trumpet player standing alongside the track while both play a 440 Hz note. The sound waves heard by a stationary observer between the two players have a beat frequency of 4.0 beats/s. What is the flatcar's speed?

59 At a certain point, two waves produce pressure variations given by $\Delta p_1 = \Delta p_m \sin \omega t$ and $\Delta p_2 = \Delta p_m \sin(\omega t - \phi)$. At this point, what is the ratio $\Delta p_r/\Delta p_m$, where Δp_r is the pressure amplitude of the resultant wave, if ϕ is (a) 0, (b) $\pi/2$, (c) $\pi/3$, and (d) $\pi/4$?

60 Two identical tuning forks can oscillate at 440 Hz. A person is located somewhere on the line between them. Calculate the beat frequency as measured by this individual if (a) she is standing still and the tuning forks move in the same direction along the line at 3.00 m/s, and (b) the tuning forks are stationary and the listener moves along the line at 3.00 m/s.

61 Figure 17-57 shows an air-filled, acoustic interferometer, used to demonstrate the interference of sound waves. Sound source S is an oscillating diaphragm; D is a sound detector, such as the ear or a microphone. Path SBD can be varied in length, but path SAD is fixed. At D, the sound wave coming along path SBD interferes with that coming along path SAD. In one demonstration, the sound intensity at D has a minimum value of 100 units at one position of the movable arm and continuously climbs to a maximum value of 900 units when that arm is shifted by 1.65 cm. Find (a) the frequency of the sound emitted by the source and (b) the ratio of the amplitude at D of the SAD wave to that of the SBD wave. (c) How can it happen that these waves have different amplitudes, considering that they originate at the same source?

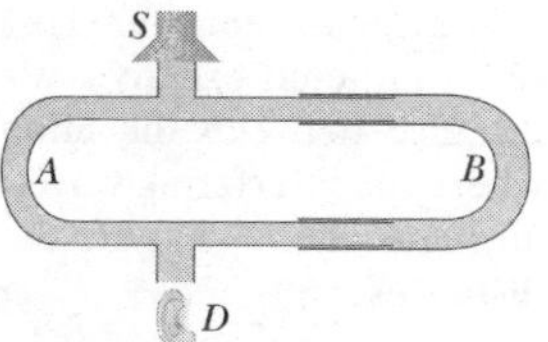

FIG. 17-57 Problem 61.

62 A bullet is fired with a speed of 685 m/s. Find the angle made by the shock cone with the line of motion of the bullet.

63 A sperm whale (Fig. 17-58*a*) vocalizes by producing a series of clicks. Actually, the whale makes only a single sound near the front of its head to start the series. Part of that sound then emerges from the head into the water to become the first click of the series. The rest of the sound travels backward through the spermaceti sac (a body of fat), reflects from the frontal sac (an air layer), and then travels forward through the spermaceti sac. When it reaches the distal sac (another air layer) at the front of the head, some of the sound escapes into the water to form the second click, and the rest is sent back through the spermaceti sac (and ends up forming later clicks).

Figure 17-58*b* shows a strip-chart recording of a series of clicks. A unit time interval of 1.0 ms is indicated on the chart. Assuming that the speed of sound in the spermaceti sac is 1372 m/s, find the length of the spermaceti sac. From such a calculation, marine scientists estimate the length of a whale from its click series.

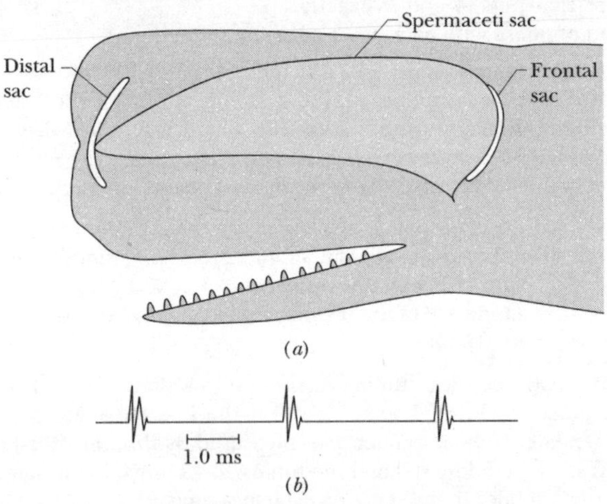

FIG. 17-58 Problem 63.

64 Straight line AB connects two point sources that are 5.00 m apart, emit 300 Hz sound waves of the same amplitude, and emit exactly out of phase. (a) What is the shortest distance between the midpoint of AB and a point on AB where the interfering waves cause maximum oscillation of the air molecules? What are the (b) second and (c) third shortest distances?

65 An avalanche of sand along some rare desert sand dunes can produce a booming that is loud enough to be heard 10 km away. The booming apparently results from a periodic oscillation of the sliding layer of sand—the layer's thickness expands and contracts. If the emitted frequency is 90 Hz, what are (a) the period of the thickness oscillation and (b) the wavelength of the sound?

66 *Waterfall acoustics*. The turbulent impact of the water in a waterfall causes the surrounding ground to oscillate in a wide range of low frequencies. If the water falls freely (instead of hitting rock on the way down), the oscillations are greatest in amplitude at a particular frequency f_m. This fact suggests that acoustic resonance is involved and f_m is the fundamental frequency. The following table gives, for nine U.S. and Canadian waterfalls, measured values for f_m and for the length L of the water's free fall. Determine how to plot the data to get the speed of sound in the water of a waterfall. From the plot, find the speed of sound if waterfall resonance is effectively like that in a tube with (a) two open ends and (b) only one open end. The speed of sound in turbulent water filled with air bubbles can be about 25% less than the speed of 1400 m/s in still water. (c) From the answers to (a) and (b), determine how many open ends are effectively involved in waterfall resonance.

WATERFALL	1	2	3	4	5	6	7	8	9
f_m (Hz)	5.6	3.8	8.0	6.1	8.8	6.0	19	21	40
L (m)	97	71	53	49	35	24	13	11	8

67 A sound wave travels out uniformly in all directions from a point source. (a) Justify the following expression for the displacement s of the transmitting medium at any distance r from the source:

$$s = \frac{b}{r} \sin k(r - vt)$$

where b is a constant. Consider the speed, direction of propagation, periodicity, and intensity of the wave. (b) What is the dimension of the constant b?

68 To search for a fossilized dinosaur embedded in rock, paleontologists can use sound waves to produce a computer image of the dinosaur. The image then guides the paleontologists as they dig the dinosaur out of the rock. (The technique is shown in the opening scenes of the movie *Jurassic Park*.) The basic idea of the detection technique is that a strong pulse of sound is emitted by a source (a seismic gun) at ground level and then detected by hydrophones that lie at evenly spaced depths in a bore hole drilled into the ground. The source and one hydrophone are shown in Fig. 17-59. If the sound wave travels from the source to the hydrophone through only rock as in Fig. 17-59, it travels at a known speed V and takes a certain time T. If, instead, it travels through a fossilized bone along the way, it takes slightly more time because it travels more slowly in the bone than in the rock. By measuring the difference Δt between the expected and measured travel times, the distance d traveled in the bone can be determined. After this procedure is repeated for many locations of the source and hydrophones, a computer can transform the many computed distances d into an image of the fossil.

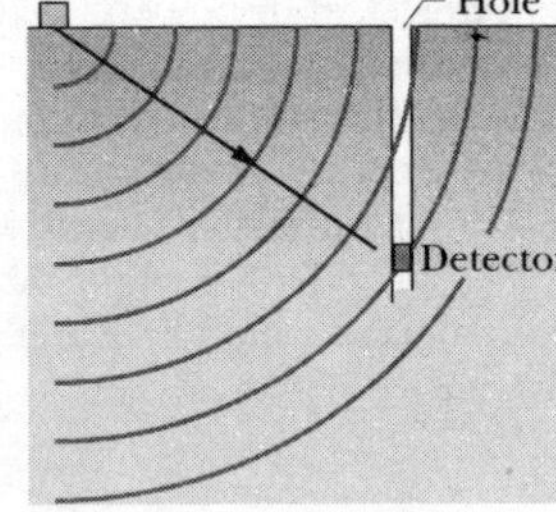

FIG. 17-59 Problem 68.

(a) Let the speed of sound through fossilized bone be $V - \Delta V$, where ΔV is small relative to V. Show that the distance d is given by

$$d \approx \frac{V^2 \Delta t}{\Delta V}$$

(b) For $V = 5000$ m/s and $\Delta V = 200$ m/s, what typical value of Δt can be expected if the sound passes along the diameter of a leg bone of an adult *T. rex*? (Estimate the bone's diameter.)

69 A listener at rest (with respect to the air and the ground) hears a signal of frequency f_1 from a source moving toward him with a velocity of 15 m/s, due east. If the listener then moves toward the approaching source with a velocity of 25 m/s, due west, he hears a frequency f_2 that differs from f_1 by 37 Hz. What is the frequency of the source? (Take the speed of sound in air to be 340 m/s.)

70 A guitar player tunes the fundamental frequency of a guitar string to 440 Hz. (a) What will be the fundamental frequency if she then increases the tension in the string by 20%? (b) What will it be if, instead, she decreases the length along which the string oscillates by sliding her finger from the tuning key one-third of the way down the string toward the bridge at the lower end?

18 Temperature and Thermal Expansion

Courtesy Hugh Thomas/BWP Media/Getty Images News and Sport Services

When a Concorde flew faster than the speed of sound, thermal expansion due to the rubbing by passing air increased the aircraft's length by about 12.5 cm. (The temperature increased to about 128°C at the aircraft nose and about 90°C at the tail, and cabin windows were noticeably warm to the touch.)

Why is the design and fuselage of supersonic aircrafts, like Concorde, different from the other airplanes?

The answer is in this chapter.

18-1 | Introduction

Temperature is one of the seven SI base quantities. Physicists measure temperature on the **Kelvin scale,** which is marked in units called *kelvins.* Although the temperature of a body apparently has no upper limit, it does have a lower limit; this limiting low temperature is taken as the zero of the Kelvin temperature scale. Room temperature is about 290 kelvins, or 290 K as we write it, above this *absolute zero.* Figure 18-1 shows a wide range of temperatures.

When the universe began 13.7 billion years ago, its temperature was about 10^{39} K. As the universe expanded it cooled, and it has now reached an average temperature of about 3 K. We on Earth are a little warmer than that because we happen to live near a star. Without our Sun, we too would be at 3 K (or, rather, we could not exist).

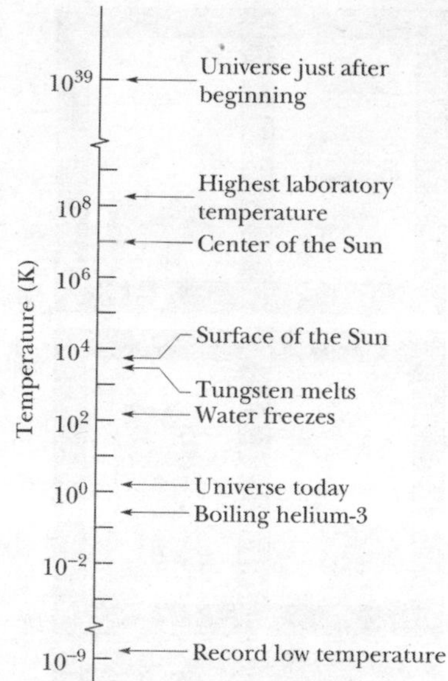

FIG. 18-1 Some temperatures on the Kelvin scale. Temperature $T = 0$ corresponds to $10^{-\infty}$ and cannot be plotted on this logarithmic scale.

18-2 | The Zeroth Law of Thermodynamics

The properties of many bodies change as we alter their temperature, perhaps by moving them from a refrigerator to a warm oven. To give a few examples: As their temperature increases, the volume of a liquid increases, a metal rod grows a little longer, and the electrical resistance of a wire increases, as does the pressure exerted by a confined gas. We can use any one of these properties as the basis of an instrument that will help us pin down the concept of temperature.

Figure 18-2 shows such an instrument. Any resourceful engineer could design and construct it, using any one of the properties listed above. The instrument is fitted with a digital readout display and has the following properties: If you heat it (say, with a Bunsen burner), the displayed number starts to increase; if you then put it into a refrigerator, the displayed number starts to decrease. The instrument is not calibrated in any way, and the numbers have (as yet) no physical meaning. The device is a *thermoscope* but not (as yet) a *thermometer.*

Suppose that, as in Fig. 18-3*a*, we put the thermoscope (which we shall call body T) into intimate contact with another body (body A). The entire system is confined within a thick-walled insulating box. The numbers displayed by the thermoscope roll by until, eventually, they come to rest (let us say the reading is "137.04") and no further change takes place. In fact, we suppose that every measurable property of body T and of body A has assumed a stable, unchanging value. Then we say that the two bodies are in *thermal equilibrium* with each other. Even though the displayed readings for body T have not been calibrated, we conclude that bodies T and A must be at the same (unknown) temperature.

Suppose that we next put body T into intimate contact with body B (Fig. 18-3*b*) and find that the two bodies come to thermal equilibrium *at the same reading of the thermoscope.* Then bodies T and B must be at the same (still unknown) temperature. If we now put bodies A and B into intimate contact (Fig. 18-3*c*), are they immediately in thermal equilibrium with each other? Experi-mentally, we find that they are.

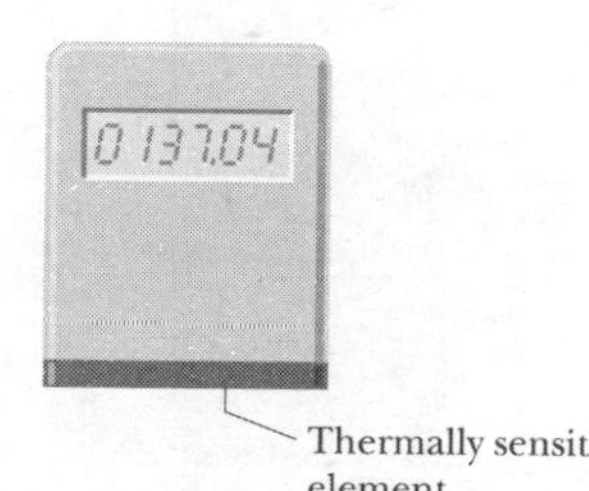

FIG. 18-2 A thermoscope. The numbers increase when the device is heated and decrease when it is cooled. The thermally sensitive element could be—among many possibilities—a coil of wire whose electrical resistance is measured and displayed.

The experimental fact shown in Fig. 18-3 is summed up in the **zeroth law of thermodynamics:**

> If bodies A and B are each in thermal equilibrium with a third body T, then A and B are in thermal equilibrium with each other.

In less formal language, the message of the zeroth law is: "Every body has a property called **temperature.** When two bodies are in thermal equilibrium, their temperatures are equal. And vice versa." We can now make our thermoscope (the third body T) into a thermometer, confident that its readings will have physical meaning. All we have to do is calibrate it.

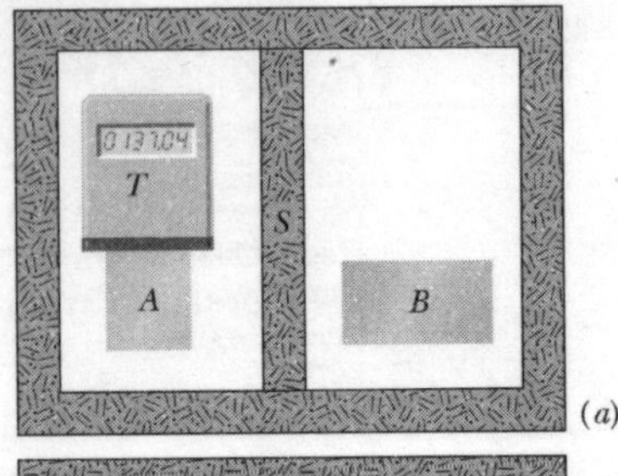

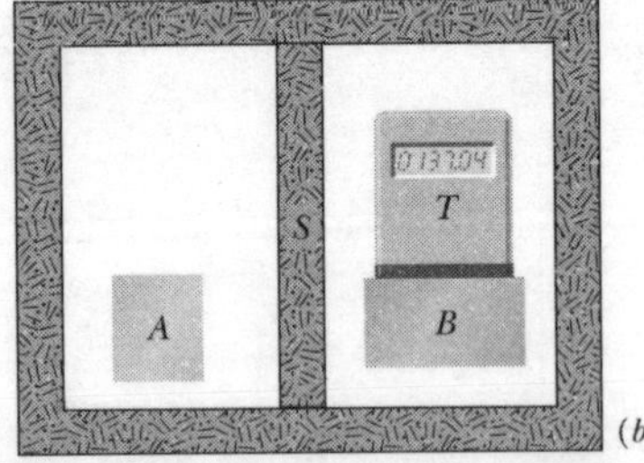

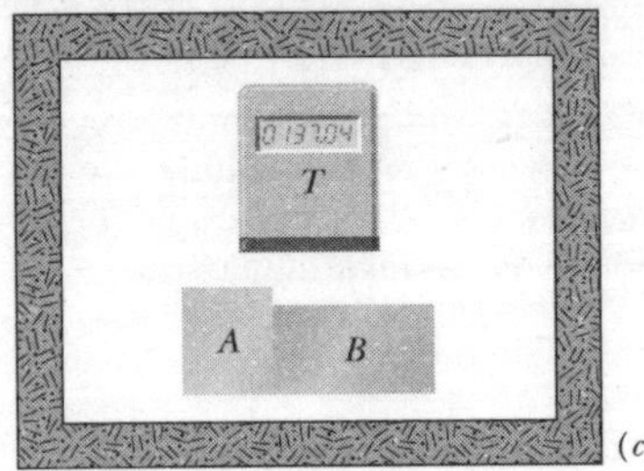

FIG. 18-3 (*a*) Body T (a thermoscope) and body A are in thermal equilibrium. (Body S is a thermally insulating screen.) (*b*) Body T and body B are also in thermal equilibrium, at the same reading of the thermoscope. (*c*) If (*a*) and (*b*) are true, the zeroth law of thermodynamics states that body A and body B are also in thermal equilibrium.

We use the zeroth law constantly in the laboratory. If we want to know whether the liquids in two beakers are at the same temperature, we measure the temperature of each with a thermometer. We do not need to bring the two liquids into intimate contact and observe whether they are or are not in thermal equilibrium.

The zeroth law, which has been called a logical afterthought, came to light only in the 1930s, long after the first and second laws of thermodynamics had been discovered and numbered. Because the concept of temperature is fundamental to those two laws, the law that establishes temperature as a valid concept should have the lowest number—hence the zero.

18-3 | Measuring Temperature

Here we first define and measure temperatures on the Kelvin scale. Then we calibrate a thermoscope so as to make it a thermometer.

The Triple Point of Water

To set up a temperature scale, we pick some reproducible thermal phenomenon and, quite arbitrarily, assign a certain Kelvin temperature to its environment; that is, we select a *standard fixed point* and give it a standard fixed-point *temperature.* We could, for example, select the freezing point or the boiling point of water but, for technical reasons, we select instead the **triple point of water.**

Liquid water, solid ice, and water vapor (gaseous water) can coexist, in thermal equilibrium, at only one set of values of pressure and temperature. Figure 18-4 shows a triple-point cell, in which this so-called triple point of water can be achieved in the laboratory. By international agreement, the triple point of water has been assigned a value of 273.16 K as the standard fixed-point temperature for the calibration of thermometers; that is,

$$T_3 = 273.16 \text{ K} \quad \text{(triple-point temperature)} \tag{18-1}$$

in which the subscript 3 means "triple point." This agreement also sets the size of the kelvin as 1/273.16 of the difference between absolute zero and the triple-point temperature of water.

Note that we do not use a degree mark in reporting Kelvin temperatures. It is 300 K (not 300°K), and it is read "300 kelvins" (not "300 degrees Kelvin"). The usual SI prefixes apply. Thus, 0.0035 K is 3.5 mK. No distinction in nomenclature is made between Kelvin temperatures and temperature differences, so we can write, "the boiling point of sulfur is 717.8 K" and "the temperature of this water bath was raised by 8.5 K."

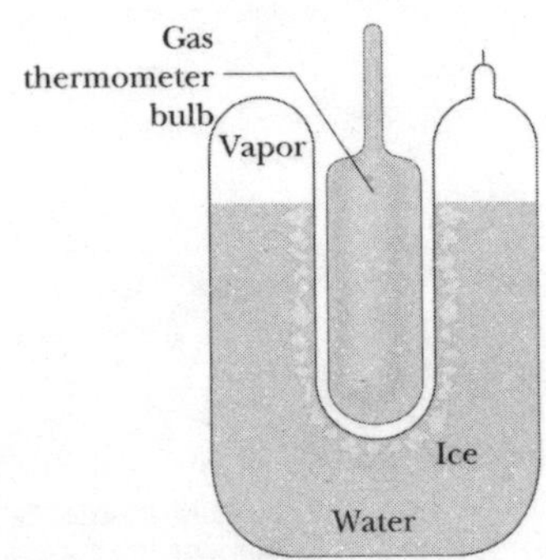

FIG. 18-4 A triple-point cell, in which solid ice, liquid water, and water vapor coexist in thermal equilibrium. By international agreement, the temperature of this mixture has been defined to be 273.16 K. The bulb of a constant-volume gas thermometer is shown inserted into the well of the cell.

The Constant-Volume Gas Thermometer

The standard thermometer, against which all other thermometers are calibrated, is based on the pressure of a gas in a fixed volume. Figure 18-5 shows such a **constant-volume gas thermometer;** it consists of a gas-filled bulb connected by a tube to a mercury manometer. By raising and lowering reservoir R, the mercury level in the left arm of the U-tube can always be brought to the zero of the scale to keep the gas volume constant (variations in the gas volume can affect temperature measurements).

The temperature of any body in thermal contact with the bulb (such as the liquid surrounding the bulb in Fig. 18-5) is then defined to be

$$T = Cp \tag{18-2}$$

in which p is the pressure exerted by the gas and C is a constant. From Eq. 14-10, the pressure p is

$$p = p_0 - \rho g h \qquad (18\text{-}3)$$

in which p_0 is the atmospheric pressure, ρ is the density of the mercury in the manometer, and h is the measured difference between the mercury levels in the two arms of the tube.* (The minus sign is used in Eq. 18-3 because pressure p is measured *above* the level at which the pressure is p_0.)

If we next put the bulb in a triple-point cell (Fig. 18-4), the temperature now being measured is

$$T_3 = C p_3 \qquad (18\text{-}4)$$

in which p_3 is the gas pressure now. Eliminating C between Eqs. 18-2 and 18-4 gives us the temperature as

$$T = T_3\left(\frac{p}{p_3}\right) = (273.16\text{ K})\left(\frac{p}{p_3}\right) \quad \text{(provisional)} \qquad (18\text{-}5)$$

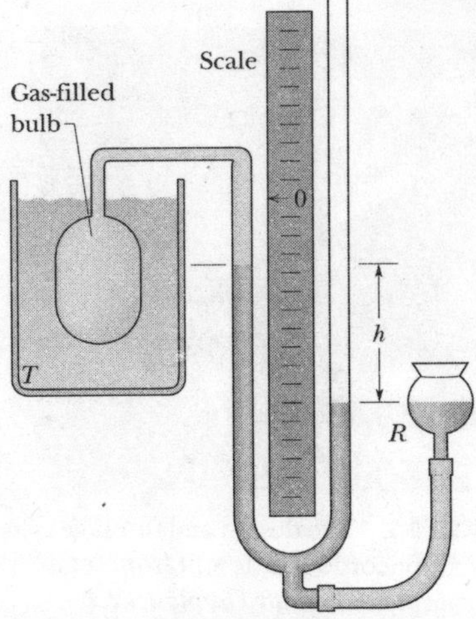

FIG. 18-5 A constant-volume gas thermometer, its bulb immersed in a liquid whose temperature T is to be measured.

We still have a problem with this thermometer. If we use it to measure, say, the boiling point of water, we find that different gases in the bulb give slightly different results. However, as we use smaller and smaller amounts of gas to fill the bulb, the readings converge nicely to a single temperature, no matter what gas we use. Figure 18-6 shows this convergence for three gases.

Thus the recipe for measuring a temperature with a gas thermometer is

$$T = (273.16\text{ K})\left(\lim_{\text{gas}\to 0} \frac{p}{p_3}\right) \qquad (18\text{-}6)$$

The recipe instructs us to measure an unknown temperature T as follows: Fill the thermometer bulb with an arbitrary amount of *any* gas (for example, nitrogen) and measure p_3 (using a triple-point cell) and p, the gas pressure at the temperature being measured. (Keep the gas volume the same.) Calculate the ratio p/p_3. Then repeat both measurements with a smaller amount of gas in the bulb, and again calculate this ratio. Continue this way, using smaller and smaller amounts of gas, until you can extrapolate to the ratio p/p_3 that you would find if there were approximately no gas in the bulb. Calculate the temperature T by substituting that extrapolated ratio into Eq. 18-6. (The temperature is called the *ideal gas temperature.*)

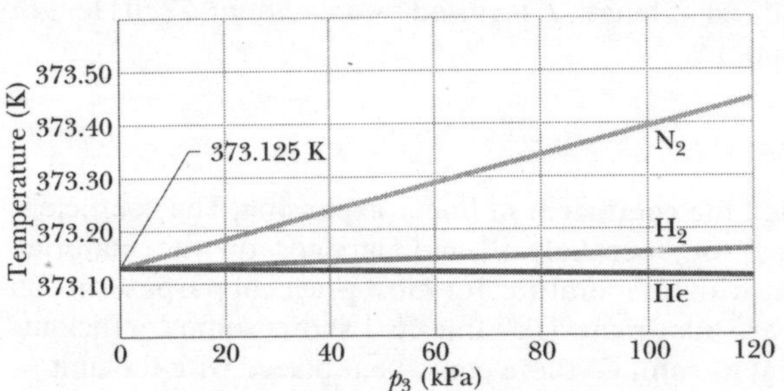

FIG. 18-6 Temperatures measured by a constant-volume gas thermometer, with its bulb immersed in boiling water. For temperature calculations using Eq. 18-5, pressure p_3 was measured at the triple point of water. Three different gases in the thermometer bulb gave generally different results at different gas pressures, but as the amount of gas was decreased (decreasing p_3), all three curves converged to 373.125 K.

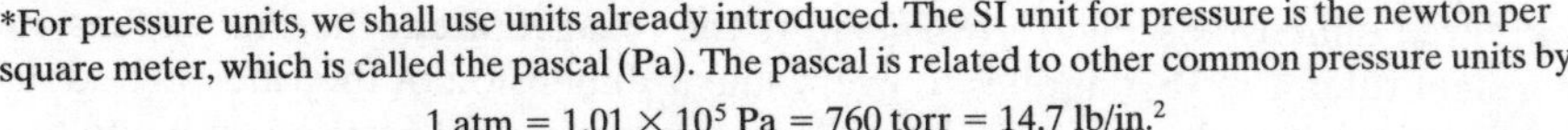

*For pressure units, we shall use units already introduced. The SI unit for pressure is the newton per square meter, which is called the pascal (Pa). The pascal is related to other common pressure units by

$$1\text{ atm} = 1.01 \times 10^5\text{ Pa} = 760\text{ torr} = 14.7\text{ lb/in.}^2$$

18-4 | Thermal Expansion

You can often loosen a tight metal jar lid by holding it under a stream of hot water. Both the metal of the lid and the glass of the jar expand as the hot water adds energy to their atoms. (With the added energy, the atoms can move a bit farther from one another than usual, against the spring-like interatomic forces that hold every solid together.) However, because the atoms in the metal move farther apart than those in the glass, the lid expands more than the jar and thus is loosened.

Such **thermal expansion** of materials with an increase in temperature must be anticipated in many common situations. When a bridge is subject to large seasonal changes in temperature, for example, sections of the bridge are separated by *expansion slots* so that the sections have room to expand on hot days without the bridge buckling. When a dental cavity is filled, the filling material must have the same thermal expansion properties as the surrounding tooth; otherwise, consuming cold ice cream and then hot coffee would be very painful. When the Concorde aircraft (Fig. 18-7) was built, the design had to allow for the thermal expansion of the fuselage during supersonic flight because of frictional heating by the passing air.

FIG. 18-7 The design and fuselage of a Concorde is different from regular airplane. *(Hugh Thomas/BWP Media/Getty Images News and Sport Services)*

Cause of Thermal Expansion

All molecules undergo oscillations due to kinetic energy associated with temperature and the oscillations in a solid are not simple harmonic. Thus, the potential energy curve between neighboring atoms, as shown in Fig. 18-8, is not simple harmonic. The energy increases faster when the atoms move close to each other than when they move apart. The horizontal lines show the range of motion of atoms for different total energy. As the energy increases, the mean position of the atoms moves apart from each other because of the asymmetric nature of the vibrations. The thermal energy increases with temperature, increasing the average separation of the atoms and thus the size of a solid sample. For a temperature change ΔT that is not too large, the resulting fractional change in length, $\Delta L/L$ is proportional to ΔT

$$\frac{\Delta L}{L} = \alpha \Delta T$$

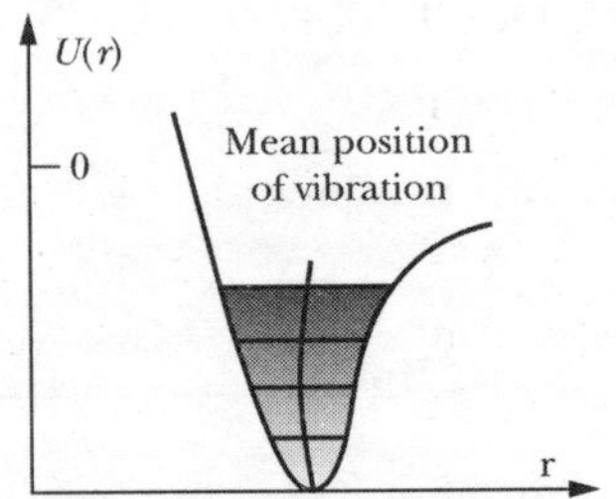

FIG. 18-8 Potential energy due to interatomic forces plotted against the distance. Mean position of vibration is also shown.

18-5 | Expansion of Solids

Linear Expansion

If the temperature of a metal rod of length L is raised by an amount ΔT, its length is found to increase by an amount

$$\Delta L = L\alpha\,\Delta T \tag{18-7}$$

in which α is a constant called the **coefficient of linear expansion.** The coefficient α has the unit "per degree" or "per kelvin" and depends on the material. Although α varies somewhat with temperature, for most practical purposes it can be taken as constant for a particular material. Table 18-1 shows some coefficients of linear expansion. Note that the unit C° there could be replaced with the unit K.

The thermal expansion of a solid is like photographic enlargement except it is in three dimensions. Figure 18-9*b* shows the (exaggerated) thermal expansion of a steel ruler. Eq. 18-7 applies to every linear dimension of the ruler, including its edge, thickness, diagonals, and the diameters of the circle etched on it and the circular hole cut in it. If the disk cut from that hole originally fits snugly in the hole, it will continue to fit snugly if it undergoes the same temperature increase as the ruler.

The constant α is called the coefficient of linear expansion for the material. Since thermal energies are very small compared with the energies of bonds between atoms the coefficients α are also small.

TABLE 18-1

Some Coefficients of Linear Expansion[a]

Substance	α (10^{-6}/C°)	Substance	α (10^{-6}/C°)
Ice (at 0°C)	51	Steel	11
Lead	29	Glass (ordinary)	9
Aluminum	23	Glass (Pyrex)	3.2
Brass	19	Diamond	1.2
Copper	17	Invar[b]	0.7
Concrete	12	Fused quartz	0.5

[a]Room temperature values except for the listing for ice.

[b]This alloy was designed to have a low coefficient of expansion. The word is a shortened form of "invariable."

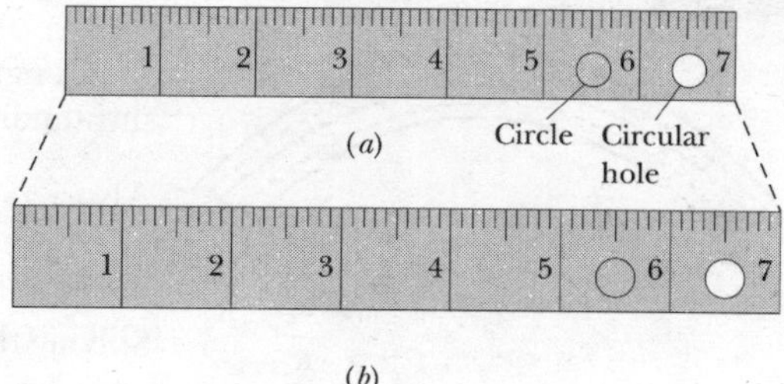

FIG. 18-9 The same steel ruler at two different temperatures. When it expands, the scale, the numbers, the thickness, and the diameters of the circle and circular hole are all increased by the same factor. (The expansion has been exaggerated for clarity.)

Sample Problem 18-1 Build your skill

A meter scale was calibrated at 0°C. If it is giving the distance between two fixed points as 12 mm, at 40°C as shown in Fig. 18-10, then what is the actual distance between them, given that coefficient of thermal expansion $\alpha = 10^{-5}\,(°\text{C})^{-1}$.

A B

FIG. 18-10 A meter scale, calibrated at 0°C, showing the distance between points *A* and *B*.

Solution: At 40°C the length of a division would have become more than 1 mm so let's call distance between two divisions as 1 mm*. Then using formula for thermal expansion we can write

Therefore, $1\text{ mm}^* = 1\text{mm}\,[1 + 10^{-5} \times 40]$

Solving we get, $1\text{ mm}^* = 1.0004\text{ mm}$

Thus, the length that our scale measured as "12 mm" is 12 mm* thus correct length is $12 \times (1.0004)$ mm

$= 12.0048$ mm (Answer)

Bimetallic Strip

Calculation of radius of curvature

The thermal expansion properties of some materials can be put to common use. Thermometers and thermostats may be based on the differences in expansion between the components of a *bimetal strip* (Fig. 18-11). Also, the familiar liquid-in-glass thermometers are based on the fact that liquids such as mercury and alcohol expand to a different (greater) extent than their glass containers.

Consider a bimetallic strip as shown in Fig. 18-12*a*. On heating it will bend as shown in Fig. 18-12*b* if $\alpha_1 > \alpha_2$ where, α_1 and α_2 are the thermal expansion coefficients of outer and inner regions and *d* is the diameter of the rod.

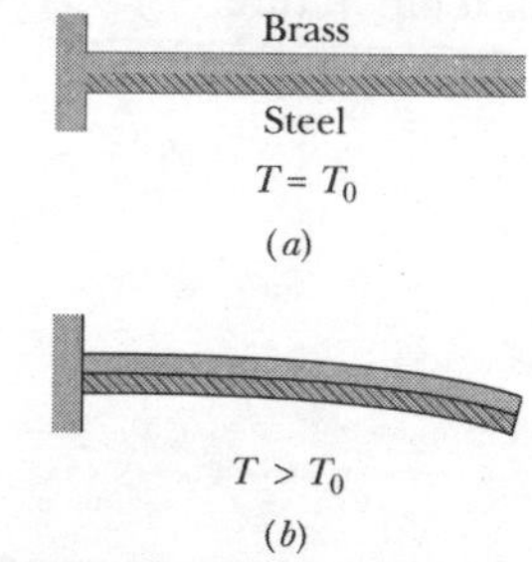

FIG. 18-11 (*a*) A bimetal strip, consisting of a strip of brass and a strip of steel welded together, at temperature T_0. (*b*) The strip bends as shown at temperatures above this reference temperature. Below the reference temperature the strip bends the other way. Many thermostats operate on this principle, making and breaking an electrical contact as the temperature rises and falls.

Length of the outer portion is l_1 where, $l_1 = (R + d/2)\,\theta$, as the rod will be substending an angle θ at the center.

$$l_1 = l\,(l + \alpha_1 \Delta t)$$

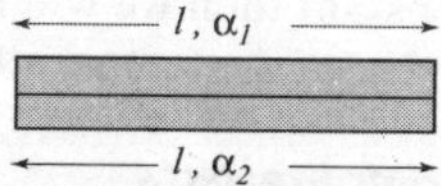

FIG. 18-12 (*a*) A bimetallic strip before thermal expansion.

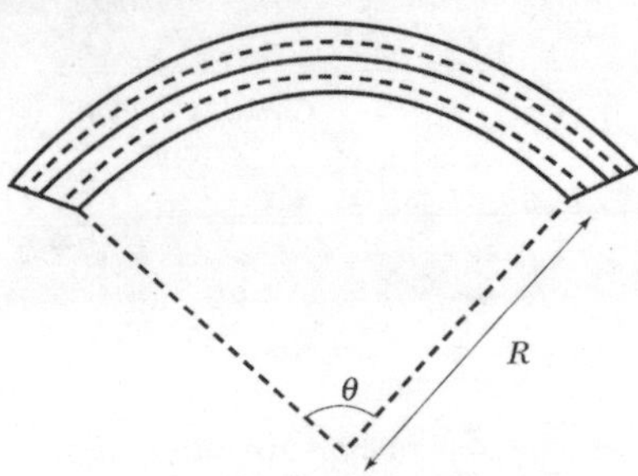

FIG. 18-12 (*b*) A bimetallic strip after thermal expansion.

Length of the inner portion is l_2, where $l_2 = (R - d/2)\,\theta$, as the rod will be substending angle θ at the center.

Also, $$l_2 = l\,(l + \alpha_2 \Delta t)$$

Comparing the two values of l_2, we have $(R - d/2)\,\theta = l\,(l + \alpha_2\Delta t)$

Solving the above equation, we get the radius of curvature R

$$R = \left(\frac{d\,(2 + (\alpha_1 + \alpha_2)\,\Delta t)}{2\,((\alpha_1 - \alpha_2)\,\Delta t)}\right)$$

Sample Problem 18-2

Thermal stress: A steel wire of 2.0 mm^2 cross section is held straight (but under no tension) by attaching it firmly to two rigid walls at a distance 1.50 m apart, at 30°C. If the temperature now decreases to −10°C, and if the end points remain fixed, what will be the tension in the wire? For steel, $Y = 2\,00\,000$ MPa.

Conceptualize: If free to do so, the wire would contract but since we have tied its ends it will not contract and maintain the original length.

Classify: Till now we have seen that when length of wire is changed it produces strain and hence stress. This situation is different as strain will be produced because of wire maintaining its length. At a lower temperature the wire will have a unstrained length smaller than the original length but due to our tieing it up it is maintaining its length, thus it is strained. Or in other words it is having larger length than what it is supposed to have at this temperature.

Compute: If free to do so, the wire would contract a distance ΔL as it cooled, where

$$\Delta L = \alpha L_0 \Delta T$$
$$= (1.2 \times 10^{-5}\,°\text{C}^{-1})\,(1.5\text{ m})\,(40°\text{C})$$
$$= 7.2 \times 10^{-4}\text{ m}$$

But the ends are fixed. As a result, forces at the ends must, in effect, stretch the wire this same length, ΔL. Therefore, from $Y = (F/A)\,/\,(\Delta L/L)$, we have tension

$$F = \frac{YA\,\Delta L}{L}$$
$$= \frac{(2 \times 10^{11}\text{ N/m}^2)(2 \times 10^{-6}\text{ m}^2)(7.2 \times 10^{-4}\text{ m})}{1.5\text{ m}}$$
$$= 192\text{ N} \qquad \text{(Answer)}$$

Conclude: Strictly, we should have substituted $(1.5 - 7.2 \times 10^{-4})$ m for L in the expression for tension. However, the error incurred in not doing so, is negligible.

CHECKPOINT 1 A thin rod of negligible mass and area of cross-section 4×10^{-6} m^2, suspended vertically from one end, has a length of 0.5 m at 100°C. The rod is cooled to 0°C, but prevented from contracting by attaching a mass at the lower end. Find (a) this mass, and (b) the energy stored in the rod. Given for the rod, Young's modulus = N/m^2, Coefficient of linear expansion = 10^{-5} K^{-1} and $g = 10$ m/s^2.

Sample Problem 18-3

A second's pendulum clock is shown in Fig.18-13. It is compensated for temperature change by using differential expansion of the light rod and the heavy bob. This keeps the center of oscillation of the pendulum at a fixed distance below the point of suspension. Find the length of the light rod, h_0 and radius r_0 of the heavy bob of this pendulum. Given that $\alpha'' \gg \alpha'$.

Conceptualize/Classify: A second's pendulum clock has the period 2 s of the pendulum. We can consider the center of the bob C as approximately the center of oscillation of the pendulum, the effective length of the pendulum is $l = h - r$. If expansion coefficients are so chosen that the difference of the lengths remain constant then we will have constant time period irrespective of the temperature change.

Compute: Now,

$$h = h_0(1 + \alpha'\Delta T)$$
$$r = r_0(1 + \alpha''\Delta T)$$

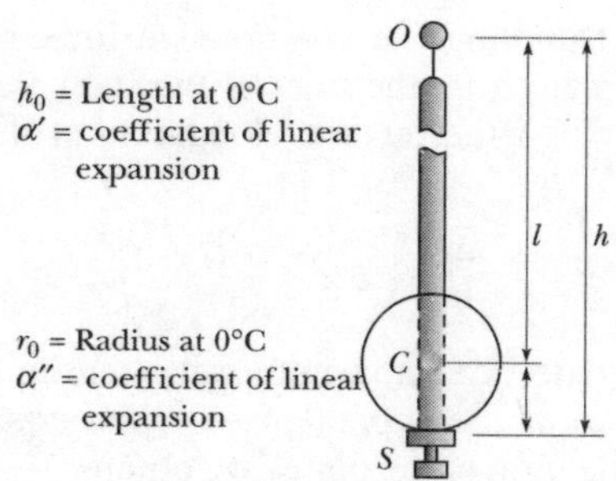

FIG. 18-13 A pendulum with differential expansion.

where $\alpha'' \gg \alpha'$. Then, $l = h_0 - r_0 + (h_0\alpha' - r_0\alpha'')\,\Delta T$, which will be independent of temperature if

$$(h_0\alpha' - r_0\alpha'') = 0.$$

Also, $$l_0 = h_0 - r_0,$$

where l_0 is the length that must be maintained. Solving these last two equations for h_0 and r_0, we get

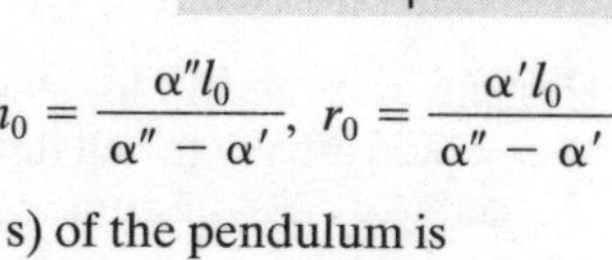

$$h_0 = \frac{\alpha'' l_0}{\alpha'' - \alpha'}, \quad r_0 = \frac{\alpha' l_0}{\alpha'' - \alpha'}$$

The period (2 s) of the pendulum is

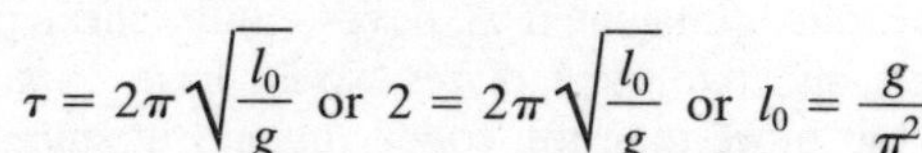

$$\tau = 2\pi\sqrt{\frac{l_0}{g}} \text{ or } 2 = 2\pi\sqrt{\frac{l_0}{g}} \text{ or } l_0 = \frac{g}{\pi^2}$$

Finally, the dimension (h_0, r_0) of the pendulum becomes

$$h_0 = \frac{\alpha'' l_0}{\alpha'' - \alpha'} = \frac{\alpha''(g/\pi^2)}{\alpha'' - \alpha'} \qquad \text{(Answer)}$$

and $$r_0 = \frac{\alpha'(g/\pi^2)}{\alpha'' - \alpha'} \qquad \text{(Answer)}$$

Conclude: If we would have used same material, that is, $\alpha'' - \alpha' = 0$, the required dimensions would have become infinite. Or in other words, using same material will not ensure the temperature independence.

CHECKPOINT 2 Why is only iron or steel used as reinforcement in concrete structures, while other metals, duralumin for example, are never employed?

Sample Problem 18-4 Build your skill

Two rods made of different materials are placed between massive walls (Fig. 18-14).

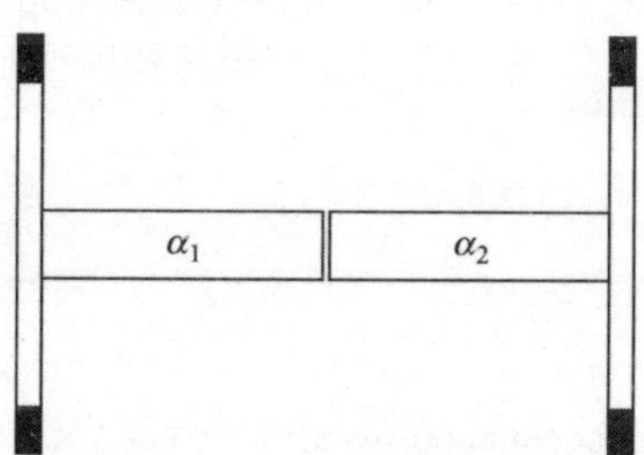

FIG. 18-14 Two composite rods kept between two fixed walls.

The cross-section of the rods is A and their respective lengths are l_1 and l_2. The temperature increases by δT.

Find the force with which the rods exert on each other if their coefficients of linear thermal expansion α_1 and α_2 and the moduli of elasticity of their materials E_1 and E_2 are known. Disregard the deformation of the walls.

Solution: When the rods are heated in a free state, their total length will increase by

$$\Delta l = \Delta l_1 + \Delta l_2 = (\alpha_1 l_1 + \alpha_2 l_2)\,t.$$

Compression by the same amount Δl will reduce the lengths of the rods by $\Delta l_1'$ and $\Delta l_2'$, where

$$\Delta l_1' + \Delta l_2' = \Delta l.$$

This requires the force

$$F = \frac{E_1 A}{l_1}\Delta l_1' = \frac{E_2 A \Delta l_2'}{l_2}$$

Upon solving this system of equations, we find that

$$F = \frac{\alpha_1 l_1 + \alpha_2 l_2}{\dfrac{l_1}{E_1} + \dfrac{l_2}{E_2}} \text{ At}$$

The rods will act upon each other with this force.

Sample Problem 18-5

A copper plate is soldered (rigidly connected) to two steel plates as shown in Fig. 18-15. What tensions will arise in the plates if the temperature is increased by δT? Given coefficient of linear thermal expansion of copper is α_c and of steel is α_s, and α_c is greater than α_s. Also the

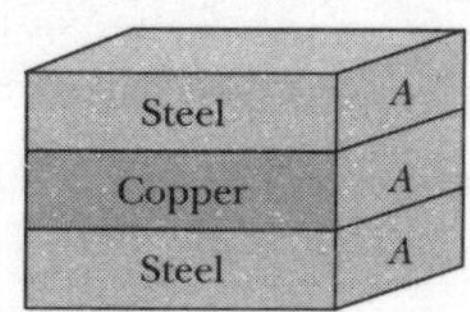

FIG. 18-15 Three plates, a copper plate between two steel plates, having cross-section area A soldered together.

coefficients of elasticity is Y_s and Y_c for steel and copper respectively. Cross-section area of the all three plates is A.

Conceptualize: Imagine if we have kept the three plates separately, the two steel plates would have expanded equally, but more than the copper plate. But since they are rigidly connected, the steel plates' expansion will be hindered by the copper plate that was unable to expand equally and similarly the copper plate will expand more because of stretching by the steel plates.

Classify: Since the coefficient of linear thermal expansion of copper α_c is greater than that of steel α_s, the increase in temperature will lead to compression of the copper plate and tension of the steel ones. Thus, to conclude the steel plates will be experiencing compressive stress and the copper plates will be experiencing tensile stress. Because they are rigidly joined, the relative elongations of all the three plates are the same.

Compute: Denoting the compressive force acting on the copper plate from the sides of the steel plates by F, we shall have for the relative elongation of the copper plate:

$$\frac{\Delta l}{l} = \alpha_c t - \frac{F}{AY_c}$$

Both steel plates are subjected to the tensile force $F/2$ from the side of the copper plate. Upon equating the relative elongation of the plates, we obtain.

$$\alpha_c t - \frac{F}{AY_c} = \alpha_c t + \frac{F}{2AY_s}$$

Hence,

$$F = \frac{2AY_c Y_c(\alpha_c - \alpha_s)t}{2Y_s + Y_c}$$

Conclude: If $\alpha_c = \alpha_s$ then we get force as zero, that is what we should expect, as both plates will have same expansion and they will not be pulling each other.

CHECKPOINT 3 Determine the lengths of an iron and a copper ruler l'_0 and l''_0 at $t = 0°C$ if the difference in their lengths at $t_1 = 50°C$ and $t_2 = 450°C$ is the same in magnitude and equal to $l = 2$ cm. The coefficient of linear expansion of iron $\alpha_1 = 12 \times 10^{-6}$ deg^{-1} and of copper $\alpha_2 = 17 \times 10^{-6}$ deg^{-1}.

The coefficient of Superficial Expansion of a substance represents the alteration in area of a sheet of the substance initially possessing unit area, when it is heated through unit difference of temperature.Its numerical value, from the above, is equal to twice the coefficient of linear expansion of the substance in question. The coefficient of superficial expansion of an isotropic solid is equal to twice the coefficient of linear expansion of the solid.

Sample Problem 18-6 Build your skill

A metallic sheet is 50 cm long and 20 cm wide at 0°C. If it is heated to 60°C, what will be its area? Given that $\alpha = 10^{-4}$ /°C.

Solution: Original area = 50 × 20 = 1000 cm^2

Let α be the coefficient of linear expansion of the metal.

Then length of sheet at 60°C = $50(1 + 60\alpha)$

Width = $20(1 + 60\alpha)$

Hence, area of sheet at 60°C = $50(1 + 60\alpha) \times 20(1 + 60\alpha)$

$= 1000(1 + 2 \times 60\alpha + (60\alpha)\,2)$

The term (60α) 2 will be very small, and may therefore be neglected. Hence,

area of sheet = $1000(1 + 2 \times 60\alpha)$

= 1012 cm^2 (Answer)

CHECKPOINT 4 The figure here shows four rectangular metal plates, with sides of L, $2L$, or $3L$. They are all made of the same material, and their temperature is to be increased by the same amount. Rank the plates according to the expected increase in (a) their vertical heights and (b) their areas, greatest first.

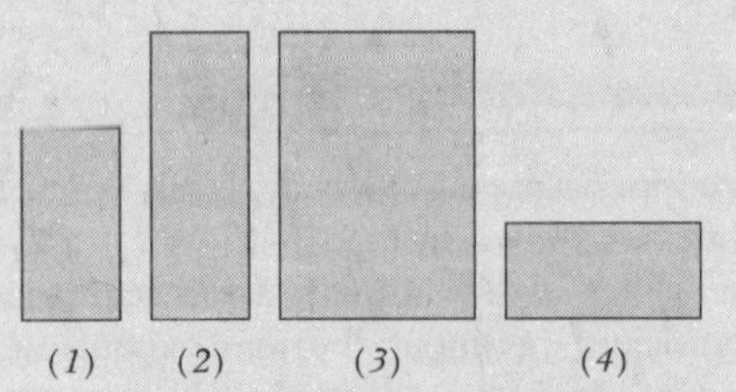

Volume Expansion

If all dimensions of a solid expand with temperature, the volume of that solid must also expand. For liquids, volume expansion is the only meaningful expansion parameter. If the temperature of a solid or liquid whose volume is V is increased by an amount ΔT, the increase in volume is found to be

$$\Delta V = V\beta\,\Delta T \tag{18-8}$$

where β is the **coefficient of volume expansion** of the solid or liquid. The coefficients of volume expansion and linear expansion for a solid are related by

$$\beta = 3\alpha \tag{18-9}$$

18-6 | Expansion of Liquids

Like solids, different liquids expand by different amounts for the same temperature rise. Fig. 18-16 is a simple set up to demonstrate the expansion in different liquids. Three flasks are filled to the brim with different (preferably colored) liquids, and identical capillary tubes attached as shown in the figure. The flasks are placed in a large trough of water. When the trough is heated, the liquids expand by different amounts, thereby rising to different heights in their respective tubes. Liquids show greater expansion than solids. The cubical expansivities of liquids are about ten times those of solids. Table gives measured coefficients of cubical expansion of some common liquids.

One of the difficulties posed when measurements are to be made on the expansion of liquids is due to the fact that liquids always need a containing vessel. When a liquid sample is heated, the container also expands. Thus measurements of the volume increase on heating must also take into account the fact that the container has also expanded, meaning the liquid now occupies a slightly larger volume than it did before heating. The following example serves to illustrate how the expansion of the containing vessel can be taken into account in problem solving.

TABLE 18-2

Coefficient of volume expansion at 20°C for some common liquids

Liquid	$\beta(\times 10^{-4})\,\mathrm{K}^{-1}$
Gasoline	9.5
Mercury	1.8
Ethyl alcohol	11.0
Glycerine	5.0
Water	2.1

FIG. 18-16 Set-up for demonstration of expansion in different liquids filled to same level in identical flasks.

Sample Problem 18-7 Build your skill

A glass flask whose volume is exactly 1000 cm^3 at 0°C is completely filled with mercury at this temperature. When the flask and mercury are heated to 100°C, it is found that 15.4 cm^3 of mercury overflows. If the coefficient of volume expansion of mercury is $1.8 \times 10^{-4}\,\mathrm{K}^{-1}$, calculate the coefficient of volume expansion of glass.

Solution: This Sample Problem represents the normal situation in which both liquid and container expand simultaneously when heated. The higher volume expansion of the liquid over the material of the container causes the overflow. We equate the overflow to the difference in the final volumes of the liquid and the container.

Data: Original volume of mercury $V_0 = 1000\ \mathrm{cm}^3$

Original temperature of mercury, $T_0 = 0°\mathrm{C} = 273\ \mathrm{K}$

Final temperature of flask and mercury $T = 100°\mathrm{C} = 373\ \mathrm{K}$

Volume of mercury overflow, $\Delta V = 15.4\ \text{cm}^3$

Volume expansivity of mercury $\beta_{Hg} = 1.8 \times 10^{-4}\ \text{K}^{-1}$

Let volume expansivity of glass be β_g. Let V_1 represent the final volume of the glass container, and V_2 that of the mercury.

$$\Delta V = V_2 - V_1$$

where the new volumes are: $V_2 = V_0 (1 + \beta_{Hg}\, \Delta T)$, and $V_1 = V_0(1 + \beta_g\, \Delta T)$

Thus $V_0 (1 + \beta_{Hg}\, \Delta T) - V_0 (1 + \beta_g\, \Delta T) = \Delta V$,

giving $1000 \times (1 + 1.8 \times 10^{-4} \times 100) - 1000 \times (1 + \beta_g \times 100) = 15.4\ \text{cm}^3$,

from which, the expansivity of glass $\beta_g = 2.6 \times 10^{-5}\ \text{K}^{-1}$. (Answer)

Sample Problem 18-8 Build your skill

A glass cylinder can contain $m_0 = 100$ g of mercury at a temperature of $t_0 = 0°\text{C}$. When $t_1 = 20°\text{C}$, the cylinder can contain $m_1 = 99.7$ g of mercury. In both cases the temperature of the mercury is assumed to be equal to that of the cylinder. Use these data to find the coefficient of linear expansion of glass α, bearing in mind that the coefficient of volume expansion of mercury $\gamma_1 = 18 \times 10^{-5}\ \text{deg.}^{-1}$

Solution: When the cylinder is heated, its volume increases according to the same law as that of the glass: $v_1 = v_0\ (1 + \gamma t_1)$, where γ is the coefficient of volume expansion of glass. If the densities of mercury at the temperatures t_0 and t_1 are denoted by ρ_0 and ρ_1, we can write that $m_0 = v_0 \rho_0$ and $m_1 = v_1 \rho_1$, where

$$\rho_1 = \frac{\rho_0}{1 + \gamma_1 t_1}$$

This system of equations will give the following expression for γ:

$$\gamma = \frac{m_1(1 + \gamma_1 t_1) - m_0}{m_0 t_1} \approx 3 \times 10^{-5}\ \text{deg}^{-1}$$

The coefficient of linear expansion $\alpha = \dfrac{\gamma}{3} \equiv 10^{-5}\ \text{deg.}^{-1}$ (Answer)

Sample Problem 18-9

A uniform capillary tube of length L, as measured by a ruler, contains some liquid. The temperature of the tube and the liquid is raised by ΔT. Show that the increase in the height of liquid column, again measured with a ruler, is $\Delta T = L(\gamma - 2\alpha)\Delta T$, where γ is the coefficient of volume expansion of the liquid and α is the coefficient of linear expansion of the tube material.

Conceptualize/Classify: As we know that the vessel and the liquid both expand so the observed increase in the height of liquid column is not representative of the increase in volume of liquid only.

Compute: Denoting the radius of the capillary by r and its cross-sectional area by A, the increase in radius due to thermal expansion is given by $dr = r\alpha dT$, where α is coefficient of linear expansion of the tube material, and dT is the temperature increase. We know that $dr/r \ll 1$.

Since $A = \pi r^2$, we find that $dA/A = 2dr/r$, or that $dA \equiv A\beta dT = A(2\alpha)dT$, where β is used as the symbol for the coefficient of area expansion.

If the temperature is changed from T to $T' \equiv T + dT$, the cross-sectional area changes from A to $A' \equiv A + dA = A(1 + 2\alpha dT)$.

The change in length from L to $L' \equiv L + dL$ of the liquid thread is governed by the volume expansion of the liquid.

Since $V' = V(1 + \gamma dT)$, where γ is the coefficient of volume expansion for the liquid, we have $L'A' = V' = V(1 + \gamma dT) = LA\,(1 + \gamma dT)$. But $A'/A = 1 + 2\,\alpha dT$, so

$$L' = L\frac{(1 + \gamma dT)}{(1 + 2\alpha dT)}$$

$$= L\,\{[1 + (\gamma - 2\alpha)]dT - 2\gamma\alpha(dT)^2\}$$

For a temperature increase ΔT, the length change $\Delta L \equiv L' - L \approx L(\gamma - 2\alpha)\,\Delta T$, and the relative change in length is

$$\frac{\Delta L}{L} \approx (\gamma - 2\alpha)\Delta T$$

Conclude: Here we have assumed that $\alpha\Delta T \ll 1$. Note that the specification that a ruler is used for the measurement is to avoid the use of scale that expands with the tube.

Density Variation on Heating

Since the volume of a liquid increases when heated, without change in mass, it follows that the density of the liquid will change on heating. How do we explain this? From the previous section, it is seen that expansion is a result of the molecules moving farther apart on the application of heat. It therefore follows that the density of a liquid will be less at a higher currents currents created in liquids when heated at the bottom. To calculate the density at the new temperature, we need to know the original density of the liquid. If we let D_0 represent the original density of the liquid, then the new density D_1 for a temperature change ΔT is given by

$$D_1 = \frac{D_0}{1 + \gamma \Delta L}$$

If value of $\gamma \Delta T$ are negligible, then: $d' = d_0(1 - \gamma \Delta T)$

Sample Problem 18-10 Build your skill

When the expansion of a liquid in a vessel is measured to obtain the coefficient γ, what is actually obtained directly is γ relative to the material of which the container is made. Fig. 18-17 illustrates an apparatus from which the correct value of γ can be found without any knowledge of γ for the container. (a) Show that $\gamma = (h_t - h_0)/h_0 t$. (b) If $h_1 - h_0 = 1.0$ cm, $h_0 = 100$ cm, and $t = 20°C$, what is the value of γ for the liquid?

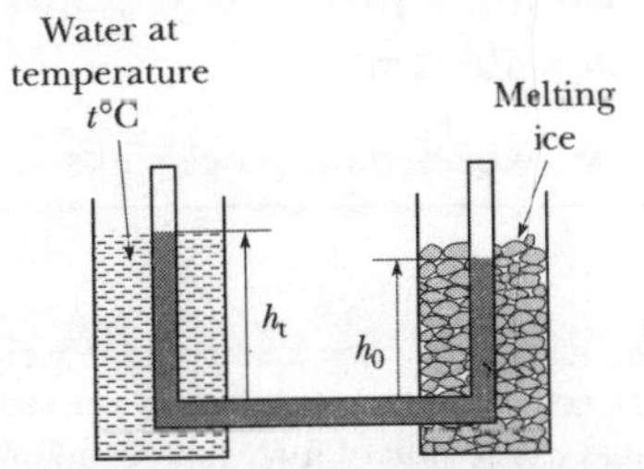

FIG. 18-17 A U tube with both arms in two different baths.

Solution: (a) Hydrostatic equlibrium of the liquid in the horizontal section of the tube implies that $\rho_t g h_t = \rho_0 g h_0$, where ρ_t is the density of the liquid in the warm column and ρ_0 is the density of the liquid in the cold column. Using the definition of the coefficient of volume expansion γ, the volumes of a given mass M of liquid at temperatures t and 0°C are related by $V_t = V_0(1 + \gamma t)$. Since $\rho_t V_t = \rho_0 V_0$, the densities are related by $\rho_0 = \rho_t(1 + \gamma t)$. But then, since $\rho_t h_t = \rho_0 h_0$, we have $h_t = h_0(1 + \gamma t)$. Solving this for γ, we find $\gamma = (h_t - h_0)/(h_0 t)$, as desired.

(b) With $h_t - h_0 = 1.0$ cm, $h_0 = 100$ cm, and $t = 20°C$, we obtain $\gamma = 1.0/[(100)(20)] = 500 \times 10^{-6}/°C$.

Sample Problem 18-11

A one liter glass flask contains some mercury. It is found that at different temperatures the volume of air inside the flask remains the same. What is the volume of mercury in this flask if coefficient of linear expansion of glass is $9 \times 10^{-6}/°C$ while volume expansion of mercury is $1.8 \times 10^{-4}/°C$?

Conceptualize/Classify: As we know that both the vessel and the liquid expand and they will expand in such that the difference of their volumes will remain unchanged or in other words the expansion of mercury will be equal to that of the whole flask.

Compute: If V is the volume of flask, V_L is mercury and V_A is air in it,

$$V = V_L + V_A$$

Now as with change in temperature volume of air remains constant, the expansion of mercury will be equal to that of the whole flask, that is

$$\Delta V = \Delta V_L$$

or $\quad V\gamma_G \Delta\theta = V_L \gamma_L \Delta\theta \qquad (\text{as}\, \Delta V = V\gamma\Delta\theta)$

Here $\quad V = 1, L = 1000$ cc and $\gamma_G = 3\alpha_G = 27 \times 10^{-6}/°C$

So $\quad V_L = (1000 \times 27 \times 10^{-6}/1.8 \times 10^{-4}) = 150$ cc

(Answer)

Sample Problem 18-12

An aluminum cube of side 20 cm floats on mercury (Fig. 18-18). How much farther will the block sink when the temperature rises from 300 to 350 K? Given that the density of aluminum and mercury at 300 K are 2.7 and 13.6 g/cc while the coefficient of volume expansion of mercury and linear expansion of aluminium are $1.8 \times 10^{-4}/°C$ and $23 \times 10^{-6}/°C$, respectively.

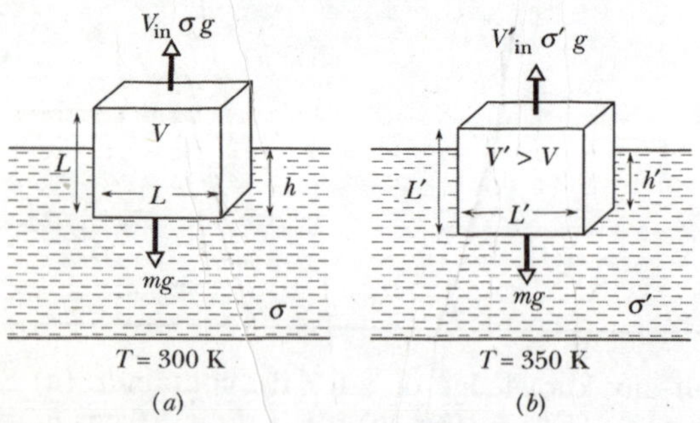

FIG. 18-18 An aluminum cube floating in mercury. The temperature of mercury is (*a*) 300 K and (*b*) 350 K.

Conceptualize/Classify: As the temperature rises the block expands and the density of the liquid decreases, so it is like we are putting a bigger block of same weight in a lighter liquid. So to apply the same buoyant force a larger fraction of the volume should sink into the liquid.

Compute: If side of cube, density of liquid (mercury) and length of the floating cube inside the liquid are L, σ, h, and L', σ', h' at 300 K and 350 K, respectively, by principle of floatation, then

$$m = V_{in}\,\sigma = V'_{in}\,\sigma' \qquad (\text{with } m = V\rho = \rho L^3)$$

that is, $hL^2\sigma = h'(L')^2\sigma'$ (as $V_{in} = hA = hL^2$)

or $$\left[\frac{h'}{h}\right] = \left[\frac{L}{L'}\right]^2 \times \left[\frac{\sigma}{\sigma'}\right]$$

Now as $L' = L\,(1 + \sigma_s\,\Delta\theta)$ and $\sigma' = \sigma\,(1 + \gamma_L\Delta\theta)$

therefore,

$$\left[\frac{h'}{h}\right] = \frac{(1+\gamma_L\Delta\theta)}{(1+\sigma_S\Delta\theta)^2} = \frac{(1+\gamma_L\Delta\theta)}{(1+2\sigma_S\Delta\theta)} = 1 + (\gamma_L - 2\sigma_S)\Delta\theta$$

so $$\Delta h = (h' - h) = h(\gamma_L - 2\alpha_S) \times \Delta\theta$$

Also from the equation $m = V_{in}\,\sigma$, we have

$$\rho L^3 = hL^2\sigma, \quad \text{that is,}$$

$$h = \left[\frac{\rho}{\sigma}\right] L = \left[\frac{2.7}{13.6}\right] \times 20 = 3.970 \text{ cm}$$

So $\Delta h = 3.970\,(1.8 \times 10^{-4} - 2 \times 23 \times 10^{-6})\,(350 - 300)$
$= 2.66 \times 10^{-2}$ cm (Answer)

Conclude: As expected the block sinks deeper.

CHECKPOINT 5 A sinker of weight W_0 has an apparent weight W_1 when weighed in a liquid at a temperature T_1 and W_2 when weighed in the same liquid at a temperature T_2. The coefficient of cubical expansion of material of sinker is γ_S. What is the coefficient of volume expansion of the liquid?

CHECKPOINT 6 A glass cylinder can contain $m_0 = 100$ g of mercury at a temperature of $t_0 = 0°C$. When $t_1 = 20°C$, the cylinder can contain $m_1 = 99.7$ g of mercury. In both cases the temperature of the mercury is assumed to be equal to that of the cylinder. Use these data to find the coefficient of linear expansion of glass α, bearing in mind that the coefficient of volume expansion of mercury $\gamma_1 = 18 \times 10^{-5}$ deg.$^{-1}$

Anamolous Expansion of Water

The most common liquid, water, does not behave like other liquids. Above about 4°C, water expands as the temperature rises, as we would expect. Between 0 and about 4°C, however, water *contracts* with increasing temperature. Thus, at about 4°C, the density of water passes through a maximum. At all other temperatures, the density of water is less than this maximum value.

This behavior of water is the reason lakes freeze from the top down rather than from the bottom up. As water on the surface is cooled from, say,

10°C toward the freezing point, it becomes denser ("heavier") than lower water and sinks to the bottom. Below 4°C, however, further cooling makes the water then on the surface *less* dense ("lighter") than the lower water, so it stays on the surface until it freezes. Thus the surface freezes while the lower water is still liquid. If lakes froze from the bottom up, the ice so formed would tend not to melt completely during the summer, because it would be insulated by the water above. After a few years, many bodies of open water in the temperate zones of Earth would be frozen solid all year round—and aquatic life could not exist.

Sample Problem 18-13

On a hot day in New Delhi, an oil trucker loaded 37 000 L of diesel fuel. He encountered cold weather on the way to Udhampur, Jammu, where the temperature was 23.0 K lower than in New Delhi, and where he delivered his entire load. How many liters did he deliver? The coefficient of volume expansion for diesel fuel is $9.50 \times 10^{-4}/\text{C}°$, and the coefficient of linear expansion for his steel truck tank is $11 \times 10^{-6}/\text{C}°$.

Conceptualize/Classify: The volume of the diesel fuel depends directly on the temperature. Thus, because the temperature decreased, the volume of the fuel did also, as given by the equation $\Delta V = V\beta\,\Delta T$.

Compute: We find

$$\Delta V = (37\,000\text{ L})(9.50 \times 10^{-4}/\text{C}°)(-23.0\text{ K}) = -808\text{ L}$$

Thus, the amount delivered was

$$V_{\text{del}} = V + \Delta V = 37\,000\text{ L} - 808\text{ L} = 36\,190\text{ L} \qquad \text{(Answer)}$$

Conclude: Note that the thermal expansion of the steel tank has nothing to do with the problem. Question: Who paid for the "missing" diesel fuel?

REVIEW & SUMMARY

Temperature; Thermometers Temperature is an SI base quantity related to our sense of hot and cold. It is measured with a thermometer, which contains a working substance with a measurable property, such as length or pressure, that changes in a regular way as the substance becomes hotter or colder.

Zeroth Law of Thermodynamics When a thermometer and some other object are placed in contact with each other, they eventually reach thermal equilibrium. The reading of the thermometer is then taken to be the temperature of the other object. The process provides consistent and useful temperature measurements because of the **zeroth law of thermodynamics:** If bodies *A* and *B* are each in thermal equilibrium with a third body *C* (the thermometer), then *A* and *B* are in thermal equilibrium with each other.

The Kelvin Temperature Scale In the SI system, temperature is measured on the **Kelvin scale,** which is based on the *triple point* of water (273.16 K). Other temperatures are then defined by use of a *constant-volume gas thermometer,* in which a sample of gas is maintained at constant volume so its pressure is proportional to its temperature. We define the *temperature T* as measured with a gas thermometer to be

$$T = (273.16\text{ K})\left(\lim_{\text{gas}\to 0} \frac{p}{p_3}\right)$$

Here T is in kelvins, and p_3 and p are the pressures of the gas at 273.16 K and the measured temperature, respectively.

Thermal Expansion All objects change size with changes in temperature. For a temperature change ΔT, a change ΔL in any linear dimension L is given by

$$\Delta L = L\alpha\,\Delta T$$

in which α is the **coefficient of linear expansion.** The change ΔV in the volume V of a solid or liquid is

$$\Delta V = V\beta\,\Delta T$$

Here $\beta = 3\alpha$ is the material's **coefficient of volume expansion.**

Heat Heat Q is energy that is transferred between a system and its environment because of a temperature difference between them. It can be measured in **joules** (J), **calories** (cal), **kilocalories** (Cal or kcal), or **British thermal units** (Btu), with

$$1\text{ cal} = 3.968 \times 10^{-3}\text{ Btu} = 4.1868\text{ J}$$

QUESTIONS

1 Figure 18-19 shows three linear temperature scales, with the freezing and boiling points of water indicated. Rank the three scales according to the size of one degree on them, greatest first.

FIG. 18-19 Question 1.

2 The initial length L, change in temperature ΔT, and change in length ΔL of four rods are given in the following table. Rank the rods according to their coefficients of thermal expansion, greatest first.

Rod	L (m)	ΔT (C°)	ΔL (m)
a	2	10	4×10^{-4}
b	1	20	4×10^{-4}
c	2	10	8×10^{-4}
d	4	5	4×10^{-4}

3 A solid cube of edge length r, a solid sphere of radius r, and a solid hemisphere of radius r, all made of the same material, are maintained at temperature 300 K in an environment at temperature 350 K. Rank the objects according to the net rate at which thermal radiation is exchanged with the environment, greatest first.

PROBLEMS

The Celsius and Fahrenheit Scales

1 At what temperature is the Fahrenheit scale reading equal to (a) twice that of the Celsius scale and (b) half that of the Celsius scale?

2 On a linear X temperature scale, water freezes at −125.0°X and boils at 375.0°X. On a linear Y temperature scale, water freezes at −70.00°Y and boils at −30.00°Y. A temperature of 50.00°Y corresponds to what temperature on the X scale?

3 Suppose that on a linear temperature scale X, water boils at −53.5°X and freezes at −170°X. What is a temperature of 340 K on the X scale? (Approximate water's boiling point as 373 K.)

Thermal Expansion

4 An aluminum flagpole is 33 m high. By how much does its length increase as the temperature increases by 15 C°?

5 Find the change in volume of an aluminum sphere with an initial radius of 10 cm when the sphere is heated from 0.0°C to 100°C.

6 An aluminum-alloy rod has a length of 10.000 cm at 20.000°C and a length of 10.015 cm at the boiling point of water. (a) What is the length of the rod at the freezing point of water? (b) What is the temperature if the length of the rod is 10.009 cm?

7 A circular hole in an aluminum plate is 2.725 cm in diameter at 0.000°C. What is its diameter when the temperature of the plate is raised to 100.0°C?

8 At 20°C, a brass cube has an edge length of 30 cm. What is the increase in the cube's surface area when it is heated from 20°C to 75°C?

9 What is the volume of a lead ball at 30.00°C if the ball's volume at 60.00°C is 50.00 cm³?

10 When the temperature of a metal cylinder is raised from 0.0°C to 100°C, its length increases by 0.23%. (a) Find the percent change in density. (b) What is the metal? Use Table 18-2.

11 An aluminum cup of 100 cm³ capacity is completely filled with glycerin at 22°C. How much glycerin, if any, will spill out of the cup if the temperature of both the cup and the glycerin is increased to 28°C? (The coefficient of volume expansion of glycerin is 5.1×10^{-4}/C°.)

12 At 20°C, a rod is exactly 20.05 cm long on a steel ruler. Both the rod and the ruler are placed in an oven at 270°C, where the rod now measures 20.11 cm on the same ruler. What is the coefficient of linear expansion for the material of which the rod is made?

13 A steel rod is 3.000 cm in diameter at 25.00°C. A brass ring has an interior diameter of 2.992 cm at 25.00°C. At what common temperature will the ring just slide onto the rod?

14 When the temperature of a copper coin is raised by 100 C°, its diameter increases by 0.18%. To two significant figures, give the percent increase in (a) the area of a face, (b) the thickness, (c) the volume, and (d) the mass of the coin. (e) Calculate the coefficient of linear expansion of the coin.

15 A vertical glass tube of length L = 1.280 000 m is half filled with a liquid at 20.000 000°C. How much will the height of the liquid column change when the tube is heated to 30.000 000°C? Take $\alpha_{glass} = 1.000\,000 \times 10^{-5}$/K and $\beta_{liquid} = 4.000\,000 \times 10^{-5}$/K.

16 In a certain experiment, a small radioactive source must move at selected, extremely slow speeds. This motion is accomplished by fastening the source to one end of an aluminum rod and heating the central section of the rod in a controlled way. If the effective heated section of the rod in Fig. 18-20 has length d = 2.00 cm, at what constant rate must the temperature of the rod be changed if the source is to move at a constant speed of 100 nm/s?

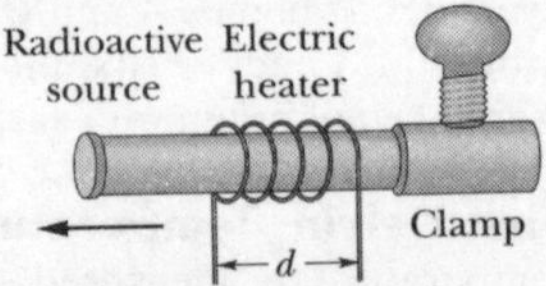

FIG. 18-20 Problem 16.

17 As a result of a temperature rise of 32 C°, a bar with a crack at its center buckles upward (Fig. 18-21). If the fixed distance L_0 is 3.77 m and the coefficient of linear expansion of the bar is 25×10^{-6}/C°, find the rise x of the center.

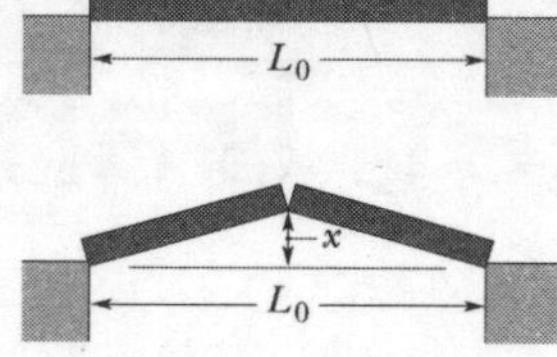

FIG. 18-21 Problem 17.

Additional Problems

18 A 0.300 kg sample is placed in a cooling apparatus that removes energy as heat at a constant rate of 2.81 W. Figure 18-22 gives the temperature T of the sample versus time t. The tem-perature scale is set by T_s = 30°C and the time scale is set by t_s = 20 min. What is the specific heat of the sample?

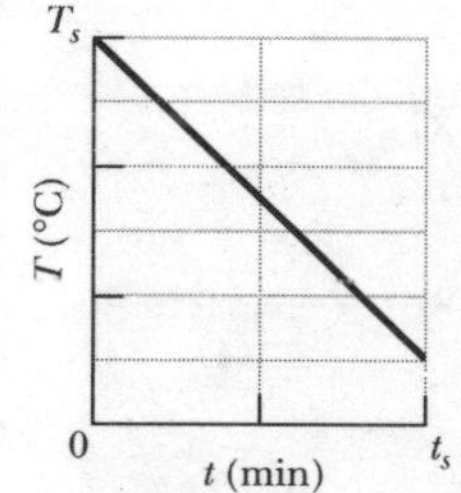

FIG. 18-22 Problem 18.

19 The temperature of a Pyrex disk is changed from 10.0°C to 60.0°C. Its initial radius is 8.00 cm; its initial thickness is 0.500 cm. Take these data as being exact. What is the change in the volume of the disk? (See Table 18-2.)

20 A glass window pane is exactly 20 cm by 30 cm at 10°C. By how much has its area increased when its temperature is 40°C, assuming that it can expand freely?

21 A steel rod at 25.0°C is bolted at both ends and then cooled. At what temperature will it rupture? Use Table 12-1.

22 Three equal-length straight rods, of aluminum, Invar, and steel, all at 20.0°C, form an equilateral triangle with hinge pins at the vertices. At what temperature will the angle opposite the Invar rod be 59.95°? See Appendix E for needed trigonometric formulas and Table 18-2 for needed data.

23 A rectangular plate of glass initially has the dimensions 0.200 m by 0.300 m. The coefficient of linear expansion for the glass is 9.00×10^{-6}/K. What is the change in the plate's area if its temperature is increased by 20.0 K?

24 Soon after Earth was formed, heat released by the decay of radioactive elements raised the average internal temperature from 300 to 3000 K, at about which value it remains today. Assuming an average coefficient of volume expansion of 3.0×10^{-5}/K, by how much has the radius of Earth increased since the planet was formed?

25 The apparatus shown in the Fig. 18-23 consists of four glass columns connected by horizontal sections. The height of two central columns B and C are 49 cm each. The two outer columns A and D are open to the atmosphere. A and C are maintained at a temperature of 95°C while the columns B and D are maintained at 5°C. The height of the liquid in A and D measured from the base line are 52.8 and 51 cm, respectively. Determine the coefficient of thermal expansion of the liquid.

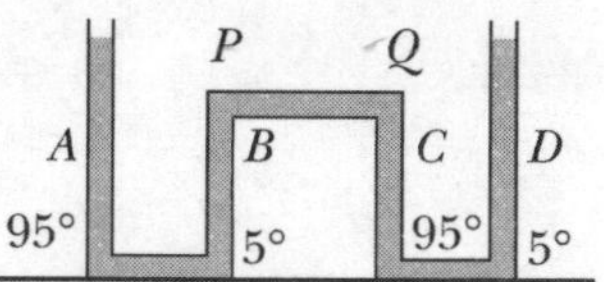

FIG. 18-23 Problem 25.

26 A pendulum clock with a pendulum made of Invar ($\alpha = 0.7 \times 10^{-6}$/°C) has a period of 0.5 s and is accurate at 25°C. If the clock is used in a country where the temperature averages 35°C, what correction is necessary at the end of a month (30 days) to the time given by the clock?

19 Heat, Calorimetery, and Heat Transfer

Courtesy Nathan Schiff, Ph. D., USDA Forest Service, Center for Bottomland Hardwoods Research, Stoneville, MS

The fairly small Melanophila *beetles are known for a bizarre behavior: They fly toward forest fires and mate near them, and then the females fly into the still smoldering ruins to lay their eggs under burnt bark. This is the ideal environment for the larvae that hatch from the eggs, because the tree can no longer protect itself from the larvae by rosin or chemical means. If a beetle were at the periphery of a fire, detecting the fire would be easy, of course. However, these beetles can detect a fairly large fire from as far away as 12 km. They do this without seeing or smelling the fire.*

How can the beetles detect a distant fire?

The answer is in this chapter.

19-1 | Temperature and Heat

One of the principal branches of physics and engineering is **thermodynamics,** which is the study and application of the *thermal energy* (often called the *internal energy*) of systems. One of the central concepts of thermodynamics is *temperature,* which we begin to explore in the next section. Since childhood, you have been developing a working knowledge of thermal energy and temperature. For example, you know to be cautious with hot foods and hot stoves and to store perishable foods in cool or cold compartments. You also know how to control the temperature inside home and car, and how to protect yourself from wind chill and heat stroke.

Examples of how thermodynamics figures into everyday engineering and science are countless. Automobile engineers are concerned with the heating of a car engine, such as during a NASCAR race. Food engineers are concerned both with the proper heating of foods, such as pizzas being microwaved, and with the proper cooling of foods, such as TV dinners being quickly frozen at a processing plant. Geologists are concerned with the transfer of thermal energy in an El Niño event and in the gradual warming of ice expanses in the Arctic and Antarctic. Agricultural engineers are concerned with the weather conditions that determine whether the agriculture of a country thrives or vanishes. Medical engineers are concerned with how a patient's temperature might distinguish between a benign viral infection and a cancerous growth.

The starting point in our discussion of thermodynamics is the concept of temperature and how it is measured.

If you take a can of cola from the refrigerator and leave it on the kitchen table, its temperature will rise—rapidly at first but then more slowly—until the temperature of the cola equals that of the room (the two are then in thermal equilibrium). In the same way, the temperature of a cup of hot coffee, left sitting on the table, will fall until it also reaches room temperature.

In generalizing this situation, we describe the cola or the coffee as a *system* (with temperature T_S) and the relevant parts of the kitchen as the *environment* (with temperature T_E) of that system. Our observation is that if T_S is not equal to T_E, then T_S will change (T_E can also change some) until the two temperatures are equal and thus thermal equilibrium is reached.

Such a change in temperature is due to a change in the thermal energy of the system because of a transfer of energy between the system and the system's environment. (Recall that *thermal energy* is an internal energy that consists of the kinetic and potential energies associated with the random motions of the atoms, molecules, and other microscopic bodies within an object.) The transferred energy is called **heat** and is symbolized Q. Heat is *positive* when energy is transferred to a system's thermal energy from its environment (we say that heat is absorbed by the system). Heat is *negative* when energy is transferred from a system's thermal energy to its environment (we say that heat is released or lost by the system).

This transfer of energy is shown in Fig. 19-1. In the situation of Fig. 19-1*a*, in which $T_S > T_E$, energy is transferred from the system to the environment, so Q is negative. In Fig. 19-1*b*, in which $T_S = T_E$, there is no such transfer, Q is zero, and heat is neither released nor absorbed. In Fig. 19-1*c*, in which $T_S < T_E$, the transfer is to the system from the environment; so Q is positive.

We are led then to this definition of heat:

> Heat is the energy transferred between a system and its environment because of a temperature difference that exists between them.

Recall that energy can also be transferred between a system and its environment as *work* W via a force acting on a system. Heat and work, unlike temperature, pressure, and volume, are not intrinsic properties of a system. They have

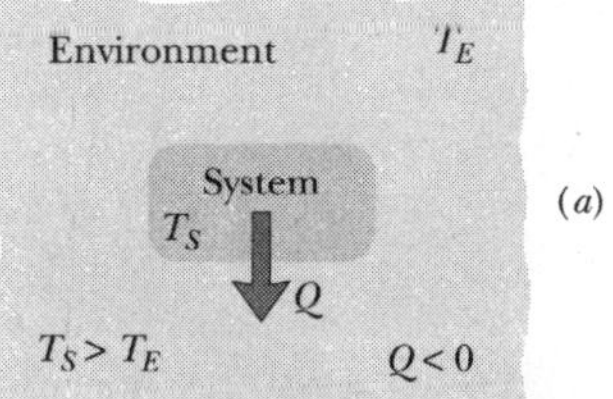

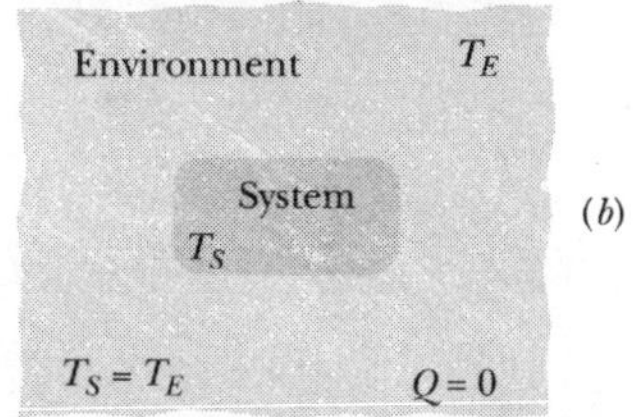

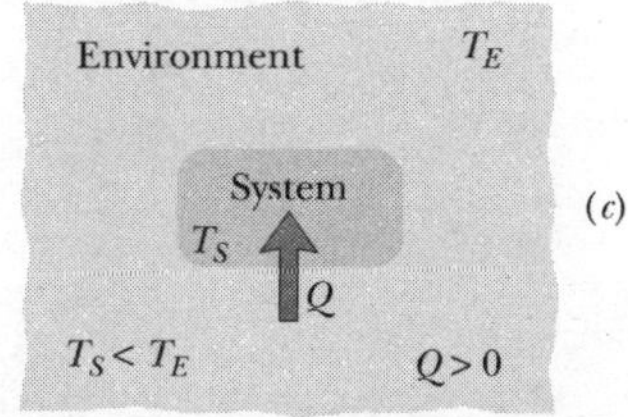

FIG. 19-1 If the temperature of a system exceeds that of its environment as in (*a*), heat Q is lost by the system to the environment until thermal equilibrium (*b*) is established. (*c*) If the temperature of the system is below that of the environment, heat is absorbed by the system until thermal equilibrium is established.

meaning only as they describe the transfer of energy into or out of a system. Similarly, the phrase "a $600 transfer" has meaning if it describes the transfer to or from an account, not what is in the account, because the account holds money, not a transfer. Here, it is proper to say: "During the last 3 min, 15 J of heat was transferred to the system from its environment" or "During the last minute, 12 J of work was done on the system by its environment." It is meaningless to say: "This system contains 450 J of heat" or "This system contains 385 J of work."

Before scientists realized that heat is transferred energy, heat was measured in terms of its ability to raise the temperature of water. Thus, the **calorie** (cal) was defined as the amount of heat that would raise the temperature of 1 g of water from 14.5°C to 15.5°C. In the British system, the corresponding unit of heat was the **British thermal unit** (Btu), defined as the amount of heat that would raise the temperature of 1 lb of water from 63°F to 64°F.

In 1948, the scientific community decided that since heat (like work) is transferred energy, the SI unit for heat should be the one we use for energy—namely, the **joule.** The calorie is now defined to be 4.1868 J (exactly), with no reference to the heating of water. (The "calorie" used in nutrition, sometimes called the Calorie (Cal), is really a kilocalorie.) The relations among the various heat units are

$$1 \text{ cal} = 3.968 \times 10^{-3} \text{ Btu} = 4.1868 \text{ J} \tag{19-1}$$

19-2 | Specific Heat and Calorimetery

The Absorption of Heat by Solids and Liquids

Heat Capacity

The **heat capacity** C of an object is the proportionality constant between the heat Q that the object absorbs or loses and the resulting temperature change ΔT of the object; that is,

$$Q = C\,\Delta T = C(T_f - T_i) \tag{19-2}$$

in which T_i and T_f are the initial and final temperatures of the object. Heat capacity C has the unit of energy per degree or energy per kelvin. The heat capacity C of, say, a marble slab used in a bun warmer might be 179 cal/C°, which we can also write as 179 cal/K or as 749 J/K.

The word "capacity" in this context is really misleading in that it suggests analogy with the capacity of a bucket to hold water. *That analogy is false,* and you should not think of the object as "containing" heat or being limited in its ability to absorb heat. Heat transfer can proceed without limit as long as the necessary temperature difference is maintained. The object may, of course, melt or vaporize during the process.

Specific Heat

Two objects made of the same material—say, marble—will have heat capacities proportional to their masses. It is therefore convenient to define a "heat capacity per unit mass" or **specific heat** c that refers not to an object but to a unit mass of the material of which the object is made. Equation 19-2 then becomes

$$Q = cm\,\Delta T = cm(T_f - T_i) \tag{19-3}$$

Through experiment we would find that although the heat capacity of a particular marble slab might be 179 cal/C° (or 749 J/K), the specific heat of marble itself (in that slab or in any other marble object) is 0.21 cal/g · C° (or 880 J/kg · K).

From the way the calorie and the British thermal unit were initially defined, the specific heat of water is

$$c = 1\ \text{cal/g}\cdot\text{C}^\circ = 1\ \text{Btu/lb}\cdot\text{F}^\circ = 4190\ \text{J/kg}\cdot\text{K} \tag{19-4}$$

Table 19-1 shows the specific heats of some substances at room temperature. Note that the value for water is relatively high. The specific heat of any substance actually depends somewhat on temperature, but the values in Table 19-1 apply reasonably well in a range of temperatures near room temperature.

TABLE 19-1

Some Specific Heats and Molar Specific Heats at Room Temperature

Substance	Specific Heat $\frac{\text{cal}}{\text{g}\cdot\text{K}}$	Specific Heat $\frac{\text{J}}{\text{kg}\cdot\text{K}}$	Molar Specific Heat $\frac{\text{J}}{\text{mol}\cdot\text{K}}$
Elemental Solids			
Lead	0.0305	128	26.5
Tungsten	0.0321	134	24.8
Silver	0.0564	236	25.5
Copper	0.0923	386	24.5
Aluminum	0.215	900	24.4
Other Solids			
Brass	0.092	380	
Granite	0.19	790	
Glass	0.20	840	
Ice (−10°C)	0.530	2220	
Liquids			
Mercury	0.033	140	
Ethyl alcohol	0.58	2430	
Seawater	0.93	3900	
Water	1.00	4180	

CHECKPOINT 1 A certain amount of heat Q will warm 1 g of material A by 3 C° and 1 g of material B by 4 C°. Which material has the greater specific heat?

Molar Specific Heat

In many instances the most convenient unit for specifying the amount of a substance is the mole (mol), where

$$1\ \text{mol} = 6.02 \times 10^{23}\ \text{elementary units}$$

of *any* substance. Thus 1 mol of aluminum means 6.02×10^{23} atoms (the atom is the elementary unit), and 1 mol of aluminum oxide means 6.02×10^{23} molecules (the molecule is the elementary unit of the compound).

When quantities are expressed in moles, specific heats must also involve moles (rather than a mass unit); they are then called **molar specific heats.** Table 19-1 shows the values for some elemental solids (each consisting of a single element) at room temperature.

An Important Point

In determining and then using the specific heat of any substance, we need to know the conditions under which energy is transferred as heat. For solids and liquids, we usually assume that the sample is under constant pressure (usually atmospheric) during the transfer. It is also conceivable that the sample is held at constant volume while the heat is absorbed. This means that thermal expansion of the sample is prevented by applying external pressure. For solids and liquids, this is very hard to arrange experimentally, but the effect can be calculated, and it turns out that the specific heats under constant pressure and constant volume for any solid or liquid differ usually by no more than a few percent. Gases, as you will see, have quite different values for their specific heats under constant-pressure conditions and under constant-volume conditions.

Heats of Transformation

When energy is absorbed as heat by a solid or liquid, the temperature of the sample does not necessarily rise. Instead, the sample may change from one *phase,* or *state,* to another. Matter can exist in three common states: In the *solid state,* the molecules of a sample are locked into a fairly rigid structure by their mutual attraction. In the *liquid state,* the molecules have more energy and move about more. They may form brief clusters, but the sample does not have a rigid structure and can flow or settle into a container. In the *gas,* or *vapor, state,* the molecules have even more energy, are free of one another, and can fill up the full volume of a container.

To *melt* a solid means to change it from the solid state to the liquid state. The process requires energy because the molecules of the solid must be freed from their rigid structure. Melting an ice cube to form liquid water is a common example. To *freeze* a liquid to form a solid is the reverse of melting and requires that energy be removed from the liquid, so that the molecules can settle into a rigid structure.

To *vaporize* a liquid means to change it from the liquid state to the vapor (gas) state. This process, like melting, requires energy because the molecules must be freed from their clusters. Boiling liquid water to transfer it to water vapor (or steam—a gas of individual water molecules) is a common example. *Condensing* a gas to form a liquid is the reverse of vaporizing; it requires that energy be removed from the gas, so that the molecules can cluster instead of flying away from one another.

The amount of energy per unit mass that must be transferred as heat when a sample completely undergoes a phase change is called the **heat of transformation** L. Thus, when a sample of mass m completely undergoes a phase change, the total energy transferred is

$$Q = Lm \tag{19-5}$$

When the phase change is from liquid to gas (then the sample must absorb heat) or from gas to liquid (then the sample must release heat), the heat of transformation is called the **heat of vaporization** L_V. For water at its normal boiling or condensation temperature,

$$L_V = 539 \text{ cal/g} = 40.7 \text{ kJ/mol} = 2256 \text{ kJ/kg} \tag{19-6}$$

When the phase change is from solid to liquid (then the sample must absorb heat) or from liquid to solid (then the sample must release heat), the heat of transformation is called the **heat of fusion** L_F. For water at its normal freezing or melting temperature,

$$L_F = 79.5 \text{ cal/g} = 6.01 \text{ kJ/mol} = 333 \text{ kJ/kg} \tag{19-7}$$

Table 19-2 shows the heats of transformation for some substances.

TABLE 19-2

Some Heats of Transformation

	Melting		Boiling	
Substance	Melting Point (K)	Heat of Fusion L_F (kJ/kg)	Boiling Point (K)	Heat of Vaporization L_V (kJ/kg)
Hydrogen	14.0	58.0	20.3	455
Oxygen	54.8	13.9	90.2	213
Mercury	234	11.4	630	296
Water	273	333	373	2256
Lead	601	23.2	2017	858
Silver	1235	105	2323	2336
Copper	1356	207	2868	4730

Sample Problem 19-1

(a) How much heat must be absorbed by ice of mass $m = 720$ g at $-10°$C to take it to liquid state at 15°C?

Conceptualize/Classify: The heating process is accomplished in three steps: (1) The ice cannot melt at a temperature below the freezing point—so initially, any energy transferred to the ice as heat can only increase the temperature of the ice, until 0°C is reached. (2) The temperature then cannot increase until all the ice melts—so any energy transferred to the ice as heat now can only change ice to liquid water, until all the ice melts. (3) Now the energy transferred to the liquid water as heat can only increase the temperature of the liquid water.

Compute: ***Warming the ice:*** The heat Q_1 needed to increase the temperature of the ice from the initial value $T_i = -10°$C to a final value $T_f = 0°$C (so that the ice can then melt) is given by Eq. 19-3 ($Q = cm\,\Delta T$). Using the specific heat of ice c_{ice} in Eq. 19-3 gives us

$$\begin{aligned} Q_1 &= c_{ice}m(T_f - T_i) \\ &= (2220\ \text{J/kg}\cdot\text{K})(0.720\ \text{kg})[0°\text{C} - (-10°\text{C})] \\ &= 15\,984\ \text{J} \approx 15.98\ \text{kJ} \end{aligned}$$

Melting the ice: The heat Q_2 needed to melt all the ice is given by equation $Q = Lm$. Here L is the heat of fusion L_F, with the value given in Eq. 19-7 and Table 19-4. We find

$$Q_2 = L_F m = (333\ \text{kJ/kg})(0.720\ \text{kg}) \approx 239.8\ \text{kJ}$$

Warming the liquid: The heat Q_3 needed to increase the temperature of the water from the initial value $T_i =$ 0°C to the final value $T_f = 15°$C is given by Eq. 19-3 (with the specific heat of liquid water c_{liq}):

$$\begin{aligned} Q_3 &= c_{liq}m(T_f - T_i) \\ &= (4190\ \text{J/kg}\cdot\text{K})(0.720\ \text{kg})(15°\text{C} - 0°\text{C}) \\ &= 45\,252\ \text{J} \approx 45.25\ \text{kJ} \end{aligned}$$

Total: The total required heat Q_{tot} is the sum of the amounts required in the three steps:

$$\begin{aligned} Q_{tot} &= Q_1 + Q_2 + Q_3 \\ &= 15.98\ \text{kJ} + 239.8\ \text{kJ} + 45.25\ \text{kJ} \\ &\approx 300\ \text{kJ} \qquad \text{(Answer)} \end{aligned}$$

Conclude: Note that the heat required to melt the ice is much greater than the heat required to raise the temperature of either the ice or the liquid water.

(b) If we supply the ice with a total energy of only 210 kJ (as heat), what then are the final state and temperature of the water?

Conceptualize/Classify: From step 1, we know that 15.98 kJ is needed to raise the temperature of the ice to the melting point. The remaining heat Q_{rem} is then 210 kJ − 15.98 kJ, or about 194 kJ. From step 2, we can see that this amount of heat is insufficient to melt all the ice. Because the melting of the ice is incomplete, we must end up with a mixture of ice and liquid; the temperature of the mixture must be the freezing point, 0°C.

Compute: We can find the mass m of ice that is melted by the available energy Q_{rem} by using Eq. 19-5 with L_F:

$$m = \frac{Q_{rem}}{L_F} = \frac{194\ \text{kJ}}{333\ \text{kJ/kg}} = 0.583\ \text{kg} \approx 580\ \text{g}$$

Thus, the mass of the ice that remains is 720 g − 580 g, or 140 g, and we have

580 g water and 140 g ice, at 0°C (Answer)

Calorimetery

To measure specific heat of a material we heat a sample to some known temperature T_m, and keep it in a vessel containing water of known mass and temperature T_w, ($T_w < T_x$) and measuring the temperature of the water after equilibrium has been reached. This method is called calorimetry, and vessel in which this energy transfer occurs is called calorimeter. If the system of the sample, water, and calorimeter is isolated, and we assume that heat capacity of the calorimeter is negligible, then the amount of energy that leaves the sample (of unknown specific heat) must be equal the amount of energy that enters the water.

$$Q_{cold} = -Q_{hot} \qquad (19\text{-}8)$$

Suppose m_m is the mass of the object composed of a substance of unknown specific heat, s_m and its initial temperature T_m. Likewise, let m_w, s_w, and T_w represent corresponding values for the water. If T_f is the final equilibrium temperature after everything is mixed, Eq. (19-8) shows that the energy transfer for the water is $m_w c_w (T_f - T_w)$, which is positive because $T_f > T_w$, and that the energy transfer for the sample of unknown specific heat is $m_x c_x (T_f - T_x)$ which is negative. Substituting these expressions into Eq. (19-8) gives.

$$m_w c_w (T_f - T_w) = -m_x c_x (T_f - T_x)$$

Solving for c_x gives

$$c_x = \frac{m_w c_w (T_f - T_w)}{m_x (T_x - T_f)}$$

Sample Problem 19-2

A copper slug whose mass m_c is 75 g is heated in a laboratory oven to a temperature T of 312°C. The slug is then dropped into a glass beaker containing a mass $m_w = 220$ g of water. The heat capacity C_b of the beaker is 45 cal/K. The initial temperature T_i of the water and the beaker is 12°C. Assuming that the slug, beaker, and water are an isolated system and the water does not vaporize, find the final temperature T_f of the system at thermal equilibrium.

Conceptualize: Because the system is isolated, the system's total energy cannot change and only internal transfers of thermal energy can occur.

Classify: Because nothing in the system undergoes a phase change, the thermal energy transfers can only change the temperatures.

Compute: To relate the transfers to the temperature changes, we can use Eqs. 19-2 and 19-3 to write

$$\text{for the water:}\quad Q_w = c_w m_w (T_f - T_i) \qquad (19\text{-}9)$$

$$\text{for the beaker:}\quad Q_b = C_b (T_f - T_i) \qquad (19\text{-}10)$$

$$\text{for the copper:}\quad Q_c = c_c m_c (T_f - T) \qquad (19\text{-}11)$$

Because the total energy of the system cannot change, the sum of these three energy transfers is zero:

$$Q_w + Q_b + Q_c = 0 \qquad (19\text{-}12)$$

Substituting Eqs. 19-9 through 19-11 into Eq. 19-12 yields

$$c_w m_w (T_f - T_i) + C_b (T_f - T_i) + c_c m_c (T_f - T) = 0 \qquad (19\text{-}13)$$

Temperatures are contained in Eq. 19-13 only as differences. Thus, because the differences on the Celsius and Kelvin scales are identical, we can use either of those scales in this equation. Solving it for T_f, we obtain

$$T_f = \frac{c_c m_c T + C_b T_i + c_w m_w T_i}{c_w m_w + C_b + c_c m_c}$$

Using Celsius temperatures and taking values for c_c and c_w from Table 19-1, we find the numerator to be

$$(0.0923\ \text{cal/g}\cdot\text{K})(75\ \text{g})(312^\circ\text{C}) + (45\ \text{cal/K})(12^\circ\text{C}) + (1.00\ \text{cal/g}\cdot\text{K})(220\ \text{g})(12^\circ\text{C}) = 5339.8\ \text{cal}$$

and the denominator to be

$$(1.00\ \text{cal/g}\cdot\text{K})(220\ \text{g}) + 45\ \text{cal/K} + (0.0923\ \text{cal/g}\cdot\text{K})(75\ \text{g}) = 271.9\ \text{cal/C}^\circ$$

We then have

$$T_f = \frac{5339.8\ \text{cal}}{271.9\ \text{cal/C}^\circ} = 19.6^\circ\text{C} \approx 20^\circ\text{C} \qquad \text{(Answer)}$$

Conclude: From the given data you can show that

$$Q_w \approx 1670\ \text{cal}, \qquad Q_b \approx 342\ \text{cal}, \qquad Q_c \approx -2020\ \text{cal}$$

Apart from rounding errors, the algebraic sum of these three heat transfers is indeed zero, as Eq. 19-12 requires.

19-3 | Conduction

Fourier's Law

Heat Transfer Mechanisms

We have discussed the transfer of energy as heat between a system and its environment, but we have not yet described how that transfer takes place. There are three transfer mechanisms: conduction, convection, and radiation.

Conduction

If you leave the end of a metal poker in a fire for enough time, its handle will get hot. Energy is transferred from the fire to the handle by (thermal) **conduction** along the length of the poker. The vibration amplitudes of the atoms and electrons of the metal at the fire end of the poker become relatively large because of the high temperature of their environment. These increased vibrational amplitudes, and thus the associated energy, are passed along the poker, from atom to atom, during collisions between adjacent atoms. In this way, a region of rising temperature extends itself along the poker to the handle.

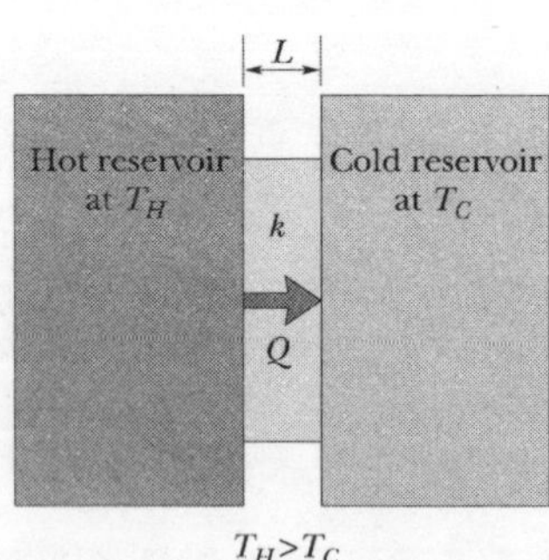

FIG. 19-2 Thermal conduction. Energy is transferred as heat from a reservoir at temperature T_H to a cooler reservoir at temperature T_C through a conducting slab of thickness L and thermal conductivity k.

Consider a slab of face area A and thickness L, whose faces are maintained at temperatures T_H and T_C by a hot reservoir and a cold reservoir, as in Fig. 19-2. Let Q be the energy that is transferred as heat through the slab, from its hot face to its cold face, in time t. Experiment shows that the *conduction rate* P_{cond} (the amount of energy transferred per unit time) is

$$P_{cond} = \frac{Q}{t} = kA\,\frac{T_H - T_C}{L} \qquad (19\text{-}14)$$

in which k, called the *thermal conductivity*, is a constant that depends on the material of which the slab is made. A material that readily transfers energy by conduction is a *good thermal conductor* and has a high value of k. Table 19-3 gives the thermal conductivities of some common metals, gases, and building materials.

TABLE 19-3

Some Thermal Conductivities

Substance	k (W/m · K)
Metals	
Stainless steel	14
Lead	35
Iron	67
Brass	109
Aluminum	235
Copper	401
Silver	428
Gases	
Air (dry)	0.026
Helium	0.15
Hydrogen	0.18
Building Materials	
Polyurethane foam	0.024
Rock wool	0.043
Fiberglass	0.048
White pine	0.11
Window glass	1.0

Thermal Resistance to Conduction (*R*-Value)

If you are interested in insulating your house or in keeping cola cans cold on a picnic, you are more concerned with poor heat conductors than with good ones. For this reason, the concept of *thermal resistance* R has been introduced into engineering practice. The R-value of a slab of thickness L is defined as

$$R = \frac{L}{k} \qquad (19\text{-}15)$$

The lower the thermal conductivity of the material of which a slab is made, the higher the R-value of the slab; so something that has a high R-value is a *poor thermal conductor* and thus a *good thermal insulator.*

Note that R is a property attributed to a slab of a specified thickness, not to a material. The commonly used unit for R (which, in the United States at least, is almost never stated) is the square foot–Fahrenheit degree–hour per British thermal unit (ft^2 · F° · h/Btu). (Now you know why the unit is rarely stated.)

Conduction Through a Composite Slab

Figure 19-3 shows a composite slab, consisting of two materials having different thicknesses L_1 and L_2 and different thermal conductivities k_1 and k_2. The temperatures of the outer surfaces of the slab are T_H and T_C. Each face of the slab has area A. Let us derive an expression for the conduction rate through the slab under the assumption that the transfer is a *steady-state* process; that is, the temperatures everywhere in the slab and the rate of energy transfer do not change with time.

In the steady state, the conduction rates through the two materials must be equal. This is the same as saying that the energy transferred through one material in a certain time must be equal to that transferred through the other material in the same time. If this were not true, temperatures in the slab would be changing and we would not have a steady-state situation. Letting T_X be the temperature of the interface between the two materials, we can now use Eq. 19-14 to write

$$P_{cond} = \frac{k_2A(T_H - T_X)}{L_2} = \frac{k_1A(T_X - T_C)}{L_1} \qquad (19\text{-}16)$$

Solving Eq. 19-16 for T_X yields, after a little algebra,

$$T_X = \frac{k_1L_2T_C + k_2L_1T_H}{k_1L_2 + k_2L_1} \qquad (19\text{-}17)$$

Substituting this expression for T_X into either equality of Eq. 19-16 yields

$$P_{cond} = \frac{A(T_H - T_C)}{L_1/k_1 + L_2/k_2} \qquad (19\text{-}18)$$

We can extend Eq. 19-18 to apply to any number n of materials making up a slab:

$$P_{cond} = \frac{A(T_H - T_C)}{\Sigma\,(L/k)} \qquad (19\text{-}19)$$

The summation sign in the denominator tells us to add the values of L/k for all the materials.

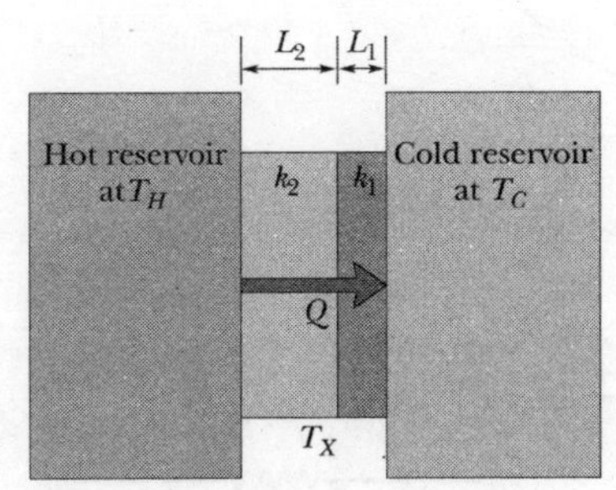

FIG. 19-3 Heat is transferred at a steady rate through a composite slab made up of two different materials with different thicknesses and different thermal conductivities. The steady-state temperature at the interface of the two materials is T_X.

Sample Problem 19-3

Figure 19-4 shows the cross-section of a wall made of white pine of thickness L_a and brick of thickness L_d ($= 2.0L_a$), sandwiching two layers of unknown material with identical thicknesses and thermal conductivities. The thermal conductivity of the pine is k_a and that of the brick is k_d ($= 5.0k_a$). The face area A of the wall is unknown. Thermal conduction through the wall has reached the steady state; the only known interface temperatures are $T_1 = 25°C$, $T_2 = 20°C$, and $T_5 = -10°C$. What is interface temperature T_4?

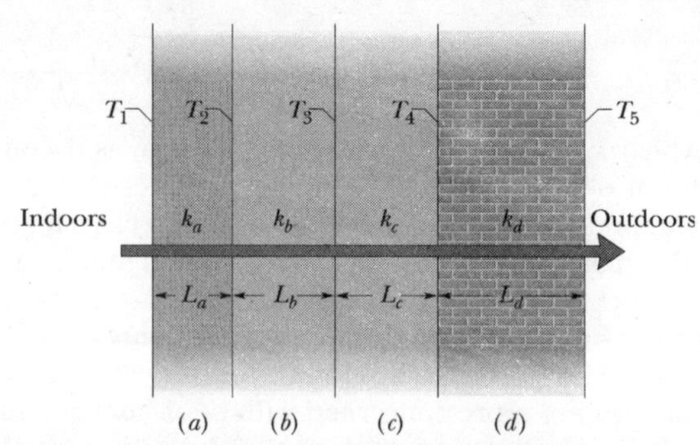

FIG. 19-4 A wall of four layers through which there is steady-state heat transfer.

Conceptualize: Temperature T_4 helps determine the rate P_d at which energy is conducted through the brick, as given by Eq. 19-14. However, we lack enough data to solve Eq. 19-14 for T_4.

Classify: Because the conduction is steady, the conduction rate P_d through the brick must equal the conduction rate P_a through the pine. That gets us going.

Compute: From Eq. 19-14 and Fig. 19-5, we can write

$$P_a = k_a A \frac{T_1 - T_2}{L_a} \quad \text{and} \quad P_d = k_d A \frac{T_4 - T_5}{L_d}$$

Setting $P_a = P_d$ and solving for T_4 yield

$$T_4 = \frac{k_a L_d}{k_d L_a}(T_1 - T_2) + T_5$$

Letting $L_d = 2.0L_a$ and $k_d = 5.0k_a$, and inserting the known temperatures, we find

$$T_4 = \frac{k_a(2.0L_a)}{(5.0k_a)L_a}(25°C - 20°C) + (-10°C)$$

$$= -8.0°C \qquad \text{(Answer)}$$

Conclude: This problem is just an extension of what we learned in theory of composite slabs.

CHECKPOINT 2 The figure shows the face and interface temperatures of a composite slab consisting of four materials, of identical thicknesses, through which the heat transfer is steady. Rank the materials according to their thermal conductivities, greatest first.

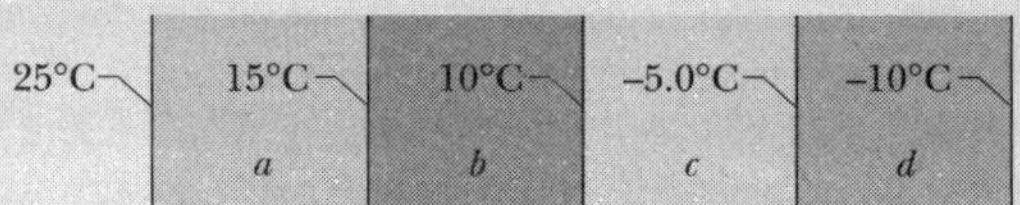

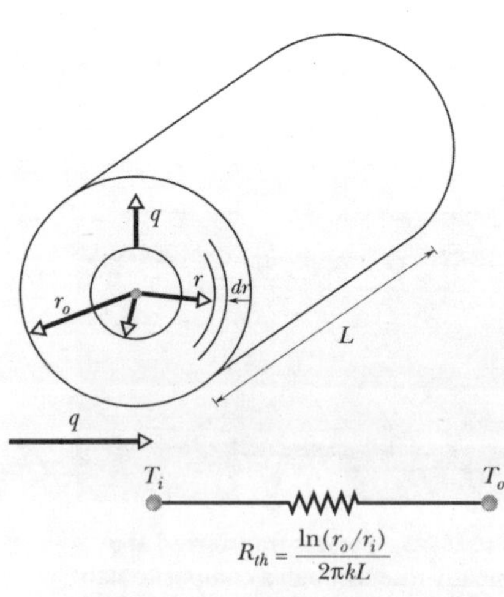

FIG. 19-5 A long cylinder with hot fluid flowing through it, acts like a resistor.

Cylinders: Consider a long cylinder of inside radius r_i, outside radius r_o, and length L, such as the one shown in Fig. 19-5. A hot fluid is flowing through the cylinder and its environment is at constant temperature T_0. Let's find rate of heat loss through the lateral surface. For a cylinder with length very much larger than diameter, it may be assumed that the heat flows only in a radial direction. Let's consider an elemental cylinder of radius r and thickness dr and length L, the area for heat flow in the cylindrical system is

$$A_r = 2\pi rL$$

so that substituting in Eq. 19-15, $q = -\,kA_r \frac{dT}{dr}$ becomes

$$q = -\,2\pi krL \frac{dT}{dr}$$

q is going to be same for all elements once steady state reaches

$$\frac{2\pi kl dT}{q} = -\frac{dr}{r}$$

integrating with the limits

$$T = T \text{ at } r = r_i$$
$$T = T_o \text{ at } r = r_o$$

We get, $$q = \frac{2\pi kL\,(T_i - T_0)}{\ln(r_o/r_i)}$$

and the thermal resistance in this case can be said to be

$$R_{th} = \frac{\ln(r_o/r_i)}{2\pi kL}$$

The thermal resistance concept may be used for multiple-layer cylindrical walls just as it was used for plane walls. For the three-layer system shown in Fig. 19-6*a* the solution is

$$q = \frac{2\pi L\,(T_1 - T_4)}{\ln(r_2/r_1)/k_A + \ln(r_3/r_2)/k_B + \ln(r_4/r_3)/k_C}$$

The thermal circuit is shown in Fig. 19-6*b*:

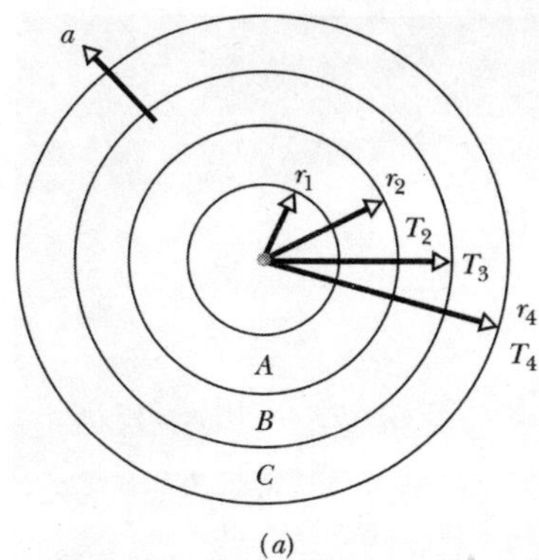

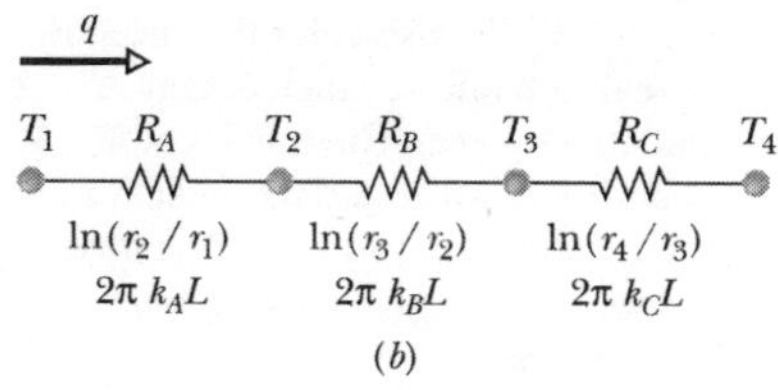

FIG. 19-6 Multiple layer cylinders with hot liquid flowing through act like a resistors in series.

CHECKPOINT 3 Derive for spherical system similar to the above discussed cylindrical system.

19-4 | Convection and Radiation

Convection

When you look at the flame of a candle or a match, you are watching thermal energy being transported upward by **convection.** Such energy transfer occurs when a fluid, such as air or water, comes in contact with an object whose temperature is higher than that of the fluid. The temperature of the part of the fluid that is in contact with the hot object increases, and (in most cases) that fluid expands and thus becomes less dense. Because this expanded fluid is now lighter than the surrounding cooler fluid, buoyant forces cause it to rise. Some of the surrounding cooler fluid then flows so as to take the place of the rising warmer fluid, and the process can then continue.

Convection is part of many natural processes. Atmospheric convection plays a fundamental role in determining global climate patterns and daily weather variations. Glider pilots and birds alike seek rising thermals (convection currents of warm air) that keep them aloft. Huge energy transfers take place within the oceans by the same process. Finally, energy is transported to the surface of the Sun from the nuclear furnace at its core by enormous cells of convection, in which hot gas rises to the surface along the cell core and cooler gas around the core descends below the surface.

Radiation

Heat from the Sun is able to pass through the atmosphere and warm the Earth's surface. This transfer of heat is obviously not by conduction, as the air is a poor conductor of heat, also the space between the Earth and the Sun is mostly vacuum. Similarly, since convection currents begin only after the air close to the Earth's surface is heated, it follows that the heat received from the Sun is not transferred by convection.

Radiation does not involve movement of atoms, as in conduction, or mass movement of molecules as in convection.

Radiant energy is in the form of electromagnetic waves, and behaves just like visible light. For example, it can be reflected and refracted.

FIG. 19-7 A false-color thermogram reveals the rate at which energy is radiated by a cat. The rate is color-coded, with white and red indicating the greatest radiation rate. The nose is cool. *(Edward Kinsman/Photo Researchers)*

The third method by which an object and its environment can exchange energy as heat is via electromagnetic waves (visible light is one kind of electromagnetic wave). Energy transferred in this way is often called **thermal radiation** to distinguish it from electromagnetic *signals* (as in, say, television broadcasts) and from nuclear radiation (energy and particles emitted by nuclei). (To "radiate" generally means to emit.) When you stand in front of a big fire, you are warmed by absorbing thermal radiation from the fire; that is, your thermal energy increases as the fire's thermal energy decreases. Observations indicate that thermal radiation is like light and that the process of heat transfer by radiation is similar to the passage of light through space. When the Sun sets, or is temporarily obscured by a dense cloud, for example, both the light and the heat diminish simultaneously. Radiant energy travels through space at the speed of light (3.0×10^8 m/s). Emissive power is defined as the thermal radiation emitted per second per unit area of the surface.

The rate P_{rad} at which an object emits energy via electromagnetic radiation depends on the object's surface area A and the temperature T of that area in kelvins and is given by

$$P_{rad} = \sigma \varepsilon A T^4 \qquad (19\text{-}20)$$

Here $\sigma = 5.6704 \times 10^{-8}\ \text{W/m}^2 \cdot \text{K}^4$ is called the *Stefan–Boltzmann constant* after Josef Stefan (who discovered Eq. 19-20 experimentally in 1879) and Ludwig Boltzmann (who derived it theoretically soon after). The symbol ε represents the *emissivity* of the object's surface, which has a value between 0 and 1, depending on the composition of the surface. A surface with the maximum emissivity of 1.0 is said to be a *blackbody radiator,* but such a surface is an ideal limit and does not occur in nature. Note again that the temperature in Eq. 19-20 must be in kelvins so that a temperature of absolute zero corresponds to no radiation. Note also that every object whose temperature is above 0 K—including you—emits thermal radiation. (See Fig. 19-7.)

The rate P_{abs} at which an object absorbs energy via thermal radiation from its environment, which we take to be at uniform temperature T_{env} (in kelvins), is

$$P_{abs} = \sigma \varepsilon A T_{env}^4 \qquad (19\text{-}21)$$

The emissivity ε in Eq. 19-21 is the same as that in Eq. 19-20. An idealized blackbody radiator, with $\varepsilon = 1$, will absorb all the radiated energy it intercepts (rather than sending a portion back away from itself through reflection or scattering).

Because an object will radiate energy to the environment while it absorbs energy from the environment, the object's net rate P_{net} of energy exchange due to thermal radiation is

$$P_{net} = P_{abs} - P_{rad} = \sigma \varepsilon A (T_{env}^4 - T^4) \qquad (19\text{-}22)$$

P_{net} is positive if net energy is being absorbed via radiation and negative if it is being lost via radiation.

FIG. 19-8 A rattlesnake's face has thermal radiation detectors, allowing the snake to strike at an animal even in complete darkness. *(David A. Northcott/Corbis Images)*

Let's now return to the story about the ability of a *Melanophila* beetle to detect a fairly large fire from a distance of 12 km without seeing or smelling it. A pair of organs along each side of the beetle's body can detect even low-level thermal radiation. Each organ contains about 70 small knob-like sensors that expand very slightly when they absorb thermal radiation from the fire; the expansion causes them to press down on sensory cells. Thus, the detector is a mechanism that transfers energy from the thermal radiation to the energy of a mechanical device. The beetle can locate the fire by orienting itself so that all four infrared-detecting organs are affected, and then it flies toward the fire so that the response of the organs increases.

Thermal radiation is also involved in the numerous medical cases of a *dead* rattlesnake striking a hand reaching toward it. Pits between each eye and nostril of a rattlesnake (Fig. 19-8) serve as sensors of thermal radiation. When, say, a mouse moves close to a rattlesnake's head, the thermal radiation from the mouse triggers these sensors, causing a reflex action in which the snake strikes the mouse with its fangs and injects its venom. The thermal radiation from a reaching hand can cause the same reflex action even if the snake has been dead for as long as 30 min because the snake's nervous system continues to function. As one snake expert advised, if you must remove a recently killed rattlesnake, use a long stick rather than your hand.

Behavior of Bodies During Heat Radiation

When radiant energy falls on a body, a part of the energy is absorbed, a part is reflected, and remaining part is transmitted. If we denote by a, r, and t the fractions absorbed, reflected, and transmitted, respectively, then

$$a + r + t = 1$$

We can use the parameters a, r, and t to classify substances in terms of their behavior toward radiant energy.

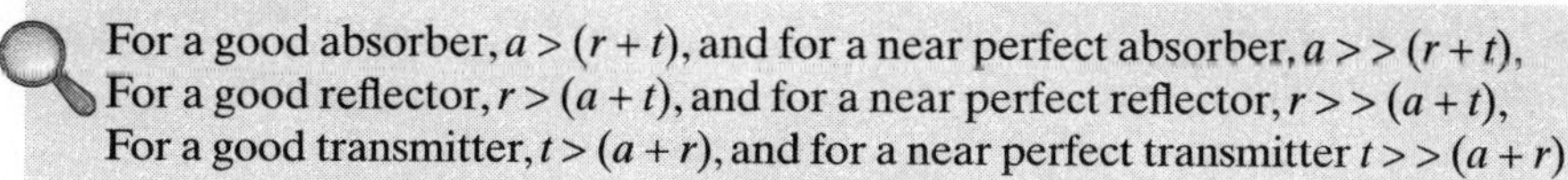

For a good absorber, $a > (r + t)$, and for a near perfect absorber, $a >> (r + t)$,
For a good reflector, $r > (a + t)$, and for a near perfect reflector, $r >> (a + t)$,
For a good transmitter, $t > (a + r)$, and for a near perfect transmitter $t >> (a + r)$.

The nature of surfaces of bodies decides the behavior of bodies toward radiation. It turns out that shiny surfaces are good reflectors, while black surfaces are good absorbers of heat. Surfaces which are transparent to light are also transparent to heat, and are hence good transmitters of heat.

Prevost's Theory of Exchanges

Let's imagine a small body A, at temperature T_A, being suspended by a nonconducting thread inside the evacuated box B whose walls are maintained at a constant, different temperature T_B as shown in Fig. 19-9. It is very clear that energy exchange between A and B can occur only by radiation. It is clear that if $T_A > T_B$, A's temperature falls until it is equal to T_B, but if $T_A < T_B$, it rises to T_B. Thus finally in any case A acquires B's temperature and it may appear that energy exchange then stops.

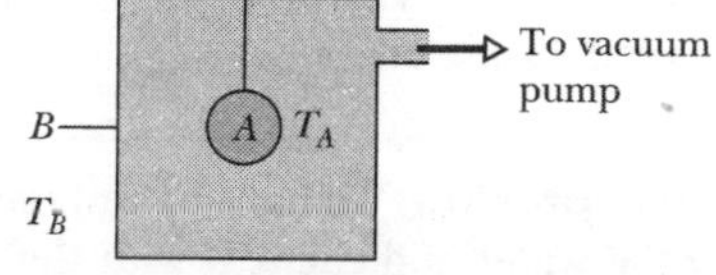

FIG. 19-9 Small body maintained at constant temperature.

Prevost suggested in 1792 that, actually, when a body is at the same temperature as its surroundings its rate of emission of radiation to the surroundings equals its rate of absorption of radiation from the surroundings. That is, there is dynamic equilibrium and energy exhange continues, at a rate depending on the temperature.

Thus a body which is a good absorber of radiation must also be a good emitter of radiation otherwise its temperature would rise above that of its surroundings. Conversely, a good emitter must be a good absorber. Experiments confirm these conclusions and indicate that a dull, black surface is the best absorber and also the best emitter.

Simultaneous Emission and Absorption of Thermal Radiation

Any object located in enviroment is simultaneously emitting and absorbing thermal radiation and net rate of heat flow due to thermal radiation is given by $P_{net} = P_{emitted} - P_{absorbed}$. Suppose an object with surface area A and temperature T is exposed to termal radiation coming from its surroundings in all directions that are at a uniform temperature T_s. Then the net rate of heat flow due to thermal radiation is

$$P_{net} = e\sigma AT^4 - e\sigma AT_s^4 = e\sigma A(T^4 - T_s^4)$$

A body emits energy even if it is at the same temperature as its surroundings; it just emits at the same rate that it absorbs, so $P_{net} = 0$. If $T > T_s$, the object emits more thermal radiation than it absorbs. If $T < T_s$, the object absorbs more thermal radiation than it emits.

The rate of absorption is proportional to the emissivity because a good emitter is also a good absorber. The emissivity e measures not only how much the object emits compared to a blackbody but it also measures how much the object absorbs compared to a blackbody. A blackbody at the same temperatue as its surroundings would have to absorb radiation at the rate $P_{absorbed} = \sigma A T_s^4$ to exactly balance the rate of emission. However, emissivity does depend on temperature. Eq. (19-22) assumes the emissivity at temperature T is the same as the emissivity at temperature T_s. If T and T_s are very different, we would have to modify Eq. (19-22) to use two different emissivities.

Caution: Do not substitute temperature in Celsius degrees into Eq. (19-22)

Sample Problem 19-4 Build your skill

During an extended wilderness hike, you have a terrific craving for ice. Unfortunately, the air temperature drops to only 6.0°C each night—too high to freeze water. However, because a clear, moonless night sky acts like a blackbody radiator at a temperature of $T_s = -23°\text{C}$, perhaps you can make ice by letting a shallow layer of water radiate energy to such a sky. To start, you thermally insulate a container from the ground by placing a poorly conducting layer of, say, foam rubber or straw beneath it. Then you pour water into the container, forming a thin, uniform layer with mass $m = 4.5$ g, top surface area $A = 9.0\text{ cm}^2$, depth $d = 5.0$ mm, emissivity $\varepsilon = 0.90$, and initial temperature 6.0°C. Find the time required for the water to freeze via radiation. Can the freezing be accomplished during one night?

Conceptualize: We have to find the total energy radiated by the water and check it with the energy that has to be lost to freeze.

Classify: The water cannot freeze at a temperature above the freezing point. Therefore, the radiation must first remove an amount of energy Q_1 to reduce the water temperature from 6.0°C to the freezing point of 0°C. The radiation then must remove an additional amount of energy Q_2 to freeze all the water. Throughout this process, the water is also absorbing energy radiated to it from the sky. We want a net loss of energy.

Conclude:

Cooling the water: Using Eq. 19-5 and Table 19-1, we find that cooling the water to 0°C requires an energy loss of

$$\begin{aligned} Q_1 &= cm(T_f - T_i) \\ &= (4190\text{ J/kg}\cdot\text{K})(4.5 \times 10^{-3}\text{ kg})(0°\text{C} - 6.0°\text{C}) \\ &= -113\text{ J} \end{aligned}$$

Thus, 113 J must be radiated away by the water to drop its temperature to the freezing point.

Freezing the water: Using Eq. 19-5 ($Q = mL$) with the value of L being L_F from Eq. 19-7 or Table 19-2, and inserting a minus sign to indicate an energy loss, we find

$$\begin{aligned} Q_2 &= -mL_F = -(4.5 \times 10^{-3}\text{ kg})(3.33 \times 10^5\text{ J/kg}) \\ &= -1499\text{ J} \end{aligned}$$

The total required energy loss is thus

$$Q_{tot} = Q_1 + Q_2 = -113\text{ J} - 1499\text{ J} = -1612\text{ J}$$

Radiation: While the water loses energy by radiating to the sky, it also absorbs energy radiated to it from the sky. In a total time t, we want the net energy of this exchange to be the energy loss Q_{tot}; so we want the power of this exchange to be

$$\text{power} = \frac{\text{net energy}}{\text{time}} = \frac{Q_{tot}}{t} \qquad (19\text{-}23)$$

The power of such an energy exchange is also the net rate P_{net} of thermal radiation, as given by Eq. 19-22; so the time t required for the energy loss to be Q_{tot} is

$$t = \frac{Q}{P_{net}} = \frac{Q}{\sigma\varepsilon A(T_s^4 - T^4)} \qquad (19\text{-}24)$$

Although the temperature T of the water decreases slightly while the water is cooling, we can approximate T as being the freezing point, 273 K. With $T_s = 250$ K, the denominator of Eq. 19-24 is

$$\begin{aligned} &(5.67 \times 10^{-8}\text{ W/m}^2\cdot\text{K}^4)(0.90)(9.0 \times 10^{-4}\text{ m}^2) \\ &\times [(250\text{ K})^4 - (273\text{ K})^4] = -7.57 \times 10^{-2}\text{ J/s}, \end{aligned}$$

and Eq. 19-24 gives us

$$\begin{aligned} t &= \frac{-1612\text{ J}}{-7.57 \times 10^{-2}\text{ J/s}} \\ &= 2.13 \times 10^4\text{ s} = 5.9\text{ h} \qquad \text{(Answer)} \end{aligned}$$

Conclude: Because t is less than a night, freezing water by having it radiate to the dark sky is feasible. In fact, in some parts of the world people used this technique long before the introduction of electric freezers.

Sample Problem 19-5 Build your skill

A copper cube with sides of length 20 mm had its surface blackened. The cube is heated up to 500 K and placed inside a room at a constant temperature of 300 K. Calculate the initial rate of temperature fall of the cube, assuming it as a perfect black-body. (Stefan's constant = 5.7×10^{-8} W/m²/K⁴; specific heat capacity of aluminum = 400 J/kg/K ; density of aluminum = 7800 kg/m³).

Conceptualize: By the theory Prevost's theory of heat exchanges, when a body is placed in an enviroment, the body absorbs heat from the enviroment and also radiates heat to the enviroment.

Classify: The net heat radiated per second P is given by:

$$P = \sigma A(T_1^4 - T_2^4) \quad (19\text{-}25)$$

where A is the surface area of the cube, T_1 is the temperature of the body, and T_2 is the temperature of the enclosure.

Compute: For the cube of side a, the area emitting radiation is, $A = 6a^2$.

Thus rate of energy radiated per second $\frac{\Delta Q}{\Delta t}$ is:

$$\frac{\Delta Q}{\Delta t} = mc\frac{\Delta T}{\Delta t} = \sigma 6a^2(T_1^4 - T_2^4) \quad (19\text{-}26)$$

where $\frac{\Delta T}{\Delta t}$ is the rate of fall of temperature, m is the mass of the cube ($m = \rho V$), ρ the density of aluminium, V the volume of the cube, and c is the specific heat capacity of the metal. We set $V = a^3$. From Eq. 19-26, we have

$$\frac{\Delta T}{\Delta t} = \frac{\sigma 6a^2(T_1^4 - T_2^4)}{mc} = \frac{\sigma 6a^2(T_1^4 - T_2^4)}{\rho a^3 c}$$

giving

$$\frac{\Delta T}{\Delta t} = \frac{\sigma 6(T_1^4 - T_2^4)}{\rho a c} \quad (19\text{-}27)$$

Substituting the given data into (19-27), we get the initial rate of fall of temperature as

$$\frac{\Delta T}{\Delta t} = \frac{6 \times 5.7 \times 10^{-8}\text{W/m}^2/\text{K}^4 \times (500^4 - 300^4)\text{K}^4}{7.8 \times 10^3\text{kg/m}^3 \times 0.020\text{m} \times 400\text{ J/kgK}}$$

$$= 0.3\text{ K/s}$$

Conclude: The rate of heat loss after this will be decreasing with time as temperature decreases.

19-5 | Approximate Surface Temperature of the Sun

Sun supplies the radiant energy to our solar system. Using Stefan's law, and considering a planet in thermal equilibrium, it is possible to estimate the temperature of the Sun. We define a quantity known as the solar constant as: solar constant is the radiant energy falling per unit time on unit area at right angles to a sunbeam. Let's find temperature of the Sun assuming we know:

1. The surface area of the Sun ($4\pi R_s^2$) is 6.07×10^{18} m².
2. The radius of the Earth's orbit round the Sun (assumed circular) is $R_0 = 1.1488 \times 10^{11}$ m.
3. Earth's ambient temperature (300 K).

The total energy P radiated by the Sun per second is

$$H_1 = H_{\text{emit by Sun}} = \sigma T_s^4 \times 4\pi R_s^2$$

$$= 3.763 \times 1026\text{ W}$$

Heat available/area of the shell of radius of the orbit of the Earth

$$\frac{H_1}{4pR_0^2} = \Sigma_{SC}$$

By calculating solar constant for Earth, Σ_{SC}, we get the value of the solar constant as 1350 W/m².

$$\text{H}_{\text{ads by Earth}} - \left[\frac{H}{4\pi R_0^2}\right] \times \pi\text{R}_E^2$$

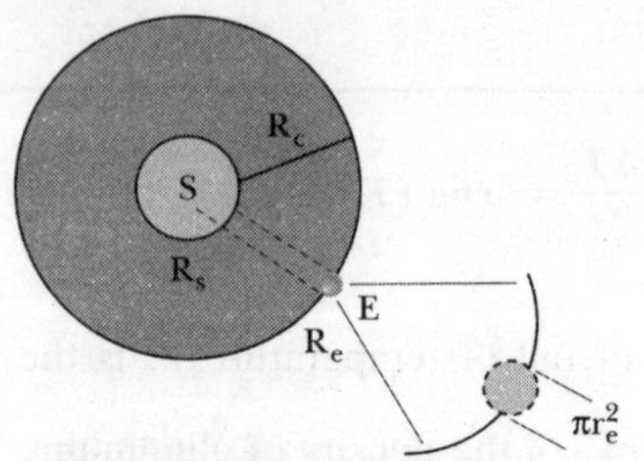

FIG. 19-10 Earth receiving small portion of the energy radiated by Sun.

(Exposed area = πr^2 and not $2\pi r^2$. Imagine if a small sphere Earth is put in the imaginary sphere of radius R_0 then only πR_E^2 area become occupied will be).

Total energy emitted by the Earth as a sphere is $\sigma T_0\, 4(4\pi R_e^2)$, as heat emitted will be from all surface of the Earth.

For thermal equilibrium energy recieved per unit time must be equal to the energy emitted per unit time.

$$\frac{\sigma T_s^4 \times 4\pi R_s^2}{4\pi R_0^2} \times \pi R_e^2 = \sigma T_0^4 = (4\pi R_e^2)$$

Solving for T_s we get 5743 K

This value is only approximate, as the distances cannot be determined accurately.

Rate of fall in temperature due to radiation for small temperature difference with surroundings

For a given object rate of heat loss due to radiation only can be written as

$$-ms\frac{d\theta}{dt} = \sigma A\,(\theta^4 - \theta_0^4)$$

$$-\frac{d\theta}{dt} = \frac{\sigma A}{ms}(\theta^4 - \theta_0^4)$$

we can write, $\theta = \theta_0 + \Delta\theta$

$$-\frac{d\theta}{dt} = \frac{\sigma A}{ms}[(\theta_0 + \Delta\theta)^4 - \theta_0^4]$$

$$-\frac{d\theta}{dt} = \frac{\sigma A\theta_0^4}{ms}\left[\left(1 + \frac{\Delta\theta}{\theta_0}\right) - 1\right]$$

If $\Delta << \theta_0$ (in kelvin)

$$= \frac{\sigma A\theta_0^4}{ms}\left[1 + \frac{4\Delta\theta_0^3}{\theta_0} - 1\right]$$

$$= \frac{4\sigma A\theta_0^3}{ms}(\theta - \theta_0)$$

$$-\frac{d\theta}{dt} = k\,(\theta - \theta_0)$$

where $k = \dfrac{4\theta A\theta_0^3}{ms}$

For an object losing heat only due to radiation, the rate of fall in temperature is directly proportional to its temperature difference with surrounding provided temperature difference that is small as compared to surrounding temperature which is expressed in kelvin.

Sample Problem 19-6

A space station is covered by an envelope which is a blackened shell. The temperature of the envelope is $T = 500$ K that is constant due to the operation of appliances of the station. Determine the temperature of the shell if the station is enveloped by a thin spherical black screen of nearly the same radius as the radius of the shell. Assume that there are no radiations falling on this space station.

Conceptualize: The total amount of heat Q emitted in space per unit time remains unchanged since it is determined by the energy liberated during the operation of the appliances of the station. As given in the question, the appliances produce heat at constant rate.

Classify: Since only the outer surface of the screen emits into space (this radiation depends only on its temperature), the temperature of the screen must be equal to the initial temperature $T = 500$ K of the station. Also it is important to remember that the screen emits the same amount of heat Q inward. This radiation reaches the envelope of the station and is absorbed by it.

Compute: Therefore, the total amount of heat supplied to the station per unit time is the sum of the heat Q liberated during the operation of the appliances and the amount of heat Q absorbed by the inner surface of the screen, that is, equal to $2Q$. According to the heat balance condition, the same amount of heat must be emiitted,

$$2Q = A\sigma T_x^4$$

and hence

$$\frac{Q}{2Q} = \frac{T^4}{T_x^4}$$

where T_x is the required temperature of the envelope of the station. Finally, we obtain

$$T_x = \sqrt[4]{2}T \equiv 600 \text{ K}$$

Conclude: The temperature of the envelope has incr-eased because to come in thermal equilibitium it must emit more energy than before as it is receiving more energy than before.

19-6 | Wien's Displacement Law

The heat radiation emitted by a body consists of different wavelengths. But some wavelengths contribute much more than the others in total radiation energy. These wavelengths are distributed continuously over a range. In Fig. 19-11*a* graph of intensity versus wavelength has been plotted using experimental data for a body at three different temperatures. We can see that intensity is not same for all wave-lengths. These graphs at a given temperature is same for all blackbodies. As the temperature of the body increases, the wavelength of dominant region decreases. At around 1100 K, the radiation has a good contribution from red region of wave-lengths and the object appears red. At temperatures around 3000 K, the radiation contains enough shorter wavelengths and the object appears white.

The peak of the wavelength distribution shifts to shorter wavelengths as the temperature increases. This behavior is described by the following relationship, called Wien's displacement law :

$$\lambda_{\max} T = 2.898 \times 10^{-3} \text{ m . K}$$

where $\lambda_{\max}$ max is the wavelength at which the curve peaks and T is the absolute temperature of the surface of the object emitting the radiation. The wavelength at the curve's peak is inversely proportional to the absolute temperature; that is, as the temperature increases, the peak is "displaced" to shorter wavelengths (Fig. 19-11*b*).

Wien's displacement law is consistent with the behavior of the object mentioned at the beginning of this section. At room temperature, the object does not appear to glow because the peak is in the infrared region of the electro-magnetic spectrum. At higher temperatures, it glows red because the peak is in the near infrared with some radiation at the red end of the visible spectrum, and at still higher temperatures, it glows white because the peak is in the visible so that all colors are emitted.

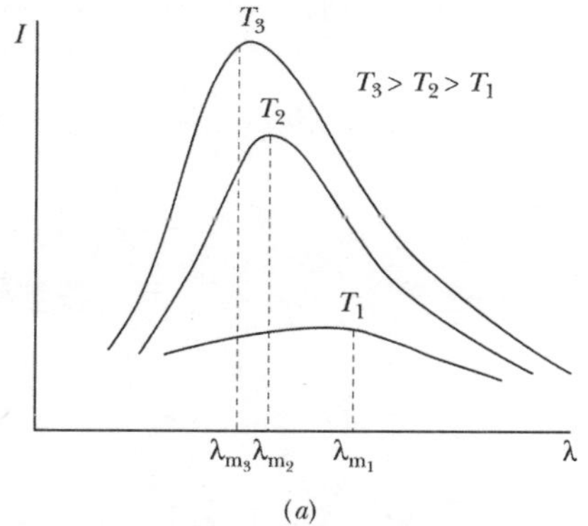

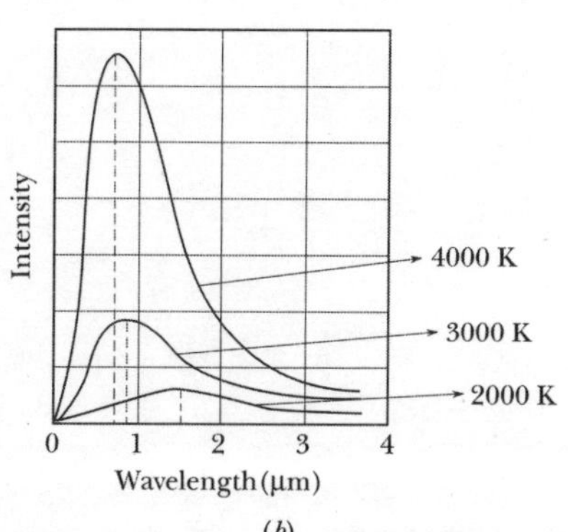

FIG. 19-11 (*a*) General variation of intensity with wavelength at different temperatures. (*b*) Variation of intensity with wavelength at different temperatures for black body.

Thus we can summarize

1. For all black bodies radiation spectrums at a given temperature is same.
2. Black body emits all wavelength from 0 to ∞.
3. Area bounded by $E_\lambda - \lambda$ curve and λ axis is the emissive power.

$$\int_0^\infty E_\lambda \quad d\lambda = E$$

Thus this area is directly propotional to the fourth power of absolute temperature.

4. With increase in temperature energy associated with each wavelength increases.

5. Wavelength that corresponds to maximum spectral emissive power (λ_m) decreases with increase in temperature. This decrease is according to Wein's law.

$$\lambda_m \propto \frac{1}{T}$$

$$\lambda_m = \frac{b}{T} \qquad b = 2.88 \times 10^{-3} \text{ m K}$$

Sample Problem 19-7 Build your skill

Visible Range: The maximum rate of emissive power from the Sun occurs in the middle of the visible range at about $\lambda = 0.5$ μm. Estimate the temperature of the Sun's surface. The evolutionists suggest this as the reason of eyes being sensitive to a particular band of the spectrum known as visible range.

Solution: We assume the Sun to be a blackbody. Then the wavelength of maximum emission and the surface temperature are related by Wien's law.

Given : $\lambda_{max} = 0.5\ \mu\text{m} = 5 \times 10^{-3}$ m·K

Then from Wien's law, we know that the product of the wavelength for maximum power emission and the corresponding temperature for the power emission is

$$\lambda_{max} T = 2.898 \times 10^{-3} \text{m} \cdot \text{K}$$

We can solve for the temperature since we know λ_{max}:

$$T = \frac{2.898 \times 10^{-3} \text{m} \cdot \text{K}}{5 \times 10^{-7} \text{m}}$$

$$= 6000 \text{ K}$$

19-7 | Newton's Law of Cooling

Netwon did an extensive study into cooling of hot bodies by convection and radiation, he formulated Newton's law of cooling, as the conclusion of his research. It states that the rate of heat loss from a body is directly proportional to the excess temperature of the body over the surroundings.

If T_r is the temperature of the surroundings, and T is the temperature of the body, and we represent the rate of heat loss by $-\frac{\Delta Q}{\Delta t}$, Newton's law of cooling can be written as

$$-\frac{\Delta Q}{\Delta t} = \text{constant} \times (T - T_r)$$

The value of the constant of proportionality depends on the area of surface exposed to the surrounding air. The larger the exposed area, the faster the body lose heat. The negative sign expressed the fact that the temperature decreases with time. Let's call the constant of propotionality as D. The result looks same as the Eq. 19-27 but the value of constants are different as the Newton's law of cooling takes both radiation and convection into account.

$$-ms\frac{d\theta}{dt} = D(\theta - \theta_0)$$

$$-\frac{d\theta}{dt} = \frac{D}{ms}(\theta - \theta_0)$$

$$-\frac{d\theta}{dt} = \frac{D}{ms}(\theta - \theta_0), \quad \text{let's say } C = \frac{D}{ms}$$

$$\int \frac{d\theta}{\theta - \theta_0} = \int C\, dt$$

$$\ln(\theta - \theta_0) = -kt + C$$

$$\ln\left(\frac{\theta - \theta_0}{\theta_{in} - \theta_0}\right) = -kt$$

$$\theta - \theta_0 = (\theta_{in} - \theta_0)\, e^{-kt}$$

$$\theta = \theta_0 + (\theta_{in} - \theta_0)\, e^{-kt}$$

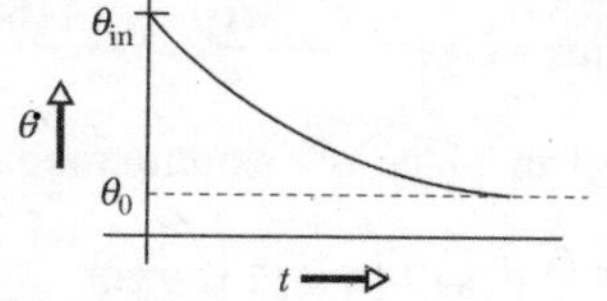

FIG. 19-12 Cooling curve based on Newton's law of cooling.

Plotting temperature of the body versus time we get, what is known as cooling curve.

19-8 | Cooling Curves

A laboratory experiment to verify Newton's law of cooling was carried out by allowing a hot solid to cool in a current of air. Temperatures of the solid were taken at regular intervals of one minute until the solid cools to about 10°C above room temperature. A graph of temperature against time was plotted. This plot is called a cooling curve. A typical cooling curve is shown in Fig. 19-13*a*.

From points along the cooling curve, tangents were drawn, and the slope of each was calculated from the ratio *a*/*b*, as shown in Fig. 19-13. The negative of this slope is proportional to the rate of heat loss, all other quantities (for example, mass, surface area) remaining unaltered. A plot of the negative slope against the temperature excess, as shown in Fig. 19-13*b*, is a straight line passing through the origin, thus verifying Newton's law of cooling.

A simple cooling curve can be obtained experimentally by heating a beaker of water to 80°C, say, and allowing it to cool to room temperature while taking readings of its temperature at regular intervals.

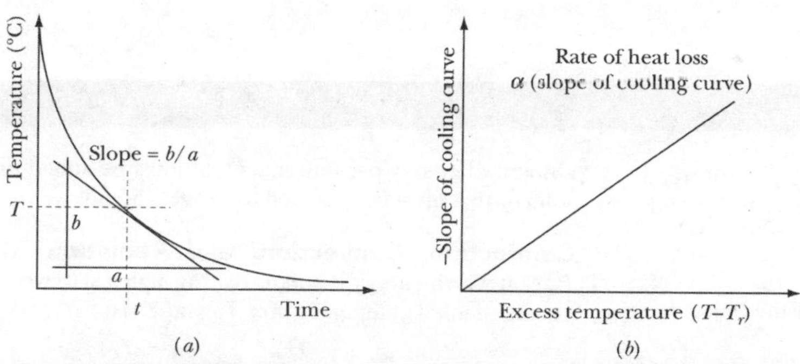

FIG. 19-13 (*a*) Cooling curve. (*b*) Plot to verify Newton's law of cooling.

Sample Problem 19-8 Build your skill

An object at temperature 70°C is placed in a surrounding medium of temperature 30°C. Its temperature decreases by 10°C in first 5 min. Find the time interval from starting in which its temperature reduces to 40°C. Assume Newton's law to be valid.

$t = 0$	$\theta = 70°C$	$\theta_0 = 30°C$
$t = 5$	$\theta = 60°C$	$\theta_0 = 30°C$
t	$\theta = 40°C$	$\theta_0 = 30°C$

Solution:

Method 1 (approximately)

$$-\frac{d\theta}{dt} = k(\theta - \theta_0)$$

can be interpreted approximately such that

$$-\frac{d\theta}{dt} = -\frac{(\theta_f - \theta_i)}{t_f - t_i}$$

Thus we get, $-\dfrac{d\theta}{dt} = -\dfrac{(60 - 70)}{5}$

and in place of instantaneous temperature θ we can write θ_{avg}, thus $\theta = \left(\dfrac{70 + 60}{2}\right)$

And, $k(\theta - \theta_0)$ becomes $k = \left(\dfrac{70 + 60}{2} - 30\right)$

$$-\left(\frac{60 - 70}{5}\right) = k\left(\frac{132}{2} - 30\right)$$

Solving for k we get $\dfrac{2}{35}$

and now applying same ideas for the change from 60 to 40, we get

$$-\left(\frac{40 - 60}{t_1}\right) = \frac{2}{35}\left(\frac{40 + 60}{2} - 30\right)$$

Solving we get $\qquad \dfrac{20}{t_1} = \dfrac{2}{35} \times 20$

$$t_1 = 17.5 \text{ min.}$$

Thus answer is $17.5 + 5 = 22.5$ min.

Method 2 (exact)

$$-\frac{d\theta}{dt} = k(\theta - \theta_0)$$

Integrating we get $\ln(\theta - \theta_0) = -kt + C$

at $t = 0, \theta = 70°C; \quad \theta_0 = 30° C$

$\ln(70 - 30) = C$ fi $C = \ln 40$

$\ln(\theta - \theta_0) = -kt + \ln 40$

at $t = 5; \theta = 60°C; \theta_0 = 30°$

$\ln 30 = -5k + \ln 40$

$$5k = \ln\left(\frac{4}{3}\right)$$

$$k = \frac{1}{5}\ln\left(\frac{4}{3}\right)$$

at $t = t_1; \theta = 40° C; \theta_0 = 30°C$

$$\ln(40 - 30) = -\frac{1}{5}\ln\left(\frac{4}{3}\right)t_1 + \ln 40$$

$$\frac{\ln(4/3)}{5}t_1 = \ln\left(\frac{40}{10}\right) = \ln 4$$

$$t_1 = \frac{5\ln 4}{\ln 4 - \ln 3} = \frac{10\ln 2}{2\ln 2 - \ln 3}$$

$= 24.1$ min

REVIEW & SUMMARY

Heat Capacity and Specific Heat If heat Q is absorbed by an object, the object's temperature change $T_f - T_i$ is related to Q by

$$Q = C(T_f - T_i)$$

in which C is the **heat capacity** of the object. If the object has mass m, then

$$Q = cm(T_f - T_i)$$

where c is the **specific heat** of the material making up the object. The **molar specific heat** of a material is the heat capacity per mole, which means per 6.02×10^{23} elementary units of the material.

Heat of Transformation Heat absorbed by a material may change the material's physical state—for example, from solid to liquid or from liquid to gas. The amount of energy required per unit mass to change the state (but not the temperature) of a particular material is its **heat of transformation** L. Thus,

$$Q = Lm$$

The **heat of vaporization** L_V is the amount of energy per unit mass that must be added to vaporize a liquid or that must be removed to condense a gas. The **heat of fusion** L_F is the amount of energy per unit mass that must be added to melt a solid or that must be removed to freeze a liquid.

Conduction, Convection, and Radiation The rate P_{cond} at which energy is *conducted* through a slab whose faces are maintained at temperatures T_H and T_C is

$$P_{cond} = \frac{Q}{t} = kA\frac{T_H - T_C}{L}$$

in which A and L are the face area and length of the slab, and k is the thermal conductivity of the material.

Convection occurs when temperature differences cause an energy transfer by motion within a fluid. *Radiation* is an energy transfer via the emission of electromagnetic energy. The rate P_{rad} at which an object emits energy via thermal radiation is

$$P_{rad} = \sigma\varepsilon AT^4$$

where σ $(= 5.6704 \times 10^{-8}\ \text{W/m}^2 \cdot \text{K}^4)$ is the Stefan–Boltzmann constant, ε is the emissivity of the object's surface, A is its surface area, and T is its surface temperature (in kelvins). The rate P_{abs} at which an object absorbs energy via thermal radiation from its environment, which is at the uniform temperature T_{env} (in kelvins), is

$$P_{abs} = \sigma\varepsilon AT_{env}^4$$

QUESTIONS

1 Materials A, B, and C are solids that are at their melting temperatures. Material A requires 200 J to melt 4 kg, material B requires 300 J to melt 5 kg, and material C requires 300 J to melt 6 kg. Rank the materials according to their heats of fusion, greatest first.

2 Figure 19-14 shows three different arrangements of materials 1, 2, and 3 to form a wall. The thermal conductivities are $k_1 > k_2 > k_3$. The left side of the wall is 20 C° higher than the right side. Rank the arrangements according to (a) the (steady state) rate of energy conduction through the wall and (b) the temperature difference across material 1, greatest first.

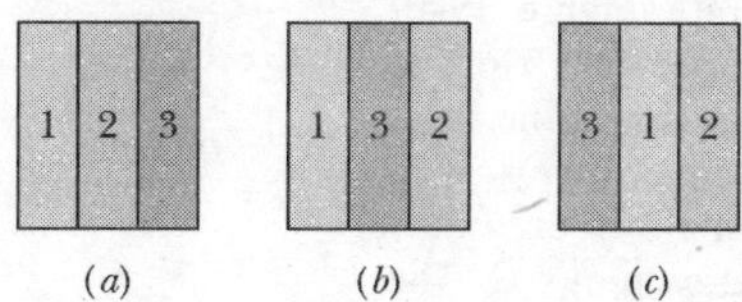

FIG. 19-14 Question 2.

3 A hot object is dropped into a thermally insulated container of water, and the object and water are then allowed to come to thermal equilibrium. The experiment is repeated twice, with different hot objects. All three objects have the same mass and initial temperature, and the mass and initial temperature of the water are the same in the three experiments. For each of the experiments, Fig. 19-15 gives graphs of the temperatures T of the object and the water versus time t. Rank the graphs according to the specific heats of the objects, greatest first.

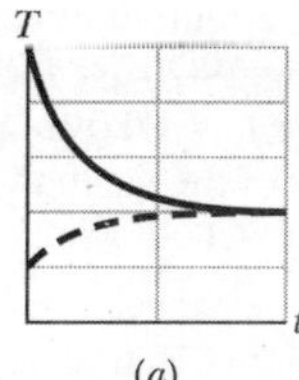

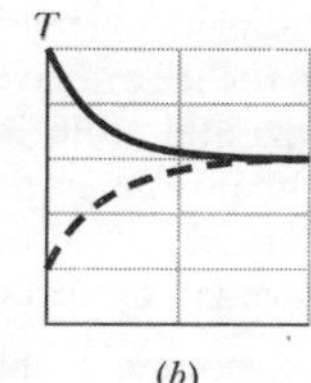

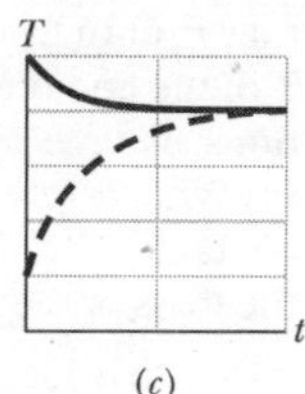

FIG. 19-15 Question 3.

4 A sample A of liquid water and a sample B of ice, of identical mass, are placed in a thermally insulated container and allowed to come to thermal equilibrium. Figure 19-16a is a sketch of the temperature T of the samples versus time t. (a) Is the equilibrium temperature above, below, or at the freezing point of water? (b) In reaching equilibrium, does the liquid partly freeze, fully freeze, or undergo no freezing? (c) Does the ice partly melt, fully melt, or undergo no melting?

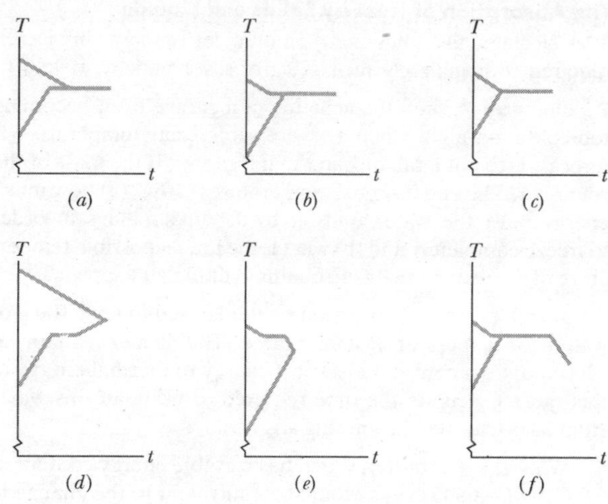

FIG. 19-16 Questions 4 and 5.

5 Question 8 continued: Graphs b through f of Fig. 19-16 are additional sketches of T versus t, of which one or more are impossible to produce. (a) Which is impossible and why? (b) In the possible ones, is the equilibrium temperature above, below, or at the freezing point of water? (c) As the possible situations reach equilibrium, does the liquid partly freeze, fully freeze, or undergo no freezing? Does the ice partly melt, fully melt, or undergo no melting?

6 A solid cube of edge length r, a solid sphere of radius r, and a solid hemisphere of radius r, all made of the same material, are maintained at temperature 300 K in an environment at temperature 350 K. Rank the objects according to the net rate at which thermal radiation is exchanged with the environment, greatest first.

7 Three different materials of identical mass are placed one at a time in a special freezer that can extract energy from a material at a certain constant rate. During the cooling process, each material begins in the liquid state and ends in the solid state; Fig. 19-17 shows the temperature T versus time t. (a) For material 1, is the specific heat for the liquid state greater than or less than that for the solid state? Rank the materials according to (b) freezing point temperature, (c) specific heat in the liquid state, (d) specific heat in the solid state, and (e) heat of fusion, all greatest first.

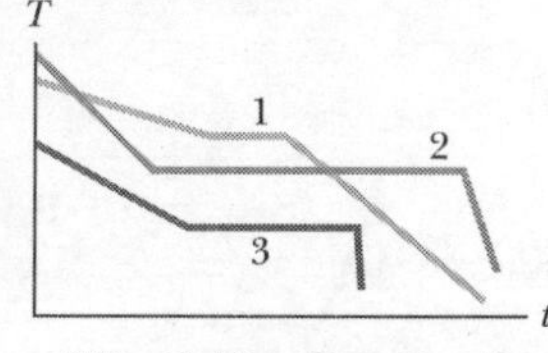

FIG. 19-17 Question 7.

PROBLEMS

The Absorption of Heat by Solids and Liquids

1 Calculate the minimum amount of energy, in joules, required to completely melt 130 g of silver initially at 15.0°C.

2 One way to keep the contents of a garage from becoming too cold on a night when a severe subfreezing temperature is forecast is to put a tub of water in the garage. If the mass of the water is 125 kg and its initial temperature is 20°C, (a) how much energy must the water transfer to its surroundings in order to freeze completely and (b) what is the lowest possible temperature of the water and its surroundings until that happens?

3 A small electric immersion heater is used to heat 100 g of water for a cup of instant coffee. The heater is labeled "200 watts" (it converts electrical energy to thermal energy at this rate). Calculate the time required to bring all this water from 23.0°C to 100°C, ignoring any heat losses.

4 What mass of butter, which has a usable energy content of 6.0 Cal/g (= 6000 cal/g), would be equivalent to the change in gravitational potential energy of a 73.0 kg man who ascends from sea level to the top of Mt. Everest, at elevation 8.84 km? Assume that the average g for the ascent is 9.80 m/s^2.

5 A 150 g copper bowl contains 220 g of water, both at 20.0°C. A very hot 300 g copper cylinder is dropped into the water, causing the water to boil, with 5.00 g being converted to steam. The final temperature of the system is 100°C. Neglect energy transfers with the environment. (a) How much energy (in calories) is transferred to the water as heat? (b) How much to the bowl? (c) What is the original temperature of the cylinder?

6 *Nonmetric version:* (a) How long does a 2.0×10^5 Btu/h water heater take to raise the temperature of 40 gal of water from 70°F to 100°F? *Metric version:* (b) How long does a 59 kW water heater take to raise the temperature of 150 L of water from 21°C to 38°C?

7 Samples A and B are at different initial temperatures when they are placed in a thermally insulated container and allowed to come to thermal equilibrium. Figure 19-18a gives their temperatures T versus time t. Sample A has a mass of 5.0 kg; sample B has a mass of 1.5 kg. Figure 19-18b is a general plot for the material of sample B. It shows the temperature change ΔT that the material undergoes when energy is transferred to it as heat Q. The change ΔT is plotted versus the energy Q per unit mass of the material, and the scale of the vertical axis is set by $\Delta T_s = 4.0$ C°. What is the specific heat of sample A?

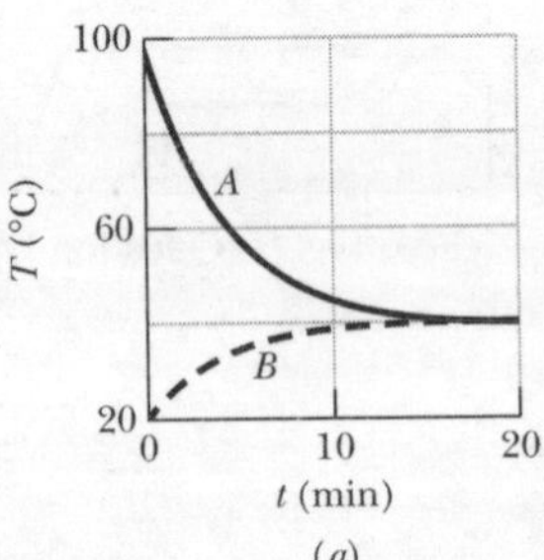

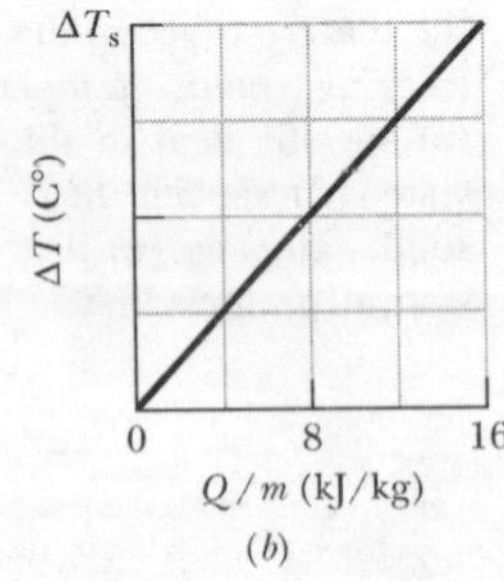

FIG. 19-18 Problem 7.

8 In a solar water heater, energy from the Sun is gathered by water that circulates through tubes in a rooftop collector. The solar radiation enters the collector through a transparent cover and warms the water in the tubes; this water is pumped into a holding tank. Assume that the effi-ciency of the overall system is 20% (that is, 80% of the incident solar energy is lost from the system). What collector area is necessary to raise the temperature of 200 L of water in the tank from 20°C to 40°C in 1.0 h when the intensity of incident sunlight is 700 W/m^2?

9 A 0.400 kg sample is placed in a cooling apparatus that removes energy as heat at a constant rate. Figure 19-19 gives the temperature T of the sample versus time t; the horizontal scale is set by $t_s = 80.0$ min. The sample freezes during the energy removal. The specific heat of the sample in its initial liquid phase is 3000 J/kg · K. What are (a) the sample's heat of fusion and (b) its specific heat in the frozen phase?

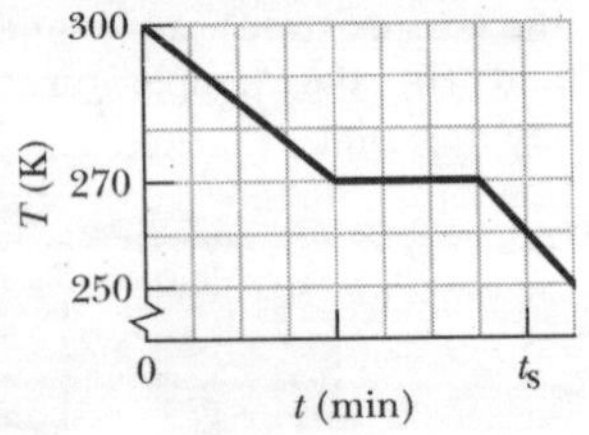

FIG. 19-19 Problem 9.

10 A 0.530 kg sample of liquid water and a sample of ice are placed in a thermally insulated container. The container also contains a device that transfers energy as heat from the liquid water to the ice at a constant rate P, until thermal equilibrium is reached. The temperatures T of the liquid water and the ice are given in Fig. 19-20 as functions of time t; the horizontal scale is set by $t_s = 80.0$ min. (a) What is rate P? (b) What is the initial mass of the ice in the container? (c) When thermal equilibrium is reached, what is the mass of the ice produced in this process?

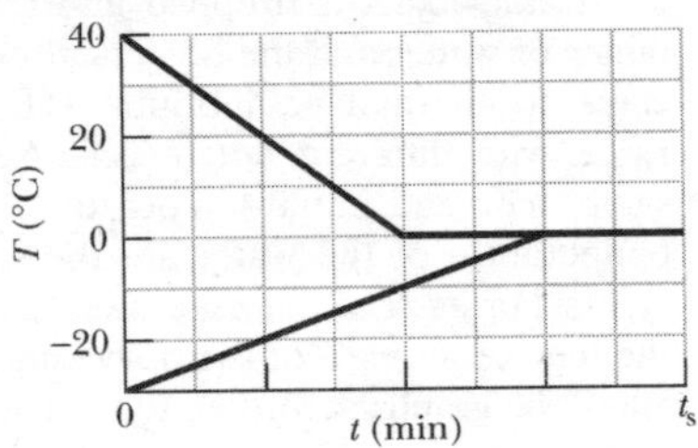

FIG. 19-20 Problem 10.

11 Ethyl alcohol has a boiling point of 78.0°C, a freezing point of −114°C, a heat of vaporization of 879 kJ/kg, a heat of fusion of 109 kJ/kg, and a specific heat of 2.43 kJ/kg· K. How much energy must be removed from 0.510 kg of ethyl alcohol that is initially a gas at 78.0°C so that it becomes a solid at −114°C?

12 The specific heat of a substance varies with temperature according to $c = 0.20 + 0.14T + 0.023T^2$, with T in °C and c in cal/g · K. Find the energy required to raise the temperature of 2.0 g of this substance from 5.0°C to 15°C.

13 A person makes a quantity of iced tea by mixing 500 g of hot tea (essentially water) with an equal mass of ice at its melting point. Assume the mixture has negligible energy exchanges with its environment. If the tea's initial temperature is $T_i = 90$°C, when thermal equilibrium is reached what are (a) the mixture's temperature T_f and (b) the remaining mass m_f of ice? If $T_i = 70$°C, when thermal equilibrium is reached what are (c) T_f and (d) m_f?

14 *Icicles.* Liquid water coats an active (growing) icicle and extends up a short, narrow tube along the central axis (Fig. 19-21). Because the water–ice interface must have a temperature of 0°C, the water in the tube cannot lose energy through the sides of the icicle or down through the tip because there is no temperature change in those directions. It can lose energy and freeze only by sending energy up (through distance L) to the top of the icicle, where the temperature T_r can be below 0°C. Take $L = 0.12$ m and $T_r = -5°C$. Assume that the central tube and the upward conduction path both have cross-sectional area A. In terms of A, what rate is (a) energy conducted upward and (b) mass converted from liquid to ice at the top of the central tube? (c) At what rate does the top of the tube move downward because of water freezing there? The thermal conductivity of ice is 0.400 W/m·K, and the density of liquid water is 1000 kg/m³.

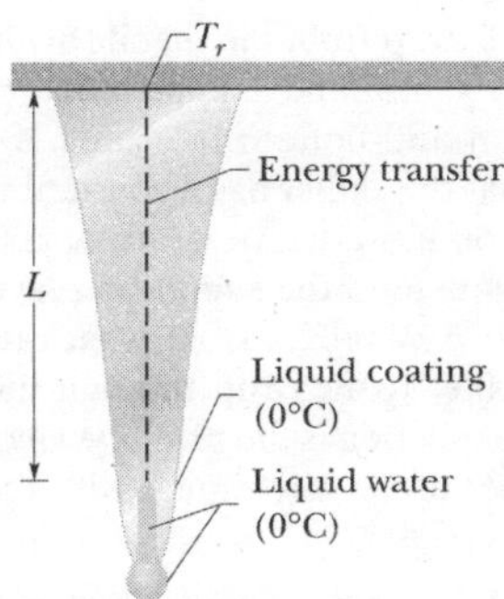

FIG. 19-21 Problem 14.

15 (a) Two 50 g ice cubes are dropped into 200 g of water in a thermally insulated container. If the water is initially at 25°C, and the ice comes directly from a freezer at −15°C, what is the final temperature at thermal equilibrium? (b) What is the final temperature if only one ice cube is used?

16 A 20.0 g copper ring at 0.000°C has an inner diameter of $D = 2.54000$ cm. An aluminum sphere at 100.0°C has a diameter of $d = 2.545\ 08$ cm. The sphere is placed on top of the ring (Fig. 19-22), and the two are allowed to come to thermal equilibrium, with no heat lost to the surroundings. The sphere just passes through the ring at the equilibrium temperature. What is the mass of the sphere?

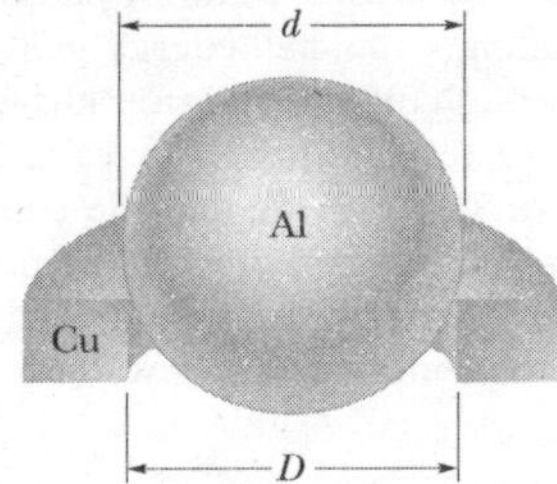

FIG. 19-22 Problem 16.

Heat Transfer Mechanisms

17 If you were to walk briefly in space without a spacesuit while far from the Sun (as an astronaut does in the movie *2001, A Space Odyssey*), you would feel the cold of space—while you radiated energy, you would absorb almost none from your environment. (a) At what rate would you lose energy? (b) How much energy would you lose in 30 s? Assume that your emissivity is 0.90, and estimate other data needed in the calculations.

18 A cylindrical copper rod of length 1.2 m and cross-sectional area 4.8 cm² is insulated to prevent heat loss through its surface. The ends are maintained at a temperature difference of 100 C° by having one end in a water–ice mixture and the other in a mixture of boiling water and steam. (a) At what rate is energy conducted along the rod? (b) At what rate does ice melt at the cold end?

19 A sphere of radius 0.500 m, temperature 27.0°C, and emissivity 0.850 is located in an environment of temperature 77.0°C. At what rate does the sphere (a) emit and (b) absorb thermal radiation? (c) What is the sphere's net rate of energy exchange?

20 A solid cylinder of radius $r_1 = 2.5$ cm, length $h_1 = 5.0$ cm, emissivity 0.85, and temperature 30°C is suspended in an environment of temperature 50°C. (a) What is the cylinder's net thermal radiation transfer rate P_1? (b) If the cylinder is stretched until its radius is $r_2 = 0.50$ cm, its net thermal radiation transfer rate becomes P_2. What is the ratio P_2/P_1?

21 In Fig. 19-23*a*, two identical rectangular rods of metal are welded end to end, with a temperature of $T_1 = 0°C$ on the left side and a temperature of $T_2 = 100°C$ on the right side. In 2.0 min, 10 J is conducted at a constant rate from the right side to the left side. How much time would be required to conduct 10 J if the rods were welded side to side as in Fig. 19-23*b*?

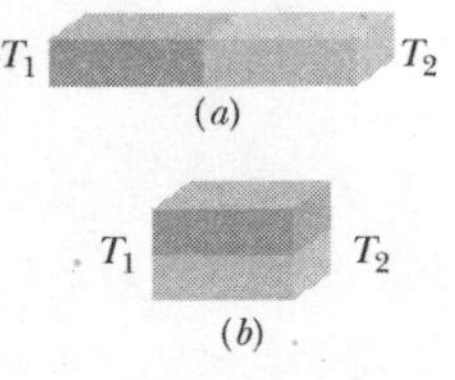

FIG. 19-23 Problem 21.

22 Figure 19-24 shows the cross section of a wall made of three layers. The thicknesses of the layers are L_1, $L_2 = 0.700L_1$, and $L_3 = 0.350L_1$. The thermal conductivities are k_1, $k_2 = 0.900k_1$, and $k_3 = 0.800k_1$. The temperatures at the left and right sides of the wall are $T_H = 30.0°C$ and $T_C = -15.0°C$, respectively. Thermal conduction is steady. (a) What is the temperature difference ΔT_2 across layer 2 (between the left and right sides of the layer)? If k_2 were, instead, equal to $1.1k_1$, (b) would the rate at which energy is conducted through the wall be greater than, less than, or the same as previously, and (c) what would be the value of ΔT_2?

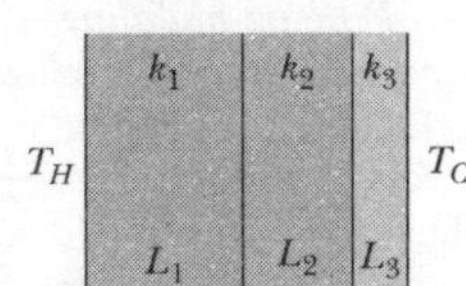

FIG. 19-24 Problem 22.

23 The giant hornet *Vespa mandarinia japonica* preys on Japanese bees. However, if one of the hornets attempts to invade a beehive, several hundred of the bees quickly form a compact ball around the hornet to stop it. They don't sting, bite, crush, or suffocate it. Rather they overheat it by quickly raising their body temperatures from the normal 35°C to 47°C or 48°C, which is lethal to the hornet but not to the bees (Fig. 19-25). Assume the following: 500 bees form a ball of radius $R = 2.0$ cm for a time $t = 20$ min, the primary loss of energy by the ball is by thermal radiation, the ball's surface has emissivity $\varepsilon = 0.80$, and the ball has a uniform temperature. On average, how much additional energy must each bee produce during the 20 min to maintain 47°C?

FIG. 19-25 Problem 23.
(© *Dr. Masato Ono, Tamagawa University*)

24 Figure 19-26 shows (in cross-section) a wall consisting of four layers, with thermal conductivities $k_1 = 0.060$ W/m·K, $k_3 = 0.040$ W/m·K, and $k_4 = 0.12$ W/m·K (k_2 is not known). The layer thicknesses are $L_1 = 1.5$ cm, $L_3 = 2.8$ cm, and $L_4 = 3.5$ cm (L_2 is not known). The known temperatures are $T_1 = 30°C$, $T_{12} = 25°C$, and $T_4 = -10°C$. Energy transfer through the wall is steady. What is interface temperature T_{34}?

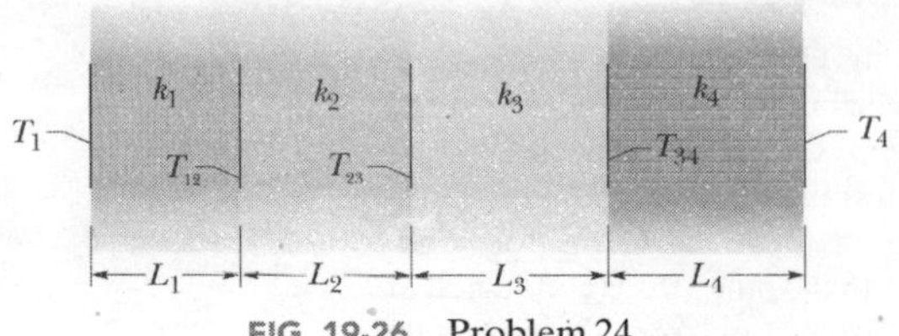

FIG. 19-26 Problem 24.

25 *Penguin huddling.* To withstand the harsh weather of the Antarctic, emperor penguins huddle in groups (Fig. 19-27). Assume that a penguin is a circular cylinder with a top surface area $a = 0.34$ m^2 and height $h = 1.1$ m. Let P_r be the rate at which an individual penguin radiates energy to the environment (through the top and the sides); thus NP_r is the rate at which N identical, well-separated penguins radiate. If the penguins huddle closely to form a *huddled cylinder* with top surface area Na and height h, the cylinder radiates at the rate P_h. If $N = 1000$, (a) what is the value of the fraction P_h/NP_r and (b) by what percentage does huddling reduce the total radiation loss?

FIG. 19-27 Problem 25.
(Alain Torterotot/Peter Arnold, Inc.)

26 Ice has formed on a shallow pond, and a steady state has been reached, with the air above the ice at −5.0°C and the bottom of the pond at 4.0°C. If the total depth of *ice + water* is 1.4 m, how thick is the ice? (Assume that the thermal conductivities of ice and water are 0.40 and 0.12 cal/m·C°·s, respectively.)

27 *Leidenfrost effect.* A water drop that is slung onto a skillet with a temperature between 100°C and about 200°C will last about 1 s. However, if the skillet is much hotter, the drop can last several minutes, an effect named after an early investigator. The longer lifetime is due to the support of a thin layer of air and water vapor that separates the drop from the metal (by distance L in Fig. 19-28). Let $L = 0.100$ mm, and assume that the drop is flat with height $h = 1.50$ mm and bottom face area $A = 4.00 \times 10^{-6}$ m^2. Also assume that the skillet has a constant temperature $T_s = 300°C$ and the drop has a temperature of 100°C. Water has density $\rho = 1000$ kg/m^3, and the supporting layer has thermal conductivity $k = 0.026$ W/m·K. (a) At what rate is energy conducted from the skillet to the drop through the drop's bottom surface? (b) If conduction is the primary way energy moves from the skillet to the drop, how long will the drop last?

FIG. 19-28 Problem 27.

28 A tank of water has been outdoors in cold weather, and a slab of ice 5.0 cm thick has formed on its surface (Fig. 19-29). The air above the ice is at −10°C. Calculate the rate of ice formation (in centimeters per hour) on the ice slab. Take the thermal conductivity of ice to be 0.0040 cal/s·cm·°C and its density to be 0.92 g/cm^3. Assume no energy transfer through the tank walls or bottom.

FIG. 19-29 Problem 28.

29 *Evaporative cooling of beverages.* A cold beverage can be kept cold even on a warm day if it is slipped into a porous ceramic container that has been soaked in water. Assume that energy lost to evaporation matches the net energy gained via the radiation exchange through the top and side surfaces. The container and beverage have temperature $T = 15°C$, the environment has temperature $T_{env} = 32°C$, and the container is a cylinder with radius $r = 2.2$ cm and height 10 cm. Approximate the emissivity as $\varepsilon = 1$, and neglect other energy exchanges. At what rate dm/dt is the container losing water mass?

Additional Problems

30 In the extrusion of cold chocolate from a tube, work is done on the chocolate by the pressure applied by a ram forcing the chocolate through the tube. The work per unit mass of extruded chocolate is equal to p/ρ, where p is the difference between the applied pressure and the pressure where the chocolate emerges from the tube, and ρ is the density of the chocolate. Rather than increasing the temperature of the chocolate, this work melts cocoa fats in the chocolate. These fats have a heat of fusion of 150 kJ/kg. Assume that all of the work goes into that melting and that these fats make up 30% of the chocolate's mass. What percentage of the fats melt during the extrusion if $p = 5.5$ MPa and $\rho = 1200$ kg/m^3?

31 In a series of experiments, block B is to be placed in a thermally insulated container with block A, which has the same mass as block B. In each experiment, block B is initially at a certain temperature T_B, but temperature T_A of block A is changed from

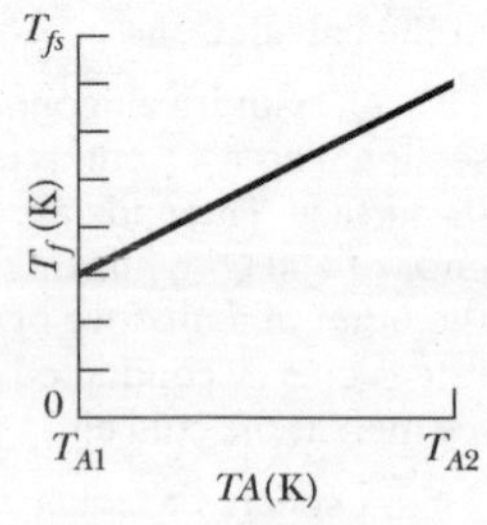

FIG. 19-30 Problem 31.

experiment to experiment. Let T_f represent the final temperature of the two blocks when they reach thermal equilibrium in any of the experiments. Figure 19-30 gives temperature T_f versus the initial temperature T_A for a range of possible values of T_A, from $T_{A1} = 0$ K to $T_{A2} = 500$ K. The vertical axis scale is set by $T_{fs} = 400$ K. What are (a) temperature T_B and (b) the ratio c_B/c_A of the specific heats of the blocks?

32 A 0.300 kg sample is placed in a cooling apparatus that removes energy as heat at a constant rate of 2.81 W. Figure 19-31 gives the temperature T of the sample versus time t. The temperature scale is set by $T_s = 30°$C and the time scale is set by $t_s = 20$ min. What is the specific heat of the sample?

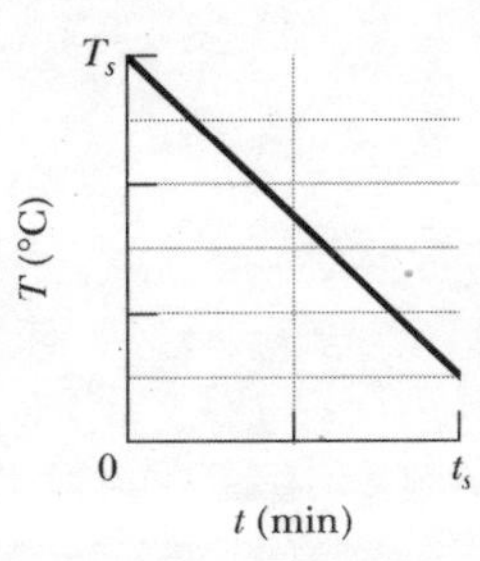

FIG. 19-31 Problem 32.

33 The average rate at which energy is conducted outward through the ground surface in North America is 54.0 mW/m², and the average thermal conductivity of the near-surface rocks is 2.50 W/m · K. Assuming a surface temperature of 10.0°C, find the temperature at a depth of 35.0 km (near the base of the crust). Ignore the heat generated by the presence of radioactive elements.

34 The temperature of a Pyrex disk is changed from 10.0°C to 60.0°C. Its initial radius is 8.00 cm; its initial thickness is 0.500 cm. Take these data as being exact. What is the change in the volume of the disk?

35 (a) Calculate the rate at which body heat is conducted through the clothing of a skier in a steady-state process, given the following data: the body surface area is 1.8 m², and the clothing is 1.0 cm thick; the skin surface temperature is 33°C and the outer surface of the clothing is at 1.0°C; the thermal conductivity of the clothing is 0.040 W/m · K. (b) If, after a fall, the skier's clothes became soaked with water of thermal conductivity 0.60 W/m · K, by how much is the rate of conduction multiplied?

36 It is possible to melt ice by rubbing one block of it against another. How much work, in joules, would you have to do to get 1.00 g of ice to melt?

37 Icebergs in the North Atlantic present hazards to shipping, causing the lengths of shipping routes to be increased by about 30% during the iceberg season. Attempts to destroy icebergs include planting explosives, bombing, torpedoing, shelling, ramming, and coating with black soot. Suppose that direct melting of the iceberg, by placing heat sources in the ice, is tried. How much energy as heat is required to melt 10% of an iceberg that has a mass of 200 000 metric tons? (Use 1 metric ton = 1000 kg.)

38 A cube of edge length 6.0×10^{-6} m, emissivity 0.75, and temperature −100°C floats in an environment at −150°C. What is the cube's net thermal radiation transfer rate?

39 A *flow calorimeter* is a device used to measure the specific heat of a liquid. Energy is added as heat at a known rate to a stream of the liquid as it passes through the calorimeter at a known rate. Measurement of the resulting temperature difference between the inflow and the outflow points of the liquid stream enables us to compute the specific heat of the liquid. Suppose a liquid of density 0.85 g/cm³ flows through a calorimeter at the rate of 8.0 cm³/s. When energy is added at the rate of 250 W by means of an electric heating coil, a temperature difference of 15 C° is established in steady-state conditions between the inflow and the outflow points. What is the specific heat of the liquid?

20 The Kinetic Theory of Gases

The interior of the railroad tank car was being cleaned with steam by a crew late one afternoon. Because the job was unfinished at the end of their work shift, they sealed the car and left for the night. When they returned the next morning, they discovered that something had crushed the car in spite of its extremely strong steel walls, as if some giant creature from a grade B science fiction movie had stepped on it during a rampage that night.

What actually crushed the railroad tank car?

The answer is in this chapter.

(Photo courtesy www.Houston.RailFan.net)

20-1 | INTRODUCTION

One of the main subjects in thermodynamics is the physics of gases. A gas consists of atoms (either individually or bound together as molecules) that fill their container's volume and exert pressure on the container's walls. We can usually assign a temperature to such a contained gas. These three variables associated with a gas—volume, pressure, and temperature—are all a consequence of the motion of the atoms. The volume is a result of the freedom the atoms have to spread throughout the container, the pressure is a result of the collisions of the atoms with the container's walls, and the temperature has to do with the kinetic energy of the atoms. The **kinetic theory of gases,** the focus of this chapter, relates the motion of the atoms to the volume, pressure, and temperature of the gas.

Applications of the kinetic theory of gases are countless. Automobile engineers are concerned with the combustion of vaporized fuel (a gas) in the automobile engines. Food engineers are concerned with the production rate of the fermentation gas that causes bread to rise as it bakes. Beverage engineers are concerned with how gas can produce the head in a glass of beer or shoot a cork from a champagne bottle. Medical engineers and physiologists are concerned with calculating how long a scuba diver must pause during ascent to eliminate nitrogen gas from the bloodstream (to avoid the *bends*). Environmental scientists are concerned with how heat exchanges between the oceans and the atmosphere can affect weather conditions.

The first step in our discussion of the kinetic theory of gases deals with measuring the amount of a gas present in a sample, for which we use Avogadro's number.

20-2 | Avogadro's Number

When our thinking is slanted toward atoms and molecules, it makes sense to measure the sizes of our samples in moles. If we do so, we can be certain that we are comparing samples that contain the same number of atoms or molecules. The *mole* is one of the seven SI base units and is defined as follows:

One mole is the number of atoms in a 12 g sample of carbon-12.

The obvious question now is: "How many atoms or molecules are there in a mole?" The answer is determined experimentally and, as you saw in Chapter 18, is

$$N_A = 6.02 \times 10^{23}\ \text{mol}^{-1} \qquad \text{(Avogadro's number)} \qquad (20\text{-}1)$$

where mol^{-1} represents the inverse mole or "per mole," and mol is the abbreviation for mole. The number N_A is called **Avogadro's number** after Italian scientist Amedeo Avogadro (1776–1856), who suggested that all gases occupying the same volume under the same conditions of temperature and pressure contain the same number of atoms or molecules.

The number of moles n contained in a sample of any substance is equal to the ratio of the number of molecules N in the sample to the number of molecules N_A in 1 mol:

$$n = \frac{N}{N_A} \qquad (20\text{-}2)$$

(*Caution:* The three symbols in this equation can easily be confused with one another, so you should sort them with their meanings now, before you end in "*N*-confusion.") We can find the number of moles n in a sample from the mass

M_{sam} of the sample and either the *molar mass* M (the mass of 1 mol) or the molecular mass m (the mass of one molecule):

$$n = \frac{M_{\text{sam}}}{M} = \frac{M_{\text{sam}}}{mN_A} \tag{20-3}$$

In Eq. 20-3, we used the fact that the mass M of 1 mol is the product of the mass m of one molecule and the number of molecules N_A in 1 mol:

$$M = mN_A \tag{20-4}$$

PROBLEM-SOLVING TACTICS

Tactic 1: Avogadro's Number of What? In Eq. 20-1, Avogadro's number is expressed in terms of mol^{-1}, which is the inverse mole, or 1/mol. We could instead explicitly state the elementary unit involved in a given situation. For example, if the elementary unit is an atom, we might write $N_A = 6.02 \times 10^{23}$ atoms/mol. If, instead, the elementary unit is a molecule, then we might write $N_A = 6.02 \times 10^{23}$ molecules/mol. Being explicit about the unit is usually the better style of writing.

The absolute zero of temperature will be reached when the linear velocities of the molecules have been reduced to zero, that is, when the molecules have been brought to rest.

20-3 | Ideal Gases

Our goal in this chapter is to explain the macroscopic properties of a gas—such as its pressure and its temperature—in terms of the behavior of the molecules that make it up. However, there is an immediate problem: which gas? Should it be hydrogen, oxygen, or methane, or perhaps uranium hexafluoride? They are all different. Experimenters have found, though, that if we confine 1 mol samples of various gases in boxes of identical volume and hold the gases at the same temperature, then their measured pressures are nearly—though not exactly—the same. If we repeat the measurements at lower gas densities, then these small differences in the measured pressures tend to disappear.

When an ideal gas is confined to a rigid container whose volume can be varied by means of a movable piston as in Fig. 20-1. We also assume that container does not leak, that is, the amount of the gas remains constant. For such system, experiments provide the following information :

1. When the gas is kept at a constant temperature, its pressure P is inversely proportional to the volume V.

$$P \alpha \frac{1}{V} \qquad \text{(Boyle's law)}$$

2. When the pressure of the gas is kept constant, the volume is directly proportional to the temperature T.

$$V \alpha T \qquad \text{(Charles's law)}$$

3. When the volume of the gas is kept constant, the pressure is directly proportional to the temperature.

$$P \alpha T \qquad \text{(Gay-Lussac's law)}$$

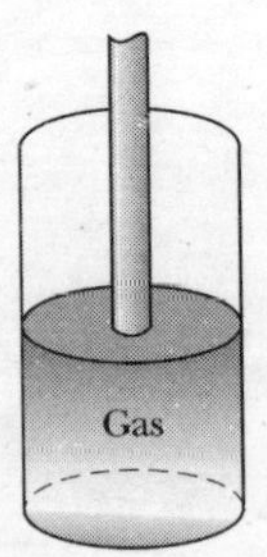

FIG. 20-1 Gas confined in a cylinder under a piston.

Further experiments show that, at low enough densities, all real gases tend to obey the relation

$$pV = nRT \qquad \text{(ideal gas law)} \tag{20-5}$$

in which p is the absolute (not gauge) pressure, n is the number of moles of gas present, and T is the temperature in kelvins. The symbol R is a constant called the **gas constant** that has the same value for all gases—namely,

$$R = 8.31 \text{ J/mol} \cdot \text{K} \tag{20-6}$$

Equation 20-5 is called the **ideal gas law.** Provided the gas density is low, this law holds for any single gas or for any mixture of different gases. (For a mixture, n is the total number of moles in the mixture.)

We can rewrite Eq. 20-5 in an alternative form, in terms of a constant called the **Boltzmann constant** k, which is defined as

$$k = \frac{R}{N_A} = \frac{8.31 \text{ J/mol} \cdot \text{K}}{6.02 \times 10^{23} \text{ mol}^{-1}} = 1.38 \times 10^{-23} \text{ J/K} \tag{20-7}$$

This allows us to write $R = kN_A$. Then, with equation $n = N/N_A$, we see that

$$nR = Nk \tag{20-8}$$

Substituting this into Eq. 20-5 gives a second expression for the ideal gas law:

$$pV = NkT \quad \text{(ideal gas law)} \tag{20-9}$$

(*Caution*: Note the difference between the two expressions for the ideal gas law—Eq. 20-5 involves the number of moles n, and Eq. 20-9 involves the number of molecules N.)

You may well ask, "What is an *ideal gas*, and what is so 'ideal' about it?" The answer lies in the simplicity of the law (Eqs. 20-5 and 20-9) that governs its macroscopic properties. Using this law—as you will see—we can deduce many properties of the ideal gas in a simple way. Although there is no such thing in nature as a truly ideal gas, *all real* gases approach the ideal state at low enough densities—that is, under conditions in which their molecules are far enough apart that they do not interact with one another. Thus, the ideal gas concept allows us to gain useful insights into the limiting behavior of real gases.

The interior of the railroad tank car in Fig. 20-2 was being cleaned with steam by a crew late one afternoon. Because the job was unfinished at the end of their work shift, they sealed the car and left for the night. When they returned the next morning, they discovered that something had crushed the car in spite of its extremely strong steel walls, as if some giant creature from a grade B science fiction movie had stepped on it during a rampage that night.

FIG. 20-2 A railroad tank car crushed overnight. *(Photo courtesy www.Houston.RailFan.net)*

With Eq. 20-9, we can explain what actually crushed the railroad tank car. When the car was being cleaned, its interior was filled with very hot steam, which is a gas of water molecules. The cleaning crew left the steam inside the car when they closed all the valves on the car at the end of their work shift. At that point the pressure of the gas in the car was equal to atmospheric pressure because the valves had been opened to the atmosphere during the cleaning. As the car cooled during the night, the steam cooled and much of it condensed, which means that the number N of gas molecules and the temperature T of the gas both decreased. Thus, the right side of Eq. 20-9 decreased, and because volume V was constant, the gas pressure p on the left side also decreased. At some point during the night, the gas pressure inside the car reached such a low value that the external atmospheric pressure was able to crush the car's steel walls. The cleaning crew could have prevented this accident by leaving the valves open, so that air could enter the car to keep the internal pressure equal to the external atmospheric pressure.

Sample Problem 20-1

A vessel of volume V is evacuated by means of a piston air pump. Upon each double stroke a piston pump sucks in a volume v_0 of air and expels it. The process is assumed to be isothermal, and the gas is ideal. When this pump is used to evacuate the air from a vessel with a volume V, it performs n double strokes. The initial pressure inside the vessel is P_0 which is equal to the atmospheric pressure.

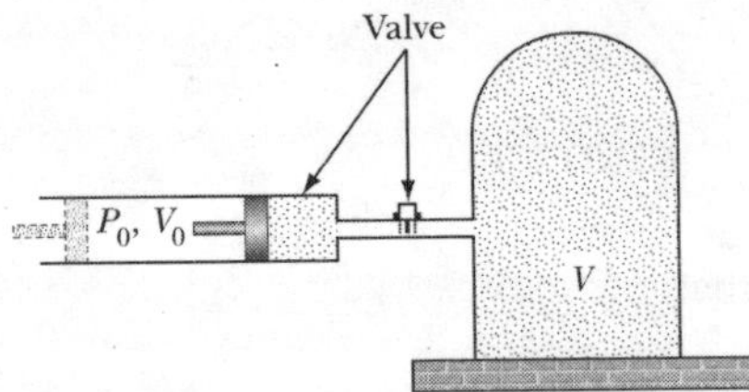

FIG. Pump used for evacuating or filling the large vessel.

Conceptualize: In the above figure we can see that when the piston comes out some of the air from the large vessel will come into the pump's chamber. Now when the piston goes in the valve connecting chamber to the vessel will close and another valve will open to atmosphere. Thus all the air inside the chamber will be thrown to the atmosphere.

Classify: We cannot say that total volume thrown out is nv_0 as number of moles being expelled will vary with every stroke. As every stroke will reduce pressure so the number of moles in chamber in each stroke will be less than the previous stroke.

Compute: When air is being pumped out of the vessel, the volume occupied by the air after one stroke will become equal to $(V + v_0)$. As it is given that the process is assumed to be isothermal, we can write

$$P_0V = P_1(V + v_0)$$

The pressure after expelling the gas will also remain P_1, as closing of the valve will not allow change in the pressure. The pressure in the vessel after one double stroke will become equal to

$$P_1 = \frac{P_0V}{V + v_0}$$

After the second double stroke, $P_1V = P_2(V + v_0)$ and, consequently,

$$P_2 = P_0\left(\frac{V}{V + v_0}\right)^2, \text{ and so on.}$$

Thus after n double strokes, the pressure in the vessel is,

$$P' = P_0\left(\frac{V}{V + v_0}\right)^n$$

Conclude: We can see that pressure inside the vessel will never become zero. Every time the vessel connects to the chamber only a fraction of the total amount goes to the pump's chamber. Thus some amount of the gas will always remain in thc vessel.

(b) After that, another pump with the same chamber volume v_0 begins to suck in the atmospheric air, also making n double strokes. What will be the pressure in side the vessel?

Conceptualize: In the figure we can see that when the piston comes out, the valve connecting chamber to the vessel will close and another valve will open to atmosphere. Thus air from the atmosphere will come into the pump's chamber. Now when the piston goes in the valve connecting chamber to the vessel will open and the other valve to atmosphere will close. Thus all the air inside the chamber will go to the vessel.

Classify: We can say that the total volume gone in is nv_0 as number of moles entering the chamber will remain constant in every stroke. Also during delivery, the pump at each double stroke sucks in air with a constant pressure p_0.

Compute: Total number of moles that will be present in the vessel are

$$(P'V + P_0nv_0)/RT.$$

If final pressure is P then we can write

$$(P'V + P_0nv_0)/RT = PV/RT$$

Solving we get,

$$P = P' + \frac{P_0nv_0}{V} = p_0\left\{\left(\frac{V}{V + v_0}\right)^n + \frac{nv_0}{V}\right\}$$

Conclude: Here $P > P'$ for any n, since during delivery the pump at each double stroke sucks in air with a pressure P', and during evacuation, volume v_0 of the air is being pumped out at pressures below P_0.

Sample Problem 20-2

A thin-walled rubber sphere of mass $M = 50$ g is filled with nitrogen at atmospheric pressure and submerged into a lake to a depth of $h = 100$ m. Find the mass m of the nitrogen filled in the sphere, if it is in a position of equilibrium. Will equilibrium be stable? The atmospheric pressure $\rho_0 = 760$ mm Hg. The temperature in the lake, $T = 4°$C. Disregard the stress of the rubber.

Conceptualize: It is easy to imagine that if we keep the sphere on the surface of the lake it will float as the density of nitrogen is at atmospheric pressure and given temperature is much less than that of water. As the sphere is sinked further down into the lake the ambient pressure around the sphere will increase, compressing it and reducing its volume and increasing its density .

Classify: Thus at some point its density will become equal to that of water and it will be in equilibrium.

Compute: From Archimedes' principle, $mg + Mg = \gamma Vg$, where γ is the density of water and V is the volume of the sphere.The equation of state gives

$$(p_0+\gamma h)V = \frac{m}{\mu} RT$$

Upon deleting V from these equations, we find that

$$m = \frac{M\mu(p_0+\gamma h)}{\gamma RT - \mu g(p_0+\gamma h)} = 0.666 \text{ g}$$

Conclude: If we push the rubber sphere down its density will become greater than that of water and it will sink and if we take it up its density will become lesser than that of water and it will rise thus equilibrium will be unstable.

Sample Problem 20-3 Build your skill

A horizontally kept cylinderical vessel closed at both ends is separated into two equal (42 cm each) parts by an adiabatic piston. Both parts contain gas having equal mass at a temperature of 27°C and a pressure of 1 atm. How much should the gas be heated in one part of the cylinder to shift the piston by 2 cm ? Find the pressure p of the gas after shifting of the piston.

Solution: Since the gas in both ends having equal mass and the piston is in equilibrium,

$$\frac{V_2}{V_1} = \frac{T_2}{T_1}$$

Hence, $T_2 = \dfrac{V_2}{V_1} T_1$

Considering h_1 and h_2 as the new lengths of the cylinder,

$$V_2 = \pi r^2 h_2, V_1 = \pi r^2 h_1$$

Calculating T_2,

$$T_2 = \frac{V_2}{V_1} T_1 = \frac{h_2}{h_1} T_1$$

$$= \frac{44}{40} \times 27°\text{C} = 30°\text{C} = 330 \text{ K}$$

Applying Boyle's law to the volume of the gas whose temperature does not change, we obtain,

$$p = \frac{p_0 V_0}{V_1}$$

Applying the values, $p_0 = 1$ atm, $V_0 = 44\pi r^2$ and $V_1 = 42 \times \pi r^2$

$$p = \frac{1 \times 44\pi r2}{42\pi r^2} = 1.05 \text{ atm} \qquad \text{(Answer)}$$

Sample Problem 20-4

Temperature of air in a tire

Before starting out on a long drive, you check the air in your car's tires to make sure they are properly inflated. The pressure gauge reads 209 kPa, and the temperature is 37°C. After a few hours of highway driving, you stop and check the pressure again. Now the gauge reads 239 kPa. What is the temperature of the air in the tires now? Assume that the volume of the tire remains constant.

Conceptualize: As a common experience we know that after driving a vehicle for a while the temperature of it's tires increase. We must use only absolute temperatures and absolute pressures when using the ideal gas law. The pressure gauge reads gauge pressure, hence to get absolute pressure we add 1 atm = 101 kPa.

Classify: As given that expansion of tire is negligible we can assume that it is isovolumetric process.

Compute: The number of moles are constant as long as the tire does not leak. The volume may actually change a bit as the tire warms up and expands, but this change is to be neglected. Since N and V are constant, we can rewrite the ideal gas law as a proportionality between P and T. We treat the air in the tire as an ideal gas. First convert the initial and final gauge pressures to absolute pressures:

$$P_i = 209 \text{ kPa} + 101 \text{ kPa} = 310 \text{ kPa}$$

$$P_f = 239 \text{ kPa} + 101 \text{ kPa} = 340 \text{ kPa}$$

Now convert the initial temperature to an absolute temperature :

$$T_i = 37°\text{C} + 273 \text{ K} = 310 \text{ K}$$

According to the ideal gas law, pressure is proportional to temperature at constant volume (Gay-Lussac Law), so

$$\frac{T_f}{T_i} = \frac{P_f}{P_i} = \frac{340\text{ kPa}}{310\text{ kPa}}$$

Then $$T_f = \frac{P_f}{P_i}T_i = \frac{340}{310} \times 310\text{ K} = 340\text{ K}$$

Now convert back to °C:

$$340\text{ K} - 273\text{ K} = 67°\text{C} \qquad \text{(Answer)}$$

Conclude: The final answer of 67°C seems reasonable since, after a long drive, the tires are noticeably hot.

CHECKPOINT 1 Suppose in the above problem, you decide to leak some air from the tires, since the manufacturer suggests keeping the pressure at 210 kPa. (The manufacturer's specification are for the tires which are "cold.") If you let out sufficient air so that the pressure returns to 210 kPa, what percentage of the air molecules did you let out of the tires? Suppose that you leave the car and go for a lunch and when you come back the tires have cooled down to 37°C. Now what is the gauge pressure?

20-4 | Pressure, Temperature, and RMS Speed

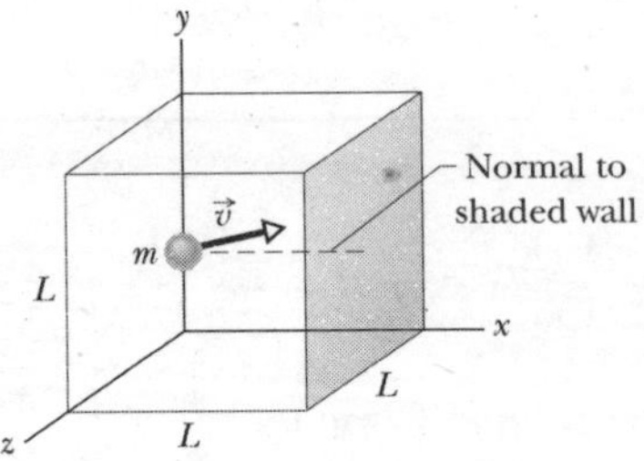

FIG. 20-3 A cubical box of edge length L, containing n moles of an ideal gas. A molecule of mass m and velocity $\vec{v}$ is about to collide with the shaded wall of area L^2. A normal to that wall is shown.

Here is our first kinetic theory problem. Let n moles of an ideal gas be confined in a cubical box of volume V, as in Fig. 20-3. The walls of the box are held at temperature T. What is the connection between the pressure p exerted by the gas on the walls and the speeds of the molecules?

The molecules of gas in the box are moving in all directions and with various speeds, bumping into one another and bouncing from the walls of the box like balls in a racquetball court. We ignore (for the time being) collisions of the molecules with one another and consider only elastic collisions with the walls.

Figure 20-3 shows a typical gas molecule, of mass m and velocity $\vec{v}$, that is about to collide with the shaded wall. Because we assume that any collision of a molecule with a wall is elastic, when this molecule collides with the shaded wall, the only component of its velocity that is changed is the x component, and that component is reversed. This means that the only change in the particle's momentum is along the x axis, and that change is

$$\Delta p_x = (-mv_x) - (mv_x) = -2mv_x$$

Hence, the momentum Δp_x delivered to the wall by the molecule during the collision is $+2mv_x$. (Because in this book the symbol p represents both momentum and pressure, we must be careful to note that here p represents momentum and is a vector quantity.)

The molecule of Fig. 20-3 will hit the shaded wall repeatedly. The time Δt between collisions is the time the molecule takes to travel to the opposite wall and back again (a distance $2L$) at speed v_x. Thus, Δt is equal to $2L/v_x$. (Note that this result holds even if the molecule bounces off any of the other walls along the way, because those walls are parallel to x and so cannot change v_x.) Therefore, the average rate at which momentum is delivered to the shaded wall by this single molecule is

$$\frac{\Delta p_x}{\Delta t} = \frac{2mv_x}{2L/v_x} = \frac{mv_x^2}{L}$$

From Newton's second law ($\vec{F} = d\vec{p}/dt$), the rate at which momentum is delivered to the wall is the force acting on that wall. To find the total force, we must add up the contributions of all the molecules that strike the wall, allowing for the possibility that they all have different speeds. Dividing the magnitude of the total force F_x by the area of the wall ($= L^2$) then gives the pressure p on that wall, where now and in the rest of this discussion, p represents pressure. Thus, using the expression for $\Delta p_x/\Delta t$, we can write this pressure as

$$p = \frac{F_x}{L^2} = \frac{mv_{x1}^2/L + mv_{x2}^2/L + \cdots + mv_{xN}^2/L}{L^2}$$

$$= \left(\frac{m}{L^3}\right)(v_{x1}^2 + v_{x2}^2 + \cdots + v_{xN}^2) \qquad (20\text{-}10)$$

where N is the number of molecules in the box.

Since $N = nN_A$, there are nN_A terms in the second set of parentheses of Eq. 20-10. We can replace that quantity by $nN_A(v_x^2)_{avg}$, where $(v_x^2)_{avg}$ is the average value of the square of the x components of all the molecular speeds. Equation 20-10 then becomes

$$p = \frac{nmN_A}{L^3}(v_x^2)_{avg}$$

However, mN_A is the molar mass M of the gas (that is, the mass of 1 mol of the gas). Also, L^3 is the volume of the box, so

$$p = \frac{nM(v_x^2)_{avg}}{V} \qquad (20\text{-}11)$$

For any molecule, $v^2 = v_x^2 + v_y^2 + v_z^2$. Because there are many molecules and because they are all moving in random directions, the average values of the squares of their velocity components are equal, so that $v_x^2 = 1/3\,v^2$. Thus, Eq. 20-11 becomes

$$p = \frac{nM(v^2)_{avg}}{3V} \qquad (20\text{-}12)$$

The square root of $(v^2)_{avg}$ is a kind of average speed, called the **root-mean-square speed** of the molecules and symbolized by v_{rms}. Its name describes it rather well: You *square* each speed, you find the *mean* (that is, the average) of all these squared speeds, and then you take the square *root* of that mean. With $\sqrt{(v^2)_{avg}} = v_{rms}$, we can then write Eq. 20-12 as

$$p = \frac{nMv_{rms}^2}{3V} \qquad (20\text{-}13)$$

Equation 20-13 is very much in the spirit of kinetic theory. It tells us how the pressure of the gas (a purely macroscopic quantity) depends on the speed of the molecules (a purely microscopic quantity).

We can turn Eq. 20-13 around and use it to calculate v_{rms}. Combining Eq. 20-13 with the ideal gas law ($pV = nRT$) leads to

$$v_{rms} = \sqrt{\frac{3RT}{M}} \qquad (20\text{-}14)$$

Table 20-1 shows some rms speeds calculated from Eq. 20-14. The speeds are surprisingly high. For hydrogen molecules at room temperature (300 K), the rms speed is 1920 m/s, or 4300 mi/h—faster than a speeding bullet! On the surface of the Sun, where the temperature is 2×10^6 K, the rms speed of hydrogen molecules would be 82 times greater than at room temperature were it not for the fact that at such high speeds, the molecules cannot survive collisions among themselves. Remember too that the rms speed is only a kind of average speed; many molecules move much faster than this, and some much slower.

The speed of sound in a gas is closely related to the rms speed of the molecules of that gas. In a sound wave, the disturbance is passed on from molecule to molecule by means of collisions. The wave cannot move any faster than the "average" speed of the molecules. In fact, the speed of sound must be somewhat less than this "average" molecular speed because not all molecules are moving in exactly the same direction as the wave. As examples, at room temperature, the rms speeds of hydrogen and nitrogen molecules are 1920 m/s and 517 m/s, respectively. The speeds of sound in these two gases at this temperature are 1350 m/s and 350 m/s, respectively.

A question often arises: If molecules move so fast, why does it take as long as a minute or so before you can smell perfume when someone opens a bottle across a room? The answer is that, each perfume molecule may have a high speed but it moves away from the bottle only very slowly because its repeated collisions with other molecules prevent it from moving directly across the room to you.

TABLE 20-1

Some RMS Speeds at Room Temperature (T = 300 K)[a]

Gas	Molar Mass (10^{-3} kg/mol)	v_{rms} (m/s)
Hydrogen (H_2)	2.02	1920
Helium (He)	4.0	1370
Water vapor (H_2O)	18.0	645
Nitrogen (N_2)	28.0	517
Oxygen (O_2)	32.0	483
Carbon dioxide (CO_2)	44.0	412
Sulfur dioxide (SO_2)	64.1	342

[a]For convenience, we often set room temperature equal to 300 K even though (at 27°C or 81°F) that represents a fairly warm room.

Sample Problem 20-5 Build your skill

Here are five numbers: 5, 11, 32, 67, and 89.

(a) What is the average value n_{avg} of these numbers?

Compute: We find this from

$$n_{avg} = \frac{5 + 11 + 32 + 67 + 89}{5} = 40.8 \quad \text{(Answer)}$$

(b) What is the rms value n_{rms} of these numbers?

Compute: We find this from

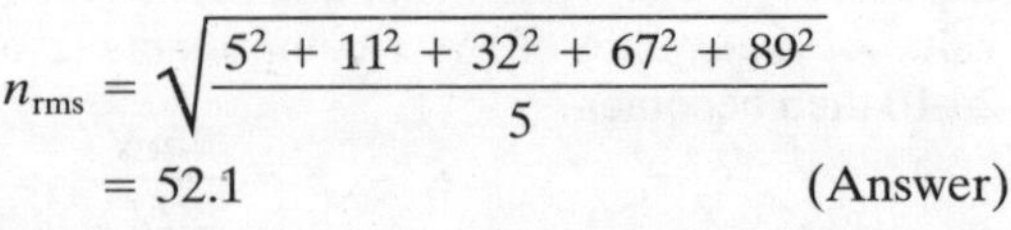

$$n_{rms} = \sqrt{\frac{5^2 + 11^2 + 32^2 + 67^2 + 89^2}{5}}$$

$$= 52.1 \quad \text{(Answer)}$$

The rms value is greater than the average value because the larger numbers—being squared—are relatively more important in forming the rms value. To test this, let us replace 89 in our set of five numbers by 300. The average value of the new set of five numbers (as you should show) is 2.0 times the previous average value. The rms value, however, is 2.7 times the previous rms value.

20-5 | Translational Kinetic Energy

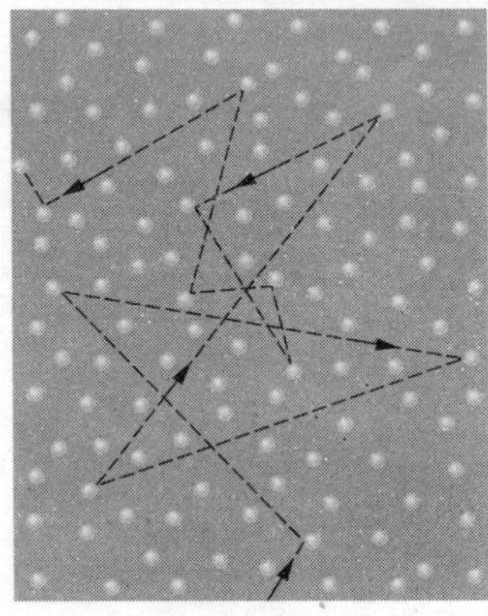

FIG. 20-4 A molecule traveling through a gas, colliding with other gas molecules in its path. Although the other molecules are shown as stationary, they are also moving in a similar fashion.

We again consider a single molecule of an ideal gas as it moves around in the box of Fig. 20-3, but we now assume that its speed changes when it collides with other molecules. Its translational kinetic energy at any instant is $\frac{1}{2}mv^2$. Its *average* translational kinetic energy over the time that we watch it is

$$K_{avg} = (\tfrac{1}{2}mv^2)_{avg} = \tfrac{1}{2}m(v^2)_{avg} = \tfrac{1}{2}mv^2_{rms} \tag{20-15}$$

in which we make the assumption that the average speed of the molecule during our observation is the same as the average speed of all the molecules at any given time. (Provided the total energy of the gas is not changing and provided we observe our molecule for long enough, this assumption is appropriate.) Substituting for v_{rms} from Eq. 20-14 leads to

$$K_{avg} = (\tfrac{1}{2}m)\frac{3RT}{M}$$

However, M/m, the molar mass divided by the mass of a molecule, is simply Avogadro's number. Thus,

$$K_{avg} = \frac{3RT}{2N_A}$$

Using Eq. $k = R/N_A$, we can then write

$$K_{avg} = \tfrac{3}{2}kT \tag{20-16}$$

This equation tells us something unexpected:

At a given temperature T, all ideal gas molecules—no matter what their mass—have the same average translational kinetic energy—namely, $\frac{3}{2}kT$. When we measure the temperature of a gas, we are also measuring the average translational kinetic energy of its molecules.

CHECKPOINT 2 A gas mixture consists of molecules of types 1, 2, and 3, with molecular masses $m_1 > m_2 > m_3$. Rank the three types according to (a) average kinetic energy and (b) rms speed, greatest first.

20-6 | The Distribution of Molecular Speeds

The root-mean-square speed v_{rms} gives us a general idea of molecular speeds in a gas at a given temperature. We often want to know more. For example, what fraction of the molecules have speeds greater than the rms value? What fraction

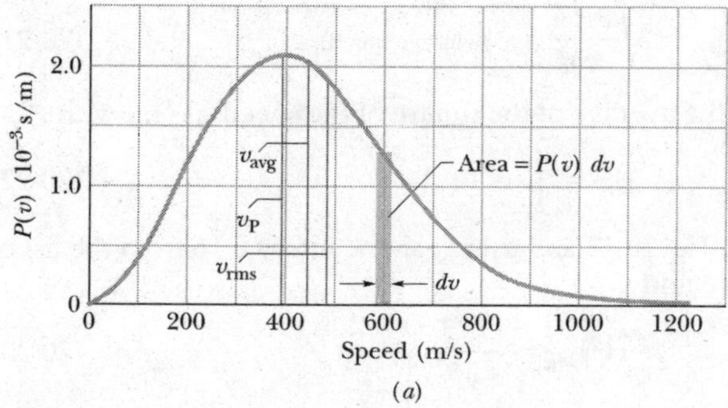

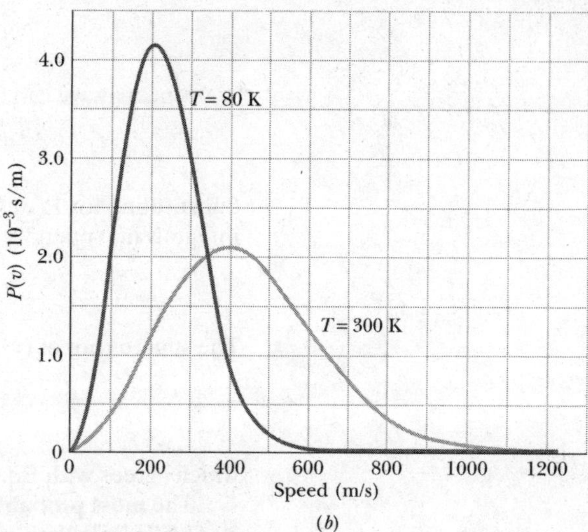

FIG. 20-5 (*a*) The Maxwell speed distribution for oxygen molecules at $T = 300$ K. The three characteristic speeds are marked. (*b*) The curves for 300 K and 80 K. Note that the molecules move more slowly at the lower temperature. Because these are probability distributions, the area under each curve has a numerical value of unity.

have speeds greater than twice the rms value? To answer such questions, we need to know how the possible values of speed are distributed among the molecules. Figure 20-5*a* shows this distribution for oxygen molecules at room temperature ($T = 300$ K); Fig. 20-5*b* compares it with the distribution at $T = 80$ K.

In 1852, Scottish physicist James Clerk Maxwell first solved the problem of finding the speed distribution of gas molecules. His result, known as **Maxwell's speed distribution law,** is

$$P(v) = 4\pi\left(\frac{M}{2\pi RT}\right)^{3/2} v^2 e^{-Mv^2/2RT} \qquad (20\text{-}17)$$

Here M is the molar mass of the gas, R is the gas constant, T is the gas temperature, and v is the molecular speed. It is this equation that is plotted in Fig. 20-5*a*, *b*. The quantity $P(v)$ in Eq. 20-17 and Fig. 20-5 is a *probability distribution function:* For any speed v, the product $P(v)\,dv$ (a dimensionless quantity) is the fraction of molecules with speeds in the interval dv centered on speed v.

As Fig. 20-5*a* shows, this fraction is equal to the area of a strip with height $P(v)$ and width dv. The total area under the distribution curve corresponds to the fraction of the molecules whose speeds lie between zero and infinity. All molecules fall into this category, so the value of this total area is unity; that is,

$$\int_0^\infty P(v)\,dv = 1 \qquad (20\text{-}18)$$

The fraction (frac) of molecules with speeds in an interval of, say, v_1 to v_2 is then

$$\text{frac} = \int_{v_1}^{v_2} P(v)\,dv \qquad (20\text{-}19)$$

Average, RMS, and Most Probable Speeds

In principle, we can find the **average speed** v_{avg} of the molecules in a gas with the following procedure: We *weight* each value of v in the distribution; that is, we multiply it by the fraction $P(v)\,dv$ of molecules with speeds in a differential interval dv centered on v. Then we add up all these values of $v\,P(v)\,dv$. The result is v_{avg}. In practice, we do all this by evaluating

$$v_{avg} = \int_0^\infty v\,P(v)\,dv \qquad (20\text{-}20)$$

Substituting for $P(v)$ from Eq. 20-17 and using generic integral 20 from the list of integrals in Appendix E, we find

$$v_{avg} = \sqrt{\frac{8RT}{\pi M}} \quad \text{(average speed)} \tag{20-21}$$

Similarly, we can find the average of the square of the speeds $(v^2)_{avg}$ with

$$(v^2)_{avg} = \int_0^\infty v^2\, P(v)\, dv \tag{20-22}$$

Substituting for $P(v)$ from Eq. 20-17 and using generic integral 16 from the list of integrals in Appendix E, we find

$$(v^2)_{avg} = \frac{3RT}{M} \tag{20-23}$$

The square root of $(v^2)_{avg}$ is the root-mean-square speed v_{rms}. Thus,

$$v_{rms} = \sqrt{\frac{3RT}{M}} \quad \text{(rms speed)} \tag{20-24}$$

which agrees with Eq. 20-14.

The **most probable speed** v_P is the speed at which $P(v)$ is maximum (see Fig. 20-5*a*). To calculate v_P, we set $dP/dv = 0$ (the slope of the curve in Fig. 20-5*a* is zero at the maximum of the curve) and then solve for v. Doing so, we find

$$v_P = \sqrt{\frac{2RT}{M}} \quad \text{(most probable speed)} \tag{20-25}$$

A molecule is more likely to have speed v_P than any other speed, but some molecules will have speeds that are many times v_P. These molecules lie in the *high-speed tail* of a distribution curve like that in Fig. 20-5*a*. We should be thankful for these few, higher speed molecules because they make possible both rain and sunshine (without which we could not exist). We next see why.

Rain The speed distribution of water molecules in, say, a pond at summertime temperatures can be represented by a curve similar to that of Fig. 20-5*a*. Most of the molecules do not have nearly enough kinetic energy to escape from the water through its surface. However, small numbers of very fast molecules with speeds far out in the high-speed tail of the curve can do so. It is these water molecules that evaporate, making clouds and rain a possibility.

As the fast water molecules leave the surface, carrying energy with them, the temperature of the remaining water is maintained by heat transfer from the surroundings. Other fast molecules—produced in particularly favorable collisions—quickly take the place of those that have left, and the speed distribution is maintained.

Sunshine Let the distribution curve of Fig. 20-5*a* now refer to protons in the core of the Sun. The Sun's energy is supplied by a nuclear fusion process that starts with the merging of two protons. However, protons repel each other because of their electrical charges, and protons of average speed do not have enough kinetic energy to overcome the repulsion and get close enough to merge. Very fast protons with speeds in the high-speed tail of the distribution curve can do so, however, and for that reason the Sun can shine.

Sample Problem 20-6

The molar mass M of oxygen is 0.0320 kg/mol.

(a) What is the average speed v_{avg} of oxygen gas molecules at $T = 300$ K?

Conceptualize/Classify: To find the average speed, we must weight speed v with the distribution function $P(v)$ of Eq. 20-17 and then integrate the resulting expression over the range of possible speeds (0 to ∞).

Compute: We end up with Eq. 20-21, which gives us

$$v_{avg} = \sqrt{\frac{8RT}{\pi M}}$$

$$= \sqrt{\frac{8(8.31\text{ J/mol}\cdot\text{K})(300\text{ K})}{\pi(0.0320\text{ kg/mol})}}$$

$$= 445\text{ m/s} \qquad \text{(Answer)}$$

Conclude: This result is plotted in Fig. 20-5*a*.

(b) What is the root-mean-square speed v_{rms} at 300 K?

Conceptualize/Classify: To find v_{rms}, we must first find $(v^2)_{\text{avg}}$ by weighting v^2 with the distribution function $P(v)$ of Eq. 20-17 and then integrating the expression over the range of possible speeds. Then we must take the square root of the result.

Compute: We end up with Eq. 20-24, which gives us

$$v_{\text{rms}} = \sqrt{\frac{3RT}{M}}$$

$$= \sqrt{\frac{3(8.31\text{ J/mol}\cdot\text{K})(300\text{ K})}{0.0320\text{ kg/mol}}}$$

$$= 483\text{ m/s} \qquad \text{(Answer)}$$

Conclude: This result, plotted in Fig. 20-5*a*, is greater than v_{avg} because the greater speed values influence the calculation more when we integrate the v^2 values than when we integrate the v values.

(c) What is the most probable speed v_P at 300 K?

Conceptualize/Classify: Speed v_P corresponds to the maximum of the distribution function $P(v)$, which we obtain by setting the derivative $dP/dv = 0$ and solving the result for v.

Compute: We end up with Eq. 20-25, which gives us

$$v_P = \sqrt{\frac{2RT}{M}}$$

$$= \sqrt{\frac{2(8.31\text{ J/mol}\cdot\text{K})(300\text{ K})}{0.0320\text{ kg/mol}}}$$

$$= 395\text{ m/s} \qquad \text{(Answer)}$$

Conclude: This result is also plotted in Fig. 20-5*a*.

20-7 | The Equipartition of Energy and Degrees of Freedom

Internal Energy E_{int}

Let us first assume that our ideal gas is a *monatomic gas* (which has individual atoms rather than molecules), such as helium, neon, or argon. Let us also assume that the internal energy E_{int} of our ideal gas is simply the sum of the translational kinetic energies of its atoms. (As explained by quantum theory, individual atoms do not have rotational kinetic energy.)

The average translational kinetic energy of a single atom depends only on the gas temperature and is given by Eq. 20-16 as $K_{\text{avg}} = \frac{3}{2}kT$. A sample of n moles of such a gas contains nN_A atoms. The internal energy E_{int} of the sample is then

$$E_{\text{int}} = (nN_A)K_{\text{avg}} = (nN_A)(\tfrac{3}{2}kT) \qquad (20\text{-}26)$$

Using Eq. $k = R/N_A$, we can rewrite this as

$$E_{\text{int}} = \tfrac{3}{2}nRT \qquad \text{(monatomic ideal gas)} \qquad (20\text{-}27)$$

The internal energy E_{int} of an ideal gas is a function of the gas temperature *only*; it does not depend on any other variable.

Degrees of Freedom

As Table 20-2 shows, the prediction that $C_V = \frac{3}{2}R$ agrees with experiment for monatomic gases but fails for diatomic and polyatomic gases. Let us try to

TABLE 20-2

Molar Specific Heats at Constant Volume

Molecule	Example		C_V (J/mol·K)
Monatomic	Ideal		$\frac{3}{2}R = 12.5$
	Real	He	12.5
		Ar	12.6
Diatomic	Ideal		$\frac{5}{2}R = 20.8$
	Real	N_2	20.7
		O_2	20.8
Polyatomic	Ideal		$3R = 24.9$
	Real	NH_4	29.0
		CO_2	29.7

explain the discrepancy by considering the possibility that molecules with more than one atom can store internal energy in forms other than translational kinetic energy.

Figure 20-6 shows common models of helium (a *monatomic* molecule, containing a single atom), oxygen (a *diatomic* molecule, containing two atoms), and methane (a *polyatomic* molecule). From such models, we would assume that all three types of molecules can have translational motions (say, moving left–right and up–down) and rotational motions (spinning about an axis like a top). In addition, we would assume that the diatomic and polyatomic molecules can have oscillatory motions, with the atoms oscillating slightly toward and away from one another, as if attached to opposite ends of a spring.

To keep account of the various ways in which energy can be stored in a gas, James Clerk Maxwell introduced the theorem of the **equipartition of energy:**

> Every kind of molecule has a certain number f of *degrees of freedom,* which are independent ways in which the molecule can store energy. Each such degree of freedom has associated with it—on average—an energy of 1/2 kT per molecule (or 1/2 RT per mole).

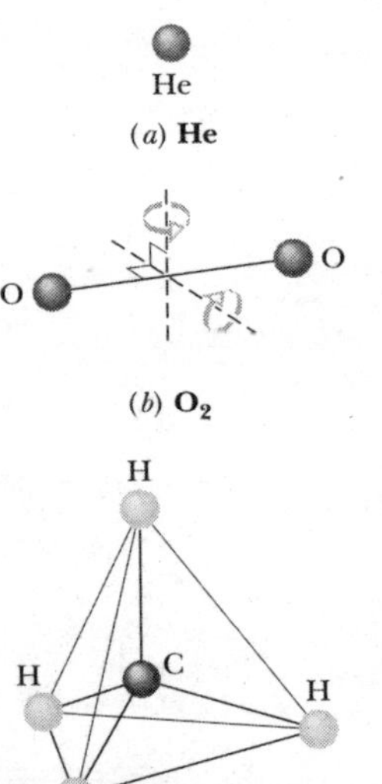

FIG. 20-6 Models of molecules as used in kinetic theory: (*a*) helium, a typical monatomic molecule; (*b*) oxygen, a typical diatomic molecule; and (*c*) methane, a typical polyatomic molecule. The spheres represent atoms, and the lines between them represent bonds. Two rotation axes are shown for the oxygen molecule.

Let us apply the theorem to the translational and rotational motions of the molecules in Fig. 20-6. (We discuss oscillatory motion in the next section.) For the translational motion, superimpose an xyz coordinate system on any gas. The molecules will, in general, have velocity components along all three axes. Thus, gas molecules of all types have three degrees of translational freedom (three ways to move in translation) and, on average, an associated energy of $3(\frac{1}{2}kT)$ per molecule.

For the rotational motion, imagine the origin of our xyz coordinate system at the center of each molecule in Fig. 20-6. In a gas, each molecule should be able to rotate with an angular velocity component along each of the three axes, so each gas should have three degrees of rotational freedom and, on average, an additional energy of $3(\frac{1}{2}kT)$ per molecule. *However,* experiment shows this is true only for the polyatomic molecules. According to *quantum theory,* the physics dealing with the allowed motions and energies of molecules and atoms, a monatomic gas molecule does not rotate and so has no rotational energy (a single atom cannot rotate like a top). A diatomic molecule can rotate like a top only about axes perpendicular to the line connecting the atoms (the axes are shown in Fig. 20-6*b*) and not about that line itself. Therefore, a diatomic molecule can have only two degrees of rotational freedom and a rotational energy of only $2(\frac{1}{2}kT3)$ per molecule.

To extend our analysis of molar specific heats to ideal diatomic and polyatomic gases, it is necessary to retrace the derivations of that analysis in detail. First, we replace Eq. $E_{int} = \frac{3}{2}nRT$ with $E_{int} = (f/2)nRT$, where f is the number of degrees of freedom listed in Table 20-3. Doing so leads to the prediction

$$C_V = \left(\frac{f}{2}\right)R = 4.16f \text{ J/mol}\cdot\text{K} \tag{20-28}$$

which agrees—as it must—with Eq. $C_V = \frac{3}{2}R$ for monatomic gases ($f = 3$). As Table 20-2 shows, this prediction also agrees with experiment for diatomic gases ($f = 5$), but it is too low for polyatomic gases ($f = 6$ for molecules comparable to CH_4).

TABLE 20-3

Degrees of Freedom for Various Molecules

Molecule	Example	Degrees of Freedom			Predicted Molar Specific Heats	
		Translational	Rotational	Total (f)	C_V (Eq. 20-28)	$C_p = C_V + R$
Monatomic	He	3	0	3	$\frac{3}{2}R$	$\frac{5}{2}R$
Diatomic	O_2	3	2	5	$\frac{5}{2}R$	$\frac{7}{2}R$
Polyatomic	CH_4	3	3	6	$3R$	$4R$

Sample Problem 20-7

A cabin of volume V is filled with air (which we consider to be an ideal diatomic gas) at an initial low temperature T_1. After you light a wood stove, the air temperature increases to T_2. What is the resulting change ΔE_{int} in the internal energy of the air in the cabin?

Conceptualize: Your initial instinct may be to conclude that the internal energy must increase as temperature increases but in this case, the amount of gas is not constant as the room is an open system.

Classify: As the air temperature increases, the air pressure p cannot change but must always be equal to the air pressure outside the room. The reason is that, because the room is not airtight, the air is not confined. As the temperature increases, air molecules leave through various openings and thus the number of moles n of air in the room decreases. Thus, we *cannot* use Eq. $\Delta E_{int} = nC_V\,\Delta T$ to find ΔE_{int}, because it requires constant n. However, we *can* relate the internal energy E_{int} at any instant to n and the temperature T with Eq. $E_{int} = nC_VT$.

Compute: From Eq. $E_{int} = nC_VT$ we can then write

$$\Delta E_{int} = \Delta(nC_VT) = C_V\,\Delta(nT)$$

Next, using Eq. $pV = nRT$, we can replace nT with pV/R, obtaining

$$\Delta E_{int} = C_V\,\Delta\left(\frac{pV}{R}\right)$$

Because p, V, and R are all constants, this yields

$$\Delta E_{int} = 0 \qquad \text{(Answer)}$$

even though the temperature changes.

Conclude: Why does the cabin feel more comfortable at the higher temperature? There are at least two factors involved: (1) You exchange electromagnetic radiation (thermal radiation) with surfaces inside the room, and (2) you exchange energy with air molecules that collide with you. When the room temperature is increased, (1) the amount of thermal radiation emitted by the surfaces and absorbed by you is increased, and (2) the amount of energy you gain through the collisions of air molecules with you is increased.

20-8 | A Hint of Quantum Theory

We can improve the agreement of kinetic theory with experiment by including the oscillations of the atoms in a gas of diatomic or polyatomic molecules. For example, the two atoms in the O_2 molecule of Fig. 20-6*b* can oscillate toward and away from each other, with the interconnecting bond acting like a spring. However, experiment shows that such oscillations occur only at relatively high temperatures of the gas—the motion is "turned on" only when the gas molecules have relatively large energies. Rotational motion is also subject to such "turning on," but at a lower temperature.

Figure 20-7 is of help in seeing this turning on of rotational motion and oscillatory motion. The ratio C_V/R for diatomic hydrogen gas (H_2) is plotted there against temperature, with the temperature scale logarithmic to cover several orders of magnitude. Below about 80 K, we find that $C_V/R = 1.5$. This result implies that only the three translational degrees of freedom of hydrogen are involved in the specific heat.

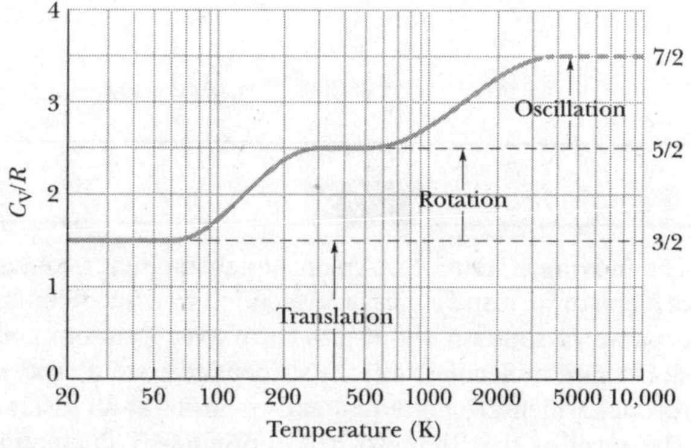

FIG. 20-7 C_V/R versus temperature for (diatomic) hydrogen gas. Because rotational and oscillatory motions begin at certain energies, only translation is possible at very low temperatures. As the temperature increases, rotational motion can begin. At still higher temperatures, oscillatory motion can begin.

As the temperature increases, the value of C_V/R gradually increases to 2.5, implying that two additional degrees of freedom have become involved. Quantum theory shows that these two degrees of freedom are associated with the rotational motion of the hydrogen molecules and that this motion requires a certain minimum amount of energy. At very low temperatures (below 80 K), the molecules do not have enough energy to rotate. As the temperature increases from 80 K, first a few molecules and then more and more obtain enough energy to rotate, and C_V/R increases, until all of them are rotating and $C_V/R = 2.5$.

Similarly, quantum theory shows that oscillatory motion of the molecules requires a certain (higher) minimum amount of energy. This minimum amount is not met until the molecules reach a temperature of about 1000 K, as shown in Fig. 20-7. As the temperature increases beyond 1000 K, more molecules have enough energy to oscillate and C_V/R increases, until all of them are oscillating and $C_V/R = 3.5$. (In Fig. 20-7, the plotted curve stops at 3200 K because there the atoms of a hydrogen molecule oscillate so much that they overwhelm their bond, and the molecule then *dissociates* into two separate atoms.)

Sample Problem 20-8 Build your skill

Five molecules have speeds of 12, 16, 32, 40, and 48 m/s. Find (a) the average speed $\vec{v}_{rms}$, and (b) the root-mean-square speed v_{rms}, for these molecules. (c) Show that for any distribution of speeds, $v_{rms} \geq \vec{v}$.

Solution: (a) $\vec{v} = \dfrac{12+16+32+40+48}{5}$

$= 29.6$ m/s (Answer)

(b) $v_{rms} = \left[\dfrac{12^2 + 16^2 + 32^2 + 40^2 + 48^2}{5}\right]^{1/2}$

$= 32.6$ m/s (Answer)

(c) Let v_i, for $i = 1 \ldots, N$, represent the various speeds. Then

$$v_{avg} = \frac{1}{N}\sum_{i=1}^{N} v_i \text{ and } v_{rms}^2 = \frac{1}{N}\sum_{i=1}^{N} v_i^2$$

Let's consider a quantity A

$$A = \frac{1}{N}\sum_{i=1}^{N} (v_i - v_{avg})^2$$

(which is the average of the squares of the deviations of the individual speeds from the average speed). *This quantity can never be negative.* By squaring and opening the bracket, and noting

$$(v_1 - v_{avg})^2 = v_i^2 - 2v_{avg}v_i + v_{avg}^2$$

we have

$$A = \frac{1}{N}\sum_{i=1}^{N} v_i^2 - \frac{2\bar{v}}{N}\sum_{i=1}^{N} v_i + \frac{1}{N}(Nv_{avg}^2)$$

or $$A = v^2_{rms} - 2v^2_{avg} + v^2_{avg}$$

$$= v^2_{rms} - v^2_{avg}$$

This implies that

$$v^2_{rms} - v^2_{avg} \geq 0$$

Thus $v_{rms} \geq v_{avg}$

When all the v_i are equal then $v_{rms} \geq v_{avg}$.

Sample Problem 20-9

The moving system of d'Arsonval galvanometer consists of a coil of wire and a mirror suspended by a fine fiber and capable of rotation about a vertical axis. Random collisions of air molecules with the suspended system produce torques which are not equal and opposite at all instants. The result is that the mirror is continuously fluctuating, see Fig. 20-8. If the root-mean-square of maximum angular displacement of the system, $\theta_{rms} = 2 \times 10^{-4}$ rad and the torque constant of a fine quartz fiber is $K = 1 \times 10^{-13}$ N m/rad, find the temperature of the air.

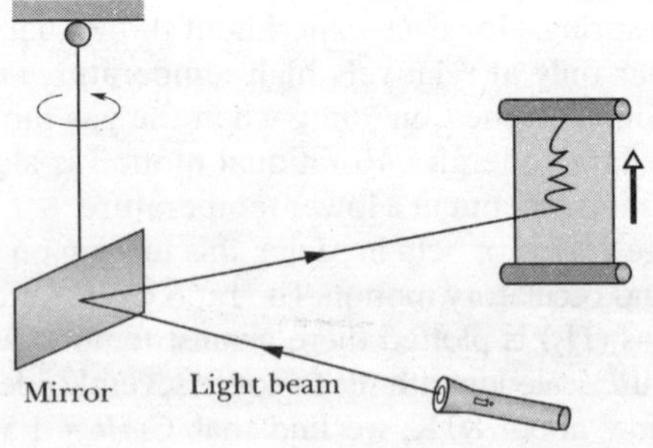

FIG. 20-8 d'Arsonval galvanometer's internal arrangement.

Conceptualize: Imagine that lots of small balls are undergoing random collisions with the mirror. These collisions will make the mirror undergo to and fro angular oscillations.

Classify: Let us assume that we have a large number of such fiber-mirror systems in air at temperature T. The total energy that a sytem possesses at maximum displacement is $1/2\ K\theta_m^2$.

We can say that the total energy that the system will posses on the average is going to be equal to the average energy being supplied by the colliding molecules.

Compute: Since we have only one fiber-mirror system, we simulate the average over a large number of them at one instant of time, by the average for one of them over many instants of time. We have a steady-state system and the motions involved are due to random collisions with air molecules, the averages should be the same. Thus if we add the random energies possessed by individual mirror systems and take an average, we will get energy as, $1/2\ K\theta_{\text{rms}}^2$. Also the momentum associated with only the normal to the mirror is being supplied to the mirror system. The energy associated with this direction is $1/2\ kT$, as we know from the law of equipartition of energy. Then, from the information given,

$$1/2\ K\theta_{\text{rms}}^2 = 1/2\ kT$$

$$T = \frac{K\theta_{\text{rms}}^2}{k} = \frac{(1 \times 10^{-13})(2 \times 10^{-4})^2}{1.38 \times 10^{-23}}$$

$$= 290\ \text{K} = 17°\text{C}$$

Conclude: In this problem we have equated energy associated with only one degree of freedom, not the total energy with the energy associated with the oscillations of the mirrors.

Variation of Atmospheric Pressure with Height

Figure 20-9 shows a thin slab in air at an altitude z. For equilibrium of the slab,

$$[p(z) - p(z + \Delta z)]\, A = \rho g A\, \Delta z$$

or

$$\frac{dp}{dz} = -\rho g$$

From the ideal gas law,

$$PV = RT$$

$$P\frac{M}{\rho} = RT$$

Thus,

$$\rho = \frac{M}{RT} P$$

where M is the average molecular mass of air and P is its density. Thus

$$\frac{dp}{dz} = -\frac{M}{RT} Pg$$

If we assume that the temperature does not vary with altitude,

$$\int_{p_0}^{p} \frac{dp}{p} = -\frac{Mg}{RT}\int_0^z dz$$

and $P = P_0 e^{-(mg/RT)z}$

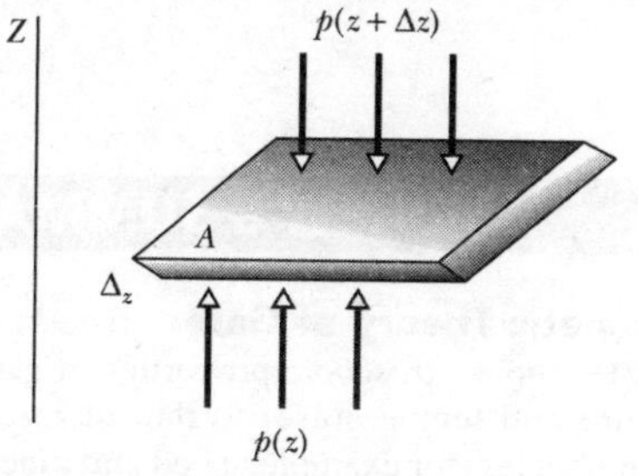

FIG. 20-9 A small slice of atmospheric air is being supported by pressure forces acting on it.

Sample Problem 20-10 Build your skill

(a) What are the average translation kinetic energies K_{avg} of the oxygen molecules and nitrogen molecules in the air that you breathe? Assume that the air is an ideal gas at a temperature of 300 K, which is the traditional value taken for room temperature.

Solution: The key idea here is that, for an ideal gas, K_{avg} depends only on the temperature and not on the type of molecule. From Eq. 20-16, the value of K_{avg} for both oxygen and nitrogen molecules is

$$K_{\text{avg}} = \frac{3}{2}kT = \left(\frac{3}{2}\right)(1.38 \times 10^{-23}\ \text{J/K})\ (300\ \text{K})$$

$$= 6.21 \times 10^{-21}\ \text{J} \qquad \text{(Answer)}$$

(b) The mass of an oxygen molecule differs from that of a nitrogen molecule. Do the oxygen molecules and the nitrogen molecules in air have the same rms speed v_{rms}?

Solution: The key idea here is that v_{rms} is related to K_{avg} by equation.

$$K_{avg} = \frac{1}{2} m v_{rms}^2$$

Although the two types of molecules have the same K_{avg}, they have different masses m and thus their rms speeds must differ.

To find their rms speeds, we solve Eq. 20-15 for v_{rms} and then substitute for molecular mass m with equation $M = mN_A$, because molar masses M can be found in Appendix F. We obtain

$$v_{rms} = \sqrt{\frac{2K_{avg}N_A}{M}} \qquad \text{(i)}$$

In the air that we breathe, oxygen and nitrogen are diatomic molecules (O_2 and N_2) – each molecule consists of two atoms. The molar mass M_{O_2} of diatomic oxygen is 2(15.9994 g/mol) ≈ 0.0320 kg/mol and the molar mass M_{N_2} of diatomic nitrogen is 2(14.0067 g/mol) ≈ 0.0280 kg/mol.

Now we can substitute known data into Eq. (i). For oxygen, we find

$$v_{rms} = \sqrt{\frac{2(6.21 \times 10^{-21}\text{J})(6.02 \times 10^{23}\text{mol}^{-1})}{0.0320\text{kg/mol}}}$$

$$= 483 \text{ m/s} \qquad \text{(Answer)}$$

Similarly, for nitrogen we find

$$v_{rms} = 517 \text{ m/s} \qquad \text{(Answer)}$$

The nitrogen molecules, with their smaller mass (and the same average kinetic energy), have the greater rms speed.

REVIEW & SUMMARY

Kinetic Theory of Gases The *kinetic theory of gases* relates the *macroscopic* properties of gases (for example, pressure and temperature) to the *microscopic* properties of gas molecules (for example, speed and kinetic energy).

Avogadro's Number One mole of a substance contains N_A (*Avogadro's number*) elementary units (usually atoms or molecules), where N_A is found experimentally to be

$$N_A = 6.02 \times 10^{23} \text{ mol}^{-1} \qquad \text{(Avogadro's number)}$$

One molar mass M of any substance is the mass of one mole of the substance. It is related to the mass m of the individual molecules of the substance by

$$M = mN_A$$

The number of moles n contained in a sample of mass M_{sam}, consisting of N molecules, is given by

$$n = \frac{N}{N_A} = \frac{M_{sam}}{M} = \frac{M_{sam}}{mN_A}$$

Ideal Gas An *ideal gas* is one for which the pressure p, volume V, and temperature T are related by

$$pV = nRT \qquad \text{(ideal gas law)}$$

Here n is the number of moles of the gas present and R is a constant (8.31 J/mol · K) called the **gas constant.** The ideal gas law can also be written as

$$pV = NkT$$

where the **Boltzmann constant** k is

$$k = \frac{R}{N_A} = 1.38 \times 10^{-23} \text{ J/K}$$

Pressure, Temperature, and Molecular Speed The pressure exerted by n moles of an ideal gas, in terms of the speed of its molecules, is

$$p = \frac{nMv_{rms}^2}{3V}$$

where $v_{rms} = \sqrt{(v^2)_{avg}}$ is the **root-mean-square speed** of the molecules of the gas. With Eq. 20-5 this gives

$$v_{rms} = \sqrt{\frac{3RT}{M}}$$

Temperature and Kinetic Energy The average translational kinetic energy K_{avg} per molecule of an ideal gas is

$$K_{avg} = \tfrac{3}{2}kT$$

Maxwell Speed Distribution The *Maxwell speed distribution* $P(v)$ is a function such that $P(v)\,dv$ gives the *fraction* of molecules with speeds in the interval dv at speed v:

$$P(v) = 4\pi\left(\frac{M}{2\pi RT}\right)^{3/2} v^2 e^{-Mv^2/2RT}$$

Three measures of the distribution of speeds among the molecules of a gas are

$$v_{avg} = \sqrt{\frac{8RT}{\pi M}} \qquad \text{(average speed)}$$

$$v_P = \sqrt{\frac{2RT}{M}} \qquad \text{(most probable speed)}$$

and the rms speed defined in the above equation for v_{rms}.

Degrees of Freedom and C_V We find C_V by using the *equipartition of energy* theorem, which states that every *degree of freedom* of a molecule (that is, every independent way it can store energy) has associated with it—on average—an energy $\frac{1}{2}kT$ per molecule ($= \frac{1}{2}RT$ per mole). If f is the number of degrees of freedom, then $E_{int} = (f/2)nRT$ and

$$C_V = \left(\frac{f}{2}\right)R = 4.16f \text{ J/mol·K}$$

For monatomic gases $f = 3$ (three translational degrees); for diatomic gases $f = 5$ (three translational and two rotational degrees).

QUESTIONS

1 An ideal diatomic gas, with molecular rotation but not oscillation, loses energy as heat Q. Is the resulting decrease in the internal energy of the gas greater if the loss occurs in a constant-volume process or in a constant-pressure process?

PROBLEMS

Avogadro's Number

1 Find the mass in kilograms of 7.50×10^{24} atoms of arsenic, which has a molar mass of 74.9 g/mol.

Ideal Gases

2 A quantity of ideal gas at 10.0°C and 100 kPa occupies a volume of 2.50 m^3. (a) How many moles of the gas are present? (b) If the pressure is now raised to 300 kPa and the temperature is raised to 30.0°C, how much volume does the gas occupy? Assume no leaks.

3 Oxygen gas having a volume of 1000 cm^3 at 40.0°C and 1.01×10^5 Pa expands until its volume is 1500 cm^3 and its pressure is 1.06×10^5 Pa. Find (a) the number of moles of oxygen present and (b) the final temperature of the sample.

4 A container encloses 2 mol of an ideal gas that has molar mass M_1 and 0.5 mol of a second ideal gas that has molar mass $M_2 = 3M_1$. What fraction of the total pressure on the container wall is attributable to the second gas? (The kinetic theory explanation of pressure leads to the experimentally discovered law of partial pressures for a mixture of gases that do not react chemically: *The total pressure exerted by the mixture is equal to the sum of the pressures that the several gases would exert separately if each were to occupy the vessel alone.*)

5 *Water bottle in a hot car.* In the American Southwest, the temperature in a closed car parked in sunlight during the summer can be high enough to burn flesh. Suppose a bottle of water at a refrigerator temperature of 5.00°C is opened, then closed, and then left in a closed car with an internal temperature of 75.0°C. Neglecting the thermal expansion of the water and the bottle, find the pressure in the air pocket trapped in the bottle. (The pressure can be enough to push the bottle cap past the threads that are intended to keep the bottle closed.)

6 Suppose 0.825 mol of an ideal gas undergoes an isothermal expansion as energy is added to it as heat Q. If Fig. 20-10 shows the final volume V_f versus Q, what is the gas temperature? The scale of the vertical axis is set by $V_{fs} = 0.30$ m^3, and the scale of the horizontal axis is set by $Q_s = 1200$ J.

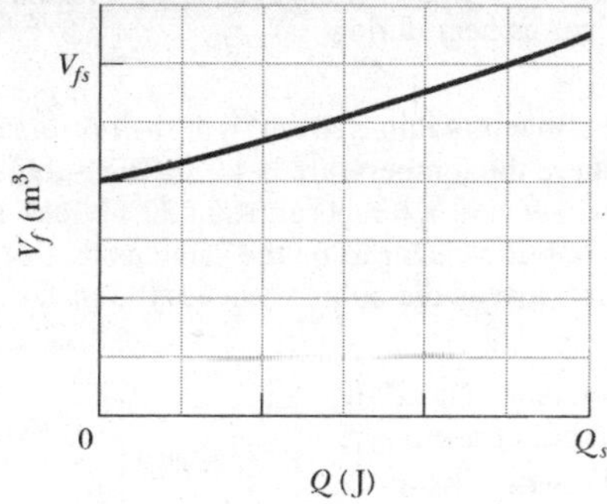

FIG. 20-10 Problem 6.

7 In the temperature range 310 K to 330 K, the pressure p of a certain nonideal gas is related to volume V and temperature T by

$$p = (24.9 \text{ J/K})\frac{T}{V} - (0.00662 \text{ J/K}^2)\frac{T^2}{V}$$

How much work is done by the gas if its temperature is raised from 315 K to 325 K while the pressure is held constant?

8 Air that initially occupies 0.140 m^3 at a gauge pressure of 103.0 kPa is expanded isothermally to a pressure of 101.3 kPa and then cooled at constant pressure until it reaches its initial volume. Compute the work done by the air. (Gauge pressure is the difference between the actual pressure and atmospheric pressure.)

9 *Submarine rescue.* When the U. S. submarine *Squalus* became disabled at a depth of 80 m, a cylindrical chamber was lowered from a ship to rescue the crew. The chamber had a radius of 1.00 m and a height of 4.00 m, was open at the bottom, and held two rescuers. It slid along a guide cable that a diver had attached to a hatch on the submarine. Once the chamber reached the hatch and clamped to the hull, the crew could escape into the chamber. During the descent, air was released from tanks to prevent water from flooding the chamber. Assume that the interior air pressure matched the water pressure at depth h as given by $p_0 + \rho g h$, where $p_0 = 1.000$ atm is the surface pressure and $\rho = 1024$ kg/m^3 is the density of seawater. Assume a surface temperature of 20.0°C and a submerged water temperature of −30.0°C. (a) What is the air volume in the chamber at the surface? (b) If air had not been released from the tanks, what would have been the air volume in the chamber at depth $h = 80.0$ m? (c) How many moles of air were needed to be released to maintain the original air volume in the chamber?

10 A sample of an ideal gas is taken through the cyclic process *abca* shown in Fig. 20-11. The scale of the vertical axis is set by $p_b = 7.5$ kPa and $p_{ac} = 2.5$ kPa. At point a, $T = 200$ K. (a) How many moles of gas are in the sample? What are (b) the temperature of the gas at point b, (c) the temperature of the gas at point c, and (d) the net energy added to the gas as heat during the cycle?

FIG. 20-11 Problem 10.

11 An air bubble of volume 20 cm^3 is at the bottom of a lake 40 m deep, where the temperature is 4.0°C. The bubble rises to the surface, which is at a temperature of 20°C. Take the temperature of the bubble's air to be the same as that of the surrounding water. Just as the bubble reaches the surface, what is its volume?

12 Container A in Fig. 20-12 holds an ideal gas at a pressure of 5.0×10^5 Pa and a temperature of 300 K. It is connected by a thin tube (and a closed valve) to container B, with four times the volume of A. Container B holds the same ideal gas at a pressure of 1.0×10^5 Pa and a temperature of 400 K. The valve is opened to allow the pressures to equalize, but the temperature of each container is maintained. What then is the pressure in the two containers?

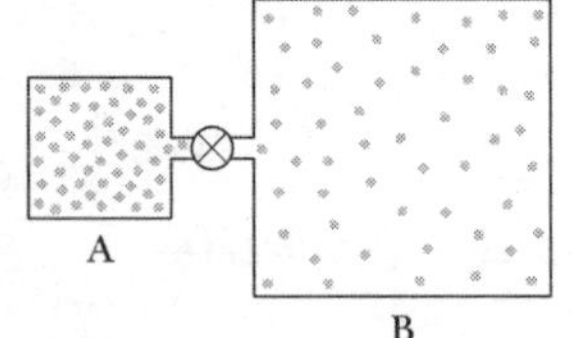

FIG. 20-12 Problem 12.

Pressure, Temperature, and RMS Speed

13 (a) Compute the rms speed of a nitrogen molecule at 20.0°C. The molar mass of nitrogen molecules (N_2) is given in Table 20-1. At what temperatures will the rms speed be (b) half that value and (c) twice that value?

14 The temperature and pressure in the Sun's atmosphere are 2.00×10^6 K and 0.0300 Pa. Calculate the rms speed of free electrons (mass 9.11×10^{-31} kg) there, assuming they are an ideal gas.

15 A beam of hydrogen molecules (H_2) is directed toward a wall, at an angle of 55° with the normal to the wall. Each molecule in the beam has a speed of 1.0 km/s and a mass of 3.3×10^{-24} g. The beam strikes the wall over an area of 2.0 cm^2, at the rate of 10^{23} molecules per second. What is the beam's pressure on the wall?

16 At 273 K and 1.00×10^{-2} atm, the density of a gas is 1.24×10^{-5} g/cm^3. (a) Find v_{rms} for the gas molecules. (b) Find the molar mass of the gas and (c) identify the gas. (*Hint:* The gas is listed in Table 20-1.)

Translational Kinetic Energy

17 What is the average translational kinetic energy of nitrogen molecules at 1600 K?

18 Water standing in the open at 32.0°C evaporates because of the escape of some of the surface molecules. The heat of vaporization (539 cal/g) is approximately equal to εn, where ε is the average energy of the escaping molecules and n is the number of molecules per gram. (a) Find ε. (b) What is the ratio of ε to the average kinetic energy of H_2O molecules, assuming the latter is related to temperature in the same way as it is for gases?

Mean Free Path

19 The mean free path of nitrogen molecules at 0.0°C and 1.0 atm is 0.80×10^{-5} cm. At this temperature and pressure there are 2.7×10^{19} molecules/cm3. What is the molecular diameter?

20 At what frequency would the wavelength of sound in air be equal to the mean free path of oxygen molecules at 1.0 atm pressure and 0.00°C? Take the diameter of an oxygen molecule to be 3.0×10^{-8} cm.

Additional Problems

21 Oxygen (O_2) gas at 273 K and 1.0 atm is confined to a cubical container 10 cm on a side. Calculate $\Delta U_g / K_{avg}$, where ΔU_g is the change in the gravitational potential energy of an oxygen molecule falling the height of the box and K_{avg} is the molecule's average translational kinetic energy.

22 The envelope and basket of a hot-air balloon have a combined weight of 2.45 kN, and the envelope has a capacity (volume) of 2.18×10^3 m^3. When it is fully inflated, what should be the temperature of the enclosed air to give the balloon a *lifting capacity* (force) of 2.67 kN (in addition to the balloon's weight)? Assume that the surrounding air, at 20.0°C, has a weight per unit volume of 11.9 N/m^3 and a molecular mass of 0.028 kg/mol, and is at a pressure of 1.0 atm.

23 During a compression at a constant pressure of 250 Pa, the volume of an ideal gas decreases from 0.80 m^3 to 0.20 m^3. The initial temperature is 360 K, and the gas loses 210 J as heat. What are (a) the change in the internal energy of the gas and (b) the final temperature of the gas?

24 At what frequency do molecules (diameter 290 pm) collide in (an ideal) oxygen gas (O_2) at temperature 400 K and pressure 2.00 atm?

25 A steel tank contains 300 g of ammonia gas (NH_3) at a pressure of 1.35×10^6 Pa and a temperature of 77°C. (a) What is the volume of the tank in liters? (b) Later the temperature is 22°C and the pressure is 8.7×10^5 Pa. How many grams of gas have leaked out of the tank?

26 At what temperature do atoms of helium gas have the same rms speed as molecules of hydrogen gas at 20.0°C? (The molar masses are given in Table 20-1.)

27 An ideal gas initially at 300 K is compressed at a constant pressure of 25 N/m^2 from a volume of 3.0 m^3 to a volume of 1.8 m^3. In the process, 75 J is lost by the gas as heat. What are (a) the change in internal energy of the gas and (b) the final temperature of the gas?

28 A parallel beam of nitrogen molecules moving with velocity $u = 400$ m/s impinges on a wall at an angle $\theta = 30°$ to its normal. The concentration of molecules in the beam $n = 0.9.10^{19}$ cm^{-3}. Find the pressure exerted by the beam on the wall assuming the molecules to scatter in accordance with the perfectly elastic collision law.

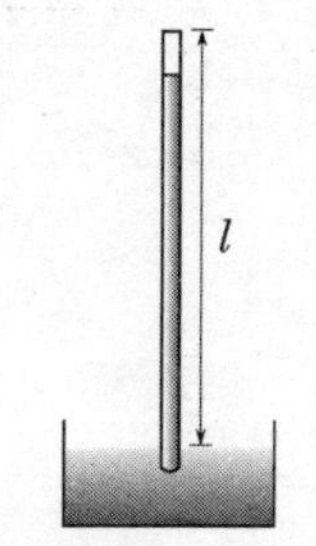

FIG. 20-13 Problem 29.

29 A barometer gives wrong readings because some air is present above the mercury column (Fig. 20-13). At a pressure of $p_{0_1} = 755$ mm Hg the barometer shows $p_1 = 748$ mm, and at $p_{0_2} = 740$ mm Hg it shows $p_2 = 736$ mm. Find the length l of the barometer tube.

30 A narrow tube open at both ends is passed through the cork of a vessel filled with water. The tube does not reach the bottom of the vessel (Mariotte's vessel shown in Fig. 20-14). Draw a diagram showing how the pressure p of the air in the vessel depends on the quantity of water Q that has flowed out.

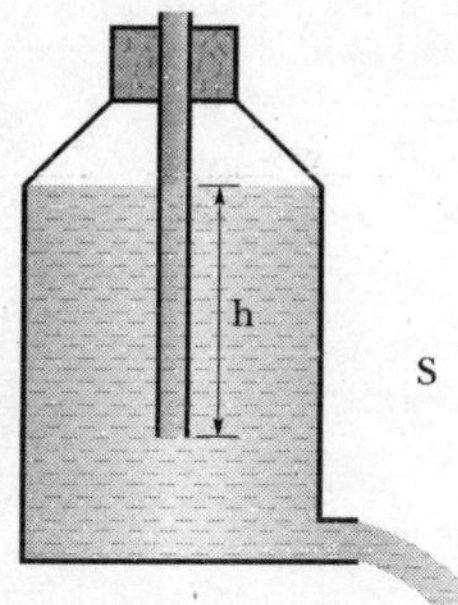

FIG. 20-14 Problem 30.

First Law of Thermodynamics

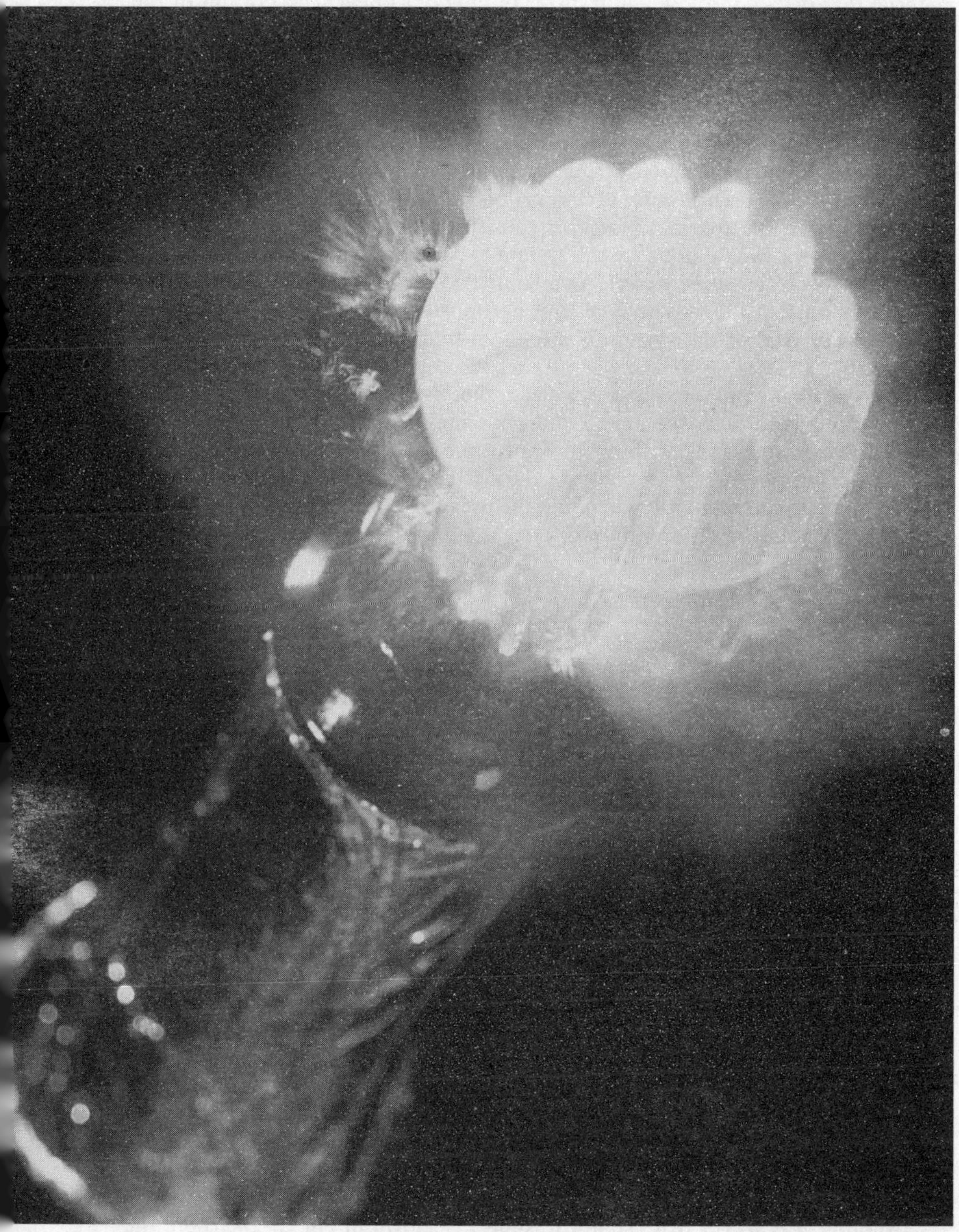

Tom Branch/Photo Researchers

When a container of cold champagne, soda pop, or any other carbonated drink is opened, a slight fog forms around the opening and some of the liquid sprays outward. In the photograph, the fog is the white cloud that surrounds the stopper, and the spray has formed streaks within the cloud.

What causes the fog?

The answer is in this chapter.

FIG. 21-1 A gas is confined to a cylinder with a movable piston. Heat Q can be added to or withdrawn from the gas by regulating the temperature T of the adjustable thermal reservoir. Work W can be done by the gas by raising or lowering the piston.

21-1 | Work and Heat

Here we look in some detail at how energy can be transferred as heat and work between a system and its environment. Let us take as our system a gas confined to a cylinder with a movable piston, as in Fig. 21-1. The upward force on the piston due to the pressure of the confined gas is equal to the weight of lead shot loaded onto the top of the piston. The walls of the cylinder are made of insulating material that does not allow any transfer of energy as heat. The bottom of the cylinder rests on a reservoir for thermal energy, a *thermal reservoir* (perhaps a hot plate) whose temperature T you can control by turning a knob.

The system (the gas) starts from an *initial state i*, described by a pressure p_i, a volume V_i, and a temperature T_i. You want to change the system to a *final state f*, described by a pressure p_f, a volume V_f, and a temperature T_f. The procedure by which you change the system from its initial state to its final state is called a *thermodynamic process.* During such a process, energy may be transferred into the system from the thermal reservoir (positive heat) or vice versa (negative heat). Also, work can be done by the system to raise the loaded piston (positive work) or lower it (negative work). We assume that all such changes occur slowly, with the result that the system is always in (approximate) thermal equilibrium (that is, every part of the system is always in thermal equilibrium with every other part).

Suppose that you remove a few lead shot from the piston of Fig. 21-1, allowing the gas to push the piston and remaining shot upward through a differential displacement $d\vec{s}$ with an upward force $\vec{F}$. Since the displacement is tiny, we can assume that $\vec{F}$ is constant during the displacement. Then $\vec{F}$ has a magnitude that is equal to pA, where p is the pressure of the gas and A is the face area of the piston. The differential work dW done by the gas during the displacement is

$$\begin{aligned} dW &= \vec{F} \cdot d\vec{s} = (pA)(ds) = p(A\,ds) \\ &= p\,dV \end{aligned} \tag{21-1}$$

in which dV is the differential change in the volume of the gas due to the movement of the piston. When you have removed enough shot to allow the gas to change its volume from V_i to V_f, the total work done by the gas is

$$W = \int dW = \int_{V_i}^{V_f} p\,dV \tag{21-2}$$

During the change in volume, the pressure and temperature of the gas may also change. To evaluate the integral in Eq. 21-2 directly, we would need to know how pressure varies with volume for the actual process by which the system changes from state i to state f.

There are actually many ways to take the gas from state i to state f. One way is shown in Fig. 21-2a, which is a plot of the pressure of the gas versus its volume and which is called a p-V diagram. In Fig. 21-2a, the curve indicates that the pressure decreases as the volume increases. The integral in Eq. 21-2 (and thus the work W done by the gas) is represented by the shaded area under the curve between points i and f. Regardless of what exactly we do to take the gas along the curve, that work is positive, due to the fact that the gas increases its volume by forcing the piston upward.

Another way to get from state i to state f is shown in Fig. 21-2b. There the change takes place in two steps—the first from state i to state a, and the second from state a to state f.

Step ia of this process is carried out at constant pressure, which means that you leave undisturbed the lead shot that ride on top of the piston in Fig. 21-1. You cause the volume to increase (from V_i to V_f) by slowly turning up the temperature control knob, raising the temperature of the gas to some higher value T_a. (Increasing the temperature increases the force from the gas on the piston, moving it upward.) During this step, positive work is done by the expanding gas (to lift the loaded piston) and heat is absorbed by the system from the thermal reservoir (in response to the arbitrarily small temperature differences that you create as you turn up the temperature). This heat is positive because it is added to the system.

Step *af* of the process of Fig. 21-2 is carried out at constant volume, so you must wedge the piston, preventing it from moving. Then as you use the control knob to decrease the temperature, you find that the pressure drops from p_a to its final value p_f. During this step, heat is lost by the system to the thermal reservoir.

For the overall process *iaf*, the work W, which is positive and is carried out only during step *ia*, is represented by the shaded area under the curve. Energy is transferred as heat during both steps *ia* and *af*, with a net energy transfer Q.

Figure 21-2*c* shows a process in which the previous two steps are carried out in reverse order. The work W in this case is smaller than for Fig. 21-2*b*, as is the net heat absorbed. Figure 21-2*d* suggests that you can make the work done by the gas as small as you want (by following a path like *icdf*) or as large as you want (by following a path like *ighf*).

To sum up: A system can be taken from a given initial state to a given final state by an infinite number of processes. Heat may or may not be involved, and in general, the work W and the heat Q will have different values for different processes. We say that heat and work are *path-dependent* quantities.

Figure 21-2*e* shows an example in which negative work is done by a system as some external force compresses the system, reducing its volume. The absolute value of the work done is still equal to the area beneath the curve, but because the gas is *compressed,* the work done by the gas is negative.

Figure 21-2*f* shows a *thermodynamic cycle* in which the system is taken from some initial state i to some other state f and then back to i. The net work done by the system during the cycle is the sum of the *positive* work done during the expansion and the *negative* work done during the compression. In Fig. 21-2*f*, the net work is positive because the area under the expansion curve (i to f) is greater than the area under the compression curve (f to i).

CHECKPOINT 1 The p-V diagram here shows six curved paths (connected by vertical paths) that can be followed by a gas. Which two of the curved paths should be part of a closed cycle (those curved paths plus connecting vertical paths) if the net work done by the gas during the cycle is to be at its maximum positive value?

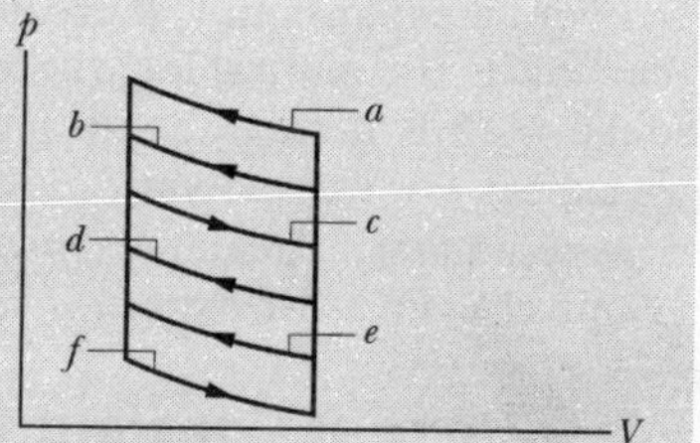

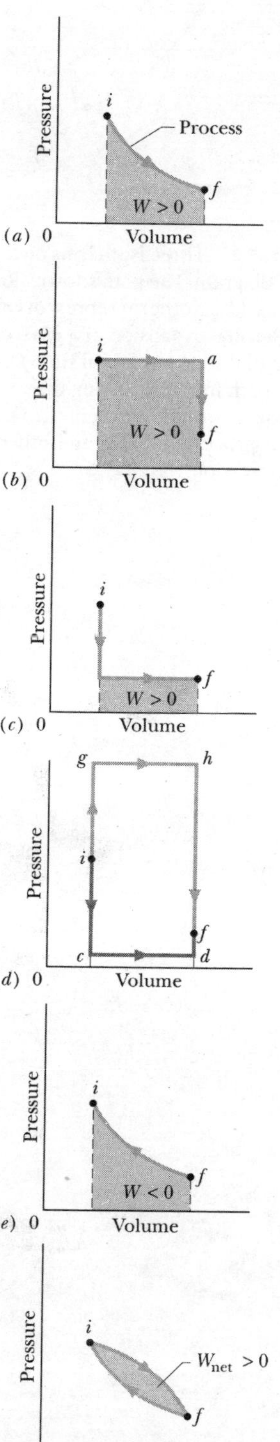

FIG. 21-2 (a) The shaded area represents the work W done by a system as it goes from an initial state i to a final state f. Work W is positive because the system's volume increases. (b) W is still positive, but now greater. (c) W is still positive, but now smaller. (d) W can be even smaller (path *icdf*) or larger (path *ighf*). (e) Here the system goes from state f to state i as the gas is compressed to less volume by an external force. The work W done *by* the system is now negative. (f) The net work W_{net} done by the system during a complete cycle is represented by the shaded area.

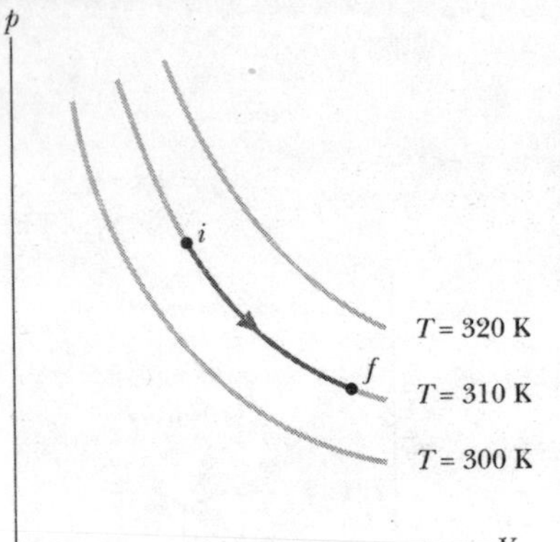

FIG. 21-3 Three isotherms on a p-V diagram. The path shown along the middle isotherm represents an isothermal expansion of a gas from an initial state i to a final state f. The path from f to i along the isotherm would represent the reverse process—that is, an isothermal compression.

Work Done by an Ideal Gas at Constant Temperature

Suppose we put an ideal gas in a piston–cylinder arrangement. Suppose also that we allow the gas to expand from an initial volume V_i to a final volume V_f while we keep the temperature T of the gas constant. Such a process, at *constant temperature,* is called an **isothermal expansion** (and the reverse is called an **isothermal compression**).

On a p-V diagram, an *isotherm* is a curve that connects points that have the same temperature. Thus, it is a graph of pressure versus volume for a gas whose temperature T is held constant. For n moles of an ideal gas, it is a graph of the equation

$$p = nRT\frac{1}{V} = (\text{a constant})\frac{1}{V} \qquad (21\text{-}3)$$

Figure 21-3 shows three isotherms, each corresponding to a different (constant) value of T. (Note that the values of T for the isotherms increase upward to the right.) Superimposed on the middle isotherm is the path followed by a gas during an isothermal expansion from state i to state f at a constant temperature of 310 K.

To find the work done by an ideal gas during an isothermal expansion, we start with,

$$W = \int_{V_i}^{V_f} p\, dV \qquad (21\text{-}4)$$

This is a general expression for the work done during any change in volume of any gas. For an ideal gas, we can use Eq. $pV = nRT$ to substitute for p, obtaining

$$W = \int_{V_i}^{V_f} \frac{nRT}{V}\, dV \qquad (21\text{-}5)$$

Because we are considering an isothermal expansion, T is constant, so we can move it in front of the integral sign to write

$$W = nRT\int_{V_i}^{V_f} \frac{dV}{V} = nRT\Big[\ln V\Big]_{V_i}^{V_f} \qquad (21\text{-}6)$$

By evaluating the expression in brackets at the limits and then using the relationship $\ln a = \ln b = \ln(a/b)$, we find that

$$W = nRT\ln\frac{V_f}{V_i} \quad \text{(ideal gas, isothermal process)} \qquad (21\text{-}7)$$

Recall that the symbol ln specifies a *natural* logarithm, which has base e.

For an expansion, V_f is greater than V_i, so the ratio V_f/V_i in Eq. 21-7 is greater than unity. The natural logarithm of a quantity greater than unity is positive, and so the work W done by an ideal gas during an isothermal expansion is positive, as we expect. For a compression, V_f is less than V_i, so the ratio of volumes in Eq. 21-7 is less than unity. The natural logarithm in that equation—hence the work W—is negative, again as we expect.

Work Done at Constant Volume and at Constant Pressure

Equation 21-7 does not give the work W done by an ideal gas during *every* thermodynamic process. Instead, it gives the work only for a process in which the temperature is held constant. If the temperature varies, then the symbol T in Eq. 21-5 cannot be moved in front of the integral symbol as in Eq. 21-6, and thus we do not end up with Eq. 21-7.

However, we can always go back to Eq. 21-4 to find the work W done by an ideal gas (or any other gas) during any process, such as a constant-volume process and a constant-pressure process. If the volume of the gas is constant, then Eq. 21-4 yields

$$W = 0 \quad \text{(constant-volume process)} \tag{21-8}$$

If, instead, the volume changes while the pressure p of the gas is held constant, then Eq. 21-4 becomes

$$W = p(V_f - V_i) = p\,\Delta V \quad \text{(constant-pressure process)} \tag{21-9}$$

CHECKPOINT 2 An ideal gas has an initial pressure of 3 pressure units and an initial volume of 4 volume units. The table gives the final pressure and volume of the gas (in those same units) in five processes. Which processes start and end on the same isotherm?

	a	b	c	d	e
p	12	6	5	4	1
V	1	2	7	3	12

Sample Problem 21-1

A cylinder contains 12 L of oxygen at 20°C and 15 atm. The temperature is raised to 35°C, and the volume is reduced to 8.5 L. What is the final pressure of the gas in atmospheres? Assume that the gas is ideal.

Conceptualize/Classify: Because the gas is ideal, its pressure, volume, temperature, and number of moles are related by the ideal gas law, both in the initial state i and in the final state f (after the changes).

Compute: We can write

$$p_iV_i = nRT_i \quad \text{and} \quad p_fV_f = nRT_f$$

Dividing the second equation by the first equation and solving for p_f yields

$$p_f = \frac{p_iT_fV_i}{T_iV_f} \tag{21-10}$$

Note here that if we converted the given initial and final volumes from liters to the proper units of cubic meters, the multiplying conversion factors would cancel out of Eq. 21-10. The same would be true for conversion factors that convert the pressures from atmospheres to the proper pascals. However, to convert the given temperatures to kelvins requires the addition of an amount that would not cancel and thus must be included. Hence, we must write

$$T_i = (273 + 20)\text{ K} = 293\text{ K}$$

and

$$T_f = (273 + 35)\text{ K} = 308\text{ K}$$

Inserting the given data into Eq. 21-10 then yields

$$p_f = \frac{(15\text{ atm})(308\text{ K})(12\text{ L})}{(293\text{ K})(8.5\text{ L})} = 22\text{ atm} \quad \text{(Answer)}$$

Sample Problem 21-2

One mole of oxygen (assume it to be an ideal gas) expands at a constant temperature T of 310 K from an initial volume V_i of 12 L to a final volume V_f of 19 L. How much work is done by the gas during the expansion?

Conceptualize/Classify: Generally we find the work by integrating the gas pressure with respect to the gas volume, using Eq. 21-4. However, because the gas here is ideal and the expansion is isothermal, that integration leads to Eq. 21-7.

Compute: Therefore, we can write

$$W = nRT \ln \frac{V_f}{V_i}$$

$$= (1\text{ mol})(8.31\text{ J/mol}\cdot\text{K})(310\text{ K}) \ln \frac{19\text{ L}}{12\text{ L}}$$

$$= 1180\text{ J} \quad \text{(Answer)}$$

The expansion is graphed in the p-V diagram of Fig. 21-4. The work done by the gas during the expansion is represented by the area beneath the curve if.

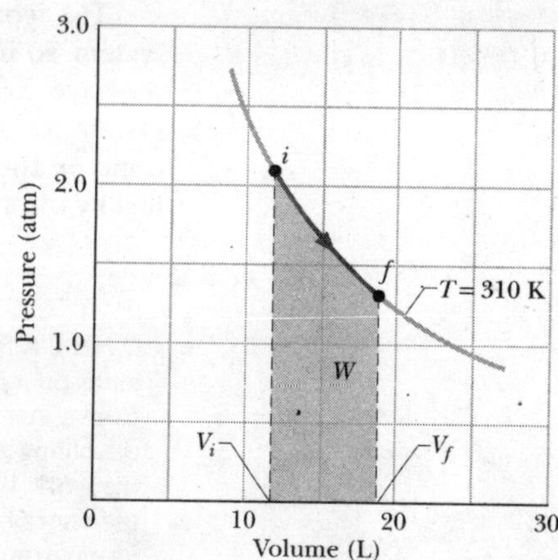

FIG. 21-4 The shaded area represents the work done by 1 mol of oxygen in expanding from V_i to V_f at a constant temperature T of 310 K.

You can show that if the expansion is now reversed, with the gas undergoing an isothermal compression from 19 L to 12 L, the work done by the gas will be −1180 J.

Conclude: Thus, an external force would have to do 1180 J of work on the gas to compress it.

21-2 | The First Law of Thermodynamics

You have just seen that when a system changes from a given initial state to a given final state, both the work W and the heat Q depend on the nature of the process. Experimentally, however, we find a surprising thing. *The quantity $Q - W$ is the same for all processes.* It depends only on the initial and final states and does not depend at all on how the system gets from one to the other. All other combinations of Q and W, including Q alone, W alone, $Q + W$, and $Q - 2W$, are *path dependent;* only the quantity $Q - W$ is not.

The quantity $Q - W$ must represent a change in some intrinsic property of the system. We call this property the *internal energy* E_{int} and we write

$$\Delta E_{int} = E_{int,f} - E_{int,i} = Q - W \quad \text{(first law)} \tag{21-11}$$

Equation 21-11 is the **first law of thermodynamics.** If the thermodynamic system undergoes only a differential change, we can write the first law as[1]

$$dE_{int} = dQ - dW \quad \text{(first law)} \tag{21-12}$$

The internal energy E_{int} of a system tends to increase if energy is added as heat Q and tends to decrease if energy is lost as work W done by the system.

We have already discussed the principle of energy conservation as it applies to isolated systems—that is, to systems in which no energy enters or leaves the system. The first law of thermodynamics is an extension of that principle to systems that are *not* isolated. In such cases, energy may be transferred into or out of the system as either work W or heat Q. In our statement of the first law of thermodynamics above, we assume that there are no changes in the kinetic energy or the potential energy of the system as a whole; that is, $\Delta K = \Delta U = 0$.

Before this chapter, the term *work* and the symbol W always meant the work done *on* a system. However, we focus on the work done *by* a system, such as the gas in Fig. 21-1.

The work done *on* a system is always the negative of the work done *by* the system, so if we rewrite Eq. 21-11 in terms of the work W_{on} done *on* the system, we have $\Delta E_{int} = Q + W_{on}$. This tells us the following: The internal energy of a system tends to increase if heat is absorbed by the system or if positive work is done *on* the system. Conversely, the internal energy tends to decrease if heat is lost by the system or if negative work is done *on* the system.

CHECKPOINT 3 The figure here shows four paths on a p-V diagram along which a gas can be taken from state i to state f. Rank the paths according to (a) the change ΔE_{int} in the internal energy of the gas, (b) the work W done by the gas, and (c) the magnitude of the energy transferred as heat Q between the gas and its environment, greatest first.

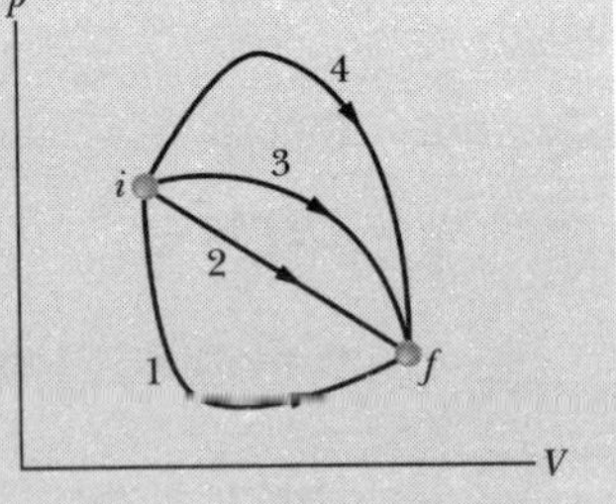

[1]Here dQ and dW, unlike dE_{int}, are not true differentials; that is, there are no such functions as $Q(p, V)$ and $W(p, V)$ that depend only on the state of the system. The quantities dQ and dW are called *inexact differentials* and are usually represented by the symbols $đQ$ and $đW$. For our purposes, we can treat them simply as infinitesimally small energy transfers.

21-3 | Some Applications of the First Law of Thermodynamics

Here we look at four different thermodynamic processes to see what consequences follow when we apply the first law of thermodynamics.

1. *Isovolumetric (Isochoric) Processes*

If the volume of a system (such as a gas) is held constant, that system can do no work. Putting $W = 0$ in the first law (Eq. 21-11) yields

$$\Delta E_{int} = Q \quad \text{(constant-volume process)} \tag{21-13}$$

Thus, if heat is absorbed by a system (that is, if Q is positive), the internal energy of the system increases. Conversely, if heat is lost during the process (that is, if Q is negative), the internal energy of the system must decrease.

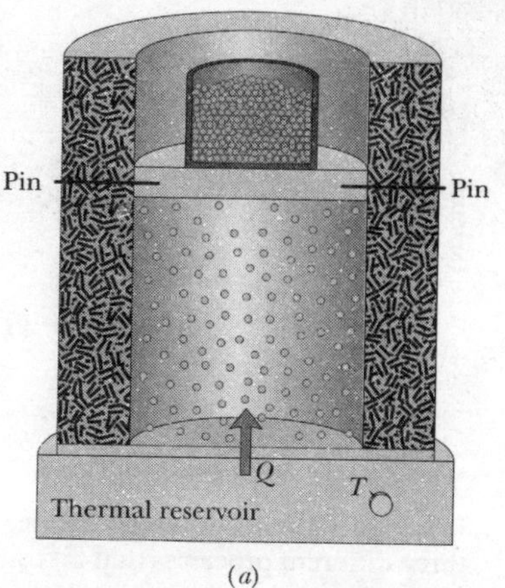

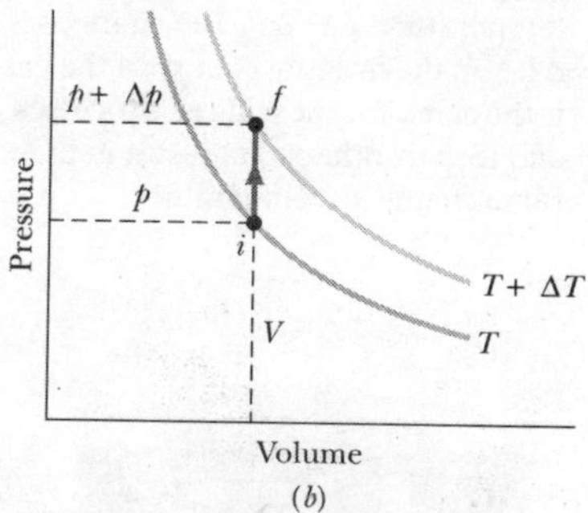

FIG. 21-5 (*a*) The temperature of an ideal gas is raised from T to $T + \Delta T$ in a constant-volume process. Heat is added, but no work is done. (*b*) The process on a *p-V* diagram.

Molar Specific Heat at Constant Volume

Figure 21-5*a* shows n moles of an ideal gas at pressure p and temperature T, confined to a cylinder of fixed volume V. This *initial state i* of the gas is marked on the *p-V* diagram of Fig. 21-5*b*. Suppose now that you add a small amount of energy to the gas as heat Q by slowly turning up the temperature of the thermal reservoir. The gas temperature rises a small amount to $T + \Delta T$, and its pressure rises to $p + \Delta p$, bringing the gas to *final state f*. In such experiments, we would find that the heat Q is related to the temperature change ΔT by

$$Q = nC_V\,\Delta T \quad \text{(constant volume)} \tag{21-14}$$

where C_V is a constant called the **molar specific heat at constant volume.** Substituting this expression for Q into the first law of thermodynamics as given by Eq. $\Delta E_{int} = Q - W$ yields

$$\Delta E_{int} = nC_V\,\Delta T - W \tag{21-15}$$

With the volume held constant, the gas cannot expand and thus cannot do any work. Therefore, $W = 0$, and Eq. 21-15 gives us

$$C_V = \frac{\Delta E_{int}}{n\,\Delta T} \tag{21-16}$$

Hence, the change in internal energy must be

$$\Delta E_{int} = \tfrac{3}{2}nR\,\Delta T \tag{21-17}$$

Substituting this result into Eq. 21-16 yields

$$C_V = \tfrac{3}{2}R = 12.5 \text{ J/mol}\cdot\text{K} \quad \text{(monatomic gas)} \tag{21-18}$$

As Table 21-1 shows, this prediction of the kinetic theory (for ideal gases) agrees very well with experiment for real monatomic gases, the case that we have assumed. The (predicted and) experimental values of C_V for *diatomic gases* (which have molecules with two atoms) and *polyatomic gases* (which have molecules with more than two atoms) are greater than those for monatomic gases.

We can now generalize Eq. $E_{int} = \frac{3}{2}nRT$ for the internal energy of any ideal gas by substituting C_V for $\frac{3}{2}R$; we get

$$E_{int} = nC_VT \quad \text{(any ideal gas)} \tag{21-19}$$

This equation applies not only to an ideal monatomic gas but also to diatomic and polyatomic ideal gases, provided the appropriate value of C_V is used. Just as with Eq. $E_{int} = \frac{3}{2}nRT$, we see that the internal energy of a gas depends on the temperature of the gas but not on its pressure or density.

TABLE 21-1

Molar Specific Heats at Constant Volume

Molecule	Example		C_V (J/mol·K)
Monatomic	Ideal		$\frac{3}{2}R = 12.5$
	Real	He	12.5
		Ar	12.6
Diatomic	Ideal		$\frac{5}{2}R = 20.8$
	Real	N_2	20.7
		O_2	20.8
Polyatomic	Ideal		$3R = 24.9$
	Real	NH_4	29.0
		CO_2	29.7

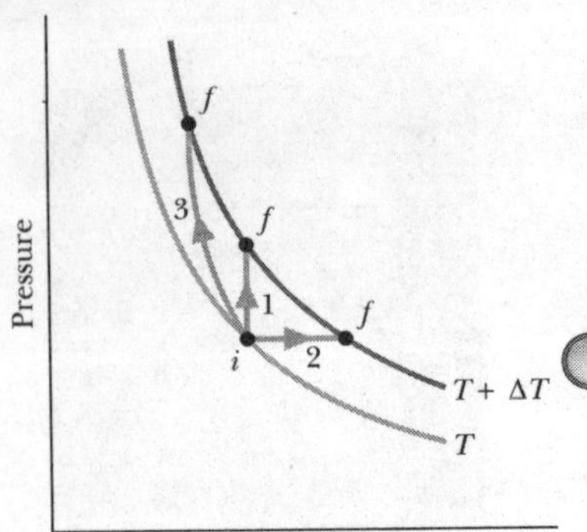

FIG. 21-6 Three paths representing three different processes that take an ideal gas from an initial state i at temperature T to some final state f at temperature $T + \Delta T$. The change ΔE_{int} in the internal energy of the gas is the same for these three processes and for any others that result in the same change of temperature.

When an ideal gas that is confined to a container undergoes a temperature change ΔT, then from either Eq. 21-16 or Eq. 21-19 we can write the resulting change in its internal energy as

$$\Delta E_{int} = nC_V\Delta T \quad \text{(ideal gas, any process)} \tag{21-20}$$

This equation tells us:

A change in the internal energy E_{int} of a confined ideal gas depends on the change in the gas temperature only; it does *not* depend on what type of process produces the change in the temperature.

As examples, consider the three paths between the two isotherms in the p-V diagram of Fig. 21-6. Path 1 represents a constant-volume process. Path 2 represents a constant-pressure process (that we are about to examine). Path 3 represents a process in which no heat is exchanged with the system's environment. Although the values of heat Q and work W associated with these three paths differ, as do p_f and V_f, the values of ΔE_{int} associated with the three paths are identical and are all given by Eq. 21-20, because they all involve the same temperature change ΔT. Therefore, no matter what path is actually taken between T and $T + \Delta T$, we can *always* use path 1 and Eq. 21-20 to compute ΔE_{int} easily.

2. Isobaric Process

Molar Specific Heat at Constant Pressure

We now assume that the temperature of our ideal gas is increased by the same small amount ΔT as previously but now the necessary energy (heat Q) is added with the gas under constant pressure. An experiment for doing this is shown in Fig. 21-7*a*; the p-V diagram for the process is plotted in Fig. 21-7*b*. From such experiments we find that the heat Q is related to the temperature change ΔT by

$$Q = nC_p\Delta T \quad \text{(constant pressure)} \tag{21-21}$$

where C_p is a constant called the **molar specific heat at constant pressure.** This C_p is *greater* than the molar specific heat at constant volume C_V, because energy must now be supplied not only to raise the temperature of the gas but also for the gas to do work—that is, to lift the weighted piston of Fig. 21-7*a*.

To relate molar specific heats C_p and C_V, we start with the first law of thermodynamics:

$$\Delta E_{int} = Q - W \tag{21-22}$$

We next replace each term in Eq. 21-22. For ΔE_{int}, we substitute from Eq. 21-20. For Q, we substitute from Eq. 21-21. To replace W, we first note that since the pressure remains constant, Eq. 21-9 tells us that $W = p\,\Delta V$. Then we note that, using the ideal gas equation ($pV = nRT$), we can write

$$W = p\,\Delta V = nR\,\Delta T \tag{21-23}$$

Making these substitutions in Eq. 21-22 and then dividing through by $n\,\Delta T$, we find

$$C_V = C_p - R$$

and then

$$C_p = C_V + R \tag{21-24}$$

This prediction of kinetic theory agrees well with experiment, not only for monatomic gases but also for gases in general, as long as their density is low enough so that we may treat them as ideal.

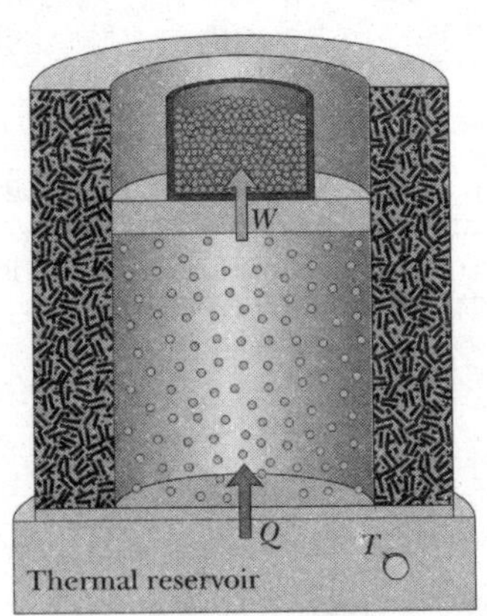

(a)

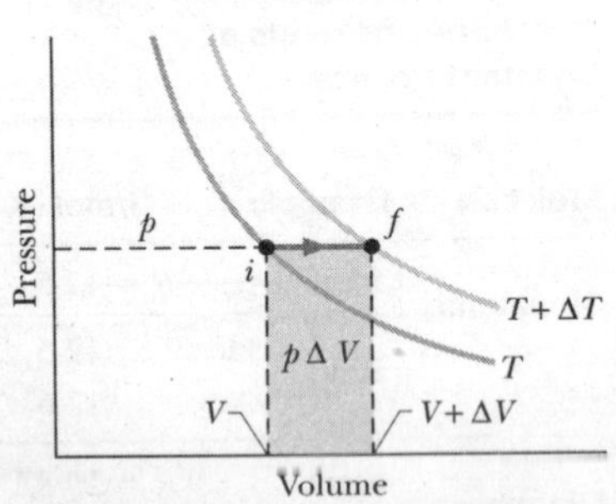

(b)

FIG. 21-7 (*a*) The temperature of an ideal gas is raised from T to $T + \Delta T$ in a constant-pressure process. Heat is added and work is done in lifting the loaded piston. (*b*) The process on a p-V diagram. The work $p\,\Delta V$ is given by the shaded area.

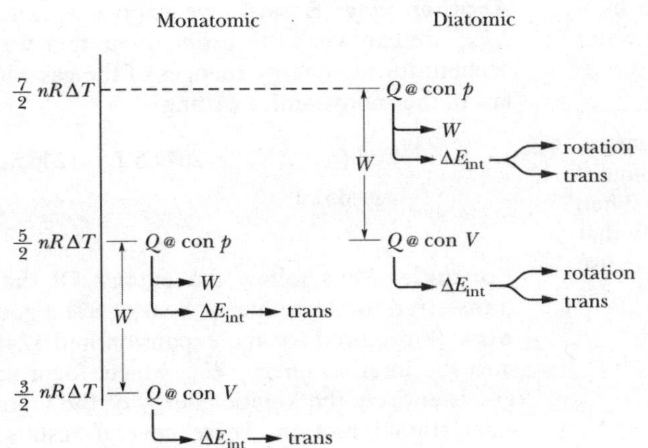

FIG. 21-8 The relative values of Q for a monatomic gas (left side) and a diatomic gas undergoing a constant-volume process (labeled "con V") and a constant-pressure process (labeled "con p"). The transfer of the energy into work W and internal energy (ΔE_{int}) is noted.

The left side of Fig. 21-8 shows the relative values of Q for a monatomic gas undergoing either a constant-volume process ($Q = \frac{3}{2}nR\,\Delta T$) or a constant-pressure process ($Q = \frac{5}{2}nR\,\Delta T$). Note that for the latter, the value of Q is higher by the amount W, the work done by the gas in the expansion. Note also that for the constant-volume process, the energy added as Q goes entirely into the change in internal energy ΔE_{int} and for the constant-pressure process, the energy added as Q goes into both ΔE_{int} and the work W.

CHECKPOINT 4 The figure here shows five paths traversed by a gas on a p-V diagram. Rank the paths according to the change in internal energy of the gas, greatest first.

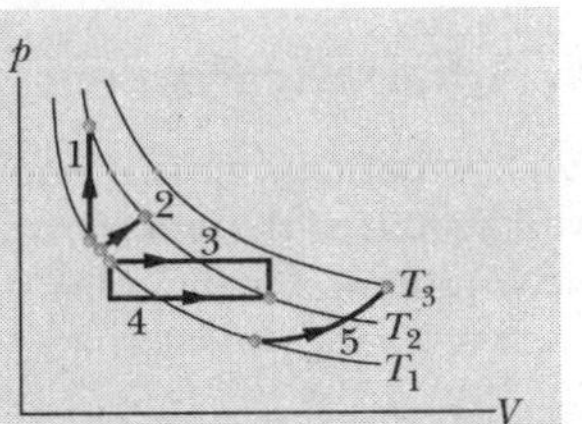

Sample Problem 21-3 Build your skill

A bubble of 5.00 mol of helium is submerged at a certain depth in liquid water when the water (and thus the helium) undergoes a temperature increase ΔT of 20.0 C° at constant pressure. As a result, the bubble expands. The helium is monatomic and ideal.

(a) How much energy is added to the helium as heat during the increase and expansion?

Conceptualize/Classify: Heat Q is related to the temperature change ΔT by a molar specific heat of the gas.

Compute: Because the pressure p is held constant during the addition of energy, we use the molar specific heat at constant pressure C_p and Eq. 21-21,

$$Q = nC_p\,\Delta T \qquad (21\text{-}25)$$

to find Q. To evaluate C_p we go to Eq. 21-24, which tells us that for any ideal gas, $C_p = C_V + R$. Then from Eq. 21-18, we know that for any *monatomic* gas (like the helium here), $C_V = \frac{3}{2}R$. Thus, Eq. 21-25 gives us

$$\begin{aligned} Q &= n(C_V + R)\,\Delta T = n(\tfrac{3}{2}R + R)\,\Delta T = n(\tfrac{5}{2}R)\,\Delta T \\ &= (5.00\ \text{mol})(2.5)(8.31\ \text{J/mol}\cdot\text{K})(20.0\ \text{C}°) \\ &= 2077.5\ \text{J} \approx 2080\ \text{J} \qquad \text{(Answer)} \end{aligned}$$

(b) What is the change ΔE_{int} in the internal energy of the helium during the temperature increase?

Conceptualize/Classify: Because the bubble expands, this is not a constant-volume process. However, the helium is nonetheless confined (to the bubble). Thus, the change ΔE_{int} is the same as *would occur* in a constant-volume process with the same temperature change ΔT.

Compute: We can now easily find the constant-volume change ΔE_{int} with Eq. 21-20:

$$\begin{aligned} \Delta E_{int} &= nC_V\,\Delta T = n(\tfrac{3}{2}R)\,\Delta T \\ &= (5.00\ \text{mol})(1.5)(8.31\ \text{J/mol}\cdot\text{K})(20.0\ \text{C}°) \\ &= 1246.5\ \text{J} \approx 1250\ \text{J} \qquad \text{(Answer)} \end{aligned}$$

(c) How much work W is done by the helium as it expands against the pressure of the surrounding water during the temperature increase?

Conceptualize/Classify: The work done by *any* gas expanding against the pressure from its environment is given by Eq. 21-4, which tells us to integrate $p\,dV$. When the pressure is constant (as here), we can simplify that to $W = p\,\Delta V$. When the gas is *ideal* (as here), we can use the ideal gas law to write $p\,\Delta V = nR\,\Delta T$.

Compute: We end up with

$$W = nR\,\Delta T = (5.00\text{ mol})(8.31\text{ J/mol}\cdot\text{K})(20.0\text{ C}^\circ) = 831\text{ J} \qquad \text{(Answer)}$$

Another way: Because we happen to know Q and ΔE_{int}, we can work this problem another way: We can account for the energy changes of the gas with the first law of thermodynamics, writing

$$W = Q - \Delta E_{int} = 2077.5\text{ J} - 1246.5\text{ J} = 831\text{ J} \qquad \text{(Answer)}$$

Conclude: Let's follow the energy. Of the 2077.5 J transferred to the helium as heat Q, 831 J goes into the work W required for the expansion and 1246.5 J goes into the internal energy E_{int}, which, for a monatomic gas, is entirely the kinetic energy of the atoms in their translational motion. These several results are suggested on the left side of Fig. 21-8.

3. Isothermal Process

The isothermal process occurs at constant temperature. Work is done at the same rate as heat is supplied, hence there is no increase of internal energy. Due to this, $\Delta U = 0$ and thus $\Delta Q = \Delta W$. We have already calculated the work done in this chapter. We have also seen that for isothermal process PV = constant. The practical way of realizing such a process is by keeping the gas in a highly conducting vessel and carrying out the process very slowly.

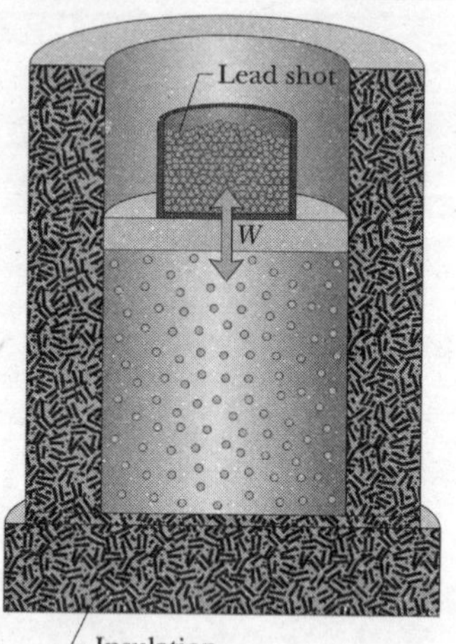

FIG. 21-9 An adiabatic expansion can be carried out by slowly removing lead shot from the top of the piston. Adding lead shot reverses the process at any stage.

4. Adiabatic Process

An adiabatic process is one that occurs so rapidly or occurs in a system that is so well insulated that *no transfer of energy as heat* occurs between the system and its environment. Putting $Q = 0$ in the first law yields

$$\Delta E_{int} = -W \qquad \text{(adiabatic process)} \qquad (21\text{-}26)$$

This tells us that if work is done *by* the system (that is, if W is positive), the internal energy of the system decreases by the amount of work. Conversely, if work is done *on* the system (that is, if W is negative), the internal energy of the system increases by that amount.

Figure 21-9 shows an idealized adiabatic process. Heat cannot enter or leave the system because of the insulation. Thus, the only way energy can be transferred between the system and its environment is by work. If we remove shot from the piston and allow the gas to expand, the work done by the system (the gas) is positive and the internal energy of the gas decreases. If, instead, we add shot and compress the gas, the work done by the system is negative and the internal energy of the gas increases.

TABLE 21-2

Degrees of Freedom for Various Molecules

		Degrees of Freedom			Predicted Molar Specific Heats	
Molecule	Example	Translational	Rotational	Total (f)	C_V	$C_p = C_V + R$
Monatomic	He	3	0	3	$\frac{3}{2}R$	$\frac{5}{2}R$
Diatomic	O_2	3	2	5	$\frac{5}{2}R$	$\frac{7}{2}R$
Polyatomic	CH_4	3	3	6	$3R$	$4R$

Sample Problem 21-4 Build your skill

We transfer 1000 J to a diatomic gas, allowing it to expand with the pressure held constant. The gas molecules rotate but do not oscillate. How much of the 1000 J goes into the increase of the gas's internal energy? Of that amount, how much goes into ΔK_{tran} (the kinetic energy of the translational motion of the molecules) and ΔK_{rot} (the kinetic energy of their rotational motion)?

Conceptualize/Classify:

1. The transfer of energy as heat Q to a gas under constant pressure is related to the resulting temperature increase ΔT via Eq. $Q = nC_p \Delta T$.
2. Because the gas is diatomic with molecules undergoing rotation but not oscillation, the molar specific heat is, from Fig. 21-8 and Table 21-2, $C_p = \frac{7}{2}R$.
3. The increase ΔE_{int} in the internal energy is the same as would occur with a constant-volume process resulting in the same ΔT. Thus, from Eq. 21-20, $\Delta E_{int} = nC_V \Delta T$. From Fig. 21-8 and Table 21-2, we see that $C_V = \frac{5}{2}R$.
4. For the same n and ΔT, ΔE_{int} is greater for a diatomic gas than a monatomic gas because additional energy is required for rotation.

Compute: Increase in E_{int}: Let's first get the temperature change ΔT due to the transfer of energy as heat. From Eq. 21-21, substituting $\frac{7}{2}R$ for C_p, we have

$$\Delta T = \frac{Q}{\frac{7}{2}nR} \qquad (21\text{-}27)$$

We next find ΔE_{int} from Eq. 21-20, substituting the molar specific heat $C_V (= \frac{5}{2}R)$ for a constant-volume process and using the same T. Because we are dealing with a diatomic gas, let's call this change $\Delta E_{int,dia}$. Equation 21-20 gives us

$$\Delta E_{int,dia} = nC_V \Delta T = n\tfrac{5}{2}R\left(\frac{Q}{\frac{7}{2}nR}\right) = \tfrac{5}{7}Q$$

$$= 0.71428Q = 714.3 \text{ J} \qquad \text{(Answer)}$$

Conclude: In words, about 71% of the energy transferred to the gas goes into the internal energy. The rest goes into the work required to increase the volume of the gas.

Increases in K: If we were to increase the temperature of a *monatomic* gas (with the same value of n) by the amount given in Eq. 21-27, the internal energy would change by a smaller amount, call it $\Delta E_{int,mon}$, because rotational motion is not involved. To calculate that smaller amount, we still use Eq. 21-20 but now we substitute the value of C_V for a monatomic gas—namely, $C_V = \frac{3}{2}R$. So,

$$\Delta E_{int,mon} = n\tfrac{3}{2}R\,\Delta T$$

Substituting for ΔT from Eq. 21-27 leads us to

$$\Delta E_{int,mon} = n\tfrac{3}{2}R\left(\frac{Q}{n\frac{7}{2}R}\right) = \tfrac{3}{7}Q$$

$$= 0.42857Q = 428.6 \text{ J}$$

Conclude: For the monatomic gas, all this energy would go into the kinetic energy of the translational motion of the atoms. The important point here is that for a diatomic gas with the same values of n and ΔT, the same amount of energy goes into the kinetic energy of the translational motion of the molecules. The rest of $\Delta E_{int,\,dia}$ (that is, the additional 285.7 J) goes into the rotational motion of the molecules. Thus, for the diatomic gas,

$$\Delta K_{trans} = 428.6 \text{ J} \quad \text{and} \quad \Delta K_{rot} = 285.7 \text{ J} \qquad \text{(Answer)}$$

The Adiabatic Expansion of an Ideal Gas

Sound waves are propagated through air and other gases as a series of compressions and expansions; these variations in the transmission medium take place so rapidly that there is no time for energy to be transferred from one part of the medium to another as heat. A process for which $Q = 0$ is an *adiabatic process.* We can ensure that $Q = 0$ either by carrying out the process very quickly (as in sound waves) or by doing it (at any rate) in a well-insulated container. Let us see what the kinetic theory has to say about adiabatic processes.

Figure 21-10*a* shows our usual insulated cylinder, now containing an ideal gas and resting on an insulating stand. By removing mass from the piston, we can allow the gas to expand adiabatically. As the volume increases, both the pressure and the temperature drop. We shall prove next that the relation between the pressure and the volume during such an adiabatic process is

$$pV^{\gamma} = \text{a constant} \qquad \text{(adiabatic process)} \qquad (21\text{-}28)$$

in which $\gamma = C_p/C_V$, the ratio of the molar specific heats for the gas. On a p-V diagram such as that in Fig. 21-10*b*, the process occurs along a line (called an

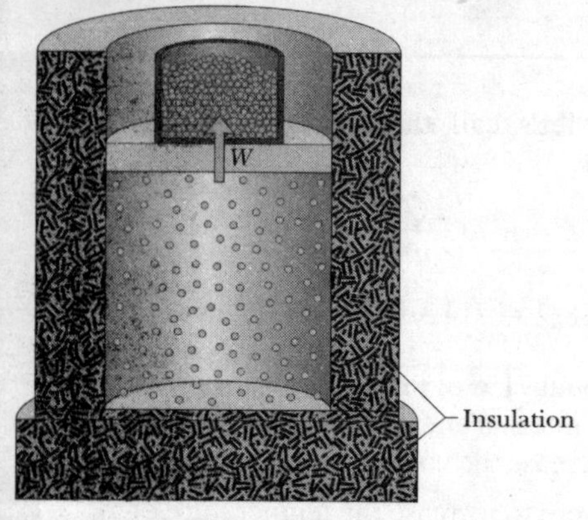

(a)

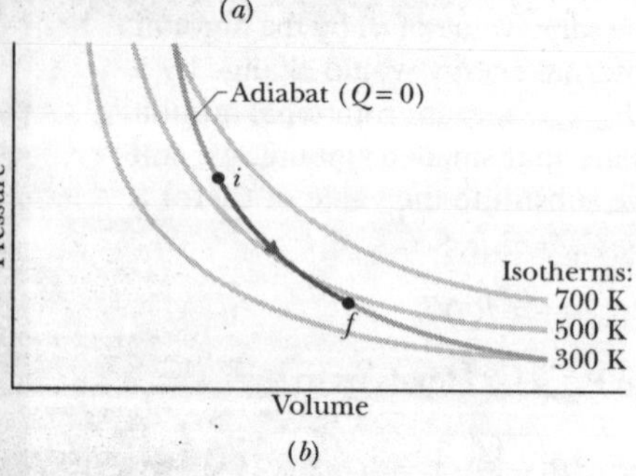

(b)

FIG. 21-10 (*a*) The volume of an ideal gas is increased by removing mass from the piston. The process is adiabatic ($Q = 0$). (*b*) The process proceeds from i to f along an adiabat on a p-V diagram.

adiabat) that has the equation $p =$ (a constant)$/V^\gamma$. Since the gas goes from an initial state i to a final state f, we can rewrite Eq. 21-28 as

$$p_i V_i^\gamma = p_f V_f^\gamma \quad \text{(adiabatic process)} \tag{21-29}$$

To write an equation for an adiabatic process in terms of T and V, we use the ideal gas equation ($pV = nRT$) to eliminate p from Eq. 21-28, finding

$$\left(\frac{nRT}{V}\right)V^\gamma = \text{a constant}$$

Because n and R are constants, we can rewrite this in the alternative form

$$TV^{\gamma-1} = \text{a constant} \quad \text{(adiabatic process)} \tag{21-30}$$

in which the constant is different from that in Eq. 19-27. When the gas goes from an initial state i to a final state f, we can rewrite Eq. 19-30 as

$$T_i V_i^{\gamma-1} = T_f V_f^{\gamma-1} \quad \text{(adiabatic process)} \tag{21-31}$$

Understanding adiabatic processes allows you to understand why popping the cork on a cold bottle of champagne (as in this chapter's opening photograph) or the tab on a cold can of soda causes a slight fog to form at the opening of the container. At the top of any unopened carbonated drink sits a gas of carbon dioxide and water vapor. Because the gas pressure is greater than atmospheric pressure, the gas expands out into the atmosphere when the container is opened. Thus, the gas volume increases, but that means the gas must do work pushing against the atmosphere. Because the expansion is rapid, it is adiabatic, and the only source of energy for the work is the internal energy of the gas. Because the internal energy decreases, the temperature of the gas also decreases, which causes the water vapor in the gas to condense into tiny drops of fog. (Note that Eq. 21-31 also tells us that the temperature must decrease during an adiabatic expansion: V_f is greater than V_i, and so T_f must be less than T_i.)

Proof of Eq. 21-27

Suppose that you remove some shot from the piston of Fig. 21-10*a*, allowing the ideal gas to push the piston and the remaining shot upward and thus to increase the volume by a differential amount dV. Since the volume change is tiny, we may assume that the pressure p of the gas on the piston is constant during the change. This assumption allows us to say that the work dW done by the gas during the volume increase is equal to $p\,dV$. From Eq. 21-12, the first law of thermodynamics can then be written as

$$dE_{\text{int}} = Q - p\,dV \tag{21-32}$$

Since the gas is thermally insulated (and thus the expansion is adiabatic), we substitute 0 for Q. Then we use Eq. 21-20 to substitute $nC_V\,dT$ for dE_{int}. With these substitutions, and after some rearranging, we have

$$nn\,dT = -\left(\frac{p}{C_V}\right)dV \tag{21-33}$$

Now from the ideal gas law ($pV = nRT$) we have

$$p\,dV + V\,dp = nR\,dT \tag{21-34}$$

Replacing R with its equal, $C_p - C_V$, in Eq. 21-34 yields

$$n\,dT = \frac{p\,dV + V\,dp}{C_p - C_V} \tag{21-35}$$

Equating Eqs. 21-33 and 21-35 and rearranging then give

$$\frac{dp}{p} + \left(\frac{C_p}{C_V}\right)\frac{dV}{V} = 0$$

Replacing the ratio of the molar specific heats with γ and integrating (see integral 5 in Appendix E) yield

$$\ln p + \gamma \ln V = \text{a constant}$$

Rewriting the left side as $\ln pV^{\gamma}$ and then taking the antilog of both sides, we find

$$pV^{\gamma} = \text{a constant} \qquad (21\text{-}36)$$

21-4 | Cyclical Processes

There are processes in which, after certain interchanges of heat and work, the system is restored to its initial state. In that case, no intrinsic property of the system—including its internal energy—can possibly change. Putting $\Delta E_{\text{int}} = 0$ in the first law yields

$$Q = W \qquad \text{(cyclical process)} \qquad (21\text{-}37)$$

Thus, the net work done during the process must exactly equal the net amount of energy transferred as heat; the store of internal energy of the system remains unchanged. Cyclical processes form a closed loop on a p-V plot, as shown in Fig. 21-2*f*.

Entropy in the Real World: Engines

A **heat engine,** or more simply, an **engine,** is a device that extracts energy from its environment in the form of heat and does useful work. At the heart of every engine is a *working substance.* In a steam engine, the working substance is water, in both its vapor and its liquid form. In an automobile engine the working substance is a gasoline–air mixture. If an engine is to do work on a sustained basis, the working substance must operate in a *cycle;* that is, the working substance must pass through a closed series of thermodynamic processes, called *strokes,* returning again and again to each state in its cycle. Let us see what the laws of thermodynamics can tell us about the operation of engines.

We have seen that we can learn much about real gases by analyzing an ideal gas, which obeys the simple law $pV = nRT$. Although an ideal gas does not exist, any real gas approaches ideal behavior if its density is low enough. Similarly, we can study real engines by analyzing the behavior of an **ideal engine.**

In an ideal engine, all processes are reversible and no wasteful energy transfers occur due to, say, friction and turbulence.

Sample Problem 21-5 Build your skill

The p – V diagram in Fig. 21-11*a* represents a series of processes, performed by an ideal gas, comprising a cyclic process of operations in which *CD* is an isothermal and *DA* is an adiabatic process. Fill in the table in Fig. 21-11*b* for this cycle, using '+' to indicate an increase in the quantity listed, '–' to indicate a decrease, and '0' to indicate no change.

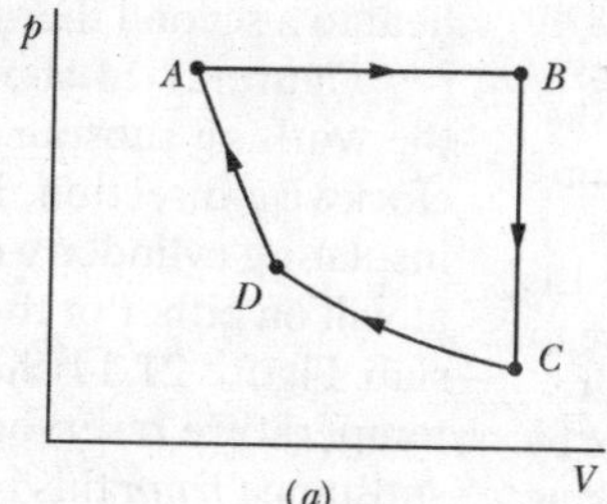

Path	ΔH	ΔW	ΔE	ΔT
AB				
BC				
CD				
DA				

(*b*)

FIG. 21-11 p-V diagram for ideal gas.

Solution:

Path *AB*: The process represents an isobaric expansion (p remains constant while V increases). Clearly the gas will do some work on the environment, so $\Delta W > 0$. In order for the pressure to remain constant with a decrease in the gas density, the temperature must increase, so $\Delta T > 0$. For an ideal gas, the energy is a function of only temperature, and E increases with T, so $\Delta E > 0$. Because $\Delta H = \Delta E + \Delta W$, we must have $\Delta H > 0$.

Path BC: The process is isovolumetric (isochoric) cooling (V remains constant while p decreases and with it T also decreases). Because the volume does not vary anywhere along the path, we have $\Delta V = 0$ and therefore $\Delta W = p\Delta V = 0$. As we already noted, $\Delta T < 0$, since that is the only way that p can decrease at constant volume. Since U is directly dependent on T, we have $\Delta E < 0$. Finally, $\Delta E + \Delta W = \Delta H < 0$.

Path CD : The process is isothermal compression, so $\Delta T = 0$. Therefore, for an ideal gas, $\Delta E = 0$. Since there is a monotonic decrease in volume ($\Delta V < 0$), so the work $\Delta W < 0$. Therefore, $\Delta E + \Delta W = \Delta H < 0$.

Path DA : The process is adiabatic compression, so that $\Delta H = 0$. There is a monotonic decrease in volume ($\Delta V < 0$), so $\Delta W < 0$. Therefore, $\Delta H - \Delta W \equiv \Delta E > 0$. The temperature of the ideal gas must increase correspondingly and so, $\Delta T > 0$. These results are summarized in Fig. 21-12.

Path	ΔH	ΔW	ΔE	ΔT
AB	+	+	+	+
BC	−	0	−	−
CD	−	−	0	0
DA	0	−	+	+

FIG. 21-12

CHECKPOINT 5 A cyclic process 1-2-3-1, performed on an ideal gas is depicted in the given V-T diagram. Show the same process on a p-V diagram and indicate the stages when the gas receives and rejects heat.

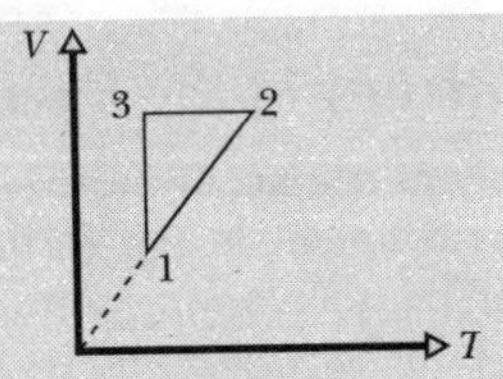

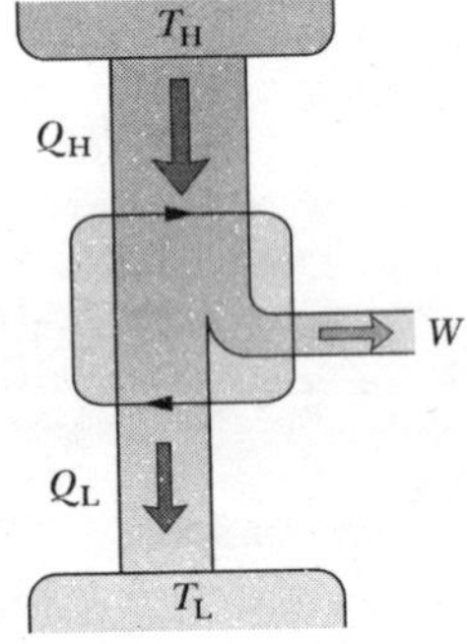

FIG. 21-13 The elements of a Carnot engine. The two black arrowheads on the central loop suggest the working substance operating in a cycle, as if on a p-V plot. Energy $|Q_H|$ is transferred as heat from the high-temperature reservoir at temperature T_H to the working substance. Energy $|Q_L|$ is transferred as heat from the working substance to the low-temperature reservoir at temperature T_L. Work W is done by the engine (actually by the working substance) on something in the environment.

21-5 | The Carnot Engine

We shall focus on a particular ideal engine called a **Carnot engine** after the French scientist and engineer N. L. Sadi Carnot (pronounced "car-no"), who first proposed the engine's concept in 1824. This ideal engine turns out to be the best (in principle) at using energy as heat to do useful work. Surprisingly, Carnot was able to analyze the performance of this engine before the first law of thermodynamics and the concept of entropy had been discovered.

Figure 21-13 shows schematically the operation of a Carnot engine. During each cycle of the engine, the working substance absorbs energy $|Q_H|$ as heat from a thermal reservoir at constant temperature T_H and discharges energy $|Q_L|$ as heat to a second thermal reservoir at a constant lower temperature T_L.

Figure 21-14 shows a p-V plot of the *Carnot cycle*—the cycle followed by the working substance. As indicated by the arrows, the cycle is traversed in the clockwise direction. Imagine the working substance to be a gas, confined to an insulating cylinder with a weighted, movable piston. The cylinder may be placed at will on either of the two thermal reservoirs, as in Fig. 21-15, or on an insulating slab. Figure 21-14 shows that, if we place the cylinder in contact with the high-temperature reservoir at temperature T_H, heat $|Q_H|$ is transferred *to* the working substance *from* this reservoir as the gas undergoes an isothermal *expansion* from volume V_a to volume V_b. Similarly, with the working substance in contact with the low-temperature reservoir at temperature T_L, heat $|Q_L|$ is transferred *from* the working substance *to* the low-temperature reservoir as the gas undergoes an isothermal *compression* from volume V_c to volume V_d.

In the engine of Fig. 21-13, we assume that heat transfers to or from the working substance can take place *only* during the isothermal processes *ab* and *cd* of Fig. 21-14. Therefore, processes *bc* and *da* in that figure, which connect the two isotherms at temperatures T_H and T_L, must be (reversible) adiabatic processes; that is, they must be processes in which no energy is transferred as heat. To ensure this, during processes *bc* and *da* the cylinder is placed on an insulating slab as the volume of the working substance is changed.

During the consecutive processes *ab* and *bc* of Fig. 21-14, the working substance is expanding and thus doing positive work as it raises the weighted piston. This work is represented in Fig. 21-14 by the area under curve *abc*. During the consecutive processes *cd* and *da*, the working substance is being compressed, which means that it is doing negative work on its environment or, equivalently, that its environment is doing work on it as the loaded piston descends. This work is represented by the area under curve *cda*. The *net work per cycle*, which is represented by W in both Figs. 21-13 and 21-14, is the difference between these two areas and is a positive quantity equal to the area enclosed by cycle *abcda* in Fig. 21-14. This work W is performed on some outside object, such as a load to be lifted.

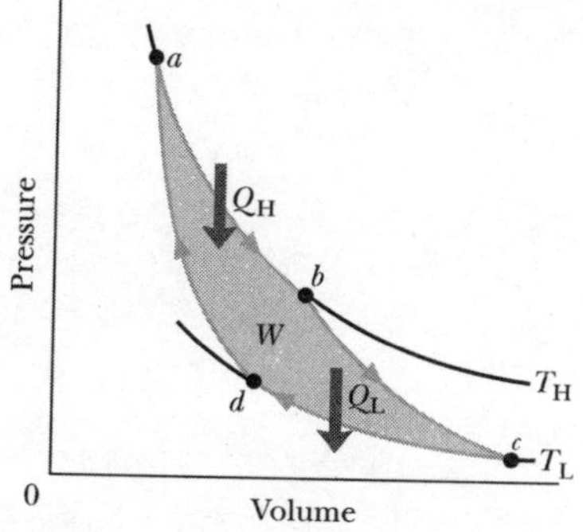

FIG. 21-14 A pressure–volume plot of the cycle followed by the working substance of the Carnot engine in Fig. 20-8. The cycle consists of two isothermal (*ab* and *cd*) and two adiabatic processes (*bc* and *da*). The shaded area enclosed by the cycle is equal to the work W per cycle done by the Carnot engine.

We can write this as

$$\varepsilon_C = 1 - \frac{T_L}{T_H} \quad \text{(efficiency, Carnot engine)} \qquad (21\text{-}38)$$

where the temperatures T_L and T_H are in kelvins. Because $T_L < T_H$, the Carnot engine necessarily has a thermal efficiency less than unity—that is, less than 100%. This is indicated in Fig. 21-13, which shows that only part of the energy extracted as heat from the high-temperature reservoir is available to do work, and the rest is delivered to the low-temperature reservoir. No real engine can have a thermal efficiency greater than that calculated from Eq. 21-38.

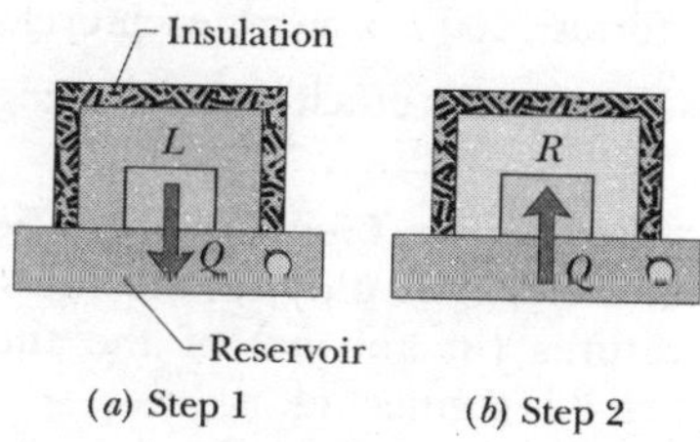

FIG. 21-15 The blocks of Fig. 21-14 can proceed from their initial state to their final state in a reversible way if we use a reservoir with a controllable temperature (*a*) to extract heat reversibly from block *L* and (*b*) to add heat reversibly to block *R*.

Inventors continually try to improve engine efficiency by reducing the energy $|Q_L|$ that is "thrown away" during each cycle. The inventor's dream is to produce the *perfect engine*, diagrammed in Fig. 21-16, in which $|Q_L|$ is reduced to zero and $|Q_H|$ is converted completely into work. Such an engine on an ocean liner, for example, could extract energy as heat from the water and use it to drive the propellers, with no fuel cost. An automobile fitted with such an engine could extract energy as heat from the surrounding air and use it to drive the car, again with no fuel cost. Alas, a perfect engine is only a dream: Inspection of Eq. 21-38 shows that we can achieve 100% engine efficiency (that is, $\varepsilon = 1$) only if $T_L = 0$ or $T_H \to \infty$, impossible requirements. Instead, experience gives the following alternative version of the second law of thermodynamics, which says in short, *there are no perfect engines:*

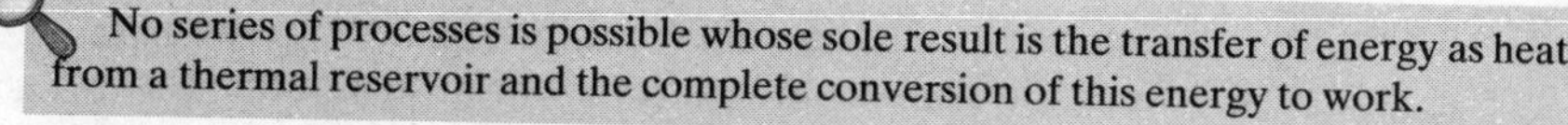

To summarize: The thermal efficiency given by Eq. 21-38 applies only to Carnot engines. Real engines, in which the processes that form the engine cycle are not reversible, have lower efficiencies. If your car were powered by a Carnot engine, it would have an efficiency of about 55% according to Eq. 21-38; its actual efficiency is probably about 25%. A nuclear power plant (Fig. 21-17), taken in its entirety, is an engine. It extracts energy as heat from a reactor core, does work by means of a turbine, and discharges energy as heat to a nearby river. If the power plant operated as a Carnot engine, its efficiency would be about 40%; its actual efficiency is about 30%. In designing engines of any type, there is simply no way to beat the efficiency limitation imposed by Eq. 21-38.

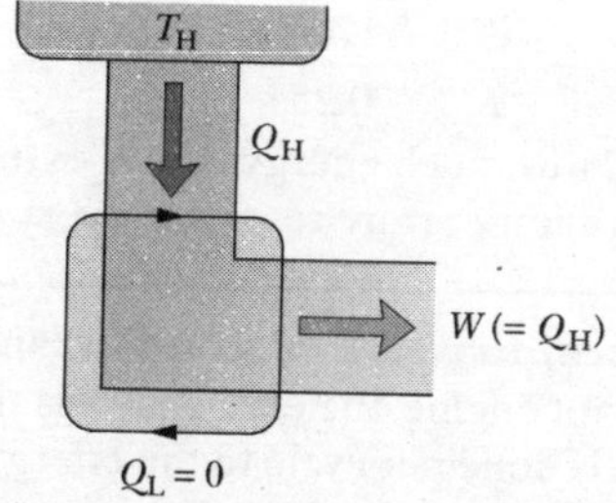

FIG. 21-16 The elements of a perfect engine—that is, one that converts heat Q_H from a high-temperature reservoir directly to work W with 100% efficiency.

FIG. 21-17 The North Anna nuclear power plant near Charlottesville, Virginia, which generates electric energy at the rate of 900 MW. At the same time, by design, it discards energy into the nearby river at the rate of 2100 MW. This plant and all others like it throw away more energy than they deliver in useful form. They are real counterparts of the ideal engine of Fig. 21-13. *(© Robert Ustinich)*

Sample Problem 21-6

Imagine a Carnot engine that operates between the temperatures $T_H = 850$ K and $T_L = 300$ K. The engine performs 1200 J of work each cycle, which takes 0.25 s.

(a) What is the efficiency of this engine?

Conceptualize/Classify: The efficiency ε of a Carnot engine depends only on the ratio T_L/T_H of the temperatures (in kelvins) of the thermal reservoirs to which it is connected.

Compute: Thus, from Eq. 21-38, we have

$$\varepsilon = 1 - \frac{T_L}{T_H} = 1 - \frac{300\text{ K}}{850\text{ K}} = 0.647 \approx 65\% \quad \text{(Answer)}$$

(b) What is the average power of this engine?

Conceptualize/Classify: The average power P of an engine is the ratio of the work W it does per cycle to the time t that each cycle takes.

Compute: For this Carnot engine, we find

$$P = \frac{W}{t} = \frac{1200\text{ J}}{0.25\text{ s}} = 4800\text{ W} = 4.8\text{ kW} \quad \text{(Answer)}$$

(c) How much energy $|Q_H|$ is extracted as heat from the high-temperature reservoir every cycle?

Conceptualize/Classify: For any engine, including a Carnot engine, the efficiency ε is the ratio of the work W that is done per cycle to the energy $|Q_H|$ that is extracted as heat from the high-temperature reservoir per cycle ($\varepsilon = W/|Q_H|$).

Compute: Here we have

$$|Q_H| = \frac{W}{\varepsilon} = \frac{1200\text{ J}}{0.647} = 1855\text{ J} \quad \text{(Answer)}$$

(d) How much energy $|Q_L|$ is delivered as heat to the low-temperature reservoir every cycle?

Conceptualize/Classify: For a Carnot engine, the work W done per cycle is equal to the difference in the energy transfers as heat: $|Q_H| - |Q_L|$.

Compute: Thus, we have

$$|Q_L| = |Q_H| - W$$
$$= 1855\text{ J} - 1200\text{ J} = 655\text{ J} \quad \text{(Answer)}$$

(e) By how much does the entropy of the working substance change as a result of the energy transferred to it from the high-temperature reservoir? From it to the low-temperature reservoir?

Conceptualize/Classify: The entropy change ΔS during a transfer of energy as heat Q at constant temperature T is given by Eq. $\Delta S = Q/T$.

Compute: Thus, for the *positive* transfer of energy Q_H from the high-temperature reservoir at T_H, the change in the entropy of the working substance is

$$\Delta S_H = \frac{Q_H}{T_H} = \frac{1855\text{ J}}{850\text{ K}} = +2.18\text{ J/K} \quad \text{(Answer)}$$

Similarly, for the *negative* transfer of energy Q_L to the low-temperature reservoir at T_L, we have

$$\Delta S_L = \frac{Q_L}{T_L} = \frac{-655\text{ J}}{300\text{ K}} = -2.18\text{ J/K} \quad \text{(Answer)}$$

Note that the net entropy change of the working substance for one cycle is zero.

Sample Problem 21-7

An inventor claims to have constructed an engine that has an efficiency of 75% when operated between the boiling and freezing points of water. Is this possible?

Conceptualize/Classify: The efficiency of a real engine (with its irreversible processes and wasteful energy transfers) must be less than the efficiency of a Carnot engine operating between the same two temperatures.

Compute: From Eq. 21-38, we find that the efficiency of a Carnot engine operating between the boiling and freezing points of water is

$$\varepsilon = 1 - \frac{T_L}{T_H} = 1 - \frac{(0 + 273)\text{ K}}{(100 + 273)\text{ K}} = 0.268 \approx 27\%$$

Thus, the claimed efficiency of 75% for a real engine operating between the given temperatures is impossible.

PROBLEM-SOLVING TACTICS

Tactic 1: The Language of Thermodynamics A rich but sometimes misleading language is used in scientific and engineering studies of thermodynamics. You may see statements that say heat is added, absorbed, subtracted, extracted, rejected, discharged, discarded, withdrawn, delivered, gained, lost, transferred, or expelled, or that it flows from one body to another (as if it were a liquid). You may also see statements that describe a body as *having* heat (as if heat can be held or possessed) or that its heat is increased or decreased. You should always keep in mind what is meant by the term *heat* in science and engineering:

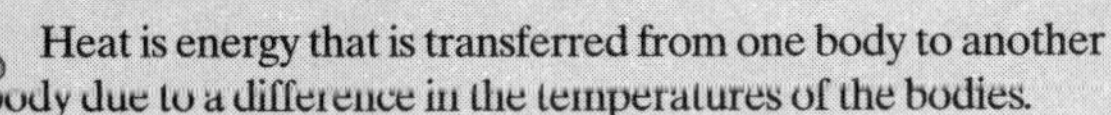

Heat is energy that is transferred from one body to another body due to a difference in the temperatures of the bodies.

When we identify one of the bodies as being our system, any such transfer of energy into it is positive heat Q and out of it is negative heat Q.

The term *work* also requires close attention. You may see statements that say work is produced or generated, or combined with heat or changed from heat. Here is what is meant by the term *work*:

Work is energy that is transferred from one body to another body due to a force that acts between them.

When we identify one of the bodies as being our system of interest, any such transfer of energy out of the system is either positive work W done *by* the system or negative work W done *on* the system. Any such transfer of energy into the system is negative work done *by* the system or positive work done *on* the system. (The preposition that is used is important.) Obviously, this can be confusing—whenever you see the term *work,* read carefully.

Sample Problem 21-8

Otto Cycle

The cycle of a petrol engine can be approximated by an Otto cycle (see Fig. 21-18). $1 \rightarrow 2$ and $3 \rightarrow 4$ are adiabatic compression and expansion, respectively; $2 \rightarrow 3$ and $4 \rightarrow 1$ are constant-volume processes. Treat the working medium as an ideal gas with constant $\gamma = C_p/C_v$.

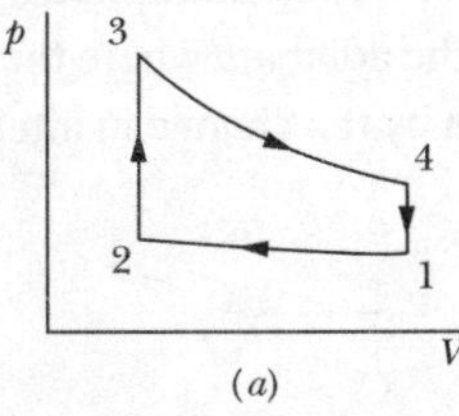

FIG. 21-18 (*a*) p-V diagram of Otto cycle. (*b*) Otto cycle showing the heat absorbed (Q_1) and heat transferred (Q_2) by the working medium.

Compute the efficiency of this cycle for $\gamma = 1.4$ and compression ratio, $r = V_i / V_f = 10$.

Conceptualize: We can see from the p-V graph that it is a cyclic process as the working medium returns to its initial state. We can see from the p-V graph that in the process $3 \rightarrow 4$, the engine is doing positive work on the surroundings and in $1 \rightarrow 2$, it is doing negative work as the gas is compressed. In other two processes, $2 \rightarrow 3$ and $4 \rightarrow 1$, work done is zero, as $\Delta V = 0$.

Classify: The Efficiency of a cyclic process is given by $\eta = W/Q_1$, where W is the work done by the cycle and Q_1 is the amount of heat absorbed by the working medium (in this case, gas). Because the working medium returns to its initial state $W = Q_1 - Q_2$, where Q_2 is the amount of heat transferred from the gas. Therefore

$$\eta = \frac{Q_1 - Q_2}{Q_1} = 1 - \frac{Q_2}{Q_1}$$

As the processes $1 \rightarrow 2$ and $3 \rightarrow 4$ are adiabatic, heat transfer can take place only during the $2 \rightarrow 3$ and $1 \rightarrow 4$ stages.

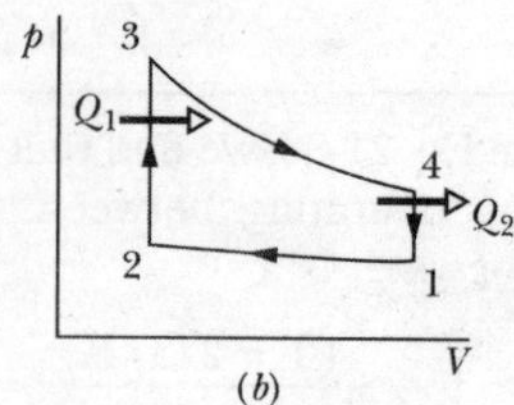

(b)

Compute: Let us calculate Q_1 and Q_2. Since both processes are occuring at a constant volume (see Fig. 21-18b), we may write

$$Q_1 = \int_2^3 dQ = c_v\int_2^3 dT = c_v(T_3 - T_2)$$

$$Q_2 = c_v\int_4^1 dT = -c_v(T_1 - T_4) = c_v(T_4 - T_1)$$

and $$\frac{Q_2}{Q_1} = \frac{T_4 - T_1}{T_3 - T_2}$$

We know that for an adiabatic process

$$pV^\gamma = \text{constant} \quad \text{or} \quad TV^{\gamma-1} = \text{constant}$$

So $$T_1V_i^{\gamma-1} = T_2V_f^{\gamma-1} \qquad \text{(i)}$$

$$T_3V_f^{\gamma-1} = T_4V_i^{\gamma-1} \qquad \text{(ii)}$$

Dividing Eq. (ii) by (i), we get

$$\frac{T_4}{T_1} = \frac{T_3}{T_2}$$

Substracting 1 from both sides and solving, gives

$$\frac{T_4 - T_1}{T_1} = \frac{T_3 - T_2}{T_2}$$

Rearranging above relation and using Eq. (i) gives

$$\frac{T_4 - T_1}{T_3 - T_2} = \frac{T_1}{T_2} = \left(\frac{V_f}{V_i}\right)^{\gamma-1}$$

and therefore the Efficiency is

$$\eta = 1 - \left(\frac{1}{r}\right)^{\gamma-1}$$

For $\gamma = 1.4$ and $r = 10$, the Efficiency is

$$\eta = 1 - (0.10)^{0.4} = 0.6 = 60\% \qquad \text{(Answer)}$$

Conclude: The maximum possible efficiency, if the cycle would have been Carnot cycle, would have been, $1 - \frac{T_2}{T_4}$, as T_2 and T_4 are the lowest and highest temperatures in the cycle. It can be seen that efficiency is less than the Carnot efficiency as the value of $\frac{T_1}{T_2}$ would be more than $\frac{T_2}{T_4}$.

Sample Problem 21-9

Joule Cycle

Find the efficiency of the Joule cycle, consisting of two adiabats and two isobars (see Fig. 21-19a). The cycle is being performed between pressures P_2 and P_1. Assume the gas to be ideal and adiabatic exponent to be γ.

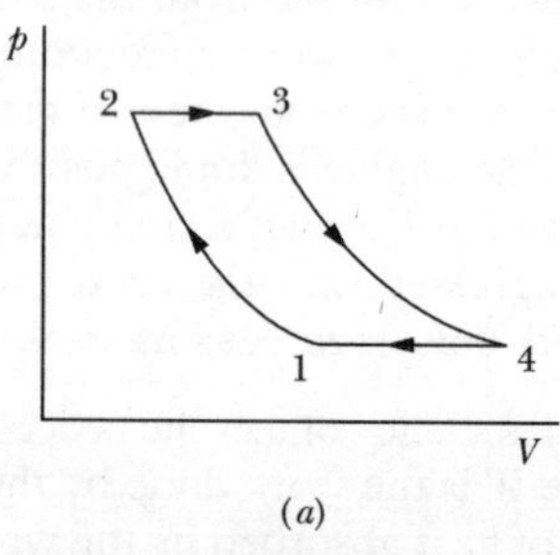

(a)

FIG. 21-19 p-V diagram of Joule cycle.

Conceptualize: It can be seen from the P-V graph that it is a cyclic process as the working medium returns to its initial state. We can see from the P-V graph that in processes $2 \to 3 \to 4$, the engine is doing positive work on the surroundings and in processes $4 \to 1 \to 2$, it is doing negative work as the gas is getting compressed.

Classify: The efficiency η of the cycle is given by the total work W, done during the cycle, divided by the heat Q absorbed in path $2 \to 3$ (see Fig. 21-19a). Total work done W can be calculated by the area enclosed by the four paths of the $P - V$ plot.

Compute: The integral $\omega = \int P\,dV$ along the paths of constant pressure $2 \to 3$ and $4 \to 1$, is simply the difference in volume of the ends, multiplied by the pressure. The work done along the adiabats, where there is no heat transfer $\delta Q = 0$, is given by the change in internal energy $C_V\,\delta T$.

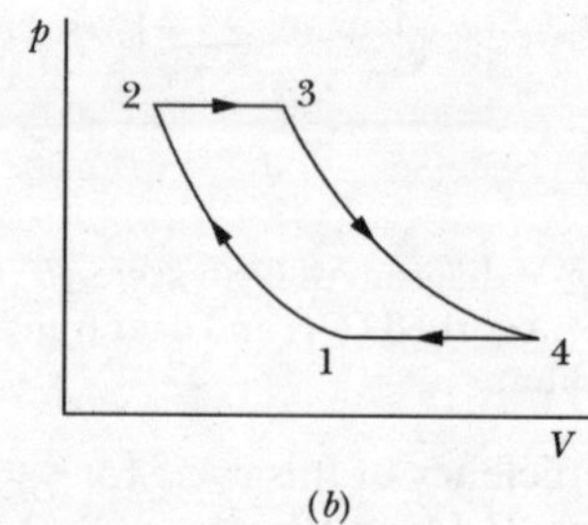

(b)

So, the total work done during the whole cycle $1 \rightarrow 2 \rightarrow 3 \rightarrow 4$, is given by

$$W = C_V[(T_3 - T_4) - (T_2 - T_1)] + P_2(V_3 - V_2) - P_1(V_4 - V_1) \quad \text{(i)}$$

Substituting the ideal gas law $PV = nRT$ into Eq. (i) and rearranging, we find

$$W = (C_V + nR)[(T_3 - T_4) - (T_2 - T_1)] = C_P[(T_3 - T_2) - (T_4 - T_1)] \quad \text{(ii)}$$

because, $\quad C_P = C_V + nR$

In the process $2 \rightarrow 3$, the gas absorbs heat Q, hence

$$Q = C_P(T_3 - T_2)$$

We now need to write W and Q in terms of P and form the quotient. Using the equation for an adiabatic process in an alternative form,

$$PV^{\gamma} = \text{constant}$$

$$TP^{(1-\gamma)/\gamma} = \text{constant}$$

we have

$$\frac{T_1}{T_2} = \left(\frac{P_1}{P_2}\right)^{(\gamma-1)/\gamma} \quad \text{(iii)}$$

and

$$\frac{T_4}{T_3} = \left(\frac{P_1}{P_2}\right)^{(\gamma-1)/\gamma} \quad \text{(iv)}$$

Substituting for T_1 and T_4 from Eq. (iii) and (iv) into Eq. (i) gives

$$W = C_p\left[(T_3 - T_2) - (T_3 - T_2)\left(\frac{P_1}{P_2}\right)^{(\gamma-1)/\gamma}\right]$$

The Efficiency η, of the Joule cycle is therefore given by

$$\eta = \frac{W}{Q} = 1 - \frac{T_4}{T_3} = 1 - \left(\frac{P_1}{P_2}\right)^{(\gamma-1)/\gamma}$$

Conclude: The maximum possible efficiency, if the cycle would have been Carnot, would be, $1 - \frac{T_2}{T_4}$, as T_2 and T_4 are the lowest and highest temperatures in the cycle. It can be seen that efficiency is less than the Carnot efficiency as the value of $\frac{T_4}{T_3}$ would be more than $\frac{T_2}{T_4}$.

Sample Problem 21-10

Cylinder with Massive Piston

Consider n moles of an ideal monoatomic gas placed in a vertical cylinder. The top of the cylinder is closed by a piston of mass M and cross section A (Fig. 21-20*a*). Initially the piston is fixed by external stops, and the gas has volume V_0 and temperature T_0. Next, the piston is released by removing stops, and after several oscillations comes to a stop. Disregarding friction and the heat capacity of the piston and cylinder, find the temperature and volume of the gas at equilibrium. The system is thermally isolated, and the pressure outside the cylinder is P_a.

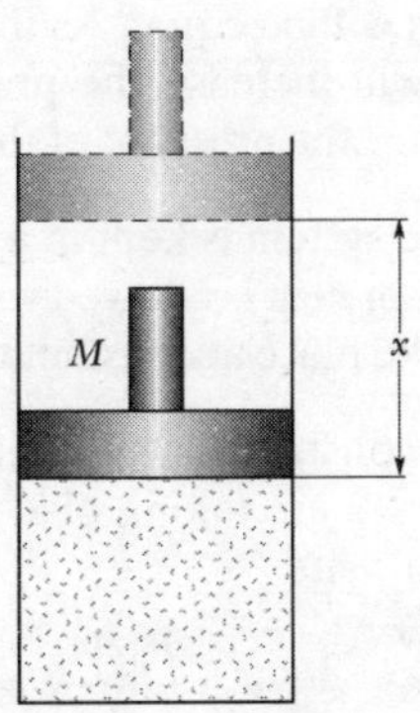

FIG. 21-20 (*a*) Cylinder with a massive piston that is fixed by external stops. (*b*) The piston has been released by removing the stops and after a few oscillations has come to a stop.

Conceptualize: When the piston is released, it will move if the forces acting on it are not balanced. Also the temperature of surroundings has no role as the system is thermally isolated. Finally the piston will come into a thermal equilibrium state.

Classify: The gas will obey the ideal gas law at both initial and final equilibrium.

Compute: Let's say that in final equilibrium, the pressure of the gas is P and the volume is V.

Also, at equilibrium, there is no net force acting on the piston (Fig. 21-20*b*), and we have

$$PA = P_aA+Mg \quad \text{(i)}$$

where, PA is the force (acting upward) exerted by the gas enclosed in the cylinder, on the piston. P_aA is the force (acting downward) exerted by the atmospheric gas on the piston. Mg is the weight (downward) of the piston due to gravitational pull of the earth.

Substituting (i) into ideal gas equation gives us

$$\left(P_a+\frac{Mg}{A}\right)V = nRT$$

We can also use energy conservation principle in this thermally insulated system. $W+\Delta U = 0$ gives the work done by gas, W, equal to reduction in its internal energy $-\Delta U$. That is, $W = -\Delta U$. For an ideal gas

$$\Delta U = nC_v(T - T_0)$$

where C_v is the heat capacity of the gas at constant volume (for a monatomic gas, $C_v = 3R/2$). The work done on the piston by the atmosphere and gravity is equal to $P_aAx+Mgx$, where x is the equilibrium position of the piston from its initial position.

Since, total work on piston must be zero, as

$$W + P_aAx + Mgx = 0$$

thus, work done by gas on piston

$$W = -(P_aA + Mg)x$$

where $x = (V_0 - V) / A$ is the distance the piston moves, and downward movement is positive.

$$\left(P_a+\frac{Mg}{A}\right)(V_0 - V) = \frac{3}{2}nR(T - T_0)$$

Solving

$$T = \frac{3}{5}T_0+\frac{2}{5}\frac{(P_a+Mg/A)V_0}{nR}$$

and $$V = \frac{2}{5}V_0+\frac{3}{5}\frac{nRT_0}{P_a+Mg/A}$$

Conclude: We may check that if $P_0 = P_a+Mg/A$, that is, the piston was initially balanced, and hence $T = T_0$ and $V = V_0$.

Sample Problem 21-11

Cylinder and Heat Bath

Consider a cylinder 1 m long with a thin massless piston clamped in such a way that it divides the cylinder into two equal parts. The cylinder is placed in a large heat bath at $T = 300$ K. The left side of the cylinder contains 1 mole of helium gas at 4 atm. The right side contains the same helium gas but at a pressure of 1 atm. Now the piston is released.

(a) What is its final equilibrium position ?

Conceptualize: It is easy to imagine that as the piston is released, it will move towards right as the larger pressure on left will push the cylinder in the opposite direction. Finally equilibrium condition is reached where, the pressure on both sides will be equal. As the piston is moving towards right, it will increase the pressure of the right chamber and reduce the pressure of the left chamber.

Classify: Since the system is kept in a constant temperature bath and flow of heat is allowed with the enviroment, the process will take place at constant temperature.

Compute: PV is constant for each side of the piston as isothermal processes are taking place. When the piston is released, we can write

$$\frac{P_{0L}V_0}{2} = PV_L, \frac{P_{0R}V_0}{2} = PV_R \quad \text{(i)}$$

where P_{0L} and P_{0R} are the initial pressures on the left and right sides of the cylinder, respectively, P is the final pressure on both sides of the cylinder, and V_L and V_R are the final volumes. From Eq. (i) we have

$$\frac{P_{0L}}{P_{0R}} = \frac{V_L}{V_R}$$

Adding 1 to both sides of the above relation and solving

$$\frac{P_{0L}+P_{0R}}{P_{0R}} = \frac{V_L+V_R}{V_R} \quad \text{(ii)}$$

Rearranging Eq. (ii) and using Eq. (i) gives

$$V_R = \frac{V_0}{1+P_{0L}/P_{0R}} = \frac{V_0}{5}$$

So, the piston ends at 20 cm from the right wall of the cylinder.

(b) How much heat will be transmitted by the bath in the process of equilibration ? (Note that $R = 8.3$ J/mole K.)

Classify: The Internal energy of the ideal gas does not change in the isothermal process, so all the work done by the gas is equal to the heat supplied by the reservoir.

$$\Delta Q = \Delta U+\Delta W$$

$$\Delta U = 0, \quad \text{thus} \quad \Delta Q = \Delta W$$

Compute: Denoting by n_L and n_R the number of moles on the left and right sides of the cylinder, respectively, and using $n_R = 1/4$ mole, we obtain the total work done and, hence, heat given by the reservoir.

$$W = \int pdv$$

Using $PV = nRT$ for ideal gases,

$$W = \int \frac{nRT}{V}\, dV = n_L RT \ln\left(\frac{V_L}{V_0/2}\right) + n_R RT \ln\left(\frac{V_R}{V_0/2}\right)$$

Since, under equilibrium,

$$V_L = \frac{4}{5} V_0 \text{ and } V_R = \frac{V_0}{5}$$

we have,

$$W = n_L RT \ln\left(\frac{4V_0/5}{V_0/2}\right) + n_R RT \ln\left(\frac{V_0/5}{V_0/2}\right)$$

$$= RT \ln\left(\frac{8}{5}\right) + \left(\frac{1}{4}\right) RT \ln\left(\frac{2}{5}\right) = 600 \text{ J} \quad \text{(Answer)}$$

Sample Problem 21-12

To find C_P/C_V of a gas, one sometimes uses the following method. A certain amount of gas with initial temperature T_0, pressure P_0, and volume V_0 is heated by a current flowing through a platinum wire for a fixed time t. The experiment is done twice: first, at a constant volume V_0 with the pressure changing from P_0 to P_1, and then at a constant pressure P_0 with the volume changing from V_0 to V_1. The time t is same in both the experiments. Explain the steps involved in calculating the ratio C_P/C_V (the gas may be considered ideal).

Conceptualize/Classify: For the gas being heated at a constant volume, the specific heat of the process is C_V and for the gas being heated at a constant pressure, the specific heat of the process is C_P. Since the current has been passed for the same duration, the heat supplied in both the processes is going to be same.

Compute: If the gas is heated at a constant volume, then the amount of heat Q transferred to the gas is

$$Q = nC_v(T - T_0) \tag{i}$$

where, n is the number of moles, and T is the temperature at pressure P_1. Using the ideal gas law, at the beginning and end of heating, gives

$$P_0V_0 = nRT_0 \tag{ii}$$

$$P_1V_0 = nRT \tag{iii}$$

where n is the number of moles of the gas. From Eq. (ii) and (iii)

$$T - T_0 = \frac{(P_1 - P_0)V_0}{nR} \tag{iv}$$

Substituting the value of $(T - T_0)$ from Eq. (iv) in Eq. (i), we get

$$Q = nC_v \frac{(P_1 - P_0)V_0}{nR} \tag{v}$$

For heating at constant pressure,

$$Q' = nC_P(T' - T_0) \tag{vi}$$

where T' is the temperature at volume V'.
Similarly

$$P_0V_0 = nRT_0 \tag{vii}$$

$$P_1V_0 = nRT' \tag{viii}$$

From Eq. (vii) and (viii), we have

$$T' - T_0 = \frac{P_0(V_1 - V_0)}{nR} \tag{ix}$$

Substituting the value of $(T' - T_0)$ from Eq. (ix) into Eq. (vi), we get

$$Q' = nC_P \frac{P_0(V_1 - V_0)}{nR} \tag{x}$$

Since the time t during which the current flows through the wire is the same in both experiments, the amount of heat transferred to the gas is also the same, that is, $Q' = Q$. Equating (v) and (x), we obtain

$$\frac{C_P}{C_V} = \frac{(P_1 - P_0)V_0}{(V_1 - V_0)P_0} = \frac{(P_1/P_0) - 1}{(V_1/V_0) - 1}$$

Conclude: In constant pressure process some part of the energy supplied by the wire is also used by the gas to expand. Thus value of C_p is always more than the value of C_v.

Sample Problem 21-13

An adiabatic rigid container contains gas at very low pressure. At some point, a small vent is opened in the container, so the air from the atmosphere starts rushing in. The temperature of the air surrounding the chamber is $T_0 = 300$ K. What is the temperature T of the gas in the chamber immediately after the vent was opened?

Conceptualize: We can imagine that the chamber will be immedietly filled with the gas from the atmosphere and the pressure will become equal to the atmospheric pressure. The air surrounding the chamber may be thought of as a very large container of gas at a constant pressure P_0 and temperature T_0. The same situation can be imagined as a piston in the chamber pushing the gas at constant pressure P_0 as shown in Fig. 21-21.

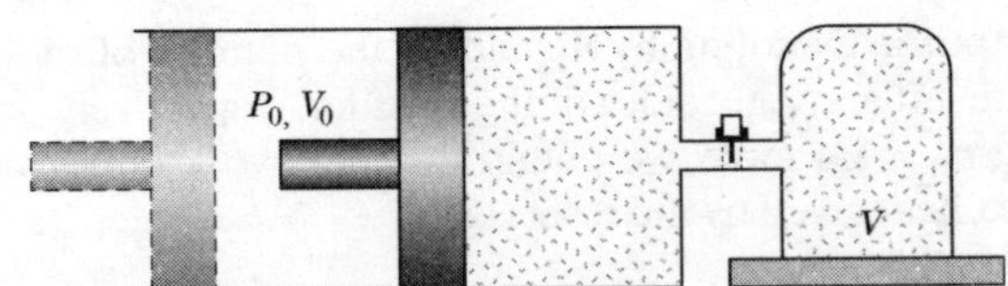

FIG. 21-21 Gas being pushed by a piston at constant pressure.

Classify: The process here can be considered as adiabatic, as the gas will be entering the vessel very fast. We can say that the internal energy of the gas in the chamber equals the sum of its energy U_0 in the reservoir plus the work done by the gas of the large reservoir at P_0 to pump the gas into the chamber.

Compute: The work may be calculated by considering the process of filling a cylinder by pushing the imaginary piston, by applying force of P_0A, A being the cross section of the piston. The final internal energy U is then given by

$$U = U_0 + P_0V_0 \qquad \text{(i)}$$

where V_0 is the volume of the gas needed to fill the volume of the chamber V. Here it is important to note that volume V is not equal to the volume V_0 because the temperature T of the gas in the chamber may not be the same as T_0 (Fig. 21-21). On the other hand,

$$\Delta U = U - U_0 = n_0c_v(T - T_0) \qquad \text{(ii)}$$

where, c_v is the heat capacity per mole, and n_0 is the number of moles. From Eq. (i) and (ii), we have

$$P_0V_0 = n_0c_v(T - T_0) \qquad \text{(iii)}$$

Using the ideal gas law,

$$P_0V_0 = n_0RT_0 \qquad \text{(iv)}$$

From Eq. (iii) and (iv), we have

$$RT_0 = c_v(T - T_0)$$

Rearranging the above equation, we have

$$T = \frac{R + c_v}{c_v}T_0 = \frac{c_p}{c_v}T_0 = \gamma T_0$$

The air is mostly nitrogen and oxygen (78% nitrogen and 21% oxygen = 99%) and both are diatomic gases, so that

$$c_v = \frac{5}{2}R \text{ and } \gamma = \frac{7}{5}$$

and therefore T = 420 K. Thus, the temperature of the gas in the chamber will increase.

Conclude: The temperature is increasing because the atmosphere is performing positive work on the gas finally present in the chamber. Note that the result does not depend on the outside pressure P_0, the volume of the chamber V, or whether it is filled to P_0.

CHECKPOINT 6 A spring having a spring constant 5 N/m is compressed 0.04 m, clamped in this configuration, and dropped into a container of acid in which the spring dissolves. How much potential energy is stored in the spring, and what happens to it when the spring dissolves ?

Sample Problem 21-14

Argon gas in a cylinder under a piston goes from a state with initial volume of V_1 = .032 m^3 and a pressure of p_1 = 4.1 × 10^5 Nm^{-2} to a state with V_2 = .09 m^3 and p_2 = 15.5 Nm^{-2}. What maximum temperature will the gas reach in the process, if the relation between p and V is linear as shown on the p - V diagram in (Fig. 21-22a)?

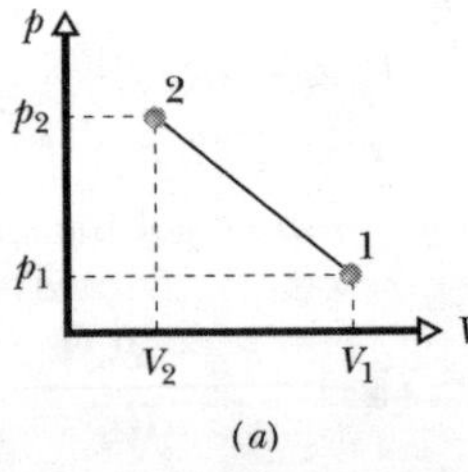

FIG. 21-22 (a) p-V diagram of Argon gas in a cylinder under a piston, going from volume V_1 to V_2 with accompanying change in pressure. (b) The relation between the temperature T and V.

Conceptualize/Classify: The process being carried out is not one of the four standard processes. So we have to begin by finding relation between p and V.

Compute: In view of the linear dependence of pressure on volume, we can write. The constants a and b can be determined from the given values of pressure and volumes of the problem:

$$p = aV + b \qquad \text{(i)}$$

$$a = \frac{p_1 - p_2}{V_1 - V_2} \equiv -\ 0.5 \times 10^8 \text{ N/m}^5$$

$$b = \frac{p_2V_1 - p_1V_2}{V_1 - V_2} \equiv 20 \times 10^5 \text{ N/m}^2$$

Multiplying Eq. (i) by V on both sides and replacing P using the equation of state of an ideal gas $PV = nRT$, we find that

$$aV^2 + bV = KT$$

where K is a constant having a value nR.

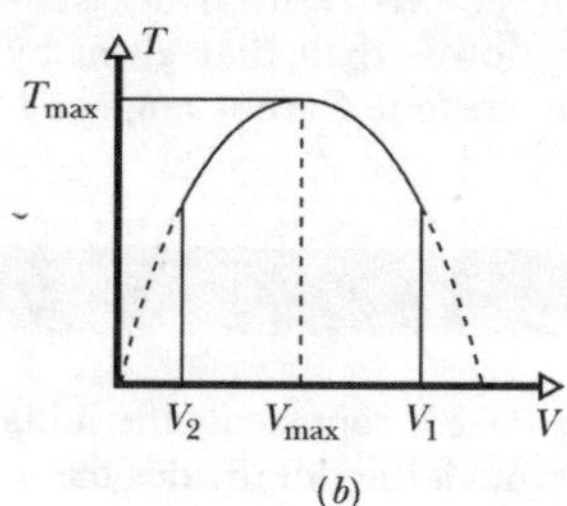

(b)

The relation between T and V (see Fig. 21-22b) is a parabola. The curve reaches its maximum at $V_{max} = -\frac{b}{2a} \equiv 20$ lit when the roots of the quadratic equation coincides

Here $$p_{max} = aV_{max} + b = \frac{b}{2} \equiv 10 \text{ atm}$$

Therefore,

$$T_{max} = \frac{p_{max}V_{max}}{nR} = 490 \text{ K} \quad \text{(Answer)}$$

Conclude: As temperature rises initially and falls finally, we see that maximum temperature is in between the initial and final state.

REVIEW & SUMMARY

Work Associated with Volume Change A gas may exchange energy with its surroundings through work. The amount of work W done *by* a gas as it expands or contracts from an initial volume V_i to a final volume V_f is given by

$$W = \int dW = \int_{V_i}^{V_f} p\, dV$$

The integration is necessary because the pressure p may vary during the volume change.

First Law of Thermodynamics The principle of conservation of energy for a thermodynamic process is expressed in the **first law of thermodynamics,** which may assume either of the forms

$$\Delta E_{int} = E_{int,f} - E_{int,i} = Q - W \quad \text{(first law)}$$

or

$$dE_{int} = dQ - dW \quad \text{(first law)}$$

E_{int} represents the internal energy of the material, which depends only on the material's state (temperature, pressure, and volume). Q represents the energy exchanged as heat between the system and its surroundings; Q is positive if the system absorbs heat and negative if the system loses heat. W is the work done *by* the system; W is positive if the system expands against an external force from the surroundings and negative if the system contracts because of an external force. *Q and W are path dependent; ΔE_{int} is path independent.*

Applications of the First Law The first law of thermodynamics finds application in several special cases:

isovolumetric processes: $W = 0, \quad \Delta E_{int} = Q$

isobaric processes: $Q = nC_P\Delta T$

adiabatic processes: $Q = 0, \quad \Delta E_{int} = -W$

cyclical processes: $\Delta E_{int} = 0, \quad Q = W$

Work in an Isothermal Volume Change The work done *by* an ideal gas during an **isothermal** (constant-temperature) change from volume V_i to volume V_f is

$$W = nRT \ln \frac{V_f}{V_i} \quad \text{(ideal gas, isothermal process)}$$

Molar Specific Heats The molar specific heat C_V of a gas at constant volume is defined as

$$C_V = \frac{Q}{n\,\Delta T} = \frac{\Delta E_{int}}{n\,\Delta T}$$

in which Q is the energy transferred as heat to or from a sample of n moles of the gas, ΔT is the resulting temperature change of the gas, and ΔE_{int} is the resulting change in the internal energy of the gas. For an ideal monatomic gas,

$$C_V = \tfrac{3}{2}R = 12.5 \text{ J/mol}\cdot\text{K}$$

The molar specific heat C_p of a gas at constant pressure is defined to be

$$C_p = \frac{Q}{n\,\Delta T}$$

in which Q, n, and ΔT are defined as above. C_p is also given by

$$C_p = C_V + R$$

For n moles of an ideal gas,

$$E_{int} = nC_VT \quad \text{(ideal gas)}$$

If n moles of a confined ideal gas undergo a temperature change ΔT due to *any* process, the change in the internal energy of the gas is

$$\Delta E_{int} = nC_V\,\Delta T \quad \text{(ideal gas, any process)}$$

in which the appropriate value of C_V must be substituted, according to the type of ideal gas.

Adiabatic Process When an ideal gas undergoes a slow adiabatic volume change (a change for which $Q = 0$), its pressure and volume are related by

$$pV^\gamma = \text{a constant} \quad \text{(adiabatic process)}$$

in which $\gamma (= C_p/C_V)$ is the ratio of molar specific heats for the gas. For a free expansion, however, pV = a constant.

Engines An **engine** is a device that, operating in a cycle, extracts energy as heat $|Q_H|$ from a high-temperature reservoir and does a certain amount of work $|W|$.

In an **ideal engine,** all processes are reversible and no wasteful energy transfers occur due to, say, friction and turbulence. A **Carnot engine** is an ideal engine that follows the cycle of Fig. 21-14. Its efficiency is

$$\varepsilon_C = 1 - \frac{T_L}{T_H}$$

in which T_H and T_L are the temperatures of the high- and low-temperature reservoirs, respectively. Real engines always have an efficiency lower than that given by this equation. Ideal engines that are not Carnot engines also have lower efficiencies.

QUESTIONS

1 For a temperature increase of ΔT_1, a certain amount of an ideal gas requires 30 J when heated at constant volume and 50 J when heated at constant pressure. How much work is done by the gas in the second situation?

2 The dot in Fig. 21-23*a* represents the initial state of a gas, and the vertical line through the dot divides the *P-V* diagram into regions 1 and 2. For the following processes, determine whether the work *W* done by the gas is positive, negative, or zero: (a) the gas moves up along the vertical line, (b) it moves down along the vertical line, (c) it moves to anywhere in region 1, and (d) it moves to anywhere in region 2.

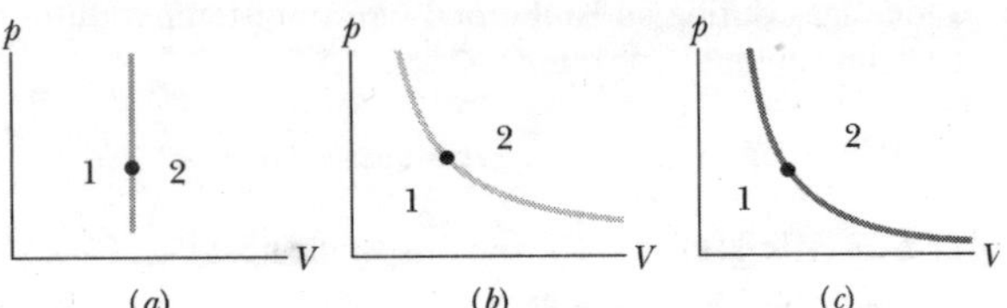

FIG. 21-23 Questions 2, 4, and 6.

3 For four situations for an ideal gas, the table gives the energy transferred to or from the gas as heat Q and either the work W done by the gas or the work W_{on} done on the gas, all in joules. Rank the four situations in terms of the temperature change of the gas, most positive first.

	a	b	c	d
Q	−50	+35	−15	+20
W	−50	+35		
W_{on}			−40	+40

FIG. 21-24 Questions 3.

4 The dot in Fig. 21-23*b* represents the initial state of a gas, and the isotherm through the dot divides the *P-V* diagram into regions 1 and 2. For the following processes, determine whether the change ΔE_{int} in the internal energy of the gas is positive, negative, or zero: (a) the gas moves up along the isotherm, (b) it moves down along the isotherm, (c) it moves to anywhere in region 1, and (d) it moves to anywhere in region 2.

5 A certain amount of energy is to be transferred as heat to 1 mol of a monatomic gas (a) at constant pressure and (b) at constant volume, and to 1 mol of a diatomic gas (c) at constant pressure and (d) at constant volume. Figure 21-25 shows four paths from an initial point to four final points on a *P-V* diagram. Which path goes with which process? (e) Are the molecules of the diatomic gas rotating?

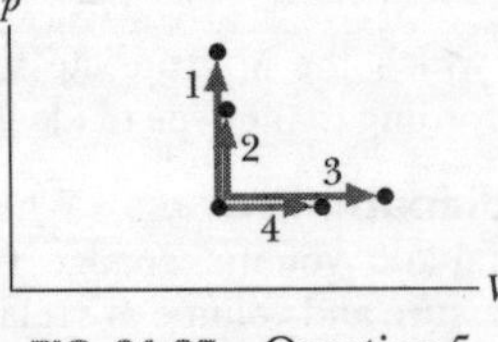

FIG. 21-25 Question 5.

6 The dot in Fig. 21-23*c* represents the initial state of a gas, and the adiabat through the dot divides the *p-V* diagram into regions 1 and 2. For the following processes, determine whether the corresponding heat Q is positive, negative, or zero: (a) the gas moves up along the adiabat, (b) it moves down along the adiabat, (c) it moves to anywhere in region 1, and (d) it moves to anywhere in region 2.

7 In the *p-V* diagram of Fig. 21-26, the gas does 5 J of work when taken along isotherm *ab* and 4 J when taken along adiabat *bc*. What is the change in the internal energy of the gas when it is taken along the straight path from *a* to *c*?

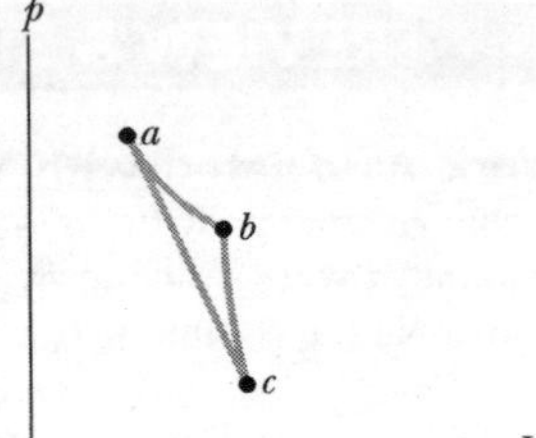

FIG. 21-26 Question 7.

8 (a) Rank the four paths of Fig. 21-16 according to the work done by the gas, greatest first. (b) Rank paths 1, 2, and 3 according to the change in the internal energy of the gas, most positive first and most negative last.

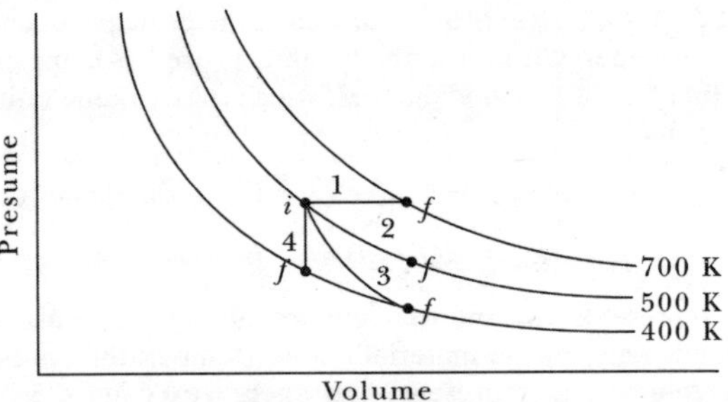

FIG. 21-27 Questions 8.

9 Does the temperature of an ideal gas increase, decrease, or stay the same during (a) an isothermal expansion, (b) an expansion at constant pressure, (c) an adiabatic expansion, and (d) an increase in pressure at constant volume?

10 Figure 21-28 shows two closed cycles on *P-V* diagrams for a gas. The three parts of cycle 1 are of the same length and shape as those of cycle 2. For each cycle, should the cycle be traversed clockwise or counterclockwise if (a) the net work *W* done by the gas is to be positive and (b) the net energy transferred by the gas as heat Q is to be positive?

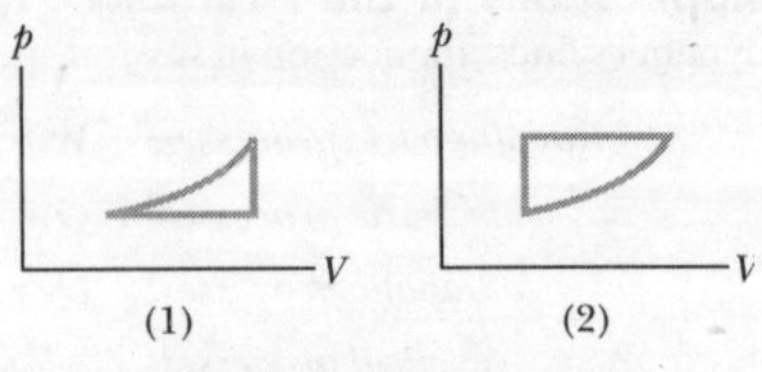

FIG. 21-28 Questions 10.

PROBLEMS

Some Special Cases of the First Law of Thermodynamics

1 A gas within a closed chamber undergoes the cycle shown in the p-V diagram of Fig. 21-29. The horizontal scale is set by $V_s = 4.0\ \text{m}^3$. Calculate the net energy added to the system as heat during one complete cycle.

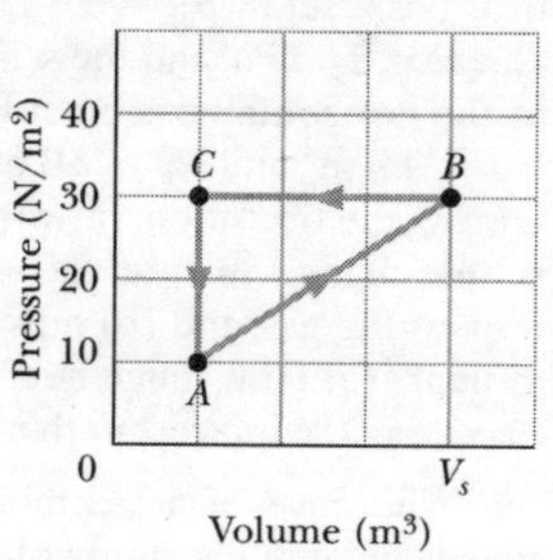

FIG. 21-29 Problem 1.

2 Suppose 200 J of work is done on a system and 70.0 cal is extracted from the system as heat. In the sense of the first law of thermodynamics, what are the values (including algebraic signs) of (a) W, (b) Q, and (c) ΔE_{int}?

3 In Fig. 21-30, a gas sample expands from V_0 to $4.0V_0$ while its pressure decreases from p_0 to $p_0/4.0$. If $V_0 = 1.0\ \text{m}^3$ and $p_0 = 40$ Pa, how much work is done by the gas if its pressure changes with volume via (a) path A, (b) path B, and (c) path C?

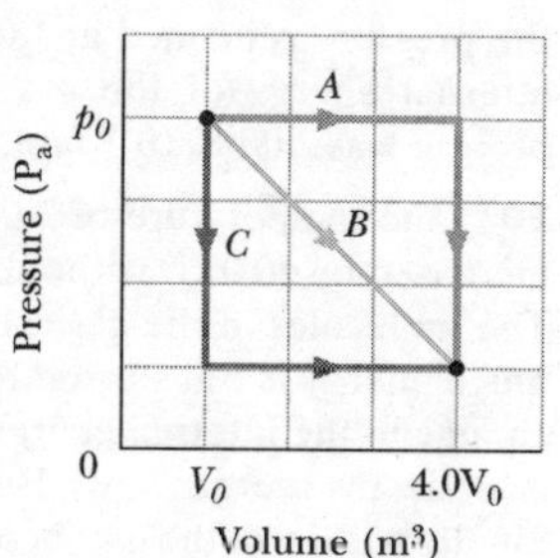

FIG. 21-30 Problem 3.

4 A thermodynamic system is taken from state A to state B to state C, and then back to A, as shown in the p-V diagram of Fig. 21-31a. The vertical scale is set by $p_s = 40$ Pa, and the horizontal scale is set by $V_s = 4.0\ \text{m}^3$. (a)–(g) Complete the table in Fig. 21-31b by inserting a plus sign, a minus sign, or a zero in each indicated cell. (h) What is the net work done by the system as it moves once through the cycle $ABCA$?

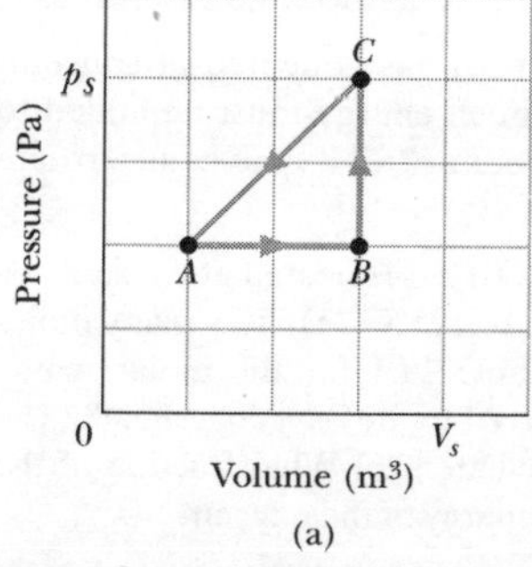

(a)

	Q	W	ΔE_{int}
$A \rightarrow B$	(a)	(b)	+
$B \rightarrow C$	+	(c)	(d)
$C \rightarrow A$	(e)	(f)	(g)

(b)

FIG. 21-31 Problem 4.

5 Figure 21-32 displays a closed cycle for a gas (the figure is not drawn to scale). The change in the internal energy of the gas as it moves from a to c along the path abc is -200 J. As it moves from c to d, 180 J must be transferred to it as heat. An additional transfer of 80 J to it as heat is needed as it moves from d to a. How much work is done on the gas as it moves from c to d?

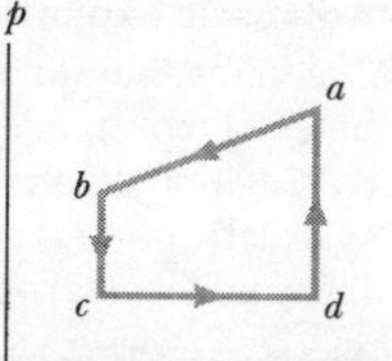

FIG. 21-32 Problem 5.

6 A sample of gas is taken through cycle $abca$ shown in the p-V diagram of Fig. 21-33. The net work done is +1.2 J. Along path ab, the change in the internal energy is +3.0 J and the magnitude of the work done is 5.0 J. Along path ca, the energy transferred to the gas as heat is +2.5 J. How much energy is transferred as heat along (a) path ab and (b) path bc?

FIG. 21-33 Problem 6.

7 When a system is taken from state i to state f along path iaf in Fig. 21-34, $Q = 50$ cal and $W = 20$ cal. Along path ibf, $Q = 36$ cal. (a) What is W along path ibf? (b) If $W = -13$ cal for the return path fi, what is Q for this path? (c) If $E_{\text{int},i} = 10$ cal, what is $E_{\text{int},f}$? If $E_{\text{int},b} = 22$ cal, what is Q for (d) path ib and (e) path bf?

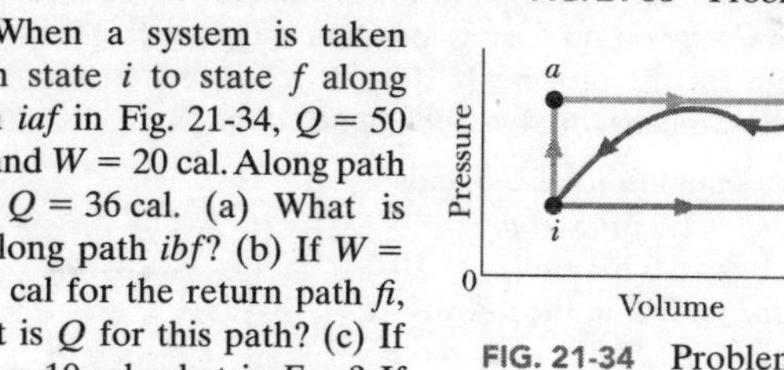

FIG. 21-34 Problem 7.

8 Gas within a chamber passes through the cycle shown in Fig. 21-35. Determine the energy transferred by the system as heat during process CA if the energy added as heat Q_{AB} during process AB is 20.0 J, no energy is transferred as heat during process BC, and the net work done during the cycle is 15.0 J.

FIG. 21-35 Problem 8.

Heat Transfer Mechanisms

9 A sample of gas undergoes a transition from an initial state a to a final state b by three different paths (processes), as shown in the p-V diagram in Fig. 21-36, where $V_b = 5.00V_i$. The energy transferred to the gas as heat in process 1 is $10p_iV_i$. In terms of p_iV_i, what are (a) the energy transferred to the gas as heat in process 2 and (b) the change in internal energy that the gas undergoes in process 3?

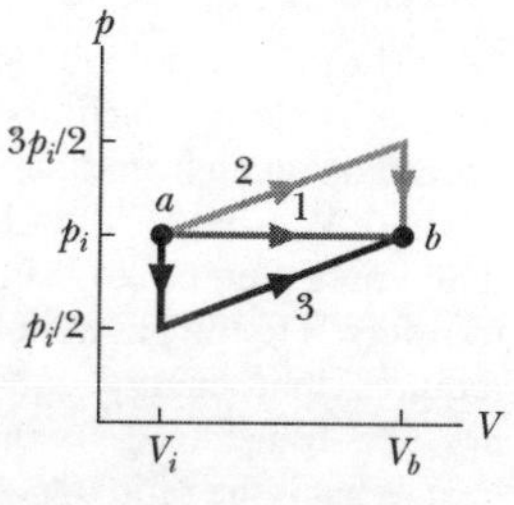

FIG. 21-36 Problem 9.

10 A sample of gas expands from an initial pressure and volume of 10 Pa and $1.0\ \text{m}^3$ to a final volume of $2.0\ \text{m}^3$. During the expansion, the pressure and volume are related by the equation $p = aV^2$, where $a = 10\ \text{N/m}^8$. Determine the work done by the gas during this expansion.

11 Figure 21-37a shows a cylinder containing gas and closed by a movable piston. The cylinder is kept submerged in an ice–water mixture. The piston is *quickly* pushed down from position 1 to position 2 and then held at position 2 until the

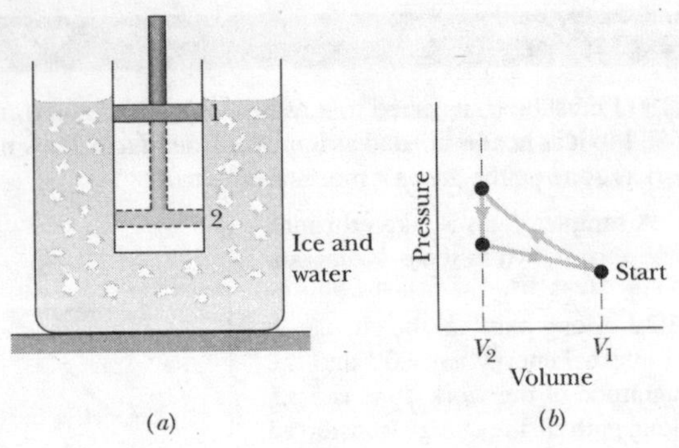

FIG. 21-37 Problem 11.

gas is again at the temperature of the ice–water mixture; it then is *slowly* raised back to position 1. Figure 21-37*b* is a *p-V* diagram for the process. If 100 g of ice is melted during the cycle, how much work has been done *on* the gas?

12 A sample of gas expands from $V_1 = 1.0\ \text{m}^3$ and $p_1 = 40$ Pa to $V_2 = 4.0\ \text{m}^3$ and $p_2 = 10$ Pa along path B in the *p-V* diagram in Fig. 21-38. It is then compressed back to V_1 along either path A or path C. Compute the net work done by the gas for the complete cycle along (a) path BA and (b) path BC.

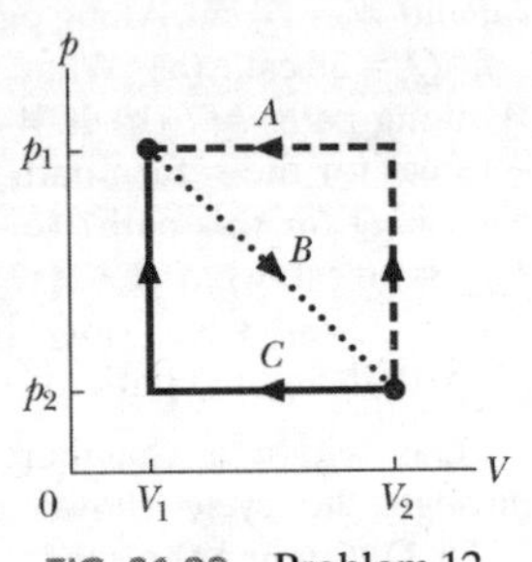

FIG. 21-38 Problem 12.

13 Figure 21-39 displays a closed cycle for a gas. The change in internal energy along path ca is -160 J. The energy transferred to the gas as heat is 200 J along path ab, and 40 J along path bc. How much work is done by the gas along (a) path abc and (b) path ab?

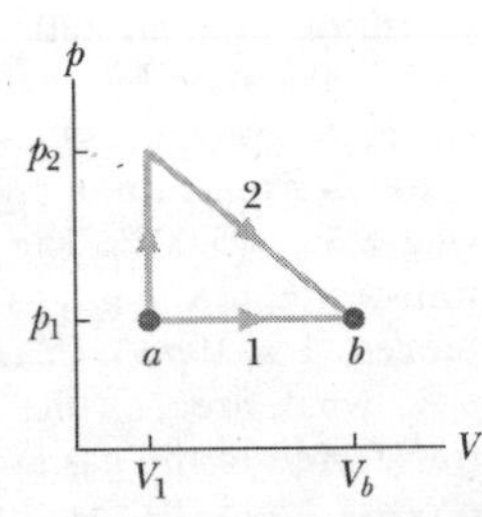

FIG. 21-39 Problem 13.

14 The *p-V* diagram in Fig. 21-40 shows two paths along which a sample of gas can be taken from state a to state b, where $V_b = 3.0\ V_1$. Path 1 requires that energy equal to $5.0\ p_1V_1$ be transferred to the gas as heat. Path 2 requires that energy equal to $5.5\ p_1V_1$ be transferred to the gas as heat. What is the ratio p_2/p_1?

FIG. 21-40 Problem 14.

The Molar Specific Heats of an Ideal Gas

15 Under constant pressure, the temperature of 2.00 mol of an ideal monatomic gas is raised 15.0 K. What are (a) the work W done by the gas, (b) the energy transferred as heat Q, (c) the change ΔE_{int} in the internal energy of the gas, and (d) the change ΔK in the average kinetic energy per atom?

16 A container holds a mixture of three nonreacting gases: 2.40 mol of gas 1 with $C_{V1} = 12.0$ J/mol·K, 1.50 mol of gas 2 with $C_{V2} = 12.8$ J/mol·K, and 3.20 mol of gas 3 with $C_{V3} = 20.0$ J/mol·K. What is C_V of the mixture?

17 One mole of an ideal diatomic gas goes from a to c along the diagonal path in Fig. 21-41. The scale of the vertical axis is set by $p_{ab} = 5.0$ kPa and $p_c = 2.0$ kPa, and the scale of the horizontal axis is set by $V_{bc} = 4.0\ \text{m}^3$ and $V_a = 2.0\ \text{m}^3$. During the transition, (a) what is the change in internal energy of the gas, and (b) how much energy is added to the gas as heat? (c) How much heat is required if the gas goes from a to c along the indirect path abc?

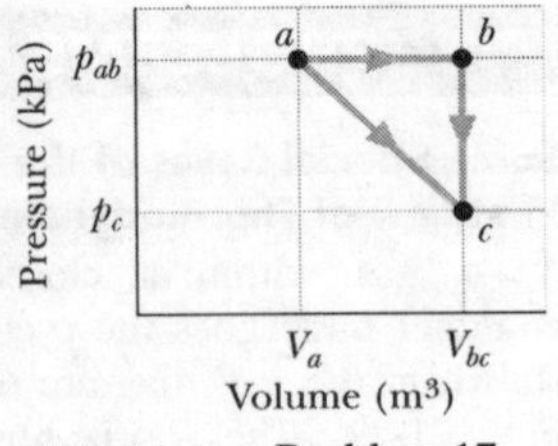

FIG. 21-41 Problem 17.

18 The mass of a gas molecule can be computed from its specific heat at constant volume c_V. (Note that this is not C_V.) Take $c_V = 0.075$ cal/g·C° for argon and calculate (a) the mass of an argon atom and (b) the molar mass of argon.

19 When 20.9 J was added as heat to a particular ideal gas, the volume of the gas changed from 50.0 cm³ to 100 cm³ while the pressure remained at 1.00 atm. (a) By how much did the internal energy of the gas change? If the quantity of gas present was 2.00×10^{-3} mol, find (b) C_p and (c) C_V.

20 The temperature of 3.00 mol of an ideal diatomic gas is increased by 40.0 C° without the pressure of the gas changing. The molecules in the gas rotate but do not oscillate. (a) How much energy is transferred to the gas as heat? (b) What is the change in the internal energy of the gas? (c) How much work is done by the gas? (d) By how much does the rotational kinetic energy of the gas increase?

Degrees of Freedom and Molar Specific Heats

21 We give 70 J as heat to a diatomic gas, which then expands at constant pressure. The gas molecules rotate but do not oscillate. By how much does the internal energy of the gas increase?

22 When 1.0 mol of oxygen (O_2) gas is heated at constant pressure starting at 0°C, how much energy must be added to the gas as heat to double its volume? (The molecules rotate but do not oscillate.)

23 Suppose 12.0 g of oxygen (O_2) gas is heated at constant atmospheric pressure from 25.0°C to 125°C. (a) How many moles of oxygen are present? (See Table 19-1 for the molar mass.) (b) How much energy is transferred to the oxygen as heat? (The molecules rotate but do not oscillate.) (c) What fraction of the heat is used to raise the internal energy of the oxygen?

24 Suppose 4.00 mol of an ideal diatomic gas, with molecular rotation but not oscillation, experienced a temperature increase of 60.0 K under constant-pressure conditions. What are (a) the energy transferred as heat Q, (b) the change ΔE_{int} in internal energy of the gas, (c) the work W done by the gas, and (d) the change ΔK in the total translational kinetic energy of the gas?

The Adiabatic Expansion of an Ideal Gas

25 We know that for an adiabatic process $pV^\gamma =$ a constant. Evaluate "a constant" for an adiabatic process involving exactly 2.0 mol of an ideal gas passing through the state having exactly $p = 1.0$ atm and $T = 300$ K. Assume a diatomic gas whose molecules rotate but do not oscillate.

26 Figure 21-42 shows two paths that may be taken by a gas from an initial point i to a final point f. Path 1 consists of an

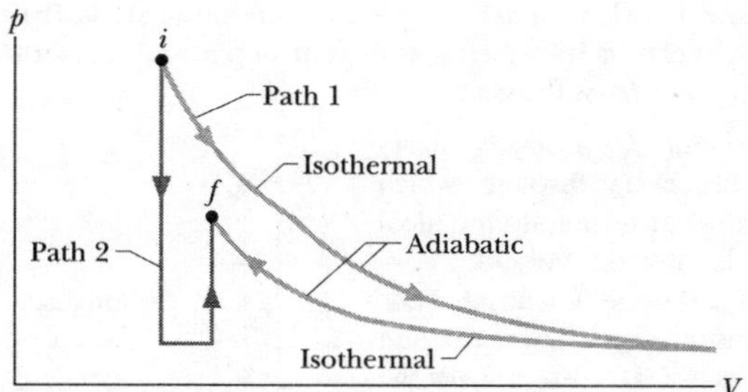

FIG. 21-42 Problem 26.

isothermal expansion (work is 50 J in magnitude), an adiabatic expansion (work is 40 J in magnitude), an isothermal compression (work is 30 J in magnitude), and then an adiabatic compression (work is 25 J in magnitude). What is the change in the internal energy of the gas if the gas goes from point i to point f along path 2?

27 *Adiabatic wind.* The normal airflow over the Rocky Mountains is west to east. The air loses much of its moisture content and is chilled as it climbs the western side of the mountains. When it descends on the eastern side, the increase in pressure toward lower altitudes causes the temperature to increase. The flow, then called a chinook wind, can rapidly raise the air temperature at the base of the mountains. Assume that the air pressure p depends on altitude y according to $p = p_0 \exp(-ay)$, where $p_0 = 1.00$ atm and $a = 1.16 \times 10^{-4}$ m^{-1}. Also assume that the ratio of the molar specific heats is $\gamma = 4/3$. A parcel of air with an initial temperature of $-5.00°$C descends adiabatically from $y_1 = 4267$ m to $y = 1567$ m. What is its temperature at the end of the descent?

28 A gas is to be expanded from initial state i to final state f along either path 1 or path 2 on a p-V diagram. Path 1 consists of three steps: an isothermal expansion (work is 40 J in magnitude), an adiabatic expansion (work is 20 J in magnitude), and another isothermal expansion (work is 30 J in magnitude). Path 2 consists of two steps: a pressure reduction at constant volume and an expansion at constant pressure. What is the change in the internal energy of the gas along path 2?

29 *Opening champagne.* In a bottle of champagne, the pocket of gas (primarily carbon dioxide) between the liquid and the cork is at pressure of $p_i = 5.00$ atm. When the cork is pulled from the bottle, the gas undergoes an adiabatic expansion until its pressure matches the ambient air pressure of 1.00 atm. Assume that the ratio of the molar specific heats is $\gamma = 4/3$. If the gas has initial temperature $T_i = 5.00°$C, what is its temperature at the end of the adiabatic expansion?

30 The volume of an ideal gas is adiabatically reduced from 200 L to 74.3 L. The initial pressure and temperature are 1.00 atm and 300 K. The final pressure is 4.00 atm. (a) Is the gas monatomic, diatomic, or polyatomic? (b) What is the final temperature? (c) How many moles are in the gas?

31 An ideal diatomic gas, with rotation but no oscillation, undergoes an adiabatic compression. Its initial pressure and volume are 1.20 atm and 0.200 m^3. Its final pressure is 2.40 atm. How much work is done by the gas?

32 Figure 21-43 shows a cycle undergone by 1.00 mol of an ideal monatomic gas. The temperatures are $T_1 = 300$ K, $T_2 = 600$ K, and $T_3 = 455$ K. For $1 \rightarrow 2$, what are (a) heat Q, (b) the change in internal energy ΔE_{int}, and (c) the work done W? For $2 \rightarrow 3$, what are (d) Q, (e) ΔE_{int}, and (f) W? For $3 \rightarrow 1$, what are (g) Q, (h) ΔE_{int}, and (i) W? For the full cycle, what are (j) Q, (k) ΔE_{int}, and (l) W? The initial pressure at point 1 is 1.00 atm ($= 1.013 \times 10^5$ Pa). What are the (m) volume and (n) pressure at point 2 and the (o) volume and (p) pressure at point 3?

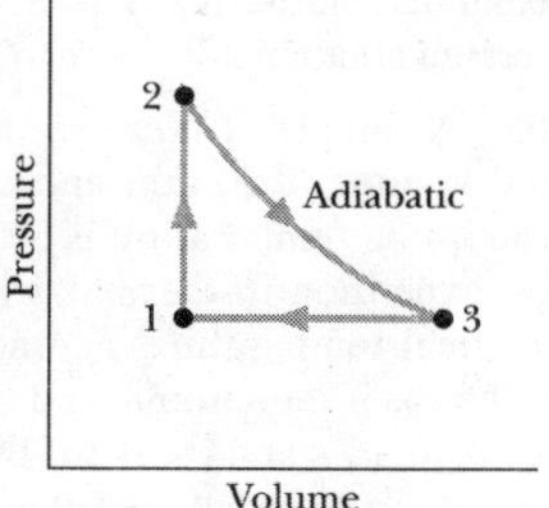

FIG. 21-43 Problem 32.

Additional Problems

33 The temperature of 3.00 mol of a gas with $C_V = 6.00$ cal/mol·K is to be raised 50.0 K. If the process is at *constant volume,* what are (a) the energy transferred as heat Q, (b) the work W done by the gas, (c) the change ΔE_{int} in internal energy of the gas, and (d) the change ΔK in the total translational kinetic energy? If the process is at *constant pressure,* what are (e) Q, (f) W, (g) ΔE_{int}, and (h) ΔK? If the process is *adiabatic,* what are (i) Q, (j) W, (k) ΔE_{int}, and (l) ΔK?

34 (a) An ideal gas initially at pressure p_0 undergoes a free expansion until its volume is 3.00 times its initial volume. What then is the ratio of its pressure to p_0? (b) The gas is next slowly and adiabatically compressed back to its original volume. The pressure after compression is $(3.00)^{1/3}p_0$. Is the gas monatomic, diatomic, or polyatomic? (c) What is the ratio of the average kinetic energy per molecule in this final state to that in the initial state?

35 The temperature of 2.00 mol of an ideal monatomic gas is raised 15.0 K in an adiabatic process. What are (a) the work W done by the gas, (b) the energy transferred as heat Q, (c) the change ΔE_{int} in internal energy of the gas, and (d) the change ΔK in the average kinetic energy per atom?

36 An ideal monatomic gas initially has a temperature of 330 K and a pressure of 6.00 atm. It is to expand from volume 500 cm^3 to volume 1500 cm^3. If the expansion is isothermal, what are (a) the final pressure and (b) the work done by the gas? If, instead, the expansion is adiabatic, what are (c) the final pressure and (d) the work done by the gas?

37 An ideal gas with 3.00 mol is initially in state 1 with pressure $p_1 = 20.0$ atm and volume $V_1 = 1500$ cm^3. First it is taken to state 2 with pressure $p_2 = 1.50\, p_1$ and volume $V_2 = 2.00\, V_1$. Then it is taken to state 3 with pressure $p_3 = 2.00\, p_1$ and volume $V_3 = 0.500\, V_1$. What is the temperature of the gas in (a) state 1 and (b) state 2? (c) What is the net change in internal energy from state 1 to state 3?

38 An ideal gas undergoes an adiabatic compression from $p = 1.0$ atm, $V = 1.0 \times 10^6$ L, $T = 0.0°$C to $p = 1.0 \times 10^5$ atm, $V = 1.0 \times 10^3$ L. (a) Is the gas monatomic, diatomic, or polyatomic? (b) What is its final temperature? (c) How many moles of gas are present? What is the total translational kinetic energy per mole (d) before and (e) after the compression? (f) What is the ratio of the squares of the rms speeds before and after the compression?

39 An ideal gas, at initial temperature T_1 and initial volume 2.0 m^3, is expanded adiabatically to a volume of 4.0 m^3, then expanded isothermally to a volume of 10 m^3, and then compressed adiabatically back to T_1. What is its final volume?

40 A sample of ideal gas expands from an initial pressure and volume of 32 atm and 1.0 L to a final volume of 4.0 L. The initial temperature is 300 K. If the gas is monatomic and the expansion isothermal, what are the (a) final pressure p_f, (b) final temperature T_f, and (c) work W done by the gas? If the gas is monatomic and the expansion adiabatic, what are (d) p_f, (e) T_f, and (f) W? If the gas is diatomic and the expansion adiabatic, what are (g) p_f, (h) T_f, and (i) W?

41 Calculate the work done by an external agent during an isothermal compression of 1.00 mol of oxygen from a volume of 22.4 L at 0°C and 1.00 atm to a volume of 16.8 L.

42 In an industrial process the volume of 25.0 mol of a monatomic ideal gas is reduced at a uniform rate from 0.616 m^3 to 0.308 m^3 in 2.00 h while its temperature is increased at a uniform rate from 27.0°C to 450°C. Throughout the process, the gas passes through thermodynamic equilibrium states. What are (a) the cumulative work done on the gas, (b) the cumulative energy absorbed by the gas as heat, and (c) the molar specific heat for the process? (*Hint:* To evaluate the integral for the work, you might use

$$\int \frac{a + bx}{A + Bx}\,dx = \frac{bx}{B} + \frac{aB - bA}{B^2}\ln(A + Bx)$$

an indefinite integral.) Suppose the process is replaced with a two-step process that reaches the same final state. In step 1, the gas volume is reduced at constant temperature, and in step 2 the temperature is increased at constant volume. For this process, what are (d) the cumulative work done on the gas, (e) the cumulative energy absorbed by the gas as heat, and (f) the molar specific heat for the process?

43 An ideal gas undergoes isothermal compression from an initial volume of 4.00 m^3 to a final volume of 3.00 m^3. There is 3.50 mol of the gas, and its temperature is 10.0°C. (a) How much work is done by the gas? (b) How much energy is transferred as heat between the gas and its environment?

44 Figure 21-44 shows a cycle consisting of five paths: AB is isothermal at 300 K, BC is adiabatic with work = 5.0 J, CD is at a constant pressure of 5 atm, DE is isothermal, and EA is adiabatic with a change in internal energy of 8.0 J. What is the change in internal energy of the gas along path CD?

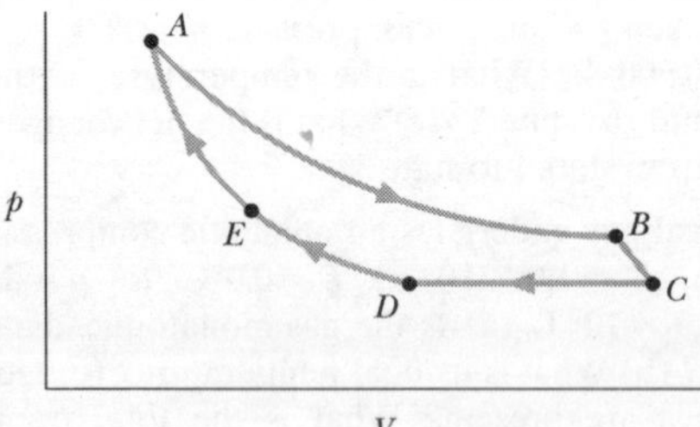

FIG. 21-44 Problem 44.

45 An ideal gas is taken through a complete cycle in three steps: adiabatic expansion with work equal to 125 J, isothermal contraction at 325 K, and increase in pressure at constant volume. (a) Draw a p-V diagram for the three steps. (b) How much energy is transferred as heat in step 3, and (c) is it transferred *to* or *from* the gas?

46 Figure 21-45 shows a reversible cycle through which 1.00 mol of a monatomic ideal gas is taken. Volume $V_c = 8.00V_b$. Process bc is an adiabatic expansion, with $p_b = 10.0$ atm and $V_b = 1.00 \times 10^{-3}$ m^3. For the cycle, find (a) the energy added to the gas as heat, (b) the energy leaving the gas as heat, (c) the net work done by the gas, and (d) the efficiency of the cycle.

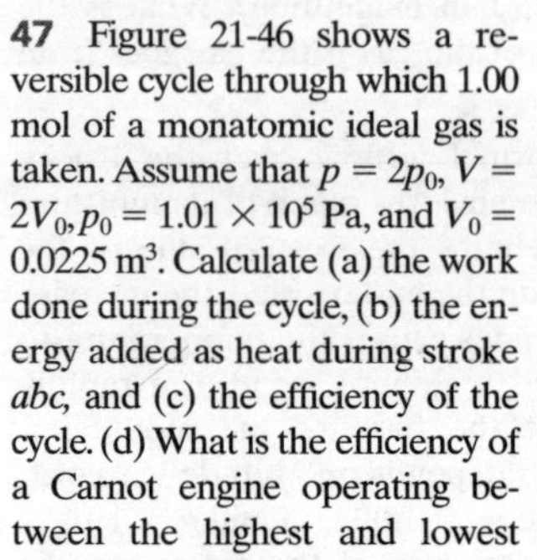

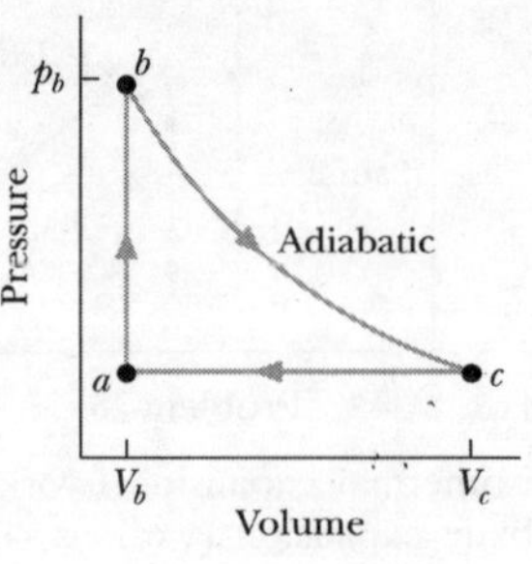

FIG. 21-45 Problem 46.

47 Figure 21-46 shows a reversible cycle through which 1.00 mol of a monatomic ideal gas is taken. Assume that $p = 2p_0$, $V = 2V_0$, $p_0 = 1.01 \times 10^5$ Pa, and $V_0 = 0.0225$ m^3. Calculate (a) the work done during the cycle, (b) the energy added as heat during stroke abc, and (c) the efficiency of the cycle. (d) What is the efficiency of a Carnot engine operating between the highest and lowest temperatures that occur in the cycle? (e) Is this greater than or less than the efficiency calculated in (c)?

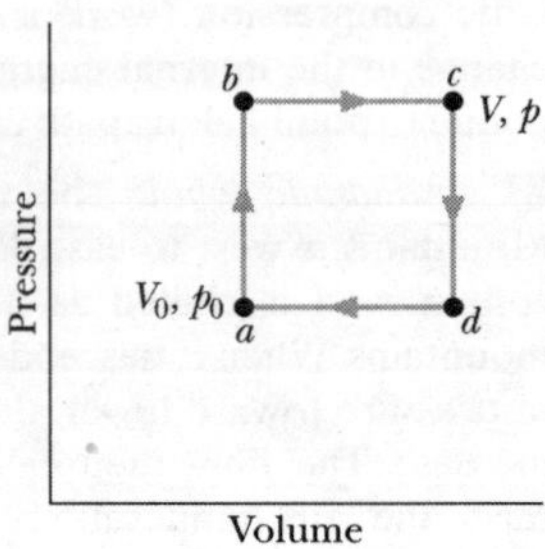

FIG. 21-46 Problem 47.

48 An ideal gas (1.0 mol) is the working substance in an engine that operates on the cycle shown in Fig. 21-47. Processes BC and DA are reversible and adiabatic. (a) Is the gas monatomic, diatomic, or polyatomic? (b) What is the engine efficiency?

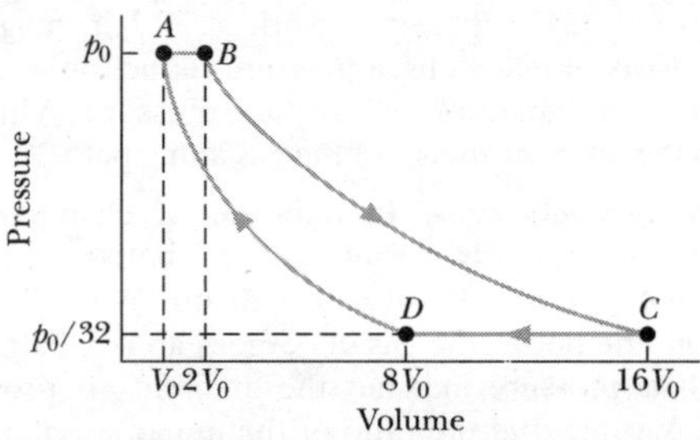

FIG. 21-47 Problem 48.

49 The efficiency of a particular car engine is 25% when the engine does 8.2 kJ of work per cycle. Assume the process is reversible. What are (a) the energy the engine gains per cycle as heat Q_{gain} from the fuel combustion and (b) the energy the engine loses per cycle as heat Q_{lost}. If a tune-up increases the efficiency to 31%, what are (c) Q_{gain} and (d) Q_{lost} at the same work value?

50 In the first stage of a two-stage Carnot engine, energy is absorbed as heat Q_1 at temperature T_1, work W_1 is done, and energy is expelled as heat Q_2 at a lower temperature T_2. The second stage absorbs that energy as heat Q_2, does work W_2, and expels energy as heat Q_3 at a still lower temperature T_3. Prove that the efficiency of the engine is $(T_1 - T_3)/T_1$.

51 The cycle in Fig. 21-48 represents the operation of a gasoline internal combustion engine. Volume $V_3 = 4.00\ V_1$. Assume the gasoline–air intake mixture is an ideal gas with $\gamma = 1.30$. What are the ratios (a) T_2/T_1, (b) T_3/T_1, (c) T_4/T_1, (d) p_3/p_1, and (e) p_4/p_1? (f) What is the engine efficiency?

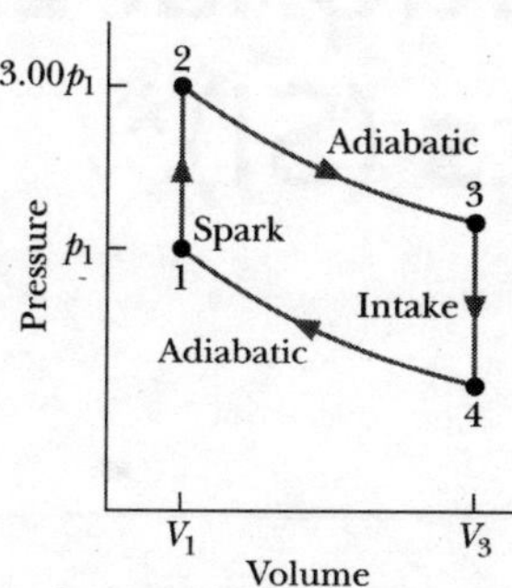

FIG. 21-48 Problem 51.

52 Figure 21-49*a* shows a cylinder containing gas closed by a movable piston. The cylinder is kept submerged in an ice-water mixture. The piston is quickly pushed down from position 1 to position 2 and then held at position 2, until the gas is again at the temperature of the ice-water mixture. It then is slowly raised back to position 1. Figure 21-49*b* is a *p-V* diagram for the process. If 100 g of ice is melted during the cycle, how much work has been done on the gas ?

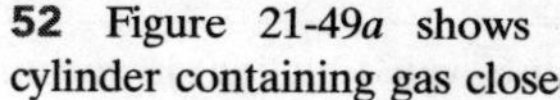

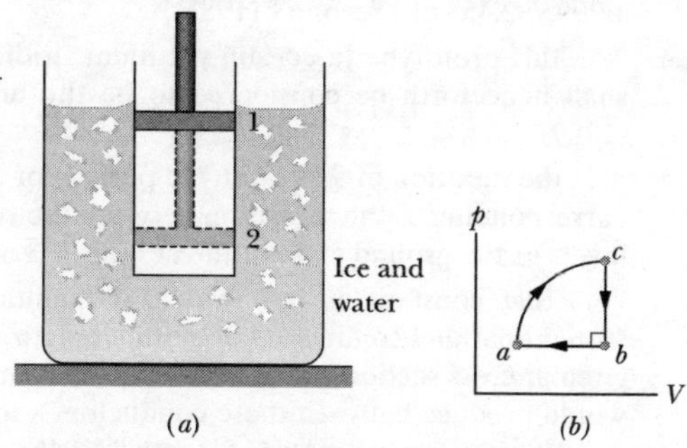

FIG. 21-49 Problem 52.

53 Figure 21-50 show a closed cycle for a gas. The change in internal energy along the path from *c* to *a* is −160 J. The energy transferred to the gas as heat is 200 J along the path from *a* to *b*, and 40 J along the path from *b* to *c*. How much work is done by the gas along (a) path *abc* and (b) path *ab*?

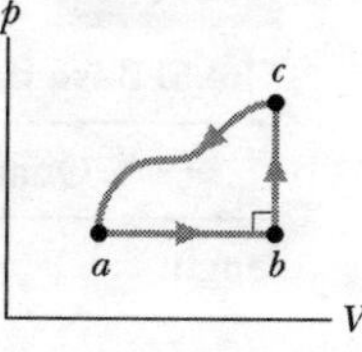

FIG. 21-50 Problem 53.

54 A closed adiabatic vessel contains ozone (O_3) at a temperature of t_1 = 527°C. After some time the ozone is completely converted into oxygen (O_2). Find the increase of the pressure in the vessel if Q = 34,000 cal have to be spent to form one gramme-molecule of ozone from oxygen. Assume that the heat capacity of one gramme-molecule of oxygen at a constant volume is equal to C_V = 5 cal/deg. mole.

The International System of Units (SI)*

A

TABLE 1

The SI Base Units

Quantity	Name	Symbol	Definition
length	meter	m	". . . the length of the path traveled by light in vacuum in 1/299,792,458 of a second." (1983)
mass	kilogram	kg	". . . this prototype [a certain platinum–iridium cylinder] shall henceforth be considered to be the unit of mass." (1889)
time	second	s	". . . the duration of 9,192,631,770 periods of the radiation corresponding to the transition between the two hyperfine levels of the ground state of the cesium-133 atom." (1967)
electric current	ampere	A	". . . that constant current which, if maintained in two straight parallel conductors of infinite length, of negligible circular cross section, and placed 1 meter apart in vacuum, would produce between these conductors a force equal to 2×10^{-7} newton per meter of length." (1946)
thermodynamic temperature	kelvin	K	". . . the fraction 1/273.16 of the thermodynamic temperature of the triple point of water." (1967)
amount of substance	mole	mol	". . . the amount of substance of a system which contains as many elementary entities as there are atoms in 0.012 kilogram of carbon-12." (1971)
luminous intensity	candela	cd	". . . the luminous intensity, in a given direction, of a source that emits monochromatic radiation of frequency 540×10^{12} hertz and that has a radiant intensity in that direction of 1/683 watt per steradian." (1979)

*Adapted from "The International System of Units (SI)," National Bureau of Standards Special Publication 330, 1972 edition. The definitions above were adopted by the General Conference of Weights and Measures, an international body, on the dates shown. In this book we do not use the candela.

TABLE 2

Some SI Derived Units

Quantity	Name of Unit	Symbol	
area	square meter	m^2	
volume	cubic meter	m^3	
frequency	hertz	Hz	s^{-1}
mass density (density)	kilogram per cubic meter	kg/m^3	
speed, velocity	meter per second	m/s	
angular velocity	radian per second	rad/s	
acceleration	meter per second per second	m/s^2	
angular acceleration	radian per second per second	rad/s^2	
force	newton	N	$kg \cdot m/s^2$
pressure	pascal	Pa	N/m^2
work, energy, quantity of heat	joule	J	$N \cdot m$
power	watt	W	J/s
quantity of electric charge	coulomb	C	$A \cdot s$
potential difference, electromotive force	volt	V	W/A
electric field strength	volt per meter (or newton per coulomb)	V/m	N/C
electric resistance	ohm	Ω	V/A
capacitance	farad	F	$A \cdot s/V$
magnetic flux	weber	Wb	$V \cdot s$
inductance	henry	H	$V \cdot s/A$
magnetic flux density	tesla	T	Wb/m^2
magnetic field strength	ampere per meter	A/m	
entropy	joule per kelvin	J/K	
specific heat	joule per kilogram kelvin	$J/(kg \cdot K)$	
thermal conductivity	watt per meter kelvin	$W/(m \cdot K)$	
radiant intensity	watt per steradian	W/sr	

TABLE 3

The SI Supplementary Units

Quantity	Name of Unit	Symbol
plane angle	radian	rad
solid angle	steradian	sr

Some Fundamental Constants of Physics* B

Constant	Symbol	Computational Value	Best (1998) Value	
			Value[a]	Uncertainty[b]
Speed of light in a vacuum	c	3.00×10^{8} m/s	2.997 924 58	exact
Elementary charge	e	1.60×10^{-19} C	1.602 176 462	0.039
Gravitational constant	G	6.67×10^{-11} m³/s² · kg	6.673	1500
Universal gas constant	R	8.31 J/mol · K	8.314 472	1.7
Avogadro constant	N_A	6.02×10^{23} mol⁻¹	6.022 141 99	0.079
Boltzmann constant	k	1.38×10^{-23} J/K	1.380 650 3	1.7
Stefan–Boltzmann constant	σ	5.67×10^{-8} W/m² · K⁴	5.670 400	7.0
Molar volume of ideal gas at STP[d]	V_m	2.27×10^{-2} m³/mol	2.271 098 1	1.7
Permittivity constant	ϵ_0	8.85×10^{-12} F/m	8.854 187 817 62	exact
Permeability constant	μ_0	1.26×10^{-6} H/m	1.256 637 061 43	exact
Planck constant	h	6.63×10^{-34} J · s	6.626 068 76	0.078
Electron mass[c]	m_e	9.11×10^{-31} kg	9.109 381 88	0.079
		5.49×10^{-4} u	5.485 799 110	0.0021
Proton mass[c]	m_p	1.67×10^{-27} kg	1.672 621 58	0.079
		1.0073 u	1.007 276 466 88	1.3×10^{-4}
Ratio of proton mass to electron mass	m_p/m_e	1840	1836.152 667 5	0.0021
Electron charge-to-mass ratio	e/m_e	1.76×10^{11} C/kg	1.758 820 174	0.040
Neutron mass[c]	m_n	1.68×10^{-27} kg	1.674 927 16	0.079
		1.0087 u	1.008 664 915 78	5.4×10^{-4}
Hydrogen atom mass[c]	$m_{^1H}$	1.0078 u	1.007 825 031 6	0.0005
Deuterium atom mass[c]	$m_{^2H}$	2.0141 u	2.014 101 777 9	0.0005
Helium atom mass[c]	$m_{^4He}$	4.0026 u	4.002 603 2	0.067
Muon mass	m_μ	1.88×10^{-28} kg	1.883 531 09	0.084
Electron magnetic moment	μ_e	9.28×10^{-24} J/T	9.284 763 62	0.040
Proton magnetic moment	μ_p	1.41×10^{-26} J/T	1.410 606 663	0.041
Bohr magneton	μ_B	9.27×10^{-24} J/T	9.274 008 99	0.040
Nuclear magneton	μ_N	5.05×10^{-27} J/T	5.050 783 17	0.040
Bohr radius	a	5.29×10^{-11} m	5.291 772 083	0.0037
Rydberg constant	R	1.10×10^{7} m⁻¹	1.097 373 156 854 8	7.6×10^{-6}
Electron Compton wavelength	λ_C	2.43×10^{-12} m	2.426 310 215	0.0073

[a]Values given in this column should be given the same unit and power of 10 as the computational value.
[b]Parts per million.
[c]Masses given in u are in unified atomic mass units, where 1 u = $1.660\,538\,86 \times 10^{-27}$ kg.
[d]STP means standard temperature and pressure: 0°C and 1.0 atm (0.1 MPa).

*The values in this table were selected from the 1998 CODATA recommended values (www.physics.nist.gov).

C Some Astronomical Data

Some Distances from Earth

To the Moon*	3.82×10^8 m	To the center of our galaxy	2.2×10^{20} m
To the Sun*	1.50×10^{11} m	To the Andromeda Galaxy	2.1×10^{22} m
To the nearest star (Proxima Centauri)	4.04×10^{16} m	To the edge of the observable universe	$\sim 10^{26}$ m

*Mean distance.

The Sun, Earth, and the Moon

Property	Unit	Sun		Earth	Moon
Mass	kg	1.99×10^{30}		5.98×10^{24}	7.36×10^{22}
Mean radius	m	6.96×10^8		6.37×10^6	1.74×10^6
Mean density	kg/m^3	1410		5520	3340
Free-fall acceleration at the surface	m/s^2	274		9.81	1.67
Escape velocity	km/s	618		11.2	2.38
Period of rotation[a]	—	37 d at poles[b]	26 d at equator[b]	23 h 56 min	27.3 d
Radiation power[c]	W	3.90×10^{26}			

[a]Measured with respect to the distant stars.
[b]The Sun, a ball of gas, does not rotate as a rigid body.
[c]Just outside Earth's atmosphere solar energy is received, assuming normal incidence, at the rate of 1340 W/m^2.

Some Properties of the Planets

	Mercury	Venus	Earth	Mars	Jupiter	Saturn	Uranus	Neptune	Pluto
Mean distance from Sun, 10^6 km	57.9	108	150	228	778	1430	2870	4500	5900
Period of revolution, y	0.241	0.615	1.00	1.88	11.9	29.5	84.0	165	248
Period of rotation,[a] d	58.7	-243[b]	0.997	1.03	0.409	0.426	-0.451[b]	0.658	6.39
Orbital speed, km/s	47.9	35.0	29.8	24.1	13.1	9.64	6.81	5.43	4.74
Inclination of axis to orbit	$<28°$	$\approx 3°$	23.4°	25.0°	3.08°	26.7°	97.9°	29.6°	57.5°
Inclination of orbit to Earth's orbit	7.00°	3.39°		1.85°	1.30°	2.49°	0.77°	1.77°	17.2°
Eccentricity of orbit	0.206	0.0068	0.0167	0.0934	0.0485	0.0556	0.0472	0.0086	0.250
Equatorial diameter, km	4880	12 100	12 800	6790	143 000	120 000	51 800	49 500	2300
Mass (Earth = 1)	0.0558	0.815	1.000	0.107	318	95.1	14.5	17.2	0.002
Density (water = 1)	5.60	5.20	5.52	3.95	1.31	0.704	1.21	1.67	2.03
Surface value of g,[c] m/s^2	3.78	8.60	9.78	3.72	22.9	9.05	7.77	11.0	0.5
Escape velocity,[c] km/s	4.3	10.3	11.2	5.0	59.5	35.6	21.2	23.6	1.1
Known satellites	0	0	1	2	60 + ring	31 + rings	21 + rings	11 + rings	1

[a]Measured with respect to the distant stars.
[b]Venus and Uranus rotate opposite their orbital motion.
[c]Gravitational acceleration measured at the planet's equator.

Conversion Factors D

Conversion factors may be read directly from these tables. For example, 1 degree = 2.778×10^{-3} revolutions, so $16.7° = 16.7 \times 2.778 \times 10^{-3}$ rev. The SI units are fully capitalized. Adapted

Plane Angle

°	′	″	RADIAN	rev
1 degree = 1	60	3600	1.745×10^{-2}	2.778×10^{-3}
1 minute = 1.667×10^{-2}	1	60	2.909×10^{-4}	4.630×10^{-5}
1 second = 2.778×10^{-4}	1.667×10^{-2}	1	4.848×10^{-6}	7.716×10^{-7}
1 RADIAN = 57.30	3438	2.063×10^{5}	1	0.1592
1 revolution = 360	2.16×10^{4}	1.296×10^{6}	6.283	1

Solid Angle

1 sphere = 4π steradians = 12.57 steradians

Length

cm	METER	km	in.	ft	mi
1 centimeter = 1	10^{-2}	10^{-5}	0.3937	3.281×10^{-2}	6.214×10^{-6}
1 METER = 100	1	10^{-3}	39.37	3.281	6.214×10^{-4}
1 kilometer = 10^{5}	1000	1	3.937×10^{4}	3281	0.6214
1 inch = 2.540	2.540×10^{-2}	2.540×10^{-5}	1	8.333×10^{-2}	1.578×10^{-5}
1 foot = 30.48	0.3048	3.048×10^{-4}	12	1	1.894×10^{-4}
1 mile = 1.609×10^{5}	1609	1.609	6.336×10^{4}	5280	1

1 angström = 10^{-10} m
1 nautical mile = 1852 m = 1.151 miles = 6076 ft
1 fermi = 10^{-15} m
1 light-year = 9.461×10^{12} km
1 parsec = 3.084×10^{13} km
1 fathom = 6 ft
1 Bohr radius = 5.292×10^{-11} m
1 yard = 3 ft
1 rod = 16.5 ft
1 mil = 10^{-3} in.
1 nm = 10^{-9} m

Area

METER^2	cm^2	ft^2	in.^{2}
1 SQUARE METER = 1	10^{4}	10.76	1550
1 square centimeter = 10^{-4}	1	1.076×10^{-3}	0.1550
1 square foot = 9.290×10^{-2}	929.0	1	144
1 square inch = 6.452×10^{-4}	6.452	6.944×10^{-3}	1

1 square mile = 2.788×10^{7} ft^2 = 640 acres
1 barn = 10^{-28} m^2
1 acre = 43 560 ft^2
1 hectare = 10^{4} m^2 = 2.471 acres

Volume

METER^3	cm^3	L	ft^3	in.^{3}
1 CUBIC METER = 1	10^6	1000	35.31	6.102×10^4
1 cubic centimeter = 10^{-6}	1	1.000×10^{-3}	3.531×10^{-5}	6.102×10^{-2}
1 liter = 1.000×10^{-3}	1000	1	3.531×10^{-2}	61.02
1 cubic foot = 2.832×10^{-2}	2.832×10^4	28.32	1	1728
1 cubic inch = 1.639×10^{-5}	16.39	1.639×10^{-2}	5.787×10^{-4}	1

1 U.S. fluid gallon = 4 U.S. fluid quarts = 8 U.S. pints = 128 U.S. fluid ounces = 231 in.^{3}
1 British imperial gallon = 277.4 in.^{3} = 1.201 U.S. fluid gallons

in part from G. Shortley and D. Williams, *Elements of Physics,* 1971, Prentice-Hall, Englewood Cliffs, NJ.

Mass

g	KILOGRAM	slug	u	oz	lb	ton
1 gram = 1	0.001	6.852×10^{-5}	6.022×10^{23}	3.527×10^{-2}	2.205×10^{-3}	1.102×10^{-6}
1 KILOGRAM = 1000	1	6.852×10^{-2}	6.022×10^{26}	35.27	2.205	1.102×10^{-3}
1 slug = 1.459×10^4	14.59	1	8.786×10^{27}	514.8	32.17	1.609×10^{-2}
1 atomic mass unit = 1.661×10^{-24}	1.661×10^{-27}	1.138×10^{-28}	1	5.857×10^{-26}	3.662×10^{-27}	1.830×10^{-30}
1 ounce = 28.35	2.835×10^{-2}	1.943×10^{-3}	1.718×10^{25}	1	6.250×10^{-2}	3.125×10^{-5}
1 pound = 453.6	0.4536	3.108×10^{-2}	2.732×10^{26}	16	1	0.0005
1 ton = 9.072×10^5	907.2	62.16	5.463×10^{29}	3.2×10^4	2000	1

1 metric ton = 1000 kg

Quantities in the colored areas are not mass units but are often used as such. For example, when we write 1 kg "=" 2.205 lb, this means that a kilogram is a *mass* that *weighs* 2.205 pounds at a location where g has the standard value of 9.80665 m/s^2.

slug/ft^3	KILOGRAM/ METER^3	g/cm^3	lb/ft^3	lb/in.^{3}
1 slug per foot^3 = 1	515.4	0.5154	32.17	1.862×10^{-2}
1 KILOGRAM per METER^3 = 1.940×10^{-3}	1	0.001	6.243×10^{-2}	3.613×10^{-5}
1 gram per centimeter^3 = 1.940	1000	1	62.43	3.613×10^{-2}
1 pound per foot^3 = 3.108×10^{-2}	16.02	16.02×10^{-2}	1	5.787×10^{-4}
1 pound per inch^3 = 53.71	2.768×10^4	27.68	1728	1

Time

y	d	h	min	SECOND
1 year = 1	365.25	8.766×10^3	5.259×10^5	3.156×10^7
1 day = 2.738×10^{-3}	1	24	1440	8.640×10^4
1 hour = 1.141×10^{-4}	4.167×10^{-2}	1	60	3600
1 minute = 1.901×10^{-6}	6.944×10^{-4}	1.667×10^{-2}	1	60
1 SECOND = 3.169×10^{-8}	1.157×10^{-5}	2.778×10^{-4}	1.667×10^{-2}	1

Speed

	ft/s	km/h	METER/SECOND	mi/h	cm/s
1 foot per second =	1	1.097	0.3048	0.6818	30.48
1 kilometer per hour =	0.9113	1	0.2778	0.6214	27.78
1 METER per SECOND =	3.281	3.6	1	2.237	100
1 mile per hour =	1.467	1.609	0.4470	1	44.70
1 centimeter per second =	3.281×10^{-2}	3.6×10^{-2}	0.01	2.237×10^{-2}	1

1 knot = 1 nautical mi/h = 1.688 ft/s   1 mi/min = 88.00 ft/s = 60.00 mi/h

Density

Quantities in the colored areas are weight densities and, as such, are dimensionally different from mass densities. See the note for the mass table.

	dyne	NEWTON	lb	pdl	gf	kgf
1 dyne =	1	10^{-5}	2.248×10^{-6}	7.233×10^{-5}	1.020×10^{-3}	1.020×10^{-6}
1 NEWTON =	10^5	1	0.2248	7.233	102.0	0.1020
1 pound =	4.448×10^5	4.448	1	32.17	453.6	0.4536
1 poundal =	1.383×10^4	0.1383	3.108×10^{-2}	1	14.10	1.410×10^2
1 gram-force =	980.7	9.807×10^{-3}	2.205×10^{-3}	7.093×10^{-2}	1	0.001
1 kilogram-force =	9.807×10^5	9.807	2.205	70.93	1000	1

1 ton = 2000 lb

Pressure

	atm	dyne/cm²	inch of water	cm Hg	PASCAL	lb/in.²	lb/ft²
1 atmosphere =	1	1.013×10^6	406.8	76	1.013×10^5	14.70	2116
1 dyne per centimeter² =	9.869×10^{-7}	1	4.015×10^{-4}	7.501×10^{-5}	0.1	1.405×10^{-5}	2.089×10^{-3}
1 inch of water[a] at 4°C =	2.458×10^{-3}	2491	1	0.1868	249.1	3.613×10^{-2}	5.202
1 centimeter of mercury[a] at 0°C =	1.316×10^{-2}	1.333×10^4	5.353	1	1333	0.1934	27.85
1 PASCAL =	9.869×10^{-6}	10	4.015×10^{-3}	7.501×10^{-4}	1	1.450×10^{-4}	2.089×10^{-2}
1 pound per inch² =	6.805×10^{-2}	6.895×10^4	27.68	5.171	6.895×10^3	1	144
1 pound per foot² =	4.725×10^{-4}	478.8	0.1922	3.591×10^{-2}	47.88	6.944×10^{-3}	1

[a]Where the acceleration of gravity has the standard value of 9.80665 m/s².

1 bar = 10^6 dyne/cm² = 0.1 MPa   1 millibar = 10^3 dyne/cm² = 10^2 Pa   1 torr = 1 mm Hg

Energy, Work, Heat

Quantities in the colored areas are not energy units but are included for convenience. They arise from the relativistic mass–energy equivalence formula $E = mc^2$ and represent the energy released if a kilogram or unified atomic mass unit (u) is completely converted to energy (bottom two rows) or the mass that would be completely converted to one unit of energy (rightmost two columns).

	Btu	erg	ft · lb	hp · h	JOULE	cal	kW · h	eV	MeV	kg	u
1 British thermal unit =	1	1.055×10^{10}	777.9	3.929×10^{-4}	1055	252.0	2.930×10^{-4}	6.585×10^{21}	6.585×10^{15}	1.174×10^{-14}	7.070×10^{12}
1 erg =	9.481×10^{-11}	1	7.376×10^{-8}	3.725×10^{-14}	10^{-7}	2.389×10^{-8}	2.778×10^{-14}	6.242×10^{11}	6.242×10^{5}	1.113×10^{-24}	670.2
1 foot-pound =	1.285×10^{-3}	1.356×10^{7}	1	5.051×10^{-7}	1.356	0.3238	3.766×10^{-7}	8.464×10^{18}	8.464×10^{12}	1.509×10^{-17}	9.037×10^{9}
1 horsepower-hour =	2545	2.685×10^{13}	1.980×10^{6}	1	2.685×10^{6}	6.413×10^{5}	0.7457	1.676×10^{25}	1.676×10^{19}	2.988×10^{-11}	1.799×10^{16}
1 JOULE =	9.481×10^{-4}	10^{7}	0.7376	3.725×10^{-7}	1	0.2389	2.778×10^{-7}	6.242×10^{18}	6.242×10^{12}	1.113×10^{-17}	6.702×10^{9}
1 calorie =	3.968×10^{-3}	4.1868×10^{7}	3.088	1.560×10^{-6}	4.1868	1	1.163×10^{-6}	2.613×10^{19}	2.613×10^{13}	4.660×10^{-17}	2.806×10^{10}
1 kilowatt-hour =	3413	3.600×10^{13}	2.655×10^{6}	1.341	3.600×10^{6}	8.600×10^{5}	1	2.247×10^{25}	2.247×10^{19}	4.007×10^{-11}	2.413×10^{16}
1 electron-volt =	1.519×10^{-22}	1.602×10^{-12}	1.182×10^{-19}	5.967×10^{-26}	1.602×10^{-19}	3.827×10^{-20}	4.450×10^{-26}	1	10^{-6}	1.783×10^{-36}	1.074×10^{-9}
1 million electron-volts =	1.519×10^{-16}	1.602×10^{-6}	1.182×10^{-13}	5.967×10^{-20}	1.602×10^{-13}	3.827×10^{-14}	4.450×10^{-20}	10^{-6}	1	1.783×10^{-30}	1.074×10^{-3}
1 kilogram =	8.521×10^{13}	8.987×10^{23}	6.629×10^{16}	3.348×10^{10}	8.987×10^{16}	2.146×10^{16}	2.497×10^{10}	5.610×10^{35}	5.610×10^{29}	1	6.022×10^{26}
1 unified atomic mass unit =	1.415×10^{-13}	1.492×10^{-3}	1.101×10^{-10}	5.559×10^{-17}	1.492×10^{-10}	3.564×10^{-11}	4.146×10^{-17}	9.320×10^{8}	932.0	1.661×10^{-27}	1

Power

	Btu/h	ft · lb/s	hp	cal/s	kW	WATT
1 British thermal unit per hour =	1	0.2161	3.929×10^{-4}	6.998×10^{-2}	2.930×10^{-4}	0.2930
1 foot-pound per second =	4.628	1	1.818×10^{-3}	0.3239	1.356×10^{-3}	1.356
1 horsepower =	2545	550	1	178.1	0.7457	745.7
1 calorie per second =	14.29	3.088	5.615×10^{-3}	1	4.186×10^{-3}	4.186
1 kilowatt =	3413	737.6	1.341	238.9	1	1000
1 WATT =	3.413	0.7376	1.341×10^{-3}	0.2389	0.001	1

Magnetic Field

	gauss	TESLA	milligauss
1 gauss =	1	10^{-4}	1000
1 TESLA =	10^{4}	1	10^{7}
1 milligauss =	0.001	10^{-7}	1

1 tesla = 1 weber/meter^2

Magnetic Flux

	maxwell	WEBER
1 maxwell =	1	10^{-8}
1 WEBER =	10^{8}	1

Mathematical Formulas E

Geometry

Circle of radius r: circumference $= 2\pi r$; area $= \pi r^2$.

Sphere of radius r: area $= 4\pi r^2$; volume $= \frac{4}{3}\pi r^3$.

Right circular cylinder of radius r and height h:
area $= 2\pi r^2 + 2\pi rh$; volume $= \pi r^2 h$.

Triangle of base a and altitude h: area $= \frac{1}{2}ah$.

Quadratic Formula

If $ax^2 + bx + c = 0$, then $x = \dfrac{-b \pm \sqrt{b^2 - 4ac}}{2a}$.

Trigonometric Functions of Angle θ

$\sin\theta = \dfrac{y}{r}$ $\quad \cos\theta = \dfrac{x}{r}$

$\tan\theta = \dfrac{y}{x}$ $\quad \cot\theta = \dfrac{x}{y}$

$\sec\theta = \dfrac{r}{x}$ $\quad \csc\theta = \dfrac{r}{y}$

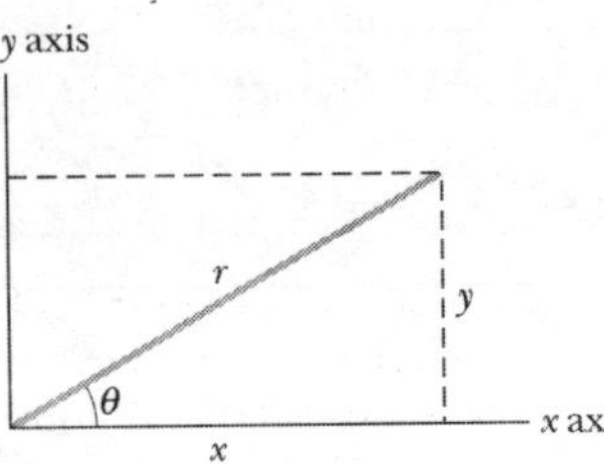

Pythagorean Theorem

In this right triangle,
$a^2 + b^2 = c^2$

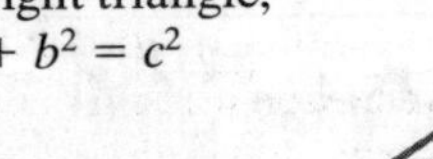

Triangles

Angles are A, B, C

Opposite sides are a, b, c

Angles $A + B + C = 180°$

$\dfrac{\sin A}{a} = \dfrac{\sin B}{b} = \dfrac{\sin C}{c}$

$c^2 = a^2 + b^2 - 2ab\cos C$

Exterior angle $D = A + C$

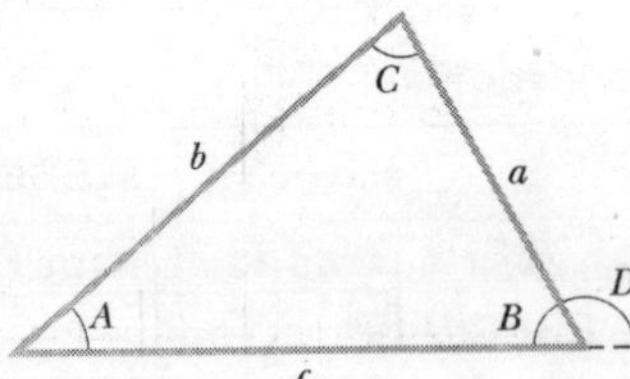

Mathematical Signs and Symbols

$=$ equals

$\approx$ equals approximately

$\sim$ is the order of magnitude of

$\neq$ is not equal to

$\equiv$ is identical to, is defined as

$>$ is greater than ($\gg$ is much greater than)

$<$ is less than ($\ll$ is much less than)

$\geq$ is greater than or equal to (or, is no less than)

$\leq$ is less than or equal to (or, is no more than)

$\pm$ plus or minus

$\propto$ is proportional to

Σ the sum of

x_{avg} the average value of x

Trigonometric Identities

$\sin(90° - \theta) = \cos\theta$

$\cos(90° - \theta) = \sin\theta$

$\sin\theta / \cos\theta = \tan\theta$

$\sin^2\theta + \cos^2\theta = 1$

$\sec^2\theta - \tan^2\theta = 1$

$\csc^2\theta - \cot^2\theta = 1$

$\sin 2\theta = 2\sin\theta\cos\theta$

$\cos 2\theta = \cos^2\theta - \sin^2\theta = 2\cos^2\theta - 1 = 1 - 2\sin^2\theta$

$\sin(\alpha \pm \beta) = \sin\alpha\cos\beta \pm \cos\alpha\sin\beta$

$\cos(\alpha \pm \beta) = \cos\alpha\cos\beta \mp \sin\alpha\sin\beta$

$\tan(\alpha \pm \beta) = \dfrac{\tan\alpha \pm \tan\beta}{1 \mp \tan\alpha\tan\beta}$

$\sin\alpha \pm \sin\beta = 2\sin\frac{1}{2}(\alpha \pm \beta)\cos\frac{1}{2}(\alpha \mp \beta)$

$\cos\alpha + \cos\beta = 2\cos\frac{1}{2}(\alpha + \beta)\cos\frac{1}{2}(\alpha - \beta)$

$\cos\alpha - \cos\beta = -2\sin\frac{1}{2}(\alpha + \beta)\sin\frac{1}{2}(\alpha - \beta)$

Binomial Theorem

$$(1+x)^n = 1 + \frac{nx}{1!} + \frac{n(n-1)x^2}{2!} + \cdots \qquad (x^2 < 1)$$

Exponential Expansion

$$e^x = 1 + x + \frac{x^2}{2!} + \frac{x^3}{3!} + \cdots$$

Logarithmic Expansion

$$\ln(1+x) = x - \tfrac{1}{2}x^2 + \tfrac{1}{3}x^3 - \cdots \qquad (|x| < 1)$$

Trigonometric Expansions (θ in radians)

$$\sin\theta = \theta - \frac{\theta^3}{3!} + \frac{\theta^5}{5!} - \cdots$$

$$\cos\theta = 1 - \frac{\theta^2}{2!} + \frac{\theta^4}{4!} - \cdots$$

$$\tan\theta = \theta + \frac{\theta^3}{3} + \frac{2\theta^5}{15} + \cdots$$

Cramer's Rule

Two simultaneous equations in unknowns x and y,

$$a_1x + b_1y = c_1 \quad \text{and} \quad a_2x + b_2y = c_2,$$

have the solutions

$$x = \frac{\begin{vmatrix} c_1 & b_1 \\ c_2 & b_2 \end{vmatrix}}{\begin{vmatrix} a_1 & b_1 \\ a_2 & b_2 \end{vmatrix}} = \frac{c_1b_2 - c_2b_1}{a_1b_2 - a_2b_1}$$

and

$$y = \frac{\begin{vmatrix} a_1 & c_1 \\ a_2 & c_2 \end{vmatrix}}{\begin{vmatrix} a_1 & b_1 \\ a_2 & b_2 \end{vmatrix}} = \frac{a_1c_2 - a_2c_1}{a_1b_2 - a_2b_1}.$$

Products of Vectors

Let $\hat{i}$, $\hat{j}$, and $\hat{k}$ be unit vectors in the x, y, and z directions. Then

$$\hat{i}\cdot\hat{i} = \hat{j}\cdot\hat{j} = \hat{k}\cdot\hat{k} = 1, \quad \hat{i}\cdot\hat{j} = \hat{j}\cdot\hat{k} = \hat{k}\cdot\hat{i} = 0,$$

$$\hat{i}\times\hat{i} = \hat{j}\times\hat{j} = \hat{k}\times\hat{k} = 0,$$

$$\hat{i}\times\hat{j} = \hat{k}, \quad \hat{j}\times\hat{k} = \hat{i}, \quad \hat{k}\times\hat{i} = \hat{j}$$

Any vector $\vec{a}$ with components a_x, a_y, and a_z along the x, y, and z axes can be written as

$$\vec{a} = a_x\hat{i} + a_y\hat{j} + a_z\hat{k}.$$

Let $\vec{a}$, $\vec{b}$, and $\vec{c}$ be arbitrary vectors with magnitudes a, b, and c. Then

$$\vec{a}\times(\vec{b}+\vec{c}) = (\vec{a}\times\vec{b}) + (\vec{a}\times\vec{c})$$

$$(s\vec{a})\times\vec{b} = \vec{a}\times(s\vec{b}) = s(\vec{a}\times\vec{b}) \qquad (s = \text{a scalar}).$$

Let θ be the smaller of the two angles between $\vec{a}$ and $\vec{b}$. Then

$$\vec{a}\cdot\vec{b} = \vec{b}\cdot\vec{a} = a_xb_x + a_yb_y + a_zb_z = ab\cos\theta$$

$$\vec{a}\times\vec{b} = -\vec{b}\times\vec{a} = \begin{vmatrix} \hat{i} & \hat{j} & \hat{k} \\ a_x & a_y & a_z \\ b_x & b_y & b_z \end{vmatrix}$$

$$= \hat{i}\begin{vmatrix} a_y & a_z \\ b_y & b_z \end{vmatrix} - \hat{j}\begin{vmatrix} a_x & a_z \\ b_x & b_z \end{vmatrix} + \hat{k}\begin{vmatrix} a_x & a_y \\ b_x & b_y \end{vmatrix}$$

$$= (a_yb_z - b_ya_z)\hat{i} + (a_zb_x - b_za_x)\hat{j} + (a_xb_y - b_xa_y)\hat{k}$$

$$|\vec{a}\times\vec{b}| = ab\sin\theta$$

$$\vec{a}\cdot(\vec{b}\times\vec{c}) = \vec{b}\cdot(\vec{c}\times\vec{a}) = \vec{c}\cdot(\vec{a}\times\vec{b})$$

$$\vec{a}\times(\vec{b}\times\vec{c}) = (\vec{a}\cdot\vec{c})\vec{b} - (\vec{a}\cdot\vec{b})\vec{c}$$

Derivatives and Integrals

In what follows, the letters u and v stand for any functions of x, and a and m are constants. To each of the indefinite integrals should be added an arbitrary constant of integration. The *Handbook of Chemistry and Physics* (CRC Press Inc.) gives a more extensive tabulation.

1. $\dfrac{dx}{dx} = 1$

2. $\dfrac{d}{dx}(au) = a\dfrac{du}{dx}$

3. $\dfrac{d}{dx}(u + v) = \dfrac{du}{dx} + \dfrac{dv}{dx}$

4. $\dfrac{d}{dx}x^m = mx^{m-1}$

5. $\dfrac{d}{dx}\ln x = \dfrac{1}{x}$

6. $\dfrac{d}{dx}(uv) = u\dfrac{dv}{dx} + v\dfrac{du}{dx}$

7. $\dfrac{d}{dx}e^x = e^x$

8. $\dfrac{d}{dx}\sin x = \cos x$

9. $\dfrac{d}{dx}\cos x = -\sin x$

10. $\dfrac{d}{dx}\tan x = \sec^2 x$

11. $\dfrac{d}{dx}\cot x = -\csc^2 x$

12. $\dfrac{d}{dx}\sec x = \tan x \sec x$

13. $\dfrac{d}{dx}\csc x = -\cot x \csc x$

14. $\dfrac{d}{dx}e^u = e^u\dfrac{du}{dx}$

15. $\dfrac{d}{dx}\sin u = \cos u\dfrac{du}{dx}$

16. $\dfrac{d}{dx}\cos u = -\sin u\dfrac{du}{dx}$

1. $\int dx = x$

2. $\int au\,dx = a\int u\,dx$

3. $\int (u + v)\,dx = \int u\,dx + \int v\,dx$

4. $\int x^m\,dx = \dfrac{x^{m+1}}{m+1} \quad (m \neq -1)$

5. $\int \dfrac{dx}{x} = \ln|x|$

6. $\int u\dfrac{dv}{dx}\,dx = uv - \int v\dfrac{du}{dx}\,dx$

7. $\int e^x\,dx = e^x$

8. $\int \sin x\,dx = -\cos x$

9. $\int \cos x\,dx = \sin x$

10. $\int \tan x\,dx = \ln|\sec x|$

11. $\int \sin^2 x\,dx = \frac{1}{2}x - \frac{1}{4}\sin 2x$

12. $\int e^{-ax}\,dx = -\dfrac{1}{a}e^{-ax}$

13. $\int xe^{-ax}\,dx = -\dfrac{1}{a^2}(ax + 1)\,e^{-ax}$

14. $\int x^2e^{-ax}\,dx = -\dfrac{1}{a^3}(a^2x^2 + 2ax + 2)e^{-ax}$

15. $\int_0^\infty x^ne^{-ax}\,dx = \dfrac{n!}{a^{n+1}}$

16. $\int_0^\infty x^{2n}e^{-ax^2}\,dx = \dfrac{1\cdot3\cdot5\cdots(2n-1)}{2^{n+1}a^n}\sqrt{\dfrac{\pi}{a}}$

17. $\int \dfrac{dx}{\sqrt{x^2 + a^2}} = \ln(x + \sqrt{x^2 + a^2})$

18. $\int \dfrac{x\,dx}{(x^2 + a^2)^{3/2}} = -\dfrac{1}{(x^2 + a^2)^{1/2}}$

19. $\int \dfrac{dx}{(x^2 + a^2)^{3/2}} = \dfrac{x}{a^2(x^2 + a^2)^{1/2}}$

20. $\int_0^\infty x^{2n+1}\,e^{-ax^2}\,dx = \dfrac{n!}{2a^{n+1}} \quad (a > 0)$

21. $\int \dfrac{x\,dx}{x + d} = x - d\ln(x + d)$

F Properties of the Elements

All physical properties are for a pressure of 1 atm unless otherwise specified.

Element	Symbol	Atomic Number Z	Molar Mass, g/mol	Density, g/cm^3 at 20°C	Melting Point, °C	Boiling Point, °C	Specific Heat, J/(g · °C) at 25°C
Actinium	Ac	89	(227)	10.06	1323	(3473)	0.092
Aluminum	Al	13	26.9815	2.699	660	2450	0.900
Americium	Am	95	(243)	13.67	1541	—	—
Antimony	Sb	51	121.75	6.691	630.5	1380	0.205
Argon	Ar	18	39.948	1.6626×10^{-3}	−189.4	−185.8	0.523
Arsenic	As	33	74.9216	5.78	817 (28 atm)	613	0.331
Astatine	At	85	(210)	—	(302)	—	—
Barium	Ba	56	137.34	3.594	729	1640	0.205
Berkelium	Bk	97	(247)	14.79	—	—	—
Beryllium	Be	4	9.0122	1.848	1287	2770	1.83
Bismuth	Bi	83	208.980	9.747	271.37	1560	0.122
Bohrium	Bh	107	262.12	—	—	—	—
Boron	B	5	10.811	2.34	2030	—	1.11
Bromine	Br	35	79.909	3.12 (liquid)	−7.2	58	0.293
Cadmium	Cd	48	112.40	8.65	321.03	765	0.226
Calcium	Ca	20	40.08	1.55	838	1440	0.624
Californium	Cf	98	(251)	—	—	—	—
Carbon	C	6	12.01115	2.26	3727	4830	0.691
Cerium	Ce	58	140.12	6.768	804	3470	0.188
Cesium	Cs	55	132.905	1.873	28.40	690	0.243
Chlorine	Cl	17	35.453	3.214×10^{-3} (0°C)	−101	−34.7	0.486
Chromium	Cr	24	51.996	7.19	1857	2665	0.448
Cobalt	Co	27	58.9332	8.85	1495	2900	0.423
Copper	Cu	29	63.54	8.96	1083.40	2595	0.385
Curium	Cm	96	(247)	13.3	—	—	—
Darmstadtium	Ds	110	(271)	—	—	—	—
Dubnium	Db	105	262.114	—	—	—	—
Dysprosium	Dy	66	162.50	8.55	1409	2330	0.172
Einsteinium	Es	99	(254)	—	—	—	—
Erbium	Er	68	167.26	9.15	1522	2630	0.167
Europium	Eu	63	151.96	5.243	817	1490	0.163
Fermium	Fm	100	(237)	—	—	—	—
Fluorine	F	9	18.9984	1.696×10^{-3} (0°C)	−219.6	−188.2	0.753
Francium	Fr	87	(223)	—	(27)	—	—
Gadolinium	Gd	64	157.25	7.90	1312	2730	0.234
Gallium	Ga	31	69.72	5.907	29.75	2237	0.377
Germanium	Ge	32	72.59	5.323	937.25	2830	0.322
Gold	Au	79	196.967	19.32	1064.43	2970	0.131

Element	Symbol	Atomic Number Z	Molar Mass, g/mol	Density, g/cm^3 at 20°C	Melting Point, °C	Boiling Point, °C	Specific Heat, $J/(g \cdot °C)$ at 25°C
Hafnium	Hf	72	178.49	13.31	2227	5400	0.144
Hassium	Hs	108	(265)	—	—	—	—
Helium	He	2	4.0026	0.1664×10^{-3}	−269.7	−268.9	5.23
Holmium	Ho	67	164.930	8.79	1470	2330	0.165
Hydrogen	H	1	1.00797	0.08375×10^{-3}	−259.19	−252.7	14.4
Indium	In	49	114.82	7.31	156.634	2000	0.233
Iodine	I	53	126.9044	4.93	113.7	183	0.218
Iridium	Ir	77	192.2	22.5	2447	(5300)	0.130
Iron	Fe	26	55.847	7.874	1536.5	3000	0.447
Krypton	Kr	36	83.80	3.488×10^{-3}	−157.37	−152	0.247
Lanthanum	La	57	138.91	6.189	920	3470	0.195
Lawrencium	Lr	103	(257)	—	—	—	—
Lead	Pb	82	207.19	11.35	327.45	1725	0.129
Lithium	Li	3	6.939	0.534	180.55	1300	3.58
Lutetium	Lu	71	174.97	9.849	1663	1930	0.155
Magnesium	Mg	12	24.312	1.738	650	1107	1.03
Manganese	Mn	25	54.9380	7.44	1244	2150	0.481
Meitnerium	Mt	109	(266)	—	—	—	—
Mendelevium	Md	101	(256)	—	—	—	—
Mercury	Hg	80	200.59	13.55	−38.87	357	0.138
Molybdenum	Mo	42	95.94	10.22	2617	5560	0.251
Neodymium	Nd	60	144.24	7.007	1016	3180	0.188
Neon	Ne	10	20.183	0.8387×10^{-3}	−248.597	−246.0	1.03
Neptunium	Np	93	(237)	20.25	637	—	1.26
Nickel	Ni	28	58.71	8.902	1453	2730	0.444
Niobium	Nb	41	92.906	8.57	2468	4927	0.264
Nitrogen	N	7	14.0067	1.1649×10^{-3}	−210	−195.8	1.03
Nobelium	No	102	(255)	—	—	—	—
Osmium	Os	76	190.2	22.59	3027	5500	0.130
Oxygen	O	8	15.9994	1.3318×10^{-3}	−218.80	−183.0	0.913
Palladium	Pd	46	106.4	12.02	1552	3980	0.243
Phosphorus	P	15	30.9738	1.83	44.25	280	0.741
Platinum	Pt	78	195.09	21.45	1769	4530	0.134
Plutonium	Pu	94	(244)	19.8	640	3235	0.130
Polonium	Po	84	(210)	9.32	254	—	—
Potassium	K	19	39.102	0.862	63.20	760	0.758
Praseodymium	Pr	59	140.907	6.773	931	3020	0.197
Promethium	Pm	61	(145)	7.22	(1027)	—	—
Protactinium	Pa	91	(231)	15.37 (estimated)	(1230)	—	—
Radium	Ra	88	(226)	5.0	700	—	—
Radon	Rn	86	(222)	9.96×10^{-3} (0°C)	(−71)	−61.8	0.092
Rhenium	Re	75	186.2	21.02	3180	5900	0.134
Rhodium	Rh	45	102.905	12.41	1963	4500	0.243
Rubidium	Rb	37	85.47	1.532	39.49	688	0.364
Ruthenium	Ru	44	101.107	12.37	2250	4900	0.239
Rutherfordium	Rf	104	261.11	—	—	—	—

Element	Symbol	Atomic Number Z	Molar Mass, g/mol	Density, g/cm³ at 20°C	Melting Point, °C	Boiling Point, °C	Specific Heat, J/(g·°C) at 25°C
Samarium	Sm	62	150.35	7.52	1072	1630	0.197
Scandium	Sc	21	44.956	2.99	1539	2730	0.569
Seaborgium	Sg	106	263.118	—	—	—	—
Selenium	Se	34	78.96	4.79	221	685	0.318
Silicon	Si	14	28.086	2.33	1412	2680	0.712
Silver	Ag	47	107.870	10.49	960.8	2210	0.234
Sodium	Na	11	22.9898	0.9712	97.85	892	1.23
Strontium	Sr	38	87.62	2.54	768	1380	0.737
Sulfur	S	16	32.064	2.07	119.0	444.6	0.707
Tantalum	Ta	73	180.948	16.6	3014	5425	0.138
Technetium	Tc	43	(99)	11.46	2200	—	0.209
Tellurium	Te	52	127.60	6.24	449.5	990	0.201
Terbium	Tb	65	158.924	8.229	1357	2530	0.180
Thallium	Tl	81	204.37	11.85	304	1457	0.130
Thorium	Th	90	(232)	11.72	1755	(3850)	0.117
Thulium	Tm	69	168.934	9.32	1545	1720	0.159
Tin	Sn	50	118.69	7.2984	231.868	2270	0.226
Titanium	Ti	22	47.90	4.54	1670	3260	0.523
Tungsten	W	74	183.85	19.3	3380	5930	0.134
Unnamed	Uuu	111	(272)	—	—	—	—
Unnamed	Uub	112	(285)	—	—	—	—
Unnamed	Uut	113	—	—	—	—	—
Unnamed	Unq	114	(289)	—	—	—	—
Unnamed	Uup	115	—	—	—	—	—
Unnamed	Uuh	116	—	—	—	—	—
Unnamed	Uus	117	—	—	—	—	—
Unnamed	Uuo	118	(293)	—	—	—	—
Uranium	U	92	(238)	18.95	1132	3818	0.117
Vanadium	V	23	50.942	6.11	1902	3400	0.490
Xenon	Xe	54	131.30	5.495×10^{-3}	−111.79	−108	0.159
Ytterbium	Yb	70	173.04	6.965	824	1530	0.155
Yttrium	Y	39	88.905	4.469	1526	3030	0.297
Zinc	Zn	30	65.37	7.133	419.58	906	0.389
Zirconium	Zr	40	91.22	6.506	1852	3580	0.276

The values in parentheses in the column of molar masses are the mass numbers of the longest-lived isotopes of those elements that are radioactive. Melting points and boiling points in parentheses are uncertain.

The data for gases are valid only when these are in their usual molecular state, such as H_2, He, O_2, Ne, etc. The specific heats of the gases are the values at constant pressure.

Source: Adapted from J. Emsley, *The Elements,* 3rd ed., 1998, Clarendon Press, Oxford. See also www.webelements.com for the latest values and newest elements.

Periodic Table G of the Elements

Metals

Metalloids

Nonmetals

Alkali metals: IA. Noble gases: 0. Transition metals: IIIB to IIB. THE HORIZONTAL PERIODS: 1 to 7.

Period	IA	IIA	IIIB	IVB	VB	VIB	VIIB	VIIIB	VIIIB	VIIIB	IB	IIB	IIIA	IVA	VA	VIA	VIIA	0
1	1 H																	2 He
2	3 Li	4 Be											5 B	6 C	7 N	8 O	9 F	10 Ne
3	11 Na	12 Mg											13 Al	14 Si	15 P	16 S	17 Cl	18 Ar
4	19 K	20 Ca	21 Sc	22 Ti	23 V	24 Cr	25 Mn	26 Fe	27 Co	28 Ni	29 Cu	30 Zn	31 Ga	32 Ge	33 As	34 Se	35 Br	36 Kr
5	37 Rb	38 Sr	39 Y	40 Zr	41 Nb	42 Mo	43 Tc	44 Ru	45 Rh	46 Pd	47 Ag	48 Cd	49 In	50 Sn	51 Sb	52 Te	53 I	54 Xe
6	55 Cs	56 Ba	57-71 *	72 Hf	73 Ta	74 W	75 Re	76 Os	77 Ir	78 Pt	79 Au	80 Hg	81 Tl	82 Pb	83 Bi	84 Po	85 At	86 Rn
7	87 Fr	88 Ra	89-103 †	104 Rf	105 Db	106 Sg	107 Bh	108 Hs	109 Mt	110 Ds	111	112	113	114	115	116	117	118

Inner transition metals

Series															
Lanthanide series *	57 La	58 Ce	59 Pr	60 Nd	61 Pm	62 Sm	63 Eu	64 Gd	65 Tb	66 Dy	67 Ho	68 Er	69 Tm	70 Yb	71 Lu
Actinide series †	89 Ac	90 Th	91 Pa	92 U	93 Np	94 Pu	95 Am	96 Cm	97 Bk	98 Cf	99 Es	100 Fm	101 Md	102 No	103 Lr

Elements 111, 112, 114, and 116 have been discovered but, as of 2003, have not yet been named. Evidence for the discovery of elements 113 and 115 has been reported. See www.webelements.com for the latest information and newest elements.

Answers

to Checkpoints, Questions and Problems

Chapter 1

P **1.** (a) 10^9 μm; (b) 10^{-4} μm; (c) 9.1×10^5 μm **2.** (a) 1.9 picas; (b) 23 points **3.** (a) 4.00×10^4 km; (b) 5.10×10^8 km^2; (c) 1.08×10^{12} km^3 **4.** 1.9×10^{22} cm^3 **5.** 3.1 μm/s **6.** 1.21×10^{12} μs **7.** (a) 52.6 min; (b) 4.9% **8.** (a) 1.43; (b) 0.864 **9.** (a) 495 s; (b) 141 s; (c) 198 s; (d) -245 s **10.** 5.2×10^6 m **11.** (a) 1.430 m^2; (b) 72.84 km **12.** (a) 1.18×10^{-29} m^3; (b) 0.282×10^{-10} m **13.** 0.260 kg **14.** 1.9×10^5 kg **15.** (a) 4.21 s; (b) 23.2 g; (c) 2.89×10^{-2} kg/min; (d) -6.05×10^{-3} kg/min **16.** 1.43 kg/min **17.** 0.3 cord **18.** (a) 3.0×10^{-26} kg; (b) 5×10^{-46} **19.** 8×10^2 km **20.** 6.0×10^{-26} **21.** 0.12 AU/min **22.** 3.8 mg/s **23.** 1.2 m **24.** 10 μ **25.** (a) 4.9×10^{-6} pc; (b) 1.6×10^{-5} ly

Chapter 2

CP **1.** (a) 7 m ($\vec{a}$ and $\vec{b}$ are in same direction); (b) 1 m ($\vec{a}$ and $\vec{b}$ are in opposite directions) **2.** c, d, f (components must be head-to-tail; $\vec{a}$ must extend from tail of one component to head of the other) **3.** (a) +, +; (b) +, −; (c) +, + (draw vector from tail of $\vec{d}_1$ to head of $\vec{d}_2$) **4.** 160 j + 120 k **5.** (a) 90°; (b) 0° (vectors are parallel—same direction); (c) 180° (vectors are antiparallel—opposite directions) **6.** 5488 **7.** $9(3x + 4)^2 + \cos x$ **Q** **1.** Either the sequence $\vec{d}_2, \vec{d}_1$ or the sequence $\vec{d}_2, \vec{d}_2, \vec{d}_3$ **3.** yes, when the vectors are in same direction **5.** (a) yes; (b) yes; (c) no **7.** all but (e) **9.** (a) $+x$ for (1), $+z$ for (2), $+z$ for (3); (b) $-x$ for (1), $-z$ for (2), $-z$ for (3) **P** **1.** (a) 13 m; (b) 7.5 m **2.** (a) 6.42 m; (b) no; (c) yes; (d) yes; (e) a possible answer: $(4.30\text{ m})\hat{i} + (3.70\text{ m})\hat{j} + (3.00\text{ m})\hat{k}$; (f) 7.96 m **3.** (a) $(3.0\text{ m})\hat{i} - (2.0\text{ m})\hat{j} + (5.0\text{ m})\hat{k}$; (b) $(5.0\text{ m})\hat{i} - (4.0\text{ m})\hat{j} - (3.0\text{ m})\hat{k}$; (c) $(-5.0\text{ m})\hat{i} + (4.0\text{ m})\hat{j} + (3.0\text{ m})\hat{k}$ **4.** (a) -70.0 cm; (b) 80.0 cm; (c) 141 cm; (d) $-172°$ **5.** 5.39 m at 21.8° left of forward **6.** 3.2 **7.** 2.2 m **8.** (a) 7.5 cm; (b) 90°; (c) 8.6 cm; (d) 48° **9.** (a) $8\hat{i} + 16\hat{j}$; (b) $2\hat{i} + 4\hat{j}$ **10.** (a) $a\hat{i} + a\hat{j} + a\hat{k}$; (b) $-a\hat{i} + a\hat{j} + a\hat{k}$; (c) $a\hat{i} - a\hat{j} + a\hat{k}$; (d) $-a\hat{i} - a\hat{j} + a\hat{k}$; (e) 54.7°; (f) $3^{0.5}a$ **11.** 0 **12.** (a) -21; (b) -9.0; (c) $5\hat{i} - 11\hat{j} - 9\hat{k}$ **13.** (a) 3.00 m; (b) 0; (c) 3.46 m; (d) 2.00 m; (e) -5.00 m; (f) 8.66 m; (g) -6.67; (h) 4.33 **14.** (a) 31 k; (b) 8.0; (c) 33; (d) 1.6 **15.** (a) 103 km; (b) 60.9° north of due west **16.** (a) $+x$; (b) $+y$; (c) 0; (d) 0; (e) $+z$; (f) $-z$; (g) d_1d_2; (h) d_1d_2; (i) $d_1d_2/4$; (j) $+z$ **17.** (a) 0; (b) 0; (c) -1; (d) west; (e) up; (f) west **18.** 32.5° **19.** 216.5 **20.** 4.1 **22.** (a) 0; (b) 4.0 m; (c) 0.82 s **23.** (a) 1.2 s; (b) 0; (c) $t > 0$; (d) $t < 0$ **24.** (a) m/s^2; (b) m/s^3; (c) 1 s; (d) 82 m; (e) (6.0 m/s^2)t – (6.0 m/s^3)t^2; (f) 0; (g) -12 m/s; (h) -36 m/s; (i) 6.0 m/s^2 – (12.0 m/s^3)t; (j) – 6.0 m/s^2; (k) – 18 m/s^2; (l) -30 m/s^2; (m) -42 m/s^2 **25.** 5.0 m/s **26.** 47 m/s **27.** (a) 18 m/s

Chapter 3

CP **1.** b and c **2.** (check the derivative dx/dt) (a) 1 and 4; (b) 2 and 3 **3.** (a) plus; (b) minus; (c) minus; (d) plus **4.** 1 and 4 ($a = d^2x/dt^2$ must be constant) **5.** (a) plus (upward displacement on y axis); (b) minus (downward displacement on y axis); (c) $a = -g = -9.8$ m/s^2 **Q** **1.** (a) all tie; (b) 4, tie of 1 and 2, then 3 **3.** (a) negative; (b) positive; (c) yes; (d) positive; (e) constant **5.** (a) positive direction; (b) negative direction; (c) 3 and 5; (d) 2 and 6 tie, then 3 and 5 tie, then 1 and 4 tie (zero) **7.** (a) 3, 2, 1; (b) 1, 2, 3; (c) all tie; (d) 1, 2, 3 **9.** (a) D; (b) E **P** **1.** (a) +40 km/h; (b) 40 km/h **2.** 48 km/h **3.** 13 m **4.** (a) 0; (b) -2 m; (c) 0; (d) 12 m; (e) 12 m; (f) 7 m/s **5.** (a) v_c; (b) 5.76×10^4 **6.** 128 km/h **7.** (a) 0.50m/s; (b) 10 s **8.** 60 km **9.** (a) 48.0 m; (b) 2.50 m/s **10.** (a) 73 km/h; (b) 68 km/h; (c) 70 km/h; (d) 0 **11.** (a) -6 m/s; (b) 1 s; (c) 6 m/s; (d) decreasing; (e) 2 s; (f) no **12.** 5.9 m **13.** (a) 28.5 cm/s; (b) 18.0 cm/s; (c) 40.5 cm/s; (d) 28.1 cm/s; (e) 30.3 cm/s **14.** (a) 54 m; (b) 18 m/s (c) -12m/s^2; (d) 64 m; (e) 4.0 s; (f) 24 m/s; (g) 2.0 s; (h) -24m/s^2; (i) 18 m/s **15.** (a) 1.10 m/s; (b) 0.00611 m/s^2; (c) 1.47 m/s; (d) 0.00611 m/s^2 **16.** 21 g **17.** (a) 10.6 m; (b) 41.5 s **18.** (a) 4.0 m/s^2; (b) $+x$ **19.** (a) 32.9 m/s; (b) 24.53 s; (c) 11.7 m/s **20.** (a) -2.5 m/s^2; (b) 4 s; (d) 0; (e) 2 **21.** (a) 2.6 s; (b) 2.1 s **22.** 40 m **23.** (a) -50 km/h; (b) -2.0 m/s^2 **24.** 0.90 m/s^2 **25.** 0.994 m/s^2 **26.** (a) 15.0 m; (b) 94 km/h **27.** (a) -12 m/s; (b) 27.1 m/s **28.** (a) 31 m/s; (b) 6.4 s **29.** (a) 5.4 s; (b) 41 m/s **30.** (a) 0.45 s; (b) 38 m/s; (c) 42 m/s **31.** 4.0 m/s **32.** 9.6 m/s **33.** (a) 20 m; (b) 59 m **34.** 3.0 m/s **35.** (a) 857 m/s^2; (b) up **36.** (a) 89 cm; (b) 22 cm **37.** (a) 3.41 s; (b) 57 m; (c) $t-1$ **38.** 2.34 m **39.** (a) 8.0 m/s^2; (b) 20 m/s **40.** 20.4 m **41.** (a) 350 ms; (b) 82 ms **42.** (a) 2.25 m/s; (b) 3.90 m/s **43.** (a) 0.13 m; (b) 0.50 m **44.** 0.56 m/s **45.** 15.6 m/s **46.** (a) 48.5 m/s; (b) 4.95 s; (c) 34.3 m/s; (d) 3.50 s **47.** 1.5 s **48.** 90 m **49.** 17 m/s **50.** (a) 1.23 cm; (b) 4 times; (c) 9 times; (d) 16 times; (e) 25 times **51.** 39 m/s **52.** 4H **53.** (a) 5.0 s; (b) 5.0 s; (c) -2.0 m/s^2; (d) 3.5 m/s; (e) 0 **54.** (a) 2.0 m/s^2; (b) 12 m/s; (c) 45 m **55.** 22.0 m/s **56.** (a) 17 s; (b) 240 m **57.** (a) 5.44 s; (b) 53.3 m/s; (c) 5.80 m **58.** (a) $v_0^2 + 2\,gh$

Chapter 4

CP **1.** (draw $\vec{v}$ tangent to path, tail on path) (a) first; (b) third **2.** (take second derivative with respect to time) (1) and (3) a_x and a_y are both constant and thus $\vec{a}$ is constant; (2) and (4) a_y is constant but a_x is not, thus $\vec{a}$ is not **3.** no **4.** $\tan\alpha + \tan\beta$, **5.** (a) v_x constant; (b) v_y initially positive, decreases to zero, and then becomes progressively more negative; (c) $a_x = 0$ throughout; (d) $a_y = -g$ throughout **6.** $u^2/g(1 + \sin\theta)$ **7.** This situation can be handled simply by thinking that our incline is making angle-θ instead of θ with horizontal. **Q** **1.** (a) $(7\text{ m})\hat{i} + (1\text{ m})\hat{j} + (-2\text{ m})\hat{k}$; (b) $(5\text{ m})\hat{i} + (-3\text{ m})\hat{j} + (1\text{ m})\hat{k}$; (c) $(-2\text{ m})\hat{i}$ **3.** (a) all tie; (b) 1 and 2 tie (the rocket is shot upward), then 3 and 4 tie (it is shot into the ground!) **5.** decreases **7.** (a) all tie; (b) all tie; (c) 3, 2, 1; (d) 3, 2, 1 **9.** (a) 0; (b) 350 km/h; (c) 350 km/h; (d) same (nothing changed about the vertical motion) **P** **1.** (a) 14 cm; (b) $-135°$;

(c) 20 cm; (d) 90°; (e) 0; (f) 0 **2.** (a) 7.59 km/h; (b) 22.5° east of due north **3.** (a) 1.08×10^3 km; (b) 63.4°; (c) 480 km/h; (d) −63.4°; (e) 644 km/h **4.** (a) 0.83 cm/s; (b) 0°; (c) 0.11 m/s; (d) −63° **5.** (a) 3.50 m/s; (b) −0.125 m/s^2 **6.** (a) (6.00 m)$\hat{i}$ − (106 m)$\hat{j}$; (b) (19.0 m/s)$\hat{i}$ − (224 m/s)$\hat{j}$; (c) (24.0 m/s^2)$\hat{i}$ − (336 m/s^2)$\hat{j}$; (d) −85.2° **7.** (a) 56.6 m; (b) −45.0°; (c) 1.89 m/s; (d) 135°; (e) 0.471 m/s^2; (f) (32 m/s)^i **8.** (a) (72.0 m)$\hat{i}$ + (90.7 m)$\hat{j}$; (b) 49.5° **9.** 60° **10.** (a) 18 cm; (b) 1.9 m **11.**(a) 5.50 s; (b) 27.4 m/s; (c) 67.5 m **12.** (a) 10.0 s; (b) 897 m **13.** (a) 202 m/s; (b) 806 m; (c) 161 m/s; (d) −171 m/s **14.** 5.8 m/s **15.** (a) 32.3 m; (b) 21.9 m/s; (c) 40.4°; (d) below **16.** (a) 95 m; (b) 31 m **17.**(a) 5.3 m; (b) 25.9 m; (c) 69 m **18.**(a) 33.7 m; (b) 26.0 m/s; (c) 71.1° **19.** 14.3° **20.** 42.0 m/s **21.** the third **22.** (a) 20 m/s; (b) 36 m/s; (c) 74m **23.** (a) 75.0 m; (b) 31.9 m/s; (c) 66.9°; (d) 25.5 m **24.** 1.67 **25.** 60° **26.**(a) 7.2 m/s; (b) 16° west of north; (c) 29 **27.** (a) (80 km/h)$\hat{i}$ − (60 km/h)$\hat{j}$; (b) 0°; (c) answers do not change **28.**(a) 24.8 m/s; (b) 83.8° north of east; (c) 0.400 m/s^2 60.0° north of east **29.** (a) (−32 km/h)$\hat{i}$ − (46 km/h)$\hat{j}$; (b) [(2.5 km) − (32 km/h)t]$\hat{i}$ + [(4.0 km) − (46 km/h)t]$\hat{j}$; (c) 0.084 h; (d) 2×10^2 m **30.** (a) 2.7 km; (b) 76° clockwise **31.** (a) 2.5 m; (b) 0.82 m; (c) 9.8 m/s^2; (d) 9.8 m/s^2 **32.** (a) 10 m/s; (b) 19.6 m/s; (c) 40 m; (d) 40 m **33.** (a) −30°; (b) 69 min; (c) 80 min; (d) 80 min; (e) 0°; (f) 60 min **34.** (−2.1$\hat{i}$ + 2.8$\hat{j}$) m/s^2 **35.** (a) 1.5; (b) (36 m, 54 m) **36.** 36 s **37.** (a) 35°; (b) 45 s; (c) 143 km/h **38.** (a) 30 m/s; (b) 4.2 s **39.** (a) 4.6×10^{12} m; (b) 2.4×10^5 s **40.** 93° from the car's direction of motion **41.** graph **42.** (a) (10 m/s)$\hat{i}$ + (10 m/s)$\hat{j}$ (b) 8.0 m/s^2; (c) 2.7 s; (d) 2.2 s

Chapter 5

CP **1.** (a) and (b) 2 N, leftward (acceleration is zero in each situation) **2.** (a) equal; (b) greater (acceleration is upward, thus net force on body must be upward) **3.** 12.2 m **4.** 0 **5.** (a) equal; (b) greater; (c) less **5.** (a) increase; (b) yes; (c) same; (d) yes **6.** 30 **7.** 0 **8.** (a) 448 N **Q** **1.** increase **3.** (a) 2 and 4; (b) 2 and 4 **5.** (a) 2, 3, 4; (b) 1, 3, 4; (c) 1, + y; 2, +x; 3, fourth quadrant; 4, third quadrant **7.** (a) 20 kg; (b) 18 kg; (c) 10 kg; (d) all tie; (e) 3, 2, 1 **9.** (a) increases from initial value mg; (b) decreases from mg to zero (after which the block moves up away from the floor) **11.** (a) M; (b) M; (c) M; (d) 2M; (e) 3M **P** **1.** (− 2 N)$\hat{i}$ + (6 n)$\hat{j}$ **2.** 9.0 m/s^2 **3.** 56° **4.** (a) 108 N; (b) 108 N; (c) 108 N **5.** (a) 2.0 N; (b) down **6.** (a) 4.0 kg; (b) 1.0 kg; (c) 4.0 kg; (d) 1.0 kg **7.** (a) −9.80$\hat{j}$ m/s^2; (b) 2.35$\hat{j}$ m/s^2; (c) 1.37 s; (d) (-5.56×10^{-3} N)$\hat{j}$; (e) (1.333×10^{-3} N)$\hat{j}$ **8.** (a) 42 N; (b) 72 N; (c) 4.9 m/s^2 **9.** (a) 11.7 N; (b) −59.0° **10.** 0.22 m/s^2 **11.** 1.2×10^5 N **12.** (a) 566 N; (b) 1.13×10^3 N **13.** (a) 0.62 m/s^2; (b) 0.13 m/s^2; (c) 2.6 m **14.** (a) (1.70 N)$\hat{i}$ + (3.06 N)$\hat{j}$; (b) zero; (c) (2.02 N)$\hat{i}$ + (2.71 N)$\hat{j}$ **15.** (a) 2.2×10^{-3} N; (b) 3.7×10^{-3} N **16.** 1.8×10^4 N **17.** (a) 1.4 m/s^2; (b) 4.1 m/s **18.** 16.0 kN **19.** (a) 1.23 N; (b) 2.46 N; (c) 3.69 N; (d) 4.92 N; (e) 6.15 N; (f) 0.250 N **20.** 176 N **21.** (a) 0.970 m/s^2; (b) 11.6 N; (c) 34.9 N **22.** (a) 2.50 m/s^2; (b) 30.0 N **23.** (a) 1.1 N; (b) 2.1 N **24.** (a) 36.8 N; (b) 0.191 m **25.** (a) 3.6 m/s^2; (b) 17 N **26.** (a) 4.9 m/s^2; (b) 2.0 m/s^2; (c) up; (d) 120 N **27.** (a) 0.735 m/s^2; (b) down; (c) 20.8 N **28.** (a) 466 N; (b) 527 N; (c) 931 N; (d) 1.05×10^3 N; (e) 931 N; (f) 1.05×10^3 N; (g) 1.86×10^3 N; (h) 2.11×10^3 N **29.** $2Ma/(a + g)$ **30.** (a) 0.653 m/s^3; (b) 0.896 m/s^3; (c) 6.50 s **31.** 81.7 N **32.** (a) 3.1 N; (b) 15 N **33.** (a) 8.0 m/s; (b) + x **34.** (a) 4.6 m/s^2; (b) 2.6 m/s^2 **35.** 4.6 N **36.** (a) 11 N; (b) 2.2 kg; (c) 0; (d) 2.2 kg **37.** (a) (5.0 m/s)$\hat{i}$ + (4.3 m/s)$\hat{j}$; (b) (15 m)$\hat{i}$ + (6.4 m)$\hat{j}$ **38.** (a) 50 kg; (b) upward; (c) 340 N; (d) upward; (e) 590 N; (f) downward **39.** 16 N **40.** (a) (-6.26 N)$\hat{i}$ − (3.23 N)$\hat{j}$; (b) 7.04 N; (c) 207° **41.** (a) 2.6 N; (b) 17°

Chapter 6

CP **1.** (a) zero (because there is no attempt at sliding); (b) 5 N; (c) no; (d) yes; (e) 8 N **2.** 70 **3.** -14/11 $\vec{a}$ $\vec{F}_N$ $\vec{F}_N$ **4.** U mg **5.** 105 **Q** **1.** (a) same; (b) increases; (c) increases; (d) no **3.** (a) decrease; (b) decrease; (c) increase; (d) increase; (e) increase **5.** (a) upward; (b) horizontal, toward you; (c) no change; (d) increases; (e) increases **7.** At first, $\vec{f}_s$ is directed up the ramp and its magnitude increases from mg sin θ until it reaches $f_{s,\max}$. Thereafter the force is kinetic friction directed up the ramp, with magnitude f_k (a constant value smaller than $f_{s,\max}$). **9.** (a) all tie; (b) all tie; (c) 2, 3, 1 **11.** 4, 3, then 1, 2, and 5 tie **P** **1.** 0.56 **2.** (a) 10.8 N; (b) 0.33 m/s^2 **3.** (a) 6.0 N; (b) 3.6 N; (c) 3.1 N **4.** (a) 12.1 m/s; (b) 19.4 m/s **5.** (a) no; (b) (−12 N)$\hat{i}$ + (5.0 N)$\hat{j}$ **6.** 0.54 **7.** (a) 19°; (b) 3.3 kN **8.** (a) (17 N)$\hat{i}$; (b) (20 N)$\hat{i}$; (c) (15 N)$\hat{i}$ **9.** 8.5 N **10.** 1.0×10^2 N **11.** 60° **12.** 0.37 **13.** 18° **14.** (a) 44 N (b) (−3.9 m/s^2)$\hat{i}$; (c) (−1.0 m/s^2)$\hat{i}$ **15.** (a) 66 N; (b) 2.3 m/s^2 **16.** 4.9×10^2 N **17.** (a) 6.1 m/s^2; (b) 0.95 m/s^2 **18.** 9.9 s **19.** 8.8 N **20.** (a) 27 N; (b) 3.0 m/s^2 **21.** (a) 1.05 N; (b) 3.62 m/s^2 **22.** $g(\sin\theta - 2^{0.5}\mu_k \cos\theta)$ **23.** (b) 240 N; (c) 0.60 (b) 1.6 m/s^2 **24.** (a) non-negative; (b) 245 N; (c) 30.0°; (d) 195 N; (e) 60.0°; (f) 158 N; (g) 103 N; (h) 81.9 N; (i) 66.4 N **25.** (a) 84.2 N; (b) 52.8 N; (c) 1.87 m/s^2 **26.** 9.1 N **27.** (a) $\mu_k mg/(\sin\theta - \mu_k \cos\theta)$; (b) $\theta_0 = \tan^{-1} \mu_s$ **28.** (a) 12 N down; (b) 10 N up; (c) 26 N down; (d) 23 N down; (e) 32 N up; (f) 23 N up **29.** (a) 0.34; (b) 0.24 **30.** (a) 90 N; (b) 70 N; (c) 0.88 m/s^2

Chapter 7

CP **1.** $g / 2\mu \cos\theta$ **2.** (a) −(4 m/s)$\hat{i}$; (b) −(8 m/s^2)$\hat{j}$ **3.** (a) This acceleration is not possible as perpendicular compound of acceleration is away from curvature; (b) This is possible but speed will be decreasing **4.** 80^2 **5.** mv^2/R **P** **1.** 21 m **2.** 0.60 **3.** 48 km/h **4.** (a) 10 s; (b) 4.9×10^2 N; (c) 1.1k N **5.** (a) 3.7×10^3 N; (b) upward; (c) 1.3×10^3 N **6.** 1.37×10^3 N **7.** 20 J (a) light; (b) 778 N; (c) 223 N; (d) 1.11 kN **8.** (a) mv^2/r^2 dr; (b) $2mv/r\ dv$ **9.** 2.2×10^3 m **10.** (a) 403 N m/s; (b) 2.50 s **11.** 1.81 m/s **12.** (a) 8.0×10^3 N; (b) 6.9×10^3 N; (c) 20 m/s; (d) 1.6×10^4 N; (e) No **13.** 2.6×10^3 N **14.** 0.078 **15.** (a) 8.74 N (b) 37.9 N; (c) 6.45 m/s; (d) leftward **16.** (a) 0.40 N; (b) 1.9 s **17.** 0.021 **18.** (a) 3.21×10^3 N; (b) 3.75×10^3 N **19.** (a) 40 N; (b) 9.5 m/s **20.** (a) 0.30 m/s; (b) 1.8 m/s^2; (d) $3.6 \times 10^-$ N; (f) 0.37 **21.** 0.021 **22.** 9.5×10^{-8} N **23.** $\tan\theta = V^2/rg$ **24.** (a) 364 N; (b) 784 N **25.** (a) 0.344%; (b) 84.4 min; (c) same **26.** $v = (rg\cot\theta)^{1/2}$ **27.** 14 m/s **28.** (a) $lk \sin\theta$; (b) $2kl(1 - \cos\theta)$ **29.** 0.97 m **30.** (a) 149 m; (b) 7.5 m/s^2 **30a.** (a) $ar = RV^2/a^2$; (b) $a\theta = 2vV/a$ **31.** 3160N **32.** 20 m **33.** (a) 2.654 kN; (b) 68.3 m **34.** N = 276.714lb **35.** v = 6.30 m/s; (b) n = 283; (b) t = 0; (c) b = 491 N **36.** 0.581 m **37.** (a) T = 1.82 N; (b) N_B = 0.844 N **38.** 104.1 N **39.** 2.83 m/s **40.** 0.969 m/s **41.** 7.394 s **42.** 1.633 m/s **43.** 3.419 lb **44.** (a) FN = 5.794 N; (b) F = 1.778 N

Chapter 8

CP **1.** N.ut **2.** $F1 \times d$ **3.** no (consider round trip on the small loop) **4.** 3, 1, 2 (see Eq. 8-6) **5.** (a) all tie; (b) all tie **6.** all tie **7.** (a) CD, AB, BC (0) (check slope magnitudes); (b) positive direction of x **8.** $-8xy\,i - (4x^2+2z^2)j - 4yzk$ **Q** **1.** (a) positive; (b) negative; (c) negative **3.** all tie **5.** all tie **7.** b (positive work), a (zero work), c (negative work), d (more negative work) **9.** (a) A; (b) B **10.** (a) 12 J; (b) −2 J **12.** (a) 3, 2, 1; (b) 1, 2, 3 **14.** 2, 1, 3 **16.** 30 J **18.** (a) increasing; (b) decreasing; (c) decreasing; (d) constant in AB and BC, decreasing in CD **P** **1.** (a) 2.4 m/s (b) 4.8 m/s **2.** 7.1 J **3.** 0.96 J **4.** (a) 1.7×10^2 N; (b) 3.4×10^2 m; (c) -5.8×10^4 J; (d) 3.4×10^2 N; (e) 1.7×10^2 m **5.** 3.5 m/s **6.** (a) 1.50 J **7.** (a) 3.00 N; (b) 9.00 J **8.** (a) 62.3°; (b) 118° **9.** (a) 1.31 J (b) 0.935 m/s **10.** 4.41 J **11.** 45 N **12.** (a) 2.59×10^4 J; (b) 2.45 N **13.** (a) 6.6 m/s; (b) 4.7 m **14.** (a) 16 J; (b) 16 J; (c) 0 J; (d) −14 J **15.** (a) 0.90 J; (b) 2.1 J; (c) 0 J **16.** (a) 8.0 N; (b) 8.0 N/m **17.** (a) 0.12 m (b) 0.36 J; (c) −0.36 J; (d) 0.060 m; (e) 0.090 J **18.** 25 J **19.** (a) $(x_o)(F_o)/2$ (b) 0 **20.** 8.0×10^2 J **21.** 5.3×10^2 J **22.** (a) 42 J; (b) 7.0 m; (c) 12 J; (d) 4.0 m; (e) $+x$ direction; (f) $+x$ direction **23.** 4.0 N/m **24.** 41.7 J **25.** 7.4×10^2 W **26.** (a) 28 W; (b) 6 m/s **27.** (a) 1.010^2 J; (b) 8.4 W **28.** (a) 32.0 J; (b) 8.00 W; (c) 12.0 m^2 **29.** 0 **30.** (a) 0; (b) 1.70×10^5 J; (c) 3.40×10^5 J; (d) 1.70×10^5 J; (e) 3.40×10^5 J **31.** (a) 13.1 J; (b) −13.1 J; (c) 13.1 J **32.** (a) 0.15 J; (b) 0.11 J; (c) 0.19 J; (d) 0.038J; (e) 0.075 J; (f) unchanged **33.** (a) 0.98 J (b) −0.98 J; (c) 3.1 N/cm **34.** (a) 7.2 J; (b) −7.2 J; (c) 0.86 m; (d) 0.26 m **35.** (a) 2.5 N; (b) 0.31 N; (c) 0.30 m **36.** (a) $27 + 12x - 3x^2$; (b) 39 J; (c) −1.6 m; (d) 5.6 m **37.** (a) 4.85 m/s (b) 2.42 m/s **38.** 0.10 m **39.** -3.2×10^{-2} J **40.** (a) 4.4 m; (b) 4.4 m **41.** (a) 0.81 m/s; (b) 0.21 m; (c) 6.3 m/s^2; (d) up **42.** (a) 39.2 J; (b) 39.2 J; (c) 4.00 m **43.** (a) 0.055 m; (b) 2.7 m/s **44.** (a) 0.35 m; (b) 1.7 m/s **45.** 0.0010 J **46.** (a) 2.40 m/s; (b) 4.19 m/s **47.** 1.25 cm **48.** − 0.018 J **49.** 9.20 m **50.** (a) 0.396 m; (b) 3.64 cm **51.** (a) 1.12; (b) positive; (c) negative **52.** (a) 2.1 m/s; (b) 10 N; (c) $+x$ direction; (d) 5.7 m; (e) 30 N; (f) $-x$ direction **53.** (a) 8.37 m/s; (b) 12.6 m/s; (c) 7.67 m; (d) 1.73 m **54.** (a) −3.7 J; (c) 1.3 m; (d) 9.1m; (e) 2.2 J; (f) 4.0 m; (h) 4.0 m **55.** (a) 5.6×10^2 J; (b) 5.6×10^2 J; **56.** (a) 105 J; (b) 30.6 J; (c) 34.4 J **57.** 75 J **58.** 0.15 **59.** 1.2 m **60.** (a) 67 J; (b) 67 J; (c) 0.46 m **61.** (a) negative; (b) 0.46 J; (c) 1.0 m/s **62.** 30 cm **63.** 20 cm **64.** 3.5 m/s **65.** (a) 7.4 m/s; (b) 90 cm; (c) 2.8 m; (d) 15 m **66.** (a) 0.29 J; (b) −1.8 J; (c) 3.5 m/s; (d) 6.942 m/s **67.** −6 J **68.** (a) 98 N; (b) 0.040 m; (c) 3.9 J; (d) −3.9 J **69.** −37 J **70.** (a) 797 N; (b) 0; (c) –1.55 kJ; (d) 0; (e) 1.55 kJ **71.** 12 J; (b) 4.0 m; (c) 18 J **72.** (a) 1.20 J; (b) 1.10 m/s **73.** (a) 2.1×10^2 J; **74.** (a) 23 mm; (b) 45 N **75.** (a) 1.0 m; (b) $(1 + \cos\theta)^{1/2}$; (c) $(1 - \cos)^{1/2}$ **76.** (a) 5 J & 8 J; (b) 6 J **77.** (b) 0; (c) 13.50 J; (d) 4.50 m; (e) 4.50 m **78.** (a) 216 J; (b) 1.8×10^3 N; (c) 432 J **79.** (a) 13 m/s; (b) 11 m/s; **80.** 15 J **81.** (a) 2.2×10^3 J; (b) 1.47×10^3 J **82.** (a) 2.7 J; (b) 1.8 J; (c) 0.39 m **83.** 25 **84.** 1.7×10^4 W **85.** (a) 0; (b) 69 hp **86.** (a) 2.1×10^6 kg; (b) 100+1.5t; (d) 6.7×10^3 m **87.** 54 % **88.** (a) $-Gm_1m_2/x$ **89.** (a) 5.00 J; (b) 9.00 J; (c) 11.00 J; (d) 3.00 J; (e) 12.00 J; (f) 2.00 J; (g) 13.00 J; (h) 1.00 J; (i) 13.00 J; (j) 1.00 J; (l) 11.00 J; (m) 0 **89.** 24 W **90.** (a) 0; (b) 0; (c) 30 J; (d) 0 **91.** (a) 4.9 N; (c) 1.5 m; (d) 13.5 m; (e) 3.5 m/s **93.** 8.80×10^8 W **94.** (a) $2gl$; (b) $5mg$; (c) $-mgl$; (d) $-2mgl$

Chapter 9

CP **1.** (a) origin; (b) fourth quadrant; (c) on y axis below origin; (d) origin; (e) third quadrant; (f) origin **2.** –L/5 **3.** (a)–(c) at the center of mass, still at the origin (their forces are internal to the system and cannot move the center of mass) **4.** (Consider slopes and Eq. 9-23.) (a) 1, 3, and then 2 and 4 tie (zero force); (b) 3 **5.** It is equal to the negative work done by the friction between the ship and the feet of the passengers **6.** (a) unchanged; (b) unchanged (see Eq. 9-32); (c) decrease (Eq. 9-35) **7.** (a) zero; (b) positive (initial p_y down y; final p_y up y); (c) positive direction of y **8.** (a) momentum cannot be conserved in vertical direction just after collision while in (b) it can be conserved just after collision **9.** (No net external force; $\vec{P}$ conserved.) (a) 0; (b) no; (c) $-x$ **10.** (a) 10 kg · m/s; (b) 14 kg · m/s; (c) 6 kg · m/s **11.** (a) 4 kg · m/s; (b) 8 kg · m/s; (c) 3 J **12.** (a) 2 kg · m/s (conserve momentum along x); (b) 3 kg · m/s (conserve momentum along y) **Q** **1.** (a) 2 N, rightward; (b) 2 N, rightward; (c) greater than 2 N, rightward **3.** (a) x yes, y no; (b) x yes, y no; (c) x no, y yes **5.** b, c, a **7.** (a) one was stationary; (b) 2; (c) 5; (d) equal (pool player's result) **9.** (a) C; (b) B; (c) 3 **11.** (a) c, kinetic energy cannot be negative; d, total kinetic energy cannot increase; (b) a; (c) b **P** **1.** (a) −0.45 cm; (b) −2.0 cm **2.** (a) 11 cm; (b) - 4.4 cm **3.** (a) 20 cm; (b) 20 cm; (c) 16 cm **4.** (a) 6.0 cm; (b) 6.0 cm; (c) 6.0 cm; (d) 2.8 cm **5.** 6.2 m **6.** (a) 28 cm; (b) 2.3 m/s **7.** (a) 22 m; (b) 9.3 m/s **8.** (a) $(2.35\hat{i} - 1.57\hat{j})$ m/s^2; (b) $(2.35\hat{i} - 1.57\hat{j})t$ m/s, with t in seconds; (d) straight, at downward angle 34° **9.** (a) 5.74 m; (b) 10.0 m/s; (c) – (3.68 m/s^2) $\hat{j}$ **10.** 53 m **11.** 58 kg **12.** 4.2 m **13.** 30.0°; (b) – (0.572 kg. m/s)$\hat{j}$ **14.** 48° **15.** 5 N **16.** (a) (30 kg.m/s)$\hat{i}$; (b) (38 kg.m/s)$\hat{i}$; (c) (6.0 m/s)$\hat{i}$ **17.** (a) 2.39×10^3N s; (b) 4.78×10^5N; (c) 1.76×10^3N s; (d) 3.52×10^5N **18.** (a) 1.00 Ns; (b) 100 N; (c) 20.0 N **19.** (a) 7.17 N s; (b) 16.0 kg.m/s **20.** 3.5 m/s **21.** (a) $-(0.15$ m/s$)\hat{i}$; (b) 0.18 m **22.** (a) 14 m/s; (b) $-y$ direction **23.** (a) 14 m/s; (b) 45° **24.** 3.4 kg **25.** (a) $(1.00\hat{i} - 0.167\hat{j})$ km/s; (b) 3.23 MJ **26.** (a) 20 J; (b) 40 J **27.** (a) 721 m/s; (b) 937 m/s **28.** 0.073 m **29.** (a) 4.4 m/s; (b) 0.80 **30.** 2.6 m **31.** (a) 2.0 m/s; (b) −1.3 J; (c) + 40 J; (d) system got energy from some source, such as a small explosion **32.** 0.33 m **33.** 25 cm **34.** (a) 1.2 kg; (b) 2.5 m/s **35.** (a) $(2.67$ m/s$)\hat{i} + (-3.00$ m/s$)\hat{j}$; (b) 4.01 m/s; (c) 48.4° **36.** −28 cm **37.** (a) – 2.47 m/s; (b) 1.23 m/s **38.** (a) 2.22 m; (b) 0.556 m **39.** (a) 0.21 kg; (b) 7.2 m **40.** 1.0 kg **41.** (a) 433 m/s; (b) 250 m/s **42.** (a) $(10\hat{i} + 15\hat{j})$ m/s; (b) -5.0×10^2 J **43.** (a) 27° **44.** 120° **45.** (a) 2.7; (b) 7.4 **46.** (a) 1.57×10^6 N; (b) 1.35×10^5 kg; (c) 2.08 km/s **47.** (a) 46 N; (b) none **48.** (a) 7.11 m/s ; (b) greater; (d) 4/9 p_{1i} **49.** (a) 1.78 m/s; (b) less; (c) less; (d) greater **50.** (a) 1.92 m; (b) 0.640 m **51.** 6.0×10^2 **52.** (a) $(7.4 \times 10^3$ N·s$)\hat{i} - (7.4 \times 10^3$ N·s$)\hat{j}$; (b) $(-7.4 \times 10^3$ N·s$)\hat{i}$; (c) 2.3×10^3N; (d) 2.1×10^4N; (e) −45° **53.** 0.57 m/s **54.** 4.4 m/s **55.** (a) 1.9 m/s; (b) −30°; (c) elastic **56.** (a) 8.0×10^4 N; (b) 27 kg/s **57.** (a) 6.9 m/s; (b) 30°; (c) 6.9 m/s; (d) −30°; (e) 2.0 m/s; (f) −180° **58.** (a) 25 mm; (b) 26 mm; (c) down; (d) 1.6×10^{-2} m/s^2 **59.** 3.0 m **60.** (a) −0.50 m/s; (b) −1.8 cm; (c) 0.50 m **61.** (b) 0.50 m/s; (c) 0 **62.** 0.0022 **63.** (a) 4.4 m/s; (b) 38 J **64.** $(-3.8$ m/s$)\hat{i}$; (b) $(7.2$ m/s$)\hat{i}$ **65.** (a) 0; (b) 0; (c) 0 **66.** (a) 0.841 m/s; (b) 0.975 m/s

Chapter 10

CP **1.** b and c **2.** (a) and (d) ($\alpha = d^2\theta/dt^2$ must be a constant) **3.** (a) yes; (b) no; (c) yes; (d) yes **4.** all tie **5.** 1, 2, 4, 3 (see Eq. 10-36) **7.** $ml^2/12$ **8.** 7/5 $Mr2$ **10.** 3 $mr^2/4$ **11.** (see Eq. 10-40) 1 and 3 tie, 4, then 2 and 5 tie (zero) **12.** (draw the vectors, use right-hand rule) (a) z; (b) y; (c) $-x$ **13.** $mg\ u \cos \theta t$ **14.** (a) downward in the figure ($\tau_{net} = 0$); (b) less (consider moment arms) **16.** (see Eq. 10-21) (a) 1 and 3 tie; then 2 and 4 tie, then 5 (zero); (b) 2 and 3 **17.** (see Eqs. 10-23 and 10-16) (a) 3, 1; then 2 and 4 tie (zero); (b) 3 **18.** (a) all tie (same, same t, thus same ΔL); (b) sphere, disk, hoop (reverse order of I) **19.** (a) decreases; (b) same (net = 0, so L is conserved); (c) increases **20.** $u/2I$
Q **1.** (a) c, a, then b and d tie; (b) b, then a and c tie, then d **3.** c, a, b **5.** larger **7.** (a) decrease; (b) clockwise; (c) counterclockwise **9.** all tie **P** **1.** 11 rad/s **2.** (a) 4.0 rad/s; (b) 28 rad/s; (c) 12 rad/s^2; (d) 6.0 rad/s2 **3.** (a) 4.0 rad/s; (b) 11.9 rad/s **4.** (a) 4.0 m/s; (b) no **5.** (a) $1.2\,t^5 - 1.33\,t^3 + 2.0$; (b) $0.20\,t^6 - 0.33\,t^4 + 2.0\,t + 1.0$ **6.** (a) 4.09 s; (b) 1.70 s **7.** (a) 44 rad; (b) 5.5 s; (c) 32 s; (d) −2.1 s; (e) 40 s **8.** (a) 1.0 rev/s^2; (b) 4.8 s; (c) 9.6 s; (d) 48 rev **9.** (a) 3.4×10^2 s; (b) -4.5×10^{-3} rad/s^2; (c) 98 s **10.** 6.9×10^{-13} rad/s **11.** (a) 3.0 rad/s; (b) 30 m/s; (c) 6.0 m/s^2; (d) 90 m/s^2 **12.** (a) 3.8×10^3 rad/s; (b) 1.9×10^2 m/s **13.** 16 s **14.** (a) 73 cm/s^2; (b) 0.075; (c) 0.11 **15.** (a) 1.5 rad/s^2; (b) 0.40 J **16.** 2.5 kg **17.** (a) 0.023 kg · m^2; (b) 11 mJ **18.** (a) 2.0 kg.m^2; (b) 6.0 kg.m^2; (c) 2.0 kg.m^2 **19.** 4.7×10^{-4} kg · m^2 **20.** (a) 1.3×10^3 g.cm^2; (b) 5.5×10^2 g.cm^2; (c) 1.9×10^2 g.cm^2; (d) 4.6 Nm **21.** −3.85 N m **22.** 12 Nm **23.** (a) 1.7 m/s; (b) 6.9 m/s^2 **24.** 2.51×10^{-4} kg · m^2 **25.** (a) 10^{-2} m/s^2 upward; (b) 4.87 N; (c) 4.54 N; (d) 1.20 rad/s^2; (e) 1.38×10^{-2} kg/m^2 **26.** (a) 6.00 cm/s^2; (b) 4.87 N; (c) 4.54 N; (d) 1.20 rad/s^2; (e) 0.0138 kg · m^2 **27.** (a) 3.0 rad/s^2; (b) 9.4 rad/s^2 **28.** (a) 4.2×10^2 rad/s^2; (b) 5.0×10^2 rad/s **29.** (a) 0.15 kg.m^2; (b) 11 rad/s **30.** 5.42 m/s **31.** (a) 11.2 mJ; (b) 33.6 mJ; (c) 56.0 mJ.; (d) 2.80×10^{-5} J.s^2/ rad^2 **32.** 9.82 rad/s **33.** 1.4 m/s **34.** 4×10^5 J **35.** (a) 5.1 h; (b) 8.1 h **36.** 3.1 rad/s **37.** (a) 2.3 rad/s^2; (b) 1.4 rad/s^2 **38.** 1.4×10^2 N · m **39.** 4.6 rad/s^2 **40.** 6.06 rad/s **41.** 17 **42.** 1.6 kg.m^2 **43.** 2.6 J **44.** 1.8 cm and 0.73 cm **45.** (a) 0.32 rad/s; (b) 1.0×10^2 km/h **46.** (a) 7.0 kg · m^2; (b) 7.2 m/s; (c) 71° **47.** (a) 3.3 J; (b) 2.9 J **48.** (a) 1.5×10^2 cm/s; (b) 15 rad/s; (c) 15 rad/s; (d) 75 cm/s; (e) 3.0 rad/s **50.** (a) 0.019 kg.m^2; (b) 0.019 kg.m^2

Chapter 11

CP **1.** (a) 59.3 rad/s; (b) 9.31 rad/s^2; (c) 70.7 m **2.** → (a) + z; (b) + y; (c) − x **3.** c, e, f **4.** (a) no; (b) at site of F1 perpendicular to plane of figure; (c) 45 N **Q** **1.** (a) 1, 2, 3 (zero); (b) 1 and 2 tie, then 3; (c) 1 and 3 tie, then 2 **3.** (a) spins in place; (b) rolls toward you; (c) rolls away from you **5.** a, then b and c tie, then e, d (zero) **7.** D, B, then A and C tie **9.** (a) same; (b) increase; (c) decrease; (d) same, decrease, increase **P** **1.** (a) 59.3 rad/s; (b) 9.31 rad/s^2; (c) 70.7 m **2.** (a) (−4.0 N) $\hat{i}$; (b) 0.60 kg · m^2 **3.** (a) 37.8 cm; (b) 1.96×10^{-2} N **4.** (a) 63 rad/s; (b) 4.0 m **5.** 7.2×10^4 kg.m^2 **6.** 4.8 m **7.** (a) 75 J; (b) 7.3 m/s **8.** 6 m; (f) 6.1 m/s **9.** 1.34 m/s **10.** 0.50 **11.** (a) 0.19 m/s^2; (c) $- 1.1 \times 10^3$ N **12.** (a) 2.7; (b) 2.7; **13.** 3.23 rev/s **14.** 3.90 rad/s and v= 2.00 m/s **15.** 95/98 L **16.** 1/3 **17.** 0.8 rad/s^2 **18.** 0.8 rad/s^2 **19.** 1.395 m/s^2 **20.** 193 ft/s^2

Chapter 12

CP **1.** d **Q** **1.** a and c (forces and torques balance) **3.** (a) 12 kg; (b) 3 kg; (c) 1 kg **5.** (a) 1 and 3 tie, then 2; (b) all tie; (c) 1 and 3 tie, then 2 (zero) **7.** increase **9.** (a) at C (to eliminate forces there from a torque equation); (b) plus; (c) minus; (d) equal **P** **1.** (a) 6.5×10^6 Nm^2; (b) 1.1×10^{-5} m; (c) 0.987 m; (d) 1.97 m **2.** (a) 7.5 X 10^{10} N/m^2; (b) 2.9 $\times 10^8$ N/m^2 **3.** (a) 6.5 106 N/m2; (b) 1.1 105 m **4.** 0.0560 J **5.** (a) 0.80; (b) 0.20; (c) 0.25 **6.** (a) equal; (b) 8.67×10^{-6} J; (c) Less than; (d) 3.42×10^{-5} J; (e) greater than **7.** (a) 1.4 109 N; (b) 75 **8.** 0.421 g **9.** (a) 1.2 10^2 N; (b) 68 N **10.** 1.3×10^7 N/m^2 **11.** (a) 1.8×10^7 N; (b) 1.4 10^7 N; (c) 16 **12.** (a) 8.0 $\times 10^{-4}$ m; (b) 0.023 m **13.** 2.4×10^9 N/m^2 **14.** (a) 1.38 kN; (b) 180 N **15.** 44 N

Chapter 13

CP **1.** all tie **2.** (a) 1, tie of 2 and 4, then 3; (b) line d **3.** (a) increase; (b) negative **4.** (a) 2; (b) 1 **5.** (a) path 1 (decreased E (more negative) gives decreased a); (b) less (decreased a gives decreased T) **Q** **1.** Gm^2/r^2, upward **3.** b and c tie, then a (zero) **5.** $3GM^2/d^2$, leftward **7.** (a) positive y; (b) yes, rotates counterclockwise until it points toward particle B **9.** 1, tie of 2 and 4, then 3 **11.** b, d, and f all tie, then e, c, a **P** **1.** 19 m **3.** $\frac{1}{2}$ **5.** $-5.00d$ **7.** 2.60×10^5 km **9.** 0.8 m **11.** (a) $M = m$; (b) 0 **13.** 8.31×10^{-9} N **15.** (a) $-1.88d$; (b) $-3.90d$; (c) $0.489d$ **17.** 2.6×10^6 m **19.** (a) 17 N; (b) 2.4 **21.** (a) 7.6 m/s^2; (b) 4.2 m/s^2 **23.** 5×10^{24} kg **25.** (a) 9.83 m/s^2; (b) 9.84 m/s^2; (c) 9.79 m/s^2 **27.** (a) $(3.0 \times 10^{-7}$ N/kg$)m$; (b) $(3.3 \times 10^{-7}$ N/kg$)m$; (c) $(6.7 \times 10^{-7}$ N/kg · m$)mr$ **29.** (a) 0.74; (b) 3.8 m/s^2; (c) 5.0 km/s **31.** (a) 0.0451; (b) 28.5 **33.** 5.0×10^9 J **35.** (a) 0.50 pJ; (b) −0.50 pJ **37.** (a) 1.7 km/s; (b) 2.5×10^5 m; (c) 1.4 km/s **39.** (a) 82 km/s; (b) 1.8×10^4 km/s **41.** -4.82×10^{-13} J **43.** 6.5×10^{23} kg **45.** 5×10^{10} stars **47.** (a) 6.64×10^3 km; (b) 0.0136 **49.** (a) 7.82 km/s; (b) 87.5 min **51.** (a) 1.9×10^{13} m; (b) $3.6R_P$ **55.** 0.71 y **57.** 5.8×10^6 m **59.** $(GM/L)^{0.5}$ **61.** (a) 2.8 y; (b) 1.0×10^{-4} **63.** (a) 3.19×10^3 km; (b) lifting **65.** (a) $r^{1.5}$; (b) r^{-1}; (c) $r^{0.5}$; (d) $r^{-0.5}$ **67.** (a) 7.5 km/s; (b) 97 min; (c) 4.1×10^2 km; (d) 7.7 km/s; (e) 93 min; (f) 3.2×10^{-3} N; (g) no; (h) yes **69.** 1.1 s **71.** (a) 1.0×10^3 kg; (b) 1.5 km/s **73.** $-0.044\hat{j}$ μN **75.** (a) 2.15×10^4 s; (b) 12.3 km/s; (c) 12.0 km/s; (d) 2.17×10^{11} J; (e) -4.53×10^{11} J; (f) -2.35×10^{11} J; (g) 4.04×10^7 m; (h) 1.22×10^3 s; (i) elliptical **77.** $0.37\hat{j}$ μN **79.** 29 pN **81.** 2.5×10^4 km **83.** (a) 2.2×10^{-7} rad/s; (b) 89 km/s **85.** 3.2×10^{-7} N **87.** (a) 0; (b) 1.8×10^{32} J; (c) 1.8×10^{32} J; (d) 0.99 km/s **89.** $GM_E m/12R_E$ **91.** (a) 1.4×10^6 m/s; (b) 3×10^6 m/s^2 **93.** $2\pi r^{1.5}G^{-0.5}(M + m/4)^{-0.5}$ **95.** 2.4×10^4 m/s **97.** −1.87 GJ **99.** (a) $GMmx(x^2 + R^2)^{-3/2}$; (b) $[2GM(R^{-1} - (R^2 + x^2)^{-1/2})]^{1/2}$ **101.** (a) Gm^2/R_i; (b) $Gm^2/2R_i$; (c) $(Gm/R_i)^{0.5}$; (d) $2(Gm/R_i)^{0.5}$; (e) Gm^2/R_i; (f) $(2Gm/R_i)^{0.5}$; (g) The center-of-mass frame is an inertial frame, and in it the principle of conservation of energy may be written as in Chapter 8; the reference frame attached to body A is noninertial, and the principle cannot be written as in Chapter 8. Answer (d) is correct. **103.** (a) 1.9×10^{11} m; (b) 4.6×10^4 m/s

Chapter 14

CP **1.** all tie **2.** (a) all tie (the gravitational force on the penguin is the same); (b) $0.95\rho_0, \rho_0, 1.1\rho_0$ **3.** The level of the water will not change because the quantity of water displaced will remain the same. **4.** The system will not topple, since according to Pascal's law the pressure on the bottom of the vessel will be the same everywhere. Thus the body will still remain in rotational equilibrium. **5.**(a) the level of the water in the glass will drop; (b) the level of the water will not change **6.** 1.5 m **7.** 13 cm³/s, outward **8.** (a) all tie; (b) 1, then 2 and 3 tie, 4 (wider means slower); (c) 4, 3, 2, 1 (wider and lower mean more pressure) **Q** **1.** *b*, then *a* and *d* tie (zero), then *c* **3.** (a) moves downward; (b) moves downward **5.** (a) downward; (b) downward; (c) same **7.** *B*, *C*, *A* **9.** (a) 1 and 4; (b) 2; (c) 3 **P** **1.** 1.1×10^5 Pa **2.** 18 N **3.** 2.9×10^4 N **4.** (a) 190 kPa; (b) 10.6 kPa **5.** 0.074 **6.** 3.8×10^4 Pa **7.** (b) 26 kN **8.** 1.90×10^4 Pa **9.** 1.08×10^3 atm **10.** 0.17 m **11.** 7.2×10^5 N **12.** 2.80 m **13.** -2.6×10^4 Pa **14.** 1.4×10^5 Pa **15.** (a) 94 torr; (b) 4.1×10^2 torr; (c) 3.1×10^2 torr **16.** 2.0 **17.** (a) 1.0×10^3 torr; (b) 1.7×10^3 torr **18.** (a) 0.019 atm; (b) 0.39 atm **19.** 0.635 J **20.** 26 torr **21.** 44 km **22.** (a) 5.0×10^6 N; (b) 5.6×10^6 N **23.** 4.69×10^5 N **24.** (a) 1.88×10^9 N; (b) 2.20×10^9 N.m; (c) 11.7 m **25.** 739.26 torr **26.** 0.39×10^{-3} atm **27.** (a) 7.9 km; (b) 16 km **28.** (a) (A/a)f; (b) 103 N **29.** 8.50 kg **30.** (a) 3.75×10^4 N; (b) 1.10×10^5 Pa; (c) 2.23×10^3 N; (d) 2.18×10^3 N **31.** (a) 2.04×10^{-2} m³; (b) 1.57 kN **32.** (a) 35.6 kN; (b) 0.330 m³ **33.** five **34.** 0.0784 m **35.** (a) 6.7×10^2 kg/m³; (b) 7.4×10^2 kg/m³ **36.** 4.11 kJ **37.** (a) 1.2 kg; (b) 1.3×10^3 kg/m³ **38.** 6.5 mm **39.** (a) 0.10; (b) 0.083 **40.** 1.5 g/cm³; (b) 2.72×10^{-3} m³ **41.** 57.3 cm **42.** 1.8 g/cm³ **43.** 0.126 m³ **44.** 1.40 m **45.** (a) 1.80 m³; (b) 4.75 m³ **46.** (a) 1.84 kg; (b) 2.01 kg **47.** (a) 637.8 cm³; (b) 5.102 m³; (c) 5.102×10^3 kg **48.** 9.7 mm **49.** 8.1 m/s **50.** (a) 3.0 m/s; (b) 2.8 m/s **51.** (a) 3.0 m/s; (b) 2.8 m/s **52.** 3.60 cm **53.** 66 W **54.** (a) 1.9 cm; (b) 1.0 **55.** (a) 2.5 m/s; (b) 2.6×10^5 Pa **56.** 1.7 MPa **57.** (a) 3.9 m/s; (b) 88 kPa **58.** (a) 2.40 m/s; (b)245 Pa **59.** (a) 1.6×10^{-3} m³/s; (b) 0.90 m **60.** (a) 2; (b) 1/2; (c) 3.00 cm **61.** 1.4×10^5 J **62.** (a) 6.4 m³; (b) 5.4 m/s; (c) 9.8×10^4 Pa. **63.** (a) 74 N; (b) 1.5×10^2 m³ **64.** (a) 0.25 m²; (b) 6.13 m³/s **65.** (a) 35 cm; (b) 30 cm; (c) 20 cm **66.** – 2.50 J **67.** (b) 2.0×10^{-2} m³/s **68.** (a) 4.1 m/s; (b) 21 m/s; (c) 8.0×10^{-3} m³/s **69.** (a) 0.0776 m³/s; (b) 69.8 kg/s **70.** (a) $\sqrt{2\rho g h/\rho_{air}}$; (b) 63.3 m/s **71.** 1.1×10^2 m/s **72.** 7.8 cm/h **73.** 44.2 g **74.** (a) 343 m/s; (b) 330 m/s **75.** 45.3 cm³ **76.** (a) 0; (b) 9.2×10^4 Pa; (c) 10.3 m **77.** (a) 3.2 m/s; (b) 9.2×10^4 Pa; (c) 10.3 m **78.** (a) 5.0%; (b) 41% **79.** 5.11×10^{-7} kg **80.** 3.82 m/s² **81.** 1.07×10^3 g **82.** 0.412 cm **83.** 6.0×10^2 kg/m³ **84.** (a) 2; (b) 3; (c) 4/3 **85.** 1.5 g/cm³

Chapter 15

CP **1.** (sketch *x* versus *t*) (a) $-x_m$; (b) $+x_m$; (c) 0 **2.** a (*F* must have the form of Eq. 15-10) **3.** (a) 5 J; (b) 2 J; (c) 5 J **4.** all tie (in Eq. 15-29, *m* is included in *I*) **5.** 1, 2, 3 (the ratio *m*/*b* matters; *k* does not) **Q** **1.** (a) 2; (b) positive; (c) between 0 and $+x_m$ **3.** a and b **5.** (a) all tie; (b) 3, then 1 and 2 tie; (c) 1, 2, 3 (zero); (d) 1, 2, 3 (zero); (e) 1, 3, 2 **7.** (a) between *D* and *E*; (b) between $3\pi/2$ rad and 2π rad **9.** (a) greater; (b) same; (c) same; (d) greater; (e) greater **11.** *b* (infinite period, does not oscillate), *c*, *a* **P** **1.** (a) **2.** (a) 1.25 X 10^5 N/m; (b) 2.68 Hz **3.** (c) **4.** −4.37 rad **5.** (c) **6.** 5.36 rad **7.** **8.** 4.00 m **9.** **10.** 2.08 h **11.** **12.** 2p(Pie)/3 **13.** **14.** 1.03 rad **15.** **16.** 54 Hz **17.** 23 cm **18.** (a) 0.525 m; (b) 0.686 s **19.** 8.3×10^2 N/m **20.** (a) 3.1 ms; (b) 4.0 m/s; (c) 0.080 J; (d) 80 N; (e) 40 N **21.** (a) 1.1 m/s; (b) 3.3 cm **22.** 0.024 m **23.** (a) 2.2 Hz; (b) 56 cm/s; (c) 0.10 kg; (d) 20.0 cm **24.** 12 s **25.** (a) 0.499 m; (b) 9.40×10^{-4} J **26.** (a) 0.205 kg·m²; (b) 47.7 cm; (c) 1.50 s **27.** 0.056 m **28.** 0.366 s **29.** 1.83 s **30.** 0.84m; (b) 0.3% **31.** (a) 0.53 m; (b) 2.1 s **32.** 0.18 s **33.** 0.0653 s **34.** (a) 0.45 m; (b) 0.16m; (c) $[(a^2 + b^2)/12]^{1/2}$ **35.** (a) 2.26 s; (b) increases; (c) same **36.** (a) 2.00 s; (b) 18.5 N m/ra **37.** 1.53 m 38. 0.19 g **39.** (a) 16.6 cm; (b) 1.23% **40.** (a) 1.72×10^{-3} s; (b) 11.2×10^{-3} s **41.** (b) k/m **42.** (a) 1.1 Hz; (b) 5.0 cm **43.** 3.5 Hz **44.** (a) 0.44 s; (b) 0.18 m **45.** 0 **46.** (a) 8.11×10^{-5} kg·m²; (b) 3.14 rad/s **47.** 1.58 **48.** (a) 0.20 s; (b) 0.20 kg; (c) –0.20 m; (d) -2.0×10^2 m/s²; (e) 4.0 J14.0° **49.** (a) 0.30 m; (b) 0.28 s; (c) 1.5×10^2 m/s²; (d) 11 J **50.** (a) 0.0625 J; (b) 3.13×10^2 J **51.** (a) 0.45 s; (b) 0.10 m above and 0.20 m below; (c) 0.15 m; (d) 2.3 J **52.**(a) 0.30 m; (b) 30 m/s2; (c) 0; (d) 4.4 s **53.** 7×10^2 N/m **54.** (a) *F*/*m*; (b) 2*F*/*mL*; (c) 0

Chapter 16

CP **1.** downwards **2.** (a) 2, 3, 1; (b) 3, then 1 and 2 tie (find amplitude of *dy*/*dt*) **3.** (a) same (independent of *f*); (b) decrease ($\lambda = v/f$); (c) increase; (d) increase **4.** 0.133 **5.** 11/360 sec **6.** 0.20 and 0.80 tie, then 0.60, 0.45 **7.** (a) 1; (b) 3; (c) 2 **8.** (a) 75 Hz; (b) 525 Hz **Q** **1.** *a*, upward; *b*, upward; *c*, downward; *d*, downward; *e*, downward; *f*, downward; *g*, upward; *h*, upward **3.** (a) 1, 4, 2, 3; (b) 1, 4, 2, 3 **5.** (a) 0, 0.2 wavelength, 0.5 wavelength (zero); (b) $4P_{avg,1}$ **7.** intermediate (closer to fully destructive) **9.** *c*, *a*, *b* **11.** *d* **P** **1.** 30 cm **2.** (a) 0.680 s; (b) 1.47 Hz; (c) 2.06 m/s **3.** (a) 22 seats/s; (b) 39 seats **4.** 1.1 ms **5.** 5.64 rad **6.** (a) 11.7 cm; (b) π rad **7.** (a) 6.0 cm; (b) 1.0×10^2 cm; (c) 2.0 Hz; (d) 2.0×10^2 cm/s; (f) 75 cm/s; (g) −2.0 cm **8.** (a) 64 Hz; (b) 1.3 m; (c) 4.0 cm; (d) 5.0 m^{-1}; (e) 4.0×10^2 s^{-1}; (f) $\pi/2$ rad; (g) minus **9.** 4.24 m/s **10.** (a) 3.0 mm; (b) 16 m^{-1}; (c) 2.4×10^2 s^{-1}; (d) minus **11.** 1.3 cm **12.** (a) negative; (b) 4.0 cm; (c) 0.31 cm^{-1}; (d) 0.63 s^{-1}; (e) π rad; (f) minus; (g) 2.0 cm/s; (h) −2.5 cm/s **13.** (a) 0.12 mm; (b) 141 m^{-1}; (c) 628 s^{-1}; (d) plus **14.** (a) 5.0 cm; (b) 0.40 m; (c) 12 m/s; (d) 0.033 s; (e) 9.4 m/s; (f) 16 m^{-1}; (g) 1.9×10^2 rad/s; (h) 0.93 rad **15.** (a) 5.0 cm; (b) 40 cm; (c) 12 m/s; (d) 0.033 s; (e) 9.4 m/s; (f) 16 m^{-1}; (g) 1.9×10^2 s^{-1}; (h) 0.93 rad; (i) plus **16.** (a) 28.6 m/s; (b) 22.1 m/s; (c) 188 g; (d) 313 g **17.** (a) *gy*; (b) l/*g* **18.** 198 Hz **19.** 3.2 mm **20.** 1.75 m/s **21.** 0.20 m/s **22.** 0.20 m/s **23.** $1.41y_m$ **24.** (a) 82.8°; (b) 1.45 rad; (c) 0.230 wavelength **25.** (a) 9.0 mm; (b) 16 m^{-1}; (c) 1.1×10^3 s^{-1}; (d) 2.7 rad; (e) plus **26.** (a) 10 W; (b) 20 W; (c) 40 W; (d) 26; (e) 0 **27.** 5.0 cm **28.** (a) p (Pie) rad; (b) 3.00 mm; (c) 0 rad; (d) 13 mm; (e) 9.4 mm **29.** 84° **30.** (a) 3.29 mm; (b) 88.8°; (c) 88.8° **31.** (a) 3.29 mm; (b) 1.55 rad; (c) 1.55 rad **32.** (a) $f_{8,b}$; (b) *t*/*u* **33.** (a) 82.0 m/s; (b) 16.8 m; (c) 4.88 Hz **34.** 10 cm **35.** (a) 144 m/s; (b) 60.0 cm; (c) 241 Hz **36.** (a) $2f_3$ **37.** (a) 105 Hz; (b) 158 m/s **38.** (a) 6.36 Hz; (b) 6.36 Hz **39.** 260 Hz **40.** (a) 4.0 m; (b) 24 m/s; (c) 1.4 kg; (d) 0.11 s **41.** (a) 0.25 cm; (b) 1.2×10^2 cm/s; (c) 3.0 cm; (d) 0 **42.** (a) 0, (b) 0.20 m; (c) 0.40 m; (d) 0.050 s; (e) 8.0 m/s; (f) 0.020 m; (g) 0 s; (h) 0.025 s; (i) 0.050 s **43.** (a) 0.50 cm; (b) 3.1 m^{-1}; (c) 3.1×10^2 s^{-1}; (d) minus **44.** (a) 0.040 m; (b) 0; (c) 0; (d) 1.0 s **45.** (a) 2.00 Hz; (b) 2.00 m; (c) 4.00 m/s; (d) 50.0 cm; (e) 150 cm; (f) 250 cm; (g) 0; (h) 100 cm; (i) 200 cm **46.** (a) 9.0 mm; (b) 16 m^{-1}; (c) 5.2×10^2 rad/s; (d) minus **47.** (a) 0.846 kg; (b) 3.68 **48.** (a) 324 Hz; (b) eight **49.** 0.845 g/m **50.** (a) $0.83y_1$; (b) 37° **51.** (a) 0.31 m; (b) 1.64 rad; (c) 2.2 mm **52.** −3.4 rad **53.** 1.2 rad **54.** (a) 54.0 cm/s; (b) $+x$ direction **55.** (a) 3.0 mm; (b) 31 m^{-1};

(c) 7.5×10^2 rad/s **56.** (a) $2P_1$; (b) $1/4\ P_1$ **57.** (a) 8.0×10^{-2} m; (b) 1.0×10^{-2} m **58.** (a) 1.33 m/s; (b) 1.88 m/s; (c) 16.7 m/s²; (d) 23.7 m/s² **59.** (a) 5.0 cm/s; (b) 3.2 cm; (c) 0.25 Hz **60.** (a) $[k\,\Delta\ell\,(\ell + \Delta\ell)/m]^{0.5}$ **61.** (a) 7.5×10^4 Hz; (b) 2.0×10^2 m; (c) 3.0×10^9 Hz **62.** (c) 2.0 m/s; (d) $-x$

Chapter 17

CP **1.** beginning to decrease (example: mentally move the curves of Fig. 17-7 rightward past the point at $x = 42$ m) **2.** (a) 1 and 2 tie, then 3 (see Eq. 17-22); (b) 3, then 1 and 2 tie (see Eq. 17-20) **3.** second (see Eqs. 17-37 and 17-39) **4.** *a*, greater; *b*, less; *c*, can't tell; *d*, can't tell; *e*, greater; *f*, less **Q** **1.** *C*, then *A* and *B* tie **3.** (a) 0, 0.2 wavelength, 0.5 wavelength (zero); (b) $4P_{avg,1}$ **5.** 150 Hz and 450 Hz **7.** *E, A, D, C, B* **9.** 1, 4, 3, 2 **P** **1.** (a) 2.6 km; (b) 2.0×10^2 **2.** 1.7×10^2 m **3.** 40.7 m **4.** 9.00 **5.** 1.9×10^3 km **6.** 44 m **7.** 0.23 ms **8.** (a) $(D \text{ Sin } \theta)v$; (b) D/v_w; (c) 13° **9.** (a) 2.3×10^2 Hz; (b) higher **10.** (a) 343 m/s; (b) 9.2 rad/m; (c) 3.1×10^3rad/s; (d) 5.9×10^{-9} m; (e) 9.8 rad/m; (f) (5.9 nm) $\cos[(9.8\ \text{m}^{-1})\,x - (3.1 \times 10^3\ \text{s}^{-1})t]$ **11.** 960 Hz **12.** (a) 14; (b) 14 **13.** 17.5 cm **14.** (a) 343 Hz; (b) 3; (c) 5; (d) 686 Hz; (e) 2; (f) 3 **15.** (a) 0.5; (b) 1.5 **16.** (a) 143 Hz; (b) 3; (c) 5; (d) 286 Hz; (e) 2; (f) 3 **17.** (a) 0; (b) 0; (c) $4\,s_m$ **18.** (a) 0; (b) fully constructive; (c) increase; (d) 128 m; (e) 63.0 m; (f) 41.2 m **19.** 15.0 mW **20.** 1.26 **21.** 36.8 nm **22.** 39.5 dB **23.** (a) 1.0×10^3; (b) 32 **24.** (a) 0.26 nm; (b) 1.5 nW/m² **25.** 2 μW **26.** 0.67 m **27.** (a) 5.97×10^{-5} W/m²; (b) 4.48 nW **28.** (a) 3.2; (b) 10 m **29.** (a) 0.34 nW; (b) 0.68 nW; (c) 1.4 nW; (d) 0.88 nW; (e) 0 **30.** (a) 86 Hz; (b) Perceptible sound of flow frequency (c) higher **31.** (a) 405 m/s; (b) 596 N; (c) 44.0 cm; (d) 37.3 cm **32.** (a) $h > 0$; (b) 0.125 m; (c) 0.375 m **33.** (a) 3; (b) 1129 Hz; (c) 1506 Hz **34.** (a) 260 Hz; (b) 4; (c) 120 Hz; (d) 7 **35.** 45.3 N **36.** (a) 71.5 Hz; (b) 64.8 N **37.** 12.4 m **38.** (a) 3; (b) 0; (c) 0.40 m; (d) 143 Hz **39.** 387 Hz **40.** 0.020 **41.** (a) 10 (b) $f_{beat} = n\Delta f, n = 1,2,3,4$ **42.** (a) 526 Hz; (b) 555 Hz **43.** 155 Hz **44.** (a) 1.58×10^3 Hz; (b) 0.208 m; (c) 2.16×10^3 Hz; (d) 0.152 m **45.** (a) 1.022 kHz; (b) 1.045 kHz **46.** 0.236 **47.** 41 kHz **48.** (a) $2\,v/3$; (b) $2\,v/3$; (c) $2\,v/3$; (d) $2\,v/3$; **49.** (a) 485.8 Hz; (b) 500.0 Hz; (c) 486.2 Hz; (d) 500.0 Hz **50.** (a) 598 Hz; (b) 608 Hz; (c) 589 Hz **51.** (a) 2.0 kHz; (b) 2.0 kHz **52.** (a) 3.3×10^2 m/s **53.** (a) 42°; (b) 11 s **54.** 3.30×10^4 m **55.** (a) 2.10 m; (b) 1.47 m **56.** (a) 572 Hz; (b) 1144 Hz **57.** 0.25 **58.** 3.1 m/s **59.** (a) 2.00; (b) 1.41; (c) 1.73; (d) 1.85 **60.** (a) 7.70 Hz; (b) 7.70 Hz **61.** (a) 5.2 kHz; (b) 2 **62.** 30° **63.** 2.1 m **64.** (a) 0; (b) 0.572 m; (c) 1.14 m **65.** (a) 11 ms; (b) 3.8 m **66.** (a) 5.5×10^2 m/s; (b) 1.1×10^3 m/s; (c) 1 **67.** (a) $b/r\,[\text{Sin}(kr - \omega t)]$; (b) length squared **68.** (b) 0.8 to 1.6 μs **69.** 4.8×10^2 Hz **70.** (a) 482 Hz; (b) 660 Hz

Chapter 18

CP **1.** 0.1 J **2.** Reinforced-concrete structures are very strong because the expansion coefficient of concrete is very close to that of iron and steel **3.** (a) 4.8 cm; (b) the iron ruler should be longer than the copper one **4.** (a) 2 and 3 tie, then 1, then 4; (b) 3, 2, then 1 and 4 tie (from Eqs. 18-9 and 18-10, assume that change in area is proportional to initial area) **6.** 10^{-5} deg^{-1} **Q** **2.** *c*, then the rest tie **P** **1.** (a) 320°F; (b) −12.3°F **2.** (a) 0.06 kPa; (b) higher **3.** −92.1°X **4.** (a) 0.011 m **5.** 29 cm³ **6.** (a) 9.996 cm; (b) 68°C **7.** 2.731 cm **8.** 11 cm² **9.** 49.87 cm³ **10.** (a) 0.69%; (b) 23×10^{-6} /°C **11.** 0.26 cm³ **12.** 23×10^{-6} / °C **13.** 360°C **14.** (a) 0.36%; (b) 0.18%; (c) 0.54%; (d) no change; (e) 1.8×10^{-5} / °C **15.** 0.13 mm **16.** 0.217 K/s **17.** 7.5 cm **18.** 4.5×10^2 J/kg·K **19.** 4.83×10^{-2} cm³ **20.** 0.32 cm² **21.** −157°C **22.** 66°C **23.** 2.16×10^{-5} m⁹² **24.** 1.7×10^2 km

Chapter 19

CP **1.** *A* (see Eq. 19-3) **2.** *b* and *d* tie, then *a*, *c* (Pcond identical; see Eq. 19-13) **Q** **1.** *B*, then *A* and *C* tie **3.** *c*, *b*, *a* **5.** (a) *f*, because ice temperature will not rise to freezing point and then drop; (b) *b* and c at freezing point, *d* above, *e* below; (c) in *b* liquid partly freezes and no ice melts; in *c* no liquid freezes and no ice melts; in *d* no liquid freezes and ice fully melts; in *e* liquid fully freezes and no ice melts **7.** (a) greater; (b) 1, 2, 3; (c) 1, 3, 2; (d) 1, 2, 3; (e) 2, 3, 1 **P** **1.** 42.7 kJ **2.** (a) 5.2×10^7 J **3.** 160 s **4.** 250 g **5.** (a) 20.3 kcal; (b) 1.11 kcal; (c) 873°C **6.** 160 s **7.** 4.0×10^2 J/kg.K **8.** 33 m² **9.** (a) 68 kJ/kg; (b) 2.3 kJ/kg°C **10.** (a) 37 W; (b) 2.0 kg; (c) 0.13 kg **11.** 742 kJ **12.** 82 cal **13.** (a) 5.3°C; (b) 0; (c) 0°C; (d) 60 g **14.** (a) (16.7*A*)W; (b) $(5.02 \times 10^{-5}A)$ kg/s; (c) 5.02×10^{-8} m/s **15.** (a) 0°C; (b) 0°C **16.** 8.71×10^{-3} kg **17.** (a) 8×10^2 W; (b) 2×10^4 J **18.** (a) 16 J/s; (b) 0.048 g/s **19.** (a) 1.23 kW; (b) 2.28 kW; (c) 1.05 kW **20.** (a) 1.4 W; (b) 3.3 **21.** 0.50 min **22.** (a) 15.8 °C; (c) 13.8 °C **23.** 0.81 J **24.** −4.2°C **25.** (a) 0.16; (b) 0.84% **26.** 1.1 m **27.** (a) 6.76 0.21 W; (b) 65 s **28.** 0.40 cm/h **29.** 0.68 mg/s **30.** 10% **31.** (a) 2.5×10^2 K; (b) 1.5 **32.** 4.5×10^2 J/kg K **33.** 766°C **34.** 4.83×10^2 cm³ **35.** (a) 2.3×10^2 J/s; (b) 23.5×10^3 J/s **36.** 333 J **37.** 0.67×10^{12} J **38.** −6.1 nW **39.** 2.5×10^3 J/kg K

Chapter 20

CP **1.** A, first; B, first and second; C, second; D, neither **P** **1.** 1.86×10^4 J **2.** 2.75 mol **3.** (a) 57.0°C; (b) −22.1 J/K; (c) + 24.9 J/K; (d) + 2.8 J/K **4.** 4.5×10^2 J/kg.K **5.** 3.5 mol **6.** (a) 320 K; (b) 0; (c) + 1.72 J/K **7.** 0.0368 J/K **8.** (a) 0.333; (b) 0.215; (c) 0.644; (d) 1.10; (e) 1.10; (f) 0; (g) 1.10; (h) 0; (i) −0.889; (j) −0.889; (k) −1.10; (l) −0.889; (m) 0; (n) 0.889; (o) 0 **9.** (a) 4.5×10^3 J; (b) 5.0×10^3 J; (c) 9.5 kJ **10.** + 0.76 J/K **11.** (a) 3.00; (b) $6.00p\,`0V_0$; (c) 0; (d) 8.64 J/K; (e) 0 **12.** (a) −943 J/K; (b) + 943 J/K; (c) yes **13.** (a) 0.693; (b) 4.50; (c) 0.693; (d) 0; (e) 4.50; (f) 23.0 J/K; (g) −0.693; (h) 7.50; (i) −0.693; (j) 3.00; (k) 4.50; (l) 23.0 J/K **14.** (a) 1.84 kPa; (b) 441 K; (c) 3.16 kJ; (d) 1.94 J/K **15.** (a) 266 K; (b) 341 K **16.** 99.99995% **17.** (a) 31%; (b) 16 kJ **18.** 97 K **19.** (a) 4.67 kJ/s; (b) 4.17 kJ/s **20.** 1.7 kJ **21.** 75 **22.** **23.** 23. 5.98 J/K **24.**

Chapter 21

CP **1.** *c and e (maximize area enclosed by a clockwise cycle)* **2.** all but c **3.** (a) all tie (*E*int depends on *i* and *f*, not on path); (b) 4, 3, 2, 1 (compare areas under curves); (c) 4, 3, 2, 1 **4.** 5 (greatest change in T), then tie of 1, 2, 3, 4 **5.** The gas rejects heat on this section **6.** 0.004 J **Q** **1.** 20 j **3.** d, then a and b tie, then c **5.** *(a) 3; (b) 1; (c) 4; (d) 2; (e) yes* **7.** (a) both clockwise; (b) both clockwise **9.** (a) 1, 2, 3, 4 (b) 1, 2, 3 **P** **1.** −30 J **2.** (a) −200 J; (b) −293 J; (c) −93 J **3.**(a) 1.2×10^2 J; (b) 75 J; (c) 30 J **4.** (a) $Q > 0$; (b) $W > 0$; (c) $W = 0$; (d) negative; (e) $Q < 0$; (f) $W < 0$; (g) $DE\text{int} < 0$; (h) −20 J **5.** 60 J **6.** (a) 8.0 J; (b) −9.3 J **7.** (a) 6.0 cal (b) – 43 cal; (c) 40 cal ; (d) 18 cal; (e) 18 cal **8.** 5.0 J **9.** (a) 11 P_iV_i (b) 7 **10.** 23 J **11.** 33.3 kJ **12.** – 45 J **13.** (a) 80 J

(b) 80 J **14.** 1.5 **15.** (a) 249 J; (b) 623 J; (c) 374 J; (d) 3.11 × 10^{-22} J **16.** 15.8 J/mol·K **17.** (a) 5.0 × 10^3 J; (b) 2.0 × 10^3 J; (c) 5.0 × 10^3 J **18.** (a) 6.6 × 10^{-23} g **19.** (a) 15.9 J; (b) 34.4 J/mol.K; (c) 26.1 J/mol·K **20.** (a) 3.49 × 10^3 J; (b) 2.49 × 10^3 J; (c) 997 J; (d) 1.00 × 10^3 J **21.** 50 J **23.** (a) 0.375 mol; (b) 1.09 × 10^3 J; (c) 0.714 **24.** (a) 6.98 × 10^3 J; (b) 4.99 × 10^3 J; (c) 1.99 × 10^3 J; (d) 2.99 × 10^3 J **25.** 1.5 × 10^3 N.m^{22} **26.** – 15 J **27.** 17°C **28.** –20 J **29.** – 87°C **30.** (a) 7/5; (b) 446 K; (c) $P_f V_f / RT_f$ **31.** –1.33 × 10^4 J **32.** (a) 3.74 × 10^3 J; (b) 3.74 × 10^3 J; (c) 0; (d) 0; (e) 1.81 × 10^3 J; (f) 1.81 × 10^3 J; (g) – 3.22 × 10^3 J; (h) – 1.93 × 10^3 J; (i) – 1.29 × 10^3 J; (j) 520 J; (k) 0; (l) 520 J; (m) 2.46 × 10^{-2}m^3; (n) 2.00 atm; (o) 1.00 atm **33.** (a) 900 cal; (b) 0; (c) 900 cal; (d) 3.0 mol; (e) 1200 cal; (f) 300 cal; (g) 900 cal; (h) 3.0 mol; (i) a diabetic; (j) −900 cal; (k) 900 cal; (l) 450 cal; **34.** (a) 0.333; (b) 4/3; (c) 1.44 **35.** (a) –374 J; (b) 0; (c) 374 J; (d) 3.11 × 10^{-22} J **36.** (a) 2.00 atm; (b) 333 J; (c) 0.961 atm; (d) 236 J **37.** (a) 122 K; (b) 365 K; (c) 0 **38.** (a) 5/3; (b) 2.7 × 10^4 K; (c) 4.5 × 10^4 mol; (d) 3.4 × 10^3 J; (e) 3.4 × 10^5 J; (f) 0.010 **39.** 5.0 m^3 **40.** (a) 8.0 atm; (b) 300 K; (c) 4.4 × 10^3 J; (d) 3.2 atm; (e) 120 K; (f) 2.9 × 10^3 J; (g) 4.6 atm; (h) 170 K; (i) 3.4 × 10^3 J **41.** 16.8/22.4 **42.** (a) 77.2 kJ; (b) 5.46 × 10^4 J; (c) .17 J/mol·K; (d) 4.32 × 10^4 J; (e) 8.86 × 10^4 J; (f) 8.38 J/ mol·K **43.** (a) –2.37 kJ; (b) –2.37 kJ **44.** –3.0 J **45.** 125 J **46.** (a) 1.47 × 10^3 J; (b) – 5.54 × 10^2 J; (c) 9.18 × 10^2 J; (d) 62.4% **47.** (a) 2.27 kJ; (b) 14.8 kJ; (c) 15.4%; (d) 75.0% **48.** (a) 5/3' (b) 75% **49.** (a) 33 kJ; (b) 25 kJ; (c) 26 kJ; (d)18 kJ **50.** $(T_1 - T_3)/T_1$ **51.** (a) 3; (b) 1.98; (c) 0.660; (d) 0.495; (e) 0.165; (f) 34.0%